AMERICAN POCKET

CHAMBERS
ENGLISH DICTIONARY

LAROUSSE

Barcelona   México   París   Buenos Aires

© MCMXCIX, Chambers Harrap Publishers Ltd.

"D. R." © MCMXCIX, por Ediciones Larousse, S. A. de C. V.
                        Renacimiento 180, Colonia San Juan Tlihuaca,
                        Delegación Azcapotzalco, C.P. 02400, México, D.F.

SEGUNDA EDICIÓN — 33ª reimpresión

ISBN 978-607-21-0082-4 (Ediciones Larousse)

Impreso en México — *Printed in Mexico*

Contents

Preface

In compiling this dictionary, the specific needs of the pocket dictionary user have been carefully considered. The wordlist is extensive and up to date, the defining style clear, and the page layout user-friendly, giving users quick answers to their questions without the loss of important information. Language features are given prominence in a text that gives inflections for all verbs and adjectives, and for irregular plurals, a wealth of examples showing headwords in use in phrases and sentences, pronunciation for difficult words, usage notes that are descriptive rather than prescriptive, plentiful and clearly presented idioms, as well as synonyms and antonyms for commonly used words. Modern and easy to use, this dictionary will be a reliable companion whenever and wherever English is written and spoken.

The Editors

Contributors

Publishing Manager
Elaine Higgleton

Senior Editors
Penny Hands
Megan Thomson

Editorial Team

John Bollard
JoAnne Chittick
George Davidson
Kaethe Ellis
Serenella Flackett
Alice Grandison
Phillip Holthaus
Barbara Kovacic

Marie McCarthy
Una McGovern
Patricia Marshall
David Replogle
James Shea
Anne Sukhanov
Holly Webber

How to use your Dictionary

ménage à trois (měn-äzh′) (*pl.* **ménages à trois**) a household consisting of three people, esp. one in which one person has a sexual relationship with both of the others.

menagerie *noun* 1 a collection of wild animals caged for exhibition. 2 a varied or confused mixture, esp. of people.

> We spell out the **past tense and present participle of all verbs** in full.

mend *verb trans., intrans.* (**mended, mending**) 1 to repair. 2 to improve, esp. in health; to heal. 3 to improve or correct: *mend one's ways.* —*noun* a repaired part or place. —**on the mend** getting better, esp. in health.

> We give examples of the **idioms** in which a headword is used, introducing them with —.

mendacity *noun* (*pl.* **mendacities**) 1 the tendency to lie; untruthfulness. 2 a lie. ▸ **mendacious** *adj.*

> **Subject labels** are given where a meaning is used within a specific area of knowledge or sphere of reference.

mendicant *noun* 1 a beggar. 2 *RC Church* a member of an order of begging monks. —*adj.* begging.

> **Help with pronunciation** is given for difficult words.

meningitis (měn,ĭn-jīt′ĭs) *noun* inflammation of the membranes covering the brain and spinal cord.

meniscus *noun* (*pl.* **menisci, meniscuses**) 1 a curved surface at the top of a liquid, caused by surface tension. 2 a lens, convex on one side and concave on the other.

menopause *noun* the time when menstruation stops permanently. ▸ **menopausal** *adj.*

menorah *noun* a seven-branched candlestick regarded as a symbol of Judaism.

> We spell out the **plural of nouns** where there could be any problem.

mensch *noun* (*pl.* **menschen, mensches**) *colloq.* a person, esp. one who is thought of as having admirable qualities.

menses (měn′sēz,) *pl. noun* blood, mucus, and other matter discharged, usu. monthly, from the uterus.

menstruate *verb intrans.* (**menstruated, menstruating**) to discharge the menses. ▸ **menstrual** *adj.* ▸ **menstruation** *noun*

> **Straightforward derivatives** are nested within their base entries.

mensuration *noun* the process of measuring.

> **Usage examples** are given in italics to illustrate meanings.

-ment *suffix* forming words denoting: 1 a process, action, or means: *repayment / treatment.* 2 a quality, state, or condition: *enjoyment / merriment.*

mental *adj.* 1 of, relating to, or done using the mind or intelligence: *mental arithmetic.* 2 *old use* of, relating to, or affected by a psychiatric or psychological illness: *a mental patient.* 3 *slang* foolish; stupid; crazy: *a mental idea.* ▸ **mentally** *adv.*

> **Usage panels** give further information on aspects of English where there is frequent uncertainty.

> *Usage* The application of *mental* to psychiatric or psychological illness or people suffering from psychiatric or psychological illness is now considered offensive.

menthol *noun* an organic compound derived from peppermint oils. ▸ **mentholated** *adj.*

mention *verb trans.* (**mentioned, mentioning**) to speak of or make reference to, esp. briefly or in passing. —*noun* **1** a brief or passing reference. **2** a reference made to an individual's merit in an official report. ▸ **mentionable** *adj.*

mentor (mĕn′tôr,, mĕnt′ər) *noun* a trusted teacher or adviser.

> After *Mentor*, a friend of Odysseus, who guides Telemachus in his search for his father

Word histories give interesting information about the word's origin.

menu *noun* **1** the range of dishes available in a restaurant, etc., or a list detailing these. **2** *Comput.* a list of optional functions displayed on a screen

meow or **mew** *noun* a crying or whining noise made by a cat. —*verb intrans.* (**meowed, meowing** or **mewed, mewing**) to make this noise.

Some entries have **additional alternative headwords**.

mercantile *adj.* of or pertaining to trade or traders; commercial.

mercenary *adj.* excessively concerned with the desire for personal gain, esp. money. —*noun* (*pl.* **mercenaries**) a soldier available for hire by a country or group.

mercerize *verb trans.* (**mercerized, mercerizing**) to treat (cotton, etc.) with a substance that strengthens it and gives it a silky appearance.

merchandise *noun* commercial goods. —*verb intrans., trans.* (*also* **merchandize**) (**merchandised, merchandising** or **merchandized, merchandizing**) to trade.

Parts of speech are marked with traditional labels. Some of the longer labels are given as abbreviations, e.g. *adj., adv., trans.*, etc.

merchant *noun* someone engaged in trading.

merchant marine the commercial fleet of a nation or those who crew and manage it.

merciful *adj.* feeling or displaying compassion. ▤ LENIENT, TOLERANT ▤ MERCILESS, INTOLERANT. ▸ **mercifully** *adv.*

Synonyms and antonyms are given for some words.

merciless *adj.* feeling or displaying no compassion. ▸ **mercilessly** *adv.*

mercurial *adj.* **1** of or containing mercury. **2** changeable.

Many derivatives are given as separate entries from their base words when they are important words in their own right.

mercury *noun* (SYMBOL Hg) a dense silvery-white metallic element, and the only metal that is liquid at room temperature.

mercy *noun* (*pl.* **mercies**) **1** compassion shown when punishment is possible or justified, or the power to be compassionate in such circumstances. **2** a relief or welcome happening. —**at the mercy of** wholly in the power of (someone or something).

mercy killing euthanasia.

mere *adj.* (*superlative* **merest**) nothing more than; no better, more important, or useful than.

We spell out the **comparative and superlative** of adjectives where there could be a problem.

Abbreviations used in the Dictionary

abbrev.	abbreviation	*i.e.*	(Latin *id est*) that is
adj.	adjective	*interj.*	interjection
adv.	adverb	*intrans.*	intransitive
Afr.	Africa(n)	*Math.*	mathematics
Amer.	America(n)	*Mech.*	mechanics
Austral.	Australia(n)	*Med.*	medicine
Aeron.	aeronautics	*Metall.*	metallurgy
Agric.	agriculture	*Meteorol.*	meteorology
Anat.	anatomy	*Microbiol.*	microbiology
Anthropol.	anthropology	*Mil.*	military
Archaeol.	archaeology	*Mus.*	music
Archit.	architecture	*Mythol.*	mythology
Astrol.	astrology	*Naut.*	nautical
Astron.	astronomy	*orig.*	originally
aux.	auxiliary	*pa p*	past participle
Biochem.	biochemistry	*pa t*	past tense
Biol.	biology	*Pathol.*	pathology
Bot.	botany	*per.*	perhaps
Brit.	British	*Philos.*	philosophy
c	century	*Photog.*	photography
c.	circa	*Phys.*	physics
Chem.	chemistry	*Physiol.*	physiology
colloq.	colloquial	*pl.*	plural
Comput.	computing	*poss.*	possibly
conj.	conjunction	*prep.*	preposition
derog.	derogatory	*prob.*	probably
Econ.	economics	*pron.*	pronoun
e.g.	(Latin *exempli gratia*) for example	*pr p*	present participle
		pr t	present tense
Electr.	electricity	*Psychol.*	psychology
Electron.	electronics	*RC Church*	Roman Catholic Church
Engin.	engineering		
Environ.	environment	*Rel.*	Religion
esp.	especially	*Scot.*	Scottish
etc.	(Latin *et cetera*) and so on	*sing.*	singular
		Sociol.	sociology
Geog.	geography	*Telecomm.*	telecommunications
Geol.	geology	*Theat.*	theatre
Geom.	geometry	*trans.*	transitive
Gram.	grammar	*usu.*	usually
Hist.	history	*Zool.*	zoology

Pronunciation Guide

Symbol	Sample Words		Symbol	Sample Words
ă	fat		ng	thing, think
ā	make, say		ō	go, toe
ä	father, bother, barn, heart		ô	law, ought
ăr, ĕr	bare, fair		oi	noise, toy
b	bib		ŏŏ	book
ch	church		ōō	boot, food
d	did		ow	now, out
ĕ	bet		p	pop, supper
ē	see, happy		r	roar, farm
f	five, photo, tough		s	source, less
g	gag		sh	ship, machine
h	high, ahead		t	type, late, pretty
hw	which, whet (in some speech)		th	thin
			th	this, then
ĭ	bit		v	valve, vivid
ī	bite, pie, aisle		w	we, wet, away
ĭr	pier, hear		y	yes
j	judge		z	zebra, raises
k	kick, can		zh	vision, pleasure
l	lip, bottle		ə	about, banana, glove, button
m	most, summer		ər	further, bird
n	no, funny, kitten			

Foreign Sounds

œ	*French* feu, *German* schön
ü	*French* tu, *German* über
KH	*German* Bach, *Scottish* loch
N	*French* bon

Stress Marks

primary stress, as in **chron**icle (krän′ĭ-kəl)

secondary stress, as in **chron**ological (krän,l-äj′ĭ-kəl), **neigh**bor**hood** (nā′bər-hŏŏd,)

Aa

A¹ *or a noun* (*pl.* **As, A's, a's**) **1** the first letter of the English alphabet. **2** (*usu.* **A**) the highest grade or quality, or a mark indicating this. **3** (**A**) *Mus.* the sixth note in the scale of C major.

A² *abbrev.* **1** ampere. **2** answer. **3** atomic: *A-bomb.*

Å *abbrev.* angstrom.

a¹ *or an indefinite article* **a** is used before words beginning with a consonant or consonant sound (e.g., *one, united, historical*), and **an** before words beginning with a vowel or vowel sound (e.g., *apple, honor*) **1** one: *Here is a book.* **2** used before a word describing quantity: *a lot of trouble.* **3** any; every: *A fire is hot.* **4** each or every; per: *once a day / 60¢ a pound.* **5** one of a stated type: *a real Romeo.*

a² *abbrev.* ante (Latin), before.

a-¹ *prefix* (*also* **an-** before a vowel) forming words denoting not, without, opposite to: *amoral / asymmetrical / agnostic.*

a-² *prefix* forming words denoting of: *akin / afresh.*

a-³ *prefix* forming words denoting **1** to or toward: *ashore.* **2** in the process of: *abuzz.* **3** on: *afire.* **4** in: *abed.*

AA *abbrev.* Alcoholics Anonymous.

AAA *abbrev.* American Automobile Association.

aardvark (ärd'värk,) *noun* an African mammal with a large snout which feeds on termites.

AB *abbrev.* artium baccalaureus (Latin), Bachelor of Arts.

aback *adv.*—**take aback** to surprise or shock.

abacus (ăb'ə-kəs) *noun* a frame with wires along which small beads can be moved, used for counting.

abaft *adv.* in or toward the stern of a ship. —*prep.* behind.

abalone (ăb'ə-lō,nē) *noun* a marine mollusk with a shell lined with mother-of-pearl.

abandon *verb trans.* (**abandoned, abandoning**) **1** to give up completely: *abandon hope.* **2** to leave behind (a person, etc.). ☒ DESERT, FORSAKE, LEAVE. **3** to leave (a place of danger or difficulty, etc.). **4** to give up to another person's control. **5** (**abandon (oneself) to (something)**) to let (oneself) be overcome by strong emotion, etc. —*noun* uncontrolled, reckless feelings. ▸ **abandonment** *noun*

abandoned *adj.* **1** having been abandoned. **2** having no sense of shame or morality.

abase *verb trans.* (**abased, abasing**) to humiliate or degrade (a person or oneself). ▸ **abasement** *noun*

abashed *adj.* embarrassed and ashamed.

abate *verb intrans., trans.* (**abated, abating**) to become or make less strong or severe. ▸ **abatement** *noun*

abattoir (ăb'ə-twär,) *noun* a slaughterhouse.

abbacy (ăb'ə-sē) *noun* (*pl.* **abbacies**) the office or authority of an abbot or abbess.

abbess (ăb'əs) *noun* a woman in charge of the nuns in an abbey.

abbey *noun* (*pl.* **abbeys**) **1** a group of monks or nuns living as a community. **2** the buildings they occupy. **3** a church associated with such a community.

abbot *noun* the head of the monks in an abbey.

abbrev. *or* **abbr.** *abbrev.* **1** abbreviated. **2** abbreviation.

abbreviate *verb trans.* (**abbreviated, abbreviating**) **1** to represent (a word) by a shortened form of it. **2** to reduce (e.g., text) in length. ▸ **abbreviation** *noun*

ABC¹ *noun* (*pl.* **ABCs, ABC's**) **1** the alphabet. **2** the basic facts about a subject.

ABC² *abbrev.* American Broadcasting Company.

abdicate *verb intrans., trans.* (**abdicated, abdicating**) **1** to give up one's right to (a throne). **2** to refuse or fail to carry out (responsibilities). ▸ **abdication** *noun*

abdomen (ăb'də-mən) *noun* the lower part of the body cavity. ▸ **abdominal** *adj.*

abduct *verb trans.* (**abducted, abducting**) to seize and hold (someone) prisoner illegally, by force. ▸ **abduction** *noun* ▸ **abductor** *noun*

abeam (ə-bēm') *adv.* in a line at right angles to the length of a ship, etc.

aberrant (ăb-ĕr'ənt, ăb'ə-rĕnt,) *adj.* not normal or accepted as standard. ▸ **aberrance** *or* **aberrancy** *noun*

aberration *noun* **1** a temporary, usu. brief, change from what is normal or accepted as standard. **2** a sudden and usu. temporary drop in standards of behavior, thought, etc.

abet (ə-bĕt') *verb trans.* (**abetted, abetting**) *esp. Law* to help or encourage (someone) to commit an offense.

abeyance (ə-bā'əns) *noun* being set aside temporarily: *hold a matter in abeyance.*

abhor verb trans. (**abhorred, abhorring**) to regard with great contempt or dislike. ▸ **abhorrence** noun ▸ **abhorrent** adj. ▸ **abhorrently** adv.

abide verb trans., intrans. (**abided, abiding**) 1 to put up with or tolerate. 2 to follow or obey (a decision, rule, etc.): abide by an agreement. 3 (pa t and pa p also **abode**) to live.

abiding adj. lasting a long time.

ability noun (pl. **abilities**) 1 the power, skill, or knowledge to do something. 2 skill or intelligence.

-ability suffix forming nouns corresponding to adjectives in -able: capability.

abject (ăb′jĕkt,) adj. 1 of conditions, etc. extremely miserable or poor. 2 of people showing lack of pride, etc. ▸ **abjectly** adv. ▸ **abjectness** noun

abjure (ăb-jŏŏr′) verb trans. (**abjured, abjuring**) to promise solemnly, esp. under oath, to stop believing or doing (something). ▸ **abjuration** noun

ablaze adj. 1 burning strongly. 2 brightly lighted. 3 (**ablaze with (something)**) feeling or displaying passionate emotion.

able adj. 1 having the necessary knowledge, power, time, opportunity, etc., to do something. 2 clever, skillful. ▸ **ably** adv.

-able suffix forming words denoting: 1 that may or must be: eatable . 2 that may be the subject of: objectionable. 3 that is suitable for or follows: seasonable. See also **-ible**.

able-bodied adj. fit and healthy.

able-bodied seaman a merchant seaman with more skills than an ordinary seaman.

ablution (ə-blŏŏ′shən) noun (usu. **ablutions**) washing parts of the body as part of a religious ceremony.

-ably suffix forming adverbs corresponding to adjectives in -able: capably.

ABM abbrev. antiballistic missile.

abnegation (ăb,nə-gā′shən) noun the act of giving something up.

abnormal (ăb-nôr′məl) adj. differing from what is usual or expected. ⊟ ABERRANT, ANOMALOUS, ATYPICAL, DEVIANT, DEVIATE, DIVERGENT, PRETERNATURAL, UNNATURAL ⊠ NORMAL, TYPICAL. ▸ **abnormality** noun ▸ **abnormally** adv.

aboard adv., prep. 1 on, onto, in, or into (a ship, train, aircraft, etc.). 2 Naut. alongside.

abode[1] noun the place where one lives.

abode[2] see abide.

abolish verb trans. (**abolished, abolishing**) to put an end to (customs, laws, etc.).

abolition (ăb,ə-lĭsh′ən) noun 1 abolishing something; the state of being abolished. 2 Hist. the abolishing of slavery.

abolitionism noun a 19th c movement to end slavery in the southern United States. ▸ **abolitionist** noun

A-bomb noun an atom bomb.

abominable (ə-băm′ə-nə-bəl) adj. 1 greatly disliked. 2 very bad. ▸ **abominably** adv.

abominable snowman a yeti.

abominate verb trans. (**abominated, abominating**) to regard with great dislike ▸ **abomination** noun.

aboriginal (ăb′ə-rĭj′ə-nəl) noun a member of a people forming the original inhabitants of a place. —adj. earliest or indigenous.

aborigine (ăb,ə-rĭj′ə-nē) noun an aboriginal.

abort verb trans., intrans. (**aborted, aborting**) 1 to expel (a fetus or embryo) spontaneously before it is viable. 2 to cause (a pregnancy) to end before the fetus is viable. 3 to stop (a plan, process, etc.) or to be stopped, before completion.

abortion noun 1 the removal of a fetus from the womb before it is viable. 2 the spontaneous expulsion of a fetus from the womb before it is viable. Also called **miscarriage**. 3 the failure of a plan, project, etc. ▸ **abortionist** noun

abortive adj. unsuccessful. ▸ **abortively** adv.

ABO system a classification of human blood into four types (A, B, AB, and O).

abound verb intrans. (**abounded, abounding**) 1 to exist in large numbers. 2 (**abound with** or in (**something**)) to be filled with (it) or rich in (it).

about prep. 1 concerning; on the subject of. 2 near to. 3 around; centering on. 4 here and there in. 5 all around. 6 occupied or busy with: While you're about it, please clean the garage. 7 in the possession of: We kept our wits about us. —adv. 1 approximately. 2 nearby. 3 scattered here and there. 4 all around; in all directions. 5 in or to the opposite direction: turn about. —adj. moving and in action: up and about after a long illness. —**about to do (something)** on the point of doing (it).

about-face noun 1 turning around so as to face in the opposite direction, as in a military formation. 2 a complete reversal, e.g., in opinion or attitude.

above prep. 1 higher than; over. 2 greater than in quantity or degree. 3 superior to in rank, importance, ability, etc. 4 too good, great, or honorable to stoop to: above petty quarrels. 5 too difficult to be understood by; beyond the abilities of. —adv. 1 at, in, or to a higher position, place, rank, etc. 2 overhead: saw black clouds above. 3 in an earlier passage of text. —adj. in a preceding passage of text. —noun colloq. something already mentioned: all of the above.

aboveboard adj. honest; open; not secret.

abracadabra noun an expression that supposedly has magic power, often used by people doing magic tricks.

abrade verb trans. (**abraded, abrading**) to scrape or wear away, esp. by rubbing. ▶ **abrasion** noun

abrasive adj. **1** of a material capable of wearing away the surface of something by rubbing and scraping. **2** of a material used to clean or smooth by rubbing. **3** of people or actions likely to offend others. —noun a substance capable of abrading.

abreast adv. side by side and facing in the same direction. —adj. (**abreast of (something)**) having the most recent information about: keep abreast of events.

abridge verb trans. (**abridged, abridging**) to shorten (a book, etc.). ▶ **abridgment** or **abridgement** noun

abroad adv. **1** in or to a foreign country. **2** in circulation; at large.

abrogate (ăb'rə-gāt͵) verb trans. (**abrogated, abrogating**) to cancel (a law, agreement, etc.) formally or officially. ▶ **abrogation** noun

abrupt adj. **1** occurring suddenly and quickly. **2** of speech, etc. sharp and rude. ▶ **abruptly** adv. ▶ **abruptness** noun

abscess (ăb'sĕs͵) noun a collection of pus in a cavity surrounded by inflamed tissues.

abscissa (ăb-sĭs'ə) noun (pl. **abscissas, abscissae**) Math. the first of a pair of numbers (x, y), known as the x coordinate, which specifies the distance of a point from the vertical or y-axis. See also **ordinate**.

abscond (ăb-skănd') verb intrans. (**absconded, absconding**) to leave quickly and usu. secretly.

absence noun **1** being away from work, etc. **2** the time that a person is away from work, etc. **3** the state of something needed or usual not being present or available.

absent adj. (ăb'sənt) **1** not in place; not present. **2** not existing, esp. where normally to be expected. **3** showing that one is not paying attention or concentrating. —verb trans. (ăb͵-sĕnt') (**absented, absenting**) to keep (oneself) away from a place. —prep. (ăb'sənt) without. ▶ **absently** adv.

absentee (ăb͵sən-tē') noun a person who is not present at a particular or required time.

absenteeism noun frequent and continued absence from work, school, etc.

absent-minded adj. forgetful or inattentive. ▶ **absent-mindedly** adv. ▶ **absent-mindedness** noun

absinthe or **absinth** (ăb'sĭnth) noun a strong green alcoholic drink flavored with substances such as aniseed and wormwood.

absolute (ăb'sə-lo͞ot͵, ăb͵sə-lo͞ot') adj. **1 a** complete; perfect. **b** devoid of any qualification. **2** having no limits; controlled by nothing or nobody else. **3** certain; undoubted. **4** measured without any comparison with other things: an absolute standard. **5** pure; mixed with nothing else. —noun a rule, standard, etc., that is thought to be true or right in all situations. ▶ **absoluteness** noun

absolutely adv. **1** completely. **2** yes; certainly.

absolute zero the lowest temperature theoretically possible, 0° K on the kelvin scale, equivalent to -459.67°F or -273.15°C.

absolution noun the formal forgiving of a person's sins, esp. by a priest.

absolutism noun government by a person who has total power. ▶ **absolutist** noun, adj.

absolve (əb-zălv', -zŏlv') verb trans. (**absolved, absolving**) **1** to pronounce (someone) free from blame or sin.

absorb (əb-sôrb', -zôrb') verb trans. (**absorbed, absorbing**) **1** to take in (heat, liquid, knowledge, etc.). **2** to receive or take in as part of itself or oneself: a country that has absorbed many immigrants. **3** to have all of the attention or interest of. ▶ **absorbency** noun ▶ **absorbent** noun, adj.

absorbed adj. engrossed: absorbed in a good novel.

absorbing adj. fully occupying the mind. ■ CAPTIVATING, CONSUMING, ENGROSSING, ENTHRALLING, GRIPPING, RIVETING, UNPUTDOWNABLE ■ BORING.

absorption noun **1** taking in, sucking up, or absorbing. **2** the state of having all one's interest or attention occupied. ▶ **absorptive** adj.

abstain verb intrans. (**abstained, abstaining**) (**abstain from (something)** or **from doing (something)**) **1** to choose not to do (it): abstain from alcohol. **2** to choose not to vote.

abstemious (ăb-stē'mē-əs) adj. taking food, alcohol, etc., in very limited amounts. ▶ **abstemiousness** noun

abstention (ăb-stĕn'chən) noun **1** the act of choosing not to do something, e.g., not to take food or alcohol. **2** a refusal to vote.

abstinence (ăb'stə-nəns) noun choosing not to do or take something, e.g., alcohol. ■ ABSTENTION, NONINDULGENCE, RESTRAINT, SELF-CONTROL, SELF-DENIAL, SOBRIETY, TEMPERANCE ■ INDULGENCE, OVERINDULGENCE. ▶ **abstinent** adj.

abstract adj. (ăb'străkt', ăb'străkt) **1** of or relating to something that exists only as an idea or a quality. **2** concerned with ideas and theory rather than with things that really exist or could exist. **3** of art forms representing the subject by shapes and patterns, etc., rather than in the shape or form it actually has. —noun (ăb'străkt) **1** a brief statement of the main points (of a book, speech, etc.). **2** an example of abstract art. —verb trans.

(**abstracted, abstracting**) **1** (ăb-străkt′) to take out or remove. **2** (ăb′străkt,) to summarize (a book, speech, etc.).

abstracted *adj.* thinking about something so much that one does not notice one's surroundings. ▸ **abstractedly** *adv.*

abstraction *noun* **1** the act or an example of abstracting. **2** a general idea rather than an actual example. **3** the state of being abstracted.

abstruse (ab-strōōs′) *adj.* hard to understand.

absurd (ab-sərd′, -zərd′) *adj.* laughably senseless. ▸ **absurdity** *noun* ▸ **absurdly** *adv.*

abundance *noun* **1** a large amount, sometimes more than is needed. **2** wealth.

abundant *adj.* **1** existing in large amounts. ▣ AMPLE, BOUNTEOUS, BOUNTIFUL, COPIOUS, PLENTEOUS, PLENTIFUL, RICH ▣ SCARCE. **2** (**abundant in** (**something**)) having or providing a large amount or variety of (something).

abundantly *adv.* **1** very; completely: *abundantly clear.* **2** in large amounts.

abuse *verb trans.* (ə-byōōz′) (**abused, abusing**) **1** to use (one's position, power, etc.) wrongly. **2** to treat (someone or something) cruelly or wrongly. **3** to speak rudely or insultingly to or about (someone). —*noun* (ə-byōōs′) **1** wrong use of one's position, power, etc. **2** misuse: *alcohol abuse.* **3** bad or cruel treatment. **4** rude or insulting words. ▸ **abuser** *noun* ▸ **abusive** *adj.*

abut *verb intrans., trans.* (**abutted, abutting**) to be next to or touching.

abutment *noun* the support at the end of an arch, e.g., in a bridge.

abuzz *adj.* in a state of noisy activity, interest, or excitement.

abysmal (ə-bĭz′məl) *adj.* **1** extremely bad. **2** very great. ▸ **abysmally** *adv.*

abyss *noun* **1** an immeasurably deep hole. **2** (**the abyss**) hell.

Ac *symbol Chem.* actinium.

ac *or* **AC** *abbrev.* alternating current.

a/c *abbrev.* **1** account. **2** air conditioning.

acacia (ə-kā′shə) *noun* a tree with small yellow flowers. *Also called* **wattle**.

academe (ăk′ə-dēm,) *noun formal* the academic world or life.

academia (ăk,ə-dēm′ē-ə) *noun* an academic community or institution.

academic (ăk,ə-dĕm′ĭk) *adj.* **1** having to do with learning, study, education, or teaching. **2** scholarly: *academic pursuits.* **3** theoretical rather than practical. **4** of no practical importance, e.g., because impossible or unreal. **5** *of a person* fond of intellectual pursuits. —*noun* a member of the teaching or research staff at a university or college. ▸ **academically** *adv.*

academician (ăk,əd-ə-mĭsh′ən) *noun* a member of scientific, literary, or artistic academy.

academy *noun* (*pl.* **academies**) **1** a school or college giving training in a particular subject or skill. **2** a secondary school, esp. a private school. **3** a society that encourages the study of science, literature, art, or music.

Academy Award an Oscar.

acanthus (ə-kăn′thəs) *noun* **1** a plant with prickly leaves and spiked purple or white flowers. **2** *Archit.* a stone carving of a leaf of this plant.

acc. *or* **acc** *abbrev.* accusative.

accede (ăk-sēd′) *verb intrans.* (**acceded, acceding**) (*often* **accede to** (**something**)) **1** to agree. **2** to take office, esp. to become a king or queen.

accelerate *verb intrans., trans.* (**accelerated, accelerating**) **1** to increase or cause to increase speed. **2** to make (something) happen sooner than expected. ▸ **acceleration** *noun*

accelerator *noun* **1** a pedal or lever that controls the speed of a motor. **2** a piece of apparatus designed to increase the velocity of charged atomic particles.

accent *noun* **1** the particular way in which words are pronounced by speakers who live in a particular region, belong to a particular social group, etc. **2** emphasis or stress on a particular syllable in speaking. **3** a mark put over or under a letter to show how it is pronounced. **4** emphasis or stress placed on certain notes or chords in a piece of music. —*verb trans.* (**accented, accenting**) to pronounce in a particular way or with stress on a particular syllable.

accentuate *verb trans.* (**accentuate, accentuating**) to emphasize or make more evident or prominent. ▸ **accentuation** *noun*

accept (ĭk-sĕpt′) *verb trans.* (**accepted, accepting**) **1** to agree to take (something offered). **2** to agree to (a suggestion, proposal, etc.). **3** to agree to do (a job, etc.) or take on (a responsibility, etc.). **4** to believe to be true or correct: *accept an explanation.* **5** to be willing to listen to and follow (advice, etc.). **6** to be willing to suffer or take (blame, etc.). **7** to take as valid or appropriate. **8** to allow into a group, treat as a colleague, etc. **9** to tolerate calmly: *accepted her fate.*

acceptable *adj.* **1** worth accepting. **2** welcome or pleasing; suitable. **3** good enough, but only just. ▣ ADEQUATE, AVERAGE, FAIR, O.K., PASSABLE, SATISFACTORY, TOLERABLE ▣ UNACCEPTABLE, UNSATISFACTORY. ▸ **acceptability** *noun* ▸ **acceptably** *adv.*

acceptance *noun* **1** the act of accepting something. **2** favorable or positive reception of something.

access (ăk'sĕs,) *noun* **1** a means of approaching or entering a place. **2** the right, opportunity, or ability to use, approach, meet with, or enter. **3** *Comput.* the right and opportunity to log onto a computer system and to read and edit files that are held within it. —*verb trans.* (**accessed, accessing**) to get and be able to use (information, files, etc.) on a computer.

accessible (ĭk-sĕs'ə-bəl) *adj.* **1** able to be reached easily. **2** easy to understand and enjoy or get some benefit from. ▸ **accessibility** *noun*

accession *noun* the act or process of taking up a new office or responsibility, esp. becoming a king or queen.

accessory *noun* (*pl.* **accessories**) **1** something additional to, but less important than, something else. **2** an item of dress, such as a hat, that goes with a dress, coat, etc. **3** *Law* a person who helps a lawbreaker before or after an illegal act.

access time the length of time it takes to get information out of a computer.

accident *noun* **1** an unexpected event that causes damage or harm. **2** chance.

accidental *adj.* determined or caused by an unknown and unpredictable element or factor. —*noun* a sign, such as a sharp or flat, put in front of a note in written music.

acclaim (ə-klām') *verb trans.* (**acclaimed, acclaiming**) **1** to praise with great enthusiasm. **2** to receive or welcome with noisy enthusiasm. —*noun* an expression of great approval. ▸ **acclamation** *noun*

acclimatize *verb trans., intrans.* (**acclimatized, acclimatizing**) to make or become accustomed to a new climate, environment, etc. ▸ **acclimatization** *noun*

acclivity *noun* (*pl.* **acclivities**) an upward slope. *See also* **declivity**.

accolade (ăk'ə-lād,) *noun* a sign or expression of great praise or approval.

accommodate *verb trans., intrans.* (**accommodated, accommodating**) **1** to provide (someone) with somewhere to stay. **2** to be large enough to hold. **3** to do what (someone) wants; to do (someone) a favor. **4** to adapt one's habits or plans in order to be more like, more acceptable to, or more helpful to, another. ▸ **accommodating** *adj.*

accommodation *noun* (**accommodations**) room and board.

accompaniment *noun* **1** something that happens or exists at the same time as something else, or that comes with something else. **2** music played to accompany or support a singer or another instrument.

accompanist *noun* a person who plays a musical instrument to accompany a singer.

accompany *verb trans.* (**accompanied, accompanying, accompanies**) **1** to come or go with. **2** to be done or found with. **3** to play a musical instrument to support (a singer).

accomplice (ə-kăm'pləs) *noun* a person who helps a lawbreaker commit an illegal act.

accomplish *verb trans.* (**accomplished, accomplishing**) to manage to do; to complete.

accomplished *adj.* **1** clever or skilled. **2** completed or finished.

accomplishment *noun* **1** a skill developed through practice. **2** a special or remarkable achievement. **3** the completion of something.

accord *verb intrans., trans.* (**accorded, according**) **1** to agree or be in harmony with another. **2** to grant (something) because of its being appropriate or called for: *accord guests the proper courtesies.* —*noun* agreement or consent; harmony. —**of (one's) own accord** willingly; without being told to or forced to.

accordance *noun* agreement or harmony: *in accordance with the law.*

according *adv.* **1** (**according to (someone)**) as said or told by. **2** (**according to (something)**) in agreement with. —*conj.* **1** (**according as**) precisely as. **2** if.

accordingly *adv.* **1** in an appropriate way: *acted accordingly.* **2** for that reason.

accordion *noun* a musical instrument consisting of two boxlike parts joined by a folding middle section which produces sound by forcing air over metal reeds. —*adj.* folded like the middle section of this instrument: *accordion blinds.* ▸ **accordionist** *noun*

accost (ə-kôst') *verb trans.* (**accosted, accosting**) to approach and speak to (someone), esp. in a threatening or aggressive way.

account *noun* **1** a description or report. **2** an explanation, esp. of one's behavior. **3** an arrangement by which a bank or business allows a person to have banking or credit privileges. **4** a statement of the money owed for goods or services. **5** (*usu.* **accounts**) a record of money received and spent. **6** an arrangement by which a shop allows a customer to buy goods on credit and pay for them later. **7** importance or value. —*verb trans.* (**accounted, accounting**) to consider (someone or something) to be (something): *accounted them all fools.* —**account for (something) 1** to give a reason or explanation for (it). **2** to make or give a reckoning of money spent, etc. **3** to be the prime reason or factor for (it). **on account of (something)** because of (it). **on (one's) own account 1** on (one's) own responsibility. **2** for (one's) own benefit. **take (something) into account** or **take account of (something)** to give consideration to (a problem, opinion, etc.) when making a decision or assessment.

accountable adj. **1** having to explain or defend one's actions or conduct. **2** that can be explained. ▸ **accountability** noun

accounting noun the skill, practice, or profession of preparing and keeping financial records. ▸ **accountancy** noun ▸ **accountant** noun

accouterments or **accoutrements** (ə-kōō'-ər-mənts, -kōō'trə-) pl. noun **1** equipment, esp. a soldier's equipment apart from clothing and weapons. **2** accessory things.

accredit verb trans. (**accredited, accrediting**) **1** to recognize (a school, college, or university) as having met the standards required. **2** to appoint (as an ambassador or diplomat) to a foreign country. **3** (**accredit (something) to (someone)** or (**someone**) **with (something)**) to attribute (a saying, action, etc.) to (one). ▸ **accreditation** noun.

accredited adj. **1** officially acknowledged. **2** of a belief, etc. generally accepted.

accretion (ə-krē'shən) noun **1** a gradual increase in size. **2** the process of separate things growing into one.

accrue (ə-krōō') verb intrans., trans. (**accrued, accruing**) **1** to come to the owner or recipient in addition, as a product, result, or gain. **2** to happen or accumulate. **3** to collect: accrued two weeks of vacation time. ▸ **accrual** noun.

acct. abbrev. (also **acct**) account.

acculturation noun the process of becoming more like another group in behavior, customs, etc., usu. because of living near them for a long time.

accumulate (ə-kyōō'myə-lāt,) verb trans., intrans. (**accumulated, accumulating**) **1** to collect or gather in an increasing quantity. **2** to increase in number or quantity. ▸ **accumulation** noun

accumulator noun **1** a person who gathers or collects things in quantity. **2** a part of a computer's memory used as a temporary store for the results of an operation.

accurate adj. **1** without mistakes. ▤ CORRECT, ERRORLESS, EXACT, FAULTLESS, PERFECT, RIGHT ▣ INACCURATE, INCORRECT, WRONG. **2** agreeing exactly with the truth or some standard. ▸ **accuracy** noun ▸ **accurately** adv.

accursed (ə-kərst', ə-kər'səd) adj. **1** disliked or hated. **2** having been cursed.

accusative (ə-kyōō'zət-ĭv) noun the grammatical case of a noun, etc., when it is the object of an action or the point toward which something is moving. —adj. of or in this case.

accuse verb trans. (**accused, accusing**) to charge (someone) with an offense. —**the accused** the one or ones charged with committing an offense. ▸ **accusation** noun ▸ **accuser** noun ▸ **accusing** adj. ▸ **accusingly** adv.

accustom verb trans. (**accustomed, accustoming**) to make familiar with or used to something.

accustomed adj. **1** (**accustomed to** (someone or something)) familiar with; experienced in. **2** usual; customary: the accustomed practice.

ac/dc abbrev. alternating current/direct current.

ace noun **1** Cards the card in each of the four suits with one symbol on it. **2** a person who is extremely good at something. **3** a fighter pilot who has shot down many enemy aircraft. **4** Tennis a serve that is so fast and well placed that the opposing player cannot hit the ball. —adj. excellent. —verb trans. (**aced, acing**) slang **1** to receive a grade of A on (e.g., an examination). **2** to gain the upper hand over (e.g., an opponent). —**an ace in the hole** a hidden or secret advantage, argument, etc., that will help to beat an opponent. **within an ace of (something)** very close to (it).

acerbic adj. bitter or harsh. ▸ **acerbity** noun

acetate noun **1** a salt of acetic acid. **2** a smooth shiny material made from cellulose acetate.

acetic (ə-sēt'ĭk) adj. of or like vinegar.

acetic acid a colorless liquid with a pungent odor, present in vinegar.

acetone (ăs'ə-tōn,) noun a colorless, flammable liquid with a pungent odor, used as a solvent.

acetylene (ə-sĕt'l-ēn,) noun a colorless, highly flammable gas, used in welding, etc.

ache verb intrans. (**ached, aching**) **1** to feel or be the source of a dull continuous pain. **2** to want something very much: ached for a few hours of rest. —noun a dull continuous pain. ▸ **achy** adj.

achieve verb trans., intrans. (**achieved, achieving**) **1** to bring to fruition (a goal, ambition, etc.), esp. through hard work. ▤ ACCOMPLISH, ATTAIN, GAIN, REACH, REALIZE. **2** to be successful. ▸ **achievable** adj. ▸ **achievement** noun ▸ **achiever** noun

Achilles' heel a person's weak or vulnerable point.

Achilles tendon the tendon that connects muscles in the leg to the heelbone.

achromatic adj. **1** colorless. **2** transmitting light without separating it into the colors that form it. ▸ **achromatically** adv.

acid noun **1** a chemical compound that has a sour or sharp taste, and that reacts with bases to form salts. **2** a sour substance. **3** *slang* LSD. —*adj.* **1** containing acid; sour to taste. **2** *of remarks, etc.* bitter or angry. ▸ **acidic** *adj.* ▸ **acidification** *noun* ▸ **acidify** *verb trans.* ▸ **acidity** *noun* ▸ **acidly** *adv.*

acid rain rain containing dissolved sulfur dioxide and nitrogen oxides released into the atmosphere by burning coal or oil.

acid test a decisive test.

acknowledge *verb trans.* (**acknowledged, acknowledging**) **1** to admit or accept the truth of (a fact or situation). **2** to recognize as valid or legal. **3** to report that one has received (what has been sent). **4** to express thanks for. **5** to show that one has noticed or recognized (someone), by greeting them, nodding one's head, etc. ▸ **acknowledgment** or **acknowledgement** *noun*

ACLU *abbrev.* American Civil Liberties Union.

acme *noun* the highest point of achievement, excellence, etc.

acne *noun* a skin disorder, esp. of the face, back, and chest, common in adolescence.

acolyte *noun* **1** a priest's assistant. **2** an assistant or attendant.

aconite (ăk′ə-nīt,) *noun* a plant with bluish-purple flowers and poisonous roots. Also called **monkshood, wolfsbane**.

acorn *noun* the nutlike fruit of the oak tree.

acorn squash a green winter squash with yellowish flesh, shaped like an acorn.

acoustic (ə-kōō′stĭk) *adj.* **1** relating to, producing, or operated by sound. **2** relating to acoustics. **3** relating to the sense of hearing. **4** *of a guitar, etc.* amplifying its sound by means of its body, not with an electrical amplifier. **5** *of building materials* designed to reduce noise. ▸ **acoustically** *adv.*

acoustics *noun* **1** (*sing.*) the scientific study of sound waves. **2** (*pl.*) the characteristics of a room, concert hall, etc., that determine the nature and quality of sounds heard within it.

acquaint *verb trans.* (**acquainted, acquainting**) **1** to make (one) familiar with. **2** to inform.

acquaintance *noun* **1** slight knowledge. **2** someone whom one knows slightly. ▸ **acquaintanceship** *noun*

acquainted *adj.* **1** knowing someone personally but only slightly. **2** familiar with something: *acquainted with her books.*

acquiesce (ăk,wē-ĕs′) *verb intrans.* (**acquiesced, acquiescing**) (**acquiesce in** or **to** (**something**)) to accept (something) or agree to (it) without objection. ▸ **acquiescence** *noun* ▸ **acquiescent** *adj.*

acquire *verb trans.* (**acquired, acquiring**) to get, gain, or develop, esp. through skill or effort. ▸ **acquirement** *noun*

acquired immune deficiency syndrome AIDS.

acquisition (ăk,wə-zĭsh′ən) *noun* **1** a thing obtained or acquired, esp. through effort. **2** the act of acquiring something.

acquisitive (ə-kwĭz′ət-ĭv) *adj.* very eager to obtain and possess things.

acquit *verb* (**acquitted, acquitting**) **1** *of a court or jury, etc.* to declare (an accused) to be innocent. **2** (**acquit** (**oneself**)) to conduct (oneself) in a particular way. ▸ **acquittal** *noun*

acre *noun* **1** a unit of measurement for land, equal to 4,840 sq. yd. (4,047 sq m). **2** (**acres**) a large expanse.

acreage *noun* a given number of acres, or land so measured.

acrid *adj.* **1** having a very strong, bitter taste or smell. **2** *of speech, manner, etc.* sharp or bitter. ▸ **acridity** *noun*

acrimonious *adj. of speech, etc.* bitter; accusatory. ▸ **acrimoniously** *adv.* ▸ **acrimony** *noun*

acrobat *noun* an entertainer, e.g., in a circus, who performs skillful balancing acts and other athletic tricks. ▸ **acrobatic** *adj.* ▸ **acrobatically** *adv.*

acrobatics *noun* **1** (*sing.*) the art or skill of an acrobat. **2** (*pl.*) acrobatic movements. **3** (*sing., pl.*) agile behavior of any sort.

acronym (ăk′rə-nĭm,) *noun* a word made from the first letters or syllables of other words.

acrophobia *noun* an abnormal fear of heights.

acropolis (ə-krăp′ə-ləs) *noun* the upper fortified part or citadel of an ancient Greek city.

across *prep.* **1** to, at, or on the other side of. **2** from one side of to the other. **3** so as to cross: *arms folded across her chest.* —*adv.* **1** to, at, or on the other side. **2** from one side to the other.

across-the-board *adj.* applying in all cases.

acrostic *noun* **1** a poem in which the first letters in each line form a word or proverb. **2** words arranged in a square in such a way that they read the same both horizontally and vertically. Also called **word square**.

acrylic (ə-krĭl′ĭk) *noun* **1** a synthetic material, esp. a type of fiber. **2** acrylic resin.

acrylic resin any of a large number of synthetic resins used to make artificial fibers, waxes, paints, adhesives, etc. Also called **acrylic**.

act *noun* **1** a thing done. **2** the process of doing something: *caught in the act.* **3** insincere behavior intended to make an impression. **4** a short piece of entertainment, usu. part of a series in a show; the one or ones performing it. **5** a major division of a play, opera, etc. See also **scene**. **6** a decree or law passed by a lawmaking body. —*verb intrans., trans.* (**acted, acting**) **1** to behave: *acted strangely.* **2** to do something: *need to act fast.* **3** (**act as** or **for**) to carry out the functions (of). **4** to perform in plays or films; to perform (a part or a play). **5** to exhibit feelings or qualities one does not really have: *Don't act so tragic.* —**act on** *or* **upon 1** to have an effect or influence on. **2** to follow (e.g., instructions) or do something because of (information, etc.). **act up** *colloq.* **1** *of a machine, etc.* to function erratically or to fail. **2** to behave badly. **get (one's) act together** *colloq.* to become organized.

acting *noun* the profession or art of performing in a play or film. —*adj.* serving temporarily in place of another.

actinide (ăk′tə-nīd,) *noun* any of the radioactive chemical elements with atomic numbers between 89 and 104, e.g., uranium and plutonium.

actinium *noun* (SYMBOL **Ac**) a silvery-white radioactive element.

action *noun* **1** the process of doing something: *put ideas into action.* **2** something done. **3** activity, force, or energy. **4** a movement or gesture. **5** the working part of a machine, instrument, etc. **6** a battle; fighting. **7** (**the action**) the events of a play, film, etc. **8** *colloq.* exciting activity: *go where the action is.* **9** a legal case.

actionable *adj.* giving cause for legal action.

activate *verb trans.* (**activated, activating**) **1** to start (something) working. **2** to increase the speed of or to cause (a chemical reaction). ▸ **activation** *noun*

activated charcoal a form of charcoal that is a very efficient absorber of gases, used in water filters, stove hoods, etc.

active *adj.* **1** moving, working, or doing things. **2** full of energy. **3** in operation. **4** having an effect: *active ingredients.* **5** *of verbs* in the form used when the subject of the sentence performs the action of the verb. *See also* **passive.** —*noun* **1** the active form of a verb. *Also called* **active voice.** *See also* **passive.** **2** a verb in this form. ▸ **actively** *adv.*

activist *noun* a person who is very active, esp. as a member of a political group.

activity *noun* (*pl.* **activities**) **1** the state of being active or busy. **2** (*often* **activities**) something done, esp. for pleasure; exercise, etc.

act of God *Law* an unforeseen or unpreventable event, e.g., an earthquake.

actor *noun* a performer in plays or films, esp. if professional.

actress *noun* a woman performer in plays or films, esp. if professional.

actual *adj.* **1** existing: *the actual world around us.* **2** real. ▨ INDISPUTABLE, REAL, TRUE, UNDENIABLE, UNQUESTIONABLE.

actuality *noun* (*pl.* **actualities**) **1** fact; reality. **2** (*usu.* **actualities**) an existing condition.

actually *adv.* **1** really; in fact. **2** as a matter of fact: *Actually, I think she's right.*

actuary (ăk′chə-wĕr,ē) *noun* (*pl.* **actuaries**) a person who calculates insurance risks and advises insurance companies, etc., on the premiums to be set. ▸ **actuarial** *adj.*

actuate *verb trans.* (**actuated, actuating**) **1** to cause (a mechanism, etc.) to go into action. **2** to cause (someone) to act in a characteristic way. ▸ **actuation** *noun*

acuity (ə-kyōō′ət-ē) *noun* sharpness or acuteness, e.g., of the mind or vision.

acumen (ə-kyōō′mən, ăk′yə-mən) *noun* the ability to judge things quickly and well.

acupressure (ăk′yə-prĕsh,ər) *noun* therapy by means of pressure on specific points of the body. ▸ **acupressurist** *noun*

acupuncture *noun* a traditional Chinese therapy by means of thin needles inserted at specific points beneath the skin. ▸ **acupuncturist** *noun*

acute *adj.* **1** severe; very bad. **2** *of the senses* sharp and penetrating. **3** *of mental powers, etc.* quick and accurate. **4** *of a disease* sudden and severe but usu. short-lived. **5** *of a sound* shrill. **6** *of an angle* of less than 90°. —*noun* (*also* **acute accent**) a mark placed over a vowel (e.g., é) in some languages to show pronunciation. ▸ **acutely** *adv.* ▸ **acuteness** *noun*

-acy *suffix* forming nouns denoting **1** a quality: *accuracy.* **2** a state, office, etc: *supremacy.*

A.D. *or* **AD** *abbrev.* Anno Domini (Latin), in the year of our Lord; used in giving dates since the birth of Christ. *See also* **B.C.**

ad *noun colloq.* an advertisement.

adage (ăd′ĭj) *noun* a long-used saying stating a general truth.

adagio (ə-däj′ē-ō,, -dăzh′-) *Mus.* *adv.* slowly. —*noun* (*pl.* **adagios**) a slow movement or piece of music.

adamant *adj.* absolutely determined or insistent. ▸ **adamantly** *adv.*

Adam's apple the slight lump of cartilage that projects at the front of a man's neck.

adapt *verb trans., intrans.* (**adapted, adapting**) to make or become suitable for a given situation or use. ▸ **adaptation** *noun*

adaptable *adj.* **1** *of a person* good at adjusting to new circumstances, etc. **2** *of a device, etc.* that can be adapted. ▸ **adaptability** *noun*

adapter *or* **adaptor** *noun* an electrical device used for connecting a plug of one type to a socket of another type, or for connecting several plugs to the same socket.

ADC *abbrev.* aide-de-camp.

add *verb trans., intrans.* (**added, adding**) **1** to calculate a total of (numbers or amounts), or to be able to do so: *add a column of figures.* **2 a** to unite or join (things) in order to increase the overall size. **b** to make an addition: *added to the deck.* **3** to say or write (something) further: *added a remark.* —**add up** *colloq.* to make sense: *Your explanation just doesn't add up.* **add up to** (something) to make or amount to (it).

addendum (ə-dĕn'dəm) *noun* (*pl.* **addenda**) an addition, esp. an appendix to a book.

adder *noun* **1** a venomous European and Asian snake of the viper family. **2** a nonvenomous N American snake.

addict (ăd'ĭkt) *noun* **1** someone dependent on a habit-forming substance. **2** *colloq.* a person who is very fond of an activity, etc.

addicted (ə-dĭkt'əd) *adj.* **1** dependent on a habit-forming substance: *addicted to cocaine.* **2** very fond of an activity, etc. ▸ **addiction** *noun* ▸ **addictive** *adj.*

addition *noun* **1** the combining of two or more numbers so as to obtain their sum. **2** the act or operation of adding. —**in addition** also. ▸ **additional** *adj.* ▸ **additionally** *adv.*

additive *noun* a substance that is added to something for some purpose, e.g., food coloring. —*adj.* relating to addition.

addle *verb trans., intrans.* (**addled, addling**) **1** to confuse. **2** *of an egg* to go bad.

add-on *noun* **1** something added to supplement something else. **2** a device added to a computer system in order to increase its capabilities.

address *noun* **1** the building, street, and town where a person lives or works. **2** a speech or lecture. **3** **a** a code that identifies where an item of data is stored in a computer memory. **b** a specific location in a computer memory. —*verb trans.* (**addressed, addressing**) **1** to put the name and address on (an envelope, etc.). **2** to make a speech, give a lecture, etc., to. **3** to speak to. **4** to give one's attention to (a problem, etc.). **5** to focus (oneself) on: *addressed myself to the matter of scheduling.* **6** to identify (a specific location) in a computer memory and either obtain data from it or store data in it.

addressee *noun* the one to whom a letter, etc., is addressed.

adduce *verb trans.* (**adduced, adducing**) to mention (a fact) as a supporting reason, piece of evidence, etc.

adenoidal *adj.* **1** relating to the adenoids. **2** sounding as if one has swollen adenoids.

adenoids (ăd'n-oidz,) *pl. noun* a pair of glands in the upper part of the throat.

adept (ə-dĕpt')*adj.* skilled; proficient. —*noun* (ăd'ĕpt,) an expert. ▸ **adeptly** *adv.*

adequate *adj.* **1** enough; sufficient. **2** good enough. ▸ **adequacy** *noun* ▸ **adequately** *adv.*

adhere *verb intrans.* (**adhered, adhering**) **1** to stick or remain fixed, e.g., with adhesive.

2 to be a loyal supporter. **3** to follow a plan, rule, etc., exactly. ▸ **adherence** *noun* ▸ **adherent** *noun, adj.*

adhesion *noun* **1** the process or condition of sticking together. **2** attraction between atoms or molecules of different substances. *See also* **cohesion**. **3** (*often* **adhesions**) fibrous tissue that develops and connects parts of the body that are normally separate, e.g., following surgery.

adhesive *adj.* able to make things stick together; sticky. —*noun* a substance used to bond two surfaces together.

ad hoc (ăd-hŏk', -hōk') *adj., adv.* for one particular purpose, situation, etc.

adieu (ə-dyōō') *noun* (*pl.* **adieus, adieux**) a good-bye. —*interj.* good-bye.

ad infinitum (ăd,ĭn-fə-nīt'əm) forever; without limit.

adipose tissue body tissue consisting of large cells that store fat and oil.

adj. *abbrev.* adjective.

adjacent *adj.* beside or near.

adjective *noun* a word that describes a noun or pronoun. ▸ **adjectival** *adj.*

adjoin *verb trans.* (**adjoined, adjoining**) to be next to and joined to (something). ▸ **adjoining** *adj.*

adjourn *verb trans., intrans.* (**adjourned, adjourning**) **1** to put off (a meeting, etc.) to another time. **2** to finish (a meeting, etc.), intending to continue it at another time or place. **3** to move to another place, e.g., for refreshment: *adjourn to the porch for coffee.* **4** to finish a meeting and separate. ▸ **adjournment** *noun*

adjudge *verb trans.* (**adjudged, adjudging**) to declare or judge officially. ▸ **adjudgment** *or* **adjudgement** *noun*

adjudicate (ə-jōōd'ĭ-kāt,) *verb intrans., trans.* (**adjudicated, adjudicating**) **1** to act as judge in a court, competition, etc. **2** to provide a decision on a disagreement. ▸ **adjudicator** *noun*

adjunct *noun* **1** a thing attached or added to something else but not an essential part of it. **2** a word or clause that adds information. —*adj.* being a subordinate or auxiliary faculty or staff member: *an adjunct professor.*

adjure *verb trans.* (**adjured, adjuring**) to request, beg, or command solemnly.

adjust *verb trans., intrans.* (**adjusted, adjusting**) **1** to alter (something), usu. only slightly, to make it more suitable, more accurate, etc. **2** to calculate or assess (the amount of money payable in an insurance claim, etc.). **3** (adjust to (something)) to change to fit in with (it) or become suited to (it). **4** to attain a psychological balance in one's life: *just couldn't adjust.* ▸ **adjustable** *adj.* ▸ **adjustment** *noun*

adjutant (ăj'ət-ənt) *noun* an army officer who does administrative work.

ad-lib *verb trans., intrans.* (**ad-libbed, ad-libbing**) to say (something) without preparation; to improvise (music, etc.). —*adj., of speeches, etc.* made up; improvised. —*noun* (**ad lib**) improvised words. —*adv.* (**ad lib**) spontaneously and unrehearsed.

Adm. *abbrev.* Admiral.

admin. *abbrev.* administration.

administer *verb trans., intrans.* (**administered, administering**) **1** to manage or direct (affairs, an organization, etc.). **2** to give out: *administer justice.* **3** to act as an administrator. **4** to cater: *administered to the child's every whim.*

administrate *verb trans., intrans.* (**administrated, administrating**) to manage (a company, organization, etc.). ▸ **administrative** *adj.* ▸ **administratively** *adv.* ▸ **administrator** *noun*

administration *noun* **1 a** the management of a company's business affairs. **b** managers as a group. **2** a period of government by a particular political party, etc. **3** (*often* **Administration**) **a** a president's time in office. **b** the Executive Branch of the US government.

admirable *adj.* **1** worthy of being admired. **2** very good. ▸ **admirably** *adv.*

admiral *noun* **1** a senior naval officer, esp. the commander-in-chief of a fleet. **2** a type of brightly colored butterfly.

admiralty *noun* **1** a court with jurisdiction over maritime law. **2** maritime law.

admire *verb trans.* (**admired, admiring**) to hold (someone or something) in high regard. ▣ ESTEEM, HONOR, RESPECT ▣ SCORN. ▸ **admiration** *noun* ▸ **admirer** *noun* ▸ **admiring** *adj.* ▸ **admiringly** *adv.*

admissible *adj.* acceptable or allowable, esp. as evidence in a court of law. ▸ **admissibility** *noun*

admission *noun* **1** the act of allowing in or being allowed in. **2** the cost of entry. **3** an act of admitting the truth of something.

admit *verb trans., intrans.* (**admitted, admitting**) **1** to agree to the truth of, or one's responsibility for, (something): *admitted his guilt.* **2** to allow to enter. **3** to accept as a member, participant, or patient.

admittance *noun* **1** the right or permission to enter. **2** the act of entering.

admittedly *adv.* as one must admit.

admixture *noun* **1** a thing added during mixing. **2** the mixing in of something extra.

admonish *verb trans.* (**admonished, admonishing**) **1** to warn. **2** to scold or reprimand firmly but mildly. **3** to advise or urge. ▸ **admonition** *noun.*

ad nauseam (ăd-nô'zē-əm) to the point of producing disgust; excessively.

ado (ə-dōō') *noun* (*pl.* **ados**) difficulty or trouble; fuss or bustle.

adobe (ə-dō'bē) *noun* **1** a building material made of clay and straw, dried in the sun. **2** a brick made from such material.

adolescent *adj.* **1** of, relating to, or being in the stage of development between child and adult. **2** *of behavior* silly; immature. —*noun* a young person between childhood and adulthood. ▸ **adolescence** *noun*

adopt *verb trans.* (**adopted, adopting**) **1** to become the legal parent of (a child of other parents). **2** to take up (a habit, position, policy, etc.). **3** to begin to follow (another person's idea, method, etc.). ▸ **adopted** *adj.* ▸ **adoption** *noun*

adoptive *adj.* that adopts: *adoptive parents.*

adorable *adj.* **1** very attractive. **2** worthy of being adored. ▸ **adorably** *adv.*

adore *verb trans.* (**adored, adoring**) **1** to love deeply. **2** to like very much. **3** to worship as a deity. ▸ **adoration** *noun* ▸ **adoring** *adj.* ▸ **adoringly** *adv.*

adorn *verb trans.* (**adorned, adorning**) **1** to provide with decorations. **2** to add beauty to. ▸ **adornment** *noun*

ADP *abbrev.* automatic data processing.

adrenal (ə-drēn'l) *adj.* **1** on or near the kidneys. **2** relating to the adrenal glands.

adrenal glands a pair of glands situated one above each kidney.

adrenaline (ə-drēn'l-ən) *noun* epinephrine.

adrift *adj., adv.* **1** drifting. **2** without help or guidance: *left the students adrift.* **3** *colloq.* without direction.

adroit *adj.* skillful. ▸ **adroitly** *adv.* ▸ **adroitness** *noun*

adsorb *verb trans.* (**adsorbed, adsorbing**) *of a solid or liquid* to hold (a layer of the atoms or molecules of a substance) on its surface. ▸ **adsorption** *noun*

adulate *verb trans.* (**adulated, adulating**) to praise or flatter too highly. ▸ **adulatory** *adj.* ▸ **adulation** *noun*

adult *adj.* **1** fully grown. **2** typical of or suitable for a fully grown person: *adult behavior.* **3** intended for grown people. **4** *of books, films, etc.* containing sexually explicit scenes. —*noun* a fully grown person or animal. ▸ **adulthood** *noun*

adulterate *verb trans.* (**adulterate, adulterating**) to make (something) impure by adding inferior or improper substances to it. ▸ **adulteration** *noun*

adultery *noun* sexual relations willingly undertaken between a married person and a person who is not his or her spouse. ▸ **adulterer** *noun* ▸ **adulteress** *noun* ▸ **adulterous** *adj.*

adumbrate *verb trans.* (**adumbrated, adumbrating**) **1** to foreshadow (something likely to happen in the future). **2** to throw a shadow over. ▸ **adumbration** *noun*

adv. *abbrev.* adverb.

advance *verb trans., intrans.* (**advanced, advancing**) **1** to put or move forward. **2** to go forward, often in a threatening way: *a platoon advancing on an enemy position.* **3** to make progress. **4** to help the progress of; to improve. **5** to suggest (an idea, etc.). **6** to put or do at an earlier time or date than orig. planned. **7** to make (money) available to (another), sometimes earlier than when due. —*noun* **1** a move forward; progress. **2** a payment made before the due date. **3** money lent. **4** (**advances**) overtures made to a person. —*adj.* done, made, or given beforehand. —**in advance** ahead in time, place, or development.

advanced *adj.* **1** having progressed well or developed far. **2** at a relatively high level: *an advanced text in chemistry.* **3** modern; new.

advancement *noun* **1** forward movement, esp. toward a goal. **2** promotion; improvement in status.

advantage *noun* **1** benefit; usefulness. **2** a favorable circumstance that may bring success, etc. **3** superiority over. **4** *Tennis* the point scored after deuce. —**take advantage of (someone** *or* **something) 1** to make use of (a situation, a person's good nature, etc.) so as to benefit oneself. **2** to seduce (someone). ▸ **advantaged** *adj.*

advantageous *adj.* giving help or benefit. ▸ **advantageously** *adv.*

advent *noun* **1** coming or arrival. **2** (**Advent**) the period before Christmas. **3** (**Advent**) the first or second coming of Christ.

adventitious *adj.* happening by chance.

adventure *noun* **1** an exciting and often dangerous experience. **2** the excitement of risk or danger: *a sense of adventure.*

adventurer *noun* **1** a person who is eager for personal adventure. **2** a person who enjoys taking risks in business.

adventurous *adj.* **1** bold or daring; enjoying adventure. **2** full of excitement, danger, daring activities, etc. ▸ **adventurously** *adv.*

adverb *noun* a word that adds to the meaning of a verb, adjective, or another adverb. ▸ **adverbial** *adj.*

adversary *noun* (*pl.* **adversaries**) **1** an opponent. **2** an enemy. ▸ **adversarial** *adj.*

adverse *adj.* **1** unfavorable. **2** opposing. ▸ **adversely** *adv.*

adversity *noun* (*pl.* **adversities**) **1** hardship or misfortune. **2** a disastrous event.

advert (ăd´-vərt´) *verb intrans.* (**adverted, adverting**) to refer or call attention to something: *adverted to the scandal.*

advertise *verb trans., intrans.* (**advertised, advertising**) **1** to draw attention to or describe (goods for sale, services offered, etc.) in newspapers, on television, etc., to encourage people to buy or use them. **2** to make known publicly or generally. **3** to ask for or seek through the use of the media or by public notice: *advertise for a maid.* ▸ **advertiser** *noun* ▸ **advertising** *noun*

advertisement (ăd,-vər-tīz´-mənt, ăd-vûr´-tīs-mənt) *noun* a public announcement, e.g., in a newspaper, or a television commercial, that advertises something.

advice (əd-vīs´) *noun* **1** suggestions about what should be done in a particular situation. **2** (*often* **advices**) information conveyed formally.

advisable *adj.* **1** recommended. **2** sensible; wise. ▸ **advisability** *noun*

advise (əd-vīz´) *verb trans., intrans.* (**advised, advising**) **1** to give advice to. **2** to recommend: *advised extreme caution.* **3** to inform. ▸ **adviser** *or* **advisor** *noun*

advised (əd-vīzd´) *adj.* (*esp. in compounds*) considered; judged: *ill-advised.*

advisedly (əd-vī´zəd-lē) *adv.* after careful thought; on purpose.

advisory *adj.* giving advice. —*noun* (*pl.* **advisories**) a memorandum offering cautionary advice.

advocacy *noun* argument for or active support of an idea, etc.

advocate (ăd´və-kĭt) *noun* **1** a person who argues or actively supports an idea, proposal, etc. **2** a person who works in another's behalf. **3** an attorney. —*verb trans.* (ăd´və-kāt,) (**advocated, advocating**) to recommend or support (an idea, proposal, etc.), esp. in public.

adz *or* **adze** *noun* a tool with a blade at right angles to its handle, used for shaping wood.

aegis (ē´jəs) *noun* —**under the aegis of (someone** *or* **something)** under the supervision and with the support of (an official organization, etc.).

aeon *noun same as* **eon.**

aerate *verb trans.* (**aerated, aerating**) **1** to force gas into (a liquid). **2** to put oxygen into (the blood) by breathing. ▸ **aeration** *noun*

aerial *noun* a wire or rod on a radio or television set, able to send or receive signals. —*adj.* **1** in or belonging to the air. **2** like air; ethereal. **3** in or from aircraft.

aerialist *noun* an acrobat who performs feats in the air, e.g., a trapeze artist.

aerie *or* **eyrie** (âr´ē, ĭr´ē) *noun* a bird's nest situated high in a tall tree or on a cliff.

aero- *combining form* forming words denoting **1** relating to air: *aerodynamics.* **2** relating to aircraft: *aerodrome.*

aerobatics *noun* **1** (*pl.*) dangerous and difficult movements of an airplane, such as flying upside down, etc. **2** (*sing.*) making an airplane perform such movements. ▸ **aerobatic** adj.

aerobic adj. **1** requiring oxygen to live: *aerobic organisms.* **2** relating to aerobics.

aerobics *sing. noun* an exercise system which increases the supply of oxygen in the blood and strengthens the heart and lungs.

aerodynamics *sing. noun* the scientific study of the movement of air or other gases relative to solid bodies immersed in them. ▸ **aerodynamic** adj. ▸ **aerodynamically** adv.

aerogram or **aerogramme** noun a piece of thin paper for airmail, designed to be folded and sealed without being put into an envelope. *Also called* **air letter.**

aeronautics *sing. noun* **1** the scientific study of navigation through Earth's atmosphere. **2** the design and building of aircraft. ▸ **aeronautic** or **aeronautical** adj.

aerosol noun **1** a cloud of fine particles of a solid or liquid suspended in a gas. **2** a can containing a product, e.g., paint, that can be sprayed to produce such a cloud.

aerospace noun Earth's atmosphere and the space beyond it. —adj. of or relating to the branch of technology or industry concerned with the flight of aircraft and spacecraft.

aesthete or **esthete** (ĕs′thēt,) noun a person who has or claims to have a special appreciation of art and beauty.

aesthetic or **esthetic** (ĕs-thĕt′ĭk) adj. **1** able to appreciate beauty. ▸ **aesthetically** adv.

aesthetics or **esthetics** *sing. noun* the branch of philosophy concerned with the principles of beauty, esp. in art.

aetiology noun same as **etiology.**

afar adv. far away.

AFB abbrev. air force base.

affable adj. pleasant and friendly in manner. ▸ **affability** noun ▸ **affably** adv.

affair noun **1** a concern, matter, or thing to be done. **2** an event or connected series of events. **3** a sexual relationship between two people, usu. when at least one of them is married to someone else. **4** (**affairs**) matters of importance and public interest: *current affairs.* **5** (**affairs**) private or public business matters.

affect verb trans. (**affected, affecting**) **1** to have an effect on. **2** to cause (someone) to feel strong emotions, esp. sadness or pity. **3** to pretend to feel or have. **4** to use, wear, etc. (something) in a way that is intended to attract attention. **5** of diseases to attack.

affected adj. **1** not genuine; false; pretended. **2** of a manner of behaving put on to impress people. ▸ **affectation** noun

affecting adj. causing people to feel strong emotion, e.g., sadness, pity, joy, etc.

affection noun **1** a feeling of love or strong liking. **2** (**affections**) feelings. ▸ **affectionate** adj. ▸ **affectionately** adv.

affianced (ə-fī′ənst) adj. engaged to be married.

affidavit noun a written statement, sworn to be true by the person who makes it, for use as evidence in a court of law.

affiliate verb trans., intrans. (ə-fĭl′ē-āt,) (**affiliated, affiliating**) (usu. **be affiliated with** or **to something**) to link or associate (a person or organization) with a group or larger body, or to be so linked or associated. —noun (ə-fĭl′ē-ət) a person or organization, etc., associated with a group or larger body. ▸ **affiliation** noun

affinity noun (pl. **affinities**) **1** (**affinity of** or **between** or **with** (**another**)) strong attraction or closeness. **2** similarity in appearance, structure, etc., esp. one suggesting relatedness.

affirm verb trans., intrans. (**affirmed, affirming**) **1** to state positively and firmly as a fact. **2** to uphold or confirm (an idea, belief, etc.). **3** in a court of law, to promise solemnly, without swearing a religious oath. ▸ **affirmation** noun

affirmative adj. expressing agreement; giving the answer yes. —noun an affirmative word or phrase. —interj. used to express the answer yes. ▸ **affirmatively** adv.

affirmative action any measure that considers race, sex, etc, to provide opportunities to people who either historically or actually have been denied opportunities.

affix verb trans. (ə-fĭks′) (**affixed, affixing**) to attach or fasten. —noun (ăf′ĭks,) a prefix or suffix.

afflict verb trans. (**afflicted, afflicting**) to cause (someone) physical or mental suffering. ▸ **affliction** noun

affluent adj. wealthy. —noun (**the affluent**) wealthy people. ▸ **affluence** noun

afford verb trans. (**afforded, affording**) **1 a** to have enough money, time, etc., to spend on (something). **b** to be able to do (something), or allow (something) to happen, without risk: *cannot afford to take chances.* **2** to give; to provide: *a room affording a view of the sea.* ▸ **affordable** adj.

afforestation noun the process of establishing a forest.

affray noun a fight in a public place.

affront noun an insult, one delivered in public. —verb trans. (**affronted, affronting**) **1** to give offense to, esp. in public. **2** to hurt the pride of; to embarrass.

Afghan (ăf′găn,) adj. of Afghanistan, its people, or their language. —noun **1** (also **Afghani**) a native or citizen of Afghanistan.

2 the official language of Afghanistan. 3 (*also* **Afghan hound**) a tall, thin dog with long, silky hair, orig. used for hunting.

aficionado (ə-fĭsh,ē-ə-näd′ō) *noun* (*pl.* **aficionados**) a person who has enthusiastic interest in a particular sport or pastime.

afield *adv.* to or at a distance: *far afield.*

afire *adj., adv.* on fire.

AFL *abbrev.* 1 American Federation of Labor. 2 American Football League.

aflame *adj.* 1 in flames. 2 very excited.

afloat *adj., adv.* 1 floating. 2 out of debt; financially secure.

afoot *adj., adv.* 1 on foot. 2 in preparation or in progress.

afore- *combining form* forming words denoting before; previously: *aforesaid.*

aforementioned *adj.* already mentioned. —*noun* (*sing.* or *pl.*) the one or ones already mentioned.

aforesaid *adj.* said or mentioned already.

aforethought *adj.* —**with malice afore-thought** *of a criminal act* done deliberately; planned beforehand.

a fortiori (ā,fōr,shē-ōr′ē, -fōrt,ē-) for an even better or stronger reason.

afraid *adj.* 1 feeling fear. 2 feeling polite regret: *I'm afraid we're going to be late.*

afresh *adv.* once more; another time, esp. from the beginning.

African *adj.* of Africa, its people, or their languages. —*noun* a person who is native to Africa or of African descent.

African-American *noun* an American of African ancestry. —*adj.* relating to Americans of African ancestry.

African violet a houseplant with violet, bluish-purple, pink, or white flowers.

Afrikaans (ăf,rĭ-käns′) *noun* one of the languages of South Africa, developed from Dutch.

Afrikaner (ăf,rĭ-kän′ər) *noun* a white inhabitant of S Africa whose native language is Afrikaans.

Afro *noun* (*pl.* **Afros**) a hairstyle consisting of thick curls standing out from the head.

Afro- *combining form* forming words denoting African: *Afro-Caribbean.*

Afro-American *noun* an African-American. —*adj.* relating to African-Americans.

aft *adv., adj.* at or toward the stern.

after *prep.* 1 coming later in time than. 2 following in position; behind. 3 next to and following in importance, order, etc. 4 because of; considering: *You can't expect to be promoted after that mistake.* 5 in spite of. 6 about: *asked after the grandchildren.* 7 in pursuit of. 8 *of a work of art* in the style or manner of (someone else). 9 given the same name as: *called her Mary after her aunt.* 10 past (an hour). —*adv.* later in time, behind in

place. —*conj.* after the time when: *The incident occurred after I had already driven off.* —*adj.* 1 later; following: *in after years.* 2 further toward the stern of a ship. —**after all** 1 in spite of all that has happened or has been said. 2 contrary to what is or was expected.

afterbirth *noun* the placenta, blood, etc., expelled from the uterus after the birth of a baby.

afterburner *noun* a device that increases the thrust of a jet engine by injecting fuel into the hot exhaust gases leaving the engine.

aftereffect *noun* a circumstance or event, usu. unpleasant, that is the result of something else.

afterglow *noun* 1 a glow remaining in the sky after the sun has set. 2 an impression or feeling, usu. pleasant, that remains when the experience that caused it is over.

after-hours *adj.* happening after an establishment has closed for the day.

afterlife *noun* the continued existence of one's spirit or soul after death.

aftermath *noun* circumstances that follow as a result of something else.

Originally a second crop coming after the main harvest

afternoon *noun* the period of the day between noon and evening.

aftershave *noun* a scented lotion for the face after shaving.

aftershock *noun* an earthquake, usu. of lesser magnitude, that follows a larger earthquake.

aftertaste *noun* the taste that remains in the mouth after eating or drinking.

afterthought *noun* an idea thought of after the main plan, etc., has been formed.

afterward *or* **afterwards** *adv.* later.

A.G. *abbrev.* attorney-general.

Ag *symbol Chem.* silver.

again *adv.* 1 once more. ⊟ AFRESH, ANEW, NEW. 2 back to a previous condition, situation, etc.: *get well again.* 3 in addition: *twice as much again.* 4 however; on the other hand: 5 further; besides.

against *prep.* 1 close to or leaning on; in contact with. 2 into collision with. 3 in opposition to: *against the law.* 4 in contrast to. 5 with a bad or unfavorable effect on: *His youth is against him.* 6 as a protection from; in anticipation of or preparation for. 7 toward the amount: *paid against the balance.* —**have something against (someone)** to have a reason for disliking (someone).

agape¹ *adj.* *of the mouth* gaping; open wide.

agape² (ä-gäp′ä, äg′ə-pä,) *noun* Christian spiritual love, as distinct from sexual love.

agar (äg′ər) *noun* a gelatinous substance

extracted from the dried stems of certain species of seaweed.

agate (ăg′ət) *noun* a fine-grained variety of chalcedony, used in jewelry and ornaments.

agave (ə-gäv′ē) *noun* an evergreen plant with tall flower stalks.

age *noun* **1** the length of time a person, animal, plant, or phenomenon has existed. **2** a particular stage in life. **3** the fact of being old or elderly. **4** in Earth's history, an interval of time during which specific life forms, physical conditions, etc., were dominant. **5** (*usu.* **ages**) *colloq.* a very long time: *waited ages.* —*verb intrans., trans.* (**aged, aging**) **1** to show signs of growing old **2** to grow old. **3** to mature. **4** to cause to seem older or look old. —**come of age** to become legally old enough to have an adult's rights and duties.

-age *suffix* forming nouns denoting: **1** a collection or set: *baggage*. **2** an action: *breakage*. **3** the result of an action or event: *wreckage*. **4** a condition: *bondage*. **5** the home, house, or place of: *orphanage*. **6** cost: *postage*.

aged (ājd, ā′jəd) *adj.* **1** having a particular age. **2** elderly. —*noun* (**the aged**) elderly people.

ageism *noun* the practice of treating people differently, usu. unfairly, on the grounds of age. ▸ **ageist** *noun, adj.*

ageless *adj.* never appearing to grow old.

age limit the age under or over which one may not do something.

agency *noun* (*pl.* **agencies**) **1** an office or business providing a particular service. **2** an active part played in bringing something about. **3** a government department providing a particular service. **4** the business of an agent.

agenda *noun* (*pl.* **agendas**) a list of things to be done or discussed.

agent *noun* **1** a person who represents and acts in behalf of an organization or another person, e.g., in business matters. **2** (*also* **secret agent**) a spy. **3** a substance that is used for producing a particular result. **4** a person who is the cause of something: *an agent of social change*.

agent provocateur (äzh′än‚prō-väk‚ə-tər′) (*pl.* **agents provocateurs**) a person employed to pretend sympathy with others in order to incite them to perform illegal acts, so making them open to arrest and punishment.

age-old *adj.* done or known for a very long time.

agglomerate *verb trans., intrans.*(ə-glăm′ə-rāt) (**agglomerated, agglomerating**) to make into or become an untidy, rounded mass. —*noun* (ə-glăm′ə-rət) **1** an untidy, rounded mass or collection of things. **2**

volcanic rock consisting of coarse fragments of lava embedded in ashy material. —*adj.* (ə-glăm′ə-rət) formed into a rounded mass. ▸ **agglomeration** *noun*

agglutinate *verb trans., intrans.* (**agglutinated, agglutinating**) to stick or glue together. ▸ **agglutination** *noun*.

aggrandize (ə-grăn′dīz‚) *verb trans.* (**aggrandized, aggrandizing**) **1** to increase the power, wealth, etc., of (a person, country, etc.). **2** to make (someone or something) seem greater than really is the case. ▸ **aggrandizement** *noun*

aggravate *verb trans.* (**aggravated, aggravating**) **1** to make (a bad situation, an illness, etc.) worse. **2** to annoy. ▸ **aggravating** *adj.* ▸ **aggravation** *noun*

aggregate *noun* (ăg′rə-gət) **1** a collection of separate units brought together; a total. **2** rock formed from a mixture of different minerals. —*adj.* (ăg′rə-gət‚ ăg′rə-gāt‚) combined together. —*verb trans., intrans.* (ăg′rə-gāt‚) (**aggregated, aggregating**) **1** to combine or be combined into a single unit or whole. **2** to amount to. ▸ **aggregation** *noun*

aggression *noun* **1** the act of attacking another person or country without being provoked. **2** the tendency to make unprovoked attacks. **3** hostile feelings or behavior. ▸ **aggressor** *noun*

aggressive *adj.* **1** ready or displaying readiness to attack. ◼ BELLIGERENT, COMBATIVE, CONTENTIOUS, HOSTILE, MILITANT, OFFENSIVE. **2** strong and determined; self-assertive. ▸ **aggressively** *adv.* ▸ **aggressiveness** *noun*

aggrieved *adj.* **1** angry or upset because one feels that one has been badly or unfairly treated. **2** having suffered because of someone else's illegal behavior.

aghast *adj.* filled with fear or horror.

agile *adj.* having or showing skill in performing quickly and with ease. ▸ **agility** *noun*

agitate *verb trans., intrans.* (**agitated, agitating**) **1** to excite and trouble (a person). **2** to stir up public opinion with respect to an issue: *agitated for an increase in taxes*. **3** to shake or stir (a liquid). ▸ **agitated** *adj.* ▸ **agitation** *noun* ▸ **agitator** *noun*

aglow *adj., adv.* shining with color or warmth.

agnostic *noun* a person who believes that nothing can be known about the existence of God. —*adj.* being an agnostic. ▸ **agnosticism** *noun*

ago *adv.* in the past; earlier.

agog *adj.* very interested and excited. —*adv.* in an eager, interested manner.

agonize *verb intrans., trans.* (**agonized, agonizing**) **1** to worry intensely about or suffer great anxiety about something. **2** to cause great anxiety or suffering to. ▶ **agonizing** *adj.*▶ **agonizingly** *adv.*

agony *noun* (*pl.* **agonies**) severe pain.

agoraphobia (ăg,ə-rə-fō'bē-ə) *noun* an abnormal fear of open and public places. ▶ **agoraphobic** *noun, adj.*

agrarian *adj.* of or concerning land and its uses, esp. farming.

agree *verb intrans.* (**agreed, agreeing**) **1** to be of the same opinion as someone else about something. **2** to say yes to a suggestion, request, or instruction. **3** to reach a joint decision about something after discussion. **4** to reach agreement about (something). **5** *usu.* of food to be suitable or good for (one): *Milk doesn't agree with me.* **6** to be consistent or compatible with something. **7** *Gram.* to have the same number, person, gender, or case.

agreeable *adj.* **1** *of things* pleasant. **2** *of people* friendly. **3** *of people* willing to accept a suggestion, etc. ▶ **agreeably** *adv.*

agreement *noun* **1** a contract or promise. **2** a joint decision made after discussion. **3** the state of holding the same opinion. **4** *Gram.* the state of having the same number, person, gender, or case.

agribusiness *noun* the production, processing, and distribution of agricultural products.

agriculture *noun* the cultivation of the land in order to grow crops or raise animal livestock as a source of food or other useful products. ▶ **agricultural** *adj.* ▶ **agriculturalist** *or* **agriculturist** *noun*

agro- *or* **agri-** *combining form* forming words denoting agricultural: *agrochemical.*

agrochemical *or* **agrichemical** *noun* a chemical used to improve the quality of farm products, e.g., a fertilizer. —*adj.* relating to the use of such chemical compounds.

agroindustry *noun* an industry embracing all the aspects of agricultural production and distribution.

agronomy *noun* the scientific study of the cultivation of crops and soil management.

aground *adj., adv.,* of ships stuck on the bottom of the sea or on rocks.

ague (ā'gyōō) *noun* **1** *old use* malaria. **2** an attack of shivering.

ah *interj.* used to express surprise, sympathy, admiration, pleasure, etc.

aha *interj.* used to express pleasure, satisfaction, triumph, or surprise.

ahead *adv.* **1** at, to, or in the front; forward. **2** for the future: *Plan ahead.* **3** at a later time: *move the deadline ahead by a week.* **4** in a position superior to others. —**get ahead** to make progress.

ahem *interj.* used to gain people's attention or express doubt or disapproval.

-aholic *or* **-oholic** *combining form* forming words denoting addicted to: *workaholic.*

ahoy *interj.* used to attract the attention of or greet another ship.

AI *abbrev.* **1** artificial insemination. **2** artificial intelligence.

aid *noun* **1** help. **2** help or support in the form of money, supplies, or services. **3 a** a person who helps do something. **b** a device that helps: *a hearing aid.* —*verb trans.* (**aided, aiding**) **1** to help or support (someone). **2** to help (something) happen; to promote.

aide *noun* **1** an aide-de-camp. **2** a helper.

aide-de-camp (ăd,dī-kămp') *noun* (*pl.* **aides-de-camp**) an officer in the armed forces who acts as assistant to a senior officer.

AIDS *noun* a severe disorder triggered by the HIV virus, causing the affected person to become very susceptible to infections and cancers. *Also called* **acquired immune deficiency syndrome.**

aikido (ī-kēd'ō) *noun* a Japanese form of self-defense.

ail *verb intrans., trans.* (**ailed, ailing**) **1** to be ill and weak. **2** to cause pain or trouble to: *What ails you today?*

aileron *noun* a hinged flap on the rear edge of each wing of an airplane, used to control roll.

ailment *noun* an illness, esp. a minor one.

aim *verb trans., intrans.* (**aimed, aiming**) **1** to turn or point (something) in a particular direction. **2** to plan, intend, or try to do something. —*noun* **1** something a person, etc., intends to do. **2** the ability to hit a target: *good aim.* —**take aim** to point a weapon at a target.

aimless *adj.* lacking purpose. ▶ **aimlessly** *adv.*

ain't *contr. nonstand.* **1** am not; is not; are not. **2** has not; have not.

> *Usage:* The use of *ain't* is widely regarded as a sign of illiteracy, notwithstanding its occurrence in set, often jocular, phrases like *Say it ain't so.*

air *noun* **1** the mixture of gases that forms Earth's atmosphere. **2** the space around Earth. **3** appearance or manner. **4** (**airs**) behavior intended to impress others: *put on airs.* **5** a tune. —*verb trans., intrans.* (**aired, airing**) **1** to hang up (laundry) to dry it or to remove smells. **2** to let fresh air into (a room, etc.). **3** to make (one's thoughts, opinions, etc.) known. **4** to broadcast or be broadcast on radio or television. —**clear the air** to lessen or remove misunderstanding or disagreement by speaking openly and honestly. **into thin air** mysteriously; without trace.

air bag *or* **airbag** a bag that inflates automatically if a vehicle is involved in a collision, preventing injury to the driver or passenger.

air base a center from which military aircraft operate.

airborne adj. 1 of aircraft flying in the air, having just taken off. 2 transported by air.

air brake a mechanism using the pressure of compressed air on a piston to stop or slow down a moving part.

airbrush noun an instrument for painting that uses compressed air to form a spray. —verb trans. (**airbrushed, airbrushing**) to paint (something) using an airbrush.

air conditioning the device or system used to control the temperature, dryness, or humidity of the air in a building, room, etc. ▸ **air-condition** verb trans. ▸ **air conditioner** noun

aircraft noun (pl. **aircraft**) a machine or device, e.g., airplane, that is designed for traveling through the air.

aircraft carrier a large naval warship with a flat deck, serving as a base for military aircraft.

aircrew noun the people who are responsible for flying an aircraft and looking after the passengers.

air-drop noun the delivery of supplies, etc., by air. —verb trans. (**air-dropped, air-dropping**) to deliver by aircraft.

airfield noun a small airport, usu. for private aircraft.

airfoil noun an aircraft structure, e.g., a wing, rudder, or propeller blade, designed to assist and control lift, direction, etc.

air force the branch of a country's defense forces that uses aircraft in combat.

air gun a gun that uses air under pressure to fire small pellets.

airhead noun slang a stupid or vague person.

airless adj. lacking fresh air; stuffy.

air letter an aerogram.

airlift noun transportation by aircraft when other routes are blocked. —verb trans. (**airlifted, airlifting**) to transport by aircraft.

airline noun a company that provides regular air transport service for passengers or cargo.

airliner noun a large passenger airplane.

airlock noun 1 a bubble of air that obstructs the flow of liquid through a pipe. 2 an airtight chamber that allows passage between two areas with different air pressures.

airmail noun the system of carrying mail by aircraft, or the mail so carried.

airman noun 1 a rank in the air force, or someone having this rank. 2 a pilot or member of the crew of an airplane.

air mile a unit of distance equal to one international nautical mile, or 6,076.115 ft., in air travel.

airplane noun a powered machine that is

supported in flight by fixed wings.

air pocket an area of reduced air pressure or a downward current that can cause an aircraft to suddenly lose height.

airport noun a place where aircraft arrive and depart, with facilities for passengers, cargo, etc.

air raid an attack by aircraft.

air rifle a rifle fired by air under pressure.

airship noun a power-driven aircraft that is lighter than air, consisting of a streamlined hull containing helium, with engines and cabins suspended from it. Also called **dirigible** or **blimp**.

airsick adj. sick because of the motion of an aircraft. ▸ **airsickness** noun

airspace noun the part of the sky directly above a country, considered part of that country.

airstrip noun a strip of ground where aircraft can land and take off but which has no facilities.

airtight adj. 1 of a container, etc. not allowing the passage of air. 2 of an argument, etc. completely sound and valid.

airtime noun time given to an item or program on television or radio.

air-to-air adj., of a weapon launched from and aimed at rockets or aircraft in flight.

airwaves pl. noun the radio waves used by radio and television stations for their broadcasts.

airway noun 1 a self-propelled covered walkway for air passengers. 2 a route regularly flown by aircraft.

airworthy adj., of aircraft in a condition to fly safely. ▸ **airworthiness** noun

airy adj. (**airier, airiest**) 1 having plenty of fresh, cool air. 2 thinking about or dealing with something in a superficial or flippant manner. 3 lively; lighthearted. ▸ **airily** adv. ▸ **airiness** noun

aisle noun a passage between rows of seats, e.g., in a church or theater.

ajar adj., adv. partly open.

a.k.a. abbrev. also known as.

akimbo adj., adv. with hand on hip and elbow bent outward.

> From an Old Norse term meaning 'bowed' or 'curved'

akin adj. 1 similar; of the same kind. 2 related by blood.

Al symbol Chem. aluminum.

-al suffix 1 forming adjectives from nouns: parental. 2 forming nouns denoting an action or occurrence: arrival.

alabaster noun a type of white stone used for ornaments, etc. —adj. of or like alabaster.

à la carte of a meal in a restaurant with each dish priced and ordered separately.

alacrity *noun* quick and cheerful enthusiasm.

à la mode 1 fashionable. **2** served with ice cream.

alarm *noun* **1** sudden fear. **2** a noise that warns of danger, or a device producing such a noise. **3** a bell, etc., that sounds to waken a person from sleep. **4** an alarm clock. —*verb trans.* (**alarmed, alarming**) **1** to frighten. **2** to warn of danger. ▸ **alarming** *adj.*

alarm clock a clock that can be set to make a noise to wake someone up.

alarmist *noun* a person who feels or spreads unnecessary alarm. —*adj.* causing unnecessary alarm.

alas *interj.* used to express grief, sadness, or dismay.

alb *noun* a long, white garment reaching to the feet, worn by some Christian priests.

Albanian *noun* **1** a native or citizen of Albania. **2** the official language of Albania. —*adj.* of Albania, its people, or their language.

albatross *noun* a large seabird having long narrow wings and white plumage.

albeit *conj.* even if; although.

albino *noun* (*pl.* **albinos**) an animal or human being having an abnormal lack of pigmentation in the hair, skin, and eyes. ▸ **albinism** *noun*

album *noun* **1** a book with blank pages for holding photographs, stamps, etc. **2** a long-playing record.

albumen *noun* the white of an egg.

albumin *noun* a protein found in egg white, milk, blood serum, etc.

alchemy *noun* the forerunner of modern chemistry, which centered mainly . on attempts to convert metals into gold. ▸ **alchemist** *noun*

alcohol *noun* **1** an organic chemical compound, e.g., ethanol, methanol, etc., used in solvents and fuels and in antiseptics. **2** ethanol. **3** a drink containing ethanol, e.g., wine, beer, spirits.

alcoholic *adj.* of, containing, or caused by alcohol. —*noun* a person who is addicted to alcoholic drinks. ▸ **alcoholism** *noun*

alcove *noun* a recess in the wall of a room or garden.

al dente (ăl-dĕn′tā) of pasta and vegetables cooked so as to remain firm when bitten.

alder *noun* a tree with catkins and toothed leaves which grows in damp areas.

alderman *noun* a member of the governing body of a city in the USA and Canada.

ale *noun* a light-colored beer flavored with hops.

aleatory (ā′lē-ə-tôr,ē) *adj.* depending on chance.

alert *adj.* **1** thinking and acting quickly. **2** (**alert to** (**something**)) watchful and aware of a danger, etc. —*noun* **1** a warning of danger.

2 the period of time covered by such a warning. —*verb trans.* (**alerted, alerting**) to warn or make aware of. —**on the alert** watchful. ▸ **alertly** *adv.* ▸ **alertness** *noun*

Aleut (ăl,ē-ōōt′) *noun* (*pl.* **Aleut, Aleuts**) **1** a member of a people inhabiting the Aleutian Islands and part of Alaska. **2** the language of this people. —*adj.* (**also Aleutian**) of the Aleut or their language.

alfalfa *noun* a plant of the pea family, an important forage crop.

alfresco *adj., adv.* in the open air.

alga *noun* (*pl.* **algae**) (*usu.* **algae**) a plant that grows in water or on moist ground.

algebra *noun* the branch of mathematics that uses letters and symbols to represent variable quantities and numbers. ▸ **algebraic** *adj.* ▸ **algebraically** *adv.*

-algia *combining form* forming words denoting pain in a part of the body: *neuralgia.*

ALGOL (ăl′gôl,) or **Algol** *noun* a computer programming language.

Algonquian (ăl-gäng′kē-ən) or **Algonkian** *adj.* denoting a family of over 30 American Indian languages. —*noun* the languages forming this family.

algorithm *noun* **1** a procedure involving a series of steps that is used to solve a problem. **2** the sequence of operations that form the basis of a computer program.

alias *noun* a false or assumed name. —*adv.* also known as: *John Smith, alias Mr. X.*

alibi *noun* **1** a plea of being elsewhere when a crime was committed. **2** *colloq.* an excuse.

alien *noun* **1** a foreign-born resident of a country who has not been naturalized. **2** an inhabitant of another planet. —*adj.* **1** foreign. **2** (**alien to** (**something** *or* **someone**)) not in keeping with (the norm); unfamiliar to (someone).

alienable *adj.* of property that can be transferred to another owner.

alienate *verb trans.* (**alienated, alienating**) **1** to make (someone) feel unwelcome or isolated. **2** to make (someone) feel estranged or hostile. **3** *Law* to transfer ownership of (property) to another party. ▸ **alienation** *noun*

alight¹ *adj.* **1** on fire. **2** showing excitement: *a face alight with wonder.*

alight² *verb intrans.* (**alighted** or **alit, alighting**) **1** to get down from or out of a vehicle. **2** to settle or land on an object.

align *verb trans., intrans.* (**aligned, aligning**) **1** to put in a straight line or bring into line. **2** to bring into agreement with others, or with a political belief, cause, etc. ▸ **alignment** *noun*

alike *adj.* having the same or almost the same characteristics. —*adv.* in a similar manner.

alimentary *adj.* relating to digestion, or to food, diet, and nutrition.

alimentary canal the tubular organ along which food passes, extending from the mouth to the anus.

alimony *noun* money for support paid by a man to his wife or by a woman to her husband when they are legally separated or divorced.

alive *adj.* **1** living; in existence. **2** lively; active. **3** (**alive to** (something)) aware of (it); responsive to (it). **4** (**alive with** (something)) full of (it); abounding in (it).

alkali *noun* a chemical compound that turns red litmus paper blue, and neutralizes acids to form salts and water. ▸ **alkaline** *adj.* ▸ **alkalinity** *noun*

all *adj.* **1** being the whole amount, number, or extent of; every. **2** being the greatest possible: *run with all speed.* **3** being any whatever: *beyond all doubt.* —*noun* one's whole strength, resources, etc. —*pron.* **1** the entire amount; the total number or quantity.**2** everyone: *freedom of speech for all.* —*adv.* **1** entirely; quite. **2** very: *went all teary-eyed.* **3** *in scores in games* on each side: *12 all.* —**all in** *colloq.* exhausted. **all in all** considering everything. **all that** *colloq.* to the expected extent or degree: *I'm not all that tired.* **at all 1** in any way: *unable to speak at all.* **2** to any extent.

Allah (ālʹə, ä-läʹ) *noun* in Islam, God.

all-American *adj.* typically American in quality, appearance, etc.

all-around *adj.* **1** having many skills. **2** including everything or everyone: *an all-around education.*

allay *verb trans.* (**allayed, allaying**) to make (pain, fear, suspicion, etc.) less intense.

all clear a signal or statement that a threat of danger is over.

allegation *noun* an unsupported statement or assertion, esp. if unfavorable.

allege *verb trans.* (**alleged, alleging**) to claim or declare to be the case, usu. without proof. ▸ **alleged** *adj.* ▸ **allegedly** *adv.*

allegiance *noun* commitment or duty to be loyal to a government, sovereign, etc.

allegory *noun* (*pl.* **allegories**) a story, play, poem, picture, etc., in which the characters represent moral or spiritual ideas or messages. ▸ **allegorical** *adj.*

allegro *Mus. adj., adv.* in a quick, lively manner. —*noun* (*pl.* **allegros**) a piece of music to be played in this way.

alleluia (ăl,ə-lōōʹyə, ăl,ä-) *or* **hallelujah** *interj.* praise the Lord.

allergen (ălʹər-jən) *noun* a substance that induces an allergic reaction in a person.

allergy *noun* (*pl.* **allergies**) **1** a reaction of the body to certain substances, causing symptoms such as asthma, hay fever, etc. **2** *colloq.* a dislike. ▸ **allergic** *adj.*

alleviate *verb trans.* (**alleviated, alleviating**) to make (pain, a problem, suffering, etc.) less severe. ▸ **alleviation** *noun*

alley *noun* (*pl.* **alleys**) **1** a narrow passage behind or between buildings. **2** a long, narrow channel used for bowling or skittles.

alliance *noun* **1** the state of being allied. **2** an agreement or treaty by which people, countries, etc., ally themselves.

allied *adj.* **1** joined by political agreement or treaty. **2** (**Allied**) of or relating to the USA and its allies in World Wars I and II. **3** similar; related.

alligator *noun* a large reptile similar to a crocodile.

alliteration *noun* the repetition of the same sound at the beginning of each word or each stressed word in a phrase. ▸ **alliterative** *adj.*

allocate *verb trans.* (**allocated, allocating**) to give, set apart, or assign (something) to someone or for a particular purpose. ▸ **allocation** *noun*

allot *verb trans.* (**allotted, allotting**) to give to (each of a group) a share of or place in (something). ▸ **allotment** *noun*

all-out *adj.* using all possible resources or means.

allow *verb trans., intrans.* (**allowed, allowing**) **1** to permit. **2** (**allow for** (something)) to take (it) into consideration. **3** to provide: *allow money for travel.* **4** to admit or agree to (a point, claim, etc.). **5** (**allow of**) to permit the existence of a possibility. ▸ **allowable** *adj.*

allowance *noun* **1** a fixed sum of money or amount given regularly. **2** something allowed. —**make allowances for** (something) to take (it) into consideration. **make allowances for** (someone) to judge another less severely because of the circumstances applying to them.

alloy *noun* a material consisting of two or more metals or a metal and a non-metal. —*verb trans.* (**alloyed, alloying**) to add (one metal or alloy) to another.

all right 1 unhurt; safe: *Are you all right?* **2** adequate; satisfactory. **3** satisfactorily; properly. **4** *colloq.* used as an intensive: *It's broken, all right.* **5** used to express agreement or approval.

all-time *adj. colloq.* best to date; unsurpassed: *an all-time diving record.*

allude *verb intrans.* (**alluded, alluding**) (**allude to** (something)) to speak of (it) indirectly or mention (it) in passing.

allure *noun* attractiveness, appeal, or charm. —*verb trans., intrans.* (**allured, alluring**) to attract or be attractive. ▸ **alluring** *adj.* ▸ **alluringly** *adv.*

allusion *noun* an indirect reference. ▸ **allusive** *adj.*

alluvium *noun* (*pl.* **alluvia**) fine particles of silt, clay, mud, and sand that are carried and deposited by rivers. ▸ **alluvial** *adj.*

ally *noun* (*pl.* **allies**) a country or person, etc., that has formally agreed to help and support another. —*verb trans., intrans.* (**allied, allying, allies**) to align oneself or be aligned politically or militarily with another, esp. by a formal agreement.

alma mater (ăl͵mə-mät'ər) the school, college, or university from which one graduated.

almanac *noun* a book, published yearly, with a calendar, information about the moon and stars, public holidays, etc., or one that provides information on a particular field.

almighty *adj.* **1** having complete power. **2** *colloq.* a very great. **b** all important: *the almighty dollar*. **3** (**the Almighty**) God.

almond *noun* **1** a tree widely grown for its pink blossom and oval edible nut. **2** the nutlike kernel of the fruit of this tree.

almost *adv.* nearly but not quite.

alms *pl. noun* donations of money, food, etc., to the poor.

almshouse *noun* a house for the poor, paid for by charity.

aloe *noun* **1** a plant with fleshy leaves and tubelike flowers. **2** (*usu.* **bitter aloes**) (*sing.*) a laxative made from the leaves of this plant.

aloe vera a species of aloe, the juice of whose leaves is supposed to have healing powers and is used in cosmetics.

aloft *adv.* **1** in the air; overhead. **2** *Naut.* in a ship's rigging.

aloha *interj.* used as a greeting or a farewell.

alone *adj., adv.* without anyone else; apart from others. —**go it alone** *colloq.* to act on one's own, without help.

along *adv.* **1** in some direction: *saw him walking along.* **2** in company with others. **3** into a more advanced state: *coming along nicely.* —*prep.* beside or over all or part of the length of. —**along with** in addition to.

alongside *prep.* close to the side of. —*adv.* to or at the side.

aloof *adj.* unfriendly and distant. —*adv.* away; apart. ▸ **aloofness** *noun*

alopecia (ăl͵ə-pē'shə) *noun* hair loss.

aloud *adv.* loud enough to be heard.

alp *noun* **1** a very high mountain. **2** (**the Alps**) a European mountain range.

alpaca *noun* **1** a hoofed mammal closely related to the llama. **2** the wool or cloth made from this animal's hair.

alpha *noun* the first letter of the Greek alphabet (A, α).

alphabet *noun* the set of letters used in writing and printing a language. ▸ **alphabetical** *adj.* ▸ **alphabetically** *adv.*

alphabetize *verb trans.* (**alphabetized, alphabetizing**) to arrange or list alphabetically.

alphanumeric *or* **alphanumerical** *adj.* **1** *Comput.* denoting characters, codes, or data that consist of letters and numerals. **2** *of a machine* using instructions that consist of letters and numbers.

alpha particle a positively charged particle.

alpine *adj.* **1** of or relating to alps. **2** (**Alpine**) of the Alps. —*noun* a plant growing in high mountain areas.

already *adv.* **1** before the present time or the time in question. **2** so soon or so early: *was already reading at the age of four.*

alright *adv. nonstand.* all right.

also *adv.* in addition; too; besides.

also-ran *noun* **1** a horse, dog, person, etc., not finishing in one of the top three places in a race. **2** an unimportant person.

altar *noun* **1** a special table at the front of a Christian church, near which the priest stands. **2** a table on which sacrifices are made to a god.

altarpiece *noun* a religious picture or carving placed above and behind an altar.

alter *verb trans., intrans.* (**altered, altering**) to make or become different. ▸ **alteration** *noun*

altercation *noun* a heated argument.

alter ego (*pl.* **alter egos**) **1** a person's second or alternative character. **2** a close and trusted friend.

alternate *adj.* (ôl'tər-nət) **1** arranged or coming one after the other by turns. **2** (*with plural nouns*) every other; one out of two: *alternate Mondays.* —*verb intrans., trans.* (ôl'tər-nāt͵) (**alternated, alternating**) **1** *of two things* to happen or cause to happen in successive turns. **2** (**alternate between** (**two things**)) to go back and forth from one thing to another. —*noun* (ôl'tər-nət) a person who substitutes for another. ▸ **alternately** *adv.* ▸ **alternation** *noun*

alternating current (ABBREV. **ac**) an electric current that reverses its direction of flow with a constant frequency. *See also* **direct current**.

alternative *adj.* **1** permitting or making a need for a choice between two or more possibilities. **2** *of a lifestyle, etc.* different from the established norm, esp. in being less conventional. —*noun* **1** the possibility of choice between two or more things. **2** any one of two or more choices or possibilities. ▸ **alternatively** *adv.*

alternative energy energy derived from sources other than nuclear power or the burning of fossil fuels such as coal, etc.

alternative medicine procedures for the treatment of disease other than those practiced in orthodox medicine.

alternator *noun* a generator that produces alternating current.

although *conj.* in spite of the fact that.

altimeter *noun* an instrument used in aircraft for measuring height above sea or ground level.

altitude *noun* 1 height, esp. above sea level. 2 *Astron.* the angular distance between a celestial body and the horizon. *See also* **azimuth.**

alto *noun* (*pl.* **altos**) 1 the lowest female singing voice. 2 the highest adult male singing voice; a countertenor. 3 a singer with voice in these ranges. 4 a part or piece of music written for a voice or instrument at this pitch. —*adj.* of a musical instrument, etc. having this pitch.

An alternative term for the female *alto* voice is **contralto**

altogether *adv.* 1 completely. 2 on the whole. 3 taking everything into consideration.

altruism *noun* an unselfish concern for the welfare of others. ▸ **altruist** *noun* ▸ **altruistic** *adj.* ▸ **altruistically** *adv.*

alum *noun* a white crystalline compound that is used in dyeing, tanning, etc.

alumina *noun Chem.* aluminum oxide.

aluminum *noun* (SYMBOL Al) a silvery-white light metallic element that is used in alloys for aircraft construction, drink cans, etc.

alumna *noun* (*pl.* **alumnae**) a female former student of a school, college, or university.

alumnus *noun* (*pl.* **alumni**) a male former student of a school, college, or university.

always *adv.* 1 at all times. 2 continually. 3 in any case; if necessary: *You can always stay.*

Alzheimer's disease a disease in which degeneration of the brain cells results in confusion, gradual loss of memory, and impairment of other mental functions.

AM *abbrev.* 1 amplitude modulation. 2 *artium magister* (Latin), Master of Arts.

am *see* be.

a.m. *abbrev. ante meridiem* (Latin), before midday; in the morning.

amalgam *noun* 1 a mixture or blend. 2 an alloy of mercury with, e.g., silver or tin, used in dentistry to fill holes in teeth.

amalgamate *verb trans., intrans.* (**amalgamated, amalgamating**) to join together or unite to form a single unit, organization, etc. ▸ **amalgamation** *noun*

amanuensis (ə-măn̩,yə-wĕn′sĭs) *noun* (*pl.* **amanuenses** -sēz) a literary assistant or secretary.

amaryllis *noun* a plant with large trumpet-shaped red, pink, or white flowers.

amass *verb trans.* (**amassed, amassing**) to gather or collect (money, possessions, knowledge, etc.) in great quantity.

amateur *noun* 1 a person who takes part in a sport, activity, etc., as a hobby and without being paid for it. 2 a person who is rather unskilled in an activity, etc. —*adj.* of, relating to, or done by amateurs as opposed to professionals. ▸ **amateurish** *adj.* ▸ **amateurishly** *adv.* ▸ **amateurism** *noun*

amatory *adj.* of or showing sexual love.

amaze *verb trans.* (**amazed, amazing**) to impress greatly with something unusual or unexpected. ▸ **amazement** *noun* ▸ **amazing** *adj.* ▸ **amazingly** *adv.*

Amazon (ăm′ə-zăn̩) *noun* 1 *Greek Mythol.* a member of a nation of women warriors from Scythia. 2 (**amazon**) an immensely strong woman.

Amazonian *adj.* 1 relating to or resembling an Amazon. 2 relating to or in the region of the Amazon River.

ambassador *noun* 1 a diplomat of the highest rank appointed by a government to represent it in other countries. 2 an unofficial representative, e.g., of good will. ▸ **ambassadorial** *adj.* ▸ **ambassadorship** *noun*

amber *noun* a transparent yellow or reddish fossilized resin. —*adj.* relating to this substance or to its color.

ambergris *noun* a pale gray waxy substance produced in the intestines of sperm whales, formerly widely used in perfumery.

ambiance or **ambience** *noun* surroundings or atmosphere.

ambidextrous *adj.* able to use both hands equally well.

ambient *adj.* of air etc. surrounding one.

ambiguous *adj.* 1 having more than one possible meaning. 2 uncertain or doubtful. ▸ **ambiguity** *noun* ▸ **ambiguously** *adv.*

ambit *noun* range, extent, or bounds.

ambition *noun* 1 a strong desire for success, fame, or power. 2 a thing one desires to do or achieve. ▸ **ambitious** *adj.* ▸ **ambitiously** *adv.*

ambivalence *noun* the state of holding two opposite views or feelings. ▸ **ambivalent** *adj.* ▸ **ambivalently** *adv.*

amble *verb intrans.* (**ambled, ambling**) to walk without hurrying; to stroll. —*noun* a leisurely walk.

ambrosia *noun* 1 a *Greek Mythol.* the food of the gods. b a dessert of orange slices and flaked coconut. 2 something with a delicious taste or smell.

ambulance *noun* a vehicle specially equipped for carrying sick or injured people to the hospital.

ambush *noun* 1 the act of lying in wait to attack someone by surprise. 2 an attack made in this way. 3 the place of concealment from which the attack is made. —*verb trans.*

(ambushed, ambushing) to lie in wait for or attack (someone) in this way.

ameliorate *verb trans., intrans.* (**ameliorated, ameliorating**) to make or become better. ▶ **amelioration** *noun*

amen (ā-měn´, ä-) *interj.*, *said at the end of a prayer or to express agreement* so be it.

amenable *adj.* 1 ready to accept advice or guidance. 2 legally responsible.

amend *verb trans.* (**amended, amending**) to correct, improve, or make minor changes to (a book, document, etc.). *See also* **emend**. —**make amends for (something)** to make up for or compensate for an injury, insult, etc.

amendment *noun* 1 a correction, improvement, or alteration. 2 the formal revision, e.g., of a constitution, and a statement of that change.

amenity *noun* (*pl.* **amenities**) 1 something that makes life more comfortable and pleasant. 2 pleasantness of situation. 3 (**amenities**) social pleasantries. 4 a public facility.

Amerasian (ăm,ə-rā´zhən) *noun* a person of American and Asian descent. —*adj.* of or relating to, or being, such a person.

American (ə-měr´ĭ-kən, -măr´-) *adj.* of the United States of America or the American continent, the people who live or were born there, and the languages they speak. —*noun* a person born or living in the United States of America or on the American continent.

American eagle the bald eagle.

American Indian a Native American.

Americanism *noun* a word, phrase, custom, etc., that is characteristic of Americans.

Americanize *verb trans., intrans.* (**Americanized, Americanizing**) 1 to incorporate into American culture, or to be so incorporated. 2 to make or become more American in style. ▶ **Americanization** *noun*

American plan a system by which a hotel guest pays a fixed price for room and meals.

Amerindian (ăm,ə-rĭn´dē-ən) *adj.* 1 Native American. 2 denoting a family of languages used by Native Americans in N, Central, and S America. —*noun* 1 a Native American. 2 the languages forming the Amerindian family.

amethyst *noun* 1 a purple variety of quartz, used as a gemstone. 2 the color of an amethyst.—*adj.* of the color of an amethyst.

Amex (ăm´ĕks,) *abbrev.* American Stock Exchange.

amiable *adj.* friendly, pleasant, and good-tempered; likeable. ▶ **amiability** *noun* ▶ **amiably** *adv.*

amicable *adj.* friendly. ▶ **amicability** *noun* ▶ **amicably** *adv.*

amid *or* **amidst** *prep.* in the middle of; among.

amide *noun* an organic chemical compound formed from ammonia.

amidships *or* **midships** *adv.* in, into, or near the middle of a ship.

amine *noun* an organic chemical compound formed from ammonia, produced by decomposing organic matter.

amino acid any of a group of organic compounds that form the individual subunits of proteins.

amiss *adj.* wrong; out of order. —*adv.* wrongly. —**take (something) amiss** to be upset or offended by (it).

amity *noun* peaceful relationship; friendship.

ammeter *noun* an instrument used to measure electric current, usu. in amperes.

ammo *noun colloq.* ammunition.

ammonia *noun* 1 a colorless, pungent gas, used in the manufacture of fertilizers and explosives. 2 a solution of ammonia in water, used for bleaching and cleaning.

ammunition *noun* 1 bullets, shells, bombs, etc., made to be fired from a weapon. 2 facts, etc., that can be used against someone in an argument.

amnesia *noun* loss or impairment of memory. ▶ **amnesiac** *noun* ▶ **amnesic** *adj.*

amnesty *noun* (*pl.* **amnesties**) 1 a general pardon, esp. for people convicted or accused of political crimes. 2 a period of time during which criminals may admit to crimes, hand in weapons, etc., with the promise of a pardon.

amniocentesis *noun* the withdrawing through a hollow needle of a sample of amniotic fluid for analysis.

amniotic fluid the clear fluid that surrounds and protects the fetus in the womb.

amoeba (ə-mē´bə) *noun* (*pl.* **amoebas, amoebae**) a microscopic animal which has no fixed shape, found in water or damp soil.

amok *adv. same as* **amuck**.

among *or* **amongst** *prep.* 1 in the middle of: *among friends.* 2 between: *divide it among them.* 3 in the group or number of: *among his best plays.* 4 with one another: *decide among yourselves.*

amoral *adj.* having no moral principles. *See also* **immoral**. ▶ **amorality** *noun*

amorous *adj.* showing, feeling, or relating to love, esp. sexual love. ▶ **amorously** *adv.*

amorphous *adj.* having no definite shape or structure.

amortize *verb trans.* (**amortized, amortizing**) to gradually pay off (a debt) by regular payments of money. ▶ **amortization** *noun*

amount *noun* a quantity, total, or extent. —*verb intrans.* (**amounted, amounting**) (**amount to (something)**) to be equal to (it) or add up to (it) in size, number, etc.

amour *noun old use* a love affair, esp. one that is kept secret.

amour-propre (ăm,ŏŏr,prŏp′, -prō′prə) *noun* self-esteem.

amp *noun* **1** an ampere. **2** *colloq.* an amplifier.

amperage *noun* the strength of an electrical current, measured in amperes.

ampere (ăm′pĭr,) *noun* (SYMBOL **A**) the SI unit of electric current, equivalent to one coulomb per second.

ampersand *noun* the sign &.

> From phrase *and per se and,* 'and by itself and'

amphetamine *noun* a potentially addictive drug that stimulates the central nervous system.

amphibian *noun* **1** a cold-blooded vertebrate animal, such as a frog, toad, or salamander. **2** a vehicle that can operate both on land and in water; an aircraft that can land and take off on either land or water.

amphibious *adj.* **1** capable of living both on land and in water. **2** *of troops and military operations* involving personnel landed from the sea.

amphitheater *noun* a round building without a roof, with tiers of seats around a central open area.

ample *adj.* **1** more than enough; plenty. **2** existing in large amounts. ▸ **amply** *adv.*

amplifier *noun* an electronic device that increases the strength of an electrical or radio signal.

amplify *verb trans., intrans.* (**amplified, amplifying, amplifies**) **1** to increase the strength of (an electrical or radio signal). **2** (**amplify on** *or* **upon (something)**) to add details or further explanation to (an account, story, etc.). ▸ **amplification** *noun*

amplitude *noun* **1** wide range or extent; spaciousness. **2** *Phys.* the maximum displacement from the mean position or average value of a wave, vibration, etc.

amplitude modulation (ABBREV. **AM**) in radio transmission, the process whereby the amplitude of the signal-carrying wave is made to vary in response to the signal being transmitted.

ampoule *or* **ampule** *noun* a small, sealed, sterile container containing one dose of a drug for injecting.

amputate *verb trans.* (**amputated, amputating**) to surgically remove (all or part of a limb). ▸ **amputation** *noun*

amputee *noun* someone who has had a limb amputated.

amt. *abbrev.* amount.

amuck *or* **amok** *adv.* in a wild, disorderly way.

> From a Malay word meaning 'fighting frenziedly'

amulet *noun* a small object or jewel worn to protect the wearer from evil or disease.

amuse *verb trans.* (**amused, amusing**) **1** to make (another) laugh. **2** to keep (another) entertained and interested. ▸ **amusement** *noun*

amusing *adj.* eliciting laughter.◨ COMICAL, FUNNY, HUMOROUS, LAUGHABLE ◨ UNAMUSING. ▸ **amusingly** *adv.*

AMVETS *abbrev.* American Veterans.

an- *see* a-[1].

an- *see* a-[1].

Anabaptist (ăn,ə-băp′tĭst) *noun* a member of a 16th c Protestant sect which advocated adult baptism. ▸ **Anabaptism** *noun*

anabolic steroid a synthetic male sex hormone that promotes tissue growth.

anachronism *noun* **1** a person, thing, or attitude that is out-of-date and old-fashioned. **2** the attribution of something to a historical period in which it did not exist. ▸ **anachronistic** *adj.*

anaconda *noun* a nonvenomous snake that kills its prey by coiling around it and squeezing it.

anaemia *noun same as* **anemia**

anaerobe (ăn′ə-rōb,) *noun* an organism that does not require oxygen to live, or that cannot survive in the presence of oxygen. ▸ **anaerobic** *adj.*

anaesthesia, anaesthetic, anaesthetist, anaesthetize *same as* **anesthesia, anesthetic, anesthetist, anesthetize.**

anagram *noun* a word, phrase, or sentence formed by rearranging the letters of another.

anal *adj.* relating to or in the region of the anus.

analgesia *noun* a reduction in or loss of the ability to feel pain, either induced by drugs or resulting from damaged nerves.

analgesic *noun* a drug or other agent that relieves pain. —*adj.* having the effect of relieving pain.

analogical *see* analogy.

analogous *adj.* **1** having the same or similar characteristics. **2** denoting structures that are similar in function but that have developed independently. *See also* **homologous.**

analogue *or* **analog** *noun* **1** a thing similar to something else. **2** a chemical compound that differs slightly in structure and properties from the compound from which it is derived. **3** an animal or plant structure that is similar in function, though not in origin, to a structure in a different organism. —*adj.*, *of a device, etc.* changing continuously rather than in discrete steps, and therefore capable of being represented by an electric voltage. *See also* **digital.**

analogue computer *or* **analog computer** a computer in which data is stored an' processed in the form of continuously varying signals, rather than in individual numerical values as in a digital computer. *See also* **digital computer**.

analogy *noun (pl.* **analogies)** **1** a likeness or similarity. **2** a way of reasoning that explains one thing by comparing it with something else.

analysis *noun (pl.* **analyses)** **1** a detailed examination of structure and content. **2** a statement of the results of such an examination. **3** psychoanalysis. ▸ **analyst** *noun* ▸ **analytic** *or* **analytical** *adj.*

analyze *verb trans.* **(analyzed, analyzing)** **1** to examine the structure or content of (something) in detail. **2** to psychoanalyze (another). ▸ **analyzable** *adj.*

anapest *or* **anapaest** *noun* in poetry, a foot consisting of two short or unstressed beats followed by one long or stressed beat.

anarchism *noun* a belief that governments and laws are unnecessary and should be abolished.

anarchist *noun* **1** a person who believes in anarchism. **2** a person who tries to overthrow a government by violence. **3** a person who tries to cause disorder of any kind. ▸ **anarchistic** *adj.*

anarchy *noun* confusion and disorder, esp. political; the failure or absence of law and government. ▸ **anarchic** *adj.*

anathema *noun* **1** a person or thing one detests. **2** *Christianity* a person or doctrine that has been cursed or denounced.

anathematize *verb trans.* **(anathematized, anathematizing)** to curse or denounce.

anatomy *noun (pl.* **anatomies)** **1 a** the science of the structure of the human or animal body, studied esp. through dissection. **b** the science of the structure of plants. **2** animal or plant structure. **3** *colloq.* a person's body. ▸ **anatomical** *adj.* ▸ **anatomically** *adv.* ▸ **anatomist** *noun*

ANC *abbrev.* African National Congress.

-ance *suffix* forming nouns denoting a state, quality, or action: *abundance*.

ancestor *noun* **1** a person from whom one is descended. **2** a forerunner. ▸ **ancestral** *adj.*

ancestry *noun (pl.* **ancestries)** one's family descent.

anchor *noun* **1** a heavy piece of metal used to restrict the movement of a ship. **2** a weight used to hold a balloon to the ground. **3** something that gives security or stability. **4** an anchorman (sense 1) or anchorwoman. **5** *Sport* an athlete running last in a relay team. *Also called* **anchorman**. —*verb trans., intrans.* **(anchored, anchoring)** **1** to fasten (a ship or balloon) using an anchor. **2** to fasten securely.

anchorage *noun* a place where a ship may anchor.

anchorite *noun* a man or woman who, for religious reasons, lives in a solitary environment.

anchorman *noun* **1** a man who presents a television program and keeps it running smoothly. *Also called* **anchor**. **2** *Sport* an anchor (sense 5).

anchorwoman *noun* a woman who presents a television program and keeps it running smoothly. *Also called* **anchor**.

anchovy *noun (pl.* **anchovies)** a small fish with a pungent flavor, used as food.

ancient *adj.* **1** dating from very long ago. **2** very old. —*noun (usu.* **ancients)** people who lived in ancient times, esp. the Greeks and Romans.

ancient history 1 the history of countries such as Greece, Asia Minor, Italy, and Egypt, up to the end of the Western Roman Empire. **2** *colloq.* information, news, etc., one has known for a long time.

ancillary *adj.* **1** helping or giving support. **2** being used as an extra. —*noun (pl.* **ancillaries)** an item that supplements another item.

-ancy *suffix* forming nouns denoting a state or quality: expectancy.

and *conj.* **1** used to show addition: *two and two*. **2** used to show a result or reason: *fall and bang one's head*. **3** used to show repetition or duration: *It rained and rained*. **4** used to show progression: *bigger and bigger*. **5** used to show variety or contrast: *There are good cars and bad cars*. **6** *colloq.* used instead of *to* after some verbs: *try and do the lesson*.

Usage: Avoid the use of *and* in the expression *try and* in formal writing.

andante *Mus. adj., adv.* played at a slow, steady tempo. —*noun* a piece of music to be played like this.

andiron *noun* an iron bar, usu. one of a pair, supporting logs and coal in a fireplace.

androgen *noun* a hormone that controls the male sex organs and male characteristics.

androgynous *adj.* **1** showing both male and female characteristics. **2** showing both male and female traits, e.g., in appearance, behavior, etc.

android *noun* a robot that looks, moves, and behaves like a human.

anecdote *noun* a short, entertaining account of an incident. ▸ **anecdotal** *adj.*

anemia *or* **anaemia** *noun Med.* a condition characterized by a reduced amount of hemoglobin in the red blood cells.

anemic *or* **anaemic** *adj.* **1** suffering from anemia. **2** pale or weak; lacking in energy.

anemometer *noun* an instrument for measuring and recording wind speed.

anemone *noun* a plant with red, purple, blue, or white cup-shaped flowers.

aneroid barometer a barometer consisting of a sealed metal box that expands or contracts as the atmospheric pressure changes.

anesthesia *noun* loss of sensation, esp. sensibility to pain, usu. induced by an inhaled gas or injected drug.

anesthesiologist *or* **anaesthesiologist** *noun* a doctor who specializes in the administration of anesthesitics to patients. ▸ **anesthesiology** *or* **anaesthesiology** *noun*

anesthetic *or* **anaesthetic** *noun* a drug or gas that causes anesthesia. ▸ **anesthetist** *or* **anaesthetist** *noun* ▸ **anesthetize** *or* **anaesthetize** *verb trans.*

aneurysm *or* **aneurism** *noun* a balloonlike swelling in the wall of an artery.

anew *adv.* 1 once more; another time. 2 in a different way.

angel *noun* 1 a *Relig.* a messenger or attendant of God. b a representation of this in human form, with a halo and wings. 2 *colloq.* a good, helpful, pure, or beautiful person. ▸ **angelic** *adj.* ▸ **angelically** *adv.*

angelfish *noun* any of various fish, so called because their pectoral fins resemble wings.

angel food cake a light sponge cake.

angelica *noun* a tall plant, the crystalized stem and leaf stalks of which are used as a food flavoring and cake decoration.

Angelus (ăn'jǝ-lǝs) *noun* 1 a Roman Catholic prayer said in the morning, at noon, and at sunset, in honor of the Incarnation. 2 a bell rung to announce these prayers.

anger *noun* great or violent displeasure. —*verb trans.* (**angered, angering**) to make angry; to displease.

angina *noun* (*in full* **angina pectoris**) a disease marked by severe chest pain induced by exertion.

angiosperm *noun Bot.* a flowering plant.

angle¹ *noun* 1 the space between two intersecting lines or planes at the place of intersection; the size or shape of this space. 2 a corner. 3 a point of view; an aspect. 4 *slang* a devious plan or scheme.—*verb trans., intrans.* (**angled, angling**) 1 to place at or move in an angle. 2 to present (a news story, information, etc.) from a particular point of view.

angle² *verb intrans.* (**angled, angling**) 1 to fish with a rod and line. 2 (**angle for (something)**) to try to get (it) in a devious or indirect way. ▸ **angler** *noun* ▸ **angling** *noun*

anglerfish *noun* a sea fish that has a dorsal fin spine modified to form a lure to attract prey.

Anglican *adj.* relating to the Church of England. —*noun* a member of an Anglican Church. ▸ **Anglicanism** *noun*

Anglicism *noun* a word or custom that is peculiar to the English.

Anglicize *verb trans., intrans.* (**Anglicized, Anglicizing**) to make or become English in character, culture, or form.

Anglo- *combining form* forming words denoting English or British: *Anglo-American.*

Anglophile *noun* a person who admires England and the English.

Anglophobe *noun* a person who hates or fears England and the English.

Anglophone *noun* an English-speaking person, esp. in states where other languages are also spoken.

Anglo-Saxon *noun* 1 a member of the Germanic tribes that settled in England and parts of Scotland in the 5th c. 2 the English language before about 1150. —*adj.* of the Anglo-Saxons or the Old English language.

angora *noun* 1 a breed of goat with soft silky wool. 2 a breed of rabbit with fine white silky wool. 3 a breed of cat with a long smooth white coat. —*adj.* made of the wool or hair of an angora goat or rabbit.

Angostura bitters *trademark* for a flavoring for alcoholic drinks.

angry *adj.* (**angrier, angriest**) 1 feeling or showing anger. 2 *of a wound* red and sore. 3 stormy: *an angry sky.* ▸ **angrily** *adv.*

angst *noun* a feeling of anxiety or foreboding.

angstrom *or* **ngstrom** *noun* (ABBREV. Å) a unit of length, sometimes used to measure wavelengths of electromagnetic radiation (e.g., light, x-rays).

anguish *noun* great pain or suffering, esp. mental. ▸ **anguished** *adj.*

angular *adj.* 1 *of a person, etc.* thin and bony; sharp or awkward in manner. 2 having an angle or angles. 3 measured by an angle: *angular distance.* ▸ **angularity** *noun*

anhydride *noun* a chemical compound formed by removing water from another compound. ▸ **anhydrous** *adj.*

aniline *noun* a colorless, oily, toxic liquid, used in the manufacture of plastics, drugs, dyes, etc.

animadversion *noun* criticism or censure. ▸ **animadvert** *verb intrans.*

animal *noun* 1 a an organism that is capable of voluntary movement, can respond rapidly to stimuli, and lacks chlorophyll. b any of these creatures except human beings. c a land-based, usu. four-legged creature, as opposed to a bird, insect, etc. 2 a rough, uncivilized person. 3 *slang* a person: *a party animal.* —*adj.* 1 of, from, or like an animal. 2 brutal; sensual. ▸ **animality** *noun.*

animalcule *noun* a microscopic organism.

animalism *noun* 1 the state of having the physical desires of an animal. 2 the belief that man is no better than other animals.

animate *verb trans.* (ăn'ĭ-māt) (**animated, animating**) 1 to give life to. 2 to make lively

3 to record (cartoons or drawings telling a story) on film in such a way as to make the images seem to move. —*adj.* (ăn'ī-mat) alive. ▸ **animation** *noun* ▸ **animator** *noun*

animated *adj.* **1** lively, spirited. **2** living. **3** moving as if alive. ▸ **animatedly** *adv.*

animism *noun* the belief that plants, rivers, mountains, etc., have souls. ▸ **animist** *noun*

animosity *noun* (*pl.* **animosities**) strong dislike or hatred.

animus *noun* strong dislike or hatred.

anion *noun* a negatively charged ion that moves toward the anode during electrolysis. *See also* **cation**.

anise *noun* a plant that produces aniseed.

aniseed *noun* the licorice-flavored seeds of anise, used in candy, drinks, and medicines.

ankh (ăngk) *noun* a T-shaped cross with a loop above the horizontal bar, a symbol of life in ancient Egypt.

ankle *noun* **1** the joint between the bones of the leg and the ankle bone. **2** the part of the leg just above the foot.

anklet *noun* a chain worn around the ankle.

ankylosis *noun* a disorder characterized by immobility or stiffening of a joint.

annals *pl. noun* **1** a record of events year by year in the order of occurrence. **2** regular reports of the work of an organization. ▸ **annalist** *noun*

anneal *verb trans., intrans.* (**annealed, annealing**) **1** to heat (a material such as metal or glass), and then slowly cool it in order to make it softer, less brittle, and easier to work. **2** to strengthen or harden or to become so. ▸ **annealing** *noun*

annelid *noun* an animal such as a worm or leech.

annex *verb trans.* (ə-nĕks', ăn'ĕks,) (**annexed, annexing**) **1** to take possession of (land, territory), esp. by conquest or occupation. **2** to add or attach (one thing) to something larger. —*noun* (ăn'ĕks,) a building added onto, or used as an addition to, another. ▸ **annexation** *noun*

annihilate *verb trans.* (**annihilated, annihilating**) **1** to destroy completely. **2** to defeat or crush, esp. in an argument. ▸ **annihilation** *noun*

anniversary *noun* (*pl.* **anniversaries**) **1** the date on which an event took place in a previous year. **2** the celebration of this event on the same date each year.

Anno Domini (ăn'ō-däm'ə-nē, -dō'mə-) in the year of our Lord, used in giving dates since the birth of Christ.

annotate *verb trans.* (**annotated, annotating**) to add notes and explanations to (a book, etc.). ▸ **annotation** *noun* ▸ **annotator** *noun*

announce *verb trans.*, (**announced, announcing**) **1** to make known publicly. **2** to make known (someone's) arrival. **3** to be a sign of. ▸ **announcement** *noun*

announcer *noun* a person who introduces programs on radio or television.

annoy *verb trans.* (**annoyed, annoying**) **1** to anger or distress. **2** to harass or pester. ▸ **annoyance** *noun* ▸ **annoyed** *adj.* ▸ **annoying** *adj.* ▸ **annoyingly** *adv.*

annual *adj.* **1** happening every year. **2** lasting for a year. —*noun* **1** a plant that germinates, flowers, produces seed, and dies within one year. *See also* **biennial, perennial**. **2** a book published every year, esp. a record of a high-school or college year. *Also called* **yearbook**. ▸ **annually** *adv.*

annualize *verb trans.* (**annualized, annualizing**) to calculate (rates of interest, inflation, etc.) for a year based on the figures for only part of it.

annuity *noun* (*pl.* **annuities**) **1** money invested providing a fixed amount of interest every year. **2** a yearly grant or allowance.

annul *verb trans.* (**annulled, annulling**) to declare publicly that (a marriage, legal contract, etc.) is no longer valid. ▸ **annulment** *noun*

annular *adj.* shaped like a ring.

annulate *adj.* formed from or marked with rings.

anode *noun* **1** the positive electrode in an electrolytic cell. **2** the negative terminal in a battery. *See also* **cathode**.

anodize *verb trans.* (**anodized, anodizing**) to coat (a metal object) with a thin protective film by making it the anode in a cell to which an electric current is applied.

anodyne *adj.* **1** able to relieve pain or distress. **2** able to prevent argument or criticism. —*noun* a painkilling medicine or drug.

anoint *verb trans.* (**anointed, anointing**) **1** to put oil or ointment on (esp. a person's head) as part of a religious ceremony, e.g., baptism. **2** to choose (another) for a position, usu. as one's successor. ▸ **anointment** *noun*

anomaly *noun* (*pl.* **anomalies**) something that is unusual or different from what is normal. ▸ **anomalous** *adj.*

anomie *or* **anomy** *noun* lack or loss of moral standards.

anon *adv. old use* soon.

anon. *abbrev.* anonymous.

anonymous *adj.* **1** having no name. **2** done by or involving a person whose name is not known or not given. ▣ NAMELESS, UNNAMED, UNSIGNED ▣ NAMED, SIGNED. **3** lacking distinctive character. ▸ **anonymity** *noun* ▸ **anonymously** *adv.*

anorak *noun* a hooded waterproof jacket.

anorexia noun 1 loss of appetite. 2 anorexia nervosa. ▸ **anorexic** adj., noun

anorexia nervosa an illness characterized by a refusal to eat because of an obsessive desire to lose weight.

another adj. 1 one more. 2 denoting a person comparable to one already known: another Mozart. 3 different. —pron. 1 one of a different kind. 2 an additional one.

anserine adj. of or like a goose.

answer noun 1 something said or done in reply. 2 the solution to a mathematical problem. —verb trans., intrans. (answered, answering) 1 to make a reply or answer to (someone). 2 to react or respond to (a doorbell, a ringing telephone, etc.). 3 (answer to (someone) for (something)) to have to account to (someone) for (it). 4 to be suitable (for something). 5 to match or be the same as (esp. a description). 6 (answer for (something)) to be punished for (it). ▸ **answerable** adj.

answering machine a machine that records telephone messages.

ant noun an insect with antennae and a narrow waist, that nests in colonies.

-ant suffix used to form words denoting: 1 a quality or function: pleasant. 2 a person who performs an action: assistant.

antacid noun a substance that relieves the pain and discomfort of excess acidity in the stomach. —adj. denoting a substance that does this.

antagonism noun openly expressed dislike or opposition. ▸ **antagonize** verb

antagonist noun an opponent or enemy. ▸ **antagonistic** adj.

Antarctic (änt-ärk′tĭk) noun (the Antarctic) the area around the South Pole. —adj. relating to this area.

ante noun 1 a stake put up by a player in poker before receiving any cards. 2 an advance payment. —verb trans. (anted or anteed, anteing) 1 to put up as a stake. 2 (ante up) to pay: anted up the bill.

ante- combining form forming words denoting before in place or time: antenatal.

anteater noun an animal that feeds on ants and termites.

antebellum adj. prewar; relating specifically to society in the slaveholding South in the decades before the Civil War.

antecedent noun 1 an event or circumstance that precedes another. 2 (usu. antecedents) a person's past. —adj. going before in time.

antechamber noun an anteroom.

antedate verb trans. (antedated, antedating) 1 to belong to an earlier period than. 2 to date (a document, letter, etc.) earlier than the actual date.

antediluvian adj. 1 from before the Flood. 2 very old or old-fashioned.

> Literally 'before the flood', in allusion to the Biblical story of Noah

antelope noun (pl. **antelope**, **antelopes**) a hoofed mammal of Africa and Asia, many having long curved antlers. See also **pronghorn antelope**.

ante meridiem see **A.M.**

antenatal adj. before birth; during pregnancy.

antenna noun 1 (pl. **antennae**) feeler (sense 2). 2 (pl. **antennas**) an aerial.

antepenultimate noun, adj. third from last.

anterior adj. 1 earlier in time. 2 at or nearer the front.

anteroom noun a small room that opens into another, usu. larger, room.

anthem noun 1 a piece of music sung by a church choir. 2 a song of praise, celebration, or patriotic sentiment: national anthem.

anther noun the structure at the tip of the stamen that contains the pollen sacs.

anthology noun (pl. **anthologies**) a collection of pieces of prose or poetry. ▸ **anthologist** noun

anthracite noun a hard shiny black coal.

anthrax noun a serious, sometimes fatal, disease of sheep and cattle, that can be transmitted to humans.

anthropo- combining form forming words denoting of or like humans.

anthropocentric adj. believing that humankind is the central element of existence.

anthropoid adj. like a human being in form.

anthropology noun the study of the origin, development, and culture of humans. ▸ **anthropological** adj. ▸ **anthropologist** noun

anthropomorphism noun the attribution of human behavior, feelings, etc. to animals, gods, etc. ▸ **anthropomorphic** adj.

anti adj. opposed to something. —noun a person who is opposed to something.

anti- combining form forming words denoting 1 opposing: antiaircraft. 2 opposite to: anticlimax.

antiaircraft adj., of a gun or missile designed to attack enemy aircraft.

antiballistic adj., of a missile designed to intercept and destroy a ballistic missile.

antibiotic noun a substance, e.g., penicillin, that is produced by or derived from a microorganism and that can destroy or inhibit bacteria and fungi.

antibody noun (pl. **antibodies**) a protein produced by white blood cells, that combines with an antigen and renders it harmless.

antic noun odd or foolish behavior.

Antichrist (ănt′ē-krīst,) noun Relig. an enemy of Christ, esp. the false Christ whom many expect to appear before the end of the world.

anticipate *verb trans.* (**anticipated, anticipating**) **1** to see what will be needed or wanted and prepare for it in advance. **2** to expect. **3** to look forward to. **4** to do, spend, etc. (something) before the proper time. ▸ **anticipation** *noun* ▸ **anticipatory** *adj.*

anticlimax *noun* a dull or disappointing end. ▸ **anticlimactic** *adj.*

anticlockwise *adv., adj.* counterclockwise.

anticyclone *noun* an area of relatively high atmospheric pressure.

antidepressant *noun* a drug used to control or treat depression.

antidote *noun* **1** a medicine that stops the harmful effects of a poison. **2** something that counteracts something bad.

antifreeze *noun* a substance added to, e.g., the water in the radiator of a motor vehicle, in order to stop it freezing.

antigen *noun* something, e.g., a bacterium, virus, etc., that stimulates the body's immune system to produce antibodies.

antihistamine *noun* a drug that counteracts the effects of allergic reactions, such as hay fever.

anti-inflammatory *adj.* reducing or eradicating inflammation. —*noun* (*pl.* **anti-inflammatories**) a drug prescribed to reduce or eradicate inflammation.

antiknock *noun* a substance added to gasoline in order to reduce knocking.

anti-lock *or* **antilock** *adj., of a braking system* designed to prevent the wheels of a motor vehicle locking when the brakes are applied.

antilogarithm *noun* the number *x* whose logarithm to a specified base is a given number *y*. Also called **antilog**.

antimatter *noun* a substance composed entirely of antiparticles.

antimony (SYMBOL **Sb**) a brittle bluish-white metal that is added to lead alloys to increase their hardness.

antioxidant *noun* a substance, e.g., a food additive, that slows down the oxidation of other substances.

antiparticle *noun* an elementary particle that has the same mass and spin as another elementary particle, but opposite electrical and magnetic properties.

antipasto *noun* (*pl.* **antipastos, antipasti**) food served at the beginning of a meal to whet the appetite.

antipathy (ăn-tĭp′ə-thē) *noun* (*pl.* **antipathies**) strong dislike or hostility. ▸ **antipathetic** *adj.* ▸ **antipathetically** *adv.*

antipersonnel *adj., of weapons* designed to attack and kill people rather than destroy buildings and other weapons.

antiperspirant *noun* a substance applied to the skin to lessen perspiration.

antiphon *noun* a hymn or psalm sung alternately by two groups of singers.

antipodes (ăn-tĭp′əd-ēz,) *pl.* *noun* places on Earth's surface exactly opposite each other, esp. (**the Antipodes**) Australia and New Zealand as being opposite Europe. ▸ **antipodean** *adj.*

antipope *noun* a pope elected in opposition to one already elected.

antipyretic *adj.* reducing fever. —*noun* a drug that reduces fever.

antiquarian *adj.* of or dealing in antiquities, antiques, and rare books. —*noun* a person who collects, studies, or deals in antiquities, antiques, and rare books. Also called **antiquary**.

antiquated *adj.* old; out-of-date; old-fashioned.

antique *noun* a piece of furniture, china, etc., that is old and often valuable, and is sought by collectors. —*adj.* **1** old and often valuable. **2** old-fashioned.

antiquity *noun* (*pl.* **antiquities**) **1** ancient times, esp. before the end of the Roman Empire. **2** great age. **3** (**antiquities**) works of art or buildings surviving from ancient times.

anti-Semitic (ănt,ĭ-sə-mĭt′ĭk) *adj.* disliking or prejudiced against Jews. ▸ **anti-Semite** *noun* ▸ **anti-Semitism** *noun*

antiseptic *adj.* killing germs and so preventing infection or disease. —*noun* a substance or drug that kills germs.

antiserum *noun* (*pl.* **antiserums, antisera**) a blood serum containing antibodies that neutralize the effects of a particular antigen, e.g., in a vaccine.

antisocial *adj.* **1** unwilling to mix socially with other people. **2** *of behavior* annoying, harmful, and destructive. **3** impolite; rude. ▸ **antisocially** *adv.*

antistatic *adj.* reducing the effects of static electricity.

antithesis *noun* (*pl.* **antitheses**) **1** a direct opposite. **2** the placing together of contrasting ideas, words, or themes, esp. for effect. ▸ **antithetical** *adj.*

antitoxin *noun* an antibody produced by the body in order to neutralize a toxin released by invading bacteria, viruses, etc.

antitrust *adj., of a law* serving to regulate business monopolies, e.g., cartels.

antiviral *adj.* destroying viruses or preventing their multiplication.

antler *noun* either of a pair of solid bony outgrowths on the head of an animal of the deer family.

antonym *noun* a word opposite in meaning to another word.

anus *noun* the opening at the end of the alimentary canal between the buttocks.

anvil *noun* a heavy iron block on which metal objects can be hammered into shape.

anxious *adj.* **1** worried, nervous, or fearful about what will or might happen. **2** causing worry, fear, or uncertainty. **3** very eager: *anxious to do well.* ▸ **anxiety** *noun* ▸ **anxiously** *adv.* ▸ **anxiousness** *noun*

any *adj.* **1** one, every, some, or all, no matter which: *Have you any apples?* **2** small in amount: *won't tolerate any nonsense.* **3** large or indefinite: *have any number of dresses.* —*pron.* any one or any amount. —*adv.* (*in questions and negative sentences*) in any way whatever.

anybody *pron.* any person, no matter which. —*noun* an important person: *Everybody who is anybody has been invited.*

anyhow *adv.* **1** in spite of what has been said, done, etc. **2** carelessly; in a state of disarray. **3** in any case.

anyone *pron.* anybody.

anyplace *adv. colloq.* anywhere.

> *Usage:* Avoid *anyplace* in formal writing. Use *anywhere.*

anything *pron.* a thing of any kind; a thing, no matter which. —*adv.* in any way; to any extent: *She isn't anything like her sister.* —*noun* someone of importance.

anyway *adv.* **1** in spite of what has been said, done, etc. **2** in any way or manner.

anywhere *adv.* **1** in, at, or to any place. **2** (**anywhere from... to...**) approximately. —*pron.* any place.

A-1 or **A-one** *adj. colloq.* first-class; of the highest quality.

aorta (ā-ôrt′ə) *noun* the main artery that carries blood from the heart to the smaller arteries.

AP *abbrev.* Associated Press.

apace *adv.* **1** quickly. **2** at the required speed.

apart *adv.* **1** in or into pieces: *come apart.* **2** separated by distance or time. **3** to or on one side. **4** (*after a noun*) leaving aside. —**apart from** except for; leaving aside.

apartheid (ə-pär′tāt,, -tīt,) *noun* an official policy of racial segregation, esp. as once practiced in South Africa.

apartment *noun* **1** a room or set of rooms for residence, usu. in a building containing many such residences. **2** a large room.

apathy *noun* lack of interest or enthusiasm. ▸ **apathetic** *adj.* ▸ **apathetically** *adv.*

ape *noun* **1** any primate that resembles humans in having no tail and in walking upright. **2** an ugly, stupid, or clumsy person. —*verb trans.* (**aped, aping**) to imitate (another's behavior, etc.).

aperitif *noun* an alcoholic drink taken before a meal to whet the appetite.

aperture *noun* **1** a small hole or opening. **2 a** the opening through which light enters, e.g., a camera or telescope. **b** the effective diameter of the lens in such an instrument.

apex *noun* (*pl.* **apexes, apices**) the highest point or tip.

aphasia *noun* loss or impairment of the ability to speak, write, or understand language, caused by brain damage.

aphelion *noun* (*pl.* **aphelia**) the point in a planet's or comet's orbit farthest from the Sun. *See also* **perihelion**.

aphid *noun* a small bug with a soft pear-shaped body and a small head. *Also called* **plant louse.**

aphorism *noun* a saying expressing a general truth. ▸ **aphoristic** *adj.*

aphrodisiac *noun* a food, drink, or drug that stimulates sexual desire. —*adj.* sexually exciting.

apiary *noun* (*pl.* **apiaries**) a place where bees are kept. ▸ **apiarist** *noun*

apical *adj.* of, at, or forming an apex.

apiculture *noun* beekeeping.

apiece *adv.* to, for, by, or from each one.

aplomb *noun* calm self-assurance and poise.

apocalypse *noun* **1** (**Apocalypse**) the last book of the New Testament. *Also called* **Revelation, Revelation of St. John**. **2** a revelation of future destruction or violence. ▸ **apocalyptic** *adj.*

Apocrypha (ə-päk′rə-fə) *pl. noun* books of the Bible excluded from modern Protestant Bibles but included in Roman Catholic and Orthodox Bibles.

apocryphal *adj., of a story, etc.* unlikely to be true.

apogee *noun Astron.* **1** the point in the orbit of the Moon or an artificial satellite around Earth when it is at its greatest distance from Earth. *See also* **perigee**. **2** the highest point.

apolitical *adj.* not interested or active in politics.

apologia *noun* a formal statement in defense of a belief or cause. ▸ **apologist** *noun*

apology *noun* (*pl.* **apologies**) **1** an expression of sorrow, e.g., for a mistake or offense. ▣ EXCUSE, REGRET. **2** a formal defense of a belief or cause. —**apology for (something)** a poor example of (it). ▸ **apologetic** *adj.* ▸ **apologetically** *adv.* ▸ **apologize** *verb*

apoplectic *adj.* **1** of or relating to apoplexy. **2** *colloq.* red-faced and very angry.

apoplexy *noun* sudden neurological impairment caused esp. by a cerebral hemorrhage; a stroke.

apostate *noun* a person who renounces a religion or belief formerly practiced or held. —*adj.* relating to or involved in renunciation of a religion or belief. ▸ **apostasy** *noun*

a posteriori *of reasoning* working from effect to cause or from particular cases to general principles. *See also* **a priori**.

apostle *noun* **1** (*often* **Apostle**) a person sent out to preach about Christ in the early Christian church, esp. one of his 12 original disciples. **2** an enthusiastic champion of a cause, etc.

apostolic *adj.* **1** relating to the Apostles in the early Christian church, or to their teaching. **2** relating to the Pope: *the Apostolic See.*

apostrophe *noun* a punctuation mark ('), used to show the omission of a letter or letters, e.g. *I'm* for *I am*, and possession, e.g., *Ann's book.*

apothecary *noun* (*pl.* **apothecaries**) *old use* a pharmacist.

apothegm (ăp′-ə-thĕm,) *noun* a saying expressing a general truth.

apotheosis *noun* (*pl.* **apotheoses**) **1** raising to the rank of god. **2** a perfect example: *He's the apotheosis of bad taste.*

appall *verb trans.* (**appalled, appalling**) to shock or horrify. ▶ **appalling** *adj.* ▶ **appallingly** *adv.*

apparatus *noun* (*pl.* **apparatus, apparatuses**) **1** equipment. **2** an organization or system made up of many different parts.

apparel *noun* clothes.

apparent *adj.* **1** easy to see or understand. **2** seeming to be real but per. not actually so.

apparently *adv.* as it seems; evidently, clearly.

apparition *noun* **1** a sudden, unexpected appearance, esp. of a ghost. **2** a supernatural being.

appeal . *verb intrans., trans.* (**appealed, appealing**) **1** to make an urgent or formal request. **2** (**appeal to (someone)**) **a** to be pleasing, interesting, or attractive. **b** to call on (someone) for support. **3** to request a higher authority or law court to review or change a decision given by a lower one. —*noun* **1** an urgent or formal request for help, money, etc. **2** *Law* the act or process of appealing. **3** the quality of attracting, interesting, or pleasing. ▶ **appealing** *adj.* ▶ **appealingly** *adv.*

appear *verb intrans.* (**appeared, appearing**) **1** to become visible or come into sight. **2** to seem. **3** to present oneself formally or in public, e.g., on the stage. **4** to be present in a law court as accused or as counsel.

appearance *noun* **1** an act or instance of appearing. **2** the way a person or thing looks, whether or not it reflects reality. —**to all appearances** so far as it can be seen.

appease *verb trans.* (**appeased, appeasing**) **1** to calm or pacify, esp. by agreeing to demands made on one. **2** to satisfy (an appetite or doubt). ▶ **appeasement** *noun*

appellant *noun* a person who makes an appeal to a higher court to review or change the decision of a lower one.

appellate *adj. Law* concerned with appeals.

appellation *noun* a name or title.

append *verb trans.* (**appended, appending**) to add or attach, esp. as a supplement to a document. ▶ **appendage** *noun*

appendectomy *noun* (*pl.* **appendectomies**) the surgical removal of the appendix.

appendicitis *noun* inflammation of the appendix.

appendix *noun* (*pl.* **appendixes, appendices**) **1** a section containing extra information, notes, etc., at the end of a book or document. **2** *Anat.* a short tubelike sac at the lower end of the cecum.

appertain *verb intrans.* (**appertained, appertaining**) to belong or relate.

appetite *noun* **1** a desire, esp. for food. **2** (**have an appetite for (something)**) to favor or enjoy (it).

appetizer *noun* a small amount of food or drink eaten before a meal.

appetizing *adj.* serving to whet the appetite, esp. by looking or smelling delicious.

applaud *verb trans., intrans.* (**applauded, applauding**) **1** to express approval of. **2** to show approval by clapping. ▶ **applause** *noun*

apple *noun* **1** a small tree with pink or white flowers and edible fruit. **2** the firm, round fruit of this tree. —**the apple of (one's) eye** a person (one) is proud or fond of.

appliance *noun* a machine, instrument, or tool.

applicable *adj.* having a bearing on the matter at hand.

applicant *noun* a person applying for a job, university admission, a grant, etc.

application *noun* **1** a formal request, e.g., for a job. **2** the act of putting something onto a surface. **3** the act of using something for a purpose. **4** hard work and effort. **5** relevance. **6** a computer program designed to perform a particular function.

applicator *noun* a device for applying something to a surface, esp. the skin.

applied *adj., of a skill, theory, etc.* put to practical use; not simply theoretical.

appliqué *noun* decoration for clothes, fabric, etc., in which material is cut into shapes that are sewn on to the clothes, etc., to make patterns and designs.

apply *verb intrans., trans.* (**applied, applying, applies**) **1** (**apply for (something)**) to make a formal request, e.g., for a job. **2** to put or spread on a surface. **3** to be relevant or suitable. **4** to put (a skill, theory, etc.) to practical use. —**apply (oneself) to (something)** to give (one's) full attention or energy to a task, etc.).

appoint *verb trans.* (**appointed, appointing**) **1** to give (a person) a job or position. **2** to fix or agree on (a date, time, or place). **3** to equip or furnish. ▸ **appointee** *noun*

appointment *noun* **1** an arrangement to meet someone. **2** the act of giving someone a job or position. **3** the job or position a person is given. **4** (**appointments**) equipment and furnishings.

apportion *verb trans.* (**apportioned, apportioning**) to divide fairly. ▸ **apportionment** *noun*

apposite *adj.* suitable; well chosen. ▸ **apposition** *noun*

appraise *verb trans.* (**appraised, appraising**) **1** to decide the value or quality of (a person's skills, ability, etc.). **2** to put a price on. ▸ **appraisal** *noun* ▸ **appraiser** *noun*

appreciable *adj.* noticeable; significant. ▸ **appreciably** *adv.*

appreciate *verb trans., intrans.* (**appreciated, appreciating**) **1** to be grateful or thankful for. **2** to have a sensitive understanding and enjoyment of (something). **3** to understand or be aware of. **4** to increase in value. ▸ **appreciation** *noun* ▸ **appreciative** *adj.* ▸ **appreciatively** *adv.*

apprehend *verb trans.* (**apprehended, apprehending**) **1** to arrest. **2** to understand. ▸ **apprehension** *noun*

apprehensive *adj.* afraid. ▸ **apprehensively** *adv.*

apprentice *noun* a young person learning a craft or trade. —*verb trans.* (**apprenticed, apprenticing**) to assign or to take on as an apprentice. ▸ **apprenticeship** *noun*

apprise *verb trans.* (**apprised, apprising**) (**apprise (someone) of (something)**) to give (someone) information about (it).

apprize *verb trans.* (**apprized, apprizing**) to value and appreciate (something).

approach *verb trans., intrans.* (**approached, approaching**) **1** to come near or nearer. **2** to ask for support from; to suggest or propose something to. **3** to begin to deal with (a problem, subject, etc.). **4** to be like or similar to: *Nothing approaches this for quality.* —*noun* **1** the act of coming near. **2** a way to or means of reaching a place. **3** a request for support, etc.; a suggestion or proposal. **4** a way of dealing with, e.g., a problem. **5** an aircraft's path to landing. **6** an approximation.

approachable *adj.* **1** friendly and ready to listen and help. **2** that can be reached.

approbation *noun* approval; consent.

appropriate *adj.* (ə-prō′prē-ət) suitable or proper. —*verb trans.* (ə-prō′prē-āt,) (**appropriated, appropriating**) **1** to take, esp. without permission. **2** to put (money) aside for a purpose. ▸ **appropriately** *adv.* ▸ **appropriateness** *noun* ▸ **appropriation** *noun*

approve *verb trans., intrans.* (**approved, approving**) **1** to agree to or permit. **2** (**approve of (someone** *or* **something**)) to be pleased with or think well of (someone or something). ▸ **approval** *noun* ▸ **approving** *adj.* ▸ **approvingly** *adv.*

approx. *abbrev.* approximately.

approximate *adj.* (ə-präk′sĭ-mət) not exact or accurate. —*verb trans., intrans.* (ə-präk′sĭ-māt,) (**approximated, approximating**) to come close to; to be almost the same as. ▸ **approximately** *adv* ▸ **approximation** *noun* .

appurtenance *noun* (*usu.* **appurtenances**) something accessory to, or a minor detail of, something larger.

APR *abbrev.* annual percentage rate.

après-ski *noun* social activities after a day's skiing.

apricot *noun* **1** a small tree with white or pale pink flowers and edible fruit. **2** the yellowish-orange fruit of this tree. —*adj.* of the color or flavor of this fruit.

April *noun* (ABBREV. **Apr.**, **Apr**) the fourth month of the year, following March.

April fool a person tricked on Apr. 1 (April Fools' Day); the trick itself.

a priori (ä p,rē-ôr′ē, äp,r-, äp,r-) *of reasoning* working from cause to effect or from general principles to particular cases. *See also* **a posteriori**.

apron *noun* **1** a piece of cloth, plastic, etc., worn over the front of clothes to protect them. **2** a hard-surface area at an airport where aircraft are loaded. **3** the part of a theater stage seen when the curtain is closed.

apropos (ăp,rə-pō,) *adj., of remarks* relevant. —*prep.* (**apropos of (something**)) with reference to (it).

apse *noun* the arched, domed east end of a church.

apt *adj.* **1** suitable. **2** inclined or tending: *apt to grow impatient.* **3** clever; quick to learn. ▸ **aptitude** *noun* ▸ **aptly** *adv.* ▸ **aptness** *noun*

aqua- *combining form* forming words denoting water: *aqualung*.

aquaculture *or* **aquiculture** *noun* the cultivation of aquatic animals and plants in the sea, a lake, or a river.

Aqua-Lung *trademark* used for an underwater breathing apparatus.

aquamarine *noun* **1** a transparent bluish-green gemstone. **2** the color of this gemstone. —*adj.* relating to this stone or its color.

aquaplane *noun* a thin board on which a person stands while being towed by a fast motor boat. —*verb intrans.* (**aquaplaned, aquaplaning**) to ride on an aquaplane.

aquarium *noun* (*pl.* **aquariums, aquaria**) a glass or plastic tank, or a building containing several such tanks, for keeping fish and other water animals.

Aquarius (ə-kwâr′ē-əs, -kwĕr′-) *noun* **1** the Water Bearer, the name of a constellation and the 11th sign of the zodiac. **2** a person born between Jan. 21 and Feb. 19, under this sign.

aquatic *adj.* **1** living or growing in water. **2** *of sports* taking place in water. —*noun* **1** an aquatic animal or plant. **2** (**aquatics**) water sports.

aquatint *noun* a picture produced by printing with a copper plate that has been etched using acid and wax.

aqua vitae (ăk,wə-vīt′ē, āk,-) a strong alcoholic drink, esp. brandy.

aqueduct *noun* a channel or canal carrying water, esp. in the form of a tall bridge across a valley.

aqueous *adj.* **1** relating to water. **2** *of a solution* containing water; in which water is the solvent.

aquifer *noun* a water-bearing rock stratum.

aquiline *adj.* **1** of or like an eagle. **2** *of a nose* curved like an eagle's beak.

Ar *symbol Chem.* argon.

Arab *noun* **1** a member of a Semitic people living in the Middle East and N Africa. **2** a breed of horse noted for its grace and speed. —*adj.* relating to Arabs or Arabia.

arabesque *noun* **1** *Ballet* a position in which the dancer stands on one leg with the other stretched out to the back. **2** a complex flowing design of leaves, flowers, etc., woven together.

Arabian *adj.* of Arabia or the Arabs.

Arabic *noun* the Semitic language of the Arabs. —*adj.* of the Arabs or their language.

Arabic numeral any of the numbers 0, 1, 2, 3, 4, 5, 6, 7, 8, and 9, based on Arabic characters. *See also* **Roman numeral**.

arable *adj.* **1** *of land* suitable or used for growing crops. **2** *of a crop* grown on plowed land, e.g., cereals, root crops.

arachnid *noun* an invertebrate such as a spider, scorpion, or daddy longlegs. —*adj.* relating to such an invertebrate.

arachnoid *adj.* relating to or resembling an arachnid.—*noun* the middle of the three membranes that cover the brain and spinal cord.

arak *noun* same as **arrack**.

Aramaic (ăr,ə-mā′ĭk) *noun* a Semitic language. —*adj.* of or in Aramaic.

arbiter *noun* **1** a person with the authority or influence to settle arguments between other people. **2** a person influential in matters of style, taste, etc.

arbitrage *noun* purchase of stocks on one market followed by immediate resale on another market, in an attempt to profit on the price discrepancy. ▸ **arbitrageur** (är,bə-trä-zhər′) *noun*

arbitrary *adj.* **1** based on subjective factors or random choice, not on objective principles. **2** *of a person* unpredictably dictatorial. ▸ **arbitrarily** *adv.* ▸ **arbitrariness** *noun*

arbitrate *verb intrans.* (**arbitrated, arbitrating**) to act as a judge in a quarrel or disagreement. ▸ **arbitration** *noun* ▸ **arbitrator** *noun*

arbor[1] *noun* a shady area in a garden formed by trees or climbing plants, usu. with a seat.

arbor[2] *noun* a shaft or axle on which a piece of machinery revolves.

arboreal *adj.* of or living in trees.

arboretum *noun* (*pl.* **arboretums, arboreta**) a botanical garden in which trees and shrubs are grown for scientific research.

arc *noun* **1** a section of a circle or other curve. **2** the graduated scale of an instrument that is used to measure angles. **3** a visible continuous electric discharge between two electrodes. *Also called* **electric arc**. —*verb intrans.* (**arced, arcing**) to form an arc.

arcade *noun* **1** a covered passage, usu. lined with shops. **2** a row of arches supporting a roof, wall, etc. **3** a business that features coin-operated games.

arcadian *adj.* pastoral and rustic.

arcane *adj.* understood only by a few; mysterious.

arch[1] *noun* **1** a curved structure forming an opening, used to support an overlying weight such as a roof or bridge, or for ornament. **2** something having this curved structure, esp. a monument. **3** the bony structure of the foot between the heel and the toes. —*verb intrans., trans.* (**arched, arching**) **1** to form an arch. **2** to span as or like an arch. ▸ **arched** *adj.*

arch[2] *adj.* self-consciously playful or coy. ▸ **archly** *adv.*

arch- *or* **archi-** *combining form* forming words denoting chief; most important: *archduke*.

archaeology *or* **archeology** *noun* the excavation and study of the remains of earlier civilizations. ▸ **archaeological** *adj.* ▸ **archaeologist** *noun*

archaic *adj.* **1** ancient; of or from a much earlier period. **2** out of date; old-fashioned. **3** *of a word, phrase, etc.* no longer in general use.

archaism *noun* **1** an archaic word or expression. **2** the deliberate use of archaic words or expressions.

archangel *noun* an angel of the highest order.

archbishop *noun* a chief bishop. *See also* **archiepiscopal**.

archdeacon *noun* in the Church of England, a member of the clergy ranking just below a bishop. *See also* **archidiaconal**.

archdiocese noun the area under the control of an archbishop.

archduke noun the title of some European princes. ▸ **archduchess** noun

archenemy noun (pl. **archenemies**) 1 a chief enemy. 2 the Devil.

archeology noun same as **archaeology**.

archer noun a person who shoots with a bow and arrows. ▸ **archery** noun

archetype noun 1 an original model; a prototype. 2 a perfect example. ▸ **archetypal** adj.

archidiaconal adj. of an archdeacon.

archiepiscopal adj. of an archbishop.

archipelago noun (pl. **archipelagos**) 1 a group or chain of islands. 2 an area of sea containing many small islands.

> From an ancient Greek term for the Aegean Sea, which translates as 'chief sea'

architect noun 1 a person who designs buildings. 2 a person responsible for creating something.

architecture noun 1 a the art of designing and constructing buildings. b a particular historical, regional, etc., style of building design. c the buildings built in a particular style. 2 set, orderly structure: the architecture of a computer system. ▸ **architectural** adj. ▸ **architecturally** adv.

architrave noun 1 a beam that rests on top of a row of columns. 2 a molded frame around a door or window.

archive noun (usu. **archives**) 1 a collection of old public documents, records, etc. 2 a place where such documents are kept. ▸ **archivist** noun

archway noun a passage or entrance under an arch or arches.

arc light an electric light in which the light source is an arc produced by an electric current flowing between two electrodes. Also called **arc lamp**.

Arctic noun (**the Arctic**) the area around the North Pole. —adj. 1 relating to the area around the North Pole. 2 (**arctic**) extremely cold.

ardent adj. 1 feeling or showing enthusiasm. 2 burning; passionate. ▸ **ardently** adv.

ardor noun great, sometimes excessive, enthusiasm.

arduous adj. 1 difficult; needing much work or energy. 2 steep: an arduous climb. ▸ **arduousness** noun

are¹ (är) see be.

are² noun a unit of land measure equal to 100 m² (119.6 sq. yd.).

area noun 1 a measure of the size of a flat surface. 2 a region, part, or section. 3 a space set aside for a particular purpose. 4 the range of a subject, activity, or topic.

arena noun 1 an area surrounded by seats, for public shows, sports contests, etc. 2 a place of great activity: the political arena. 3 the open area in the middle of an amphitheater.

arena stage a theater-in-the-round.

aren't contr. 1 are not: They aren't coming. 2 (in questions) am not: Aren't I lucky?

areola noun (pl. **areolae**) a faintly colored circular area, esp. that around a nipple.

argon noun Chem. (SYMBOL **Ar**) a colorless, odorless gas, 0.93% of the air, used in light bulbs, fluorescent tubes, etc.

argot noun slang used and understood by a particular group of people.

arguable adj. 1 capable of being disputed. 2 of a proposition, etc. capable of being maintained. ▸ **arguably** adv.

argue verb intrans., trans. (**argued, arguing**) 1 to exchange views, esp. heatedly. 2 to suggest reasons for or against (something): declined to argue the point. 3 (**argue** (**someone**) **into** or **out of** (**something**)) to persuade (someone) to do or not to do (something). 4 to suggest or be evidence for.

argument noun 1 a quarrel or unfriendly discussion. 2 a reason for or against an idea, etc. 3 the use of reason in making decisions. 4 a summary of the subject of a book, etc.

argumentation noun sensible and methodical reasoning.

argumentative adj. fond of arguing; ready to quarrel. ▸ **argumentatively** adv.

aria noun Mus. a long, accompanied song for one voice, esp. in an opera or oratorio.

arid adj. 1 dry and barren; having very little water. 2 lacking interest; dull. ▸ **aridity** noun

Aries (är'ēz, ĕr'-) noun 1 the Ram, the name of a constellation and the first sign of the zodiac. 2 a person born between Mar. 21 and Apr. 20, under this sign.

aright adv. correctly: hear aright.

arise verb intrans. (pa t **arose**; pa p **arisen**; pr p **arising**) 1 to come into being. 2 (**arise from** or **out of** (**something**)) to result from (it) or be caused by (it). 3 to get up or stand up. 4 to come to one's notice.

aristocracy noun (pl. **aristocracies**) 1 the highest social class; the nobility. 2 government by this class. 3 the best representatives of something. ▸ **aristocrat** noun ▸ **aristocratic** adj.

Aristotelian (ăr,ə-stə-tē'lē-ən) adj. relating to the Greek philosopher Aristotle or his ideas. —noun a student or follower of Aristotle.

arithmetic noun (ə-rĭth'mə-tĭk) 1 the branch of mathematics that solves problems by the processes of addition, subtraction, multiplication, and division. 2 ability in performing such mathematical operations: My arithmetic is poor. —adj. (ăr,ĭth-mĕt'ĭk) relating to arithmetic. ▸ **arithmetical** adj. ▸ **arithmetician** noun

arithmetic mean mean³ (sense 2b).

arithmetic progression a sequence of numbers in which each differs from the preceding and following ones by a constant amount, e.g. 2, 4, 6, 8, 10.

ark noun 1 Bible the ship built by Noah in which his family and animals survived the Flood. 2 (**Ark**) Judaism a chest in a synagogue in which the law scrolls are kept.

arm¹ noun 1 either of the two upper limbs of the body, from the shoulders to the hands. 2 anything shaped like or similar to a human arm: an arm of the sea. 3 the sleeve of a garment. 4 the part of a chair, etc., that supports a person's arm. 5 a section or division of a larger group. 6 power and influence: the long arm of the law. —**arm in arm** with arms linked together. **with open arms** with a very friendly welcome.

arm² noun 1 a weapon, e.g., a firearm. 2 a branch of a military force. 3 (**arms**) fighting; soldiering. 4 (**arms**) the heraldic design that is the symbol of a family, country, etc. —verb trans., intrans. (**armed, arming**) 1 to equip, or be or become equipped, with weapons. 2 (**arm (someone) with (something)**) to supply (someone) with whatever is needed. —**up in arms** openly angry and protesting.

armada noun a fleet of ships.

armadillo noun (pl. **armadillos**) a small nocturnal burrowing mammal covered with horny plates.

Armageddon (är,mə-gĕd'n) noun the final battle between good and evil before the Day of Judgment.

armament noun 1 (usu. **armaments**) weapons and military equipment. 2 preparation for war.

armature noun 1 the moving part of an electromagnetic device, e.g., the rotating wire-wound coil of an electric motor or generator. 2 a piece of soft iron placed across the two ends of a magnet that is not in use, in order to preserve its magnetic properties. 3 a wire framework around which a sculpture is modeled.

armband noun a strip of cloth worn around the arm, usu. to indicate an official position or as a sign of mourning.

armchair noun a comfortable chair with arms at each side. —adj. taking no active part: armchair warriors.

armed adj. 1 supplied with arms. 2 provided with means of defense.

armed forces the military forces of a country, such as the army and navy. Also called **armed services**.

Armenian noun 1 a member of the people of Armenia. 2 an Indo-European language spoken in Armenia, parts of Turkey, and the Middle East. —adj. of Armenia, its people, or their language.

armful noun (pl. **armfuls**) an amount that can be held in one's arms.

armhole noun the opening at the shoulder of a garment through which the arm is put.

armistice noun a stopping of hostilities; a truce.

armlet noun a band or bracelet worn around the arm.

armor noun 1 Hist. a metal suit or covering worn by men or horses as a protection against injury in battle. 2 metal covering to protect ships, tanks, etc. 3 armored fighting vehicles. 4 a protective covering on some animals and plants. ► **armored** adj.

armorer noun a person who makes or repairs arms and armor.

armorial adj. relating to heraldry or coats of arms.

armor-plate noun strong metal or steel for protecting ships, tanks, etc. ► **armor-plated** adj.

armory noun (pl. **armories**) 1 a place where weapons are kept. 2 a collection of weapons.

armpit noun the hollow under the arm at the shoulder.

arms race a contest between countries for weapons superiority.

army noun (pl. **armies**) 1 a large number of people armed and organized for fighting on land. 2 the military profession. 3 a very large number.

aroma noun a distinctive, usu. pleasant smell.

aromatherapy noun a form of therapy involving the use of plant oils, generally in combination with massage. ► **aromatherapist** noun

aromatic adj. having a strong, but sweet or pleasant smell.

arose see arise.

around adv. 1 on every side. 2 in or to the opposite direction, position, or opinion: win someone around. 3 here and there; in different directions or to different places: drove around for a while. 4 in a circle; round. 5 in circumference or perimeter: measures 16 ft. around. 6 from one person to another: pass it around. 7 to a specified place. 8 near the current location: wait around for an express train. —prep. 1 on all sides of. 2 at or to different points in. 3 somewhere in or near. 4 approximately in or at; about. 5 a so as to encircle: put an arm around her waist. b so as to move or revolve about a center or axis and return to the starting point. 6 to or on the farther side of: drove around the corner. 7 a extant; in existence: Their old tomcat is still around. 2 present: Is a doctor around?

arouse verb trans., intrans. (**aroused, arousing**) 1 to cause or produce (an emotion, sexual desire, etc.), or to undergo such a reaction. **2** to awaken or to cause to become awake or active. ▸ **arousal** noun

arpeggio (är-pěj′ē-ō,) noun (pl. **arpeggios**) a chord whose notes are played in rapid succession.

arr. abbrev. **1** Mus. arranged by. **2** arrival; arrived:

arrack (är′ək, ə-răk′) or **arak** noun an alcoholic drink made from grain or rice.

arraign verb trans. (**arraigned, arraigning**) **1** to bring into a court of law, usu. to face serious charges. **2** to find fault with. ▸ **arraignment** noun

arrange verb trans., intrans. (**arranged, arranging**) **1** to put into the proper order. **2** to plan (something) in advance or to make plans. **3** to come to an agreement with someone about something. **4** to make (a piece of music) suitable for particular voices or instruments. ▸ **arrangement** noun

arrant adj. out-and-out; notorious: an arrant liar.

arras (är′əs) noun a tapestry for hanging on a wall or concealing an alcove.

array noun **1** a large, impressive number or collection. **2** a well-ordered arrangement: troops in battle array. **3** Comput. elements of data arranged in such a way that any element can be located and retrieved. **4** fine clothes. —verb trans. (**arrayed, arraying**) **1** to put in order, e.g. for battle. **2** to dress (someone or oneself) in fine clothes.

arrears pl. noun money that still needs to be paid. —**in arrears** late in paying money owed.

arrest verb trans. (**arrested, arresting**) **1** to take (a person) into custody, esp. by the police. **2 a** to stop or slow the development of (a disease, etc.). **b** to stop. **3** to catch or attract (a person's attention). —noun **1** the act of taking, or being taken, into custody, esp. by the police. **2** a stopping or stoppage: cardiac arrest. —**under arrest** having been arrested by the police.

arresting adj. strikingly individual or attractive.

arrive verb intrans. (**arrived, arriving**) **1** to reach a place. **2** (**arrive at (something)**) to come to a conclusion, decision, etc. **3** to be successful. **4** of a time to occur. ▸ **arrival** noun

arrogant adj. offensively self-assertive; having or showing too high an opinion of one's abilities or importance. ▸ **arrogance** noun ▸ **arrogantly** adv.

arrogate verb trans. (**arrogated, arrogating**) to claim (a responsibility, power, etc.) for someone or oneself without having any legal right to it. ▸ **arrogation** noun

arrow noun **1** a thin, straight stick with a point at one end and feathers at the other, fired

from a bow. **2** an arrow-shaped sign.

arrowhead noun the pointed tip of an arrow.

arrowroot noun **1** a plant cultivated in the West Indies for its tubers. **2** the digestible starch obtained from the tubers of this plant

arsenal noun **1** a factory or store for weapons, explosives, etc. **2** the weapons, etc., available to a country or group.

arsenic noun (är′sn ĭk) **1** (SYMBOL As) a chemical element. **2** a poisonous oxide of arsenic.

arson noun the crime of deliberately setting fire to a building, etc. ▸ **arsonist** noun

art[1] noun **1** the creation of works of beauty. **2 a** (**the arts**) music, painting, literature, etc., considered as a group. **b** any one of these creative activities. **3** (**arts**) the branches of learning linked to creative skills, e.g., languages, literature, and history. **4** human skill and work as opposed to nature. **5** a skill, esp. gained through practice. ▤ CRAFT, EXPERTISE, KNACK, TECHNIQUE. **6** (**arts**) colloq. cunning schemes.

art[2] verb old use the form of the present tense of the verb be used with thou.

artefact noun same as **artifact**.

arterial adj. **1** of or like an artery. **2** of a road, etc. connecting large towns or cities.

arteriosclerosis noun (pl. **arterioscleroses**) a disorder of the arteries, e.g., atherosclerosis.

artery noun (pl. **arteries**) **1** a blood vessel that carries blood from the heart to the body tissues. **2** a main road, rail line, or shipping lane.

artesian well a deep well in which underground water trapped under pressure is forced upward.

artful adj. **1** able to achieve what one wants, often by illicit or underhand means. **2** skillful. ▸ **artfully** adv. ▸ **artfulness** noun

arthritis noun inflammation of a joint in the body, with swelling, pain, and often restricted movement of the affected part. ▸ **arthritic** adj., noun

arthropod (är′thrə-păd,) noun an invertebrate animal such as an insect, crustacean, arachnid, or myriapod.

artichoke noun **1 a** a tall plant cultivated for food and as an ornamental. Also called **globe artichoke**. **b** the fleshy base of the immature flower head of this plant, eaten as a vegetable. **2 a** a plant cultivated for its edible tubers. Also called **Jerusalem artichoke**. **b** the tuber of this plant, eaten as a vegetable.

article noun **1** a thing: articles of clothing. **2** a usu. short written composition in a newspaper or magazine. **3** a clause or paragraph in a document, legal agreement, etc. **4** the definite article the or the indefinite article a or an.

articular *adj.* relating to the joints in the body.

articulate *verb trans., intrans.* (är-tĭk′yə-lāt,) (**articulated, articulating**) **1** to pronounce (words) or speak clearly and distinctly. **2** to express (thoughts, feelings, etc.) clearly. —*adj.* (är-tĭk′yə-lət) **1** able to express thoughts clearly. **2** *of speech* pronounced clearly and distinctly. **3** having one or more joints. ▸ **articulated** *adj.* ▸ **articulately** *adv.* ▸ **articulation** *noun*

artifact *or* **artefact** *noun* an object made by human effort, e.g., a tool, esp. one with historical or archaeological interest.

artifice *noun* **1** a clever trick. **2** clever skill and tricks; cunning.

artificer (är-tĭf′ĭ-sər, ärt′ə-fĭs,ər) *noun* a skilled craftsperson, esp. a mechanic in the army or navy.

artificial *adj.* **1** made by human effort; not occurring naturally. **2** made in imitation of a natural product, synthetic. **3** *of a person, behavior, etc.* not genuine or sincere. ▸ **artificiality** *noun* ▸ **artificially** *adv.*

artificial intelligence *noun* (ABBREV. AI) the development and use of computer systems that can mimic human intelligence.

artificial respiration breathing that is stimulated and maintained by a person or machine by forcing air in and out of someone's lungs when normal spontaneous breathing has stopped.

artillery *noun* (*pl.* **artilleries**) **1** large guns for use on land. **2** the part of an army equipped with such guns.

artisan *noun* a person who does skilled work with his or her hands.

artist *noun* **1** a person who produces works of art, esp. paintings. **2** a person who is skilled at a particular thing. **3** an artiste.

artiste (är-tēst′) *noun* a performer in a theater, circus, etc.

artistic *adj.* **1** liking or skilled in painting, music, etc. **2** made or done with skill and good taste. ▸ **artistically** *adv.*

artistry *noun* artistic skill and imagination.

artless *adj.* **1** simple and natural in manner. **2** honest. ▸ **artlessness** *noun*

artwork *noun* illustrations, drawings, etc., produced for reproduction in a book, magazine, etc.

arty *adj.* (**artier, artiest**) *colloq.* affectedly or ostentatiously artistic.

-ary *suffix* forming adjectives or nouns denoting of or connected with: *budgetary.*

Aryan (ăr′ē-ən, ĕr′-, är′-) *noun* **1** a member of the peoples speaking Indo-European languages, now esp. the Indo-Iranian languages. **2** *Hist., in Nazi Germany* a Caucasian, esp. of a northern European type. —*adj.* of the Aryans or Aryan languages.

AS *abbrev.* American Samoa.

As *symbol Chem.* arsenic.

as *conj.* **1** when; while; during. **2** because; since. **3** in the manner that: *behave as one likes.* **4** that which; what: *do as one's told.* **5** although. **6** for instance: *large books, as this one, for example.* —*prep.* **1** in the role of: *speaking as her friend.* **2** in a way similar to. —*adv.* to whatever extent or amount. —*pron.* **1** that, who, or which also: *I have the same dress as you have.* **2** a fact that: *as you know.* —**as from** *or* **as of** starting at (a particular time). **as it were** in a way; to some extent.

asafetida (ăs,ə-fĭt′əd-ē, -fĕt′əd-ə) *or* **asafoetida** *noun* a resin with an unpleasant smell.

ASAP *or* **asap** *abbrev.* as soon as possible.

asbestos *noun* a fibrous mineral that is resistant to heat.

asbestosis *noun* a lung disease caused by inhalation of asbestos dust.

ascend *verb trans., intrans.* (**ascended, ascending**) to climb, go, or rise up.

ascendant *or* **ascendent** *adj.* having more influence or power than formerly. —*noun* an increasing influence or power. ▸ **ascendancy** *or* **ascendency** *noun*

ascension *noun* **1** an ascent. **2** (**Ascension**) *Christianity* Christ's ascent to heaven after his Resurrection.

ascent *noun* **1** the act of climbing, ascending, or rising. **2** an upward slope.

ascertain *verb trans.* (**ascertained, ascertaining**) to discover (the truth, etc.).

ascetic *noun* a person who avoids all physical comfort and pleasure, e.g., for religious reasons. —*adj.* avoiding physical pleasure and comfort; self-denying. ▸ **ascetically** *adv.* ▸ **asceticism** *noun*

ASCII (ăs′kē) *noun Comput.* the American Standard Code for Information Interchange, a standard for representing text characters by binary code in digital computing systems.

ascorbic acid a vitamin that occurs in citrus fruits and green vegetables, and which prevents and cures scurvy. *Also called* **vitamin C.**

ascribe *verb trans.* (**ascribed, ascribing**) to think of (something) as done, made, or caused by another: *ascribed her success to hard work.* ▸ **ascription** *noun*

aseptic *adj.* free from harmful bacteria; sterile.

asexual *adj.* **1** denoting asexual reproduction. **2** without functional sexual organs. **3** not sexually attracted to others. ▸ **asexually** *adv.*

ash¹ *noun* (*pl.* **ashes**) **1** the dust that remains after something is burned. **2** (**ashes**) the remains of a human body after cremation.

ash² *noun* **1** a tree or shrub with winged fruits. **2** the strong timber obtained from this tree.

ashamed *adj.* **1** (*often* **ashamed of (some-**

one or **something**)) feeling shame or embarrassment because of (another person, an act, etc.). **2 (ashamed to (do something**)) hesitant or reluctant to do (it) through shame or a fear of disapproval.

ashcan noun a container for trash.

ashen adj., of a face very pale, as from shock.

ashore adv. on or onto the shore or land.

ashram noun esp. in India, a hermitage for a holy man, or a place of retreat for a religious community.

ashtray noun a container for ash, esp. cigarette ash.

ashy adj. (**ashier, ashiest**) **1** covered in ash. **2** gray; ashen.

Asian noun **1** a person born and living in Asia. **2** a person of Asian descent. —adj. of Asia, its people, languages, and culture.

> Usage: Asian is the preferred term for people of SE Asian ancestry, as opposed to Oriental and the often offensive Asiatic.

Asian-American noun an American of Asian ancestry. —adj. relating to Americans of Asian ancestry.

Asiatic adj. Asian.

> Usage: Often considered offensive when used to refer to people.

aside adv. **1** on or to one side. **2 (aside from (something**)) apart from (it). —noun **1** words said by a character in a play which the audience hears, but the other characters supposedly do not. **2** a remark unrelated to the main subject of a conversation.

asinine adj. of or like an ass, esp. in being stupid and stubborn.

ask verb trans., intrans. (**asked, asking**) **1** to put a question to (someone) or call for an answer to (a question). **2** to inquire about: ask the way. **3** (often **ask for (something**)) to make a request for (it); to seek (it). **4** to invite. **5** (**ask (something**) of (**someone**)) to expect (it) of (the person asked).

askance adv. sideways. —**look askance at (something** or **someone**) to regard (someone or something) with suspicion or disapproval.

askew adj., adv. not straight or level.

aslant adj., adv. in a slanting position.

asleep adj., adv. **1** in or into a sleeping state: fall asleep. **2** of limbs numb.

asocial adj. **1** not sociable. **2** hostile to, or against the interests of, society.

asp noun a venomous snake.

asparagus noun **1** a plant with cylindrical green shoots, cultivated as a vegetable. **2** the edible shoots of this plant.

aspartame (ăs′pər-tām,) noun an artificial sweetener, much sweeter than sugar.

aspect noun **1** a particular or distinct part or element of a problem, subject, etc. **2** a particular way of considering a matter. **3** look or appearance. **4** the direction in which a building faces. **5** Astron. the position of a planet in relation to the Sun as viewed from Earth.

aspen noun a tree with grayish-green leaves that tremble in the breeze. Also called **quaking aspen**.

asperity noun (pl. **asperities**) roughness, bitterness, or harshness, esp. of temper.

aspersion noun a damaging or spiteful remark.

asphalt noun a brown or black semisolid material used for roofing, paving and road-surfacing. —adj. relating to or containing this material. —verb trans. (**asphalted, asphalting**) to cover with asphalt.

asphyxia (ăs-fĭk′sē-ə) noun suffocation caused by choking, drowning, inhaling poisonous gases, etc. ▸ **asphyxiate** verb trans. ▸ **asphyxiation** noun

aspic noun a savory jelly, made from meat or fish, used as a glaze.

aspidistra (ăs,pə-dĭs′trə) noun a houseplant with broad leathery leaves.

aspirant noun a person who aspires to something.

aspirate noun (ăs′pə-rət) the sound represented by the letter h. —verb trans., intrans. (ăs′pə-rāt,) (**aspirated, aspirating**) **1** to pronounce (a word, etc.) with a breath at the beginning. **2** Med. to remove (liquid or gas) from a cavity by suction.

aspiration noun **1** eager desire; ambition. **2** Med. the removal of fluid from the mouth or body by suction using an aspirator.

aspirator noun Med. an instrument used to suck liquid, gas, or solid debris from a cavity of the body.

aspire verb intrans. (**aspired, aspiring**) to have a strong desire to achieve or reach an objective or ambition. ▸ **aspiring** adj.

aspirin noun a pain-relieving drug, also used to reduce inflammation and fever.

ass[1] noun **1** a hoofed animal, resembling a horse but with a smaller body, longer ears, and a characteristic bray. **2** colloq. a stupid person.

ass[2] noun coarse slang the buttocks or the anus.

assail verb trans. (**assailed, assailing**) **1** to make a strong physical or verbal attack on. **2** to trouble greatly: assailed by doubts. ▸ **assailant** noun

assassin noun a killer, esp. for political or religious reasons.

> Literally 'hashish eater', after an Islamic sect during the Crusades who consumed the drug before assassinating Christians

assassinate *verb trans.* (**assassinated, assassinating**) **1** to murder, esp. for political or religious reasons. **2** to destroy the good reputation of (someone). ▸ **assassination** *noun*

assault *noun* **1** a violent physical or verbal attack. **2** rape. —*verb trans.* (**assaulted, assaulting**) to make an assault on.

assault and battery *Law* an attack causing physical injury to the victim.

assault course an obstacle course with walls, pools, nets, etc., used for training soldiers.

assay *noun* the analysis and assessment of the composition of an ore or mineral or of a chemical compound. —*verb trans., intrans.* (**assayed, assaying**) **1** to perform such an analysis; to determine the value of an ore or mineral on the basis of such an analysis. **2** to evaluate.

assemblage *noun* **1** a collection of people or things. **2** a gathering together.

assemble *verb trans., intrans.* (**assembled, assembling**) **1** to gather or collect together. **2** to put together the parts of (a machine, etc.).

assembler *noun* **1** a worker who puts together parts of a product on an assembly line. **2** a computer program designed to convert another program written in assembly language into one written in machine code.

assembly *noun* (*pl.* **assemblies**) **1** a group of people gathered together, esp. for a meeting. **2** the act of assembling.

assembly language a programming language that uses short sequences of letters to represent machine code programs in a form that can be easily understood by the user.

assembly line a continuous series of machines and workers along which an article, product, etc., passes in its manufacturing stages.

assent *noun* consent; approval. —*verb intrans.* (**assented, assenting**) to agree to something.

assert *verb trans.* (**asserted, asserting**) **1** to state firmly: *asserted her innocence.* **2** to insist on or defend (one's rights, etc.). **3** to put (oneself) forward boldly and with self-assurance, e.g., in order to win an argument. ▸ **assertion** *noun* ▸ **assertive** *adj.* ▸ **assertively** *adv.* ▸ **assertiveness** *noun*

assess *verb trans.* (**assessed, assessing**) **1** to judge the quality or importance of. **2** to estimate the cost, value, etc., of. **3** to fix a fine or tax at a stated amount. ▸ **assessment** *noun* ▸ **assessor** *noun*

asset *noun* **1** a valuable skill, quality, thing, or person. **2** (**assets**) the property and possessions of a person or company.

asset-stripping *noun* the practice of buying an unsuccessful company at a low price and selling off its assets separately for a profit.

asseverate *verb trans.* (**asseverated, asseverating**) to state solemnly.

asshole *noun coarse slang* **1** the anus. **2** a stupid or contemptible person.

assiduous *adj.* **1** hard-working. **2** done carefully and exactly. ▸ **assiduity** *noun* ▸ **assiduously** *adv.* ▸ **assiduousness** *noun*

assign *verb trans.* (**assigned, assigning**) **1** to give (a task, etc.) to someone or to appoint (someone) to a position or task. **2** to fix (a time, place, etc.) for a purpose. **3** to give (one's property, etc.) to another party by contract. ▸ **assignee** *noun* ▸ **assignment** *noun*

assignation (ăs,ĭg-nā′shən) *noun* a secret appointment to meet, esp. one made between lovers.

assimilate *verb trans., intrans.* (**assimilated, assimilating**) **1** to take in and understand (facts, information, etc.) completely. *2 to become part of, or make (people) part of, a larger group, esp. of a different race or culture. **3** to become or make (something) like, or more like, something else. ▸ **assimilation** *noun*

assist *verb trans., intrans.* (**assisted, assisting**) **1** to help (someone) with (something). —*noun* **1** an act of helping. **2 a** *Baseball* a fielding or throwing of the ball so as to help put a runner out. **b** *Sport* a pass of a basketball, soccer ball, or ice hockey puck that helps to score a goal. ▸ **assistance** *noun*

assistant *noun* **1** a person employed to help someone of higher rank, position, etc. **2** a person who serves customers in a shop.

assistantship *noun* a university or college academic position given to a student for part-time teaching and research.

assistant professor a university or college teacher ranking below associate professor and above instructor.

assize *noun* **1** a session of a court of law, or a decree rendered by it. **2** a judicial inquest, the writ instituting it, or the verdict rendered.

assoc. *abbrev.* **1** associated. **2** association.

associate *verb trans., intrans.* (ə-sō′shē-āt) (**associated, associating**) **1** to connect in the mind: *associate lambs with spring.* **2** to mix socially: *Don't associate with them.* **3** to involve (oneself) in a group because of shared views or aims. **4** to join with people for a common purpose. —*noun* (ə-sō′shē-ət, -sē) **1** a business partner. **2** a colleague or friend. **3** a person admitted to a society without full membership. —*adj.* (ə-sō′shē-ət, -sē) **1** joined with another, esp. in a business: *an associate director.* **2** not having full membership of a society or club.

associate professor a university or college teacher ranking below professor and above assistant professor.

association noun **1** an organization or club. **2** friendship or partnership. **3** a connection made mentally. **4** the act of associating.

assonance noun **1** the rhyming of vowel sounds but not consonants, as in *load* and *cold*. **2** the use of a consonant or consonants with different vowel sounds, as in *milled* and *mulled*.

assorted adj. **1** of or containing various different kinds; mixed. **2** arranged in sorts; classified. ▸ **assortment** noun

assuage (ə-swāj′) verb trans. (**assuaged, assuaging**) to make (a pain, sorrow, hunger, etc.) less severe.

assume verb trans. (**assumed, assuming**) **1** to accept (something) without proof; to take (something) for granted. **2** to take upon oneself (a responsibility, duty, etc.). **3** to take on or adopt (an appearance, quality, etc.). **4** to pretend to have or feel.

assumed adj. **1** false: *an assumed name*. **2** accepted as true without proof.

assuming adj. arrogant; presumptuous. —conj. on the assumption that.

assumption noun **1** something accepted as true without proof. **2** accepting something as true without proof. **3** the act of assuming: *assumption of great power*.

assurance noun **1** a promise, guarantee, or statement that a thing is true. **2** confidence: *answered all questions with assurance*.

assure verb trans. (**assured, assuring**) **1** to state positively and confidently. **2** to convince (someone) of the truth or validity of (something). **3** to make (an outcome, etc.) certain: *assured the success of the fundraiser*.

assured adj. **1** of a person confident. **2** certain to happen. ▸ **assuredly** adv.

aster noun a flower consisting of a central yellow disk surrounded by blue, purple, pink, or white rays.

asterisk noun a star-shaped mark (*) used in printing and writing. —verb trans. (**asterisked, asterisking**) to mark with an asterisk.

astern adv., adj. **1** in or toward the stern. **2** backward or backwards. **3** behind.

asteroid noun a small rocky object that revolves around the Sun, mainly between Mars and Jupiter. *Also called* **minor planet**.

asthma (ăz′mə) noun a respiratory disorder which causes breathlessness and wheezing. ▸ **asthmatic** adj., noun ▸ **asthmatically** adv.

astigmatism noun a defect in a lens, esp. of the eye, causing distortion of the image seen. ▸ **astigmatic** adj.

astir adj., adv. **1** awake and out of bed. **2** in a state of motion or excitement.

astonish verb trans. (**astonished, astonishing**) to surprise greatly. ▸ **astonishing** adj. ▸ **astonishingly** adv. ▸ **astonish-**

ment noun

astound verb trans. (**astounded, astounding**) to surprise, impress, or shock greatly. ▸ **astounding** adj. ▸ **astoundingly** adv.

astrakhan noun dark, tightly curled wool from lambs, used to make cloth.

astral adj. of or like the stars.

astray adj., adv. out of the right or expected way. —**go astray** to become lost.

astride adv. **1** with a leg on each side. **2** with legs apart. —prep. **1** with a leg on each side of. **2** stretching across.

astringent adj. **1** severe and harsh. **2** of a substance causing cells to shrink. —noun a substance that causes cells to shrink, used, e.g., in medications to stop bleeding from minor cuts. ▸ **astringency** noun.

astro- combining form forming words denoting stars or space.

astrology noun the study of the movements of the stars and planets and their purported influence on people's lives. ▸ **astrologer** noun ▸ **astrological** adj. ▸ **astrologically** adv.

astronaut noun a person trained for space travel.

astronautics sing. noun the science of space travel.

astronomical adj. **1** of numbers, amounts, etc. very large; extreme. **2** relating to astronomy. ▸ **astronomically** adv.

astronomical unit (ABBREV. **A.U.**) the mean distance between Earth and the Sun, about 93 million mi. (149.6 million km).

astronomy noun the scientific study of the planets, stars, and galaxies and the universe as a whole. ▸ **astronomer** noun

astrophysics sing. noun the branch of physics concerned with the nature and behavior of stars, galaxies, etc. ▸ **astrophysical** adj. ▸ **astrophysicist** noun

astute adj. able to judge intelligently and act decisively. ▸ **astutely** adv. ▸ **astuteness** noun

asunder adv. apart or into pieces.

asylum noun (pl. **asylums**) **1** a place of safety or protection. **2** the granting of protection. *See also* **political asylum**. **3** a mental hospital.

asymmetry noun a lack of symmetry. ▸ **asymmetric** or **asymmetrical** adj.

at prep. **1** in, on, or near (the position or location specified). **2** to or toward the direction or site of: *Look at the book*. **3** when it is (a given time). **4** in the state or occupation of: *children at play*. **5** during the time of: *work at night*. **6** with (a given rate or level): *work at speed*. **7** to the point or amount of, in cost: *sell at $10 each*. **8** on account of; by: *shocked at his behavior*.

atavism noun **1** a resemblance to ancestors

rather than immediate parents. **2** reversion to an earlier, esp. more primitive, type. ▸ **atavistic** adj.

ataxia noun the loss of the ability to control muscle movements.

ate see **eat**.

-ate suffix **1** forming verbs denoting cause to be: hyphenate. **2** forming nouns denoting rank, profession, or group: doctorate. **3** forming nouns denoting a salt: carbonate. See also **-ide**, **-ite** (sense 5). **4** forming adjectives denoting having, showing features of; like or related to: passionate.

atelier noun a workshop or artist's studio.

atheism (ā'thē-ĭz,əm) noun the belief that there is no God. ▸ **atheist** noun ▸ **atheistic** adj.

atherosclerosis noun a form of arteriosclerosis in which cholesterol and other substances are deposited on the inner walls of arteries, eventually obstructing the flow of blood.

athlete noun **1** a person who is good at sports, esp. track-and-field events, such as running. **2** a healthy person with athletic ability.

athlete's foot a contagious fungal disease that damages the skin between the toes.

athletic adj. **1** of people physically fit and strong. **2** relating to athletics..

athletics sing. noun competitive track-and-field sports, such as running, jumping, etc.

athwart adv., prep. across, from side to side (of).

-ation suffix forming nouns denoting the process or result of: expectation. See also **-ion**.

-ative suffix forming adjectives denoting a particular attribute or tendency: talkative.

Atlantic (ət-lăn'tĭk) adj. **1** in or relating to the area of the Atlantic Ocean. **2** of or relating to North American and European countries bordering on the Atlantic Ocean.

atlas noun a book of maps and geographical charts.

After the mythological Atlas, punished by the Greek gods by having to carry the heavens on his shoulders

ATM abbrev. automated teller machine.

atmosphere noun **1** the layer of gas surrounding a planet. **2** the air in a particular place. **3** the mood of a place, book, etc. **4** a unit of atmospheric pressure, equal to normal air pressure at sea level. ▸ **atmospheric** adj.

atmospherics sing. noun electromagnetic radiation in Earth's atmosphere that interferes with radio communications. Also called **atmospheric interference**.

atoll (ă'tôl,) noun a ring-shaped coral reef surrounding a lagoon.

atom noun the smallest unit of a chemical element that can display the properties of that element.

atom bomb or **atomic bomb** a powerful explosive device that derives its force from the sudden release of enormous amounts of energy during nuclear fission. Also called **A-bomb**.

atomic adj. **1** relating to atoms. **2** obtained by atomic phenomena, esp. nuclear fission: atomic energy. ▸ **atomically** adv.

atomic number Chem.· (SYMBOL Z) the number of protons in the nucleus of an atom of a particular element.

atomic weight relative atomic mass.

atomize verb trans. (**atomized, atomizing**) **1** to reduce to atoms or small particles. **2** to reduce (a liquid) to a spray or mist of fine droplets by passing it through a nozzle under pressure. ▸ **atomizer** noun

atonal adj. Mus. lacking tonality; not written in a particular key. ▸ **atonality** noun

atone verb intrans. (**atoned, atoning**) to make amends for a wrongdoing.

atonement noun an act of atoning.

atop (ə-tăp') prep. on top of.

atrium noun (pl. **atria, atriums**) **1** a central court or entrance hall in an ancient Roman house. **2** a central courtyard in a modern building, usu. with a skylight.

atrocious adj. very bad; wicked or horrible. ▸ **atrociously** adv. ▸ **atrociousness** noun

atrocity noun (pl. **atrocities**) **1** extreme cruelty. **2** (usu. **atrocities**) an act or acts of extreme cruelty.

atrophy verb trans., intrans. (**atrophied, atrophying, atrophies**) to make· or become weak and thin through lack of use or nourishment. ——noun the process of atrophying: muscle atrophy.

atropine or **atropin** noun a poisonous drug obtained from deadly nightshade. Also called **belladonna**.

attach verb trans., intrans. (**attached, attaching**) **1** to fasten or join. **2** to associate (oneself) with or join. **3** to attribute or assign: attach great importance to detail. **4** to be connected with or form part of something. **5** to seize (property) by legal authority: attach a tax dodger's salary. ——**be attached to** (**someone** or **something**) to be fond of (the one specified).

attaché (ăt,ə-shā', ă,tă,-) noun a junior official in an embassy.

attaché case a small rigid leather case for documents, etc.

attachment noun **1** an act or means of fastening. **2** liking or affection. **3** an extra part that can be fitted to a machine. **4** a legal seizure of property.

attack verb trans., intrans. (**attacked, attacking**) **1** to make a sudden, violent attempt to hurt, damage, or capture. **2** to criticize strongly. **3** to begin to do (something) with enthusiasm or determination. **4** to begin to damage. **5** to take the initiative in a game, contest, etc., to attempt to win or score points. —*noun* **1** an act of attacking. **2** a sudden spell of illness. ▸ **attacker** *noun*

attain *verb trans.* (**attained, attaining**) **1** to bring to fruition (a goal, ambition, etc.), esp. through hard work. **2** to reach with effort. ▸ **attainable** *adj.* ▸ **attainment** *noun*

attar (ăt'ər, ä'tär,) *noun* a fragrant oil made from rose petals.

attempt *verb trans.* (**attempted, attempting**) **1** to try. **2** to try to climb or master (a mountain, problem, etc.). —*noun* an endeavor to achieve something: *a brave attempt at skiing.* —**an attempt on (someone's) life** an attempt to kill (someone).

attend *verb trans., intrans.* (**attended, attending**) **1** to be present at (something): *attend a dance.* **2** to go regularly to (e.g., a school). **3** (**attend to (something** *or* **someone**)) to devote oneself to or take action about (something or someone). **4** to accompany. **5** to serve or wait on.

attendance *noun* **1** the act of attending. **2** the number attending. **3** regularity of attending.

attendant *noun* **1** a person employed to help, esp. the public. **2** a servant. —*adj.* **1** giving attendance. **2** accompanying: *the attendant complications of a train strike.*

attention *noun* **1** the act of concentrating or directing the mind. **2** special care and consideration. **3** (**attentions**) an act of politeness or courtship. **4** *Mil.* a position in which one stands rigidly erect with heels together and hands by one's sides.

attentive *adj.* **1** with sharply focused concentration. **2** polite and courteous. ▸ **attentively** *adv.* ▸ **attentiveness** *noun*

attenuate *verb trans., intrans.* (**attenuated, attenuating**) **1** to make or become thin and weak. **2** to reduce the strength or value of. **3** to decrease in intensity. ▸ **attenuation** *noun*

attest *verb trans., intrans.* (**attested, attesting**) to affirm, be proof of, or certify the truth or validity of. ▸ **attested** *adj.* ▸ **attestation** *noun*

attic *noun* a space or room under the roof of a house.

From *Attica* in ancient Greece, famous for a type of square architectural column used in upper storeys of classical buildings

attire *noun* clothing. —*verb trans.* (**attired, attiring**) to clothe.

attitude *noun* **1** a way of thinking or behaving. **2** a position of the body. **3** a pose, esp. if adopted for dramatic effect. **4** *slang* independence and impudence.

attitudinize *verb intrans.* (**attitudinized, attitudinizing**) to adopt an opinion or position for effect.

attorney *noun* (*pl.* **attorneys**) a lawyer.

attorney general (*pl.* **attorneys general, attorney generals**) **1** (**Attorney General**) the head of the US Department of Justice. **2** the chief legal counsel and law officer of the government of a US state.

attract *verb trans.* (**attracted, attracting**) **1** to cause to come or stay close. **2** to arouse or draw to oneself. **3** to arouse liking or admiration in (someone).

attraction *noun* **1** the act or power of attracting. **2** a person or thing that attracts.

attractive *adj.* **1** capable of attracting attention; appealing. **2** good-looking. ▸ **attractively** *adv.* ▸ **attractiveness** *noun*

attribute *verb trans.* (ə-trĭb'yŏot) (**attributed, attributing**) to believe that (something) was written, made, said, or caused by a particular person. —*noun* (ă'trĭbyŏot,) a distinguishing element, esp. of a person's character. ▸ **attributable** *adj.* ▸ **attribution** *noun*

attributive *adj. of an adjective or noun* placed before the noun that it modifies. *See also* **predicative** (sense 1).

attrition *noun* **1** rubbing together; friction. **2** wearing away, esp. by continual friction. **3** making weaker, esp. by continual attacks: *a war of attrition.*

attune *verb trans.* (**attuned, attuning**) **1** to adjust to or prepare for a situation, etc. **2** to put (e.g. a musical instrument) into tune.

atty. gen. *abbrev.* attorney general.

ATV *abbrev.* all-terrain vehicle.

atypical *adj.* departing from the typical or the normal. ▸ **atypically** *adv.*

Au *symbol Chem.* gold.

auburn *adj., esp. of hair* reddish-brown.

auction *noun* a public sale in which each item is sold to the person who offers the most money. —*verb trans.* (**auctioned, auctioning**) to sell by auction: *auctioned off the antique silver.* ▸ **auctioneer** *noun*

audacious *adj.* **1** bold and daring. **2** disrespectful; impudent. ▸ **audaciously** *adv.* ▸ **audacity** *noun*

audible *adj.* loud enough to be heard. ▸ **audibility** *noun* ▸ **audibly** *adv.*

audience *noun* **1** a group of people watching a performance. **2** the people reached by a film, television or radio broadcast, book, etc. **3** a formal interview with an important person.

audio *adj.* relating to hearing, sound, or the recording and broadcasting of sound. —*noun* (*pl.* **audios**) **1** the part of television or movie equipment that relates to sound. **2** the reproduction, broadcasting, or reception of sound.

audio book a book read aloud and reproduced in cassette form.

audiocassette *noun* a cassette, or a tape recording produced in cassette form.

audiotape *noun* **1** a narrow magnetic tape that is used for recording sound. **2** a recording of sound using such tape. —*verb trans.* (**audiotaped, audiotaping**) to record (sounds) on tape.

audiotyping *noun* the typing of material recorded on a dictating machine. ▸ **audiotypist** *noun*

audiovisual *adj.* using both sound and vision. —*noun* something that uses sound and graphics to convey information.

audit *noun* an official inspection of accounts. —*verb trans., intrans.* (**audited, auditing**) to examine (accounts) officially or to be so examined. ▸ **auditor** *noun*

audition *noun* a short performance to test the suitability of an actor, singer, musician, etc., for a particular part or role. —*verb trans., intrans.* (**auditioned, auditioning**) to test or be tested by means of an audition.

auditorium *noun* (*pl.* **auditoriums, auditoria**) a large building or large room intended to seat an audience.

auditory *adj.* relating to hearing.

aught *pron.* anything.

augment *verb trans., intrans.* (**augmented, augmenting**) to make or become greater in size, number, strength, etc. ▸ **augmentation** *noun*

au gratin (ō-grät'n, -grät'n) *of food* covered and cooked with bread crumbs and often grated cheese.

augur *verb intrans.* (**augured, auguring**) to be a sign of the future.

augury *noun* (*pl.* **auguries**) **1** a sign or omen. **2** the practice of predicting the future.

August (ô'gəst) *noun* (ABBREV. **Aug., Aug**) the eighth month of the year.

august (ô-gəst') *adj.* noble; imposing.

auk (ôk) *noun* a small diving seabird with a heavy body and black and white plumage.

auld lang syne days of long ago.

aunt (ănt, änt) *noun* the sister of one's father or mother, or the wife of one's uncle.

au pair (ō'pâr', ō'pĕr) a young person from abroad who lives with a family and helps with housework, babysitting, etc., in return for room and board.

aura *noun* (*pl.* **auras, aurae**) **1** a distinctive character or quality associated with or surrounding a person or place. **2** a light supposedly coming from and surrounding a person's body.

aural *adj.* relating to the sense of hearing or the ears.

> *Usage:* Aural is often confused with *oral*, which refers to the mouth and speech.

aureole *or* **aureola** *noun* **1** in painting, a bright light surrounding the head or body of a holy figure. **2** a corona (sense 1).

au revoir (ōr,əv-wär') good-bye.

auricle *noun* the outer part of the ear. ▸ **auricular** *adj.*

aurora *noun* (*pl.* **auroras, aurorae**) **1** the aurora borealis or the aurora australis. **2** *poetic* the dawn.

aurora australis (ô-strā'ləs) bands or curtains of light in the night sky in the southern hemisphere. *Also called* **southern lights**.

aurora borealis (bôr,ē-ăl'əs) bands or curtains of light in the night sky in the northern hemisphere. *Also called* **northern lights**.

AUS *abbrev.* Army of the United States.

auscultation *noun* the practice of listening, usu. with a stethoscope, to the sounds produced in esp. the heart and lungs, as a means of diagnosis.

auspices *pl. noun* protection; patronage.

auspicious *adj.* promising success; favorable. ▸ **auspiciousness** *noun*

austere *adj.* **1** severely simple and plain. **2** serious; severe; stern. **3** severe in self-discipline. ▸ **austerely** *adv.* ▸ **austerity** *noun*

Australasian *adj.* of or relating to Australia, New Zealand, and the nearby Pacific islands.

Australian *adj.* of Australia, its people, or their languages. —*noun* a native or citizen of Australia.

autarchy (ô'tär,kē) *noun* (*pl.* **autarchies**) government by a ruler who has absolute power.

authentic *adj.* **1** undoubtedly original, real, or true. **2** reliable; trustworthy. ▸ **authentically** *adv.* ▸ **authenticity** *noun*

authenticate *verb trans.* (**authenticated, authenticating**) to prove to be true or genuine. ▸ **authentication** *noun*

author *noun* **1** the writer of a book, article, etc. **2** the creator or originator of an idea, event, etc. —*verb trans.* (**authored, authoring**) to write (a report, etc.). ▸ **authorship** *noun*

authoritarian *adj.* in favor of, or insisting on, strict authority. —*noun* a person who insists upon strict obedience to authority. ▸ **authoritarianism** *noun*

authoritative *adj.* **1** accepted as a reliable source of knowledge. **2** having authority; official. ▸ **authoritatively** *adv.*

authority *noun* (*pl.* **authorities**) **1** the power or right to control or judge others. **2** (*often* **authorities**) the person or people with power, esp. political or administrative. **3** a position that has such a power or right. **4** a public agency: *a turnpike authority*. **5** the ability to influence others, usu. because of knowledge or expertise. **6** an expert.

authorize *verb trans.* (**authorized, authorizing**) 1 to give (someone) the power or right to do something. 2 to give permission for. ▸ **authorization** *noun*

autism *noun* a mental disorder that develops in early childhood, characterized by inability to relate to other people, repetitive body movements, etc. ▸ **autistic** *adj.*

auto *noun (pl.* **autos**) an automobile.

auto- *combining form* forming words denoting of or by oneself or itself: *automatic.*

autobiography *noun (pl.* **autobiographies**) the story of a person's life written by that person. ▸ **autobiographical** *adj.*

autocracy *noun (pl.* **autocracies**) absolute government by one person; dictatorship. ▸ **autocrat** *noun* ▸ **autocratic** *adj.*

autocross *noun* a car competition that tests the drivers' speed and skills.

auto-da-fé (ôt,ōd-ə-fā') *noun (pl.* **autos-da-fé**) *Hist.* 1 the ceremonial sentencing of heretics by the Spanish Inquisition. 2 the public burning of a heretic.

autograph *noun* 1 a person's signature, esp. a famous person's, kept as a souvenir. 2 a manuscript in the author's handwriting. —*verb trans.* (**autographed, autographing**) to sign (a photograph, etc.).

autoimmunity *noun* the body's production of antibodies that attack its own tissues as if they were foreign material.

Automat (ôt'ə-măt,) *trademark* used for automatic restaurant services whereby food is served from vending machines.

automate *verb trans., intrans.* (**automated, automating**) to convert (a factory, etc.) to automation or to make use of automation.

automated teller machine an electronic device in a public place from which a customer, using a card, can withdraw cash, etc. *Also called* **cash machine.**

automatic *adj.* 1 of a machine, etc. capable of operating on its own, requiring little human control. 2 a of an action done without thinking; unconscious; spontaneous. b of a person's actions done merely as a duty or in the usual or expected way, without care or feeling. 3 happening as a necessary and inevitable result. 4 of a firearm able to reload itself and so able to fire continuously. 5 of a motor vehicle having an automatic transmission. —*noun* 1 an automatic firearm. 2 a vehicle with automatic transmission. ▸ **automatically** *adv.*

automatic pilot an electronic control device that automatically steers a vehicle, esp. an aircraft, a space vehicle, or a ship. *Also called* **autopilot.**

automatic transmission in a motor vehicle, a system that allows the gears to be selected and engaged automatically.

automation *noun* the use of automatic machinery requiring little or no human intervention.

automaton *noun (pl.* **automatons, automata**) 1 a robot. 2 a person who acts like a machine.

automobile *noun* a usu. four-wheeled passenger vehicle powered by its own engine, used for land transport.

automotive *adj.* relating to motor vehicles.

autonomy *noun (pl.* **autonomies**) 1 the power or right of self-government. 2 personal freedom. ▸ **autonomous** *adj.* ▸ **autonomously** *adv.*

autopilot *noun* automatic pilot.

autopsy *noun (pl.* **autopsies**) examination of a corpse to determine the cause of death. *Also called* **post-mortem.**

autosuggestion *noun* a form of psychotherapy that involves repeating ideas to oneself in order to change attitudes or habits.

autumn *noun* 1 the season of the year, between summer and winter; fall. 2 a period of maturity before decay or death. ▸ **autumnal** *adj.*

auxiliary *adj.* 1 helping or supporting. 2 additional or extra. —*noun (pl.* **auxiliaries**) 1 a helper. 2 (**auxiliaries**) foreign troops helping another nation at war. 3 an auxiliary verb.

auxiliary verb a verb that shows the tense, voice, or mood of the main verb in a phrase, e.g., *should, will, can.*

AV *abbrev.* audiovisual.

avail *verb trans.* (**availed, availing**) to help. —*noun* use; advantage: *of no avail.*

available *adj.* able to be obtained; ready to be used. ▸ **availability** *noun* ▸ **availably** *adv.*

avalanche *noun* 1 the rapid movement of a large mass of snow or ice down a mountain slope. 2 a sudden appearance of a large number of people or things.

avant-garde (äv,änt,gärd') *noun* those writers, painters, musicians, etc., whose techniques and ideas are the most modern or advanced. —*adj.,* of a work of art, etc. employing or supporting the most modern and advanced techniques and ideas.

avarice *noun* a great desire for money, possessions, etc. ▸ **avaricious** *adj.*

avatar (äv'ə-tär,) *noun* in Hinduism, a god appearing in human or animal form.

avdp. *abbrev.* avoirdupois.

Ave. *abbrev.* avenue.

Ave Maria (ä'vä,mə-rē'ə) *or* **Ave** *R C Church* Hail Mary.

avenge *verb trans.* (**avenged, avenging**) to punish (someone) in return for (harm done). ▸ **avenger** *noun*

avenue *noun* **1** a broad road or street, often with trees along the sides. **2** a tree-lined approach to a house. **3** a means or way.

aver *verb trans.* (**averred, averring**) to state firmly.

average *noun* **1** the usual or typical amount or number. **2** the result obtained by adding together two or more numbers and then dividing the total by the number of numbers added. —*adj.* **1** usual or ordinary. **2** estimated by taking an average. **3** good enough; mediocre. —*verb trans., intrans.* (**averaged, averaging**) **1** to obtain the average of. **2** to amount to on average. **3** to have as an average.

averse *adj.* strongly reluctant or opposed.

aversion *noun* **1** a strong dislike. **2** an object of strong dislike.

aversion therapy a form of therapy that aims to eliminate an undesirable habit or form of behavior by repeatedly linking it with an unpleasant feeling.

avert *verb trans.* (**averted, averting**) **1** to turn away: *avert one's eyes.* **2** to prevent by acting in advance.

aviary *noun* (*pl.* **aviaries**) a large enclosed area in which birds are kept.

aviation *noun* **1** the science or practice of flying in aircraft. **2** the aircraft industry.

aviator *noun* an aircraft pilot.

avid *adj.* **1** enthusiastic. **2** (**avid for (something**)) eagerly wanting (it). ▸ **avidity** *noun* ▸ **avidly** *adv.*

avionics *noun* **1** (*sing.*) the scientific study of the development and use of electronic and electrical devices for aircraft and spacecraft. **2** (*pl.*) the electronic and electrical devices so studied and used.

avocado *noun* (*pl.* **avocados**) **1** a tropical tree with edible pear-shaped fruit. **2** (*also* **avocado pear**) the fruit of this tree. **3** the greenish-brown color of an avocado. —*adj.* of the greenish-brown color of an avocado.

avocation *noun old use* **1** a pastime or hobby. **2** a vocation.

avocet *noun* a wading bird with long legs, and a long slender bill.

avoid *verb trans.* (**avoided, avoiding**) **1** to keep away from (a place, person, action, etc.). **2** to stop, prevent, manage not to, or escape. ▸ **avoidable** *adj.* ▸ **avoidably** *adv.* ▸ **avoidance** *noun*

avoirdupois (ăv,ər-də-poiz′) *noun* (ABBREV. **avdp.**) a system of weights based on a pound weighing 16 oz.

avow *verb trans.* (**avowed, avowing**) to state openly; to declare; to admit. ▸ **avowal** *noun* ▸ **avowed** *adj.* ▸ **avowedly** *adv.*

avuncular *adj.* of or like an uncle, esp. in being kind and caring.

AWACS (ā′wăks,) *abbrev.* Airborne Warning and Control System.

await *verb trans., intrans.* (**awaited, awaiting**) **1** to wait for. **2** to be certain to happen to (someone) in the future. **3** to be certain to occur: *A long night awaits.*

awake *verb intrans., trans.* (*pa* t **awoke** *or* **awaked**; *pa p* awaked *or* **awoken**; *pr p* **awaking**) **1** to stop sleeping or cause to stop sleeping. **2** to become active or cause to become active. —*adj.* **1** not sleeping. **2** alert or aware.

awaken *verb trans., intrans.* (**awakened, awakening**) **1** to awake. **2** to start feeling or be aware of. ▸ **awakening** *noun*

award *verb trans.* (**awarded, awarding**) to give, esp. as a payment or prize: *awarded her a silver bowl.* —*noun* **1** a payment, prize, etc., awarded. **2** a legal judgment.

aware *adj.* **1** (*often* **aware of (something** *or* **someone**)) knowing about (something or someone); conscious of (something or someone). **2** well informed. ▸ **awareness** *noun*

awash *adj.* **1** covered or flooded by water. **2** (**awash with (something**)) covered by or having a large amount of (it).

away *adv.* **1** (*often* **away from (something**)) showing distance or movement from (a place, person, or time). **2** in or to another, usual, or proper place: *put the books away.* **3** gradually into nothing: *fade away.* **4** continuously: *work away.* **5** as one wishes: *ask away.* —*adj.* **1** not present. **2** distant. **3** of a sports event played on the opponent's ground. **4** *Baseball* being out.

awe *noun* admiration, fear, and wonder. —*verb trans.* (**awed, awing**) to fill with awe.

aweigh *adv.*, of an anchor being raised.

awesome *adj.* **1** causing awe; dreaded: *an awesome plague.* **2** expressive of awe. **3** *slang* outstanding; remarkable.

awestruck *or* **awestricken** *adj.* filled with awe.

awful *adj.* **1** very bad. **2** *colloq.* very great. **3** terrible or shocking; awe-inspiring. —*adv. colloq.* very. ▸ **awfulness** *noun*

awfully *adv.* **1** very badly. **2** *colloq.* very; extremely.

awhile *adv.* for a short time.

> *Usage: Awhile* should not be preceded by a preposition like *for*, although the two-word expression *a while* may be, e.g., sat *awhile* in the sun; sat *for a while* in the sun.

awkward *adj.* **1** clumsy and ungraceful. **2** embarrassed or embarrassing. **3** difficult, dangerous, or inconvenient to deal with. ▸ **awkwardly** *adv.* ▸ **awkwardness** *noun*

awl *noun* a pointed tool for making small holes, esp. in leather.

awning *noun* a covering that projects over an entryway or a window and gives shelter from sun or rain.

awoke, awoken *see* **awake**.

AWOL (ā'wôl,) *abbrev.* absent without leave.

awry (ə-rī') *adj., adv.* **1** in a crooked or twisted position or posture. **2** wrong; amiss.

ax *or* **axe** *noun* **1** a tool with a long handle and a heavy metal blade, for cutting down trees, etc. **2** *colloq.* a severe cut in spending or staff. —*verb trans.* (**axed, axing, axes**) **1** to get rid of or dismiss. **2** to reduce (costs, services, etc.). —**have an ax to grind** to have a selfish reason for doing something.

axial *adj.* of, forming, or placed along, an axis.

axiom *noun* **1 a** a principle that is generally accepted as true. **b** a saying that expresses a general truth. **2** a self-evident statement. ▸ **axiomatic** *adj.*

axis *noun* (*pl.* **axes**) **1** an imaginary line around which an object, e.g., a planet, rotates. **2** an imaginary line about which a body is symmetrical. **3** one of the lines of reference used to specify the position of points on a graph, e.g., the horizontal x-axis and vertical y-axis.

axle *noun* a rod that carries a wheel or wheels.

axolotl (ăk'sə-lät,l) *noun* a rare salamander found in certain lakes in Mexico. *Also called* **mole salamander**.

ayatollah (ī,ə-tō'lə, -těl'ə) *noun* a Shiite religious leader in Iran.

aye¹ (ī) *or* **ay** *interj.* yes. —*noun* a vote in favor.

aye² (ā) *adv. poetic* always.

AYH *abbrev.* American Youth Hostels.

ayurveda (ī'ər-vād,ə) *noun* a traditional Indian system of medicine.

azalea *noun* a garden shrub related to the rhododendron with clusters of variously colored flowers.

azimuth *noun* in astronomy and surveying, the direction of an object measured in degrees around the observer's horizon clockwise from north. *See also* **altitude**.

Aztec (ăz'těk,) *noun* **1** a member of a Mexican Indian people whose great empire was overthrown by the Spanish in the 16th c. **2** Nahuatl, the language of the Aztecs.—*adj.* of the Aztecs, or their language.

azure *adj.* of a deep sky-blue color. —*noun* a deep sky-blue color.

Bb

B¹ *or* **b** *noun* (*pl.* **Bs, B's, b's**) **1** the second letter of the English alphabet. **2** (*usu.* **B**) the second highest grade or quality, or a mark indicating this. **3** (B) *Mus.* the seventh note in the scale of C major.

B² *abbrev* byte.

B³ *symbol Chem.* boron.

b. *abbrev* born.

BA *abbrev* Bachelor of Arts.

baa *noun* the cry of a sheep. —*verb intrans.* (**baaed, baaing**) to make this cry.

baba *noun* a small sponge cake soaked in a rum-flavored syrup.

babble *verb trans., intrans.* (**babbled, babbling**) **1** to say or talk quickly, imulsively, or indistinctly. **2** to talk foolishly. **3** to make a low murmuring sound: *a babbling brook.* **4** to give away (a secret) carelessly.

babe *noun* **1** *slang* a girl or young woman. **2** a baby. **3** a naive, unsophisticated person.

babel *noun* **1** a confused sound of voices. **2** a scene of noise and confusion.

baboon *noun* **1** a large ground-dwelling monkey with a long doglike muzzle and long tail. **2** *slang* a clumsy or stupid person.

baby *noun* (*pl.* **babies**) **1** a newborn or very young child or animal. **2** an unborn child. **3** the youngest member of a group. **4** a childish person. **5** *slang* a girl or young woman. **6** *slang* a person's own particular project, responsibility, etc. —*verb trans.* (**babied, babying, babies**) to treat as a baby. —*adj.* **1** of or intended for a baby: *baby clothes.* **2** childish. **3** very small: *baby peas.* ▸ **babyhood** *noun* ▸ **babyish** *adj.*

baby carriage a four-wheeled carriage for wheeling an infant around.

baby-sit *verb trans., intrans.* (**baby-sat, baby-sitting**) to look after a child in the absence of the parent or parents. ▸ **baby sitter**

baby-walker *noun* a frame with a seat and wheels in which a baby can sit while learning to walk.

baccalaureate (băk,ə-lôr'ē-ət) *noun* **1** a bachelor's degree. **2** a farewell sermon given to a graduating class.

baccarat (băk,ə-rä', băk,-) *noun* a card game in which players bet money against the banker.

bacchanal *noun* **1** a noisy and drunken party. **2** a follower of Bacchus (or Dionysus), the god of wine and pleasure in ancient Greece and Rome. ▶ **bacchanalian** *adj.*

bachelor *noun* 1 an unmarried man. 2 a person with a bachelor's degree. ▶ **bachelorhood** *noun*

bachelor's degree an academic degree conferred by a university or college on students who have successfully completed the undergraduate curriculum. *Also called* **baccalaureate.**

bacillus *noun* (*pl.* **bacilli**) any rod-shaped bacterium.

back *noun* 1 a the rear part of the human body from the neck to the base of the spine. b the upper part of an animal's body. 2 the spine. 3 the part of an object that is opposite to or farthest from the front. 4 the side of an object that is not normally seen or used. 5 the upright part of a chair, sofa, etc. 6 *Sport* a player taking a position behind the front line of the team. —*adj.* 1 located or situated behind or at the rear. 2 of or from an earlier date: *a back issue of a newspaper.* 3 away from centers of activity: *back roads.* —*adv.* 1 to or toward the rear. 2 in or into an original position or condition. 3 in return or in response: *hit back.* 4 in or into the past: *look back to happier days.* —*verb trans., intrans.* (**backed, backing**) 1 to help or support, usu. with money. 2 to substantiate; to verify: *back an assertion with hard facts.* 3 to bet on the success of (a horse, etc.). 4 to provide a back or support for. 5 to accompany (a singer) with music. —**back away** to retreat or withdraw. **back down** to concede an argument or claim, esp. under pressure or opposition. **back off** to move backward in retreat or withdrawal. **back up** 1 to accumulate or cause to accumulate: *Traffic has backed up on the turnpike.* 2 to copy (computer data) onto a disk or tape. **back to front** 1 with the back where the front should be. 2 in the wrong order.

backbeat *noun* the loud, steady beat that is characteristic of rock music.

backbench *adj.* relating to freshmen members of the US Congress.

backbite *verb intrans.* (*pa t* **backbit**; *pa p* **backbitten**; *pr p* **backbiting**) to speak unkindly about someone who is absent.

backboard *noun* 1 a board placed beneath an injured person's back to preclude further injury when he or she is being carried. 2 *Basketball* the board on which the basket is mounted.

backbone *noun* 1 the spine. 2 a main support: *They form the backbone of the club.* 3 firmness and strength of character.

backbreaking *adj.,* of a task, etc. extremely hard or tiring.

back burner *colloq.* a position of low priority: *put a project on the back burner.*

backcomb *verb trans.* (**backcombed, backcombing**) to comb (the hair) toward the roots to make it look thicker.

backcourt *noun* 1 *Sport* a in net games, e.g., tennis, the zone of the court between the service and base lines. b in court games, e.g., handball, the zone of the playing area farthest from the target wall or the goal. 2 *Basketball* a that half of the court defended by a team. b the two guards who defend that area.

backdate *verb trans.* (**backdated, backdating**) 1 to put a date on (a document, etc.) that is earlier than the actual date. 2 to make effective from a date in the past.

backdoor *noun* 1 the rear door to a building. 2 a clandestine or illicit means of achieving an objective. —*adj.* denoting an activity done secretly, often dishonestly: *backdoor political deals.*

backdrop *noun* the painted curtain at the back of a stage, forming part of the scenery.

backer *noun* someone who gives financial support to a project, etc.

backfield *noun* 1 *Football* a the zone of the playing field behind the line of scrimmage. b the players who line up in this zone. 2 *Sport* the defense in soccer, field hockey, and rugby.

backfire *verb intrans.* (**backfired, backfiring**) 1 of an engine or vehicle to produce a loud bang caused by the explosion of unburned gases in the exhaust or intake system. 2 of a plan, etc. to go wrong and have a bad effect on the originator.

back-formation *noun* 1 the making of a new word as if it were the root of an existing word. 2 a word made in this way, e.g., *edit* from *editor.*

backgammon *noun* a board game for two people, with pieces moved according to the throws of dice.

background *noun* 1 the space behind the main figures in a picture. 2 a position less noticeable or less public than others: *stay in the background.* 3 the events or circumstances that precede and help to explain an event, etc. 4 a person's social origins, education, etc. 5 soft music accompanying the dialogue, e.g., in a movie.

backhand *noun* 1 a tennis stroke made with the back of the hand turned toward the ball. *See also* **forehand.** 2 handwriting with the letters sloping backward.

backhanded *adj.* 1 made with or as if a backhand. 2 ambiguous or doubtful in effect: *backhanded compliments.*

backing *noun* 1 support, esp. financial. 2 material, etc., that supports the back of something else.

backlash *noun* **1** a sudden violent reaction to an action, situation, etc. **2** jarring or recoil between parts of a machine that do not fit together properly.

backlight *verb trans.* (**backlighted** *or* **backlit, backlighting**) to illuminate (a subject) from behind.

backlist *noun* published titles still kept in print by a publishing house.

backlog *noun* a quantity of uncompleted work.

backpack *noun* a pack worn on a person's back, e.g., to carry camping equipment. —*verb intrans.* (**backpacked, backpacking**) to go hiking with a pack on one's back. ▸ **backpacker** *noun*

backpedal *verb intrans.* (**backpedaled, backpedaling**) to withdraw rapidly or suddenly from one's previous opinion or course of action.

backroom *noun* **1** a room at the rear of a building. **2** a place where a power group can meet in privacy. —*adj.* taking place in an inconspicuous way: *backroom political maneuvering.*

back seat an inferior or unimportant position.

backside *noun colloq.* the buttocks.

backslide *verb intrans.* (**backslid, backsliding**) to relapse into former bad behavior, habits, etc. ▸ **backslider** *noun*

backspace *verb intrans.* (**backspaced, backspacing**) to move the carriage of a typewriter or a computer cursor back one or more spaces. —*noun* the key on a typewriter or computer keyboard used for backspacing.

backspin *noun Sport* the spinning of a ball in the direction opposite to the one in which it is traveling, thereby reducing its speed upon hitting a surface. *See also* **sidespin, topspin.**

backstab *verb trans., intrans.* (**backstabbed, backstabbing**) to attack (another) in an underhanded manner. ▸ **backstabber** *noun*

backstage *adj., adv.* **1** behind a theater stage. **2** not seen by the public.

backstop *noun* **1** *Baseball* the catcher. **2** *Sport* a barrier preventing a ball from leaving the playing area. **3** someone who supports another. —*verb trans.* (**backstopped, backstopping**) to support (another); to serve as a substitute for (another).

backstreet *noun* a street away from the main streets. —*adj.* secret or illicit: *a backstreet abortion.*

backstroke *noun* a swimming stroke performed on the back.

back talk impudent retorts.

backtrack *verb intrans.* (**backtracked, backtracking**) **1** to return the way one came. **2** to reverse one's previous opinion.

backup *noun* **1** support; assistance. **2** a copy of a computer program or data, stored separately in case the original is lost or damaged.

backward *adj.* **1** directed behind or toward the back. **2** less advanced than others in mental or physical development. **3** reluctant or shy. —*adv.* (*also* **backwards**) **1** toward the back or rear. **2** with one's back facing the direction of movement. **3** in reverse order. **4** in or into a worse state. ▸ **backwardness** *noun*

backwater *noun* **1** a pool of stagnant water connected to a river. **2** an isolated place, untouched by what is happening elsewhere.

backwoods *noun* (*sing., pl.*) **1** a remote uncleared forest area. **2** a remote region. ▸ **backwoodsman** *noun*

baclava *noun see* **baklava.**

bacon *noun* meat from the back and sides of a pig, usu. salted and smoked.

bacteria *see* **bacterium.**

bacteriology *noun* the scientific study of bacteria and their effects. ▸ **bacteriologist** *noun*

bacterium *noun* (*pl.* **bacteria**) any of a large group of microscopic, usu. single-celled organisms, some species of which are responsible for infectious diseases. ▸ **bacterial** *adj.*

bad *adj.* (**worse, worst**) **1** not measuring up to a required standard. **2** wicked; immoral. **3** naughty. **4** (**bad at (something)**) not skilled or clever at (some activity). **5** (**bad for (someone)**) harmful to (someone). **6** unpleasant; unwelcome. **7** rotten; decayed. **8** serious; severe: *a bad nosebleed.* **9** unhealthy; injured; painful. **10** sorry, upset, or ashamed. **11** not valid; worthless: *passed bad checks.* **12** undergoing mechanical malfunction: *bad television reception.* **13** (**badder, baddest**) *slang* very good. —*adv. colloq.* badly. —*noun* **1** unpleasant events. **2** evil; badness: *take the good with the bad.* ▸ **badness** *noun*

Usage The adverb *bad* is often used colloquially where *badly* is preferred in formal prose: *My leg* throbbed *so* badly (*not* bad) *after the skiing accident that I had to see a doctor. See note at* **badly.**

---

bad blood angry or bitter feelings.

bad debt a debt that will never be repaid.

bade *see* **bid.**

badge *noun* **1** a small emblem or mark worn to show rank, membership, etc. **2** a distinguishing feature or mark.

badger *noun* a small gray burrowing mammal with a white head with two black stripes. —*verb trans.* (**badgered, badgering**) to pester or worry.

badlands *noun* (*sing., pl.*) barren, roughly eroded land with peaks, mesas, and ridges.

badly *adv.* (**worse, worst**) **1** poorly; inefficiently. **2** unfavorably. **3** extremely; severely: *They are badly in arrears.*

Usage Those who wish to convey the notion of emotional, rather than physical, distress may use *badly* rather than *bad* after verbs such as *feel*, e.g., *We feel badly* about the air crash. See note at **bad**.

badminton *noun* a game for two or four players played with rackets and a shuttlecock that is hit across a high net.

Although based on a 16th-century game, this was first played in its modern form in *Badminton* House in Avon in Great Britain

badmouth *verb trans.* (**badmouthed, badmouthing**) *slang* to criticize or malign.

bad news *slang* a person or thing regarded as dangerous, irritating, or otherwise troubling.

baffle *verb trans.* (**baffled, baffling**) 1 to confuse or puzzle. 2 to hinder. —*noun* a device for controlling the flow of gas, liquid, or sound through an opening. ▶ **bafflement** *noun* ▶ **baffling** *adj.* ▶ **bafflingly** *adv.*

bag *noun* 1 a container made of a soft material with an opening at the top, for carrying things. 2 the amount a bag will hold. 3 a woman's handbag. 4 an amount of fish or game caught. 5 *offensive slang* a woman, esp. an unpleasant or ugly one. 6 *slang* an area of expertise or special interest: *Computer science is not my bag.* —*verb trans., intrans.* (**bagged, bagging**) 1 to put (something) into a bag: *bagged groceries after school.* 2 to kill (game). 3 *esp. of clothes* to hang loosely or bulge.

bagatelle (băg,ə-tĕl´) *noun* 1 a game played on a board with holes into which balls are rolled. 2 an unimportant thing.

bagel *noun* a hard, glazed, ring-shaped roll.

baggage *noun* 1 a traveler's luggage. 2 unnecessary, unimportant, yet burdensome factors, traits, practices, or rules.

baggy *adj.* (**baggier, baggiest**) hanging loose or bulging. ▶ **bagginess** *noun*

bagpipes *pl. noun* a musical instrument consisting of a bag into which air is blown through a pipe and from which air flows through other pipes to make sound.

baguette *noun* a long narrow loaf of French bread.

bail¹ *noun* money required as security for an accused person's temporary release while awaiting trial. —*verb trans.* (**bailed, bailing**) 1 to provide bail for. 2 *colloq.* to get (someone) out of a messy situation: *had to bail the youngster out of trouble with the neighbors.* —**jump bail** to fail to return for trial after being released on bail. **on bail** released once bail money has been given to the court.

bail² *verb trans., intrans.* (**bailed, bailing**) to remove (water) from (a boat) with a bucket.

—**bail out** to escape from an airplane by jumping out.

bailiff *noun* an officer of a court of law, esp. one empowered to keep order at trials.

bait *noun* 1 food put on a hook or in a trap to attract fish or animals. 2 something intended to attract or tempt. —*verb trans.* (**baited, baiting**) 1 to put food on or in (a hook or trap). 2 to harass or tease willfully. 3 to set dogs on (another animal).

baize *noun* a usu. green woolen cloth used as a covering on pool and card tables.

bake *verb trans., intrans.* (**baked, baking**) 1 to cook (cakes, bread, vegetables, etc.) in an oven. 2 to dry or harden by heat from the sun or a fire. 3 *colloq.* to be extremely hot.

baker *noun* a person who bakes and sells bread, cakes, etc. ▶ **bakery** *noun*

baker's dozen thirteen.

baking powder a powder containing baking soda, used to make cakes, etc., rise.

baking soda a white crystalline compound, used to make baking powder and mineral water, and in fire extinguishers. *Also called* **bicarbonate of soda, sodium bicarbonate**.

baklava *or* **baclava** *noun* a rich cake made of layers of flaky pastry with a filling of honey, nuts, and spices.

balaclava *noun* a knitted hat that covers the head and neck, with an opening for the face.

balance *noun* 1 a weighing instrument, usu. with two dishes hanging from a bar supported in the middle. 2 a state of stability in which the weight of a body is evenly distributed. 3 mental or emotional stability. 4 a a state of equality between two opposite forces. b something needed to create such equality. 5 the amount by which the money spent and money received in an account differ. 6 an amount left over. —*verb trans., intrans.* (**balanced, balancing**) 1 to be or put into a state of physical balance. 2 to compare (two or more things) in one's mind. 3 to find the difference between money put into an account and money taken out of it, and to make them equal: *balance the books.* 4 to be or become equal in amount: *The two accounts balance out.* —**in the balance** not yet decided.

balance beam a raised horizontal beam, used in gymnastics for balancing exercises. *See* **gymnastics**.

balcony *noun* (*pl.* **balconies**) 1 a platform surrounded by a wall or railing, projecting from the wall of a building. 2 an upper tier in a theater or auditorium.

bald *adj.* 1 *of a person* having little or no hair on the head. 2 *of birds or other animals* having no feathers or fur. 3 bare or plain. ▶ **balding** *adj.* ▶ **baldness** *noun*

bald eagle a large eagle with dark body plumage and white head, neck, and tail, which is the national emblem of the USA. *Also called* **American eagle.**

balderdash *noun* nonsense.

baldly *adv.* in a plain and often hurtful way.

bale[1] *noun* a large tied bundle of, e.g., hay. —*verb trans.* (**baled, baling**) to make or put into bales.

bale[2] *noun old use* evil; suffering.

baleful *adj.* **1** strongly suggesting evil or harm. **2** threatening; gloomy. ▸ **balefully** *adv.* ▸ **balefulness** *noun*

balk *or* **baulk** *verb intrans., trans.* (**balked, balking**) **1** (*usu.* **balk at (something)**) to hesitate or refuse to go on because of an obstacle or impediment. **2** to check or block. ▸ **balky** *adj.*

Balkan (böl'kən) *adj.* **1** of the peninsula in SE Europe surrounded by the Adriatic, Aegean, and Black seas. **2** relating to the peoples or countries of this region.

ball[1] *noun* **1 a** a round or roundish object used in some sports. **b** *Baseball* a pitched ball that does not travel through the strike zone and is not swung at by the person at bat. **2** anything round or nearly round in shape: *a ball of dough.* **3** a rounded fleshy part of the body: *the ball of the foot.* —*verb trans., intrans.* (**balled, balling**) to form or gather into a ball.

ball[2] *noun* **1** a formal social gathering for dancing. **2** *colloq.* an enjoyable time: *have a ball.*

ballad *noun* **1** a slow, usu. romantic song. **2** a poem or song with short verses, which tells a popular story.

ballast *noun* **1** heavy material used to keep a balloon or a ship steady. **2** broken rocks or stones used as a base for roads and railway lines.

ball bearing *noun* **1** a device consisting of a ring of steel balls whose rolling action in the spherical grooves between a fixed housing and a rotating shaft serves to minimize friction. **2** one of these balls.

ballcock *noun* a floating ball attached to a hinged rod, by which the level of water in a tank or cistern operates a valve and controls the inflow of water.

ballerina *noun* a female ballet dancer.

ballet *noun* **1** a classical style of dancing and mime, using set steps and body movements. **2** a performance of this style of dance. ▸ **balletic** *adj.*

ball game 1 a baseball game. **2** *colloq.* a situation: *a whole new economic ball game.* **a** a situation: *a whole new economic ball game.* **b** a competitive situation: *a senatorial candidate who lost the entire ball game over a single issue.*

ballistic missile a type of missile that initially is guided but then drops on its target pulled by gravity.

ballistics *sing. noun* the scientific study of the movement, behavior, and effects of bullets, rockets, guided missiles, etc. ▸ **ballistic** *adj.*

balloon *noun* **1** a small rubber pouch with a neck, filled with air or other gas and used as a toy or decoration. **2** an aircraft consisting of a large bag filled with hot air or a light gas, and having a basket or gondola for passengers suspended beneath it. **3** an outline contain-ing the words or thoughts of characters in a cartoon. —*verb intrans.* (**ballooned, ballooning**) **1** to swell out like a balloon. **2** to increase dramatically: *The costs started to balloon alarmingly.* **3** to travel by balloon. ▸ **ballooning** *noun* ▸ **balloonist** *noun*

ballot *noun* **1** a method or act of voting, usu. in secret, by pulling levers on a voting machine or by putting a marked paper into a container. **2** the total number of votes recorded in an election. **3** a piece of paper, etc., used in voting. —*verb intrans., trans.* (**balloted, balloting**) **1** to vote by ballot. **2** to take a ballot of.

ballpark *noun* **1** a baseball stadium and its playing field. **2** *colloq.* a range of possibilities, probabilities, parameters, and alternatives: *a sales forecast that was way out of the ballpark.* —*adj.* approximate; rough: *a ballpark sales estimate.*

ballpoint *noun* a pen having a tiny ball as the writing point.

ballroom *noun* a large hall where dances are held.

ballyhoo *noun colloq.* **1** a noisy, confused situation. **2** noisy or sensational publicity.

balm *noun* **1** a pleasant-smelling oil obtained from certain trees, used in healing or reducing pain. **2** a source of comfort to body or spirit.

balmy[1] *adj.* (**balmier, balmiest**) *of the air* warm and soft. ▸ **balminess** *noun*

balmy[2] *adj.* (**balmier, balmiest**) strange; eccentric.

baloney *noun same as* **bologna.**

balsa *noun* **1** a large fast-growing tree of tropical America. **2** the light, soft timber of this tree. *Also called* **balsa-wood.**

balsam *noun* an oily, resinous substance obtained from certain trees, and used in medicines and perfumes.

baluster *noun* each of a series of posts or pillars supporting a rail.

balustrade *noun* a row of posts or pillars, joined by a rail, on the edge of a balcony, staircase, bridge, etc.

bamboo *noun* **1** a tall grass, found mainly in tropical regions, with jointed hollow woody stems. **2** the stem of this grass, used in making furniture, in building, etc.

bamboozle *verb trans.* (**bamboozled, bamboozling**) *colloq.* **1** to trick or cheat. **2** to confuse.

ban *noun* an official order that something may not be done. —*verb trans.* (**banned, banning**) to forbid or prevent, esp. officially or formally.

banal *adj.* lacking freshness and originality, usu. through overuse. ▣ BROMIDIC, CLICHÉD, HACKNEYED, STALE, TRITE ▣ FRESH, ORIGINAL, IMAGINATIVE. ▸ **banality** *noun*

banana *noun* **1** a large treelike plant with large oar-shaped leaves. **2** the long, yellow, curved, edible fruit of this plant.

band¹ *noun* **1** a flat narrow strip of cloth, metal, paper, etc. **2** a stripe of color or strip of material differing from its surroundings. **3** a group or range of radio frequencies: *waveband.* —*verb trans.* (**banded, banding**) to fasten or mark with a band. ▸ **banded** *adj.*

band² *noun* **1** a group of people with a common purpose or interest. **2** a group of musicians. —*verb trans., intrans.* (**banded, banding**) to assemble (individuals) into a group: *We banded the scouts into three patrols.*

bandage *noun* a strip of cloth for winding around a wound or a broken limb. —*verb trans.* (**bandaged, bandaging**) to wrap (a wound or a broken limb) in a bandage.

bandana or **bandanna** *noun* a large brightly colored cotton or silk square, folded and worn around the neck or head.

bandicoot *noun* a nocturnal ratlike Australasian marsupial with long hind legs and a long flexible snout.

bandit *noun* an armed robber.

band saw a saw consisting of a blade with teeth attached to a metal band that moves very fast around two wheels.

bandstand *noun* a platform, sometimes with a roof, on which bands play music.

bandwagon *noun colloq.* a trend, fad, cause, or organization that enjoys ever increasing interest.

bandy¹ *verb trans.* (**bandied, bandying, bandies**) **1** to pass (a story, information, etc.) from one person to another. **2** to mention (something) casually. **3** to exchange (words).

bandy² *adj.* (**bandier, bandiest**) of legs curved or bending wide apart at the knee. ▸ **bandy-legged** *adj.*

bane *noun* the cause of trouble or evil: *the bane of my existence.* ▸ **baneful** *adj.*

bang¹ *noun* **1** a sudden loud explosive noise. **2** a heavy blow. **3** *slang* a big thrill. —*verb trans., intrans.* (**banged, banging**) **1** to make a loud noise by hitting, dropping,

closing violently, etc. **2** to hit sharply, esp. by accident. **3** to make or cause to make the sound of an explosion. —*adv. colloq.* **1** exactly: *bang on time.* **2** suddenly.

bang² *noun* (*usu.* **bangs**) hair cut in a straight line across the forehead.

bangle *noun* a piece of jewelry in the form of a solid band, worn round the arm or leg.

banian *noun same as* **banyan**.

banish *verb trans.* (**banished, banishing**) **1** to send (someone) away from a place, usu. his or her country of origin. **2** to put (thoughts, etc.) out of one's mind. ▸ **banishment** *noun*

banister or **bannister** *noun* a row of posts and the handrail they support, running up the side of a staircase.

banjo *noun* (*pl.* **banjos, banjoes**) a stringed musical instrument with a long neck and a round body. ▸ **banjoist** *noun*

bank¹ *noun* **1** a long raised pile of earth, snow, etc. **2** the side or slope of a hill. **3** the ground at the edge of a river, lake, etc. **4** a raised area of sand under the sea. —*verb trans., intrans.* **1** to form or rise into a bank or banks. **2** to cover (a fire) with a large amount of coal or ash to keep it burning low. **3** of an aircraft **a** to change direction, with one wing higher than the other. **b** to tilt (an aircraft) laterally while turning.

bank² *noun* **1** a financial institution that keeps money in accounts for its clients, lends money, exchanges currency, etc. **2** a box in which money can be saved. **3** a place in which something is stored or collected for later use: *a blood bank.* **4** in some games, a stock of money controlled by one of the players. —*verb trans., intrans.* (**banked, banking**) to put (money) into a bank.

bank³ *noun* a set of similar items arranged in one or more rows: *a bank of switches.*

bankbook *noun* a book recording the amounts of money deposited in and withdrawn from a bank account.

bankcard *noun* a card issued by a bank to a depositor, used, e.g., for operating an automated teller machine.

banker *noun* **1** the owner or manager of a bank. **2** the person in charge of the bank in some games.

banking *noun* the business done by a bank or by bankers.

bank note a single piece of paper money.

bankroll *noun* money or cash resources. —*verb trans.* (**bankrolled, bankrolling**) *colloq.* to finance (e.g., a new business venture).

bankrupt *noun* someone who is legally recognized as not being able to pay debts. —*adj.* **1** not having the money to pay one's debts. **2** deficient in a specified quality:

morally bankrupt. —*verb trans.* (**bankrupted, bankrupting**) to make bankrupt. ▸ **bankruptcy** *noun*

banner *noun* 1 a large piece of cloth or cardboard with a design, slogan, etc.. 2 a military flag.

banns *pl. noun* a public announcement in church of a couple's intention to marry.

banquet *noun* a sumptuous formal meal. ▣ FEAST, REPAST. —*verb trans., intrans.* (**banqueted, banqueting**) to entertain with, or take part in, a banquet.

bantam *noun* 1 a small breed of farm chicken. 2 a small but forceful person.

bantamweight *noun* 1 a class for boxers, wrestlers, and weightlifters of not more than a specified weight (120 lbs./54 kg in professional boxing; slightly more in the other sports). 2 a boxer, etc., of this weight.

banter *noun* lighthearted, friendly talk. —*verb intrans.* (**bantered, bantering**) to tease or joke.

Bantu (băn'tōō,) *noun* 1 a group of languages spoken in southern and central Africa. 2 (*pl.*) the group of peoples who speak these languages. 3 *offensive* a speaker of one of these languages. —*adj.* of the Bantu languages or Bantu-speaking people.

banyan *or* **banian** *noun* a large tree with roots that grow downward from its branches, giving the appearance of a thicket of separate trunks.

baobab (bow'băb,, bā'ə-băb,) *noun* a large African tree with a trunk that serves as a water store.

baptism *noun* the religious sacrament of baptizing a person. ▸ **baptismal** *adj.*

baptist *noun* 1 a person who baptizes. 2 (**Baptist**) a member of a Christian denomination that believes that only people who are able to profess their religious beliefs should be baptized.

baptistery (băp'tə-strē) *or* **baptistry** *noun* (*pl.* **baptisteries**) 1 the part of a church where baptisms are carried out. 2 a font for baptisms.

baptize *verb trans., intrans.* (**baptized, baptizing**) 1 to sprinkle with or dip in water as a sign of having become a Christian. 2 to administer baptism. 3 to name during the sacrament of baptism.

bar *noun* 1 a block of a solid substance: *a bar of soap.* 2 a long piece of a strong rigid material used as a weapon, obstruction, etc. 3 something that prevents or hinders. 4 a line, stripe, or band of color, light, etc. 5 a room, counter, or establishment where alcoholic drinks are sold and drunk. 6 an establishment where drinks and snacks are served: *a coffee bar.* 7 a a vertical line marked on music, dividing it into sections of

equal value. b one of these sections. 8 (**the Bar**) a the legal profession. b attorneys as a group. —*verb trans.* (**barred, barring**) 1 to fasten or obstruct with a bar. 2 to prevent or forbid (someone) from entering a place. 3 to prevent (progress). 4 to mark with a stripe or bar. —*prep.* except for: *her best score, bar none.*

barb *noun* a point on a hook facing in the opposite direction to the main point.

barbarian *noun* 1 a cruel and wild person. 2 an uncivilized and uncultured person. —*adj.* cruel and wild; uncivilized.

barbaric *adj.* 1 cruel and brutal. 2 coarse and rude. ▸ **barbarically** *adv.*

barbarism *noun* 1 the state of being uncivilized, coarse, etc. 2 a coarse or ignorant act. 3 an utterance considered coarse or ungrammatical.

barbarous *adj.* 1 uncultured and uncivilized. 2 extremely cruel or brutal. 3 coarse or rude. ▸ **barbarity** *noun*

barbecue *noun* 1 a frame, pit, or outdoor oven on or in which food is grilled over coals. 2 food cooked in this way. 3 a party held outdoors at which food is so cooked. —*verb trans., intrans.* (**barbecued, barbecuing**) to cook on a barbecue.

> From a Haitian creole term for a wooden grid or frame

barbed wire fence wire with short, sharp points twisted on at intervals.

barbel (bär'bəl) *noun* a fleshy whiskerlike outgrowth on the mouths or nostrils of some fishes, e.g., catfish.

barbell *noun* a bar with heavy metal weights at each end, used for weightlifting exercises.

barber *noun* a person who cuts and styles men's hair, and shaves their beards.

barberry *noun* (*pl.* **barberries**) a shrub with small yellow or orange flowers and red, yellow, black, or blue berries.

barbiturate *noun* a sedative and hypnotic drug used, e.g., in sleeping pills and anesthetics.

bar chart *or* **bar graph** a graph in which rectangular blocks are used to represent data. *See also* **pie chart**.

bar code a series of numbers and black parallel lines of varying thickness, commonly used on food packaging and book jackets.

bard *noun* a poet. ▸ **bardic** *adj.*

bare *adj.* 1 not covered by clothes. 2 being without the usual or natural covering: *bare trees.* 3 empty: *The cupboard was bare.* 4 simple; plain: *the bare facts.* 5 basic; essential: *the bare necessities.* —*verb trans.* (**bared, baring**) to uncover: *bare a deep secret.* ▸ **bareness** *noun*

bareback *adv., adj.* without a saddle.

barefaced *adj.* having no shame or regret.

barefoot *or* **barefooted** *adj., adv.* not wearing shoes or socks.

bareheaded *adj., adv.* not wearing a hat.

barelegged (băr'lĕg'ĭd, -lĕg'd') *adj., adv.* with the legs uncovered.

barely *adv.* **1** scarcely or only just: *barely enough.* **2** plainly; simply; *barely furnished.*

bargain *noun* **1** an agreement made between people buying and selling things, offering and accepting services, etc.: *strike a bargain.* **2** something offered for sale, or bought, at a low price. —*verb intrans.* (**bargained, bargaining**) to discuss the terms for buying or selling, etc. —**bargain for (something)** to be prepared for (it): *I didn't bargain for all this work.* **into the bargain** in addition; besides.

barge *noun* **1** a long flat-bottomed boat used on rivers and canals. **2** a large boat, often decorated, used in ceremonies, celebrations, etc. —*verb intrans.* (**barged, barging**) **1** to move in a clumsy, ungraceful way: *barged about, knocking over vases.* **2** (**barge into (something)**) to hit or knock (it) clumsily. **3** to make one's way rudely or roughly: *barged past me.* **4** (**barge in**) to create a rude intrusion or interruption: *barged into my office.*

baritone *noun* **1** the second lowest male singing voice, between bass and tenor. **2** a singer with such a voice. **3** a part written for such a voice.

barium *noun* (SYMBOL **Ba**) a soft silvery-white metal.

bark¹ *noun* the short sharp cry of a dog, fox, etc. —*verb intrans., trans.* (**barked, barking**) **1** to make this cry. **2** to speak or say loudly and sharply: *barked at the troops.*

bark² *noun* the tough protective outer layer of the stems and roots of trees. —*verb trans.* (**barked, barking**) **1** to scrape or rub off the skin from (a part of the body): *barked my shins.* **2** to strip or remove the bark from (a tree).

bark³ *or* **barque** *noun* **1** a small three-masted sailing ship. **2** *literary* a boat.

barker *noun* a person employed by a circus or carnival to shout to attract customers.

barley *noun* **1** a cereal that bears a dense head of grains with long slender bristles. **2** the grain of this plant. *Also called* **barleycorn.**

barley sugar a kind of hard orange-colored candy.

barman *noun* a male bartender.

bar mitzvah **1** a Jewish ceremony in which a boy accepts full religious responsibilities. **2** a boy for whom this ceremony is conducted.

barn *noun* **1** a building in which grain, hay, etc., is stored, or for cattle, etc. **2** a large, bare building.

barnacle *noun* a marine crustacean that cements itself firmly to rocks, boats, etc.

barn owl an owl with a pale heart-shaped face.

barnstorm *verb intrans.* (**barnstormed, barnstorming**) **1** to tour a country, stopping briefly in each town to give theatrical performances. **2** to travel about the country making political speeches just before an election.

barnyard *noun* the area around a barn.

barometer *noun* an instrument for measuring atmospheric pressure. *See also* **aneroid barometer.** ▸ **barometric** *adj.*

baron *noun* **1** a man holding the lowest rank in the British nobility. **2** a leading or dominant figure in a field: *an oil baron.* ▸ **baronial** *adj.*

baroness *noun* **1** a baron's wife. **2** a woman holding the title equivalent to baron in her own right.

baronet (băr'ə-nət, băr'ə-nĕt') *noun* (ABBREV. **Bart.**) in the UK, a title below that of baron, hereditary but not part of the peerage. ▸ **baronetcy** *noun*

barony *noun* (*pl.* **baronies**) **1** the rank of baron. **2** land belonging to a baron.

baroque *noun* (*usu.* **Baroque**) a complex decorative style of architecture, art, decoration, and music, popular in Europe from the late 16th c to the early 18th c. **2** (*usu.* **the Baroque**) this period in European cultural history. —*adj.* (*usu.* **Baroque**) written or executed in such a style.

barperson *noun* a person who prepares and serves drinks in a bar.

barque *noun* same as **bark³.**

barrack *noun* (**barracks**) a building or buildings for housing troops. —*verb trans.* (**barracked, barracking**) to house (soldiers).

barracuda *noun* (*pl.* **barracuda, barracudas**) a large predatory marine fish.

barrage *noun* **1** a long burst of gunfire that keeps an enemy back while soldiers move forward. **2** a large number of questions, criticisms, etc., coming en masse. **3** a human-made barrier across a river.

barre (băr) *noun* a rail fixed to a wall at waist level, used by ballet dancers to balance themselves while exercising.

barred *adj.* **1** having bars. **2** closed off; blocked.

barrel *noun* **1** a large, round, usu. wooden container with a flat top and bottom and curving out in the middle. **2** the amount a barrel will hold. **3** a measure of capacity, esp. of oil. **4** the long tube-shaped part of a gun, etc. —*verb trans., intrans.* (**barreled or barrelled, barreling or barrelling**) **1** to put in barrels. **2** *slang* to move very fast: *barreling along the freeway at 90 mph.*

barren *adj.* **1 a** unable to bear offspring. **b** producing no offspring. **2** having or producing no vegetation. **3** devoid of the expected characteristic: *barren of courage.* **4** dull; uninteresting: *barren dialogue.* ▸ **barrenness** *noun*

barricade *noun* a barrier made of material that can be piled up quickly, e.g., to block a street. —*verb trans.* (**barricaded, barricading**) **1** to block or defend with a barricade. **2** to shut in or out by using a barricade.

barrier *noun* **1** a structure, such as a fence, gate, bar, etc., put up to defend, block, protect, separate, etc. **2** an obstruction or impediment: *a barrier to arms limitation.*

barrier reef a long, narrow, actively growing coral reef separated from the land by a wide, deep lagoon.

barring *prep.* except for; leaving out of consideration: *Barring further delays, we'll meet the schedule.*

barroom *noun* an establishment where alcoholic drinks are served.

barrow¹ *noun* **1** a small one-wheeled cart. **2** a cart with two or four wheels, from which goods are often sold in the street.

barrow² *noun* a large pile of earth over an ancient grave.

Bart. *abbrev* (*also* **Bart**) Baronet.

bartender *noun* a person who prepares and serves drinks at a bar.

barter *verb trans., intrans.* (**bartered, bartering**) to trade or exchange (goods or services) without using money. —*noun* trade by exchanging goods rather than using money.

baryon *noun* a heavy subatomic particle.

basal *adj.* at or forming a base.

basalt *noun* a fine-grained dark volcanic rock.

base¹ *noun* (*pl.* **bases**) **1** the lowest part or bottom; the part supporting another thing. **2** the origin, root, or foundation of something. **3** a headquarters; a center of activity or operations. **4** a starting point. **5** the main part of a mixture: *Rice forms the base of this dish.* **6** a chemical compound that can neutralize an acid to form a salt and water. **7** *Baseball* any one of four points at the corners of the infield that runners must touch in order to score a run. **8** in a numerical system, the number of different symbols used. **9** in logarithms, the number that when raised to a certain power has a logarithm equal in value to that power. —*verb trans.* (**based, basing**) **1** to form, provide, or find the basis for: *based my conclusions on the facts.* **2** to assign to a particular place: *troops based in France.* —*adj.* **1** serving as a base: *the base layer of paint.* **2** located near or at the bottom, e.g., of a mountain: *the hikers' base lodge.*

base² *adj.* (**baser, basest**) **1** lacking morals; wicked. **2** impure. **3** low in value. ▸ **baseness** *noun*

baseball *noun* **1** a game for two teams of nine players each, played with a bat and ball on a diamond-shaped infield. **2** the ball used in this game.

base hit *Baseball* a hit enabling the batter to get to first base.

baseless *adj.* lacking valid cause or foundation: *baseless fears.*

baseline *noun* **1** one of the two lines that mark the ends of a tennis court. **2** *Baseball* the area of the infield within which base runners must stay when going from one base to another. **3** an amount or value taken as a basis for comparison.

baseman *noun Baseball* a player guarding first, second, or third base.

basement *noun* the lowest floor of a building, usu. below ground level.

base on balls *Baseball* an advance to first base given to a batter who has taken four pitches judged as balls.

base runner *Baseball* a player on the team at bat who is attempting to get to a base or has safely touched one.

bases *see* **base**¹, **basis.**

bash *verb trans.* (**bashed, bashing**) **1** to hit with a crushingly heavy blow. **2** *colloq.* to criticize harshly. —*noun* **1** a crushingly heavy, physical blow. **2** *slang* a party.

bashful *adj.* lacking confidence; shy. ▸ **bashfully** *adv.* ▸ **bashfulness** *noun*

BASIC (bā'sĭk) *or* **Basic** *noun* a high-level computer programming language.

basic —*adj.* **1** of or forming the base or basis. **2** at a very simple or low level: *a basic course in math.* **3** without additions: *basic pay.* —*noun* (*usu.* **basics**) the essential parts or facts; the simplest principles. ▸ **basically** *adv.*

basil *noun* a bushy aromatic plant widely cultivated as a culinary herb.

basilica *noun* **1** an ancient Roman public hall, with a rounded wall at one end and a row of stone pillars along each side. **2** a church shaped like this building.

basilisk (bǎs'ə-lĭsk, bǎz'-) *noun* a forest-dwelling lizard of Central and S America.

basin *noun* **1** a shallow, round container in which to hold liquid. **2** a sink; a washbasin. **3** a partly enclosed body of water, usu. not much affected by tides. **4** an area that is drained by one river or river system.

basis *noun* (*pl.* **bases**) **1** a principle on which an idea, theory, etc., is based. **2** a starting point: *a basis for discussion.* **3** the main part of a mixture.

bask *verb intrans.* (**basked, basking**) **1** to lie in comfort, esp. in warmth or sunshine. **2**

to take great pleasure: *basking in her approval.*

basket *noun* **1** a container made of woven strips of wood, cane, etc. **2** the amount a basket will hold. **3** *Basketball* **a** one of two elevated nets through which the ball is thrown to score goals. **b** the goal so scored.

basketball *noun* **1** a game for two teams of five players, who score by throwing a ball through a bottomless net mounted on a board at the end of the opposing team's side of a rectangular court. **2** the ball used in this game.

basketful *noun* (*pl.* **basketfuls**) the amount a basket will hold.

basketry·*noun* the art or craft of making baskets.

bas mitzvah *same as* **bat mitzvah**.

Basque (bǎsk) *noun* **1** a member of a people living in the western Pyrenees. **2** the language of the people. —*adj.* of the Basque people or their language.

basque *noun* a tight-fitting garment for women, covering the body between the shoulders and the hips.

bas-relief (bä,rǐ-lēf') *noun* a technique of cutting and shaping stone or wood so that the figures on it are slightly raised from the background.

bass¹ (bǎs) *noun* (*pl.* **bass**, **basses**) **1** a marine fish having a greenish-gray body with silvery sides, and spiny fins. **2** any of various similar fishes.

bass² (bās) *noun* **1** the lowest male singing voice. **2** a singer with such a voice. **3** a part written for such a voice or for an instrument of the lowest range. **4** *colloq.* a bass guitar or double bass.

basset hound a dog with a long body, a black, tan, and white coat, short legs, and long pendulous ears .

bass guitar *or* **bass** an electric guitar that plays the bass part. ▸ **bassist** *noun*

bassoon *noun* a woodwind instrument consisting of a long jointed wooden tube fitted with metal keys and a curved crook with a double reed. ▸ **bassoonist** *noun*

bastard *noun* **1** *offensive* a child born of parents not married to each other. **2** *coarse slang* used as a term of abuse or sympathy for a man. —*adj.* **1** *offensive* born to parents not married to each other. **2** not genuine, standard, or pure.

bastardize *verb trans.* (**bastardized**, **bastardizing**) to debase.

baste¹ *verb trans.* (**basted**, **basting**) to pour hot fat or butter over (esp. roasting meat).

baste² *verb trans.* (**basted**, **basting**) to sew with temporary loose stitches.

baste³ *verb trans.* (**basted**, **basting**) to beat or thrash.

bastion *noun* **1** a tower that juts at an angle from a castle wall. **2** a person, place, or thing that is regarded as a defender of a principle, etc.: *a bastion of freedom.* ◨ BULWARK, CITADEL, FORTRESS, STRONGHOLD.

bat¹ *noun Sport* a shaped piece of, e.g., metal or wood, for hitting the ball in baseball, table tennis, etc. See also **racket¹**. —*verb trans.*, *intrans.* (**batted**, **batting**) **1 a** *Sport* to take a turn at hitting the ball with a bat. **b** *Baseball* to have as one's batting average. **2** to hit with, or as if with, a bat.

bat² *noun* a nocturnal flying mammal, with wings of skin.

bat³ *verb trans.* (**batted**, **batting**) to open and close (one's eyes) very quickly. —**not bat an eye** *or* **eyelid** *colloq* to show no surprise or emotion.

batboy *noun Baseball* a boy hired by a team to take care of its equipment.

batch *noun* a number of things or people prepared, delivered, dealt with, etc., at the same time.

bate *verb trans.* (**bated**, **bating**) to moderate or lessen the force of. —**with bated breath** feeling anxiety, excitement, or fear.

batgirl *noun Baseball* a girl hired by a team to take care of its equipment.

bath *noun* **1** a large open container in which to wash the whole body. **2** an act of washing the body in a bath. **3** the water filling a bath: *run a bath.* **4** (**baths**) a resort that offers bathing for therapy; a spa. **5** a liquid, or its container, in which something is washed, usu. as part of a technical process.

bathe (bā<u>th</u>) *verb intrans.*, *trans.* (**bathed**, **bathing**) **1** to swim in the sea, etc., for pleasure. **2** to have a bath. **3** to wash or treat (part of the body) with water, a liquid, etc., to clean it or to lessen pain. **4** to cover and surround (e.g., in light); to suffuse. ▸ **bather** *noun*

bathing suit a swimsuit.

bathos *noun* **1** in speech or writing, a sudden change from very important, serious, or beautiful ideas to very ordinary or trivial ones, generating a ridiculous effect. **2** grossly sentimental pity or sympathy.

bathrobe *noun* a loose, coatlike garment typically used before and after taking a bath.

bathroom *noun* a room containing a toilet and also usu. a bathtub, shower, and sink.

bath salts a substance in the form of grains that perfumes and softens the water in a bath.

bathtub *noun* a receptacle for a bath.

bathyscaphe (bǎth'ə-skǎf,, -skǎf,) *or* **bathyscaph** *or* **bathyscape** *noun* an electrically powered vessel with a spherical observation cabin on its underside, used for exploring the ocean depths.

batik *rioun* **1** a technique of printing on cloth, in which those parts not to be colored or dyed are covered with wax. **2** cloth colored in this way.

bat mitzvah (băt-mĭts′və, bäs-) **1** a Jewish ceremony in which a girl accepts full religious responsibilities. **2** a girl for whom this ceremony is performed.

baton *noun* **1** a light, thin stick used by the conductor of an orchestra. **2** a short, heavy stick carried by a police officer as a weapon. **3** *Sport* a short stick passed from one runner to another in a relay race. **4** a stick carried by a person at the head of a marching band.

battalion *noun* an army unit typically made up of a headquarters company and two or more companies or other subunits.

batten *noun* **1** a long flat piece of wood used for keeping other pieces in place. **2** a strip of wood or metal used to fasten the covers over a ship's hatches. —*verb trans.* (**battened, battening**) to fasten or shut with battens.

batter¹ *verb trans., intrans.* (**battered, battering**) **1** to strike or hit hard and often, or continuously. **2** to damage or wear through continual use.

batter² *noun* a mixture of eggs, flour, and milk or water, beaten together and used in cooking.

batter³ *noun Baseball* a person who bats or is batting.

battering ram a large wooden beam with a metal head, formerly used in war for breaking down walls or gates.

battery *noun* (*pl.* **batteries**) **1** a device that converts chemical energy into electrical energy. **2** a number of similar items or things: *a battery of questions.* **3** unlawful offensive or harmful striking or touching of a person by another person. **4** a group of heavy guns and the place at which they are mounted. **5** *Baseball* the pitcher and the catcher.

battle *noun* **1** a fight between opposing armies or people. **2** a competition between opposing groups or people: *a battle of wits.* **3** a long or difficult struggle: *a battle for equality.* —*verb intrans., trans.* (**battled, battling**) **1** to fight. **2** to struggle or to campaign vigorously or defiantly against: *battled urban crime.*

battle-ax or **battle-axe** *noun* **1** a heavy ax formerly used in warfare. **2** *colloq.* a fierce and domineering woman.

battle cry 1 a shout given by people charging into battle. **2** a slogan.

battlement *noun* a low wall around the top of a castle, etc., with gaps for shooting through.

battleship *noun* the largest type of warship.

batty *adj.* (**battier, battiest**) *colloq.* crazy; eccentric.

bauble *noun* a small cheap ornament or piece of jewelry.

baulk *verb same as* **balk**.

bauxite *noun* a white, yellow, red, or brown claylike substance, the main ore of aluminum.

bawdy *adj.* (**bawdier, bawdiest**) *of language, writing, etc.* containing coarsely humorous references to sex. ▸ **bawdiness** *noun*.

bawl *verb intrans., trans.* (**bawled, bawling**) to cry or shout loudly. —**bawl (someone) out** *colloq.* to scold (another) angrily.

bay¹ *noun* a body of water that forms a wide-mouthed indentation in a coastline.

bay² *noun* **1** a small area of a room set back into a wall. **2** an area for parking vehicles, or for loading and unloading them. **3** a compartment for storing or carrying: *a baggage bay.*

bay³ *adj.* of a horse reddish-brown in color. —*noun* a bay-colored horse.

bay⁴ *noun* a tree, the dried leaves of which are used to flavor soups and stews.

bay⁵ *verb intrans.* (**bayed, baying**) to make a deep howling bark: *wolves and dogs baying at the moon.* —**at bay 1** not able to escape; forced to face an attacker. **2** at a distance: *keep poverty at bay.*

bayonet *noun* a steel knife fixed to the end of a combat rifle. —*verb trans.* (**bayoneted, bayoneting**) to stab with a bayonet.

bay window a three-sided or rounded window that juts from the wall of a building.

bazaar *noun* **1** *in Middle Eastern countries* a market. **2** a sale of goods, etc., usu. to raise money for a particular organization or purpose.

BBS *abbrev Comput.* bulletin board system.

BC *abbrev* British Columbia.

B.C. or **BC** *abbrev.* Before (the birth of) Christ: used in dates. *See also* **A.D.**

B.C.E. or **BCE** *abbrev.* before the common era: sometimes used instead of **B.C.** in dates.

> *Usage* **B.C.E.** (Before the Common Era), which is culturally neutral, is sometimes used instead of **B.C.**

BD *abbrev* Bachelor of Divinity.

Be *symbol Chem.* beryllium.

be *verb intrans., aux.* (*pr t* **am, are, is, are**; *pr p* **being**; *pa t* **was, were**; *pa p* **been**) **1** to exist or be alive: *I think, therefore I am.* **2** to occur or take place: *Lunch is in an hour.* **3** to occupy a position in space: *She is at home.* **4** (*in past tense*) to go: *He's never been to Italy.* **5** to remain or continue without change: *Let it be.* **6** used to link a subject and what is said about it: *He is ill.* **7** used with the infinitive form of a verb to express a possibility, command, intention, outcome, etc.: *We are to come tomorrow.* —*verb aux.* **1** used as an auxiliary with the past participle of a verb to form a passive: *The movie was shown last night*. **2** used as an auxiliary with a present participle to form the continuous tenses: *He was running*.

be- *prefix* forming words denoting **1** all over or all around; thoroughly or completely: *beset / bedazzle*. **2** considering as or causing to be: *befriend / benumb*. **3** having or covered with; affected by: *bejeweled*. **4** affecting someone or something by an action: *bereave*.

beach *noun* the sandy or stony shore of a sea or lake. —*verb trans*. (**beached, beaching**) to push or pull (e.g., a boat) onto a beach.

beachcomber *noun* a person who searches beaches for things of interest or value.

beacon *noun* **1** a fire on a hill or mountain, lighted as a signal. **2** a warning or guidance device for aircraft or ships, e.g., a lighthouse. **3** a source of inspiration.

bead *noun* **1** a small ball or cylinder of glass, stone, etc., strung with others, e.g., in a necklace. **2** (**beads**) **a** a string of beads worn as jewelry. **b** a string of beads used when praying. **3** a small drop of liquid: *beads of sweat*. —*verb trans*. (**beaded, beading**) to decorate with beads.

beady *adj*. (**beadier, beadiest**) *of eyes* small, round, and bright.

beagle *noun* a dog with pendulous ears and usu. a short white, tan, and black coat.

beak *noun* **1** the horny projecting jaws of a bird. *Also called* **bill**. **2** any pointed projection that resembles this.

beaker *noun* **1** a large drinking glass or handleless plastic cup. **2** a deep glass container with a lip, used in chemistry.

beam *noun* **1** a long, straight, thick piece of wood, used, e.g., in a building. **2** the widest part of a ship or boat. **3** a ray of light. **4** a balance beam in gymnastics. —*verb intrans., trans*. (**beamed, beaming**) **1** to smile broadly with pleasure. **2** to shine. **3** to send out (rays of light, radio waves, etc.).

bean *noun* **1** the edible kidney-shaped seed of various plants of the pea family. **2** a plant that bears such seeds. **3** a seed that superficially resembles such seeds, e.g., coffee bean.

bean sprouts young bean shoots, esp. of the mung bean, used as food.

bear¹ *verb trans., intrans*. (*pa t* **bore**; *pa p* **borne**; *pr p* **bearing**) **1** to carry, bring, or take: *bear gifts*. **2** to support (a weight). **3** to produce: *bear fruit*. **4** (*pa p* in the passive is **born** when not followed by an object or by *by* and a name) to give birth to: *Has she borne children? / He was born in 1960*. **5** to take or accept: *bear the blame*. **6** to put up with or like. **7** to show or be marked by: *bear the traces of tears*. **8** to carry in thought or memory: *bear a grudge*. **9** to turn slightly in a given direction: *bear left*. **10** to have: *bear no resemblance to*. **11** to behave: *bear oneself well*. —**bear down on (someone)** to move toward (another) threateningly. **bear (something or someone) out** to support or confirm (something or someone). **bear up** to remain strong, brave, etc., under strain. **bear with (someone)** to be patient with (another).

bear² *noun* **1** a large carnivorous animal, having a heavily built body, thick fur and strong claws. **2** a rough, ill-mannered person.

bearable *adj*. able to be suffered or tolerated. ▸ **bearably** *adv*.

beard *noun* **1** the hair that grows on a man's chin and neck. **2** a beardlike growth on some animals, esp. goats. —*verb trans*. (**bearded, bearding**) to oppose or confront openly or boldly. ▸ **bearded** *adj*.

bearer *noun* **1** one that bears or carries. **2** a person who helps carry equipment on an expedition. **3** a person who holds a banknote, check, or other money order that can be exchanged for money.

bear hug *colloq*. a rough, tight squeeze with the arms.

bearing *noun* **1** the way a person stands, walks, etc. **2** a relation or effect: *Your remark has no bearing on the situation*. **3** the horizontal direction of a fixed point or the path of a moving object, usu. expressed in degrees clockwise from the north. **4** (*usu*. **bearings**) position, or a calculation of position: *a ship's bearings*. **5** (**bearings**) *colloq*. a sense or awareness of one's own position or surroundings: *lose one's bearings*. **6** a part of a machine or other device that supports another part and allows free movement between the two parts.

bearish *adj. of a person* bad-tempered.

bearskin *noun* **1** the skin of a bear. **2** a tall fur military hat.

beast *noun* **1** a large wild animal, esp. a four-footed one. **2** a cruel, brutal person. **3** *colloq*. a difficult or unpleasant person or thing.

beastly *adj*. (**beastlier, beastliest**) **1** fierce or brutal. **2** *colloq*. unpleasant; horrid.

beat *verb trans., intrans*. (*pa t* **beat**; *pa p* **beaten**; *pr p* **beating**) **1** to hit violently and repeatedly. **2** to strike repeatedly, e.g., to remove dust or make a sound. **3** to knock or strike repeatedly: *rain beating against the door*. **4 a** to do something better than (another); to defeat. **b** *colloq*. to be superior to or more desirable than (an alternative): *Flying beats driving*. **c** *colloq*. to circumvent by prior planning: *Let's leave early and beat the rush hour*. **d** *colloq*. to

get to a destination earlier than (another): *She beat me to the office.* **5** to be too difficult to be solved or understood by: *This puzzle beats me.* **6** to mix or stir thoroughly: *beat eggs.* **7** to make or shape (something) by striking the raw material. **8** to vibrate with a strong, regular rhythm. **9** to mark or show musical time: *beat out time.* **10** to move rhythmically up and down. **11** to push, drive, or force (someone or something) away: *beat off an intruder.* **12** to strike (bushes, trees, etc.) to force birds or animals into the open for shooting. —*noun* **1** a regular stroke, or its sound: *the beat of a heart.* **2** the main accent in music. **3** a regular or usual course or journey, esp. one made by a police officer. —*adj. slang* exhausted; tired: *I'm really beat.* —**beat around** *or* **about the bush** to talk tediously about a subject without coming to the main point. **beat it** *slang* to go away.
▶ **beater** *noun* ▶ **beating** *noun*

beatific (bē̗,ə-tĭf´ĭk) *adj.* showing great blessedness or happiness.

beatify *verb trans.* (**beatified, beatifying, beatifies**) **1** *RC Church* to declare the blessed status of (someone who has died), usu. as the first step toward canonization. **2** to make extremely happy. ▶ **beatification** *noun*

beatnik *noun* a young person, esp. in the 1950s, who rejected conventional social and political ideas and attire.

beat-up *adj. slang* old and worn; in very bad condition.

beau *noun* (*pl.* **beaus, beaux**) **1** a boyfriend or male lover. **2** a man who thinks a lot about his clothes and appearance.

beauteous *adj.* beautiful.

beautician *noun* a person who styles women's hair, applies their make-up, etc., esp. in a beauty parlor.

beautiful *adj.* delightful to the senses: *a beautiful garden.* ▣ BEAUTEOUS, GORGEOUS, LOVELY, RAVISHING ▣ UGLY. ▶ **beautifully** *adv.*

beautify *verb trans.* (**beautified, beautifying, beautifies**) to make beautiful. ▶ **beautification** *noun*

beauty *noun* (*pl.* **beauties**) **1** a quality pleasing to the senses. **2** a beautiful woman or girl. **3** *slang* an outstandingly good example: *a beauty of a car.*

beauty mark a small, dark mark on the face.

beauty parlor a place that offers hairdressing, make-up, etc. *Also called* **beauty salon**.

beauty queen the winner in a beauty contest.

beaver *noun* **1** a large aquatic rodent that has brown fur, a flat broad tail, and sharp teeth with which it can cut down trees and branches. **2** the fur of this rodent.

became *see* **become**.

because *conj.* for the reason that. —*prep.* (**because of**) on account of: *couldn't come because of rain.*

> *Usage* Avoid the redundant expression the reason is because, as in *The reason the President was not reelected was because he was unpopular.* Rewrite it: *The reason the President was not reelected was that he was unpopular* or *The reason the President was not reelected was his unpopularity*

beck *noun* —**at (someone's) beck and call** having to be always ready to carry out (someone's) orders or wishes.

beckon *verb trans., intrans.* (**beckoned, beckoning**) to call (someone) toward oneself, esp. by making a hand signal.

become *verb intrans., trans.* (*pa t* **became**; *pa p* **become**; *pr p* **becoming**) **1** to come or grow to be. **2** (**become of (someone** *or* **something)**) to happen to: *Whatever became of Donald?* **3** to suit or look good on: *That hat becomes you.*

becoming *adj.* **1** attractive. **2** suitable or proper.

becquerel *noun* (SYMBOL **Bq**) the unit of radioactivity in the International System, equivalent to one disintegration of a radioactive source per second.

bed *noun* **1** a piece of furniture for sleeping on. **2** the bottom of a river, lake, or sea. **3** an area of ground in a garden, for growing plants: *a flower bed.* **4** a support or foundation. **5** a layer, esp. of rock. —*verb trans., intrans.* (**bedded, bedding**) **1** to provide (someone) with a bed, bedding, or a sleeping place: *bedded them down on the sofa.* **2** to have sex with. **3** to plant (something) in a garden. **4** to place or fix firmly.

bedazzle *verb trans.* (**bedazzled, bedazzling**) **1** to impress greatly. **2** to confuse.

bedbug *noun* a wingless household pest that infests bedding and feeds on human blood.

bedclothes *pl. noun* the sheets, blankets, etc., used to cover a bed.

bedcover *noun* a top cover for a bed.

bedding *noun* mattresses, blankets, etc.

bedeck *verb trans.* (**bedecked, bedecking**) to provide with decorations.

bedevil *verb trans.* (**bedeviled, bedeviling**) **1** to cause continual difficulties or trouble to. **2** throw into utter confusion. ▶ **bedevilment** *noun*

bedfellow *noun* **1** a person with whom one shares a bed. **2** a partner or associate.

bedlam *noun* a noisy, confused situation.

> After St Mary of *Bethlehem* Hospital, a former mental asylum in London

bedpan *noun* a wide, shallow pan used as a toilet by people who are unable to get out of bed.

bedraggled *adj.* 1 wet and limp: *bedraggled hair.* 2 dirty and deteriorating: *bedraggled buildings in a seedy neighborhood.*

bedridden *adj.* unable to get out of bed.

bedrock *noun* 1 the solid rock forming the lowest layer under soil and rock fragments. 2 the basic principle, idea, etc., on which something else rests.

bedroom *noun* a room in which people sleep.

bedside *noun* the place or position next to a bed, esp. of a sick person. —*adj.* relating to or near a bed, esp. that of a sick person: *a physician's bedside manner.*

bedsore *noun* an ulcer on a person's skin, caused by lying in bed for long periods.

bedspread *noun* a top cover for a bed.

bedstead *noun* the frame of a bed.

bee *noun* 1 a flying, stinging insect that makes honey. 2 a meeting of friends or neighbors for work or enjoyment: *a knitting bee.*

beech *noun* 1 a tree with smooth gray bark. 2 the wood of this tree. —*adj.* made from the wood of the beech tree.

beef *noun* (*pl.* **beeves, beef**) 1 a the flesh of a bull, steer, cow, or ox, used as food. b a fully grown bull, steer, cow, or ox. 2 *colloq.* muscle; strength. 3 (*pl.* **beefs**) *slang* a complaint. —*verb intrans.* (**beefed, beefing**) *colloq.* to complain. —**beef** (**something**) **up** *colloq.* to make (something) stronger or greater than before.

beefsteak *noun* a thick slice of beef for grilling or frying.

beefy *adj.* (**beefier, beefiest**) 1 of or like beef. 2 having a lot of fat or muscle.

beehive *noun* a box or hut in which bees are kept, and where they store their honey.

beekeeper *noun* a person who keeps bees for their honey. *Also called* **apiarist.** ▸ **beekeeping** *noun.*

beeline *noun* a straight line between two places.

been *see* **be.**

beep *noun* a short high-pitched sound. —*verb intrans., trans.* (**beeped, beeping**) to produce or cause to produce a beep.

beeper *noun* a paging device that beeps.

beer *noun* 1 a an alcoholic drink that is prepared by the slow fermentation of malted cereal grains, usu. barley, flavored with hops. b a glass, can, or bottle of this beverage. 2 another fermented liquor, e.g., ginger beer. ▸ **beery** *adj.*

beeswax *noun* a solid yellowish substance produced by bees for making the cells in which they live, used as a polish.

beet *noun* a plant with an edible large root, used as food or for making sugar.

beetle[1] *noun* a winged insect with thickened forewings that form hard cases that cover and protect the hindwings.

beetle[2] *noun* a tool with a heavy head for crushing, beating, etc.

befall *verb intrans., trans.* (*pa t* **befell**; *pa p* **befallen**; *pr p* **befalling**) to happen; to happen to.

befit *verb trans.* (**befitted, befitting**) to be suitable or right for.

before *prep.* 1 earlier than: *before noon.* 2 ahead of; in front of: *stand before the table.* 3 in the presence of; for the attention of: *the question before us.* 4 in the face of: *draw back before the blast.* 5 rather than; in preference to: *put money before friendship.* —*conj.* 1 earlier than the time when: *Do it before you forget.* 2 rather than; in preference to: *I'd die before I'd surrender.* —*adv.* 1 in front; ahead: *go before.* 2 previously; in the past: *Haven't we met before?*

beforehand *adv.* early; in advance; in preparation.

befriend *verb trans.* (**befriended, befriending**) to become the friend of.

beg *verb intrans., trans.* (**begged, begging**) (*usu.* **beg for** (**something**)) 1 to ask for (money, food, etc.). 2 to ask earnestly or humbly.

began *see* **begin.**

beget *verb trans.* (*pa t* **begot**; *pa p* **begotten** *or* **begot**; *pr p* **begetting**) 1 to be the father of. 2 to cause: *social conditions that begot revolution.*

beggar *noun* 1 a person who lives by begging. 2 *colloq.* a man or boy: *Cheeky beggar!* ▸ **beggarly** *adj.*

begin *verb trans., intrans.* (*pa t* **began**; *pa p* **begun**; *pr p* **beginning**) 1 to start. 2 to bring or come into being. ▸ **beginner** *noun* ▸ **beginning** *noun*

begonia *noun* a tropical plant with brightly colored waxy flowers.

begrudge *verb trans.* (**begrudged, begrudging**) 1 to do, give, or allow unwillingly or with regret. 2 to envy or resent (another) for his or her possession of (something): *He begrudged her her success.*

beguile *verb trans.* (**beguiled, beguiling**) 1 to charm, trick, or deceive. ▸ **beguiling** *adj.* ▸ **beguilingly** *adv.*

begun *see* **begin.**

behalf *noun* interest and support.

behave *verb intrans., trans.* (**behaved, behaving**) 1 to act in a specified way: *children who behave well.* 2 to act or conduct (oneself) in a suitable, polite, or orderly way: *Behave yourself at the party.*

behavior *noun* way of behaving; manners: *good behavior.* ▸ **behavioral** *adj.*

behaviorism *noun* an approach to psychology that studies only observable behavior rather than thoughts and emotions. ► **behaviorist** *noun*

behead *verb trans.* (**beheaded, beheading**) to cut off the head of (someone), usu. as a punishment.

beheld *see* **behold**.

behind *prep.* **1** at or toward the back of or the far side. **2** later or slower than; after in time: *behind schedule.* **3** supporting: *We're all behind you.* **4** in the past with respect to: *Those problems are all behind me now.* **5** not as far advanced as. **6** being the cause of: *reasons behind the decision.* —*adv.* **1** in or to the back or far side. **2** remaining: *leave something behind.* **3** following: *run behind.* —*noun colloq.* the buttocks.

behold *verb trans., intrans.* (**beheld, beholding**) to look at; to see. —*interj.* look. ► **beholder** *noun*

beige *adj.* of a pale pinkish-yellow color. —*noun* a pale pinkish-yellow color.

being *noun* **1** existence; life. **2** a living person or thing. —*verb see* **be**.

bejeweled *adj.* decorated with jewels.

bel *noun* (**SYMBOL B**) a quantity equal to 10 decibels.

belabor *verb trans.* (**belabored, belaboring**) to argue about or discuss to excessive lengths.

belated *adj.* happening, or coming, or having been done late or too late. ► **belatedly** *adv.*

belay *verb trans.* (**belayed, belaying**) **1** *Mountaineering* to make (a climber) safe by tying his or her rope to a rock or pin. **2** *Naut.* to make (a rope) secure by winding it around a cleat, peg, etc.

belch *verb intrans., trans.* (**belched, belching**) **1** to give out air noisily from the stomach through the mouth. **2** *of a chimney, etc.* to send out smoke, etc. —*noun* an act of belching.

beleaguer *verb trans.* (**beleaguered, beleaguering**) **1** to surround and lay siege to. **2** to cause (someone) bother or worry. ► **beleaguered** *adj.*

belfry *noun* (*pl.* **belfries**) **1** a tower for bells, usu. attached to a church. **2** the upper part of such a tower, containing the bells.

belie *verb trans.* (**belied, belying, belies**) **1** to show to be untrue or false. **2** to give a false idea or impression of.

belief *noun* **1** intellectual acceptance of the reality or truth of something: *That accusation is unworthy of belief.* **2** a firm opinion. ☒ CONVICTION, FEELING, OPINION, POSITION, SENTIMENT, VIEW ☒ DISBELIEF. **3** trust or confidence: *has no belief in people.* **4** a person's religious faith: *belief in the afterlife.*

believe *verb trans., intrans.* (**believed, believing**) **1** to accept (something) as true. **2** to accept what is said by (a person) as true. **3** to think, assume, or suppose. **4 a** to have religious faith or strong conviction about (it). **b** to consider (it) right or good: *believe in telling the truth.* **5** (**believe in** (**someone**)) to have trust or confidence in (another). ► **believable** *adj.* ► **believer** *noun*

belittle *verb trans.* (**belittled, belittling**) to treat as unimportant, esp. disparagingly.

bell *noun* **1** a deep hollow object, usu.. of metal, rounded at one end and wide and open at the other, with a small hammer or clapper inside, which gives a ringing sound when struck. **2** the sound made by such an object. **3** any other device that makes a ringing sound. **4** something shaped like a bell. **5** the ringing of a bell on board ship to tell the time, or the number of times such a device is rung.

belladonna *noun* **1** a poisonous herb with purple-colored, bell-shaped flowers and shiny black berries. *Also called* **deadly nightshade**. **2** atropine.

bellboy *noun* a man or boy who works in a hotel, carrying guests' bags, etc. *Also called* **bellhop**.

belle *noun* a beautiful woman: *the belle of the ball.*

bellhop *noun* a bellboy.

bellicose *adj.* likely or wanting to cause an argument or war.

belligerent *adj.* **1** of a person or action ready or displaying readiness to attack. **2** fighting a war. —*noun* a person or country fighting a war. ► **belligerence** ► **belligerently** *adv.*

bellow *verb intrans., trans.* (**bellowed, bellowing**) **1** to make a loud deep cry like that of a bull. **2** to shout (words) loudly or angrily. —*noun* a loud deep sound or cry.

bellows *noun* (*sing., pl.*) a device consisting of or containing a baglike or boxlike part with folds in it that is squeezed to create a current of air.

belly *noun* (*pl.* **bellies**) **1** the part of the body below the chest containing the organs used for digesting food. **2** *colloq.* the stomach. **3** a hollow interior at the bottom of a structure. —*verb intrans.* (**bellied, bellying, bellies**) to swell out; to bulge.

bellyache *noun* a pain in the belly. —*verb intrans.* (**bellyached, bellyaching**) *slang* to complain noisily or repeatedly.

bellybutton *noun colloq.* the navel.

bellydance *noun* an erotic Middle Eastern dance performed by women, in which the belly and hips are moved around, often very fast. —*verb intrans.* (**bellydanced, bellydancing**) to perform a bellydance. ► **bellydancer** *noun*

bellyful *noun* (*pl.* **bellyfuls**) enough to eat. —**have had a bellyful of (something** *or* **someone)** *colloq.* to have put up with more of (something or someone) than is really bearable.

belong *verb intrans.* (**belonged, belonging**). **1 (belong to)** to be the property or right of. **2 (belong to)** to be a native of (a place), member of (a group), etc. **3 (belong with** *or* **in** (**something**)) to have a proper place; to go together.

belongings *pl. noun* personal possessions.

beloved *adj.* much loved. —*noun* a much-loved person.

below *prep.* **1** lower in position, rank, amount, etc., than. **2** not worthy of. —*adv.* **1** at, to, or in a lower place, point, or level. **2** farther on in a book, etc.: *see page 23 below.* **3** in temperature measurement, below zero: *30 below.*

belt *noun* **1** a long, narrow piece of leather, plastic, or cloth worn around the waist to keep clothing in place or for decoration. **2** an area, usu. relatively long and narrow: *a rain belt.* **3** a band of rubber, etc., moving the wheels, or around the wheels, of a machine. **4** *slang* a hard blow. —*verb trans., intrans.* (**belted, belting**) **1** to put a belt around. **2** to beat with a belt. **3** *slang* to sing loudly: *belt out a torch song.*

beltway *noun* a freeway encircling an urban area.

belvedere *noun* a pavilion, or a raised turret or lantern on the top of a house, built to provide a view or admit light and air.

bemuse *verb trans.* (**bemused, bemusing**) to puzzle or confuse.

bench *noun* **1** a long seat, typically having no back. **2** a worktable for a carpenter, scientist, etc. **3 (the bench)** a judge's seat in court. **4 (the Bench)** judges and magistrates as a group.

benchmark *noun* **1** a mark on a post, etc., giving the height above sea level of the land at that spot. **2** a standard or point of reference: *high office as the benchmark of professional success.*

bend *verb trans., intrans.* (pa t and pa p **bent**; *pr p* **bending**) **1** to make or become angled or curved. **2** to move or stretch in a curve: *a road bending to the left.* **3** to move the top part of the body forward and down. **4** to submit or force to submit: *bent them to her will.* —*noun* **1** a curved or bent part. **2** the act of curving or bending. **3 (the bends)** (*sing., pl.*) decompression sickness.

beneath *prep.* **1** under; below. **2** not worthy of. —*adv.* below; underneath.

Benedictine (bĕn,ə-dīk′tən, -tēn,) *noun* **1** a member of the Christian community that follows the teachings of St. Benedict. **2** a strong greenish-yellow alcoholic drink first made by Benedictine monks in France in the 16th c. —*adj.* relating to the Benedictines or to St. Benedict.

benediction *noun* **1** a prayer giving blessing, esp. at the end of a religious service. **2** *RC Church* a short service in which the congregation is blessed.

benefactor *noun* a person who gives financial help to an institution or cause.

benefice *noun* a position as priest or a church office, and the income (from land, buildings, etc.) that is attached to it.

beneficent *adj.* actively kind and generous. ▸ **beneficence** *noun*

beneficial *adj.* having good results or benefits.

beneficiary *noun* (*pl.* **beneficiaries**) **1** a person who benefits from something. **2** a person who receives money, etc., in a will.

benefit *noun* **1** something good gained or received. **2** advantage or sake: *for your benefit.* **3** (*often* **benefits**) a payment made by a government or insurance company, usu. to someone who is ill or out of work. **4** a game, performance at a theater, etc., from which the profits are given to a worthy cause. —*verb intrans., trans.* (**benefited, benefiting**) (**1 (benefit from** *or* **by (something)**) to gain an advantage or receive something good. **2** to do good to.

benevolent *adj.* showing kindness and generosity. ▸ **benevolence** *noun*

Bengali (bĕn-gô′lē, -gä′lē) *noun* **1** a member of a people living in Bangladesh and the state of West Bengal in India. **2** the language of this people. —*adj.* of the Bengalis or their language.

benign *adj.* **1** kind; gentle. **2** favorable. **3** *of a disorder* not having harmful effects, esp. being noncancerous. *See also* **malignant.** ▸ **benignly** *adv.*

bent *adj.* **1** not, or no longer, straight. **2 (bent on (something))** with one's attention or energy strongly focused on (it) —*noun* a natural liking or aptitude. —*verb see* **bend.**

benumb *verb trans.* (**benumbed, benumbing**) to make numb.

benzene *noun* a colorless flammable liquid used as a solvent and in the manufacture of plastics, dyes, drugs, etc.

benzine *noun* a motor fuel obtained from petroleum.

benzoin *noun* a resin used to make perfumes.

bequeath *verb trans.* (**bequeathed, bequeathing**) to leave (personal belongings) to (someone) in a will.

bequest *noun* **1** an act of leaving personal belongings to someone in a will. **2** something left or bequeathed in a will.

berate *verb trans.* (**berated, berating**) to scold severely.

bereaved *adj.* having recently suffered the death of a close friend or relative. ▸ **bereavement** *noun*

bereft *adj.* (**bereft of (something)**) deprived of (it); having had (it) taken away.

beret *noun* a round, flat, soft cap.

beriberi *noun* a disease caused by lack of vitamin B1, resulting in inflammation of the nerves, paralysis, edema, and heart failure.

berry *noun* (*pl.* **berries**) **1** a fruit in which the seeds are surrounded by a single fleshy receptacle, e.g., the grape, cucumber, or tomato. **2** any small fruit, such as a raspberry or strawberry.

berserk *adj.* violently angry; wild and destructive.

berth *noun* **1** a place in which to sleep on a ship, train, etc. **2** a place in a port where a ship or boat can be tied up.—*verb trans.,* *intrans.* (**berthed, berthing**) to tie up (a ship) in its berth; to arrive at a designated berth: *The destroyer berthed at midnight.*

beryl *noun* a green, blue, yellow, or white mineral often used as a gemstone.

beryllium *noun* (SYMBOL **Be**) a silvery-grey metal, used in x-ray tubes and alloys.

beseech *verb trans.* (**besought** or **beseeched, beseeching, beseeches**) to ask earnestly; to beg.

beset *verb trans.* (**beset, besetting**) to attack on all sides; worry: *We were beset with problems.*

beside *prep.* **1** by the side of or near; next to. **2** compared with. **3** not relevant to: *beside the point.* —**beside (oneself)** in a state of uncontrollable anger or other emotion.

besides *prep.* **1** in addition to; as well as. **2** except for. —*adv.* also; as well.

besiege *verb trans.* (**besieged, besieging**) **1** to surround (a town or stronghold) with an army in order to force it to surrender. **2** to gather around in a crowd: *besieged by members of the press.* **3** to annoy constantly; bother: *We were besieged with questions.*

besotted *adj.* **1** foolishly infatuated. **2** confused, esp. through being drunk.

besought *see* **beseech.**

best *adj.* **1** most excellent, suitable, or desirable: *wanted the best grades.* **2** most successful, clever, etc.: *the best student in the class.* **3** greatest; most: *The best part of the day was spent in meetings.* **4** *see* **good. 5** *see* **well**[1]. —*adv.* **1** most successfully, etc.: *Who did best on the exam?* **2** more than all others: *I like her best.* **3** *see* **good. 4** *see* **well**[1]. —*noun* **1** the most excellent or suitable person or thing; the most desirable quality, etc.: *the best of the bunch.* **2** the greatest effort: *do one's best.* **3** a person's finest clothes: *our Sunday best.*

4 victory or success: *get the best of an opponent.* —*verb trans.* (**bested, besting**) to beat or defeat. —**at best** considered in the most favorable way; in the best circumstances. **for the best** likely or intended to have the best results possible.

bestial *adj.* **1** of or like an animal. **2** cruel. ▸ **bestiality** *noun*

bestir *verb trans.* (**bestirred, bestirring**) to rouse (oneself).

best man a bridegroom's main male attendant at a wedding.

bestow *verb trans.* (**bestowed, bestowing**) **1** to confer as an honor or gift: *bestow an award.* **2** to direct, focus, or apply: *bestowed considerable thought on the issue.* ▸ **bestowal** *noun*

bestseller *noun* a book or other item that sells in large numbers. ▸ **bestselling** *adj.*

bet *verb trans., intrans.* (**bet** or **betted, betting**) **1 a** to risk (usu. money) on predicting the outcome or result of a future event, esp. a race or other sporting event. **b** to engage in making bets. **2** to feel sure or confident: *I bet they'll be late.* —*noun* **1** an act of betting. **2** a sum of money bet. **3** an opinion.

beta *noun* **1** the second letter of the Greek alphabet (Β, β). **2** the second unit or item in a classification series.

beta particle an electron or positron produced when a neutron inside an unstable radioactive nucleus turns into a proton, or a proton turns into a neutron.

betel *noun* an Asian climbing plant, whose leaves are wrapped around the seeds of the plant and chewed.

betel nut the dried seed of the betel palm, chewed for its mild stimulatory properties.

béte noire (bĕt-nwär′) *noun* (*pl.* **bétes noires**) a person or thing that especially bothers, annoys, or frightens one.

betide *verb trans., intrans.* (**betided, betiding**) **1** to happen to (one). **2** to occur; to take place.

betray *verb trans.* (**betrayed, betraying**) **1** to aid and abet an enemy of (e.g., one's country); to commit treason against. **2** to break (a promise, etc.) or be unfaithful to (someone): *betray one's spouse.* **3** to reveal (a secret, etc.): *betray confidences.* **4** to be evidence of: *Her face betrayed her unhappiness.* ▸ **betrayal** *noun*

betrothed *adj.* engaged to marry someone. ▸ **betrothal** *noun*

better[1] *adj.* **1** good to a greater extent, or more excellent, suitable, desirable, etc., than others. **2** (**better at (something)**) more successful, etc., in doing (it). **3** partly or fully recovered from illness: *feel better.* **4** greater: *the better part of a day.* **5** *see* **good. 6** *see*

well¹. —*adv.* **1** more excellently, successfully, etc., than another or others. **2** in or to a greater degree than others or than before. **3** *see* **good. 4** *see* **well** —*noun* (*often* **betters**) a person superior in quality, rank, etc.: *one's elders and betters.* —*verb trans., intrans.* (**bettered, bettering**) **1** to improve on; to beat. **2** to make or become better. **3** to improve one's position or social standing: *better oneself by getting an education.* —**better off** more affluent or fortunate than others or than before. **had better** ought to: *We'd better hurry or we'll be late.* ▸ **betterment** *noun*

bettor *or* **better²** *noun* a person who bets.

between *prep.* **1** in, to, through, or across the space dividing (two people, places, times, etc.). **2** to and from: *a regular bus service between Baltimore and Annapolis.* **3** in combination; acting together: *Between them, they bought a private plane.* **4** shared out among: *divide the money between them.* **5** involving choice: *choose between right and wrong.* **6** including; involving: *a fight between rivals.* —*adv.* (**in between**) in, into the middle of (two points in space, time, etc.). —**between you and me** as a matter of confidence.

> *Usage* The expression *between you and I* is considered incorrect; the correct wording is *between you and me.*

betwixt *prep., adv.* between. —**betwixt and between** undecided; in a middle position.

bevel *noun* **1** a sloping edge. **2** a tool that makes a sloping edge on wood or stone. —*verb trans., intrans.* (**beveled, beveling**) **1** to give a bevel or slant to. **2** to slope at an angle.

beverage *noun formal* a drink.

bevy *noun* (*pl.* **bevies**) a group of women or girls, or of birds such as quail.

beware *verb intrans., trans.* (**bewared, bewaring**) to be careful of or on one's guard against (someone or something): *Beware of the dog.* / *Beware the Ides of March.*

bewilder *verb trans.* (**bewildered, bewildering**) to confuse or puzzle. ▸ **bewilderment** *noun*

bewitch *verb trans.* (**bewitched, bewitching**) **1** to cast a spell on. **2** to charm.

beyond *prep.* **1** on the far side of: *beyond the hills.* **2** farther on than (something) in time or place. **3** out of the range, reach, power, understanding, possibility, etc., of: *It's quite beyond me.* **4** greater or better than in amount, size, or level. **5** other than; apart from: *unable to help beyond giving money.* —*adv.* farther away; to or on the far side of.

bhp *abbrev.* brake horsepower.

Bi *symbol Chem.* bismuth.

bi- *prefix* forming words denoting **1** having, involving, etc., two: *bifocal.* **2** happening once every two: *biweekly.* **3** on or from both sides: *bilateral.* **4** *Chem.* used nontechnically for an acid salt: *bicarbonate.*

> *Usage* The prefix *bi-* plus *monthly* or *weekly* means once *every* two (months or weeks); the prefix *semi-*, when so used, means twice a (month or week).

biannual *adj.* occurring twice a year; semiannual. ▸ **biannually** *adv.*

> *Usage* This word is often confused with *biennial*, which means occurring every two years.

bias *noun* **1 a** a disposition to favor or disfavor one side against another. **b** a policy, set of procedures, or act that derives from and exhibits prejudice. **2** a line cut across the grain of a fabric. —*verb trans.* (**biased** *or* **biassed, biasing** *or* **biassing**) **1** to influence or prejudice. **2** to give a bias to.

biathlon *noun* a sporting event in which competitors cross a course on skis, stopping at intervals to shoot at targets with rifles.

Bib. *abbrev.* Bible.

bib *noun* a piece of cloth or plastic fastened esp. under a child's chin to protect the clothes while eating.

Bible *noun* **1** the sacred writings of the Christian Church, consisting of the Old and New Testaments. **2** a copy of these writings. **3** (**bible**) an authoritative and comprehensive book on a subject. ▸ **Biblical** *or* **biblical** *adj.*

bibliography *noun* (*pl.* **bibliographies**) **1** a list of books by one author or on one subject. **2** a list of books used as the sources of another book and usu. given in a list at the back of it. ▸ **bibliographical** *adj.*

bibulous *adj.* liking alcohol too much, or drinking too much of it.

bicameral *adj.* made up of two legislative houses or chambers.

bicarbonate of soda baking soda.

bicentenary *noun* (*pl.* **bicentenaries**) a bicentennial. —*adj.* denoting a bicentenary.

bicentennial *noun* a 200th anniversary, esp. a cause for celebration. *Also called* **bicentenary.** —*adj.* denoting a bicentennial.

biceps *noun* (*pl.* **biceps, bicepses**) a muscle with two points of origin, esp. the one at the front of the upper arm.

bicker *verb intrans.* (**bickered, bickering**) to argue or quarrel, esp. about trivial matters.

bicoastal *adj.* **1** of or relating to the East and West coasts of the USA, or those traveling to and from them. **2** from one coast of the USA to another: *bicoastal business calls.*

bicycle noun a vehicle consisting of a metal frame with two wheels, one behind the other, and a seat, driven by turning pedals with the feet. —verb intrans. (**bicycled, bicycling**) to ride a bicycle. ▸ **bicyclist** noun

bid verb trans., intrans. (pa t **bade** or **bid**; pa p **bidden** or **bid**; pr p **bidding**) **1** to command. **2** to invite: bid her to start. **3** to express a wish, greeting, etc.: bid him welcome. **4** (pa t and pa p **bid**) to offer (an amount of money) when trying to buy something, esp. at an auction. **5** (pa t and pa p **bid**) Cards to state in advance (the number of tricks one will try to win). **6** (pa t and pa p **bid**) to state a price one will charge for work to be done. —noun **1** an offer of a price, esp. at an auction. **2** Cards a statement of how many tricks one hopes to win. **3** an attempt to obtain something: make a bid for freedom. ▸ **bidder** noun

biddable adj. compliant; docile.

bide verb intrans. (pa t **bided** or **bode**; pa p **bided**; pr p **biding**) to wait or stay.

bidet (bĭ-dā′) noun a small low basin with faucets, on which one sits to wash the genital area.

biennial adj. **1** occurring once every two years. **2** lasting two years. —noun a plant that takes two years to complete its life cycle. See also **annual, perennial.** ▸ **biennially** adv.

> **Usage** This word is often confused with *biannual*, which means occurring twice a year.

bier noun a movable stand on which a coffin rests or is transported.

bifocal adj. denoting eyeglasses or contact lenses having two separate sections with different focal lengths.

bifocals pl. noun a pair of eyeglasses with bifocal lenses.

bifurcate verb intrans. (**bifurcated, bifurcating**) of roads, etc. to divide into two parts; to fork.

big adj. (**bigger, biggest**) **1** large or largest in size, weight, or number. **2** significant; important. **3** powerful or successful: the big four. **4** older: my big sister. **5** generous: That was big of you. **6** extravagant: big ideas. **7** in the advanced stage of pregnancy: big with child. —adv. colloq. **1** in a boastful or extravagant way: she talked big. **2** in a far-seeing way: need statesmen who think big.

bigamy noun (pl. **bigamies**) the crime of being married to two wives or husbands at the same time. ▸ **bigamist** noun ▸ **bigamous** adj.

Big Bang theory a hypothetical model of the origin of the universe that postulates that all matter and energy were once concentrated into a dense mass, which underwent a gigantic explosion between 13 and 20 billion years ago.

big cat a large member of the cat family, such as the lion, tiger, or leopard.

big game large animals, such as lions, tigers, etc., that are hunted for sport.

bighead noun colloq. a conceited or arrogant person. ▸ **big-headed** adj.

big-hearted adj. thoughtful and generous.

bighorn noun (pl. **bighorn** or **bighorns**) a wild sheep that inhabits mountains, esp. cliffs, in N America and Siberia.

bight noun **1** a stretch of gently curving coastline. **2** a loop in a length of rope.

big mouth slang a boastful, talkative person.

bigot noun an extremely prejudiced person who refuses to tolerate the opinions of others. ▸ **bigoted** adj. ▸ **bigotry** noun

big-ticket adj. colloq. costly.

big time colloq. success in an activity or profession, esp. in show business: hit the big time.

big top a large round tent in which a circus performs.

bigwig noun colloq. an important person.

bijou (bē′zhōō,) noun (pl. **bijoux**) a small delicate jewel or similar object.

bike noun a bicycle, motorcycle, or motorbike.

biker noun **1** a person who rides a motorcycle. **2** a member of a motorcycle gang.

bikini noun a brief, two-piece swimsuit for women.

> Named after *Bikini* Atoll atomic test site, because of its supposedly dynamic effect on viewers

bilateral adj. **1** of or on two sides. **2** affecting, or signed or agreed by, two countries, groups, etc.: a bilateral trade agreement. ▸ **bilateral** adv.

bilberry noun (pl. **bilberries**) the blueberry (sense 1).

bile noun **1** a thick yellowish-green fluid produced by the liver, which helps in the breakdown and absorption of fats during digestion. **2** anger or bad temper. See also **bilious.**

bilge noun **1** the broadest part of a ship's bottom. **2** the dirty water that collects in a ship's bilge. Also called **bilge water. 3** slang nonsense.

bilingual adj. able to speak two languages fluently. —noun a person who speaks two languages fluently. ▸ **bilingualism** noun

bilious adj. **1** relating to bile or marked by excessive secretions of it. **2** sickly. **3** similar to bile, esp. in color. **4** bad-tempered. ▸ **biliously** adv.

bill[1] noun **1** a printed or written statement of the amount of money owed for goods or services received. **2** a written plan for a proposed law. **3** a banknote. **4** an advertising poster or public notice. **5** a list of items, events, performers, etc. —*verb trans.* (**billed, billing**) **1** to send a bill to (someone), requesting payment for goods, etc. **2** to ad-vertise or announce (a person or event) on a poster, etc.

bill² *noun* a beak (sense 1).

billboard *noun* a large board on which advertising posters are displayed.

billet *noun* **1** a formal order to provide lodgings for a soldier. **2** a house, often a private home, where soldiers are given food and lodging. —*verb trans.* (**billeted, billeting**) to give lodging to (soldiers, etc.).

billfold *noun* a wallet.

billiards *sing. noun* a game played on a cloth-covered table with pockets at the sides and corners, in which colored balls must be struck against each other or into the pockets with long thin sticks. *See also* **snooker, pool¹** (sense 5).

billing *noun* the importance of a performer in a play or concert, esp. as shown by the position of the name on the advertising poster: *top billing*.

billion *noun* **1** a thousand million. **2** *colloq.* a very great number: *billions of problems*. —*adj.* a thousand million. ▸ **billionth** *noun, adj.*

billionaire *noun* a person owning money and property worth at least a billion dollars.

bill of exchange a written order to one party to pay a specified sum of money to another party on a certain date or when payment is asked for.

bill of fare a menu.

bill of goods 1 a consignment of items for sale. **2** *colloq.* a deceptive or misleading offer.

bill of rights 1 a written declaration of the rights of the citizens of a country. **2** (**Bill of Rights**) the first 10 amendments of the US Constitution (1791) that are intended to guard certain rights of US citizens.

bill of sale a document stating that something has been sold by one party to another.

billow *noun* **1** a large wave. **2** an upward-moving mass of smoke, mist, etc. —*verb intrans.* (**billowed, billowing**) **1** to move in large waves or clouds. **2** (**billow out**) to swell or bulge like a sail in the wind. ▸ **billowy** *adj.*

billy club a short club carried by police officers. *Also called* **billy.**

billy goat a male goat. *See also* **nanny goat.**

bimetallic *adj.* made of or using two metals.

bimonthly *adj.* **1** occurring once every two months. **2** semimonthly. —*adv.* **1** every two months. **2** semimonthly.

bin *noun* a container for storing some kinds of food: *a bread bin.*

binary *adj.* **1** consisting of or containing two parts or elements. **2** denoting a system that consists of two components, esp. a number system which uses the digits 0 and 1. —*noun* (*pl.* **binaries**) a thing made up of two parts.

bind *verb trans., intrans.* (**bound, binding**) **1** to tie or fasten tightly. **2** (**bind (something) up**) to tie or pass strips of cloth, bandage, etc., around (it). **3** to control or prevent from moving. **4** to make (someone) promise (to do something). **5** to require or oblige (to do something). **6** to fasten together and put a cover on (the separate pages of a book). **7** to put a strip of cloth on the edge of (something) to strengthen it. **8** to cause (dry ingredients) to stick together. **9** to stick together. —*noun colloq.* a difficult or boring situation.

binder *noun* **1** one who binds books. **2** a hard, booklike cover in which loose pieces of paper can be kept in order. **3** a cementing agent that causes loose particles of a mixture to adhere.

binding *noun* **1** the part of a book cover onto which the pages are attached. **2** cloth, etc., used to bind something. —*adj.* formally or legally obliging (a party) to do (something).

binge *noun* a bout of extravagant eating and/or drinking. —*verb intrans.* (**binged, binging** *or* **bingeing, binges**) to indulge in a binge.

bingo *noun* a game in which players have cards marked with rows of numbered squares; as one person calls out numbers at random, players mark their cards, and the first to mark a full row wins. —*interj.* used to express completion of a row in bingo, or success or sudden pleasure.

binocular *adj.* relating to the use of both eyes simultaneously.

binoculars *pl. noun* an optical instrument designed for viewing distant objects, and consisting of two small telescopes arranged side by side so that the observer is able to use both eyes at once. *Also called* **field glasses.**

binomial *noun* an algebraic expression that contains two variables. —*adj.* containing two variables.

bio- *combining form* forming words denoting life or living things: *biology.*

biochemistry *noun* the scientific study of the chemical compounds and chemical reactions that occur within living organisms. ▸ **biochemical** *adj.* ▸ **biochemist** *noun*

biodegradable *adj.* capable of being broken down by living organisms. *See also* **photodegradable.** ▸ **biodegradation** *noun*

biofeedback *noun* the technique of learning to control body functions, e.g., heart rate, by seeing them monitored and displayed on electronic instruments.

biography *noun* (*pl.* **biographies**) **1** an account of a person's life, usu. written by someone else and intended for publication. **2** the art of writing biographies. ▸ **biographer** *noun* ▸ **biographical** *adj.*

biological *adj.* **1** relating to biology. **2** of or relating to physiology. **3** *of a detergent* containing enzymes that are said to remove dirt of organic origin. ▸ **biologically** *adv.*

biology *noun* the scientific study of living organisms. ▸ **biologist** *noun*

biomedicine *noun* the branch of medical science that applies biological and physiological principles to clinical medicine.

bionic *adj.* **1** relating to or using bionics. **2** *colloq.* having extraordinary powers of speed, strength, etc.

biophysics *sing. noun* the science that applies the ideas and methods of physics to the study of biological processes. ▸ **biophysicist** *noun*

biopsy *noun* (*pl.* **biopsies**) the removal of a small piece of living tissue from part of the body in order to determine the nature or presence of a suspected disease.

biorhythm *noun* **1** a periodic change in the behavior or physiology of many animals and plants, e.g., winter hibernation, spring flowering. **2** a circadian rhythm associated, e.g., with sleep, independent of day length.

biosphere *noun* that part of Earth's surface and its atmosphere in which living organisms exist. *Also called* **ecosphere.**

biotin (bī′ə-tĭn) *noun* a member of the vitamin B complex. *Also called* **vitamin H.**

bipartite *adj.* **1** consisting of two parts. **2** involving or agreed upon by two parties.

biped *noun* an animal with two feet, e.g., a human being. ▸ **bipedal** *adj.*

biplane *noun* an airplane or glider with two sets of wings, one above the other.

bipolar *adj.* having two poles or extremes.

birch *noun* **1** a tree with smooth bark that often peels in long papery strips. **2** a bundle of birch twigs, used for punishment.

bird *noun* **1** a warm-blooded, egg-laying, feathered animal with a beak, usu. able to fly. **2** a person, esp. a strange one: *an odd bird.*

birdie *Golf noun* a score of one stroke less than par for a particular hole.

bird of paradise a bird native to New Guinea and neighboring islands, the male of which has brightly colored plumage.

biretta *noun* a stiff square cap worn by Roman Catholic clergy.

birth *noun* **1** the act or process of being born or of bearing children. **2** family history or origin: *of humble birth.* **3** beginning; origins: *the birth of socialism.*

birth control the prevention of pregnancy, esp. by means of contraception.

birthday *noun* the anniversary of the day on which a person was born, or the day on which one is born.

birthmark *noun* a mark that is present on the skin at birth.

birthplace *noun* **1** the place where a person was born. **2** the place where something began: *the birthplace of medicine.*

birthright *noun* a right that may be claimed by a person at birth.

biscuit *noun* a small round piece of pastry made with flour, salt, water or milk, shortening, and baking powder.

bisect *verb trans., intrans.* (**bisected, bisecting**) to divide or be divided into two equal parts. ▸ **bisection** *noun*

bisexual *adj.* **1** sexually attracted to both males and females. **2** having the sexual organs of both male and female. —*noun* a bisexual person or organism. ▸ **bisexuality** *noun*

bishop *noun* **1** a senior Christian priest or minister in the Roman Catholic, Episcopal, and Eastern Orthodox Churches, in charge of a diocese. **2** *Chess* a piece shaped like a bishop's miter at the top, which may only be moved diagonally across the board.

bismuth *noun* (**SYMBOL Bi**) a hard silvery-white metallic element with a pinkish tinge.

bison *noun* (*pl.* **bison**) a type of shaggy wild cattle with large heads and short horns.

bisque *noun* a thick, rich soup, usu. made from shellfish, cream, and sherry.

bistro (bē′strō, bĭs′trō) *noun* (*pl.* **bistros**) a club open at night for drinking, dancing, etc.

bit¹ *noun* a small piece. —**a bit 1** a short time or distance: *wait a bit.* **2** a little; slightly; rather: *a bit of a fool.* **3** a lot: *takes a bit of doing.* — **bit by bit** gradually.

bit² *see* **bite.**

bit³ *noun* the metal bar in a bridle that a horse holds in its mouth.

bit⁴ *noun* a binary digit with a value of either 0 or 1, representing the smallest piece of information that can be dealt with by a computer.

bitch *noun* **1** a female animal of the dog family. **2** *offensive slang* an unpleasant, spiteful woman. **3** *coarse slang* a difficult or unpleasant thing. —*verb intrans.* (**bitched, bitching, bitches**) *coarse slang* **1** to speak scathingly or spitefully. **2** to complain. ▸ **bitchy** *adj.* ▸ **bitchiness** *noun*

bite *verb trans., intrans.* (*pa t* **bit**; *pa p* **bitten** or **bit**; *pr p* **biting**) **1** to grasp, seize, or tear (something) with the teeth. **2** to penetrate (a victim's skin) with teeth, fangs, etc. **3** to be caught on the hook on a fishing line: *Are the fish biting today?* **4** to start to have an adverse effect: *The spending cuts are* *beginning to bite.* **5** *of a screw, etc.* to grip firmly. —*noun* **1** an act of biting. **2** a wound caused by biting. **3** a small amount of food: *a bite to eat.* **4** sharpness or bitterness of taste: *a citrus punch that has a bite to it.* **5** strength; sharpness: *a political speech with bite.* —**bite the bullet** *slang* to confront a bad situation stoically and try to carry on. **bite the dust** *slang* **1** to be confounded or defeated utterly: *The plan bit the dust.* **2** to be killed, esp. in a battle.

biting *adj.* **1** bitterly and painfully cold: *a biting wind.* **2** *of a remark* sharp and hurtful.

bitter *adj.* **1** having a sharp, acid, and often unpleasant taste. **2** feeling or causing sadness or pain: *bitter memories.* **3** difficult to accept: *a bitter disappointment.* **4** showing an intense dislike, hatred, or opposition: *bitter criticism.* **5** extremely cold. —*noun* **1** something bitter. **2** (**bitters**) a liquid made of bitter herbs or roots, used to flavor certain alcoholic drinks. ▸ **bitterly** *adv.* ▸ **bitterness** *noun*

bittern *noun* a bird of the heron family, with a booming call.

bittersweet *adj.* pleasant and unpleasant at the same time.

bitty *adj.* (**bittier, bittiest**) *colloq.* very small; tiny.

bitumen *noun* a black, solid or tarry substance used for surfacing roads, pavements, etc. ▸ **bituminous** *adj.*

bivalent *adj. same as* **divalent**.

bivalve *adj.*, *of a mollusk* having a shell composed of two parts hinged together. —*noun* a mollusk having a shell composed of two parts hinged together, e.g., a clam.

bivouac (bĭv′wăk,) *noun* a temporary camp without tents. —*verb intrans.* (**bivouacked, bivouacking**) to camp out temporarily at night without a tent.

bizarre *adj.* weirdly odd or strange. ▸ **bizarrely** *adv.*

blab *verb intrans.*, *trans.* (**blabbed, blabbing**) **1** to tell a secret, etc. **2** to chatter foolishly.

blabber *verb intrans.* (**blabbered, blabbering**) to talk nonsense, esp. without stopping.

blabbermouth *noun* a person who talks foolishly and indiscreetly.

black *adj.* **1** of the color of coal, etc. **2** lacking light. **3** (*usu.* **Black**) relating to, concerning, or belonging to a racial group that has brown to black skin, esp. one of African origin. **4** (*usu.* **Black**) African-American. **5** angry, threatening: *black looks.* **6** dirty: *They came in from the garden with their hands black.* **7** sad, gloomy, or depressed: *a black mood.* **8** wicked or grotesquely sinister: *black humor.* —*noun* **1** the color of coal, the night sky, etc. **2** something that is

black in color. **3** (*usu.* **Black**) a person belonging to a racial group that has brown to black skin, esp. one of African origin. **4** (*usu.* **Black**) an African-American. **5** the dark clothes worn in mourning. —*verb trans.*, *intrans.* (**blacked, blacking**) **1** to make black. **2** to clean with black polish. —**black out 1** to lose consciousness. **2** to deprive (someone or something) of light: *a power failure that blacked out the theater.* **3** to prevent (information) from being broadcast or published. **in the black** with assets on the credit side of an account. ▸ **blackness** *noun*

blackball *verb trans.* (**blackballed, blackballing**) **1** to vote against (a candidate for membership). **2** to refuse to speak to (someone).

black belt 1 a belt indicating that the wearer has reached the highest level of skill in a martial art. **2** a person who is entitled to wear such a belt.

blackberry *noun* **1** a plant having prickly stems and edible fruit resembling dark-colored raspberries. **2** a berry from this plant.

blackbird *noun* any of various species of N American, European, and Asian birds, the males of which have black feathers.

blackboard *noun* a dark-colored board for writing on with chalk, esp. used in schools.

black box a flight recorder.

blacken *verb trans.*, *intrans.* (**blackened, blackening**) **1** to make or become black or very dark in color. **2** to speak evil or badly of: *tried to blacken their name.*

Black English the varieties of English used by African-Americans.

black eye an eye with darkened swollen skin around it, usu. caused by a blow.

black-eyed Susan a N American herb having flowers with orange-yellow petals.

blackguard (blăg′ərd) *noun old use* a rogue or villain.

blackhead *noun* a mass of fatty material blocking a sebaceous duct in the skin. Also called **comedo**.

black hole a region in space believed to be formed when a star has collapsed in on itself.

blackjack *noun* **1** a card game, the object of which is to accumulate cards having a higher count than those held by the dealer but not in excess of 21. Also called **twenty-one, vingt-et-un**. **2** a length of hard flexible leather, esp. used as a weapon.

black lead graphite.

blacklist *noun* a list of people suspected of something, or not approved of. —*verb trans.* (**blacklisted, blacklisting**) to put (a person, etc.) on such a list.

black magic magic that performs evil by the power of the devil.

blackmail *verb trans.* (**blackmailed, blackmailing**) **1** to extort money from (a person) by threatening to reveal damaging information about the person. **2** to try to influence (a person), using unfair pressure. —*noun* an act of blackmail. ▶ **blackmailer** *noun*

black market the illegal buying and selling, at high prices, of goods that are scarce or in great demand. ▶ **black-marketeer** *noun*

Black Muslim a member of a predominately African-American group, the Nation of Islam, that adheres to the religion of Islam.

blackout *noun* **1** a loss of memory or consciousness. **2** a suppression of information. **3** a period during which lights are turned out over an area as a precaution during a night air raid.

black pepper pepper produced by grinding the dried fruits of the pepper plant without removing their dark outer covering.

Black Power racial pride and social equality, achieved among African-Americans through creation of African-American cultural, scholarly, and political entities and institutions.

black sheep a member of a family or group whose behavior is disapproved of by the rest of the family or group.

blacksmith *noun* a person who makes and repairs by hand things made of iron, such as horseshoes.

blacksnake *noun* any of several dark, nonvenomous snakes native to N America.

blackthorn *noun* a thorny shrub or small tree with sour, bluish-black fruits known as *sloes*.

black-tie (blăk′tī′) *noun* a black bow tie. —*adj.*, *of a function* very formal, with guests expected to wear evening dress.

blacktop *noun* the material, e.g., asphalt, used in road paving.

black widow a venomous spider.

bladder *noun* a hollow organ in which urine is collected before being discharged.

blade *noun* **1** the cutting part of a knife, sword, etc. **2** the flat, usu. long and narrow part of a leaf or petal. **3** the wide, flat part of an oar, etc. **4** a flat bone, esp. in the shoulder.

blame *verb trans.* (**blamed, blaming**) **1** to consider (a person or thing) responsible for (something bad or undesirable). **2** to find fault with (a person). —*noun* responsibility for something bad or undesirable. ▶ **blameless** *adj.* ▶ **blameworthy** *adj.*

blanch *verb trans., intrans.* (**blanched, blanching**) **1** to make or become white, esp. through fear. **2** to prepare (vegetables) for cooking or freezing by boiling in water for a few seconds.

bland *adj.* **1** having a very mild taste. **2** mild or gentle in manner; showing no strong emotions. **3** lacking interest; insipid.

blandish *verb trans.* (**blandished, blandishing**) to persuade by gentle flattery; to cajole. ▶ **blandishments** *pl. noun*

blank *adj.* **1** *of paper* not written or printed on. **2** *of magnetic tape, etc.* having no sound or pictures yet recorded on it. **3** having spaces left for details, information, etc.: *a blank form.* **4** expressionless and uninterested: *a blank look.* **5** lacking thoughts and ideas: *My mind was blank.* **6** lacking distinguishing features or breaks in texture: *a blank wall.* —*noun* **1** an empty space. **2** an empty space left on forms, etc., to be filled in with particular information. **3** a printed form with blank spaces. **4** the state of having no thoughts or ideas: *My mind was a complete blank.* **5** a dash written in place of a word or letter. **6** a blank cartridge: *fire blanks.* —*verb* (**blanked, blanking**). ▶ **blankly** *adv.* ▶ **blankness** *noun*

blank check a check that has been signed but on which the amount to be paid has been left blank.

blanket *noun* **1** a cover of wool or other material, used on a bed for warmth. **2** a thick layer or mass that envelops: *a blanket of fog.* —*adj.* applying to or covering all cases, general: *a blanket condemnation of human-rights violations.* —*verb trans.* (**blanketed, blanketing**) to cover with or as if with a blanket.

blank verse poetry that does not rhyme.

blare *verb intrans., trans.* (**blared, blaring**) **1** to make the sound of a trumpet or a similar loud sound. **2** to sound or say loudly and harshly. ▤ BLAST, BOOM, ROAR ▤ WHISPER. —*noun* a loud, harsh sound such as that of a trumpet.

blarney *noun* flattering words used to persuade or deceive. —*verb* (**blarneyed, blarneying**) to persuade using flattery.

blasé (blä-zā′) *adj.* lacking enthusiasm, esp. through overfamiliarity.

blasphemy *noun* (*pl.* **blasphemies**) disrespectful remarks about God or sacred matters; profanity using the name of God. ▶ **blaspheme** *verb intrans., trans.* ▶ **blasphemer** *noun* ▶ **blasphemous** *adj.*

blast *noun* **1** an explosion, or the strong shockwaves from one. **2** a strong, sudden stream or gust (of air, wind, etc.). **3** a loud, sudden sound of a trumpet, car horn, etc. **4** a sudden, violent outburst of anger or criticism. **5** *slang* an exciting or greatly enjoyed experience. —*verb trans., intrans.* (**blasted, blasting**) **1** to blow up (a tunnel, rock, etc.) with explosives. **2** to destroy: *blast one's hopes.* **3** to wither or cause to shrivel up. **4** to criticize severely. **5** to emit loud noise: *portable radios blasting out at the beach.* **6** to sound or say loudly and harshly. —*interj. colloq.* an expression of annoyance, etc. —**blast off** *of a spacecraft* to take off.

blast furnace a furnace that is used to extract iron from ores, and in which the temperature is raised by a blast of hot, dry air.

blast-off *noun, of a spacecraft* take-off.

blatant (blāt′nt) *adj.* very noticeable and obtrusive, and intentionally so. ▸ **blatantly** *adv.*

Usage Blatant stresses the intentional failure to conceal an undesirable act. It is sometimes confused with *flagrant*, which denotes the seriousness of a wrongdoing, as in a *flagrant lie* or *flagrant violations of the arms treaty.*

---

blather *or* **blether** *verb intrans.* (**blathered, blathering**) to talk foolishly.

blaze[1] *noun* **1** a bright, strong fire or flame. **2** a sudden, sharp burst of feeling or emotion. **3** a brilliant display. —*verb intrans.* (**blazed, blazing**) **1** to burn or shine brightly. **2** to show great emotion, esp. anger.

blaze[2] *noun* **1** a white mark on an animal's face. **2** a mark made on the bark of a tree, esp. to show a route or path. —*verb trans.* (**blazed, blazing**) to mark (a tree, path, etc.) with blazes.

blaze[3] *verb trans.* (**blazed, blazing**) to make (news or information) widely known.

blazer *noun* a light jacket, often in the colors of a school or club.

blazon *verb trans.* (**blazoned, blazoning**) **1** to make public. **2 a** to describe (a coat of arms) in technical terms. **b** to paint names, designs, etc., on (a coat of arms). —*noun* a coat of arms or a shield.

bleach *verb trans., intrans.* ▪ (**bleached, bleaching**) to whiten or remove color from (something) by exposure to sunlight or certain chemicals; to become white or colorless. —*noun* a liquid chemical used to whiten or remove color from cloth, paper, hair, etc.

bleak *adj.* **1** exposed and desolate: *bleak moors.* **2** cold and unwelcoming: *a bleak smile.* **3** offering little or no hope: *bleak economic forecasts.* ▸ **bleakly** *adv.* ▸ **bleakness** *noun*

bleary *adj.* (**blearier, bleariest**) *of a person's eyes* red and dim, usu. from fatigue or crying.

bleat *noun* the cry of a sheep, goat, or calf. —*verb intrans., trans.* (**bleated, bleating**) to make the cry of a sheep, goat, or calf.

bleed *verb intrans., trans.* (**bled, bleeding**) **1** to let out or lose blood. **2** to remove or take blood from. **3** *of plants, etc.* to lose juice or sap. **4** to empty liquid or air from (a radiator, etc.).

bleep *noun* a short, high sound, usu. made by an electronic device. —*verb intrans., trans.* (**bleeped, bleeping**) **1** to give out a bleep. **2** to edit out (e.g., objectionable material) from a broadcast. ▸ **bleeper** *noun*

blemish *noun* a stain, mark, or fault. —*verb trans.* (**blemished, blemishing**) to stain or spoil the beauty of.

blench *verb intrans.* (**blenched, blenching**) to start back or move away, esp. in fear.

blend *verb trans., intrans.* (**blended, blending**) **1 a** to mix (different sorts or varieties) into one. **b** to combine or be combined into a whole. **2** (**blend in** *or* **with (something)**) to form a mixture or harmonious combination; to go well together. **3** *esp. of colors* to shade gradually one into another: *the blue of the sea blending into the sky.* —*noun* a mixture or combination.

blender *noun* a machine for mixing food or making it into a liquid.

blenny *noun* (*pl.* **blennies**) a small fish with a long, tapering, slimy body and no scales.

bless *verb trans.* (**blessed** *or* **blest, blessing**) **1** to ask for divine favor or protection for. **2** to make or pronounce holy; consecrate. **3** to praise; to give honor or glory to. **4** to thank or be thankful for: *I bless the day I met you.*

blessed (blĕs′əd) *adj.* **1** holy. **2** *RC Church, of a deceased person* pronounced holy by the Pope, usu. as the first stage of being named a saint. **3** *colloq.* damned: *I can't solve this blessed puzzle.*

blessing *noun* **1** a wish or prayer for happiness or success. **2** a cause of happiness; a benefit or advantage. **3** approval or good wishes. **4** a short prayer said before or after a meal.

blether *verb same as* **blather.**

blew *see* **blow**[1].

blight *noun* **1** a fungal disease of plants. **2** a person or thing that causes decay or destruction, or spoils things. —*verb trans., intrans.* (**blighted, blighting**) **1** to affect with blight. **2** to harm or destroy. **3** to disappoint or frustrate: *hopes blighted by poverty.*

blimp *noun* a large balloon or airship, used for publicity, observation, or defense.

blind *adj.* **1** unable to see. **2** (**blind to (something)**) unable or unwilling to understand or appreciate (something unwelcome). **3** done without preparation or previous knowledge. **4** devoid of reason or purpose; unthinking: *blind hatred.* **5** hidden from sight: *a blind driveway.* **6** not allowing sight of what is beyond: *a blind summit.* **7** *in flying* using instruments only, without visual contact. **8** closed at one end: *a blind alley.* —*adv.* **1** without being able to see or to use visual references: *flying blind.* **2** without thinking ahead: *entered into the contract blind.* —*noun* **1** a screen to stop light coming through a window. **2** a person, action, or thing that hides the truth or deceives. —*verb trans.* (**blinded, blinding**) **1** to make blind. **2** to make unreasonable, foolish, etc.: *blinded by your anger.* **3** (**blind (someone) with (something)**) to confuse or dazzle (another): *Don't try to blind me with your excuses.* ▸ **blindly** *noun* ▸ **blindness** *noun*

blind date 1 a date with a person one has not met before. **2** the person met on such a date.

blinder (blīn´dər) *noun* (**blinders**) the two small flat pieces of leather attached to a horse's bridle to prevent it from seeing sideways.

blindfold *noun* a piece of cloth used to cover the eyes to prevent the wearer from seeing. —*adj., adv.* with the eyes covered. —*verb trans.* (**blindfolded, blindfolding**) to cover the eyes of (another) to prevent (the one so covered) from seeing.

blindside *verb trans.* (**blindsided, blindsiding**) **1** to attack or hit (a victim) from the side away from which the person's attention is directed. **2** to catch (someone) by surprise, with harmful results.

blind spot 1 a small area on the retina of the eye from which no visual images can be transmitted. **2** an area of poor or no visibility, esp. in the window area of a motor vehicle. **3** a subject in which a person lacks understanding.

blink *verb intrans., trans.* **1** to close and open (an eye or the eyes) quickly. **2** *of a light* to flash on and off or shine unsteadily. —*noun* an act of blinking.

blip *noun* **1** a sudden, sharp sound produced by a machine. **2** a spot of light on a screen showing the position of an object. **3** a sudden, fleeting deviation from what is normal or correct.

bliss *noun* **1** very great happiness. **2** the special happiness of heaven. ▸ **blissful** *adj.* ▸ **blissfully** *adv.*

blister *noun* **1** a small swelling containing fluid on or just beneath the surface of the skin. **2** a bubble in a coating of paint, varnish, etc., or on the surface of metal or plastic. —*verb trans., intrans.* (**blistered, blistering**) **1** to cause a blister on (skin, a surface, etc.). **2** to erupt in blisters.

blistering *adj.* **1** extreme: *blistering heat.* **2** angry and aggressive: *blistering criticism.*

blister pack a bubble pack.

blithe (blīth, blĭth) *adj.* **1** airily happy. **2** marked by lack of serious thought; casual: *blithe disregard for danger.* ▸ **blithely** *adv.*

blitz *noun* **1** a sudden strong attack, or period of such attacks, esp. from the air. **2** (**the Blitz**) the German air raids on Britain in 1940. **3 a** a period of hard work, etc., to get something finished. **b** an intense, aggressive campaign: *a political media blitz.* —*verb trans.* (**blitzed, blitzing**) to attack, damage, or destroy as if by a blitz or air raid.

blizzard *noun* **1** a severe snowstorm characterized by low temperatures and strong winds. **2** a torrent: *a blizzard of complaints.*

bloat *verb trans., intrans.* (**bloated, bloating**) to cause to swell or puff out with air, pride, etc. ▸ **bloated** *adj.*

blob *noun* **1** a small, soft, round mass: *a blob of jam.* **2** a small drop of liquid.

bloc *noun* a group of countries, people, etc., who have a common interest, purpose, or policy: *the Asian trade bloc.*

block *noun* **1** a mass of solid wood, stone, ice, or other hard material, usu. with flat sides. **2** a piece of wood, stone, etc., used for chopping and cutting on. **3** (*usu.* **blocks**) a set of wooden or plastic cubes, used as a child's toy. **4** a large building containing offices, apartments, etc. **5** a group of buildings with roads on all four sides. **6** a group of seats, tickets, etc., thought of as a single unit. **7** something that causes or acts as a stoppage of movement, thought, etc. **8** a piece of wood or metal that has been cut to be used in printing. **9** a series of ropes and wheels for lifting things, or pulleys, mounted in a case. *See also* **block and tackle**. **10** *slang* a person's head. —*verb trans., intrans.* (**blocked, blocking**) **1** to obstruct or impede. **2** *Sport* to impede (an opponent or the ball) by physical interference.

blockade *noun* the closing off of a port, region, etc., by military means in order to stop people, goods, etc., from passing in and out. —*verb trans.* (**blockaded, blockading**) to put a blockade around (a port, etc.).

blockage *noun* **1** something that causes passage to be obstructed or stopped. **2** the state of being blocked.

block and tackle a series of ropes and wheels used for lifting heavy objects. *See also* **block** (sense 9).

blockbuster *noun colloq.* **1** a highly popular and successful movie, book, etc. **2** an extremely powerful bomb; used in demolition.

blockhead *noun colloq.* a stupid person.

block letter a sans-serif printed letter.

bloke *noun Brit. colloq.* a man.

blond *adj.* **1** *of a person* having pale yellow hair and light-colored skin. **2** *of hair* pale yellow.

blonde (bländ) *noun* a woman with pale yellow hair. —*adj., of a woman* having pale yellow hair.

blood *noun* **1** the red fluid that circulates in the arteries, veins, and capillaries of the body. **2**

relationship through belonging to the same family, race, etc.: *of royal blood*. **3** near family: *my own flesh and blood*. **4** someone seen as adding new strength to an existing group: *new blood*. —**in cold blood** deliberately and cruelly, showing no concern or passion.

blood bank a place where the blood collected from donors is stored, categorized and tested, prior to transfusion.

bloodbath *noun* a massacre.

blood count a numerical calculation to determine the number of red or white blood cells in a known volume of blood.

bloodcurdling *adj.* causing great fear.

bloodhound *noun* a large dog, having a powerful body, a tan or black and tan coat, long pendulous ears, and a keen sense of smell.

bloodletting *noun Hist.* the treating of sick people by removing some of their blood.

blood money 1 money paid for committing murder. **2** money paid in compensation to the relatives of a murdered person.

blood poisoning a serious systemic condition caused by the presence of either bacterial toxins or large numbers of bacteria in the bloodstream. *Also called* **septicemia.**

bloodshed *noun* the shedding of blood or the killing of people.

bloodshot *adj. of the eyes* sore and red.

blood sports sports that involve the killing of animals.

bloodstain *noun* a stain that is made by blood. ▸ **bloodstained** *adj.*

bloodstream *noun* the flow of blood through the arteries, veins, and capillaries.

bloodsucker *noun* **1** an animal, e.g., the leech, that sucks blood. **2** *colloq.* a person who extorts money from another.

bloodthirsty *adj.* **1** eager for or fond of killing or violence. **2** *of a movie, etc.* including much violence and killing.

blood vessel an artery, vein, or capillary.

bloody *adj.* (**bloodier, bloodiest**) **1** stained or covered with blood. **2** involving or including much killing. **3** *slang* used as an intensive to express annoyance, etc.: *a bloody fool.* —*adv. slang* extremely. —*verb trans.* (**bloodied, bloodying, bloodies**) to stain or cover with blood.

bloom *noun* **1** a flower, esp. on a plant valued as an ornamental. **2** the state of flowering: *in bloom.* **3** a state of perfection or great beauty: *an operatic career in full bloom.* **4** a glow or flush on the skin: *the bloom of a young child's face.* **5** a fine white powder on leaves, fruit, etc. —*verb intrans.* (**bloomed, blooming**) **1** to be in flower. **2** to be in or achieve a state of great beauty or perfection. **3** to be healthy; to flourish.

bloomers *pl. noun old colloq.* women's underpants or knickers.

> After Amelia *Bloomer*, 19th-century US feminist who promoted the use of bloomers for women

blooper *noun* **1** *colloq.* a silly mistake or clumsy error. **2** *Baseball* **a** a high pitch that is lobbed directly to the batter. **b** a ball that is so weakly hit that it goes only just past the infield.

blossom *noun* **1** a flower or mass of flowers, esp. on a fruit tree. **2** the state of flowering: *in blossom.* —*verb intrans.* (**blossomed, blossoming**) **1** to develop flowers. **2** to grow well or develop nicely.

blot *noun* **1** a spot or stain, esp. of ink. **2** a spot or blemish which spoils the beauty of something. **3** a stain on a person's reputation or character. —*verb trans.* (**blotted, blotting**) **1** to make a spot or stain on, esp. with ink. **2** to dry with blotting paper.

blotch *noun* a large colored or sore spot or mark on the skin, etc. —*verb trans.* (**blotched, blotching**) to cover or mark with blotches. ▸ **blotchy** *adj.*

blotter *noun* a large sheet or pad of blotting paper with a hard backing.

blotting paper soft, thick paper used for drying wet ink when writing.

blouse (blows, blowz) *noun* **1** a woman's shirtlike garment. **2** a tunic or coat that is part of the uniform of some branches of the US armed forces. —*verb trans.* (**bloused, blousing**) to arrange in loose folds.

blow¹ *verb intrans., trans.* (*pa t* **blew**; *pa p* **blown**; *pr. p* **blowing**) **1** *of a current of air, wind, etc.* to be moving, esp. rapidly. **2** to move or be moved by a current of air, wind, etc.: *leaves blowing along the sidewalk.* **3** to send (air) from the mouth. **4** to form or shape by blowing air from the mouth: *blow bubbles.* **5** to shatter or destroy by an explosion: *The blast blew the chimney from the roof.* **6** to operate (a noise-making device): *blow a whistle.* **7** to breathe heavily. **8** to clear (nasal passages) by blowing through: *blow one's nose.* **9** **a** to cause (a fuse) to break. **b** *of a fuse* to break, causing an interruption in the flow of current. **c** to cause (air) to be suddenly ejected from (a tire). **10** to break into (a safe, etc.) using explosives. **11** *colloq.* to spoil or bungle (an opportunity, etc.): *He had his chance, but he blew it.* **12** *colloq.* to spend a large amount of money: *blew $20 on a round of drinks.* **13** *slang* to leave (a place) quickly and suddenly: *blow town after the robbery.*—*noun* **1** an act or example of blowing. **2** a windstorm: *a big blow coming up the coast.* —**blow over** *of an incident, threat, etc.* to pass over without harmful effect. **blow up 1** to explode. **2** to fill up or swell up with air or gas. **3** *colloq.* to lose one's temper. **blow (something) up 1** to produce a larger version of (a photograph, etc.). **2** *colloq.* to make (something) seem more serious or important than it really is.

blow² *noun* **1** a stroke or knock with the hand or a weapon. **2** a sudden shock or misfortune.

blow-by-blow *adj.*, *of an account, etc.* giving all the details in the right order.

blow-dry *verb trans.* (**blow-dried**, **blow-drying**, **blow-dries**) to dry (hair) in a particular style with an electric dryer.

blowhole *noun* a nostril on the head of a whale, through which a stream of water droplets and air is released as the animal surfaces.

blown *see* **blow¹**.

blowout *noun* **1** the bursting of a tire on a motor vehicle. **2** a violent escape of gas, etc., esp. on an oil rig. **3** *slang* a large party.

blowtorch *noun* a device for producing and directing an intensely hot flame at a particular spot, used for burning off paint, etc.

blowup *noun* **1** an enlargement of a photograph. **2** an explosion. **3** a sudden argument.

blowy *adj.* (**blowier, blowiest**) blustery; windy.

blowzy or **blowsy** (blow′zē) *adj.* (**blowzier, blowziest**) **1** bloated and red-faced. **2** generally unkempt: *blowzy attire.*

BLT *noun* a bacon, lettuce and tomato sandwich.

blubber *noun* **1** a thick insulating layer of fat beneath the skin of whales, seals, etc. **2** too much body fat. —*verb trans.*, *intrans.* (**blubbered, blubbering**) to weep convulsively.

bludgeon *noun* a club with a heavy end. —*verb trans.* (**bludgeoned, bludgeoning**) **1** to hit with, or as if with, a bludgeon. **2** to force or bully into doing something.

blue *adj.* **1** of the color of a clear, cloudless sky. **2** sad or depressed. **3** *of a movie, joke, etc.* pornographic or indecent. **4** having skin that is pale blue or purple because of the cold. —*noun* **1** the color of a clear, cloudless sky. **2** paint or dye of this color. **3** material or clothes of this color: *dressed in blue.* **4** (**blues**) the dress uniform of the US Army. —*verb trans.*, *intrans.* (**blued, bluing**) to make blue. —**out of the blue** without warning; unexpectedly.

bluebell *noun* any of various plants with blue bell-shaped flowers.

blueberry *noun* (*pl.* **blueberries**) **1** a shrub with bluish-black edible berries. *Also called* **bilberry. 2** the fruit of this plant.

bluebird *noun* any of various birds, the males of which have blue plumage on their back.

blue blood royal or noble blood or descent.

bluebottle *noun* a large fly that lays its eggs in rotting flesh, so called because its abdomen has a metallic blue sheen.

blue-collar *adj.*, *of workers* doing manual or unskilled work. *See also* **white-collar**.

bluegrass *noun* **1** a style of folk music started in the southern states of the USA, usu. played on guitars and banjos and marked by fast tempos and improvisations similar to those in jazz. **2** a lawn and pasture grass, e.g., Kentucky bluegrass.

blue law a law that forbids certain businesses from opening on Sundays or that restricts their hours of operation on Sunday.

blueprint *noun* **1** a photographic print of plans, designs, etc., consisting of white lines on a blue background. **2** a detailed plan of work to be done.

blues *noun* (*sing., pl.*) **1** (*usu.* **the blues**) a feeling of sadness or depression. **2** slow melancholy jazz of Southern US African-American origin.

bluestocking *noun* a highly educated woman who is interested in serious academic subjects.

blue whale a large species of whale, the largest living animal.

bluff¹ *verb intrans., trans.* (**bluffed, bluffing**) to try to deceive (someone) by pretending to be stronger, cleverer, more determined, etc., than one really is. —*noun* an act of deceit or trickery through false displays of confidence.

bluff² *noun* a steep cliff or bank of ground. —*adj.* **1** *usu. of a cliff or the bow of a ship* steep and upright. **2** rough, cheerful, and honest in manner.

blunder *verb intrans.* (**blundered, blundering**) **1** to make a foolish, usu. serious, mistake. **2** to move about awkwardly and clumsily. —*noun* a foolish, usu. serious, mistake. ⊟ BLOOMER, BLOOPER, BONER, FAUX PAS, FUMBLE, GOOF, MISCUE, STUMBLE. ▸ **blunderer** *noun*

blunderbuss *noun Hist.* a shotgun with a short wide barrel.

blunt *adj.* **1** not sharp. **2** honest and direct in a rough way. —*verb trans., intrans.* (**blunted, blunting**) to make (something), or become, blunt. ▸ **bluntly** *adv.* ▸ **bluntness** *noun*

blur *noun* **1** a thing not clearly seen or heard. **2** a smear or smudge. —*verb trans., intrans.* (**blurred, blurring**) **1** to make or become less clear or distinct. **2** to rub over and smudge. **3** to make (one's memory, judgment, etc.) less clear. ▸ **blurry** *adj.*

blurb *noun* a brief description of or commentary on a book, usu. printed on the jacket in order to promote it.

blurt *verb trans.* (**blurted, blurting**) to say suddenly or without thinking of the effect or result: *blurted out the truth*.

blush *noun* **1** a red or pink glow on the skin of the face, caused by shame, embarrassment, etc. **2** a pink, rosy glow. —*verb intrans.* (**blushed, blushing**) **1** to become red or pink in the face because of shame, embarrassment, etc. **2** to feel ashamed or embarrassed.

blusher *noun* a pink or pale orange cream or powder used to give color to the cheeks.

bluster *verb intrans.* (**blustered, blustering**) **1** to speak in a boasting, angry, or threatening way, often to hide fear. **2** *of the wind, waves, etc.* to blow or move roughly. —*noun* **1** speech that is ostentatiously boasting, angry, or threatening. **2** the roaring noise of the wind or sea on a rough day. ▸ **blustery** *adj.*

blvd. *abbrev.* boulevard.

B.O. *abbrev.* body odor.

boa *noun* **1** a snake that coils around its prey and kills it by suffocation rather than crushing. One species is the **boa constrictor.** **2** a woman's long, thin scarf, usu. made of fur or feathers.

boar *noun* **1** a wild ancestor of the domestic hog. *Also called* **wild boar.** **2** a mature uncastrated male hog.

board *noun* **1** a long, flat strip of wood. **2** a piece of material resembling a long, flat strip of wood, made from compressing fibers together. **3** a flat piece of wood, etc., intended for a stated purpose, e.g., for listing scores, for diving, etc. **4** thick, stiff card used, e.g., for binding books. **5** a person's meals, provided in return for money. **6** an official group of people controlling or managing an organization, etc., or examining or interviewing candidates. **7** (**the boards**) a theater stage: *tread the boards*. —*verb trans., intrans.* (**boarded, boarding**) **1** to enter or get onto (a ship, airplane, etc.). **2** to receive accommodation and meals in someone else's house, in return for payment. **3** to provide (someone) with accomodation and meals in return for payment. **4** (*also* **board** (**something**) **up**) to cover (a gap or entrance) with boards. —**on board** on or into a ship, airplane, etc. **take** (**something**) **on board** to understand or accept (new ideas, responsibilities, etc.).

boarder *noun* **1** a person who receives accommodation and meals in someone else's house, in return for payment. **2** a student who lives at school during the term.

boarding *noun* **1** a collection of wooden boards laid next to each other. **2** the act of boarding a ship, airplane, etc.

boarding house a house where people live and take meals as paying guests.

boarding school a school where pupils may live during the term.

boardroom *noun* a room in which the directors of a company meet.

boardwalk *noun* a walkway of planks, esp. along a shore.

boast *verb intrans., trans.* (**boasted, boasting**) **1** to talk with excessive pride about one's own abilities, achievements, etc. **2** *colloq.* to own or have (something it is right to be proud of): *The hotel boasts magnificent views across the valley.* —*noun* **1** an act of boasting. **2** a thing one is proud of. ▸ **boastful** *adj.*

boat *noun* **1** a small vessel for traveling over water. **2** *colloq.* any water-traveling vessel; a ship or submarine. **3** a boat-shaped dish for serving gravy, etc. —*verb intrans.* (**boated, boating**) to sail in a boat for pleasure. —**in the same boat** in the same difficult circumstances. ▸ **boater** *noun.*

boathouse *noun* a building at water's edge where boats are stored, esp. by a lake or river.

boatman *noun* a man in charge of a small boat that carries passengers.

boatswain (bō'sən), **bo's'n** *or* **bos'n** *or* **bosun** *noun* a ship's officer, who is in charge of the lifeboats, ropes, sails, etc., and deck crew.

bob[1] *verb intrans., trans.* (**bobbed, bobbing**) **1** to move up and down quickly. **2** to curtsy. **3** to move (the head) up and down, usu. as a greeting. —*noun* **1** an up-and-down bouncing movement. **2** a curtsy.

bob[2] *noun* **1** a short hairstyle for women and children, with the hair cut square across the face and evenly all round the head. **2** a bobsled. —*verb trans., intrans.* (**bobbed, bobbing**) to cut (hair) in a bob.

bobbin *noun* a small cylindrical object on which thread is wound.

bobby pin a small metal clip for holding hair in place.

bobcat *noun* a N American wild cat that has reddish-brown spotted fur, a short tail, and tufts on its ears.

bobolink *noun* an American songbird.

bobsled *noun* a sled with metal runners used in crossing, and sometimes racing on, snow and ice.

bobwhite *noun* a small brown-and-white N American quail.

bock *noun* a dark, strong, malty, sweet beer.

bod *noun slang* one's physique.

bodacious (bō-dā'shəs) *adj. dialect* **1** extraordinary; outstanding. **2** daring; audacious.

bode[1] *verb trans.* (**boded, boding**) to be a sign of. —**bode ill** *or* **well** to be a bad or good sign for the future.

bode[2] *see* **bide.**

bodice (băd′əs) *noun* **1** the part of a dress covering the upper part of the body. **2** a woman's close-fitting outer garment, worn over a blouse.

bodily *adj.* of or concerning the body. —*adv.* **1** as a whole. **2** in person.

bodkin *noun* a large blunt needle.

body *noun* (*pl.* **bodies**) **1** the whole physical structure of a person or animal. **2** the physical structure of a person or animal excluding the head and limbs. **3** a corpse. **4** a main or central part. **5** a substantial section or group: *a body of opinion.* **6** a group of people thought of as a single unit. **7** a quantity: *a body of water.* **8** of wine, music, etc. a full or strong quality or tone. **9** a person.

bodybuilding *noun* physical exercise designed to develop the muscles and strengthen the body. ▸ **bodybuilder** *noun*

bodyguard *noun* a person or group of people guarding another person.

body language the communication of information by means of gestures, facial expressions, etc.

body-piercing *noun* the practice of inserting metal studs or rings through parts of the body for decoration.

body politic all the people of a nation in their political capacity.

body-snatcher *noun* a person who robs graves of their corpses and then sells them, usu. for dissection.

body stocking a garment worn next to the skin, covering all of the body and often the arms and legs.

body suit a close-fitting, one-piece garment for women.

bodywork *noun* the outer painted structure of a motor vehicle.

Boer (bōr, bôr) *noun* a descendant of the early Dutch settlers in South Africa. —*adj.* of or relating to these descendants.

boffo *adj. slang* hugely successful.

bog *noun* an area of wet, spongy, poorly drained ground, composed of peat and slowly decaying plant material. —*verb trans., intrans.* (**bogged, bogging**) to cause to slow down or sink, as if becoming stuck in a bog. ▸ **boggy** *adj.*

bogey¹ (bŏŏg′ē, bō′gē) *noun* same as **bogy.**

bogey² (bō′gē) *noun* (*pl.* **bogeys**) *Golf* a score for a hole (or a course) of one stroke more than par (for each hole).

bogeyman (bŏŏg′ē-măn,) or **bogyman** *noun* a cruel or frightening person, existing or imaginary, used to deter or frighten children.

boggle *verb intrans.* (**boggled, boggling**) to be amazed at something, or unable to understand or imagine it: *The mind boggles at the very idea.*

bogus *adj.* not genuine; false.

bogy (bō′gē) or **bogey** *noun* (*pl.* **bogies** or **bogeys**) **1** a supernatural being or form. **2** something especially feared. **3** *slang* an unidentified aircraft, esp. in a combat situation.

bogyman *noun* same as **bogeyman.**

bohemian *noun* **1** (**Bohemian**) a person from Bohemia in the Czech Republic. **2** a person, esp. a writer or an artist, who lives in a way that ignores standard rules of social behavior. —*adj.* **1** (**Bohemian**) of Bohemia. **2** ignoring standard customs and rules of social behavior.

boil¹ *verb intrans., trans.* (**boiled, boiling**) **1** to change from a liquid to a vapor on reaching a boiling point. **2** *of a container* to have its contents at boiling point: *Is the pot boiling yet?* **3** to cause (a liquid) to reach its boiling point. **4** *of food* to cook or be cooked by boiling. **5** *colloq.* **a** to be very hot. **b** to be extremely upset, angry, or otherwise disturbed. **6** to treat with boiling water, esp. to clean. **7** *of the sea, etc.* to move and bubble. —*noun* the act or point of boiling. —**boil down to (something)** to have as the most important part or factor; to mean. **boil over** to be heated to boiling and then flow over the edge of a container.

boil² *noun* a reddened, painful swelling of the skin, containing pus.

boiler *noun* **1** a closed vessel that is used to convert water into steam, esp. by burning coal, oil, or other fuel, used to drive steam turbines, engines, etc. **2** an apparatus for heating a building's hot water supply.

boiling point 1 (ABBREV. **bp**) the temperature at which a particular substance boils. **2** a point at which emotions can no longer be controlled.

boisterous *adj.* very lively, noisy, and cheerful. ▸ **boisterously** *adv.*

bold *adj.* **1** daring or brave. **2** not showing respect; impudent. **3** striking and clearly marked. **4** *Printing* printed in boldface. ▸ **boldly** *adv.* ▸ **boldness** *noun*

boldface *noun* *Printing* thicker, stronger letters, as used in the word **boldface.**

bole *noun* the trunk of a tree.

bolero *noun* (*pl.* **boleros**) **1** a traditional Spanish dance, or the music for it. **2** a short, open jacket reaching not quite to the waist.

bollard *noun* a short but strong post on a ship, quay, etc., around which ropes are fastened.

boll-weevil *noun* a gray, long-snouted beetle that attacks cotton bolls.

bologna (bə-lō′nē) or **baloney** *noun* a smoked sausage made of mixed meats.

Bolshevik (bŏl′shə-vĭk,) *noun* **1** *Hist.* a member of the radical faction of the Russian socialist party, which became the Communist Party in 1918. **2** a Russian communist. —*adj.*

of the Bolsheviks. ▸ **Bolshevism** *noun* ▸ **Bolshevist** *noun, adj.*

A Russian word based on *bolshe* 'greater', because of the majority held by the Bolsheviks in the Social Democratic Congress of 1903

bolster *noun* **1** a long, narrow pillow. **2** a pad or support. —*verb trans.* (**bolstered, bolstering**) to support, make stronger, or hold (something) up: *a pep talk that bolstered our morale.*

bolt[1] *noun* **1** a bar to fasten a door, gate, etc. **2** a small, thick, round bar of metal with a screw thread, used with a nut to fasten things together. **3** a flash of lightning. **4** a sudden movement or dash away, esp. to escape: *made a bolt for the door.* **5** a roll of cloth. —*verb trans., intrans.* (**bolted, bolting**) **1** to fasten (a door, window, etc.) with a bolt. **2** to eat very quickly. **3 a** to run or dash away suddenly and quickly. **b** to move with speed, impetuously and often needlessly. **4** *of a horse* to run away out of control.

bolt[2] *verb trans.* (**bolted, bolting**) **1** to pass (flour, etc.) through a sieve. **2** to examine or investigate.

bomb *noun* **1** a device containing substances capable of causing explosions, fires, etc. **2** (**the bomb**) the atomic bomb. **3** *Football* a long forward pass. **4** *colloq.* a failure: *The movie was a real bomb.* —*verb trans., intrans.* (**bombed, bombing**) **1** to attack, damage, etc., with a bomb or bombs. **2** *colloq.* to fail badly.

bombard *verb trans.* (**bombarded, bombarding**) **1** to attack with large heavy guns or bombs. **2** to direct questions or abuse at (someone) very quickly and without stopping. **3** *Phys.* to subject (a target, esp. an atom) to a stream of high-energy particles. ▸ **bombardment** *noun*

bombardier *noun* the member of a combat aircraft crew who releases the bombs.

bombast *noun* pretentious, boastful, or insincere words having little real meaning. ▸ **bombastic** *adj.*

bomber *noun* **1** an airplane built for bombing. **2** a person who bombs something.

bomber jacket a short jacket gathered tightly at the waist.

bombshell *noun* a piece of surprising and usu. disappointing news.

bombsite *noun* an area where buildings have been destroyed by a bomb.

bona fide *adj.* undoubtedly original, real, or true. —*adv.* genuinely or sincerely.

bonanza *noun* **1** an unexpected and sudden source of good luck or wealth. **2** a large amount, esp. of gold from a mine.

bonbon *noun* a piece of candy.

bond *noun* **1** something, e.g., a cord, used for tying, binding, or holding. **2** (*usu.* **bonds**) something that restrains or imprisons (a person): *break the bonds of poverty.* **3** something that unites or joins people together: *a bond of friendship.* **4** a binding agreement or promise. **5** a certificate issued by a government or a company, which promises to pay back money borrowed at a fixed rate of interest at a stated time. **6** *Law* **a** a written agreement to pay money or carry out the terms of a contract. **b** an amount put up as bail. **7** *Chem.* the strong force of attraction between atoms in a molecule. —*verb trans., intrans.* (**bonded, bonding**) **1** to join or tie together. **2** to hold or stick together. **3** to unite (two or more people) in a close personal relationship, or to become so united.

bondage *noun* **1** slavery. **2** the state of being confined, imprisoned, etc.

bone *noun* **1** the dense, hard tissue that forms the skeleton of vertebrates. **2** any one of the components of the skeleton. **3** (**bones**) the skeleton. **4** a substance similar to human bone, such as ivory, whalebone, etc. —*verb trans.* (**boned, boning**) **1** to take bones out of (meat, etc.). **2** to make (a piece of clothing) stiff by adding pieces of bone or some other hard substance. ▸ **boneless** *adj.* ▸ **bony** *adj.*

bone china fine china made from clay mixed with ash from burned bones.

bone-dry *adj.* completely dry.

bone marrow marrow (sense 1).

bone meal dried and ground bones, used as a plant fertilizer and animal feed.

boner *noun colloq.* a foolish, usu. embarrassing mistake.

bonfire *noun* a large outdoor fire, often burned as a celebration or signal.

bong *noun* a long, deep sound such as is made by a large bell. —*verb trans., intrans.* (**bonged, bonging**) to make a bong.

bongo (bǎng'gō) *noun* (*pl.* **bongos, bongoes**) each of a pair of small drums held between the knees and played with the hands. *Also called* **bongo drums.**

bonhomie *noun* an easy, friendly nature.

bonito (bə-nēt'ō) *noun* (*pl.* **bonito, bonitos**) a marine game and food fish related to the tuna.

bon mot (bōn-mō') (*pl.* **bons mots**) a short, clever remark.

bonnet *noun* **1** a hat fastened under the chin with ribbon, formerly worn by women but now worn esp. by babies. **2** *Brit.* the hood of a motor vehicle.

bonsai (bŏn-sī') *noun* (*pl.* **bonsai**) **1** the ancient Japanese art of cultivating artificially miniaturized trees in small containers. **2** a miniature tree cultivated in this way.

bonus noun (pl. **bonuses**) **1** an extra sum of money given on top of what is due as interest or wages. **2** an unexpected extra benefit.

bon vivant (bŏN′-vē-vän′) (pl. **bons vivants**) a person who enjoys good food and wine.

bon voyage (bŏN′vwĭ-äzh′) used to express good wishes to a traveler.

boo noun (pl. **boos**) a hooting sound made to express disapproval. —interj. used to express disapproval, or to frighten or surprise (someone). —verb intrans., trans (**booed, booing, boos**) to shout boo to express disapproval (of).

boob[1] noun colloq. a stupid or foolish person. Also called **booby**.

boob[2] noun coarse slang a woman's breast.

boo-boo or **booboo** noun (pl. **boo-boos**) a mistake or blunder.

booby noun (pl. **boobies**) **1** boob. **2** a large seabird of the gannet family, native to tropical waters.

booby prize a prize for the lowest score, the person coming last, etc., in a competition.

booby trap 1 a bomb or mine disguised so that it is set off by the victim. **2** something placed as a trap, e.g., a bucket of water put above a door so as to fall on the person who opens the door. ▸ **booby-trap** verb trans.

boodle noun slang money, gained dishonestly, made by counterfeiting, or used as a bribe.

boogie (bŏŏg′ē) slang verb intrans. (**boogied, boogieing** or **boogying, boogies**) to dance to pop or jazz music. —noun a dance to pop or jazz music.

book noun **1** a number of printed pages bound together along one edge and protected by covers. **2** a rather lengthy piece of written work intended for publication. **3** a number of sheets of blank paper bound together. **4** (usu. **books**) a record of the business done by a company, a society, etc.: audited the books. **5** a major division of a long literary work. **6** a number of stamps, matches, checks, etc., bound together. **7** a record of bets. —verb trans., intrans. (**booked, booking**) **1** to reserve (a ticket, seat, etc.), or engage (a person's services) in advance. **2** to enter (a person's name, etc.) in a book or list. **3** to set down the charges against (a person) in police records. ▸ **bookable** adj. ▸ **booking** noun

bookcase noun a set of shelves or a cabinet for books.

bookend noun each of a pair of supports used to keep a row of books standing upright.

bookie noun colloq. a bookmaker.

bookish adj. **1** devoted to reading. **2** learned and serious.

bookkeeping noun the keeping of financial accounts. ▸ **bookkeeper** noun

booklet noun a pamphlet.

bookmaker noun a person who takes bets on horseraces, etc., and pays out winnings.

bookmark noun a strip of flat material put into a book to mark a place.

bookplate noun a decorated paper stuck on at the front of a book and bearing the owner's name.

bookstall noun a small shop in a station, etc., where books, newspapers, etc., are sold.

bookworm noun **1** colloq. a person devoted to reading. **2** a small insect that feeds on the paper and glue in books.

boom[1] noun a deep resounding sound, like that made by a large drum or gun. —verb intrans., trans. (**boomed, booming**) **1** to make a deep resounding sound. **2** to say (something) with a deep booming voice.

boom[2] noun a sudden increase or growth in business, prosperity, etc. —verb intrans. to prosper rapidly.

boom[3] noun **1** a spar attached to a mast, on which the foot of the ship's sail is attached. **2** a heavy pole or chain, etc., across the entrance to a harbor. **3** a long pole with a microphone attached to one end, allowing the microphone to be held above the heads of people being filmed.

boomerang noun **1** a piece of flat, curved wood used by Australian Aborigines for hunting, which when thrown to a distance, it returns to the thrower. —verb intrans. (**boomeranged, boomeranging**) to go wrong and harm the perpetrator rather than the intended victim; to backfire.

boon[1] noun an advantage, benefit, or blessing.

boon[2] adj. close, intimate, or favorite: a boon companion.

boondoggle noun counterproductive, time-consuming work.

boor noun an uncivilized and uncultured person. ⊟ BARBARIAN, PHILISTINE, YAHOO. ▸ **boorish** adj.

boost verb trans. (**boosted, boosting**) **1** to improve or encourage. **2** to make greater, to increase: boost profits. **3** to promote by advertising. —noun **1** help or encouragement, etc. **2** a push upward. **3** a rise or increase.

booster noun **1** a person or thing that boosts. **2** a dose of vaccine that is given in order to renew or increase the immune response to a previous dose. **3 a** an engine in a rocket that provides additional thrust at some stage of the vehicle's flight. **b** a rocket that is used to launch a space vehicle, before another engine takes over. Also called **booster rocket**.

boot[1] noun **1** an outer covering for the foot and lower part of the leg. **2** Brit. the trunk of a car. **3** colloq. a hard kick. **4** (**the boot**)

colloq. dismissal from a job: *get the boot.*
—*verb trans.* (**booted, booting**) **1** to kick.
2 to start (a computer) by loading the programs that control its basic functions.

boot² *noun* —**to boot** as well; in addition.

bootee *noun* a soft knitted boot for a baby.

booth *noun* **1** a small temporary roofed structure, or a tent, esp. at a fair. **2** a small building or structure for a stated purpose: *a polling booth.*

bootlace *noun* a long, slender, sturdy cord that is used to fasten boots.

bootleg *verb trans.* (**bootlegged, bootlegging**) to make, distribute, or sell (a product, e.g. liquor) illegally. —*adj.* illegally produced or transported. ▶ **bootlegger** *noun*

bootlicker *noun colloq.* a person who tries to gain the favor of someone in authority by flattery, etc.

bootstrap *Comput. noun* a short program used to boot up a computer by transferring the disk-operating system program from storage on disk into a computer's working memory. —*verb trans., intrans.* (**bootstrapped, bootstrapping**) to boot up (a computer) by activating the bootstrap program.

booty *noun* (*pl.* **booties**) valuable goods taken in wartime or by force.

booze *slang noun* alcoholic drink. —*verb intrans.* (**boozed, boozing**) to drink a lot of, or too much, alcohol. ▶ **boozer** *noun* ▶ **boozy** *adj.*

bop¹ *verb intrans.* (**bopped, bopping**) *colloq.* to dance to popular music. —*noun colloq.* bebop. ▶ **bopper** *noun*

bop² *verb trans.* (**bopped, bopping**) *colloq.* to hit lightly.

boracic *adj.* same as **boric.**

borage (bôr'ĭj) *noun* a plant cultivated as a herb for use in salads and medicinally.

border *noun* **1** a band or margin along an edge. **2** the boundary of a country. **3** the land on either side of a country's border. **4** a narrow strip of ground planted with flowers, surrounding a small area of grass. **5** a decorated or ornamental edge. —*verb trans., intrans.* (**bordered, bordering**) **1** to provide with a border. **2** to be a border to or on the border of. **3** (**border on (something)**) to be nearly the same as: *actions bordering on stupidity.*

borderland *noun* **1** land at or near the country's border. **2** a condition between two states.

borderline *noun* **1** the border between one thing, country, etc., and another. **2** a line dividing two opposing conditions: *the borderline between passing and failing.* —*adj.* on the border between one thing, state, etc., and another.

bore¹ *verb trans., intrans.* (**bored, boring**) **1** to make a hole in (something) by drilling. **2** to produce (a tunnel, mine, etc.) by drilling. —*noun* **1** the hollow barrel of a gun. **2** the diameter of the barrel of a gun, esp. as showing which size of bullets the gun requires.

bore² *verb trans.* (**bored, boring**) to make (someone) feel tired and uninterested, by being dull, uninteresting, unimaginative, etc. —*noun* a dull, uninteresting, tedious person or thing. ▶ **bored** *adj.* ▶ **boredom** *noun* ▶ **boring** *adj.* ▶ **boringly** *adv.*

bore³ *noun* a solitary high wave of water, resembling a wall, that moves rapidly upstream.

bore⁴ *see* **bear¹.**

boric *or* **boracic** *adj.* **1** of or containing borax. **2** of or containing boron.

boric acid *or* **boracic acid** a white or colorless crystalline solid that is used in pharmaceutical products, enamels, etc.

born *adj.* **1** brought into being by birth. **2** having a natural quality or ability: *a born leader.* **3** destined to do something stated: *born to lead others.* —*verb see* **bear¹.**

borne *see* **bear¹.**

boron *noun* (SYMBOL **B**) a nonmetallic element used in semiconductors and as a component of control rods and shields in nuclear reactors.

borough *noun* **1** an administrative division of New York City. **2** a self-governing incorporated town, e.g., in New Jersey. **3** a county in Alaska.

borrow *verb trans., intrans.* **1 a** to take (something) temporarily, usu. with permission and with the intention of returning it. **b** to get money in this way. **2** to take, adopt, or copy (words, ideas, etc.) from another language, person, etc. ▶ **borrower** *noun*

borscht (bôrsht) *noun* beet soup served with sour cream.

borzoi *noun* a breed of dog with a tall slender body, a long thin muzzle, and a long soft coat.

bosh *noun, interj. colloq.* nonsense.

bos'n *or* **bo's'n** *noun* same as **boatswain.**

bosom *noun* **1** a person's, esp. a woman's, chest or breast. **2** (*usu.* **bosoms**) a woman's breasts. **3** a loving or protective center: *the bosom of the family.*

boss¹ *colloq. noun* a person who employs or who is in charge of others. —*verb trans.* to give orders to (others) in a domineering way. —*adj.* fine; excellent.

boss² *noun* a round raised decorative knob, e.g., on a shield.

bossy *adj.* (**bossier, bossiest**) *colloq.* prone to give orders; domineering. ▶ **bossiness** *noun*

bosun *noun* same as **boatswain.**

botanical garden *or* **botanic gardens** a garden in which a collection of plants is developed and maintained for educational, scientific, and conservation purposes.

botany *noun* the scientific study of plants. ▸ **botanical** *or* **botanic** *adj.* ▸ **botanist** *noun*

botch *colloq. verb trans.* (**botched, botching**) **1** to do (something) badly and without skill. **2** to repair, (something) carelessly or badly: *botched up the renovation.* —*noun* a badly or carelessly done piece of work, repair, etc.

both *adj., pron.* the two. —*adv.* as well.

bother *verb trans.* *intrans.* (**bothered, bothering**) **1** to excite and trouble (a person). **2** to take the time or trouble to consider (something). **3** (**bother about** (**something**)) to worry about (it). —*noun* **1** a minor trouble or worry. **2** a person or thing that causes bother. —*interj.* used to express annoyance or impatience. ▸ **bothersome** *adj.*

bottle *noun* **1** a hollow glass or plastic container with a narrow neck, for holding liquids. **2** the amount a bottle will hold. **3** (*usu.* **the bottle**) *slang* the drinking of alcohol, esp. to excess: *hit the bottle.* —*verb trans.* (**bottled, bottling**) **1** to put into or store in bottles. **2** (*usu.* **bottle** (**something**) **up** *or* **in**) to restrain or suppress (one's feelings).

bottleneck *noun* **1** an impediment to the movement of traffic, esp. a narrow part of a road. **2** an obstacle to progress.

bottom *noun* **1** the lowest position or part. **2** the point farthest away from the front, top, most important or most successful part: *bottom of the class.* **3** the part of the body on which a person sits. **4** the base on which something stands. **5** the seat of a chair. **6** the ground underneath a sea, river, or lake. **7** the part of a ship that is under the water. —*adj.* lowest or last. —*verb trans., intrans.* (**bottomed, bottoming**) **1** to put a bottom on. **2** of a ship to reach or touch the bottom. ▸ **bottomless** *adj.*

bottom line 1 the last line of a financial statement showing profit or loss. **2** *colloq.* the most important part of a situation.

botulism *noun* a severe form of food poisoning.

boudoir (bōō-wär′) *noun* a woman's private sitting room or bedroom.

bouffant (bōō-fänt′, bōō′fänt,) *adj.,* of a *hairstyle or dress, etc.* very full and puffed out.

bougainvillea *or* **bougainvillaea** *noun* a climbing shrub with conspicuous flower heads.

bough (bow) *noun* a branch of a tree.

bought *see* **buy.**

bouillon (bōō'yən, bōō'yän,) *noun* a thin, clear soup made by boiling meat and vegetables in water, often used as a basis for thicker soups.

boulder *noun* a large piece of rock that has been rounded and worn smooth by weathering and abrasion.

boulevard *noun* a broad, tree-lined street.

bounce *verb intrans., trans.* (**bounced, bouncing**) **1** *of a ball, etc.* to spring or jump back from a solid surface. **2** to make (a ball, etc.) spring or jump back from a solid surface. **3** (**bounce about** *or* **up**) to move or spring suddenly: *bounce about the room.* **4** (**bounce in** *or* **out**) to rush noisily, angrily, with a lot of energy, etc. **5** *colloq., of a check* to be returned without being paid, because of lack of funds in a bank account. —*noun* **1** the act of springing back from a solid surface. **2** the ability to spring back or bounce well. **3** a jump or leap. **4** *colloq.* energy and liveliness.

bouncer *noun* a person employed by clubs and restaurants, etc., to stop unwanted guests entering and to remove people who cause trouble.

bouncy *adj.* (**bouncier, bounciest**) **1** able to bounce well. **2** *of a person* lively and energetic. ▸ **bounciness** *noun*

bound[1] *adj.* **1** tied with, or as if with, a rope, etc. **2** (*in compounds*) restricted to or by the thing specified: *housebound.* **3** *of a book* fastened with a permanent cover. —*verb see* **bind.**

bound[2] *adj.* **1** (**bound for** (**a place**)) going to or toward (it). **2** (*in combination*) going in a specified direction: *southbound.*

bound[3] *noun* (*often* **bounds**) **1** a limit or boundary. **2** a limitation or restriction. —*verb trans., intrans.* (**bounded, bounding**) **1** to form a boundary of. **2** to set limits to; to restrict.

bound[4] *noun* a jump or leap upward. —*verb intrans.* (**bounded, bounding**) **1** to move energetically; to spring or leap. **2** to move with leaps.

boundary *noun* (*pl.* **boundaries**) a line or border marking the farthest limit of an area, etc.

bounden *adj.* obligatory: *my bounden duty.*

boundless *adj.* having no limits; extensive: *boundless energy.*

bounteous *adj.* **1** existing in large amounts. **2** freely given.

bountiful *adj.* **1** generous. **2** existing in large amounts.

bounty *noun* (*pl.* **bounties**) **1** the giving of things generously; generosity. **2** a generous gift. **3** a reward given, esp. by a government, as encouragement, e.g., to kill or capture criminals, etc.

bouquet *noun* **1** a bunch of flowers. **2 a** a sweet odor. **b** the delicate smell of wine.

bourbon (bər′bən) *noun* whiskey made from corn, malt, and rye.

bourgeois (bŏōrzh′wä., bŏōzh′-) *noun* (*pl.* **bourgeois**) a member of the middle class, esp. regarded as politically conservative and socially self-interested. —*adj.* of or like the conservative middle class.

bourgeoisie *noun* the middle class, esp. regarded as politically conservative and socially self-interested.

bout *noun* 1 a period or turn of activity: *a drinking bout*. 2 a period of illness: *a bout of flu*. 3 a boxing or wrestling match.

boutique *noun* a small shop, esp. one selling fashionable clothes.

bovine *adj.* 1 of or like cattle. 2 of *people* dull or stupid.

bow¹ (bow) *verb intrans., trans.* (**bowed, bowing**) 1 to bend the head or the upper part of the body forward and downward, usu. as a sign of greeting, respect, etc., or to acknowledge applause. 2 to bend (the head or the upper part of the body) forward and downward. 3 (**bow to** (**something**)) to accept or submit to (it), esp. unwillingly: *bow to the inevitable*. —*noun* an act of bowing. —**bow out** to stop taking part; to withdraw.

bow² (bō) *noun* 1 a knot with a double loop. 2 a curved weapon for shooting arrows. 3 a long, thin piece of wood with horsehair stretched along its length, for playing the violin, etc. —*verb trans., intrans.* (**bowed, bowing**) to use a bow on (a violin, etc.).

bow³ (bow) *noun* (*often* **bows**) the front part of a ship or boat.

bowdlerize *verb trans.* (**bowdlerized, bowdlerizing**) to remove passages or words from (a book, play, etc.) that are considered morally or socially offensive.

> After Thomas *Bowdler*, who produced an expurgated edition of Shakespeare in the 19th century

bowel *noun* 1 (*often* **bowels**) the intestines. 2 (*usu.* **bowels**) the depths or innermost part, esp. when deep or mysterious: *the bowels of a mine*.

bower *noun* a place in a garden that is shaded from sun by plants and trees.

bowl¹ *noun* 1 a round, deep dish. 2 the amount a bowl will hold. 3 the round hollow part of a spoon or pipe. 4 *Football* a post-season game that is played by teams, usu. winning teams during the regular season.

bowl² *noun* 1 *Sport* a a large wooden or plastic ball designed to roll in a curve. b a throw or a roll of the ball in the game of bowling. 2 (**bowls**) lawn bowling. —*verb trans., intrans.* (**bowled, bowling**) 1 to roll (a ball, hoop, etc.) smoothly along the ground. 2 to engage in the game of bowling; to score (specified points) in bowling. —**bowl** (**someone**) **over** *colloq.* to surprise or impress (another) greatly.

bow-legged *adj.*, of a person having legs that curve out at the knees.

bowler¹ *noun* 1 a person who bowls a ball. 2 a person who engages in bowling.

bowler² *noun* a man's hard, round felt hat with a narrow brim. *Also called* **bowler hat**.

bowline (bō′lən) *noun* a knot that makes a loop that will not slip at the end of a piece of rope.

bowling *noun* 1 a game played indoors, in which a ball is rolled along an alley at a group of pins, the object being to knock over as many as possible. 2 the game of bowls.

bowling alley 1 a long, narrow channel, or lane, made of wooden boards, used in bowling. 2 a building containing several of these lanes.

bowling green an area of smooth grass set aside for the game of lawn bowling.

bowsprit (bow′sprĭt,) *noun* a pole projecting forward from the front of a ship, with stays and lines from the mast and sails fastened to it.

bow tie a tie that is secured in a double loop to form a horizontal bow at the collar.

box¹ *noun* 1 a usu. square or rectangular container made from wood, cardboard, plastic, etc., and usu. having a lid. 2 the amount a box will hold. 3 a separate compartment for a particular purpose, e.g., for a group of people in a theater or a witness in a court of law. 4 a small enclosed area for a particular purpose: *a telephone box*. 5 *Sport* a section on a field, rink, etc., marked out by straight lines: *a penalty box*. —*verb trans.* (**boxed, boxing, boxes**) 1 (**box** (**something**) **up**) to put (it) into or provide with a box or boxes. 2 (**box** (**someone** *or* **something**) **in** *or* **up**) to stop (someone) from moving; confine or enclose (someone or something).

box² *verb trans., intrans.* (**boxed, boxing, boxes**) 1 to fight with the fists, protected by padded leather gloves, esp. as a sport. 2 to hit (esp. someone's ears) with the fist. —*noun* a punch with the fist, esp. on the ears.

box³ *noun* a small tree with dark shiny leaves. *Also called* **boxwood**.

boxer *noun* 1 a person who boxes, esp. as a sport. 2 a large breed of dog.

boxing *noun* the sport or practice of fighting with the fists, esp. in padded gloves.

box office 1 an office that sells theater tickets. 2 theatrical entertainment regarded in terms of its commercial value.

box pleat a large double pleat on a skirt.

box score *Sport* a printed game summary listing players, positions, performance ratings, and scores.

boxwood *noun* box³.

boy *noun* 1 a male child. 2 a man, esp. regarded as immature. —*interj.* used to express excitement, surprise, or pleasure. ▸ **boyhood** *noun* ▸ **boyish** *adj.* ▸ **boyishly** *adv.*

boycott *verb trans.* (**boycotted, boycotting**) to refuse to have any business or social dealings with (a company, a country, etc.), esp. as a form of disapproval or coercion. —*noun* an act of boycotting.

After Charles *Boycott*, British estate manager ostracized by the Irish Land League in the 19th century

boyfriend *noun* a person's regular male companion, with whom one has a romantic relationship.

Boy Scout a member of an international organization of boys and young men, devoted to service, character building, and good citizenship.

bpi *abbrev.* 1 bits per inch. 2 bytes per inch.

Br¹ *abbrev.* British.

Br² *symbol Chem.* bromine.

bra *noun* a brassiere.

brace *noun* 1 a device that supports, strengthens, or holds two things together. 2 a wire device worn on the teeth to straighten them. 3 (*pl.* **brace**) a pair or couple, esp. of game birds. 4 *Printing* either of two symbols, {or}. —*verb trans.* (**braced, bracing**) 1 to make tight or stronger, usu. by supporting in some way. 2 (**brace (oneself)**) to prepare (oneself) for a blow, shock, etc.

bracelet *noun* a band or chain worn as a piece of jewelry round the arm or wrist.

bracing *adj.*, of the wind, air, etc. stimulatingly cold and fresh.

bracken *noun* a species of fern with tall fronds.

bracket *noun* 1 each of a pair of symbols, ( ), { }, or [ ], used to group together or enclose words, figures, etc. *See also* **brace** (sense 4), **parenthesis**. 2 a group or category falling within a certain range: *out of my price bracket.* 3 an L-shaped piece of metal or strong plastic, used for attaching shelves, etc., to walls. —*verb trans.* (**bracketed, bracketing**) 1 to enclose or group together (words, etc.) in brackets. 2 to put (people, things, etc.) into a group or category.

brackish *adj.*, of water tasting slightly salty.

bract *noun* a modified leaf above which a flower develops.

brad *noun* a thin, flat nail with a small head.

brag *verb intrans.* (**bragged, bragging**) to talk boastfully about oneself, what one has done, etc. —*noun* 1 a boastful statement; boastful talk. 2 a card game like poker.

braggart *noun* a person who brags a lot.

braid *noun* 1 a band or tape, often made from threads of gold and silver twisted together, used as a decoration on uniforms, etc. 2 a length of hair consisting of several lengths interwoven together. —*verb trans.* (**braided, braiding**) 1 to interweave (several lengths of thread, hair) together. 2 to decorate with braid.

Braille *noun* a system of printing for the blind, in which raised dots represent printed characters.

Named after its inventor, French teacher Louis *Braille*

brain *noun* 1 the mass of nervous tissue enclosed in the skull of humans and higher animals, that controls thoughts and activities. 2 (**brains**) *colloq.* cleverness; intelligence. 3 *colloq.* a very clever person. 4 (also **brains**) *colloq.* the person responsible for devising a plan, etc. —*verb trans.* (**brained, braining**) *colloq.* to hit hard on the head. — **have (something) on the brain** *colloq.* to be preoccupied with (it). ▸ **brainless** *adj.* ▸ **brainy** *adj.*

brainchild *noun* one person's particular theory, idea, or plan.

brain death the functional death of the centers in the brain that control breathing and other vital reflexes. ▸ **brain-dead** *adj.*

brainstem *noun* the part of the brain that is connected to the top of the spinal cord.

brainstorm *noun* 1 a sudden clever idea. 2 a sudden loss of the ability to think clearly and act properly. —*verb intrans., trans.* (**brainstormed, brainstorming**) to engage in group problem-solving and generation of new ideas and strategies.

brainwash *verb trans.* (**brainwashed, brainwashing**) to force (someone) to change his or her beliefs, ideas, etc., by continually applying mental pressure.

brainwave *noun* a wave representing the pattern of electrical activity in the brain, recorded by electrodes placed on the scalp.

braise *verb trans.* (**braised, braising**) to cook (meat, etc.) slowly with a small amount of liquid in a closed dish.

brake¹ *noun* 1 a device that is used to slow down or stop a moving vehicle or machine. 2 something that makes something stop, prevents progress, etc.: *put a brake on public spending.* —*verb intrans.* (**braked, braking**) to apply or use a brake.

brake² *noun* 1 an area of wild, rough ground covered with low bushes, etc. 2 a thicket.

brake horsepower (ABBREV. **bhp**) the power developed by an engine as measured, e.g., by the force that must be applied to a friction brake in order to stop it.

bramble *noun* a prickly bush that produces blackberries.

bran *noun* the outer covering of cereal grain, an important source of vitamin B and dietary fiber.

branch *noun* **1** an offshoot from the trunk of a tree or the main stem of a shrub. **2** a main division of a railroad line, river, road, or mountain range. **3** a division in a family, subject, etc. **4** a local office of a large company or organization. —*verb intrans.* **(branched, branching)** (*also* **branch off**) **1** to send out branches. **2** to divide from the main part: *a road branching off to the left.*

brand *noun* **1** a maker's name or trademark. **2** a variety or type: *a special brand of humor.* **3** an identifying mark on cattle, etc., usu. burned on with a hot iron. **4** a sign of disgrace or shame. **5** a piece of burning or smoldering wood. —*verb trans.* **(branded, branding) 1** to mark a brand on (cattle, etc.). **2** to make a permanent impression on (another). **3** to give (someone) a bad name or reputation: *branded him a liar.*

brandish *verb trans.* **(brandished, brandishing)** to wave (a weapon, etc.) as a threat or display.

brand name a trade name (sense 1).

brand-new *adj.* completely new.

brandy *noun* (*pl.* **brandies**) a strong alcoholic drink made from wine or fermented fruit juice.

brash *adj.* **1** very loud or showy. **2** rude; impudent. ▸ **brashness** *noun*

brass *noun* **1** an alloy of copper and zinc. **2** objects, tools, etc., made of brass. **3** a wind instruments made of brass, such as the trumpet. **b** the people who play brass instruments in an orchestra. **4** a small, flat, brass ornament with a design on it, for a horse's harness. **5 (top brass)** *colloq.* people in authority or of high military rank. —*adj.* made of brass.

brass band a band consisting mainly of brass instruments.

brasserie *noun* a small, usu. inexpensive restaurant, esp. one serving French food.

brass hat *colloq.* a high-ranking military officer.

brassica *noun* a plant such as a cabbage, cauliflower, broccoli, brussels sprout, or turnip.

brassiere (brə-zîr') *noun* an undergarment worn by women to support the breasts.

brass tacks *colloq.* the essential details: *Let's get down to brass tacks.*

brassy *adj.* **(brassier, brassiest) 1** like brass in appearance, esp. in color. **2** like a brass musical instrument in sound. **3** *colloq.* loudly confident and rude. **4** flashy or showy. ▸ **brassiness** *noun*

brat *noun* a rude or badly behaved child.

bravado (brə-väd'ō) *noun* a display of confidence or daring, often boastful and insincere.

brave *adj.* having or displaying no fear in the face of danger or adversity. —*verb trans.* **(braved, braving)** to meet or face up to (danger, pain, etc.): *brave the storm.* —*noun Hist.* a Native American warrior. ▸ **bravely** *adv.* ▸ **bravery** *noun*

bravo *interj.* well done! excellent! —*noun* (*pl.* **bravos**) a cry expressing hearty approval.

bravura (brə-vyŏŏr'ə, -vŏŏr'ə) *noun* **1** a display of great spirit or daring. **2** a piece of music, esp. for the voice, requiring considerable technical ability.

brawl *noun* a noisy quarrel or fight, esp. in public. —*verb intrans.* **(brawled, brawling)** to quarrel or fight noisily. ▸ **brawler** *noun*

brawn *noun* muscle or physical strength. ▸ **brawny** *adj*

bray *noun* the loud, harsh sound made by a donkey. —*verb intrans., trans.* **(brayed, braying)** to make the braying sound of a donkey.

braze *verb trans.* **(brazed, brazing)** to join (two pieces of metal) by means of an alloy with a lower melting point.

brazen *adj.* **1** bold, impudent, and shameless. **2** of or like brass. —*verb trans.* **(brazened, brazening)** to face (an embarrassing or difficult situation) boldly and without shame. ▸ **brazenly** *adv.*

brazier[1] (brā'zhər) *noun* a metal frame for holding a fire, used esp. outside in cold weather.

brazier[2] *noun* a worker of brass.

Brazil nut a long, three-sided, edible white nut from a S American tree.

breach *noun* **1** a breaking (of a law, promise, etc.) or failure to carry out (a duty). **2** a serious disagreement. **3** a gap, break, or hole. —*verb trans.* **(breached, breaching) 1** to break (a promise, etc.) or fail to carry out (a duty). **2** to make an opening or hole in.

breach of the peace a riot or other public disturbance.

bread *noun* **1** a solid food prepared from flour mixed with water or milk, kneaded into a dough with yeast to make it rise, and baked. **2** food and other things one needs to live: *earn one's bread.* **3** *slang* money. —*verb trans.* **(breaded, breading)** to cover (food) with breadcrumbs.

breadbasket *noun* **1** a basket for holding bread. **2** an area that produces large amounts of grain for export.

breadfruit *noun* **1** a tall tropical tree cultivated for its large edible fruit. **2** the fruit of this tree, which has a texture similar to that of bread.

breadth noun 1 the measurement from one side of an object to the other. 2 openness and willingness to understand and respect other people's opinions, beliefs, etc.: *breadth of vision*.

breadwinner noun the person who earns the money to support a family.

break verb trans., intrans. (pa t **broke**; pa p. **broken**; pr p **breaking**) 1 to divide or become divided into two or more parts as a result of stress or a blow. 2 *of a machine or tool, etc.* to damage or become damaged, so as to stop working and be in need of repair. 3 to do something not allowed by (a law, promise, etc.). 4 to stop work, etc., for a short period of time: *break for lunch*. 5 to achieve better than (a sports record, etc.). 6 *of news, etc.* to make or become known. 7 *of the weather* to change suddenly, esp. after a bad spell. 8 to make or become weaker: *tried to break his spirit*. 9 to defeat or destroy: *break a strike*. 10 to make (the force of something) less: *The trees broke her fall*. 11 to decipher: *break a code*. 12 to come into being: *day breaking over the hills*. 13 *of a storm* to begin violently. 14 *of a boy's voice* to become lower in tone on his reaching puberty. 15 to lose or disrupt the order or form of: *break ranks*. —noun 1 an act of or result of breaking. 2 a brief pause in work, etc. 3 a change: *a break in the weather*. 4 *colloq.* an unexpected or sudden opportunity. —**break away** 1 to escape from control. 2 to put an end to one's connection with a group, etc. **break down** 1 *of a person* to give way to one's emotions. 2 *of a machine, etc.* to stop working properly. **break even** to make neither profit nor loss in a transaction. **break in** 1 to enter a building by force, esp. to steal things. 2 to interrupt a conversation, etc. 3 to train. **break off** 1 to stop talking. 2 to become detached. 3 to come to an end abruptly. **break out** 1 to escape from a prison, etc. 2 to begin suddenly and usu. violently: *war broke out*. **break up** 1 to break into pieces. 2 to come to an end; to finish. 3 *a of people* to end a relationship or marriage. b *of a marriage, etc.* to come to an end. ▸ **breakable** adj., noun

breakage noun 1 the act of breaking. 2 a broken object.

breakaway npun an act of breaking away or escaping from control.

breakdown noun 1 a failure in a machine or device. 2 *of a person* a mental collapse. 3 a failure or collapse of a process: *a breakdown in communications*.

breaker noun 1 a person or thing that breaks something. 2 a large wave that breaks on rocks or the beach.

breakfast noun the first meal of the day. —verb intrans. (**breakfasted, breakfasting**) to have breakfast.

break-in noun an illegal entry by force into a building, esp. to steal things.

breakneck adj. extremely fast.

breakout noun forceful emergence, e.g., from confinement.

breakthrough noun a decisive advance or discovery.

breakup noun 1 termination, e.g., of a relationship or situation. 2 a dispersal or scattering.

breakwater noun a wall built on a beach to break the force of the waves.

breast noun 1 the upper front part of the human body. 2 in adult females, each of the two milk-producing glands forming soft protuberances on the chest. 3 the source or seat of emotions. —verb trans. (**breasted, breasting**) to face or oppose: *breast the wind*. —**make a clean breast of** (**something**) to be frank and honest about (something one has done, etc.).

breastbone noun the sternum.

breastfeed verb trans. (**breastfed, breastfeeding**) to feed a (baby) with milk from the breast.

breastplate noun a piece of armor that protects the chest.

breaststroke noun a style of swimming in which the arms are pushed out in front and then pulled backward together.

breastwork noun a temporary dirt wall for defense, reaching up to a person's chest.

breath noun 1 the air drawn into and forced out of the lungs. 2 an act of breathing air in. 3 a faint breeze. 4 a slight hint, suggestion, or rumor: *Not a breath of scandal follows him.*

Breathalyzer (brĕth'ə-lī,zər) trademark used for a piece of equipment that measures a person's blood alcohol concentration.

breathe verb intrans., trans. (**breathed, breathing**) 1 to draw air into, and force it out of, the lungs. 2 to say: *I won't breathe a word.* 3 to take breath or pause. —**breathe down (someone's) neck** to watch or supervise (someone) so closely that the person feels uncomfortable. ▸ **breathing** noun

breather noun colloq. a short rest or break from work.

breathless adj. 1 having difficulty in breathing normally, either from illness or from hurrying, etc. 2 very eager or excited. ▸ **breathlessly** adv. ▸ **breathlessness** noun

breathtaking adj. very surprising, exciting, or impressive. ▸ **breathtakingly** adv.

breathy adj. (**breathier, breathiest**) *of the voice* producing a sound of breathing when speaking.

bred see **breed**.

breech noun the back part of a gun barrel, where it is loaded.

breech birth the birth of a baby buttocks first instead of the normal head-first position. Also called **breech delivery**.

breeches (brĭch′ĭz) pl. noun **1** short trousers fastened below the knee. **2** colloq. trousers.

breechloading adj., of a firearm intended to be loaded from behind the barrel.

breed verb (**bred**, **breeding**) **1** to reproduce or cause to reproduce; to keep (animals or plants) for the purpose of producing offspring. **2** to train or educate. **3** to cause or produce (usu. something bad): Dirt breeds disease. —noun **1** a subdivision within a species, esp. of farm livestock or pet animals, produced by domestication and selective breeding. **2** a race or lineage. **3** a kind or type.

breeder noun **1** a person who breeds animals or plants, esp. for a living. **2** an animal used for breeding.

breeder reactor a nuclear reactor that produces more fissionable material than it consumes as fuel.

breeding noun **1** control of the manner by which plants or animals reproduce, so that certain characteristics are passed on to the next generation. **2** the result of education and training.

breeze noun **1** a gentle wind. **2** colloq. a job, etc., that is easily done. —verb intrans. (**breezed**, **breezing**) colloq. **1** to move briskly and confidently: breezed into the room. **2** (**breeze through (something)**) to do (it) easily and quickly: breezed through the exam. ▸ **breezily** adv. ▸ **breeziness** noun ▸ **breezy** adj.

breezeway noun a passage that links two structures or two parts of a single structure, e.g., a garage and a house.

brethren see **brother** (sense 3).

Breton (brĕt′n) noun **1** a person from Brittany in France. **2** the Celtic language of Brittany. —adj. of Brittany, its people, or their language.

breve (brēv, brĕv) noun **1** Mus. a note that is the equivalent of two whole notes. **2** a mark {ă} sometimes put over a vowel to show that it is short or unstressed.

breviary (brē′vē-ĕr,ē) noun (pl. **breviaries**) RC Church a book containing the hymns, prayers, and psalms that form the daily service.

brevity noun **1** the use of few words; conciseness. **2** shortness of time.

brew verb trans., intrans. (**brewed**, **brewing**) **1** to make (beer or other alcoholic beverages) by fermentation of barley malt. **2** to make (tea, coffee, etc.) by mixing the leaves, grounds, etc., with boiling water. **3** to become threatening: There's a storm brewing. —noun **1** a drink produced by brewing, e.g., beer. **2** an amount of beer, etc., produced by brewing: last year's brew. **3** the quality of what is brewed: a good strong brew of coffee. ▸ **brewer** noun ▸ **brewing** noun

brewery noun (pl. **breweries**) a place where beer, etc., is brewed.

briar[1] or **brier** noun a prickly shrub, esp. a wild rose bush.

briar[2] or **brier** noun **1** a shrub whose woody root is used to make tobacco pipes. **2** a pipe made from the root.

bribe noun a gift, usu. of money, offered to someone to persuade him or her to do something illegal or improper. —verb trans. (**bribed**, **bribing**) to offer or promise a bribe, etc., to (someone). ▸ **bribery** noun

bric-a-brac noun small objects of little financial value kept as decorations or ornaments.

brick noun **1** a rectangular block of baked clay used for building. **2** the material used for making bricks. **3** a child's plastic or wooden rectangular or cylindrical toy for building. —adj. **1** made of bricks. **2** of the dull red color of bricks. —verb trans. (**bricked**, **bricking**) to close or fill in with bricks.

brickbat noun **1** an insult or criticism. **2** a piece of brick, or another hard object, thrown at someone or something.

bricklayer noun a person who builds with bricks. ▸ **bricklaying** noun

brickwork noun that part of a building, e.g., the walls, that is made of brick.

bride noun a woman who has just been married, or is about to be married. ▸ **bridal** adj.

bridegroom noun a man who has just been married, or is about to be married; a groom.

bridesmaid noun a girl or unmarried woman attending the bride at a wedding.

bridge[1] noun **1** a structure joining the two sides of a road, railway, river, etc., to allow people, vehicles, etc., to cross. **2** a structure joining or connecting two separate things. **3** the narrow raised platform or an enclosed area above the main deck of a vessel from which the captain directs its course. **4** the hard bony upper part of the nose. **5** a small piece of wood on a violin, guitar, etc., that keeps the strings tightly stretched. **6** bridgework. —verb trans. (**bridged**, **bridging**) **1** to form or build a bridge over. **2** to close (a gap, etc.).

bridge[2] noun a card game for four people playing in pairs, in which players gain points by winning tricks.

bridge loan a short-term loan, usu. from a bank, to provide or extend financing for a temporary period of time.

bridgework *noun* a plate with false teeth, which is connected to the real teeth on either side of it. *Also called* **bridge.**

bridle *noun* **1** the leather straps on a horse's head that help the rider control the horse. **2** a control or a restraint. —*verb trans., intrans.* (**bridled, bridling**) **1** to put a bridle on (a horse). **2** to bring under control: *bridle one's anger.* **3** to become insulted or take offense: *bridled at the criticism.*

brief *adj.* **1** lasting only a short time. **2** short; small. **3** *of writing or speech* using few words. —*noun* **1** (**briefs**) underpants without legs. **2** a summary. **3** *Law* a summary of the facts and legal points relative to a case. **4** instructions for a job or task. —*verb trans.* (**briefed, briefing**) (**brief** (**someone**) **on** (**something**) to give (a person) advance information or instructions: *brief him on the procedure.* ▸ **briefly** *adv.* ▸ **briefness** *noun*

briefcase *noun* a light, usu. flat case for carrying papers, etc.

briefing *noun* **1** a meeting at which information and instructions are given. **2** the information or instructions given at a meeting.

brier *noun same as* **briar¹, briar².**

brig *noun* **1** a sailing ship with two masts and square sails. **2** a naval prison.

brigade *noun* **1** a division of an army, typically commanded by a brigadier general. **2** a group of people organized for a particular purpose: *a fire brigade.*

brigadier general in the US army, an officer ranking above a colonel. *Also called* **brigadier.**

brigand *noun* a member of a band of robbers.

brigantine *noun* a sailing ship with two masts, with square sails on the main mast, and sails set lengthwise on the second mast.

bright *adj.* **1** giving out or shining with much light. **2** *of a color* strong, light, and clear. **3** lively; cheerful. **4** good or quick at learning and understanding. —*adv.* **brightly:** *a fire burning bright.* ▸ **brighten** *verb trans., intrans.* ▸ **brightly** *adv.* ▸ **brightness** *noun*

brilliant *adj.* **1** very bright and sparkling. **2** *of a color* bright and vivid. **3** of outstanding intelligence or talent. **4** making a great display or show: *a brilliant display of flowers.* —*noun* a diamond cut to have a lot of facets so that it sparkles brightly. ▸ **brilliance** *noun* ▸ **brilliantly** *adv.*

brilliantine *noun old use* a perfumed oil used by men to make the hair shiny.

brim *noun* **1** the top edge or lip of a cup, glass, bowl, etc. **2** the projecting edge of a hat. —*verb intrans.* (**brimmed, brimming**) to be full to the brim: *Her eyes were brimming with tears.*

brimstone *noun old use* sulfur.

brindled *adj.,* *of animals* brown or gray, and marked with stripes of a darker color.

brine *noun* **1** very salty water, used for preserving food. **2** *literary* the sea. ▸ **briny** *adj.*

bring *verb* (**brought, bringing**) **1** to carry or take (something or someone) to a stated or implied place or person. **2** to cause or result in: *War brings misery.* **3** to cause to be in or reach a certain state: *Can't I bring you to your senses?* **4** to make or force (oneself): *I can't bring myself to tell her.* **5** to be sold for; to produce as income. —**bring** (**something**) **about** to cause (it) to happen. **bring** (**something**) **off** *colloq.* to succeed in doing (something difficult). **bring** (**something**) **on** **1** to cause (it) to happen or appear. **2** to help (it) to develop or progress. **bring** (**something**) **out** **1** to emphasize or clarify (it). **2** to publish (it). **bring** (**someone**) **up** to care for and educate (a person) when young. **bring** (**something**) **up** to introduce (a subject) for discussion.

brink *noun* **1** the edge or border of a steep, dangerous place or of a river. **2** the point immediately before the start of a dangerous, unknown, or exciting event.

brinkmanship *noun* the art of going to the very edge of a dangerous situation before moving back or withdrawing.

brioche (brē-ōsh´, -ōsh´) *noun* a breadlike cake made with a yeast dough, eggs, and butter.

briquette (brĭ-kĕt´) *noun* a brick-shaped block made from coal dust, used for fuel.

brisk *adj.* **1** lively, active, or quick: *a brisk walk.* **2** *of the weather* pleasantly cold and fresh. ▸ **briskly** *adv.* ▸ **briskness** *noun*

brisket *noun* the breast of an animal, esp. of a bull or cow, when eaten as food.

brisling *noun* a small marine fish of the herring family that is usu. processed and canned in oil.

bristle *noun* **1** a short stiff hair on an animal or plant. **2** a piece of short, stiff, synthetic material, used, e.g., for brushes. —*verb intrans., trans.* (**bristled, bristling**) **1** *of hair* to stand or cause it to stand upright. **2** to show anger, rage, etc. **3** (**bristle with** (**people** *or* **things**)) to be covered with or full of (the people or things specified): *bristling with weeds.* ▸ **bristly** *adj.*

Brit *noun colloq.* a British person.

Brit. *abbrev.* **1** Britain. **2** British.

Britannic (brĭ-tăn´ĭk) *adj. formal* of Britain; British: *Her Britannic Majesty.*

British *adj.* of Great Britain or its people. —*noun* (**the British**) people from Great Britain.

British thermal unit (ABBREV. **Btu**) the amount of heat required to raise the temperature of one pound of water by 1°F.

Briton (brĭt'n) *noun* **1** one of the Celtic people living in S Britain before the Roman conquest. **2** a British person.

brittle *adj.* **1** hard but easily broken or likely to break. **2** sharp or hard in quality: *a brittle laugh.*

broach *verb trans.* (**broached, broaching, broaches**) **1** to raise (a subject, esp. one likely to cause arguments or problems) for discussion. **2** to open (a bottle or barrel, etc.) to remove liquid. —*noun* a tool for making holes.

broad *adj.* **1** large in extent from one side to the other. **2** wide and open; spacious. **3** general: *a broad inquiry.* **4** clear: *in broad daylight.* **5** strong; obvious: *a broad hint.* **6** tolerant or liberal: *take the broad view.* **7** of an accent or speech strongly marked by local features. —*noun* **1** the wide part of anything: *the broad of my hand.* **2** *offensive slang* a woman. ▸ **broaden** *verb trans., intrans.* ▸ **broadly** *adv.*

broad bean 1 a plant cultivated for its large edible seeds borne in long pods. **2** one of the seeds of this plant.

broadcast *verb trans., intrans.* (**broadcast** or **broadcasted, broadcasting**) **1** to send out (a program) by radio or television. **2** to make (something) widely known: *Let's not broadcast that piece of gossip.* **3** to scatter (seed) by hand. —*noun* a television or radio program. —*adj.* **1** communicated or sent out by radio or television. **2** concerning or involving the electronic media: *broadcast journalists.* ▸ **broadcaster** *noun*

broadcloth *noun* a thick cloth made from wool, cotton, or silk.

broad-minded *adj.* tolerant of others opinions, etc.

broadsheet *noun* **1** a large sheet of paper usu. printed on one side only, for advertisements, etc. **2** a newspaper printed on large sheets of paper. *See also* **tabloid**.

broadside *noun* **1** the firing of all guns on one side of a warship. **2** a strong verbal attack.

broadsword *noun* a heavy sword with a broad blade.

brocade *noun* a heavy silk material with a raised design on it.

broccoli *noun* **1** a cabbage grown for its heads of immature flower buds, which are eaten as a vegetable. **2** the immature buds of this plant.

brochure *noun* a short book or pamphlet, often used in advertising or in conveying product data.

brogue[1] *noun* a strong outdoor shoe.

brogue[2] *noun* a strong but gentle accent, esp. of the Irish speaking English.

broil *verb trans.* (**broiled, broiling**) to grill (food), often with the source of heat above the food being broiled.

broiler *noun* **1** a small chicken suitable for broiling. **2** a grill.

broke *adj. colloq.* having no money. —*verb* *see* **break**.

broken *adj.* **1** smashed or fractured. **2** disturbed or interrupted: *broken sleep.* **3** not working properly: *The food processor is broken.* **4** of a promise, etc. not kept. **5** of language, esp. speech lacking fluency: *broken English.* **6** weakened or tired out, esp. through illness or misfortune. —*verb* *see* **break**.

broken-down *adj.* **1** out of working order. **2** in poor condition or health.

brokenhearted *adj.* overwhelmed with sadness or grief.

broker —*noun* **1** someone employed to buy and sell securities or bonds for others. **2** a middleman or negotiator. —*verb trans.* (**brokered, brokering**) to manage or arrange (something) in the manner of a broker: *brokered a peace settlement.*

brokerage *noun* **1** the business done by a broker. **2** the profit or fee charged by a broker.

bromide *noun* **1** a salt of hydrobromic acid, used, e.g., as a sedative. **2** an overused, trite statement or phrase.

bromine *noun* (SYMBOL Br) a nonmetallic element consisting of a dark red liquid with a pungent smell, that gives off a reddish-brown vapor.

bronchi *see* **bronchus**.

bronchial (brăng'kē-əl) *adj.* relating to the two large air tubes leading to the lungs, or the smaller tubes into which they divide.

bronchitis (brăng-kīt'ĭs) *noun* inflammation of the mucous membrane of the bronchi, also affecting the throat and larynx. ▸ **bronchitic** *adj.*, *noun*

bronchus *noun* (*pl.* **bronchi**) either of the two main branching airways to the lungs.

bronco *noun* (*pl.* **broncos**) a wild or half-tamed horse of the western USA.

bronze *noun* **1** an alloy of copper and tin, sometimes also containing small amounts of lead and zinc. **2** the dark red-brown color of bronze. **3** a work of art made of this alloy. —*adj.* **1** made of an alloy of copper and tin. **2** of the color of bronze. —*verb trans., intrans.* (**bronzed, bronzing**) **1** to give a bronze color or surface to: *sun bronzing the skin.* **2** to become the color of bronze.

Bronze Age (usu. **the Bronze Age**) the period in human history when tools, weapons, etc., were made out of bronze, between about 3000 and 1000 B.C.

bronze medal a medal given to the person who comes third in a race, etc.

brooch *noun* a decoration or a piece of jewelry, fastened to clothes by a pin.

brood noun **1** a number of young animals, esp. birds, that are produced or hatched at the same time, or that are being cared for by adults. **2** all the children in a family. —verb intrans. (**brooded, brooding**) **1** of a bird to sit on eggs in order to hatch them. **2** (**brood about, on** or **over** (**something**)) to think anxiously or resentfully about (it) for a period of time.

broody adj. (**broodier, broodiest**) **1** of a bird ready and wanting to brood. **2** deep in anxious thought.

brook¹ noun a small stream.

brook² verb trans. (**brooked, brooking**) to tolerate or accept: brook no criticism.

broom noun **1** a brush with a long handle for sweeping the floor. **2** a shrubby plant with yellow, white, or purple flowers.

broomstick noun the long handle of a broom.

Bros. abbrev. Brothers.

broth noun a thin, clear soup made by boiling meat, fish, or vegetables.

brothel noun a house of prostitution.

Originally brothel-house, brothel being a general term of abuse that was later applied specifically to prostitutes

brother noun (pl. **brothers**) **1** a boy or man with the same parents as another person or people. **2** a man belonging to the same society, church, trade union, etc., as another or others. **3** (pl., also often **brethren**) a man who is a member of a religious group, esp. a monk. ▸ **brotherly** adj.

brotherhood noun **1** the state of being a brother. **2** friendliness felt toward people with whom one has something in common. **3** an association of men for a particular, esp. religious, purpose.

brother-in-law noun (pl. **brothers-in-law**) **1** the brother of one's husband or wife. **2** the husband of one's sister. **3** the husband of the sister of one's own wife or husband.

brought see **bring**.

brouhaha (brōō'hä,hä,) noun noisy, excited, and confused activity.

brow noun **1** (usu. **brows**) an eyebrow. **2** the forehead. **3** the top (of a hill, etc.).

browbeat verb trans. (pa t **browbeat**; pa p **browbeaten**; pr p **browbeating**) to frighten (someone) by speaking angrily or looking fierce; to bully.

brown adj. **1** of the color of coffee or dark wood. **2** made from wholemeal flour. **3** having a dark skin or complexion. **4** having a skin tanned from being in the sun. —noun **1** any of various dark colors similar to that of coffee, dark wood, etc. **2** brown paint, dye, material, or clothes. —verb trans., intrans. (**browned, browning**) to make or become brown by cooking, burning in the sun, etc.

brownie noun **1** Folklore a friendly goblin or fairy. **2** (**Brownie**) a member of the junior branch of the Girl Scout movement. **3** a small, square chocolate cake, usu. with nuts.

brownout noun a cutback in electric power.

brown rice rice that has not had its outer covering removed.

brownstone noun a brownish sandstone, or a building constructed of it.

brown sugar sugar that has not been completely refined.

browse verb, intrans. (**browsed, browsing**) **1** to read a book or look around a shop, etc. casually or haphazardly. **2** of animals to feed by nibbling on plants. —noun **1** an act of browsing. **2** young shoots, twigs, leaves, etc., used as food for cattle.

browser noun Comput. software that acts as an interface between the user and the content on the Internet or other network.

bruise noun an area of skin discoloration and swelling, caused by injury. —verb trans., intrans. (**bruised, bruising**) **1** to mark and discolor (the surface of the skin) by injury, e.g., a blow. **2** to develop bruises. **3** to hurt or be hurt emotionally or mentally.

bruiser noun colloq. a big, strong person.

brunch noun a meal eaten late in the morning combining breakfast and lunch.

brunette noun a woman with brown or dark hair and a fair skin.

brunt noun the main force or shock of a blow, attack, etc.

brush noun **1** a tool with lengths of stiff nylon, wire, hair, bristles, etc., for grooming the hair, cleaning, painting, etc. **2** an act of brushing. **3** a short episode: a brush with the law. **4** a fox's brushlike tail. **5** brushwood. —verb trans., intrans. (**brushed, brushing**) **1** to rub (something) with an object, e.g., a brush, to remove dirt, dust, etc. **2** (**brush against** (**something**)) to touch (it) lightly in passing. —**brush** (**something**) **up** or **brush up on** (**something**) to improve or refresh one's knowledge of a subject, language, etc.

brushfire noun **1** a fire of dead and dry bushes and trees, which usu. spreads quickly. **2** slang a minor crisis or problem that, in recurring quantity, can cause serious trouble.

brushoff noun colloq. an abrupt dismissal; a rebuff or rejection.

brushwood noun **1** dead and broken branches, etc., from trees and bushes. **2** small trees and bushes on rough land. **3** rough land covered by such trees and bushes. Also called **brush**.

brusque adj. blunt and often impolite. ▸ **brusquely** adv. ▸ **brusqueness** noun

Brussels sprouts the small, round, cabbage-like buds of a plant of the cabbage family, eaten as a vegetable.

brut *adj.* *of champagne* extremely dry.

brutal *adj.* **1** savagely cruel or violent. **2** ruthlessly harsh. ▸ **brutality** *noun* ▸ **brutally** *adv.*

brutalize *verb trans.* (**brutalized, brutalizing**) **1** to make brutal. **2** to treat brutally. ▸ **brutalization** *noun*

brute *noun* **1** an animal other than a human being. **2** a cruel and violent person. —*adj.* **1** unable to use reason or intelligence. **2** uncivilized and coarse in behavior. ▸ **brutish** *adj.*

B.S. *abbrev.* Bachelor of Science.

BSA *abbrev.* Boy Scouts of America.

B.Sc. *abbrev.* Bachelor of Science.

Btu *abbrev.* British thermal unit.

bubble *noun* **1** a thin film of liquid forming a hollow sphere filled with air or gas, esp. one that floats in liquid. **2** a ball of air or gas that has formed in a solid: *an air bubble in glass.* **3** an unrealistic or overambitious plan or scheme. —*verb intrans.* (**bubbled, bubbling**) **1** to form or rise in or as if in bubbles. **2** (**bubble away**) to make the sound of bubbling liquid. ▸ **bubbly** *adj.*

bubble bath a scented liquid put into bath water to make bubbles.

bubble gum chewing gum that can be blown into bubbles.

bubble pack a clear plastic bubble, usu. on cardboard, in which goods for sale are packed. *Also called* **blister pack**.

bubo *noun* (*pl.* **buboes**) a swollen tender lymph node, esp. in the armpit or groin, commonly developing as a symptom of, e.g., syphilis or gonorrhoea.

bubonic plague the most common form of plague, one symptom of which is painful swelling of the lymph nodes.

buccaneer *noun* a pirate.

buck[1] *noun* **1** the male of some animals, e.g., the deer. **2** an act of bucking. —*verb intrans., trans.* (**bucked, bucking**) **1** *of a horse* to make a series of rapid jumps into the air, with the back arched and legs held stiff, esp. in an attempt to throw a rider. **2** *of a horse* to throw (a rider) from its back in this way. **3** *colloq.* to oppose or resist (an idea, etc.). —**buck up** *colloq.* to become more cheerful than before. **buck (someone) up** to make (someone) more cheerful than before.

buck[2] *noun colloq.* a dollar.

bucket *noun* **1** a round, open-topped container for holding or carrying liquids, sand, etc. **2** the amount a bucket will hold. **3** the scoop of a dredging machine or an earthmover. —*verb intrans.* (**bucketed, bucketing**) to move with speed: *trucks bucketing along the road.*

bucket seat a small seat with a round back, for one person, e.g., in a car.

buckeye *noun* a poisonous tree with large, shiny, brown seeds.

buckle *noun* a flat piece of metal attached to one end of a strap or belt, with a pin in the middle that goes through a hole in the other end of the strap or belt to fasten it. —*verb trans., intrans.* (**buckled, buckling**) **1** to fasten or be fastened with a buckle. **2** *of metal* to bend or become bent, esp. as a result of great heat or force. **3** to begin to collapse, e.g., from physical exhaustion or stress: *After the accident, my knees buckled.* —**buckle down (to)** to begin working seriously (at something).

buckler *noun* a small, round shield.

buckram *noun* stiffened cotton or linen.

buckshot *noun* large lead shot used in hunting.

buckskin *noun* **1** the skin of a deer. **2** a soft leather made from deerskin.

bucktooth *noun* a tooth that sticks out in front.

buckwheat *noun* **1** a fast-growing plant cultivated in cool temperate regions as a substitute for cereals. **2** the nutritious seeds of this plant.

bucolic *adj.* concerned with or reflective, in atmosphere, of the countryside.

bud *noun* **1 a** in a plant, a knoblike shoot that will develop into a leaf or flower. **b** a flower or leaf that is not yet fully open. **2** in an embryo, an outgrowth from which a limb develops. **3** the origin of something: *a tiny bud of an idea.* —*verb intrans.* (**budded, budding**) **1** to put out buds. **2** to reproduce by the production of buds.

Buddhism (boōd'iz,əm, bood'-) *noun* the religion founded by the Buddha, Gautama, in the 6th c B.C., which teaches a path of deliverance from suffering ▸ **Buddhist** *adj., noun*

budding *adj.* developing, beginning to show talent: *a budding pianist.* —*noun* **1** the formation of buds on a plant shoot, or the artificial propagation of a plant by grafting a bud. **2** a method of reproduction involving the production of outgrowths that develop into new individuals.

buddy *colloq. noun* (*pl.* **buddies**) a friend or companion.

budge *verb intrans., trans.* (**budged, budging**) **1** to move or cause to move. **2** to change or cause to change one's mind or opinions: *Nothing you say will make me budge.*

budgerigar (bəj'ə-rē-gär,) *noun* a small Australian long-tailed parrot, a popular cagebird that readily mimics human speech.

budget *noun* **1** a plan, esp. for a particular period of time, showing how money will be spent. **2** the amount of money set aside for a particular purpose. —*verb intrans., trans.* (**budgeted, budgeting**) **1** to calculate how much money one is earning and spending, so that one does not spend more than one has. **2** (**budget for** (**something**)) to allow for (it) in a budget: *Next year we'll budget for a new car.* **3** to provide (an amount of money) in a budget: *budget $2,000 for a vacation.* ▸ **budgetary** *adj.*

budgie *noun colloq.* a budgerigar.

buff *noun* **1** a dull yellow color. **2** a soft, undyed leather. **3** *colloq.* a person who is enthusiastic about and knows much about a subject: *an opera buff.* —*adj.* of a dull yellow color. —*verb trans.* (**buffed, buffing**) to polish with a piece of soft material: *buff up the brass and silver.*

The later meaning of 'enthusiast' derives from the *buff*-colored uniforms once used by volunteer firefighters in New York

buffalo *noun* (*pl.* **buffalo, buffaloes, buffalos**) **1** the N American bison. **2** a member of the cattle family native to S and E Africa. *Also called* **African buffalo.**

buffer *noun* **1** an apparatus, esp. one using springs, on railway cars, etc., or a cushion of rope on a ship, that takes the shock when the car or ship hits something. **2** a person or thing that protects from harm or shock. **3** *Comput.* a temporary storage area for data that is being transmitted from the central processing unit to an output device such as a printer.

buffet[1] (bə-fā´) *noun* **1** a sideboard or cupboard for holding china, glasses, etc. **2** a meal set out on tables from which people help themselves.

buffet[2] (bəf´ĭt) —*noun* a blow with the hand. —*verb trans.* (**buffeted, buffeting**) **1** to strike or knock with the fist. **2** to knock about: *a ship buffeted by the waves.*

buffoon *noun* **1** a person who does amusing or foolish things. **2** a clumsy fool. ▸ **buffoonery** *noun*

bug *noun* **1** an insect, e.g., an aphid or bedbug, that has a flattened oval body and mouthparts modified for piercing and sucking. **2** *colloq.* an insect. **3** *colloq.* a bacterium or virus that causes infection or illness: *a stomach bug.* **4** *colloq.* a small microphone hidden so as to eavesdrop on conversations. **5** *colloq.* a fault in a computer program or hardware. **6** *colloq.* an obsession or craze: *get the skiing bug.* —*verb trans.* (**bugged, bugging**) **1** *colloq.* to hide a microphone in (a room, etc.) so as to eavesdrop on conversations. **2** *slang* to annoy or worry.

bugaboo *noun* (*pl.* **bugaboos**) an imaginary thing that causes fear.

bugbear *noun* a cause of fear or annoyance.

bug-eyed *adj.* having eyes that protrude, esp. in astonishment.

buggy *noun* (*pl.* **buggies**) **1** a light, open carriage pulled by one horse. **2** a baby carriage.

bugle *noun* a brass instrument like a small trumpet, used mainly for military signals. —*verb intrans.* (**bugled, bugling**) to sound a bugle. ▸ **bugler** *noun*

build *verb trans.* (*pa t* and *pa p* **built**; *pr p* **building**) **1** to make or construct from parts. **2** to develop gradually. **3** to make in a particular way or for a particular purpose. —*noun* physical form, esp. of the human body: *of slim build.* —**build up 1** to increase gradually in size, strength, amount, etc. **2** to build (something) in stages: *built up a marketing strategy.* ▸ **builder** *noun*

building *noun* **1** the business of constructing houses, etc. **2** a structure with walls and a roof, such as a house.

building block any of the separate parts out of which something else is built.

buildup *noun* **1** a gradual increase. **2** a gradual approach to a conclusion or climax: *the buildup of a plot in a novel.* **3** publicity or praise of something or someone given in advance of a launch of a product or a personal appearance.

built *see* **build.**

built-up *adj.* **1** of land, etc. covered with buildings, esp. houses. **2** increased in height by additions. **3** made up of separate parts.

bulb *noun* **1** in certain plants, e.g., the tulip or the onion, a swollen underground organ that functions as a food store between one growing season and the next. **2** a flower grown from a bulb. **3** *Electr.* the airtight glass envelope that encloses the electric filament of an incandescent lamp, the electrodes of a vacuum tube, etc. **4** a pear-shaped object. ▸ **bulbous** *adj.*

Bulgarian *noun* **1** a native or citizen of Bulgaria. **2** the official language of Bulgaria. —*adj.* of Bulgaria, its people, or their language.

bulge *noun* **1** a swelling, esp. where one would expect to see something flat. **2** a sudden, usu. temporary, increase. —*verb intrans.* (**bulged, bulging**) to swell outward.

bulimia (byoō-lĭm´ē-ə, -lē´mē-ə) *noun* **1** compulsive overeating. **2** bulimia nervosa.

bulimia nervosa a psychological disorder in which bouts of excessive eating are followed by self-induced vomiting or laxative abuse in an attempt to avoid weight gain. *Also called* **bulimia.**

bulk *noun* **1** size, esp. when large or awkward. **2** the greater or main part: *The bulk of the task is routine.* **3** a large body, shape, or person. **4** a large quantity: *buy in bulk.* **5** roughage. —*adj.* in large quantity: *bulk shipments.*

bulkhead noun a wall in a ship or aircraft that separates one section from another.

bulky adj. (**bulkier, bulkiest**) large in size and awkward to carry or move.

bull¹ noun 1 the uncastrated male of animals in the cattle family. 2 the male of the elephant, whale, and some other large animals. 3 Stock Exchange a person who buys commodities or securities because of expectations of rising prices. 4 coarse slang nonsense.

bull² noun an official letter or written instruction from the Pope.

bulldog noun a breed of dog with a heavy body, a short brown coat, and a large square head.

bulldoze verb trans. (**bulldozed, bulldozing**) 1 to use a bulldozer to move, flatten, or demolish. 2 (**bulldoze (someone) into (something)**) to force (someone) to do (something) the person does not want to do.

bulldozer noun a large, powerful tractor with a vertical blade at the front, for pushing heavy objects, clearing ground, etc.

bullet noun a small metal cylinder with a pointed end, for firing from hand guns and rifles.

bulletin noun 1 a short official statement of news. 2 a short, printed newspaper or leaflet, esp. one produced regularly by a group or organization.

bulletin board a board onto which small items of news or reminders are tacked.

bulletproof adj. strong enough to prevent bullets from passing through: bulletproof vests.

bullfight noun a public show, esp. in Spain and Mexico, in which men bait and kill a bull. ▸ **bullfighter** noun ▸ **bullfighting** noun

bullfrog noun the largest N American frog.

bullheaded adj. refusing to change or compromise.

bullhorn noun a portable microphone connected to a loudspeaker.

bullion noun gold or silver in large bars.

bullish adj. 1 like a bull, esp. in heaviness or muscularity. 2 Stock Exchange causing, linked with, or expecting a rise in prices. 3 very confident about the future.

bull-necked adj., of a person having a short, thick, strong neck.

bullock noun a castrated bull, or a young male ox.

bullpen noun Baseball the area in which relief pitchers warm up.

bullring noun an arena where bullfights take place.

bull session colloq. an informal gathering for discussion.

bull's-eye noun 1 the small circular center of a target used in shooting, darts, etc. 2 a shot hitting this part of a target. 3 colloq. something that hits its target, achieves its aim, etc. 4 a thick round disk of glass forming a window, esp. on a ship. 5 a thick round boss in a sheet of glass.

bull terrier a breed of dog with a heavy body, a short, usu. white coat, and a broad head.

bullwhip noun a long rawhide whip with a knot on its end. —verb trans. (**bullwhipped; bullwhipping**) to beat or strike with a bullwhip.

bully¹ noun (pl. **bullies**) a person who hurts or frightens weaker or smaller people. —verb trans. (**bullied, bullying, bullies**) 1 to act like a bully toward. 2 (**bully (someone) into (something)**) to force (someone) to do (something) the person does not want to do. —adj. very good; excellent.

> Originally a term of affection that developed to mean 'pimp' and so to someone who harasses others

bully² noun corned beef. Also called **bully beef**.

bully-boy noun colloq. a rough person employed to bully and threaten people.

bulrush noun 1 a tall waterside plant with long narrow grayish leaves and one or two thick spikes of tightly packed dark brown flowers. 2 Bible a papyrus plant.

bulwark noun 1 a wall built as a defense, often made of dirt. 2 a person, place, or thing regarded as a defender of a principle, etc. 3 (usu. **bulwarks**) the side of a ship projecting above the deck.

bum colloq. noun 1 a person who lives by begging. 2 a person who is lazy and shows no sense of responsibility. —verb (**bummed, bumming**) to get by begging, borrowing, or cadging: bum a lift.

bumble verb intrans. (**bumbled, bumbling**) 1 to speak in a confused or confusing way. 2 to move in an awkward or clumsy way.

bumblebee noun a large, hairy, black and yellow bee.

bumbling adj. inept; blundering.

bump verb trans., intrans. (**bumped, bumping**) 1 to knock or hit. 2 to hurt or damage by hitting. 3 of two moving objects to collide. 4 to move or travel along with jerky or bumpy movements: bump along the road. —noun 1 a knock, jolt, or collision. 2 a dull sound caused by a knock, collision, etc. 3 a lump or swelling on the body, esp. one caused by a blow. —**bump into (someone)** colloq. to meet (another person) by chance. **bump (someone) off** slang to kill (someone).

bumper noun a bar on the front or back of a motor vehicle, intended to lessen the shock or damage if the vehicle hits something.

bumpkin noun colloq. an awkward, simple, or stupid person, esp. one from the country.

bumptious adj. offensively or irritatingly conceited.

bumpy adj. (**bumpier, bumpiest**) 1 having a lot of bumps: a bumpy road. 2 affected by bumps: a bumpy flight.

bun¹ noun 1 a small, round, sweetened roll, often containing currants. 2 a mass of hair fastened in a round shape on the back of the head.

bun² noun slang (usu. **buns**) a buttock.

bunch noun colloq. a group or collection: a bunch of old books. —verb trans., intrans. (**bunched, bunch-ing**) to group together in or form a bunch.

bundle noun 1 a number of things loosely fastened or tied together. 2 slang a large amount of money. —verb trans. (**bundled, bundling**) to make into a bundle.

bung noun a small, round piece of wood, rubber, cork, etc., that closes a hole in the bottom of a barrel, a small boat, etc.

bungalow noun a single-story house.

bungee jumping the sport of jumping from a height with a strong rubber cable attached to the ankles.

bunghole noun a hole by which a barrel, etc., is emptied or filled.

bungle verb trans., intrans. (**bungled, bungling**) to do (something) carelessly or badly. —noun carelessly or badly done work; a mistake. ▸ **bungler** noun

bunion noun a painful swelling on the first joint of the big toe.

bunk noun a narrow bed attached to the wall, e.g., in a ship's cabin or a railroad sleeping car. —verb intrans. (**bunked, bunking**) to lie down and go to sleep, esp. in an improvised place.

bunk bed each of a pair of narrow beds fixed one on top of the other.

bunker noun 1 a large container or cupboard for storing coal. 2 Golf a sand trap. 3 an underground shelter. 4 a reinforced-concrete shelter above ground, used, e.g., for observing rocket launches.

bunkhouse noun a building with many beds, usu. for workers.

bunkum noun colloq. nonsense; foolish talk.

> From *Buncombe* county in N Carolina, whose representative once gave a rambling speech in Congress

bunny noun (pl. **bunnies**) a young rabbit.

Bunsen burner a gas burner, used mainly in chemistry laboratories.

bunt Baseball verb intrans., trans. (**bunted, bunting**) to bat (a pitched ball) with light force so that it rolls in front of the infielders. —noun the action of bunting; a bunted ball.

bunting¹ noun 1 a row of small cloth or paper flags and other decorations. 2 thin, loosely woven cotton used to make flags, esp. for ships.

bunting² noun a small finchlike bird.

buoy noun a brightly-colored floating object fastened to the bottom of a body of water by an anchor, to warn boats and ships of rocks, etc. —verb trans. (**buoyed, buoying**) to mark with a buoy or buoys.

buoyant adj. 1 of an object able to float in a liquid. 2 of a person cheerful. ▸ **buoyancy** noun

bur or **burr** noun 1 a seed or fruit that bears numerous hooks or prickles. 2 a plant that produces such seeds or fruits. 3 a small rotary drill used by a dentist or surgeon.

burbot (bar'bat) noun (pl. **burbot, burbots**) a large fish of the cod family.

burden¹ noun 1 something to be carried; a load. 2 a duty, obligation, etc., that is difficult, time-consuming, costly, etc. —verb trans. (**burdened, burdening**) to load with a burden, difficulty, problem, etc. ▸ **burdensome** adj.

burden² noun 1 the main theme (of a book, speech, etc.). 2 a line repeated at the end of each verse of a song.

burdock noun a plant with flower heads composed of many tiny purple flowers and fruits that are burs.

bureau noun (pl. **bureaus, bureaux**) 1 a chest of drawers. 2 an office or department for business, esp. for collecting and supplying information. 3 a government or newspaper agency or department: the Bureau of Standards.

bureaucracy noun (pl. **bureaucracies**) 1 a a system of government by unelected officials who are responsible solely to their department heads. b these officials as a group, esp. when regarded as needlessly clerical or downright oppressive. c a country governed by officials. 2 a system of administration in which matters are complicated by excessive paperwork and trivial rules.

bureaucrat noun 1 a government official. 2 an official who follows rules rigidly, thereby creating delays and difficulties. ▸ **bureaucratic** adj. ▸ **bureaucratically** adv.

burette (byŏŏ-rĕt') noun Chem. a long vertical glass tube marked with a scale and having a tap at the bottom, used to deliver controlled volumes of liquid.

burgeon verb intrans. (**burgeoned, burgeoning**) 1 to grow or develop buds quickly. 2 to begin to grow or flourish. ▸ **burgeoning** adj.

burger noun 1 a hamburger. 2 an item of food shaped like a hamburger but made of something different: a soybean burger.

burgher *noun* a citizen of a town or borough, esp. in Europe.

burglar *noun* a person who enters a building, etc., illegally with intent to steal. ▶ **burglarize** *verb* ▶ **burglary** *noun* ▶ **burgle** *verb*

burgundy *noun* (*pl.* **burgundies**) a deep or purplish red color.

burial *noun* the burying of a corpse in a grave.

burlesque *noun* 1 a piece of literature, acting, etc., that exaggerates and mocks a serious subject or art form. 2 theatrical entertainment involving humorous sketches, songs, and usu. striptease. —*adj.* being or resembling a burlesque. —*verb trans.* (**burlesqued, burlesquing**) to make fun of (something) using burlesque.

burly *adj.* (**burlier, burliest**) *of a person* strong and heavy in build; big and sturdy. ▶ **burliness** *noun*

Burmese (bər-mēz', -mēs') *noun* 1 (*pl.* **Burmese**) a native or citizen of Burma (Myanmar). 2 the official language of Burma. —*adj.* of Burma, its people, or their language.

burn *verb trans., intrans.* (**burned** or **burnt, burning**) 1 to be set on fire or on fire. 2 to damage or injure, or be damaged or injured, by fire or heat. 3 to use as fuel. 4 to make (a hole, etc.) by or as if by fire, heat, etc. 5 to kill or die by fire. 6 to be or feel hot: *My face is burning.* 7 to feel or cause to feel a stinging pain: *Vodka burns my throat.* 8 to feel strong emotion: *burn with shame.* 9 *colloq.* to want to do something very much: *is burning for revenge.* —*noun* 1 an injury or mark caused by fire, heat, acid, etc. 2 an act of burning. **burn out** 1 to be completely burned and reduced to nothing. 2 *of a rocket engine* to stop working when the fuel is used up. 3 *of a person* to become totally exhausted as the result of overwork or unremitting stress. **burn up** to be destroyed by fire, heat, acid, etc.

burner *noun* the part of a gas lamp, stove, etc., that produces the flame.

burnish *verb trans.* (**burnished, burnishing**) to make (metal) bright by polishing.

burnoose or **burnous** *noun* a long cloak with a hood, worn by Arabs.

burnout *noun* 1 physical or emotional exhaustion caused by overwork or unremitting stress. 2 the point at which a rocket engine stops working when the fuel is used up.

burnt *see* **burn.**

burp *colloq. verb intrans., trans.* (**burped, burping**) 1 to let air escape noisily from one's stomach through one's mouth. 2 to help (a baby) get rid of air in its stomach. —*noun* a belch.

burr¹ *noun same as* **bur.**

burr² *noun* 1 in some accents of English, a rough *r* sound. 2 a continual humming sound. 3 a rough edge on metal or paper. —*verb intrans., trans.* (**burred, burring**) 1 to make a burring sound. 2 to pronounce with a burr.

burro *noun* (*pl.* **burros**) a small donkey.

burrow *noun* a hole or tunnel dug by rabbits etc. for shelter. —*verb intrans., trans.* (**burrowed, burrowing**) 1 to make a hole or tunnel in or under (something). 2 to search or investigate (some-thing): *A special prosecutor was burrowing into his financial dealings.*

bursar *noun* a school, college, or university treasurer.

burst *verb intrans., trans.* (**burst, bursting**) 1 to break open or into pieces, usu. suddenly and violently. 2 to make one's way suddenly or violently: *burst into the room.* 3 to appear suddenly and be immediately important or noteworthy: *burst onto the political scene.* 4 **a** to be quite full: *The sack is bursting with apples.* **b** to break open, overflow, etc. **c** to be consumed with emotion, vitality, etc.: *She's bursting with life.* 5 to begin (an action, e.g., laughing or crying) with great suddenness: *burst out laughing.* —*noun* 1 an instance of, or the place of, bursting or breaking open. 2 a sudden brief period of something: *a burst of gunfire.*

bury (bĕr'ē) *verb trans.* (**buried, burying, buries**) 1 to place (a corpse) into a grave. 2 to hide (something) in the ground: *a dog burying a bone.* 3 to put out of sight; to cover: *buried her face in her hands.* —**bury the hatchet** to stop quarreling and become friends again.

bus *noun* (*pl.* **buses** or **busses**) a usu. large road vehicle that carries passengers to and from established stops along a fixed route for payment. —*verb intrans., trans.* (**bused** or **bussed, busing** or **bussing, buses** or **busses**) 1 to go by or take a bus. 2 to transport (children) by bus to schools in different areas.

busby *noun* (*pl.* **busbies**) a tall military fur hat.

bush *noun* 1 a low woody perennial plant, esp. one having branches originating at or near ground level. 2 a dense group of such plants. 3 something that looks like a bush, esp. in thickness or density. 4 (*usu.* **the bush**) wild uncultivated land, esp. in Australia and Africa. ▶ **bushiness** *noun* ▶ **bushy** *adj.*

bushed *adj. colloq.* extremely tired.

bushel *noun* a unit of measurement for weighing grains, fruit, liquid, etc., equivalent to 4 pecks, 2,150.42 cu. in., or 35.24 liters.

bushman *noun* a person who lives or travels in the bush in Australia or New Zealand.

bushmaster noun a large poisonous snake.

bushwhack verb, trans. (**bushwhacked, bushwhacking**) to attack suddenly from a hiding place, usu. in rough country. ▸ **bushwhacker** noun

business (bĭz'nəs) noun 1 the buying and selling of goods and services. 2 a shop, firm, commercial company, etc. 3 one's regular occupation, trade, or profession. 4 the things that are one's proper or rightful concern: Mind your own business. 5 serious work or activity: Let's get down to business. 6 an affair; a matter: a nasty business.

business card a card carried by business people showing their name and business address.

business class seats between standard and first class in price and quality on a commercial aircraft.

businesslike adj. 1 practical and efficient. 2 professional and unemotional in demeanor.

businessman, businessperson or **businesswoman** noun a person who works in business.

busman's holiday leisure time spent doing what one normally does at work.

busses, bussing see bus.

bust¹ noun 1 the upper front part of a woman's body. 2 a sculpture of a person's head, shoulders, and chest.

bust² verb trans., intrans. (**busted, busting**) 1 slang to break or burst. 2 slang to arrest: bust a narcotics dealer. 3 slang to raid or search: bust an after-hours club. 4 to cause to go into bankruptcy or to be bank-rupt. —noun 1 slang a police raid. 2 slang a drinking bout; a spree. 3 the state of being bankrupt. —**go bust** to go bankrupt.

bustier (bōos-tyā') noun a sleeveless, usu. strapless, form-fitting woman's top, worn, e.g., as evening attire.

bustle¹ verb intrans., trans. (**bustled, bustling**) to busy oneself noisily and energetically: bustled around cleaning the house. —noun hurried, noisy, and excited activity.

bustle² noun Hist. a frame or pad for holding a skirt out from the back of the waist.

busty adj. (**bustier, bustiest**) colloq., of a woman having large breasts.

busy adj. (**busier, busiest**) 1 having much work to do; fully occupied. 2 full of activity. 3 of a telephone line in use. 4 constantly working or occupied. 5 fussy and tending to interfere in the affairs of others. —verb trans. (**busied, busying, busies**) (**busy (someone) with (something)**) to occupy (someone) with (a task, etc.). ▸ **busily** adv. ▸ **busyness** noun

busybody noun a person who is always interfering in other people's affairs.

but conj. 1 contrary to expectation: She fell down but didn't hurt herself. 2 in contrast: You've been to Spain but I haven't. 3 other than: can do nothing but wait. —prep. except: They are all here but him. —adv. only: I can but try. —noun an objection or doubt: Do what I say, and no buts about it!

> **Usage** But may be used to begin sentences, whether in formal or informal prose.

butane noun a colorless highly flammable gas, used in compressed liquid form as a fuel for portable stoves, etc.

butch adj. slang tough and masculine in appearance or demeanor.

butcher noun 1 a person or shop that sells meat. 2 a person who kills animals for food. 3 a person who kills people savagely. —verb trans. (**butchered, butchering**) 1 to kill and prepare (an animal) for sale as food. 2 to kill cruelly. 3 to ruin or spoil: a copyeditor who butchered my book. ▸ **butchery** noun

butler noun the head male servant in a house, in charge of the wine cellar, dining table, etc.

butt¹ verb trans., intrans. (**butted, butting**) 1 to push or hit hard or roughly with the head like a ram or goat. 2 to join or be joined end-to-end. —noun 1 a blow with the head or horns. 2 the place where two edges join. —**butt in** colloq. to interrupt or interfere. **butt out** slang to remove oneself from a situation of no concern to one.

butt² noun a large barrel for beer, rain, etc.

butt³ noun 1 a person who is often a target (of jokes, ridicule, etc.). 2 a mound of earth behind a target on a shooting range.

butt⁴ noun 1 the thick, heavy, or bottom end of a tool or weapon. 2 the unused end of a finished cigar, cigarette, etc. 3 colloq. the buttocks.

butte (byōot) noun dialect an isolated flat-topped hill with steep sides.

butter noun 1 a solid yellow food made by churning from the fats contained in milk. 2 any of various substances that resemble this food, e.g., peanut butter —verb trans. (**buttered, buttering**) to put butter on or in. —**butter up** colloq. to flatter, esp. in order to gain a favor.

butter bean dialect 1 a lima bean. 2 a wax bean.

buttercup noun a plant with cup-shaped, usu. yellow flowers.

butterfat noun the fat derived from milk, from which butter is made.

butterfingers sing. noun a person who often drops things, or who does not manage to catch things.

butterfly noun (pl. **butterflies**) 1 an insect having four large, often brightly colored wings. 2 (**butterflies**) a nervous feeling. 3 the butterfly stroke.

butterfly stroke a swimming stroke in which both arms are brought out of the water and over the head at the same time.

buttermilk noun the slightly sharp-tasting liquid left after all the butter has been removed from milk.

butternut noun 1 a walnut tree of-eastern N America having nuts enclosed in sticky, aromatic, egglike husks. 2 the edible nut of this tree.

butternut squash a bell-shaped winter squash with a tan rind and yellow flesh.

butterscotch noun a hard candy made from butter and brown sugar.

buttock noun (usu. **buttocks**) each of the fleshy parts of the body between the back and the legs.

button noun 1 a small, usu. round piece of metal, plastic, etc., sewn onto clothes, which fastens them by being passed through a slit or hole. 2 a small disk pressed to operate a door, bell, etc. 3 a small object similar to a button. —verb trans., intrans. (**buttoned**, **buttoning**) 1 to fasten (something) using a button or buttons: button a blouse. 2 to be capable of being fastened by buttons: a blouse that buttons easily.

buttonhole noun a small slit or hole through which a button is passed to fasten a garment. —verb trans. (**buttonholed**, **buttonholing**) to stop and force conversation on (a usu. reluctant person).

buttress noun 1 a support built on to the outside of a wall. 2 a support or prop. —verb trans. (**buttressed**, **buttressing**) 1 to support (a wall, etc.) with buttresses. 2 to support or encourage (an argument, etc.).

buxom adj., of a woman attractively plump and healthy-looking.

buy verb trans., intrans. (**bought**, **buying**) 1 to obtain (something) by paying a sum of money for (it). 2 to be a means of obtaining (something): There are some things money can't buy. 3 to obtain by giving up or sacrificing something: success that was bought at the expense of happiness. 4 colloq. to believe or accept as true: I just don't buy your excuses. 5 to bribe (someone). —noun a thing bought: a good buy. —**buy (someone) off** to get rid of (a threatening person, etc.) by paying money. **buy (someone) out** to buy all the shares held by (someone) in a company.

buyer noun 1 a person who buys; a customer. 2 a person employed by a shop or firm to buy merchandise.

buyout noun the purchase of all the shares in a company in order to gain control of it.

buzz verb intrans., trans. (**buzzed**, **buzzing**, **buzzes**) 1 to make a continuous humming or rapidly vibrating sound. 2 to be filled with activity or excitement: buzzing with activity. 3 colloq. to call (someone) on the telephone or on an intercom. 4 colloq. to call (someone) using a buzzer. 5 colloq., of an aircraft to fly very low over or very close to (a building, etc.). —noun 1 a humming or rapidly vibrating sound, e.g., as made by a bee. 2 a low murmuring sound, e.g., as made by many people talking. 3 colloq. a telephone call. 4 colloq. a sense of activity, excitement, etc. 5 colloq. a rumor. —**buzz off** colloq. to go away.

buzzard noun 1 a N American vulture, esp. the turkey vulture. 2 colloq. a mean, avaricious person.

buzzer noun an electrical or electronic device that makes a buzzing sound.

buzzword noun colloq. a fashionable new word or expression, often in a particular subject or social group.

by[1] prep. 1 next to; beside; near. 2 past: drive by the house. 3 through, along, or across: enter by the window. 4 used to show the person or thing that does, causes, produces, etc., something: bitten by a dog / a play by Shakespeare. 5 used to show method or means: travel by air. 6 not later than: be home by midnight. 7 during: escape by night. 8 used to show extent or amount: bigger by six feet. 9 used in stating rates of payment, etc.: paid by the hour. 10 according to: by my watch. 11 used in giving measurements, compass directions, etc.: a room measuring six feet by ten. 12 used to show the number that must perform a mathematical operation on another: divide six by two. 13 with regard to: did my duty by them. —adv. 1 near: live close by. 2 past: drive by without stopping. 3 aside; away; in reserve: put money by. —**by and by** after a short time.

bye[1] or **by**[2] noun a pass to the next round of a competition given to a competitor or team that has not been given an opponent in the current round. —**by the bye** while I think about it; incidentally.

bye[2] or **bye-bye** interj. colloq. goodbye.

by-election noun an election held to fill a seat that has become empty because the member has died or resigned.

bygone adj. past; former. —noun (usu. **bygones**) a past event or argument. —**let bygones be bygones** to agree to forget past disagreements.

bylaw noun a law or rule that governs an organization.

byline noun a line under the title of a newspaper or magazine article that has the bylining) to write (an article) under a byline.

bypass *noun* **1** a road that avoids a busy area or town. **2** the redirection of blood flow around a blocked or diseased blood vessel, usu. by grafting a blood vessel taken from another part of the body. —*verb trans.* (**bypassed, bypassing**) **1** to avoid (a place) by taking a road that goes around it. **2** to leave out (a step in a process) or ignore and not discuss something with (a person). **3** to provide with a bypass.

by-play *noun* less important action happening at the same time as the main action, e.g., in a play.

byproduct *noun* **1** a secondary product that is formed at the same time as the main product during a chemical reaction or manufacturing process. **2** an unexpected, extra result.

byroad *noun* a minor road. *Also called*

byway.

bystander *noun* a person who watches but does not take part in what is happening.

byte *noun* (ABBREV. **B**) *Comput.* **1** a group of usu. eight adjacent bits that are handled as a single unit. **2** the amount of storage space occupied by such a group.

byway *noun* a byroad.

byword *noun* a person or thing well known as a prime example.

Byzantine (bĭz′ən-tēn, bə-zăn′-, -tīn,) *adj.* **1** relating to Byzantium (now Istanbul in Turkey) or the eastern part of the Roman Empire from A.D. 395 to 1453. **2** of the style of architecture or painting developed by the Byzantine Empire. **3** complex and impenetrable; secret. —*noun* an inhabitant of Byzantium.

Cc

C¹ *or* **c** *noun* (*pl.* **Cs, C's, c's**) **1** the third letter of the English alphabet. **2** (*usu.* **C**) the third highest grade or quality, or a mark indicating this. **3** (**C**) *Mus.* **a** the note on which the Western system of music is based. **b** a musical key with the note C as its base.

C² *noun* a programming language used on microcomputers.

C³ *abbrev.* **1** calorie; kilocalorie. **2** Celsius. **3** centigrade. **4** *slang* cocaine.

C⁴ *symbol* **1** the Roman numeral for 100. **2** *Electr.* capacitance. **3** *Chem.* carbon. **4** coulomb.

c *abbrev.* **1** *Math.* constant. **2** cubic.

c. *abbrev.* **1** cent. **2** century. **3** *circa* (Latin), approximately.

© *symbol* copyright.

Ca *symbol Chem.* calcium.

cab *noun* **1** a taxi. **2** the driver's compartment in a truck, train engine, etc.

cabal (kə-băl′, -bäl′) *noun* **1** a small group formed within a larger body, for secret discussion or planning. **2** a secret plan with an evil or illegal goal.

cabaret *noun* **1** a nightclub with live entertainment. **2** this entertainment.

cabbage *noun* **1** a plant with a compact head of edible leaves, usu. green. **2** these leaves eaten as a vegetable.

cabby *or* **cabbie** *noun* (*pl.* **cabbies**) a taxi driver.

caber *noun Scot.* a heavy wooden pole that is carried upright and then tipped end over end,

usu. in competitions of strength.

cabin *noun* **1** a small house, esp. one made of wood. **2** a small room on a ship. **3** an airplane passenger section.

cabin cruiser a large power-driven boat.

cabinet *noun* **1** a piece of furniture with shelves and doors, for storage or display. **2** (**Cabinet**) the senior ministers or department heads of a government.

cable *noun* **1** a strong wire cord or rope. **2** protected electrical wires used to transmit electricity, etc. **3** cable television. **4** a cablegram. **5** *Naut.* a unit of length or depth, about 600ft (220m). —*verb intrans., trans.* (**cabled, cabling**) to send a cable, or send (a message) to (a recipient) by cable.

cable car an electric railcar operating on a circular cable.

cablegram *noun* a telegram sent by cable.

cable television a television broadcasting system in which the signals are relayed directly by means of cables. *Also called* **cable, cableTV**.

caboodle *noun colloq.* (**the whole caboodle**) everything.

caboose *noun* a freight train car, for use by the crew.

cabriolet (kăb,rē-ə-lā′) *noun* **1** a light two-wheeled carriage drawn by one horse. **2** an automobile with a folding roof.

cacao *noun* a tropical tree whose seeds are used to produce cocoa and chocolate.

cache *noun* **1** a hiding place, e.g., for weapons or illicit drugs. **2** a collection of hidden things.

cache memory *Comput.* a memory subsystem providing fast access to frequently used data.

cachet (kăsh-ā') *noun* **1** something that brings one respect or admiration. **2** a distinguishing mark, e.g. an official seal or special postmark.

cackle *noun* **1** the shrill sound that a hen or goose makes. **2** a laugh resembling this sound. —*verb intrans.* (**cackled, cackling**) to laugh shrilly.

cacophony (kə-kăf'ə-nē) *noun* a combination of loud, discordant noises or voices. ► **cacophonous** *adj.*

cactus *noun* (*pl.* **cacti, cactuses**) a spiny desert plant.

CAD *abbrev.* computer-aided design.

cad *noun* a man who behaves discourteously or dishonorably. ► **caddish** *adj.*

cadaver *noun* a dead body, esp. a human one. ► **cadaverous** *adj.*

caddie *or* **caddy** *noun* (*pl.* **caddies**) someone who carries a golfer's clubs. —*verb intrans.* (**caddied, caddying, caddies**) to act as a caddy.

caddy[1] *noun* (**caddies**) a small container for tea.

caddy[2] *noun, verb* same as **caddie**.

cadence *noun* **1** a fall in pitch. **2** the rising and falling of the voice in speaking. **3** rhythm or beat. **4** the close of a musical passage.

cadenza *noun* an elaborate solo variation at the end of a concerto movement, etc.

cadet *noun* a trainee, esp. in the armed services.

cadge *verb trans., intrans.* (**cadged, cadging**) to beg or scrounge. ► **cadger** *noun*

cadmium *noun Chem.* (SYMBOL **Cd**) a soft bluish-white metallic element.

cadre *noun* an inner group of politically active people, e.g., within a political party.

caecum *noun Anat.* same as **cecum**.

caesarean *noun Med.* same as **cesarean**.

caesium *noun Chem.* same as **cesium**.

caesura *noun* (*pl.* **caesuras, caesurae**) a pause in a line of poetry.

café *or* **cafe** *noun* a small restaurant.

cafeteria *noun* a self-service restaurant.

caffeine (kă-fēn') *noun* a bitter alkaloid, found in coffee, tea, etc., that acts as a stimulant.

caftan *or* **kaftan** *noun* a long loose-fitting garment worn orig. by men in Middle Eastern countries.

cage *noun* a container with bars, etc., where captive birds or animals are kept. —*verb trans.* (**caged, caging**) to put or keep in a cage.

cagey *adj.* (**cagier, cagiest**) *colloq.* not speaking openly; secretive and cautious. ► **cagily** *adv.* ► **caginess** *noun*

cahoots *pl. noun colloq.* close, often secret, partnership.

caiman *or* **cayman** *noun* (*pl.* **caimans**) a Central and S American reptile closely related to the alligator.

cairn *noun* **1** a heap of stones piled up as a monument or marker. **2** a small dog with short legs, a thick shaggy brown coat, and erect ears. *Also called* **cairn terrier.**

caisson *noun* **1** a watertight chamber used to protect construction workers when underwater. **2** a wheeled, horse-drawn vehicle, once used to haul artillery ammunition.

caisson disease a condition affecting divers who have decompressed too quickly, characterized by pain, nausea, and paralysis.

cajole *verb trans.* (**cajoled, cajoling**) to persuade by persistent appeals, flattery, etc.: *cajoled me into skydiving.* ► **cajolery** *noun*

Cajun (kā'jən) *noun* **1** a member of a people of S Louisiana who are descendants of the French colonists exiled in the 18th c from Acadia. **2** (*often* **Cajan**) a member of a people of S Alabama and SE Mississippi whose ancestry is a combination of Native American and African-American.

cake *noun* **1** a sweet food made by baking a mixture of flour, fat, eggs, sugar, etc. **2** a solid block, e.g., of soap. —*verb intrans., trans.* (**caked, caking**) to form into or cover in a thick crust. —**a piece of cake** *colloq.* a very easy task, etc.

cakewalk *noun* **1** a dance performed in minstrel shows. **2** *colloq.* something accomplished with extreme ease.

calabash *noun* a tropical American tree or its large round gourdlike fruit.

calaboose *noun colloq.* a jail.

calamine *noun* zinc carbonate, or sometimes zinc oxide, used in soothing lotions and creams.

calamity *noun* (*pl.* **calamities**) a catastrophe, disaster, or other serious misfortune. ► **calamitous** *adj.* ► **calamitously** *adv.*

calcareous *adj.* containing or relating to calcium carbonate; chalky.

calcify *verb trans., intrans.* (**calcified, calcifying, calcifies**) to harden or become hardened as a result of the deposit of calcium. ► **calcification** *noun*

calcite *noun* crystalline calcium carbonate.

calcium *noun* (SYMBOL **Ca**) a soft silvery-white metallic element occurring in chalk, limestone, and bone.

calculate *verb trans., intrans.* (**calculated, calculating**) **1** to work out, find out, or estimate, esp. by mathematical means. ▣ COMPUTE, RECKON. **2** to plan, intend, or guess. ► **calculable** *adj.* ► **calculably** *adv.* ► **calculation** *noun*

calculated *adj.* carefully planned; deliberate; intentional.

calculating *adj.* coldly shrewd and scheming. ► **calculatingly** *adv.*

calculator *noun* a small electronic device used to perform numeric calculations.

calculus *noun* (*pl.* **calculi, calculuses**) **1** the branch of mathematics concerned with the differentiation and integration of functions. **2** a hard mass or stone, e.g., a gallstone.

caldron *or* **cauldron** *noun* a large metal pot for boiling or heating liquids.

calendar *noun* **1** a booklet or device showing the months and days of the year. **2** a system by which the divisions of the year are fixed: *the Julian calendar*. **3** a timetable of important appointments, etc.

calender *noun* a machine with heated rollers for pressing cloth or paper. —*verb trans.* (**calendered, calendering**) to press (cloth or paper) in this machine.

calends *or* **kalends** *noun* (*pl.* **calends**) the first day of the month in the calendar of ancient Rome.

calf[1] *noun* (*pl.* **calves**) **1** the young of a cow, elephant, whale, etc. **2** calfskin.

calf[2] *noun* (*pl.* **calves**) the fleshy back part of the human leg below the knee.

calfskin *noun* leather made from the skin of a calf.

caliber *noun* **1** the diameter of the bore of a gun or of a bullet or shell. **2** quality; ability.

calibrate *verb trans.* (**calibrated, calibrating**) **1** to mark a scale on (a measuring instrument). **2** to correct or adjust (the scale or instrument). ▸ **calibration** *noun*

calico *noun* (*pl.* **calicoes, calicos**) brightly painted, coarse cotton cloth.

> Originally *Calicut cloth*, after the port in SW India from where it was exported

californium *noun* (SYMBOL Cf) a synthetic radioactive metallic element.

caliper *or* **calliper** *noun* (**calipers**) a measuring instrument with two prongs, used to measure diameter.

caliph *or* **khalif** *noun* a Muslim civil and religious leader. ▸ **caliphate** *noun*

calisthenics *noun* (*pl.*) physical exercises for increasing the body's strength and grace. ▸ **calisthenic** *adj.*

call *verb trans., intrans.* (**called, calling**) **1** to shout or speak loudly. **2** to ask (someone) to come, esp. with a shout. **3** to ask for a professional visit from. **4** to summon or invite. **5** to telephone. **6** to make a visit. **7** to give a name to: *called her Mary.* **8** to regard or consider (something) as: *call that strange.* **9** to announce or declare. **10** of a bird, etc. to make a characteristic sound. —*noun* **1** a shout or cry. **2** the characteristic cry of a bird or animal. **3** an invitation; a summons. **4** a telephone communication. **5** a brief visit. **6** a signal blown on a bugle, etc. ▸ **caller** *noun*

call girl a prostitute contacted by telephone.

calligraphy *noun* **1** handwriting as an art. **2** decorative handwriting. ▸ **calligrapher** *noun*

calling *noun* **1** a profession or career. **2** an urge to follow a particular profession.

calling card a visiting card.

callosity *noun* (*pl.* **callosities**) callus.

callous *adj.* lacking concern for others. ▸ **callously** *adv.* ▸ **callousness** *noun*

callow *adj.* young and inexperienced.

callus *noun* (*pl.* **calluses**) a thickening of skin on the palm of the hand or sole of the foot.

calm *adj.* **1** relaxed and in control. ▤ COMPOSED, SERENE, UNRUFFLED ▤ DISTURBED, UPSET. **2** of the weather, etc. still and peaceful. —*noun* peace, quiet, and tranquillity. —*verb trans., intrans.* (**calmed, calming**) to make or become calm. ▸ **calmly** *adv.* ▸ **calmness** *noun*

calorie *noun* a measure of heat and of the energy value of food. *Also called* **small calorie**. *See also* **kilocalorie**. ▸ **calorific** *adj.*

calumet (kăl′yə-mĕt,, -mət) *noun* a Native American ceremonial smoking pipe.

calumniate *verb trans.* (**calumniated, calumniating**) to slander. ▸ **calumniator** *noun* ▸ **calumniation** *noun.*

calumny *noun* (*pl.* **calumnies**)an untrue and malicious spoken statement about a person. ▸ **calumnious** *adj.*

calve (kăv) *verb intrans.* (**calved, calving**) to give birth to a calf.

calves *pl. noun see* **calf**[1], **calf**[2].

Calvinism *noun* the teachings of John Calvin, a strict branch of Protestantism. ▸ **Calvinist** *noun* ▸ **Calvinistic** *adj.*

calyx *noun* (*pl.* **calyxes, calyces**) the outermost whorl of a flower, consisting of the sepals.

CAM *abbrev.* computer-aided manufacturing.

cam *noun Engineering* an irregular projection on a wheel or rotating shaft, which transmits regular movement to another part.

camaraderie (kăm,ə-räd′ə-rē) *noun* a feeling of friendship within a group. ▤ ESPRIT DE CORPS.

camber *noun* a slight arching of the upper surface of a road, etc.

cambium *noun* a layer of cellular tissue in the roots and stems of woody plants..

cambric *noun* a fine white cotton or linen cloth.

camcorder *noun* a portable video camera, used to record images and sound.

came *verb see* **come.**

camel *noun* a large plant-eating mammal with one or two humps on its back.

camellia *noun* an evergreen shrub with white, pink, or crimson flowers and glossy leaves.

Camembert (kăm′əm-bĕr,) *noun* a soft white French cheese.

cameo *noun* (*pl.* **cameos**) **1** a gemstone with a raised design, esp. a head, carved on it. **2** a small part in a play or movie performed by a well-known actor. **3** a short descriptive piece of writing.

camera *noun* **1** a device used for taking photographs, or for making movies or television broadcasts. **2** the private chamber of a judge. —**in camera** in complete privacy.

From Latin word 'room' or 'chamber'

cameraman *noun* a man who operates a television or movie camera.

camera obscura a darkened room with an opening through which light reflected from an exterior scene is projected onto a wall.

cameraperson *noun* a cameraman or a camerawoman.

camera-shy *adj.* having a dislike of being photographed.

camerawoman *noun* a woman who operates a television or movie camera.

camisole *noun* a woman's garment with narrow shoulder straps for the top half of the body.

camomile *noun same as* **chamomile**.

camouflage (kăm′ə-fläzh,, -fläj,) *noun* **1** coloring used on military equipment, vehicles, etc., that imitates the colors of nature, making them difficult for an enemy to see. **2** coloring on an animal or bird that blends with its natural surroundings, making it difficult to see. **3** anything used as a disguise. —*verb trans.* (**camouflaged, camouflaging**) to disguise or conceal.

camp[1] *noun* **1** a site on which tents are erected. **2** a collection of buildings, huts, etc., used as temporary accommodation. **3** a permanent site where troops are housed or trained. **4** a group having a particular set of opinions, beliefs, etc. —*verb intrans.* (**camped, camping**) to stay in a tent.

camp[2] *colloq. adj.* theatrical and exaggerated, esp. amusingly so.

campaign *noun* **1** an organized series of actions to gain support for or build up opposition to a particular practice, group, etc. **2** military operations directed at achieving a particular goal or objective. —*verb intrans.* (**campaigned, campaigning**) (*usu.* **campaign for** or **against**) to take part in a drive in support of or against (something). ▸ **campaigner** *noun*

campanile (kăm,pə-nē′lē) *noun* a bell tower standing by itself.

campanula (kăm-păn′yə-lə) *noun* a plant with bell-shaped, *usu.* blue, flowers.

camp bed a light folding bed.

camper *noun* **1** a person who camps, e.g., in a tent. **2** a motor vehicle equipped with sleeping, cooking, and washing facilities.

camp follower 1 a person who supports a particular group, party, etc., only because it

is fashionable. **2** a person who travels about with an army in order to earn money, e.g., as a prostitute.

campground *noun* a place with facilities for camping.

camphor *noun* a strong-smelling white crystalline compound found in the leaves of an evergreen tree or manufactured artificially, and used as a medicinal liniment and inhalant. ▸ **camphorated** *adj.*

campsite *noun* a piece of land on which to camp.

campus *noun* the grounds of a college or university.

can[1] *verb, aux.* (*pa t* **could**) **1** to be able to. **2** to know how to. **3** *colloq.* to have permission to: *Can I take an apple?*

Usage In formal American English *can* should be used to express one's capacity to do something; *may* should be used to express permission: *May I take an apple? Can you reach the apple on the tree?*

can[2] *noun* **1** a sealed metal container for preserving food or drink. **2** a large container for holding liquids, e.g., oil or paint. **3** *slang* prison. **4** *slang* a toilet or bathroom. —*verb trans.* (**canned, canning**) **1** to seal (food or drink) in metal containers. **2** *slang* to dismiss from a job; fire. **3** *slang* to stop (an activity).

Canada goose a N American wild goose.

Canadian (kənăd′ē-ən) *noun* a native or citizen of Canada. —*adj.* of Canada, or its people, or their form of the French language.

canal *noun* **1** an artificial channel or waterway for ships, barges, etc., or for irrigation. **2** a tubular passage that conveys air, fluids, or food from one part of the body to another. ▸ **canalize** *verb* ▸ **canalization** *noun*

canapé (kăn′ə-pē, -pā,) *noun* a small piece of bread or a cracker with a savory topping.

canard (kə-närd′, -när′) *noun* an untrue piece of news; a rumor or hoax.

canary *noun* (*pl.* **canaries**) a small songbird with bright yellow plumage, often kept as a pet.

canasta *noun* a card game similar to rummy but played with two packs.

cancan *noun* a lively dance performed by women, who execute high kicks, raising their skirts at the same time.

cancel *verb trans., intrans.* (**canceled** *or* **cancelled, canceling** *or* **cancelling**) **1** to stop (something) from taking place or from continuing. **2** to cross out; to delete. **3** to put an official stamp on (e.g., a postage stamp) so that it cannot be reused. —**cancel out** to remove the effect of (something). ▸ **cancellation** *noun*

Cancer *noun* **1** the Crab, the name of a constellation and the fourth sign of the zodiac. **2** a person born between June 22 and July 22, under this sign.

cancer *noun* **1** a malignant tumor. **2** an area of tissue affected by cancer.

candelabrum *noun* (*pl.* **candelabra, candelabrums**) a decorative candleholder with branches for several candles.

candid *adj.* expressing one's views forthrightly and sincerely. ◳ FORTHRIGHT, FRANK, STRAIGHTFORWARD ◳ EVASIVE, FURTIVE. ▶ **candidly** *adv.* ▶ **candidness** *noun*

candidate *noun* **1** a person who is seeking a job, political office, etc. **2** a person taking an examination. ▶ **candidacy** *noun*

> From a Latin word meaning 'dressed in white', because of the white togas worn by electoral candidates in ancient Rome

candied *adj.* preserved or encrusted with sugar.

candle *noun* a stick or block of wax surrounding a wick which is burned to provide light.

Candlemas (kăn'dl-məs) *noun* a Christian festival on Feb. 2 celebrating the purification of the Virgin Mary.

candlepin *noun* **1** (*often* **candlepins**) (*sing.*) a type of bowling using pins and a ball that are smaller than those of tenpins. **2** a slender pin used in this game.

candlestick *noun* a holder for a candle.

candlewick *noun* **1** a wick of a candle. **2** a cotton fabric with a tufted surface.

can-do *adj. colloq.* assertively willing or determined.

candor *noun* frankness and honesty.

C & W *abbrev. Mus.* country and western.

candy *noun* (*pl.* **candies**) **1** a sugar-based confection. **2** a piece of this confection. —*verb trans., intrans.* (**candied, candying, candies**) **1** to preserve (fruit, peel, etc.) by boiling in sugar or syrup. **2** to coat with sugar.

candy striper a hospital volunteer, usu. a teenager.

cane *noun* **1** the hollow stem of certain large plants, e.g., bamboo. **2** sugar cane. **3** thin stems, etc., for weaving into baskets, etc. **4** a walking stick. **5** a long slim stick, esp. for supporting plants. —*verb trans.* (**caned, caning**) **1** to beat with a cane. **2** to construct or mend with cane.

cane sugar sucrose obtained from sugar cane.

canine *adj.* relating to or like a dog. —*noun* an animal of the dog family.

canine tooth a long, sharp, pointed tooth. Also called **eye tooth**.

canister *noun* **1** a container for dry foods. **2** a metal cylinder filled with gas or metal shot, which explodes when thrown or fired.

canker *noun* **1** an ulceration or ulcerous disease. **2** an evil, destructive influence. ▶ **cankerous** *adj.*

cannabis *noun* a narcotic drug prepared from the hemp plant.

canned *adj.* **1** preserved in cans. **2** *colloq.* previously recorded: *canned applause.*

cannelloni (kăn,l-ō'nē) *noun* tubular pieces of pasta filled with, usu. meat, cheese, etc.

cannery *noun* (*pl.* **canneries**) a factory where goods are canned.

cannibal *noun* **1** a person who eats human flesh. **2** an animal that eats others of its kind. ▶ **cannibalism** *noun* ▶ **cannibalistic** *adj.*

cannibalize *verb trans.* (**cannibalized, cannibalizing**) to take parts from (a machine, vehicle, etc.) to repair another.

cannon *noun* (*pl.* **cannon, cannons**) **1** a large mounted weapon that fires projectiles. **2** a rapid-firing gun on an aircraft or ship. —*verb trans., intrans.* (**cannoned, cannoning**) to fire a cannon (at).

cannonade *noun* continuous bombardment by heavy guns.

cannonball *noun* a round projectile, usu. of iron, for shooting from a cannon.

cannon fodder *colloq.* soldiers regarded merely as material to be sacrificed in combat.

cannot *verb, aux.* can not.

canny *adj.* (**cannier, canniest**) astute, wary, or prudent. ◳ CUNNING, SHARP, SLICK, WILY. ▶ **cannily** *adv.* ▶ **canniness** *noun*

canoe *noun* a light, narrow boat propelled by paddles. —*verb intrans.* (**canoed, canoeing, canoes**) to travel by canoe. ▶ **canoeing** *noun* ▶ **canoeist** *noun*

canon *noun* **1** a basic law, rule, or principle. **2** a member of the clergy attached to a cathedral. **3** an officially accepted collection of religious writings, or of works considered to be by a particular writer. ▶ **canonical** *adj.*

canonize *verb trans.* (**canonized, canonizing**) to declare (someone) officially to be a saint. ▶ **canonization** *noun*

canopy *noun* (*pl.* **canopies**) a suspended or projected covering, e.g., over a shop window.

cant[1] (kănt) *noun* **1** insincere talk, esp. with a false display of moral or religious principles. **2** the private slang or jargon of a particular group of people, e.g., thieves. —*verb intrans.* (**canted, canting**) **1** to talk in a preachy, whining way. **2** to speak using jargon or private slang.

cant[2] *noun* **1** a slope. **2** a sloping or tilting position or plane. —*verb trans., intrans.* (**canted, canting**) to tilt, slope, or tip up.

can't (kănt, känt) *contr.* cannot.

cantabile (kăn-täb'ĭ-lā,) *adj., adv. Mus.* in an easy, flowing, melodious style.

cantaloupe *or* **cantaloup** (kănt'l-ōp,) *noun* a melon with orange-colored flesh.

cantankerous adj. bad-tempered; irritable.
▸ **cantankerously** adv. ▸ **cantankerousness** noun

cantata noun a sung musical work, esp. on a religious theme.

canteen noun **1** a cafeteria attached to a factory, office, etc. **2** a shop selling food and drink on a military installation. **3** a flask for water, etc., carried by campers or soldiers.

canter noun the pace of a horse between trotting and galloping. —verb intrans., trans. (**cantered**, **cantering**) to move, or cause to move, at a pace between the trot and the gallop.

> Originally Canterbury gallop, referring to the pace at which pilgrims rode to the town

canticle noun a hymn with words from the Bible.

cantilever noun Eng. a beam that is fixed at one end only.

cantilever bridge a fixed bridge consisting of two outer spans that project toward one another.

canto noun (pl. **cantos**) a section of a long poem.

canton noun a division of a country, esp. Switzerland.

Cantonese (kăn'tn-ēz', -ēs') noun **1** the dialect of Chinese used in the Guangzhou (Canton) area of China. **2** a resident or the residents of Guangzhou. —adj. belonging to Guangzhou.

cantonment noun a permanent military station.

cantor noun **1** a person who leads a synagogue service. **2** a person who leads a choir in a Christian service.

canvas noun **1** a thick, heavy cloth used for sails, tents, etc., and on which to do oil paintings. **2** a painting done on canvas, or a piece of canvas prepared for painting.

canvasback noun a N American wild duck .

canvass verb trans., intrans. (**canvassed**, **canvassing**) **1** to ask for votes or support from (someone) for a person or proposal. **2** to find out the opinions of, on a particular matter. **3** to discuss or examine (a question) in detail. ▸ **canvasser** noun

canyon noun a deep gorge.

cap¹ noun **1** a peaked hat. **2** a lid, cover, or top. **3** a small paper case containing gunpowder, that explodes when struck, used in toy guns. **4** a final or ultimate limit: a cap on military spending. —verb trans. (**capped**, **capping**) **1** to put a cap on or cover with a cap. **2** to be or form the top of. **3** to do better than, improve on, or outdo. **4** to set an upper limit on. —**cap in hand** humbly.

cap² noun colloq. a capital letter in printing.

capable adj. **1** having the ability to do a task or meet an objective. **2** clever; able; efficient. capability noun

capacious adj. having plenty of room for, holding things. ▸ **capaciously** adv. ▸ **capaciousness** noun

capacitance noun (SYMBOL **C**) the ability of a capacitor to store electric charge.

capacitor noun a device with a large capacitance. Also called **condenser**.

capacity noun (pl. **capacities**) **1** the amount that something can hold. **2** the amount that a factory, etc., can produce. **3** (**capacity for**) the ability to achieve (something). **4** function; role.

caparison noun **1** Hist. a decorative covering, harness, etc., for a horse. **2** formal a fine set of clothes. —verb trans. (**caparisoned**, **caparisoning**) **1** to put a caparison on (a horse). **2** formal to dress (another) in finery.

cape¹ noun a short cloak.

cape² noun a part of the coast that projects into the sea.

caper¹ verb intrans. (**capered**, **capering**) to jump or dance about playfully. —noun **1** a playful jump. **2** a playful trick or joke.

caper² noun a prickly shrub whose flower buds are pickled for use as flavoring.

capillary noun (pl. **capillaries**) **1** a tube with a very small diameter. **2** in vertebrates, the narrowest type of blood vessel. —adj. **1** of a tube having a very small diameter. **2** of or relating to the surface tension of liquid. **3** slender and fine like a hair. ▸ **capillarity** noun

capital¹ noun **1** the chief city of a country, state, or province, usu. where the government is based. **2** a capital letter. **3** the total amount of money or wealth possessed by a person or business, esp. when used to produce more wealth. —adj. **1** principal; chief. **2** of a letter of the alphabet in its large form, as used at the beginnings of names and sentences. **3** of a crime punishable by death.

> Usage The chief city of a country or state and the one where its government is based is the capital; the building in which its legislature convenes is the capitol.

capital² noun slab of stone, etc., usu. ornamentally carved, that forms the top of a column or pillar.

capital gains profit from the sale of assets.

capital-intensive adj. of an industry, etc. needing substantial capital to keep it going. See also **labor-intensive**.

capitalism noun an economic system based on private rather than state ownership of businesses, factories, transport services, etc.

capitalist noun **1** a person who believes in and supports capitalism. **2** a wealthy person. —adj. believing in, supporting, or marked by capitalism. ▸ **capitalistic** adj.

capitalize *verb trans.* (**capitalized, capitalizing**) **1** to write with a capital letter. **2** to sell (property) in order to raise money. **3** to supply (a business, etc.) with needed capital. **4** (usu. **capitalize on**) to use (something) to one's own advantage. ▸ **capitalization** *noun*

capital punishment the death penalty.

capitation *noun* a tax levied at a rate per person.

capitol a building in which a legislature convenes.

> *Usage* See note at **capital¹**

capitulate *verb intrans.* (**capitulated, capitulating**) to surrender, usu. on agreed conditions. ▸ **capitulation** *noun*

capon *noun* a castrated chicken that has been fattened for eating.

cappuccino (kăp‚ô-chē'nō) *noun* (*pl.* **cappuccinos**) espresso coffee mixed with steamed milk, often topped with frothy milk.

capriccio (kə-prē'chō) *noun* (*pl.* **capriccios**) *Mus.* **1** a free-form, improvisational instrumental work. *Also called* **caprice**. **2** a prank or whim.

caprice *noun* **1** a sudden, whimsical, impulsive change of mind. ☰ FANCY, MAGGOT, NOTION, WHIM, WHIMSY. **2** the tendency to change one's mind on impulse. ▸ **capricious** *adj.* ▸ **capriciously** *adv.* ▸ **capriciousness** *noun*

> Originally meaning 'horror', from an Italian word which translates as 'hedgehog head'

Capricorn (kăp'rĭ-kôrn‚) *noun* **1** the Goat, the name of a constellation and the tenth sign of the zodiac. **2** a person born between Dec. 23 and Jan. 19, under this sign.

capsicum *noun* pepper (sense 2).

capsize *verb intrans., trans.* (**capsized, capsizing**) **1** to tip over completely; to overturn. **2** to cause (a boat, etc.) to capsize.

capstan *noun* a cylinder-shaped apparatus that is turned to wind a heavy rope or cable, e.g., that of a ship's anchor.

capsule *noun* **1** a soluble gelatin case containing a single dose of a drug. **2** a space capsule. **3** a dry seed-case that splits to release the seeds. ▸ **capsular** *adj.*

Capt. *abbrev.* Captain.

captain *noun* **1** a leader; chief. **2** the commander of a ship. **3** the commander of a company of troops in the US Army or Marine Corps. **4** a US Navy or Coast Guard officer below commodore and above commander in rank. **5** a US Army, Air Force, or Marine Corps officer below major and above first lieutenant. **6** the first officer of a commercial aircraft. **7** the leader of a team. —*verb trans.* (**captained, captaining**) to be captain of. ▸ **captaincy** *noun*

caption *noun* **1** the words that accompany a photograph, a cartoon, etc., to explain it. **2** wording appearing on a television or movie screen as part of a broadcast or film. —*verb trans.* (**captioned, captioning**) to provide with a caption or captions.

captious *adj.* inclined to look for and point up faults. ▸ **captiously** *adv.* ▸ **captiousness** *noun*

captivate *verb trans.* (**captivated, captivating**) to delight, charm, or fascinate. ▸ **captivation** *noun*

captivating *adj.* fully occupying the mind and seizing the imagination. ▸ **captivatingly** *adv.*

captive *noun* a person or animal that has been caught or taken prisoner. —*adj.* **1** kept captive or prisoner. **2** forced into a certain state or role: *a captive audience.* ▸ **captivity** *noun*

captor *noun* one who captures a person or animal.

capture *verb trans.* (**captured, capturing**) **1** to take prisoner; to catch. **2** to gain control of. **3** to succeed in recording (a subtle quality, etc.). —*noun* **1** the capturing of someone or something. **2** the person or thing captured. ▸ **capturer** *noun*

Capuchin (kăp'yə-shĭn) *noun* a member of an order of Franciscan monks.

capuchin (kăp'yə-shĭn, kə-pyōō'chĭn) a S American monkey with a long prehensile tail.

capybara *noun* a large semiaquatic rodent, native to Central and S America.

car *noun* **1** an automobile. **2** *combining form* a railroad car: *a box-car.* **3** a passenger compartment in e.g., an airship, elevator, or cable railway.

carafe *noun* a wide-necked bottle for wine, etc.

caramel (kăr'məl, kăr'ə-mĕl‚) *noun* **1** boiled and slightly burnt sugar used as flavoring. **2** a chewy candy.

caramelize *verb trans., intrans.* (**caramelized, caramelizing**) **1** to change (sugar) into caramel. **2** to turn into caramel. ▸ **caramelization** *noun*

carapace *noun* a hard thick shell that covers the upper part of the body of some reptiles, e.g., tortoises, and crustaceans, e.g., crabs.

carat (kăr'ət) *noun* **1** a unit of weight used for precious stones, equal to 200 mg. **2** *same as* **karat.**

caravan *noun* **1** a group of trucks, vehicles, or animals traveling in single-file. **2** a group of travelers, etc., usu. with camels, crossing the desert in company for safety. **3** *Brit.* a trailer for recreational travel.

caravansaray *or* **caravanserai** (kăr‚ə-văn'sə-rī‚) *noun* (*pl.* **caravansaries, caravanserais**) an inn where caravans crossing the desert, etc. can stay.

caraway *noun* a plant with clusters of small white flowers, or its strong-flavored seed, used as a flavoring.

carbide *noun* a chemical compound consisting of carbon and another element, widely used as an abrasive.

carbine *noun* a short light rifle. ▸ **carbineer** *noun*

carbohydrate *noun* any of a group of organic compounds of carbon with hydrogen and oxygen, an important source of energy for both plants and animals.

carbolic acid *Chem.* phenol (sense 1).

carbon *noun* **1** (SYMBOL C) a nonmetallic element that occurs naturally as coal, coke, and charcoal, and as diamond and graphite. **2** a sheet of carbon paper, or a carbon copy.

carbonate *noun* a salt of carbonic acid. —*verb trans.* (**carbonated, carbonating**) to charge (e.g., a drink) with carbon dioxide. ▸ **carbonate** *adj.* ▸ **carbonation** *noun*

carbonated water soda water.

carbon black *Chem.* finely divided carbon, used in pigments and printer's ink.

carbon copy 1 a copy made using carbon paper. **2** a person or thing that looks exactly like someone or something else. **3** *Comput.* (ABBREV. **cc**) a directive in an e-mail message to send an exact copy to one or more other recipients.

carbon dating a scientific method of estimating the age of archeological specimens by measuring the amount of the radioactive isotope carbon-14 they contain. *Also called* **radiocarbon dating**.

carbon dioxide a colorless odorless tasteless gas; dry ice.

carbonize *verb trans., intrans.* (**carbonized, carbonizing**) **1** to turn into or reduce to carbon, by heating. **2** to coat with carbon. ▸ **carbonization** *noun*

carbon monoxide a poisonous colorless odorless gas.

carbon paper paper coated on one side with an inklike substance for making copies of written or typed text.

carbon tetrachloride a poisonous liquid used in fire extinguishers and as a cleaning solvent.

Carborundum *trademark* used for an abrasive made of silicon carbide crystals.

carboy *noun* a large round bottle, usu. with an outer case made of basketwork, etc.

carbuncle *noun* **1** a large boil on the skin. **2** a round red gemstone, esp. a garnet.

carburetor *noun* a device in an internal combustion engine where liquid fuel and air are mixed and vaporized before being sucked into the cylinders.

carcass *noun* a dead body of an animal.

carcinogen (kär-sĭn′ə-jən) *noun* a substance that causes cancer. ▸ **carcinogenic** *adj.*

carcinoma (kär‚sə-nō′mə) *noun* a cancer that occurs in body tissue.

card¹ *noun* **1** a thick stiff paper or thin cardboard. **2 a** a playing card. **b** (**cards**) a game played using playing cards. **3** a small rectangular piece of card or plastic, showing, e.g., one's identity. **4** a small rectangular piece of stiff plastic issued by a bank, etc., to a customer, used for operating an automated teller machine, etc. **5** *Comput.* a magnetic card. **6** a greeting card. **7** a post card. **8** an amusing, usu. somewhat odd, person. **9** a program for sports, esp. a racing event. —*verb trans.* (**carded, carding**) to check (e.g., a patron's identification), esp. to determine legal age.

card² *noun* a comblike device for removing tangles from sheep's wool, etc., before spinning, or for pulling across the surface of cloth to make it fluffy. —*verb trans.* (**carded, carding**) to treat with a card.

cardamom *or* **cardamon** *noun* a seed of a tropical shrub, used as a spice.

cardboard *noun* a stiff material manufactured from paper pulp, used for making boxes, etc.

card-carrying *adj.* **1** officially registered as a member of a political party, etc. **2** *colloq.* strongly supporting.

cardholder *noun* the holder or owner of a card, esp. a credit card.

cardiac *adj.* **1** relating to or affecting the heart. **2** relating to the upper part of the stomach.

cardiac arrest the stopping of the heartbeat.

cardigan *noun* a long-sleeved knitted sweater or jacket that fastens down the front.

> Named after the 19th-century Earl of *Cardigan* who advocated the use of buttonable woollen jackets

cardinal *noun* **1** *RC Church* one of the group of prelates who elect and advise the pope. **2** a cardinal number. **3** a N American songbird. **4** a bright red color. —*adj.* of the highest importance.

cardinalate *noun* *RC Church* **1** the rank or office of a cardinal. **2** cardinals as a body.

cardinal number a number expressing quantity, such as 1, 2, or 3. *See also* **ordinal number**.

cardinal point *noun* any of the four main points of the compass: north, south, east, and west.

cardio- *combining form* belonging or relating to the heart.

cardiogram *noun* an electrocardiogram.

cardiograph *noun* an electrocardiograph. ▸ **cardiography** *noun*

cardiology *noun* the branch of medicine concerned with the study of diseases of the heart. ▸ **cardiologist** *noun*

cardiopulmonary *adj.* relating to the heart and lungs.

cardiopulmonary resuscitation (ABBREV. **CPR**) an emergency medical procedure, used to restart the heart after cardiac arrest.

cardiovascular adj. (ABBREV. **CV**) relating to both the heart and the blood vessels.

cardsharp or **cardsharper** noun a person who cheats at card games played for money.

care noun 1 thorough, serious attentiveness. ⊟ HEED, REGARD. 2 regard for safety; caution and gentleness. 3 the activity of looking after someone or something. 4 a disquieted mental state. ⊟ ANXIETY, CONCERN, DISQUIET, DISQUIETUDE, PERTURBATION, UNEASE, UNEASINESS, WORRY. 5 a cause for worry; a responsibility. —verb intrans. (**cared, caring**) 1 to mind or be upset by something. 2 to concern oneself about a person or a matter. 3 (**care for**) to have affection or a wish for (someone or something). 4 to wish or be willing.

careen verb intrans. (**careened, careening**) 1 of a ship to lean over to one side. 2 colloq. to rush headlong; career.

Usage Substitution of *careen* for *career* in the sense to rush is objected to by some linguistic conservatives, but its use has become so prevalent as to be regarded as unexceptionable by most critics today.

---

career noun 1 a job, occupation, or profession. 2 a calling or vocation. 3 a swift or headlong course. —verb intrans. (**careered, careering**) to rush in a headlong way.

careerist noun a person who is totally interested in his or her own advancement or promotion. ▸ **careerism** noun

carefree adj. having few worries; cheerful.

careful adj. 1 giving or showing care and attention to detail. ⊟ CONSCIENTIOUS, EXACT, METICULOUS, PAINSTAKING, PUNCTILIOUS, SCRUPULOUS. 2 exhibiting prudence and caution. ▸ **carefully** adv. ▸ **carefulness** noun

caregiver noun someone who looks after a dependent child or adult, usu. voluntarily.

careless adj. 1 giving no care or attention to detail. ⊟ NEGLIGENT, SLACK, SLIPSHOD, SLOPPY ⊟ CAREFUL, METICULOUS, PAINSTAKING, PUNCTILIOUS, SCRUPULOUS. 2 lacking, or showing a lack of, a sense of responsibility. 3 effortless: careless charm. ▸ **carelessly** adv. ▸ **carelessness** noun

caress verb trans. (**caressed, caressing**) to touch or stroke gently and lovingly. —noun a gentle, loving touch.

caret noun a mark (‸) made on written or printed material to show where a missing word, letter, etc., should be inserted.

caretaker noun a person employed to look after a public building. —adj. taking temporary responsibility: a caretaker government.

careware noun Comput. software that can be downloaded from the Internet free, although the user can make a discretionary payment to a, usu. named, charity.

careworn adj. showing signs of anxiety or worry.

carfare noun a charge for riding a bus or streetcar.

cargo noun (pl. **cargoes**) the goods carried by a ship, aircraft, or other vehicle.

caribou noun (pl. **caribou, caribous**) a large deer of N America and Siberia.

caricature noun a representation, esp. a drawing, of a subject, with the subject's most distinctive features exaggerated for comic effect. —verb trans. (**caricatured, caricaturing**) to make a caricature of. ▸ **caricaturist** noun

caries noun decay, esp. of the teeth or bones. ▸ **carious** adj.

carillon noun 1 a set of bells played by means of a keyboard or mechanically. 2 a tune played on such bells.

caring adj. showing concern for others; sympathetic and helpful.

carjack verb trans. (**carjacked, carjacking**) to steal (a motor vehicle) from its driver.

carmine noun a deep red color; crimson.

carnage noun great slaughter.

carnal adj. 1 relating or belonging to the body or the flesh; as opposed to the spirit or intellect. 2 sexual. ▸ **carnally** adv.

carnal knowledge sexual relations.

carnation noun 1 a strongly scented red, white, or pink flower. 2 a deep pink color.

carnelian noun a reddish semiprecious stone.

carnival noun 1 a period of public festivity with street processions, colorful costumes, and singing and dancing. 2 a circus or fair.

carnivore noun an animal that feeds mainly on the flesh of other animals. See also **herbivore.** ▸ **carnivorous** adj.

carob noun an evergreen tree or its large reddish-brown seedpod, rich in sugars and gums. Also called **locust tree.**

carol noun a religious song sung at Christmas. —verb intrans. (**caroled** or **carolled, caroling** or **carolling**) 1 to sing carols. 2 to sing joyfully.

carom noun Billiards a stroke in which the cue ball strikes the other balls one after the other.

carotene or **carotin** noun a yellowish-orange pigment found in carrots, etc., and a rich source of vitamin A.

carotid noun either of the two arteries that supply blood to the head and neck.

carousal (kə-row′zəl) noun a drinking bout or party.

carouse verb intrans. (**caroused, carousing**) to take part in a noisy drinking party.

carousel (kăr,ə-sĕl') *noun* **1** a revolving luggage belt in an airport, etc. **2** a revolving slide case in a film projector. **3** a merry-go-round.

carp¹ *noun* (*pl.* **carp, carps**) an edible freshwater fish.

carp² *verb intrans.* (**carped, carping**) to complain, find fault, or criticize, esp. unnecessarily. ▸ **carper** *noun*

carpal *noun* any of the wrist bones.

car park *Brit.* a parking lot.

carpel *noun* the female reproductive part of a flowering plant.

carpenter *noun* a skilled worker in wood, e.g., in building houses. ▸ **carpentry** *noun*

carpenter ant a large ant that makes nests in and destroys wood.

carpet *noun* **1** a floor covering made of heavy, usu. woven and tufted fabric. **2** something that completely covers a surface. —*verb trans.* (**carpeted, carpeting**) to cover with or as if with a carpet.

carpetbag *noun* an old-fashioned traveling bag made of carpeting.

carpetbagger *noun* a Northerner who went to the defeated South after the Civil War to take advantage of the opportunities offered by the reconstruction.

carpeting *noun* **1** fabric for making carpets. **2** carpets in general.

car phone a cellular telephone for use in a motor vehicle.

carpool *noun* an arrangement among a group of commuters to travel together in a single vehicle, each person contributing to the cost of gas, etc. —*verb intrans.* (**carpooled, carpooling**) to travel by means of such an arrangement.

carport *noun* a shelter for an automobile, often attached to the side of a house.

carpus *noun* (*pl.* **carpi**) the set of bones forming the wrist.

carrel *or* **carrell** *noun* a small compartment or desk in a library, for private study.

carriage *noun* **1** a wheeled vehicle. **2** the process or cost of transporting goods. **3** a moving section of a machine, e.g., a typewriter. **4** the way one holds oneself in standing or walking.

carriage trade wealthy customers considered as a group.

carrier *noun* **1** a person or thing that carries. **2** a person or firm that transports goods. **3** an aircraft carrier. **4** a person or animal that, without showing symptoms of a disease, is still capable of passing it on to others.

carrier pigeon a homing pigeon that has been bred and trained to transport messages.

carrion *noun* dead and rotting animal flesh.

carrot *noun* **1** a plant with a tapering orange root, eaten as a vegetable. **2** something offered as an incentive. ▸ **carroty** *adj.*

carry *verb trans., intrans.* (**carried, carrying, carries**) **1** to hold in one's hands or have in a bag etc., while moving from one place to another. **2** to bring, take, or convey. **3** to have on one's person. **4** to be the means of spreading (a disease, etc.). **5** to support: *The walls carry the roof.* **6** to be pregnant with. **7** to hold (oneself or a part of one's body) in a certain way. **8** to bear (responsibilities, etc.). **9** to print or broadcast. **10** to stock or sell. **11** to have or involve, etc.: *a crime carrying the death penalty.* **12** *of a sound* to be able to be heard a distance away. **13** to pass or agree to by majority vote. —**be** *or* **get carried away** *colloq.* to become overexcited or overenthusiastic. **carry on 1** to keep going; to continue. **2** to make a fuss. **3** to conduct or engage in business, etc.

carryon *noun* a piece of luggage small enough to be carried on to a commercial airplane.

carsick *adj.* feeling sick as a result of traveling in a car. ▸ **carsickness** *noun*

cart *noun* a two- or four-wheeled horse-drawn vehicle for carrying goods or passengers. **2** a light vehicle pushed or pulled by hand: *a shopping cart.* —*verb trans.* (**carted, carting**) to carry or transport in a cart.

carte blanche (kärt-blänsh') complete freedom of action or discretion.

cartel (kär-tĕl') *noun* a group of firms that agree, esp. illegally, on similar fixed prices for their products, so as to reduce competition and keep profits high.

cartilage *noun* a tough flexible material found in the larynx, nose, etc., and around the ends of bones at joints. ▸ **cartilaginous** *adj.*

cartography *noun* the art or science of making maps. ▸ **cartographer** *noun* ▸ **cartographic** *adj.*

carton *noun* **1** a plastic or cardboard container for food, milk, etc. **2** a cardboard box.

cartoon *noun* **1** a humorous drawing, often ridiculing a subject. **2** an animated film. **3** a strip of, usu. humorous, drawings in a newspaper, etc. **4** a preparatory drawing. ▸ **cartoonist** *noun*

cartouche *noun Hist.* **1** a paper case containing the explosive charge for a gun, etc.; a cartridge. **2** *Archit.* a scroll-like ornament or decorative border with rolled ends.

cartridge *noun* **1** a small case containing the explosive charge and bullet for a gun. **2** a plastic case containing tape, larger than a cassette. **3** a plastic case containing photographic film, for loading directly into a camera. **4** the part of the pickup arm of a record player that contains the needle or stylus. **5** a tube containing ink for loading into a fountain pen, inkjet printer, etc.

cartwheel noun an acrobatic movement with a wheel-like action, putting weight on each hand and foot in turn.

carve verb trans., intrans. (**carved, carving**) **1 a** to cut (wood, stone, etc.) into a shape. **b** to make (something) from wood or stone by cutting into it. **c** to produce (a design, inscription, etc.) in wood or stone. **2** to cut (meat) into slices. **3** (**carve out**) to establish or create (an opportunity, etc.) for oneself through personal effort. ▶ **carver** noun

carving noun a figure or pattern, etc., produced by carving.

car wash a place for washing motor vehicles.

Casanova (kăs′ə-nō′və, kăz′-) noun a man with a reputation for having many love affairs.

cascade noun **1** a waterfall or series of waterfalls. **2** something resembling a waterfall. —verb intrans. (**cascaded, cascading**) to fall in the manner of a waterfall.

case[1] noun **1** a box, container, or cover for storage or protection. **2** a suitcase or briefcase. —verb trans. (**cased, casing**) **1** to put in a case. **2** slang to have a good look at (a building) with the intention of breaking into it. —**case the joint** slang to stake out a robbery target.

case[2] noun **1 a** a particular occasion, situation, or set of circumstances. **b** reality; fact. **2** an example, instance, or occurrence: a case of flu. **3** a person receiving treatment or care. **4** a matter requiring investigation. **5** a matter to be decided in a law court. **6** an argument for or against, with the relevant facts fully presented. **7** the relationship of a noun, pronoun, or adjective to other words in a, sentence. **8** an eccentric person.

caseharden verb trans. (**casehardened, casehardening**) to harden the surface layer of (metal) by heat.

casein (kā′sēn,, -sē-ən) noun a milk protein that is the main constituent of cheese.

casement noun a window that opens outward like a door.

cash noun **1** coins or paper money, as distinct from checks, credit cards, etc. **2** colloq. money in any form. —verb trans. (**cashed, cashing**) to obtain or give cash in return for (a check, traveler's check, etc.). —**cash in** to exchange (tokens, vouchers, etc.), for money. **cash on delivery** (ABBREV. **C.O.D.** or **c.o.d.**) with payment for goods immediately on delivery.

cash-and-carry noun a large store where accredited customers pay for goods in cash and take them away immediately.

cash cow slang a source of continuing high income or profits.

cashew noun a tropical American tree, or its edible comma-shaped nut.

cash flow the amount of money coming into, and going out of, a business, etc.

cashier[1] noun a person in a bank, shop, or other business who is responsible for handling cash.

cashier[2] verb trans. (**cashiered, cashiering**) to dismiss in disgrace.

cashier's check a check that is drawn on a bank's own funds.

cashless adj. using payment by credit card or electronic transfer of money, rather than by cash or check.

cash machine same as **ATM**.

cashmere (kăzh′mĭr,, kăsh′-) noun very fine soft wool from a long-haired Asian goat.

cash register a machine that calculates and records the amount of each sale and from which change and a receipt are usu. given.

casing noun a protective covering.

casino (kə-sē′nō) noun (pl. **casinos**) a public building or room for gambling.

cask noun **1** a barrel for holding liquids, esp. alcohol. **2** the amount contained by a cask.

casket noun **1** a coffin. **2** a small case for holding jewels, etc.

cassava (kə-sä′və) noun **1** a tropical shrubby plant with edible roots. Also called **manioc**. **2** a starchy substance obtained from the root of this plant, used in tapioca.

casserole noun **1** an ovenproof dish with a lid, in which meat, vegetables, etc., can be baked and served. **2** the food baked in such a dish.

cassette noun **1** a small plastic case containing magnetic tape, that can be inserted into an audio or video tape recorder or player, for recording or playback. **2** a lightproof plastic cartridge containing photographic film for loading into a camera.

cassette player a machine that plays or records material on cassette.

cassock noun a long garment worn in church by clerics.

cassowary noun (pl. **cassowaries**) a large flightless bird of New Guinea and N Australia.

cast verb trans., intrans. (pa t and pa p **cast**; pr p **casting**) **1** to throw. **2** to turn, direct, shed, or cause to fall or arise. **3** to throw (a fishing line) out into the water. **4** of animals to get rid of or shed (a skin, horns, etc.). **5** (usu. **cast off, aside** or **out**) to get rid of (something). **6** to give (a performer) a part in a play or film; to distribute the parts in (a film, play, etc.). **7** to shape (metal, plastic, plaster, etc.) by pouring it in a molten or liquid state into a mold; to create (an object) by this means. **8** to give or record (a vote). —noun **1** an act of throwing; a throw. **2** an object shaped in a mold. **3** a covering of plaster molded, when wet, around a broken limb to support it while it heals. Also called **plaster cast**. **4** the set of performers in a film, play, etc. **5** type, form, shape, or **6** a slight tinge. **7** a slight squint in the eye.

castanets (kăs,tə-nĕts') *pl. noun* two small pieces of wood or plastic struck together rhythmically, e.g., by Spanish dancers.

> From a Spanish word for 'chestnuts', because of their shape

castaway *noun* a shipwrecked person or object.

caste *noun* **1** any of the four hereditary social classes into which Hindus are divided. **2** a system of social division based on inherited rank or wealth.

castellated *adj.* having turrets and battlements. ▶ **castellation** *noun*

caster *or* **castor** *noun* **1** a closed container with holes in its lid, used for sprinkling, e.g., sugar or flour. **2** a small swiveling wheel attached to the leg of a piece of furniture.

castigate *verb trans.* (**castigated, castigating**) to criticize or punish severely. ▶ **castigation** *noun*

casting *noun* **1** the process of forming a solid object by pouring molten material, e.g., metal or plastic, into a mold and allowing it to cool and solidify. **2** an object formed in this way.

casting vote a deciding vote, e.g., that of a chairperson, used when votes are equally divided.

castiron *adj.* **1** made of cast iron. **2** very strong. **3** firm and very rigid; not to be altered. **4** devoid of loopholes or faulty reasoning.

cast iron an alloy of iron containing more carbon than steel.

castle *noun* **1** a large, fortified, esp. medieval, building with battlements and towers. **2** *Chess* a piece that can be moved any number of squares forward, backward, or sideways. *Also called* **rook²**. —*verb intrans.* (**castled, castling**) *Chess* to make a move involving both the king and a castle. —**castles in the air** grand but impossible schemes; daydreams.

castoff *noun* something, esp. a garment, discarded or no longer wanted.

castor *same as* **caster** (senses 1, 2).

castor oil from the seeds of a tropical plant, used as a lubricant and as a laxative.

castrate *verb trans.* (**castrate, castrating**) **1** to remove the testicles of. **2** to deprive of masculinity or strength. ▶ **castration** *noun*

casual *adj.* **1** happening by chance. **2** showing no particular interest or concern; careless. **3** lacking serious purpose or intention. **4** informal in design. **5** not permanent or regular; occasional. —*noun* someone working without a permanent contract. ▶ **casually** *adv.* ▶ **casualness** *noun*

casualty *noun* (*pl.* **casualties**) **1** a person killed or hurt in an accident or war. **2** an accident that results in serious loss of human life or injury. **3** something lost, destroyed, sacrificed, etc., as a result of some event.

casuist *noun* a person who uses specious arguments. ▶ **casuistic** *adj.* ▶ **casuistry** *noun*

casus belli (kăs,əs-bĕl'ē) a circumstance or situation that causes a war.

CAT *abbrev.* computerized axial tomography.

cat¹ *noun* **1** any of a wide range of carnivorous mammals, including the lion, tiger, and lynx, as well as the common domestic cat. **2** *offensive colloq.* a woman with a spiteful tongue. **3** the cat-o'-nine-tails.

cat² *noun colloq.* catalytic converter.

catabolism *noun* the metabolic processes whereby complex organic compounds in living organisms are broken down into simple molecules.

cataclysm *noun* **1** an event causing tremendous change or upheaval. **2** a terrible tragedy or disaster. ▶ **cataclysmic** *adj.*

catacomb *noun* (*usu.* **catacombs**) an underground tunnel containing burial places.

catafalque (kăt'ə-fôlk,) *noun* a platform on which the coffin of a monarch or other important person is placed for the funeral.

catalepsy *noun* a state of unconsciousness with complete rigidity of the body. ▶ **cataleptic** *adj.*

catalog *or* **catalogue** *noun* **1** a list of items arranged in a systematic order, esp. alphabetically. **2** a brochure containing a list of items for sale. **3** a list or series of things. —*verb trans.* (**cataloged, cataloging**) **1** to make a list of or enter in a systematic list. **2** to list or mention one by one. ▶ **cataloger** *or* **cataloguer** *noun*

catalpa (kə-tăl'pə, -tôl'-) *noun* a deciduous tree with white flower clusters.

catalysis *noun* the speeding up of a chemical reaction by a catalyst.

catalyst *noun* **1** a substance that changes the rate of a chemical reaction, esp. by increasing it. **2** someone or something that causes change. ▶ **catalytic** *adj.* ▶ **catalize** *verb trans.*

catalytic converter a device designed to reduce toxic emissions from the engine of a motor vehicle.

catamaran *noun* **1** a boat with two parallel hulls. **2** a raft made of logs or boats lashed together.

catapult *noun* **1** *Hist.* a weapon of war designed to launch boulders. **2** an apparatus on an aircraft carrier for launching aircraft. **3** a slingshot. —*verb trans., intrans.* (**catapulted, catapulting**) **1** to fire or propel into the air with, or as if with, a catapult. **2** to leap.

cataract *noun* **1** an opaque area within the lens of the eye that produces blurring of vision. **2 a** a succession of steep waterfalls within a river. **b** an immense rush of water.

catarrh *noun* inflammation of the lining of the nose and throat, or the discharge of mucus it causes. ▸ **catarrhal** *adj.*

catastrophe (kə-tăs′trə-fē) *noun* a great disaster. ▸ **catastrophic** *adj.* ▸ **catastrophically** *adv.*

catatonia *noun* an abnormal mental state characterized either by stupor and immobility, or by violent or uncoordinated activity. ▸ **catatonic** *adj.*

cat burglar a burglar who breaks into buildings by climbing walls, water pipes, etc.

catcall *noun* a long, shrill whistle expressing disagreement or disapproval.

catch *verb trans., intrans.* (pa t and pa p **caught**; *pr p* **catching**) **1** to stop (a moving object) and hold it. **2** to manage to get hold of or trap, esp. after a hunt or chase. **3** to be in time to see, get, reach, etc. **4** to overtake or draw level with. **5** to see or surprise (someone, esp. when doing something wrong). **6** to trick or trap. **7** to become infected with. **8** to become, or cause to become, accidentally attached or held. **9** to hit. **10** to manage to hear, see, or understand. **11** to attract (attention, etc.). **12** to succeed in recording (a subtle quality, etc.). **13** *Baseball* to serve as catcher. —*noun* **1** an act of catching. **2** a device for keeping a lid, door, etc., closed. **3** something caught. **4** the total amount of fish, for example, caught. **5** a hidden problem or disadvantage; a snag. **6** one whom it would be advantageous to get hold of, e.g., a certain person as a spouse. **7** a children's game of throwing and catching a ball.

Catch-22 *or* **catch-22** *noun* (*pl.* **Catch-22s** *or* **catch-22s**) a problematic situation where any change or action will result in an equally undesirable outcome.

catchall *adj.* covering all possibilities.

catcher *noun Baseball* a player who stands behind home base and who tries to catch pitched balls.

catching *adj.* infectious.

catchpenny *adj.* poor in quality but designed to appeal to the eye and sell quickly.

catch phrase a frequently used phrase or slogan.

catchup *noun* same as **ketchup**.

catchword *noun* **1** a much-repeated, well-known word. **2** a guide word.

catchy *adj.* (**catchier, catchiest**) easily remembered. ▸ **catchiness** *noun*

catechism (kăt′ə-kĭz′əm) *noun* a series of questions and answers about the Christian religion, used for instruction. ▸ **catechize** *verb trans.*

catechumen (kăt,ə-kyōō′mən) *noun* a person who is being taught the main beliefs of Christianity.

categorical *or* **categoric** *adj.* absolute or definite; giving no room for doubt or argument. ▸ **categorically** *adv.*

category *noun* (*pl.* **categories**) a group of things, people, or concepts classed together. ▸ **categorize** *verb trans.* ▸ **categorization** *noun*

cater *verb intrans.* (**catered, catering**) **1** to supply food or entertainment, esp. as a business. **2** to be esp. or unduly solicitous: *catered to the V.I.P.'s every whim.* ▸ **caterer** *noun*

caterpillar *noun* the larva of a butterfly or moth.

> Based on a Latin phrase which translates as 'hairy cat'

caterwaul *verb intrans.* (**caterwauled, caterwauling**) to wail or shriek like a cat. —*noun* a loud, high wail.

catfish *noun* (*pl.* **catfish, catfishes**) a large fish with whiskerlike growths around its mouth.

catharsis *noun* (*pl.* **catharses**) **1** the emotional relief, e.g., from allowing repressed feelings to surface or from an intensely dramatic experience. **2** a purging of the bowels. ▸ **cathartic** *adj.*

cathedral *noun* the principal church of a diocese.

catheter *noun* a tube inserted into a body part, esp. the bladder, to drain off fluids. ▸ **catheterize** *verb trans.*

cathode *noun* **1** the negative electrode in an electrolytic cell. **2** the positive terminal of a battery. *See also* **anode**.

cathode rays streams of negatively charged electrons issuing from the cathode of a vacuum tube.

cathode-ray tube (ABBREV. **CRT**) a vacuum tube in which the electrons are made to act on a fluorescent screen to produce an image.

catholic *adj.* **1** (**Catholic**) relating to the Roman Catholic Church or to certain other Christian Churches. **2** broad; wide-ranging: *a catholic taste in music.* —*noun* (**Catholic**) a member of the Roman Catholic Church. ▸ **Catholicism** *noun*

catholicity *noun* **1** universality. **2** liberality or breadth of view.

cation (kăt′ī,ən) *noun* a positively charged ion. *See also* **anion**.

catkin *noun* a dangling flowering part in trees such as the willow, hazel, etc.

catnap *noun* a short sleep. —*verb intrans.* (**catnapped, catnapping**) to doze.

catnip *noun* a plant of the mint family, attractive to cats.

cat-o'-nine-tails *noun* a whip with nine knotted rope lashes, used as an instrument of punishment.

CAT-scan *noun* an x-ray image of cross-sectional segments of the body.

CAT scanner a computerized axial tomography scanner that produces x-ray images of cross-sections of the brain.

cat's-eye noun (pl. **cat's-eyes**) a semiprecious stone.

cat's-paw noun (pl. **cat's-paws**) a person used by another to do an unpleasant job.

catsup noun same as **ketchup**.

cattail noun a marsh herb with a cluster of tiny flowers and fruits. Also called **reedmace**.

cattle pl. noun large, heavy, grass-eating mammals that are raised for dairy products and meat.

catty adj. (**cattier, cattiest**) spitefully malicious. ▸ **cattily** adv. ▸ **cattiness** noun

catwalk noun 1 a narrow walkway, usu. at a high level, e.g., alongside a bridge or above a factory floor. 2 the narrow stage along which models walk at a fashion show.

Caucasian (kô-kā′zhən) adj. belonging or relating to one of the light-skinned peoples. —noun a light-skinned person.

Caucasoid (kô′kə-zoid,) adj. old use Caucasian.

caucus noun (pl. **caucuses**) 1 a group of members of a political party, or a meeting of such a group for a specific purpose. 2 a group of politicians or legislators representing a special-interest group. —verb intrans. to hold a meeting to discuss party policies.

caudal adj. relating to or resembling a tail.

caudate adj. having a tail.

caught verb see **catch**.

caul noun 1 the membrane in which a human fetus is enclosed. 2 the part of this membrane, sometimes found over a baby's head at birth.

cauldron noun same as **caldron**.

cauliflower (kô′lǐ-flow,ər, käl′ǐ-) noun a variety of cabbage with an edible white flower, eaten as a vegetable.

cauliflower ear an ear permanently swollen and misshapen by injury, esp. from repeated blows.

caulk (kôk) verb trans. (**caulked, caulking**) to make (a boat, etc.) watertight.

causal adj. 1 relating to or being a cause. 2 relating to cause and effect. ▸ **causally** adv.

causality noun the relationship or principle governing cause and effect.

causation noun 1 causality. 2 the process of causing.

causative adj. making something happen; producing an effect. ▸ **causatively** adv.

cause noun 1 something that produces an effect. 2 a reason or justification. 3 an ideal, principle, aim, etc., that people support and work for. 4 a matter that is to be settled by a lawsuit; the lawsuit itself. —verb trans. (**caused, causing**) to produce as an effect; to bring about.

'cause conj. colloq. because.

cause célèbre (kôz,sə-lĕb′, -lĕb′rə) noun (pl. **causes célèbres**) something, e.g., a legal case that attracts great attention.

causeway noun 1 a raised roadway. 2 a paved road.

caustic adj. 1 strongly alkaline and corrosive to living tissue. 2 sarcastic; cutting; bitter. —noun a caustic substance. ▸ **caustically** adv. ▸ **causticity** noun

caustic soda sodium hydroxide.

cauterize verb trans. (**cauterized, cauterizing**) to burn away (infected or damaged body tissue, using a heated instrument, a caustic chemical, etc.

caution noun 1 care in avoiding danger; prudent wariness. 2 a warning. —verb trans., intrans. (**cautioned, cautioning**) to warn (someone) or to give a warning. ▸ **cautionary** adj.

cautious adj. having or showing caution; careful and wary. ▸ **cautiously** adv. ▸ **cautiousness** noun

cavalcade noun a ceremonial procession of vehicles or horseback riders.

cavalier noun 1 old use a horseman or knight. 2 old use a courtly gentleman. —adj. not having or displaying due concern; thoughtless. ▸ **cavalierly** adv.

cavalry noun (pl. **cavalries**) 1 the part of an army consisting of soldiers in armored vehicles. 2 the part of an army consisting of soldiers on horseback. ▸ **cavalryman** noun

cave noun a large natural hollow chamber either underground or in the side of a mountain. —**cave in** 1 to collapse inward. 2 to give way to persuasion or opposition.

caveat (kăv′ē-ät,, kăv′-) noun 1 a warning. 2 an official request that a court should not take a particular action without first hearing the person making the request.

caveat emptor (ĕmp′tər) the principle that the buyer of merchandise is solely responsible for ascertaining its quality prior to purchase.

cave-in noun a collapse, e.g., of a mine shaft, or the site at which it occurs.

caveman noun 1 a prehistoric cave-dweller. 2 colloq. a man of crude, brutish behavior.

cavern noun a large dark cave.

cavernous adj. 1 deep and vast. 2 full of caverns. ▸ **cavernously** adv.

caviar or **caviare** noun the roe of the sturgeon, used as food and considered a delicacy.

cavil verb intrans. (**caviled** or **cavilled, caviling** or **cavilling**) to raise objections or find fault, esp. trivially or unnecessarily. —noun a trivial objection. ▸ **caviler** noun ▸ **caviling** adj.

caving noun the sport of exploring caves.

cavity noun (pl. **cavities**) 1 a hollow or hole. 2 a hole in a tooth, caused by decay.

cavort verb intrans. (**cavorted, cavorting**) to jump, prance, or caper about.

caw noun the loud harsh cry of a crow. —verb intrans. (**cawed, cawing**) to make this cry.

cay (kē, kā) noun a small, low-lying island formed chiefly of coral or sand.

cayenne pepper a hot spice made from the seeds of certain types of capsicum. Also called **red pepper**.

cayman noun same as **caiman**.

CB abbrev. citizens band

CBC abbrev. Canadian Broadcasting Corporation.

cc abbrev. **1** carbon copy. **2** cubic centimeter.

CCTV abbrev. closed-circuit television.

CD abbrev. **1** certificate of deposit. **2** compact disk.

Cd symbol Chem. cadmium.

CD-i or **CDI** abbrev. compact disk interactive, a multimedia compact disk that stores sound, text, graphics, animation, and video in a single format.

CD+MM abbrev. compact disk plus multimedia, an enhanced CD, an audio compact disk having a portion playable on a multimedia computer.

Cdr. abbrev. Commander.

CD-ROM (sē,dē,räm′) abbrev. compact disk read-only memory, a facility allowing examination, but not alteration, of data on compact disk.

CDT abbrev. Central Daylight Time.

CD tower a narrow, vertical case in which to store compact disks.

C.E. abbrev. **1** civil engineer. **2** Common Era.

Ce symbol Chem. cerium.

cease verb trans., intrans. (**ceased, ceasing**) to bring or come to an end.

cease-fire noun a break in armed hostilities, agreed to by both combatants.

ceaseless adj. continuous; going on without a pause or break. ▸ **ceaselessly** adv. ▸ **ceaselessness** noun

cecum or **caecum** noun (pl. **ceca, caeca**) the pouch at the junction of the small and large intestines, to which the appendix is attached.

cedar noun a tall coniferous tree.

cede verb trans., intrans. (**ceded, ceding**) **1** to hand over or give up formally. **2** to yield or give way: cede to a higher authority.

cedilla noun a mark (₎) put under c to show that it is to be pronounced like s, not like k.

ceiling noun **1** the inner roof of a room. **2** an upper limit. **3** the maximum height that a particular aircraft can reach.

celebrate verb trans., intrans. (**celebrated, celebrating**) **1** to mark (e.g., a success or other happy occasion) with festivities. **2** to do something enjoyable to mark a happy occasion. **3** to give public praise or recognition to. **4** to conduct (a religious ceremony). ▸ **celebrant** noun ▸ **celebration** noun ▸ **celebrator** noun ▸ **celebratory** adj.

celebrated adj. famous.

celebrity noun (pl. **celebrities**) **1** a widely known person. ◘ LUMINARY, NAME, PERSONAGE, SUPERSTAR. **2** the condition of being widely known. See syn at **fame**.

celeriac (sə-lěr′ē-ăk,) noun a variety of celery whose swollen base is eaten as a vegetable.

celery noun (**celeries**) a plant with crisp juicy stalks eaten as a vegetable.

celesta (sə-lěs′tə) noun a keyboard instrument that produces soft, bell-like sounds when struck with hammers.

celestial adj. **1** belonging to or relating to the sky. **2** heavenly; divine.

celiac or **coeliac** adj. relating to the abdomen.

celibate adj. **1** unmarried, esp. in obedience to a religious vow. **2** abstaining from sexual relations. —noun **1** a person who is unmarried, esp. because of a religious vow. **2** a person who abstains from sexual relations. ▸ **celibacy** noun

cell noun **1** a small room for a prisoner or a member of a religious community. **2** a basic structural unit of living organisms. **3** a device containing electrodes and an electrolyte for producing electricity by chemical energy; a battery. **4** Comput. a self-contained unit at a point in a spreadsheet where a row and column intersect.

cellar noun **1 a** a room, usu. underground, for storage, e.g., of wine. **b** a basement to a building, esp. a private residence. **2** a stock of wines.

cellblock noun a section or unit of a prison.

cello (chěl′ō) noun (pl. **cellos**) a large stringed musical instrument, played with a bow while sitting. Also called **violoncello**. ▸ **cellist** noun

cellophane (sěl′ə-fān,) noun thin transparent sheeting, used as a wrapping.

cellphone noun a cellular telephone.

cellular adj. **1** composed of cells, or divided into cell-like compartments. **2** knitted with an open pattern.

cellular telephone noun a mobile radio-telephone that uses a network of short-range transmitters found in cells throughout a single geographical area. Also called **cellphone**.

cellulite noun a deposit of fat cells that gives the skin a dimpled, pitted appearance.

celluloid noun a transparent plastic material, formerly used in photographic film.

cellulose noun the main constituent in plant cell walls, an important ingredient of paper, synthetic fibers, etc.

Celsius (sěl′sē-əs) noun (ABBREV. **C**) a scale of temperature in which the freezing point of water is 0°C and its boiling point is 100°C.

Celt or **Kelt** (kĕlt, sĕlt) *noun* a member of one of the ancient peoples who inhabited most parts of Europe in pre-Roman and Roman times, or of the peoples descended from them.

Celtic (kĕl'tĭk, sĕl'-) *adj.* relating to the Celts or their languages. —*noun* the group of languages spoken by the Celts, including Gaelic, Irish, Manx, Welsh, Cornish, and Breton.

cement *noun* **1** a fine powder that hardens when mixed with water, used in building as an ingredient of mortar and concrete. **2** any of various substances used as adhesives. —*verb trans., intrans.* (**cemented, cementing**) **1** to stick together with cement. **2** to make stronger (e.g., a friendship).

cemetery *noun* (*pl.* **cemeteries**) a burial ground.

cenobite or **coenobite** (sĕn'ɔ-bīt,) *noun* a member of a monastic community. ▸ **cenobitic** *adj.* ▸ **cenobitism** *noun*

cenotaph *noun* a tomblike monument erected in honor of a person or people buried elsewhere.

censer *noun* a container in which incense is burned.

censor (sĕn'sər) *noun* an official who examines books, movies, etc., and has the power to cut out any parts thought undesirable and to forbid publication or showing altogether. —*verb trans.* (**censored, censoring**) to alter or cut out parts of, or to forbid publication or showing of. ▸ **censorship** *noun*

censorious *adj.* inclined to find fault; severely critical. ▸ **censoriously** *adv.* ▸ **censoriousness** *noun*

censure (sĕn'chər) *noun* severe criticism or disapproval. —*verb trans.* (**censured, censuring**) to criticize severely or express strong disapproval of. ▸ **censurable** *adj.*

census *noun* an official count and survey, carried out at intervals, of a population.

cent *noun* a coin worth one-hundredth of a US dollar.

cent. *abbrev.* **1** centigrade. **2** century.

centaur (sĕn'tôr,) *noun Greek Mythol.* a creature with a man's head, arms, and trunk joined to the body of a horse.

centenarian *noun* a person who is 100 years old or more.

centenary *noun* (*pl.* **centenaries**) a centennial. —*adj.* centennial.

centennial *noun* the 100th anniversary of an event, or the celebration of it. —*adj.* **1** relating to a period of 100 years. **2** occurring every 100 years.

center *noun* **1 a** a part at the middle. **b** the innermost or essential part. **2** a point inside a circle or sphere that is an equal distance from all points on the circumference or surface, or a point on a line at an equal distance from either end. **3** a point or an axis around which a body revolves or rotates. **4** a central area. **5** a place in which a particular activity is concentrated or particular facilities are available. **6** a point from which activities radiate and are controlled. **7** (*often* **Center**) a position that is at neither extreme in politics. **8** in some sports, a position in the middle of the field, or a player in this position. —*adj.* at the center; central. —*verb trans., intrans.* (**centered, centering**) **1** to place in or at the center. **2** to adjust or focus, e.g., one's thoughts. **3** to be concentrated in a given area.

centerboard *noun* a movable plate in a sail boat that can be let down through the keel to prevent sideways drift.

centered *adj.* well-balanced and self-confident: *a centered personality.*

centerfold *noun* the sheet that forms the two central facing pages of a magazine, or a picture, etc., occupying it. *Also called* **center spread.**

centi- *combining form* denoting a hundred.

centigrade *noun* same as Celsius.

centimeter *noun* the 100th part of a meter.

centipede *noun* a small insect-like creature with many legs.

central *adj.* **1** at, or forming, the center. **2** near the center; easy to reach. **3** principal or most important. ▸ **centrality** *noun* ▸ **centrally** *adv.*

centralism *noun* the policy of bringing the administration of a country under central control, with a decrease in local administrative power. ▸ **centralist** *noun, adj.*

centralize *verb trans., intrans.* (**centralized, centralizing**) to bring or be under central control. ▸ **centralization** *noun*

central nervous system (ABBREV. **CNS**) the brain and the spinal cord.

central processing unit (ABBREV. **CPU**) the part of a computer that performs arithmetical and logical operations on data, and controls the other units contained in the system. *Also called* **central processor, microprocessor**

centri- *combining form* denoting a center or middle.

-centric *combining form* having a stated center, focus, basis, etc.

centrifugal *adj.* acting or moving away from the center of a circle.

centrifugal force a force that seems to exert an outward pull on an object that is moving in a circular path. *See also* **centripetal force.**

centrifuge *noun* a rotating device used to separate solid or liquid particles by spinning them in a horizontal circle at speed in a tube.

centripetal (sĕn-trĭp′ət-l) *adj.* acting or moving toward the center of a circle.

centripetal force the force that is required to keep an object moving in a circular path. It is directed inward toward the center of the circle. *See also* **centrifugal force**.

centrism *noun* the holding of moderate political opinions. ► **centrist** *adj., noun*

centurion *noun Hist.* a Roman officer in charge of a century.

century *noun* (*pl.* **centuries**) **1** any of the 100-year periods counted forward or backward from an important event, esp. the birth of Christ. **2** a period of 100 years. **3** *Hist.* in ancient Rome, a company orig. of 100 foot soldiers.

CEO *abbrev.* Chief Executive Officer.

cephalic (sə-făl′ĭk) *adj.* relating to the head.

ceramic *noun* a hard, brittle material produced by firing a nonmetallic substance, such as, clay, at a high temperature. —*adj.* relating to or made of such material, or to pottery in general.

ceramics *pl. noun* **1** (*sing.*) the art of making pottery. **2** (*pl.*) pottery articles.

cereal *noun* **1** a plant that yields an edible grain. **2** the grain produced. **3** a breakfast food prepared from grain. —*adj.* relating to edible grains.

cerebellum *noun* (*pl.* **cerebella**) the main part of the hindbrain. ► **cerebellar** *adj.*

cerebra *see* **cerebrum**.

cerebral *adj.* **1** relating to the brain. **2** requiring use of or appealing to the intellect.

cerebral palsy a condition, often characterized by weakened limbs and intellectual impairment, usu. caused by injury to the brain, esp. around the time of birth.

cerebrate *verb intrans.* (**cerebrated**, **cerebrating**) to think. ► **cerebration** *noun*

cerebrum *noun* (*pl.* **cerebrums**, **cerebra**) the part of the brain that coordinates all voluntary activity.

ceremonial *adj.* relating to, used for, or involving a ceremony. —*noun* a ceremony or set of ceremonies. ► **ceremonially** *adv.*

ceremonious *adj.* elaborately formal. ► **ceremoniously** *adv.*

ceremony *noun* (*pl.* **ceremonies**) **1** a ritual performed to mark a particular, esp. public or religious, occasion. **2** formal politeness.

cerise (sə-rēs′, -rēz′) *noun* a vivid purplish-red color. —*adj.* of a vivid purplish-red color.

cerium *noun* (SYMBOL **Ce**) a soft silvery-gray metallic element.

certain *adj.* **1** known beyond doubt. **2** having no doubt; absolutely sure. **3** definitely going to happen. **4** particular, and, though known, not named or specified: *a certain friend of yours.* **5** used before a person's name to indicate either the person's obscurity or unfamiliarity with the person. **6** undeniably present without being clearly definable: *The beard gave his face a certain authority.* **7** some, though not much: *That's true to a certain extent.*

certainly *adv.* **1** without any doubt; of course. **2** definitely.

certainty *noun* (*pl.* **certainties**) **1** something that cannot be doubted or is bound to happen. **2** freedom from doubt; the state of being sure. **3** the state of being bound to happen.

certificate (sər-tĭf′ĭ-kət) *noun* an official document that formally acknowledges or witnesses a fact. (sər-tĭf′ĭ-kāt,) —*verb trans.* (**certificate**, **certificated**) to provide with a certificate.

certify *verb trans.* (**certified**, **certifying**, **certifies**) **1** to declare or confirm officially. **2** to declare (someone) insane. **3** to declare to have reached a required standard, passed certain tests, etc. ► **certifiable** *adj.* ► **certification** *noun* ► **certified** *adj.*

certitude *noun* a feeling of certainty.

cervical *adj.* relating to or in the region of the cervix.

cervix *noun* (*pl.* **cervixes**, **cervices**) **1** the neck of a body part, esp. the uterus. **2** *Anat.* the neck.

cesarean or **caesarean** (sĭ-zâr′ē-ən, -zĕr′-) *noun* a surgical operation in which a baby is delivered through an incision in the lower abdomen.

cesium or **caesium** *noun* (SYMBOL **Cs**) a soft silvery-white metallic element.

cessation *noun* a stopping or a ceasing.

cession *noun* the giving up or yielding of territories, rights, etc., to another.

cesspit *noun* a pit for garbage or sewage material.

cesspool *noun* a covered hole, pit, or other depression for collection and drainage of sewage, e.g., from a dwelling.

cetacean *adj.* relating to whales, dolphins, etc.

Cf *symbol Chem.* californium.

CFC *abbrev.* chlorofluorocarbon.

cha-cha *noun* a Latin American dance, or music for it.

chafe *verb trans., intrans.* (**chafed**, **chafing**) **1** to make or become sore or worn by rubbing. **2** to anger or irritate.

chafer *noun* a large nocturnal beetle.

chaff[1] *noun* **1** the husks or shells separated from grain during threshing. **2** chopped hay and straw used to feed cattle. **3** worthless material.

chaff[2] *noun* lighthearted joking or teasing. —*verb trans.* (**chaffed**, **chaffing**) to tease or make fun of.

chaffinch *noun* a songbird, the male having a pinkish body and gray head.

chafing dish a metal dish set into a stand over a source of heat and used to warm food.

chagrin *noun* acute annoyance or disappointment.

chain *noun* **1** a series of connected links or rings, esp. of metal. **2** a series or progression: *a chain of events.* **3** a number of shops, hotels, etc., under common ownership or management. —*verb trans.* (**chained, chaining**) to fasten, bind, or restrict with, or as if with, chains. —**in chains** bound by chains, as a prisoner or slave.

chain gang a group of prisoners chained together for working outside the prison.

chain letter a letter copied to a large number of people, each recipient being asked to copy the letter to a stated number of acquaintances.

chain mail *Hist.* close-fitting, flexible body armor made of metal links or scales.

chain reaction 1 a chemical reaction in which a change in one molecule causes many other molecules to undergo change. **2** a series of events, each causing another, successive event.

chainsaw *noun* a power-driven saw, the blade of which is a fast-revolving chain composed of metal teeth.

chain-smoke *verb trans., intrans.* (**chain-smoked, chain-smoking**) to smoke (cigarettes, etc.) continuously or to engage in such smoking. ▸ **chain-smoker** *noun*

chain store one of a series of stores owned by the same company and selling the same goods.

chair *noun* **1** a seat for one person, with a back-support and four legs. **2** the office of chairman or chairwoman, or the person holding this office. **3** a professorship. **4** (**the chair**) *slang* the electric chair. —*verb trans.* (**chaired, chairing**) to control or conduct (a meeting) as chairman or chairwoman.

chairlift *noun* a series of seats suspended from a moving cable, for carrying people up a slope.

chairman *noun* (*pl.* **chairmen**) a man who presides over a committee, board, meeting, or debate.

chairperson *noun* a chairman or a chairwoman.

chairs *pl. noun* a waiting area, esp. in a hospital.

chairwoman a woman who presides over a committee, board, meeting, or debate.

chaise (shāz) *noun Hist.* an open two-wheeled horse-drawn carriage. *Also called* **shay.**

chaise longue (shāz'lông') *noun* (*pl.* **chaise longues** or **chaises longues**) a long seat with a back and one armrest, on which one can recline at full length.

chalcedony (kăl-sĕd'n-ē, chăl-) *noun* (*pl.* **chalcedonies**) a variety of quartz, several varieties of which are semiprecious stones.

chalet (shə-lā') *noun* a small house, built of wood, with shutters and a sloping roof.

chalice *noun* **1** a goblet. **2** a cup used for serving the wine at Communion or Mass.

chalk *noun* **1** a soft fine-grained porous rock, composed of calcium carbonate, often pure white or very light in color. **2** a material similar to this, or a stick of it, used for writing and drawing, esp. on a board. —*verb trans.* (**chalked, chalking**) to write or mark in chalk. —**chalk up** to add (an item) to one's list of successes or experiences.

chalkboard *noun* a board, typically on the wall of a classroom, for writing on in chalk.

chalky *adj.* (**chalkier, chalkiest**) **1** like or consisting of chalk. **2** very pale. ▸ **chalkiness** *noun*

challenge *verb trans.* (**challenged, challenging**) **1** to call on (someone) to settle a matter by, or as if by, contest. ◼ DARE. **2** to cast doubt on or call into question. **3** to test, esp. in a stimulating way. **4** to order (someone) to stop and show official proof of identity, etc. **5** to object to the inclusion of (a person) on a jury. —*noun* **1** an invitation to a contest. **2** the questioning or doubting of something. **3** a problem or task that stimulates effort and interest. **4** an order from a guard or sentry to stop and prove identity. **5** an objection to the inclusion of (someone) on a jury.

challenged *adj.* **1** having a specified impairment. **2** often used facetiously, having a specified difficulty, personal shortcoming, etc.: *vertically challenged/cerebrally challenged.*

challenger *noun* **1** a person who issues a challenge. **2** *Sport* an athlete, e.g., in boxing, who challenges a title holder to a match.

challenging *adj.* difficult but rewarding; demanding. ▸ **challengingly** *adv.*

chamber *noun* **1 a** a room, esp. a bedroom. **b** a room or compartment with a particular function: *a decompression chamber.* **2** a hall for the meeting of an assembly, esp. a legislative or judicial body. **3** (**chambers**) a suite of rooms used by, e.g., a judge. **4** an enclosed space or hollow; a cavity.

chamberlain *noun* **1** a person who manages a royal or noble household. **2** the treasurer of a municipality.

chambermaid *noun* a woman in a hotel, etc., who cleans the bedrooms.

chamber music pieces composed for a small group of musicians

chamber pot a receptacle for urine, etc., for use in a bedroom.

chambray *noun* a lightweight, strong fabric that is woven with white thread over a colored warp.

chameleon *noun* **1** a lizard whose skin changes color rapidly in response to changes in its environment, acting as camouflage. **2** a fickle, usu. unreliable, person.

chamfer *verb trans.* **(chamfered, chamfering)** to give a smooth, rounded shape to (an edge or corner). —*noun* a rounded or beveled edge.

chamois (shăm'ē) *noun* (*pl.* **chamois**) **1** a small goatlike antelope of mountainous regions of Europe and SW Asia. **2** (*also* **shammy**) soft suede leather made from the skin of this antelope, used esp. as a polishing cloth.

chamomile *or* **camomile** *noun* a plant whose flowers can be crushed to make drinks, etc., e.g., for medicinal purposes.

champ¹ . *verb trans., intrans.* **(champed, champing)** to munch noisily or to chew (food) noisily. —*noun* the sound of noisy munching. ·—**champ at the bit** to be impatient to act.

champ² *noun colloq.* a champion.

champagne *noun* a sparkling white wine traditionally drunk at celebrations.

champion *noun* **1** a competitor that has defeated all others in a game, competition, etc. **2** the supporter or defender of a person or cause. —*adj.* holding the winning place; superior to all others. —*verb trans.* **(championed, championing)** to support strongly or defend (a person or cause).

championship *noun* **1** a contest held to find the champion. **2** the title or position of champion. **3** the strong defense or support of a cause or person.

chance *noun* **1 a** the unforeseen, unplanned element that can be inherent in events or occurrences. **b** an unforeseen, unplanned occurrence. **2** (*often* **chances**) a possibility or probability. **3** a possible or probable success. **4** an opportunity. **5** a risk or hazard. —*verb trans., intrans.* **(chanced, chancing)** **1** to risk. **2** to do or happen by chance: / *chanced to meet her.* —*adj.* determined or caused by an unknown, unforeseen, and unpredictable element. ⊟ ACCIDENTAL, FLUKY, FORTUITOUS ⊟ PLANNED.

chancel *noun* the eastern part of a church, where the altar is.

chancellery *noun* (*pl.* **chancelleries**) **1 a** the rank of a chancellor. **b** a chancellor's department or staff. **c** the offices or residence of a chancellor; a chancery. **2** the office of an embassy or consulate.

chancellor *noun* **1** the head of the government in certain European countries. **2** a legal or state official of various kinds, e.g., a presiding judge in some US state courts. **3** the president of some universities or colleges. ► **chancellorship** *noun*

chancery *noun* (*pl.* **chanceries**) the offices or residence of a chancellor; a chancellory.

chancre (shăng'kər) *noun* a small hard sore, an initial sign of syphilis. ► **chancrous** *adj.*

chancroid *noun* a sexually transmitted disease that is characterized by ulceration and enlargement of the lymph nodes in the groin.

chancy *adj.* **(chancier, chanciest)** risky; uncertain. ► **chanciness** *noun*

chandelier (shăn,də-lîr') *noun* an ornamental light fixture hanging from the ceiling, with branching holders for candles or light bulbs.

chandler *noun* a dealer in ship's supplies and equipment. ► **chandlery** *noun*

change *verb trans., intrans.* **(changed, changing)** **1** to make or become different. **2** to give, leave, or substitute .one thing for another. **3** to exchange or replace: *changed the baby's diaper / changed into her swimsuit / changed dollars for francs.* —*noun* **1** the process of changing or an instance of it. **2** the replacement of one thing with another. **3** something different. **4 a** coins, as distinct from notes. **b** coins or notes given in exchange for ones of higher value. **c** money left over or returned from the amount given in payment. —**change of life** *colloq.* the menopause.

changeable *adj.* inclined or liable to change often. ► **changeability** *noun* ► **changeably** *adv.*

changeling *noun* a child, usu. a newborn, who is secretly substituted for another.

changeover *noun* a change from one preference or situation to another.

channel *noun* **1** a watercourse, e.g., the bed of a stream, or an irrigation channel. **2** the part of a river, waterway, etc., that is deep enough for navigation by ships. **3** a wide stretch of water, esp. between an island and a continent. **4** a frequency for radio or television signals. **5** a groove, furrow, or a long narrow cut, esp. one along which something moves. **6** *Comput.* the path along which electrical signals or data flow. **7** (**channels**) a means by which information, etc., is communicated, obtained, or received. —*verb trans.* **(channeled** *or* **channelled, channeling** *or* **channelling)** **1** to make a channel in. **2** to convey (a liquid, information, etc.) through, or as if through, a channel. **3** to direct (a resource) into a course or project.

channel-surf *verb* to flit from one television channel to another looking for something interesting to watch.

chant *verb trans., intrans.* **(chanted, chanting)** **1** to recite in a singing voice. **2** to keep repeating, esp. loudly and rhythmically.

—*noun* **1** the singing used in religious services for passages in prose, with a simple melody and several words sung on one note. **2** a phrase or slogan constantly repeated, esp. loudly and rhythmically. ▸ **chanter** *noun*

chanterelle (shănt‚ə-rĕl′, shănt‚-) *noun* an edible yellow mushroom with a trumpet-shaped cap.

chantey, chanty, shantey *or* **shanty** (shănt′ē, chănt′ē) *noun* (*pl.* **chanteys, chanties, shanteys, shanties**) a rhythmical song of a kind formerly sung by sailors working in unison.

Chanukkah (кнän′ə-kə, hän′-) *noun* same as **Hanukkah**.

chaos *noun* **1** complete confusion; utter disorder. **2** *Phys.* a state of disorder and irregularity that is an intermediate stage between highly ordered motion and entirely random motion. ▸ **chaotic** *adj.* ▸ **chaotically** *adv.*

chap¹ *noun colloq.* a man or boy; a fellow.

chap² *verb trans., intrans.* (**chapped, chapping**) *of skin* to make or become roughened, sore, and red from rubbing or exposure to cold.

chaparral (shăp‚ə-răl′, -rĕl′) *noun* an area of dense undergrowth, shrubs, and small trees.

chapel *noun* **1** a recess within a church or cathedral, with its own altar. **2** a place of worship attached to a house, school, etc.

chaperone *or* **chaperon** *noun* **1** *formerly* an older woman accompanying a younger unmarried one on social occasions, for respectability's sake. **2** an older person accompanying and supervising a group of young people. —*verb trans.* (**chaperoned, chaperoning**) to act as chaperone to.

chaplain *noun* a cleric attached to a school, hospital, or other institution, or to the armed forces. ▸ **chaplaincy** *noun*

chaplet *noun* **1** a wreath of flowers or a band of gold, etc., for the head. **2** a string of beads.

chaps (chăps) *pl. noun* a ranch hand's protective leather riding leggings, worn over the pants.

chapter *noun* **1** one of the sections into which a book is divided. **2** a period associated with certain happenings: *an unfortunate chapter in my life.* **3** a branch of a society, or its meeting. **4** the body, or a meeting, of canons of a cathedral.

chapter house 1 a building used for meetings of a cathedral chapter. **2** a building used to house members of a fraternity or sorority, and where their meetings are held.

char¹ *verb trans., intrans.* (**charred, charring**) **1** to blacken by burning. **2** *of wood* to turn into charcoal by partial burning.

char² *verb intrans.* (**charred, charring**) *Brit.* to do paid cleaning work.

char³ *or* **charr** *noun* (*pl.* **char; charr, chars, charrs**) a fish related to the salmon.

charabanc (shăr′ə-băng‚) *noun* a single-decker bus for tours, sightseeing, etc.

character *noun* **1** the combination of qualities forming a person's personality and way of thinking. ⊟ FIBER, NATURE. **2** a combination of typifying qualities. **3** type or kind. **4** strong, admirable qualities. **5** interesting qualities that make for individuality: *a house with character.* **6** a person in a story, play, etc. **7** a person, esp. an odd or amusing person. **8** a letter, number, or other written or printed symbol.

characteristic *adj.* **1** typical. **2** distinctive. —*noun* a distinguishing element. ▸ **characteristically** *adv.*

characterize *verb trans.* (**characterized, characterizing**) **1** to be the identifying or distinguishing trait or feature of. **2** to depict or describe the qualities of. ▸ **characterization** *noun*

characterless *adj.* lacking individuality; dull; uninteresting.

charade *noun* **1** a ridiculous pretense; a farce. **2** (**charades**) (*sing., pl.*) a party game in which players act out each syllable of a word, or each word of a book title, etc.

charbroil *verb trans.* (**charbroiled, charbroiling**) to broil (e.g., meat) on a grill over charcoal.

charcoal *noun* **1** partially burnt wood, used for drawing and as a fuel. **2** a drawing done using this material. **3** a dark gray color.

charge *verb trans., intrans.* (**charged, charging**) **1** to ask for (an amount) as the price of something. **2** to ask (someone) to pay an amount for something. **3** to record (an amount) as a debt against (someone). **4** to accuse (someone) officially of a crime. **5** to rush at in attack. **6** to move with speed, impetuously and often heedlessly. **7** to order officially. **8** to load (a gun, etc.). **9** *old use, formal* to fill up: *Charge your glasses, gentlemen!* **10** *of a battery, etc.* to store up, or cause to store up, electricity. —*noun* **1** an amount charged; a price, fee, or cost. **2** control or responsibility; supervision or guardianship. **3** a thing or person in the care of someone else. **4** an illegal act of which one is accused. **5** a rushing attack. **6** the electricity carried or stored. ▸ **chargeable** *adj.*

charge account a credit arrangement by which customers receive merchandise and pay for it later.

charge card a credit card.

charge-coupled device (ABBREV. **CCD**) **1** *Comput.* a memory unit in which information is stored using electrically charged particles. **2** a sensor in a video camera, made up of a mosaic of minute diodes.

chargé d'affaires (shär-zhăd,ə-făr', -fĕr') (*pl.* **chargés d'affaires**) a deputy to, or substitute for, an ambassador.

charger *noun* a strong horse used by a knight in battle, etc.

chariot *noun* a two-wheeled vehicle pulled by horses, used in ancient times for warfare or racing. ▸ **charioteer**

charisma (kə-rĭz'mə) *noun* a strong ability to attract people, and inspire loyalty and admiration. ⊟ GLAMOUR, MAGNETISM.

charismatic *adj.* 1 relating to or having charisma. 2 *Relig.* relating to the charismatic movement.

charismatic movement a Christian movement that emphasizes the power of the Holy Spirit at work within individuals.

charitable *adj.* 1 kind and understanding. 2 relating to or of the nature of a charity: *charitable institutions.* ▸ **charitably** *adv.*

charity *noun* (*pl.* **charities**) 1 assistance given to those in need. 2 an organization established to provide such assistance. 3 kindness and understanding.

charlatan *noun* a person posing as an expert in a profession, e.g., medicine. ▸ **charlatanism** *noun*

Charleston *noun* a vigorous dance popular in the 1920s.

charley horse *colloq.* a cramp, esp. in the upper part of the leg.

charm *noun* 1 the power of delighting, attracting, or fascinating. 2 a particularly attractive quality a person, place, or thing has. 3 an object believed to have magical powers. 4 a magical spell or saying. —*verb trans.* (**charmed, charming**) 1 to delight, attract, or fascinate. 2 to influence or persuade by charm. ▸ **charming** *adj.* ▸ **charmingly** *adv.*

charmer *noun* 1 *colloq.* a person with an attractive, winning manner. 2 a person who can charm animals: *a snake charmer.*

charnel house *Hist.* a building where corpses or bones are stored.

charr *noun same as* char³.

chart *noun* 1 a map, esp. one designed as an aid to navigation, or one on which weather developments are shown. 2 a record of progress, change, etc. —*verb trans., intrans.* (**charted, charting**) to make a map or record of.

charter *noun* 1 a document guaranteeing rights, privileges, etc. 2 a document detailing the constitution, principles, etc. of an organization. —*verb trans.* (**chartered, chartering**) 1 to hire (an aircraft, boat, etc.) for private use. 2 to grant a charter to. ▸ **chartered** *adj.* ▸ **charterer** *noun*

chartreuse *noun* a green or yellow liqueur made from brandy and herbs.

chary *adj.* (**charier, chariest**) cautious; wary. ▸ **charily** *adv.* ▸ **chariness** *noun*

chase¹ *verb trans., intrans.* (**chased, chasing**) 1 to follow or go after in an attempt to catch. 2 to drive or force away. 3 to move with speed. —*noun* 1 a pursuit. 2 (**the chase**) the hunting of animals, e.g., foxes.

chase² *verb trans.* (**chased, chasing**) to decorate (metal) with engraved or embossed work.

chaser *noun colloq.* a drink taken after one of a different kind, e.g., beer after whiskey.

chasm *noun* 1 a deep crack in the ground. 2 a very great divergence in opinion, feeling, etc.

chassis *noun* (*pl.* **chassis**) 1 the structural framework of a motor vehicle. 2 a supporting framework.

chaste *adj.* 1 a totally virtuous and clean. ⊟ IMMACULATE, PURE ⊟ IMPURE, UNCHASTE. b refraining from sexual relations. 2 simple; plain; unadorned. ▸ **chastely** *adv.* ▸ **chasteness** *noun*

chasten *verb trans.* (**chastened, chastening**) to discipline or punish.

chastise *verb trans.* (**chastised, chastising**) 1 to punish severely, e.g., by beating. 2 to scold; reprove. ▸ **chastisement** *noun*

chastity *noun* the quality or state of being chaste.

chasuble *noun* a priest's long sleeveless garment.

chat *verb intrans.* (**chatted, chatting**) to talk or converse in a friendly, informal way. —*noun* informal, familiar talk; a friendly conversation. —**chat up** *colloq.* to speak to (someone) in a light, casual manner.

chateau (shă-tō') *noun* (*pl.* **chateaus, chateaux**) 1 a large castle or country estate, esp. in France.

chatelaine (shăt'l-ēn,) *noun* 1 the mistress of a large house. 2 *Hist.* a chain hanging from the belt, worn by women.

chat group a group of people who share interests and engage in discussions on the Internet.

chat room an Internet site where people with similar interests communicate.

chat show a TV or radio program where invited guests are interviewed by the presenter.

chattel *noun Law* a moveable possession.

chatter *verb intrans.* (**chattered, chattering**) 1 to talk rapidly, unceasingly, and heedlessly, usu. about trivial matters. 2 *of the teeth* to knock together as a result of cold or fear. 3 *of monkeys or birds* to make high-pitched noises. —*noun* rapid, noisy talk or a sound similar to it. ▸ **chatterer** *noun*

chatterbox *noun* a person who is inclined to chatter.

chatty *adj.* (**chattier, chattiest**) *colloq.* 1 given to amiable chatting. 2 *of writing* informal in style. ▸ **chattily** *adv.*

chauffeur (shō-fər', shō'fər) *noun* a person employed to drive an automobile for someone else. —*verb trans.* (**chauffeured, chauffeuring**) to act as a driver for (someone else).

chauvinism *noun* an unreasonable belief, esp. if aggressively expressed, in the superiority of one's own nation, gender, etc. ▸ **chauvinist** *noun* ▸ **chauvinistic** *adj.*

> After Nicholas *Chauvin*, Napoleonic French soldier and keen patriot

cheap *adj.* **1** not costly. ▣ INEXPENSIVE, LOW, LOW-COST, LOW-PRICED, REASONABLE ▣ COSTLY, EXPENSIVE, HIGH, PRICEY. **2** poor in quality. ▣ CHEAPJACK, CHEESY, SHODDY ▣ FINE, PRECIOUS. **3** of little worth; valueless. **4** mean; stingy. **5** undeserving of respect. —*adv. colloq.* cheaply: *Good houses don't come cheap.* ▸ **cheaply** *adv.* ▸ **cheapness** *noun*

cheapen *verb trans., intrans.* (**cheapened, cheapening**) **1** to diminish, or cause to diminish, in price, value, respectability, reputation, etc.

cheapskate *noun colloq.* a mean, miserly person.

cheat *verb trans., intrans.* (**cheated, cheating**) **1** to trick, deceive, swindle. **2** to deprive (someone) of (something) by deceit or trickery. **3** to act dishonestly so as to gain an advantage. **4** (**cheat on**) *colloq.* to be unfaithful to (a spouse or partner, esp. sexually). **5** to escape (something unpleasant) by luck or skill. —*noun* **1** a person who cheats. **2** a dishonest trick.

check *verb trans., intrans.* (**checked, checking**) **1** to examine or establish, esp. by investigation or inquiry. **2** to hold back, prevent, or stop. **3** to indicate (something) with a check mark. **4** to deposit for safekeeping. **5** of *information, etc.* to be consistent; to agree with other information. **6** *Chess* to put (the opposing king) into check. —*noun* **1** an inspection or investigation. **2** a standard or test for checking something. **3** a stoppage in, or a control on, progress or development. **4** a pattern of squares. **5** a mark written next to something, e.g., an item on a list. **6** a written order to a bank telling it to pay a specified amount to the payee. **7** a restaurant bill. **8** a ticket or token for claiming an item left in safekeeping. **9** *Chess* the position of the king when directly threatened by an opposing piece. —**check in 1** to report one's arrival at an airport or hotel. **2** to register or record the arrival of (esp. guests at a hotel or passengers at an airport). **3** to hand in (luggage for weighing and loading) at an airport. **check out 1** to register one's

departure, esp. from a hotel upon paying the bill. **2** to investigate (something or someone) thoroughly. ▸ **checkable** *adj.*

checkbook *noun* a book of blank, personalized checks.

checkbook journalism the practice of paying high prices for exclusive rights, esp. to sensational material for newspaper or magazine stories.

checked *adj.* having a pattern of squares.

checker *noun* **1** a person who checks. **2** a person who operates a store checkout counter. **3** (**checkers**) (*sing.*) a game that is played with 24 round pieces on a checkerboard by two participants.

checkerboard *noun* a board divided into 64 squares of two alternating colors on which checkers and chess are played.

checkered *adj.* **1** patterned with squares or patches of alternating color. **2** *of a person's life, career, etc.* eventful, with both good and bad fortune.

check-in *noun* an airport desk where passengers' tickets are checked and luggage weighed and accepted for loading.

checklist *noun* a list of things to be done or systematically checked off.

checkmate *noun* **1** *Chess* a winning position, i.e., the putting of one's opponent's king under inescapable attack. **2** frustration or defeat. —*verb trans.* (**checkmated, checkmating**) **1** *Chess* to put (the opposing king) into checkmate. **2** to foil or outwit.

checkout *noun* a place, time, or act of checking out, e.g., in a supermarket or hotel.

checkpoint *noun* a place where vehicles are stopped and travel documents checked.

checkup *noun* a thorough examination, esp. a medical one.

cheddar *noun* a smooth, hard, yellow cheese.

cheek *noun* **1** either side of the face below the eye. **2** the state or quality of being boldly impolite.

cheeky *adj.* (**cheekier, cheekiest**) impudent; disrespectful. ▸ **cheekily** *adv.* ▸ **cheekiness** *noun*

cheep *verb intrans.* (**cheeped, cheeping**) *esp. of young birds* to make high-pitched noises. —*noun* a high-pitched sound.

cheer *noun* **1** a shout of approval or encouragement. **2** mood; spirits: *Be of good cheer.* **3** merriment. —*verb trans., intrans.* (**cheered, cheering**) to give approval or encouragement by shouting. —**cheer on** to encourage (someone) by shouting. **cheer up** to make or become cheerful or more cheerful.

cheerful *adj.* **1** happy; optimistic. **2** bright and cheering. ▸ **cheerfully** *adv.* ▸ **cheerfulness** *noun*

cheerio *interj. Brit. colloq.* good-bye.

cheerleader *noun* a person who leads organized cheering, esp. at sports events.

cheerless *adj.* dismal, depressing, or dull. ▸ **cheerlessly** *adv.* ▸ **cheerlessness** *noun*

cheers *interj. colloq.* used as a toast before drinking.

cheery *adj.* (**cheerier, cheeriest**) cheerful; lively; jovial. ▸ **cheerily** *adv.*

cheese *noun* a solid or soft creamy food that is prepared from the curds of milk. —**cheese off** *colloq.* to annoy, irritate, or frustrate.

cheeseburger *noun* a hamburger served with a slice of cheese.

cheesecake *noun* a sweet food made with soft cheese.

cheesecloth *noun* a thin, coarse, cotton cloth.

cheesy *adj.* (**cheesier, cheesiest**) **1** relating to or like cheese. **2** *colloq.* poor in quality.

cheetah *noun* a large fast-running cat with a tawny or gray body covered with black spots.

chef *noun* a head cook.

chef-d'oeuvre (shā-dœv', -dœv'rə) *noun* (*pl.* **chefs-d'oeuvre**) a masterpiece.

chemical *adj.* relating to, or made using, chemistry or chemicals. —*noun* a substance produced by or used in chemistry. ▸ **chemically** *adv.*

chemical warfare the use of toxic chemical or biological substances against an enemy.

chemin de fer (shə-măn,də-fĕr') *Cards* a variation of baccarat.

chemise *noun* a woman's shirt or loose-fitting dress.

chemistry *noun* **1** the science of elements and compounds and the ways in which they act on, or combine with, each other. **2** the emotional and psychological interaction experienced in a relationship. ▸ **chemist** *noun*

chemo (kē'mō) *noun* (*pl.* **chemos**) *colloq.* chemotherapy.

chemotherapy *noun* the treatment of disease, esp. cancer, by means of drugs or other chemical compounds. ▸ **chemotherapeutic** *adj.*

chenille (shə-nēl') *noun* a soft, shiny, velvety fabric.

cherish *verb trans.* (**cherished, cherishing**) **1** to care for lovingly. **2** to take great care to keep (a tradition, etc.) alive. **3** to cling fondly to (a hope, belief, or memory).

cheroot (shə-rōōt') *noun* a cigar cut square at both ends.

cherry *noun* (*pl.* **cherries**) **1** a small tree or its edible, usu. red fruit with a single stone. **2** the wood of this tree, used in furniture-making. **3** a bright red color.

cherry picker a mobile crane with a basket that allows an electrician or a tree surgeon, etc. to work at great heights.

cherrystone *noun* a small, immature, edible clam.

cherry tomato a small round red or yellow tomato.

cherub *noun* **1** (*pl.* **cherubim**) an angel, represented in painting and sculpture as a winged child. **2** (*pl.* **cherubs**) a sweet, innocent, beautiful child. ▸ **cherubic** *adj.* ▸ **cherubically** *adv.*

chervil *noun* an herb whose aniseed-flavored leaves are used in salads, etc.

chess *noun* a board game for two people, who each start with 16 playing pieces.

chessboard *noun* the board, divided into 64 squares of alternating colors, on which chess is played.

chessman *noun* a piece used in playing chess.

chest *noun* **1** the front part of the body between the neck and the waist. **2** a large, strong, box used for storage or transport. **3** a small cabinet, e.g., for medicines. —**get (something) off one's chest** *colloq.* to reveal (a troublesome secret, burden, etc.) to relieve anxiety.

chesterfield *noun* **1** a large sofa. **2** a man's overcoat.

chestnut *noun* **1** a deciduous tree or its shiny, reddish-brown nut encased in a prickly husk. **2** the wood of this tree. **3** a reddish-brown color. **4** an often-repeated joke or anecdote.

chest of drawers a piece of furniture with drawers, esp. for holding clothes.

chesty *adj.* (**chestier, chestiest**) *colloq.* **1** arrogantly self-absorbed and conceited. **2** *slang, of a woman* having large breasts. ▸ **chestily** *adv.* ▸ **chestiness** *noun*

cheval glass (shə-văl') a full-length pivoting mirror on a stand.

chevalier *noun* **1** a member of a modern order in France, such as the Legion of Honor, or of one of the historical French orders of knighthood. **2** *old use* a chivalrous man; a knight.

chevron *noun* a V-shaped mark or symbol, e.g., one indicating military rank.

chew *verb trans., intrans.* (**chewed, chewing**) **1** to use the teeth to break up (food) before swallowing. **2** to keep biting or nibbling at or on something. **3** to crush, damage, or destroy by, or as if by, chewing. —*noun* **1** an act of chewing. **2** something for chewing, e.g., a chewy candy. —**chew over** *colloq.* to consider or discuss (something) at length. **chew the fat** *slang* to engage in casual, lengthy conversation. ▸ **chewy** *adj.* ▸ **chewiness** *noun*

chewing gum a sticky, flavored substance, chewed but not swallowed.

chi (chē) *noun* same as **qi**.

chic (shēk) *adj.* appealingly elegant or fashionable. ⊟ **MODISH, SMART, STYLISH, SWANK, SWANKY** ⊟ **DOWDY.** ▸ **chicly** *adv.* ▸ **chicness** *noun*

Chicana (chĭ-kän'ä, shĭ-) noun a Mexican-American woman or young girl.

> **Usage** See note at *Chicano*.

chicanery noun (pl. **chicaneries**) trickery; deception.

Chicano (chĭ-kän'ō, shĭ-) noun (pl. **Chicanos**) a Mexican-American man or youth.

> **Usage** In some parts of the USA, *Chicano* and *Chicana* are regarded by those denoted as terms indicative of ethnic pride; in other regions, these same terms can be regarded as derogatory. Writers and speakers using the terms should do so with care. See note at *Hispanic*.

chick noun 1 a baby bird. 2 *slang* a young woman.

chickadee noun a small, plump bird of N America, with a dark crown on its head.

chicken noun 1 a domestic fowl, bred for its meat and eggs. 2 the flesh of a chicken used as food. 3 a cowardly person. 4 *slang* a youthful person: *He's no chicken.* —*adj. colloq.* having or displaying a contemptible lack of courage. —*verb intrans.* (**chickened**, **chickening**) *slang* to avoid or withdraw from (an activity or commitment) because of a lack of nerve.

chicken feed 1 food for poultry. 2 *slang* a paltry sum of money.

chicken-hearted adj. colloq. having or displaying a contemptible lack of courage.

chickenpox noun an infectious viral disease, characterized by fever and a rash, that mainly affects children.

chicken wire light wire netting for fences, etc.

chickpea noun a plant of the pea family, or its edible seed.

chickweed noun a low-growing plant with oval pointed leaves and tiny white flowers.

chicory noun a blue-flowered plant whose dried root is blended with coffee, and whose leaves are eaten raw as a salad vegetable.

chide verb (pa t **chided** or **chid**; pa p **chided**, **chid** or **chidden**; pr p **chiding**) to scold; rebuke.

chief noun 1 the head, e.g., of a tribe or clan. 2 a leader. 3 the person in charge of a group, organization, or department. —*adj.* 1 used in titles, etc. first in rank; leading. 2 most important; principal or main. ▸ **chiefly** adv.

Chief Executive the US President.

chief executive officer (ABBREV. **CEO**) the highest-ranking company officer who reports only to the board of directors and the stockholders.

chief justice (abbrev. **CJ**) the presiding judge, e.g., of the US Supreme Court or an appellate court.

chief of staff (pl. **chiefs of staff**) the senior officer of the US Army and the US Air Force.

chieftain noun 1 the head of a clan or tribe. 2 a leader or commander. ▸ **chieftancy** noun

chiffon (shĭ-fän') noun a very fine, transparent silk or nylon fabric.

chiffonier (shĭf,ə-nĭr') noun a tall chest of drawers, often with an attached mirror.

chigger or **chigoe** noun 1 a tropical flea that burrows into the skin, causing irritating sores. 2 a larva from a mite whose bite produces severe itching. *Also called* **harvest mite.**

chignon (shēn'yän,) noun a soft bun or coil of hair worn at the back of the head.

chigoe noun same as **chigger**.

chihuahua noun the smallest domestic breed of dog.

chilblain noun a painful red itchy swelling of the skin, esp. on the fingers, toes, or ears, caused by exposure to cold.

child noun (pl. **children**) 1 a boy or girl between birth and physical maturity. 2 one's son or daughter. —**child's play** colloq. a basic or simple task. **with child** old use pregnant. ▸ **childless** adj. ▸ **childlessness** noun ▸ **childlike** adj.

child abuse physical, mental, or emotional maltreatment of a child.

childbirth noun the process whereby a mother gives birth to a child at the end of pregnancy.

child-care or **childcare** noun provision of supervised care for children.

childhood noun the state or time of being a child.

childish adj. 1 silly; immature. 2 relating to children or childhood; like a child. ▸ **childishly** adv. ▸ **childishness** noun

childproof adj. designed to prevent access, operation, etc. by a child. *Also called* **child-resistant.**

children see **child**.

chili noun (pl. **chilies**) 1 the dried or fresh fruit of the capsicum, used as a spice in cooking. 2 chili con carne.

chili con carne a spicy dish of minced meat and beans.

chill noun 1 a feeling of coldness. 2 a feverish cold. —*verb trans., intrans.* (**chilled**, **chilling**) 1 to make or become cold. 2 to cause to feel cold, scared, depressed, or discouraged. —**chill out** slang to relax, esp. after a period of hard work, stress, or exercise.

chiller noun a terrifying tale or film.

chill factor see **wind-chill factor**.

chilly adj. (**chillier**, **chilliest**) 1 rather cold. 2 unfriendly; hostile. ▸ **chillily** adv. ▸ **chilliness** noun

chime noun 1 a set of tuned bells; the sound made by them. 2 (**chimes**) a percussion instrument consisting of hanging metal tubes that are struck with a hammer. —*verb intrans., trans.* (**chimed, chiming**) **1** *of bells* to ring. **2** *of a clock* to indicate (the time) by sounding. **3** to agree or harmonize. —**chime in 1** to add a remark, esp. in agreement.

chimera *noun* **1** *Mythol.* a female monster with a lion's head, goat's body, and serpent's tail. **2** a wild, impossible idea. ▸ **chimerical** *adj.*

chimney *noun* (*pl.* **chimneys**) **1** a narrow vertical shaft for the escape of smoke from a fire or furnace; the top part of this shaft, rising from a roof. **2** a narrow vertical cleft in a rock face.

chimneypot *noun* a rounded fitting on top of a chimney to improve the draft.

chimney sweep a person who cleans chimneys.

chimp *noun colloq.* a chimpanzee.

chimpanzee *noun* a large anthropoid ape with long, coarse, black hair.

chin *noun* the front central part of the lower jaw.

china *noun* articles made from a fine, translucent earthenware or similar materials.

China syndrome a hypothetical effect of the meltdown of a nuclear reactor, resulting in its sinking deep into the ground.

chinchilla *noun* **1** a small S American rodent, or its soft, gray fur.

chine *noun* **1** *old use* the backbone, particularly that of an animal. **2** a cut, esp. of pork, consisting of part of t. e backbone and adjoining parts. **3** a steep-sioed ridge.

Chinese (chī-nēz', -nēs') *noun* (*pl.* **Chinese**) **1** a native or citizen of China, or a person of Chinese descent. **2** the language of China. —*adj.* of China, its people, descendants, or their language.

Chinese cabbage a plant with a head of crisp whitish leaves, eaten as a vegetable.

Chinese checkers (*sing., pl.*) a game played by moving pegs or marbles on a star-shaped board.

Chinese gooseberry kiwi (sense 2).

Chinese lantern a collapsible paper lantern.

chink¹ *noun* **1** a small slit or crack. **2** a narrow beam of light shining through such a crack.

chink² *noun* a faint, short ringing noise; a clink. —*verb intrans., trans.* (**chinked, chinking**) to make, or cause to make, this noise.

chino *noun* **1** a strong, twilled cotton fabric. **2** a garment, esp. casual pants, made from this.

chinook *noun* **1** a warm dry wind blowing east of the Rocky Mountains, or a warm moist wind blowing to the west of them. **2** (**Chinook**) a Native North American people, or a member of these people.

chintz *noun* a glazed cotton material, usu. printed in bright colors on a light background.

From a Hindi word for painted or multi-coloured cotton

chintzy *adj.* (**chintzier, chintziest**) *colloq.* trashy and cheap.

chip *verb trans., intrans.* (**chipped, chipping**) **1** to knock or strike (small pieces) from (a hard object). **2** to break off in small pieces. **3** to form by taking small pieces away. —*noun* **1** a small piece chipped off. **2** a place from which a piece has been chipped off. **3** a potato chip. **4** a plastic counter used as a token in gambling. **5** a small piece of silicon, on which a large amount of information can be stored electronically. *Also called* **microchip, silicon chip.** —**chip in** *colloq.* to contribute: *chipped in to buy the present.* **have a chip on one's shoulder** *colloq.* to feel resentful (about something), esp. unreasonably.

chipmunk *noun* a small ground squirrel with striped fur.

chipper *adj. colloq.* cheerful and lively.

chirography *or* **cheirography** *noun* the study of handwriting.

chiromancy *noun* palmistry.

chiropody *noun* podiatry. ▸ **chiropodist** *noun*

chiropractic *noun* a system of medical treatment involving manipulating the vertebrae of the spine. ▸ **chiropractor** *noun*

chirp *verb intrans., trans.* (**chirped, chirping**) **1** *of birds, grasshoppers, etc.* to produce a short, high, unmusical sound. **2** to chatter or say (something) merrily. —*noun* a chirping sound.

chirrup *verb intrans.* (**chirruped, chirruping**) to chirp, esp. in little bursts. —*noun* a burst of chirping.

chisel¹ *noun* a hand tool with a flat steel blade, used for cutting wood, stone, or metal. —*verb trans., intrans.* (**chiseled** *or* **chiselled, chiseling** *or* **chiselling**) **1** to cut with a chisel. **2** *slang* to cheat.

chit¹ *noun* a short note, recording money owed or paid, etc.

chit² *noun* a cheeky young girl.

chitchat *noun* idle chatter. —*verb intrans.* (**chitchatted, chitchatting**) to chatter idly.

chitterlings (chĭt'lĭnz), **chitlins** *or* **chit-lings** *pl. noun* a pig's intestines, prepared as a food.

chivalry *noun* **1** courtesy, gallantry, and protectiveness. **2** the medieval system of knighthood. ▸ **chivalrous** *adj.* ▸ **chival-rously** *adv.* ▸ **chivalrousness** *noun*

chive *noun* a plant of the onion family with long thin hollow leaves used as a flavoring or garnish.

chivvy *or* **chivy** *verb trans.* (**chivvying, chivvied, chivvies**) to keep urging on or nagging (another), esp. to hurry or to get a task done.

chlamydia *noun* (*pl.* **chlamydiae**) a common sexually transmitted disease.

chlor- *or* **chloro-** *combining form* **1** green. **2** chlorine.

chloral hydrate a colorless crystalline compound used as a sedative. *Also called* **trichloroethanal**

chloride a compound containing chlorine and another chemical element or group.

chlorinate *verb trans.* (**chlorinated**, **chlorinating**) **1** to introduce (chlorine) into an organic chemical compound. **2** to treat (a substance, esp. water) with chlorine. ▸ **chlorination** *noun*

chlorine *noun* (SYMBOL **Cl**) a poisonous gaseous element with a pungent smell, widely used as a disinfectant and a bleach.

chloro- *see* **chlor-**.

chlorofluorocarbon (klôr͵ō-flŏŏr͵ō-kär′bən) *noun* (ABBREV. **CFC**) a chemical compound composed of chlorine, fluorine, and carbon, used as an aerosol propellant, and in refrigeration systems.

chloroform *noun* a colorless volatile sweet-smelling liquid, formerly used as an anesthetic.

chlorophyll *noun* the green pigment in plants that absorbs the energy from the sun needed for the process of photosynthesis.

chocaholic (chäk͵ə-häl′ĭk, chô͵kə-hŏ′lĭk) *or* **chocoholic** *noun* a person who is addicted to or craves chocolate.

chock *noun* a heavy block or wedge used to prevent movement of a wheel, etc.

chockablock *adj.* holding or containing as many or as much as possible.

chock-full *adj.* absolutely full.

chocolate (chäk′lət, chô′klət) *noun* **1** a food product made from cacao seeds. **2** a candy made from or coated with this substance. **3** a drink made by dissolving a powder prepared from this substance in hot water or milk. **4** a dark brown color.

choice *noun* **1** the act or process of choosing. **2** the right, power, or opportunity to choose. ▤ OPTION, SELECTION. **3** something or someone chosen. **4** a variety of things available for choosing. —*adj.* (**choicer**, **choicest**) of esp. good quality. ▸ **choiceness** *noun*

choir (kwīr) *noun* **1** an organized group of trained singers, esp. one that performs in church. **2** the area occupied by the choir esp. in a cathedral or large church.

choirmaster *noun* the trainer of a choir.

choke *verb trans., intrans.* (**choked**, **choking**) **1** to prevent, or be prevented, from breathing by an obstruction in the throat, fumes, etc. **2** to stop or interfere with breathing in this way.

3 to make or become speechless from emotion. **4** to fill up, block, or restrict. —*noun* a valve in the carburetor of an engine that reduces the air supply and so gives a richer fuel /air mixture while the engine is still cold. —**choke back** to suppress (tears, laughter, or anger). **choke up** to be overcome by emotion.

choker *noun* a close-fitting necklace or broad band of velvet, etc. worn around the neck.

choler *noun old use* anger; irritability. ▸ **choleric** *adj.*

cholera *noun* an acute, potentially fatal bacterial infection of the small intestine.

cholesterol (kə-lĕs′tə-rôl͵) *noun* a crystalline substance found mainly in animal tissues, esp. in fat, blood, etc.

chomp *verb trans., intrans.* (**chomped**, **chomping**) to munch noisily.

choose *verb trans., intrans.* (*pa t* **chose**; *pa p* **chosen**; *pr p* **choosing**) **1** to take or select (one or more things or people) from a larger number. **2** to decide.

choosy *adj.* (**choosier**, **choosiest**) *colloq.* difficult to please; fussy.

chop¹ *verb* (**chopped**, **chopping**) **1** to cut (something) with a vigorous slicing action, with an ax, knife, etc. **2** to hit (a ball) with a sharp downward stroke. —*noun* **1** a slice of pork, lamb, or mutton containing a bone. **2** a chopping action, movement, or stroke.

chop² *verb intrans.* (**chopped**, **chopping**) (*usu.* **chop and change**) to vacillate or change from one direction to another.

chopper *noun* **1** *colloq.* a helicopter. **2** *colloq.* a customized motorcycle. **3** a device used for chopping, e.g., vegetables.

choppy *adj.* (**choppier**, **choppiest**) of the sea, etc. marked by short, irregular wave motion. ▸ **choppily** *adv.* ▸ **choppiness** *noun*

chops *pl. noun* the jaws or mouth.

chopsticks *pl. noun* a pair of slender wooden, plastic, or ivory sticks, used as cutlery.

> Literally 'quick sticks', from Pidgin English *chop* for 'quick'

chop suey a Chinese-American dish of chopped meat and vegetables fried in a sauce.

choral (kôr′əl) *adj.* relating to, or to be sung by, a choir or chorus. ▸ **chorally** *adv.*

chorale (kə-räl′, -räl′) *noun* **1** a hymn tune with a slow, dignified rhythm and strong harmonization. **2** a choir or choral society.

choral society a group that meets regularly to practice and perform choral music.

chord¹ *noun* a combination of musical notes played together.

chord² *noun* **1** *poetic* a string of a musical instrument. **2** *same as* **cord** (sense 2). **3** *Geom.* a straight line joining two points on a curve. —**strike a chord** to prompt a feeling of recognition or familiarity.

chore noun 1 a boring and laborious task. 2 (**chores**) routine housework.

chorea (kə-rē′ə) noun a disorder of the nervous system causing rapid involuntary movements of the limbs and face.

choreography noun 1 the arrangement of the sequence and pattern of movements in dancing. 2 the art of dance. ► **choreograph** verb trans. ► **choreographer** noun ► **choreographic** noun

chorister noun a singer in a choir.

chortle verb intrans. (**chortled, chortling**) to give a half-suppressed, amused, or triumphant laugh.

chorus noun 1 a set of lines in a song, sung after each verse. 2 a large choir. 3 a piece of music for such a choir. 4 the group of singers and dancers supporting the soloists in an opera or musical show. 5 something uttered by a number of people at the same time: a chorus of objections. 6 a group of actors, always on stage, who comment on the developments in the plot, orig. in classical Greek drama. —verb trans. (**chorused, chorusing**) to say, sing, or utter together.

chose verb see **choose**.

chosen verb see **choose**. —adj. preferred over all the rest: the chosen few.

chow[1] noun a dog with thick fur, a curled tail, and a blue tongue.

chow[2] noun slang food.

chowder noun a thick soup containing clams or fish and vegetables.

chow mein (chow-mān′) a Chinese-American dish of chopped meat and vegetables served with fried noodles.

chrism noun holy oil used in the Roman Catholic and Orthodox Churches for anointing.

Christ (krīst) noun 1 the Messiah or anointed one whose coming is prophesied in the Old Testament. 2 Jesus of Nazareth, or Jesus Christ, believed by Christians to be the Messiah.

christen (krĭs′ən) verb trans. (**christened, christening**) 1 to baptize and receive into the Christian Church. 2 to give a name or nickname to. ► **christening** noun

Christendom (krĭs′ən-dəm) noun 1 all Christians. 2 the parts of the world in which Christianity is the recognized religion.

Christian noun a person who believes in and follows the teachings and example of Jesus Christ. —adj. relating to Jesus Christ, the Christian religion, or Christians. ► **Christianity** noun

christian name 1 the personal name given to a Christian at baptism. 2 a person's first or given name.

Christian Science a system of religion in which spiritual or divine power is relied on for healing, rather than medicines or surgery.

Christmas (krĭs′məs) noun 1 the annual Christian festival commemorating the birth of Christ, held on Dec. 25. 2 the period of celebration surrounding this date. ◼ NATIVITY, NOEL, XMAS, YULETIDE.

chromatic adj. 1 relating to colors; colored. 2 Mus. relating to notes from the 12-note scale (chromatic scale) that includes semitones. See also **diatonic**. ► **chromatically** adv.

chromato- see **chromo-**.

chromatography noun a technique for separating and analyzing the components of a substance.

chrome noun chromium or one of its compounds; esp. when present in a dye or pigment, or used as a plating for other metals.

chromium (krō′mē-əm) noun (SYMBOL **Cr**) a hard silvery metallic element that is used in alloys with iron and nickel, and as an electroplated coating on other metals, esp. steel.

chromo- or **chromato-** combining form color.

chromosome noun a microscopic threadlike structure containing, in the form of DNA, all the necessary genetic information. ► **chromosomal** adj.

chron- or **chrono-** combining form forming words denoting time.

chronic adj. 1 of long duration. See also **acute**. 2 habitual. ► **chronically** adv. ► **chronicity** noun

chronicle noun (often **chronicles**) a record of events year by year in the order of occurrence. ◼ ANNALS, HISTORY. —verb trans. (**chronicled, chronicling**) to record (events) in a chronicle. ► **chronicler** noun

chrono- see **chron-**.

chronological adj. arranged in order of occurrence. ► **chronologically** adv.

chronology noun (pl. **chronologies**) 1 the science of determining the correct order of historical events. 2 the arrangement of events in order of occurrence. ► **chronologist** noun

chronometer (krə-năm′ət-ər) noun a very accurate watch or clock, used esp. at sea.

chrysalis (krĭs′ə-lĭs) noun 1 the pupa of insects that undergo metamorphosis, e.g., butterflies, moths. 2 the protective case that surrounds the pupa.

chrysanthemum noun a garden plant with large bushy flowers.

chrysolite noun a light yellowish-green gemstone.

chub noun (pl. **chubs, chub**) a freshwater or marine fish.

chubby adj. (**chubbier, chubbiest**) plump, esp. in a childishly attractive way. ► **chubbily** adv. ► **chubbiness** noun

chuck[1] verb trans. (**chucked, chucking**) **1** colloq. to throw or fling. **2** to give (a child, etc.) an affectionate tap under the chin. **3** slang to abandon or reject (someone or something).

chuck[2] noun **1** beef cut from the area between the neck and shoulder. **2** a device for holding a piece of work in a lathe; or for holding the blade or bit in a drill.

chuckle verb intrans., trans. (**chuckled, chuckling**) to laugh quietly, esp. in a half-suppressed private way. —noun a little laugh.

chug verb intrans. (**chugged, chugging**) of a vehicle to progress with a labored, thudding noise. —noun a labored, thudding noise.

chukka boot a leather ankle boot.

chukker or **chukkar** noun one of the periods of play in the game of polo.

chum[1] noun colloq. a close friend. ► **chummy** adj.

chum[2] noun ground-up, oily fish scattered on water for bait.

chump noun colloq. an idiot; a fool.

chunk noun **1** a thick, esp. irregularly shaped, piece. **2** colloq. a large or considerable amount.

chunky adj. (**chunkier, chunkiest**) **1** stockily or strongly built; thick-set. **2** solid and strong: chunky furniture.

church noun **1** a building for public Christian worship. **2** the religious services held in a church: go to church. **3** (**Church**) a Christian denomination with its own doctrines, style of worship, etc.

churchgoer noun a person who attends church services regularly.

churchman noun a man who is a member of the clergy or of a church.

Church of Jesus Christ of Latter-Day Saints the Mormon Church.

churchwoman noun a woman who is a member of the clergy or of a church.

churchyard noun the yard and sometimes the burial ground around a church.

churlish adj. bad-tempered; rude; ill-mannered. ► **churlishly** adv. ► **churlishness** noun

churn noun a machine in which milk is shaken about to make butter. —verb trans., intrans. (**churned, churning**) **1** to make (butter) in a churn, or to turn (milk) into butter in a churn. **2** to shake or agitate (something) violently or to be agitated. —**churn out** to keep producing (something of tedious similarity).

chute[1] noun **1** a sloping channel down which to send water, trash, etc. **2** a slide in a playground or swimming pool.

chute[2] noun colloq. a parachute.

chutney noun an Indian condiment consisting of pickles mixed with fruit, vinegar, spices, and sugar.

chutzpah (кноот'spə, hoŏt'-, -spä,) noun impudent, bold self-assurance; audacity.

chyle (kīl) noun a milky digestive fluid produced by the small intestine.

ciabatta noun (pl. **ciabattas**) an Italian bread made using olive oil.

CIA abbrev. Central Intelligence Agency.

ciao (chow) interj. hello; farewell.

cicada (sĭ-kā'də, -kä') noun a large insect that makes a loud, rhythmic chirping noise.

cicatrix (sĭk'ə-trĭks,, sĭ-kā'trĭks) noun (pl. **cicatrices**) a scar left by a wound after healing.

CID abbrev. Criminal Investigation Department.

-cide combining form forming nouns denoting: **1** the act of killing; murder: homicide. **2** a person, substance, or thing that kills: insecticide.

cider noun juice pressed from apples, often fermented to give an alcoholic drink.

cigar noun a roll of tobacco leaves, for smoking.

cigarette noun a tube of finely cut tobacco rolled in thin paper, for smoking.

cilium noun (pl. **cilia**) a short hair or hair-like structure, e.g., an eyelash, a propelling appendage in protozoans, etc. ► **ciliary** adj.

C-in-C abbrev. Commander in Chief.

cinch (sĭnch) noun **1** colloq. **a** an easily accomplished task. **b** a certainty. **2** a girth used to secure a saddle or pack. —verb **1** to fasten, secure, or tighten with a cinch. **2** colloq. to make certain of: a perfomance that cinched victory.

cinchona (sĭng-kō,nə, sĭn-chō'-) noun a tropical tree or its dried bark, used as a source of quinine.

cincture noun a belt or girdle, esp. one on a monk's habit.

cinder noun **1** a piece of burned coal or wood. **2** (**cinders**) ashes.

cinder block a building block made of coal cinders mixed with concrete.

cinema noun **1** (usu. **the cinema**) movies in general, or the art or business of making movies. **2** a movie theater. ► **cinematic** adj.

cinematography noun the art of movie photography. ► **cinematographer** noun ► **cinematographic** adj.

cinéma vérité (sĭn'ə-mə-věr,ĭ-tā') the art or process of making movies in a very realistic way, or such movies collectively.

cinnabar noun a bright red mineral form of mercuric sulfide that is the principal source of mercury.

cinnamon noun **1** a spice obtained from the inner bark of a SE Asian tree. **2** a brownish-orange color.

CIO abbrev. Congress of Industrial Organizatons.

cipher *noun* **1 a** a secret code. **b** matter written or transmitted in code. **c** the key to a code. **2** *old use* the symbol 0. **3** a person or thing of little importance. **4** any Arabic numeral. —*verb trans.* (**ciphered, ciphering**) to write (a message, etc.) in code.

> Originally meaning 'zero' and later 'number', because of the early use of numbers in encoded documents

circa (sər'kə, sĭr'-) *prep.* (ABBREV. **c.**) *used esp. with dates* about; approximately.

circle *noun* **1** a perfectly round plane figure that is bordered by a line on which all points are an equal distance from the centre. **2** something in round form. **3** a curved upper floor of seats in a theater. **4** a series of events, steps, or developments, ending at the point where it began. **5** a group of associated people. —*verb trans., intrans.* (**circled, circling**) **1** to move in a circle; to move in a circle around (another or others). **2** to draw a circle around.

circuit *noun* **1** a complete course, journey, or route around something. **2** an association of competitors: *the pro tennis circuit*. **3** a path consisting of various electrical devices joined together by wires so that an electric current can flow continuously through it. **4** the places or venues visited in turn and regularly by entertainers, etc.

circuit breaker a device that automatically interrupts an electric current when a fault occurs.

circuitous (sər-kyoo'ət-əs) *adj.* taking a long, complicated route; indirect; roundabout. ▸ **circuitously** *adv.* ▸ **circuitousness** *noun*

circuitry *noun* (*pl.* **circuitries**) *Electr.* a plan or system of circuits.

circular *adj.* **1** having the form of a circle. **2** moving or going around in a circle. —*noun* a letter or notice sent to a number of people. ▸ **circularity** *noun* ▸ **circularly** *adv.*

circular saw a power saw with a rotating disk-shaped toothed blade.

circulate *verb trans., intrans.* (**circulated, circulating**) **1** to move or cause to move around freely, esp. in a fixed route. **2** to pass around; to spread: *circulate the report*. **3** to move around talking to different people, e.g., at a party.

circulation *noun* **1** the act or process of circulating. **2** the flow of a fluid, etc., around a system, esp. of the blood around the body. **3** the extent of distribution of a newspaper or magazine, or the number of copies of it that are sold.

circulatory *adj.* relating to circulation, esp. of the blood.

circum- *combining form* round about: *circumnavigate*.

circumcise *verb trans.* (**circumcised, circumcising**) **1** to cut away the foreskin of (a male), as a religious rite or medical necessity. **2** to cut away the clitoris of (a female), or the skin covering it, for the same reasons. ▸ **circumcision** *noun*

circumference (sər-kəm'fə-rəns, -frəns) *noun* **1** the length of the boundary of a circle or other closed curve, or the length of a path around a sphere at its widest point. **2** the boundary of an area of any shape. ▸ **circumferential** *adj.*

circumflex *noun* a mark (ˆ) placed over a vowel, denoting pronunciation.

circumlocution *noun* deliberate long-windedness or evasion of a point in speech or writing. ▸ **circumlocutory** *adj.*

circumnavigate *verb trans.* (**circumnavigated, circumnavigating**) to sail or fly around (the world). ▸ **circumnavigation** *noun* ▸ **circumnavigator** *noun*

circumscribe *verb trans.* (**circumscribed, circumscribing**) **1** to put a line or boundary around. **2** to limit or restrict. ▸ **circumscription** *noun*

circumspect *adj.* cautious or discreet. ▤ GUARDED, WARY ▨ RASH. ▸ **circumspectly** *adv.*

circumstance *noun* **1** a fact, occurrence, or condition, esp. when relating to an act or event. **2** (**circumstances**) one's financial situation. **3** events that one cannot control; fate: *a victim of circumstance*. **4** ceremony: *pomp and circumstance*.

circumstantial *adj. of an account of an event* full of detailed description, etc. ▸ **circumstantially** *adv.*

circumstantial evidence *Law* details or facts that give a statement etc. the appearance of truth, but do not prove it.

circumvent *verb trans.* (**circumvented, circumventing**) **1** to find a way of getting around or evading (a rule, law, etc.). **2** to outwit or frustrate (someone or something). ▸ **circumvention** *noun*

circus *noun* **1** a traveling company of performers including acrobats, clowns, and often trained animals, etc. **2** *colloq.* a scene of noisy confusion or a disorderly group.

cirrhosis (sə-rō'sĭs) *noun* a disease, esp. of the liver, where normal tissue is replaced by abnormal lumpy tissue.

cirrus *noun* (*pl.* **cirri**) a commonly occurring high cloud with a wispy appearance.

CIS *abbrev.* Commonwealth of Independent States.

cistern *noun* **1** a tank for storing rain water. **2** an underground reservoir.

citadel *noun* a stronghold or fortress close to or dominating the center of a city.

citation *noun* **1** the quoting or citing of something as example or proof. **2** a passage quoted from a book, etc. **3** *Law* an order to appear in court. **4** a special, official commendation or award for merit, bravery, etc.

cite *verb trans.* (**cited, citing**) **1** to quote (a book, author, etc.) as an example. **2** to mention as an example or illustration. **3** *Law* to summon (a person) to appear in court.

citizen *noun* **1** an inhabitant of a city or town. **2** a native of a country or state, or a naturalized member of it. ▸ **citizenship** *noun*

citizenry *noun* the citizens of a town, country, etc.

citizens' band (ABBREV. **CB**) a band of radio frequencies that the public can use for personal or business communication.

citric acid an organic acid present in the juice of citrus fruit.

citron *noun* **1** a fruit resembling a large lemon. **2** the candied rind of this fruit.

citrus *noun* **1** a tropical tree or shrub, e.g., the orange, lemon, grapefruit, etc. **2** (also **citrus fruit**) the edible, juicy, thick-skinned fruit of one of these trees or shrubs.

city *noun* (*pl.* **cities**) **1** a population center of some importance. **2** (*usu. in combination*) *slang* a place with a specified characteristic: *Our yard was ice city after two days of sleet.*

city desk a department in a newspaper office that handles local news.

city father a member of a city council.

city hall the local government of a city, or the building in which it is housed.

city slicker *colloq.* a city dweller.

civet *noun* **1** a small mammal related to the mongoose. **2** a substance secreted by this animal's glands and used as a perfume fixer.

civic *adj.* **1** relating to a city, citizen, or citizenship. **2** relating to the community. ▸ **civically** *adv.*

civics *noun* (*sing.*) the study of local government and of the duties of citizenship.

civil *adj.* **1** relating to the community: *civil affairs.* ▤ CIVIC, NATIONAL, PUBLIC. **2** relating to or occurring between citizens: *civil disturbances.* **3** relating to ordinary citizens; not military, legal, or religious. **4** *Law* relating to cases about individual rights, etc., not criminal cases. **5** civilized or polite. ▸ **civilly** *adv.*

civil defense (ABBREV. **CD**) ordinary citizens trained to assist the armed forces in wartime.

civil disobedience the refusal to obey regulations, pay taxes, etc., as a form of nonviolent protest.

civil engineering the branch of engineering concerned with the design, construction, and maintenance of roads, bridges, etc. ▸ **civil engineer** *noun*

civilian *noun* someone who is not a member of the armed forces or the police. —*adj.* relating to civilians.

civility *noun* (*pl.* **civilities**) polite, civilized behavior.

civilization *noun* **1 a** the state of being civilized; the act of civilizing. **b** a stage of development in human society that is socially, politically, culturally, and technologically advanced. **c** the parts of the world that have reached such a stage. **2** a people and their society and culture. **3** built-up, heavily populated areas.

civilize *verb trans.* (**civilized, civilizing**) **1** to lead to an advanced stage of social development. **2** to educate and enlighten morally, intellectually, and spiritually.

civilized *adj.* **1** socially, politically, and technologically advanced. **2** agreeably refined, sophisticated, or comfortable.

civil law law that deals with citizens' rights, etc., not with crimes.

civil liberty an individual's right to freedom, esp. in thought, speech, and action.

civil rights the personal rights of a citizen, including civil liberty, freedom from discrimination, and equal protection under the law.

civil service 1 the permanent branches of a country's administration, excluding the legislative, judicial, and military departments. **2** people employed in these branches, whose jobs do not depend on affiliation with any political party ▸ **civil servant**

civil war an internal war between citizens of a country.

civvies *pl. noun colloq.* ordinary civilian clothes.

Cl *symbol Chem.* chlorine.

clack *noun* a sharp noise made by one hard object striking another. —*verb trans., intrans.* (**clacked, clacking**) **1** to make, or cause to make, a sharp, abrupt noise. **2** to talk noisily.

clad *adj.* **1** clothed. **2** covered: *fields clad in green.*

cladding *noun* a covering, e.g., applied to the external surface of a building.

cladistics *noun* (*sing.*) a system of animal and plant classification by analysis of common ancestral characteristics.

claim *verb trans., intrans.* (**claimed, claiming**) **1** to state (something) firmly, insisting on its truth. **2** to assert: *claim one's innocence.* **3** to demand or assert as a right. **4** to have a right to; to deserve: *this problem claims our immediate attention.* —*noun* **1** a statement purporting to be the truth. **2 a** a demand, esp. for something that one has, or believes one has, a right to. **b** a demand for money in connection with an insurance policy. **3** a right to or reason for: *his claim to fame.* **4** something one has claimed, e.g., a piece of land. ▸ **claimant** *noun*

clairvoyance *noun* the ability, claimed by some, to see into the future, or know things that cannot be discovered through the normal range of senses. ▸ **clairvoyant** *adj.,* *noun*

clam *noun* **1** a burrowing, bivalve mollusk. **2** *colloq.* an uncommunicative person. —*verb intrans.* (**clammed, clamming**) **1** to dig for clams. **2** (**clam up**) *colloq.* to stop talking.

clambake *noun* **1** a shore picnic with clams, lobster, corn, fish, etc. that are baked on hot stones covered with seaweed. **2** a social gathering of any kind.

clamber *verb intrans.* (**clambered, clambering**) to climb, esp. using hands as well as feet.

clammy *adj.* (**clammier, clammiest**) moist or damp, esp. unpleasantly so. ▸ **clammily** *adv.* ▸ **clamminess** *noun*

clamor *noun* **1** a noise of shouting or loud talking. **2** loud protesting or loud demands. —*verb intrans.* (**clamored, clamoring**) to make noisy demands. ▸ **clamorous** *adj.*

clamp *noun* **1** a tool with adjustable jaws for gripping things firmly or pressing parts together. **2** a reinforcing or fastening device, used in woodwork, etc. —*verb trans.* (**clamped, clamping**) **1** to fasten together or hold with a clamp. **2** to hold, grip, shut, or press tightly. —**clamp down on** to put a stop to or to exercise strict control over (something or someone).

clan *noun* **1** a group of families, in Scotland or of Scots origin, generally with the same surname. **2** one's family or relations. **3** a group of people who have similar interests, concerns, etc. ▸ **clansman** *noun* ▸ **clanswoman** *noun*

> From Scottish Gaelic *clann* meaning 'children'

clandestine *adj.* **1** kept secret; concealed. **2** furtive; sly; surreptitious. ▸ **clandestinely** *adv.*

clang *verb intrans., trans.* (**clanged, clanging**) to make, or cause to make, a loud, deep, ringing sound. —*noun* a loud, deep, ringing sound.

clangor *noun* a continuous, loud, confused, and intrusive noise.

clank *verb intrans., trans.* (**clanked, clanking**) to make, or cause to make, a sharp sound of metal striking metal or some other hard surface. —*noun* a sharp, metallic sound.

clannish *adj.,* of *a group of people* closely united, with little interest or trust in people not belonging to the group. ▸ **clannishly** *adv.* ▸ **clannishness** *noun*

clap *verb intrans., trans.* (**clapped, clapping**) **1** to strike (esp. the palms of one's hands) together with a loud noise, to applaud (someone), gain attention, etc. **2** to strike (someone) with the palm of the hand, usu. as a friendly gesture. **3** to place forcefully. —*noun* **1** an act of clapping. **2** the sudden, loud explosion of noise that thunder makes.

clapboard *noun* a long board that overlaps with other boards to form the outer wall, e.g., of a frame house. *Also called* **weatherboard.**

clapper *noun* the part inside a bell that strikes against the side to make it ring.

clapperboard *noun* a pair of hinged boards clapped together in front of the camera before and after shooting a piece of film, to synchronize sound and vision.

claptrap *noun* meaningless, insincere, or pompous talk.

claque (klăk) *noun* a group of people paid to applaud a speaker, performer, etc.

claret (klăr'ət) *noun* **1** a red wine, esp. from Bordeaux. **2** the deep reddish-purple color of claret.

clarify *verb trans., intrans.* (**clarified, clarifying, clarifies**) **1** to make or become clearer or easier to understand. **2** *of butter, fat, etc.* to make or become clear by heating. ▸ **clarification** *noun*

clarinet *noun* a woodwind instrument with a cylindrical tube and a single reed. ▸ **clarinetist** *noun*

clarion *noun* a trumpet with a shrill sound, formerly used to call men to arms, etc.

clarity *noun* **1** the quality of being clear and pure. **2** the quality of being easy to see, hear, or understand. **3** clearness and accuracy of thought, reasoning, and expression.

clash *noun* **1** a loud noise, like that of metal objects striking each other. **2** a serious disagreement. **3** a fight, battle, or match. —*verb intrans., trans.* (**clashed, clashing**) **1** *of metal objects, etc.* to strike against each other noisily. **2** to fight or disagree violently. **3** *of colors, styles, etc.* to be unpleasing or unharmonious together.

clasp *noun* **1** a fastener on jewelry, a bag, etc. **2** a firm grip; an act of gripping. —*verb trans.* (**clasped, clasping**) **1** to hold or take hold of firmly. **2** to fasten or secure with a clasp.

class *noun* **1 a** a lesson or lecture. **b** a number of pupils taught together. **2** a category, kind, or type. **3** a social grouping into which people fall. **4** *colloq.* stylishness in dress, behavior, etc.; good quality. —*verb trans.* (**classed, classing**) to regard as belonging to a certain class; to put into a category.

class act *slang* someone or something of the highest order.

class action *Law* a suit brought by one or more plaintiffs for a large number of others sharing the same interest in redress.

classic *adj.* **1** of the highest quality; established as the best. **2** entirely typical. **3** simple, neat, and elegant, esp. in a traditional style. —*noun* **1** an established work of literature. **2** (*often* **classics**) the literature and history of ancient Greece and Rome. **3** an outstanding example of a type.

classical *adj.* **1** of ancient Greece and Rome. **2** having an established, traditional, and somewhat formal style and form: *classical music*. **3** *of a language* relating to or having an older, often literary, form. ▸ **classically** *adv.*

classicism *noun* purtiy and simplicity of style.

classicist *noun* someone who has studied classics, esp. as a university subject.

classification *noun* **1** the arrangement and division of things and people into classes. **2** a group or division in a classifying system.

classified *adj.* **1** arranged in groups or classes. **2** *of information* kept secret.

classified ad a small advertisement in a newspaper offering something for sale, advertising a job, etc. *Also called* **classified**, **classified advertisement**.

classify *verb* (**classified, classifying, classifies**) **1** to put into a particular class or group. **2** to declare (information) secret. ▸ **classifiable** *adj.*

classy *adj.* (**classier, classiest**) *colloq.* stylish; fashionable.

clatter *noun* a loud noise made by, or as if by, hard objects striking each other or falling onto a hard surface. —*verb intrans., trans.* (**clattered, clattering**) to make, or cause to make, a loud, hard noise.

clause *noun* **1** *Gram* a part of a sentence that at least has its own subject and verb. **2** a stipulation, condition, etc. in a contract, will, or legislative act.

claustrophobia *noun* an abnormal or morbid fear of confined spaces. ▸ **claustrophobic** *adj., noun*

clavichord *noun* an early keyboard instrument with a soft tone.

clavicle *noun* either of two slender bones linking the shoulderblades with the top of the breastbone. *Also called* **collarbone**.

claw *noun* **1 a** a hard, curved, pointed nail on the end of each digit of the foot in birds, most reptiles, and many mammals. **b** a structure resembling a claw, e.g., the pincer of a crab or lobster. **2** something with the shape or action of a claw, e.g., part of a mechanical device. —*verb trans., intrans.* (**clawed, clawing**) to tear, scratch, or pull with claws, nails, or fingers.

clay *noun* fine-grained, sticky soil, used to make pottery, bricks, etc.

clay court a tennis court with a hard surface of clay or a similar substance.

clean *adj.* **1** free from dirt. **2** not containing anything harmful to health; pure. **3** pleasantly fresh. **4** hygienic in habits. **5** unused; unmarked: *a clean sheet of paper*. **6** neat and even: *a clean cut*. **7** simple and elegant. **8 a** clear of legal offenses. **b** *slang* not carrying drugs or offensive weapons. **9** not offensive or obscene. **10** fair: *a clean fight*. —*adv.* **1** *colloq.* completely: *clean forgot*. **2** encountering no obstruction; straight: *sailed clean through the window*. —*verb trans., intrans.* (**cleaned, cleaning**) to make or become free from dirt. —*noun* an act of cleaning. —**come clean** *colloq.* to admit or tell the truth about something that one has previously concealed. ▸ **cleanness** *noun*

clean-cut *adj.* **1** pleasingly regular in outline or shape. **2** neat; respectable.

cleaner *noun* **1** a person employed to clean inside buildings. **2** a machine or substance used for cleaning. **3** (*also* **cleaners**) a shop where clothes, etc., are dry-cleaned.

clean-living *adj.* leading a decent, healthy existence.

cleanly (klĕn′lē) *adv.* **1** in a clean way. **2** efficiently; easily. ▸ **cleanliness** *noun*

clean room a room or area that is kept free from contamination, e.g., in a laboratory, or in the production of electronic or aerospace parts, etc.

cleanse (klĕnz) *verb trans.* (**cleansed, cleansing**) **1** to clean. **2** to remove sin or guilt from; to purify. ▸ **cleanser** *noun*

cleansing *noun* an act or. the process of ridding an area, country, etc. of people deemed undesirable, esp. by force: *social cleansing/ ethnic cleansing*

clean-shaven *adj.* without a beard or mustache.

clear *adj.* **1** transparent; easy to see through. **2** not misty or cloudy. **3** *of the skin* unblemished by spots, etc.; healthy. **4** easy to see, hear, or understand. **5** bright; sharp; well-defined. **6** having no doubts or confusion; certain; convinced. **7** free of doubt, ambiguity, or confusion; definite. **8** capable of, or resulting from, accurate observation, logical thinking, etc. **9** evident; obvious. **10** free from guilt, etc. —*verb, trans. intrans.* (**cleared, clearing**) **1** to make or become clear, free of obstruction, etc. **2** to remove or move out of the way. **3** to prove to be innocent. **4** to get over or past without touching. **5** to make as a profit over expenses. **6** to give or get official permission for (a plan, etc.). **7** to approve (someone) for a special assignment, access to secret information, etc. **8** to pass (a check), or (*of a check*) to pass from one bank to another through a clearing house.

9 to pay (a debt). —**clear off** *colloq.* to go away. **clear up 1** to brighten after rain, a storm, etc. **2** to straighten up (a mess, room, etc.). **3** to solve (a mystery, etc.). **4** to make (something) better. **in the clear** no longer under suspicion, in difficulties, or in danger. ▸ **clearly** *adv.* ▸ **clearness** *noun*

clearance *noun* **1** the act of clearing. **2** a big sale held by a store, etc. **3** the distance between one object and another passing object. **4** permission, or a document granting it.

clear-cut *adj.* clear; sharp.

clear-headed *adj.* capable of or showing clear, logical thought. ▸ **clear-headedly** *adv.* ▸ **clear-headedness** *noun*

clearing *noun* an area, in a forest, etc., that has been cleared of trees, underbrush, etc.

clearing-house *noun* **1** a banking establishment that deals with transactions among its members. **2** a central agency that collects, organizes, and distributes information.

clear-sighted *adj.* capable of, or showing, accurate observation and good judgment. ▸ **clear-sightedly** *adv.* ▸ **clear-sightedness** *noun*

cleat *noun* **1** a small strip, e.g., of metal or wood, used to support or strengthen the surface it is attached to. **2** (**cleats**) shoes with projecting metal or hard rubber parts on the soles for added traction.

cleavage (klē'vij) *noun* **1** an act, or the process or result of splitting or division. **2** *colloq.* the hollow between a woman's breasts, esp. as revealed by a dress with a low neck.

cleave[1] *verb trans., intrans.* (pa t **cleaved** or **clove**; pa p **cleft**, **cleaved** or **cloven**; pr p **cleaving**) **1** to split or divide. **2** to cut or slice.

cleave[2] *verb intrans.* (pa t and pa p **cleaved**; pr p **cleaving**) **1** to cling or stick. **2** to be or remain faithful.

cleaver *noun* a knife with a large square blade, used by butchers, etc.

clef *noun Mus.* a symbol placed on a staff to indicate the pitch of the notes written on it.

cleft *noun* a split, crack, or deep indentation. —*adj.* split; divided.

clematis *noun* a climbing woody plant with pink, purple, or white flowers.

clement *adj.* **1** mild: *a clement climate.* **2** merciful. ▸ **clemency** *noun* ▸ **clemently** *adv.*

clementine *noun* a citrus fruit like a small tangerine.

clench *verb trans.* (**clenched, clenching**) **1** to close (one's teeth or one's fists) tightly, esp. **2** to hold or grip firmly.

clerestory or **clearstory** *noun* (*pl.* **clerestories** or **clearstories**) an upper row of windows in the nave wall above the roof of the aisle in a church.

clergy *noun* (*pl.* **clergies**) the ordained ministers of the Christian church or the priests of any religion, considered collectively. ▸ **clergyman** *noun* ▸ **clergywoman** *noun*

cleric (klĕr'ĭk) *noun* a minister.

clerical *adj.* **1** relating to the clergy. **2** relating to clerks, office workers, or office work.

clerk *noun* **1** a person in an office or bank who deals with letters, records, files, etc. **2** in a court of law, a person who keeps records or accounts. **3** a shop assistant or hotel receptionist. **4** *old use* a scholar or cleric.

clever *adj.* **1** good or quick at learning and understanding. ▣ BRIGHT, INTELLIGENT, SHARP, SMART ▣ DUMB, STUPID, UN-INTELLIGENT. **2** skillful, dexterous, nimble, or adroit. **3** well thought out; ingenious. ▸ **cleverly** *adv.* ▸ **cleverness** *noun*

clew *noun* **1** *Naut.* the corner of a ship's sail. **2** *old use* a ball of thread.

cliché (klē-shā', klĕ'shā,) *noun* **1** a phrase that has become stale and feeble through repetition. **2** a too-frequently used idea or image; a stereotype. ▸ **clichéd** *adj.*

> From a French word for 'stereotype', in the sense of a fixed printing plate

click *noun* a short sharp sound. —*verb intrans., trans.* (**clicked, clicking**) **1** to make, or cause to make, a click. **2** *colloq.* to become clear or understood. **3** *colloq.* to become mutually friendly. **4** *Comput.* to press and release (a mouse button) to select or deselect, an item, or to activate a program, etc.

clickstream *noun* the path that a user takes from site to site while browsing the Internet or the World Wide Web.

client *noun* **1** a person or an organization using the professional services of, e.g., a lawyer, bank manager, etc. **2** a customer.

clientele (klī,ən-tĕl', klĕ,-) *noun* the group of clients of a professional person or the body of customers of a business.

client/server network a system where a network of personal computers use programs and data stored in the server.

cliff *noun* a high, steep rock face, esp. on a coast.

cliffhanger *noun* **1** a story, movie, etc. that keeps one in suspense up to the end. **2** an exciting situation, contest, etc. where the conclusion is in doubt until the very last minute. ▸ **cliffhanging** *adj.*

climate *noun* **1** the general weather conditions of a particular region of the world. **2** a current trend in general feeling, opinion, etc. ▸ **climatic** *adj.* ▸ **climatically** *adv.*

climatology *noun* the scientific study of climate. ▸ **climatological** *adj.* ▸ **climatologist** *noun*

climax *noun* **1** the culmination of a series of events or of an experience. **2** the turning point, or a point of culminating intensity in, e.g., a play or novel. **3** a sexual orgasm. —*verb intrans., trans.* (**climaxed, climaxing**) to come or bring to a climax. ▸ **climactic** *adj.* ▸ **climactically** *adv.*

climb (klīm) *verb trans., intrans.* **1** to go toward the top of. **2** (**climb down, in, out,** etc.) to get to a specified position, esp. by using the hands and feet. **3** to rise or go up. **4** to increase. —*noun* an act of climbing. ▸ **climbable** *adj.*

climb-down *noun* a dramatic or humiliating change of mind or concession.

climber *noun* **1** a climbing plant. **2** a mountaineer.

climbing *noun* the sport of climbing rock faces, esp. with the help of ropes and other devices.

clime *noun* climate, or a part of the world characterized by a certain climate.

clinch *verb trans., intrans.* (**clinched, clinching**) **1** to bend and hammer down the projecting point of (a nail that has been driven through a piece of wood, etc.). **2** *Boxing* to hold (each other) in a firm grip. **3** *colloq.* to embrace. **4** to settle (an argument or bargain) finally and decisively. —*noun* **1** an act of clinching. **2** *colloq.* an embrace.

clincher *noun colloq.* a point, argument, or circumstance that finally settles a matter.

cling *verb intrans.* (pa t and pa p **clung**; pr p **clinging**) **1** to hold firmly or tightly; to stick. **2** to be emotionally overdependent. **3** to refuse to drop or let go. ▸ **clinger** *noun* ▸ **clingy** *adj.* ▸ **clinginess** *noun*

clingstone *adj., of a peach* having a stone that sticks to the flesh.

clinic *noun* **1 a** a hospital facility that specializes in the diagnosis, treatment, and medical care of outpatients. **b** a medical facility that is run by several specialists who work together. **c** a session during which patients are given medical treatment or advice. **2** a session in which an expert is available for consultation: *a golf clinic*.

clinical *adj.* **1** *of medical studies* relating to direct observation and treatment of a patient. **2** impersonal; unemotional; detached. **3** *of surroundings, etc.* severely plain and simple, with no personal touches. ▸ **clinically** *adv.*

clinician *noun* a physician, psychiatrist, or psychologist who works directly with patients.

clink¹ *noun* a short, sharp, ringing sound. —*verb intrans., trans.* (**clinked, clinking**) to make, or cause to make, a clink.

clink² *noun slang* a prison.

clinker *noun* **1** a mass of fused ash or slag left unburned in a furnace. **2** the cindery crust on a lava flow. **3** *slang* a highly visible failure.

clip¹ *verb trans.* (**clipped, clipping**) **1** to cut (hair, wool, etc.). **2** to trim or cut off the hair, wool, or fur of. **3** to cut (an article, etc.) from a newspaper, etc. **4** *colloq.* to hit or strike sharply. —*noun* **1** an act of clipping. **2** a short movie sequence. **3** *colloq.* a sharp blow. **4** *colloq.* speed.

clip² *noun* **1** a small device for holding things together or in position. **2** a container for bullets attached to a gun. —*verb trans., intrans.* (**clipped, clipping**) to fasten with a clip.

clip art *Comput.* illustrations stored on disk that may be inserted into word processing documents.

clipboard *noun* **1** a board serving as a portable writing surface, with a clip at the top for holding paper or forms. **2** *Comput.* a memory facility where the text, etc. of the last copy or paste action is stored for potential reuse.

clip joint *slang* a bar, restaurant, nightclub, etc. charging excessively high prices.

clip-on *adj.* fastening with a clip: *a clip-on microphone*.

clipped *adj. of speaking styles* tending to shorten vowels, omit syllables, etc.

clipper *noun Hist.* a fast sailing ship with large sails.

clippers *pl. noun* a clipping instrument.

clipping *noun* a piece clipped off, e.g. from a newspaper, etc.

clique (klēk, klĭk) *noun* a group of friends, colleagues, etc., who stick together and are hostile toward outsiders. ▤ COTERIE, IN-GROUP, RING. ▸ **cliquey** *adj.* ▸ **cliquiness** *noun*

clitoris *noun* a small, erectile organ in female mammals located in front of the vagina. ▸ **clitoral** *adj.*

cloak *noun* **1** a loose outer garment, usu. sleeveless. **2** a covering or disguise. —*verb trans.* (**cloaked, cloaking**) to cover up or conceal.

cloak-and-dagger *adj.* full of mystery, plots, spying, etc.

cloakroom *noun* a room in a theater, restaurant, etc., where coats, hats, etc., may be left.

clobber *verb trans.* (**clobbered, clobbering**) *colloq.* **1** to hit. **2** to defeat completely. **3** to criticize severely.

cloche (klōsh) *noun* **1** a transparent covering for protecting young plants, e.g., from frost. **2** a woman's close-fitting, dome-shaped hat.

clock¹ *noun* **1** an instrument for measuring and indicating time. **2** a device that controls the speed of the central processing unit in a computer. **3** a device in a vehicle for showing distance traveled or speed of travel. **4** an instrument for recording employees' times of arrival and departure. *Also called* **time**

clock. —verb trans. (clocked, clocking) 1 to measure or record time using an instrument. 2 to record the speed of (an athelete, motorist, etc.). —against the clock with a time deadline. around the clock throughout the day and night. beat the clock to finish before the time limit or deadline. clock in to record one's time of arrival at a place of work. clock out or off to record one's time of departure from a place of work. put or turn back the clock to seek to return to the conditions of an earlier period.

clock² noun a decoration on the side of a sock.

clockwise adj. adv. moving, etc., in the same direction as the hands of a clock.

clockwork noun a mechanism like that of a clock, working by means of gears and a spring that must be wound periodically. —adj. operated or carried out by, or as if by, clockwork. —like clockwork smoothly and with regularity; without difficulties.

clod noun 1 a lump of earth, clay, etc. 2 colloq. a stupid person. ► cloddish adj. ► cloddishly adv. ► cloddishness noun

clodhopper noun colloq. 1 a clumsy person. 2 a large, heavy boot or shoe.

clog noun a wooden shoe, or a shoe with a thick wooden sole. —verb trans., intrans. (clogged, clogging) 1 to obstruct or become obstructed so that movement is difficult or impossible. 2 to perform a clog dance.

clog dance a dance characterized by heavy, stamping steps, performed by people wearing clogs.

cloisonné (kloi,zə-nā') noun decoration for vases, etc., the pattern being formed in wire and filled in with colored enamel.

cloister noun 1 a covered walk built against the wall of a church, college, etc., with arches along its other side. 2 a place of religious retreat. —verb trans. (cloistered, cloistering) to keep (someone) away from the problems of normal life in the world. ► cloistral adj.

clone noun 1 any of a group of genetically identical cells or organisms derived from a single parent cell or organism by asexual reproduction. 2 Comput. a usu. cheaper imitation of an existing computer or software product, produced by a different manufacturer. 3 colloq. a person or thing that looks like a replica of another. —verb trans., intrans. (cloned, cloning) 1 to produce a set of identical cells or organisms from a single parent cell or organism. 2 to produce a replica of. ► clonal adj.

clop noun the hollow sound of a horse's hooves on hard ground. —verb intrans. (clopped, clopping) to walk along making a hollow, hard sound.

close (klōs) adj. 1 near in space or time; at a short distance. 2 a near in relationship or connection. b on amicable terms with (someone). 3 dense or compact. 4 thorough; searching. 5 of a contest, etc. with little difference between entrants. 6 about to happen. 7 similar to the original, or to something else. 8 uncomfortably warm; stuffy. 9 secretive. 10 mean. —adv. in a close manner; closely. —verb trans., intrans. (klōz) (closed, closing) 1 to shut. 2 to block (a road, etc.) so as to prevent its use. 3 of shops, etc. to stop or cause to stop being open to the public for a period of time. 4 of a factory, business, etc. to stop or cause to stop operating permanently. 5 to come or bring to an end; to finish. 6 to join up or come together; to cause the edges, etc., of something to come together. 7 to settle or agree on. 8 of currency, shares, etc. to be worth at the end of a period of trading: Gold closed high today. 9 (close on) to catch up with (someone). —noun 1 an end or conclusion. 2 an enclosed area; a quadrangle. —a close call or shave a narrow or lucky escape.

closed (klōzd) adj. 1 having been shut or blocked. 2 of a community or society with membership restricted to a chosen few. —behind closed doors in private.

closed book a person or subject that one cannot understand.

closed circuit 1 a complete electrical circuit through which current flows when voltage is applied. 2 closed-circuit television.

closed-circuit television (ABBREV. CCTV) a television system serving a limited number of receivers, e.g., within a building, the signal being transmitted by wires.

closed-loop adj. denoting a computer system in which performance is controlled by comparing an amount of output with an expected standard.

closed shop a union shop.

close-fisted (klōs'fĭs'tĭd) adj. colloq. mean; miserly.

close-knit (klōs'nĭt') adj., of a group, community, etc. closely bound together.

closet noun 1 an enclosed space or cabinet, used for storage. 2 a state of complete privacy. —adj. not openly declared; secret. —verb trans. (closeted, closeting) to shut (another or oneself) away in private.

close-up (klōs'əp,) noun 1 a photograph, television shot, etc., taken at close range. 2 a detailed look at, or examination of, something.

closure (klō'zhər) noun 1 the act of closing something, e.g., a business or a transport route. 2 a device for closing or sealing something.

clot *noun* a soft mass, esp. of solidified liquid matter such as blood. —*verb intrans.*, *trans.* (**clotted**, **clotting**) to form into clots.

cloth *noun* **1** woven, knitted, or felted material. **2** a piece of fabric for a special use. **3** (**the cloth**) the clergy.

clothe (klōth) *verb* (*pa t and pa p* **clothed** or **clad**; *pr p* **clothing**) **1** to cover or provide with clothes. **2** to dress.

clothes (klōz, klōthz) *pl. noun* **1** articles of dress for covering the body. ≡ APPAREL, ATTIRE, CLOTHING, RAIMENT, TOGS. **2** bedclothes.

clotheshorse *noun* **1** a hinged frame on which to dry or air clothes indoors. **2** *colloq.* a person who loves clothes and buys a lot of them.

clothesline *noun* a rope suspended usu. outdoors, on which to hang clothes to dry.

clothespin *noun* a small cliplike device for securing clothes to a clothesline.

clothier *noun old use* a person who makes, sells, or deals in clothing.

clothing *noun* articles of dress for covering the body.

cloture (klō'chər) *noun* a parliamentary procedure for cutting short a debate and taking an immediate vote.

cloud *noun* **1** a visible floating mass of small water droplets or ice crystals suspended in the atmosphere above Earth's surface. **2** a visible mass of particles of dust or smoke in the atmosphere. **3** a state of gloom, depression, or suspicion. —*verb intrans.*, *trans.* (**clouded**, **clouding**) **1** to become overcast with clouds. **2** to make or become misty or cloudy. **3** to develop a troubled expression. **4** to make confused. **5** to affect with something discreditable. —**on cloud nine** *colloq.* extremely happy. ▸ **cloudless** *adj.*

cloudburst *noun* a sudden downpour of rain.

cloudy *adj.* (**cloudier**, **cloudiest**) **1** full of clouds; overcast. **2** not clear; milky. **3** confused; muddled. ▸ **cloudily** *adv.* ▸ **cloudiness** *noun*

clout *colloq. noun* **1** a blow. **2** *colloq.* influence or power. —*verb trans.* (**clouted**, **clouting**) to hit.

clove[1] *noun* the strong-smelling dried flower bud of a tropical tree, used as a spice.

clove[2] *noun* one of the sections into which a bulb, esp. of garlic, naturally splits.

clove[3] *verb see* **cleave**[1].

cloven *verb see* **cleave**[1].

cloven hoof the partly split hoof of cattle, sheep or goats, and, in folklore, etc., of the Devil.

clover *noun* a small herbaceous plant with leaves divided into three or four leaflets. —**in clover** *colloq.* in great comfort, luxury, and contentment.

cloverleaf *noun* an interchange at the junction of two or more freeways or highways, the entrance and exit ramps of which form a complex resembling a four-leaf clover.

clown *noun* **1** a comic performer in a circus or pantomime, usu. wearing ridiculous clothes and makeup. **2** someone who behaves comically. **3** *slang* a boor. —*verb intrans.* (**clowned**, **clowning**) to behave ridiculously. ▸ **clownish** *adj.* ▸ **clownishly** *adv.*

cloy *verb intrans.* (**cloyed**, **cloying**) to become distasteful through excess, esp. of sweetness.

club *noun* **1** a stick used as a weapon. **2** *Golf* a stick with a specially shaped head, for driving the ball or putting. **3** an athletic team, often professional. **4 a** a society or association. **b** the place where such a group meets. **5** a nightclub. **6 a** a playing card with a black cloverleaf-shaped symbol on it. **b** (**clubs**) a suit of cards with such symbols on them. —*verb trans.*, *intrans.* (**clubbed**, **clubbing**) **1** to beat or strike with a club. **2** (**club together**) to contribute money jointly for a special purpose.

clubfoot *noun* a physical deformity in which the foot is turned inward.

club sandwich two or three slices of bread with tomato, lettuce, usu. bacon, and dressing, all stacked together in layers.

club soda soda water.

cluck *noun* the sound that a hen makes. —*verb intrans.* (**clucked**, **clucking**) **1** *of a hen* to make clucks. **2** to express disapproval by making a similar sound with the tongue.

clue *noun* something that helps solve a mystery, a crime, a crossword puzzle, etc.

clueless *adj.* completely stupid, incompetent, or ignorant.

clump *noun* a group of, e.g., trees, plants, or people close together. —*verb intrans.*, *trans.* (**clumped**, **clumping**) **1** to walk or move with a heavy tread. **2** to form into clumps. ▸ **clumpiness** *noun* ▸ **clumpy** *adj.*

clumsy *adj.* (**clumsier**, **clumsiest**) **1** unskillful with the hands or ungainly in movement. **2** badly or awkwardly made; unwieldy. **3** embarrassingly inept.

clung *verb see* **cling**.

clunk *noun* the sound of a heavy, esp. metal, object striking something. —*verb intrans.*, *trans.* (**clunked**, **clunking**) to make or cause to make this sound.

clunker *noun colloq.* an utter flop.

clunky *adj.* (**clunkier**, **clunkiest**) heavy, awkward, and clumsy in configuration or movement.

cluster *noun* **1** a small group or gathering. **2** a number of flowers growing together on one stem. —*verb trans.*, *intrans.* (**clustered**, **clustering**) to form into a cluster or clusters.

clutch¹ *verb trans., intrans.* (**clutched, clutching**) 1 to grasp tightly. 2 (**clutch at**) to try to grasp (something). —*noun* 1 a (*usu.* **clutches**) control or power. b a critically tense situation. 2 a a device in a motor vehicle that connects or disconnects two revolving shafts, thereby passing, or preventing the passing of, the driving force from engine to gearbox. b the pedal operating this device. —**clutch at straws** to try anything, however unlikely, in desperation.

clutch² *noun* 1 a number of eggs laid at the same time. 2 a brood of chickens.

clutter *noun* a messy, unsightly accumulation of objects, or the confused, overcrowded state caused by it. —*verb* (**cluttered, cluttering**) (**clutter up**) to overcrowd or make messy with accumulated objects.

Clydesdale (klīdz′dāl,) *noun* a very large, powerful draft horse.

Cm *symbol Chem.* curium.

cm *abbrev.* centimeter.

CNN *abbrev.* Cable News Network.

Co *symbol Chem.* cobalt.

co- *prefix* forming words denoting with, together, jointly: *costar / co-opt / cooperate.*

coach *noun* 1 a closed horse-drawn carriage or a stagecoach. 2 a a trainer of sports people. b a tutor or an instructor. —*verb trans., intrans.* (**coached, coaching**) to train in a sport, etc., or teach privately.

coachman *noun* the driver of a horse-drawn coach.

coagulate (kō-ăg′yə-lāt,) *verb intrans., trans.* (**coagulated, coagulating**) to pass, or cause to pass, from a liquid state to a semisolid one; to curdle or clot. ▸ **coagulant** *noun* ▸ **coagulation** *noun*

coal *noun* 1 a hard, combustible rock consisting mainly of carbon and used as fuel. 2 a piece of this rock.

coalesce *verb intrans.* (**coalesced, coalescing**) to come together so as to form a single mass. ▸ **coalescence** *noun* ▸ **coalescent** *adj.*

coalition *noun* 1 a combination or temporary alliance, e.g., between countries, political parties, factions, or people. 2 a union.

coal tar a thick black liquid obtained as a byproduct during the manufacture of coke.

coarse *adj.* 1 rough or open in texture. 2 indecent; vulgar. 3 lacking refined manners and sensitivity. ▤ CRUDE, GROSS, RAW, UNCOUTH, VULGAR ▤ REFINED. ▸ **coarsely** *adv.* ▸ **coarseness** *noun* ▸ **coarsen** *verb trans., intrans.*

coast *noun* 1 the zone of land that borders on a sea; the seashore. 2 (**the Coast**) the US Pacific Coast. —*verb intrans.* (**coasted, coasting**) 1 to travel downhill, e.g., on a bicycle or in a motor vehicle, using no kind of propelling power. 2 to progress smoothly and satisfactorily without much effort. ▸ **coastal** *adj.*

coaster *noun* 1 a vessel that sails along a coast taking goods to coastal ports. 2 a sled or other device, used for sliding down snowy hills. 3 a small mat or tray placed under a glass, decanter, etc., to protect a table.

coast guard or **Coast Guard** (ABBREV. **C.G.**) the branch of a country's armed forces concerned with coastal defense, rescue, etc.

coastline *noun* the shape of a coast, esp. as seen on a map, or from the sea.

coat *noun* 1 an outer garment typically reaching to the knees and with long sleeves. 2 a jacket. 3 the hair, fur, or wool of an animal. 4 a covering or application of something, e.g., paint, sugar, etc. —*verb trans.* (**coated, coating**) to cover with a layer (of something). ▸ **coating** *noun*

coathanger *noun* a shaped piece of wood, plastic, or metal, with a hook, on which to hang clothes.

coat of arms the heraldic emblem of a family or organization.

coauthor *noun* one of two or more people who have jointly written something. —*verb trans.* (**coauthored, coauthoring**) to write (a book, etc.) with one or more others.

coax (kōks) *verb trans.* (**coaxed, coaxing**) 1 to persuade with flattery, kind words, etc. 2 to get by coaxing: *coaxed a smile out of the grouchy baby.*

coaxial (kō-ăk′sē-əl) *adj.* 1 having or mounted on a common axis. 2 *of a cable* consisting of a conductor in the form of a metal tube surrounding and insulated from a second conductor.

cob *noun* 1 a corncob. 2 a strong horse with short legs. 3 a male swan.

cobalt *noun* 1 *Chem.* (SYMBOL **Co**) a silvery-white metallic element that is commonly used in the form of an alloy, e.g., stainless steel. 2 a a mixture of cobalt oxide and alumina that is used as a bright blue pigment in paints, ceramics, etc. b the color of this compound. *Also called* **cobalt blue.** ▸ **cobaltic** *adj.*

cobble¹ *noun* a cobblestone.

cobble² *verb trans., intrans.* (**cobbled, cobbling**) 1 to mend (shoes). 2 (**cobble together**) to construct or concoct roughly or hastily.

cobbler¹ *noun* a person who mends shoes.

cobbler² *noun* a deep-dish pie of fruit with a thick crust of pastry.

cobblestone *noun* a rounded stone used esp. in earlier times to pave streets.

COBOL or **Cobol** (kō′bôl,) *abbrev.* Common Business Orientated Language.

cobra *noun* a venomous snake found in Africa and Asia.

cobweb *noun* a web formed of fine sticky threads spun by a spider. ▸ **cobwebby** *adj.*

cobweb site *Comput.* a web site that is no longer in use or that has not been updated for a long time.

coca *noun* the dried leaves of a S American shrub, chewed as a stimulant or processed for the extraction of cocaine.

cocaine *noun* an alkaloid drug obtained from the leaves of the coca plant, used recreationally as a stimulant and sometimes medicinally as a local anesthetic.

coccyx (kăk′sĭks) *noun* (*pl.* **coccyges**) a small triangular bone at the base of the spine.

cochineal *noun* a bright red pigment widely used as a food coloring, e.g., in alcoholic drinks.

cochlea (kŏ′klē-ə, kăk′lē-ə) *noun* (*pl.* **cochleae, cochleas**) a hollow, spirally coiled structure in the inner ear. ▸ **cochlear** *adj.*

cock[1] *noun* **1** a male bird, esp. an adult male chicken. **2** a stopcock for controlling the flow of liquid, gas, etc. —*verb trans.*, *intrans.* (**cocked, cocking**) **1** to turn in a particular direction. **2** to draw back the hammer of (a gun).

cock[2] *noun* a small pile of hay, etc.

cockade *noun* a feather or a rosette of ribbon worn on the hat as a badge.

cock-a-hoop *adj. colloq.* jubilant; exultant.

cockamamie *or* **cockamamy** *adj. slang* absurd; crazy; ridiculous.

cock-and-bull story *noun slang* an unlikely story, esp. one used as an excuse or explanation.

cockatoo *noun* a parrot with a large, brightly colored crest on its head.

cockatrice *noun Mythol.* a monster, part cock and part snake.

cockchafer *noun* a large brown beetle of Europe and Asia.

cock-crow *noun* early morning; dawn.

cocked hat a three-cornered hat with upturned brim. —**knock into a cocked hat** *colloq.* to wreck utterly.

cocker *noun* a small, esp. copper-colored, spaniel. *Also called* **cocker spaniel**.

cockerel *noun* an immature rooster.

cockeyed (kăk′īd,) *adj.* **1** crooked; lopsided. **2** senseless; crazy; impractical.

cockfight *noun* a fight between roosters armed with sharp metal spurs, illegal in most US jurisdictions. ▸ **cockfighting** *noun*

cockle *noun* an edible shellfish with a rounded, ribbed, hinged shell in two equal halves. —**warm the cockles of one's heart** *colloq.* to delight and gladden.

cockney *noun* (*pl.* **cockneys**) **1** (*often* **Cockney**) a native of London, esp. of the East End. **2** the dialect used by Cockneys. —*adj.* relating to Cockneys or their dialect.

Literally 'cock's egg', an old word for a misshapen egg which was later applied to an effeminate person, and so to a soft-living city-dweller

cockpit *noun* **1** the compartment for the pilot and crew aboard an aircraft. **2** the driver's seat in a racing car. **3** the part of a small yacht, etc., containing the wheel and tiller. **4** *Hist.* a pit into which cocks were put to fight each other.

cockroach *noun* a large insect with a flattened body, a serious pest in houses.

cocksure *adj.* foolishly overconfident.

cocktail *noun* **1** a mixed drink of spirits and other liquors. **2** an appetizer usu. of seafood.

cocky *adj.* (**cockier, cockiest**) cheekily self-confident. ▸ **cockily** *adv.* ▸ **cockiness** *noun*

cocoa (kŏ′kō) *noun* **1** the seed of the cacao tree, used in the making of chocolate. *Also called* **cocoa bean**. **2** a powder prepared from the seeds of the cacao tree. **3** a drink prepared by mixing this powder with hot milk or water.

cocoa butter a pale yellow fat obtained from cocoa beans, used as a base in the manufacture of chocolate and in cosmetics.

coconut *noun* the large fruit of a tropical palm tree, with a thick fibrous outer husk and white edible flesh.

Based on a Portuguese word meaning 'grimace', because of the resemblance of the three holes on the base of the fruit to a human face

cocoon *noun* **1** the protective silky covering that many animals, e.g., spiders, earthworms, spin around their eggs; a similar covering that a larva spins around itself before it develops into a pupa. **2** *slang* a protective wall. —*verb trans., intrans.* (**cocooned, cocooning**) to wrap up as if in a cocoon.

cocotte (kô-kôt′) *noun* a prostitute.

C.O.D. *or* **c.o.d.** *abbrev.* cash on delivery.

cod *noun* (*pl.* **cod, cods**) a large, edible, soft-finned fish.

coda (kŏd′ə) *noun* a passage added at the end of a musical movement or piece.

coddle *verb trans.* (**coddled, coddling**) **1** to cook (eggs) gently in hot, rather than boiling, water. **2** to pamper or overprotect.

code *noun* **1** a system of words, letters, or symbols, used in place of those really intended, for secrecy's or brevity's sake. **2** a set of signals for sending messages, etc. **3** a a set of symbols that represent numbers, letters, etc., in binary form so that information can be stored or exchanged between different computer systems. **b** the set of written instructions or statements that make up a computer program. **4** a set of principles of behavior or dress. **5** a systematically organized set of laws. —*verb trans.* (**coded, coding**) **1** to put (a message, etc.) into a code; to encode. **2** *Comput.* to generate a set of written instructions or statements that make up a program.

codeine (kō′dēn) *noun* a morphine derivative that relieves mild to moderate pain.

codex *noun* (*pl.* **codices**) an ancient manuscript bound in book form.

codfish *noun* a cod.

codger *noun colloq.* a man, esp. an old and strange man.

codicil (kăd′ə-sĭl) *noun* a short addition to a will, added after the will has been written.

codify *verb trans.* (**codified, codifying, codifies**) to arrange (laws, etc.) into a systematic code. ▸ **codification** *noun*

cod-liver oil a medicinal oil obtained from the liver of the cod and related fish, rich in vitamins A and D.

codpiece *noun Hist.* a flap of material attached to a man's breeches, covering his genitals.

coed *or* **co-ed** (kō′ĕd,) *noun colloq.* a woman student at a coeducational institution. —*adj.* coeducational.

coeducation *noun* the education of students of both sexes in the same school or college. ▸ **coeducational** *adj.*

coefficient *noun* in an algebraic expression, a number placed before and multiplying another quantity.

coeliac *adj. same as* **celiac.**

coenobite *noun same as* **cenobite.**

coequal *adj.* equal, e.g., in power, rank, or magnitude. —*noun* one of two or more coequal people or things. ▸ **coequally** *adv.*

coerce (kō-ûrs′) *verb trans.* (**coerced, coercing**) to force or compel, using threats, etc. ▸ **coercion** *noun* ▸ **coercive** *adj.*

coeval (kō-ē′vəl) *adj. formal* of the same age or period of time.

coexist *verb intrans.* (**coexisted, coexisting**) to exist together or simultaneously. ▸ **coexistence** *noun* ▸ **coexistent** *adj.*

coextensive *adj.* covering the same distance or time.

coffee *noun* **1** an evergreen tree or shrub with red fleshy fruits or its seeds, roasted whole or ground to a powder. **2** a drink prepared from this. **3** a mid-brown color.

coffee bean a seed of the coffee plant.

coffeehouse *noun* an establishment where coffee and other light refreshments are served, usu. also functioning as a place for people to socialize.

coffee mill a device for grinding coffee beans.

coffee table a long, narrow, low table, typically positioned in front of a sofa.

coffee-table book a large, expensive, highly illustrated book.

coffer *noun* **1** a large chest for holding valuables. **2** (**coffers**) a treasury or supply of funds.

cofferdam *noun* a caisson used for underwater ship or pier repair.

coffin *noun* a box in which to bury a corpse.

cog *noun* one of a series of teeth on the edge of a wheel that engage with another series of teeth to bring about motion.

cogeneration *noun* an industrial process where waste energy is used to fuel another process.

cogent *adj.* strong; persuasive; convincing. ▸ **cogency** *noun* ▸ **cogently** *adv.*

cogitate *verb intrans.* (**cogitated, cogitating**) to think deeply; to ponder. ▸ **cogitation** *noun* ▸ **cogitative** *adj.*

cognac *noun* a high-quality brandy from *Cognac* in SW France.

cognate *adj.* related; akin. —*noun* something related to another.

cognition *noun* the combination of mental activities that enable a person to experience and learn about his or her environment. ▸ **cognitive** *adj.* ▸ **cognitively** *adv.*

cognizance *noun* **1** knowledge; understanding; perception; awareness. **2** the range or scope of one's awareness or knowledge. ▸ **cognizant** *adj.*

cognomen *noun* **1** a Roman's third name, often an epithet. **2** a nickname or surname.

cognoscenti (kăg,nə-shĕnt′ē, kän,yə-) *pl. noun* knowledgeable or refined people; connoisseurs.

cogwheel *noun* a wheel with cogs.

cohabit *verb intrans.* (**cohabited, cohabiting**) to live together as, or as if, spouses. ▸ **cohabitation** *noun* ▸ **cohabiter** *noun*

cohere *verb intrans.* (**cohered, cohering**) **1** to stick together. **2** to have a clear, logical connection or development; to be consistent. ▸ **coherence** *noun* ▸ **coherent** *adj.* ▸ **coherently** *adv.*

cohesion *noun* **1** the tendency to stick together. **2** the force with which the particles of a liquid or solid stick together. *See also* **adhesion.** ▸ **cohesive** *adj.*

cohort *noun* **1** in the ancient Roman army, one of the 10 divisions of a legion. **2** a band of warriors. **3** a follower, supporter, or companion.

> *Usage* The word *cohort* meaning a follower, supporter, or companion, once frowned on in this sense, has gained such widespread currency in the prose of the best writers that it can no longer be questioned.

cohost *noun* one of two or more hosts, e.g., on a broadcast. —*verb trans.* (**cohosted, cohosting**) to act as a cohost.

coif (koif, kwäf) *noun* a close-fitting cap worn esp. by women in medieval times or by nuns under a veil. —*verb trans.* (kwäf) (**coiffed, coiffing**) to dress (the hair).

coiffeur (kwä-fər′) *noun* a male hairdresser.

coiffeuse (kwä-fy o͞oz′) *noun* a female hairdresser.

coiffure (kwä-fy o͞or′) *noun* a hairstyle.

coil *verb trans., intrans.* (**coiled, coiling**) to wind around and around in loops to form rings or a spiral. —*noun* **1** something looped into rings or a spiral. **2** a single loop in such an arrangement. **3** a wound length of wire for conducting electricity.

coin *noun* a small metal disk stamped for use as money. —*verb trans.* (**coined, coining**) **1** to manufacture (coins) from metal; to make (metal) into coins. **2** to invent (a new word or phrase).

coinage *noun* **1** the process of coining. **2** coins. **3** a newly invented word or phrase. **4** the official currency of a country.

coincide *verb intrans.* (**coincided, coinciding**) **1** to happen at the same time. **2** to be the same; to agree. **3** to occupy the same position.

coincidence *noun* **1** the occurrence of events together or in sequence in a startling way, without any causal connection. **2** the fact of being the same.

coincident *adj.* **1** coinciding in space or time. **2** in agreement. ▸ **coincidental** *adj.* ▸ **coincidentally** *adv.*

coir *noun* fiber from coconut shells, used for making ropes, matting, etc.

coition *or* **coitus** *noun* sexual intercourse.

coke[1] *noun* the solid fuel that remains after gases have been extracted from coal.

coke[2] *noun colloq.* cocaine.

Col. *abbrev.* Colonel.

col *noun* a pass between two adjacent mountain peaks.

col- *prefix* forming words denoting together, joint, jointly and used before *l: collateral*.

cola *noun* **1** (**kola**) an evergreen tree whose seeds (cola nuts) contain caffeine. **2** a soft drink flavored with the extract obtained from cola seeds.

colander *noun* a perforated bowl in which to drain the water from cooked vegetables, etc.

cold *adj.* **1** low in temperature. **2** lower in temperature than is normal, comfortable, or pleasant. **3** cooked, but not eaten hot. **4** unfriendly. **5** unenthusiastic. **6** *of colors* not producing a feeling of warmth. **7** *colloq.* far from an answer, hidden object, etc. **8** *of a trail or scent* too old to follow; not fresh. —*adv.* without preparation or rehearsal: *gave the speech cold.* —*noun* **1** lack of heat or warmth; cold weather. **2** a common

contagious viral infection that causes inflammation of the mucous membranes of the nose, throat, and bronchial tubes. —**catch cold** to become ill with a cold. **the cold shoulder** *colloq.* a rebuff. **get cold feet** *colloq.* to lose courage. **in cold blood** deliberately and unemotionally. ▸ **coldly** *adv.* ▸ **coldness** *noun*

cold-blooded *adj.* **1** *of an animal* having a body temperature that varies with the temperature of the surrounding environment. *Also called* **poikilothermic**. **2** lacking emotion; callous and often cruel. ▸ **cold-bloodedly** *adv.* ▸ **cold-bloodedness** *noun*

cold boot *Comput.* a reboot activated by completely shutting off a computer and restarting it from the power source.

cold calling a marketing technique in which a sales representative telephones potential customers without advance warning.

cold cash *colloq.* money at hand, as opposed to checks or credit cards.

cold comfort very limited comfort or sympathy, if that.

cold cream face cream for cleaning the skin and keeping it soft.

cold duck a drink made of sparkling burgundy and champagne.

cold fish *colloq.* an unresponsive, aloof, cold person.

cold frame a glass-covered frame for protecting young plants growing outdoors.

cold front the edge of a cold air mass pushing against a warm air mass.

cold-hearted *adj.* unkind. ▸ **cold-heartedly** *adv.* ▸ **cold-heartedness** *noun*

cold sore a patch of small blisterlike spots around or near the mouth.

cold storage 1 the storage of food, etc., under refrigeration. **2** the state of being put aside or saved until another time; postponement or abeyance.

cold sweat the condition of or as if sweating as a result of fear or nervousness.

cold turkey *slang* the acute discomfort felt by someone withdrawing from an addictive drug.

cold war *or* **Cold War** a state of hostility and antagonism, e.g., between nations or parties without actual warfare or overt hostilities. ▸ **cold warrior** *noun*

cole *noun* kale.

coleslaw *noun* a salad made with finely-cut raw cabbage, carrots, and mayonnaise.

colic *noun* severe abdominal pain. ▸ **colicky** *adj.*

coliseum *noun* a large stadium or amphitheater for sports events or other entertainments.

colitis *noun* inflammation of the lining of the large intestine.

collaborate *verb intrans.* (**collaborated, collaborating**) **1** to work together with another or others. **2** to cooperate with or otherwise help an enemy occupying one's country. ▸ **collaboration** *noun* ▸ **collaborative** *adj.* ▸ **collaboratively** *adv.* ▸ **collaborator** *noun*

collage (kə-läzh′, kô-) *noun* **1** a design or picture made up of pieces of paper or cloth, or parts of photographs, etc., attached to a background surface. **2** the art of producing such works.

collagen (käl′ə-jən) *noun* a tough fibrous protein that is the main constituent of connective tissue found in skin, bones, etc.

collapse *verb intrans., trans.* (**collapsed, collapsing**) **1** to fall, give way, or cave in. **2** to drop unconscious, exhausted, or helpless; to faint. **3** to break down emotionally. **4** to fail suddenly. **5** to fold up compactly. —*noun* the process of collapsing. ▸ **collapsible** *adj.* ▸ **collapsibility** *noun*

collar *noun* **1** a neck of a garment or a band around it. **2** a band worn around the neck by a dog, etc., or by a horse to ease the strain of pulling a vehicle.**3** *colloq.* an arrest. —*verb trans.* (**collared, collaring**) **1** to seize by the collar. **2** *colloq.* to catch or capture. ▸ **collarless** *adj.*

collarbone *noun same as* **clavicle.**

collate *verb trans.* (**collated, collating**) **1** to examine and compare (texts, evidence, etc.) electronically or manually. **2** to check and arrange in order (sheets of paper, pages of a book, etc.), ready for fastening together. ▸ **collator** *noun*

collateral *adj.* **1** descended from a common ancestor, but through a different branch of the family. **2** secondary in importance; additional or subsidiary. —*noun* assets offered to a creditor as security for a loan. ▸ **collaterally** *adv.*

collation *noun* **1** the act of collating. **2** a light meal.

colleague *noun* a fellow worker, esp. in a profession.

collect (kə-lĕkt′) *verb trans., intrans.* **1** to bring or come together; to gather or accumulate. **2** to accumulate (antiques, books, stamps, etc.) as a hobby or for study, etc. **3** to call for, fetch, or pick up. **4** to get (e.g., money owed or voluntary contributions) from people. **5** to calm or control (oneself). —*adj. of a telephone call* paid for by the person receiving it. —*adv. of the manner of placing a telephone call* reversing the charges. (käl′ĕkt) —*noun Christianity* (*usu.* **the Collect**) a short form of prayer used in the Episcopal and Roman Catholic Churches. ▸ **collector** *noun* ▸ **collection** *noun*

collected *adj.* **1** of a *writer's works* published

together in a single volume or a uniform set of volumes. **2** calm; self-possessed. ▸ **collectedly** *adv.* ▸ **collectedness** *noun·*

collectible *or* **collectable** *noun* something worthy of collecting. *Also called* **collector's item.**

collective *adj.* of, belonging to, or involving all the members of a group. —*noun* a business operation owned and controlled by its workers. ▸ **collectively** *adv.*

collective bargaining talks between a labor union and a company's management to settle questions of pay, hours of work, and working conditions.

collective noun *Gram.* a noun that stands for a group of people, animals, etc., and that usu. takes a singular verb.

collectivism *noun* the socialist economic theory that industry should be state owned and financed.

collectivize *verb trans.* (**collectivized, collectivizing**) to group (farms, factories, etc.) into larger units and bring under state control and ownership. ▸ **collectivization** *noun*

colleen *noun Irish* a girl.

college *noun* **1 a** an institution of higher education. **b** one of a number of self-governing establishments that make up certain universities. **c** the staff and students of a college. **2** a body of people with particular duties and rights.

collegiate *adj.* **1** relating to or suitable for a college, or college staff or students. **2** *of a university* comprised of several colleges. **3** *of a group of churches* allied, esp. in sharing the same pastors.

collide *verb intrans.* (**collided, colliding**) **1** to crash together, or crash into someone or something. **2** to disagree or clash.

collie *noun* a long-haired black- or tan-and-white dog used for herding sheep, etc.

collier (käl′yər) *noun* **1** a coal miner. **2** a ship that transports coal.

colliery *noun* (*pl.* **collieries**) a coal mine with its buildings.

collinear *adj.* lying on the same straight line.

collision *noun* **1** an act, or the process or result of colliding; a crash. **2** a disagreement or conflict.

collocate *verb intrans.* (**collocated, collocating**) **1** to place side by side or arrange in a particular order. **2** *Gram. of a word* to occur frequently alongside another word. ▸ **collocation** *noun*

colloquial *adj.*, relating or appropriate to everyday speech. ▸ **colloquialism** *noun* ▸ **colloquially** *adv.*

colloquium *noun* (*pl.* **colloquiums, colloquia**) an academic conference; a seminar.

colloquy (kăl'ə-kwē) *noun* (*pl.* **colloquies**) *formal* **1** a conversation; talk. **2** a debate or conference.

collude *verb intrans.* to conspire together, usu. with illegal or fraudulent intent. ▸ **collusion** *noun* ▸ **collusive** *adj.*

cologne *noun* eau de cologne.

colon¹ (kō'lən) *noun* the large intestine. ▸ **colonic** *adj.*

colon² *noun* a punctuation mark (:), used to introduce a list, an example, or an explanation.

colonel (kərn'l) *noun* a military officer ranking below a brigadier general and above a lieutenant colonel. ▸ **colonelcy** *noun*

colonial *adj.* **1** relating to, belonging to, or living in a colony. **2** possessing colonies. —*noun* an inhabitant of a colony. ▸ **colonialism** *noun* ▸ **colonialist** *noun* ▸ **colonially** *adv.*

colonize *verb trans. intrans.* (**colonized, colonizing**) **1** to establish a colony in (an area or country). **2** to settle (people) in a colony. ▸ **colonization** *noun*

colonnade *noun* a row of columns.

colony *noun* (*pl.* **colonies**) **1** a settlement abroad founded and controlled by the founding country; the settlers living there; the territory they occupy. **2** a group of the same nationality or occupation forming a distinctive community within a city, etc. **3** a group of animals or plants of the same species living together in close proximity.

colophon *noun* a publisher's ornamental mark or device.

color *noun* **1** a property that surfaces have when light falls on them, arising from their capacity to reflect or absorb light waves. **2** any of these variations or colors, often with the addition of black and white. **3** a substance, esp. paint, that conveys or applies a hue. **4** pinkness of the face or cheeks. **5** lively or convincing detail. **6** (**colors**) the flag of a nation, etc. **7** (**colors**) ribbons or other devices that are worn to represent, e.g., a college, team, etc. —*verb trans.* (**colored, coloring**) **1** to put color on; to paint or dye. **2** (*also* **color in**) to fill in (an outlined area or a black-and-white picture) with color. **3** to influence. **4** to blush.

colorant *noun* a substance used for coloring.

coloration *noun* arrangement or combination of colors; coloring.

coloratura *noun* **1** an elaborate and intricate passage or style in singing. **2** a soprano specializing in such singing.

colorblind *adj.* unable to distinguish between certain colors. ▸ **colorblindness** *noun*

color-coded *adj.* marked by a system of colors for the purposes of identification or classification, e.g., in electrical wiring.

colored *adj.* **1** having color, or a specified color. **2** (*often* **Colored**) *offensive* belonging to a dark-skinned people; African-American. **3** biased.

colorfast *adj.* dyed with colors that will not run when washed.

colorful *adj.* **1** full of, esp. bright, color. **2** full of interest or character; lively and vivid. ▸ **colorfully** *adv.*

coloring *noun* **1** a substance used to give color, e.g., to food. **2** arrangement or combination of color. **3** facial complexion, esp. in combination with eye and hair color.

colorize *verb trans.* (**colorized, colorizing**) to add color to (a movie film made in black and white), usu. with the aid of a computer. ▸ **colorization** *noun*

colorless *adj.* **1** lacking color. **2** uninteresting; dull; lifeless. **3** pale. ▸ **colorlessly** *adv.*

colossal *adj.* of exceedingly or excessively large size. ▸ **colossally** *adv.*

colossus (kə-läs'əs) *noun* (*pl.* **colossi, colossuses**) **1** a gigantic statue. **2** someone or something of great importance.

colostomy *noun* (*pl.* **colostomies**) an operation to create an artificial opening in the abdomen through which the colon can be emptied.

colostrum *noun* a yellowish milky fluid secreted by the mammary glands in mammals immediately before and after giving birth.

colt *noun* a young male horse.

coltish *adj.* youthfully awkward in movement or behavior. ▸ **coltishly** *adv.*

columbine (kăl'əm-bīn,) *noun* a wildflower with spurred flowers. *Also called* **aquilegia**.

columbium *noun old use* niobium.

column *noun* **1** *in classical architecture* a cylindrical, sometimes square pillar with a base and capital. **2** a long, more or less cylindrical mass or structure shaped similar to this. **3** a vertical row of numbers. **4** a vertical strip of print on a newspaper or magazine page, etc. **5** a regular section in a newspaper or magazine, concerned with a particular topic, or by a regular writer. **6** a troop of soldiers or vehicles standing or moving a few abreast. ▸ **columnar** (kə-ləm'nər) *adj.*

columnist (kăl'əm-nĭst) *noun* a person who writes a regular section in a newspaper.

com- *see* **con-**.

coma *noun* a prolonged state of deep unconsciousness, caused by brain damage, infection, etc.

comatose *adj.* **1** in a coma. **2** *colloq.* in a deep sleep.

comb *noun* **1** a toothed device for disentangling and arranging the hair. **2** a toothed tool for disentangling and cleaning strands of wool or cotton. **3** a honeycomb. **4** the fleshy crest on the head of a male chicken or other male bird. —*verb trans.* (**combed, combing**) **1** to arrange, smooth, or clean with a comb. **2** to search (a place) thoroughly.

combat *noun* a struggle or contest. —*verb trans.* (**combated** *or* **combatted, combating** *or* **combatting**) to fight against; to oppose. —*adj.* of, relating to, or intended for combat. ▸ **combatant** *noun, adj.*

combination *noun* **1** the process of combining or the state of being combined. **2** two or more things, people, etc., combined; the resulting mixture or union. **3** a set of numbers or letters for opening a keyless lock.

combine —*verb trans., intrans.* (**combined, combining**) **1** to join together; to unite. **2** to possess (two contrasting qualities, etc.); to manage or achieve (two different things) at the same time. —*noun* **1** a group of people or businesses associated for a common purpose. **2** *colloq.* a combine harvester. ▸ **combinatorial** *adj.*

combine harvester a machine that can both reap and thresh crops.

combining form *noun* a word form that occurs in combinations or compounds.

combo *noun* (*pl.* **combos**) *colloq.* **1** a small jazz dance band. **2** a combination of two or more things: *I'll have the crab and shrimp combo.*

combustion *noun* the process of catching fire and burning. ▸ **combustible** *adj.*

come *verb intrans.* (*pa t* **came**; *pa p* **come**; *pr p* **coming**) **1** to move toward or approach. **2** to reach. **3** to total. **4** (**come from**) to have as a source or place of origin. **5** to happen. **6** to become or to turn out. —*prep.* when (a particular time) arrives: *Come next Tuesday I'll be free.* —*interj.* used to reassure or admonish: *Oh, come now, don't exaggerate!* —**come across 1** to make a certain impression. **2** to meet or discover. **come around 1** to regain consciousness. **2** to change one's opinion. **come off 1** to succeed. **2** to take place. **come over 1** to change one's opinion or side. **2** to make a certain impression. **3** to affect them. **come through** to survive. **come to** to regain consciousness.

comeback *noun* **1** a return after a period of retirement, obscurity, etc. **2** a retort.

comedian *noun* an entertainer who writes or tells jokes, performs comic sketches, etc.

comedy *noun* (*pl.* **comedies**) **1** a light, amusing play, movie, etc. **2** light, amusing drama. **3** collectively funny incidents or situations.

comely *adj.* (**comelier, comeliest**) wholesomely attractive. ▸ **comeliness** *noun*

come-on *noun colloq.* sexual encouragement: *give someone the come-on.*

comestible (kə-mĕs′tə-bəl) *noun* (*usu. in pl.*) something to eat.

comet *noun* a body with a frozen nucleus and tail-like trail, that travels around the Sun.

comeuppance *noun colloq.* a well-deserved punishment or retribution.

comfit *noun* candy composed of a sugar-coated nut or fruit.

comfort *noun* **1** a state of contentedness or well-being. **2** relief from suffering or consolation in grief. **3** a person who provides relief or consolation. **4** (*usu.* **comforts**) something that makes for ease and physical well-being. —*verb trans.* (**comforted, comforting**) to console or soothe.

comfortable *adj.* **1** being in a state of physical well-being; at ease. **2** providing comfort. **3** *colloq.* financially secure. **4** in a stable, generally pain-free condition. **5** quite large: *won by a comfortable margin.* ▸ **comfortably** *adv.*.

comforter *noun* **1** a person who comforts. **2** a warm scarf. **3** a quilt.

comfort station a public toilet, esp. one in a park or along an interstate highway.

comfrey *noun* a bristly plant with bell-shaped blue flowers, formerly used medicinally. *Also called* **healing herb.**

comfy *adj.* (**comfier, comfiest**) *colloq.* comfortable.

comic *adj.* **1** relating to comedy; intended to amuse. **2** funny. —*noun* **1** a comedian. **2** a paper or magazine that includes strip cartoons, illustrated stories, etc. *Also called* **comic book.** ▸ **comical** *adj.* ▸ **comically** *adv.*

comic opera a lighthearted opera with spoken dialogue as well as singing.

comic strip a brief story or episode told through a short series of pictures, in a newspaper, etc.

coming *noun* an arrival; an approach. —*adj.* approaching: *in the coming months.* —**comings and goings** *colloq.* bustle.

comity *noun* civility; courtesy, esp. between nations.

comma *noun* a punctuation mark (,) indicating a slight pause or break.

command *verb trans., intrans.* (**commanded, commanding**) **1** to order (another or others) formally or to engage in giving orders. **2** to have authority over. **3** to deserve or be entitled to. **4** to look down over. —*noun* **1** an order. **2** control; charge: *second in command.* **3** knowledge of and ability to use something. **4** a military unit, or a district, under a specified person's command. **5** a specialized section of an army, air force, etc. **6** a group of high-ranking army officers, etc. **7** an instruction to a computer to carry out an operation.

commandant (käm'ən-dănt, -dänt,) *noun* a commanding officer, e.g., of a prisoner-of-war camp, a military training installation, etc.

commandeer (käm,ən-dīr') *verb trans.* (**commandeered, commandeering**) **1** to seize (property) for military use in wartime, etc. **2** to seize without justification.

commander *noun* **1** a person who commands. **2** in the US Navy and Coast Guard, an officer ranking below captain and above lieutenant commander. **3** a high-ranking police or fire department officer.

commander-in-chief *noun* (*pl.* **commanders-in-chief**) the officer in supreme command of a nation's forces or of a coalition of such forces.

commanding *adj.* **1** powerful; leading; controlling. **2** in charge. **3** inspiring respect or awe. **4** giving good views all around.

commandment *noun* **1** (**Commandment**) a divine command. **2** a formal or stern edict.

command module the self-contained unit in a spacecraft from which operations are directed.

commando *noun* (*pl.* **commandos, commandoes**) a member of a unit of military personnel specially trained to carry out dangerous and difficult attacks or raids.

command post a temporary military headquarters.

commemorate *verb trans.* (**commemorated, commemorating**) **1** to honor the memory of (a person or event) with a ceremony, etc. **2** to be a memorial to. ▶ **commemoration** *noun* ▶ **commemorative** *adj.*

commence *verb trans., intrans.* (**commenced, commencing**) to begin.

commencement *noun* **1** a beginning. **2** a graduation ceremony.

commend *verb trans.* (**commended, commending**) **1** to praise. **2** to entrust (someone or something) to someone. **3** to recommend. ▶ **commendable** *adj.* ▶ **commendably** *adv.* ▶ **commendatory** *adj.*

commendation *noun* **1** praise; approval. **2** an award or honor.

commensurable *adj.* (*often* **commensurable with** *or* **to** (**something**) **1** having a common factor. **2** measurable by a common standard.

commensurate *adj.* (**commensurate with**) **1** in proportion to; appropriate to. **2** equal to in extent, quantity, etc. ▶ **commensurately** *adv.*

comment (käm'ĕnt,) *noun* **1** a remark or observation. **2** talk, discussion, or gossip. —*verb trans., intrans.* (**commented, commenting**) to make a passing remark or give an observation.

commentary *noun* (*pl.* **commentaries**) **1** a continuous, esp. broadcast, report on an event, match, etc., as it actually takes place. **2** an explanation.

commentate *verb intrans.* (**commentated, commentating**) *colloq.* to give a running commentary.

> *Usage* This back-formation of *commentator* has never gained widespread approval among linguistic conservatives; those writers wanting to avoid criticism would be best advised to avoid use of it in formal prose.

commentator *noun* **1** a broadcaster giving a commentary on a match, event, etc. **2** a writer of a textual commentary.

commerce *noun* **1** large scale buying and selling of commodities and services. **2** social or intellectual dealings or communication.

commercial *adj.* **1** relating to, engaged in, or used for commerce. **2** having profit as the chief aim. **3** paid for by advertising. —*noun* a radio or television advertisement. ▶ **commerciality** *noun* ▶ **commercially** *adv.*

commercialism *noun* **1** commercial attitudes and aims. **2** strong emphasis on making a profit.

commercialize *verb trans.* (**commercialized, commercializing**) **1** to exploit for profit. **2** to make commercial. ▶ **commercialization** *noun*

commiserate (kə-mĭz'ə-rāt,) *verb intrans.* (**commiserated, commiserating**) to express sympathy for. ▶ **commiseration** *noun*

commissar *noun* the head of a former Soviet government department.

commissariat *noun* **1** a department in an army responsible for food supplies. **2** a government department in the former Soviet Union until the year 1946.

commissary *noun* (*pl.* **commissaries**) **1** a supermarket on a military installation that sells groceries, etc. **2** a canteen serving a movie studio, etc.

commission *noun* **1** a request to perform a task or duty; the authority to perform it; the task or duty. **2** a government document conferring the rank of a commissioned officer in the armed forces. **3** an order for a piece of work, esp. a work of art. **4** a board or committee entrusted with a particular task. **5** a fee or percentage given to an agent arranging a sale. **6** the act of committing, e.g., a crime. —*verb trans.* (**commissioned, commissioning**) **1** to give a commission or authority to. **2** to grant commissioned-officer rank to. **3** to request (someone) to do something. **4** to place an order for (a work of art, etc.). **5** to prepare (a ship) for active service. —**out of commission** not in use.

commissioned officer a military officer who holds a commission. *See also* **noncommissioned officer.**

commissioner *noun* **1** a representative of the government in a district, department, etc. **2** a member of a commission. ‣ **commissionership** *noun*

commit *verb trans., intrans.* (**committed**, **committing**) **1** to carry out (a crime, etc.). **2** to have (someone) put in prison or a psychiatric hospital, etc. **3 a** to promise or engage (esp. oneself) for some undertaking. **b** to obligate (oneself) totally. **4** to dedicate (oneself) to a cause, etc. **5** to entrust or give, e.g., facts, to memory or thought to paper.

commitment *noun* **1** the act of committing. **2** dedication or devotion; strong conviction. **3** an undertaking or responsibility.

committal *noun* the act of committing someone to a prison or psychiatric hospital, etc.

committee *noun* a group of people selected to undertake administrative work, an investigation, inquiry, etc.

commode *noun* **1** a chest of drawers. **2 a** a toilet. **b** a chair with a hinged seat covering a chamber pot.

commodious *adj.* comfortably spacious. ‣ **commodiousness** *noun*

commodity (kə-mäd′ət-ē) *noun* (*pl.* **commodities**) **1** something bought and sold, esp. a manufactured product or raw material. **2** a useful thing.

commodore (käm′ə-dôr,) *noun* a US Navy rank that is above captain and below rear admiral.

common *adj.* **1** often met with; familiar. **2** shared by two or more people, things, etc. **3** of an expected standard. **4** widespread. **5** lacking taste or refinement; vulgar. **6** ordinary —*noun* **1** a piece of land that is publicly owned or available for public use. **2** (**commons**) a college or university dinnig hall, or the food served there. **3** (**the Commons**) (*sing., pl.*) the House of Commons in Great Britain. —**in common** *of interests, etc.* shared. ‣ **commonly** *adv.* ‣ **commonness** *noun*

common denominator 1 a multiple of each of the denominators of two or more fractions. *See also* **lowest common denominator**. **2** something that enables comparison, agreement, etc., between people or things.

commoner *noun* a person who is not a member of the nobility.

common fraction a fraction expressed as one number above another, rather than in decimal form. *Also called* **vulgar fraction**. *See also* **decimal fraction**.

common ground an area of agreement between people, as a starting point for discussion.

common law law based on custom and judicial decisions, as distinct from written statutes.

common-law *adj.* denoting a relationship of two people living together as spouses but not legally married.

Common Market the European Community.

common *noun* a noun that is not a proper name. *See also* **proper noun**:

commonplace *adj.* **1** ordinary; everyday. **2** lacking individuality; trite or unoriginal. —*noun* **1** a trite comment; a cliché. **2** an everyday occurrence.

common sense sound judgement in practical matters. ‣ **commonsense** *or* **commonsensical** *adj.*

common stock ordinary shares in a corporation.

commonwealth *noun* **1** a country or state. **2** an association of states that have joined together for their common good.

commotion *noun* **1** a disturbance or tumult. **2** noisy confusion; an uproar or a din.

communal (kə-myōōn′l) *adj.* **1** relating to, or belonging to, a community. **2** owned in common; shared. ‣ **communally** *adv.*

commune[1] (käm′yōōn, käm-yōōn′) *noun* a number of unrelated families and individuals living as a mutually supportive community. **2** (käm′yōōn) a local administrative unit in some European countries.

commune[2] (käm-yōōn′) *verb intrans.* (**communed**, **communing**) **1** to communicate intimately or confidentially. **2** to get close to or relate spiritually to (e.g., nature).

communicable *adj.* **1** capable of being communicated. **2** infectious or contagious.

communicant *noun* **1** a person who receives Communion. **2** an informant.

communicate *verb trans., intrans.* (**communicated**, **communicating**) **1** to impart (information, ideas, etc.); to get in touch. **2** to pass on or transmit (a disease, feeling, etc.). **3** to understand someone; to have a comfortable social relationship. **4** *of rooms, etc.* to be connected.

communication *noun* **1** the exchanging or imparting of ideas and information, etc. **2** a piece of information, a letter, or a message. **3** (**communications**) the systems involved in transmission of information, etc., esp. by electronic means or radio waves. **4** (**communications**) the science and activity of transmitting information, etc.

communications satellite an artificial satellite that relays radio, television, and telephone signals.

communicative *adj.* **1** sociable; talkative. **2** relating to communication. ‣ **communicatively** *adv.*

communion *noun* **1** the sharing of thoughts or feelings. **2** (**Communion**) a sacrament in the Christian Church during which bread and wine are taken as symbols of Christ's body and blood; the consecrated bread and wine.

communiqué (kə-myoō,nǐ-kā') *noun* an official bulletin or announcement.

communism *noun* a political theory advocating that land, factories, etc. should be collectively owned and controlled by the people. ▸ **communistic** *adj.*

communist *noun* **1** a supporter of or believer in communism. **2** (*often* **Communist**) a member of a communist political party. —*adj.* **1** relating to communism. **2** believing in or favoring communism.

community *noun* (*pl.* **communities**) **1** the group of people living in a particular locality. **2** a group of people bonded together by a common religion, nationality, or occupation. **3** the fact of being shared or common: *a community of interests.*

commute *verb intrans., trans.* (**commuted, commuting**) **1** to travel regularly between home and work. **2** to reduce (a criminal sentence). ▸ **commutable** *adj.* ▸ **commutation** *noun* ▸ **commuter** *noun*

comp *noun colloq.* a commercial item, e.g. a ticket, etc. given to a person free of charge.

compact¹ (kəm-păkt') *adj.* **1** firm and dense in form or texture. **2** small, but with all essentials neatly contained. **3** neatly concise. —*verb trans.* (**compacted, compacting**) to compress. (kăm'păkt,) —*noun* **1** a small case for women's face powder, usu. including a mirror. **2** an automobile bigger than a subcompact but smaller than an intermediate. ▸ **compaction** *noun* ▸ **compactly** *adv.* ▸ **compactness** *noun*

compact² (kăm'păkt,) *noun* a contract or agreement.

compact disk *or* **compact disc** (kăm,-păkt,dĭsk') (ABBREV. **CD**) a disk that is used to store and access digital data, mainly recorded music, but also computer data.

compact disk interactive (ABBREV. **CD-I**) a type of CD-ROM that responds intelligently to instructions given by the user, and is used in conjunction with a computerized reader.

compact disk read-only memory (ABBREV. **CD-ROM**) a facility that allows large amounts of data stored on compact disk to be read (but not altered) on a visual display unit by passing a low-power laser beam over the disk.

compactor *or* **compacter** *noun* a device that compresses garbage into small bundles for easy disposal.

companion *noun* **1** a friend or frequent associate. **2** one who accompanies another on a journey. **3** a person paid to live or travel with, and be company for, another. **4** a book of advice; a handbook or guide. **5** one of a pair of matching objects. ▸ **companionship** *noun*

companionable *adj.* friendly; sociable. ▸ **companionably** *adv.*

companionway *noun* a staircase between decks on a vessel.

company *noun* (*pl.* **companies**) **1** another person or other people e.g. guests, friends or associates. **2** a business organization. **3** a troupe of actors or entertainers. **4** a subdivision of a battalion or regiment. **5** a ship's crew. —**be in good company** to be not the only one in a situation. **in company with** together with; along with. **part company** to separate.

comparable *adj.* **1** able to be, or worthy of being compared. **2** similar. ▸ **comparably** *adv.*

comparative (kəm-păr'ət-ĭv) *adj.* **1** judged by comparison; as compared with others. **2** as observed by comparing one another: *their comparative strengths.* **3** of adjectives and adverbs in the form denoting a greater degree of the quality in question. —*noun* the comparative form of a word. ▸ **comparatively** *adv.*

compare *verb trans., intrans.* (**compared, comparing**) **1** to examine (people or things of the same kind) to see their differences. **2** (**compare with**) to stand comparison.

comparison *noun* **1** the process of, an act of, or a reasonable basis for, comparing. **2** the positive, comparative, and superlative forms of adjective and adverbs.

compartment *noun* **1** a section separated or closed off from another larger section. **2** any of several enclosed sections into which a railroad car is divided. ▸ **compartmental** *adj.* ▸ **compartmentalize** *verb trans.* ▸ **compartmentalization** *noun*

compass *noun* **1** an instrument for finding direction, esp. one consisting of a magnetized needle that swings freely on a pivot and points to magnetic North. See **gyrocompass.** **2** an instrument consisting of two hinged arms, for drawing circles, etc. *Also called* **pair of compasses.** **3** range or scope.

compassion *noun* a feeling of sorrow and pity for someone in trouble. ▸ **compassionate** *adj.* ▸ **compassionately** *adv.*

compatible *adj.* **1** able to associate or coexist agreeably. **2** of a program or device capable of being used with a particular computer system, esp. one produced by another manufacturer. ▸ **compatibility** *noun* ▸ **compatibly** *adv.*

compatriot *noun* someone from one's own country; a fellow citizen.

compeer *noun* a companion or comrade; an equal.

compel *verb trans.* (**compelled, compelling**) to force or bring about by force. ⊟ CONSTRAIN, DRIVE, FORCE, OBLIGE ⊟ COAX, WHEEDLE.

compelling *adj.* irresistibly fascinating or powerful. ▸ **compellingly** *adv.*

compendium *noun* (*pl.* **compendiums, compendia**) **1** a concise summary; an abridgment. **2** a collection, e.g., of short stories. ▸ **compendious** *adj.* ▸ **compendiously** *adv.*

compensate (käm′pən-sāt,) *verb trans., intrans.* (**compensated, compensating**) **1** (**compensate (someone) for (something)**) to make amends to (another) for (loss, injury, or wrong), esp. by a suitable payment. **2** (**compensate for (something)**) to make up for (a disadvantage, loss, etc.).

compensation *noun* **1** the process of compensating. **2** something that compensates. **3 a** a sum of money given to make up for loss, injury, etc. **b** payment given for services rendered. ▸ **compensatory** (kəm-pĕn′sə-tôr,ē) *adj.*

compete *verb intrans.* (**competed, competing**) **1** to take part in a contest. **2** to strive or struggle.

competence *noun* **1** capability; efficiency. **2** sufficient income to live comfortably.

competent *adj.* **1** efficient. **2** having sufficient skill or training to do something. ▸ **competently** *adv.*

competition *noun* **1** an event in which people compete. **2** the process or fact of competing. **3** rivals, e.g., in business, or their products.

competitive *adj.* **1** involving rivalry. **2** enjoying rivalry; aggressive and ambitious. **3** comparing well, e.g., in price, with market rivals. ▸ **competitively** *adv.* ▸ **competitiveness** *noun*

competitor *noun* **1** a person, team, etc. that competes. **2** a rival.

compilation *noun* **1** the process of compiling. **2** a compiled work.

compile *verb trans.* (**compiled, compiling**) **1** to collect and organize (information, etc.); to produce (a reference book, etc.) from information collected. **2** to devise (a set of instructions) from a programming language by means of a compiler.

compiler *noun* **1** a person who compiles information, etc. **2** a program for converting a programming language into a language usable with a particular computer.

complacent *adj.* **1** self-satisfied; smug. **2** too easily satisfied; disinclined to worry. ▸ **complacence** *or* **complacency** *noun* ▸ **complacently** *adv.*

complain *verb intrans.* (**complained, complaining**) **1** to express dissatisfaction or displeasure. **2** (**complain of**) to say that one is suffering from (a pain, disease, etc.). **3** *Law* to make or bring a formal charge. ▸ **complainer** *noun*

complainant *noun* a plaintiff.

complaint *noun* **1** an expression of dissatisfaction; a cause for it. **2** a disorder or illness.

complaisant *adj.* wanting to please; quite obliging or amenable. ▸ **complaisance** *noun* ▸ **complaisantly** *adv.*

complement *noun* **1** something that completes or perfects. **2** the number or quantity, e.g., the crew of a ship, that is necessary to fill a requirement. **3** *Gram.* a word or phrase added to a verb to complete the predicate of a sentence. —*verb trans.* (**complemented, complementing**) to be a complement to.

complementary *adj.* **1** serving as a complement to something else. **2** complementing each other. ▸ **complementarily** *adv.*

complete *adj.* **1 a** with nothing missing; whole. **b** having been brought to completion; finished. **2** thorough; utter. —*verb trans.* (**completed, completing**) **1** to make whole, with nothing missing. **2** to bring to a finish. **3** to fill in (a form, etc.). ▸ **completely** *adv.* ▸ **completeness** *noun* ▸ **completion** *noun*

complex (käm-plĕks′, käm′plĕks,) *adj.* **1** composed of many interrelated parts. **2** complicated; involved. **3** *of a sentence* having a main clause and one or more subordinate clauses. *See also* **simple** (sense 7).—*noun* (käm′plĕks,) **1** something made of interrelating parts, e.g., a multipurpose building. **2** a set of repressed thoughts and emotions that strongly influence a person's behavior and attitudes. **3** *colloq.* an obsession or phobia.

complexion *noun* **1** the color or appearance of the skin, esp. of the face. **2** character or appearance.

complexity *noun* (*pl.* **complexities**) **1** the quality of being complex. **2** a complication; an intricacy.

complex number the sum of a real and an imaginary number.

compliant *adj.* inclined to comply with or yield to the wishes of others; obedient. ▸ **compliance** *noun* ▸ **compliantly** *adv.*

complicate *verb trans.* (**complicated, complicating**) to add difficulties or intricacies to; to make complex or involved.

complicated *adj.* **1** difficult to understand or deal with. **2** intricate; complex.

complication *noun* **1** something that causes difficulties. **2** a second disease or disorder that arises during the course of an existing disease or disorder.

complicity *noun* participation in a crime or wrongdoing.

compliment *noun* **1** an expression of praise, admiration, or approval. **2** (**compliments**) formal regards accompanying a gift, etc. —*verb trans.* (**complimented, complimenting**) to praise or give a compliment to.

complimentary (käm,plə-měnt'ə-rē) *adj.* **1** paying a compliment; admiring or approving. **2** given free.

complimentary care alternative medical therapy.

comply *verb intrans.* (**complied, complying, complies**) (*often* **comply with**) to act in obedience (to an order, request, etc.).

component *noun* one of the parts that make up a larger structure or entity. —*adj.* being one of the parts of something else.

comport *verb trans., intrans.* (**comported, comporting**) **1** (**comport (oneself)**) to behave in a specified way. **2** (**comport with**) to suit or be appropriate to (something).

comportment *noun* behavior; bearing.

compose *verb trans., intrans.* (**composed, composing**) **1** to create (music). **2** to write (a poem, letter, etc.). **3** to make up or constitute. **4** to arrange as a balanced, artistic whole. **5** to calm (oneself); to get (one's thoughts, etc.) under control. **6** to settle (a dispute among people). **7** to arrange (type) or set (a page, etc.) in type ready for printing.

> *Usage* See note at *comprise.*

composed *adj.* relaxed and in control. ▸ **composedly** *adv.*

composer *noun* one who composes, esp. music.

composite *adj.* **1** made up of different parts, materials, or styles. **2** belonging to a family of plants with flower heads composed of many small flowers. —*noun* a member of this family of plants. ▸ **compositely** *adv.*

composition *noun* **1** something composed, esp. a musical or literary work. **2** the process of composing. **3** arrangement, esp. with regard to balance and visual effect. **4** a school or college essay. **5** the totality or consistency of something, or the elements thast combine to form something. ▸ **compositional** *adj.*

compositor *noun* a person who sets pages of type ready for printing.

compost (käm'pŏst,) *noun* rotting vegetable matter, etc., used for enriching soil.

composure *noun* mental and emotional calmness; self-control.

compound¹ (käm'pownd,) *noun* **1** a sub-stance composed of two or more chemical elements combined in fixed proportions. **2** something composed of two or more ingredients or parts. **3** a term made up of two or more words.—*adj.* (käm-pownd') **1** composed of a number of parts or ingredients. **2** *of a sentence* made up of two or more main clauses. *See also* **simple** (sense 7). **3** *of a bone fracture* accompanied by damage to blood vessels, nerves, or organs. —*verb trans. intrans.* (**compounded, compounding**) **1** to make (esp. something bad) much worse; to complicate or add to (a difficulty, error, etc.). **2** to mix or combine (ingredients); to make up (a mixture, etc.) by so doing.

compound² (käm'pownd,) *noun* **1** an area enclosed by a wall or fence and containing a house; set of dwellings, etc. **2** an enclosed area in a prison.

compound interest interest on the principal and on any accrued interest. *See also* **simple interest**.

comprehend *verb trans.* (**comprehended, comprehending**) **1** to understand. **2** *formal* to include.

comprehensible *adj.* capable of being understood. ▸ **comprehensibility** *noun* ▸ **comprehensibly** *adv.*

comprehension *noun* the process or power of understanding; the scope or range of one's knowledge or understanding.

comprehensive *adj.* covering or including everything or a great deal. ▸ **comprehensiveness** *noun*

compress (kəm-prěs') *verb trans.* (**compressed, compressing**) **1** to press together, squeeze, or squash. **2** to decrease (something) in length or scope. **3** to pack (data) into the minimal possible space in computer memory.—*noun* (käm'prěs,) a pad pressed against a part of the body to reduce swelling, stop bleeding, etc. ▸ **compressible** *adj.* ▸ **compressibility** *noun* ▸ **compression** *noun*

compressor *noun* a device that compresses a gas, esp. air, by raising its pressure and decreasing its volume.

comprise *verb trans.* (**comprised, comprising**) to contain, include, or consist of.

> *Usage* Proper use of *comprise* is best illustrated by this easily remembered rule: the whole (e.g., the Union) *comprises* (i.e., consists of) the parts: The Union *comprises* the 50 US states. Conversely, the parts (e.g., the states) *compose* (i.e., make up or constitute) the whole: The 50 US states *compose* (not *comprise*) the Union.

compromise (käm'prə-mīz,) *noun* **1** the resulting agreement after concessions have been made on each side of an issue or dispute. **2** an intermediate stage, course, option, etc. —*verb intrans., trans.* (**compromised, compromising**) **1** to make concessions; to reach a compromise. **2** to expose (another), e.g., to scandal or danger, by acting indiscreetly. **3** to relax (one's principles, etc.).

comptroller (kən-trō′lər, kămp′trō͵lər) *noun same as* **controller** (sense 2).

compulsion *noun* **1** the condition of being compelled. **2** an irresistible urge to perform a certain action, esp. an irrational one. **3** a specific action or ritual that is repeated many times and usu. represents a form of obsession.

compulsive *adj.* **1** *of an action* resulting from a compulsion. **2** *of a person* acting on compulsion. **3** *of a book, film, etc.* holding one's attention. ▸ **compulsively** *adv.*

compulsory *adj.* required by rules, law, etc.; obligatory. ▸ **compulsorily** *adv.*

compunction *noun* a feeling of guilt, remorse, or regret; qualms.

compute *verb trans., intrans.* (**computed, computing**) to work out, find out, or estimate, esp. by mathematical means. ▸ **computable** *adj.* ▸ **computation** *noun* ▸ **computational** *adj.* ▸ **computationally** *adv.*

computer *noun* an electronic device that is capable of accepting data, processing it at great speed according to a set of instructions stored within the device, and presenting the results.

computer generation any of five broad groups denoting the different eras of technological development of digital computers.

computer graphics the use of computers to display and manipulate information in graphic or pictorial form; the forms so produced.

computerize *verb trans.* (**computerized, computerizing**) **1** to transfer (a business procedure, system, etc.) to control by computer. **2** to equip with computers. ▸ **computerization** *noun*

computer language a defined set of numbers, symbols, or words used to write a computer program.

computer literacy the condition of being competent or fully versed in the use of computers.

computer memory the part of a computer system that stores the programs and data and is connected to the central processing unit (CPU) of the computer.

computer science the study of the development, operations, and applications of computers. ▸ **computer scientist**

comrade (kăm′răd͵, -rəd) *noun* **1** a friend or companion; a fellow worker, etc. **2** (usu.

Comrade) a fellow communist or socialist. ▸ **comradely** *adj.* ▸ **comradeship** *noun*

Comsat (kăm′săt͵) *trademark* used for a communications satellite.

con[1] *slang noun* a deception, trick, or bluff. —*verb trans.* (**conned, conning**) to swindle or trick (someone), esp. after winning trust.

con[2] *verb trans., intrans.* (**conned, conning**) to read over and learn by heart.

con[3] *verb trans.* (**conned, conning**) to direct the steering of (a ship). —*noun* the post or station of the crew member who steers a ship.

con[4] *noun slang* a convict.

con[5] *adv.* in disagreement with or in opposition to.

con- or **com-** *prefix, found usu. in words derived from Latin*, forming words denoting with or together: *condone, convene.* See *also* **cor-, col-.**

concatenate *verb trans.* (**concatenated, concatenating**) to link up into a connected series. ▸ **concatenation** *noun*

concave (kăn-kāv′, kăn′kāv͵) *adj.* inward-curving, like the inside of a bowl. *See also* **convex.** ▸ **concavity** (kăn-kăv′ət-ē) *noun*

conceal *verb trans.* (**concealed, concealing**) **1** to place out of sight; to hide. **2** to keep secret. ▸ **concealment** *noun*

concede *verb intrans., trans.* (**conceded, conceding**) **1** to admit that something is true or correct. **2** to yield. **3** to give or grant. **4** to admit (defeat) in (a contest).

conceit *noun* **1** too high an opinion of oneself. ⊟ EGOISM, EGOTISM, NARCISSISM, PRIDE, VAINGLORY, VAINNESS, VANITY ⊟ MODESTY. **2** an ingenious thought or idea.

conceited *adj.* having too high an opinion of oneself. ▸ **conceitedly** *adv.*

conceivable *adj.* imaginable; possible: *tried every conceivable ploy.* ▸ **conceivability** *noun* ▸ **conceivably** *adv.*

conceive *verb intrans., trans.* (**conceived, conceiving**) **1** to become pregnant (with offspring). **2** to form (an idea, etc.). **3** (**conceive of**) to think of or imagine (an idea, etc.).

concentrate *verb intrans., trans.* (**concentrated, concentrating**) **1** (**concentrate on**) to give all one's attention and energy to (something or someone). **2** to focus. **3** to bring or come together in one place. **4** to make a substance denser or purer. —*noun* a concentrated liquid.

concentration *noun* **1** intense mental effort devoted to something. **2** the state of being concentrated. **3** a concentrate.

concentration camp a prison camp for political prisoners, prisoners of war, or enemy aliens, typically run in violation of human rights.

concentric *adj.* denoting two or more circles of different sizes but with a common center. ▸ **concentrically** *adv.* ▸ **concentricity** *noun*

concept *noun* an abstract or general idea; a notion.

conception *noun* 1 an idea or notion. 2 the origin or start, esp. of something intricate. 3 the act of conceiving. 4 fertilization representing the start of pregnancy.

conceptual *adj.* relating to or existing as concepts or conceptions. ▸ **conceptually** *adv.*

conceptualize *verb trans., intrans.* (**conceptualized, conceptualizing**) to form a concept of. ▸ **conceptualization** *noun*

concern *verb trans., intrans.* (**concerned, concerning**) 1 to have to do with; to be about. 2 to worry, bother, or interest. 3 to affect; to involve. —*noun* 1 a disquieted mental state or a cause of this. 2 one's business or responsibility. 3 a company or business; an organization.

concerned *adj.* 1 worried. 2 involved or interested in a matter.

concerning *prep.* about; regarding.

concert *noun* (kän′sərt,) a musical performance given before an audience. —*verb trans., intrans.* (kən-sərt′) (**concerted, concerting**) to endeavor or plan by arrangement; to act in close harmony. —**in concert** 1 jointly; in cooperation. 2 in a live performance.

concerted (kən-sərt′ĭd) *adj.* planned and carried out jointly.

concertina *noun* a musical instrument resembling a small accordion.

concerto (kən-chĕrt′ō) *noun* (*pl.* **concertos, concerti**) a musical composition for one or more solo instruments and orchestra.

concession *noun* 1 the act of conceding. 2 something conceded. 3 a the right to conduct a business from within a larger concern. b a business located in or forming part of a larger entity.

concessionaire *noun* the holder of a business concession.

conch (känk) *noun* (*pl.* **conchs, conches**) a large spiral shell or an edible shellfish having such a shell.

concierge (kôn-syĕrzh′) *noun* a member of a hotel or apartment-house staff who handles luggage storage, entertainment reservations, and tour arrangements.

conciliate *verb trans.* (**conciliated, conciliating**) 1 to overcome the hostility of; to placate. 2 to reconcile (people in dispute, etc.). ▸ **conciliation** *noun* ▸ **conciliator** *noun* ▸ **conciliatory** *adj.*

concise *adj.* brief, but covering essential points. ▸ **concisely** *adv.* ▸ **conciseness** *noun* ▸ **concision** *noun*

conclave *noun* 1 a private or secret meeting. 2 *RC Church* the body of cardinals gathered to elect a new pope.

conclude *verb trans., intrans.* (**concluded, concluding**) 1 to come or bring to an end. 2 to reach an opinion based on reasoning. 3 to settle or arrange.

conclusion *noun* 1 an end. 2 a reasoned judgment; an opinion based on reasoning. 3 the settling of terms, an agreement, etc. —**in conclusion** finally; lastly.

conclusive *adj.* decisive and convincing; leaving no room for doubt. ▸ **conclusively** *adv.* ▸ **conclusiveness** *noun*

concoct *verb trans.* (**concocted, concocting**) 1 to make, esp. with skill and resourcefulness, from a variety of ingredients. 2 to invent (a story, excuse, etc.); to contrive. ▸ **concoction** *noun*

concomitant *adj.* accompanying. —*noun* something that serves to accompany. ▸ **concomitantly** *adv.*

concord (kän′kôrd,, käng′-) *noun* 1 peace or harmony; agreement. 2 a treaty; a pact.

concordance (kən-kôrd′ns) *noun* 1 a state of harmony. 2 an alphabetical index of words used by an author or in a book, giving the reference points and usu. the meanings. ▸ **concordant** *adj.*

concordat (kon-kôr′dăt,) *noun* an agreement, esp. between church and state.

concourse *noun* 1 a large open area for people, in a railroad station, airport, etc. 2 a throng; a gathering.

concrete (kän′krēt,, kän-krēt′) *noun* a building material consisting of cement, sand, and gravel mixed with water, that forms a hard, rocklike mass when dry. (kän-krēt′, kən-) —*adj.* 1 relating to such a material. 2 able to be felt, touched, or seen. 3 definite or positive. 4 of a noun denoting a physical thing. —*verb trans., intrans.* (**concreted, concreting**) to cover with concrete. ▸ **concretely** *adv.* ▸ **concreteness** *noun*

concretion *noun* a hard, stony mass occurring in a body tissue or natural cavity.

concubine *noun* a woman who lives with a man and has sexual relations with him, without being married to him. ▸ **concubinage** *noun*

concupiscence *noun* strong sexual desire. ▸ **concupiscent** *adj.*

concur *verb intrans.* (**concurred, concurring, concurs**) 1 to agree. 2 to happen at the same time; to coincide.

concurrent *adj.* running in parallel; happening or taking place simultaneously. ▸ **concurrence** *noun* ▸ **concurrently** *adv.*

concussion *noun* temporary injury to the brain caused by a blow or fall, usu. producing temporary unconsciousness. ▸ **concuss** *verb*

condemn (kən-dĕm´) *verb trans.* (**condemned, condemning**) **1** to declare to be wrong or evil. **2** to find guilty; to convict. **3** (**condemn to**) a to sentence (someone) to a punishment, esp. death. **b** to be the cause of (someone's disagreeable fate). **4** to declare (a building) unfit to be used or lived in. ▸ **condemnation** (kăn,dəm-nā'shən, -dĕm-) *noun* ▸ **condemnatory** *adj.*

condensation *noun* the process whereby a gas or vapor turns into a liquid as a result of cooling.

condense *verb trans., intrans.* (**condensed, condensing**) **1** to decrease the volume, size, or density of (a substance). **2** to be reduced in volume, size, or density. **3** to decrease (something) in length or scope. **4** to undergo or cause to undergo (condensation).

condensed milk milk concentrated and thickened by evaporation, and to which sugar has been added.

condenser *noun* **1** a capacitor. **2** an apparatus for changing a vapor into a liquid by cooling it and allowing it to condense.

condescend *verb intrans.* (**condescended, condescending**) **1** to act in a gracious manner to those one considers one's inferior. **2** to be gracious enough to do something, esp. as though it were a favor. ▸ **condescension** *noun*

condescending *adj.* **1** patronizingly gracious. **2** displaying an offensively superior attitude. ▸ **condescendingly** *adv.*

condign *adj.* well deserved.

condiment *noun* a seasoning, e.g., salt, pepper, used at table to give flavor to food.

condition *noun* **1** a particular state. **2** a state of health, fitness, or suitability for use. **3** an ailment or disorder. **4** (**conditions**) circumstances. **5** a requirement or qualification. —*verb trans.* (**conditioned, conditioning**) **1** to accustom or train to behave or react in a particular way. **2** to affect or control; to determine. **3** to get (an animal, one's hair, skin, muscles, etc.) into good condition.

conditional *adj.* dependent on a particular circumstance or set of circumstances. ▸ **conditionally** *adv.*

conditioner *noun* a substance for improving the condition of something else: *hair conditioner.*

conditioning *noun* **1** the process of making or becoming conditioned. **2** a reflex response to a stimulus that depends on the former experience of the individual.

condo *noun* (*pl.* **condos**) *colloq.* a condominium.

condole *verb intrans.* (**condoled, condoling**) (**condole with**) to express sympathy to (someone) esp. after a bereavement, etc.

condolence (kən-dō´ləns, kăn´də-) *noun* (*often* **condolences**) sympathy, or an expression of it.

condom (kăn´dəm, kən´-) *noun* a contraceptive consisting of a thin rubber or latex sheath worn on the penis during sexual intercourse.

condominium *noun* **1** a block of individually owned apartments or a freestanding house in a complex. **2** joint control of a state by two or more other states.

condone *verb trans.* (**condoned, condoning**) to pardon or overlook (an offense or wrong). ▸ **condonable** *adj.*

condor *noun* a large S American vulture.

conduce *verb intrans.* (**conduced, conducing**) (**conduce to**) to help or tend toward (a result, esp. a desirable one).

conducive *adj.* (**conducive to (something)**) likely to achieve (a desirable result, etc.); encouraging.

conduct (kən-dəkt´) *verb trans., intrans.* (**conducted, conducting**) **1** to lead or guide. **2** to manage; to control. **3** to direct the performance of an orchestra or choir by movements of the hands or a baton. **4** to transmit (heat or electricity) by conduction. **5** to direct, channel, or convey. **6** to behave (oneself) in a specified way. —*noun* (kăn´dəkt,) **1** behavior. **2** the managing or organizing of something.

conductance *noun* the ability of a material to conduct heat or electricity.

conduction *noun* the process by which heat or electricity is transmitted through a material, body, etc.

conductivity *noun* **1** a measure of the ability of a material to conduct electricity. **2** the ability of a material to conduct heat.

conductor *noun* **1** the director of a choir or orchestra. **2** a material that conducts heat or electricity. **3** a person who collects fares from passengers on a bus, streetcar, or train.

conduit *noun* **1** a channel, trough, or pipe carrying water or electric cables. **2** a channel through which something, e.g., information or gossip, is transmitted.

cone *noun* **1** a solid figure with a flat base in the shape of a circle or ellipse, and a curved upper surface that tapers to a fixed point. **2** something similar to this geometric figure in shape. **3** the pointed oval fruit of a conifer, consisting of many overlapping woody scales. *Also called* **strobilus.**

confab *noun colloq.* a casual conversation.

confabulate *verb intrans.* (**confabulated, confabulating**) to talk, discuss, or confer, casually. ▸ **confabulation** *noun*

confection *noun* **1** a sweet food, e.g., a cake, a piece of candy. **2** a fancy or elaborate garment.

confectioner noun a person who makes or sells candy and cakes.

confectionery noun (pl. **confectioneries**) 1 candy and cakes. 2 the art or business of a person who makes or sells candy and cakes.

confederacy noun (pl. **confederacies**) 1 a league or alliance of states. 2 (**the Confederacy**) the union of 11 US southern states that seceded from the USA in 1860–1861, so causing the Civil War.

confederate (kən-fĕd′ə-rət) noun 1 a member of a confederacy. 2 a friend or an ally; an accomplice or a fellow conspirator. 3 (**Confederate**) a supporter of the Confederacy of US states that seceded in 1860–61. —adj. 1 allied; united. 2 (**Confederate**) belonging to the Confederacy. —verb trans., intrans. (kən-fĕd′ə-rāt,) (**confederated, confederating**) to form into or to unite into a confederacy.

confederation noun 1 the uniting of states into a league. 2 the league so formed.

confer verb intrans., trans. (**conferred, conferring**) 1 to consult. 2 to grant (an honor or distinction).

conference noun 1 a formally organized gathering for the discussion of matters of common interest or concern. 2 the formal exchanging of views; consultation. 3 an assembly of representatives of a church denomination, etc. 4 an association of teams, e.g., college football teams. —verb intrans. (**conferenced, conferencing**) to take part in a conference or a conference call.

conference call a multiple-party telephone call, with each of the parties hooked up via a central switching unit.

conferencing noun the practice of going to conferences or of holding conference calls.

confess verb trans., intrans. (**confessed, confessing**) 1 to own up to (a fault, wrongdoing, etc.); to admit (a disagreeable fact, etc.) reluctantly. 2 to recount (one's sins) to a priest, in order to gain absolution. 3 of a priest: to hear the confession of (someone).

confession noun 1 the admission of a fault, crime, etc. 2 the formal act of confessing one's sins to a priest.

confessional noun the small, enclosed stall in a church where a priest sits when hearing confessions.

confessor noun a priest who hears confessions and gives spiritual advice.

confetti pl. noun (sing.) tiny pieces of colored paper traditionally thrown at a newly wed couple by wedding guests.

confidant or **confidante** (kän′fə-dänt,, -dänt,, -dənt) noun a friend with whom one discusses personal matters.

confide verb intrans., trans. (**confided, confiding**) 1 (**confide in**) to speak freely with (someone) about personal matters. 2 to tell (a secret, etc.) to someone.

confidence noun 1 trust in or reliance on a person or thing. 2 faith in one's own ability; self-assurance. 3 a secret, entrusted to another. 4 a relationship of mutual trust. —**in confidence** in secret; confidentially.

confidence game see con game

confidence man see con man

confident adj. 1 certain; sure. 2 self-assured.

confidential adj. 1 not to be divulged; secret. 2 trusted with private matters. ▸ **confidentiality** noun ▸ **confidentially** adv.

configuration noun 1 the positioning or distribution of the parts of a whole relative to one another. 2 an outline or an external shape. 3 Comput. the internal and external components of a system, and how they relate to one another, esp. in terms of their optimum efficiency.

configure verb trans. Comput. to arrange (internal and external components of a system), esp. to do a specified task or to achieve optimum efficiency.

confine (kən-fīn′) verb trans. (**confined, confining**) 1 to restrict; to limit. 2 to prevent the spread of (e.g., a fire). 3 to hold prisoner or keep from moving. (kän′fīn,, kən-fīn′) —noun (**confines**) limits or restrictions.

confined (kən-fīnd′) adj. narrow; restricted.

confinement noun 1 the state of being shut up or kept in an enclosed space. 2 old use the period surrounding childbirth.

confirm verb trans. (**confirmed, confirming**) 1 to provide support for the truth or validity of (something). 2 to make final or definite (a reservation, an arrangement, etc.). 3 to make firmer or to strengthen (e.g., a belief). 4 to accept (someone) formally into full membership of a church. ▸ **confirmation** noun

confirmed adj. so settled into a specified state or condition as to be unlikely to change: a confirmed bachelor.

confiscate verb trans. (**confiscated, confiscating**) to take away (something) from someone, as a penalty. ▸ **confiscation** noun

conflagration noun a fierce, destructive blaze.

conflate verb trans. (**conflated, conflating**) to blend or combine (e.g., two different versions of a text, story, etc.) into a single whole. ▸ **conflation** noun

conflict (kän′flĭkt,) noun 1 fierce argument; disagreement. 2 a clash between different aims, interests, or ideas. 3 a fight, battle, or war. —verb intrans. (kən-flĭkt′, kän′flĭkt,) (**conflicted, conflicting**) to be incompatible or in opposition.

confluence (kăn'flŏo,əns, kən-flŏo'-) noun 1 the place at which one river flows into another. 2 the juncture at which two things co-occur. ▸ confluent adj.

conform verb intrans. (conformed, conforming) 1 to behave, dress, etc. in obedience to a standard considered normal by a majority. 2 (conform to) to obey (rules, etc.); to meet or comply with (standards). ▸ conformist noun

conformation noun a shape, structure, or arrangement.

conformity noun 1 obedience to rules and standards, etc. 2 accordance; compliance.

confound (kən-fownd') verb trans. (confounded, confounding) 1 to puzzle; to baffle. 2 to mix up or confuse (one thing with another).

confounded (kən-fown'dĭd, kăn'fown,dĭd) adj. used to indicate annoyance: a confounded nuisance. ▸ confoundedly adv.

confrere noun a fellow member of one's profession, etc.; a colleague.

confront verb trans. (confronted, confronting) 1 to face, esp. defiantly or accusingly. 2 (confront with) to bring (someone) face to face with (something). ▸ confrontation noun

Confucianism noun the teachings of the Chinese philosopher Confucius. ▸ Confucian noun, adj. ▸ Confucianist noun

confuse verb trans., intrans. (confused, confusing) 1 to cause to be unable to think clearly or act intelligently. 2 to fail to distinguish; to mix up. 3 to puzzle or bewilder. ▸ confused adj. ▸ confusedly adv. ▸ confusing adj. ▸ confusingly adv.

confusion noun 1 the state of being confused. 2 disorder. 3 mental bewilderment.

confute (kən-fyŏot') verb trans. (confuted, confuting) to prove (a person) wrong, or (a theory, etc.) false. ▸ confutation noun

Cong. abbrev. Congress or Congressional.

conga noun 1 an orig. Cuban dance performed in single file, with three steps followed by a kick. 2 a large drum beaten with the fingers. —verb intrans. (congaed, congaing) to dance the conga.

con game slang swindle.

congeal verb trans., intrans. (congealed, congealing) to thicken, coagulate, or solidify, esp. through cooling. ▸ congealment noun

congenial adj. 1 having a personality and interests that fit well with one's own; companionable. 2 pleasant or agreeable. ▸ congeniality noun ▸ congenially adv.

congenital adj. present at or before birth. ▸ congenitally adv.

conger noun a large sea eel. Also called conger eel

congest verb trans., intrans. (congested, congesting) to make or become crowded or overfull.

congested adj. 1 too full; crowded. 2 overfull of blood or other matter. 3 obstructed with mucus. ▸ congestion noun

conglomerate (kən-glăm'ə-rət) noun 1 a mass formed from things of different kinds. 2 a sedimentary rock consisting of small rounded pebbles embedded in a matrix of sand or other fine-textured material. 3 a business composed of a large number of merged firms. —adj. composed of things of different kinds formed into a mass. —verb intrans. (kən-glăm'ə-rāt,) (conglomerated, conglomerating) to accumulate and form into a mass. ▸ conglomeration noun

congrats pl. noun colloq. congratulations.

congratulate (kən-grăch'ə-lăt,, -grăj'-) verb trans. (congratulated, congratulating) 1 to express pleasure to (someone) upon the person's good fortune or happiness. 2 to consider (oneself) lucky or clever to have managed something. ▸ congratulatory adj.

congratulation noun 1 the act or an expression of congratulating. 2 (also congratulations) an expression of praise and pleasure accorded to another.

congregate verb trans., intrans. (congregated, congregating) to gather together into a crowd.

congregation noun 1 a gathering of people, e.g., for worship in church. 2 the people regularly attending a particular church, synagogue, or mosque.

congregational adj. 1 relating to a congregation. 2 (Congregational) belonging or relating to Congregationalism.

Congregationalism noun a Protestant denomination in which the affairs of each individual church are run by its own congregation. ▸ Congregationalist adj.

congress noun 1 a large, esp. international assembly of delegates, gathered for discussion. 2 (Congress) the national law-making body of the USA. ▸ congressional adj.

congressman noun a male member of Congress.

congressperson noun a member of Congress.

congresswoman noun a female member of Congress.

congruent (kən-grŏo'ənt, kăng'grŏo-ənt) adj. 1 of geometric figures identical in size and shape. 2 (congruent with) suitable or appropriate to (someone or something). ▸ congruence or congruency noun ▸ congruently adv.

congruous adj. (congruous with) fitting; suitable; proper. ▸ congruity noun

conic *adj.* relating to a cone.

conical *adj.* shaped like a cone.

conic section the curved geometric figure produced when a plane intersects a cone.

conifer *noun* a cone-bearing tree or shrub, usu. evergreen with needle-like leaves. ▸ **coniferous** *adj.*

conj. *abbrev.* conjunction.

conjecture *noun* **1** an opinion based on incomplete evidence. **2** the process of forming such an opinion. *—verb trans., intrans.* (**conjectured, conjecturing**) to guess or surmise. ▸ **conjectural** *adj.* ▸ **conjecturally** *adv.*

conjoin *verb trans., intrans.* (**conjoined, conjoining**) to join together, combine, or unite.

conjoint *adj.* joint; associated; united. ▸ **conjointly** *adv.*

conjugal *adj.* relating to marriage or to the relationship between spouses. ▸ **conjugality** *noun* ▸ **conjugally** *adv.*

conjugate (kän'jə-gāt,) *verb trans., intrans.* (**conjugated, conjugating 1** to give the inflected forms of (a verb). **2** of a verb to have inflected forms. *—adj.* (kän'jə-gət) joined, connected, or coupled.

conjugation *noun* **1** the inflection of a verb. *See also* **declension**. **2** a uniting, joining, or fusing.

conjunction *noun* **1** a word that links sentences, clauses, or words. **2** a joining together; combination. **3** the coinciding of two or more events. **—in conjunction with** together with. ▸ **conjunctive** *adj., noun* ▸ **conjunctively** *adv.*

conjunctiva (kän,jəngk-tī'və, kən-) *noun* (*pl.* **conjunctivas, conjunctivae**) a membrane that covers the eyeball and the inside of the eyelid. ▸ **conjunctival** *adj.*

conjunctivitis (kən-jəngk,tī-vīt'ĭs) *noun* inflammation of the conjunctiva.

conjuncture *noun* a combination of circumstances, esp. one leading to a crisis.

conjure *verb intrans., trans.* (**conjured, conjuring**) **1** to practice conjuring. **2 a** to summon (a spirit, demon, etc.) to appear. **b** to call up, evoke, or stir (images, memories, etc.). **3** *old use* to beg (someone) earnestly to do something. **—conjure up** to produce as though from nothing. ▸ **conjurer** or **conjuror** *noun*

conk *noun slang* the human head. *—verb trans., intrans.* (**conked, conking**) *slang* **1** to hit (someone) on the head. **2** (*usu.* **conk out**) to cease functioning. **3** (*usu.* **conk out**) to suddenly fall asleep from great fatigue.

con man *slang* a swindler.

connect *verb trans., intrans.* (**connected, connecting**) **1** to join; to link. **2** to associate or involve. **3** to associate or relate mentally. **4** a to join by telephone, fax, or computer. **b** to plug (an electrical appliance or device) into a socket. **—well connected** with important or aristocratic relatives. ▸ **connectible** or **connectable** *adj.* ▸ **connective** *adj.* ▸ **connector** *noun*

connection *noun* **1** the state of being connected. **2** something that connects; a link. **3** a relationship. **4** an influential person; a contact.

connective tissue tissue, usu. containing collagen, that provides the body and its internal organs with structural support.

conning tower 1 the raised part of a submarine containing the periscope. **2** the wheelhouse of a warship.

connive *verb intrans.* (**connived, conniving**) **1** (**connive at**) to pretend not to notice (a wrongdoing), and thereby share responsibility for it. **2** to conspire. ▸ **connivance** *noun* ▸ **conniver** *noun*

connoisseur (kän,ə-sər', -sŏŏr') *noun* a person who is knowledgeable about, and a good judge of, the arts, wine, food, etc.

connote *verb trans.* (**connoted, connoting**) **1** *of a word* to suggest, in addition to its literal meaning. **2** to mean; to imply. ▸ **connotation** *noun* ▸ **connotational** *adj.*

connubial *adj.* of or relating to marriage or to relations between spouses. ▸ **connubially** *adv.*

conquer *verb trans., intrans.* (**conquered, conquering**) **1** to gain possession or dominion over (a people, territory, etc.) by force. **2** to defeat. **3** to overcome or put an end to (a failing, difficulty, evil, etc.). ▸ **conquering** *adj.* ▸ **conqueror** *noun*

conquest *noun* **1** the act of defeating or conquering. **2** a conquered territory. **3** something won by effort or force. **4** a person whose affection or admiration one has won.

conquistador (kông-kē'stə-dôr,) .*noun* (*pl.* **conquistadors, conquistadores**) 16th c Spanish conqueror of Peru and Mexico.

consanguineous (kän,săng,gwĭn'ē-əs) *adj.* descended from a common ancestor. ▸ **consanguinity** *noun*

conscience (kän'shəns) *noun* the sense of moral right and wrong.

conscientious *adj.* **1** giving or showing care and attention. **2** guided by conscience. ▸ **conscientiously** *adv.* ▸ **conscientiousness** *noun*

conscientious objector a person who refuses, on moral grounds, to serve in the armed forces.

conscious *adj.* **1** awake and aware of one's surroundings. **2** aware; knowing. **3** deliberate: *a conscious effort.* **4** (*often in compounds*) concerned, esp. too concerned, with: *class-conscious*. —*noun* (*often* **the conscious**) the component of waking awareness that is perceptible by a person at any given instant. ▸ **consciously** *adv*. ▸ **consciousness** *noun*

conscript (kən-skrĭpt′) *verb trans.* (**conscripted, conscripting**) to enroll in compulsory military service. —*noun* (kän′-skrĭpt,) a person who has been conscripted.

consecrate (kän′sĭ-krāt,) *verb trans.* (**consecrated, consecrating**) **1** to set apart for a holy use; to dedicate to God. **2** to devote to a special use. ▸ **consecration** *noun*

consecutive (kən-sĕk′yət-ĭv) *adj.* following one after the other. ▸ **consecutively** *adv*.

consensus *noun* general feeling or opinion; a majority view.

> *Usage* The expressions *general consensus, overall consensus,* and *consensus of opinion,* though often used, are redundant, given the intrinsic meaning of *consensus*: general feeling or opinion.

consent *verb intrans., trans.* (**consented, consenting**) **1** (**consent to**) to give permission for; to agree to. **2** to agree to do something. —*noun* agreement; permission.

consequence (kän′sĭ-kwəns, -kwĕns,) *noun* **1** something that follows from, or is caused by, an action or set of circumstances. **2** a conclusion reached from reasoning. **3** importance: *of no consequence*.

consequent *adj.* **1** resulting **2** following, esp. logically. —*noun* something that results from, follows on from, or is dependent on another. ▸ **consequently** *adv..*

consequential *adj.* **1** having great significance, value, or effect. **2** consequent.

conservancy *noun* (*pl.* **conservancies**) **1** an area under special environmental protection. **2** a body concerned with environmental conservation.

conservation *noun* **1** the act of conserving. **2** the management of the environment in such a way that that its wildlife, natural resources, and quality are preserved and protected. **3** the preservation of historical artifacts for future generations. ▸ **conservationist** *noun*

conservative *adj.* **1** favoring the keeping of what is established or traditional; disliking change. **2** of an estimate or calculation deliberately low, for the sake of caution. **3** of clothing, etc. avoiding the flamboyant; restrained. **4** (**Conservative**) relating to a Conservative Party. —*noun* **1** a traditionalist. **2** (**Conservative**) a member or supporter of a Conservative Party. ▸ **conservatism** *noun* ▸ **conservatively** *adv*.

Conservative Party in Britain, Canada, and Australia, a political party on the right of the political spectrum, advocating support of established customs and institutions, opposition to socialism, and usu. favoring free enterprise. ▸ **Conservatism** *noun*

conservatory *noun* (*pl.* **conservatories**) **1** a greenhouse for plants. **2** a school specializing in music or any of the fine arts.

conserve (kən-sɔrv′) *verb trans., intrans.* (**conserved, conserving**) to keep safe from damage, deterioration, or undesirable change. —*noun* (kän′sərv,) a jam made esp. from fresh fruit. ▸ **conservable** *adj.*

consider *verb trans., intrans.* (**considered, considering**) **1** to ponder, study, or look at thoughtfully. **2** to call to mind for comparison, etc. **3** to contemplate doing something. **4** to have as one's opinion; to think. **5** to take into account; to make allowances for.

considerable *adj.* **1** large; great. **2** significant. ▸ **considerably** *adv*.

considerate *adj.* careful not to hurt or inconvenience others; thoughtful. ▸ **considerately** *adv.* ▸ **considerateness** *noun*

consideration *noun* **1** thoughtfulness for others' feelings. **2** careful thought. **3** a fact or circumstance to be taken into account. **4** a payment, reward, or recompense.

considered *adj.* **1** carefully thought about: *my considered opinion*. **2** deliberate.

considering *conj.* taking into account. —*adv.* taking the circumstances into account: *It's pretty good, considering*.

consign *verb trans.* (**consigned, consigning**) **1** to hand over; to entrust. **2** to send, commit, or deliver. **3** to send (goods). ▸ **consignee** (kän,sə-nē′, kən-sī,-) *noun* ▸ **consignor** (kän,sə-nōr′, kən-sī,-) *noun*

consignment *noun* **1** a load of goods, etc., sent or delivered. **2** the act of consigning.

consist *verb intrans.* (**consisted, consisting**) **1** (**consist of**) to be composed of (several elements or ingredients). **2** (**consist in**) to have as an essential feature.

consistency *noun* (*pl.* **consistencies**) **1** texture or composition, with regard to density, solidity, etc. **2** the quality of being consistent. **3** agreement; harmony.

consistent *adj.* **1** (**consistent with**) in agreement or in keeping with. **2** unchanging, regular, or steady. ▸ **consistently** *adv.*

consistory *noun* (*pl.* **consistories**) an ecclesiastical council or its meeting place.

consolation *noun* **1** something or someone that offers some comfort. **2** the act of consoling.

consolation prize a prize given to a competitor who falls short of winning.

console[1] (kən-sōl′) *verb trans.* (**consoled, consoling**) to comfort in distress, grief, or disappointment. ▸ **consolable** *adj.*

console² (kän'sōl,) *noun* **1** the part of an organ with the keys, pedals, and panels of stops. **2** a panel of dials, switches, etc., for operating an electronic machine. **3** a freestanding cabinet for audio or video equipment. **4** an ornamental bracket for a shelf, etc.

consolidate *verb trans., intrans.* (**consolidated, consolidating**) **1** to make or become solid or strong. **2** to combine or merge. ▸ **consolidation** *noun* ▸ **consolidator** *noun*

consommé (kän,sə-mā') *noun* thin, clear soup made from meat stock.

consonant¹ (kän'sə-nənt) *noun* **1** a speech sound produced by obstructing the passage of the breath. **2** a letter representing such a sound. ▸ **consonance** *noun*

consonant² *adj.* (**consonant with**) in harmony or agreement with.

consort¹ (kän'sôrt,) *noun* **1** a spouse, esp. of a reigning sovereign. **2** an accompanying ship. (kən-sôrt', kän'sôrt,) —*verb intrans.* (**consort with**) to associate or keep company with (another esp. an enemy).

consort² (kän'sôrt,) *noun* a group of players, singers, or instruments, esp. specializing in early music.

consortium (kən-sôrt'ē-əm, -sôr'shəm) *noun* (*pl.* **consortia, consortiums**) an association or combination of several banks, businesses, etc.

conspectus *noun* (*pl.* **conspectuses**) a survey or report; a summary.

conspicuous *adj.* **1** very noticeable; obvious. **2** notable; striking; glaring. ▸ **conspicuously** *adv.* ▸ **conspicuousness** *noun*

conspiracy *noun* (*pl.* **conspiracies**) **1** the activity of plotting secretly together for an evil or illegal purpose. **2** a secret plan with an evil or illegal goal. ▸ **conspirator** *noun* ▸ **conspiratorial** *adj.* ▸ **conspiratorially** *adv.*

conspiracy theory a theory that attempts to explain something as a plot rather than as an accident or the work of a single person.

conspire *verb intrans.* (**conspired, conspiring**) **1** to plot secretly together, esp. for an unlawful purpose. **2** *of events* to seem to be working together to thwart one.

constable *noun* a law-enforcement officer.

constabulary (kən-stăb'yə-lĕr,ē) *noun* (*pl.* **constabularies**) the police force of a district or county. —*adj.* of or relating to the police.

constant *adj.* **1** never stopping. **2** frequently recurring. **3** unchanging. **4** faithful; loyal. —*noun Math.* a symbol (usu. a numeral) that remains unchanged. ▸ **constancy** *noun* ▸ **constantly** *adv.*

constellation *noun* **1** a group of stars that often form a distinctive shape in the sky. **2** a group of associated people or things.

consternation *noun* alarm or anxiety.

constipation *noun* a condition in which the feces become hard and difficult to pass from the bowels. ▸ **constipate** *verb*

constituency *noun* (*pl.* **constituencies**) **1** the district represented by an elected legislator. **2** the voters in the district of an elected legislator.

constituent *adj.* forming part of a whole. —*noun* **1** a necessary part. **2** a voter in a given district.

constitute *verb trans.* (**constituted, constituting**) **1** to go together to make; to be. **2** to establish; to appoint.

constitution *noun* **1** a set of rules governing an organization; the supreme laws and rights of a country's people, etc. **2** the way in which something is formed or made up. **3** one's physical makeup, health, etc.

constitutional *adj.* **1** legal according to a given constitution. **2** relating to, or controlled by, the law of the land. **3** relating to one's physical makeup, health, etc. —*noun* a regular walk taken for the sake of one's health. ▸ **constitutionally** *adv.*

constrain *verb trans.* (**constrained, constraining**) **1** to make (someone or something) give in to pressure. **2** to limit the freedom, scope, or range of. ▸ **constraint** *noun*

constrict *verb trans.* (**constricted, constricting**) **1** to squeeze or compress; to cause to tighten. **2** to inhibit. ▸ **constriction** *noun* ▸ **constrictive** *adj.* ▸ **constrictor** *noun*

construct (kən-strəkt') *verb trans.* (**constructed, constructing**) **1** to build. **2** to form, compose, or put together. —*noun* (kän'-strəkt,) **1** something constructed. **2** a mental image, concept, or idea. ▸ **constructor** *noun*

construction *noun* **1** the process of building or constructing. **2** something, e.g., a building, that is built or constructed. **3** the arrangement of words in a particular grammatical relationship, to form a sentence, clause, etc. **4** an interpretation. ▸ **constructional** *adj.*

constructionist *noun* one who interprets a law or a legal text in a given manner.

constructive *adj.* **1** helping toward progress or development; useful and practical. **2** *Law* based on an interpretation and not expressed directly. ▸ **constructively** *adv.*

construe *verb trans.* (**construed, construing**) **1** to interpret or explain. **2 a** to analyze the grammatical structure of (a sentence, etc.). **b** to translate word for word.

consul *noun* **1** an official repesentative of a state, stationed in a foreign country to look after the interests of fellow citizens living there. **2** a chief magistrate in ancient Rome.

consulate (kän'sə-lət) *noun* the post or official residence of a diplomatic consul.

consult *verb trans., intrans.* (**consulted, consulting**) **1** to ask the advice of. **2** to refer to (a map, book, etc.). **3** to consider. **4** (**consult with**) to have discussions with (another).

consultant *noun* a person or firm that gives professional advice. ▸ **consultancy** *noun*

consultation *noun* **1** the act or process of consulting. **2** a meeting for the obtaining of advice or for discussion. ▸ **consultative** *adj.*

consulting *adj.* acting as an adviser: *a consulting architect.*

consume *verb trans., intrans.* (**consumed, consuming**) **1** to eat or drink. **2** to use up. **3** to destroy. **4** (**be consumed with**) to be obsessed or overcome by (a feeling, etc.). ▸ **consumable** *adj.*

consumer *noun* **1** the one who uses a product; any member of the public buying and using goods and services. **2** one that consumes.

consumer goods goods bought to satisfy personal needs, as distinct from, e.g., machinery and other equipment used in the production of goods.

consumerism *noun* **1** protection of the interests of consumers. **2** the buying of goods, esp. just for the sake of it, or a preoccupation with shopping and materialism.

consuming *adj.* fully occupying the mind.

consummate (kän'sə-mät,) *verb trans.* (**consummated, consummating**) **1** to finish, perfect, or complete. **2** to complete (a marital union) in its full legal sense through the first act of sexual intercourse. —*adj.* (kän'sə-mət, kən-sʌɪ'ət) **1** skilled or accomplished to a supreme degree. **2** complete; utter. ▸ **consummately** *adv.* ▸ **consummation** (kän,sə-mä'shən) *noun*

consumption *noun* **1** the act or process of consuming. **2** an amount consumed. **3** the buying and using of goods. **4** *old use* tuberculosis of the lungs.

consumptive *adj.* **1** relating to consumption; wasteful or destructive. **2** suffering from tuberculosis of the lungs. —*noun* a person suffering from tuberculosis of the lungs.

contact (kän'täkt,) *noun* **1** the condition of physically touching. **2** communication or a means of it. **3** an acquaintance whose influence or knowledge may prove useful, esp. in business. **4** an electrical connection that allows the passage of a current. **5** (*often* **contacts**) a contact lens, or a set of these. —*verb trans.* (**contacted, contacting**) to get in touch with; to communicate with. ▸ **contactable** *adj.*

contact lens (kän'täkt,) a small lens worn in direct contact with the front of the eyeball for the correction of visual defects.

contact sport a sport, e.g., soccer or football, that involves physical contact among the players as part of normal play.

contagion *noun* **1** the transmission of a

disease by direct physical contact with an infected person. **2** *old use* a disease that is transmitted in this way. **3** spreading social evil; a corrupting influence.

contagious *adj.* **1** *of a disease* transmitted by direct contact. **2** *of a mood, laughter, etc* spreading from person to person.

contain *verb trans.* (**contained, containing**) **1** to hold or have; to consist of. **2** to control or prevent the spread of. **3** to control (oneself or one's feelings). **4** to enclose or surround. ▸ **containable** *adj.*

container *noun* **1** an object designed for holding or storing. **2** a huge, sealed metal box of standard size and design for carrying goods by truck, rail, or ship.

containerize *verb trans.* (**containerized, containerizing**) to put (cargo) into containers. ▸ **containerization** *noun*

containment *noun* the action of preventing the expansion of a hostile power.

contaminate *verb trans.* (**contaminated, contaminating**) **1** to pollute or infect; to make impure. **2** to make radioactive through exposure to radioactive material. ▸ **contaminant** *noun* ▸ **contamination** *noun*

contemn (kən-těm') *verb trans.* (**contemned, contemning**) to despise or scorn.

contemplate *verb trans., intrans.* (**contemplated, contemplating**) **1** to think about; to go over (something) mentally. **2** to look thoughtfully at. **3** to consider as a possibility. ▸ **contemplation** *noun* ▸ **contemplative** *adj.*

contemporaneous (kən-těm,pə-rā'nē-əs) *adj.* existing or happening at the same time or period as something else. ▸ **contemporaneity** (kən-těm,pə-rə-nē'ət-ē, -nā'-) *noun* ▸ **contemporaneously** *adv.*

contemporary *adj.* **1** belonging to the same period or time as something else. **2** of the same age as someone else. **3** modern. —*noun* (*pl.* **contemporaries**) **1** a person who lives or lived, or thing that exists or existed, at the same time as another. **2** a person of about the same age as another.

contempt *noun* **1** scorn. **2** disregard of, disrespect for, or disobedience to the rules of a court of law. —**hold in contempt** to despise. ▸ **contemptible** *adj.* ▸ **contemptibly** *adv.*

contemptuous *adj.* showing or feeling contempt. ▸ **contemptuously** *adv.*

contend *verb intrans., trans.* (**contended, contending**) **1** to struggle or compete. **2** to argue earnestly. **3** to say, maintain, or assert.

contender *noun* a contestant or competitor.

content[1] (kən-těnt') *adj.* satisfied; happy; uncomplaining. —*verb trans.* (**contented, contenting**) **1** to satisfy. **2** (**content oneself) with**) to limit (oneself) to (a particular choice or course of action). —*noun* peaceful satisfaction; peace of mind. ▸ **contentment** *noun*

content² (kăn'tĕnt,) *noun* 1 the subject matter of a book, speech, etc. 2 the proportion in which a particular ingredient is present. 3 (**contents**) the things contained. 4 (**contents**) a summary of the text of a book by chapters, etc., given at the beginning.

contented *adj.* peacefully happy or satisfied. ▸ **contentedly** *adv.* ▸ **contentedness** *noun*

contention *noun* 1 a point asserted or maintained in an argument. 2 argument or debate.

contentious *adj.* 1 controversial and liable to provoke dissent, argument, etc. 2 argumentative or quarrelsome. ▸ **contentiously** *adv.*

contest (kăn'tĕst,) *noun* 1 a competition. 2 a struggle. —*verb trans., intrans.* (kən-tĕst') (pronounced with stress on the last syllable) (**contested, contesting**) 1 to enter the competition or struggle for. 2 to dispute (a claim, someone's will, etc.). ▸ **contestable** *adj.*

contestant *noun* a person who takes part in a contest; a competitor.

context *noun* 1 the passage in a text or speech within which a particular word, statement, etc., occurs. 2 circumstances, background, or setting. ▸ **contextual** *adj.*

contiguous *adj.* (**contiguous with** *or* **to**) 1 touching; neighboring or adjacent to. 2 near or next in order or time. ▸ **contiguity** *noun* ▸ **contiguously** *adv.*

continence *noun* 1 the ability to control the bowels and bladder. 2 control over one's appetites and passions; self-control.

continent¹ *noun* 1 a any of the seven main land masses of the world. b the mainland portion of one of these land masses. 2 (**the Continent**) the mainland of Europe.

continent² *adj.* 1 able to control one's bowels and bladder. 2 self-controlled.

continental *adj.* 1 relating to any of the continents of the world. 2 (**Continental**) belonging or relating to the mainland of the continent of Europe.

contingency (kən-tĭn'jən-sē) *noun* (*pl.* **contingencies**) 1 something that is liable, but not certain, to occur; a chance happening. 2 something dependent on a future chance happening.

contingent *noun* 1 a body of troops. 2 any body of people. —*adj.* 1 (**contingent on** *or* **upon**) dependent on (some uncertain circumstance). 2 liable, but not certain, to occur; accidental.

continual *adj.* 1 constantly happening or done; frequent. 2 never ceasing; constant. ▸ **continually** *adv.*

continuance *noun* 1 the act or state of continuing. 2 duration. 3 *Law* adjournment to a future date.

continuation *noun* 1 the act or process of continuing. 2 something that adds to something or carries it on.

continue *verb trans., intrans.* (**continued, continuing**) 1 to go on without stopping. 2 to last or cause to last. 3 to carry on or start again after a break.

continuity *noun* 1 the state of being continuous, unbroken, or consistent. 2 the arrangement of scenes in a movie or television program so that one progresses smoothly from another.

continuous *adj.* 1 uninterrupted, as in extent or sequence. 2 physically attached in a series of units; unbroken. ▸ **continuously** *adv.*

continuum (kən-tĭn'yə-wəm) *noun* (*pl.* **continua, continuums**) a continuous sequence; an unbroken progression.

contort *verb trans., intrans.* (**contorted, contorting**) to twist violently out of shape. ▸ **contortion** *noun*

contortionist *noun* an entertainer who is able to twist his or her body into spectacularly unnatural positions.

contour (kăn'tŏŏr,) *noun* 1 (*usu.* **contours**) a distinctive outline. 2 a line on a map joining points of the same height or depth. *Also* called **contour line**. —*verb trans.* (**contoured, contouring**) 1 to shape the contour of. 2 to mark the contour lines on (a map).

contra- *prefix* forming words denoting: 1 against: *contraception*. 2 opposite: *contraflow*.

contraband *noun* the smuggling of goods prohibited from being imported or exported, or the goods so smuggled. —*adj.* prohibited from being imported or exported; smuggled.

contrabass *noun* double bass.

contrabassoon *noun* a double bassoon that sounds an octave lower than the standard instrument.

contraception *noun* the prevention of pregnancy by the use of birth-control devices or drugs.

contraceptive *noun* a device or drug that prevents pregnancy. —*adj.* serving to prevent pregnancy.

contract *noun* (kăn'trăkt,) 1 an agreement, esp. a legally binding one. 2 *slang* an agreement where someone is to be murdered. —*verb intrans., trans.* (kən-trăkt', kăn'-trăkt,) (**contracted, contracting**) 1 to make or become smaller. 2 of *muscles* to bend a joint, etc. 3 to catch (a disease). 4 to enter into (an alliance, legal contract, or a marriage). 5 to incur or accumulate (a debt).

contraction *noun* **1** the process of contracting or state of being contracted. **2** a tightening of a muscle or set of muscles, esp. those of the uterus in the period of labor before childbirth. **3** a shortened form of a word or phrase.

contractor *noun* a person or firm that undertakes work on contract, esp. connected with building.

contractual *adj.* relating to a contract or other binding agreement. ▸ **contractually** *adv.*

contradict *verb trans.* (**contradicted, contradicting**) **1** to assert the opposite of (a statement, etc.) **2** to assert the opposite of a statement, etc. made by (a person, etc.) **3** *of a statement, etc.* to disagree or be inconsistent with (another). ▸ **contradiction** *noun* ▸ **contradictory** *adj.*

contradistinction *noun* a distinction made in terms of a contrast between qualities, properties, etc.

contrail (kän'trāl,) *noun* a vapor trail seen in the wake of a jet aircraft.

contraindicate *verb trans.* (**contraindicated, contraindicating**) to be a reason for not using (a medical treatment, operation, etc.). ▸ **contraindication** *noun*

contralto (kən-trăl'tō) *noun* (*pl.* **contraltos**) the lowest female singing voice, or a singer with this voice.

contraption *noun colloq.* a machine or apparatus.

contrapuntal *adj.* relating to, or arranged as, counterpoint. ▸ **contrapuntally** *adv.*

contrariwise *adv.* **1** in the opposite way around. **2** in a perverse manner; waywardly.

contrary *adj.* **1** quite different; opposite; opposed. **2** obstinate, self-willed, or wayward. —*noun* (*pl.* **contraries**) an extreme opposite. —**contrary to** in opposition or contrast to something. **on the contrary** in opposition or contrast to what has just been said. ▸ **contrariety** *noun* ▸ **contrarily** *adv.*

contrast (kän'trăst) *noun* **1** difference or dissimilarity between things or people being compared. **2** a person or thing that is strikingly different from another. **3** the degree of difference between the light and dark parts of a photograph or television picture. —*verb trans., intrans.* (kən-trăst', kän'trăst,) (**contrasted, contrasting**) **1** to place in opposition so as to reveal contrasts or differences. **2** to be distinct from; to exhibit contrasts or differences.

Usage The noun *contrast* may be followed by the pronouns *with, to,* or *between.* When used transitively, the verb *contrast* takes the prepositions *with* and, less commonly, *to.*

contravene *verb trans.* (**contravened, contravening**) to break or disobey (a law or rule). ▸ **contravention** *noun*

contretemps (kän'trə-tän,, kŏn,trə-tän') *noun* (*pl.* **contretemps**) **1** an awkward or embarrassing moment or happening. **2** a slight disagreement.

contribute *verb trans., intrans.* (**contributed, contributing**) **1** to give for a joint purpose. **2** to be one of the causes of (something). **3** to supply (e.g., an article) for publication in a newspaper, anthology, or magazine. ▸ **contribution** *noun* ▸ **contributor** *noun*

contributory *adj.* having partial responsibility.

contrite *adj.* sorry for something one has done. ▸ **contritely** *adv.* ▸ **contrition** *noun*

contrivance *noun* **1** the act or power of contriving. **2** a device or apparatus. **3** an instance of cunning; a scheme.

contrive *verb trans.* (**contrived, contriving**) **1** to manage or succeed. **2** to bring about. **3** to make or construct, esp. with difficulty.

contrived *adj.* forced or artificial.

control *noun* **1** authority or charge; power to influence or guide. **2** a means of limitation. **3** (**controls**) the levers, switches, etc., by which a machine, etc., is operated. **4** the people in charge of an operation: *mission control.* —*verb trans.* (**controlled, controlling**) **1** to have or exercise control over. **2** to regulate. **3** to limit. **4** to check or verify against a standard. ▸ **controllable** *adj.* ▸ **controllability** *noun*

controlled substance a chemical substance or drug, whose use and possession are regulated by the government.

controller *noun* **1** a person or thing that controls. **2** (*also* **comptroller**) an official in charge of a government's currency.

control tower a tall building at an airport or air base from which takeoff and landing instructions are given.

controversy *noun* (*pl.* **controversies**) a usu. longstanding disagreement or dispute. ▸ **controversial** *adj.* ▸ **controversially** *adv.*

contumacy (kən-tyōō'mə-sē) *noun* obstinate refusal to obey; resistance to authority. ▸ **contumacious** *adj.* ▸ **contumaciously** *adv.*

contumely (kän-tyōō'mə-lē, kän'tyə-mē,lē, kän'tyōōm,lē) *noun* (*pl.* **contumelies**) scornful or insulting treatment or words. ▸ **contumelious** *adj.*

contuse (kən-tyōōz', -tōōz') *verb trans.* (**contused, contusing**) to bruise. ▸ **contusion** *noun*

conundrum (kə-nən'drəm) *noun* **1** a confusing problem. **2** a riddle.

conurbation *noun* an extensive built-up area, consisting of several towns whose outskirts have merged.

convalesce (kăn,və-lĕs′) *verb intrans.* (**convalesced, convalescing**) to recover one's strength after an illness, operation or injury, esp. by resting.

convalescent *adj.* recovering from an illness. —*noun* a person who is recovering from an illness or injury. ▸ **convalescence** *noun*

convection *noun* the transmission of heat through liquids or gases by means of currents that begin to circulate as heated particles rise from the cooler areas to the warmer areas.

convector *noun* a heating apparatus that circulates warm air by convection.

convene *verb trans., intrans.* (**convened, convening**) to assemble or summon to assemble.

convenience *noun* 1 the quality of being convenient. 2 an appliance or device that enhances personal comfort or ease of work.

convenience food any food that has been partially or entirely prepared by the manufacturer, and requires only to be cooked or thawed and then served.

convenience store a small retail store that operates long hours, selling groceries, toiletries, etc.

convenient *adj.* 1 fitting in with one's plans, etc.; not causing trouble or difficulty. 2 saving time and trouble; useful. 3 at hand; available. ▸ **conveniently** *adv.*

convent *noun* 1 a community of nuns, or the building occupied by them. 2 a school where the teaching is done by nuns.

convention *noun* 1 a large, formal conference or assembly. 2 a formal treaty or agreement. 3 a custom or generally accepted practice.

conventional *adj.* 1 traditional; normal; customary. 2 conservative or unoriginal. 3 *of weapons or warfare* not nuclear. ▸ **conventionality** *noun* ▸ **conventionalize** *verb* ▸ **conventionally** *adv.*

converge *verb intrans.* (**converged, converging**) 1 (**converge on** *or* **upon**) to move toward or meet at one point. 2 *of opinions* to coincide. ▸ **convergence** *noun* ▸ **convergent** *adj.*

conversant *adj.* (**conversant in** *or* **with**) having a thorough knowledge of something.

conversation *noun* informal talk. ▸ **conversational** *adj.* ▸ **conversationalist** *noun*

converse¹ (kən-vərs′) *verb intrans.* (**conversed, conversing**) to hold a conversation; to talk to another or others.

converse² (kən-vərs′, kăn′vərs,) *adj.* reversed; opposite. —*noun* (kăn′vərs,) an opposite. ▸ **conversely** *adv.*

conversion *noun* 1 the act of converting. 2 something converted to another use. 3 *Football* a score that is made when trying

for a point or points after a touchdown has been made.

convert (kən-vərt′) *verb trans., intrans.* (**converted, converting**) 1 to change (something) in form or function. 2 to win over, or be won over, as to another religion or opinion. —*noun* (kăn′vərt,) a person who has been converted to a new religion or practice.

converter *or* **convertor** *noun* something or someone that converts, esp. an electrical or electronic device for converting a current or signal.

convertible *adj.* capable of being converted. —*noun* an automobile having a top that can be folded or rolled back or removed.

convex *adj.* outward-curving, like the upper surface of a dome. *See also* **concave**. ▸ **convexity** *noun*

convey *verb trans.* (**conveyed, conveying**) 1 to carry; to transport. 2 to communicate; to impart (a specified meaning or sense). 3 *Law* to transfer the ownership of (property). ▸ **conveyable** *adj.*

conveyance *noun* 1 the process of conveying. 2 a transport vehicle of any kind. 3 *Law* the transfer of the ownership of property.

conveyancing *noun Law* the act or process of transferring the ownership of property. ▸ **conveyancer** *noun*

conveyer *or* **conveyor** *noun* one that conveys.

conveyor belt an endless moving belt for conveying articles, e.g., in a factory.

convict (kən-vĭkt′) *verb trans.* (**convicted, convicting**) to prove or declare (a party) guilty of a crime. —*noun* (kăn′vĭkt,) a person serving a prison sentence.

conviction *noun* 1 the act of convicting; the state of being convicted. 2 a the state of being convinced. b something that is accepted by a person as true, not always proved.

convince *verb trans.* (**convinced, convincing**) to cause (another) to believe (something) by force of argument or persuasion. ▸ **convincing** *adj.* ▸ **convincingly** *adv.*

convivial *adj.* 1 jovial, sociable, and cheerful. 2 festive. ▸ **conviviality** *noun* ▸ **convivially** *adv.*

convocation *noun* 1 the act of summoning together. 2 an assembly.

convoke *verb trans.* (**convoked, convoking**) to call together.

convoluted *adj.* 1 coiled and twisted. 2 complicated. ▸ **convolution** *noun*

convoy (kăn′voi,) *noun* a group of vehicles, merchant ships, etc. traveling together, or under escort. —*verb trans.* (kăn′voi,, kən-voi′) (**convoyed, convoying**) to accompany for protection.

convulse *verb trans., intrans.* (**convulsed, convulsing**) to jerk or distort violently.

convulsion *noun* **1** the state of being convulsed. **2** (*often* **convulsions**) a violent, involuntary contraction of the muscles of the body, or a series of such contractions. **3** (**convulsions**) *colloq.* spasms of laughter.

convulsive *adj.* **1** causing or affected by convulsions. **2** spasmodic. ▸ **convulsively** *adv.*

coo *noun* the soft murmuring call of a dove. —*verb intrans., trans.* (**cooed, cooing**) **1** to make the soft murmur of a dove. **2** to murmur affectionately.

cook *verb trans., intrans.* (**cooked, cooking**) to prepare or be prepared by heating. —*noun* a person who prepares food by heating and other procedures.

cookbook *noun* a book of recipes.

cookery (kook'ə-rē) *noun* the art or practice of cooking food.

cookie or **cooky** *noun* (*pl.* **cookies**) **1** a small, crisp, flat cake. **2** *slang* a person: *a tough cookie.* **3** *Comput.* a packet of data that records and relays information about a user's habits of accessing a particular Web site.

cookout *noun* an outdoor meal where food is cooked, e.g., on a barbecue grill.

cool *adj.* **1** fairly cold. **2** pleasantly fresh: *a cool breeze.* **3** calm. **4** lacking enthusiasm; unfriendly. **5** *of a large sum* at least. **6** *slang* excellent. **7** *of colors* suggestive of coolness, typically containing blue. **9** *colloq.* all right: *Cool, I'll see you at 8.* —*noun* **1** a part, place, or period that is fairly cold. **2** *slang* self-control; composure: *Keep your cool.* —*verb trans., intrans.* (**cooled, cooling**) **1** to become cool. **2** to become less interested or enthusiastic. **3** (**cool down** or **off**) to make cool. —**cool it** *slang* to calm down. **play it cool** *slang* to deal with a situation calmly but warily. ▸ **coolly** *adv.* ▸ **coolness** *noun*

coolant *noun* a liquid or gas used as a cooling agent, esp. a fluid used to remove heat from a working engine.

cooler *noun* **1** a container or device for cooling things. **2** *slang* a jail or prison.

cooling-off period an interval for reflection and negotiation before taking action.

cooling tower a tall structure in which water heated in an industrial process is cooled for reuse.

coon *noun colloq.* a raccoon.

coop (koop) *noun* a cage for hens. —**coop up** to confine in a small space or to be so confined.

co-op (kō'āp,) *noun colloq.* a cooperative apartment or business.

cooper *noun* a person who makes or repairs barrels.

cooperate *verb intrans.* (**cooperated, co-operating**) **1** to work together. **2** to be

helpful or willing to fit in with others' plans. ▸ **cooperation** *noun* ▸ **cooperator** *noun*

cooperative *adj.* **1** relating to or giving cooperation. **2** jointly owned by residents or workers, with profits shared equally. —*noun* a cooperative building, business, or farm. ▸ **cooperatively** *adv.*

co-opt (kō-äpt') *verb trans.* (**co-opted, co-opting**) **1** *of the members of a body* to choose as an additional member. **2** to appropriate as one's own. **3** to manage to win over (e.g., an opposing minority) by assimilating it into the main group. ▸ **co-option** *noun* ▸ **co-optive** *adj.*

coordinate (kō-ôrd'n-āt,) *verb trans., intrans.* (**coordinated, coordinating**) **1** to combine, integrate, and adjust (a number of different parts or processes) so as to relate smoothly one to another. **2** to work or function together in a harmonious manner. —*adj.* (kō-ôrd'n-ət,) **1** relating to or involving coordination or coordinates. **2** *of clauses* equal in status, as when joined by *and* or *but.* —*noun* (pronounced -nat) **1** *Math* one of a pair of numbers taken from a vertical and horizontal axis which together establish the position of a fixed point, e.g., on a map. **2** (**coordinates**) garments designed to be worn together. ▸ **coordinator** *noun*

coordination *noun* **1** ordered, concerted action. **2** balanced or skillful movement.

coot *noun* **1** a water bird with a white patch above the beak. **2** *colloq.* a fool or an eccentric.

cootie *noun slang* a parasitic louse that infests the human body.

cop¹ *noun slang* a police officer.

cop² *verb trans.* (**copped, copping**) *slang* **1** to catch. **2** to steal. —**cop a plea** *slang* to admit guilt to a lesser charge in order to avoid trial for a more serious one.

cope *verb intrans.* (**coped, coping**) **1** (**cope with**) to deal with successfully in spite of difficulty. **2** to manage; to get by.

copier *noun* a machine for making copies, esp. photocopies.

copilot *noun* the assistant pilot, or the second officer, of an aircraft.

coping *noun* the top row of stones in a wall.

copious *adj.* existing in large amounts.

cop-out *noun slang* **1** avoidance of a responsibility; an escape or withdrawal. **2** a flimsy excuse.

copper¹ *noun* **1** *Chem.* (SYMBOL **Cu**) a soft reddish-brown metallic element, used to make electric cables, wire, and coins. **2** a coin of low value made of copper or bronze. ▸ **coppery** *adj.*

copper² *noun slang* a police officer.

copperhead *noun* a poisonous American pit viper.

coppice (käp´ĭs) *noun* an area of woodland in which trees are regularly cut back to ground level.

copra (kō´prə) *noun* the dried kernels of the coconut, yielding coconut oil.

copse *noun* a coppice.

copula (käp´yə-lə) *noun* a verb that links subject and complement.

copulate (käp´yə-lāt,) *verb intrans.* (**copulated, copulating**) to have sexual intercourse. ▸ **copulation** *See also* **cop-**.

copy *noun* (*pl.* **copies**) **1** an imitation or reproduction. **2** one of the many specimens of a book, or of a particular issue of a newspaper, etc. **3** written material for printing. **4** the wording of an advertisement. **5** material suitable for a newspaper article. —*verb trans., intrans.* (**copied, copying, copies**) **1** to imitate. **2** to make a copy of. **3** to reproduce; to photocopy. **4** *Comput.* to duplicate data, etc. and send it to another file, computer, etc., without altering it.

copybook *noun* a book of handwriting examples for copying. —*adj.* unoriginal: *copybook prose.*

copycat *colloq. noun* a mere imitator. —*adj.* imitating another: *copycat crimes.*

copyedit *verb trans.* (**copyedited, copyediting, copyedits**) to correct and prepare (a manuscript) for publication.

copyright *noun* the sole right to print, publish, translate, perform, film, or record a literary, dramatic, musical, or artistic work.

copywriter *noun* a person who writes advertising copy.

coquette (kō-kĕt´) *noun* a flirtatious woman. ▸ **coquettish** *adj.* ▸ **coquettishly** *adv.* ▸ **coquettishness** *noun* .

cor- *prefix, found usu. in words derived from Latin,* forming words denoting with or together: *correlation. See also* **con-**.

coracle (kôr´ə-kəl, kär´-) *noun* a small, oval rowboat made of wicker covered with hides.

coral *noun* **1** a tiny invertebrate marine animal, consisting of a hollow tube with a mouth, surrounded by tentacles. **2** a hard mass formed from the skeletons of this animal. **3** a pinkish-orange color.

coral snake an American venomous snake, usu. with bands of black, yellow, and red.

corbel (kôr´bəl) *noun* a stone or timber projecting from a wall, taking the weight of a parapet, arch, or bracket. *Also called* **truss**. —*verb* (**corbeled, corbeling**) to support on corbels.

cord *noun* **1** thin rope or thick string. **2** *Anat.* a long flexible structure resembling a thin rope. **3** the cable of an electrical appliance. **4** a ribbed fabric, esp. corduroy. **5** (**cords**) corduroy pants. **6** a unit of measurement for cut wood equal to 128 cu. ft. (3.63 cu m).

cordial (kôr´jəl) *adj.* **1** warm and affectionate. **2** heartfelt; profound. —*noun* a fruit-flavored drink. ▸ **cordiality** *noun* ▸ **cordially** *adv.*

cordite *noun* a smokeless explosive, used as a propellant in, eg., firearms and big guns.

cordless *adj.* of an appliance operating without an electrical cord.

cordon (kôrd´n, kôr´dän,) *noun* **1** a line of police or soldiers encircling an area so as to prevent passage into or out of it. **2** a ribbon bestowed as a mark of honor. —*verb trans.* (**cordoned, cordoning**) (**cordon off**) to close off (an area) with a cordon.

cordon bleu (kôr-dôɴ´blœ´) a cook of the highest standard. —*adj.* denoting first class cookery.

> Literally 'blue ribbon' in French, after the ribbon worn by the Knights of the Holy Ghost

corduroy *noun* **1** a thick, ribbed, cotton fabric. **2** (**corduroys**) pants made of corduroy.

CORE *abbrev.* Congress of Racial Equality.

core *noun* **1** the fibrous case at the center of some fruits, containing the seeds. **2** the central, essential, or unchanging part of something. ⊟ CENTER, HEART, PITH **3** *Comput.* the main memory of a computer, where instructions and data are stored in such a way that they are available for immediate use. *Also called* **core memory**. —*verb trans.* (**cored, coring**) to remove the core of (an apple, etc.).

corespondent (kō,rə-spän´dənt) *noun* in divorce cases, a person said to have committed adultery with the partner against whom the case is being brought.

corgi (kôr´gē) *noun* a small dog with very short legs.

coriander *noun* a European plant whose strong-smelling leaves and seeds are used as a flavoring.

cork *noun* **1** a layer of tissue that forms below the epidermis in the stems and roots of woody plants, e.g., trees. **2** a piece of this tissue used as a stopper for a bottle, etc. —*verb trans.* (**corked, corking**) **1** to stop (a bottle, etc.) with a cork. **2** to suppress (one's feelings, etc.).

corkage (kôr´kĭj) *noun* a fee charged by a restaurant for serving wine bought elsewhere.

corked *adj.*, *of wine* spoiled as a result of having a faulty cork.

corker *noun slang* something or someone regarded as remarkable.

corkscrew *noun* an implement with a spiral spike for screwing into bottle corks to remove them. —*adj.* shaped like a spiral. —*verb intrans.* (**corkscrewed, corkscrewing**) to move spirally.

corm *noun* in certain plants, a swollen underground stem, rounded in shape and bearing roots on its lower surface.

cormorant *noun* a large seabird.

corn[1] *noun* **1 a** any of various cultivated forms of a tall annual cereal grass that bears kernels on large ears. **b** the kernels of one of these plants, eaten as food·by humans and livestock. **c** an ear formed on this plant. *Also called* **Indian corn, maize. 2** *slang* something old-fashioned, stale, or trite. .

corn[2] *noun* a small patch of hardened skin, esp. on a toe.

cornbread *noun* bread that is made of cornmeal, milk, butter, and eggs.

corncob *noun* the core part of an ear of corn, to which the kernels are attached.

cornea (kôr'nē-ə) *noun* the transparent covering of the eyeball. ▸ **corneal** *adj.*

corned beef beef that has been salted, cooked, and packaged.

corner *noun* **1** a point or place where lines or surface edges meet; the inside or outside of the angle so formed. **2** an intersection between roads. **3** a quiet or remote place. **4** an awkward situation. **5** either of the angles of a boxing ring used as a base between rounds by contestants. —*verb trans., intrans.* (**cornered, cornering**) **1** to force into a place or position from which escape is difficult. **2** to gain control of (a market). **3** *of a driver or vehicle* to turn a corner. —**cut corners** to spend less money, effort, time, etc., on something than one should.

cornerstone *noun* **1** a stone built into the corner of the foundation of a building. **2** a crucial or indispensable part; a basis.

cornet (kôr-nĕt') *noun* a brass musical instrument similar to a trumpet. ▸ **cornetist** *noun*

corn flakes flaky, crisp, coarse cornmeal made into a cereal product.

cornflower *noun* a plant with deep blue flowers. *Also called* **bachelor's buttons.**

cornice *noun* **1** a decorative border of molded plaster around a ceiling. **2 a** the lower section of the horizontal layer of masonry surmounting a row of columns. **b** a projecting molding at the top of an external wall.

cornmeal *noun* ground meal from corn kernels, used in cooking.

corn oil a light yellow liquid obtained from the embryos of grains of corn, used in cooking.

cornrow *verb trans.* (**cornrowed, cornrowing**) to fix (hair) by dividing into sections, then braiding in rows close to the scalp. ▸ **cornrow** *noun*

corn silk the silky tuft or tassel·that forms on an ear of corn.

cornstarch *noun* a starch, obtained from corn, used in cooking as a thickener.

cornucopia *noun* a horn full to overflowing with fruit and other produce, used as a symbol of abundance. ▸ **cornucopian** *adj.*

corny *adj.* (**cornier, corniest**) *colloq.* **1** old and stale. **2** embarrassingly old-fashioned or sentimental. ▸ **cornily** *adv.* ▸ **corniness** *noun*

corolla (kə-rāl'ə, -rō'lə) *noun* the petals of a flower, which may be separate, or fused to form a tube.

corollary (kôr'ə-lĕr,ē) *noun* (*pl.* **corollaries**) **1** something that follows from another thing that has been proved. **2** a natural·or obvious consequence.

corona *noun* (*pl.* **coronas, coronae**) **1** a ring of light around the Sun or moon. *Also called* **aureole. 2** the glowing region surrounding a high-voltage conductor. **3** a halo or crown.

coronary (kôr'ə-nĕr,ē, kär'-) *adj.* denoting the arteries supplying blood to the heart muscle. —*noun* (*pl.* **coronaries**) *colloq.* a heart attack.

coronary thrombosis the formation of a blood clot in a coronary artery, which results in death of part of the heart muscle.

coronation *noun* the ceremony of crowning a king, queen, or consort.

coroner *noun* an officer empowered to investigate by inquest deaths believed to be other than naturally caused.

coronet *noun* **1** a small crown. **2** a circlet of jewels for the head.

corporal[1] (kôr'prəl, -pə-rəl) *noun* a noncommissioned rank in the US Army that is above private first class and below sergeant, and, in the US Marine Corps, is above lance corporal and below sergeant.

corporal[2] *adj.* relating to the human body.

corporal punishment physical punishment, such as beating or caning.

corporate *adj.* **1** shared by members of a group; joint. **2** belonging or relating to a corporation. ▸ **corporately** *adv.*

corporation *noun* a body of people acting jointly.

corporeal (kôr-pôr'ē-əl) *adj.* **1** relating to actual matter or to actuality. **2** relating to the body as distinct from the soul. ▸ **corporeality** *noun* ▸ **corporeally** *adv.*

corps (kôr) *noun* (*pl.* **corps**) **1 a** a group of students constituting the student body at a military school or college. **b** an army ground unit composed of two divisions or more. **2** a body of people engaged in particular work: *the diplomatic corps.*

corps de ballet (kôrd,ə-bă-lā') a company of ballet dancers.

corpse (kôrps) *noun* the dead body of a human being.

corpulent *adj.* extremely fat; obese. ▸ **corpulence** *noun*

corpus *noun* (*pl.* **corpora**) **1** a body of writings, e.g., by a particular author. **2** a body of written and/or spoken material for language research. **3** any of various structures within the body.

corpuscle *noun* a small particle or cell within a tissue or organ, esp. a blood cell. ▸ **corpuscular** *adj.*

corral (kə-rãl') *noun* an enclosure into which horses or cattle are driven. —*verb trans.* (**corralled, corralling**) to herd or pen into, or as if into, a corral.

correct *verb trans.* (**corrected, correcting**) **1** to set or put right; to remove errors from. **2** to mark the errors in. **3** to adjust or make better. **4** to rebuke or punish. —*adj.* **1** containing or having no mistakes. **2** right; proper; appropriate. **3** conforming to accepted standards. ▸ **corrective** *adj., noun* ▸ **correctly** *adv.* ▸ **correctness** *noun*

correction *noun* **1** the act of correcting. **2** an alteration that corrects something. **3** (**corrections**) the system of incarceration, rehabilitation, probation, and parole used with respect to lawbreakers.

correlate *verb intrans., trans.* (**correlated, correlating**) **1** to have a connection or correspondence; to relate one to another. **2** to combine, compare, show relationships between (information, reports, etc.). ▸ **correlation** *noun*

correlative *adj.* **1** mutually linked. **2** *of words* used as an interrelated pair, like *either* and *or*.

correspond *verb intrans.* (**corresponded, corresponding**) **1** (**correspond to**) to be similar or equivalent to. **2** (**correspond with** or **to**) to be in agreement; to match. **3** to write to and receive letters (from another).

correspondence *noun* **1** similarity; equivalence. **2** communication by letters; letters received or sent.

correspondence course a course of study conducted by mail or electronic means.

correspondent *noun* **1** a person who writes letters. **2** a person employed by a newspaper, radio station, etc. to send reports from a particular part of the world, or on a particular topic.

corridor *noun* **1** a passageway. **2** a strip of land through foreign territory, giving access, e.g., to a port.

corrigendum (kôr,ĭ-jěn'dəm, kär,-) *noun* (*pl.* **corrigenda**) an error for correction, e.g., in a book.

corroborate (kə-rãb'ə-rāt,) *verb trans.* (**corroborated, corroborating**) to confirm (e.g., a statement, evidence, etc.). ▸ **corroboration** *noun* ▸ **corroborative** *adj.* ▸ **corroborator** *noun*

corrode *verb trans., intrans.* (**corroded, corroding**) **1 a** *of rust, chemicals, etc.* to eat away (a material or an object) little by little. **b** *of a material or object* to be gradually eaten away. **2** to destroy gradually.

corrosion *noun* **1** an act or the process or effect of corroding. **2** a corroded part or patch. ▸ **corrosive** *adj.*

corrugate *verb trans.* (**corrugated, corrugating**) to fold into parallel ridges, so as to make stronger. ▸ **corrugation** *noun*

corrupt *verb trans.* (**corrupted, corrupting**) **1** to change for the worse, esp. morally. **2** to spoil, deform, or make impure. **3** to bribe. —*adj.* **1** morally evil and dishonest. **2** accepting bribes. **3** *of a text* so full of errors and alterations as to be unreliable. **4** *of a program or data* containing errors arising, e.g., from a fault in the hardware or software. ▸ **corruptible** *adj.* ▸ **corruptibility** *noun* ▸ **corruptive** *adj.* ▸ **corruptly** *adv.*

corruption *noun* **1** the process of corrupting or condition of being corrupt. **2** a deformed form of a word or phrase.

corsage (kôr-säzh', -säj') *noun* a small spray of flowers for wearing on a garment.

corsair *noun old use* a pirate or pirate ship.

corselet *noun* **1** (*also* **corslet**) *Hist.* a protective garment or piece of armor for the upper part of the body. **2** (*also* **corselette**) a woman's undergarment combining girdle and brassière.

corset *noun* a tightly fitting undergarment stiffened by strips of bone or plastic, for shaping, or supporting the figure.

cortège (kôr-tĕzh') *noun* a procession, esp. a funeral procession.

cortex *noun* (*pl.* **cortices, cortexes**) the outer layer of an organ or tissue, e.g., of the brain. ▸ **cortical** *adj.*

cortisone *noun* a naturally occurring steroid hormone, used to treat rheumatoid arthritis, certain eye and skin disorders, etc.

corundum *noun* an extremely hard aluminum oxide mineral, used as an abrasive powder, and, in the form of ruby, sapphire, etc., as a gemstone.

coruscate (kôr'ə-skăt,) *verb intrans.* (**coruscated, coruscating**) to sparkle. ▸ **coruscation** *noun*

cos *noun* a crisp lettuce. *Also called* **romaine**.

cosmetic *adj.* **1** used to beautify the face, body, or hair. **2** improving only superficially, for the sake of appearances. —*noun* a beautifying application, esp. for the face. ▸ **cosmetically** *adv.*

cosmic *adj.* **1** relating to the Universe. **2** coming from outer space. **3** *colloq.* large or significant. ▸ **cosmically** *adv.*

cosmic rays or **cosmic radiation** radiation consisting of streams of high-energy particles from outer space, traveling at about the speed of light.

cosmogony (kăz-măg′ə-nē) *noun* (*pl.* **cosmogonies**) the study of the origin and development of the Universe.

cosmology *noun* the scientific study of the origin, nature, structure, and evolution of the Universe. ▸ **cosmological** *adj.* ▸ **cosmologist** *noun*

cosmonaut *noun* a Russian astronaut.

cosmopolitan *adj.* **1** belonging to, or representative of, all parts of the world. **2** international in experience and outlook. —*noun* a citizen of the world.

cosmos *noun* the Universe seen as an ordered system.

Cossack (kăs′ăk,) *noun* a member of a people of Ukraine and the southern parts of Russia, notable as cavalrymen. —*adj.* belonging or relating to this people.

cosset *verb trans.* (**cosseted, cosseting**) to treat too kindly; to pamper.

cost *verb intrans., trans.* (*pa t and pa p* **cost**; *pr p* **costing**) **1** to require (a specified monetary amount). **2** to cause to lose. **3** (*pa t and pa p* **costed**) to estimate or decide the cost of. —*noun* **1** the amount that something costs. **2** loss or sacrifice.

costar *or* **co-star** *noun* a person who shares a leading role in a film, play, etc. —*verb intrans.* (**costarred, costarring**) **1** *of a performer* to appear alongside another star. **2** *of a production* to feature as fellow stars.

cost-effective *adj.* giving acceptable value for money expended.

costive *adj.* constipated or causing constipation.

costly *adj.* (**costlier, costliest**) **1** of great monetary price. **2** involving major losses or sacrifices. ▸ **costliness** *noun*

costume *noun* **1** a set of clothing of a special kind, esp. of a particular historical period or particular country. **2** a garment or an outfit for a special activity.

costume jewelry jewelry made of inexpensive or artificial materials.

costumer *or* **costumier** *noun* a person who makes or supplies costumes.

cosy *adj., noun, verb same as* **cozy**.

cot *noun* a camp bed.

cote *noun* a small shelter for birds or animals.

coterie (kō′tə-rē) *noun* a group of friends, professional colleagues, etc., who stick together and are hostile toward outsiders.

cottage *noun* a small country house.

cottage cheese a soft, white cheese made from sour milk.

cottage industry a craft industry such as knitting or weaving, employing workers in their own homes.

cotton *noun* **1** a shrubby plant with creamy-white, yellow, or reddish flowers and egg-shaped seed pods. **2** the soft, white fiber obtained from this plant. **3** cloth that is woven from fibers obtained from this plant and spun into yarn. —*verb intrans.* (**cottoned, cottoning**) (**cotton to** *or* **cotton up to**) colloq. to take a liking to (someone or something). ▸ **cottony** *adj.*

cotton candy threaded sugar, often tinted with food coloring and twirled around a stick, eaten as a confection.

cottonmouth *noun* an American pit viper. *Also called* **moccasin, water moccasin.**

cottontail *noun* a brown-to-gray N American rabbit with a fluffy white tail.

cottonwool *noun* soft, fluffy wadding used in treating injuries, applying cosmetics, etc.

cotyledon (kăt,l-ēd′n) *noun* in flowering plants, one of the leaves produced by the embryo.

couch (kowch) *noun* **1** a sofa. **2** a bedlike seat with a headrest. —*verb trans.* (**couched, couching**) to express (something) in words, esp., of a specified kind.

couchette (kōō-shĕt′) *noun* a sleeping berth on a European passenger train; a railroad car with such berths.

couch potato *slang* one who spends most of his or her leisure time sitting inactive in front of the television.

cougar (kōō′gər) *noun* a mountain lion.

cough (kôf) *verb intrans.* (**coughed, coughing**) **1** to expel air, mucus, etc., from the throat or lungs with a rough, sharp noise. **2** *of an engine, etc.* to make a rough, irregular noise. —*noun* **1** an act or sound of coughing. **2** a condition of lungs or throat causing coughing. —**cough up 1** *slang* to provide (something wanted). **2** to bring up (mucus, phlegm, blood, etc.) by coughing.

cough drop a small, sweetened, and medicated lozenge for relieving coughing.

could *verb aux. past tense of* **can**[1].

coulomb (kōō′lăm,, -lōm,) *noun* (SYMBOL **C**) a unit of electric charge, equal to the amount of charge transported by a current of one ampere in one second.

council *noun* **1** a body of people whose function is to advise, administer, or legislate. **2** the elected body of people directing the governmental affairs of, e.g., a city or town.

councilman *noun* a man serving on a council.

councilor *or* **councillor** *noun* a member of a council, esp. of a city or town.

councilwoman *noun* a woman serving on a council.

counsel *noun* **1** advice. **2** consultation, discussion, or deliberation: *take counsel.* **3** a lawyer or group of lawyers giving legal advice. —*verb trans.* (**counseled** *or* **counselled, counseling** *or* **counselling**) to advise.

counselor *or* **counsellor** *noun* **1** an adviser. **2** a lawyer.

count¹ *verb intrans., trans.* (**counted, counting**) **1** to say numbers in order. **2** to find the total amount of, by adding up item by item. **3** to include. **4** to be important or to matter. —*noun* **1** an act of counting. **2** the number counted. **3** a charge brought against an accused person. —**count on** to rely or depend on (someone *or* something). **out for the count** fast asleep. ▶ **countable** *adj.*

count² *noun* a European nobleman.

countdown *noun* a count backward, with zero as the moment for action, used, e.g., in launching a rocket.

countenance *noun* expression or appearance; face. —*verb trans.* (**countenanced, countenancing**) to allow; to tolerate.

counter¹ *noun* **1** a long flat-topped surface in a shop, cafeteria, etc., over which goods are sold or food is served. **2** a small flat disk used as a playing-piece in various board games. **3** a disk-shaped token used as a substitute coin. **4** a device for counting something.

counter² *verb trans., intrans.* (**countered, countering**) to oppose, act against, or hit back. —*adv.* (**counter to**) in the opposite direction to; in contradiction to. —*noun* an opposite.

counter- *prefix* forming words denoting: **1** against: *counterattack.* **2** in competition or rivalry: *counterdemonstration.* **3** matching or corresponding: *counterpart.*

counteract *verb trans.* (**counteracted, counteracting**) to reduce or prevent the effect of. ▶ **counteraction** *noun* ▶ **counteractive** *adj.*

counterattack *noun* an attack in response to another attack. —*verb intrans.* (**counterattacked, counterattacking**) to attack in return.

counterbalance *noun* a weight, force, or circumstance that balances another and cancels it out. —*verb trans.* (**counterbalanced, counterbalancing**) to act as a counterbalance to; to neutralize or cancel out.

countercharge *noun* an accusation made in response to one made against oneself.

counterclaim *noun* a claim or assertion made in opposition to one made by someone else.

counterclockwise *adj., adv.* in the opposite direction to that in which the hands of a clock move.

counterculture *noun* a culture that rejects or opposes the values of the culture of the majority.

counterespionage *noun* activities undertaken to detect, frustrate, and interdict enemy spying.

counterfeit *adj.* **1** made in imitation of a genuine article, esp. with the purpose of deceiving; forged. **2** not genuine; insincere. —*verb trans.* (**counterfeited, counterfeiting**) to copy for a dishonest purpose; to forge.

counterfoil *noun* the section of a check, ticket, etc., retained as a record by the person who issues it.

counterinsurgency *noun* military action taken against insurgents or rebels.

counterintelligence *noun* counterespionage.

countermand *verb trans.* (**countermanded, countermanding**) to cancel (a previously issued order or command).

counteroffensive *noun* an aggressive move made in response to an initial attack.

counterpane *noun* a bedspread.

counterpart *noun* a person or thing matching or corresponding to another person or thing; an opposite number.

counterpoint *noun* **1** the combining of two or more melodies. *See also* **contrapuntal.** **2** a parallel, yet contrasting, theme or element.

counterpoise *noun* **1** a state of balance between two weights. **2** an influence, factor, or force that serves to counteract equally another influence, factor, or force.

counterproductive *adj.* tending to undermine productiveness and efficiency; having the opposite effect to that intended.

counterrevolution *noun* a revolution to overthrow a system of government established by a previous revolution. ▶ **counterrevolutionary** *adj., noun*

countersign *verb trans.* (**countersigned, countersigning**) to sign (a document, etc., already signed by someone else) by way of confirmation. —*noun* a password. ▶ **countersignature** *noun*

countersink *verb trans.* (*pa t* **countersunk**; *pa p* **countersunk**; *pr p* **countersinking**) **1** to widen the upper part of (a screw hole) so that the top of the screw when inserted will be level with the surrounding surface. **2** to insert (a screw) into such a hole.

counterspy *noun* (*pl.* **counterspies**) an espionage agent who works in opposition to enemy espionage forces.

countertenor *noun* an adult male singer who sings falsetto.

counterweight *noun* a counterbalancing weight.

countess *noun* **1** the wife or widow of an earl or count. **2** a woman with the rank of earl or count.

countless *adj.* so many as to be impossible to count.

count noun a noun that can be used with *a* or *an*, or in the plural.

countrified adj. rustic in appearance or style; rural.

country (kən'trē) noun (pl. **countries**) 1 the land of any of the nations of the world. 2 the population of such land. 3 one's native land. 4 open land, with hills, fields, etc., as distinct from towns. 5 country music.

country and western country music.

country club a suburban or rural club with facilities for golf, tennis, etc.

country music popular music whose melodies and lyrics are based on the folk style of the cowboys and the southern rural areas of the USA.

countryside noun land away from or outside towns.

countrywide adj., adv. all over the country.

county (kownt'ē) noun (pl. **counties**) the main administrative subdivision of a US state. —adj. relating to a county.

coup (kōō) noun 1 a successful move. 2 a coup d'état.

coup de grâce (kōōd,ə-gräs') a final decisive blow.

coup d'état (kōōd,ä-tä') noun (pl. **coups d'état**) the sudden, usu. violent, overthrow of a government.

coupe (kōōp, kōō-pā') or **coupé** noun a closed, two-door car.

couple (kəp'əl) noun 1 a pair of people romantically attached. 2 a pair of partners, e.g., for dancing. 3 two, or a few. —verb trans., intrans. (**coupled, coupling**) 1 to link; to connect. 2 to have sexual intercourse.

couplet noun a pair of consecutive lines of verse, esp. rhyming.

coupling noun 1 a link for joining things together. 2 sexual intercourse.

coupon noun 1 a slip of paper entitling one to something, e.g., a discount. 2 a detachable order form, competition entry form, etc.

courage noun 1 bravery. 2 power or ability to face danger etc. without fear.

courageous adj. having or displaying no fear in the face of danger or adversity. ▣ BRAVE, DAUNTLESS, FEARLESS, VALIANT ▣ COWARDLY, CRAVEN, YELLOW. ▸ **courageously** adv. ▸ **courageousness** noun

courier noun 1 a a commercial package-delivery service. b a person sent with a message. 2 a guide who travels with, and looks after, groups of tourists.

course noun 1 the path that someone or something moves in, takes, etc. 2 the channel, e.g., of a river. 3 the passage of a period of time. 4 a series of lessons. 5 a prescribed treatment, e.g., medicine to be taken, over a given period. 6 any of the successive parts of a meal. 7 the ground over which a game is played or a race run. —verb intrans., trans. (**coursed, coursing**) 1 to

move or flow. 2 to hunt (game) using dogs. —**of course** without doubt; naturally; certainly.

courser noun 1 a person who courses rabbits, etc., or a hound used for it. 2 poetic a swift horse. 3 an Asian or African running bird related to the plover.

coursing noun hunting rabbits or other small game with dogs.

court noun 1 the judge, law officers, and members of the jury gathered to hear and decide on a legal case. Also called **court of law**. 2 the room or building used for such a hearing. 3 an area marked out for a particular game. 4 an open space or square surrounded by houses or by sections of a building. 5 the palace, household, attendants, and advisers of a sovereign. —verb trans., intrans. (**courted, courting**) 1 to try to win the love of. 2 to try to win the favor of. 3 to seek (popularity, etc.). 4 to risk or invite.

courteous adj. polite; considerate; respectful. ▸ **courteously** adv.

courtesan (kôrt'ə-zən, -zăn,) noun Hist. a prostitute with wealthy or noble clients.

courtesy noun (pl. **courtesies**) 1 courteous behavior; politeness. 2 a courteous act.

courthouse a building with courts of law and often other government offices.

courtier (kôrt'ē-ər) noun 1 a person in attendance at a royal court. 2 an elegant flatterer.

courtly adj. having fine manners.

court-martial noun (pl. **courts-martial**) a trial, by a group of officers, of a member of the armed forces, for a breach of military law. —verb trans. (**court-martialed, court-martialing, court-martials**) to try by a military or naval court.

courtroom noun the room in which a court of law sits.

courtship noun the wooing of an intended spouse; the period for which this lasts.

courtyard noun an open space surrounded by buildings or walls.

couscous (kōōs'kōōs,) noun a N African dish of crushed wheat steamed and served, e.g., with meat.

cousin (kəz'ən) noun a son or daughter of one's uncle or aunt. Also called **first cousin**.

couture (kōō-tōōr') noun the designing, making, and selling of fashionable clothes.

couturier (kōō-tōōr'ē-ā,, -ē-ər) noun a fashion designer.

couturière (kōō-tōōr'ē-ĕr,, -ē-ər) noun a woman fashion designer.

cove noun a small, usu. sheltered bay or inlet on a rocky coast.

coven (kəv'ən) noun a gathering or band of witches, usu. 13.

covenant (kŏv'ə-nənt) *noun* a formal binding agreement or compact. —*verb trans.*, *intrans.* (**covenanted, covenanting**) to agree by covenant to do something. ▸ **covenanter** (kŏv'ə-nănt,ər) *noun*

cover *verb trans., intrans.* (**covered, covering**) **1** to form a layer over. **2** to protect or conceal by putting something over. **3** to clothe. **4** to extend over. **5** to sprinkle, spatter, mark all over, etc. **6** to deal with (a subject). **7** *of a news reporter* to investigate and then write about (a topic). **8** to have as one's area of responsibility. **9** to travel (a given distance). **10** to be adequate to pay. **11** to insure; to insure against. **12** to aim a gun at while backing up another. **13** *of a bird* to sit (on eggs). —*noun* **1** something, e.g., a piece of material or a lid, that covers. **2** (**covers**) the sheets, blankets, and spread covering a bed. **3** the protective paper or board that encases a book or magazine. **4** shelter; protection. **5** a prétense or a false identity. **6** a place setting. —**under cover** in secret.

coverage (kŏv'rĭj, -ə-rĭj) *noun* an amount covered; the fullness of treatment of a news item in any of the media, etc.

coveralls *pl. noun* a one-piece protective work garment worn over normal clothes.

cover charge a charge made in a bar, disco, etc. for enertainment.

cover girl a girl or woman whose photograph is shown on a magazine cover.

covering *noun* something that covers, esp. a blanket or protective casing.

covering letter *or* **cover letter** a letter accompanying and explaining documents or goods.

coverlet *noun* a thin top cover for a bed; a bedspread.

covert (kŏ'vərt, kō-vərt') *adj.* secret; clandestine.—*noun* (kŏv'ərt, kō'vərt) a thicket providing cover for game. ▸ **covertly** *adv.*

cover-up *or* **coverup** *noun* an act of concealing or withholding information about something suspect or illicit.

covet *verb trans.* (**coveted, coveting**) to long to possess (esp. something belonging to someone else). ▸ **covetous** *adj.* ▸ **covetously** *adv.* ▸ **covetousness** *noun*

covey *noun* (*pl.* **coveys**) a small flock of partridge or quail.

cow[1] *noun* **1** a female of any species of cattle. **2** a female of other large animals, e.g., the elephant, whale, etc.

cow[2] *verb trans.* (**cowed, cowing**) to frighten into submission.

coward *noun* someone easily frightened, or lacking courage to face danger or difficulty.

cowardice *noun* lack of courage.

cowardly *adj.* having or displaying a contemptible lack of courage. ▣ CHICKEN, CHICKEN-HEARTED, CRAVEN, GUTLESS, POLTROONISH, YELLOW, YELLOW-BELLIED ▣ BRAVE, COURAGEOUS, FEARLESS, VALIANT. ▸ **cowardliness** *noun*

cowboy *noun* **1** in the western USA, a man in charge of cattle. *Also called* **cowman**. **2** *slang* a reckless person.

cowboy boot a boot with a high arch and high Cuban heel.

cowboy hat a relatively high-crowned hat with a wide brim, worn chiefly with western attire. *Also called* **ten-gallon hat**.

cowcatcher *noun* a guard on the front of a railroad engine.

cower *verb intrans.* (**cowered, cowering**) to shrink in fear.

cowgirl *noun* in the Western USA, a woman in charge of cattle.

cowhand *noun* a cowboy or cowgirl.

cowhide *noun* a cow's hide made into leather.

cowl *noun* **1** a monk's large, loose hood or hooded habit. **2** a cowling.

cowlick *noun* a lock of hair standing up stiffly from the forehead.

cowling *noun* a removable metal covering for the engine of a vehicle or aircraft.

cowman *noun* a person who owns cattle.

coworker (kō-wər'kər, kō'wər,-) *or* **co-worker** *noun* a fellow worker; a colleague.

cowpox *noun* a viral infection of the udders of cows that can be transmitted to humans and causes mild symptoms similar to smallpox .

cowrie *noun* **1** a marine snail with a colorful egg-shaped shell. **2** the brightly colored egg-shaped shell of this animal, a popular collector's item, and used as currency in parts of Africa and S Asia.

cowslip *noun* the marsh marigold.

coxcomb *noun* a foolishly vain or conceited man.

coxswain (kăk'sən) *noun* **1** the person in a racing shell whose job it is to direct its crew. **2** the person who steers a ship's small boat and has charge of its crew.

coy *adj.* affectedly bashful; shy; modest: uncommunicative. ▸ **coyly** *adv.* ▸ **coyness** *noun*

coyote (kī'ōt,, kī-ōt'ē) *noun* (*pl.* **coyotes**, **coyote**) a N American carnivore resembling, but smaller than, a wolf. *Also called* **prairie wolf**.

coypu (koi'pōō) *noun* (*pl.* **coypus**) a S American rodent similar to a beaver.

cozy *or* **cosy** *adj.* (**cozier, coziest**) **1** warm and comfortable. **2** friendly, intimate, and confidential. —*noun* (*pl.* **cozies**) a warm cover, e.g., for a teapot. ▸ **cozily** *adv.* ▸ **coziness** *noun*

CPR *abbrev.* cardiopulmonary resuscitation.

CPU *abbrev. Comput.* central processing unit.

Cr *symbol* chromium.

crab *noun* 1 an edible crustacean with a hard, flattened shell. 2 (**Crab**) the sign of the zodiac and constellation Cancer. —*verb intrans.* (**crabbed, crabbing**) to catch crabs.

crab apple *or* **crabapple** a small, sour, wild apple.

crabbed (krăb'əd) *adj.* 1 bad-tempered. 2 *of handwriting* cramped and hard to decipher.

crabby *adj.* (**crabbier, crabbiest**) *colloq.* bad-tempered.

crabgrass *or* **crab grass** *noun* a grass, considered a lawn pest.

crack *verb trans., intrans.* (**cracked, cracking**) 1 to fracture partially without falling to pieces. 2 to split. 3 to make or cause to make a sudden, sharp noise. 4 to strike sharply. 5 to give way or cause to give way. 6 to force open (a safe). 7 to solve (a code or problem). 8 to tell (a joke). —*noun* 1 a sudden, sharp sound. 2 a partial fracture in a material. 3 a narrow opening. 4 a resounding blow. 5 a joke. 6 *slang* a highly addictive derivative of cocaine. —*adj. colloq.* expert: *a crack shot.* —**crack down on** *colloq.* to take firm action against (someone or something).

crackdown *noun* a firm action taken against someone or something.

cracked *adj.* 1 *colloq.* crazy. 2 having cracks.

cracker *noun* 1 a thin, crisp, unsweetened biscuit or wafer. 2 a small, noisy firework. 3 a toy that, when pulled apart reveals party favors. 4 *offensive* a poor white person, a farmer of SE USA. 5 *slang* a computer hacker who engages in criminal activity, e.g., on the networks.

crack house a place where crack cocaine is sold and used.

crackle *verb intrans.* (**crackled, crackling**) to make a faint, continuous snapping or popping sound. —*noun* a snapping or popping noise. ▸ **crackly** *adj.*

crackling *noun* the crisp skin of roast pork.

crackpot *colloq. adj.* crazy. —*noun* a crazy person.

-cracy *combining form* denoting rule, government, or domination by a particular group: *democracy.*

cradle *noun* 1 a bed with rockers for a small baby. 2 a place of origin: *the cradle of civilization.* 3 the support for the receiver on a telephone. —*verb trans.* (**cradled, cradling**) to rock or hold gently.

craft *noun* 1 (*also in compounds*) a skill or occupation, esp. one requiring the use of the hands. 2 **a** a skill, esp. gained through practice. **b** skilled ability. 3 cunning. 4 (*pl.* **craft**) a vehicle, e.g., a boat, ship, or airplane. —*verb trans.* (**crafted, crafting**) to make skillfully.

craftsman *noun* a man skilled at a craft. ▸ **craftsmanship** *noun*

craftsperson *noun* a craftsman or a craftswoman.

craftswoman *noun* a woman skilled at a craft.

crafty *adj.* (**craftier, craftiest**) clever, cunning, or sly. ▸ **craftily** *adv.* ▸ **craftiness** *noun*

crag *noun* a rocky peak or jagged outcrop of rock. ▸ **craggy** *adj.*

cram *verb trans., intrans.* (**crammed, cramming**) 1 to stuff full. 2 (**cram in** *or* **together**) to push or pack (something) tightly. 3 to study intensively for an examination. ▸ **crammed** *adj.*

cramp[1] *noun* 1 the painful involuntary contraction of a muscle. 2 (**cramps**) severe abdominal pain. —*verb trans.* (**cramped, cramping**) to restrict tiresomely. ▸ **cramped** *adj.*

crampon (krăm'păn,) *noun* a spiked iron attachment for climbing boots, to improve grip on ice or rock.

cranberry *noun* (*pl.* **cranberries**) an evergreen shrub or one of its edible red, acidic berries.

crane *noun* 1 a machine with a long pivoted arm from which lifting gear is suspended. 2 a large wading bird with a long neck and long legs. —*verb trans., intrans.* (**craned, craning**) to stretch (one's neck), or lean forward, in order to see better.

crane fly a long-legged, slender-bodied, two-winged insect. *Also called* **daddy longlegs**.

cranium *noun* (*pl.* **craniums, crania**) the dome-shaped part of the skull that encloses and protects the brain. ▸ **cranial** *adj.*

crank *noun* 1 an arm projecting at right angles from a shaft, for communicating motion to or from the shaft. 2 a tool bent at right angles for starting an engine by hand. 3 *colloq.* an eccentric person.

crankshaft *noun* a shaft driving, or driven by, a crank, e.g., in a vehicle engine.

cranky *adj.* (**crankier, crankiest**) *colloq.* bad-tempered.

cranny *noun* (*pl.* **crannies**) a narrow opening; a cleft or crevice.

craps *noun* (*sing., pl.*) a gambling game in which the player rolls two dice.

crapulence *noun* sickness caused by excessive drinking. ▸ **crapulent** *adj.*

crash *verb trans., intrans.* (**crashed, crashing**) 1 to fall or strike with a banging or smashing noise. 2 to collide, or cause to collide, with. 3 to move noisily. 4 *of a business or stock exchange* to collapse. 5 *of a computer or program* to fail completely, because of a malfunction, etc. 6 to gatecrash. 7 *slang* **a** to find a place to spend the night. **b** to fall asleep or go to bed exhausted. —*noun* 1 a violent impact or breakage, or the sound of it. **2** a deafening noise. **3** a traffic or aircraft accident; a collision. **4** the collapse of a business or a stock exchange. **5** *Comput.* the failure of a computer or program. —*adj.* concentrated or intensive.

crash dive a rapid emergency dive by a submarine. ▸ **crash-dive** *verb*

crash helmet a protective helmet worn, e.g., by motorcyclists.

crash-land *verb trans., intrans.* (**crash-landed, crash-landing**) to land in an emergency with the risk of crashing. ▸ **crash landing**

crass *adj.* **1** lacking all delicacy and sensitivity. **2** incredibly stupid. ▸ **crassly** *adv.* ▸ **crassness** *noun*

-crat *combining form* forming nouns and adjectives corresponding to words in -*cracy*: *democrat.*

crate *noun* a strong case for carrying breakable or perishable goods. —*verb trans.* (**crated, crating**) to pack in a crate.

crater *noun* **1** the bowl-shaped mouth of a volcano. **2** a hole left in the ground where a bomb or mine has exploded. **3** a circular depression in the surface of the moon.

cratic *combining form* forming adjectives corresponding to nouns in -*cracy*: *democratic.*

cravat (krə-văt′) *noun* a formal neckerchief worn by men instead of a tie.

From a French word for 'Croat', because of the linen neckbands worn by 17th-century Croatian soldiers

crave *verb trans.* (**craved, craving**) **1** to long for (something). **2** *old formal use* to ask for politely.

craven *adj.* displaying a contemptible lack of courage. —*noun* a coward. ▸ **cravenly** *adv.* ▸ **cravenness** *noun*

craving *noun* an overwhelming desire.

craw *noun* the crop of a bird or an insect.

crawfish *noun* (*pl.* **crawfish, crawfishes**) *same as* **crayfish.**

crawl *verb intrans.* (**crawled, crawling**) **1** of insects, worms, etc. to move along the ground. **2** to move along on hands and knees. **3** to progress very slowly. **4** to be, or feel as if, covered with crawling insects. **5** *colloq.* to behave in an overly humble way to someone whose approval one wants. —*noun* **1** a crawling motion. **2** a very slow pace. **3** a swimming stroke with an alternate overarm action.

crayfish *or* **crawfish** *noun* (*pl.* **crayfish, crayfishes**) a freshwater crustacean resembling a small lobster.

crayon *noun* a colored stick of wax for drawing. —*verb trans., intrans.* (**crayoned, crayoning**) to draw or color with a crayon.

craze *noun* an intense but passing enthusiasm or fashion. —*verb trans., intrans.* (**crazed, crazing**) to make crazy.

crazy *adj.* (**crazier, craziest**) **1** mad; insane. **2** foolish; absurd. **3** (**crazy about**) madly enthusiastic about (someone or something) ▸ **crazily** *adv.* ▸ **craziness** *noun*

creak *noun* the squeaking noise made typically by an unoiled hinge. —*verb intrans.* (**creaked, creaking**) to make a creak.

creaky *adj.* (**creakier, creakiest**) **1** emitting squeaks; squeaky. **2** dilapidated. ▸ **creakily** *adv.* ▸ **creakiness** *noun*

cream *noun* **1 a** the yellowish fatty substance that rises to the surface of milk, and yields butter when churned. **b** a food that resembles this substance in consistency or appearance. **2** a cosmetic substance that resembles cream in texture or consistency. **3** the best part; the pick. **4** a yellowish-white color. —*verb trans.* (**creamed, creaming**) **1** to beat (e.g., butter and sugar) until creamy. **2** to remove the cream from (milk). **3** *colloq.* to beat (someone). ▸ **creamy** *adj.*

creamer *noun* **1** a powdered milk substitute used in coffee. **2** a small pitcher or jug for serving cream.

creamery *noun* (*pl.* **creameries**) a place where dairy products are made or sold.

cream of tartar a white crystalline powder used together with sodium bicarbonate in baking powder to lighten the texture of cakes etc.

crease *noun* a line made by folding, pressing, or crushing. —*verb trans., intrans.* (**creased, creasing**) to make a crease or creases in; to develop creases.

create *verb trans., intrans.* (**created, creating**) **1** to form from nothing. **2** to bring into existence. **3** to cause. **4** to produce or contrive. **5** to raise to an honorable rank: *was created a peer.*

creation (krē-ā′shən) *noun* **1** the act of creating. **2** something created. **3** all created things; the universe.

creative *adj.* inventive or imaginative. ▸ **creatively** *adv.* ▸ **creativity** *noun*

creator *noun* **1** a person who creates. **2** (**the Creator**) God.

creature (krē′chər) *noun* **1** a bird, beast, or fish. **2** a person. **3** a slavish underling or puppet.

creature comforts comforts such as food, clothes, and warmth.

crèche (krĕsh) *noun* **1** a representation of the birth of Christ, using statues, a manger, etc. **2** a children's day-care center or facility.

credence *noun* faith or belief.

credentials *pl. noun* personal qualifications and achievements; documents or other evidence of such.

credenza *noun* a rectangular, low bookcase or cabinet.

credible *adj.* **1** capable of being believed. **2** reliable; trustworthy. ▸ **credibility** *noun* ▸ **credibly** *adv.*

credit *noun* **1** faith placed in something. **2** honor or a cause of honor: *To her credit, she didn't say anything.* **3** acknowledgment, recognition, or praise. **4** (**credits**) a list of acknowledgments to those who have helped in the preparation of a book, movie, etc. **5** a trust given to someone promising to pay later for goods already supplied: *buy goods on credit.* **b** one's financial reliability, esp. as a basis for such trust. **c** the amount of money available to one at one's bank. **d** an entry in a bank account acknowledging a payment. *See also* **debit.** **6** official acknowledgment of a student's completion of a course of instruction. —*verb trans.* (**credited, crediting**) **1** to place faith in; to believe. **2** to enter a sum as a credit on someone's account, or allow someone a sum as credit. **3** (**credit with**) to attribute (a quality or achievement) to (someone): *We credited you with more sense.*

creditable *adj.* praiseworthy; laudable. ▸ **creditably** *adv.*

credit card a card authorizing one to purchase goods or services on credit. *Also called* **charge card.**

creditor *noun* a party to whom money is owed. *See also* **debtor.**

credit rating an assessment of a party's creditworthiness.

creditworthy *adj.* judged as deserving financial credit. ▸ **creditworthiness** *noun*

credo (krēd'ō, krăd'ō) *noun* (*pl.* **credos**) a creed.

credulity *noun* a tendency to believe something without proper proof.

credulous (krĕj'ə-ləs) *adj.* too ready to believe; too trusting. ▸ **credulously** *adv.*

creed *noun* **1** (*often* **Creed**) a statement of the main points of Christian belief. **2** a set of beliefs or principles, personal or religious.

creek (krēk, krĭk) *noun* a small river or tributary.

creel *noun* a basket for carrying fish.

creep *verb intrans.* (pa t and pa p **crept**; pr p **creeping**) **1** to move slowly, with stealth or caution. **2** to move with the body close to the ground; to crawl. **3** *of a plant* to grow along the ground, up a wall, etc. **4** to enter barely noticeably. **5** to develop little by little. —*noun* an unpleasantly sly or sinister person. —**give one the creeps** *colloq.* to disgust or repel one.

creeper *noun* a creeping plant.

creepy *adj.* (**creepier, creepiest**) *colloq.* slightly scary; spooky or eerie. ▸ **creepily** *adv.*

cremate *verb trans.* (**cremated, cremating**) to burn (a corpse) to ashes, as an alternative to burial. ▸ **cremation** *noun*

crematorium *noun* (*pl.* **crematoriums, crematoria**) a place where corpses are cremated.

crème de la crème (krĕm,də-lä-krĕm') the very best.

crenelated *or* **crenellated** (krĕn'l-āt,ĭd) *adj.* having battlements. ▸ **crenelation** *noun*

creole (krē'ōl,) *noun* **1** a pidgin language that has become the accepted language of a region. **2** (**Creole**) the French-based pidgin spoken in some US states, e.g., Louisiana. **3** (**Creole**) a West Indian or Latin American of mixed European and African blood; a French or Spanish native of the Gulf states.

creosote (krē'ə-sōt,) *noun* **1** a dark brown oil distilled from coal tar, used for preserving wood. **2** a transparent oil distilled from wood tar, used as an antiseptic.

crepe (krāp, krĕp) *noun* **1** a thin, finely wrinkled, silk fabric. **2** rubber with a wrinkled surface, used for shoe soles. **3** a thin pancake.

crepe paper (krāp) paper with a wrinkled, elastic texture, used for making decorations.

crept *see* **creep.**

crepuscular *adj.* of or relating to twilight; dim.

crescendo (krə-shĕn'dō) *noun* (*pl.* **crescendos**) **1** *Mus.* a gradual increase in loudness. **2** *colloq.* a high point or climax. —*adj., adv. Mus.* played with increasing loudness. *See also* **diminuendo.**

> *Usage* Though widely used to mean a high point or climax, the noun *crescendo*, when so used, can be faulted by those conversant with the musical sense.

crescent *noun* **1** the moon in its first quarter; the new moon. **2** something sickle-shaped, like this phase of the moon.

cress *noun* a plant whose sharp-tasting leaves are used in salads.

crest *noun* **1** a comb or tuft on the head of certain birds or animals. **2** a plume on a helmet. **3** the part of a coat of arms that appears above the shield. **4** the top part of a mountain, wave, etc . ▸ **crested** *adj.*

crestfallen *adj.* dejected.

cretin *noun* **1** a person who has a congenital malfunction of the thyroid gland, resulting in mental impairment. ▸ **cretinous** *adj.* ▸ **cretinism** *noun*

cretonne (krē'tän,, krĭ-tän') *noun* a strong cotton material.

crevasse *noun* a deep vertical crack in a glacier.

crevice *noun* a narrow opening; a crack.

crew[1] *noun* **1** the team of people operating a ship, aircraft, train, etc. **2** a team engaged in an operation: *a camera crew.* **3** *colloq.* a bunch of people: *a strange crew.* —*verb intrans., trans.* (**crewed, crewing**) to serve as a crew member on (a yacht, etc.).

crew² see **crow.**

crewcut *noun* a closely cropped hairstyle for men.

crewel *noun* thin, loosely twisted yarn for tapestry or embroidery.

crew neck a firm, round neckline on a sweater.

crib *noun* 1 a baby's bed or cradle. 2 something copied or plagiarized from another's work. —*verb trans., intrans.* (**cribbed, cribbing**) to copy or plagiarize.

cribbage *noun* a card game for two to four players, who each try to be first to score a certain number of points.

crib death sudden infant death syndrome.

crick *noun colloq.* a painful spasm or stiffness, esp. in the neck.

cricket¹ *noun* an outdoor game for two teams of eleven players each, played with a ball, bats, and wickets. ▶ **cricketer** *noun*

cricket² *noun* an insect related to the grasshopper.

crime *noun* 1 an illegal act, punishable by law. 2 illegal activities in general. 3 a gravely wrong moral act.

criminal *noun* a person who has committed a crime. —*adj.* 1 against the law. 2 of or relating to crime. 3 *colloq.* very wrong; wicked. ▶ **criminality** *noun* ▶ **criminally** *adv.*

criminology (krĭm,ə-näl′ə-jē) *noun* the study of crime and criminals. ▶ **criminologist** *noun*

crimp *verb trans.* (**crimped, crimping**) 1 to press into small, regular ridges; to corrugate. 2 to wave or curl (hair) with a curling iron or with heated tongs.

crimson (krĭm′zən) *adj.* of a deep purplish red color: —*noun* a deep purplish red color.

cringe *verb intrans.* (**cringed, cringing**) 1 to cower away in, or as if in, fear. 2 to behave in a submissive, overly humble way. 3 to wince in embarrassment, etc. ▶ **cringer** *noun*

crinkle *verb trans., intrans.* (**crinkled, crinkling**) to wrinkle or crease. —*noun* a wrinkle or crease; a wave. ▶ **crinkly** *adj.*

crinoline (krĭn′l-ĭn) *noun Hist.* a hooped petticoat for making skirts stand out.

cripple *verb trans.* (**crippled, crippling**) 1 to make lame; to disable. 2 to damage, weaken, or undermine. —*noun* a physically disabled or emotionally damaged person.

crisis *noun* (*pl.* **crises**) 1 a crucial or decisive moment. 2 a turning point, e.g., in a disease. 3 a time of great difficulty or distress.

crisp *adj.* 1 dry and brittle. 2 firm and fresh. 3 of weather fresh; bracing. 4 firm; decisive; brisk. —*verb trans., intrans.* to make or become crisp. ▶ **crisply** *adv.* ▶ **crispy** *adj.*

crisscross —*adj.* 1 of lines crossing one

another in different directions. 2 of a pattern consisting of crisscross lines. —*adv.* running or lying one another. —*noun* a pattern of crisscross lines. —*verb trans., intrans.* (**crisscrossed, crisscrossing**) to form or mark with a crisscross pattern.

criterion *noun* (*pl.* **criteria**) a standard or principle on which to base a judgment.

> *Usage* Note that *criteria* is a plural form; a *criteria*, though often heard, is incorrect.

critic *noun* 1 a professional reviewer of literature, art, drama, or music. 2 a person who finds fault with or disapproves of something.

critical *adj.* 1 relating to criticism. 2 inclined to look for and point up faults. ▤ CAPTIOUS, CARPING, CAVILING. 3 involving analysis and assessment. 4 decisive; crucial. 5 so ill or seriously injured as to be at risk of dying. ▶ **critically** *adv.*

critical mass the smallest amount of a given fissile material that is needed to sustain a nuclear chain reaction.

criticism *noun* 1 reasoned analysis and assessment, esp. of art, literature, music, or drama; the art of such assessment. 2 fault finding.

criticize *verb trans., intrans.* (**criticized, criticizing**) 1 to analyze and assess. 2 to find fault; to express disapproval of.

critique *noun* a critical analysis; a criticism.

> *Usage* Though frequently used, the verb *critique* is frowned upon by many people as an example of pretentious jargon; the verbs *criticize, review,* or *analyze* or a combination of them are appropriate substitutions.

croak *noun* the harsh, throaty noise typically made by a frog or crow. —*verb intrans., trans.* (**croaked, croaking**) 1 to make the harsh, throaty noise of a frog or crow. 2 *slang* to die or kill.

croaker *noun* a frog, or a fish that makes grunting or croaking noises.

crochet (krō-shā′) *noun* decorative work consisting of intertwined loops, made with wool or thread and a hooked needle. —*verb intrans., trans.* (**crocheted, crocheting**) to work, or produce something in crochet.

crock *noun* a vessel made of earthenware.

crockery *noun* earthenware or china dishes.

Crock-Pot *trademark* used to denote an electric cooking pot that maintains a low temperature.

crocodile *noun* a large aquatic reptile with powerful jaws, and a thick scaly skin.

crocodile tears a show of pretended grief.

crocus *noun* (*pl.* **crocuses**) a small plant with an underground corm, and a single yellow, purple, or white flower.

croissant (kwä-säN′) *noun* a crescent-shaped bread roll, flaky in consistency.

cromlech (krăm′lĕk,, -lĕκн,) *noun* a prehistoric circle of standing stones or burial mound.

crone *noun offensive* an old woman; a hag.

crony *noun* (*pl.* **cronies**) a close friend.

cronyism *noun* favoritism toward one's close friends and long-term associates.

crook *noun* 1 a bend or curve. 2 a hooked staff. 3 a hooked fitting. 4 *colloq.* a thief or swindler.

crooked *adj.* 1 bent or twisted. 2 tipped at an angle; not straight. 3 *colloq.* dishonest. ► **crookedly** *adv.* ► **crookedness** *noun*

croon *verb intrans., trans.* (**crooned, crooning**) to sing in a subdued tone and reflective or sentimental style. ► **crooner** *noun*

crop *noun* 1 a a plant that is cultivated to produce food. for humans, fodder for animals, or raw materials. b the total yield produced by or harvested from such a plant, or from a field. 2 a batch; a bunch: *this year's crop of graduates.* 3 a short haircut. 4 a horseback rider's short whip. 5 the thin-walled pouch in the gullet of a bird. —*verb trans., intrans.* (**cropped, cropping**) 1 to decrease (something) in length or scope. 2 of animals) to feed on grass, etc. 3 (*usu.* **crop up**) to occur or appear unexpectedly or on occasion.

cropduster *or* **crop duster** *noun* a light airplane that sprays fields with fungicides and insecticides.

cropper *noun* a fall or failure. —**come a cropper** to fail disastrously.

croquet (krō-kā′) *noun* a game played on a lawn, in which mallets are used to drive wooden balls through a sequence of hoops.

croquette (kro-kĕt′) *noun* a ball or roll of minced meat or potato, coated in bread-crumbs and fried.

crosier *or* **crozier** (krō′zhər) *noun* a bishop's hooked staff.

cross *noun* 1 a mark, structure, or symbol composed of two lines, one crossing the other in the form + or ×. 2 a a vertical post with a horizontal bar fixed to it, on which criminals were crucified in antiquity. b (**the Cross**) the cross on which Christ was crucified or a representation of it, used as a symbol of Christianity. 3 a burden or affliction. 4 a plant or animal produced by crossing two different breeds. 5 a mixture or combination. —*verb trans., intrans.* (**crossed, crossing**) 1 to move, pass, or get across. 2 to place (one) across (the other). 3 to meet; to intersect. 4 (**cross (oneself)**) to make the sign of the Cross. 5 (*also* **cross out** *or* **off**) to delete or cancel (something) by drawing a line through. 6 to crossbreed. 7 to

frustrate or thwart. —*adj.* 1 in a bad temper; angry. 2 opposing; contrary: *at cross purposes.*

crossbar *noun* a horizontal bar, strip, or line.

crossbones *pl. noun* a pair of crossed femurs used to symbolize piracy.

crossbow *noun* a bow placed crosswise on a stock, with a crank to pull back the bow, and a trigger to release arrows.

crossbreed *Biol. verb trans., intrans.* (**crossbred, crossbreeding**) to mate (two animals of different pure breeds). —*noun* a cross-bred animal.

crosscheck *verb trans.* (**crosschecked, crosschecking**) to check (information) from an independent source.

cross-country *adj.* 1 moving from one side of a country to the other. 2 *Sport* (ABBREV. **XC, X-C**) moving across open country rather than on an established course or run. *See* **skiing.**

cross cut a transverse or diagonal cut.

crossdress *verb intrans.* (**crossdressed, crossdressing**) to wear clothes associated with the opposite sex. ► **crossdresser** *noun*

cross-examine *verb trans.* (**cross-examined, cross-examining**) to question (esp. a witness for the opposing side in court) so as to develop or throw doubt on his or her statements. ► **cross-examination** *noun* ► **cross-examiner** *noun*

cross-eyed *adj.* having one or both eyes turned inward toward the nose.

crossfire *noun* 1 gunfire coming from different directions. 2 a bitter or excited exchange of opinions or arguments.

crosshatch *verb trans.* (**crosshatched, cross-hatching**) to shade with intersecting lines.

crossing *noun* 1 a place for crossing a river, road, etc. 2 a journey across water.

cross-legged (krôs′lĕg′əd) *adj., adv.* sitting with the ankles crossed and knees wide apart.

cross-pollinate *verb trans.* (**cross-pollinated, cross-pollinating**) to transfer pollen from (one flower) to (another). ► **cross-pollination** *noun*

cross-question *verb trans.* (**cross-questioned, cross-questioning**) to cross-examine.

cross-refer *verb intrans., trans.* (**cross-referred, cross-referring**) to direct (the reader) to refer from one part of a text to another.

cross-reference *noun* a reference from one part of a text to another. —*verb trans.* (**cross-referenced, cross-referencing**) to supply with cross-references.

crossroads *noun* (*sing.*) 1 the point where two or more roads cross or meet. 2 a point at which an important choice has to be made.

cross section or **cross-section** noun **1** the surface revealed when a solid object is sliced through, esp. at right angles to its length. **2** a representative sample. ▸ **cross-sectional** adj.

cross-stitch noun an embroidery stitch made by two crossing stitches. ▸ **cross-stitch** verb

crosswalk noun a section of pavement marked off for a pedestrian crossing.

crosswind noun a wind blowing across the path of a vehicle or aircraft.

crosswise or **crossways** adj., adv. lying or moving across, or so as to cross.

crossword puzzle a puzzle in which clues yield words that cross vertically and horizontally within a grid of squares.

crotch or **crutch** noun the place where the body or a pair of trousers forks into the two legs.

crotchet noun **1** an odd notion or a stubbornly held opinion or idea. **2** a quarter note.

crotchety adj. irritable; peevish.

crouch verb intrans. (**crouched, crouching**) to bend low or squat with the legs close to the chest.

croup (kroop) noun. inflammation of the trachea and larynx in children, causing difficulty in breathing and a hoarse cough. ▸ **croupy** adj.

croupier (kroo′pē-ər, -ā,) noun a person who presides over a gaming table, collecting the stakes and paying the winners.

croûton (kroo′tän,) noun a small cube of fried bread, served in soups and on salads.

crow noun **1** a large, black bird. **2** the shrill, long-drawn-out cry of a rooster. —verb intrans. (pa t **crowed** or **crew, crowing**) **1** of a rooster to cry shrilly. **2** to exult gleefully and loudly, e.g., over another's defeat or misfortune. —**as the crow flies** in a straight line.

crowbar noun a heavy iron bar with a bent, flattened end, used as a lever.

crowd noun **1** a large number of people gathered together. **2** a set or group of people having some specified characteristic: a fast crowd. **3** the general mass of people: Don't just follow the crowd. —verb intrans., trans. (**crowded, crowding**) **1** to gather or move in a large, usu. tightly packed, group. **2** to fill. **3** to pack; to cram. **4** to press around (someone) too closely.

crowded adj. full of people; thronged.

crown noun **1** the circular, usu. jeweled, gold headdress of a sovereign. **2** (**Crown**) the sovereign as head of state; the authority or jurisdiction of a sovereign. **3** a wreath for the head. **4** a highest point of achievement. **5** the part of a tooth projecting from the gum; an artificial replacement for it. —verb trans., intrans. (**crowned, crowning**) **1** to place a crown ceremonially on the head of; to make king or queen. **2** to be on or around the top of. **3** to make complete or perfect. **4** to put an artificial crown on (a tooth). **5** colloq. to hit on the head. —**to crown it all** colloq. as the finishing touch to a series of esp. unfortunate events.

crown prince a male heir to a throne.

crown princess 1 the wife of a crown prince. **2** a female heir to a throne.

crow's foot noun (pl. **crow's-feet**) a wrinkle at the outer corner of the eye.

crow's-nest noun a platform for a lookout, situated near the top of a ship's mast.

crozier noun same as **crosier**.

CRT abbrev. cathode-ray tube.

cruces see **crux**.

crucial (kroo′shəl) adj. **1** decisive; critical. **2** very important; essential. **3** slang very good; great. ▸ **crucially** adv.

crucible noun an earthenware pot in which to heat metals or other substances.

crucifix noun a representation, esp. a model, of Christ on the cross.

crucifixion noun **1** execution by crucifying. **2** (**Crucifixion**) the crucifying of Christ, or a representation of this.

cruciform adj. cross-shaped.

crucify (kroo′sī-fī,) verb trans. (**crucified, crucifying, crucifies**) **1** to put to death by fastening to a cross by the hands and feet. **2** to torment or persecute.

crud noun slang **1** dirt. **2** something worthless or shoddy. **3** nonsense. ▸ **cruddy** adj.

crude adj. **1** in its natural, unrefined state: crude oil. **2** rough or undeveloped. **3** lacking refined manners and sensitivity. ▸ **crudely** adv. ▸ **crudity** noun

cruel (kroo′əl) adj. **1** deliberately and pitilessly causing pain or suffering. **2** painful; distressful. ▸ **cruelly** adv. ▸ **cruelty** noun

cruet (kroo′ĭt) noun **1** a small container for salt, pepper, vinegar, etc., for use at the table. **2** a stand for a set of such jars.

cruise verb intrans., trans. (**cruised, cruising**) **1** to sail about for pleasure, calling at a succession of places. **2** to go at a steady, comfortable speed. **3** slang to search a (public place) looking for a sexual partner. **4** slang to drive around.

cruise missile a low-flying, long-distance, computer-controlled winged missile.

cruiser noun **1** a large, fast warship. **2** a cabin cruiser. **3** a police automobile.

crumb noun **1** a particle of dry food, esp. bread. **2** a small amount: not a crumb of comfort. **3** slang an obnoxious person.

crumble verb trans., intrans. (**crumbled, crumbling**) **1** to break into crumbs or powdery fragments. **2** to collapse, decay, or disintegrate. ▸ **crumbly** adj.

crummy adj. (**crummier, crummiest**) slang shoddy or inferior. ▸ **crumminess** noun

crumpet noun a thick, round cake made of soft light dough, eaten toasted and buttered.

crumple verb trans., intrans. (**crumpled, crumpling**) 1 to make or become creased or crushed. 2 of a face to pucker in distress. 3 to give way; to collapse.

crunch verb trans., intrans. 1 to crush or grind noisily between the teeth or under the foot. 2 slang to process or otherwise manipulate (arithmetic numbers). —noun 1 a crunching action or sound. 2 colloq. the moment of decision or crisis: when it comes to the crunch. ▸ **crunchy** adj.

crusade (krōō-sād′) noun a strenuous campaign in aid of a cause. —verb intrans. (**crusaded, crusading**) to engage in a crusade; to campaign. ▸ **crusader** noun

crush verb trans., intrans. (**crushed, crushing**) 1 to damage or injure by compressing violently. 2 to grind into powder, crumbs, etc. 3 to crumple or crease. 4 to defeat, subdue, or humiliate. —noun 1 violent compression. 2 a dense crowd. 3 a drink made from the juice of crushed fruit. 4 colloq. an infatuation. ▸ **crusher** noun

crust noun 1 the hard-baked outer surface of a loaf of bread; a piece of it. 2 the pastry covering a pie, etc. 3 a crisp or brittle covering. 4 the solid, outermost layer of Earth. —verb trans., intrans. (**crusted, crusting**) to cover with, or form, a crust.

crustacean noun an invertebrate, mainly aquatic, animal with a shell, e.g. a crab.

crusty adj. (**crustier, crustiest**) 1 having a crisp crust. 2 irritable, snappy, or cantankerous. ▸ **crustily** adv.

crutch noun 1 a stick, used as a support by a disabled or injured person. 2 a support, help, or aid. 3 same as **crotch**.

crux (kraks′) noun (pl. **crux, cruces**) the decisive, essential, or crucial point.

cry verb intrans., trans. (**cried, crying, cries**) 1 to shed tears; to weep. 2 to shout or shriek. 3 to exclaim. 4 of an animal or bird to utter its characteristic noise. —noun (pl. **cries**) 1 a shout or shriek. 2 an excited utterance or exclamation. 3 an appeal or demand. 4 a rallying call or slogan. 5 a bout of weeping. 6 the characteristic utterance of an animal or bird.

crybaby noun colloq. a person who weeps or whines at the slightest upset.

cryogenics (krī,ə-jěn′ĭks) noun (sing., pl.) the branch of physics concerned with the study of very low temperatures.

crypt noun an underground chamber or vault, esp. one beneath a church used for burials.

cryptic adj. puzzling, mysterious, or enigmatic. ▸ **cryptically** adv.

crypto- combining form forming words denoting: 1 hidden or obscure: cryptogram. 2 secret or undeclared: crypto-Nazi.

cryptogram (krĭp′tə-grăm,) noun something written in a code or cipher.

cryptography (krĭp-tăg′rə-fē) noun the study or art of writing in and deciphering, codes. ▸ **cryptographer** noun ▸ **cryptographic** adj.

crystal noun 1 colorless, transparent quartz. Also called **rock crystal**. 2 a globe of rock crystal or glass used for fortune-telling. Also called **crystal ball**. 3 a brilliant, highly transparent glass used for cut glass; cut-glass articles. 4 any solid substance consisting of a regularly repeating arrangement of atoms, ions, or molecules. 5 a crystalline element that functions as a transducer or oscillator in an electronic device. —adj. like crystal in brilliance and clarity. —**crystal clear** as clear or obvious as can be. ▸ **crystalline** adj.

crystallize verb trans., intrans. (**crystallized, crystallizing**) 1 to form crystals. 2 to coat or preserve (fruit) in sugar. 3 of plans, ideas, etc. to make or become clear and definite. ▸ **crystallization** noun

Cs symbol cesium.

C.S.A. abbrev. Confederate States of America.

CST abbrev. Central Standard Time.

Cu symbol copper.

cu. or **cu** abbrev. cubic.

cub noun 1 the young of certain animals, e.g., the fox, bear, and wolf. 2 (**Cub**) a member of the Cub Scouts. 3 colloq. a beginner; a novice. 4 old use an impudent young man.

cubbyhole noun colloq. a tiny room, a cupboard, nook, or recess.

cube noun 1 a solid figure having six square faces of equal area. 2 the product of any number or quantity multiplied by its square. 3 a block having the shape of six equal square faces. —verb trans., intrans. (**cubed, cubing**) 1 to raise (a number or quantity) to the third power. 2 to form or cut into cubes.

cube root the number of which a given number is the cube.

cubic adj. (ABBREV. **cu., cu**) 1 relating to or resembling a cube. 2 having three dimensions. 3 of or involving a number or quantity that is raised to the third power.

cubical adj. cubic (senses 1, 2).

cubicle noun a small compartment for work, e.g., in an open-office setting.

Cubism or **cubism** (kyōō′bĭz,əm) noun an early 20th c movement in painting, with objects represented in geometrical shapes. ▸ **Cubist** noun

cubit noun an old measure, equal to the length of the forearm from the elbow to the tip of the middle finger.

Cub Scouts the junior division of the Boy Scouts.

cuckold (kǝk'ǝld, -ōld,) *noun old use* a man whose wife is unfaithful. —*verb trans.* (**cuckolded, cuckolding**) to make a cuckold of.

cuckoo (kōō'kōō, kŏŏk'ōō) *noun* (*pl.* **cuckoos**) a bird with a distinctive two-note call. —*adj. slang* insane; crazy.

cuckoo clock a clock from which a model cuckoo springs on the hour.

cucumber *noun* a creeping plant or its long, green, edible fruit eaten raw in salads. —**cool as a cucumber** *colloq.* calm and composed.

cud *noun* the partially digested food that a cow or other ruminant animal brings back into the mouth from the stomach to chew again.

cuddle *verb* **1** *trans., intrans.* (**cuddled, cuddling**) to hug or embrace affectionately. **2** to lie close and snug; to nestle. —*noun* an affectionate hug.

cuddlesome *adj.* cuddly or affectionate.

cuddly *adj.* (**cuddlier, cuddliest**) pleasant to cuddle; attractively soft and plump.

cudgel *noun* a heavy club used as a weapon. —*verb* (**cudgeled** *or* **cudgelled, cudgeling** *or* **cudgelling**) to beat with a cudgel.

cue¹ *noun* **1** the final words of an actor's speech that serve as a prompt for another to say or do something. **2** a signal or hint to do something. —*verb trans.* (**cued, cueing**) **1** to give a cue to. **2** to prepare (a tape or other recording) for immediate play, e.g., in a radio broadcast. —**on cue** at precisely the right moment.

cue² *noun* **1** a stick tapering to a point, used to strike the ball in billiards, snooker, and pool. **2** *old use* a pigtail.

cue ball the white ball in billiards and pool that is moved by the cue.

cuff¹ *noun* **1** a band or folded-back part at the lower end of a sleeve, usu. at the wrist. **2** the turned-up part of a pant leg. **3** (**cuffs**) *slang* handcuffs. —**off the cuff** *colloq.* without preparation or previous thought.

cuff² *noun* a blow with the open hand. —*verb trans.* (**cuffed, cuffing**) to hit with an open hand.

cufflink *noun* one of a pair of decorative fasteners for shirt cuffs.

cuirass (kwĭ-răs', kyōō-) *noun* a piece of armor; a breastplate.

cuisine (kwĭ-zēn') *noun* **1** a style of cooking. **2** the range of food served at a restaurant, etc.

cul-de-sac (kŭl'dĭ-săk', kŏl'dĭ-săk') *noun* (*pl.* **culs-de-sac, cul-de-sacs**) a street closed at one end.

culinary *adj.* relating to cooking or the kitchen.

cull *verb trans.* (**culled, culling**) **1** to gather or pick up (information or ideas). **2** to select and kill (weak or surplus animals) from a group in order to keep the population under control. —*noun* an act of culling or something culled.

culminate *verb intrans.* (**culminated, culminating**) (**culminate in**) to reach the highest point or climax. ▸ **culmination** *noun*

culottes (kōō'lăts, kyōō'-) *noun* (*pl.*) widely flared pants for women.

culpable *adj.* deserving blame. ▸ **culpability** *noun* ▸ **culpably** *adv.*

culprit *noun* a person guilty of a misdeed or offense.

cult *noun* **1** a system of religious belief or the sect following such a system. **2** a fashion, craze, or fad.

cultivate (kŭl'tǝ-vāt,) *verb trans.* (**cultivated, cultivating**) **1 a** to prepare and use (land or soil) for crops. **b** to grow (a crop, plant, etc.). **2** to develop or improve. **3** to try to develop a friendship with (someone), esp. for personal advantage. ▸ **cultivated** *adj.* ▸ **cultivation** *noun*

cultivator *noun* a machine for breaking up ground.

culture (kŭl'chǝr) *noun* **1** the customs, ideas, art, etc., of a particular civilization, society, or social group. **2** appreciation of art, music, literature, etc. **3** improvement and development through care and training. **4** a population of microorganisms, esp. bacteria, cells, or tissues, grown for scientific study or medical diagnosis. —*verb trans.* (**cultured, culturing**) to grow (microorganisms, cells, or tissues) for study. ▸ **cultural** *adj.* ▸ **culturally** *adv.*

cultured *adj.* **1** having refined tastes and manners; well educated. **2** *of a pearl* formed by an oyster around a foreign body deliberately inserted into its shell.

culture shock disorientation caused by a change from a familiar environment to another that is radically different.

culvert *noun* a covered drain or channel carrying water under a roadway or railroad.

-cum- *combining form* forming words denoting combined with; also used as: *kitchen-cum-dining room.*

cumbersome *adj.* heavy, unwieldy, or unmanageable.

cumin *noun* a plant whose seeds are used as a food flavoring.

cum laude (kōōm-lowd'ǝ, -ē) with honors.

cummerbund *noun* a waist sash, esp. one worn with a dinner jacket.

cumulative *adj.* increasing in amount, effect, or strength. ▸ **cumulatively** *adv.*

cumulus (kyōōm'yǝ-lǝs) *noun* (*pl.* **cumuli**) a fluffy, heaped cloud.

cuneiform (kyŏŏ-nē'ə-fôrm,, kyōō'nə-) *adj.* of or in an ancient Middle Eastern script with impressed, wedge-shaped characters.

cunning *adj.* 1 astute but unprincipled. 2 ingenious, skillful, or subtle. —*noun* 1 the quality or condition of being sly or wily. 2 skill; expertise. ▸ **cunningly** *adv.*

cup *noun* 1 a small round container with a handle, from which to drink liquids. 2 the amount a cup will hold, used as a measure in cooking. 3 a container shaped like a cup, or something else having this shape. 4 an ornamental, usu. silver, vessel awarded as a prize in sports competitions, etc. —*verb trans.* (**cupped, cupping**) to form (e.g., one's hands) into a cup shape. ▸ **cupful** *noun*

cupboard (kəb'ərd) *noun* a piece of furniture or a recess with doors, shelves, etc., for storing provisions or personal effects.

cupidity *noun* greed for wealth and possessions.

cupola (kyōō'pə-lə, -lŏ,) *noun* 1 a small dome or turret on a roof. 2 a furnace used in iron foundries.

cur *noun* 1 a mongrel dog considered undesirable or unattractive. 2 a scoundrel.

curable *adj.* capable of being cured. ▸ **curability** *noun*

curare (kyōō-rär'ē, kōō-) *noun* a paralyzing poison smeared on arrow tips by S American hunters, and which also has medicinal uses as a muscle relaxant.

curate (kyōōr'ət) *noun* an assistant to a vicar or rector.

curative *adj.* able, or tending, to cure. —*noun* a substance that cures.

curator (kyōōr'āt,ər, kyōō-rāt'-) *noun* a person who has responsibility for a museum or other collection.

curb *noun* 1 the row of jointed stones forming the edging of a pavement. 2 something that restrains or controls. —*verb trans.* (**curbed, curbing**) 1 to restrain or control. 2 to lead (a dog) away from the sidewalk and to the gutter to urinate or defecate.

curd *noun* (*often* **curds**) milk thickened or coagulated by acid.

curdle *verb trans., intrans.* (**curdled, curdling**) to turn into curds.

cure *verb trans.* (**cured, curing**) 1 to restore (someone) to health or normality. 2 to get rid of (an illness, harmful habit, or other evil). 3 to preserve (meat) by soaking it in a salt solution and then removing it in order to dehydrate it. 4 to preserve (leather, tobacco, etc.), by drying. —*noun* 1 a remedy. 2 restoration to health. 3 a course of healing or remedial treatment.

cure-all *noun* a universal remedy; a panacea.

curettage (kyōōr,ə-täzh') *noun* the process of removing tissue from a body cavity by surgical scraping.

curette *or* **curet** (kyōō-rĕt') *noun* a spoon-shaped instrument used to scrape tissue or growths from a body cavity.

curfew *noun* 1 a an order forbidding people to be in the streets after a certain hour, e.g., when martial law is in force. b the time at which such an order applies. 2 the ringing of a bell as a signal for the start of a curfew.

curie *noun* a unit of radioactivity.

curio *noun* (*pl.* **curios**) a usu. small article valued for its rarity or unusualness.

curiosity *noun* (*pl.* **curiosities**) 1 eagerness to know. 2 something rare, exotic, or unusual.

curious *adj.* 1 informal strange; odd. 2 eager or interested. 3 inquisitive. ▸ **curiously** *adv.*

curium (kyōōr'ē-əm) *noun* (**SYMBOL Cm**) a radioactive element formed by bombarding plutonium-239 with alpha particles.

curl *verb trans., intrans.* (**curled, curling**) 1 to twist, roll, or wind (hair) into coils or ringlets; to grow in coils or ringlets. 2 to move in or form into a spiral, coil, or curve. 3 to take part in the game of curling. —*noun* 1 a small coil or ringlet of hair. 2 a spiral, coil, or curve. ▸ **curly** *adj.* ▸ **curliness** *noun*

curler *noun* a device for curling the hair.

curlew *noun* a large wading bird with a slender downward-curving bill.

curlicue *noun* a fancy twist or curl; a flourish made with a pen.

curling *noun* a team game, played on ice with heavy, smooth stones with handles, which are slid toward a circular target marked on the ice.

curmudgeon (kər-məj'ən) *noun* a bad-tempered or mean person. ▸ **curmudgeonly** *adj.*

currant *noun* 1 a small, dried, seedless grape. 2 a shrub, such as the redcurrant or one of its small, soft, edible berries.

currency *noun* (*pl.* **currencies**) 1 the coins and notes in use in a country. 2 general acceptance or popularity, esp. of an idea, theory, etc.

current *adj.* 1 generally accepted. 2 of or belonging to the present. —*noun* 1 a continuous flow of water, air, or heat in a particular direction. 2 a flow of an electrical charge. *Also called* **electric current.** 3 a popular trend or tendency. ▸ **currently** *adv.*

curriculum *noun* (*pl.* **curricula, curriculums**) a course, esp. of study at a school or university.

curriculum vitae (*pl.* **curricula vitae**) (**ABBREV. CV**) a written summary of one's personal details and the main events of one's education and career. *Also called* **résumé.**

curry[1] *noun* (*pl.* **curries**) a dish, orig. Indian, of meat, fish, or vegetables cooked with usu. hot spices.

curry² *verb trans.* (**curried, currying, curries**) **1** to groom (a horse). **2** to treat (tanned leather) to improve its flexibility, strength, and waterproof quality. —**curry favor with** to use flattery to gain (someone's) approval.

curry powder a selection of ground spices used in making curry dishes.

curse *noun* **1** a blasphemous or obscene expression, usu. of anger; an oath. **2 a** an appeal to a divine power to harm another. **b** the resulting harm suffered by another. **3** a cause of harm; an evil. —*verb trans., intrans.* (**cursed, cursing**) **1** to utter a curse against; to revile with curses. **2** to use violent, abusive language; to swear.

cursed *adj.* **1** (kər'sĭd) under a curse. **2** (kərst') damnable; hateful.

cursive *adj.* of writing with letters joined up, not printed separately. ▸ **cursively** *adv.*

cursor *noun* a usu. blinking indicator on a computer screen that marks the insertion point of the next character, etc.

cursory *adj.* hasty and superficial. ▸ **cursorily** *adv.*

curt *adj.* rudely brief; dismissive or abrupt. ▸ **curtly** *adv.* ▸ **curtness** *noun*

curtail (kər-tāl') *verb trans.* (**curtailed, curtailing**) **1** to cut short. **2** to restrict, reduce, or clampdown on. ▸ **curtailment** *noun*

curtain (kərt'n) *noun* **1** a hanging cloth or drapery over a window or in front of a stage. **2** something resembling a hanging cloth or drapery. **3** (**curtains**) *colloq.* the end; death. —*verb trans.* (**curtained, curtaining**) **1** to surround or enclose (something) with, or as if with, curtains or a curtain. **2** to supply (windows, etc.) with curtains.

curtsy *or* **curtsey** *noun* (*pl.* **curtsies, curtseys**) a slight bend of the knees with one leg behind the other, performed as a formal gesture of respect by women. —*verb intrans.* (**curtsied** *or* **curtseyed, curtsying** *or* **curtseying, curtsies** *or* **curtseys**) to perform a curtsy.

curvaceous (kər-vā'shəs) *adj. colloq.* of a woman having a shapely figure.

curvature *noun* the condition of being curved.

curve *noun* a line no part of which is straight, or a surface no part of which is flat. —*verb intrans., trans.* (**curved, curving**) to form, or form into, a curve. ▸ **curvy** *adj.*

curve ball *Baseball* a confusingly veering ball.

curvilinear (kər-və-lĭn'ē-ər) *adj.* consisting of or bounded by a curved line.

cushion (kŏŏsh'ən) *noun* **1** a stuffed fabric case used for making a seat comfortable, etc. **2** something that gives protection from shock, reduces unpleasant effects, etc. **3** the padded inner rim of a billiard, etc. table.

—*verb trans.* (**cushioned, cushioning**) **1** to protect from shock, injury, or the extremes of distress. **2** to provide with cushions.

cushy *adj.* (**cushier, cushiest**) *colloq.* comfortable and luxurious. ▸ **cushiness** *noun*

cusp *noun* **1** either point of a crescent moon. **2** a sharp, raised point on the grinding surface of a molar tooth. **3** the point of transition between one sign of the zodiac and the next.

cuss *colloq. noun* **1** a curse. **2** a person or animal, esp. if stubborn. —*verb intrans., trans.* (**cussed, cussing**) to curse.

cussed *adj. colloq.* infuriatingly stubborn or awkward.

custard *noun* a dish or sauce of baked eggs and milk, flavoring, and sugar.

custodial (kə-stōd'ē-əl) *adj.* relating to or involving custody.

custodian *noun* a person who has the care of something or someone, e.g., a public building or an underage child; a guardian. ▸ **custodianship** *noun*

custody (kəs'təd-ē) *noun* **1** the guardianship of a child, awarded to someone by a court of law. **2** the condition of being held by the police.

custom *noun* **1** a traditional activity or practice. **2** a personal habit. **3** the body of established practices of a community; convention. **4** the trade or business that one gives to a shop, etc., by regular purchases. —*adj.* made according to a purchaser's orders.

customary *adj.* according to custom; usual; traditional. ▸ **customarily** *adv.*

custom-built *or* **custom-made** *adj.* built or made to an individual customer's requirements; custom.

customer *noun* **1** a person who purchases goods from a shop, uses the services of a business, etc. **2** *colloq.* a difficult person with whom to deal: *He's one tough customer.*

customhouse *or* **customshouse** the office at a port, etc., where customs are paid or collected and where entering and departing ships are cleared.

customize *verb trans.* (**customized, customizing**) to adjust or make (something) as per the purchaser's or owner's orders. ▸ **customization** *noun*

customs *noun* **1** (*pl.*) taxes or duties paid on imports. **2** (*sing.*) the government department that collects these taxes. **3** (*sing.*) the place at a port, airport, etc., where baggage is inspected for goods on which duty must be paid.

customs union an economic agreement where nations adopt common excise duties, thereby eliminating the need for customs checks along their common borders.

cut verb trans., intrans. (pa t and pa p **cut**, **cutting**) 1 to slit, slice, or sever. 2 to divide by cutting. 3 to trim (hair, nails, etc.), mow (grass), etc. 4 to make or form by cutting. 5 Comput. to remove (selected text, etc.), often prior to re-inserting, either at a different place in the same document or in another document. See also **paste**. 6 to shape the surface of (a gem) into facets or decorate (glass) by cutting. 7 to shape the pieces of (a garment). 8 to bring out (a record or disk). 9 to injure or wound with a sharp edge or instrument. 10 to hurt. 11 to reduce (e.g., prices, wages, etc.). 12 a to decrease (something) in length or scope. ⊟ ABBREVIATE, ABRIDGE, COMPRESS, CON- DENSE, CROP, PRUNE, REDUCE, SHORTEN ⊟ AMPLIFY, EXPAND, LENGTHEN. **b** to delete or omit. 13 a to stop filming. b of a film or camera to change directly to another shot. 14 to cross or intersect. 15 to reject or renounce. 16 to ignore or pretend not to recognize (a person). 17 to absent oneself from: cut classes. 18 of a baby to grow (teeth). 19 to dilute (e.g., an alcoholic drink) or adulterate (a drug). —noun 1 the act of cutting; a cutting movement or stroke. 2 a slit, incision, or injury made by cutting. 3 a reduction. 4 slang one's share of the profits. 5 a piece of meat cut from an animal. 6 the style in which clothes or hair are cut. —**a cut above** colloq. superior to (something). **cut and dried** decided; definite. **cut and paste** Comput. to cut or copy (data or graphic files) and then insert it into another place. **cut both ways** to have advantages and disadvantages. **cut in 1** to interrupt. **2** of a vehicle to overtake and squeeze in front of another vehicle. **cut out** for or to be having the qualities needed for (something). **cut up** colloq. to behave playfully or comically; to clown around.

cutaway (kat'ə-wã,) adj. 1 of a diagram, etc. having outer parts omitted so as to show the interior. 2 of a coat with the front part cut away below the waist.

cutback noun a reduction in spending, use of resources, etc.

cute adj. colloq. 1 attractive; pretty. 2 clever; cunning; shrewd. ▸ **cutely** adv. ▸ **cuteness** noun

cutesy adj. (**cutesier, cutesiest**) colloq. cloyingly or preciously cute and highly affected.

cut glass glass with patterns cut into its surface.

cuticle noun 1 the outer layer of the skin. 2 the hardened skin at the base of the fingernails and toenails.

cutlass (kat'ləs) noun a short, broad, slightly curved sword.

cutlery noun knives, forks, and spoons.

cutlet noun 1 a thin piece of meat usu. without a bone attached. 2 a flat croquette of minced meat or vegetables.

cutoff noun 1 the point at which something is cut off. 2 a stopping of a flow or supply. 3 (**cutoffs**) pants that have been cut off at about the knees and made into shorts.

cutout noun 1 something cut out of a newspaper, etc. 2 a safety device for breaking an electrical circuit.

cut-rate adj. on sale or sold at a reduced price.

cutter noun 1 someone or something that cuts. 2 a a small, usu. lightly armed vessel used by the Coast Guard. b a ship's boat, often motorized. c a small, single-masted sailing ship.

cutthroat adj. very keen and aggressive: cutthroat competition. —noun a murderer.

cutting noun 1 a piece cut from a plant for rooting or grafting. 2 a piece cut from a newspaper etc. —adj. hurtful; sarcastic.

cutting edge adj. innovative; avant-garde.

cuttlefish noun (pl. **cuttlefish, cuttlefishes**) a mollusk related to the squid and octopus, having a shield-shaped body.

CV abbrev. curriculum vitae.

cwt. or **cwt** abbrev. hundredweight.

cyan (sī'ắn,) noun a greenish-blue color.

cyanide (sī'ə-nīd,) noun a salt of hydrocyanic acid, esp. the highly poisonous potassium cyanide.

cyanogen (sī-ắn'ə-jən) noun a compound of carbon and nitrogen, a colorless inflammable poisonous gas.

cyanosis noun blueness of the skin caused by lack of oxygen in the blood. ▸ **cyanotic** adj.

cybernetics (sī,bər-nĕt'ĭks) noun (sing.) the comparative study of communication and automatic control processes in mechanical or electronic systems and biological systems. ▸ **cybernetic** adj.

cybercafé or **Cyber café** noun 1 a coffee shop providing customers with accesss to the Internet, e-mail facilities, etc. 2 an Internet virtual café where visitors can chat, post messages, etc.

cyberspace noun 1 the three-dimensional artificial environment of virtual reality. See also **virtual reality**. 2 the space in which electronic communication takes place over computer networks.

cyclamate (sī'klə-māt,) noun a chemical compound formerly used as an artificial sweetening agent.

cyclamen (sī'klə-mən, sĭk'lə-) noun a plant with white, pink, purple, or red flowers.

cycle (sī'kəl) noun 1 a constantly repeating series of events or processes. 2 one of a regularly repeated set of similar changes, e.g., in the movement of a wave. 3 a bicycle or motorcycle. —*verb intrans.* (**cycled,** **cycling**) to ride a bicycle. ▸ **cyclist** *noun*

cyclic (sī′klĭk, sĭk′lĭk) *or* **cyclical** *adj.* **1** recurring in cycles. **2** *of a compound* having molecules containing one or more closed rings of atoms. ▸ **cyclically** *adv.*

cycling *noun* the activity of riding a bicycle for pleasure, transport, or sport.

cyclo- *combining form* forming words denoting: **1** circle; ring; cycle. **2** cyclic compound.

cyclone (sī′klōn,) *noun* **1** an area of low atmospheric pressure in which winds spiral inward toward a central low. *Also called* **depression.** **2** a violent tropical storm caused by such an area of low atmospheric pressure, and accompanied by torrential rains and extremely strong winds. ▸ **cyclonic** *adj.*

cyclotron *noun* an apparatus for accelerating charged atomic particles in a magnetic field.

cygnet (sĭg′nət) *noun* a young swan.

cylinder *noun* **1** a solid geometric figure of uniform circular cross section, in which the curved surface is at right angles to the base. **2** a container, machine part, or other object of this shape. **3** in an internal combustion engine, the tubular part inside which the piston moves. ▸ **cylindrical** *adj.*

cymbal *noun* a platelike brass percussion instrument, either beaten with a drumstick, or used as one of a pair that are struck together to produce a ringing clash. ▸ **cymbalist** *noun*

cynic (sĭn′ĭk) *noun* a person who habitually doubts or questions human goodness or

sincerity. ▸ **cynical** *adj.* ▸ **cynically** *adv.* ▸ **cynicism** *noun*

cynosure (sī′nə-shŏŏr,) *noun* the focus of attention.

cypress *noun* a coniferous evergreen tree.

cyst (sĭst) *noun* an abnormal body sac that contains fluid, semisolid material, or gas. ▸ **cystic** *adj.*

cystic fibrosis a hereditary disease in which the exocrine glands produce abnormally thick mucus.

cystitis *noun* inflammation of the urinary bladder.

-cyte *combining form* forming words denoting a mature cell: *leucocyte.*

cyto- *combining form* forming words denoting a cell or cells: *cytoplasm.*

cytology (sī-tăl′ə-jē) *noun* the study of plant and animal cells. ▸ **cytological** *adj.* ▸ **cytologist** *noun*

cytoplasm *noun* the part of a living cell, excluding the nucleus, that is enclosed by the cell membrane.

CZ *abbrev.* Canal Zone.

czar (zär, sär, tsär) *noun same as* **tsar.**

czarina (zär-ē′nə, sär-, tsär-) *noun same as* **tsarina.**

czaritsa (zär-ĭt′sə, sär-, tsär-) *noun same as* **tsaritsa.**

Czech (chĕk) —*noun* **1** a native of the former Czechoslovakia or the Czech Republic. **2** one of the two principal languages of the Czechs. —*adj.* of or relating to the former Czechoslovakia, the Czech Republic, the Czechs, or their language.

Dd

D¹ *or* **d** *noun* (*pl.* **Ds, D's, d's**) **1** the fourth letter of the English alphabet. **2** (**D**) *Mus.* **a** the second note in the scale of C major. **b** a musical key with the note D as its base. **3** (**D**) something shaped like a D.

D² *abbrev.* **1** Democrat. **2** *Cards* diamonds.

D³ *symbol* **1** the Roman numeral for 500. **2** *Chem.* deuterium.

'd *contr.* **1** would: *I'd go.* **2** had: *He'd gone.* **3,** did: *Where'd she go?*

D.A. *abbrev.* district attorney.

dab¹ *verb intrans., trans.* (**dabbed, dabbing**) **1** to touch lightly and usu. repeatedly with a cloth, etc. **2** (**dab** (**something**) **on** *or* **off**) to spread (it) on or remove (it) with light touches of a cloth, etc. —*noun* **1** a small

amount of something creamy or liquid. **2** a light, gentle touch.

dab² *noun* a small brown flatfish.

dabble *verb trans., intrans.* (**dabbled,** **dabbling**) **1** to move or shake (a hand, foot, etc.) about in water, esp. playfully. **2** (**dabble at** *or* **in** (**something**)) to do (it) or study (it) without serious effort. ▸ **dabbler** *noun*

dabchick *noun* a small bird of the grebe family.

dab hand an expert.

da capo (dä-käpō) *Mus.* an instruction to go back to the beginning of the piece.

dace *noun* (*pl.* **dace, daces**) a small river fish.

dacha (däch′ə) *noun* a Russian country house.

dachshund (dăk'sənd, dăks'hŏŏnt,) *noun* a dog with a long body and short legs.

dactyl (dăk'təl) *noun Poetry* a metrical foot of one stressed syllable followed by two unstressed syllables. ▶ **dactylic** *adj.*

dad *noun colloq.* a father.

Dada *noun* an art movement that rejected traditional art values and replaced them with seemingly irrational images.

daddy *noun (pl.* **daddies**) *colloq.* a father.

daddy longlegs 1 an arachnid with a small body and long slender legs. **2** the crane fly.

dado (dād'ō) *noun (pl.* **dadoes**) **1** the lower part of the wall of a room when decorated differently from the upper part. **2** *Archit.* the part of a pedestal in a classical building between the base and the cornice.

daemon *noun same as* **demon** (sense 4).

daffodil *noun* a spring-flowering plant with a single yellow trumpet-shaped flower.

daft *adj.* silly or foolish. ▶ **daftness** *noun*

dagger *noun* **1** a knife or short sword with a pointed end, used for stabbing. **2** *Printing* the reference symbol †. *Also called* **obelisk, obelus.**

daguerreotype *noun* **1** a type of early photograph produced on chemically treated silver.

dagwood *or* **Dagwood** *noun* a sandwich with many layers and various fillings.

dahl *noun same as* **dal.**

dahlia *noun* a herbaceous perennial plant with large colorful flowers.

> Named after Anders *Dahl*, 18th-century Swiss botanist

daily *adj.* **1** happening, appearing, done, etc. every day or during the day. **2** relating to a single day. —*adv.* every day. —*noun (pl.* **dailies**) a newspaper published every weekday or every day.

dainty *adj.* (**daintier, daintiest**) **1** small, pretty, and usu. delicate. **2** small and neat. **3** excessively sensitive or fastidious. —*noun (pl.* **dainties**) a delicacy, esp. a small cake. ▶ **daintily** *adv.* ▶ **daintiness** *noun*

daiquiri (dī'kə-rē, dăk'ə-) *noun* a drink made with rum, lime juice, and sugar.

dairy *noun (pl.* **dairies**) **1** a business that processes, bottles, and distributes milk, often also manufacturing other milk products. **2 a** a farm that concentrates on raising milk cows. **b** a farm building where butter and cheese are made and stored. ▶ **dairymaid** *noun* ▶ **dairyman** *noun*

dais (dā'əs, dī'əs) *noun* a raised platform for speakers.

daisy *noun (pl.* **daisies**) **1** a common flowering plant, such as the oxeye daisy or the white daisy. **2** a low-growing plant that has a flower head with a yellow center surrounded by white bracts. *Also called* **English daisy.**

> Literally 'day's eye', so called because of its opening during the day

dal, dahl *or* **dhal** *noun* a dish made from split pulses and spices.

Dalai Lama (dăl,ī-läm'ə) the title traditionally given to the Tibetan spiritual and political leader, prior to Chinese rule in Tibet.

dale *noun* a valley.

dally *verb intrans.* (**dallied, dallying, dallies**) **1** to waste time. **2** (**dally with** (**someone**)) to flirt with (someone). ▶ **dalliance** *noun*

Dalmatian *noun* a large dog with a smooth white coat and black or brown spots.

dalton *noun Chem.* an atomic mass unit.

dam¹ *noun* **1** a barrier built across a river to hold back the flow of water. **2** the water confined behind such a structure. —*verb trans.* (**dammed, damming**) to hold back with or as if with a dam.

dam² *noun* a female parent of a four-footed animal.

damage *noun* **1** harm or injury, or loss caused by injury. **2** (**damages**) *Law* payment due for loss or injury caused by another party. —*verb trans.* (**damaged, damaging**) to cause harm, injury, or loss to.

damask (dăm'əsk) *noun* cloth with a woven pattern, used for upholstery, tablecloths, etc.

> After *Damascus* in Syria, from where it was exported in the Middle Ages

dame *noun* **1** *slang* a woman. **2** *Brit.* a title of honor awarded to a woman for service or merit. **3** a woman who has such a title. *See also* **knight** (sense 4).

damn *verb trans.* (**damned, damning**) **1** *Relig.* to sentence to eternal punishment in hell. **2** to declare to be useless or worthless. **3** to suggest or prove the guiltiness of. —*interj.* used to express annoyance or contempt. —*adj.* annoying; contemptible: *the damn cold.* —*adv.* used to express annoyance or contempt: *It's damn cold.* ▶ **damnable** *adj.* ▶ **damnably** *adv.*

damnation *noun Relig.* **1** eternal punishment in hell. **2** the act of condemning or state of being condemned to such punishment. —*interj.* used to express annoyance, frustration, contempt, etc.

damned *adj.* **1** *Relig.* sentenced to damnation. **2** annoying; frustrating; contemptible. —*adv.* extremely; very.

damp *adj.* slightly wet. —*noun* slight wetness, e.g., in walls or the air. —*verb trans.* (**damped, damping**) **1** to make slightly wet. **2** to depress (spirits, confidence, etc.). ▶ **damply** *adv.* ▶ **dampness** *noun*

dampen verb trans., intrans. (**dampened, dampening**) **1** to make or become slightly wet. **2** to make or become less strong.

damper noun **1** something that lessens enthusiasm, interest, etc. **2** a movable plate for regulating the flow of air to a fire, etc. **3** a facility in keyboard instruments for regulating string vibrations.

damsel noun old use, literary a girl or young woman.

damson noun **1** a small deciduous tree grown for its small oval blue-black plum-like fruits. **2** a fruit of this tree.

dance verb intrans., trans. (**danced, dancing**) **1** to make a series of rhythmic steps or movements, usu. in time to music. **2** to perform (a particular series of such steps or movements): dance a waltz. **3** (usu. **dance about** or **around**) to move or jump quickly up and down or from side to side. —noun **1** a series of fixed steps, usu. made in time to music. **2** a social gathering for dancing. **3** a piece of music for dancing. —adj. denoting a type of modern music, with an insistent beat, popular in club culture. ▸ **dancer** noun.

dandelion noun a plant, regarded as a lawn weed, that has a single yellow flower head.

From the French phrase dent de lion, meaning 'lion's tooth'

dander noun ire; wrath; temper.

dandle verb trans. (**dandled, dandling**) to bounce (usu. a small child) on one's knee.

dandruff noun whitish flakes of dead skin from the scalp.

dandy noun (pl. **dandies**) a man who dresses very fashionably or elegantly. —adj. colloq. (**dandier, dandiest**) good; fine.

Dane (dān) noun a native or citizen of Denmark.

danger noun **1** a situation or state likely to lead to harm, injury, loss, etc. ▣ ENDANGERMENT, HAZARD, IMPERILMENT, JEOPARDY, PERIL, RISK ▣ SAFETY, SECURITY. **2** something that may cause harm, injury, or loss. **3** a possibility of something unpleasant happening.

dangerous adj. likely to or able to cause harm, injury, etc. ▸ **dangerously** adv.

dangle verb intrans., trans. (**dangled, dangling**) to hang, or cause something to hang, loosely.

Danish (dā'nish) —adj. of Denmark, its inhabitants, or their language. —noun **1** the official language spoken in Denmark. **2** (**the Danish**) the people of Denmark. See also **Dane**.

Danish pastry a pastry cake with a sweet topping.

dank adj. unpleasantly wet and cold. ▸ **dankness** noun

dapper adj. **1** neat and smart in appearance. **2** lively in movement.

dapple verb trans. to mark with differently colored spots. ▸ **dappled** adj.

dare verb trans., intrans. **1** to be brave enough to do something frightening, difficult, or dangerous. **2** to challenge (someone) to do something. —noun a challenge (to do something dangerous, etc.).

daredevil noun a reckless person who does dangerous things. —adj. reckless and dangerous.

daresay or **dare say** verb trans., intrans. (used in the first person singular present tense) to express probability; to suppose: I daresay you're right.

daring adj. bold, courageous, or adventurous. —noun boldness; courage. ▸ **daringly** adv.

dark adj. **1** deficient in or without light or brightness: a dark corridor. ▣ DIM, DUSKY, LIGHTLESS, UNILLUMINATED, UNLIT ▣ BRIGHT, ILLUMINATED, LIGHTED, LIT. **2** of a color neither light nor pale: dark blue. **3** not light or fair: dark hair. **4** sad or gloomy. **5** evil or sinister: dark powers. **6** mysterious and unknown: a dark secret. —noun **1** (usu. **the dark**) the absence of light. **2** the time when night begins: after dark. **3** a dark color. —**in the dark** not knowing or aware of something.

darken verb trans., intrans. (**darkened, darkening**) to make or become dark or darker.

dark horse an unlikely successful candidate.

darkroom noun a darkened room used for developing photographic film.

darling noun **1** a dearly loved or lovable person or thing. **2** a form of address used to a dearly loved person. —adj. **1** well loved. **2** delightful; charming.

darn¹ verb trans., intrans. (**darned, darning**) to mend or engage in mending by sewing with rows of stitches that cross each other. —noun a mended part in something.

darn² colloq. interj. used to express disgust, displeasure, dismay, etc. —adv., adj. used to express irritation, frustration, etc.: a darn expensive mistake.

darned adv., adj. colloq. used to express irritation, frustration, etc.: This darned car won't start.

dart noun **1** a narrow, pointed weapon or missile, thrown, fired, or used in the game of darts. **2** a sudden quick movement. **3** a fold sewn in clothing to make it fit neatly. —verb intrans., trans. (**darted, darting**) **1** to move or travel suddenly and quickly. **2** to throw or thrust suddenly.

darts noun (sing., pl.) a game in which darts are thrown at a circular target (dartboard).

dash verb intrans., trans. (**dashed, dashing**) **1** to move with speed. **2** to crash or smash violently, esp. in order to shatter. **3** to destroy or put an end to (hopes, etc.). **4** (*usu.* **dash (something) off**) to write or draw (it) quickly. —*noun* **1** a quick run or sudden rush. **2** a small amount of something added, esp. a liquid. **3** a patch of color. **4** a short line (—) used to show a break in a sentence, etc. **5** confidence, enthusiasm, and stylishness. *Sport* a short, fast race.

dashboard *noun* an instrument panel facing the driver of a vehicle, boat, etc.

dashing *adj.* **1** smart; stylish. **2** lively and enthusiastic. ▶ **dashingly** *adv.*

dastardly *adj.* cowardly, mean, and cruel.

DAT *abbrev.* digital audio tape.

data (dāt′ə, dăt′ə, dät′ə) *pl. noun* (*sing., pl.*) **1** pieces of information or facts, esp. obtained by scientific observation. **2** a collection of information in the form of numbers, electrical signals, etc. that can be processed by a computer. *See also* **datum.**

> *Usage* Data, the plural of the Latin singular *datum*, something that has been given, is regarded by conservative grammarians as a true plural and only that, one that must take a plural verb: 'All the *data* on the various homes for sale *have* (not *has*) been studied.' But in the literature of science, where *data* has been in essence redefined to mean a unitary collection, e.g., of various items (each one a datum), *data* is used with a singular verb: The *data* on the new syndrome has not yet been studied.

database *noun Comput.* an organized collection of coded and stored computer data that can be easily and widely accessed.

data communications *Comput.* the sending of digitally encoded data between computers by means of communication lines.

data processing *Comput.* the performance of operations on data by a computer system.

date¹ *noun* **1** the month, the day of that month, and/or the year, recorded by a number or series of numbers or by words and numbers. **2** a statement on a letter, document, etc., giving usu. the day, the month, and the year when it was written, sent, etc. **3** a particular period of time in history: *costumes of an earlier date.* **4 a** a planned meeting or social outing. **b** a person one is meeting socially or going out with. **5** an agreed time and place of performance. —*verb trans., intrans.* (**dated, dating**) **1** to put a date on. **2** to find, decide on, or guess the date of. **3** to have begun or originated at a specified time: *The evidence dates to 1980. / The documents date back to 1980.* **4** to become old-fashioned. **5** to go out (with a person), esp. regularly, socially, and romantically. —**to date** up to the present time.

date² *noun* a brown sticky, sweet dried fruit of the date palm.

dated *adj.* old-fashioned.

dateline *noun* a line, usu. at the top of a newspaper article, giving the date and place of writing.

date palm a tall tree cultivated for its edible fruits.

date rape rape committed by someone known to the victim while on a date.

dative *noun Gram.* a case indicating the indirect object. —*adj.* of or in this case.

datum (dāt′əm, dăt′-, dät′-) *noun* (*pl.* **data**) a single piece of information. *See also* **data.**

> *Usage* See note at **data.**

daub (dôb) *verb trans., intrans.* (**daubed, daubing**) **1** to spread roughly or unevenly on to or over a surface: *daubed paint on the walls.* **2** to cover (a surface) with a soft, sticky substance or liquid. **3** to paint carelessly or without skill. —*noun* **1** soft, sticky material such as clay, often used as a covering for walls. **2** an unskillful or carelessly done painting.

daughter *noun* **1** a female child considered in relation to her parents. **2** a woman closely associated with, involved with, or influenced by a person, thing, or place: *a faithful daughter of the Church.* ▶ **daughterly** *adj.*

daughterboard *noun Comput.* a supplementary circuit board linked to another, larger circuit board to give extra capabilities. *See also* **motherboard.**

daughter cell a cell formed as a result of cell division.

daughter-in-law *noun* (*pl.* **daughters-in-law**) the wife of one's son.

daunt *verb trans.* (**daunted, daunting**) to frighten, worry, or discourage.

daunting *adj.* intimidating; discouraging. ▶ **dauntingly** *adv.*

dauntless *adj.* having or displaying no fear in the face of danger or adversity.

dauphin (dō-făn′, dô′fĭn) *noun* **1** a title given to the eldest son of the French king during the period 1349–1830. **2** (**the dauphin**) a person holding this title.

davenport *noun* **1** a large sofa, sometimes converting into a bed. **2** a small desk.

davit (dă′vĭt, dăv′ĭt) *noun* a small crane on a ship, esp. one of a pair that a lifeboat is suspended from.

dawdle *verb trans., intrans.* (**dawdled, dawdling**) **1** to walk slowly. **2** to take one's time or waste (time): *dawdled over a drink / dawdled the hours away.* ▶ **dawdler** *noun*

dawn *noun* **1** the time when the sun rises. **2** the beginning (of something): *the dawn of a new era.* —*verb intrans.* (**dawned, dawning**) **1** *of the day* to start; to become light. **2** to begin to be understood or taken into account: *It suddenly dawned on me.*

day *noun* **1 a** a period of 24 hours. **b** the time the Earth takes to rotate once on its axis. **2** the period from sunrise to sunset. **3** the time during any 24-hour period normally spent doing something: *a working day.* **4** (**day** or **days**) a particular period of time, usu. in the past: *It never happened in my day.* —**call it a day** to decide not to continue with something.

daybreak *noun* dawn.

daycare *noun* supervision and care given by trained staff to young children or disabled people during the day.

daydream *noun* pleasant distracting thoughts. —*verb intrans.* (**daydreamed** or **daydreamt, daydreaming**) to indulge in daydreams. ▸ **daydreamer** *noun*

daylight *noun* **1** light from the sun, esp. as contrasted with artificial light. **2** dawn.

daylight-saving time (ABBREV. **DST, D.S.T.**) a system, during late spring, summer, and early fall, where clocks are set an hour or more ahead of standard time to take advantage of more daylight.

day nursery a place where young children are looked after during the day, e.g., while their parents are at work.

daytime *noun* the time between sunrise and sunset. —*adj.* happening in or associated with the period between sunrise and sunset.

daze *verb trans.* (**dazed, dazing**) to make (someone) feel confused or unable to think clearly (e.g., by a blow or shock). —*noun* a confused or inattentive state of mind.

dazzle *verb trans.* (**dazzled, dazzling**) **1** to cause (someone) to be unable to see properly, with or because of a strong light. **2** to impress greatly, e.g., by beauty, charm, skill, etc. ▸ **dazzlingly** *adv.*

de- *prefix* forming words denoting: **1** down or away: *depress / deport.* **2** reversal or removal: *delouse.*

deacon or **deaconess** *noun* a cleric or layperson who assists a priest, minister, etc.

deactivate *verb trans.* (**deactivated, deactivating**) to make (a bomb, virus, etc.) inactive or harmless. ▸ **deactivation** *noun*

dead *adj.* **1** no longer living; not alive. **2** no longer in use or existence; extinct: *a dead language.* **3** not functioning or lacking power, electrical charge, etc.: *the phone's dead.* **4** lacking interest, excitement, or activity, etc. **5** numb. **6** complete; absolute: *dead silence.* —*noun* **1** (**the dead**) a dead person or dead people: *don't speak ill of the dead.* **2** the most intense period of something: *the dead of night.* —*adv.* **1** completely: *You're dead wrong.* **2** suddenly and abruptly: *stopped dead.*

deadbeat *noun slang* **1 a** person who fails to pay debts. **2** an idle or useless person.

dead duck *colloq.* someone or something with no chance of success or survival.

deaden (dĕd'n) *verb trans.* (**deadened, deadening**) to lessen, weaken, or make less sharp or strong.

dead end 1 a road closed off at one end. **2** a situation or activity with no possibility of further progress or movement.

dead-end *adj.* allowing no progress.

deadhead *informal verb trans., intrans.* (**deadheaded, deadheading**) **1** to remove withered or dead flowers from (plants). **2** to drive or pilot a vehicle or aircraft without freight or passengers. —*noun* **1** a person attending an event, etc. on a free ticket or without paying. **2** a person who is considered boring.

dead heat a race, competition, etc. where the outcome is a draw.

deadline *noun* a time by which something must be done.

> Originally a line in a military prison, the penalty for crossing which was death

deadlock *noun* a situation in which no further progress toward an agreement is possible; a standstill. —*verb trans., intrans.* (**deadlocked, deadlocking**) to cause or come to a total standstill.

deadly *adj.* (**deadlier, deadliest**) **1** causing or likely to cause death. **2** absolutely accurate: *a deadly shot.* **3** relentless, unforgiving, merciless: *deadly enemies.* **4** *informal* tediously dull. —*adv.* extremely; absolutely: *deadly serious.* ▸ **deadliness** *noun*

deadpan *adj.* lacking animation, expression, emotion, etc.

dead ringer *colloq.* a person or thing almost identical to another.

deadwood *noun* someone or something that is burdensome, superfluous, or useless.

deaf (dĕf) *adj.* **1** unable to hear properly. **2** (**deaf to (something)**) refusing or unwilling to listen to advice, etc. —*noun* (**the deaf**) (*pl.*) hearing-impaired people.

deafen *verb trans.* (**deafened, deafening**) **1** to make deaf or temporarily unable to hear. **2** to soundproof. ▸ **deafening** *adj.*

deaf-mute *noun offensive* a person who is both deaf and unable to speak.

> **Usage** Because of the associations with mental impairment that this term now has, it should be avoided and the term *profoundly deaf* should be used instead.

deafness *noun* partial or total loss of hearing.

deal *noun* **1 a** bargain, transaction, agreement, or arrangement, etc.: *a business deal / a raw deal.* **2** an act of distributing cards to the players in a card game. —*verb intrans., trans.* (*pa t and pa p* **dealt**; *pr p* **dealing**) **1** (**deal in** (**something**)) to buy and sell (it). **2** (*also* **deal out**) to distribute cards to the players in a card game. **3** to give (something) out to a number of people, etc. —**a good** *or* **great deal 1** a large quantity. **2** very much or often: *She sees them a good deal.* **deal** (**someone**) **a blow** to hit or strike (another). **deal with** (**something** *or* **someone**) **1** to take action regarding (the one specified). **2** to be concerned with (the one specified).

dealer *noun* **1** a person or firm buying or selling goods. **2** a person who distributes the cards in a card game.

dealing *noun* **1 a** (**dealings**) business activities and transactions. **b** contact. **2** conduct.

dealt *see* **deal.**

dean *noun* **1** a senior official in a university or college. **2** a senior cleric in an Anglican or Episcopal cathedral. **3** a senior member, e.g., of a diplomatic corps.

deanery *noun* (*pl.* **deaneries**) the house, office, or jurisdiction of a dean.

dear *adj.* **1** lovable; attractive. **2** (**dear to**) greatly loved by, or very important or precious to (someone or something): *very dear to me.* **3** used to address someone at the start of a letter, e-mail, etc. **4** costing a 'lot of money or costing more than is reasonable. *See* **syn** *at* **expensive.** —*noun* **1** a charming or lovable person. **2** a term of affection for someone loved. —*adv.* affectionately or fondly. —*interj.* used to express dismay, etc. ▸ **dearly** *adv.*

dearth (därth) *noun* an extreme scarcity or lack (of something specified).

death *noun* **1** the time, act, or manner of dying, or the state of being dead. **2** something that causes a person to die. **3** an end, cessation, or destruction: *the death of the mining industry.* **4** (*usu.* **Death**) a personification of death or its inevitability, usu. in the form of a skeletal figure carrying a scythe.

deathly *adj., adv.* suggestive of or relating to death.

death row a section of a prison for inmates who have been sentenced to death.

deathtrap *noun* a building, vehicle, etc., that is very unsafe.

deathwatch beetle a small brownish beetle whose larvae bore holes in timber.

debacle (dǐ-bäk'əl, dä-bäk') *noun* **1** an utter, and often sudden or unexpected, failure, or fiasco. **2** a sudden break-up of ice, a log jam, etc. on a river.

debar *verb trans.* (**debarred, debarring**) to stop (someone) from joining, taking part in, doing, etc., something. ▸ **debarment** *noun*

debase *verb trans.* (**debased, debasing**) to degrade the value, quality, or status (of something). ▸ **debasement** *noun* ▸ **debaser** *noun*

debatable *adj.* doubtful; uncertain.

debate *noun* **1** a formal discussion, often for the presentation of two opposing views on a subject and usu. in front of an audience. **2** an ongoing discussion, argument, etc. —*verb trans., intrans.* (**debated, debating**) **1** to discuss (a topic); to hold or take part in a formal discussion. **2** to consider the arguments for or against (something). ▸ **debater** *noun*

debauch (dǐ-bôch', -bäch') *verb trans.* (**debauched, debauching**) **1** to corrupt or ruin (someone). **2** to take part in hedonistic or immoral activities. —*noun* a time spent indulging in hedonistic or immoral activities. ▸ **debauched** *adj.* ▸ **debauchee** *noun* ▸ **debauchery** *noun*

debenture (dǐ-běn'chər) *noun* **1** an unsecured bond. **2** a document acknowledging a debt.

debilitate *verb trans.* (**debilitated, debilitating**) to make weak or weaker. ▸ **debilitation** *noun*

debility *noun* (*pl.* **debilities**) weakness.

debit *noun* **1** an entry in an account recording what is owed or has been spent. **2** a sum taken from a bank account, etc.. **3** a deduction made from a bill or account. *See also* **credit** (sense 5d). —*verb trans.* (**debited, debiting**) **1** to take from (an account, etc.). **2** to record (something) in a debit entry.

debonair *or* **debonaire** (děb,ə-när', -něr') *adj.* cheerful, charming, and elegant, and showing good manners. ▸ **debonairly** *adv.*

debrief *verb trans.* (**debriefed, debriefing**) to gather information after a battle, event, mission, etc. (from someone directly involved). ▸ **debriefing** *noun*

debris *or* **débris** (də-brē', dä-) *noun* **1** the smashed remains of something. **2** trash or garbage.

debt (dět) *noun* **1** something that is owed. **2** (**in debt**) owing something.

debtor *noun* someone who owes something. esp. money. *See also* **creditor.**

debug *verb trans.* (**debugged, debugging**) **1** to locate and remove concealed microphones from (e.g., a room). **2** *Comput.* to locate and remove errors in (a program,etc.).

debunk *verb trans.* (**debunked, debunking**) to show (a claim, etc.) to be false.

debut *or* **début** (dā'byōō,, dā-byōō') *noun* a first public performance or appearance. —*verb trans., intrans.* (**debuted, debuting**) to present (someone or something) as a debut or to make a debut. ▸ **debutant** *noun*

deca- *combining form* forming words denoting ten: *decahedron*.

decade (dĕk′ād′, -dĕ-kād′) *noun* **1** a period of 10 years. **2** a group or series of 10 things.

decadence *noun* **1** a process, time, or state of deterioration, e.g., in morals, art, etc. **2** dissipation or self-indulgence.

decadent (dĕk′əd-ənt) *adj.* **1** living in a dissipated or self-indulgent way. **2** marked by or showing signs of deterioration. ▸ **decadently** *adv.*

decaf *colloq. adj.* decaffeinated. —*noun* decaffeinated coffee.

decaffeinate *verb trans.* (**decaffeinated, decaffeinating**) to remove all or part of the caffeine from (e.g., coffee or a soft drink). ▸ **decaffeinated** *adj.*

decagon (dĕk′əgăn,) *noun* a polygon with 10 sides and 10 angles.

decahedron (dĕk,ə-hē′drən) *noun* a solid figure with 10 faces.

Decalogue (dĕk′ə-lôg,, -lăg,) *noun* the Ten Commandments.

decamp *verb intrans.* (**decamped, decamping**) to go away suddenly, esp. secretly.

decant *verb trans.* (**decanted, decanting**) to pour (wine, etc.) from one bottle or container to another, leaving any sediment behind.

decanter *noun* an ornamental bottle for wine, sherry, whiskey, etc.

decapitate *verb trans.* (**decapitated, decapitating**) to cut off the head of. ▸ **decapitation** *noun*

decathlon (dĭ-kăth′lăn,) *noun* an athletic competition with 10 different track-and-field events.

decay *verb trans., intrans.* (**decayed, decaying**) to make or become rotten, ruined, etc. —*noun* **1** dead or decomposing organic matter. **2** a gradual decrease in health, power, quality, etc.

decease *noun* death. —*verb intrans.* (**deceased, deceasing**) to stop living.

deceased *adj.* dead. —*noun* (**the deceased**) a dead person, or dead people.

deceit *noun* **1** an act of deceiving or misleading. **2** dishonesty; deceitfulness.

deceitful *adj.* **1** tending to deceive, esp. habitually. **2** intended to deceive. ▸ **deceitfully** *adv.* ▸ **deceitfulness** *noun*

deceive *verb trans., intrans.* (**deceived, deceiving**) **1** to lie to or mislead (someone or something). **2** to give a false or misleading impression. ▸ **deceiver** *noun*

decelerate *verb trans., intrans.* (**decelerated, decelerating**) to slow down or cause to slow down. ▸ **deceleration** *noun*

December (dĭ-sĕm′bər) *noun* (ABBREV. **Dec.**, **Dec**) (*pl.* **Decembers**) the 12th month of the year.

decency *noun* (*pl.* **decencies**) **1** decent behavior or character. **2** (**decencies**) the generally accepted rules of respectable or moral behavior.

decennial *adj.* **1** happening every 10 years. **2** consisting of 10 years.

decent *adj.* **1** respectable; not vulgar or immoral. **2** kind or likable. **3** fairly good. ▸ **decently** *adv.*

decentralize *verb trans., intrans.* (**decentralized, decentralizing**) to split up the departments, offices, etc. (of a government, large organization, etc.) to promote their greater autonomy. ▸ **decentralization** *noun*

deception *noun* **1** an act of deceiving or misleading. **2** something that deceives or misleads.

deceptive *adj.* deceiving; misleading. ▸ **deceptively** *adv.*

deci- *combining form* forming words denoting one-tenth: *deciliter*.

decibel (dĕs′ĭ-bĕl,) *noun* (ABBREV. **dB**) a unit for comparing levels of sound.

decide *verb intrans., trans.* (**decided, deciding**) **1** to make up one's mind, esp. after some thought: *decided to go / decided it was a good idea*. **2** to make a choice, esp. from a number of options: *decided on the chilli burger*. **3** to settle or determine (something, esp. an outcome): *A single goal decided the match*. **4** to make a formal judgment about (something): *A panel of judges will decide the case*.

decided *adj.* **1** unmistakable. **2** determined. ▸ **decidedly** *adv.*

decider *noun* something that decides the result of something else.

deciduous (dĭ-sĭj′ə-wəs) *adj.* **1** of a plant, esp. a tree shedding leaves annually. See also **evergreen** (sense 1). **2** of leaves, antlers, etc. falling out or dropping off after a period of time.

decimal *adj.* **1** based on the number 10; relating to powers of 10 or the base 10. **2** denoting a system of measurement, etc., with units that are related to each other by multiples of 10. —*noun* a decimal fraction.

decimal fraction a fraction expressed in the form of an integer followed by a decimal point, followed by one or more digits. See also **common fraction**.

decimalize *verb trans.* (**decimalized, decimalizing**) to convert (numbers, a currency, etc.) to a decimal system, esp. the metric system. ▸ **decimalization** *noun*

decimate *verb trans.* (**decimated, decimating**) **1** to kill a large number of (a group or force). **2** *colloq.* to inflict great damage on. ▸ **decimation** *noun*

Usage The commonly occurring usage of *decimate* to mean to inflict great damage on, as in 'Termites have *decimated* the beams in the house' is objected to by many and should be avoided in formal prose or speech by those who wish to avoid criticism.

decipher *verb trans.* (**deciphered, deciphering**) **1** to translate (a message, etc. written in code) into ordinary language. **2** to work out the meaning of (something obscure or difficult to read). ▸ **decipherable** *adj.*

decision *noun* **1** the act of deciding. **2** something decided. **3** determination: *a woman of decision.*

decisive *adj.* **1** conclusive. **2** acting with firmness. **3** beyond doubt. ▸ **decisively** *adv.* ▸ **decisiveness** *noun*

deck[1] *noun* **1** a floor on a ship. **2** a pack of playing cards. **3** the turntable of a record player or the part of a tape recorder where tapes are placed to be played. **4** (**decks**) record players used for mixing, esp. dance music. —*verb trans.* (**decked, decking**) *slang* to knock (someone) down with a violent blow or blows.

deck[2] *verb trans.* (**decked, decking**) (*also* **deck** (**someone** *or* **something**) **out**) to decorate (e.g., a house, etc.).

declaim (dĭ-klām') *verb trans., intrans.* (**declaimed, declaiming**) **1** to make (a speech) in an impressive and dramatic manner. **2** (**declaim against** (**something**)) to protest about (it) loudly and passionately. ▸ **declamation** *noun* ▸ **declamatory** *adj.*

declaration *noun* a formal statement or announcement.

declare *verb trans., intrans.* (**declared, declaring**) · **1** to announce publicly or formally: *declare war.* **2** to say firmly or emphatically.

declassify *verb trans.* (**declassified, declassifying, declassifies**) to take (an official document, etc.) off a list of classified information and allow public access to it. ▸ **declassification** *noun*

declension *noun* **1** a set of the different grammatical forms a noun, adjective, or pronoun can take. *See also* **conjugation** (sense 1), **decline** (sense 4). **2** decline, descent, or deterioration.

decline *verb trans., intrans.* (**declined, declining**) **1** to refuse (an invitation, etc.), esp. politely. **2** to become less strong or healthy. **3** to become lower in quality or less in quantity. **4** to state the set of the different grammatical forms (a noun, adjective, or pronoun) can take. *See also* **conjugate** (sense 1), **declension**. **5** to move down from a higher to a lower place or position.

—*noun* a lowering or lessening of strength, health, quality, or quantity. ▸ **declination** *noun*

declivity (dĭ-klĭv'ĭt-ē) *noun* (*pl.* **declivities**) a downward slope. *See also* **acclivity**.

decode *verb trans.* (**decoded, decoding**) to translate (a coded message) into ordinary language. ▸ **decoder** *noun*

décolletage (dĕk,lə-täzh') *noun* a low-cut dress or neckline.

décolleté *or* **décolletée** (dĕk,lə-tā') *adj.* **1** having a low-cut neckline **2** wearing a low-cut garment.

decompose *verb intrans., trans.* (**decomposed, decomposing**) **1** to rot. **2** to separate into smaller or simpler parts. ▸ **decomposition** *noun*

decongestant *noun* a drug, etc. that reduces nasal congestion.

decontaminate *verb trans.* (**decontaminated, decontaminating**) to make (something) safe by removing germs, poisons, radioactivity, etc. ▸ **decontamination** *noun*

decor *or* **décor** (dĭ-kôr') *noun* the style of decoration, furnishings, etc., in a room or house.

decorate (dĕk'ə-rāt,) *verb trans.* (**decorated, decorating**) **1** to make (something) attractive or more attractive by adding something. ▣ ADORN, BEDECK, EMBELLISH, ORNAMENT. **2** to put paint or wallpaper on. **3** to give (someone) a medal or badge as an honor. ▸ **decoration** *noun* ▸ **decorative** *adj.* ▸ **decorator** *noun*

decorous (dĕk'ə-rəs) *adj.* correct or socially acceptable. ▸ **decorously** *adv.*

decorum (dĭ-kôr'əm) *noun* correct or socially acceptable behavior.

decoy *verb trans.* (**decoyed, decoying**) to lead or lure into a trap, etc. —*noun* someone or something used to lead or lure a person or animal into a trap, etc.

decrease *verb trans., intrans.* (dĭ-krēs') (**decreased, decreasing** to make or become less. —*noun* (dē' krēs) a lessening or loss.

decree *noun* a formal order, ruling, law, etc. made by a high authority, e.g., a monarch, court of law, etc. —*verb trans.* (**decreed, decreeing**) to order or decide (something) formally or officially.

decrepit *adj.* weak or worn out because of old age or long use: *a decrepit old man / a decrepit lawnmower.* ▸ **decrepitude** *noun*

decriminalize *verb trans.* (**decriminalized, decriminalizing**) to remove the illegal status of (something, esp. a drug).

decry *verb* (**decried, decrying, decries**) to criticize or express disapproval of.

dedicate *verb trans.* (**dedicated, dedicating**) **1** to give or devote (oneself or one's time, money, etc.) to a purpose, etc.: *dedicated himself to his work.* **2** to address (a book, piece of music, etc.) to someone as a token of affection or respect. **3** to set apart for a sacred purpose. ▸ **dedication** *noun*

dedicated *adj.* **1** very conscientious or devoted. **2** *Comput.* designed to carry out one particular task or function. **3** built or designed for, or assigned to, a single purpose: *dedicated telephone wires.*

deduce *verb trans.* (**deduced, deducing**) to think out or judge on the basis of what is known. ▸ **deducible** *adj.*

deduct *verb trans.* (**deducted, deducting**) to take away (a number, amount, etc.). ▸ **deductible** *adj., noun*

deduction *noun* **1** the act or process of deducting. **2** something, esp. money, deducted. **3** the act, process, or result of deducing, esp. of deducing a particular fact from what is known or thought to be generally true. *See also* **induction** (sense 3). ▸ **deductive** *adj.*

deed *noun* **1** something someone has done. **2** a legal document that records the terms of an agreement.

deejay *colloq. noun* a disc jockey. —*verb intrans.* (**deejayed, deejaying**) to work as a deejay.

deem *verb trans.* (**deemed, deeming**) to judge, think, or consider.

deep *adj.* **1** extending, coming from, or being relatively far down, within, etc. **2** very serious, long-standing, etc. **3** *of a color* strong and relatively dark. **4** absorbed: *deep in thought.* **5** low in pitch. **6** difficult; obscure: *a deep book.* **7** mysterious: *deep, dark secrets.* **8** sincere: *with deepest sympathy.* —*adv.* **1** in a deep manner: *drink deep.* **2** far down or into: *dig deep.* **3** late on in or well into: *deep in the night.* —*noun* **1** (**the deep**) the ocean. **2** a huge, immeasurable extent: *the deep of outer space.* —**deep down** in reality, though not in appearance. ▸ **deeply** *adv.*

deepen *verb trans., intrans.* (**deepened, deepening**) to make or become deeper, greater, more intense, etc.

deep-dish *adj.* baked in a dish with high sides to allow for plenty of filling or for a thick base. —*noun* a pizza with a thick base.

deep-freeze *verb trans.* to preserve (perishable material, esp. food) by storing it in a frozen state.

deep-fry *verb trans.* to fry by complete submersion in hot oil or fat.

deep-rooted *adj.* firmly established.

deep-seated *adj.* **1** deep-rooted. **2** *of a disease, etc.* difficult to detect or treat, because of being sited well inside a structure, etc.: *deep-seated psychiatric problems.*

deep-set *adj., of eyes, etc.* in relatively deep sockets.

deer *noun* (*pl.* **deer**) a hoofed ruminant mammal, many species of which have antlers, esp. the males. *See also* **venison.**

deface *verb trans.* (**defaced, defacing**) to mar or spoil (something), often deliberately.

de facto (dā-fāk'tō) *adj., adv.* actual or actually. *See also* **de jure.**

defame *verb trans.* (**defamed, defaming**) to damage the good reputation of (someone). ▸ **defamation** (děf,ə-mā'shən) *noun* ▸ **defamatory** (dĭ-fām'ə-tôr,ē) *adj.*

default *verb intrans.* (**defaulted, defaulting**) **1** to fail to do something, esp. some financial or legal obligation: *defaulted on the loan.* **2** (*usu.* **default to**) *of a computer program* to go automatically to (a particular option) unless the user selects to do otherwise. —*noun* **1** a failure to fulfill a financial or legal obligation. **2** an option that a computer program automatically goes to when a user gives no alternative instruction. ▸ **defaulter** *noun*

defeat *verb trans.* (**defeated, defeating**) **1** to beat, win a victory over, e.g., in a war, competition, game, or argument. **2** to confuse or make it impossible to understand. —*noun* an act of defeating or the state of being defeated. ▣ BEATING, CONQUEST ▣ VICTORY, WIN.

defeatism *noun* a state of mind where defeat or failure is too readily accepted. ▸ **defeatist** *noun, adj.*

defecate *verb intrans.* (**defecated, defecating**) to expel feces from the body through the anus. ▸ **defecation** *noun*

defect *noun* (dē'fěkt,, dĭ-fěkt') a flaw, fault, or imperfection. —*verb intrans.* (dĭ-fěkt') (**defected, defecting**) to leave a country, political party, group, etc., esp. with the intention of going over to another. ▸ **defection** *noun* ▸ **defector** *noun*

defective *adj.* having a defect or defects.

defend *verb trans., intrans.* (**defended, defending**) **1** to guard or protect against danger or attack. **2** to justify or argue in support of (someone or something). **3** to represent (an accused person) at a trial.

defendant *noun* a party charged in a court of law. *See also* **plaintiff.**

defender *noun* a person who defends against attack, esp. in military and sporting contexts.

defense *noun* **1** an act, means, or method of resisting attack. **2** (**defenses**) fortifications. **3** a justification for an action, etc. or to an accusation. **4 a** a defendant and a lawyer or team of lawyers representing the defendant at a trial. **b** an argument and any supporting evidence presented by or on behalf of a defendant at a trial. **5** *Sport* (**the defense**) the team or the players on a team who try to prevent their opponents from scoring. ▸ **defenseless** *adj.*

defensible *adj.* able to be defended or justified. ▸ **defensibly** *adv.*

defensive *adj.* 1 defending or ready to defend. 2 attempting to justify actions, etc. —**on the defensive** defending oneself or prepared to defend oneself against attack or criticism. ▸ **defensively** *adv.* ▸ **defensiveness** *noun*

defer[1] *verb trans.* (**deferred, deferring**) to put off or leave until a later time.

defer[2] *verb intrans.* (**deferred, deferring**) (**defer to (someone**)) to yield to (another's) wishes, opinions, or orders.

deference (dĕf'ə-rəns) *noun* 1 willingness to consider or respect the wishes, etc., of others. 2 the act of deferring. —**in deference to (someone** *or* **something**) deferring to (the one or thing specified).

deferential (dĕf'ə-rĕn'chəl) *adj.* respectful. ▸ **deferentially** *adv.*

defiance *noun* 1 open disobedience; contempt of authority. 2 a challenge to fight. ▸ **defiant** *adj.* ▸ **defiantly** *adv.*

deficient (dĭ-fĭsh'ənt) *adj.* failing to meet standards or requirements; not good enough. ▸ **deficiency** *noun*

deficit (dĕf'ĭ-sĭt) *noun* an amount something is short of what is required or expected.

defile[1] (dĭ-fīl') *verb trans.* (**defiled, defiling**) 1 to dirty or pollute. 2 to spoil the purity, holiness, etc., of. ▸ **defiler** *noun*

defile[2] (dĭ-fīl', dē'fīl,) *noun* a narrow mountain pass. —*verb intrans.* (**defiled, defiling**) to march in file.

define *verb trans.* (**defined, defining**) 1 to fix or state the exact meaning of (a word, etc.). 2 to fix, describe, or explain (opinions, duties, etc.). ▸ **definable** *adj.*

definite (dĕf'ə-nĭt) *adj.* 1 fixed or firm; unlikely to change. 2 sure; certain. 3 clear and precise. ▸ **definitely** *adv.*

definite article *Gram.* a word, *e.g., the* in English, that is used before another to denote something already mentioned, known, etc. *See also* **indefinite article**.

definition *noun* 1 a statement of the meaning of a word or phrase. 2 the act of defining a word or phrase. 3 the degree of clarity, precision, resolution, etc.

definitive (dĭ-fĭn'ət-ĭv) *adj.* 1 conclusive; final. 2 most complete or authoritative. ▸ **definitively** *adv.*

deflate *verb trans., intrans.* (**deflated, deflating**) 1 to remove air from (a tire, etc.); to grow smaller through loss of air. 2 to reduce the size or importance of (e.g. hopes, self-confidence, etc.). 3 to lower (prices, etc.). *See also* **inflate** (sense 3), **reflate**. ▸ **deflation** *noun* ▸ **deflationary** *adj.*

deflect *verb intrans., trans.* (**deflected, deflecting**) to turn aside or away or cause to turn aside or away. ▸ **deflection** *noun*

deflower *verb trans., old literary* (**deflowered, deflowering**) to be the first person to have sexual intercourse with (a virginal woman).

defog *verb trans.* (**defogged, defogging**) to clear (a windshield) of condensed water vapor. ▸ **defogger** *noun*

defoliate *verb trans.* (**defoliated, defoliating**) to remove the leaves from (a plant, esp. a tree). ▸ **defoliant** *noun, adj.* ▸ **defoliation** *noun*

deforest *verb trans.* (**deforested, deforesting**) to clear (an area) of its forests or trees. ▸ **deforestation** *noun*

deform *verb trans., intrans.* (**deformed, deforming**) 1 to distort the shape of (something), esp. by making it look ugly. 2 to become misshapen. ▸ **deformation** *noun*

deformed *adj.* misshapen.

deformity *noun* (*pl.* **deformities**) 1 a deformed thing, esp. a body part. 2 the state of being deformed.

defraud *verb trans.* (**defrauded, defrauding**) to deprive (someone) of money, rights, etc., by dishonest means.

defray *verb trans.* (**defrayed, defraying**) to provide the money to pay (costs or expenses). ▸ **defrayal** *noun* ▸ **defrayment** *noun*

defrock *verb trans.* (**defrocked, defrocking**) to remove (a priest) from office.

defrost *verb trans., intrans.* (**defrosted, defrosting**) 1 to clear ice from (e.g., a windshield) or become clear of ice. 2 to thaw (frozen food) or become thawed.

deft *adj.* skillful; able to do something quickly and easily. ▸ **deftly** *adv.* ▸ **deftness** *noun*

defunct *adj.* no longer living, existing, active, usable, or in use.

defuse *verb trans.* (**defused, defusing**) 1 to remove the fuse from (a bomb, etc.). 2 to make (a situation, etc.) less dangerous.

defy *verb* (**defied, defying, defies**) 1 to disobey blatantly or with contempt. 2 to dare or challenge (someone).

degaussing (dē-gow'sĭng) *noun* a process of neutralizing a magnetic field.

degenerate *adj.* (dĭ-jĕn'ə-rət) degraded, esp. in moral terms. —*noun.* a degenerate person. —*verb intrans.* (dĭ-jĕn'ə-rāt,) (**degenerated, degenerating**) to go from a normal or acceptable state to an inferior one. ▸ **degeneracy** *noun* ▸ **degeneration** *noun* ▸ **degenerative** *adj.*

degrade *verb trans., intrans.* (**degraded, degrading**) 1 to disgrace or humiliate. 2 to downscale in rank or grade. 3 to break down chemically. ▸ **degradable** *adj.* ▸ **degradation** *noun*

degrading *adj.* humiliating.

degree *noun* **1** an amount or extent. **2** *Phys.* (SYMBOL°) a unit of temperature. **3** *Geom.* (SYMBOL°) a unit by which angles are measured. **4** a title or an award given by a university or college. **5** *Law* the comparative severity or seriousness of a crime: *assault in the first degree.*

dehiscent (dĭ-hĭs'ənt) *adj. Bot.* denoting a plant part, e.g., a fruit that bursts open to release seeds, pollen, etc. ▶ **dehiscence** *noun*

dehumanize *verb trans.* (**dehumanized, dehumanizing**) to deprive of all desirable human qualities. ▶ **dehumanization** *noun*

dehydrate *verb trans., intrans.* (**dehydrated, dehydrating**) **1** to remove water from. **2** to lose or cause to lose too much water. ▶ **dehydration** *noun*

deice *verb trans.* (**deiced, deicing**) to remove ice or frost from (a vehicle windshield, etc.) by scraping or using a chemical substance.

deicer *noun* a scraping device or a chemical substance for removing ice or frost.

deify (dē'ə-fī,) *verb trans.* (**deified, deifying, deifies**) **1** to raise to the status of a god. **2** to regard or worship (someone or something) as a god. ▶ **deification** *noun*

deign (dān) *verb intrans.* (**deigned, deigning**) to condescend: *didn't even deign to reply.*

deism *noun* belief in the existence of God. *See also* **theism.** ▶ **deist** *noun*

deity (dē'ət-ē) *noun* (*pl.* **deities**) *formal* **1** a god or goddess. **2** the state of being divine.

déjà vu (dā,zhä,vōō') a feeling of having experienced something before although it is actually being experienced for the first time.

dejected *adj.* sad; miserable. ▶ **dejectedly** *adv.* ▶ **dejection** *noun*

de jure (dē-jōōr'ē, dā-yōōr'ē) *Law* according to law; by right. *See also* **de facto.**

delay *verb trans., intrans.* (**delayed, delaying**) **1** to slow down or cause to be late. **2** to put off to a later time. —*noun* **1** the act of delaying or state of being delayed. **2** the amount of time by which someone o. something is delayed.

delectable *adj.* very pleasant. ▶ **delectably** *adv.* ▶ **delectation** *noun*

delegate *verb trans., intrans.* (dĕl'ə-gāt,) (**delegated, delegating**) **1** to give or entrust (a task, responsibility, etc.) to someone else. **2** to send or name (a person) as a representative, etc. —*noun* (dĕl'-ə-gət, -gāt,) someone sent, named, or chosen as a representative for another.

delegation *noun* **1** a group of delegates. **2** the act of delegating or the state of being delegated.

delete *verb trans.* (**deleted, deleting**) to take out or erase (esp. something written or printed). ▶ **deletion** *noun*

deleterious *adj.* harmful or destructive.

delft *noun* earthenware, typically white with a blue design.

deli *noun colloq.* a delicatessen.

deliberate *adj.* (dĭ-lĭb'ə-rət) **1** done on purpose. **2** slow and careful. —*verb trans., intrans.* (dĭ-lĭb'ə-rāt,) (**deliberated, deliberating**) to think about something carefully. ▶ **deliberately** *adv.* ▶ **deliberation** *noun*

delicacy *noun* (*pl.* **delicacies**) **1** the state or quality of being delicate. **2** a food that is particularly delicious or highly valued.

delicate (dĕl'ĭ-kət) *adj.* **1** easily damaged or broken. **2** not strong or healthy. **3** small and attractive; dainty. **4** requiring tact and careful handling. **5** *of colors, flavors, etc.* not dark or strong. ▶ **delicately** *adv.*

delicatessen *noun* a food store specializing in salads, cooked meats, cheeses, etc. *Also called* **deli.**

delicious *adj.* **1** having a very pleasing taste or smell. ⊟ DELECTABLE, LUSCIOUS, SAVORY, SCRUMPTIOUS, TASTY, TOOTHSOME, YUMMY ⊟ DISTASTEFUL, INEDIBLE, UNPALATABLE. **2** giving great pleasure. ▶ **deliciously** *adv.*

delight *verb trans., intrans.* (**delighted, delighting**) **1** to please greatly. **2** (**delight in**) to take great pleasure in (something). —*noun* **1** great pleasure. **2** someone or something that gives great pleasure.

delighted *adj.* highly pleased; thrilled. ▶ **delightedly** *adv.*

delightful *adj.* giving great pleasure. ▶ **delightfully** *adv.*

delimit *verb trans.* (**delimited, delimiting**) to mark or fix the limits or boundaries of (e.g., powers). ▶ **delimitation** *noun*

delineate *verb trans.* (**delineated, delineating**) to show by drawing or by describing in words. ▶ **delineation** *noun*

delinquent *noun* a person who habitually commits minor crimes, or who is in arrears, etc. —*adj.* **1** guilty of a crime or misdeed. **2** in arrears. ▶ **delinquency** *noun*

deliquesce (dĕl,ĭ-kwĕs') *verb intrans.* (**deliquesced, deliquescing**) to melt; to become liquid by absorbing moisture from the air. ▶ **deliquescence** *noun* ▶ **deliquescent** *adj.*

delirious *adj.* **1** affected by delirium. **2** very excited or happy. ▶ **deliriously** *adv.*

delirium *noun* (*pl.* **deliriums, deliria**) **1** a temporarily disordered state of mind. **2** extreme excitement or joy.

deliver *verb trans., intrans.* (**delivered, delivering**) **1** to carry (goods, letters, etc.) to a person or place. **2** to hurl, throw, or direct (a ball, a blow, criticism, etc.). **3** to give or make (a speech, etc.). **4** (**deliver from**) to set free or rescue. **5** to help at a birth or to give birth to. **6** to keep or fulfill a promise, etc. ▸ **deliverer** *noun*

deliverance *noun* an act of rescue, or the state of being rescued.

delivery *noun* (*pl.* **deliveries**) **1 a** an act of carrying of (goods, letters, etc.) to a person or place. **b** a thing or things delivered. **2** the process or a manner of giving birth. **3** an act or manner of making, a speech, etc. **4** an act or manner of throwing a ball, esp. in some sports.

dell *noun* a small valley or hollow, usu. with trees.

delphinium *noun* (*pl.* **delphiniums**) a tall plant with spikes of usu. blue flowers. *Also called* **larkspur**.

> From a Greek word translating as 'little dolphin', because of the shape of the flower-heads

delta *noun* **1** a usu. triangular silty area at the mouth of a river. **2** the fourth letter of the Greek alphabet (Δ, δ).

> Originally from a Hebrew word meaning 'tent door'

deltoid *noun* a triangular shoulder muscle. —*adj.* triangular

delude *verb trans.* (**deluded, deluding**) to deceive or mislead.

deluge *noun* **1** a flood. **2** a downpour of rain. **3** a great quantity. —*verb trans.* (**deluged, deluging**) **1** to come or arrive in great quantities or numbers. **2** to cover in water; to flood.

delusion *noun* **1** a false belief. **2** an act of deluding or the state of being deluded. **3** a persistently held false or mistaken belief, esp. one that is symptomatic of mental illness. ▸ **delusive** *adj.* ▸ **delusory** *adj.*

delusions of grandeur an overinflated belief in one's own importance.

deluxe *or* **de luxe** (dĭ-lŭks′, -lŏŏks′, -lōōks′) *adj.* very high quality; luxurious.

delve *verb intrans.* (**delved, delving**) **1** (**delve into** (**something**)) to search (it) for information, etc. **2** (**delve through** (**something**)) to search through (it).

demagogue (dĕm′ə-gäg,) *noun* a political leader who relies on alarmist tactics to win support. ▸ **demagogic** *adj.* ▸ **demagoguery** *noun* ▸ **demagogy** *noun*

demand *verb trans.* (**demanded, demanding**) **1** to ask or ask for firmly, forcefully, or urgently. **2** to require or need. **3** to claim as a right. —*noun* **1** a forceful request or order. **2** an urgent claim. **3** people's desire or ability to buy or obtain goods etc.: *a slump in demand*.

demanding *adj.* **1** requiring a lot of effort, ability, etc.; *a demanding job*. **2** needing or

expecting a lot of attention: *a demanding child*.

demarcate (dĭ-mär′kāt, dĕ′mär,-) *verb trans.* (**demarcated, demarcating**) to mark out the limits or boundaries of. ▸ **demarcation** *noun*

demean *verb trans.* (**demeaned, demeaning**) to lower the dignity of or lessen respect for (someone, esp. oneself).

demeaning *adj.* humiliating.

demeanor *noun* behavior; manner; bearing.

demented *adj.* mad; crazy. ▸ **dementedly** *adv.*

dementia (dĭ-mĕn′chə) *noun* a mental disorder due to brain disease or injury. *See also* **senile dementia**.

demerit *noun* a fault or failing, or a recorded mark indicating this.

demi- *combining form* forming words denoting half or partly: *demigod*.

demigod *noun* **1** *Mythol.* a person who is part human and part god. **2** a very highly regarded person.

demijohn *noun* a large bottle for storing wine, oil, etc.

demilitarize *verb trans.* (**demilitarized, demilitarizing**) **1** to remove armed forces from (an area, etc.). **2** to transfer (an area, etc.) from military to civilian control. ▸ **demilitarization** *noun*

demimonde (dĕm′ĭ-mänd,) *noun* **1** a group or class of wealthy prostitutes. **2** a group of people considered to be on the margins of respectability.

demise (dĭ-mīz′) *noun* **1** death. **2** the end (of something): *the demise of the typewriter*. —*verb trans., intrans.* (**demised, demising**) *Law* to transfer (an estate, etc.), usu. by a will.

demobilize *verb trans.* (**demobilized, demobilizing**) to release from service in the armed forces, e.g., after a war. ▸ **demobilization** *noun*

democracy *noun* (*pl.* **democracies**) **1** a form of government elected by the people. **2** a country, state, or other body with such a form of government. **3** equality among people in society, at work, etc.

democrat *noun* **1** a person who believes in political democracy. **2** a person who believes in equality in society, at work, etc. **3** (**Democrat**) a member or supporter of the Democratic Party of the USA. *See also* **republican** (sense 2). ▸ **democratic** *adj.* ▸ **democratically** *adv.*

demodulate *verb trans.* (**demodulated, demodulating**) *Radio* to extract (a modulating signal) from a carrier wave of a radio broadcast. ▸ **demodulation** *noun*

demography *noun* the scientific study of populations. ▸ **demographer** *noun* ▸ **demographic** *adj.*

demolish *verb* *trans.* (**demolished, demolishing**) 1 to pull down (a building, etc.). 2 to break into pieces; to ruin. ▸ **demolition** *noun*

demon *noun* 1 an evil spirit. 2 an evil or tormenting person, factor, or force. 3 a person who shows enthusiasm or skill (in a particular field). 4 (*also* **daemon**) a good or friendly spirit. ▸ **demoniac** *adj.* ▸ **demoniacal** *adj.* ▸ **demonic** *adj.* ▸ **demonically** *adv.*

demonstrable *adj.* capable of being proven or shown. ▸ **demonstrability** *noun* ▸ **demonstrably** *adv.*

demonstrate (děm'ən-strāt,) *verb trans., intrans.* (**demonstrated, demonstrating**) 1 to show or prove by reasoning or providing evidence. 2 to show how something is done, operates, etc. 3 to show (support, opposition, etc.) by protesting, marching, etc., in public. ▸ **demonstration** *noun* ▸ **demonstrator** *noun*

demonstrative (dĭ-mǎn'strə-tĭv) *adj.* 1 showing feelings openly. 2 (**demonstrative of (something)**) showing (it) or proving (it) to be so: *words demonstrative of anger.* ▸ **demonstratively** *adv*

demonstrative pronoun *Gram.* a word, e.g., in English, *this, that, these,* and *those,* indicating a person or thing referred to or already known.

demoralize *verb trans.* (**demoralized, demoralizing**) to take away the confidence, courage, or enthusiasm of; to dishearten. ▸ **demoralization** *noun*

demote *verb trans.* (**demoted, demoting**) to reduce in rank, grade, importance, etc. ▤ DEGRADE, DOWNGRADE, REDUCE ▣ ELEVATE, PROMOTE, UPGRADE. ▸ **demotion** *noun*

demotic *adj.* relating to or used by ordinary people; popular. —*noun* colloquial language.

demur (dĭ-mər') *verb intrans.* (**demurred, demurring**) to object mildly. —*noun* an objection. ▸ **demurral** *noun*

demure (dĭ-myŏŏr') *adj.* quiet; modest; prim and proper. ▸ **demurely** *adv.* ▸ **demureness** *noun*

den *noun* 1 a place, esp. a cave, where a wild animal lives. 2 a place where illegal or immoral activities go on: *a den of iniquity.* 3 a study, playroom, etc. in a house.

dendrite *noun* a cytoplasmic projection radiating outward from a neuron. *See also* **neuron.**

dendrochronology (děn,drō,krə-nǎl'ə-jē) *noun* the study or science of analyzing annual growth rings in trees.

dendrology (děn-drǎl'ə-jē) *noun* the scientific study of trees. ▸ **dendrologist** *noun*

denial *noun* 1 an act of declaring something to be untrue. 2 *Psychol.* a subconscious defense mechanism where a person does not or cannot acknowledge something distressing. 3 a refusal, esp. to grant, allow, accept, or acknowledge something or someone.

denier (děn'yər) *noun* a unit for grading the fineness of silk, rayon, or nylon thread.

denigrate (děn'ĭ-grāt,) *verb trans.* (**denigrated, denigrating**) to attack, belittle, scorn, or criticize. ▸ **denigration** *noun* ▸ **denigrator** *noun*

denim *noun* 1 a hard-wearing, usu. blue, cotton cloth. 2 (**denims**) denim jeans.

denizen (děn'ĭ-zən) *noun* an inhabitant.

denominate *verb trans.* (**denominated, denominating**) to give a specific name or title to (something).

denomination *noun* 1 a religious group. 2 a unit of value of a postage stamp, coin, or banknote. 3 a name. ▸ **denominational** *adj.*

denominator *noun* *Math.* the number below the line in a common fraction that is the divisor, e.g., in $\frac{3}{5}$, "5" is the denominator. *See also* **numerator.**

denote *verb trans.* (**denoted, denoting**) 1 to be a sign of. 2 to designate. ▸ **denotation** *noun*

denouement *or* **dénouement** (dā,nōō,mäN') *noun* a resolution, e.g., of a plot in a story, play, movie, etc.

> Literally 'untying' or 'unraveling', from French

denounce *verb trans.* (**denounced, denouncing**) 1 to accuse (someone) formally or publicly, esp. of some wrongdoing. 2 to condemn (an action, proposal, idea, etc.) strongly and openly.

dense *adj.* 1 closely packed or crowded together. 2 thick. 3 *colloq.* slow to understand; stupid. ▸ **densely** *adv.* ▸ **denseness** *noun*

density *noun* (*pl.* **densities**) 1 the state of being dense, or a specified degree of denseness. 2 the ratio of the mass of a substance to its volume. 3 the number of things or people within a specific area, etc. 4 *Comput.* the number of bits that can be stored on one track of a disk, or within a specific area of magnetic tape, etc.

dent *noun* a hollow made by pressure or a blow. —*verb trans., intrans.* (**dented, denting**) 1 to make a dent or dents in. 2 to become dented.

dental *adj.* concerned with or for the teeth.

dental floss a soft thread for cleaning between the teeth.

dental hygienist a person who practices preventive dental procedures.

dentin or **dentine** (dĕnt'n) noun a material, covered in enamel, that forms the bulk of a tooth.

dentist noun a person who practices dentistry.

dentistry noun the branch of medical science concerned with the mouth and teeth.

dentition (dĕn-tǐsh'ən) noun 1 the number, arrangement, and type of teeth in a human or animal. 2 the cutting of teeth.

denture (dĕn'chər) noun 1 a removable plate with a false tooth or teeth. 2 (**dentures**) a full set of removable teeth for both jaws.

denude verb trans. (**denuded, denuding**) to make completely bare; to strip.

denunciation noun a public condemnation or accusation.

Denver boot a wheel clamp used to prevent a vehicle from being driven, esp. because of a parking violation.

deny verb trans. (**denied, denying, denies**) 1 to declare (something) to be untrue. 2 to refuse, esp. to grant, allow, accept, or acknowledge something or someone. —**deny** (**oneself**) to do without.

deodar (dē'ə-där,) or **deodara** (-där,ə) noun a tall evergreen tree.

deodorant (dē-ōd'ə-rənt) noun a substance used to conceal unpleasant smells.

deodorize verb trans. (**deodorized, deodorizing**) to conceal the unpleasant smell of. ▸ **deodorization** noun

depart verb intrans., trans. (**departed, departing**) 1 to leave (a place). 2 to die. 3 to deviate. ▸ **departure** noun

departed adj. dead. —noun (**the departed**) a dead person or people.

department noun 1 a section, esp. of an organization. 2 a person's special skill or particular responsibility. ▸ **departmental** adj.

department store a large store with many different departments selling a wide variety of goods.

depend verb. intrans. (**depended, depending**) (**depend on** or **upon**) 1 to rely on (something or someone). 2 to be contingent upon (something). 3 to have a dependence on (a drug, etc.).

dependable adj. trustworthy or reliable. ▸ **dependability** noun ▸ **dependably** adv.

dependant noun a person who is kept or supported financially by another.

dependence noun 1 the state of being dependent on someone or something. 2 trust or reliance.

dependency noun (pl. **dependencies**) 1 a territory governed or controlled by another. 2 dependence.

dependent adj. 1 relying on someone or something. 2 contingent upon someone or something.

depict verb trans. (**depicted, depicting**) 1 to paint or draw. 2 to describe. ▸ **depiction** noun

depilatory (dĭ-pĭl'ə-tôr,ē) noun (pl. **depilatories**) a substance used to remove hair. —adj. capable of hair removal.

deplane verb intrans. (**deplaned, deplaning**) to exit an aircraft.

deplete verb trans. (**depleted, depleting**) to reduce or use up (supplies, money, energy, resources, etc.). ▸ **depletion** noun

deplore verb trans. (**deplored, deploring**) to feel or express great disapproval of or regret for. ▸ **deplorable** adj. ▸ **deplorably** adv.

deploy verb trans., intrans. (**deployed, deploying**) 1 to spread out and position (troops, ships, supplies, etc.) ready for battle. 2 to organize (resources, arguments, etc.) and bring into use. ▸ **deployment** noun

depopulate verb trans. (**depopulated, depopulating**) to reduce the number of people living in (an area, country, etc.). ▸ **depopulation** noun

deport[1] verb trans. (**deported, deporting**) to expel (a person) from a country. ▸ **deportation** noun ▸ **deportee** noun

deport[2] verb trans. (**deported, deporting**) (**deport** (**oneself**)) formal to behave (oneself) in a particular way. ▸ **deportment** noun

depose verb trans. (**deposed, deposing**) to remove from high office.

deposit verb trans. (**deposited, depositing**) 1 to put or leave. 2 to put (money, etc.), e.g., in a bank, for safekeeping or to earn interest. 3 to give (a sum of money) as the first part of the payment for something. 4 to pay (a sum of money) as a guarantee against loss or damage. —noun 1 a sum of money, etc., deposited, e.g., in a bank, as a down payment, or paid as a guarantee against loss or damage. 2 an accumulation of material, e.g., sediments, etc. ▸ **depositor** noun

depositary noun (pl. **depositaries**) formal a person, etc., to whom something is given for safekeeping.

deposition noun 1 the act of deposing or the process of being deposed. 2 a sworn statement or testimony.

depository noun (pl. **depositories**) 1 a place where things are stored. 2 a depositary.

depot (dē'pō, dĕp'ō) noun 1 a bus or railroad station. 2 a military headquarters. 3 a storehouse or warehouse.

deprave (dĭ-prāv') verb trans. (**depraved, depraving**) to corrupt. ▸ **depravity** noun

deprecate (dĕp'rĭ-kāt,) verb trans. (**deprecated, deprecating**) 1 to express disapproval of; to deplore. 2 to belittle. ▸ **deprecation** noun ▸ **deprecatory** adj.

Usage The word *deprecate*, whose prime meaning is to deplore (sense 1 here), has also taken on a second sense, to belittle, a sense that it shares with the verb *depreciate*: Don't *deprecate* (or *depreciate*) the child's efforts.

---

depreciate (dĭ-prē'shē-āt,) *verb trans., intrans.* (**depreciated, depreciating**) **1** to fall or cause to fall in value. **2** to belittle. ▸ **depreciatory** *adj.*

Usage See note at *deprecate*.

---

depreciation *noun* **1** a fall in value of a currency in relation to that of other currencies. **2** a reduction in the value of fixed assets through use or age. **3** the act of depreciating.

depredation *noun* (*often* **depredations**) damage, destruction, or violent robbery.

depress *verb trans.* (**depressed, depressing**) **1** to make sad and gloomy. **2** to make lower. **3** to press down.

depressant *adj.* of a drug, etc. reducing mental or physical activity. —*noun* something, e.g., a barbiturate or alcohol, that reduces physical or mental activity. *See also* **antidepressant**.

depressed *adj.* **1** sad and gloomy. **2** suffering from a mental disorder that causes depression. **3** of an area, etc. characterized by low standards of living. **4** pressed down, lowered, or slightly hollowed.

depressing *adj.* causing low spirits. ▸ **depressingly** *adv.*

depressive *noun* a person who is frequently affected by psychological depression.

deprive (dĭ-prīv') *verb trans.* (**deprived, depriving**) **1** to take away, divest, or withhold from. **2** to prevent from enjoying, possessing, etc. ▸ **deprivation** *noun* ▸ **deprived** *adj.*

depth *noun* **1** distance measured from top to bottom, front to back, or from a surface inward. **2** of feelings, understanding, colors, etc. intensity, strength, extent, or profundity. **3** (*also* **depths**) a very deep, distant, intense place, time, etc.: *ocean depths / the depth of winter / the depths of despair.* —**in depth** deeply; thoroughly: *thought about it in depth.*

depth charge an explosive device timed to detonate underwater, used to attack submarines.

deputation *noun* a group of people representing others.

depute (dĭ-pyōōt') *verb trans.* (**deputed, deputing**) *formal* **1** to appoint (someone) formally to do something. **2** (**depute** (**something**) **to** (**someone**)) to give (work, etc.) to someone else to do.

deputize *verb intrans., trans.* (**deputized, deputizing**) **1** to act as a deputy for another. **2** to appoint as a deputy.

deputy *noun* (*pl.* **deputies**) a person appointed to act on behalf of or as an assistant to someone else.

derail *verb intrans., trans.* (**derailed, derailing**) **1** to leave, or cause (a train, etc.) to leave the rails. **2** to cause (something) to go off course. ▸ **derailment** *noun*

derange *verb trans.* (**deranged, deranging**) **1** to make insane. **2** to disrupt or throw into disorder or confusion.

derby (dar'bē) *noun* (*pl.* **derbies**) **1** a horse race. **2** a felt hat with a small, upturned brim and a rounded crown.

deregulate *verb trans.* (**deregulated, deregulating**) to remove controls from (a business, etc.). ▸ **deregulation** *noun*

derelict (dĕr'ə-lĭkt,) *adj.* **1** abandoned and in ruins. **2** neglectful of responsibilities, duties, etc. —*noun* a homeless person. ▸ **dereliction** *noun*

deride *verb trans.* (**derided, deriding**) to ridicule or make fun of. ▸ **derision** *noun* ▸ **derisive** *adj.* ▸ **derisively** *adv.*

de rigueur (də-rĭ-gər') obligatory.

derisory *adj.* **1** ridiculous, laughable, esp. in being too small: *a derisory contribution.* **2** derisive. ▸ **derisorily** *adv.*

derivation *noun* **1** the act of deriving or the state or process of being derived. **2** a source or origin, esp. of a word.

derivative *adj.* lacking originality. —*noun* **1** something that is derived from something else. **2** a word formed by adding an affix.

derive *verb intrans., trans.* (**derived, deriving**) **1** to arise from (something). **2** to trace (something) back to a source or origin.

dermatitis *noun* inflammation of the skin.

dermato- *or* **dermat-** *or* **-derm** *combining form* forming words denoting of the skin.

dermatology *noun* the branch of medicine concerned with the skin and its diseases. ▸ **dermatologist** *noun*

derogate *verb intrans.* (**derogated, derogating**) *formal* **1** to cause (something) to appear inferior. **2** to belittle. ▸ **derogation** *noun*

derogatory *adj.* disapproving, scornful, or lacking respect. ▸ **derogatorily** *adv.*

derrick *noun* **1** a crane with a movable arm. **2** a framework over an oil well for raising and lowering the drill.

Named after *Derrick*, a famous 17th-century hangman in Tyburn, England

---

derring-do *noun* daring deeds.

Based on a misprint of a medieval English phrase *dorring dò*, meaning 'daring to do'

---

derringer (dĕr'ĭn-jər) *noun* a small pistol.

dervish *noun* **1** a member of a Muslim group, some of whom perform spinning dances as part of their religious ritual. **2** a person with plenty of energy.

desalinate (dē-săl'ĭ-nāt,) *verb trans.* (**desalinated, desalinating**) to remove salt from (esp. seawater).

descant noun (dĕs'kănt,) a melody played or harmony sung above the main tune. —*verb trans.* (dĕs'kănt,, dĕs-kănt') **1** to sing. **2** to talk at length.

descend *verb trans., intrans.* (**descended, descending**) **1** to go or move down from a higher to a lower place or position. **2** to lower oneself. **3** to lead or slope downward. **4** (**descend on** *or* **upon**) to invade or attack (a target). —**be descended from** to have (someone) as an ancestor.

descendant noun someone or something that is descended from a specified ancestor.

descent noun **1** an act or the process of coming or going down. **2** a slope downward. **3** ancestry.

describe *verb trans.* (**described, describing**) **1** to portray orally or in writing. **2** to draw, represent, or outline.

description noun **1** an act of describing. **2** an oral, written, or drawn account. **3** *colloq.* a sort, type, or kind.

descriptive adj. **1** serving to describe. **2** vividly told. ▸ **descriptively** adv.

descry *verb trans.* (**descried, descrying, descries**) *formal* **1** to see or glimpse. **2** to discover by looking carefully.

desecrate *verb trans.* (**desecrated, desecrating**) to treat (something sacred) sacrilegiously or behave disrespectfully in (a holy place). ▸ **desecration** noun

desegregate *verb trans.* (**desegregated, desegregating**) to end segregation, esp. racial segregation, in. ▸ **desegregation** noun

desensitize *verb trans.* (**desensitized, desensitizing**) to make insensitive or less sensitive. ▸ **desensitization** noun

desert¹ (dĭ-zɜrt') *verb trans., ˋ intrans.* (**deserted, deserting**) **1** to leave (someone or something) behind. **2** to leave, esp. the army, without permission. ▸ **desertion** noun

desert² (dĕz'ərt) noun a barren region, esp. a dry sandy area.

deserted adj. abandoned.

deserter noun someone who deserts from the armed forces.

deserts (dĭ-zɜrts') pl. noun something deserved, usu. something bad.

deserve *verb trans.* (**deserved, deserving**) to be entitled to or worthy of (something). ▸ **deservedly** adv. ▸ **deserving** adj.

deshabille noun same as **dishabille**.

desiccate *verb trans.* (**desiccated, desiccating**) to dry or remove the moisture from (something, esp. food), in order to preserve (it). ▸ **desiccation** noun

desideratum noun (pl. **desiderata**) formal something wanted or required.

design *verb trans.* (**designed, designing**) **1** to prepare a plan, etc. of (something) before it is built or made. **2** to plan, intend, or develop for a particular purpose. —noun **1** a plan, etc. showing how something is to be made. **2** the art or job of making such drawings, plans, etc. **3** the way in which something has been made. **4** a picture, pattern, arrangement of shapes, etc., used e.g., as decoration. **5** a plan, purpose, or intention. ▸ **designer** adj., noun

designate (dĕz'ĭg-nāt,) *verb trans.* (**designated, designating**) **1** to name, choose, or specify for a particular purpose or duty. **2** to mark or indicate. **3** to be a name or label for. ▸ **designation** noun

designing adj. cunning or crafty.

desire noun **1** a longing or wish. **2** strong sexual interest and attraction. **3** something wished for. —*verb trans.* (**desired, desiring**) **1** to want. **2** to long for or feel sexual desire for. **3** formal to ask or command. ▸ **desirability** noun ▸ **desirable** adj. ▸ **desirably** adv. ▸ **desirous** adj.

desist (dĭ-zĭst', -sĭst') *verb intrans.* (**desisted, desisting**) to stop.

desk noun **1** a table for writing, reading, etc. **2** a counter in a hotel, public building, etc. where service is provided. **3** a department, e.g., in a newspaper, media, government, etc. office.

desktop publishing (ABBREV. **DTP**) the production of documents, etc. using specialized software that gives a print quality close to that of typeset texts.

desolate adj. (dĕs'ə-lət, dĕz'-) **1** of a place deserted, barren, and lonely. **2** of a person deeply sad; in despair. **3** lacking pleasure or comfort: *a desolate life.* —*verb trans.* (dĕs'ə-lāt,, dĕz'-) (**desolated, desolating**) to make desolate. ▸ **desolation** noun

despair *verb intrans.* (**despaired, despairing**) to lose or lack hope. —noun the state of having lost hope. ▸ **despairing** adj. ▸ **despairingly** adv.

despatch verb, noun same as **dispatch**.

desperado (dĕs,pə-rād'ō, -räd'ō) noun (pl. **desperadoes, desperados**) a bandit or outlaw.

desperate (dĕs'pə-rət, dĕs'prət) adj. **1** characterized by extreme anxiousness, fear, despair, etc.. **2** recklessly frantic, eager, etc. **3** very great, serious, difficult, dangerous, hopeless, urgent, etc. ▸ **desperately** adv. ▸ **desperation** noun

despicable (dĭ-spĭk'ə-bəl, dĕs'pĭk-) adj. deserving contempt. ▸ **despicably** adv.

despise *verb trans.* (**despised, despising**) to hold in utter contempt.

despite (dĭ-spīt′) *prep.* in spite of: *drove on despite the blizzard.*

despoil *verb trans.* (**despoiled, despoiling**) *literary* to plunder. ▸ **despoiler** *noun* ▸ **despoliation** *noun*

despondent *adj.* deeply sad and dejected. ▸ **despondency** *noun* ▸ **despondently** *adv.*

despot (dĕs′pət, -pŏt,) *noun* an oppressively cruel ruler. ▸ **despotic** *adj.* ▸ **despotically** *adv.* ▸ **despotism** *noun*

dessert (dĭ-zərt′) *noun* a course, usu. of sweet food, served at the end of a meal.

destabilize *verb trans.* (**destabilized, destabilizing**) to make unstable. ▸ **destabilization** *noun*

destination *noun* a place where someone or something is going or being sent.

destine (dĕs′tĭn) *verb trans.* (**destined, destining**) 1 to determine or decide beforehand. 2 to appoint a specified use. 3 to direct to a specified place.

destiny *noun* (*pl.* **destinies**) 1 the future as decided by, or as if by, fate or God. 2 something that is in store in the future.

destitute *adj.* 1 lacking money, food, shelter, etc.; extremely poor. 2 (**destitute of**) completely lacking in (something needed or desirable). ▸ **destitution** *noun*

destroy *verb trans.* (**destroyed, destroying**) 1 to break into pieces; to ruin. 2 to kill or put an end to.

destroyer *noun* 1 someone or something that destroys or causes destruction. 2 a small, fast warship.

destruct *verb trans., intrans.* (**destructed, destructing**) to destroy or be destroyed, esp. for safety reasons.

destruction *noun* 1 the act or process of destroying or being destroyed. 2 a means of destroying or of being destroyed. ▸ **destructible** *adj.* ▸ **destructibility** *noun*

destructive *adj.* 1 causing serious damage or destruction. 2 intended to discredit; hurtful. ▸ **destructively** *adv.*

desultory (dĕs′əl-tôr,ē, dĕz′-) *adj.* jumping haphazardly or randomly from one thing to another. ▸ **desultorily** *adv.*

detach *verb trans.* (**detached, detaching**) 1 to unfasten or separate. 2 *Mil.* to select and send (a group of soldiers, etc.) on a mission. ▸ **detachable** *adj.*

detached *adj.* 1 of a building not joined to another. 2 of a person a feeling no personal or emotional involvement. **b** showing no prejudice or bias. ▸ **detachedly** *adv.*

detachment *noun* 1 the state of being emotionally detached or free from prejudice. 2 a group (e.g., of soldiers) sent on a mission. 3 an act of detaching or the state or process of being detached.

detail (dĭ-tāl′, dē′tāl,) *noun* 1 a single feature, part, etc. 2 a group, e.g. of soldiers or other personnel, on a special duty. —*verb trans.* (**detailed, detailing**) 1 to describe or list fully. 2 to appoint (someone) to do a particular task. —**in detail** thoroughly.

detailed *adj.* 1 intricate. 2 thorough.

detain *verb trans.* (**detained, detaining**) 1 to stop, hold back, keep waiting, or delay. 2 to keep in prison or custody. ▸ **detention** *noun*

detect *verb trans.* (**detected, detecting**) to discover (something that is not obvious or that has been obscured). ▸ **detectable** *adj.* ▸ **detection** *noun* ▸ **detector** *noun*

detective *noun* a person whose job is investigating crimes.

deter (dĭ-tər′) *verb trans.* (**deterred, deterring**) 1 to prevent by acting in advance. 2 to discourage or prevent.

detergent *noun* a cleaning agent.

deteriorate *verb intrans.* (**deteriorated, deteriorating**) to grow worse. ▸ **deterioration** *noun*

determinate (dĭ-tər′mĭ-nət) *adj.* definite; fixed.

determination *noun* 1 firmness of will, purpose, or character. 2 an act of determining or the process of being determined.

determine *verb trans., intrans.* (**determined, determining**) 1 to fix, settle, or decide. 2 to reach or cause (someone) to reach a conclusion, etc.

determined *adj.* 1 firmly intent on doing something. 2 displaying or characterized by an unwavering manner.

determiner *noun* a word that comes before a noun or noun phrase, and limits its meaning in some way, e.g., *a*, *the*, *this*, *every*, *some*.

deterrent *noun* something that deters.

detest (dĭ-tĕst′) *verb trans.* (**detested, detesting**) to loathe. ▸ **detestable** *adj.* ▸ **detestably** *adv.* ▸ **detestation** *noun*

dethrone *verb trans.* (**dethroned, dethroning**) to remove from a reigning or powerful position. ▸ **dethronement** *noun*

detonate (dĕt′n-āt,) *verb trans., intrans.* (**detonated, detonating**) to explode or cause to explode. ▸ **detonation** *noun*

detonator *noun* a substance or device used to make a bomb, etc. explode.

detour (dē′tŏŏr,, dĭ-tŏŏr′) *noun* a route other than the most direct one. —*verb intrans.* (**detoured, detouring**) to make a detour.

detox (dē-tăks′, dē′tăks,) *verb trans.* (**detoxed, detoxing, detoxes**) *colloq.* to detoxify. —*noun* a session or the process of detoxifying, or a place someone goes to detoxify: *been in detox for three weeks.*

detoxify *verb trans.* (**detoxified, detoxifying, detoxifies**) to remove toxic substances or their effects from.

detract *verb intrans.* (**detracted, detracting**) to reduce the attractiveness, value,

importance, etc. of. ▸ **detraction** *noun*
▸ **detractor** *noun*

detriment (dĕ'trə-mənt) *noun* harm or loss.
▸ **detrimental** *adj.* ▸ **detrimentally** *adv.*

detritus (dĭ-trīt'əs) *noun* (*pl.* **detritus**) 1 *Geol.* loose fragments of eroded rock. 2 bits and pieces of trash.

deuce¹ (dōōs, dyōōs) *noun* a tied score in a tennis game or set. *See also* **two** (sense 5).

deuce² *noun* *colloq.* (**the deuce**) used in expressions of annoyance, confusion, etc.

deus ex machina (dā,əs-ĕks,mäk'ĭ-nə, -mäk'-) 1 a god in classical drama who resolves problems, decides the final outcome, etc. 2 someone or something introduced to a plot to resolve matters.

> Literally a 'god from a machine' referring to the pulley device used in ancient Greek theaters to lower the character of a god onto the stage

deuterium (dōō-tîr'ē-əm, dyōō-) *noun* (SYMBOL D) a heavy isotope of hydrogen.

Deutschmark (doich'märk,) *noun* (ABBREV. **DM**) the standard unit of currency in Germany, equal to 100 pfennigs.

devalue *verb trans., intrans.* (**devalued, devaluing**) to reduce the value of (a currency, a person's importance, etc.). *Also called* **devaluate.** ▸ **devaluation** *noun*

devastate *verb trans.* (**devastated, devastating**) 1 to cause great destruction in or to. 2 to overwhelm with grief, shock, etc. ▸ **devastated** *adj.* ▸ **devastating** *adj.* ▸ **devastation** *noun*

develop *verb trans., intrans.* (**developed, developing**) 1 to make or become more mature, advanced, complete, etc. 2 to begin to have. 3 to process a photographic film, etc. 4 to expand or bring into use or into fuller use: *developed her argument.*

developer *noun* 1 a chemical agent used in processing photographic film, etc. 2 someone who builds on land or improves and increases the value of buildings.

development *noun* 1 the act of developing or the process of being developed. 2 a new stage, event, or situation. 3 a result or consequence. 4 land that has been or is being developed, or the buildings built or being built on it. ▸ **developmental** *adj.*

deviant *adj.* deviating from what is accepted or normal. —*noun* a person who deviates from an accepted or normal way of behaving. ▸ **deviance** *noun*

deviate *verb intrans.* (dē'vē-āt,) (**deviated, deviating**) to turn aside or move away from an accepted or normal way of behaving, thinking, etc. —*noun* (dē'vē-ət, -āt,) a deviant. —*adj.* departing from the norm. ▸ **deviation** *noun*

device *noun* 1 an object, e.g., a tool or an instrument, that is made for a special purpose. 2 a plan or scheme, sometimes one involving trickery or deceit. 3 a sign, pattern, heraldic symbol, etc.

devil *noun* 1 (**the Devil**) the most powerful evil spirit; Satan. 2 any evil or wicked spirit. 3 *colloq.* a mischievous or bad person. 4 *colloq.* a person of a stated type: *a lucky devil.* 5 someone or something difficult to deal with: *a devil of a problem.* 6 a person with a specified talent, interest, etc. 7 (**the devil**) used to express surprise, indignation, etc.: *What the devil is she doing?* —*verb* (**deviled** or **devilled, deviling** or **devilling**) 1 to prepare or cook with a spicy seasoning. 2 *colloq.* to annoy, bother, or harass. ▸ **devilish** *adj.* ▸ **devilishly** *adv.* ▸ **devilry** *noun*

devilment (dĕv'əl-mənt) *noun* mischievous fun.

devil's advocate a person who argues for or against something simply to encourage discussion or argument.

devil's food cake a rich chocolate layer cake.

devious *adj.* 1 deceitful; cunning; crafty. 2 indirect; circuitous. ▸ **deviously** *adv.* ▸ **deviousness** *noun*

devise (dĭ-vīz,) *verb trans.* (**devised, devising**) 1 to invent, make up, etc. 2 *Law* to leave (property, such as land or buildings) to another in a will. *See also* **bequeath.** ▸ **deviser** *noun*

devoid *adj.* (*usu.* **devoid of**) free from, lacking, or empty of (something).

devolve *verb intrans., trans.* (**devolved, devolving**) 1 to transfer (duties, power, etc.) to another. 2 *Law* to pass (a title, estate, etc.) by succession to. ▸ **devolution** *noun* ▸ **devolutionist** *noun*

devote *verb trans.* (**devoted, devoting**) 1 to use or give up (oneself, time, money, etc.) to something. 2 to dedicate (something) for a specified use, etc.

devoted *adj.* 1 loving and loyal. 2 dedicated: *a devoted teacher.* ▸ **devotedly** *adv.*

devotee (dĕv,ə-tē', -tā') *noun* 1 an enthusiastic follower or supporter. 2 a strong, active believer in a religion.

devotion *noun* 1 great love or loyalty; enthusiasm for or willingness to do what is required. 2 devoting or being devoted. 3 religious enthusiasm and piety. 4 (**devotions**) *Relig.* worship and prayers. ▸ **devotional** *adj.*

devour *verb trans.* (**devoured, devouring**) 1 to eat up greedily. 2 to destroy thoroughly. 3 to read eagerly. 4 to take over totally: *was devoured by guilt.*

devout *adj.* 1 sincerely religious. 2 earnest. ▸ **devoutly** *adv.* ▸ **devoutness** *noun*

dew (doo, dyoo) *noun* tiny water droplets on the ground and objects close to the ground, condensed from the air on cool nights. ▸ **dewy** *adj.*

dewclaw *noun* a rudimentary claw or toe on the foot of a dog.

dewdrop *noun* a drop of dew.

dewlap *noun* a flap of loose skin hanging down from the throats of certain cattle, dogs, and other animals.

dewy-eyed *adj.* naive.

dexterity (děk-stěr'ət-ē) *noun* manual or mental skill or adroitness. ▸ **dexterous** *adj.* ▸ **dexterously** *adv.* ▸ **dextrous** *adj.*

dextrin *noun Biochem.* a polysaccharide produced during the partial breakdown of starch or glycogen.

dextrose (děk'strōs,, -strōz,) *noun* a form of glucose occurring naturally in plant and animal tissue, and that can be synthetically derived from starch.

dhal *noun* same as **dal**.

dhoti (dōt'ē) *noun* (*pl.* **dhotis**) a garment consisting of a long strip of cloth wrapped around the waist and between the legs.

dhow (dow) *noun* a sailing ship used around the Indian Ocean.

di- *prefix* forming words denoting two, twice, or double: *dicotyledon* / *dioxide*.

dia- or **di-** *prefix* forming words denoting 1 through: *diachronic*. 2 across: *diatinic*.

diabetes (dī,ə-bēt'ēz, -əs) *noun* a metabolic disorder characterized by thirst and excessive production of urine.

diabetic (dī,ə-bět'ĭk) *noun* a person with diabetes. —*adj.* 1 relating to or affected with diabetes. 2 designed or intended esp. for people who have diabetes.

diabolical (dī,ə-bäl'ĭ-kəl) or **diabolic** *adj.* 1 devilish. 2 very shocking, annoying, bad, cruel, wicked, etc. ▸ **diabolically** *adv.*

diacritic (dī'ə-krĭt'ĭk) *noun* a mark over, under, or through a letter to show that it is pronounced in a particular way.

diadem *noun* a crown or jeweled headband.

diaeresis (dī,ə-rē'sĭs) *noun* same as **dieresis**.

diagnose *verb trans.* (**diagnosed, diagnosing**) to detect and identify (a disease, fault, etc.).

diagnosis *noun* (*pl.* **diagnoses**) the detection and identification of a disease, fault, etc. ▸ **diagnostic** *adj.* ▸ **diagnostician** *noun*

diagonal (dī-ăg'ən-l) *adj.* 1 denoting a straight line joining any two nonadjacent corners in a polygon. 2 sloping or slanting. —*noun* a diagonal line. ▸ **diagonally** *adv.*

diagram *noun* a plan, graph, etc. showing how something functions, etc. ▸ **diagrammatic** *adj.* ▸ **diagrammatically** *adv.*

dial *noun* 1 a disk on a clock, radio, meter, etc., with numbers, measurements, etc. and an indicator for gauging speed, time, etc. 2 the numbered dialing plate on some telephones. —*verb trans., intrans.* (**dialed** or **dialled**, **dialing** or **dialling**) to use a telephone keypad or its rotary disk to call (a number).

dialect *noun* a form of a language spoken in a particular region or by a certain social group. ▸ **dialectal** *adj.*

dialectic *noun* 1 the art or practice of logical discussion. 2 (**dialectics**) (*sing.*) inquiry into opposing theories. ▸ **dialectical** *adj.*

dialogue *noun* 1 a discussion or conversation, esp. a formal one. 2 words spoken by a literary character.

dial tone the steady, low tone heard in a telephone receiver and indicating that a number may be dialed.

dialysis (dī-ăl'ə-sĭs) *noun* (*pl.* **dialyses**) separation of particles of different sizes in a solution by passing the solution through a semipermeable membrane.

diameter (dī-ăm'ət-ər) *noun* 1 a straight line drawn through a circle, passing through its center. 2 the length of such a line.

diametrical or **diametric** *adj.* 1 of or along a diameter. 2 of opinions, etc. directly opposed; very far apart. ▸ **diametrically** *adv.*

diamond *noun* 1 a a crystalline allotrope of carbon, the hardest known mineral. b a piece of this used as a gemstone. c a piece of this used in cutting tools, etc. 2 a four-sided lozenge-shaped geometric figure. 3 *Cards* a a playing card with a red lozenge-shaped symbol on it. b (**diamonds**) a suit of cards with such symbols on them. 4 *Baseball* the infield or the entire playing field.

diamondback *noun* a large, poisonous rattlesnake with diamond-shaped markings on its back.

diaper (dī'pər, -ə-pər) *noun* 1 cloth or paper fitted around a baby's buttocks for absorbing and containing excrement. 2 a diamond patterned linen or cotton cloth.

> Originally a kind of decorated white silk. The current US meaning was used in British English in the 16th century

diaphanous (dī-ăf'ə-nəs) *adj.* thin or fine enough as to be transparent.

diaphragm (dī'ə-frăm,) *noun* 1 a muscular sheet separating the thorax from the abdomen. 2 any thin partition, such as the vibrating disk that converts sound waves to electric signals in a microphone, etc. 3 a contraceptive device that fits over the neck of the uterus.

diarrhea or **diarrhoea** (dī,ə-rē'ə) *noun* abnormally frequent discharge of usu. liquid feces.

diary (dī'ə-rē, dī'rē) *noun* (*pl.* **diaries**) **1** a written record of events in a person's life. **2** a book containing such a record. ▸ **diarist** *noun*

diastole (dī-ăs'tə-lē) *noun* the period between two rhythmic heart contractions when the muscles relax, allowing the chambers to fill with blood. *See also* **systole**. ▸ **diastolic** *adj.*

diatom (dī'ə-täm,) *noun* a one-celled microscopic alga found in salt and fresh water.

diatonic *adj. Mus.* involving only the notes proper to a particular key, with no chromatic alteration. *See also* **chromatic**.

diatribe *noun* a bitter critical attack.

diazepam (dī-ăz'ə-păm,) *noun* a tranquilizing drug that relieves anxiety and acts as a muscle relaxant.

dibble *noun* a short, pointed implement used to make holes in the ground for seeds, etc.

dibs *pl. noun slang* a claim or a right.

dice *noun* **1** a pair or set of small cubes with different numbers of spots, from 1 to 6, on each of the sides or faces, used in certain games of chance. **2** a game of chance played with one or more of these cubes. *See also* **die²** (sense 2). —*verb trans., intrans.* (**diced, dicing**) **1** to cut (vegetables, etc.) into small cubes. **2** to play or gamble with dice.

dicey *adj.* (**dicier, diciest**) *colloq.* risky.

dichotomy (dī-kät'ə-mē) *noun* (*pl.* **dichotomies**) a division or separation into two parts.

dick *noun slang* a detective.

dickens *noun colloq.* (**the dickens**) the devil: *What the dickens are you doing?*

dicker *verb intrans.* (**dickered, dickering**) to argue about the price or cost of something. —*noun* a haggling session.

dickey or **dickie** *noun* (*pl.* **dickeys, dickies**) **1** a man's false shirt front, worn esp. with evening dress. **2** a woman's false blouse front, worn esp. under a suit jacket or a low-necked outer garment.

dicta *see* **dictum**.

dictate *verb trans., intrans.* (dīk'tāt,, dīk-tāt') (**dictated, dictating**) **1** to say or read out (something) for someone else to take down. **2** to lay down (rules, terms, etc.) with authority. **3** to command. —*noun* (dīk'tāt,) **1** an order or instruction. **2** a guiding principle. ▸ **dictation** *noun*

dictator *noun* **1** a ruler with complete and unrestricted power. **2** an authoritarian person. ▸ **dictatorial** *adj.* ▸ **dictatorially** *adv.* ▸ **dictatorship** *noun*

diction *noun* **1** the way someone speaks, including the choice of words. **2** enunciation, esp. the quality or clarity of pronunciation.

dictionary *noun* (*pl.* **dictionaries**) **1** a book listing words and their meanings, etc. in alphabetical order. **2** a book listing words of one language with their translations in a second language. **3** a book listing the vocabulary with its meanings of a particular subject.

dictum *noun* (*pl.* **dictums, dicta**) **1** a formal or authoritative statement of opinion. **2** a saying that articulates a general truth.

did *see* **do¹**.

didactic *adj.* **1** instructive. **2** instructive in an overly patronizing or moralistic way.

diddle¹ *verb trans.* (**diddled, diddling**) *slang* to cheat or swindle. ▸ **diddler** *noun*

diddle² *verb trans., intrans.* (**diddled, diddling**) *slang* to waste time.

didn't *contr.* did not.

die¹ *verb intrans.* (**died, dying, dies**) **1** to stop living. ▤ DECEASE, DEMISE, DEPART, EXPIRE, PASS (AWAY or ON), SUCCUMB ▤ LIVE. **2** to come to an end or stop working. **3** (**die for**) to need or want (something) badly: *I'm dying for a drink.* **4** (**die of** or **from**) to be overcome by the effects of (something): *almost died from shock / die of boredom.* —**to die for** deeply coveted or wanted: *leather boots to die for.*

die² *noun* **1** (*pl.* **dies**) a stamp for embossing designs, etc. **2** (*pl.* **dice**) *Games* a small numbered cube used in certain games of chance. *See also* **dice** (sense 1).

diehard or **die-hard** *noun* a person who stubbornly refuses to accept new ideas or changes. —*adj.* conservative, esp. in holding onto outmoded ideas, etc.

dielectric *noun* a nonconducting material. —*adj.* denoting such a material.

dieresis or **diaresis** (dī,ə-rē'sĭs) *noun* a mark (¨) placed over a vowel to show that it is to be pronounced separately from the vowel before it, as in *naïve.*

diesel *noun* **1** an internal combustion engine in which air is compressed until it reaches a sufficiently high temperature to ignite the fuel. **2** a fuel suitable for use in a diesel engine. **3** a train, etc., driven by a diesel engine.

diet¹ (dī'ət) *noun* **1** the food and drink habitually consumed by a person or animal. **2** a planned or prescribed selection of food and drink, esp. one designed for weight loss, maintenance of good health, or the control of a medical disorder. —*adj.* denoting a food or drink that contains fewer calories than the standard version. —*verb intrans.* (**dieted, dieting**) to restrict the quantity or type of food that one eats, esp. in order to lose weight. ▸ **dietary** *adj.* ▸ **dieter** *noun*

diet² *noun* **1** the legislative assembly of certain countries, e.g., Japan. **2** *Hist.* a conference held to discuss political or church affairs.

dietetics noun (sing.) the scientific study of dietary regulation. ▸ **dietetic** adj.

dietitian or **dietician** noun a scientist who specializes in dietetics.

differ verb intrans. (**differed, differing**) 1 to be different or unlike (another) in some way. 2 (**differ from**) to be different from or unlike (something else). 3 (**differ with**) to disagree with (another).

difference noun 1 a dissimilarity. 2 the state of being unalike. 3 a change from an earlier state. 4 the amount by which something is more or less than something else. 5 a quarrel or disagreement.

different adj. 1 dissimilar. 2 separate; distinct; various. 3 colloq. unusual. ▸ **differently** adv.

> *Usage* Different is commonly followed by *from* in US and British usage: This situation is *different from* that one. *Different* is also commonly and unexceptionally followed by *than* in US usage, esp. when a full clause ensues, e.g., This situation is *different than* the situation we had last year. *Different* followed by *to*, as in She is so *different to* Rebecca is British usage.

differential (dif'ə-rĕn'chəl) adj. of, showing, or based on a difference. —noun 1 a difference between comparable things. 2 a gear arrangement in a vehicle allowing the outer wheels to turn faster when the vehicle is cornering. 3 Math. a function that expresses the difference between two potential values of a variable.

differentiate verb intrans., trans. (**differentiated, differentiating**) 1 to establish, constitute, etc. a difference (between). 2 to be able to distinguish (one from another). ▸ **differentiation** noun

difficult adj. 1 requiring great skill, intelligence, or effort. 2 of a person not easy to please; awkward, uncooperative. 3 of a problem, situation, etc. potentially embarrassing; hard to resolve or get out of.

difficulty noun (pl. **difficulties**) 1 the state or quality of being difficult. 2 a difficult thing to do or understand. 3 a problem, obstacle, or objection. 4 (usu. **difficulties**) trouble or embarrassment, esp. financial.

diffident adj. lacking confidence; overly modest or shy. ▸ **diffidence** noun ▸ **diffidently** adv.

diffract verb trans., intrans. (**diffracted, diffracting**) to undergo or cause to undergo diffraction. ▸ **diffractive** adj.

diffraction noun a change in the direction of light or sound waves after they pass an obstacle or emerge from a small aperture.

diffuse verb trans., intrans. (dĭ-fyōōz') (**diffused, diffusing**) to spread or send out in all directions. —adj. (dĭ-fyōōs') 1 widely spread; not concentrated. 2 using too many words. ▸ **diffusely** adv. ▸ **diffuseness** noun ▸ **diffusion** noun

dig verb trans., intrans. (pa t and pa p **dug**; pr p **digging**) 1 to turn up or move (e.g., earth, etc.), esp. with a spade. 2 to make (e.g., a hole) by digging. 3 to poke or prod. 4 slang to appreciate or understand. —noun 1 a ridiculing, critical, etc. remark. 2 a place where archeologists are digging. 3 a poke. 4 an act of digging.

digest¹ (dĭ-jĕst', də-) verb trans., intrans. (**digested, digesting**) 1 to convert and absorb (food) for assimilation in the cells. 2 to take in (information, etc.) and think about it. ▸ **digestible** adj. ▸ **digestion** noun. ▸ **digestive** adj.

digest² (dī'jĕst,) noun a collection of summaries or shortened versions.

digger noun 1 a machine used for digging and excavating. 2 a person who digs, esp. a gold miner.

digit (dĭj'ĭt) noun 1 a single figure representing a number under ten. 2 a finger or toe.

digital adj. 1 showing numerical information in the form of a set of digits, rather than by means of a pointer on a dial: a digital watch. 2 of a process or device operating by processing information that is supplied and stored in combinations of binary digits: a digital recording / a digital computer program. 3 of an electronic circuit responding to and producing signals that at any given time are in one of two possible states. 4 of or involving digits. See also analogue.

digital audio tape Electron. (ABBREV. **DAT**) 1 a magnetic audio tape onto which sound has been recorded after it has been converted into a digital code. 2 sound so recorded, affording greater clarity and less distortion than conventional recording.

digital computer Comput. a computer that operates by processing data represented as digits, usu. in the form of a series of binary digits. See also analogue computer.

digitalis (dĭj,ĭ-tăl'ĭs) noun 1 a plant such as the purple foxglove. 2 an extract from the dried leaves of the foxglove used as a heart stimulant.

digitize verb trans. (**digitized, digitizing**) to convert (data) into binary form. ▸ **digitization** noun

digitizer noun a device that converts analog data into digital form. Also called **analog-to-digital converter**.

dignified adj. showing dignity; stately and serious.

dignify verb trans. (**dignified, dignifying, dignifies**) 1 to make (something) impressive or dignified. 2 to make (something) seem more important or impressive than it really is.

dignitary noun (pl. **dignitaries**) a person of high rank or position, esp. in public life.

dignity noun 1 stateliness, seriousness, and formality of manner and appearance. 2 goodness and nobility of character. 3 calmness and self-control. 4 elevated professional or social position. ▤ PRESTIGE, RANK, STANDING, STATURE, STATUS.

digraph noun a pair of letters that represent a single sound, as in the ph of digraph.

digress verb intrans. (**digressed, digressing**) to wander from the point. ▸ **digression** noun

dihedral (dī-hē′drəl) adj. having, formed by, or bounded by two planes.

dike or **dyke** noun a wall to prevent or control flooding.

dilapidated adj. of furniture, buildings, etc. falling to pieces because of neglect or age; in great need of repair. ▸ **dilapidation** noun

dilate (dī-lāt′, dǐ′lāt,) verb (**dilated, dilating**) to widen, expand, or distend. ▸ **dilatation** noun ▸ **dilation** noun

dilatory (dǐl′ə-tôr,ē) adj. inclined to or causing delay. ▸ **dilatorily** adv. ▸ **dilatoriness** noun

dildo noun (pl. **dildos, dildoes**) an object shaped like an erect penis, used for sexual stimulation.

dilemma noun 1 a situation with choices that are equally undesirable. 2 colloq. a problem or difficult situation.

> *Usage* Though commonly used, this meaning of dilemma (sense 2 here) can incur criticism; careful writers and speakers are best advised to avoid it, at least in formal speech and writing.

dilettante (dǐl′ə-tänt,, -tänt,) noun (pl. **dilettantes**) a person who has a superficial or casual interest in or knowledge of a subject. ▸ **dilettantism** noun

diligent adj. 1 hard-working, careful, and committed. 2 showing or done with care and serious effort. ▸ **diligence** noun ▸ **diligently** adv.

dill noun an aromatic herb used as a flavoring.

dilly-dally verb intrans. (**dilly-dallied, dilly-dallying, dilly-dallies**) colloq. 1 to be slow or waste time. 2 to dither.

diluent (dǐl′yə-wənt) noun a fluid used to dilute another.

dilute verb trans. (**diluted, diluting**) to decrease the concentration, strength, influence, or effect of. ▸ **dilution** noun

diluvial or **diluvian** adj. 1 of, pertaining to, or caused by a flood. 2 relating to debris swept along or deposited by a flood.

dim adj. (**dimmer, dimmest**) 1 lacking light or brightness. 2 faint. 3 colloq. not very intelligent. —verb trans., intrans. (**dimmed,**

dimming) to make or become dim. ▸ **dimly** adv. ▸ **dimness** noun

dime noun a coin worth 10 cents or one tenth of a dollar.

dime novel an inexpensive paperback book, usu. a romance or adventure story.

dimension noun 1 a measurement of length, width, or height. 2 (often **dimensions**) size or extent.

-dimensional combining form forming words denoting having a certain number of dimensions: two-dimensional.

dime store same as **five-and-dime**.

diminish verb trans., intrans. (**diminished, diminishing**) to make or become smaller, less important, less valuable, less satisfactory, etc. ▸ **diminution** noun

diminuendo (də-mǐn,yə-wěn′dō) Mus. noun (pl. **diminuendos**) 1 a gradual lessening of volume. 2 a passage with gradually lessening sound. —adj., adv. with gradually lessening sound. See also **crescendo**.

diminutive adj. very small. —noun an ending added to a word to indicate smallness, e.g., -let in booklet.

dimmer noun a switch used to reduce the brightness of light.

dimple noun a small hollow, esp. in the skin of the cheeks, chin, etc.

dim sum (dǐm′soom′) a Chinese dish of savory dumplings, usu. served as a snack.

dimwit noun slang a stupid person. ▸ **dimwitted** adj.

din noun a loud, continuous, and unpleasant noise.

dinar (dǐ-när′, dē′när,) noun the standard unit of currency in the former Yugoslavia and several Arab countries.

dine verb intrans., trans. (**dined, dining**) to eat dinner or give dinner to (someone). —**dine out on** to use (an entertaining or interesting story, experience, etc.) to amuse people, esp. several times: dined out on meeting the President for weeks.

diner noun 1 a person who dines. 2 a dining car on a train. 3 a small, inexpensive restaurant.

ding noun 1 a ringing sound. 2 a small dent in a car. —verb intrans. (**dinged, dinging**) to make dings or a ding.

dingbat noun colloq. 1 a silly, stupid person. 2 a typographical symbol.

ding-dong noun 1 the sound of bells ringing. 2 slang a stupid person. —adj. going quickly and furiously back and forth between people: a ding-dong battle.

dinghy (dǐng′ē, -gē) noun (pl. **dinghies**) a small boat, usu. propelled by oars.

dingo (dǐng′gō) noun (pl. **dingoes**) a wild Australian dog.

dingy (dǐn′jē) adj. (**dingier, dingiest**) faded, dirty-looking, or dark. ▸ **dinginess** noun

dinky *adj.* (**dinkier, dinkiest**) *colloq.* **1** insignificant. **2** poor in quality.

dinner *noun* **1** the main meal of the day. **2** a formal meal, esp. a celebratory one.

dinner jacket a man's formal jacket. *Also called* **tuxedo**.

dinosaur *noun* **1** an extinct reptile. **2** a thing or person that is outmoded or hopelessly obsolete.

> Coined in the 19th century, from Greek words which translate as 'terrible lizard'

dint *noun* **1** a dent. **2** a power; force.

diocese *noun* the district under the authority of a bishop. ▸ **diocesan** *adj.*

diode *noun Electron.* a device used as a rectifier.

dioxide *noun Chem.* an oxide with two atoms of oxygen per molecule.

dip *verb trans., intrans.* (**dipped, dipping**) **1** to put into a liquid for a short time. **2** to go briefly into or under something. **3** to drop. **4** to slope downward. **5** to immerse (an animal) in an insecticide, etc. —*noun* **1** an act of dipping. **2** a downward slope (e.g., in a road, etc.) or a downturn (e.g., in sales, etc.). **3** a short swim. **4** a liquid for dipping animals. **5** a sauce that food is dipped in.

diphtheria (dǐf-thǐr'ē-ə, dǐp-) *noun* a serious infectious disease of the throat which makes breathing and swallowing difficult.

diphthong (dǐf'thông, dǐp'-) *noun* a complex speech sound where one vowel moves to another within a single syllable, e.g., *ou* in *sound*.

diploma *noun* a document certifying that a school, college, or university course has been successfully completed.

> From a Greek word meaning a letter folded double

diplomacy *noun* **1** the art or profession of negotiating agreements, treaties, etc., esp. between countries. **2** tact.

diplomat (dǐp'lə-mǎt,) *noun* **1** a government official or representative engaged in diplomacy. **2** a very tactful person.

diplomatic *adj.* **1** concerning or involved in diplomacy. **2** tactful. ▸ **diplomatically** *adv.*

dipole (dī'pōl,) *noun Phys.* a separation of electric charge, in which two equal and opposite charges are separated from each other by a small distance.

dipper *noun* a ladle.

dipsomania *noun* an extreme form of alcoholism. ▸ **dipsomaniac** *noun*

dipstick *noun* a rod used to measure the level of liquid in a container, esp. oil in an engine.

diptych (dǐp'tǐk) *noun* a pair of pictures or carvings on two hinged wooden panels. *See also* **triptych**.

dire *adj.* **1** dreadful; terrible. **2** very serious; extreme. **3** urgent and desperate.

direct *adj.* **1** following the quickest and shortest path from beginning to end or to a destination; straight. **2** open, straightforward, and honest. **3** exact; complete. —*verb trans., intrans.* (**directed, directing**) **1** to turn (something) in a particular direction. **2** to show the way. **3** to order or instruct. **4** to control or manage; to be in charge of (something). **5** to plan and supervise the production of (a play or movie. —*adv.* by the quickest or shortest path; directly. ▸ **directness** *noun*

direct current (ABBREV. **dc**) an electric current that flows in one direction. *See also* **alternating current**.

direction *noun* **1** the place or point toward which someone or something is moving or facing. **2** the way that someone or something is going or developing. **3** (*usu.* **directions**) information, instructions, or advice, e.g., on how to construct or operate a piece of equipment. **4** (**directions**) instructions about the way to go to reach a place. **5** management or supervision. **6** the act, style, etc., of directing a play or movie. ▸ **directional** *adj.*

directive *noun* an official instruction issued by a higher authority, e.g., a government.

directly *adv.* **1** in a direct manner; by a direct route. **2** at once; immediately.

direct object a noun, noun phrase, or pronoun that is directly affected by the action of a transitive verb, as *the dog* in *The boy patted the dog*. *See also* **indirect object**.

director *noun* **1** a person controlling the operations of a corporation or other institution. **2** a person directing a play, movie, etc. ▸ **directorial** *adj.* ▸ **directorship** *noun*

directorate *noun* a group of directors.

directory *noun* (*pl.* **directories**) **1** a book with a *usu.* alphabetical list of names and addresses of people or organizations. **2** *Comput.* a named grouping of files.

dirge (dərj') *noun* **1** a funeral song, hymn, or march. **2** a slow, sad piece of music.

dirigible (də-rǐj'ə-bəl, dǐr'ǐj-ə-bəl) *noun* an airship.

dirk *noun* a small knife or dagger.

dirndl (dərn'dəl) *noun* **1** a traditional full-skirted peasant dress. **2** a skirt that is tight at the waist and wide at the bottom.

dirt *noun* **1** an unclean substance, e.g., mud or dust. **2** soil; earth. **3** excrement. **4** obscene speech or writing. **5** *colloq.* spiteful gossip; scandal.

dirt-cheap *adj., adv. colloq.* very cheap or cheaply.

dirty *adj.* (**dirtier, dirtiest**) **1** soiled. **2** involving or becoming soiled with dirt: *a* *dirty job.* **3** unfair; dishonest: *dirty tricks.* **4** offensive to accepted standards of decency and modesty. · **5** showing dislike or disapproval: *a dirty look.* **6** unsportingly rough or violent: *dirty play.* —*verb trans.* (**dirtied, dirtying, dirties**) to make dirty. —*adv.* in an unsportingly rough manner: *fight dirty.* ▸ **dirtily** *adv.* ▸ **dirtiness** *noun*

dirty linen personal information that, if publicized, could cause embarrassment. —**wash (one's) dirty linen** to expose to public comment personally embarrassing information about (oneself).

dirty word 1 an indecent or vulgar word. **2** *colloq.* an unpopular concept or point of view: *Ambition is a dirty word.*

dis *verb trans.* (**dissed, dissing, disses**) *slang* to act or speak disrespectfully toward.

dis- *prefix* forming words denoting: **1** the opposite of the simplex (the simple word): *disagree / dislike.* **2** reversal of the action of the simplex: *disassemble.* **3** removal or undoing: *dismember / disrobe.*

disability *noun* (*pl.* **disabilities**) **1** the state of being disabled. **2** a physical deficiency or disadvantage.

disable *verb trans.* (**disabled, disabling**) **1** to deprive of a physical or mental ability. **2** to make (e.g., a machine) unable to work; to make useless. ▸ **disablement** *noun*

disabuse (dĭs,ə-byōōz′) *verb trans.* (**disabused, disabusing**) (**disabuse (someone) of (something)**) to rid (someone) of (a mistaken idea, impression, etc.).

disadvantage *noun* **1** a difficulty, drawback, or weakness. **2** an unfavorable situation. —*verb trans.* (**disadvantaged, disadvantaging**) to put at a disadvantage. ▸ **disadvantaged** *adj.* ▸ **disadvantageous** *adj.*

disaffected *adj.* no longer loyal or committed because of dissatisfaction or rebelliousness. ▸ **disaffection** *noun*

disagree *verb intrans.* **1** to differ, conflict, or quarrel. **2** (**disagree with**) to have a different opinion from (someone) or be opposed to (something). ▸ **disagreement** *noun*

disagreeable *adj.* unpleasant; bad-tempered; unfriendly. ▸ **disagreeably** *adv.*

disallow *verb trans.* to refuse to allow. ▸ **disallowance** *noun*

disappear *verb intrans.* to go out of sight or existence. ▸ **disappearance** *noun*

disappoint *verb trans., intrans.* (**disappointed, disappointing**) to fail to fulfill the hopes, expectations, etc. of. ▸ **disappointment** *noun*

disapprove *verb trans., intrans.* **1** (*usu.* **disapprove of**) to condemn. **2** to refuse to sanction. ▸ **disapproval** *noun*

disarm *verb trans., . intrans.* (**disarmed, disarming**) **1** to deprive of weapons, mi-

litary power, etc. **2** to take away the anger or suspicions of. ▸ **disarmament** *noun*

disarming *adj.* taking away anger or suspicion; quickly winning confidence or affection. ▸ **disarmingly** *adv.*

disarrange *verb trans.* to make messy or disordered. ▸ **disarrangement** *noun*

disarray *noun* a state of disorder or confusion. —*verb trans.* (**disarrayed, disarraying**) to throw into disorder.

disassociate *verb trans.* same as **dissociate**.

disaster (dĭz-ăs′tər, dĭs-) *noun* **1** an event causing great damage, injury, or loss of life. **2** a total failure. ▸ **disastrous** *adj.* ▸ **disastrously** *adv.*

disavow *verb trans.* (**disavowed, disavowing**) to deny knowledge of, a connection with, or responsibility for. ▸ **disavowal** *noun*

disband *verb trans., intrans.* (**disbanded, disbanding**) to stop operating as a group; to break up. ▸ **disbandment** *noun*

disbar *verb trans.* (**disbarred, disbarring**) to remove the right of (a lawyer) to practice. ▸ **disbarment** *noun*

disbelief *noun* an inability or refusal to believe.

disbelieve *verb trans., intrans.* **1** to refuse to believe. **2** to have no religious faith.

disburse *verb trans.* (**disbursed, disbursing**) to pay out, esp. from a fund. ▸ **disbursement** *noun*

disc *noun, verb* same as **disk**.

discard *verb trans.* (dĭs-kärd′, dĭs′kärd,) (**discarded, discarding**) **1** to get rid of. **2** *Cards* to put down (a card of little value) esp. when unable to follow suit. —*noun* (dĭs′kärd,) *Cards* a playing card that has been discarded.

discern (dĭ-sərn′, dĭz-) *verb trans.* (**discerned, discerning**) to distinguish, perceive, or discriminate. ▸ **discernible** *adj.* ▸ **discernment** *noun*

discerning *adj.* having or showing good judgment.

discharge *verb trans., intrans.* (**discharged, discharging**) **1** to send away, dismiss, free, or absolve. **2** to carry out (duties, etc.) in a specified way. **3** to flow out or cause to flow out. **4** to fire (a gun, etc.). **5** to unload (cargo, passengers, etc.). —*noun* **1** an act of discharging. **2** something discharged.

disciple (dĭs-ī′pəl) *noun* **1** a person who believes in and follows the teachings of another. **2** (**Disciple**) one of the 12 original followers of Christ.

disciplinarian *noun* a person who enforces strict discipline.

disciplinary *adj.* **1** of, relating to, or enforcing discipline. **2** intended as punishment.

discipline (dĭs′ə-plĭn) *noun* **1** strict enforcement of rules, etc. **2** punishment intended to engender obedience. **3** an area of learning, esp. a subject of academic study. —*verb trans.* (**disciplined, disciplining**) **1** to train. **2** to punish.

disc jockey (ABBREV. **DJ**) a person who presents a program of recorded popular music on the radio, at a disco, or at a private party.

disclaim *verb trans.* (**disclaimed, disclaiming**) to deny; to renounce.

disclaimer *noun* **1** a written statement denying legal responsibility. **2** a denial.

disclose *verb trans.* (**disclosed, disclosing**) to make known. ▸ **disclosure** *noun*

disco *noun* (*pl.* **discos**) a discotheque.

discolor *verb trans., intrans.* to stain or dirty; to change in color. ▸ **discoloration** *noun*

discomfit *verb trans.* (**discomfited, discomfiting**) **1** to embarrass, frustrate, or perplex. ▸ **discomfiture** *noun*

discomfort *noun* a slight physical pain or mental uneasiness. —*verb trans.* (**discomforted, discomforting**) to make physically uncomfortable or mentally uneasy.

discompose *verb trans.* to unsettle, disturb, or trouble. ▸ **discomposure** *noun*

disconcert *verb trans.* (**disconcerted, disconcerting**) to make (someone) anxious, uneasy, flustered, etc.

disconnect (dĭs̸kə-nĕkt′) *verb trans.* **1** to interrupt, break, or cut off a connection to (something). **2** to cut off the supply of (a public utility, etc.). ▸ **disconnection** *noun*

disconsolate (dĭs-kăn′sə-lət) *adj.* deeply sad or disappointed; inconsolable. ▸ **disconsolately** *adv.*

discontent (dĭs̸kən-tĕnt′) *noun* lack of contentment; dissatisfaction.

discontented *adj.* dissatisfied; unhappy.

discontinue *verb trans., intrans.* to stop or suspend. ▸ **discontinuance** *noun* ▸ **discontinuation** *noun*

discontinuity *noun* a lack of continuity; interruption.

discontinuous *adj.* having breaks or interruptions.

discord (dĭs′kôrd̸) *noun* **1** disagreement or conflict. **2** *Mus.* lack of harmony. **3** uproarious noise. ▸ **discordant** *adj.*

discotheque (dĭs′kə-tĕk̸, dĭs̸kə-tĕk′) *noun* formerly a nightclub with dancing to recorded pop music.

discount *noun* (dĭs′kownt̸) a deduction. —*verb trans.* (dĭs-kownt′, dĭs′kownt̸) (**discounted, discounting**) **1** to regard (something) as unworthy of consideration. **2** to deduct from (a price).

discourage *verb trans.* (**discouraged, discouraging**) **1** to deprive of confidence, hope, or the will to continue. **2** to seek to prevent (something). ▸ **discouragement** *noun*

discourse *noun* (dĭs′kôrs̸, dĭs-kôrs′) a formal speech or serious conversation. —*verb intrans.* (dĭs-kôrs′, dĭs̸kôrs̸) (**discoursed, discoursing**) to speak or write at length, formally, or with authority.

discourteous *adj.* lacking or exhibiting a lack of respect or manners. ▸ **discourteously** *adv.* ▸ **discourtesy** *noun*

discover *verb trans.* (**discovered, discovering**) **1** to be the first person to find. **2** to find by chance, esp. for the first time.

discovery *noun* (*pl.* **discoveries**) **1** an act or the process of discovering. **2** a person or thing discovered.

discredit *noun* loss of good reputation, or the cause of it. —*verb trans.* (**discredited, discrediting**) **1** to cause (someone or something) to be disbelieved or regarded with doubt or suspicion. **2** to damage the reputation or reliability of. ▸ **discreditable** *adj.*

discreet *adj.* **1** careful to prevent suspicion or embarrassment; tactful. **2** deliberately inconspicuous or unobtrusive.

Usage Discreet is often confused with *discrete.*

discrepancy *noun* (*pl.* **discrepancies**) a lack of correspondence, e.g., between amounts, etc. that should tally or be the same. ▸ **discrepant** *adj.*

discrete *adj.* **1** separate; distinct. **2** discontinuous.

Usage Discrete is often confused with *discreet.*

discretion *noun* **1** the quality of behaving in a discreet way. **2** wise judgment or the power or freedom to decide. ▸ **discretionary** *adj.*

discriminate *verb intrans.* (**discriminated, discriminating**) **1** to differentiate. **2** to make a distinction, esp. an unjust or prejudiced one, between people or groups, e.g., on grounds of race, gender, etc. ▸ **discrimination** *noun* ▸ **discriminatory** *adj.*

discriminating *adj.* showing good judgment; able to recognize even slight differences.

discursive *adj.* **1** wandering from the main point or from one topic to another. **2** based on reason.

discus (dĭs′kəs) *noun* (*pl.* **discuses**) **1** a heavy metal disk thrown in athletic competitions. **2** the competition itself.

discuss (dĭs-kəs′) *verb trans.* (**discussed, discussing, discusses**) to examine or consider in speech or writing. ▸ **discussion** *noun*

disdain (dĭs-dān′) *noun* dislike arising out of lack of respect; contempt. —*verb trans.* (**disdained, disdaining**) **1** to refuse or reject out of lack of respect. **2** to regard with contempt or lack of respect. ▸ **disdainful** adj. ▸ **disdainfully** adv.

disease noun an abnormal or unhealthy condition or a cause of this. —verb trans. (**diseased, diseasing**) to infect or affect with disease.

disembark verb trans., intrans. to take or go from a ship to land. ▸ **disembarkation** noun

disembowel verb trans. (**disemboweled** or **disembowelled, disemboweling** or **disembowelling**) to remove the internal organs of, as a punishment, torture, etc. ▸ **disembowelment** noun

disempower verb trans. to deprive of influence or power. ▸ **disempowerment** noun

disenchant verb trans. 1 to free from illusion. 2 to make dissatisfied or discontented. ▸ **disenchantment** noun

disenfranchise verb trans. (**disenfranchised, disenfranchising**) same as **disfranchise.** ▸ **disenfranchisement** noun

disengage verb trans., intrans. 1 to release or detach from a connection. 2 to withdraw (troops) from combat. ▸ **disengagement** noun

disentangle verb trans. to free from complication, difficulty, confusion, etc. ▸ **disentanglement** noun

disfigure verb trans. (**disfigured, disfiguring**) to spoil the beauty or general appearance of. ▸ **disfigurement** noun

disfranchise or **disenfranchise** verb trans. (**disfranchised, disfranchising**) to deprive of the right to vote. ▸ **disfranchisement** noun

disgorge (dĭs-gôrj') verb trans. (**disgorged, disgorging**) 1 to vomit. 2 to discharge or pour out.

disgrace noun loss of respect or favor, or the cause of it. —verb trans. (**disgraced, disgracing**) to bring shame upon.

disgraceful adj. bringing shame; degrading. ▸ **disgracefully** adv.

disgruntled adj. annoyed and dissatisfied.

disguise verb trans. (**disguised, disguising**) 1 to hide the identity of, esp. by a change of appearance. 2 to conceal the true nature of (e.g., intentions, etc.). —noun 1 concealment. 2 something, esp. clothes, makeup, a wig, etc., intended to disguise.

disgust verb trans. (**disgusted, disgusting**) to provoke intense dislike or disapproval in; to sicken. —noun intense dislike; loathing.

disgusting adj. causing a feeling of intense dislike or revulsion.

dish noun 1 a container that food is served or cooked in. 2 a particular kind of food. 3 (**dishes**) the plates and other utensils used for a meal: —verb trans. (**dished, dishing**) to hol-low (something) out. —**dish out** to

distribute (something). **dish up** to serve (food).

dishabille or **deshabille** (dĭs,ə-bēl', -bĕ', -bĭl') noun the state of being slovenly dressed or of being only partly dressed.

dish antenna same as **satellite dish**.

disharmony noun disagreement. ▸ **disharmonious** adj.

dishearten verb trans. (**disheartened, disheartening**) to dampen the courage, hope, or confidence of. ▸ **disheartenment** noun

dishevelled (dĭsh-ĕv'əld) adj., of clothes or hair in a messy or untidy state. ▸ **dishevelment** noun

dishonest (dĭs-ăn'ĭst) adj. likely to deceive or cheat; not honest; insincere. ▸ **dishonestly** adv. ▸ **dishonesty** noun

dishonor noun loss of respect or favor, or the cause of it. —verb trans. (**dishonored, dishonoring**) 1 to bring dishonor on. 2 to treat with no respect. 3 to refuse to honor (a check). ▸ **dishonorable** adj.

dishonorable discharge (abbrev. **D.D.**) discharge from the armed forces because of being guilty of a grave offense, e.g., espionage, sabotage, or cowardice.

dishwasher noun 1 a machine that washes and dries dishes. 2 a person employed to wash dishes, e.g., in a restaurant.

dishwater noun water in which dirty dishes have been washed.

disillusion verb trans. (**disillusioned, disillusioning**) to correct the mistaken beliefs or illusions of. ▸ **disillusionment** noun

disincentive noun something that discourages or deters.

disinclination noun a state of being unwilling

disinclined adj. unwilling.

disinfect verb trans. (**disinfected, disinfecting**) to clean with a substance that kills germs.

disinfectant noun a germ-killing substance.

disinformation noun false information intended to deceive or mislead.

disingenuous (dĭs,ĭn-jĕn'yə-wəs) adj. not entirely sincere or open; creating a false impression of frankness. ▸ **disingenuously** adv. ▸ **disingenuousness** noun

disinherit verb trans. to deprive legally of an inheritance. ▸ **disinheritance** noun

disintegrate (dĭs-ĭnt'ə-grāt,) verb trans., intrans. (**disintegrated, disintegrating**) 1 to break or cause (something) to break, into tiny pieces; to shatter or crumble. 2 to break up. 3 Phys. to undergo or cause to undergo nuclear fission. ▸ **disintegration** noun

disinter (dĭs,ĭn-tər') verb trans. 1 to dig up (esp. a corpse from a grave). 2 to discover; to unearth.

disinterested adj. **1** lacking bias or self-interest; impartial; objective. **2** colloq. showing no interest; uninterested; indifferent. ▸ **disinterest** noun

> Usage Use of disinterested as defined in sense 2 is often disapproved of.

disjointed adj. not properly connected; incoherent.

disjunctive adj. marked by breaks; discontinuous.

disk or **disc** noun **1** a flat, thin, circular object. **2** Comput. a magnetic circular-shaped medium used to record and store data in a computer. See also **floppy disk, hard disk. 3** a circular-shaped recording medium, e.g., a compact disk or phonograph record.

disk drive Comput. the device that controls the transfer of information onto and from a disk.

diskette (dĭs-kĕt′) noun Comput. a floppy disk.

disk-operating system (ABBREV. **DOS**) Comput. an operating system that controls storage and retrieval of information, file management, etc.

dislike verb trans. to consider unpleasant or unlikable. —noun **1** aversion; distaste. **2** something disliked.

dislocate (dĭs′lō-kāt,, dĭs-lō′-) verb trans. (**dislocated, dislocating**) **1** to dislodge (a bone) from its normal position. **2** to disturb or disrupt. ▸ **dislocation** noun

dislodge verb trans. to force out.

disloyal adj. displaying or feeling no loyalty or faithfulness. ▸ **disloyalty** noun

dismal (dĭz′məl) adj. **1** sad; gloomy. **2** very bad; lacking in merit: a dismal failure. ▸ **dismally** adv.

> Based on a Latin phrase dies mali 'evil days', referring to two days each month which were believed to be unusually unlucky

dismantle verb trans. (**dismantled, dismantling**) to take to pieces, esp. bit by bit; to demolish.

dismay noun a feeling of sadness arising from deep disappointment or discouragement. —verb trans. (**dismayed, dismaying**) **1** to destroy (someone's) courage, etc. **2** to disillusion.

dismember verb trans. (**dismembered, dismembering**) **1** to tear or cut the arms and legs from. **2** to divide up. ▸ **dismemberment** noun

dismiss verb trans. (**dismissed, dismissing**) **1** to refuse to consider or accept. **2** to discharge (someone) from a job, duty, etc. **3** to send away; to allow to leave. **4** Law to refuse to continue (a court case). ▸ **dismissal** noun

dismissive adj. (often **dismissive of**) giving no consideration or respect; showing no willingness to believe.

dismount verb intrans., trans. **1** to get off a horse, bicycle, etc. **2** to force (someone) off a horse, bicycle, etc. **3** to remove from a stand or frame.

disobey verb trans., intrans. to act contrary to the orders of; to refuse to obey. ▸ **disobedience** noun ▸ **disobedient** adj.

disobliging adj. unwilling to help; disregarding or tending to disregard wishes or requests.

disorder noun **1** lack of order; confusion or disturbance. **2** unruly or riotous behavior. **3** a disease or illness. ▸ **disorderly** adj.

disorganize verb trans. to disturb the order or arrangement of; to throw into confusion. ▸ **disorganization** noun

disorient verb trans. (**disoriented, disorienting**) to cause to lose all sense of position, direction, or time. ▸ **disorientation** noun

disown verb trans. to deny having any relationship to or connection with; to refuse to recognize or acknowledge. ▸ **disownment** noun

disparage (dĭs-păr′ĭj) verb trans. (**disparaged, disparaging**) to speak of with contempt. ▸ **disparagement** noun

disparate (dĭs-păr′ət, dĭs-pə-rət) adj. completely different; too different to be compared.

disparity (dĭs-păr′ət-ē) noun (pl. **disparities**) a great or fundamental difference; inequality.

dispassionate adj. **1** calm; unemotional. **2** not influenced by personal feelings; impartial.

dispatch or **despatch** (dĭs-păch′) verb trans. (**dispatched, dispatching**) **1** to send to a place for a particular reason. **2** to finish off or deal with quickly. **3** to kill. —noun **1** (often **dispatches**) an official (esp. military or diplomatic) report. **2** a journalist's report sent to a newspaper. **3** the act of dispatching; the fact of being dispatched. **4** speed or haste. ▸ **dispatcher** noun

dispel verb trans. (**dispelled, dispelling**) to drive away or banish (thoughts or feelings).

dispensable adj. **1** not absolutely necessary; expendable. **2** able to be dispensed.

dispensary noun (pl. **dispensaries**) **1** a place where medicines are given out. **2** a public clinic.

dispensation noun **1** special exemption from a rule or obligation. **2** an act or the process of dispensing.

dispense verb trans. (**dispensed, dispensing**) **1** to give out (e.g., advice). **2** to prepare and distribute (medicine). **3** to administer (e.g., the law). —**dispense with** to do without (someone or something).

disperse (dĭs-pərs') verb trans., intrans. (**dispersed, dispersing**) **1** to spread out over a wide area. **2** to break up or cause (a crowd) to break up and leave. **3** to vanish or cause to vanish. **4** to scatter (seeds, etc.) in all directions over a wide area. ▸ **dispersal** noun ▸ **dispersion** noun

dispirit (dĭs-pĭr'ĭt) verb trans. (**dispirited, dispiriting**) to dishearten or discourage.

displace verb trans. **1** to put or take out of the usual place. **2** to take the place of. **3** to remove from a post. ▸ **displacement** noun

display (dĭs-plā') verb trans. (**displayed, displaying**) **1** to put on view. **2** to show, esp. in a way that is intended to attract attention. **3** to show evidence of; to make manifest or known: displayed great courage. —noun **1** an act of displaying. **2** an exhibition; a show of talent; an arrangement of objects on view. **3** a visual unit linked to a computer, or a liquid-crystal unit, used in watches, calculators, etc.

displease verb trans. to annoy or offend. ▸ **displeasure** noun

disport verb trans., intrans. (**disported, disporting**) literary to indulge in or indulge (oneself) in lively amusement.

disposable adj. **1** intended to be thrown away or destroyed after use. **2** of income or assets available to be used.

dispose (dĭs-pōz') verb intrans., trans. (**disposed, disposing**) **1** (**dispose of**) **a** to get rid of (something or someone). **b** to deal with or settle (something). **2** to place in an arrangement or order. **3** (**dispose to**) to incline to: I am not disposed to try. ▸ **disposal** noun

disposition noun **1** a tendency; temperament; personality. **2** arrangement; position; distribution.

dispossess verb trans. (**dispossess of**) to take (esp. property) away from (someone). ▸ **dispossession** noun

disproof noun **1** the act of disproving. **2** something that disproves.

disproportionate adj. (**disproportionate to**) unreasonably large or small in comparison with (something else). ▸ **disproportion** noun ▸ **disproportionately** adv.

disprove verb trans. to show to be false or wrong.

dispute (dĭs-pyōōt') verb trans., intrans. (**disputed, disputing**) **1** to question or deny the accuracy or validity of. **2** to quarrel over rights to or possession of. **3** to argue about (something). —noun an argument. ▸ **disputable** adj. ▸ **disputation** noun

disqualify verb trans. **1** to remove from a competition, esp. for breaking rules. **2** to make unsuitable or ineligible. ▸ **disqualification** noun

disquiet verb trans. (**disquieted, disquieting**) to cause (someone) to feel anxious, uneasy, troubled, etc. —noun an anxious, etc. frame of mind. ▸ **disquieting** adj. ▸ **disquietude** noun

disquisition noun formal a long, detailed, oral or written discussion of a subject.

disregard verb trans. to pay no attention to; to dismiss as unworthy of consideration. —noun dismissive lack of attention or concern.

disrepair noun bad condition or working order.

disreputable (dĭs-rĕp'yət-ə-bəl) adj. suffering from or leading to a bad reputation. ▸ **disreputably** adv.

disrepute (dĭs,rĭ-pyōōt') noun a state of having a bad or damaged reputation.

disrespect noun lack of respect; impoliteness; rudeness. —verb trans., intrans. to display a lack of respect. ▸ **disrespectful** adj. ▸ **disrespectfully** adv.

disrupt verb trans. (**disrupted, disrupting**) to disturb the order or peaceful progress of. ▸ **disruption** noun ▸ **disruptive** adj.

dissatisfy verb trans. to fail to satisfy; to make discontented. ▸ **dissatisfaction** noun

dissect (dĭs-ĕkt', dĭ-sĕkt') verb trans. (**dissected, dissecting**) **1** to cut apart; to cut into small pieces. **2** to cut open (an animal, plant, or human corpse, etc) for the purpose of scientific, medical, or forensic study. **3** to examine in minute detail, esp. critically. ▸ **dissection** noun

dissemble (dĭs-ĕm'bəl) verb trans., intrans. (**dissembled, dissembling**) to conceal or disguise (true feelings or motives); to assume false appearances. ▸ **dissemblance** noun

disseminate verb trans. (**disseminated, disseminating**) to cause (e.g., news) to be widely circulated. ▸ **dissemination** noun

dissent (dĭs-ĕnt') noun disagreement; discord. —verb intrans. (**dissented, dissenting**) **1** to differ in opinion; to disagree. **2** to break away, esp. from a national church. ▸ **dissension** noun ▸ **dissenter** noun

dissertation noun **1** a very long essay; a thesis. **2** a formal lecture on a particular subject.

disservice (dĭs-ər'vĭs, dĭs-sər'-) noun a wrong; an injurious action.

dissident noun a person who disagrees publicly, esp. with a government. —adj. disagreeing; dissenting. ▸ **dissidence** noun

dissimilar (dĭs-sĭm'ə-lər) adj. different. ▸ **dissimilarity** noun

dissipate (dĭs'ĭ-pāt,) verb trans., intrans. (**dissipated, dissipating**) **1** to separate and scatter or cause to separate and scatter. **2** to use up carelessly; to squander. **3** to act or live in a debauched way. ▸ **dissipation** *noun*

dissociate (dĭs-ō'shē-āt,, -sē-) *verb trans., intrans.* (**dissociated, dissociating**) to separate or regard as separate. **2** to declare (someone or oneself) to be unconnected with. ▸ **dissociation** *noun*

dissoluble *adj.* able to be dissolved; soluble.

dissolute (dĭs'ə-lōōt,) *adj.* indulging in pleasures considered immoral; debauched. ▸ **dissoluteness** *noun*

dissolution *noun* **1** the formal breaking up or ending of something, esp. a meeting, parliament, monarchy, marriage, business, etc. **2** the process of breaking up or ending something.

dissolve (dĭz-ôlv', -ŏv', -ālv', -äv') *verb trans., intrans.* (**dissolved, dissolving**) **1** to break up and merge with a liquid; to melt or become liquid. **2** to bring (a meeting, parliament, monarchy, marriage, business, etc.) to an end. **3** to disappear or cause to disappear. **4** to collapse emotionally: *dissolved into tears.* **5** of a film or television *image* to fade out as a second image fades in. —*noun* a fading out of one film or television image as a second is simultaneously faded in.

dissonance (dĭs'ə-nəns) *noun* **1** *Mus.* an unpleasant combination of sounds or notes; lack of harmony. **2** disagreement; incompatibility. ▸ **dissonant** *adj.*

dissuade (dĭs-wād') *verb trans.* (**dissuaded, dissuading**) (**dissuade (someone) from doing (something)**) to deter (someone) with advice or persuasion. ▸ **dissuasion** *noun*

dissyllable *noun same as* **disyllable**.

distaff (dĭs'tăf,) *noun* the rod on which a bunch of wool, flax, etc., is held ready for spinning by hand. —**the distaff side** the female line of descent in a family. *See also* **spear**.

distance *noun* **1** the measured length between two points in space; the fact of being apart. **2** a faraway point or place; the farthest visible area. **3** coldness of manner. —*verb trans.* (**distanced, distancing**) **1** to put at a distance. **2** (*usu.* **distance (oneself)**) to declare (oneself) to be unconnected or unsympathetic to (something or someone else).

distant *adj.* **1** far away or far apart in space or time. **2** cold and unfriendly. ▸ **distantly** *adv.*

distaste *noun* dislike; aversion. ▸ **distasteful** *adj.*

distemper[1] *noun* an infectious disease of animals, esp. dogs and cats.

distemper[2] *noun* a water-based paint used for poster painting or murals. —*verb trans.* (**distempered, distempering**) to paint with distemper.

distend *verb trans., intrans.* (**distended, distending**) to make or become swollen, inflated, or stretched. ▸ **distensible** *adj.* ▸ **distension** *noun* ▸ **distention** *noun*

distill *or* **distil** (dĭs-tĭl') *verb trans.* (**distilled, distilling**) **1 a** to purify a liquid by the process of distillation. **b** to produce alcoholic spirits in this way. **2** to extract the pertinent facts from.

distillation *noun* a method of purifying a liquid by heating it to boiling point and condensing the vapor formed to a liquid (the *distillate*), which is then collected, e.g., in the production of whiskey, etc. ▸ **distillate** *noun*

distillery *noun* (*pl.* **distilleries**) a place where alcoholic spirits are produced by distillation. ▸ **distiller** *noun*

distinct (dĭs-tĭngkt') *adj.* **1** easily seen, heard, or recognized; clear or obvious. **2** noticeably different or separate. ▸ **distinctly** *adv.*

distinction *noun* **1** exceptional ability or achievement, or an honor awarded in recognition of this. **2** an act of differentiating. **3** the state of being noticeably different. **4** a distinguishing feature.

distinctive *adj.* easily recognized because of very individual characteristics. ▸ **distinctiveness** *noun*

distinguish *verb trans., intrans.* (**distinguished, distinguishing**) **1** to mark or recognize as being different. **2** to see the difference between (things or people). **3** to make out or identify. **4** to cause to be considered outstanding. ▸ **distinguishable** *adj.*

distinguished *adj.* **1** famous and greatly respected. **2** having a noble or dignified appearance.

distort *verb trans.* (**distorted, distorting**) **1** to twist out of shape. **2** to change the meaning or tone of by inaccurate retelling. **3** to alter the quality of (sound). ▸ **distortion** *noun*

distract *verb trans.* (**distracted, distracting**) **1** to divert the attention of. **2** to entertain or amuse. **3** to confuse, worry, or anger. ▸ **distraction** *noun*

distraught (dĭs-trôt') *adj.* being in an extremely troubled state of mind; highly agitated.

distress *noun* **1** mental or emotional pain. **2** financial difficulty; hardship. **3** great danger. —*verb trans.* (**distressed, distressing, distresses**) to cause distress to; to upset. ▸ **distressful** *adj.*

distressed *adj.* **1** suffering distress. **2** of *furniture, etc.* given an antique appearance.

distribute (dĭs-trĭb'yət) *verb trans.* (**distributed, distributing**) **1** to give out. **2** to supply or deliver (goods). **3** to spread out widely; to disperse. ▸ **distribution** *noun*

distributor (dĭs-trĭb′yət-ər) *noun* **1** a person or company that distributes goods. **2** a device, e.g., in a vehicle engine, that sends electricity to the spark plugs.

district *noun* an area or region, esp. one forming an administrative or geographical unit.

district attorney (ABBREV. **D.A.**) a prosecuting officer of a judicial district.

distrust *verb trans.* (**distrusted, distrusting**) to have no trust in; to doubt. —*noun* suspicion; lack of trust. ▸ **distrustful** *adj.* ▸ **distrustfulness** *noun*

disturb *verb trans.* (**disturbed, disturbing**) **1** to interrupt. **2** to inconvenience. **3** to upset the order or arrangement of. **4** to trouble.

disturbance *noun* **1** an outburst of noisy or violent behavior. **2** an interruption. **3** an act of disturbing or process of being disturbed.

disturbed *adj. colloq.* exhibiting symptoms of psychiatric instability or illness.

disturbing *adj.* causing anxiety; unsettling.

disuse *noun* the state of no longer being used, practiced, or observed; neglect.

disyllable *or* **dissyllable** (dī′sĭl,ə-bəl, dī-sĭl′-) *noun* a word of two syllables. ▸ **disyllabic** *adj.*

ditch *noun* a narrow channel for drainage or irrigation, or acting as a boundary. —*verb trans., intrans.* (**ditched, ditching**) *slang* **1** to get rid of. **2** to crash-land (an aircraft) in water, or to engage in this emergency procedure.

dither *verb intrans.* (**dithered, dithering**) to act in a nervously uncertain manner; to waver. —*noun* a state of nervous indecision. ▸ **ditherer** *noun* ▸ **dithery** *adj.*

ditsy *adj. slang* scatterbrained; flighty.

ditto *noun* (*pl.* **dittos**) *noun* the same thing; the above: a mark (″) indicating this. —*adv.* the same; likewise.

ditty *noun* (*pl.* **ditties**) a short simple song or poem.

diuretic (dī,yə-rĕt′ĭk) *noun* a drug, etc. that increases the volume of urine produced. —*adj.* increasing the production of urine.

diurnal (dī-ərn′l) *adj. formal* **1** daily. **2** occurring during the daytime. *See also* **nocturnal**. ▸ **diurnally** *adv.*

diva (dē′və) *noun* (*pl.* **divas, dive**) a great female singer, esp. in opera.

divalent *or* **bivalent** *adj. Chem, of an atom* having a valence of two.

divan (də-văn′, dī-) *noun* a long sofa, usu. without a back or sides.

dive[1] *verb intrans.* (**dived** *or* **dove, dived, diving**) **1** to go downward headfirst, esp. into water. **2** to become submerged. **3** to fall steeply through the air. **4** to plummet, esp. in price or value. **5** to throw oneself to the side or to the ground. **6** to jump into an activity

with vigor and enthusiasm. —*noun* **1** an act of diving. **2** *slang* a dirty or disreputable place, esp. a bar or club.

dive[2] *see* **diva**.

diver *noun* **1** someone or something that dives. **2** a person who swims, works, etc. underwater. **3** a diving water bird.

diverge (də-vərj′, dī-) *verb intrans.* (**diverged, diverging**) **1** to separate and go in different directions. **2** to differ. **3** (**diverge from**) to depart or deviate from (a usual route, etc.). ▸ **divergence** *noun* ▸ **divergent** *adj.* ▸ **divergently** *adv.*

divers (dī′vərz) *adj. old use, literary* various.

diverse (də-vərs′, dī-) *adj.* **1** various; assorted. **2** different; dissimilar.

diversify *verb trans., intrans.* (**diversified, diversifying, diversifies**) **1** to make diverse. **2** to branch out. ▸ **diversification** *noun*

diversion (də-vər′zhən, dī-) *noun* **1** an act of diverting; the state of being diverted. **2** a detour from a usual route. **3** something intended to draw attention away from a focal point. **4** amusement. ▸ **diversionary** *adj.*

diversity *noun* **1** variety in kind. **2** difference.

divert (də-vərt′, dī-) *verb trans.* (**diverted, diverting**) **1** to cause to change direction. **2** to draw away (esp. attention). **3** to amuse.

divest (dī-vĕst′, də-) *verb trans.* (**divested, divesting**) **1** (**divest of**) to take (something, e.g., a title, rights, property, etc.) from (someone). **2** to undress. ▸ **divestment** *noun*

divide (də-vīd′) *verb trans., intrans.* (**divided, dividing**) **1** to split up or cause to split up into two or more parts. **2** (**divide up, between, among**) to share. **3** to calculate how many times one number is contained in (another). **4** to cause separation or disagreement between: *an issue that divides academics.* —*noun* **1** a dividing point; a gap or split. **2** a ridge of high land.

dividend (dĭv′ĭd-ĕnd,) *noun* **1** a portion of a company's profits paid to a shareholder. **2** a benefit. **3** a number to be divided by another number.

dividers *pl. noun* a V-shaped device with movable arms, used in geometry, navigation, etc., for measuring.

divination (dĭv,ĭ-nā′shən) *noun* the practice or art of supposedly foretelling the future by supernatural means.

divine (də-vīn′) *adj.* **1** of, from, or relating to a god. **2** extremely pleasant; excellent. —*verb trans., intrans.* (**divined, divining**) **1** to foretell by divination or intuition. **2** to search for (underground water) with a divining rod. —*noun* a member of the clergy who is an expert in theology. ▸ **divinely** *adv.*

diving *noun* the activity or sport of plunging into water, esp. from a platform or board at the end of a swimming pool.

divining rod a stick held near the ground that, supposedly, will twitch when underground water is present.

divinity (də-vĭn'ət-ē) *noun* (*pl.* **divinities**) 1 theology. 2 a god.

divisible (də-vĭz'ə-bəl) *adj.* able to be divided, esp. without leaving a remainder.

division *noun* 1 the act of dividing; the state of being divided. 2 something that divides or separates; a gap or barrier. 3 one of the parts into which something is divided. 4 the process of determining how many times one number is contained in another. ▸ **divisional** *adj.*

divisive (də-vī'sĭv, -vĭs'ĭv) *adj.* tending to cause disagreement or conflict. ▸ **divisiveness** *noun*

divisor (də-vī'zər) *noun* a number by which another number is to be divided.

divorce *noun* 1 the legal ending of a marriage. 2 a complete separation: *the divorce of church and state.* —*verb trans., intrans.* (**divorced, divorcing**) 1 to obtain a legal ending to a marriage. 2 to separate: *divorce personal matters from business.*

divorcé (də-vôr-sā', -sē') *noun* a divorced man.

divorcée (də-vôr-sā', -sē') *noun* a divorced woman.

divot (dĭv'ət) *noun* a clump of grass and dirt, esp. one loosened from the ground by the blade of a golf club or the hoof of a horse.

divulge (də-vəlj', dī-) *verb trans.* (**divulged, divulging**) to make (something secret) known. ▸ **divulgence** *noun*

divvy *slang noun* (*pl.* **divvies**) a share. —*verb trans.* (**divvied, divvying, divvies**) (*often* **divvy up**) to divide or share.

Dixie (dĭk'sē) *noun* the southern and eastern states of the USA, esp. those that constituted the Confederacy during the Civil War.

dizzy *adj.* (**dizzier, dizziest**) 1 experiencing or causing a spinning sensation resulting in a loss of balance: *felt dizzy / dizzy heights.* 2 *colloq.* unreliable or irresponsible; silly. ▸ **dizzily** *adv.* ▸ **dizziness** *noun*

DJ *abbrev.* disc jockey.

djinni *or* **djinny** *noun* same as **jinni**.

DNA *abbrev. Biochem.* deoxyribonucleic acid, a nucleic acid that carries essential genetic information.

do¹ (dōo) *verb trans., intrans., aux.* (*pa t* **did**; *pa p* **done**; *pr p* **doing**; *3d person sing. present* **does**) 1 to carry out, perform, or commit. 2 to finish or complete. 3 to be enough or suitable. 4 to work at or study. 5 to be in a particular state: *doing well.* 6 to put in order or arrange. 7 to act or behave. 8 to provide as a service. 9 to cause or produce. 10 to travel (a distance); to travel at (a speed). 11 *colloq.* to cheat or swindle. 12 *colloq.* to copy the behavior of; to mimic. 13 to visit as a tourist. 14 *colloq.* to assault, injure, or murder. 15 *colloq.* to spend (time) in prison. 16 *slang* to take (drugs). —*verb aux.* 1 used in questions and negative statements or commands: *Do you smoke? / I don't like wine. / Don't do that!* 2 used to avoid repetition of a verb: *She eats as much as I do.* 3 used for emphasis: *She does know you've arrived.* —*noun* (*pl.* **do's, dos**) *colloq.* 1 a gathering; a party. 2 a fracas, scuffle, or commotion. —**do away with** 1 to murder. 2 to abolish (an institution, etc.). **do in** *slang* 1 to kill (someone). 2 to exhaust (someone). **do up** *colloq.* 1 to repair, clean, or improve (a home, building, etc.). 2 to fasten; to tie or wrap (a present, parcel, etc.). 3 to dress up.

do² (dō) *noun* the first note of the scale in the solfeggio system of music notation.

DOA *abbrev.* dead on arrival. —*noun* (*pl.* **DOAs**) a person who is declared dead on arrival at a hospital or emergency room.

doable (dōo'ə-bəl) *adj.* able to be done.

DOB *abbrev.* date of birth.

Doberman pinscher (dō'bər-mən) a large dog with a lean body and a glossy black and tan coat. *Also called* **Doberman**.

doc *noun colloq.* a medical doctor, veterinarian, or dentist.

docile (däs'əl, -īl,) *adj.* easy to manage or control; submissive. ▸ **docilely** *adv.* ▸ **docility** *noun*

dock¹ *noun* 1 a harbor where ships are loaded, unloaded, and repaired. 2 (**docks**) the area surrounding a working harbor. —*verb trans., intrans.* (**docked, docking**) 1 to bring or come into a dock. 2 *of space vehicles* to link up in space.

dock² *verb trans.* (**docked, docking**) 1 to cut off all or part of (an animal's tail). 2 to make deductions from (esp. pay); to deduct (an amount).

dock³ *noun* sorrel¹.

dock⁴ *noun* the enclosure in a court of law where the accused sits or stands. —**in the dock** under intense scrutiny or on trial.

docker *noun* a laborer who loads and unloads ships.

docket *noun* 1 *Law* a court calendar listing forthcoming cases. 2 a label or note accompanying a parcel, etc. —*verb trans.* (**docketed, docketing**) 1 *Law* to enter (a case) into a court calendar. 2 to fix a label to; to record the contents or delivery of.

dockyard *noun* a shipyard.

doctor *noun* 1 a person trained and qualified to practice medicine; a physician. 2 a person holding a doctorate. —*verb trans., intrans.* (**doctored, doctoring**) **1** to rig; repair. **2 a** to falsify (e.g., information); to tamper with; to drug (food or drink). **b** to modify: *doctored the script for mass appeal.* **3** *colloq.* **a** to give medical treatment to. **b** to practice medicine.

doctorate *noun* a high academic degree, awarded esp. for research. ▸ **doctoral** *adj.*

> *Usage* The expression *doctorate degree* is redundant and should be avoided. Use either simply *doctorate*, or *doctoral degree*.

doctrinaire (dăk,trĭ-năr′, -nĕr′) *adj.* adhering rigidly or demanding rigid adherence to theories or principles, often regardless of practicalities or appropriateness.

doctrine *noun* a belief or principle or a set of beliefs or principles, esp. as held by a religious, political, or academic, etc. group. ▸ **doctrinal** *adj.*

docudrama *noun* a play or movie based on real events and characters.

document *noun* **1** a piece of writing of an official nature, e.g., a certificate. **2** *Comput.* a text file, graphic, spreadsheet, etc produced by a computer. —*verb trans.* (**documented, documenting**) **1** to record, esp. in written form. **2** to provide written evidence to support or prove.

documentary (dăk,yə-mĕnt′ərē, -mĕn′trē) *noun* (*pl.* **documentaries**) a movie, or television or radio program presenting real people in real situations. —*adj.* **1** connected with or consisting of documents. **2** of the nature of a documentary; undramatized.

documentation *noun* documents or documentary evidence, or the provision or collection of them.

dodder *verb intrans.* (**doddered, doddering**) to walk or move in an unsteady way. ▸ **dodderer** *noun*

doddery *adj.* unsteady or trembling

dodecagon (dō-dĕk′ə-gän,) *noun* a polygon with 12 sides and 12 angles.

dodecahedron (dō-dĕk,ə-hē′drən) *noun* a polyhedron with 12 plane faces.

dodge *verb trans., intrans.* (**dodged, dodging**) **1** to avoid by moving quickly away, esp. sideways. **2** to escape or avoid, esp. by cleverness or deceit. —*noun* **1** a sudden movement aside. **2** a trick or stratagem to escape or avoid something unwanted. ▸ **dodger** *noun*

dodgy *adj.* (**dodgier, dodgiest**) *Brit. colloq.* **1** difficult or risky. **2** dishonest, or dishonestly obtained; untrustworthy. **3** slightly broken; unstable.

dodo *noun* (*pl.* **dodoes, dodos**) **1** a large extinct flightless bird. **2** *colloq.* an old-

fashioned person or thing. **3** *colloq.* a stupid person.

doe (dō) *noun* (*pl.* **doe, does**) the adult female of several mammals, e.g., deer or hare.

doer (dōo′ər) *noun* **1** a person who does something. **2** an active person; an achiever.

does (dəz′) *See* **do** (sense 1).

doesn't *contr.* does not.

doff *verb trans.* (**doffed, doffing**) **1** to take off (a piece of clothing). **2** to lift (one's hat) in greeting or in respect.

dog *noun* **1 a** a carnivorous wild mammal, e.g., a wolf, jackal, fox, etc. **b** a domesticated relation kept as a pet or worked on farms, etc. **2** a mechanical gripping device. **3** *slang* an unattractive or contemptible person. **4** *slang* a fellow: *you lucky dog.* **5** *slang* something very inferior: *His first novel was a real dog.* —*verb trans.* (**dogged, dogging**) **1** to follow very closely; to track. **2** to trouble or plague. —**go to the dogs** to degenerate: *This neighborhood's gone to the dogs.* **put on the dog** to make an ostentatious display.

dog days the hottest period of the summer. ·

doge (dōj) *noun* the chief magistrate in the former republics of Venice and Genoa.

dog-ear *verb trans., intrans.* (**dog-eared, dog-earing**) **1** to turn (a page or pages) down at the corners. **2** to fray or become frayed, esp. through use. —*noun* a turned down corner of a page or a frayed part of something.

dog-eat-dog *adj.* highly and ruthlessly competitive and aggressive.

dogfight or **dog fight** *noun* a battle at close quarters, esp. between two fighter aircraft.

dogfish *noun* (*pl.* **dogfish, dogfishes**) a small shark.

dogged (dô′gĭd) *adj.* very determined; resolute. ▸ **doggedly** *adv.* ▸ **doggedness** *noun*

doggerel (dô′gə-rəl, -grəl) *noun* **1** badly written poetry. **2** poetry with an irregular rhyming pattern for comic effect.

doggy *adj.* (**doggier, doggiest**) of, like, or relating to dogs. —**doggie** *noun* (*pl.* **doggies**) *informal* a dog.

doggy bag or **doggie bag** a bag for taking home leftovers, esp. from a restaurant.

doghouse *noun* a small house for a dog. —**in the doghouse** *slang* completely out of favor; in trouble.

dogie or **dogy** *noun* (*pl.* **dogies**) a stray or motherless calf.

dogleg *noun* a sharp bend, e.g., in a road, river, golf fairway, etc.

dogma *noun* **1** a belief or principle laid down by an authority as unquestionably true. **2** a set of such beliefs or principles.

dogmatic (dôg-măt′ĭk) *adj.* **1** forcefully and arrogantly stated as if unquestionable. **2**

tending to make such statements of opinion. ▸ **dogmatically** adv. ▸ **dogmatism** noun ▸ **dogmatist** noun

dog tag 1 a metal identification tag worn around a dog's neck. **2** slang a metal identification tag worn by a US service person.

dogtooth violet a wild plant that flowers in early spring.

dogtrot noun a gentle trotting pace.

dogwood noun a tree with with small green flowers surrounded by large attractive pink or white bracts.

doily noun (pl. **doilies**) a piece of lace or lacelike paper used as a decorative mat.

> Originally a light summer fabric, named after Doily's drapery shop in 17th-century London

do it yourself (ABBREV. **DIY**) household repairs, home decorating, etc., done without professional help. ▸ **do-it-yourself** adj.

Dolby (dŏl′bē, dôl′-) or **Dolby system** Trademark a system of noise reduction in audio recordings, broadcasting, cinema, etc.

dolce (dŏl′chä) adj., adv. Mus. an instruction to play gently or sweetly.

doldrums (dŏl′drəmz, däl′-, dôl′-) pl. noun (sing., pl.) (**the doldrums**) **1** a depressed mood; low spirits. **2** a state of inactivity. **3** (also **Doldrums**) Meteorol. regions on either side of the Equator where there tends to be little or no wind.

> The doldrums take their name from an area of the ocean about the Equator famous for calms and variable winds

dole noun **1** alms. **2** (**the dole**) Brit. colloq. benefit money for the unemployed. —verb trans. (**doled, doling**) to hand out.

doleful adj. expressing or suggesting sadness; mournful and sad. ▸ **dolefully** adv. ▸ **dolefulness** noun

doll noun **1** a toy in the form of a human being. **2** offensive a woman or girl, esp. one considered attractive. —verb trans. (**dolled, dolling**) (**doll up**) to dress (usu. oneself).

dollar noun (SYMBOL **$**) the standard unit of currency in the USA, Canada, Australia, etc., divided into 100 cents.

dollop noun colloq. a small shapeless mass of something, esp. a semi-solid food.

dolly noun (pl. **dollies**) **1** colloq. a doll. **2** a frame with wheels that a movie or television camera is mounted on for filming action scenes.

dolmen noun a simple prehistoric monument consisting of a large flat stone supported by two or more upright stones.

dolomite noun a mineral composed of calcium magnesium carbonate.

dolor noun poetic sorrow or grief.

dolorous (dŏ′lə-rəs) adj. literary causing, involving, or suggesting sorrow or grief.

dolphin noun **1** a small marine mammal related to the whale. **2** a marine game fish.

dolt noun a stupid person. ▸ **doltish** adj.

-dom suffix forming words denoting: **1** a state or rank: serfdom / dukedom. **2** an area ruled or governed: kingdom. **3** a group of people with a specified characteristic: officialdom.

domain noun **1** the scope of a subject or area of interest. **2** a territory owned or ruled by one person or government.

domestic adj. **1 a** of or relating to the home, the family, or private life. **b** liking home life. **2** of an animal kept as a pet or farm animal. **3** relating to one's country, as opposed to being foreign. —noun a household servant.

domesticate (də-měs′tĭ-kāt,) verb trans. (**domesticated, domesticating**) to train (an animal) for life in the company of people. ▸ **domestication** noun

domesticity (dŏ,měs,tĭs′ət-ē, däm,ěs,-, də-měs,-) noun home life.

dominant adj. **1** most important, evident, prevalent, or active; foremost. **2** tending or seeking to command or influence. ▸ **dominance** noun

dominate (däm′ə-nāt,) verb trans., intrans. (**dominated, dominating**) **1** to have command or influence over. **2** to be the most important, evident, prevalent, or active of (a group). ▸ **domination** noun

domineer (däm,ə-nĭr′) verb trans., intrans. (**domineered, domineering**) **1** to behave in an arrogantly dominant way. **2** to control (someone or something) forcefully or in an overbearing way.

domineering adj. overbearing.

dominion noun **1** rule; power; influence. **2** a territory or country governed by a single ruler or government; formerly, a self-governing colony within the British Empire.

Dominion Day July the first, a holiday in Canada.

domino noun (pl. **dominoes, dominos**) **1 a** one of a set of 28 rectangular tiles divided into two halves, each of which carries a number of spots, varying from none to six. **b** (**dominoes** or **dominos**) (sing., pl.) a game of skill played with these tiles. **2** a black cloak with a hood and mask attached, worn at masked balls.

domino effect a scenario where things happen as a direct result of an initial event, etc.

Don (dän) noun **1** used in Spanish as the equivalent of Mr. **2** a head of a Mafia family.

don¹ noun Brit. a university lecturer, esp. at Oxford or Cambridge.

don² verb trans. (**donned, donning**) to put on (clothing).

donate *verb trans., intrans.* (**donated, donating**) to give, esp. to charity.

donation *noun* a formal gift, usu. of money; an amount given as a gift.

done (dŭn) *adj.* **1** finished. **2** *of food* fully cooked: *The turkey is done.* **3** socially acceptable: *It's just not done.* **4** *colloq.* exhausted: *At the end of the day I'm done.* —*interj.* expressing agreement or completion of a deal.' —*verb see* **do**[1].

donjon (dŏn′jŏn, dän′-) *noun* a. heavily fortified central tower in a medieval castle.

donkey *noun* (*pl.* **donkeys**) **1** a domestic ass, used for riding, pulling equipment, and carrying loads. **2** *colloq.* a stupid or obstinate person.

donor (dō′nər) *noun* a person who donates something, e.g., money, blood, semen, living tissue, organs, etc.

don't (dōnt) *contr.* do not. —*noun colloq.* something that must not be done: *dos and don'ts.*

donut *noun same as* **doughnut**.

doodad *noun colloq.* an unnamed thing or something whose name has been forgotten.

doodle *verb intrans.* (**doodled, doodling**) to scrawl or scribble aimlessly and meaninglessly. —*noun* a meaningless scribble.

doom *noun* inescapable death, ruin, or other unpleasant fate. —*verb trans.* (**doomed, dooming**) to condemn to death or another dire fate.

doomsday *noun* the last day of the world.

door *noun* **1** a hinged or sliding barrier that allows entrance and exit, e.g., to a room, closet, vehicle, etc. **2** any means or opportunity of entry, entrance, exit, etc.

doorman *noun* a person whose job is to stand at the entrance to an apartment building, a hotel, a restaurant, nightclub, etc. and give assistance to people going in or out.

doorstep *noun* a step positioned immediately in front of a door.

doorway *noun* an entrance to a building or room, esp. the space filled by a door.

doozy *or* **doozie** *noun* (*pl.* **doozies**) *slang* something extraordinarily unusual or bizarre.

dopamine *noun* an important chemical compound whose reduction is thought to be associated with Parkinson's disease.

dope *noun* **1** *colloq.* **a** a recreational drug, esp. cannabis. **b** a drug of any kind, esp. one given to athletes or horses to affect performance. **2** *colloq.* a stupid person. **3** (**the dope**) *slang* information, esp. when confidential. —*verb trans.* (**doped, doping**) to drug, esp. dishonestly or furtively. —**dope out** *colloq.* to work out.

dopey *or* **dopy** *adj.* (**dopier, dopiest**) *colloq.* **1** sleepy or inactive, as if drugged. **2** stupid. ▸ **dopily** *adv.* ▸ **dopiness** *noun*

doppelgänger *or* **doppelganger** (dô′pəl-gĕng,ər, dăp′əl-) *noun* a person's double.

Doppler effect the change in wavelength observed when the distance between a source of waves and the observer is changing.

dork *noun slang* a person who is considered stupid, useless, or geeky.

dorm *noun colloq.* a dormitory.

dormant (dôr′mənt) *adj.* in a temporarily inactive or resting state, esp. under certain conditions: *a dormant volcano / The hedgehog is dormant in winter.* ▸ **dormancy** *noun*

dormer *noun* a window fitted vertically into an extension built out from a sloping roof. *Also called* **dormer window**.

dormitory *noun* (*pl.* **dormitories**) a building or large room that sleeps numerous people, e.g., in a boarding school, etc.

dormouse *noun* (*pl.* **dormice**) a small nocturnal rodent with rounded ears, large eyes, velvety fur, and a bushy tail.

dorsal *adj.* relating to or lying near the back, esp. of a person's, animal's, etc. body.

dory[1] *noun* (*pl.* **dories**) **1** a sea fish with long spines on the dorsal fin and a compressed body. *Also called* **John Dory**. **2** walleye (sense 2).

dory[2] *noun* (*pl.* **dories**) a small, narrow flat-bottomed fishing boat.

DOS (däs) *abbrev. Comput.* disk operating system, any of several operating systems that are loaded from a disk device when a computer system is turned on or re-booted.

dose *noun* **1** a prescribed measure of medicine, etc. **2** *colloq.* a bout, esp. of an illness or something else unpleasant: *a dose of the flu.* —*verb trans.* (**dosed, dosing**) (*usu.* **dose** (**someone**) **up with**) to give (a prescribed measure of medicine, etc.) to. ▸ **dosage** *noun*

do-si-do *noun* (*pl.* **do-si-dos**) in square dancing, a movement during which two dancers approach one another, circle back to back, and then go back to their original places.

dosimeter (dō-sĭm′ət-ər) *noun* an instrument for measuring a dose of radiation, etc.

doss *verb intrans.* (**dossed, dossing, dosses**) *Brit. slang* (*also* **doss down**) to sleep, esp. on an improvised bed.

dossier (dô′sē-ā,, däs′ē-) *noun* a file containing information on a person or subject.

dost (dəst) *verb old use* the form of *do*[1] used with *thou.*

dot *noun* **1** a small round mark; a spot; a point. **2** *Comput.* a small round punctuation mark used to separate elements in an e-mail address, as in *.com.* —*verb trans., intrans.*

(dotted, dotting) 1 to put dots or a dot on. **2** to scatter or cover with a scattering of: *a hillside dotted with houses.* —**on the dot** exactly on time.

dotage (dōt′ij) *noun* physical and mental deterioration, esp. in old age; senility.

dotard *noun* a person in his or her dotage.

dote *verb intrans.* **(doted, doting) (dote on)** to have or show a great fondness for (someone or something).

dotty *adj.* **(dottier, dottiest)** *colloq.* **1** silly; crazy. **2 (dotty about)** infatuated or obsessed with (someone or something). ▸ **dottily** *adv.* ▸ **dottiness** *noun*

double (dəb′əl) *adj.* **1** made up of two similar parts; paired; in pairs. **2** of twice the usual weight, size, etc. **3** ambiguous: *a double meaning.* —*adv.* **1** twice. **2** with one half over the other: *folded double.* —*noun* **1** a size, quantity, etc. twice the regular amount. **2** a duplicate or look-alike. **3** an actor's stand-in, used esp. in dangerous scenes. **4** a measure of alcoholic spirits twice the usual, or the single, measure. **5 (doubles)** a game, e.g., of tennis, badminton, etc., with two players on each side. —*verb trans., intrans.* **(doubled, doubling) 1** to make or become twice as large in size, number, etc. **2** to fold one half over another. **3** to have a second use. —**on** or **at the double** very quickly. ▸ **doubly** *adv.*

double-cross *verb trans.* **(double-crossed, double-crossing, double-crosses)** to cheat or deceive, esp. by deliberately doing something other than what was promised, etc. —*noun* an act of deliberate betrayal. ▸ **double-crosser** *noun*

double-decker *noun* **1** a bus with two levels. **2** *colloq.* something with two levels or layers: *a double-decker sandwich.*

double-entendre (dōōb,län-tänd′, dəb,əl-än-tän′drə) *noun* a remark with two possible meanings.

double-jointed *adj.* having extraordinarily flexible body joints.

doublet (dəb′lət) *noun* **1** a man's close-fitting jacket. **2** a pair of objects of any kind, or one of them.

double take an initial inattentive reaction followed swiftly by a sudden full realization.

doubloon (də-blōōn′) *noun* a former gold coin of Spain.

doubt (dowt) *verb trans., intrans.* **(doubted, doubting) 1** to feel uncertain, suspicious, or undecided. **2** to be inclined to disbelieve. —*noun* **1** a feeling of uncertainty, suspicion, or mistrust. **2** an inclination to disbelieve; a reservation. ▸ **doubter** *noun*

doubtful *adj.* **1** feeling doubt. **2** uncertain. **3** unlikely. ▸ **doubtfully** *adv.*

doubtless *adv.* certainly. —*adj.* certain.

douche (dōōsh) *noun* **1** a powerful jet of water that is used to clean a body part. **2** an apparatus for producing such a jet. —*verb trans., intrans.* **(douched, douching)** to apply a douche to, or treat with a douche.

doughnut or **donut** (dō′nət,, -nət) *noun* a spongy ring-shaped cake, usu. deep-fried, and often with a sweet coating.

doughty (dowt′ē) *adj.* **(doughtier, doughtiest)** brave; strong. ▸ **doughtily** *adv.* ▸ **doughtiness** *noun*

dour *adj.* **(dourer, dourest)** sullen; harshly stern.

douse or **dowse** (dows, dowz) *verb trans., intrans.* **(doused, dousing) 1** to immerse in water or throw water over. **2** to extinguish (a light or fire).

dove[1] (dəv) *noun* **1** a bird of the pigeon family, often used as a symbol of peace. **2** a person favoring peace. *See also* **hawk**[1].

dove[2] (dōv) *See* **dive**[1].

dovecote or **dovecot** (dəv′kōt,) *noun* a place where doves or domestic pigeons are kept.

dovetail (dəv′tāl,) *noun* a corner joint, esp. in wood, made by inserting v-shaped pegs into corresponding slots. *Also called* **dovetail joint.** —*verb trans., intrans.* **(dovetailed, dovetailing)** to fit or combine neatly.

dowager (dow′ə-jər) *noun* **1** an aristocrat's widow. **2** *colloq.* an elderly lady of social prominence.

dowdy *adj.* **(dowdier, dowdiest)** dull, plain, and unfashionable. ▸ **dowdily** *adv.* ▸ **dowdiness** *noun*

dowel *noun* a pin used to join two pieces of wood or stone together.

down *adv.* **1** toward or in a low or lower position, level, or state; on or to the ground. **2** from a greater to a lesser size, amount, or level. **3** toward or in a more southerly place. —*prep.* **1** at a further position on, by, or through. **2** from the top to, or toward, the bottom. —*adj.* **1** in low spirits; sad. **2** going toward or reaching a lower position. **3** reduced; lowered. **4** *of a computer, etc.* not functioning, esp. temporarily. —*verb trans.* **(downed, downing) 1** to drink quickly, esp. in one gulp. **2** to force to the ground. —*noun* **1** downward movement. **2** *Football* one of a series of four plays during which a team has to advance itself no fewer than 10 yds. in order to retain the ball.

downcast *adj.* **1** glum; dispirited. **2** *of eyes* looking downward.

downer *noun slang* **1** a state of depression. **2** a tranquilizing or depressant drug.

downfall *noun* failure or ruin, or its cause.

downgrade *verb trans.* **(downgraded, downgrading)** to downscale in rank or grade.

downhearted *adj.* dispirited, discouraged, or dismayed.

downhill *adv.* **1** down a slope, etc.: *skied downhill.* **2** to or toward a worse condition: *sales are going downhill.* —*adj.* **1** sloping down. **2** becoming worse; deteriorating. **3** of or pertaining to the sport of skiing down a mountain: *a downhill race.*

downlink *verb trans.* (**downlinked, downlinking**) to transmit (signals) from a satellite to an earthbound receiver and back.

download *verb trans.* (**downloaded, downloading**) *Comput.* to get or transfer (data, a program, etc.) from one source to another: *downloaded the software from the Internet.*

down-market *adj.* cheap, of poor quality, or lacking prestige.

down payment an initial payment for something to be paid off by installments.

downplay *verb trans.* (**downplayed, downplaying**) to minimize the importance of.

downpour *noun* a very heavy fall of rain.

downright *adj.* devoid of any qualification. —*adv.* with no qualification; utterly.

downscale *verb trans., intrans.* (**downscaled, downscaling**) to reduce the size of (a company, its output, work force, etc.).

downshift *verb trans., intrans.* (**downshifted, downshifting**) to put (a vehicle's) gear) into a lower range.

downside *noun* **1** the lower or under side. **2** *colloq.* a negative aspect; a disadvantage.

downsize *verb trans.* (**downsized, downsizing**) to reduce (something, e.g. a company's work force) in size.

Down's syndrome *same as* **Down syndrome.**

downstage *adj., adv.* at or toward the front of a theater stage.

downstairs *adv.* to or toward a lower floor; down the stairs. —*adj.* on a lower or ground floor. —*noun* a lower or ground floor.

Down syndrome a congenital disorder giving rise to slowness in mental and physical development, rather flattened facial features and skull shape, and slightly slanted eyes. *Also called* **trisomy 21.**

Usage The former name for this condition, *mongolism,* is now considered offensive and should be avoided.

downtime *noun* the length of time something, esp. a computer, is not working.

down-to-earth *adj.* **1** sensible and practical. **2** devoid of all pretensions. **3** plain-speaking.

downtown *adj., adv.* in or relating to the lower or business part of a city. —*noun* the lower or business part of a city.

downtrodden *adj.* oppressed.

downturn *noun* a decline, esp. in economic activity.

downward *adv.* (**downwards**) **1** to or toward a lower position or level. **2** from a prior source or from an earlier period. —*adj.* leading or moving down. ▸ **downwardly** *adv.*

downwind *adv.* in or toward the direction in which the wind is blowing; with the wind from behind.

dowry *noun* (*pl.* **dowries**) money, goods, etc. that a woman brings to a marriage.

dowse[1] (dowz) *verb intrans.* (**dowsed, dowsing**) to search for underground water with a divining rod. ▸ **dowser** *noun*

dowse[2] *verb same as* **douse.**

doxology (dăk-săl'ə-jē) *noun* (*pl.* **doxologies**) a hymn, etc. praising God.

doyen (doi'ĕn,, -ən) *noun* the most senior and most respected male member of a group or profession.

doyenne (doi-ĕn') *noun* the most senior and most respected female member of a group or profession.

doze *verb intrans.* (**dozed, dozing**) to sleep lightly. —*noun* a brief period of light sleep.

dozy *adj.* (**dozier, doziest**) **1** sleepy. **2** *colloq.* slow to understand; not alert; stupid. ▸ **dozily** *adv.* ▸ **doziness** *noun*

drab *adj.* (**drabber, drabbest**) **1** dull; dreary. **2** of a dull greenish-brown color. ▸ **drably** *adv.* ▸ **drabness** *noun*

drachma (drăk'mə) *noun* (*pl.* **drachmas, drachmae**) the standard unit of currency in Greece.

draft *noun* **1** a current of air, esp. indoors. **2** a quantity of liquid swallowed at one gulp. **3** a written plan; a preliminary sketch. **4** a written order requesting a bank to pay out money, esp. to another bank. **5** (**the draft**) conscription into the armed forces. —*verb trans.* (**drafted, drafting**) **1** to set out in preliminary sketchy form. **2** to select and send off (personnel) to perform a specific task. **3** to conscript. —*adj.* **1** used for pulling heavy loads: *draft horses.* **2** *of beer* drawn from a keg, as opposed to being bottled. *Also* **draught.**

draft dodger *colloq.* a person who avoids conscription into the armed forces.

drafter *noun* someone who drafts the designs, plans, etc., for structures, machines, and other things. *Also* **draughtsman** and **draughtswoman.**

drafts *or* **draughts** *noun* (*sing.*) *Brit.* the game of checkers.

drafty *adj.* (**draftier, draftiest**) prone to or suffering drafts of air.

drag *verb trans., intrans.* (**dragged, dragging**) **1** to pull roughly, violently, or with force. **2** (*also* **drag along**) to move or cause to move slowly, heavily, reluctantly, etc. **3** to make an underwater search (of a lake; etc.). —*noun* **1** an act of dragging; a dragging effect. **2** *colloq.* a draw on a cigarette, etc. **3** *colloq.* a dull or tedious person or thing. **4** *colloq.* clothes of one gender worn by someone of the opposite sex, esp. women's clothes worn by a man. **5** *colloq.* a street. **6** the resistance that a moving object traveling through a liquid or gas is subjected to. —**in drag** wearing the clothing of the opposite sex.

dragnet *noun* **1** a system of highly coordinated forces and methods for apprehending a criminal or suspect at large. **2** a heavy net pulled along the bottom of a river, lake, etc., in a search for something.

dragonfly *noun* (*pl.* **dragonflies**) an insect with a long slender body and gauzy wings.

dragoon (drə-gōōn') *noun Hist.* a heavily armed mounted soldier. —*verb trans,* (**dragooned, dragooning**) to force or bully (someone) into doing something.

drag strip a short, straight, paved course for drag racing.

drain *verb trans., intrans.* (**drained, draining**) **1** to cause or allow (liquid) to escape. **2** to remove liquid from (something). **3** to disappear or flow away or cause to disappear or flow away. **4** to drink the contents of (a glass, etc.). —*noun* **1** a device, esp. a pipe, for carrying away liquid. **2** something that exhausts or seriously depletes (someone or something).

drainage (drā'nĭj) *noun* a process, method, or system of draining.

drake *noun* a male duck.

dram *noun* **1** *colloq.* a small amount of alcoholic spirits, esp. whiskey. **2 a** a measure of weight equal to $\frac{1}{16}$ oz. **b** $\frac{1}{8}$ of a fluid ounce.

drama (dräm'ə, drăm'ə) *noun* **1 a** a work performed by actors; a play. **b** plays as a literary genre. **2** excitement and emotion; an exciting situation: *high political drama.*

dramatic *adj.* **1** of or relating to plays, the theater, or acting in general. **2** exciting. **3** sudden and striking; drastic. **4** *of behavior, etc.* flamboyantly emotional. ► **dramatically** *adv.*

dramatics *noun* (*sing., pl.*) **1** the activity associated with the staging and performing of plays. **2** exaggeratedly emotional behavior.

dramatis personae (drăm,ət-ĭs-pər-sō'nē, drăm,-, -nī,) a list of the characters in a play.

dramatist *noun* a writer of plays.

dramatize *verb trans.* (**dramatized, dramatizing**) **1** to make into a work for public performance. **2** to treat as or cause to seem more exciting or important than is actually the case. ► **dramatization** *noun*

drank *See* **drink**.

drape *verb trans., intrans.* (**draped, draping**) **1** to hang (cloth, one's body, etc.) loosely over (something): *draped herself over the sofa.* **2**

to hang loosely. —*noun* **1** a window curtain. **2** material, e.g., of disposable quality, for use in covering a patient during an operation or a medical examination.

drapery *noun* (*pl.* **draperies**) **1** fabric; textiles. **2** (*often* **draperies**) curtains and other hanging fabrics. ► **draper** *noun*

drastic *adj.* extreme; severe. ► **drastically** *adv.*

draught *and* **draughts** (drăfts) *noun; verb Brit. same as* **draft** *and* **drafts.**

draw *verb trans., intrans.* (pa t **drew**; pa p **drawn**; pr p **drawing**) **1** to make a picture of (something or someone), esp. with a pencil. **2** to pull out, take out, or extract. **3** to move or proceed: *drew nearer.* **4** (**draw on**) to make use of (something or someone). **5** to open or close (curtains). **6** to attract (e.g., attention, criticism, etc.). **7** to end (a game) with neither side winning; to finish on equal terms with an opponent. **8** to choose or be given as the result of random selection. **9** to take (cards or a card) from a stack or a dealer. **10** to arrive at (a conclusion, etc.). **11 a** to suck air, e.g., through a cigarette, etc. **b** *of a chimney* to cause air to flow through a fire, allowing burning. **12** to disembowel: *hanged, drawn, and quartered.* —*noun* **1** a result in which neither side is the winner; a tie. **2** an act or the process of making of a random selection, e.g., of the winners of a competition; a competition with winners chosen at random. **3** the potential to attract many people, or a person or thing having this potential. **4** the act of drawing a gun. —**draw back** to retreat, cower, or flinch.

drawback *noun* a disadvantage.

drawbridge *noun* a bridge that can be lifted or swung aside to allow access beneath, or to prevent passage across.

drawer (drôr, drô'ər) *noun* **1** (drôr) a person who draws. •**2** (drô'ər) a sliding lidless storage box fitted as part of a piece of furniture. **3** (**drawers**) underpants, knickers, or panties.

drawing *noun* a picture made up of lines, esp. one drawn in pencil.

drawing board a board that paper is attached to for drafting or drawing, e.g., a design. —**go back to the drawing board** to return to the planning stages, esp. to devise a more successful approach.

drawing room a formal reception or sitting room where guests are entertained.

drawl *verb trans., intrans.* (**drawled, drawling**) to speak in a slow, manner, esp. with prolonged vowel sounds. —*noun* a drawling accent or way of speaking.

drawn *adj.* showing signs of mental strain or tiredness. —*verb see* **draw**.

-drawn *combining form* forming words meaning pulled by: *horse-drawn*.

drawn-out *adj.* tedious; prolonged.

dray *noun* a low horse-drawn cart used for heavy loads.

dread (drĕd) *noun* great fear or apprehension. —*verb trans.* (**dreaded, dreading**) to look ahead to (something) with dread. —*adj.* inspiring awe or great fear.

dreaded *adj.* 1 greatly feared. 2 *loosely* much disliked.

dreadful *adj.* 1 inspiring great fear; terrible. 2 very bad, unpleasant, or extreme. ▸ **dreadfully** *adv.*

dreadlocks *pl. noun* thin braids of hair tied tightly all over the head, worn esp. by Rastafarians.

dream *noun* 1 images or ideas that are experienced during sleep. 2 a completely engrossed state. 3 a distant ambition, esp. unattainable. 4 *colloq.* an extremely pleasing person or thing. —*adj.* ideal: *my dream house.* —*verb trans., intrans.* (pa t and pa p **dreamed** or **dreamt**; pr p **dreaming**) 1 to experience images or ideas during sleep. 2 (*usu.* **dream of**) to have a distant ambition, hope, etc. 3 to be lost in thought. —**dream up** to devise or invent (something) unusual or absurd. **like a dream** *colloq.* extremely well, easily, or successfully.

dreamer *noun* a person who dreams, esp. of unrealistic schemes.

dreamy *adj.* (**dreamier, dreamiest**) 1 unreal, as in a dream. 2 having a wandering mind or exhibiting symptoms of it. 3 *colloq.* lovely. ▸ **dreamily** *adv.* ▸ **dreaminess** *noun*

dreary *adj.* (**drearier, dreariest**) 1 gloomy and depressing. 2 dull, boring, or uninteresting. ▸ **drearily** *adv.* ▸ **dreariness** *noun*

dredge¹ *verb trans., intrans.* (**dredged, dredging**) to clear the bottom of or deepen (a river, etc.) by bringing up mud and waste. —*noun* a machine for dredging.

dredge² *verb trans.* (**dredged, dredging**) to sprinkle (food), e.g., with sugar or flour.

dregs *pl. noun* 1 solid particles in a liquid that settle to the bottom. 2 worthless or contemptible elements.

drench *verb trans.* (**drenched, drenching**) to wet thoroughly.

dress *verb trans., intrans.* (**dressed, dressing**) 1 to put clothes on; to wear or cause (someone) to wear clothes (of a certain kind). 2 to treat and bandage (wounds). —*noun* 1 a woman's garment with top and skirt in one piece. 2 clothing: *evening dress.* —*adj.* for wearing in the evenings or formal occasions: *a dress jacket.* —**dress down** to scold (someone) harshly, usu. in public. **dress up** 1 to put on fancy dress. 2 to put

on smart clothes or cause (someone) to put on smart clothes.

dressage (drĕ-säzh´, drə-) *noun* the training of a horse to do set maneuvers or an example of a horse showing these maneuvers.

dress circle the first balcony in a theater, etc.

dress code a group of regulations, e.g., at a school, that indicates the nature of approved or disapproved attire.

dress-down day a day of the week, often Friday, when office workers and management wear casual clothes to work.

dresser *noun* 1 a low chest of drawers, often with a mirror. 2 a freestanding kitchen cupboard with shelves above, for storing and displaying dishes, etc. 3 a theater assistant employed to help actors with their costumes. 4 a person who dresses in a particular way: *a flashy dresser.*

dressing *noun* 1 a sauce added, esp. to salad. 2 a covering for a wound. 3 a stuffing for poultry or fish.

dressing-down *noun* a harsh, sometimes public, reprimand.

dressing gown a loose robe worn informally indoors, esp. over nightclothes.

dressing table a piece of bedroom furniture typically with drawers and a large mirror.

dressmaker *noun* a person who makes or alters women's clothes. ▸ **dressmaking** *noun*

dress rehearsal a last rehearsal of a play, opera, etc. with full costumes, lighting and other effects.

dressy *adj.* (**dressier, dressiest**) 1 dressing stylishly. 2 *of clothes* for formal wear; elegant. ▸ **dressily** *adv.* ▸ **dressiness** *noun*

drew *see* draw.

dribble *verb intrans., trans.* (**dribbled, dribbling**) 1 to fall or flow, or let (something) fall or flow, in drops. 2 to drool. 3 *Sport* to move along keeping (a ball, esp. a basketball or soccer ball) in close control. —*noun* 1 a small quantity of liquid, esp. saliva. 2 *Sport* an act of dribbling a ball.

dribs and drabs very small quantities at a time.

drier or **dryer** *noun* a device or substance that dries hair, laundry, paint, etc.

drift *noun* 1 a general movement or tendency to move. 2 the direction in which something moves. 3 a water current. 4 a general or essential meaning: *the drift of a conversation.* —*verb intrans.* (**drifted, drifting**) 1 to float or be blown along or into heaps. 2 to move aimlessly from one place or job to another. 3 to move off course.

drifter *noun* a person who moves from place to place, or job to job.

drift net a large fishing-net allowed to drift with the tide.

driftwood *noun* wood floating near or washed up on a shore.

drill¹ *noun* **1** a tool for boring holes in metal, wood, teeth, etc. **2** a training exercise or session. **3** *colloq.* correct procedure; routine. —*verb trans. intrans.* (**drilled, drilling**) **1** to make (a hole) with a drill; to make a hole in (something) with a drill. **2** to exercise or teach through repeated practice.

drill² *noun* thick strong cotton cloth used for work clothes.

drill³ *noun* **1** a shallow furrow where seeds are sown; the seeds so sown. **2** a machine for sowing seeds in rows. —*verb trans.* (**drilled, drilling**) to sow in rows.

drink *verb trans., intrans.* (*pa t* **drank**; *pa p* **drunk**; *pr p* **drinking**) **1** to swallow (a liquid); to consume (a liquid) by swallowing. **2 a** to consume alcohol. **b** to consume alcohol habitually. **c** (**drink to**) to toast (someone or something): *Let's drink to the happy couple.* —*noun* **1** an act of drinking; a liquid suitable for drinking. **2** alcohol of any kind. **3** a glass or amount of something to drink. **4** (**the drink**) *colloq.* the sea. ▸ **drinkable** *adj.* ▸ **drinker** *noun*

drip *verb trans., intrans.* (**dripped, dripping**) to release or fall, or cause a liquid to be released or to fall, in drops. —*noun* **1** an act or noise of dripping. **2** *colloq.* a person who is regarded as unattractive or boring.

drive *verb trans., intrans.* (*pa t* **drove**; *pa p* **driven**; *pr p* **driving**) **1** to be at the controls of (a vehicle). **2** to travel in a vehicle. **3** to take or transport in a vehicle. **4** to urge or force to move: *drive cattle.* **5** to produce motion in; to cause to function: *steam drives this engine.* **6** to make (someone or something) give in to pressure. **7** to conduct or dictate: *drove a hard bargain.* **8** to hit a golf ball from the tee. —*noun* **1** a trip in a vehicle; travel by road. **2** a driveway. **3** energy and enthusiasm. **4** an organized campaign; a group effort. **5** operating power, or a device supplying it. **6** a process of rounding up and a moving cattle, e.g., to take them to market or to a new pasture. **7** *See* **disc drive**. **8** a golf shot where the ball is hit from the tee. —**drive at** to intend or imply as a meaning or conclusion.

drive-by *adj. slang* carried out from a moving vehicle: *drive-by shootings.*

drive-in *noun* a facility that provides service for customers remaining seated in their vehicles. ▸ **drive-in** *adj.*

drivel (drĭv'əl) *noun* nonsense. —*verb intrans.* (**drivel** *or* **drivelled, driveling** *or* **drivelling**) **1** to talk nonsense. **2** to slaver.

driver *noun* **1** a person who drives a vehicle. **2** *Golf* a large-headed club for hitting long shots from the tee.

driver's seat *colloq.* a position of authority and control.

driveway *noun* a private stretch of road, esp. leading from a residence or garage to the public street.

driving *noun* the act, practice, or way of driving vehicles. —*adj.* **1** producing or transmitting operating power. **2** heavy and windblown: *a driving rain.* **3** very determined or energetic: *a driving ambition.*

drizzle *noun* fine, light rain. —*verb intrans.* (**drizzled, drizzling**) to rain lightly.

droll (drōl) *adj.* oddly amusing or comical. ▸ **drollery** *noun* ▸ **drolly** *adv.*

dromedary (dräm'ə-dĕr,ē, drŭm'-) *noun* (*pl.* **dromedaries**) a single-humped camel.

drone *verb intrans.* (**droned, droning**) **1** to make a low humming noise. **2** (**drone on**) to talk at length in a tedious, monotonous voice. —*noun* **1** a deep humming sound. **2** a male honeybee. *See also* **worker** (sense 4). **3** a lazy person, esp. one living off others.

drool *verb intrans.* (**drooled, drooling**) **1** to dribble or slaver. **2** (**drool over**) to show uncontrolled admiration for (something).

droop *verb intrans.* (**drooped, drooping**) **1** to hang loosely; to sag. **2** to be weak with fatigue or dejectedness. ▸ **droopy** *adj.*

drop *verb trans. intrans.* (**dropped, dropping**) **1** to go or move, or cause someone or something to go or move, from a higher to a lower place or position. **2** to decline or cause to decline. **3** to lower or weaken, or cause something, to lower or weaken. **4** to give up or abandon (someone or something). **5** (*usu.* **drop off**) to deliver (someone or something) from a vehicle or at a destination. **6** to leave or take out: *dropped me from the team.* **7** *of an animal* to give birth to. —*noun* **1** a small round or pear-shaped mass of liquid, esp. one falling. **2** a small amount of something, esp. a liquid. **3** a descent, decrease, decline, or fall. **4** a vertical distance. —**drop in** *or* **by** to pay a brief unexpected visit. **drop off** *colloq.* to fall asleep. **drop out 1** to withdraw from an activity. **2** *colloq.* to adopt an unconventional lifestyle.

drop-dead *slang adj.* spectacularly impressive. —*adj.* extremely: *drop-dead gorgeous.*

droplet *noun* a tiny drop of liquid.

dropout *noun* **1** a student who quits before completing a course of study. **2** a person who adopts an unconventional lifestyle.

dropper *noun* a tube with a flexible bulb on one end, used for applying liquid in drops.

droppings *pl. noun* animal feces.

dropsy *noun* used formerly for *edema*, an abnormal accumulation of fluid in the body tissues. ▸ **dropsical** *adj.*

dross (drôs, dräs) *noun* **1** waste, e.g., from coal. **2** scum that forms on molten metal. **3** any worthless substance; rubbish.

drought (drowt) *noun* a prolonged lack of rainfall.

drove¹ *See* **drive.**

drove² *noun* **1** a moving herd of animals, esp. cattle. **2** a large number, esp. a moving crowd: *tourists arriving in droves.*

drover *noun* a person who drives sheep or cattle.

drown *verb intrans., trans.* (**drowned, drowning**) **1** to die, or kill a person, by the inhalation of liquid, esp. water, into the lungs. **2** to apply an excessive amount of liquid to; to soak or flood: *drowned the gin with too much tonic.* **3** (**drown out**) to suppress the effect of (one sound) with a louder one.

drowse *verb intrans.* (**drowsed, drowsing**) to sleep lightly for a short while; to be in a pleasantly sleepy state.

drowsy *adj.* (**drowsier, drowsiest**) **1** causing sleepiness; sleepy. **2** lethargic. **3** quiet and peaceful. ▸ **drowsily** *adv.* ▸ **drowsiness** *noun*

drub *verb trans., intrans.* (**drubbed, drubbing**) **1** to defeat severely. **2** to thump, stamp, or throb.

drubbing *noun* a complete defeat; a beating.

drudge *verb intrans.* (**drudged, drudging**) to do hard, tedious, or menial work. —*noun* a person engaged such work.

drudgery *noun* hard, tedious, or menial work.

drug *noun* **1** a chemical substance taken into the body or applied externally to alleviate or cure something. **2** a narcotic or other substance taken recreationally. —*verb trans.* (**drugged, drugging**) **1** to administer a drug or drugs to. **2** to poison or stupefy with a drug or drugs. **3** to put a drug or drugs into (a drink, food, etc).

druggist *noun* a pharmacist.

drugstore *noun* a shop that fills prescriptions and sells sundries.

drum *noun* **1** a percussion instrument consisting of a hollow frame with a membrane stretched across it which is struck with sticks or the hands to produce a sound. **2** a cylindrical container: *an oil drum.* **3** an eardrum. **4** a bony fish. —*verb intrans., trans.* (**drummed, drumming**) **1** to beat a drum. **2** to make continuous tapping sound: *drummed his fingers on the desk.* —**drum in** *or* **into** to force (something) into the mind of another through constant repetition. **drum up** to achieve or attract (something) by energetic persuasion: *drum up support for a cause.* ▸ **drummer** *noun*

drum machine a piece of equipment, esp. a programmable electronic device, that produces the sound of percussion instruments.

drum major the male leader of a marching band, esp. a military one.

drum majorette the female leader of a marching band, or one of a group of baton twirlers.

drumstick *noun* **1** a stick used for beating a drum. **2** the lower leg of a cooked fowl.

drunk *verb see* **drink.** —*adj.* **1** intoxicated. **2** (**drunk with**) intoxicated or obsessed with (something): *drunk with power.* —*noun* an intoxicated person.

drunkard *noun* a person who is often drunk.

drunken *adj.* **1** intoxicated through consuming alcohol. **2** relating to, or brought on by, alcoholic intoxication. ▸ **drunkenness** *noun*

drupe *noun* a fruit, e.g., a plum, cherry, peach, etc, containing a stone.

dry *adj.* (**drier** *or* **dryer, driest** *or* **dryest**) **1** containing, experiencing, or having been freed from moisture or wetness. **2** thirsty; parched. **3** *of wine, etc.* not sweet. **4** *of humor* expressed in a quietly sarcastic or matter-of-fact way. **5** forbidding the sale and consumption of alcohol. **6** dull; uninteresting. —*verb trans., intrans.* (**dried, drying, dries**) **1** to make or become dry. **2** to preserve (food) by removing all moisture. —*noun* (*pl.* **drys**) *old colloq.* use a prohibitionist. —**dry out 1** to make or become completely dry. **2** *colloq.* to receive treatment to cure addiction to alcohol; to have one's addiction cured. **dry up 1** to run out of a supply; to become depleted. **2** *slang* to shut up or be quiet. ▸ **dryly** *or* **drily** *adv.* ▸ **dryness** *noun*

dryad *noun Greek Mythol.* a woodland nymph.

dry cell a battery containing a moist paste, e.g., ammonium chloride, instead of a liquid.

dry-clean *verb trans.* (**dry-cleaned, dry-cleaning**) to clean (esp. clothes) with liquid chemicals. ▸ **dry cleaner** *noun*

dry dock a dock which can be pumped dry to allow work on a ship's lower parts.

dryer *noun same as* **drier.**

dry ice solid carbon dioxide used as a refrigerating agent.

dry rot 1 timber decay caused by a fungus. **2** a fungal disease of plants.

dry run a rehearsal or practice.

dual (dōō′əl, dyōō′-) *adj.* **1** consisting of or representing two separate parts. **2** double. ▸ **duality** *noun*

dub¹ *verb trans.* (**dubbed, dubbing**) to give a name, e.g., a nickname, to.

dub² *verb trans.* (**dubbed, dubbing**) **1** to add a new soundtrack to (e.g., a movie), esp. one in a different language. **2** to add sound effects or music to (e.g., a movie). —*noun* a form of modern music that involves remixing original tracks, esp. reggae ones, to give prominence to instrumental parts.

dubbin *noun* a mixture of oil and tallow for softening and waterproofing leather.

dubious *adj.* **1** feeling doubt; unsure or uncertain. **2** arousing suspicion; potentially dishonest or dishonestly obtained. ► **dubiety** *noun* ► **dubiously** *adv.*

ducal (dōō'kəl, dyōō'-) *adj.* relating to a duke or to a dukedom.

duchess *noun* **1** the wife or widow of a duke. **2** a woman who holds the rank of duke.

duchy *noun* (*pl.* **duchies**) the territory owned or ruled by a duke or duchess.

duck¹ *noun* **1 a** a wild or domesticated water bird with webbed feet. **b** the female of such a water bird. **2** the flesh of this water bird used as food. **3** *colloq.* used as a term of endearment or of address for a likable person.

duck² *verb intrans. trans.* (**ducked, ducking**) **1** to lower the head or body suddenly, e.g., to avoid someone or something. **2** to push or go briefly under water. **3** *colloq.* (**duck out of**) to avoid (something unpleasant or unwelcome).

duck-billed platypus a platypus.

duckling *noun* a young duck.

duckpins *noun* (*sing.*) a bowling game using pins that are shorter than tenpins and a smaller ball.

ducky *colloq. adj.* (**duckier, duckiest**) attractive or pleasing; excellent. —*noun* used as a term of endearment to someone liked.

duct *noun* **1** a tube in the body. **2** a casing or shaft in a building for pipes, electrical cables, ventilation, air conditioning, etc.

ductile (dək'təl, -tīl,) *adj.* **1** of copper, *etc.* capable of being drawn out into a thin wire or thread. **2** easily influenced by others. ► **ductility** *noun*

dud *colloq. noun* **1** something counterfeit or that fails to function properly. **2** a bomb or other projectile that fails to go off. **3** (**duds**) clothes. —*adj.* **1** useless. **2** counterfeit.

dude *noun slang* **1** a man, esp. a city man or an Easterner who lives in a city, but vacations on a Western ranch. **2** a man preoccupied with dressing smartly. **3** a person: *a cool dude*.

dude ranch a Western-style resort patterned on a working ranch that offers paying guests trail rides and other outdoor activities.

dudgeon *noun* an indignant or angry mood. —**in high dudgeon** very angry, resentful, or indignant.

due (dōō, dyōō) *adj.* **1** payable at once; owed or owing. **2** expected according to a timetable or prearrangement. **3** proper: *due respect*. —*noun* **1** something owed, required, or expected. **2** (**dues**) a fee for membership. —*adv.* in a direct, unwavering line or course: *due north*. —**due to** caused by or because of (someone or something). **give (someone) his** *or* **her due** to acknowledge (a person's) qualities or achievements, esp. when other aspects may be unsatisfactory or lacking.

duel (dōō'əl) *noun* a prearranged fight to the death between two people, to settle a matter of honor. —*verb intrans.* (**dueled** *or* **duelled, dueling** *or* **duelling**) to fight a duel. ► **duelist** *noun*

duet (dōō-ĕt', dyōō-) *noun* **1** music for two singers or players. **2** a pair of musical performers.

duffel *or* **duffle** *noun* a thick, coarse, woolen fabric.

> After *Duffel,* a town in Belgium where the fabric was first made

duffel bag a cylindrical canvas shoulder bag with a drawstring fastening.

duffel coat a heavy, esp. hooded, coat made of duffel, typically with toggle fastenings.

duffer *noun colloq.* a clumsy or incompetent person.

dug¹ *See* **dig.**

dug² *noun* an animal's udder or nipple.

dugong (dōō'gông, -gäng,) *noun* a whale-like plant-eating tropical sea mammal.

dugout *noun* **1** a canoe made from a hollowed-out log. **2** a shelter dug into a slope or bank, or in a trench. **3 a** *Sport* a shelter at the side of a pitch where the trainer, substitutes, etc. sit during a match. **b** *Baseball* either of two sunken shelters set to the sides of the field, used by players when they are off the field.

duke *noun* **1** *Brit.* **a** (**Duke**) a hereditary title ranking immediately below that of prince. **b** a nobleman who has such a title. **2** a ruler of a small state or principality. **3** (*often* **dukes**) *slang* a fist: *He put up his dukes and prepared to fight.* ► **dukedom** *noun*

dulcet (dəl'sət) *adj. literary,* of sounds sweet and pleasing to the ear.

dulcimer (dəl'sĭ-mər) *noun* a musical instrument consisting of a box with tuned strings stretched across, struck with small hammers.

dull *adj.* **1** lacking brightness or clearness. **2** deep and low; muffled: *a dull thud.* **3** cloudy; overcast: *dull skies.* **4** lacking a sharp edge; blunt. **5** slow to learn or understand; stupid. **6** lacking liveliness; uninteresting. **7** not keenly felt: *a dull pain.* —*verb trans., intrans.* (**dulled, dulling**) to make or become dull. ► **dully** *adv.* ► **dullness** *noun*

dullard *noun* a stupid person.

dulse *noun* a red seaweed having large, tough, edible fronds.

duly *adv.* **1** in the proper way. **2** at the proper or expected time.

dumb *adj.* **1** *offensive* not having the power of speech. **2** silent. **3** *colloq.* foolish; unintelligent. **4** *Comput.* having no data-processing capability: *dumb terminals.* ▸ **dumbly** *adv.* ▸ **dumbness** *noun*

> *Usage* The third sense of this word has so overwhelmed the original meaning that it is now preferable to use *speech-impaired* when referring to someone who does not have the power of speech.

dumbbell *noun* **1** a weight, consisting of a metal bar with heavy disks on each end, used in muscle-developing exercises. **2** *slang* a stupid person.

dumbfound *or* **dumfound** *verb trans.* (**dumbfounded, dumbfounding**) to astonish or confound.

dumbwaiter *noun* a small elevator for transporting laundry, dirty dishes, etc. between floors, esp. in a hotel, etc.

dummy *noun* (*pl.* **dummies**) **1** a model of the human body, used for displaying clothes, by a ventriloquist, etc.. **2** *Football* a heavy cylindrical bag used in tackling and blocking practice. **3** a realistic copy of something. **4** *slang* a stupid person. **5** *Cards* a partner in bridge whose hand of cards is exposed. **6** the hand of cards so exposed. —*adj.* false, sham, or counterfeit.

dump *verb trans., intrans.* (**dumped, dumping**) **1** to put down heavily or carelessly. **2** to dispose of trash and garbage. **3** *slang* to spurn or reject (esp. a friend or romantic or sexual partner). **4** a *Stock Exchange* to put (shares of stock) up for sale in large quantities. **b** *Econ.* to sell (goods) abroad very cheaply and in quantity to keep domestic prices high. **5** *Comput.* to copy and transfer (stored data) to another location, usu. as a safeguard against its loss. —*noun* **1** a place where trash or garbage may be deposited. **2** a military store, e.g., of weapons. **3** *Comput.* an act or the process of copying and transferring data from one location to another. **4** *slang* a dirty or dilapidated place or residence.

dumpling *noun* a boiled ball of dough.

dumps *pl. noun* low spirits. —**down in the dumps** in low spirits; depressed.

Dumpster *(dəmp'stər) trademark* used to denote a container where trash and garbage are deposited.

dumpy *adj.* (**dumpier, dumpiest**) short and plump.

dun¹ *noun* a dark grayish brown color.

dun² *verb trans.* (**dunned, dunning**) to press (a debtor) persistently for payment. —*noun* a demand for payment.

dunce *noun* a stupid person; a slow learner.

> Originally a term of abuse applied to followers of the medieval Scottish philosopher, John *Duns Scotus*

dunderhead *noun* a stupid person.

dune *noun* a ridge or hill formed by the accumulation of windblown sand.

dune buggy a recreational four-wheeled motor vehicle often on an open chassis and having fat tires for use on beaches. *Also called* **beach buggy.**

dung *noun* animal excrement.

dungarees *pl. noun* pants or overalls made of denim, worn casually or for working.

dungeon *(dən'jən) noun* a prison cell, esp. underground.

dunk *verb trans.* (**dunked, dunking**) **1** to submerge. **2** to dip (food) into a liquid prior to eating it.

duo *(dōō'ō, dyōō'ō) noun* (*pl.* **duos**) a pair, esp. of performers.

duodecimal *adj.* relating to the number 12, or multiples of it.

duodenum *(dōō-ād'n-əm, dyōō-) noun* (*pl.* **duodena, duodenums**) the first part of the small intestine. ▸ **duodenal** *adj.*

dupe *verb trans.* (**duped, duping**) to trick or deceive. —*noun* a person who is deceived.

duple *adj.* double; twofold.

duplex *noun* an apartment divided into two living units or on two floors. —*adj.* **1** double; twofold. **2** *Electron., Comput.* allowing communication and transmission of signals in both directions simultaneously.

duplicate *adj. (dōō'pli-kət, dyōō')* identical to another. —*noun* **1** an exact copy. **2** another of the same kind; a spare. —*verb trans. (dōō'pli-kāt, dyōō'-)* (**duplicated, duplicating**) **1** to make or be an exact copy or copies of. **2** to repeat. —**in duplicate** in the form of two exact copies. ▸ **duplicator** *noun* ▸ **duplication** *noun*

duplicity *noun* deception; trickery; double-dealing. ▸ **duplicitous** *adj.*

durable *adj.* lasting a long time; enduring. —*noun* something expected to last a long time. ▸ **durability** *noun* ▸ **durably** *adv.*

duration *noun* the length of time that something lasts or continues.

duress *(də-rĕs', dyə-) noun* the influence of force or threats; coercion.

during *prep.* **1** throughout the time of. **2** in the course of.

dusk *noun* the period of semi-darkness before night; twilight.

dusky *adj.* (**duskier, duskiest**) **1** deficient in or without light or brightness. **2** dark-colored. ▸ **duskiness** *noun*

dust *noun* **1** earth, sand, or household dirt in the form of a fine powder. **2** a substance in

powder form. —*verb trans., intrans.*
(**dusted, dusting**) **1** to remove dust from
(furniture, etc.). **2** to sprinkle with a substance in powdered form.

duster *noun* **1** a cloth for removing household
dust. **2** a work smock to protect the wearer's
clothing underneath.

dust jacket a loose protective paper cover on a
book, carrying the title and other information. *Also called* **dust cover.**

dustpan *noun* a handled container for
collecting swept-up dust.

dusty *adj.* (**dustier, dustiest**) **1** covered with
or containing dust. **2** of a color dull: *dusty
rose.* **3** old-fashioned; dated. **4** lacking
liveliness; flat. ▸ **dustily** *adv.*

Dutch *noun* **1** the official language of the
Netherlands. *See also* **Afrikaans.** **2** (**the
Dutch**) (*pl.*) the people of the Netherlands.
—*adj.* of the Netherlands, its people, or
their language. —**go Dutch** *colloq.* to pay
one's own share of expenses, esp. for a
restaurant meal, etc. **in Dutch** in trouble.

Dutch auction an auction at which the price is
gradually lowered until someone agrees to
buy.

Dutch courage artificial courage gained by
drinking alcohol.

duteous (dōōt'ē-əs, dyōōt'-) *adj. literary*
dutiful.

dutiable *adj.*, *of goods* subject to import
duties.

dutiful *adj.* having or showing a sense of duty.
▸ **dutifully** *adv.* ▸ **dutifulness** *noun*

duty *noun* (*pl.* **duties**) **1** something one is or
feels obliged to do; a moral or legal
responsibility, or an awareness of it. **2** a task
to be performed, esp. in connection with a
job. **3** a tax on goods, esp. on imports.

duty bound obliged by a sense of duty.

duty-free *adj.*, *of goods, esp. imports* not
subject to tax.

duvet (dōō-vā', dyōō-) *noun* a thick quilt.

dwarf *noun* (*pl.* **dwarfs, dwarves**) **1** a
person, animal, plant, etc. that is smaller
than average. **2** a mythical humanlike
creature with magic powers. —*verb trans.*
(**dwarfed, dwarfing**) **1** to cause to seem
small or unimportant. **2** to stunt the growth
of. ▸ **dwarfish** *adj.* ▸ **dwarfism** *noun*

dweeb *noun slang* **1** a flunky or other very
subservient person. **2** a bookish or nerdy
person.

dwell *verb intrans.* (*pa t and pa p* **dwelt,
dwelled**; *pr p* **dwelling**) **1** to reside. **2**
(**dwell on** *or* **upon**) to think or speak about
(something) obsessively. ▸ **dweller** *noun*

dwelling *noun* a place of residence; a house.

dwindle *verb trans., intrans.* to shrink, or
cause (something) to shrink, gradually in
size, number, intensity, etc., esp. until there
is little or none left.

dye *verb trans., intrans.* (**dyed, dyeing**) to
color or stain, esp. permanently. —*noun* a
substance used to impart color to or change
the color of another material. ▸ **dyer** *noun*

dyed-in-the-wool *adj.* of firmly fixed opinions; out-and-out.

dying *verb see* **die¹.** —*adj.* relating to,
expressed at, etc. the time immediately
before death or the end of something:
*dying soldiers / dying wishes / the dying
days of a failed administration.*

dyke¹ *noun, verb same as* **dike.**

dyke² *noun offensive slang* a lesbian.

dynamic *adj.* **1** full of energy, enthusiasm, and
new ideas. **2** relating to dynamics. ▸ **dynam-
ically** *adv.*

dynamics *noun* **1** (*sing.*) the branch of
mechanics that deals with motion and the
forces that produce motion. **2** (*pl.*)
movement or change in any sphere, or the
forces causing this: *political dynamics.* **3**
(*sing.*) the ways in which people work
together in a group.

dynamism *noun* limitless energy and
enthusiasm.

dynamite *noun* **1** a powerful blasting
explosive. **2** *slang* a thrilling or dangerous
person or thing. —*verb trans.* (**dynamited,
dynamiting**) to blow up with dynamite. —
adj. slang excellent; fantastic.

dynamo *noun* (*pl.* **dynamos**) a device that
converts mechanical energy into electricity.

dynamometer (dī'nə-mäm'ət-ər) *noun* an
instrument for measuring mechanical force
or power.

dynasty (dī'nə-stē) *noun* (*pl.* **dynasties**) **1** a
succession of rulers from the same family;
their period of rule. **2** a succession of
members of a powerful family or other
connected group. ▸ **dynastic** *adj.*

dysentery (dĭs'ən-tĕr,ē) *noun* an intestinal
disease characterized by severe diarrhea.

dysfunction *noun* impaired or abnormal
function, e.g., of a physiological system or
organ. ▸ **dysfunctional** *adj.*, *noun*
▸ **dysfunctionally** *adv.*

dyslexia (dĭs-lĕk'sē-ə) *noun* a disorder
characterized by an impaired ability to read,
write, and spell. ▸ **dyslexic** *adj.*, *noun*

dyspepsia *noun* impaired digestion.
▸ **dyspeptic** *adj.*

dysprosium (dĭs-prō'zē-əm) *noun* (SYMBOL
Dy) a soft silvery metallic element of the
lanthanide series.

dystrophy (dĭs'trə-fē) *noun* a degenerative
disorder caused by poor nutrition. *See also*
muscular dystrophy.

Ee

E¹ *or* **e** *noun* (*pl.* **Es, E's, e's**) **1** the fifth letter of the English alphabet. **2** (*usu.* **E**) the fifth highest grade or quality; or a mark indicating this. **3** *Mus.* **a** the third note in the scale of C major. **b** a musical key with the note E as its base.

E² *abbrev.* **1** East. **2** *Phys.* electromotive force. **3** (*also* **e**) electronic: *E-mail.* **4** *Phys.* energy.

e *or* **e.** *abbrev. Baseball* error.

each *adj.* every one of two or more. —*pron.* every single one of two or more people, animals, or things. —*adv.* to, for, or from each one: *give them one each.* —**each other** used as the object of a verb or preposition when an action takes place between two (or more than two) people, etc.: *They were talking to each other. See also* **one another.**

eager *adj.* anxious to do for; keen: *eager for riches.* ▸ **eagerly** *adv.* ▸ **eagerness** *noun*

eagle *noun* **1** a large bird of prey noted for its soaring, graceful flight and keen eyesight. **2** a golf score of two under par. —**eagle-eyed** having exceptionally good eyesight.

eaglet *noun* a young eagle.

ear¹ *noun* **1** the sense organ on each side of the human head that makes hearing possible **2** the sense of hearing **3** the act of listening; attention: *give ear to.* —**be all ears** *colloq.* to listen attentively or with great interest. **up to (one's) ears (in something)** *colloq.* deeply involved in or occupied with (it).

ear² *noun Bot.* a spike of eg. corn.

earache *noun* continuous or intermittent pain in the ear.

eardrum *noun Anat.* the membrane that separates the outer ear from the middle ear.

earl (**ərl´**) *noun* a male member of the British nobility ranking below a marquess and above a viscount. ▸ **earldom** *noun*

earlobe *noun* the soft piece of flesh that forms the lower part of the human ear.

early *adv., adj.* (**earlier, earliest**) **1** near the beginning of a period of time. **2** happening or occurring before the expected time: *early arrivals.* ▣ PREMATURE ▣ LATE. **3** in the near future. **4** in the far-off past. **early on** at or near the beginning of a period of time, etc. ▸ **earliness** *noun*

earmark *verb trans.* (**earmarked, earmarking**) to set aside or intend for a particular purpose.

earmuffs *pl. noun* coverings worn over the ears to protect them from cold or noise.

earn *verb trans., intrans.* (**earned, earning**) **1** to gain (money, wages, or one's living) by working. **2** to gain. **3** to be worthy of (something): *earned her promotion.* **4** to yield, e.g., as profits. ▸ **earner** *noun*

earnest *adj.* **1** serious or overly serious. **2** showing determination, sincerity, or strong feeling. —**in earnest** serious or seriously. ▸ **earnestly** *adv.* ▸ **earnestness** *noun*

earnings *pl. noun* money earned, e.g., wages or business profits.

earphones *pl. noun* headphones.

earplug *noun* a piece of wax, rubber, etc., placed in the ear to keep out noise, cold, or water.

earring *noun* a piece of jewelry worn attached to the ear.

earshot *noun* the distance at which sound can be heard: *within earshot.*

earsplitting *adj.* making an extremely loud and irritating sound.

earth *noun* **1** (*often* **Earth**) the third planet in order from the Sun. **2** the material world. **3** the land and sea as opposed to the sky. **4** dry land as opposed to the sea. **5** soil; dirt. —**come back** *or* **down to earth** to become aware of the realities of life. **on earth** used as an intensive: *What on earth is that?*

earthen *adj.* **1** of a floor, etc. made of dirt or soil. **2** of a pot, etc. made of baked clay.

earthenware *noun* pottery made of baked clay.

earthling *noun* in science fiction, a native of Earth.

earthly *adj.* **1** of or belonging to this world; not spiritual. **2** *colloq.* used for emphasis: *We have no earthly chance of winning.*

earthmover *noun* a piece of heavy equipment used for excavating and moving soil.

earthquake *noun* a series of shock waves that pass through the Earth, that may cause damage. ▣ QUAKE, TEMBLOR, TREMBLOR, TREMOR.

earth science a science concerned with the study of Earth and its atmosphere.

earthshaking *adj.* of great importance or consequence. ▸ **earthshakingly** *adv.*

earth-shattering *adj.* earthshaking. ▸ **earth-shatteringly** *adv.*

earthwork noun Technical **1** (often in pl.) a human-made bank of earth, used formerly as a fortification. **2** an artwork constructed by alteration of a usu. large area of land.

earthworm noun a worm with a ringed body and no backbone, living in damp earth.

earthy adj. (**earthier, earthiest**) **1** of or like earth or soil. **2** coarse or crude; lacking politeness. ▸ **earthily** adv. ▸ **earthiness** noun

earwig noun an insect named after the mistaken belief that it enters the ear of a sleeping person.

ease noun **1** freedom from pain or anxiety. **2** absence of difficulty. **3** freedom from embarrassment. **4** absence of restriction. —verb trans., intrans. (**eased, easing**) **1** to free from pain, trouble, or anxiety. **2** (**ease off** or **up**) to become less intense; to relax. **3** (**ease (something) in** or **out**) to move (something) gently or gradually in or out of position.

easel noun a stand for supporting an artist's canvas.

east noun **1** (ABBREV. **e, E**) (also **the east** or **the East**) the direction from which the Sun rises. **2** (**the East** or **East**) **a** the eastern part of a country **b** the countries of Asia, east of Europe. —adj. (ABBREV. **E**) **1** in the east. **2** coming from the direction of the east: an east wind. —adv. (ABBREV. **E**) toward the east.

eastbound adj. going or leading toward the east.

Easter (ē′stər) noun a Christian religious festival celebrating the resurrection of Christ.

easterly adj. **1** of a wind, etc. coming from the east. **2** looking, lying, etc., toward the east. —adv. to or toward the east. —noun (pl. **easterlies**) an easterly wind.

eastern adj. (ABBREV. **E**) **1** of or in the east. **2** facing or directed toward the east.

eastward adv., adj. toward the east. ▸ **eastwardly** adv., adj. ▸ **eastwards** adv.

easy adj. (**easier, easiest**) **1** presenting no difficulty. **2** free from pain, anxiety, etc. **3** lacking formality; friendly. **4** exhibiting or presenting no strain; leisurely. **5** colloq. having no strong preferences: Do what you want; I'm easy. **6** sexually promiscuous. —adv. colloq. in a slow, calm, or relaxed way. ▸ **easiness** noun ▸ **easily** adv.

easygoing or **easy-going** adj. relaxed and tolerant.

eat verb trans., intrans. (pa t **ate**; pa p **eaten**; pr p **eating**) **1** to chew, and swallow (food). **2** (**eat (something) away** or **eat into (something)**) to erode or corrode. **3** (**eat into** or **through (something)**) to use (it) up gradually. **4** colloq. to trouble or worry: What's eating you? —**eat (one's) words** to admit that (one) is or was wrong. ▸ **eatable** adj.

eater noun one that eats, usu. in the manner specified: He is a noisy eater.

eau de cologne (ōd,ə-kə-lōn′) a mild perfume. Also called **cologne**.

eaves (ēvz) pl. noun the part of a roof that sticks out beyond the wall.

eavesdrop verb intrans. (**eavesdropped, eavesdropping**) (**eavesdrop on**) to listen secretly to a private conversation. ▸ **eavesdropper** noun

ebb verb intrans. (**ebbed, ebbing**) **1** of the tide: to recede. **2** to grow smaller or weaker. —noun **1** the lowering of the tide. **2** a decline: His health is on the ebb.

ebony (ĕb′ə-nē) noun a hard, heavy, jet-black wood. —adj. **1** made of ebony. **2** literary black in color: ebony skies at night.

ebullience (ĭ-bŏŏl′yəns, -bəl′-) or **ebulliency** noun enthusiasm; cheerfulness. ▸ **ebullient** adj. ▸ **ebulliently** adv.

EC abbrev. **1** European Commission. **2** European Community.

eccentric (ĭk-sĕn′trĭk) adj. **1** of a person, behavior, etc. odd; unusual; strange. **2** technical, of a wheel, etc. not having the axis at the center. **3** Geom. denoting two circles that do not have a common center. —noun a bizarre or odd person. ▸ **eccentrically** adv.

eccentricity (ĕk,sĕn,trĭs′ət-ē) noun (pl. **eccentricities**) a bizarre or odd manner or characteristic.

ecclesiastic noun formal a cleric.

ecclesiastical adj. of or relating to a church or the clergy. ▸ **ecclesiastically** adv.

ECG abbrev. **1** electrocardiogram. **2** electrocardiograph.

echelon (ĕsh′ə-lŏn) noun **1** a level or rank in an organization **2** a roughly V-shaped formation, used by ships, planes, birds in flight, etc.

echinoderm (ĭ-kē′nə-dərm,) noun Zool. a marine animal characterized by five-rayed symmetry, e.g., the starfish.

echo noun (pl. **echoes**) **1** the reflection of a sound wave by the surface of a nearby object. **2** a person who imitates or repeats. **3** an imitation or repetition. **4** (often **echoes**) something that brings to mind thoughts. —verb intrans., trans. (**echoed, echoing, echoes**) **1** to sound loudly with an echo. **2** to repeat or imitate. ▸ **echoic**

echolocation noun the perception of objects by means of reflected sound waves.

éclair (ā-klâr,, -klĕr′) noun a long, cream-filled cake of light pastry, with chocolate icing.

éclat (ā-klä′) noun brilliance; dazzling effect.

eclectic (ĭ-klĕk′tĭk) adj., selecting material or ideas from a wide range of sources. ▸ **eclectically** adv. ▸ **eclecticism** noun

eclipse noun **1** the obscuring of light from a celestial body, e.g., the Sun when the Moon comes between it and Earth or the Moon when Earth's shadow falls across it. **2** a loss of fame or importance. —*verb trans.* (**eclipsed, eclipsing**) **1** to cause an eclipse of. **2** to outshine.

ecliptic *noun* (**the ecliptic**) *Astron.* the path that the Sun appears to follow through the stars. —*adj.* relating to an eclipse or the ecliptic.

eclogue (ĕk'lôg,, -läg,) *noun* a short poem in the form of a dialogue or soliloquy.

eco- (ē,kō, ĕk,ō) *combining form* forming words denoting ecology or the environment: *ecology / ecotourism.*

ecofriendly or **eco-friendly** *adj.* doing no harm to the environment.

ecology (ĭ-kăl'ə-jē) *noun* the study of the relationship between living organisms and their natural environment. ▸ **ecologist** *noun* ▸ **ecological** *adj.* ▸ **ecologically** *adv.*

econ. *abbrev.* **1** economic. **2** economics. **3** economy.

economic (ĕk,ə-năm'ĭk, ē,kə-) *adj.* **1** of or concerned with the economy of a nation, etc. **2** *of a business practice, etc.* likely to bring a profit. **3** of or relating to economics, the science.

economical *adj.* not wasting money or resources. ▸ **economically** *adv.*

economics *noun* **1** (*sing.*) the study of the production, distribution, and consumption of money, goods, and services. **2** (*pl.*) financial aspects. ▸ **economist** *noun.*

economize (ĭ-kăn'ə-mīz,) *verb intrans.* (**economized, economizing**) to cut down on spending or waste. ▸ **economization** *noun*

economy *noun* (*pl.* **economies**) **1** the organization of money and resources within a nation, etc. **2** careful management of money or other resources. —*adj.* larger than the standard or basic size, and proportionally cheaper: *an economy bag of potatoes.*

ecosphere *noun* biosphere.

ecosystem *noun* *Biol.* a self-contained community of plants and animals and the physical environment with which it interacts.

ecotourism *noun* tourism in areas of unspoiled natural beauty.

ecstasy (ĕk'stə-sē) *noun* (*pl.* **ecstasies**) **1** a feeling of immense joy. **2** *Psychol.* a mental state of extreme well-being and trancelike elation. **3** a drug taken for its stimulant and hallucinogenic properties. ▸ **ecstatic** *adj.* ▸ **ecstatically** *adv.*

ECT *abbrev. Med.* electroconvulsive therapy.

ecto- *combining form* forming words meaning outside: *ectopic. See also* **endo-, ento-, exo-.**

-ectomy *combining form Med.* forming words denoting removal by surgery: *hysterectomy.*

ectopic pregnancy the development of a fetus outside the uterus.

ectoplasm (ĕk'tə-plăz,əm) *noun* the substance thought to be given off by the body of a medium during a trance.

ecu or **ECU** (ā'kyōō,, ā'kōō,, ĕk'yōō,, ĕk'ōō,) *noun* a European currency unit based on the combined values of several European currencies.

ecumenical (ĕk,yə-mĕn'ĭ-kəl) *adj.* promoting or reflecting unity among all or many churches and religious faiths. ▸ **ecumenically** *adv.* ▸ **ecumenicalism** or **ecumenism** *noun*

eczema (ĕg'zə-mə, ĕk'sə-, ĭg-zē'-) *noun Med.* acute or chronic inflammation of the outer layer (*epidermis*) of the skin.

ed. *abbrev.* **1 a** edited. **b** edition. **c** editor. **2** educated. **3** education.

-ed *suffix* **1** used to form past tenses and past participles: *talked / waited.* **2** used to form adjectives from nouns: *bearded / bald-headed.*

Edam *noun* a mild yellow cheese, usu. shaped into balls and covered with red wax.

eddy *noun* (*pl.* **eddies**) a circular or swirling movement that develops within a current of water or air. —*verb intrans., trans.* (**eddied, eddying, eddies**) to move or cause to move in a circular or swirling way.

edelweiss (ād'l-wīs, -vīs,) *noun* a small white alpine plant.

edema or **oedema** (ĭ-dē'mə) (*pl.* **edemas, edemata**) *Med. noun* an abnormal buildup of fluid in the tissues in the body, causing swelling.

Eden (ēd'n) *noun* **1** the biblical place where Adam and Eve lived. *Also called* **Garden of Eden. 2** a beautiful region; a place of delight.

edge *noun* **1** a border or boundary. **2** the brink. **3** the cutting side of an instrument. **4** severity or sharpness: *a cold wind with an edge to it.* —*verb trans., intrans.* (**edged, edging**) **1** to form or make a border to. **2** to move or cause to move gradually and carefully. —**on edge** nervous and irritable; uneasy.

edgewise or **edgeways** *adv.* sideways.

edging *noun* a decorative border.

edgy *adj.* (**edgier, edgiest**) feeling or exhibiting anxiety and nervous tension. ▸ **edgily** *adv.* ▸ **edginess** *noun*

edible (ĕd'ə-bəl) *adj.* fit to be eaten; suitable to eat. ▸ **edibility** *noun*

edict (ē'dĭkt) *noun* an order issued by a monarch or government.

edifice *noun* a building, esp. a large, impressive one.

edify (ĕd'ə-fī,) *verb trans.* (**edified, edifying, edifies**) to improve the mind or morals of.

edit *verb trans.* (**edited, editing**) **1** to prepare (a book, program, etc.), for publication or broadcast. **2** to be in charge of the process of producing (a book, etc.) **3** to prepare (a movie, or a program) by putting together material previously photographed or recorded. **4** *Comput.* to manipulate (data). —*noun* a period or instance of editing. ▸ **editor** *noun*

edition *noun* **1** a number of copies of a book, etc., printed at one time. **2** the form in which a book, etc., is published: *a paperback edition*. **3** a specified issue of a newspaper: *the evening edition*. **4** the entire set of like items manufactured and sold.

editorial *adj.* of or relating to editors or editing. —*noun* an article written by or on behalf of the editor of a newspaper or magazine, usu. offering an opinion. ▸ **editorially** *adv.*

editorialize *verb intrans.* (**editorialized, editorializing**) **1** to write an editorial. **2** to introduce personal opinion into what is meant to be factual reporting.

EDP *abbrev.* electronic data processing.

EDT *or* **E.D.T.** *abbrev.* Eastern Daylight Time.

educable (ĕj′ə-kə-bəl) *adj.* capable of being educated.

educate (ĕj′ə-kāt,) *verb trans.* (**educated, educating**) **1** to train and teach. **2** to provide school instruction for. **3** to train and improve (one's taste, etc.). ▸ **educator** *noun*

educated *adj.* **1** having received an above-average education. **2** produced by or suggesting a good education. **3** based on experience or knowledge: *educated guesses*.

education *noun* **1 a** the process of teaching and training. **b** the instruction received. **2** the study of methods of instruction and learning. ▸ **educational** *adj.* ▸ **educationally** *adv.*

educe (ĭ-dōōs′, -dyōōs′) *verb trans.* (**educed, educing**) *formal* to bring or draw out (something reserved or hidden). ▸ **educible** *adj.* ▸ **eduction** *noun*

Edwardian (ĕd-wôrd′ē-ən, -wärd′-) *adj.* of or characteristic of King Edward VII of England or of his reign.

E.E. *abbrev.* **1** electrical engineer. **2** electrical engineering.

-ee *suffix* forming nouns denoting: **1** the person who is the object of the action of a verb: *payee / employee*. **2** a person in a stated condition: *absentee / escapee / refugee*. **3** a person with a stated association or connection: *townee*.

EEC *abbrev.* European Economic Community (the former name of the European Community).

EEG *abbrev. Med.* **1** electroencephalogram. **2** electroencephalograph.

eel *noun* (*pl.* **eel, eels**) a fish with a long, slender, snakelike body.

EEO *abbrev.* Equal Employment Opportunity.

-eer *suffix* **1** forming nouns denoting a person concerned with a stated activity: *auctioneer / mountaineer*. **2** forming verbs denoting

actions or behavior associated with a stated activity: *electioneer*.

eerie (ĭr′ē) *or* **eery** *adj.* (**eerier, eeriest**) strangely disturbing or frightening. ▸ **eerily** *adv.* ▸ **eeriness** *noun*

> Originally a Scots word meaning 'afraid' or 'cowardly'

efface (ĭ-fās′) *verb trans.* (**effaced, effacing**) **1** to rub or wipe out. **2** to block out (a memory, etc.). **3** to avoid drawing attention to (oneself). ▸ **effacement** *noun*

effect *noun* **1** a result. **2** an impression given or produced. **3** working state; operation: *put the new regulations into effect*. **4** (*usu.* **effects**) property. **5** (*usu.* **effects**) lighting and sound devices, used in a movie, etc. —*verb trans.* (**effected, effecting**) to do, cause to happen, or bring about. —**in effect** in reality; practically speaking. **take effect** to come into force

> *Usage* The word *effect* is often confused with *affect*.

effective *adj.* **1** producing a desired result. **2** producing a pleasing effect. **3** in operation; active. ▸ **effectiveness** *noun*

effectively *adv.* **1** in an effective way. **2** for all practical purposes; in reality.

effectual *adj.* producing the intended result. ▸ **effectually** *adv.*

effectuate (ĭ-fĕk′chə-wāt,) *verb trans.* (**effectuated, effectuating**) to carry out. ▸ **effectuation** *noun*

effeminate *adj.*, *of a man* having features of appearance or behavior more typical of a woman than of a man. ▸ **effeminately** *adv.* ▸ **effeminacy** *noun*

efferent *adj. Anat.* **1** leading away from a central point. **2** carrying nerve impulses from the central nervous system to the muscles, glands, etc.

effervesce (ĕf,ər-vĕs′) *verb intrans.* (**effervesced, effervescing**) **1** to give off bubbles of gas. **2** to be lively and energetic. ▸ **effervescence** *noun* ▸ **effervescent** *adj.*

effete (ĕ-fēt′, ĭ-) *adj.* lacking strength, energy, or force of character. ▸ **effeteness** *noun*

efficacious (ĕf,ĭ-kā′shəs) *adj.* producing, or certain to produce, the intended result. ▸ **efficaciously** *adv.* ▸ **efficacy** *noun*

efficient (ĭ-fĭsh′ənt) *adj.* **1** producing satisfactory results with an economy of effort. **2** *of a person* capable of doing competent work within a relatively short time. ▸ **efficiently** *adv.* ▸ **efficiency** *noun*

effigy (ĕf′ə-jē) *noun* (*pl.* **effigies**) **1** a crude model of a person, on which contempt for the person can be expressed, e.g., by burning. **2** *formal* a likeness of a person (esp. sculptured).

effloresce *verb intrans.* (**effloresced, efflorescing**) 1 *Chem.*, of a crystalline salt to lose water and become powdery on exposure to air. 2 *Bot.*, of a flower to produce flowers. ▶ **efflorescent** *adj.* ▶ **efflorescence** *noun*

effluent (ĕf'loo͝o‚ənt, ě-floo͝o'-) *noun* 1 an outflow of sewage, waste, etc., into a river, lake, or sea. 2 *Geog.* a stream or river flowing from a larger body of water. —*adj. technical* flowing out.

effluvium *noun* (*pl.* **effluvia, effluviums**) an unpleasant smell or vapor given off, e.g., by decaying matter.

efflux *noun* the act of flowing out; something that flows out.

effort *noun* 1 hard mental or physical work, or something that requires it. 2 an act of trying hard. 3 the result of an attempt; an achievement.

effortless *adj.* done without effort. ▶ **effortlessly** *adv.*

effrontery *noun* (*pl.* **effronteries**) shameless rudeness.

effulgent *adj. literary* shining brightly; brilliant. ▶ **effulgently** *adv.* ▶ **effulgence** *noun*

effusion (ĭ-fyoo͞o'zhən, ě-) *noun* 1 a pouring or flowing out. 2 *derog.* an uncontrolled flow of speech or writing.

effusive (ĭ-fyoo͞o'sĭv, ě-, -zĭv) *adj. derog.* gushing, emotional. ▶ **effusively** *adv.* ▶ **effusiveness** *noun*

e.g. *or* **eg** *abbrev. exempli gratia* (Latin), for example.

egalitarian (ĭ-găl‚ĭ-tār'ē-ən, těr'-) *adj.* relating to the principle of equality for all. —*noun* a person who upholds this principle. ▶ **egalitarianism** *noun*

egg[1] *noun* 1 *Biol.* an ovum. 2 *Zool.* a rounded body laid by, e.g., a bird, from which a young one is hatched. 3 such a body laid by a hen, used as food.

egg[2] *verb trans.* (**egged, egging**) (**egg (someone) on**) to encourage (someone) to action; to incite.

egghead *noun colloq.* a highbrow; an intellectual. ▶ **eggheaded** *adj.*

eggnog *noun* a drink made from raw eggs, milk, sugar, and rum or brandy or both.

eggplant *noun* a plant widely cultivated for its edible dark purple fruit. *Also called* **aubergine.**

egg roll a deep-fried pastry consisting of a cylinder-shaped casing of thin egg dough filled, e.g., with minced meat, seafood, and vegetables.

eggshell *noun* the hard, thin covering of an egg. —*adj.* 1 of paint or varnish having a slightly glossy finish. 2 of articles of china very thin and fragile.

ego (ē'gō, ěg'ō) *noun* (*pl.* **egos**) 1 personal

pride. 2 self-centeredness or conceit. 3 *Psychol.* the part of the mind that maintains conscious contact with the outside world. *See also* **id, superego.**

egocentric *adj.* interested only in oneself. ▶ **egocentrically** *adv.* ▶ **egocentricity** *noun*

egoism *noun* 1 *Philos.* the principle that self-interest is the basis of morality. 2 selfishness. 3 too good an opinion of oneself. ▶ **egoist** *noun* ▶ **egoistical** *adj.* ▶ **egoistically** *adv.*

egomania *noun Psychol.* extreme self-interest. ▶ **egomaniac** *noun*

egotism *noun* 1 the fact of having a very high opinion of oneself. 2 the habit of speaking too much about oneself. ▶ **egotist** *noun* ▶ **egotistic** *or* **egotistical** *adj.*

egotistic *or* **egotistical** *adj.* speaking too much about oneself; boastful. ▶ **egotistically** *adv.*

ego trip *slang* an action undertaken to enhance one's own reputation. ▶ **ego-trip** *verb*

egregious (ĭ-grē'jəs) *adj.* shockingly bad; outrageous. ▶ **egregiously** *adv.* ▶ **egregiousness** *noun*

egress (ē'grěs‚) *noun* 1 the act of leaving. 2 an exit.

egret (ē'grət) *noun* a wading heron noted for its long pointed bill and long neck.

Egyptian (ĭ-jĭp'shən) *noun* 1 a native or citizen of Egypt. 2 the language of ancient Egypt. —*adj.* relating or belonging to Egypt.

eider *noun* any large sea duck with extremely soft down used for filling duvets, pillows, etc.

eiderdown *noun* 1 the soft feathers of the eider. 2 a quilt filled with down.

eight (āt) *noun* 1 the number or figure 8. 2 the age of 8. 3 a garment or a person, whose size is denoted by the number 8. 4 8 o'clock. 5 a set of 8 people or things. —*adj.* 1 8 in number. 2 aged 8.

eight ball *Billiards* the black ball that bears the numeral 8. —**be behind the eight ball** *slang* in a disadvantageous or uncomfortable spot or position.

eighteen (āt-tēn', ā-) *noun* 1 the number or figure 18. 2 the age of 18. 3 a garment or a person, whose size is denoted by the number 18. 4 a set of 18 people or things. —*adj.* 1 18 in number. 2 aged 18.

eighteenth *noun, adj.* the position in a series corresponding to 18 in a sequence of numbers.

eighth (āth, āth) *noun, adj.* 1 the position in a series corresponding to 8 in a sequence of numbers. 2 one of eight equal parts.

eighties *pl. noun* the numbers eighty to eighty-nine.

eightieth *noun, adj.* the position in a series corresponding to 80 in a sequence of numbers.

eighty *noun* (*pl.* **eighties**) **1** the number or figure 80. **2** the age of 80. **3** a set of 80 people or things. —*adj.* **1** 80 in number. **2** aged 80.

einsteinium *noun* (SYMBOL **Es**) a synthetic radioactive metallic element.

either (ē'thər, ī'-) *adj.* **1** any one of two. **2** each of two; both: *a garden with a fence on either side.* —*pron.* any one of two things, people, etc. —*adv.* (*used in negative statements*) also; as well. —**either... or...** introducing two choices or possibilities: *Either you come or I don't go.*

ejaculate *verb intrans., trans.* (pronounced *-late*) (**ejaculated, ejaculating**) **1** *of a male* to discharge semen. **2** to exclaim. —*noun* (pronounced *-lat*) semen. ▸ **ejaculation** *noun* ▸ **ejaculatory** *adj.*

eject *verb trans., intrans.* (**ejected, ejecting**) **1** to throw out with force. **2** to force to leave. ▸ **ejection** *noun* ▸ **ejective** *adj.* ▸ **ejector** *noun*

ejection seat a seat designed to eject a pilot from the aircraft in an airborne emergency.

eke (ēk) *verb trans.* (**eked, eking**) (**eke out**) to make (a supply) last longer than normally.

EKG *abbrev.* **1** electrocardiogram. **2** electrocardiograph.

elaborate (ĭ-lăb'-rət, -ə-rət) *adj.* complicated in design; complex. —*verb intrans., trans.* (**elaborated, elaborating**) (ĭ-lăb'ə-rāt,) (**elaborate on** *or* **upon** (**something**)) to add detail to (it). ▸ **elaborately** *adv.* ▸ **elaboration** *noun*

élan (ā-län') *noun* impressive and energetic style.

eland (ē'lənd, -lănd,) *noun* (*pl.* **eland, elands**) a large African antelope with spirally twisted horns.

elapse *verb intrans.* (**elapsed, elapsing**) to pass: *Two weeks have elapsed since then.*

elastic *adj.* **1** *of a material* able to return to its original shape or size after being pulled or pressed out of shape. **2** able to be changed; flexible. **3** made of elastic. —*noun* stretchable cord or fabric. ▸ **elastically** *adv.* ▸ **elasticity** *noun*

elastic band a rubber band.

elasticize *verb trans.* (**elasticized, elasticizing**) to make elastic.

elate (ĭ-lāt') *verb trans.* (**elated, elating**) to make intensely happy. ▸ **elated** *adj.* ▸ **elatedly** *adv.* ▸ **elation** *noun*

elbow *noun* **1** **a** the joint where the arm bends. **b** the part of a garment that covers this. **2** a sharp turn or bend. —*verb trans.* (**elbowed, elbowing**) **1** to push with the elbow. **2** to jostle.

elbow grease *colloq.* hard physical work.

elbow room *noun* space enough for moving or doing something.

elder[1] *adj.* **1** older. **2** superior in rank. —*noun* **1** a person who is older. **2** an office-bearer in some presbyterian churches.

elder[2] *noun* a shrub or tree, the flowers and fruits of which are used to make wine, preserves, and jellies.

elderberry *noun* (*pl.* **elderberries**) the fruit of the elder bush or tree.

elderly *adj.* rather old. —*noun* (**the elderly**) senior citizens considered as a group. ▸ **elderliness** *noun*

eldest *adj.* oldest. —*noun* a person who is the oldest of three or more.

elect *verb trans.* (**elected, electing**) **1** to choose by vote. **2** (**elect to do** (**something**)) to do (it) by choice. —*adj.* **1** (*following the noun, usu. hyphenated*) elected to a position, but not yet formally occupying it: *the senator-elect.* **2** specially chosen. —*noun* (**the elect**) **1** *Relig.* people chosen for salvation. **2** the chosen ones. ▸ **elected** *adj.* ▸ **electable** *adj.* ▸ **electability** *noun*

election *noun* the process or act of choosing people for office by taking a vote.

electioneer *verb intrans.* (**electioneered, electioneering**) to take an active part in a political election campaign.

elective *adj.* **1** *of a position.* to which someone is appointed by election. **2** having the power to elect. **3** optional. —*noun* an academic subject that is optional. ▸ **electively** *adv.*

elector *noun* **1** a person who has the right to vote in an election. **2** a member of the US Electoral College. ▸ **electoral** *adj.*

Electoral College the body of people who elect the US President, having themselves been elected by popular vote.

electorate *noun* (**the electorate**) all the qualified voters of a city, country, etc.

electric (ĭ-lĕk'trĭk) *adj.* **1** of electricity. **2** having or causing great excitement. —*noun* (*often* **electrics**) electrical appliances.

electrical *adj.* related to or operated by electricity. ▸ **electrically** *adv.*

electric chair a chair for executing criminals sentenced to death under the law.

electric eel a S American freshwater fish resembling an eel, and able to deliver electric shocks of up to 550 volts.

electric eye *colloq.* a photoelectric cell.

electric guitar a guitar with an electrical amplifier.

electrician (ĭ-lĕk-trĭsh'ən) *noun* a person whose job is to install and repair electrical equipment.

electricity (ĭ-lĕk-trĭs'ət-ē) *noun* **1** **a** the manifestation of a form of energy associated with separation or movement of charged particles. **b** an electric charge or current used for operating various devices. **2** excitement, tension, or expectation.

electrify (ĭ-lĕk′trə-fī,) *verb trans.* (**electrified, electrifying, electrifies**) **1** to give an electric charge to. **2** to adapt (e.g. a railroad system) for operation by electricity. **3** to cause to feel an exciting sensation. ▸ **electrification** *noun* ▸ **electrifying** *adj.* ▸ **electrifyingly** *adv.*

electro- *combining form* forming words denoting electricity: *electrocute.*

electrocardiogram *noun Med.* (ABBREV. **ECG, EKG**) a recording of the electrical activity of the heart muscle. *Also called* **cardiogram.**

electrocardiograph (ĭ-lĕk,trō-kärd′ē-ə-grăf,) *noun Med.* (ABBREV. **ECG, EKG**) a recording instrument used to record the electrical activity of the heart muscle. *Also called* **cardiograph.** ▸ **electrocardiography** *noun*

electroconvulsive therapy *Med.* (ABBREV. **ECT**) a treatment for psychological disorders in which a low-voltage electric current is passed through the brain.

electrocute *verb trans.* (**electrocuted, electrocuting**) **1** to kill accidentally by electric shock. **2** to execute (a prisoner) by means of electricity. ▸ **electrocution** *noun*

electrode *noun Electr.* either of the two conducting elements through which an electric current enters or leaves e.g. a battery.

electroencephalogram *noun Med.* (ABBREV. **EEG**) a diagram or tracing produced by an electroencephalograph. *Also called* **encephalogram.**

electroencephalograph *noun Med.* (ABBREV. **EEG**) an apparatus that registers, as a diagram or tracing, the electrical activity of the brain. *Also called* **encephalograph.**

electrolysis (ĭ-lĕk′trə-trăl′ə-sĭs) *noun* **1** *Chem.* the separation of a chemical compound using an electric current. **2** the removal of tumors, hair roots, etc., by means of an electric current.

electrolyte (ĭ-lĕk′trə-līt,) *noun* **1** *Chem.* a chemical substance that can conduct electricity when in its molten state or when dissolved. **2** *Physiol.* an atom or group of atoms (ions) needed by cells to regulate the electric charge and flow of molecules across the cell membrane. ▸ **electrolytic** *adj.*

electromagnet *noun Phys.* a temporary magnet consisting of a coil of insulated wire wrapped around a soft iron or steel core. ▸ **electromagnetic** *adj.*

electromagnetism *noun* magnetic forces produced by the flow of electric current, rather than by a permanent magnet.

electromotive *adj. Phys.* relating to or producing an electric current.

electromotive force (ABBREV. **emf, EMF**) *Phys.* the energy that forces a current to flow in an electrical circuit.

electron *noun Phys.* a fundamental particle that carries a negative electric charge.

electronic *adj. of a device* of or involving electrons or electronics. ▸ **electronically** *adv.*

electronic mail *Comput.* the sending of messages via computer systems. *Also called* **E-mail.**

electronic publishing *Comput.* the publishing of computer-readable texts on disk, CD-ROM, etc.

electronics *noun* **1** (*sing.*) the scientific study of the conduction of electricity. **2** (*pl.*) the electronic parts of a machine or system.

electron microscope *Biol.* a microscope that uses a beam of electrons instead of light rays to produce a highly magnified images.

electroplate *verb trans.* (**electroplated, electroplating**) to plate or coat (a metal surface) with a thin layer of another metal by electrolysis. —*noun* electroplated articles.

electroscope *noun Phys.* a device for detecting the presence of an electric charge and estimating its amount.

electroshock *noun Med.* electroconvulsive therapy.

electrostatic field *Phys.* an electric field associated with stationary electric charges.

electrostatics *noun* (*sing.*) *Phys.* the scientific study of fields and potentials caused by stationary electric charges.

elegant *adj.* **1** having or showing good taste, combined with graceful refinement. **2** *of a movement* graceful. ▸ **elegantly** *adv.* ▸ **elegance** *noun*

elegize *verb trans., intrans.* (**elegized, elegizing**) **1** to write an elegy about. **2** to produce mournful or thoughtful writings or songs.

elegy (ĕl′ə-jē) *noun* (*pl.* **elegies**) a mournful or thoughtful song or poem, esp. one whose subject is death or loss. ▸ **elegiac** *adj.* ▸ **elegiacally** *adv.*

element *noun* **1** a component of a whole: *a key element of a strategy.* **2** *Chem.* a chemical element. **3** a high-resistance wire through which an electric current is passed in order to produce heat. **4** a component in an electric circuit. **5** *Math.* a member of a set. **6** any one of the four basic substances (earth, air, fire, and water) **7** (**the elements**) weather conditions, esp. when severe. **8** (**the elements**) basic facts or skills. ▸ **elemental** *adj.*

elementary (ĕl,ə-mĕn′trē, -mĕnt′ə-rē) *adj.* **1** dealing with simple or basic facts; fundamental. **2** pertaining to elementary education or to elementary schools.

elementary particle *Phys.* a subatomic particle that does not appear to be divisible into smaller units.

elementary school a school encompassing the first six or eight grades. *Also called* **grammar school, grade school**.

elephant *noun* an animal with thick gray skin, large ears, tusks, and a flexible muscular trunk.

elephantiasis (ĕl,ə-fən-tī'ə-sĭs, -făn-) *noun Med.* a chronic disease causing thickening of the skin, usu. in the legs.

elephantine (ĕl,ə-făn'tēn,, ĕl'ə-fən-, -tīn,) *adj.* **1** of or like an elephant. **2** of exceedingly or excessively large size.

elevate (ĕl'ə-vāt,) *verb trans.* (**elevated, elevating**) **1** to raise or lift. **2** to promote. **3** to improve (a person's mind). **4** to make more cheerful. ▸ **elevated** *adj.* ▸ **elevating** *adj.*

elevation *noun* **1** the act of elevating or state of being elevated. **2** *technical* height, e.g., of a place above sea level. **3** *technical* a drawing or diagram of one side of a building, machine, etc. **4** *formal* a high place.

elevator *noun* **1** a device for moving people or objects up and down in a building. **2** a tall building in which grain is stored. **3** a movable flap at the tail of an aircraft, by means of which the aircraft climbs or descends.

eleven (ĭ-lĕv'ən) *noun* **1** the number or figure 11. **2** the age of 11. **3** a garment or a person, whose size is denoted by the number 11. **4** 11 o'clock. **5** a set of 11 people or things. **6** a score of 11 points. —*adj.* **1** 11 in number. **2** aged 11.

eleventh *noun, adj.* the position in a series corresponding to 11 in a sequence of numbers.

elf *noun* (*pl.* **elves**) **1** in folklore, a tiny fairy with a tendency to play tricks. **2** a mischievous child. ▸ **elfish** *or* **elvish** *adj.*

elfin *adj.* **1** of *physical features, etc.* small and delicate. **2** small and mischievous but charming; elfish.

elicit (ĭ-lĭs'ĭt) *verb trans.* (**elicited, eliciting**) **1** to bring or draw out (something reserved or hidden). ≡ EDUCE, EVINCE, EVOKE, EXTRACT. **2** to cause: *remarks that elicited hostility.* ▸ **elicitation** *noun* ▸ **elicitor** *noun*

elide *verb trans.* (**elided, eliding**) **1** *Gram.* to omit (a vowel or syllable) at the beginning or end of a word. **2** to omit (a part ,of something). ▸ **elision** (ĭ-lĭzh'ən) *noun*

eligible *adj.* (*often* **eligible for** (**something**)) **1** suitable or deserving to be chosen (e.g., for a job). **2** having a right. ▸ **eligibility** *noun*

eliminate *verb trans.* (**eliminated, eliminating**) **1** to get rid of or exclude. **2** *slang* to kill. ▸ **elimination** *noun* ▸ **eliminator** *noun*

elite (ĭ-lēt', ā-) *or* **élite** *noun* **1** the most influential people within society. **2** the best of a group or profession. —*adj.* most influential ▸ **elitism** *noun* ▸ **elitist** *noun, adj.*

elixir (ĭ-lĭk'sər) *noun* **1** *Med.* a sweetened liquid used to mask the taste of an unpalatable medicine. **2** in alchemy, a chemical preparation that was claimed to be a universal remedy.

Elizabethan (ĭ-lĭz,ə-bē'thən) *adj.* relating to or typical of the reign of Queen Elizabeth I of England (1558–1603). —*noun* a person who lived during the time of Elizabeth I.

elk *noun* (*pl.* **elk, elks**) **1** the moose. **2** wapiti.

ellipse (ĭ-lĭps') *noun Geom.* a plane curve shaped like an oval. ▸ **elliptic** *or* **elliptical** *adj.* ▸ **elliptically** *adv.*

ellipsis *noun* (*pl.* **ellipses**) **1** *Gram.* the omission of a word or words, needed for the sense or grammar, but understood. **2** a set of three dots that indicate the omission of a word or words.

ellipsoid *noun Geom.* a smooth closed surface formed by rotation of an ellipse about one of its axes.

elm *noun* a tall tree with broad serrated leaves and clusters of small flowers.

elocution *noun* the art of speaking clearly and effectively. ▸ **elocutionary** *adj.*

elongate (ĭ-lông'gāt,) *verb trans., intrans.* (**elongated, elongating**) to lengthen or stretch out ▸ **elongation** *noun* ▸ **elongated** *adj.*

elope (ĭ-lōp') *verb intrans.* (**eloped, eloping**) to run away secretly, esp. to get married. ▸ **elopement** *noun* ▸ **eloper** *noun*

eloquence *noun* **1** the art or power of using speech to impress, move, or persuade. **2** fine and persuasive language. ≡ EXPRESSION, EXPRESSIVENESS. ▸ **eloquent** *adj.* ▸ **eloquently** *adv.*

else *adj., adv.* different from the person or thing mentioned: *I'd like something else.* —**or else** or if not . .; otherwise: *Hurry up, or else we'll be late.*

elsewhere *adv.* to or in a different place.

elucidate (ĭ-lōō'sĭ-dāt,) *verb trans., intrans.* (**elucidated, elucidating**) to make clear or explain. ▸ **elucidation** *noun* ▸ **elucidatory** *adj.*

elude *verb trans.* (**eluded, eluding**) **1** to escape by quickness or cleverness. **2** to escape the memory or understanding. ▸ **elusive** *adj.* ▸ **elusively** *adv.* ▸ **elusiveness** *noun*

> *Usage* Elude and allude are often confused. *Elude*, meaning to escape the memory or understanding, is correctly used here: His name *eludes* me. *Allude*, meaning to contain indirect references, is correctly used here: The essay *alludes* to the excesses of the French revolution.

elver *noun* a glass eel.

elves *see* **elf**.

elvish *adj. see* **elf**.

Elysium (ĭ-lĭzh′əm, ĭ-lĭz′ē-əm) *noun* 1 *Greek Mythol.* the place where the good remain after death in perfect happiness. 2 *poetic* a state or place of perfect happiness. ▸ **Elysian** *adj.*

em- *prefix* a form of *en-* used before b, m, and p.

'em (əm) *contr. colloq.* them.

emaciate (ĭ-mā′shē-āt,) *verb trans.*, *intrans.* (**emaciated, emaciating**) to make or become extremely thin. ▸ **emaciation** *noun*

E-mail *or* **e-mail** *noun Comput.* electronic mail.

emanate *verb intrans.* (**emanated, emanating**) 1 of *an idea, etc.* to emerge or originate. 2 of *light, gas* to flow; to issue. ▸ **emanation** *noun*

emancipate (ĭ-măn′sĭ-pāt,) *verb trans.* (**emancipated, emancipating**) to deliver from slavery, or restraint. ▸ **emancipation** *noun*

emasculate *verb trans.* (**emasculated, emasculating**) 1 to reduce the strength or effectiveness of. 2 to remove the testicles of; to take away the masculinity of. ▸ **emasculation** *noun* ▸ **emasculatory** *adj.* ▸ **emasculated** *adj.*

embalm *verb trans.* (**embalmed, embalming**) to preserve (a corpse) from decay by treatment with chemicals. ▸ **embalmment** *noun* ▸ **embalmer** *noun*

embankment *noun* a bank or wall of dirt made to enclose a waterway, or to carry a road or railroad.

embargo *noun* (*pl.* **embargoes**) 1 an official order forbidding something, esp. trade with another country. 2 a restriction or prohibition. —*verb trans.* (**embargoed, embargoing, embargoed**) to place under embargo.

embark *verb trans.*, *intrans.* (**embarked, embarking**) 1 to go or put on board ship. 2 (**embark on** (**something**)) to begin (a lengthy task). ▸ **embarkation** *noun*

embarrass (ĭm-băr′əs) *verb trans.*, *intrans.* (**embarrassed, embarrassing**) 1 to cause to feel, or to become, self-conscious or ashamed. 2 to impede. 3 (**be embarrassed**) to be in financial difficulties. ▸ **embarrassed** *adj.* ▸ **embarrassing** *adj.* ▸ **embarrassingly** *adv.* ▸ **embarrassment** *noun*

embassy (ĕm′bə-sē) *noun* (*pl.* **embassies**) 1 the official residence of an ambassador. 2 an ambassador and his or her staff. 3 a deputation.

embattled *adj.* 1 prepared for battle. 2 troubled by problems or difficulties.

embed *verb trans.* (**embedded, embedding**) to set or fix firmly and deeply.

embellish *verb trans.* (**embellished, embellishing**) 1 to add details to (a story, etc.) to make it more interesting. 2 to provide with decorations. ▸ **embellishment** *noun*

ember *noun* (*usu.* **embers**) glowing or smoldering coal or wood.

embezzle *verb trans.* (**embezzled, embezzling**) to take dishonestly (money with which one has been entrusted). ▸ **embezzlement** *noun* ▸ **embezzler** *noun*

embitter *verb trans.* (**embittered, embittering**) to cause (someone) to feel bitter. ▸ **embitterment** *noun*

emblazon (ĭm-blā′zən) *verb trans.* (**emblazoned, emblazoning**) 1 to decorate, e.g., with a coat of arms. 2 to display prominently. ▸ **emblazonment** *noun*

emblem *noun* an object chosen to represent an idea, a country, etc. ▸ **emblematic** *adj.*

embody *verb trans.* (**embodied, embodying, embodies**) 1 to typify or personify. 2 to have as part of a larger whole. ▸ **embodiment** *noun*

embolden *verb trans.* (**emboldened, emboldening**) to make bold.

embolism (ĕm′bə-lĭz,əm) *noun* the blockage of a blood vessel by a blood clot.

emboss *verb trans.* (**embossed, embossing**) to mold a raised design on (a surface).

embrace *verb trans.*, *intrans.* (**embraced, embracing**) 1 to hold closely in the arms; to hug. 2 to take or accept. 3 to include. —*noun* a hug.

embrasure (ĭm-brā′zhər) *noun* an opening in the wall through which to shoot a weapon.

embrocation *noun* a lotion for rubbing into the skin to ease muscular pain.

embroider *verb trans.*, *intrans.* (**embroidered, embroidering**) 1 to decorate (cloth) with sewn designs. 2 to make (a story, etc.) more interesting by adding fictitious details. ▸ **embroiderer** *noun* ▸ **embroidery** *noun*

embroil *verb trans.* (**embroiled, embroiling**) 1 to involve (someone) in (a quarrel or in a difficult situation). 2 to throw into confusion. ▸ **embroilment** *noun*

embryo (ĕm′brē-ō,) *noun* (*pl.* **embryos**) 1 a young animal or plant in its earliest stages in seed, protective tissue, egg or womb. 2 something in its earliest stages: *the embryo of revolution.* ▸ **embryonic** *adj.*

embryology *noun* the scientific study of the formation and development of embryos. ▸ **embryological** *adj.* ▸ **embryologist** *noun*

emend *verb trans.* (**emended, emending**) to edit (a text). ▸ **emendation** *noun*

emerald *noun* 1 a green gemstone. 2 the color of this stone.

emerge *verb intrans.* (**emerged, emerging**) 1 to come out into view. 2 to become known. 3 to survive a difficult situation. ▸ **emergence** *noun* ▸ **emergent** *adj.* ▸ **emerging** *adj.*

emergency *noun* (*pl.* **emergencies**) an unexpected happening requiring immediate action.

emeritus *adj. masc.* (ĭ-mĕr′ət-əs), **emerita** *adj. fem.* (ĭ-mĕr′ət-ə) retired, but retaining a former title as an honor.

emery *noun* a mixture of fine-grain minerals, used as an abrasive.

emetic (ĭ-mĕt′ĭk) *adj.* inducing vomiting. —*noun* a medicine used to induce vomiting.

emf *or* **EMF** *abbrev. Phys.* electromotive force.

emigrate (ĕm′ĭ-grāt,) *verb intrans.* (**emigrated, emigrating**) to leave one's native country and settle in another. ▸ **emigrant** *noun* ▸ **emigration** *noun*

émigré (ĕm′ĭ-grā,) *noun* a person who has emigrated, usu. for political reasons.

eminence *noun* **1** distinction. **2** an area of high ground. **3** (**Eminence**) a title of honour for a cardinal.

eminent *adj.* famous and admired. ▸ **eminently** *adv.*

eminent domain *Legal* a government's legal right to appropriate private property for public use.

emir (ĭ-mîr′, ā-) *or* **amir** *noun* used as a title for various Muslim rulers.

emirate (ĭ-mîr′ət) *noun* the position, or the territory ruled by, an emir.

emissary *noun* (*pl.* **emissaries**) a person sent on a mission, esp. on behalf of a government.

emit *verb trans.* (**emitted, emitting**) to give out (light, heat, a sound, a smell, etc.). ▸ **emission** *noun*

emollient *adj.* **1** softening or soothing the skin. **2** *formal* advocating a more peaceful attitude. —*noun* a substance that softens or soothes the skin.

emolument (ĭ-mäl′yə-mənt) *noun formal* money earned from employment.

emote *verb intrans.* (**emoted, emoting**) to display exaggerated or insincere emotion.

emotion *noun* strong, intense feelings.

emotional *adj.* **1** of the emotions. **2** *of a person* tending to express emotions easily or excessively. ▸ **emotionally** *adv.* ▸ **emotionalism** *noun*

emotive *adj.* tending, or designed, to excite emotion. ▸ **emotively** *adv.*

empanel *verb Legal same as* **impanel**.

empathy (ĕm,pə-thē) *noun* the ability to share and understand another person's feelings. ▸ **empathetic** *adj.* ▸ **empathize** *verb*

emperor *noun* the male ruler of an empire.

emphasis *noun* (*pl.* **emphases**) **1** (**emphasis on** (**something**)) special importance or attention given to (it). **2** stress put on words. ▸ **emphatic** *adj.* ▸ **emphatically** *adv.*

emphasize *verb trans.* (**emphasized, emphasizing**) to put emphasis on.

emphysema (ĕm,fə-zē′mə, -sē′-) *noun Med.* an abnormal increase in the size of air spaces in the lungs, causing labored breathing.

empire (ĕm′pīr,) *noun* **1** a group of states, etc. under the control of a single ruler or ruling power **2** a large commercial or industrial organization controlling many separate firms.

empirical (ĕm-pīr′ĭ-kəl) *adj.* based on experiment, observation, or experience, rather than on theory. ▸ **empirically** *adv.* ▸ **empiricism** *noun* ▸ **empiricist** *noun*

emplacement *noun* **1** *Mil.* a strongly defended position for a weapon. **2** *formal* location.

employ *verb trans.* (**employed, employing**) **1** to give (usu. paid) work to. **2** to occupy the time and attention of. **3** to use. —*noun* employment: *in the employ of the state.* ▸ **employable** *adj.* ▸ **employed** *adj.*

employee *or* **employe** (ĭm-ploi,ē′, ĕm-, -ploi′ē,) *noun* a person who works for another in return for payment.

employer *noun* a person, company, or other entity or group that employs workers.

employment *noun* **1** the act of employing or the state of being employed. **2** an occupation.

emporium *noun* (*pl.* **emporiums, emporia**) a large shop selling a wide variety of goods.

empower *verb trans.* (**empowered, empowering**) (**empower** (**someone**) **to do** (**something**)) to give (someone) authority to do (it). ▸ **empowerment** *noun*

empress (ĕm′prəs) *noun* **1** the female ruler of an empire. **2** the wife or widow of an emperor.

empty *adj.* (**emptier, emptiest**) **1** having nothing inside. **2** unoccupied. **3** unlikely to be carried out: *empty promises.* **4** without, devoid of: *a life empty of meaning.* —*verb trans., intrans.* (**emptied, emptying, empties**) to make or become empty. —*noun* (*pl.* **empties**) *colloq.* an empty container, esp. a drink can or bottle. ▸ **emptily** *adv.* ▸ **emptiness** *noun*

empty-handed *adj.* **1** carrying nothing. **2** having gained or achieved nothing.

empyrean *noun literary* (*usu.* **the empyrean**) the sky. ▸ **empyreal** *adj.*

EMT *abbrev.* emergency medical technician.

emu (ē′myōō,) *noun* a large flightless Australian swift-running bird, related to the ostrich.

emulate (ĕm′yə-lāt,) *verb trans.* (**emulated, emulating**) **1** to strive to equal or be better than. **2** to imitate. ▸ **emulation** *noun*

emulsify *verb trans., intrans.* (**emulsified, emulsifying, emulsifies**) to make or become an emulsion. ▸ **emulsifier** *noun*

emulsion *noun Chem.* a milky liquid obtained by mixing, e.g. oil and water.

en- *prefix* **1** forming verbs with the meaning put into, on, or onto: *entrust / enthrone.* **2**

forming verbs with the meaning cause to be: *enrich*. **3** forming verbs with the meaning in, into: *entangle*.

-en *suffix* **1** forming verbs with the meaning make or become (more): *deepen*. **2** forming verbs with the meaning give, endow with: *strengthen*. **3** forming adjectives with the meaning made or consisting of: *wooden*.

enable *verb trans.* (**enabled, enabling**) to make able.

enact *verb trans.* (**enacted, enacting**) **1** to act or perform, e.g., on stage or in real life. **2** to establish by law. ▸ **enactment** *noun*

enamel *noun* **1** a hardened glasslike substance applied as a covering to metal or glass. **2** a glossy paint. **3** the hard white material that covers the teeth. —*verb trans.* (**enameled** *or* **enamelled, enameling** *or* **enamelling**) to cover or decorate with enamel.

enamored *adj.* (**enamored with (someone** *or* **something)**) in love with or very fond of.

en bloc (ān-blăk′) *adv.* all together; as one unit.

enc. *abbrev.* **1** enclosed. **2** enclosure.

encamp *verb trans., intrans.* (**encamped, encamping**) to settle in a camp. ▸ **encampment** *noun*

encapsulate *verb trans., intrans.* (**encapsulated, encapsulating**) **1** to express concisely but sufficiently. **2** to enclose in, or as if in, a capsule. ▸ **encapsulation** *noun*

encase *verb trans.* (**encased, encasing**) to enclose in, or as if in, a case. ▸ **encasement** *noun*

-ence *suffix* forming nouns denoting: **1** a state or quality: *confidence / diligence*. **2** an action: *reference*.

encephalitis (ĕn-sĕf′ə-līt′ĭs) *noun* inflammation of the brain.

encephalo- *or* **encephal-** *combining form* Anat. forming words denoting the brain: *encephalitis*.

encephalogram (ĕn-sĕf′ə-lə-grăm,) *noun* Med. electroencephalogram.

encephalograph *noun* Med. electroencephalograph.

enchant *verb trans.* (**enchanted, enchanting**) **1** to charm or delight. **2** to put a magic spell on. ▸ **enchanter** *noun* ▸ **enchanted** *adj.* ▸ **enchanting** *adj.* ▸ **enchantment** *noun*

enchantress *noun* **1** a sorceress. **2** a woman of great mysterious charm.

enchilada (ĕn,chə-läd′ə) *noun* a Mexican dish consisting of a tortilla with a meat and cheese filling, served with a chili-flavored sauce.

encircle *verb trans.* (**encircled, encircling**) to surround or form a circle around. ▸ **encirclement** *noun*

encl. *abbrev.* **1** enclosed. **2** enclosure.

enclave (ĕn′klāv,, än′-) *noun* a piece of

territory entirely enclosed within foreign territory.

enclose *verb trans.* (**enclosed, enclosing**) **1** to put inside a letter or its envelope. **2** to shut in or surround. ▸ **enclosure** *noun*

encode *verb trans.* (**encoded, encoding**) to express in or convert into code.

encomium *noun* (*pl.* **encomiums, encomia**) *formal* an expression of very high praise. ▸ **encomiastic** *adj.*

encompass *verb trans.* (**encompassed, encompassing**) **1** to have or incorporate as part of a larger whole. **2** to surround. **3** to bring about.

encore (än′kôr,) *noun* a repetition of a performance. —*interj.* an enthusiastic call for such a repeat. —*verb trans.* (**encored, encoring**) to call for an extra performance of or from.

encounter *verb trans.* (**encountered, encountering**) **1** to meet, esp. unexpectedly. **2** to meet with (difficulties, an enemy, etc.). —*noun* **1** a chance meeting. **2** a fight.

encourage *verb trans.* (**encouraged, encouraging**) **1** to give courage or hope to. **2** to urge (someone) to do (something). ▸ **encouragement** *noun* ▸ **encouraging** *noun* ▸ **encouragingly** *adv.*

encroach *verb intrans.* (**encroached, encroaching**) (*usu.* **encroach on (someone** *or* **something)**) **1** to intrude, esp. little by little on (e.g., someone else's land, etc.). **2** to go beyond the fair limits of a right, etc. ▸ **encroachment** *noun*

encrust *verb trans.* (**encrusted, encrusting**) to cover with a thick, hard coating, e.g., of jewels or ice. ▸ **encrustation** *noun*

encumber *verb trans.* (**encumbered, encumbering**) **1** to prevent the free and easy movement of; to hamper or impede. **2** to burden with a load or debt. ▸ **encumbrance** *noun*

-ency *suffix* forming nouns denoting a state or quality: *efficiency / inconsistency*.

encyclical (ĭn-sĭk′lĭkəl, ĕn-) *noun* a letter sent by a pope to all bishops.

encyclopedia *or* **encyc-lopaedia** (ĭn-sī,klə-pēd′ē-ə) *noun* a comprehensive reference work containing information on the majc, branches of knowledge. ▸ **encyclopedic** *adj.*

end *noun* **1** the last point or part. **2** a finish. **3** a piece left over. **4** death: *meet one's end.* **5** an object or purpose. **6** *Football* one of the two players assigned the outermost position in a line of scrimmage. —*verb trans., intrans.* (**ended, ending**) to finish or cause to finish. —**in the end** after much discussion, work, etc.; finally.

endanger *verb trans.* (**endangered, endangering**) to put in danger. ▸ **endangerment** *noun*

endangered adj. in danger of extinction.

endear verb trans. (**endeared, endearing**) (**endear (oneself** or **someone) to (some-one** or **something)**) to cause (the one specified) to be beloved or liked. ▸ **endearing** adj. ▸ **endearingly** adv. ▸ **endearment** noun

endeavor (ĭn-dĕv'ər) verb trans., intrans. (**endeavored, endeavoring**) 1 (**endeavor to do (something)**) to try hard to do (it). 2 to work toward a specific goal. —noun a determined attempt or effort.

endemic adj. of a disease, etc. regularly found within a particular population or geographical region. —noun an endemic disease or plant.

ending noun 1 the end, esp. of a story, poem, etc. 2 Gram. the end part of a word, esp. an inflection.

endive noun a salad plant related to chicory.

endless (ĕn'dləs, ĕn'-ləs) adj. having or seeming to have no end. ▸ **endlessly** adv. ▸ **endlessness** noun

endmost adj. nearest the end.

endo- combining form internal; inside. See also ecto-, ento-, exo-.

endocrine (ĕn'də-krĭn, -krīn,, -krēn,) adj. of a gland making hormones and releasing them into the bloodstream. See also exocrine. ▸ **endocrinology** noun

endogamy (ĕn-dăg'ə-mē) noun the practice or rule of marrying only within one's own group.

endometriosis (ĕn,də-mē,trē-ō'sĭs) noun Med. a painful condition caused by the presence of uterus-lining tissue growing outside the uterus.

endoplasm noun Biol. the central portion of the cytoplasm of a cell.

endorphin (ĕn-dôr'fĭn) noun Biochem. any of a group of chemicals that occur naturally in the brain and have pain-relieving properties.

endorse verb trans. (**endorsed, endorsing**) 1 to write one's signature on the back of (a check, etc.). 2 to state one's approval of; to support. ▸ **endorsement** noun

endoscope (ĕn'də-skōp,) noun Med. a long, thin, flexible instrument used for viewing internal body cavities and organs. ▸ **endoscopic** adj. ▸ **endoscopy** noun

endow (ĭn-dow') verb trans. (**endowed, endowing**) 1 to provide a source of income for (e.g. a hospital). 2 (**be endowed with (something)**) to have a quality, ability, etc. ▸ **endowment** noun

endue (ĭn-dōō', -dyōō') verb trans. (**endued, enduing**) (**endue (someone) with (something)**) to provide with a certain quality.

endure verb trans., intrans. (**endured, enduring**) 1 to bear patiently; to put up with. 2 to continue to exist; to last.

▸ **endurable** adj. ▸ **endurance** noun ▸ **enduring** adj. ▸ **enduringly** adv.

endwise or **endways** adv. 1 with the end forward or upward. 2 end to end.

enema (ĕn'ə-mə) noun Med. a liquid medicine injected into the rectum.

enemy noun (pl. **enemies**) 1 a person, force or nation who is actively opposed to another. 2 an opponent. —adj. belonging to a hostile nation or force.

energetic adj. forceful; vigorous. ▸ **energetically** adv.

energize verb trans. (**energized, energizing**) to stimulate; provide energy for.

energy noun (pl. **energies**) 1 the capacity for vigorous activity. 2 force or forcefulness. 3 Phys. the capacity to do work.

enervate (ĕn'ər-vāt,) verb trans. (**enervated, enervating**) to take strength or vigor from. ▸ **enervating** adj. ▸ **enervation** noun

enfeeble verb trans. (**enfeebled, enfeebling**) formal to make weak. ▸ **enfeeblement** noun

enfilade (ĕn'fə-lād,, -lād,) Mil. noun gunfire sweeping across a line of enemy soldiers. —verb trans. (**enfiladed, enfilading**) to direct an enfilade at.

enfold verb trans. (**enfolded, enfolding**) 1 to wrap up or enclose. 2 to embrace.

enforce verb trans. (**enforced, enforcing**) 1 to cause (a law or decision) to be carried out. 2 (**enforce (something) on (someone)**) to impose (one's will, etc.) on another. 3 to strengthen (an argument). ▸ **enforcement** noun

enfranchise verb trans. (**enfranchised, enfranchising**) 1 to give voting rights to. 2 to set free. ▸ **enfranchisement** noun

engage (ĭn-gāj') verb trans., intrans. (**engaged, engaging**) 1 to take on as a worker. 2 to reserve. 3 to involve or occupy in. 4 Mil. to come or bring into battle. 5 to cause to interlock. ▸ **engagement** noun

engaged adj. 1 (**engaged to (someone)**) bound by a promise to marry (the one specified). 2 (**engaged in (something)**) busy or occupied with (it). 3 of a room, etc. being used; occupied.

engaging adj. charming or attractive. ▸ **engagingly** adv.

engender verb trans. (**engendered, engendering**) to produce or cause (esp. feelings or emotions).

engine (ĕn'jĭn) noun 1 a machine in which heat or other energy is used to produce motion. 2 a railroad locomotive.

engineer noun 1 a person who designs, makes, or works with machinery. 2 a person who designs or constructs roads, bridges, etc. 3 an officer in charge of a ship's engines. 4 a member of the armed forces who designs and builds military apparatus. —*verb trans.* (**engineered, engineering**) **1** to arrange or bring about by skill or cunning. **2** to design or construct as an engineer. ▸ **engineering** *noun*

English (ĭng'glĭsh, -lĭsh) *noun* **1** a native or citizen of England. **2** the official language of Britain, N America, most of the British Commonwealth, and some other countries, — *adj.* **1** of England or its people. **2** of the English language.

English horn a woodwind instrument similar to but lower in pitch than the oboe.

engorged *adj.* **1** crammed full. **2** *Med.* blocked by blood.

engrave *verb trans.* (**engraved, engraving**) **1** to carve (letters or designs) on stone, wood, metal, etc. **2** to decorate (stone, etc.) in this way. **3** to fix or impress deeply (on the mind, etc.). ▸ **engraver** *noun*

engraving *noun* **1** the art of carving designs on stone, etc. **2** a piece of stone, etc., decorated in this way. **3** a print taken from an engraved metal plate.

engross *verb trans.* (**engrossed, engrossing**) to take up completely the attention and interest of. ▸ **engrossed** *adj.* ▸ **engrossing** *adj.*

engulf *verb trans.* (**engulfed, engulfing**) to swallow up completely.

enhance *verb trans.* (**enhanced, enhancing**) to improve or increase the value, quality, or intensity of. ▸ **enhancement** *noun*

enigma (ĭ-nĭg'mə) *noun* a puzzling statement, quality or thing. ▸ **enigmatic** *adj.* ▸ **enigmatically** *adv.*

enjoin *verb trans.* (**enjoined, enjoining**) **1** to order (someone) to do something. **2** to forbid.

enjoy *verb trans.* (**enjoyed, enjoying**) **1** to find pleasure in. **2** to have the benefit of (something good): *The room enjoys sunlight all day.* ▸ **enjoyable** *adj.* ▸ **enjoyably** *adv.* ▸ **enjoyment** *noun*

enkindle *verb trans.* (**enkindled, enkindling**) **1** *literary* to set fire to. **2** to stir up (feelings) or to arouse strong feelings in.

enlarge *verb trans., intrans.* (**enlarged, enlarging**) **1** to make or become greater. **2** to reproduce (a photograph, etc.) in a larger form. **3** (**enlarge on** or **upon** (**something**)) to speak or write about (it) at greater length. ▸ **enlargement** *noun*

enlighten *verb trans.* (**enlightened, enlightening**) **1** to give more information to. **2** to free from ignorance or superstition. ▸ **enlightened** *adj.* ▸ **enlightening** *adj.* ▸ **enlightenment** *noun*

enlist *verb intrans., trans.* (**enlisted, enlisting**) **1** to join one of the armed forces. **2** to

obtain the support and help of. ▸ **enlistment** *noun*

enliven *verb trans.* (**enlivened, enlivening**) to make more lively, or cheerful than before. ▸ **enlivenment** *noun*

en masse (än-măs', än-) all together; as a mass or group.

enmesh *verb trans.* (**enmeshed, enmeshing**) to catch or trap in, or as if in, a net.

enmity (ĕn'mĭt-ē) *noun* ill will; hostility.

ennoble *verb trans.* (**ennobled, ennobling**) **1** to make (something) noble. **2** to make (someone) a member of the nobility. ▸ **ennoblement** *noun*

ennui (än-wē') *noun* boredom.

enormity *noun* (*pl.* **enormities**) **1** wickedness. **2** an outrageous or wicked act.

> *Usage* The use of *enormity* to mean *enormousness* (as in the *enormity* of the building) is usually regarded as incorrect.

enormous *adj.* of exceedingly or excessively large size. *See syn at* **huge.** ▸ **enormously** *adv.* ▸ **enormousness** *noun*

enough *adj.* in the number or quantity needed: *enough food to eat.* —*adv.* to the necessary degree or extent: *Has it warmed up enough?* —*pron.* the amount needed. —*interj.* used to indicate exasperation, surfeit, or impatience.

enquire *verb same as* **inquire.**

enquiry *noun same as* **inquiry.**

enrage *verb trans.* (**enraged, enraging**) to make extremely angry.

enrapture (ĭn-răp'chər) *verb trans.* (**enraptured, enrapturing**) to give intense pleasure or joy to.

enrich *verb trans.* (**enriched, enriching**) **1** to make rich or richer, esp. in quality, flavor, etc. **2** to make wealthy or wealthier. ▸ **enrichment** *noun*

enroll or **enrol** *verb trans., intrans.* (**enrolled, enrolling, enrolls** or **enrols**) **1** to add the name of (a person) to a list. **2** to add one's own name to such a list.

en route (än-rōōt', ĕn-, än-) on the way to a place.

Ens. or **ENS** *abbrev.* ensign.

ensconce (ĭn-skäns') *verb trans.* (**ensconced, ensconcing**) to settle comfortably or safely.

ensemble *noun* **1** a small group of musicians who play together. **2** a passage in opera, performed by all the singers together. **3** an outfit. **4** all the parts of a thing considered as a whole.

enshrine *verb trans.* (**enshrined, enshrining**) to enclose in, or as if in, a shrine.

enshroud *verb trans.* (**enshrouded, enshrouding**) to cover completely in, or as if in, a shroud.

ensign (ĕn'sən) *noun* **1** the flag of a nation,

regiment, etc. **2** the lowest ranking commissioned officer in the US Navy.

enslave *verb trans.* (**enslaved, enslaving**) **1** to make into a slave. **2** to subject to a dominating influence. ▸ **enslavement** *noun*

ensnare *verb trans.* (**ensnared, ensnaring**) to catch in, or as if in, a trap.

ensue (ĭn-sōō′) *verb intrans.* (**ensued, ensuing**) to follow; to happen after; to result from. ▸ **ensuing** *adj.*

en suite (äN-swēt′) attached as part of a set: *an en suite bathroom.*

ensure (ĭn-shōōr′) *verb trans.* (**ensured, ensuring**) to make certain; to assure or guarantee.

ENT *abbrev.* ear, nose, and throat.

-ent *suffix* forming adjectives and nouns denoting an action, activity, or function: *resident / different.*

entail *verb trans.* (**entailed, entailing**) **1** to have as a necessary result. **2** *Law* to limit (inherited property) to a specified heir. —*noun Law* **1** the practice of entailing property, property so entailed. **2** the successive heirs to property. ▸ **entailment** *noun*

entangle *verb trans.* (**entangled, entangling**) **1** to cause to get caught in an obstacle, e.g., a net. **2** to involve in difficulties. **3** to make complicated or confused. ▸ **entanglement** *noun*

enter *verb intrans., trans.* (**entered, entering**) **1** to go or come in or into. **2** to register in a competition. **3** to record in a book, diary, etc. **4** to join (a profession, society, etc.): *enter the ministry.* **5** (**enter into**) to begin to take part in.

enteric (ĕn-tĕr′ĭk) *adj. Med.* of or pertaining to the intestines.

enteritis (ĕnt′ə-rīt′ĭs) *noun Med.* inflammation of the intestines.

entero- *or* **enter-** *combining form* forming words denoting the intestine: *enteritis.*

enterprise *noun* **1** a project; an undertaking, esp. one that requires boldness. **2** initiative and boldness. **3** a business firm. ▸ **enterprising** *adj.* ▸ **enterprisingly** *adv.*

entertain *verb trans., intrans.* (**entertained, entertaining**) **1** to provide amusement for. **2** to give hospitality to (a guest). **3** to consider (e.g. an idea). ▸ **entertaining** *adj.* ▸ **entertainment** *noun*

entertainer *noun* a person who provides amusement, esp. professionally.

enthrall (ĭn-thrôl′) *verb* (**enthralled, enthralling**) **1** to hold as if by a spell. **2** to enslave. ▸ **enthrallment** *noun* ▸ **enthralling** *adj.*

enthrone *verb trans.* (**enthroned, enthroning**) to place on a throne. ▸ **enthronement** *noun*

enthuse *verb intrans., trans.* (**enthused, enthusing**) to be, or make another, enthusiastic.

> *Usage* Though in use since at least the early 1800s, this back-formation has never gained wide acceptance, and careful writers are best advised to avoid it.

enthusiasm *noun* lively or passionate interest.

enthusiast (ĭn-thōō′zē-əst, -thyōō′-, -ăst,) *noun* a person filled with enthusiasm; a fan.

enthusiastic *adj.* feeling or exhibiting enthusiasm. ▣ ARDENT, FERVENT, KEEN, WARM ▣ APATHETIC, UNENTHUSIASTIC, UNINTERESTED. ▸ **enthusiastically** *adv.*

entice (ĭn-tīs′) *verb trans.* (**enticed, enticing**) to tempt or persuade, by arousing hopes or desires or by promising a reward. ▸ **enticement** *noun* ▸ **enticing** *adj.* ▸ **enticingly** *adv.*

entire *adj.* **1** whole; complete. **2** absolute; total. ▸ **entirely** *adv.*

entirety (ĭn-tī′rət-ē, -tīrt′ē) *noun* (*pl.* **entireties**) **1** wholeness: *read the book in its entirety.* **2** the whole amount or extent.

entitle *verb trans.* (**entitled, entitling**) **1** (**entitle** (someone) **to** (something)) to give (someone) a right to have or to do (it). **2** to give a title or name to (a book, etc.). ▸ **entitlement** *noun*

entity *noun* (*pl.* **entities**) **1** something that exists. **2** *Philos.* the fact or quality of existing.

ento- *combining form* forming words denoting inside. *See also* **ecto-, endo-, exo-.**

entomb *verb trans.* (**entombed, entombing**) to bury in, or as if in, a tomb. ▸ **entombment** *noun*

entomology *noun* the scientific study of insects. ▸ **entomological** *adj.* ▸ **entomologist** *noun*

entourage (än,tōō-räzh′) *noun* a group of followers or assistants.

entr'acte (äN′träkt,, -träkt,) *noun* **1** an interval between the acts of a play. **2** entertainment provided during this interval.

entrails *pl. noun* the internal organs of an animal or a person.

entrance¹ (ĕn′trəns) *noun* **1** a way in, e.g., a door. **2** the act of entering: *gain entrance.* **3** the right to enter.

entrance² (ĭn-trăns′) *verb trans.* (**entranced, entrancing**) to fill with rapturous delight. ▸ **entrancement** *noun*

entrant *noun* a person who enters, esp. a competition.

entrap *verb trans.* (**entrapped, entrapping**) **1** to catch in, or as if in, a trap. **2** *Law* to trick (someone) into committing an illegal act. ▸ **entrapment** *noun*

entreat *verb trans.* (**entreated, entreating**) to beg for earnestly. ▸ **entreaty** *noun*

entrecôte (äɴ'trə-kōt,) *noun* a boneless steak cut from between two ribs.

entrée (än'trā, än-trā') *noun* **1** a main course of a meal. **2** the right of entry.

entrench *verb trans.* (**entrenched, entrenching**) **1** to fix or establish firmly. **2** to fortify with trenches. ▸ **entrenchment** *noun*

entrepreneur (än,trə-prə-nûr', -nŏŏr') *noun* a person who engages in business enterprises, usu. with some personal financial risk. ▸ **entrepreneurial** *adj.* ▸ **entrepreneurship** *noun*

entropy (ĕn'trə-pē) *noun* (*pl.* **entropies**) *Phys.* a measure of the amount of disorder in a system, or of the unavailability of energy for doing work.

entrust *verb trans.* (**entrusted, entrusting**) (**entrust** (**something**) **to** (**someone**) *or* (**someone**) **with** (**something**)) to give (it) to (someone) to take care of or deal with.

entry *noun* (*pl.* **entries**) **1** the act of coming or going in. **2** the right to enter. **3** a place of entering. **4** an item written on a list, in a book, etc.

entwine *verb trans.* (**entwined, entwining**) to wind or twist (two things) together.

enumerate (ĭ-nōō'mə-rāt, -nyōō'-) *verb trans.* (**enumerated, enumerating**) **1** to list one by one. **2** to count. ▸ **enumerative** *adj.*

enunciate (ĭ-nən'sē-āt,) *verb* (*trans., intrans.*) (**enunciated, enunciating**) **1** to pronounce (words) clearly. **2** to state formally. ▸ **enunciation** *noun*

enuresis (ĕn,yə-rē'sĭs) *noun Med.* involuntary urination, esp. during sleep. ▸ **enuretic** *adj.*

envelop (ĭn-vĕl'əp) *verb trans.* (**enveloped, enveloping**) **1** to cover by wrapping. **2** to obscure or conceal: *an event that was enveloped in mystery.* ▸ **envelopment** (ĭn-vĕl'əp-mənt) *noun*

envelope (ĕn'və-lōp, än'-) *noun* **1** a cover, esp. for a letter. **2** a cover or wrapper of any kind.

enviable *adj.* likely to cause envy; highly desirable. ▸ **enviably** *adv.*

envious *adj.* feeling or showing envy. ▸ **enviously** *adv.*

environment (ĭn-vī'rən-mənt, -vīrn'mənt) *noun* **1** surroundings. **2** surrounding conditions, esp. as influencing development and growth. **3** (*usu.* **the environment**) the natural conditions in which we live. ▸ **environmental** *adj.* ▸ **environmentally** *adv.* ▸ **environmentalism** *noun* ▸ **environmentalist** *noun*

environmentally friendly posing no threat of harm to the environment.

environs *pl. noun* surrounding areas, esp. the outskirts of a town or city.

envisage (ĭn-vĭz'ĭj) *verb trans.* (**envisaged, envisaging**) **1** to picture in the mind. **2** to consider as likely in the future.

envoy (ĕn'voi,, än'-) *noun* a person sent on a mission, esp. on behalf of a government. ▣ EMISSARY, INTERNUNCIO.

envy *noun* **1** a feeling of discontent at another's better fortune or success. **2** something that arouses envy. —*verb trans.* (**envied, envying, envies**) to feel envy against: *envy them their good luck.*

enzyme *noun* a specialized protein molecule that acts as a catalyst for the biochemical reactions that occur in living cells.

eon (ē'än,, -ən) *or* **aeon** *noun* **1** a very long period of time. **2** *Geol.* the largest unit of geological time, consisting of a number of eras.

eosin (ē'ə-sĭn) *noun Biol.* a red acidic dye used in biology to stain cells.

EPA *abbrev.* Environmental Protection Agency.

epaulet (ĕp,ə-lĕt') *or* **epaulette** *noun* a decoration on the shoulder of a garment, esp. a uniform.

épée (ĕp'ā,, ā-pā') *noun* a sword with a narrow flexible blade, used in fencing.

ephedrine (ĭ-fĕ'drĭn) *noun Med.* an alkaloid drug used as a nasal decongestant.

ephemera (ĭ-fĕm'ə-rə) *pl. noun* things that are valid only for a short time. ▸ **ephemeral** *adj.*

epi- *combining form* forming words denoting above, over, upon: *epicenter.*

epic *noun* **1** a long story telling of heroic acts. **2** a long adventure story, movie, etc. —*adj.* of or like an epic.

epicene (ĕp'ĭ-sēn,) *adj.* **1** having characteristics of both sexes, or of neither sex. **2** effeminate.

epicenter *noun* the point on Earth's surface directly above the origin of an earthquake.

epicure (ĕp'ĭ-kyŏŏr') *noun* a person who has refined taste, esp. in food and drink. ▸ **epicurean** *noun*

epicurism *noun* the pursuit of pleasure, esp. as found in good food and drink.

epidemic *noun* a sudden widespread outbreak of infectious disease. —*adj.* of or constituting an epidemic: *epidemic typhus.*

epidermis *noun Biol.* the outermost protective layer of the skin. ▸ **epidermal** *adj.*

epidural *adj. Med.* the membrane enveloping the brain and the spinal cord. —*noun Med.* an anesthetic administered into this membrane to reduce sensation below the waist.

epiglottis *noun Anat.* the moveable flap of cartilage hanging at the back of the tongue. ▸ **epiglottal** *adj.*

epigram *noun* a witty or sarcastic saying or short poem. ▸ **epigrammatic** *adj.*

epigraph *noun* **1** a quotation at the beginning of e.g. a book. **2** an inscription on a monument or building.

epigraphy (ĭ-pĭg'rə-fĕ) *noun* the study of inscriptions.

epilepsy (ĕp'ə-lĕp,sē) *noun* a disorder of the nervous system characterized by periodic loss of consciousness with or without convulsions. ▸ **epileptic** *adj. noun*

epilogue (ĕp'ə-lôg, -lăg,) *or* **epilog** *noun* **1** the closing section of a book, program, etc. **2** a speech addressed to the audience at the end of a play.

epinephrine (ĕp,ə-nĕf'rĭn) *noun* a hormone that constricts certain blood vessels, diverting blood away from the intestines and toward the muscles; adrenaline

epiphany (ĭ-pĭf'ə-nē) *noun* (*pl.* **epiphanies**) (*usu.* **Epiphany**) a Christian festival on Jan. 6, commemorating the showing of Christ to the three wise men.

epiphyte *noun Bot.* an air plant.

episcopacy *noun* (*pl.* **episcopacies**) **1** the government of a church by bishops. **2** episcopate (sense 2). **3** episcopate (sense 1).

episcopal (ĭ-pĭs'kə-pəl) *adj.* **1** relating to or governed by bishops. **2** (**Episcopal**) of or pertaining to the Episcopal Church.

episcopalian *adj.* **1** relating to or advocating church government by bishops. **2** (**Episcopalian**) of or pertaining to the Episcopal Church. —*noun* (**Episcopalian**) a member of the Episcopal Church.

episcopate *noun* **1** the position or period of office of a bishop. *Also called* **episcopacy**. **2** bishops as a group. *Also called* **episcopacy**. **3** an area under the care of a bishop; a diocese or bishopric.

episiotomy (ĭ-pĭz,ē-ät'ə-mē) *noun* (*pl.* **episiotomies**) *Med.* a surgical cut made at the opening of the vagina during childbirth, to assist the delivery of the baby.

episode *noun* **1** one of several events or distinct periods making up a longer sequence. **2** one of the separate parts in which a story is broadcast. ▸ **episodic** *adj.* ▸ **episodically** *adv.*

epistemology (ĭ-pĭs,tə-mäl'ə-jē) *noun* the branch of philosophy that is concerned with the study of the nature of knowledge.

epistle (ĭ-pĭs'əl) *noun* **1** *literary* a long letter dealing with important matters. **2** (*usu.* **Epistle**) in the Bible, a letter from an apostle. ▸ **epistolary** *adj*

epitaph *noun* an inscription on a gravestone.

epithet *noun* an adjective capturing the particular quality of the noun it describes: *Tszar Ivan IV was given the epithet The Terrible.*

epitome (ĭ-pĭt'ə-mē) *noun* **1** a person or thing that is a perfect example of, e.g., a quality, etc. **2** a short summary.

epitomize *verb trans.* (**epitomized, epitomizing**) **1** to typify or personify. **2** to summarize or shorten.

epoch (ĕp'ək, -äk,) *noun* a major period of history, a person's life, etc. ▸ **epochal** *adj.*

eponym (ĕp'ə-nĭm,) *noun* a person after whom something is named. ▸ **eponymous** (ĭ-pän'ĭ-məs) *adj.*

epoxy *Chem. noun* (*pl.* **epoxies**) an industrially prepared chemical resin, used in laminates and as an adhesive.

epsilon *noun* the fifth letter of the Greek alphabet (E).

Epsom salts (ĕp'səm) hydrated magnesium sulfate, used for clearing the bowels and as an anti-inflammatory agent.

equable *adj.* **1** of a climate not extreme. **2** of a person even-tempered. ▸ **equability** *noun* ▸ **equably** *adv.*

equal *adj.* **1** the same in size, amount, value, etc. **2** evenly balanced; displaying no advantage or bias. **3** having or entitled to the same rights. **4** (**equal to** (**something**)) having the necessary ability or strength for (it). —*noun* a person or thing of the same age, rank, ability, worth, etc. —*verb* (**equaled** *or* **equalled, equaling** *or* **equalling**) **1** to be the same in amount, value, size, etc., as. **2** to be as good as; to match. ▸ **equally** *adv.* ▸ **equality** *noun*

equalize *verb trans., intrans.* (**equalized, equalizing**) to make or become equal. ▸ **equalization** *noun* ▸ **equalizer** *noun*

equanimity (ĕk,wə-nĭm'ət-ē, ē,kwə-) *noun* calmness of temper; composure.

equate *verb trans., intrans.* (**equated, equating**) **1** (**equate** (**one thing**) **with** *or* **to** (**another**)) to consider (them) as equivalent. **2** to be or appear to be equal: *The two salary scales equate.*

equation *noun* **1** *Math.* a statement that two things are equal or the same. **2** *Chem.* a formula expressing a chemical reaction. **3** a set of variables.

equator *noun* (**the Equator**) the imaginary great circle that passes around Earth at latitude 0° at an equal distance from the North and South Poles. ▸ **equatorial** (ĕk,wə-tôr'ē-əl, ē,kwə-) *adj.*

equerry (ĕk'wə-rē) *noun* (*pl.* **equerries**) an official attending a member of a royal family.

equestrian *adj.* **1** pertaining to horseback riding or to horses. **2** performed on horseback. —*noun* a horseback rider or performer. ▸ **equestrianism** *noun*

equi- *combining form* forming words denoting equal or equally: *equidistant.*

equiangular *adj.* having equal angles.

equidistance *noun* equality of distance. ▸ **equidistant** *adj.*

equilateral *adj.* having all sides of equal length.

equilibrium *noun* (*pl.* **equilibriums, equilibria**) a state of equal balance between weights or forces, or between opposing powers or influences, etc.

equine *adj.* of, relating to, or like a horse or horses.

equinox (ē'kwə-nāks,, ĕk'wə-) *noun* the time when the sun crosses the equator, making night and day equal in length, about March 21 and September 23. ► **equinoctial** (ē,kwə-nāk'shəl, ĕk,wə-) *adj.*

equip *verb trans.* (**equipped, equipping**) to fit out with the necessary equipment.

equipment *noun* ► the clothes, machines, tools, instruments, etc., necessary for a particular kind of work or activity.

equipoise (ĕk'wə-poiz,, ē'kwə-) *noun formal* 1 a state of balance. 2 a counterbalancing weight.

equitable *adj.* fair and just.

equitation *noun formal* the art of riding a horse.

equity *noun* (*pl.* **equities**) 1 fair or just conditions; the spirit of justice that helps in interpreting the law. 2 ordinary shares.

equivalent *adj.* equal in value, power, meaning, etc. —*noun* an equivalent thing, amount, etc. ► **equivalence** *noun* ► **equivalently** *adv.*

equivocal (ĭ-kwĭv'ə-kəl) *adj.* 1 of doubtful meaning; ambiguous. 2 of an uncertain nature. ► **equivocally** *adv.*

equivocate (ĭ-kwĭv'ə-kāt,) *verb intrans.* (**equivocated, equivocating**) to use words ambiguously, esp. in order to mislead. ► **equivocation** *noun*

-er¹ *suffix* used to form the comparative of adjectives and adverbs: *happier / sooner.*

-er² *suffix* 1 forming words denoting the person or thing performing the action of the verb: *driver.* 2 forming words denoting a person from a particular town or city: *New Yorker.*

ER *abbrev.* emergency room.

Er *symbol Chem.* erbium.

ERA *abbrev.* 1 *Baseball* earned run average. 2 Equal Rights Amendment.

era (ĭr'ə, ĕr'ə) *noun* a distinct period in history marked by or beginning at an important event.

eradicate *verb trans.* (**eradicated, eradicating**) to get rid of completely. ► **eradication** *noun*

erase *verb trans.* (**erased, erasing**) 1 to rub out (pencil marks, etc.). 2 to remove all trace of. ► **eraser** *noun* ► **erasure** *noun*

erbium *noun Chem.* (**SYMBOL Er**) a soft silvery metal that absorbs neutrons and has a high electrical resistivity.

ere (ĕr, ăr) *prep., conj. poetic* before.

erect *adj.* 1. not bent or leaning; upright. 2 *Physiol.* enlarged and rigid. —*verb trans.* (**erected, erecting**) 1 to put up or build. 2 to set up or establish.

erectile *adj. Physiol.*, of an organ, etc. capable

of becoming erect.

erection *noun* 1 the act of erecting or the state of being erected. 2 a building or structure. 3 an erect sexual organ, esp. an erect penis. ► **erectly** *adv.* ► **erectness** *noun*

erg (ərg') *noun Phys.* a unit of work.

ergo (ĕr'gō, ər'-) *conj.* therefore; consequently.

ergonomics *noun* (*sing.*) the study of the relationship between people and their working environment. ► **ergonomic** *adj.* ► **ergonomically** *adv.* ► **ergonomist** *noun*

ergot (ər'gət, -gắt,) *noun* 1 a fungus that affects rye and other cereals. 2 the disease caused by this fungus. 3 a medicine obtained from this fungus.

ermine *noun* 1 a weasel whose coat in winter turns white except for the tip of the tail. 2 the highly-prized fur of this weasel.

erode *verb trans., intrans.* (**eroded, eroding**) to wear away, destroy, or be destroyed gradually. ► **erosion** *noun* ► **erosive** *adj.*

erogenous *adj.*, of part of the body sensitive to sexual stimulation.

erotic *adj.* of or arousing sexual desire, or giving sexual pleasure. ► **erotically** *adv.* ► **eroticism** *noun*

erotica *pl. noun* erotic literature, pictures, and other such materials.

err *verb intrans.* (**erred, erring**) 1 to make a mistake; to be wrong. 2 to sin.

errand *noun* 1 a short journey made in order to get or do something. 2 the purpose of such a journey.

errant *adj. literary* 1 doing wrong; erring. 2 wandering in search of adventure: *a knight errant.* 3 aimless in movement: *errant breezes.* ► **errantly** *adv.* ► **errantry** *noun*

erratic *adj.* 1 wandering. 2 unpredictable in behavior. ► **erratically** *adv.*

erratum *noun* (*pl.* **errata**) an error in writing or printing.

erroneous *adj.* wrong or mistaken. ► **erroneously** *adv.*

error *noun* 1 a mistake, inaccuracy, or misapprehension. 2 the state of being mistaken.

errorless *adj.* having no mistakes.

ersatz *noun* a cheap substitute. —*adj.* substitute; imitation: *ersatz coffee.*

Erse (ərs') *noun* Gaelic. —*adj.* relating to or spoken or written in this language.

erstwhile *adj.* former; previous.

eructation *noun* the act of belching, or a belch.

erudite *adj.* showing or having a great deal of knowledge. ► **eruditely** *adv.* ► **erudition** *noun*

erupt *verb intrans.* (**erupted, erupting**) 1 *of a volcano* to throw out lava, ash, and gases. 2 to break out suddenly and violently. 3 *of a* *blemish* to appear on the skin. ▸ **eruption** *noun*

erysipelas (ĕr,ə-sĭp'ə-ləs) *noun* a contagious disease of the skin characterized by inflammation of the face and the scalp and fever.

erythrocyte *noun Med.* a red blood cell.

erythromycin (ə-rĭth,rō-mī'sən) *noun Med.* an antibiotic used esp. in patients who are allergic to penicillin.

-ery *or* **-ry** *suffix* **1** denoting a place for an activity of the stated kind: *brewery.* **2** denoting a class, group, or type: *greenery.* **3** denoting an art, skill, or practice: *dentistry.* **4** denoting behavior of the stated kind: *bravery.* **5** denoting something connected with the stated person or thing: *popery.*

-es *suffix same as* **-s¹**.

Es *symbol Chem.* einsteinium.

escalate *verb intrans., trans.* (**escalated, escalating**) to increase or be increased rapidly. ▸ **escalation** *noun*

escalator *noun* a mechanized moving staircase.

escallop *noun, verb same as* **scallop**.

escapade *noun* a daring, adventurous, mischievous, or unlawful act.

escape *verb intrans., trans.* (**escaped, escaping**) **1** to gain freedom from captivity. **2** to manage to avoid (something unpleasant): *escaped the flu this year.* **3** to elude (one). **4** of a gas, liquid, etc. to leak out or get out. —*noun* **1** an act or means of escaping. **2** avoidance of danger: *a narrow escape.* **3** a leak.

escapee (ĭ-skā,pē', ĕs,kā,-) *noun* a person who has escaped, esp. from prison.

escapism *noun* the tendency to try to escape unpleasant reality by daydreaming, fantasizing, etc. ▸ **escapist** *adj. noun*

escarpment *noun* the steep side of a hill or rock.

eschew *verb trans.* (**eschewed, eschewing**) *formal* to avoid, keep away from: *eschewed violence.* ▸ **eschewal** *noun*

escort *noun* (ĕs'kôrt,) one or more people, vehicles, etc., accompanying another or others for protection, guidance or courtesy. —*verb trans.* (ĭs-kôrt', ĕs'kôrt,) (**escorted, escorting**) to accompany as an escort.

escritoire (ĕs'krə-twär,) *noun* a writing desk.

escrow *noun* something, esp. money, handed over to a third party only upon fulfillment of certain conditions.

escudo (ĭs-kōōd'ō) *noun* (*pl.* **escudos**) the standard unit of currency in Portugal.

escutcheon *noun* **1** a shield decorated with a coat of arms. **2** a small metal plate around a keyhole.

-ese *suffix* forming nouns and adjectives denoting: **1** a stated country or place:

Japanese. **2** the people or language of a stated country: *Chinese.* **3** the typical style or language of a particular group or profession: *journalese.*

Eskimo (ĕs'kĭ-mō,) *noun* (*pl.* **Eskimo, Eskimos**) **1** *now often offensive* a member of any of several peoples inhabiting Arctic North America, Greenland and Siberia. **2** the family of languages spoken by these peoples. —*adj.* relating to these peoples or to their language.

> *Usage* Although *Eskimo* is the established English name for the people, the people themselves often find it offensive and prefer the name *Inuit*.

ESL *abbrev.* English as a second language.

esophagus *or* **oesophagus** (ĭ-sãf'ə-gəs) *noun* (*pl.* **esophagi**) the narrow, muscular tube by means of which food is conveyed to the stomach.

esoteric (ĕs,ə-tĕr'ĭk) *adj.* understood only by those who have the necessary knowledge; secret; mysterious. ▸ **esoterically** *adv.*

ESP *abbrev.* extra sensory perception.

esp. *abbrev.* especially.

espadrille (ĕs'pə-drĭl,) *noun* a light canvas shoe with a sole made of rope or other plaited fiber.

espalier (ĭ-spăl'yər, -yā,) *noun* **1** a trellis against which a fruit tree is trained to grow flat. **2** a shrub or tree growing flat.

especial *adj.* special.

especially *adv.* more than in other cases; principally.

Esperanto (ĕs,pə-rän'tō, -rănt'ō) *noun* a language invented for international use.

espionage (ĕs'pē-ə-näzh,, -näj,) *noun* the activity of spying, or the use of spies.

esplanade (ĕs'plə-näd,) *noun* a long wide pavement or stretch of grass next to the shore.

espouse *verb trans.* (**espoused, espousing**) **1** to adopt or give one's support to (a cause, etc.). **2** to marry, or to give (e.g., a daughter) in marriage. ▸ **espousal** *noun*

espresso *or* **expresso** *noun* (*pl.* **espressos**) coffee made by forcing steam through ground coffee beans.

esprit (ĭs-prē') *noun* liveliness or wit.

esprit de corps (ĭs-prēd,ə-kôr') a common feeling of friendship and loyalty.

espy *verb trans.* (**espied, espying, espies**) *literary* to catch sight of; to observe.

-esque *suffix* forming words denoting: **1** in the style or fashion of: *Byronesque.* **2** like or similar to: *picturesque.*

esquire *noun* **1** (ABBREV. **Esq.**) a title used in its abbreviated form after the surname of an attorney or consul: *Lee Gordon, Esq.* **2** an English country gentleman.

-ess *suffix* forming words denoting a female of the type or class: *lioness / duchess*.

essay (ĕs′ā,) *noun* **1** a short formal piece of writing. **2** an attempt. (ĕ-sā′, ĕs′ā,) —*verb trans.* (**essayed, essaying, essays**) to attempt. ▸ **essayinst** *noun*

essence *noun* **1** the basic distinctive nature of anything. **2** a liquid obtained from a plant, drug, etc., in concentrated form.

essential *adj.* **1** absolutely necessary. **2** of the basic or inner nature of something. —*noun* **1** something necessary. **2** a basic or fundamental element. ▸ **essentially** *adv.* ▸ **essentiality** *noun*

EST *or* **E.S.T.** *abbrev.* Eastern Standard Time.

est. *abbrev.* **1** established. **2** estimated.

-est *suffix* forming the superlative of adjectives and some adverbs: *quickest / soonest*.

establish *verb trans.* (**established, establishing**) **1** to settle (someone) firmly in a position. **2** to set up (e.g., a business). **3** to find, show, or prove: *established the motive*. **4** to cause people to accept (e.g., an idea). ▸ **established** *adj.*

establishment *noun* **1** the act of establishing. **2** a business, its premises, or its staff. **3** a public or government institution: *a research establishment*. **4** (**the Establishment**) the group of people in power in a society.

estate *noun* **1** a large piece of land owned by a person or group of people. **2** *Law* a person's total possessions. **3** *Brit.* an area of land developed for building. **4** *old use* a condition or state: *the holy estate of matrimony*.

esteem *verb trans.* (**esteemed, esteeming**) **1** to hold in high regard. **2** *formal* to consider to be. —*noun* respect.

ester *noun* *Chem.* an organic compound formed by the reaction of an alcohol with an organic acid.

esthete *noun same as* **aesthete**.

esthetic *adj. same as* **aesthetic**.

esthetics *noun same as* **aesthetics**.

estimable *adj.* highly respected; worthy of respect.

estimate *verb trans.* (ĕs′tə-māt,) (**estimated, estimating**) **1** to calculate roughly or without measuring. **2** to judge the worth of. —*noun* (ĕs′tə-mət) **1** a rough assessment (of size, etc.). **2** a calculation of the probable cost of a job. ▸ **estimation** *noun* ▸ **estimator** *noun*

estrange *verb trans.* (**estranged, estranging**) to cause (someone) to break away from a previously friendly state. ▸ **estrangement** *noun*

estrogen *or* **oestrogen** *noun* *Biochem.* a hormone produced mainly by the ovaries, that controls the growth and functioning of the female sex organs.

estrus *or* **oestrus** *noun* *Physiol.* a regularly recurring period of fertility and sexual preparedness in many female mammals.

estuary (ĕs′chə-wĕr,ē) *noun* (*pl.* **estuaries**) the broad mouth of a river that flows into the sea.

ET *or* **E.T.** *abbrev.* Eastern Time.

ETA *abbrev.* estimated time of arrival.

et al. *abbrev. et alia* or *et alii* (Latin), and other things or people.

etc. *abbrev.* et cetera.

et cetera (ət-sĕt′ə-rə, -sĕ′trə) (Latin), and the rest; and so on.

etch *verb trans., intrans.* (**etched, etching**) **1** to make designs on (metal, glass, etc.), using an acid. **2** to make a deep impression. ▸ **etcher** *noun* ▸ **etching** *noun*

ETD *abbrev.* estimated time of departure.

eternal *adj.* **1** having no beginning and no end; everlasting. **2** unchanging: *eternal truths*. **3** *colloq.* frequent; endless. ▸ **eternally** *adv.*

eternity *noun* (*pl.* **eternities**) **1** an endless, or seemingly endless, period of time. **2** the state of being eternal. **3** *Relig.* timeless existence after death. **4** *colloq.* an extremely long time.

-eth *suffix same as* **-th¹**.

ethane *noun* *Chem.* a colorless odorless gas used as a fuel and refrigerant.

ethanol *noun* *Chem.* ethyl alcohol.

ether *noun* **1** a compound of sulfuric acid and alcohol used as a solvent, and as an anesthetic. **2** *poetic* the clear upper air or a clear sky.

ethereal (ĭ-thîr′ē-əl) *adj.* **1** of an unreal lightness; fairylike. **2** heavenly or spiritual. ▸ **ethereally** *adv.*

ethic *noun* **1** the set of principles particular to a certain person, community, etc. **2** (**ethics**) (*sing.*) the study of morals. **3** (**ethics**) (*sing., pl.*) rules or principles of behavior: *medical ethics*. ▸ **ethical** *adj.* ▸ **ethically** *adv.*

ethnic *adj.* **1** having a common national, racial, linguistic, religious, or cultural tradition: *ethnic groups from Africa*. **2** distinctive of such a group: *ethnic clothes*. **3** involving different racial groups: *ethnic violence*. —*noun* a member of a specified ethnic group. ▸ **ethnically** *adv.* ▸ **ethnicity** *noun*

ethnocentric *adj.* relating to or holding the belief that one's own ethnic group is superior to all others. ▸ **ethnocentricity** *noun* ▸ **ethnocentricism** *noun*

ethnography *noun* a detailed description of the culture of a particular society based on fieldwork and participation in the life of the society.

ethnology *noun* the scientific study of different races and cultural traditions. ▸ **ethnological** *adj.* ▸ **ethnologist** *noun*

ethology (ē-thăl′ə-jē) *noun* *Zool.* the study of animal behavior.

ethos (ē'thäs,) *noun* the typical spirit, character, values, and attitudes of a group, period, community, etc.

ethyl *noun Chem.* an organic radical.

ethyl alcohol a colorless flammable liquid, derived from the fermentation of sugar and starch, and used in drugs, and in intoxicating beverages.

ethylene *noun* a colorless flammable gas used in the manufacture of organic chemicals.

ethylene glycol *Chem.* a thick liquid alcohol used as an antifreeze.

etiology (ēt,ē-äl'ə-jē) *or* **aetiology** *noun (pl.* **etiologies**) **1** the study of the origins or causes of disease. **2** the origin or the cause of a given disease.

etiquette *noun* conventions of correct or polite social behavior.

-ette *suffix* forming words denoting: **1** *often offensive* a female of the stated type: *majorette.* **2** a small thing of the type: *cigarette.* **3** an imitation: *leatherette.*

etude (ā'tood,, ā'tyood,) *noun Mus.* a short piece written for a single instrument.

ety. *abbrev.* etymology.

etymology *noun (pl.* **etymologies**) **1** the study of the origin and development of words and their meanings. **2** an explanation of the history of a particular word. ▸ **etymologist** *noun* ▸ **etymological** *adj.*

EU *abbrev.* European Union.

Eu *symbol Chem.* europium.

eucalyptus *noun (pl.* **eucalyptuses, eucalypti**) a large Australian evergreen tree, yielding timber, oils, and gum.

Eucharist (yoo'kə-rĭst) *noun* Christianity (the bread and wine administered at) the sacrament of the Lord's supper. *Also called* **Holy Communion, Mass.** ▸ **Eucharistic** *adj.*

euchre (yoo'kər) *noun Cards* a game for two, three, or four players, played with 32 cards.

eugenics *noun (sing.)* the principle or practice of improving the human race by selective breeding. ▸ **eugenic** *adj.* ▸ **eugenically** *adv.*

eulogize *verb trans.* (**eulogized, eulogizing**) to praise highly; often at a funeral.

eulogy *noun (pl.* **eulogies**) **1** a speech or piece of writing in praise of someone, esp. one who has died. **2** extremely high praise. ▸ **eulogistic** *adj.* ▸ **eulogistically** *adv.*

eunuch (yoo'nək) *noun* **1** a man who has been castrated. **2** *derog.* a person who lacks power or effectiveness.

euphemism *noun* a mild or inoffensive term used in place of one considered offensive. ▸ **euphemistic** *adj.* ▸ **euphemistically** *adv.*

euphonious *adj.* pleasing to the ear. ▸ **euphoniously** *adv.*

euphonium *noun* a large brass instrument of the tuba family.

euphony (yoo'fə-nē) *noun (pl.* **euphonies**) **1** a pleasing sound. **2** pleasantness of sound.

euphoria *noun* a feeling of wild happiness and well-being. ▸ **euphoric** *adj.* ▸ **euphorically** *adv.*

euphuism *noun* a pompous and affected style of writing.

Eur. *abbrev.* Europe; European.

Eurasian (yŏŏr-ā'zhən, -ā'shən) *adj.* **1** of mixed European and Asian descent. **2** of or relating to Europe and Asia. —*noun* a person of mixed European and Asian descent.

eureka *interj.* used to express triumph at finding something, solving a problem, etc.

Euro- *combining form* forming words denoting Europe; European: *Eurodollars.*

Eurocurrency *noun* convertible currencies held in banks in W Europe outside the country of origin.

Eurodollars *pl. noun* US currency held in European banks to assist trade.

European (yŏŏr,ə-pē'ən) *adj.* **1** of Europe, its people, or their languages. **2** favoring cooperation between the countries of Europe. —*noun* **1** a native or citizen of Europe. **2** a person who favors cooperation between the countries of Europe.

europium *noun Chem.* (SYMBOL **Eu**) a soft silvery metal used as a neutron absorber in nuclear reactors.

eustachian tube *or* **Eustachian tube** (yŏŏ-stā'shē-ən, -kē-ən) either of the two tubes that connect the middle ear to the pharynx.

euthanasia *noun* the act or practice of ending the life of a patient who is suffering from an incurable illness.

evacuate *verb trans., intrans.* (**evacuated, evacuating**) **1 a** to leave (a place), esp. because of danger. **b** to leave hurriedly because of danger. **c** to cause (people) to leave a place, esp. because of danger. **2** *Med.* to empty (the bowels). ▸ **evacuation** *noun*

evacuee *noun* an evacuated person.

evade *verb trans.* (**evaded, evading**) **1** to escape or avoid by trickery or skill: *evaded capture.* **2** to avoid answering (a question). ⊟ DODGE, EQUIVOCATE, HEDGE, PUSSYFOOT, SIDESTEP, TERGIVERSATE, WEASEL ⊟ CONFRONT

evaluate *verb trans.* (**evaluated, evaluating**) **1** to form a judgment about the worth of. **2** *Math.* to calculate the value of. ▸ **evaluation** *noun*

evanesce (ĕv,ə-nĕs') *verb intrans.* (**evanesced, evanescing**) to go gradually out of sight. ▸ **evanescence** *noun* ▸ **evanescent** *adj.*

evangelical (ē,văn,jĕl'ĭ-kəl, ĕv,ən-) *adj.* **1** based on the Gospels. **2** of a group within the Protestant church stressing the authority of the Bible, and seeking the con-

version of sinners. ▸ **evangelically** adv.
▸ **evangelicalism** noun

evangelism noun **1** the act or practice of evangelizing. **2** evangelicalism. ▸ **evangelistic** adj.

evangelist noun **1** a person who preaches Christianity, esp. at large public meetings. **2** (usu. **Evangelist**) each of the writers of the four Biblical Gospels.

evangelize verb trans., intrans. (**evangelized, evangelizing**) **1** to preach the gospel to. **2** to attempt to convert. ▸ **evangelization** noun

evaporate verb trans., intrans. (**evaporated, evaporating**) **1** to change or cause to change from a liquid into a vapor. **2** to disappear, or cause to disappear. ▸ **evaporation** noun

evasion noun **1** the act of evading. **2** a trick used to evade a question, etc.

> Usage See note at **avoidance**

evasive adj. **1** having the purpose of evading. **2** displaying a lack of openness. ▸ **evasively** adv. ▸ **evasiveness** noun

eve noun **1** the evening or day before a notable event. **2** the period immediately before something is to happen: the eve of war.

even[1] adj. **1** smooth and flat. **2** constant or regular: traveling an even 50 mph. **3** divisible by 2, with nothing left over. **4** (**even with**) on the same plane or at the same height; level. **5** equal: an even chance. **6** of temper calm. —adv. **1** still, yet: He's good, but she's even better. **2** used to emphasize: She looked sad, even depressed. **3** used to introduce a surprising piece of information: Even John was there! **4** (**even if** or **though**) in spite of the fact that. —verb trans., intrans. (**evened, evening**) **1** to make even. **2** (**even out**) to become level or regular. —noun (usu. **evens**) an even number or something designated by one. ▸ **evenness** noun ▸ **evenly** adv.

even[2] noun old use, poetic evening.

evenhanded adj. fair; unbiased. ▸ **evenhandedly** adv. ▸ **evenhandedness** noun

evening noun **1** the last part of the day. **2** the latter part of something: the evening of the old admiral's life.

evensong noun a service of evening prayer; vespers.

event noun **1** something that occurs or happens; an incident. **2** an item in a sports program, etc.: various Olympic events.

eventful adj. full of important or significant events. ▸ **eventfully** adv.

eventide noun poetic evening.

eventual adj. happening at the end of a period of time, process, etc. ▸ **eventually** adv.

eventuality noun (pl. **eventualities**) a possible happening or result.

eventuate verb intrans. (**eventuated, eventuating**) formal to result; to turn out.

ever adv. **1** at any time. **2** formal always; continually: She was ever the dignified monarch. **3** used for emphasis: She's ever so beautiful!

everglade noun a large marsh, typically under water.

evergreen adj. of certain trees and shrubs bearing leaves all the year round. —noun a tree or shrub that bears leaves all the year round.

everlasting adj. without, or seemingly without end; continual. —noun **1** any of several kinds of flowers that keep their shape and color when dried. **2** eternity. ▸ **everlastingly** adv.

evermore adv. for all time to come; eternally.

every adj. **1** each single, omitting none. **2** all possible: We're making every effort to avoid war. —adv. at, in, or at the end of each stated period of time, distance, etc.: every fourth week. —**every now and again** or **every so often** from time to time; occasionally.

everybody pron. every person.

everyday adj. **1** happening, done, used, etc., daily. **2** common or usual.

everyone pron. every person.

everything pron. **1** all things; all. **2** the most important thing.

everywhere adv. in or to every place.

evict verb trans. (**evicted, evicting**) to put out of a house, etc., or off land by force of law. ▸ **eviction** noun

evidence noun **1** information, etc., that gives grounds for belief. **2** Law written or spoken testimony used in a court of law. —verb trans. (**evidenced, evidencing**) to be evidence of; to prove. ▸ **evidential** adj. ▸ **evidentially** adv.

evident adj. clear to see or understand; obvious; apparent.

evidently adv. **1** obviously; apparently: He is evidently drunk. **2** as it appears; so it seems: Evidently they don't believe us.

evil adj. **1** morally bad or offensive. **2** harmful. **3** colloq. very unpleasant: an evil stench. —noun **1** wickedness, sin. **2** harm. **3** something bad or unpleasant. ▸ **evilly** adv.

evildoer noun a person who does evil things.

evil eye (the evil eye) **1** the supposed power of causing harm by a look. **2** a glare, superstitiously thought to cause harm.

evince verb trans. (**evinced, evincing**) to show or display (a personal quality) clearly.

eviscerate (ĭ-vĭs′ə-rāt,) verb trans. (**eviscerated, eviscerating**) **1** to tear out the bowels of. **2** to take away the essential quality or meaning of. ▸ **evisceration** noun

evoke verb trans. (**evoked, evoking**) **1** to bring or draw out (something reserved or hidden). **2** to bring to the mind. ▸ **evocation** noun ▸ **evocative** adj.

evolution noun **1** the process of evolving. **2** a gradual development. **3** the teaching that higher forms of life have gradually arisen out of lower. **4** Chem. the giving off of a gas. ▸ **evolutionary** adv. ▸ **evolutionism**

evolutionism noun **1** belief in the theory of evolution. **2** a 19th c belief that organisms were intrinsically bound to improve themselves, and that acquired characters could be transmitted genetically. ▸ **evolutionist** noun

evolve verb trans., intrans. (**evolved, evolving**) **1** to develop or produce gradually. **2** to develop from a primitive into a more complex or advanced form. **3** Chem. to give off (heat, etc.).

ewe (yōō) noun a female sheep.

ewer noun a large water jug with a wide mouth.

ex¹ noun (pl. **exes, ex's**) colloq. a former husband, wife, or lover.

ex² prep. **1** direct from: ex warehouse. **2** excluding: ex dividend.

ex- prefix forming words denoting: **1** former: ex-wife. **2** outside: exogamy.

exacerbate (ĭg-zăs′ər-bāt,) verb trans. (**exacerbated, exacerbating**) to make (pain, emotion, a bad situation, etc.) worse. ▸ **exacerbation** noun

exact adj. completely accurate; correct; precise —verb trans. (**exacted, exacting**) **1** (**exact (something) from** or **of (someone)**) to demand (e.g., payment, loyalty) from (the one or ones specified). **2** to insist on (a right, etc.). ▸ **exactly** adv. ▸ **exactitude** noun ▸ **exactness** noun

exacting adj. making difficult or excessive demands. ▸ **exactingly** adv.

exaction noun **1** the act of demanding payment, or the payment demanded. **2** illegal demands for money.

exaggerate verb trans., intrans. (**exaggerated, exaggerating**) **1** to describe something as being greater or better than it really is. **2** to go beyond the truth. ▸ **exaggeration** noun ▸ **exaggerator** noun

exalt verb trans. (**exalted, exalting**) **1** to praise highly. **2** to fill with great joy. **3** to give a higher rank or position to. ▸ **exaltation** noun

exalted adj. **1** very moral; noble. **2** too high; exaggerated. ▸ **exaltedly** adv.

exam noun colloq. an examination (senses 1 and 2).

examination noun **1** a test of knowledge or ability. **2** an inspection of a person's state of health. **3** the act or process of examining. **4** formal questioning.

examine verb trans. (**examined, examining**) **1** to inspect, consider, or look into closely. **2** to check the health of. **3** to test the knowledge or ability of (a person). **4** to question formally in a court of law. ▸ **examinee** noun ▸ **examiner** noun

example noun **1** a specimen. **2** an illustration of a fact or rule. **3** a model to be, or not to be, copied: set a good example / a poor example in planning.

exasperate verb trans. (**exasperated, exasperating**) to make (someone) annoyed and frustrated. ▸ **exasperation** noun

excavate verb trans. (**excavated, excavating**) **1** to dig up or uncover (esp. historical remains). **2** to dig up (a piece of ground, etc.). ▸ **excavation** noun ▸ **excavator** noun

exceed verb trans. (**exceeded, exceeding**) **1** to be greater than. **2** to go beyond.

exceedingly adv. to a high degree; very; extremely.

excel verb intrans., trans. (**excelled, excelling**) **1** (**excel in** or **at (something)**) to be exceptionally good at (it). **2** to be better than: She excels her sister in math.

Excellency noun (pl. **Excellencies**) used with His, Her, or Your as a title of honor given to, e.g., an ambassador.

excellent adj. of very high quality; extremely good. ▸ **excellence** noun ▸ **excellently** adv.

except prep. leaving out; not including. —verb trans., intrans. (**excepted, excepting**) to leave out or exclude.

excepting prep. not including or counting; leaving out.

exception noun **1** a person or thing not included. **2** someone or something that does not follow a general rule. **3** an act of excluding. **4** a formal objection. —**take exception to** to object to.

exceptionable adj. **1** likely to cause disapproval or offense. **2** open to objection.

exceptional adj. **1** remarkable or outstanding. **2** being an exception. ▸ **exceptionally** adv.

excerpt noun (ĕk′sərpt, ĕg′zərpt,) a short passage taken from a book, film, etc. —verb trans. (ĕk-sərpt′, ĕg-zərpt′) (**excerpted, excerpting**) to select extracts from (a book, etc.).

excess noun **1** going beyond normal or suitable limits. **2** an extreme amount. **3** the amount by which one quantity, etc., exceeds another; an amount left over. **4** (often **excesses**) over-indulgence. —adj. greater than is usual, necessary, or permitted. —**in excess of** going beyond. ▸ **excessive** adj.

exchange verb trans. (**exchanged, exchanging**) **1** to give, or give up, in return for something else. **2** to give and receive. —noun **1** the giving and taking of one thing for another. **2** a thing exchanged. **3** giving and receiving in return. **4** a conversation or argument. **5** the act of changing the currency of one country for that of another. **6** a place where shares are traded, or international financial deals carried out. **7** a central telephone system. —**in exchange for** in return for. ▶ **exchangeable** adj.

exchequer noun **1** Brit. (often **Exchequer**) the government department in charge of financial affairs. **2** financial resources and funding.

excise¹ (ĕk'sīz,, -sīs,) noun the tax on goods, etc., produced and sold within a country, and on certain licences. —verb trans. (**excised, excising**) to charge excise on (goods, etc.).

excise² (ĭk-sīz') verb trans. (**excised, excising**) **1** to remove (e.g., a passage from a book). **2** to cut out or cut off by surgery. ▶ **excision** noun

excitable adj. easily excited, flustered, frantic, etc. ▶ **excitability** noun ▶ **excitably** adv.

excite verb trans. (**excited, exciting**) **1** to cause to feel lively expectation or a pleasant tension and thrill. **2** to arouse (feelings, emotions, sensations; etc.). **3** to provoke (e.g., action). **4** to arouse sexually. ▶ **excitation** noun ▶ **excitement** noun ▶ **excited** adj. ▶ **excitedly** adv. ▶ **exciting** adj. ▶ **excitingly** adv.

exclaim verb trans., intrans. (**exclaimed, exclaiming**) to call or cry out suddenly, e.g., in surprise. ▶ **exclamation** noun

exclamation point the punctuation mark ! used to indicate an exclamation. Also called **exclamation mark**.

exclamatory adj. containing or expressing exclamation.

exclude verb trans. (**excluded, excluding**) **1** to shut out or keep out. **2** to omit or leave out of consideration. ▶ **exclusion** noun ▶ **exclusionary** adj.

excluding prep. not counting; without including.

exclusive adj. **1** rejecting everything else: mutually exclusive statements. **2** (**exclusive to**) limited to only one place, group, or person. **3** select; snobbish. **4** fashionable and expensive. —noun a report or story published in only one newspaper or magazine. ▶ **exclusively** adv. ▶ **exclusiveness** noun

excommunicate verb trans. (**excommunicated, excommunicating**) to remove (someone) from membership in a church by ecclesiastical edit or authority. ▶ **excommunication** noun

excoriate (ĭk-skôr'ē-āt,) verb trans. (**excoriated, excoriating**) **1** to strip the skin from (a person or animal). **2** to criticize severely. ▶ **excoriation** noun

excrement noun waste matter passed out of the body, esp. feces. ▶ **excremental** adj.

excrescence noun **1** an abnormal outgrowth

on the surface of the body or on an organ. **2** an unsightly addition.

excreta pl. noun excreted matter; feces or urine.

excrete verb trans. (**excreted, excreting**) of a plant or animal to eliminate (waste products). ▶ **excretion** noun ▶ **excretory** adj.

excruciating adj. **1** extremely painful. **2** colloq. extremely bad or irritating. ▶ **excruciatingly** adv.

exculpate verb trans. (**exculpated, exculpating**) formal to remove from guilt or blame. ▶ **exculpation** noun

excursion noun **1** a short trip, usu. one made for pleasure. **2** a digression.

excursive adj. formal tending to wander from the main point.

excuse (ĭk-skyōōz') verb trans. (**excused, excusing**) **1** to pardon or forgive. **2** to ask permission to absent oneself **3** to free (from an obligation, a duty, etc.). **4** to allow to leave (a room, etc.). —noun (ĭk-skyōōs') **1** a justifying explanation for a mistake or wrongdoing. **2** a very poor example: You'll never sell this excuse for a painting! ▶ **excusable** adv. ▶ **excusably** adv.

execrate verb trans. (**execrated, execrating**) **1** to regard with great contempt or dislike. **2** to curse. ▶ **execrable** adv. ▶ **execrably** adv. ▶ **execration** noun

execute (ĕk'sĭ-kyōōt,) verb trans. (**executed, executing**) **1** to put to death by order of the law. **2** to perform or carry out: execute a duty. **3** Law to make valid by signing. **4** to carry out instructions contained in (a will or contract). ▶ **execution** noun

executioner noun a person who carries out a sentence of death.

executive (ĭg-zĕk'yət-ĭv) adj. **1** concerned with management or administration of a business operation. **2** relating to the branch of a government responsible for administering and carrying out its laws. —noun **1** the executive branch of a business. **2** the executive branch of government.

executor (ĭg-zĕk'yət-ər) noun a person appointed to carry out instructions stated in a will.

executrix (ĭg-zĕk'yə-trĭks) noun (pl. **executrixes, executrices**) a woman appointed to carry out instructions stated in a will.

exegesis (ĕk,sə-jē'sĭs) noun (pl. **exegeses**) a critical explanation of a text, esp. of the Bible. ▶ **exegetic** or **exegetical** adj.

exemplar (ĭg-zĕm'plär,, -plər) noun **1** a model worth copying. **2** a typical example.

exemplary adj. **1** serving as an illustration or warning. **2** worth following as an example.

exemplification noun provision of an example or examples; illustration.

exemplify verb trans. (**exemplified, exemplifying, exemplifies**) 1 to be an example of. 2 to show an example of; to show by means of an example.

exempt verb trans. (**exempted, exempting**) to free from a duty or obligation that applies to others. —adj. free from an obligation; not liable. ▸ **exemption** noun

exercise noun 1 physical or mental training. 2 an activity intended to develop a skill. 3 a task that tests ability. 4 formal the act of putting into practice: the exercise of one's duty. 5 (usu. **exercises**) Mil. training and practice for soldiers. —verb intrans., trans. (**exercised, exercising**) 1 to give exercise to; to train. 2 to use: exercise the right to vote. 3 to worry or make anxious.

exert verb trans. (**exerted, exerting**) 1 to bring into use or action forcefully: exert one's authority. 2 to force (oneself) to make a strenuous, esp. physical, effort. ▸ **exertion** noun

exhale verb trans., intrans. (**exhaled, exhaling**) 1 to breathe out. 2 to give off or be given off. ▸ **exhalation** noun

exhaust (ĭg-zôst') verb trans. (**exhausted, exhausting**) 1 to make very tired. 2 to use up completely: exhaust a supply of fuel. 3 to say all that can be said about (a subject, etc.). —noun 1 the waste gases from an engine. 2 the part of an engine through which waste gases escape. ▸ **exhausted** adj. ▸ **exhausting** adj. ▸ **exhaustible** adj. **exhaustion** noun

exhaustive adj. very thorough; complete: an exhaustive search. ▸ **exhaustively** adv.

exhibit (ĭg-zĭb'ĭt) verb trans. (**exhibited, exhibiting**) 1 to present for public appreciation. 2 to manifest (a quality, etc.): exhibits politeness. —noun 1 an object displayed publicly. 2 an object produced in a court of law as part of the evidence.

exhibition (ĕk,sə-bĭsh'ən) noun 1 a public display, e.g., of works of art. 2 the act or an instance of showing, e.g., a quality.

exhibitionism noun the tendency to behave so as to attract attention to oneself. ▸ **exhibitionist** noun ▸ **exhibitionistic** adj.

exhibitor (ĭg-zĭb'ĭt-ər) noun one that provides an exhibit for public display.

exhilarate (ĭg-zĭl'ə-rāt,) verb trans. (**exhilarated, exhilarating**) to fill with lively cheerfulness. ▸ **exhilaration** noun

exhort (ĭg-zôrt') verb trans. (**exhorted, exhorting**) to urge or advise strongly and sincerely. ▸ **exhortation** noun

exhume (ĭg-zōōm') verb trans. (**exhumed, exhuming**) to dig up (a corpse) from a grave. ▸ **exhumation** noun

exigency (ĭg-zĭj'ən-sē) noun (pl. **exigencies**) 1 (**exigencies**) urgent needs: the exigencies of life. 2 an emergency.

exigent (ĕk'sĭ-jənt) adj. 1 pressing; urgent. 2 demanding and difficult.

exiguous (ĭg-zĭg'yə-wəs) adj. meager: an exiguous budget. ▸ **exiguity** noun ▸ **exiguously** adv. ▸ **exiguousness** noun

exile (ĕg'zīl', ĕk'sīl,) noun 1 enforced absence from one's country. 2 a person suffering enforced absence from his or her country. —verb trans. (**exiled, exiling**) to banish.

exist verb intrans. (**existed, existing**) 1 to be. 2 to occur or be found: fossils existing in cold climes. 3 to manage to stay alive.

existence noun 1 the state of existing or being. 2 a life, or a way of living. 3 everything that exists.

existent adj. having an actual being; existing.

existential adj. 1 relating to human existence. 2 Philos. relating to existentialism.

existentialism noun a philosophy that emphasizes freedom of choice and personal responsibility for one's own actions. ▸ **existentialist** adj. noun

exit (ĕg'sĭt, ĕk'sĭt) noun 1 a way out, e.g., of a building. 2 an act of going out. 3 a performer's departure from the stage. —verb intrans. (**exited, exiting**) 1 to go out, leave, or depart. 2 as a stage direction (he or she) leaves the stage.

exo- combining form forming words denoting out or outside: exobiology. See also **ecto-, endo-, ento-**.

exocrine noun of a gland discharging its secretions through a duct. See also **endocrine**.

exodus (ĕg'zəd-əs, ĕk'səd-) noun 1 a mass departure of people. 2 (**Exodus**) the departure of the Israelites from Egypt.

ex officio (ĕk,sə-fĭsh'ē-ō,) adv. by virtue of one's official position.

exogamy (ĕk-săg'ə-mē) noun the practice of marrying only outside one's own group.

exogenous adj. Biol. originating outside a cell, organ, or organism.

exonerate verb trans. (**exonerated, exonerating**) to free from blame; acquit. ▸ **exoneration** noun

exorbitance noun excessiveness of prices or demands.

exorbitant (ĭg-zôr'bĭt-ənt) adj., of prices or demands very high, excessive, or unfair. ▸ **exorbitance** adj. ▸ **exorbitantly** adv.

exorcise (ĕk'sər-sīz,) verb trans. (**exorcised, exorcising**) to drive away (an evil spirit). ▸ **exorcism** noun ▸ **exorcist** noun

exordium noun (pl. **exordiums, exordia**) formal an introductory part, esp. of a formal speech or piece of writing.

exosphere noun Astron. the outermost layer of Earth's atmosphere.

exotic (ĭg-zăt'ĭk) adj. 1 introduced from a

foreign country. **2** interestingly different; colorful and rich. —*noun* an exotic person or thing. ▸ **exotically** *adv.*

expand *verb trans., intrans.* (**expanded, expanding**) **1** to make or become larger. **2** (**expand on** *or* **upon** (**something**)) to give additional information. **3** to unfold or spread out. **4** to write out in full. ▸ **expandable** *adj.*

expanse *noun* a wide area or space.

expansible *adj.* able to expand or be expanded.

expansion *noun* **1** the act of expanding or the state of having been expanded. **2** the amount by which something expands.

expansionism *noun* the act or practice of increasing territory or political influence. ▸ **expansionist** *noun, adj.*

expansive *adj.* **1** ready or eager to talk; open; effusive. **2** wide-ranging; comprehensive. **3** able or tending to expand. ▸ **expansively** *adv.* ▸ **expansiveness** *noun*

expatiate (ĭk-spā′shē-āt,) *verb intrans.* (**expatiated, expatiating**) *formal* to talk or write at length. ▸ **expatiation** *noun*

expatriate *adj.* (ĕk-spā′trē-ət, -āt,) **1** living in a foreign land. **2** having been exiled. —*noun* (ĕk-spā′trē-āt,) a person living or work-ing in a foreign land. —*verb trans.* (pro-nounced -ate) (**expatriated, expatriating**) **1** to banish or exile. **2** to deprive of citizenship.

expect *verb trans., intrans.* (**expected, expecting**) **1** to think of as likely to happen or come: *expect trouble.* **2** (**expect** (**something**) **from** *or* **of** (**someone**)) to regard (it) as normal or reasonable. **3** *colloq.* to suppose. **4** (in the progressive) to be pregnant: *She's expecting.*

expectancy *noun* (*pl.* **expectancies**) **1** the act or state of expecting. **2** a future chance or probability: *life expectancy.*

expectant *adj.* **1** eagerly waiting; hopeful. **2** expecting to be, esp. a mother or father. ▸ **expectantly** *adv.*

expectation *noun* **1** the state of expecting. **2** (**expectations**) one's prospects, whether good or bad.

expectorant *Med. adj.* causing the coughing up of phlegm. —*noun* a medicine that causes the coughing up of phlegm.

expectorate (ĭk-spĕk′tə-rāt,) *verb trans., intrans.* (**expectorated, expectorating**) *Med.* to cough up and spit out (phlegm).

expedient (ĭk-spēd′ē-ənt) *adj.* **1** suitable or appropriate. **2** practical or advantageous, rather than morally correct. —*noun* a suitable method or solution, esp. one quickly thought of to meet an urgent need. ▸ **expediency** *or* **expedience** *noun* ▸ **expediently** *adv.*

expedite (ĕk′spə-dīt,) *verb trans.* (**expedited, expediting**) **1** to speed up, or assist

the progress of. **2** to carry out quickly.

expedition *noun* **1** an organized journey with a purpose, or the group making it. **2** *formal* speed; promptness. ▸ **expeditionary** *adj.*

expeditious *adj. formal* carried out with speed and efficiency. ▸ **expeditiously** *adv.*

expel *verb trans.* (**expelled, expelling**) **1** to dismiss. **2** to get rid of; to force out.

expend *verb trans.* (**expended, expending**) to use or spend (time, supplies, effort, etc.).

expendable *adj.* **1** that may be given up. **2** not valuable enough to be worth preserving.

expenditure *noun* **1** the act of expending. **2** an amount, esp. of money, that is expended.

expense *noun* **1** money spent. **2** something on which money is spent. **3** (**expenses**) charges incurred by an employee. —*verb trans.* (**expensed, expensing**) to write (something) off as an expense.

expensive *adj.* of great monetary price. ▣ COSTLY, DEAR, HIGH, STEEP ▣ CHEAP, INEXPENSIVE, LOW. ▸ **expensively** *adv.*

experience *noun* **1** practice in an activity. **2** knowledge or skill gained through practice or observation. **3** an event that affects or involves one. —*verb trans.* (**experienced, experiencing**) **1** to have practical acquaintance with. **2** to feel or undergo. ▸ **experienced** *adj.*

experiential *adj.*, based on direct experience. ▸ **experientially** *adv.*

experiment *noun* (ĭk-spĭr′ə-mənt) **1** a trial carried out in order to test a theory, a machine's performance, etc. **2** an attempt at something original. —*verb intrans.* (ĭk-spĭr′ə-mĕnt,) (**experimented, experimenting**) to carry out an experiment. ▸ **experimental** *adj.* ▸ **experimentally** *adv.* ▸ **experimentation** *noun* ▸ **experimenter** *noun*

expert *noun* a person who is skilled through long practice. —*adj.* **1** highly skilled or extremely knowledgeable. **2** relating to or done by an expert or experts. ▸ **expertly** *adv.*

expertise (ĕk,spər-tēz′, -tēs′) *noun* a skill, esp. one gained through practice or knowledge.

expiate (ĕk′spē-āt,) *verb trans.* (**expiated, expiating**) to make amends for (a wrong). ▸ **expiation** *noun*

expire *verb intrans.* (**expired, expiring**) **1** to come to an end; cease to be valid. **2** to breathe out; to exhale. **3** to stop living; to cease to be alive. ▸ **expiration** *noun*

expiry *noun* (*pl.* **expiries**) the ending of the duration or validity of, e.g., a contract.

explain *verb trans., intrans.* (**explained, explaining**) **1** to make clear or easy to understand: *explained the theorem.* **2** to give, or be, a reason for: *Let me explain my reasons for objecting.* ▸ **explanatory** *adj.*

explanation *noun* **1** the act or process of explaining. **2** a statement or fact that explains.

expletive *noun* an oath or exclamation.

explicable (ĭk-splĭk′ə-bəl) *adj.* able to be explained.

explicate (ĕk′splĭ-kāt,) *verb trans.* (**explicated, explicating**) to explain (esp. a literary work) in depth. ▸ **explication** *noun*

explicit (ĭk-splĭs′ĭt) *adj.* **1** stated or shown fully and clearly. **2** showing or otherwise depicting sexual activity or nudity in graphic detail. ▸ **explicitly** *adv.* ▸ **explicitness** *noun*

explode *verb intrans., trans.* (**exploded, exploding**) **1** to cause or undergo an explosion. **2** to suddenly show a strong or violent emotion, esp. anger. **3** to disprove (a theory, etc.) with vigor. **4** *of population* to increase rapidly.

exploit *noun* (ĕk′sploit,) a daring act or feat. —*verb trans.* (ĭk-sploit′) (**exploited, exploiting**) **1** to take unfair advantage of. **2** to make good use of: *exploit oil resources.* ▸ **exploitation** *noun*

explore *verb trans.* (**explored, exploring**) **1** to search or travel through (a place) for the purpose of discovery. **2** to examine carefully. ▸ **exploration** *noun* ▸ **exploratory** *adj.* ▸ **explorer** *noun*

explosion *noun* **1** *Chem.* **a** a sudden, violent increase in pressure that generates heat and destructive shock waves that are heard as a loud bang. **b** the sudden loud noise that accompanies such a reaction. **2** a sudden display, e.g., of strong feelings. **3** a sudden great increase, e.g., in a population.

explosive (ĭk-splō′sĭv, -zĭv) *adj.* **1** tending to explode. **2** having a tendency towards emotional outbursts. **3** likely to result in an outburst of feeling: *an explosive situation.* —*noun* a substance capable of producing an explosion. ▸ **explosively** *adv.*

expo *noun* (*pl.* **expos**) *colloq.* a large public exposition.

exponent (ĭk-spō′nənt) *noun* **1** *Math.* a symbol showing the power to which a quantity is to be taken. **2** a supporter of, e.g., a belief. **3** one that interprets something or otherwise expounds upon it.

exponential (ĕk,spə-nĕn′chəl) *Math. adj.* involving an ever more rapid increase. ▸ **exponentially** *adv.*

export *verb trans.* (ĕk-spôrt′, ĕk′spôrt,) (**exported, exporting**) to send or take (goods, etc.) to another country, esp. for sale. —*noun* (ĕk′spôrt,) **1** the act or business of exporting. **2** a product or a set of products exported. ▸ **exportation** *noun* ▸ **exporter** *noun*

expose *verb trans.* (**exposed, exposing**) **1** to remove cover from: *a deck exposed to high winds.* **2** (**expose (someone) to (some-**thing)) to subject (one) to **3** to discover or make known (e.g., a criminal or crime). **4** to subject (film) to the action of light.

exposé (ĕk,spō-zā′, -spə-) *noun* a formal statement of facts, esp. one introducing an argument.

exposition *noun* **1** an in-depth explanation or account (of a subject). **2** a large public exhibition.

expostulate (ĭk-späs′chə-lāt,) *verb intrans.* (**expostulated, expostulating**) (**expostulate with** (**someone**)) to argue or reason with (someone). ▸ **expostulation** *noun*

exposure *noun* **1** the act of exposing or the state of being exposed. **2** the harmful effects on the body of extreme cold. **3** the number or regularity of appearances in public, e.g., on television. **4 a** the act of exposing photographic film or paper to light. **b** film exposed in this way.

expound *verb trans., intrans.* (**expounded, expounding**) **1** to explain in depth: *expound a theory.* **2** to talk at length about a topic.

express *verb trans.* (**expressed, expressing**) **1** to put into words. **2** to indicate or represent. **3** to show or reveal. **4** to press or squeeze out: *express juice from a lemon.* **5** to send by fast delivery service. —*adj.* **1** *of a train or bus* traveling fast, with few stops. **2** sent by a fast delivery service. **3** clearly stated: *her express wish.* **4** particular; clear: *with the express purpose of leaving.* —*noun* **1** an express train or bus. **2** an express delivery service. —*adv.* by express delivery service. ▸ **expressible** *adj.*

expression *noun* **1 a** the act of expressing. **b** the indication of feeling, e.g., in a manner of speaking. **2** a word or phrase. **3** a look on the face that displays feelings. **4** *Math.* a set of symbols that represents a quantity.

Expressionism (ĭk-sprĕsh′ə-nĭz,əm) *noun* a movement in art, architecture, and literature that aims to communicate the internal emotional realities of a situation. ▸ **Expressionist** *noun*

expressionless *adj.* showing no feeling; impassive.

expressive *adj.* **1** showing meaning or feeling in a clear or lively way. **2** (**expressive of** (**something**)) expressing a feeling or emotion. ▸ **expressively** *adv.* ▸ **expressiveness** *noun* ▸ **expressivity** *noun*

expressly *adv.* **1** clearly and definitely. **2** particularly; specifically.

expresso *noun* same as **espresso**.

expressway *noun* a freeway.

expropriate (ĭk-sprō′prē-āt,) *verb trans.* (**expropriated, expropriating**) *of a state* to take (money, property, etc.) away from its owner.

expulsion noun **1** the act of expelling from school, a club, etc. **2** the act of forcing or driving out. ▸ **expulsive** adj.

expunge verb trans. (**expunged, expunging**) **1** to cross out or delete (e.g., a passage from a book). **2** to cancel out or destroy.

expurgate (ĕk'spər-gāt,) verb trans. (**expurgated, expurgating**) to revise (a book) by removing objectionable or offensive words or passages. ▸ **expurgation** noun

exquisite (ĕk-skwĭz'ĭt, ĕk'skwĭz,-) adj. **1** extremely beautiful or skillfully produced. **2** of pain, pleasure, etc. extreme. ▸ **exquisitely** adv.

ext. abbrev. **1** extension. **2** exterior. **3** external; externally.

extant (ĕk'stənt, ĭk-stănt') adj. still existing or living.

extemporaneous adj. spoken, done, etc., without preparation; impromptu. ▸ **extemporaneously** adv.

extempore (ĭk-stĕm'pə-rē) adv., adj. without planning or preparation.

extemporize verb trans., intrans. (**extemporized, extemporizing**) to speak or perform without preparation. ▸ **extemporization** noun

extend verb trans., intrans. (**extended, extending**) **1** to make longer or larger. **2** to reach or stretch in space or time: a view extending across the desert. **3** to hold out (a hand, etc.). **4** to offer (kindness, etc.).

extendable or **extendible** adj. extensible.

extensible adj. capable of being extended or made longer.

extension noun **1** the process of extending, or the state of being extended. **2** an added part, making the original larger or longer. **3** a subsidiary or extra telephone.

extensive adj. large in area, amount, range, or effect. ▸ **extensively** adv.

extensor noun Physiol. any of various muscles that straighten out limbs.

extent noun **1** the area over which something extends. **2** amount, scope, or degree.

extenuate (ĭk-stĕn'yə-wāt,) verb trans. (**extenuated, extenuating**) to reduce the seriousness of (an offense) by giving an explanation that partly excuses it. ▸ **extenuation** noun ▸ **extenuating** adj.

exterior adj. on, from, or for use on the outside. —noun **1** an outside part or surface. **2** an outward appearance.

exterminate verb trans. (**exterminated, exterminating**) to get rid of or completely destroy (living beings). ▸ **extermination** noun ▸ **exterminator** noun

external (ĕk-stərn'l) adj. **1** of, for, from, or on the outside. **2** of the world: external realities. **3** involving foreign nations; foreign.

—noun (**externals**) outward appearances, features, or circumstances. ▸ **externally** adv.

externalize verb trans. (**externalized, externalizing**) to express (thoughts, feelings, ideas, etc.) in words.

extinct adj. **1** of a species of animal, etc. no longer in existence. **2** of a volcano no longer active.

extinction noun **1** the process of making or becoming extinct; elimination or disappearance. **2** Biol. the total elimination or dying out of any plant or animal species, or a whole group of species, worldwide.

extinguish verb trans. (**extinguished, extinguishing**) **1** to put out (a fire, etc.). **2** to kill off or destroy (e.g., passion). ▸ **extinguisher** noun

extirpate (ĕk'stər-pāt,) verb trans. (**extirpated, extirpating**) **1** to destroy completely. **2** to uproot; to root out. **3** to remove surgically. ▸ **extirpation** noun

extn. abbrev. extension.

extol (ĭk-stōl') verb trans. (**extolled, extolling**) to praise enthusiastically. ▸ **extolment** noun

extort verb trans. (**extorted, extorting**) to obtain (money, information, etc.) by threats or violence. ▸ **extortion** noun ▸ **extortionist** noun

extortionate (ĭk-stôr'shə-nət) adj. **1** of a price unreasonably high or great. **2** using extortion. ▸ **extortionately** adv.

extra adj. more than is usual or necessary; additional —noun **1** an additional or unexpected thing. **2** a performer employed temporarily in a small part in a movie. **3** a special edition of a newspaper containing later news. —adv. unusually; exceptionally.

extra- prefix forming words denoting outside or beyond: extra-curricular.

extract verb trans. (ĭk-străkt) (**extracted, extracting**) **1** to bring or draw out (something reserved or hidden). **2** to separate a substance from a liquid or solid mixture. **3** to obtain (money, etc.) by threats or violence. **4** to select (passages from a book, etc.). **5** Dentistry to pull (a tooth). —noun (ĕk'străkt,) **1** a passage selected from a book, etc. **2** Chem. a concentrated substance that is drawn from a liquid or solid mixture by heat, distillation, etc. ▸ **extractor** noun ▸ **extraction** noun

extracurricular adj. not belonging to the subjects studied in a school's or college's main teaching curriculum.

extradite verb trans. (**extradited, extraditing**) to return (a person accused of a crime) for trial in the country where the crime was committed. ▸ **extraditable** adj. ▸ **extradition** noun

extramarital adj., esp. of sexual relations taking place outside marriage.

extramural adj. 1 of courses, etc. for people who are not full-time students at a college, etc. 2 outside the scope of normal studies.

extraneous (ĭk-strā'nē-əs) adj. 1 not relevant or related; not belonging. 2 coming from outside. ▸ **extraneously** adv.

extraordinary (ĭk-strôrd'n-ĕr,ē, ĕk,strə-ôrd'-) adj. 1 unusual; surprising; remarkable. 2 not usual or regular. 3 (following the noun) employed to do additional work: ambassador extraordinary. ▸ **extraordinarily** adv.

extrapolate (ĭk-străp'ə-lāt,) verb trans., intrans. (**extrapolated, extrapolating**) to make (an estimate) based on known facts. ▸ **extrapolation** noun

extrasensory perception (ABBREV. ESP) perception realized by means other than the five senses.

extraterrestrial adj. coming from outside Earth or its atmosphere. —noun a being not of Earth.

extravagant adj. 1 using, spending, or costing too much. 2 unreasonably or unbelievably great: extravagant claims. ▸ **extravagance** noun ▸ **extravagantly** adv.

extravaganza (ĭk-străv,ə-găn'zə) noun a spectacular display, performance, or production.

extravert (ĕk'strə-vərt,) noun, adj. same as **extrovert**.

extreme adj. 1 very high, or highest, in degree or intensity. 2 very far, or farthest, in any direction, esp. out from the center. 3 very violent or strong; not moderate. —noun 1 either of two things as different as possible from each other. 2 the greatest degree of any state or condition. ▸ **extremely** adv.

extremism noun support for extreme opinions, esp. in politics. ▸ **extremist** noun

extremity (ĭk-strĕm'ət-ē) noun (pl. **extremities**) 1 the highest degree. 2 a situation of great danger. 3 (**extremities**) the hands and feet.

extricate (ĕk'strə-kāt,) verb trans. (**extricated, extricating**) to free from difficulties; to disentangle. ▸ **extrication** noun ▸ **extricable** adj.

extrovert or **extravert** (ĕk'strə-vərt,) noun a person who is sociable, outgoing, and talkative. —adj. having the temperament of an extrovert. See also **introvert**.

extroverted adj. sociable and outgoing.

extrude verb trans. (**extruded, extruding**) to squeeze or force out. ▸ **extrusion** noun

exuberant adj. 1 in very high spirits. 2 enthusiastic and energetic. 3 healthy. ▸ **exuberance** noun ▸ **exuberantly** adv.

exude (ĭg-zōōd') verb trans., intrans. (**exuded, exuding**) 1 to give off or give out (an odor or sweat). 2 to show by one's behavior: exuded friendliness. 3 to ooze out. ▸ **exudate** verb ▸ **exudation** noun

exult (ĭg-zəlt') verb intrans. (**exulted, exulting**) 1 (**exult in** or at (something)) to be intensely joyful about (it). 2 (**exult over** (something)) to enjoy a feeling of triumph. ▸ **exultant** adj. ▸ **exultation** noun

eye noun 1 the sense organ by which we see. 2 (often **eyes**) sight; vision. 3 attention, gaze, or observation: kept my eye on the gauge. 4 the ability to appreciate and judge: an eye for beauty. 5 judgment; opinion: in the eyes of the law. 6 Bot. the bud of a tuber such as a potato. 7 an area of calm at the center of a tornado, etc. 8 the hole in a needle. —verb trans. (**eyed, eyeing**) 1 to look at carefully. 2 to observe (something): eyed the pedestrians with indifference. —see **eye to eye (with someone)** to be in agreement (with another). (**be) up to the** or **one's eyes in** (something) (to be) busy or deeply involved in (work, a commitment, etc.).

eyeball noun the globe of the eye.

eyebrow noun the arch of hair on the bony ridge above each eye.

eye-catching adj. drawing attention, esp. by being strikingly attractive.

eyeful (ī'fŏŏl,) noun colloq. 1 an interesting or beautiful sight. 2 a look or view.

eyelash noun any of the short hairs growing from the edge of the eyelids.

eyelet (ī'lət) noun a small hole through which a lace, etc., is passed.

eyelid noun the protective fold of skin that can be closed to cover the eyeball.

eye opener colloq. a surprising or revealing sight, experience, etc.

eyepiece noun the lens of a telescope, etc. to which the eye is applied.

eyesight noun the ability to see.

eyesore noun derog. an ugly thing, esp. a building.

eye tooth one of the two upper canine teeth.

eyewash noun 1 liquid for soothing sore eyes. 2 derog. colloq. nonsense.

eyewitness (ī'wĭt'nəs) noun a person who sees an incident, esp. a crime, happen.

eyrie (ĕr'ē, ĭr'ē) noun same as **aerie**.

Ff

F¹ or **f** *noun (pl.* **Fs, F's, f's**) **1** the sixth letter of the English alphabet. **2** (*usu.* **F**) fail. **3** (**F**) **a** the fourth note in the scale of C major. **b** a musical key with the note F as its base.

F² *abbrev.* **1** Fahrenheit. **2** Fellow. **3** franc.

f *abbrev. Mus.* forte.

f. *abbrev.* **1** fathom. **2** female. **3** feminine. **4** focal length. **5** folio. **6** following.

fa or **fah** *noun* the fourth note of the scale in the solfeggio system of music notation.

fab *adj. slang* fabulous.

fable *noun* **1** a story with a moral, usu. with animals as characters. **2** a myth or legend. **3** a lie. ▸ **fabled** *adj.*

fabric *noun* **1** cloth. **2** quality; texture. **3** the walls, floor, and roof of a building. **4** orderly structure.

fabricate (făb′rĭ-kāt,) *verb trans.* (**fabricated, fabricating**) **1** to invent (a false story, etc.). **2** to make. ▸ **fabrication** *noun* ▸ **fabricator** *noun*

fabulous *adj.* **1** marvelous. **2** immense; amazing. **3** legendary; mythical. ▸ **fabulously** *adv.*

façade or **facade** (fə-säd′) *noun* **1** the front of a building. **2** a false or superficial appearance.

face *noun* **1** the front part of the head. **2** a facial expression, or facial features. **3** a surface or side. **4** the exposed surface from which coal, etc. is mined. **5** a general look or appearance. **6** impudence. —*verb* (**faced, facing**) **1** to be opposite to. **2** to turn to look at or look in some direction. **3** to confront, tackle, or accept (esp. problems, difficulties, etc.). **4** to cover a surface (with something). —**on the face of it** at first glance.

face card a playing card with the image of a king, queen, or jack.

faceless *adj.* lacking identity; impersonal or anonymous.

face-lift *noun* **1** cosmetic surgery that tightens the facial skin in order to minimize wrinkles. **2** improvement of the appearance of something.

face-off *noun* **1** the start of play, e.g., in ice hockey. **2** a confrontation.

face-saving *adj.* preventing a loss of dignity, pride, etc.

facet (făs′ĭt) *noun* **1** a small surface on a cut jewel. **2** an aspect, e.g., of a topic.

facetious (fə-sē′shəs) *adj.* playful, amusing or witty, sometimes unsuitably so. ▸ **facetious-**

ly *adv.* ▸ **facetiousness** *noun*

face value **1** the stated value on a coin, stamp, etc. **2** apparent meaning or implication.

facial *adj.* relating or belonging to the face. —*noun* a treatment for improving the appearance of the skin of the face and neck.

facile (făs′əl) *adj.* **1** accomplished without difficulty. **2** lacking careful thought. **3** skilled; performed with ease. ▸ **facilely** *adv.*

facilitate (fə-sĭl′ĭ-tāt,) *verb trans.* (**facilitated, facilitating**) to make (a process, etc.) easier. ▸ **facilitation** *noun* ▸ **facilitator** *noun*

facility *noun* (*pl.* **facilities**) **1** skill, talent, or ability. **2** fluency; ease. **3** an arrangement, feature, attachment, etc., that enables the performance of a given function. **4** (*usu.* **facilities**) a building, service, or piece of equipment for a particular activity.

facing *noun* material used for stiffening or decorating.

facsimile (făk-sĭm′ə-lē) *noun* **1** an exact copy of a manuscript, drawing. **2** fax.

fact *noun* **1** something known to be true, to exist, or to have happened. **2** truth or reality, as distinct from mere statement or belief. **3** an assertion; a piece of information. —**in (point of) fact** actually.

faction¹ *noun* **1** a divisive group within a larger organization. **2** discord within a group. ▸ **factional** *adj.*

faction² *noun* a film or literary work that contains elements of both fact and fiction.

factitious *adj.* deliberately contrived.

fact of life **1** an unavoidable, usu. unpleasant, truth. **2** (**the facts of life**) basic information about sex and reproduction.

factor (făk′tər) *noun* **1** a circumstance that contributes to a result. **2** *Math.* one of two or more numbers that will divide exactly into another given number. **3** an agent acting for another person. **4** the amount, quality or extent of something: *wind-chill factor.* —*verb, trans.* (**factored, factoring**) to act as an agent. —**factor in** to take into account. ▸ **factorial** *adj.*

factory (făk′trē, -tə-rē) *noun* (*pl.* **factories**) a building or buildings with equipment for the large-scale manufacture of goods.

factotum *noun* (*pl.* **factotums**) a person employed to do a number of different jobs.

factual *adj.* concerned with or based on facts. ▸ **factually** *adv.*

faculty *noun* (*pl.* **faculties**) **1** a mental or physical power. **2** a particular talent or aptitude. **3 a** the teaching staff of a school, college, or university. **b** a section of a college or university.

fad *noun* a short-lived fashion; a craze.

fade *verb trans., intrans.* (**faded, fading**) **1** to cause to lose or to undergo loss of strength, freshness, or color. **2** *of a sound or image* to disappear gradually. —*noun Cinema, Broadcasting* a gradual lessening of the brightness of a picture or the volume of the soundtrack of a film or broadcast. —**fade (something) in** or **out** *Cinema, Broadcasting* to cause a sound or picture to become gradually louder and more distinct, or to become fainter and disappear.

fag¹ *noun slang* a cigarette. —*verb trans., intrans.* (**fagged, fagging**) **1** to tire out. **2** to work hard, often to exhaustion.

fag² *noun offensive slang* a gay man.

faggot *noun* **1** (*also* **fagot**) a bundle of sticks. **2** *offensive slang* a gay man.

fah *noun same as* **fa**.

Fahrenheit (făr′ən-hīt,) *noun* a temperature scale on which the freezing point of water is +32° and the boiling point is +212°. —*adj.* on or of this scale.

fail *verb intrans., trans.* (**failed, failing**) **1** be unsuccessful. **2 a** to get a grade below the minimum required to pass. **b** to judge (a candidate) not good enough to pass a test, etc.. **3** to stop working or functioning. **4** to neglect (to do something). **5** to let (someone) down. **6** *of courage, strength, etc.* to desert (one) at the time of need. **7** to become gradually weaker. **8** *of a business, etc.* to collapse. **without fail** for certain.

failing *noun* a fault. —*prep.* in the absence of.

fail-safe *adj.* **1** automatically counteracting the effects of any failure. **2** designed or guaranteed not to go wrong.

failure *noun* **1** a the act of failing; lack of success. **b** the act or the result of not passing a test. **2** an unsuccessful person or thing.

faint *adj.* **1** pale; dim; indistinct; slight. **2** on the verge of losing consciousness. **3** feeble. —*verb intrans.* (**fainted, fainting**) to lose consciousness; to collapse. —*noun* a sudden loss of consciousness. ▸ **faintly** *adv.* ▸ **faintness** *noun*

faint-hearted *adj.* timid; cowardly.

fair¹ *adj.* **1** not dishonest or biased. **2** in accordance with the rules or laws. **3** having light-colored hair and skin; light-colored. **4** beautiful. **5** good enough, but usu. only just. **6 a** *of the weather* fine. **b** *of the wind* favorable. —*adv.* **1** in a just way; in accordance with the rules or laws. **2** squarely. **fair and square** honest and open. ▸ **fairness** *noun*

fair² *noun* **1** a collection of sideshows and amusements. **2** a market for the sale of produce, livestock, etc., with or without sideshows. **3** an indoor exhibition of goods to promote trade. **4** a sale of goods to raise money for charity, etc.

fairly *adv.* **1** in a just manner; honestly. **2** quite; rather. **3** actually; absolutely.

fair play honorable behavior; just treatment.

fairway *noun Golf* a broad strip of short grass extending between a tee and its green.

fair-weather *adj.* loyal or supportive only when things are going well.

fairy *noun* (*pl.* **fairies**) a supernatural being with magical powers and human shape.

fairy tale **1** a story about fairies, magic, etc.. **2** a fanciful, fictitious explanation or story.

fait accompli (făt,ə-kăm,plē′, fĕt,-) (*pl.* **faits accomplis**) something done and unalterable; an established fact.

faith *noun* **1** trust or confidence. **2** strong belief, e.g., in God. **3** a religion. **4** loyalty to a promise, etc. —**in good faith** from good or sincere motives.

faithful *adj.* **1** having or showing faith. **2** loyal and true. **3** accurate. **4** reliable; constant. —*noun* **1** (**the faithful**) the believers in a particular religion. **2** (*also* **the faithful**) a supporter; supporters in general. ▸ **faithfully** *adv.* ▸ **faithfulness** *noun*

faith healer a person who claims or is reputed to heal others by the power of religion. ▸ **faith healing** *noun*

faithless *adj.* **1** disloyal; treacherous. **2** having no religious faith. ▸ **faithlessly** *adv.* ▸ **faithlessness** *noun*

fake *noun* **1** a person, thing, or act that is not genuine. **2** *Sport* a sudden change in direction intended to confuse an opponent. —*adj.* not genuine or authentic; false. —*verb trans., intrans.* (**faked, faking**) **1** to alter dishonestly; to falsify or make up. **2** to pretend to feel (an emotion) or have (an illness). **3** *Sport* to confuse or mislead (an opponent); to perform a misleading move or motion. ▸ **faker** *noun* ▸ **fakery** *noun*

fakir (fə-kîr′, fā′kər) *noun* a Hindu or Muslim holy man.

falcon (făl′kən, fôl′-, fô′-) *noun* a small bird of prey, often used as a trained hunter. ▸ **falconer** *noun*

fall *verb intrans.* (*pa t* **fell**; *pa p* **fallen**; *pr p* **falling**) **1 a** to go or move down from a higher to a lower place or position. ▨ DECLINE, DESCEND, DROP, LOWER ▨ CLIMB, RISE. **b** to descend or drop by force of gravity, esp. accidentally. **c** (*also* **fall over** *or* **down**) to drop to the ground after losing balance. **d** *of rain, snow, etc.* to come down. **2 a** *of a government, etc.* to lose power. **b** *of a stronghold* to be captured. **c** *of defenses or* *barriers* to be lowered or broken down. **3 a** of *value, temperature, sound, etc.* to become less; to diminish. **b** of *silence, darkness, night, etc.* to arrive. **4** to die or be badly wounded in battle, etc. **5** to pass into a certain state: *fall asleep.* **6** to be grouped or classified in a certain way. **7** to occur at a certain time or place. **8** of *someone's face* to show disappointment. —*noun* **1 a** an act of falling. **b** a way or type of falling: *a thick fall of snow.* **2** something, or an amount, that falls. **3** (**falls**) a waterfall. **4** a drop in quality, quantity, value, temperature, etc. **5** a defeat or collapse. **6** (*usu.* **Fall**) the period of the year between summer and winter; autumn. —*fall* **apart** to break into pieces; to collapse. **fall behind** to fail to keep up with another or others, with one's work, or with financial obligations. **fall for (someone)** to fall in love with (someone). **fall for (something)** to be deceived or taken in by (it). **fall in** of *soldiers, etc.* to take up their place in a military formation. **fall in with (something)** to agree to (it); to support (it). **fall off** to decline in quality or quantity. **fall out** of *soldiers, etc.* to come out of military formation. **fall out with (someone)** to quarrel with (someone). **fall short** to prove inadequate or insufficient. **fall through** of *a plan, etc.* to come to nothing; to fail. **fall to pieces 1** to break up; to disintegrate. **2** to experience an emotional collapse.

fallacy (făl′ə-sē) *noun* (*pl.* **fallacies**) **1** a mistaken notion. **2** a mistake in reasoning. ▸ **fallacious** *adj.* ▸ **fallaciously** *adv.*

fallen *adj.* **1** having lost one's virtue, honor or reputation. **2** killed in battle. **3** having dropped or overturned. —*verb see* **fall.**

fall guy *slang* **1** someone easily cheated. **2** someone left to take the blame.

fallible *adj.* capable of making mistakes. ▸ **fallibility** *noun*

fallopian tubes *or* **Fallopian tubes** (fə-lō′pē-ən) the two ducts that eggs travel along as they pass from the ovaries to the womb.

fallout *noun* **1** particles of radioactive material released after a nuclear explosion. **2** usu. unwanted side effects or consequences.

fallow *adj.* of plowed *farmland* left unplanted.

false *adj.* **1** of a *statement, etc.* untrue. **2** of *an idea, etc.* mistaken. **3** not genuine; artificial. **4** of *words, promises, etc.* insincere. **5** treacherous; disloyal. **6** of *a plant* resembling, but wrongly so called: *false indigo.* —**under false pretenses** by giving a deliberately misleading impression. ▸ **falsely** *adv.* ▸ **falseness** *noun* ▸ **falsity** *noun*

false alarm 1 an alarm given unnecessarily. **2** a warning or cry for help that is unwarranted.

falsehood *noun* a lie.

false start 1 an invalid start to a race caused by

one or more competitors beginning before the starting signal has been given. **2** a failed attempt to begin something.

falsetto (fôl-sĕt′ō) *noun* (*pl.* **falsettos**) an artificially high voice.

falsify *verb trans.* (**falsified, falsifying, falsifies**) to alter or make up, in order to deceive or mislead. ▸ **falsification** *noun*

falter *verb intrans.* (**faltered, faltering**) **1** to move unsteadily; to stumble. **2** to start functioning unreliably. **3** to lose strength or conviction; to hesitate or break down in speaking. ▸ **falteringly** *adv.*

fame *noun* **1** the condition of being widely known. ▣ CELEBRITY, RENOWN, REPUTE ▣ OBLIVION, OBSCURITY. **2** reputation. ▸ **famed** *adj.*

familiar *adj.* **1** well known or recognizable. **2** (**familiar with (something)**) well acquainted with (it); having a thorough knowledge of (it). **3** on amicable terms with (someone). **4** excessively informal; overly friendly. —*noun* **1** a close friend. **2** a demon or spirit, esp. in the shape of an animal, allegedly serving a witch. ▸ **familiarity** *noun* ▸ **familiarize** *verb trans.* ▸ **familiarization** *noun* ▸ **familiarly** *adv.*

family (făm′lē, -ə-lē) *noun* (*pl.* **families**) **1 a** a group typically consisting of parents or a parent and children. **b** a set of relatives. **c** a person's children. **d** a household of people. **2** all those descended from a common ancestor. **3** a related group. **4** an independent, local crime group, esp. one with mafia connections. ▸ **familial** *adj.*

family planning 1 the control of the number and spacing of children born, using contraception. **2** *informal* contraception.

family tree the relationships within a family through several generations, or a diagram showing these relationships.

famine (făm′ĭn) *noun* **1** a severe or disastrous shortage of food. **2** extreme hunger.

famished *adj.* **1** starving. **2** very hungry.

famous *adj.* **1** well known; renowned. **2** great; glorious. ▸ **famously** *adv.*

fan¹ *noun* **1** a hand-held device made of paper, silk, etc., for creating a current of air. **2** any similar mechanical or electrical device. —*verb trans., intrans.* (**fanned, fanning**) **1** to create a current of air, esp. as a means of cooling. **2** (**fan out**) to spread out. **3** to rouse or agitate. **4** *Baseball* to strike out.

fan² *noun colloq.* an enthusiastic supporter or devoted admirer.

fanatic *noun* someone with an extreme, excessive, or zealous enthusiasm for something. ▸ **fanatical** *adj.* ▸ **fanatically** *adv.* ▸ **fanaticism** *noun*

fancier *noun* a breeder or grower of a certain kind of animal or plant.

fanciful adj. 1 imaginative or overly imaginative. 2 imaginary. 3 designed in a curious way. ▸ **fancifully** adv.

fancy noun (pl. **fancies**) 1 imagination. 2 a an image, idea, or whim. b a sudden, whimsical change of mind. c a sudden liking or desire. —adj. 1 elaborate. 2 of special, unusual, or superior quality. 3 colloq. too high: fancy prices. —verb trans. (**fancied, fancying, fancies**) 1 to think or believe. 2 to have a desire for. 3 to imagine: Fancy him getting married at last! ▸ **fancily** adv

fanfare noun 1 a flourish on trumpets to announce an important event or arrival. 2 a great public display.

fang noun 1 a sharp tooth. 2 in snakes, a grooved tooth that venom is injected through.

fantasize verb intrans. (**fantasized, fantasizing**) to have pleasant, but unlikely, fantasies or daydreams.

fantastic adj. 1 wonderful; great. 2 colloq. enormous; amazing. 3 of a story, etc. absurd; unlikely. ▸ **fantastically** adv.

fantasy noun (pl. **fantasies**) 1 a longed-for but unlikely happening. 2 a product of the imagination. 3 a mistaken notion.

FAQ abbrev. Comput. frequently asked questions.

far (**farther, farthest** or **further, furthest**) adv. 1 at, to, or from a great distance. 2 to or by a great extent. 3 at or to a distant time. —adj. 1 distant; remote. 2 more distant than another: the far corner. 3 extreme, e.g., in political views. —**be a far cry from** (**something**) to differ greatly from (it). **go far** to achieve great things.

faraway adj. 1 distant and remote. 2 of a look or expression dreamy; abstracted.

farce noun 1 a ridiculous comedy; comedies of this type. 2 an absurd situation. ▸ **farcical** adj. ▸ **farcically** adv.

fare noun 1 the price paid by a passenger to travel on public transportation. 2 a passenger who is transported for a fee. 3 a particular type of food or drink. —verb intrans. (**fared, faring**) to get along in a certain way: fared well after surgery.

farewell interj. good-bye. —noun a parting or an act of saying good-bye. —adj. parting or closing: farewell speech.

far-fetched adj. unlikely or unconvincing, esp in terms of being bizarre or unrealistic.

far-flung adj. distant and remote.

farm noun 1 an area of land used for growing crops and/or raising livestock. 2 a place specializing in breeding and growing particular animals or plants for food. —verb trans., intrans. (**farmed, farming**) to prepare and use land to grow crops, raise and/or breed livestock, etc. —**farm** (**something**

or **someone**) **out** to give (work, children, etc.) to another to do, look after, etc. ▸ **farmer** noun ▸ **farming** noun

farmstead (färm'stĕd,) noun a farmhouse and the buildings around it.

far-out adj. slang strange; weird; outlandish.

farrier noun a person who shoes horses.

farrow noun a sow's litter of piglets. —verb trans., intrans. (**farrowed, farrowing**) of a sow to give birth to (piglets).

farsighted or **far-sighted** adj. 1 (also **farseeing**) wise; prudent; forward-looking. 2 of a person only able to see distant objects clearly. ▸ **farsightedness** noun

farther adv., adj. (with reference to physical distance) a comparative of **far**.

farthest adv., adj. (with reference to physical distance) a superlative of **far**.

fascia (fā'shə) noun (pl. **fasciae**) 1 Archit. a long flat band or surface between moldings. 2 Anat. a sheet of fibrous connective tissue. ▸ **fascial** adj.

fascinate verb trans., intrans. (**fascinated, fascinating**) 1 a to interest strongly. b to be spellbinding. 2 to hold spellbound; to enchant irresistibly. ▸ **fascinating** adj. ▸ **fascinatingly** adv. ▸ **fascination** noun

fascism or **Fascism** (făsh'ĭzəm) noun a rightwing totalitarian, nationalistic, and militaristic form of government.

fascist noun 1 (also **Fascist**) a supporter of fascism. 2 a dictatorial person. —adj. 1 (also **Fascist**) supporting fascism. 2 dictatorial. ▸ **fascistic** adj.

fashion noun 1 style, esp. the latest style, e.g., in clothes. 2 a currently popular style or practice; a trend. 3 a manner of doing something. 4 the way something is made or constructed. —verb trans. (**fashioned, fashioning**) 1 to form or shape, esp. with the hands. 2 to mold or influence. —**after a fashion** in some way, particularly to only a limited extent: ski, after a fashion. **in** (or **out of**) **fashion** currently (or no longer) fashionable. ▸ **fashionable** adj. ▸ **fashionably** adv.

fast[1] adj. 1 moving or able to move quickly. 2 taking a relatively short time. 3 of a clock, etc. showing the time in advance of the correct time. 4 of a person or lifestyle characterized by hedonism, promiscuity, or recklessness. 5 firmly fixed or caught. 6 of friends firm; close. 7 of fabric colors not liable to run or fade. —adv. 1 rapidly. 2 in quick succession: thick and fast. 3 tightly. 4 deeply. —**pull a fast one** (**on someone**) colloq. to cheat or deceive (the person). ▸ **fastness** noun

fast[2] verb intrans. (**fasted, fasting**) to abstain from food completely or to restrict one's diet. —noun abstinence from food; time spent abstaining from food.

fasten *verb trans., intrans.* (**fastened, fastening**) to make or become firmly closed or fixed. **—fasten on (something)** to concentrate on (it) eagerly; to dwell on (it).

fastener *noun* a device that fastens something. *Also called* **fastening**.

fast food food, e.g., hamburgers, fried chicken, pizza, etc. that is quickly prepared for eating on the premises or for taking away.

fastidious *adj.* **1** particular in matters of taste, detail, cleanliness, esp. excessively so. **2** easily disgusted. ▸ **fastidiously** *adv.* ▸ **fastidiousness** *noun*

fast lane 1 the passing lane on a four-lane, or multiple-lane highway or freeway. **2** *slang* a dissipated, reckless way of living.

fast time *same as* **daylight-saving time**.

fast track *colloq.* **1** a way of accelerating a proposal, etc., through its formalities. **2** a quick but competitive route to advancement, esp. in the workplace.

fat *noun* **1** a greasy substance that occurs naturally in animals and plants. **2** a layer of this in the body. —*adj.* (**fatter, fattest**) **1** having too much fat on the body. **2** containing a lot of fat. **3** thick, wide, or large: *made a fat profit.* **4** tiny; minimal: *a fat lot of good that did you.* **—chew the fat** *colloq.* to talk. ▸ **fatness** *noun*

fatal *adj.* **1** causing death; deadly. **2** causing tragedy, ruin, or great destruction. **3** destined; unavoidable. **4** *Comput., of an error, etc.* causing a program to crash. —*noun slang* an accident involving loss of life. ▸ **fatally** *adv.*

fatalism *noun* the belief that fate controls everything. ▸ **fatalist** *noun* ▸ **fatalistic** *adj.* ▸ **fatalistically** *adv.*

fatality *noun* (*pl.* **fatalities**) **1** an accidental or violent death. **2** the quality of being fatal. **3** the quality of being controlled by fate.

fat cat *slang* a wealthy person.

fate *noun* **1** (*also* **Fate**) the alleged power that determines the course of events, over which humans supposedly have no control. **2** a future or ultimate outcome. ▤ DESTINY, LOT. **3** death, downfall, destruction, or doom. ▸ **fated** *adj.*

fateful *adj.* **1** *of a remark, etc.* prophetic. **2** having significant results; decisive; critical. **3** bringing disaster. ▸ **fatefully** *adv.*

fathead (făt'hĕd,) *noun slang* a fool. ▸ **fatheaded** *adj.*

father *noun* **1** a natural or adoptive male parent. **2** (**fathers**) one's ancestors. **3** a founder, inventor, originator, pioneer, or early leader. **4** (**Father**) used as a title or form of address for a priest. **5** (**Father**) God. **6** (**fathers**) the leading or senior men of a city, etc. **7** (**Father**) used as a title in per-

sonifying something ancient or venerable: *Father Time.* —*verb trans., intrans.* (**fathered, fathering**) **1** to be the father of. **2** to invent or originate. ▸ **fatherhood** *noun* ▸ **fatherless** *adj.* ▸ **fatherly** *adj.* ▸ **fatherliness** *noun*

father figure an older man, esp. one that acts as a role model or substitute parent.

father-in-law *noun* (*pl.* **fathers-in-law**) the father of one's wife or husband.

fatherland *noun* one's native country.

fathom (făth'əm) *noun* a unit of measurement of the depth of water equal to 6 ft. (1.83 m). —*verb trans.* (**fathomed, fathoming**) **1** (*usu.* **fathom** (**something**) **out**) to solve (a problem or mystery). **2** to measure the depth of (water).

fathomless *adj.* **1** too deep to be measured. **2** too difficult or mysterious to understand.

fatigue *noun* **1** extreme tiredness. **2** (**fatigues**) clothes worn for military or work purposes. —*verb trans., intrans.* (**fatigued, fatiguing**) to exhaust or to become exhausted.

fatten *verb trans., intrans.* (**fattened, fattening**) (*also* **fatten up**) to make or become fat. ▸ **fattening** *adj.*

fatty *adj.* (**fattier, fattiest**) **1** containing fat. **2** greasy; oily. —*noun* (*pl.* **fatties**) *offensive* a fat person. ▸ **fattiness** *noun*

fatuous *adj.* foolish, esp. in a self-satisfied way; empty-headed. ▸ **fatuity** *noun* ▸ **fatuously** *adv.* ▸ **fatuousness** *noun*

fatwa *noun* an edict.

faucet *noun* a device that controls the flow of water, esp. on a washbasin, bathtub, etc.

fault *noun* **1** a weakness, flaw, or defect. **2** responsibility or cause for something wrong: *all my fault.* **3** a weakness or break in the Earth's crust. **4** in tennis and other racket games, an incorrectly placed or delivered serve. **—to a fault** to too great an extent. ▸ **faultless** *adj.* ▸ **faultlessly** *adv.*

faulty *adj.* (**faultier, faultiest**) having faults or a fault; not working correctly.

fauna *noun* (*pl.* **faunas, faunae**) the animals associated with a particular habitat, region, or geological period. *See also* **flora**.

faux *adj.* imitation: *a faux leopard skin coat.*

faux pas (fō-pä') *noun* (*pl.* **faux pas**) an embarrassing, esp. social, blunder.

favor *noun* **1** a kind or helpful action. **2** liking, approval, or goodwill. **3** a small, decorative gift given to a guest at a party. —*verb trans.* (**favored, favoring**) **1** to regard with goodwill. **2** to treat with preference or overindulgence. **3** to prefer; to support. **4** to look like (a particular member of one's family).

favorable *adj.* **1** showing or giving agreement or consent. **2** pleasing. **3** *of a wind* following. ▸ **favorably** *adv.*

favorite *adj.* preferred. —*noun* **1** a preferred or favored person or thing. **2** a horse expected to win a race.

favoritism *noun* preferential help or support, esp. when undeserved or unfair.

fawn[1] *noun* **1** a young deer. **2** beige.

fawn[2] *verb intrans.* (**fawned, fawning**) (*also* **fawn over** *or* **on (someone)**) (*of a dog, etc.* to show affection by licking, nuzzling, etc. **2** to try to win approval or favor by behaving obsequiously or showing excess reverence.

fax *noun* **1** a machine that sends a copy of a document by telephone. **2** a copy sent by fax. —*verb trans.* to send by fax.

faze *verb trans.* (**fazed, fazing**) to disconcert.

FBI *abbrev.* Federal Bureau of Investigation.

fear *noun* **1** a anxiety and distress caused by the awareness of danger or expectation of pain. **b** a cause of this feeling. **2** religious awe or dread. —*verb trans., intrans.* (**feared, fearing**) **1** to be afraid of. **2** (**fear for (something)**) to be frightened or anxious about (it).

fearful *adj.* **1** afraid. **2** frightening. ▸ **fearfully** *adv.* ▸ **fearfulness** *noun*

fearless *adj.* having or displaying no fear. ▸ **fearlessly** *adv.* ▸ **fearlessness** *noun*

fearsome *adj.* frightening.

feasible *adj.* capable of being done. ▸ **feasibility** *noun* ▸ **feasibly** *adv.*

feast *noun* **1** a lavish meal. **2** a source of great satisfaction or pleasure. **3** a festival or saint's day. —*verb intrans., trans.* (**feasted, feasting**) **1** (**feast on** *or* **upon (something)**) to eat or experience (it) with enjoyment. **2** to entertain (someone) with a specific food.

feat *noun* a deed or achievement, esp. a remarkable one.

feather *noun* any of the parts that form a bird's plumage.

featherweight *noun* **1** *Sport* **a** a class for boxers, wrestlers, and weight lifters of not more than a specified weight (126 lbs., or 57 kg) in professional boxing, similar weights in the other sports). **b** a boxer, etc., of this weight. **2** someone who weighs very little.

feature *noun* **1** **a** a part of the face, e.g., the eyes, nose, mouth, etc. **b** (**features**) the human face itself. **2** **a** a noticeable part or quality. **b** a distinguishing element, esp. of a person's character. **3** a non-news article in a newspaper. —*verb trans.* (**featured, featuring**) to include or give prominence to (someone or something). ▸ **featureless** *adj.*

febrile (fĕb′rĭl, fē′brĭl) *adj.* relating to or caused by fever; feverish.

February *noun* (ABBREV. **Feb., Feb**) (*pl.* **Februaries**) the 2d month of the year.

feces (fē′sēz) *pl. noun* the solid waste matter discharged through the anus. ▸ **fecal** *adj.*

feckless *adj.* **1** irresponsible; aimless. **2** help-less; clueless. ▸ **fecklessly** *adv.* ▸ **fecklessness** *noun*

fecund *adj.* richly productive; fruitful; fertile. ▸ **fecundity** *noun*

fed[1] *noun slang* an FBI agent.

fed[2] *verb see* **feed**.

federal (fĕd′rəl, -ə-rəl) *adj.* **1** consisting of states independent in local matters but united under a central government for other purposes. **2** relating to the central government of a federal union. **3** (**Federal**) *Hist.* relating to or supporting the Union during the Civil War. ▸ **federalism** *noun* ▸ **federalist** *noun* ▸ **federalize** *verb trans., intrans.*

federation *noun* **1** a federal union of states. **2** a union of business organizations, etc. **3** the act of uniting in a league. ▸ **federate** *verb intrans., trans.* ▸ **federative** *adj.*

fee *noun* **1** a charge made for professional services. **2** a charge for, e.g., membership, admission, etc. **3** (*usu.* **fees**) payment for school or college education, etc.

feeble *adj.* **1** lacking strength; weak. **2** lacking power, influence, or effectiveness: *a feeble excuse.* ▸ **feebleness** *noun* ▸ **feebly** *adv.*

feeble-minded *adj.* **1** exhibiting no prior thought or little thought: *a feeble-minded argument.* **2** lacking in intelligence; stupid.

feed *verb intrans., trans.* (*pa t and pa p* **fed**; *pr p* **feeding**) **1** (**feed on (something)**) to eat (it), esp. as a regular diet. **2** to give food to or prepare food for. **3** (**feed on (something)**) to be fueled by (it). **4** to give as food. —*noun* **1** an act or session of feeding. **2** any of various types of fodder for livestock. **3** *colloq.* a meal, esp. a hearty one. —**fed up** *colloq.* bored and impatient. ▸ **feeder** *noun*

feedback *noun* **1** information about the suitability or adequacy of a particular product, performance, etc. given to guide future adjustments or improvements. **2** the partial return to a microphone, amplifier, etc. of its own sound output, or the unwanted noise produced by this.

feel *verb trans., intrans.* (*pa t and pa p* **felt**; *pr p* **feeling**) **1** to become aware of or investigate by touching. ▣ FINGER, TOUCH. **2** to sense (something) or experience (an emotion). ▣ KNOW, SAVOR, TASTE. **3** to react intuitively, emotionally, empathetically to something: *I feel it's wrong.* **4** to give the impression of being (soft, hard, rough, etc.). **5** to be or seem to be. —*noun* **1** a sensation or impression produced by touching. **2** an impression or atmosphere. **3** an act of feeling with the fingers, etc. **4** *informal* an aptitude or talent (for something).

feeler *noun* a sensory or tactile organ, such as the antenna of certain invertebrates. —**put out feelers** *colloq.* to test for possible reactions, before taking action.

feeling noun 1 a sensation or emotion. 2 (**feelings**) an opinion or attitude. 3 an instinct not based on reason. 4 strong emotion: *spoke with feeling*. 5 (**feelings**) emotions or sensibilities. —adj. sensitive; sympathetic. ▸ **feelingly** adv.

feet see foot.

feign (fān) verb trans. (**feigned, feigning**) to pretend to have (an illness, etc.) or to feel (an emotion, etc.). ▸ **feigned** adj.

feint noun 1 in boxing, fencing, or other sports, a movement, e.g., a mock attack, intended to deceive or distract an opponent. 2 a cunning means to an end. ▤ DODGE, GAMBIT, JIG, PLOY, RUSE, SHENANIGAN, SLEIGHT, STRATAGEM, TRICK.

feisty adj. (**feistier, feistiest**) colloq. 1 spirited; lively. 2 irritable; quarrelsome.

feldspar (fĕld'spär,) or **felspar** noun a mineral found in igneous and metamorphic rocks.

felicitate verb trans. (**felicitated, felicitating**) to congratulate.

felicitations pl. noun congratulations.

felicitous adj. 1 elegantly apt. 2 appropriately pleasant or happy. ▸ **felicitously** adv. ▸ **felicitousness** noun ▸ **felicity** noun

feline adj. 1 of or relating to cats. 2 catlike, esp. in being quiet or stealthy.

fell¹ see fall.

fell² verb trans. (**felled, felling**) 1 to cut down (a tree). 2 to knock down. 3 to kill (someone).

fell³ —at or in one fell swoop with a single, quick action.

fellow noun 1 a man or boy. 2 a companion or equal. 3 a person sharing the same situation, condition, status, etc. as oneself. 4 a postgraduate research student financed by a fellowship. 5 a member of a learned society. —adj. of the same kind, class, etc.

fellow feeling sympathy for someone with experiences similar to one's own.

fellowship noun 1 friendly companionship. 2 commonness or similarity of interests. 3 the status of being a fellow of a college, society, etc. 4 a grant paid for study or research, usu. at postgraduate level.

felony noun (pl. **felonies**) a serious crime. ▸ **felon** noun ▸ **felonious** adj.

felspar noun same as feldspar.

felt¹ see feel.

felt² noun a fabric formed by matting or pressing together fibers of wool, etc. —verb trans., intrans. (**felted, felting**) to form into felt; to become matted like felt.

female adj. 1 denoting the sex that gives birth to young, produces eggs, etc. 2 denoting the reproductive structure of a plant that contains an egg cell. 3 of, relating to, or belonging to a woman or to women. 4 denoting a piece of machinery into which another part (the male) fits. —noun 1 a woman or girl. 2 a female animal or plant:

feminine adj. 1 relating to, typical of, or suitable for a woman. 2 relating to the gender of nouns and adjectives that in some languages are conventionally treated as female. ▸ **femininity** noun

feminism noun a belief or movement advocating the cause of women's rights and opportunities. ▸ **feminist** noun

femme fatale (fĕm,fə-täl', -tăl') (pl. **femmes fatales**) an irresistibly attractive woman who leads men into dangerous situations.

femur (fē'mər) noun (pl. **femurs, femora**) 1 the human leg bone between the hip and the knee joint. Also called **thighbone**. 2 the corresponding bone in the hind limb of four-limbed vertebrates. ▸ **femoral** adj.

fen noun a waterlogged area of low-lying land.

fence noun 1 a barrier, e.g., of wood or wire, for enclosing land. 2 slang a person who receives and disposes of stolen goods. —verb trans., intrans. (**fenced, fencing**) 1 (**fence (something) in** or **off**) to enclose or separate (it) with, or as if with, a fence. 2 Sport to engage in fencing. —on the fence not supporting either side in a dispute, etc. ▸ **fencer** noun ▸ **fencing** noun

fend verb trans., intrans. 1 (**fend off (something** or **someone**)) to deflect (questions, blows, etc.). ▤ DEFLECT, PARRY. 2 (**fend for**) to provide for (esp. oneself).

fender noun 1 a guard over a vehicle's wheel, for deflecting mud or water. 2 a low guard around a fireplace. 3 a bundle of rope, etc. at a ship's side to protect it when in contact with piers, etc.

feng shui (fŭng'shwē') ancient Chinese beliefs regarding the good and evil influences inherent in natural features, esp. in the siting and design of homes, offices, etc.

fennel noun a plant used in cooking with a flavor similar to aniseed.

fenugreek (fĕn'yə-grēk,) noun a plant with strong-smelling seeds used as flavoring.

feral (fīr'əl; fĕr'-) adj. 1 living wild, having previously been domesticated or cultivated. 2 wild, savage, or ferocious.

ferment (fŭr'mĕnt) noun 1 agitation or excitement. 2 fermentation. —verb trans., intrans. (fər-mĕnt') (**fermented, fermenting**) 1 to undergo fermentation, or to cause to do so. 2 to make or become agitated.

fermentation noun conversion from sugar to alcohol.

fern noun a nonflowering plant that reproduces by means of spores.

ferocious adj. fierce; cruel; savage. ▸ **ferociously** adv. ▸ **ferociousness** noun ▸ **ferocity** noun

-ferous combining form forming words denoting bearing or containing: *carboniferous*.

ferret (fĕr′ət) *noun* **1** a variety of polecat. **2** an inquisitive and persistent investigator. —*verb intrans. trans.* (**ferreted, ferreting**) **1** (**ferret about** *or* **around**) to search busily; to rummage. **2** (**ferret** (**something**) **out**) to find (it) out through persistent investigation.

ferric *adj.* of or relating to iron.

Ferris wheel *or* **ferris wheel** (fĕr′ĭs) *noun* an amusement-park ride consisting of a large wheel with seats hanging from its rim.

ferrous *adj.* containing or derived from iron.

ferrule *noun* a metal tip at the end of an umbrella or a walking stick.

ferry *noun* (*pl.* **ferries**) a boat that carries passengers and often cars. —*verb trans., intrans.* (**ferried, ferrying, ferries**) to transport or go by ferry or other vehicle.

fertile (fərt′l) *adj.* **1** of *soil* or *land* able to support an abundant growth of crops or other plants. **2** producing or capable of producing living offspring. **3** *of the mind* rich in ideas. ▸ **fertility** *noun*

fertilize *verb trans.* (**fertilized, fertilizing**) **1** to introduce sperm into (an egg) or pollen into (a plant) so that reproduction occurs. **2** to put extra nutrients onto (soil or land) to increase the yield of crops. ▸ **fertilization** *noun* ▸ **fertilizer** *noun*

fervent *adj.* feeling or exhibiting enthusiasm. ▸ **fervently** *adv.*

fervid *adj.* full of fiery passion or zeal. ▣ FEVERISH, FIERY, HOT, IMPASSIONED, PERFERVID ▣ DISPASSIONATE, UNEMOTIONAL, UNIMPASSIONED. ▸ **fervidly** *adv.* ▸ **fervor** *noun*

-fest *colloq. suffix* forming words denoting an indulgent spree or a gathering for a specific purpose: *a food-fest.*

fester *verb intrans.* (**festered, festering**) **1** of *a wound* to become infected. **2** to rot. **3** of *anger* or *resentment* to become more bitter.

festival *noun* **1** a day or period of celebration, esp. one kept traditionally. **2** a saint's day or a feast. **3** a program of cultural events.

festive *adj.* of or suitable for a celebration; lively and cheerful.

festivity *noun* (*pl.* **festivities**) **1** celebration; merrymaking. **2** (**festivities**) celebrations.

festoon *noun* a decorative chain of flowers, ribbons, etc., looped between two points. —*verb trans.* (**festooned, festooning**) to decorate, esp. with festoons.

feta (fĕt′ə) *noun* a soft crumbly white cheese made from ewes' or goats' milk.

fetal *or* **foetal** (fĕt′l) *adj.* relating to a fetus.

fetal position a curled-up body position with the head bent forward, and the limbs are drawn up to the chest.

fetch *verb trans., intrans.* (**fetched, fetching**) **1** to go and get, and bring back. **2** to be sold for (a certain price).

fetching *adj. old, colloq.* charming; attractive. ▸ **fetchingly** *adv.*

fete *or* **fête** (fāt) *noun* an outdoor entertainment with competitions, stalls, etc. —*verb trans.* (**feted, feting**) to entertain or honor lavishly.

fetid *or* **foetid** *adj.* having a disgusting smell.

fetish *noun* **1** an object worshipped for its magical powers. **2** a ritual followed obsessively, or an object of obsessive devotion. ▸ **fetishism** *noun* ▸ **fetishist** *noun* ▸ **fetishistic** *adj.*

fetlock *noun* a projection on a horse's leg above the hoof, or the tuft of hair on it.

fetter *noun* (*usu.* **fetters**) a chain or shackle fastened to the ankle. —*verb trans.* (**fettered, fettering**) to restrain with fetters.

fettle *noun* spirits or condition: *in fine fettle.*

fettuccine *or* **fettucini** (fĕt͵ə-chē′nē) *pl. noun* pasta in the form of flat ribbons or a dish containing this kind of pasta.

fetus *or* **foetus** (fĕt′əs) *noun* an embryo during the later stages of development.

> *Usage* The spelling *fetus* is standard in technical contexts, and in N America generally; the variant spelling *foetus* is widely used in general context in British English.

feud (fyōōd) *noun* a protracted, bitter quarrel. —*verb intrans.* (**feuded, feuding**) to be involved in a feud.

feudal *adj. Hist.* of, relating to, or constituting the social system under which lords granted people the use of lands, and, in return, the people were obliged to serve their lords in battle. ▸ **feudalism** *noun*

fever *noun* **1** a rise in body temperature; an illness causing this. **2** a state of agitation or excitement. ▸ **fevered** *adj.*

feverish *adj.* **1** affected by or showing symptoms of fever. **2** agitated or restless. **3** full of passion and zeal. ▸ **feverishly** *adv.*

fever pitch a state of great excitement.

few *adj.* not many; hardly any. —*pron.* hardly any things, people, etc. —**a few** a small number; some. **quite a few** several; many. **the few** the minority, or the discerning people, as distinct from the many.

> *Usage* See note at *less.*

fez *noun* (*pl.* **fezzes**) a tasseled hat shaped like a flat-topped cone.

ff *abbrev. Mus.* fortissimo.

ff. *abbrev.* following: *page 102 ff.*

fiancé (fē͵än-sā′, fē-än′sā͵) *noun* a man to whom a woman is engaged to be married.

fiancée (fē͵än-sā′, fē-än′sā͵) *noun* a woman to whom a man is engaged to be married.

fiasco (fē-ǎs′kō) *noun* (*pl.* **fiascos, fiascoes**) a ludicrous, humiliating, usu. confused failure.

☰ BOONDOGGLE, BOTCH, HASH, WASH-OUT.

> Based on an Italian phrase far fiasco 'make a bottle', meaning forget your lines on stage

fiat (fē′ät,, -ät,) *noun* 1 an official command; a decree. 2 a formal authorization.

fib *colloq. noun* a lie. —*verb intrans.* (**fibbed, fibbing**) to tell lies. ▸ **fibber** *noun*

fiber *noun* 1 a thin strand: *muscle fibers.* 2 material or cloth made from fibers: *acrylic fiber.* 3 plant parts that are hard to digest; dietary fiber. 4 a particular personal quality or attribute: *moral fiber.*

fiberboard *noun* board made of compressed wood chips or other organic fiber.

fiberglass *noun* a strong, durable, synthetic material consisting of fine flexible glass fibers. *Also called* **glass fiber.**

fiber optics (*sing.*) the technique of using flexible glass fibers to carry information in the form of light signals. *See also* **optical fiber.** ▸ **fiber-optic** *adj.*

fibrillate (fĭb′rə-lāt,, fī′brə-) *verb intrans.* (**fibrillated, fibrillating**) *of the heart* to have an abnormal rapid, irregular beat. ▸ **fibrillation** *noun*

fibroid *adj.* composed of fibrous tissue; resembling fibers. —*noun* a benign tumor consisting of fibrous tissue.

fibrosis *noun* the formation of excess fibrous tissue in an organ or body part.

fibrous *adj.* consisting of, containing, or like fiber.

fibula (fĭb′yə-lə) *noun* (*pl.* **fibulae, fibulas**) 1 the narrower of the two human leg bones between the knee and the ankle. 2 the corresponding bone in the hind limb of four-limbed vertebrates. ▸ **fibular** *adj.*

fickle *adj.* changeable; inconstant, esp. in loyalties. ☰ LUBRICIOUS, MERCURIAL, VARIABLE ☰ CONSTANT, LOYAL, STEADY, STEADFAST, UNCHANGING. ▸ **fickleness** *noun*

fiction *noun* 1 literature concerning imaginary characters or events. 2 a pretense or lie. ▸ **fictional** *adj.* ▸ **fictionally** *adv.*

fictitious *adj.* 1 invented; not real. 2 of or occurring in fiction. ▸ **fictitiously** *adv.*

fiddle *noun* 1 *colloq.* a violin. 2 *colloq.* a dishonest arrangement; a fraud. —*verb intrans., trans.* (**fiddled, fiddling**) 1 a to move the hands or move something with the hands without any purpose. b (*often* **fiddle with**) to play about (with something) aimlessly. 2 (**fiddle around**) to waste time. 3 to falsify accounts, etc.; to engage in dishonest manipulation. 4 to play a violin. ▸ **fiddler** *noun*

fiddling *adj.* unimportant; trifling.

fidelity (fĭ-dĕl′ət-ē, fī-) *noun* 1 loyalty; faithfulness. 2 accuracy in sound reproduction, or in reporting, describing, or copying something.

fidget *verb intrans.* (**fidgeted, fidgeting**) 1 to move restlessly. 2 (*often* **fidget with**) to play with or move something distractedly. —*noun* 1 a person who moves restlessly or plays about with something distractedly. 2 (**the fidgets**) nervous restlessness. ▸ **fidgety** *adj.*

fiduciary (fĭ-dōō′shē-ĕr,ē) *Law adj.* given or held in trust. —*noun* (*pl.* **fiduciaries**) a person or an institution entrusted with, e.g., the funds of others.

fief (fēf) *noun Hist.* land granted to a vassal under the feudal system by his lord in return for military service, etc.

field *noun* 1 an area of land, often enclosed, used for growing crops or grazing livestock. 2 a marked-off area for a sport, etc.: *a football field.* 3 (*in compounds*) a an area rich in a particular mineral, etc.: *coalfield.* b an expanse: *snowfields.* 4 an area of knowledge, interest, or study. 5 an inclusive area; the range over which a force, effect, etc., extends: *a magnetic field.* 6 a specific area where related information is stored or recorded. 7 the contestants, horses, etc. in a race, competition, etc. 8 a place of battle. 9 the background to the design on a flag, coin, etc. —*verb trans., intrans.* (**fielded, fielding**) 1 *Sport* to put forward as (a team or player) for a game or match. 2 *Sport* to catch or retrieve (a ball). 3 to deal with a succession of (inquiries, etc.).

field day 1 a day set aside for sports and games. 2 a day of military exercises and maneuvers. 3 *colloq.* an occasion of great success, enjoyment, satisfaction, etc.

fielder *noun Baseball* a member the team not at bat or a member of the outfield.

field event *Athletics* a discipline involving jumping, throwing, etc. *See also* **track event.**

field glasses binoculars.

field goal 1 in football, a score made by kicking the ball between the goal posts. 2 in basketball, a score made by throwing the ball through the opponent's basket.

field hockey a game for two teams of 11 players each, in which curved sticks are used to pass the ball and points are scored when the ball is driven into the opponent's goal.

field marshal an army officer of the highest rank in some European armies.

field-test *verb trans.* (**field-tested, field-testing**) to test (e.g., a product) under actual conditions of use.

field trip an excursion made to a place of educational interest.

fieldwork *noun* 1 practical work or research carried out away from the laboratory or place of work. 2 *Mil.* a temporary fortification. ▸ **field-worker** *noun*

fiend (fēnd) *noun* 1 an evil spirit; a devil. 2 *colloq.* an extremely cruel, mean person. 3 *colloq.* an enthusiast or person who indulges in a specified thing, activity, etc.

fiendish *adj.* 1 like or of a fiend. 2 a so unpleasant as to be suggestive of hell itself. b extremely cruel and mean. 3 *colloq.* extremely difficult. ▸ **fiendishly** *adv.*

fierce (fīrs) *adj.* 1 violent and aggressive. 2 intense; strong;. severe; extreme. ▸ **fiercely** *adv.* ▸ **fierceness** *noun*

fiery (fīr'ē) *adj.* (**fierier, fieriest**) 1 consisting of fire; like fire. 2 easily enraged. 3 full of passion and zeal. 4 *of food* very spicy. ▸ **fierily** *adv.* ▸ **fieriness** *noun*

fiesta (fē-ĕs'tə) *noun* a religious festival or holiday.

fife *noun* a small flute played in military bands.

fifteen *noun* 1 the number or figure 15. 2 the age of 15. 3 any person or thing denoted by the number 15. 4 a set of 15 people or things. 5 a score of 15 points. —*adj.* 1 15 in number. 2 aged 15.

fifteenth *noun, adj.* 1 the one numbered 15 in a series. 2 one of 15 equal parts.

fifth (fĭfth, fĭth) *noun, adj.* 1 the one numbered 5 in a series. 2 one of 5 equal parts.

fifth column a group whose members are prepared to cooperate with an enemy.

fifties *pl. noun* 1 the period of time between one's 50th and 60th birthdays. 2 the range of temperatures between 50° and 60° F. 3 the period of time between the 50th and 60th years of a century.

fiftieth *noun, adj.* 1 the one numbered 50 in a series. 2 one of 50 equal parts.

fifty *noun* (*pl.* **fifties**) 1 the number or figure 50. 2 the age of 50. 3 any person or thing denoted by the number 50. 4 a set of 50 people or things. 5 a score of 50 points. —*adj.* 1 50 in number. 2 aged 50.

fifty-fifty *adj., of a chance* equal either way. —*adv., adj.* divided equally between two.

fig *noun* a large shrub or small tree with large shiny leaves and edible fruits; the fleshy fruit of this tree. —**not give** *or* **care a fig** *colloq.* not to care in the least.

fig. *abbrev.* figure.

fight *verb trans., intrans.* (pa t and pa˙p **fought;** *pr p* **fighting**) 1 a to attack physically; to engage in a battle. b to quarrel or argue. 2 to campaign (for or against something). —*noun* 1 a a violent physical attack or struggle; a battle. b a quarrel or argument. 2 ability or willingness to fight. 3 a contest, esp. a boxing match, or a campaign.

fighter *noun* 1 a person who fights, esp. a professional boxer. 2 a person with determination. 3 an aircraft equipped to attack other aircraft.

fighting chance a chance to succeed dependent chiefly on determination.

figment *noun* something imagined or invented.

figurative *adj.* 1 metaphorical. 2 full of figures of speech. 3 *of art* showing things as they look. ▸ **figuratively** *adv.*

figure *noun* 1 a shape or form, esp. an indistinct human one. 2 the shape of a particular human body. 3 a a symbol or number representing an amount or price, etc. b (**figures**) arithmetical or mathematical calculations. c (**figures**) statistics. 4 a well-known person. 5 an impression that one makes. 6 a a representation of the human form. b a diagram or illustration. c an image, design, pattern, geometric shape; etc. 7 a set pattern of steps or movements in dancing, skating, etc. 8 a figure of speech. —*verb intrans., trans.* (**figured, figuring**) 1 (**figure in** (**something**)) to play a part in a story, incident, etc. 2 *colloq.* to think, reckon, or guess. 3 to calculate. —**figure on** *colloq.* 1 to intend or plan on. 2 to expect or depend on. **figure out** to work (something) out; to begin to understand (it).

figurehead *noun* 1 a leader in name only. 2 *Hist.* a wooden figure fixed to a ship's prow.

figure of speech (*pl.* **figures of speech**) a rhetorical device, such as a metaphor, simile, etc. *Also called* **figure.**

figure skating a type of ice skating that involves performing elaborate figures.

figurine (fĭg,yə-rēn') *noun* a little statue.

filament (fĭl'ə-mənt) *noun* 1 a fine thread or fiber. 2 a fine wire with a high resistance that emits heat and light when current is passed through it. 3 the stalk of a stamen.

filch *verb trans.* (**filched, filching**) to steal (something small or trivial), usu. furtively.

file¹ *noun* a tool with a rough surface, used to smooth metal, wood, etc. —*verb trans.* (**filed, filing**) to smooth using this tool.

file² *noun* 1 a folder or box that loose papers, etc. can be kept in, or its contents. 2 a collection of stored computer data that can be handled as a single unit. 3 a line of people or things. —*verb trans., intrans.* (**filed, filing**) 1 to put (papers, computer records, etc.) into a file. 2 to make a formal application to a court of law. 3 to move along one behind the other. —**on file** retained in a file for reference; on record.

file-server *noun* a computer that handles files from several linked computers.

filial (fĭl'ē-əl) *adj.* relating to or suitable to a

son or daughter.

filibuster *noun* **1** making long speeches in a legislative body in order to delay the passing of laws. **2** a person who does this. —*verb intrans.* (**filibustered, filibustering**) to obstruct the passage of legislation by making long speeches.

filigree *noun* delicate work in gold or silver wire, used in jewelry, etc.

filing cabinet a piece of furniture with drawers, etc., for holding files.

filings *pl. noun* pieces of wood, metal, etc., rubbed off with a file.

fill *verb trans., intrans.* (**filled, filling**) **1** to make or become full. **2** to take up the space in. **3** to occupy (time). **4** to appoint someone to or be appointed to (a job, etc) **5** to put material into (a hole, cavity, etc.) to level the surface. —*noun* a satisfactory or tolerable amount: *ate my fill.* —**fill in 1** *colloq.* to give (someone) new or needed information. **2** to enter information (esp. on a form). **3** to do another's work temporarily. **fill out 1** to become plumper. **2** to enter information (esp. on a form).

filler *noun* a substance used for filling cracks or holes.

fillet (fĭ-lā´, fĭl´ət) *noun* **1** (*also* **filet**) a boneless piece of meat or fish. **2** a broad ribbon or headband. **3** *Archit.* a narrow flat band. —*verb trans.* (**filleted, filleting**) (*also* **filet** (**fileted, fileting**)) to remove the bones from; to divide into fillets.

filling *noun* **1** the material used to fill a hole in a tooth. **2** food put inside a pie, sandwich, etc.

filling station a gas station.

fillip *noun* something that has a stimulating or brightening effect; a boost.

filly *noun* (*pl.* **fillies**) a young female horse or pony.

film *noun* **1** a strip of thin flexible plastic or other substance, coated so as to be light-sensitive and exposed inside a camera to produce still or moving pictures. **2 a** a motion picture. **b** movies collective, esp. as an art form or field of study. **3** a thin coating. —*verb trans., intrans.* (**filmed, filming**) **1** to photograph with or operate a movie or video camera. **2** (**film over**) to become covered with a fine skin or coating.

filmography *noun* (*pl.* **filmographies**) **1** a list of the movies of a specified actor or director. **2** a body of writings about various movies.

filmstrip a series of photographs on a strip of film, for separate projection as slides.

filmy *adj.* (**filmier, filmiest**) thin, light, and transparent. ▸ **filminess** *noun*

filo (fē´lō, fĭl´ō) *noun* same as **phyllo**.

filter *noun* **1** a porous material through which a liquid or gas is passed in order to remove suspended matter. **2** a plate of glass or other semitransparent material placed over a camera lens, etc.. **3** in electronics, a device that allows signals of only certain frequencies to pass. —*verb trans., intrans.* (**filtered, filtering**) **1** to pass through a filter. **2** to pass little by little. —**filter out** *or* **through** of news or information to leak out. **filter (something) out** to remove (impurities, etc.) by filtering.

filth *noun* **1** repulsive dirt; disgusting rubbish. **2 a** obscene vulgarity. **b** obscenity. ▸ **filthy** *adj.* ▸ **filthily** *adv.* ▸ **filthiness** *noun*

filtrate (fĭl´trāt,) *noun* a clear liquid obtained after any impurities have been filtered out of it. —*verb trans., intrans.* (**filtrated, filtrating**) to filter or be filtered. ▸ **filtration** *noun*

fin *noun* **1** a winglike projection in fish or other aquatic animals. **2** a fixed or adjustable airfoil attached to the rear of an airplane for increased stability.

final *adj.* **1** occurring at the end; last. **2** having been completed; finished. **3** *of a decision, etc.* not to be altered; definite; conclusive. —*noun* **1** the last round of a competition. **2** (**finals**) the examinations held at the end of an academic course. ▸ **finalist** *noun* ▸ **finality** *noun* ▸ **finally** *adv.*

finale *noun* a grand conclusion to a show, etc.

finalize *verb trans.* (**finalized, finalizing**) *colloq.* **1** to decide on or agree to, finally. **2** to complete; to finish. ▸ **finalization** *noun*

finance *noun* (fə-năns´, fī´năns,) **1** monetary matters and affairs; their study or management. **2** the money needed or used to pay for something. **3** (**finances**) financial resources or revenues. —*verb trans.* (fī-năns´) (**financed, financing**) to provide funds for. ▸ **financial** *adj.* ▸ **financially** *adv.*

finance company a business that lends money.

financier (fĭn,ən-sĭr´, fə-năn,-, fī,năn,-) *noun* **1** a person engaged in large financial transactions; a banker or capitalist. **2** a person who finances an operation.

finch *noun* a small, usu. colorful, bird, e.g., the sparrow, canary, or goldfinch, with a short beak adapted for cracking seeds.

find *verb trans., intrans.* (*pa t and pa p* **found;** *pr p* **finding**) **1** to discover, locate, become aware of, etc. through search, inquiry, mental effort, or chance. **2** to arrive at (a result or conclusion). **3** to consider, think, or decide. **4** *Law* to declare (a person guilty or not guilty). —*noun* something that has been found, esp. an important discovery. ▸ **finder** *noun*

finding *noun* (*usu.* **findings**) a conclusion reached as a result of an investigation, etc.

fine[1] *adj.* **1** of high quality; excellent; splendid. **2** beautiful; handsome. **3** *of weather* bright.

4 healthy. **5** satisfactory. **6** pure. **7** delicate; subtle. —*adv.* **1** satisfactorily. **2** into fine pieces; finely. ▸ **finely** *adv.* ▸ **fineness** *noun*

fine² *noun* money to be paid as a penalty. —*verb trans.* (**fined, fining**) to exact a fine from.

fine arts painting, sculpture, music, and architecture.

fine print 1 deliberately ambiguous or obscure material. **2** a section of a legal document, e.g., a contract, containing stipulations and qualifications in small typeface, sometimes in obscure language. *Also called* **small print.**

finery *noun* elaborate or expensive clothing, jewelry, etc.

finespun (fĭn'spən,) *adj.* overly subtle.

finesse (fĭ-nĕs') *noun* **1** skillful elegance or expertise. **2** tact and poise.

fine-tune *verb trans.* (**fine-tuned, fine-tuning**) to make slight adjustments to (a machine, etc.) to make it work perfectly.

finger (fĭng'gər) *noun* **1** one of the five jointed extremities of the hand; any of the four of these other than the thumb. **2** something, such as a glove part, similar in shape to one of these extremities. **3** *Comput.* an Internet facility that allows a user to obtain certain information about other users. —*verb trans.* (**fingered, fingering**) **1** to investigate or touch with the fingers. **2** to play (a musical instrument) with the fingers. **3** *slang* to identify (a criminal) to the police, etc. **4** *Comput.* to obtain information using a finger program. **keep (one's) fingers crossed** to hope that all will turn out well or as planned. **twist (someone) around (one's) little finger** *colloq.* to manipulate someone in order to get one's own way.

fingerboard *noun* the neck of a violin, etc.

fingerbowl *noun* a small bowl of water for cleaning one's fingers at the table.

fingering *noun* the correct positioning of the fingers for playing a particular musical instrument or piece of music.

fingerprint *noun* **1** a unique impression made by the pattern of ridges at the tips of a finger or thumb, used for identification. **2** any other accurate identifying feature or means of identifying a person. —*verb trans.* (**fingerprinted, fingerprinting**) to take an impression of a person's fingerprints.

fingertip *noun* the tip of a finger. —**have (something) at (one's) fingertips 1** to know (a subject) thoroughly. **2** to have (it) readily at hand.

finial (fĭn'ē-əl) *noun* a decorative feature on top of a gable, spire, pillar, etc.

finicky *adj.* overly fussy or too concerned with trivial details. ▣ **FUSSY, PERNICKETY, PERSNICKETY, PICKY.**

finish *verb trans., intrans.* (**finished,**

finishing) **1** to bring or come to an end. **2** to complete or perfect. **3** to use, eat, drink, etc., (the last of something). **4** (*often* **finish up**) to reach or end up in a certain position or situation. **5** (**finish (something** *or* **someone) off**) *colloq.* to exhaust (the one or ones specified); to defeat or kill. **6** to give a particular treatment to the surface of (cloth, wood, etc.). —*noun* **1** the last stage; the end. **2** the last part, e.g., of a race. **3** perfecting touches given to a product. **4** the surface texture given to cloth, wood, etc. ▸ **finisher** *noun*

finished *adj.* **1** completed or perfected. **2** very accomplished.

finishing school a girls' private school where the emphasis is on culture and social skills.

finite *adj.* having an end or limit.

fiord *noun same as* **fjord.**

fir *noun* **1** an evergreen tree with needlelike leaves. **2** the timber from this type of tree.

fire *noun* **1** the flames, heat, and usu. smoke produced by something burning. **2** a destructive instance of burning. **3** a pile of burning wood, coal, etc. in a grate, stove, boiler, etc., used for warmth, cooking, or power. **4** a gas or electric heater. **5** a discharge of firearms. —*verb trans., intrans.* (**fired, firing**) **1 a** to shoot (a gun); to send off (a bullet, arrow, or other missile. **b** *of a firearm* to be discharged. **2** to launch (a rocket or missile). **3** to detonate (an explosive). **4** to direct (e.g., questions) in quick succession at someone. **5** *colloq.* to dismiss from employment. **6** to start or cause to start burning. **7** to inspire or stimulate. **8** to bake (pottery or bricks) in a kiln. —**catch fire 1** to begin to burn. **2** to gain sudden popularity: *The idea caught fire.* **cease fire** to stop fighting. **play with fire** *colloq.* to take risks; to act recklessly.

firearm *noun* a gun, pistol, revolver, or rifle.

fireball *noun* **1** a mass of hot gases at the center of a nuclear explosion. **2** a ball-shaped flash of lightning. **3** a brilliant meteor.

firebomb *noun* an incendiary bomb. —*verb trans.* (**firebombed, firebombing**) to attack with an incendiary bomb.

firebrand *noun* **1** a piece of burning wood. **2** someone who stirs up unrest.

firebreak *noun* a cleared strip in a forest to stop the spread of a fire.

fire brigade a team of people called out to fight fires.

firebug *noun colloq.* an arsonist.

firecracker *noun* a firework.

fire department a body responsible for controlling and extinguishing fires.

fire drill the routine to be followed in case of fire, or a practice of this routine.

fire-eater *noun* **1** a performer who pretends

to swallow fire from flaming torches. **2** an aggressive or quarrelsome person.

fire engine a firefighting vehicle.

fire escape a way by which people can escape from a burning building.

fire extinguisher a portable device for putting out a fire.

firefighter *noun* a person who puts out fires. ▸ **firefighting** *noun*

firefly *noun* (*pl.* **fireflies**) a small winged beetle that can emit light. *Also called* **lightning bug.**

fireguard *noun* a protective metal or wire-mesh screen for putting around an open fire.

firelighter *noun* a block of flammable material used to help light a fire.

fireplace *noun* **1** a recess in a room for an open fire, usu. consisting of a grate with a chimney above it. **2** the external structure that surrounds or conceals this.

fireplug *noun* a hydrant.

firepower *noun* the destructive capacity of an armed force.

fireproof *adj.* resistant to fire and high heat. —*verb trans.* (**fireproofed, fireproofing**) to make resistant to fire and high heat.

fire sale the sale of goods damaged by fire.

fireside *noun* the area around a fireplace.

fire station a fire department's building.

firestorm *noun* **1** a huge fire, esp. one fed by strong winds. **2** an intense outburst, e.g., of criticism.

firetrap *noun* a building likely to burn easily or with inadequate escape routes in case of fire.

firewall *noun* a fireproof barrier, e.g., in a building or a mechanical device.

firewater *noun slang* strong liquor, esp. cheap whiskey.

firework *noun* **1** a device designed to produce spectacular colored sparks, flares, bangs, etc. **2** (**fireworks**) a show at which such devices are let off for entertainment. **3** (**fireworks**) *colloq.* a show of anger or bad temper.

firing line 1 the front line of battle. **2** a prominent position, esp. one that could lead to criticism.

firing pin the part in a firearm that detonates the explosive charge propelling the projectile.

firing squad a detachment of people whose duty is to shoot a condemned person.

firm[1] *adj.* **1** steady: *a firm deck.* **2** solid. **3** definite; determined; resolute. —*adv.* firmly. —*verb trans.* (**firmed, firming**) to make firm or secure. **firm (something) up** to make (it) firmer or more definite. ▸ **firmly** *adv.* ▸ **firmness** *noun*

firm[2] *noun* a business company.

firmament *noun old literary use* the sky.

firmware *noun* software permanently held in a computer's read-only memory.

first *adj.* **1** earliest or foremost in time, order,

importance, etc. **2** basic: *first principles.* —*adv.* before anything or anyone else or before doing anything else. —*noun* **1** a first person or thing. **2** a first occurrence of something; something never done before. **3** the one numbered 1 in a series. —**at first** at or in the beginning.

first aid immediate emergency treatment given to an injured or ill person.

first base 1 *Baseball* **a** the first of the three bases, exclusive of home plate. **b** the position guarded by the first baseman. **2** *slang* the very first of several stages along the way to completion of a project or success. ▸ **first baseman**

first-born *noun* the eldest child in a family. —*adj.* eldest.

first class the highest grade, e.g., of traveling accommodations.

first-class *adj.* **1** of the first class. **2** excellent. —*adv.* by first-class mail or transport.

first cousin a child of an aunt or uncle.

first-day cover a stamped envelope postmarked with the stamp's or the set of stamps' date of issue.

first-degree *adj.* **1** *of a burn* showing damage to only the outer layer of the skin. **2** *of a crime, esp. murder* very serious, esp. in being premeditated.

first floor 1 the ground floor of a structure. **2** *Chiefly Brit.* the floor above the ground floor.

first-generation *adj.* denoting the first or earliest stage in technological development.

firsthand *adj.* from the original source; direct.

firstly *adv.* in the first place; first of all.

fiscal *adj.* **1** relating to government finances or revenue. **2** relating to financial matters generally. ▸ **fiscally** *adv.*

fiscal year the 12-month period for which a business or other organization plans the use of its funds.

fish *noun* (**fish, fishes**) **1. a** a cold-blooded aquatic vertebrate that has fins and breathes through gills. **b** the flesh of a fish used as food. **2** a water-inhabiting creature such as a jellyfish. **3** *colloq.* a person: *an odd fish.* —*verb intrans., trans.* (**fished, fishing**) **1** to try to catch (fish). **2** to try to catch fish in (a body of water). **3** to search for or seek out (something). ▸ **fisher** *noun* ▸ **fishing** *noun*

fishbowl *noun* **1** a clear bowl in which pet fish are kept. **2** a place with no privacy.

fisherman *noun* **1** a man who fishes. **2** a commercial fishing boat, e.g., a trawler.

fishery *noun* (*pl.* **fisheries**) **1** an area of sea where fishing takes place. **2** the business of catching fish. **3** a fish hatchery.

fisheye lens a camera lens with an extremely wide angle and a small focal length.

fishhook *noun* a hook with barbs for gripping the jaw of a fish taking the bait.

fishing line a strong line with a fish hook.

fishing rod a flexible rod to which a fishing line is attached.

fish ladder a series of steplike pools alongside a waterway enabling migratory fish to move upstream around a dam.

fish story *colloq.* a boasting, implausible tale.

fishtail *verb intrans.* (**fishtailed, fishtailing**) *of a vehicle* to sway from side to side.

fishwife *noun* **1** a woman who guts or sells fish. **2** a loud coarse-mannered woman.

fishy *adj.* (**fishier, fishiest**) **1** of or like a fish. **2** *colloq.* odd; suspicious.

fissile (fĭs′əl, -ĭl,) *adj.* **1** capable of undergoing nuclear fission. **2** of rocks easily split.

fission (fĭsh′ən, fĭzh′-) *noun* **1** a splitting or division. **2** the splitting of atomic nuclei. ▸ **fissionable** *adj.*

fissure (fĭsh′ər) *noun* **1** a narrow cleft or groove. **2** a long narrow crack or fracture, e.g., in a rock, the Earth's surface, or a volcano. —*verb intrans., trans.* (**fissured, fissuring**) to crack or divide.

fist *noun* a clenched hand.

fisticuffs *pl. noun* fighting with the fists.

fistula (fĭs′chə-lə) *noun* (*pl.* **fistulas, fistulae**) an abnormal passage in the body.

fit¹ *verb trans., intrans.* (*pa t* **fitted** *or* **fit;** *pa p* **fitted;** *pr p* **fitting**) **1** to be, or be made to be, the right shape or size for. **2** to be small or few enough to go into (a space, etc.). **3** to be appropriate for or compatible with (something). **4** to insert, place, or install (something) in position. **5** to equip or supply. —*noun* the way something fits: *a good fit.* —*adj.* (**fitter, fittest**) **1** suited to or good enough for (someone or something). **2** healthy. **3** about to do something: *looked fit to collapse.* —**fit in 1** to be suitable. **2** to find time to deal with (someone or something). ▸ **fitly** *adv.* ▸ **fitness** *noun*

fit² *noun* **1** an epileptic convulsion or sudden attack of e.g., coughing. **2** a burst or bout.

fitful *adj.* irregular or spasmodic. ▸ **fitfully** *adv.*

fitted *adj.* made to fit closely.

fitter *noun* **1** a person who installs or repairs gas pipes, plumbing, etc.. **2** a person who fits clothes.

fitting *adj.* suitable. —*noun* an act of trying on a specially made garment to see if any adjustment is necessary. ▸ **fittingly** *adv.*

five *noun* **1** the number or figure 5. **2** the age of 5. **3** any person or thing denoted by the number 5. **4** 5 o'clock. **5** a set of 5 people or things. **6** a score of 5 points. —*adj.* **1** 5 in number. **2** aged 5.

five-and-dime *or* **five-and-ten** *noun* a store where a variety of reasonably priced items can be purchased. *Also called* **dime store**.

fiver *noun colloq.* a five-dollar bill.

fix *verb trans.* (**fixed, fixing**) **1** to attach firmly. **2** to repair. **3** to direct or transfix. **4** to arrange, agree or establish (a time, etc.). **5** to arrange the result of (a race, trial, etc.) dishonestly. **6** to make (a dye or photographic image, etc.) permanent. **7** to prepare (a meal, etc.). **8** to neuter or spay (an animal). —*noun* **1** a difficulty or predicament. **2** *slang* an act of injecting a drug, etc. **b** a dose of a drug injected or to be injected. **3** *slang* a solution to a problem, etc. ▸ **fixed** *adj.* ▸ **fixedly** *adv.*

fixated *adj.* obsessively attached to someone or something. ▸ **fixation** *noun*

fixative (fĭk′sət-ĭv) *noun* **1** a liquid sprayed on a drawing, painting, or photograph to preserve and protect it. **2** a substance used for holding something in place.

fixture *noun* **1** a fixed piece of furniture or equipment. **2** someone who is closely associated with a particular activity or area.

fizz *verb intrans.* (**fizzed, fizzing**) to bubble noisily. —*noun* a fizzing sound or sensation.

fizzle *verb intrans.* (**fizzled, fizzling**) **1** to make a faint hiss. **2** (**fizzle out**) to come to a feeble end.

fizzy *adj.* (**fizzier, fizziest**) effervescent. ▸ **fizziness** *noun*

fjord *or* **fiord** (fē-ôrd′) *noun* a long, narrow, steep-sided inlet of the sea.

fl *abbrev.* fluid.

flab *noun colloq.* excess fat on the body.

flabbergast *verb trans.* (**flabbergasted, flabbergasting**) to amaze; to astonish.

flabby *adj.* (**flabbier, flabbiest**) **1** lacking firmness. **2** lacking vigor; feeble; ineffective. ▸ **flabbily** *adv.* ▸ **flabbiness** *noun*

flaccid (flăs′ĭd, flăk′sĭd) *adj.* limp and soft. ▸ **flaccidity** *noun* ▸ **flaccidly** *adv.*

flag¹ *noun* a piece of cloth, often with a distinctive design, used to represent a country, political party, etc., mark a boundary, etc., or for signaling. —*verb trans.* (**flagged, flagging**) **1** to mark or signal with a flag, or other symbol. **2** (**flag (someone** *or* **something) down**) to signal (a driver or vehicle) to stop.

flag² *verb intrans.* (**flagged, flagging**) to grow tired or feeble.

flag³ *noun* a flagstone.

flagellate (flăj′ə-lāt,) *verb trans.* (**flagellated, flagellating**) to whip, as a religious discipline or for sexual stimulation. ▸ **flagellant** *noun* ▸ **flagellation** *noun*

flagon *noun* a large bottle or jug with a narrow neck, usu. with a spout and handle.

flagpole *noun* the pole from which a flag is flown. *Also called* **flagstaff**.

flagrant (flā′grənt) *adj.* **1** glaringly and obviously bad. **2** brazen. ▸ **flagrancy** *noun* ▸ **flagrantly** *adv.*

Usage See note at *blatant*.

flagship *noun* **1** the ship that carries and flies the flag of a fleet commander. **2** a company's leading product, premises, etc.

flagstaff *noun* a flagpole.

flagstone *noun* a large flat paving stone.

flail *noun* a hand-held threshing tool. —*verb intrans., trans.* (**flailed, flailing**) **1** (**flail about or around**) to wave about violently. **2** to thresh or beat with a flail, etc.

flair *noun* **1** a natural ability or talent. **2** stylishness.

flak *noun* **1** antiaircraft fire. **2** *colloq.* criticism.

flake *noun* **1** a small flat particle. **2** *slang* an odd or eccentric person. —*verb intrans., trans.* (**flaked, flaking**) to come off in flakes or break (something) into flakes. —**flake out** *slang* to fall asleep or pass out.

flak jacket a metal-reinforced jacket worn for protection by police or soldiers.

flaky *adj.* (**flakier, flakiest**) **1** made of or tending to form flakes. **2** odd; eccentric.

flambé (flām-bā′) *adj.* of food soaked in brandy and set on fire before serving.

flamboyant (flăm-boi′ənt) *adj.* colorful, bright, or exuberant. ▸ **flamboyance** *noun* ▸ **flamboyantly** *adv.*

flame *noun* **1** a flickering stream of hot luminous gas or vapor produced by burning. **2** a strong passion. **3** a bright reddish-orange color. —*verb trans., intrans.* (**flamed, flaming**) **1** to burn with flames. **2** to shine brightly. **3** to explode with anger. **4** to become red and hot. ▸ **flaming** *adj.*

flamingo (flə-mĭng′gō) *noun* (*pl.* **flamingos, flamingoes**) a large wading bird with white, red, or pink plumage, a long neck and long legs.

flammable *adj.* liable to catch fire.

Usage In the USA at least, the word *flammable* has all but replaced *inflammable*.

flan *noun* an open pastry with a fruit, custard, or cheese filling.

flange (flănj) *noun* a broad, flat, projecting rim.

flank *noun* **1** the side of an animal or human body, between the ribs and hip. **2** the side of something. —*verb trans.* (**flanked, flanking**) to be or move beside.

flannel *noun* **1** a soft woolen cloth. **2** (**flannels**) trousers made of this cloth.

flannelette (flăn‚l-ĕt′) *noun* cotton cloth with a soft brushed surface.

flap *verb trans., intrans.* (**flapped, flapping**) **1** to wave up and down or backward and forward. **2** of a bird to move (the wings) in this way. **3** *colloq.* to become flustered. —*noun* **1** a part that is attached along one edge and hangs loosely from something else. **2** an act or sound of flapping. **3** *colloq.* a flustered state.

flapjack *noun* a pancake.

flare *verb intrans., trans.* (**flared, flaring**) **1** to burn with sudden brightness. **2** to explode into anger. **3** to widen towards the edge. —*noun* **1** a sudden blaze of bright light. **2** a device for producing a blaze of light, used as a distress signal or emergency illumination. **3** a device for burning off superfluous combustible gas or oil safely. **4** a flared edge. —**flare up 1** to blaze suddenly. **2** to explode into anger. ▸ **flare-up** *noun*

flash *noun* **1** a sudden brief blaze of light, flame, etc. **2** an instant. **3** a brief but intense occurrence, look, etc. **3** a brief news announcement. —*verb intrans., trans.* (**flashed, flashing**) **1** to shine or sparkle briefly or brightly. **2** to appear, move, or pass quickly. **3** *colloq., of a man* to expose the genitals in public. —*adj.* **1** sudden and severe: *flash floods.* **2** quick. **3** *colloq.* smart, expensive, and ostentatious. —**a flash in the pan** *colloq.* something that is only momentarily successful. ▸ **flasher** *noun*

flashback *noun* a return to the past, esp. a scene in a movie, etc.

flashbulb *noun* a small bulb used to produce a brief bright light in photography.

flashing *noun* sheet metal for weatherproofing and reinforcing the angles and joints of a roof.

flashlight *noun* a small, battery-powered lamp.

flashpoint *noun* a stage in a tense situation when tempers are likely to be lost or violence is liable to erupt.

flashy *adj.* (**flashier, flashiest**) *colloq.* ostentatious; gaudy. ▸ **flashily** *adv.* ▸ **flashiness** *noun*

flask *noun* **1** a small container for alcoholic spirits. **2** a glass or metal container with a long narrow neck.

flat *adj.* (**flatter, flattest**) **1** without hollows or bumps. **2** not bent or crumpled. **3** dull; toneless; off key. **4** definite; emphatic: *flat refusal.* **5** of a tire lacking sufficient air. **6** of a drink having lost its effervescence. **7** of a battery lacking electrical charge. **8** unvarying: *charge a flat rate.* **9** of paint not glossy. —*adv.* **1** stretched out. **2** exactly or only: *in two minutes flat.* **3** bluntly and emphatically. —*noun* **1** an apartment. **2** something flat; a flat surface or part. **3** *colloq.* a tire lacking sufficient air. **4** *Mus.* a note lowered by a half step; a sign (♭) indicating it. —**flat out** *colloq.* with maximum speed and energy. ▸ **flatly** *adv.*

flatcar *noun* a flat railroad freight car.

flatfish *noun* (*pl.* **flatfish, flatfishes**) a fish with a wide, horizontally flat body.

flatfoot *noun* 1 (*pl.* **flatfeet**) a foot condition in which the arch of the instep has dropped. ▸ **flat-footed** *adj.*

flatline *verb intrans., colloq.* 1 to die. 2 to become useless. ▸ **flatliner** *noun*

flatten *verb trans., intrans.* (**flattened, flattening**) 1 to make or become flat. 2 *colloq.* to knock to the ground. 3 *colloq.* to crush or subdue completely.

flatter *verb trans.* (**flattered, flattering**) 1 to compliment excessively or insincerely. 2 to represent in an overly favorable manner. ▸ **flatterer** *noun* ▸ **flattery** *noun*

flattop *noun colloq.* an aircraft carrier.

flatulent *adj.* 1 suffering from or caused by an accumulation of gas in the stomach or intestines. 2 pompous. ▸ **flatulence** *noun*

flatware *noun* 1 knives, forks, and spoons. 2 plates and platters.

flaunt (flônt) *verb trans.* (**flaunted, flaunting**) to put on view ostentatiously, esp. to attract envy or admiration. ▣ DISPLAY, DISPORT, EXHIBIT, FLASH, PARADE, SHOW (OFF) ▣ HIDE.

> **Usage** The verb *flaunt* is often confused with *flout*.

flautist (flôt′Ist, flowt′-) *noun* a flutist.

flavor *noun* 1 the taste of a food or drink. 2 a characteristic quality or atmosphere. —*verb trans.* (**flavored, flavoring**) to impart flavor to. ▸ **flavoring** *noun*

flaw *noun* a fault, defect, or mistake. ▸ **flawed** *adj.* ▸ **flawless** *adj.* ▸ **flawlessly** *adv.*

flax *noun* a blue-flowered plant whose stem yields a fiber used for making linen, and whose seeds are used to make linseed oil.

flaxen *adj.*, of hair very fair.

flay *verb trans.* (**flayed, flaying**) 1 to strip the skin from. 2 to whip or beat violently. 3 to criticize harshly.

flea *noun* a wingless blood-sucking parasitic insect. —**a flea in one's ear** *colloq.* 1 a severe scolding. 2 an annoying hint.

flea market a street market selling second-hand goods or clothes.

fleck *noun* a spot or speck. ▸ **flecked** *adj.*

fled see **flee**.

fledged (flējd) *noun* 1 of a young bird able to fly. 2 qualified; trained.

fledgling *or* **fledgeling** *noun* 1 a young bird that has just grown its feathers. 2 an inexperienced person. — *adj.* new or inexperienced.

flee *verb intrans., trans.* (*pa t and pa p* **fled**; *pr p* **fleeing**) to run away (from something); to take to flight.

fleece *noun* 1 the coat of a sheep or similar animal. 2 the wool shorn from a single sheep at one time. 3 a soft cozy jacket. —*verb trans.* (**fleeced, fleeci g**) *slang* to rob, swindle, or overcharge. ▸ **fleecy** *adj.*

fleet[1] *noun* 1 a number of ships under one command. 2 a navy. 3 a group of buses, taxis, etc. under the same ownership.

fleet[2] *adj.* swift. ▸ **fleetness** *noun*

fleeting *adj.* brief. ▸ **fleetingly** *adv.*

flesh *noun* 1 the soft muscular tissue of the body of a human or animal. 2 the soft tissue of an animal used as food. 3 the soft edible tissue of a fruit or vegetable. 4 the body as distinct from the soul or spirit. 5 a yellowish-pink color. —**flesh and blood** 1 bodily or human nature. 2 (one's) **flesh and blood** (one's) family or relations. **flesh** (**something**) **out** to add descriptive detail to (it). **in the flesh** in person.

fleshpot *noun* (*often* **fleshpots**) an area of adult or hedonistic entertainment.

fleshy *adj.* (**fleshier, fleshiest**) plump. ▸ **fleshiness** *noun* ▸ **fleshly** *adv.*

fleur-de-lis *or* **fleur-de-lys** (flərd,l-ē′, floōrd,-) *noun* (*pl.* **fleurs-de-lis, -lys**) a three-petal representation of a lily or iris.

flew see **fly**[2].

flex *verb trans., intrans.* (**flexed, flexing**) 1 to bend (a limb or joint) or to be so bent. 2 to contract (a muscle).

flexible *adj.* 1 bending easily; pliable. 2 readily adaptable to suit circumstances. ▸ **flexibility** *noun* ▸ **flexibly** *adv.*

flextime *noun* a system allowing workers to choose when they put in their hours. *Also called* **flexible time, flexitime**.

flick *verb trans., intrans.* (**flicked, flicking**) 1 to move or touch with a quick, light movement. 2 (**flick through (something)**) to look quickly through (a book, etc.). —*noun* 1 a quick, light movement or action. 2 *slang* a movie.

flicker[1] *verb intrans., trans.* (**flickered, flickering**) 1 to burn or shine unsteadily. 2 to move lightly to and fro; to flutter. —*noun* 1 a brief or unsteady light. 2 a fleeting appearance or occurrence.

flicker[2] *noun* a large woodpecker.

flier *or* **flyer** *noun* 1 someone or something that flies. 2 someone or something that moves fast. 3 an advertising leaflet.

flight[1] *noun* 1 an act of flying. 2 the movement of a vehicle, bird, insect, etc. through the air. 3 an air or space journey; the distance, course, etc. of such a journey. 4 a set of steps or stairs. 5 an extravagant or implausible notion or account: *a flight of fancy*. —**in flight** flying.

flight[2] *noun* the act of fleeing. —**put to flight** to cause to flee. **take flight** to flee.

flight attendant a member of the cabin crew on a passenger aircraft.

flightless *adj.*, of birds or insects unable to fly.

flighty *adj.* (**flightier, flightiest**) easily

excited; frivolous or silly.

flimsy *adj.* (**flimsier, flimsiest**) **1** light and thin. **2** insubstantial; frail. **3** *of an excuse, etc.* inadequate or unconvincing. ▸ **flimsily** *adv.* ▸ **flimsiness** *noun*

flinch *verb intrans.* (**flinched, flinching**) **1** to jump in pain or fright. **2** (**flinch from** (**something**)) to shrink from or avoid (something unpleasant).

fling *verb* (*pa t and pa p* **flung**; *pr p* **flinging**) **1** to throw, esp. strongly or vigorously. **2** (**fling** (**something**) **away**) to discard (it). —*noun* **1** *colloq.* a spell of doing something enjoyable. **2** a lively dance, esp. a reel.

flint *noun* **1** a hard, dark gray or black form of quartz. *Also called* **chert.** **2** a trimmed piece of this used as a tool. **3** a piece of this or of a hard metal alloy used for obtaining a spark.

flinty *adj.* (**flintier, flintiest**) **1** made of or containing flint. **2** rigid or stubborn.

flip *verb trans., intrans.* (**flipped, flipping**) **1** to toss or turn over in midair. **2** (*also* **flip** (**one's**) **lid**) *colloq.* to go crazy or lose one's temper. —*noun* **1** a flipping action. **2** an alcoholic drink containing beaten egg. —*adj. colloq.* flippant; impertinent.

flip-flop *noun colloq.* **1** a rubber or plastic sandal. **2** a reversal, e.g., of a decision, opinion, policy, etc.—*verb trans., intrans.* (**flip-flopped, flip-flopping**) **1** to walk or move with a flapping noise. **2** to reverse (a decision, opinion, policy, etc.).

flippant (flĭp'ənt) *adj.* disrespectful; taking or treating serious things too casually or lightly. ▸ **flippancy** *noun* ▸ **flippantly** *adv.*

flipper *noun* **1 a** a broad, flat limb adapted for swimming. **b** a similar rubber foot covering worn for swimming and diving. **2** a lever in a pinball machine that moves the ball.

flip side *colloq.* the opposite side, e.g., of an issue or other matter of discussion.

flirt *verb intrans.* (**flirted, flirting**) **1** (*also* **flirt with** (**someone**)) to indicate a romantic or sexual interest (in someone) without serious intentions. **2** (**flirt with** (**something**)) to toy with (it) or take a fleeting interest in (it). —*noun* someone who flirts. ▸ **flirtation** *noun* ▸ **flirtatious** *adj.*

flit *verb intrans.* (**flitted, flitting**) to dart lightly from place to place.

flitch *noun* a salted and cured side of pork.

float *verb trans., intrans.* (**floated, floating**) **1** to rest or move, or cause to rest or move, on a liquid. **2** to drift about or hover in the air. **3** to move about in an aimless or disorganized way. **4** to start up (a company, scheme, etc.). **5** to offer (stocks) for sale. **6** to allow (a currency) to vary in value in relation to other currencies. —*noun* **1** a floating device. **2** a decorated vehicle in a parade. ▸ **floater** *noun*

floating *adj.* **1** not fixed, esp. in time or place. **2** *of a currency* varying in value in relation to other currencies.

flock[1] *noun* **1** a group of creatures, esp. birds or sheep, or a crowd of people. **2** a congregation. —*verb intrans.* (**flocked, flocking**) to gather or move in a crowd.

flock[2] *noun* **1** a tuft of wool, etc. **2** fine fibers of wool, etc. applied to paper or cloth to create a pattern.

floe *noun* a mass of ice floating in the sea.

flog *verb trans.* (**flogged, flogging**) **1** to beat; to whip. **2** *colloq.* to publicize (something) insistently and aggressively.

flood *noun* **1** a flow of water over land. **2** (**Flood**) the flood from which Noah took refuge in the Ark (Genesis 7-8). **3** a great flow or quantity. —*verb trans., intrans.* **1** to cover with a flood; to cause a flood. **2** to come in large numbers. **3** to file with a large quantity of something.

floodgate *noun* a gate for controlling the flow of a large amount of water. —**open the floodgates** to remove all restraints.

floodlight *noun* a powerful light used to illuminate extensive areas. —*verb trans.* (**floodlighted** *or* **floodlit, floodlighting**) to illuminate with floodlights.

floor (flôr) *noun* **1** the lower interior surface of a room, vehicle, etc. **2** all the rooms on the same level in a building. —*verb trans.* (**floored, flooring**) **1** to construct a floor. **2** *colloq.* to knock (someone) down. **3** *colloq.* to baffle completely.

flooring *noun* material for constructing floors.

floorshow *noun* a series of entertainments at a nightclub or restaurant.

floorwalker *noun* a sales supervisor in a department store.

floozy *or* **floozie** *noun* (*pl.* **floozies**) *slang* a disreputable or immodest woman or girl.

flop *verb intrans.* (**flopped, flopping**) **1** to fall or move heavily. **2** *colloq.* to fail. —*noun* **1** a flopping movement or sound. **2** *colloq.* a failure.

floppy *adj.* (**floppier, floppiest**) hanging loose. ▸ **floppily** *adv.* ▸ **floppiness** *noun*

floppy disk a small flexible plastic disk for storing computer data. *Also called* **diskette.** *See also* **hard disk.**

flora *noun* (*pl.* **floras, florae**) the plants of a particular place or geological period. *See also* **fauna.**

floral *adj.* of, relating to, or patterned with flowers. ▸ **florally** *adv.*

floret (flôr'ət) *noun* **1** a single flower in the head of a composite flower. **2** a branch in the head of cauliflower or of broccoli.

florid *adj.* **1** overly elaborate. **2** pink or ruddy in complexion. ▸ **floridly** *adv.*

florist *noun* a person or firm that grows or sells flowers.

floss *noun* 1 strands of thin, strong thread for cleaning between the teeth, etc. 2 strands of silky material. 3 embroidery thread. —*verb trans., intrans.* (**flossed, flossing**) to clean using floss. ▸ **flossy** *adj.*

flotation *noun* 1 the launching of a commercial company with a sale of shares to raise money. 2 the action or capability of floating in a liquid.

flotilla (flə-tĭl′ə) *noun* a small fleet, or a fleet of small ships.

flotsam (flăt′səm) *noun* wreckage or cargo from a shipwreck, found floating on the sea. *See also* **jetsam**.

flounce[1] *verb intrans.* (**flounced, flouncing**) 1 to move in petulant or indignant way. 2 to swagger. —*noun* a flouncing movement.

flounce[2] *noun* a deep frill.

flounder[1] *verb intrans.* (**floundered, floundering**) 1 to struggle or thrash about helplessly. 2 to be in difficulties or at a loss.

flounder[2] *noun* (*pl.* **flounder, flounders**) a small, grayish-brown marine flatfish.

flour (flowr) *noun* 1 the finely ground meal of a cereal grain, esp. wheat. 2 a dried powdered form of any other vegetable material. —*verb trans.* (**floured, flouring**) to cover or sprinkle with flour. ▸ **floury** *adj.*

flourish (flûr′ĭsh) *verb intrans., trans.* (**flourished, flourishing**) 1 to be strong and healthy; to do or grow well; to prosper. 2 to wave or brandish. —*noun* a decorative twirl in handwriting, a sweep of the hand, a musical fanfare, etc.

flout (flowt) *verb trans.* (**flouted, flouting**) to ignore or defy blatantly or deliberately. ▣ DEFY, SCOUT (AT).

> *Usage* The verb *flout* is often confused with *flaunt*.

flow *verb intrans.* (**flowed, flowing**) 1 to move along, like water. 2 to circulate. 3 to keep coming or moving. —*noun* 1 the action or rate of flowing. 2 a continuous stream or outpouring.

flow chart a diagram representing the nature and sequence of operations to be carried out.

flower (flow′ər, flowr) *noun* 1 a a plant's reproductive structure, esp. one with brightly colored petals. b a plant that has flowers. 2 the best part; the cream. —*verb intrans.* (**flowered, flowering**) 1 to produce flowers; to bloom. 2 to reach a peak; to develop to full maturity. —**in flower** with flowers fully out.

flowerpot *noun* a clay or plastic container in which to grow plants.

flowery *adj.* (**flowerier, floweriest**) 1 relating to or decorated with flowers. 2 excessively elaborate: *flowery prose*.

flown *see* **fly**[2].

fl oz *or* **fl. oz.** *abbrev.* fluid ounce.

flu *noun colloq.* influenza.

fluctuate *verb intrans.* (**fluctuated, fluctuating**) to vary in amount, value, level, etc.; to rise and fall. ▸ **fluctuation** *noun.*

flue *noun* a duct for smoke, gas, heat, etc.

fluent (flōō′ənt) *adj.* 1 *of a person* having full command of a language. 2 *of a language* spoken or written with ease. 3 *of a person* speaking or writing in an easy flowing style. ▸ **fluency** *noun* ▸ **fluently** *adv.*

fluff *noun* 1 small bits of soft woolly or downy material. 2 *colloq.* a mistake, e.g., in speaking or reading aloud. —*verb trans., intrans.* (**fluffed, fluffing**) 1 (*usu.* **fluff** (something) **out** *or* **up**) to shake or arrange (it) into a soft mass. 2 to make a mistake in (one's lines, etc.); to bungle (something). ▸ **fluffy** *adj.*

fluid *noun* any non-solid form of matter, such as gas or liquid. —*adj.* 1 capable of flowing freely and readily changing shape. 2 altering easily; adaptable. ▸ **fluidity** *noun*

fluid ounce (ABBREV. **fl oz, fl. oz.**) 1 unit of liquid measurement equal to 1.804 cu. in. (29.57 ml).

fluke[1] *noun* a success achieved by accident. ▸ **fluky** *adj.*

fluke[2] *noun* a flounder, or other flatfish.

fluke[3] *noun* 1 the barb on the end of a harpoon. 2 the part of an anchor that catches and digs into the bed of the sea or river. 3 the lobe of a whale's tail.

flume *noun* a channel for water.

flummox (flŭm′əks) *verb trans.* (**flummoxed, flummoxing**) *colloq.* to bewilder.

flung *see* **fling**.

flunk *verb trans., intrans.* (**flunked, flunking**) *colloq.* to fail (a test, examination, student, etc.). —**flunk out** to be forced to leave a school or college because of academic failure.

flunky *or* **flunkey** *noun* (*pl.* **flunkies, flunkeys**) 1 a slavish follower. 2 a person doing a menial job. 3 a manservant.

fluorescence *noun* the emission of radiation, usu. light, by an object after it has absorbed electrons or radiation of a different wavelength. ▸ **fluoresce** *verb intrans.* ▸ **fluorescent** *adj.*

fluorescent light an electric light consisting of a glass tube containing mercury vapor or a chemically inert gas. *Also called* **fluorescent lamp**.

fluoridation *noun* the addition of small amounts of fluoride salts to drinking-water supplies to help prevent tooth decay.

fluoride (flŏŏr′ĭd,, flôr′-) *noun* a compound of fluorine and another element.

fluorine (flŏŏr′ēn,, flôr′-) *noun* (SYMBOL **F**) a poisonous pale yellow gaseous element.

flurry *noun* (*pl.* **flurries**) 1 a sudden gust; a

brief shower of snow, etc. **2** a bustle or rush.
—*verb trans., intrans.* (**flurried, flurrying, flurries**) to agitate or confuse.

flush¹ *verb intrans., trans.* (**flushed, flushing**) **1** to blush or cause to blush or get red in the face. **2** to clean out (something) or get rid of (something) with a powerful rush of water. **3** to drive (a bird or animal) from a hiding place —*noun* **1** a redness or rosiness, esp. of the face; a blush. **2** a rush of water for cleaning something or the mechanism that controls it. **3** a sudden rush, esp. of emotion. **4** a time when something is particularly fresh, blooming, or vigorous.

flush² *adj.* **1** level with an adjacent surface. **2** *colloq.* having plenty of money. —*adv.* so as to be level with an adjacent surface.

flush³ *noun* a hand in cards consisting of a single suit.

fluster *noun* a state of confusion or agitation. —*verb trans., intrans.* (**flustered, flustering**) to make or become agitated or confused.

flute *noun* **1** a tubular woodwind instrument. **2** *Archit.* a rounded groove in wood or stone. —*verb trans., intrans.* (**fluted, fluting**) **1** to speak with a vibrating, often high-pitched, voice. ▶ **fluting** *noun* ▶ **fluty** *adj.*

flutist a flute player. *Also called* **flautist**

flutter *verb trans., intrans.* (**fluttered, fluttering**) **1** to fly with rapid wing movements or drift with a twirling motion. **2** to move about in a restless way. **3** *of the heart* to race, e.g., from excitement or a disorder. —*noun* **1** agitation; excitement. **2** sudden irregular movement.

fluvial (floo′vē-əl) *adj.* relating to rivers.

flux *noun* **1** constant change; instability. **2** a substance added to another, e.g., to aid the process of melting, to combine with impurities, to remove oxides, etc. **3** the rate of flow of particles, energy, mass, etc. across a given area. ▶ **fluxion** *noun*

fly¹ *noun* (*pl.* **flies**) **1** a two- or four-winged flying insect. **2** a fishhook make to look like a fly.

fly² *verb intrans., trans.* (pa t **flew**; pa p **flown**; pr p **flying**; 3d person sing. present **flies**) **1** to travel through the air or through space. **2** to travel or convey in an aircraft, spacecraft, etc. **3** to operate and control (an aircraft, spacecraft, kite, etc.). **4 a** to raise (a flag, etc.). **b** *of a flag, etc.* to blow in the wind. **6** to move fast or to depart quickly. **7** (**fly at**) to attack angrily. **8** to flee (a country, etc.); to escape. **9** (*3d person sing. past* **flied**) *Baseball* to hit a fly. —*noun* (*pl.* **flies**) **1** a zip or set of buttons fastening the front of pants or trousers, or the flap covering this fastener. **2** a flap covering the entrance to a tent. **3** (**flies**) the space above a stage from

which scenery is lowered. **4** *Baseball* a ball batted in a high arc, usu. into the outfield.

flyblown *noun* **1** contaminated with fly eggs or larvae. **2** shabby, dirty, or dingy.

fly-by-night *adj.* unreliable or untrustworthy. —*noun* an unreliable person, esp. one who fails to pay creditors.

flycatcher *noun* a small insectivorous bird, esp. one that catches its food on the wing.

flyer *noun same as* **flier**.

fly-fishing *noun* fishing using artificial flies.

flying *noun* **1** flight. **2** the activity of piloting, navigating, or traveling in an aircraft or spacecraft. —*adj.* **1** hasty; brief: *a flying visit.* **2** designed or organized for fast movement. **3** relating to, adapted for, or capable of flight or gliding.

flying boat a large seaplane..

flying fish a tropical fish with winglike fins that can rise above the water.

flying fox a large fruit-eating bat.

flying saucer a circular flying object, believed by some to be from outer space.

flying squirrel a squirrel with a large flap of skin between the front and hind legs, which allows it to glide between trees.

flyleaf *noun* a blank page at the beginning or end of a book.

flypaper *noun* sticky paper for trapping and killing flies.

fly swatter a long-handled implement with a large flat end, used for killing insects.

flyweight *noun* **1** a class for boxers, wrestlers, and weight lifters of not more than a specified weight (112 lbs., or 50.8 kg, in professional boxing, similar weights in the other sports). **2** a boxer, etc., of this weight.

flywheel *noun* a heavy wheel on a revolving shaft that regulates the action of a machine.

foal *noun* a young horse, donkey, etc. —*verb intrans.* (**foaled, foaling**) to give birth to a foal.

foam *noun* **1** a mass of frothy bubbles. **2** a light cellular material, used in insulation, packaging, upholstery, etc. —*verb intrans.* (**foamed, foaming**) to produce frothy bubbles. ▶ **foamy** *adj.*

fob¹ *verb trans.* (**fobbed, fobbing**) **1** (**fob something off**) to pass off or sell (something inferior). **2** (**fob someone off**) to appease deceitfully.

fob² *noun* **1** a chain attached to a watch. **2** a small watch pocket.

focaccia (fō-käch′ə) *noun* a flat Italian bread topped with olive oil and herbs.

focal point 1 the meeting-point of rays of light reflected by a mirror or passing through a lens. *Also called* **focus. 2** a center of attraction.

fo'c'sle (fōk′səl) *noun same as* **forecastle**.

focus *noun* (*pl.* **focuses, foci**) **1** focal point (sense 1). **2** the center of an earthquake. **3** a

center of interest or attention. —*verb trans.,
intrans.* (**focused** or **focussed, focusing** or
focussing) **1** to bring or be brought into
focus. **2** to adjust the eye or a lens to obtain
the sharpest possible image. ▸ **focal** *adj.*

fodder *noun* feed for livestock esp. hay or
straw

foe *noun old use* an enemy or opponent.

foetid (fĕt′ĭd) *adj. same as* **fetid**.

foetus (fēt′əs) *noun same as* **fetus**.

fog *noun* (fŏg, fȁg) **1** a thick mist. **2** a state of
confusion or bewilderment. —*verb trans.,
intrans.* (**fogged, fogging**) **1** to make or
become obscure with fog or condensation
2 to confuse or perplex. ▸ **foggy** *adj.*

fogbound *adj.* **1** brought to a standstill by fog.
2 totally enshrouded in fog.

fogey (fō′gē) *noun same as* **fogy**.

foghorn *noun* a horn that sounds a warning at
regular intervals to ships in fog.

fogy or **fogey** (fō′gē) *noun* (*pl.* **fogies,
fogeys**) an old-fashioned person.

foible *noun* ◼ a slight personal weakness or
eccentricity. ◼ **FAILING, FRAILTY, IMPERFEC-
TION, SHORTCOMING.**

foil[1] *verb trans.* (**foiled, foiling**) to prevent,
thwart, or frustrate (a person or an attempt).

foil[2] *noun* **1** metal beaten or rolled out into
very thin sheets. **2** something or someone
that forms a contrast to another.

foil[3] *noun* a long slender sword with its point
protected by a button, used in fencing.

foist *verb trans.* (**foisted, foisting**) to give
(something unwanted or inferior) to (someone).

fold[1] *verb trans., intrans.* (**folded, folding**) **1**
to double (something) over so that one part
lies on top of another. **2** to be able to be
folded. **3** to cross (arms, wings, petals. etc.)
over a body part or over each other. **4** to
wrap up. **5** to clasp (someone) in one's arms,
etc. **6** *colloq.* to collapse, fail, or admit defeat.
—*noun* a doubling of one layer over another
or the crease made by doing this.

fold[2] *noun* a walled or fenced enclosure for
sheep or cattle.

-fold *suffix* forming words denoting multiplied
by a stated number: *threefold.*

folder *noun* a cardboard or plastic cover for
loose papers.

foliage (fō′lē-ĭj, -lĭj) *noun* the leaves on a tree
or plant.

folic acid (fō′lĭk) a member of the vitamin B
complex.

folio (fō′lē-ō,) *noun* (*pl.* **folios**) **1** a leaf of a
manuscript, etc., numbered on one side. **2**
Hist. a sheet of paper folded once; a book of
the largest size, composed of such sheets.

folk (fōk) *noun* (*pl.* **folk, folks**) **1** people. **2**
(*usu.* **folks**) *colloq.* one's family or parents.
—*adj.* traditional; of popular origin.

folk dance a traditional dance or its music.

folklore *noun* the customs, beliefs, stories,
traditions, etc., of a particular people.

folksong *noun* an old song reflecting a
people's oral tradition, or one composed to
resemble this. ▸ **folksinger** *noun*

folksy *adj.* (**folksier, folksiest**) simple and
plain: *a politician with folksy mannerisms.*

folktale *noun* a legend or story handed down
orally from one generation to another.

follicle *noun Anat.* a small cavity or sac.

follow *verb trans., intrans.* (**followed,
following**) **1** to go or come after (another).
2 to pursue. **3** to accept as leader or
authority. **4** to be as a consequence. **5** to go
along (a road, etc.). **6** to watch. **7** to practice,
copy, obey, or conform to: *follow a trade/
example.* **8** to understand. **9** to take an
active interest in (a sport, etc.).

follower *noun* **1** a person who comes after
others. **2** a person who copies another or
others. **3** a supporter or enthusiast.

following *noun* a body of supporters. —*adj.*
coming after; next. —*prep.* after.

follow-up *noun* a further action or
investigation.

folly *noun* (*pl.* **follies**) **1** a foolish act;
foolishness. **2** a building without any real
purpose.

foment *verb trans.* (**fomented, fomenting**)
to encourage or promote (ill feeling, etc.). ◼
INCITE, INSTIGATE, STIR ◼ **DISCOURAGE.**
▸ **fomentation** *noun*

fond *adj.* **1** (**fond of** (**someone** or
something)) having a liking for (the person
or thing specified). **2** loving. **3** foolishly
impractical. ▸ **fondly** *adv.* ▸ **fondness** *noun*

fondant (fǎn′dənt) *noun* a soft candy or paste
made with sugar and water.

fondle *verb trans., intrans.* (**fondled,
fondling**) to caress affectionately.

fondue (fǎn-dōō′, -dyōō′) *noun* **1** a dish
where pieces of ˙bread, meat, etc. are
dipped into a sauce or cooked in oil at the
table. **2** a soufflé or baked pudding.

font[1] *noun* a basin for baptismal water.

font[2] *noun* a set of printing type of the same
design and size.

fontanel or **fontanelle** (fǎnt,n-ĕl′) *noun* a
gap between the bones of the skull in a
young child or animal.

food *noun* **1** substances taken into the body to
provide energy. **2** solid substances taken as
nourishment. **3** something that stimulates:
food for thought.

food poisoning a illness, caused by
consuming contaminated food or water.

food processor an apparatus for chopping,
blending, slicing, and puréeing food.

foodstuff *noun* a substance used as food.

fool[1] *noun* **1** a person lacking common sense

or intelligence. 2 *Hist.* a jester. —*verb trans.,
intrans.* (**fooled, fooling**) 1 to deceive
(someone). 2 (*also* **fool around**) to joke or
behave stupidly or playfully. ▸ **foolery** *noun.*

fool² *noun* a dessert of puréed fruit mixed
with cream or custard.

foolhardy *adj.* (**foolhardier, foolhardiest**)
rash; reckless. ▸ **foolhardiness** *noun*

foolish *adj.* unwise; senseless. ▸ **foolishly**
adv. ▸ **foolishness** *noun*

foolproof *adj.* guaranteed to be effective.

foot *noun* (*pl.* **feet**) 1 the end part of the leg
on which a human being or animal stands or
walks. 2 the part of a sock, stocking, etc.,
that fits over the foot. 3 a bottom or lower
part of, e.g., a bed. 4 (*pl.* **feet, foot**) a
measure of length equal to 12 in. (30.48 cm).
5 a unit of rhythm in poetry. —**foot it**
colloq. to walk. 2 *old use* to dance. **foot
the bill** to pay a bill. **get off on the wrong
foot** to make a bad start.

footage (fŏŏt'ĭj) *noun* 1 measurement in feet.
2 a length of film or videotape.

football *noun* 1 a a game for two teams of 11
players, in which the object is to advance the
ball across the opponents' goal line by
running, passing, or kicking. b an oval,
inflated ball used in this game. 2 *Brit.* rugby
or soccer or the ball used in these games.

footfall *noun* the sound of a footstep.

foothill (fŏŏt'hĭl,) *noun* a lower hill on the
approach to a high mountain or range.

foothold (fŏŏt'hōld,) *noun* a secure place.

footing *noun* 1 stability on the ground. 2 basis
or status. 3 relationship.

footlights *pl. noun* a row of lights set along
the front edge of a stage to illuminate it.

footloose *adj.* free to go where, or do as, one
likes.

footman (fŏŏt'mən) *noun* a uniformed male
attendant.

footnote *noun* a note, e.g., at the bottom of a
page or at the end of a chapter.

footprint *noun* 1 the mark or impression of a
foot or shoe. 2 the space taken up by a
computer and its hardware on a desk, etc.

footsore *adj.* having painful feet, esp. from
prolonged walking.

footstep *noun* the sound or print of a foot or
shoe. —**follow in the footsteps of**
(**someone**) to do as was done earlier by
(another); to copy or succeed (another).

footwear *noun* shoes, boots, socks, etc.

footwork *noun* the agile use of the feet.

fop *noun* a man who is too unwisely elegant
in his dress and manners; a dandy.

for *prep.* 1 intended to be given or sent to. 2
toward: *heading for home.* 3 throughout (a
time or distance). 4 in order to have, get, etc.:
fight for freedom. 5 at a cost of: *sells for
$20,000.* 6 as reward, payment, or penalty

appropriate to: *got seven months for
stealing.* 7 with a view to: *train for the race.*
8 on behalf of; representing: *the candidate
for Greenfield.* 9 to the benefit of: *What
can I do for you?* 10 in favor of: *for the
proposal.* 11 because of: *famous for its fine
views.* 12 appropriate to: *books for
children.* 13 on the occasion of: *got it for my
birthday.* 14 meaning: *the German word for
lazy.* 15 in place of: *translated word for word.*
16 in proportion to: *one chair for every two
people.* 17 up to: *It's for him to decide.* 18 as
being: *know for a fact.* 19 with regard to:
can't beat that for quality. 20 considering
what one would expect: *warm for winter.* 21
aimed at; about. 22 in spite of: *quite nice for
all her faults.* 23 available to be disposed of
or dealt with by: *not for sale.* 24 a at or on:
an appointment for 12:00 p.m. b in order to
start at: *7:30 for 8:00.* 25 in honor of.

forage (fôr'ĭj) *noun* 1 a crop grown as fodder.
2 a search for something, esp. food. —*verb
intrans., trans.* (**foraged, foraging**) to
search around, esp. for food.

foray (fôr'ā, fŏr-ā') *noun* 1 a raid or attack. 2 a
venture.

forbad, forbade *see* **forbid**.

forbear¹ (fôr-bĕr', -bâr') *verb trans., intrans.*
(*pa t* **forbore**; *pa p* **forborne**; *pr p* **forbear-
ing**) to stop oneself going as far as (doing
something). ▸ **forbearance** *noun* ▸ **forbear-
ing** *adj.*

forbear² *noun* same as **forebear**.

forbid *verb trans., intrans.* (*pa t* **forbade** or
forbad; *pa p* **forbidden** or **forbid**; *pr p*
forbidding) 1 to order (someone) not to do
something. 2 to debar from doing. 3 to
refuse access to. 4 to prevent or not allow.

forbidding *adj.* threatening; grim. ▸ **forbid-
dingly** *adv.*

forbore, forborne *see* **forbear¹**.

force *noun* 1 a capacity or ability to exert
effort, strength, power, etc. or the result of
such exertion. 2 compulsion, esp. with
threats or violence. 3 strength of feeling,
passion, earnestness, etc. 4 a person or
thing seen as an influence: *a force for good.*
5 *Phys.* an external agent that produces a
change in the speed or direction of a moving
object, or that causes a stationary object to
move. 6 an irresistible power or agency: *the
forces of nature.* 7 meaning or importance. 8
(**forces**) a nation's armed services. —*verb
trans.* (**forced, forcing**) 1 to compel
(someone or something) using pressure. 2
to obtain or produce (something) using
pressure or effort. 3 to inflict: *force one's
opinions on people.* 4 to cause (a plant) to
grow or (fruit) to ripen unnaturally quickly.
—**in force** 1 of a law, etc. valid; effective. 2
in large numbers.

forced *adj.* **1** unnatural; not spontaneous. **2** compulsory. **3** caused by an emergency.

forceful *adj.* powerful; effective; influential. ▸ **forcefully** *adv.* ▸ **forcefulness** *noun*

forceps (fôr'sĕps,, -saps) *noun* (*pl.* **forceps**) a surgical instrument like pincers, for gripping.

forcible *adj.* **1** done by or involving force. **2** powerful. ▸ **forcibly** *adv.*

ford *noun* a shallow crossing place in a river or stream. —*verb trans.* (**forded, fording**) to ride, drive, or wade across (a stream, etc.).

fore *adj.* toward the front. —*noun* the front part. —*interj. Golf* used to warn that a ball has been hit in the direction of other players.

fore- *prefix* forming words denoting: **1** before or beforehand: *forewarn.* **2** in front: *foreleg.*

forearm¹ (fôr'ärm,) *noun* the lower part of the arm between wrist and elbow.

forearm² (fôr-ärm′) *verb trans.* to prepare or arm beforehand.

forebear *or* **forebear** (fôr'bĕr,, -bär,) *noun* an ancestor.

forebode *verb trans.* to be a sign of (esp. something bad); to foretell.

foreboding *noun* a feeling of approaching trouble.

forecast *verb trans.* (fôr'kăst,, fôr-kăst′) to gauge or estimate (weather, statistics, etc.) in advance; to predict. —*noun* (fôr'kăst,) a warning, prediction, or advance estimate.

forecastle *or* **fo'c's'le** (fōk'səl) *noun* the bow section of a ship.

foreclose *verb intrans. of a bank, etc.* to repossess a mortgaged property, etc., usu. because the mortgagor has failed to keep up payments. ▸ **foreclosure** *noun*

forecourt *noun* a courtyard or paved area in front of a building.

forefather *noun* an ancestor.

forefinger *noun* the finger next to the thumb.

forefoot *noun* either of the two front feet of a four-legged animal.

forefront *noun* **1** the very front. **2** the most prominent or active position.

forego (fôr-gō) *verb trans.* (*pa t* **forewent;** *pa p* **foregone;** *pr p* **foregoing**) **1** to do without; to sacrifice or give up. **2** to precede in time, place; etc.

foregoing (fôr-gō'ĭng) *adj.* just mentioned. —*noun* the one just mentioned.

foregone (fôr,gŏn,) *adj.* **1** having gone before. **2** already settled or agreed. —*verb see* **forego.**

foreground *noun* the part of a view or picture nearest to the viewer.

forehand *noun Tennis* a stroke made with palm facing forward. *See also* **backhand.**

forehead (făr'əd, fôr'əd, fôr'hĕd,) *noun* the part of the face between the eyebrows and hairline.

foreign (fôr'ən, făr'-) *adj.* **1** of, from, relating to, or belonging to another country or countries. **2** occurring out of place. **3** (**foreign to (someone)**) **a** unfamiliar. **b** uncharacteristic. ▸ **foreigner** *noun*

foreknow (fôr-nō′) *verb trans.* to see or know in advance. ▸ **foreknowledge** *noun*

foreleg *noun* either of the two front legs of a four-legged animal.

forelock *noun* a lock of hair growing or falling over the brow.

foreman *noun* **1** a man in charge of workers. **2** the spokesman of a jury.

foremost (fôr'mōst,) *adj.* leading; best. —*adv.* coming first; leading.

forensic (fə-rĕn'zĭk, -sĭk) *adj.* relating to or belonging to courts of law, or to the work of a lawyer in court. ▸ **forensically** *adv.*

foreperson *noun* **1** the spokesperson of a jury. **2** a person in charge of workers.

foreplay *noun* sexual stimulation, usu. prior to sexual intercourse.

forerunner *noun* an earlier type or version; a predecessor.

foresee (fôr-sē′) *verb trans.* to see or know in advance. ▣ FOREKNOW, PREKNOW. ▸ **foreseeable** *adj.*

foreshadow *verb trans.* to be an advance sign of.

foresight *noun* **1** the ability to foresee. **2** consideration taken or provisions made for the future.

foreskin *noun* the loose skin at the tip of the penis, which is removed in circumcision. *Also called* **prepuce.**

forest (fôr'əst, fär'-) *noun* a large area of trees.

forestall (fôr-stôl′) *verb trans.* to prevent by acting in advance. ▣ AVERT, DETER, PRECLUDE, STAVE (OFF), WARD (OFF) ▣ LET, PERMIT.

forestry *noun* the care and management of forests. ▸ **forester** *noun*

foretaste *noun* a brief experience of what is to come.

foretell *verb trans.* (*pa t* and *pa p* **foretold;** *pr p* **foretelling**) to predict or prophesy.

forethought *noun* **1** deliberate, prior planning. **2** consideration taken or provision made for the future.

foretold *see* **foretell.**

forever *adv.* **1** always; eternally. **2** continually.

forewarn *verb trans.* to warn beforehand.

forewent *see* **forego.**

forewoman (fôr'wŏŏm,ən) *noun* **1** a woman in charge of workers. **2** the spokeswoman of a jury.

foreword (fôr'wərd) *noun* an introduction to a book.

forfeit (fôr'fĭt) *noun* something that is surrendered as a penalty. —*adj.* surrendered or liable to be surrendered as a penalty.

—*verb trans.* (**forfeited, forfeiting**) **1** to hand over as a penalty. **2** to give up or do without voluntarily. ▸ **forfeiture** *noun*

forgave *see* **forgive.**

forge[1] (fôrj) *noun* **1** a furnace for heating metal prior to shaping it. **2** the workshop of a blacksmith. —*verb intrans., trans.* (**forged, forging**) **1** to shape metal by heating and hammering. **2** to make an imitation of (a signature, document, banknote, etc.) for a dishonest purpose. ▸ **forgery** *noun*

forge[2] *verb intrans.* (**forged, forging**) to move steadily. —**forge ahead 1** to progress swiftly. **2** to take the lead.

forget (fər-gĕt', fôr-) *verb trans., intrans.* (*pa t* **forgot**; *pa p* **forgotten**; *pr p* **forgetting**) **1** to fail to or be unable to remember (something). **2** to stop being aware of; to neglect or overlook; to leave behind accidentally. **3** to lose control over (oneself). ▸ **forgetful** *adj.* ▸ **forgetfully** *adv.* ▸ **forgetfulness** *noun*

forget-me-not *noun* a low-growing plant with blue flowers.

forgivable *adj.* able or likely to be forgiven. ▸ **forgivably** *adv.*

forgive *verb trans., intrans.* (**forgave, forgiven, forgiving**) **1** to stop being angry with (someone) or about (an offense). **2** to pardon. ▸ **forgiveness** *noun* ▸ **forgiving** *adj.*

forgot, forgotten *see* **forget.**

fork *noun* **1** an implement with prongs, for spearing and lifting food. **2** a pronged digging or lifting tool. **3** a point in a road, river, tree, etc. where it divides into two branches; the branch itself. —*verb intrans., trans.* (**forked, forking**) **1** *of a road, etc.* to divide into two branches. **2** *of a person or vehicle* to follow one such branch: *fork left.* **3** to lift or move with a fork.

forked (fôrkt, fôr'kĭd) *adj.* **1** divided into two branches or parts. **2** forming a zigzag, as lightning does at times.

forklift *noun* a small vehicle with two horizontal prongs that can be raised or lowered to move or stack goods.

forlorn *adj.* **1** pathetically unhappy or alone. **2** deserted; forsaken. **3** desperate and without any expectation of success. ▸ **forlornly** *adv.* ▸ **forlornness** *noun*

forlorn hope 1 a desperate but impractical hope. **2** a hopeless undertaking.

form *noun* **1** shape or outward appearance. **2** a human or other figure, esp. an indistinct one. **3** kind, type, variety, or manifestation. **4** a document with spaces for the insertion of information. **5** a way, esp. the correct way, of doing or saying something. **6** a way that a word can be spelled or grammatically inflected. **7** physical condition. —*verb*

trans., intrans. (**formed, forming**) **1** to organize or set up. **2** to come into existence; to take shape. **3** to make (a shape); to shape. **4** to take on the shape or function of. **5** to make up, constitute, or develop. **6** to influence or mold.

-form *combining form* forming words denoting: **1** having the appearance or structure of. **2** in so many forms:

formal *adj.* **1** conventional; suitable for a conventional occasion. **2** overly polite. **3** valid; official; explicit. —*noun* something, e.g., an evening gown, intended for a formal occasion. ▸ **formally** *adv.*

formaldehyde (fôr-mǎl'də-hīd/, fər-) *noun* a disinfectant and preservative.

formalism *noun* concern, esp. excessive concern, with outward form. ▸ **formalist** *noun*

formality *noun* (*pl.* **formalities**) **1** a procedure gone through as a requirement of etiquette, the law, etc., or merely for the sake of correctness or legality. **2** strict attention to the rules of social behavior.

formalize *verb trans.* (**formalized, formalizing**) to make official, e.g., by putting in writing, etc.; to give definite or legal form to. ▸ **formalization** *noun*

format *noun* **1** the general style, appearance, size, shape, etc. of something. **2** *Comput.* a specific arrangement of data on a disk. —*verb trans.* (**formatted, formatting**) **1** to design, shape, or organize in a particular way. **2** *Comput.* **a** to organize (e.g., data) in a particular format. **b** to prepare a new disk for use.

formation *noun* **1** the process of forming, making, developing, or establishing. **2** a particular arrangement, pattern, or order. **3** a shape or structure.

formative *adj.* **1** relating to development or growth. **2** having an effect on development.

former *adj.* **1** belonging to an earlier time. **2** having previously been or functioned as: *former colleagues.* ▪ LATE, ONETIME, QUONDAM, WHILOM ▪ CURRENT. —**the former** the first of two people or things mentioned. ▸ **formerly** *adv.* ▪

formic acid a colorless irritant and corrosive acid found in ants and stinging nettles.

formidable *adj.* **1** awesomely impressive. **2** *of a task, problem, etc.* enormous; difficult to overcome. ▸ **formidably** *adv.*

formless *adj.* lacking a clear shape or structure. ▸ **formlessly** *adv.* ▸ **formlessness** *noun*

formula *noun* (*pl.* **formulas, formulae**) **1** a combination of chemical or mathematical symbols. **2** the ingredients used in a product, etc. **3** a method or rule, esp. a successful one. **4** powdered milk for babies. ▸ **formulaic** (fôrm/yə-lā'ĭk) *adj.*

formulate *verb trans.* (**formulated, formulating**) **1** to express in terms of a formula. **2** to express (something) in words. ▸ **formulation** *noun*

fornicate *verb intrans.* (**fornicated, fornicating**) to have sexual intercourse outside marriage. ▸ **fornication** *noun*

forsake *verb trans.* (*pa t* **forsook**; *pa p* **forsaken**; *pr p* **forsaking**) to abandon or leave behind.

forswear *verb trans., intrans.* (*pa t* **forswore**; *pa p* **forsworn**; *pr p* **forswearing**) **1** to give up or renounce, esp. under oath. **2** to perjure (oneself).

fort *noun* (ABBREV. **ft., Ft.**) a fortified military building, enclosure, or position; an army post. —**hold the fort** to keep things running in someone's absence.

forte¹ (fōrt, fōr'tā) *noun* something one does particularly well. ▣ MÉTIER, OYSTER.

forte² (fōr'tā) *Mus. adj.* played loud. —*adv.* in a loud manner; loudly.

forth *adv.* **1** into existence or view. **2** forward. **3** out: *set forth on a journey.* **4** onward: *from this day forth.* —**and so forth** and so on.

forthcoming *adj.* **1** happening or appearing soon. **2** *of a person* willing to talk; communicative. **3** available on request.

forthright *adj.* expressing one's views freely, straightforwardly, sincerely, and firmly. ▸ **forthrightly** *adv.* ▸ **forthrightness** *noun*

forthwith *adv.* right away; immediately.

forties *pl. noun* **1** the period of time between one's 40th and 50th birthdays. **2** the range of temperatures between 40° and 50°. **3** the period of time between the 40th and 50th years of a century.

fortieth *noun, adj.* the position in a series corresponding to 40 in a sequence of numbers.

fortify *verb trans.* (**fortified, fortifying, fortifies**) **1** **a** to strengthen in preparation for an attack. **b** to make strong or stronger. ▣ REINFORCE, STRENGTHEN ▣ UNDERMINE. **2** to add extra alcohol to (wine). ▸ **fortification** *noun*

fortissimo (fōr-tĭs'ĭ-mō,) *Mus. adj.* played very loud. —*adv.* very loudly.

fortitude *noun* power to endure pain or misfortune.

fortnight *noun* a period of 14 days. ▸ **fortnightly** *adv.*

fortress *noun* a fortified town or a large fort.

fortuitous (fōr-tōō'ĭt-əs) *adj.* accidental; determined not by planning but by an unpredictable factor. ▸ **fortuitously** *adv.* ▸ **fortuitousness** *noun*

Usage Fortuitous is often confused with *fortunate.*

fortunate (fōr'chə-nət) *adj.* **1** favored by fate; lucky. **2** timely; opportune. ▸ **fortunately** *adv.*

Usage See note at **fortuitous.**

fortune (fōr'chən) *noun* **1** fate. **2** luck. **3** a large sum of money. **4** (**fortunes**) unpredictable happenings.

fortuneteller *noun* a person who claims to be able to tell people their destinies.

forty *noun* (*pl.* **forties**) **1** the number or figure 40. **2** the age of 40. **3** any person or thing denoted by the number 40. **4** a set of 40 people or things. **5** a score of 40 points. —*adj.* **1** 40 in number. **2** aged 40.

forty winks (*sing., pl.*) *colloq.* a short sleep.

forum *noun* **1** a public square or market place. **2** a place, program, or publication in which opinions can be aired and discussed.

forward *adv.* **1** in the direction in front or ahead. **2** on or onward. **3** to an earlier time: *bring the wedding forward.* **4** into view or public attention: *put forward suggestions.* —*adj.* **1** in the direction in front or ahead. **2** near or toward the front. **3** advanced. **4** concerning the future: *forward planning.* **5** brash, bold, or presumptuous. —*noun Sport* a front player, as opposed to a defender. —*verb trans.* (**forwarded, forwarding**) **1** to send (mail, etc.) on to another address. **2** to help or encourage. ▸ **forwardly** *adv.* ▸ **forwardness** *noun*

forward-looking *adj.* viewing issues and problems in a progressive, assertive manner.

fossil *noun* **1** the remains, impression, or cast of an animal or plant preserved within the earth's crust. **2** an antiquated or outdated person or thing. ▸ **fossilize** *verb trans., intrans.* ▸ **fossilization** *noun*

fossil fuel a fuel, such as coal, petroleum, and natural gas, derived from the fossilized remains of plants and animals.

foster *verb trans.* (**fostered, fostering**) **1** to bring up (a child that is not one's own). **2** to encourage the development of (ideas, feelings, etc.). —*adj.* relating to or concerned with fostering.

fought *see* **fight.**

foul *adj.* **1** disgusting, soiled, filthy, or contaminated. **2** very unkind or unpleasant. **3** *of language* obscene. **4** unfair: *by fair means or foul.* **5** **a** *Baseball* outside the legal bounds. **b** *Sport* against the rules. **6** clogged. **7** entangled: *foul deck lines.* **8** *of weather* stormy. —*noun Sport* a breach of the rules. —*verb intrans., trans.* (**fouled, fouling**) **1** *Sport* to commit a foul (against an opponent). **2** to make (something) dirty or polluted. **3** to become entangled or become entangled with (something). —**fall foul of** to get into trouble or conflict with. ▸ **foulness** *noun*

foul-mouthed *adj.* using offensive or obscene language.

foul play treachery or criminal violence.

foul-up *noun* a bungled situation.

found¹ *see* **find.**

found² *verb trans.* (**founded, founding**) 1 to start or establish (an organization, institution, city, etc.). 2 to base (an argument, the foundation of a building, etc.). ► **founder** *noun*

found³ *verb trans.* (**founded, founding**) 1 to cast (metal or glass) by melting and pouring into a mold. 2 to produce (articles) by this method.

foundation *noun* 1 the act of founding or establishing, e.g., an institution; the institution, etc., founded or the fund providing for it. 2 (*also* **foundations**) an underground structure supporting a building. 3 the basis on which a theory, etc., rests or depends. 4 a skin cream, etc., used as a base for other cosmetics.

founder *verb intrans.* (**foundered, foundering**) 1 *of a ship* to go under water. 2 *of a vehicle, etc.* to get stuck in mud, etc. 3 *of a horse* to go lame. 4 *of a business, scheme, etc.* to fail.

foundling *noun* an abandoned child of unknown parents.

foundry *noun* (*pl.* **foundries**) a place where metal or glass castings are produced.

fount *noun* 1 a spring or fountain. 2 a source.

fountain *noun* 1 a jet or jets of water for drinking or for ornamental effect, or a structure supporting this. 2 a spring of water.

fountainhead *noun* 1 a spring from which a stream flows. 2 a principal source.

fountain pen a metal-nibbed pen with a reservoir of ink.

four *noun* 1 the number or figure 4. 2 the age of 4. 3 any person or thing denoted by the number 4. 4 4 o'clock. 5 a set of 4 people or things. 6 a score of 4 points. —*adj.* 1 4 in number. 2 aged 4. —**on all fours** on hands and knees.

four-poster *noun* a large bed with a post at each corner, often supporting a canopy.

fourscore *adj., noun* eighty.

foursome (fōr'səm) *noun* a set of four people.

four-square *adj.* 1 having four equal sides. 2 solidly based; strong and steady. —*adv.* in a strong, forthright manner; squarely.

fourteen (fōrt-tēn', fōr-) *noun* 1 the number or figure 14. 2 the age of 14. 3 any person or thing denoted by the number 14. 4 a set of 14 people or things. —*adj.* 1 14 in number. 2 aged 14.

fourteenth (fōrt-tēnth, fōr-) *noun, adj.* 1 the one numbered 14 in a series. 2 one of 14 equal parts.

fourth *noun, adj.* 1 the one numbered 4 in a series. 2 one of four equal parts.

fourth dimension time regarded as a dimension.

Fourth of July a public holiday in the USA, commemorating the adoption of the Declaration of Independence in 1776. *Also called* **Independence Day.**

fowl *noun* (*pl.* **fowl, fowls**) 1 a farm bird, e.g., a chicken or turkey. 2 any bird, esp. if eaten as meat or hunted as game. —*verb intrans.* (**fowled, fowling**) to hunt or trap wild birds. ► **fowler** *noun*

fox *noun* (*pl.* **foxes, fox**) 1 a carnivorous mammal of the dog family, with a pointed muzzle and a long bushy tail. b the fur of this animal. 2 *colloq.* a cunning person. 3 *slang* an attractive young woman. —*verb trans., intrans.* (**foxed, foxing**) 1 to baffle. 2 to deceive, trick, or outwit.

foxtrot *noun* a ballroom dance with gliding steps or the music for it. —*verb intrans.* (**foxtrotted, foxtrotting**) to perform this dance.

foxy *adj.* (**foxier, foxiest**) 1 relating to or like a fox. 2 *slang, of a woman* sexually attractive. 3 cunning; sly.

foyer (foi'ər, foi'ā,) *noun* 1 the entrance hall of a theater, hotel, etc. 2 the hallway of a house, apartment, or apartment building.

fracas (frā'kəs, frăk'əs) *noun* (*pl.* **fracas**) *colloq.* a noisy quarrel; a fight or brawl.

fraction *noun* 1 a numerical quantity that is not a whole number. 2 a part.

fractional *adj.* 1 of, relating to, or constituting a fraction or fractions. 2 tiny; insignificant. ► **fractionally** *adv.*

fractious *adj.* inclined to quarrel or complain. ► **fractiously** *adv.* ► **fractiousness** *noun*

fracture (frăk'chər) *noun* a breakage or cracking of something hard. —*verb trans., intrans.* (**fractured, fracturing**) to break or crack or become broken or cracked.

fragile (frăj'əl, -ĭl,) *adj.* easily broken, damaged or destroyed. ► **fragility** *noun*

fragment *noun* (frăg'mənt) 1 a piece broken off; a small piece of something that has broken. 2 something incomplete; a small part remaining. —*verb trans., intrans.* (frăg'mĕnt,) (**fragmented, fragmenting**) 1 to break or cause to break into pieces. ▣ PULVERIZE, SHATTER, SPLINTER. 2 *Comput.*, *of a file* to split or be split into sections on different parts of a floppy disk, making access slower. ► **fragmentary** (frăg'mən-tĕr,ē) *adj.* ► **fragmentation** *noun*

fragrance *noun* a sweet or pleasant smell. ▣ BOUQUET, PERFUME, REDOLENCE, SCENT ▣ STENCH, STINK. ► **fragrant** *adj.* ► **fragrantly** *adv.*

frail *adj.* 1 easily broken or destroyed; delicate or fragile. 2 in poor physical health. ▣

FRAGILE, INFIRM, WEAK ◨ ROBUST, STRONG. **3** morally weak; easily tempted. ▸ **frailness** noun ▸ **frailty** noun

frame noun **1** a structure that supports or surrounds something or that has other parts attached to it. **2** a single picture in a strip of film or a comic strip, etc. **3** a glass structure for protecting young plants growing out of doors. —verb trans. (**framed, framing**) **1** to put a frame around (something) or to act as a frame for (something). **2** to compose or design. **3** colloq. to incriminate (someone innocent).

frame of mind an outlook or state of the mind. ◨ HUMOR, MOOD, TEMPER.

framework noun **1** a basic supporting structure; a frame. **2** a basic plan or system. **3** a structure of horizontal and vertical bars.

franc (frănk) noun the standard unit of currency in France, Belgium, Switzerland, and several other French-speaking countries.

franchise (frăn'chīz,) noun **1** the right to vote. **2** a right, privilege, exemption from a duty, etc. **3** an agreement by which a company gives the right to market its products in an area; the business so operated. —verb trans. (**franchised, franchising**) to grant a franchise to.

francophone or **Francophone** (frăng'kə-fōn,) noun a French-speaking person.

frank[1] adj. **1** open and honest in speech or manner. **2** expressing one's views freely, forthrightly, and sincerely. **3** openly visible; undisguised. —verb trans. (**franked, franking**) to mark (a letter) to show that it can be sent without charge or that postage has been paid. —noun a franking mark. ▸ **frankly** adv. ▸ **frankness** noun

frank[2] noun a frankfurter.

Frankenstein (frăng'kən-stīn,) noun a creation or creature that destroys its creator.

frankfurter noun a red, spicy, smoked beef or beef and pork sausage.

frankincense (frăng'kĭn-sĕns,) noun a sweet-smelling gum resin used as incense.

frantic adj. frenzied, wild, or desperate, e.g., with fear, anxiety, excitement, etc. ◨ FRENETIC, FRENZIED, FURIOUS ◨ PLACID, UNPERTURBED. ▸ **frantically** adv.

fraternal adj. **1** brotherly. **2** of twins not identical. **3** relating to a fraternity. ▸ **fraternally** adv.

fraternity noun (pl. **fraternities**) **1** a group of people with common interests. **2** the fact of being brothers; brotherly feeling. **3** a social society for male students. See also **sorority. 4** a religious brotherhood.

fraternize (frăt'ər-nīz,) verb intrans. (**fraternized, fraternizing**) to meet, associate, or collaborate as friends.

fratricide noun **1** the murder of a brother. **2** a

person who murders his or her brother. ▸ **fratricidal** adj.

fraud (frôd) noun **1** a trick or deliberate deception. **2** someone who dishonestly pretends to be something he or she is not. ▸ **fraudulent** adj. ▸ **fraudulence** noun ▸ **fraudulently** adv.

fraught (frôt) adj. **1** (**fraught with (something)**) full of, e.g., danger, difficulties, and problems. **2** characterized by anxiety or worry: a fraught relationship.

fray[1] verb intrans., trans. (**frayed, fraying**) **1** to wear away or become worn away. **2** to make or become edgy and strained.

fray[2] noun **1** a fight, quarrel, or argument. **2** a scene of lively action.

frazzle noun **1** a state of nervous and physical exhaustion. **2** an exhausted state. —verb trans., intrans. (**frazzled, frazzling**) to tire out physically and emotionally.

freak noun **1** someone or something odd, unusual, or abnormally shaped. **2** slang an enthusiast; someone who indulges excessively in something. **3** a whim. —adj. abnormal. —verb intrans., trans. (**freaked, freaking**) (often **freak out** or **freak (someone) out**) slang **1** to become or make overexcited, esp. by taking hallucinatory drugs. **2** to become or make angry. ▸ **freakish** adj. ▸ **freaky** adj.

freckle noun a small yellowish-brown benign spot on the skin. ▸ **freckly** adj.

free adj. (**freer, freest**) **1** able to do, move, go as one pleases. **2** of a country independent. **3** sold or bought for no charge. **4** open or available to all. **5** available for use, consultation, etc.: I'm free this afternoon. **6** not having, affected by, etc. (a specified condition, etc.): free from care. **7** (**free with (something)**) generous or liberal with (it). **8** of a translation not verbatim or exact. **9** lacking obstruction: given free passage. **10** of a person's manner disrespectful, overly familiar, or presumptuous. —adv. **1** without charge. **2** without restriction. —verb trans. (**freed, freeing**) **1** to release from restraint, prison, etc. ◨ EMANCIPATE, ENFRAN-CHISE, LIBERATE, MANUMIT, RELEASE, UNCHAIN, UNSHACKLE ◨ ENTHRALL, SHACKLE, SUBJUGATE. **2** to rid or relieve (someone) of (something). ▸ **freely** adv.

-free combining form forming words denoting: **1** not paying: rent-free. **2** not affected or troubled by; not having: fat-free / cancer-free.

freebie noun slang something given or provided without charge.

freeborn adj. born as a free citizen.

freedman (frĕd'mən, -măn,) noun a freed male slave.

freedom noun **1** the condition of being free to

act, move, etc., without restriction. ⊟ INDEPENDENCE, LIBERTY ⊟ ENSLAVEMENT, SLAVERY. **2** a right that comes with being free: *freedom of speech*. **3** the state of being without or exempt from something. **4** unrestricted access to or use of. **5** honorary citizenship of a place, entitling one to certain privileges. **6** candor; frankness. **7** overfamiliarity; presumptuous behavior.

freedwoman *noun* a freed female slave.

free-for-all *noun* a fight, argument, or discussion in which everybody is free to join.

freehand *adj. adv., of a drawing, etc.* done without the help of a ruler, compass, etc.

freehold *adj., of land, property, etc.* belonging to the owner for life and without limitations. —*noun* land, property, etc. of this kind. *See also* **leasehold.** ▸ **freeholder** *noun*

freelance *noun* a self-employed person offering his or her services to any employer. —*adj., adv.* of, or as, a freelance. —*verb intrans.* (**freelanced, freelancing**) to work as a freelance. ▸ **freelancer** *noun*

freeload *verb intrans.* (**freeloaded, freeloading**) *slang* to eat, live, etc. at the expense of someone else. ▸ **freeloader** *noun*

freeman (frē'mən, -măn,) *noun* a person not in slavery or in serfdom.

Freemason (frē'mā,sən) *noun* a member of an international secret male society. *Also called* **Mason.** ▸ **freemasonry** *noun*

free-range *adj.* **1** *of livestock* able to move about freely and graze or feed naturally. **2** *of eggs, meat, etc.* laid by or produced from livestock that have been kept this way.

freesia (frē'zhə) *noun* a plant with fragrant white, yellow, purple, or crimson flowers.

free speech the right to express any opinion freely and publicly.

freestanding *adj.* not attached to or supported by a wall or other structure.

freestyle *Sport adj.* permitting, allowing, or employing any maneuver, swimming stroke, etc. —*noun* **1** a competition in which participants are allowed to choose their own style, maneuvers, swimming stroke, or program. **2** the crawl swimming stroke.

freethinker *noun* someone who forms his or her own ideas, rather than accepting the view of an authority or a majority.

free verse poetry with no regular pattern of rhyme, rhythm, or line length.

freeware *noun Comput.* software that is available free of charge.

freeway *noun* an expressway.

freewheel *verb intrans.* (**freewheeled, freewheeling**) **1** to travel, usu. downhill, on a bicycle, in a car, etc., without using mechanical power. **2** to act or drift about unhampered by responsibilities.

free will the power of making choices without the constraint of fate.

freeze *verb trans., intrans.* (**froze, frozen, freezing**) **1** to change (a liquid) or be changed into a solid by cooling to below freezing point. **2** to cover or become covered with frost or ice. **3** to be at or below the freezing point of water. **4** *colloq.* to be very cold or make (someone or something) very cold. **5** to preserve (food, sperm, etc.) by bringing it to and storing it below the freezing point of water. **6** to fix (prices, wages, a moving film, etc.) at a certain level, point, etc. **7** to prevent (money, shares, etc.) from being used. **8** to anesthetize (a part of the body). —*noun* **1** a period of very cold weather with temperatures below freezing point. *Also called* **freeze-up. 2** a period when wages, prices, etc. are kept at a certain level. —**freeze out** to exclude (someone) from an activity, conversation, negotiation, etc..

freeze-dry *verb trans.* (**freeze-dried, freeze-drying, freeze-dries**) to preserve by rapid freezing and drying under high-vacuum conditions.

freezer *noun* a cabinet or in which to preserve food at below freezing point.

freezing *adj.* extremely cold.

freight *noun* **1** transportation of goods by rail, road, sea, or air. **2** the goods transported in this way. **3** the cost of such transport. **4** a train carrying goods. —*verb trans.* (**freighted, freighting**) **1** to transport (goods) by freight. **2** to load with goods.

freighter *noun* a ship that carries cargo.

French *noun* **1** (**the French**) the people of France. **2** the official language of France. —*adj.* of France, its people, or their language.

French dressing a salad dressing made from oil, spices, and lemon juice or vinegar.

French fries thin strips of potato that are fried in deep fat.

French horn a brass wind instrument with valves.

French leave leave from work without permission.

Frenchman (frĕnch'mən) *or* **Frenchwoman** *noun* a native or citizen of France.

French toast sliced bread dipped into a mixture of beaten egg and milk, then browned in a frying pan.

frenetic *adj.* uncontrollably excited. ▸ **frenetically** *adv.*

frenzy *noun* (*pl.* **frenzies**) **1** violent mental disturbance. **2** wild agitation or excitement. **3** a frantic burst of activity. ▸ **frenzied** *adj.*

frequency *noun* (*pl.* **frequencies**) **1** the condition of happening often. **2** the rate at which an event, a phenomenon, etc. recurs.

frequency modulation (ABBREV. **FM**) a method of radio transmission in which the wavelength frequency is alternated to prevent distortion noise.

frequent adj. (frē'kwənt) **1** recurring at short intervals. **2** habitual. —verb trans. (frĕkwĕnt', frē'kwǒnt) (**frequented, frequenting**) to visit or attend often. ▸ **frequently** adv.

fresco noun (pl. **frescoes, frescos**) a picture painted on a wall while the plaster is damp.

fresh adj. **1** having or retaining an original quality, color, etc.: fresh paint. **2** having just arrived; straight. **3** young and inexperienced. **3** different; clean: a fresh sheet of paper. **4** new; additional. **5** original. **6 a** of fruit, vegetables, etc. not canned, frozen, preserved, etc. **b** of food recently made, cooked, picked, slaughtered, etc. **7** bright and alert: a fresh mind. **8** of air, a breeze, etc. cool, refreshing, bracing, etc. **9** of water containing no salt. **10** of the face o' complexion youthfully healthy. **11** colloq., of behavior impudent; offensively informal. —adv. not long ago; recently. ▸ **freshly** adv. ▸ **freshness** noun

freshen verb trans., intrans. (**freshened, freshening**) **1** to make fresh or fresher. **2** (also **freshen up** or **freshen (someone) up**) to get washed and clean; to wash and clean. **3** of a wind to become stronger.

freshman (frĕsh'mən) noun a first-year student in a high school, college, etc.

freshwater adj. denoting water that contains less than 0.2% dissolved salt.

fret[1] verb (**fretted, fretting**) **1** to worry, esp. unnecessarily; to show or express anxiety. **2** to worry or agitate (another). **3** to wear away or consume by rubbing or erosion. ▸ **fretful** adj. ▸ **fretfully** adv. ▸ **fretfulness** noun

fret[2] noun a narrow metal ridge across the neck of a guitar or similar musical instrument.

fret[3] noun an ornamental repeated pattern used as a border, etc. —verb trans. (**fretted, fretting**) to decorate with a fret, or carve with fretwork.

fretsaw noun a saw with a narrow blade for cutting designs in wood or metal.

fretwork noun decorative carved openwork in wood or metal.

Freudian slip a slip of the tongue taken as revealing an unexpressed thought.

friable (frī'ə-bəl) adj. easily broken; easily reduced to powder. ▸ **friability** noun

friar noun (ABBREV. **Fr.**) a member of any of various Roman Catholic religious orders.

friary noun (pl. **friaries**) a building where friars live.

fricassee (frĭk'ə-sē,, frĭk,ə-sē') noun a dish made with pieces of meat or chicken served in a cream sauce.

friction noun **1** the rubbing of one thing against another. **2** the resistance met with by an object that is moving against another or through liquid or gas. **3** quarreling; disagreement; conflict. ▸ **frictional** adj.

Friday (frīd'ē, -ā) noun (ABBREV. **Fri.**) the sixth day of the week.

fridge noun colloq. a refrigerator.

fried see **fry**[1].

friend (frĕnd) noun **1** a person whom one knows and likes. **2** a person who gives support or help. **3** (**Friend**) a Quaker. ▸ **friendless** adj. ▸ **friendship** noun

friendly adj. (**friendlier, friendliest**) **1** amicable and approachable; kind. **2** (**friendly with (someone)**) on amicable terms with (someone). ⊟ CLOSE, FAMILIAR, TIGHT ⊟ DISTANT, HOSTILE, UNFRIENDLY. **3** Sport, of a match, etc. played for enjoyment or practice and not as part of a competition. —noun (pl. **friendlies**) Sport a friendly match. ▸ **friendliness** noun

-friendly combining form forming words denoting made easy or convenient: user-friendly.

friendly fire Mil. the accidental firing on one's own or one's allies' forces.

frier noun same as **fryer**.

fries see **fry**[1].

frieze (frēz) noun **1** a decorative strip running along a wall. **2** Archit. a horizontal band between the cornice and capitals of a classical temple, or the sculpture filling it.

frigate (frĭg'ət) noun a small warship.

fright noun **1** sudden fear; a shock. **2** colloq. a person or thing that looks ridiculous.

frighten verb trans., intrans. (**frightened, frightening**) **1** to make afraid. **2** (**frighten away** or **off**) to scare away.

frightened adj. feeling fear. ⊟ AFRAID, APPREHENSIVE, SCARED ⊟ UNAFRAID.

frightful adj. **1** serious; shocking. **2** colloq. bad; awful; great; extreme. ▸ **frightfully** adv. ▸ **frightfulness** noun

frigid adj. **1** cold and unfriendly. **2** sexually or emotionally unresponsive. **3** extremely cold. ⊟ ARCTIC, BITTER, FREEZING, GELID, GLACIAL, ICY, POLAR ⊟ SCALDING, SCORCHING, SIZZLING, WHITE-HOT. ▸ **frigidity** noun

frill noun **1** a gathered or pleated strip of cloth attached to a garment, etc., as a trimming. **2** (usu. **frills**) something extra serving no very useful purpose. ▸ **frilly** adj.

fringe noun **1** a border of loose threads on a carpet, tablecloth, garment, etc. **2** hair covering the forehead. **3** the part, group, point of view, etc. that is farthest from the center or mainstream, etc. —verb trans. (**fringed, fringing**) **1** to decorate with fringe. **2** to form a fringe around.

fringe benefits benefits given in addition to wages or salary.

frippery *noun* (*pl.* **fripperies**) unnecessary finery or adornment.

Frisbee (frĭz'bē) *noun trademark* a light plastic disk thrown from one person to another.

frisk *verb intrans., trans.* (**frisked, frisking**) **1** to jump or run about happily. **2** *slang* to search (a person) for something concealed. —*noun slang* an act of searching a person for concealed weapons, etc.

frisky *adj.* (**friskier, friskiest**) lively and playful. ◨ FROLICSOME, GAMESOME, IMPISH, PLAYFUL, PUCKISH, SPORTIVE. ▸ **friskily** *adv.* ▸ **friskiness** *noun*

fritter[1] *noun* a piece of meat, vegetable, etc., coated in batter and fried.

fritter[2] *verb trans.* (**frittered, frittering**) to waste (e.g., time) on unimportant things.

frivolous (frĭv'ə-ləs) *adj.* **1** lightheartedly silly. ◨ GIDDY, LIGHTHEADED, SCATTERBRAINED ◨ DEEP, SUBSTANTIVE. **2** trifling or unimportant. ▸ **frivolity** *noun* ▸ **frivolously** *adv.*

frizz *noun* a mass of tight curls. —*verb trans., intrans.* (**frizzed, frizzing**) to form or cause to form a frizz. ▸ **frizzy** *adj.*

frizzle[1] *verb trans., intrans.* (**frizzled, frizzling**) to cook noisily.

frizzle[2] *verb trans.* (**frizzled, frizzling**) to frizz (hair). —*noun* **1** a curl. **2** a frizz.

fro *adv. old use* back or from.

frock *noun* **1** a woman's or girl's dress. **2** a priest's or monk's long garment.

frog (frŏg, frăg) *noun* **1** a tailless amphibian with powerful hind legs and webbed feet. **2** a plate that allows a train or streetcar to cross from one set of rails to another. **3** a decorative-looped fastener. **4** a device for holding cut flowers. —**a frog in one's throat** an accumulation of phlegm that interferes with one's speech.

frogman *noun* a swimmer wearing a rubber suit and flippers, and using breathing equipment.

frogspawn *noun* a mass of frog's eggs.

frolic *verb intrans.* (**frolicked, frolicking**) to run about playfully. —*noun* a spell of happy playing. ▸ **frolicsome** *adj.*

from *prep.* indicating: **1** a starting point, progression, or movement out of, distance away. **2** a viewpoint. **3** separation; removal: *took it away from her.* **4** point of attachment. **5** exclusion: *omitted from the sample.* **6** source or origin. **7** change of condition: *translate from French into English.* **8** cause: *exhaustion from overwork.* **9** deduction as a result of observation. **10** distinction: *can't tell one twin from the other.* **11** prevention, protection, exemption, immunity, release, escape, etc.: *safe from harm.*

fromage frais a mild, smooth, white, low-fat cheese.

frond *noun* a large leaf, esp. of a fern or palm.

front (frŭnt) *noun* **1** the part of something that faces or is nearest the viewer. **2** the most important side or part of something, esp. the side of a building with the main door. **3** a piece of land along a bay, river, lake, etc. or a promenade beside the sea. **4** the area where fighting is taking place. **5** a field of activity, concern, or interest: *the economic front.* **6** a boundary between two air masses with different temperatures: *a warm front.* **7** an outward appearance, bearing, etc. —*verb trans., intrans.* (**fronted, fronting**) **1** *of a building* to have the front facing or beside something specified. **2** to be a leader, representative, presenter, etc. of (a group, radio or television program, etc.). **3** (**front for**) to provide a cover or excuse for (an illegal activity, etc.).

frontage (frŭnt'ĭj) *noun* the front of a building.

frontal *adj.* **1** relating to the front. **2** relating to the forehead.

frontier (frŭn-tîr') *noun* **1** a border between countries or the area along the border. **2** an outer limit. **3** an area beyond civilization.

frontiersman *and* **frontierswoman** *noun* a person who lives on the edges of the civilized part of a country.

frontispiece (frŭnt'ĭ-spēs,) *noun* a picture at the beginning of a book, facing the title page.

frontline *noun* (*usu.* **the frontline**) **1** the area where important or pioneering work is going on. **2** the area closest to the enemy.

front-runner *noun* the person most likely to win an election or a competition.

frost *noun* **1** frozen water vapor forming patterns on glass and a white powdery deposit on other surfaces. **2** an air temperature below freezing point. —*verb trans., intrans.* (**frosted, frosting**) **1** to cover or become covered with frost. **2** to damage (plants) with frost. **3** to cover (a cake, etc.) with frosting.

frostbite *noun* damage to the body tissues, usu. of the extremities, caused by exposure to very low temperatures. ▸ **frostbitten** *adj.*

frosted *adj., of glass* patterned or roughened to make it difficult to see through it.

frosting *noun* icing for cakes, etc.

frosty *adj.* (**frostier, frostiest**) **1** covered with frost. **2** cold enough for frost to form. **3** cold and unfriendly. **4** *of hair* gray or graying. ▸ **frostily** *adv.* ▸ **frostiness** *noun*

froth *noun* **1** a mass of tiny bubbles. **2** something that has no serious content or purpose. —*verb intrans., trans.* (**frothed, frothing**) to produce or cause to produce froth. ▸ **frothy** *adj.*

frown verb intrans. (**frowned, frowning**) 1 to wrinkle the forehead while drawing the eyebrows together as an expression of disapproval, worry, confusion, etc. ▣ GLOWER, LOWER, SCOWL ▣ SMILE. 2 (**frown on (something)**) to disapprove of (something). —noun a frowning expression.

frowzy or **frowsy** adj. (**frowzier, frowziest**) untidy and slovenly. ▸ **frowziness** noun

froze see **freeze**.

frozen adj. 1 covered with ice or made of ice. 2 preserved in a freezer. 3 paralyzed by fear. 4 not able to be utilized. —verb see **freeze**.

fructose (frɘk'tōs, frŏŏk'-, frōŏk'-) noun a very sweet sugar found in fruit, honey, etc.

frugal (frōŏ'gəl) adj. 1 thrifty and economical. 2 not costing much money. ▸ **frugality** noun ▸ **frugally** adv.

fruit noun (pl. **fruit, fruits**) 1 a a ripe ovary of a flowering plant, containing one or more seeds. b an edible part of a plant that is generally sweet and juicy. c plant products generally. 2 (also **fruits**) something gained as a result of hard work, etc. 3 offspring; young. —verb intrans. (**fruited, fruiting**) to produce fruit. —**in fruit** bearing fruit.

fruitcake noun 1 a cake containing dried fruit, nuts, and candied fruit. 2 slang a crazy or eccentric person.

fruitful adj. producing good or useful results. ▸ **fruitfully** adv. ▸ **fruitfulness** noun

fruition (frōŏ-ĭsh'ən) noun 1 the realization of a goal, plan, hope, etc. 2 the bearing of fruit.

fruitless adj. useless; unsuccessful; in vain. ▸ **fruitlessly** adv. ▸ **fruitlessness** noun

fruity adj. (**fruitier, fruitiest**) 1 full of fruit. 2 having the taste or appearance of fruit. ▸ **fruitily** adv. ▸ **fruitiness** noun

frump noun a dowdy or unattractive person. ▸ **frumpish** adj. ▸ **frumpy** adj.

frustrate (frəs'trāt,) verb trans. (**frustrated, frustrating**) 1 to prevent (someone) from doing or getting something; to thwart or foil (a plan, attempt, etc.). 2 to make (someone) feel disappointed, useless, etc. ▸ **frustration** noun

fry[1] verb trans., intrans. (**fried, frying, fries**) to cook or be cooked in hot oil or fat. —noun (pl. **fries**) 1 a dish of something fried. 2 a gathering at which fried food is served.

fry[2] pl. noun 1 young fish. 2 youngsters.

fryer or **frier** noun 1 a frying pan, or a deep vessel for the deep-fat frying of foods. 2 a young, small chicken for frying.

frying pan a long-handled shallow pan in which to fry food. —**out of the frying pan (and) into the fire** from a bad situation into a worse one.

ft. abbrev. foot; feet.

fuchsia (fyōō'shə) noun 1 a shrub with drooping purple, red, or white flowers. 2 a reddish purple color.

fuddle verb trans. (**fuddled, fuddling**) to muddle the wits of; to stupefy. —noun a state of confusion or intoxication.

fuddy-duddy colloq. adj. quaintly old-fashioned or prim. —noun (pl. **fuddy-duddies**) a quaintly old-fashioned person.

fudge noun 1 a soft rich candy made from butter and sugar, and often chocolate. 2 colloq. nonsense. —verb intrans., trans. (**fudged, fudging**) colloq. 1 to avoid stating a clear opinion. 2 to invent, concoct, or distort (an excuse, information, etc.).

fuel (fyōō'əl, fyōōl) noun 1 a material that releases energy when it is burned. 2 something that feeds an argument or inflames passions. —verb trans., intrans. (**fueled** or **fuelled, fueling** or **fuelling**) 1 to fill or feed with fuel. 2 to take on fuel. 3 to inflame (an argument, anger, etc.).

fug (fŭg') noun a stale-smelling, stuffy atmosphere. ▸ **fuggy** adj.

fugitive noun a person who is fleeing. —adj. 1 fleeing. 2 lasting only briefly; fleeting.

fugue (fyōōg) noun a musical composition in which a theme is introduced in one part and developed as successive parts take it up.

-ful combining form 1 (pl. **-fuls**) forming nouns denoting an amount held by a container: mugfuls. 2 forming adjectives denoting: a full of: eventful. b characterized by: graceful. c having the qualities of: youthful. d in accordance with: lawful. e showing an inclination to: forgetful.

fulcrum (fŏŏl'krəm, fəl'-) noun (pl. **fulcrums, fulcra**) a fixed point about which a lever moves or pivots.

fulfill or **fulfil** (fŏŏl-fĭl') verb trans. (**fulfilled, fulfilling**) 1 to carry out or perform (a task, promise, etc.). 2 to satisfy (requirements). 3 to achieve (an aim, ambition, etc.). ▸ **fulfillment** noun

full[1] (fŏŏl) adj. 1 holding, containing, or having as much as possible. ▣ BRIMMING, CHOCKABLOCK, CRAMMED, · LOADED, PACKED ▣ EMPTY. 2 complete. 3 including everything necessary; detailed; thorough. 4 occupied: My hands are full. 5 having eaten until one wants no more. 6 plump; fleshy. 7 of clothes made with a large amount of material. 8 rich and strong. 9 rich and varied. 10 having all possible rights, etc.: a full member. 11 of the Moon appearing as a complete disk. —adv. 1 at maximum capacity; completely. 2 exactly; directly. ▸ **fullness** noun

full[2] verb trans. (**fulled, fulling**) to shrink and beat (cloth) to thicken it. ▸ **fuller** noun

fullback noun 1 Football an offensive player in the backfield. 2 Sport a defense player in the backfield.

full-blooded adj. 1 of pure breed; not of mixed blood. 2 vitally vigorous. ▸ **full-bloodedness** noun

full-blown adj. having all the expected or necessary features.

full-bodied adj. having a rich flavor or quality.

fuller's earth a green, blue, or yellowish-brown clay.

full-fledged adj. 1 completely trained or qualified. 2 of a bird having adult feathers.

full house 1 a theater or movie audience of maximum size. 2 a set of five cards, esp. in poker, consisting of three cards of one kind and two of another.

fully adv. 1 to the greatest possible extent. 2 completely. 3 in detail. 4 at least; quite.

fulminate (fŏŏl'mə-nāt,) verb intrans., trans. (**fulminated, fulminating**) (**fulminate against (something)**) to utter angry criticism or condemnation. ▸ **fulmination** noun

fulsome (fŏŏl'səm) adj. excessively or distastefully cloying. ▸ **fulsomely** adv. ▸ **fulsomeness** noun

fumble verb intrans., trans. (**fumbled, fumbling**) 1 to handle things, or grope, clumsily. 2 Sport to fail to hold (a ball). —noun an act or instance of fumbling.

fume noun (usu. **fumes**) smoke, gas, or vapor, esp. when strong-smelling or toxic —verb intrans. (**fumed, fuming**) 1 to be furious. 2 to give off smoke, gas, or vapor.

fumigate (fyŏŏ'mĭ-gāt,) verb trans. (**fumigated, fumigating**) to expose (clothing, buildings, etc.) to a disinfectant or pesticidal gas or vapor. ▸ **fumigation** noun

fun noun 1 enjoyment. 2 a source of amusement. —adj. colloq. enjoyable.

function noun 1 the special purpose or task of somebody or something. 2 an organized event, such as a party, reception, meeting, etc. 3 Math. a value that varies in relation to another value. —verb intrans. (**functioned, functioning**) 1 to work; to operate. 2 to serve or act.

functional adj. 1 designed for efficiency rather than decorativeness. ▤ PRACTICAL, USEFUL, UTILE ▤ ABSTRACT, IMPRACTICAL. 2 being in working order; operational. ▸ **functionally** adv.

functionalism noun the belief that the intended or actual function of something should determine its design.

functionary noun (pl. **functionaries**) a minor official, e.g. in the government, etc.

fund noun 1 a sum of money for a special purpose. 2 (**funds**) money available for spending. 3 a large store or supply. —verb trans. (**funded, funding**) 1 to provide money for. 2 to make (a debt) permanent, with fixed interest.

fundamental adj. 1 basic; underlying. 2 large; important. 3 essential; necessary. —noun (usu. **fundamentals**) a basic rule, principle, etc. ▤ ELEMENTS, PRINCIPLES, RUDIMENTS. ▸ **fundamentally** adv.

fundamentalism noun in religion, politics, etc., strict adherence to traditional teachings. ▸ **fundamentalist** noun

funeral (fyŏŏn'rəl, fyŏŏ'nə-rəl) noun a ceremony to mark the burial or cremation of a deceased person. ▸ **funerary** adj.

funeral director an undertaker.

funeral parlor an undertaker's place of business.

funereal (fyŏŏ-nîr'ē-əl) adj. 1 relating to or suitable for a funeral. 2 mournful; dismal. ▸ **funereally** adv.

fungicide (fən'jĭ-sīd,, fəng'gĭ-) noun an agent that kills or limits the growth of fungi. ▸ **fungicidal** adj.

funicular (fyŏŏ-nĭk'yə-lər) adj., of a mountain railroad, etc. operated by machine-driven cables. —noun a funicular railway.

funk[1] noun colloq. 1 a a state of nervousness, fear, or panic. b a severe emotional depression. 2 a coward.

funk[2] noun colloq. jazz or rock music with a strong rhythm and repeating bass pattern.

funky adj. (**funky, funkier, funkiest**) 1 of jazz or rock music strongly rhythmical and soulful. 2 unconventional. 3 having a strong earthy or musty smell.

funnel (fən'l) noun 1 a cone-shaped utensil for directing a liquid, etc. into a narrow-necked container. 2 a large vertical chimney on a steamship or steam engine. —verb intrans., trans. (**funneled** or **funnelled, funneling** or **funnelling**) 1 to rush through a narrow space. 2 to transfer (liquid, etc.) from one vessel to another using a funnel.

funny adj. (**funnier, funniest**) 1 eliciting laughter. 2 strange; odd; mysterious. —noun (**the funnies**) newspaper comic strips. ▸ **funnily** adv.

funny bone the area near the elbow which, if accidentally struck, sends out a tingling sensation.

fur noun 1 the soft, fine hairs covering the body of many mammals. 2 dressed animal skin with the hair attached, or an imitation of this, used in clothing. 3 a coat, etc. made of or trimmed with natural or imitation fur. 4 a coating, e.g., on a tongue, kettle, etc. —verb trans., intrans. (**furred, furring**) to cover, trim, or line with fur or to be so covered, trimmed, or lined.

furbelow (fər'bə-lō,) noun 1 a pleated strip, ruffle, or flounce on a garment. 2 a fussy ornamentation.

furbish verb trans. (**furbished, furbishing**) to restore, decorate, or clean.

furious *adj.* **1** violently or intensely angry. **2** raging; stormy. **3** uncontrollably excited. ▸ **furiously** *adv.*

furl *verb trans., intrans.* (**furled, furling**) to roll up (a flag, sail, etc.) or be rolled up.

furlong *noun* a measure of distance equal to 220 yds. (201.2 m), now generally used only in horseracing.

furlough (fər'lō) *noun* **1** leave of absence from military duty. **2** a temporary layoff.

furnace (fər'nəs) *noun* an enclosed chamber where coal etc. is burned for industrial purposes, e.g., smelting.

furnish *verb trans.* (**furnished, furnishing**) **1** to provide (a house, etc.) with furniture. **2** to supply (someone) with what is necessary.

furnishings *pl. noun* furniture, appliances, carpets, curtains, etc.

furniture (fər'nĭ-chər) *noun* movable equipment such as tables, chairs, beds, desks, etc.

furor (fyŏŏr'ôr,, -ər) *noun* a general outburst of excitement or indignation.

furrier *noun* someone who sells furs or makes garments out of fur.

furrow (fər'ō, fə'rō) *noun* **1** a groove or trench cut into the earth by a plow; a rut. **2** a wrinkle, e.g., in the forehead. —*verb trans., intrans.* (**furrowed, furrowing**) **1** to plow (land) into furrows. **2** to become wrinkled.

furry *adj.* (**furrier, furriest**) **1** covered with fur. **2** made of or like fur.

further *adj.* **1** more distant or remote in time, space, or degree: *at a further date.* **2** more extended: *further delay.* **3** additional. —*adv.* **1** at or to a more advanced or more distant point. **2** to a greater extent or degree: *modified even further.* **3** moreover; furthermore. —*verb trans.* (**furthered, furthering**) to help the progress of.

furtherance *noun* an advancement or continuation.

furthermore *adv.* in addition; moreover.

furthermost *adj.* most distant or remote.

furthest *adj.* most distant or remote in time, space, or degree. —*adv.* **1** (with reference to physical distance) *a superlative of* **far. 2** at or to the most advanced point or the greatest distance.

furtive (fûr'tĭv) *adj.* sly, stealthy, or secretive. ▸ **furtively** *adv.* ▸ **furtiveness** *noun*

fury (fyŏŏr'ē) *noun* (*pl.* **furies**) **1** violent or frenzied anger. **2** violence: *the fury of the* wind. **3** a frenzy: *a fury of activity.*

fuse¹ (fyŏŏz) *noun* a safety device in an electric circuit consisting of a length of wire that melts and breaks the circuit if the current exceeds a certain value. —*verb trans., intrans.* (**fused, fusing**) **1** to melt as a result of the application of heat. **2** to join by or as if by melting together. **3** *of an electric circuit or appliance* to cease to function as a result of the melting of a fuse.

fuse² *noun* a cord or cable containing combustible material, used for detonating a bomb or explosive charge.

fuselage (fyŏŏ'sə-läzh,, -zə-) *noun* the main body of an aircraft.

fusillade (fyŏŏ'sə-läd,, -läd,) *noun* a discharge of firearms.

fusion *noun* **1** melting or liquefying by the application of heat. **2** joining together. **3** nuclear fusion.

fuss *noun* **1** agitation and excitement, esp. over something trivial. **2** a commotion, disturbance, or bustle. —*verb intrans.* (**fussed, fussing**) **1** to worry needlessly. **2** to be overly concerned with trivial matters. **3** to agitate. ▸ **fussy** *adj.* ▸ **fussily** *adv.* ▸ **fussiness** *noun*

fusty *adj.* (**fustier, fustiest**) **1** old and musty. **2** old-fashioned. ▸ **fustiness** *noun*

futile (fyŏŏt'l, fyŏŏ'tīl,) *adj.* unproductive, ineffective, vain, or pointless. ▸ **futilely** *adv.* ▸ **futility** *noun*

futon (fŏŏ'tän,) *noun* a thin mattress that can be rolled up when not in use.

future (fyŏŏ'chər) *noun* **1** the time to come; events that are still to occur. **2** prospects. —*adj.* **1** yet to come or happen. **2** about to become.

futurism *noun* belief in or concern with the importance of the future. ▸ **futurist** *noun*

futuristic *adj.* **1** relating to futurism. **2** *of design, etc.* ultramodern. ▸ **futuristically** *adv.*

futurity *noun* (*pl.* **futurities**) **1** the future. **2** a future event.

futurology *noun* the forecasting of future events from present tendencies.

fuzz¹ *noun* a mass of fine fibers or hair.

fuzz² *noun slang* the police or a police officer.

fuzzy *adj.* (**fuzzier, fuzziest**) **1** covered with fuzz. **2** forming a mass of tight curls. **3** obscured or made unclear by or as if by a vaporous mist. ▸ **fuzzily** *adv.*

Gg

G¹ *or* **g** *noun (pl.* **Gs, G's, g's) 1** the seventh letter of the English alphabet. **2 (G)** *Mus.* **a** the fifth note on the scale of C major. **b** a musical key with the note G as its base.

G² *noun (pl.* **G's)** *slang* 1,000 dollars.

G³ *noun, of a movie rating* allowing admission to people of all ages.

G⁴ *abbrev.* giga-.

g *abbrev.* **1** gallon. **2** gram. **3 a** gravity. **b** acceleration due to gravity.

gab *slang noun* idle talk; chat. —*verb intrans.* (**gabbed, gabbing**) to talk idly, esp. at length. —**the gift of the gab** *colloq.* the ability to speak persuasively and with ease.

gabardine *or* **gaberdine** (găb'ər-dēn,) *noun* **1** a closely woven fabric, esp. of wool or cotton. **2** *Brit.* a coat or loose cloak made from this fabric.

gabble *verb intrans., trans.* (**gabbled, gabbling**) to talk or say quickly and unclearly. —*noun* fast indistinct talk.

gaberdine *noun same as* **gabardine**.

gable *noun* **1** the triangular upper part of a side wall between the sloping parts of a roof. **2** a triangular canopy above a door or window.

gad¹ *verb intrans.* (**gadded, gadding**) *colloq.* (**gad about** *or* **around**) to go from place to place, esp. in the pursuit of amusement or pleasure.

gad² *or* **Gad** *interj.* used to express surprise or mild dismay.

gadabout *noun* a person who goes from place to place, esp. seeking pleasure or amusement.

gadfly *noun (pl.* **gadflies) 1** any of various large flies that inflict painful bites. **2** a person who deliberately annoys others.

gadget *noun* a small device or appliance.

gadgetry *noun* gadgets collectively.

Gaelic (gā'lĭk, găl'ĭk) *noun* any of the closely related Celtic languages spoken in the Scottish Highlands and Islands, parts of Ireland, and, formerly, on the Isle of Man. —*adj.* of or relating to these Celtic languages or the people who speak them.

gaff *noun* **1** a long pole with a hook for landing large fish. **2** a vertical spar to which sails are attached. —*verb trans.* (**gaffed, gaffing**) to seize (a fish) with a gaff.

gaffe (găf) *noun* a socially embarrassing action or remark.

gaffer *noun* **1** the senior electrician on a film or television set. **2** *Brit. colloq.* a boss or foreman.

gag *verb trans., intrans.* (**gagged, gagging**) **1** to silence (someone) by putting something in or over the mouth. **2** to deprive of free speech. **3** to retch or choke. —*noun* **1** something put into or over a person's mouth to impose silence. **2** censorship or obstruction of free speech. **3** a joke or a practical joke.

gaga *adj. colloq.* **1** weak-minded; senile. **2** silly; foolish. **3** wildly enthusiastic.

gage¹ *noun* **1** an object given as security or a pledge. **2** *Hist.* an object or item, e.g., a glove, that is thrown down to signal a challenge.

gage² *verb, noun same as* **gauge**.

gage³ *noun* the greengage.

gaggle *noun* **1** a flock of geese. **2** *colloq.* a group of noisy people.

gaiety *noun* **1** the condition of being merry. **2** attractively bright appearance. **3** the state of making merry; fun.

gaily *adv.* **1** in a lighthearted, merry way. **2** in a bright or colorful manner.

gain *verb trans., intrans.* (**gained, gaining**) **1** to get, obtain, or earn: *gain recognition.* **2** (**gain from**) to benefit or profit from (something). **3** to experience an increase in: *gain speed.* **4** *of a clock, etc.* to go too fast by (a given amount of time). **5** to reach (a place), esp. after difficulties. **6** (**gain on**) to catch up with (someone or something). —*noun* **1** (*often* **gains**) something gained, e.g., profit. **2** an increase, e.g., in weight. **3** an instance of gaining.

gainer *noun Sport* a dive executed by leaving the diving board face forward, then completing a backward somersault.

gainful *adj.* **1** profitable. **2** *of employment* paid. ▸ **gainfully** *adv.*

gainsay *verb trans.* (*pa t and pa p* **gainsaid**; *pr p* **gainsaying**) *formal* to deny or contradict.

gait *noun* **1** a way of walking. **2** an animal's leg movements at a particular speed.

gaiter *noun* a covering for the lower leg and ankle.

gal *noun colloq.* a girl.

gal. *abbrev.* gallon.

gala (gā'lə, gă'lə) *noun* **1** a lavish social event, e.g., a grand ball. **2** *Brit.* a meeting for sports, esp. swimming, competitions.

galactose noun Biochem. a simple sugar that occurs together with glucose in lactose.

galantine noun a dish of boneless cooked white meat or fish served cold in jelly.

galaxy noun (pl. **galaxies**) **1** Astron. any of a large number of huge concentrations of stars, dust, and gas. **2** (**the Galaxy**) the vast spiral arrangement of stars to which our Sun belongs, known as the Milky Way. **3** a fabulous gathering or array, e.g., of famous people. ▸ **galactic** adj.

gale noun **1** a very strong wind. **2** a sudden loud burst, e.g., of laughter.

gall[1] noun **1** the state or quality of being boldly impolite. **2** the quality or condition of feeling bitter. **3** something unpleasant. **4** old a bitter liquid produced in the liver to aid digestion; bile.

gall[2] noun Bot. a round abnormal growth on the stem or leaf of a plant.

gall[3] noun **1** a sore or painful swelling on the skin caused by chafing. **2** something annoying or irritating. **3** a state of being annoyed. —verb trans. (**galled, galling**) **1 a** to chafe (the skin). **b** of the skin to become chafed. **2** to annoy.

gallant (gə-lănt′, gə-länt′, găl′ənt) adj. **1** brave. **2** splendid, grand, or fine. **3** of a man courteous and attentive to women. —noun **1** a woman's lover. **2** a handsome young man who pursues women. ▸ **gallant** adv. ▸ **gallantry** noun

gallbladder or **gall bladder** noun a small muscular sac lying beneath the liver, in which bile is stored.

galleon noun a large Spanish ship used for war or trade from the 15th to the 18th c.

gallery noun (pl. **galleries**) **1** a room or building used to display works of art. **2** a balcony along an inside upper wall. **3** the upper floor in a theater; the part of the audience seated there. **4** a long narrow room or corridor.

galley noun (pl. **galleys**) **1** a long single-deck ship propelled by sails and oars. **2** the kitchen on a ship. **3** Printing a tray holding arrangements of individual metal letters. **4** Printing a galley proof.

galley proof a preliminary printing of part of a book, etc., on which corrections can be made.

galliard noun a lively dance in triple time; also, a piece of music for it. See also **pavane**.

Gallic (găl′ĭk) adj. **1** typically or characteristically French. **2** of ancient Gaul or the Gauls.

Gallicism noun a French word or expression used in another language.

galling adj. irritating.

gallivant verb intrans. (**gallivanted, gallivanting**) to roam idly in search of amusement.

galion noun (ABBREV. **gal.**) **1** a unit of liquid

measurement in the US, equal to eight pints (3.78 liters). **2** a unit of liquid measurement in the British Imperial System, equal to eight pints (4.54 liters).

gallop noun **1** a fast pace, esp. of a horse. **2** an unusually fast speed. —verb intrans., trans. (**galloped, galloping**) **1** to move, or cause to move, at a gallop. **2** to move, progress, or increase very quickly.

gallows noun (pl. **gallows, gallowses**) **1** a wooden frame on which criminals are put to death by hanging. **2** (**the gallows**) execution by hanging until dead.

gallstone noun a small hard mass of cholesterol and salts formed in the gallbladder.

galop (găl′əp, gă-lō′) noun a lively 19th-c dance for couples, or a piece of music for it.

galore adv. in large amounts or numbers: books galore.

> Based on an Irish Gaelic phrase go leór, meaning 'sufficient'

galosh noun a waterproof overshoe.

galumph verb intrans. (**galumphed, galumphing**) colloq. to walk in a heavy, ungainly manner.

galvanic adj. **1** Physics **a** relating to or producing an electric current. **b** of an electric current produced by chemical means. **2** of behavior, etc. startlingly energetic.

> Named after the Italian physicist, Luigi Galvani

galvanize verb trans. (**galvanized, galvanizing**) **1** to protect (metal, esp. iron or steel) from corrosion with a zinc coating. **2** to stimulate by applying an electric current. **3** to stimulate or rouse (someone) to action. ▸ **galvanism** noun ▸ **galvanized** adj. ▸ **galvanization** noun

galvanometer noun an instrument for measuring small amounts of electric currents.

gambit noun **1** a chess move in which a piece is sacrificed in order to gain an overall advantage. **2** an initial action or remark establishing a point of view. **3** a cunningly devised means to an end.

gamble verb trans., intrans. (**gambled, gambling**) **1** to bet (usu. money) on the result of a card game, horserace, etc. **2** (**gamble on**) to take a chance or risk on (something). —noun **1** an act of gambling; a bet. **2** a risk or a situation involving risk. ▸ **gambler** noun ▸ **gambling** noun

gamboge (găm-bōj′, -bōōzh′) noun a gum resin obtained from various tropical Asian trees.

gambol verb intrans. (**gamboled, gamboling**) to jump around playfully. —noun an act of leaping around playfully.

game[1] noun **1** an amusement or pastime. **2** a

competitive activity with rules. **3** a match. **4** in some sports, a division of a match. **5** (**games**) an event consisting of competitions in various, esp. sporting, activities. **6** certain birds and animals that are killed for sport; the flesh of these creatures. **7** *colloq.* a scheme, trick, or intention: *Don't give the game away.* —*adj. colloq.* **1** (**game for**) ready and willing to undertake (something): *game for a try.* **2** having plenty of fighting spirit; plucky. —*verb intrans.* (**gamed, gaming**) to gamble. —**play the game** to behave fairly.

game² *adj.* lame: *my game leg.*

Game Boy or **Game Girl** *Trademark* a hand-held device for playing computer games.

gamecock *noun* a cock trained for cock-fighting.

gamekeeper *noun* a person employed to take care of wildlife.

gamely *adv.* in a brave way; sportingly.

game plan 1 *Sport* the strategy used in the hope of winning an event or competition. **2** *slang* any strategy chosen to meet an objective.

gamesmanship *noun* the art or practice of winning games.

gamete *noun* a reproductive sex cell, esp. an ovum or sperm.

gamey *adj. same as* **gamy.**

gamine (gă-mēn') *noun* a girl or young woman with a mischievous, boyish appearance. ▸ **gamine** *adj.*

gamma (găm'ə) *noun* **1** the third letter of the Greek alphabet (Γ, γ). **2** a mark indicating the third highest grade or quality.

gamma rays *Physics* high-frequency photons, often produced during radioactive decay.

gammon *noun* **1** cured meat from a pig. **2** the back part of a side of bacon.

gamut *noun* **1** the whole range; the full extent. **2** *Mus.* a scale of notes; the range of notes produced by a voice or instrument.

> From the name of the medieval 6-note musical scale, two notes of which were *gamma* and *ut*

gamy or **gamey** (gā'mē). *adj.* (**gamier, gamiest**) **1** *of meat* having the strong taste or smell of game that has been kept for a long time. **2** plucky. **3** corrupt, sleazy, or scandalous. ▸ **gaminess** *noun*

gander *noun* **1** a male goose. **2** *colloq.* a look: *took a gander at their new car.*

gang *noun* **1** a group, e.g. of criminals, friends, workers, etc. **2** a group of machines, etc. working together. —*verb trans.* (**ganged, ganging**) to arrange (tools) for simultaneous use. —**gang up on** (**someone**) to act as a group against (a targeted person, etc.).

gangland *noun* the world of organized crime.

gangling *adj.* tall and thin, and usu. awkward in movement.

ganglion (găng'glē-ən) *noun* (*pl.* **ganglia, ganglions**) **1** a group of nerve-cell bodies in the central nervous system. **2** a cyst or swelling that forms on the tissue surrounding a tendon.

gangly (găng'glē) *adj.* (**ganglier, gangliest**) gangling.

gangplank *noun* a movable plank for accessing a ship.

gangrene *noun* the death and subsequent decay of part of the body caused, e.g., by lack of blood supply. ▸ **gangrenous** *adj.*

gangsta (găng'stə) *noun* **1** a style of rap music characterized by violent lyrics or subject matter. **2** *slang* a gangster.

gangster *noun* a member of a gang of usu. armed criminals.

gangway *noun* **1** a small movable bridge used for boarding and leaving a ship. **2** *Brit.* a passage between rows of seats

ganja (găn'jə, găn'-) *noun* marijuana.

gannet *noun* a large seabird with a heavy body and white plumage.

gantlet¹ (gônt'lət, gănt'-) *noun same as* **gauntlet¹.**

gantlet² *noun same as* **gauntlet².**

gantry *noun* (*pl.* **gantries**) a large metal supporting framework.

gaol (jāl) *noun Brit.* a jail.

gap *noun* **1** a break or open space **2** a break in time; an interval. **3** a difference or disparity: *a generation gap.* **4** a ravine or gorge.

gape *verb intrans.* (**gaped, gaping**) **1** to stare with the mouth open, esp. in surprise. **2** to be or become wide open. **3** to open the mouth wide. —*noun* **1** a wide opening. **2** an open-mouthed stare.

garage *noun* **1** a building in which motor vehicles are kept. **2** an establishment where motor vehicles are bought, sold, and repaired, often selling fuel, etc. **3** a style of pop music played in a loud, energetic style.

garb *noun* **1** clothing, esp. as worn by people in a particular job or position. **2** outward appearance. —*verb trans.* (**garbed, garbing**) to dress or clothe.

garbage *noun* **1** domestic trash; refuse. **2** worthless or poor-quality articles or matter. **3** nonsense. **4** *Comput.* erroneous, irrelevant, or meaningless data. —**garbage in, garbage out** (ABBREV. **GIGO**) *Comput.* computer data output can be only as valid and as accurate as the input will allow.

garble *verb trans.* (**garbled, garbling**) **1** to mix up unintentionally the details of. **2** to distort deliberately the meaning of.

> Originally meaning 'sift', which gradually developed into the sense of confusing by leaving out too much

garçon (gär-sôn´) *noun* a waiter in a French restaurant or café.

garden *noun* **1** a piece of ground attached to or near a house. **2** (*usu.* **gardens**) a large area where plants are grown and displayed for public enjoyment. —*verb intrans.* (**gardened, gardening**) to work at the care of a garden and its plants, usu. as a hobby. —**lead up** *or* **down the garden path** *colloq.* to mislead or deceive (another) deliberately. ▶ **gardener** *noun* ▶ **gardening** *noun*

gardenia (gär-dēn´yə) *noun* a shrub with glossy leaves and large white flowers.

Named after US botanist and physician, Dr. Alexander *Garden*

gargantuan *adj.* of exceedingly or excessively large size.

Named after *Gargantua*, a giant with an enormous appetite in an 18th-century French novel by Rabelais

gargle *verb intrans., trans.* (**gargled, gargling**) to cleanse the throat by blowing air from the lungs through a liquid held in the throat. —*noun* **1** an act of gargling or the sound so produced. **2** the liquid used in gargling.

gargoyle *noun* a grotesque, open-mouthed figure acting as a rainwater spout from a roof gutter.

garish *adj.* unpleasantly bright or colorful; very gaudy. ▶ **garishly** *adv.* ▶ **garishness** *noun*

garland *noun* a wreath of flowers or leaves. —*verb trans.* (**garlanded, garlanding**) to decorate with a garland.

garlic *noun* a plant cultivated for its underground bulb, widely used as a flavoring in cooking. ▶ **garlicky** *adj.*

garment *noun* an article of clothing.

garner *verb trans.* (**garnered, garnering**) to collect and store (information, knowledge, etc.).

garnet *noun* a deep red, semiprecious stone.

garnish *verb trans.* (**garnished, garnishing**) to decorate (esp. food). —*noun* a decoration, esp. one added to food.

garnishee *Legal noun* a third party, notified that money has been seized by legal writ. —*verb trans.* (**garnisheed, garnisheeing**) to seize by legal writ.

garret *noun* an attic or a room in an attic.

garrison *noun* **1** a permanently established military base. **2** the troops stationed there.

garrote *or* **garrotte** (gə-rät´, -rōt´) *noun* **1** a wire loop or metal collar tightened around the neck to cause strangulation. **2** this method of murder or execution. —*verb trans.* (**garroted, garroting**) to murder or execute (a victim) using a garrotte.

garrulous (găr´ə-ləs) *adj.* **1** tending to talk a

lot, esp. about trivial things. **2** *of a speech, etc.* long and wordy. ▶ **garrulousness** *noun*

garter *noun* a band of elastic worn on the leg to hold up a stocking or sock.

gas *noun* (*pl.* **gases, gasses**) **1** an airlike form of matter that will expand to occupy all the space available. **2** a substance or mixture of substances that is in this state at ordinary temperatures. **3** natural gas used as fuel. **4** a mixture of explosive gases occurring naturally in coal mines; firedamp. **5** a poisonous gas used as a weapon in war. **6** gasoline. **7** *slang* an amusing or enjoyable event or situation. **8** *slang* foolish, boasting talk. —*verb trans.* (**gassed, gassing, gases** *or* **gasses**) **1** to poison or kill with gas. **2** (*also* **gas up**) to fill (the fuel tank of a motor vehicle) with gasoline. **3** *slang* to chat boastfully of or about trivial things. ▶ **gaseous** *adj.*

gasbag *noun slang* a person who talks a lot or too much, usu. boastfully.

gas chamber a room that can be filled with poisonous gas, used for executing people or killing animals.

gash *noun* a deep open cut or wound. —*verb trans.* (**gashed, gashing**) to make a gash in.

gasify *verb trans., intrans.* (**gasified, gasifying, gasifies**) **1** to convert into gas. **2** to produce gas, esp. from coal. ▶ **gasification** *noun*

gasket *noun* a thin, flat, shaped ring or sheet of rubber sealing a gap between two metal surfaces.

gaslight *noun* a lamp powered by gas, or the light from it.

gas mask a mask that filters out poisonous gas.

gasohol (găs´ə-hôl´, -häl´) *noun* a fuel mixture consisting of ethanol and gasoline.

gasoline *or* **gasolene** (găs´ə-lēn´) *noun* a liquid fuel distilled from petroleum, and used as a fuel for motor vehicles.

gasp *verb intrans., trans.* (**gasped, gasping**) **1** to take in a sharp breath, through surprise, sudden pain, etc. **2** to say breathlessly. —*noun* a sharp intake of breath.

gas station a place selling fuel for motor vehicles and where servicing of the vehicles may also be done.

gassy *adj.* (**gassier, gassiest**) **1** like gas; full of gas. **2** *slang* talking a lot, esp. in a boastful way. ▶ **gassiness** *noun*

gasteropod (găs´tə-rə-päd´) *noun same as* **gastropod**.

gastr- *combining form same as* **gastro-**.

gastrectomy *noun* the surgical removal of all or part of the stomach.

gastric *adj.* relating to or affecting the stomach.

gastritis *noun* inflammation of the lining of the stomach.

gastro- or **gastr-** combining form forming words denoting the stomach.

gastroenteritis (găs,trō-ĕnt,ə-rīt'ĭs) noun inflammation of the lining of the stomach and intestine, resulting in vomiting and diarrhea.

gastronome or **gastronomer** noun a person who appreciates good food and wine.

gastronomy noun the practice, study, or art of appreciating or preparing good food and wine. ▸ **gastronomic** adj.

gastropod (găs'trə-păd,) or **gasteropod** noun a mollusk, such as a snail or slug, with a spiral coiled shell, or no shell.

gastroscope noun an instrument used to inspect the interior of the stomach.

gasworks noun (sing.) a place where gas is manufactured.

gate noun **1** a usu. hinged door moved to open or close an entrance in a wall, fence, etc.; the entrance itself. **2** any of the numbered exits at an airport via which passengers can board or leave an aircraft. **3 a** the total number of people attending a sports event or other entertainment. **b** the total money paid in admission fees. **4** slang dismissal, esp. from employment: got the gate. —verb trans. (**gated, gating**) Brit. to confine (pupils) to school after hours.

-gate combining form forming words denoting a scandal: Monicagate.

gateau or **gâteau** (gă-tō') noun (pl. **gateaux, gâteaux**) a large rich cake, esp. filled with cream and decorated.

gatecrash verb trans., intrans. (**gatecrashed, gatecrashing**) slang to gain entry to (a party, meeting, etc.) uninvited or without paying. ▸ **gatecrasher** noun

gateleg adj., of a table having a hinged or framed leg that can swing inward to let down a leaf.

gateway noun **1** an entrance, esp. to a city, park, etc., with a gate across it. **2** a way to or into a place. **3** a means of acquiring something: a gateway to success. **4** Comput. a device connecting networks using different communication protocols and allowing the transfer of mutually compatible information.

gather verb trans., intrans. (**gathered, gathering**) **1** (also **gather together**) to bring or come together in one place. **2** to collect, pick, or harvest (something). **3** to increase in (speed or force). **4** to accumulate or become covered with (e.g., dust). **5** to learn, understand, or presume. **6** to pull, and often stitch, (material) into small folds. **7** to draw together or muster (e.g., strength). —noun a small fold in material, often stitched.

gathering noun a meeting or assembly.

GATT (găt) abbrev. General Agreement on Tariffs and Trade.

gauche (gōsh) adj. tactless and awkward, esp. in social situations. ▸ **gauchely** adv. ▸ **gaucherie** noun

> Taken from the French word for 'left', because of the supposed awkwardness of using the left hand

gaucho (gow'chō) noun (pl. **gauchos**) a modern cowboy of the S American plains.

gaudy (gôd'ē) adj. (**gaudier, gaudiest**) coarsely and brightly colored or decorated. ▸ **gaudily** adv. ▸ **gaudiness** noun

gauge or **gage** (gāj) verb trans. (**gauged** or **gaged, gauging** or **gaging**) **1** to measure accurately. **2** to estimate or guess (e.g., a measurement, size, etc.). **3** to judge. —noun **1** an instrument used to measure quantity. **2** each of a series of standard sizes, e.g., of wire, bullets, etc. **3** the distance between the rails of a railroad track. **4** a standard measurement. **5** a standard against which other things are measured or judged.

gaunt adj. thin or thin-faced; lean, haggard. ▸ **gauntness** noun

gauntlet[1] or **gantlet** noun **1** a metal or metal-plated glove worn by medieval soldiers. **2** a heavy protective leather glove loosely covering the wrist. —**take up** or **throw down the gauntlet** to accept or make a challenge.

gauntlet[2] or **gantlet** noun **1** a form of military punishment in which a person must scramble along between two rows of men while receiving hard blows from them. **2** hostile treatment or criticism.

gauze noun **1** thin, transparent cloth, esp. cotton used to dress wounds. **2** thin wire mesh. ▸ **gauzy** adj.

gave verb see **give**.

gavel noun a small hammer used by a judge, auctioneer, etc.

gavotte (gə-vät') noun a lively old French country dance, or a piece of music for it.

gawk colloq. verb intrans. (**gawked, gawking**) to stare blankly or stupidly; to gawp. —noun an awkward, clumsy or stupid person.

gawky adj. (**gawkier, gawkiest**) awkward-looking. ▸ **gawkiness** noun

gawp verb intrans. (**gawped, gawping**) to stare stupidly, esp. open-mouthed; to gape.

gay adj. **1** homosexual. **2** happily carefree. **3** bright and attractive. —noun a homosexual. ▸ **gayness** noun

> **Usage** Gay is the term of choice in reference to the US homosexual community, esp. in contexts emphasizing the sociocultural aspects of homosexuality.

gaze verb intrans. (**gazed, gazing**) to stare fixedly. —noun a fixed stare.

gazebo (gə-zē'bō) noun (pl. **gazebos, gazeboes**) a small summer house or open structure, esp. in a garden.

gazelle *noun* (*pl.* **gazelles, gazelle**) a swift-moving antelope.

gazette *noun* **1** a newspaper. **2** *Brit.* an official newspaper giving government, military, and legal notices. —*verb trans.* (**gazetted, gazetting**) *Brit. formal* to announce or publish in an official gazette.

gazetteer *noun* a dictionary of place names.

gazpacho (gə-späch′ō) *noun* a Spanish vegetable soup, served cold.

gazump *verb trans.* (**gazumped, gazumping**) *Brit., colloq.* to go back on a verbal agreement to sell one's house to (a prospective buyer). ▸ **gazumper** *noun*

GB *or* **G.B.** *abbrev.* Great Britain.

gear *noun* **1 a** a toothed wheel or disk that engages with another, transmitting motion or changing speed. **b** the combination of such wheels or disks that is currently in use. **2** the equipment or tools needed for a particular job, sport, etc. **3** *colloq.* clothes. —*verb trans.* (**geared, gearing**) **1** to adapt or design to suit a particular need. **2** to supply with or connect by gears. **3** (**gear up**) to become or make ready or prepared.

gear shift a lever or mechanism in a motor vehicle used to change gears.

gecko *noun* (*pl.* **geckos, geckoes**) a small lizard with an ability to climb smooth walls.

gee[1] *interj.* used to encourage a horse to move ahead or turn right.

gee[2] *interj. colloq.* used to express surprise, admiration, or enthusiasm.

geek *noun* **1** *slang* a ridiculous, unpleasant person. **2** a performer in a carnival sideshow.

geese *pl. noun see* **goose.**

gee whiz *interj. colloq* same as **gee[2].**

gee-whiz *adj. colloq.* exhibiting an air of naive wonder: *a gee-whiz attitude.*

geezer (gē′zər) *noun colloq.* a man, esp. an old man.

Geiger counter (gī′gər) an instrument used to detect and measure the intensity of radiation.

> Named after German physicist Hans Wilhelm *Geiger*

geisha (gā′shə, gē′-) *noun* (*pl.* **geisha, geishas**) **1** a Japanese woman who entertains people, esp. men. **2** a Japanese prostitute.

gel *noun* **1** *Chem.* a jellylike substance formed by a solid dispersing through a liquid. **2** a substance used to hold hair in place. Also called **styling gel.** —*verb intrans., trans.* (**gelled, gelling**) **1** to become, or cause to become, like a gel. **2** to take on a definite form; to jell.

gelatin *or* **gelatine** (jĕl′ət-n) *noun* a clear jellylike substance formed by boiling animal bones and hides, used in foods, glues, and photographic film. ▸ **gelatinous** *adj.*

gelatinize *verb trans., intrans.* (**gelatinized, gelatinizing**) to make or become like gelatin

or jelly.

geld (gĕld) *verb trans.* (**gelded, gelding**) to remove the testicles of (esp. a male horse).

gelding *noun* a gelded horse.

gelid *adj.* extremely cold.

gelignite *noun* a powerful explosive, used esp. in mining.

gem *noun* **1** a precious stone cut and polished for use in jewelry, etc. **2** *colloq.* a person or thing that one values.

geminate (jĕm′ə-nət) *adj. of leaves, etc.* arranged in pairs. ▸ **gemination** *noun*

Gemini (jĕm′ə-nī, -nē,) *noun* **1** the Twins, the name of a constellation and the third sign of the zodiac. **2** a person born between May 21 and Jun. 20, under this sign.

gemstone *noun* same as **gem** (sense 1).

-gen *or* **-gene** *combining form* forming words denoting something that causes or produces: *carcinogen / phosgene.*

gendarme (zhän′därm,) *noun* a member of an armed police force in France and French-speaking countries.

gender *noun* **1** *Gram.* **a** the system in some languages of dividing nouns and pronouns into different classes. **b** any of these classes, e.g., masculine, feminine, or neuter. **2** the condition of being male or female; sex.

gender-bender *noun colloq.* someone who adopts a sexually ambiguous image and style of dress, etc.

gender-neutral *adj.* devoid of explicit or implicit gender markers.

gene *noun* the basic unit of inheritance, responsible for the passing on of one or more specific characteristics from parents to offspring.

-gene *combining form same as* **-gen.**

genealogy (jē,nē-äl′ə-jē, -ăl′-) *noun* (*pl.* **genealogies**) a person's line of descent from an ancestor, or a diagram or scheme showing it; the study of such matters. ▸ **genealogical** *adj.* ▸ **genealogist** *noun*

gene pool the collection of genes contained by all of the individuals of an interbreeding population of organisms.

genera *pl. noun see* **genus.**

general *adj.* **1** of, involving, or applying to all or most parts, people, or things; widespread. **2** not detailed or definite; rough; vague. **3** broad, and not specialized: *general knowledge.* **4** chief: *general manager.* —*noun* **1** a senior officer, e.g., in the US Army. **2** the commander of an army. —**in general** usually; mostly.

general anesthetic an anesthetic that induces total loss of consciousness and a lack of sensation in the entire body.

general assembly 1 a US state legislature. **2** (**General Assembly**) the main deliberative body of the UN.

general election an election in which the voters of all or most state or national constituencies choose candidates for public office.

generalissimo (jĕn′ə-rə-līs′ĭ-mō,) *noun* (*pl.* **generalissimos**) a supreme military commander.

generality *noun* (*pl.* **generalities**) **1** the quality of being general. **2** a general rule or principle. **3** the majority.

generalize *verb intrans., trans.* (**generalized**, **generalizing**) **1** to speak in general terms or form general opinions. **2** to make more general. ▸ **generalization** *noun*

generally *adv.* **1** usually. **2** without considering details; broadly. **3** as a whole; collectively.

general practitioner (ABBREV. **G.P.**, **GP**) a physician providing basic treatment for all common illnesses, not specializing in any one area of medicine.

generate (jĕn′ə-rāt,) *verb trans.* (**generated**, **generating**) to produce or create.

generation *noun* **1** of *living organisms* the act or process of producing offspring. **2** the act of producing (e.g., electricity, heat, etc.). **3** all the offspring produced at a particular stage in the natural descent of humans or animals: *the younger generation*. **4** the average period between the birth of a person or animal and the birth of any offspring. **5** any period of technological development or innovation: *a new generation of computers*.

Generation X people who share a common skepticism about the value of traditionally held beliefs, lifestyles, etc. ▸ **Generation Xer** *noun*

generative (jĕn′ə-rət-ĭv) *adj. formal* **1** able to produce or generate. **2** relating to production or creation.

generator *noun* a machine that converts mechanical energy into electrical energy.

generic *adj.* **1** of or relating to any member of a general class or group. **2** not marketed under a specific brand name. **3** *Biol.* of, relating to, or belonging to a genus: *a generic name*. **4** of *computers, software, etc.* belonging to the same family; interchangeable.

generous *adj.* **1** giving or willing to give or help unselfishly. **2** of *a donation, etc.* large and given unselfishly. **3** large; ample; plentiful: *generous portions*. **4** willing to forgive; kind: *of generous spirit*. ▸ **generosity** *noun* ▸ **generously** *adv.*

genesis (jĕn′ə-sĭs) *noun* (*pl.* **geneses**) a beginning or origin.

genetic *adj.* **1** of or relating to genes or genetics; inherited: *a genetic defect*. **2** of or relating to origin. ▸ **genetically** *adv.*

genetically modified having one or more genes altered for a specific purpose, esp. in order to increase productivity, improve taste,

appearance, etc., or lengthen shelf-life: *genetically modified tomatoes*.

genetic engineering alteration of an organism's genes by a method other than conventional breeding.

geneticist *noun* a person who studies or is an expert in genetics.

genetics *noun* (*sing.*) the scientific study of the mechanisms whereby characteristics are transmitted from one generation to the next.

genial *adj.* **1** cheerful; friendly; sociable. **2** of *a climate* pleasantly warm or mild. ▸ **geniality** *noun* ▸ **genially** *adv.*

-genic *combining form* forming words denoting causing or producing: *carcinogenic*.

genie (jē′nē) *noun* (*pl.* **genies**) in fairy stories, a spirit with the power to grant wishes.

genital *adj.* of, relating to, or affecting the genitals.

genitals or **genitalia** *pl. noun* the external sexual organs.

genitive *Grammar noun* **1** the form or case of a noun, pronoun, or adjective which shows possession or association, e.g., 'John's'. **2** a noun, etc. in this case. —*adj.* of or belonging to this case.

genius *noun* (*pl.* **geniuses**) **1** a person of outstanding creative or intellectual ability. **2** such ability.

genocide *noun* the deliberate and systematic killing of a whole nation, ethnic group, etc. ▸ **genocidal** *adj*

genome (jē′nōm,) *noun* the complete set of genetic material of a living organism.

genotype *noun* the genetic makeup of a particular organism.

genre (zhän′rə, zhăn′-) *noun* **1** a particular kind of literature, music, or other artistic work. **2** *Art* a type of painting featuring scenes from everyday life.

gent *noun colloq.* a gentleman.

genteel (jĕn-tēl′) *adj.* **1** polite or refined. **2** well-mannered. **3** affectedly and snobbishly refined. ▸ **genteelly** *adv.*

gentian (jĕn′chən) *noun* **1** an ornamental plant with deep blue flowers. **2** a tonic prepared from the bitter-tasting roots of this plant.

gentile (jĕn′tīl,) *adj.* **1** (*often* **Gentile**) not Jewish. **2** relating to a nation or tribe. —*noun* (*often* **Gentile**) a person who is not Jewish.

gentility *noun* **1** good manners and respectability. **2** people of noble birth.

gentle *adj.* **1** not stern, coarse, or violent; mild of manner. **2** not harsh, loud, strong; light and soft: *a gentle caress* / *a gentle breeze*. **3** moderate; mild: *a gentle reprimand*. **4** of *hills, etc.* rising gradually. **5** *old use* of the upper classes; noble. ▸ **gentleness** *noun* ▸ **gently** *adv.*

gentlefolk *pl. noun old use* people of good breeding.

gentleman *noun* **1** a man. **2** a polite, well-mannered, respectable man. **3** a man from the upper classes.

gentlemanly *adj.* **1** polite and well-mannered. **2** suitable for, or typical of, a gentleman.

gentlewoman *noun old use* **1** a polite, well-mannered, respectable woman. **2** a woman from the upper classes.

gentrify *verb trans.* (**gentrified, gentrifying, gentrifies**) to renovate (an area) to conform to relatively wealthy taste. ▶ **gentrification** *noun*

gentry *pl. noun* **1** people belonging to the class directly below the nobility in the UK. **2** people of good breeding.

genuflect *verb intrans.* (**genuflected, genuflecting**) to bend the knee, esp. in worship or as a sign of respect. ▶ **genuflection** *noun*

genuine (jĕn'yə-wĭn, -wĭn,) *adj.* **1** undoubtedly original, real, or true: *a genuine Picasso.* ▣ AUTHENTIC, BONA FIDE ▣ COUNTERFEIT, FAKE, SPURIOUS. **2** honest; sincere. ▶ **genuinely** *adv.* ▶ **genuineness** *noun*

genus (jē'nəs) *noun* (*pl.* **genera**) *Biol.* a group of closely related species in plant and animal classification.

geo- *combining form* forming words denoting associated with the Earth: *geochemistry.*

geocentric *adj.* **1** having the Earth as a center. **2** measured from the center of the Earth.

geode (jē'ōd,) *noun Geol.* a hollow cavity within a rock, lined with crystals.

geodesic (jē,ə-dĕs'ĭk, -dē'sĭk) *Math. noun* the shortest line between two points, e.g.; a straight line on a plane. —*adj.* denoting an artificial structure made up of a large number of identical components; e.g., a dome.

geodesy (jē-ŏd'ə-sē) *noun* the scientific study of the Earth's exact shape and size.

geography *noun* **1** the scientific study of Earth's surface, esp. its physical features, climate, and population. **2** *colloq.* the layout of a place. ▶ **geographer** *noun* ▶ **geographic** *or* **geographical** *adj.* ▶ **geographically** *adv.*

geology *noun* **1** the scientific study of the Earth, including its origin, history, structure, and composition. **2** the history, composition, and structure of the rocks of a particular region. ▶ **geological** *or* **geologic** *adj.* ▶ **geologically** *adv.* ▶ **geologist** *noun*

geomagnetism *noun Physics* Earth's magnetic field.

geometry *noun* the branch of mathematics concerned with the properties of lines, angles, shapes, etc. and their relationships. ▶ **geometric** *or* **geometrical** *adj.*

geophysics *noun* (*sing.*) the study of the physical properties of the Earth, and the physical

processes that determine its structure.

geopolitics *noun* (*sing.*) the study of geographical factors as a basis of the power of nations. ▶ **geopolitical** *adj.*

Georgian[1] *adj.* **1** of *architecture, painting, or furniture* from or suggestive of the period 1714–1830. **2** of *literature* from the period 1910–20.

Georgian[2] *noun* **1** a native or citizen of the Republic of Georgia. **2** the official language of the Republic of Georgia. —*adj.* of the Republic of Georgia, its people, or their language.

geothermal *adj. Geol.* relating to, or using the energy that can be extracted from, the internal heat of the Earth.

geranium *noun* **1** a plant that has large pink or purple flowers and fruit initially resembling the bill of a crane. Also called **cranesbill**. **2** a plant with hairy stems, fragrant leaves, and scarlet, pink, or white flowers.

gerbil *noun* a small burrowing rodent, popular as a pet.

geriatric (jĕr,ē-ă'trĭk) *adj.* relating to the elderly. —*noun colloq.* a very old person.

geriatrics *noun* (*sing.*) the branch of medicine concerned with the care and treatment of the elderly. ▶ **geriatrician** (jĕr,ē-ə-trĭsh'ən) *noun*

germ *noun* **1** a microorganism that causes disease. **2** a living structure that is capable of developing into a complete organism, e.g., a seed. **3** the embryo of a plant, esp. wheat. ▣ BUD, EMBRYO, KERNEL, NUCLEUS, SEED.

German (jar'mən) *noun* **1** a native or citizen of Germany. **2** the official language of Germany, Austria, and parts of Switzerland. —*adj.* of Germany, its people, or their language. ▶ **Germanic** *adj.*

german *adj.* (*following the noun*) **1** having both parents the same: *brother german.* **2** having both grandparents the same on one side of the family: *cousin german.*

germane (jər-mān') *adj.*, of *ideas, remarks, etc.* having a bearing on the matter at hand.

German measles rubella.

German shepherd a large wolflike dog, often used as a guard dog or by the police.

germicide (jar'mĭ-sīd,) *noun* an agent that destroys germs. ▶ **germicidal** *adj.*

germinal *adj.* in the earliest stage of development.

germinate (jər'mĭ-nāt,) *verb trans., intrans.* (**germinated, germinating**) to begin, or cause to begin, to grow or come into existence. ▶ **germination** *noun*

gerontology *noun* the scientific study of the psychological, sociological, and biological aspects of old age. ▶ **gerontological** (jĕr,ənt-l-äj'ī-kəl) *adj.* ▶ **gerontologist** (jĕr,ən-täl'ə-jĭst) *noun*

gerrymander (jĕr'ē-măn,dər, gĕr'-) *verb trans.* (**gerrymandered, gerrymandering**) to change the boundaries of (an electoral district) so as to favor one political party. —*noun* the practice or result of this.

After US governor Elbridge *Gerry*, who rearranged the map of Massachusetts in 1811 to a shape resembling that of a sala*mander*

gerund (jĕr'ənd) *noun Grammar* a noun formed from a verb, e.g., *Smoking* damages your health.

gestalt *noun* (**gestalts** *or* **gestalten**) *Psychol.* a whole pattern or structure perceived as something greater than the sum of its constituent parts.

Gestapo (gə-stäp'ō) *noun* the political police during the German Third Reich.

gestate (jĕs'tāt,) *verb trans., intrans.* (**gestated, gestating**) 1 *of a mammal* to carry, or undergo development, in the womb. 2 to develop (an idea, etc.) slowly in the mind. ▸ **gestation** *noun*

gesticulate *verb intrans., trans.* (**gesticulated, gesticulating**) to express (something) using bold gestures. ▸ **gesticulation** *noun*

gesture (jĕs'chər) *noun* 1 a movement of a part of the body as an expression of meaning. 2 something done to communicate feelings or intentions. —*verb intrans., trans.* (**gestured, gesturing**) 1 to make gestures. 2 to express with gestures. ▸ **gestural** *adj*

get *verb trans., intrans.* (pa t and pa p **gotten** *or* **got**; pr p **getting**) 1 to receive or obtain. 2 to have or possess. 3 to go or cause (another) to go, move, travel, or arrive as specified: *I tried to get past him. / We got to Paris on Friday.* 4 to fetch, take, or bring (something) as specified: *got the book down from the shelf.* 5 to put into a particular state or condition: *Don't get your feet wet. / got me into trouble.* 6 to become: *got angry.* 7 to catch (a disease, etc.): *got the measles.* 8 to order or persuade: *got him to help us.* 9 *colloq.* to receive as punishment: *got 10 years for armed robbery.* 10 *slang* to wreak revenge onto: *I'll get you for that!* 11 *colloq.* (**get to**) to annoy (another): *You shouldn't let them get to you.* 12 *colloq.* to understand: *They just don't get it.* 13 *colloq.* to baffle: *You've got me there.* —**get away** to escape: *The fugitive got away again.* **get away with** to commit (an offense or wrongdoing) without being caught or punished. **get by** to manage to live. **get off** *colloq.* to escape, or cause to escape, with no punishment, or with only the stated punishment: *was charged but got off / managed to get him off with a warning.* **get on** *colloq.* 1 to make progress or be successful. 2 *of a person* to grow old. 3 *of time,*

etc. to grow late. **get on with** 1 to have a friendly relationship with (someone). 2 to continue working on or dealing with (something). **get through to** 1 to make contact with (someone) by telephone or fax. 2 to make (another) understand (something). **get up** 1 to get out of bed. 2 *of the wind, etc.* to become strong.

getaway *noun* an escape, esp. after committing a crime.

get-go *noun colloq.* the very start, origin, or beginning. —**from the get-go** *colloq.* from the outset.

get-together *noun colloq.* an informal meeting.

get-tough *adj. slang* resolutely austere or aggressive: *a new get-tough policy on drugs.*

getup *noun colloq.* an outfit, esp. when considered strange or remarkable.

get-up-and-go *noun colloq.* energy.

gewgaw (gōō'gô,, gyōō'-) *noun* a brightly-colored trinket.

geyser (gī'zər) *noun* 1 *Geol.* a spring that intermittently spouts hot water and steam into the air. 2 *Brit.* a domestic appliance for heating water rapidly.

ghastly *adj.* (**ghastlier, ghastliest**) 1 extremely and disturbingly frightening. ▣ GRIM, GRISLY, GRUESOME, HIDEOUS, HORRIBLE, HORRIFIC, MACABRE, TERRIBLE, TERRIFYING. 2 *colloq.* very unpleasant: *a ghastly cocktail party.* ▸ **ghastliness** *noun*

ghee (gē) *noun* clarified butter made from cow's or buffalo's milk.

gherkin (gər'kĭn) *noun* a variety of cucumber with very small fruits, often used for pickling.

ghetto *noun* (*pl.* **ghettos, ghettoes**) 1 a slum area. 2 any marginalized area, group, activity, etc. 3 *Hist.* a Jewish area of a city.

ghetto blaster *colloq.* a large, portable stereo.

ghost *noun* 1 a supernatural being. ▣ APPARITION, BOGY, HAUNT, PHANTASM, PHANTOM, SHADE, SPECTER, SPIRIT, SPOOK, VISITANT, WRAITH. 2 a suggestion, hint, or trace: *a ghost of a chance.* —*verb intrans., trans.* (**ghosted, ghosting**) to be a ghostwriter for (someone), or of (a written work). —**give up the ghost** *colloq.* to die.

ghostly *adj.* relating to or suggesting the presence of ghosts.

ghost town a formerly thriving town, now deserted.

ghostwriter a person who writes books, speeches, etc. on behalf of another person who is credited as the author.

ghoul (gōōl) *noun* 1 a person interested in morbid or disgusting things. 2 a grave robber. ▸ **ghoulish** *adj.*

GHQ *abbrev.* General Headquarters.

GI *noun* (*pl.* **GIs, GI's**) a soldier in the US Army.

giant *noun* **1** an unusually large person or animal. **2** a person, group, etc. of exceptional ability or importance. **3** in fairy stories, a huge, extremely strong, often cruel creature of human form. —*adj.* **1** of exceedingly or excessively large size. **2** of a particularly large species: *the giant tortoise.*

giantess *noun* a female giant.

gibber *verb intrans.* (**gibbered, gibbering**) **1** to talk so fast that one cannot be understood. **2** to talk foolishly.

gibberish *noun* **1** fast unintelligible talk. **2** foolish talk; nonsense.

gibbet *noun Hist.* **1** a frame on which the bodies of executed criminals were hung as a public warning. **2** a gallows. —*verb trans.* (**gibbeted, gibbeting**) **1** *Hist.* to hang on a gibbet. **2** to expose to public ridicule.

gibbon *noun* the smallest of the apes, and the only one to walk upright habitually.

gibbous *adj.* **1** *of the moon or a planet* more than half illuminated. **2** humpbacked. **3** swollen; bulging.

gibe *or* **jibe** *verb intrans.* (**gibed** *or* **jibed, gibing** *or* **jibing**) to mock, scoff, or jeer. —*noun* a jeer.

giblets *pl. noun* the heart, liver, and other edible internal organs of a chicken or other fowl.

giddy *adj.* (**giddier, giddiest**) **1** suffering a spinning sensation. **2** causing such a sensation. **3** overwhelmed by excitement or pleasure. **4** lightheartedly silly. ▸ **giddily** *adv.* ▸ **giddiness** *noun*

gift *noun* **1** something given; a present. **2** a natural ability. **3** *colloq.* something easily obtained. —*verb trans.* (**gifted, gifting**) **1** *colloq.* to give (something) as a present to (someone).

Usage The colloquial use of the verb *gift* is heavily stigmatized in formal writing, owing to its long association with the language of advertising, and so it is best avoided in formal contexts. See also note at **free.**

gifted *adj.* having a great natural ability or exceptional intelligence: *classes for gifted children.* ▸ **giftedness** *noun*

gig¹ *noun* **1** *Hist.* a small, open, two-wheeled, horse-drawn carriage. **2** a long lightweight rowboat.

gig² *slang noun* a band's, musician's, etc. booking to play a concert, or the performance itself. —*verb intrans.* (**gigged, gigging**) to play a gig or gigs.

giga- *combining form* (ABBREV. **G**) **1** used in the metric system to denote 10 to the power of nine (10^9), i.e., one thousand million: *gigahertz.* **2** *Comput.* two to the power of 30 (2^{30}): *gigabyte.*

gigantic *adj.* of exceedingly or excessively large size. ▸ **gigantically** *adv.*

giggle *verb intrans.* (**giggled, giggling**) to laugh quietly in short bursts or in a nervous or silly way. —*noun* **1** such a laugh. **2** (**the giggles**) a fit of laughing. ▸ **giggly** *adj.*

GIGO (gī′gō, gē′-) *abbrev. Comput.* garbage in, garbage out.

gigolo (jĭg′ə-lō,) *noun* (*pl.* **gigolos**) **1** the paid male companion, and often lover, of a rich woman. **2** a hired professional dancing partner.

gigot (jĭg′ət, zhē-gō′) *noun* a leg of lamb or mutton.

gigue (zhēg) *noun* same as **jig.**

gila monster (hē′lə) a venomous lizard, native to America. Its bite is seldom fatal.

gild *verb* (*pa t* and *pa p* **gilded, gilt;** *pr p* **gilding**) to cover with a thin coating of gold or similar material. —**gild the lily** to try to improve something already beautiful, often spoiling it.

gill¹ (gĭl) *noun* a respiratory organ in fishes and many other aquatic animals.

gill² (jĭl) *noun* a unit of liquid measure equal to a quarter of a pint.

gilt (gĭlt) *adj.* covered with a thin coating of gold. —*noun.* **1** gold or a goldlike substance used in gilding. **2** (**gilts**) gilt-edged securities. —*verb see* **gild.**

gilt-edged securities government securities with a fixed rate of interest, that can be sold at face value.

gimbals *pl. noun* a device which allows a navigation instrument to remain in a horizontal position at sea or in the air.

gimcrack *adj.* cheap, gaudy, and poorly made. —*noun* a cheap, gaudy, poorly made article.

gimlet *noun* **1** a T-shaped hand tool for boring holes in wood. **2** a cocktail of lime juice and gin or vodka.

gimlet-eyed *adj.* having a piercing look or stare.

gimmick *noun* a scheme or object used to attract publicity. ▸ **gimmickry** *noun* ▸ **gimmicky** *adj*

gimp¹ *noun* a strip of silk with a wire core, used as a decoration in dressmaking.

gimp² *noun* **1** a limp. **2** one who limps.

gin¹ *noun* an alcoholic spirit made from barley, rye, or corn, flavored with juniper berries.

gin² *noun* **1** a snare or trap for catching game. **2** a hoisting machine. **3** a device used to separate seeds from raw cotton. —*verb trans.* (**ginned, ginning**) **1** to snare or trap (game) in a gin. **2** to remove (the seed) from raw cotton using a gin.

gin³ *.noun Cards* gin rummy.

ginger *noun* **1** an aromatic, spicy root that is used as a flavoring and in some medicines. **2** a reddish-brown color. **3** *colloq.* energy; liveliness. —*adj.* **1** flavored with ginger. **2** *Brit.,* of hair reddish-brown in color. —*verb trans.*

(gingered, gingering) *colloq.* to make lively, active, or efficient.

ginger ale a nonalcoholic sparkling drink flavored with ginger.

gingerbread *noun* cake flavored with molasses and ginger.

gingerly *adv.* with delicate caution.

ginger snap a ginger-flavored cookie.

gingham (gĭng′əm) *noun* striped or checked cotton cloth.

gingivitis (jĭn,jə-vīt′ĭs) *noun* inflammation of the gums.

ginkgo or **gingko** *noun* (*pl.* **ginkgoes, gingkoes**) a cone-bearing plant with fan-shaped leaves, native to SW China. Also called **maidenhair tree**.

gin rummy *Cards* a version of rummy allowing a finish by a player whose unmatched cards total 10 points or fewer.

ginseng (jĭn′săng,, -sĕng,) *noun* **1** a plant with round red fruits, widely used as a tonic, stimulant, and medicine. **2** a medicinal preparation made from the root of this plant.

gip *verb, noun slang* same as **gyp**.

Gipsy *noun* same as **Gypsy**.

giraffe (jə-răf′) *noun* the tallest living animal, with an extremely long neck and legs, a small head, and a blotchy coat.

Called a *camelopard* until the 17th century

gird (gərd) *verb trans.* (*pa t* and *pa p* **girded, girt**; *pr p* **girding**) to encircle or fasten with, or as if with, a belt. —**gird up (one's) loins** to prepare for action.

girder *noun* a large supporting beam of iron, steel, or wood.

girdle *noun* **1** a woman's close-fitting undergarment worn over the waist and thighs. **2** a belt or cord worn around the waist. **3** a surrounding part, esp. such a part of the body: *pelvic girdle.* —*verb trans.* (**girdled, girdling**) to surround with, or as if with, a girdle.

girl *noun* **1** a female child. **2** a daughter. **3** a young woman.

girlfriend *noun* **1** a person's regular female companion, often with whom one has a romantic or sexual relationship. **2** a female friend, esp. of a woman.

girlhood *noun* the period of life when a person is a girl.

girlie or **girly** *adj. colloq.*, of a magazine etc. featuring naked or nearly naked young women in erotic poses.

girlish *adj.* like a girl in appearance or behavior. ▸ **girlishly** *adv.* ▸ **girlishness** *noun*

Girl Scout a member of an organization, the Girl Scouts of America, of girls and young women, devoted to good citizenship.

girt *verb see* **gird**.

girth *noun* **1** the distance around something. **2** a strap around a horse's belly that holds a

saddle in place.

gist (jĭst) *noun* the general meaning; the main point.

give *verb trans., intrans.* (*pa t* **gave**; *pa p* **given**; *pr p* **giving**) **1** to transfer ownership of; to transfer possession of temporarily: *I gave her my watch.* **2** to provide or administer: *give advice / give medicine.* **3** to produce: *Cows give milk.* **4** to perform (an action, service, etc.): *give a smile / gave a lecture.* **5** to pay: *gave $20 for it.* **6** to make a donation: *Please give generously.* **7** (also **give up**) to sacrifice: *gave her life for her country.* **8** to yield or break: *give under pressure.* **9** to organize at one's own expense: *give a party.* **10** to have as a result: *4 into 20 gives 5.* **11** *colloq.* used to state a preference: *Give me jazz any day.* —*noun* capacity to yield; flexibility. —**give away 1** to present (a bride) to a bridegroom at a wedding ceremony. **2** to hand (something) over as a gift: *gave all her money away.* **give in** to yield. **give off** to produce or emit (e.g., a smell). **give up 1** to admit defeat and yield. **2** to renounce or quit (a habit, etc.): *give up smoking.* **give way 1** to give priority. **2** to collapse under pressure. **give as good as one gets** *colloq.* to respond to an attack with equal effect.

give-and-take *noun* cooperation between people who are prepared to compromise.

giveaway *noun colloq.* **1** an act of accidentally revealing secrets, etc. **2** something obtained extremely easily or cheaply. ▸ *adj.*

given *adj.* **1** stated or specified. **2** (**given to**) prone to (something). —*prep.* accepting as a basis for discussion: *Given the problems, can you do the job?* —*verb see* **give**.

given name the name that is given to a person either at birth or at baptism, or both.

gizmo *noun* (*pl.* **gizmos**) *slang* a gadget, etc., the name for which is unknown.

gizzard *noun* **1** a muscular chamber in certain animals that is specialized for grinding up indigestible food. **2** *colloq.* the stomach.

glacé (glä-sā′) *adj.* **1** coated with a sugary glaze: *glacé cherries.* **2** frozen, or covered with ice.

glacial (glā′shəl) *adj.* **1** relating to or resembling a glacier; caused by the action of a glacier. **2** extremely cold. ▸ **glacially** *adv.*

glaciate (glā′shē-āt,) *verb trans.* (**glaciated, glaciating**) of land, etc. to become covered with glaciers or ice sheets. ▸ **glaciation** *noun*

glacier (glā′shər) *noun* a slow-moving body of ice that occurs on land.

glad *adj.* (**gladder, gladdest**) **1** (**glad about**) happy or pleased about (something). **2** (**glad of**) grateful for (something): *I was glad of your support.* **3** very willing: *We are glad to* help. ▸ **gladly** adv. ▸ **gladness** noun

gladden verb trans. (**gladdened, gladdening**) to make happy or pleased.

glade noun an open space in woods or a forest.

gladiator noun a man trained in ancient Rome to fight against other men or animals in an arena. ▸ **gladiatorial** adj.

gladiolus (glăd,ē-ō′ləs) noun (pl. **gladioli, gladioluses**) an ornamental plant with sword-shaped leaves and funnel-shaped flowers. Also called **gladiola**.

glad rags slang one's best clothes.

glair noun egg-white, or a similar substance, used as a glaze or an adhesive.

glamorize verb trans. (**glamorized, glamorizing**) 1 to make glamorous. 2 to romanticize.

glamour or **glamor** (glăm′ər) noun great beauty or sexual charm, esp. created by make-up, stylish clothes, etc. ▸ **glamorous** adj.

A variant of *grammar*, from the medieval association of magic with learning

glance verb intrans. (**glanced, glancing**) 1 to look quickly (at someone or something). 2 (**glance off**) to be deflected by (something). —noun 1 a brief look, often indirect. 2 a deflection. 3 a brief flash of light. —**at a glance** at once; from one brief look.

gland noun an organ in animals that produces a specific chemical substance. ▸ **glandular** adj.

glandular fever infectious mononucleosis.

glare verb intrans., trans. (**glared, glaring**) 1 to stare angrily. 2 to be unpleasantly bright or shiny. —noun 1 an angry stare. 2 dazzling light.

glaring adj. 1 unpleasantly bright. 2 obvious. ▸ **glaringly** adv.

glasnost (glăs′nəst, -nôst, -nōst) noun openness and willingness on the part of a government to provide information.

glass noun 1 a hard, brittle material that is usu. transparent or translucent. 2 an article made from this material, e.g., a mirror, a lens, or esp. a drinking vessel. 3 (**glasses**) a pair of optical lenses used to protect the eyes or to correct vision. —adj. made of glass. —verb trans. (**glassed, glassing**) to supply or cover with glass.

glasshouse noun Brit. a greenhouse.

glasspaper noun paper coated with finely ground glass, used as an abrasive.

glassy adj. (**glassier, glassiest**) 1 like glass. 2 expressionless: a cold, glassy stare.

glaucoma (glow-kō′mə, glô-) noun a disease of the eye that causes impaired vision.

glaze verb trans., intrans. (**glazed, glazing**) 1 to put glass into (a window, door, etc.). 2 to

give a hard, shiny, transparent coating to (e.g., pottery). 3 (usu. **glaze over**) of the eyes to become fixed and expressionless. 4 to apply a shiny coating of milk, eggs, or sugar to (e.g., pastry). —noun 1 a hard glassy coating on pottery. 2 a shiny coating of milk, eggs, or sugar on food. ▸ **glazed** adj.

glazier (glā′zhər, -zē-ər) noun a person employed to glaze windows, doors, etc.

gleam noun 1 a gentle glow. 2 a brief flash of esp. reflected light. 3 a brief appearance or sign. —verb intrans. (**gleamed, gleaming**) 1 to glow gently. 2 to shine with brief flashes of light.

glean verb trans., intrans. (**gleaned, gleaning**) to collect (information, etc.) bit by bit, often with difficulty. ▸ **gleaner** noun

glee noun 1 great delight; joy. 2 a song in three or four parts. ▸ **gleeful** adj. ▸ **gleefully** adv.

glen noun a long narrow valley, esp. in Scotland.

glib adj. (**glibber, glibbest**) speaking or spoken readily, but unsincerely: glib politicians / glib explanations. ▸ **glibly** adv. ▸ **glibness** noun

glide verb intrans. (**glided, gliding**) 1 to move smoothly. 2 to travel through the air smoothly or gently. 3 to travel through the air by glider.

glider noun an aircraft designed to glide in air currents without using any form of engine power.

glimmer verb intrans. (**glimmered, glimmering**) to glow faintly. —noun 1 a faint glow; a twinkle. 2 a hint or trace: not a glimmer of hope.

glimpse noun a very brief look. —verb trans. (**glimpsed, glimpsing**) to see momentarily.

glint verb intrans. (**glinted, glinting**) to give off flashes of bright light. —noun a brief flash of light.

glissando (glis-än′dō) noun (pl. **glissandi, glissandos**) Mus. a sliding from one note to another.

glisten (glĭs′ən) verb intrans. (**glistened, glistening**) usu. of something wet, icy, etc. to shine or sparkle.

glitch noun colloq. a sudden brief irregularity or failure to function.

glitter verb intrans. (**glittered, glittering**) to sparkle. —noun 1 sparkle. 2 colloq. sparkle attractiveness. 3 tiny pieces of shiny material, used for decoration.

glitterati (glĭt,ə-rät′ē) pl. noun colloq. famous, fashionable, and beautiful people.

glitz noun flashy appearance; garishness. ▸ **glitzy** adj.

Originally a Yiddish word meaning 'glitter'

gloaming noun poetic. dusk; twilight.

gloat verb intrans. (**gloated, gloating**) (often

gloat over) to feel or show smug or vindictive satisfaction. —*noun* an act of gloating.

glob *noun colloq.* a small amount of thick liquid; a blob or dollop.

global *adj.* 1 affecting the whole world. 2 including everything; total. 3 *Comput.* relating to, affecting, or performed on an entire document, file, program, etc. ▸ **globally** *adv.*

global warming a gradual increase in the average temperature of the Earth's surface and its atmosphere, attributed to the greenhouse effect.

globe *noun* 1 (**the globe**) the Earth. 2 a sphere with a map of the world on it. 3 a ball-shaped object.

globe artichoke an artichoke (sense 1a).

globetrotter *noun colloq.* a person who travels all over the world. ▸ **globetrotting** *noun*

globin (glō′bĭn) *noun* a soluble protein in animals present in red blood cells and muscle cells.

globular (glăb′yə-lər) *adj.* 1 shaped like a globe or globule. 2 consisting of globules.

globule (glăb′yo͞ol,) *noun* a small drop, esp. of liquid.

globulin (glăb′yə-lĭn) *noun* a single protein, found in blood plasma, eggs, and milk.

glockenspiel (glăk′ən-shpēl,) *noun* a musical instrument consisting of tuned metal plates played with two small hammers.

gloom *noun* 1 a state of near darkness. 2 a state of sadness or despair. ▸ **gloomy** *adj.* ▸ **gloomily** *adv.*

glorify *verb trans.* (**glorified, glorifying, glorifies**) 1 to exaggerate the importance of. 2 to praise or worship (God). ▸ **glorification** *noun*

glorious *adj.* 1 having or bringing glory. 2 splendidly beautiful. 3 outstanding. ▸ **gloriously** *adv.*

glory *noun* (*pl.* **glories**) 1 great honor and prestige. 2 great beauty or splendor. 3 praise and thanks given to God. —*verb intrans.* (**gloried, glorying, glories**) to feel or show great delight or pride (in something).

gloss[1] (glôs, gläs) *noun* 1 shiny brightness on a surface. 2 a superficial pleasantness. 3 a. substance that adds shine. —*verb trans.* (**glossed, glossing, glosses**) 1 to give a shiny finish to. 2 to paint with gloss. —**gloss over** to conceal, esp. by treating briefly and dismissively. ▸ **glossy** *adj.* ▸ **glossily** *adv.* ▸ **glossiness** *noun*

gloss[2] *noun* a short explanation of a word, phrase, etc. in a text. —*verb trans.* (**glossed, glossing, glosses**) to provide a gloss of (a word, etc.).

glossary (glô′sə-rē, gläs′ə-) *noun* (*pl.* **glossaries**) a list of glosses, often at the end of a book.

glottis *noun* (*pl.* **glottises, glottides**) the space between the two vocal cords at the entrance to the windpipe, controlling voice modulation.

glove (glŭv) *noun* a covering for the hand, usu. with a separate sheath for each finger. —**fit like a glove** to fit perfectly.

glow (glō) *verb intrans.* (**glowed, glowing**) 1 to give out a steady heat or light without flames. 2 to shine brightly, as if very hot; *cheeks glowing with health*. 3 to feel or show contentment or well-being: *glow with pride*. —*noun* 1 a steady flameless heat or light. 2 bright, shiny appearance. 3 intensity of esp. pleasant feeling.

glower (glow′ər) *verb intrans.* (**glowered, glowering**) to draw the eyebrows together, e.g., in disapproval. —*noun* an angry stare; a scowl.

glowworm *noun* a small nocturnal beetle, the female of which gives out a bright greenish light.

gloxinia (glăk-sĭn′ē-ə) *noun* a plant with large white, pink, red, or purple flowers.

glucagon *noun* a hormone that increases blood glucose levels.

glucose (glo͞o′kōs,) *noun* 1 a sugar that is the main form in which energy is transported round the bloodstream. 2 a concentrated sugary solution used in confectionery.

glue *noun* an adhesive. —*verb trans.* (**glued, gluing**) 1 to join with glue. 2 *colloq.* to put or stay very close to; to fix on: *Her eyes were glued to the window.* ▸ **gluey** *adj.*

glue sniffing the practice of breathing in fumes from some types of glue to produce hallucinatory or intoxicating effects. ▸ **glue sniffer** *noun*

glum *adj.* (**glummer, glummest**) in low spirits; sullen. ▸ **glumly** *adv.* ▸ **glumness** *noun*

glut *noun* 1 an excessive supply. 2 an act of eating to excess. —*verb trans., intrans.* (**glutted, glutting**) 1 to feed or supply to excess. 2 to block or choke up.

gluten *noun* a mixture of two proteins that occurs in wheat flour, giving bread dough elastic properties.

glutinous *adj.* having the properties of glue; sticky.

glutton[1] (glŭt′n) *noun* a person who eats too much. —**a glutton for punishment** a person who is eager to undertake difficult or arduous tasks. ▸ **gluttonous** *adj.* ▸ **gluttony** *noun*

glutton[2] *noun* a wolverine.

glycerin or **glycerine** (glĭs′ə-rĭn) *noun* glycerol or a preparation containing it.

glycerol (glĭs′ə-rôl,, -rōl,) *noun Chem.* a colorless viscous liquid with a sweet taste, an important constituent of fats and oils.

GM *abbrev.* general manager.

gm *abbrev.* gram.

GMT *abbrev.* Greenwich Mean Time.

gnarled (närld) *adj.*, of trees, branches, human hands, etc. having knots and lumps, usu. as a result of age.

gnarly *adj.* (**gnarlier, gnarliest**) **1** gnarled. **2** *Sport slang*, of an ocean wave in surfing excellent to ride.

gnash *verb trans., intrans.* (**gnashed, gnashing**) to grind (the teeth) together, esp. in anger.

gnat *noun* a small biting fly.

gnaw *verb trans., intrans.* (**gnawed, gnawing**) **1** to bite (something) with a scraping action. **2** (*usu.* **gnaw at**) of pain, anxiety, etc. to trouble (one) persistently.

gneiss (nīs) *noun* a banded, coarse-grained metamorphic rock.

gnocchi (nyô′kē) *pl. noun* an Italian dish of small dumplings made with flour, cooked potato, or semolina.

gnome[1] *noun* **1** in fairy-tales a small misshapen man who lives underground, often guarding treasure. **2** a statue of such a creature, esp. as a garden ornament. ▸ **gnomish** *adj.*

gnome[2] *noun* a maxim, saying, or aphorism. ▸ **gnomic** *adj.*

gnostic (näs′tĭk) *adj.* **1** relating to knowledge, esp. mystical or religious knowledge. **2** (*usu.* **Gnostic**) relating to early Christian heretics. —*noun* (*usu.* **Gnostic**) an early Christian heretic. ▸ **Gnosticism** *noun*

GNP *abbrev.* gross national product.

gnu (nōō, nyōō) *noun* (*pl.* **gnus, gnu**) either of two species of large grazing antelopes. Also called **wildebeest**.

go[1] *verb intrans.* (*pa t* **went**; *pa p* **gone**; *pr p* **going**; *3d person sing. present* **goes**) **1** to walk, move, or travel in the direction specified. **2** to lead or extend: *The path goes across the field.* **3** to visit or attend something, once or regularly: *Go to the movies / Go to school.* **4** to leave or move away. **5** to be destroyed or taken away; to disappear: *The old door had to go.* **6** to proceed or fare in a given manner: *The project is going well.* **7** to be used up: *money going for drink.* **8** to be given or sold for a stated amount: *went for $200.* **9** to leave or set out for a stated purpose: *Go for a ride. / Go on vacation.* **10** to perform (an action) or produce (a sound): *Go like this when you perform a swan dive.* **11** to break, break down, or fail: *The old TV finally went.* **12** to work or be in working order: *The fan is going at last.* **13** to pass into a certain condition; to become: *go mad.* **14** to be placed correctly; to belong: *Where does this top go?* **15** to fit, or be contained: *Four into three just won't go.* **16** to continue in a certain state: *The population is going hungry.* **17** of time to pass. **18** (*often* **go with**) of colors, etc. to match or blend. **19** *slang, usu. with*

quoted speech to say: *She goes, 'Why are you dating my boyfriend?'.* —*noun* (*pl.* **goes**) **1** a turn or spell: *It's my go.* **2** an attempt: *have a go.* **3** energy; liveliness: *a gymnast who lacks go.* **4** *colloq.* a success: *made a go of it.* —**go back on** to break (an agreement, etc.). **go down 1** to fall or sink. **2** *colloq.* to be accepted or received: *The joke went down well.* **3** *colloq.* to happen: *What's going down, man?* **go for** *colloq.* **1** to be attracted by: *I really go for smart people.* **2** to choose: *went for the red shoes instead.* **go off 1** to explode. **2** to emit a loud noise: *My alarm clock goes off at five.* **go out with** to spend time with (someone) socially, esp. romantically. **go places** *colloq.* to be in the process of achieving success. **go to pieces** to have a nervous breakdown or to suffer loss of one's health. **go under** *colloq.* to fail or be ruined: *The new business went under.* **no go** *colloq.* not possible; in vain. **on the go** *colloq.* busily active. **to go** ready to be taken out, e.g. from a restaurant: *ordered four pizzas to go.*

go[2] *noun* a Japanese board game for two players.

goad *verb trans.* (**goaded, goading**) to urge or provoke. —*noun* **1** a sharp-pointed stick used for driving cattle, etc. **2** a source or mechanism for provoking or inciting.

go-ahead *colloq. adj.* energetically ambitious and farsighted. —*noun* (**the go-ahead**) permission to start doing something.

goal *noun* **1 a** the posts through which the ball is struck in football, etc. **b** an act of scoring in this way; the point or points scored. **2** an aim or purpose.

goalkeeper *noun* the player guarding the goal in various sports. Also called **goalie, goaltender.**

goat *noun* **1** an animal related to the sheep, characterized by the presence of a beard in the male. **2** *colloq.* a lecherous man. **3** *colloq.* a foolish person. **4** (**the Goat**) the name of a constellation and the tenth sign of the zodiac. **5** a person born between Dec. 23 and Jan. 19, under this sign. Also called **Capricorn**. —**get (someone's) goat** *colloq.* to annoy or irritate (the one specified).

goatee (gō-tē′) *noun* a pointed beard growing only on the front of a man's chin.

gob *noun* **1** *slang* the mouth. **2** a soft wet lump. **3** *colloq.* (*often* **gobs**) a large amount or a great number: *has gobs of money.*

gobbet *noun* **1** a lump or chunk. **2** a drip or drop.

gobble *verb trans., intrans.* (**gobbled, gobbling**) **1** to eat (something) hurriedly and noisily. **2** of a male turkey to make a loud gurgling noise in the throat. —*noun* the loud gurgling sound made by a male turkey.

gobbledygook or **gobbledegook** noun colloq. 1 official jargon, meaningless to ordinary people. 2 nonsense; rubbish.

gobbler noun a male turkey.

go-between noun a messenger between two people or sides; an intermediary.

goblet noun a drinking cup with a base and stem but no handles.

goblin noun in folk tales an evil or mischievous spirit in the form of a small man.

go-cart noun a small wagon that a child can ride in or pull.

god noun 1 a divine or superhuman being with power over nature and the human race, and often an object of worship. 2 (**God**) the supreme being and creator of the universe and the human race, worshiped by believers, e.g., Christians. 3 a man greatly admired, esp. for his fine physique or wide influence.

godchild noun a child for whom a godparent is responsible.

goddaughter noun a female godchild.

goddess noun 1 a superhuman feminine being with power over nature and humans, and often an object of worship. 2 a woman greatly admired for her beauty or wide influence.

godfather noun 1 a male godparent. 2 slang the head of an organized crime group.

God-forsaken adj. remote and desolate.

godless adj. 1 having no religious faith; believing in no god. 2 wicked; immoral. ▶ **godlessness** noun

godlike adj. resembling a god.

godly adj. (**godlier, godliest**) religious; pious. ▶ **godliness** noun

godmother noun a female godparent.

godparent noun a person with responsibility for the religious education of another, esp. a child, or for a child's upbringing in the event of the death of the parents.

godsend noun a person or thing whose arrival is unexpected but extremely welcome.

godson noun a male godchild.

goer noun (usu. in compounds) a person who makes regular visits: moviegoers.

gofer noun slang one who runs errands in an office setting.

go-getter noun colloq. an ambitious, enterprising person.

goggle verb intrans, trans. (**goggled, goggling**) 1 to look with wide staring eyes. 2 to roll (the eyes). 3 of the eyes to stick out. —noun a wide-eyed stare.

goggles pl. noun protective eyeglasses with the edges fitting closely against the face.

going noun 1 an act of leaving; a departure. 2 the condition of the terrain under one's feet: The going was easy on flat ground. 3 progress: slow going at the beginning of the task. 4 colloq. general situation or conditions: when the going gets rough. —adj. 1 flourishing: a going concern. 2 usual or accepted: the going rate. —verb see **go**[1].

going-over noun (pl. **goings-over**) colloq. 1 a beating. 2 a harsh reprimand or severe criticism. 3 a close inspection.

goings-on pl. noun colloq. events or happenings, esp. if strange, disapproved of, or illegal.

goiter noun abnormal enlargement of the thyroid gland, often resulting in a large swelling in the neck.

gold noun 1 a (SYMBOL Au) a soft, dense, yellow precious metal that does not tarnish. b articles made from it, esp. jewelry and coins. c its value, used as a standard for the value of currency. d its deep yellow color. —adj. 1 made of gold. 2 gold-colored.

golden adj. 1 gold-colored. 2 made of or containing gold. 3 prosperous or thriving; happy: golden years. 4 extremely valuable; excellent: a golden opportunity. 5 denoting a 50th anniversary.

golden eagle a large eagle with a wingspan of up to 6.5 ft. (2 m).

goldenrod or **golden rod** noun a N American plant with long pointed leaves, and spikes of tiny golden yellow flowers.

goldfinch noun a small finch, the male of which has yellow plumage and a black forehead.

goldfish noun (pl. **goldfish, goldfishes**) a freshwater fish belonging to the carp family.

gold leaf gold rolled or beaten into very thin sheets, used to decorate books, etc.

gold plate 1 a thin coating of gold, esp. on silver. 2 articles, e.g., spoons and dishes, made of gold.

gold-plate verb trans. (**gold-plated, gold-plating**) to coat (another metal) with gold.

gold rush the rapid influx of prospectors to an area reputed to be rich in gold.

goldsmith noun a person who makes articles out of gold.

gold standard a monetary standard or system according to which the unit of currency has a precise value in gold.

golf noun a game played on a large outdoor course, the object being to hit a small ball into each of a series of holes. —verb intrans. (**golfed, golfing**) to play golf. ▶ **golfer** noun

golf club noun 1 any of the set of long-handled clubs used to play golf. 2 an association of players of golf, or its premises with a golf course attached.

golf course a tract of land designed for playing golf.

-gon combining form Math. forming words denoting a geometrical figure: polygon / hexagon.

gonad (gō′năd,) noun an organ in animals in which eggs or sperm are produced.

gondola (găn'də-lə) *noun* **1** a long, narrow boat with pointed upturned ends, used on the canals of Venice. **2** the passenger cabin suspended from an airship, balloon, or cable railroad.

gondolier (găn,də-lĭr') *noun* a person who rows a gondola on a canal.

gone *adj.* **1** departed. **2** lost. **3** dead. **4** *colloq.* pregnant: *four months gone.* **5** *colloq.* in ecstasy. **6** *colloq.* (**gone on**) infatuated or obsessed with (someone or something).—*verb see* go[1].

goner *noun slang* a person or thing beyond hope of recovery.

gong *noun* a hanging metal plate that sounds when struck.

gonorrhea (găn,ə-rē'ə) *noun* a sexually transmitted disease.

goo *noun colloq.* **1** a sticky substance. **2** excessive sentimentality.

goober *noun* a peanut.

good *adj.* (**better, best**) **1** having desirable or necessary qualities; admirable. **2** (**good at**) competent in doing (something); talented. **3** morally correct; virtuous. **4** (**good for**) beneficial to (someone or something). **5** kind and generous. **6** bringing happiness or pleasure: *good news.* **7** well behaved. **8** wise; advisable: *a good buy.* **9** thorough. **10** finest among others: *my good cups.* **11** adequate; satisfactory: *a good supply.* **12** enjoyable: *having a good time.* **13** valid: *Your ticket is good for 30 days.* **14** at least; considerable: *lasted a good month.* —*noun* **1** moral correctness; virtue. **2** benefit; advantage: *do you good.* —*interj.* used to express approval or satisfaction. —*adv.* (**better, best**) *colloq.* well. —**as good as** almost; virtually: *He's as good as dead.* **good and** *colloq.* very; completely or absolutely: *I'll do it when I'm good and ready.* **make good** to be successful.

good-bye, goodbye *or* **good-by** *interj.* used to express farewell. —*noun* an act of saying farewell.

good-for-nothing *adj.* lazy and irresponsible. —*noun* a lazy and irresponsible person.

Good Friday *noun* the Friday before Easter.

goodies *pl. noun colloq.* pleasant or desirable things.

goodish *adj.* good enough, but usu. only just.

goodly *adj.* (**goodlier, goodliest**) adequate or plentiful. ► **goodliness** *noun*

goodness *noun* **1** the state or quality of being good; generosity, kindness, or moral correctness. **2** *in exclamations* God: *Goodness knows when we'll be done with this.* **3** nourishing quality. —*interj.* used to express surprise or relief.

goods *pl. noun* **1** articles for sale; merchandise. **2** personal possessions: *all my worldly goods.*

good Samaritan a person who helps others.

goodwill *noun* **1** a feeling of kindness toward others. **2** the good reputation of an established business, seen as having value.

goody *colloq. interj.* used to express happiness or pleasure.

goody-goody *colloq.* —*adj.* virtuous in an ostentatious or self-satisfied way. —*noun* (*pl.* **goody-goodies**) an ostentatiously virtuous person.

gooey *adj.* (**gooier, gooiest**) sticky.

goof *slang noun* **1** a silly or foolish person. **2** a foolish mistake. —*verb intrans.* (**goofed, goofing**) **1** to make a stupid mistake. **2** (**goof around**) to spend time idly or foolishly. ► **goofy** *adj.*

goon *noun slang* **1** a hired thug. **2** a silly person.

goose *noun* (*pl.* **geese**) **1 a** a large waterfowl, with a stout body, long neck, webbed feet, and a broad flat bill. *See also* **gander. b** the female of this bird. **2** the flesh of this waterfowl cooked as food. **3** a silly person. —*verb trans.* (**goosed, goosing**) *slang* to poke (someone) on or between the buttocks.

gooseberry (gōōs'bĕr,ē, gōōz'-) *noun* (*pl.* **gooseberries**) a yellowish-green or reddish edible berry used to make jam, pies, etc.

goose bumps a condition of the skin caused by cold or fear, in which the hairs become erect, causing small bumps to appear on the surface. Also called **goose flesh, goose pimples**.

goose step a military marching step in which the legs are kept rigid and swung very high. ► **goosestep** *verb*

GOP *abbrev.* Grand Old Party.

gopher *noun* **1** a rodent with two external fur-lined cheek pouches. **2** a prairie ground squirrel.

gore[1] *noun* blood from a wound, esp. when clotted.

gore[2] *verb trans.* (**gored, goring**) to pierce with the horn or tusk.

gore[3] *noun* a triangular piece of material, e.g., a section of an umbrella.

gorge *noun* **1** a deep, narrow valley, usu. containing a river. **2** the contents of the stomach. **3** a spell of greedy eating. **4** the throat or gullet. —*verb intrans., trans.* (**gorged, gorging**) **1** to eat or swallow greedily. **2** (*usu.* **gorge oneself**) to stuff oneself with food.

gorgeous *adj.* **1** having an appearance or qualities that delight the senses. **2** *colloq.* extremely pleasant; excellent. ► **gorgeously** *adv.* ► **gorgeousness** *noun*

gorilla *noun* the largest of the apes, with a heavily built body, long arms, and black skin covered with dense fur.

gorse *noun* a wild thorny evergreen shrub with yellow flowers. Also called **furze, whin.**

gory adj. (**gorier, goriest**) 1 causing or involving bloodshed. 2 unpleasant: the gory details. 3 covered with gore.

gosh interj. colloq. used to express mild surprise.

goshawk (gäs'hôk,) noun a large hawk with grey or brownish plumage.

gosling (gäs'lǐng, -lǐn) noun a young goose.

gospel noun 1 the life and teachings of Christ. 2 (usu. **Gospel**) each of the New Testament books. 3 lively, religious music associated with evangelism, blending folk music, jazz, and African-American spirituals. —**the gospel truth** the absolute truth.

gossamer (gäs'ə-mər) noun 1 fine, filmy, spider-woven threads. 2 a very soft, fine, almost transparent material.

gossip noun 1 talk or writing about the private affairs of others, often spiteful and untrue. 2 a person who engages in such talk or writing. 3 casual and friendly talk. —verb intrans. (**gossiped, gossiping**) to chat or engage in malicious gossip. ▸ **gossipy** adj.

> Originally godsibb, meaning 'godparent'

got verb see **get**.

Goth (gäth) noun one of a Germanic nation that invaded the Roman Empire.

Gothic (gäth'ǐk) adj. 1 of the Goths or their language. 2 of a style of architecture featuring high pointed arches. 3 of a genre of literature dealing with mysterious or supernatural events. —noun 1 architecture or literature in the Gothic style. 2 (**gothic**) a printing type style without serifs. 3 the extinct Germanic language of the Goths.

gotten verb see **get**.

Gouda noun a flat, round, mild Dutch cheese.

gouge noun 1 a chisel with a rounded hollow blade, used for cutting grooves or holes in wood. 2 a groove or hole made using this tool. —verb trans. (**gouged, gouging**) 1 to cut (something) out with, or as if with, this tool. 2 to force or press (something) out of position.

goulash (gōō'läsh,) noun a thick meat stew heavily seasoned with paprika, orig. from Hungary.

gourd (gôrd, gŏŏrd) noun 1 a plant related to the squash. 2 its fruit, used as a drinking vessel, container, etc.

gourmand (gŏŏr'mänd,) noun 1 a greedy eater; a glutton. 2 a person who enjoys good food and wines.

gourmet (gŏŏr-mā') noun a person with expert knowledge of good food and wine.

gout noun a disease causing recurrent attacks of acute arthritis, most commonly of the big toe. ▸ **gouty** adj.

gov. abbrev. 1 government. 2 (**Gov.**) governor.

govern verb trans., intrans. (**governed, governing**) 1 to control and direct the affairs of (a country, state, or organization). 2 to guide or influence; to control or restrain: governed her temper. ▸ **governable** adj. ▸ **governance** noun

governess noun a woman employed to teach, and perhaps look after, children in their home.

government (gəv'ər-mənt, -ərn-) noun 1 a governing body. 2 the way in which the control of a nation or state's affairs is executed. 3 the act or practice of ruling. ▸ **governmental** adj.

governor (gəv'ə-nər, -ər-) noun 1 (also **Governor**) the elected head of a US state. 2 the head of an institution, e.g., a prison. 3 a member of a governing body of a school, hospital, college, etc. 4 (also **Governor**) the head of a colony or province. 5 a device for maintaining or controlling uniform speed in an engine or vehicle.

gown noun 1 a woman's long formal dress. 2 an official robe worn by, e.g., lawyers and academics on formal occasions. 3 a protective overall worn by surgical staff in a hospital.

G.P. or **GP** abbrev. general practitioner.

GPA abbrev. grade point average.

GPO abbrev. general post office.

GQ abbrev. general quarters.

gr. or **gr** abbrev. 1 grade. 2 grain. 3 gram. 4 gross.

grab verb trans., intrans. (**grabbed, grabbing**) 1 to seize (something) suddenly and often with violence. 2 to take greedily. 3 to take hurriedly or without hesitation: grab a snack. —noun 1 an act of taking suddenly or greedily. 2 a mechanical device used, e.g., for excavation. —**up for grabs** slang available, esp. easily or cheaply.

grace noun 1 elegance and beauty of form or movement. 2 decency; politeness: had the grace to say thank you. 3 a short prayer before or after a meal. 4 a delay allowed before a deadline. 5 a pleasing or attractive characteristic: social graces. 6 Relig. mercy shown by God. 7 (**His Grace, Her Grace** or **Your Grace**) used in addressing or speaking of a non-royal duke or duchess or an archbishop. —verb trans. (**graced, gracing**) 1 to honor, e.g., with one's presence. 2 to add beauty or charm to.

graceful adj. having or showing elegance and beauty of form or movement. ▸ **gracefully** adv. ▸ **gracefulness** noun

graceless adj. 1 awkward in form or movement. 2 bad-mannered. ▸ **gracelessly** adv. ▸ **gracelessness** noun

gracious adj. 1 kind and polite. 2 of God merciful. 3 luxurious and elegant. —interj. used to express surprise. ▸ **graciously** adv. ▸ **graciousness** noun

gradation noun 1 the act or process of forming grades or stages. **2** a series of gradual, successive stages. **3** the gradual change or movement from one state to another. ▸ **gradational** adj.

grade noun **1** a stage or level on a scale of quality, rank, size, etc. **2 a** a class or year in school, or the level of work taught in it. **b** (**grades** or **the grades**) elementary school. **3** a slope or gradient. —verb trans. (**graded, grading**) **1** to arrange in different grades. **2** to evaluate and determine the quality of (a student's work). **3** to produce a gradual blending of (esp. colors). **4** to make level (e.g., road surfaces). —**make the grade** colloq. to reach the required standard. ▸ **grader** noun

grade point average (ABBREV. **GPA**) a student's average grade earned in a course.

gradient (grād'ē-ənt) noun **1** the steepness of a slope. **2** a slope.

gradual (grăj'ə-wəl) adj. **1** developing or happening slowly, by degrees: gradual improvement. ▣ STEP-BY-STEP ▣ ABRUPT, SUDDEN. **2** of a slope not steep; gentle. ▸ **gradually** adv.

graduate verb intrans., trans. (grăj'ə-wāt,) (**graduated, graduating**) **1** to receive an academic degree. **2** to move up to a higher level, often in stages. **3** to mark (e.g., a thermometer) with units of measurement. **4** to arrange into regular groups. —noun (grăj'ə-wət) the recipient of a diploma or an academic degree. ▸ **graduation** noun

> **Usage** Avoid the transitive use of graduate, as in 'They graduated college'. Write instead 'They graduated from college'.

Graeco- combining form same as **Greco-**.

graffito (grə-fēt'ō) noun (pl. **graffiti**) a drawing or inscription on walls etc., in public places.

graft¹ noun **1** a shoot of a plant, attached to another plant. **2** the surgical transfer of an organ or tissue from one individual or site to another. **3** material transferred in this way. —verb trans., intrans. (**grafted, grafting**) **1** to attach a graft in; to attach as a graft. **2** to attach grafts.

graft² noun slang the use of illegal or unfair means to gain profit; the profit gained. —verb intrans., trans. (**grafted, grafting**) slang to gain profit through corruption.

graham cracker a rectangular, sweet, whole wheat cracker.

grain noun **1** a single small hard fruit, resembling a seed. **2** any of the cereal plants, e.g., wheat, corn, that produce such fruits. **3** a small hard particle. **4** a very small amount: a grain of truth. **5** the smallest unit of avoirdupois weight, equal to 0.0026 oz. (0.065 g). **6** the arrangement, size, and direction of the

fibers in wood. **7** the main direction of the threads in a woven fabric. —verb trans., intrans. (**grained, graining**) **1** to paint or stain with a pattern like the grain of wood. —**go against the grain** to be against one's principles. **with a grain of salt** with skepticism. ▸ **grainy** adj

gram noun (ABBREV. **g, gm, gr., gr**) one thousandth of a kilogram.

-gram combining form denoting something written or recorded in a specified way: diagram / telegram.

grammar noun **1** the accepted rules by which words are formed and combined into sentences. **2** the branch of language study dealing with these. **3** a description of these rules as applied to a particular language; a book containing it. **4** writing or speech judged according to these rules: bad grammar.

grammarian noun an expert in grammar.

grammar school 1 an elementary school. **2** Brit. a secondary school emphasizing the study of academic subjects.

grammatical adj. **1** relating to grammar. **2** correct according to the rules of grammar. ▸ **grammatically** adv.

gramme (grăm) noun Brit. gram.

gramophone noun Brit., old a record player.

grampus noun (pl. **grampuses**) a large sea mammal related to the dolphin.

granary (grăn'ə-rē, grā'nə-) noun (pl. **granaries**) a building in which grain is stored.

grand adj. **1** large or impressive. **2** dignified; self-important. **3** intended to impress. **4** in full; complete: a grand total. **5** very pleasant; excellent. **6** highest ranking; greatest: Grand Master. —noun **1** slang **a** a thousand dollars. **b** Brit. a thousand pounds. **2** colloq. a grand piano. ▸ **grandly** adv.

grand- combining form indicating a family relationship that is one generation more remote than that of the base word: grandparents.

grandchild noun a child of one's son or daughter.

granddaughter noun a daughter of one's son or daughter.

grandee (grăn-dē') noun **1** a Spanish or Portuguese nobleman of the highest rank. **2** a well-respected or high-ranking person.

grandeur (grăn'jər) noun **1** greatness of character. **2** impressive beauty; magnificence.

grandfather noun the father of one's father or mother. —verb trans. (**grandfathered, grandfathering**) to exempt (a party already involved) from new regulations.

grandfather clock noun a clock built into a tall freestanding wooden case, operated by a long pendulum.

grandiloquent adj. speaking, spoken, or written in a pompous, self-important style. ▸ **grandiloquence** noun ▸ **grandiloquently** adv.

grandiose adj. 1 splendid; magnificent; impressive. 2 exaggeratedly impressive or imposing.

grand mal a serious form of epilepsy.

grandmother noun the mother of one's father or mother.

Grand Old Party (ABBREV. **GOP**) the Republican Party of the USA.

grandparent noun either parent of one's father or mother.

grand piano a large piano in which the strings are arranged horizontally.

grand slam 1 a Sport the winning in one season of every part of a competition, or of all major competitions. **b** Baseball a home run that is hit when there are already three runners on the three bases. **2** Cards esp. in bridge, the winning of all 13 tricks by one player or side, or the contract to do so.

grandson noun a son of one's son or daughter.

grandstand noun the largest covered stand at a sports ground, providing the best view. —verb intrans. (**grandstanded**, **grandstanding**) slang to engage in ostentatious behavior intended to impress.

grange noun 1 (**Grange**) an association of US farmers, or a local lodge in this association. 2 Brit. a country house with farm buildings attached.

granite (grăn′ĭt) noun Geol. a hard coarse-grained igneous rock, widely used in the construction of buildings and roads. ▸ **granitic** (grə-nĭt′ĭk) adj.

granola (grə-nō′lə) noun a breakfast cereal made of rolled oats, brown sugar, nuts, and dried fruits.

grant verb trans. (**granted**, **granting**) 1 to give, allow, or fulfill. 2 to admit to be true. —noun 1 something granted, esp. an amount of money from a public fund. 2 Law the transfer of property by deed.

grantee noun the party to which a grant is made.

grantor (grănt′ər, grăn′tôr,) noun the party making a grant.

granular (grăn′yə-lər) adj. 1 made of or containing tiny particles or granules. 2 of appearance or texture rough. ▸ **granularity** (grăn-yə-lă′rĭ-tĭ) noun

granulate verb trans., intrans. (**granulated**, **granulating**) 1 to break down into small particles or granules. 2 to give a rough appearance or texture to. ▸ **granulation** noun

granule noun a very small particle or grain.

grape noun 1 a pale green or purplish-black, edible berry, widely used in wine-making. 2 literary (the grape) wine.

grapefruit noun (pl. **grapefruit**, **grapefruits**) a large edible citrus fruit with juicy acidic pale yellow or pink flesh.

grape hyacinth a plant with grasslike leaves and blue flowers hanging in clusters.

grapeshot noun ammunition in the form of small iron balls, spreading when fired from a cannon.

grapevine noun 1 a vine on which grapes grow. 2 colloq. informal conversation between people: I heard it on the grapevine.

graph noun 1 a diagram consisting of two axes, with points representing different sets of data plotted in the areas between them. 2 a bar or pie chart. —verb trans. (**graphed**, **graphing**) to represent with a graph.

-graph combining form forming words denoting: 1 an instrument that writes or records: telegraph. 2 something written or recorded: autograph.

graphic or **graphical** adj. 1 described or shown vividly and in detail: graphic violence. 2 of the branch of the arts concerned with drawing, printing, and lettering: graphic design. 3 relating to graphs; shown using a graph. ▸ **graphically** adv.

-graphic or **-graphical** combining form forming adjectives corresponding to nouns in -graph and -graphy: telegraphic / geographical.

graphics noun 1 (sing.) the art or science of drawing according to mathematical principles. 2 (pl.) the photographs and illustrations used in a magazine. 3 (sing., pl.) Comput. the use of computers to manipulate information in graphic form or the images generated by this.

graphic user interface (ABBREV. **GUI**) Comput. a system that uses icons on the screen to represent programs, files, and menu choices.

graphite noun a soft black carbon used in lubricants, paints, and lead pencils.

graphology noun the study of handwriting, esp. as a way of analyzing the writer's character. ▸ **graphologist** noun

-graphy combining form 1 a type of writing or method of representing: biography / lithography. 2 a descriptive science or art: geography / choreography.

grapnel (grăp′nəl) noun 1 a large multi-pointed hook, used for securing heavy objects. 2 a light anchor for small boats.

grappa (grăp′ə) noun a brandy distilled from the grape residue left in a wine press.

grapple verb intrans., trans. (**grappled**, **grappling**) 1 (**grapple with**) to struggle with (something or someone). 2 to secure with a hook, etc. —noun 1 a device, e.g., a hook, for securing. 2 an act of gripping, as in wrestling; a way of gripping.

grasp verb trans., intrans. (**grasped**, **grasping**) 1 to take a firm hold of, or to attempt to do so; to clutch. 2 to understand: couldn't grasp the lecture. —noun 1 a grip or hold. 2 ability to reach, achieve, or obtain: in one's *grasp.* **3** ability to understand: *a lecture beyond their grasp.*

grasping *adj.* greedy or miserly.

grass *noun* **1 a** a plant typically with long narrow leaves with parallel veins and a jointed upright stem. **b** an area planted with or growing such plants, e.g., a lawn or meadow. **2** *slang* marijuana. **3** *Brit. slang* a person who betrays others, esp. to the police. —*verb intrans.* (**grassed, grassing**) *Brit. slang* (*often* **grass on**) to inform, esp. to the police. ▸ **grassy** *adj.*

grasshopper *noun* a large jumping insect with long, powerful, hind legs, and short antennae.

grass roots (*sing., pl.*) **1** ordinary people, as opposed to those in political power. **2** the bare essentials; the fundamental principles: *get to the grass roots of the issue.* ▸ **grass-roots** *adj.*

grass snake a harmless snake with black and yellow patches on the back of its neck.

grate[1] *noun* a framework of iron bars for holding coal, etc., in a fireplace or furnace.

grate[2] *verb trans., intrans.* (**grated, grating**) **1** to cut (food) into shreds by rubbing against a rough surface. **2** to make, or cause to make, a harsh grinding sound by rubbing. **3** (**grate on**) to irritate or annoy (another or a person's nerves). ▸ **grater** *noun*

grateful *adj.* **1** feeling thankful; showing or giving thanks. **2** pleasant and welcome: *grateful sleep.* ▸ **gratefully** *adv.* ▸ **gratefulness** *noun*

gratify *verb trans.* (**gratified, gratifying, gratifies**) **1** to please. **2** to satisfy or indulge (e.g., a desire). ▸ **gratification** *noun*

grating[1] *noun* a framework of metal bars set, e.g., over a window or over a drain.

grating[2] *adj.*, of sounds, etc. harsh and irritating. —*noun* a harsh, irritating sound.

gratis (grăt'ĭs, grăt'-) *adv., adj.* without charge; free.

gratitude *noun* thankfulness or the expression of it.

gratuitous (grə-tōō'ə-təs) *adj.* **1** unnecessary or unjustified. **2** given or received without charge; voluntary. ▸ **gratuitously** *adv.*

gratuity (grə-tōō'ət-ē, -tyōō'-) *noun* (*pl.* **gratuities**) a sum of money given for good service; a tip.

grave[1] *noun* **1 a** a deep trench dug in the ground for burying a corpse. **b** the site of an individual burial. **2** (**the grave**) death: *rose from the grave.* —**dig one's own grave** to be the cause of one's own downfall.

grave[2] *adj.* **1** giving cause for great concern. **2** very important in terms of the consequences: *a grave decision.* ▪ HEAVY, SEVERE, SOBER, WEIGHTY ▫ LIGHT, TRIFLING, TRIVIAL. **3** solemn and serious in manner. ▸ **gravely** *adv.*

grave[3] (gräv, grāv) *noun* a mark placed over a vowel (e.g., *à, è*) in some languages to indicate a particular pronunciation.

gravel *noun* a mixture of small loose rock fragments. —*verb trans.* (**graveled** *or* **gravelled, graveling** *or* **gravelling**) to cover (e.g., a road) with gravel.

gravelly *adj.* **1** full of, or containing, small stones. **2** *of a voice* rough and usu. deep.

graven (grā'vən) *adj.* **1** carved or engraved. **2** firmly fixed in the mind.

gravestone *noun* a stone marking a grave.

graveyard *noun* a cemetery.

gravid (grăv'ĭd) *adj. Medicine* pregnant.

gravimeter (grə-vĭm'ət-ər, grăv'ĭ-mēt,ər) *noun Geol.* an instrument for measuring specific gravity.

gravitas (grăv'ĭ-täs,) *noun literary* seriousness of manner; solemnity.

gravitate (grăv'ĭ-tāt,) *verb intrans.* (**gravitated, gravitating**) **1** to be drawn under the force of gravity. **2** to move or be drawn gradually. ▸ **gravitation** *noun* ▸ **gravitational** *adj.*

gravity[1] *noun* **1** the observed effect of the force of attraction that exists between two massive bodies.

gravity[2] *noun* **1** dangerous nature; seriousness: *Are you aware of the gravity of this situation?* **2** serious tone; solemnity: *the gravity of a state funeral.*

gravlax (grăv'lăks,) *or* **gravadlax** *noun* a Scandanavian dish made with dry-cured salmon and dill.

gravure (grə-vyŏŏr') *noun* **1** a method of printing using etched cylinders. **2** an image produced by this process. *See also* **photogravure.**

gravy *noun* (*pl.* **gravies**) **1** the juices released by meat as it is cooking. **2** a sauce made by thickening and seasoning these juices. **3** *slang* easily obtained money.

gray[1] *or* **grey** *adj.* **1** of a color between black and white. **2** *of the weather* dull and cloudy. **3 a** *of a person's hair* turning white. **b** *of a person* having gray hair. **4** anonymous or uninteresting. —*noun* **1** a color between black and white. **2** dull light. —*verb trans., intrans.* (**grayed, graying**) to make or become gray. ▸ **grayness** *noun*

grayhound *noun same as* **greyhound.**

gray matter 1 the tissue of the brain and spinal cord. **2** *colloq.* intelligence or common sense.

graze[1] *verb intrans., trans.* (**grazed, grazing**) *of animals* to eat grass.

graze[2] *verb trans.* (**grazed, grazing**) **1** to suffer a break in the skin through scraping. **2** to brush against lightly in passing. —*noun* **1** an area of grazed skin. **2** the act of grazing the skin.

grease *noun* **1** animal fat softened by melting.

2 a thick oily substance, esp. a lubricant for machinery. —*verb trans.* (**greased, greasing**) **1** to lubricate or soil with grease. **2** to ease the progress of.

greasepaint *noun* waxy makeup used by actors.

greaser *noun* a person whose job it is to grease machinery.

greasy *adj.* (**greasier, greasiest**) **1** containing or covered with grease. **2** having an oily appearance or texture. **3** *colloq.* insincerely friendly or flattering. ▸ **greasiness** *noun*

great (grāt) *adj.* **1** outstandingly talented, and much admired and respected. **2** very large in size, quantity, intensity, or extent. **3** *colloq.* very enjoyable; excellent or splendid. **4** *colloq.* (**great at**) clever at doing (something); talented. **5** most important: *the great advantage of it.* **6** *colloq.* used to emphasize other adjectives describing size, esp. *big*: *a great big dog.* —*noun* a person who has achieved lasting fame: *the all-time greats of classical music.* ▸ **greatly** *adv.* ▸ **greatness** *noun*

great- *combining form* indicating a family relationship that is one generation more remote than that of the base word: *great-grandmother.*

greatcoat *noun* a heavy overcoat.

Great Dane one of the largest breeds of dogs, with a short smooth coat, long powerful legs, and a square head.

greater or **Greater** *adj.* considered or being part of the environs of a major urban center: *the greater metropolitan area of Chicago / Greater Newark.*

grebe *noun* a ducklike waterbird with lobed toes and sometimes colorful plumes.

Grecian (grē'shən) *adj., of a design, etc.* in the style of ancient Greece.

Greco- or **Graeco-** *combining form* forming words relating to Greece or Greek: *Greco-Roman.*

greed *noun* **1** selfish desire in general, e.g., for money. **2** an excessive desire for food. ▸ **greedy** *adj.* ▸ **greedily** *adv.* ▸ **greediness** *noun*

Greek (grēk) *noun* **1** a native or citizen of Greece. **2** the language of Greece. **3** *colloq.* language one cannot understand. —*adj.* of Greece, its people, or their language.

green *adj.* **1** of the color of the leaves of most plants, between yellow and blue in the spectrum. **2** covered with grass, bushes, etc.: *green areas of the city.* **3** consisting mainly of leaves: *a green salad.* **4** of fruit yet to ripen. **5** *colloq., of people* young and inexperienced: *green recruits.* ☐ FRESH, INEXPERIENCED, RAW, UNSEASONED ☒ EXPERIENCED, HARDENED, MATURE, SEASONED. **6 a** designed to be harmless to

the environment: *green cars.* **b** (*often* **Green**) supporting a global political movement that is concerned with the protection of the Earth's environment. **7** extremely jealous or envious. —*noun* **1** the color of the leaves of most plants, between yellow and blue in the spectrum. **2** an area of grass, esp. in a public place. **3** (**greens**) vegetables with edible green leaves and stems. **5** (*often* **Green**) a person who supports actions or policies designed to benefit the environment. —*verb trans., intrans.* (**greened, greening**) to make or become green in color.

greenback *noun colloq.* a US currency note.

green bean any variety of bean of which the unripe pod and contents are eaten whole.

greenbelt open land surrounding a town or city, where building or development is strictly controlled.

green card a document issued to aliens by the US Government, permitting them to work legally.

greenery *noun* green plants or their leaves.

green-eyed *adj. colloq.* jealous; envious.

greenfly *noun* (*pl.* **greenfly, greenflies**) any of various species of aphids that feed by sucking plant sap.

greengage *noun* a small round edible fruit resembling a plum, but with greenish-brown flesh.

greengrocer *noun Brit.* a person or shop selling fruit and vegetables. ▸ **greengrocery** *noun*

greenhorn *noun colloq.* an inexperienced person; a novice.

greenhouse *noun* a building, usu. made of glass or clear plastic, for growing plants that need special protection or conditions.

greenhouse effect the warming of the Earth's surface as a result of the trapping of long-wave radiation in the Earth's atmosphere.

green light 1 a signal to move forward. **2** *colloq.* (**the green light**) permission to proceed: *We've got the green light to proceed with the deal.*

green pepper a green unripe sweet pepper, eaten as a vegetable. *See also* **red pepper**.

greenroom *noun* a room in a theater, concert hall, etc. where performers prepare to go on stage.

green thumb *colloq.* natural skill at growing plants successfully.

Greenwich Mean Time (ABBREV. **GMT**) the local time at the line of 0° longitude used to calculate times in most other parts of the world.

greet *verb trans.* (**greeted, greeting**) **1** to address or welcome, esp. in a friendly way. **2** to react to in a certain way: *remarks that were greeted with dismay.*

greeting *noun* 1 a friendly expression or gesture used upon meeting someone. 2 (**greetings**) a good wish; a friendly message.

gregarious *adj.* 1 *of a person* liking the company of other people. ▣SOCIABLE, SOCIAL ▣ REMOTE, UNSOCIAL, WITHDRAWN. 2 *of an animal* tending to live in groups. ▸ **gregariousness** *noun*

gremlin *noun* an imaginary mischievous creature blamed for faults in machinery or electronic equipment.

grenade *noun* a small bomb thrown by hand or fired from a rifle.

> From a French word for 'pomegranate', because of its shape

grenadier (grĕn,ə-dîr′) *noun* a member of a regiment of soldiers formerly trained in the use of grenades.

grenadine (grĕn′ə-dēn,) *noun* a syrup made from pomegranate juice.

grew *verb see* **grow**.

grey *adj., noun, verb same as* **gray**.

greyhound *or* **grayhound** *noun* a tall breed of dog with a slender body, short coat, arched back and long powerful legs.

grid *noun* 1 a network of lines superimposed on a map, used to identify specific points. 2 a system of electrical distribution serving a region. 3 a framework of metal bars, esp. one covering a drain. 4 *Electron.* an electrode that controls the flow of electrons in a vacuum tube.

griddle *noun* a flat pan or iron plate heated for baking or frying.

griddlecake *noun* a pancake.

gridiron *noun* 1 a frame of iron bars used for grilling food over a fire. 2 *Football* a the playing field. b the sport itself.

gridlock *noun* 1 a situation where large numbers of motor vehicles have come to a halt or are moving only slowly. 2 a situation where progress is being hampered.

grief *noun* 1 great sorrow and unhappiness, esp. at a person's death. 2 an event causing great sorrow. 3 *colloq.* trouble or bother. —**come to grief** to end in failure; to have an accident.

grievance *noun* 1 a real or perceived cause for complaint. 2 a formal complaint, esp. made in the workplace.

grieve *verb intrans., trans.* (**grieved, grieving**) 1 to feel grief, esp. upon the death of a friend or loved one. 2 to upset or distress.

grievous *adj.* 1 very severe or painful. 2 causing or likely to cause grief. 3 showing grief. 4 extremely serious or evil.

griffin *or* **gryphon** *noun Mythol.* a winged monster with an eagle's head and a lion's body.

grill *verb trans.* (**grilled, grilling**) 1 a to cook under radiated heat. b to broil, e.g., on a grid-

iron. 2 *colloq.* to interrogate. —*noun* 1 a device on a stove that radiates heat downward. 2 a metal frame for cooking food over a fire. 3 a dish of grilled food. 4 a restaurant specializing in grilled food.

grille *or* **grill** *noun* a protective framework of metal bars or wires, e.g., over a window.

grilling *noun colloq.* an interrogation.

grim *adj.* (**grimmer, grimmest**) 1 stern and unsmiling. 2 extremely and disturbingly frightening. 3 resolute; dogged: *grim determination.* 4 depressing; gloomy. ▸ **grimly** *adv.* ▸ **grimness** *noun*

grimace (grĭm′əs, grə-mās′) *noun* an ugly twisting of the face. —*verb intrans.* (**grimaced, grimacing**) to twist the face into an ugly expression.

grime *noun* thick ingrained dirt or soot. —*verb trans.* (**grimed, griming**) to soil heavily. ▸ **griminess** *noun* ▸ **grimy** *adj.*

grin *verb intrans., trans.* (**grinned, grinning**) to smile broadly, showing the teeth. —*noun* a broad smile, showing the teeth. —**grin and bear it** *colloq.* to endure something unpleasant without complaining.

grind *verb trans., intrans.* (pa t and pa p **ground;** *pr p* **grinding**) 1 to crush into small particles or powder between two hard surfaces. 2 to sharpen or polish by rubbing against a hard surface. 3 to rub together with a jarring noise. 4 to operate by turning a handle. 5 (**grind down**) to crush the spirit of; to oppress. —*noun* 1 *colloq.* steady, dull, and laborious routine. 2 the act or sound of crushing, sharpening, or polishing. 3 the size or texture of crushed particles. —**grind to a halt** to stop completely and abruptly.

grinder *noun* 1 a person or machine that grinds. 2 a molar. 3 *colloq. same as* **submarine sandwich**.

grindstone *noun* a revolving stone wheel used for sharpening and polishing. —**put one's nose to the grindstone** *colloq.* to work hard and with commitment.

gringo (grĭng′gō) *noun* (*pl.* **gringos**) *derog. slang* an English-speaking foreigner in Latin America, esp. Mexico.

grip *verb trans.* (**gripped, gripping**) 1 to take or keep a firm hold of. 2 to capture the imagination or attention of. —*noun* 1 a firm hold; the action of taking a firm hold. 2 a way of holding firmly. 3 a handle or part that can be held firmly. 4 *Brit.* a hairpin. 5 a suitcase. 6 understanding. 7 control; mastery: *lost her grip of the situation.* 8 a stagehand or member of a film crew. —**come to grips with (something)** to begin to deal successfully with (something).

gripe *verb intrans., trans.* (**griped, griping**) 1 *colloq.* to complain persistently. 2 to feel, or cause to feel, intense stomach pain. —*noun* 1

gripping *adj.* fully occupying the mind.

grisly *adj.* (**grislier, grisliest**) extremely and disturbingly frightening. ▸ **grisliness** *noun*

grist *noun* cereal grain that is to be, or that has been, ground into flour in a mill. —**grist for one's** *or* **the mill** something that is, or that will prove to be, useful or profitable; a useful contribution.

gristle (grĭs′əl) *noun* cartilage, esp. in meat. ▸ **gristly** *adj.*

grit *noun* 1 small particles or grains of rock. 2 courage and determination. —*verb trans.* (**gritted, gritting**) 1 to clench (the teeth). 2 to treat or cover (something) with grit.

grits *noun* (*sing., pl.*) coarsely ground grain, esp. oats, with the husks removed.

gritty *adj.* (**grittier, grittiest**) 1 full of, covered with, or like grit. 2 resolute and determined.

grizzled *adj.* 1 *of the hair* gray or graying. 2 *of a person* having gray or graying hair.

grizzly *adj.* (**grizzlier, grizzliest**) gray or graying; grizzled. —*noun* (*pl.* **grizzlies**) *colloq.* a grizzly bear.

grizzly bear the largest of the bears, having dark brown fur frosted with white.

groan *verb intrans., trans.* (**groaned, groaning**) 1 to make a long deep sound expressing pain, distress, etc. 2 to creak loudly. 3 to be weighed down or almost breaking. —*noun* an act or the sound of groaning.

groats *noun* (*sing., pl.*) crushed grain, esp. oats, with the husks removed.

grocer (grō′sər) *noun* a person selling food and general household goods.

grocery (grō′sə-rē) *noun* (*pl.* **groceries**) 1 the trade or premises of a grocer. 2 (**groceries**) merchandise, esp. food, sold in a grocery store.

grog (grăg) *noun* a mixture of alcoholic spirits, esp. rum and water.

groggy *adj.* (**groggier, groggiest**) *colloq.* weak, dizzy, and unsteady on the feet, e.g., from fatigue, illness, or alcohol. ▸ **groggily** *adv.* ▸ **grogginess** *noun*

> Originally meaning 'drunk', from *grog*, a mixture of rum and water

groin *noun* the part of the body where the abdomen joins the thigh.

grommet *or* **grummet** *noun* a reinforced eyelet in fabric.

groom (grŏŏm, grŏŏm) *noun* 1 a person who takes care of horses and cleans stables. 2 a bridegroom. —*verb trans.* (**groomed, grooming**) 1 to clean and brush (e.g., a horse). 2 to keep (a person) clean, neat, and tidy. 3 to train or prepare for a specific purpose or job.

groove *noun* 1 a long narrow channel, esp. one cut with a tool. 2 the long spiral cut in a phonograph record. 3 *colloq.* a set routine. 4 *slang* a pleasurable experience. —*verb trans., intrans.* (**grooved, grooving**) 1 to cut grooves or a groove in. 2 *slang* to enjoy oneself: *just grooving through a Sunday afternoon.* ▸ **groovy** *adj.*

grope *verb intrans., trans.* (**groped, groping**) 1 to search by feeling about, e.g., in the dark. 2 to search with difficulty: *groping for answers.* 3 to find (one's way) by feeling: *groped my way down the pitch-black corridor.* 4 *colloq.* to touch or fondle (someone) sexually. —*noun colloq.* an act of sexual fondling.

grosbeak (grōs′bēk‚) *noun* a finch with a stout conical beak.

gross (grōs) *adj.* 1 total, with no deductions: *gross weight / gross wages.* 2 very great; flagrant; glaring: *gross negligence.* 3 vulgar; coarse. 4 obese; fat. 5 *colloq.* very unpleasant. —*noun* 1 (*pl.* **gross**) 12 dozen or 144. 2 (*pl.* **grosses**) the total amount or weight, without deductions. —*verb trans.* (**grossed, grossing**) to earn as income or profit, before tax is deducted. —**gross out** *slang* to disgust or repel: *His behavior grossed us out.* ▸ **grossly** *adv.* ▸ **grossness** *noun*

gross national product (ABBREV. **GNP**) the total value of goods and services produced by a country's economy over a specified period.

grotesque *adj.* 1 so unnatural or strange as to cause fear. 2 so absurd as to elicit ridicule. ▸ **grotesquely** *adv.* ▸ **grotesqueness** *noun*

grotto *noun* (*pl.* **grottoes, grottos**) 1 a cave, esp. a small and picturesque one. 2 an artificial cavelike structure, esp. in a garden or park.

grotty *adj.* (**grottier, grottiest**) *Brit. colloq.* 1 unpleasantly dirty or shabby. 2 ill. ▸ **grottiness** *noun*

grouch *colloq. verb intrans.* (**grouched, grouching**) to grumble or complain. —*noun* 1 a complaining person. 2 a bad-tempered complaint; the cause of such a complaint.

grouchy *adj.* (**grouchier, grouchiest**) bad-tempered and complaining.

ground[1] *noun* 1 the solid surface of the Earth, or any part of it; soil; land. 2 (*often* **grounds**) an area of land attached to or surrounding a building. 3 an area of land used for a specific purpose: *a burial ground.* 4 the substance of a discussion: *We covered a lot of ground in the meeting.* 5 (*usu.* **grounds**) a reason or justification: *grounds for requesting a mistrial.* 6 (**grounds**) sediment or dregs, esp. of coffee. 7 an electrical connection with the

Earth. —*verb trans.*, *intrans.* (**grounded**, **grounding**) **1** to base (an argument, complaint, etc.). **2** (**ground in**) to give basic instruction to (someone) in (a given subject). **3** to hit or cause (a ship) to hit the seabed and remain stuck. **4** to refuse to allow (a pilot or airplane) to fly. **5** *colloq.* to restrict (e.g., a teenager) to the home as punishment. **6** *Electr.* to connect to the Earth electrically. **7** *Baseball* to strike a ground ball. —*adj.* on or relating to the ground: *ground forces.* —**get off the ground** to make a start on (something).

ground[2] *verb see* **grind**.

ground ball *Baseball* a ball that, when hit by the batter, bounces and rolls along the ground.

groundbreaking *adj.* new, original, and innovative. ▸ **groundbreaker** *noun*

ground control the control and monitoring from the ground of the flight of aircraft or spacecraft.

grounder *noun Baseball* a ground ball.

ground floor the floor of a building at or nearest to the level of the ground outside.

groundhog *noun* a woodchuck.

grounding *noun* a foundation of basic knowledge or instruction.

groundless *adj.* having no reason or justification.

groundling (grown'dlǐng) *noun* **1** a small freshwater fish that lives close to the bottom of a river or lake. **2** a low-growing or creeping plant.

groundnut *noun Brit.* a peanut.

ground rule (*often* **ground rules**) a basic principle.

groundsel (grownd'səl) *noun* a plant with bright green leaves and small yellow flowers.

ground squirrel a burrowing rodent with yellowish-brown fur.

groundswell *noun* **1** a broad high swell of the sea. **2** a sudden and rapid growth, esp. of public opinion.

ground water *Geol.* water distributed in the rocks beneath the surface of the Earth.

ground work essential preparatory work.

ground zero the point where a nuclear weapon detonates.

group *noun* **1** a number of people or things gathered, placed, or classed together. **2** a band of musicians and singers, esp. playing rock music. —*verb trans.*, *intrans.* (**grouped**, **grouping**) to form or make into a group.

Usage Use a singular verb with the collective noun *group* when the things or the people constituting it are being thought of as a single unit: The fighter *group* is ready for combat operations. Use a plural verb when the things or the people constituting

the *group* are being thought of separately: The *group are* fighting among themselves.

group captain *Brit.* an air force officer equivalent to a US Army colonel.

grouper (grōō'pər) *noun* a large game and food fish that inhabits warm seas.

groupie *noun slang* an ardent follower of a touring rock group, often a young woman seeking a sexual relationship with them.

group therapy a form of psychotherapy that involves the joint participation of several people.

grouse[1] (grows) *noun* (*pl.* **grouse, grouses**) a ground-living game bird with a plump body, short wings, and a short curved bill.

grouse[2] *colloq.* *verb intrans.* (**groused**, **grousing**) to complain in a bad-tempered way. —*noun* a complaint or period of complaining.

grout *noun* thin mortar applied to the joints between bricks or ceramic tiles. —*verb trans.* (**grouted**, **grouting**) to apply grout to the joints of.

grove *noun* **1** a small group of trees. **2** an area planted with fruit trees: *orange groves.*

grovel (grəv'əl, grăv'-) *verb intrans.* (**groveled** *or* **grovelled**, **groveling** *or* **grovelling**) **1** to act with exaggerated respect or humility. **2** to lie or crawl face down, in fear or respect. ▸ **groveler** *noun*

grow *verb intrans.*, *trans.* (*pa t* **grew**; *pa p* **grown**; *pr p* **growing**) **1** of a *living thing* to develop into a larger more mature form. **2** of *hair, nails, etc.* to increase or allow to increase in length. **3** to increase in size, intensity, or extent. **4** to cultivate (plants). **5** to become gradually: *Over the years they grew very lazy.* **6** (**grow to**) to come gradually: *grew to hate him.* —**grow on** to come gradually to be liked. **grow up 1** to become or to be in the process of becoming an adult. **2** to behave in an adult way.

growl *verb intrans.*, *trans.* (**growled**, **growling**) **1** to make a deep rough sound in the throat, showing hostility or displeasure. **2** to complain in a bad-tempered, surly way. —*noun* an act or the sound of growling.

grown *adj.* mature: *a grown woman.* —*verb see* **grow**.

grownup *or* **grown-up** (grō'nəp,) *colloq.* —*adj.* adult. —*noun* an adult.

growth *noun* **1** the process or rate of growing. **2** an increase: *growth in a population.* **3** a tumor.

grub *noun* **1** the wormlike larva of an insect, esp. a beetle. **2** *colloq.* food. —*verb intrans.*, *trans.* (**grubbed**, **grubbing**) **1** to dig or search in the soil. **2** to search generally. **3** to engage in laborious toil.

grubby *adj.* (**grubbier**, **grubbiest**) *colloq.* dirty. ▸ **grubbily** *adv.* ▸ **grubbiness** *noun*

grudge *verb trans.* (**grudged, grudging**) **1** to feel a sense of unfairness or resentment at. **2** to be unwilling to give; to give or admit unwillingly. —*noun* deeply felt resentment.

grudging *adj.* **1** unwilling. **2** resentful. ▸ **grudgingly** *adv.*

gruel (grōō′əl) *noun* thin porridge.

grueling (grōō′ə-lĭng) *adj.* exhausting; punishing.

gruesome (grōō′səm) *adj.* extremely and disturbingly frightening.

> Originally a Scots word, from *grue*, 'be terrified', popularized by Walter Scott

gruff *adj.* **1** *of a voice* deep and rough. **2** rough, unfriendly, or surly in manner. ▸ **gruffly** *adv.* ▸ **gruffness** *noun*

grumble *verb intrans., trans.* (**grumbled, grumbling**) **1** to complain in a bad-tempered way. ▣ GROUSE, GROWL, MUTTER. **2** to rumble. —*noun* **1** a complaint. **2** a rumbling sound. ▸ **grumbler** *noun*

grummet *noun* same as **grommet**.

grump *noun colloq.* **1** a grumpy person. **2** a fit of bad temper or sulking.

grumpy *adj.* (**grumpier, grumpiest**) bad-tempered; surly. ▸ **grumpily** *adv.* ▸ **grumpiness** *noun*

grunge *noun colloq.* **1** dirt; grime; trash. **2** an unpleasant or nasty substance. **3** a crude style of dress; rejecting current fashions.

grungy *adj.* (**grungier, grungiest**) dirty and grimy. ▸ **grunginess** *noun*

grunt *verb intrans., trans.* (**grunted, grunting**) **1** *of animals, esp. pigs* to make a low rough sound in the back of the throat. **2** *of people* to make a low rough sound in the back of the throat, e.g., indicating unwillingness to speak fully. —*noun* an act or the sound of grunting.

Gruyère (grōō-yĕr′, grē-ĕr′) *noun* a pale yellow cheese with holes, orig. made in *Gruyère*, in Switzerland.

gryphon *noun Mythol.* same as **griffin**.

GSA *abbrev.* Girl Scouts of America.

G-string *noun* a thin strip of cloth covering the genital area, attached with a string around the waist.

G-suit *noun* a close-fitting garment, worn by astronauts, that prevents blackout caused by the conditions of high acceleration.

guacamole (gwäk,ə-mō′lē) *noun* a traditional Mexican dish of seasoned and mashed avocado.

guano (gwän′ō) *noun* (*pl.* **guanos**) the droppings of bats, sea birds, or seals, used as a fertilizer.

guarantee (găr,ən-tē′, găr,-) *noun* **1** a formal, usu. written promise, esp. by a manufacturer, to repair or replace an article found to be faulty within a stated period of time. **2** something assuring a given result: *Hard work is often a guarantee of success.* **3** guaranty (senses 1 and 3). —*verb trans.* (**guaranteed, guaranteeing**) **1** to act as, or give, a guarantee for. **2** to promise. **3** to ensure.

guarantor (găr,ən-tôr′, găr′ən-tər) *noun* a party that gives a guarantee.

guaranty (găr′ən-tē, găr′-) *noun* (*pl.* **guaranties**) **1** an agreement, usu. written, to take on another party's responsibility or debt if the party neglects it. *Also called* **guarantee**. **2** a person making such an agreement; a guarantor. **3** something undertaken to be handed over if a contract or agreement is broken. *Also called* **guarantee**. —*verb trans.* (**guarantied, guarantying, guaranties**) to guarantee.

guard *verb trans.* **1** to protect from danger or attack. **2** to prevent from escaping. **3** (**guard against**) to take precautions to prevent (something). —*noun* **1** a person whose job is to provide protection or to prevent escape. **2** *Brit.* a person in charge of a railroad train. **3** a wary or alert state: *on one's guard.* **4 a** *Football* one of the two offensive linemen either side of the center. **b** *Basketball* one of the two players in the back part of the court. **5** something designed to prevent injury.

guarded *adj.* **1** carefully prudent. **2** restrained. ▸ **guardedly** *adv.* ▸ **guardedness** *noun*

guardhouse *noun* a building for guards on duty.

guardian *noun* **1** a person legally responsible for the care of another, esp. a child. **2** a guard, defender, or protector.

guardsman *noun* **1** a guard. **2** a person who serves in the National Guard. **3** a member of a regiment of soldiers known as guards.

guava (gwäv′ə) *noun* a yellow pear-shaped fruit with sweet juicy pulp rich in vitamin C.

gubernatorial (gōō,bər-nə-tôr′ē-əl, -bə-) *adj.* of or relating to a governor.

gudgeon *noun* a metal pivot.

Guernsey (gərn′zē) *noun* (*pl.* **Guernseys**) a breed of dairy cattle that produces high yields of rich creamy milk.

guerrilla *or* **guerilla** (gə-rĭl′ə) *noun* a member of a small armed force making surprise attacks.

guess *verb trans., intrans.* (**guessed, guessing**) **1** to make an estimate based on little or no information. **2** to estimate correctly. **3** to think or suppose: *I guess I'm OK.* —*noun* an estimate based on little or no information.

guesstimate *or* **guestimate** *colloq. noun* (gĕs′tĭ-mət) a rough estimate, based on little knowledge. —*verb trans., intrans.* (gĕs′tĭ-māt,) (**guesstimated, guesstimating**) to make such an estimate of.

guesswork *noun* the process or result of guessing.

guest noun **1** a person who receives hospitality from another. **2** a person staying at a hotel, motel, etc. **3** a person specially invited to take part: *a guest on a talk show.* —verb intrans. (**guested, guesting**) to appear as a guest, e.g., on a television show.

guesthouse noun a private home offering accommodations to paying guests.

guest worker a worker from one country, permitted or invited to work in another country.

guff noun colloq., nonsense.

guffaw noun a loud coarse laugh. —verb intrans. (**guffawed, guffawing**) to make a loud coarse laugh.

GUI abbrev. Comput. graphic user interface.

guidance noun **1** help, advice, or counseling; the act of guiding. **2** direction or leadership.

guide verb trans. (**guided, guiding**) **1** to lead, direct, or show the way to. **2** to control or direct the movement or course of. **3** to advise or influence. —noun **1** a person who leads the way for, e.g., tourists. **2** a device used to direct movement. **3** a guidebook.

guidebook noun a book containing information on a particular subject or place.

guide dog a dog specially trained to guide a sightless person safely.

guideline noun a statement laying out what kind of action is required.

guild noun **1** a medieval association of merchants or craftsmen. **2** an association of people with a common purpose, often supporting a church or museum.

guile noun the ability to deceive or trick; craftiness or cunning. ▸ **guileful** adj. ▸ **guileless** adj.

guillemot (gĭl´ĭ-mät,) noun a black-and-white sea bird with a long narrow bill.

guillotine (gĭl´ə-tēn, gē,ə-tēn´) noun **1** a heavy-bladed instrument for beheading. **2** a device with a large blade to cut paper or metal. —verb trans. (**guillotined, guillotining**) to behead or cut with, or as if with, a guillotine.

> Named after Joseph *Guillotin*, a French doctor who recommended its use during the French Revolution

guilt noun **1** a feeling of shame or remorse. **2** the state of having done wrong or having broken a law. **3** blame.

guiltless adj. innocent.

guilty adj. (**guiltier, guiltiest**) (often **guilty of**) **1** responsible for (a crime or wrongdoing), or judged to be so. **2** feeling, showing, or involving guilt: *a guilty look.* ▸ **guiltily** adv. ▸ **guiltiness** noun

guinea noun **1** an obsolete British gold coin worth 21 shillings. **2** the sum of 21 shillings, now valued at £1.05, used in the calculation

of professional services, the sale of race-horses, and at auctions.

guinea fowl a domesticated bird related to the pheasant, with speckled grayish plumage.

guinea pig 1 a small tailless rodent kept as a pet or used in scientific experiments. **2** colloq. a person used as the subject of an experiment.

guise (gīz) noun **1** outward appearance; intended to deceive or hide. **2** a style or way of dressing.

guitar (gĭ-tär´) noun a musical instrument with a long fretted neck, and usu. six strings that are plucked or strummed. ▸ **guitarist** noun

gulag (gŏŏ´läg,) noun a network of political prisons or labor camps, esp. in the former Soviet Union; one of these prisons or camps.

gulch noun a narrow rocky ravine.

gulf noun **1** a very large inlet of the sea. **2** a vast difference or separation. **3** a deep hollow in the ground; a chasm.

gulfweed noun a brown-colored seaweed with rounded air bladders, found floating in masses. *Also called* **sargasso**.

gull[1] noun a sea bird with a stout body, white or grayish plumage, and a hooked bill.

gull[2] old use verb trans. (**gulled, gulling**) to cheat or deceive. —noun an easily fooled person.

gullet noun the esophagus or throat.

gullible adj. easily tricked or fooled. ▸ **gullibility** noun

gully noun (pl. **gullies, gulleys**) noun a small channel with steep sides, formed by running water.

gulp verb trans., intrans. (**gulped, gulping**) **1** to swallow (food, drink, etc.) in large mouthfuls. **2** to make a swallowing motion, e.g., because of fear. —noun **1** a swallowing motion. **2** an amount swallowed at once; a mouthful.

gum[1] noun the firm fibrous fleshy tissue surrounding the roots of the teeth.

gum[2] noun **1 a** a sticky substance found in the stems and branches of certain plants. **b** this substance or a similar one used as glue. **2** chewing gum. —verb trans. (**gummed, gumming**) to glue with gum.

gum arabic thick, sticky, water-soluble gum exuded by certain acacia trees.

gumball a small, ball-shaped piece of chewing gum coated with a colored sugary substance.

gumbo noun (pl. **gumbos**) **1** a thick soup or stew made from meat or fish, okra, and other vegetables. **2** okra.

gumboil noun a small abscess on the gum.

gumboot noun a long rubber waterproof boot.

gumdrop noun a candy made from hard, transparent jelly.

gummy adj. (**gummier, gummiest**) 1 producing gum. 2 sticky.

gumption noun colloq. 1 common sense; initiative. 2 courage.

gumshoe noun 1 a rubber overshoe; a galosh. 2 slang a detective.

gun noun 1 a weapon that fires bullets or shells from a metal tube. 2 an instrument that forces something out under pressure: a spray gun. 3 colloq. a hired gunman; a shooter. 4 the signal to start, e.g., a race. —verb trans., intrans. (**gunned, gunning**) 1 (**gun down**) to shoot (someone) with a gun. 2 to hunt, using a gun. 3 to accelerate (an engine) by opening its throttle. —**gun for** to try to obtain (something): We're gunning for a pay rise. **jump the gun** to do something before the proper time. **stick to one's guns** to maintain one's position firmly, in an argument, etc.

gunboat noun a small warship with large mounted guns.

gunboat diplomacy diplomacy consisting of threats of military attack.

gun cotton a highly explosive material formed by treating clean cotton with nitric acid and sulfuric acid. Also called **cellulose nitrate, nitrocellulose.**

gun dog a dog trained to find birds or small animals that have been shot.

gunfight noun a fight involving the use of firearms. ▸ **gunfighter** noun

gunfire noun 1 the act of firing guns. 2 the bullets so fired. 3 the sound of the firing of guns.

gung ho extremely enthusiastic or eager.

> Based on a Chinese phrase meaning 'work together'

gunk noun colloq. any slimy semi-solid substance.

gunman noun 1 an armed criminal. 2 an assassin.

gunmetal noun 1 a an alloy of copper, tin, and zinc. b a metal used to make guns. 2 a dark gray color.

gunnel noun Naut. same as **gunwale.**

gunner noun 1 any member of an armed force who operates a heavy gun. 2 Brit. a soldier in an artillery regiment.

gunnery noun 1 the use of guns. 2 the science of designing guns.

gunny noun (pl. **gunnies**) 1 thick coarse jute cloth, used esp. for sacking. 2 a sack made from this.

gunpoint noun the end of the barrel of a gun that points to a target. —**at gunpoint** under the threat of a gun.

gunpowder noun an explosive used in guns.

gunrunning noun the act of smuggling arms into a country. ▸ **gunrunner** noun

gunshot noun 1 bullets fired from a gun. 2 the distance over which a gun can fire a bullet: within gunshot. 3 a sound of a gun firing.

gunwale or **gunnel** (gən'l) noun the upper edge of the side of a ship.

guppy noun (pl. **guppies**) a small brightly-colored freshwater fish.

gurgle verb intrans., trans. (**gurgled, gurgling**) 1 of water to make a bubbling noise when flowing. 2 to make or express with a bubbling noise in the throat: —noun a watery bubbling noise.

gurney noun (pl. **gurneys**) a metal wheeled stretcher for transporting patients.

guru (gŏŏr'ōō, gə-rōō') noun 1 a Hindu or Sikh spiritual leader or teacher. 2 a greatly respected and influential leader or mentor.

gush verb intrans., trans. (**gushed, gushing**) 1 of a liquid to flood out suddenly and violently. 2 to speak or act with an affected and exaggerated emotion. —noun 1 a sudden violent flooding. 2 exaggerated emotion or enthusiasm.

gusher noun an oil well from which oil flows under great pressure without the use of pumps.

gusset noun a piece of material sewn into a garment for added strength or to allow for freedom of movement.

gussy verb trans. (**gussied, gussying, gussies**) slang (often **gussy up**) to dress in an elaborate manner; to overdress.

gust noun 1 a sudden blast or rush, e.g., of wind or smoke. 2 an emotional outburst. —verb intrans. (**gusted, gusting**) of the wind to blow in sudden rushes. ▸ **gusty** adj.

gusto (gəs'tō) noun enthusiastic enjoyment; vigor.

gut noun 1 the alimentary canal, or a section of it. 2 (**guts**) colloq. the insides of a person or animal. 3 colloq. the stomach or abdomen. 4 colloq. a fat stomach; a paunch. 5 (**guts**) colloq. courage or determination. 6 a strong thread made from animal intestines; catgut. —verb trans. (**gutted, gutting**) 1 to take the guts out of (e.g., fish). 2 to destroy the insides of: Fire gutted the building. —adj. based on instinct and emotion: a gut reaction. —**hate someone's guts** colloq. to have a violent dislike for (the one specified).

gutless adj. having or displaying a contemptible lack of courage. ▸ **gutlessly** adv. ▸ **gutlessness** noun

gutsy adj. (**gutsier, gutsiest**) colloq. courageous and determined.

gutta-percha noun a whitish rubbery substance, obtained from certain tropical trees, used in dentistry and in the manufacture of golf balls.

gutter noun 1 a channel for carrying away surface water. 2 (**the gutter**) a state of poverty and social deprivation. —*verb intrans., trans.* **(guttered, guttering) 1 a** *of a candle* to melt away. **b** to flicker. **2** to wear away channels in.

guttering *noun* **1** gutters collectively. **2** material for making roof gutters.

guttersnipe *noun* a raggedly dressed or ill-mannered person, esp. a street child.

guttural (gŭt′ə-rəl) *adj.* **1** *of sounds* produced deep in the throat. **2** *of a language* having or using such sounds. ▸ **gutturally** *adv.*

guy¹ (gī) *noun* **1** *colloq.* a man or boy. **2** *Brit.* a crude model of a man, burned in Britain on a bonfire on Guy Fawkes Day, Nov. 5. —*verb trans.* **(guyed, guying)** to tease.

guy² *noun* a rope or wire used to hold something, esp. a tent, firm or steady. —*verb trans.* **(guyed, guying)** to secure with guys.

guzzle *verb trans., intrans.* **(guzzled, guzzling)** to drink or eat greedily. ▸ **guzzler** *noun*

gybe (jīb) *verb, noun Naut.* same as **jibe¹**.

gym (jĭm) *noun* **1** a gymnasium. **2** a course in physical education, taken in school. **3** a frame used by children in outdoor play.

gymkhana (jĭm-kän′ə) *noun* a local public event consisting of competitions in horse riding.

gymnasium (jĭm-nā′zē-əm) *noun* (*pl.* **gymnasiums, gymnasia**) **1** a building or room with equipment for physical exercise. **2** in various European countries, a top-grade secondary school.

gymnastics *noun* (*pl.*) physical exercises designed to strengthen the body and improve agility, usu. using special equipment. ▸ **gymnast** *noun* ▸ **gymnastic** *adj.*

gymnosperm *noun* any plant that produces seeds borne on the surface of special leaves, e.g. in cones.

gym shoe a light, canvas, usu. rubber-soled, shoe.

gynecology *noun* the branch of medicine concerned with the treatment of diseases and disorders that affect the female reproductive organs. ▸ **gynecological** *adj.* ▸ **gynecologist** *noun*

gyp or **gip** (jĭp) *slang verb* **(gypped** or **gipped, gypping** or **gipping)** to cheat or swindle. —*noun* a cheat.

gypsophila (jĭp-säf′ə-lə) *noun* a plant with branching heads of small white flowers, widely used by florists.

gypsum *noun* a soft mineral used to make plaster of Paris, cement, rubber, and paper.

Gypsy or **Gipsy** (jĭp′sē) *noun* (*pl.* **Gypsies, Gipsies**) **1** a member of a traveling people, orig. from NW India, now scattered throughout Europe and N America. *See also* **Romany**. **2** (*gypsy*) a person whose lifestyle is nomadic and unconventional.

> Based on *Egyptian*, because of the belief that the Romanies came originally from Egypt

gypsy moth a moth with hairy caterpillars that are highly destructive to trees.

gyrate *verb intrans.* **(gyrated, gyrating)** to move with a circular or spiraling motion. ▸ **gyration** *noun*

gyrene (gī-rēn′) *noun slang* a US Marine.

gyrfalcon (jər′făl,kən, -fôl,-) *noun* a large falcon with plumage ranging from grayish-brown to white.

gyro¹ (zhĭr′ō, jĭr′ō, yĭr′ō) *noun* (*pl.* **gyros**) a sandwich of pita bread stuffed with roasted lamb, tomato, and onion.

gyro² (jī′rō) *noun* (*pl.* **gyros**) *slang* **1** a gyroscope. **2** a gyrocompass.

gyrocompass *noun* a nonmagnetic compass containing a spinning disk that registers true north.

gyroscope (jī′rə-skōp,) *noun* a device that can rotate freely at high speed in any direction; used in ship stabilizers and navigation systems. ▸ **gyroscopic** *adj.*

Hh

H¹ or **h** *noun* (**Hs, H's, h's**) the eighth letter of the English alphabet.

H² or **h** *abbrev.* hospital.

H³ *symbol* **1** *Phys.* henry. **2** *Chem.* hydrogen.

h. or **h** *abbrev.* **1** hardness. **2** height.

ha¹ *interj.* used to express surprise, happiness, triumph, etc.

ha² or **ha.** *abbrev.* hectare.

habeas corpus (hā′bē-əs-kôr′pəs) *Law* a writ requiring a party to be brought into court for a judge to decide if the party has been unlawfully jailed.

haberdasher *noun* **1** a shop selling men's furnishings. **2** *Brit.* a shop dealing in small items used for sewing.

haberdashery *noun* (*pl.* **haberdasheries**)

1 a haberdasher's shop, business, or department. **2** the merchandise sold by a haberdasher.·

habit noun **1** a usual or regular practice or tendency. **2** a practice, sometimes bad, which is hard to give up. **3** mental attitude or constitution. **4** a long, loose garment worn by friars and nuns. ▸ **habit-forming** adj.

habitable adj. suitable for living in. ▸ **habitability** noun

habitat noun the natural home of an animal or plant.

habitation noun **1** the act of living, e.g., in a building. **2** a house or home.

habitual (hə-bĭch′ə-wəl) adj. **1** seen, done, etc., regularly. **2** done or doing something by habit. ▸ **habitually** adv.

habituate (hə-bĭch′ə-wāt,) verb trans. (**habituated, habituating**) to make (someone or something) accustomed to something. ▸ **habituation** noun

habitué (hə-bĭch′ə-wā,) noun a regular or frequent visitor to a place, e.g., a restaurant.

hack¹ verb trans., intrans. (**hacked, hacking**) **1** to cut or chop roughly. **2** (often **hack** (**something**) **out**) to cut (a path, etc.) roughly. **3** colloq. (**hack into**) to obtain access to computer files without authority. **4** slang to be able to bear or suffer. **5** to cough in a rough, dry, harsh manner. —noun **1** a wound or rough cut, esp. from a kick. **2** a hoe.

hack² noun **1 a** a horse kept for general riding, esp. one for hire. **b** a ride on horseback. **2 a** writer, journalist, etc., who produces dull, mediocre, or routine work. —verb intrans. (**hacked, hacking**) to travel on horseback at a leisurely pace, usu. for pleasure.

hacker noun colloq. **1** a skilled computer user who gains unauthorized access to other computer systems. **2** a computer enthusiast or a skilled computer programmer.

hacking noun colloq. the act of gaining access to computer files without permission. —adj., of a cough rough, dry, and harsh.

hackles pl. noun the hairs on the back of the neck of a dog or cat, that rise when angered or alarmed. —**get** (**someone's**) **hackles up** to make (someone) irritated or insulted.

hackney noun (pl. **hackneys**) a· horse for general riding.

hackneyed adj., of a word or phrase lacking freshness and originality.

hacksaw noun a saw used for cutting metal.

had see **have.**

haddock (hăd′ək) noun (pl. **haddock, haddocks**) a small food fish related to the cod.

hadn't contr. had not.

haem-, haemato- or **haemo-** combining form same as **hem-, hemato-, hemo-.**

hafnium (hăf′nē-əm) noun (SYMBOL Hf) a silvery metal used mainly in tungsten alloys for filaments in light bulbs and electrodes.

haft noun a handle, e.g. of a knife, sword or ax.

hag noun **1** offensive an ugly old woman. **2** a witch.

haggard adj. looking very tired and thin-faced.

> Originally a falconer's term for an untamed hawk

haggle verb intrans. (**haggled, haggling**) to argue over, e.g., a price. ▸ **haggler** noun

hagiography (hăg,ē-äg′rə-fē, hăj,-) noun (pl. **hagiographies**) the writing of stories about the lives of saints. ▸ **hagiographer** noun

hail¹ noun **1** precipitation that consists of pellets of ice. **2** a large number or amount of individual items, e.g., words, questions, missiles. —verb intrans., trans. (**hailed, hailing**) **1** of hail to fall. **2** to shower with e.g. words, questions, missiles.

hail² verb trans., intrans. (**hailed, hailing**) **1** to call out to in order to attract attention; to signal. **2** to greet. **3** to recognize or describe as being or representing. **4** to come from or belong to a place.

hailstone noun a single pellet of hail.

hailstorm noun a storm during which hail falls.

hair noun **1 a** each of many long threadlike structures that grow out from the skin of mammals. **b** a mass of these, esp. on a person's head. **c** something resembling one of these. **d** a threadlike cell growing from the surface of a plant. **2** a tiny or minute distance. —**get in** (**someone's**) **hair** colloq. to annoy or irritate (someone). **split hairs** to make small, unnecessary distinctions. ▸ **hairless** adj.

hairbrush noun a brush for smoothing the hair.

haircut noun **1** the cutting of a person's hair. **2** the shape or style in which it is cut.

hairdo (hăr′dōō,, hĕr′-) noun (pl. **hairdos**) **1** a style of hairdressing. **2** a woman's haircut or style.

hairdresser noun **1** a person who cuts, washes, and styles hair. **2** a shop providing these services. ▸ **hairdressing** noun

hairdryer or **hairdrier** noun an electric apparatus that dries a person's hair by blowing hot air over it.

hairline noun the line along the forehead where the hair begins to grow. —adj., of a crack very thin.

hairnet noun a fine-meshed net, worn to keep the hair in place.

hairpin noun a thin, flat, U-shaped piece of wire for keeping the hair in place. —adj., of a road bend very sharp and U-shaped.

hair-raising adj. extremely frightening.

hairspray noun liquid sprayed on the hair for keeping it in place.

hairspring *noun* a very small spring that regulates a watch or a clock.

hairstyle *noun* the way in which a person's hair is cut or shaped.

hairy *adj.* (**hairier**, **hairiest**) **1** covered with hair. **2** *colloq.* dangerous, frightening, and exciting. ▸ **hairiness** *noun*

hake *noun* (*pl.* **hake**, **hakes**) a food fish, closely related to the cod.

halcyon (hăl'sē-ən) *adj.* peaceful, calm, and happy.

> From the Greek word for 'kingfisher' in the phrase 'kingfisher days', a period of calm weather in mid-winter

hale *adj.* having, showing, or enjoying good health.

half (hăf, häf) *noun* (*pl.* **halves**) **1** one of two equal parts that together form a whole. **2** the fraction equal to one divided by two. **3** one of two equal periods of play in a sport. —*adj.* forming or equal to half. —*adv.* **1** to the extent or amount of one half. **2** to some extent; almost; partly. **3** 30 minutes past the hour stated.

half-and-half *adv.*, *adj.* in equal parts.

halfback *noun* **1** (ABBREV. **hb**, **h.b.**) *Football* a player or position behind the line of scrimmage near the flanks. **2** *Sport* a soccer or hockey player or position immediately behind the forwards.

half-baked *adj. colloq.*, *of an idea or plan* not properly or completely thought out.

half-breed *noun*, *offensive* a person whose parents are of different ethnic types.

half brother a brother with whom one has only one parent in common.

half-caste *noun*, *offensive* a person having parents of different races.

half-dollar *noun* a US coin worth 50 cents.

halfhearted *adj.* feeling or showing no eagerness or enthusiasm. ▸ **halfheartedly** *adv.* ▸ **halfheartedness** *noun*

half-hour *noun* a period of 30 minutes. ▸ **half-hourly** *adv.*

half-mast *noun* the position halfway up a flagpole, at which flags are flown as a mark of respect for a deceased person.

half-moon *noun* **1 a** the Moon in its first or last quarter, when half of its disk is illuminated. **b** the time at which this occurs. **2** anything shaped like a half-moon.

half note *Mus.* a note that has half the value of a whole note. *Also called* **minim**.

half-price *adj.*, *adv.* being or at half the usual price.

half sister a sister with whom one has only one parent in common.

halftime *noun* (ABBREV **HT**) *Sport* an interval between the two halves of a game.

half-truth *noun* a statement that is only partially true. ▸ **half-true** *adj.*

halfway *adj.* equally distant from two points. —*adv.* to, or at, half the distance.

halfwit *noun offensive* a foolish or stupid person. ▸ **halfwitted** *adj.* ▸ **halfwittedly** *adv.*

halibut *noun* (*pl.* **halibut**, **halibuts**) a large flatfish used for food.

halitosis *noun* bad breath.

hall *noun* **1** a room or passage just inside the entrance to a house or apartment. **2** a building or large room, used, e.g., for concerts. **3** a large country house. **4** a building where university or college students live.

hallelujah (hăl,ə-loo'yə) *interj. same as* **alleluia**.

hallmark *noun* **1** an official mark on a gold or silver article guaranteeing its quality. **2** a typical or distinctive feature, esp. of quality. —*verb trans.* (**hallmarked**, **hallmarking**) to stamp with a hallmark.

hallowed (hăl'ōd, hăl'ə-wəd) *adj.* holy; revered.

hallucination *noun* the apparent perception of something that does not really exist. ▸ **hallucinate** *verb intrans.* ▸ **hallucinatory** *adj.*

hallway *noun* an entrance hall.

halo *noun* (*pl.* **halos**, **haloes**) a ring of light around the head of a saint, angel, etc., in paintings, etc.

halogen *noun* any of the five non-metallic chemical elements fluorine, chlorine, bromine, iodine, or astatine.

halt *noun* **1** a short or temporary stop. **2** *Brit.* a small railroad station without a building. —*verb trans.*, *intrans.* (**halted**, **halting**) to stop, or cause to stop.

halter *noun* **1** a rope or strap for holding and leading a horse by its head. **2** a bodice for a girl or woman that ties around the neck and waist. —*verb trans.* (**haltered**, **haltering**) to put a halter on.

haltertop *noun* a woman's top or dress with a halter bodice.

halting *adj.* pausing a lot; hesitant. ▸ **haltingly** *adv.*

halvah (häl-vä', häl'və) *or* **halva** *noun* a sweetmeat containing sesame seeds, honey, nuts, rosewater, and saffron.

halve *verb trans.* (**halved**, **halving**) **1** to divide into two equal parts. **2** to reduce (costs, problems, etc.) by half.

halves *see* **half**.

ham[1] *noun* **1** the top part of the back leg of a hog, salted and smoked and used as food. **2** the back of the thigh.

ham[2] *colloq. noun* **1** a bad actor, esp. one who overacts. **2** an amateur radio operator. —*verb intrans.*, *trans.* (**hammed**, **hamming**) (*also* **ham** (**something**) **up**) to overact.

hamburger *noun* a flat, round cake of finely chopped beef, usu. served in a soft roll.

ham-fisted *or* **ham-handed** *adj. colloq.* clumsy.

hamlet *noun* a small village.

hammer *noun* 1 a tool for driving nails or breaking hard substances. 2 the part of a bell, piano, etc., that hits against another part, making a noise. 3 *Sport* a metal ball on a chain, thrown in competitions. —*verb trans., intrans.* (**hammered, hammering**) 1 to hit with a hammer. 2 *slang* to defeat.

hammerhead *noun* a shark with a hammer-shaped head.

hammock *noun* a piece of netting or canvas hung by the corners and used as a bed.

hamper¹ *verb trans.* (**hampered, hampering**) to hinder the progress or movement of.

hamper² *noun* a large basket with a lid, used for carrying food.

hamster *noun* a small short-tailed rodent, popular as a domestic pet.

hamstring *noun Anat.* a tendon at the back of the knee. —*verb (pa t and pa p* **hamstrung;** *pr p* **hamstringing**) 1 to lame by cutting the hamstring. 2 to make powerless or to hinder.

hand *noun* 1 the part of the body with a thumb, four fingers and a palm. 2 (*often* **hands**) control, agency, or influence. 3 help; assistance. 4 a part or influence in an activity: *had a hand in the victory.* 5 a needle or pointer on, e.g. a clock. 6 *colloq.* applause. 7 a manual worker. 8 a person skillful in an activity. 9 a way of doing something: *have a light hand at pastry.* 10 *Cards* the cards dealt to a player in one round of a game. 11 a position in relation to an object or (*in compounds*) to a point in time: *on the right hand.* 12 a person's handwriting or its style. 13 a promise to marry. 14 a unit of measurement, equal to four inches, used for measuring the height of horses. —*verb trans.* (**handed, handing**) to deliver or give using the hands. —**at hand** near by; about to happen. **by hand** 1 with a person's hand or tools held in the hands. 2 delivered by messenger, not by mail. **hand (something) in** to return (something) to someone entitled to hold it, e.g., lost property. **hand in hand** 1 holding (someone's) hand. 2 in close association. **hand it to (someone)** *colloq.* to give (the one specified) due credit. **in hand** 1 under control. 2 being done or prepared. **on hand** available for use; near. **out of hand** unable to be controlled. **to hand** within reach.

handbag *noun* a woman's purse.

handball *noun* 1 a game in which players hit a small ball with their gloved hands. 2 the ball used in this game.

handbook *noun* a short manual or guidebook.

handbrake *noun* a brake on a motor vehicle which is operated by hand.

handcart *noun* a small light cart which can be moved by hand.

handcrafted *adj.* made by skilled crafting with the hands.

handcuff *verb trans.* (**handcuffed, handcuffing**) to put handcuffs on (a person). —*noun* (**handcuffs**) a pair of steel rings, joined by a short chain, for locking around the wrists of prisoners.

handful (hănd'fŏŏl,) *noun* (*pl.* **handfuls**) 1 the number or amount that can be held in one hand. 2 a small number or amount. 3 *colloq.* one that is difficult to control: *these kids are a handful.*

handicap *noun* 1 a physical or mental disability. 2 a disadvantage given to a superior competitor in a contest, race, etc. 3 a race or competition in which some competitors are given a handicap. —*verb trans.* (**handicapped, handicapping**) 1 to give a handicap to. 2 to make something difficult for (someone).

> Originally a gambling game in which wagers were drawn by hand from a cap

handicapped *adj.* physically or mentally disabled. —*pl. noun* people who are physically or mentally disabled.

handicraft *noun* 1 an activity that requires skillful use of the hands. 2 (*usu.* **handicrafts**) an object or objects produced by such craft.

handiwork *noun* 1 work, esp. skillful, done by the hands. 2 something bad done or caused by a particular person.

handkerchief (hăng'kər-chĭf, -chēf,) *noun* (*pl.* **handkerchiefs, handkerchieves**) a small, usu. square piece of cloth or soft paper used for wiping one's nose, mouth, etc.

handle *noun* 1 the part of an object by which it is held so that it may be used or operated. 2 an advantage or opening given to an opponent. 3 *slang* a person's name. —*verb trans., intrans.* (**handled, handling**) 1 to touch, hold, move, or operate with the hands. 2 to deal with or manage, esp. successfully or in the correct way. 3 to buy, sell, or deal in (goods). 4 to respond to control in the way stated: *this car that handles well.* —**fly off the handle** *colloq.* to become suddenly angry.

handlebars *pl. noun* a usu. curved metal bar with handles at each end, for steering a bicycle or motorcycle.

handler *noun* 1 a person who trains and controls an animal, esp. a dog. 2 a person who handles something.

handmade *adj.* made with a person's hands or with tools held in the hands, not by machine.

hand-me-down *noun colloq.* a secondhand garment, toy, etc.

handoff *noun Football* a play during which one player hands the ball to another player.

handout *noun* **1** money, food, etc., given to people who need it. **2** a leaflet given out as publicity for something. **3** a statement given as a substitute for an oral address.

handpick *verb trans.* (**handpicked, handpicking**) to choose carefully, esp. for a particular purpose.

handrail *noun* a narrow rail running along stairs, etc., for support.

handset *noun* a telephone mouthpiece and earpiece together in a single unit.

handshake *noun* the act of holding or shaking a person's hand, esp. as a greeting.

hands-off *adj.* marked by nonintervention.

handsome (hăn'səm) *adj.* **1** good-looking. **2** dignified, healthy, and attractive in appearance. **3** substantial; generous. ▸ **handsomely** *adv.* ▸ **handsomeness** *noun*

hands-on *adj.* involving practical experience rather than just theory.

handspring *noun* a somersault or cartwheel.

handstand *noun* an act of balancing one's body upside down on one's hands.

hand-to-hand *adj., of fighting* involving direct physical contact with an opponent.

hand-to-mouth *adj.* possessing or providing only the bare essentials for life.

handwriting *noun* **1** writing with a pen or pencil. **2** the way a person writes.

handy *adj.* (**handier, handiest**) **1** conveniently placed and ready to use. **2** easy to use or handle. **3** clever with one's hands. ▸ **handily** *adv.* ▸ **handiness** *noun*

handyman *noun* a person skilled at or employed to do odd jobs.

hang *verb trans., intrans.* (*pa t and pa p* **hung**; *pr p* **hanging**) **1** to fasten or be fastened from above, esp. with the lower part free. **2** *e.g., of a door* to fasten or be fastened with hinges so that it can move freely. **3** (*pa t and pa p* **hanged**) to suspend or be suspended from a rope around the neck until dead. **4** to remain without moving, esp. in the air or in a threatening way: *The threat of war hung over the nation.* **5** to droop or cause to droop. **6** to attach (wallpaper) to a wall. **7** to decorate (a room, wall, etc.) with pictures or other hangings. **8** to depend on (another factor). —*noun* the way something hangs, falls, or droops. —**get the hang of (something)** *colloq.* to learn or begin to understand how to do (it). **hang about or around** *colloq.* **1** to stand around doing nothing. **2** (**hang around or about with (someone)**) to spend a lot of time with (the

one or ones specified). **hang back** to be reluctant to do something. **hang on** *colloq.* **1** to wait. **2** to persevere, in spite of problems or difficulties. **hang out 1** *slang* to spend much time in a place. **2** to stand around. **hang tough** *colloq.* to remain steadfast. **hang up 1** to finish a telephone conversation by replacing the receiver. **2** to hang (something) on a hook or hanger. **3** to delay.

hangar *noun* a building in which aircraft or spacecraft are housed and maintained.

hangdog *adj.* showing shame or guilt.

hanger *noun* **1** a frame on which garments are hung. **2** a person who hangs something.

hanger-on *noun* (*pl.* **hangers-on**) a fan or follower, esp. one who is not wanted.

hang glider 1 an unpowered aircraft consisting of a small glider with a light framework from which the operator is suspended in a harness. **2** the pilot of a hang glider. ▸ **hang gliding** *noun*

hanging *noun* **1** execution by hanging. **2** (*usu.* **hangings**) tapestries, etc., hung on walls.

hangman *noun* an official who executes convicted criminals by hanging.

hangout *noun slang* a place in which one spends much time.

hangover *noun* **1** unpleasant physical symptoms following a period of heavy drinking. **2** something that remains from an earlier time.

hang-up *noun colloq.* an emotional or psychological problem or obsession.

hanker *verb intrans.* (**hankered, hankering**) (**hanker after or for (something)**) to long for or crave (it). ▸ **hankering** *noun*

hankie *or* **hanky** *noun* (*pl.* **hankies**) *colloq.* a handkerchief.

hanky-panky *noun slang* **1** slightly improper sexual behavior. **2** dishonest dealings.

Hanukkah *or* **Chanukkah** a Jewish festival commemorating the rededication of the Temple at Jerusalem.

haphazard (hăp-hăz'ərd) *adj.* governed by chance. ▣ HIT-OR-MISS, RANDOM, SPOT ▣ PLANNED, PURPOSIVE. —*adv.* at random. ▸ **haphazardly** *adv.*

hapless *adj.* unlucky; unfortunate.

happen *verb intrans.* (**happened, happening**) **1** to take place or occur. **2** (**happen to (someone)**) *esp. of something unwelcome* to be done to someone, or be experienced by the one specified. **3** to have the good or bad luck to. **4** (**happen on (something)**) to encounter (it), esp. by chance.

happening *noun* **1** an event. **2** a public performance, esp. one which has not been fully planned.

happy *adj.* (**happier, happiest**) **1** feeling or showing pleasure. **2** causing pleasure. **3** suitable; fortunate: *a happy coincidence.*

—**happy event** the birth of a child. ▸ **happily** adv. ▸ **happiness** noun

happy-go-lucky adj. carefree.

harangue noun a loud, forceful speech. —verb trans. (**harangued, haranguing**) to deliver such a speech.

harass (hə-răs′, hăr′əs) verb trans. (**harassed, harassing**) 1 to annoy or trouble (a person) constantly or frequently. 2 to make frequent attacks on (an enemy). ▸ **harassment** noun

harassed adj. troubled, worried, or overburdened.

harbinger (här′bĭn-jər) noun a person or thing that is a sign of something that is to come.

harbor noun 1 a place of shelter for ships. 2 a refuge. —verb trans. (**harbored, harboring**) 1 to give shelter or protection to (e.g., a criminal). 2 to have (usu. bad thoughts or feelings): harbor a grudge.

hard adj. 1 of a substance resistant to scratching or indentation. ◳ FIRM, FLINTY, GRANITIC, SOLID ◳ SOFT. 2 difficult to do, understand, solve, or explain. 3 using or needing a great deal of effort. 4 harsh; cruel. 5 suffering hardship. 6 of information, etc. proven and reliable. 7 of water containing salts which produce an insoluble scum with soap. 8 of a drug highly addictive. 9 being a spirit rather than beer or wine. 10 politically extreme: the hard right. 11 of currency with a stable value and exchange rate. —adv. 1 with great effort or energy. 2 in such a manner as to cause hardship or damage. 3 earnestly or intently. —**hard and fast** permanent or absolute. **hard of hearing** partially deaf. **hard put** experiencing difficulty (in doing). **hard up** colloq. short of money. ▸ **hardness** noun

hardback noun a book with a hard cover. —adj. having a hard cover.

hardball noun Sport the game of baseball. —**play hardball** slang to use any and all means possible to meet an objective.

hardboard noun light, strong board made by compressing wood pulp.

hard-boiled adj. 1 of eggs boiled until the yolk is solid. 2 of a person tough; cynical.

hard copy any form of computer output that is printed on paper.

hard-core or **hardcore** adj. 1 having longlasting, strong, unchanging beliefs. 2 of pornography sexually explicit.

hard disk Comput. a rigid aluminum disk, coated with magnetic material and permanently sealed within the disk drive, that is used to store data. See also **floppy disk**.

harden verb trans., intrans. (**hardened, hardening**) 1 to make or become hard or harder. 2 to become or make less sympathetic or understanding.

hardened adj. toughened through experience: a hardened criminal.

hardhat noun a protective hat worn, e.g., by construction workers.

hardheaded adj. 1 refusing to compromise. 2 practical; not influenced by emotion.

hardhearted adj. feeling no pity or kindness. ▸ **hardheartedly** adv. ▸ **hardheartedness** noun

hard-hitting adj. frankly critical; direct.

hardihood noun courage and daring.

hard line a strong opinion, decision, or policy unlikely to be changed. ▸ **hard-line** adj. ▸ **hard-liner** noun

hardly adv. 1 only with difficulty; scarcely. 2 probably not: They'll hardly come now.

hard-nosed adj. colloq. not influenced by emotion; tough.

hard-pressed adj. having problems; difficulties.

hard sell an aggressive way of promoting, selling, or advertising.

hardship noun severe suffering and pain, or a cause of this.

hardware noun 1 metal goods such as pots, cutlery, etc. 2 Comput. the electronic, electrical, magnetic, and mechanical components of a computer system. See also **software**.

hard-wired adj. 1 of a computer having functions that are controlled by hardware and cannot be altered by software programs. 2 having direct electrical connections.

hardy adj. (**hardier, hardiest**) 1 tough; strong. 2 of a plant able to survive outdoors in winter.

hare noun a mammal belonging to the same family as the rabbit, but with longer ears and hind legs than a rabbit.

hare-brained adj. foolish; rash.

harem (hăr′əm, hĕr′-) noun 1 the part of a traditional Muslim house where the women live. 2 the women living in this area.

haricot (hăr′ĭ-kō, är′-) noun a small, white, dried bean, used as food.

harm noun physical, mental, or moral injury or damage. —verb trans. (**harmed, harming**) to cause harm to. —**in** or **out of harm's way** in a dangerous (or safe) place. ▸ **harmful** adj. ▸ **harmfully** adv. ▸ **harmfulness** noun ▸ **harmless** adj. ▸ **harmlessly** adv. ▸ **harmlessness** noun

harmonic adj. of or relating to harmony; harmonious. —noun a note produced on a stringed instrument by touching one of the strings lightly at one of the points that divide the string into exact fractions.

harmonica noun a small musical instrument played by blowing through metal reeds situated along one side. Also called **mouth organ**.

harmonious *adj.* **1** pleasant-sounding and tuneful. **2** forming a pleasing whole: *harmonious colors.* **3** devoid of disagreement or bad feeling. ▸ **harmoniously** *adv.* ▸ **harmoniousness** *noun*

harmonize *verb intrans., trans.* (**harmonized, harmonizing**) **1** to be or bring into musical harmony. **2** to add notes to (a simple tune) to form harmonies. **3** to form or be made to form a pleasing whole. ▸ **harmonization** *noun*

harmony *noun* (*pl.* **harmonies**) **1** a pleasing combination of musical notes or sounds produced simultaneously. **2** a pleasing arrangement of parts or things; *harmony of color.* **3** agreement in opinions and feelings.

harness *noun* a set of leather straps used to attach a cart to a horse, and to control the horse's movements. —*verb trans.* (**harnessed, harnessing**) to put a harness on.

harp *noun* a large upright musical instrument played by plucking strings stretched vertically from a curved neck to a soundboard. —**harp on** *colloq.* to talk repeatedly and tediously about something. ▸ **harpist** *noun*

harpoon *noun* a barbed spear fastened to a rope; used for catching whales. —*verb. trans.* (**harpooned, harpooning**) to strike (a whale, etc.) with a harpoon.

harpsichord *noun* a keyboard instrument in which the strings are plucked mechanically when the player presses the keys.

harrier[1] *noun* **1** a cross-country runner. **2** a hound used orig. for hunting hares.

harrier[2] *noun* a hawk with an owl-like head, broad wings, and long legs and tail.

harrowing (hăr'ə-wĭng) *adj.* causing great distress, agony, and misery.

harry *verb* (**harried, harrying, harries**) **1** to ravage or destroy. **2** to annoy or worry (a person).

harsh *adj.* **1** unpleasant to the senses; rough; grating. **2** strict, cruel, or severe. ▸ **harshly** *adv.* ▸ **harshness** *noun*

harum-scarum *adj.* wild and thoughtless; reckless. —*adv.* in a reckless manner.

harvest *noun* **1** the gathering in of ripened crops. **2** the season when this takes place. **3** the crops gathered. **4** the product or result of some action. —*verb trans., intrans.* (**harvested, harvesting**) to gather as a harvest. ▸ **harvester** *noun*

harvest moon the full moon nearest to the autumnal equinox, usu. Sep. 22 or 23.

has *see* have.

has-been *noun colloq.* a person who is no longer successful, important, or influential.

hash *noun* **1** a dish of cooked meat and vegetables chopped up together and recooked. **2** *colloq.* a ludicrous, humiliating, usu. confused failure. —*verb trans.* (**hashed, hashing**) to make into a hash.

hasn't *contr.* has not.

hasp *noun* a metal fastening held shut by a pin or padlock.

hassle *colloq. noun* **1** trouble, annoyance, or inconvenience, or a cause of it. **2** a fight or an argument. —*verb trans., intrans.* (**hassled, hassling**) **1** to annoy or bother, esp. repeatedly. **2** to argue or fight.

hassock *noun* **1** a firm cushion on which to kneel in church. **2** a tuft of grass.

haste *noun* **1** urgency of movement. **2** too much speed. —**make haste** to hurry.

hasten (hā'sən) *verb trans., intrans.* (**hastened, hastening**) **1** to cause to move or to move with speed. **2** (**hasten to do (something)**) to do (it) eagerly and promptly.

hasty *adj.* (**hastier, hastiest**) **1** occurring suddenly and quickly: *a hasty departure.* ▣ ABRUPT, PRECIPITATE, SUDDEN ▣ DELIBERATE, LEISURELY. **2** carelessly and thoughtlessly done: *a hasty, messy paint job.* ▸ **hastily** *adv.* ▸ **hastiness** *noun*

hat *noun* **1** a covering for the head. **2** *colloq.* a role or capacity: *wearing her vet's hat.* —**hat in hand** in a supplicating manner. **old hat** *colloq.* so well known or familiar as to be tedious and uninteresting. **pass the hat around** to collect money for a cause. **take (one's) hat off to (someone)** *colloq.* to admire or praise (another).

hatch[1] *noun* **1** a narrow or confined opening in a ship, aircraft, or spacecraft; the lid or cover of this opening. **2** a hatchway. **3** an opening in a wall between a kitchen and dining room, used esp. for serving food.

hatch[2] *verb intrans., trans.* (**hatched, hatching**) **1** to break out of an egg. **2** *of an egg* to break open, allowing young to emerge. **3** to cause (the young of various animals) to emerge from an egg. **4** to plan or devise (a plot, scheme, etc.), esp. in secret. —*noun* **1** the act of hatching. **2** a group of newly hatched animals.

hatchback *noun* a car with a sloping door at the back that opens upward.

hatchet *noun* a small ax.

hatchway *noun* an opening in a ship's deck through which to load cargo.

hate *verb trans.* (**hated, hating**) **1** to regard with great contempt or dislike. ▣ ABHOR, ABOMINATE, DESPISE, DETEST, EXECRATE ▣ ADORE, LOVE. **2** to regret: *I hate to bother you.* —*noun* **1** great dislike. **2** a greatly disliked person or thing.

hateful *adj.* causing or deserving great dislike. ▸ **hatefully** *adv.* ▸ **hatefulness** *noun*

hatpin *noun* a long metal pin, used to keep a hat in place.

hatred *noun* great dislike.

hatstand *noun* a piece of furniture for hanging hats, coats, umbrellas, etc.

hatter *noun* a person who makes or sells hats. —**mad as a hatter** extremely mad or eccentric.

haughty *adj.* (**haughtier, haughtiest**) arrogantly proud. ⊟ CAVALIER, HIGH-AND-MIGHTY, LORDLY, SUPERCILIOUS ⊟ LOWLY, SUBSERVIENT. ▸ **haughtily** *adv.* ▸ **haughtiness** *noun*

haul *verb trans., intrans.* (**hauled, hauling**) 1 to drag with some effort. 2 to transport by road, e.g., in a truck. —*noun* 1 the distance to be traveled. 2 the act of dragging with effort. 3 an amount gained at any one time.

haunch *noun* the fleshy part of the human hip and buttock.

haunt *verb trans.* (**haunted, haunting**) 1 *of a ghost or spirit* to be present in (a place) or visit (a person or place) regularly. 2 *of unpleasant thoughts, etc.* to keep coming back to a person's mind. 3 *colloq.* to visit (a place) frequently. —*noun dialect* a supernatural being or form.

haunting *adj.* making a very strong and moving impression. ▸ **hauntingly** *adv.*

have *verb trans., aux.* (pa t and pa p **had**; pr p **having**; 3d person sing. PRESENT **has**) 1 to possess. 2 to receive, obtain, or take: *have a drink.* 3 to think of or hold in the mind: *have an idea.* 4 to experience, enjoy, or suffer: *have a good time.* 5 to be in a specified state: *have a page missing.* 6 to hold or take part in: *have a party.* 7 to cause, order, or invite someone to do something or something to be done. 8 (**have to be** *or* **do** (**something**)) to be required to be or do (it). 9 to eat or drink. 10 to gain an advantage over. 11 *colloq.* to cheat or deceive. 12 to show or feel: *have pity.* 13 to accept or tolerate: *I'm not having that!* 14 to receive as a guest. 15 to be pregnant with or give birth to: *had a baby.* 16 *coarse slang* to have sexual intercourse with. —*verb aux.* used with past participles of verbs to show that an action has been completed: *have made the cake.* —*noun* (*often* **haves**) *colloq.* those who have wealth: *the haves and the have-nots.* —**have had it** *colloq.* 1 to be exhausted or disgusted. 2 to have missed one's opportunity. **have it in for** (**someone**) *colloq.* to feel hostile toward (the one or ones specified). **have it out** to settle, e.g., an dispute, with an argument.

haven (hā'vən) *noun* 1 a place of safety or rest. 2 a harbor.

have-not *noun* (*often* **have-nots**) one or ones who have little or no wealth.

haven't *contr.* have not.

haversack *noun* a canvas bag carried over one shoulder or on the back.

havoc *noun* 1 great destruction or damage. 2 chaos. —**play havoc with** (**something**) to cause damage to (it) or to create confusion around (it).

hawk[1] *noun* 1 a bird of prey with short rounded wings and very good eyesight. 2 *Politics* a person who favors hostilities or warfare rather than peace. *See also* **dove**[1] (sense 2). ▸ **hawker** *noun*

hawk[2] *verb trans., intrans.* (**hawked, hawking**) to carry (goods) around, usu. from door to door, trying to sell them; to engage in this. ▸ **hawker** *noun*

hawk[3] *verb intrans., trans.* (**hawked, hawking**) 1 to clear the throat noisily. 2 to bring (phlegm) up from the throat.

hawk-eyed *adj.* having very keen eyesight.

hawthorn *noun* a shrub or small tree with pink or white flowers.

hay *noun* grass that has been cut and allowed to dry in the field, used as food for livestock.

hay fever an allergic response to pollen, characterized by sneezing, itching, watery eyes, and a running or stopped-up nose.

haystack *noun* a large stack of hay built in an open field. *Also called* **hayrick**.

haywire *adj., adv. slang* in or into a state of great confusion.

hazard *noun* 1 a risk of harm or danger. 2 a situation or state in which one is exposed to harm, injury, or loss. 3 an obstacle on a golf course. —*verb trans.* (**hazarded, hazarding**) 1 to put forward (a guess or suggestion). 2 to risk.

hazardous *adj.* damaging to safety or health; dangerous. ▸ **hazardously** *adv.* ▸ **hazardousness** *noun*

haze *noun* 1 a thin mist or vapor that obscures visibility. 2 a feeling of confusion or not understanding. —*verb intrans.* (**hazed, hazing**) to become covered in a thin mist.

hazel *noun* a nut-producing tree of the birch family. —*adj.* of a greenish-brown color.

hazelnut *noun* the nut produced by the hazel tree.

hazy *adj.* (**hazier, haziest**) obscured or made unclear by or as if by vaporous mist: *a hazy view / a hazy recollection.* ⊟ FOGGY, FUZZY, MISTY, VAGUE ⊟ CLEAR, DISTINCT. ▸ **hazily** *adv.* ▸ **haziness** *noun*

H-bomb *noun Mil.* a hydrogen bomb.

He *symbol Chem.* helium.

he *pron.* 1 a male person or animal already referred to. 2 a person or animal of unknown sex. —*noun* (*pl.* **hes**) a male person or animal: *Is the puppy a he or a she?*

head *noun* 1 the part of an animal's body containing the brain and the organs of sight, smell, hearing, and taste. 2 intelligence; imagination or ability: *He has a good head* *for math.* **3** the top of a device, e.g., a tool. **4 a** the person with the most authority in an organization, country, etc. **b** the position of being in charge. **c** a principal teacher. **5** the top or upper part, e.g., of a bed. **6** the front or forward part, e.g., of a line of people. **7** the foam on top of a glass of beer. **8** the top part of a plant that produces leaves or flowers. **9** a crisis or turning point in a sequence of events. **10** (*pl.* **head**) a group of animals or individuals: *60 head of cattle.* **11** *colloq.* a headache. **12** the source of a body of fresh water. **13** the height or length of a head, used as a measurement: *won by a head.* **14** the pressure produced by water or steam in an enclosed space. **15** the device in a tape recorder, video recorder, etc., which records onto tapes or disks. **16** the side of a coin bearing the head of a president, etc. **17** a headline. —*verb trans., intrans.* (**headed, heading**) **1** to be at the front of or top of. **2** to be in charge of. **3** to move in a certain direction: *head for home.* **4** to put or write (a title or headline) at the beginning of a story, chapter, etc. **5** *Soccer* to hit (the ball) with the head. —**head (someone) off** to get ahead of (the one or ones specified) so as to intercept and turn (them) back. **head over heels 1** rolling over completely with the head first. **2** completely: *head over heels in love.* **keep (one's) head** to remain calm and sensible in a crisis. **lose (one's) head** to become angry, or to act foolishly in a crisis. **off (one's) head** *colloq.* mad; crazy. ▸ **headless** *adj.*

headache *noun* **1** a pain in the head. **2** *colloq.* a worry or annoyance. ▸ **headachy** *adj.*

headband *noun* a band worn around the head.

headboard *noun* a board at the top end of a bed.

headdress *noun* a covering for the head, esp. one that is decorative.

header *noun* **1** *colloq.* a fall or dive forward. **2** *Soccer* the hitting of the ball with the head.

headfirst *adv.* **1** moving quickly with one's head bent forward. **2** without thinking; rashly.

headgear *noun* something worn on the head.

headhunting *noun* **1** the practice of taking the heads of one's dead enemies as trophies. **2** the practice of trying to recruit personnel by attracting people away from their present jobs. ▸ **headhunter** *noun*

heading *noun* a title at the top of e.g., a page, letter, or section of a report.

headlamp *noun* a headlight.

headland *noun* a high, steep area of land jutting into the sea.

headlight *noun* a powerful light on the front of a vehicle. *Also called* **headlamp**.

headline *noun* **1** the title or heading of a newspaper article, printed in large type above the article. **2** (**headlines**) the most important points in a television or radio news broadcast.

headlong *adj., adv.* **1** moving esp. quickly with one's head bent forward. **2** quickly and usu. without thinking.

headmaster *noun* a man who is the principal in charge of a usu. private school.

headmistress *noun* a woman who is the principal in charge of a usu. private school.

head-on *adv., adj.* **1** with the front of one vehicle hitting the front of another: *a head-on collision.* **2** in open, direct opposition.

headphones *pl. noun* a pair of small sound-receiving devices worn over the ears and connected to a radio, cassette player, etc. *Also called* **earphones**.

headquarters *noun* (*sing., pl.*) the center of an organization or group, e.g., in an army, from which operations are controlled.

headrest *noun* a cushion that supports the head, attached to the top of a car seat, etc.

headscarf *noun* (*pl.* **headscarfs**, **head-scarves**) a scarf worn over the head and tied under the chin.

headset *noun* a set of headphones, typically with an attached microphone.

head start an advantage at the beginning of a race or competition.

headstone *noun* an inscribed stone at the head of a grave.

headstrong *adj.* obstinately and recklessly willful and determined.

headway *noun* **1** forward movement, esp. to a goal: *made headway with the backlog.* **2** *Naut.* a ship's movement forward.

headwind or **head wind** *noun* a wind blowing directly against the course of a ship, aircraft, etc.

headword *noun* a word forming a heading, esp. for a dictionary or encyclopedia entry.

heady *adj.* (**headier, headiest**) **1** tending to make one intoxicated quickly. **2** rash; impetuous.

heal *verb trans.* (**healed, healing**) **1** to cause to become healthy again; to cure. **2** to return to good health. **3** to put right: *healed the family rift.* ▸ **healer** *noun* ▸ **healing** *noun*

health (hĕlth) *noun* **1** a state of physical, mental, and social well-being. **2** a person's general mental or physical condition.

healthy *adj.* (**healthier, healthiest**) **1** having, showing, or enjoying good health. ▣ HALE, SOUND, WELL ▣ ILL, INFIRM, SICK, UNHEALTHY. **2** causing good health: *a healthy environment.* **3** in a good state: *a healthy economy.* **4** wise. **5** large; considerable. ▸ **healthily** *adv.* ▸ **healthiness** *noun*

heap noun 1 a collection of things in a messy pile. 2 (usu. **heaps**) colloq. a large amount or number. 3 slang something, esp. a motor vehicle, that is very old and not working properly. —verb trans., intrans. (**heaped, heaping**) 1 to collect or be collected together in a heap. 2 to give (something) to (someone) in large amounts: heaped praise on him.

hear verb trans., intrans. (pa t and pa p **heard**; pr p **hearing**) 1 to perceive (sounds) with the ear. 2 to listen to. 3 (**hear about** or **of** (**something**)) to be told about (it) or informed of (it). 4 (**hear from**) to be reached by (the one or ones specified), esp. by letter or telephone. **hear** (**someone**) **out** to allow (the one specified) to finish speaking or explaining.

hearing noun 1 the sense that involves the perception of sound. 2 the distance within which something or someone can be heard. 3 an opportunity to state one's case. 4 Law a court case.

hearing aid a small electronic device worn in or just behind the ear to aid hearing.

hearsay noun rumor; gossip.

hearse (hɔrs) noun a motor vehicle used for carrying a coffin to a funeral.

heart noun 1 a the hollow muscular organ that pumps blood through the blood vessels. b this organ considered as the center of a person's thoughts, emotions, conscience, etc. 2 ability to feel tenderness or pity. 3 courage and enthusiasm. 4 the innermost, central, essential, or unchanging part. 5 the compact inner part of some vegetables, e.g., artichokes, lettuce. 6 a usu. red symbol representing the heart, with two rounded lobes at the top curving down to meet in a point at the bottom. 7 Cards a a playing card with a red heart-shaped symbol on it. b (**hearts**) a suit of cards with such shapes on them. —**by heart** by or from memory. **heart and soul** with all one's attention and energy; completely. **lose heart** to become discouraged. **take heart** to become encouraged or more confident. **take** (**something**) **to heart** to pay great attention to (it) or be very affected by (it).

heartache noun great sadness or suffering.

heart attack a sudden failure of the heart to function properly, causing severe chest pain and sometimes death.

heartbeat noun 1 the regular throb of the heart as it pumps blood around the body. 2 a single pumping action of the heart.

heartbreak noun very great sorrow or grief. ▸ **heartbroken** adj. ▸ **heartbreaking** adj.

hearten verb trans., intrans. (**heartened, heartening**) to make or become more cheerful or encouraged. ▸ **heartening** adj.

▸ **hearteningly** adv.

heartfelt adj. sincere; earnest.

hearth (härth) noun 1 the floor of a fireplace, or the area surrounding it. 2 the home.

hearthrug noun a rug placed on the floor in front of a hearth.

heartless adj. very unkind; cruel. ▸ **heartlessly** adv. ▸ **heartlessness** noun

heart-rending adj. causing great sorrow or pity. ▸ **heart-rendingly** adv.

heartsick adj. very sad or disappointed.

heartstrings pl. noun one's deepest feelings of love, sympathy, or pity: tugging at my heartstrings.

heart-throb noun slang 1 a person whom a lot of people find very attractive, esp. a male actor or singer. 2 one's sweetheart.

heart-to-heart adj., of a conversation intimate, sincere, and candid. —noun an intimate and candid conversation.

heartwarming adj. emotionally moving; pleasing.

hearty (härt'ē) adj. (**heartier, heartiest**) 1 very friendly and warm in manner. 2 strong, vigorous, or enthusiastic. 3 of a meal or appetite large. ▸ **heartily** adv. ▸ **heartiness** noun

heat noun 1 the state of being hot. 2 a high temperature. 3 hot weather. 4 warmth of feeling, esp. anger or excitement: the heat of the argument. 5 the most intense part: the heat of battle. 6 Sport a preliminary race or contest that eliminates competitors. 7 a period of sexual receptivity in some female mammals. 8 prickly heat. —verb trans., intrans. (**heated, heating**) to make or become hot or warm.

heated adj. 1 having been made hot or warm. 2 angry or excited. ▸ **heatedly** adv. ▸ **heatedness** noun

heater noun a device for heating something.

heath noun 1 an area of open, flat land, often covered with shrubs. 2 a shrub with needlelike leaves and white, pink, or yellow flowers.

heathen (hē'thən) noun 1 a person who is not a Christian, Jew, or Muslim. 2 colloq. a person who is felt to be ignorant or uncivilized. —adj. of, relating to, or characteristic of irreligious or uncivilized people.

heather (heth'ər) noun 1 a bushy shrub with small leaves and small pinkish-purple flowers. Also called **ling**. 2 used loosely for a heath.

heating noun a system for heating a room or building.

heat stroke a severe condition of collapse and fever brought on by continuous exposure to heat. Also called **sunstroke**.

heat wave a prolonged period of unusually hot, dry weather.

heave (hēv) *verb trans.*, *intrans.* (*pa t and pa p* **heaved**; *pr p* **heaving**) **1** to lift or pull with great effort. **2** *colloq.* to throw (something heavy). **3** to utter: *heave a sigh.* **4** to rise and fall heavily or rhythmically. **5** to retch or vomit. **6** (*pa t and pa p* **hove**) *of a ship* to move: *heave into sight.* —*noun* an act of heaving.

heaven (hēv'ən) *noun* **1** the place believed to be the abode of God, the angels, and the righteous after death. **2** (*usu.* **heavens**) the sky. **3** a feeling of immense joy. ▸ **heavenliness** *noun.* ▸ **heavenly** *adj.*

heavy *adj.* (**heavier, heaviest**) **1** having great weight. **2** having a great or relatively high density. **3** great in size, amount, force, power, etc.: *heavy traffic.* **4** severe, intense, or excessive. **5** hard to bear or endure. **6** *of sky* dark and cloudy. **7** needing a lot of physical or mental effort. **8 a** *of literature* serious in tone and content. **b** very important in terms of the consequences. **c** *slang* extremely profound. **9** *of food* difficult to digest. **10** *of breathing* loud, because of excitement, exhaustion, etc. **11** striking or falling with force; powerful: *heavy rain.* **12** sad or dejected. **13** ungraceful and coarse: *heavy features.* **14** fat; solid. **15** *colloq.* strict; severe. **16** *of weapons* large and powerful. —*noun* (*pl.* **heavies**) **1** *slang* **a** a large, violent, and usu. not very intelligent man. **b** a goon; a mobster. **2** *slang* a villain in a play, film, etc. **3** *slang* a very important and influential person: *political heavies.* —**heavy going** difficult or slow progress. ▸ **heavily** *adv.* ▸ **heaviness** *noun*

heavy-duty *adj.* made to withstand very hard wear or use.

heavy-handed *adj.* **1** clumsy. **2** excessively severe or strict. ▸ **heavy-handedly** *adv.* ▸ **heavy-handedness** *noun*

heavy-hearted *adj.* sad; dejected.

heavy metal loud, flamboyant rock music, usu. dominated by the electric guitar.

heavyset *adj.* stocky and compact in physique.

heavyweight *noun* **1 a** the class for the heaviest competitors, e.g., in boxing or wrestling. **b** a boxer, etc., of this weight. **2** *colloq.* an important, powerful, or influential person. **3** a person who is heavier than average. —*adj.* of the specified weight.

hebdomadal (hĕb-dăm'əd-l) *adj.* weekly. ▸ **hebdomadally** *adv.*

Hebraic (hĭ-brā'ĭk) *adj.* of the Hebrews or the Hebrew language or culture.

Hebrew (hē'brōō,) *noun* **1** the ancient Semitic language of the Hebrews. **2** a member of an ancient Semitic people. —*adj.* of the Hebrew language or people.

heckle *verb trans.*, *intrans.* (**heckled,**

heckling) to interrupt (a speaker) with critical or abusive shouts. ▸ **heckler** *noun*

hectare (hĕk'tăr,, -tär,) *noun* (ABBREV. **ha**) a unit of area in the metric system, most commonly for land, equal to 2.47 acres (100 ares or 10,000 m²).

hectic *adj.* marked by intense, busy activity, haste, and confusion. ▸ **hectically** *adv.*

hecto- *combining form* forming words denoting one hundred: *hectometer.*

hector *verb trans.* to bully, intimidate, or threaten. —*noun* a bully.

> After *Hector*, the Trojan hero in the Iliad

he'd *contr.* **1** he had. **2** he would.

hedge *noun* **1** a boundary formed by shrubs planted close together. **2** a protection against loss. —*verb intrans.*, *trans.* (**hedged, hedging**) **1** to avoid answering (a question) by speaking evasively. **2** to enclose (an area of land) with a hedge.

hedgehog *noun* a small mammal having a body covered with spines, and a short tail.

hedonism (hēd'n-ĭz,əm) *noun* the belief that pleasure is the most important aim in life. ▸ **hedonist** *noun* ▸ **hedonistic** *adj.* ▸ **hedonistically** *adv.*

heebie-jeebies *pl. noun slang* feelings of nervousness or anxiety.

heed *verb trans.* (**heeded, heeding**) to pay attention to or take notice of (e.g., advice). —*noun* **1** notice; attention. **2** thorough, serious attentiveness. ▸ **heedful** *adj.* ▸ **heedless** *adj.* ▸ **heedlessly** *adv.* ▸ **heedlessness** *noun*

heel[1] *noun* **1** the rounded back part of the foot. **2** the part of a sock, stocking, shoe, etc., that covers or supports the heel. **3** *slang* a generally untrustworthy person. —*verb trans.*, *intrans.* (**heeled, heeling**) **1** to put a new heel on (a shoe, etc.). **2** *Rugby* to kick the ball backward with the heel. **3** *of a dog* to walk at or go to a person's side. —**on the heels of** following close behind. **take to (one's) heels** to run away. **turn on (one's) heel** to turn around suddenly or sharply.

heel[2] *verb intrans.* (**heeled, heeling**) (*often* **heel over**) *of a ship* to lean over to one side.

hefty *adj.* (**heftier, heftiest**) **1** *of a person* big and strong. **2** *of an object, blow, etc.* large, heavy, or powerful. **3** *colloq.* large in amount. ▸ **heftily** *adv.* ▸ **heftiness** *noun*

hegemony *noun* (*pl.* **hegemonies**) leadership or control by one state within a group of states or alliance.

heifer (hĕf'ər) *noun* a female cow over one year old that has not calved, or that has calved only once.

height *noun* **1** the distance from bottom to top. **2** a distance above the ground from a recognized point, esp. above sea level. **3**

relatively high altitude. **4** a high place or rising ground. **5** the highest point; the summit. **6** the most intense part: *the height of battle.* **7** a very good, bad, or serious example: *the height of stupidity.*

heighten *verb trans., intrans.* (**heightened, heightening**) to make or become higher, greater, etc.

heinous (hā′nəs) *adj.* very wicked or horrible. ► **heinously** *adv.* ► **heinousness** *noun*

heir (ăr, ĕr) *noun* a person who by law receives wealth, a title, etc., when the owner or holder dies.

heiress *noun* a woman who by law receives wealth, a title, etc., when the owner or holder dies.

heirloom *noun* an object that has been handed down in a family from parents to children over many years.

heist *slang noun* a robbery. —*verb trans.* (**heisted, heisting**) to rob at weaponpoint; to steal.

held *see* **hold**[1].

helical (hĕl′ĭ-kəl, hē′lĭ-) *adj.* of or like a helix; coiled.

helicopter *noun* an aircraft with two or more rotating blades that allow it to take off and land vertically.

A coinage based on Greek words meaning 'spiral wing'

heliotrope *noun* **1** a small shrub with small bluish-violet fragrant flowers. **2** the purple color of these flowers.

helipad *noun* a landing area for a helicopter, usu. a square marked with a cross or a large H.

heliport *noun* a place where helicopters take off and land.

helium *noun Chem.* (SYMBOL **He**) a colorless odorless inert gas used to fill balloons and airships.

helix *noun* (*pl.* **helixes, helices**) **1** a spiral or coiled structure, e.g., the thread of a screw. **2** *Geom.* a spiral-shaped curve that lies on the lateral surface of a cylinder or cone.

hell *noun* **1** the abode of evil spirits and the place or state of punishment for the wicked after death. **2** the abode of the dead. **3** a place or state that is the cause of intense pain and misery. —*interj. colloq.* used to express strong annoyance. —**for the hell of it** *colloq.* just for fun.

he'll *contr.* he will; he shall.

hellbent *adj.* (**hellbent on (something)**) *colloq.* determined to do (it).

hellebore (hĕl′ə-bôr,) *noun* a plant with white, greenish-white or purplish flowers.

Hellene (hĕl′ēn,) *noun* a Greek. ► **Hellenic** *adj*

Hellenism (hĕl′ə-nĭz,əm) *noun* Greek character or culture, esp. that of ancient Greece. ► **Hellenist** *noun* ► **Hellenistic** *adj.*

hellish *adj. colloq.* so unpleasant as to be suggestive of hell itself. ► **hellishly** *adv.* ► **hellishness** *noun*

hello *interj.* used as a greeting, to attract attention, or to start a telephone conversation.

helm *noun* the wheel or tiller by which a ship is steered. —**at the helm** in a controlling position; in charge.

helmet *noun* a protective hard covering for the head.

helmsman *noun* the one who steers a ship.

help *verb trans., intrans.* (**helped, helping**) **1** to assist. **2** to improve (a situation). **3** to refrain from. **4** to prevent or control: *I can't help the bad weather.* **5 a** serve (oneself) food or a portion of food. **b** to take something without permission: *helped himself to my money.* —*noun* **1** an act of helping. **2** a person or thing that helps. **3 a** a domestic servant. **b** *offensive* one's employees. **4** a remedy or relief. —**help out** to offer help, usu. for a short time. ► **helper** *noun.*

helpful *adj.* giving help; useful. ► **helpfully** *adv.* ► **helpfulness** *noun*

helping *noun* a single portion of food.

helpless *adj.* **1** unable to do anything for oneself. **2** weak and defenseless. ► **helplessly** *adv.* ► **helplessness** *noun*

helpmate *noun* a friend or partner, esp. a spouse.

helter-skelter *adj.* careless and confused. —*adv.* in a careless and confused manner.

hem[1] *noun* a bottom edge of a piece of clothing, folded over and sewn down. —*verb trans.* (**hemmed, hemming**) to make a hem on.

hem[2] *noun* a sound made when clearing the throat. —*verb intrans.* (**hemmed, hemming**) to clear the throat or cough slightly.

hem-, hemato-, hemo-, haem-, haemato- or **haemo-** *combining form* forming words denoting blood.

he-man *noun colloq.* a very strong, virile man.

hematology *noun Med.* the study of diseases and disorders of the blood.

hemi- *combining form* forming words denoting half: *hemisphere.*

hemisphere (hĕm′ĭs-fîr,) *noun* **1** one half of a sphere. **2** each half of Earth's sphere. **3** cerebral hemisphere. ► **hemispherical** *adj.*

hemline *noun* the level at which the hem of a garment hangs.

hemlock *noun* **1** a poisonous plant with small white flowers and a spotted stem. **2** a poisonous drug derived from this plant.

hemoglobin (hē′mə-glō,bĭn) *noun Biol.* the substance in red blood cells that carries oxygen round the body.

hemophilia (hē͵mə-fĭl′ē-ə) *noun* a hereditary disease, usu. only affecting males, in which the blood fails to clot. ► **hemophiliac** *noun*

hemorrhage (hĕm′ə-rĭj) *noun* the escape of large amounts of blood, esp. from a ruptured blood vessel. —*verb intrans.* (**hemorrhaged, hemorrhaging**) to suffer a hemorrhage.

hemorrhoid (hĕm′ə-roid͵) *noun* a swollen vein around the inside or outside of the anus.

hemp *noun* 1 a plant grown for its stem fibers (hemp) and for its leaves and flowers. *Also called* **Indian hemp.** 2 any narcotic drug, e.g., cannabis or marijuana, obtained from this plant. 3 the coarse tough fiber obtained from the stem of this plant.

hen *noun* a female bird of any kind, esp. the domestic fowl.

hence *adv.* 1 for this reason. 2 from this time. 3 *old use* from this place.

henceforth *adv.* from now on.

henchman *noun* a faithful supporter, esp. one who obeys without question.

henna *noun* reddish-brown dye obtained from a tropical shrub. —*verb trans.* (**hennaed, hennaing**) to dye or stain using henna.

henpecked *adj. colloq.,* of a man constantly harassed and criticized, esp. by a spouse.

heparin *noun Biochem.* a chemical substance, formed in most tissues of the body that prevents the clotting of blood.

hepatic (hĭ-păt′ĭk) *adj. Anat.* relating to or affecting the liver.

hepatitis (hĕp͵ə-tīt′ĭs) *noun* a serious disease in which the liver becomes inflamed, usu. caused by a viral infection

hepta- *combining form* forming words denoting seven: *heptagonal.*

heptagon *noun* a plane figure with seven sides and seven angles. ► **heptagonal** *adj.*

her *pron.* the form of *she* used as the object of a verb or after a preposition: *We all like her.* —*adj.* of or belonging to a female person or animal, or to a thing personified or thought of as female, e.g., a ship: *went to her house.*

herald *noun* 1 a person who announces important news. 2 a person or thing that is a sign of what is to come. —*verb trans.* (**heralded, heralding**) to be a sign of the approach of; to proclaim. ► **heraldic** *adj.*

herb (ərb′, hərb) *noun* 1 *Bot.* a plant with a soft stem, which dies back at the end of the growing season. 2 a plant that has aromatic leaves or other parts, used for flavoring food or making medicines.

herbaceous *adj.* 1 relating to or resembling herbs. 2 denoting a plant with a stem that is soft, not hard and woody.

herbal *adj. Bot.* relating to herbs. —*noun Bot.* a book describing the different uses of herbs.

herbalist *noun* a person who prescribes and uses plant extracts for medical purposes.

herbivore *noun* an animal that only eats plants. *See also* **carnivore.** ► **herbivorous** *adj.*

herd *noun* 1 a group of animals, esp. cattle, that are kept together on a farm. 2 a person who looks after a herd. 3 a large group of people. —*verb trans., intrans.* (**herded, herding**) 1 to gather or be gathered together in a herd. 2 to look after a herd of animals, or to group animals together. ► **herdsman** *noun*

here *adv.* 1 at, in, or to this place. 2 at this time; at this point in an argument. 3 used after a noun for emphasis: *this book here.* —*noun* this place. —*interj.* 1 used to call for someone's attention. 2 used to call attention to one's own presence. —**here and now** 1 at this time; immediately. 2 (**the here and now**) the present time. **here and there** in or to various places. **neither here nor there** of no importance.

> *Usage* When the adverb *here* occurs between a noun and *this* or *that,* the usage is nonstandard; avoid constructions such as *This here book is torn.* Say, instead, *This book here is torn* or simply *This book is torn.*

hereabouts *adv.* near this place.

hereafter *adv. formal* after this; from now on. —*noun* (**the hereafter**) life after death; the future.

hereby *adv. formal* by means of; as a result of this.

hereditary *adj.* 1 relating to by heredity. 2 *of a characteristic* genetically transmittable from parents to offspring.

heredity *noun* (*pl.* **heredities**) 1 the transmission of genetic characteristics from one generation to the next. 2 the genetic constitution of a living organism.

herein *adv.* in this place, document, or matter.

hereinafter *adv. formal* from this point on.

hereof *adv. Law formal* of or concerning this.

heresy (hĕr′ə-sē) *noun* (*pl.* **heresies**) 1 an opinion or belief that is contrary to official doctrine held by the religious community to which one belongs. 2 an opinion contrary to that which is normally accepted.

heretic *noun* a person who is guilty of heresy. ▤ INFIDEL, UNBELIEVER ▨ BELIEVER, ORTHODOX. ► **heretical** *adj.*

hereto *adv. formal* to this place, document, or matter.

heretofore *adv. formal* before this time; formerly.

hereupon *adv. Law formal* after or as a result of this.

herewith adv. formal with this; enclosed with this letter or other document.

heritable adj. 1 of property that may be passed on from parent to child. 2 of people able to inherit property. 3 denoting a characteristic that can be transmitted from one generation to the next.

heritage (hĕr'ət-ĭj) noun 1 that which is inherited. 2 the characteristics, qualities, property, etc., that one inherits at birth. 3 a nation's historic buildings, countryside, cultural traditions, etc.

heritance noun things or a set of things inherited.

hermaphrodite (hər-măf'rə-dīt,) noun a plant or animal possessing both male and female reproductive organs. —adj. possessing both male and female reproductive organs. ▸ **hermaphroditic** adj.

hermetic adj. closed very tightly so that no air gets in or out. ▸ **hermetically** adv.

hermit noun a person who lives alone, esp. for religious reasons.

hermitage noun 1 the place where a hermit lives. 2 a secluded place or retreat.

hernia noun (pl. **hernias, herniae**) a medical condition in which an organ sticks out through a weak spot in the wall of its surroundings.

hero noun (pl. **heroes**) 1 a person who is admired for bravery, courage, and other noble qualities. 2 the main male character, e.g., in a story or play.

heroic adj. 1 very brave. 2 of or about heroes or heroines. —noun (**heroics**) (pl.) overly dramatic speech or behavior. ▸ **heroically** adv.

heroin (hĕr'ō-wĭn) noun a highly addictive drug, formed from morphine, used medically to relieve pain, and illegally for recreation.

heroine (hĕr'ə-wĭn) noun 1 a woman who is admired for bravery, courage, and other noble qualities. 2 the main female character, e.g., in a story or play.

heroism noun the qualities of a hero or heroine, esp. great bravery.

heron noun a large wading bird with long legs, a long neck, and a long pointed bill.

herpes (hər'pēz) noun a viral skin disease characterized by clusters of small blisters.

herring noun (pl. **herring, herrings**) a small fish with a long silvery body, used as food.

herringbone noun a zigzag pattern woven into cloth.

hers pron. the one or ones belonging to her.

herself pron. 1 the reflexive form of her and she: She made herself a dress. 2 used for emphasis: She herself did it. 3 her normal self: She isn't herself this morning. 4 without help; alone: She won the victory by herself.

hertz (hərts') noun (pl. **hertz**) (ABBREV. Hz) the SI unit of frequency, equal to one cycle per second.

he's contr. 1 he is. 2 he has.

hesitant adj. holding back; hesitantly uncertain. ▸ **hesitancy** noun ▸ **hesitantly** adv.

hesitate verb intrans. (**hesitated, hesitating**) 1 to be slow in speaking or acting, esp. because of uncertainty. 2 to be unwilling to do or say something. ▸ **hesitation** noun

hetero- combining form forming words denoting other; different: heterosexual.

heterodox adj. having a belief or beliefs different from what is commonly accepted.

heterosexual adj. 1 sexually attracted to people of the opposite sex. 2 of a relationship involving sexual or romantic partners of opposite sexes. —noun a heterosexual person. ▸ **heterosexuality** noun

heuristic (hyŏŏr-ĭs'tĭk, yŏŏr-) adj. 1 of a teaching method encouraging learners to find their own solutions. 2 Comput., of a program capable of modifying itself or learning from its mistakes or the response of a user. ▸ **heuristically** adv.

hew verb trans., intrans. (pa t **hewed**; pa p **hewn**; pr p **hewing**) 1 to cut or hit (a person or thing) with an ax, sword, etc. 2 to carve or shape (figures, etc.) out of wood or stone.

hexa- combining form forming words denoting six: hexagram.

hexadecimal adj. Comput. denoting a number system having 16 as its base.

hexagon noun a plane figure with six sides and six angles. ▸ **hexagonal** adj.

hexameter (hĕk-săm'ət-ər) noun Poetry a line or verse with six measures or feet.

hey interj. colloq. used to attract attention, or to express joy, surprise, a question, or dismay.

heyday noun a time of greatest success, power, importance, strength, popularity, prosperity, etc.

> From an old English expression heyda, meaning 'hurrah'. The -day ending and current sense developed much later

HF abbrev. high frequency.

Hf symbol Chem. hafnium.

Hg symbol Chem. mercury.

hgt. abbrev. height.

hgwy. abbrev. highway.

HH abbrev. 1 His Holiness. 2 His or Her Highness.

HHFA abbrev. Housing and Home Finance Agency.

HHS abbrev. (Department of) Health and Human Services.

hi interj. used to express a greeting or to attract attention.

hiatus (hī-āt'əs) *noun* (*pl.* **hiatuses**) a break in something which should be continuous.

hibernate *verb intrans.* (**hibernated, hibernating**) *of many mammals* to pass the winter in a sleeplike state. ▶ **hibernation** *noun*

hibiscus *noun* (*pl.* **hibiscuses**) a shrub with large brightly colored flowers.

hiccup *or* **hiccough** *noun* **1** a sudden involuntary breathing in of air caused by a spasm in the diaphragm. **2** (**hiccups**) the frequent repetition of this. **3** *colloq.* a minor, usu. temporary, problem. —*verb intrans., trans.* (**hiccuped, hiccuping**) **1** to make a hiccup or hiccups. **2** to say with a hiccup.

hick *noun colloq.* an unsophisticated person from the country.

hickey *noun* (*pl.* **hickeys**) *slang* a red mark on someone's skin caused, e.g., by biting and sucking while petting. *Also called* **strawberry**.

hickory *noun* (*pl.* **hickories**) **1** a tall tree related to the walnut, with edible nuts. **2** the wood of this tree.

hidden *adj.* difficult to see, find, or understand.

hide[1] *verb trans., intrans.* (*pa t* **hid**; *pa p* **hidden**; *pr p* **hiding**) **1** to put (a person, thing, etc.) into a place where one cannot easily see or find (that person, thing, etc.). **2** to go to or be in a place where one cannot be seen or easily found. **3** to keep (information, feelings, etc.) secret. **4** to make (something) difficult to see; to obscure.

hide[2] *noun* **1** the skin of an animal. **2** *colloq.* the human skin.

hide-and-seek *noun* a children's game in which one child searches for the others who have hidden themselves.

hideaway *noun* a hiding place or refuge. *Also called* **hideout**.

hidebound *adj.* unwilling to accept new ideas or opinions.

hideous (hĭd'ē-əs) *adj.* **1** so ugly and unpleasant as to be repulsive. **2** extremely and disturbingly frightening. ▶ **hideously** *adv.* ▶ **hideousness** *noun*

hideout *noun* a hideaway.

hie (hī) *verb intrans.* (**hied, hieing** *or* **hying, hies**) to go quickly.

hierarchy (hī'ə-rär,kē, hī'rär,-) *noun* (*pl.* **hierarchies**) **1** an arrangement, esp. of people or things in a group, in order of rank or importance. **2** the people who control an organization. ▶ **hierarchical** *adj.*

hieroglyphics *noun* (*sing., pl.*) **1** a form of writing using pictures or symbols to represent a word, syllable, or sound, used in ancient Egypt. **2** *colloq.* writing that is difficult to read. ▶ **hieroglyphic** *adj.*

hifalutin *adj. colloq. same as* **high-falutin**.

hi-fi *noun colloq.* an electronic system that reproduces recorded music or speech with minimal distortion. ▶ **hi-fi** *adj.*

higgledy-piggledy *adv., adj. colloq.* in confusion; in a muddle.

high *adj.* **1** inclined to such a sharp degree as to be almost perpendicular: *high hills.* **2** of relatively great vertical, upward length or extension. **3** of a particular height: *three feet high.* **4** at a relatively great distance from the ground. **5** great; intense. **6** greater than average height. **7** of great monetary price. **8** very important or exalted: *high art.* **9** of sound acute in pitch. **10** extremely emotional: *high drama.* **11** luxurious: *high living.* **12** elated. **13** *colloq.* under the influence of drugs or alcohol. —*adv.* at or to a height; in or into a raised position. —*noun* **1** a high point. **2** an area of high pressure; an anticyclone. **3** *colloq.* a state of great excitement or happiness, sometimes produced by drugs or alcohol. —**high and dry 1** stranded or helpless. **2** *of boats* out of the water. **high and low** everywhere. ▶ **highly** *adv.*

high-and-mighty *adj. colloq.* arrogantly proud.

highball *noun* an alcoholic drink of spirits and soda served in a tall glass.

highbrow *noun* an intellectual or cultured person. —*adj., of art, literature, etc.* intellectual or cultured.

highchair *noun* a baby's or young child's tall chair, used esp. at the table.

high-class *adj.* of high quality or elevated social class.

high court *Law* (*often* **the high court**) the Supreme Court of the United States.

high-falutin (hī,fə-lōōt'n) *or* **hifalutin** *adj. colloq.* pompous or pretentious.

high fidelity hi-fi.

high-five *noun slang* a sign of greeting or celebration, consisting of slapping together raised palms.

highflier *or* **high-flier** *noun* **1** an ambitious person likely to be successful. **2** a person with proven talent in a career field.

high-flying *adj.* extremely ambitious; extremely successful.

high frequency (ABBREV. **HF**) a radio frequency between 3 and 30 megahertz.

highhanded *adj.* behaving or carried out without thought or consideration for others. ▶ **highhandedly** *adv.* ▶ **highhandedness** *noun*

highjack *verb same as* **hijack**.

high jinks *colloq.* boisterous fun; mischief.

high jump **1** an athletic event in which competitors jump over a bar raised higher as the event progresses. *See* **track and field athletics**. **2** *Brit. colloq.* a severe punishment: *be for the high jump.*

highland noun 1 (often **highlands**) a high mountainous area. 2 (**the Highlands**) the mountainous area of N and W Scotland. —adj. (also **Highland**) of, pertaining to, or characteristic of a highland or highlands, or the Scottish Highlands. ▸ **highlander** noun

high-level adj. involving people at a high stratum of management, etc.

highlight noun 1 the best or most memorable event, experience, or part of something. 2 a light streak in one's hair, usu. produced artificially. —verb trans. (**highlighted, highlighting**) to draw attention to or emphasize.

high-minded adj. having or showing noble ideals and principles. ▸ **high-mindedness** noun

highness noun 1 (**Highness**) used as a title when addressing or speaking about a member of a royal family: Your Highness. 2 the state or quality of being high.

high-pitched adj. 1 of a sound high in tone. 2 of a roof steeply angled.

high point the best or most exalted state reached: the high point of a day.

high-powered adj. very powerful or energetic.

high-pressure adj. 1 having, using, etc., air, water, etc., at a high pressure. 2 colloq. very forceful and persuasive. 3 involving considerable effort or stress.

high-profile adj. extremely famous or well known.

high-rise adj., of a building having many floors.

high-risk adj. dangerous.

highroad or **high road** noun 1 the easiest course of action. 2 the most positive attitude or course of action. 3 Brit. a main road.

high school (ABBREV. **HS, H.S.**) a secondary school encompassing, usu. grades 9–12 or 10–12. ▸ **high-school** adj.

high seas the open waters of a sea, not under the control of any country.

high season (usu. **the high season**) the busiest time of year at a resort.

high-sounding adj. pretentious; pompous.

high-spirited adj. lively, cheerful, and vivacious.

high-strung adj. very nervous and easily upset or excited.

high tech colloq. advanced, esp. electronic equipment. ▸ **high-tech** adj.

high-tension adj. (ABBREV. **HT**) 1 of cables, etc. carrying high-voltage electrical currents. 2 operating at or requiring a high voltage, usu. hundreds or thousands of volts.

high tide 1 the highest level reached by a rising tide. Also called **high water**. 2 the time when the tide is farthest up the shore.

high treason treason against one's country or one's monarch.

high water high tide (sense 1).

highway noun a public road, esp. a large or main one.

highwayman noun Hist. a robber, usu. on horseback, who attacks and robs people traveling on public roads.

high wire a tightrope high above the ground.

hijack or **highjack** verb trans. (**hijacked, hijacking**) 1 to take control of (a moving vehicle, esp. an aircraft) and force it to go to a different destination. 2 to stop and rob (a vehicle). ▸ **hijacker** or **highjacker** noun ▸ **hijacking** or **highjacking** noun

hike noun a long walk, usu. in the country. —verb intrans., trans. (**hiked, hiking**) 1 to go on a hike. 2 to pull up or raise (something) with a jerk. 3 to increase (prices) suddenly. —**take a hike** slang to leave because of being unwelcome. ▸ **hiker** noun

hilarious adj. extremely funny. ▸ **hilariously** adv. ▸ **hilariousness** noun

hilarity noun great laughter and amusement.

hill noun 1 any natural elevation of the ground, lower than a mountain. 2 a slope on a road. 3 a heap or mound. —**over the hill** colloq. past one's prime; too old. ▸ **hilly** adj. ▸ **hilliness** noun

hillbilly noun (pl. **hillbillies**) 1 an unsophisticated person from a remote, mountainous country area. 2 country and western music.

hillock noun a small hill.

hillside noun the sloping side of a hill.

hilt noun the handle, e.g., of a sword, dagger, or knife. —**up to the hilt** thoroughly.

him pron. the form of he used as the object of a verb or after a preposition: We all like him.

himself pron. 1 the reflexive form of him or he: He made himself a sandwich. 2 used for emphasis: He did it himself. 3 his normal self: He isn't himself this morning. 4 without help; alone: He won the victory by himself.

hind[1] noun a female deer.

hind[2] adj. situated at the back: hind legs.

hinder verb trans. (**hindered, hindering**) to delay or keep back; to prevent progress.

Hindi (hĭn′dē) noun 1 one of the main languages of India. 2 a group of languages spoken in N India.

hindmost adj. farthest behind; last.

hindquarters pl. noun the back legs and buttocks of a four-legged animal.

hindrance (hĭn′drəns) noun 1 a person or thing that hinders. 2 the act of hindering.

hindsight noun wisdom or knowledge after the event.

Hindu (hĭn′dōō) noun a person who practices Hinduism. —adj. of Hindus or Hinduism.

Hinduism *noun* the main religion of India, which includes worship of many gods, a belief in reincarnation, and the arrangement of people in society in social castes.

Hindustani (hĭn'dŏŏ-stän'ē) *noun* a form of Hindi used as a lingua franca in much of India. —*adj.* relating to Hindustani.

hinge *noun* **1** the movable joint by means of which a door can turn on a frame. **2** a principle or fact on which something else depends. —*verb intrans., trans.* (**hinged, hinging**) **1** to hang or turn on. **2** (**hinge on (something)**) to depend on (it).

hint *noun* **1** a statement that passes on information without giving it openly or directly. **2** a helpful piece of advice. **3** a very small amount. —*verb intrans., trans.* (**hinted, hinting**) **1** (**hint at (something)**) to suggest or imply (it), esp. indirectly. **2** to indicate (something) indirectly. —**take a** or **the hint** *colloq.* to understand what a person is hinting at, and do what that person wants.

hinterland *noun* the land that lies inland from a coast or the banks of a river.

hip[1] *noun* the haunch, or upper fleshy part of the thigh just below the waist.

hip[2] *noun* the large, red, cup-shaped fruit produced by some esp. wild roses.

hip[3] *interj.* used to call for a united cheer: *Hip, hip hooray!*

hip[4] *adj.* (**hipper, hippest**) *colloq.* following current fashions in music, fashion, etc.

hippie or **hippy** *noun* (*pl.* **hippies**) *colloq.* a young person, esp. in the 1960s, typically wearing brightly colored casual clothes and long hair, advocating freedom of thought and esp. cultural and sexual expression.

hippo *noun* (*pl.* **hippos**) *colloq.* a hippopotamus.

hippopotamus *noun* (*pl.* **hippopotamuses, hippopotami**) a large African mammal having a thick hairless body, massive head, and short legs.

> Based on a Greek word which translates as 'river horse'

hippy *noun* same as **hippie**.

hire *verb trans.* (**hired, hiring**) **1** to get the temporary use of (something that belongs to someone else) in exchange for payment. **2** (**hire (oneself or something) out**) to offer (one's) services or give someone the temporary use of (something) in exchange for payment. **3** to employ (someone) for wages. —*noun* **1** an act of hiring. **2** payment for services. **3** *colloq.* a person hired.

hirsute (hər'sōōt, hĭr'-) *adj.* hairy.

his *pron.* the one or ones belonging to him. —*adj.* of or belonging to a male person or animal, or to a thing personified or thought of as male: *went to his house.*

Hispanic (hĭ-spăn'ĭk) *adj.* of Spain, the Spanish, or other Spanish-speaking countries and peoples. —*noun* a Spanish-speaking American of Latin-American descent.

hiss *noun* a sharp sound like that of a prolonged *s.* —*verb, intrans., trans.* (**hissed, hissing**) **1** to make a hiss, esp. as a sign of disapproval or anger. **2** to show one's disapproval (of a person, etc.) by hissing.

histamine *noun Biochem.* a chemical compound present in most body tissues, released into the blood during allergic reactions.

histogram *noun* a chart in which vertical rectangles are used to represent the amount or frequency of a given variable.

historian *noun* a person who studies or writes about history.

historic (hĭs-tôr'ĭk, -tär'-) *adj.* famous or important in history; significant.

> ***Usage*** The adjective *historic* denotes that which is significant or famous in history.

historical *adj.* of or relating to history; of or about people or events from history: *historical novels.* ▸ **historically** *adv.*

> ***Usage*** The adjective *historical* denotes that which existed in the past, important or unimportant; it also denotes anything relating to history or the study of it.

historiography *noun* the study of the writing of history. ▸ **historiographer** *noun*

history *noun* (*pl.* **histories**) **1** the study of events, etc., that happened in the past. **2** a record of past events and developments. **3** everything that is known about past events connected with a particular nation, the world, a person, etc. **4** a past full of events and of more than usual interest.

histrionic *adj.* **1** of behavior, etc. showing too much emotion; theatrical. **2** of or pertaining to actors or acting. —*noun* (**histrionics**) (*pl.*) theatrical or dramatic behavior that conveys excessive, insincere emotion. ▸ **histrionically** *adv.*

hit *verb trans., intrans.* (pa t and pa p **hit**; pr p **hitting**) **1** to strike (a person or thing) with a blow, missile, etc. **2** to knock (something) against something else, esp. hard or violently. **3** to cause to suffer or affect badly: *The news hit her hard.* **4** to direct a blow. **5** *colloq.* to find (esp. an answer) by chance: *You've hit it!* **6** to reach or arrive at. **7** *Sports* to drive (a ball) with a stroke of a bat, etc. —*noun* **1 a** a blow, stroke, or shot. **b** *Comput.* an act or instance of accessing e.g. a website. **2** a shot that is successful. **3** *colloq.* something popular or successful. —**hit it off with (someone)** to get on well with (another or others). **hit the nail on the**

head to be exactly correct. **hit the roof** or **ceiling** slang to explode into anger. **hit the spot** colloq. to be exactly what is needed or appropriate.

hit-and-run adj., of a motor vehicle accident where the driver leaves the scene immediately, without stopping, reporting the accident, or helping the injured.

hitch verb trans., intrans. (**hitched, hitching**) 1 to fasten with a piece of rope, etc.; to tether. 2 to pull (something) up with a jerk: hitched up his trousers. 3 colloq. to hitchhike. —noun 1 a minor, temporary delay or difficulty. 2 a slight jerk. 3 a knot for attaching two pieces of rope together.

hitchhike verb intrans. (**hitchhiked, hitchhiking**) to travel by means of free rides in other people's vehicles. ▸ **hitchhiker** noun

hither adv. to this place.

hitherto adv. up to this or that time.

hit man slang a hired assassin.

hit-or-miss adj. governed not by plan but by chance.

HIV abbrev. Med. human immunodeficiency virus, the virus responsible for AIDS.

hive noun 1 a box for housing bees, esp. honeybees. 2 a colony of bees, esp. honeybees. 3 a place where people are working very busily: a hive of activity.

HM abbrev. Her or His Majesty.

HMO abbrev. health maintenance organization.

HMS abbrev. Her or His Majesty's Ship.

Ho symbol Chem. holmium.

hoagie noun dialect see **submarine sandwich**.

hoar adj. white or grayish-white, esp. with age.

hoard noun an often secret store of money, food, or treasure, usu. hidden away for use in the future. —verb trans., intrans. (**hoarded, hoarding**) to store (food, money, etc.), often in secret and esp. for use in the future. ▸ **hoarder** noun

hoarfrost noun the white frost that forms on grass, etc., in the morning after a cold night.

hoarse adj. 1 of the voice rough and croaking. 2 of a person having a hoarse voice. ▸ **hoarsely** adv. ▸ **hoarseness** noun

hoary adj. (**hoarier, hoariest**) 1 white or gray with age. 2 ancient. ▸ **hoariness** noun

hoax noun a trick played to deceive people, done either humorously or spitefully. —verb trans. (**hoaxed, hoaxing**) to trick or deceive with a hoax. ▸ **hoaxer** noun

hob noun 1 the flat surface for heating pots, etc., on top of a stove. 2 a small shelf next to a fireplace on which pots, etc., may be kept hot.

hobble verb intrans., trans. (**hobbled, hobbling**) 1 to walk with difficulty, taking short, unsteady steps. 2 to tie the legs of (a

horse) together, to stop it from straying.

hobby noun (pl. **hobbies**) an activity or occupation done in one's spare time for pleasure or relaxation.

> Originally hobby-horse, a horse used in morris dances and therefore for amusement or pleasure

hobbyhorse noun 1 a stick with a horse's head at one end, used as a toy. 2 a subject which a person talks about frequently.

hobnail noun a short nail with a heavy head for protecting the soles of boots and shoes.

hobnob verb intrans. (**hobnobbed, hobnobbing**) (**hobnob with** (**someone**)) to spend time with (another or others) socially.

hobo noun (pl. **hoboes, hobos**) a tramp or other homeless person.

hock[1] noun in horses and other hoofed mammals, the joint on the hind leg between the knee and the fetlock.

hock[2] slang verb trans. (**hocked, hocking**) to pawn. —noun the condition of being pawned.

hockey noun 1 field hockey. 2 ice hockey.

hocus-pocus noun colloq. 1 words, actions, etc., that are intended to deceive or mislead. 2 trickery in general.

hod noun 1 a V-shaped box on a pole, used for carrying bricks. 2 a container for coal.

hodgepodge noun a jumble of miscellaneous, dissimilar items.

hoe noun a long-handled tool with a metal blade at one end, used to loosen soil, control weeds, etc. —verb trans., intrans. (**hoed, hoeing**) 1 to use a hoe to loosen soil and control weeds. 2 to use a hoe.

hoedown noun a square dance, or a party at which square dancing is done.

hog noun 1 a any domesticated pig, esp. a castrated male, reared for slaughter. b a pig. 2 slang a greedy person. —verb trans. (**hogged, hogging**) colloq. to take, use, or occupy selfishly.

hogshead (hŏgz'hĕd,, hägz'-) noun a large cask.

hog-tie verb trans. (**hog-tied, hog-tieing** or **hog-tying**) 1 to tie together (the legs of someone). 2 colloq. to obstruct or impede.

hogwash noun colloq. nonsense.

hog-wild adj. colloq. wildly, often irrationally enthusiastic.

hoi polloi (usu. **the hoi polloi**) the common people; the masses.

> Taken from a Greek phrase for 'the people'

hoist verb trans. (**hoisted, hoisting**) 1 to lift or heave up (esp. something heavy). 2 to raise or lift using ropes and pulleys. —noun 1 equipment for lifting heavy objects. 2 colloq. an act of hoisting.

hoity-toity *adj. colloq.* arrogant; haughty.

hokey *adj.* (**hokier, hokiest**) *slang* corny; maudlin.

hold¹ *verb trans., intrans.* (*pa t and pa p* **held**; *pr p* **holding**) **1 a** to have in one's hand or hands. **b** to have in one's possession under one's control. **2** (**hold (something) down** *or* **up**) to support or keep in a particular position. **3** to keep or stay in a particular state. **4** to remain in position, fixed and unbroken, esp. when under pressure. **5** to detain or restrain. **6** to contain or be able to contain. **7** to cause to take place; to conduct. **8** to have (a position of responsibility, job, etc.): *holds office.* **9** to have or possess as a result of, e.g., a competition: *hold the world record.* **10** to keep (a person's attention). **11** *of good weather* to continue. **12** to consider to be. **13** to continue to be valid or apply. **14** (**hold (someone) to (something)**) to compel (someone) to keep (e.g., a promise). **15** to defend from the enemy. **16** to be able to drink (alcohol) without feeling any bad effects. **17** to stop: *hold fire.* **18** to continue to sing or play (a musical note). **19** *of a telephone caller* to wait without hanging up while the person being called comes or returns to the telephone. —*noun* **1** the act of holding; a grasp. **2** power; influence: *have a hold over him.* **3** a way of restraining someone, esp. in certain sports. **4** a thing to hold onto. —**hold back 1** to restrain oneself; to hesitate. **2** to restrain (someone) from doing something. **hold forth** to give one's opinions about something, usu. loudly and at great length. **hold (something) in** to restrain or check (it). **hold out 1** to continue to stand firm. **2** to last. **hold (someone) up** to stop and rob (someone). **hold (something) up 1** to delay (it). **2** to use (it) as a good example for others to follow. ▸ **holder** *noun*

hold² *noun* the place where cargo is stored in ships and aircraft.

holding *noun* **1** land held by lease. **2** the amount of land, shares, etc., that a person or company owns.

holdup *noun* **1** a delay or setback. **2** a robbery, usu. at weaponpoint.

hole *noun* **1** an opening or gap in or through something. **2** a hollow area in something solid. **3** an animal's burrow. **4** *colloq.* an unpleasant, gloomy, or dirty place. **5** *colloq.* an awkward or difficult situation. **6** a fault or mistake. **7** *Golf* a round can-shaped hollow in the middle of each green, into which the ball is hit. ▸ **holey** *adj.*

hole-and-corner *adj.* secretive; underhand.

holiday *noun* **1** a day when one does not have to work, as dictated by law or custom. **2** *Brit.* (often **holidays**) a vacation.

holiness *noun* **1** the state of being holy. **2** (**Holiness**) used as a title for the Pope and certain other religious leaders.

holistic *adj.* denoting an approach to medical treatment that considers a person as a whole. ▸ **holistically** *adv.*

holler *colloq. verb intrans., trans.* (**hollered, hollering**) to shout or cry loudly. —*noun* a shout.

hollow *adj.* **1** containing an empty space; not solid. **2** sunken: *hollow cheeks.* **3** *of a sound* echoing as if made in an empty place. **4** worthless; insincere. —*noun* **1** a hollow or sunken space. **2** a small valley or depression in the land. —*verb trans.* (**hollowed, hollowing**) (**hollow (something) out**) to make a hole or hollow in (it); to form (it) by making a hollow. ▸ **hollowly** *adv.* ▸ **hollowness** *noun*

holly *noun* (*pl.* **hollies**) a tree or shrub with dark, shiny evergreen leaves, usu. with prickly edges, and red berries.

hollyhock *noun* a tall garden plant with colorful flowers.

holmium *noun* (SYMBOL **Ho**) a soft, silvery, metallic element.

holocaust *noun* **1** large-scale destruction, esp. by fire. **2** (**Holocaust**) **a** the mass murder of Jews by the Nazis during the Second World War. **b** a massive slaughter.

hologram *noun Photog.* a three-dimensional image of an object recorded on a photographic plate by the process of holography.

holography *noun Photog.* a photographic technique that uses beams of laser light to produce a three-dimensional image of an object. ▸ **holograph** *noun* ▸ **holographic** *adj.* ▸ **holographically** *adv.*

holster *noun* a leather case for a pistol, usu. worn attached to a belt.

holy *adj.* (**holier, holiest**) **1** belonging to or associated with God or gods; sacred. **2** morally pure; saintly. ▸ **holily** *adv.*

Holy Ghost the Holy Spirit.

holy water water blessed by a priest.

Holy Week in the Christian Church, the week before Easter Sunday.

homage *noun* a display of great respect.

home *noun* **1** the place where one lives. **2** the country or area one comes from. **3** a place where a thing first occurred or was first invented. **4** an institution where people who need care or rest live. **5** *Baseball* home plate. **6** *Sport* the finishing point in some games and races. —*adj.* **1** of one's home, country, or family. **2** made or done at home or in one's own country. **3** *Sport* played on one's own ground: *home games.* —*adv.* **1** at or to a person's home. **2** to the place, position, etc., aimed at: *hit the point home.* **3** as far as possible: *hammer the nail home.* **4** *Sport* on one's own ground. —*verb intrans.* (**homed, homing**) **1** *of a bird* to return home safely. **2** (**home in on** (**something**)) to be directed toward a destination or target. —**bring** (**something**) **home to** (**someone**) to make (it) clear or obvious to (someone). **make** (**oneself**) **at home** to behave as one would in one's own home.

home base 1 *Baseball* home plate. **2** a headquarters.

homecoming *noun* the return home of a person who has been away for a long time.

home economics (*sing., pl.*) the art or science of household management. ▶ **home economist**

homeland (hōm′lănd′, -lənd) *noun* the country where a person is born, or from where his or her ancestors come.

homeless *adj.* having no home; having nowhere to live. —*noun* (**the homeless**) (*pl.*) people having no place to live. ▶ **homelessness** *noun*

homely *adj.* (**homelier, homeliest**) **1** simple but pleasant. **2** making someone feel at home. **3** *of a person* plain and unattractive. ▶ **homeliness** *noun*

homemade *adj., of food, etc.* made at home.

homemaker *noun* the one who manages a domestic household.

homeopathy (hō′mē-ăp′ə-thē) *noun* a system of alternative medicine in which an illness is treated by giving the patient very small doses of drugs which induce the same symptoms as the disease. ▶ **homeopath** *noun* ▶ **homeopathic** *adj.* ▶ **homeopathically** *adv.*

homeostasis (hō′mē-ō-stā′sĭs) *or* **homeostasis** *noun Biol.* the maintenance by a living organism of a constant internal environment that is independent of change in the external environment.

home plate *Baseball* the base on which the batter stands and which the base runners must finally step on or otherwise touch in order to score a run. *Also called* **home, home base.**

homer *noun Baseball* a home run. ▶ **homer** *verb*

home rule government of a country by its own citizens.

home run *Sport* a hit in baseball and softball that permits the batter to make a complete circuit of all the bases and make a score.

homesick *adj.* sad and depressed at being away from one's home and family. ▶ **homesickness** *noun*

homespun *adj. of advice, thinking, etc.* simple and straightforward.

homestead *noun* **1** a house, esp. a farmhouse, with the land and other buildings which belong to it. **2** an area of land granted to a settler for development as a farm.

homestretch *noun* **1** *Sport* the last part of a racecourse just before the finish. **2** the final stages of any project or venture.

hometown *noun* the town where one was born, is living, or has a home.

homeward *adj.* going home. —*adv.* (*also* **homewards**) toward home.

homework *noun* work or study done at home, esp. by students.

homey *or* **homy** *adj.* (**homier, homiest**) like a home, esp. in being warm and comfortable.

homicidal *adj.* **1** of or pertaining to homicide. **2** *of a person* psychologically disposed to commit murder.

homicide (hăm′ə-sīd′, hō′mə-) *noun* **1** the killing of one person by another. **2** a person who kills another person.

homily (hăm′ə-lē) *noun* (*pl.* **homilies**) **1** a sermon. **2** a long, boring talk, usu. telling someone else how to behave.

homing *adj.* **1** *of a pigeon* able to find its way home. **2** *of a missile* able to guide itself to its target.

hominy *noun* coarsely ground corn, boiled with water or milk to make a soft breakfast food.

hommos *noun* same as **hummus.**

homo- *combining form* forming words denoting same: *homosexual.*

homoeopathy *noun Brit.* homeopathy.

homogeneity (hō′mə-jə-nē′ĭ-tē, -nā′-) *noun* the quality of being homogeneous.

homogeneous (hō′mə-jē′nē-əs) *adj.* made of parts that are all of the same kind. ▶ **homogeneously** *adv.*

homogenize (hə-măj′ə-nīz′) *verb trans.* (**homogenized, homogenizing**) **1** to break up the fat droplets of a liquid, esp. milk, so that they are evenly distributed throughout the liquid. **2** to make homogeneous.

homogenous *adj. Biol.* similar, owing to common descent.

homogeny *noun Biol.* similarity of structure due to common descent or origin.

homograph (hăm′ə-grăf′, hō′mə-) *noun* a word with the same spelling as another but with a different meaning and origin and sometimes a different pronunciation, e.g., *entrance* (a way in; stressed on *en-*) and *entrance* (to bewitch; stressed on *-trance*).

homologous *adj.* **1** having a related or similar function or position. **2** *Biol.* denoting plant or animal structures that have a common origin, but have developed different forms and functions. *See also* **analogous.** ▶ **homology** *noun*

homonym *noun* a word having the same sound and spelling as another word but a different meaning, e.g., *kind* (helpful) and *kind* (sort).

homophobia *noun* an intense dislike or fear of homosexuals. ▸ **homophobic** *adj., noun*

homophone *noun* a word having the same sound as another word but a different spelling and meaning, e.g., *bear/bare*.

homosexual *noun* a person who is sexually attracted to people of the same sex. —*adj.* of or concerning a homosexual or homosexuals. ▸ **homosexuality** *noun*

homy *adj.* same as **homey**.

Hon. *abbrev.* Honorable.

honcho *slang noun* (*pl.* **honchos**) a leader. —*verb trans.* (**honchoed, honchoing, honchos**) to lead, manage, or otherwise direct.

hone *noun* a smooth stone for sharpening tools and knives. —*verb trans.* (**honed, honing**) to sharpen with or as if with a sharpening tool; to whet.

honest (ăn′əst) *adj.* 1 truthful; trustworthy. 2 sincere and respectable. 3 just or fair: *an honest wage.* 4 ordinary and undistinguished. ▸ **honestly** *adv.* ▸ **honesty** *noun*

honey *noun* (*pl.* **honeys**) 1 the edible, thick, sweet substance made by bees. 2 a dark, dull, yellow color. 3 *colloq.* used as a term of endearment. 4 *colloq.* a person or thing that is excellent of its kind.

honeybee *noun* any of several varieties of bee which live in hives and make honey.

honeycomb *noun* 1 the structure formed by the rows of hexagonal cells of beeswax, in which bees store honey. 2 a structure resembling a honeycomb.

honeyed (hŭn′ēd) *adj.* ingratiatingly pleasing, flattering, or soothing: *a honeyed voice.*

honeymoon *noun* 1 a vacation taken by a newly married couple. 2 a period of goodwill and enthusiasm at the beginning, e.g., of a new business relationship or political administration. —*verb intrans.* (**honeymooned, honeymooning**) to spend a honeymoon. ▸ **honeymooner** *noun*

honeysuckle *noun* a climbing garden shrub with sweet-smelling flowers.

honk *noun* 1 the sound made by a horn, e.g., on a motor vehicle. 2 the cry of a wild goose. —*verb trans., intrans.* (**honked, honking**) to make or cause to make a honking noise.

honky *or* **honkie** *or* **honkey** *noun* (*pl.* **honkies, honkeys**) *offensive slang* a white person.

honky-tonk *noun colloq.* 1 a style of popular piano music based on ragtime. 2 a cheap, seedy nightclub.

honor (ăn′ər) *noun* 1 great respect or public regard. 2 the quality of doing what is right and having a high standard of moral behavior. 3 fame or glory, often achieved through bravery. 4 a source of fame, glory, or distinction, e.g., for one's country. 5 the pleasure or privilege. 6 *old use* a woman's chastity or her reputation for being chaste. 7 (**honors**) a a special college or university program for exceptional students. b special recognition for outstanding academic achievements: *graduated with honors in English.* 8 (**His, Her** *or* **Your Honor**) used as a title of respect for judges and mayors. 9 (**honors**) in some card games, any of the top four or five cards. 10 *Golf* the right to play from the tee first. —*verb trans.* (**honored, honoring**) 1 to hold (someone or something) in high regard; to have a high opinion of. 2 to give (someone) an award, title, or honor as a mark of respect for (an ability or achievement, etc.). 3 a to pay (a bill, debt, etc.) when it falls due. b to accept (e.g., a check) as good. 4 to keep (a promise).

honorable *adj.* 1 deserving or worthy of honor. 2 having high moral principles. 3 (**Honorable, The Honorable** *or* **The Hon.**) used as a courtesy title before the full names of some high officials. ▸ **honorably** *adv.*

honorary *adj.* 1 given to a person as a mark of respect, without the usual requirement having been met or privileges extended: *an honorary degree.* 2 of an official position not providing any payment; voluntary.

honor-bound *adj.* obliged to do something out of duty or moral considerations.

honorific *adj.* showing or giving respect.

hood¹ *noun* 1 a covering for the whole head, often attached to a coat at the collar. 2 a folding, usu. removable, roof or cover, e.g., on a car. 3 a hinged lid that covers a motor or engine compartment on a motor vehicle. ▸ **hooded** *adj.*

hood² *noun slang* a hoodlum.

-hood *suffix* 1 denoting a state or condition: *manhood.* 2 denoting a collection or group: *priesthood.*

hoodlum (hood′ləm, hood′-) *noun* 1 a criminal. 2 a young, violent, destructive, or badly behaved person.

hoodoo (hood′oo) *noun* 1 voodoo. 2 bad luck, or the thing or person bringing it. —*verb trans.* (**hoodooed, hoodooing, hoodoos**) to bring bad luck to.

hoodwink (hood′wĭngk,) *verb trans.* (**hoodwinked, hoodwinking**) to trick or deceive.

hooey *noun slang* nonsense.

hoof (hoof, hoof) *noun* (*pl.* **hoofs, hooves**) the horny structure at the end of the feet of horses, cows, etc. —*verb trans.* (**hoofed, hoofing, hoofs**) to trample with the hoofs.

hoo-ha *noun slang* a commotion, usu. an angry one.

hook *noun* 1 a small piece of metal, etc., shaped like a J, used for catching and holding things. **2** a curved tool for cutting grain, branches, etc. **3** a sharp bend or curve, e.g., in a river. **4** a *Boxing* a swinging punch with the elbow bent. **b** *Golf* a shot that sends the ball to the right-handed player's left. **c** *Basketball* a shot that is made over one's head and shoulders in a high, arcing movement while moving sideways to the basket. —*verb trans., intrans.* (**hooked, hooking**) **1** to catch with or as if with a hook. **2** (*also* **hook up** *or* **hook (something) up**) to fasten or be fastened to (something else) by means of a hook or hooks. **3** *Golf* to hit (the ball) out around the other side of one's body, i.e., to the left if one is right-handed. —**by hook or by crook** by some means or other, proper or improper. **hook, line, and sinker** *colloq.* completely. **off the hook 1** *colloq.* excused of the blame for something. **2** *of a telephone receiver* not on its rest. ▸ **hooked** *adj.*

hookah (hōōk′ə) *noun* a tobacco pipe that passes through water, cooling the smoke before it is drawn into the mouth.

hooker *noun slang* a prostitute.

hookey (hōōk′ē) *noun slang* absence from school without permission.

hookup *noun* **1** a temporary linking up of separate broadcasting stations for a special broadcast. **2** an arrangement of circuits or other components for a particular purpose.

hooligan *noun* a violent, destructive, or badly behaved young person. ▸ **hooliganism** *noun*

hoop *noun* **1 a** a thin ring of metal, wood, etc., esp. one used around casks. **b** a circular earring shaped like a ring. **2** a large ring, esp. one made of light wood or plastic, used as a toy. **3 a** *Sport* a metal arch that the ball is hit through in croquet. **b** *Basketball* the basket through which the ball is thrown; the game of basketball itself. —*verb trans.* (**hooped, hooping**) to bind with a hoop or hoops.

hoopla *noun slang* great commotion, excitement, or publicity.

hooray (hə-rā′) *interj. same as* **hurrah**.

hoot *noun* **1** the call of an owl. **2** the sound of a car horn, siren, whistle, etc. **3** a loud shout of laughter, scorn, or disapproval. **4** *slang* a highly amusing person, event, or thing. —*verb intrans., trans.* (**hooted, hooting**) **1** to make a hoot. **2** to sound (a car horn, etc.). **3** to shout or laugh loudly, expressing disapproval, scorn, etc. **4** to force (a performer) off the stage by hooting.

hooter *noun* **1** an instrument that makes a hooting sound. **2** *Brit. colloq.* the human nose. **3** *coarse slang* a woman's breast.

hooves *see* **hoof**.

hop¹ *noun* **1** a tall climbing plant. **2** (*usu.* **hops**) the female flower of this plant, used for

flavouring beer. —*verb trans.* (**hopped, hopping**) to flavor (beer) with hops.

hop² *verb intrans., trans.* (**hopped, hopping**) **1** *of a person* to jump on one leg, esp. repeatedly. **2** *of certain small animals* to jump on both or all legs simultaneously. **3** to jump over. **4** to move in a lively way. **5** *colloq.* to make a short journey, esp. by air: *hopped over to France from Scotland.* —*noun* **1** an act of hopping; a short jump. **2** *colloq.* a short journey by air. **3** an informal dance. —**hop to it** *colloq.* to start doing something without further delay.

hope *noun* **1** a desire for something, esp. when there is a measure of confidence in obtaining it. **2** a person, thing, or event that one is relying on. **3** a reason for believing that the thing desired will still happen. **4** that which is desired or hoped for. —*verb trans., intrans.* (**hoped, hoping**) **1** to wish or desire that something may happen, esp. with some reason to believe that it will: *hope for peace.* **2** to want and expect. ▸ **hopeful** *adj.* ▸ **hopefulness** *noun*

hopefully *adv.* **1** in a hopeful way. **2** *colloq.* it is to be hoped.

hopeless *adj.* **1** not likely to be successful. **2** *colloq.* (**hopeless at (something)**) not competent to do (it). **3** unable to be stopped or cured. ▸ **hopelessly** *adv.* ▸ **hopelessness** *noun*

hopper *noun* **1** a person or thing that hops. **2** a funnel-shaped container used for feeding e.g. grain into another container below.

hopscotch *noun* a children's game in which players take turns at throwing a stone into one of a series of squares drawn on the ground and hopping in the others around it.

horde *noun* a crowd or large group, esp. a noisy one.

horizon *noun* **1** the line at which Earth or the sea and the sky appear to meet. **2** the limit of a person's knowledge, interests, or experience.

horizontal *adj.* **1** at right angles to vertical; level or flat. **2** applying equally to all members of a group or all aspects of a situation. —*noun* a horizontal line or position. ▸ **horizontally** *adv.*

hormone *noun* **1** a substance produced by a part of a plant or animal body, and which has a specific effect on that body. **2** a synthetic chemical which has the same effects as a natural hormone. ▸ **hormonal** *adj.*

horn *noun* **1** one of a pair of hard, hollow, usu. pointed structures that grow on the heads of cattle, sheep, etc. **2** the bony substance of which horns are made. **3** something that looks like a horn in shape. **4** *Mus.* **a** a wind instrument made of brass. **b** a French horn. **5** an apparatus for making a warning sound, esp. on a vehicle. —*verb trans.* (**horned**, **horning**) **1** to fit with a horn or horns. **2** to injure or gore with horns. ▸ **horned** *adj.*

hornet *noun* a large wasp that can sting severely. —**stir up a hornet's nest** to cause a strong or hostile reaction.

hornpipe *noun* **1** a lively, solo sailor's jig. **2** the music for this dance.

horny *adj.* (**hornier, horniest**) **1** of or like horn, esp. in being hard. **2** *slang* sexually excited.

horology *noun* the art of measuring time or making clocks and watches. ▸ **horological** *adj.* ▸ **horologist** *noun*

horoscope *noun* **1** a description of a person's future based on the position of the stars and planets at the time of his or her birth. **2** a diagram showing the positions of the stars and planets at a particular moment in time.

horrendous *adj.* causing great shock, fear, or terror; horrifying. ▸ **horrendously** *adv.* ▸ **horrendousness** *noun*

horrible (hôr'ə-bəl, här'-) *adj.* **1** extremely and disturbingly frightening. **2** unpleasant.

horribly *adv.* **1** in a horrible way. **2** badly; very.

horrid *adj.* **1** revolting; detestable. **2** unpleasant; disagreeable. ▸ **horridly** *adv.* ▸ **horridness** *noun*

horrific *adj.* **1** causing fear, disgust, or horror; terrible. **2** *colloq.* very bad. ▸ **horrifically** *adv.*

horrify *verb trans.* (**horrified, horrifying, horrifies**) to shock greatly. ▸ **horrifying** *adj.* ▸ **horrifyingly** *adv.*

horror *noun* **1** intense fear. **2** intense dislike, loathing, or disgust. **3** a person or thing causing intense fear, loathing, or disgust. **4** *colloq.* a bad or ridiculous person or thing. **5.** (*attributive*) of literature, films, *etc.* based on horrifying or frightening themes.

hors d'oeuvre (ôr-dərv') *noun* a small appetizer served at the beginning of a meal.

horse *noun* **1** a large hoofed four-legged animal with a long mane and tail, used e.g. for pulling carts and carrying people. **2** an adult male horse. **3** cavalry. **4** *Sport* a piece of apparatus used for vaulting. **5** a clotheshorse. —**straight** or **right from the horse's mouth** directly from a reliable source.

horseback *adj., adv.* on the back of a horse.

horse chestnut chestnut (sense 3).

horseflesh *noun* **1** the meat of a horse. **2** horses as a group.

horsefly *noun* (*pl.* **horseflies**) a large fly that bites horses and cattle.

horseman (hôr'smən) *noun* **1** a male rider. **2** a skilled male rider. ▸ **horsemanship** *noun*

horseplay *noun* rough, noisy play.

horsepower *noun* (ABBREV. **HP, hp**) the US Customary System unit of power, equal to

745.7 watts or 33,000 foot-pounds per minute.

horseracing *noun* the competitive sport of racing horses around a track. ▸ **horserace** *noun*

horseradish *noun* a plant with a long, white sharp-tasting root which is used to make a sauce, usu. eaten with beef.

horse sense plain good sense.

horseshoe *noun* **1** a piece of curved iron nailed to the bottom of a horse's hoof to protect the foot. **2** something in this shape, esp. as a symbol of good luck.

horsetail *noun* **1** the tail of a horse. **2** a plant with a hollow, green, jointed stem and whorls of small scalelike leaves.

horsewhip *noun* a whip for encouraging horses. —*verb trans.* (**horsewhipped, horsewhipping**) to whip, esp. severely, usu. as a punishment.

horsewoman *noun* **1** a female rider. **2** a skilled female rider.

horsy or **horsey** *adj.* (**horsier, horsiest**) **1** of or relating to horses. **2** suggestive of a horse. **3** *colloq.* very interested in or devoted to horses.

horticulture *noun* the science and art of cultivating fruit, vegetables, flowers, etc.. ▸ **horticulturally** *adv.* ▸ **horticulturist** *noun*

hosanna (hō-zăn'ə) *noun, interj.* used to shout adoration or praise to God.

hose *noun* **1** (*pl.* **hoses**) a flexible tube for directing water. **2** (*pl.*) women's stockings or men's socks. —*verb trans.* (**hosed, hosing**) (**hose (something) down**) to direct water at (something) or clean (it) with a hose.

hosiery (hō'zhə-rē) *noun* stockings or socks.

hospice (hăs'pĭs) *noun* a program that specializes in the care of the terminally ill and provides support for their families.

hospitable *adj.* showing kindness to guests or strangers. ▸ **hospitably** *adv.*

hospital *noun* (ABBREV. **H, h**) an institution where people who are physically or mentally ill receive medical or surgical care and nursing.

hospitality (hăs,pĭ-tăl'ət-ē) *noun* a friendly welcome for guests or strangers, which usu. includes offering them food and drink.

hospitalize *verb trans.* (**hospitalized, hospitalizing**) to take or admit or send (a person) into a hospital for treatment. ▸ **hospitalization** *noun*

host¹ (hōst) *noun* **1** a person who receives and entertains guests in his or her own home. **2** *old use* an innkeeper or hotel manager. **3** a person who introduces performers, etc., on a television or radio show. **4** *Biol.* a plant or animal on which a parasite lives and feeds. —*verb trans., intrans.* (**hosted, hosting**) to act as a host to (people) or be the host of (an event or program).

host² *noun* **1** a very large number. **2** an army.

host³ or **Host** *noun* the bread or wafer of the Eucharist.

hostage (hăs'tĭj) *noun* a person who is held prisoner as a guarantee that demands will be met.

hostel *noun* **1** a building that provides overnight accommodations as a charity, esp. for the homeless. **2** a youth hostel. **3** *old use* an inn.

hostess *noun* **1** a woman who receives and entertains guests in her own home. **2** a woman employed to greet and seat customers in a restaurant or hotel dining room. **3** a woman who introduces performers, etc., on a television or radio show.

hostile (hăs'təl, -tīl,) *adj.* **1** *of a person or an action* ready or displaying readiness to attack. **2** of or belonging to an enemy. **3** (**hostile to** (**something**)) strongly opposed to (it).

hostility *noun* (*pl.* **hostilities**) **1** aggression; opposition. **2** (**hostilities**) acts of war.

hot *adj.* (**hotter, hottest**) **1** having a relatively high temperature. **2** producing or giving off heat. **3** highly radioactive. **4** *of food* causing a burning sensation on the tongue; spicy. **5** easily angered; excitable. **6 a** full of passion or zeal. **b** feeling sexual desire. **7** *of a contest or fight* intense; animated. **8** *of news* recent; fresh. **9** strongly favored: *a hot favorite.* **10** *of music* having strong, exciting rhythms. **11** *of colors* bright; fiery. **12** *slang, of goods* stolen, esp. recently stolen. **13** *slang, of information* up to date and reliable. **14** *colloq., of a situation* difficult, unpleasant, or dangerous: *made life hot for him.* **15** in a game, etc., very close to guessing correctly or finding the thing sought. —*noun* (**the hots**) *slang* strong sexual desire. —**hot and bothered** *colloq.* anxious and confused. **in hot pursuit** chasing as fast or as closely as one can. ▸ **hotly** *adv.*

hot air *colloq.* empty or boastful talk.

hotbed *noun* a place or situation that allows something, esp. something bad, to grow quickly: *a hotbed of discontent.*

hot-blooded *adj.* having strong, esp. sexual, feelings.

hotcake *noun* a pancake. —**sell like hotcakes** *colloq.* to sell quickly and in high volume.

hotchpotch *noun* **1** a hodgepodge. **2** a mutton stew with vegetables.

hot dog 1 a hot frankfurter in a long, soft bread roll. **2** *slang* a person who does dangerous athletic stunts.

hotel (hō-tĕl') *noun* a building providing lodging, meals, and other services to paying guests.

hotelier (hō-tĕl'yər, ōt,l-yā') *noun* a person who owns or manages a hotel.

hot flash 1 a sudden, short sensation of heat felt typically over the entire body. **2** *slang* an important newsbrief.

hotfoot *verb intrans.* (**hotfooted, hotfooting**) *colloq.* (**hotfoot it**) to rush.

hothead (hăt'hĕd,) *noun* a person easily angered. ▸ **hotheaded** *adj.* ▸ **hotheadedness** *noun*

hothouse *noun* **1** a greenhouse that is kept warm for growing tender or tropical plants. **2** (*attributive*) *of a plant* suitable for growing in a greenhouse.

hot key *Comput.* a key that activates a program when pressed, either alone or in combination with other keys.

hot line 1 a direct, exclusive telephone line, esp. for use by political leaders in crisis situations. **2** an emergency telephone number for receiving inquiries and providing help regarding personal problems or crises.

hot potato *colloq.* a difficult, controversial problem or situation.

hot rod a car modified to generate high power and great speed.

hot seat 1 *colloq.* an uncomfortable or difficult position. **2** *slang* the electric chair.

hotshot *noun slang* a very daring, successful person.

hot spot *colloq.* an area where there is likely to be trouble, esp. political or military.

hot stuff *colloq.* **1** a person who has outstanding ability. **2** a person who is sexually exciting.

hot-tempered *adj.* quick to anger.

hot tub a very large tub in which one or more people may soak.

hot water *colloq.* trouble; bother.

hot-wire *verb trans.* (**hot-wired, hot-wiring**) *slang* to start (a vehicle engine) by touching together electrical wires rather than using the ignition switch.

hound *noun* **1** (*often in compounds*) a hunting-dog. **2** *colloq.* a despicable person. **3** *colloq.* one who eagerly pursues an objective. —*verb trans.* (**hounded, hounding**) to chase or bother relentlessly.

hour *noun* **1** one of 24 units of time in a day, equal to 60 minutes, or 3,600 seconds. **2** any of the points on a clock or watch that shows the hour. **3** a point in time: *an early hour.* **4** the time allowed or fixed for an activity: *office hours.* **5** the distance traveled in an hour.

hourglass *noun* an instrument which measures an hour by the running of sand from one glass chamber to another. —*adj.* curving in at the waist or middle like an hourglass: *an hourglass figure.*

hourly *adj.* **1** happening or done every hour. **2** measured by the hour. **3** frequent; continual.

—*adv.* **1** every hour. **2** at any hour: *expect news hourly.* **3** by the hour. **4** frequently.

house *noun* **1 a** a building in which people live. **b** the people living in such a building. **2** (*in compounds*) a building used for a particular purpose: *an opera house.* **3** (**House**) a legislative body that makes laws, or the place where it meets. **4** a business firm: *a publishing house.* **5** the audience in a theater, a theater itself, or a performance given there. **6** (*often* **House**) a family, esp. an important or noble one. **7** *Astrol.* one of the 12 divisions of the heavens. —*verb trans.* (**housed, housing**) **1** to provide with a house or similar shelter. **2** to store. **3** to protect (a part) by covering. —**on the house** of food, drink, *etc.* paid for by the manager or owner; free.

house arrest confinement in one's own home, rather than prison, by court order.

houseboat *noun* a boat that is built to be lived in or for cruising or both.

housebreak *verb trans.* (**housebroke, housebroken, housebreaking**) to train (e.g., a puppy) to acquire excretory habits suitable to living chiefly indoors.

housebreaking *noun* the unlawful breaking into a building in order to steal. ▸ **housebreaker** *noun*

housefly *noun* a common fly, often found in houses.

household *noun* the people who live together in a house. —*adj.* of or relating to a house or the people living in one. ▸ **householder** *noun*

househusband *noun* a husband who does the work usu. done by a housewife.

housekeeper *noun* a person who is paid to look after the management of a (usu. large) house and household.

housekeeping *noun* **1** the management of a house or household. **2** money set aside to pay for the expenses of running a house.

housemaid *noun* a maid employed to keep a house or other building clean and tidy.

housemate *noun* a person with whom one shares a house.

House of Commons in the UK, the lower elected assembly of Parliament, or the building where this assembly meets.

House of Lords in the UK, the upper assembly of Parliament, made up of peers and bishops.

house-proud *adj.* taking a lot of pride in the condition and appearance of one's house.

housesit *verb intrans.* (**housesat, housesitting**) to live in and take care of a house while its owner is away. ▸ **housesitter** *noun*

housewarming *noun* a party given to celebrate moving into a new house.

housewife *noun* (*pl.* **housewives**) a woman who looks after her house, her husband, and

her family, and who often does not have a job outside the home. ▸ **housewifely** *adj.*

housework *noun* the work of keeping a house clean and tidy.

housing (how'zĭng) *noun* **1** houses as a group. **2** the act or job of providing housing for people. **3** the hard cover around a machine.

hove *see* **heave** (sense 6).

hovel (hŏv'əl, hăv'-) *noun* a small, dirty dwelling.

hover *verb intrans.* (**hovered, hovering**) **1** of a bird, helicopter, *etc.* to remain in the air without moving in any direction. **2** to move around while still remaining near a person or thing. **3** (**hover between**) to be undecided. —*noun* an act or state of hovering or waiting to make a decision.

hovercraft *noun* a vehicle that is able to move over land or water on a cushion of air.

how *adv.* **1** in what way; by what means: *How did it happen?* **2** to what extent: *How old is he?* **3** in what condition, esp. of health: *How is she feeling now?* **4** to what extent is something good, successful, *etc.*. *How was your vacation?* **5** using whatever means are necessary: *Do it how best you can.* —*conj.* *colloq.* that: *He told me how he'd done it on his own.* —*noun* a manner or means of doing something: *the how and why.* —**how about?** would you like?; what do you think of? **how come?** *colloq.* for what reason?

howdy *interj.* used to express hello.

however *adv.* **1** in spite of that; nevertheless. **2** *esp.* implying surprise in what way?; by what means?: *However did you do that?* **3** by whatever means: *Do it however you want to.* **4** to no matter what extent: *You must finish this however long it takes.*

howl *noun* **1** the long, loud, plaintive cry of a wolf or dog. **2** a long, loud cry made, e.g., by the wind. **3** a cry of pain or distress. **4** a loud yell of laughter. **5** *slang* something extremely funny. —*verb intrans., trans.* (**howled, howling**) **1** to make a long, loud, plaintive cry or similar wailing noise. **2** to cry or laugh loudly. **3** to shout or shriek (instructions, orders, etc.).

howler *noun colloq.* a glaring mistake.

howling *adj. colloq.* very great: *a howling success.*

howsoever *adv.* in whatever way; to whatever extent.

how-to *adj.* offering detailed instructions and advice: *a how-to guide to home repairs.* ▸ **how-to** *noun*

hoy *interj.* used to attract attention.

hoyden (hoid'n) *noun* a wild, lively girl. ▸ **hoydenish** *adj.*

hp *abbrev.* horsepower.

HQ *abbrev.* headquarters.

HR *abbrev.* House of Representatives.

hr *abbrev.* hour.

HRH or **H.R.H.** *abbrev.* His or Her Royal Highness.

HS or **H.S.** *abbrev.* high school.

HST or **H.S.T.** *abbrev.* Hawaiian Standard Time.

hub *noun* **1** the center of a wheel, propeller, fan, or other circular rotating part. **2** the main point of activity, interest, etc.

hubbub *noun* a confused noise of many sounds. ⊟ HULLABALOO, PANDEMONIUM, TUMULT, UPROAR.

> Originally meaning 'battle' or 'war cry', based on an Irish Gaelic word

hubby *noun (pl.* **hubbies)** *colloq.* a husband.

hubcap *noun* the metal cover over the hub of a wheel.

hubris (hyōō'brĭs) *noun* arrogance or overconfidence, esp. when likely to end in disaster or ruin.

huckster *noun* **1** a street trader. **2** an aggressive seller or advertiser.

HUD (hŭd') *abbrev.* (Department of) Housing and Urban Development.

huddle *verb (trans., intrans.)* **(huddled, huddling) 1 (huddle together** or **up)** to crowd together closely. **2** to sit curled up. **3** to curl (oneself) up. —*noun* **1** a confused mass or crowd. **2** a secret or private conference: *go into a huddle.*

hue *noun* **1** a color or shade. **2** the feature of a color that makes it different from other colors. **3** aspect or appearance in general.

huff *noun* a fit of anger or annoyance. —*verb intrans., trans.* **(huffed, huffing) 1** to blow or puff loudly. **2** to give or take offense. ▸ **huffy** *adj.* ▸ **huffily** *adv.* ▸ **huffiness** *noun*

hug *verb trans.* **(hugged, hugging) 1** to hold tightly in one's arms, esp. to show love. **2** to keep close to: *a ship hugging the shore.* **3** to hold (a belief, etc.) very firmly. —*noun* a tight grasp with the arms, esp. to show love.

huge *adj.* of exceedingly or excessively large size. ⊟ COLOSSAL, CYCLOPEAN, DINO-SAURIC, ELEPHANTINE, ENORMOUS, GARGANTUAN, GIANT, GIGANTIC, HER-CULEAN, HUMONGOUS, IMMENSE, LEVI-ATHAN, MAMMOTH, MASSIVE, MASTO-DONIC, MONSTER, MONSTROUS, MONU-MENTAL, MOUNTAINOUS, PRODIGIOUS, PYTHONIC, Titan, TITANIC, TREMEND-OUS ⊟ LITTLE, MINIATURE, SMALL, TINY. ▸ **hugely** *adv.* ▸ **hugeness** *noun*

huh *interj. colloq.* used to express disgust, disbelief, or inquiry.

hulk *noun* **1** the stripped body of an old ship. **2** a ship that is or looks difficult to steer. **3** a large, awkward person or thing.

hulking *adj.* large and awkward.

hull *noun* **1** the floating body or frame of a ship. **2** the outer covering or husk of a fruit or seed. **3** the calyx at the base of certain fruits, e.g., the strawberry. —*verb trans.* **(hulled, hulling)** to remove (the outer casing) from a fruit or seed.

hullabaloo *noun* a confused noise of many sounds.

hullo *interj.* hello.

hum *verb intrans., trans.* **(hummed, humming) 1** to make a low, steady murmuring sound like a bee. **2** to sing (a tune) with one's mouth shut. **3** to speak indistinctly or stammer, esp. through embarrassment. **4** to be full of activity. —*noun* **1** a low, steady murmuring sound. **2** busy activity. —*interj.* used to express hesitation or contemplation.

human (hyōō'mən, yōō'-) *adj.* **1** of or belonging to people. **2** having or showing the qualities, esp. the weaknesses, of people as opposed to God, animals, or machines. **3** thoughtful. —*noun* a human being.

human being *noun* a person.

humane (hyōō-mān', yōō-) *adj.* **1** kind; sympathetic. **2** *of a branch of learning* likely to civilize or make more elegant. ▸ **humanely** *adv.* ▸ **humaneness** *noun*

humanitarian *adj.* concerned about improving, or likely to improve, people's lives. —*noun* a person who tries to do this by means of political and social reform, charity, etc. ▸ **humanitarianism** *noun*

humanity *noun (pl.* **humanities) 1** the human race. **2** the nature of human beings. **3** kindness or mercy. **4 (the humanities)** subjects involving the study of human culture, esp. language, literature, and philosophy.

humanize *verb trans.* **(humanized, humanizing)** to make caring, thoughtful, and compassionate. ▸ **humanization** *noun*

humankind *noun* human beings as a whole.

humanly *adv.* within human power: *a task not humanly possible.*

humble *adj.* **1** having a modest opinion of oneself and one's abilities, etc.; not proud. **2** having a low position in society. **3** lowly; modest. —*verb trans.* **(humbled, humbling)** to make humble, modest, or of less importance. ▸ **humbleness** *noun* ▸ **humbly** *adv.*

humbug *noun* **1** something done to deceive; a trick. **2** nonsense; rubbish. **3** a dishonest person. —*interj.* used to express contempt or disgust.

humdinger *noun slang* an exceptionally good person or thing.

humdrum *adj.* dull; ordinary; monotonous.

humerus *noun (pl.* **humeri)** the bone of the upper arm, extending from the shoulder to the elbow in humans.

humid *adj.* damp; moist. ▸ **humidity** *noun*

humidifier *noun* a device for adding moisture

to dry air to increase the humidity or maintain it at a desirable level, esp. in a home or office.

humidify verb trans. (**humidified, humidifying, humidifies**) to make (the air or atmosphere) damp or humid.

humiliate (hyōō-mĭl′ē-āt,, yōō-) verb trans. (**humiliated, humiliating**) to make (someone) feel ashamed or look foolish. ▸ **humiliating** adj. ▸ **humiliatingly** adv. ▸ **humiliation** noun

humility noun 1 the state or quality of being humble. 2 lowliness of mind; modesty.

hummingbird noun a small brightly-colored bird which beats its wings rapidly making a humming noise.

hummock noun a low hill.

hummus (həm′əs, hōōm′-), **humus** or **hommos** noun a Middle Eastern hors d'oeuvre or dip consisting of pureed cooked chickpeas and tahini paste, flavored with lemon juice and garlic.

humongous (hyōō-məng′gəs, yōō-) or **humungous** adj. slang of exceedingly or excessively large size.

humor (hyōō′mər, yōō′-) noun 1 the quality of being amusing. 2 the ability to amuse or be amused. 3 a state of the mind and emotions: in good humor. 4 writing, plays, speech, etc., that are amusing or funny. 5 any of various fluids in the body. —verb trans. (**humored, humoring**) to please (someone) by doing what that person wishes. ▸ **humorist** noun ▸ **humorless** adj.

humorous adj. funny; amusing. ▸ **humorously** adv. ▸ **humorousness** noun

humour Brit. noun, verb humor.

hump noun 1 a large, rounded lump of fat on the back of a camel. 2 a lump on a person's back caused by an abnormality of the spine. 3 a rounded lump on a road. —verb trans., intrans. (**humped, humping**) 1 (**hump (something) about** or **around**) to carry (esp. something awkward or heavy) with difficulty. 2 coarse slang to have sexual intercourse with (someone). —**over the hump** colloq. having gotten beyond the hardest stage or part.

humpback noun 1 a back with a hump. 2 a hunchback. 3 a whale with a humplike dorsal fin. —adj. (also **humpbacked**) rising and falling in the shape of a hump; having a hump.

humph interj. used to express doubt or displeasure.

humungous adj. slang same as **humongous**.

humus[1] (hyōō′məs, yōō-) noun dark brown substance produced in soil as a result of decomposing plant and animal matter.

humus[2] (həm′əs, hōōm′-) noun same as **hummus**.

Hun noun 1 Hist. a member of a powerful and warlike people who invaded Europe in the 4th and 5th centuries. 2 offensive slang a German.

hunch noun 1 an idea or belief based on one's feelings, suspicions, or intuition rather than on clear evidence. 2 a hump. —verb trans., intrans. (**hunched, hunching**) 1 to bend or arch. 2 (also **hunch up**) to sit with one's body curled up or bent.

hunchback noun a person with a large round lump on his or her back, usu. caused by an abnormality of the spine.

hundred noun (pl. **hundreds, hundred**) 1 the number or figure 100. 2 the age of 100. 3 any person or thing denoted by the number 100. 4 a set of 100 people or things. 5 a score of 100 points. 6 (usually **hundreds**) colloq. very many: hundreds of people. —adj. 1 100 in number. 2 aged 100. ▸ **hundredth** noun, adj.

hundredweight noun (pl. **hundredweight, hundredweights**) 1 a measure of weight in the US Customary system equal to 100 pounds (45.36 kg). Also called **short hundredweight**. 2 a measure of weight in the British Imperial system equal to 112 pounds (50.80 kg). Also called **long hundredweight**.

hung verb see **hang**. —**hung over** colloq. suffering from a hangover. **hung up on** colloq. extremely anxious or obsessed about (something or someone), esp. needlessly.

Hungarian (həng-găr′ē-ən) adj. of Hungary or its official language. —noun 1 a citizen of or person from Hungary. 2 the official language of Hungary.

hunger noun 1 the desire or need, esp. very great, for food. 2 a strong desire. —verb intrans. (**hungered, hungering**) (**hunger for** or **after (something)**) to have a strong desire for (it).

hungry (həng′grē) adj. (**hungrier, hungriest**) 1 wanting or needing food. 2 (**hungry for (something)**) having a strong desire for (it). 3 reflecting or expressing greed or desire: hungry eyes. ▸ **hungrily** adv. ▸ **hungriness** noun

hunk noun 1 a lump broken or cut off from a larger piece. 2 slang a strong, muscular, sexually attractive man. ▸ **hunky** adj.

hunker verb intrans. (**hunkered, hunkering**) (usu. **hunker down**) 1 to squat; crouch. 2 to refuse to yield.

hunky-dory adj. slang excellent.

hunt verb trans., intrans. (**hunted, hunting**) 1 to chase and kill (animals) for food or for sport. 2 to hunt foxes using hounds, and on horseback. 3 (**hunt for (something)**) to search for (it); to look for (it). 4 (**hunt (someone or something) down** or **out**) to search for and find or capture (the one or ones specified). —noun 1 an act or instance of hunting. **2** a group of people meeting together on horses to hunt foxes. ▸ **hunter** *noun* ▸ **hunting** *noun* ▸ **huntress** *noun*

huntsman (hŏnt'smən) *noun* **1** a male hunter. **2** an official who manages the hounds during a fox hunt.

hurdle *noun* **1** *Sport* one of a series of light barriers to be jumped in a race. **2** (**hurdles**) *Sport* a race with hurdles. **3** a problem or difficulty. —*verb trans., intrans.* (**hurdled, hurdling**) to jump (hurdles) in a race. ▸ **hurdler** *noun*

hurdy-gurdy *noun* (*pl.* **hurdy-gurdies**) a musical instrument with strings that make a droning noise when they are sounded by a wheel turned by a handle.

hurl *verb trans.* (**hurled, hurling**) **1** to throw violently. **2** to speak (esp. words of abuse or insults) with force and spite.

hurly-burly *noun* the noisy activity of crowds.

hurrah *or* **hooray** *noun, interj.* used to express great joy, enthusiasm, or pleasure at a victory.

hurricane *noun* an intense cyclonic tropical storm with wind speeds in excess of 74 mph (119 kph).

hurried *adj.* done quickly, esp. too quickly. ▸ **hurriedly** *adv.* ▸ **hurriedness** *noun*

hurry *verb intrans., trans.* (**hurried, hurrying, hurries**) **1** to move or cause to move or act quickly. **2** to cause to move or progress too quickly. —*noun* **1** great haste or speed. **2** the need for haste or speed. —**hurry up** *or* **hurry** (**someone**) **up** to move or try to cause to move more quickly than before. **in a hurry 1** hurrying; rushed; impelled by haste or urgency. **2** readily; willingly: *I won't do that again in a hurry.*

hurt *verb trans., intrans.* (pa t and pa p **hurt**; pr p **hurting**) **1** to injure or cause physical pain to. **2** to upset. **3** to be injured or painful. **4** to have an adverse or negative effect. **5** *colloq.* to be in a state of need or distress: *He's hurting after losing his job.* —*noun* **1** an injury or wound. **2** mental pain or suffering. —*adj.* **1** injured. **2** upset; distressed. ▸ **hurtful** *adj.* ▸ **hurtfully** *adv.* ▸ **hurtfulness** *noun*

hurtle *verb trans., intrans.* (**hurtled, hurtling**) to move or throw very quickly and violently.

husband (hŭz'bənd) *noun* a man to whom a woman is married. —*verb trans.* (**husbanded, husbanding**) to use (money, resources, etc.) wisely and with economy.

husbandry *noun* **1** the practice or occupation of farming. **2** the economic management of resources.

hush *interj.* used to indicate that another or others ought to be quiet or still. —*noun* silence. —*verb trans., intrans.* (**hushed, hushing**) to make or become quiet or still.

hushed *adj.* very quiet; silent and still.

hush-hush *adj. colloq.* secret.

hushpuppy *noun* (*pl.* **hushpuppies**) a small, usu. oblong or rounded ball of deep-fat fried cornmeal.

husk *noun* the thin, dry, outer covering of certain fruits and seeds. —*verb trans.* (**husked, husking**) to remove (the husk) from a fruit or seed.

husky[1] *adj.* (**huskier, huskiest**) **1** *of a voice* rough and dry in sound. **2** *colloq.* big and strong: *husky football players.* ▸ **huskily** *adv.* ▸ **huskiness** *noun*

husky[2] *noun* (*pl.* **huskies**) any of various breeds of dog with a thick coat and a curled tail, used in the Arctic region to pull sleds. *Also called* **Eskimo dog.**

hussy *noun* (*pl.* **hussies**) an immoral or immodest girl or woman.

hustings *pl. noun* **1** the platform, etc., from which speeches are made during a political election campaign. **2** the speeches, etc., made during an election campaign.

hustle *verb trans., intrans.* (**hustled, hustling**) **1** to push roughly; to jostle. **2** to coerce (someone) to act or deal with something quickly: *hustled us into agreeing.* **3** *slang* to sell (goods) aggressively. —*noun* **1** lively activity. **2** *slang* a swindle. ▸ **hustler** *noun*

hut *noun* a small house or shelter, usu. made of wood.

hutch *noun* **1** a box with a wire front for small animals, e.g., rabbits. **2** a cupboard with open shelves on top and drawers below.

hyacinth (hī'ə-sĭnth) *noun* a plant which grows from a bulb and has sweet-smelling flowers.

hyaena *noun same as* **hyena.**

hybrid *noun* **1** an animal or plant produced by crossing two species, varieties, or breeds. **2** something produced by combining elements from different sources. —*adj., of an animal or plant* produced by crossing two species, varieties, or breeds. ▸ **hybridism** *noun* ▸ **hybridization** *noun* ▸ **hybridize** *verb*

hydr- *combining form same as* **hydro-.**

hydra *noun* **1** a freshwater polyp with a tubelike body and tentacles around the mouth. **2** something hard to finish, get rid of, or destroy.

hydrangea (hī-drān'jə) *noun* a garden shrub with clusters of pink or blue flowers.

hydrant *noun* a pipe connected to the main water supply, esp. in a street, with a nozzle for attaching a hose when fighting fires. *Also called* **fire hydrant, fireplug.**

hydrate (hī'drāt,) *noun Chem.* a chemical compound that contains a fixed number of molecules of water of crystallization. (hī-drāt')—*verb intrans., trans.* (**hydrated,**

hydrating) 1 to form such a compound. **2** to cause a substance to absorb water. **hydration** noun

hydraulic (hī-drô'līk) adj. **1** of, relating to, or using a liquid or liquids in motion. **2** of or relating to the pressure generated when a liquid, such as water or oil, is forced through a pipe. **3** of or relating to a machine or device that is operated by this pressure. **4** relating to hydraulics. ▸ **hydraulically** adv.

hydraulics noun (sing.) Eng. the study of the mechanical properties of fluids, esp. water, at rest or in motion, and how to use them.

hydro noun (pl. **hydros**) a hydroelectric power plant.

hydro- or **hydr-** combining form forming words meaning: **1** of or by means of water: hydroelectricity. **2** combined with hydrogen: hydrocarbon.

hydrocarbon noun Chem. an organic compound of hydrogen and carbon.

hydrocephalus (hī,drī-sĕf'ə-ləs) noun Med. a condition of having an abnormal amount of fluid in the brain, causing the head to be enlarged. ▸ **hydrocephalic** adj.

hydrochloric acid Chem. a solution of the gas hydrogen chloride in water, creating a powerful acid used in industry.

hydroelectric adj. generating electricity by means of the pressure of falling water. ▸ **hydroelectrically** adv. ▸ **hydroelectricity** noun

hydrofoil noun **1** a device on a boat that lifts it out of the water as its speed accelerates. **2** a boat fitted with such a device.

hydrogen (hī'drə-jən) noun (SYMBOL H) the first and lightest element in the periodic table, and by far the most abundant element in the universe.

hydrogenate (hī-drăj'ə-nāt,) verb intrans., trans. (**hydrogenated, hydrogenating**) Chem. **1** of hydrogen to combine with another substance. **2** to cause (a substance) to undergo a reaction with hydrogen. ▸ **hydrogenation** noun

hydrogen bomb Mil. the most powerful form of nuclear bomb, which releases vast amounts of energy as a result of the nuclear fusion of deuterium and tritium. Also called **H-bomb**. See also **thermonuclear bomb**.

hydrogenous adj. relating to or consisting of hydrogen.

hydrogen peroxide Chem. a colorless viscous liquid, H_2O_2, it is used in antiseptics, disinfectants, and bleaches for hair and textiles. Also called **peroxide**.

hydrology noun the study of the movement and properties of water, and its resources on Earth.

hydrolysis (hī-drăl'ə-sĭs) noun the chemical decomposition or alteration of a compound as a result of its reaction with water.

hydrometer (hī-drăm'ət-ər) noun Phys. a floating instrument used to measure the density of a liquid.

hydropathy (hī-drăp'ə-thē) noun a way of treating disease or illness using water both internally and externally. ▸ **hydropathic** adj.

hydrophobia noun **1** the fear of water. **2** the inability to swallow water, especially as a symptom of rabies. **3** rabies. ▸ **hydrophobic** adj.

hydroplane noun **1** a light, flat-bottomed motorboat which, at high speeds, skims along the surface of the water. **2** a finlike device on a submarine which allows it to rise and fall in the water.

hydrosphere noun the water, e.g., seas and rivers, on the surface of Earth.

hydrotherapy noun Med. the treatment of diseases and disorders by the external use of water.

hydrous adj. containing water.

hydroxide (hī-drăk'sīd,) noun Chem. a chemical compound that contains the hydroxide (OH⁻) ion or the hydroxyl (-OH) group.

hydroxyl group Chem. the (-OH) group, in a chemical compound, consisting of a hydrogen atom and an oxygen atom bonded together.

hyena (hī-ē'nə) or **hyaena** noun a doglike carnivorous mammal with a shrill cry.

hygiene (hī'jēn,) noun the practice or study of health and cleanliness. ▸ **hygienic** adj. ▸ **hygienically** adv.

hygrometer (hī-grăm'ət-ər) noun Meteorol. an instrument for measuring humidity.

hymen noun Anat. a thin membrane that covers the opening of the vagina at birth.

hymn (hĭm) noun a song of praise, esp. to God.

hymnal (hĭm'nəl) noun a book of hymns.

hype¹ colloq. noun intensive, exaggerated, and usu. misleading publicity or advertising. —verb trans. (**hyped, hyping**) to promote or advertise (something) intensively.

hype² verb intrans. (**hyped, hyping**) slang to inject oneself with a drug. —**hyped up** slang highly excited, esp. as if by drugs.

hyper adj. slang overexcited or overactive.

hyper- combining form forming words denoting over, beyond, more than normal: hyperactive.

hyperactive adj., esp. of a child abnormally or excessively active. ▸ **hyperactivity** noun

hyperbola (hī-pər'bə-lə) noun (pl. **hyperbolas, hyperbolae**) Geom. a plane curve produced when a section is cut in a cone at a steeper angle to its base than its side. ▸ **hyperbolic** adj.

hyperbole (hī-pər'bə-lē) noun the use of an overstatement or exaggeration to produce an effect. ▸ **hyperbolic** adj.

hypercritical adj. overly critical. ▶ **hypercritically** adv.

hyperglycemia noun Med. a condition in which the glucose (sugar) concentration in the blood is abnormally high.

hypermarket noun a very large supermarket.

hypersensitive adj. very sensitive, or more sensitive than is normal. ▶ **hypersensitivity** noun

hypersonic adj. Aeron. having a speed more than five times the speed of sound.

hypertension noun Med. abnormally high blood pressure.

hypertext noun Comput. computer-readable text in which cross-reference links have been inserted, enabling the user to call up relevant data from other files, or parts of the same file, by clicking on a coded word or symbol, etc.

hypertrophy noun (pl. **hypertrophies**) Biol. an abnormal enlargement of an organ or cell.

hyperventilation noun Med. the abnormal increase in the speed and depth of breathing.

hyphen noun a punctuation mark (-) used to join two words to form a compound (booby-trap, double-barreled) or, esp. in printing, to split a word syllabically between the end of one line and the beginning of the next. —verb trans. (**hyphened, hyphening**) to hyphenate.

hyphenate (hī′fə-nāt,) verb trans. (**hyphenated, hyphenating**) to join (two words or parts of a word) with a hyphen. ▶ **hyphenation** noun

hypnosis (hĭp-nō′sĭs) noun (pl. **hypnoses**) a sleeplike state in which the subject is deeply relaxed and acts only on the suggestion of another person. ▶ **hypnotism** noun ▶ **hypnotist** noun

hypnotherapy noun the treatment of illness or habits such as smoking by hypnosis.

hypnotic (hĭp-nät′ĭk) adj. **1** of, relating to, causing, or produced by hypnosis. **2** causing sleepiness or sleep. —noun a drug that induces sleep. ▶ **hypnotically** adv.

hypnotize verb trans. (**hypnotized, hypnotizing**) **1** to put (someone) in a state of hypnosis. **2** to fascinate or bewitch.

hypo (hī′pō) noun (pl. **hypos**) colloq. a hypodermic syringe or injection.

hypo- combining form forming words denoting under, beneath, inadequate: hypotension.

hypochondriac (hī,pə-kän′drē-ăk,) noun one who is excessively concerned about one's health. —adj. excessively concerned about one's health. ▶ **hypochondria** noun

hypocrisy (hĭ-päk′rə-sē) noun (pl. **hypocrisies**) the act or state of pretending to have feelings or beliefs that one does not actually have, or of hiding one's true character.

hypocrite (hĭp′ə-krĭt,) noun a person who pretends to have feelings or beliefs he or she does not actually have, or who hides his or her true character. ▶ **hypocritical** adj. ▶ **hypocritically** adv.

hypodermic (hī,pə-dər′mĭk) adj., of an instrument or drug for injecting under the skin. —noun **1** a hypodermic syringe. **2** an injection of a drug under the skin.

hypodermic syringe a syringe with a fine hollow needle, used for injecting drugs under the skin or taking blood samples.

hypoglycemia noun Med. an abnormal reduction of glucose in the blood.

hypotension noun abnormally low blood pressure.

hypotenuse (hī-pät′n-yoōs,, -noōs,) noun Math. the longest side of a right-angled triangle, opposite the right angle.

hypothermia noun Med. a condition caused by exposure to cold, in which the body temperature falls below normal.

hypothesis (hī-päth′ə-sĭs) noun (pl. **hypotheses**) a statement or proposition assumed to be true and on which an argument, etc., may be based. ▶ **hypothesize** verb intrans., trans.

hypothetical adj. based on a hypothesis; assumed. ▶ **hypothetically** adv.

hyrax noun a mammal that resembles a large guinea pig, with a pointed muzzle and round ears.

hyssop noun a small shrubby plant with narrow leaves and long spikes of bluish-violet flowers.

hysterectomy noun (pl. **hysterectomies**) the surgical removal of the uterus.

hysteria noun **1** Psychol. a mental disorder characterized by symptoms such as hallucinations and uncontrolled weeping. **2** any uncontrolled emotional state caused by acute stress or a traumatic experience.

> Based on a Greek word for 'womb', because originally thought to be caused by womb disease or abnormalities

hysteric noun a hysterical person.

hysterical adj. **1** of or suffering from hysteria. **2** colloq. very funny. ▶ **hysterically** adv.

hysterics noun **1** (sing. pl.) a fit of hysteria. **2** colloq. uncontrollable laughter.

Hz abbrev. hertz.

Ii

I¹ or **i** *noun* (*pl.* **Is**, **I's**, **i's**) the ninth letter of the English alphabet.

I² *pron.* used by the speaker or writer to refer to himself or herself as the subject of an actual or implied verb.

> *Usage* See note at **between**.

I³ *abbrev.* **1** Institute. **2** Interstate. **3** Island.

I⁴ *symbol* **1** *Chem.* iodine. **2** the Roman numeral for one.

-ial *suffix* **1** forming adjectives denoting of, relating to: *managerial*. **2** forming nouns denoting the action of: *tutorial*.

iamb (ī'ăm،, -ămb،) or **iambus** *noun* (*pl.* **iambs**, **iambuses** or **iambi**) *Poetry* a metrical foot containing one short or unstressed syllable followed by one long or stressed one. ▸ **iambic** *adj.*, *noun*

-ian *suffix* **1** forming adjectives denoting relating to, similar to: *Dickensian*. **2** forming nouns denoting a person interested or skilled in: *historian*.

ib. or **ibid.** *abbrev.* ibidem.

Iberian (ī-bîr'ē-ən) *noun* a native or citizen of the Iberian Peninsula; a Spaniard or Portuguese. —*adj.* of the Iberian Peninsula, its people, or their languages.

ibex (ī'běks،) *noun* (*pl.* **ibex**, **ibexes**) a bearded wild goat having a gray or yellowish-brown coat and large backward-curving horns with prominent ridges.

ibidem (ĭb'ə-děm،) *adv.* in the place in a book, article, passage, etc., previously mentioned or cited.

-ible *suffix* forming words denoting "that may be or is capable of being": *expressible*. See also **-able**.

IBS *abbrev. Med.* irritable bowel syndrome.

ibuprofen *noun* an anti-inflammatory drug used esp. to treat arthritis.

-ic *suffix* **1** (*also* **-ical**) forming words denoting relating to: *photographic*. **2** *Chem.* forming words denoting formed with an element in its higher valence: *sulfuric*.

ICBM *abbrev.* intercontinental ballistic missile.

ice *noun* **1** water in its solid frozen state. **2** a sheet of frozen water, e.g., on the surface of a road. **3** ice cream or water ice, or a portion of it. **4** *slang* diamonds. **5** coldness of manner; reserve. —*verb trans.*, *intrans.* (**iced**, **icing**) **1** to chill with ice. **2** (*often* **ice over** or **up**) to freeze: *The bridge has iced over.* **3** to cover (a cake) with icing. —**break the ice** to relax feelings of reserve, shyness, or formality, esp. between strangers. **on ice** to be used later, or awaiting further attention.

Ice Age 1 any of several periods of time in Earth's history when ice sheets and glaciers covered large areas of Earth.

iceberg *noun* a huge mass of ice floating in the sea, only a part of which projects above the surface.

iceboat *noun* **1** an icebreaker (sense 1). **2** a sharp-runnered vehicle with a sail and a tiller, used for sailing across ice.

icebox *noun* **1** a refrigerator compartment where food is kept frozen and ice is made. **2** a refrigerator.

icebreaker *noun* **1** a ship designed to cut channels through floating ice. Also called **iceboat**. **2** *colloq.* something said or done to relax an otherwise formal or uncomfortable situation.

icecap *noun* a thick mass of ice or snow that permanently covers the polar regions of a planet, the peak of a mountain, etc.

ice cream a sweet, creamy frozen dessert, made either from cream or a substitute, and flavored.

ice cube a small block of ice used for cooling drinks, etc.

ice hockey a form of hockey played on ice by two teams of skaters, using long wooden sticks and a puck instead of a ball, in which each team tries to shoot the puck into the opposing team's goal.

Icelandic *noun* the language of Iceland. —*adj.* of Iceland, its people, or their language.

ice milk a smooth, sweet, cold food like ice cream but made with skim milk.

ice pack 1 pack ice. **2** a bag filled with crushed ice, applied to the body to reduce swelling.

ice pick a small tool with a pointed end for breaking ice into small pieces for drinks.

ice skate a skate with a metal blade for use on ice. ▸ **ice-skate** *verb intrans.* ▸ **ice-skater** *noun* ▸ **ice-skating** *noun*

ice storm a winter storm in which ice pellets fall, or rain or snow freezes on contact, forming a coating of ice on surfaces.

ichthyology (ĭk،thē-ăl'ə-jē) *noun* the study of fish. ▸ **ichthyological** *adj.* ▸ **ichthyologist** *noun*

icicle (ĭ'sĭk-əl) *noun* a long, hanging spike of ice, formed by water freezing as it drops.

icing *noun* a mixture of sugar, egg whites, water, and flavoring, used to form a coating on cakes and other pastries.

icon (ī'kăn) or **ikon** *noun* **1** an image of Christ, the Virgin Mary, or a saint, usu. painted on wood, esp. in the Orthodox Church. **2** a picture, image, or representation. **3** *Comput.* a small picture or symbol, displayed on the screen of a computer, that represents a particular command or operation.

iconoclast *noun* **1** a person who destroys religious images and is opposed to their use in worship. **2** a person who attacks traditional and cherished beliefs and superstitions. ▸ **iconoclasm** *noun* ▸ **iconoclastic** *adj.*

-ics *suffix* forming singular or plural nouns denoting subjects of study or activities: *athletics* / *mathematics. See also* **-ic**.

icy *adj.* (**icier, iciest**) **1** extremely cold. **2** covered with ice. **3** unfriendly; hostile. ▸ **icily** *adv.* ▸ **iciness** *noun*

ID or **Id.** *abbrev.* identification.

I'd *contr.* **1** I had. **2** I would.

id *noun Psychol.* the part of the unconscious mind that is regarded as the source of primitive biological instincts and urges for survival and reproduction, and governs the unconscious. *See also* **ego, superego**.

-ide *suffix Chem.* denoting a compound of an element with some other element, etc.: *chloride. See also* **-ate, -ite.**

idea *noun* **1** a thought, image, or concept formed by the mind. **2** a plan or intention. **3** a main aim, purpose, or feature. **4** a vague notion or fancy: *have no idea of the work required.* **5** a conception of what is the best or perfect example: *not my idea of fun.*

ideal *adj.* **1 a** highest and best; perfect. **b** exactly right or appropriate. ▣ MODEL, PERFECT, VERY ▣ INAPPROPRIATE, WRONG. **2** existing only in the mind; imaginary; visionary. —*noun* **1** the highest standard of behavior, perfection, beauty, etc. **2** a person or thing considered to be perfect. ▸ **ideally** *adv.*

idealism *noun* **1** a tendency to present things in an ideal or idealized form. **2** the practice of forming and living according to ideals. **3** *Philos.* the theory that material objects and the external world do not really exist but are products of the mind. *See also* **realism** (sense 3). ▸ **idealist** *noun* ▸ **idealistic** *adj.* ▸ **idealistically** *adv.*

idealize *verb trans., intrans.* (**idealized, idealizing**) to regard or treat (a person, thing, etc.) as perfect or ideal. ▸ **idealization** *noun*

idem (ĭd'əm, ĭd'-, ēd'-) *pron.* the same author, place, etc., as previously mentioned.

identical *adj.* **1** being exactly alike in every respect. **2** being one single one instead of another or others: *sat in the identical chair at every meal.* **3** *of twins* developed from the same fertilized egg. ▸ **identically** *adv.*

identify *verb trans.* (**identified, identifying, identifies**) **1** to establish the identity of. **2** to associate (one person, thing, or group) with another. **3** (**identify with (someone)**) to feel understanding for a person because of shared characteristics or experiences. **4** to see clearly or pinpoint (a problem, etc.). ▸ **identifiable** *adj.* ▸ **identification** *noun*

identity *noun* (*pl.* **identities**) **1** the state or quality of being a specified person or thing: *The winner's identity is not yet known.* **2** the individual characteristics by which a person or thing can be identified. **3** the state of being exactly the same.

ideogram *noun* a written symbol designed to convey an abstract concept, or that stands for a real object without being a direct representation of it. *Also called* **logograph, pictograph.**

ideology *noun* (*pl.* **ideologies**) **1** the set of ideas and beliefs forming the basis for a social, economic, or political system. **2** the opinions, beliefs, and way of thinking characteristic of a particular person, group of people, or nation. ▸ **ideological** *adj.* ▸ **ideologically** *adv.* ▸ **ideologist** *noun*

idiocy *noun* (*pl.* **idiocies**) **1** the state of being an idiot or extremely retarded mentally. **2** a foolish action or foolish behavior.

idiom *noun* **1** an expression with a meaning that cannot be guessed at or derived from the meanings of the individual words that form it. **2** the syntax, grammar, and forms of expression peculiar to a language or a variety of language. **3** the language, vocabulary, forms of expression, etc., used by a particular person or group of people. ▸ **idiomatic** *adj.* ▸ **idiomatically** *adv.*

idiosyncrasy (ĭd,ē-ō-sĭng'krə-sē) *noun* (*pl.* **idiosyncrasies**) a personal peculiarity or eccentricity. ▸ **idiosyncratic** *adj.* ▸ **idiosyncratically** *adv.*

idiot *noun* **1** *colloq.* a foolish or stupid person. **2** a person who is severely mentally retarded. ▸ **idiotic** *adj.* ▸ **idiotically** *adv.*

idle (īd'l) *adj.* **1** not in use. **2** lazy. **3** without cause, basis, or good reason: *idle rumor.* —*verb trans., intrans.* (**idled, idling**) **1** to spend time doing nothing. **2** to do nothing: *youngsters idling at malls.* **3** *of an engine, etc.* to run slowly, esp. when out of gear. **4** to cause (an engine, etc.) to idle. ▸ **idleness** *noun* ▸ **idler** *noun* ▸ **idly** *adv.*

idol (īd'l) *noun* **1** an image or symbol used as an object of worship. **2** an object of excessive love, honor, or devotion.

idolatry *noun* (*pl.* **idolatries**) **1** the worship of idols. **2** excessive love, honor, admiration, or devotion. ▸ **idolater** *noun* ▸ **idolatrous** *adj.* ▸ **idolatrously** *adv.*

idolize *verb trans.* (**idolized, idolizing**) **1** to love, honor, admire, etc., (a person) too much. **2** to make an idol of. ▸ **idolization** *noun* ▸ **idolizer** *noun*

idyll (īd'l) or **idyl** *noun* **1** a short poem or prose work describing a simple, pleasant, usu. pastoral scene. **2** a story or scene suitable for such a work, e.g., one of happy innocence or love. ▸ **idyllic** *adj.* ▸ **idyllically** *adv.*

i.e. *abbrev. id est* (Latin), that is to say.

if *conj.* **1** in the event that. **2** although; even though. **3** whenever. **4** whether. **5** used to express a wish: *If only it would stop raining.* **6** used to make a polite request or suggestion: *if you wouldn't mind stopping just a minute.* —*noun* a condition or supposition: *too many ifs and buts.*

iffy *adj.* (**iffier, iffiest**) *colloq.* uncertain; doubtful; dubious.

igloo *noun* a dome-shaped house built with blocks of snow and ice.

igneous *adj.* **1** of or resembling fire. **2** *Geol.* denoting rocks that are formed by the solidification of molten magma. *See also* **metamorphic, sedimentary.**

ignis fatuus (ĭg,nĭs-făch'ə-wəs) (*pl.* **ignes fatui**) phosphorescent light that hovers over swampy land at night. *Also called* **wildfire, will-o'-the-wisp.**

ignite *verb trans., intrans.* (**ignited, igniting**) **1** to burn, or cause to start burning. **2** to excite (feelings, emotions, etc.). ▸ **ignitable** *adj.*

ignition *noun* **1** the act or instance of igniting. **2** *Engineering* a system that produces a spark, igniting an explosive mixture of fuel and air in an internal combustion engine.

ignoble *adj.* **1** causing shame; dishonorable; mean. **2** of humble or low birth. ▸ **ignobility** *noun* ▸ **ignobleness** *noun* ▸ **ignobly** *adv.*

ignominy *noun* **1** loss of respect or favor, or the cause of it. **2** dishonorable conduct. ▸ **ignominious** *adj.* ▸ **ignominiously** *adv.* ▸ **ignominiousness** *noun*

ignoramus *noun* (*pl.* **ignoramuses**) an ignorant person.

ignorant *adj.* **1** lacking education or knowledge. **2** (**ignorant of (something)**) knowing little or nothing about (it). **3** rude; ill-mannered. ▸ **ignorance** *noun* ▸ **ignorantly** *adv.*

ignore *verb trans.* (**ignored, ignoring**) to take no notice of deliberately.

iguana (ĭg-wän'ə) *noun* a large gray-green tree-dwelling lizard with a row of spines along its back.

ikon *noun same as* **icon.**

il- *prefix* a form of *in-*.

ileum *noun* (*pl.* **ilea**) the lowest part of the small intestine.

ilium *noun* (*pl.* **ilia**) the hip bone. ▸ **iliac** *adj.*

ilk *noun* —**of that ilk** of that type or kind.

I'll *contr.* **1** I will. **2** I shall.

ill *adj.* (**worse, worst**) **1** being in poor health. **2** of health in a state that is or was unsound. **3** bad or harmful: *ill effects.* **4** hostile; unfriendly. **5** causing bad luck: *an ill omen.* **6** of manners incorrect; improper. —*adv.* (**worse, worst**) **1** with difficulty; not easily. **2** in a mean manner; harshly: *spoke ill of me.* —*noun* **1** evil; harm. **2** injury; ailment.

ill-advised *adj.* done with little thought or consideration.

ill at ease anxious or embarrassed.

ill-bred *adj.* badly brought up or educated; rude.

ill-considered *adj.* badly thought out; not well planned.

illegal *adj.* against the law. ▸ **illegality** *noun* ▸ **illegally** *adv.*

illegible (ĭl-ĕj'ə-bəl) *adj.* difficult or impossible to read; not legible. ▸ **illegibility** *noun* ▸ **illegibly** *adv.*

illegitimate *adj.* **1** born of parents not married to each other. **2** against the law. ▸ **illegitimacy** *noun* ▸ **illegitimately** *adv.*

ill-equipped *adj.* poorly provided with the necessary tools, abilities, etc.

ill-fated *adj.* ending in or bringing bad luck or ruin.

ill-favored *adj.* not attractive, esp. in appearance; objectionable.

ill feeling bad or hostile feeling; animosity.

ill-founded *adj.* having no sound basis or reason.

ill-gotten *adj.* obtained dishonestly: *ill-gotten gains.*

ill-humored *adj.* irritable; bad-tempered; quick-tempered.

illiberal *adj.* having strict opinions about morality, behavior, etc.; narrow-minded; prejudiced. ▸ **illiberality** *noun* ▸ **illiberally** *adv.*

illicit (ĭl-ĭs'ĭt) *adj.* **1** forbidden by social custom. **2** against the law. ▸ **illicitly** *adv.* ▸ **illicitness** *noun*

illiterate *adj.* unable to read and write. —*noun* a person who is unable to read and write. ▸ **illiteracy** *noun* ▸ **illiterately** *adv.*

ill-mannered *adj.* lacking or exhibiting a lack of social manners.

ill-natured *adj.* surly; mean.

illness *noun* **1** a disease. **2** the state of being sick or unwell.

illogical *adj.* **1** not based on careful thinking or reason. **2** following no principles of logic. ▸ **illogicality** *noun* ▸ **illogically** *adv.*

ill-starred *adj.* marked by bad luck; bound to fail.

ill-tempered *adj.* bad-tempered; surly.

ill-treat *verb trans.* (**ill-treated, ill-treating**) to treat badly or cruelly; to abuse. ▸ **ill-treatment** *noun*.

illuminate (ĭ-lōō′mĭ-nāt,) *verb trans.* (**illuminated, illuminating**) 1 to light up or make bright. 2 to decorate with lights. 3 to make more easily understood. 4 to decorate (a manuscript). ▸ **illumination** *noun*

illumine *verb trans.* (**illumined, illumining**) *poetic, literary* to illuminate.

illusion *noun* 1 a deceptive or misleading appearance. 2 a false or misleading impression, belief, or understanding. 3 a misleading perception of an object or experience. ▸ **illusive** *adj.* ▸ **illusory** *adj.*

> *Usage* The word *illusion* is often confused with *allusion*.

illustrate (ĭl′ə-strāt,) *verb trans.* (**illustrated, illustrating**) 1 to provide (a book, text, etc.) with pictures and diagrams. 2 to make (a statement, etc.) clearer, esp. by providing examples. 3 to be an example of. ▸ **illustration** *noun* ▸ **illustrative** (ĭ- əs′trət-ĭv) *adj.* ▸ **illustratively** *adv.* ▸ **illustrator** *noun*

illustrious *adj.* distinguished; renowned; celebrated. ▸ **illustriously** *adv.*

ill will wishing that distress, injury, or pain will befall another.

ILO *abbrev.* International Labor Organization.

I'm *contr.* I am.

im- *prefix* a form of *in-*.

image *noun* 1 a likeness of a person or thing, esp. in the form of a portrait or statue. 2 a person or thing that resembles another person or thing closely. 3 an idea or picture in the mind. 4 an optical reproduction of a physical object formed by light reflected in a mirror. 5 the visual display reproduced by a television receiver. 6 the impression that people in general have of someone's character, behavior, etc. 7 a typical example or embodiment. —*verb trans.* (**imaged, imaging**) 1 to form an image of. 2 to form a likeness of in the mind; to imagine.

imagery *noun* (*pl.* **imageries**) 1 the use of figures of speech in writing, literature, etc. 2 mental images.

imaginary *adj.* 1 existing only in the mind or imagination; not real. 2 consisting of, involving, or containing an imaginary number.

imaginary number the square root of a negative number.

imagination *noun* 1 the ability to form or the process of forming mental images of things which are not real or known. 2 the creative ability of the mind. 3 the ability to cope resourcefully with unexpected events.

imaginative *adj.* 1 showing, done with, or created by imagination. 2 having a lively imagination. ▸ **imaginatively** *adv.* ▸ **imaginatively** *noun*

imagine *verb trans., intrans.* (**imagined, imagining**) 1 to formulate a picture of (something) in the mind. 2 to see or hear, etc. (something that is not true or does not exist). 3 to think, suppose, or guess. 4 to use the imagination. ▸ **imaginable** *adj.*

imago (ĭm-ā′gō, -äg′ō) *noun* (*pl.* **imagos, imagines**) the final stage in the life cycle of an insect, when it is sexually mature.

imam (ĭ-mäm′) *noun* 1 a leader of prayers in a mosque. 2 (**Imam**) a Muslim leader.

imbalance *noun* a lack of balance or proportion; inequality.

imbecile (ĭm′bə-sīl) *noun* a fool. —*adj.* stupid; foolish. ▸ **imbecility** *noun*

imbibe *verb trans., intrans.* (**imbibed, imbibing**) 1 to drink (esp. alcoholic drinks). 2 to take in or absorb (ideas, etc.).

imbroglio (ĭm-brōl′yō) *noun* (*pl.* **imbroglios**) a confused and complicated situation.

imbue (ĭm-byōō′) *verb trans.* (**imbued, imbuing**) 1 (**imbue** (**someone**) **with** (**something**)) to fill or inspire (the one specified). 2 to soak or saturate, esp. with dye.

IMF *abbrev.* International Monetary Fund.

imitate *verb trans.* (**imitated, imitating**) 1 to copy the behavior, manners, appearance, etc. of. 2 to mimic. 3 to make a copy of. ▸ **imitable** *adj.*

imitation *noun* 1 an act of imitating. 2 something that is produced by imitating; a copy. —*adj.* cheaply made to look or function like something more expensive. ▸ **imitative** *adj.* ▸ **imitatively** *adv.* ▸ **imitativeness** *noun* ▸ **imitator** *noun*

immaculate *adj.* 1 perfectly clean and neat. 2 free from blemish or error; pure. 3 totally virtuous and clean. ▸ **immaculately** *adv.*

immanent *adj.* existing or remaining within. ▸ **immanence** *noun*

immaterial *adj.* having no importance or significance.

immature *adj.* 1 not fully grown or developed; not ripe. 2 not fully developed emotionally or intellectually. ▸ **immaturely** *adv.* ▸ **immaturity** *noun*

immeasurable *adj.* very great; immense. ▸ **immeasurably** *adv.*

immediate (ĭm-ēd′ē-ət) *adj.* 1 happening or done at once. 2 nearest or next in space, time, or relationship. 3 of the current time; urgent. 4 having a direct, uninterrupted effect. ▸ **immediacy** *noun*

immediately *adv.* at once or without delay —*conj.* as soon as.

immemorial adj. extending far back in time beyond anyone's memory: a custom since time immemorial. ▸ **immemorially** adv.

immense adj. **1** very large. **2** colloq. very good. ▸ **immensely** adv. ▸ **immenseness** noun ▸ **immensity** noun

immerse verb trans. (**immersed, immersing**) **1** to dip (something) completely into or under the surface of a liquid. **2** to baptize (someone) by submerging the whole body in water. **3** (**be immersed in (something)**) to be occupied or involved deeply in (it); to be absorbed. ▸ **immersible** adj. ▸ **immersion** (ĭm-ər'zhən, -shən) noun

immigrate (ĭm'ə-grāt,) verb intrans. (**immigrated, immigrating**) to come to a foreign country with the intention of settling in it. See also **emigrate**. ▸ **immigrant** noun, adj. ▸ **immigration** noun

imminent adj. likely to happen in the near future. ▸ **imminence** noun

immobile (ĭm-ō'bəl, -bēl,, -bĭl,) adj. **1** not able to move or be moved. **2** not moving; motionless. ▸ **immobility** noun

immobilize verb trans. (**immobilized, immobilizing**) to make or keep immobile. ▸ **immobilization** noun

immoderate adj. going far beyond normal or reasonable limits. **2** **immoderacy** noun ▸ **immoderately** adv. ▸ **immoderateness** noun

immodest adj. **1** lacking modesty; indecent or improper. **2** boastful and conceited. ▸ **immodestly** adv. ▸ **immodesty** noun

immolate (ĭm'ə-lāt,) verb trans. (**immolated, immolating**) to kill or offer in sacrifice. ▸ **immolation** noun

immoral adj. **1** morally wrong or bad; evil. **2** not conforming to the established moral standards of society. ▸ **immorality** noun ▸ **immorally** adv.

immortal adj. **1** living forever. **2** lasting forever; perpetual. —noun a person who will live forever, or who will always be remembered. ▸ **immortality** noun

immortalize verb trans. (**immortalized, immortalizing**) to make (a person, event, etc.) famous forever, esp. by inclusion in a work of art.

immovable adj. **1** impossible to move. **2** steadfast; unyielding. ▸ **immovability** noun ▸ **immovably** adv.

immune (ĭm-yōōn') adj. **1** (**immune to (something)**) protected by inoculation from or having a natural resistance to (a particular disease). **2** (**immune from (something)**) exempt or protected from (it). ▸ **immunity** noun

immunize (ĭm'yə-nīz,) verb trans. (**immunized, immunizing**) to produce artificial immunity to a disease in (a person) by injecting an antiserum, etc. ▸ **immunization** noun

immunodeficiency (ĭm,yə-nō,dĭ-fĭsh'ən-sē) noun (pl. **immunodeficiencies**) a deficiency or breakdown in the body's ability to fight infection.

immure (ĭm-yōōr') verb trans. (**immured, immuring**) **1** to enclose or imprison within walls. **2** to shut (someone or oneself) away.

immutable adj. that cannot be changed or will not change. ▸ **immutability** noun ▸ **immutably** adv.

imp noun **1** a small mischievous or evil spirit. **2** a mischievous or annoying child.

impact noun (ĭm'păkt,) **1** the act of an object hitting another object; a collision. **2** the force of such a collision. **3** a strong effect or impression. —verb trans., intrans. (ĭm-păkt') (**impacted, impacting**) **1** to strike (something) with force or to force (one object) into (another). **2** colloq. to have an impact or effect on (someone or something).

> **Usage** The verb impact in its second sense, to have an impact or effect on someone or something, as in Budget cuts have impacted the poor, is criticized by many people as being an example of bureaucratese. Writers and speakers not wishing to incur such criticism are best advised to avoid the usage, substituting have an impact on or simply affect.

impacted adj. **1** firmly pressed or wedged together. **2** denoting a tooth that is unable to erupt through the gum into a normal position because it is firmly wedged between the jawbone and another tooth.

impair verb trans. (**impaired, impairing**) to damage or weaken, esp. in quality. ▸ **impairment** noun

impala (ĭm-pǎl'ə, -pǎl'ə) noun a graceful medium-sized antelope.

impale verb trans. (**impaled, impaling**) to pierce with or as if with a long pointed object. ▸ **impalement** noun

impanel (ĭm-pǎn'l) or **empanel** verb trans. (**impaneled** or **impanelled, impaneling** or **impanelling**) **1** to enter (the names of prospective jurors) on a list. **2** to select (a jury) from such a list.

impart verb **1** to make (information, knowledge, etc.) known. **2** to give or transmit (a particular quality). ▸ **impartation** noun

impartial adj. not favoring one person, etc., more than another; fair and unbiased. ▸ **impartiality** noun ▸ **impartially** adv.

impassable adj. that cannot be passed through or traveled along. ▸ **impassability** noun ▸ **impassableness** noun ▸ **impassably** adv.

impasse (ĭm'păs,, ĭm-păs') *noun* a situation in which progress is impossible.

impassioned *adj.* full of passion or zeal.

impassive *adj.* **1** incapable of feeling and expressing emotion. **2** showing no feeling or emotion. ▸ **impassively** *adv.* ▸ **impassiveness** *noun*

impasto (ĭm-păs'tō, -päs'-) *noun* in painting and pottery, the technique of laying the paint or pigment on thickly.

impatient *adj.* **1** unwilling to wait or delay. **2** restlessly eager and anxious. ▸ **impatience** *noun* ▸ **impatiently** *adv.*

impeach *verb trans.* (**impeached, impeaching**) to accuse (a public or government official) of misconduct while in office. ▸ **impeachable** *adj.* ▸ **impeachment** *noun*

impeccable *adj.* free from fault or error. ▸ **impeccably** *adv.*

impecunious *adj.* having little or no money; poor. ▸ **impecuniously** *adv.* ▸ **impecuniousness** *noun*

impedance (ĭm-pēd'ns) *noun* (SYMBOL Z) the effective resistance of an electric circuit or circuit component to the passage of an electric current.

impede *verb trans.* (**impeded, impeding**) to prevent or delay the start or progress of (an activity, etc.).

impediment (ĭm-pĕd'ĭ-mənt) *noun* **1** a thing or person that delays or prevents the start or progress of something. **2** a minor defect in a person's speech.

impel *verb trans.* (**impelled, impelling**) **1** to push or urge forward; to propel. **2** to force or urge into action.

impend *verb intrans.* (**impended, impending**) to be about to happen. ▸ **impending** *adj.*

impenetrable *adj.* **1** incapable of being passed through. **2** difficult to understand. ▸ **impenetrability** *noun* ▸ **impenetrably** *adv.*

imperative *adj.* **1** requiring immediate action. **2** having or showing authority. **3** of or being the mood of a verb used to give orders. —*noun* **1 a** the imperative mood. **b** a verb in the imperative mood. **2** something that is imperative. ▸ **imperatively** *adv.*

imperceptible *adj.* too small or slight to be seen, heard, etc. ▸ **imperceptibility** *noun* ▸ **imperceptibly** *adv.*

imperfect *adj.* **1** having faults; not perfect. **2** lacking the full number of parts; incomplete. **3** of or being the verb tense expressing a continuing state or incomplete action. —*noun* **1** the imperfect tense. **2** a verb in the imperfect tense. ▸ **imperfection** *noun* ▸ **imperfectly** *adv.*

imperial (ĭm-pĭr'ē-əl) *adj.* **1** of or suitable for an empire, emperor, or empress. **2** commanding; august. **3** regal; magnificent. ▸ **imperially** *adv.*

imperialism *noun* the policy or principle of having and extending control over the territory of other nations. ▸ **imperialist** *noun, adj.* ▸ **imperialistic** *adj.*

imperil (ĭm-pĕr'əl) *verb trans.* (**imperiled** or **imperilled, imperiling** or **imperilling**) to put in peril or danger. ▸ **imperilment** *noun*

imperious (ĭm-pĭr'ē-əs) *adj.* arrogant and domineering. ▸ **imperiously** *adv.* ▸ **imperiousness** *noun*

imperishable *adj.* that will not decay and will last forever.

impermanent *adj.* not lasting or remaining. ▸ **impermanence** or **impermanency** *noun*

impermeable *adj.* not allowing esp. liquids to pass through or penetrate. ▸ **impermeability** *noun*

impersonal *adj.* **1** having no reference to any particular person; objective. **2** without or unaffected by personal or human feelings, warmth, etc.. **3** lacking personality. ▸ **impersonality** *noun* ▸ **impersonally** *adv.*

impersonate *verb trans.* (**impersonated, impersonating**) to pretend to be, or copy the behavior and appearance of, (another person). ▸ **impersonation** *noun* ▸ **impersonator** *noun*

impertinent (ĭm-pərt'n-ənt) *adj.* not showing respect; insolent and rude. ▸ **impertinence** *noun* ▸ **impertinently** *adv.*

imperturbable (ĭm,pər-tər'bə-bəl, -pə-tər'-) *adj.* not easily worried or upset; always calm. ▸ **imperturbability** *noun* ▸ **imperturbably** *adv.*

impervious *adj.* **1** not allowing fluids to pass through. **2** (**impervious to** (something)) not affected by (it). ▸ **imperviously** *adv.* ▸ **imperviousness** *noun*

impetigo (ĭm,pə-tī'gō, -tē'-) *noun* a highly contagious skin disease.

impetuous (ĭm-pĕch'ə-wəs) *adj.* **1** acting or done hurriedly and without thinking. **2** moving or acting forcefully. ▸ **impetuosity** *noun* ▸ **impetuously** *adv.* ▸ **impetuousness** *noun*

impetus *noun* (*pl.* **impetuses**) **1** the force or energy with which something moves. **2** a driving force. **3** incentive or encouragement.

impiety (ĭm-pī'ət-ē) *noun* (*pl.* **impieties**) lack of piety or devotion.

impinge *verb intrans.* (**impinged, impinging**) (**impinge against** or **on** (**something** or **someone**)) **1** to encroach on (something or someone). **2** to come into contact with (something or someone). **3** to make an impression on (someone). ▸ **impingement** *noun*

impious (ĭm'pē-əs, ĭm-pī'-) *adj.* lacking respect or reverence, esp. for a divine being. ▸ **impiously** *adv.* ▸ **impiousness** *noun*

impish *adj.* marked by or given to lively playfulness. ▸ **impishly** *adv.* ▸ **impishness** *noun*

implacable *adj.* impossible to satisfy or appease. ▸ **implacability** *noun* ▸ **implacableness** *noun* ▸ **implacably** *adv.*

implant *verb trans.* (ĭm-plănt') (**implanted, implanting**) **1** to fix or plant securely. **2** to fix (ideas, beliefs, etc.) in a person's mind. **3** to graft or insert (an object, tissue, or substance) into the body, esp. by surgery. —*noun* (ĭm'plănt,) an object, tissue, or substance that is implanted. ▸ **implantation** *noun*

implausible *adj.* not likely to be true. ▸ **implausibility** *noun* ▸ **implausibly** *adv.*

implement *noun* (ĭm'plə-mənt) a tool or utensil. —*verb trans.* (ĭm'plə-měnt,) (**implemented, implementing**) to carry out or perform. ▸ **implementation** *noun*

implicate *verb trans.* (**implicated, implicating**) to show or suggest that (a person) is involved, esp. in a crime.

implication *noun* **1** the state of being implicated. **2** the act of implying. **3** something that is implied.

implicit *adj.* **1** conveyed indirectly, without words or direct references. **2** unquestioning; complete. ▸ **implicitly** *adv.* ▸ **implicitness** *noun*

implode *verb intrans., trans.* (**imploded, imploding**) to collapse or burst inward in a violent manner.

implore *verb trans.* (**implored, imploring**) **1** to entreat or beg (a person). **2** to beg for earnestly. ▸ **imploringly** *adv.*

implosion *noun* a violent collapse or bursting inward. ▸ **implosive** *adj.*

imply *verb trans.* (**implied, implying, implies**) **1** to suggest or express indirectly; to hint at. **2** to suggest or involve as a necessary result or consequence.

impolite *adj.* lacking social manners. ▸ **impolitely** *adv.* ▸ **impoliteness** *noun*

imponderable *adj.* that cannot be measured or determined. —*noun* something imponderable.

import *verb trans.* (ĭm-pôrt', ĭm'pôrt,) (**imported, importing**) **1** to bring (goods, etc.) in from another country. **2** to signify or portend. —*noun* (ĭm'pôrt,) **1** something imported. **2** the act or business of importing goods. **3** importance. **4** meaning. ▸ **importation** *noun* ▸ **importer** *noun*

important *adj.* **1** having great significance, value, or effect. **2** of high social rank or status; eminent. **3** pompous. ▸ **importance** *noun* ▸ **importantly** *adv.*

importunate (ĭm-pôr'chə-nət) *adj.* persistent or excessively demanding. ▸ **importunately** *adv.*

importune (ĭm,pôr-tōōn', -tyōōn') *verb trans., intrans.* (**importuned, importuning**) **1** to make persistent, usu. annoying, requests of (another). **2** to irritate; to vex. ▸ **importunity** *noun*

impose *verb trans., intrans.* (**imposed, imposing**) **1** (**impose (something) on** *or* **upon (someone)**) to make payment of (a tax, fine, etc.) or (performance of a duty) compulsory; to enforce (it). **2** (**impose (oneself) on** *or* **upon (someone)**) to force (oneself, one's opinions, etc.) on (another). **3 a** (**impose on** *or* **upon (someone)**) to take advantage of (another). **b** to engage in taking unfair advantage. ▸ **imposition** *noun*

imposing *adj.* impressive, esp. because of large size, dignity, etc. ▸ **imposingly** *adv.*

impossible *adj.* **1** that cannot be done or cannot happen. **2** that cannot be true; difficult to believe. **3** *colloq.* unacceptable, unsuitable, or difficult to bear: *an impossible situation.* ▸ **impossibility** *noun* ▸ **impossibly** *adv.*

impostor *noun* a person who pretends to be someone else in order to deceive others.

imposture *noun* **1** deception, esp. by pretending to be someone else. **2** an act of deception.

impotent *adj.* **1** lacking the necessary strength; powerless. **2** *of an adult male* unable to achieve or maintain an erection and therefore unable to perform sexual intercourse. ▸ **impotence** *noun* ▸ **impotently** *adv.*

impound *verb trans.* (**impounded, impounding**) **1** to shut (e.g., an animal) up in or as if in a pound. **2** to take legal possession of; to confiscate.

impoverish *verb trans.* (**impoverished, impoverishing**) **1** to make poor. **2** to reduce the quality or fertility of (e.g., soil). ▸ **impoverished** *adj.* ▸ **impoverishment** *noun*

impracticable *adj.* not able to be done, put into practice, or used. ▸ **impracticability** *noun* ▸ **impracticably** *adv.*

impractical *adj.* incapable of dealing sensibly with practical matters. ▸ **impracticality** *noun* ▸ **impractically** *adv.*

imprecate (ĭm'prə-kāt,) *verb trans.* (**imprecated, imprecating**) to invoke evil upon (someone). ▸ **imprecation** *noun*

imprecise *adj.* not precise; inaccurate. ▸ **imprecision** *noun*

impregnable *adj.* **1** impossible to be seized or taken by force. **2** unable to be affected by criticism, doubts, etc. ▸ **impregnability** *noun* ▸ **impregnably** *adv.*

impregnate (ĭm-prĕg′nāt,) verb trans. (**impregnated, impregnating**) **1** to permeate completely or saturate. **2** to make pregnant; to fertilize. ▸ **impregnation** noun

impresario (ĭm,prə-sär′ē-ō,, -sär′-) noun (pl. **impresarios**) an organizer of public entertainments, e.g., concerts.

impress[1] verb trans., intrans. (ĭm-prĕs′) (**impressed, impressing**) **1** to produce a strong and usu. favorable impression on (someone). **2** (**impress on** or **upon** (**someone**)) to make very clear or emphasize to (another). **3** to make or stamp (a mark) on by applying pressure. **4** (**impress** (**something**) **on** or **upon** (**someone**)) to fix (a fact, etc.) firmly in (another's) mind or memory. —noun (ĭm′prĕs,) **1** the act of impressing. **2** something that is made by impressing or being impressed, such as a mark.

impress[2] (ĭm-prĕs′) verb trans. (**impressed, impressing**) to force (a person) to serve, e.g., in a navy, or other military unit.

impression noun **1** an (esp. favorable) idea or effect produced in the mind or made on the senses. **2** a vague or uncertain idea or belief. **3** the act or process of impressing. **4** a mark produced by or as if by pressure. **5** an imitation of a person, done for entertainment. **6** the number of copies of a book, newspaper, etc., printed at one time.

impressionable adj. easily impressed or influenced. ▸ **impressionability** noun ▸ **impressionably** adv.

Impressionism noun a 19th c style of art, music, or literature that aims to give a general impression of feelings and events rather than a formal or structural treatment of them. ▸ **Impressionist** noun, adj.

impressionistic adj. based on impressions or personal observation as distinct from definite facts or particular knowledge. ▸ **impressionistically** adv.

impressive adj. capable of making a deep impression on a person's mind, feelings, etc.; causing admiration or approval. ▸ **impressively** adv. ▸ **impressiveness** noun

imprimatur (ĭm,prə-mä′tŏŏr,) noun a licence or permission to print or publish a book, granted esp. under conditions of censorship.

imprint noun (ĭm′prĭnt,) **1** a mark produced by or as if by pressure. **2** a permanent effect produced by some experience or event. **3** a publisher's name and address, printed at the bottom of a book's title page. —verb trans. (ĭm-prĭnt′, ĭm′prĭnt,) (**imprinted, imprinting**) **1** to mark or print an impression of (something). **2** to fix firmly in the mind.

imprison verb trans. (**imprisoned, imprisoning**) to put into prison. ▸ **imprisonment** noun

improbable adj. **1** not likely to happen. **2** hard to believe. ▸ **improbability** noun ▸ **improbably** adv.

impromptu (ĭm-prămp′tŏŏ, -tyŏŏ) adj. made or done without preparation; spontaneous. —adv. without preparation; spontaneously. —noun **1** something improvised or spontaneous. **2** a piece of music that suggests improvisation.

improper adj. **1** not conforming to accepted standards of modesty and moral behavior; indecent. **2** not correct; wrong. **3** not suitable. ▸ **improperly** adv.

improper fraction a fraction in which the numerator has a value equal to or higher than that of the denominator. See also **proper fraction**.

impropriety noun (pl. **improprieties**) **1** an improper act. **2** an improper use of a word. **3** the state of being improper; indecency.

improve (ĭm-prŏŏv′) verb trans., intrans. (**improved, improving**) **1** to make or become better. **2** (**improve on** (**something**)) to produce something better than (a previous example). **3** to increase the value or beauty of (land or property) by laying out gardens, building, etc. ▸ **improvement** noun

improvident adj. not considering or providing for likely future needs. ▸ **improvidence** noun ▸ **improvidently** adv.

improvise (ĭm′prə-vīz,) verb trans., intrans. (**improvised, improvising**) **1** to compose, recite, or perform (music, verse, etc.) without advance preparation. **2** to make or provide quickly, without advance preparation, and using whatever materials are at hand. ▸ **improvisation** noun ▸ **improviser** noun

imprudent (ĭm-prŏŏd′nt) adj. showing a lack of good sense or caution; rash. ▸ **imprudence** noun ▸ **imprudently** adv.

impudence (ĭm′pyəd-əns) noun the state or quality of being boldly impolite. ◨ AUDACITY, BRASS, CHEEK, GALL, NERVE. ▸ **impudent** adj. ▸ **impudently** adv.

impugn (ĭm-pyŏŏn′) verb trans. (**impugned, impugning**) to call into question or raise doubts about (a person's honesty, integrity, etc.); to criticize. ▸ **impugnable** adj. ▸ **impugnment** noun

impulse (ĭm′pəls,) noun **1** a sudden push forward; a force producing sudden movement forward. **2** a sudden urge to do something without thinking of the consequences. **3** an electrical stimulus in a nerve or muscle.

impulsive adj. **1** acting without any prior thought or deliberation. **2** likely to take action suddenly and on impulse. ▸ **impulsively** adv. ▸ **impulsiveness** noun

impunity noun freedom or exemption, e.g., from punishment or loss.

impure adj. **1** mixed with something else, typically a substance of inferior quality. **2** dirty. **3** not chaste; immoral. ▸ **impurity** noun

impute verb trans. (**imputed, imputing**) (**impute (something) to (someone)**) to believe (something) to be caused by (a person or thing). ▸ **imputation** noun

in prep. **1** used to express the position of a person or thing with regard to what encloses, surrounds, or includes it, him, etc. **2** into. **3** after (a period of time). **4** during; while. **5** used to express arrangement or shape. **6** from; out of. **7** by the medium or means of; using. **8** wearing. **9** used to describe a state or manner. **10** used to state an occupation. **11** used to state a purpose. —adv. **1** to or toward the inside; indoors. **2** at a place, e.g., an office or a house. **3** so as to be added or included. **4** so as to enclose or conceal. **5** in or into political power or office. **6** Baseball to home plate; in such a way as to score. **7** in a good position; in favor. **8** (in compounds) expressing prolonged activity, esp. by large numbers of people: a sit-in. —adj. **1** internal; inside. **2** fashionable. **3** in power or office. **4** (also in compounds) shared by a group of people.

in. abbrev. inch.

in-¹ prefix (also **il-** before words beginning with l, **im-** before words beginning with b, m, and p, **ir-** before words beginning with r) forming words that are the negative or opposite of the root word, or words denoting a lack of the quality implied by the root word: inhospitable / illogical / immature / irrelevant.

in-² prefix (also **il-** before words beginning with l, **im-** before words beginning with b, m, and p, **ir-** before words beginning with r) forming words denoting in, on, toward: intrude / imprison.

inability noun (pl. **inabilities**) the lack of sufficient power, means, or ability.

in absentia (ĭn,ăb-sĕn'chə) (Latin), in his, her, or their absence.

inaccessible (ĭn,ək-sĕs'ə-bəl) adj. **1** difficult or impossible to approach, reach, or obtain. **2** difficult to understand or influence; unapproachable. ▸ **inaccessibility** noun ▸ **inaccessibly** adv.

inaccurate (ĭn-ăk'yə-rət) adj. containing errors; not correct or accurate. ▸ **inaccuracy** noun ▸ **inaccurately** adv.

inaction noun lack of action; sluggishness.

inactive adj. **1** taking little or no exercise; idle. **2** no longer operating or functioning. ▸ **inactively** adv. ▸ **inactivity** noun

inadequate (ĭn-ăd'ə-kwət) adj. **1** not sufficient or adequate. **2** of a person not competent or capable. ▸ **inadequacy** noun ▸ **inadequately** adv.

inadmissible adj. not allowable or acceptable.

inadvertent adj. **1** unintentional. **2** not paying proper attention. ▸ **inadvertence** noun ▸ **inadvertently** adv.

inadvisable adj. not wise; not to be advised. ▸ **inadvisability** noun

inalienable adj. that cannot be taken or given away.

inane (ĭn-ān') adj. having no real meaning or point; silly. ▸ **inanely** adv. ▸ **inanity** noun

inanimate adj. devoid of life; not living.

inanition (ĭn,ə-nĭsh'ən) noun a condition characterized by exhaustion, weakness, and weight loss, caused by lack of nutrients in the blood

inapplicable adj. not applicable or suitable. ▸ **inapplicably** adv.

inappropriate adj. not suitable or appropriate. ▸ **inappropriately** adv.

inarticulate adj. unable to express oneself clearly or speak distinctly. ▸ **inarticulately** adv. ▸ **inarticulateness** noun

inattention noun a lack of attention. ▸ **inattentive** adj.

inaudible adj. not loud enough to be heard.

inaugural adj. **1** relating to a ceremony officially marking the beginning of something, e.g., a new government administration. **2** of a speech, etc. given by a person on taking office.

inaugurate (ĭn-ô'gyə-rāt,) verb trans. (**inaugurated, inaugurating**) **1** to place (a person) in office with a formal ceremony. **2** to mark the beginning of (an activity) with a formal ceremony. **3** to mark the opening of (a new building or service). ▸ **inauguration** noun

inauspicious adj. not promising future success; unlucky.

inboard adj., adv. situated within the hull or interior of a boat or ship. See also **outboard**.

inborn adj. possessed by a person from birth.

inbound adj., of a flight coming toward its destination; arriving.

inbred adj. **1** inborn. **2** denoting a plant or animal that is the result of inbreeding.

inbreed verb trans. to breed (plants or animals) by allowing reproduction between closely related members of a species. ▸ **inbreeding** noun

Inc. abbrev. Incorporated.

incalculable adj. too great to be measured. ▸ **incalculably** adv.

incandescent (ĭn,kən-dĕs'ənt) adj. **1** white hot or glowing with intense heat. **2** emitting light as a result of being heated to a high temperature. **3** exhibiting brilliance or emotion. ▸ **incandescence** noun ▸ **incandescently** adv.

incantation noun **1** words said or sung as a spell; a magical formula. **2** the use of spells and magical formulas.

incapable adj. 1 (**incapable of (something)**) not capable of doing (it). 2 unable or unfit to do anything, esp. look after one's own affairs. ▶ **incapably** adv.

incapacitate verb trans. (**incapacitated, incapacitating**) 1 to make (someone) unfit (for). 2 to disqualify legally. ▶ **incapacitated** adj. ▶ **incapacitation** noun

incapacity noun (pl. **incapacities**) a lack of the necessary strength, power, or ability.

incarcerate verb trans. (**incarcerated, incarcerating**) to shut in or keep in prison. ▶ **incarceration** noun

incarnate adj. (ĭn-kär'nət, -nāt,) 1 in bodily, esp. human, form: God incarnate. 2 personified; typified: evil incarnate. —verb trans. (ĭn-kär'nāt,) (**incarnated, incarnating**) 1 to give bodily, esp. human, form to. 2 to personify or typify. ▶ **incarnation** noun

incautious adj. acting or done without thinking; heedless. ▶ **incautiously** adv. ▶ **incautiousness** noun

incendiary (ĭn-sĕn'dē-ĕr,ē, -dyə-rē) adj. 1 of or relating to the deliberate and illegal burning of property or goods. 2 capable of burning readily or designed to start fires. 3 of or relating to ammunition or other devices designed to set fire to a target. 4 tending to cause violence. —noun (pl. **incendiaries**) 1 a person who deliberately and illegally sets fire to buildings or property. 2 a bomb containing a highly flammable substance, designed to burst into flames upon striking its target. Also called **incendiary bomb**. 3 a person who stirs up violence.

incense[1] (ĭn'sĕns,) noun 1 a spice or other substance that gives off a pleasant odor when burned. 2 the odor or smoke given off by burning spices, etc. —verb trans. (**incensed, incensing**) 1 to offer incense to (a god). 2 to perfume with incense.

incense[2] (ĭn-sĕns') verb (**incensed, incensing**) to make (someone) very angry.

incentive (ĭn-sĕn't'ĭv) noun a source of motivation or encouragement. —adj. serving to motivate or encourage.

inception noun a beginning.

incessant adj. going on without stopping; continual. ▶ **incessantly** adv.

incest (ĭn'sĕst,) noun sexual relations between people who are too closely related to be allowed to marry. ▶ **incestuous** adj. ▶ **incestuously** adv. ▶ **incestuousness** noun

inch noun 1 a measure of length equal to one twelfth of a foot. 2 formerly, the amount of rain or snow that will cover a surface to the depth of one inch. —verb intrans., trans. (**inched, inching**) to move slowly, carefully, and by degrees. —**every inch** completely; in every way.

inchoate (ĭn-kō'āt,) adj. 1 at the earliest stage of development; just beginning. 2 not fully developed; rudimentary. ▶ **inchoately** adv.

inchworm noun a measuring worm.

incidence noun 1 the frequency with which something happens or the extent of its influence. 2 the way in which something moving in a line comes into contact with a surface.

incident (ĭn'səd-ənt, -sə-dĕnt,) noun 1 an event or occurrence. 2 an event or occurrence that is dependent on or a consequence of something else. 3 a relatively minor event or occurrence that might have serious consequences. —adj. 1 (**incident to (something)**) belonging naturally to (it) or being a natural consequence of (it). 2 Law (**incident to (something)**) dependent on (it).

incidental (ĭn,sə-dĕnt'l) adj. 1 happening, etc., by chance in connection with something else, and of secondary or minor importance. 2 occurring or likely to occur as a minor consequence. ▶ **incidentally** adv.

incinerate (ĭn-sĭn'ə-rāt,) verb trans. (**incinerated, incinerating**) to burn to ashes. ▶ **incineration** noun

incinerator noun a furnace or machine for burning trash.

incipient (ĭn-sĭp'ē-ənt) adj. beginning to exist; in an early stage. ▶ **incipiently** adv. ▶ **incipience** or **incipiency** noun

incise (ĭn-sīz', -sĭs') verb trans. (**incised, incising**) 1 to cut into. 2 to engrave (an inscription, stone, etc.).

incision noun 1 a cut, esp. one made by a surgeon. 2 an act of cutting, esp. by a surgeon.

incisive (ĭn-sī'sĭv) adj. clear, crisp, and keen. ▣ PENETRATING, TRENCHANT ▣ DULL, UNINCISIVE. ▶ **incisively** adv. ▶ **incisiveness** noun

incisor (ĭn-sī'zər) noun any of the sharp chisel-shaped teeth at the front of the mouth.

incite (ĭn-sīt') verb trans. (**incited, inciting**) 1 to encourage or promote (ill feeling, etc.). 2 to stir (someone) up or provoke (someone) to action. ▶ **incitement** noun

incivility noun (pl. **incivilities**) rudeness.

incl. abbrev. 1 including. 2 inclusive.

inclement adj. stormy or severe. ▶ **inclemency** noun

inclination noun 1 a particular tendency or liking. 2 an act of inclining. 3 a slope. 4 the degree at which an object slopes away from a horizontal or vertical line or plane.

incline verb trans., intrans. (ĭn-klīn') (**inclined, inclining**) 1 to lean or cause to lean toward a particular opinion or conduct. 2 to slope or cause to slope. 3 to bow or bend (the head, one's body) forward or downward. —noun (ĭn'klīn,) a slope.

include verb trans. (**included, including**) 1 to take in or consider along with others as part of a group. 2 to have or incorporate as part of a larger whole. ▣ EMBODY, EMBRACE, ENCOMPASS, INVOLVE ▣ EXCLUDE, OMIT. ▸ **inclusion** noun

inclusive adj. 1 including everything. 2 including the stated limits: *March to August inclusive.* ▸ **inclusively** adv.

incognito (ĭn,kăg,nĕt'ō, ĭn-kăg'nət-ō,) adv., adj. keeping one's identity a secret, e.g., using a disguise and a false name.

incoherent (ĭn,kō-hĭr'ənt, -hĕr'-) adj. 1 not expressed clearly or logically; difficult to understand and follow. 2 unable to speak clearly and logically. ▸ **incoherence** noun ▸ **incoherently** adv.

income noun money received as payment for work, etc., or as interest or profit from shares or investment.

income tax a tax levied on one's personal income or on a business income.

incoming adj. 1 coming in or approaching 2 ready to take office.

incommode verb trans. (**incommoded, incommoding**) to cause trouble or inconvenience to. ▸ **incommodious** adj.

incommunicado (ĭn,kə-myōō,nĭ-kăd'ō) adj., adv. not allowed to communicate with other people or not wishing to do so.

incomparable (ĭn-kăm'pə-rə-bəl, ĭn,kəm-păr'ə-bəl) adj. 1 having no peer or equal. 2 not to be compared. ▸ **incomparability** noun ▸ **incomparably** adv. ▸ **incomparableness** noun

incompatible adj. 1 of people unable to live and work together in harmony. 2 (**incompatible with** (**something**)) not in agreement; inconsistent. ▸ **incompatibility** noun ▸ **incompatibly** adv.

incompetent adj. lacking the necessary skill, ability, or qualifications. ▸ **incompetence** noun ▸ **incompetently** adv.

incomplete adj. not complete or finished. ▸ **incompletely** adv. ▸ **incompleteness** noun

incomprehensible adj. difficult or impossible to understand. ▸ **incomprehension** noun

inconceivable adj. unable to be believed or conceived by the mind. ▸ **inconceivability** noun ▸ **inconceivably** adv.

inconclusive adj. leading to no definite result or decision. ▸ **inconclusively** adv. ▸ **inconclusiveness** noun

incongruous (ĭn-kăng'grə-wəs) adj. out of place; unsuitable or inappropriate. ▸ **incongruity** (ĭn,kən-grōō'ət-ē) noun ▸ **incongruously** adv. ▸ **incongruousness** noun

inconsequent adj. 1 not following logically; illogical. 2 irrelevant. 3 not connected or related.

inconsequential adj. 1 of no importance or value. 2 illogical. ▸ **inconsequentially** adv.

inconsiderable adj. small, e.g., in amount or value.

inconsiderate (ĭn,kən-sĭd'ə-rət) adj. thoughtless, esp. in not considering the feelings of others.

inconsistent adj. 1 (**inconsistent with** (**something**)) not in agreement or accordance with (it). 2 having contradictory elements. 3 not always behaving in accord with the same principles. ▸ **inconsistency** noun ▸ **inconsistently** adv.

inconsolable adj. unable to be comforted. ▸ **inconsolably** adv.

inconspicuous adj. attracting little attention; not easily noticed. ▸ **inconspicuously** adv. ▸ **inconspicuousness** noun

inconstant adj. changeable, esp. in one's loyalties. ▸ **inconstancy** noun

incontinent adj. 1 unable to control one's bowels or bladder or both. 2 lacking restraint or control. ▸ **incontinence** noun

incontrovertible (ĭn-kän,trə-vərt'ə-bəl) adj. not able to be disputed or doubted. ▸ **incontrovertibly** adv.

inconvenience noun trouble or difficulty. —verb trans. (**inconvenienced, inconveniencing**) to cause trouble or difficulty to.

inconvenient adj. not convenient, esp. causing trouble or difficulty. ▸ **inconveniently** adv.

incorporate (ĭn-kôr'pə-rāt,) verb trans., intrans. (**incorporated, incorporating**) 1 to contain as part of a whole. 2 to include or be included as part of a whole. 3 to combine or be united thoroughly in a single mass. 4 to form into a legal corporation. 5 to form a legal corporation. ▸ **incorporation** noun

incorrect adj. 1 not accurate; wrong. 2 not in accord with normal or accepted standards. ▸ **incorrectly** adv. ▸ **incorrectness** noun

incorrigible (ĭn-kôr'ĭ-jə-bəl) adj. not able to be improved or reformed, usu. because of being too bad. ▸ **incorrigibility** noun

incorruptible adj. incapable of being bribed or otherwise morally corrupted.

increase verb trans., intrans. (ĭn-krēs', ĭn'krēs,) (**increased, increasing**) to make or become greater in size, number, strength, etc. ▣ AUGMENT, ENLARGE, EXPAND, MULTIPLY ▣ DECREASE, REDUCE. —noun (ĭn'krēs,, ĭn-krēs') 1 the act of increasing. 2 the amount by which something increases or is increased. ▸ **increasingly** adv.

incredible adj. 1 difficult or impossible to believe. 2 unusually good; amazing. ▸ **incredibility** noun ▸ **incredibly** adv.

incredulous (ĭn-krĕj'ə-ləs) adj. unwilling or unable to believe or accept something as true. ▸ **incredulity** (ĭn,krə-dōō'lət-ē,

-dyŏŏ'-) noun ▸ **incredulously** adv. ▸ **incredulousness** noun

increment (ĭng'krǝ-mǝnt, ĭn'-) noun **1** an increase of one point on a fixed scale; e.g., a regular increase in salary. **2** the amount by which something is increased. **3** a usu. small increase or addition. ▸ **incremental** (ĭng,krǝ-mĕnt'l, ĭn,-) adj. ▸ **incrementally** adv.

incriminate (ĭn-krĭm'ǝ-nāt,) verb trans. (**incriminated, incriminating**) to show that (someone) was involved in a crime or fault. ▸ **incrimination** noun ▸ **incriminatory** adj.

incubate (ĭng'kyǝ-bāt,) verb trans., intrans. (**incubated, incubating**) **1** of birds to brood (eggs), esp. by sitting on them. **2** to hatch (eggs). **3** to encourage (the growth of bacteria or other microorganisms) in a culture medium under favorable conditions, esp. in an incubator. ▸ **incubation** noun

incubator noun **1** a transparent boxlike container in which a premature baby can be nurtured under controlled conditions. **2** a cabinet or room that can be maintained at a constant preset temperature, used for culturing bacteria, hatching eggs, etc.

incubus (ĭng'kyǝ-bǝs) noun (pl. **incubuses, incubi**) **1** an evil male spirit believed by some to have sexual intercourse with sleeping women. See also **succubus**. **2** something that oppresses or weighs heavily on one, esp. a nightmare.

inculcate (ĭn-kǝl'kāt,, ĭn'kǝl-) verb trans. (**inculcated, inculcating**) (**inculcate** (**something**) **in** (**someone**)) to teach or fix (ideas, habits, etc.) firmly in (someone's) mind by constant repetition. ▸ **inculcation** noun

inculpate (ĭn-kǝl'pāt,, ĭn'kǝl-) verb trans. (**inculpated, inculpating**) to blame or show to be guilty of a crime.

incumbent adj. **1** (**incumbent on** or **upon** (**someone**)) imposed as a duty on (the one specified). **2** occupying a specified position. —noun a holder of a governmental or ecclesiastical office. ▸ **incumbency** noun

incur verb trans. (**incurred, incurring**) to bring (something unpleasant) upon oneself; to become liable for (debts, etc.).

incurable adj. that cannot be cured or corrected. ▸ **incurably** adv.

incurious adj. showing no interest; lacking a normal curiosity; indifferent. ▸ **incuriously** adv.

incursion noun **1** a brief or sudden attack made into enemy territory. **2** the act or fact of entering: an incursion on our privacy.

incus (ĭng'kǝs) noun (pl. **incudes**) Anat. a small anvil-shaped bone in the middle ear. See also **malleus, stapes**.

Ind. abbrev. **1** Independent. **2** India; Indian.

indebted adj. (often **indebted to** (**someone**)) **1** having reason to be obliged to (the one specified). **2** owing (someone else) money. ▸ **indebtedness** noun

indecent adj. **1** offensive to accepted standards of decency and modesty. **2** being in bad taste; improper. ▸ **indecency** noun ▸ **indecently** adv.

indecipherable adj. that cannot be read or understood.

indecision noun inability to decide; uncertainty.

indecisive adj. **1** producing no clear or definite decision or result. **2** unable to make a firm decision; hesitating. ▸ **indecisively** adv. ▸ **indecisiveness** noun

indeed adv. **1** without any question; in truth. **2** in fact; actually. —interj. used to express surprise, disbelief, etc., or acknowledgment.

indefatigable (ĭn,dĭ-făt'ĭ-gǝ-bǝl) adj. **1** never tiring. **2** never stopping; unremitting. ▸ **indefatigably** adv.

indefensible adj. that cannot be defended or justified.

indefinable adj. that cannot be clearly, fully, or exactly described.

indefinite adj. **1** having no fixed or exact limits. **2** vague; imprecise. ▸ **indefinitely** adv. ▸ **indefiniteness** noun

indefinite article a or an. See also **definite article**.

indelible adj. **1** of a mark, etc. unable to be removed or rubbed out. **2** of a pen, etc. making indelible marks. ▸ **indelibly** adv.

indelicate adj. **1** tending to embarrass or offend. **2** slightly coarse; rough. ▸ **indelicacy** noun ▸ **indelicately** adv.

indemnify verb trans. (**indemnified, indemnifying, indemnifies**) **1** (**indemnify** (**someone**) **against** (**something**)) to provide (the one specified) with security against (loss or misfortune). **2** (**indemnify** (**someone**) **for** (**something**)) to pay (the one specified) money in compensation for (esp. loss or damage). ▸ **indemnification** noun

indemnity noun (pl. **indemnities**) **1** compensation, e.g., money paid, for loss or damage. **2** security against loss or damage. **3** legal exemption from liabilities.

indent[1] verb trans., intrans. (ĭn-dĕnt') (**indented, indenting**) **1** to begin (a line or paragraph) several spaces in from the margin. **2** to make a notch in. —rioun (ĭn-dĕnt', ĭn'dĕnt,) an indented line or paragraph.

indent[2] (ĭn-dĕnt') verb trans. (**indented, indenting**) to form a dent in.

indentation (ĭn,dĕn,tā'shǝn, -dǝn-) noun **1** a mark produced by or as if by pressure. **2** a deep inward curve or recess, e.g., in a coastline. **3** a cut or notch.

indenture (ĭn-dĕn′chər) *noun* **1** (*usu.* **indentures**) a contract binding an apprentice to a master. **2** an indented agreement or contract. —*verb trans.* (**indentured, indenturing**) to bind (e.g., an apprentice) by indentures.

independence *noun* the condition of being free to act, move, etc., without restriction.

Independence Day Fourth of July.

independent *adj.* **1** not under the control or authority of others, esp. (of a country or state) self-governing. **2** not relying on others for financial support, care, or guidance. **3** thinking and acting for oneself and not under obligation to others. **4** not related to or affected by others. **5** (*often* **Independent**) not belonging to any political party. ▸ **independently** *adv.*

in-depth *adj.* thorough; exhaustive.

indescribable *adj.* that cannot be described, often because too extreme. ▸ **indescribably** *adv.*

indestructible *adj.* that cannot be destroyed.

indeterminable *adj.* that cannot be fixed, decided, or measured.

indeterminate (ĭn,dĭ-tər′mĭ-nət) *adj.* **1** not precisely or exactly fixed or settled. **2** doubtful; vague. ▸ **indeterminacy** *noun.* ▸ **indeterminately** *adv.* ▸ **indeterminateness** *noun*

index *noun* (*pl.* **indexes, indices**) **1** an alphabetical list of names, subjects, etc., dealt with in a book, usu. given at the end of that book, and with the page numbers on which each item appears. **2** a catalog or a computerized database, e.g., in a library, that lists each book, etc., alphabetically and gives details of where it is shelved. **3** something that identifies or highlights a particular trend or condition. **4** a scale of numbers that shows changes in price, wages, etc.. **5** a hand or pointer on a dial or scale. **6** *Math.* exponent (sense 1). —*verb trans.* (**indexed, indexing**) **1** to provide (a book) with an index. **2** to list in an index.

index finger the finger next to the thumb.

India ink a black ink.

Indian *noun* **1** a native or citizen of India. **2** **a** a Native American. **b** a member of any of the various peoples native to Central and S America. **3** any of the languages spoken by Native Americans or by peoples indigenous to Central and S America. —*adj.* **1** of India or the Indian subcontinent, its people, or their languages. **2** relating to Native Americans or to their languages; Native American.

Indian corn corn¹.

Indian summer a period of unusually warm, dry weather in late autumn.

indicate (ĭn′dĭ-kāt,) *verb trans.* (**indicated, indicating**) **1** to point out or show. **2** to be a sign or symptom of. **3** *of a gauge, dial, etc.* to show as a reading. ▸ **indication** *noun*

indicative *adj.* **1** (**indicative of (something)**) being a sign or indication of (it). **2** *Gram.* being the mood or in the mood that is used to state facts or ask questions. —*noun Gram.* the indicative mood.

indicator *noun* **1** an instrument, or a needle or pointer on a device, that shows the level of temperature, fuel, pressure,. etc. **2** a sign, condition, etc., that shows or illustrates.

indices *see* index.

indict (ĭn-dīt′) *verb* (**indicted, indicting**) to accuse formally of a crime or other offense.

indictment (ĭn-dīt′mənt) *noun* **1** a formal written accusation or charge, drawn up by a prosecutor. **2** severe criticism or censure.

indifferent *adj.* **1** (**indifferent to (someone or something)**) showing no interest in (the one specified). **2 a** neither good nor bad; mediocre. **b** inferior. ▸ **indifference** *noun*

indigenous (ĭn-dĭj′ə-nəs) *adj.* belonging naturally to a country or area; native.

indigent (ĭn′dĭ-jənt) *adj.* very poor; needy. ▸ **indigence** *noun*

indigestible (ĭn,də-jĕs′tə-bəl, -dĭ-) *adj.* **1** difficult or impossible to digest. **2** not easily understood; complicated. ▸ **indigestibility** *noun*

indigestion (ĭn,də-jĕs′chən,-dĭ-) *noun* discomfort or pain in the abdomen or chest, caused by difficulty in digesting food.

indignant (ĭn-dĭg′nənt) *adj.* feeling or showing anger or a sense of ill-treatment. ▸ **indignantly** *adv.* ▸ **indignation** *noun*

indignity *noun* (*pl.* **indignities**) **1** an act or treatment that causes the victim to feel shame; disgrace or dishonor. **2** a feeling of shame, disgrace, or dishonor.

indigo (ĭn′dĭ-gō,) *noun* (*pl.* **indigos, indigoes**) **1** a violet-blue dye. **2** the violet-blue color of this dye. —*adj.* of the violet-blue color of this dye.

indirect *adj.* **1** not straight or direct. **2** not direct in expression or behavior. **3** not directly aimed at or intended. ▸ **indirectly** *adv.* ▸ **indirectness** *noun*

indirect object a noun, noun phrase, or pronoun that is affected indirectly by the action of a verb. *See also* **direct object.**

indiscreet *adj.* **1** giving away too many secrets or too much information. **2** not wise or cautious. ▸ **indiscreetly** *adv.*

indiscretion *noun* **1** lack of discretion or caution. **2** an act or remark showing a lack of discretion.

indiscriminate (ĭn,dĭs-krĭm′ĭ-nət) *adj.* making or showing no careful choices or discrimination. ▸ **indiscriminately** *adv.* ▸ **indiscriminateness** *noun*

indispensable *adj.* that cannot be done without; essential.

indisposed *adj.* **1** slightly ill. **2** reluctant or unwilling. ▶ **indisposition** *noun*

indisputable *adj.* agreeing with or corresponding to fact. ▶ **indisputably** *adv.*

indissoluble (in‚dĭs-äl′yə-bəl) *adj.* incapable of being dissolved; permanent.

indistinct *adj.* unclear to a person's eye, ear, or mind; dim. ▶ **indistinctly** *adv.*

indistinguishable *adj.* incapable of being distinguished or told apart.

individual *adj.* **1** relating to a single person or thing. **2** particular to one person; showing or having unique qualities or characteristics. **3** separate; single. —*noun* **1** a particular person, animal, or thing, esp. in contrast to the group to which it belongs. **2** *colloq.* a person. ▶ **individually** *adv.*

individualism *noun* behavior governed by the belief that individual people should lead their lives as they want and should be independent. ▶ **individualist** *noun* ▶ **individualistic** *adj.*

individuality *noun* (*pl.* **individualities**) **1** the qualities that distinguish one person or thing from others. **2** a separate and distinct existence.

individualize *verb trans.* (**individualized, individualizing**) **1** to give (someone or something) a distinctive character or personality. **2** to make suitable for a particular person, thing, or situation. ▶ **individualization** *noun*

indivisible *adj.* incapable of being divided or separated.

Indo- *combining form* denoting Indian; India: *Indo-European.*

indoctrinate (ĭn-dăk′trĭ-nāt‚) *verb trans.* (**indoctrinated, indoctrinating**) to teach (an individual or group) to accept and believe a particular set of beliefs uncritically. ▶ **indoctrination** *noun*

Indo-European (ĭn‚dō-yŏor‚ə-pē′ən) *adj.* denoting the family of languages spoken throughout Europe and in many parts of Asia.

indolent (ĭn′də-lənt) *adj.* **1** lazy. **2** causing little or no pain. ▶ **indolence** *noun*

indomitable (ĭn-dăm′ĭt-ə-bəl) *adj.* impossible to conquer or defeat. ▶ **indomitability** *noun* ▶ **indomitably** *adv.*

Indonesian *noun* **1** a native or citizen of Indonesia or the Malay archipelago. **2 a** the languages spoken in the Malay archipelago. **b** Bahasa Indonesian, the official language of Indonesia. —*adj.* relating to Indonesia, its people, or their languages.

indoor (ĭn′dôr‚) *adj.* used, done, etc., inside a building.

indoors (ĭn-dôrz′) *adv.* in or into a building.

indubitable (ĭn-dōō′bĭt-ə-bəl, -dyōō′-) *adj.* that cannot be doubted; certain. ▶ **indubitably** *adv.*

induce *verb trans.* (**induced, inducing**) **1** to persuade, influence, or cause to do something. **2** to cause to happen or appear. **3** during childbirth, to initiate or hasten (labor) by artificial means. **4** to infer or come to (e.g., a general conclusion) from particular cases. ▶ **inducement** *noun*

induct *verb trans.* (**inducted, inducting**) **1** to place (e.g., a priest) formally in an official position. **2** to initiate as a member of, e.g., a society or profession. **3** to enroll for military service or training.

inductance *noun* the property of an electric circuit that causes an electromotive force to be generated in it by changing the current.

induction *noun* **1** the act of inducting, e.g., into office. **2** during childbirth, the initiation of labor by artificial means. **3** the process of forming a general conclusion from particular cases. *See also* **deduction** (sense 3). **4** the production of an electrified or magnetic state in an object in close proximity to another, already electrified or magnetic, object. ▶ **inductive** *adj.*

indulge *verb trans., intrans.* (**indulged, indulging**) **1** (**indulge in (something)** *or* **indulge (someone) in (something)**) to permit or allow (oneself or someone else) pleasure or the particular pleasure of (something). **2** to allow (someone) to have anything he or she wants; to spoil. **3** *colloq.* to drink alcohol, esp. without restraint.

indulgence *noun* **1** the act of indulging a person, desire, etc. **2** *RC Church* remission from the punishment that remains due after the sin has been absolved.

indulgent *adj.* too quick to overlook or forgive faults or gratify the wishes of others. ▶ **indulgently** *adv.*

industrial *adj.* **1** relating to or used in industry. **2** *of a country, etc.* having highly developed industry.

industrialist *noun* a person who owns a large industrial organization.

industrialize *verb trans., intrans.* (**industrialized, industrializing**) to make or become industrially developed. ▶ **industrialization** *noun*

industrial park an area that is developed and zoned for industry and business.

industrial relations relations between management and workers.

Industrial Revolution the rapid development of a country's industry, characterized by a change from small-scale production to increased mechanization and mass production.

industrious *adj.* busy and hard-working. ▶ **industriously** *adv.* ▶ **industriousness** *noun*

industry (ĭn'də-strē, -dəs,trē) *noun* (*pl.* **industries**) **1** the business of producing goods; all branches of manufacturing and trade. **2** a branch of manufacturing and trade that produces a particular product. **3** hard work or effort; diligence.

-ine *suffix* forming words denoting like, relating to: *Alpine*.

inebriate *verb trans.* (ĭ-nē'brē-āt,) (**inebriated, inebriating**) **1** to make drunk. **2** to exhilarate greatly. —*noun* (ĭ-nē'brē-ət) a person who is drunk, esp. habitually. ▸ **inebriation** *noun* ▸ **inebriety** (ĭn,ĭ-brī'ət-ē) *noun*

inedible *adj.* unfit or not suitable to be eaten.

ineffable *adj.* too great to be described or expressed in words. ▸ **ineffability** *noun* ▸ **ineffably** *adv.*

ineffective *adj.* having no effect; not producing a result or the intended result. ▸ **ineffectiveness** *noun*

ineffectual *adj.* **1** not producing the intended result. **2** lacking the ability to achieve results; weak. ▸ **ineffectually** *adv.*

inefficient *adj.* not working or producing the required results, etc., in the best way. ▸ **inefficiency** *noun* ▸ **inefficiently** *adv.*

inelegant *adj.* lacking elegance or good taste; awkward. ▸ **inelegance** *noun* ▸ **inelegantly** *adv.*

ineligible *adj.* not qualified; not allowed. ▸ **ineligibility** *noun*

ineluctable (ĭn,ĭ-lək'tə-bəl) *adj.* that cannot be avoided or escaped from.

inept *adj.* **1** done without or not having skill. **2** not suitable or fitting. ▸ **ineptly** *adv.* ▸ **ineptitude** *noun* ▸ **ineptness** *noun*

inequality (ĭn,ĭ-kwäl'ət-ē) *noun* (*pl.* **inequalities**) **1** a lack of equality, fairness, or evenness. **2** a dissimilarity or disparity.

inequitable (ĭn-ĕk'wĭt-ə-bəl) *adj.* unfair or unjust. ▸ **inequitably** *adv.*

inequity (ĭn-ĕk'wĭt-ē) *noun* (*pl.* **inequities**) **1** lack of fairness. **2** an unjust action.

inert *adj.* **1** tending to remain in a state of rest or uniform motion. **2** not wanting to move, act, or think; sluggish. **3** chemically unreactive. ▸ **inertness** *noun*

inertia (ĭn-ər'shə) *noun* **1** the tendency of an object to remain at rest, or to continue to move in the same direction at constant speed unless it is acted on by an external force. **2** the state of not wanting to move, act, or think; sluggishness.

inescapable *adj.* impossible to avoid. ▸ **inescapably** *adv.*

inestimable (ĭn-ĕs'tĭ-mə-bəl) *adj.* too great to be measured or fully appreciated.

inevitable *adj.* impossible to avoid; certain to happen. ▸ **inevitability** *noun* ▸ **inevitably** *adv.*

inexact *adj.* not correct, exact, or true.

inexcusable *adj.* too bad to be excused or tolerated. ▸ **inexcusably** *adv.*

inexhaustible (ĭn,ĭg-zôs'tə-bəl) *adj.* incapable of being used up (esp. because too big).

inexorable (ĭn-ĕk'sə-rə-bəl, -ĕg'zə-) *adj.* that cannot be moved by entreaty or persuasion; unrelenting. ▸ **inexorably** *adv.*

inexpensive *adj.* not costly.

inexperience *noun* lack of experience or of the skill gained from experience. ▸ **inexperienced** *adj.*

inexpert *adj.* not skilled; not expert.

inexplicable *adj.* impossible to explain or account for. ▸ **inexplicably** *adv.*

inextricable (ĭn,ĭk-strĭk'ə-bəl, -ĕk'strĭk-) *adj.* that cannot be disentangled. ▸ **inextricably** *adv.*

infallible *adj.* **1** never making a mistake; incapable of error. **2** not likely to fail. ▸ **infallibility** *noun* ▸ **infallibly** *adv.*

infamous (ĭn'fə-məs) *adj.* having a notoriously bad reputation. ▸ **infamously** *adv.* ▸ **infamy** *noun*

infancy *noun* (*pl.* **infancies**) **1** the time of being an infant. **2** an early period of existence and development.

infant *noun* **1** a very young child in the first period of life. **2** *Law* a person who is under the legal age of maturity.

infanticide (ĭn-fănt'ĭ-sīd,) *noun* **1** the murder of a young child. **2** a person who murders a young child.

infantile (ĭn'fən-tīl,) *adj.* **1** of or relating to infants. **2** very childish; immature.

infantry (ĭn'fən-trē) *noun* (*pl.* **infantries**) soldiers who fight on foot.

infantryman *noun* a soldier in the infantry.

infatuate (ĭn-făch'ə-wāt,) *verb trans.* (**infatuated, infatuating**) to cause to feel a passionate and unreasonable love or admiration. ▸ **infatuated** *adj.* ▸ **infatuation** *noun*

infect *verb trans.* (**infected, infecting**) **1** to contaminate (a living organism) with a bacterium, virus, etc., and thereby cause disease. **2** to pass a feeling or opinion to (someone). ▸ **infection** *noun*

infectious *adj.* **1** caused by bacteria, viruses, etc., and therefore capable of being transmitted by infection. **2** *of a feeling, opinion, etc.* likely to be passed on to others. ▸ **infectiously** *adv.* ▸ **infectiousness** *noun*

infer (ĭn-fər') *verb trans.* (**inferred, inferring**) **1 a** to conclude from facts, observation, and deduction. **b** to lead to as a conclusion. **2** *colloq.* to suggest or hint.

Usage The use of *infer* in sense 2 is regarded by some critics as incorrect, and so it is usu. advisable to use *imply* instead.

inference (ĭn'fə-rəns, -frəns) *noun* **1** an act of inferring. **2** something that is inferred, esp. a conclusion. ▸ **inferential** *adj.*

inferior *adj.* (*often* **inferior to** (**something** or **someone**)) **1** poor or poorer in quality. **2** low or lower in rank or status. **3** low or lower in position. —*noun* a person who is lower, e.g., in rank or level of accomplishment, than another. ▸ **inferiority** (ĭn-fîr,ē-ôr'ət-ē) *noun*

infernal *adj.* **1** of or relating to hell. **2** wicked; evil. ▣ DEVILISH, DIABOLICAL, FIENDISH, HELLISH ▣ HEAVENLY. ▸ **infernally** *adv.*

inferno *noun* (*pl.* **infernos**) **1** (*often* **Inferno**) hell. **2** a raging fire.

infertile (ĭn-fûrt'l) *adj.* unable to produce offspring; sterile. ▸ **infertility** *noun*

infest *verb trans.* (**infested**, **infesting**) to be present in large numbers on or within (an animal, plant, etc.). ▸ **infestation** *noun*

infidel (ĭn'fəd-l, -fə-dĕl,) *noun* a person who is totally unorthodox in personal beliefs, esp. one guilty of religious heresy.

infidelity *noun* (*pl.* **infidelities**) **1 a** unfaithfulness to someone, e.g., a spouse. **b** an instance of it. **2** lack of belief in a religion.

infield *noun* **1** *Baseball* the diamond-shaped playing area bounded by the four bases. **2** the defensive base playing positions of first, second, third, and shortstop, regarded as a group. *See also* **outfield.** ▸ **infielder** *noun*

in-fighting *noun* fighting or competition between members of the same group.

infiltrate (ĭn-fĭl'trāt,, ĭn'fĭl-) *verb trans., intrans.* (**infiltrated**, **infiltrating**) **1** of troops, agents, *etc.* to pass into (territory or an organization held by the enemy or rivals) secretly, to gain influence or information. **2** of a liquid to flow slowly into (the pores of a solid). ▸ **infiltration** *noun* ▸ **infiltrator** *noun*

infinite (ĭn'fĭ-nĭt) *adj.* **1** having no boundaries or limits. **2 a** too great to be measured or counted. **b** very great. —*noun* something that has no limits, boundaries, etc. ▸ **infinitely** *adv.* ▸ **infiniteness** *noun*

infinitesimal (ĭn,fĭ-nĭ-tĕs'ĭ-məl) *adj.* infinitely small. ▸ **infinitesimally** *adv.*

infinitive *noun* a verb form that expresses an action but does not refer to a particular subject or time, in English often used with *to.* —*adj.* having this form.

infinity *noun* **1** the quality of being infinite. **2** space, time, or quantity that is without limit or boundaries, or is too great to be measured. **3** *Math.* a number that is larger than any finite value.

infirm *adj.* in poor physical health; debilitated.

infirmary (ĭn-fər'mə-rē) *noun* (*pl.* **infirmaries**) a hospital.

infirmity *noun* (*pl.* **infirmities**) **1** the state of being sick, weak, or infirm. **2** a disease or illness.

inflame *verb trans.* (**inflamed**, **inflaming**) **1** to arouse strong or violent emotion in. **2** to cause to burst into flames. **3** to produce inflammation in (part of the body).

inflammable (ĭn-flăm'ə-bəl) *adj.* easily set on fire. ▸ **inflammability** *noun*

> *Usage* See note at *flammable.*

inflammation (ĭn-flə-mā'shən) *noun* the state of being or process of becoming red, swollen, and painful.

inflammatory (ĭn-flăm'ə-tôr,ē) *adj.* likely to cause strong or violent emotion, esp. anger.

inflatable *adj.* that can be filled with air. —*noun* an object that can be filled with air, e.g., a rubber boat.

inflate *verb trans., intrans.* (**inflated**, **inflating**) **1** to swell or cause to swell or expand with air or gas. **2** to exaggerate the importance or value of. **3** to increase (prices generally) artificially or to increase (the volume of money in circulation). *See also* **deflate, reflate.** ▸ **inflated** *adj.*

inflation *noun* **1** the process of inflating. **2** a general increase in the level of prices accompanied by a fall in the purchasing power of money, caused by an increase in the amount of money in circulation and credit available. *See also* **deflation, reflation.** ▸ **inflationary** *adj.*

inflect *verb trans., intrans.* (**inflected**, **inflecting**) **1 a** to change the form of (a word) to show, e.g., tense, gender, etc. **b** of a word to change to show tense, gender, etc. **2** to vary the tone or pitch of (the voice). **3** to bend inward.

inflection *noun* **1** an act of inflecting or state of being inflected. **2 a** the change in the form of a word that shows tense, gender, etc. **b** an inflected form of a word. **3** a change in the tone, pitch, etc., of the voice. **4** a change in a curve from being convex to concave, or vice versa. ▸ **inflectional** *adj.* ▸ **inflective** *adj.*

inflexible *adj.* **1** incapable of being bent; rigid. **2** never giving way; obstinate. ▸ **inflexibility** *noun*

inflict *verb trans.* (**inflicted**, **inflicting**) (**inflict** (**something**) **on** (**someone**)) to impose on or cause to suffer (something unpleasant). ▸ **infliction** *noun*

inflorescence *noun* **1** the head of a flowering plant. **2** an arrangement of flowers on the main stem of a flowering plant.

influence (ĭn'flo͞o,əns, ĭn-flo͞o'əns) *noun* (*often* **influence on** or **over** (**someone**) or (**something**)) **1 a** the power that one person or thing has to affect another. **b** a person or thing that has such a power. **2** power resulting from political or social position, wealth, etc. —*verb trans.* (**influenced**,

influencing) to have an effect on (a person, events, etc.). **—under the influence** *colloq.* intoxicated.

influential (ĭn,flə-wĕn'chəl) *adj.* **1** having influence or power. **2** making an important contribution. ▸ **influentially** *adv.*

influenza (ĭn,flə-wĕn'zə) *noun* a viral infection whose main symptoms include fever, muscular aches and pains, and inflammation of the respiratory passages.

influx *noun* **1** a continual stream of large numbers of people or things. **2** a flowing in.

info *noun colloq.* information.

inform *verb trans., intrans.* (**informed, informing**) **1** (**inform (someone) about** *or* **of (something)**) to give (someone) knowledge or information on (a specific topic). **2** (**inform against** *or* **on** (**someone**)) to give incriminating evidence about (the specific party) to the authorities.

informal *adj.* **1** lacking ceremony or formality; relaxed and friendly. **2** *of clothes, etc.* suitable for relaxed, everyday situations. ▸ **informality** *noun* ▸ **informally** *adv.*

informant *noun* someone who informs, e.g., against another person.

information *noun* **1** knowledge gained or given; facts; data. **2** the communicating or receiving of knowledge. **3** an accusation made by a public officer instead of by way of indictment by a grand jury.

information superhighway systems and networks of computers and telecommunication devices enabling fast, global communications among users.

information technology (ABBREV. **IT**) the use of a range of technologies, esp. computer systems and telecommunications, to store, process, and transmit information.

informative (ĭn-fôr'mət-ĭv) *adj.* giving useful information; instructive. ▸ **informatively** *adv.* ▸ **informativeness** *noun*

informed *adj.* having or showing knowledge, esp. in being educated and intelligent.

informer *noun* a person who informs against another, esp. to law-enforcement agencies, usu. for a reward.

infra- *combining form* forming words denoting below, beneath: *infrared.*

infraction *noun* the breaking of a law, rule, etc.

infrared (ĭn,frə-rĕd') *adj.* (ABBREV. **IR**) **1** denoting electromagnetic radiation with wavelengths in the region between the red end of the visible spectrum and microwaves and radio waves. **2** using or sensitive to such radiation. **—noun** infrared radiation.

infrastructure *noun* **1** the basic structure of a society, organization, or system. **2** the permanent services and equipment, e.g., the roads, factories, and schools, needed for a country to be able to function properly.

infrequent (ĭn-frē'kwənt) *adj.* occurring only occasionally. ▸ **infrequency** *noun* ▸ **infrequently** *adv.*

infringe *verb trans., intrans.* (**infringed, infringing**) **1** to break or violate (e.g., a law or an oath). **2** (**infringe on** *or* **upon** (**something**)) to affect (a person's rights, freedom, etc.) in such a way as to limit or reduce them. ▸ **infringement** *noun*

infuriate (ĭn-fyŏŏr'ē-āt,) *verb trans.* (**infuriated, infuriating**) to make very angry. ▸ **infuriatingly** *adv.*

infuse (ĭn-fyŏŏz') *verb trans., intrans.* (**infused, infusing**) **1** (**infuse (something) into (someone)** *or* **infuse (someone) with (something)**) to inspire (the one specified) with (a positive feeling, quality, etc.). **2** to soak or cause (e.g., tea leaves) to be soaked in hot water to release their flavor or other qualities. ▸ **infusion** *noun*

-ing¹ *suffix* forming nouns, esp. from verbs, usu. expressing the action of the verb, its result or product, etc.: *building / driving.*

-ing² *suffix* used to form the present participle of verbs: *charming / walking.*

ingenious (ĭn-jē'nē-əs) *adj.* showing skill and inventive cleverness. ▸ **ingeniously** *adv.* ▸ **ingeniousness** *noun*

> **Usage** The adjective *ingenious* is often confused with *ingenuous.*

ingénue (ăn'jə-nŏŏ,, än'jə-, ăn'zhə-) *noun* **1** a naive and unsophisticated young woman. **2** an actress playing the role of a naive, artless young woman.

ingenuity (ĭn,jə-nŏŏ'ət-ē, -nyŏŏ'-) *noun* inventive cleverness or skill.

ingenuous (ĭn-jĕn'yə-wəs) *adj.* innocent and childlike. ▸ **ingenuously** *adv.* ▸ **ingenuousness** *noun*

> **Usage** The adjective *ingenuous* is often confused with *ingenious.*

ingest *verb trans.* (**ingested, ingesting**) to take (food or liquid) into the body by swallowing. ▸ **ingestible** *adj.* ▸ **ingestion** *noun*

inglorious *adj.* **1** not glorious or noble; ordinary. **2** bringing shame. ▸ **ingloriously** *adv.* ▸ **ingloriousness** *noun*

ingot (ĭng'gət) *noun* a brick-shaped mass of metal, esp. of gold.

ingrained *adj.* fixed firmly; difficult to remove.

ingrate *noun* an ungrateful person.

ingratiate (ĭn-grā'shē-āt,) *verb trans.* (**ingratiated, ingratiating**) (**ingratiate (oneself) with (someone)**) to gain or try to gain someone's favor or approval. ▸ **ingratiating** *adj.* ▸ **ingratiatingly** *adv.*

ingratitude *noun* lack of proper gratitude.

ingredient *noun* a component of a mixture or compound, esp. in cooking.

ingress (ĭn'grĕs,) *noun* the act of going in or entering or the right to do so.

ingrown *adj.* that has grown inward.

inhabit *verb trans.* (**inhabited, inhabiting**) to live in or occupy (a place).

inhabitant *noun* a person or animal that lives permanently in a place.

inhalant (ĭn-hā'lənt) *noun* a medicinal preparation that is inhaled, used esp. to relieve nasal congestion.

inhale (ĭn-hāl') *verb trans., intrans.* (**inhaled, inhaling**) to draw (air, tobacco smoke, etc.) into the lungs; to breathe in. ▸ **inhalation** (ĭn,hə-lā'shən, ĭn,ə-) *noun*

inhaler *noun* a device for administering a medicinal preparation by inhalation, esp. to reduce nasal congestion.

inhere (ĭn-hĭr') *verb intrans.* (**inhered, inhering**) (*often* **inhere in** (**something** *or* **someone**)) to be an essential or permanent part.

inherent (ĭn-hĕr'ənt, -hĭr'-) *adj., of a quality, etc.* belonging naturally or being an essential or permanent part. ▸ **inherently** *adv.*

inherit (ĭn-hĕr'ĭt) *verb trans., intrans.* (**inherited, inheriting**) **1** to receive (property, a title, etc.) from a member of one's family on his or her death, or through legal descent from a predecessor. **2** to receive genetically transmitted characteristics from the previous generation. ▸ **inheritable** *adj.* ▸ **inheritance** *noun* ▸ **inheritor** *noun*

inhibit (ĭn-hĭb'ĭt) *verb trans.* (**inhibited, inhibiting**) **1** to hold back or prevent (an action, progress, etc.). **2** to make (a person) feel nervous or frightened about acting freely or spontaneously. **3** to prohibit or forbid (someone) from doing something. ▸ **inhibited** *adj.* ▸ **inhibitedly** *adv.*

inhibition (ĭn,ĭ-bĭsh'ən) *noun* **1** a feeling of fear or embarrassment which prevents one from acting, thinking, etc., freely or spontaneously. **2** an act of inhibiting.

inhospitable *adj.* **1** not friendly or welcoming. **2** offering little shelter (e.g., from harsh weather). ▸ **inhospitably** *adv.*

inhuman *adj.* **1** cruel and unfeeling; brutal. **2** not human. ▸ **inhumanly** *adv.*

inhumane *adj.* showing no kindness, sympathy, or compassion. ▸ **inhumanely** *adv.* ▸ **inhumanity** *noun*

inimical (ĭn-ĭm'ĭ-kəl) *adj.* **1** tending to discourage; unfavorable. **2** not friendly; hostile. ▸ **inimically** *adv.*

inimitable (ĭn-ĭm'ĭt-ə-bəl) *adj.* too good, etc., to be satisfactorily imitated by others; unique. ▸ **inimitably** *adv.*

iniquitous (ĭn-ĭk'wĭ-təs) *adj.* **1** grossly unjust or unreasonable. **2** wicked. ▸ **iniquitously** *adv.* ▸ **iniquity** *noun*

initial *adj.* of or at the beginning. —*noun* the first letter of a word, esp. of a proper name. —*verb trans.* (**initialed** *or* **initialled, initialing** *or* **initialling**) to mark or sign with the initials of one's name, esp. as a sign of approval. ▸ **initially** *adv.*

initiate *verb trans.* (ĭ-nĭsh'ē-āt,) (**initiated, initiating**) **1** to cause to begin. **2** (**initiate** (**someone**) **into** (**something**)) to accept (a new member) into (a society, organization, etc.). **3** to give (someone) instruction in the basics of, e.g., a skill, science, etc. —*noun* (ĭn-ĭsh'ē-ət) a person who has recently been or is soon to be initiated. ▸ **initiation** *noun* ▸ **initiator** *noun*

initiative (ĭn-ĭsh'ət-ĭv) *noun* **1** the ability or skill to make decisions or act resourcefully. **2** a first step or move toward an end.

inject *verb trans.* (**injected, injecting**) **1** to introduce (a fluid) into a cavity in the body of a person or animal by the process of injection. **2** to introduce (a quality, element, etc.).

injection *noun* **1** the act or process of introducing fluid into a cavity under pressure. **2** the fluid injected by this process, esp. a drug introduced into the body for medicinal purposes.

injudicious *adj.* not wise.

injunction *noun* **1** a court order forbidding something, or commanding that something be done. **2** an authoritative order or warning. ▸ **injunctive** *adj.*

injure (ĭn'jər) *verb trans.* (**injured, injuring**) **1** to do physical harm or damage to. **2** to spoil or weaken. **3** to do an injustice or wrong to.

injurious (ĭn-jŏŏr'ē-əs) *adj.* causing injury or damage; harmful. ▸ **injuriously** *adv.*

injury *noun* (*pl.* **injuries**) **1** physical harm or damage. **2** a wound. **3** a wrong or injustice.

injustice *noun* unfairness or lack of justice.

ink *noun* **1** a liquid used for writing, drawing, or printing. **2** a dark liquid ejected by octopus, squid, etc., in order to confuse predators. —*verb trans.* (**inked, inking**) **1** to mark with ink. **2** to cover with ink.

inkjet printer a computer printer that produces characters on paper by means of a fine spray of ink.

inkling *noun* a vague idea or suspicion; a hint.

inkwell *noun* a small container for ink, esp. one that fits into a hole in a desk.

inky *adj.* (**inkier, inkiest**) **1** covered with ink. **2** black or very dark. ▸ **inkiness** *noun*

inlaid *adj.* **1** *of a design* set into a surface. **2** *of an object* having a design set into its surface.

inland (ĭn'lənd, -lănd,) *adj.* of or in that part of a country which is not beside the sea. —*adv.* in or toward the inner regions of a country.

in-law (ĭn'lô,) *noun* (*pl.* **in-laws**) *colloq.* a relative by marriage.

inlay *verb trans.* (ĭn-lā′, ĭn′lā,) **1** to embed (e.g., pieces of wood, metal, etc., in another material) so that the surfaces are flat. **2** to decorate (e.g., a piece of furniture) by setting flat pieces of different colored wood, ivory, etc., in the surface. —*noun* (ĭn′lā,) **1** a decoration or design made by inlaying. **2** the pieces used to create an inlaid design. **3** a filling shaped to fit a cavity in a tooth.

inlet (ĭn′lĕt,, -lət) *noun* a narrow opening in a coastline.

inmate *noun* a person living in an institution, esp. a prison or a hospital.

inmost *adj.* **1** farthest in. **2** most secret or private.

inn *noun* a public house or small hotel.

innards (ĭn′ərdz) *pl. noun colloq.* **1** the inner organs of a person or animal. **2** the inner workings of a machine.

innate (ĭn-āt′) *adj.* existing in a person from birth; natural rather than acquired. ▸ **innately** *adv.* ▸ **innateness** *noun*

inner *adj.* **1** situated inside; farther in. **2** secret, hidden, and profound.

inner city the central, typically older, area of a city, often densely populated. ▸ **inner-city** *adj.*

innermost *adj.* **1** farthest within. **2** most secret or hidden.

inner tube an inflatable rubber tube inside a tire.

inning *noun Baseball* a period of a game during which each team has its turn at bat.

innings *pl. noun* a period during which a person has an opportunity for action or achievement.

innkeeper *noun* a person who owns or manages an inn.

innocent *adj.* (*often* **innocent of (something)**) **1** free from sin; pure. **2** not guilty (e.g., of a crime). **3** not intending to cause harm. **4** lacking something. **5** simple and trusting. —*noun* an innocent person. ▸ **innocence** *noun* ▸ **innocently** *adv.*

innocuous (ĭn-äk′yə-wəs) *adj.* harmless; inoffensive. ▸ **innocuously** *adv.* ▸ **innocuousness** *noun*

innovate (ĭn′ə-vāt,) *verb intrans., trans.* (**innovated, innovating**) **1** to make changes; to introduce new methods, etc. **2** to introduce (something) as new. ▸ **innovation** *noun* ▸ **innovative** *adj.* ▸ **innovator** *noun*

innuendo (ĭn,yə-wĕn′dō) *noun* (*pl.* **innuendoes**) **1** an indirect, usu. slightly unpleasant, critical or rude remark, esp. about someone's reputation or character. **2** the act of making such remarks.

Innuit *noun same as* **Inuit**.

innumerable *adj.* too many to be counted; a great many. ▸ **innumerably** *adv.*

innumerate (ĭn-nōō′mə-rət, -nyōō′-) *adj.* having no knowledge or understanding of mathematics or science. ▸ **innumeracy** *noun*

inoculate (ĭn-äk′yə-lāt,) *verb trans.* (**inoculated, inoculating**) **1** to produce a mild form of a particular infectious disease in (a person or animal), followed by immunity to it, by injecting a harmless form of an antigen. **2** to introduce an idea into the mind of (a person). ▸ **inoculation** *noun*

inoffensive *adj.* not likely to offend; harmless.

inoperable *adj.* unsuitable for surgical procedures.

inoperative (ĭn-äp′ə-rət′ĭv) *adj.* **1** not working or functioning; having no effect. **2** no longer in force.

inopportune *adj.* not convenient or suitable; poorly timed. ▸ **inopportunely** *adv.*

inordinate *adj.* greater than reasonable; beyond acceptable limits. ▸ **inordinately** *adv.*

inorganic *adj.* not composed of material that has or formerly had the structure and characteristics of living organisms.

inpatient (ĭn′pā,shənt) *noun* a patient who has been admitted to hospital to receive treatment necessitating at least one overnight stay.

input *noun* (ĭn′pŏŏt,) **1** the data transferred from a disk, tape, or input device into the main memory of a computer. **2** something put or taken in, e.g., a contribution to a discussion. **3** the power, labor, etc., required to produce something, esp. the power put into a machine. —*verb trans.* (ĭn′pŏŏt,, ĭn-pŏŏt′) to transfer (data) from a disk, tape, or input device into the main memory of a computer.

inquest (ĭn′kwĕst,) *noun* **1** a judicial investigation, esp. an inquiry into a sudden and unexpected death, usu. held before a jury. **2** any investigation.

inquietude *noun* mental restlessness or uneasiness.

inquire (ĭn-kwīr′) *or* **enquire** *verb intrans., trans.* (**inquired, inquiring**) **1** to request information about something by asking a question. **2** (**inquire about (someone)**) to ask about (someone's) health or happiness. **3** (**inquire into (something)**) to try to discover the facts of (a crime, etc.). ▸ **inquirer** *noun*

inquiring *or* **enquiring** *adj.* **1** eager to discover or learn things. **2** appearing to be asking a question. ▸ **inquiringly** *adv.*

inquiry (ĭn-kwī′rē, ĭn′kwə-rē) *or* **enquiry** *noun* (*pl.* **inquiries**) **1** the act of asking for information or inquiring. **2** an investigation.

inquisition (ĭn,kwĭ-zĭsh′ən) *noun* **1** an intensive inquiry or investigation. **2** a judicial or otherwise official inquiry. **3 (Inquisition)** a former papal tribunal for the prosecution of heresy. ▸ **inquisitor** noun

inquisitive adj. **1** overly eager to find out things, esp. about other people's affairs. **2** eager for knowledge or information. ▸ **inquisitively** adv. ▸ **inquisitiveness** noun

inroad (ĭn'rōd,) noun **1** (usu. **inroads into (something)**) a large or significant encroachment. **2** a hostile attack or raid.

insane adj. **1** mentally ill. **2** extremely foolish; stupid. **3** of or intended for the mentally ill. —noun, **(the insane)** people who are mentally ill to a severe extent. ▸ **insanely** adv. ▸ **insanity** noun

insanitary (ĭn-săn'ĭ-tĕr,ē) adj. so dirty as to be dangerous to health.

insatiable (ĭn-sā'shə-bəl) adj. unable to be satisfied; extremely greedy.

inscribe verb trans. **(inscribed, inscribing) 1** to write, print, or engrave (words) on (paper, metal, stone, etc.). **2** to enter (a name) on a list or in a book. **3 (inscribe (something) to (someone))** to dedicate (a book, etc.) to (someone), usu. by writing in the front of it.

inscription noun words written, printed, or engraved, e.g., as an epitaph on a gravestone. ▸ **inscriptive** adj.

inscrutable adj. **1** hard to understand or explain. **2** mysterious; enigmatic. ▸ **inscrutability** noun ▸ **inscrutably** adv.

insect noun **1** an invertebrate animal, e.g., a fly, beetle, or bee. **2** an insignificant or worthless person.

insecticide (ĭn-sĕk'tĭ-sīd,) noun a substance used to kill insects.

insectivore (ĭn-sĕk'tĭ-vôr,) noun a living organism that feeds on insects. ▸ **insectivorous** (ĭn,sĕk,tĭv'ə-rəs) adj.

insecure adj. **1** not firmly fixed; unstable. **2** lacking confidence. **3** not guarded to a satisfactory extent. ▸ **insecurely** adv. ▸ **insecurity** noun

inseminate verb trans. **(inseminated, inseminating) 1** to introduce semen into the vagina of (a female). **2** to sow (seeds, ideas, etc.). ▸ **insemination** noun

insensate (ĭn-sĕn'sāt,) adj. **1** unable to perceive physical sensations; inanimate. **2** insensitive and unfeeling. ▸ **insensately** adv. ▸ **insensateness** noun

insensible adj. **1** unable to feel pain or experience consciousness; unconscious. **2 (insensible to (something))** unaware of (it); not caring about (it). **3** incapable of feeling emotion. **4** too slight to be noticed; imperceptible. ▸ **insensibility** noun ▸ **insensibly** adv.

insensitive adj. **(often insensitive to (something)) 1** not capable of responding sympathetically, esp. to other people's feelings. **2** not reacting to stimulation. ▸ **insensitively** adv. ▸ **insensitivity** noun

inseparable adj. **1** incapable of being separated. **2** of friends, etc. constantly together. ▸ **inseparability** noun ▸ **inseparably** adv.

insert verb trans. (ĭn-sərt') **(inserted, inserting) 1** to put or fit (something) inside something else. **2** to introduce (text, words, etc.) into the body of other text, words, etc. —noun (ĭn'sərt,) something inserted. ▸ **insertion** noun

inset noun (ĭn'sĕt,) **1** something set in or inserted. **2** a small map or picture put into the corner of a larger one. —verb (ĭn'sĕt,, ĭn-sĕt') to put in or insert.

inshore adv., adj. in or on the water, and close to or toward the shore.

inside noun **1** the inner surface or part; the internal parts. **2** the part of a path away from an edge. **3 (insides)** colloq. the inner organs, esp. the stomach and bowels. —adj. **1** of, on, or near the inside. **2** colloq. coming from or planned by someone within an organization. —adv. on or to the inside; indoors. —prep. **1** on or to the inside of; within. **2** in less than. See also **outside**. —**inside out 1** with the inside surface turned out. **2** colloq. thoroughly; completely.

insider noun a recognized or accepted member of an organization or group who has access to secret information.

insidious (ĭn-sĭd'ē-əs) adj. **1** developing gradually without being noticed but causing very great harm. **2** attractive but harmful; treacherous. ▸ **insidiously** adv. ▸ **insidiousness** noun

insight noun **1** the ability to gain a relatively rapid, clear, and deep understanding of the real nature of a situation, problem, etc. **2** an instance of this. ▸ **insightful** adj.

insignia (ĭn-sĭg'nē-ə) noun (pl. **insignia, insignias**) a badge or emblem of office.

insignificant adj. **1** of little or no meaning or importance. **2** relatively small. ▸ **insignificance** noun ▸ **insignificantly** adv.

insincere adj. not sincere or genuine; false. ▸ **insincerely** adv. ▸ **insincerity** noun

insinuate (ĭn-sĭn'yə-wāt,) verb trans. **(insinuated, insinuating) 1** to suggest or hint (something unpleasant) indirectly. **2** to introduce (e.g., an idea) in an indirect or devious way. **3 (insinuate (someone) into (something))** to gain acceptance or favor for (esp. oneself) by gradual, often cunning means. ▸ **insinuatingly** adv. ▸ **insinuation** noun

insipid adj. **1** lacking liveliness; boring. **2** lacking taste or flavor. ▸ **insipidly** adv. ▸ **insipidness** noun

insist verb intrans., trans. **(insisted, insisting) 1** to maintain or assert firmly. **2 (insist on or**

upon (something)) to demand (it) firmly. ► **insistence** noun ► **insistent** adj. ► **insistently** adv.

in situ (ĭn-sī′tyōō, -sī′-) done, carried out, etc., while remaining in place.

insofar as to the extent that.

insole (ĭn′sōl,) noun 1 a loose inner sole that can be put into a shoe to make it slightly smaller. 2 a fixed inner sole of a shoe.

insolent (ĭn′sə-lənt) adj. insultingly rude; showing a gross lack of respect. ► **insolence** noun ► **insolently** adv.

insoluble adj. 1 unable to be dissolved. 2 impossible to resolve. ► **insolubility** noun

insolvent adj. not having enough money to pay one's debts. ► **insolvency** noun

insomnia (ĭn-säm′nē-ə) noun chronic inability to sleep. ► **insomniac** noun, adj.

insomuch as 1 to such an extent or degree as. **2** given that; because of the fact that.

insouciant (ĭn-sōō′sē-ənt) adj. without cares or worries; lighthearted. ► **insouciance** noun

inspect verb trans. (**inspected, inspecting**) 1 to look at or examine closely. 2 to look at or examine officially. ► **inspection** noun ► **inspector** noun

inspiration noun 1 a supposed power that stimulates the mind, esp. to creativity. 2 a person or thing that inspires or the state of being inspired. 3 a brilliant or inspired idea. ► **inspirational** adj.

inspire verb trans., intrans. (**inspired, inspiring**) 1 to stimulate (a person), esp. to creative activity. 2 to fill (a person) with a feeling of confidence and encouragement. 3 (**inspire (someone) with (something)**) to create a particular feeling in (someone). 4 to be the origin or source of (a poem, piece of music, etc.). ► **inspiring** adj.

inst. abbrev. instant.

instability noun lack of steadiness or stability.

install verb trans. (**installed, installing**) 1 to put (equipment, machinery, etc.) in place and make it ready for use. 2 to place (a person) in office with a formal ceremony. ► **installation** noun

installment or **instalment** noun 1 one of a series of parts into which a debt is divided for payment. 2 one of several parts published, broadcast, etc., at regular intervals.

instance noun 1 an example. 2 a stage in a process. 3 formal a request. —**for instance** for example.

instant adj. 1 immediate. 2 quickly and easily prepared. 3 of or occurring in the current month. —noun 1 a particular moment in time, esp. the present: this instant. 2 a very brief period of time. ► **instantly** adv.

instantaneous adj. done or occurring at once

or in an instant. ► **instantaneously** adv.

instead (ĭn-stĕd′) adv. as a substitute or alternative. —**instead of** in place of or as an alternative to.

instep noun the prominent arched middle section of the human foot.

instigate (ĭn′stĭ-gāt,) verb trans. (**instigated, instigating**) 1 a to encourage or promote (ill feeling, etc.). b to urge on or incite (someone), esp. to do something wrong. 2 to set in motion or initiate (e.g., an inquiry). ► **instigation** noun ► **instigator** noun

instill (ĭn-stĭl′) or **instil** verb trans. (**instilled, instilling**) 1 (**instil (something) in** or **into (someone)**) to impress (ideas, feelings, etc.) gradually into (a person's mind). 2 to pour (a liquid) into, drop by drop. ► **instiller** noun ► **instillment** noun

instinct noun 1 a natural and usu. fixed way of responding to particular stimuli without having to think 2 a natural, involuntary, and usu. unconscious reaction, response, or impulse. 3 intuition. ► **instinctive** adj. ► **instinctively** adv.

institute noun 1 a society or organization that promotes research, education, or a particular cause. 2 an institution of higher learning that focuses chiefly on technical subjects. —verb trans. (**instituted, instituting**) to set up, establish, or organize.

institution noun 1 an organization or public body founded esp. for charitable or educational purposes, or as a hospital. 2 a place in which the homeless, the destitute, etc., are housed and given care. 3 a custom or tradition. 4 a familiar and well-known person or object. 5 the act of instituting. ► **institutional** adj.

institutionalize verb trans. (**institutionalized, institutionalizing**) 1 to place in an institution. 2 to make into an institution.

instruct verb trans. (**instructed, instructing**) 1 to cause (a person) to acquire skill or knowledge in (a subject or activity). 2 to direct or order.

instruction noun 1 (often **instructions**) a direction or command. 2 (**instructions**) a set of detailed guidelines, e.g., on how to operate a machine. 3 an element in a computer program or language that activates a specific operation. 4 teaching.

instructive adj. giving knowledge or information. ► **instructiveness** noun

instructor noun 1 a person who gives instruction. 2 a university or college teacher ranking below assistant professor.

instrument noun 1 a tool, esp. one used for delicate scientific work. 2 a device inside a vehicle or aircraft that shows and controls speed, temperature, etc. 3 a device that can be made to produce music. 4 a thing or person used as a means of achieving or doing something. **5** a legal document.

instrumental *adj.* **1** (*often* **instrumental in** (**something**)) responsible for (it) or an important factor in (it). **2** performed by or written or arranged for musical instruments. —*noun* a piece performed by or written for musical instruments.

instrumentalist *noun* a person who plays a musical instrument.

instrumentation *noun* **1** the particular way in which a piece is written or arranged to be played by instruments. **2** the use or provision of instruments or tools.

insubordinate (ĭn,sə-bôrd'n-ət) *adj.* unwilling to comply with orders. ▸ **insubordinately** *adv.* ▸ **insubordination** *noun*

insubstantial *adj.* **1** not solid or strong. **2** not real.

insufferable *adj.* too unpleasant or annoying to bear. ▸ **insufferably** *adv.*

insufficient *adj.* not enough or not adequate. ▸ **insufficiency** *noun* ▸ **insufficiently** *adv.*

insular (ĭn'sə-lər, -syə-) *adj.* **1** of or belonging to an island. **2** not influenced by or responsive to contact with other people, cultures, etc. ▸ **insularity** (ĭn,sə-lăr'ət-ē, -syə-) *noun*

insulate (ĭn'sə-lāt,) *verb trans.* (**insulated, insulating**) **1** to surround (a body, device, or space) with a material that prevents or slows down the flow of heat, electricity, or sound. **2** to remove or set (someone or something) apart; to isolate. ▸ **insulation** *noun* ▸ **insulator** *noun*

insulin (ĭn'sə-lĭn) *noun* a hormone which controls the concentration of glucose, deficiency of which causes diabetes mellitus.

> Based on the Latin word for 'island', because insulin is secreted by cells called the *islets of Langerhans*

insult *verb trans.* (ĭn-sŏlt') (**insulted, insulting**) to give offense to. ▣ AFFRONT, OFFEND, OUTRAGE. —*noun* (ĭn'sŏlt,) **1** a rude and offensive remark or action. **2** an affront. ▸ **insulting** *adj.* ▸ **insultingly** *adv.*

insuperable *adj.* so difficult as to be virtually impossible to overcome. ▸ **insuperability** *noun* ▸ **insuperably** *adv.*

insupportable *adj.* too unpleasant, annoying, etc., to be tolerated.

insurance (ĭn-shŏŏr'əns, ĭn'shŏŏr,-) *noun* **1 a** an agreement by which one party promises to pay another party money in the event of theft, damage to property, death, etc. **b** the business of providing such agreements for clients. **2** any measure taken to try to prevent disappointment, problems, etc.

insure (ĭn-shŏŏr') *verb trans., intrans.* (**insured, insuring**) (*often* **insure against** (**something**)) **1** to arrange for the payment

of an amount of money in the event of theft, damage to (property), or the death of (someone), etc., by paying regular amounts of money to an insurance company. **2** to provide insurance; to underwrite. **3** to take measures to try to prevent (damage, difficulties, etc.). ▸ **insurable** *adj.* ▸ **insurer** *noun*

insured *noun* (**the insured**) a person whose life, health, or property is covered by insurance.

insurgent *adj.* opposed to and fighting against the government of the country. —*noun* a rebel. ▸ **insurgence** (ĭn-sər'jəns) or **insurgency** *noun*

insurmountable *adj.* impossible to overcome. ▸ **insurmountability** *noun*

insurrection (ĭn,sə-rĕk'shən) *noun* rebellion against authority, esp. active, violent opposition to a nation's government. ▸ **insurrectionary** *adj.* ▸ **insurrectionist** *noun*

int. *abbrev.* **1** internal. **2** international.

intact (ĭn-tăkt') *adj.* not broken or damaged; whole.

intaglio (ĭn-tăl'yō, -tăl'-) *noun* **1** the art or process of engraving designs into the surface of objects, esp. jewelry. **2** printmaking using engraved plates.

intake (ĭn'tāk,) *noun* **1** the act of taking in: *intake of food.* **2** a thing or quantity taken in or accepted.

intangible *adj.* **1** incapable of being felt or otherwise perceived by the senses. **2** difficult to understand. ▸ **intangibility** *noun* ▸ **intangibly** *adv.*

integer (ĭnt'ə-jər) *noun* any of the whole numbers, or zero.

integral (ĭnt'ĭ-grəl, ĭn-tĕg'rəl) *adj.* **1** being a necessary part of a whole. **2** forming a whole; supplied as part of a whole. **3** whole; complete. **4** denoting a number that is an integer.

integrate (ĭnt'ə-grāt,) *verb trans., intrans.* (**integrated, integrating**) **1** to fit (parts) together to form a whole. **2** to mix or cause to mix freely with other groups in society, etc. ▸ **integration** *noun*

integrated circuit a miniature electronic circuit consisting of several separate semiconductor devices printed into a large silicon chip.

integrity (ĭn-tĕg'rət-ē) *noun* **1** strict adherence to moral values and principles. **2** the quality or state of being whole and unimpaired.

intellect (ĭnt'l-ĕkt,) *noun* the part of the mind that uses both memory and intelligence.

intellectual (ĭnt,l-ĕk'chə-wəl) *adj.* **1** of, involving or appealing to the intellect. **2** having a highly developed ability to think, reason, and understand. —*noun* a person with a highly developed intellect and great mental ability. ▸ **intellectually** *adv.*

intelligence *noun* **1** the ability to use memory, knowledge, reasoning, etc.. **2** news or information. **3 a** the gathering of secret information about an enemy. · **b** the government department or group of people responsible for gathering such information.

intelligence quotient (ABBREV. IQ) a measure of a person's intellectual ability.

intelligent *adj.* **1 a** having or exhibiting highly developed mental acumen. **b** good or quick at learning and understanding. **2** *of a computer, etc.* able to vary its behavior according to the situation. ▸ **intelligently** *adv.*

intelligentsia (ĭn-tĕl,ə-jĕnt'sē-ə, -gĕnt'-) *noun* (*usu.* the **intelligentsia**) the most highly educated and cultured people in a society.

intelligible *adj.* **1** able to be understood; clear. **2** able to be understood only by the intellect and not by the senses or feelings. ▸ **intelligibility** *noun* ▸ **intelligibly** *adv.*

intemperate (ĭn-tĕm'pə-rət) *adj.* **1** not controlled or restrained. **2** habitually drinking too much alcohol. **3** having extreme, severe temperatures. *See also* **temperate**. ▸ **intemperance** *noun* ▸ **intemperately** *adv.*

intend *verb trans., intrans.* (**intended, intending**) **1** to plan or have in mind as one's purpose or aim. **2** to create or design (something) for a particular purpose. **3** (**intend (something) for (someone** *or* **something)**) to set (it) aside or destine (it) to (some specified person or thing). **4** to mean.

intended *adj.* done on-purpose, or planned. —*noun colloq.* one's future spouse.

intense *adj.* **1** very great or extreme. **2** feeling or expressing emotion deeply. ▸ **intensely** *adv.* ▸ **intensity** *noun* .

intensifier *noun* an adverb or adjective that adds emphasis to the word or phrase that follows it. ·

intensify *verb trans., intrans.* (**intensified, intensifying, intensifies**) to make or become intense. ▸ **intensification** *noun*

intensive *adj.* **1** (*often in compounds*) using or requiring considerable amounts of effort, time, etc., within a relatively short period: *labor-intensive*. **2** thorough; intense; concentrated. **3** *of an adverb or adjective* adding force or emphasis. —*noun* an intensive adverb or adjective. ▸ **intensively** *adv.* ▸ **intensiveness** *noun*

intent *noun* something aimed at or intended; a purpose. —*adj.* **1** (**intent on** *or* **upon** (**something**)) firmly determined to do (it). **2**

(**intent on (something)**) having one's attention firmly fixed on (it); concentrating hard on (it). **3** showing concentration; absorbed. ▸ **intently** *adv.* ▸ **intentness** *noun*

intention *noun* **1** something that one plans or intends to do; an aim or purpose. **2** (**intentions**) *colloq.* someone's purpose with regard to marriage. ▸ **intentional** *adj.*

inter (ĭn-tər') *verb trans.* (**interred, interring**) to bury (a dead person, etc.).

inter- *combining form* forming words denoting: **1** between or among: *interstate* ·*commerce.* **2** mutual or reciprocal: *intermingling.*

interact *verb intrans.* (**interacted, interacting**) to act with or on one another. ▸ **interaction** *noun*

interactive *adj.* **1** being a situation in which the people, things, etc., interact. **2** involving or allowing a continuous exchange of information between a computer and its user.

intercalary (ĭn-tər'kə-lĕr,ē, ĭnt,ər-kăl'ə-rē) *adj.* **1** *of a day* added to a calendar month to make the calendar year match the solar year. **2** *of a year* containing such a day.

intercede *verb intrans.* (**interceded, interceding**) **1** to act as a peacemaker between (two parties, countries, etc.). **2** (**intercede for (someone)**) to plead or make an appeal on (someone's) behalf.

intercept ·*verb trans.* (ĭnt,ər-sĕpt') (**intercepted, intercepting**) **1** to stop or catch (e.g., a person, missile, etc.) on his, its, etc., way from one place to another. **2** to cut off (part of a line or plane) with another line or plane that crosses it. —*noun* (ĭnt'ər-sĕpt,) the part of a line or plane that is cut off by another line or plane crossing it. ▸ **interception** *noun* ▸ **interceptive** *adj.*

interceptor *noun* a fighter aircraft used to intercept and destroy approaching enemy aircraft.

intercession *noun* **1** the act of interceding. **2** a prayer or request to God on behalf of someone else. ▸ **intercessional** *adj.*

intercessor (ĭnt,ər-sĕs'ər) *noun* a person who intercedes; a mediator.

interchange *verb intrans., trans.* (ĭnt,ər-chānj') (**interchanged, interchanging**) to change or cause to change places with something or someone. —*noun* (ĭnt'ər-chānj,) **1** the act of interchanging; an exchange. **2** a road junction, esp. leading to or from a freeway. ▸ **interchangeable** *adj.* ▸ **interchangeability** *noun* ▸ **interchangeably** *adv.*

intercity *adj.* pertaining to or moving between two or more cities.

intercom (ĭnt'ər-kăm,) *noun* a system consisting of microphones and loudspeakers that allow communication within a building, aircraft, etc.

interconnect *verb trans., intrans.* (**interconnected, interconnecting**) to connect (two things), or be connected together or with one another. ▸ **interconnection** *noun*

intercontinental *adj.* traveling between or connecting different continents.

intercourse (ĭnt′ər-kôrs,) *noun* 1 sexual intercourse. 2 communication or dealings between people, countries, etc.

interdependent *adj.* depending on one another. ▸ **interdependence** *noun* ▸ **interdependently** *adv.*

interdict *noun* (ĭnt′ər-dĭkt,) 1 a court order forbidding someone to do something. 2 *RC Church* a sentence or punishment removing the right to most sacraments from the people of a place. —*verb trans.* (ĭnt,ər-dĭkt′) (**interdicted, interdicting**) to place under an interdict; to forbid. ▸ **interdiction** *noun* ▸ **interdictory** *adj.*

interdisciplinary *adj.* involving two or more subjects of study.

interest (ĭn′trəst, ĭnt′ə-rĕst,, ĭnt′ə-rəst) *noun* 1 the desire to learn or know about someone or something. 2 the power to attract a person's attention and curiosity. 3 something that arouses a person's attention and curiosity; a pastime. 4 money paid as a charge for borrowing money or using credit. 5 (*often* **interests**) advantage, benefit, or profit. 6 a claim to a business and its profits. —*verb trans.* (**interested, interesting**) 1 to attract the attention and curiosity of. 2 (**interest (someone) in (something)**) to cause (someone) to take a part in (some activity).

interested *adj.* 1 (*often* **interested in (something** *or* **someone)**) showing or having an interest in (the one specified). 2 personally involved and therefore not impartial.

interesting *adj.* attracting interest; holding the attention. ▸ **interestingly** *adv.*

interface *noun* 1 a surface forming a common boundary between two regions, things, etc. 2 a common boundary between two different systems or processes. 3 a a device consisting of hardware together with software programs to drive it, that links a computer to a printer, etc. b the physical connection between a computer and the user. —*verb trans., intrans.* (**interfaced, interfacing**) to connect (a piece of equipment, etc.) with another by means of an interface.

interfere (ĭnt,ər-fîr′) *verb intrans.* (**interfered, interfering**) 1 (**interfere in** *or* **with (something)**) to involve oneself in matters that do not concern one. 2 (**interfere with (something)**) to slow

down or hinder the progress of (something).

interference *noun* 1 the act of interfering. 2 the distortion of radio or television signals by an external power source.

interferon (ĭnt,ər-fîr′ŏn,) *noun* any of various proteins produced by the body to prevent the growth of a hostile virus.

interim (ĭnt′ə-rĭm) *adj.* serving or lasting for only a limited period of time. —**in the interim** in the meantime.

interior *adj.* 1 on, of, acting in, or coming from the inside; inner. 2 away from the shore; inland. 3 concerning the domestic affairs of a country. 4 of or relating to mental or spiritual life. —*noun* 1 an internal or inner part; the inside. 2 the part of a country or continent that is farthest from the coast.

interj. *abbrev.* interjection.

interject *verb trans.* (**interjected, interjecting**) to say or add abruptly.

interjection *noun* 1 an exclamation. 2 the act of interjecting.

interlace *verb trans., intrans.* (**interlaced, interlacing**) 1 to join by lacing or by crossing over. 2 to mix or blend.

interlard *verb trans.* (**interlarded, interlarding**) to add foreign words, unusual phrases, etc., to (a speech or piece of writing).

interleave (ĭnt,ər-lēv′) *verb trans.* (**interleaved, interleaving**) to insert a usu. blank leaf of paper between.

interline[1] *verb trans.* (**interlined, interlining**) to insert (words) between the lines of (a document, book, etc.).

interline[2] *verb trans.* (**interlined, interlining**) to put an extra lining between the first lining and the fabric (of a garment). ▸ **interlining** *noun*

interlink *verb trans., intrans.* (**interlinked, interlinking**) to join or connect together.

interlock *verb trans., intrans.* (**interlocked, interlocking**) to fit, fasten, or connect together. —*noun* a device or mechanism that connects and coordinates the functions of the parts or components of, e.g., a machine.

interlocution *noun* dialogue; conversation. ▸ **interlocutory** (ĭnt,ər-läk′yə-tôr,ē) *adj.* ▸ **interlocutor** *noun*

interloper *noun* a person who meddles or interferes with other people's affairs; an intruder.

interlude *noun* 1 a short period of time between two events. 2 a short break between the acts of a play or opera. 3 a short item of entertainment played during such a break.

intermarry *verb intrans.* (**intermarried, intermarrying, intermarries**) 1 *of different races, religious groups, etc.* to become connected by marriage. 2 to marry someone from one's own family. ▸ **intermarriage** (ĭnt′ər-măr′ĭj) noun

intermediary (ĭnt,ər-mēd′ē-ĕr,ē) noun (pl. **intermediaries**) a person who mediates between two people or groups.

intermediate adj. (ĭnt,ər-mēd′ē-ət) in the middle; placed between two points or extremes. —noun an intermediate person, e.g., in terms of skill. —verb intrans. (ĭnt,ər-mēd′ē-āt,) (**intermediated, intermediating**) to act as an intermediary. ▸ **intermediately** adv. ▸ **intermediation** noun

interment (ĭn-tər′mənt) noun a burial.

intermezzo (ĭnt,ər-mĕt′sō) noun (pl. **intermezzos, intermezzi**) a short instrumental piece usu. performed between the sections of an opera or other dramatic musical entertainment.

interminable (ĭn-tər′mĭ-nə-bəl) adj. seeming to have no end, esp. because of being extremely dull. ▸ **interminably** adv.

intermingle verb trans., intrans. (**intermingled, intermingling**) to combine or to be combined into a whole.

intermission noun a short pause between two things, e.g., between two parts of a film.

intermittent (ĭnt,ər-mĭt′nt) adj. happening occasionally; stopping for a while and then starting again. ▸ **intermittence** noun ▸ **intermittently** adv.

intern¹ (ĭn′tərn,) or **interne** noun an advanced student or graduate who is gaining practical professional experience by working, esp. a graduate of a medical school working under close supervision in a hospital. ▸ **internship** noun

intern² (ĭn-tərn′) verb trans. (**interned, interning**) to confine (a person) within a country or prison. ▸ **internee** (ĭn-tər,nē′) noun ▸ **internment** noun

internal (ĭn-tərn′l) adj. 1 of, in, or suitable for the inside. 2 of or relating to a nation's domestic affairs. 3 of or relating to the inner nature or feelings. ▸ **internally** adv.

internal combustion engine an engine that produces power by the combustion of a mixture of fuel and air inside it.

internalize verb trans. (**internalized, internalizing**) to make (a type of behavior, characteristic, etc.) part of one's personality. ▸ **internalization** noun

international (ĭnt,ər-năsh′ən-l) adj. 1 involving or used by two or more nations. 2 going beyond national frontiers or cultures. ▸ **internationality** noun ▸ **internationally** adv.

internationalism noun the view that the nations of the world should cooperate and work toward greater mutual understanding. ▸ **internationalist** noun

internationalize verb trans. (**internationalized, internationalizing**) to make international, esp. to bring under the control of two or more countries. ▸ **internationalization** noun

interne (ĭn′tərn,) noun same as **intern¹**.

internecine (ĭnt,ər-nĕs′ēn,, -nē′sĭn,) adj. of a war, etc. destructive and damaging to both sides. 2 involving or being a conflict or struggle within a group or organization.

internet (ĭnt′ər-nĕt,) noun a computer network that links several other networks, allowing the transfer of messages between them.

interpersonal adj. concerning the relationships between people.

interplay noun the action and influence of two or more things on each other.

Interpol (ĭnt′ər-pôl,) noun an international law-enforcement organization.

interpolate (ĭn-tər′pə-lāt,) verb trans. (**interpolated, interpolating**) 1 to add (words) to a book or manuscript, esp. so as to make the text misleading or corrupt. 2 to interrupt a conversation, etc., with (a remark or comment). ▸ **interpolation** noun

interpose (ĭnt,ər-pōz′) verb trans., intrans. (**interposed, interposing**) 1 a to put (something) between two other things. b to come between two other things. 2 to act as mediator; to intervene. ▸ **interposition** (ĭnt,ər-pə-zĭsh′ən) noun

interpret (ĭn-tər′prət) verb trans., intrans. (**interpreted, interpreting**) 1 to explain the meaning of (a foreign word, a dream, etc.). 2 a to express (something) in another language, with the same meaning. b to act as an interpreter. 3 to consider or understand (behavior, a remark, etc.). 4 to bring out one's idea of the meaning of (e.g., a piece of music) in one's performance. ▸ **interpretation** noun ▸ **interpreter** noun ▸ **interpretive** or **interpretative** adj.

interregnum noun (pl. **interregnums, interregna**) an interval or pause in a continuous sequence of events.

interrelate (ĭnt′ə-rĭ-lāt′) verb intrans., trans. (**interrelated, interrelating**) to be in or be brought into a mutually dependent relationship. ▸ **interrelationship** noun

interrogate (ĭn-tĕr′ə-gāt,) verb trans. (**interrogated, interrogating**) to question closely and thoroughly. ▸ **interrogation** noun ▸ **interrogator** noun ▸ **interrogatory** (ĭnt,ə-răg′ə-tôr,ē) adj.

interrogative (ĭnt,ə-răg′ət-ĭv) adj. 1 asking a question. 2 of an adjective or pronoun used to ask a question. —noun an interrogative word, sentence, or construction. ▸ **interrogatively** adv.

interrupt verb trans., intrans. (**interrupted, interrupting**) 1 to break into (a conversation or monologue). **2** to make a break in the continuous activity of (an event). ▸ **interruption** noun ▸ **interruptive** adj.

intersect (ĭnt,ər-sĕkt′) verb trans., intrans. (**intersected,. intersecting**) **1** to divide (lines, an area, etc.) by passing or cutting through. **2** of lines, roads, etc. to run through or cut across each other. ▸ **intersection** noun

intersperse (ĭnt,ər-spərs′) verb trans. (**interspersed, interspersing**) **1** to scatter or insert (something) here and there. **2** to diversify or change with scattered things.

interstate adj. (ĭnt,ər-stāt′) (often **Interstate**) occurring, involving, or between two or more states. —noun (ĭnt′ər-stāt,) (often **the Interstate**) a major four-lane (or more) highway crossing state boundaries.

interstellar adj. happening or existing in the space between stars.

interstice noun a very small space between two things.

intertwine verb trans., intrans. (**intertwined, intertwining**) to twist or be twisted together.

interval (ĭnt′ər-vəl) noun **1** a period of time between two events. **2** a distance between two things. **3** the difference in pitch between two musical notes.

intervene (ĭnt,ər-vēn′) verb intrans. (**intervened, intervening**) **1** (**intervene in** (**something**)) to involve oneself in (something that is happening) in order to affect the outcome. **2** to interfere in a dispute between other people in order to settle it. **3** to occur between two things in place or time. ▸ **intervention** noun

interventionism noun the belief that the government of a country should be allowed to interfere in the economic affairs of the country or in the internal affairs of other countries. ▸ **interventionist** noun, adj.

interview (ĭnt′ər-vyōō,) noun **1** a formal meeting and discussion with someone, esp. one between an employer and a prospective employee. **2** a conversation that aims at obtaining information, esp. one in which a journalist asks questions of a famous person. —verb trans. (**interviewed, interviewing**) to hold an interview with. ▸ **interviewee** (ĭnt,ər-vyōō,ē′) noun ▸ **interviewer** noun

interweave verb trans., intrans. to weave or be woven together.

intestate (ĭn-tĕs′tāt,, -tət) adj. dying without having made a valid will. —noun a person who dies without making a valid will. ▸ **intestacy** (ĭn-tĕs′tə-sē) noun

intestine (ĭn-tĕs′tən) noun the muscular, tubelike part of the alimentary canal that extends from the stomach to the anus. ▸ **intestinal** (ĭn-tĕs′tən-l) adj.

intimacy noun (pl. **intimacies**) **1** a close personal friendship. **2** an intimate or personal remark. **3** the state of being intimate.

intimate[1] (ĭnt′ə-mət) adj. **1** marked by or sharing a close and affectionate friendship. **2** very private or personal. **3** of a place small and quiet with a warm, friendly atmosphere. **4** (**intimate with** (**someone**)) sharing a sexual relationship with (another). **5** of knowledge deep and thorough. —noun a close friend. ▸ **intimately** adv.

intimate[2] (ĭnt′ə-māt,) verb trans. (**intimated, intimating**) to hint or suggest indirectly. ▸ **intimation** noun

intimidate (ĭn-tĭm′ĭ-dāt,) verb trans. (**intimidated, intimidating**) (**intimidate** (**someone**) **into** (**something**)) to coerce or frighten (another) into doing (what one wants). ▸ **intimidating** adj. ▸ **intimidation** noun

into prep. **1** to or toward the inside or middle of. **2** into contact or collision with; against. **3** so as to be: form into groups. **4** used to express division: divide 4 into 20. **5** slang interested in or enthusiastic about.

intolerable adj. too bad, difficult, etc., to be put up with. ▸ **intolerably** adv.

intolerant adj. (often **intolerant of** (**something**)) refusing or unwilling to accept (ideas, beliefs, etc., different from one's own). ▸ **intolerance** noun ▸ **intolerantly** adv.

intonation noun **1** the rise and fall of the pitch of the voice in speech. **2** the act of intoning. **3** the correct pitching of musical notes.

intone (ĭn-tōn′) verb trans., intrans. (**intoned, intoning**) **1** to recite (a prayer, etc.) in a solemn, monotonous voice or in singing tones. **2** to say (something) with a particular intonation.

in toto (ĭn-tōt′ō) totally; completely.

intoxicant noun something, esp. an alcoholic beverage, that causes intoxication.

intoxicate (ĭn-tăk′sĭ-kāt,) verb trans. (**intoxicated, intoxicating**) **1** to make drunk. **2** to excite or elate to the point at which self-control is lost. ▸ **intoxicating** adj. ▸ **intoxication** noun

intra- prefix forming words denoting within, inside, on the inside: intrauterine.

intractable adj. **1** refusing to change or compromise. **2** difficult to solve or deal with. ▸ **intractability** noun ▸ **intractably** adv.

intramural (ĭn,trə-myōōr′əl) adj. within or among the people in an institution, esp. a school or university. ▸ **intramurally** adv.

intransigent (ĭn-trăn′zə-jənt) adj. refusing to change or compromise. —noun a rigid, stubborn person. ▸ **intransigence** noun ▸ **intransigently** adv.

intransitive *adj.* (ABBREV. **intrans.**) *of a verb* not having a direct object. *See also* **transitive.** ▸ **intransitively** *adv.*

intrauterine (ĭn,trə-yōōt′ə-rən, -rīn,) *adj.* located or occurring within the womb.

intrauterine device a contraceptive device that is inserted into the womb to prevent pregnancy.

intravenous (ĭn,trə-vē′nəs) *adj.* located within or introduced into a vein. ▸ **intravenously** *adv.*

intrepid (ĭn-trĕp′ĭd) *adj.* bold and daring; brave. ▸ **intrepidity** (ĭn,trə-pĭd′ət-ē) *noun* ▸ **intrepidly** *adv.*

intricate (ĭn′trĭ-kət) *adj.* full of complicated or tangled details or parts and therefore difficult to understand or sort out. ▸ **intricacy** *noun* ▸ **intricately** *adv.*

intrigue *noun* (ĭn′trēg,, ĭn-trēg′) **1** secret plotting. **2** a secret plot or plan. **3** a secret love affair. —*verb trans., intrans.* (ĭn-trēg′) (**intrigued, intriguing**) **1** to arouse the curiosity or interest of. **2** to plot secretly. ▸ **intriguing** *adj.* ▸ **intriguingly** *adv.*

intrinsic (ĭn-trĭn′zĭk, -sĭk) *adj.* (**intrinsic to (something)**) belonging to (it) as an inherent and essential part of (its) nature. ▸ **intrinsically** *adv.*

intro *noun* (*pl.* **intros**) *colloq.* an introduction.

intro- *prefix* forming words denoting within, into, inward: *introvert.*

introduce (ĭn,trə-dōōs′, -dyōōs′) *verb trans.* (**introduced, introducing**) **1** to make (one) familiar with. ▣ ACQUAINT, PRESENT. **2** to announce or present (e.g., a television program) to an audience. **3** to bring (esp. something new) into a place, situation, etc., for the first time. **4** to bring into operation, practice, or use. **5** (**introduce (someone) to (something)**) to cause (a person) to experience (something) for the first time. **6** to start or preface. **7** (**introduce (one thing) into (another)**) to insert or put (something) into (something else).

introduction *noun* **1** the act of introducing or the process of being ·introduced. **2** a presentation· of one person to another or others. **3** a section at· the beginning of a book that explains briefly what it is about, etc. **4** a book that outlines the basic principles of a subject. **5** a short musical passage beginning a piece. **6** something that has been introduced. ▸ **introductory** *adj.*

introspection *noun* an examination of one's own thoughts, feelings, and intuition. ▸ **introspective** *adj.*

introvert (ĭn′trə-vərt,) *noun* **1** a person who is more concerned with his or her inner thoughts and feelings than with the outside world. **2** a person who is not sociable or talkative. —*verb trans.* (**introverted, intro-**verting) to turn (one's thoughts) inward to concentrate on oneself. *See also* **extrovert.**

introverted *adj.* not sociable or talkative.

intrude *verb intrans., trans.* (**intruded, intruding**) **1** to force oneself where one is unwanted and unwelcome. **2** to force (something) in, without invitation or in an inappropriate way. ▸ **intruder** *noun*

intrusion *noun* an act of intruding or process of being intruded, esp. on someone else's property. ▸ **intrusive** *adj.* ▸ **intrusively** *adv.* ▸ **intrusiveness** *noun*

intuit (ĭn-tōō′ət, -tyōō′ət) *verb trans.* (**intuited, intuiting**) *colloq.* to know (something) by intuition.

> *Usage* Though often used, the verb *intuit* still has not gained widespread acceptance.

intuition (ĭn,tə-wĭsh′ən, -tyə-) *noun* **1** the power of understanding ·or realizing something without conscious rational thought. **2** immediate, instinctive understanding or belief. ▸ **intuitive** *adj.* ▸ **intuitively** *adv.* ▸ **intuitiveness** *noun*

Inuit (ĭn′yə-wĭt, ĭn′ə-) *or* **Innuit** *noun* (*pl.* **Inuits, Inuit**) **1** a native people of the Arctic and sub-Arctic regions of Canada, Greenland, Alaska, and Siberia (also known as Eskimos). **2** any of the languages of this people.

inundate (ĭn′ən-dāt,) *verb trans.* (**inundated, inundating**) to overwhelm with or as if with water. ▸ **inundation** *noun*

inure (ĭn-yōōr′, -ōōr′) *verb trans.* (**inured, inuring**) (**inure (someone) to (something)**) to accustom (someone or oneself) to (something unpleasant). ▸ **inurement** *noun*

invade *verb trans., intrans.* (**invaded, invading**) **1** to enter (a country) by force with an army. **2** to overrun. **3** to interfere with (a person's privacy, etc.). ▸ **invader** *noun*

invalid[1] (ĭn′və-lĭd) *noun* a person who is ill or disabled. —*adj.* suitable for or being an invalid. ▸ **invalidity** *noun*

invalid[2] (ĭn-văl′ĭd) *adj.* **1** having no legal force. **2** based on a mistake and therefore not valid or reliable. ▸ **invalidity** *noun* ▸ **invalidly** *adv.*

invalidate (ĭn-văl′ĭ-dāt,) *verb trans.* (**invalidated, invalidating**) to make (something, e.g., an argument) invalid. ▸ **invalidation** *noun*

invaluable *adj.* having a value too great to be measured. ▸ **invaluably** *adv.*

invariable *adj.* not changing; always the same. ▸ **invariably** *adv.*

invasion *noun* the act of invading or the process of being invaded.

invasive (ĭn-vā′sĭv, -zĭv) *adj.* **1** invading; aggressive. **2** entering; penetrating, e.g., during a medical procedure.

invective *noun* angry attacking words, often including abuse and swearing.

inveigh (ĭn-vā′) *verb intrans.* (**inveighed, inveighing**) to speak passionately against someone or something.

inveigle (ĭn-vā′gəl) *verb trans.* (**inveigled, inveigling**) (**inveigle** (**someone**) **into** (**something**)) to cajole (someone) into doing (something). ▸ **inveiglement** *noun*

invent *verb trans.* (**invented, inventing**) 1 to be the first person to make or use (a machine, method, etc.). 2 to think or make up (an excuse, etc.). ▸ **inventor** *noun*

invention *noun* 1 something invented, esp. a device, machine, etc. 2 the act of inventing. 3 inventiveness. 4 *colloq.* a lie.

inventive *adj.* skilled at inventing; creative. ▸ **inventiveness** *noun*

inventory (ĭn′vən-tôr,ē) *noun* (*pl.* **inventories**) a formal and complete list of the articles, goods, etc., found in a particular place. —*verb trans.* (**inventoried, inventorying, inventories**) to make an inventory of; to list in an inventory.

inverse *adj.* (ĭn-vərs′, ĭn′vərs,) opposite or reverse in order, direction, etc. —*noun* (ĭn′vərs,, ĭn-vərs′) a direct opposite. ▸ **inversely** *adv.*

inversion *noun* 1 the act of turning upside down or inside out. 2 the state of being turned upside down or inside out. 3 a reversal of order, direction, etc.

invert (ĭn-vərt′) *verb trans.* (**inverted, inverting**) 1 to turn upside down or inside out. 2 to reverse in order, direction, etc.

invertebrate (ĭn-vərt′ə-brət, -brāt,) *noun* an animal that does not possess a backbone. —*adj.* relating to an animal that does not possess a backbone.

invest *verb trans., intrans.* (**invested, investing**) 1 to put (money) into a company or business in order to make a profit. 2 (**invest in** (**something**)) to buy (it). 3 to devote (time, effort, etc.) to something. 4 (**invest** (**someone**) **with** (**something**)) to give someone the symbols of power, rank, etc., officially. 5 (**invest** (**something**) **in** (**someone**)) to place (power, rank, etc.) in (someone). 6 to besiege (a stronghold). ▸ **investor** *noun*

investigate (ĭn-vĕs′tĭ-gāt,) *verb trans., intrans.* (**investigated, investigating**) to carry out a thorough, detailed, and often official inquiry into (something or someone). ▸ **investigation** *noun* ▸ **investigative** *adj.* ▸ **investigator** *noun* ▸ **investigatory** *adj.*

investiture *noun* a formal ceremony conferring a rank or office on someone.

investment *noun* 1 a sum of money invested. 2 something in which one invests money, time, effort, etc. 3 the act of investing.

inveterate (ĭn-vĕt′ə-rət) *adj.* firmly fixed in a habit by long practice. ▸ **inveterately** *adv.*

invidious (ĭn-vĭd′ē-əs) *adj.* 1 likely to cause envy, resentment, or indignation. 2 unfair; discriminatory. ▸ **invidiousness** *noun*

invigorate (ĭn-vĭg′ə-rāt,) *verb trans.* (**invigorated, invigorating**) to give fresh life, energy, and health to; to strengthen. ▸ **invigoration** *noun*

invincible *adj.* that cannot be defeated. ▸ **invincibility** *noun* ▸ **invincibleness** *noun* ▸ **invincibly** *adv.*

inviolable (ĭn-vī′ə-lə-bəl) *adj.* that must not or cannot be broken or violated; sacred. ▸ **inviolability** *noun* ▸ **inviolably** *adv.*

inviolate (ĭn-vī′ə-lət) *adj.* not broken, violated, or injured.

invisible *adj.* 1 that cannot be seen. 2 inconspicuous. 3 not shown in regular financial statements. ▸ **invisibility** *noun* ▸ **invisibly** *adv.*

invitation *noun* 1 the act of inviting. 2 a request to a person to go somewhere, e.g., to a party. 3 encouragement; enticement

invite *verb trans.* (ĭn-vīt′) (**invited, inviting**) 1 to request the presence of (someone) at a party, etc. 2 to ask formally for (e.g., comments, etc.). 3 to bring on or encourage (something unwanted or undesirable). —*noun* (ĭn′vīt,) *colloq.* an invitation.

inviting *adj.* attractive or tempting. ▸ **invitingly** *adv.*

in vitro (ĭn-vē′trō) performed outside a living organism by means of scientific equipment, e.g., in a test tube: *in vitro fertilization.*

invocation (ĭn,və-kā′shən) *noun* 1 the act of invoking. 2 a prayer calling on God, a saint, etc., for blessing or help. ▸ **invocatory** (ĭn-văk′ə-tôr,ē) *adj.*

invoice (ĭn′vois,) *noun* a list of goods supplied, giving details of price and quantity. —*verb trans.* (**invoiced, invoicing**) to send an invoice to (a customer).

invoke *verb trans.* (**invoked, invoking**) 1 to make an appeal to (God, etc.) for help or support. 2 to appeal to (a law, etc.) as an authority or reason for, e.g., one's behavior. 3 to make an earnest appeal for (help, support, inspiration, etc.). 4 to put (a law, etc.) into effect.

involuntary *adj.* 1 done or acting by compulsion, not by free will. 2 *of a movement* not produced or controlled by the will. ▸ **involuntarily** *adv.*

involve (ĭn-vălv′, -vôlv′) *verb trans.* (**involved, involving**) 1 a to require as a necessary part. b to have or incorporate as part of a larger whole. 2 (**involve** (**someone**) **in** (**something**)) to cause (someone) to take part or be implicated in (it). **3** to have an effect on. **4** to complicate. ▸ **involvement** noun

invulnerable adj. that cannot be hurt, damaged, or attacked. ▸ **invulnerability** noun ▸ **invulnerably** adv.

inward adj. **1** placed or being within. **2** moving toward the inside. **3** of or relating to the mind or soul. —adv. **1** toward the inside or the center. **2** into the mind, thoughts, or soul.

inwardly adv. **1** on the inside; internally. **2** in one's thoughts; secretly.

in-your-face adj. slang aggressively, often insolently, assertive.

I/O abbrev. input/output.

iodine (ī′ə-dīn, -dēn) noun **1** (SYMBOL I) a nonmetallic element, used in photography and medicine. **2** a solution of iodine in ethanol, used as an antiseptic.

iodize verb trans. (**iodized, iodizing**) to treat (a substance) with iodine.

ion (ī′ən, ī′ăn) noun an atom or group of atoms that has acquired a positive electrical charge by losing one or more electrons, or a negative charge by gaining one or more electrons.

-ion suffix forming nouns denoting a process, state, result, etc.: completion / contrition / pollution. See also **-ation**.

ionize verb trans. (**ionized, ionizing**) to cause to produce ions. ▸ **ionization** noun

ionizer noun a device that produces negatively charged ions.

ionosphere (ī-ăn′ə-sfīr) noun the layer of Earth's atmosphere that extends from about 30 mi. (50 km) to about 300 mi. (500 km) above Earth's surface. ▸ **ionospheric** adj.

iota (ī-ōt′ə) noun **1** the ninth letter of the Greek alphabet (Ι ι). **2** a very small amount.

IOU noun (pl. **IOUs, IOU's**) colloq. a written and signed note of a debt.

ipecac (ĭp′ə-kăk) noun a medicinal preparation used to induce vomiting.

ipso facto (Latin) because of that very fact.

IQ abbrev. intelligence quotient.

Ir symbol Chem. iridium.

ir- prefix a form of in-.

IRA abbrev. **1** Individual Retirement Account. **2** Irish Republican Army.

Iranian (ī-rän′ē-ən, -rän′-, -răn′-) noun **1** a native or citizen of Iran. **2** a branch of the Indo-European family of languages. —adj. of Iran, its people, or their languages.

irascible adj. easily made angry; irritable. ▸ **irascibility** noun ▸ **irascibly** adv.

irate (ī-rāt′, ī′rāt,) adj. very angry; enraged. ▸ **irately** adv. ▸ **irateness** noun

ire noun anger.

iridescent adj. having many bright, rainbowlike colors that seem to shimmer and change constantly. ▸ **iridescence** noun ▸ **iridescently** adv.

iridium (ī-rĭd′ē-əm) noun (SYMBOL Ir) a silvery metal that is resistant to corrosion.

iris noun **1** (pl. **irises**) a plant with large brilliantly colored flowers. **2** the colored, central membrane in the eye which controls the size of the pupil.

Irish (ī′rĭsh) noun **1** a native or citizen of Ireland. **2** (in full **Irish Gaelic**) the Celtic language of Ireland. —adj. of Ireland, its people, their Celtic language, or their dialect of English.

Irishman noun a man who is Irish by birth or descent.

Irish setter a setter with a silky, reddish-brown coat.

Irish stew a stew made from mutton, potatoes, and onions.

Irish wolfhound the tallest domestic breed of dog, having a long, usu. gray coat.

Irishwoman noun a woman who is Irish by birth or descent.

irk (ərk′) verb trans. (**irked, irking**) to annoy.

irksome adj. annoying, irritating, or boring. ▸ **irksomely** adv.

iron (ī′ərn) noun **1** (SYMBOL Fe) a strong hard silvery-white metallic element that is naturally magnetic. **2** a tool, weapon, or other implement made of this material. **3** a triangular, flat-bottomed, now usu. electrical, household tool used for pressing clothes. **4** a golf club with an angled iron head. **5** (**irons**) chains; fetters. —adj. **1** made of iron. **2** resembling iron, esp. in being inflexible or unyielding. —verb trans., intrans. (**ironed, ironing**) to press (e.g., clothes) with an iron. —**iron out** to remove or put right (difficulties, problems, etc.). **iron(s) in the fire** a commitment or commitments.

Iron Age the period in history following the Bronze Age, when weapons and tools were made of iron, from about 1,000 B.C.

Iron Curtain from 1945 to 1989, a political, ideological, and military barrier between countries in W Europe and the communist countries of E Europe.

ironic (ī-răn′ĭk) or **ironical** adj. **1** containing or expressing irony. **2** given to frequent use of irony. ▸ **ironically** adv.

ironing (ī′ər-nĭng) noun clothes and household linen, etc., that need to be or have just been ironed.

iron lung a respirator, used to provide artificial respiration in paralyzed patients, consisting of an airtight metal chamber that encloses the body from the neck down.

ironstone noun hard, white earthenware that is ovenproof.

ironwork noun things made of iron, such as gates and railings.

irony (ī′rə-nē, ī′ər-nē) noun (pl. **ironies**) **1** a linguistic device or form of humor that takes its effect from stating or implying the opposite of what is intended. **2** awkward or perverse circumstances applying to a situation that is in itself satisfactory or desirable.

irradiate *verb trans.* (**irradiated, irradiating**) **1** to expose (a part of the body) to radiation for diagnostic or therapeutic purposes. **2** to preserve (food) by exposing it to radiation in order to destroy bacteria and other microorganisms. ▶ **irradiation** *noun*

irrational *adj.* **1** unable to think logically and clearly. **2** not the result of clear, logical thought. ▶ **irrationality** *noun* ▶ **irrationally** *adv.*

irreconcilable *adj.* **1** not agreeing or able to be brought into agreement; incompatible. **2** hostile and opposed. ▶ **irreconcilably** *adv.*

irredeemable *adj.* incapable of being recovered, repaired, or cured. ▶ **irredeemably** *adv.*

irreducible *adj.* that cannot be reduced or made simpler. ▶ **irreducibly** *adv.*

irrefutable (ĭr͵ĭ-fyŏŏt′ə-bəl, ĭr-ĕf′yət-) *adj.* not able to be denied or proved false. ▶ **irrefutably** *adv.*

irregardless *adv. nonstand., considered an illiteracy* regardless.

> *Usage* This word is so heavily stigmatized that it is best avoided.

irregular *adj.* **1** not happening or occurring at regular intervals. **2** not smooth or balanced. **3** not conforming to rules, accepted behavior, or routine. **4** *of a word* departing from the usual patterns of inflection. **5** not belonging to a regular army. ▶ **irregularity** *noun* ▶ **irregularly** *adv.*

irrelevant *adj.* not connected with or applying to the subject in hand. ▶ **irrelevance** or **irrelevancy** *noun* ▶ **irrelevantly** *adv.*

irreligious *adj.* **1** having no religion. **2** lacking respect for religion.

irremediable (ĭr͵ĭ-mēd′ē-ə-bəl) *adj.* that cannot be made better or corrected. ▶ **irremediably** *adv.*

irreparable (ĭr-ĕp′ə-rə-bəl) *adj.* that cannot be restored or put right. ▶ **irreparability** *noun* ▶ **irreparably** *adv.*

irreplaceable *adj.* not able to be replaced, esp. because of being too valuable. ▶ **irreplaceably** *adv.*

irrepressible *adj.* not able to be restrained or repressed, esp. because of being too lively. ▶ **irrepressibly** *adv.*

irreproachable *adj.* free from faults; blameless. ▶ **irreproachably** *adv.*

irresistible *adj.* too strong, tempting, or attractive to be resisted. ▶ **irresistibleness** *noun* ▶ **irresistibly** *adv.*

irresolute *adj.* hesitating or doubtful; not able

to make firm decisions. ▶ **irresolutely** *adv.*

irrespective *adj.* (**irrespective of (something)**) without considering or taking (it) into account.

irresponsible *adj.* **1** done without or showing no concern for the consequences; reckless. **2** not able to bear responsibility; not trustworthy. ▶ **irresponsibility** *noun* ▶ **irresponsibly** *adv.*

irretrievable *adj.* not able to be recovered or put right. ▶ **irretrievably** *adv.*

irreverent *adj.* lacking respect or reverence. ▶ **irreverence** *noun* ▶ **irreverently** *adv.*

irreversible *adj.* that cannot be changed back to a former state. ▶ **irreversibly** *adv.*

irrevocable (ĭr-ĕv′ə-kə-bəl, ĭr͵ĭ-vō′kə-) *adj.* that cannot be changed or undone. ▶ **irrevocably** *adv.*

irrigate (ĭr′ĭ-gāt͵) *verb trans.* (**irrigated, irrigating**) **1** to provide (land) with a supply of water. **2** to wash out (a wound, the colon, etc.), with a continuous flow of water or antiseptic solution. ▶ **irrigation** *noun*

irritable (ĭr′ĭt-ə-bəl) *adj.* easily annoyed. ▶ **irritability** *noun* ▶ **irritableness** *noun* ▶ **irritably** *adv.*

irritable bowel syndrome a condition in which the mucous membrane lining the colon becomes inflamed, causing abdominal pain, with constipation or diarrhea.

irritant *noun* **1** an agent that produces an esp. inflammatory response in a susceptible body tissue. **2** something that causes irritation. —*adj.* causing irritation.

irritate (ĭr′ĭ-tāt͵) *verb trans.* (**irritated, irritating**) **1** to make annoyed. **2** to make (part of the body) sore and swollen or itchy. ▶ **irritating** *adj.* ▶ **irritatingly** *adv.* ▶ **irritation** *noun*

irrupt (ĭr-əpt′) *verb intrans.* (**irrupted, irrupting**) to burst into or enter a place suddenly with speed and violence. ▶ **irruption** *noun* ▶ **irruptive** *adj.*

IRS *abbrev.* Internal Revenue Service.

is *see* **be.**

-isation *suffix same as* **-ization.**

-ise *suffix same as* **-ize.**

> *Usage* In British English verbs such as *categorize* and their derived forms such as *categorization* are typically spelled *-ise, -isation*; i.e., *categorise, categorisation.*

-ish *suffix* forming adjectives denoting: **1** having a trace of; fairly: *reddish / autumnish.* **2** having the qualities of; like: *childish.* **3** having as a nationality: *Swedish.* **4** approximately; about: *fiftyish.*

isinglass (ī′zən-glăs͵, -zĭng-) *noun* **1** gelatin made from the dried air bladders of certain fish. **2** thin transparent sheets of mica used in furnace and stove doors.

Islam (ĭs-läm', ĭs'läm, ĭz'läm,) *noun* **1** the religion that originated in Arabia during the 7th c A.D. through the Prophet Muhammad. **2** the nations and peoples who practice Islam. ▸ **Islamic** *adj.*

island (ī'lənd) *noun* **1** an area of land entirely surrounded by water. **2** something like an island, esp. in its isolation. ▸ **islander** *noun*

isle (īl) *noun* an island.

islet (ī'lət) *noun* a small island.

ism (ĭz'əm) *noun colloq.* a distinctive and formal set of ideas, principles, or beliefs.

-ism *suffix* forming nouns denoting: **1** a formal set of beliefs, ideas, principles, etc.: *feminism.* **2** a quality or state: *heroism.* **3** an activity or practice: *criticism.* **4** discrimination or prejudice on the grounds of: *ageism.* **5** an illness caused by, causing resemblance to, or named after (something or someone stated): *alcoholism / dwarfism.* **6** a characteristic of (a specified language or type of language): *regionalism.*

isn't *contr.* is not.

ISO *abbrev.* International Standards Organization.

iso- *combining form* forming words denoting same, equal: *isobar.*

isobar (ī'sə-bär,) *noun* a line drawn on a weather chart connecting points that have the same atmospheric pressure at a given time.

isolate (ī'sə-lāt,) *verb trans.* (**isolated, isolating**) **1** to separate from others; to cause to be alone. **2** to place in quarantine. **3** to separate, esp. to allow closer examination: *isolate a problem.* **4** to separate so as to obtain in a pure form. ▸ **isolation** *noun*

isolationism *noun* the policy of not joining with other countries in international political and economic affairs. ▸ **isolationist** *noun, adj.*

isomer (ī'sə-mər) *noun* one of two or more chemical compounds that have the same chemical formula but different structures. ▸ **isomeric** (ī,sə-mĕr'ĭk) *adj.*

isometric (ī,sə-mĕ'trĭk) *adj.* **1** having equal size or measurements. **2** of or relating to muscular contraction that generates tension but does not produce shortening of the muscle fibers. **3** denoting a system of exercises involving pushing one or more limbs against a stationary object.

isometrics *noun* (*sing., pl.*) a system of physical exercises in which the muscles are pushed either together or against an immovable object.

isosceles (ī-säs'ə-lēz,) *adj., of a triangle* having two sides of equal length.

isotherm *noun* a line on a weather map connecting places where the temperature is the same at a particular time or where the average is the same for a particular period.

isotope (ī'sə-tōp,) *noun* one of two or more atoms of the same chemical element that contain the same number of protons but different numbers of neutrons in their nuclei.

Israeli (ĭz-rā'lē, ĭz,rə-ā'lē) *noun* a native or citizen of the modern state of Israel. —*adj.* of the modern state of Israel or its people.

Israelite (ĭz'rē-ə-līt, ĭz'rə-līt,) *noun Hist.* a native or citizen of the ancient kingdom of Israel (922 B.C.–721 B.C.). —*adj.* of the ancient kingdom of Israel or its people.

issue (ĭsh'ōō) *noun* **1 a** the publishing, distributing, or circulating of materials, e.g., magazines and stamps. **b** the materials so published, distributed, or circulated. **c** one copy of a periodical. **2** a subject for discussion. **3** a result or consequence. **4** *formal* children; offspring. —*verb trans., intrans.* (**issued, issuing**) **1 a** to publish, distribute, or circulate. **b** to distribute or otherwise make available, esp. officially. **2** (*often* **issue forth** *or* **out**) to flow or come out, esp. in large quantities. **3 issue from** (**someone** *or* **something**)) to be produced or caused by (the one specified). **4** (**issue** (**someone**) **with** (**something**)) to present (the one specified) with (something required). —**at issue 1** in dispute or disagreement. **2** under discussion. **make an issue of** (**something**) to make (it) the explicit subject of an argument or disagreement. **take issue with** (**someone**) to disagree with (that person).

-ist *suffix* forming words denoting: **1** a believer in a formal system of ideas, principles, or beliefs: *feminist.* **2** a person who carries out an activity or practices an art: *novelist.*

isthmus (ĭs'məs) *noun* (*pl.* **isthmuses, isthmi**) a narrow strip of land joining two larger areas of land.

IT *abbrev.* information technology.

it *pron.* **1** the thing, animal, infant, or group already mentioned. **2** the person in question: *Who is it?* **3** used as the subject with impersonal verbs and when describing the weather, etc. **4** used as the grammatical subject of a sentence when the real subject comes later: *It's not a very good idea running away.* **5** used to refer to a general situation: *How's it going?* **6** exactly what is needed, suitable, or available. —*noun* **1** one person in a children's game who has to oppose all the others, e.g., by trying to catch them. **2** *old colloq. use* sex appeal. **3** *colloq.* sexual intercourse.

Italian (ĭ-tăl'yən) *noun* **1** a native or citizen of Italy. **2** the language of Italy and parts of Switzerland. —*adj.* of Italy, its people, or their language.

italic *adj.* **1** of or in a typeface with characters that slope to the right. **2** (**Italic**) of ancient

Italy. —noun (*usu.* **italics**) a typeface with characters that slope to the right.
italicize verb trans. (**italicized, italicizing**) to print or write in italics. ▸ **italicization** noun
itch noun **1** an unpleasant irritation on the surface of the skin that makes one want to scratch. **2** a skin disease or condition which causes a constant unpleasant irritation, esp. scabies. **3** *colloq.* a strong desire. —verb intrans., trans. (**itched, itching**) **1** to have an itch and want to scratch. **2** to cause (someone) to feel an itch. **3** *colloq.* to feel a strong desire: *I'm just itching to take a cruise.*
itchy adj. (**itchier, itchiest**) affected with or causing an itch. —**itchy feet** *colloq.* restlessness, or a strong desire to travel. ▸ **itchiness** noun
it'd contr. **1** it had. **2** it would.
-ite suffix forming nouns denoting: **1** a place, origin, or national group: *Israelite.* **2** a follower of or believer in: *Mennonite.* **3** a fossil: *ammonite.* **4** a mineral: *graphite.* **5** a salt of a certain formula: *nitrite.* See also **-ate** (sense 3), **-ide.** **6** an explosive: *dynamite.*
item noun **1** a separate item, object, or unit, esp. one on a list. **2** a separate piece of information or news.
itemize verb trans. (**itemized, itemizing**) to list (things) separately, e.g., on a bill. ▸ **itemization** noun
iterate (ĭt'ə-rāt,) verb trans. (**iterated, iterating**) to say again. ▸ **iteration** noun ▸ **iterative** adj.
itinerant (ī-tĭn'ə-rənt) adj. traveling from place to place. —noun an itinerant person.
itinerary noun (pl. **itineraries**) a plan of one's route for a journey.
it'll contr. **1** it will. **2** it shall.
its adj. belonging to it. —pron. the one or ones belonging to it.

Usage Note that there is no apostrophe; *it's* means it is or it has.

it's contr. **1** it is. **2** it has.

Usage See note at *its.*

itself pron. **1** the reflexive form of *it.* **2** used for emphasis: *The committee itself made the decision to move forward.* **3** (*also* **by itself**) without help; alone.
itsy-bitsy or **itty-bitty** adj. colloq. very small.
-ity suffix forming words denoting a state or quality, or an instance of it: *irregularity.*
IUD noun (pl. **IUDs, IUD's**) an intrauterine device.
I've contr. I have.
-ive suffix forming words denoting a quality, action, etc., or a person associated with it: *creative / detective.*
IVF abbrev. in vitro fertilization.
ivory (ī'və-rē, ī'vrē) noun **1 a** a hard white material that forms the tusks of the elephant, walrus, etc., formerly used to make ornaments and piano keys. **b** the creamy-white color of ivory. **2** (**ivories**) *slang* the keys on a piano. —adj. of or resembling the material forming the tusks of certain animals, esp. in color.
ivory tower a place where one can be secluded from the unpleasant realities of life.
ivy noun (pl. **ivies**) **1** a woody climbing or trailing plant with glossy, dark green leaves. **2** any of several other climbing plants, e.g., poison ivy.
-ization or **-isation** suffix forming nouns of action corresponding to verbs in *-ize* or *-ise.*
-ize or **-ise** suffix forming verbs denoting: **1** to make or become: *equalize.* **2** to treat or react to (in a stated way): *criticize.* **3** to engage in (a stated activity): *theorize.*

Usage See note at *-ise.*

Jj

J¹ or **j** noun (pl. **Js, J's, j's**) the tenth letter of the English alphabet.
J² abbrev. joule.
jab verb trans., intrans. (**jabbed, jabbing**) to poke or prod. —noun **1** a poke or prod. **2** colloq. an injection or inoculation. **3** a sharp, cutting remark.
jabber verb intrans., trans. (**jabbered, jabbering**) to talk rapidly and indistinctly. —noun rapid indistinct speech.

jabot (zhă-bō') noun a lace ruffle for a shirt front.
jacaranda (jăk,ə-răn'də) noun a tropical American tree with pale purple flowers.
jack noun **1** a device for lifting heavy objects, e.g., motor vehicles, off the ground. **2** *Cards* the face card of least value, bearing a picture of a page. *Also called* **knave.** **3** *Bowling* a pin used in some games. **4** a small national flag flown at the bow of a ship. **5** one

of the playing pieces used in the game of jacks. **6** *Electr.* a socket taking a plug at one end and configured so that it can attach to electric circuitry at the other end. **7** the male of certain animals, e.g., the donkey. —*verb trans., intrans.* (**jacked, jacking**) (*often* **jack (something) up**) to raise (it) with or as if with a jack. —**every man jack** *colloq.* everybody.

jackal *noun* a doglike animal that mainly feeds on the remains of creatures killed by other animals.

jackass *noun* **1** a male ass or donkey. **2** *colloq.* a foolish person.

jackboot *noun* a leather knee-high military boot.

jackdaw *noun* a bird of the crow family known for stealing bright objects.

jacket *noun* **1** a short coat, esp. a long-sleeved, hip-length one. **2** something worn over the top half of the body, e.g., a life jacket. **3 a** a loose cover on a book. **b** a cardboard cover for a phonograph record. **c** the cardboard or plastic container for a floppy disk.

jackhammer *noun* a hand-held drill for breaking up concrete or paving material.

jack-in-the-box *noun* (*pl.* **jack-in-the-boxes, jacks-in-the-box**) a box containing a doll attached to a spring, that leaps out when the lid is opened, used as a child's toy.

jackknife *noun* **1** a large pocket knife with a folding blade. **2** a dive in which the body is bent double and then straightened before entering the water. —*verb intrans., trans.* (**jackknifed, jackknifing, jackknifes**) *of a trailer truck* to go out of control in such a way that the trailer swings around against the cab; to cause (a trailer truck) to go out of control in this manner.

jack-of-all-trades *noun* (*pl.* **jacks-of-all-trades**) a person who does a variety of jobs.

jack-o'-lantern *noun* a pumpkin, hollowed out, with eyes, a nose, and a mouth cut into its side, used as a Halloween decoration.

jackpot *noun* the maximum win to be made in a lottery, card game, etc. —**hit the jackpot** *colloq.* to have a remarkable financial win or stroke of luck.

jackrabbit *noun* a long-eared hare with a brown coat, long hind legs, and large ears with black tips.

jacks *noun* (*sing., pl.*) a game in which playing pieces (orig. small bones or pebbles) are tossed and caught on the back of the hand.

Jacobean (jǎk,ɔ-bē'ɔn) *adj.* relating or belonging to the reign of James I of England (VI of Scotland) (1603–25).

Jacuzzi (jɔ-kōō'zē) *noun* used for a large bath equipped with underwater jets that massage and invigorate the body.

jade¹ *noun* **1** a very hard, usu. green

semiprecious stone. **2** the intense green color of jade. —*adj.* of the intense green color of jade.

jade² *noun old use* **1** a disreputable or ill-natured woman. **2** a worn-out old horse.

jaded *adj.* dull and bored; fatigued.

jag¹ *noun* a sharp projection. —*verb trans.* (**jagged, jagging**) to prick, sting, or pierce.

jag² *noun slang* a bout of indulgence: *a shopping jag.*

jagged *adj.* having a rough or sharp uneven edge. ▸ **jaggedly** *adv.* ▸ **jaggedness** *noun*

jaguar *noun* a large spotted S American animal of the cat family.

jail *noun* a secure place of confinement for prisoners in custody. —*verb trans.* (**jailed, jailing**) to imprison.

jailbird *noun slang* a person in prison, esp. habitually so.

jailbreak *noun* an escape from jail.

jailer *or* **jailor** *noun* a person in charge of prisoners in a jail.

jalapeño (hǎl,ɔ-pān'yō, hāl,-) *noun* (*pl.* **jalapeños**) an esp. hot type of capsicum pepper, used in Mexican cooking.

jalopy (jɔ-lǎp'ē) *noun* (*pl.* **jalopies**) *colloq.* an old worn-out car.

jam¹ *noun* a thick sticky food made from fruit boiled with sugar, used as a spread on bread, etc.

jam² *verb trans., intrans.* (**jammed, jamming**) **1** to stick or wedge so as to be immovable. **2** *of machinery, etc.* to stick or cause (it) to stick and stop working. **3** to act upon by steady thrusting force. **4** (*also* **jam (something) up**) to fill (e.g., a street) so full that movement comes to a stop. **5** to cause interference to (a radio signal, etc.), esp. deliberately. **6** *colloq.* to play in a jam session.

jamb *noun* the vertical post at the side of a door, window, or fireplace.

jamboree *noun* **1** *colloq.* a large, lively gathering. **2** a large rally of Boy or Girl Scouts.

jam-packed *adj. colloq.* packed tight.

jam session *slang* a session of live, esp. improvised, jazz or other popular music.

jangle *verb trans., intrans.* (**jangled, jangling**) **1** to make or cause to make a discordant ringing noise. **2** to upset or irritate. ▸ **jangly** *adj.*

janitor *noun* **1** a caretaker, e.g., of a building. **2** a doorman, e.g., of an apartment building.

January (jǎn'ū-wěr,ē) *noun* (ABBREV. **Jan., Jan**) the first month of the year.

japan *noun* a hard glossy black lacquer, orig. from Japan, used to coat wood and metal. —*verb trans.* (**japanned, japanning**) to lacquer with japan.

Japanese (jǎp,ɔ-nēz', -nēs') *noun* **1** (*pl.* **Japanese**) a native or citizen of Japan. **2** the language of Japan. —*adj.* relating or belonging to Japan, or its people or language.

jape *noun* a trick, prank, or joke.

jar¹ *noun* a wide-mouthed cylindrical container, usu. of glass; the contents of it.

jar² *verb intrans., trans.* (**jarred, jarring**) **1** to have a harsh effect; to grate. **2** to jolt or vibrate. **3** to make or cause to make a harsh sound. **4** (**jar with (something)**) to clash or conflict with (it). —*noun* a jarring sensation, shock, or jolt. ‣ **jarring** *adj.* ‣ **jarringly** *adv.*

jardinière (järd͵n-ĭr′, zhärd͵n-yĕr′) *noun* an ornamental pot or stand for flowers.

jargon *noun* **1** the specialized vocabulary of a particular trade, profession, group, or activity. **2** confusing or meaningless talk.

jasmine (jăz′mĭn) *noun* a shrub or climbing plant with fragrant white or yellow flowers.

jasper *noun* a usu. red semiprecious gemstone.

jaundice *noun* a condition in which there is an excess of bile in the blood, the pigment of which causes the skin and the whites of the eyes to become yellow.

jaundiced *adj.* **1** affected by jaundice. **2** *of a person or attitude* bitter or resentful; cynical.

jaunt *noun* a short journey for pleasure. —*verb intrans.* (**jaunted, jaunting**) to go for a jaunt.

jaunty *adj.* (**jauntier, jauntiest**) **1** breezy and exuberant. **2** smart; stylish. ‣ **jauntily** *adv.* ‣ **jauntiness** *noun*

javelin (jăv′ə-lĭn) *noun* **1** a light spear for throwing as a weapon in sports. **2** the throwing of the javelin as an athletic event.

jaw *noun* **1** either of the two hinged parts of the skull in which the teeth are set. **2** the lower part of the face around the mouth and chin. **3** (**jaws**) the mouth, esp. of an animal. **4** (**jaws**) a threshold, esp. of something fearful: *the jaws of death.* **5** (**jaws**) *of a machine or tool* a pair of opposing parts used, e.g., for gripping or crushing. **6** *slang* a long conversation; a talking-to; talk; chatter. —*verb intrans.* (**jawed, jawing**) *slang* to chatter, gossip, or talk.

jawbone *noun* the bone that forms the lower jaw. —*verb trans., intrans.* (**jawboned, jawboning**) to attempt to persuade (another) by constant conversation and urging.

jawbreaker *noun* **1** a piece of hard candy. **2** *slang* a word hard to pronounce.

jay *noun* a bird of the crow family with a loud, harsh call, brightly-colored plumage, and usu. a crested head.

jaywalk *verb intrans.* (**jaywalked, jaywalking**) to cross streets carelessly, without regard to oncoming traffic or pedestrian crossings. ‣ **jaywalker** *noun*

jazz *noun* **1** popular music of African-American origin, with strong, catchy rhythms, performed with much improvisation. **2** *colloq.* talk; nonsense; business, stuff, etc. —*verb* (*usu.* **jazz (something) up**) *slang* **1** to enliven or brighten (it). **2** to give (it) a jazzy rhythm. —**and all that jazz** *colloq.* and all that sort of thing: *philosophy and all that jazz.*

jazzy *adj.* (**jazzier, jazziest**) **1** in the style of or like jazz. **2** *slang* showy; flashy; stylish. ‣ **jazzily** *adv.*

JCS *or* **J.C.S.** *abbrev.* Joint Chiefs of Staff.

JD *abbrev.* **1** (*juris doctor*) (Latin), doctor of law. **2** Justice Department. **3** juvenile delinquent.

jealous (jĕl′əs) *adj.* (*often* **jealous of (someone** *or* **something)**) **1** envious of (someone else, his or her possessions, success, talents, etc.). **2** suspicious and resentful of (possible rivals); possessive. **3** anxiously protective of (something one has). **4** caused by jealousy: *a jealous fury.* ‣ **jealously** *adv.* ‣ **jealousy** *noun*

jeans *pl. noun* casual denim pants, esp. blue.

jeep *noun* a light military vehicle with four-wheel drive, capable of traveling over rough terrain.

jeer *verb trans., intrans.* (**jeered, jeering**) **1** to mock or deride (a speaker, performer, etc.). **2** (**jeer at**) to laugh unkindly: *They jeered at his accent.* —*noun* a taunt, insult, or hoot of derision.

jeez *interj. slang* used to express annoyance or surprise.

jehad *noun* same as **jihad**.

jejune (jǐ-jōōn′) *adj.* **1** dull, banal, unoriginal, and empty of imagination. **2** childish; naive.

> From a Latin word meaning 'hungry' or 'fasting'

jell *verb intrans.* (**jelled, jelling**) **1** to become firm; to set. **2** to take definite shape.

jellied *adj.* set in jelly: *jellied eels.*

jelly *noun* (*pl.* **jellies**) **1** a clear jam made by boiling and straining fruit. **2** meat stock or other medium set with gelatin. **3** a jellylike substance.

jellybean *noun* a small, chewy, colored, oval piece of candy.

jellyfish *noun* (*pl.* **jellyfish, jellyfishes**) **1** a free-swimming sea creature, usu. with an umbrella-shaped translucent body and trailing tentacles containing stinging cells. **2** *slang* a weakling; a spineless person.

jellyroll *noun* a thin sponge cake topped with jelly and then rolled up.

jenny *noun* (*pl.* **jennies**) **1** the female of certain animals or birds, esp. the donkey, owl, or wren. **2** a spinning jenny.

jeopardize *verb trans.* (**jeopardized, jeopardizing**) to put at risk.

jeopardy (jĕp'ərd-ē) *noun* a situation or state in which one is exposed to possible harm, injury, or loss.

> Originally a gambling term, based on French *jeu parti*, meaning 'even chance'

jerboa (jər-bō'ə) *noun* a small, ratlike animal of N Africa and Asia, with long hind legs adapted for jumping.

jeremiad (jĕr,ə-mī'əd, -ăd,) *noun* a lengthy and mournful tale of woe, often containing a prediction of impending disaster.

jerk *noun* **1** a quick tug or pull. **2** a sudden movement; a jolt. **3** *slang* a stupid person. —*verb trans., intrans.* (**jerked, jerking**) **1** to pull or tug sharply. **2** to move with sharp suddenness. ▸ **jerkily** *adv.* ▸ **jerky** *adj.*

jerkin *noun* a short, close-fitting, esp. sleeveless jacket.

jerkwater *adj. colloq.* remote, and small in size: *a jerkwater town.*

jeroboam (jĕr,ə-bō'əm) *noun* a large wine bottle holding the equivalent of six standard bottles (or four of champagne).

jerrybuild *verb trans.* (**jerrybuilt, jerrybuilding**) to put up (flimsy buildings) cheaply and quickly. ▸ **jerrybuilder** *noun*

jersey *noun* (*pl.* **jerseys**) **1** a knitted garment worn on the upper part of the body; a pullover. **2** a fine knitted fabric used for clothing. **3** (**Jersey**) a breed of dairy cattle with a tan to dark gray coat.

jest *noun* a joke or prank. —*verb intrans.* (**jested, jesting**) to make jokes. —**in jest** as a joke; not seriously. ▸ **jestingly** *adv.*

jester *noun Hist.* a colorfully dressed professional clown employed to amuse the court.

jet[1] *noun* a hard black mineral that takes a high polish and is used in jewelry, etc.

jet[2] *noun* **1** a strong fast stream of liquid, gas, etc. forced under pressure from a narrow opening such as the orifice of a nozzle. **2** an orifice, nozzle, or pipe emitting such a stream. **3** a device powered by such a stream of liquid or gas, esp. a jet engine used on an aircraft. **4** a jet aircraft. —*verb intrans., trans.* (**jetted, jetting**) **1** *colloq.* to travel or transport by jet aircraft. **2** to emit or cause to emit (liquid or gas) in a jet; to spurt.

jet engine an engine which ejects a stream of rapidly expanding hot gases to obtain forward thrust.

jet lag the fatigue and lethargy that result from the body's inability to adjust to the rapid changes of time zone that go with high-speed, long-distance air travel.

jet-propelled *adj.* **1** driven by jet propulsion. **2** *slang* fast. ▸ **jet propulsion**

jetsam (jĕt'səm) *noun* goods jettisoned from a ship and washed up on the shore. *See also* **flotsam**.

jet set *colloq.* wealthy people who lead a life of fast travel and expensive enjoyment. ▸ **jet-setter** *noun*

jet stream a narrow current of rapidly moving air blowing from a westerly direction at speeds often of more than 250 m.p.h. (400 kph) per hour at altitudes of 10–15 mi. (15–25 km).

jettison *verb trans.* (**jettisoned, jettisoning**) **1** to throw (cargo) overboard to lighten a ship, aircraft, etc., in an emergency. **2** to abandon, reject, or get rid of.

jetty *noun* (*pl.* **jetties**) **1** a wooden or stone wharf. **2** a stone barrier built out into the sea to protect a harbor from currents and high waves.

Jew (jōō) *noun* **1** a member of the now widely dispersed people who are orig. descended from the ancient Hebrews and who share an ethnic heritage that is grounded in Judaism. **2** a person who practices Judaism.

jewel (jōō'əl) *noun* **1** a precious stone. **2** a personal ornament made with precious stones and metals. **3** a gem used in the machinery of a watch. **4** someone or something greatly prized.

jeweled *adj.* set or decorated with jewels.

jeweler *noun* a person who deals in or makes or repairs jewelry, watches, and objects of gold and silver.

jewelry (jōō'əl-rē, jōōl'rē) *noun* articles worn for personal adornment, e.g., bracelets, necklaces, brooches, rings, etc.

Jewish *adj.* relating or belonging to the Jews or to Judaism.

Jewry (jōōr'ē, jōō'rē) *noun* the Jewish people.

jibe[1] *verb intrans.* (**jibed, jibing**) *colloq.* to be in a state of conformity or factual agreement: *Her report jibes with her actual expenditures.*

jibe[2] *noun, verb* same as **gibe**.

jiffy *noun* (*pl.* **jiffies**) *colloq.* a moment.

jig *noun* **1** a lively country dance or folk dance; music for this. **2** a device that holds a piece of work in position and guides the tools being used on it. **3** a cunningly devised means to an end. **4** a metal fishing lure with one or multiple hooks, designed to be deployed on or near the bottom of a body of water, and jiggled by the person using it. —*verb intrans., trans.* (**jigged, jigging**) **1** to dance a jig. **2** to jump, move, or bob up and down.

jigger *noun* **1** a small quantity of alcoholic spirits, or a glass for measuring it. **2** *colloq.* a thing whose name is not known or not remembered.

jiggery-pokery *noun colloq.* trickery or deceit.

jiggle *verb intrans., trans.* (**jiggled, jiggling**) **1** to move, bob, or jump up and down. **2** to cause to move in a jerking, rapid manner. —*noun* a jiggling movement.

jigsaw *noun* **1** a fine-bladed saw for cutting intricate patterns. **2** a jigsaw puzzle.

jigsaw puzzle a picture mounted on wood or cardboard and sawn into irregularly shaped interlocking pieces, taken apart for later reassembly into the picture.

jihad (jĭ-häd′, -hăd′) *or* **jehad** *noun* a holy war fought by Muslims in behalf of Islam.

jilt *verb trans.* (**jilted, jilting**) to discard (a lover).

Jim Crow *slang noun* the policy of discriminating against and suppressing African-Americans. —*adj.* supporting and practicing discrimination against and suppression of African-Americans.

jimmies *pl. noun* tiny particles of candy, often multicolored, sprinkled on ice cream.

jimmy *noun* (*pl.* **jimmies**) a small crowbar used by burglars for forcing open windows.

jimsonweed *noun* a poisonous, coarse weed with large, trumpetlike white or purple blossoms.

jingle *noun* **1** a ringing or clinking sound, as of small bells, coins, or keys. **2** a simple rhyming verse or song. —*verb trans., intrans.* (**jingled, jingling**) to make or cause to make a ringing or clinking sound.

jingoism *noun* overly enthusiastic or belligerent nationalism or patriotism. ▸ **jingoist** *noun* ▸ **jingoistic** *adj.*

jinni (jĭn′ē) *or* **jinnee** *or* **djinni** *noun* (*pl.* **jinn** *or* **djinn**) in Muslim folklore, a supernatural being able to adopt human or animal form.

jinx *noun* an evil spell or influence, held responsible for misfortune. —*verb trans.* (**jinxed, jinxing, jinxes**) to put a jinx on.

> Probably from the *Jynx* bird which was once invoked in spells and charms

jitney *noun* a small van or bus used typically to transport passengers on airport-to-hotel routes and back.

jitter *colloq. verb intrans.* (**jittered, jittering**) to shake with nerves. —*noun* (**the jitters**) an attack of nervousness.

jitterbug *noun* an energetic dance involving two-step movements, twirls, and sometimes semiacrobatic maneuvers. —*verb intrans.* (**jitterbugged, jitterbugging**) to dance the jitterbug.

jittery *adj.* feeling or exhibiting anxiety and nervous tension.

jiujitsu *noun* same as **jujitsu**.

jive *noun* **1** lively jazz or swing music. **2** a jazz musicians' jargon. **b** *slang* glib talk. **c** *slang* nonsense. —*verb intrans., trans.* (**jived, jiving**) **1** to dance to jive music. **2** *slang* **a** to speak nonsense. **b** to tease (another). **c** to engage in idle conversation.

job (jäb) *noun* **1** a person's regular paid employment. ▣ OCCUPATION, WORK **2** a piece of work. **3** a completed task: *did a good job of the pruning.* **4** a function or responsibility: *It's not my job to tidy up.* **5** *colloq.* a problem; difficulty: *It was a job to finish in time.* **6** a crime, esp. a burglary: *an inside job.* **7** an underhand scheme: *a put-up job.* **8** *Brit. colloq.* an event, affair, etc.: *The wedding was a proper church job.* **9** *slang* a surgical operation, usu. involving plastic surgery: *a nose job.* **10** *colloq.* a manufactured product, or other object: *smart little jobs, these calculators.* —*verb intrans., trans.* (**jobbed, jobbing**) **1** to do casual jobs. **2** to function as a jobber. **3** to hire or rent for a period or a job. ▸ **jobless** *adj.*

job action a slowdown or a strike, both temporary, effected by workers as a means of protest.

jobber *noun* a firm or person that purchases goods from manufacturers and then sells the goods to retailers.

job lot a mixed collection of objects sold as one item at an auction, etc.

jock[1] *noun* **1** *Sport* a jockey. **2** a disc jockey.

jock[2] *noun* **1** *slang* a person who excels in and is interested chiefly in athletics. **2** a jockstrap. **3** *slang* an excessively macho man.

jockey *noun* (*pl.* **jockeys**) a rider, esp. professional, in horseraces. —*verb trans., intrans.* (**jockeyed, jockeying**) **1** to ride (a horse) in a race. **2** (**jockey (someone) into (something), out of (something)**) to manipulate (the one or ones specified) deviously.

jockstrap *noun* a garment for supporting the genitals, worn by male athletes.

jocose (jə-kōs′, jō-) *adj.* eliciting or intended to elicit amusement and laughter: *a jocose analysis of a senate debate.* ▣ JOCULAR, WITTY ▣ SOBER, SOLEMN. ▸ **jocosely** *adv.* ▸ **jocosity** *noun*

jocular (jăk′yə-lər) *adj.* **1** given to joking; good-humored. **2** eliciting or intended to elicit amusement and laughter. ▸ **jocularity** *noun* ▸ **jocularly** *adv.*

jocund (jăk′ənd) *adj.* cheerful; merry; good-humored. ▸ **jocundity** *noun*

jodhpurs (jäd′pərz) *pl. noun* riding breeches that are loose-fitting over the buttocks and thighs and tight-fitting from knee to calf.

jog *verb trans.* (**jogged, jogging**) **1** to knock slightly. **2** to prompt (the memory). **3** (**jog along**) to progress slowly and steadily; to plod. **4** to run at a gentle, steady pace, for exercise. —*noun* **1** the act or activity of jogging or the time spent doing this. **2** a nudge, knock, or jolt. ▸ **jogger** *noun* ▸ **jogging** *noun*

joggle verb intrans., trans. (**joggled, joggling**) to move in a jolting or wobbling way; to cause to move in this way. —noun a shake or jolt.

john noun slang **1** (usu. **the john**) a toilet. **2** the male customer of a prostitute.

John Doe 1 used in legal proceedings to designate n unidentified or unidentifiable male. **2** a rather undistinguished, average male.

Johnny-come-lately noun (pl. **Johnny-come-latelies, Johnnies-come-lately**) colloq. a latecomer.

joie de vivre (zhwäd'ə-vēv', -vē'vrə) enthusiasm for living; exuberant spirits.

join verb trans., intrans. (**joined, joining**) **1** to connect, attach, link, or unite. **2** to become a member of (a society, firm, etc.). **3** of roads, rivers, etc. to meet. **4** to come together with; to enter the company of: joined them for supper. **5** to take part in: joined the festivities. **6** to do the same as, for companionship: Who'll join me in a drink? —noun a seam or joint. —**join in** to participate in; to take part. **join up** to enlist as a member of an armed force.

joiner noun **1** a person who makes and fits wooden doors, window frames, stairs, shelves, etc. **2** colloq. a sociable person who likes joining clubs and being a member of a group. ▸ **joinery** noun

joint noun **1** the place where two or more pieces join. **2** the point of contact or articulation between two or more bones, together with the ligaments that surround it. **3** a piece of meat, usu. containing a bone, for cooking or roasting. **4** slang a cheap, shabby cafe, bar, nightclub, etc. **5** slang a marijuana cigarette. —verb trans. (**jointed, jointing**) **1** to connect by the use of joints. **2** to divide (the meat of a bird or other animal) into, or at, the joints, for cooking. —adj. **1** owned, done, etc., in common; shared. **2** working together: joint naval and air force operations. —**out of joint 1** of a bone dislocated. **2** colloq. **a** in disorder. **b** in a bad temper. ▸ **jointly** adv.

joist noun any of the beams supporting a floor or ceiling.

jojoba (hə-hō'bə) noun a shrub whose seeds yield a waxy oil, used in the manufacture of cosmetics and lubricants.

joke noun **1** a humorous story. **2** something said or done in jest. **3** an amusing situation. **4** something or someone ludicrous. **5** slang something so poorly made or badly done as to be laughable: Their attempt at comedy was a joke. —verb intrans. (**joked, joking**) **1** to make jokes. **2** to speak in jest, not in earnest. ▸ **jokey** adj. ▸ **jokiness** noun ▸ **jokingly** adv.

joker noun **1** Cards an extra card in a pack, usu. bearing a picture of a jester. **2** a cheerful person, always full of jokes. **3** slang an irresponsible or incompetent person. **4** slang a person: Some joker vandalized my car.

jollification noun merriment; fun.

jollity noun (pl. **jollities**) merriment.

jolly adj. (**jollier, jolliest**) **1** good-humored; cheerful. **2** happy; enjoyable; convivial. —adv. Brit. colloq. very. —**jolly well** Brit. colloq. used for emphasis: You jolly well deserved it. ▸ **jolliness** noun

jolt verb intrans., trans. (**jolted, jolting**) **1** to move along jerkily and sharply. **2** to undergo heavy vibration or jolting, particularly as the result of a physical shock. —noun **1** a jarring, sharp shake. **2** an emotional shock.

josh colloq. verb trans., *intrans. (**joshed, joshing**) to tease. —noun a bit of teasing.

jostle verb intrans., trans. (**jostled, jostling**) **1** to push and shove; to push against (someone) roughly. **2** to compete aggressively.

jot noun the least bit: Haven't you a jot of compassion? —verb trans. (**jotted, jotting**) (often **jot (something) down**) to write (it) down hastily.

jotting noun (usu. **jottings**) something jotted down.

joule (jōōl, jowl) noun Physics (ABBREV. **J**) a unit of energy or work.

jounce verb trans., intrans. (**jounced, jouncing**) to move or to cause to move with rough bounces and jolts.

journal (jərn'l) noun **1** a periodical, e.g., a magazine, that deals with a specialized subject. **2** a diary in which one recounts one's daily activities.

journalese noun the language, judged as shallow and full of clichés and jargon, used in some newspapers and magazines.

journalism noun the profession of writing for newspapers and magazines, or for radio and television. ▸ **journalist** noun ▸ **journalistic** adj.

journey noun (pl. **journeys**) **1** the process of traveling from one place to another or an instance of it. **2** the distance covered by or the time taken for a trip from one place to another. **3** a day's work. —verb intrans. (**journeyed, journeying, journeys**) to make a journey.

journeyman noun (pl. **journeymen**) **1** a craftsperson qualified in a particular trade and working for an employer. **2** an experienced and competent worker.

joust noun Hist. a contest between two mounted knights armed with lances. —verb intrans. (**jousted, jousting**) **1** Hist. to take part in a joust. **2** to engage in a personal competition with an opponent.

jovial adj. good-humored; merry; cheerful.
▸ **joviality** noun ▸ **jovially** adv.

jowl noun 1 the lower jaw. 2 (**jowls**) the cheeks. 3 loose flesh under the chin.

joy noun a feeling of happiness or a cause of it.
▸ **joyless** adj.

joyful adj. 1 full of joy; happy. 2 expressing or causing joy. ▸ **joyfully** adv.

joyous adj. filled with, causing, or showing joy.
▸ **joyously** adv. ▸ **joyousness** noun

joyride noun a jaunt, esp. a reckless drive in a motor vehicle. —verb intrans. (past tense **joyrode**; past participle **joyridden**; present participle **joyriding**) to go for such a reckless ride. ▸ **joyrider** noun

joystick noun 1 slang the control lever of an airplane, machine, etc. 2 Comput. slang a lever for controlling the movement of the cursor on the screen.

J.P. or **JP** abbrev. Justice of the Peace.

Jr. abbrev. (used after a name) Junior: John Smith, Jr.

jubilant adj. showing and expressing triumphant joy. ▸ **jubilantly** adv.

jubilation noun 1 a triumphant rejoicing. 2 a great celebration.

jubilee noun 1 a special anniversary, esp. the 25th (silver jubilee), 50th (golden jubilee), or 60th (diamond jubilee) of a significant event. 2 the celebrating of such an event.

> From a Hebrew word for 'ram's horn', which was blown to announce the start of a celebratory Jewish year

Judaic (jōō-dā'ĭk) adj. relating to the Jews or Judaism.

Judaism (jōō'dē-ĭz-əm, jōō'də-) noun the religion of the Jews, central to which is the belief in one god, having its basis in the Old Testament and the Talmud.

Judas (jōō'dəs) noun a traitor, esp. to one's friends.

judder verb intrans. (**juddered, juddering**) of a vehicle to jolt, shake, shudder, or vibrate. —noun a shuddering vibration.

judge noun 1 a public officer who hears and decides cases in a court of law. 2 a person appointed to decide the winner of a contest. 3 someone who assesses something: a good judge of character. 4 the person who decides or assesses: I'll be the judge of that. —verb trans., intrans. (**judged, judging**) 1 to hear and decide (a case) in a court of law as judge. 2 to decide the winner of (a contest). 3 to act as judge or adjudicator. 4 to form an opinion; to assess. 5 to estimate: judged the speed of the car as being around 65 mph. 6 to consider or state: judged her fit to travel. 7 to criticize, esp. severely; to condemn.

judgment (jəj'mənt) or **judgement** noun 1
the decision of a judge in a court of law. 2 the act or process of judging. 3 the ability to make wise or sensible decisions; good sense. 4 an opinion: in my judgment. 5 punishment regarded as sent by divine providence.

judgmental adj. 1 involving judgment. 2 apt to pass judgment.

judicature (jōō'dĭ-kə-chōōr, -chər) noun 1 the administration of justice by legal trial. 2 the office of a judge. 3 a body of judges. 4 a court or system of courts.

judicial (jōō-dĭsh'əl) adj. of or relating to a court of law, judges, or their decisions.
▸ **judicially** adv.

judiciary (jōō-dĭsh'ē-ĕr,ē, -dĭsh'ə-rē) noun (pl. **judiciaries**) 1 the branch of government concerned with the legal system. 2 a body of judges and the courts of law in which they hear cases.

judicious adj. shrewd, sensible, wise, or tactful. ▸ **judiciously** adv. ▸ **judiciousness** noun

judo (jōō'dō) noun a Japanese sport and form of physical training that employs principles of balance and leverage taken over from jujitsu.

jug noun 1 a deep container for liquids with a handle and a shaped lip for pouring. 2 the amount that a jug can hold. 3 slang prison. —verb trans. (**jugged, jugging**) to stew (hare) in an earthenware container.

juggernaut noun a mighty force sweeping away and destroying everything in its path.

> From a Hindi word for a large wagon used to carry the image of the god Krishna in religious processions

juggle verb intrans., trans. (**juggled, juggling**) 1 to keep several objects simultaneously in the air by skillful throwing and catching. 2 (usu. **juggle with** (**something**)) to adjust (facts or figures) to create a misleading impression. 3 to do (many tasks) at once, keeping (them) under control: juggled a career and motherhood.
▸ **juggler** noun

jugular (jəg'yə-lər) adj. relating to the neck or throat. —noun Anat. any of several veins that carry blood from the head to the heart. Also called **jugular vein**.

juice noun 1 liquid from fruit or vegetables. 2 (usu. **juices**) the body's natural fluids: digestive juices. 3 slang power or fuel, esp. electricity or gasoline.

juicy adj. (**juicier, juiciest**) 1 full of juice; rich and succulent. 2 colloq., of gossip intriguing; spicy. 3 colloq. profitable; lucrative.
▸ **juiciness** noun

jujitsu (jōō-jĭt'sōō) or **jiujitsu** noun a system of unarmed self-defence, developed in Japan.

jujube (jōō'jōō-bē,) noun a small, firm, fruit-flavored candy made with gelatin.

jukebox *noun* a coin-operated machine that plays whatever recording is selected.

julep *noun* an iced drink of spirits and sugar, flavored esp. with mint.

July (jŏŏ-lī′) (ABBREV. **Jul., Jul**) *noun* the seventh month of the year.

jumble *verb trans.* (**jumbled, jumbling**) **1** to mix or confuse (things). **2** to throw (things) together untidily. —*noun* a confused mass.

jumbo *colloq. adj.* extra-large. —*noun* (*pl.* **jumbos**) an extra-large person or thing.

jump *verb intrans., trans.* (**jumped, jumping**) **1** to spring off the ground, pushing off with the feet. **2** to leap or bound. **3** to get over or across by leaping. **4** to make (esp. a horse) leap. **5** *of prices, levels, etc.* to rise abruptly. **6** to make a startled movement. **7** to twitch, jerk, or bounce. **8** **a** to pass directly from one point to another, omitting intermediate matter or essential steps: *jump to conclusions.* **b** *colloq.* to upscale (another) in rank: *Management decided to jump a junior editor to a supervisory position.* **9** to omit; to skip: *jump the next chapter.* **10** *colloq.* to pounce on. **11** *colloq.* to board and travel on (esp. a train) without paying. **12** to start (a motor vehicle), using jumpers. —*noun* **1** the act of jumping. **2** an obstacle to be jumped, esp. a fence by a horse. **3** the height or distance jumped. **4** a jumping contest: *the high jump.* **5** a sudden rise in amount, cost, or value. **6** an abrupt change or move. **7** a startled movement; a start.

jumper¹ *noun* **1** a sleeveless dress worn typically over a pullover sweater or a blouse. **2** *Brit.* a pullover sweater.

jumper² *noun* **1** a person or animal that jumps. **2** *Electr.* a short length of conductor, e.g., wire, used to make a usu. temporary connection.

jump shot *Basketball* a shot to the basket made by a player while at the highest elevation of a jump.

jump-start *noun* the act of jump-starting a vehicle. —*verb trans.* (**jump-started, jump-starting**) **1** to start the engine of (a motor vehicle) by using jumpers or by pushing (it) and engaging the gears while it is moving. **2** *slang* to energize (an otherwise sluggish or immobile state of affairs): *tried to jump-start the economy.*

jumpsuit *noun* a one-piece garment combining pants and top.

jumpy *adj.* (**jumpier, jumpiest**) **1** nervy; anxious. **2** moving jerkily. ▸ **jumpily** *adv.* ▸ **jumpiness** *noun*

junction *noun* a place at which roads or railroad lines meet; an intersection.

juncture (jəngk′chər, -shər) *noun* a point in time, esp. if critical.

June (jŏŏn) *noun* (ABBREV. **Jun., Jun**) the sixth month of the year.

jungle *noun* **1** an area of dense vegetation. **2** *colloq.* a tropical rain forest. **3** a mass of complexities difficult to penetrate: *the jungle of medical insurance regulations.* **4** a complex or hostile environment where toughness is needed for survival: *the urban jungle.*

junior (jŏŏn′yər) *adj.* **1** (*often* **junior to** (**someone**)) **a** low or lower in rank. **b** younger. **2** of, relating to, or being a student in the third year of a US high school, college, or university. —*noun* **1** a person of low or lower rank in a profession, organization, etc. **2** a third-year US high-school, college, or university student. **3** a person younger than the one in question: *She's three years his junior.* **4** (**Junior**) a name used for referring to a son with the same name as his father.

junior college a two-year college.

junior high school a public secondary school offering classes to youngsters in the seventh, eighth, and sometimes ninth grades.

juniper *noun* an evergreen shrub of northern regions with purple berries used as a medicine and for flavoring gin.

junk¹ *noun colloq.* **1** worthless or rejected material; trash. **2** old or secondhand articles sold cheaply. **3** nonsense. —*adj.* cheap and worthless: *junk jewelry.*

junk² *noun* an Asian flat-bottomed, square-sailed boat.

junket *noun* **1** a dessert made from sweetened and curdled milk. **2** a feast or celebration. **3** a trip made by a government official and paid for out of public funds. —*verb intrans.* (**junketed, junketing**) **1** to feast, celebrate, or make merry. **2** to go on a usu. political junket.

junk food prepackaged food with little nutritional value and usu. a high caloric content.

junkie *or* **junky** *noun* (*pl.* **junkies**) *slang* **1** a drug addict. **2** an avid fan of a particular product or activity: *a fitness junkie.*

junk mail third-class mail addressed to Occupant or Resident sent by advertisers.

junta (hŏŏn′tə, jənt′ə) *noun derog.* a group, clique, or faction, usu. of army officers, in control of a country after a coup d'état.

juridical (jŏŏ-rĭd′ĭ-kəl) *adj.* of or relating to the law or the administration of justice.

jurisdiction *noun* **1** the right or authority to apply laws and administer justice. **2** the district or area over which this authority extends. **3** authority generally.

jurisprudence *noun* **1** the science and philosophy of law. **2** a department or a division of law: *medical jurisprudence.* ▸ **jurisprudential** *adj.*

jurisprudence *noun* **1** the science and philosophy of law. **2** a department or a division of law: *medical jurisprudence.*
▸ **jurisprudential** *adj.*

jurist *noun* an expert in law.

juristic *adj.* **1** relating to jurists. **2** relating to law or the study of law.

juror (jŏōr'ər, -ôr,) *noun* a member of a jury in a court of law.

jury¹ *noun* (*pl.* **juries**) **1** a body of people sworn to give an honest verdict on the evidence presented to a court of law on a particular case. **2** a group of people selected to judge a contest.

jury² *adj.* Naut. makeshift; temporary: *a jury mast.*

just¹ *adj.* **1** fair; impartial. **2** based on justice; reasonable. **3** deserved: *your just reward.*
▸ **justly** *adv.* ▸ **justness** *noun*

just² *adv.* **1** exactly; precisely. **2** a short time before: *He had just gone.* **3** at this or that very moment: *She was just leaving.* **4** and no earlier, more, etc.: *only just enough.* **5** barely; narrowly: *The blow just missed his ear.* **6** only; merely; simply: *just a brief note.* **7** colloq. used for emphasis: *That's just not true.* **8** colloq. absolutely: *just marvelous.*
—just as well 1 fortunate; lucky: *It's just as well you came.* **2** advisable: *It would be just as well to wait.* **just the same** nevertheless.

justice (jəs'tĭs) *noun* **1** the quality of being just; just treatment; fairness. **2** the quality of being reasonable. **3** the law, or administration of or conformity to the law: *a miscarriage of justice.* **4** (**Justice**) used as a

title for a judge at the appellate level: *Mr. Justice Marshall.* **5** a justice of the peace. **6** a judge. **—bring to justice** to arrest and try (a party). **do justice to 1** to treat fairly or properly. **2** to show the full merit, etc., of (the one or ones specified). **do justice to** (**oneself**) to fulfill (one's) potential.

justice of the peace (*pl.* **justices of the peace**) (ABBREV. J.P., JP) a magistrate of the lowest level in some US state court systems, who is authorized to judge minor offenses, remit cases to higher courts for trial, and perform wedding ceremonies.

justification *noun* **1** the act of justifying. **2** something that justifies.

justify *verb trans.* (**justified, justifying, justifies**) **1** to prove or show to be right, just, or reasonable. **2** Printing to arrange (text) so that the margins are even-edged.
▸ **justifiable** *adj.* ▸ **justifiably** *adv.*

jut *verb intrans.* (**jutted, jutting**) (*also* **jut out**) to stick out; to project.

jute *noun* fiber from certain tropical barks used for making sacking, ropes, etc.

juvenile (jōō'və-nīl,, -vən-l) *adj.* **1** young; youthful. **2** suitable for young people. **3** childish; immature: *juvenile pranks.* **—noun 1** a young person. **2** a young animal. **3** an actor playing youthful parts.

juvenile delinquent a young person who is guilty of a crime or who engages in antisocial behavior.

juxtapose *verb trans.* (**juxtaposed, juxtaposing**) to place side by side. ▸ **juxtaposition** *noun*

Kk

K¹ *or* **k** *noun* (*pl.* **Ks, K's, k's**) the 11th letter of the English alphabet.

K² *noun* (*pl.* **K**) **1** *slang* 1,000. **2** *slang* one thousand dollars. **3** Comput. a unit of memory equal to 1,024 bits, bytes, or words.

K³ *abbrev.* **1** Physics kelvin. **2** kilo-. **3** Chess, Cards king.

K⁴ *symbol* Chem. potassium.

Kaffir (kăf'ər) *noun offensive* **1** a black African in South Africa. **2** the Xhosa language.

kaftan *noun same as* **caftan.**

Kaiser (kī'zər) *noun* Hist. the emperor of Germany, Austria, or the Holy Roman Empire.

kale *noun* a crinkly-leaved type of cabbage.

kaleidoscope (kə-līd'ə-skōp,) *noun* **1** an optical device, usu. consisting of mirrors fixed at angles to one another inside a tube

containing small pieces of plastic, glass, or paper, forming changing symmetrical patterns as the tube is shaken or rotated, viewed through one end. **2** a colorful, constantly changing scene or succession of events.
▸ **kaleidoscopic** *adj.* ▸ **kaleidoscopically** *adv.*

kamikaze (käm,ĭ-käz'ē) *noun* **1** a Japanese plane in World War II, loaded with explosives and deliberately crashed by its pilot on an enemy target. **2** the pilot of such an aircraft. **—adj.** colloq., of exploits, missions, etc. suicidally dangerous.

kana *noun* either of two Japanese syllabic writing systems.

kangaroo *noun* (*pl.* **kangaroo, kangaroos**) an Australian marsupial animal with large powerful hind legs adapted for leaping, and a thick muscular tail.

kaolin (kā'ə-lĭn) *noun* a soft white clay used for making pottery and as a medicine.

kapok *noun* a light, cottonlike fiber obtained from the pods of a tropical tree and used as padding or as stuffing for toys, etc.

kappa *noun* the 10th letter of the Greek alphabet (K κ).

kaput *adj. colloq.* **1** broken or destroyed. **2** having been totally incapacitated.

karaoke *noun* an orig. Japanese form of entertainment in which amateur performers sing pop songs to the accompaniment of prerecorded music from a machine.

karat *or* **carat** *noun* (ABBREV. **k, kt.**) a measure of the purity of gold, pure gold being 24 karats.

karate *noun* an orig. Japanese art of self-defense, using blows and kicks.

karate chop a sharp downward blow delivered with the side of the hand.

karma *noun Buddhism, Hinduism* one's lifetime's actions, seen as governing one's fate in one's next life.

kart *noun colloq.* a miniature race car.

katydid *noun* a large N American grasshopper.

kayak *noun* **1** a sealskin-covered canoe used by the Inuit. **2** a similar canvas-covered or fiberglass craft used in the sport of canoeing.

kayo *Boxing noun* (*pl.* **kayos**) a knockout. —*verb trans.* (**kayoed, kayoing, kayos**) to knock (an opponent) out.

kazoo *noun* (*pl.* **kazoos**) a wind instrument consisting of a short metal tube into which one hums, causing a buzzing effect.

KC *abbrev.* **1** *Legal* King's Counsel **2** (**K.C.**) Knight of Columbus.

kebab *noun* a dish of small pieces of meat and vegetable, esp. (*shish kebab*) grilled on a skewer.

kedge *verb trans., intrans.* (**kedged, kedging**) *of a ship* to maneuver by means of a hawser attached to a light anchor. —*noun* a light anchor used for kedging.

kedgeree *noun* an orig. E Indian dish, now usu. a mixture of rice, fish, and eggs.

keel *noun* the timber or metal strut extending from stem to stern along the base of a ship, from which the hull is built up. —*verb intrans.* (**keeled, keeling**) (**keel over**) **1** *of a ship* to tip over sideways. **2** *colloq.* to fall over, e.g., in a faint. —**on an even keel** calm and steady.

keelboat *noun* a shallow-drafted boat that was propelled by poling or rowing, or sometimes towed by animals along a riverbank.

keen[1] *adj.* **1** eager; willing. **2** feeling or exhibiting enthusiasm. **3** *of competition, rivalry, etc.* fierce. **4** *of the wind* bitter. **5** *of a* blade, etc. sharp. **6** *of the mind or senses* quick; acute. ▸ **keenly** *adv.* ▸ **keenness** *noun*

keen[2] *verb intrans.* (**keened, keening**) to lament or mourn in a loud wailing voice. —*noun* a lament for the dead.

keep *verb trans., intrans.* (*pa t and pa p* **kept**; *pr p* **keeping**) **1** to have in one's possession or under one's control: *kept the rare books.* ◼ HOLD, RESERVE, RETAIN, WITHHOLD ◻ RELINQUISH, SURRENDER, YIELD. **2** to continue to have; not to part with; to save. **3** to maintain or retain: *kept his temper.* **4** to store. **5** to remain or cause to remain in a certain state, position, place, etc. **6** to continue or be frequently (doing something): *keep smiling.* **7** *of a shopkeeper, etc.* to have regularly in stock: *keeps rain hats and umbrellas.* **8** to own (an animal, etc.) for use or pleasure: *keep horses.* **9** to own or run (a shop, boardinghouse, etc.). **10** to look after: *keep house.* **11** *of food* to remain fit to be eaten: *Shellfish don't keep.* **12** to maintain (a record, diary, accounts, etc.). **13** (**keep from** (**doing something**)) to hold back (doing it): *couldn't keep from smiling at the thought.* **14** to obey (the law, etc.). **15** to preserve (a secret). **16** to stick to (a promise or appointment). **17** to celebrate (a festival, etc.). **18** to support financially. **19** to protect: *kept them from harm.* **20** *Sport* to guard (the goal) in soccer or (the wicket) in cricket. **21** to remain firm on: *managed to keep his footing.* —*noun* the cost of one's food and other daily expenses: *earn one's keep.* —**for keeps** *colloq.* for good; permanently: *Marriage used to be for keeps.*

keeper *noun* **1** a person who looks after something, e.g., animals in a zoo or a collection in a museum. **2** *colloq.* a warden or guard in a prison. **3** *Sport* a goalkeeper or wicketkeeper.

keepsake *noun* something kept in memory of the giver.

keg *noun* a small barrel for transporting and storing beer.

kelp *noun* **1** a large brown seaweed. **2** the ash obtained by burning this seaweed, used as a fertilizer and a source of iodine.

Kelt *noun* same as **Celt**.

kelvin *noun* (ABBREV. **K**) *Physics* the unit on the Kelvin scale for measuring temperature, with zero at absolute zero. ▸ **kelvin** *adj.*

kennel *noun* **1** a shelter for a dog. **2** (*often* **kennels**) an establishment where dogs are bred or boarded. —*verb trans.* (**kenneled** *or* **kennelled, kenneling** *or* **kennelling**) to put or keep in a kennel.

kept *verb see* **keep.** —*adj., of a man or woman* supported financially by someone in return for being available to that person for sexual relations.

keratin *noun* *Biol.* a tough fibrous protein which is the main component of hair, nails, claws, horns, feathers, and the dead outer layers of skin cells.

kerchief *noun* **1** a cloth or scarf for wearing over the head or around the neck. **2** a handkerchief.

kernel *noun* **1** *Bot.* **a** the inner part of a seed, e.g., the edible part of a nut. **b** in cereal plants such as corn, the entire grain or seed. **2** the important, essential part.

kerosene *noun* a paraffin oil obtained mainly by distillation of petroleum, used for heating systems and lamps, and as a fuel for jet aircraft.

kestrel *noun* a type of small falcon.

ketch *noun* a small two-masted sailboat.

ketchup *or* **catsup** *noun* a thick sauce made from tomatoes, vinegar, spices, etc.

> Based on a Chinese word for 'fish brine'

ketone *noun* *Chem.* one of a class of organic chemical compounds that includes acetone.

kettle *noun* a kitchen vessel with a spout, lid, and handle, for, e.g., boiling water.

kettledrum *noun* a large copper or brass cauldron-shaped drum mounted on a tripod.

key¹ *noun* **1** an instrument for opening or closing a lock, winding up, turning, tightening, or loosening. **2** one of a series of buttons or levers pressed to sound the notes on a musical instrument, or to print or display a character on a computer, typewriter, calculator, etc. **3** *Mus.* a system of notes related to one another in a scale. **4** pitch, tone, or style: *spoke in a low key.* **5** something that provides an answer or solution. **6** a means of achievement: *the key to success.* **7** a set of answers, e.g., at the back of a book of puzzles. **8** a table explaining signs and symbols used on a map, etc. **9** *Electr.* a leverlike switch that makes or breaks a circuit for as long as the handle is depressed. **10** a pin or wedge for fixing something. **11** *Basketball* one of two areas, each at the end of the court between the base and foul lines that includes the circle at the foul line where jump balls are made. —*adj.* centrally important: *key questions.* —*verb trans.* (**keyed, keying**) **1** to enter (data) into a computer, calculator, etc., by means of a keyboard. **2** to lock or fasten with a key. **3** (**key (one thing) to (another thing)**) to adjust or harmonize (it). —**keyed up** *colloq.* excited; tense; anxious.

key² *noun* a small low island or reef formed of mud, sand, coral, or rock.

keyboard *noun* **1** the set of keys on a piano, etc., or the bank of keys for operating a computer or typewriter. **2** *Mus.* an instrument with a keyboard, e.g., one connected to an amplifier or a synthesizer. —*verb intrans., trans.* (**keyboarded, keyboarding**) **1** to operate the keyboard of a computer. **2** to set (text) using a computer keyboard. ▸ **keyboarder** *noun*

keycard *noun* a plastic card with a magnetically encoded strip that is electronically scanned, e.g., to access an automatic teller machine or open doors.

keyhole *noun* the hole through which a key is inserted into a lock.

keynote *noun* **1** *Mus.* the note on which a scale or key is based. **2** a central theme of a speech, feature of an occasion, etc.

keypad *noun* **1** a small device with pushbutton controls, e.g., a television remote control unit. **2** a small cluster of usu. numeric keys positioned to one side of a keyboard or on a separate keyboard.

keypunch *noun* a device, operated by a keyboard, that transfers data on to cards by punching holes in them.

key signature *Mus.* the sharps and flats shown on the staff at the start of a piece of music, indicating its key.

keystone *noun* **1** the central supporting stone at the high point of an arch. **2** the point in a theory or argument on which the rest depends.

keystroke *noun* a single press of a key, e.g., on a typewriter or computer.

kg *abbrev.* kilogram.

KGB *abbrev.* *Komitet Gosudarstvennoi Bezopastnosti* (Russian), Committee of State Security, the Russian and former Soviet secret police.

khaki *noun* **1** a brownish-green color. **2** brownish-green cloth, or military uniforms made of it. —*adj.* of a brownish-green color.

> From an Urdu word meaning 'dusty'

khan (kän, кнän) *noun* **1** a ruler or prince in Central Asia. **2** in ancient Persia, a governor.

kHz *abbrev.* kilohertz.

kibbutz (kǐ-boots′) *noun* (*pl.* **kibbutzim**) a farm or other concern in Israel owned and run jointly by its workers. ▸ **kibbutznik** *noun*

kibitz *verb intrans.* (**kibitzed, kibitzing, kibitzes**) to watch an activity and offer unsolicited advice; to talk, converse, or chat generally.

kibosh (kǐ′bäsh,) *noun* a terminating, checking, or controlling element or factor. —**put the kibosh on** *or* **to** (**something**) to put an end to (it).

kick *verb trans., intrans.* (**kicked, kicking**) **1** to hit (a person, etc.) or propel (a ball, etc.) with the foot. **2** to swing or jerk (the leg) vigorously. **3** *of a gun* to recoil when fired. **4**

to get rid of (a habit, etc.). **5** to score (a goal) with a kick. **6** to argue against something; to protest: *started kicking when taxes rose.* —*noun* **1** a blow with the foot. **2** *Sport* a the action of kicking a ball. **b** the ball so kicked. **3** a swing of the leg: *high kicks.* **4** *Swimming* any of various leg movements. **5** the recoil of a gun after firing. **6** *colloq.* a **a** thrill of excitement. **b** (**kicks**) enjoyment; fun. **7** *colloq.* a strong effect; power: *a drink with a kick.* **8** *colloq.* a brief enthusiasm: *We're on a culture kick.*

kickback *noun* money paid for help or favors, esp. if illegally given.

kickboxing *noun* the sport and martial art of defense and attack, executed in a boxing ring, and mixing elements of boxing and karate. ▸ **kickboxer** *noun*

kicker *noun* one that kicks, esp. in a sport such as football or soccer.

kickoff *noun* **1** *Sport* a place kick, e.g., in football or soccer, by which the play starts or resumes. **2** *colloq.* the start of something.

kick-start *noun* **1** a pedal on a motorcycle that is kicked vigorously downward to start the engine. **2** the starting of an engine with this pedal. —*verb trans.* (**kick-started, kick-starting**) to start (a motorcycle) using this pedal.

kid¹ *noun* **1** *colloq.* a young person; a child. **2** a young goat, antelope, or other related animal. **3** the smooth, soft leather made from the skin of such an animal. —*adj. colloq.* younger: *my kid sister.*

kid² *verb trans., intrans.* (**kidded, kidding**) *colloq.* **1** to fool or deceive, esp. light-heartedly or in fun. **2** to bluff; to pretend. **3** to tease. —**kid (oneself)** to fool (oneself) about (something). ▸ **kidder** *noun*

kidnap *verb trans.* (**kidnapped, kidnapping**) to seize and hold (someone) prisoner illegally, usu. demanding money for the victim's safe release: *kidnapped the heiress.* ■ ABDUCT, SNATCH ◙ RANSOM.

kidney *noun* (*pl.* **kidneys**) **1** one of a pair of abdominal organs whose function is to filter waste products from the blood, which are then excreted in the urine. **2** animal kidneys eaten as food.

kidney bean a dark red, kidney-shaped bean eaten as a vegetable.

kill *verb trans., intrans.* (**killed, killing**) **1 a** to deprive of life. **b** to cause the death of (a human being) illegally, with malice. **c** to be fatal: *Excessive speeds kill.* **2** *colloq.* to cause pain to: *My feet are killing me.* **3** *colloq.* to cause to fail; to put an end to: *how to kill a conversation.* **4** *colloq.* to deaden (pain, noise, etc.). **5** to pass (time), esp. aimlessly, while waiting for a later event. —*noun* **1** an act of killing. **2** prey killed.

—**dressed to kill** captivatingly or impressively dressed. ▸ **killer** *noun*

killer whale a toothed whale with a black body, white underparts and white patches on its head.

killing *colloq., noun* **1** an act of slaying. **2** *colloq.* a financial windfall; a great deal of money in terms of earnings or profits: *made a killing.* —*adj.* **1** exhausting. **2** highly amusing.

killjoy *noun* someone who spoils others' pleasure.

kiln (kĭln, kĭl) *noun* an oven for baking pottery or bricks, or for drying grain.

kilo (kē′lō) *noun* (*pl.* **kilos**) **1** a kilogram. **2** a kilometer.

kilo- *combining form* forming words denoting one thousand: *kilobyte.*

kilobyte *noun Comput.* 1,024 bytes.

kilocalorie *noun* (ABBREV. **C**) the amount of heat required to raise the temperature of one kilogram of water by 1°C, often used to express the energy content of food.

kilocycle *noun old use* a kilohertz.

kilogram *noun* (ABBREV. **kg**) the unit of mass in the International System, equal to 1,000 g (2.2 lbs.)

kilohertz *noun* (*pl.* **kilohertz**) (ABBREV. **kHz**) a unit of frequency equal to 1,000 hertz or 1,000 cycles per second, used to measure the frequency of sound and radio waves. *Also called* **kilocycle.**

kiloliter *noun* (ABBREV. **kl**) a unit of liquid measure equal to 1,000 liters.

kilometer (kǐ-lăm′ət-ər, kǐl′ə-mēt,ər) *noun* (ABBREV. **km**) a unit of length equal to 1,000 m (0.62 mi).

kiloton *noun* (ABBREV. **kT**) a unit of explosive force equivalent to that of 1,000 metric tons of TNT.

kilowatt *noun* (ABBREV. **kW**) a unit of electrical power equal to 1,000 watts or about 1.34 horsepower.

kilowatt hour (ABBREV. **kWh**) a unit of electricity consumption, equal to the energy used when an electrical appliance with a power of one kilowatt is run for one hour.

kilt *noun* a pleated, knee-length, tartan skirt, traditionally worn by men as part of Scottish Highland dress.

kilter *noun colloq.* good working condition: *The video is out of kilter.*

kimono *noun* (*pl.* **kimonos**) **1** a long, loose, wide-sleeved, Japanese garment fastened by a sash at the waist. **2** a dressing gown in this style.

kin *noun* one's relations. —*adj.* related: *kin to the President.* —**next of kin** one's nearest relative.

-kin *suffix* forming words denoting a diminutive: *lambkin.*

kind¹ *noun* **1** a group, class, sort, or type. **2** nature, character, or distinguishing quality: *differ in kind.* —**kind of** *colloq.* somewhat; slightly: *kind of old-fashioned.*

kind² *adj.* **1** friendly, helpful, generous, benevolent, or considerate. **2** warm; cordial: *kind regards.* ▸ **kindness** *noun*

kindergarten *noun* a school for young children, usu. ones aged between four and six.

kindhearted *adj.* kind; generous; good-natured. ▸ **kindheartedly** *adv.* ▸ **kind-heartedness** *noun*

kindle *verb trans., intrans.* (**kindled, kindling**) **1** a to cause to start burning. **b** to start burning. **2** *of feelings* to stir or be stirred.

kindling (kĭn′dlĭng, kĭn′lĭn) *noun* dry wood, leaves, etc., for starting a fire.

kindly *adv.* **1** in a kind manner. **2** please: *Would you . kindly sign here?* —*adj.* (**kindlier, kindliest**) kind, friendly, generous, or good-natured. ▸ **kindliness** *noun*

kindred *noun* **1** one's relations. **2** relationship by blood. —*adj.* **1** related. **2** having qualities in common: *kindred arts.*

kindred spirit someone who shares one's tastes, opinions, etc..

kine *pl. noun* old use cattle.

kinematics *noun* (*sing.*) *Physics* the science of the motion of objects.

kinetic (kə-nĕt′ĭk) *adj.* of or relating to motion. ▸ **kinetically** *adv.*

kinetic energy *Physics* the energy that an object has in relation to its motion.

kinetics *noun* (*sing.*) **1** *Chem.* the scientific study of the rates of chemical reactions. **2** *Physics* the study of the relationship between moving objects, their masses, and the forces acting on them.'

kinfolk *or* **kinsfolk** *pl. noun* one's relatives.

king *noun* **1** a male ruler of a nation. **2** a ruler or chief. **3** someone or something considered supreme in a group: *the lion, the king of beasts.* **4** a leading or dominant figure in a field, e.g., a wealthy manufacturer: *a steel king.* **5** *Cards* the face card bearing the image of a king. **6 a** *Chess* the most important piece, the one that must be protected from checkmate. **b** in checkers, a piece that, having crossed the board safely, has been crowned, and may move both forward and backward. ▸ **kingliness** *noun* ▸ **kingly** *adj.* ▸ **kingship** *noun*

kingdom *noun* **1** a country or region ruled by a monarch. **2** *Biol.* the highest rank in the classification of plants and animals. **3** the domain in which something is thought of as existing or operating: *the kingdom of the imagination.*

kingfisher *noun* a bird with brilliant blue and orange plumage that dives for fish.

kingpin *noun* **1** the central pin in bowling. **2** the most important person in an organization, team, etc. **3** *Mech.* a bolt serving as a pivot.

King's English standard written or spoken English.

king-size *or* **king-sized** *adj.* of a large, or larger-than-standard, size.

kink *noun* **1** a bend or twist, e.g., in a string, rope, or wire. **2** *colloq.* an oddness of personality; an eccentricity; a sexual preference regarded as strange. —*verb trans., intrans.* (**kinked, kinking**) to develop or cause to develop a kink or kinks.

kinky *adj.* (**kinkier, kinkiest**) *colloq.* intriguingly odd or eccentric, esp. in a sexual way. ▸ **kinkiness** *noun*

kinsfolk *pl. noun* same as **kinfolk.**

kinship *noun* family relationship.

kinsman *noun* one's male relation.

kinswoman *noun* one's female relation.

kiosk *noun* a booth or stall for the sale of candy, newspapers, etc.

kipper *noun* a herring split open, salted, and smoked.

kirsch (kĭrsh) *noun* a clear liqueur distilled from black cherries.

kismet *noun* **1** fate. **2** one's destiny.

kiss *verb trans.* (**kissed, kissing**) **1** to touch with the lips, as a greeting or sign of affection. **2** *of two people* to kiss each other on the lips. —*noun* **1** an act of kissing. **2** a gentle touch.

kissable *adj.* **1** that can be kissed. **2** desirable.

kit¹ *noun* **1** a set of instruments, equipment, etc., needed for a purpose, esp. if kept in a container. **2** a set of special clothing and equipment, e.g., for a soldier. **3** a set of parts ready for assembling. —**the (whole) kit and caboodle** *colloq.* the entire set, lot, or collection: *threw the whole kit and caboodle out.*

kit² *noun* a kitten.

kitchen *noun* a room in which food is prepared and cooked.

kite *noun* **1** a bird of prey of the hawk family, with a long, often forked, tail. **2** a light frame covered in paper or some other light material, with a long holding string attached to it, for flying in the air for fun, etc. —*verb trans.* (**kited, kiting**) to use (a bad check) to keep credit afloat or to raise funding.

kith and kin friends and relations.

kitsch *noun* art, design, writing, moviemaking, etc., that is characterized by often pretentious poor taste and by sentimentality. ▸ **kitschy** *adj.*

kitten *noun* **1** a young cat. **2** the young of various other small mammals, e.g., the rabbit. —**have kittens** *colloq.* to become extremely agitated.

kittenish *adj.* like a kitten; playful.

kitty¹ *noun (pl.* **kitties) 1** a fund contributed to jointly, for communal use by a group of people. **2** *Cards* a pool of money used in certain games.

kitty² *noun (pl.* **kitties)** *colloq.* a cat or kitten.

kiwi *noun* **1** a flightless, tailless, long-beaked bird, native to New Zealand. *Also called* **apteryx. 2 a** a woody Chinese vine. **b** the fruit of this tree, having a fuzzy skin and a sweet, green pulp. *Also called* **Chinese gooseberry.**

kJ *abbrev.* kilojoule.

KKK *abbrev.* Ku Klux Klan.

kl *abbrev.* kiloliter.

Klaxon (klăk′sən) *trademark* used to denote a loud electric horn that serves as a warning signal, e.g., on ambulances, fire engines, etc.

kleptomania *noun Psychol.* the irresistible urge to steal, esp. objects that are not desired for themselves, and are of little monetary value. ▸ **kleptomaniac** *noun*

klutz *noun slang* a stupid, clumsy, inept person.

km *abbrev.* kilometer.

knack *noun* **1** a skill, esp. gained through practice. **2** an expedient method.

knapsack *noun* a hiker's or traveler's canvas bag for food, clothes, etc., carried on the back or over the shoulder.

knave *noun old use* **1** *Cards* jack (sense 2). **2** a scoundrel. ▸ **knavery** *noun* ▸ **knavish** *adj.* ▸ **knavishly** *adv.*

knead *verb trans.* (**kneaded, kneading**) **1** to work (dough) with one's fingers and knuckles. **2** to massage (flesh) with firm finger movements.

knee *noun* **1** the joint between the thigh and the shin. **2** the upper surface of a sitting person's thigh; the lap. **3** the part of a garment covering the knee. —*verb trans.* (**kneed, kneeing**) to strike or nudge with the knee.

kneecap *noun* the small lens-shaped plate of bone covering the front of the knee joint. —*verb trans.* (**kneecapped, kneecapping**) to shoot or otherwise damage the kneecaps of (a person) as a form of revenge or unofficial punishment.

kneel *verb intrans.* (*pa t and pa p* **knelt** or **kneeled**; *pr p* **kneeling**) (*also* **kneel down**) to support one's weight on, or lower oneself onto, one's knees.

knee-length *adj.* coming down, or up, as far as the knees.

kneeler *noun* a cushion on which to kneel, esp. in a church.

knell *noun* **1** the tolling of a bell announcing a death or funeral. **2** something that signals an end. —*verb trans., intrans.* (**knelled, knelling**) **1** to announce or summon by or as

if by tolling. **2** to ring or toll solemnly and slowly.

knelt *see* **kneel**.

knew *see* **know**.

knickers *pl. noun* **1** *Brit.* an undergarment for women and girls, covering the lower abdomen and buttocks, with separate legs or leg holes. **2** full breeches that are banded just below the wearer's knees.

> Short for *knickerbockers*: named after Diedrich *Knickerbocker*, a fictional Dutchman invented by US author Washington Irving in the 19th century

knickknack *noun* a little trinket or ornament.

knife *noun (pl.* **knives)** a cutting instrument or weapon, typically in the form of a blade fitted into a handle. —*verb trans.* (**knifed, knifing, knifes**) to stab or kill with a knife. —**twist the knife in the** *or* **a wound** to increase deliberately another person's distress or embarrassment by constant reminders of the circumstances that caused it. **under the knife** *colloq.* undergoing a surgical operation: *The patient was under the knife for seven hours.*

knife-edge *noun* the cutting edge of a knife. —**on a** *or* **the knife-edge** in a state of extreme uncertainty.

knifepoint *noun* the sharp, pointed end of a knife. —**at knifepoint** in a position where one is being threatened by someone with a knife: *was robbed at knifepoint.*

knight *noun* **1** *Hist.* a man-at-arms of high social standing, usu. mounted, serving a feudal lord. **2** *Hist.* the armed champion of a lady, devoted to her service. **3** *Chess* a piece shaped like a horse's head. **4** *Brit.* a man who has been awarded the title 'Sir'. *See also* **Dame.** —*verb trans.* (**knighted, knighting**) *Brit.* to confer the title 'Sir' on. ▸ **knightly** *adj.*

knight-errant *noun (pl.* **knights-errant)** *Hist.* a knight traveling about in search of opportunities for daring and chivalrous deeds.

knighthood *noun Brit.* the rank of a knight.

knish (kə-nĭsh′) *noun* dough stuffed with meat, potatoes, or cheese, then fried or baked.

knit *verb trans., intrans.* (*pa t and pa p* **knit** or **knitted**; *pr p* **knitting**) **1** to produce a fabric composed of interlocking loops of yarn, using a pair of knitting needles or a machine; to make (garments, etc.) by this means. **2** to make (a stitch) in plain knitting. **3** to unite: *a closely knit family.* **4** of a broken bone to grow or cause it to grow together again. **5** to draw (one's brows) together in a frown. —*noun* **1** a fabric or garment created by knitting. **2** the manner in which a fabric has

been created by knitting: *a tight knit.*
▸ **knitter** *noun* ▸ **knitting** *noun*

knitting needle an implement like a long, stout pin, made of wood, plastic, or metal, used for knitting.

knitwear *noun* knitted garments.

knives *see* **knife**.

knob *noun* 1 a hard, rounded projection. 2 a handle, esp. rounded, on a door or drawer. 3 a button on mechanical or electrical equipment, pressed or rotated to operate it. 4 a small, roundish lump. ▸ **knobby** *adj.*

knock *verb intrans., trans.* (**knocked, knocking**) 1 to tap or rap with the knuckles or another object. 2 (**knock** (**something**) **down** *or* **over**) to strike and so push (it), esp. accidentally. 3 to put into a certain condition by hitting: *knocked him senseless.* 4 to make by striking. 5 (**knock against** *or* **into** (**something** *or* **someone**)) to strike, bump, or bang against (something or someone). 6 *colloq.* to find fault with, esp. unfairly: *Don't keep knocking her efforts.* —*noun* 1 the act or an instance of knocking. 2 a tap or rap. 3 *colloq.* a cutting, critical remark. —**knock around** *or* **about** *colloq.* 1 *of a person* to wander about casually: *students knocking about in Europe during the summer.* 2 to discuss: *knocked the idea around for a while.* **knock** (**someone**) **around** *or* **about** to treat (the one specified) roughly. **knock** (**someone**) **back** to cost (someone) a specified amount: *The dinner knocked me back $200.* **knock** (**someone**) **down** to deliver a blow that strikes (another) to the ground. **knock** (**something**) **down** 1 to demolish (a building, etc.). 2 *colloq.* to reduce the price of (merchandise). **knock** (**someone**) **out** 1 **a** to strike (someone) unconscious. **b** *Boxing* to hit (an opponent) so as to be incapable of rising in the required time. **c** *Boxing* to defeat (an opponent) in a knockout competition. 2 *colloq.* to amaze (someone); to impress (someone) greatly.

knockdown *adj. colloq.* 1 low; cheap: *knockdown prices.* 2 *of furniture* able to be taken to pieces easily. 3 *of an argument or a fight* overwhelmingly strong.

knocker *noun* 1 a doorknocker. 2 (**knockers**) *coarse slang* a woman's breasts.

knock knees a condition in which the knees touch when a person is standing with feet slightly apart. ▸ **knock-kneed** *adj.*

knockoff *noun* a copy or an imitation, usu. cheap and done without permission.

knockout *noun* 1 *colloq.* someone or something stunning. 2 a competition in which the defeated competitors are dropped after each round. 3 *Boxing* the act of knocking out an opponent.

knoll *noun* a small, round hill.

knot *noun* 1 a join or tie in string, etc., made by looping the ends around each other and pulling tight. 2 a bond or uniting link. 3 a coil or bun in the hair. 4 a decoratively tied ribbon. 5 a tangle in hair or string. 6 a difficulty or complexity. 7 a hard mass in a tree trunk where a branch has grown out from it; the resultant patch in timber. 8 a small gathering or cluster, e.g., of people. 9 a unit of speed at sea, a nautical mile, about 1.15 statute mph (1.85 kph). 10 a tight feeling in the belly, caused by nervousness. —*verb trans., intrans.* (**knotted, knotting**) 1 to tie in a knot. 2 to tangle. —**tie the knot** *colloq.* to get married. ▸ **knotty** *adj.*

knothole *noun* a hole left in a piece of wood where a knot has fallen out.

know *verb trans., intrans.* (*pa t* **knew**; *pa p* **known**; *pr p* **knowing**) 1 (**know** (**something**) *or* **know of** *or* **about** (**something**)) to be aware of (it); to be certain about (it). 2 to have learned. 3 to have an understanding or grasp of. 4 to be familiar with: *know her well.* 5 to be able to recognize or identify. 6 to have enough experience or training: *knew not to question her further.* 7 to think of (someone or something) in a certain way: *knew them as kindly folk.* 8 **a** to experience (an emotion). **b** to undergo, experience, or be subject to (e.g., a given state or set of circumstances): *know poverty.* —**in the know** *colloq.* having information not known to most. **know** (**something**) **backwards and forwards** *colloq.* to know (it) thoroughly. ▸ **knowable** *adj.*

know-how *noun* skill and ability.

knowing *adj.* 1 cunningly shrewd. 2 indicating the possession of private or secret information: *a knowing look.* 3 intentional; deliberate: *a knowing attempt to deceive us.* —*verb see* **know.** ▸ **knowingly** *adv.* ▸ **knowingness** *noun*

knowledge *noun* 1 the fact of knowing; awareness; understanding. 2 that which one knows; the information one has acquired through learning or experience. 3 learning; the sciences: *a branch of knowledge.* —**to the best of** (**one's**) **knowledge** as far as (one) knows.

knowledgeable *adj.* knowing a great deal. ▸ **knowledgeably** *adv.*

knuckle *noun* a joint of a finger, esp. the one at its base. —**knuckle down** (**to something**) to begin to work hard: *had to knuckle down and try harder.* **knuckle under** *colloq.* to submit, yield, or give way.

knucklehead *noun colloq.* a stupid person.

KO *slang, noun* a knockout, esp. in boxing. —*verb trans.* (**KO'd, KO'ing, KO's**) to knock out, esp. in boxing.

koala (kō-äl'ə) *noun* an Australian tree-climbing marsupial animal with thick gray fur and large ears, that feeds on eucalyptus leaves. *Also called* **koala bear.**

kohl *noun* a cosmetic in the form of a powder, used particularly by women in the Middle East to darken the eyelids.

kola *noun same as* **cola** (sense 1).

kook *noun slang* a crazy or eccentric person. ▸ **kooky** *or* **kookie** *adj.*

Koran (kə-rän') *or* **Qur'an** *noun* the holy book of Islam, believed by Muslims to be composed of the revelations of Allah to Muhammad. ▸ **Koranic** *adj.*

Korean (kə-rē'ən) *noun* **1** a native or citizen of North or South Korea. **2** the official language of North and South Korea. —*adj.* of Korea, its people, or their language.

kosher *adj.* **1** in accordance with Jewish law. **2** of food prepared as prescribed by Jewish dietary laws. **3** *colloq.* genuine; legitimate. —*noun* kosher food, or a shop selling it.

kowtow *verb intrans.* (**kowtowed, kowtowing**) **1** to defer to another, esp. in an overly submissive or obsequious way. **2** to touch the forehead to the ground in a gesture of submission. —*noun* an act of deference or submission.

> Based on a Chinese phrase meaning 'to prostrate yourself before the emperor'

kph *abbrev.* kilometers per hour.

Kr *symbol Chem.* krypton.

kremlin *noun* **1** the citadel of a Russian town. **2** (**the Kremlin**) the government of the former Soviet Union, housed in the citadel of Moscow.

krill *noun* a tiny shrimplike shellfish, eaten by whales, etc.

krona (krōō'nə, krō'-) *noun* **1** (*pl.* **kronor**) the standard unit of Swedish currency. **2** (*pl.* **kronur**) the standard unit of Icelandic currency.

krone (krō'nə) *noun* (*pl.* **kroner**) the standard unit of Danish and Norwegian currency.

krypton *noun Chem.* (**SYMBOL Kr**) a colorless, odorless gas, used in fluorescent lighting and lasers.

kt. *abbrev.* karat.

kudos (kōō'däs,, kyōō'-, -dōs,) *noun colloq.* credit, honor, or prestige.

kumquat (kəm'kwät,) *noun* **1** a small spiny evergreen shrub or tree, native to China, that bears fragrant white flowers and small, edible citrus fruits. **2** the small, round, orange citrus fruit produced by this plant.

kung fu a Chinese martial art with similarities to karate and judo.

Kurdish (kərd'ĭsh) *noun* the Iranian language that is spoken by the Kurds.

kW *abbrev.* kilowatt.

kWh *abbrev.* kilowatt hour.

Ll

L¹ *or* **l** *noun* (*pl.* **Ls, L's, l's**) the 12th letter of the English alphabet.

L² *abbrev.* **1** lake. **2** Latin. **3** licentiate. **4** (*also* **l**) lira; lire.

L³ *symbol* the Roman numeral for 50.

l *abbrev.* **1** left. **2** length. **3** line. **4** liter.

La *symbol Chem.* lanthanum.

la *or* **lah** *noun Mus.* the sixth note of the scale in the solfeggio system of music notation.

lab *noun colloq.* a laboratory.

label *noun* **1** a note attached to a parcel, object, etc., giving details of its contents, owner, destination, etc. **2** a word or short phrase used to describe a person or thing. **3** a strip of material on a garment, giving the maker's or designer's name. **4** a recording company's trademark. —*verb trans.* (**labeled** *or* **labelled, labeling** *or* **labelling**) **1** to attach a label to; to describe in a label. **2** to

describe in a certain way: *were labeled as rebels:*

labia *see* **labium.**

labial *adj.* relating to the lips, or to the labia.

labile (lā'bĭl,, -bəl) *adj.* receptive to change; adaptable: *a labile personality.*

labium *noun* (*pl.* **labia**) a lip or liplike structure, esp. one of the folds of skin of the vulva.

labor *noun* **1** strenuous and prolonged work. **2** (*usu.* **labors**) a difficult task. **3** working people or their efforts. **4** the process of childbirth. —*verb intrans.; trans.* (**labored, laboring**) **1** to work hard or with difficulty. **2** to progress or move slowly and with difficulty. **3** to strive earnestly. **4** to inflict a burden on: *labored them with requests.* ▸ **laborer** *noun*

laboratory (lăb'rə-tôr,ē) *noun* (*pl.* **laboratories**) a room or building equipped for conducting scientific experiments and research, for preparing chemicals, etc., or for teaching science.

Labor Day a public holiday held on the first Monday in September in the USA and Canada and on May 1 in many other countries, in honor of working people.

labored *adj.* **1** showing effort or difficulty: *labored breathing.* **2** not natural or spontaneous: *a labored style of prose.*

labor-intensive *adj.* of an industry, etc. needing a lot of workers. *See also* **capital-intensive.**

laborious (lə-bôr′ē-əs) *adj.* **1** requiring hard work or much effort. **2** not looking or sounding natural; not fluent. ▸ **laboriously** *adv.*

labyrinth (lăb′ə-rĭnth) *noun* **1** a complicated network of passages. **2** a complicated arrangement. ▸ **labyrinthine** *adj.*

lac *noun* a resinous substance in varnish.

lace *noun* **1** a delicate material made from fine thread woven into netlike patterns. **2** a string or cord drawn through holes, used for fastening shoes, etc. —*verb trans., intrans.* (**laced, lacing**) **1** (*also* **lace up**) to fasten or be fastened with a lace. **2** to trim with lace. **3** to weave in and out of; to intertwine. **4** to flavor or strengthen with alcohol: *punch laced with rum.* ▸ **lacy** *adj.*

lacerate (lăs′ə-rāt,) *verb trans.* (**lacerated, lacerating**) **1** to tear or cut (flesh) roughly. **2** to wound or hurt (a person's feelings). ▸ **laceration** *noun*

lachrymal (lăk′rə-məl) *or* **lacrimal** *adj.* relating to tears or the tear glands.

lachrymose (lăk′rə-mōs,) *adj. literary* **1** crying very easily and very often. **2** very sad; likely to make a person cry.

lack *noun* **1** the absence of what is needed or usual: *a lack of time.* ■ ABSENCE, DEARTH, DEFICIENCY, WANT ☒ ABUNDANCE. **2** something missing or in short supply. —*verb trans., intrans.* (**lacked, lacking**) **1** to be completely without or to have too little of. **2** (**lack for** (**something**)) to be in need of (something): *did not lack for money.*

lackadaisical (lăk,ə-dā′zĭ-kəl) *adj.* displaying a lack of energy, interest, or enthusiasm. ▸ **lackadaisically** *adv.*

lackey *noun* (*pl.* **lackeys**) **1** a groveling or servile follower. **2** *old use* a male servant.

lackluster *adj.* lacking in energy or brightness.

laconic *adj.* using few words. ▸ **laconically** *adv.*

lacquer (lăk′ər) *noun* a solution of resins or other substances that can be applied to surfaces in order to provide a hard, glossy, transparent coating. —*verb trans.* (**lacquered, lacquering**) to apply lacquer to (a surface).

lacrimal *adj. same as* **lachrymal.**

lacrosse (lə-krôs′) *noun* a game for two teams of ten players using long sticks with nets at one end to hurl a small ball into their opponents' net.

lactate (lăk′tāt,) *verb intrans.* (**lactated, lactating**) *of the mammary glands* to secrete milk. ▸ **lactation** *noun*

lactic *adj.* of or derived from milk.

lacuna (lə-kōō′nə, -kyōō′-) *noun* (*pl.* **lacunae, lacunas**) a gap or space where something is missing, esp. in printed text.

lad *noun* a boy or youth.

ladder *noun* **1** a piece of equipment consisting of rungs or steps between two long supports, used for climbing up or down. **2** a means or route of progress or advancement: *the social ladder.*

laden *adj.* **1** loaded with cargo. **2** heavily loaded. **3** *of one's mind, conscience, etc.* oppressed with guilt, worry, etc.

ladies' room a women's public toilet.

lading *noun* **1** a cargo or load carried. **2** the act of loading cargo or goods.

ladle *noun* a large spoon with a long handle and deep bowl, for serving or transferring liquid. —*verb trans.* (**ladled, ladling**) to serve or transfer with a ladle.

lady *noun* (*pl.* **ladies**) **1** a woman regarded as well-mannered, elegant, or refined. **2** a polite word for a woman. **3** (**Lady**) *Brit.* a title of honor for peeresses and for some other women of importance, e.g., mayoresses. **4** a woman in a position of authority or control: *the lady of the house.*

> *Usage* **Lady,** when used to modify another noun (lady doctors; lady executives) is now considered offensive, in that such usages convey the impression that the speaker or writer considers it unusual for a woman to be in a profession or position (e.g., medicine, management) typically or traditionally dominated by men.

ladybug *noun* a small beetle that is usu. reddish with black spots, and that feeds on aphids. *Also called* **ladybird.**

lady-in-waiting *noun* (*pl.* **ladies-in-waiting**) a woman attending a queen or princess.

ladylike *adj.* polite and elegant.

Ladyship *noun Brit.* (*usu.* **Your** *or* **Her Ladyship**) used as a title to address peeresses, etc.

lag¹ *verb intrans.* (**lagged, lagging**) to move or progress too slowly and become left behind: *lagging behind.* —*noun* **1** a lagging behind; a delay. **2** the amount by which one thing is delayed behind another.

lag² *verb trans.* (**lagged, lagging**) to cover (water pipes, a boiler, etc.) with a thick covering to keep the heat in. —*noun* lagging. ▸ **lagging** *noun*

lager *noun* a light beer.

laggard *noun* someone who lags behind.

lagoon *noun* 1 a relatively shallow body of water separated from the open sea by a reef or bank of sand or shingle. 2 a body of liquid waste, e.g., at a dump site.

lah *noun Mus. same as* **la**.

laid *see* **lay**[1]. —**laid up** *colloq.* confined to bed because of illness.

laid-back *adj. colloq.* relaxed and easygoing.

lain *see* **lie**[2].

lair *noun* a wild animal's den.

laissez-faire (lĕs,ā-fâr′, lĕz,- -fĕr′) *or* **laisser-faire** *noun* a policy of not interfering in what others are doing.

laity (lā′ət-ē) *noun (usu.* **the laity**) ordinary people who are not members of a particular profession, esp. not members of the clergy.

lake *noun* a large area of water surrounded by land.

lam *verb trans.* (**lammed, lamming**) *slang* to beat or thrash.

lamb *noun* 1 a young sheep. 2 the flesh of a lamb or sheep, eaten as food. 3 a person who is kind, gentle, and good. —*verb intrans.* (**lambed, lambing**) 1 to give birth to a lamb. 2 to tend lambing ewes. ▸ **lambing** *noun, adj.*

lambaste (lăm-bāst′, -băst′) *verb trans.* (**lambasted, lambasting**) 1 to thrash or beat severely. 2 to scold severely.

lambent *adj.* 1 *of a flame or light* flickering over a surface. 2 *of eyes, etc.* gently sparkling. 3 *of wit* light and brilliant. ▸ **lambency** *noun*

lame *adj.* 1 unable to walk properly, esp. because of an injury or physical defect. 2 *of an excuse, etc.* not convincing; weak. —*verb trans.* (**lamed, laming**) to make lame. ▸ **lameness** *noun*

lamé (lăm-ā′) *noun* a fabric that has gold and silver threads woven into it.

lament (lə-mĕnt′) *verb trans., intrans.* (**lamented, lamenting**) to feel or express regret or sadness. —*noun* 1 an expression of, e.g., sadness, grief, or regret. 2 a poem, song, etc., that expresses great grief, esp. following a death. ▸ **lamentation** *noun*

lamentable *adj.* regrettable, shameful, or deplorable. ▸ **lamentably** *adv.*

laminate *verb. trans., intrans.* (lăm′ĭ-nāt,) (**laminated, laminating**) 1 to beat (a material, esp. metal) into thin sheets. 2 to form (a composite material) by bonding or gluing together two or more thin sheets of that material. 3 to separate or be separated into thin layers. — *noun* (lăm′ĭ-nət, -nāt,) a sheet of material formed by laminating two or more thin sheets of that material. ▸ **laminated** *adj.* ▸ **lamination** *noun*

lamp *noun* an appliance that serves as a source of artificial light.

lampblack *noun* soot obtained from burning carbon, used as a pigment.

lampoon *noun* a personal, satirical attack. —*verb trans.* (**lampooned, lampooning**) to attack or laugh at in lampoons. ▸ **lampooner** *noun* ▸ **lampoonist** *noun* ▸ **lampoonery** *noun*

lamppost *noun* a tall post supporting a street lamp.

lamprey *noun* (*pl.* **lampreys**) a jawless, scaleless, eel-like fish with a round suckerlike mouth and horny teeth.

lampshade *noun* a shade placed over a lamp or light bulb to soften or direct the light coming from it.

lance *noun* a long spear used as a weapon by horsemen. —*verb trans.* (**lanced, lancing**) 1 to cut open (a boil, etc.) with a lancet. 2 to pierce with, or as if with, a lance.

lance corporal (ABBREV. **L.Cpl.**) a non-commissioned officer of a rank above private first class and below corporal.

lancet *noun* 1 a small surgical knife with a point. 2 *Archit.* a high, narrow, pointed arch or window. *Also called* **lancet arch, lancet window**.

land *noun* 1 the solid part of Earth's surface. 2 ground, esp. in terms of its use or quality: *building land.* 3 a country, state, or region: *your native land.* 4 (**lands**) estates. —*verb intrans., trans.* (**landed, landing**) 1 to come to rest on the ground, on water, etc., after flight through the air. 2 to bring onto land from a ship. 3 (**land** (someone *or* oneself) **in** (something)) *colloq.* to put (someone) or find (oneself) in (a given position or situation), usu. unwelcome or unfavorable: *landed themselves in big trouble.* 4 *colloq.* to succeed in acquiring (a job, prize, etc.).

landed *adj.* 1 owning land: *the landed gentry.* 2 consisting of or derived from land: *landed estates.*

landfall *noun* an approach to land, or the land approached, after a journey by sea or air.

landfill *noun* a site used for the disposal of solid waste.

landing *noun* 1 the process of coming to rest on shore or on the ground. 2 a place for disembarking, esp. from a ship. 3 the level part of a staircase between flights of steps, or at the very top.

landlady *noun* 1 a woman who owns property that is rented to a tenant. 2 a woman who keeps an inn, a rooming house, or a hotel.

landlocked *adj., of a country* almost or completely enclosed by land.

landlord *noun* 1 a man or organization that owns property that is rented to a tenant. 2 a man who keeps an inn, a rooming house, or a hotel.

landlubber *noun Naut.* a person who has no experience of the sea.

landmark *noun* 1 a conspicuous or well-known object that serves as a guide to travelers. 2 an event marking a significant stage in the history or development of something. —*adj.* of great importance, esp. in terms of history or consequence: *a landmark decision.*

landmass *noun* a large area of land unbroken by seas.

land mine a mine laid on or near the surface of the ground.

land office a government office that maintains records of the sale of public lands.

landscape *noun* 1 the area and features of land that can be seen in a broad view. 2 a picture showing a view of the countryside.

landslide *noun* 1 the sudden downward movement of a mass of soil and rock, esp. in mountainous areas. *Also called* **landslip.** 2 an overwhelming victory in an election.

landward *adj.* lying or facing toward the land. —*adv.* (**landward** or **landwards**) toward land: *turned landward.*

lane *noun* 1 a narrow road or street. 2 a division of a road for a single line of traffic. 3 a regular course across the sea taken by ships or through the air by aircraft.

language *noun* 1 the system of spoken and written human communication. 2 the speech and writing of a particular nation or group. 3 the faculty of speech. 4 a style of speech or expression with words: *elegant language.* 5 a way of communicating without written or spoken words: *sign language.* 6 professional or specialized vocabulary: *the language of science.* 7 *Comput.* computer language.

languid *adj.* 1 lacking energy or vitality. 2 slow-moving; sluggish. ▸ **languidly** *adv.*

languish *verb intrans.* (**languished, languishing**) 1 to lose energy or vitality; to grow weak. 2 to look sorrowful. 3 to pine.

languor *noun* 1 a lack of energy; dullness. 2 tender softness or sentiment. 3 a stuffy, suffocating atmosphere or stillness. ▸ **languorous** *adj.*

lank *adj.* 1 long and thin. 2 *of hair* long, straight, and limp. ▸ **lankness** *noun*

lanky *adj.* (**lankier, lankiest**) thin and tall, esp. in an ungainly way. ▸ **lankiness** *noun*

lanolin (lăn'l-ĭn) *noun* a yellowish substance derived from the grease in sheep's wool.

lantern *noun* a lamp or light contained in a transparent case so that it can be held or carried.

lanthanum *noun Chem.* (SYMBOL **La**) a silvery-white metallic element.

lap¹ *verb trans., intrans.* (**lapped, lapping**) 1 to drink by scooping (liquid) up with the tongue. 2 *of water* to wash or flow against a shore, etc., with a light splashing sound. —*noun* 1 the act of lapping or the amount lapped up. 2 the sound of water lapping.

lap² *noun* 1 the front part of the body, from waist to knees, when sitting. 2 the part of clothing that covers this part.

lap³ *noun* 1 one circuit of a racecourse or other track. 2 one section of a journey. 3 a part that overlaps or the amount by which it overlaps. —*verb trans., intrans.* (**lapped, lapping**) 1 to get ahead of (a competitor) in a race by one or more laps. 2 to fold (a piece of clothing, etc.) around (someone). 3 to wrap a (person) in (clothing, etc.), esp. protectively.

lapdog *noun* a small dog kept as a pet.

lapel *noun* the part of a coat or jacket joined to the collar and folded back across the chest.

lapidary *noun* (*pl.* **lapidaries**) a person who cuts and polishes gemstones. —*adj.* 1 relating to stones. 2 engraved on stone.

lapis lazuli (lăp'ĭs-lăzh'ə-lē, -lăz'-) 1 a deep blue gemstone. 2 the color of this stone.

lapse *noun* 1 a slight mistake or failure: *a lapse of memory.* 2 a decline in standards of behavior. 3 a passing of time: *after a lapse of two years.* 4 *Law* the loss of a right or privilege by failing to renew a claim to it. —*verb intrans.* (**lapsed, lapsing**) 1 to fail to behave properly or morally. 2 (**lapse into** (**something**)) to pass into or return to (a bad or less welcome state). 3 *Law, of a right or privilege* to be no longer valid because the claim to it has not been renewed.

laptop *noun* a portable personal computer small enough to be used on a person's lap.

larceny (lär'sə-nē) *noun* (*pl.* **larcenies**) *Law* theft of personal property. ▸ **larcenist** *noun*

larch *noun* 1 a coniferous tree with egg-shaped cones. 2 the wood of this tree.

lard *noun* soft, white fat from hogs. —*verb trans.* (**larded, larding**) 1 to stuff (meat) with bacon or pork. 2 to fill (e.g., a piece of writing) with details, technical words, etc.

larder *noun* 1 a cool room or cupboard for storing food. 2 a store of food.

large *adj.* 1 great in size, extent, or amount. 2 broad; wide-ranging. 3 generous. 4 in a big way; extensive. —*adv.* to a prominent or significant extent: *problems that loomed large.* —**at large** 1 having escaped captivity and roaming the country at liberty: *escaped convicts now at large.* 2 in general; as a whole. ▸ **largeness** *noun*

largely *adv.* 1 mainly or chiefly. 2 to a great extent.

largess (lär-jĕs', -zhĕs') or **largesse** *noun* 1 generosity. 2 gifts, money, etc., generously given.

largo *Mus. adv.* slowly and with dignity. —*adj.* slow and dignified. —*noun* (*pl.* **largos**) a piece of music to be played in this way.

lark[1] *noun* a small, ground-nesting bird, often singing in flight as it soars upward.

lark[2] *noun colloq.* a joke or piece of fun. —*verb intrans.* (**larked, larking**) (**lark about** *or* **around**) *colloq.* to play or fool around frivolously.

larva *noun* (*pl.* **larvae**) the immature stage of many insects, amphibians, and fish that hatches from the egg, e.g., a caterpillar or tadpole. ▸ **larval** *adj.*

laryngitis (lăr,ĭn-jīt′ĭs) *noun* inflammation of the larynx, often accompanied by coughing, hoarseness, or complete loss of voice.

larynx *noun* (*pl.* **larynges, larynxes**) the upper part of the windpipe. *Also called* **voice box.** ▸ **laryngeal** *adj.*

lasagna (lə-zän′yə) *or* **lasagne** *noun* pasta in the form of thin, flat sheets.

lascivious (lə-sĭv′ē-əs) *adj.* without sexual restraint. ▸ **lasciviously** *adv.*

laser *noun* a device that produces a narrow beam of light powerful enough to cut metal.

> An acronym of 'light amplification by stimulated emission of radiation'

lash *noun* **1** a strike or blow with a whip. **2** the flexible part of a whip. **3** (*usu.* **lashes**) an eyelash. —*verb trans., intrans.* (**lashed, lashing, lashes**) **1** to hit or beat with a lash. **2** to beat or strike with great force: *waves lashing the shore.* **3** to fasten with a rope or cord. **4** to make a sudden whiplike movement.

lashing *noun* **1** a rope for tying things fast. **2** a beating with a whip.

lassitude *noun* lack of energy and enthusiasm.

lasso (lăs′ō, lă-sōō′) *noun* (*pl.* **lassos, lassoes**) a long rope with a loop which tightens when the rope is pulled, used for catching animals, etc. —*verb* (**lassoed, lassoing, lassos** *or* **lassoes**) to catch with a lasso.

last[1] *adj.* **1** coming after all others. **2** most recent; next before the present. **3** coming or remaining after all the others. **4** least likely or suitable: *the last person you'd expect to help.* **5** lowest in rank; worst. —*adv.* **1** after all others. **2** most recently. **3** lastly. —*noun* **1** the last person or thing. **2** the end or last moment. **3** (**the last**) the final appearance or mention: *We haven't heard the last of him.* —**at** (**long**) **last** in the end, esp. after a long delay. ▸ **lastly** *adv.*

last[2] *verb intrans., trans.* (**lasted, lasting**) **1** to continue for a long time, or for a specified time. **2** to be adequate for (someone) for (a length of time). ▸ **lasting** *adj.*

last-ditch *adj.* done as a last resort.

last rites religious rites for a dying person.

last straw an often insignificant addition to a mounting difficulty or burden, which finally makes all of it intolerable: *Losing my keys*

was the last straw.

latch *noun.* **1** a door catch consisting of a bar that is lowered or raised from its notch by a lever or string. **2** a door lock by which a door may be opened from the inside using a knob or handle, and from the outside by using a key. —*verb trans., intrans.* (**latched, latching**) to fasten or be fastened with a latch.

latchkey *noun* a key for an outer door with a latch.

late *adj.* **1** coming, arriving, etc., after the expected or usual time. **2** far on in a period of time: *late afternoon.* **3** occurring, ripening, etc., towards the end of the season: *late potatoes.* **4** having died, esp. recently: *his late father.* **5** having been such previously. **6** most recent. —*adv.* **1** after the expected or usual time. **2** far on in a period of time. **3** at an advanced time: *late in the season.* **4** recently: *The letter was sent as late as this morning.* ▸ **lateness** *noun*

lately *adv.* not long ago.

latent *adj.* **1** present but hidden and not yet developed. **2** in an inactive state, esp. one unlikely to last. ▸ **latency** *noun*

later *adj., adv.* at some time after, or in the near future.

lateral *adj.* at, to, or from the side. —*noun* a side part, esp. a branch. ▸ **laterally** *adv.*

latest *adj.* most recent. —*noun* (**the latest**) the most recent news, occurrence, fashion, etc.

latex *noun* (*pl.* **latices, latexes**) **1** a whitish milky fluid produced by certain trees and plants (e.g., rubber tree). **2** a suspension of fine particles of rubber or plastic in water.

lath *noun* a thin, narrow strip of wood, esp. used to support plaster in a building.

lathe *noun* a machine tool that is used to cut, drill, or polish a piece of metal, wood, or plastic by rotating it against the shaping edge of the tool.

lather *noun* **1** a foam made by mixing water and soap. **2** foamy sweat. —*verb intrans., trans.* (**lathered, lathering**) **1** to form a lather. **2** to cover with lather. ▸ **lathery** *adj.*

Latin (lăt′n) *noun* **1** the language of ancient Rome and its empire. **2** an inhabitant of ancient Latium in Central Italy. —*adj.* **1** relating to or in the Latin language. **2** *of a language* derived from Latin, as Italian and Spanish are. **3** relating to the Roman Catholic Church.

Latina (lə-tē′nə, lă-) *noun* a woman of Latin American descent, esp. in N America.

Latin America the republics of South and Central America where Latin languages, esp. Spanish, are spoken. ▸ **Latin American** *noun, adj.*

Latino (lə-tē′nō, lă-) *noun* (*pl.* **Latinos**) a man of Latin American descent, esp. in N America.

latitude *noun* **1** *Geog.* any of the imaginary circles drawn around Earth parallel to the Equator. *See also* **longitude**. **2** (*usu.* **latitudes**) a region or area in terms of its distance from the Equator or its climate: *warm latitudes.* **3** scope for freedom of action or choice. ▸ **latitudinal** *adj.* ▸ **latitudinally** *adv.*

latrine (lə-trēn′) *noun* a communal toilet, esp. in a barracks or in the field.

latter *adj.* **1** nearer to the end: *the latter part of the holiday.* **2** being the second of two people or things mentioned, or the last of several. —*noun* (**the latter**) the second of two people or things mentioned, or the last of several. ▸ **latterly** *adv.*

latter-day *adj.* recent or modern.

Latter-day Saint a Mormon.

lattice *noun* **1** an open frame made from crossed narrow strips of wood or metal, used esp. for gates and fences. *Also called* **latticework.** **2** a window with small diamond-shaped panels of glass formed by strips of lead. *Also called* **lattice window.**

laud —*verb trans.* (**lauded, lauding**) to praise, esp. in a loud or formal way. —*noun* praise. ▸ **laudability** *noun* ▸ **laudable** *adj.* ▸ **laudatory** *adj.*

laudanum (lôd′n-əm) *noun Med.* a solution of morphine in alcohol, formerly often taken as a painkiller.

laugh *verb intrans., trans.* (**laughed, laughing**) **1** to make spontaneous sounds associated with happiness, amusement, scorn, etc. **2** to express by laughing: *He laughed his contempt.* —*noun* **1** an act or sound of laughing. **2** *colloq.* a person or thing that is amusing or causes laughter. —**laugh (something) off** to treat (an injury, embarrassment, etc.) trivially. ▸ **laughingly** *adv.*

laughable *adj.* **1** eliciting laughter. **2** deserving to be laughed at. ▸ **laughably** *adv.*

laughing gas *colloq.* nitrous oxide.

laughingstock *noun* someone who is laughed at or ridiculed.

laughter *noun* the act or sound of laughing.

launch¹ *verb trans., intrans.* (**launched, launching**) **1** to send (a boat or ship) into the water, esp. for the first time. **2** to send (a spacecraft, missile, etc.) into the air. **3** to start (a person, project, etc.) on a course. —*noun* the act of launching a spacecraft, missile, ship, etc. ▸ **launcher** *noun*

launch² *noun* a large motorboat.

launch pad *or* **launching pad** a platform for launching a spacecraft or rocket.

launder *verb trans.* (**laundered, laundering**) **1** to wash and iron (clothes or linen). **2** *slang* to transfer (money obtained illegally) through banks or legitimate businesses to hide its origins. ▸ **laundress** *noun*

laundromat *noun* an establishment with coin-operated machines for customers to wash and dry clothes.

laundry *noun* (*pl.* **laundries**) **1** a place where clothes and linen are washed. **2** clothes and linen for washing or newly washed.

laureate (lôr′ē-ət, lär′-) *adj.* crowned with laurel leaves as a sign of honor or distinction. —*noun* a person honored for artistic or intellectual achievement, esp. a poet laureate.

laurel *noun* **1 a** a tree or shrub with leaves that have a spicy scent and are used for flavoring. **b** any of various unrelated trees and shrubs with laurel-like foliage. **2** (**laurels**) honor; praise.

lava *noun* **1** hot molten rock that has flowed from a volcano or fissure in Earth's surface. **2** the solid rock that forms as a result of cooling and solidification of this material.

lavatory *noun* (*pl.* **lavatories**) **1** a toilet (sense 1). **2** a room containing one or more toilets.

lavender *noun* **1** a plant with spikes of lilac or mauve flowers, widely cultivated for its fragrant oil. **2** the dried flowers from this plant, used to perfume clothes or linen. **3** the pale bluish-purple color of the flowers. —*adj.* of a pale bluish-purple color

lavish *adj.* **1** spending or giving generously. **2** gorgeous or luxurious. —*verb trans.* (**lavished, lavishing**) to spend (money) or give (praise, etc.) freely or generously. ▸ **lavishly** *adv.* ▸ **lavishness** *noun*

law *noun* **1 a** a rule allowing or prohibiting certain actions. **b** a collection of such rules according to which people live, a country or state is governed, or an activity is regulated. **c** the control which such rules exercise: *law and order.* **2** *colloq.* the police or a member of the police. **3** (**laws**) jurisprudence. **4** the legal system as a recourse; litigation: *went to law on the issue.* **5** a rule in science, philosophy, etc., based on observation, that says that under certain conditions certain things will always happen. **6** (**the Law**) the first five books of the Bible.

law-abiding *adj.* obeying the law.

lawbreaker *noun* a person who breaks the law.

lawful *adj.* **1** allowed by or according to law. **2** just or rightful. ▸ **lawfully** *adv.* ▸ **lawfulness** *noun*

lawless *adj.* **1 a** ignoring or breaking the law, esp. violently. **b** against the law. **2** having no laws; not governed by laws. ▸ **lawlessly** *adv.* ▸ **lawlessness** *noun*

lawmaker *noun* one who is engaged in the making and enacting of laws; a member of a legislature. ▸ **lawmaking** *adj.*

lawn¹ *noun* an area of smooth mown grass.

lawn² *noun* fine linen or cotton.

lawnmower noun a machine for cutting grass on lawns.

lawn tennis tennis (sense 1).

law of nations international law.

lawsuit noun an argument or disagreement taken to a court of law to be settled.

lawyer noun a person who knows the law, who gives legal advice and help, and represents clients in legal matters and in court.

lax adj. **1** lacking care or concern in one's behavior or morals. **2** loose, slack, or flabby. ▸ **laxity** or **laxness** noun ▸ **laxly** adv.

laxative noun a medicine or food that stimulates movement of the bowels. —adj. having the effect of stimulating bowel movements.

lay¹ verb trans. (**laid, laying**) **1** to place on a surface, esp. horizontally. **2** to put or place: laid her hand on my arm. **3** to design, arrange, or prepare: lay plans. **4** to put plates and cutlery, etc., on (a table) ready for a meal. **5** of a female bird to produce (eggs). **6** to present: laid her case before the court. **7** colloq. to place (a bet). —noun the way or position in which something is resting horizontally or flat: the smooth lay of a rug. —**lay (something) by** to put (it) away for future use. **lay (something) down 1** to give up or sacrifice (something): laid down his life for his country. **2** to formulate or devise (something): lay down a plan of action. **lay (something) in** to get and store a supply of (it). **lay (people) off** to dismiss (employees) when there is no work available. **lay (something) out 1** to plan and arrange (land or natural features). **2** to spread out or display something: laid out their wares at the yard sale. **3** colloq. to spend (money). **lay (someone) up** colloq., of an illness to force (a person) to stay in bed or at home. **lay waste** to destroy or devastate completely: a storm that laid waste to the East Coast.

Usage The verbs lay and lie are often confused, esp. in their inflected forms. Remember first of all that lay is a transitive verb, therefore taking an object, and that lie is an intransitive verb, therefore taking no object. Recalling the basic meanings of the words also helps: lay means to place on a surface, while lie means to be located, to recline. Finally, note the inflected forms of the two verbs. Lay (laid, laying) is used correctly in these examples: She laid (not lay) the heavy volumes on the shelf and The table has been laid (not lay) for a late supper. Lie (lay, lain, lying) is used correctly in these examples: The heavy volumes have lain (not laid) on the shelf for years and When she lay (not laid) down she immediately fell asleep.

---

lay² see **lie²**

lay³ adj. **1** relating to or involving people who are not members of the clergy. **2** having no specialized or professional knowledge in a particular subject.

lay⁴ noun a short narrative or lyric poem, esp. one intended to be sung.

layabout noun a lazy or idle person.

layaway noun **1** a method of payment by which a purchaser puts some money down on the desired item, pays for it in increments, and takes possession of it after the final payment. **2** an item so purchased.

layer noun **1** a thickness or covering, esp. one of several on a surface. **2** a hen regularly laying eggs. —verb trans. (**layered, layering**) to arrange or cut in layers.

layette noun a complete set of clothes, blankets, etc., for a baby.

layman noun see **layperson**.

layoff noun a dismissal of employees when there is no work available.

layout noun **1 a** an arrangement or plan of how land, buildings, pages of a book, etc., are to be set out. **b** the things displayed or arranged in this way. **2** the general appearance of a printed page.

laypeople pl. noun laymen and laywomen.

layperson, layman or **laywoman** noun **1** someone who is not a member of the clergy. **2** someone who has no specialized or professional knowledge in a subject.

lay-up noun Basketball a one-handed shot made close to the basket by a player who has driven into that area of the court.

laywoman noun see **layperson**.

laze verb intrans. (**lazed, lazing**) to do nothing. —noun a period of time spent lazing.

lazy adj. (**lazier, laziest**) **1** disinclined to work or do anything requiring effort. **2** of or causing idleness. ▸ **lazily** adv. ▸ **laziness** noun

lazybones noun (sing.) colloq. a lazy person.

lazy Susan a tray or plate that revolves.

lb. abbrev. pound¹ (sense 1).

lc or **l.c.** abbrev. **1** loco citato (Latin), in the place cited. **2** Printing lowercase.

LCD abbrev. Math (also **l.c.d.**) lowest common denominator.

LCM or **l.c.m.** abbrev. Math lowest common multiple.

L.Cpl. abbrev. lance corporal.

lea noun land temporarily under grass, that will be plowed and used to grow crops.

leach verb trans., intrans. (**leached, leaching**) to remove (a soluble substance) out of (a solid) by allowing a solvent to percolate through it. ▸ **leaching** noun

lead¹ (lĕd) verb trans., intrans. (**led, leading**) **1** to guide by going in front. **2** to guide or cause to go in a certain direction by holding or pulling with the hand, etc. **3** to direct or be in control (of). **4** to cause to act, feel, or think in a certain way: *What led you to say that?* **5** to pass or experience: *lead a miserable existence*. **6** to go or take in a certain direction: *The road leads to the village*. **7** to have as a consequence: *lead to problems*. **8** to be foremost or first, the most important or most influential: *lead the world in engineering*. **9** *Cards* to begin a round of cards by playing (the first card, esp: of a particular suit): *led with hearts*. —*noun* **1** guidance: *We're waiting for you to give us the lead*. **2** the first or most prominent place; leadership. **3** the amount by which a person, etc., is in front of others in a race, contest, etc. **4** a strap or chain for leading or holding a dog, etc. **5** a clue or piece of information that might help solve a problem, mystery, etc. **6** *Cards* an act of playing the first card in a game; the first card played. **7** a wire, cable, or other conductor used to connect two points in an electric circuit, or to allow the passage of electric current from a voltage source to an appliance. —**lead off** to begin. **lead (someone) on** to persuade (someone) to go further than intended. **lead up to (something) 1** to prepare to do (something), for (something to happen, etc.), by gradual steps or stages. **2** to be an underlying cause of (something). ▸ **leader** *noun* ▸ **leadership** *noun* ▸ **leading** *noun, adj.*

lead² (lĕd) *noun* **1** *Chem.* (SYMBOL **Pb**) a soft, heavy, bluish-gray, highly toxic metallic element. **2** graphite. **3** a thin stick of graphite, or some other colored substance, used in pencils. **4** a lump of lead attached to a line, used for measuring the depth of the water, esp. at sea. —*adj.* made of lead. —*verb trans.* (**leaded, leading**) to cover, weight, fit, or surround with lead.

leaden *adj.* **1** made of lead. **2** dull gray in color. **3** heavy or slow. **4** depressing; dull.

lead-time *noun* **1** the time needed between the conception or design of a product and its production. **2** the time taken for delivery of goods after an order has been placed.

lead-up *noun* something that introduces or causes something else, or the process involved: *the lead-up to full-scale war*.

leaf *noun* (*pl.* **leaves**) **1** a usu. green, flat outgrowth from the stem of a plant. **2** something shaped like a leaf. **3** the condition of having leaves: *trees in leaf*. **4** a single sheet of paper forming two pages in a book. **5** a metal, esp. gold, in very thin sheets. —*verb trans., intrans.* (**leafed, leafing, leafs**) **1** (usu. **leaf through**) to turn the pages of a book quickly, glancing at the contents. **2** of

plants to produce leaves. ▸ **leafy** *adj.*

leafage (lē'fĭj) *noun* the leaves of plants.

leaflet (lē'flət) *noun* **1** a sheet of paper, or several sheets folded together, giving information, advertising products, etc. **2** a small leaf or leaflike part. —*verb trans., intrans.* (**leafleted, leafleting**) to distribute leaflets to.

league¹ *noun* **1** a union of persons, nations, etc., formed for the benefit of the members. **2** a group of sports teams that compete over a period of time for a championship. **3** a class or group, considered in terms of ability, importance, etc.: *They're not in the same league with us.* —*verb trans., intrans.* (**leagued, leaguing**) to form or be formed into a league.

league² *noun old use* about 3 mi. (4.8 km).

leak *noun* **1** an unwanted crack or hole in a container, pipe, etc., that allows liquid or gas to pass in or out. **2** liquid or gas that has escaped in this way: *Can you smell a leak?* **3** a divulging of secret information, esp. if unauthorized. —*verb intrans., trans.* (**leaked, leaking**) **1** *of liquid, gas, etc.* to pass accidentally in or out of a crack, hole, etc. **2** to allow (liquid, gas, etc.) to leak. **3** to make known (something that should be concealed). **4** *of secret information* to become known. ▸ **leakage** *noun* ▸ **leakiness** *noun* ▸ **leaky** *adj.*

lean¹ *verb intrans., trans.* (**leaned, leaning**) **1** to slope or be placed in a sloping position. **2** to rest or be rested against something for support. **3** to have an inclination or preference for or tendency toward. —*noun* an act of leaning; the condition of leaning.

lean² *adj.* **1** *of a person or animal* having no superfluous fat; thin. **2** *of meat* containing little or no fat. **3** producing very little food, money, etc.: *the lean years of the late 1920s*. ▸ **leanness** *noun*

leaning *noun* a liking or preference.

lean-to *noun* (*pl.* **lean-tos**) a shed or light construction built against a wall.

leap *verb* (*pa t and pa p* **leaped** *or* **leapt**; *pr p* **leaping**) **1** to jump suddenly or with force. **2** to jump over. **3** (**leap at (something)**) to accept (it) eagerly. **4** *of prices* to go up suddenly and quickly. —*noun* **1** an act of leaping or jumping. **2** the distance leaped.

leapfrog *noun* a game in which one player bends over for another player to vault over with legs parted. —*verb trans., intrans.* (**leapfrogged, leapfrogging**) to vault over (a person's back) with the vaulter's legs parted.

leap year a year of 366 days.

learn *verb trans., intrans.* (*pa t and pa p* **learned** *or* **learnt**; *pr p* **learning**) **1** to gain knowledge of or skill in (something) through study, teaching, or experience. **2** to get to know by heart; to memorize. **3** (**learn of** or **about (something)**) to acquire information about (something). ▸ **learner** noun

learned (lɜr'nɪd) adj. having great knowledge or learning, esp. through years of study. ▸ **learnedly** adv.

learning noun knowledge gained through study.

lease noun a contract by which the owner of a house, land, piece of equipment, etc., agrees to let another person use it for a stated period of time in return for payment. —verb trans. (**leased, leasing**) to give or borrow (a building, equipment, or land) on lease.

leasehold noun **1** the holding of land or buildings by lease. **2** the land or building held by lease. —adj. held by lease. See also **freehold**. ▸ **leaseholder** noun

leash noun a strip of heavy woven material, leather, or chain used for leading or holding a dog or other animal. —verb trans. (**leashed, leashing**) **1** to put a leash on. **2** to control or restrain.

least adj. **1** smallest; slightest. **2** see **little**. —adv. **1** in the smallest or lowest degree. **2** see **little**. —pron. the smallest amount. —**at least 1** at all events; anyway: You could at least say Thank you. **2** not less than. **not in the least** or **not the least bit**, not at all.

leather noun the tanned skin of an animal. ▸ **leathery** adj.

leatherjacket noun the leathery-skinned larva of some crane flies.

leatherneck noun slang a US Marine.

leave¹ verb trans., intrans. (**left, leaving, leaves**) **1** to go away (from); to move out (of). **2** (also **leave behind**) to go without taking; to cause to remain behind: left her keys on the table. **3** to allow to remain in a particular state or condition: leave the window open. **4** to stop going to, belonging to, or working at: decided to leave the company. **5** to have as a remainder: Three minus one leaves two. **6** (also **leave (something) to (someone)**) to make a gift of (something) to (someone else) in one's will: left the antique silver to her niece. **leave off doing (something)** to stop doing (it); to come or bring to an end.

leave² noun **1** a permission to be absent, esp. from work or military duties. **b** the length of time this lasts. **2** permission to do something. —**take (one's) leave of** to say goodbye to.

leaven (lĕv'ən) noun **1** a substance that causes fermentation in dough and batter, producing gas that causes it to rise. Also called **leavening**. **2** an influence or cause of change. —verb trans. (**leavened, leaven-**

ing) **1** to use (a fermenting substance) to cause (dough) to rise. **2** to influence or cause change in.

leaves see **leaf, leave¹**.

leavings pl. noun colloq. things that have been left: the leavings from a meal.

lecherous adj. **1** ignoring sexual restraint. **2** having or showing great or excessive sexual desire, esp. in offensive ways. ▸ **lecher** noun ▸ **lecherously** adv. ▸ **lechery** noun

lectern noun a stand with a sloping surface for holding a book to be read from, esp. in a lecture hall or church.

lecture noun **1** a formal talk on some subject. **2** a long, tedious scolding. —verb trans., intrans. (**lectured, lecturing**) **1** to give or read a lecture (to a group of people). **2** to scold (someone) at length.

lecturer noun **1** a professional speaker. **2** a college or university faculty member who ranks below assistant professor. ▸ **lecture-ship** noun

LED abbrev. Electron. light-emitting diode.

led see **lead¹**.

ledge noun a narrow, horizontal shelf or shelflike part.

ledger noun an office's or shop's main account book.

lee noun Naut. the sheltered side, away from the wind. Also called **lee side**.

leech noun **1** a bloodsucking annelid with a cylindrical or flattened body bearing suckers at each end. **2** a person who befriends another in the hope of personal gain.

leek noun a vegetable related to the onion, with a white cylindrical bulb and broad, flat, green leaves.

leer noun a lecherous grin or sneer. —verb intrans. (**leered, leering**) to grin or sneer lecherously. ▸ **leeringly** adv.

leery adj. (**leerier, leeriest**) (**leery of (someone)**) not having great trust in (someone).

lees pl. noun the sediment at the bottom of a cask or bottle of wine.

leeward (lē'wərd, lōō'ərd) Naut. adj., adv. in or toward the direction in which the wind blows. —noun the sheltered side.

leeway noun scope for freedom of movement or action.

left¹ see **leave¹**.

left² adj. **1** relating to the side that is toward the west when a person or thing is facing north. **2** on or close to a spectator's left side: stage left. **3** relating to the political left. —adv. on or toward the left side. —noun **1** the left side, part, direction, etc. **2** the members of any political party holding the most liberal or radical views. **3** (**the Left**) people, political parties, etc., in favor of liberal or radical positions and actions.

left field 1 *Baseball* the third of the outfield to the left. **2** *slang* a position that is out of the ordinary or bizarre. ▸ **left fielder** *noun*

left-hand *adj.* **1** on or toward the left. **2** done with the left hand.

left-handed *adj.* **1** having the left hand stronger and more dexterous than the right. **2** for use by left-handed people, or the left hand. **3** awkward, clumsy. ▸ **left-handedness** *noun* ▸ **left-hander** *noun*

leftist *noun* a supporter of the political left. —*adj.* relating to or characteristic of the political left. ▸ **leftism** *noun*

leftover *adj.* not used up, eaten, etc. —*noun* (**leftovers**) food that remains uneaten at the end of a meal.

left wing 1 the members of a political party who hold the most liberal or radical opinions. **2** *Sport* **a** the left side of a team in a field game. **b** a player playing on this side. **3** the left side of an army. ▸ **left-wing** *adj.* ▸ **left-winger** *noun*

lefty *noun* (*pl.* **lefties**) *colloq.* **1** a person who is left-handed. **2** a political left-winger.

leg *noun* **1** either of the two lower limbs of the human body. **2 a** a similar appendage in animals that is used for walking or standing. **b** a cut of meat from this part of an animal, esp. the thigh. **3** the part of a piece of clothing that covers a leg. **4** a long narrow support of a table, chair, etc. **5** a distinct part or stage of a course or journey. —*verb intrans.* (**legged, legging**) *colloq.* to walk or run quickly: *legged it to the station.* —**pull (someone's) leg** *colloq.* to try to make (someone) believe something untrue, esp. as a joke.

legacy *noun* (*pl.* **legacies**) **1 a** something that is inherited: *the legacy of freedom.* ≡ HERITAGE, HERITANCE, INHERITANCE. **b** *Law* property or money left in a will. **2** something handed on or left unfinished by someone: *a legacy of unpaid bills.*

legal *adj.* **1** allowed by the law. **2** of or relating to the law or to lawyers. ▸ **legality** *noun* ▸ **legally** *adv.*

legalism *noun* strict adherence to the law. ▸ **legalist** *noun* ▸ **legalistic** *adj.*

legalize *verb trans.* (**legalized, legalizing**) to make legal or lawful. ▸ **legalization** *noun*

legate *noun* an ambassador or representative.

legatee (lĕg,ə-tē′) *noun* a person who is left a legacy in a will.

legation *noun* **1** a diplomatic mission or group of delegates. **2** the official residence of such a mission or group.

legato (lə-gät′ō) *Mus. adv.* smoothly, with the notes running into each other. —*adj.* smooth and flowing. —*noun* (*pl.* **legatos**) **1** a piece of music to be played in this way. **2** a legato style of playing.

legend (lĕj′ənd) *noun* **1 a** a traditional story, popularly regarded as true. **b** such stories collectively. **2** a famous person about whom popularly believed stories are told: *a legend in her own lifetime.* **3** an inscription on a coin, medal, or coat of arms. ▸ **legendary** *adj.*

legerdemain (lĕj,ər-də-mān′) *noun* skill to deceive or conjure with the hands.

leggy *adj.* (**leggier, leggiest**) **1** *esp. of a woman* having attractively long, slim legs. **2** *of a plant* having a long stem.

legible *adj., esp. of handwriting* clear enough to be read. ▸ **legibility** *noun* ▸ **legibly** *adv.*

legion *noun* **1** *Hist.* a unit in the Roman army, between 3,000 and 6,000 soldiers. **2** a very great number. —*adj.* great in number: *Books on this subject are legion.* ▸ **legionary** *noun, adj.*

legionnaire (lē,jə-năr′, -nĕr′) *noun* a member of a legion, esp. of the French Foreign Legion.

legislate *verb intrans.* (**legislated, legislating**) **1** to make laws. **2** (**legislate for** (**something**)) to make provision for (it). ▸ **legislation** *noun* ▸ **legislative** *adj.* ▸ **legislator** *noun*

legislature *noun* the part of the government that has the power to make laws.

legitimate *adj.* (lə-jĭt′ə-mət) **1** lawful. **2** born to parents who are married to each other. **3** *of an argument, conclusion, action, etc.* reasonable; logical; justifiable. —*verb trans.* (lə-jĭt′ə-māt,) (**legitimated, legitimating**) to make lawful or legitimate. ▸ **legitimacy** *noun* ▸ **legitimately** *adv.*

legitimize *verb trans.* (**legitimized, legitimizing**) **1** to make lawful or legal. **2** to make (an illegitimate child) the legal heir to its parents. ▸ **legitimization** *noun*

legroom *noun* space for one's legs, esp. in a motor vehicle or aircraft.

legume (lĕg′yōōm,, lĭ-gyōōm′) *noun Bot.* **1** a plant that produces a fruit in the form of a pod. **2** the fruit of this plant, containing the seeds. ▸ **leguminous** *adj.*

leisure (lē′zhər, lĕzh′ər) *noun* time to relax and do as one wishes. —**at (one's) leisure** at a time convenient to one.

leisurely *adj.* not hurried; relaxed. —*adv.* without hurrying and taking plenty of time.

leitmotif *or* **leitmotiv** *noun* a theme associated with a particular person, idea, etc., which recurs throughout a piece of music, novel, etc.

lemming *noun* a small rodent, native to northern regions, noted for periodical mass migrations.

lemon *noun* **1 a** a small, oval, yellow citrus fruit with pointed ends and acidic juicy flesh. **b** the tree that bears this fruit. **2** a pale yellow color. **3** *colloq.* a worthless thing or person. —*adj.* of a pale yellow color.

lemonade *noun* a drink made from lemon juice, water, and sugar, served cold.

lemur *noun* a nocturnal tree-dwelling primate found in Madagascar.

lend *verb trans.* (**lent, lending**) **1** to give (someone) the use of (something) on the understanding that it is to be returned. **2** to allow (someone) the use of (money), esp. in return for interest paid on it. **3** to give or add (interest, beauty, etc.) to (something or someone): *lend an air of elegance.* —**lend a hand** to help. ▸ **lender** *noun*

> *Usage* See note at *loan.*

length *noun* **1** the distance from one end of an object to the other. **2** the distance by which a thing extends: *the length of an arm.* **3** a period of time. **4** the quality of being long. **5** a given piece or a stated amount, in terms of being long: *a 200-ft length of wire.* **6** (*usu.* **lengths**) trouble or effort: *went to great lengths to help us.* —**at length 1** in detail. **2** for a considerable time.

lengthen *verb trans., intrans.* (**lengthened, lengthening**) to make or become longer.

lengthwise *adv., adj.* in the direction of a thing's length.

lengthy *adj.* (**lengthier, lengthiest**) **1** measuring a great distance; lasting or continuing a long time. **2** *of a speech, etc.* long and tedious.

lenient *adj.* **1** feeling or displaying charitable patience. **2** loath to discipline or to punish: *lenient parents.* ▸ **lenience** *or* **leniency** *noun* ▸ **leniently** *adv.*

lens *noun* **1** a piece of glass, clear plastic, etc., curved on one or both sides, that changes the direction of a beam of light, and that is used in cameras, telescopes, microscopes, glasses, etc. **2** a transparent structure in the eye that focuses light from an object onto the retina, forming an image.

Lent *noun Christianity* the weeks before Easter, a period of prayer, penance, and abstinence.

lent *see* **lend**.

lentil *noun* **1** a plant cultivated for its edible seeds that are produced in pods. **2** a seed of this plant.

lento *Mus. adv.* slowly. —*adj.* slow. —*noun* (*pl.* **lentos**) a piece of music to be performed in this way.

Leo (lē′ō) *noun* the Lion, the name of a constellation and the fifth sign of the zodiac. **2** a person born between Jul. 21 and Aug. 22, under this sign.

leonine *adj.* of or resembling a lion.

leopard *noun* a large wild cat with tawny yellow fur covered with small black spots.

leopardess *noun* a female leopard.

leotard *noun* a tight-fitting, one-piece garment worn for dancing and exercise.

leper *noun* **1** a person who has leprosy. **2** a person who is avoided: *a social leper.*

lepidopterist *noun* a person who studies or collects butterflies and moths.

leprosy *noun* an infectious bacterial disease of the skin, mucous membranes, and nerves. ▸ **leprous** *adj.*

lesbian *noun* a woman who is sexually attracted to other women. —*adj.* relating to lesbians. ▸ **lesbianism** *noun*

lesion *noun* **1** an injury or wound. **2** a scar, ulcer, abscess, etc.

less *adj.* **1** smaller in amount, duration, etc.. **2** *colloq.* smaller in number: *in 1,000 words or less.* **3** *see* **little**. —*adv.* **1** not so much; to a smaller extent. **2** *see* **little**. —*noun* a smaller amount or number. —*prep.* minus; without.

> *Usage Less* is generally used with words that indicate measurable extent: *less* humidity today; *less* money. *Fewer*, on the other hand, is generally used with other words that denote things that can be counted: *fewer* than 15 members; *fewer* dollar bills in the cash register today. As the example given at sense 2 of the adjective *less* clearly indicates, however, certain colloquial usages have become so widespread (as in 10 items or *less*) that they are, unofficially at least, regarded as idiomatic English. The same holds with the idiom *less than*, e.g., *less than* 40 miles to go.

-less *combining form* forming words denoting: **1** free from; lacking; without: *heartless / godless.* **2** not subject to the action of the verb: *countless.*

lessee (lĕs-ē′) *noun* a person granted the use of property by lease.

lessen *verb trans., intrans.* (**lessened, lessening**) to make or become less.

lesser *adj.* smaller in size, quantity, or importance.

lesson *noun* **1** an amount taught or learned at one time. **2** a period of teaching. **3** an experience or example that one should take as a warning or encouragement: *Let that be a lesson to you.* **4** (*often* **Lesson** *or the* **Lesson**) a passage from the Bible read during a church service.

lessor (lĕs-ôr′, lĕs-ôr′) *noun* a person who rents out property by lease.

lest *conj. formal, literary* for fear that: *Speak quietly lest they hear us.*

let¹ *verb trans.* (**let, letting**) **1** to allow, permit, or cause to do something. **2** (*usu. in the imperative*) to give orders, requests, warnings, permission, etc., and to show assumptions: *Let him go.* **3** to rent (e.g., a room). —**let (something** *or* **someone) down 1** to lower. **2** to disappoint or fail to help (someone) when necessary. **let go of (something)** to stop holding (it). **let (someone) in on (something)** colloq. to share (a secret, etc.) with (someone). **let (someone) off** to allow (someone) to go without punishment. **let (something) off** 1 to fire (a gun), explode (a bomb), etc. 2 to release (liquid or gas). **let up** to become less strong or violent: *The strong winds have finally let up.*

let² noun Tennis, Squash an obstruction of the ball, e.g., by the net, requiring it to be served again.

-let suffix forming words denoting a small or young example of the thing specified: *piglet / leaflet.*

letdown noun a disappointment.

lethal adj. causing or enough to cause death. ▸ **lethally** adv.

lethargic adj. lacking in energy or vitality. ▣ LISTLESS, SLUGGISH, TORPID ▣ ENERGETIC, SPIRITED. ▸ **lethargically** adv.

lethargy noun lack of interest, enthusiasm, or energy.

letter noun 1 a written symbol used to express a speech sound. 2 a written or printed message normally sent by mail in an envelope. ▣ EPISTLE, MISSIVE. 3 **(the letter)** the strict, literal meaning of words: *the letter of the law.* 4 **(letters)** literature; knowledge of books. —verb trans. (**lettered, lettering**) to write or mark letters on.

lettered adj. 1 well educated; literary. 2 marked with letters.

letterhead noun a printed heading on stationery or notepaper, giving a person's or company's name, address, etc.

lettering noun 1 the act of forming letters or the way in which they are formed. 2 letters that have been written, painted, or inscribed.

lettuce noun 1 a plant with an oblong or rounded head of edible green leaves. 2 the leaves, eaten in salads.

leukemia noun a malignant disease that affects the bone marrow and other blood-forming organs, causing an increased production of abnormal white blood cells.

leukocyte or **leucocyte** noun Anat. a white blood cell.

levee noun 1 an embankment. 2 a quay.

level noun 1 a horizontal plane or line. 2 a height, value, or extent. 3 position, status, or importance in a scale of values: *discussions at the ambassadorial level.* 4 a stage or degree of progress. 5 an aspect or way: *on a practical level.* 6 a flat area of land. 7 a spirit level —adj. 1 having a flat, smooth, even surface. 2 horizontal. 3 having the same height as something else. 4 having the same standard as something else; equal to it. 5 steady; constant; regular: *keep*

one's body temperature level. —verb trans., intrans. (**leveled** or **levelled, leveling** or **levelling**) 1 to make flat, smooth, or horizontal. 2 to make equal. 3 to point (something, e.g., a gun) in a particular direction. 4 to pull down or demolish. 5 **(level (something) at** or **against (someone))** to direct (an accusation, criticism, etc.) to (a given person). —**level off** to make or become flat, even, steady, regular, etc. **level out** to make or become level. ▸ **levelness** noun

levelheaded adj. sensible.

lever noun 1 a rigid bar that rests on a fixed point, one end being raised by pushing down on the other. 2 a strong bar for moving heavy objects, prying things open, etc. 3 a handle for operating a machine. 4 something that can be used to gain an advantage. —verb (**levered, levering**) to move, open, or use as a lever.

leverage (lĕv'rĭj, lēv'-) noun 1 the mechanical power or advantage gained by using a lever. 2 the action of levering. 3 power or advantage.

leveret (lĕv'ə-rət) noun a young hare.

levitate (lĕv'ĭ-tāt,) verb intrans., trans. (**levitated, levitating**) to float or cause to float in the air in what appears to be a supernatural defiance of gravity. ▸ **levitation** noun

levy verb trans. (**levied, levying, levies**) to raise or collect, esp. taxes or troops for an army. —noun (pl. **levies**) 1 the act of levying. 2 taxes or troops collected by order.

lewd adj. sexually rude, offensive, o: unrestrained. ▣ LASCIVIOUS, LECHEROUS, LIBERTINE, LIBIDINOUS, LICENTIOUS, LUSTFUL, RANDY, SALACIOUS, SATYRIC ▣ DECENT, MORAL, PURE. ▸ **lewdness** noun

lexical adj. 1 relating to the words of a language. 2 relating to a lexicon. ▸ **lexically** adv.

lexicography noun the writing of dictionaries ▸ **lexicographer** noun ▸ **lexicographic** adj

lexicology noun the study of vocabulary.

lexicon noun 1 a dictionary. 2 the vocabulary of a person, a field of knowledge, or a language.

Li symbol Chem. lithium.

liability noun (pl. **liabilities**) 1 the state of being legally liable or responsible. 2 (often **liabilities**) a debt or obligation: *a company's assets and liabilities.* 3 a person or thing one is responsible for. 4 a person or thing that is or causes a problem.

liable adj. 1 legally bound or responsible. 2 (**liable to (something)**) likely to have, get, suffer from (it). 3 (**liable to do (something)**) likely to do (it)

liaise (lē-āz') verb intrans. (**liaised, liaising**) (**liaise between** or **with**) to have or establish a close working relationship with or between other people.

liaison (lē'ā-zän,, lē-ā'-) *noun* **1** communication or cooperation between groups. **2** a romantic relationship that is kept secret, esp. when adulterous or otherwise illicit.

liana (lē-än'ə, -än'ə) *or* **liane** *noun* a climbing, twisting plant found in tropical forests.

liar *noun* a person who tells lies.

lib *noun colloq.* liberation, used esp. in the names of movements: *gay lib.*

libation *noun* **1 a** the pouring out of wine, etc., in honor of a god. **b** the drink so poured. **2** *colloq.* an alcoholic beverage.

libel *noun* an untrue and malicious statement about a person, in words, signs, or pictures; the act of making one. ≡ CALUMNY, DEFAMATION, SLANDER. —*verb* (**libeled** *or* **libelled, libeling** *or* **libelling**) **1** to commit a libel against (someone). **2** to accuse wrongly and spitefully. ▸ **libelous** *or* **libellous** *adj.* ▸ **libelously** *or* **libellously** *adv.*

liberal *adj.* **1** given or giving generously, freely, or abundantly. **2** tolerant of different opinions; open-minded. **3** in favor of social and political reform. **4** (**Liberal**) of, relating to, or being a member of a political party, e.g., in Canada and the UK, that is grounded in the principles of sociopolitical liberalism. —*noun* **1** a liberal person. **2** (**Liberal**) a member or supporter of a Liberal party. ▸ **liberalism** *or* **Liberalism** *noun* ▸ **liberality** *noun* ▸ **liberalization** *noun* ▸ **liberalize** *verb* ▸ **liberally** *adv.*

liberate *verb trans.* (**liberated, liberating**) to deliver from slavery, imprisonment, or some other social or political restraint. ▸ **liberation** *noun* ▸ **liberator** *noun*

libertine (lĭb'ər-tēn,) *noun old use* a person who leads an immoral or amoral life. —*adj.* **1** leading a dissolute life. **2** ignoring sexual restraint.

liberty *noun* (*pl.* **liberties**) **1** freedom to act, move, etc., as one pleases. **2** an action or utterance thought of as too familiar or presumptuous. —**at liberty** allowed or permitted to.

libidinous *adj.* ignoring sexual restraint.

libido (lə-bēd'ō) *noun* (*pl.* **libidos**) **1** intensity of sexual desire. **2** in psychoanalysis, the sexual drive which is said to be a fundamental source of energy for mental events and behavior. ▸ **libidinal** *adj.*

Libra (lē'brə) *noun* **1** the Scales, the name of a constellation and the seventh sign of the zodiac. **2** a person born between Sep. 23 and Oct. 22, under this sign. ▸ **Libran** *noun, adj.*

librarian *noun* a person employed in or in charge of a library. ▸ **librarianship** *noun*

library *noun* (*pl.* **libraries**) **1** a collection of books for public or private use. **2** the room, rooms, or building housing a collection of books. **3** a collection of films, records, etc., or the place where it is kept.

libretto (ləbrĕt'ō) *noun* (*pl.* **librettos, libretti**) the words or text of an opera, an oratorio, or a musical comedy. ▸ **librettist** *noun*

lice *see* **louse** (sense 1).

license *noun* **1** a document giving official permission to own a dog, gun, etc., or to drive a motor vehicle, sell alcohol, etc. **2** permission or leave. **3** excessive freedom of action or speech. **4** a departure from a rule or convention, esp. by a writer or artist, for effect: *poetic license.* —*verb trans.* (**licensed, licensing**) to give a license or permit for (something) or to (someone).

licensee (lī,sən-sē') *noun* a person to whom a license is given.

licentious *adj.* lacking sexual restraint. ▸ **licentiously** *adv.* ▸ **licentiousness** *noun*

lichee *noun* same as **lychee**.

lichen (lī'kən) *noun* a composite organism formed by a fungus and an alga.

licit *adj.* lawful; permitted. ▸ **licitly** *adv.*

lick *verb trans.* (**licked, licking**) **1** to pass the tongue over to moisten, taste, or clean. **2** to flicker over or around. **3** *slang* to defeat. **4** *slang* to hit repeatedly. —*noun* **1** an act of passing the tongue over. **2** *slang* a small amount. **3** *slang* a quick speed: *at a lick.* **4** *slang* a sharp blow.

licorice (lĭk'ə-rĭsh, -rĭs) *noun* **1** a plant cultivated for its roots. **2** the dried root of this plant, used medicinally and in confectionery. **3** a black, sticky candy made from the juice of roots of this plant.

lid *noun* **1** a removable or hinged cover, e.g., for a pot or box. **2** an eyelid.

lie¹ *noun* **1** a false statement made with the intention of deceiving. **2** something misleading; a fraud: *live a lie.* —*verb intrans.* (**lied, lying, lies**) **1** to say things that are not true with the intention of deceiving. **2** to give a wrong or false impression: *The camera never lies.*

lie² *verb intrans.* (*pa t* **lay**; *pa p* **lain**; *pr p* **lying**; *3d person sing. present* **lies**) **1** to be in or on a flat, more or less horizontal position on a supporting surface. **2** to remain undiscussed: *let matters lie.* **3** to be or remain in a particular state: *lie dormant.* **4** to be situated. **5** to stretch or be spread out to view. —*noun* **1** the way or direction in which something is lying. **2** an animal's or bird's hiding place. —**lie low** *or* **lay low** to stay in hiding; to keep out of sight.

Usage See note at *lay*¹

liege (lēj) *Hist. adj.* **1** entitled to receive feudal service or homage from a vassal. **2** bound to give feudal service or homage to a superior. —*noun* **1** a feudal superior, lord, or sovereign. *Also called* **liege lord.** **2** a feudal subject or vassal.

lien (lēn) *noun Law* a right to keep another person's money or property until the owner pays a debt.

lieu (lōō) *noun* —**in lieu of** instead of.

lieutenant (lōō-tĕn'ənt) *noun* **1** a deputy acting for a superior. **2** (ABBREV. **Lt.**) **a** an officer in the US Army, Air Force, or Marines ranking next below captain. **b** an officer in the US Navy or Coast Guard ranking below lieutenant commander and above lieutenant junior grade. **3** a police officer or firefighter ranking below captain. ▸ **lieutenancy** *noun*

lieutenant colonel (ABBREV. **Lt. Col.**) an officer ranking below colonel.

lieutenant commander (ABBREV. **Lt. Comdr., LCDR**) an officer in the US Navy or Coast Guard ranking below commander and above lieutenant.

lieutenant general (ABBREV. **Lt. Gen.**) an officer in the US Army ranking below general and above major general.

lieutenant governor (ABBREV. **Lt. Gov.**) **1** a US elected state official ranking second to a governor **2** a Canadian nonelected chief of government in a province.

lieutenant junior grade (ABBREV. **Lt. (j.g.), LTJG**) an officer in the US Navy or Coast Guard ranking below lieutenant and above ensign.

life · *noun* (*pl.* **lives**) **1 a** what distinguishes living organisms from dead ones and from matter that has never been alive. **b** the state or fact of being alive. **2** the period between birth and death. **3** the period of time during which machinery, etc. is functional. **4** living organisms collectively: *marine life.* **5** a living person: *endangered many lives.* **6** a way or manner of living: *a joyless life.* **7** an aspect of a person's life: *one's love life.* **8** a source of liveliness, energy, or high spirits: *a director who was the life of the movie company.* **9** a written account of a person's life. **10** *colloq.* a sentence in which the convicted person is to be imprisoned for the rest of his or her life. —**not on your life** *colloq.* on no account.

life belt a ring that floats in water, used to support people in danger of drowning.

lifeblood *noun* an essential part or factor.

lifeboat *noun* **1** a boat for rescuing people in trouble at sea. **2** a small boat carried on a ship for use in emergencies.

life buoy a float for supporting a person in water.

lifeguard *noun* an person employed at a swimming pool or beach to rescue people in danger of drowning.

life jacket an inflatable, sleeveless jacket for supporting a person in water.

lifeless *adj.* **1** dead. **2** inanimate. **3** having no energy or vivacity. ▸ **lifelessly** *adv.* ▸ **lifelessness** *noun*

lifelike *adj.*, *of a portrait, etc.* very like the person or thing represented.

lifeline *noun* **1** a rope for support in dangerous operations or for saving lives. **2** a vital means of communication or support.

lifelong *adj.* lasting the whole of a life.

lifer *noun slang* a person who is sentenced to prison for life.

life raft a raft kept on a ship, for use in emergencies.

lifesaver *noun* a person or thing that saves lives, or that saves a person from difficulty. ▸ **lifesaving** *adj.*

life-size *or* **life-sized** *adj.*, *of a copy, drawing, etc.* as large as the original.

lifestyle *noun* a way of living.

lifetime *noun* the duration of a person's life.

lift *verb trans., intrans.* (**lifted, lifting**) **1** to raise or rise to a higher position. **2** to move (esp. one's eyes or face) upward. **3** to take and carry away. **4** to raise to a better or more agreeable level: *lift one's spirits.* **5** *of cloud, fog, etc.* to clear. **6** to remove (a barrier or restriction). **7** *colloq.* to plagiarize. —*noun* **1** an act of lifting. **2** the upward force of the air on an aircraft, etc. **3** *Brit.* an elevator (sense 1). **4** a ride in a car or other vehicle: *gave me a lift to the airport.* **5** a boost to the spirits or sudden feeling of happiness.

liftoff *noun* the launching of a spacecraft or rocket.

ligament *noun* a band of tough fibrous connective tissue that holds two bones together at a joint.

ligature *noun* **1** something that binds or ties. **2** *Mus.* a smooth link between a sequence of notes. **3** *Printing* a character formed from two or more characters joined together. —*verb trans.* (**ligatured, ligaturing**) to bind (a blood vessel, etc.).

light¹ *noun* **1** the part of electromagnetic radiation that can be seen. **2** a source of light, such as the Sun, a lamp, etc. **3** brightness; a shine or gleam. **4** daylight; dawn. **5** (*often* **lights**) a traffic light or a set of them. **6** a flame or spark for igniting. **7** a means, such as a match, of producing a flame for igniting. **8** a way in which something is regarded. **9** a glow in the eyes or on the face as a sign of energy, liveliness, happiness, or excitement. **10** an eminent person: *one of the lights of the movies in the 1950s.* —*adj.* **1** having light; not dark. **2** *of a color* closer to white than black; pale. —*verb trans., intrans.* (**lighted** *or* **lit, lighting**) **1** to bring light to.

2 a to cause to start burning. ⊟ IGNITE, KINDLE ⊟ DOUSE, PUT (OUT). **b** to begin to burn. **3** to guide or show (someone) the way, or (someone's way), using a light or flashlight. **—in the light of (something)** taking (it) into consideration. **light up 1** to become bright. **2** *of a person* to become lively and excited. **3** *colloq.* to light a cigarette, etc., and begin smoking.

light² *adj.* **1** not heavy. **2** low in amount or density: *light rain.* **3** easy to bear, suffer, or do: *light work.* **4** of less weight than is correct or proper. **5** without problems, sorrow, etc.; cheerful. **6** graceful and quick. **7** not serious or profound, but for amusement only: *light reading.* **8** thoughtless or trivial: *a light remark.* **9** dizzy; giddy. **10** *of food* easily digested. **11** *of cakes, pastry, etc.* spongy and well risen. **—adv. 1** in a light manner. **2** with little luggage. ▸ **lightly** *adv.* ▸ **lightness** *noun*

light³ *verb* (**lighted** or **lit, lighting**) **1** (**light on** or **upon**) to come upon or find by chance. **2** *esp. of birds* to come to rest after flight. **—light into** *colloq.* to attack (someone) harshly.

light-emitting diode *Electron.* (ABBREV. **LED**) a semiconductor diode that gives out light when an electric current is passed through it, used to display numerals and letters in calculators, watches, etc.

lighten¹ *verb trans., intrans.* **1** (**lightened, lightening**) to make or become brighter. **2** to cast light on. **3** to shine or glow.

lighten² *verb trans., intrans.* (**lightening, lightened**) **1** to make or become less heavy. **2** (*often* **lighten up**) to make or become happier or more cheerful. **3** to make (a problem, unhappy mood, etc.) less.

lighter¹ *noun* a device for lighting, e.g., cigarettes.

lighter² *noun* a large, open boat used for transferring goods to and from ships.

lightheaded *adj.* **1** dizzy. **2** lightheartedly silly. ▸ **lightheadedly** *adv.* ▸ **lightheadedness** *noun*

lighthearted *adj.* **1** happy and carefree. **2** cheerful and amusing. ▸ **lightheartedly** *adv.* ▸ **lightheartedness** *noun*

lighthouse *noun* a tall building on a coast or on an island, having a flashing light to guide ships or warn of rocks, etc.

lighting *noun* **1** equipment for providing light. **2** the quality or type of light produced.

lightning *noun* a gigantic spark produced, e.g., between a cloud and Earth's surface, accompanied by thunder. **—adj.** very quick and sudden.

lightning bug a firefly.

lightning rod a metal rod on the roof of a building that protects the building from lightning by diverting electrical discharge.

lights *pl. noun* the lungs of an animal, used for food.

lightweight *adj.* **1** light in weight. **2** having little importance or authority. **—noun 1** a person or thing having little importance or authority. **2** a person or thing of little physical weight. **3** a boxer, wrestler, or weightlifter of not more than a specified weight, 135 lbs. (57–61 kg).

light-year *noun* the distance traveled by a beam of light in one year, equal to about 5.88 trillion mi. or 9.46 trillion km.

lignite *noun* a soft, brown coal. *Also called* **brown coal.**

like¹ *adj.* having the same or almost the same characteristics: *like opinions.* ⊟ ALIKE, ANALOGOUS, COMPARABLE, SIMILAR ⊟ DIFFERENT, DISSIMILAR, UNALIKE, UNLIKE. **—prep. 1** typical of: *It's just like them to forget.* **2** in the same manner as; to the same extent as: *studied like mad.* **—adv. 1** *old use* likely: *She'll be on time, like as not.* **2** *nonstand.* used for emphasis or to insert a pause: *Like, I really don't want to do this.* **—conj. 1** *colloq.* as if. **2** as. **—noun** the equal of a person or thing: *compare like with like.*

like² *verb trans.* (**liked, liking**) **1** to be pleased with; to find pleasant or agreeable. **2** to be fond of. **3** to prefer: *She likes her tea without sugar.* **4** to wish, or wish for: *Would you like to help?* **—noun** (*often* **likes**) a thing liked. ▸ **likeable** or **likable** *adj.*

-like *combining form* forming words denoting resembling, suitable for, or characteristic of: *childlike.*

likely *adj.* **1** probable. **2** suitable or useful for a particular purpose. **—adv.** probably. ▸ **likelihood** *noun*

like-minded *adj.* having similar opinions, tastes, or purposes.

liken *verb trans.* (**likened, likening**) (**liken (one thing) to (another)**) to think or speak of two things as comparable.

likeness *noun* **1** a similarity. **2** a person or thing that is like someone or something else. **3** a portrait.

likewise *adv.* **1** in the same or a similar manner. **2** also.

liking *noun* **1** a taste or preference: *a liking for chocolates.* **2** satisfaction.

lilac (lɪˈlăk, -lək) *noun* **1** a small tree that has large, dense, conical, drooping heads of small purple or white flowers. **2** a pale pinkish-purple color. **—adj.** of a lilac color.

lilt *noun* **1 a** a light, graceful, swinging rhythm. **b** a tune, song, or voice with such a rhythm. **2** a springing, swinging walk. **—verb intrans.** (**lilted, lilting**) to speak, sing, or move with a lilt. ▸ **lilting** *adj.*

lily *noun* (*pl.* **lilies**) **1** a plant that grows from bulbs, with narrow leaves and white or brightly colored flowers on tall stems. **2** a flowering plant, e.g., the water lily, that resembles a true lily. —*adj.* pale; white.

lima bean (lī'mə) **1** a plant widely cultivated for its broad, flat, edible seeds. **2** a seed of the plant. *Also called* **butter bean**.

limb *noun* **1** an arm, leg, or wing. **2** a main branch on a tree. **3** a branch or section of an organization. ▸ **limbed** *adj.* ▸ **limbless** *adj.*

limber *adj.* **1** having an elastic, resilient character or quality. **2** exhibiting ease and freedom in body movements. —*verb trans., intrans.* (**limbered, limbering**) (*often* **limber up**) to stretch and warm up before exercise.

limbo *noun* (*pl.* **limbos**) **1** *Christianity* an area between heaven and hell, reserved for the unbaptized dead. **2** a state of uncertainty or waiting. **3** a place of oblivion or neglect.

lime¹ *noun* **1** calcium oxide. **2** calcium hydroxide (slaked or hydrated lime). —*verb trans.* (**limed, liming**) to apply (ground limestone) as a fertilizer to soil. ▸ **limy** *adj.*

lime² *noun* **1** a citrus tree cultivated for its small green or yellowish-green fruits. **2** the edible fruit of this tree, which has sour juicy flesh. **3** the green color of this fruit. —*adj.* of a lime-green color. ▸ **limy** *adj.*

lime³ *noun* **1** the linden. **2** the wood of this tree.

limelight *noun* the glare of publicity.

limerick *noun* a humorous poem of five lines with an *aabba* rhyme-scheme.

After Limerick in Ireland, the name of which was repeated in nonsense songs in an old Victorian parlor game

limestone *noun* a rock composed mainly of calcium carbonate, e.g., chalk.

limit *noun* **1** a point, degree, or amount beyond which something does not or may not pass. **2** (*often* **limits**) the boundary or edge of an area. **3** the greatest or smallest extent, degree, etc., allowed. **4** (**the limit**) *colloq.* an intolerable or extremely annoying person, thing, or situation. —*verb trans.* (**limited, limiting**) to bound; to restrict. ▸ **limitation** *noun* ▸ **limitless** *adj.*

limited *adj.* **1** having a limit. **2** restricted; incomplete.

limited company (ABBREV. **Ltd.**) a business company owned by shareholders who are responsible for its debts only to the extent of the money they have put into it. *Also called* **limited liability company**.

limousine (lĭm'ə-zēn,, lĭm,ə-zēn') *noun* a large, luxurious automobile, esp. one with a screen separating the driver and passengers. *Also called colloq.* **limo**.

Named after a type of cloak worn in Limousin in France, because the car's roof was supposedly similar in shape

limp¹ *verb intrans.* (**limped, limping**) **1** to walk with an awkward or uneven step, because one leg is weak or injured. **2** *of a damaged ship or aircraft* to move with difficulty. —*noun* a limping walk. ▸ **limpingly** *adv.*

limp² *adj.* **1** not stiff or firm; hanging loosely. **2** having little or no energy or vitality; drooping. ▸ **limply** *adv.* ▸ **limpness** *noun*

limpet *noun* **1** a marine mollusk with a ridged conical shell, that clings firmly to rocks, etc. **2** a person difficult to get rid of.

limpid *adj., of water, eyes, etc.* clear; transparent. ▸ **limpidity** *noun* ▸ **limpidly** *adv.*

limy *see* **lime¹,²**

linage (lī'nĭj) *noun* **1** the number of lines to a page. **2** payment by the line.

linchpin *or* **lynchpin** *noun* **1** a pin-shaped rod passed through an axle to keep a wheel in place. **2** a person or thing essential to a business, plan, etc.

line¹ *noun* **1** a long, narrow mark, streak, or stripe. **2** the use of such marks in art. **3** a length of thread, rope, wire, etc., esp. for a specific purpose. **4** a wrinkle or furrow, esp. in the skin. **5** the path that a moving object is considered to leave behind it. **6** (*often* **lines**) an outline or shape: *a car noted for its clean lines.* **7** a row. **8** a row of words. **9** (**lines**) the words of an actor's part. **10** *Mus.* **a** any one of the five horizontal marks forming a staff. **b** a series of notes forming a melody. **11** *colloq.* a short letter. **12** a series of people coming one after the other, esp. in the same family or profession: *comes from a long line of doctors.* **13** a field of activity or interest: *one's line of business.* **14** the manufacturing process: *a production line.* **15** a boundary. **16 a** *Sport* one of several white marks showing a playing area, racetrack, etc., on a field. **b** *Football* the line of scrimmage, or the linemen regarded collectively. **17 a** a continuous system, e.g., of telephone cables. **b** a telephone connection. **18** a row of people waiting, e.g., for entry, exit, or for transportation. —*verb trans., intrans.* (**lined, lining**) **1** to mark or cover with or as if with lines. **2** to form a line along. —**in line for** likely to get. **lay it on the line** to speak frankly. **out of line** unruly and uncalled for; wrong.

line² *verb trans.* (**lined, lining**) **1** to cover the inside of (e.g., a garment or box) with another material. **2** to cover as if with a lining: *lined the walls with books.* ▸ **liner** *noun*

lineage (lĭn'ē-ĭj) *noun* ancestry.

lineal (lĭn'ē-əl) *adj.* **1** of *family descent* in a direct line. **2** linear (sense 1). ▸ **lineally** *adv.*

lineament (lĭn'ē-ə-mənt) *noun* (*usu.* **lineaments**) a feature or distinguishing mark, esp. on the face.

linear (lĭn'ē-ər) *adj.* **1** of, consisting of, or like a line or lines. **2** relating to length. **3** *Math.* involving one dimension only. ▸ **linearity** *noun*

line drive *Baseball* a ball that is batted hard, and that moves in a straight line. *Also called* **frozen rope.**

lineman *noun* **1** *Football* a player who is positioned on the forward line. **2** a person employed to install or fix telecommunications and electrical lines.

linen (lĭn'ən) *noun* **1** cloth made from flax. **2** household articles made from linen. **3** underclothes, orig. made from linen. —*adj.* of or resembling linen.

line of scrimmage (ABBREV. **LOS**) *Football* an imaginary line on a football field, upon which the ball is positioned and to which players in both teams line up to start or restart the play.

line printer *Comput.* an output device that prints a complete line of characters at a time.

liner *noun* **1** one that makes or draws lines. **2** a large passenger ship or aircraft.

linesman *noun* an official at a boundary line in some sports, whose job is to indicate when the ball has gone out of play or out of bounds or that violations have occurred.

lineup *noun* **1** a line of things or people. **2** *Sport* players selected to start a game. **3** a group of people, including a suspect, positioned in a row for possible identification by a witness to a crime.

-ling *suffix* forming words denoting: **1** a young, small, or minor person or thing: *duckling.* **2** a person connected with something or having a stipulated quality: *earthling / weakling.*

linger *verb intrans.* (**lingered, lingering**) **1** to be slow to depart; to delay. **2** (**linger over** (**something**)) to spend a long time with (it) or doing (it). ▸ **lingerer** *noun* ▸ **lingering** *adj.* ▸ **lingeringly** *adv.*

lingerie (län'jə-rā', län'zhə-) *noun* women's underwear and nightclothes.

lingo *noun* (*pl.* **lingos**) *colloq.* **1** language. **2** the specialized vocabulary of a particular group of people or profession.

lingua franca (lĭng'gwə-frăng'kə) (*pl.* **lingua francas**) a language used as a means of mutual communication by speakers of other languages.

lingual *adj.* **1** relating to the tongue. **2** of or relating to speech or languages. ▸ **lingually** *adv.*

linguist *noun* **1** a person who has a good knowledge of languages. **2** a person who studies linguistics.

linguistics *noun* (*sing.*) the scientific study of language. ▸ **linguistic** *adj.* ▸ **linguistically** *adv.*

liniment *noun* a medicated liquid rubbed onto the skin.

lining *noun* a piece of material used to line garments, boxes, etc.

link *noun* **1** a ring of a chain. **2** a person or thing that serves to connect. —*verb trans.*, *intrans.* (**linked, linking**) **1** to connect or join. **2** to be or become connected.

linkage (lĭng'kĭj) *noun* **1** the act or process of linking. **2** in negotiations, making agreement on one issue contingent upon progress on another issue.

links *pl. noun* a golf course.

linkup *noun* a connection or union, esp. of two different systems.

linoleum (lĭn-ō'lē-əm) *noun* a smooth, hard-wearing floor covering, made of canvas coated with linseed oil and cork.

linseed oil a pale yellow oil, extracted from flax seed (linseed), which hardens on exposure to air, and is used in paints, varnishes, enamels, etc.

lint *noun* fine, very small pieces of wool, cotton, etc.; fluff.

lintel *noun* a horizontal beam placed over a doorway or window.

lion *noun* **1** a large African wild cat with a tawny coat and tufted tail. **2** a brave or celebrated person. **3** (**the Lion**) the constellation and sign of the zodiac Leo. —**the lion's share** the largest share.

lioness *noun* a female lion.

lionhearted *adj.* very brave.

lionize *verb trans.* (**lionized, lionizing**) to treat as a celebrity or hero.

lip *noun* **1** either of the two fleshy folds around the opening to the mouth. **2** a structure that resembles this, e.g., the projecting part of the rim of a jug. **3** *slang* insolent remarks or retorts. ▸ **lipped** *adj.*

liposuction (lĭ,pō-sək'shən) *noun* removal of excess subcutaneous fat from parts of the body by means of suction.

lip-read *verb intrans.* (**lip-read, lip-reading**) *esp. of a hearing-impaired person* to understand what another person is saying by watching the movement of the lips. ▸ **lip-reader** *noun*

lip service expressed approval, loyalty, or agreement that is unsupported by actual conviction or serious action.

lipstick *noun* cosmetic coloring for the lips; a stick of this.

liquefy *verb trans.*, *intrans.* (**liquefied, liquefying, liquefies**) to make or become liquid. ▸ **liquefaction** *noun*

liqueur (lĭ-kər', -kyŏŏr') *noun* a strong, sweet, alcoholic drink, taken esp. at the end of a meal.

liquid *noun* a substance, e.g., water, in a state in which it readily flows, changes shape, and forms a level surface. —*adj.* **1** being or relating to a liquid. **2** *of assets* easily changed into cash. ► **liquidize** *verb trans.*

liquidate *verb trans.* (**liquidated, liquidating**) **1** to settle (the business affairs of, e.g., a corporation or firm) and have its debts and assets calculated. **2** to turn (assets) into cash. **3** to pay off (a debt). **4** to kill. ► **liquidation** *noun* ► **liquidator** *noun*

liquor (lĭk'ər) *noun* **1** strong alcoholic drink. **2** liquid produced in cooking.

lira (lĭr'ə, lē'rə) *noun* (*pl.* **lire, liras**) the standard unit of currency in Italy and Turkey.

lisp *verb intrans., trans.* (**lisped, lisping**) **1** to pronounce *s* as *th* in *thin* and *z* as *th* in *this*, as a speech defect. **2** to pronounce (something) in this way. —*noun* the act or habit of lisping.

lissome or **lissom** *adj.* graceful and supple in shape and movement.

list[1] *noun* a series of names, numbers, prices, etc., written down or said one after the other. —*verb trans.* (**listed, listing**) **1** to make a list of. **2** to add to a list.

list[2] *verb intrans.* (**listed, listing**) *esp. of ships* to lean over to one side. —*noun* the act of listing or a listing position.

listen *verb intrans.* (**listened, listening**) **1** to give attention so as to hear something. **2** to follow advice: *he wouldn't listen to me.* —*noun* an act or period of listening. ► **listener** *noun*

listless *adj.* lacking in energy or vitality. ► **listlessly** *adv.* ► **listlessness** *noun*

lit *see* **light**[1], **light**[3].

litany (lĭt'n-ē) *noun* (*pl.* **litanies**) **1** a series of prayers or supplications with a response repeated several times by a church congregation. **2** a long, tedious list.

litchi *noun same as* **lychee**.

liter (lēt'ər) *noun* (ABBREV. **l**) the basic unit of volume in the metric system, equal to about 1.056 liquid quarts, 0.908 dry quart, or 0.264 gallon.

literacy *noun* the ability to read and write. ► **literate** *adj.*

literal *adj.* **1** following the exact meaning of words or a text. **2** *of a translation* exactly following the words of the original. **3** a factual and objective. **b** exact: *the literal truth.* ► **literally** *adv.* ► **literalness** *noun*

> *Usage* Though sense 2 is often regarded as incorrect, it is nevertheless the more common usage.

literary *adj.* **1** relating to or concerned with

literature or the writing of books. **2** *of a person* knowing a great deal about literature. **3** *of a word* used esp. in older literature.

literate *see* **literacy**.

literature *noun* **1** novels, poems, and plays that are valued for language and content. **2** the written works of a particular country or period in time. **3** *colloq.* printed matter, esp. advertising leaflets.

lithe (līth, lĭth) *adj.* **1** bending easily; elastic and resilient. **2** exhibiting ease and freedom in body movements: *a lithe modern dancer.* ⊟ LIMBER, LISSOME, SUPPLE ⊟ STIFF, WOODEN. ► **lithely** *adv.* ► **litheness** *noun*

lithium *noun Chem.* (SYMBOL **Li**) a soft silvery metal.

litho *noun* (*pl.* **lithos**) **1** a lithograph. **2** lithography. —*adj.* lithographic. —*verb trans.* (**lithoed, lithoing, lithoes**) to lithograph.

lithography *noun* a method of printing using a stone or metal plate which has been treated so that the ink adheres only to the design or image to be printed. ► **lithograph** *noun, verb* ► **lithographer** *noun* ► **lithographic** *adj.* ► **lithographically** *adv.*

litigate (lĭt'ĭ-gāt,) *verb intrans., trans.* (**litigated, litigating**) *Law* **1** to be involved in a lawsuit. **2** to contest (a claim, etc.) in a lawsuit. ► **litigant** *noun* ► **litigation** *noun*

litigious (lĭ-tĭj'əs) *adj. Law* **1** relating to litigation or lawsuits. **2** often taking legal action over arguments, problems, etc. ► **litigiously** *adv.*

litmus *noun Chem.* a dye which turns red in acid solutions and blue in alkaline ones.

litmus paper paper impregnated with litmus.

litmus test 1 a test using litmus paper. **2** a test or trial that uses a single issue to determine the result: *Attitude to gun control became the litmus test of electability.*

litter *noun* **1** a mess of paper, trash, etc., in a public place. **2** a scattered or confused collection of objects. **3** a straw, hay, etc., used as bedding for livestock. **b** an absorbent material used to cover the bottom of an animal's excretory box or its cage. **4** a number of animals born to the same mother at one time. —*verb trans., intrans.* (**littered, littering**) **1** to make (a place) messy by spreading trash or objects. **2** *of objects* to lie messily around (a place).

litterbug *noun colloq.* a person who drops litter in public places.

little *adj.* (**littler, littlest; less, least**) **1** small in size, extent, or amount. **2** young or younger. **3** small in importance; trivial, petty: *funny little ways.* **4** small-minded or mean. —*noun* something small in size, amount, or extent. —*adv.* (**less, least**) **1** (a

little) to a small degree or extent. **2** not much or at all.

littoral (lĭt'ə-rəl, lĭt,ə-răl') adj. relating to the shore of a lake, sea, etc. —noun a shore or coastal strip of land.

liturgy (lĭt'ər-jē) noun (pl. **liturgies**) the standard form of service in a church. ▸ **liturgical** adj. ▸ **liturgically** adv.

livable adj. **1** of a house, etc. fit to live in. **2** of life worth living; tolerable.

live¹ (lĭv) verb intrans., trans. (**lived, living**) **1** to have life; to be alive. **2** to continue to be alive; to escape death. **3** to continue or last. **4** (**live with (something)**) to continue to, suffer from or be haunted by the memory of (it): He will live with the mistake for the rest of his life. **5** to have a home or dwelling. **6** to lead one's life in a certain way: live well. **7** (**live by, on** or **off**) to support one's life; to make a living: live by farming / live on rice / live off the land. ▸ **liver** noun

live² (lĭv) adj. **1** of an organism showing the characteristics of life; alive. **2** of a radio or television broadcast heard or seen as the actual event takes place, and not from a recording. **3** of a record, CD, etc. recorded during a performance. **4** of a wire connected to an active source of electrical power. —adv. at, during, or as a live performance.

livelihood noun a means of living, esp. of earning money to live on.

livelong adj. in all its length: sang the livelong day.

lively adj. (**livelier, liveliest**) **1** full of life, energy, and high spirits. **2** brisk: a lively tune. **3** vivid; bright. ▸ **liveliness** noun

liven verb trans., intrans. (**livened, livening**) (usu. **liven up**) to make or become lively.

liver noun a large, dark red organ in the abdominal cavity, whose main function is to regulate the composition of the blood.

liverwort noun a plant closely related to moss.

livery (lĭv'ə-rē) noun (pl. **liveries**) **1** a distinctive uniform. **2** the feeding, care, stabling, and renting of horses for money: a livery stable. ▸ **liveried** adj.

lives noun see **life**.

livestock noun domesticated animals, esp. cattle, sheep, horses, hogs, and poultry.

live wire colloq. a person who is full of energy and enthusiasm.

livid adj. **1** of a bruise black and blue. **2** white or very pale. **3** colloq. extremely angry.

living adj. **1** alive. **2** currently in existence, use, or activity. **3** of a likeness exact. —noun **1** livelihood. **2** a manner of life: fast living.

living room noun a room in a house, etc., for social and recreational purposes. Also called **sitting room**.

lizard noun a usu. fairly small and very active four-legged, long-tailed reptile.

'll contr. shall; will: I'll / they'll.

llama (läm'ə, yäm'ə) noun a domesticated hoofed mammal of S America, related to the camel, with a long shaggy coat.

LL.B. abbrev. legum baccalaureus (Latin), Bachelor of Laws.

LL.D. abbrev. legum doctor (Latin), Doctor of Laws.

load noun **1** something carried; a burden. **2** something that is or can be carried at one time. **3** (**loads**) colloq. a large amount. **4** work, duties, feelings, etc., that are oppressive and heavy to bear. —verb trans., intrans. (**loaded, loading**) **1** to put (an amount or quantity of something) on or in (a ship, vehicle, washing machine, etc.). **2** (**load up**) to take or pick up a load. **3** to be a weight on or burden to. **4** (**load (someone) with (something)**) to give (something) in great amounts to (someone). **5** to put (film, etc.) into a (camera, etc.). **6** to put (ammunition) into (a firearm).

loaded adj. **1 a** carrying a load. **b** holding, containing, or having as much as possible: waiters holding loaded trays. **2** of a gun containing bullets. **3** of a person **a** colloq. rich. **b** slang drunk. **4** of a question intended to elicit a particular response by the way it is phrased or by an implicit assumption contained in it.

loadstar noun same as **lodestar**.

loadstone noun same as **lodestone**.

loaf¹ noun (pl. **loaves**) **1** a mass of bread for baking or when baked. **2** a quantity of food, e.g., meat, formed into a regular shape.

loaf² verb intrans., trans. (**loafed, loafing**) **1** to do nothing. ◼ IDLE, LAZE, LOLL, LOUNGE. **2** to spend or pass idly. ▸ **loafer** noun

loam noun a dark, fertile, easily worked soil. ▸ **loamy** adj.

loan noun something that is lent, esp. money. —verb trans. (**loaned, loaning**) to lend (esp. money).

> **Usage** The transitive usage of the verb loan is now considered acceptable in contexts where a physical transaction is stipulated (He loaned me some money). In figurative contexts, lend is the word of choice (Darkness lends an air of mystery to the film).

loanword noun a word taken into one language directly from another.

loath (lōth, lōth) adj. unwilling; reluctant.

loathe (lōth) verb trans. (**loathed, loathing**) to feel intense dislike or disgust for. ▸ **loathing** noun

loathsome adj. causing intense dislike or disgust.

loaves see **loaf¹**.

lob *noun Tennis* a ball hit in a high overhead path. —*verb trans.* (**lobbed, lobbing**) to hit or send (e.g., a ball) in a high path.

lobby *noun* (*pl.* **lobbies**) 1 a small entrance hall, passage, or waiting room from which several rooms open. 2 a group of people who try to influence politicians, etc., in favor of a particular cause. —*verb trans.* (**lobbied, lobbying, lobbies**) to try to influence (the government, politicians, etc.) in favor of a particular cause. ▸ **lobbyist** *noun*

lobe *noun* 1 an earlobe. 2 a usu. rounded subdivision of an organ or gland of the body, esp. the lungs, liver, or brain. ▸ **lobed** *adj.*

lobotomy (lə-băt′ə-mē) *noun* (*pl.* **lobotomies**) the surgical operation of cutting into a lobe of any organ of the body, esp. the brain.

lobster *noun* a large, long, marine crustacean with four pairs of legs and a pair of large claws, also used as food.

local *adj.* 1 of or belonging to a particular place. 2 of or belonging to one's home area or neighborhood. 3 of a train or bus stopping at all the stations or stops in a neighborhood or small area. 4 *Med.* affecting or confined to a small area or part: *a local anesthetic.* —*noun* 1 a person living in a particular area. 2 a bus or train which stops at all the stations in a neighborhood or small area. 3 a local anesthetic. ▸ **locally** *adv.*

locale (lō-kăl′) *noun* the scene of some event or occurrence.

locality (lō-kăl′ət-ē) *noun* (*pl.* **localities**) a district or neighborhood.

localize (lō′kə-līz,) *verb trans.* (**localized, localizing**) 1 to restrict to a place or area. 2 to mark with the characteristics of a particular place. ▸ **localization** *noun*

locate (lō′kāt,) *verb trans.* (**located, locating**) 1 to set in a particular place or position. 2 to find the exact position of. 3 to establish in a proper place or position. 4 to establish oneself in business or residence in an area: *The company plans to locate in New Jersey.*

location *noun* 1 a position or situation. 2 the act of locating or process of being located. 3 an authentic setting for making a movie or broadcast, as distinct from an artificial setting in a studio: *made on location in Spain.*

loc. cit. *abbrev. loco citato* (Latin), in the passage just quoted.

loci *see* **locus**.

lock¹ *noun* 1 a device that fastens shut a door or lid, prevents a machine operating, etc. 2 an enclosed section of a canal or river in which the water level can be raised or lowered. 3 a state of being jammed or locked together, and completely immovable. 4 the part of a

gun that explodes the charge. —*verb trans.*, *intrans.* (**locked, locking**) 1 to fasten (a door, box, etc.) with a lock. 2 *of a door, etc.* to have the means to be locked. 3 to shut up or secure (a building) by locking the doors and windows. 4 to jam or cause to jam. 5 to fasten or cause to be fastened so as to prevent movement. 6 to hold closely in an embrace or tussle. ▸ **lockable** *adj.*

lock² *noun* 1 a section or curl of hair. 2 (**locks**) hair.

locker *noun* a small, lockable cupboard.

locker room a room furnished with lockers, e.g., for workers or players of sports to change clothes and stow equipment.

locket *noun* a small, ornamented case for holding a personal photograph or memento, worn on a chain round the neck.

lockjaw *noun* 1 tetanus (sense 1). 2 difficulty in opening the mouth caused by spasm of the jaw muscles.

lockout *noun* the exclusion of employees by the management from their place of work during a labor dispute. *Also called* **shutout.**

locksmith *noun* a person or a firm that makes and repairs locks.

loco *adj. slang* crazy; mad.

locomotion *noun* the ability to move, or act of moving, from place to place. ▸ **locomotor** *adj.*

locomotive *noun* a railroad engine for pulling trains. —*adj.* relating to or causing locomotion.

locoweed *noun* a plant that causes severe poisoning in livestock.

locus *noun* (*pl.* **loci**) an exact place or location.

locust *noun* 1 a a large grasshopper. b the cicada. 2 a a tree that has drooping clusters of white sweet-smelling flowers and hard wood. b the wood of a locust tree.

locution *noun* 1 a style of speech. 2 a word, phrase, or sentence.

lode *noun* a deposit of ore occurring as one or more veins in rock.

lodestar *or* **loadstar** *noun* 1 a star that can be used as a guide, esp. the Pole Star. 2 a guide or guiding principle.

lodestone *or* **loadstone** *noun* a naturally occurring variety of iron oxide that has magnetic properties.

lodge *noun* 1 a small house at the gate to the grounds of a large house. 2 a small house in the country for hunters, fishers, or skiers. 3 the meeting place of a branch of a fraternity or other society; the members of the branch. —*verb intrans.*, *trans.* (**lodged, lodging**) 1 a to live in rented accommodations, esp. in someone else's home, usu. temporarily. b to provide with rented, usu. temporary accommodations, esp. in one's home. 2 to bring (a charge or accusation), or make (an official complaint), against someone. **3** to become or cause to become firmly fixed. **4** (**be lodged in** or **with** (**someone**)) of power, authority, etc. to belong to (someone).

lodging noun **1** (usu. **lodgings**) a room or rooms rented in someone else's home. **2** temporary accommodations. ▸ **lodger** noun

loft noun **1** a large room or space under a roof. **2** a gallery in a church or hall. **3** an upper room used for storage. **b** an area over a stable or in the top of a barn for storing hay. **4** Golf a stroke that causes a golf ball to rise high. —verb trans. (**lofted, lofting**) to strike, kick, or throw (a ball, etc.) high in the air.

lofty adj. (**loftier, loftiest**) **1** of great or imposing height. **2** of high or noble character. **3** proud or haughty. ▸ **loftily** adv. ▸ **loftiness** noun

log¹ noun **1** part of a tree trunk or thick branch, e.g., when cut for firewood. **2** a detailed record of events occurring during a voyage. **3** a logbook. —verb trans., intrans. (**logged, logging**) **1** to record (distances covered, events, etc.) in a book or logbook. **2** to cut (trees, etc.) into logs. **3** to cut logs. —**log in** or **on** Comput. to gain access to a system by keying in an appropriate command. **log out** or **off** Comput. to relinquish access to a system by keying in a closing command.

log² noun Math. a logarithm.

loganberry noun (pl. **loganberries**) **1** a trailing prickly plant cultivated for its edible fruit. **2** the reddish-purple fruit.

logarithm noun Math. the power to which a number a must be raised in order to give another number b. ▸ **logarithmic** adj. ▸ **logarithmically** adv.

logbook noun a book containing an official record of the voyage of a ship, aircraft, etc., including details of crew and any incidents that occur.

loggerhead noun a large marine turtle with a beaked head. —**at loggerheads** arguing or disagreeing fiercely.

logic noun **1** the science of reasoning. **2** correct or incorrect use of reasoning; the ability to reason soundly. **3** Comput. the arrangement of circuit elements within a computer that enables it to perform arithmetical and logical operations. ▸ **logician** noun

logical adj. **1** of or according to logic. **2** correctly reasoned or thought out. **3** able to reason correctly. **4** following reasonably or necessarily from facts or events. ▸ **logicality** noun ▸ **logically** adv.

-logical or **-logic** combining form forming adjectives corresponding to nouns in -logy: archeological / pathological.

logistics noun (sing., pl.) the art of moving and supplying troops and military equipment. ▸ **logistic** or **logistical** adj. ▸ **logistically** adv.

logjam noun **1** a jam caused by logs being floated down a river. **2** a complete stopping of movement or progress.

logo (lō'gō) noun (pl. **logos**) a small design used as the symbol of an organization.

logograph or **logogram** noun an ideogram.

-logy or **-ology** combining form forming words denoting: **1** a science or study: geology. **2** writing or speech: trilogy.

loin noun **1** the lower back and sides of the body. **2** a cut of meat from this part of an animal. **3** (**loins**) the hips and the top of the legs, esp. the crotch.

loincloth noun a piece of material worn around the hips, esp. as a sole garment.

loiter verb intrans. (**loitered, loitering**) **1** to work slowly and idly. **2** to stand around or pass one's time doing nothing. ▸ **loiterer** noun.

loll verb intrans. (**lolled, lolling**) **1** (**loll about**) to lie or sit about lazily; to lounge or sprawl. **2** of the tongue to hang down or out.

lollipop noun hard, boiled candy on a stick.

lone adj. **1** of a person alone. **2** of a place lonely. **3** of a thing standing alone.

lonely adj. (**lonelier, loneliest**) **1** of a person sad because without companions or friends. **2** without companionship. **3** of a place isolated and unfrequented. ▸ **loneliness** noun

loner noun a person who prefers to be alone and who avoids close relationships.

lonesome adj. **1** sad and lonely. **2** of a place lonely.

long¹ adj. **1** measuring a great distance from end to end or lasting for an extended period of time. ▣ ELONGATE, ELONGATED, EXTENDED, LENGTHY ▣ BRIEF, SHORT. **2** measuring a specified amount in space or time: six feet long. **3** having a large number of items. **4** measuring more than average, expected, or wanted: a long sermon. **5** greater in value, amount, etc., than usual or expected. **6** Phonetics, of a vowel or syllable having the greater of two recognized lengths. —adv. **1** for, during, or by an extended period of time: long ago. **2** throughout the whole time: all night long. —noun something that is long, esp. a long period of time. —**as long as** or **so long as 1** provided that. **2** during the time that; while. **no longer** not now, although in the past.

long² verb intrans. (**longed, longing**) (**long for** (**something** or **someone**)) to want (someone or something) intensely. ▸ **longing** adj., noun ▸ **longingly** adv.

longbow noun a large bow drawn by hand.

longevity noun great length of life.

longhand *noun* ordinary handwriting.

long haul the carrying of cargo or passengers over a long distance.

long horn a breed of cattle with long horns.

longhouse *noun* a long communal dwelling of Native Americans.

longitude (län'jĭ-tood,, lŏn'-, -tyōōd,) *noun* any of a series of imaginary circles that pass around Earth through both poles. *See also* **latitude** (sense 1) ▸ **longitudinal** *adj.* ▸ **longitudinally** *adv.*

long jump a track-and-field event in which competitors jump as far as possible along the ground from a running start.

long-playing *adj., of a phonograph record* with each side playing for 20 to 30 minutes, turning at 33⅓ revolutions per minute.

long-range *adj.* 1 able to reach remote or far-off targets or destinations. 2 *of a weather forecast* covering a period of several weeks or more.

longshoreman *noun* a person who loads and unloads ships at a port.

long shot *colloq.* a guess, attempt, etc., that is unlikely to be successful.

long-standing *adj.* having existed or continued for a long time.

long-suffering *adj.* patiently tolerating difficulties and hardship.

long-term *adj., of a plan, etc.* occurring in or concerned with the distant future.

long ton a ton (sense 2).

long wave an electromagnetic wave, esp. a radio wave, with a wavelength greater than 1,000 m.

long-winded *adj.* using too many words. ▸ **long-windedly** *adv.* ▸ **long-windedness** *noun*

loofa or **loofah** *noun* the long, thin, dried inner part of a tropical fruit, used as a sponge.

look *verb intrans., trans.* (**looked, looking**) 1 (**look at**) to turn the eyes toward (someone or something) so as to see. 2 to seem to be or appear. 3 to face or be turned toward: *a window looking south.* 4 (**look for (something))** to search for (it). 5 (**look into (something))** to investigate (it). —*noun* 1 an act of looking; a glance or view. 2 the general appearance of a thing or person. 3 (**looks**) beauty; attractiveness. —*interj.* (*also* **look here**) used to call attention to something or to express protest. —**look after (someone** or **something)** to attend to or take care of (someone or something). **look on** to watch without taking part. **look out** to keep watch and be careful. **look (something) over** to check (it) cursorily. **look up** to show signs of improving. **look (someone) up** *colloq.* to visit (someone), often after having not seen the person for a long time. **look (something)**

up to search for (an item of information) in a reference book.

looker *noun colloq.* an attractive person.

look-in *noun* 1 a quick glance at something. 2 a short visit.

looking glass a mirror.

lookout *noun* 1 a a careful watch. b a place from which such a watch can be kept. 2 a person set to watch, e.g., on board ship.

look-see *noun colloq.* a brief look around or inspection.

loom¹ *noun* a weaving machine.

loom² *verb intrans.* (**loomed, looming**) 1 to appear, usu. in a large or threatening form. 2 *of an event* to be imminent, esp. in a menacing or threatening way.

loon *noun* a diving ducklike bird with a slender body, a sharp beak, and a laughlike call.

loony *slang noun* (*pl.* **loonies**) an insane person or a person who behaves in a very bizarre manner. —*adj.* (**loonier, looniest**) crazy; insane.

loop *noun* 1 an oval coil in a piece of rope, chain, etc., formed as it crosses over itself. 2 a similar oval or U-shaped bend, e.g., in a river. 3 *Comput.* a sequence of instructions in a program that is executed a fixed number of times, or repeatedly performed until a predetermined condition has been satisfied. —*verb trans.* (**looped, looping**) 1 to fasten with or enclose in a loop. 2 to form into loops or a loop.

loophole (loop'hōl,, loo'pōl,) *noun* a means, usu. based on a legal weakness or oversight, of avoiding obeying a rule or law or fulfilling a contract without formally breaking it.

loopy *adj.* (**loopier, loopiest**) *slang* mad; crazy; bizarre.

loose (loos) *adj.* 1 not or no longer tied or held in confinement; free. 2 not tight or close-fitting. 3 not held together; not fastened or firmly fixed in place. 4 not tightly packed or compact. 5 vague or inexact: *a loose translation.* 6 immoral or promiscuous. 7 indiscreet: *loose talk.* 8 *Sport, of a ball, etc.* in play but not under a player's control. —*verb trans., intrans.* (**loosed, loosing**) 1 to release or set free. 2 to unfasten or untie. 3 to make less tight, compact, or dense. 4 to relax: *loose one's hold on a rope.* 5 to discharge (a gun, bullet, arrow, etc.). ▸ **loosely** *adv.* ▸ **looseness** *noun*

loosen *verb trans., intrans.* (**loosened, loosening**) 1 to make or become loose or looser. 2 (**loosen up**) to make or become less tense, rigid, or stiff.

loot *noun* 1 stolen goods, esp. those stolen from an enemy in wartime. 2 *slang* money. —*verb trans., intrans.* (**looted, looting**) to steal; to steal from (e.g., an enemy in wartime, or a place). ▸ **looter** *noun*

lop verb trans. (**lopped, lopping**) **1** (**lop off**) to cut off, esp. tree branches. **2** (**lop** (**something**) **off** or **away**) to cut away unnecessary parts of (something).

lope verb intrans. (**loped, loping**) to run with long, bounding steps. —noun a bounding leap.

lopsided adj. **1** with one side smaller, lower, or lighter than the other. **2** leaning over to one side; unbalanced.

loquacious adj. formal highly talkative. ► **loquaciously** adv. ► **loquaciousness** noun ► **loquacity** noun

lord noun **1** a master or ruler. **2** Hist. a feudal superior. **3** Brit. **a** a male member of the nobility. **b** (**Lord**) used as a title to address some noblemen. **4** (**Lord, the Lord**, or **Our Lord**) God, or Christ. —interj. (**Lord**) used to express surprise or dismay.

lordly adj. (**lordlier, lordliest**) arrogantly proud. ► **lordliness** noun

Lordship noun Brit. (**His** or **Your Lordship**) used as a title to address bishops, judges, and all peers except dukes.

Lord's Prayer a popular prayer of Christian worship, derived from Matthew 6:9–13. Also called **Our Father, Pater Noster**.

lore noun the whole body of knowledge, esp. traditional knowledge, on a subject.

lorgnette (lôrn-yĕt') noun eyeglasses or opera glasses on a long handle.

lorry noun (pl. **lorries**) Brit. a large truck.

lose (lōōz) verb trans., intrans. (**lost, losing**) **1** to no longer have, or to fail to keep or obtain, esp. by accident or through carelessness. **2** to be bereaved of. **3** to leave accidentally or be unable to find: lose one's way. **4** to fail to use or get; to miss: lose a good opportunity. **5** to fail to win (a game, battle, etc.). **6** to fail or cease to hear, see, or understand: lost the thread of his argument. **7** to waste (time, money, etc.); to use to no purpose. **8** to be in a worse position or suffer as the result of something. —**lose out** or **lose out on** (**something**) colloq. **1** to suffer loss or to be at a disadvantage. **2** to fail to get something one wants. ► **loser** noun

loss noun **1** the act or fact of losing or of being lost. **2** the thing, amount, etc., lost. **3** the detriment resulting from losing: a great loss to our company. —**at a loss** puzzled and uncertain.

loss-leader noun an item on sale at less than cost price, as a means of attracting customers for a wider range of goods.

lost verb see **lose**. —adj. **1** no longer to be found; missing. **2** unable to find one's way. **3** confused; puzzled.

lot noun **1** colloq. (often **a lot of** or **lots of**) a great number or amount. **2 a** something, e.g., a slip of paper, drawn from among several as a way of reaching a decision by chance: draw/cast lots. **b** this way of making a decision. **3** that which is in store in the future. **4** an item or set of items for sale by auction. **5** an area of land.

lotion noun a liquid for healing or cleaning the skin.

lottery noun (pl. **lotteries**) a system of raising money by selling tickets and giving prizes for those tickets drawn at random.

lotto noun a game like bingo.

lotus (lōt'əs) noun **1** a shrub whose fruit was thought by the ancient Greeks to produce a state of forgetfulness. **2** a water lily.

loud adj. **1 a** making noise. **b** making a great sound. ◼ EARSPLITTING, STENTORIAN, STENTORIOUS, THUNDEROUS ◼ LOW, SOFT. **c** capable of making a great sound. **2** shrill and insistent: loud complaints. **3** of colors or a design too bright; gaudy. **4** of behavior aggressively noisy and coarse. —adv. in a noisy manner. ► **loudly** adv. ► **loudness** noun

loudmouthed adj. colloq. noisily and aggressively boastful.

loudspeaker noun an electronic device that converts electrical signals into audible sound waves, used in radios, televisions, telephone receivers, hi-fi systems, etc.

lounge verb intrans. (**lounged, lounging**) **1** to lie or recline comfortably. **2** to do nothing. —noun **1** a room in a public building, e.g., in an airport, in which people wait; a waiting room. **2** a bar in which cocktails are served. **3** a long, backless sofa, often with a headrest at one end. ► **lounger** noun

lour (lowr) verb same as **lower**²

louse (lows) noun **1** (pl. **lice**) a small wingless insect that lives on the bodies of animals and birds, feeding on skin, blood, etc. **2** (pl. **louses**) slang a despicable person. —verb trans. (**loused, lousing**) (**louse** (**something**) **up**) to ruin or bungle (something).

lousy (low'zē) adj. (**lousier, lousiest**) **1** having lice. **2** slang very bad, unpleasant, or disgusting. ► **lousily** adv. ► **lousiness** noun

lout noun an aggressively rough, coarse male. ► **loutish** adj.

louver or **louvre** (lōō'vər) noun any one of a set of horizontal, sloping, overlapping slats in a door, etc., that let air in but keep rain and light out.

love noun **1** great affection for and devotion to another person. **2** strong sexual attraction. **3** sexual passion; sexual relations: one's love life. **4** a strong liking for something. **5** a person one loves. **6** Tennis, Squash no score. —verb trans. (**loved, loving**) **1** to feel great affection for. **2** to enjoy very much; to like. —**in love** (**with**) feeling love and sexual attraction for (someone). ► **lov-**

able or loveable adj. ▸ loveless adj.
▸ loving adj. ▸ lovingly adv.

lovebird noun 1 a small tropical parrot that mates for life. 2 (**lovebirds**) a couple deeply in love.

lovelorn adj. left by or pining for the person with whom one is in love.

lovely adj. (**lovelier, loveliest**) delighting the senses. ▸ **loveliness** noun

lovemaking noun sexual activity.

lover noun 1 a person in love with another, esp. a person having a romantic and sexual relationship. 2 (**lovers**) two people who are in love with one another or who are sharing a sexual relationship. 3 a person who is fond of something specified: a lover of dogs.

lovesick adj. sad or pining because of love.

loving cup a large, two-handled drinking cup.

low[1] (lō) adj. 1 less than average in height; not reaching 'to a high level. 2 situated close to the ground, to sea level, or to the horizon. 3 (**low in** (**something**)) containing less than the average amount. 4 of numbers small or reduced in amount. 5ʹa with little value or quality. b not costly. 6 (**low on** (**something**)) not having much left of (it). 7 of humble rank or position. 8 of sounds produced by slow vibrations and having a deep pitch. 9 unfavorable: a low opinion of them. —adv. 1 in or to a low position, state, or manner. 2 in a small quantity or to a small degree. 3 with a low voice; quietly. 4 at or in a low pitch. —noun 1 the position, level, etc., that is low or lowest. 2 Meteorol. an area of low atmospheric pressure. ▸ **lowness** noun

low[2] verb intrans. (**lowed, lowing**) to moo. —noun the mooing made by cattle.

low-born adj. of humble birth.

lowboy noun a relatively low chest of drawers.

lowbrow adj. having or involving tastes that are relatively popular and unintellectual. —noun a person with such tastes.

low-down colloq. adj. mean and dishonorable. —noun information, esp. when disreputable or acquired surreptitiously.

lower[1] (lō'ər) adj. not as high as something else in position, status, height, value, etc. —adv. in or to a position lower than usual or required or below that of others. —verb trans., intrans. (**lowered, lowering**) 1 a to make or become lower in amount, value, status, sound, etc. b to go or move down from a higher to a lower place or position. 2 to pull or let down.

lower[2] (low'ər, lō'ər) or **lour** verb intrans. (**lowered, lowering**) 1 to wrinkle one's forehead and draw one's eyebrows together, e.g., in disapproval, worry, etc. 2 of the sky, etc. to become dark or threaten inclement weather.

lower case Printing small letters as opposed to capitals. ▸ **lowercase** or **lower-case** adj.

lower class the social class regarded as being below the middle class. ▸ **lower-class** adj.

lowest common denominator Math. (ABBREV. **LCD, l.c.d.**) in a group of fractions, the lowest common multiple of all the denominators.

lowest common multiple Math. (ABBREV. **LCM, l.c.m.**) the smallest number into which every member of a group of numbers will divide exactly.

low frequency a radio frequency between 30 and 300 kilohertz.

low-key adj. 1 restrained and subdued: low-key publicity. 2 of a person not easily excited.

lowland noun (usu. **lowlands**) land that is low-lying in comparison with other areas. —adj. of or relating to low-lying land areas. ▸ **lowlander** noun

lowly adj. (**lowlier, lowliest**) 1 humble in rank, status, or behavior. 2 simple, modest, and unpretentious. ▸ **lowliness** noun

low profile a deliberate avoidance of publicity and attention.

low tide the lowest level reached by a falling tide.

loyal adj. 1 faithful and true. 2 personally devoted to a government, leader, sovereign, friend, etc. ▸ **loyally** adv. ▸ **loyalty** noun

loyalist noun a loyal supporter, esp. of a sovereign or an established government.

lozenge (läz'ənj) noun 1 a small medicated candy that dissolves in the mouth, used, e.g., to relieve a sore throat. 2 a rhombus that is not a true square.

LP noun (pl. **LP's, LPs**) a long-playing phonograph record.

LPG abbrev. liquefied petroleum gas.

LSD noun a habit-forming, highly toxic hallucinogen. Also called **acid**.

Lt. abbrev. lieutenant.

Lt.Col. abbrev. lieutenant colonel.

Lt.Comdr. abbrev. lieutenant commander.

Ltd. abbrev. limited company.

Lt.Gen. abbrev. lieutenant general.

Lt.(j.g.) or **LTJG** abbrev. lieutenant, junior grade.

lube colloq. noun the act or process of lubricating the engine of a motor vehicle. —verb trans. (**lubed, lubing**) to lubricate (the engine of a motor vehicle).

lubricate (lōō'brĭ-kāt,) verb trans. (**lubricated, lubricating**) 1 to apply a lubricant, such as oil or grease, to (e.g., moving parts of machinery) to reduce friction. 2 to make smooth, slippery, or greasy. ▸ **lubricant** noun, adj. ▸ **lubrication** noun ▸ **lubricator** noun

lubricious adj. 1 smooth and slippery in quality or texture. 2 changeable, esp. in one's loyalties. 3 literary lewd. ▸ **lubricity** noun

lucid *adj.* **1** expressed, or expressing something, clearly. **2** *of a person's state of mind* sane and sound. **3** bright; shining. ▸ **lucidity** *noun* ▸ **lucidly** *adv.*

Lucifer (loo'sĭ-fər) *noun* Satan.

luck *noun* **1** chance, esp. when thought of as bringing good fortune. **2** good fortune.

luckless *adj.* unlucky, esp. habitually so.

lucky *adj.* (**luckier, luckiest**) **1** having good luck. **2** bringing good luck. **3** fortunate: *a lucky coincidence.* ▸ **luckily** *adv.* ▸ **luckiness** *noun*

lucrative *adj.* affording financial gain; profitable. ▸ **lucratively** *adv.*

lucre (loo'kər) *noun* (*often* **filthy lucre**) money, profits, or financial gain in general.

ludicrous *adj.* laughably senseless. ▸ **ludicrously** *adv.*

lug¹ *verb trans.* (**lugged, lugging**) to drag or carry with great effort or difficulty.

lug² *noun* **1** a projection, esp. one by which the thing to which it is attached may be carried or turned. **2** *slang* a dumb person.

luge (loozh) *noun* a light toboggan on which the rider sits or lies face up. —*verb intrans.* (**luged, lugeing**) to travel on a luge.

luggage *noun* suitcases, bags, etc., used in traveling.

lugubrious *adj.* sad and gloomy. ▸ **lugubriously** *adv.*

lugworm *noun* a large marine worm.

lukewarm *adj.* **1** moderately warm. **2** *of interest, support, etc.* lacking any real or strong enthusiasm. ▸ **lukewarmly** *adv.*

lull *verb trans., intrans.* (**lulled, lulling**) **1** to make or become calm or quiet. **2** to deceive (someone) into feeling unsuspiciously secure. —*noun* a period of calm and quiet.

lullaby *noun* (*pl.* **lullabies**) a soothing song to lull children to sleep.

lumbago *noun* chronic pain in the lower region of the back.

lumbar *adj.* relating to or located in the lower back.

lumber¹ *noun* timber, esp. when partly cut up ready for use. —*verb intrans., trans.* (**lumbered, lumbering**) to fell trees and saw the wood into timber for transporting.

lumber² *verb intrans.* (**lumbered, lumbering**) to move about heavily and clumsily.

lumberjack *noun* a person employed to fell, saw up, and move trees.

luminary *noun* (*pl.* **luminaries**) **1** a widely known person. **2** an expert or authority. —*adj.* of or relating to light or enlightenment.

luminescence *noun* the emission of light by a substance in the absence of a rise in temperature, e.g., *fluorescence.* ▸ **luminescent** *adj.*

luminous *adj.* **1** radiating or reflecting light; glowing or shining. **2** giving out light in the dark; phosphorescent. ▸ **luminosity** *noun* ▸ **luminously** *adv.*

lump¹ *noun* **1** a small, solid, shapeless mass. **2** a swelling or tumor. **3** a feeling of tightening or swelling, esp. in the throat. **4** the total number of things taken as a single whole. —*verb trans., intrans.* (**lumped, lumping**) to form or collect into a lump. ▸ **lumpily** *adv.* ▸ **lumpiness** *noun* ▸ **lumpy** *adj.*

lump² *verb colloq.* (**lumped, lumping**) to accept or put up with (something bad or unwanted): *like it or lump it.*

lumpectomy *noun* (*pl.* **lumpectomies**) the surgical removal of a tumor from the breast.

lunacy (loo'nə-sē) *noun* (*pl.* **lunacies**) **1** insanity. **2** great foolishness or stupidity.

lunar *adj.* **1** resembling the Moon. **2** relating to or caused by the Moon.

lunatic *adj.* **1** insane. **2** foolish. **3** wildly eccentric. **4** for the insane. —*noun* **1** an insane person. **2** a foolish person. **3** a highly eccentric person.

lunch *noun* a meal eaten in the middle of the day. —*verb intrans.* (**lunched, lunching**) to eat lunch.

luncheon (lŭn'chən) *noun* a lunch, esp. a formal one.

lunchroom *noun* **1** a small restaurant that serves simple meals. *Also called* **luncheonette.** **2** a cafeteria, esp. in a school.

lung *noun* a large spongy organ, usu. one of a pair, that removes carbon dioxide from the blood and replaces it with oxygen.

lunge *noun* **1** a sudden plunge forward. **2** *Fencing* a sudden thrust with a sword. —*verb intrans.* (**lunged, lunging**) to make a lunge.

lupine *adj.* relating to or resembling a wolf.

lurch¹ *verb intrans.* (**lurched, lurching**) to move or stagger unsteadily, esp. rolling slightly to one side. —*noun* a sudden roll to one side.

lurch² *noun* —**leave (someone) in the lurch** *colloq.* to leave (someone) in a difficult situation and without help.

lure *verb trans.* (**lured, luring**) (**lure (someone) away** *or* **into (something)**) to tempt, attract, or entice (someone). —*noun* **1** a person or thing that tempts, attracts, or entices. **2** (**the lure of (something)**) its attractive or tempting qualities. **3** *Angling* a metal or plastic bait with hooks attached.

lurid *adj.* **1** glaringly bright. **2** horrifying or sensational. **3** pale or wan. ▸ **luridly** *adv.* ▸ **luridness** *noun*

lurk *verb intrans.* (**lurked, lurking**) **1** to lie in wait, esp. in ambush. **2** to linger unseen or furtively; to be latent.

luscious *adj.* **1** having a very pleasing taste. **2** attractive in a voluptuous way. ▸ **lusciously** *adv.* ▸ **lusciousness** *noun*

lush¹ *adj.* **1** green and growing abundantly. **2** luxurious. ▸ **lushness** *noun*

lush² *noun slang* a drunkard or alcoholic.

lust *noun* **1** strong sexual desire. **2** enthusiasm; relish: *a lust for life.* —*verb intrans.* (**lusted, lusting**) (**lust after** *or* **for** (**someone** *or* **something**)) to have a strong desire for (someone or something). ▸ **lustful** *adj.* ▸ **lustfully** *adv.* ▸ **lustfulness** *noun*

luster *noun* **1** shiny appearance. **2** brightness or gloss. **3** splendor and glory, on account of beauty, accomplishments, etc. ▸ **lustrous** *adj.* ▸ **lustrously** *adv.*

lusty *adj.* (**lustier, lustiest**) **1** vigorous or loud. **2** strong and healthy. ▸ **lustily** *adv.*

lute *noun* a stringed instrument with a pear-shaped body and a long neck with a bent-back pegbox. ▸ **lutenist** *noun*

Lutheran (lōō'thə-rən) *noun* a follower of the German Protestant reformer Martin Luther, or a member of the Lutheran Church. —*adj.* relating to Martin Luther, his teachings, or the Church based on these.

luxuriant *adj.* **1** very elaborate; extravagant; flowery. **2** growing abundantly; lush. **3** luxurious. ▸ **luxuriance** *noun* ▸ **luxuriantly** *adv.*

luxuriate (ləg-zhŏŏr'ē-āt,, lək-shŏŏr'-) *verb intrans.* (**luxuriated, luxuriating**) (**luxuriate in** (**something**)) to enjoy (it) greatly or revel in (it).

luxurious *adj.* **1** supplied or furnished with luxuries. **2** enjoying or providing luxury. ▸ **luxuriously** *adv.* ▸ **luxuriousness** *noun*

luxury (lŭg'zhə-rē, lək'shə-) *noun* (*pl.* **luxuries**) **1** expensive, rich, extremely comfortable surroundings and possessions. **2** habitual indulgence in or enjoyment of luxurious surroundings. **3** something pleasant and enjoyable but not essential.

-ly *suffix* used: **1** to form adverbs: *cleverly / hopefully.* **2** to form adverbs and adjectives denoting at intervals of: *daily.* **3** to form adjectives denoting like: *brotherly.*

lyceum (lī-sē'əm) *noun* a place or building where concerts, etc. are presented.

lychee (lē'chē), **lichee,** *or* **litchi** *noun* **1** a tree cultivated for its edible fruit. **2** the fruit of this tree, consisting of a hard seed surrounded by a sweet juicy whitish pulp.

lye *noun* a concentrated solution of sodium or potassium hydroxide.

lying *see* **lie¹·².**

Lyme disease (līm) an inflammatory disease causing a skin rash, aches in joints and muscles, headache, fever, fatigue, etc.

lymph *noun* a colorless fluid derived from blood, that cleanses body tissues and prevents the spread of infection.

lymphatic *adj.* of or relating to lymph or the lymphatic system. —*noun* any vessel that transports lymph.

lymphatic system the network of lymph vessels and lymph nodes.

lymph node a small rounded body found in the lymphatic system that produces antibodies in immune responses and filters bacteria and foreign bodies from the lymph. *Also called* **lymph gland.**

lymphocyte *noun* a white blood cell present in lymphatic tissues and involved in immune responses in the body.

lymphoma *noun* a malignant tumor of the lymph nodes.

lynch *verb trans.* (**lynched, lynching**) to condemn and put to death, usu. by hanging, without a legal trial, usu. by a mob.

Named after William Lynch, 19th-century Virginian planter who organized unofficial trials of suspected criminals

lynchpin *noun same as* **linchpin.**

lynx *noun* a member of the cat family, having yellowish-gray or reddish fur, a stubby tail and tufted ears.

lynx-eyed *adj.* sharp-sighted.

lyre *noun* a U-shaped, harplike instrument used esp. in ancient Greece.

lyric (lĭr'ĭk) *adj.* **1** of *poems or poets* expressing personal, private, or individual emotions. **2** having the form of a song; meant to be sung, orig. to the lyre. —*noun* **1** a short lyric poem or a song. **2** (*usu.* **lyrics**) the words of a song. ▸ **lyricist** *noun*

lyrical *adj.* **1** like a song; lyric. **2** full of enthusiastic praise. ▸ **lyrically** *adv.*

Mm

M¹ *or* **m** *noun* (*pl.* **Ms, M's, m's**) the 13th letter of the English alphabet.

M² *or* **M.** *abbrev.* **1** Majesty. **2** mark (German currency). **3** Master. **4** (**M.**) (French) Monsieur. **5** *Brit.* Motorway.

M³ *symbol* the Roman numeral for 1,000.

m *abbrev.* **1** male. **2** married. **3** masculine. **4** meter. **5** million. **6** minute. **7** month.

m. *abbrev.* **1** *meridiem* (Latin), noon. **2** mile.

ma *noun colloq.* mother.

ma'am (măm) *noun* used as a polite form of direct address to a woman.

Mac *noun slang* used to address a man whose name is unknown: *Hey, Mac, move your car!*

macabre (mə-käb', -käb'rə) *adj.* **1** extremely and disturbingly frightening. **2** relating to death.

macadam (mə-kăd'əm) *noun* **1** a road-paving material consisting of small stones bound together with tar or asphalt. **2** a road surface made with this. *See also* **tarmacadam.**

macadamia (măk͵ə-dā'mē-ə) an Australian tree, now also cultivated in Hawaii, or its hard-shelled edible nut.

macaque (mə-kăk') *noun* a short-tailed monkey native to S Asia and NW Africa.

macaroni *noun* (*pl.* **macaroni**) pasta in the form of short hollow tubes, or a dish made from this.

macaroon *noun* an almond-flavored cake or cookie.

macaw (mə-kô') *noun* a large, brilliantly colored, long-tailed parrot.

mace[1] *noun* **1** a heavy club, usu. with a spiked metal head, used as a weapon in medieval times. **2** a ceremonial rod carried as a symbol of authority.

mace[2] *noun* a spice ground from the dried fleshy covering around the nutmeg seed.

macerate (măs'ə-rāt͵) *verb intrans., trans.* **(macerated, macerating)** to break up or become soft, or cause to break up or become soft, by soaking. ▸ **maceration** *noun*

Mach (mäk) *noun* the ratio of the speed of an object such as an aircraft to the speed of sound, e.g., Mach 2 is twice the speed of sound. *Also called* **Mach number.**

machete (mə-shĕt'ē) *noun* a long, heavy, broad-bladed knife.

Machiavellian *adj.* cunning and unscrupulous, esp. in seeking power or advantage at any price.

machinate (măk'ĭ-nāt͵, măsh'-) *verb intrans.* **(machinated, machinating)** to plot or scheme, usu. with intent to do harm. ▸ **machination** *noun*

machine *noun* **1** a device designed to transmit or modify forces or energy in order to perform useful work. **2** a group of people or institutions. **3** *colloq.* an engine-powered vehicle, esp. a motorcycle. **4** *colloq.* a person with no initiative; a tireless or mechanically efficient worker. —*verb trans.* **(machined, machining) 1** to make, shape, cut, or finish (an object) with a machine. **2** to print or sew (an object) with a machine.

machine code *Comput.* the numeric, usu. binary, code system that gives instructions to a computer.

machine gun a portable gun capable of firing a continuous stream of bullets.

machinery *noun* **1** a group of machines, etc. esp. one designed to work together to perform a specific function. **2** the working parts of a machine. **3** a system or group of things or people that fit, work, etc. together.

machinist *noun* **1** a person who operates a machine. **2** a person who makes or repairs machines.

machismo (mä-chēz'mō, -kēz'-, -kĭz'-) *noun* masculinity, now usu. an over-exaggerated or aggressive sense of male pride.

Mach number *see* **Mach.**

macho (mäch'ō) *colloq. adj.* exaggeratedly or aggressively manly. —*noun* (*pl.* **machos**) **1** a man exhibiting aggressive, exaggerated masculinity. **2** machismo.

macintosh *noun same as* **mackintosh.**

mackerel *noun* (*pl.* **mackerel, mackerels**) **1** an important food fish related to the tuna. **2** the oily edible flesh of this fish used as food.

mackerel sky a sky with ripples of cloud resembling a mackerel's skin markings.

mackintosh *or* **macintosh** *noun* a waterproof raincoat.

macramé (măk'rə-mā͵) *noun* coarse open lacework made by knotting string or thread into patterns.

macro *noun* (*pl.* **macros**) *Comput.* a set of recorded and saved keystrokes and instructions that have been allocated a single key code.

macro- *or* **macr-** *combining form* forming words denoting large, long, or large-scale.

macrobiotics *noun* (*sing.*) the science or practice of prolonging life, esp. through diet. ▸ **macrobiotic** *adj.*

macrocosm *noun* **1** the universe. **2** a large or complex system or structure made up of similar smaller systems or structures.

macron (mā'krän͵, măk'-) *noun* a mark (¯) placed over a letter to show that it is a long vowel. *See also* **breve.**

macroscopic *adj.* large enough to be seen by the naked eye.

mad *adj.* **(madder, maddest) 1** psychologically or psychiatrically disturbed; insane. **2** foolish or senseless; extravagantly carefree. **3** *colloq.* (*also* **mad at** *or* **with**) very angry. **4** *colloq.* (*usu.* **mad about**) extremely enthusiastic; fanatical; infatuated. **5** marked by extreme confusion, haste, excitement, etc.: *a mad rush.* **6** of a dog infected with rabies. ▸ **madly** *adj.* ▸ **madness** *noun*

madam (măd'əm) *noun* **1 a** (*pl.* **Mesdames**) a polite form of address to a woman. **b** (**Madam**) a polite form of address to a woman holding a specified office or rank. **2** a formal salutation at the start of a letter, etc. to a woman whose name is unknown. **3** a woman who manages a brothel.

Madame (mə-dăm´, -däm´) *noun* (*pl.* **Mes-dames**) (ABBREV. **Mme.**) a French title equivalent to *Mrs.*

madcap *adj.* foolishly impulsive or reckless. —*noun* a foolishly impulsive person.

madden *verb trans.* (**maddened, maddening**) to make mad, esp. to enrage.

madder *noun* a plant with a red fleshy root; its root, used as a source of a red dye; a red dye obtained from its root.

made *adj.* artificially produced. —*verb see* **make.** —**have it made** *colloq.* to enjoy or be assured of complete success or happiness. **made for** ideally suited to (someone or something): *They're made for each other.*

-made *combining form* forming words denoting produced, constructed, or formed in a specified way: *handmade.*

Madeira (mə-dīr´ə, -dĕr´ə) *noun* a fortified wine.

Madeira cake a rich sponge cake.

madeleine *noun* a small sponge cake.

made-up *adj.* **1** wearing makeup. **2** not true; invented.

madhouse *noun* **1** *old use* a psychiatric hospital. **2** *colloq.* a place of great confusion and noise.

madman *noun* an insane or foolish man.

Madonna (mə-dän´ə) *noun* a picture or statue of the Virgin Mary.

madras *noun* a cotton fabric, usu. with a bold striped or checked pattern.

madrigal *noun* an unaccompanied part song.

madwoman *noun* an insane or foolish woman.

maelstrom (māl´strəm, -sträm,) *noun* **1** a violent whirlpool. **2** a state of utter confusion.

maestro (mī´strō) *noun* (*pl.* **maestros, maestri**) a distinguished and talented man in the field of the arts, esp. music.

Mafia (mäf´ē-ə, măf´-) *noun* (**the Mafia**) a criminal organization, orig. based in Sicily, but now allegedly involved in illegal activities worldwide, esp. in the USA.

Mafioso (mäf´ē-ō´sō, măf´-, -zō) *noun* (*pl.* **Mafiosi**) a member of the Mafia.

mag *noun colloq.* a magazine.

magazine *noun* **1** a periodical, usu. illustrated. **2** a regular television or radio program, usu. featuring topical discussion. **3** a supply compartment, e.g., for gun cartridges, photographic slides, etc. **4** a storeroom, esp. for ammunition, explosives, etc.

> The sense of *magazine* as a periodical developed from the military use, being intended as a storehouse or treasury of information

maggot *noun* a wormlike larva of various flies. ▸ **maggoty** *adj.*

magic *noun* **1** the supposed art or practice of using supernatural forces to affect people, objects, and events. **2** the art or practice of performing entertaining illusions and conjuring tricks. **3** the quality of being wonderful, charming, or delightful. —*adj.* **1** of, used in, or using sorcery or conjuring. **2** excellent; fantastic. —*verb trans.* (**magicked, magicking, magics**) to produce, transform, or otherwise affect, using sorcery or conjuring.

magical *adj.* **1** relating to magic. **2** fascinating; wonderful; charming. ▸ **magically** *adv.*

magic bullet a drug or remedy that works without any harmful side effects.

magician *noun* **1** a performer of illusions; a conjurer. **2** a person supposedly invested with supernatural powers.

magic lantern an early form of slide projector.

magic square a square filled with rows of figures so arranged that the sums of all the rows (vertical, horizontal, and diagonal) will be the same.

magisterial *adj.* **1** relating to or administered by a magistrate. **2** authoritative; commanding; dictatorial. **3** relating to a teacher, etc. ▸ **magisterially** *adv.*

magistrate (măj´ə-strāt,, -strət) *noun* **1** a judge in a local court of law dealing with minor criminal offenses and exerting limited jurisdiction. **2** a justice of the peace. ▸ **magistracy** *noun*

magma *noun* (*pl.* **magmas, magmata**) *Geol.* hot molten material lying below the Earth's crust. *See also* **lava.**

magnanimous *adj.* having or showing admirable generosity of spirit not spoiled by petty feelings. ▸ **magnanimity** *noun*

magnate (măg´nāt,, -nət) *noun* a leading or dominant figure in a field, esp. a successful, wealthy manufacturer. ▣ BARON, CZAR, KING, MOGUL, PRINCE, TYCOON.

magnesia *noun* magnesium oxide.

magnesium *noun* (SYMBOL **Mg**) a silvery-gray metallic element.

magnet *noun* **1** a piece of metal, esp. iron, capable of attracting other iron-containing metals and of aligning itself in a magnetic field. **2** a person or thing that attracts. ▸ **magnetic** *adj.* ▸ **magnetically** *adv.*

magnetic field *Phys.* the space surrounding a magnet, electromagnetic wave, or current-carrying conductor, within which magnetic forces may be detected.

magnetic north the direction indicated by the north end of a magnetic compass needle.

magnetism *noun* **1** the cause of the properties of attraction possessed by magnets. **2** the phenomena associated with magnets. **3** the scientific study of magnetic fields. **4** an ability to attract other people.

magnetize verb trans., intrans. (**magnetized**, **magnetizing**) 1 to make or become magnetic. 2 to attract through charm or influence. ▸ **magnetization** noun

magneto (măg-nēt′ō) noun (pl. **magnetos**) an electric generator that produces power by means of a rotating magnet.

magnetron (măg′nə-trän,) noun a device for generating microwaves.

magnet school a school whose students come from all parts of a city and who qualify for attendance by having high grades or great artistic talent.

magnificent adj. 1 splendidly impressive in size or extent. 2 excellent; admirable. ▸ **magnificence** noun ▸ **magnificently** adv.

magnify verb (**magnified**, **magnifying**, **magnifies**) 1 to cause (something) to appear larger by using a microscope, etc. 2 to increase in size. 3 to exaggerate. ▸ **magnification** noun ▸ **magnifier** noun

magniloquent adj. speaking or spoken in a grand or pompous style. ▸ **magniloquence** noun

magnitude noun 1 importance, extent, size, or largeness. 2 a measure of the brightness of a star or other celestial object.

magnolia noun 1 a shrub or tree with large, glossy, dark green leaves and large cup-shaped fragrant flowers. 2 a pale pinkish-white color.

magnum noun a wine bottle holding twice the normal amount

magnum opus (pl. **magnum opuses** or **magna opera**) an important or large work of art, esp. one considered to be the best work of a particular composer, artist, etc.

magpie noun 1 a white-and-dark bird of the crow family. 2 a chattering person.

> Originally *maggot pie*, meaning 'pied Margaret'

Magyar noun 1 a member of the predominant people in Hungary. 2 same as **Hungarian**. —adj. of the Magyars or their language.

maharajah or **maharaja** (mä′hə-räj′ə, -räzh′ə) noun an Indian prince.

maharani or **maharanee** (mä′hə-rän′ē) noun the wife or widow of a maharajah, or a woman of the same rank as a maharajah.

maharishi (mä,hə-rē′shē,¯ mə-här′ē-shē,) noun a Hindu guru or spiritual leader.

mahatma (mə-hät′mə, -hăt′-) noun 1 a wise and holy Hindu leader. 2 a title of respect among Hindus.

mah-jong or **mah-jongg** (mä-zhŏng′) noun a game, orig. Chinese, for four players, using small tiles.

mahlstick or **maulstick** (môl′stĭk,) noun a padded stick an artist uses to steady the painting hand.

mahogany noun (pl. **mahoganies**) 1 a tall tropical tree. 2 its hard, reddish-brown timber used in furniture making, etc. 3 a reddish-brown color.

mahout noun a person who looks after and drives a working elephant.

maid noun 1 a female servant. 2 old use, literary an unmarried woman.

maiden noun 1 old use, literary a young unmarried woman. 2 old use, literary a virgin. 3 a horse, male or female, that has never won a race. —adj. 1 first ever: the ship's maiden voyage. 2 literary unused; fresh. 3 of a horse race open to maidens only. 4 never having been married: a maiden aunt. ▸ **maidenly** adj. ▸ **maidenhood** noun

maidenhair noun a fern with dark wiry stems and feathery fronds.

maiden name a married woman's surname before marriage.

maid of honor (pl. **maids of honor**) 1 an unmarried woman attending a bride. See also **matron of honor**. 2 an unmarried female servant of a queen or princess.

mail[1] noun 1 a postal service. 2 letters, parcels, etc., sent via the postal service. —verb trans. (**mailed**, **mailing**) to send by mail.

mail[2] noun chain mail.

mail order a system of buying and selling goods by mail. ▸ **mail-order** adj.

maim verb trans. (**maimed**, **maiming**) to wound seriously; to disable or cripple.

main adj. chief, esp. in size, importance, etc. —noun 1 (**mains**) a chief pipe or cable in a branching system. 2 old use the open sea: the Spanish main. 3 great strength: with might and main. ▸ **mainly** adv.

main clause a clause that can stand alone as a sentence.

mainframe noun a large computer, usu. with many smaller linked computers.

mainland noun a land mass, as distinct from a nearby island or islands.

mainline verb trans., intrans. (**mainlined**, **mainlining**) slang to inject (a drug) into a principal vein.

mainspring noun 1 a chief spring in a watch or clock. 2 a chief motive, reason, or cause.

mainstay noun the chief support.

mainstream noun the prevailing trend of thought in an intellectual, cultural, etc. field. —verb trans. (**mainstreamed**, **mainstreaming**) to integrate (e.g., students with learning difficulties) into regular school classes.

maintain (mān-tān′) verb trans., intrans. (**maintained**, **maintaining**) 1 to continue; to keep in existence. 2 to keep in good condition. 3 to support financially. 4 to continue to argue; to assert to be true. ▸ **maintenance** noun

maître d'hôtel (mä,trə-dō-tĕl', mĕ,-) *or* **maître d'** (*pl.* **maîtres d'hôtel, maîtres d's**) **1** a headwaiter. **2** the manager of a hotel or restaurant.

maize *noun Brit.* corn¹.

majestic *or* **majestical** *adj.* dignified; stately and grand. ▸ **majestically** *adv.*

majesty *noun* (*pl.* **majesties**) **1** great dignity. **2** stately splendor. **3** (**Majesty**) a monarch's title.

majolica *noun* glazed or enameled earthenware, usu. colorfully decorated.

major *adj.* **1** great or greater: *the major share.* **2** very serious, important, etc.: *a major disaster.* **3** *of a key or scale* having two full tones between the first and third notes. **4** having reached legal age. —*noun* **1** (*also* **Major**) a rank in the US Army, Air Force, or Marine Corps above captain; a person who holds this rank. **2** *Mus.* a major key, chord, or scale. **3 a** a college or university student's main subject of study: *French is her major.* **b** a student taking such a subject: *She's a French major.* —*verb intrans.* (**majored, majoring**) (**major in**) to take (a subject) as the main part of one's study at college or university.

major-domo *noun* (*pl.* **major-domos**) a chief servant in charge of a household.

majorette *noun* a marching girl, esp. one who performs displays of baton-twirling.

major general (*also* **Major General**) a rank in the US Army, Air Force, or Marine Corps above brigadier general; a person who holds this rank.

majority *noun* (*pl.* **majorities**) **1** the greater number; the largest group; the bulk. **2 a** a number that is more than half the total number. **b** the winning margin of votes in an election. **3** the age at which a person legally becomes an adult.

major league a principal league in professional sports. *Also called* **big league.** ▸ **major-league** *adj.* ▸ **major-leaguer** *noun*

major medical insurance that pays most or all of the medical bills of a patient that result from a prolonged illness.

make *verb trans., intrans.* (*pa t and pa p* **made**; *pr p* **making**) **1** to form, create, manufacture, or produce. **2** to cause to be or become. **3** to cause, bring about, or create. **4** to force, induce, or cause. **5** to transform or convert. **6** to be suitable for. **7** to appoint. **8** to cause to appear. **9** to gain, earn, or acquire. **10** to add up to; to calculate, judge, or estimate to be. **11** to arrive at, reach, or succeed in achieving, reaching, or gaining. **12** to propose. **13** to engage in; to perform, carry out, or produce. **14** to show an intention of doing. **15** *slang* to identify: *made him as the thief.*

—*noun* **1** a manufacturer's brand. **2** the way in which something is made. —**make away with 1** to kill (someone). **2** to steal (something). **make believe** to pretend. **make do with** to make the best use of (something, esp. a second or an inferior choice). **make do without** to manage without (something). **make it** *colloq.* **1** to be successful. **2** to survive. **make of** to understand or interpret (someone or something): *What do you make of their comments?* **make off with** to run off with (someone or something); to steal or kidnap. **make out 1** to pretend: *made out he was ill.* **2** *colloq.* to make progress: *How did they make out?* **3** *colloq.* to manage, succeed, or survive: *made out on a small income.* **4** *slang* to neck or pet. **5** to begin to discern, esp. to see or hear (something): *make out a figure in the distance.* **6** to write or fill in a document, etc.: *make out a check.* **make up 1** to resolve a disagreement: *kiss and make up.* **2** to apply cosmetics to (the face). **3** to invent: *made up an excuse.* **4** to constitute. **make up for** to compensate or serve as an apology for: *some flowers to make up for what I did.* **on the make** *colloq.* **1** seeking a large or illegal profit. **2** aggressively seeking a sexual partner.

make-believe *noun* pretense, esp. when playful or innocent. —*adj.* pretended; imaginary.

make-or-break *adj.* determining success or failure.

make-over *noun* a complete change in a person's style of dress, makeup, etc.

makeshift *adj.* serving as a temporary and, usu. less adequate, substitute.

makeup *or* **make-up** *noun* **1** cosmetics. **2** the combination of characteristics or ingredients that form or constitute something, e.g., a personality.

makings *pl. noun* **1** components or ingredients. **2** potential, talent, etc. necessary for: *has the makings of a professional footballer.*

mal- *combining form* forming words denoting: **1** bad or badly: *maladapted.* **2** incorrectly: *malfunction.*

malachite *noun* a bright green copper mineral used as a gemstone.

maladjusted *adj.* **1** poorly fitting or badly adjusted. **2** unable to cope with everyday situations, social and personal relationships, etc. ▸ **maladjustment** *noun*

malady *noun* (*pl.* **maladies**) *formal* an illness or disease.

malaise (mə-lāz', -lĕz') *noun* a general feeling of illness, uneasiness, discontent, etc.

malapropism *noun* the misuse of a word, usu. with comic effect, through confusion with another that sounds similar but has a different meaning; a word so misused.

malaria *noun* a disease transmitted by mosquitoes, and characterized by anemia and recurring bouts of fever. ▸ **malarial** *adj.*

> From an Italian phrase meaning 'bad air', malarial fever being originally thought to be caused by poisonous marsh gases

malarkey *noun colloq.* nonsense; rubbish.

Malay (mə-lā', mā'lā,) *noun* **1** a member of a people inhabiting Malaysia, Singapore, and Indonesia. **2** the official language of of Malaysia. —*adj.* of the Malays or their language.

malcontent *adj.* dissatisfied. —*noun* a dissatisfied person.

male *adj.* **1** of the sex that produces sperm, fertilizes eggs, etc. **2** of the reproductive structure of a plant that produces the male gamete. **3** relating or belonging to a man or to men. **4** denoting a piece of machinery that fits into another part (the female). —*noun* **1** a man or boy. **2** a male animal or plant.

male bonding a process or session where two or more men form close friendships.

male chauvinism the belief that men are superior to women. ▸ **male chauvinist** *noun*

malediction (măl,ə-dĭk'shən) *noun* an act of cursing; a curse. ▸ **maledictory** *adj.*

malefactor (măl'ə-făk,tər) *noun formal* a criminal; a wrongdoer. ▸ **malefaction** *noun*

male menopause *colloq.* a crisis of confidence in some middle-aged men caused by fear of aging, etc.

malevolent (mə-lĕv'ə-lənt) *adj.* wishing to do evil to others. ▸ **malevolence** *noun*

malformation *noun* **1** the state of being badly or wrongly formed or shaped. **2** a badly or wrongly formed part. ▸ **malformed** *adj.*

malfunction *noun* the act or instance of working imperfectly or failing to work. —*verb intrans.* (**malfunctioned, malfunctioning**) to work imperfectly; to fail to work.

malice *noun* **1** a disposition or desire to cause distress, injury, pain, etc. to another. ▣ ILL WILL, MALEVOLENCE, MALIGNITY, SPITE, SPITEFULNESS, SPLEEN ▣ BENEVOLENCE, BENIGNANCY. **2** evil intent. ▸ **malicious** *adj.* ▸ **maliciousness** *noun*

malign *verb trans.* (**maligned, maligning**) to say or write unpleasant things about (someone or something). —*adj.* evil or harmful.

malignant (mə-lĭg'nənt) *adj.* **1** threatening harm or danger. **2** of a tumor, etc. resistant to treatment; cancerous. *See also* **benign**. ▸ **malignancy** *noun* ▸ **malignity** *noun*

malinger *verb intrans.* (**malingered,**

malingering) to pretend to be ill. ▸ **malingerer** *noun*

mall *noun* **1** a large covered shopping precinct, often also including cinemas, restaurants, etc. *Also called* **shopping mall**. **2** a public promenade or walkway. **3** *same as* **maul**.

mallard *noun* (*pl.* **mallard, mallards**) a wild duck, the male having a dark green glossy head.

malleable *adj.* **1** of *esp.* a metal capable of being easily stretched by beating, hammering, rolling, etc. **2** willing to adapt; easily influenced. ▸ **malleability** *noun*

mallet *noun* **1** a hammer with a large wooden head. **2** a long-handled wooden hammer for playing croquet or polo.

malleus *noun* (*pl.* **mallei**) *Anat.* a small hammer-shaped bone in the middle ear. *See also* **incus, stapes**.

mallow *noun* a plant or shrub with pink or white flowers.

malnutrition *noun* poor nutrition caused by insufficient food, a lack of protein, vitamins, etc. in the diet, or an inability to absorb nutrients from food.

malodorous *adj. formal* having a foul smell.

malpractice *noun* improper, negligent, or illegal conduct.

malt *noun* **1** a mixture prepared from barley or wheat grains that have been soaked in water, allowed to sprout, and then dried in a kiln. **2** beer or ale made from malt. **3** malted milk. —*verb trans.* (**malted, malting**) to make into malt; to treat or combine with malt.

malted milk **1** a mixture of dried milk and malted barley. **2** a drink made with this powder, milk, flavoring, and ice cream.

maltose *noun* a sugar that forms starch and glycogen.

maltreat *verb trans.* (**maltreated, maltreating**) to treat roughly or cruelly. ▸ **maltreatment** *noun*

mama *or* **mamma** *noun colloq.* mother.

mamba *noun* a venomous African snake.

mambo *noun* (*pl.* **mambos**) a Latin American rhythmic dance, or a piece of music for this.

mammal *noun* a warm-blooded vertebrate whose young are fed on milk secreted from mammary glands. ▸ **mammalian** *adj.*

mammary gland a milk-producing gland of a female mammal.

mammography *noun* x-ray examination of the breast, usu. to detect any abnormality in the tissues, esp. cancer.

Mammon (măm'ən) *noun* **1** riches, personified as a false god. **2** (**mammon**) wealth considered as a source of evil.

mammoth *noun* an extinct hairy prehistoric elephant. —*adj.* very large: *a mammoth task.*

man *noun* (*pl.* **men**) **1** an adult male human. **2**

human beings as a whole. **3** a human being. **4** an adult male human displaying typical masculine qualities. **5** *colloq.* a husband or boyfriend. **6** an employee, worker, or member of the armed forces, not a manager or an officer. **7** one of the movable pieces in various board games. **8** a male member of a team. **9** *old use* a male servant, esp. a valet. **10** *colloq.* used as a form of address indicating friendship, impatience, etc. **11** (**the Man**) *slang* a person in a powerful or authoritative position. —*verb trans.* (**manned, manning**) **1** to provide with sufficient workers. **2** to operate. —*interj. colloq.* used to intensify a statement: *Man! It's cold outside.*

-man *combining form* forming words denoting: **1** a man associated with a specified activity: *postman.* **2** a native of a specified country or place: *Englishman.*

manacle *noun* a handcuff. —*verb trans.* (**manacled, manacling**) to handcuff.

manage *verb trans., intrans.* (**managed, managing**) **1** to be in overall control or charge of. **2** to deal with or handle successfully or competently. **3** to succeed in doing or producing (something). **4** to have enough room, time, etc., for. ‣ **manageable** *adj.*

management *noun* **1** the skill or practice of controlling something, esp. a commercial enterprise. **2** the managers of a company, etc., as a group.

manager *noun* a person in charge, esp. of a commercial enterprise. ‣ **managerial** *adj.*

mañana (măn-yän'ə) *noun, adv. colloq.* some later time; tomorrow.

man-at-arms *noun* (*pl.* **men-at-arms**) *Hist.* a soldier, esp. when heavily armed and mounted.

manatee *noun* a large aquatic mammal. *Also called* **sea cow.**

mandarin *noun* **1** (**Mandarin**) the official spoken language of China. *Also called* **Mandarin Chinese. 2** *Hist.* a senior official in the Chinese empire. **3** a high-ranking official. **4** a small citrus tree or one of its orange edible fruits.

mandate (măn'dāt,) *noun* **1** a right given to a nation, person, or political party to act on behalf of others. **2** an order given by a superior. —*verb trans.* (**mandated, mandating**) **1** to give authority or power to. **2** to assign (territory) to a nation under a mandate.

mandatory *adj.* **1** compulsory. **2** relating to a mandate.

mandible *noun* **1** the lower jaw of a vertebrate. **2** one of a pair of jawlike mouthparts in insects, crustaceans, etc.

mandolin *noun* a musical instrument like a small guitar.

mandrake *noun* a plant with pale blue or violet flowers and poisonous roots.

mandrill *noun* a large African baboon with red and blue coloring on its face and rump.

mane *noun* long coarse hair around the neck of mammals, such as the horse and the lion.

man-eater *noun* **1** a tiger, shark, etc. that has been known to kill and eat humans. **2** *colloq.* an aggressively domineering woman, esp. one who has had many male sexual partners.

maneuver (mə-nōō'vər) *noun* **1 a** a tactical military or naval movement. **b** (*usu.* **maneuvers**) a military or naval exercise. **2** a skilled movement or series of movements. —*verb, intrans., trans.* (**maneuvered, maneuvering**) **1** to engage in military exercises. **2** to make a series of skilled movements or cause (a vehicle, etc.) to do so. ‣ **maneuverability** *noun* ‣ **maneuverable** *adj.*

man Friday (*pl.* **men Friday, men Fridays**) an efficient and dedicated male worker, esp. one who does various tasks.

manful *adj.* brave and determined; manly. ‣ **manfully** *adv.* ‣ **manfulness** *noun*

manganese *noun* (SYMBOL **Mn**) a brittle metallic chemical element.

mange (mānj) *noun* a contagious skin disease causing intense itching and loss of hair.

mangel-wurzel *noun* a variety of beet with a large yellowish root, used as animal fodder.

manger (mān'jər) *noun* an open box or trough for animal feed.

mangle[1] *verb trans.* (**mangled, mangling**) **1** to damage or destroy by cutting, crushing, or tearing. **2** to spoil.

mangle[2] *noun* an ironing machine. —*verb trans.* (**mangled, mangling**) to press (clothing, fabric, or laundry) with a mangle.

mango (măng'gō) *noun* (*pl.* **mangoes, mangos**) a tree with glossy leaves and small fragrant yellow or red flowers, or the edible oblong fruit of this tree.

mangrove (măn'grōv., măng'-) *noun* a tree whose roots often become tangled with those of other mangroves to form a mangrove swamp.

mangy *adj.* (**mangier, mangiest**) **1** affected with mange. **2** shabby; seedy. ‣ **mangily** *adv.* ‣ **manginess** *noun*

manhandle *verb trans.* (**manhandled, manhandling**) **1** to treat roughly. **2** to move or transport using manpower, not machinery.

manhole *noun* an opening, esp. in a road, to give a person access, e.g., to a sewer, etc.

manhood *noun* **1** the state of being an adult male. **2** manly qualities.

man-hour *noun* a unit of work that can be done by one person in one hour.

manhunt *noun* a concentrated, usu. large-scale search for a person, esp. a criminal.

mania *noun* **1** a psychological or psychiatric disorder characterized by unpredictable behavior, excitability, hyperactivity, etc. **2** a great desire or enthusiasm: *a mania for chocolate*.

-mania *combining form* forming words denoting: a great love, enthusiasm, or compulsion for: *kleptomania*.

maniac *noun* **1** *colloq.* a person who behaves wildly or who is avidly enthusiastic about something. **2** a person affected by mania. ▸ **maniacal** (mə-nī′ə-kəl) *or* **maniac** *adj.*

-maniac *combining form* forming nouns denoting a person affected with a mania: *kleptomaniac*.

manic *adj.* **1** relating to or suffering from mania. **2** *colloq.* very energetic or active.

manic-depressive *adj.* suffering from a psychological or psychiatric disorder marked by alternating episodes of extreme euphoria and severe depression. —*noun* a person suffering from this disorder.

manicure *noun* a cosmetic treatment of the hands, esp. the fingernails. —*verb trans.* (**manicured, manicuring**) to give a manicure to (a person or hand). ▸ **manicurist** *noun*

manifest *verb trans.* (**manifested, manifesting**) **1** to show or display clearly. **2** to be evidence or proof of. —*adj.* easily seen; obvious. —*noun* a list of a ship's or plane's cargo or passengers. ▸ **manifestation** *noun* ▸ **manifestly** *adv.*

manifesto (măn,ə-fĕs′tō) *noun* (*pl.* **manifestoes, manifestos**) a declaration of policies or intentions, esp. by a political party or candidate.

manifold *adj.* **1** of many different kinds; many and various. **2** having many different features or functions. —*noun* **1** something with many different forms or functions. **2** a pipe with several inlets and outlets.

manikin *or* **mannikin** *noun* **1** *old use* an abnormally small person. **2** a model of the human body, used in teaching art and anatomy.

manila *or* **manilla** *noun* a thick, strong, brown paper.

manioc *noun same as* **cassava** (sense 1).

manipulate *verb trans.* (**manipulated, manipulating**) **1** to handle, esp. skillfully. **2** to control or influence cleverly and unscrupulously, esp. to one's own advant-age. **3** to apply treatment with the hands to (a part of the body). ▸ **manipulation** *noun* ▸ **manipulative** *adj.*

mankind *noun old use* the human race as a whole.

> *Usage* It is now preferable to use *human-kind*.

manly *adj.* (**manlier, manliest**) displaying qualities considered admirable in a man. ▸ **manliness** *noun*

manna *noun* **1** in the Old Testament, the food miraculously provided by God for the Israel-ites in the wilderness. **2** an unexpected gift.

mannequin (măn′ĭ-kən) *noun* **1** a fashion model. **2** a life-size dummy of the human body, used in making or displaying clothes.

manner *noun* **1** way; fashion. **2** (**manners**) polite or socially accepted behavior. **3** style. **4** kind or kinds. —**to the manner born** accustomed, esp. to a privileged lifestyle, from birth.

mannered *adj. formal* unnatural and artificial; affected: *a mannered prose style.*

-mannered *combining form* forming ad-jectives denoting a specified kind of social behavior: *ill-mannered*.

mannerism *noun* an individual characteristic.

mannikin *noun same as* **manikin**.

mannish *adj. of a woman* dressing, behaving, etc. in a way that is more typical of a man.

man-of-war *or* **man-o'-war** *noun* (*pl.* **men-of-war, men-o'-war**) *Hist.* a warship with sails.

manometer (mə-năm′ət-ər) *noun* an in-strument for measuring the pressure of liquids or gases. ▸ **manometric** *adj.*

manor *noun* a European, esp. English, country estate, or the main house on such an estate. ▸ **manorial** *adj.*

manpower *noun* **1** the number of people available, e.g., for work, etc. **2** human effort.

manqué (măn-kā′) *adj.* unfulfilled or un-successful, esp. in terms of promise or potential shown at an earlier time: *an artist manqué.*

mansard (măn′särd,, -sərd) *noun* a roof in two sections, with the lower part sloping almost vertically and the top part hardly sloping at all.

manse *noun* the house of a cleric.

mansion *noun* a large, stately house.

manslaughter *noun* the crime of killing someone without intent to do so.

manta ray a giant ray that lives in tropical and subtropical seas.

mantel *noun* **1** an ornamental fireplace facing. **2** a mantelpiece.

mantelpiece *noun* the top part of a mantel that forms a shelf over a fireplace. *Also called* **mantelshelf**.

mantilla (măn-tē′ə) *noun* **1** a woman's lace or silk head covering, often supported by a decorative comb, worn esp. in Spanish-speaking communities. **2** a short, light-weight cape or cloak.

mantis *noun* (*pl.* **mantises**, **mantes**) a carnivorous insect resembling a grass-hopper, that rests with the two front legs raised. *Also called* **praying mantis**.

mantissa *noun Math.* the decimal part of a logarithm. *See also* **characteristic**.

mantle *noun* **1** a fireproof mesh around a gas or oil lamp. **2** a cloak or loose outer garment. **3** the part of Earth between the crust and the core. —*verb trans.* (**mantled, mantling**) to cover.

mantra (măn′trə, măn′-) *noun* a word or sound repeated during meditation.

manual *adj.* **1** relating to or using the hand or hands. **2** worked, controlled, or operated by hand; not automatic. —*noun* **1** a book of instructions. **2** an organ keyboard. ▸ **manually** *adv.*

manufacture *verb trans.* (**manufactured, manufacturing**) **1** to make (goods) from raw materials, esp. in large quantities using machinery. **2** to invent or fabricate. —*noun* the practice or process of manufacturing. ▸ **manufacturer** *noun*

manumission *noun* release from slavery.

manumit *verb trans.* (**manumitted, manumitting**) to release from slavery, or from some other restraint.

manure *noun* natural waste material, esp. animal dung, used as a fertilizer.

manuscript *noun* **1** an author's text in its unpublished form. **2** any handwritten text, e.g., a book, document, piece of music, etc.

Manx cat a breed of tailless cat.

many *adj.* (**more, most**) numerous. —*pron.* a great number. —*noun* (**the many**) the majority of people.

Maori (mowr′ē) *noun* (*pl.* **Maori, Maoris**) **1** a member of a New Zealand aboriginal people. **2** the language of this people. —*adj.* of this people or their language.

map *noun* **1** a diagram of the Earth's surface or part of it, esp. one showing geographical features, positions of towns, roads, etc. **2** a similar diagram of the surface of the Moon or a planet. **3** a diagram showing the positions of the stars in the sky. —*verb trans.* (**mapped, mapping**) **1** to make a map of. **2** (*usu.* **map out**) to outline or plan: *mapped out his cost-cutting ideas.*

maple *noun* **1** a tree with a large canopy, some species of which are grown for their timber and for their sugary sap. **2** the timber of this tree, used to make furniture, etc.

mar *verb trans.* (**marred, marring**) **1** to spoil. **2** to injure or damage.

maraca *noun* a hollowed-out gourd filled with beans, pebbles, etc. and used as a percussion instrument.

maraschino (măr′ə-skē′nō, -shē′-) *noun* (*pl.* **maraschinos**) a liqueur made from cherries, with a taste like bitter almonds.

maraschino cherry a cherry preserved in maraschino or a similar liqueur, used for decorating cocktails, cakes, etc.

marathon *noun* **1** a running race, usu. 26 mi., 385 yd. (42.195 km). **2** any lengthy and difficult task.

> After the distance run by a Greek soldier from *Marathon* to Athens with news of the victory over the Persians

maraud *verb intrans., trans.* (**marauded, marauding**) to go in search of people to attack and property to plunder. ▸ **marauder** *noun*

marble *noun* **1** a hard rock used in sculpture and architecture. **2** a small hard, usu. glass, ball. **3** (**marbles**) (*sing.*) a game played with these small hard balls.

marbled *adj.* streaked with different colors, etc.: *black and gray marbled fur.*

marcasite *noun* a pale yellow mineral used for jewelry and in manufacturing sulfuric acid.

March *noun* (ABBREV. **Mar., Mar**) (*pl.* **Marches**) the third month of the year.

march¹ *verb intrans., trans.* (**marched, marching**) **1** to walk, or cause (someone, esp. a soldier) to walk, at a brisk pace and in step with others. **2** to walk, or cause (someone) to walk, in a brisk, determined way: *marched the culprits to the principal's room.* —*noun* **1** an act of marching; a distance traveled by marching. **2** progress from one place, thing, etc to another. **3** an organized mass protest or demonstration. **4** a piece of marching music. —**steal a march on** to get an advantage over (someone), esp. by acting quickly, secretly, underhandedly, etc. ▸ **marcher** *noun*

march² *noun* **1** a boundary or border. **2** a border district, esp. a border claimed by two countries.

marchioness *noun* the wife or widow of a marquis, or a woman who holds the same rank as a marquis.

Mardi Gras (mär′dē-grä,, -grô,) *noun* Shrove Tuesday or a celebration held on this day.

mare¹ (măr, mĕr) *noun* an adult female member of the horse family.

mare² (mär′ā) *noun* (*pl.* **maria**) a huge plain on the surface of the Moon, Mars, etc.

mare's nest (*pl.* **mare's nests, mares' nests**) **1** something illusionary or that proves to be untrue or without value. **2** a complex or muddled situation.

mare's tail (*pl.* **mare's tails, mares' tails**) **1** a water plant with tiny flowers and whorled leaves. **2** a long, narrow, trailing cloud.

margarine *noun* a butter substitute, usu. made from vegetable oil.

margin *noun* **1** a blank area at the edge of a page or a line indicating where this begins. **2** an edge, border, or boundary: *living on the margins of civilization.* **3** a difference between one thing and another: *won by a* *margin of two points.* **4** a concession, esp. to ensure something succeeds or meets a requirement, etc.: *a margin for error.*

marginal *adj.* **1** small and unimportant. **2** appearing in the margin of a page of text. **3** very close to a limit, esp. a low one: *scraped a marginal pass in the exam.* ▸ **marginally** *adv.*

marginalize *verb trans.* (**marginalized, marginalizing**) to confine or relegate to an outer or lower area, limit, or edge, esp. of society.

marguerite *noun* a garden plant that has large white or pale yellow flowers with yellow centers.

maria *noun see* **mare²**.

mariachi *noun* (*pl.* **mariachis**) **1** a Mexican band, esp. one that plays music for dancing in the streets. **2** the music played by such bands. **3** a member of one of these bands.

marigold *noun* a plant of the daisy family.

marijuana *or* **marihuana** (măr͏ʹĭ-wän͏ʹə, -hwän͏ʹə) *noun* a hemplike plant whose leaves and flowers can be eaten or smoked to give a feeling of euphoria. *Also called* **cannabis** *or* **pot.**

marimba *noun* a type of xylophone that originated in Africa.

marina *noun* a small harbor, esp. one for yachts and pleasure boats.

marinade *noun* a liquid mixture in which food, esp. meat or fish, is soaked to add flavor before cooking. —*verb trans., intrans.* (**marinaded, marinading**) to be soaked in a marinade, or to soak (food) in a marinade.

marinate (măr͏ʹĭ-nāt͏ʹ) *verb trans., intrans.* (**marinated, marinating**) to marinade.

marine *adj.* **1** of, concerned with, or found in the sea. **2** of or relating to ships, the shipping trade, or the navy. —*noun* **1 a** a soldier trained to serve on land or at sea. **b** (**Marine**) a member of the US Marine Corps. **2** the merchant or naval ships of a nation.

mariner *noun* a sailor.

marionette *noun* a puppet with jointed limbs moved by strings.

marital *adj.* of or relating to marriage. ▸ **maritally** *adv.*

maritime *adj.* **1** of or relating to the sea or ships, esp. to merchant ships. **2** living or growing near the sea.

marjoram *noun* an aromatic herb used in salads and cooking.

mark¹ *noun* **1** a blemish. **2** a grade or rating, or a letter used to denote one. **3** a sign or symbol. **4** an indication or representation. **5** an object or thing aimed at; a target. **6** a required standard. —*verb trans., intrans.* (**marked, marking**) **1** to make a mark on. **2** to award a grade to. **3** to show; to be a sign of. **4** to make a note of or pay close attention to. **5** to characterize or label. —**mark time 1**

to move the feet up and down as if marching, but without going forward. **2** to keep things going while waiting to speed up or progress.

mark² *noun* **1** *same as* **Deutschmark.** **2** a European unit of weight for gold and silver.

markdown *noun* an amount subtracted from a price, e.g., in a sale.

marked *adj.* **1** obvious or noticeable. **2** doomed. ▸ **markedly** *adv.*

marker *noun* **1** something used as a mark, e.g. of the position of something, etc. **2** *slang* a promissory note, esp. a handwritten IOU.

market *noun* **1 a** a gathering of people to buy and sell various goods. **b** the building or other public place where this goes on. **c** a store. **2** potential customers; demand; level of trade. —*verb trans., intrans.* (**marketed, marketing**) **1** to offer for sale; to promote. **2** to trade or deal. ▸ **marketable** *adj.*

marketing *noun* business techniques, processes, etc. used for selling or promoting a product.

marketplace *or* **market place** *noun* **1** an open space where a market is held. **2** the commercial world of buying and selling.

market research investigation into the habits, needs, preferences, etc. of customers.

marksman *or* **markswoman** *noun* a person skilled in shooting, esp. a trained soldier or police officer. ▸ **marksmanship** *noun*

markup *noun* an amount added to a cost price to give a profit.

marlin *noun* (*pl.* **marlin, marlins**) a large game fish with a spearlike beak. *Also called* **spearfish.**

marlinespike *or* **marlinspike** *noun Naut.* a pointed metal tool used in rope splicing.

marmalade *noun* a preserve made from citrus fruit, esp. oranges.

marmoreal *adj. formal* of or like marble.

marmoset *noun* a small monkey.

marmot *noun* any of various large burrowing rodents, such as the woodchuck .

maroon¹ *noun* a dark brownish-red or purplish-red hue.

maroon² *verb trans.* (**marooned, marooning**) **1** to leave in isolation in a deserted place, esp. on an island. **2** to leave helpless.

marquee (mär-kē͏ʹ) *noun* **1** a very large tent used for circuses, parties, etc. **2** a rooflike structure, typically with a sign on it, that projects over the entrance to a theater.

marquess *noun* in the UK, a nobleman above an earl and below a duke in rank.

marquetry *noun* a decorative effect made by setting different woods into the surface of wooden furniture, etc., or the art or practice of producing this effect.

marquis (mär͏ʹkwĭs) *noun* in European countries, a nobleman next in rank above a count; a marquess.

marquise (mär-kēz') *noun* in various countries, a marchioness.

marriage *noun* **1 a** the state or relationship of being spouses. **b** an act or ceremony of becoming spouses. **2** a joining together; a union. ▸ **marriageable** *adj.*

marrow *noun* **1** the soft tissue that fills the internal cavities of bones. *Also called* **bone marrow**. **2** a plant with large prickly leaves or its large oblong fruit, eaten as a vegetable. *Also called* **vegetable marrow**. **3** the innermost, essential, or best part.

marrowbone *noun* an animal bone containing edible marrow, used for making stock, etc.

marrowfat *noun* a pea plant cultivated for its large edible seeds or the seed of one of these plants. *Also called* **marrow pea**.

marry *verb trans., intrans.* (**married, marrying, marries**) **1** to take (someone) as one's spouse. **2** to perform a wedding ceremony. **3** to become spouses.

Marsala (mär-säl'ə) *noun* a fortified wine.

marsh *noun* a poorly drained, low-lying area. ▸ **marshy** *adj.*

marshal *noun* **1** an officer, e.g., in the armed forces, assigned to a judicial district, in the fire department, etc. **2** an official who organizes parades, etc. —*verb trans.* (**marshalled** *or* **marshaled, marshalling** *or* **marshaling**) **1** to arrange (facts, etc.) in order. **2** to direct, lead, or show the way to.

marsh gas a colorless, tasteless gas consisting mainly of methane.

marsh hawk a N American hawk with a white patch on its rump.

marshmallow *noun* a spongy pink or white confection.

marsh marigold a plant with large, yellow, cup-shaped flowers. *Also called* **cowslip**.

marsupial *noun* a mammal, e.g., a kangaroo, wallaby, etc., that carries and suckles its young in an external pouch on the abdomen.

mart *noun* a market.

marten (*pl.* **marten, martens**) *noun* **1** a nocturnal, tree-dwelling, carnivorous mammal. **2** the fine, soft fur of this animal.

martial *adj.* of, relating to, or suitable for war, the armed forces, etc.

martial art any of various fighting sports or self-defense techniques, e.g., karate, judo.

martial law army rule, esp. when ordinary civil law has broken down.

Martian (mär'shən) *adj.* relating to or supposedly coming from the planet Mars. —*noun* a fictional inhabitant of Mars.

martin *noun* a small bird of the swallow family.

martinet *noun* a person who maintains strict discipline.

Named after Jean *Martinet*, a 17th-century French officer who invented a type of military drill

martini *noun* a cocktail made with gin or vodka, and dry vermouth.

martyr *noun* a person who suffers, is tortured, or is put to death because of his or her beliefs. —*verb trans.* (**martyred, martyring**) to torture or put to death as a martyr. ▸ **martyrdom** *noun*

marvel *noun* an astonishing or wonderful person or thing. —*verb intrans., trans.* (**marveled** *or* **marvelled, marveling** *or* **marvelling**) (**marvel at**) to be amazed by (someone or something). ▸ **marvelous** *adj.* ▸ **marvelously** *adv.*

Marxism *noun* Karl Marx's and Friedrich Engels's economic and political theories, esp. that socialism would lead on to the worldwide adoption of Communism and the end of capitalism. ▸ **Marxist** *adj., noun*

marzipan *noun* a sweet paste made from crushed almonds, sugar, and egg whites, used to decorate cakes, make candy, etc.

mascara *noun* a cosmetic for darkening the eyelashes.

mascarpone *noun* a soft Italian cream cheese.

mascot *noun* someone or something thought to bring good luck.

masculine *adj.* **1** relating to, typical of, or suitable for a man. **2** denoting or belonging to the gender of nouns and adjectives that in some languages are conventionally treated as male. ▸ **masculinity** *noun*

maser *noun* a device that amplifies microwaves.

MASH *abbrev.* Mobile Army Surgical Hospital.

mash *verb trans.* (**mashed, mashing, mashes**) to crush or pound into a pulpy mass. —*noun* **1** a mixture of grain and water used to feed farm animals. **2** a mixture of crushed malt and hot water, used in brewing. **3** a soft pulpy mass.

mask *noun* **1** a covering for the face, worn for amusement, for protection, or as a disguise. **2** something that disguises or covers up the truth. —*verb trans.* (**masked, masking**) to disguise, conceal, or cover up.

masochism *noun* pleasure, esp. sexual pleasure, derived from one's own suffering. ▸ **masochistic** *adj.*

After Leopold von Sacher-*Masoch*, 19th-century Austrian novelist

mason *noun* **1** a stonemason. **2** (**Mason**) a Freemason.

Masonic (mə-sän'ĭk) *adj.* relating to Freemasons.

Mason-Dixon line a surveying line that runs along the border between Pennsylvania and Maryland and which, prior to the Civil War, was regarded as dividing the slave states from the free states.

masonry *noun* **1** stonework. **2** (**Masonry**) Freemasonry.

masque *noun* a dramatic entertainment performed to music by masked actors.

masquerade *noun* **1** a disguise or false appearance or impression. **2** a formal dance where guests wear masks and costumes. —*verb intrans.* (**masqueraded, masquerading**) (*often* **masquerade as**) to disguise (oneself); to pretend to be (someone or something else).

Mass *or* **mass** *noun* a church service, esp. in the Roman Catholic Church.

mass *noun* **1** *Phys.* **a** the amount of matter that an object contains. **b** a measure of the quantity of matter in a body. **2** a large, usu. shapeless, quantity; a lump. **3** *colloq.* (*also* **masses**) a large quantity or number. **4** majority; bulk. **5** (**the masses**) ordinary people. —*adj.* involving a large number of people or things: *a mass exodus.* —*verb intrans., trans.* (**massed, massing, masses**) to gather or cause to gather in large numbers.

massacre *noun* **1** the violent killing of large numbers of people or animals. **2** *colloq.* an overwhelming defeat. —*verb trans.* (**massacred, massacring**) **1** to kill violently and in large numbers. **2** *colloq.* to defeat overwhelmingly.

massage *noun* **1** rubbing, kneading, etc. body parts with the hands, esp. for easing stiff or painful muscles, or as a means of easing stress. **2** a session of such treatment. —*verb trans.* (**massaged, massaging**) to give (a person or body part) such treatment. ▸ **masseur** *noun* ▸ **masseuse** *noun*

massif *noun* a distinct group of mountains within a range.

massive *adj.* **1** very solid, big, and heavy. **2** exceedingly or excessively large in size. ▸ **massively** *adv.*

mass-market *adj.* of, pertaining to, or intended for mass consumption or purchase: *mass-market paperbacks.*

mass media (*pl.*) those forms of communication that reach large numbers of people, e.g., television and newspapers.

mass-produce *verb trans.* (**mass-produced, mass-producing**) to produce (consumer goods, etc.) in a standard form in large quantities, esp. using mechanization. ▸ **mass production**

mast[1] *noun* an upright supporting pole, esp. one carrying the sails of a ship or used to house a radio or television aerial.

mast[2] *noun* the fruit of the oak, beech, and other forest trees.

mastectomy *noun* (*pl.* **mastectomies**) surgical removal of a human breast.

master *noun* **1** a person who commands or controls. **2** a male owner of an animal, etc. **3** a person with outstanding skill in a particular activity. **4** the commanding officer of a merchant ship. *Also called* **master mariner**. **5** a fully qualified craftsman, allowed to train others. **6** a male teacher. —*adj.* **1** fully qualified; highly skilled; expert. **2** main; principal. —*verb trans.* (**mastered, mastering**) **1** to overcome or defeat. **2** to become skilled in.

masterful *adj.* showing authority, skill, or power.

masterly *adj.* showing the skill of a master. ▸ **masterly** *adv.*

mastermind *noun* a person responsible for devising or planning something. —*verb trans.* (**masterminded, masterminding**) to devise or plan.

master of ceremonies (*pl.* **masters of ceremonies**) (ABBREV. **MC**) an announcer esp. one introducing speakers at formal occasions.

masterpiece *noun* an extremely skillful or brilliant piece of work. *Also called* **masterwork**. ▣ MAGNUM OPUS, TOUR DE FORCE.

master sergeant (ABBREV. **M.Sgt., MSGT**) a noncommissioned officer in the US Army or Air Force.

masterstroke *noun* a very clever, well-timed action.

mastery *noun* skill, knowledge, or control.

masthead *noun* **1** the top of a ship's mast. **2** the title of a newspaper or periodical, usu. at the top of its front page, often with details of its owner, address, price, etc.

mastic *noun* **1** an aromatic shrub or a resin obtained from its sap. *Also called* **mastic gum**. **2** a waterproof putty-like cement.

masticate (măs′tĭ-kāt,) *verb trans., intrans.* (**masticated, masticating**) to chew (food). ▸ **mastication** *noun*

mastiff *noun* a large dog with a powerful body and a short-haired tan or brindled coat.

mastitis *noun* inflammation of a woman's breast or an animal's udder.

mastodon *noun* a large extinct mammal related to the elephant.

mastoid *adj.* **1** resembling a nipple or breast. **2** of or relating to a mastoid. —*noun* a bony outgrowth situated behind and below the ear. *Also called* **mastoid process**.

masturbate *verb intrans., trans.* (**masturbated, masturbating**) to rub or stroke the genitals (of oneself or someone else) for sexual arousal. ▸ **masturbation** *noun* ▸ **masturbatory** *adj.*

mat[1] *noun* **1** a floor-covering. **2** a piece of protective or decorative fabric, cork, etc.: *a place mat*. **3** a dense, untidy tangle, e.g., of vegetation, hair, etc. —*verb intrans., trans.* (**matted, matting**) to become, or cause to become, tangled into a dense, untidy mass.

mat[2] *noun* **1** a decorative border around a picture, drawing, etc. **2** (*also* **matte**) a dull surface. —adj. (also **matte**) having or producing a dull surface. —verb trans. (**matted, matting**) **1** to surround (a picture, drawing, etc.) with a decorative border. **2** to apply a dull finish to, or produce a dull finish on (something).

matador noun the principal toreador who kills the bull in bullfighting.

match[1] noun a piece of wood or strip of cardboard with a tip that ignites when struck against a rough surface.

match[2] noun **1** a contest or game. **2** an equal or peer. **3** a person or thing that is the same as or similar to another, or that corresponds to, combines well with, or suits another. **4** a partnership or pairing. —verb trans., intrans. (**matched, matching**) **1** (also **match up** or **match** (**something**) **up**) to be the same as or similar to another, or to correspond to, combine well with, or suit another. **2** to fit or put (people or things that match) together. **3** to equal.

matchless adj. having no equal; superior to all.

matchmaker noun a person who arranges romantic partnerships between people.

mate[1] noun **1** an animal's breeding partner. **2** a person's sexual partner. **3** colloq. a companion or friend, usu. male. **4** (in compounds) a person with whom one has something in common: a workmate. **5** one of a pair. **6** an officer on a merchant ship. —verb intrans., trans. (**mated, mating**) **1** of animals to copulate. **2** to bring (animals) together for breeding. **3** to marry. **4** to join as a pair.

mate[2] noun Chess a checkmate.

material noun **1** a substance for making something. **2** cloth; fabric. —adj. **1** relating to physical things or to actuality. **2** important or essential.

materialism noun great or excessive interest in possessions, financial success, etc. ▸ **materialist** noun ▸ **materialistic** adj. ▸ **materialistically** adv.

materialize verb intrans. (**materialized, materializing**) **1** to become real, visible, or tangible; to appear. **2** to become fact; to happen. ▸ **materialization** noun

materially adv. formal importantly or significantly.

maternal adj. **1** of, typical of, or like a mother. **2** related on the mother's side of the family. ▸ **maternally** adv.

maternity noun the state of being or becoming a mother. —adj. relating to pregnancy or giving birth.

math noun colloq. mathematics.

mathematical adj. **1** of, relating to, or using mathematics. **2** very exact or accurate. ▸ **mathematically** adv.

mathematics noun (sing.) the science of measurements, numbers, quantities, and shapes.

matinee or **matinée** (măt,n-ā′) noun a movie, play, etc. put on in the afternoon.

matri- combining form forming words denoting of a woman or a mother: matricide.

matriarch (mā′trē-ärk,) noun a female head of a family, community, or people. ▸ **matriarchal** adj.

matriarchy noun (pl. **matriarchies**) a social system run by women, often with property, power, etc. being handed down from mother to daughter.

matrices pl. noun see **matrix**.

matricide (mā′trĭ-sīd,, măt′-) noun **1** the killing of a mother by her own child. **2** a person who kills his or her own mother. ▸ **matricidal** adj.

matriculate verb trans., intrans. (**matriculated, matriculating**) to enrol or be enrolled at a university or college. ▸ **matriculant** noun ▸ **matriculation** noun

matrimony noun (pl. **matrimonies**) **1** the state of being married. **2** a wedding ceremony. ▸ **matrimonial** adj.

matrix noun (pl. **matrices, matrixes**) **1** Math. a square or rectangular arrangement of symbols or numbers. **2** a substance or place where something develops or is formed.

matron noun **1** a woman in charge of the nursing, domestic, etc. arrangements in an institution. **2** a middle-aged to elderly woman.

matronly adj., of a woman dignified; authoritative.

matron of honor (pl. **matrons of honor**) a bride's main married attendant at a wedding. See also **maid of honor** (sense 1).

matte noun same as **mat**[2] (sense 2). —adj. same as **mat**[2].

matted adj., of hair, etc. tangled.

matter noun **1** the substance from which all physical things are made. **2** material of a particular kind: vegetable matter. **3** a subject or topic; a concern, affair, or question: Matters of principle are important. **4** content as distinct from style or form. **5** an approximate amount: in a matter of minutes. **6** pus —verb intrans. (**mattered, mattering**) to be important or significant. —**be the matter** (**with**) to be the trouble, difficulty, or thing that is wrong: What's the matter with your car? **for that matter** as far as that is concerned. **no matter** regardless of: No matter when she comes, we'll be ready to greet her.

matter-of-fact adj. unemotional; straightforward or commonplace. ▸ **matter-of-factly** adv. ▸ **matter-of-factness** noun

matting noun material of rough, woven fibers for making mats.

mattock *noun* a pickax with a blade that is flattened horizontally at one end.

mattress *noun* a large, flat, fabric-covered pad for sleeping on.

maturate (măch′ə-rāt,) *verb trans., intrans.* (**maturated, maturating**) to suppurate.

mature (mə-tŏŏr′, -chŏŏr′) *adj.* **1** fully grown or developed. **2** relating to or appropriate for adults, or comprising adults. **3** showing or having grown-up traits; not childish: *a mature outlook.* **4** *of cheese, wine, etc.* having a fully developed flavor. **5** *of an insurance policy, etc.* paying out, or beginning to pay out, money to the holder. —*verb trans., intrans.* (**matured, maturing**) **1** to make or become fully grown or developed. **2** *of a life insurance policy, etc.* to begin to produce a return. ▸ **maturity** *noun*

maudlin *adj.* foolishly or drunkenly gloomy or sentimental. ▣ MAWKISH, MUSHY, SAPPY, SCHMALTZY, SLOPPY, SLUSHY, SOPPY ▣ DISPASSIONATE, UNEMOTIONAL.

From Mary *Magdalene*, who was frequently depicted crying in paintings

maul *verb trans.* (**mauled, mauling**) **1** to attack fiercely, usu. tearing flesh. **2** to handle roughly or clumsily. —*noun* a long-handled, heavy hammer.

maulstick *noun* same as **mahlstick**.

maunder *verb intrans.* (**maundered, maundering**) to talk or move in a rambling or aimless way.

mausoleum *noun* (*pl.* **mausoleums, mausolea**) a grand or monumental tomb.

mauve *noun* a pale purple color.

maven *noun* an expert in a given field.

maverick *noun* **1** an unbranded stray animal, esp. a calf. **2** a dissenter or nonconformist.

After Samuel *Maverick*, Texas rancher who never branded his cattle

maw *noun* a throat or gullet.

mawkish *adj.* foolishly or drunkenly gloomy or sentimental.

max *slang noun* the maximum. —*adj.* maximal. —*adv.* maximally. —*verb intrans.* (**maxed, maxing, maxes**) (*also* **max out**) to get to a specified limit, etc., e.g., of one's endurance, or where no further development, improvement, etc. is possible.

max. *abbrev.* maximum.

maxi- *combining form* forming words denoting larger or longer than average or normal.

maxilla *noun* (*pl.* **maxillae, maxillas**) **1** one of a pair of bones in the upper jaw of a vertebrate. **2** a mouthpart, esp. of an insect, crustacean, etc. ▸ **maxillary** *adj.*

maxim *noun* **1** a saying, esp. one that succinctly expresses a general truth. ▣ APHORISM, AXIOM, TRUISM. **2** a general rule or principle.

maximal *adj.* of a maximum; of the greatest possible size, value, etc.

maximize *verb trans., intrans.* (**maximized, maximizing**) to make or become as high, great, etc., as possible. ▸ **maximization** *noun*

maximum *adj.* being the greatest possible. —*noun* the greatest possible number, quantity, degree, etc.

May *noun* (*pl.* **Mays**) the fifth month of the year.

may *verb aux.* (*pa t* **might**) used to denote possibility, permission, a wish, dependency, or contingency.

maybe *adv.* perhaps; possibly.

May Day May 1, a national holiday in many countries, often accompanied by spring celebrations and sometimes honoring labor organizations.

mayday *or* **Mayday** *noun* an international distress signal.

mayfly (*pl.* **mayflies**) *noun* a short-lived slender fragile insect, usu. found near water.

mayhem *noun* **1** chaos. **2** an act or the process of violently injuring someone or a crime involving maiming someone.

mayonnaise *noun* a cold, creamy sauce made of egg yolk, oil, vinegar or lemon juice, and seasoning. *Also called colloq.* **mayo.**

mayor *noun* the head of the local government of a city, town, or municipal corporation. ▸ **mayoral** *adj.* ▸ **mayoralty** *noun*

maypole *noun* a tall pole set up for dancing around on May Day.

maze *noun* **1** a labyrinth. **2** a confusingly complicated system, procedure, etc.

McCoy (mə-koi′) *noun* (*usu.* **the (real) McCoy**) the genuine article, not an imitation.

me *pron.* the object form of *I.*

Usage See note at **between.**

mea culpa (mā,ə-kŏŏl′pə, -kəl′-) admittance of an error or fault.

mead[1] *noun* a spicy alcoholic drink made by fermenting honey.

mead[2] *noun old use, poetic* a meadow.

meadow *noun* a field of grass, typically used for grazing animals or making hay.

meadowlark a yellow-breasted songbird.

meager *adj.* **1** lacking in quality or quantity; inadequate; scanty. **2** *of a person* thin, esp. unhealthily so.

meal[1] *noun* **1** an occasion on which food is eaten. **2** an amount or type of food eaten on one occasion.

meal[2] *noun* (*often in compounds*) **1** edible grain ground to a coarse powder. **2** any other ground substance. ▸ **mealy** *adj.*

meal ticket 1 a ticket that entitles its holder to a meal. **2** *slang* someone or something used as a source of income or other means of support.

mealy-mouthed *adj.* speaking evasively or insincerely.

mean[1] *verb, trans., intrans.* (pa t and pa p **meant;** *prp* **meaning**) **1** to express or intend to express, show, or indicate. **2** to have as a purpose. **3** to be serious or sincere about. **4** to represent, entail, result in, or involve.

mean[2] *adj.* **1** not generous. **2** unkind; despicable. **3** of inferior quality. **4** *colloq.* malicious or nasty. **5** *slang* good; skillful. ▸ **meanly** *adv.* ▸ **meanness** *noun*

mean[3] *noun* **1** a midway position, course, etc. **2** a mathematical or statistical average. —*adj.* **1** midway. **2** average.

meander (mē-ăn'dər) *verb intrans.* (**meandered, meandering**) **1** *of a river, road, etc.* to have a winding course. **2** to wander aimlessly. —*noun* a winding course.

> After the winding *Maeander* river in Turkey

meanie *or* **meany** *noun colloq.* **1** a selfish or ungenerous person. **2** a nasty, often cruel, person.

meaning *noun* **1** a sense of a word, phrase, etc. **2** significance, importance, or purpose. —*adj.* significant.

meaningful *adj.* significant or important in value, influence, effect, etc. ▸ **meaningfully** *adv.*

meaningless *adj.* lacking meaning, importance, or purpose.

means *noun* **1** (*sing., pl.*) an instrument, method, etc. used to achieve an end. **2** (*pl.*) resources, esp. financial.

meant *verb see* **mean[1]**.

meantime *noun* the time or period between one thing and another. —*adv.* meanwhile.

meanwhile *adv.* during the time in between; at the same time.

measles *noun* (*sing., pl.*) a highly infectious disease, common in children, characterized by fever, a sore throat, and a blotchy red rash.

measly *adj.* (**measlier, measliest**) **1** *slang, of an amount or value* very small; miserable; paltry. **2** relating to, or suffering from, measles.

measure *noun* **1** a standardized unit for determining the dimensions, quantity, etc. of something. **2** a dimension, quantity, etc. ascertained using such a standardized unit, or an act or the process of ascertaining it. **3** any standard or ascertainable amount. **4** (*often in compounds*) an instrument for determining the dimensions, quantity, etc. of anything: *a tape-measure.* **5** (*usu.* **measures**) an action or step: *drastic measures.* **6** a unit of rhythm or time in

music or poetry. —*verb trans. intrans.* (**measured, measuring**) **1** to determine or show the dimensions, quantity, etc. of something. **2** to be a specified size. ▸ **measurable** *adj.*

measured *adj.* **1** slow and steady. **2** carefully chosen or considered.

measurement *noun* **1** (*often* **measurements**) a size, amount, etc., determined by measuring. **2** an act of measuring.

measuring worm a caterpillar. *Also called* **inchworm**.

meat *noun* **1** animal flesh used as food. **2** the basic, most important part of something.

meaty *adj.* (**meatier, meatiest**) **1** relating to, full of, containing, etc. meat. **2** full of interesting information or ideas. ▸ **meatiness** *noun*

mecca *noun* a place of outstanding importance, esp. one much visited.

mechanic *noun* someone who repairs or maintains machinery, engines, etc.

mechanical *adj.* **1** of or concerning machines. **2** worked by or performed with machinery. **3** automatic; lacking feeling, sincerity, etc. ▸ **mechanically** *adv.*

mechanics *noun* **1** (*sing.*) the scientific study of motion and forces causing motion. **2** (*sing., pl.*) machine design, construction, and utilization. **3** (*pl.*) the elements or properties of a system, etc. that make it function.

mechanism *noun* **1** two or more moving parts that interact to perform a specific function. **2** the specific arrangement of moving parts in a machine. **3** the arrangement and action by which a result is produced. **4** a philosophy that regards the phenomena of life as explainable by mechanical forces. ▸ **mechanistic** *adj.*

mechanize *verb trans.* (**mechanized, mechanizing**) **1** to convert to a mechanical process or cause to operate with or be operated by machines. **2** to supply (troops) with motor vehicles. ▸ **mechanization** *noun*

medal *noun* a metal disc, usu. with an inscription, presented to someone in recognition of an achievement, bravery, etc. ▸ **medalist** *noun*

medallion *noun* **1** a large medal-like piece of jewelry, usu. worn on a chain. **2** an oval or circular decorative feature in architecture or on textiles. **3** a thin circular cut of meat.

Medal of Honor the highest US military decoration.

meddle *verb intrans.* (**meddled, meddling**) to interfere in or tamper with (something). ▸ **meddler** *noun* ▸ **meddlesome** *adj.*

media *pl. noun see* **medium**.

mediaeval *adj. same as* **medieval**.

medial *adj.* of or situated in the middle; intermediate. ▸ **medially** *adv.*

median *noun* a middle point or part. —*adj.* situated in or passing through the middle.

median strip a paved or landscaped area in the middle of a highway.

mediate (měd′ē-āt,) *verb intrans., trans.* (**mediated, mediating**) 1 to try to reconcile two sides or people in dispute. 2 to try to settle (a dispute, etc.) by acting as an intermediary. ▸ **mediation** *noun* ▸ **mediator** *noun*

medic *noun colloq.* 1 a military medical corps member. 2 a physician or a medical student.

Medicaid (měd′ĭ-kād,) *noun* a US government program to reimburse physicians, hospitals, etc. for treating people who are unable to meet their medical expenses themselves.

medical *adj.* 1 of or relating to the science or practice of medicine. 2 of or relating to treatment by means of drugs, etc., as opposed to surgery. 3 of a substance, treatment, etc. therapeutic or medicinal. —*noun colloq.* a medical examination. ▸ **medically** *adv.*

medical examiner (ABBREV. **ME**) a physician who ascertains the cause of deaths occurring under other than natural circumstances.

medicament *noun* formal a medicine.

Medicare (měd′ĭ-kăr,, -kĕr,) *noun* a US government program for the medical care of the elderly or disabled.

medicate (měd′ĭ-kāt,) *verb trans.* (**medicated, medicating**) to treat with medicine. ▸ **medication** *noun*

medicine *noun* 1 the science or practice of treating or preventing diseases, etc. 2 a drug, etc. used to prevent or treat disease. ▸ **medicinal** *adj.* ▸ **medicinally** *adv.*

medicine ball a heavy ball thrown from person to person as a form of exercise.

medicine man a person believed to have magic powers, used for healing or sorcery.

medico *noun* (*pl.* **medicos**) *slang* a physician or a medical student.

medieval *or* **mediaeval** *adj.* relating to or characteristic of the Middle Ages.

medievalist *or* **mediaevalist** *noun* a person who studies or is an expert in the medieval period.

mediocre *adj.* ordinary or average; rather inferior. ▸ **mediocrity** *noun*

meditate *verb intrans., trans.* (**meditated, meditating**) 1 to think deeply, esp. in a spiritual way. 2 to consider carefully. ▸ **meditation** *noun* ▸ **meditative** *adj.*

medium *noun* (*pl.* **media, mediums**) 1 something by or through which an effect is produced. 2 (*pl.* **media**) (*often* **the media**) **a** a means of communicating to a wide audience, e.g., television, radio, the press, etc. **b** (*sing., pl.*) broadcast and print journalists as a group. 3 (*pl.* **mediums**) a person who acts as a means for the living to contact the dead. 4 a substance in which specimens are preserved, bacteria are grown, etc. 5 a middle position, condition, or course: *a happy medium.* 6 a particular type or category of materials used in art: *works, in the medium of oils.* —*adj.* 1 intermediate; midway; average. 2 moderate.

medlar *noun* a small deciduous tree or shrub or its edible fruit.

medley *noun* (*pl.* **medleys**) 1 a selection of songs, tunes, etc. played together. 2 a mixture. 3 a race with different stages.

meek *adj.* 1 having a mild, gentle temperament. 2 submissive or unassertive. ▸ **meekly** *adv.* ▸ **meekness** *noun*

meerschaum (mĭr′shəm, -shŏm,) *noun* 1 a claylike mineral. *Also called* **sepiolite.** 2 a tobacco pipe with a bowl made of this.

meet[1] *verb trans., intrans.* (*pa t and pa p* **met**; *pr p* **meeting**) 1 to come together with (someone) by chance or arrangement. 2 to be introduced to (someone) for the first time. 3 to be present at the arrival of: *met the train.* 4 (*often* **meet with**) to encounter a specified action, response, etc.: *Our ideas met with approval.* 5 to come into contact with; to join: *where the paths meet.* 6 to satisfy: *meet your requirements.* 7 to pay: *meet the costs.* —*noun* a sporting event or an assembly of hunters, etc. before a fox hunt.

meet[2] *adj.* old use proper, fitting, correct, or suitable. ▸ **meetly** *adv.*

meeting *noun* 1 an act of coming together. 2 an assembly or gathering. 3 a sporting event, esp. in athletics or horse racing.

meetinghouse *noun* a building used for religious services.

mega *adj. slang* excellent.

mega- *combining form* forming words denoting: 1 a million: *megawatt.* 2 *Comput.* 2^{20} *megabit.* 3 *colloq.* great; huge amounts of: *a megastar* / *earns mega-bucks.*

megabit *noun Comput.* (ABBREV. **Mb**) a data unit equal to 2^{20} or 1,048,576 bits.

megabyte *noun Comput.* (ABBREV. **MB**) a data unit equal to 2^{20} or 1,048,576 bytes.

megahertz *noun* (ABBREV. **MHz**) one million cycles per second, used as a unit of measuring radio frequencies.

megalith *noun* a very large stone, esp. one forming part of a prehistoric monument. ▸ **megalithic** *adj.*

megalomania *noun* 1 delusions of grandeur, power, wealth, etc. 2 *colloq.* an excessive craving or need for power. ▸ **megalomaniac** *noun*

megalopolis *noun* a very large city or a large city with densely populated suburban areas.

megaphone *noun* a funnel-shaped voice-amplifying device.

meiosis (mī-ō′sĭs) *noun* (*pl.* **meioses**) a process of cell division that results in the number of original chromosomes being halved. *Also called* **reduction division**. *See also* **mitosis**.

melamine *noun* a crystalline compound used in the manufacture of artificial resins that are resistant to heat, water, chemicals, etc.

melancholia *noun old use same as* **depression** sense 1.

melancholic *adj.* relating to or affected by melancholia or melancholy.

melancholy *noun* **1** prolonged and deep sadness. **2** a sad, pensive state of mind.

mélange *or* **melange** (mā-länzh′, -länj′) *noun* a mixture.

melanin *noun* a dark pigment that gives hair, skin, etc. their color.

melanoma *noun* (*pl.* **melanomas, melanomata**) a dark skin tumor often associated with excessive exposure to sunlight.

Melba toast very thin crisp toast.

meld *verb intrans., trans.* (**melded, melding**) to merge or cause to merge.

melee *or* **mêlée** *noun* **1** a riotous brawl involving large numbers of people. **2** a confused or muddled collection.

mellifluous *adj., of sounds, speech, etc.* having a smooth, sweet, flowing quality. ▸ **mellifluously** *adv.* ▸ **mellifluousness** *noun*

mellow *adj.* **1** *colloq., of a person or character* calm and relaxed. **2** *of sound, color, light, etc.* soft, rich, and pure. **3** *of wine, cheese, etc.* fully flavored with age. **4** *of fruit* sweet and ripe. **5** *colloq. of a person, atmosphere, etc.* pleasantly relaxed or relaxing. —*verb trans., intrans.* (**mellowed, mellowing**) to make or become mellow.

melodic *adj.* **1** relating to melody. **2** tuneful; melodious. ▸ **melodically** *adv.*

melodious *adj.* **1** pleasant to listen to. **2** having a recognizable melody. ▸ **melodiousness** *noun*

melodrama *noun* **1** a film, play, etc. with a sensational plot, exaggerated action, and usu. a sentimental ending. **2** excessively dramatic behavior.

melodramatic *adj.* exaggerated or sensational in expressing emotion. ▸ **melodramatically** *adv.* ▸ **melodramatics** *pl. noun*

melody *noun* (*pl.* **melodies**) **1** a tune. **2** pleasantness of sound; tuneful music. **3** pleasant arrangement or combination of sounds, esp. in poetry.

melon *noun* a plant of the gourd family, or the large round or oval edible fruit it produces.

melt *verb trans., intrans.* (**melted, melting**) **1** to make or become liquid as a result of heat. **2** to dissolve. **3** to dwindle or disappear. **4** *colloq.* to make or become emotionally or romantically tender or sympathetic: *a sight that would melt the hardest of hearts.*

meltdown *noun* **1** the melting of all or most of the core of a nuclear reactor. **2** *slang* a major disaster or failure.

melting pot a place or situation where different communities, beliefs, ideas, cultures, etc., come together, usu. with a degree of assimilation and acceptance.

member *noun* **1** a person who belongs to or who is elected to a group, organization, governing body, etc. **2** a plant or animal belonging to a specified taxonomic classification. **3** a part of a whole, esp. a limb or a petal. ▸ **membership** *noun*

membrane *noun* **1** a thin sheet of animal or plant tissue, e.g., enclosing an organ, connecting parts, forming a boundary, or enclosing individual structures. **2** a thin sheet of permeable or semi-permeable material used as a filter. ▸ **membranous** *adj.*

memento *noun* (*pl.* **mementos, mementoes**) a physical object serving as a reminder of the past; a souvenir.

memo *noun* (*pl.* **memos**) a memorandum.

memoir (mĕm′wär, -wôr) *noun* **1** a written record of past events. **2** (**memoirs**) an account of a person's life history; an autobiography.

memorabilia *pl. noun* souvenirs of people or events.

memorable *adj.* worth remembering; easily remembered. ▸ **memorably** *adv.*

memorandum *noun* (*pl.* **memorandums, memoranda**) **1** a note of something to be remembered. **2** a statement or record, esp. one circulated for the attention of colleagues.

memorial *noun* something commemorating a person, an event, etc. —*adj.* serving to commemorate.

Memorial Day a US national holiday, observed on the last Monday in May in honor of the war dead.

memorize *verb trans.* (**memorized, memorizing**) to learn thoroughly, so as to be able to reproduce exactly from memory.

memory *noun* (*pl.* **memories**) **1** the ability to remember, or the store of things remembered. **2** the processes involved in remembering or something recalled by remembering. **3** commemoration: *in memory of our dead.* **4** computer memory.

men *pl. noun see* **man**.

menace *noun* **1** a source of threatening danger. **2** a show of hostility; a threat. —*verb trans.* (**menaced, menacing**) to show an intention to cause damage or harm to; to threaten.

ménage *noun* a group of people living together; a household.

ménage à trois (měn-äzh′) (pl. **ménages à trois**) a household consisting of three people, esp. one in which one person has a sexual relationship with both of the others.

menagerie noun **1** a collection of wild animals caged for exhibition. **2** a varied or confused mixture, esp. of people.

mend verb trans., intrans. (**mended, mending**) **1** to repair. **2** to improve, esp. in health; to heal. **3** to improve or correct: mend one's ways. —noun a repaired part or place. —**on the mend** getting better, esp. in health.

mendacity noun (pl. **mendacities**) **1** the tendency to lie; untruthfulness. **2** a lie. ► **mendacious** adj.

mendicant noun **1** a beggar. **2** RC Church a member of an order of begging monks. —adj. begging.

menfolk pl. noun men collectively, esp. the male members of a family or group.

menhir noun a prehistoric monument in the form of a single standing stone.

menial adj., of work unskilled, uninteresting, and of low status. —noun a domestic servant.

meningitis (měn،ĭn-jīt′ĭs) noun inflammation of the membranes covering the brain and spinal cord.

meniscus noun (pl. **menisci, meniscuses**) **1** a curved surface at the top of a liquid, caused by surface tension. **2** a lens, convex on one side and concave on the other.

menopause noun the time when menstruation stops permanently. ► **menopausal** adj.

menorah noun a seven-branched candlestick regarded as a symbol of Judaism.

mensch noun (pl. **menschen, mensches**) colloq. a person, esp. one who is thought of as having admirable qualities.

menses (měn′sēz،) pl. noun blood, mucus, and other matter discharged, usu. monthly, from the uterus.

menstruate verb intrans. (**menstruated, menstruating**) to discharge the menses. ► **menstrual** adj. ► **menstruation** noun

mensuration noun the process of measuring.

-ment suffix forming words denoting: **1** a process, action, or means: repayment / treatment. **2** a quality, state, or condition: enjoyment / merriment.

mental adj. **1** of, relating to, or done using the mind or intelligence: mental arithmetic. **2** old use of, relating to, or affected by a psychiatric or psychological illness: a mental patient. **3** slang foolish; stupid; crazy: a mental idea. ► **mentally** adv.

> **Usage** The application of mental to psychiatric or psychological illness or people suffering from psychiatric or psychological illness is now considered offensive.

mentality noun (pl. **mentalities**) **1** a certain way of thinking, an outlook. **2** intellectual ability.

menthol noun an organic compound derived from peppermint oils. ► **mentholated** adj.

mention verb trans. (**mentioned, mentioning**) to speak of or make reference to, esp. briefly or in passing. —noun **1** a brief or passing reference. **2** a reference made to an individual's merit in an official report. ► **mentionable** adj.

mentor (měn′tôr،, měnt′ər) noun a trusted teacher or adviser.

> After Mentor, a friend of Odysseus, who guides Telemachus in his search for his father

menu noun **1** the range of dishes available in a restaurant, etc., or a list detailing these. **2** Comput. a list of optional functions displayed on a screen.

meow or **mew** noun a crying or whining noise made by a cat. —verb intrans. (**meowed, meowing** or **mewed, mewing**) to make this noise.

mercantile adj. of or pertaining to trade or traders; commercial.

mercenary adj. excessively concerned with the desire for personal gain, esp. money. —noun (pl. **mercenaries**) a soldier available for hire by a country or group.

mercerize verb trans. (**mercerized, mercerizing**) to treat (cotton, etc.) with a substance that strengthens it and gives it a silky appearance.

merchandise noun commercial goods. —verb intrans., trans. (also **merchandize**) (**merchandised, merchandising** or **merchandized, merchandizing**) to trade.

merchant noun someone engaged in trading.

merchant marine the commercial fleet of a nation or those who crew and manage it.

merciful adj. feeling or displaying compassion. ▣ LENIENT, TOLERANT ▣ MERCILESS, INTOLERANT. ► **mercifully**.adv.

merciless adj. feeling or displaying no compassion. ► **mercilessly** adv.

mercurial adj. **1** of or containing mercury. **2** changeable.

mercury noun (SYMBOL Hg) a dense silvery-white metallic element, and the only metal that is liquid at room temperature.

mercy noun (pl. **mercies**) **1** compassion shown when punishment is possible or justified, or the power to be compassionate in such circumstances. **2** a relief or welcome happening. —**at the mercy of** wholly in the power of (someone or something).

mercy killing euthanasia.

mere[1] adj. (superlative **merest**) nothing more than; no better, more important, or useful than.

mere[2] noun a lake or pool.

merely adv. only; simply.

meretricious adj. superficially attractive, but actually of no real value.

merganser noun a large diving duck that feeds on fish. Also called **sheldrake**.

merge verb trans., intrans. (**merged, merging**) 1 to be, or cause something to be, absorbed, combined, or joined with something else. 2 Comput. to combine two or more files, lists, etc.

merger noun a joining together, esp. of business firms.

meridian noun 1 an imaginary line on the Earth's surface passing through the poles at right angles to the Equator; a line of longitude. 2 a peak, e.g., of success. ▸ **meridional** adj.

meringue (mǝ-răng') noun a crisp cooked mixture of sugar and egg whites, or a cake made from this.

merino noun (pl. **merinos**) a breed of domestic sheep, its fine silky wool, or yarn or fabric made from its wool.

merit noun 1 worth, excellence, or praiseworthiness. 2 (often **merits**) a good point or quality. —verb trans. (**merited, meriting**) to be worthy of. ▣ DESERVE, EARN.

meritocracy noun (pl. **meritocracies**) government or leadership by people of great talent or intelligence. ▸ **meritocrat** noun ▸ **meritocratic** adj.

meritorious adj. deserving reward or praise.

merlin noun a small falcon. Also called **pigeon hawk**.

mermaid noun a mythical sea creature with a woman's head and upper body and a fish's tail.

merman noun a mythical sea creature with a man's head and upper body and a fish's tail.

merry adj. (**merrier, merriest**) 1 cheerful and lively. 2 colloq. slightly drunk. ▸ **merrily** adv. ▸ **merriment** noun

merry-go-round noun a revolving amusement ride with rising and falling seats in the form of horses or other figures.

merrymaker noun a reveler. ▸ **merrymaking** noun

mesa noun a flat-topped hill.

mésalliance (mā,zăl,yăns', mā,zǝ-lī'ǝns) noun a marriage where one party is socially inferior.

mescal noun a small round spineless cactus or the hallucinogenic drug or intoxicating drink made from it. Also called **peyote**.

mescaline or **mescalin** noun a hallucinogenic compound derived from the mescal cactus. Also called **peyote**.

Mesdames pl. noun see **madam** (sense 1a), **Madame**.

mesh noun 1 netting, or a piece of netting. 2 an opening between the threads of a net. —verb intrans., trans. (**meshed, meshing**) 1 of the teeth on gear wheels to engage. 2 to work or fit together, or cause to work or fit together. 3 to become entangled.

mesmerize verb trans. (**mesmerized, mesmerizing**) 1 old use to hypnotize. 2 to fascinate. ▸ **mesmeric** adj. ▸ **mesmerism** noun ▸ **mesmerist** noun

An earlier term than hypnotize, the word comes from the name of the 18th-century Austrian doctor, Franz Anton Mesmer, who claimed to be able to cure disease through the influence of his will on patients

mesolithic adj. (also **Mesolithic**) of or relating to the middle period of the Stone Age.

meson noun an unstable, strongly interacting subatomic particle.

mesosphere noun the layer of the Earth's atmosphere above the stratosphere.

Mesozoic (měz,ǝ-zō'ĭk, měs,-) adj. relating to the time when dinosaurs flourished and then became extinct, and the first mammals, birds, and flowering plants appeared.

mess noun 1 an untidy or dirty state. 2 a state of disorder or confusion. 3 a badly damaged state. 4 something in a damaged or disordered state. 5 a communal dining room, esp. in the armed forces. —verb intrans., trans. (**messed, messing**) 1 colloq. to interfere: Stop messing in something that doesn't concern you. 2 (also **mess up**) to put into an untidy, dirty, or damaged state. 3 of soldiers, etc. to eat, or live, together. 4 (**mess with**) colloq. to become involved in argument or conflict with (someone). —**mess up** slang to bungle something; to make a mistake. ▸ **messy** adj. ▸ **messily** adv.

message noun 1 a spoken or written communication sent from one person to another. 2 a moral of a story, etc. —**get the message** colloq. to understand.

messenger noun a person sent with a message. ▣ CARRIER, COURIER, EMISSARY

Messiah (mǝ-sī'ǝ) noun (**the Messiah**) 1 Christianity Jesus Christ. 2 Judaism the anticipated redeemer of the Jewish people. ▸ **Messianic** adj.

Messieurs pl. noun (ABBREV. **Messrs.**) see **Monsieur.**

Messrs. abbrev. see **Mr.**

mestiza noun a woman of mixed European and Native American descent.

mestizo noun (pl. **mestizos**) a person of mixed European and Native American descent.

met verb see **meet**[1].

meta- combining form forming words denoting: 1 a change: metabolism. 2 an area of study related to another subject of

study, but going beyond it: *metalinguistics.*
3 a position behind or beyond: *metacarpal.*

metabolism *noun* the chemical reactions that occur within the cells of a living organism. ▸ **metabolic** *adj.*

metabolite *noun* a substance essential to, or produced during, metabolism.

metacarpus *noun* (*pl.* **metacarpi**) the bones or part of the human hand between the wrist and the fingers, or the corresponding bones or part in an animal's forelimb. ▸ **metacarpal** *adj.*

metal *noun* **1** a chemical element, e.g., iron, copper, tin, gold, silver, mercury, etc. **2** a metallic alloy.

metallic *adj.* relating to, made of, or characteristic of metal.

metalloid *noun Chem.* a chemical element that has both metallic and nonmetallic properties.

metallurgy *noun* the scientific study of metals. ▸ **metallurgist** *noun*

metalwork *noun* **1** the craft or practice of shaping metal. **2** articles made of metal. ▸ **metalworker** *noun*

metamorphic *adj.* **1** relating to metamorphosis or metamorphism. **2** denoting rocks that have been formed as a result of intense heat or pressure. *See also* **igneous, sedimentary** (sense 2).

metamorphism *noun* a process of change in the structure or composition of a rock as a result of intense heat or pressure.

metamorphosis (mĕt,ə-môr′fə-sĭs) *noun* (*pl.* **metamorphoses**) a complete or significant change in form, appearance, structure, or character. ▸ **metamorphose** *verb*

metaphor *noun* a figure of speech where a word, etc. is used to denote or refer to something else and thereby imply a similarity between the two. ▸ **metaphorical** *adj.* ▸ **metaphorically** *adv.*

metaphysics *noun* (*sing.*) the branch of philosophy dealing with the nature of existence and the basic principles of truth and knowledge. ▸ **metaphysical** *adj.* ▸ **metaphysically** *adv.*

metastasis *noun* (*pl.* **metastases**) **1** *Med.* the spread of a disease, esp. a malignant tumor, from one part of the body to another. **2** a secondary tumor that has developed in this way.

metatarsus *noun* (*pl.* **metatarsi**) the bones or part of the human foot between the ankle and the toes, or the corresponding bones or part in an animal's hind leg. ▸ **metatarsal** *adj.*

metazoan (mĕt,ə-zō′ən) *noun* a multicellular animal whose cells are organized into specialized tissues and organs. —*adj.* of or relating to metazoans.

mete *verb trans.* (**meted, meting**) to give out or dispense (esp. punishment).

meteor *noun* a small particle of matter from space that comes into Earth's atmosphere, where it burns up with the emission of a brief flash or streak of light. *Also called* **falling star, shooting star.**

meteoric *adj.* **1** of or relating to meteors. **2** *of success, etc.* very rapid. ▸ **meteorically** *adj.*

meteorite *noun* a lump of rock or metal from outer space that is large enough to fall to the Earth's surface without burning up as it passes through the atmosphere.

meteoroid *noun* a small moving solid object orbiting the Sun.

meteorology *noun* the scientific study of the Earth's atmosphere, esp. in relation to short-term weather forecasting. ▸ **meteorological** *adj.* ▸ **meteorologist** *noun*

meter¹ *noun* (ABBREV. **m**) *noun* **1** the unit of length in the International System, approximately equal to 39.37 in. **2** an instrument for measuring and recording, esp. quantities of electricity, gas, water, etc., used. —*verb trans.* (**metered, metering**) to measure and record using a meter.

meter² *noun* **1** *Poetry* the arrangement of words and syllables in a rhythmic pattern according to their length and stress. **2** *Mus.* the basic, repeating pattern of note values, accents, and beats per measure, as indicated by a time signature.

-meter *combining form* forming words denoting: **1** an instrument for measuring: *thermometer.* **2** a line of poetry with a specified number of units of stress, or feet: *pentameter.*

methadone *or* **methadon** *noun* a synthetic narcotic drug used esp. as a substitute drug in the treatment of morphine and heroin users wanting to end their addiction.

methane *noun* a colorless odorless flammable gas, the main component of natural gas.

methanol *noun* a colorless flammable toxic liquid. *Also called* **methyl alcohol, wood alcohol.**

method *noun* **1** a way of doing something, esp. an ordered set of procedures. **2** good planning; efficient organization. **3** (*often* **methods**) a technique used in a particular activity: *farming methods.*

methodical *adj.* efficient and orderly; done in an orderly way. ▸ **methodically** *adv.*

Methodist (mĕth′əd-ĭst) *noun* a member of the Methodist Church, a Protestant denomination. —*adj.* relating to Methodists or their church. ▸ **Methodism** *noun*

methodology *noun* (*pl.* **methodologies**) **1** the system of methods and principles used in a particular activity. **2** the study of method and procedure. ▸ **methodological** *adj.*

methyl alcohol *Chem.* methanol.

methylated spirits *or* **methylated spirit** ethanol mixed with small quantities of methanol and pyridine to make it undrinkable.

meticulous *adj.* giving or showing care and attention to detail. ▸ **meticulousness** *noun*

métier (mĕ′tyă,, mĕ-tyā′) *noun* something that one does well.

metre *noun* meter².

metric¹ *adj.* of or based on the meter or the metric system.

metric² *or* **metrical** *adj.* Poetry of or in verse as distinct from prose.

-metric *combining form* forming words denoting scientific measurement: *thermometric*.

metrically *adv.* **1** in or with the metric system of measurement. **2** in terms of meter; in meter.

metricate (mĕ′trĭ-kāt,) *or* **metricize** *verb trans.* (**metricated**, **metricating**, *or* **metricized**, **metricizing**) to convert to the metric system. ▸ **metrication** *noun*

metric system a standard system of measurement, based on decimal units.

metric ton a ton (sense 3).

metro¹ *noun* (*pl.* **metros**) an urban subway system.

metro² *noun* (*pl.* **metros**) an urban area; a metropolitan area.

metronome *noun* a device that indicates musical tempo by means of a ticking pendulum.

metropolis *noun* (*pl.* **metropolises**) a large city, esp. the capital city of a nation or region.

metropolitan *adj.* **1** of, typical of, or situated in a large city. **2** of or referring to a country's mainland, as opposed to its overseas territories. —*noun* **1** a bishop (usu. an archbishop) with authority over all the bishops in a province. **2** an inhabitant of a metropolis.

-metry *combining form* forming words denoting a science involving measurement: *geometry*.

mettle *noun* character, esp. courage, determination, stamina, etc.

mettlesome *adj.* high-spirited; lively.

mew *verb, noun* see **meow**.

mews *noun* (*pl.* **mews, mewses**) a group of stables around a yard.

> Originally a cage for hawks, *mews* took on its present meaning after royal stables were built in the 17th century on a site formerly used to house the king's hawks.

Mexican (mĕk′sĭ-kən) *adj.* of Mexico, its people, or their language. —*noun* a native or citizen of Mexico.

mezzanine *noun* **1** a small story between between main stories in a building. **2** the lowest of a theater's or stadium's balconies.

mezzo-soprano *noun* (*pl.* **mezzo-sopranos**) **1** a singing voice with a range between soprano and contralto. **2** a singer with this voice.

mezzotint *noun* a method of engraving a metal plate by polishing and scraping to produce areas of light and shade; a print from a plate engraved in this way.

mi *noun* the third note of the scale in the solfeggio system of music notation.

miasma (mī-ăz′mə, mē-) *noun* (*pl.* **miasmas, miasmata**) **1** a thick, foul-smelling vapor, esp. as given off by swamps, etc. **2** an evil influence or atmosphere. ▸ **miasmal** *adj.*

mica *noun* a silicate mineral readily split into thin flexible sheets.

mice *pl. noun* see **mouse.**

Mickey Finn *slang* a drink, esp. an alcoholic one, that has had a drug secretly added to it; a drug added to a drink in this way.

Mickey Mouse *adj. slang* petty, unimportant, or trivial.

micro *noun* (*pl.* **micros**) **1 a** a microcomputer. **b** a microprocessor. **2** a microwave oven.

micro- *combining form* forming words denoting: **1** very small: *microchip*. **2** one millionth part: *micrometer*.

microbe *noun* a microorganism, esp. a bacterium that is capable of causing disease. ▸ **microbial** *adj.* ▸ **microbic** *adj.*

microbiology *noun* the scientific study of microorganisms. ▸ **microbiological** *adj.* ▸ **microbiologist** *noun*

microchip *noun* Comput. chip (sense 6).

microcircuit *noun* a miniature electronic circuit consisting of a number of components mounted on a single chip of silicon or other semiconductor material.

microcomputer *noun* a small computer for use in the home or by a small business. *Also called* **personal computer**.

microcosm *noun* a structure or system that contains, in miniature, all the features of the larger structure or system of which it is a part. ▸ **microcosmic** *adj.*

microdot *noun* **1** a photograph, e.g., of secret documents, reduced to the size of a pinhead. **2** a tiny pill, esp. one impregnated with LSD, etc.

microeconomics *noun* (*sing.*) the branch of economics concerned with the financial circumstances of individual households, firms, industries, etc., and the way individual elements in an economy (such as specific products, commodities, or consumers) behave.

microfiche (mī′krō-fēsh,, -fīsh,) *noun* a film that has large amounts of photographically reduced information on it.

microfilm *noun* photographic film used in the preparation of microfiches and other types of microphotography.

micrometer (mī-krăm′ət-ər) *noun* **1** a device used in measuring small diameters, thicknesses, etc. to a high degree of accuracy. **2** a unit of length equal to one millionth of a meter.

micron *noun* (SYMBOL μ) *no longer used technically* micrometer (sense 2).

micronutrient *noun Biol.* a trace element, vitamin, or other essential nutrient required in minute quantities by a living organism.

microorganism *noun* a living organism, e.g., a bacterium, virus, protozoan, etc., visible only through a microscope.

microphone *noun* an electronic device that converts sound waves into electrical signals that can be amplified, recorded, or transmitted over long distances, used in radio and television broadcasting, telephone receiver mouthpieces, etc.

microphotography *noun* photography of documents, plans, etc. that produces greatly reduced images, which need to be magnified or enlarged by projection to be viewed.

microprocessor *noun Comput.* a central processing unit on a single chip.

microscope *noun* an instrument with a system of magnifying lenses for viewing objects that are too small to be seen with the naked eye. *See also* **electron microscope**.

microscopic *adj.* **1** too small to be seen without the aid of a microscope. **2** extremely small. **3** of or by means of a microscope. ► **microscopically** *adv.*

microsecond *noun* a unit of time equal to one millionth part of a second.

microsurgery *noun* a delicate surgical procedure requiring the use of a powerful microscope and small specialized instruments.

microwave *noun* **1** an electromagnetic wave with a wavelength shorter than a radio wave, but longer than those of infrared radiation, used in radar, communications, and cooking. **2** a microwave oven. —*verb trans.* (**microwaved**, **microwaving**) to cook (food) in a microwave.

microwave oven an oven that uses microwaves to cook food more rapidly than is possible in a conventional oven.

mid[1] *adj.* (*often in compounds*) being the part at or in the middle: *in mid-sentence.*

mid[2] *prep.* amid.

midair *adj.* occurring in the air: *a midair collision.*

midday *noun* the middle of the day; twelve o'clock.

middle *adj.* **1** equally placed between or distant from two points, extremes, limits, etc. **2** intermediate, not senior or chief: *middle management.* **3** moderate, not extreme: *a middle course.* —*noun* **1** the center; a

middle point, part, or position. **2** *colloq.* the area of the body around the waist. —**be in the middle of** to be busy doing (something).

middle age the years between youth and old age, usu. between ages 45 and 60. ► **middle-aged** *adj.*

Middle Ages the period in European history roughly between the decline of the Roman Empire in the 5th c. A.D. and the start of the Italian Renaissance in the 15th c. A.D., but sometimes restricted to the period between 1000 and 1400 A.D.

Middle America 1 the section of US people thought of as having relatively high incomes, and good educations, and being fairly conservative in their opinions, etc. **2** the heartland of the USA, esp. those areas made up of small towns and cities.

middle class a social class between working class and upper class.

middle ear the part of the ear where sound waves are transmitted from the outer ear to the inner ear.

Middle East a loosely defined geographical region stretching east from the Mediterranean Sea to Afghanistan and including the Arabian peninsula and sometimes the eastern parts of N Africa. ► **Middle Eastern** *adj.*

middleman *noun* an intermediary, esp. someone who buys goods directly from a manufacturer and then sells them on to a retailer, or to a customer, etc.

middle-of-the-road *adj.* neutral; not extreme, esp. in opinions, outlook, politics, etc.

middle school a school between elementary and high school, with grades five through to eight.

middleweight *noun* **1** a class for professional boxers who weigh between 147 lbs. and 160 lbs., or for amateur boxers, wrestlers, and weight lifters whose weight is roughly similar. **2** a boxer, etc., of this weight.

middling *colloq. adj.* average; moderate; mediocre.

midge *noun* a small, delicate fly.

midget *noun* **1** a person who is smaller than average in stature, often someone whose skeleton and features are in proportion. **2** any small thing of its kind.

midi *combining form* forming words denoting medium size, length, etc.

MIDI, Midi *or* **midi** *noun* a computer interface for connecting and controlling electronic musical instruments, etc.

midiron *noun Golf* a club used chiefly for long approach shots.

midland *noun* the central inland part of a country.

midlife *noun* middle age.

mid-life crisis a period of anxiety, doubt, and unease experienced by some people during middle age.

midnight *noun* 12 o'clock at night. —*adj.* of or at 12 o'clock at night.

midnight sun a phenomenon that occurs during the summer north of the Arctic circle and south of the Antarctic circle, where the Sun remains visible for 24 hours a day.

midpoint *noun* a point at or near the middle in distance or time.

midrib *noun* a rib that runs along the center of a leaf and forms an extension of the leaf stalk.

midriff *noun* the part of the body between the chest and the waist.

midshipman *noun* (*pl.* **midshipmen**) a trainee naval officer, typically one attending a naval academy or college.

midships *adv.* same as **amidships**.

midst *noun* (*usu.* **in the midst of**) an interior or central position, etc.

midstream *noun* an area of water in the middle of a river or stream.

midsummer *noun* the middle of the summer, esp. the period around the summer solstice.

midway *adj.*, *adv.* halfway between two points in distance, time, etc.

Midwest (mǐd-wěst′) or **Middle West** *noun* the north central states of the USA. ▸ **Midwestern** *adj.*

midwife *noun* (*pl.* **midwives**) a person medically trained to assist in childbirth. ▸ **midwifery** (mǐd-wǐf′ə-rē, -wǐ′fə-rē) *noun*

Meaning literally 'with-woman'

midwinter *noun* the period in the middle of winter, around Dec. 22.

mien (mēn) *noun* an appearance, expression, manner, etc.

miff *colloq.* *verb trans.* (**miffed, miffing**) to offend.

might¹ *verb*, *aux.* (*pr t* **may**) used to denote possibility, permission, a wish, dependency, or contingency.

might² *noun* the capacity or ability to exert effort.

mighty *adj.* (**mightier, mightiest**) **1** powerful. **2** very large. —*adv. informal* very: *mighty pretty*. ▸ **mightily** *adv.* ▸ **mightiness** *noun*

migraine *noun* a severe headache, usu. affecting only one side of the head.

migrate *verb intrans.* (**migrated, migrating**) **1** to move from one location to another, esp. on a regular basis in response to seasonal changes: *Swallows migrate south in winter.* **2** to leave one region or country and settle in another: *Our family migrated from Poland to the USA.* ▸ **migrant** *noun* ▸ **migration** *noun* ▸ **migratory** *adj.*

mikado *noun* (*pl.* **mikados**) (*often* **Mikado**) a former title of an emperor of Japan.

mike *noun colloq.* a microphone.

mil *noun* one thousandth of an inch.

milch (mǐlk, mǐlch) *adj.*, of cattle producing milk.

mild *adj.* **1** gentle in temperament or behavior. **2** not sharp or strong in flavor or effect. **3** not great or severe: *a mild allergic reaction.* **4** of a climate, weather, etc. not characterized by extremes; rather warm. ▸ **mildly** *adv.* ▸ **mildness** *noun*

mildew *noun* a fungus that produces a fine white powdery coating on the surface of infected plants, or on things made from plant or animal material. —*verb trans.*, *intrans.* (**mildewed, mildewing**) to affect or become affected by mildew.

mile *noun* **1** a unit of distance on land equal to 1,760 yd. (1.61 km). Also called **statute mile**. **2** a unit of distance at sea equal to 2025 yd. (1.85 km). Also called **nautical mile**.

mileage *noun* **1** the number of miles traveled or to be traveled. **2** the number of miles a motor vehicle will travel on a fixed amount of fuel. **3** an allowance for travel expenses.

milepost *noun* a post indicating the distance in miles, esp. on a highway.

miler *noun* an athlete or horse that runs races of one mile.

milestone *noun* **1** a stone pillar at a roadside showing distances in miles to various places. **2** a very important event , e.g., in the life of a person, the progress of something, a nation's history, etc.

milieu (mēl-yər′, -yōō′) *noun* (*pl.* **milieus, milieux**) an environment or set of surroundings.

militant (mǐl′ǐ-tənt) *adj.* **1** ready, or displaying readiness, to attack. **2** *formal* engaged in warfare. **3** favoring or displaying extreme, violent, or confrontational action, esp. in support of a cause. —*noun* a militant person. ▸ **militancy** *noun*

militarism *noun* an aggressive readiness to engage in warfare; the vigorous pursuit of military aims and ideals. ▸ **militarist** *noun* ▸ **militaristic** *adj.*

militarize *verb trans.* (**militarized, militarizing**) to equip or prepare for war. ▸ **militarization** *noun*

military *adj.* relating to, done by, characteristic of, or for the armed forces: *under military rule.* —*noun* (**the military**) the armed forces. ▸ **militarily** *adv.*

militate (mǐl′ə-tāt,) *verb intrans.* (**militated, militating**) (**militate for** or **against**) to act, or have a strong influence, in favor of or against (something).

Usage **Militate** is often confused with *mitigate.*

militia (mə-lǐsh′ə) *noun* a body of citizens

that can be called up to serve as soldiers, etc. in an emergency. ▸ **militiaman** *noun* ▸ **militiawoman** *noun*

milk *noun* **1** a white or yellowish liquid that is secreted by the mammary glands of female mammals for the nourishment of their young. **2** a liquid that resembles this, e.g., the juice of a coconut. —*verb trans.* (**milked, milking**) **1** to take milk from (an animal). **2** *colloq.* to obtain money, information, or other benefit from, cleverly or relentlessly.

milkmaid *noun old use* a woman who milks cows or works in a dairy.

milk of magnesia a suspension of magnesium hydroxide in water, used as an antacid and a laxative.

milk shake a drink consisting of a mixture of milk, flavoring, and usu. ice cream, whipped until creamy.

milksop *noun* a weak or ineffectual man or youth.

milk tooth any of a child's or animal's first teeth. *Also called* **deciduous tooth**.

milky *adj.* (**milkier, milkiest**) **1** resembling or containing milk. **2** white. ▸ **milkiness** *noun*

Milky Way 1 a band of diffuse light in the night sky formed by the light from billions of stars. **2** the Galaxy to which our Sun belongs.

mill *noun* **1** a building or factory where paper, textiles, steel, etc., are made, or where materials, e.g., timber, etc. are processed. **2** a machine or device for grinding cereals into flour, or peppercorns, coffee beans, etc. into powdered form, etc. **3** a device for cutting, rolling, finishing metal, etc. —*verb trans., intrans.* (**milled, milling**) **1** to grind, pulverize, or press in a mill. **2** to manufacture or process in a mill. **3** to cut, roll, or finish in a mill. **4** *colloq.* (**mill about** *or* **around**) to move in an aimless or confused way. —**go** *or* **put** (**someone**) **through the mill** to undergo or cause to undergo an unpleasant experience or difficult test.

millenarianism *noun* the doctrine or belief that a period of 1,000 years of blessedness, signalled by the second coming of Christ, is imminent. ▸ **millenarian** *noun*

millennium *noun* (*pl.* **millennia**) **1** a period of a thousand years. **2** (**the millennium**) a period of 1,000 years of blessedness, signalled by the second coming of Christ, that some Christians believe to be imminent. ▸ **millennial** *adj.*

millennium bug *noun Comput.* a potential cause of computer failure happening at the start of the year 2000, and affecting computers whose operating systems cannot recognize dates of years other than those between 1900 and 1999.

millepede *noun same as* **millipede**.

miller *noun* a person who owns or operates a mill.

millet *noun* a cereal grass cultivated as an important food and fodder crop in parts of Africa and Asia.

milli- *combining form* forming words denoting a thousandth part: *millisecond*.

millibar *noun* (ABBREV. **mb**) a unit of atmospheric pressure, equal to one thousandth of a bar.

milligram *noun* (ABBREV. **mg**) a unit of weight, equal to one thousandth of a gram.

milliliter *noun* (ABBREV. **ml**) a unit of volume, equal to one thousandth of a liter.

millimeter *noun* (ABBREV. **mm**) a unit of length, equal to one thousandth of a meter.

milliner *noun* a person who makes or sells women's hats. ▸ **millinery** *noun*

million *noun* (*pl.* **millions, million**) **1 a** a thousand thousands. **b** a numeral, figure, or symbol representing this, e.g., 1,000,000. **2** *colloq.* a great number: *millions of books*.

millionaire *noun* a person worth a million dollars, etc., or more; a very rich person.

millionth *noun, adj.* a thousand thousandth.

millipede *or* **millepede** *noun* an insect with a cylindrical segmented body and many legs.

millrace *noun* a current of water driving a mill, esp. one that grinds cereals, or the channel carrying a current of this kind.

millstone *noun* **1** either of the large heavy stones between which grain is ground in a mill. **2** a heavy burden, e.g., a duty or responsibility.

milquetoast (mĭlk′tōst,) *noun* a timid, weak person.

milt *noun* the testes or sperm of a fish.

mime *noun* **1** the theatrical art of acting using only movements and gestures. **2** a play or dramatic sequence performed in this way. —*verb trans., intrans.* (**mimed, miming**) to act (feelings, etc.) in this way or to engage in the performance of mime.

mimeograph *noun* a machine that produces copies of printed or handwritten material from a stencil; a copy produced in this way. —*verb trans.* (**mimeographed, mimeographing**) to copy in this way.

mimic *verb trans.* (**mimicked, mimicking**) **1** to imitate, esp. for comic effect. **2** to copy. —*noun* someone or something that imitates or copies another.

mimicry *noun* **1** the skill or practice of mimicking. **2** the close resemblance of one animal or plant to another, or to its natural environment, as a defense mechanism.

mimosa *noun* a tropical tree or shrub with clusters of small, typically yellow, flowers.

mina *noun same as* **myna**.

minaret *noun* a tower on a mosque from which Muslims are called to prayer.

mince *verb trans., intrans.* (**minced, mincing**) **1** to cut or shred (esp. meat) into very small pieces. **2** to talk in an evasive or euphemistic way. **3** to walk or speak with affected delicateness. —*noun* minced meat, esp. beef.

mincemeat *noun* a spiced mixture of dried fruits, used as a filling for pies. —**make mincemeat of** *colloq.* to defeat or destroy (someone or something) completely.

mincing *adj.* overly delicate and affected. ▸ **mincingly** *adv.*

mind *noun* **1** the power of thinking and understanding; the site at which thoughts and feelings exist; the intelligence. **2** memory; recollection. **3** opinion; judgment. **4** attention. **5** wish; inclination. **6** a very intelligent person. **7** sanity. —*verb trans., intrans.* (**minded, minding**) **1** to look after, care for, or keep safe. **2** to be upset, bothered, or concerned (by). **3** to be careful or wary of. **4** to take notice of or pay attention to. —**never mind** don't worry; it doesn't matter.

mind-blowing *adj. colloq.* **1** very surprising, shocking, or exciting. **2** hallucinogenic.

mind-boggling *adj. colloq.* too difficult, large, strange, etc., to imagine or understand.

minded *adj.* **1** having an intention or desire; inclined. **2** (*in compounds*) having a certain kind of mind or attitude: *open-minded.*

mindful *adj.* (*usu.* **mindful of**) keeping (something) in mind; attentive to (something). ▸ **mindfulness** *noun*

mindless *adj.* **1** done without a reason; senseless. **2** needing no effort of mind. ▸ **mindlessly** *adv.*

mind reading the process of supposedly apprehending the thoughts of another. ▸ **mind reader**

mindset *or* **mind-set** *noun* a predisposition or a fixed mental attitude.

mine[1] *pron.* something or someone belonging to, or connected with, me.

mine[2] *noun* **1** an opening or excavation in the ground where minerals, metal ores, coal, etc. can be removed. **2** an explosive device placed beneath the ground or in water for the destruction of tanks, personnel, ships, etc. that come into contact with it. **3** a rich source: *a mine of information.* —*verb trans., intrans.* (**mined, mining**) **1** to dig for (minerals, etc.) in (an area). **2** to lay explosive devices in (land or water). **3** to destroy with explosive devices.

minefield *noun* **1** an area of land or water where explosives devices have been laid. **2** a subject or situation presenting many hidden problems or dangers.

miner *noun* a person who works in a mine.

mineral *noun* **1** a naturally occurring inorganic substance, e.g., quartz. **2** a substance obtained by mining, including, e.g., coal, natural gas, petroleum. —*adj.* relating to or consisting of a mineral or minerals.

mineralogy *noun* the scientific study of minerals. ▸ **mineralogical** *adv.* ▸ **mineralogist** *noun*

mineral oil an oil that is obtained from mineral sources, esp. petroleum or one of its liquid derivatives.

mineral water water that is naturally high in dissolved mineral salts or gases, or water that has had such substances added to it.

minestrone (mĭn,ə-strō'nē, -strōn,) *noun* thick soup containing vegetables and pasta.

minesweeper *noun* a ship equipped to clear mines from an area.

mingle *verb intrans., trans.* (**mingled, mingling**) **1** (*often* **mingle with**) to become or cause to become blended. **2** to associate or have dealings (with).

mini *colloq. noun* something small or short, esp. a miniskirt. —*adj.* small or short of its kind; miniature.

mini- *prefix* forming words denoting something smaller or shorter than the standard: *miniskirt / minisubmarine.*

miniature *noun* **1** a small copy or model. **2** a very small painting, esp. a portrait. —*adj.* small-scale.

miniaturize *verb trans.* (**miniaturized, miniaturizing**) to make very small or on a small scale.

minibus *noun* a small bus.

minicam *noun* a small hand-held video camera.

minicomputer *noun* a computer that is between a mainframe and a microcomputer in size, speed, and capability.

minim *noun* **1** a unit of liquid volume, equal to $\frac{1}{60}$ of a fluid dram (0.06 ml). **2** *Mus.* a half note.

minimal *adj.* **1** relating to a minimum. **2** negligible. ▸ **minimally** *adv.*

minimalism *noun* the philosophy or style of employing the simplest forms, patterns, etc., often with little or no use of color. ▸ **minimalist** *noun, adj.*

minimize *verb trans.* (**minimized, minimizing**) **1** to reduce to a minimum. **2** to treat as being of little importance or significance.

minimum *noun* (*pl.* **minimums, minima**) the lowest possible number, value, quantity, or degree, or the lowest reached or allowed.

minimum wage *noun* the lowest wage an employer is allowed to pay by law.

minion *noun* **1** a subordinate. **2** an employee or follower, esp. when fawning or subservient.

miniscule (mĭn'ĭ-skyōōl,) *adj., noun* same as **minuscule**.

miniseries *noun* a short series of related television programs, usu. broadcast over consecutive days or weeks.

miniskirt *noun* a very short skirt.

minister *noun* 1 a member of the clergy. 2 a high-ranking diplomat. 3 a senior politician. —*verb intrans.* (**ministered, ministering**) 1 (**minister to**) to provide help or a service for. 2 to perform the duties of a cleric. ▸ **ministerial** *adj.*

ministration *noun formal* 1 the act of ministering. 2 (*usu.* **ministrations**) help or services given.

ministry *noun* (*pl.* **ministries**) 1 a government department or its premises. 2 (**the ministry**) the profession, duties, or period of service of a cleric; clerics collectively.

mink *noun* (*pl.* **mink, minks**) a semiaquatic mammal, its fur, or a garment made from its fur.

minneola *noun* a citrus fruit that is a cross between a grapefruit and a tangerine.

minnow *noun* a small freshwater fish.

minor *adj.* 1 not as great in importance or size as others; fairly small or insignificant. 2 below the age of legal majority or adulthood. 3 *Mus.*, of a scale having a semitone between the second and third, fifth and sixth, and seventh and eighth notes; based on such a scale. —*noun* 1 a person below the age of legal majority. 2 *Mus.* a minor key, chord, or scale.

minority *noun* (*pl.* **minorities**) 1 a small number; the smaller of two groups. 2 a group of people who are regarded as being different, esp. in terms of race or religion, from most of the other people. 3 the state of being the smaller of two groups: *in a minority.* 4 the state of being below the age of legal majority.

minor league a professional sports club, particularly in baseball, outside the major leagues.

minster *noun Brit.* a large church or cathedral.

minstrel *noun* a traveling poet and singer in the Middle Ages.

mint¹ *noun* 1 an aromatic plant. 2 the leaves of this plant used as a flavoring. 3 a sweet flavored with an extract of these leaves, or a synthetic substitute. ▸ **minty** *adj.*

mint² *noun* 1 a place where coins are produced under government authority. 2 *colloq.* a large sum of money. —*verb trans.* (**minted, minting**) to manufacture (coins). —**in mint condition** brand new; never or hardly used.

minuet (mĭn,yə-wĕt′) *noun* a slow, formal dance, or a piece of music for it.

minus *prep.* 1 made smaller by. 2 *colloq.* without. —*noun* 1 a sign (-) indicating a negative quantity, or indicating that a following quantity is to be subtracted. *Also called* **minus sign.** 2 *colloq.* a negative point; a disadvantage. —*adj.* 1 negative or less than zero. 2 *colloq.* of the nature of a disadvantage. 3 of a student's grade slightly below that indicated by the letter: *got a B minus for my essay.*

minuscule (mĭn′ə-skyōōl,, mĭ-nəs′-) *or* **miniscule** *adj.* 1 extremely small. 2 of a letter lowercase, not uppercase or capital. —*noun* a lowercase letter.

minute¹ (mĭn′ət) *noun* 1 $\frac{1}{60}$ of an hour; 60 seconds. 2 *colloq.* a short while: *Wait a minute.* 3 a particular point in time: *at that minute.* 4 the distance that can be traveled in a minute: *a house five minutes away.* 5 *Geom.* $\frac{1}{60}$ of a degree; 60 seconds. 6 (*usu.* **minutes**) the official written record of what is said at a formal meeting. —*verb trans.* (**minuted, minuting**) to make an official written record of. —**up to the minute** modern or recent.

minute² (mī-nōōt′, -nyōōt′) *adj.* 1 very small; tiny. 2 *formal* precise; detailed. 3 *formal* petty. ▸ **minutely** *adv.*

Minuteman (mĭn′ət-măn,) *noun* a militiaman, particularly one involved in the American Revolution before there was a regular army.

minutiae (mə-nōō′shē-ē,, -nyōō′-, -shē-ī,) *pl. noun* small, unimportant details.

minx *noun* a cheeky or flirtatious young woman.

MIPS *or* **mips** *abbrev. Comput.* millions of instructions per second.

miracle *noun* 1 an act or event attributed to something supernatural. 2 *colloq.* a fortunate or amazing thing or event.

miraculous *adj.* 1 relating to or of the nature of a miracle. 2 *colloq.* wonderful; amazing.

mirage (mə-räzh′) *noun* an optical illusion, esp. one seen in a desert.

mire *noun* 1 deep mud; a boggy area. 2 trouble; difficulty. —*verb intrans., trans.* (**mired, miring**) 1 to sink or cause to sink in or as if in a mire. 2 to involve, or become involved, in trouble or difficulty.

mirror *noun* 1 a smooth, highly polished reflecting surface, esp. one used for checking one's appearance. 2 a faithful representation or reflection. —*verb trans.* (**mirrored, mirroring**) 1 to reflect as in a mirror. 2 to represent or depict faithfully.

mirror image 1 a reflected image as produced by a mirror. 2 an object that matches another as if it were its image as seen in a mirror.

mirth *noun* laughter; merriment.

MIS *abbrev. Comput.* management information system.

mis- *prefix* forming words denoting: 1 wrong or wrongly; bad or badly: *misconceive.* 2 a lack or absence of something: *mistrust.*

misadventure *noun* an unfortunate happening; bad luck.

misanthrope (mĭs'ən-thrōp,) or **misanthropist** noun a person who hates or distrusts all people. ▸ **misanthropic** adj. ▸ **misanthropy** noun

misapprehend verb trans. to misunderstand. ▸ **misapprehension** noun

misappropriate verb trans. to take (something, esp. money) dishonestly for oneself; to put to a wrong use. ▸ **misappropriation** noun

misbegotten adj. 1 illegally obtained. 2 foolishly planned or thought out. 3 illegitimate.

misbehave verb intrans. to behave badly. ▸ **misbehavior** noun

miscalculate verb trans., intrans. to calculate or estimate wrongly. ▸ **miscalculation** noun

miscarriage noun 1 abortion (sense 2). 2 a failure of a plan, etc., to reach a desired objective. 3 (in full **miscarriage of justice**) a failure of a judicial system to serve the ends of justice in a particular case.

miscarry verb intrans. 1 to have an abortion (sense 2). 2 to fail.

miscegenation (mĭs-ĕj,ə-nā'shən) noun interbreeding between people of different races, esp. of different skin colors.

miscellaneous adj. made up of various kinds.

miscellany noun (pl. **miscellanies**) a mixture of various kinds, esp. a collection of writings on different subjects, or by different authors.

mischance noun bad luck, or an instance of it.

mischief noun 1 behavior that irritates but causes no serious harm, or an inclination to behave like this. 2 a source or example of damage or harm. ▸ **mischievous** adj. ▸ **mischievously** adj.

miscible adj. of liquids capable of dissolving or mixing together. ▸ **miscibility** noun

misconceive verb trans., intrans. 1 to misunderstand. 2 to plan or think out badly. ▸ **misconception** noun

misconduct noun 1 improper or unethical behavior. 2 deliberate wrongdoing, esp. by someone in a position of authority.

misconstrue verb trans. to interpret wrongly or mistakenly. ▸ **misconstruction** noun

miscreant (mĭs'krē-ont) noun a malicious person; a rogue or scoundrel.

miscue noun a foolish, usu. serious mistake. ▸ **miscue** verb

misdeed noun an evil or wicked action.

misdemeanor noun 1 a wrongdoing. 2 Law a crime less serious than a felony.

misdirect verb trans. 1 to send to the wrong place. 2 to use (esp. funds) for an unsuitable purpose. 3 Law, of a judge to give (a jury) an erroneous framework on which to base a verdict, etc. ▸ **misdirection** noun

miser (mī'zər) noun a person who hoards money; an ungenerous person. ▸ **miserly** adj. ▸ **miserliness** noun

miserable (mĭz'ə-rə-bəl, mĭz'rə-) adj. 1 very unhappy. 2 marked by great unhappiness. 3 causing unhappiness or discomfort. 4 marked by poverty or squalor. ▸ **miserably** adv

misery (mĭz'ə-rē, mĭz'rē) noun (pl. **miseries**) 1 great unhappiness, or a cause of it. 2 poverty or squalor.

misfire verb intrans. 1 of a gun, car engine, etc. to fail to fire at all or at the correct time. 2 to be unsuccessful; to produce the wrong effect: a joke that misfired. —noun an instance of failing to fire, ignite, or produce an effect as wanted.

misfit noun 1 a person not suited to a particular situation or environment. 2 something that fits badly or not at all.

misfortune noun an unfortunate incident; bad luck.

misgiving noun (often **misgivings**) a feeling of uneasiness, doubt, or suspicion.

misguided adj. acting from or showing mistaken ideas or bad judgment. ▸ **misguidedly** adv.

mishandle verb trans. 1 to deal with carelessly or without skill. 2 to handle roughly; to mistreat.

mishap noun an unfortunate, esp. minor, accident; bad luck.

mishear verb trans. to hear incorrectly.

mishmash (mĭsh'măsh,, -mäsh,) noun, colloq. a disordered collection or mixture.

misinform verb trans. to give incorrect or misleading information to. ▸ **misinformation** noun

misinterpret verb trans. to understand or explain incorrectly or misleadingly. ▸ **misinterpretation** noun

misjudge verb trans. to judge wrongly; to have an unfairly low opinion of. ▸ **misjudgment** noun

miskey verb trans. Comput. to key (data on a keyboard, etc.) incorrectly.

mislay verb trans. to lose (something), usu. temporarily, esp. by forgetting where it was put.

mislead (mĭs-lēd') verb trans. to cause to take a wrong or undesirable course of action; to deceive or cause to have a false impression or belief.

mismanage verb trans. to manage or handle badly or carelessly. ▸ **mismanagement** noun

mismatch verb trans. (mĭs-măch') to match unsuitably or incorrectly. —noun (mĭs'-măch,) an unsuitable or incorrect match.

misnomer noun a wrong or unsuitable name; an act of using a wrong or unsuitable name.

misogynist (mĭ-säj'ə-nĭst) noun a person who hates women. ▸ **misogynous** adj. ▸ **misogyny** noun

misplace *verb trans.* 1 to lose (something), usu. temporarily, esp. by forgetting where it was put. 2 to give (trust, affection, etc.) unwisely or inappropriately. 3 to put in the wrong place.

misprint *noun* (mĭs′prĭnt′) a mistake in printing. —*verb trans.* (mĭs-prĭnt′) to print wrongly.

misprision *noun Law* deliberate concealment of one's knowledge of a serious crime.

mispronounce *verb trans.* to pronounce (words, etc.) incorrectly. ▸ **mispronunciation** *noun*

misquote *verb trans.* to quote inaccurately. ▸ **misquotation** *noun*

misread *verb* 1 to read incorrectly. 2 to misunderstand or misinterpret.

misrepresent *verb trans.* to give a false or misleading account or impression of, often intentionally. ▸ **misrepresentation** *noun*

misrule *noun* 1 bad or unjust government. 2 civil disorder. —*verb trans., intrans.* to govern in a disorderly or unjust way.

miss[1] *verb trans., intrans.* 1 to fail to hit, catch, arrive in time for, take advantage of, etc. (something). 2 to regret or notice the absence of: *I've really missed you.* 3 to fail to hear or see. 4 to avoid, escape, fail to attend, etc. (something): *I missed class.* —*noun* a failure to hit or catch something.

miss[2] *noun* 1 a girl or unmarried woman. 2 (**Miss**) a title or form of address for an unmarried woman or girl. *See also* **Ms.** 3 a girl or young woman with a specified attribute: *thinks she's little Miss Perfect.*

misshapen *adj.* badly shaped.

missile *noun* any weapon or object that is thrown or fired.

missing *adj.* absent, lost, or unaccounted for.

missing link *noun* 1 something needed to complete a series. 2 (**the missing link**) a hypothetical extinct primate linking the evolutionary development of apes and humans.

mission *noun* 1 a purpose or end for which a person or group of people is sent. 2 a journey made for a scientific, military, or religious purpose, or the people sent on such a journey. 3 a group of people sent to a foreign country to conduct diplomacy or engage in negotiations. 4 a purpose or calling in life. 5 a group of missionaries or a building occupied by them.

missionary *noun* (*pl.* **missionaries**) a person who goes to spread the teachings of a religion to people in another country or who have different beliefs.

mission statement a declaration made by a company or organization outlining its aims, procedures, guiding principles, etc.

missis *noun colloq. same as* **missus**.

missive *noun* a written or printed message.

misspell *verb trans.* to spell incorrectly.

misspend *verb trans.* to spend wastefully or foolishly.

missus *or* **missis** *noun colloq.* 1 *humorous* a wife. 2 *old use* the female head of the household.

missy *noun old colloq. use* a term used to address a girl or young woman.

mist *noun* 1 a slight fog. 2 a fine spray, such as very small droplets of rain, or a squirt from an aerosol, etc. 3 condensed water vapor, a watery film, or something that has an obscuring effect: *a mist of tears / the mists of time.* —*verb trans., intrans.* (misted, misting) (*also* mist up *or* over) to cover or become covered with or as if with mist.

mistake *verb trans., intrans.* (*pa t* mistook; *pa p* mistaken; *pr p* mistaking) 1 to identify incorrectly. 2 to misunderstand or misinterpret. 3 to be in the wrong or in error. —*noun* an error in identification, action, judgment, etc.

mistaken *adj.* 1 understood or identified wrongly. 2 having failed to understand or interpret correctly. ▸ **mistakenly** *adv.*

mister *noun* (ABBREV. **Mr.**) 1 used usu. in abbreviated form as a title before the full name or the surname of a man. 2 *colloq.* used as a term of address for an adult male stranger.

mistime *verb trans.* (mistimed, mistiming) to do or say (something) at a wrong or unsuitable time.

mistletoe *noun* a small evergreen parasitic shrub with white berries, often used as a Christmas decoration.

mistook *verb see* **mistake**.

mistreat *verb trans.* to treat cruelly or without care. ▸ **mistreatment** *noun*

mistress *noun* 1 a woman in a commanding or controlling position; a female head or owner. 2 a female teacher. 3 *old use* the female lover of a married man.

mistrial *noun Law* a trial not conducted properly according to the law, and hence declared invalid.

mistrust *verb trans.* to have no trust in; to be suspicious of. —*noun* lack of trust. ▸ **mistrustful** *adj.* ▸ **mistrustfully** *adv.*

misty *adj.* (mistier, mistiest) 1 obscured or made unclear by or as if by mist. 2 *of the eyes* filled with tears. ▸ **mistily** *adv.* ▸ **mistiness** *noun*

misunderstand *verb trans., intrans.* to fail to understand properly.

misunderstanding *noun* 1 a failure to understand properly. 2 a disagreement.

misunderstood *adj., of a person, motive, etc.* not properly understood or appreciated. —*verb see* **misunderstand**.

misuse *noun* (mĭsh-ōōs′ mĭs-yōōs′) improper or inappropriate use. —*verb trans.* (mĭsh-ōōz′, mĭs-yōōz′) **1** to put to improper or inappropriate use. **2** to treat badly.

mite¹ *noun* a tiny, often microscopic, free-living or parasitic arachnid.

mite² *noun* **1** any small person or animal, esp. a child. **2** a small amount.

miter *noun* **1** a ceremonial headdress worn by a bishop, etc. **2** a corner joint between two lengths of wood, etc., made by fitting two equal sloping surfaces together. *Also called* **miter joint.** —*verb trans.* (mitered, mitering) to join with a miter.

mitigate (mĭt′ĭ-gāt,) *verb trans., intrans.* (mitigated, mitigating) **1** to partially excuse or make less serious. **2** to make or become less severe.

mitosis (mī-tō′sĭs) *noun* cell division that results in the production of two daughter cells with identical nuclei. *See also* **meiosis.**

mitt *noun* **1** a mitten. **2** *slang* a hand. **3** a baseball glove.

mitten *noun* a glove that encloses the four fingers together and has a separate part for the thumb.

mix *verb trans., intrans* (mixed, mixing) **1** to combine or to be combined. ⊟ BLEND, MINGLE ⊟ DIVIDE, PART, SEPARATE. **2** to meet with people socially. **3** to manipulate various music tracks to form a single piece of music, esp. by using computer software. **4** (*often* **mix up**) **a** to confuse: *I mixed him up with his brother.* **b** to cause (someone) to be upset or emotionally unstable. *See also* **mixed-up.** —*noun* **1** a collection of different things or people. **2** a final version of a song, etc., esp. one that has been produced by mixing.

mixed *adj.* **1** consisting of different, often opposite kinds: *mixed feelings.* **2** done, used, etc., by people of both sexes.

mixed metaphor a combination of two or more metaphors giving an inconsistent or incongruous mental image.

mixed-up *adj.* **1** mentally or emotionally confused. **2** badly adjusted in terms of social behavior.

mixer *noun* **1** a machine or device for mixing. **2** a device for blending sounds, music, etc. **3** a soft drink suitable for adding to an alcoholic one.

mixture *noun* **1** a blend of ingredients: *a cough mixture.* **2** a combination: *a mixture of sadness and relief.* **3** the act of mixing.

mix-up *or* **mixup** *noun* a confusion or misunderstanding, e.g., mistaking of one person or thing for another.

mizzenmast *noun* the third mast from the front of the ship, or the aft mast on a yawl or ketch.

mnemonic (nĕ-män′ĭk) *noun* an aid to memory. ▸ **mnemonically** *adv.*

moan *noun* **1** a low, prolonged sound expressing sadness, grief, pain, etc. **2** *colloq.* a complaint. —*verb intrans.* (moaned, moaning) **1** to utter or produce a moan. **2** *colloq.* to complain, esp. without good reason. ▸ **moaner** *noun*

moat *noun* a deep defensive trench, often filled with water, surrounding a castle, etc.

mob *noun* **1** a large, disorderly crowd. **2** *colloq.* any group or gang. **3** *colloq.* (**the mob**) ordinary people; the masses. —*verb trans., intrans.* (mobbed, mobbing) **1** to attack as a mob. **2** to crowd around curiously or admiringly.

mobile *adj.* **1** moving form place to place, or willing to move to another location. **2** capable of moving or able to be moved. —*noun* **1** a hanging decoration moved around by air currents. **2** *colloq.* a mobile phone. ▸ **mobility** *noun*

mobile home a large trailer equipped with utility-connections, and often used as a residence on a relatively permanent site.

mobile phone *or* **mobile telephone** a small portable telephone.

mobilize *verb trans., intrans.* (mobilized, mobilizing) **1** to organize or prepare for use. **2** to assemble and make or become ready for war. ▸ **mobilization** *noun*

mobster *noun slang* a member of an organized group of criminals.

moccasin *noun* **1** a soft hide or leather shoe. **2** a cottonmouth.

mocha (mō′kə) *noun* **1** dark brown coffee of fine quality. **2** a flavoring made from coffee and chocolate.

mock *verb trans., intrans.* (mocked, mocking) **1** to ridicule. **2** to mimic. —*adj.* false; sham: *mock sincerity.*

mockery *noun* (*pl.* **mockeries**) **1** an act of ridicule. **2** a distortion of something worthy.

mockingbird *noun* a bird noted for its ability to mimic the songs of other birds.

mock orange a shrub whose scented flowers resemble those of the orange.

mock turtle soup a soup made with a calf's head, veal, or other meat and seasoned to taste like turtle soup.

mockup *noun* a full-size model or replica built for experimental purposes.

mod *adj. colloq.* modern.

mode *noun* **1** a way of doing, living, operating, etc. **2** a fashion or style, e.g., in clothes or art. ▸ **modal** *adj.* ▸ **modality** *noun*

model *noun* **1** a small-scale representation used as a guide to construction. **2** a small-scale replica. **3** one of several types or designs of a manufactured article. **4** a person who displays clothes to potential buyers by wearing them. **5** a person who sits as a subject for an artist, photographer, etc. **6** something used as an example or a basis. **7** an example worthy of being admired or copied. —*verb trans., intrans.* (**modeled** *or* **modelled, modeling** *or* **modelling**) **1** to work as a fashion model or a model for an artist, photographer, etc. **2** to make a replica, representation, etc. **3** to shape into a particular form: *model clay*. **4** to plan, build, or create according to a model. —*adj.* exactly right or appropriate.

modem (mōd'əm, mō'dĕm,) *noun Comput.* an electronic device that can transmit data between two computers, using a telephone line.

moderate *adj.* (mäd'ə-rət) **1** not extreme, strong, or violent. **2** average. —*noun* a person holding moderate views, esp. in politics. —*verb trans., intrans.* (mäd'ə-rāt,) (**moderated, moderating**) **1** to make or become less extreme or less violent. **2** to preside over a meeting, etc. ▸ **moderately** *adv.* ▸ **moderation** *noun* ▸ **moderator** *noun*

moderato (mäd,ə-rät'ō) *adv., adj. Mus.* to be played at a restrained and moderate tempo.

modern *adj.* **1** relating or belonging to the present or to recent times. —*noun* à person who keeps up with the latest trends. ▸ **modernity** *noun*

Modernism *noun* an experimental movement in literature, art, and music started at the beginning of the 20th c. ▸ **Modernist** *noun*

modernize *verb trans., intrans.* (**modernized, modernizing**) **1** to bring up to modern standards. **2** to switch to more modern methods or techniques. ▸ **modernization** *noun*

modest *adj.* **1** humble. **2** not large; moderate: *a modest income*. **3** *of clothing, appearance, etc.* plain and restrained; not offending standards of decency: *a modest dress*. ▸ **modestly** *adv.* ▸ **modesty** *noun*

modicum *noun formal* a small amount.

modify *verb trans.* (**modified, modifying, modifies**) **1** to change the form or quality of, usu. slightly. **2** *Gram., of a word* to qualify or describe (another word). ▸ **modification** *noun* ▸ **modifier** *noun*

modish *adj. formal* appealingly elegant or fashionable.

modiste (mō-dēst') *noun* a person who designs or sells fashionable clothes, hats, etc.

modular *adj.* **1** relating to or consisting of modules. **2** relating to modulation.

modulate *verb trans.* (**modulated, modulating**) **1** to alter the tone or volume of (a sound or one's voice). **2** *formal* to change or alter. **3** *Radio* to cause modulation of a carrier wave. ▸ **modulator** *noun*

modulation *noun Radio* an act or the process of increasing or decreasing the frequency, amplitude, etc. of a carrier wave in response to variations in the signal being transmitted. *See also* **amplitude modulation, frequency modulation.**

module (mäj'ōōl,) *noun* **1** a standard unit of measurement, esp. used in coordinating dimensions of buildings, etc. **2** a self-contained unit, e.g., in computer hardware or software, an academic course, a spacecraft, etc.

modus operandi (mōd'əs-äp,ə-răn'dī,, -dē) (*pl.* **modi operandi**) (ABBREV. **MO, M.O.**) a way of working; the way something operates.

modus vivendi (vī-věn'dē, -dī,) (*pl.* **modi vivendi**) a way of living.

mogul *noun* **1** a leading or dominant figure in a field, e.g., a wealthy manufacturer. **2** (**Mogul**) a Muslim ruler of India between the 16th and 19th c.

mohair *noun* the long, soft hair of the angora goat; a yarn or fabric made of this.

moiety *noun* (*pl.* **moieties**) a half.

moiré (mwä-rä') *noun* watered silk.

moist *adj.* slightly damp. ▸ **moisten** *verb* ▸ **moistness** *noun*

moisture *noun* liquid in vapor or spray form, or condensed as droplets.

moisturize *verb trans.* (**moisturized, moisturizing**) to make less dry, esp. to add moisture to (the skin) by rubbing in a cream. ▸ **moisturizer** *noun*

molar *noun* a tooth near the back of the mouth, with a relatively large surface area for grinding food.

molasses *sing. noun* a thick brown syrup produced during the refining of sugar.

mold[1] *noun* a fungus that produces a woolly growth on decaying matter, esp. food. ▸ **moldy** *adj.*

mold[2] *noun* **1** a hollow, shaped container that a liquid substance is poured into to set and which gives it a solid form. **2** something that has been produced using this kind of container. **3** distinctive nature, character, or personality. —*verb trans., intrans.* (**molded, molding**) to shape (something) using a mold, the hands, or by exerting a controlling influence.

mold[3] *noun* loose soft earth.

molder *verb intrans.* (**moldered, moldering**) to become rotten with age; to decay.

molding *noun* **1** a shaped decorative strip, esp. of wood or plaster. **2** something produced from a mold.

mole[1] *noun* a pigmented spot or mark on the skin.

mole[2] *noun* **1** a small insectivorous burrowing mammal. **2** *colloq.* someone who has inside access to the secret information of a company, organization, etc. and who passes it to outside sources.

mole³ *noun* a pier, causeway, or breakwater made of stone; a harbor protected by any of these.

molecule (mǎl'ə-kyōōl,) *noun* **1** the smallest particle of a chemical element or compound that can exist independently and participate in a chemical reaction. **2** a very small part or particle. ▸ **molecular** *adj.*

molehill *noun* a little pile of earth thrown up by a burrowing mole.

moleskin *noun* **1** the fur of a mole. **2** a a heavy, twilled cotton fabric with a short nap. **b** (**moleskins**) trousers made of this fabric.

molest *verb trans.* (**molested, molesting**) **1** to subject (someone) to unwanted or improper sexual advances. **2** to disturb, upset, or irritate; to interfere with. ▸ **molestation** *noun*

moll *noun* a gangster's girlfriend.

mollify *verb trans.* (**mollified, mollifying, mollifies**) **1** to make calmer or less angry. **2** to soothe or ease. ▸ **mollification** *noun*

mollusk *noun* an invertebrate animal such as a snail, slug, oyster, clam, or octopus.

mollycoddle *verb trans.* (**mollycoddled, mollycoddling**) *colloq.* to treat with fussy care and protection.

Molotov cocktail a small, crude bomb for throwing, consisting of a bottle filled with gasoline, usu. with a burning cloth as a fuse.

molt (mōlt) *verb intrans.* (**molted, molting**) to shed feathers, hair, or skin to make way for a new growth. —*noun* the process of molting, or the time taken to molt.

molten *adj.* in a melted state.

molybdenum (mə-lǐb'də-nəm) *noun Chem.* (SYMBOL **Mo**) a hard silvery metal that is used as a hardening agent in various alloys.

mom *noun, colloq.* mother.

mom-and-pop store a small neighborhood business, esp. a grocery store, owned and run by a family.

moment *noun* **1** a short while or a particular point in time. **2** importance or significance.

momentarily *adv.* **1** for a moment. **2** *colloq.* in a moment.

momentary *adj.* lasting for only a moment.

momentous *adj.* having great significance, value, influence, or effect. ▸ **momentousness** *noun*

momentum *noun* **1** *Phys.* the product of the mass and the velocity of a moving object. **2** continuous speed of progress; impetus: *The campaign gained momentum.*

mommy *noun* (*pl.* **mommies**) *colloq.* a mother.

mon- *see* **mono-**.

monandrous *adj.* **1** having or allowing only one

husband or male sexual partner at a time. **2** having only one stamen in each flower. *See also* **polyandrous**. ▸ **monandry** *noun*

monarch (mǎn'ork, -ärk,) *noun* a king, queen, or other sovereign with a hereditary right to rule. ▸ **monarchic** *adj.* ▸ **monarchical** *adj.* ▸ **monarchism** *noun* ▸ **monarchist** *noun*

monarchy *noun* (*pl.* **monarchies**) a government with a monarch as head of state, or a country governed by a monarch.

monastery *noun* (*pl.* **monasteries**) the home of a community of monks or sometimes nuns.

monastic *adj.* **1** of or relating to monasteries, monks, or nuns. **2** marked by simplicity and self-discipline, like life in a monastery. ▸ **monastically** *adv.* ▸ **monasticism** *noun*

Monday (mən'dě, -dā) *noun* (ABBREV. **Mon.**) the second day of the week.

monetarism *noun* the basing of an economy on control of the supply of money in circulation. ▸ **monetarist** *noun, adj.*

monetary *adj.* of or relating to money.

moneybags *noun* (*sing.*) *colloq.* a very rich person.

moneyed *adj.* wealthy.

money market trade in short-term, low-risk securities.

money order a written order for the transfer of money from one person to another, through a post office or bank.

-monger *combining form* **1** a trader or dealer: *ironmonger.* **2** a person who spreads or promotes something: *scandalmonger.*

mongol *noun old use, now offensive* a person affected by Down Syndrome. ▸ **mongolism** *noun* ▸ **mongoloid** *adj.*

> *Usage* See note at *Down Syndrome.*

mongoose *noun* (*pl.* **mongooses**) a small carnivorous mammal noted for its ability to kill snakes.

mongrel *noun* **1** a dog of mixed breeding. **2** a person or thing of mixed origin or nature. —*adj.* of mixed origin or nature.

moniker *noun slang* a name or nickname.

monition *noun* **1** a warning or admonition. **2** an official or legal notice; a court order.

monitor *noun* **1** an instrument designed to check, record, or control something on a regular basis. **2** a high-quality screen used in closed-circuit television systems, as a visual display unit in computing, etc. **3** a pupil who helps with specific tasks, or oversees other pupils. —*verb trans.* (**monitored, monitoring**) to check, record, or control something on a regular basis; to observe.

monitory *adj. formal* serving as a warning.

monk *noun* a member of a religious community of men living disciplined, austere lives devoted to worship. ▸ **monkish** *adj.*

monkey *noun* (*pl.* **monkeys**) **1** a primate other

than a human, ape, chimpanzee, lemur, etc. **2**
colloq. a mischievous child. —*verb intrans.*
(**monkeyed, monkeying, monkeys**)
colloq. (often **monkey about** *or* **around**)
to play, fool, interfere, etc.

monkey business *colloq.* illegal activities;
mischief.

monkey jacket a fitted, waist-length jacket
worn as part of a military full-dress uniform.

monkey-puzzle *noun* a large coniferous
evergreen tree with a tangle of branches.
Also called **Chile pine.**

monkey wrench a hand tool with movable
jaws; an adjustable wrench.

monkshood *noun* a plant with violet hooded
flowers. *See also* **aconite.**

mono *colloq. adj.* monophonic. —*noun*
monophonic sound reproduction.

mono- *or* **mon-** *combining form* forming
words denoting one or single.

monochrome *adj.* using only black and white
or shades of only one color. ▸ **mono-
chromatic** *adj.*

monocle (măn′ə-kəl) *noun* a lens for correcting sight in one eye only.

monogamy (mə-năg′ə-mē) *noun* having only
one spouse at any one time. *See also*
polygamy. ▸ **monogamous** *adj.*

monogram *noun* a design made up of
interwoven letters, usu. a person's initials,
often used on personal belongings, etc.

monograph *noun* a book or essay dealing
with one particular subject or aspect of
it.

monolingual *adj.* **1** able to speak only one
language. **2** expressed in or dealing with a
single language.

monolith *noun* a single tall block of stone,
often shaped into a column or pillar.

monolithic *adj.* **1** relating to or resembling a
monolith. **2** *of an organization, etc.* large,
powerful, impersonal, and impenetrable.

monologue *or* **monolog** *noun* **1** a long
speech by one actor in a film or play. **2** a
drama for one actor. **3** a long, uninterrupted
speech delivered to discourage others from
participating.

monomania *noun* **1** a mental disorder characterized by extreme preoccupation with a
single thought or idea. **2** domination of the
mind by a single subject or concern; an
obsession. ▸ **monomaniac** *noun, adj.*

mononucleosis *noun* the presence of an
abnormally large number of white blood
cells with a kidney-shaped nucleus in the
blood.

monophonic *adj.* recording or reproducing
sound using one channel only between the
sound source and the loudspeaker.

monoplane *noun* an airplane with only one
pair of wings.

monopoly (mə-năp′ə-lē) *noun* (*pl.*
monopolies) **1** exclusive right or control,
etc., esp. over a particular commodity,
service, etc. **2** an exclusively controlled
commodity, service, etc., or a company that
has exclusive control over something.
▸ **monopolist** *noun* ▸ **monopolistic** *adj.*
▸ **monopolize** *verb trans.* ▸ **monopoliza-
tion** *noun*

monorail *noun* **1** a railroad system in which the
trains run on, or are suspended from, a single
rail. **2** a train running on this type of railroad.

monosodium glutamate a chemical substance used as a flavor enhancer.

monosyllable *noun* a word consisting of only
one syllable. ▸ **monosyllabic** *adj.*

monotheism *noun* the doctrine, belief, or
worship of a single god. ▸ **monotheist** *noun*
▸ **monotheistic** *adj.*

monotone *noun* **1** a single, unvarying tone in
speech or sound. **2** a sequence of soundings
of the same tone. **3** sameness, esp. in color.
—*adj.* lacking in variety; unchanging.

monotonous (mə-năt′n-əs) *adj.* lacking in
variety; tediously unchanging. ▸ **monotonously** *adv.* ▸ **monotony** *noun*

Monsieur (məs-yœ′, məsh-yər′) *noun* (*pl.*
Messieurs) (ABBREV. **M.**) a French title
equivalent to *Mr.*

Monsignor (măn-sēn′yər, mən-) *noun* (*pl.*
Monsignors) (ABBREV. **Msgr.**) *RC Church*
a title for various high-ranking priests.

monsoon *noun* **1** a S Asian wind or the heavy
rains accompanying it. **2** *colloq.* an extremely
heavy fall of rain.

monster *noun* **1** any large, frightening,
imaginary creature. **2** a cruel or evil person.
3 an unusually large object. —*adj.* exceedingly or excessively large.

monstera *noun* a tall climbing tropical plant
that has large heart-shaped leaves with
deep notches and sometimes holes. *Also
called* **Swiss cheese plant.**

monstrance *noun* *RC Church* a large gold or
silver cup in which the host is displayed to
the congregation during Mass.

monstrosity *noun* (*pl.* **monstrosities**) **1** an
ugly or outrageous thing. **2** the quality or
condition of being monstrous.

monstrous *adj.* **1** exceedingly or excessively
large. **2** flagrantly wicked or horrible. **3**
extremely cruel; evil. ▸ **monstrously** *adv.*

montage (măn-tăzh′, môN-) *noun* a picture
made by piecing together elements from
other pictures, photographs, etc., or the art
or process of making such a picture.

month *noun* **1** any of the 12 named divisions of
the year. **2** a period of roughly four weeks or
30 days; the period between identical dates
in consecutive months.

monthly *adj.* happening, published, etc., once

a month; lasting one month. —*adv.* once a month. —*noun* (*pl.* **monthlies**) a monthly periodical.

monument *noun* 1 something, e.g., a statue, tomb, tombstone, etc., erected in memory of a person or event. 2 a notable or excellent example, esp. one that is enduring or that has been preserved, e.g. a building, an outstanding work of art, etc.: *ancient Greek monuments*.

monumental *adj.* 1 relating to a monument. 2 of exceedingly or excessively large size.

moo *noun* the sound made by a cow. —*verb intrans.* (**mooed, mooing, moos**) to make this sound.

mooch *verb trans., intrans.* (**mooched, mooching, mooches**) *slang* 1 to get (things) for nothing by asking directly; to cadge. 2 to hang about without a purpose.

mood[1] *noun* 1 a state of the mind, esp. one where a particular emotion is dominant. 2 a temporary grumpy state of mind: *went off in a mood*. 3 an atmosphere.

mood[2] *noun Gram.* a form of a verb or verbal inflection indicating a specific grammatical or semantic category: *the subjunctive mood*.

moody *adj.* (**moodier, moodiest**) 1 tending to change mood often. 2 frequently difficult to get on with or bad-tempered. ▸ **moodily** *adv.* ▸ **moodiness** *noun*

moon *noun* 1 (*usu.* **the Moon**) the Earth's only natural satellite. 2 a natural satellite of any planet. —*verb intrans.* (**mooned, mooning**) 1 (**moon around** or **about**) to wander aimlessly; to spend time idly. 2 *slang* to bare one's buttocks in public. —**over the moon** *colloq.* thrilled; delighted.

moonbeam *noun* a ray of moonlight.

Moonie *noun* (*pl.* **Moonies**) a member of the Unification Church.

moonlight *noun* light from the Moon. —*adj.* illuminated by light from the Moon: *a moonlight swim*. —*verb intrans.* (*pa t and pa p* **moonlighted**; *pr p* **moonlighting**) *colloq.* to work at a second job outside the working hours of the main job. ▸ **moonlighter** *noun*

moonlit *adj.* illuminated by moonlight.

moonshine *noun colloq.* 1 smuggled or illegally distilled alcoholic spirit. 2 foolish talk; nonsense. ▸ **moonshiner** *noun*

moonstone *noun* a form of feldspar used as a semiprecious stone.

moonstruck *adj. colloq.* wildly excited or crazy.

Moor *noun* a member of a NW African people who established themselves in Spain between the 8th c. and the 15th c. A.D. ▸ **Moorish** *adj.*

moor[1] *noun* a large area of open uncultivated land.

moor[2] *verb trans., intrans.* (**moored, mooring**) 1 to tie up (a ship or boat) by a rope, cable, or anchor. 2 to be fastened in this way.

mooring *noun* 1 a place where a boat is moored. 2 (**moorings**) the ropes, anchors, etc., used to moor a boat.

moose *noun* (*pl.* **moose**) a large deer with big broad antlers. *Also called* **elk.**

moot *verb trans.* (**mooted, mooting**) to bring up for discussion; to suggest. —*adj.* open to argument; debatable: *a moot point*.

moot court a mock court where law students are trained to try hypothetical cases.

mop *noun* 1 a long-handled tool for cleaning floors, or a similar, smaller tool for washing dishes by hand. 2 *colloq.* a thick, often untidy, mass of hair. —*verb trans.* (**mopped, mopping**) 1 to clean (a floor, etc.) with a mop. 2 to wipe or dab: *mopped his brow*.

mope *verb intrans.* (**moped, moping**) to behave in a depressed, sulky, or aimless way.

moped (mō′pěd,) *noun* a lightweight bicycle with a small engine.

moppet *noun* a doll or small child, esp. a little girl.

moquette (mō-kět′) *noun* thick velvety material used to make carpets and upholstery.

moraine *noun* an accumulation of rock fragments carried from its place of origin and deposited by a glacier or ice sheet.

moral (môr′əl) *adj.* 1 of or relating to the principles of good and evil, or right and wrong. 2 conforming to what is considered by society to be good, right, or proper. 3 having a psychological effect: *moral support*. 4 considered in terms of psychological effect rather than outward appearance: *a moral victory*. 5 capable of distinguishing between right and wrong. —*noun* 1 a principle to be learned from a story or event. 2 (**morals**) a sense of right and wrong, or a standard of behavior based on it.

morale (mə-răl′, -räl′) *noun* level of confidence or optimism; spirits.

moralist *noun* 1 a person who lives according to strict moral principles. 2 a person who tends to lecture others on their low moral standards. ▸ **moralistic** *adj.*

morality *noun* (*pl.* **moralities**) 1 the quality of being right or wrong; behavior in relation to accepted moral standards. 2 a particular system of moral standards.

morality play an allegorical drama, originating in the Middle Ages, in which the characters act out a conflict between good and evil.

moralize *verb intrans., trans.* (**moralized, moralizing**) 1 to write or speak, esp. critically, about moral standards. 2 to explain in terms of morals. ▸ **moralizer** noun

morass (mɔ-răs′) noun 1 an area of wet, spongy ground saturated and often partially covered with water. 2 a dangerous or confused situation, esp. one that is difficult to escape from.

moratorium noun (pl. **moratoriums, moratoria**) 1 an agreed temporary break in an activity. 2 a legally authorized postponement of payment of a debt.

moray noun a large predatory tropical marine eel. Also called **moray eel**.

morbid adj. 1 displaying an unhealthy interest in unpleasant things, esp. death. 2 relating to or indicating the presence of disease. ▸ **morbidity** noun

mordant adj. 1 sharply sarcastic or critical; biting. 2 characterized by having the property of fixing colors. —noun a chemical compound used to fix color on textiles.

more adj. being greater or additional in number or quantity. See **many**. See **much**. —adv. 1 to a greater degree; with a greater frequency. 2 again. 3 See **much**. —pron. (pl.) a greater, or additional, number or quantity of people or things.

morel (mɔ-rĕl′) noun an edible mushroom.

morello noun (pl. **morellos**) a deciduous cherry tree or its dark red edible fruit that is used in cooking and making cherry brandy. Also called **morello cherry**.

moreover adv. and what is more important; also.

mores (môr′āz) pl. noun social customs reflecting the basic moral and social values of a particular society.

morganatic adj., of marriage occurring between a person of high social rank and one of lower rank.

From early German morgengabe 'morning gift', a present given to a spouse on the morning after the wedding

morgue noun 1 a building where corpses are kept until buried or cremated. 2 a store of miscellaneous information for reference.

moribund adj. 1 near the end of existence; dying. 2 lacking strength or vitality.

Mormon (môr′mən) noun a member of the Church of Jesus Christ of Latter-Day Saints. Also called **Latter-Day Saint**. ▸ **Mormonism** noun

morn noun poetic morning.

mornay adj. served in a cheese sauce: cod. mornay.

morning noun 1 the part of the day from sunrise to midday, or from midnight to midday. 2 sunrise; dawn. —adj. taken or taking place in the morning: morning coffee.

morning-after pill a contraceptive drug taken after unprotected sex.

morning glory (pl. **morning glories**) a tropical climbing plant with bright blue funnel-shaped flowers with a yellow throat.

morning sickness nausea and vomiting during the early stages of pregnancy, esp. in the morning.

morocco noun soft, fine goatskin leather.

moron noun 1 colloq. a very stupid person. 2 offensive, old use a person with a mild degree of mental disability. ▸ **moronic** adj.

morose adj. silently gloomy or bad-tempered. ▸ **moroseness** noun

morphine noun a highly-addictive narcotic drug obtained from opium.

morphing noun Cinema the use of computer graphics to blend one image into another, e.g., to transform or manipulate an actor's body.

morphology noun the scientific study of form and structure, esp. of biological organisms. ▸ **morphological** adj.

morris dance a traditional English folk dance.

Originally a Moorish dance brought from Spain

morrow noun old use, poetic (**the morrow**) the following day.

Morse code a code formerly used for sending messages, each letter being represented as a series of short or long radio signals or flashes of light.

morsel noun a small piece, esp. of food.

mortal adj. 1 certain to die. 2 of or causing death. 3 extreme: mortal danger. 4 characterized by intense hostility: mortal enemies. —noun a living being.

mortality noun 1 the state of being mortal. 2 the number of deaths, e.g., in a war or caused by a disease. 3 loss of life.

mortal sin RC Church a sin that is so grave that it will lead to a loss of sanctifying grace and certain damnation unless confessed and forgiven. See also **venial sin**.

mortar noun 1 a bonding mixture used in building. 2 the small dish in which substances are ground with a pestle. 3 a short-barreled artillery piece for firing shells over short distances.

mortarboard noun 1 a flat board used by bricklayers to hold mortar. 2 a flat-topped cap worn by academics, graduating students, etc.

mortgage (môr′gĭj) noun 1 a legal agreement by which a financial institution grants a client a loan for the purpose of buying property, ownership of the property being held by the institution until the loan has been repaid. 2 the money borrowed, or the regular amounts repaid. 3 any loan for which property is used as security. —verb trans. (**mortgaged, mortgaging**) to give ownership of property as security for a loan.

mortice *noun, verb* same as **mortise**.

mortician *noun* an undertaker.

mortify *verb trans., intrans.* (**mortified, mortifying, mortifies**) **1** to cause to feel humiliated or ashamed. **2** *Relig.* to subject (the body or physical desires) to control through self-discipline. **3** *of a wound, etc.* to become gangrenous. ▶ **mortification** *noun*

mortise *or* **mortice** *noun* a hole cut in a piece of wood, into which a tenon, or shaped end of a second piece, fits to form a joint. —*verb trans.* (**mortised, mortising**) to cut a mortise in; to join with a mortise and tenon joint.

mortuary *noun* (*pl.* **mortuaries**) a building, esp. a funeral home, or room where corpses are kept until buried or cremated.

mosaic *noun* a design or picture formed by fitting together small pieces of colored stone, glass, etc.

Moselle (mō-zěl′) *noun* a dry white wine.

mosey *verb intrans.* (**moseyed, moseying, moseys**) (*often* **mosey along**) *colloq.* to walk in a leisurely way; to saunter or amble.

Moslem (măz′ləm, măs′-) *noun, adj.* same as **Muslim**.

mosque *noun* a Muslim place of worship.

mosquito *noun* (*pl.* **mosquitoes, mosquitos**) a small, biting, blood-sucking insect that can transmit diseases, including malaria.

mosquito net a fine mesh net designed to keep away mosquitoes, often hung over a bed at night.

moss *noun* a plant typically found growing in dense tufts or spreading clusters in moist shady habitats. ▶ **mossy** *adj.*

most *adj.* being the greatest part, amount, or number. *See* **many**. *See* **much**. —*adv.* **1** (**the most**) to the greatest degree; with the greatest frequency. **2** extremely. **3** *See* **more**. **4** *See* **much**. —*pron.* the greatest number or quantity, the majority of people or things, or the greatest part or segment. —**make the most of** to take the greatest possible advantage of (something).

-most *combining form* forming words denoting a superlative: *foremost / southernmost.*

mostly *adv.* usually; mainly.

mote *noun* a speck, esp. of dust.

motel *noun* an inn with extensive parking, mainly used by passing motorists on overnight stops.

motet *noun* a short piece of usu. sacred music for several voices.

moth *noun* a winged insect related to the butterfly, and mostly nocturnal.

mothball *noun* a small ball of camphor or naphthalene used for keeping clothes moths away. —*verb trans.* (**mothballed, mothballing**) **1** to take (a ship, etc.) out of operational service and put in storage. **2** *colloq.* to defer (a plan, project, etc) indefinitely.

moth-eaten *adj.* **1** *of clothes, etc.* damaged by clothes moths. **2** *colloq.* old and worn.

mother *noun* **1** a natural or adoptive female parent. **2** (**Mother** *or* **Mother Superior**) the head of a female religious, esp. Christian, community. **3** a cause, origin, or most extreme example. —*adj.* like a mother in being protect-ive, or in being a source from which others spring. —*verb trans., intrans.* (**mothered, mothering**) **1** to give birth to; to give rise to. **2** to treat with care and protection. **3** to assume the parental role of mother. ▶ **motherhood** *noun* ▶ **motherless** *adj.* ▶ **motherly** *adj.* ▶ **motherliness** *noun*

motherboard *noun Comput.* a main printed circuit board of a microcomputer, that other circuit boards, etc. can be plugged into.

mother country one's native country.

Mothering Sunday *Brit.* the fourth Sunday in Lent, traditionally a day on which children honor their mothers with gifts. *See also* **Mother's Day**.

mother-in-law *noun* (*pl.* **mothers-in-law**) the mother of one's wife or husband.

motherland *noun* one's native country.

mother-of-pearl *noun* a pearly layer of the shell of certain mollusks, e.g., oysters. *Also called* **nacre**.

Mother's Day the day on which mothers are honored: in the USA, Canada, and Australia, it is the second Sunday in May; in the UK, it is Mothering Sunday.

mother tongue one's native language.

motif (mō-tēf′) *noun* **1** a shape repeated many times within a pattern; a single design or symbol, e.g., on clothing. **2** something that recurs, often in a developed form, in a work of art, e.g., a passage of music in a symphony, or a théme in a novel or film. 🔳 SUBJECT, THEME.

motile *adj. of a living organism* capable of spontaneous movement.

motion *noun* **1** an act, state, or way of moving. **2** a single movement, esp. of the body. **3** the ability to move a part of the body. **4** a proposal for formal discussion at a meeting. —*verb trans., intrans.* (**motioned, motioning**) to give (someone) a signal or direction. —**go through the motions** to perform a task mechanically or half-heartedly; to pretend.

motionless *adj.* without moving; completely still.

motion picture a movie (sense 1).

motivate (mōt′ĭ-vāt‚) *verb trans.* (**motivated, motivating**) **1** to be the motive of. **2** to cause or stimulate (a person) to act. ▶ **motivation** *noun*

motive (mōt'ĭv) *noun* a reason for or underlying cause of an action, etc. —*adj.* **1** causing motion: *motive power.* **2** stimulating action: *motive force.*

motley *adj.* **1** made up of many different kinds: *a motley crew.* **2** many-colored. —*noun* a jester's multicolored costume.

motocross *noun* (ABBREV. **MX**) a cross-country motorcycle race or the sport of cross-country motorcycle racing.

motor *noun* **1** a device that powers or operates something, esp. one that converts electrical, steam, etc. energy into mechanical energy, e.g., in domestic appliances, industry machinery, etc. **2** an engine, esp. the internal combustion engine of a vehicle or machine. **3** *colloq.* a car. —*adj.* **1** of or relating to cars or other road vehicles: *a motor show.* **2** driven by a motor. —*verb intrans.* (**motored, motoring**) **1** to travel by motor vehicle, esp. by private car. **2** *colloq.* to move, work, etc., fast and effectively.

motorbike *noun colloq.* a lightweight motorcycle, or a bicycle having a small motor.

motorboat *noun* a boat driven by an engine or electric motor. *Also called* **powerboat.**

motorcade *noun* a procession of cars carrying important, esp. political figures.

motorcar an automobile.

motorcycle *noun* a two-wheeled road vehicle powered by a gasoline engine. ▸ **motorcycle** *verb* ▸ **motorcyclist** *noun*

motorist *noun* a person who drives a car.

motorize *verb trans.* (**motorized, motorizing**) **1** to fit a motor to. **2** to supply with motor vehicles.

motor scooter scooter (sense 2).

motorway *noun Brit.* a major multilane highway.

Motown (mō'town,) a style of music combining the styles of pop and rhythm and blues.

mottled *adj.* having a pattern of different-colored blotches or streaks.

motto *noun* (*pl.* **mottoes, mottos**) a phrase or word adopted as a guiding principle: *'Do your best' is my motto.*

mound *noun* **1** a natural or artificial hill, bank of earth, etc. **2** a heap or pile.

mount¹ *verb trans., intrans.* (**mounted, mounting**) **1** to go up: *mounted the stairs.* **2** to get up on (a horse, bicycle, etc.). **3** (*also* **mount up**) to increase in quantity, level, intensity, etc. **4** to put in a frame or on a background for display, etc. **5** to organize or hold (a campaign, etc.). **6** to carry out (e.g., an attack). —*noun* **1** a support or backing on which a thing is placed for display. **2** a horse that is ridden.

mount² *noun* a mountain.

mountain *noun* **1** a natural upward projection of the Earth's surface, higher and steeper than a hill. **2** *colloq.* a great quantity, heap, or mass: *a mountain of work.* **3** a huge surplus of a commodity: *a butter mountain.*

mountain ash a slender deciduous European tree with bunches of small fleshy fruits. *Also called* **rowan.**

mountain bike a sturdy bicycle with thick, deep-tread tires, suitable for riding off-road.

mountaineer *noun* a person who climbs mountains. —*verb intrans.* (**mountaineered, mountaineering**) to climb mountains. ▸ **mountaineering** *noun*

mountain goat a long-haired antelope with curved black horns. *Also called* **Rocky Mountain goat.**

mountain laurel an evergreen shrub with leathery poisonous leaves.

mountain lion a large, tawny-colored wild cat living in mountain regions of the Western hemisphere. *Also called* **cougar, panther, puma.**

mountainous *adj.* **1** containing many mountains. **2** of exceedingly or excessively large size.

mountebank (mownt'ĭ-băngk,) *noun* **1** a person who goes from place to place selling quack medicines. **2** a cheat or swindler.

> Originally a street pedlar who climbed on a mound or bench to sell his goods

mounted *adj.* **1** on horseback. **2** hung on a wall, or placed in a frame or on a background.

mourn *verb trans., intrans.* (**mourned, mourning**) to feel or show deep sorrow at the death or loss of (a person or thing). ▸ **mourner** *noun*

mournful *adj.* **1** feeling or expressing grief. **2** suggesting sadness or gloom. ▸ **mournfully** *adv.*

mourning *noun* **1** grief felt or shown over a death. **2** a symbol of grief, esp. black clothes. **3** a period of time during which one mourns or grieves.

mouse *noun* (*pl.* **mice**) **1** a small rodent with a gray or brown coat, a pointed muzzle and bright eyes, sharp teeth, and a long naked tail. **2** *colloq.* a very shy, quiet person. **3** (*pl.* **mice, mouses**) *Comput.* a hand-operated computer input device with one or more selection buttons. It is used for moving the cursor to the desired place, choosing options displayed on menus, etc. *See also* **trackball.** —*verb intrans.* (**moused, mousing**) **1** to hunt mice. **2** (**mouse around**) *Comput. slang* to explore public portions of a large computer system, looking for material to download without permission. **3** (**mouse across, mouse one's way, mouse over**) *Comput.* to move around a computer screen using a mouse: *moused across to the toolbar / Mouse your way to that window and click. / Mouse over the icon and a menu will appear.*

mouse deer the chevrotain.

mouse potato *colloq.* a person who spends a lot of time in front of a computer screen, esp. playing computer games or accessing Internet sites.

mouser *noun* a cat used for, or adept at, catching mice.

mousetrap *noun* a mechanical trap for catching and often killing mice. —*verb trans.* (**mousetrapped, mousetrapping**) to ensnare in or as if in a trap for mice.

moussaka (mōō,sə-kä') *noun* an oven-cooked dish of minced meat and vegetables, esp. eggplant, covered with a cheese sauce.

mousse (mōōs) *noun* **1** a dessert made from a whipped mixture of cream, eggs and flavoring, eaten cold. **2** a similar meat or fish dish. **3** a frothy hair preparation applied to make styling easier. *Also called* **styling mousse**.

moustache *noun see* **mustache**.

mousy *or* **mousey** *adj.* (**mousier, mousiest**) **1** of or like a mouse. **2** *of hair* of a dull, light brown color. **3** shy or quiet, esp. tiresomely so. ▶ **mousiness** *noun*

mouth *noun* (mowth) **1** an opening in the head of many animals, including humans, through which food is taken in and sounds are emitted. **2** a opening resembling this, e.g., the opening of a jar, etc., the entrance to a cave, the point where a river flows into a sea, etc. —*verb trans., intrans.* (mowth) (**mouthed, mouthing**) **1** to form (words) without actually speaking. **2** to speak pompously or without sincerity.

-mouthed *combining form* forming words denoting: **1** using a certain kind of language: *foul-mouthed.* **2** having a certain kind of mouth: *wide-mouthed.*

mouthful (mowth'fōōl,) *noun* (*pl.* **mouthfuls**) **1** as much as fills the mouth. **2** a small quantity, esp. of food. **3** *colloq.* a word or phrase difficult to pronounce. **4** *colloq.* an outburst of forceful, often abusive language: *let fly with a mouthful.*

mouth organ a harmonica (sense 1).

mouthpiece *noun* **1** the part of a musical instrument, telephone receiver, tobacco pipe, etc., held in or against the mouth. **2** a person or publication expressing the views of a group.

mouth-to-mouth *adj.* denoting a method of artificial respiration in which a person administering first aid covers the patient's mouth with his or her own and breathes out sharply and rhythmically in order to force air into the patient's lungs.

mouthwash *noun* an antiseptic liquid gargled to freshen the mouth.

mouthwatering *adj.* **1** *of food* having a delicious appearance or smell. **2** *colloq.* highly desirable.

movable *or* **moveable** *adj.* **1** able or designed to be moved. ⊟ MOBILE, PORTABLE, UNFIXED ⊟ FIXED, IMMOVABLE, SET. **2** *of a religious festival* taking place on a different date each year: *Easter is a movable feast.*

move *verb trans., intrans.* (**moved, moving**) **1** to change or cause to change position or go from one place to another. **2** to make progress of any kind: *move toward a political solution.* **3** (**move on, out,** *or* **away**) to change (one's place of living, working, operating, etc.). **4** to affect the feelings or emotions of. **5** (**move (someone) to do (something)**) to affect or inspire (the one specified) so that they do (it): *What moved him to say that?* **6** to change the position of (a piece in a board game). **7** *formal* (**move for (something)**) to propose or request (it) formally. **8** to spend time; to associate with people: *move in fashionable circles.* **9** *colloq.* to progress speedily. **10** *colloq.* to sell or be sold. **11** *said of the bowels* to be evacuated or cause them to be evacuated. —*noun* **1 a** an act of moving the body. **b** the manner in which the body is moved. **2** an act of moving a piece in a board game, or the rules governing how the pieces are moved; any of a series of actions taken as part of an overall strategy. **3** an act of relocating one's residence. —**get a move on** *or* **get moving** *colloq.* to hurry up. **make a move 1** to take a step; to begin to proceed. **2** *colloq.* to leave. **move heaven and earth** to make strenuous efforts to achieve something. **move in** to begin to occupy new premises. **move in on 1** to advance toward (someone), esp. threateningly. **2** to take steps toward controlling (another) or usurping (that person's) position, etc. **on the move 1** moving from place to place. **2** advancing or making progress.

movement *noun* **1** a process or act of changing position or going from one point to another. **2** an organization or association, esp. one promoting a particular cause. **3** a general tendency. **4** the theatrical art of moving the body gracefully or with expression. **5** (**movements**) a person's actions during a particular time. **6** the moving parts of a watch or clock. **7** an act of evacuating the bowels; the waste matter evacuated. **8** a section of a piece of music, e.g., a symphony, sonata, or string quartet.

mover *noun* a person or thing that moves. —**mover and shaker** an influential, powerful person in a specific area of endeavor.

movie *noun* **1** a series of photographs that are projected onto a screen fast enough to create the illusion of continuity and motion. **2** a cinematic narrative created using this technique. **3** a theater showing movies. **4** ((the) movies) **a** a showing of a movie. **b** the movie industry.

moving *adj.* **1** having an effect on the emotions; touching; stirring. **2** in motion; not static: *a moving staircase*.

moving sidewalk a conveyor on which pedestrians are transported over flat, long areas, e.g., in large airports. *Also* called **people mover**.

mow (mō) *verb trans.* (pa t **mowed**; pa p **mowed** or **mown**, pr p **mowing**) to cut (grass or a crop) with a machine or by hand. —**mow down** *colloq.* **1** to drive a motor vehicle and knock (someone or something) down with it. **2** to kill in large numbers.

mower *noun* a machine with blades for cutting grass.

moxie *noun slang* aggressive skill, courage, or spirit.

mozzarella (māt‚sə-rĕl′ə) *noun* a soft, white Italian cheese, often used as a pizza topping.

mph *abbrev.* miles per hour.

Mr. *noun* (*pl.* **Messrs.**) a title used before the full name or the surname of a man, or before a word designating a man's official position: *Mr. Clooney / Mr. Chairman.*

Ms. (mǐz) *noun* (*pl.* **Mss., Mss**) a title before the first name and surname or the surname only of a woman, married or not: *Ms. Brown.*

MS-DOS (ĕm‚ĕs‚däs′) *trademark* the standard operating system for all IBM-compatible computers.

much *adj.* (**more, most**) great in quantity, extent, or degree. —*adv.* (**more, most**) **1** by a great deal or to a great degree. **2** almost. **3** often. —*pron.* a considerable quantity, amount, etc.

muchacha *noun* (*pl.* **muchachas**) a girl or young woman.

muchacho *noun* (*pl.* **muchachos**) a boy or young man.

mucilage (myōō′sə-lǐj) *noun* **1** a gumlike plant secretion. **2** an adhesive. ▸ **mucilaginous** *adj.*

muck *noun* **1** *colloq.* dirt. **2** animal dung; manure. **3** *colloq.* anything disgusting, or of very poor quality. —*verb trans., intrans.* (**mucked, mucking**) **1** (*usu.* **muck out**) to clear dung from (a farm building): *mucked out the barn.* **2** to treat (soil) with manure. ▸ **mucky** *adj.*

muckrake *verb intrans.* (**muckraked, muckraking**) to seek out and expose scandal. ▸ **muckraker** *noun*

mucus *noun* a thick, slimy, protective or lubricating substance, e.g., on the lining of the nasal passages and other body cavities. ▸ **mucous** *adj.*

mud *noun* **1** soft, wet earth. **2** slanderous attacks; insults.

muddle *verb trans.* (**muddled, muddling**) (*also* **muddle up**) **1** to put into a disordered or confused state. **2** to confuse the mind of; to confuse (different things) in the mind. —*noun* a state of disorder or mental confusion.

muddle-headed *adj.* incapable of clear thinking; confused.

muddy *adj.* (**muddier, muddiest**) **1** covered with or containing mud. **2** not clear; vague. —*verb trans.* (**muddied, muddying, muddies**) to make muddy, esp. in the sense of unclear, or difficult to understand. ▸ **muddiness** *noun*

mudguard *noun* a shield over or behind a vehicle's wheel to stop mud, dirty rainwater, etc. from splashing up.

mudslinger *noun* a person who makes slanderous allegations to discredit another. ▸ **mudslinging** *noun*

muesli (mōōz′lē, myōōz′-) *noun* a mixture of grains, nuts, and dried fruit, eaten with milk, esp. for breakfast.

muezzin (myōō-ĕz′ĭn, mwĕz′-) *noun* the Muslim official who calls worshippers to prayer, usu. from a minaret.

muff¹ *noun* a fur tube for keeping the hands warm.

muff² *colloq. verb trans.* (**muffed, muffing**) **1** *Sport* to miss (a catch); to perform (a stroke) awkwardly or unsuccessfully. **2** to miss (an opportunity, etc.). —*noun* a failure, esp. to hold a catch.

muffin *noun* a small, round, flat, cake usu. eaten hot with butter.

muffle *verb trans.* (**muffled, muffling**) **1** to make quieter; to suppress (sound). **2** to prevent (someone) from saying (something).

muffler *noun* a thick scarf.

mufti *noun* civilian clothes worn by people who usu. wear a uniform.

mug¹ *noun* a drinking cup with a handle, used without a saucer.

mug² *noun* **1** *colloq.* a face or mouth. **2** a hood'um or street thug. —*verb trans., intrans.* (**mugged, mugging**) to attack and rob violently or under threat of violence. ▸ **mugger** *noun* ▸ **mugging** *noun*

muggy *adj.* (**muggier, muggiest**) *of the weather* unpleasantly warm and damp; close. ▸ **mugginess** *noun*

mug shot *colloq.* a photograph of a person's face, taken for police records.

mugwump *noun* someone who is politically independent.

mulatto (myə-lăt′ō, -lăt′ō) *noun* (*pl.* **mulattos, mulattoes**) ·*old use, now usu. offensive* a person of mixed race.

mulberry *noun* (*pl.* **mulberries**) **1** a tree or shrub whose leaves are used as food for silkworms, or its edible fruit. **2** a dark purple color.

mulch *noun* decaying leaves, straw, etc. used as a protection around the base of plants or trees, or to provide extra nutrients to soil. —*verb trans.* (**mulched, mulching**) to cover (the soil surface) with mulch.

mulct *noun* a fine or penalty. —*verb trans.* (**mulcted, mulcting**) **1** to fine, or deprive (someone) of something as a fine. **2** to swindle.

mule¹ *noun* **1** an offspring of a male donkey and a female horse. **2** any hybrid animal. **3** a machine that spins cotton into yarn. **4** a stubborn person. **5** *slang* a courier of illegal drugs.

mule² *noun* a shoe or slipper with no back part covering the heel.

muleskinner *noun colloq.* a muleteer.

muleteer *noun* a person who drives mules.

mulish *adj.* stubborn.

mull¹ *verb trans., intrans.* (**mulled, mulling**) to consider (something) carefully.

mull² *verb trans.* (**mulled, mulling**) to spice, sweeten, and warm (wine or beer).

mullah *noun* a Muslim scholar and adviser in Islamic religion and sacred law.

mullet *noun* a marine or freshwater fish.

mulligatawny (məl,ĭ-gə-tô′nē) *noun* (*pl.* **mulligatawnies**) a thick, spicy soup.

mullion *noun* a vertical bar or post separating the panes or casements of a window.

multi- *combining form* forming words denoting many: *multicolored*.

multifarious *adj. formal* having many different parts.

multilateral *adj.* **1** involving or affecting several people, groups, or nations. **2** many-sided.

multilingual *adj.* written or expressed in, or able to speak, several different languages.

multimedia *adj.* of a computer, etc. designed or able to present and manipulate data in a variety of forms, e.g., text, graphics, and sound, often simultaneously.

multimillionaire *noun* a person whose wealth is valued at several million dollars.

multinational *adj.* operating in several different countries. —*noun* a business or other organization that operates in several different countries.

multiple *adj.* having, involving or affecting many parts. —*noun Math.* an number or expression for which a given number or expression is a factor, e.g., 24 is a multiple of 12.

multiple-choice *adj.*, *of an exam* giving a selection of possible answers, including the right one, after each question from which candidates attempt to choose the correct one.

multiple sclerosis (ABBREV. **MS**) a degenerative disease of the central nervous system.

multiplex *adj. formal* having very many parts; complex. —*noun* a large movie theater with several screens showing a variety of different movies.

multiplicand (məl,tĭ-plĭ-kănd′) *noun Math.* a number to be multiplied by another.

multiplication *noun Math.* a mathematical operation where two or more numbers are multiplied, usu. denoted as $x \times y$. **2** an act or the process of multiplying or increasing in number.

multiplicity *noun* (*pl.* **multiplicities**) a great number and variety.

multiplier *noun Math.* a number or quantity by which another is to be multiplied.

multiply *verb trans., intrans.* (**multiplied, multiplying, multiplies**) **1** *Math.* to add a number, etc. to itself a specified number of times: *Two multiplied by four equals eight.* **2** to increase, or cause to increase, in number, quantity, size, etc.

multipurpose *adj.* having many uses.

multiracial *adj.* of, for, or including people of many different races.

multistory *adj.*, *of a building* having many floors. —*noun* (*pl.* **multistories**) *colloq.* a building with many floors.

multitasking *noun Comput.* a mode of operating where a computer can be seen to be carrying out one function on-screen, while the operating system is also doing another task or tasks in the background.

multitude *noun* **1** a great number. **2** a huge crowd of people. ▸ **multitudinous** *adj.*

multiuser *Comput. adj.*, *of a computer system* consisting of several terminals linked to a central computer, allowing access by several users at the same time.

mum *adj. colloq.* not speaking; silent. —**mum's the word** *colloq.* an exhortation to secrecy.

mumble *verb trans., intrans.* (**mumbled, mumbling**) to speak unclearly, esp. with the mouth partly closed. —*noun* unclear or hushed speech.

mumbo jumbo (*pl.* **mumbo jumbos**) *colloq.* **1** foolish talk, esp. of a religious or spiritual kind. **2** baffling jargon. **3** something, e.g., a statue, foolishly treated as an object of worship.

mummer *noun* **1** an elaborately costumed and masked performer or merrymaker, e.g., in a festival. **2** an actor.

mummery *noun* (*pl.* **mummeries**) **1** a performance of mumming. **2** ridiculous or pretentious ceremony.

mummify *verb trans.* (**mummified, mummifying, mummifies**) to preserve (a corpse) as a mummy. ▸ **mummification** *noun*

mummy *noun* a corpse, esp. in ancient Egypt, preserved with spices and bandaged.

mumps *noun* (*sing., pl.*) an infectious viral disease, mainly affecting children, causing painful swelling of the salivary glands.

munch *verb trans., intrans.* (**munched, munching**) to chew with a steady movement of the jaws, esp. noisily.

munchies *pl. noun colloq.* **1** snacks, esp. potato chips and other packaged foods. **2** (**the munchies**) a sudden strong craving for this kind of food.

mundane *adj.* **1** ordinary; dull; everyday. **2** of this world, only.

mung bean a bushy plant or its edible pods and nutritious seeds.

municipal *adj.* of, relating to, or controlled by government at a local level. ▸ **municipally** *adv.*

municipality *noun* (*pl.* **municipalities**) a town or region having its own local government; the local government itself.

munificence *noun* magnificent generosity.

munificent *adj. formal* extremely generous.

munitions *pl. noun* military equipment, esp. ammunition and weapons.

muon (myōō'ăn,) *noun* an elementary particle that behaves like a heavy electron, but decays to form an electron and neutrinos.

mural *noun* a painting executed directly onto a wall. —*adj.* of or relating to a wall or walls. ▸ **muralist** *noun*

murder *noun* **1** the act of unlawfully and intentionally killing a person. **2** *colloq.* something or a situation that causes hardship or difficulty. —*verb trans., intrans.* (**murdered, murdering**) **1** to cause the death of (someone) illegally, with malice. ▤ KILL, OFF, SLAY. **2** *colloq.* to spoil or ruin: *took a classic song and murdered it.* **3** *colloq.* to defeat easily and by a huge margin: *Our team murdered the visitors.* ▸ **murderer** *noun* ▸ **murdereress** *noun* ▸ **murderous** *adj.*

murk *noun* gloom or darkness.

murky *adj.* (**murkier, murkiest**) **1** dark; gloomy. **2** *of water* dark and dirty. **3** suspiciously vague or unknown; shady: *her murky past.* ▸ **murkiness** *noun*

murmur *noun* **1** a quiet continuous sound or a low, indistinct voice. **2** a complaint. **3** *Med.* a abnormal body sound, esp. of the heart. *Also called* **heart murmur.** —*verb trans., intrans.* (**murmured, murmuring**) **1** to

speak (words) softly and indistinctly. **2** to complain or grumble. **3** to make a sound that, in its quiet continuousness, is likened to that of the sound of low voices. ▸ **murmurous** *adj.*

Murphy's Law (mər'fěz) a maxim stating that if something can go wrong, it will go wrong.

murrain *noun* a disease of cattle.

muscatel (mŭs,kə-těl') , **muscat** *or* **muscadel** *noun* **1** a variety of sweet white grape or a grapevine that produce such grapes. **2** a wine made from these grapes.

muscle *noun* **1 a** an animal tissue composed of bundles of fibers that are capable of contracting and so produce movement. **b** a body structure composed of this tissue, e.g., the biceps. **2** bodily strength. **3** *slang* power, influence, coercion or someone who uses any of these. —*verb intrans.* (**muscled, muscling**) (*usu.* **muscle in**) *colloq.* to force one's way, presence, etc. (in): *tried to muscle his way to the front of the queue / wanted to muscle in on the deal.*

muscle-bound *adj.* having overly enlarged muscles that are stiff and difficult to move.

Muscovite (mŭs'kə-vīt,) *noun* a native or citizen of Moscow. —*adj.* of Moscow or its citizens.

muscular *adj.* **1** of, relating to, or consisting of muscle. **2** having well-developed muscles; strong. ▸ **muscularity** *noun*

muscular dystrophy a hereditary disease characterized by progressive muscle wasting.

musculature *noun* the system or arrangement of muscles.

Muse (myōōz) *noun* **1** one of the nine mythical Greek goddesses of the arts. **2** (**muse**) a guiding spirit or a source of any kind of inspiration.

muse *verb intrans., trans.* (**mused, musing**) to reflect or ponder.

museum *noun* a place where objects of artistic, scientific, or historic interest are displayed for the public.

mush¹ *noun* **1** a soft, half-liquid mass. **2** *colloq.* sloppy sentimentality.

mush² *interj.* used to urge on a dogsled team. —*verb intrans.* (**mushed, mushing**) to travel on a dogsled.

mushroom *noun* a fungus, esp. an edible one. —*verb intrans.* (**mushroomed, mushrooming**) to develop or increase quickly.

mushy *adj.* (**mushier, mushiest**) **1** soft and pulpy. **2** foolishly sad or sentimental.

music *noun* **1 a** the art of making sound in a rhythmically organized harmonious form, either sung or produced with instruments. **b** this type of sound. **2** any written form in which such sound is expressed.

musical *adj.* **1** of, relating to, or producing music. **2** pleasant to hear; melodious. **3**

having a talent for playing music. —*noun* (*also* **musical comedy**) a play or movie with singing and dancing. ▸ **musically** *adv.* ▸ **musicality** *noun*

musician *noun* a person skilled in performing or composing music. ▸ **musicianship** *noun*

musicology *noun* the academic study of music in all its aspects. ▸ **musicologist** *noun*

musings *pl. noun* thoughts.

musk *noun* a strong-smelling animal secretion much used in perfumery.

musket *noun* a gun loaded through the barrel.

musketeer *noun* a soldier armed with a musket.

musketry *noun* **1** firing practice. **2** troops armed with muskets.

muskmelon *noun* a sweet melon, e.g., the cantaloupe.

musk ox (*pl.* **musk oxen**) a large mammal with a long, shaggy, dark brown coat.

muskrat (*pl.* **muskrat, muskrats**) *noun* a large aquatic rodent or its soft, dense, silvery-brown to black fur. *Also called* **musquash.**

musky *adj.* (**muskier, muskiest**) of, or like the smell of, musk. ▸ **muskiness** *noun*

Muslim *or* **Moslem** (mŏŏz′lǎm, mŏŏs′-) *noun* a follower of the religion of Islam. —*adj.* relating to Muslims or to Islam.

muslin *noun* a fine cotton cloth with a gauzelike appearance.

musquash *noun* a muskrat.

muss *verb* (*often* **muss up**) to make untidy; to ruffle.

mussel *noun* a bivalve mollusk.

must[1] *verb, aux.* expressing: **1** need. **2** duty or obligation. **3** certainty. **4** determination. **5** probability. —*noun* something essential.

must[2] *noun* the juice of grapes or other fruit before it is fermented to become wine.

mustache *or* **moustache** *noun* a line of unshaven hair on the upper lip.

mustachio (mə-stăsh′ē-ō,) *noun* (*pl.* **mustachios**) an elaborately curled and groomed mustache. ▸ **mustachioed** *adj.*

mustang *noun* a small, sturdy, feral horse.

mustard *noun* **1** a plant cultivated for its seeds. **2** a hot-tasting paste made from the powdered seeds of this plant. **3** a light yellow or brown color.

mustard gas a highly poisonous gas, used as a chemical warfare agent, esp. in World War I.

muster *verb trans., intrans.* (**mustered, mustering**) **1** to gather (esp. troops) together for duty or inspection. **2** (*also* **muster up**) to summon or gather (e.g., courage or energy). —*noun* an assembly or gathering, esp. of troops for duty or inspection. —**pass muster** to be accepted as satisfactory.

musty *adj.* (**mustier, mustiest**) **1** moldy or damp. **2** smelling or tasting stale. ▸ **mustiness** *noun*

mutable *adj.* subject to change; variable. ▸ **mutability** *noun*

mutate (mōō′tāt,, myōō-tāt′) *verb trans., intrans.* (**mutated, mutating**) **1** *Biol.* to cause to undergo or to undergo mutation. **2** to change. ▸ **mutant** *noun, adj.*

mutation *noun* **1** a sudden change in genetic structure that can result in a change in appearance, or behavior of the organism. **2** *formal* a change of any kind.

mutatis mutandis (mōō-tät′ĭs-mōō-tän′dĭs) with all necessary adjustments having been made.

mute *adj.* **1** *of a person* physically or psychologically unable to speak; dumb. **2** silent. —*noun* **1** *offensive* a person who is unable to speak. **2** a device that softens or deadens sound, esp. of a musical instrument. —*verb trans.* (**muted, muting**) to soften or deaden the sound of.

muted *adj.* of sound, color, etc. not loud or harsh; soft; mild.

mutilate (myōōt′l-āt,) *verb trans.* (**mutilated, mutilating**) to cause severe injury to, esp. by removing a limb. ▸ **mutilation** *noun*

mutineer *noun* a person who mutinies.

mutinous *adj.* **1** of or relating to mutiny. **2** insubordinate or disobedient.

mutiny (myōōt′n-ē) *noun* (*pl.* **mutinies**) rebellion, or an act of rebellion, against established authority, esp. in the armed services. —*verb intrans.* (**mutinied, mutinying, mutinies**) to engage in mutiny.

mutt *noun colloq.* **1** a dog, esp. a mongrel. **2** a foolish person.

mutter *verb trans., intrans.* (**muttered, muttering**) **1** to utter (words) in a quiet, barely audible voice. **2** to complain in a bad-tempered, surly way. —*noun* **1** a soft, barely audible tone of voice. **2** a complaint.

mutton *noun* the flesh of an adult sheep, used as food.

muttonchops *pl. noun* men's long side whiskers.

mutual (myōō′chə-wəl) *adj.* **1** felt by each of two or more people about the other or others; reciprocal. **2** of, to, or having the same relationship toward each other. **3** *colloq.* shared by each of two or more; common: *a mutual friend.* ▸ **mutuality** *noun* ▸ **mutually** *adv.*

mutual fund an investment company that pools the funds of its shareholders and invests in a diversified portfolio of stocks and shares.

Muzak (myōō′zǎk,) *trademark* a system for playing recorded music in public places, e.g., restaurants, malls, elevators, etc., or the music itself

muzzle *noun* **1** the jaws and nose of an animal, e.g., a dog. **2** a device fitted around an animal's jaws to prevent it from biting. **3** the open end of a gun barrel. —*verb trans.* (**muzzled, muzzling**) **1** to put a muzzle on (e.g., a dog). **2** to prevent from speaking; to silence or gag.

muzzy *adj.* (**muzzier, muzziest**) **1** not thinking clearly; confused. **2** blurred; hazy. ▸ **muzzily** *adv.* ▸ **muzziness** *noun*

my *adj.* **1** of or belonging to me. **2** used with nouns in various exclamations: *My goodness!* —*interj.* used to express surprise: *My, how healthy you look!*

myalgia (mī-ăl′ja) *noun* pain in the muscles.

myalgic encephalomyelitis (ABBREV. ME) a disorder characterized by extreme fatigue, muscular pain, lack of concentration, memory loss, and depression.

myasthenia *noun* a condition characterized by abnormally weak muscles.

mycology *noun* the scientific study of fungi.

myelitis *noun* **1** inflammation of the spinal cord. **2** inflammation of the bone marrow. *Also called* **osteomyelitis**.

Mylar (mī′lăr,) *trademark* a thin, strong, polyester film.

myna, mynah *or* **mina** *noun* a bird of the starling family noted for its ability to imitate human speech.

myocardium *noun* (*pl.* **myocardia**) the muscular tissue of the heart. ▸ **myocardial** *adj.*

myopia *noun* **1** inability to see distant objects; shortsightedness. **2** inability to see or appreciate the point of view of others. ▸ **myopic** *adj.*

myriad *noun, adj.* denoting an exceedingly great number: *a myriad of stars / her myriad admirers.*

myrrh (mər′) *noun* **1** a deciduous shrub or small tree, or the transparent aromatic resin obtained from it. **2** a plant that smells strongly of aniseed, and is widely cultivated as a seasoning. *Also called* **sweet cicely**.

myrtle *noun* an evergreen shrub or its edible aromatic bluish-black berry.

myself *pron.* **1** the reflexive form of *me*: *I did myself a favor. / I said to myself.* **2** used for emphasis: *I, myself, prefer tea.* **3** my normal self: *I am not myself this morning.* **4** without help; alone: *I did it myself. / I did it by myself.*

mysterious *adj.* **1** difficult or impossible to understand or explain; deeply curious. **2** creating or suggesting mystery. ▸ **mysteriously** *adv.*

mystery *noun* (*pl.* **mysteries**) **1** something that cannot be, or has not been, explained. **2** the quality of being difficult or impossible to explain or understand. **3** a person about whom very little is known. **4** a story about a crime that is difficult to solve.

mystery play a medieval play based on the life of Jesus, or of a saint.

mystic *noun* a person who practices mysticism. —*adj.* **1** relating to or practicing mysticism. **2** occult. **3** mysterious. ▸ **mystical** *adj.*

mysticism *noun* spiritual enlightenment achieved through prayer or deep meditation, etc., or the practice of achieving this.

mystify *verb trans.* (**mystified, mystifying, mystifies**) **1** to puzzle or bewilder. **2** to make mysterious. ▸ **mystification** *noun*

mystique (mī-stēk′) *noun* a charismatically mysterious quality possessed by a person or thing.

myth *noun* **1** an ancient story featuring gods and heroes, or such stories collectively. **2** a commonly held notion that is actually untrue. **3** a nonexistent person or thing. ▸ **mythical** *adj.* ▸ **mythically** *adv.*

mythology *noun* (*pl.* **mythologies**) **1** myths, esp. of a particular culture, collectively. **2** a collection of myths. ▸ **mythological** *adj.*

Nn

N¹ *or* **n** *noun* (*pl.* **Ns, N's, n's**) the 14th letter of the English alphabet.

N² *abbrev.* **1** North; Northern.

N³ *symbol* **1** *Chem.* nitrogen.

n *abbrev.* noun.

Na *symbol Chem.* sodium.

n/a *abbrev.* nonapplicable.

nab *verb trans.* (**nabbed, nabbing**) **1** to arrest (a wrongdoer). **2** to grab, take, or snatch.

nabob *noun colloq.* a wealthy, influential person.

nacho *noun* (*pl.* **nachos**) a tortilla chip topped with chilis and melted cheese.

nacre *noun* mother-of-pearl. ▸ **nacreous** *adj.*

NAFTA (năf′tə) *or* **Nafta** *abbrev.* North American Free Trade Agreement.

nag¹ *noun derog.* a broken-down old horse.

nag² *verb trans., intrans.* (**nagged, nagging**) **1** to scold (someone) constantly; to keep finding fault. **2** (**nag into**) to keep urging (someone) to do (something). **3** (**nag at**) to cause (someone) anxiety: *The problem keeps nagging at me.* **4** *of pain* to persist. —*noun* a person who nags.

nagging *adj.* constantly worrying or causing concern: *a nagging suspicion.*

nail *noun* **1** the horny plate covering the upper surface of the tip of a finger or toe. **2** a metal spike hammered into an object or surface, e.g., to join two objects together. —*verb trans.* (**nailed, nailing**) **1** (*also* **nail down** or **together**) to fasten (something) with or as if with nails or a nail. **2** *slang* to catch, trap, or corner. **3** *slang* to detect, identify, or expose (a lie, deception, etc.).

—**nail down** *slang* **1** to extract a definite decision from (someone). **2** to define or identify (something) clearly.

naive *or* **naïve** (nă-ēv´) *adj.* **1** simple, innocent, or unsophisticated. **2** too trusting. ▸ **naively** *adv.* ▸ **naiveté** *or* **naïveté** *noun*

naked *adj.* **1** wearing no clothes. **2** without fur, feathers, or foliage. **3** blatant or flagrant: *naked greed.* ▸ **nakedly** *adv.* ▸ **nakedness** *noun*

namby-pamby *adj.* **1** feebly sentimental; soppy. **2** overly demure; prim.

> Originally a nickname of the 18th-century sentimental English poet, *Ambrose Philips*

name *noun* **1** a word or words by which a person, place, or thing is identified and referred to. **2** reputation: *get a bad name.* **3** a widely known person: *the big name in fashion design.* —*verb trans.* (**named, naming**) **1** to give a name to. **2** to mention or identify by name. **3** to specify; to decide on. **4** (**name as**) to choose or appoint: *has been named as the lead attorney in the case.* —**in the name of 1** by the authority of (the one specified). **2** for the sake of; using as justification: *tortured in the name of religion.* **in name only** officially, but not in practice.

name-dropping *noun* the practice of casually referring to well-known people as if they were friends. ▸ **name-drop** *verb intrans.* ▸ **name-dropper** *noun*

nameless *adj.* **1** having no name. **2** *of an act, piece of writing, etc.* used by or involving a person whose name is not known or not given. **3** too awful to specify: *nameless horror.*

namely *adv.* used to introduce an expansion on what has just been mentioned: *Her intention, namely, to discredit her associates, has become obvious.*

namesake *noun* a person with the same name as oneself.

nanny *noun* (*pl.* **nannies**) someone trained to look after young children. —*verb trans.* (**nannied, nannying, nannies**) to over-protect or oversupervise.

nanny goat a female goat. *See also* **billy goat.**

nano- *combining form* forming words denoting: **1** in the metric system, 10; one thousand-millionth: *nanometer.* **2** something microscopic in size: *nano-plankton.*

nap[1] *noun* a short sleep. —*verb intrans.* (**napped, napping**) to have a short sleep.

nap[2] *noun* the raised surface on cloth such as velvet, corduroy, etc.

napalm *noun* a highly flammable jelly, used in incendiary bombs and flamethrowers. —*verb trans.* (**napalmed, napalming**) to attack or destroy with a bomb made of this material.

nape *noun* the back of the neck.

napery *noun* (*pl.* **naperies**) household linen, esp. for the table.

naphtha (năf´thə, năp´-) *noun* a highly flammable liquid obtained from coal and petroleum, used as a solvent.

naphthalene *noun* a white crystalline substance obtained from coal tar, used e.g. in dyes and mothballs.

napkin *noun* **1** a piece of cloth or paper for wiping one's mouth and fingers at mealtimes. **2** a sanitary napkin.

narcissism *noun* too good an opinion of or admiration for oneself. ▸ **narcissistic** *adj.*

narcissus *noun* (*pl.* **narcissuses, narcissi**) a plant, similar to the daffodil, that grows from a bulb and has white or yellow flowers.

narcolepsy *noun* a disorder characterized by a sudden and uncontrollable tendency to fall asleep for brief periods.

narcosis *noun* (*pl.* **narcoses**) a state of insensibility produced by a narcotic or anesthetic.

narcotic *noun* a potentially addictive drug that causes numbness and drowsiness, and also relieves pain.

naris (năr´ĭs) *noun* (*pl.* **nares**) *Anat.* a nostril.

narrate *verb trans.* (**narrated, narrating**) **1** to tell (a story); to relate. **2** to give a running commentary on (a movie, etc.). ▸ **narrator** *noun*

narration *noun* an oral or written account of the circumstances surrounding an event or the details of an event or series of events. ▣ DESCRIPTION, RECOUNTING.

narrative *noun* **1** an account of events. **2** those parts of a book, etc. that recount events. —*adj.* **1** telling a story; recounting events: *narrative poetry.* **2** relating to the telling of stories: *narrative skills.*

narrow *adj.* **1** of little breadth, esp. in comparison with length. **2** *of interests or* *experience* restricted; limited. **3** *of attitudes or ideas* intolerant or bigoted. **4** close; only just achieved: *a narrow victory*. —*noun* **(narrows)** a narrow part, e.g., of a channel or river. —*verb intrans., trans.* **(narrowed, narrowing) 1** to make or become narrow. **2** (also **narrow down**) *of a range of possibilities, etc.* to reduce or be reduced or limited. ▸ **narrowly** *adv.* ▸ **narrowness** *noun*

narrow-minded *adj.* intolerant; prejudiced. ▸ **narrow-mindedness** *noun*

NASA (năs'ə) *abbrev.* National Aeronautics and Space Administration.

nasal *adj.* **1** relating to the nose. **2** *of a sound* pronounced through, or partly through, the nose. **3** *of a voice, etc.* exceptionally full of nasal sounds.

nascent *adj.* in the process of coming into being; in the early stages of development.

nasturtium *noun* (*pl.* **nasturtiums**) a climbing garden plant with flat round leaves and red, orange, or yellow trumpet-like flowers.

nasty *adj.* (**nastier, nastiest**) **1** unpleasant; disgusting. **2** malicious; ill-natured. **3** worrying; serious: *a nasty wound*. **4** *of weather* wet or stormy. ▸ **nastily** *adv.* ▸ **nastiness** *noun*

nation *noun* **1 a** a country. **b** the people living in, belonging to, and together forming, a single country. **c** the government of a sovereign country. **2 a** a Native American people, or federation of peoples. **b** the territory occupied by such a people or federation.

national *adj.* **1** belonging to a particular nation. **2** concerning or covering a whole nation. **3** relating to the community. —*noun* a citizen of a particular nation: *foreign nationals*. ▸ **nationally** *adv.*

national anthem a song adopted as a nation's official song.

National Guard (ABBREV. **NG, N.G.**) the military reserves of each of the US states, subject to federal or state call-up in times of emergency.

nationalism *noun* **1** extreme pride in the history, culture, successes, etc., of one's nation. **2** a movement aiming at national unity or independence. ▸ **nationalist** *noun* ▸ **nationalistic** *adj.* ▸ **nationalistically** *adv.*

nationality *noun* (*pl.* **nationalities**) **1** the status of belonging to a particular nation. **2** the racial or national group to which one belongs.

nationalize *verb trans.* (**nationalized, nationalizing**) to bring (e.g., an industry) under state ownership. ▸ **nationalization** *noun*

nationwide *adj., adv.* extending throughout an entire nation.

native *adj.* **1** being or belonging to the place of one's upbringing. **2** born a citizen of a particular place: *a native Italian*. **3** inborn or innate: *native wit*. **4** having a particular language as one's first tongue. **5** originating in a particular place: *native to China*. **6** *of old use* belonging to the original inhabitants of a country: *native Balinese music*. —*noun* **1** a person born in a certain place. **2** a plant or animal originating in a particular place. **3** *offensive* one of the original inhabitants of a place as distinct from later, esp. European, settlers.

Native American an indigenous inhabitant of North America.

nativity *noun* (*pl.* **nativities**) **1** birth, advent, or origin. **2** (**Nativity**) **a** the birth of Christ. **b** the period of celebration surrounding Dec. 25th.

natter *verb intrans.* (**nattered, nattering**) *colloq.* to chat busily. —*noun* an intensive chat.

natty *adj.* (**nattier, nattiest**) *colloq.* **1** *of clothes* flashily smart. **2** clever; ingenious. ▸ **nattily** *adv.*

natural (năch'rəl, năch'ə-rəl) *adj.* **1** normal; unsurprising. **2** not learned; instinctive. **3** born in one; innate: *a natural talent*. **4** being such because of inborn qualities: *a natural communicator*. **5** *of manner, etc* simple, easy, and direct; not artificial. **6** *of looks* not or apparently not improved artificially. **7** relating to nature, or to parts of the physical world not made or altered by humans: *areas of natural beauty*. **8** following the normal course of nature: *died a natural death*. **9** uncultivated. **10** related to one by blood: *one's natural parents*. **11** *Mus.* not sharp or flat. —*noun* **1** *colloq.* a person with an inborn feel for something: *She's a natural when it comes to acting*. **2** *Mus.* a sign (♮) indicating that a note that is not to be played sharp or flat. ▸ **naturalness** *noun*

natural history the scientific study of plants, animals, and minerals.

naturalism *noun* the view that rejects supernatural explanations of phenomena, maintaining that all must be due to natural causes. ▸ **naturalist** *noun*

naturalistic *adj.* characterized by the realistic treatment of subjects in art and literature. ▸ **naturalistically** *adv.*

naturalize *verb trans.* (**naturalized, naturalizing**) **1** to confer citizenship on (a foreigner). **2** to admit (a word) into a language, or (a custom) among established traditions. **3** to cause (an introduced species of plant or animal) to adapt to the local environment. ▸ **naturalization** *noun*

naturally *adv.* **1** of course; not surprisingly. **2** in accordance with the normal course of things. **3** by nature; as a natural characteristic:

Kindness comes naturally to her. **4** by means of a natural process, as opposed to being produced by an artificial or human-made process: *elements that occur naturally.* **5** in a relaxed or normal manner.

nature *noun* **1** (*often* **Nature**) the physical world not made by humans; the forces that have formed and control it. **2** that which something is or consists of. **3** the fundamental tendencies, attitudes, and outlook, e.g., of a group, taken as a whole: *human nature.* **4** a kind or type: *situations of that nature.*

naturism *noun* nudism. ▸ **naturist** *noun*

naught *or* **nought** (nôt, nät) *noun* **1** nothing. **2** zero.

naughty *adj.* (**naughtier, naughtiest**) **1** mischievous; disobedient. **2** mildly shocking or indecent. ▸ **naughtily** *adv.* ▸ **naughtiness** *noun*

nausea (nô′zē-ə, nô′zhə) *noun* **1** an inclination to vomit. **2** disgust; revulsion.

nauseate (nô′zē-āt,, -zhē-) *verb trans.* (**nauseated, nauseating**) **1** to cause to feel nausea. **2** to disgust. ▸ **nauseated** *adj.* ▸ **nauseating** *adj.* ▸ **nauseatingly** *adv.*

nauseous *adj.* involving or causing nausea.

nautical *adj.* relating to ships or sailors. ▸ **nautically** *adv.*

nautilus *noun* (*pl.* **nautiluses, nautili**) a mollusk with a spiral chambered shell, which is lined with mother-of-pearl.

naval *adj.* relating to a navy or to ships.

nave *noun* the main central part of a church, where the congregation sits.

navel *noun* a place on the abdomen where the umbilical cord was attached to the body of the fetus.

navigable *adj.* **1** of a river, channel, etc. able to be sailed along or through. **2** of a vessel or craft that can be steered; steerable. ▸ **navigability** *noun*

navigate (năv′ĭ-gāt,) *verb intrans., trans.* (**navigated, navigating**) **1** to direct the course of a ship, aircraft, or other vehicle. **2** to find one's way and hold one's course. **3** to steer (a ship or aircraft). ▸ **navigation** *noun* ▸ **navigational** *adj.* ▸ **navigator** *noun*

navy *noun* (*pl.* **navies**) **1 a** the warships of a state, usu. considered together with the officers and other personnel operating them. **b** the organization to which they belong, one of the armed services. **2** a body or fleet of ships with their crews. **3** a dark blue color, typically used for naval uniforms.

nay *interj.* **1** no. **2** to put it more strongly: *misfortune, nay, a tragedy.* —*noun* a negative response or vote: *The nays were 50 and the yeas were 40.*

NB *abbrev.* (*also* **n.b.**) *nota bene* (Latin), note well.

Nb *symbol Chem.* niobium.

NBA *abbrev.* National Basketball Association.

NCAA *or* **N.C.A.A.** *abbrev.* National Collegiate Athletic Association.

NCO *or* **N.C.O.** *abbrev.* noncommissioned officer.

Nd *symbol Chem.* neodymium.

NE *abbrev.* northeast; northeastern.

Ne *symbol Chem.* neon.

Neanderthal (nē-ăn′dər-thôl,, -tôl,) *noun* a species of human of the early Stone Age in Europe.

near *prep.* **1** at a short distance from. **2** close to (in amount, etc.): *was near tears.* —*adv.* **1** (**near to**) close: *came near to hitting the other car.* **2** *colloq.* almost; nearly: *nowhere near enough.* —*adj.* **1** being a short distance away; close: *The exit is near.* **2** closer of two: *the near exit.* **3** similar; comparable. **4** closely related to one: *a near relative.* **5** almost amounting to or almost turning into: *a near tragedy.* —*verb trans., intrans.* (**neared, nearing**) to approach. ▸ **nearness** *noun*

nearby *adj., adv.* a short distance away; close at hand.

nearly *adv.* almost.

nearsighted *adj.*, only able to see close objects clearly.

neat *adj.* **1** tidy; clean; orderly. **2** pleasingly small or regular. **3** elegantly or cleverly simple: *a neat explanation.* **4** skillful or efficient: *Neat work!* **5** *slang* excellent: *had a neat time.* **6** consisting of itself only: *neat vodka.* ▸ **neaten** *verb trans.* ▸ **neatly** *adv.* ▸ **neatness** *noun*

nebbish *noun* a weak-willed, timid person.

nebulous *adj.* lacking distinct shape or nature.

necessarily *adv.* as a necessary or inevitable result.

necessary *adj.* **1** needed; essential. **2** inevitable: *a necessary evil.* **3** logically required or unavoidable. —*noun* (*pl.* **necessaries**) something that is necessary.

necessitate *verb trans.* (**necessitated, necessitating**) to make necessary or unavoidable.

necessity *noun* (*pl.* **necessities**) **1** something necessary or essential. **2** circumstances that make something necessary, obligatory, or unavoidable: *from necessity rather than choice.* **3** a pressing need: *no necessity to rush.* **4** poverty; want; need.

neck *noun* **1** the part of the body between the head and the shoulders. **2** the part of a garment at or covering the neck. **3** a narrow connecting part, or strip of land. **4** *Horse Racing* a head-and-neck's length; a small margin: *won by a neck.* —*verb intrans.* (**necked, necking**) *slang* to hug and kiss amorously. —**neck and neck** of competitors, e.g., in a race exactly level. **up to**

one's neck in *colloq.* deeply involved in (something); busy.

neckerchief *noun* (*pl.* **neckerchiefs, neckerchieves**) a cloth for wearing around the neck.

necklace (nĕk′ləs) *noun* a string of beads or jewels, etc., or a chain, worn around the neck as jewelry.

neckline *noun* the shape of a garment at the neck.

necktie *noun* a narrow band of fabric worn around the neck under the collar of a shirt, tied in a bow or knot.

necromancy *noun* 1 divination or prophecy through alleged communication with the dead 2 black magic; sorcery.

necropolis (nə-krăp′ə-lĭs) *noun* a cemetery, esp. an elaborate large one in an ancient city.

necrosis *noun* (*pl.* **necroses**) the death of cells or tissue as a result of disease or injury. ▸ **necrotic** *adj.*

nectar *noun* 1 the sticky liquid produced in flowers, which bees use to make honey. 2 *Greek Mythol.* the special drink of the gods. 3 a delicious drink. 4 something that is delightfully welcome to the senses.

nectarine *noun* a peach-like fruit with a shiny, downless skin.

née (nā) *adj.* born, used in giving a woman's maiden name.

need *verb trans., intrans.* (**needed, needing**) 1 to have want of; to require. 2 to be required or obliged to do something. —*noun* 1 something one requires. 2 (**need of** *or* **for**) a condition of lacking or requiring (something); an urge or desire. 3 (**need for**) necessity or justification.

needful *adj.* necessary.

needle *noun* 1 a a slender pointed steel sewing instrument with a hole for thread. b a longer, thicker implement of metal, wood, plastic, etc., with no hole, used for knitting, crocheting, etc. 2 a hypodermic syringe, or its pointed end. 3 a stylus for a record player. 4 the moving pointer on a compass or other instrument. 5 a needle-shaped leaf of a tree such as the pine or fir. —*verb trans.* (**needled, needling**) *colloq.* to provoke or irritate, esp. deliberately.

needless *adj.* unnecessary. ▸ **needlessly** *adv.*

needlework *noun* sewing and embroidery.

needs *adv. old use* of necessity; inevitably.

needy *adj.* (**needier, neediest**) in severe need; poverty-stricken.

nefarious *adj.* wicked; evil. ▸ **nefariousness** *noun*

negate (nĭ-gāt′) *verb trans.* (**negated, negating**) 1 to cancel or destroy the effect of. 2 to deny the existence of. ▸ **negation** *noun*

negative *adj.* 1 expressing denial, refusal, or prohibition. 2 *of people, attitudes, etc.*

unenthusiastic, defeatist, or pessimistic. 3 *Math.* a denoting a number or quantity that is less than zero; minus. b being or measured in the opposite direction to whatever is regarded as positive. 4 contrary to or canceling the effect of whatever is regarded as positive. 5 denoting an electric charge produced by an excess of electrons. 6 of or relating to a photographic negative, an image that is the reverse of a positive. 7 denoting a test that indicates the absence of the disease or condition being investigated. —*noun* 1 a word, statement, or grammatical form expressing denial: *replied in the negative.* 2 a trait, characteristic, or feature regarded as detrimental: *The candidate's past is a big negative.* 3 a piece of photographic film or a photographic plate bearing an image in which the light and dark areas are reversed. —*verb trans.* (**negatived, negativing**) to reject; to veto. ▸ **negatively** *adv.*

neglect *verb trans.* (**neglected, neglecting**) 1 to give improper care and attention to. 2 to leave (duties, etc.) undone. 3 to fail or omit (to do something). —*noun* 1 lack of proper care. 2 a state of disuse or decay: *a farm that fell into neglect.*

neglectful *adj.* inattentive or negligent.

negligee *or* **négligée** (nĕg′lĭ-zhā„, nĕg„lĭ-zhā′) *noun* a woman's thin light dressing gown.

negligence *noun* 1 lack of proper attention or care; carelessness. 2 *Law* failure to use reasonable care under a given set of circumstances. ▸ **negligent** *adj.*

negligible *adj.* small or unimportant enough to ignore.

negotiable *adj.* 1 open to discussion: *The salary is still negotiable.* 2 *of a cash order or other asset* able to be transferred to another person in exchange for its value in money. 3 *of a hazard or obstacle* able to be negotiated.

negotiate (nĭ-gō′shē-āt,) *verb trans., intrans.* (**negotiated, negotiating**) 1 (**negotiate with**) to confer with (someone) to reach agreement on terms affecting both parties. 2 to bring about (an agreement) or arrange (a treaty, price, etc.) by conferring. 3 to pass safely (a hazard, etc.). ▸ **negotiation** *noun* ▸ **negotiator** *noun*

Negro (nē′grō) *noun* (*pl.* **Negroes**) *often offensive* a person belonging to one of the black-skinned peoples. —*adj.* relating or belonging to these peoples.

neigh *noun* the characteristic cry of a horse. —*verb intrans.* (**neighed, neighing**) to make this cry.

neighbor *noun* 1 a person living near or next door to one. 2 an adjacent territory, person, etc. 3 any of one's fellow humans.

neighborhood *noun* **1** a district or locality. **2** the area near something or someone. —**in the neighborhood of** roughly: *It cost in the neighborhood of $500.*

neighborly *adj.* friendly, esp. to the people around one. ▸ **neighborliness** *noun*

neither (nē′thər, nī′-) *adj., pron.* not the one nor the other (thing or person): *Neither proposal is acceptable.* —*conj.* (*introducing the first of two or more alternatives;* usu. paired with *nor*) not: *I neither know nor care.* —*adv.* also not; nor: *If you won't, neither will I* —**neither here nor there** irrelevant; unimportant.

> *Usage* Neither is normally followed by a singular verb, e.g., *Neither of them is coming.* However, in more informal usage, the plural is common, e.g., *Neither of them are coming.*

nematode *noun* a long, thin, unsegmented, cylindrical worm, occurring as a parasite in plants and animals as well as in soil or sediment.

nemesis *noun* **1 a** a retribution or just punishment. **b** something that brings retribution or just punishment. **2** an unbeatable opponent.

neo- *combining form* forming words denoting new, a new form, or modern: *neoclassical.*

neoclassical *adj., of an artistic or architectural style* imitating or adapting the styles of the ancient classical world. ▸ **neoclassicism** *noun*

neodymium (nē͵ō-dĭm′ē-əm) *noun* (SYMBOL **Nd**) a soft silvery metallic element, used in lasers and astronomical lenses.

Neolithic *or* **neolithic** (nē͵ə-lĭth′ĭk) *adj.* of or relating to the last period of the Stone Age.

neologism (nē-ăl′ə-jĭz′əm) *noun* a new word or expression.

neon *noun* (SYMBOL **Ne**) a colorless, odorless gas that glows red when electricity is passed through it, used, e.g., in illuminated signs and advertisments.

neophyte *noun* **1** a beginner. **2** a new convert to a religious faith.

neoplasm *noun* an abnormal mass or tissue; a malignant or benign tumor.

nephew *noun* the son of one's brother or sister, or of one's brother- or sister-in-law.

nephritis *noun* inflammation of the kidneys.

nepotism (nĕp′ə-tĭz′əm) *noun* the practice of favoring one's relatives, esp. in making official appointments.

neptunium *noun* (SYMBOL **Np**) a silvery-white radioactive metallic element that is usu. obtained during the production of plutonium.

nerd *noun slang* an annoying person, esp. one who apparently studies excessively.

nerve *noun* **1** a bundle of fibers carrying instructions for movement and information on sensation between the brain or spinal cord and other parts of the body. **2** *colloq.* the state or quality of being boldly impolite or cheeky. **3** (**nerves**) *colloq.* tension or stress; nervousness. **4** *colloq.* capacity to cope with stress or excitement. —*verb trans.* (**nerved, nerving**) (**nerve oneself for**) to prepare oneself for (a challenge or an ordeal).

nerve cell a neuron.

nerve center 1 a group of neurons associated with a specific body function. **2** the center of control, e.g., within an organization.

nerveless *adj.* **1** lacking feeling or strength; inert. **2** fearless.

nerve-racking *or* **nerve-wracking** *adj.* causing one to feel highly tense and anxious.

nervous *adj.* **1** easily agitated; timid. **2** apprehensive; uneasy. **3** relating to the nerves: *nervous illnesses.* **4** consisting of nerves. ▸ **nervously** *adv.* ▸ **nervousness** *noun*

nervous breakdown *colloq.* a psychological or psychiatric illness usu. characterized by intense anxiety, low self-esteem, and loss of concentration.

nervous system the network of communication consisting of the brain, nerves, and spinal cord, controlling all one's mental and physical functions.

nervy *adj.* (**nervier, nerviest**) **1** brazenly and arrogantly impudent. **2** brave and bold.

-ness *suffix* forming nouns denoting a state, condition, or degree: *darkness.*

nest *noun* **1** a structure built by birds, reptiles, fish, etc., in which to lay eggs or give birth to and rear young. **2** a large group of animals of the same species occupying the same structure or site: *a nest of hornets.* **3** a cozy habitation or retreat. **4** a den or haunt (e.g., of thieves) or secret center (e.g., of vice or crime). **5** a set of things that fit together or one inside the other: *a nest of mixing bowls.* —*verb intrans., trans.* (**nested, nesting**) **1** to build and occupy a nest, esp. in order to lay and subsequently incubate eggs. **2** to fit together compactly: *bowls that nest neatly.* **3** to go in search of birds' nests.

nest egg *colloq.* a sum of money saved up for the future; one's savings.

nestle *verb intrans.* (**nestled, nestling**) (**nestle down** *or* **together**) to lie or settle snugly.

net[1] *noun* **1 a** an openwork material made of thread, cord, etc., knotted, twisted, or woven so as to form regularly shaped meshes. **b** a piece of this in any of various shapes or qualities appropriate to such uses as catching fish or insects. **2 a** a strip of openwork material dividing a tennis or badminton court. **b** the net-backed goal, e.g., in hockey or soccer. **3** a snare or trap. **4** a radio, television, or computer network. **5 (the Net)** *colloq.* the Internet. —*verb trans., intrans.* **(netted, netting) 1** to catch in or as if in a net. **2** *Sport* to hit, kick, etc., (the ball) into the net or goal.

net² *adj.* **1** *of profit* remaining after all expenses, etc., have been paid. **2** *of weight* not including packaging or container. —*verb trans.* **(netted, netting)** to produce or earn as clear profit.

nether *adj.* lower or under.

netiquette *noun* the standards of acceptable behavior followed on-line by users of the Internet, the World Wide Web, etc.

netizen *noun* a regular user of the Internet.

netting *noun* material with meshes, made by knotting or twisting, e.g., thread, cord, wire. *Also called* **network**.

nettle *noun* a plant covered with hairs that sting if touched. —*verb trans.* **(nettled, nettling)** to offend or irritate.

network *noun* **1** a system resembling a mass of crisscrossing lines: *a network of streets*. **2** a system of interconnected telephone lines, electrical supply lines, etc., that allow information to be passed from one location to another. **3** a group of radio or television stations that broadcast the same programs at the same time. **4** *Comput.* a system of two or more computer terminals that are linked to each other, enabling users to share facilities and to communicate with other users. **5** netting. —*verb trans., intrans.* **(networked, networking) 1** to broadcast on a network. **2** *of computer users* to communicate with other network users. **3** *of people generally* to interact with others, esp. as a way of providing and receiving useful job information and other assistance.

neural (nŏŏr′əl, nyŏŏr′-) *adj.* relating to a nerve, the nerves, or the nervous system.

neuralgia *noun* a severe spasmodic burning or stabbing pain, often along the course of one or more nerves. ▸ **neuralgic** *adj.*

neuro- *or* **neur-** *combining form* forming words denoting the nerves: *neurosurgery.*

neurology *noun* the study of the structure, functions, and diseases and disorders of the nervous system.

neuron *noun* a nerve cell, esp. one that transmits nerve impulses. *See also* **dendrite.**

neurosis *noun* (*pl.* **neuroses**) **1** a disorder causing obsessive fears, depression, and unreasonable behaviour. **2** *colloq.* an anxiety or obsession.

neurotic (nŏŏ-răt′ĭk, nyŏŏ-) *adj.* **1** relating to or affected by a neurosis. **2** *colloq.* overly

anxious, sensitive, or obsessive. —*noun* a person affected by a neurosis.

neuter *adj.* **1** denoting a gender of nouns that are neither masculine nor feminine. **2 a** denoting animals in which the reproductive organs are not fully developed or are absent in the adult, e.g., the worker bee. **b** denoting an animal that has been sterilized. —*noun* **1 a** the neuter gender. **b** a neuter word. **2 a** neuter plant, animal, or insect, e.g., a worker bee or ant. —*verb trans.* **(neutered, neutering)** to sterilize (an animal) by castration or spaying.

neutral *adj.* **1** not taking sides in a war or quarrel. **2** not belonging or relating to either of two, usu. different, sides: *neutral ground.* **3** *of colors* indefinite enough to blend easily with brighter ones. **4** having no strong, noticeable qualities: *a neutral tone of voice.* **5** having no net positive or negative electrical charge. **6** *of a substance* neither acidic nor alkaline. —*noun* **1** a person or nation taking no part in a war or quarrel. **2** the position in which the gears of an engine, etc. are disengaged, so that no power can be transmitted to the moving parts. ▸ **neutrality** *noun*

neutralize *verb trans.* **(neutralized, neutralizing) 1** to cancel out the effect of; to make useless or harmless. **2** to make neutral. ▸ **neutralization** *noun*

neutron *noun* any of the electrically uncharged particles in the nucleus of an atom, similar in mass to a proton.

never *adv.* **1** not ever; at no time. **2** not: *I never realized that.* **3** emphatically not: *This will never do.* **4** surely not: *Those two are never twins!*

nevermore *adv.* never again.

nevertheless *adv.* in spite of that.

nevus (nē′vəs) *noun* (*pl.* **nevi**) a birthmark or mole on the skin.

new *adj.* **1** recently made, bought, built, or opened. **2** recently discovered. **3** never having existed before; just invented, etc. **4** fresh; additional; supplementary. **5** recently arrived or installed. **6 (new to)** unfamiliar with; experienced or experiencing for the first time: *He's new to the work.* **7** changed physically, mentally, or morally for the better: *a new woman since her operation.* **8** renewed: *gave us new hope.* **9** modern: *the new generation.* —*adv.* **1** only just; freshly. **2** once more; another time. ▸ **newness** *noun*

New Age a movement that embraces mysticism, alternative medicines, environmentalism, and an interest in non-Western philosophies. ▸ **New Ager** *noun* ▸ **New Agey** *adj.*

newborn *adj.* newly or recently born. —*noun* a newly born infant.

newcomer *noun* someone recently arrived.

newfangled *adj. colloq.* modern, esp. objectionably so.

Newfoundland *noun* a very large dog with a thick, shaggy coat.

newly *adv.* **1** only just; recently. **2** again; anew.

newlyweds *pl. noun* a recently married couple.

news *noun (sing.)* **1** information about recent events, esp. as reported in the media. **2** (**the news**) a radio or television broadcast report of news. **3** fresh, interesting information. **4** a currently celebrated person, thing, or event.

newsbreak *noun* **1** an urgent item of news. **2** a news flash.

newscast *noun* a radio or television broadcast of news items. ▸ **newscaster** *noun*

news flash a brief announcement of urgent news interrupting a radio or TV broadcast. *Also called* **newsbreak**.

newshound *noun colloq.* a newspaper reporter.

newsletter *noun* a sheet containing news issued to members of a society, etc.

newsmagazine *noun* **1** a weekly magazine reporting on current events. **2** a weekly or nightly television program focusing on newsworthy events.

newspaper *noun* **1** a daily or weekly publication containing news, advertisements, topical articles, correspondence, etc. **2** the printed paper that makes up such a publication.

newspeak *noun* the ambiguous language, full of the latest distortions and euphemisms, used by some politicians, etc.

newsprint *noun* **1** the paper on which newspapers are printed. **2** the ink used to print newspapers.

newsreel *noun* a film of news events, once a regular movie feature.

newsroom *noun* an office in a newspaper office or broadcasting station where news stories are received and edited for publication or broadcasting.

newsstand *noun* a small shop or a stall selling newspapers, magazines, etc.

newsworthy *adj.* interesting or important enough to be reported as news.

newsy *adj.* (**newsier, newsiest**) full of news.

newt *noun* a small amphibious animal with a long body and tail and short legs.

New Testament (ABBREV. **NT**, **N.T.**) the second part of the Christian Bible, concerned with the teachings of Christ and his earliest followers. *See also* **Old Testament**.

newton *noun* the unit of force equal to the force required to give a mass of one kilogram an acceleration of one meter per second per second.

New Year the first day of the year or the days immediately following or preceding it.

New Year's Day Jan. 1, the first day of a New Year.

New Year's Eve Dec. 31, the last day of a passing year.

New York minute *slang* a very brief period of time.

next *adj.* **1** following in time or order: *the next day.* **2** following this one: *next week.* **3** adjoining; neighboring: *in the next apartment.* **4** first, counting from now: *the very next person I meet.* —*noun* someone or something that is next: *The next said no.* —*adv.* **1** immediately after that or this: *What happened next?* **2** on the next occasion: *when I next saw her.* **3** following, in order of degree: *the next longest river after the Amazon.* —**next to 1** beside or close by (someone or something). **2** after (something) in order of degree: *Next to swimming I like dancing.* **3** almost: *wearing next to nothing.*

next door in or to the neighboring structure, e.g., a house. ▸ **next-door** *adj.*

next of kin (*pl.* **next of kin**) one's closest relative.

nexus *noun* (*pl.* **nexus, nexuses**) **1** a connected series or group. **2** a bond or link.

NFC *abbrev.* National Football Conference.

NFL *abbrev.* National Football League.

NHL *abbrev.* National Hockey League.

Ni *symbol Chem.* nickel.

niacin *noun* a white crystalline acid which is a member of the vitamin B complex. *Also called* **nicotinic acid**.

nib *noun* the writing point of a pen.

nibble *verb trans., intrans.* (**nibbled, nibbling**) **1** (*also* **nibble at**) to take very small bites of (something). **2** to bite gently. —*noun* an act of nibbling or something nibbled. ▸ **nibbler** *noun*

nice *adj.* **1** pleasant. **2** good; satisfactory. **3** fine; subtle: *nice distinctions.* **4** exacting; particular. ▸ **niceness** *noun*

nicely *adv.* **1** in a nice or satisfactory way. **2** precisely; carefully: *judged it nicely.* **3** suitably; effectively: *That will do nicely.*

nicety (nɪˈsət-ē) *noun* (*pl.* **niceties**) **1** precision. **2** a subtle point of detail.

niche *noun* **1** a shallow recess in a wall, suitable for holding a lamp, ornament, etc. **2** a position in life in which one feels fulfilled or at ease.

nick *noun* a small cut. —*verb trans.* (**nicked, nicking**) to make a small cut in; to cut slightly. —**in the nick of time** at the last possible moment; just in time.

nickel *noun* **1** (SYMBOL **Ni**) a silvery-white metal used esp. in alloys and for plating. **2** a coin worth five cents in the U.S. and Canada.

nickname *noun* a name, usu. additional to the real one, given to a person or place for fun, in affection, or to show contempt. —*verb* *trans.* (**nicknamed, nicknaming**) to give a nickname to.

nicotine *noun* a poisonous alkaloid compound contained in tobacco.

Named after Jean *Nicot*, 16th-century French ambassador who sent tobacco samples back from Portugal

nicotinic acid niacin.

niece *noun* the daughter of one's brother or sister, or of one's brother- or sister-in-law.

nifty *adj.* (**niftier, niftiest**) **1** clever; adroit; agile. **2** stylish.

niggard *noun* a stingy person. ▸ **niggardly** *adj.* ▸ **niggardliness** *noun*

niggle *verb intrans., trans.* (**niggled, niggling**) **1** to complain about unimportant details. **2** to bother, slightly but continually. —*noun* **1** a slight nagging worry. **2** a small complaint or criticism. ▸ **niggler** *noun*

nigh *adv.* near. —**nigh on** *or* **well nigh** nearly; almost: *It was nigh on midnight.*

night *noun* **1** the time of darkness between sunset and sunrise, during which most people sleep. **2** nightfall. **3** darkness: *taillights vanishing into the night.* **4** evening: *stayed at home last night.* **5** an evening on which a particular activity or event takes place: *my aerobics night.*

night blindness abnormally reduced vision in dim light or darkness.

nightcap *noun* **1** a drink, esp. alcoholic, taken before going to bed. **2** a cap formerly worn in bed at night.

nightclub *noun* a club open at night for drinking, dancing, and other entertainment. ▣ CABARET, NIGHTSPOT, WATERING HOLE.

nightfall *noun* the beginning of night; dusk.

nightgown *or* **nightdress** *noun* a loose garment worn in bed by women and girls.

nightie *noun* (*pl.* **nighties**) *colloq.* a night-gown.

nightingale *noun* a small bird with a melodious song, heard esp. at night.

nightlife *noun* entertainment available in a city, etc., late into the night.

nightlong *adj., adv.* throughout the night.

nightly *adj., adv.* every night.

nightmare *noun* **1** a frightening dream. **2** an intensely distressing experience or situation. ▸ **nightmarish** *adj.*

The *-mare* ending comes from an old English word meaning 'incubus', nightmares being thought to be caused by an evil spirit pressing on the body

night owl a person who likes to stay up late at night.

night school an institution providing educational evening classes.

nightshade *noun* a wild plant, e.g., the belladonna or deadly nightshade.

night shift 1 a period of working during the night. **2** the people who work during this period.

nightshirt *noun* a long shirtlike garment, usu. for men, worn in bed.

nightspot *noun* a club open at night for drinking, dancing, and other entertainment.

nightstick *noun* a police truncheon.

nighttime *noun* the time between sunset and sunrise. —*adj.* happening in or associated with this time.

nihilism *noun* **1** rejection of moral and religious principles. **2** the view that nothing has real existence; extreme skepticism. ▸ **nihilist** *noun* ▸ **nihilistic** *adj.*

-nik *suffix* forming nouns denoting someone concerned or associated with a certain cause, activity, etc.: *peacenik.*

nil *noun* in games, etc., a score of nothing.

nimble *adj.* **1** a quick and light in movement. **b** having or showing skill in performing with ease. **2** *of a person's wits* sharp; alert. ▸ **nimbleness** *noun* ▸ **nimbly** *adv.*

nimbus *noun* (*pl.* **nimbi, nimbuses**) **1** a cloud, usu. dark gray, that produces precipitation, esp. rainfall; a rain cloud. **2** a luminous mist or halo surrounding the head of a divine or saintly person in artistic representation.

NIMBY *abbrev.* not in my back yard.

nincompoop *noun* a fool; an idiot.

nine *noun* **1** the number or figure 9. **2** the age of 9. **3** any person or thing denoted by the number 9. **4** 9 o'clock. **5** a set of 9 people or things. **6** a score of 9 points. **7** *Cards* a playing-card with 9 spots. —*adj.* **1** 9 in number.

ninepins *noun* (*sing.*) bowling in which players use a wooden ball and nine pins arranged in a triangle. *See also* **bowling** (sense 1).

nineteen *noun* **1** the number or figure 19. **2** the age of 19. **3** any person or thing denoted by the number 19. **4** a set of 19 people or things. —*adj.* **1** 19 in number. **2** aged 19.

nineteenth *noun, adj.* **1** the one numbered 19 in a series. **2** one of 19 equal parts.

nineties *pl. noun* **1** the period of time between one's 90th and 100th birthdays. **2** the range of temperatures between 90 and 100 degrees. **3** the period of time between the 90th and 100th years of a century.

ninetieth *noun, adj.* **1** the one numbered 90 in a series. **2** one of 90 equal parts.

ninety *noun* (*pl.* **nineties**) **1** the number or figure 90. **2** the age of 90. **3** any person or thing denoted by the number 90. —*adj.* **1** 90 in number. **2** aged 90.

ninja *noun* (*pl.* **ninja, ninjas**) a person trained in Japanese martial arts and stealth.

ninny *noun* (*pl.* **ninnies**) a foolish person.

ninth *noun, adj.* **1** the one numbered 9 in a series. **2** one of 9 equal parts.

niobium *noun* (SYMBOL **Nb**) a soft grayish-blue metal with a brilliant luster.

nip¹ *verb trans., intrans.* **1** to pinch or squeeze sharply. **2** to give a sharp little bite to. **3** to sting; to cause smarting. **4** to halt the growth or development of: *nipped all opposition in the bud.* —*noun* **1** a pinch or squeeze. **2** a sharp little bite. **3** a sharp, biting coldness; a sharp, stinging quality.

nip² *noun* a small quantity of alcoholic spirits: *a nip of brandy.*

nipper *noun* **1** the claw, e.g., of a crab or lobster. **2** (**nippers**) a gripping tool, eg pincers, tweezers, etc. **3** *colloq.* a child.

nipple *noun* **1** the colored pointed protuberance on a breast, which, in the female, is the outlet of the milk ducts. **2** the teat on a baby's bottle. **3** any structure resembling a nipple in appearance or function.

nippy *adj.* (**nippier, nippiest**) *colloq.* **1** cold; chilly. **2** quick-moving; nimble.

nirvana *noun* (*also* **Nirvana**) **1** *Buddhism, Hinduism* the ultimate state of spiritual tranquility attained through release from everyday concerns and extinction of individual passions. **2** *colloq.* a place or state of perfect bliss.

nit *noun* *colloq.* the egg or young of a louse, found, e.g., in human hair.

niter *noun* potassium nitrate.

nitpicking *noun* petty criticism or faultfinding. ‣ **nit-picker** *noun*

nitrate *noun* **1** a salt or ester of nitric acid. **2** sodium nitrate or potassium nitrate used as a soil fertilizer. —*verb trans., intrans.* (**nitrated, nitrating**) **1** to treat with nitric acid or a nitrate. **2** to convert into a nitrate. ‣ **nitration** *noun*

nitric acid a colorless, caustic, and corrosive acid, used as an oxidizing agent and for making explosives, fertilizers, and dyes.

nitride *noun* a compound of nitrogen with another element, usu. a metal.

nitro- *combining form* forming words denoting: **1** relating to or containing a nitro group. **2** relating to or containing nitrogen.

nitrogen (nīˈtrə-jən) *noun* (SYMBOL **N**) a colorless, odorless, tasteless gas that represents about 78% of the Earth's atmosphere by volume.

nitroglycerin or **nitroglycerine** *noun* a toxic, oily, yellow, explosive liquid, used e.g., in dynamite and as a rocket fuel.

nitrous oxide a colorless, sweet-tasting gas used as an anesthetic; laughing gas.

nitty-gritty *noun* *colloq.* (**the nitty-gritty**) the fundamental issue or essential part of a matter, situation, activity, etc.

nitwit *noun* a stupid person.

nix *slang noun* nothing. —*interj.* no.

NL *abbrev.* National League.

NLRB *abbrev.* National Labor Relations Board.

No *symbol Chem.* nobelium.

No. *or* **no.** *abbrev.* (usu. followed by a numeral) number: *No. 3.*

no¹ *interj.* **1** a negative reply, expressing denial, refusal, or disagreement. **2** an astonished rejoinder: *No! You don't say!* —*adv.* **1** (*with comparative*) not any: *no bigger than his thumb.* **2** not: *whether she's willing or no.* —*noun* (*pl.* **noes**) a negative reply or vote.

no² *adj.* **1** not any. **2** certainly not a; far from a: *She's no fool.* **3** hardly any: *We did it in no time.* **4** not allowed: *no smoking.* —**no way** *colloq.* definitely not; no: *Will you go? No way!*

nobelium *noun* (SYMBOL **No**) a synthetic radioactive metallic element produced artificially from the element curium.

nobility *noun* **1** the quality of being noble in character, conduct, or rank. **2** (**the nobility**) the class of people of noble birth.

noble *adj.* **1** honorable. **2** generous. **3** of high rank or birth. —*noun* a person of noble rank. ‣ **nobleness** *noun* ‣ **nobly** *adv.*

nobleman *noun* a male member of the nobility.

noblesse oblige (nō-blĕs,ə-blēzhˈ) honorable, benevolent behavior regarded as the duty of those who are privileged.

noblewoman *noun* a female member of the nobility.

nobody *pron.* no person; no one. —*noun* (*pl.* **nobodies**) a person of no significance.

nocturnal *adj.* **1** of animals, etc. active at night. **2** happening at night. **3** of, belonging to, or relating to the night.

nocturne *noun* **1** a dreamy musical composition, usu. for the piano. **2** *Art* a night or moonlight scene.

nod *verb intrans., trans.* (**nodded, nodding**) **1** to make a brief bowing gesture with the head, in agreement, greeting, etc.; to bow (the head) briefly. **2** to let the head droop with sleepiness; to become drowsy. **3** to indicate or direct by nodding: *nodded her approval.* **4** of flowers, etc. to sway or bob about.

node *noun* **1** a small lump or mass of tissue, e.g., a lymph node. **2** a swelling where a leaf is attached to a stem. **3** *Phys.* in a system of standing waves, a point, line, or surface where there is minimum disturbance. ‣ **nodal** *adj.*

nodule *noun* a small round lump. ‣ **nodular** *adj.*

Noel (nō-ĕlˈ) *noun* the period of celebration surrounding Dec. 25.

no-frills *adj.* *colloq.* having no extra features: *a no-frills apartment.*

noggin noun **1** a small measure or quantity of alcoholic spirits. **2** a small mug or wooden cup. **3** colloq. a human head.

no-go adj. **1** impossible; too difficult, dangerous, etc. to proceed. **2** forbidden: a no-go area.

noise noun **1** a sound, esp. a harsh or disagreeable one. **2** a series of unpleasant or confused sounds, causing a continuous din. **3** unwanted, often random, interference. **4** vague murmuring, etc.: He's making noises about leaving. —verb trans. (**noised, noising**) **1** to make generally known; to spread (a rumor, etc.) about. **2** (usu. **noise off**) colloq. to grumble: noising off about his boss.

noiseless adj. lacking noise. ▣ QUIET, SILENT, STILL ▣ LOUD, NOISY.

noisome (noi'səm) adj. **1** disgusting; offensive; stinking. **2** harmful; poisonous: noisome fumes.

noisy adj. (**noisier, noisiest**) **1** making noise: noisy revelers. ▣ LOUD ▣ NOISELESS, QUIET, SILENT, STILL. **2** full of noise: noisy streets. ▸ **noisily** adv.

nomad noun **1** a member of a people without permanent home, who travel from place to place. **2** a wanderer. ▸ **nomadic** adj.

no man's land 1 unclaimed land; wasteland. **2** neutral territory between opposing forces or between two countries with a common border.

nom de plume (näm,dĭ-plōōm') (pl. **noms de plume**) a pseudonym used by a writer; a pen name.

nomenclature noun **1** a classified system of names, esp. in scientific terminology. **2** a list or set of names.

nominal adj. **1** in name only: a nominal head of state. ▣ SO-CALLED, TITULAR ▣ ACTUAL. **2** very small in comparison to actual cost or value: nominal rent. **3** of, being, or relating to a noun. ▸ **nominally** adv.

nominate (näm'ĭ-nāt,) verb trans. (**nominated, nominating**) **1** (**nominate for**) to propose (someone) formally as a candidate for (e.g., election, a job). **2** (**nominate to**) to appoint (someone) to (a post or position). ▸ **nomination** noun.

nominative adj. denoting the case used, in inflected languages such as Latin, for the subject of the verb. —noun **1** the case used for the subject of a verb. **2** a word in this case.

nominee noun a person who is nominated.

non- prefix forming words denoting the opposite; not: nonexistent / nonfiction.

nonage (nän'ĭj, nō'nĭj) noun Law the condition of being under age; the period of immaturity.

nonagenarian noun someone between 90 and 99 years old.

nonaligned adj., of a country not allied to any of the major powers in world politics. ▸ **nonalignment** noun

nonce noun the present occasion. —**for the nonce** for the time being; for the present.

nonchalant adj. calmly and indifferently unconcerned. ▸ **nonchalance** noun ▸ **nonchalantly** adv.

noncommissioned officer (ABBREV. NCO, N.C.O.) an enlisted person in the armed forces, such as a corporal or petty officer, who leads other enlisted people.

noncommittal adj. avoiding expressing a definite opinion or decision. ▸ **noncommittally** adv.

non compos mentis (nän,käm,pəs-mĕnt'əs, nōn,-) not of sound mind.

nonconductor noun a substance or an object that does not readily conduct heat, electricity, or sound.

nonconformist noun someone who refuses to conform to generally accepted practice. —adj. of or relating to nonconformists. ▸ **nonconformity** noun

nondescript adj. lacking any strongly noticeable characteristics or distinctive features: a man of nondescript features. ▣ FEATURELESS, ORDINARY, UNREMARKABLE ▣ DISTINCTIVE, MEMORABLE, REMARKABLE.

none (nən') pron. **1** not any. **2** no one.

> *Usage* When referring to a plural noun, *none* may be followed by either a singular or a plural verb, whichever is logically appropriate. If the emphasis is on the individuals in a group (and *none* is equivalent to *no one* or *not one*), the verb should be singular, e.g., *None of us has the answer*, but if the emphasis is on the individuals constituting a group, the verb is typically plural, e.g., *None of us speak French*. When *almost* qualifies *none*, the pronoun is usu. treated as a plural, e.g., *Almost none of the guests have arrived yet.*

nonentity noun (pl. **nonentities**) a person of no significance, character, ability, etc.

nonetheless (nən,thə-lĕs') adv. in spite of that; nevertheless.

nonevent noun an event one has been greatly looking forward to that turns out to be a disappointment.

nonfiction noun literature other than fiction, including biography, reference books, etc.

nonflammable adj. not liable to catch on fire or burn easily.

nonintervention noun Politics a policy of systematic abstention from interference in the affairs of other nations.

noninvasive adj. **1** not invading healthy living tissue. **2** not penetrating the body: a noninvasive surgical procedure.

nonissue *noun* a matter of no import.

nonmetal *noun* a chemical element that does not have the properties of metal, e.g. sulfur or hydrogen.

no-no *noun* (*pl.* **no-noes**) *colloq.* something that must not be done, said, etc.

nonobservance *noun* failure to observe, e.g., a custom, rule.

no-nonsense *adj.* **1** sensible; practical; efficient. **2** tolerating no distractions or irrelevancies.

nonpareil (nän,pə-rĕl′) *adj.* having no equal. —*noun* a person or thing having no peers or equals.

nonperson *noun* a person whose existence is officially denied or ignored, often by removal of his or her name from official records.

nonplus *verb trans.* (**nonplussed, nonplussing**) to puzzle; to disconcert.

nonproliferation *noun* the policy of limiting the production and ownership of nuclear or chemical weapons.

nonreturnable *adj.* **1** *of merchandise* not able to be returned to the place of purchase. **2** *of bottles* not able to be exchanged for a deposit fee.

nonsense (nän′sĕns,, -səns) *noun* **1** words or ideas that make no sense. **2** silly behavior; foolishness. —*interj.* used to express strong disagreement with what someone else says. ► **nonsensical** *adj.*

non sequitur (nän-sĕk′wĭt-ər) **1** a conclusion that does not follow from the premises. **2** a statement that does not follow from what has just been said.

nonsexist *adj.* displaying no sexist discrimination or stereotyping.

nonsmoking *adj.* **1** engaging in no tobacco smoking. **2** reserved for the use of those who do not smoke tobacco. **3** of or pertaining to abstinence from tobacco smoking. ► **nonsmoker** *noun*

nonstandard *adj., of the use of language* not generally accepted as correct.

nonstarter *noun* a person, thing, idea, etc. that has no chance of success.

nonstick *adj.,of a pan, etc.* having a coating to which food does not stick during cooking.

nonstop *adj., adv.* without a stop.

nonunion *adj.* **1** not belonging to a labor union. **2** employing or produced by workers not belonging to a labor union.

nonviolence *noun* **1** a lack of violence. **2** the doctrine or practice of seeking peaceful solutions to disputes, etc.

noodle[1] *noun* (*usu.* **noodles**) a thin strip of pasta, made with egg.

noodle[2] *noun colloq.* **1** a human head. **2** a simpleton.

nook (nŏŏk) *noun* **1** a corner or recess. **2** a

secluded retreat. —**every nook and cranny** absolutely everywhere.

noon *noun* the time of 12 o'clock in the daytime; midday.

no one no person; nobody.

noose *noun* a loop made at the end of a rope, etc., with a sliding knot, used, e.g., for killing by hanging.

nope *interj. colloq.* used to express a negative answer; no.

nor *conj.* **1** used to introduce alternatives after *neither*: *He neither knows nor cares.* **2** *and…not*: *It didn't look appetizing, nor was it.* —*adv.* not either: *She's not going, nor shall I.*

Nordic (nôrd′ĭk) *adj.* **1** of or belonging to Scandinavia or its inhabitants. **2** tall, blond, and blue-eyed. **3** *of skiing* comprising crosscountry and jumping disciplines.

norm *noun* **1** (**the norm**) a typical pattern or situation. **2** an accepted way of behaving, etc.: *social norms.*

normal *adj.* **1** not extraordinary; usual; typical. **2** *colloq.* free from any physical, psychological, emotional, etc. defect. —*noun* **1** what is average or usual. **2** a norm. ► **normalcy** *noun* ► **normality** *noun* ► **normally** *adv.*

normalize *verb trans., intrans.* (**normalized, normalizing**) to make or become normal or regular. ► **normalization** *noun*

Norman (nôr′mən) *noun* **1** a person from Normandy. **2** the form of French spoken in Normandy. —*adj.* relating to the Normans, their language, or their culture.

normative *adj.* establishing a guiding standard or rules: *normative grammar.*

Norse (nôrs) *adj.* **1** of or belonging to ancient or medieval Scandinavia. **2** Norwegian. —*noun* **1** (*pl.*) *Hist.* the Scandinavians, esp. the Norwegians. **2** the language of these peoples. Also called **Old Norse.**

north (ABBREV. **N**) *noun* (also **the north** or **the North**) the direction to one's left when one faces the rising Sun. —*adj.* **1** in the north; on the side that is on or nearest the north. **2** coming from the direction of the north: *a north wind.* —*adv.* toward the north.

northeast (nôr-thēst′, nôr-ēst′) (ABBREV. **NE**) *noun* the direction midway between north and east. —*adj.* **1** in the northeast. **2** from the direction of the northeast: *a northeast wind.*

northeaster (nôr-thēs′tər, nôr-ēs′-) *noun* a wind blowing from the northeast. ► **northeasterly** *adj., adv.*

northeastern *adj.* (ABBREV. **NE**) to the northeast.

northerly *adj.* **1** *of a wind, etc.* coming from the north. **2** looking, lying, etc., toward the north. —*adv.* to or toward the north. —*noun* (*pl.* **northerlies**) a northerly wind.

northern *adj.* (ABBREV. **N**) **1** of or in the north. **2** facing or directed toward the north.

northerner *or* **Northerner** *noun* a person who lives in or comes from the north, esp. the northern part of the USA.

northern lights (**the northern lights**) the aurora borealis.

North Pole 1 (**the North Pole**) the northernmost point of the Earth's axis of rotation, at 90°N, longitude 0°. **2** (**north pole**) the north-seeking pole on a straight magnet.

northward *adv., adj.* toward the north. ‣ **northwardly** *adv., adj.* ‣ **northwards** *adv.*

northwest (nôrth-wĕst', nôr-) (ABBREV. **NW**) *noun* the direction midway between north and west. —*adj.* **1** in the northwest. **2** from the direction of the northwest.

northwester (nôrth-wĕs'tər, nôr-) *noun* a wind blowing from the northwest. ‣ **northwesterly** *adj., adv.*

northwestern *adj.* (ABBREV. **NW**) to the northwest.

Norwegian (nôr-wē'jən) *noun* **1** a native or citizen of Norway. **2** the official language of Norway. —*adj.* of Norway, its people, or their language.

Nos. *or* **nos.** *abbrev.* numbers.

nose *noun* **1** the projecting organ above the mouth with which one smells and breathes. **2** an animal's snout or muzzle. **3** the sense of smell. **4** (**a nose for**) a faculty for detecting or recognizing (something). **5** a scent or aroma, esp. the bouquet of a wine. **6** a front or projecting part, e.g., of a motor vehicle or of an aircraft. —*verb trans., intrans.* (**nosed, nosing**) of a vehicle or its driver to move carefully and slowly forward. —**under one's** (**very**) **nose** of something sought prominently in front of one.

nosebleed *noun* bleeding from the nose, usu. caused by physical injury.

nose cone the conical front section of a spacecraft or missile.

nosedive *noun* **1** a steep, rapid plunge by an aircraft, with the nose pointed down. **2** a sharp plunge or fall. **3** a sudden drop, e.g., in prices. —*verb intrans.* (**nosedived** *or* **nosedove, nosediving**) to plunge or fall suddenly.

nosegay *noun* a small bouquet of flowers.

nosey *adj. same as* **nosy.**

nosh *slang noun* food. —*verb intrans.* (**noshed, noshing, noshes**) to eat a light meal.

nostalgia (nô-stăl'jə) *noun* **1** a yearning for the past. **2** homesickness. ‣ **nostalgic** *adj.* ‣ **nostalgically** *adv.*

nostril *noun* either of the two openings in the

nose, through which one breathes, smells, etc.

nostrum *noun* a medicine, esp. a quack one.

nosy *or* **nosey** *adj.* (**nosier, nosiest**) unduly or inappropriately inquisitive.

not *adv.* (*with auxiliary and modal verbs, often shortened to -n't and joined to the verb*) **1** used to make a negative statement, etc.: *That isn't fair.* **2** used with verbs of opinion, intention, etc., to make the clause or infinitive following the verb negative: *I don't think he's right* (I think he is not right). **3** used in place of a negative clause or predicate: *I might be late, but I hope not.* **4** used to indicate surprise, an expectation of agreement, etc.: *Haven't you heard?* **5** used to contrast the untrue with the true: *It's a cloud, not a mountain.* **6** barely: *He stood with his face not two inches from mine.* **7** (**not a**) absolutely no: *Not a sound was to be heard in the theater.* **8** by no means: *Not everyone would agree.* **9** used with *only, just,* etc., to introduce what is usu. the lesser of two points, etc.: *Not just her family, but her wider public, disagrees with her decision.* —*interj.* used standing alone, followed by an exclamation point to express strong opposition or disagreement: *That was a great movie—not!*

notable *adj.* **1** worth noting; significant. **2** distinguished. **3** (**notable for**) famous on account of (something): *Maryland is notable for its fresh seafood.* —*noun* a famous person. ‣ **notability** *noun* ‣ **notably** *adv.*

notary (nōt'ə-rē) *noun* (*pl.* **notaries**) *Law* a notary public.

notary public (*pl.* **notaries public**) (ABBREV. **N.P.**) *Law* a public officer with the legal power to draw up and witness official documents.

notation *noun* **1** the representation of quantities, numbers, musical sounds, movements, etc., by symbols. **2** a set of such symbols.

notch *noun* a small V-shaped cut. —*verb trans.* (**notched, notching**) to cut a notch in. —**notch up** to record (something) as a score; to achieve (something).

note *noun* **1** (*often* **notes**) a brief record made for later reference: *lecture notes.* **2** a short informal letter. **3** a brief comment explaining a textual point, etc. **4** a short account or essay. **5** a formal, esp. diplomatic, communication. **6** attention; notice: *buildings worthy of note.* **7** distinction; eminence: *women of note.* **8** *Mus.* a written symbol indicating the pitch and length of a sound; the sound itself. **9** an impression conveyed; feeling; mood: *with a note of optimism.* —*verb trans.* (**noted, noting**) **1** (*also* **note**

down) to write (something) down. **2** to be aware of; to notice: *I noted the change in his attitude.* —**compare notes** to exchange ideas and opinions. **strike the right note** to act or speak appropriately.

notebook *noun* **1** a small book in which to write notes. **2** a laptop computer small enough to fit into a briefcase.

noted *adj.* well known.

notepad *noun* a pad of paper for jotting down notes.

notepaper *noun* paper for writing letters.

noteworthy *adj.* worthy of notice; remarkable.

nothing *noun* **1** no thing; not anything. **2** very little; something that is of no importance or is not very impressive. **3** the number 0. **4** absence of anything: *heard a shriek and then nothing.* —*adv.* not at all: *She looks nothing like her mother.* ▸ **nothingness** *noun*

notice *noun* **1** an announcement displayed or delivered publicly. **2** one's attention: *It escaped their notice.* **3** a warning or notification given, e.g., before leaving, or dismissing someone from, a job: *give one's notice.* **4** a review of a performance, book, etc. —*verb trans.* (**noticed, noticing**) **1** to apprehend by sight. **2** to remark on. —**at or on short notice** with little warning, time for preparation, etc.

noticeable *adj.* easily perceived, felt, or seen; clearly apparent. ▸ **noticeably** *adv.*

notifiable *adj.* denoting any disease or injury that must be reported to public-health authorities.

notify *verb trans.* (**notified, notifying, notifies**) (**notify of**) to inform or warn (someone) about (something). ▸ **notification** *noun*

notion *noun* **1** an impression, conception, or understanding. **2** a belief or principle. **3** an inclination, whim, or fancy. **4** (**notions**) pins, needles, and other small items used in sewing.

notional *adj.* existing only in the mind or imagination. ▣ IMAGINARY, SHADOWY, UNREAL ▣ ACTUAL, PHYSICAL, REAL.

notorious *adj.* famous, usu. for something disreputable. ▸ **notoriety** *noun* ▸ **notoriously** *adv.*

notwithstanding *prep.* in spite of. —*adv.* in spite of everything; nonetheless. —*conj.* in spite of the fact that.

nougat (nŏō'gət) *noun* a chewy confection containing nuts, etc.

nought *noun same as* **naught.**

noun *noun* (ABBREV. **n.**) a word used as the name of a person, animal, thing, place, or quality.

nourish *verb trans.* (**nourished, nourishing**)

1 to supply with food needed for survival and growth. **2** to encourage the growth of; to foster (an idea, etc.). ▸ **nourishing** *adj.* ▸ **nourishment** *noun*

nouveau riche (nŏō,vō,rēsh') (*pl.* **nouveaux riches**) a person who has recently acquired wealth, but lacks the breeding to go with it.

novel[1] (nǎv'əl) *noun* a book-length fictional story usu. involving relationships between characters and events concerning them. ▸ **novelist** *noun*

novel[2] *adj.* new and original.

novelette *noun* a short, esp. trite or sentimental novel.

novella *noun* a piece of fiction longer than a short story.

novelty *noun* (*pl.* **novelties**) **1** the quality of being new and intriguing. **2** something new and strange. **3** a small cheap toy or souvenir.

November (nō-věm'bər) *noun* (ABBREV. **Nov., Nov**) the eleventh month of the year, following October.

novice *noun* **1** a beginner. **2** a person who has joined a religious community but not yet taken vows.

novitiate *noun* **1** the period of being a novice in a religious community. **2** the novices' quarters in such a community.

NOW (now) *abbrev.* National Organization for Women.

now *adv.* **1** at the present time or moment: *is now at home.* **2** immediately: *Leave now!* **3** in narrative then: *She now turned from journalism to fiction.* **4** in these circumstances; as things are: *I planned to go, but now I can't.* **5** up to the present: *He has now been teaching 13 years.* **6** used conversationally to accompany explanations, warnings, etc.: *Careful, now!* —*noun* the present time: *Up to now, he's been living in Greenwich Village.* —*conj.* (**now that**) because at last; because at this time: *Now that we're all here, we can begin.*

nowadays *adv.* in these present times.

nowhere *adv.* in or to no place; not anywhere.

no-win *adj. colloq.* sure to result in disappointment or failure: *a no-win situation.*

noxious *adj.* harmful; poisonous.

nozzle *noun* a fitting attached as an outlet to the end of a hose, etc.

N.P. *abbrev.* notary public.

Np *symbol Chem.* neptunium.

NSC *abbrev.* National Security Council.

NT *or* **N.T.** *abbrev. Bible* New Testament.

nth (ĕnth) *adj.* **1** denoting an indefinite position in a sequence: *to the nth degree.* **2** denoting an item or occurrence that is at many removes from the first in a sequence: *I'm telling you for the nth time.*

nuance (nŏō'äns,, nyŏō'-) *noun* a subtle variation, e.g., in color, meaning, expression.

nub *noun* the central, most important issue.

nubile *adj.*, *of a young woman* **1** physically mature. **2** sexually attractive.

nuclear (nōō'klē-ər, nyōō'-) *adj.* **1** having the nature of a nucleus: *the nuclear family.* **2** of or relating to the nucleus of an atom or the nuclei of atoms. **3** relating to or powered by the energy released by the fission or fusion of atomic nuclei: *nuclear weapons.* **4** relating to or caused by]warfare involving the deployment and use of nuclear weapons: *nuclear devastation.*

nuclear bomb a completely assembled bomb in which detonation results from the energy released by reactions involving atomic nuclei, either fission or fusion, or both.

nuclear energy the energy released during a nuclear reaction, esp. fission or fusion.

nuclear family a family consisting of mother, father, and children only.

nuclear reaction a reaction involving a change in an atomic nucleus, as in nuclear fission.

nuclear reactor a device that produces nuclear energy in the form of a controlled chain reaction.

nucleate *verb trans.*, *intrans.* (**nucleated, nucleating**) (nōō'klē-āt, nyōō'-) to form or to form into a nucleus. —*adj.* (nōō'klē-ət, nyōō'-) **1** having a nucleus. **2** being in the form of or resembling a nucleus.

nucleic acid (nōō-klē'ĭk, nyōō-, -klā'-) either of the acids DNA or RNA, found in all living cells.

nucleon *noun* a proton or neutron, esp. one present in the nucleus of an atom.

nucleonics *noun* (*sing.*) the study of the uses of radioactivity and nuclear energy.

nucleus *noun* (*pl.* **nuclei**) **1** the positively charged central part of an atom, consisting of neutrons and protons and surrounded by electrons. **2** the central part of a plant or animal cell, containing the substances that control its development and characteristics. **3** a core around which things accumulate.

nude *adj.* wearing no clothes; naked. —*noun* **1** a representation of a naked figure in painting, sculpture, etc. **2** someone naked. **3** the state of being naked: *in the nude.* ▸ **nudity** *noun*

nudge *verb trans.* (**nudged, nudging**) **1** to knock slightly. ▣ JOG, PROD. **2** to push slightly or little by little: *nudged the project along.* —*noun* a gentle prod.

nudism *noun* the practice of not wearing clothes, as a matter of principle. *Also called* **naturism.** ▸ **nudist** *noun*

nugatory *adj.* **1** worthless; trifling; valueless. **2** ineffective; futile. **3** invalid.

nugget *noun* **1** a lump, esp. of gold. **2** a small piece of something precious: *nuggets of wisdom.*

nuisance *noun* **1** an annoying or troublesome person, thing, or circumstance. **2** something obnoxious to the community or an individual, that is disallowed by law.

nuke *slang verb trans.* (**nuked, nuking**) **1** to attack with nuclear weapons. **2** to cook (food) in a microwave oven. —*noun* a nuclear weapon.

null *adj.* **1** legally invalid: *declared the will null and void.* **2** nonexistent. ▸ **nullity** *noun*

nullify *verb trans.* (**nullified, nullifying, nullifies**) **1** to cause or declare to be legally invalid. **2** to make ineffective; to cancel out. ▸ **nullification** *noun*

numb *adj.* **1** deprived completely, or to some degree, of sensation. **2** *of a limb, etc.* unable to move; paralyzed. **3** too stunned to feel emotion; stupefied: *numb with fear.* —*verb trans.* (**numbed, numbing**) to make numb; to deaden. ▸ **numbly** *adv.* ▸ **numbness** *noun*

number *noun* **1** the means or system by which groups, sets, etc., of individual things, etc., are counted; a quantity calculated in units. **2** *Math.* one or more arithmetical symbols representing such a quantity; a numeral or set of numerals. **3** a numeral or set of numerals identifying something or someone within a series: *telephone numbers.* **4** (*followed by a numeral*) the person, animal, vehicle, etc., identified by the numeral: *Number 21 is pulling ahead.* **5** a single issue, e.g., of a magazine. **6** a quantity of individuals. **7** an act or turn in a programme. **8** a piece of popular music or jazz. **9** *colloq.* an article or person considered appreciatively: *drives a white sports number.* **10** a group of people: *isn't one of our number.* **11** (**numbers**) numerical superiority: *by sheer weight of numbers.* **12** *Gram.* the property of expressing, or classification of word forms into, singular and plural. —*verb trans.* (**numbered, numbering**) **1** to give a number to; to mark with a number. **2** to include: *I number her among my closest friends.* **3** to amount to: *a crowd numbering about 500.* —**one's days are numbered** one is soon to suffer or die. **safety in numbers** security or comfort afforded in difficult circumstances by the support of others.

numberless *adj.* too many to count; innumerable.

numbskull *noun colloq.* same as **numskull.**

numeracy *noun* **1** the state of being numerate; the ability to use numbers, esp. to solve arithmetical problems. **2** some understanding of mathematics and science.

numeral *noun* a symbol or group of symbols used to represent a number in written form.

—*adj.* relating to, consisting of, or denoting a number.

numerate *adj.* (nōō'mə-rət, nyōō'-) **1** able to use numbers, esp. to solve arithmetical problems. **2** having some understanding of mathematics and science. —*verb trans.* (nōō'məbrāt,, nyōō'-) (**numerated, numerating**) **1** to read off (something or a group of things) as numbers (from figures). **2** to list (numbers) in their natural order, from smallest to largest; to enumerate. ▸ **numeration** *noun*

numerator *noun* the number shown above the line in a fraction. *See also* **denominator**.

numerical *adj.* relating to, using, or consisting of numbers: *numerical superiority.* ▸ **numerially** *adv.*

numerology *noun* the study of numbers as an alleged influence on human affairs.

numerous *adj.* **1** many. **2** containing a large number of people.

numinous *adj.* **1** mysterious; awe-inspiring. **2** characterized by the sense of a deity's presence.

numismatics *noun* (*sing.*) the study or collecting of coins and medals. ▸ **numismatic** *adj.* ▸ **numismatist** *noun*

numskull or **numbskull** *noun colloq.* a stupid person.

nun *noun* a member of a religious order of women living, in obedience to certain vows, in a community.

nunnery *noun* (*pl.* **nunneries**) a house in which a group of nuns live.

nuptial (nəp'shəl, -chəl) *adj.* relating to marriage. —*noun* (*usu.* **nuptials**) a marriage ceremony.

nurse *noun* **1** a person who is trained to care for sick or injured people, esp. in a hospital. **2** a person, esp. a woman, who looks after small children in a household. —*verb trans., intrans.* (**nursed, nursing**) **1** to look after (sick or injured people) esp. in a hospital. **2 a** to feed (a baby) at the breast. **b** *of an infant* to feed at the breast. **3** to tend with concern: *was at home nursing a cold.* **4** to encourage (a feeling) in oneself: *nursing her resentment.*

nursery *noun* (*pl.* **nurseries**) **1** a place where children are looked after while their parents are at work, etc. **2** a room in a house reserved for young children. **3** a place where plants are grown for sale.

nursery rhyme a short simple traditional rhyme for children.

nursery school a school for children aged between three and five.

nursing *noun* the profession of a nurse, and the tasks and the health care performed by a nurse.

nursing home a private institution that offers living accommodations, meals, recreation, and health care to the elderly or the chronically ill.

nurture *noun* care, nourishment, and encouragement given to a growing child, animal, or plant. —*verb trans.* (**nurtured, nurturing**) **1** to nourish and tend (a growing child, animal, or plant). **2** to encourage the development of (a project, idea, feeling, etc.).

nut *noun* **1** a fruit consisting of a kernel contained in a hard shell; the kernel itself. **2** a small, usu. hexagonal, piece of metal with a hole through it, used for screwing on the end of a bolt. **3** *colloq.* **a** a person's head. **b** a person regarded as insane.

nutcase *noun colloq.* a person regarded as insane.

nutcracker *noun* a utensil for cracking nuts.

nutmeg *noun* the hard aromatic seed of the fruit of an Asian Indian tree, used ground or grated as a spice.

nutrient *noun* a nourishing substance. —*adj.* nourishing.

nutriment *noun* nourishment; food.

nutrition *noun* **1** the process of nourishment. **2** the scientific study of nutrients, the nutritional value of food, and the body's dietary needs. **3** a source of nourishment; food. ▸ **nutritional** *adj.* ▸ **nutritive** *adj.*

nutritious *adj.* providing nutrition; nourishing.

nuts *adj. colloq.* **1** insane; crazy. **2** (**nuts about**) infatuated with or extremely fond of (someone or something).

nutshell *noun* the hard shell surrounding the kernel of a nut. —**in a nutshell** concisely or very briefly expressed.

nutty *adj.* (**nuttier, nuttiest**) **1** full of or tasting of nuts. **2** *colloq.* crazy.

nuzzle *verb trans., intrans.* (**nuzzled, nuzzling**) (**nuzzle up** or **against**) *usu. of animals* to push or rub (someone or something) with the nose.

NW *abbrev.* northwest; northwestern.

nylon *noun* **1** a synthetic material used in the manufacture of clothing, hosiery, ropes, brushes, etc. **2** (**nylons**) a woman's stockings made of this material. —*adj.* relating to such a material.

nymph *noun* **1** *Mythol.* a goddess inhabiting e.g., water or trees. **2** *poetic* a beautiful young woman. **3** an immature larval form of certain insects.

NYSE *abbrev.* New York Stock Exchange.

NZ or **N.Z.** *abbrev.* New Zealand.

Oo

O¹ *or* **o** *noun* (*pl.* **Os, O's, o's**) **1** the 15th letter of the English alphabet. **2** a zero.

O² *or* **oh** *interj.* **1** (*usu.* **oh**) used to express surprise, admiration, etc. **2** used in addressing a person or thing.

O³ *abbrev.* Old.

oaf *noun* a stupid or awkward person. ▶ **oafish** *adj.*

oak *noun* **1** a tree with fruit in the form of *acorns*. **2** the hard durable wood of this tree. ▶ **oaken** *adj.*

oakum *noun* pieces of old rope pulled apart, used to fill small holes in wooden ships.

oar *noun* **1** a long pole with a broad, flat blade, used for rowing a boat. **2** a rower.

oarlock *noun* a device for holding an oar in place. *See also* **thole.**

oarsman *noun* a man who rows. ▶ **oarsmanship** *noun*

oarswoman *noun* a woman who rows. ▶ **oarswomanship** *noun*

OAS *abbrev.* Organization of American States.

oasis (ō-ā'sĭs) *noun* (*pl.* **oases**) **1** a fertile area in a desert where water is found and plants grow. **2** a place of rest or pleasure in the middle of problems or trouble.

oast *noun* a kiln for drying hops.

oat *noun* **1** (*also* **oats**) a cereal cultivated as a food crop. **2** (**oats**) the seeds of this plant, used as a food. —**sow (one's) wild oats** *colloq.* to indulge in excessive drinking, promiscuity, etc., during youth. ▶ **oaten** *adj.*

oater *noun slang* a western movie.

oath *noun* **1** a solemn promise, usu. naming God as a witness. **2** a swearword or a blasphemy. —**on** *or* **under oath** having sworn to tell the truth, e.g., in a court of law.

oatmeal *noun* oats ground into meal, typically eaten hot with milk or water, as a breakfast food.

OAU *abbrev.* Organization of African Unity.

ob. *abbrev. obiit* (Latin), he or she died.

obbligato (äb,lĭ-gät'ō) *noun* (*pl.* **obbligatos, obbligati**) an accompaniment forming an essential part of a piece of music.

obdurate (äb'də-rət, -dyə-) *adj.* **1** hardhearted. **2** difficult to influence, esp. morally. ▶ **obduracy** *noun*

obedient *adj.* ready and willing to obey. ▶ **obedience** *noun* ▶ **obediently** *adv.*

obeisance (ō-bē'səns, ō-bā'-) *noun* an act or expression indicating obedience or respect, e.g., a bow.

obelisk *noun* **1** a tapering, needlelike stone pillar. **2** *Printing* a dagger (sense 2).

obese *adj.* very fat. ▶ **obesity** *noun*

obey *verb trans., intrans.* (**obeyed, obeying, obeys**) **1** to do what one is told to do by (someone else). **2** to carry out (a command). **3** to be controlled by (a force, impulse, etc.).

obfuscate (äb'fə-skāt,) *verb trans.* (**obfuscated, obfuscating**) to confuse or make difficult to understand. ▶ **obfuscation** *noun* ▶ **obfuscatory** (äb-fəs'kə-tôr,ē) *adj.*

obiter dictum (ō'bĭt-ər-dĭk'təm) (*pl.* **obiter dicta**) a remark that is related to but inessential to the main argument.

obituary *noun* (*pl.* **obituaries**) an announcement of a person's death, often with a short account of his or her life.

object¹ *noun* (äb'jikt) **1** something that is inanimate, yet has demonstrable physical bulk and existence. **2** an aim or purpose. **3** the person or thing to which action, feelings, or thought are directed. **4** the noun, noun phrase, or pronoun affected by the action of verb, or a preposition. *See also* **subject** (sense 6), **direct object, indirect object.** —**be no object** to constitute no difficulty.

object² *verb intrans., trans.* (**objected, objecting** (äb-jĕkt') **object to (something)**) to feel or express dislike or disapproval for (it). ▣ KICK, PROTEST, REMONSTRATE ▣ PROPONE.

objection *noun* **1** an expression of disapproval. **2** (**objection to (something)**) a reason for disapproving of (it).

objectionable *adj.* likely to cause offense; unpleasant.

objective *adj.* **1** influenced by no personal opinions or prejudices. **2 a** having existence outside the mind. *See also* **subjective** (sense 1). **b** relating to actual matter or to actuality. **3** *Gram.* indicating the object; in the relation of object to a verb or preposition. —*noun* **1** a thing aimed at or wished for; a goal. **2** *Gram.* the objective case. **3** the lens in a camera, telescope, etc., that is nearest the object being viewed. ▶ **objectivity** *noun*

object lesson an experience that gives a practical example of a principle or ideal.

objector *noun* a person who objects, e.g., to military service.

objet d'art (ōb,zha,där') (*pl.* **objets d'art**) a small object of artistic value.

oblate (äb'lāt,, äb-lāt') *adj.* flattened at the poles, like Earth.

oblation *noun* a sacrifice or religious offering.

obligate (äb'lĭ-gāt,) *verb trans.* (**obligated, obligating**) to bind by duty or moral obligation.

obligation *noun* 1 a moral or legal duty or tie. 2 the binding power of such a duty or tie. 3 a debt of gratitude for a service.

obligatory *adj.* legally or morally binding.

oblige *verb trans., intrans.* (**obliged, obliging**) 1 a to make (someone or something) give in to pressure. b to bind morally or legally. 2 to bind by a service or favor. —**much obliged** used to express gratitude.

obliging *adj.* willing to help others. ▸ **obligingly** *adv.*

oblique (ō-blēk', ō-blīk') *adj.* 1 sloping. 2 deviating from the straight or direct in expression or behavior. ⊟ INDIRECT, ROUNDABOUT ⊟ DIRECT, FORTHRIGHT, FRANK, STRAIGHTFORWARD. 3 not at a right angle. ▸ **obliquely** *adv.*

obliterate *verb trans.* (**obliterated, obliterating**) 1 to destroy completely. 2 to cover and prevent from being seen. ▸ **obliteration** *noun*

oblivion *noun* 1 the state of having forgotten or being unconscious. 2 the state of being forgotten.

oblivious *adj.* (**oblivious of** *or* **to** (**something** *or* **someone**)) unaware or forgetful of (the one specified). ▸ **obliviously** *adv.* ▸ **obliviousness** *noun*

oblong *adj.* rectangular with adjacent sides unequal. —*noun* a rectangular figure.

obloquy (äb'lə-kwē) *noun* (*pl.* **obloquies**) 1 abuse or censure. 2 loss of respect or favor.

obnoxious *adj.* offensive; objectionable.

oboe *noun* a wind instrument with a double reed and a penetrating tone. ▸ **oboist** *noun*

obscene *adj.* 1 offensive to accepted standards of decency and modesty. ⊟ DIRTY, FOUL, INDECENT, RAUNCHY, SCATOLOGICAL, SMUTTY ⊟ CLEAN, DECENT. 2 *colloq.* indecent; disgusting: *made an obscene salary.* ▸ **obscenely** *adv.* ▸ **obscenity** *noun*

obscurantism *noun* opposition to inquiry or the spreading or use of new knowledge, etc. ▸ **obscurantist** *noun, adj.*

obscure *adj.* 1 dark; dim. 2 not clear; difficult to see. 3 not well known. 4 difficult to understand. —*verb trans.* (**obscured, obscuring**) to make dark or difficult to see or understand. ▸ **obscurity** *noun*

obsequies (äb'sə-kwēz) *pl. noun* funeral rites.

obsequious (əb-sē'kwē-əs) *adj.* submissively obedient; fawning.

observable *adj.* discernible; perceptible.

observance *noun* 1 the act of obeying rules, keeping customs, etc. 2 a custom or religious rite observed.

observant *adj.* 1 quick to notice. 2 carefully attentive. ▸ **observantly** *adv.*

observation *noun* 1 the act of noticing or watching. 2 ability to observe; perception. 3 a remark or comment. 4 the noting of symptoms, phenomena, etc., as they occur, esp. before analysis or diagnosis. ▸ **observational** *adj.*

observation car a railroad car with large windows to allow passengers to view the scenery.

observatory *noun* (*pl.* **observatories**) a room, building, or site specially equipped for making systematic observations of the stars and other celestial objects.

observe *verb trans., intrans.* (**observed, observing**) 1 to apprehend (an image) by using the faculty of vision. 2 to watch carefully. 3 to examine and note (symptoms, phenomena, etc.). 4 to obey or keep (a law, custom, etc.). 5 to make a remark or comment. ▸ **observer** *noun*

obsess *verb trans., intrans.* (**obsessed, obsessing**) 1 to occupy or haunt the mind of (someone) persistently or constantly. 2 to be totally preoccupied with and fixated on someone or something.

obsession *noun* 1 a persistent or dominating idea. ⊟ FETISH, FIXATION, MANIA, THING. 2 a recurring thought, feeling, or impulse that preoccupies a person and is a source of constant anxiety ▸ **obsessional** *adj.*

obsessive *adj.* 1 relating to or resulting from an obsession. 2 affected by an obsession. ▸ **obsessively** *adv.*

obsessive-compulsive disorder neurosis in which a person becomes preoccupied with an obsession.

obsidian *noun* the commonest type of volcanic glass, usu. black.

obsolescent *adj.* going out of use; becoming out of date. ▸ **obsolescence** *noun*

obsolete *adj.* no longer in use; out of date.

obstacle *noun* a person or thing that prevents progress.

obstacle race a race in which runners have to climb over, crawl through, etc., obstacles.

obstetrics *noun* (*sing.*) the branch of medicine that deals with pregnancy and childbirth. ▸ **obstetric** *adj.* ▸ **obstetrician** *noun*

obstinate (äb'stĭ-nət) *adj.* 1 refusing to change or compromise. ⊟ BULLHEADED, HARDHEADED, INCOMPLIANT, INTRACTABLE, INTRANSIGENT, MULISH, PERTINACIOUS, PIGHEADED, REFRACTORY, SELF-WILLED,

STUBBORN, WRONGHEADED ⚌ COM-
PLIANT, PLIABLE, PLIANT, TRACTABLE. 2
difficult to remove or treat. ▸ **obstinacy**
noun ▸ **obstinately** *adv.*

obstreperous *adj.* noisy and hard to control.

obstruct *verb trans.* (**obstructed, obstructing**) 1 to block or close. 2 to prevent or
hinder the progress of. ▸ **obstruction** *noun*

obstructionism *noun* the practice of
obstructing legislative or legal action. ▸ **ob-
structionist** *noun*

obstructive *adj.* causing or designed to cause
an obstruction.

obtain *verb trans., intrans.* (**obtained, obtaining**) 1 to become the owner or come
into possession of. 2 to be established or to
hold good.

obtrude *verb intrans., trans.* (**obtruded,
obtruding**) 1 to be unpleasantly noticeable
or prominent. 2 (**obtrude (something) on
or upon (someone)**) to push (oneself, one's
opinions, etc.), forward, esp. when unwelcome.

obtrusive *adj.* unpleasantly noticeable.

obtuse (äb-tōōs′, -tyōōs′) *adj.* 1 not pointed or
sharp. 2 *colloq.* stupid and slow to
understand. 3 denoting an angle that is
greater than 90° and less than 180°
▸ **obtuseness** *noun*

obverse *noun* 1 the side of a coin with the
head or main design on it. *See also* **reverse**
(sense 4). 2 an opposite or counterpart.

obviate (äb′vē-āt,) *verb trans.* (**obviated, ob-
viating**) to prevent or remove (a potential problem, etc.) in advance.

obvious *adj.* easily seen or understood.
▸ **obviously** *adv.* ▸ **obviousness** *noun*

ocarina *noun* a small wind instrument with an
egg-shaped body.

occasion *noun* 1 a particular event or
happening. 2 a special event or celebration.
3 a suitable opportunity. 4 a reason: *have
no occasion to be angry.* 5 an event that
determines the time at which something
else happens, but which is not the cause of
it. —*verb trans.* (**occasioned, occa-
sioning**) to cause. —**on occasion** from
time to time. **rise to the occasion** to
produce the extra energy or ability needed
by unusual circumstances.

occasional *adj.* 1 happening irregularly and
infrequently. 2 produced on or for a special
occasion.

occasionally *adv.* on occasion; now and then.

Occident (äk′səd-ənt, -sə-dĕnt,) *noun* (**the
Occident**) the countries in the west, esp.
those in Europe and America. ▸ **occidental**
adj., noun

occiput (äk′sĭ-pət) *noun* (*pl.* **occipita, oc-
ciputs**) the back of the head. ▸ **occipital**
(äk-sĭp′ĭt-l) *adj.*

occlude *verb trans.* (**occluded, occluding**) 1
to block up or cover (e.g., a pore). 2 *of a
solid* to absorb a gas. 3 to shut in or out.
▸ **occlusion** *noun*

occult (ə-kəlt′, äk′əlt,) *adj.* 1 involving or
dealing with magical, mystical, or supernatural matters. 2 beyond ordinary understanding. 3 secret or esoteric. —*noun* (**the
occult**) the knowledge and study of magical, mystical, or supernatural matters.
▸ **occultism** *noun* ▸ **occultist** *noun*

occultation *noun* a phenomenon that is
observed when one celestial body passes
directly in front of another, so obscuring it.

occupancy *noun* (*pl.* **occupancies**) 1 the act
of occupying, e.g., a house. 2 a period of
time during which a house, etc., is occupied.

occupant *noun* a person who occupies or
takes possession of something.

occupation *noun* 1 a person's regular paid
employment. 2 an activity that occupies a
person's free time, etc. 3 the act of
occupying or state of being occupied. 4 the
act of taking and keeping control of a
foreign country, using military power.
▸ **occupational** *adj.* ▸ **occupationally** *adv.*

occupational hazard a risk or danger caused
by the working conditions of a particular job.

occupational therapy a form of rehabilitation
in which patients are encouraged to
participate in selected activities that will
equip them to function independently in
everyday life. ▸ **occupational therapist**

occupy *verb trans.* (**occupied, occupying,
occupies**) 1 to have possession of or live in
(a house, etc.). 2 to be in or fill (time, space,
etc.). 3 to take possession of (a building, a
foreign country, etc.) by force. 4 to keep
(oneself, one's mind, etc.) busy; to fill in
(time). 5 to hold (a post or office).
▸ **occupier** *noun*

occur *verb intrans.* (**occurred, occurring**) 1 to
happen or take place. 2 (**occur to
(someone)**) to come into the mind. 3 to be
found or exist.

occurrence *noun* 1 something that occurs; an
event. 2 the act of occurring.

ocean (ō′shən) *noun* 1 a the continuous
expanse of salt water that covers about 70%
of Earth's surface. b any one of its five main
divisions, the Atlantic, Indian, Pacific, Arctic,
and Southern. c the sea. 2 (*often* **oceans**) a
very large quantity. ▸ **oceanic** *adj.*

oceangoing *adj.* built to sail on the seas rather
than on rivers, etc.

oceanography *noun* the scientific study of the
oceans. ▸ **oceanographer** *noun* ▸ **oceano-
graphic** *adj.*

ocelot (äs′ə-lät, ō′sə-) *noun* a medium-sized
wild cat that has a pale coat with large dark
spots.

och (äкн) *interj. Scottish, Irish* used to express surprise, impatience, etc.

ocher (ō'kər) *or* **ochre** *noun* **1** fine earth or clay, used as a yellow, red, or brown dye. **2** a pale brownish-yellow color. —*adj.* of a pale brownish-yellow color.

o'clock *adv.* used after a number in specifying the time.

OCR *abbrev.* **1** optical character reader. **2** optical character recognition.

OCS *abbrev.* Officer Candidate School.

oct- *or* **octa-** *combining form same as* **octo-**.

octagon *noun* a two-dimensional figure with eight sides and eight angles. ▸ **octagonal** *adj.*

octahedron *noun* (*pl.* **octahedrons**, **octahedra**) a solid figure with eight plane faces. ▸ **octahedral** *adj.*

octane *noun* a colorless liquid belonging to the alkane series of hydrocarbons.

octane number a numeric system for classifying motor fuels according to their resistance to knocking. *Also called* **octane rating.**

octant *noun* one eighth of the circumference of a circle.

octave (äk'tĭv) *noun* **1 a** the series of notes between the first note and the eighth note on a major or minor scale. **b** a note that is an eighth above or below another. **2 a** a verse or stanza with eight lines. **b** the first eight lines of a sonnet.

octavo (äk-tā'vō, -täv'ō) *noun* (*pl.* **octavos**) a size of book or page produced by folding a standard-sized sheet of paper three times to give eight leaves.

octet (äk-tět') *noun* **1** a group of eight, e.g., musicians, lines in a poem, etc. **2** a piece of music written for eight musicians or singers. **3** the first eight lines in a sonnet.

octo-, oct- *or* **octa-** *combining form* forming words denoting eight.

October (äk-tō'bər) *noun* (ABBREV. **Oct.,** **Oct**) the tenth month of the year, following September.

octogenarian *noun* someone between 80 and 89 years old.

octopus *noun* (*pl.* **octopuses, octopi**) a marine mollusk with a soft rounded body and eight arms.

octoroon *noun* a person whose ancestry is an eighth black.

ocular *adj.* of or related to the eyes or vision.

oculist *noun* an optician or ophthalmologist.

OD *slang noun* (*pl.* **ODs, OD's**) an overdose of drugs. —*verb intrans.* (**OD'd, OD'ing**) to take a drug overdose.

O.D. *abbrev.* **1** officer of the day. **2** (*often* **o/d**) overdraft.

odalisque (ōd'l-ĭsk,) *or* **odalisk** *noun* a female slave in a harem.

odd *adj.* **1** left over when others have been put into groups or pairs. **2** not matching: *odd socks.* **3** not exactly divisible by two. **4** unusual; strange. **5** not regular; occasional: *odd jobs.* **6** (*in compounds with a number*) being a little more than the number stated: *20-odd replies.* —**odd man out** a person or thing that is different from others. ▸ **oddly** *adv.* ▸ **oddness** *noun*

oddball *noun colloq.* a strange or eccentric person.

oddity *noun* (*pl.* **oddities**) a strange person or thing.

oddments *pl. noun* pieces left over from something much larger.

odds *pl. noun* **1** the chance or probability, expressed as a ratio, that something will or will not happen. **2** the difference between the amount placed as a bet and the money that might be won, expressed as a ratio. **3** an advantage that is thought to exist. **4** likelihood. —**against all (the) odds** in spite of great difficulty or disadvantage. **at odds** in disagreement. **odds and ends** *colloq.* small objects of different kinds.

odds-on *adj.* having better than an even chance of winning.

ode *noun* a usu. long lyric poem.

odious *adj.* extremely unpleasant or offensive.

odium *noun* hatred or disapproval.

odometer (ō-däm'ət-ər) *noun* an instrument for measuring the distance traveled by a motor vehicle.

odor *noun* **1** a distinctive smell. **2** reputation; standing: *in bad odor with his voting public.* ▸ **odorless** *adj.*

odoriferous *adj.* giving off a pleasant smell.

odorous *adj.* giving off a distinctive odor.

odyssey *noun* (*pl.* **odysseys**) a long and adventurous journey.

Oedipus complex (ĕd'ĭ-pəs, ēd'-) the repressed sexual desire of a son for his mother. ▸ **Oedipal** *adj.*

OEM *abbrev.* original equipment manufacturer.

o'er *prep., adv. poetic, old use* over.

of *prep.* **1** used to show origin, cause, or authorship. **2** belonging to; connected with. **3** used to specify a component, ingredient, etc. **4** at a given distance or amount of time from. **5** about; concerning. **6** belonging to or forming a part. **7** existing, happening, etc., at, in, or during. **8** used with words denoting loss, removal, etc. **9** used to show the connection between a verbal noun and the person who is performing or who is the object of the action stated. **10** before a stated hour; to: *a quarter of one.*

off *adv.* **1** at or to a distance; away. **2** in or into a position that is not attached; loose. **3** ahead in time. **4** in or into a state of no longer working or operating. **5** in or into a state of sleep. **6** to the end, so as to be completely finished. **7** away from work or one's duties. **8** away from a course; aside. **9** situated as regards money: *well off.* —*adj.* **1** remote in terms of coming into being: *on the off chance.* **2** nearest the center of the road. **3** not good; not up to standard: *an off day.* **4** not operating. **5** having been canceled. **6** not up to par; slack. **7** inaccurate. **8** on the way to see (someone) or do (something). —*prep.* **1** away from; from. **2** removed from. **3** leading from. **4** not wanting; no longer attracted by. **5** not up to the usual standard: *She's off her game today.* **6** out to sea from. —*verb trans.* (**offed, offing**) *slang* to cause the death of (a human being). —**off and on** now and then; occasionally.

off-air *adj.* delivered or occurring not during a broadcast.

offal *noun* the heart, brains, liver, etc., of an animal, used as food.

offbeat *adj. colloq.* not conventional; eccentric.

Off-Broadway *noun* theatrical productions in smaller theaters in New York City, which are often avant-garde or experimental. —*adj.* denoting such productions.

off-color *adj.* **1** not in good health; unwell. **2** *of humor* dirty; smutty.

offend *verb trans., intrans.* (**offended, offending**) **1** to give offense to. **2** to be unpleasant or annoying to (someone). **3** (**offend against (someone** or **something)**) to commit a sin or crime. ▸ **offended** *adj.* ▸ **offending** *adj.*

offender *noun* a person who has committed an offense.

offense (ə-fĕns', ô'fĕns,) *noun* **1 a** the breaking of a law or rule. **b** a crime. **2** a cause of displeasure or annoyance. **3** displeasure or annoyance. **4** (pronounced with stress on the first syllable) the team that has possession of a ball or puck. —**give offense** to cause displeasure or annoyance. **take offense at (something)** to be offended by (it).

offensive *adj.* **1** giving or likely to give offense; insulting. **2** disgusting or repulsive, esp. to the senses. **3** a ready to attack. **b** used for attacking. **4** (pronounced with stress on the first syllable) of or pertaining to the team in possession of a ball or puck. —*noun* **1** an aggressive action or attitude: *go on the offensive.* **2** an attack. **3** a great or aggressive effort to achieve a goal. ▸ **offensively** *adv.* ▸ **offensiveness** *noun*

offer *verb trans.* (**offered, offering**) **1** to put forward (a gift, suggestion, etc.) to be accepted, refused, or considered. **2** to provide. **3** to

state one's willingness (to do something). **4** to present for sale. **5** to provide an opportunity for. **6** to propose (a sum) as payment (to someone). **7** (also **offer (something) up**) to present (a prayer or sacrifice) to God. **8** to show (resistance, etc.). —*noun* **1** an act of offering. **2** something that is offered, esp. an amount of money offered to buy something. —**on offer** for sale.

offering *noun* **1** a gift of money given to a church, usu. during a religious service, used for charity, etc. **2** a sacrifice made to God.

offertory *noun* (*pl.* **offertories**) **1 a** the offering of bread and wine to God during the Eucharist. **b** a hymn sung while this is happening. **2** money collected during a church service.

offhand or **offhanded** *adj.* casual or careless, often with the result of being rude.

office *noun* **1** the room or building in which the business of a firm is done. **2** a room or building used for a particular kind of business. **3** a local center or department of a large business. **4** a position of authority, esp. in the government: *run for office.* **5** forming the government: *out of office.* **6** the group of people working in an office. **7** a function or duty. **8** (usu. **offices**) an act of kindness or service: *through her good offices.* **9** an authorized form of Christian worship or service.

officeholder *noun* a person who holds an official position or job.

officer *noun* **1** a person who holds a commission in the armed forces of a nation. **2** a person holding an official position in an organization or government department. **3** a person serving in a law-enforcement or espionage agency.

official *adj.* **1** of or relating to an office or position of authority. **2** given or authorized by a person in authority. —*noun* a person who holds office or who is in a position of authority. ▸ **officially** *adv.*

officialdom *noun* officials and bureaucrats as a group.

officialese *noun* the language of the government, etc., regarded as being unclear, wordy, and sometimes euphemistic.

officiate (ə-fĭsh'ē-āt,) *verb intrans.* (**officiated, officiating**) **1** to act in an official capacity; to perform official duties, esp. at a particular function. **2** to conduct a religious service.

officious *adj.* offering help, advice, etc., when it is not wanted. ▸ **officiously** *adv.*

offing *noun* the more distant part of the sea that is visible from the shore. —**in the offing** likely to happen soon.

off-key *adj., adv.* **1** out of tune. **2** not quite suitable.

off-limits *adj.* not to be entered.

off-line *adj.* not connected to or served by a computer or telecommunications network. *See also* **on-line**.

offload *verb trans.* **1** to remove (e.g., cargo) from a vehicle or aircraft. **2** to get rid of (esp. something unpleasant) by giving it to someone else. **3** *Comput.* to move (data) to a peripheral device.

off-off-Broadway *noun* theatrical productions in small, multipurpose venues outside the commercial theaters centered on Broadway, which are highly avant-garde or experimental. —*adj.* denoting such theatrical productions.

off-peak *adj.* used at a time when there is little demand, and therefore usu. cheaper.

offprint *noun* a copy of an article forming part of a larger magazine or periodical.

off-putting *adj. colloq.* disturbing; disconcerting.

off-road *adj.* designed for rugged terrain.

off-screen *or* **offscreen** *adj., adv.* relating to information not displayed on a television or computer screen.

off-season *noun* the less popular and less busy period.

offset *noun* (ŏf'sĕt,) **1** a printing process in which an image is inked on to a rubber roller which then transfers it to paper, etc. **2** something that compensates or is a counterbalance for something else. —*verb trans.* (ŏf'sĕt,, ôf-sĕt') (pa t and pa p **offset**; pr p **offsetting**) **1** to compensate for or counterbalance (something). **2** to print (something) using an offset process.

offshoot *noun* **1** a shoot growing from a plant's main stem. **2** something that has developed from something else.

offshore *adv., adj.* **1** situated in or on the sea, not far from the coast. **2** *of the wind* blowing away from the coast, out to sea.

offside *or* **offsides** *adj., adv.* in an illegal position between the ball or puck and the opponents' goal.

offspring *noun* (*pl.* **offspring**) **1** a person's child or children. **2** the young of an animal.

off-stage *adj., adv.* not on the stage, so unable to be seen by the audience.

off-the-rack *adj.* ready to wear; readymade.

off-the-wall *adj. colloq.* very unusual, or exhibiting bizarre behavior.

off-track betting a system for placing bets, e.g., on horseraces.

off-white *noun* a yellowish- or grayish-white color. —*adj.* of a yellowish- or grayish-white color.

oft *adv. old use, poetic* often.

often (ôf'ən, -tən) *adv.* **1** many times; frequently. **2** in many cases. —**as often as not** quite often; in about half the cases.

every so often now and then; sometimes. **more often than not** in most cases; usually.

ogee *noun* an S-shaped curve.

ogle *verb trans., intrans.* (**ogled, ogling**) to look or stare at (a person) expressing sexual desire with the eyes.

ogre *noun* **1** in fairy stories, a frightening, cruel, man-eating male giant. **2** a frightening man. ▸ **ogreish** *adj.* ▸ **ogress** *noun*

oh *interj.* same as **O²**.

ohm *noun* the unit of electrical resistance .

-oholic *combining form* same as **-aholic**.

-oid *suffix* forming nouns and adjectives denoting having the form of: *humanoid.*

-oidal *suffix* forming adjectives corresponding to nouns in *-oid.*

oil *noun* **1** a viscous substance that is liquid at room temperature and insoluble in water, used as a fuel, lubricant, or food. **2 a** (*often* **oils**) oil paint. **b** a picture painted with this substance. —*verb trans.* (**oiled, oiling**) to apply oil to; to lubricate. —**oil the wheels** to do something in order to make things go more smoothly. **pour oil on troubled waters** to soothe or calm a person or situation. ▸ **oiled** *adj.*

oilcloth *noun* canvas coated with oil to make it waterproof.

oil color an oil paint.

oiler *noun* a ship used to refuel other vessels.

oilfield *noun* an area of land containing reserves of oil.

oil-fired *adj.* using oil as a fuel.

oil paint a paint made by mixing ground pigment with oil. *Also called* **oil color**.

oil painting a picture painted with oil paints.

oil rig the complete installation, including the equipment, machinery, etc., required for oil drilling. *Also called* **rig**.

oilseed rape a plant with yellow cross-shaped flowers, whose seeds contain an edible oil.

oilskin *noun* **1** a cloth treated with oil to make it waterproof. **2** (*often* **oilskins**) a garment made of this cloth.

oil slick a patch of oil forming a film on the surface of water, e.g., as a result of discharge from an oil tanker.

oil tanker a large ship for carrying oil in bulk.

oil well a usu. vertical hole bored into the land surface or into a seabed in order to extract oil.

oily *adj.* (**oilier, oiliest**) **1** of, containing, or like oil. **2** covered with oil. **3** unpleasantly polite; servile and flattering.

oink *noun* the characteristic noise of a pig. —*verb intrans.* (**oinked, oinking**) to make this noise.

ointment *noun* a greasy semisolid preparation that can be applied to the skin in order to heal, soothe, or protect it.

O.K., OK or **okay** *slang adj.* good enough, but usu. only just. —*adv.* well; satisfactorily. —*interj.* used to express agreement. —*noun (pl.* **O.K.'s, OKs, okays)** approval, sanction, or agreement. —*verb trans.* (**O.K.'d, OK'd** or **okayed, O.K.'ing, OK'ing** or **okaying, O.K.'s, OK's** or **okays)** to approve or pass as satisfactory.

okapi *noun (pl.* **okapi, okapis)** a mammal, related to the giraffe but smaller and with a shorter neck.

okay *adj., adv., interj., noun, verb same as* **O.K.**

okra *noun* **1** a tall plant with edible long green seed pods. **2** the long green seed pod of this plant, eaten as a vegetable.

old *adj.* **1** advanced in age; having existed for a long time. **2** having a stated age: *five years old.* **3** of or relating to the terminal period of a long life: *old age.* **4** worn out through long use. **5** no longer in use; out of date. **6** belonging to the past. **7** former or earlier. **8** of long standing or long existence. —**of old** a long time ago; formerly.

old age the later part of life.

olden *adj.* former; past: *in olden days.*

old-fashioned *adj.* **1** in a style common some time ago; out of date. **2** in favor of or living according to the moral views of the past. —*noun* a cocktail of whiskey, bitters, fruit, and sugar, served over ice cubes.

old flame *colloq.* a person with whom one used to be in love.

old guard or **Old Guard** *(usu.* **the old guard)** the original or most conservative members of a society or organization.

old hat *colloq.* something tediously familiar or well known.

oldie *noun colloq.* a once popular song.

old lady *slang* a person's wife or mother.

old man *slang* a person's husband or father.

old master a great painter or painting from the period stretching from the Renaissance to about 1800.

oldster *noun colloq.* an elderly person.

Old Testament (ABBREV. **OT, O.T.**) the first part of the Christian Bible, containing the Hebrew scriptures. *See also* **New Testament.**

old-time *adj.* belonging to or typical of the past.

old-timer *noun* a person who has been in a job, position, etc., for a long time.

old wives' tale an ancient belief considered foolish and unscientific.

Old World the eastern hemisphere, constituting Europe, Asia, and Africa.

oleaginous (ō,lē-ăj′ĭ-nəs) *adj.* of, like, or producing oil.

oleander (ō′lē-ăn,dər)· *noun* an evergreen shrub with pink, red, or white flowers. *Also called* **rosebay.**

oleomargarine *noun* margarine.

olfactory *adj.* relating to the sense of smell.

oligarchy (ăl′ĭ-gär′kē, ō′lĭ-) *noun (pl.* **oligarchies) 1** government by a small group of people. **2** a small group of people that forms a government. ▸ **oligarchic** or **oligarchical** *adj.*

oligo- or **olig-** *combining form* forming words denoting few in number: *oligarchy.*

olive *noun* **1** a small evergreen tree cultivated for its edible fruit. **2** the small oval edible fruit of this tree, which has a hard stone and bitter oily flesh. **3** the dull yellowish-green color of unripe olives. *Also called* **olive drab, olive green.** —*adj.* **1** of the dull yellowish-green color of unripe olives. **2** *of a complexion* light brown.

olive branch a gesture toward peace or reconciliation.

olive drab the dull gray-green color of US Army uniforms.

olive oil the pale yellow oil obtained by pressing ripe olives, used as a cooking and salad oil, and in ointments, etc.

-ology *combining form same as* **-logy.**

Olympiad (ō-lĭm′pē-əd, -ăd,) *noun* **1** the celebration of the modern Olympic Games. **2** the period between Olympic Games, used by the ancient Greeks as a way of reckoning time.

Olympic (ō-lĭm′pĭk) *adj.* of or relating to the Olympic Games.—*noun* (**the Olympics)** the Olympic Games.

Olympic Games 1 games celebrated every four years in Olympia in ancient Greece, including athletic, musical, and literary competitions. **2** a modern international sports competition held every four years.

-oma *suffix* forming words denoting a tumor: *melanoma.*

ombudsman *noun (pl.* **ombudsmen) 1** an official appointed to investigate complaints against public authorities or government departments. **2** a person who mediates complaints brought, e.g., by consumers against corporations.

> From a Swedish word meaning 'administration man', introduced into English in the 1960s

omega *noun* the last letter of the Greek alphabet (Ω, ω).

omelet or **omelette** (ăm′lət) *noun* a dish of beaten eggs fried in a pan, folded around a filling.

omen *noun* a sign of a future event.

ominous *adj.* containing a warning of something bad that will happen; threatening. ▸ **ominously** *adv.*

omission *noun* **1** something that has been left out. **2** the act of leaving something out.

omit *verb trans.* (**omitted, omitting**) **1** to leave-out. **2** to fail (to do something).

omni- *combining form* forming words denoting all, every: *an omnidirectional antenna.*

omnibus *noun* (*pl.* **omnibuses**) **1** a large passenger-carrying bus. **2** a book containing a number of novels or stories by a single author. —*adj.* made up of -or bringing together several different items.

omnipotent (ăm-nĭp'ət-ənt) *adj.* having absolute power. ▸ **omnipotence** *noun*

omnipresent *adj.* present everywhere at the same time. ▸ **omnipresence** *noun*

omniscient *adj.* knowing everything. ▸ **omniscience** *noun*

omnivore *noun* an animal or plant that eats any type of food.

omnivorous *adj.* **1** eating any type of food, esp. both meat and vegetable matter. **2** reading, using, etc., everything.

on *prep.* **1** touching, supported by, or enclosing. **2** in or into (a vehicle, etc.). **3** carried with: *I've got no money on me.* **4** very near to or along the side of: *a house on the shore.* **5** at or during (a certain day, etc.). **6** immediately after or at: *He found the letter on his return.* **7** within the (given) limits of: *a picture on page 12.* **8** about: *a book on Jane Austen.* **9** through contact with: *I cut myself on the broken bottle.* **10** in the state or process of: *on fire.* **11** using as a means of transport. **12** using as a means or medium: *talk on the telephone.* **13** having as a basis or source: *on good authority.* **14** working for or being a member of: *on the committee.* **15** at the expense of: *The joke's on you.* **16** supported by: *lived on bread and cheese.* **17** regularly taking or using. **18** staked as a bet: *put money on a horse.* —*adv.* **1** of *clothes* covering. **2** ahead, forward, or toward. **3** without interruption; continuously. **4** in or into operation or activity. —*adj.* **1** working, broadcasting, or performing: *Which films are on this week?* **3** *colloq.* talking continuously, esp. to complain or nag: *She's always on at him to try harder.* **4** in favor of a win: *odds of 3 to 4 on.* —**be on to** *slang* to be aware of (usu. something negative). **on and off** now and then; occasionally. **on and on** at length; continually. **on time** at the right time; promptly.

onager (ăn'ĭ-jər) *noun* (*pl.* **onagers, onagri**) a wild ass, native to S and W Asia.

on-air *adj.* delivered or occurring during a broadcast.

onanism (ō'nə-nĭz,əm) *noun* **1** sexual intercourse in which the penis is withdrawn from the vagina before ejaculation. **2** masturbation.

once *adv.* **1** a single time; on one occasion. **2** at some time in the past. **3** at any time; ever. —*conj.* as soon as. —*noun* one time or occasion. —**all at once** without warning; suddenly. **at once** immediately. **once again** or **once more** one more time, as before. **once and for all** for the last time. **once in a while** only on occasion. **once or twice** a few times. **once upon a time** *used to begin stories for children* at a certain time in the past.

once-over *noun colloq.* a quick, often casual examination.

oncoming *adj.* approaching; advancing.

one (wŭn) *adj.* **1** being a single unit, number, or thing. **2** being a particular person or thing, esp. as distinct from others of the same kind. **3** being a particular but unspecified instance or example. **4** being the only such: *the one woman who can beat her.* **5** same; identical. **6** forming a single whole. **7** first: *page one.* **8** aged 1. —*noun* **1** the number or figure 1. **2** the age of 1. **3** a unit. **4** a garment or a person whose size is denoted by the number 1. **5** 1 o'clock. **6** *colloq.* a story or joke: *Have you heard the one about the singing monkey?* **7** *colloq.* (**one for**) an enthusiast. **8** *colloq.* a drink, esp. an alcoholic beverage: *a quick one.* **9** a score of 1 point. —*pron.* **1** (often referring to a noun already mentioned or implied) an individual person, thing, or instance: *the blue one.* **2** anybody: *One can't do better than that.* **3** I; me: *One doesn't like to pry.* —**be one up on (someone)** *colloq.* to have an advantage over (another). **for one** as one person: *I for one don't agree.* **one and all** everyone. **one and only** only: *my one and only copy of the article.* **one another** used as the object of a verb or preposition when an action takes place between two (or more than two) people, etc.: *love one another. See also* **each other.** **one by one** individually. **one or two** *colloq.* a few.

one-armed bandit *slang* a slot machine.

one-horse *adj. colloq.* small, poor, and of little importance: *a one-horse town.*

one-liner *noun colloq.* a short amusing remark made in a single sentence.

one-man *adj.* done by one man.

one-night stand 1 a performance given only once in any place. **2** *colloq.* a brief sexual encounter.

one-piece *adj.* made in a single piece as opposed to separate parts.

onerous (ăn'ə-rəs, ō'nə-) *adj.* hard to bear or do; demanding a lot of effort.

oneself *pron.* **1** the reflexive form of *one.* **2** used for emphasis: *One can do it oneself.* **3** one's normal self: *One can hardly be feeling oneself after an operation.*

one-sided adj. **1** of a competition with one side having an advantage over the other. **2** seeing, representing, or favoring only one side of a subject; unfair.

onetime adj. having been such previously.

one-to-one adj. in which a person is involved with only one other person.

one-track mind colloq. a mental state that is marked by an obsession with one activity or idea.

one-upmanship noun colloq. the art of gaining social or professional advantages over other people.

one-way adj. **1** of a street being one on which traffic can move only in one direction. **2** of a ticket valid for travel in one direction only, not back again.

one-woman adj. done by one woman.

ongoing adj. in progress; continuing.

onion noun **1** a plant with an edible bulb consisting of white fleshy scales, surrounded by a brown papery outer layer. **2** the bulb of this plant, eaten as a vegetable.

on-line adj., adv. connected to or available through a computer or telecommunications network. See also **off-line.**

on-load verb trans. (**on-loaded, on-loading**) to place (e.g., cargo) on board a vehicle or aircraft.

onlooker noun a person who watches and does not take part.

only adj. **1** without any others of the same type. **2** having no siblings. **3** colloq. best: Flying is the only way to travel. —adv. **1** not more than; just. **2** alone; solely. **3** not longer ago than: only a minute ago. **4** merely: I arrived only to find that they had already left. —conj. **1** but; however: Come if you want to, only don't complain if you're bored. **2** if it were not for the fact that: I'd come with you on the boat only I know I'd be sick. —**if only** I wish. **only too** very; extremely.

onomatopoeia (än,ɔ-mät,ɔ-pē'ɔ, -mät,-) noun the formation or use of a word that imitates the sound or action represented. ▸ **onomatopoeic** adj.

onrush noun a sudden, strong movement forward.

on-screen or **onscreen** adj., adv. relating to information displayed on a television or computer screen.

onset noun **1** a beginning, esp. of something unpleasant. **2** an attack.

onshore adj., adv. **1** of the wind blowing toward the shore. **2** situated in or on the shore.

onside adj., adv. in a position where a ball or puck may legally be played.

onslaught noun a fierce attack.

on-stage adj., adv. on the stage and able to be seen by the audience.

on-stream adj. adv. in operation or ready to go into operation.

on-the-record adj., adv. delivered with the understanding that the one imparting the information may be named or quoted.

onto prep. to a position upon.

ontogeny (än-täj'ɔ-nē) noun the history of the development of a living organism, from fertilization of the ovum to sexual maturity.

ontology noun the branch of philosophy that deals with the nature of being. ▸ **ontological** adj.

onus noun (pl. **onuses**) a responsibility or burden.

onward adj. moving forward in place or time. —adv. (also **onwards**) **1** toward or at a place or time which is advanced or in front. **2** forward.

onyx noun a very hard variety of agate with alternating bands of colors.

oodles pl. noun colloq. lots.

ooh interj. used to express pleasure, surprise, or excitement.

oomph noun slang **1** energy; enthusiasm. **2** personal attractiveness, esp. sex appeal.

oops interj. slang used to express surprise or apology when a person makes a mistake, etc.

ooze[1] noun **1** on the ocean floor, a deposit of fine organic sediments. **2** soft, marshy ground.

ooze[2] verb intrans., trans. (**oozed, oozing**) **1** to flow or leak out gently or slowly. **2** to give out moisture. **3** to give out (a liquid, etc.) slowly. **4** to overflow with (a quality or feeling). —noun something that oozes, e.g., wet mud or pus.

oozy adj. (**oozier, ooziest**) like ooze; slimy.

op noun colloq. a surgical or military operation.

opacity (ō-păs'ɔt-ē) noun the state of being difficult to understand.

opal noun a milky-white form of silica with iridescent reflections.

opalescent adj. reflecting different colors as the surrounding light changes. ▸ **opalescence** noun

opaque (ō-pāk') adj. **1** allowing little or no light to pass through. **2** difficult to understand.

Op Art (äp') a modern art movement that exploits the illusions created by abstract compositions of spirals, grids, etc.

op. cit. abbrev. opere citato (Latin), in the work already quoted.

OPEC (ō'pěk,) abbrev. Organization of Petroleum Exporting Countries.

open adj. **1** allowing things or people to go in or out; not closed. **2** of a container having no seal. **3** not enclosed, confined, or restricted. **4** not covered, guarded, or protected. **5** spread out or unfolded. **6** receiving customers; ready for business. **7** generally known; public. **8** able to be attacked or questioned: *open to criticism.* **9** allowing anyone to compete or take part, esp. both amateurs and professionals. **10** free from restraint or restrictions. **11** still being discussed. **12** ready to consider new ideas: *an open mind.* **13** ready and willing to talk honestly. **14** having many small gaps: *an open weave.* —*verb trans., intrans.* (**opened, opening**) **1** to make or become open. **2** to unfasten or become unfastened to allow access. **3** (*also* **open out** *or* **open** (**something**) **out**) to spread out or be spread out or unfolded. **4** to start or begin working. **5** to declare open with an official ceremony. **6** to begin or start speaking, writing, etc. **7** (**open into** *or* **onto** (**something**)) to provide access to (it). **8** to arrange (a bank account), usu. by making an initial deposit. **9** to make a preliminary statement about a case before beginning to call witnesses. —*noun* **1** (**the open**) an area of open country. **2** (**the open**) public notice or attention. **3** (**Open**) a sports contest in which both amateurs and professionals may enter. —**open and above board** thoroughly honest or legal. **open out** *or* **up** to begin to reveal one's feelings and thoughts or to behave with less restraint. **open up 1** to open a door. **2** to start firing weapons. **3** *of a game, etc.* to become more interesting as it develops. **open** (**something**) **up 1** to make (it) more accessible or available. **2** to increase the speed of (an engine, vehicle, etc.). **open up** (**one's**) **thoughts, mind,** *etc.,* **to** (**someone**) to reveal (one's feelings, etc.). ▸ **openness** *noun*

open admissions (*sing., pl.*) a college policy that allows student enrollment regardless of academic qualifications. *Also called* **open enrollment.**

open air unenclosed space outdoors. ▸ **open-air** *adj.*

open-and-shut *adj.* easily proved or solved.

open book a person who keeps no secrets.

open-ended *adj.* having no limits or restrictions, e.g., of time, set in advance.

open enrollment open admissions.

opener *noun* **1** a device for opening something. **2** the first item on a program. —**for openers** *colloq.* to start with.

openhanded *adj.* generous.

open-heart surgery surgery performed on a heart that has been stopped and opened up while the blood circulation is maintained by a heart-lung machine.

open house a social event in which a residence is open to invited guests for a certain period of time, refreshments being served.

opening *noun* **1** a hole; a gap. **2** the act of making or becoming open. **3** a beginning. **4** the first performance, e.g., of a play. **5** an opportunity or chance. —*adj.* of, relating to, or forming an opening; first.

open letter a letter, esp. one of protest, addressed to a person or organization, etc., but intended also for publication in a newspaper or magazine.

openly *adv.* in a direct and honest manner.

open market a market in which buyers and sellers are allowed to compete freely without restriction.

open-minded *adj.* willing to consider or receive new ideas. ▸ **open-mindedness** *noun*

open-plan *adj.* having few internal walls and large, undivided rooms.

open shop a firm that does not oblige its employees to belong to a labor union. *See also* **union shop.**

openwork *noun* work in cloth, wood, etc., so constructed as to have gaps or holes in it, for decoration.

opera[1] (äp′rə, äp′ə-rə) *noun* **1** a dramatic work set to music, in which the singers are usu. accompanied by an orchestra. **2** such work considered as an art form. **3** a theater where such works are performed. **4** a company that performs such works. ▸ **operatic** (äp,ə-rät′ĭk) *adj.*

opera[2] *see* **opus.**

operable (äp′rə-bəl, äp′ə-rə-) *adj.* **1** that can be treated by surgery. **2** that can be put into effective operation.

opera glasses small binoculars used at the theater or opera.

opera house a theater specially built for the performance of operas.

operate (äp′ə-rāt,) *verb trans., intrans.* (**operated, operating**) **1** to cause to function or work, or to function. **2** to produce an effect or have an influence. **3** to manage or direct (e.g., a business). **4** (**operate on** (**someone** *or* **something**)) to treat (a patient) with surgery.

operating room (ABBREV. **OR**) the specially equipped room, e.g., in a hospital, where surgical operations are performed.

operating system (ABBREV. **OS**) a group of programs that control all the main activities of a computer.

operating table a special table on which surgery is performed.

operation *noun* **1** an act or process of working or operating. **2** the state of working or being active: *The factory is not yet in operation.* **3** an activity: *the operation of moving a family from coast to coast.* **4** a surgical procedure performed in order to treat a damaged or diseased part of the body. **5** (*often* **operations**) one of a series of military, naval, etc., actions performed as part of a much larger plan. **6** *Math.* a specific procedure, such as addition or multiplication, whereby one numerical value is derived from another value. **7** a series of actions that are specified by a single computer instruction. ▸ **operational** adj. ▸ **operationally** adv.

operative (ăp'rət-ĭv, ăp'ə-rāt'ĭv) adj. **1** in action; working. **2** of a word especially important or significant. **3** of or relating to a surgical operation. —noun **1** a worker, esp. one with special skills. **2** a private detective.

operator noun **1** a person who operates a machine or apparatus. **2** a person who operates a telephone switchboard. **3** a person who runs a business. **4** a symbol used to indicate that a particular mathematical operation is to be carried out. **5** colloq. a calculating, manipulative person.

operetta noun a short opera whose subject matter is not serious. Also called **light opera.**

ophthalmic adj. of or relating to the eye.

ophthalmology (ăf,thə-măl'ə-jē, ăp,-) noun the branch of medicine that is concerned with the study of diseases and defects of the eye. ▸ **ophthalmologist** noun

ophthalmoscope (ăf-thăl'mə-skōp,) noun an instrument that is used to examine the interior of the eye.

opiate (ō'pē-ət) noun **1** any of a group of drugs containing or derived from opium, used medicinally to relieve severe pain. **2** something that dulls physical or mental sensation.

opine verb trans. (**opined, opining**) to suppose or express as an opinion.

opinion noun **1** something that is accepted by a person as true. **2** a professional judgment given by an expert: medical opinion. **3** estimation or appreciation. —a matter of opinion a matter about which people have different opinions. **be of the opinion that** to think or believe that.

opinionated adj. having very strong opinions that one stubbornly refuses to change.

opinion poll a test of public opinion made by questioning a representative sample of the population. Also called **poll.**

opium noun **1** a highly addictive narcotic drug derived from a poppy. **2** something that has a soothing or dulling effect on people's minds.

opossum noun (pl. **opossum, opossums**) a nocturnal marsupial with thick fur and a grasping prehensile tail.

opponent noun a person who belongs to the opposing side in an argument, battle, etc.

opportune adj. **1** happening at a time that is suitable or correct. **2** of a time suitable.

opportunism noun the practice of regulating actions by favorable opportunities rather than by consistent principles. ▸ **opportunist** noun

opportunistic adj. **1** characterized or deter-

mined by opportunism. **2** of an infection not affecting healthy people but attacking those whose immune systems are weak.

opportunity noun (pl. **opportunities**) an occasion offering a possibility; a chance.

oppose verb trans., intrans. (**opposed, opposing**) **1** to resist or fight against by force or argument. **2** to object. **3** to compete in a game, etc., against another person or team. **4** to place opposite or in contrast to. —as opposed to in contrast to; as distinct from. ▸ **opposing** adj.

opposite adj. **1** being on the other side of or at the other end of a line or space. **2** facing in a directly different direction. **3** completely or diametrically different. **4** of leaves, etc. arranged in pairs on a stem, so that the two members of a pair are exactly opposite each other. —noun an opposite person or thing. —adv. in or into an opposite position. —prep. **1** across from and facing. **2** of an actor in a role that complements that taken by another actor: played opposite Olivier.

opposite number a person with an equivalent position or job, e.g., in another company.

opposition noun **1** the act of resisting or fighting against someone or something by force or argument. **2** the state of being hostile or in conflict. **3** a person or group of people who are opposed to something. **4** (**Opposition**) a political party that opposes the party in power. **5** an act of opposing or being placed opposite.

oppress verb trans. (**oppressed, oppressing**) **1** to govern with cruelty and injustice. **2** to worry, trouble, or make anxious. ▸ **oppression** noun ▸ **oppressor** noun

oppressive adj. **1** cruel, tyrannical, and unjust. **2** causing worry or mental distress. **3** hot and sultry. ▸ **oppressively** adv.

opprobrium noun loss of respect or favor.

oppugn (ə-pyōon') verb trans. (**oppugned, oppugning**) to call into question; to dispute.

ops pl. noun Mil. operations.

opt verb intrans. (**opted, opting**) (**opt for (something)**) to decide between (several possibilities). —opt out of (something) to choose not to take part in (something).

optic adj. of or concerning the eye or vision.

optical adj. **1** of or concerning sight or what one sees. **2** of or concerning light or optics. **3** of a lens designed to help visual acuity.

optical character reader (ABBREV. OCR) a device used in optical character recognition.

optical character recognition (ABBREV. OCR) the process whereby printed characters are optically scanned and identified by means of a photoelectric device attached to a computer.

optical fiber a thin, flexible strand of glass or plastic that transmits light, used, e.g., for transmitting computer data. *See also* **fiber optics.**

optical illusion a thing which has an appearance that deceives the eye.

optician (ăp-tĭsh'ən) *noun* a person who fits and sells glasses and contact lenses.

optics *noun* (*sing.*) the branch of physics that is concerned with the study of light.

optimal *adj.* being the best or most favorable.

optimism *noun* 1 a tendency to take a hopeful view and expect the best possible outcome. 2 the theory that good will ultimately triumph over evil. ▸ **optimist** *noun* ▸ **optimistic** *adj.* ▸ **optimistically** *adv.*

optimize *verb trans.* (**optimized, optimizing**) to make the most efficient use of.

optimum *noun* (*pl.* **optima, optimums**) the most favorable condition or situation. —*adj.* being the best or most favorable.

option *noun* 1 something that is or may be chosen. 2 the right or opportunity to choose. 3 the exclusive right to buy or sell something at a fixed price and within a specified time limit. —**keep** *or* **leave** (**one's**) **options open** to avoid making a choice or committing (oneself) to a particular course of action. ▸ **optional** *adj.*

optometrist (ăp-tăm'ə-trĭst) *noun* a person who is licensed and qualified to examine the eyes and to prescribe glasses and contact lenses.

opulent *adj.* 1 rich; wealthy. 2 luxurious. 3 abundant. ▸ **opulence** *noun*

opus *noun* (*pl.* **opera, opuses**) an artistic work, esp. a musical composition.

OR *abbrev.* operating room.

or *conj.* used to introduce 1 alternatives: *red or pink*. 2 a synonym or explanation: *a puppy or young dog*. 3 an afterthought: *She's laughing, or is she crying?* 4 the second part of an indirect question: *Ask her whether she thinks he'll come or not.* 5 because if not; or else: *Run or you'll be late!* 6 and not: *never joins in or helps.* —**or else** 1 otherwise. 2 *colloq.* expressing a threat or warning: *Give it to me now, or else!* **or rather** or to be more accurate. **or so** roughly: *We had been there two hours or so.*

-or *suffix* forming words denoting a person or thing that performs an action or function: *actor / elevator.*

oracle (ôr'ə-kəl) *noun* 1 a a holy place in ancient Greece or Rome where a god was believed to give advice and prophecy. b a priest or priestess at an oracle, through whom the god was believed to speak. c the advice or prophecy given at an oracle. 2 a person who is believed to have great wisdom. ▸ **oracular** (ə-răk'yə-lər) *adj.*

oral *adj.* 1 spoken, not written. 2 of, relating to, or located in the mouth. 3 *of a medicine* taken by mouth. —*noun* a spoken test or examination. ▸ **orally** *adv.*

> *Usage* **Oral** is often confused with *aural*, which refers to the ear and hearing.

orange *noun* 1 a round citrus fruit with a tough reddish-yellow outer rind enclosing sweet or sharp-tasting juicy flesh. 2 the evergreen tree that bears this fruit. 3 the reddish-yellow color of this fruit. 4 an orange-flavored drink. —*adj.* 1 of the reddish-yellow color of an orange. 2 orange-flavored.

orangeade *noun* an orange-flavored drink, typically carbonated.

Orangeman *noun* (*pl.* **Orangemen**) a member of a society founded in 1795 to support Protestantism in Ireland.

orangutan *or* **orangoutang** (ə-răng'ə-tăn, -tăng) *noun* a great ape, found in tropical forests in Borneo and Sumatra, with long reddish hair.

> Based on a Malay phrase which translates as 'wild man'

oration *noun* a formal public speech.

orator (ôr'ət-ər, är'-) *noun* a person who is skilled in persuading or exciting people through public speech.

oratorical *adj.* 1 of or relating to an orator. 2 resembling oratory, esp. in using rhetoric.

oratorio *noun* (*pl.* **oratorios**) a theme or story, usu. on a religious topic, set to music and sung by soloists and a chorus accompanied by an orchestra.

oratory (ôr'ə-tôr,ē) *noun* (*pl.* **oratories**) 1 the art of speaking well in public, esp. using elegant rhetorical devices. 2 a small place or chapel for private prayer.

orb *noun* 1 a globe decorated with jewels, carried by the monarch during important ceremonies. 2 an object in the shape of a globe. 3 *poetic* a star, the Sun, or a planet. 4 an eyeball.

orbit *noun* 1 the path of one celestial body around another or the path of an artificial satellite around a celestial body. 2 a sphere of influence. 3 one of the two bony hollows in which the eyeball is situated. —*verb intrans., trans.* (**orbited, orbiting**) to follow an orbital path around (an object). ▸ **orbital** *adj.*

orchard *noun* a piece of land or garden where fruit trees are grown.

orchestra (ôr'kə-strə, -kĕs,trə) *noun* a usu. large group of musicians who play a variety of different instruments. ▸ **orchestral** (ôr-kĕs'trəl) *adj.*

orchestra pit pit¹ (sense 4).

orchestrate (ôr'kə-strāt,) *verb trans.* (**orchestrated, orchestrating**) 1 to arrange or compose (a piece of music) for an orchestra.

2 to organize or arrange (something) so as to get the desired best result. ▸ **orchestration** *noun* ▸ **orchestrator** *noun*

orchid (ôr′kĭd) *noun* a plant that bears complex and exotic flowers.

ordain *verb trans.* (**ordained, ordaining**) 1 to make (someone) a priest, minister, etc. 2 to order or command formally.

ordeal *noun* a difficult, painful, or testing experience.

order *noun* 1 a state in which everything is in its proper place; tidiness. 2 an arrangement of objects according to importance, value, etc. 3 a command, instruction, or direction. 4 a state of peace and harmony in society. 5 the condition of being able to function properly: *out of order.* 6 a an instruction to a manufacturer, supplier, etc., to provide something. b the goods, food, etc., supplied. 7 an established system of society: *a new world order.* 8 a category in the classification of animals and plants which is below a class and above a family. 9 the usual procedure followed at official meetings and during debates: *a point of order.* 10 a (**Order**) a religious community living according to a particular rule and bound by vows. *Also called* **Religious Order.** b (**orders**) holy orders. 11 (**Order**) a group of people to which new members are admitted as a mark of honor or reward. —*verb trans., intrans.* (**ordered, ordering**) 1 to give a command (to). 2 a to instruct a manufacturer, supplier, or waiter to supply or provide (something). b to give a command, request, or order, esp. to a waiter for food. 3 to arrange or regulate: *order one's affairs.* —*interj.* (**Order! Order!**) a call for quiet, calm, proper behavior to be restored, esp. during a debate. —**in order** 1 in accordance with the rules; properly arranged. 2 suitable or appropriate. 3 in the correct sequence. **in the order of** approximately (the number stated). **in order that** so that. **in order to** so as to be able to. **order (someone) around** *or* **about** to give (someone) orders continually and officiously. **order (someone) off** to order (a player) to leave the field because of illegal behavior. **out of order** not correct, proper, or suitable. ▸ **ordered** *adj.*

orderly *adj.* 1 in good order; nicely arranged. 2 properly behaved; quiet. —*noun* (*pl.* **orderlies**) 1 an attendant, usu. without medical training, who does various jobs in a hospital. 2 a soldier who performs various clerical or personal tasks for an officer. ▸ **orderliness** *noun*

ordinal (ôrd′n-əl) *noun* an ordinal number. —*adj.* denoting a position in a sequence.

ordinal number a number expressing position, or order, in a sequence, such as *first, second,* or *third.* See also **cardinal number**.

ordinance *noun* a law, order, or ruling.

ordinary *adj.* 1 usual; normal. 2 lacking any strongly noticeable characteristics. —**out of the ordinary** unusual; strange. ▸ **ordinarily** *adv.*

ordination *noun* the act or ceremony of ordaining a priest or minister.

ordnance *noun* 1 heavy guns and military ammunition, etc. 2 (**Ordnance**) the branch of the US Army responsible for storage, maintenance, etc., of heavy weapons and the equipment associated with them.

ordure (ôr′jər) *noun* waste matter from the bowels; excrement.

ore *noun* a solid mineral deposit from which one or more metals can be extracted.

oregano (ə-rĕg′ə-nō,) *noun* the dried aromatic leaves of a variety of wild marjoram, used as a culinary herb.

organ *noun* 1 a part of a body or plant that has a special function. 2 a a large musical instrument with a keyboard and pedals, in which sound is produced by air being forced through pipes. b any similar instrument without pipes, such as one producing sound electronically. 3 a means of spreading information, such as a newspaper. 4 the penis. ▸ **organist** *noun*

organdy *or* **organdie** (ôr′gən-dē) *noun* a very fine cotton fabric that has been stiffened.

organic *adj.* 1 relating to an organ of the body. 2 relating to living organisms. 3 relating to farming practices that avoid the use of chemical fertilizers, pesticides, etc., or to crops so produced. 4 being an inherent or natural part. 5 systematically organized. 6 relating to the branch of chemistry concerned with compounds that contain carbon, or relating to such compounds. ▸ **organically** *adv.*

organism *noun* 1 a living structure, such as a plant or animal, capable of growth and reproduction. 2 an establishment, system, or whole made up of parts that depend upon each other.

organization *noun* 1 a group of people formed into a society, union, or esp. business. 2 the act of organizing or the state of being organized. ▸ **organizational** *adj.*

organize *verb trans., intrans.* (**organized, organizing**) 1 to give an orderly structure to. 2 to arrange, provide, or prepare. 3 a to form or enroll (people) into a labor union. b to form a labor union.

organizer *noun* 1 someone or something that organizes. 2 a small bag or wallet, or a file case for personal notes and information; an electronic device that serves a similar function.

organza (ôr-găn′zə) *noun* a very fine dress material made of silk or synthetic fibers.

orgasm *noun* the climax of sexual excitement, experienced as an intense, extremely pleasurable, sensation. ▸ **orgasmic** *adj.*

orgy (ôr′jē) *noun* (*pl.* **orgies**) 1 a wild party involving excessive drinking and unrestrained sexual activity. 2 an act of excessive indulgence. ▸ **orgiastic** *adj.*

oriel (ôr′ē-əl) *noun* a window projecting from the wall of a house, usu. at an upper story.

orient *noun* (ôr′ē-ənt, -ĕnt,) (**the Orient**) the countries in the east, esp. those of E Asia. —*verb trans.* (ôr′ē-ĕnt,) (**oriented, orienting**) 1 to place in a definite position in relation to the points of the compass or another fixed point. 2 to acquaint (oneself or someone) with the position relative to points known, or with details of a situation. ▸ **oriental** (ôr,ē-ĕnt′l) *adj., noun*

> *Usage* See note at *Asian.*

orientation *noun* 1 the act or an instance of orienting or of being oriented. 2 a position relative to a fixed point. 3 a person's position or attitude relative to his or her situation. 4 a meeting giving information or training needed for a new situation. ▸ **orientate** (ôr′ē-ən-tāt,) *verb trans., intrans.*

oriented *adj.* interested in something.

orienteering *noun* a sport in which contestants race over an unfamiliar cross-country course.

orifice (ôr′ə-fĭs) *noun* an opening, esp. in the body.

origami (ôr′ĭ-gäm′ē) *noun* the orig. Japanese art of folding paper into shapes.

origin *noun* 1 a beginning or starting point. 2 (**origins**) a person's family background or ancestors.

original *adj.* 1 existing from the beginning; first. 2 of an idea fresh or new. 3 of a person creative or inventive. 4 being the first form from which copies or reproductions are made. —*noun* 1 the first example of something that is copied or reproduced. 2 a model from which a painting, etc., is made. 3 an odd or eccentric person. ▸ **originality** *noun* ▸ **originally** *adv.*

originate *verb trans., intrans.* (**originated, originating**) to bring or come into being; to start. ▸ **origination** *noun* ▸ **originator** *noun*

oriole (ôr′ē-əl, -ōl,) *noun* a brightly colored songbird.

ormolu *noun* a gold-colored alloy, used to decorate furniture and to make ornaments.

ornament *noun* 1 something that decorates or adds beauty. 2 a small decorative object. 3 a person whose talents add honor to the group to which he or she belongs. —*verb trans.* (**ornamented, ornamenting**) to provide

with decorations.. ▸ **ornamental** *adj.* ▸ **ornamentation** *noun*

ornate (ôr-nāt′) *adj.* 1 highly decorated. 2 using many elaborate literary words or expressions. ▸ **ornately** *adv.*

ornery *adj.* (**ornerier, orneriest**) *colloq.* mean, stubborn, and difficult to deal with.

ornithology *noun* the scientific study of birds. ▸ **ornithological** *adj.* ▸ **ornithologist** *noun*

orogeny (ô-răj′ə-nē) *or* **orogenesis** *noun* the process of mountain building.

orotund *adj.* 1 of the voice full, loud, and grand. 2 of speaking self-important; pompous. ▸ **orotundity** *noun*

orphan *noun* a child who has lost both parents. —*verb trans.* (**orphaned, orphaning**) to cause to become an orphan.

orphanage (ôr′fə-nĭj) *noun* a home for orphans.

orrery (ôr′ə-rē) *noun* (*pl.* **orreries**) a clockwork model of the Sun and the planets that revolve around it.

orris *noun* an iris with white flowers and fragrant fleshy rhizomes, which are used in perfume.

ortho- *combining form* forming words denoting correct, straight, upright: *orthodontics.*

orthodontics *noun* (*sing.*) the branch of dentistry that is concerned with the correction of irregularities in the alignment of the teeth. ▸ **orthodontist** *noun*

orthodox *adj.* 1 believing in or conforming with established or generally accepted opinions; conventional. 2 (**Orthodox**) of, relating to, or being a member of an Orthodox church. 3 (**Orthodox**) of, relating to, or adhering to the doctrines of the branch of Judaism that keeps to strict, traditional interpretations of scripture. ▸ **orthodoxy** *noun*

Orthodox Church the Eastern Orthodox Church.

orthogonal (ôr-thăg′ən-l) *adj.* right-angled; perpendicular.

orthography *noun* (*pl.* **orthographies**) correct or standard spelling. ▸ **orthographic** *or* **orthographical** *adj.*

orthopedics (ôr,thə-pēd′ĭks) *noun* (*sing.*) the branch of medicine that is concerned with the treatment of conditions and disorders arising from injury or disease of the bones and joints. ▸ **orthopedic** *adj.* ▸ **orthopedist** *noun*

ortolan (ôrt′l-ən) *noun* 1 a small bunting, native to Europe, Asia, and N Africa. 2 any one of several New World birds, e.g., the bobolink.

-ory[1] *suffix* forming nouns denoting a place for a specified activity: *dormitory.*

-ory[2] *suffix* forming adjectives and occasionally nouns with the sense of relating to or involving the action of the verb: *depository.*

oryx *noun* a grazing antelope with very long, slender horns.

OS *abbrev.* operating system.

Os *symbol Chem.* osmium.

Oscar (ăs'kər) *noun* each of a number of golden statuettes awarded annually by the American Academy of Motion Picture Arts and Sciences for outstanding acting, directing, etc., in films during the previous year. *Also called* **Academy Award.**

oscillate (ăs'ə-lāt,) *verb trans., intrans.* **(oscillated, oscillating) 1** to cause to swing or to swing backward and forward in the manner of a pendulum. **2** to vary between opinions, choices, etc. ▸ **oscillation** *noun* ▸ **oscillator** *noun*

From Latin *oscillum*, literally 'small face', a mask of the god Bacchus which hung in Roman vineyards and swayed in the wind

oscilloscope (ă-sĭl'ə-skōp,) *noun* an instrument that measures the rapidly changing values of an electric current and displays the varying electrical signals graphically on the fluorescent screen of a cathode-ray tube. *Also called* **cathode-ray oscilloscope.**

osier *noun* a willow tree whose stems are used to make baskets, etc.

-osis *suffix (pl.* **-oses)** forming nouns denoting **1** a condition or process: *hypnosis.* **2** a diseased or disordered state: *neurosis.*

osmium *noun* (SYMBOL Os) a dense, very hard, bluish-white metallic element used as a hardening agent in alloys with platinum, etc.

osmosis *noun (pl.* **osmoses) 1** the gradual passing of liquid through a membrane, sometimes so as to make the concentration of the solution on either side of the membrane equal. **2** a gradual process of absorption.

osprey (ăs'prē, -prā,) *noun (pl.* **ospreys)** a large bird of prey that feeds on fish.

OSS *abbrev.* Office of Strategic Services.

osseous *adj.* of, resembling, or formed from bone.

ossify *verb intrans., trans.* **(ossified, ossifying, ossifies)** to turn into or cause to turn into bone. ▸ **ossification** *noun*

ossuary (ăsh'ə-wĕr,ē) *noun (pl.* **ossuaries)** an oven or an urn for keeping the bones of a dead person.

ostensible *adj.* stated or claimed, but not necessarily true. ▸ **ostensibly** *adv.*

ostentation *noun* pretentious display of wealth, knowledge, etc. ▸ **ostentatious** *adj.* ▸ **ostentatiously** *adv.*

osteoarthritis *noun* a form of arthritis in which degeneration of the cartilage overlying the bones at a joint leads to stiffness, swelling, and eventually deformity of the affected joint.

osteopathy *noun* a system of medicine involving manipulation of the bones and joints, etc. ▸ **osteopath** *noun*

osteoporosis *noun* a disease in which the bones become porous, brittle, and liable to fracture, owing to the loss of calcium from the bone substance.

ostracism *noun* social exclusion. ▸ **ostracize** *verb trans.*

Based on *ostrakon*, a piece of pottery used in ancient Greece to cast votes to decide if someone was to be exiled

ostrich *noun* the largest living bird, which is incapable of flight and is found in E Africa.

OT *or* **O.T.** *abbrev.* Old Testament.

OTB *abbrev.* off-track betting.

other *adj.* **1** remaining from a group of two or more when one or some have been specified already. **2** different from the one or ones already mentioned or implied. **3** additional; further. **4** far or opposite. —*pron.* another person or thing. —*adv. colloq.* otherwise; differently. —**every** each alternate. **other than** except for; apart from. **the other day, week,** *etc.* a few days, weeks, etc., ago.

otherwise *conj.* or else; if not. —*adv.* **1** in other respects. **2** in a different way. **3** under different circumstances. —**or otherwise** or the opposite; or not.

otherworldly *adj.* concerned with spiritual or intellectual matters.

otic *adj.* of or relating to the ear.

otiose *adj.* **1** serving no purpose; useless. **2** lazy.

otitis *noun* inflammation of the ear.

OTS *or* **O.T.S.** *abbrev.* Officers' Training School.

otter *noun* an aquatic mammal with a long body, short legs, and a stout tail.

Ottoman (ăt'ə-mən) *noun (pl.* **Ottomans) 1** an inhabitant of the Ottoman Empire; a Turk. **2** (**ottoman**) a long, low, upholstered seat without a back or arms.

oubliette (ōō,blē-ĕt') *noun* a secret dungeon with a single opening at the top.

ouch *interj.* used to express sudden sharp pain.

ought *verb aux.* used to express **1** duty or obligation. **2** advisability. **3** probability or expectation. **4** shortcoming or failure. —**ought not (to)** used to express moral disapproval.

Ouija (wē'jə, -jē) *trademark* used for a board with a pointer that spells out alleged messages from spirits.

ounce[1] *noun* **1** (ABBREV. **oz.**) a unit of avoirdupois weight equal to one sixteenth of a pound (28.36 g). **2** a unit of weight equal to one twelfth of the pound troy, equal to 480 grains. **3** a fluid ounce.

ounce² *noun* the snow leopard.

our *adj.* 1 of, belonging to, or associated with us. 2 *formal* used by a sovereign to mean my.

Our Lady the Virgin Mary.

ours *pron.* the one or ones belonging to us. —**of ours** of or belonging to us.

ourselves *pron.* 1 the reflexive form of *we.* 2 used for emphasis: *We did it ourselves.* 3 our normal selves: *We can relax and be ourselves.* 4 without help; alone.

-ous *suffix* forming adjectives denoting 1 having a particular quality or nature: *venomous.* 2 *Chem.* formed with an element in its lower valence: *ferrous.*

oust *verb trans.* (**ousted, ousting**) to force (someone) out of a position and take that person's place.

out *adv., adj.* 1 away from the inside; not in or at a place. 2 not in one's home or place of work. 3 to or at an end. 4 aloud. 5 with, or taking, care. 6 in all directions from a central point. 7 to the fullest extent or amount. 8 to public attention or notice; revealed. 9 a *of a person batting* no longer able to bat, e.g., because of having the ball caught by an opponent. b *Baseball* having been counted out of the game. 10 in or into a state of being removed, omitted, or forgotten. 11 not to be considered; rejected. 12 having been removed; dislocated. 13 not in authority; not having political power. 14 into unconsciousness: *passed out.* 15 in error: *Your total is out by three.* 16 in bloom. 17 just published. 18 visible: *The moon is out.* 19 no longer in fashion. 20 on strike. 21 of a jury considering its verdict. 22 of a young woman introduced into fashionable society as a debutante. 23 of a tide at or to the lowest level of water. —*noun* a way out; an excuse: *couldn't find an easy out.* —*verb intrans., trans.* (**outed, outing**) 1 to become publicly known: *Murder will out.* 2 to make public the homosexuality of (a famous person who has been attempting to keep his or her homosexuality secret). —**out of date** old-fashioned and no longer of use; obsolete. **out of doors** in or into the open. **out of it** *slang* 1 not part of a group, activity, etc. 2 unable to behave normally or control oneself, usu. because of alcohol or drugs. **out of pocket** having spent more money than one can afford. **out of (something)** 1 from inside (it). 2 not in or within (it). 3 having exhausted a supply of (it). 4 from among several: *two out of three.* 5 from a material. 6 because of (it): *did it out of anger.* 7 beyond the scope or bounds of (it). 8 excluded from (it). 9 no longer in a stated condition: *out of practice.* **out of the way** 1 difficult to reach or arrive at. 2 unusual; uncommon. **out to lunch** *slang, of*

a *person* slightly crazy; in a dream world.

out- *combining form* forming words denoting 1 external; separate; from outside: *outpatient.* 2 away from the inside, esp. as a result: *output.* 3 going away or out of; outward: *outboard.* 4 so as to excel or surpass: *outrun.*

outage (owt'ïj) *noun* a period of time during which a power supply fails.

out-and-out *adj.* devoid of any qualification.

outback *noun* isolated, remote areas of a country, esp. Australia.

outbalance *verb trans.* (**outbalanced, outbalancing**) to weigh more than or be more important than.

outbid *verb trans.* (pa t **outbid**; pa p **outbidden** or **outbid**; pr p **outbidding**) to offer a higher price than (someone else), esp. at an auction.

outboard *adj.* of a motor or engine situated outside the hull or interior of a boat, ship, or aircraft. See also **inboard.**

outbound *adj.,* of a vehicle, flight, etc. going away from its destination; departing.

outbreak *noun* a sudden beginning or occurrence, usu. of something unpleasant.

outbuilding *noun* a building such as a barn or stable that is separate from a main house but within its grounds.

outburst *noun* a sudden violent expression of strong emotion.

outcast *noun* a person who is avoided. ⊟ ISHMAEL, LEPER, PARIAH, UNTOUCHABLE.

outclass *verb trans.* to be much better than.

outcome *noun* a result; a consequence.

outcrop *noun* a rock that sticks out above the surface of the ground.

outcry *noun* (pl. **outcries**) a widespread public show of anger or objection.

outdated *adj.* no longer useful or in fashion.

outdistance *verb trans.* (**outdistanced, outdistancing**) to leave (a competitor) far behind.

outdo *verb* to do much better than.

outdoor *adj.* done, taking place, etc., in the open air.

outdoors *adv.* in or into the open air. —*noun* (sing.) the open air.

outer *adj.* 1 belonging to or for the outside. 2 farther from the center or middle.

outermost *adj.* farthest from the center.

outer space space (sense 5).

outerwear *noun* garments for wear out of doors.

outface *verb trans.* 1 to stare at (someone) until he or she looks away. 2 to fight or deal with (someone) bravely.

outfield *noun Baseball* 1 the area of the playing field beyond the diamond where the bases are laid out. 2 the defensive positions played by team members assigned to this area. *See also* **infield** (sense 1).

outfit *noun* 1 a set of clothes worn together, esp. for a particular occasion. 2 a set of tools, equipment, etc., for a particular task. 3 *colloq.* a group of people working as a team. —*verb trans.* (**outfitted, outfitting**) to provide with an outfit, esp. clothes.

outflank *verb trans.* to go around the side of (an enemy's) position and attack from behind.

outfox *verb trans.* to get the better of (someone else) by being more cunning.

outgoing *adj.* 1 friendly and sociable. 2 leaving, e.g., an office or a job.

outgrow *verb trans.* 1 to grow too large for (one's clothes). 2 to become too old for (children's games, etc.). 3 to grow larger or faster than (something).

outgrowth *noun* 1 a natural product. 2 something that grows out of something else.

outhouse (owt'hows,) *noun* 1 a small structure enclosing an outdoor toilet. 2 a small building, such as a shed, built close to a house.

outing *noun* a short pleasure trip.

outlandish *adj.* very strange; odd.

outlast *verb trans.* to last or live longer than (another or others).

outlaw *noun* a criminal who is a fugitive from the law. —*verb trans.* (**outlawed, outlawing**) 1 to make (someone) an outlaw. 2 to debar from doing.

outlay *noun* money, or occasionally time, spent on something.

outlet *noun* 1 a way or passage out, esp. for water or steam. 2 a way of releasing or using energy, talents, etc. 3 a market for a store that sells the goods produced by a particular manufacturer.

outline *noun* 1 a line forming or marking the outer edge of an object. 2 a drawing with only the outer lines and no shading. 3 the main points, etc., without the details. 4 (*usu.* **outlines**) the most important features. —*verb trans.* (**outlined, outlining**) 1 to draw the outline of. 2 to give a brief description of the main features of.

outlive *verb trans.* to live or survive longer than (another).

outlook *noun* 1 a view from a particular place. 2 a person's mental attitude. 3 a prospect for the future.

outlying *adj.* away from, e.g., a city.

outmaneuver *verb trans.* to gain an advantage over by more skillful maneuvering.

outmoded *adj.* no longer in fashion.

outnumber *verb trans.* to be more in number than (others).

out-of-state *adj.* from another US state.

outpace *verb trans.* to move or progress faster than.

outpatient *noun* a patient who receives treatment at a hospital but does not stay there overnight.

outplacement *noun* the processes involved in helping a laid-off employee find another job, paid for by the former employing company.

outplay *verb trans.* to play better than (an opponent) in a sports contest.

outpost *noun* 1 a group of soldiers stationed at a distance from a main force. 2 a distant or remote settlement.

outpouring *noun* (*usu.* **outpourings**) a powerful or violent show of emotion.

output *noun* 1 a quantity or amount produced. 2 the data transferred from the main memory of a computer to a disk, tape, or output device. —*verb* (*pa t and pa p* **outputted** or **output**; *pr p* **outputting**) 1 to produce (information, power, etc.) as output. 2 to transfer (data) from the main memory of a computer to a disk, tape, or output device.

output device a device that displays computer-processed data to the user in an intelligible form, e.g., a VDU or printer.

outrage (owt'rāj,) *noun* 1 an act of great cruelty or violence. 2 an act that breaks accepted standards of morality and decency. 3 great anger or resentment. —*verb trans.* (**outraged, outraging**) to give offense to.

outrageous *adj.* 1 grossly immoderate in behavior; extravagant. 2 flagrantly wicked or horrible. ⊟ ATROCIOUS, HEINOUS, INIQUITOUS, MONSTROUS, SHOCKING. ▶ **outrageously** *adv.*

outrank *verb trans.* to have a higher rank than.

outré (ōō-trā') *adj.* not conventional; eccentric; shocking.

outreach *noun* (owt'rēch,) 1 extent of reach. 2 a concerted attempt to provide, e.g., social services to a broad group of recipients. —*verb trans.* (owt-rēch') to be greater than.

outrider *noun* an attendant or guard who rides a horse or motorcycle at the side or ahead of a carriage or car conveying an important person.

outrigger *noun* a beam or framework sticking out from the side of a boat to help balance the vessel and prevent it from capsizing.

outright *adv.* 1 at once; immediately: *was killed outright.* 2 in an open, frank way; honestly. —*adj.* 1 devoid of any qualification. 2 clear: *the outright winner.* 3 open; honest: *outright disapproval.*

outrun *verb trans.* 1 to run faster or further than. 2 to do better than.

outsell *verb* to be sold more quickly or in greater quantities than.

outset *noun* a beginning or start.

outshine *verb* 1 to shine brighter than. 2 to be very much better than.

outside *noun* **1** the outer surface; the external parts. **2** everything that is not inside or within the bounds of something else. **3** the farthest limit. —*adj.* **1** of, on, or near the outside. **2** not forming part of a group, organization, etc.: *outside interests.* **3** unlikely; remote: *an outside chance.* —*adv.* on or to the outside. —*prep.* **1** on or to the outside of. **2** beyond the limits of. **3** apart from; except. —**at the outside** at the most. *See also* **inside.**

outsider *noun* **1** a person who is not part of a group, etc., or who refuses to accept the general values of society. **2** *in a race, etc.* a competitor who is not expected to win.

outsize *adj.* (*also* **outsized**) over normal or standard size. —*noun* something that is larger than standard, e.g., a garment.

outskirts *pl. noun* the outer parts of a city or town.

outsmart *verb trans.* (**outsmarted, outsmarting**) *colloq.* to get the better of by being cleverer than.

outsource *verb trans.* (**outsourced, outsourcing**) to give (work) to an outside manufacturer, in an attempt to cut costs and overhead.

outspoken *adj.* saying exactly what one thinks; frank. ▸ **outspokenness** *noun*

outstanding *adj.* **1** excellent; remarkable. **2** not yet paid, done, etc. ▸ **outstandingly** *adv.*

outstare *verb trans.* to discomfort by staring; to beat in staring.

outstation *noun* a position, post, or station in a remote area.

outstay *verb* **1** to stay longer than the length of (one's invitation, etc.). **2** to stay longer than (other people).

outstretch *verb trans.* to stretch or spread out.

outstrip *verb trans.* **1** to go faster than. **2** to surpass.

outtake *noun* a sequence of film removed from the final edited version of a motion picture or video.

out tray a shallow basket used in offices for letters, etc., that are ready to be sent out.

outvote *verb trans.* to defeat by a majority of votes.

outward *adj.* **1** on or toward the outside. **2** *of a journey* away from a place. **3** apparent or seeming. —*adv.* (*also* **outwards**) toward the outside; in an outward direction.

outwardly *adv.* in appearance.

outweigh *verb trans.* to be greater than in weight, value, or importance.

outwit *verb trans.* (**outwitted, outwitting**) to get the better by being cleverer than.

outworks *pl. noun* defenses outside the main line of a set of fortifications.

outworn *adj.* no longer useful or in fashion.

ouzel (ōō'zəl) *noun* a water ouzel.

ouzo (ōō'zō) *noun* (*pl.* **ouzos**) a Greek alcoholic drink flavored with aniseed.

ova *see* **ovum.**

oval *adj.* shaped like an egg. —*noun* an egg-shaped figure or object.

ovary *noun* (*pl.* **ovaries**) in a female animal, the reproductive organ in which the eggs are produced. ▸ **ovarian** *adj.*

ovation *noun* cheering or applause.

oven *noun* an enclosed compartment in which food may be baked or roasted.

ovenproof *adj.* *of dishes, etc.* made of material that will not crack when subjected to high temperatures.

over *adv.* **1** above and across. **2** outward and downward: *I knocked him over.* **3** across a space; to or on the other side. **4** from one person, side, or condition to another. **5** through, from beginning to end: *read the letter over.* **6** in repetition: *do it twice over.* **7** at an end. **8** so as to cover completely. **9** beyond a limit; in excess. **10** remaining. —*prep.* **1** in or to a position above or higher in place, importance, etc. **2** above and from one side to another. **3** so as to cover. **4** out and down from. **5** throughout the extent of. **6** during: *over the weekend.* **7** more than. **8** concerning; about: *argued over who would pay.* **9** recovered from the effects of: *is over the accident.* **10** divided by. —*adj.* **1** surplus; extra. **2** outer. **3** excessive. —*interj.* used during two-way radio conversations to show that one has finished speaking. —**be all over (someone)** to make a great fuss about (someone). **over and above (something)** in addition to (it). **over and over again** again and again; repeatedly.

over- *combining form* forming words denoting **1** excessively: *overconfident.* **2** in a higher position or authority: *overlord.* **3** across the surface; covering: *overcoat.* **4** away from an upright position; down: *overturn.* **5** to a complete extent: *overwhelm.*

overact *verb intrans., trans.* to act (a theatrical part) with too much expression or emotion.

overage[1] (ō,və-rāj') *adj.* beyond the usual or required age.

overage[2] (ō'və-rĭj) *noun* a surplus or an excess, e.g., of goods or money.

overall *noun* (ō'və-rôl,) (**overalls**) a one-piece garment with pants, worn to protect clothes. —*adj.* (ō'və-rôl, ō,və-rôl') **1** including everything: *the overall total.* **2** from end to end: *the overall length of the frigate.* —*adv.* (ō,və-rôl') as a whole; in general.

overarm *adj., adv.* executed with the hand and arm raised and moving around the shoulder.

overawe *verb trans.* (**overawed, overawing**) to make silent by filling with awe, fear, or astonishment.

overbalance *verb intrans.* to lose one's balance and fall.

overbearing *adj.* too powerful and proud; domineering.

overblown *adj.* 1 self-important and pretentious. 2 *of flowers* past their prime; beginning to wilt.

overboard *adv.* over the side of a ship into the water. —**go overboard** *colloq.* to be too enthusiastic.

overbook *verb trans., intrans.* to make or allow more reservations (for an aircraft, hotel, etc.) than there are seats or rooms available.

overburden *verb trans.* to give (someone) too much to do, carry, or think about.

overcame *see* **overcome.**

overcast *adj.* cloudy.

overcharge *verb trans.* to charge too much.

overcoat *noun* a warm, heavy coat worn in winter.

overcome *verb* 1 to deal successfully with; to defeat. 2 to affect strongly; to overwhelm.

overcrowd *verb trans.* to cause too many people or things to be in (a place).

overdo *verb intrans., trans.* to do (something) too much. —**overdo it** to work too hard.

overdose *noun* (ō′vər-dōs,) an excessive, sometimes fatal, dose of a drug. —*verb intrans.* (ō,vər-dōs′) to take an overdose.

overdraft *noun* 1 a state in which one has taken more money out of one's bank account than what was in it. 2 the excess of money taken from one's account over the sum that was in it.

overdraw *verb trans., intrans.* 1 to draw more money from (one's bank account) than one has in it. 2 to exaggerate in describing. ▸ **overdrawn** *adj.*

overdress *verb trans., intrans.* to wear or put on clothes that are too formal for the occasion.

overdrew *see* **overdraw.**

overdrive *noun* an additional very high gear in a motor vehicle, which saves fuel when traveling at high speeds.

overdue *adj.* not yet paid, delivered, etc., though the date for doing this has passed.

overestimate *verb trans.* to estimate, judge, etc., too highly. —*noun* too high an estimate. ▸ **overestimation** *noun*

overexpose *verb trans.* to expose (photographic film) to too much light.

overflow *verb trans., intrans.* (ō,vər-flō′) 1 to flow over (a brim) or go beyond (the edge of). 2 to be filled so full that the contents spill over. 3 (**overflow with (something)**) to be full of (it): *overflowing with gratitude.* —*noun* (ō′vər-flō,) 1 the act of flowing over. 2 something that overflows. 3 an outlet for spare water.

overgrown *adj.* 1 dense with plants that have grown too large and thick. 2 grown larger than usual.

overhand *adj., adv.* thrown, done, etc., with the hand brought down from above the shoulder.

overhang *verb trans., intrans.* (ō,vər-hăng′) 1 to project or hang out over. 2 to threaten. —*noun* (ō′vər-hăng,) 1 a piece of rock that overhangs. 2 the amount by which something overhangs.

overhaul *verb trans.* 1 to examine carefully and repair. 2 to catch up with and pass. —*noun* (ō′vər-hôl,) a thorough examination and repair.

overhead *adv., adj.* (ō,vər-hĕd′) over one's head; above. —*noun* (ō′vər-hĕd,) the regular costs of a business, such as rent, wages, and electricity.

overhead projector a projector designed to stand on a desk or table and project an enlarged image of a transparency onto a screen behind a speaker.

overhear *verb trans., intrans.* to hear (someone or something) without the speaker's knowledge.

overheat *verb trans., intrans.* to make or become too hot.

overheated *adj.* angry and excited; passionate.

overjoyed *adj.* very glad; elated.

overkill *noun* 1 action, behavior, treatment, etc., that is far in excess of what is required. 2 the capability to destroy or kill an enemy or a victim using a much greater force than is actually needed.

overland *adv., adj.* across land.

overlap *verb trans., intrans.* (ō,vər-lăp′) 1 to cover partly (another object). 2 *of two parts* to have one part partly covering the other. 3 to have something in common; to partly coincide. —*noun* (ō′vər-lăp,) an overlapping part.

overlay¹ *verb trans.* (ō,vər-lā′) (**overlay (one thing) with (another)**) to cover (it) with a usu. thin layer of (something else), esp. for decoration. —*noun* (ō,vər-lā′) something that is laid over something else, esp. for decoration.

overlay² *see* **overlie.**

overleaf *adv.* on the other side of the page.

overlie *verb trans.* 1 to lie on. 2 to smother and kill (a baby or small animal) by lying on it.

overload (ō,vər-lōd′) *verb trans.* 1 to load too heavily. 2 to put too great an electric current through (a circuit).

overlook *verb trans.* 1 to give a view of from a higher position. 2 to fail to notice. 3 to allow (a mistake, crime, etc.) to go unpunished. 4 to supervise.

overlord *noun* a lord or ruler with supreme power.

overly *adv. formal* too much; excessively.

overmuch *adv., adj.* too much.

overnight *adv.* (ō,vər-nīt') **1** during the night. **2** for the duration of the night. **3** suddenly. —*adj.* (ō'vər-nīt,) **1** done or occurring in the night. **2** sudden: *an overnight success.* **3** for use overnight: *an overnight case.* —*noun* (ō'vər-nīt,) an overnight visit

overpass *noun* a bridge that takes a freeway, pedestrian walkway, etc. over another freeway, etc.

overplay *verb trans.* to exaggerate or over-emphasize. —**overplay (one's) hand** to overestimate (one's) talents, etc.

overpower *verb trans.* (**overpowered, overpowering**) **1** to defeat by great strength. **2** to weaken or reduce to help-lessness. ▸ **overpowering** *adj.*

overran *see* overrun.

overrate *verb trans.* to think too highly of.

overreach *verb trans., intrans.* to defeat (oneself) by trying to do too much, be too clever, etc.

overreact *verb intrans.* (**overreact to (something))** to react too strongly to (it). ▸ **over-reaction** *noun*

override *verb trans.* (ō,vər-rīd') **1** to annul or set aside, esp. to cancel the functioning of. **2** to be of more importance than. —*noun* (ō'vər-rīd,) the process or a means of overriding.

overriding *adj.* most important; dominant.

overrule *verb trans.* **1** to rule against or cancel (esp. a previous decision) by higher authority. **2** to impose a decision on (a person) by higher authority.

overrun *verb trans., intrans.* **1** to spread over or through (something); to infest. **2** to invade and take possession of (another country) quickly and by force. **3** to go beyond (a fixed limit).

overseas *adv.* abroad. —*adj.* across or from beyond the sea; foreign.

oversee *verb* to supervise. ▸ **overseer** *noun*

oversexed *adj.* having unusually strong sexual urges.

overshadow *verb trans.* **1** to seem much more important than. **2** to cast a shadow over; to make seem more gloomy.

overshoe *noun* a shoe made of plastic or rub-ber, worn over normal shoes in wet weather.

overshoot *verb trans.* to go farther than (an area or a target aimed at).

oversight *noun* **1** a mistake made through a failure to notice something. **2** careful scru-tiny and supervision.

oversimplify *verb trans., intrans.* to simplify (something) so much as to cause a dis-tortion. ▸ **oversimplification** *noun*

oversize *noun* (ō'vər-sīz,) a size or a thing larger than the norm. —*adj.* (ō,vər-sīz') (*also* **oversized**) larger than the norm.

oversleep *verb intrans.* to sleep longer than one intended.

overspend *verb intrans.* to spend too much money.

overstate *verb trans.* to state too strongly or with unnecessary emphasis. ▸ **overstate-ment** *noun*

overstay *verb trans.* to stay longer than the length of (one's invitation, etc.).

overstep *verb trans.* to go beyond (a limit). —**overstep the mark** to go beyond what is prudent or reasonable.

overstretched *adj.* stretched too far; extended to the limit.

overstrung *adj.* too sensitive and nervous.

oversubscribed *adj.* having too few places, etc., to meet demand.

overt *adj.* not hidden or secret; open. ▸ **overtly** *adv.*

overtake *verb trans.* **1** to draw level with and begin to do better than. **2** to come upon (someone) suddenly or without warning.

overtax *verb trans.* (**overtaxed, overtaxing, overtaxes**) **1** to put too great a strain on (someone or oneself). **2** to tax (e.g., a population) to an excessive degree.

over-the-counter *adj. of a drug* that can be legally sold without a physician's prescription.

overthrow *verb trans.* (ō,vər-thrō') **1** to bring about the total collapse and downfall of (e.g., a government). **2** to upset or overturn. —*noun* (ō'vər-thrō,) a collapse; a downfall.

overtime (ō'vər-tīm,) *noun* **1** time spent working at one's job beyond one's regular hours. **2** the money paid for this extra time. —*adv.* in addition to one's regular hours.

overtone *noun* **1** (*usu.* **overtones**) a subtle hint, suggestion, or meaning. **2** a musical tone that contributes toward the sound and adds to its quality.

overture *noun* **1** an orchestral introduction to an opera, oratorio, or ballet. **2** (*usu.* **overtures**) a proposal or offer intended to open a discussion.

overturn *verb trans., intrans.* **1** to turn or be turned over or upside down. **2** to bring down or destroy (a government). **3** to overrule or cancel (a court's previous decision).

overview *noun* a brief general account or description.

overweening *adj.* **1** arrogant. **2** *of pride* inflated and excessive.

overweight *adj.* being above the desired, required, or usual weight.

overwhelm *verb trans.* (**overwhelmed, over-whelming**) **1** to overpower (a person's) emotions, thoughts, etc. **2** to defeat by

overwork *verb intrans., trans.* **1** to work too hard. **2** to make (someone) work too hard. **3** to make too much use of. —*noun* the act of working too hard. ▸ **overworked** *adj.*

overwrite *verb trans. Comput.* to write new information over (existing data), thereby destroying it.

overwrought *adj.* very nervous or excited.

oviduct *noun* a tube that conveys egg cells from the ovary to the uterus or to the outside of the body.

ovine *adj.* of or resembling sheep.

oviparous *adj.* laying eggs that develop and hatch outside the mother's body. *See also* **viviparous** (sense 1).

ovoid *adj.* shaped like an egg.

ovulate (äv′yə-lāt,, ōv′-) *verb intrans.* (**ovulated, ovulating**) to release an ovum, or egg cell, from the ovary. ▸ **ovulation** *noun*

ovule *noun* the structure in flowering and cone-bearing plants that develops into a seed after fertilization.

ovum *noun* (*pl.* **ova**) an unfertilized reproductive cell produced by the ovary. *Also called* **egg**.

ow *interj.* used to express sudden, usu. mild, pain.

owe *verb trans., intrans.* (**owed, owing**) **1** to be under an obligation to pay (money) to (someone). **2** to feel required by duty or gratitude to do or give. **3** to have or enjoy as a result of: *She owes her promotion to her own hard work.*

owing *adj.* still to be paid; due. —**owing to** (something) because of (it).

owl *noun* a nocturnal bird of prey with a flat face, large eyes, and a short hooked beak.

owlet *noun* a young owl.

own *adj.* belonging to or for oneself or itself. —*pron.* one or something belonging to oneself or itself: *a room of one's own.* —*verb trans.* (**owned, owning**) to have as a possession or property. —**on one's own 1** alone. **2** without help. **own up** to confess. **own up to** (something) to admit to or confess (a wrongdoing). ▸ **owner** *noun*

owner-occupier *noun* a person who owns the property he or she is living in.

ownership *noun* **1** the status of owner. **2** legal claim or right: *took ownership of the apartment house.* ▣ POSSESSION, POSSESSORSHIP, PROPRIETORSHIP.

ox *noun* (*pl.* **oxen**) **1** a bovine mammal, esp. the male or female of common domestic cattle. **2** an adult castrated male of a domesticated species of cattle.

oxalic acid (ăk-săl′ĭk) a highly poisonous white crystalline solid, used in tanning, bleaching, etc.

oxbow *noun* a shallow curved lake found on a flat floodplain alongside a meandering river.

oxen *see* **ox**.

oxeye daisy a daisy with long white petals and a dark yellow center.

oxidant *noun* an oxidizing agent.

oxidation *noun* a chemical reaction that involves the addition of oxygen to form a substance.

oxide *noun* a compound of oxygen and another element.

oxidize *verb trans., intrans.* (**oxidized, oxidizing**) to undergo or cause to undergo a chemical reaction with oxygen. ▸ **oxidization** *noun*

oxtail *noun* the tail of an ox, used esp. in soups and stews.

oxyacetylene *noun* a mixture of oxygen and acetylene, which burns with an extremely hot flame, used in torches for cutting and welding metals.

oxygen *noun* (SYMBOL O) a colorless odorless tasteless gaseous element, an essential requirement of most forms of life. ▸ **oxygenate** (ăk′sə-jə-nāt,) *verb trans.*

oxygen mask a masklike breathing apparatus that covers the nose and mouth and is used to supply oxygen on demand.

oxygen tent a tentlike enclosure erected around the bed of a patient, into which oxygen can be pumped in order to aid breathing.

oxymoron (ăk,sĭ-môr′ăn,) *noun* a figure of speech in which contradictory terms are used together.

oyez (ō-yā′, ō-yěs′) *or* **oyes** *interj.* used to call for silence and attention.

oyster *noun* **1** an edible marine bivalve mollusk with a soft fleshy body enclosed by a hinged shell. **2** the pale grayish-beige or -pink color of an oyster. —*adj.* of the pale grayish-beige or -pink color of an oyster. —**the world is (one's) oyster** (one) has everything (one) needs or wants within (one's) grasp.

oyster bed a place where oysters breed or where they are cultivated as a source of food or pearls.

oystercatcher *noun* a large wading bird with black-and-white plumage and a long straight orange-red bill.

oz. *abbrev.* ounce[1] (sense 1).

ozone *noun* **1** a pungent unstable bluish gas that is a form of oxygen. **2** *colloq.* fresh, bracing sea air.

ozone-friendly *adj.* denoting a product that does not contain chemicals that deplete the ozone layer.

ozone layer a layer of the upper atmosphere, where ozone is formed, which filters harmful ultraviolet radiation from the Sun and prevents it from reaching Earth.

Pp

P¹ or **p** noun (*pl.* **Ps, P's, p's**) the 16th letter of the English alphabet.

P² *abbrev.* **1** parking. **2** *Chess* pawn. **3** *of airline transportation* first class.

P³ *symbol Chem.* phosphorus.

P⁴ *symbol, of airline transportation* first class.

P. *abbrev.* Priest.

p. or **p** *abbrev.* **1** page. **2** penny; pence. **3** pint. **4** population. **5** pro.

PA *abbrev.* **1** personal assistant. **2** public-address (system).

P.A. *abbrev.* (*also* **PA**) *Law* prosecuting attorney.

Pa¹ *abbrev.* pascal.

Pa² *symbol Chem.* protactinium.

p.a. *abbrev. per annum* (Latin), per year.

Pac. *abbrev.* Pacific.

pace noun **1** a single step. **2** the distance covered by a single step. **3** rate of movement or progress: *work at one's own pace.* **4** a manner of walking or running. **5** a horse's gait in which both feet on one side leave and touch the ground together. —verb intrans., trans. (**paced, pacing**) **1** to keep walking around: *paced the floor all night.* **2** to walk steadily. **3** to set the pace for (others), e.g., in a race.

pacemaker noun **1** an electronic device, inserted in the body, used to correct weak or irregular heart rhythms. **2** a pacesetter.

pacesetter noun a person who sets the pace; a leader in some field. *Also called* **pace-maker.**

pachyderm (păk′ĭ-dərm,) noun **1** a large thick-skinned hoofed mammal, esp. the elephant, rhinoceros, or hippopotamus. **2** an elephant.

pacific adj. tending to afford or make peace: *a pacific foreign policy.* ▣ PACIFICA-TORY, PEACEABLE ▣ BELLICOSE, UN-PACIFIC.

Pacific Standard time (ABBREV. **PST, P.S.T.**) standard time in the eighth time zone west of Greenwich. *Also called* **Pacific time.**

pacifier noun a baby's rubber nipple on which to suck.

pacifist noun someone who refuses to take part in war. ▸ **pacifism** noun

pacify verb trans. (**pacified, pacifying, pacifies**) **1** to calm, soothe, or appease. **2** to restore to a peaceful condition. ▸ **pacifi-cation** noun ▸ **pacificatory** adj.

pack noun **1** things tied into a bundle for carrying. **2** a backpack. **3** a set of playing cards. **4** a troop of animals hunting together, e.g., dogs or wolves. **5** a compact package, e.g., of equipment: *an air pack for firefighters.* **6** a group or number: *a pack of fools/lies.* **7** a medicinal or cosmetic skin preparation: *a face pack.* —verb trans., intrans. (**packed, packing**) **1** (*also* **pack (something) up**) to stow (goods, clothes, etc.) in cases, boxes, etc. **2** to put (one's belongings) into (a traveling bag, etc.) ready for a trip. **3 a** (*also* **pack (something) in**) to cram (it) in. **b** to fill (something) tightly. **4** *colloq.* to carry (a gun). **5** *of animals* to form a pack.

package (păk′ĭj) noun **1** a parcel. **2** *Comput.* a group of programs designed to perform a particular function and meeting the requirements of a large number of users. —verb trans. (**packaged, packaging**) to wrap up in a parcel.

packaging noun **1** the wrappers or containers in which goods are packed. **2** the manner in which a proposal, a product, a candidate for public office, etc., is presented to the public.

packet noun **1** a paper, cardboard, or plastic container; a small pack or package. **2** a mail boat also carrying cargo and passengers.

packing noun materials used for padding or wrapping goods for transport, etc.

pact noun an agreement reached between two or more groups, states, etc.

pad¹ noun **1** a wad of material used to cushion, shape, or clean. **2** a block of sheets of paper. **3** a rocket-launching platform. **4** the fleshy underside of an animal's paw. **5** a large leaf on a water lily. **6** *slang* one's living quarters. —verb trans. (**padded, padding**) **1** to cover, fill, cushion, or shape with layers of soft material. **2** to include unnecessary or irrelevant material in a piece of writing, speech, etc., to make it longer. ▸ **padding** noun

pad² verb intrans., trans. (**padded, padding**) **1** to walk softly or with a muffled tread. **2** to travel along (a road) on foot.

paddle¹ verb intrans., trans. (**paddled, pad-dling**) to walk about or barefoot in shallow water. —noun a period of paddling.

paddle² noun **1** a short light oar with a blade at one or both ends. **2** one of the slats on a paddle wheel. **3** a light, round, wooden racket used to play table tennis. —*verb trans., intrans.* (**paddled, paddling**) **1** to propel (a canoe, etc.) with paddles. **2** to move through water using, or as if using, a paddle or paddles.

paddle wheel a large engine-driven wheel at the side or back of a ship that propels the ship through the water as the wheel turns.

paddock *noun* **1** a small enclosed field in which to keep a horse. **2** an enclosure beside a racetrack where horses are saddled and walked around before a race.

paddy *noun* (*pl.* **paddies**) a field filled with water in which rice is grown. *Also called* **paddy field**.

padlock *noun* a detachable lock with a U-shaped bar that pivots at one side so that it can be passed through a ring or chain and locked in position. —*verb trans.* (**padlocked, padlocking**) to fasten with a padlock.

pagan *adj.* **1** not a Christian, Jew, or Muslim. **2** lacking religious belief. —*noun* a person who follows a pagan religion. ▸ **paganism** *noun*

page[1] *noun* (ABBREV. **pg.**) one side, or both sides, of a leaf in a book, etc. —*verb trans.* (**paged, paging**) to paginate (a text).

page[2] *noun* **1** a young person who carries, e.g., messages: *Congressional pages.* **2** *Hist.* a boy attendant serving a knight and training for knighthood. —*verb trans.* (**paged, paging**) to summon through a public-address system or by way of a pager.

pageant (păj'ənt) *noun* **1** a series of dramatic scenes, usu. depicting historical events. **2** a colorful and varied spectacle. ▸ **pageantry** *noun*

pageboy *noun* a male page. —*adj.* denoting a smooth, jaw-length hairstyle with the ends curling under.

pager *noun* a small radio receiver and transmitter that enables its user to receive a signal or to send a signal to another person.

paginate (păj'ĭ-nāt,) *verb trans.* (**paginated, paginating**) to give number the pages of (a text). ▸ **pagination** *noun*

paid *see* **pay**.

pail *noun* **1** a bucket. **2** the amount contained in a bucket.

pain *noun* **1** a distressing, uncomfortable, or agonizing sensation in the body. **2** emotional suffering. **3** (**pains**) trouble taken or efforts made: *take pains to do something.* —*verb trans.* (**pained, paining**) to cause distress to. ▸ **pained** *adj.*

painful *adj.* **1** causing pain or distress. **2** laborious. ▸ **painfully** *adv.*

painkiller *noun* a drug that relieves pain.

painless *adj.* inflicting or affected by no pain or distress. ▸ **painlessly** *adv.*

painstaking *adj.* giving or showing care and attention to detail.

paint *noun* **1 a** a liquid coloring matter for applying to a surface. **b** a dried coating of it. **2** a tube or tablet of coloring matter for creating pictures. **3** face makeup. —*verb trans., intrans.* (**painted, painting**) **1 a** to apply a coat of paint to (walls, woodwork, etc.). **b** to turn (something) a certain color by this means. **2 a** to make (pictures) using liquid coloring matter. **b** to depict (a person, place, or thing) in paint. **3** to put makeup on. ▸ **painter** *noun.*

paintbox *noun* a box of paints in a variety of colors, for painting pictures.

paintbrush *noun* a brush used for applying paint.

painting *noun* **1** the art or process of applying paint to, e.g., walls. **2** the art of creating pictures in paint. **3** a painted picture.

pair *noun* **1** two identical or corresponding things, e.g., shoes, gloves, etc., intended for use together. **2** something consisting of two joined and corresponding parts: *a pair of scissors.* **3** one of a matching pair. **4** two people associated in a relationship. —*verb trans., intrans.* (**paired, pairing**) **1** (*also* **pair off**) to divide into pairs. **2** (**pair up with** (**someone**)) to join with (someone) for a purpose.

pajamas *pl. noun* nightwear consisting of a loose top and pants.

pal *colloq. noun* a friend. —*verb intrans.* (**palled, palling**) to be friends with (someone).

palace *noun* **1** the official residence of a sovereign, bishop, archbishop, or president. **2** a spacious, magnificent residence or other building.

palae- *or* **palaeo-** *combining form same as* **paleo-**.

palatable *adj.* **1** having a pleasant taste. **2** acceptable; agreeable.

palate *noun* **1** the roof of the mouth. **2** the sense of taste.

palatial *adj.* like a palace, e.g., in magnificence or size. ▤ NOBLE, REGAL.

palaver *noun colloq.* idle talk.

pale[1] *adj.* **1** of a face, etc. having less color than normal. **2** of a color closer to white than black; light: *pale green.* **3** lacking brightness or vividness: *pale sunlight.* —*verb intrans.* (**paled, paling**) to become pale. ▸ **paleness** *noun*

pale[2] *noun* **1** a post used for making fences. **2** a fence made of fencing posts; a boundary fence. —**beyond the pale** outside the limits of acceptable behavior.

paleo-, pale-, palae- *or* **palaeo-** *combining form* forming words denoting old, ancient, former: *paleography.*

paleography *noun* the study of ancient writing and manuscripts. ▸ **paleographer** *noun*

paleontology *noun* the scientific study of extinct life forms by interpretation of fossil remains. ▸ **paleontologist** *noun*

Palestinian *noun* a native or citizen, esp. an Arab, of ancient or modern Palestine. —*adj.* relating to ancient or modern Palestine.

palette (păl'ət). *noun* **1** a hand-held board on which an artist mixes colors. **2** the colors used by an artist, in a particular picture, etc.

palindrome *noun* a word or phrase that reads the same backward and forward, e.g., *radar.* ▸ **palindromic** *adj.*

> From Greek *palindromos*, meaning 'running back'

paling *noun* any of a row of wooden posts fixed edge to edge to form a solid fence; a fence of this kind.

palisade *noun* a fence of pointed wooden stakes fixed edge to edge, for defense or protection.

pall¹ *noun* **1 a** the cloth that covers a coffin at a funeral. **b** the coffin itself. **2** gloom: *The remark cast a pall over the meeting.*

pall² *verb intrans.* (**palled, palling**) to begin to bore or seem tedious.

palladium *noun Chem.* (**SYMBOL Pd**) a soft, silvery-white metal used in electrical components, catalytic converters, and, combined with gold, to form the alloy white gold.

pallet *noun* a small wooden platform on which goods can be stacked for lifting and transporting by forklifts.

palliate (păl'ē-āt,) *verb trans.* (**palliated, palliating**) **1** to ease the symptoms of (a disease) without curing it. **2** to lessen the gravity of (an offense, etc.). **3** to reduce the effect of (something disagreeable). ▸ **palliative** *adj., noun*

pallid *adj.* **1** pale, esp. unhealthily so. **2** lacking vigor or conviction.

pallor *noun* paleness, esp. of complexion.

palm *noun* **1** the inner surface of the hand between the wrist and the fingers. **2** the part of a glove covering this part of a human hand. —*verb trans.* (**palmed, palming**) to conceal in the palm of the hand.

palmistry *noun* the art or practice of telling a person's fortune by the lines on his or her palm. ▸ **palmist** *noun*

palmtop *noun* a personal computer even smaller than a laptop.

palmy *adj.* (**palmier, palmiest**) *colloq.* characterized by effortless success and prosperity.

palpable *adj.* **1** easily detected; obvious. **2** *Med.* able to be felt. ▸ **palpably** *adv.*

palpate (păl'pāt,) *verb trans.* (**palpated, palpating**) to examine (the body or a part of it) by touching or pressing, in order to diagnose medical disorders.

palpitate (păl'pĭ-tāt,) *verb intrans.* (**palpitated, palpitating**) **1** *of the heart* to beat abnormally rapidly. **2** to tremble or throb. ▸ **palpitation** *noun*

palsy *noun* loss of control or feeling, or paralysis, in a part of the body.

paltry (pôl'trē) *adj.* (**paltrier, paltriest**) meager; trivial. ▸ **paltriness** *noun*

pamper *verb trans.* (**pampered, pampering**) to treat overindulgently and overprotectively.

pamphlet *noun* a booklet or leaflet providing information, or dealing with a current topic.

pan¹ *noun* **1** a usu. metal pot used for cooking. **2** either dish on a pair of scales. **3** a shallow hollow in the ground: *a salt pan.* —*verb intrans., trans.* (**panned, panning**) **1** to wash (river gravel) in a shallow metal vessel in search of gold. **2** *colloq.* to criticize or review harshly.

pan² *verb trans., intrans.* (**panned, panning**) *of a movie camera, etc.* to swing around so as to follow a moving object or show a panoramic view. —*noun* a panning movement or shot by a movie camera.

pan- *combining form* forming words denoting all, entire: *Pan-African.*

panacea (păn,ə-sē'ə) *noun* a universal remedy for any illness or problem.

panache (pə-năsh', -näsh') *noun* flamboyant self-assurance.

panama *noun* a lightweight brimmed hat for men made from plaited leaves.

pancake *noun* a round of batter cooked on both sides in a frying pan or on a griddle. *Also called* **flapjack, griddlecake, hotcake.**

pancreas (păng'krē-əs, păn'-) *noun* a large gland, lying between the duodenum and the spleen, that has hormonal and digestive functions.

panda *noun* the giant panda.

pandemonium (păn,də-mō'nē-əm) *noun* a scene of confusion and noise.

> The name of the capital of Hell in Milton's *Paradise Lost* (1667)

pander *verb intrans.* (**pandered, pandering**) (**pander to (someone)**) to indulge or gratify (someone) or (someone's wishes or tastes).

> After *Pandarus*, who acts as a go-between in the story of Troilus and Cressida

pane *noun* a sheet of glass, esp. one fitted into a window or door.

panegyric (păn,ə-jĭ'rĭk) *noun* a speech or piece of writing in praise of someone or something.

panel *noun* **1** a separate, esp. ornamental, section of a wall or door. **2** one of several strips of fabric making up a garment. **3** a metal section of the bodywork of a vehicle.

4 a board bearing the instruments and dials for controlling an aircraft, etc. **5** people selected to judge a contest or participate in a discussion, quiz, etc. before an audience. **6** a list of jurors. —*verb trans.* (**paneled** *or* **panelled, paneling** *or* **panelling**) to fit (a wall or door) with panels.

paneling *or* **panelling** *noun* panels in walls or doors, or material for making them.

panelist *noun* a member of a panel.

pang *noun* a painfully acute feeling of, e.g., hunger, remorse, etc.

panhandle *noun* territory that consists of a narrow strip of land projecting like the handle of a pan from a larger area.

panic *noun* a sudden overpowering fear. —*verb intrans., trans.* (**panicked, panicking**) to feel or cause to feel panic. ▸ **panicky** *adj.*

Panjabi *noun, adj. same as* **Punjabi**.

panoply *noun* (*pl.* **panoplies**) **1** the full, splendid assemblage arranged for a ceremony, etc.: *the full panoply of a society wedding.* **2** *Hist.* a full set of armor and weapons.

panorama *noun* **1** an open, extensive, or all-round view. **2** a view in all its range and variety: *the panorama of history.* ▸ **panoramic** *adj.*

panpipes *pl. noun* a musical instrument consisting of pipes of graded lengths bound together, played by blowing along their open ends.

pansy *noun* (*pl.* **pansies**) a plant having flat flowers with five rounded petals in a variety of color combinations.

pant *verb intrans., trans.* (**panted, panting**) **1** to breathe in gasps as a result of exertion. **2** to say breathlessly. —*noun* a gasping breath.

pantaloons *pl. noun* baggy pants gathered at the ankle.

pantheism (păn'thē-ĭz,əm) *noun* the belief that equates all the matter and forces in the universe with God. ▸ **pantheist** *noun* ▸ **pantheistic** *adj.*

pantheon (păn'thē-än,, -ən) *noun* **1** all the gods of a particular people. **2** a temple sacred to all the gods. **3** a public building containing memorabilia relating to a nation's honored heroes.

panther *noun* **1** a black leopard. **2** a mountain lion.

panties *pl. noun* thin light underpants for women and girls.

pantomime *noun* a Christmas entertainment usu. based on a popular fairytale, with songs, dancing, comedy acts, etc.

pantry *noun* (*pl.* **pantries**) a room or cupboard for storing food.

pants *pl. noun* **1** outerwear for covering the legs. **2** underpants.

pantsuit, pant suit *or* **pants suit** *noun* a suit for women consisting of long pants and a jacket.

pantyhose *pl. noun* women's stockings and stretchable underpants forming a single undergarment.

pap *noun* **1** soft semiliquid food, e.g. for babies. **2** trivial or worthless spoken or written material or entertainment.

papa *noun* a father.

papacy *noun* (*pl.* **papacies**) **1** the position, power, or period of office of a pope. **2** government by popes.

papal *adj.* of or relating to the pope or the papacy.

paparazzo (păp,ə-rät'sō) *noun* (*pl.* **paparazzi**) a newspaper photographer who follows famous people around in the hope of photographing them in unguarded moments.

papaw *or* **pawpaw** *noun* **1** a tree that has edible, fleshy, black-skinned fruit. **2** the fruit. **3** the papaya (sense 2).

papaya (pə-pī'ə) *noun* **1** a small tree with yellow flowers and large, edible, yellow or orange fruit. **2** the fruit. *Also called* **papaw**.

paper *noun* **1** a thin material used for writing and printing on, to wrap things, etc. **2** a single piece of paper. **3** wallpaper. **4** a newspaper. **5** a set of questions in a written examination. **6** (**papers**) personal documents establishing one's identity, nationality, etc. —*verb trans.* (**papered, papering**) to decorate with wallpaper. ▸ **papery** *adj.*

paperback *noun* a book with a paper binding.

paperboy *noun* a boy who delivers or sells newspapers.

paper clip a metal or plastic clip for holding papers together.

papergirl *noun* a girl who delivers or sells newspapers.

paperknife *noun* a knife for slitting open envelopes, etc.

paper tiger something or someone more apparently threatening than actually dangerous.

paperweight *noun* a heavy, usu. ornamental, object for holding papers down.

paperwork *noun* routine written work, e.g., keeping files, writing letters and reports, etc.

papier-mâché (pă,pər-mə-shā', păp,yā,mə-) *noun* pulped paper mixed with glue and sometimes other substances, molded into shapes while wet.

papilla *noun* (*pl.* **papillae**) *Biol.* a small nipplelike projection from the surface of something.

papoose *noun* a Native American baby or young child.

paprika *noun* a powdered seasoning for food, made from red peppers.

pap smear *Pathol.* the collection of a cell sample from the *cervix* for examination in order to detect any changes indicative, e.g., of cancer. *Also called* **Pap test**.

papyrus *noun* (*pl.* **papyruses, papyri**) **1** a tall plant. **2** the writing material prepared from this plant. **3** an ancient manuscript written on this material.

par *noun* **1** a normal level or standard. **2** *Golf* the standard number of strokes that a good golfer would take for a certain course or hole.

par. *or* **para.** *abbrev.* paragraph.

para- *or* **par-** *combining form* forming words denoting **1** alongside: *parathyroid*. **2** beyond: *parapsychology*. **3** resembling: *paramilitary*. **4** auxiliary: *paramedical*. **5** abnormal: *paraesthesia*.

parable *noun* a story whose purpose is to convey a moral or religious lesson.

parabola *noun* a shape produced when a plane intersects a cone parallel to its sloping side. ▸ **parabolic** *adj.*

parachute *noun* a loose canopy of light fabric with a harness, for slowing the fall of a person or package dropped from an aircraft. —*verb intrans., trans.* (**parachuted, parachuting**) to drop by parachute. ▸ **parachutist** *noun*

parade *noun* **1** a ceremonial procession of people, vehicles, etc. **2** of *soldiers, etc.* **a** the state of being drawn up in ranks for formal marching or inspection: *on parade*. **b** soldiers, etc., drawn up in this way. **3** a self-advertising display: *made a parade of her generosity.* —*verb intrans., trans.* (**paraded, parading**) **1** to walk or cause to walk or march in procession. **2** to put on view in such a way as to get special attention.

paradigm *noun* an example, model, or pattern. ▸ **paradigmatic** *adj.*

paradise (păr′ə-dīs,, -dīz,) *noun* **1** heaven. **2 a** a place of utter bliss or delight. **b** a feeling of immense joy. **3** (**Paradise**) the Garden of Eden.

paradox *noun* **1** a statement that contradicts, or seems to contradict, itself. **2** a situation involving apparently contradictory elements. ▸ **paradoxical** *adj.* ▸ **paradoxically** *adv.*

paraffin *noun* **1** alkane. **2** paraffin wax. **3** *Brit.* kerosene.

paragon *noun* a model of excellence or perfection.

paragraph *noun* **1** a section of a piece of writing, starting on a fresh, often indented, line, and dealing with a distinct point or idea. **2** a short report in a newspaper. **3** (*also* **paragraph mark**) *Printing* a sign (¶), indicating the start of a new paragraph. —*verb trans.* (**paragraphed, paragraphing**) to divide (text) into paragraphs.

parakeet *noun* a small, brightly colored parrot with a long pointed tail.

parallax *noun* the apparent change in the position of an object, relative to a distant background, when it is viewed from two different positions.

parallel *adj.* (*often* **parallel to** (**something**)) **1** of *lines* or *planes* being at every point the same distance apart. **2** equivalent; corresponding; similar. —*adv.* (*often* **parallel to** (**something**)) alongside and at an unvarying distance from (something). —*noun* **1** *Geom.* a line or plane parallel to another. **2** a corresponding or equivalent instance: *without parallel.* **3** *Geog.* a line of latitude. —*verb trans.* (**paralleled, paralleling**) **1** to equal. **2** to correspond to or be equivalent to. ▸ **parallelism** *noun*

parallelogram *noun* *Geom.* a four-sided, two-dimensional figure in which opposite sides are parallel and equal in length.

Paralympics (păr′ə-lĭm,pĭks) *noun* an Olympic competition for people with physical disabilities.

paralysis *noun* **1** a temporary or permanent loss of muscular function or sensation in any part of the body. **2** a state of immobility; a standstill. ▸ **paralytic** *adj., noun*

paralyze *verb trans.* (**paralyzed, paralyzing**) **1** to affect (a person or body part) with paralysis. **2** of *fear, etc.* to have an immobilizing effect on. **3** to disrupt or bring (something) to a standstill.

paramedic *noun* a person, such as a technician or member of an ambulance crew, who is trained to assist doctors and other medical staff and to give emergency medical treatment.

parameter (pə-răm′ət-ər) *noun* **1** (*often* **parameters**) factors that define the scope of a task, project, discussion, etc. **2** *Math.* a constant or variable that, when altered, affects the form of the mathematical expression in which it appears.

paramilitary *adj.* organized as a military force but composed of private citizens. —*noun* (*pl.* **paramilitaries**) a member of a paramilitary force.

paramount *adj.* of supreme importance; foremost.

paranoia *noun* a strong feeling that one is being persecuted by others. ▸ **paranoiac** *adj., noun* ▸ **paranoid** *adj., noun*

paranormal *adj.* of occurrences beyond the normal scope of scientific explanation. —*noun* (**the paranormal**) paranormal occurrences.

parapet *noun* a low wall along the edge of a bridge, balcony, etc.

paraphernalia (păr,ə-fə-nāl′yə, -fər-) *pl. noun* **1** the equipment and accessories associated with an activity, etc. **2** personal belongings.

Originally a woman's property outwith her dowry, which remained her own after marriage

paraphrase *noun* a rewording or rephrasing of something while conveying the same meaning. —*verb trans.* (**paraphrased, paraphrasing**) to express in other words.

paraplegia *noun* paralysis of the lower half of the body, including both legs. ▸ **paraplegic** *adj., noun.*

parasite *noun* **1** a plant or animal that obtains food and physical protection from a different organism. **2** *derog.* a person who lives at the expense of others. ▸ **parasitic** *or* **parasitical** *adj.* ▸ **parasitism** *noun*

parasol *noun* a light umbrella used as a protection against sunlight.

paratroops *pl. noun* troops trained to parachute into enemy territory or a battle zone. ▸ **paratrooper** *noun*

parboil *verb trans.* (**parboiled, parboiling**) to boil until partially cooked.

parcel *noun* **1** an object wrapped in paper, etc., and secured with string or tape. **2** a portion, e.g., of land. **3** a lot or portion of merchandise for sale. —*verb* (**parceled** *or* **parcelled, parceling** *or* **parcelling**) **1** to divide into portions and share out. **2** to wrap (something) up in a parcel.

parch *verb trans.* (**parched, parching**) **1** to deprive (soil, plants, etc.) of water. **2** to make thirsty.

parchment *noun* **1 a** a material formerly used for bookbinding and for writing on, made from goatskin, calfskin, or sheepskin. **b** a piece of it, or a manuscript written on it. **2** stiff off-white writing paper.

pardon *verb trans.* (**pardoned, pardoning**) **1** to forgive or excuse (someone) for (a fault or offense). **2** to cancel the punishment of. —*noun* **1** forgiveness. **2** the cancelation of a punishment. ▸ **pardonable** *adj.* ▸ **pardoner** *noun*

pare *verb trans.* (**pared, paring**) **1** to trim off (skin, etc.) in layers. **2** to cut (fingernails or toenails). **3** to peel (fruit). **4** to reduce (expenses, funding, etc.), gradually, in order to economize. ▸ **paring** *noun*

parent *noun* **1** a father or mother. **2** an animal or plant that has produced offspring. **3** a source or origin. —*verb intrans., trans.* (**parented, parenting**) to be, act as, or care for as a parent. ▸ **parental** *adj.* ▸ **parenthood** *noun*

parentage (păr'ənt-ĭj) *noun* family or ancestry.

parenthesis *noun* (*pl.* **parentheses**) **1** a word or phrase inserted into a sentence as a comment, usu. marked off by brackets or dashes. **2** (**parentheses**) a pair of round

brackets ( ) used, e.g., to enclose such a comment. ▸ **parenthetic** *or* **parenthetical** *adj.*

par excellence (pär,ĕk,sə-läns') to the highest degree; in the truest sense: *a diplomat par excellence.*

parfait (pär-fā') *noun* a cold dessert made of layers of various kinds of ice cream, sauces, and garnish, served in a tall, frosty glass.

pariah (pə-rī'ə) *noun* **1** a person who is avoided. **2** in S India and Burma, a person of no, or low, caste.

Originally a member of a low caste in southern India

parietal (pə-rī'ət-l) *adj.* relating to, or forming, the wall of a body cavity, e.g., the skull: *the parietal bones.*

parish *noun* **1** a district or an area served by its own church and priest or minister. **2** in Louisiana, an administrative subdivision corresponding to a county in other US states. **3** the inhabitants of a parish. ▸ **parishioner** *noun*

parity *noun* (*pl.* **parities**) **1** equality, e.g., in pay. **2** precise equivalence; exact correspondence.

park *noun* **1** a public recreation area in a town, with grass and trees. **2** an area of land kept as a nature reserve, etc.: *a wildlife park.* **3** the woodland and pasture forming the estate of a large country house. **4** a sports field or stadium: *a baseball park.* **5** a parking lot. —*verb trans., intrans.* (**parked, parking**) **1** to place or leave (a vehicle) temporarily at the side of the road or in a parking lot. **2** *colloq.* to install or sit (oneself).

parka *noun* a windproof jacket, esp. quilted with a fur-trimmed hood.

parkland *noun* pasture and woodland forming part of a country estate.

parkway *noun* (ABBREV. **pkwy., pky.**) a broad highway that incorporates grassy areas and is lined with trees.

parlance *noun* a particular style of using words: *in legal parlance.*

parlay (pär'lā,, -lē) *verb trans.* (**parlayed, parleying, parlays**) to bet (a wager made earlier, along with its winnings) on a subsequent event.

parley (pär'lē) *verb intrans.* (**parleyed, parleying, parleys**) to discuss peace terms, etc., with an enemy. —*noun* (*pl.* **parleys**) a meeting with an enemy to discuss peace terms, etc.

parliament (pär'lə-mənt) *noun* **1** the highest law-making assembly of a nation. **2** (**Parliament**) in Britain, the House of Commons and House of Lords. ▸ **parliamentary** *adj.*

parliamentarian *noun* **1** an expert in parliamentary procedure. **2** an experienced parliamentary debater.

parlor noun **1** a sitting room for receiving visitors. **2** a shop or commercial premises providing particular goods or services: *an ice-cream parlor.*

parochial (pə-rō'kē-əl) *adj.* concerned only with local affairs; limited, or provincial in outlook. ▸ **parochialism** noun ▸ **parochially** adv.

parody noun (pl. **parodies**) **1** a comic or satiric imitation of a work or of the style of a particular writer, composer, etc. **2** a contemptibly mocking distortion of something worthy. —verb trans. (**parodied, parodying, parodies**) to ridicule or mimic by parody.

parole noun **1** the release of a prisoner before the end of his or her sentence, on condition of sustained law-abiding behavior. **2** the length of time of this conditional release. —verb trans. (**paroled, paroling**) to release or place (a prisoner) on parole. ▸ **parolee** noun

> From French parole meaning 'word' because prisoners are released on their word of honour

paroxysm noun **1** a sudden emotional outburst, e.g., of laughter. **2** a spasm or convulsion, e.g., of acute pain. ▸ **paroxysmal** adj.

parricide noun the killing of, or a person who kills, a parent. ▸ **parricidal** adj.

parrot noun a bird with a strong hooked bill, usu. bright plumage, and an ability to mimic human speech.

parry verb trans., intrans. (**parried, parrying, parries**) to defend (oneself) from (questions, blows, etc.) by or as if by turning them aside. —noun (pl. **parries**) an act of parrying.

parse verb trans., intrans. (**parsed, parsing**) **1** to analyze (a sentence) grammatically. **2** Comput. to analyze (input symbols) in terms of the computing language being used. ▸ **parser** noun

parsec noun a unit of distance in space equal to 3.26 light-years, 1.918×10^{13} mi., or 3.09×10^{13} km.

parsimony noun **1 a** extreme care in spending money. **b** praiseworthy economy. **c** the condition or quality of being very stingy. **2** meanness. ▸ **parsimonious** adj. ▸ **parsimoniously** adv.

parsley noun a plant with curly aromatic leaves used either fresh as a garnish or as a herb in cooking.

parsnip noun **1** a plant grown for its edible root. **2** the long, thick, creamy-white, sweet root of this plant.

parson noun **1** an Anglican parish priest. **2** a cleric, esp. a Protestant one.

parsonage (pär'sə-nĭj) noun the residence of a parson.

part noun **1** a portion, piece, or bit. **2** one of two or more equal divisions or amounts that compose a whole: *Mix five parts cement with two of sand.* **3** an essential piece; a component. **4 a** a performer's role in a play, etc. **b** the words, actions, etc., belonging to the role. **5** the melody, etc., given to a particular instrument or voice in a musical work. **6** (usu. **parts**) a region: *foreign parts.* **7** a line of exposed scalp on the human head, dividing hair brushed or combed in opposite directions. —verb trans., intrans. (**parted, parting**) **1** to become or cause to become disunited. **2** (**part with** or **from (someone)**) to leave or separate from (someone). **3** of more than one person to leave one another. **4** (**part with (something)** or **be parted from (it)**) to give (it) up or hand (it) over. ▸ **parting** noun

partake verb intrans. (pa t partook; pa p partaken; pr p partaking) **1** (usu. partake in (something)) to participate in (something). **2** (usu. partake of (something)) to eat or drink.

partial adj. **1** in part only; incomplete. **2** (**partial to (something)**) having a liking for (it). **3** favoring one side or person unfairly. ▸ **partiality** noun ▸ **partially** adv.

participate (pär-tĭs'ĭ-pāt,) verb intrans. (**participated, participating**) (often **participate in (something)**) to take part or be involved in (it). ▸ **participant** noun ▸ **participation** noun ▸ **participatory** adj.

participle (pärt'ə-sĭp,əl) noun Gram. a word formed from a verb and used as an adjective or to form tenses, e.g., a present participle such as *going* and *hitting*, or a past participle such as *gone, bitten*, and *swum*). ▸ **participial** adj. ▸ **participially** adv.

particle noun **1** a tiny piece. **2** Phys. a tiny unit of matter such as a molecule or atom. **3** the least bit: *not a particle of sympathy.* **4** Gram. **a** an uninflected word, e.g., a preposition, conjunction, or interjection. **b** an affix, such as *un-* and *-ly*.

particular adj. **1** individually known or referred to; specific. **2** more than usual: *took particular care.* **3** difficult to satisfy; exacting. **4** exact; detailed. —noun **1** a single, usu. small feature, constituent, or characteristic of a whole. **2** (**particulars**) details: *took down the particulars of the story.* —**in particular** especially; specifically. ▸ **particularly** adv.

particularize verb trans., intrans. (**particularized, particularizing**) **1** to specify individually. **2** to give specific examples of. ▸ **particularization** noun

partisan (pärt'ə-zən, -zăn,) noun **1** an enthusiastic supporter. **2** a member of a resistance group in a country occupied by an enemy. —adj. strongly loyal to one side, esp. blindly so. ▸ **partisanship** noun

partition *noun* **1** a screen or thin wall dividing a room. **2** the dividing of a country into two or more independent states. —*verb trans.* (**partitioned, partitioning**) **1** to divide (a country) into independent states. **2** to separate (something) off with a partition.

partly *adv.* in part, or in some parts.

partner *noun* **1** one of two or more people jointly owning or running a business, etc. on an equal footing. **2** a person with whom one dances. **3** a person who is on the same side as oneself in a game. **4** a person with whom one has a sexual relationship. —*verb trans.* (**partnered, partnering**) to act as a partner to. ▸ **partnership** *noun*

partook *see* **partake.**

partridge *noun* (*pl.* **partridge, partridges**) **1** a ground-dwelling game bird.

part-time *adj., adv.* during only part of the working day. ▸ **part-timer** *noun*

partway *adv. colloq.* in part; to a degree or distance.

party *noun* (*pl.* **parties**) **1** a social gathering, esp. of invited guests. **2** a group of people involved in some activity together. **3** an organization of people united by a common political aim. **4** *Law* each of the individuals or groups concerned in an agreement, lawsuit, etc. —*verb intrans.* (**partying, parties**) *slang* to engage in revelry.

party wall a wall that divides two houses, etc.

parvenu *noun* a person who has recently acquired substantial wealth but lacks the social refinement to go with it.

pascal *noun* (ABBREV. **Pa**) the unit of pressure in the International System, equal to a force of one newton per square meter.

pass *verb trans., intrans.* (**passed, passing**) **1** to come alongside and go past (someone or something going in the opposite direction). **2** to run, flow, progress, etc.: *the blood passing through our veins.* **3** (*also* **pass** *or* **pass** (**something**) **through, into,** *etc.*) to go or cause (it) to go, penetrate, etc.: *pass it through a filter.* **4** to move lightly across, over, etc.: *pass a duster over the furniture.* **5** to go from one state or stage to another: *pass from the larval to the pupal stage.* **6** to exceed or surpass: *pass the target.* **7** of a vehicle to overtake. **8** a· to achieve the required standard in (a test, etc.). **b** to award (a student, etc.) the marks required for success in a test, etc. **9** to take place: *What passed between them must remain secret.* **10** *of time* **a** to go by. **b** to use up (time) in an activity,· etc. **11** (**pass** *or* **be passed around, on,** *etc.*) to hand or transfer; to be transferred. **12** (**pass down** *or* **pass** (**something**) **down**) to be inherited; to hand it down. **13** *Sport* to throw, kick, or hit (a ball, etc.) to another player on one's team. **14** to

vote (a law) into effect: *passed the legislation.* **15** *of a judge or court of law* to pronounce (judgment): *passed sentence on him.* **16** to go away after a while: *Her nausea finally passed.* **17** to be accepted, tolerated, or ignored: *Let's just let it pass.* **18** to choose not to answer in a quiz, etc., or bid in a card game. **19** to discharge (urine or feces). —*noun* **1** a route through a gap in a mountain range. **2** an official card or document permitting one to enter, be absent from duty, etc. **3** a successful result in an examination, but usu. without distinction or honors. **4** *Sport* a throw, kick, hit, etc., to another player on one's team. **5** a state of affairs: *This is a sorry pass!* **6** a decision not to answer in a quiz, etc., or not to bid in a card game. —**pass away** *or* **on** to die. **pass out** to faint.

passable *adj.* **1** good enough, but usu. only just. **2** *of a road, etc.* able to be traveled along, crossed, etc. ▸ **passably** *adv.*

passage (păs'ĭj) *noun* **1** a corridor, narrow street, or channel. **2** a piece of a text or musical composition. **3** the process of passing: *the passage of time.* **4** a journey by boat. **5** permission or freedom to pass through a territory, etc.

passageway *noun* a narrow passage or way, usu. with walls on each side.

passbook *noun* a book in which the amounts of money put into and taken out of a bank account, etc., are recorded.

passé (păs-ā') *adj.* no longer popular; outmoded.

passenger *noun* a traveler in a motor vehicle, boat, airplane, etc., driven, sailed, or piloted by another.

passerby *noun* (*pl.* **passersby**) a person walking past; a passing observer of an incident.

passerine *Zool. adj.* relating to or belonging to the perching birds. —*noun* a perching bird.

passim *adv.* occurring frequently throughout the literary or academic work in question.

passing *adj.* **1** lasting only briefly: *passing showers.* **2** casual: *a passing glance.*

passion *noun* **1** a violent emotion, e.g., hate or envy. **2** a fit of anger. **3** sexual love or desire. **4** something for which one has great enthusiasm. **5** great, sometimes excessive, enthusiasm. **6** (**the Passion**) **a** the suffering and death of Christ. ▸ **passionate** *adj.* ▸ **passionately** *adv.*

passive *adj.* **1** lacking positive or assertive qualities; submissive. **2** lethargic; inert. **3** *Gram.,* *of verbs* in the form that is used when the subject of the sentence undergoes, rather than performs, the action of the verb, as in *it has been bought. See also* **active** (sense 5). —*noun Gram.* a passive verb. ▸ **passively** *adv.* ▸ **passiveness** *noun*

passkey *noun* a key designed to open all of a set of locks.

Passover (păs′ō,vər) *noun* an annual Jewish festival commemorating the deliverance of the Israelites from bondage in Egypt. *Also called* **Pesach**.

passport *noun* a document issued by a government, giving proof of the holder's identity and nationality, and permission to travel abroad.

password *noun* **1** a secret word allowing entry to a high-security area or past a checkpoint, etc. **2** *Comput.* a set of characters that a user inputs to gain access to a computer or network.

past *adj.* **1** of an earlier time. **2** just gone by: *the past year.* **3** over; finished: *That relationship is past.* **4** former; previous: *past presidents.* **5** *Gram.,* of the tense of a verb indicating a past action or condition. —*prep.* **1** up to and beyond: *went past me.* **2** after in time or age: *He's well past 60.* **3** beyond the reach of: *past help.* —*adv.* **1** so as to pass by: *go past.* **2** ago: *two months past.* —*noun* **1** the time before the present; events, etc., belonging to this former time. **2** one's earlier life or career. **3** *Gram.* the past tense.

pasta *noun* **1** dough made with flour, water, and eggs, and shaped into various forms. **2** a cooked dish of this dough, usu. with a sauce.

paste *noun* **1** a stiff, moist, semisolid mixture. **2** a spread for sandwiches, etc., made from ground meat or fish. **3** a fine doughlike mixture: *almond paste.* **4** a hard, brilliant glass used in making imitation gems. —*verb trans.* (**pasted, pasting**) to stick with paste. ▸ **pasting** *noun*

pasteboard *noun* stiff board built up from sheets of paper pasted together.

pastel (păs-tĕl′) *noun* **1** a chalklike crayon made from ground pigment. **2** a picture drawn with these crayons. —*adj.,* of colors delicately pale.

pasteurization *noun* the partial sterilization of a food, esp. milk, by heating. ▸ **pasteurize** *verb*

Named after Louis *Pasteur,* the 19th-century French chemist who invented the process

pastille (păs-tĕl′) *noun* a small fruit-flavored, esp. medicinal, candy.

pastime *noun* a spare-time pursuit; a hobby.

pastor *noun* a member of the clergy, esp. in Protestant churches. ▸ **pastorate** *noun*

pastoral (păs′tə-rəl, -trəl) *adj.* **1** of, e.g., a poem, painting, etc. relating to or depicting the countryside or country life. **2** relating to a member of the clergy. —*noun* **1** a pastoral poem or painting. **2** *Mus.* same as **pas-torale**. **3** a letter from a bishop to the clergy

and people of the diocese.

pastry *noun* (*pl.* **pastries**) **1** dough made with flour, fat, and water, used for pie crusts. **2** a pie, tart, etc.

pasturage (păs′chə-rĭj) *noun* land on which livestock are allowed to graze.

pasture (păs′chər) *noun* an area of grassland suitable or used for the grazing of livestock. —*verb trans., intrans.* (**pastured, pasturing**) **1** to put (animals) in a pasture to graze. **2** of animals to graze.

pasty (pā′stē) *adj.* (**pastier, pastiest**) of a person's complexion unhealthily pale. ▸ **pastiness** *noun*

pat *verb trans.* (**patted, patting**) **1** to touch lightly or affectionately with one's hand. **2** to shape by striking lightly, e.g. with one's hand: *Pat the pillows into shape.* —*noun* **1** a light, esp. affectionate, touch with one's hand. **2** a small, flattish mass: *a pat of butter.* —*adv., esp. of things said* immediately and fluently, as if memorized: *pat answers.* —*adj.,* of answers, etc. quickly and easily supplied.

patch *noun* **1** a piece of material sewn or applied to, e.g., clothing, to cover a hole or reinforce a worn part. **2** a plot of ground: *a vegetable patch.* **3** a cover worn over an injured eye. **4** a small expanse contrasting with its surroundings: *patches of ice.* **5** a scrap or shred. —*verb trans.* (**patched, patching**) **1** to mend (a hole or garment) by sewing patches on. **2** (*also* **patch (something) up**) to repair (it) hastily and temporarily. **3** to connect or to be connected, e.g., by telephone, in a temporary manner: *patched the police officers through to headquarters.*

patchwork *noun* **1** needlework done by sewing together pieces of contrastingly patterned fabric. **2** a variegated expanse: *a patchwork of fields.*

patchy *adj.* (**patchier, patchiest**) **1** forming or occurring in patches: *patchy clouds.* **2** uneven or variable in quality. ▸ **patchiness** *noun*

pate *noun* the human head: *a bald pate.*

pâté (pă-tā′, pä-) *noun* a spread made from ground or chopped meat or fish blended with herbs, spices, etc.

patella (pə-tĕl′ə) *noun* (*pl.* **patellae**) the kneecap.

patent (păt′nt) *noun* **1** an official license granting the sole right to make and sell a particular article. **2** the right so granted. **3** the invention so protected. —*verb trans.* (**patented, patenting**) to obtain a patent for (an invention, design, etc.). —*adj.* **1** (also pronounced pay- in this sense) very evident: *patent misrepresentation.* **2** concerned with the granting of, or protection by, patents. **3** *of a product* made or protected under

patent. **4** open for inspection: *letters patent.*
▸ **patentee** *noun* ▸ **patently** *adv.*

patent leather (păt'nt) glossy varnished leather.

paternal (pə-tərn'l) *adj.* **1** relating to, appropriate to, or like a father. **2** *of a relation or ancestor* related on one's father's side. ▸ **paternally** *adv.*

paternalism *noun* governmental or managerial benevolence, esp. if taken to excessive overprotectiveness and authoritarianism. ▸ **paternalistic** *adj.*

paternity *noun* **1** fatherhood. **2** the identity of a child's father. **3** authorship, source, or origin.

Pater Noster *or* **pater-noster** (păt,ər-năs'tər, păt,-) *noun* the Lord's Prayer.

path *noun* **1** a track on which to walk. **2** the line along which something is traveling: *the path of Jupiter.*

path- *combining form same as* **patho-**.

-path *combining form* forming words denoting: **1** a sufferer from a disorder: *psychopath.* **2** a practitioner of a therapy: *osteopath.*

pathetic *adj.* **1** moving one to pity. **2** hopelessly inadequate: *a pathetic attempt.* ▸ **pathetically** *adv.*

-pathic *combining form* forming adjectives corresponding to nouns in *-pathy: homeopathic.*

patho- *or* **path-** *combining form* forming words denoting disease: *pathology.*

pathogen *noun* a bacterium, virus, etc. that causes disease. ▸ **pathogenic** *adj.*

pathological *adj.* **1** relating to pathology. **2** *colloq.* compulsive; habitual: *a pathological liar.* ▸ **pathologically** *adv.*

pathology *noun* **1** the study of the nature, causes, and consequences of disease. **2** the manifestations of disease. **3** a marked, abnormal departure from what is considered normal. ▸ **pathologist** *noun*

pathos (pā'thäs,, -thôs,, -thôs,) *noun* a quality in a situation, etc., that moves one to pity.

pathway *noun* a way someone or something travels; a path.

-pathy *combining form* forming words denoting **1** feeling: *telepathy.* **2** disease or disorder: *psychopathy.* **3** a method of treating disease: *homeopathy.*

patient *adj.* showing an ability to endure delay, trouble, pain, or hardship calmy. —*noun* a person who receives treatment or other care from a physician, dentist, etc. ▸ **patience** *noun* ▸ **patiently** *adv.*

patio (păt'ē-ō,) *noun* (*pl.* **patios**) an open paved area beside a house.

patois (pă-twä') *noun* (*pl.* **patois**) **1** the local dialect of a region. **2** jargon.

patriarch (pā'trē-ärk,) *noun* **1 a** the male head

of a family, community, or tribe. **b** a venerable elderly man. **2 a** in the Orthodox Church, any of the five senior bishops, of Constantinople, Antioch, Alexandria, Moscow, and Jerusalem. **b** *RC Church* the pope. ▸ **patriarchal** *adj.*

patriarchy *noun* (*pl.* **patriarchies**) a social system in which men are the heads of families or tribes, and descent is traced through the male line.

patrician *noun* an aristocrat.

patricide *noun* **1** the act of killing one's father. **2** a person who kills his or her father. ▸ **patricidal** *adj.*

patrimony *noun* (*pl.* **patrimonies**) property inherited from one's father or ancestors. ▸ **patrimonial** *adj.*

patriot (pā'trē-ət, -ăt,) *noun* someone who loves and serves his or her country devotedly. ▸ **patriotic** *adj.* ▸ **patriotism** *noun*

patrol *verb trans., intrans.* (**patrolled**, **patrolling**) to make a regular systematic tour of (an area) to maintain security or surveillance. —*noun* **1** one or more people patrolling an area. **2** the act of patrolling: *on patrol.*

patrolman *or* **patrolwoman** *noun* a police officer of the lowest rank.

patron *noun* **1** a person who gives financial support and encouragement, e.g., to an artist, the arts, etc. **2** a regular customer.

patronage (pā'trə-nĭj) *noun* **1** support given by a patron. **2** regular business given by customers.

patronize *verb trans.* (**patronized**, **patronizing**) **1** to treat condescendingly. **2** to give esp. regular business to (e.g., a shop, theater, etc.). ▸ **patronizing** *adj.*

patron saint the guardian saint of a country, profession, craft, etc.

patronymic (pă,trə-nĭm'ĭk) *noun* a name derived from one's father's or a male ancestor's name.

patter[1] *verb intrans.* (**pattered, pattering**) *of rain, footsteps, etc.* to make a light, rapid, tapping noise. —*noun* the light, rapid tapping of footsteps or rain.

patter[2] *noun* the fast persuasive talk of a salesperson, or the quick speech of a comedian. —*verb intrans., trans.* (**pattered, pattering**) to say or speak rapidly or glibly.

pattern *noun* **1** a model, guide, or set of instructions for making something. **2** a decorative design, e.g., on wallpaper or fabric. **3** a sample, e.g., of fabric. **4** an excellent example. **5** a coherent series of occurrences or set of features: *a pattern of events.* —*verb trans.* (**patterned, patterning**) to model (something) on (another type, design, etc.). ▸ **patterned** *adj.*

paucity *noun* smallness of quantity.

paunch *noun* a large fat belly. ▸ **paunchy** *adj.*

pauper *noun* a poverty-stricken person, esp. one who is eligible to live, or who is living, on public charity. ▸ **pauperism** *noun*

pause *noun* 1 a short break in activity. 2 *Mus.* the prolonging of a note or rest beyond its normal duration, or a sign indicating to do so. —*verb intrans.* (**paused, pausing**) 1 to have a short break. 2 to hesitate.

pave *verb trans.* (**paved, paving**) to surface (a road, street, etc.) with, e.g., concrete or asphalt.

pavement *noun* 1 a smooth, hard surface, e.g., of concrete or asphalt, on which to walk or ride. 2 road-surfacing material.

pavilion *noun* 1 a sports arena. 2 a light temporary building in which to display exhibits at a trade show, etc. 3 a summerhouse. 4 a building or wing connected to an even bigger structural complex.

paving *noun* 1 material that is used to pave a surface. 2 a paved surface.

paw *noun* 1 an animal's clawed foot or hand. 2 *colloq.* a hand. —*verb trans., intrans.* (**pawed, pawing**) 1 *of an animal* to scrape or strike (it) or at (it) with its paw or paws. 2 a to finger or handle clumsily. b to touch (someone) with unwelcome familiarity.

pawn[1] *verb trans.* (**pawned, pawning**) to deposit (an article of value) with a pawnbroker as a pledge for a sum of money borrowed. —*noun* 1 the condition of being pawned: *in pawn.* 2 a pawned article.

pawn[2] *noun* 1 a chess piece of the lowest value. 2 a person manipulated by others.

pawnbroker *noun* a person who lends money in exchange for pawned articles.

pawnshop *noun* a pawnbroker's place of business.

pawpaw *noun* same as **papaw**.

pay *verb trans., intrans.* (**paid, paying**) 1 to give (money) to (someone) in exchange for goods, services, etc. 2 to give money to settle (a bill, debt, etc.). 3 to give (wages or salary) to an employee. 4 to make a profit; to make as profit: *businesses that don't pay.* 5 to be worthwhile: *It pays to be polite.* 6 (also **pay for (something)**) to suffer or be punished for (it). —*noun* money given or received for work, etc. —**pay off** to have profitable results. —**pay (something) off** to finish paying (a debt, etc.). ▸ **payable** *adj.* ▸ **payee** *noun* ▸ **payer** *noun*

PAYE *or* **P.A.Y.E.** *abbrev.* pay as you enter.

payload *noun* 1 the revenue-earning part of a vehicle's load. 2 the quantity of goods, passengers, etc., carried by an aircraft.

paymaster *noun* an official in charge of the payment of wages and salaries, esp. in the armed forces.

payment *noun* 1 a sum of money paid. 2 the act of paying or process of being paid.

payoff *noun colloq.* 1 a bribe. 2 a final settling of accounts. 3 a climax, outcome, or final resolution.

payroll *noun* 1 a register of employees listing the wage due to each. 2 the total amount of money required for employees' wages.

Pb *symbol Chem.* lead[2] (sense 1).

PC *abbrev.* 1 *Comput.* personal computer. 2 politically correct.

Pd *symbol Chem.* palladium.

pd. *abbrev.* paid.

PDT *or* **P.D.T.** Pacific Daylight Time.

P.E. *abbrev.* physical education.

pea *noun* 1 a climbing plant cultivated for its round, green, edible seeds, which are produced in long pods. 2 the seed of this plant.

peace *noun* 1 freedom from war. 2 a treaty or agreement ending a war. 3 freedom from noise, disturbance, or disorder. 4 freedom from mental agitation: *peace of mind.* ▸ **peaceable** *adj.* ▸ **peaceably** *adv.*

peaceful *adj.* 1 calm and quiet. 2 unworried; serene. 3 free from war, violence, disturbance, or disorder. ▸ **peacefully** *adv.* ▸ **peacefulness** *noun*

peacemaker *noun* a person who makes or brings about peace.

peace officer a law-enforcement officer.

peace pipe a long ornate pipe smoked by Native Americans as a token of peace.

peach *noun* 1 a a small tree cultivated for its edible fruit. b the fruit of this tree, consisting of a hard stone, sweet juicy yellow or white flesh, and a yellowish-pink, usu. velvety skin. 2 the color of this fruit. ▸ **peachy** *adj.*

peacock *noun* (*pl.* **peacocks, peacock**) a male peafowl, which has green and gold eye-spot tail-feathers that it forms into a large fan during courtship.

peafowl *noun* same as **peacock**.

peahen *noun* a female peacock.

peak *noun* 1 a pointed summit of a mountain or hill. 2 a maximum, e.g., in consumer use: *electricity consumed at peak periods.* —*verb intrans.* (**peaked, peaking**) 1 to reach a maximum. 2 to reach the height of one's powers or popularity.

peal *noun* 1 the ringing of a bell or bells. 2 a set of bells, each with a different note. 3 a burst of noise: *peals of laughter.* —*verb intrans., trans.* (**pealed, pealing**) to ring or resound.

peanut *noun* 1 a low-growing plant cultivated for its edible nutlike seeds, which are produced in wrinkled yellowish underground pods. 2 the seed of this plant, consisting of hard, white flesh surrounded by a reddish-brown papery skin.

pear *noun* **1** a tree cultivated for its edible fruit. **2** the usu. cone-shaped fruit of this tree, with sweet, juicy, white pulp and a usu. yellowish-green skin.

pearl *noun* **1** a bead of smooth, hard, lustrous material found inside the shell of certain mollusks, e.g., oysters. **2** mother-of-pearl. **3** something valued or precious. —*adj.* **1** like a pearl in color or shape. **2** made of or set with pearls or mother-of-pearl. ▶ **pearly** *adj.*

peasant *noun* in poor agricultural societies, a farm worker or small farmer. ▶ **peasantry** *noun*

peat *noun* **1** a mass of plant material formed in a waterlogged environment, used in compost and manure, and in dried form as a fuel. **2** a cut block of this material. ▶ **peaty** *adj.*

peat moss a moss that grows in wet places; also, the partly carbonized remains of such a moss that are widely used as mulch.

pebble *noun* a small, roundish, smooth stone. ▶ **pebbly** *adj.*

pecan *noun* **1** a tree with an edible nut. **2** the oblong reddish-brown nut of this tree.

peccadillo (pĕk′ə-dĭl′ō) *noun* (*pl.* **peccadilloes, peccadillos**) a minor misdeed.

peck[1] *verb intrans., trans.* (**pecked, pecking**) **1** (**peck at (something)** or **peck (something)**) *of a bird* to strike, nip, or pick at (it) with the beak. **2** (**peck at (something)**) usu. *of a person* to eat (food) desultorily and without relish. **3** to kiss perfunctorily: *pecked me on the cheek.* —*noun* **1** a tap or nip with the beak. **2** a perfunctory kiss.

peck[2] *noun* a unit of dry capacity or volume equal to 8 qts. or about 537.6 cu. in.

pectin *noun* a carbohydrate found in and between plant cell walls that is used in jam-making.

pectoral *adj.* of or relating to the breast or chest.

peculiar *adj.* **1** strange; odd. **2** (**peculiar to (someone** or **something)**) exclusively associated with (someone or something): *habits peculiar to cats.* **3** especial; particular: *of peculiar interest.* ▶ **peculiarity** *noun* ▶ **peculiarly** *adv.*

pecuniary *adj.* concerning, or consisting of money.

ped- *combining form same as* **pedi-**.

-ped or **-pede** *combining form forming words denoting foot: quadruped / millipede.*

pedagogue (pĕd′ə-gäg.) *noun* a teacher.

pedagogy (pĕd′ə-gō.jē, -gäj.ē) *noun* the science, principles, or work of teaching. ▶ **pedagogic** or **pedagogical** *adj.*

pedal *noun* a lever operated by the foot, e.g., on a machine, vehicle, or musical instrument. —*verb trans., intrans.* (**pedaled** or **pedalled, pedaling** or **pedalling**) to move or operate by means of a pedal or pedals.

pedant *noun* someone overly concerned with correctness of detail. ▶ **pedantic** *adj.* ▶ **pedantically** *adv.* ▶ **pedantry** *noun*

peddle *verb trans., intrans.* (**peddled, peddling**) to go from place to place selling (small items of merchandise). ▶ **peddler** *noun*

-pede *combining form same as* **-ped.**

pedestal *noun* the base on which a statue or column is mounted.

pedestrian *noun* a person traveling on foot, esp. in a street. —*adj.* of or for pedestrians.

pedi- or **ped-** *combining form forming words denoting foot: pedicure.*

pediatrics *noun* (*sing.*) the branch of medicine concerned with the care of children, and the treatment of childhood diseases. ▶ **pediatric** *adj.* ▶ **pediatrician** *noun*

pedicure *noun* medical or cosmetic treatment of the feet and toenails.

pedigree *noun* **1** a person's ancestry, esp. if long and distinguished; proof of an animal's pure breeding. **2** a genealogical table or family tree.

> Literally 'crane's foot', because the forked feet of the bird were thought to resemble the lines of a family tree

pedo-, ped-, paed- or **paedo-** *combining form forming words denoting child or children: pediatrics.*

peek *verb intrans.* (**peeked, peeking**) to glance briefly and surreptitiously. —*noun* a brief, usu. furtive glance.

peel *verb trans., intrans.* (**peeled, peeling**) **1** to strip the skin or rind off (a fruit or vegetable); to be able to be peeled. **2** (*also* **peel (something) away** or **off**) to strip off (an outer layer). **3** *of skin, paint, etc.* to flake off in patches. **4** *of a wall or other surface* to shed its coating in flaky strips. —*noun* the skin or rind of vegetables or fruit, esp. citrus fruit. ▶ **peeler** *noun* ▶ **peelings** *pl. noun*

peep[1] *verb intrans.* (**peeped, peeping**) **1** to look quickly or covertly. **2** to emerge briefly or partially: *the sun peeping from behind the clouds.* —*noun* a quick covert look.

peep[2] *noun* the high-pitched cry of a baby bird, etc. —*verb intrans.* (**peeped, peeping**) **1** *of a young bird, etc.* to utter a high-pitched cry. **2** *colloq.* to sound or cause to sound: *peep the horn.*

peephole *noun* a hole, crack, etc., through which to look, usu. surreptitiously.

peer[1] *noun* **1** an equal, contemporary, companion, or fellow. **2** a member of the nobility.

peer[2] *verb intrans.* (**peered, peering**) **1** (**peer at (something** or **someone)**) to look hard at (someone or something), esp. as if having difficulty in seeing. **2** to peep out or emerge briefly or partially: *the sun peered from behind the clouds.*

peerage (pǐr'ǐj) noun the title or rank of a peer.

peeress noun 1 the wife or widow of a peer. 2 a female peer in her own right.

peerless adj. without equal. ▸ **peerlessly** adv.

peeve verb trans. (**peeved, peeving**) colloq. to irritate, annoy, or offend. ▸ **peeved** adj.

peevish adj. irritable; cantankerous. ▸ **peevishly** adv. ▸ **peevishness** noun

peg noun 1 a little shaft of wood, metal, or plastic shaped for any of various fixing, fastening, or marking uses. 2 a coat hook. 3 a clothespin. 4 a pin on a stringed instrument, turned to tune it. —verb trans. (**pegged, pegging**) 1 to insert a peg into. 2 to fasten with a peg or pegs.

PEI or **P.E.I.** abbrev. Prince Edward Island.

pejorative adj. disapproving, derogatory, or disparaging. —noun a word or affix with derogatory force. ▸ **pejoratively** adv.

pelican noun (pl. **pelicans**) an aquatic bird with an enormous beak with a pouch below it that is used to scoop up fish.

pellet noun 1 a small rounded mass of compressed material. 2 a piece of small shot for an air rifle, etc.

pell-mell adv. in confused haste.

pellucid (pə-loo'sĭd) adj. 1 clear: the pellucid waters of the lake. 2 absolutely clear in expression and meaning: a pellucid statement.

pelt[1] verb trans. (**pelted, pelting**) 1 to bombard with missiles. 2 (also pelt down) of rain, etc. to fall fast and heavily. —noun an act or spell of pelting.

pelt[2] noun the furry skin of a dead animal.

pelvis noun 1 the basin-shaped bony cavity into which the base of the spine fits. 2 the pelvic bones. ▸ **pelvic** adj.

pen[1] noun 1 a small enclosure for animals. 2 a small enclosure or area of confinement: a playpen. —verb trans. (**penned** or **pent, penning**) to enclose or confine in or as if in a pen.

pen[2] noun a writing instrument that uses ink. —verb trans. (**penned, penning**) to compose and write with a pen.

pen[3] noun colloq. a prison.

pen[4] noun a female swan.

penal adj. relating to punishment, esp. by law: the penal code. ▸ **penally** adv.

penalize verb trans. (**penalized, penalizing**) 1 to impose a penalty on for wrongdoing, breaking a rule, etc. 2 to disadvantage: penalized by the new tax laws. ▸ **penalization** noun

penalty noun (pl. **penalties**) 1 a punishment for wrongdoing, breaking a contract or rule, etc. 2 a fine. 3 Sport a handicap imposed for an infringement of the rules, in team games an advantage awarded to the opposing side.

penance noun 1 repentance or atonement for wrongdoing; an act of repentance: do penance. 2 RC Church a sacrament involving confession, repentance, forgiveness, and absolution.

pence Brit. see penny (sense 2).

penchant noun a liking or tendency.

pencil noun 1 a writing and drawing instrument consisting of a wooden shaft containing a stick of graphite or other material. 2 a similar object used, e.g., to darken the eyebrows. —verb trans. (**penciled** or **pencilled, penciling** or **pencilling**) to write, draw, or mark with a pencil.

pendant noun an ornament suspended from a neck chain, bracelet, etc.; a necklace with such an ornament hanging from it.

pendent adj. 1 suspended; dangling. 2 jutting; overhanging. 3 undetermined or undecided.

pending adj. 1 waiting to be decided or dealt with. 2 of a patent about to come into effect: patent pending. —prep. until; awaiting: held in prison pending trial.

pendulum noun a swinging lever used to regulate the movement of a clock.

penetrate (pĕn'ə-trāt,) verb trans., intrans. (**penetrated, penetrating**) 1 to find a way in; to enter with difficulty. 2 to infiltrate (an organization, etc.). 3 to find a way through; to pierce: penetrated the silence. 4 to be understood: The news didn't penetrate at first. ▸ **penetrable** adj. ▸ **penetration** noun

penetrating adj. 1 all too loud and clear; strident. 2 clear, crisp, and keen: a penetrating intellect. 3 piercing: a penetrating look.

penguin noun a stout, usu. black and white, flightless sea bird found esp. in the Antarctic region.

penicillin noun an antibiotic widely used to treat bacterial infections.

peninsula noun a piece of land almost surrounded by water or projecting into water from a larger landmass. ▸ **peninsular** adj.

penis noun (pl. **penises, penes**) the male organ of reproduction.

penitent adj. regretful for wrong one has done. —noun a repentant person, esp. one doing penance. ▸ **penitence** noun ▸ **penitently** adv.

penitentiary (pĕn,ĭ-tĕn'chə-rē) noun (pl. **penitentiaries**) a prison. —adj. of or relating to punishment, penance, or incarceration.

penknife noun a pocket knife with blades that fold into the handle.

pen name a pseudonym used by a writer.

pennant noun a small, narrow, triangular flag.

penniless adj. having no money at all.

penny noun (pl. **pennies**) 1 one cent, or a copper coin of this value. 2 Brit. (pl. **pence, pennies**) in the UK, a hundredth part of fl1, or a bronze coin of this value. **3** a coin of low value in certain other countries.

penny-pincher *noun* a miser. ▸ **penny-pinching** *adj., noun*

penology (pĭ-nǎl′ə-jē) *noun* the study of crime and punishment. ▸ **penologist** *noun*

pension *noun* a sum of money that is paid to a retired person. —*verb trans.* (**pensioned, pensioning**) to grant a pension to. ▸ **pensionable** *adj.* ▸ **pensioner** *noun*

pensive *adj.* preoccupied with one's thoughts. ▸ **pensively** *adv.* ▸ **pensiveness** *noun*

pent *verb see* pen¹. —*adj.* held in: *a mass of pent emotions*. —**pent up** *of feelings, energy, etc.* repressed or stifled.

penta- *or* **pent-** *combining form* forming words denoting five: *pentatonic*.

Pentagon (pĕnt′ə-gän,) the US military establishment.

pentagon *noun* a two-dimensional figure with five sides and five angles. ▸ **pentagonal** *adj.*

pentagram *noun* a five-pointed star, esp. as a magic symbol.

pentameter (pĕn-tăm′ət-ər) *noun* a line of verse with five metrical feet.

pentathlon (pĕn-tăth′lən, -län,) *noun Sport* an athletic competition composed of five events, the modern pentathlon being made up of swimming, cross-country riding and running, fencing, and pistol-shooting.

penthouse (pĕnt′hows,) *noun* a usu. luxurious apartment on the roof of a high building.

penultimate (pĭ-nəl′tĭ-mət) *adj.* the last but one.

penumbra (pə-nəm′brə) *noun* (*pl.* **penumbrae, penumbras**) a rim of lighter shadow around the shadow proper of a body; an area where dark and light blend.

penurious *adj.* **1** miserly. **2** poor; impoverished. ▸ **penuriously** *adv*

penury *noun* **1** extreme poverty. **2** lack; scarcity.

people *pl. noun* **1** men and women in general. **2** (**the people**) ordinary citizens. **3** (**the people**) voters as a body. **4** subjects or supporters of a monarch, etc. **5** *colloq.* parents or relations. —*noun* (*pl.* **peoples**) a nation or race. —*verb trans.* (**peopled, peopling**) to fill (a region) with people; to inhabit.

pep *noun colloq.* energy; vitality. —*verb trans.* (**pepped, pepping**) to enliven or invigorate (someone or something).

pepper *noun* **1 a** a shrub cultivated for its pea-sized red berries. **b** a pungent seasoning prepared from the dried berries of this plant. **2 a** a shrub cultivated for its large green, red, or yellow edible fruits. **b** the hollow fruit of this plant, eaten as a vegetable. *Also called* **capsicum.** —*verb trans.* (**peppered,**

peppering) **1** to bombard (with missiles). **2** to sprinkle liberally: *a text peppered with errors*. **3** to season with pepper (sense 1b).

peppercorn *noun* the dried berry of the pepper plant (sense 1).

peppermint *noun* **1 a** a species of mint cultivated for its aromatic oil, which is used in confectionery, etc. **b** this flavoring. **2** a candy flavored with peppermint.

peppery *adj.* **1** well seasoned with, or tasting of, pepper. **2** short-tempered; irascible.

pep talk a brief talk intended to raise morale.

peptic *adj.* **1** relating to or promoting digestion. **2** relating to the digestive juices.

per *prep.* **1** out of every. **2** for every. **3** in every: *100 accidents per week*.

perambulate *verb trans., intrans.* (**perambulated, perambulating**) to walk about (a place): *perambulated the streets*. ▸ **perambulation** *noun*

per annum for each year; by the year.

per capita for each person: *income per capita*.

perceive *verb trans.* (**perceived, perceiving**) **1** to apprehend (an image) by sight. **2** to understand, interpret, or view: *perceived her role as teacher, not disciplinarian*. ▸ **perceivable** *adj.*

percent *or* **per cent** (SYMBOL **%**) *adv.* **1** in or for every 100. **2** on a scale of 1 to 100: *90 percent certain*. —*noun* (*usu.* **percent**) **1** a percentage or proportion. **2** one part on every 100: *half a percent*.

percentage (pər-sĕnt′ĭj) *noun* **1** an amount, number, or rate stated as a proportion of one hundred. **2** a proportion.

Usage When preceded by the definite article *the*, the word *percentage*, followed by *of* and a count noun, takes a singular verb. When preceded by the indefinite article *a* and followed by a count noun, *percentage* takes a plural verb: *The percentage of successful candidates is quite low. / A small percentage of the candidates were successful.* If the noun following a *percentage* is a mass noun, not a count noun, a singular verb is the choice: *A large percentage of the potato crop has been hit by blight.*

perceptible *adj.* able to be perceived; noticeable; detectable. ▸ **perceptibility** *noun*

perception *noun* **1** *Psychol.* the organization and interpretation of information about one's environment that is received by the senses. **2** one's powers of observation and discernment. **3** one's view or interpretation.

perceptive *adj.* quick to notice or discern; astute. ▸ **perceptively** *adv.*

perch¹ *noun* **1** a branch, stick, etc. above ground on which a bird can rest. **2** a place selected, esp. temporarily, as a seat. **3** a high

position or vantage point. —*verb intrans.,
trans.* (**perched, perching**) **1** of a bird to
alight and rest on a perch. **2** to sit, esp.
insecurely or temporarily.

perch² *noun* (*pl.* **perch, perches**) an edible
freshwater fish with spiny fins.

percolate *verb intrans., trans.* (**percolated,
percolating**) **1** to pass through a porous
material; to ooze, trickle, or filter. **2** of
coffee to make it, or to be made, in a
percolator. ▸ **percolation** *noun*

percolator *noun* a coffee pot in which boiling
water circulates up through a tube and down
through ground coffee beans.

percussion *noun* **1** the striking of one hard
object against another. **2** *Mus.* **a** instruments played by striking, e.g., drums,
cymbals, etc. **b** these instruments as a
section of an orchestra. ▸ **percussionist**
noun ▸ **percussive** *adj.*

peregrinate (pĕr'ə-grĭ-nāt,) *verb intrans.*
(**peregrinated, peregrinating**) to travel,
voyage, or roam. ▸ **peregrination** *noun*

peremptory *adj.* **1** of an order expecting
immediate compliance. **2** of a tone or
manner arrogantly impatient. **3** of a statement, conclusion, etc. allowing no denial or
discussion. ▸ **peremptorily** *adv.*

perennial *adj.* **1** of a plant living for several or
many years. **2** lasting throughout the year. **3**
constant; continual. —*noun* a perennial
plant. See also **annual** (sense 1), **biennial**.
▸ **perennially** *adv.*

perfect (pər'fĭkt) *adj.* **1** complete in all essential elements. **2** a faultless; flawless. **b** without mistakes: a perfect translation. **3** exactly
right or suitable. **4** exact: drew a perfect
circle. **5** absolute; utter: perfect nonsense.
6 Gram., of the tense of a verb denoting
completed action. —*noun Gram.* the perfect tense, in English formed with the auxiliary verb have and the past participle.
—*verb trans.* (pər-fĕkt') (**perfected,
perfecting**) **1** to improve, make perfect. **2** to
make final; to complete. **3** to develop (a technique, etc.) to a reliable standard. ▸ **perfec-
tible** *adj.* ▸ **perfection** *noun* ▸ **perfectly** *adv.*

perfectionism *noun* an expectation of the
very highest standard. ▸ **perfectionist** *noun*

perfidious *adj.* treacherous or disloyal. ▸ **per-
fidiously** *adv.* ▸ **perfidy** *noun*

perforate (pər'fə-rāt,) *verb trans.* (**perforated, perforating**) **1** to make a hole or
holes in. **2** to make a row of holes in (e.g.,
paper) for ease of tearing. ▸ **perforation**
noun

perform *verb trans., intrans.* (**performed,
performing**) **1** to carry out (a task, job,
etc.), fulfill (a function), or provide (a service,
etc.). **2** to entertain an audience. **3** to conduct oneself: performs well in interviews.

▸ **performer** *noun*

performance *noun* **1** the performing of a play,
part, dance, piece of music, etc. **2** the
performing of a task, etc. **3** a level of
achievement, success, or profitability.

perfume *noun* **1** a sweet odor. **2** a fragrant
liquid for applying to the skin. —*verb trans.*
(**perfumed, perfuming**) to apply perfume
to.

perfumery *noun* (*pl.* **perfumeries**) **1** perfumes. **2** a place where perfumes are made
or sold.

perfunctory *adj.* done merely as a duty, etc.
without genuine care, effort, or feeling. ◨
AUTOMATIC, MECHANICAL, ROUTINE.
▸ **perfunctorily** *adv.*

perhaps *adv.* possibly; maybe.

peril *noun* **1** a situation or state in which one is
exposed to harm, injury, or loss. **2** a hazard.
▸ **perilous** *adj.*

perimeter (pə-rĭm'ət-ər) *noun* **1** the boundary
of an enclosed area, e.g., of a two-
dimensional figure. **2** its length.

perinatal (pĕr,ĭ-nāt'l) *adj.* relating to or occurring between the 28th week of pregnancy
and about a month after childbirth.

period *noun* **1** a portion of time. **2** a phase or
stage, e.g., in history or development. **3** any
long interval of geological time, e.g., the
glacial period. **4** any of the sessions into
which the school day is divided. **5** a punctuation mark (.), used at the end of a
sentence and to mark an abbreviation. Also
called **full stop**. **6** the monthly discharge of
blood during a woman's menstrual cycle.
—*adj.* dating from or designed in the style
of the historical time or era in question:
period costumes.

periodic *adj.* happening at intervals, usu.
regular intervals. ▸ **periodically** *adv.* ▸ **peri-
odicity** *noun*

periodical *adj.* periodic. —*noun* a magazine
published weekly, monthly, quarterly, etc.

periodic table *Chem.* a table of all the chemical elements arranged in order of increasing
atomic number.

peripatetic (pĕr,ĭ-pə-tĕt'ĭk) *adj.* traveling
about from place to place. —*noun* an
itinerant. ▸ **peripatetically** *adv.*

peripheral *adj.* **1** relating to or belonging to
the outer edge or outer surface: peripheral
nerves. **2** not central to (the issue in hand).
—*noun Comput.* a device, e.g., a printer or
mouse, that is connected to a computer
system and controlled by it, but is not part of
the central processing unit.

periphery *noun* (*pl.* **peripheries**) **1** an edge or
boundary. **2** an external surface.

periscope *noun* a device that enables the user
to view objects above eye level. ▸ **periscopic**
adj.

perish *verb intrans., trans.* **(perished, perishing)** to be destroyed or ruined; to die.

perishable *adj.,* of esp. *food* liable to go bad quickly. —*noun* (*usu.* **perishables**) a perishable commodity, esp. food. ▸ **perishability** *noun*

periwinkle[1] *noun* a plant with slender trailing stems and bluish-purple flower.

periwinkle[2] *noun* a small marine snail with a spirally coiled shell.

perjure *verb trans.* **(perjured, perjuring)** *Law* to lie while under oath to tell the truth in a court of law. ▸ **perjurer** *noun* ▸ **perjury** *noun*

perk[1] *verb intrans., trans.* **(perked, perking)** (*also* **perk up** *or* **perk (someone) up**) to become or make more lively and cheerful.

perk[2] *noun colloq.* a benefit, additional to income, derived from employment, such as the use of a company car.

perm *noun* a hair treatment using chemicals that give a long-lasting wave or curl. —*verb trans.* **(permed, perming)** to curl or wave (hair) with a perm.

permafrost *noun* an area of subsoil or rock that has remained below freezing point for at least a year.

permanent *adj.* **1** lasting or intended to last indefinitely: *a permanent promotion.* ▣ EN-DURING ▣ TEMPORARY. **2** of a condition, *etc.* unlikely to alter. ▸ **permanence** *or* **permanency** *noun* ▸ **permanently** *adv.*

permeate (pər′mē-āt,) *verb trans., intrans.* **(permeated, permeating) 1** of a *liquid* to penetrate, pass or seep through, (a fine or porous material, a membrane, etc.). **2** of a smell, gas, *etc.* to spread through a room or other space. ▸ **permeable** *adj.* ▸ **permeability** *noun*

permissive *adj.* allowing great, usu. excessive, freedom, esp. in sexual matters. ▸ **permissively** *adv.* ▸ **permissiveness** *noun*

permit (pər-mĭt′) *verb trans.* **(permitted, permitting) 1** to give consent, permission, or authorization to (someone) for (something); to allow (someone) (something). **2** (**permit (something)** *or* **permit of (something)**) to enable (it) to happen or take effect: *an outrage that permits* (of) *no excuses.* (pər′mĭt, pər-mĭt′) —*noun* a document authorizing something. ▸ **permissible** *adj.* ▸ **permissibility** *noun* ▸ **permission** *noun*

permute *verb trans.* **(permuted, permuting)** to rearrange (a set of things) in different orders, esp. in every possible order in succession. ▸ **permutation** *noun*

pernicious *adj.* harmful; destructive; deadly. ▸ **perniciously** *adv.*

pernickety *or* **persnickety** *adj.* overly particular and given to fussing over details.

peroxide *noun Chem.* **1** a chemical that releases hydrogen peroxide when treated with acid. **2** hydrogen peroxide, used as a bleach for hair and textiles. —*verb trans.* **(peroxided, peroxiding)** to bleach (hair) with hydrogen peroxide.

perpendicular *adj.* **1** vertical; upright. **2** being at right angles. —*noun* a perpendicular line, position, or direction. ▸ **perpendicularity** *noun*

perpetrate (pûr′pə-trāt,) *verb trans.* **(perpetrated, perpetrating)** to commit, or be guilty of (a crime, error, etc.). ▸ **perpetration** *noun* ▸ **perpetrator** *noun*

perpetual (pər-pĕch′ə-wəl) *adj.* **1** permanent: *in perpetual bliss.* **2** continual: *perpetual quarrels.*

perpetuate (pər-pĕch′ə-wāt,) *verb trans.* **(perpetuated, perpetuating)** to cause to last or continue: *perpetuate a feud.* ▸ **perpetuation** *noun* ▸ **perpetuity** *noun*

perplex *verb trans.* **(perplexed, perplexing) 1** to confuse, or baffle. **2** to complicate. ▸ **perplexing** *adj.* ▸ **perplexity** *noun*

perquisite (pûr′kwĭ-zĭt) *noun* **1** same as **perk**[2]. **2** something regarded as due to one by right.

per se in itself; intrinsically.

persecute *verb trans.* **(persecuted, persecuting) 1** to ill-treat or oppress, esp. on the grounds of religious or political beliefs. **2** to harass or bother continually. ▸ **persecution** *noun* ▸ **persecutor** *noun*

persevere *verb intrans.* **(persevered, persevering)** to keep on striving for (something). ▸ **perseverance** *noun*

Persian *noun* **1** a native or citizen of Persia (Iran). **2** the language of Persia. —*adj.* relating to Persia, its people, or their language.

persist *verb intrans.* **(persisted, persisting) 1** (**persist in** *or* **with (something)**) to continue (it) in spite of resistance, discouragement, etc. **2** of *rain, etc.* to continue steadily. ▸ **persistence** *noun* ▸ **persistent** *adj.* ▸ **persistently** *adv.*

person *noun* **1** an individual human being. **2** one's body: *concealed on his person.* **3** *Gram.* each of the three classes into which pronouns and verb forms fall, *first person* denoting the speaker (or the speaker and others), *second person* the person addressed (with or without others) and *third person* the person(s) or thing(s) spoken of.

persona *noun* (*pl.* **personas, personae**) one's character as one presents it to other people.

personable *adj.* attractive physically, and likable.

personage (pûr′sə-nĭj) *noun* a widely known person.

personal *adj.* **1** coming from someone as an individual: *my personal opinion.* **2** done, attended to, etc., by the person in question: *gave it my personal attention.* **3** relating to oneself in particular: *a personal triumph.* **4** relating to one's private concerns: *her personal life.* **5** of remarks referring, often disparagingly, to an individual's physical or other characteristics.. ▸ **personally** *adv.*

personal computer (ABBREV. **PC**) a micro-computer.

personality *noun* (*pl.* **personalities**) **1** a person's nature, disposition, or character. **2** strength or distinctiveness of character: *lots of personality.* **3** a celebrity.

personalize *verb trans.* (**personalized, personalizing**) **1** to mark as the property of a particular person. **2** to personify.

persona non grata (pər-sō͞,nə-nän,grät'ə, -grät'ə) a person who is not wanted or welcome within a particular group or in a nation-state.

personify *verb trans.* (**personified, personifying, personifies**) **1** in literature, etc., to represent (an abstract quality, etc.) as a human or as having human qualities. **2** to embody in human form; to be the perfect example of: *She personifies patience.* ▸ **personification** *noun*

personnel (pər,sə-nĕl') *noun* **1** (*pl.*) the people employed in a business or other organization. **2** a department within such an organization dealing with matters concerning employees.

perspective *noun* **1** the observer's view of objects in relation to one another. **2** a sensible, balanced, objective view of a situation: *kept the problem in perspective.* **3** an individual way of regarding a situation.

perspicacious *adj.* shrewd, astute, or discerning. ▸ **perspicacity** *noun*

perspicuous *adj.*, of speech or writing clearly expressed and easily understood. ▸ **perspicuity** *noun* ▸ **perspicuously** *adv.*

perspire *verb intrans.* (**perspired, perspiring**) to sweat. ▸ **perspiration** *noun*

persuade *verb trans.* (**persuaded, persuading**) to urge successfully; to prevail on (someone) to do something. ▸ **persuadable** or **persuasible** *adj.* ▸ **persuader** *noun* ▸ **persuasive** *adj.* ▸ **persuasively** *adv.*

persuasion *noun* **1** the act of persuading. **2** a creed, conviction, or set of beliefs.

pert *adj.* **1** impudent; cheeky. **2** *of clothing or style* jaunty; saucy. ▸ **pertly** *adv.* ▸ **pertness** *noun*

pertain *verb intrans.* (**pertained, pertaining**) (*often* **pertain to** (**someone** *or* **something**)) **1** to have something to do with. **2** to belong to: *skills pertaining to the job.* **3** to be appropriate; to apply.

pertinacious *adj.* refusing to change or compromise. ▸ **pertinaciously** *adv.* ▸ **pertinacity** *noun*

pertinent *adj.* relevant. ▸ **pertinence** or **pertinency** *noun*

perturb *verb trans.* (**perturbed, perturbing**) to excite and trouble (a person). ▸ **perturbation** *noun*

peruse (pə-ro͞oz') *verb trans.* (**perused, perusing**) to examine or study attentively. ▸ **perusal** *noun*

pervade *verb trans.* (**pervaded, pervading**) to spread or extend throughout. ▸ **pervasive** *adj.*

perverse *adj.* deliberately and unreasonably differing or disagreeing. ▸ **perversely** *adv.* ▸ **perversity** *noun*

perversion *noun* **1** the process of perverting or condition of being perverted. **2** an instance of abnormal sexual activity.

pervert *verb trans.* (pər-vərt') (**perverted, perverting**) **1** to divert illicitly from what is normal or right. **2** to distort or misinterpret (words, etc.). —*noun* (pər'vərt,) someone who is morally or sexually perverted.

Pesach (pä'säкн, pĕs'äкн,) *noun* Passover.

peseta (pə-sāt'ə) *noun* the standard unit of currency in Spain.

pesky *adj.* (**peskier, peskiest**) *colloq.* troublesome or infuriating. ▸ **peskily** *adv.*

peso *noun* (*pl.* **pesos**) the standard unit of currency in many Central and S American countries and the Philippines.

pessimism *noun* **1** the tendency to emphasize the gloomiest aspects, and to expect the worst. **2** the belief that there is more evil in the world than good. ▸ **pessimist** *noun* ▸ **pessimistic** *adj.*

pest *noun* **1** an insect, fungus, weed, etc. that has a damaging effect on livestock, crops, or stored produce. **2** an irritating person or thing

pester *verb trans.* (**pestered, pestering**) **1** to annoy constantly. **2** to harass or hound with requests.

pesticide *noun* a chemical compound that is used to kill pests, e.g., insects or weeds.

pestle (pĕs'əl, -təl) *noun* a clublike utensil for pounding substances in a mortar.

pet *noun* **1** a tame animal or bird kept as a companion. **2** someone's favorite. —*adj.* **1** kept as a pet. **2** of or for pets. **3** own special; favorite. —*verb trans., intrans.* (**petted, petting**) **1** to pat or stroke (an animal, etc.). **2** to fondle and caress sexually.

petal *noun* one of the often scented and usu. brightly colored leaflike parts of a flower head.

petard (pə-tär', -tärd') *noun* —**hoist with one's own petard** being the victim of one's own trick or cunning.

peter *verb intrans.* (**petered, petering**) (**peter out**) to dwindle away to nothing.

petite (pə-tēt′) *adj.*, *of a woman or girl* small and dainty.

petition *noun* **1** a formal written request to an authority to take an action, signed by a large number of people. **2** an appeal to a higher authority. —*verb trans.*, *intrans.* (**petitioned, petitioning**) to address a petition to (someone) for (some cause); to make an appeal or request. ▸ **petitioner** *noun*

petitjury *or* **pettyjury** (pĕt′ē-jŏŏr,ē) *noun* a civil or a criminal trial jury.

petrel (pĕ′trəl, pē′-) *noun* a sea bird with a hooked bill and external tube-shaped nostrils.

petrifaction *or* **petrification** *noun* a fossilization process in which wood, shell, bone, etc. are turned into stone.

petrify *verb trans.*, *intrans.* (**petrified, petrifying, petrifies**) **1** to terrify. **2** *of organic material* to undergo petrifaction.

petrol *noun Brit.* gasoline.

petroleum *noun* a naturally occurring oil consisting of a thick black, brown, or greenish liquid mixture of hydrocarbons.

petroleum jelly a greasy jellylike substance obtained from petroleum, used in ointments and as a lubricant.

petrology *noun* the scientific study of the structure, origin, distribution, etc. of rocks. ▸ **petrologist** *noun*

petticoat *noun* a woman's slip or underskirt.

pettifogger *noun* **1** a lawyer dealing with unimportant cases, esp. deceitfully or quibblingly. **2** someone who quibbles over trivial details. ▸ **pettifog** *verb* ▸ **pettifogging** *noun, adj.*

petty *adj.* (**pettier, pettiest**) **1** of minor importance; trivial. **2** small-minded or childishly spiteful.

petty cash money kept for small everyday expenses in an office, etc.

petty jury *same as* **petitjury**.

petty officer (ABBREV. **PO, P.O.**) a non-commissioned naval officer.

petulant *adj.* ill-tempered; peevish. ▸ **petulance** *noun* ▸ **petulantly** *adv.*

petunia *noun*. a plant with large, funnel-shaped, brightly colored flowers.

pew *noun* a long church bench.

pewter *noun* an alloy of tin and lead, silvery with a bluish tinge.

pfennig (fĕn′ĭg, -ĭk) *noun* a German unit of currency worth a hundredth of a mark.

PG *abbrev.*, *as a film classification* parental guidance.

pg. *abbrev.* page[1].

PG–13 *abbrev.*, *as a film classification* parental guidance (for children under 13).

pH *noun Chem.* a measure of the relative acidity or alkalinity of a solution. *Also called* **pH value.**

phalanges (fə-lăn′jēz) *pl. noun* (*sing.* **phalanx**) *Anat.* the bones of the fingers and toes.

phalanx (fā′lăngks,) *noun* **1** a solid body of people, esp. when representing united support or opposition. **2** *Anat. see* **phalanges.**

phallus *noun* (*pl.* **phalli, phalluses**) a representation or image of an erect penis. ▸ **phallic** *adj.*

phantasm *noun* **1** an illusion or fantasy. **2** a supernatural being or form. ▸ **phantasmal** *adj.*

phantom *noun* **1** a supernatural being or form. **2** an illusory image or vision. —*adj.* of the nature of a phantom; imaginary.

pharaoh (făr′ō, fā′rō) *noun* a king of ancient Egypt.

Pharisee (făr′ĭ-sē,) *noun* **1** a member of an ancient Jewish sect that was greatly concerned with rules. **2** a self-righteous or hypocritical person. ▸ **Pharisaic** *or* **pharisaic** (făr,ə-sā′ĭk) *adj.*

pharmacist *noun* a person trained to prepare and dispense drugs and medicines.

pharmacology *noun* the scientific study of medicines and drugs, and their effects and uses. ▸ **pharmacologist** *noun*

pharmacy *noun* (*pl.* **pharmacies**) **1** the mixing and dispensing of drugs and medicines. **2** a drugstore.

pharyngitis *noun Med.* inflammation of the mucous membrane of the pharynx, with sore throat and fever.

pharynx (făr′ĭngks) *noun* (*pl.* **pharynges, pharynxes**) *Anat.* the throat. ▸ **pharyngeal** (fə-rĭn′jē-əl) *adj.*

phase *noun* **1** a stage or period in growth or development. **2** any of the stages in a recurring cycle of changes. —*verb trans.* (**phased, phasing**) to organize or carry out in stages. —**phase** (**something**) **in** *or* **out** to introduce (it), or get rid of (it), in stages.

Ph.D. *abbrev. philosophiae doctor* (Latin), Doctor of Philosophy.

pheasant (fĕz′ənt) *noun* (*pl.* **pheasant, pheasants**) a large, long-tailed game bird related to the domestic chicken.

phenomenal *adj.* **1** remarkable; extraordinary; abnormal. **2** of the nature of a phenomenon. **3** relating to phenomena. ▸ **phenomenally** *adv.*

phenomenon *noun* (*pl.* **phenomena**) **1** a happening perceived through the senses, esp. if unusual or scientifically explainable. **2** an extraordinary or abnormal person or thing.

> *Usage* Note that *phenomena* is a plural form; *a phenomena* is incorrect, though often heard.

pheromone *noun* a chemical secreted by an animal or insect, which affects the behavior of others of the species.

phial *noun* a little medicine bottle.

phil- *or* **philo-** *combining form* forming words denoting fondness or liking: *philanthropy*.

-phil *combining form same as* **-phile**.

philander *verb intrans.* (**philandered, philandering**) to flirt, or have casual love affairs, with women. ▸ **philanderer** *noun*

philanthropy *noun* concern for one's fellow human beings; esp. benevolence to those in need. ▸ **philanthropic** *adj.* ▸ **philanthropist** *noun*

philately *noun* the study and collecting of postage stamps. ▸ **philatelist** *noun*

-phile *or* **-phil** *combining form* forming words denoting fondness or attraction: *bibliophile / pedophile*.

philharmonic *adj.* dedicated to music.

-philia *combining form* forming words denoting: **1** a tendency: *hemophilia*. **2** an unnatural liking: *necrophilia*.

-philiac *combining form* forming nouns and adjectives corresponding to nouns in *-philia*: *hemophiliac*.

Philistine *or* **philistine** (fĭl'ə-stēn,) *adj.* having no interest in or appreciation of art, literature, music, etc. —*noun* a person who is uncivilized and uncultured.

> After a people of ancient Palestine, enemies of the Israelites

philo- *see* **phil-**.

philosophical *adj.* **1** of or relating to philosophy or philosophers. **2** calmly resigned, stoic, or patient in the face of adversity. ▸ **philosophically** *adv.*

philosophize *verb intrans.* (**philosophized, philosophizing**) **1** to form philosophical theories. **2** to take a calm, dispassionate view in the face of adversity.

philosophy *noun* (*pl.* **philosophies**) **1** the search for truth and knowledge by means of reflection and reasoning. **2** a particular system or set of beliefs established as a result of this. **3** a set of principles serving as a basis for making judgments and decisions: *one's philosophy of life.* ▸ **philosopher** *noun*

phlegm (flĕm) *noun* **1** sputum. **2** calmness or impassiveness; stolidity or sluggishness of temperament. ▸ **phlegmatic** *adj.*

-phobe *combining form* forming words denoting a person affected by a particular form of phobia: *Russophobe*.

phobia *noun* an obsessive, persistent fear of a specific object or situation. ▸ **phobic** *adj.*

-phobia *combining form* forming nouns denoting obsessive and persistent fears: *claustrophobia*.

phon- *combining form same as* **phono-**.

phone *noun* a telephone. —*verb trans., intrans.* (**phoned, phoning**) to telephone.

-phone *combining form* forming words denoting: **1** an instrument transmitting or reproducing sound: *microphone*. **2** a musical instrument: *saxophone*. **3** a speech sound: *homophone*.

phoneme (fō'nēm,) *noun* the smallest unit of sound in a language that distinguishes one word from another. ▸ **phonemic** *adj.*

phonetic *adj.* **1** of or relating to the sounds of a spoken language. **2** of, e.g., spelling intended to represent pronunciation. **3** denoting a pronunciation system using symbols that each represent one sound only. ▸ **phonetically** *adv.*

phonetics *noun* (*sing.*) the branch of linguistics that deals with the production and perception of speech sounds.

phoney *adj., noun same as* **phony**.

phono- *or* **phon-** *combining form* forming words denoting sound or voice: *phonology*.

phonograph *noun* a record player.

phonology *noun* (*pl.* **phonologies**) **1** the study of speech sounds. **2** the system of speech sounds of a particular language. ▸ **phonological** *adj.* ▸ **phonologist** *noun*

phony *or* **phoney** *adj.* (**phonier, phoniest**) fake, sham, bogus, or insincere. —*noun* (*pl.* **phonies** *or* **phoneys**) someone or something fake, bogus, or insincere. ▸ **phoniness** *noun*

phosphorescence *noun* **1** the emission of light from a substance that has absorbed energy ultraviolet radiation, x-rays, etc., and continuing after the energy source has been removed. **2** the emission of light by a substance without a significant rise in temperature. ▸ **phosphorescent** *adj.*

phosphorus (făs'fə-rəs) *noun Chem.* (SYMBOL P) a nonmetallic element that exists in a toxic yellowish-white form and also in red and black forms.

photo *noun* (*pl.* **photos**) *colloq.* a photograph.

photo- *combining form* forming words denoting: **1** photography: *photomontage*. **2** light: *photoelectric*.

photocell *noun* a photoelectric cell.

photocopier *noun* a machine that makes copies on paper of documents, etc. by any of various photographic techniques. ▸ **photocopy** *noun, verb*

photoelectric cell a device activated by photoelectricity, used, e.g., in burglar alarms. *Also called* **electric eye, photocell**.

photoelectricity *noun* electrical or electronic activity triggered by light or other electromagnetic radiation. ▸ **photoelectric** *adj.*

photogenic *adj.* looking attractive in photographs.

photograph *noun* a permanent record of an image produced by photography. —*verb trans., intrans.* (**photographed, photo-**

graphing) to take a photograph of (a person, thing, etc.). ▸ **photographer** noun

photographic adj. 1 relating to or similar to photographs or photography. 2 of memory retaining images in exact detail. ▸ **photographically** adv.

photography noun the process of recording an image on light-sensitive film or another sensitized material.

photon noun a particle of electromagnetic radiation that travels at the speed of light.

photosensitive adj. reacting to light or other electromagnetic radiation. ▸ **photosensitivity** noun

photosynthesis noun the process whereby plants manufacture carbohydrates from carbon dioxide and water, using the energy from sunlight trapped by the chlorophyll. ▸ **photosynthesize** verb

phrase noun 1 a group of words expressing a single idea, forming part of a sentence but not constituting a clause. 2 an idiomatic expression. 3 Mus. a run of notes forming a distinct part of a melody. —verb trans. (**phrased, phrasing**) 1 to express (something) in words. 2 Mus. to bring out the phrases in (music) as one plays. ▸ **phrasal** adj.

phraseology (frā,zē-ăl'ə-jē) noun one's choice of words and way of combining them, in expressing oneself.

phrenology noun the former practice of assessing a person's character and aptitudes by examining the shape of the skull. ▸ **phrenologist** noun

phyla Biol. see **phylum**.

phylactery noun (pl. **phylacteries**) 1 either of two small boxes containing religious texts worn on the arm and forehead by Jewish men during prayers. 2 a charm or amulet.

phyllo or **filo** noun a type of pastry made in thin sheets and layered with oil or butter for cooking.

phylum noun (pl. **phyla**) Biol. each of the major groups into which the animal kingdom is divided.

physi- combining form same as **physio-**.

physical adj. 1 of the body: physical exercise. 2 relating to actual matter or to actuality: the physical world. 3 relating to nature or to the laws of nature: a physical impossibility. ▸ **physicality** noun ▸ **physically** adv.

physical education (ABBREV. P.E., phys. ed.) instruction in sport and gymnastics as part of a school or college curriculum.

physical science any of the sciences dealing with nonliving matter, e.g., astronomy, physics, chemistry, and geology.

physical therapy (ABBREV. P.T.) treatment of bodily injuries or physical dysfunction, using therapeutic exercise and other restorative regimens. Also called **physiotherapy**.

▸ **physical therapist**

physician noun a medical doctor, esp. one engaged in general medicine as opposed to surgery.

physics noun (sing.) the scientific study of the properties and interrelationships of matter and energy. ▸ **physicist** noun

physio- or **physi-** combining form forming words denoting physical or physiological: physiotherapy.

physiognomy (fĭz,ē-ăg'nə-mē, -ăn'ə-) noun (pl. **physiognomies**) the face or features, esp. as a supposed key to personality.

physiology noun the study of the internal processes and functions of living organisms, such as respiration and reproduction. ▸ **physiological** adj. ▸ **physiologist** noun

physiotherapy noun physical therapy. ▸ **physiotherapist** noun

physique (fĭ-zēk') noun the structure of the body with regard to size, shape, proportions, and muscular development.

pi noun 1 the 16th letter of the Greek alphabet (Π, π). 2 Math. this symbol as a representation of the ratio of the circumference of a circle to its diameter, in numerical terms approximately 3.14159.

piano[1] noun (pl. **pianos**) a large musical instrument with a keyboard, the keys being pressed down to operate a set of hammers that strike tautened wires to produce the sound. Also called **pianoforte**. ▸ **pianist** noun

piano[2] adj., adv. Mus. played softly.

pianoforte (pē-ăn'ə-fôrt,, -fôrt,ē) noun a piano[1].

picaresque (pĭk,ə-rĕsk') adj., of a novel, etc. telling of the adventures of a usu. likable rogue in separate, only loosely connected, episodes.

picayune (pĭk,ē-yōōn') adj. trifling; paltry; insignificant. —noun slang something of little or no value.

piccolo noun (pl. **piccolos**) a small flute.

pick[1] verb trans., intrans. (**picked, picking**) 1 to choose or select. 2 to detach and gather (flowers from a plant, fruit from a tree, etc.). 3 (**pick** (something) **up, off, out,** etc.) to lift, remove, detach, or extract (it): picked a crumb off the carpet. 4 to open (a lock) with a device other than a key. 5 to steal money or valuables from (someone's pocket). 6 to undo; to unpick. 7 to provoke (a fight, quarrel, etc.) with someone. —noun 1 the best of a group: the pick of the bunch. 2 one's own preferred selection. —**pick on** (**someone**) 1 to blame (someone) unfairly. 2 to bully (someone). **pick up** of a person's health, a situation, etc. to recover or improve. **pick** (**someone**) **up** to arrest or seize (someone): picked up by the police.

pick (something) up 1 to lift or raise (it) from a surface. **2** to learn or acquire (a skill, language, etc.) over time. **3** *Telecomm.* to receive a signal, program, etc. ▸ **picker** *noun*

pick² *noun* **1** a tool with a long metal head pointed at one or both ends, for breaking ground, rock, ice, etc. **2** a plectrum. ·

pickax *noun* a long-handled pick (sense 1).

picket *noun* **1** a person or group stationed outside a place of work to persuade other employees not to go in during a strike. **2** a body of soldiers on patrol or sentry duty. **3** a stake fixed in the ground, e.g., as part of a fence. —*verb trans., intrans.* (**picketed, picketing**) **1** to station pickets, or act as a picket, at (e.g., a factory). **2** to guard or patrol with or as a military sentry.

pickle *noun* **1** a preserve of vegetables in vinegar, salt water, or a tart sauce. **2** a vegetable so preserved. **3** the liquid used. —*verb trans.* (**pickled, pickling**) to preserve in vinegar, salt water, etc. ·

pickpocket *noun* a thief who steals from people's pockets.

pickup *noun* **1** the stylus on a record player. **2** a pickup truck. **3** a halt to load goods or passengers; the goods or passengers so loaded.

pickup truck a lightweight truck with a cab and low-sided open body.

picky *adj.* (**pickier, pickiest**) *colloq.* overly particular and given to fussing over details.

picnic *noun* an outing on which one takes food for eating in the open; the food so taken or eaten. —*verb intrans.* (**picnicked, picnicking**) to have a picnic. ▸ **picnicker** *noun*

pictograph or **pictogram** *noun* **1** an ideogram. **2** a pictorial or diagrammatic representation of values, statistics, etc.

pictorial *adj.* relating to, or consisting of, pictures. —*noun* a periodical with a high proportion of pictures. ▸ **pictorially** *adv.*

picture *noun* **1** a drawing, painting, or photograph. **2** a mental image; a view: *a clear picture of the battle.* **3** a situation or outlook: *a gloomy financial picture.* **4** a visible embodiment: *the picture of happiness.* **5** the image received on a television screen. **6** a movie. —*verb trans.* (**pictured, picturing**) **1** to imagine or visualize. **2** to describe vividly. **3** to represent or show in a picture.

picturesque (pĭk,chə-rĕsk′) *adj.* of places or buildings charming to look at, esp. if rather quaint.

pidgin *noun* a simplified language used between speakers of different languages. See also **creole**.

pie *noun* a quantity of food with a covering and/or base of pastry.

piebald (pī′bôld,) *adj.* having contrasting patches of color, esp. black and white. —*noun* a piebald horse.

piece *noun* **1** a bit; a portion taken from a whole. **2** a component; an item in a set. **3** one item of a class of things: *a piece of fruit.* **4** a specimen: *a fine piece of Chippendale.* **5** an instance: *a piece of nonsense.* **6** a musical or artistic work. **7** an article in a newspaper, etc. **8** a cannon or firearm. —*verb trans.* (**pieced, piecing**) (**piece (something** or **things) together**) to join (something or things) together to form a whole.

pièce de résistance (pyĕs,də-rə-zē,stäɴs′) (*pl.* **pièces de résistance**) the best or most impressive item.

piecemeal *adj.* developing or happening a bit at a time. —*adv.* a bit at a time.

pie chart a diagram consisting of a circle divided into sectors, used to display statistical data.

pied (pīd) *adj.*, *of a bird* having variegated, esp. black and white, plumage.

pier (pĭr) *noun* **1** a structure projecting into the sea or a lake for use as a landing or a breakwater. **2** a pillar supporting a bridge or arch.

pierce *verb trans., intrans.* (**pierced, piercing**) (**pierce (something)** or **pierce through (something)**) **1** to make (a hole) in or through (something). **2** to penetrate: *The wind pierced through her clothing.* **3** *of light or sound* to burst through (darkness or silence). ▸ **piercing** *adj.*

piety (pī′ət-ē) *noun* piousness.

piffle *noun* nonsense; rubbish.

pig *noun* **1** a hoofed mammal with a heavy, stout body and a protruding, flattened snout. **2** a greedy, dirty or selfish person. **3** *offensive slang* a male chauvinist. **4** *offensive slang* a police officer. **5** an oblong block of metal. ▸ **piggish** *adj.* ▸ **piggishness** *noun* ▸ **piggy** *adj.*

pigeon *noun* a medium-sized bird related to the dove.

pigeonhole *noun* any of a set of compartments for filing letters or papers. —*verb trans.* (**pigeonholed, pigeon-holing**) **1** to put into a pigeonhole. **2** to put mentally into a category.

piggyback *noun* a ride on someone else's back. —*adv.* on someone else's back.

pigheaded *adj.* refusing to change or compromise. ▸ **pigheadedness** *noun*

pig iron an impure form of iron produced by smelting, so called because it is cast into *pigs*.

piglet *noun* a young pig.

pigment *noun* (pĭg′mənt) **1** coloring matter used to color paint, paper, etc. **2** a colored substance in plant and animal tissues. —*verb trans.* (pĭg′mənt, -mĕnt,) (**pigmented, pigmenting**) to color or stain. ▸ **pigmentation** *noun*

pigmy *noun, adj. same as* **pygmy**.

pigsty (pĭg'stī,) *noun* (*pl.* **pigsties**) **1** a pen for pigs; a sty. **2** a place of filth and disorder.

pigtail *noun* a plaited length of hair.

pike[1] *noun* (*pl.* **pike, pikes**) a large predatory freshwater game and food fish of lakes and rivers.

pike[2] *noun Hist.* a weapon resembling a spear.

pilaster *noun* a rectangular column standing out in relief from the façade of a building.

pilchard (pĭl'chərd) *noun* a small sea fish of the herring family.

pile[1] *noun* **1** a number of things on top of one another; a heap or mound. **2** *colloq.* a large quantity. **3** a pyre. **4** a nuclear reactor. —*verb trans.* (**piled, piling**) **1** (*usu.* **pile up** or **pile (something) up**) to accumulate into a pile. **2** (**pile in**) to move in a crowd or confused bunch.

pile[2] *noun* the soft thick surface of carpeting, velvet, etc.

pile[3] *noun* (*usu.* **piles**) a hemorrhoid.

pileup *noun* a multivehicle collision.

pilfer *verb trans., intrans.* (**pilfered, pilfering**) to steal in small quantities. ▶ **pilferer** *noun*

pilgrim *noun* **1** a person who makes a journey to a holy place as an act of reverence and religious faith. **2** a traveler. ▶ **pilgrimage** *noun*

pill *noun* **1** a small tablet of medicine for swallowing. **2** (**the pill**) an oral contraceptive.

pillage (pĭl'ĭj) *verb trans., intrans.* (**pillaged, pillaging**) to plunder or loot. —*noun* **1** an act of pillaging. **2** loot, plunder, or booty. ▶ **pillager** *noun*

pillar *noun* **1** a vertical post of wood, stone, metal, or concrete serving as a support. **2** a strong, reliable supporter of a cause or organization.

pillbox *noun* **1** a small round container for pills. **2** *Mil.* a small, usu. circular, concrete shelter.

pillion *noun* a seat for a passenger on a motorcycle or horse, behind the rider.

pillory *noun* (*pl.* **pillories**) *Hist.* a wooden frame with holes for the hands and head into which wrongdoers were locked as a punishment and publicly ridiculed.

pillow *noun* a cushion for the head on a bed.

pillowcase *noun* a washable cover for a pillow. *Also called* **pillowslip**.

pilot *noun* **1** a person who flies an aircraft. **2** a person employed to take ships into and out of harbors. **3** a guide. **4** a pilot light. **5** a television program produced to test public reaction to a possible series. —*adj.* (*attributive*) *of a scheme* experimental. —*verb trans.* (**piloted, piloting**) **1** to act as pilot to. **2** to direct, guide, or steer (a project, etc.).

pilot light a small permanent gas flame, e.g., on a gas stove, that ignites the main burners when they are switched on.

pimp *noun* a man who finds customers for a prostitute. —*verb intrans.* (**pimped, pimping**) to act as a pimp.

pimple *noun* a small, raised, pus-containing swelling on the skin. ▶ **pimply** *adj.*

PIN (pĭn) *noun, abbrev.* personal identification number.

pin *noun* **1** a short, slender implement with a sharp point and small, round head, used for fastening, attaching, etc. **2** a fastening device consisting of or incorporating a slender metal or wire shaft. **3** a narrow brooch. **4** *Bowling* a club-shaped object set upright for toppling with a ball. **5** the clip on a grenade, removed before throwing. —*verb trans.* (**pinned, pinning**) **1** to secure (something) with a pin. **2** (**pin (something) on (someone)**) *colloq.* to put the blame for (a crime or offense) on (someone).

pinafore *noun* a sleeveless dress for wearing over a blouse, sweater, etc.

pinball *noun* a game played on a device in which a small metal ball is propelled round a course, the score depending on what hazards it avoids and targets it hits.

pince-nez (păn-snā') *pl. noun* spectacles that are held in position by gripping the nose instead of being supported over the ears.

pincers (pĭn'sərz, -chərz) *pl. noun* **1** a hinged tool with clawlike jaws for gripping things. **2** a crab's or lobster's claw.

pinch *verb trans., intrans.* (**pinched, pinching, pinches**) **1** to squeeze the flesh of (someone) between thumb and finger. **2** *of tight shoes* to hurt or chafe. **3** *colloq.* to steal. —*noun* **1** an act of pinching. **2** a quantity that can be held between thumb and finger.

pincushion *noun* a pad into which to stick dressmaking pins for convenient storage.

pine[1] *noun* a tree with narrow needlelike leaves and woody cones; its wood.

pine[2] *verb intrans.* (**pined, pining**) to long or yearn.

pineapple *noun* **1** a tropical plant having a large yellowish-brown spiny fruit with a rosette of pointed green leaves. **2** the edible fruit of this plant.

ping *noun* a sharp ringing sound. —*verb intrans., trans.* (**pinged, pinging**) to make or cause to make this sound.

Ping-Pong *trademark* used for table tennis and the equipment for playing it.

pinion[1] *verb trans.* (**pinioned, pinioning**) **1** to immobilize by holding or binding the arms of; to hold or bind (someone's arms). **2** to hold fast or bind: *was pinioned against a wall.*

pinion² *noun* a small cogwheel that engages with a larger wheel or rack.

pink¹ *noun* **1** a color between red and white. **2** a plant, such as a carnation, having slightly frilled petals. —*adj.* **1** of the color pink. **2** slightly left-wing in views.

pink² *verb trans.* (**pinked, pinking**) to cut (cloth) with a notched or serrated edge.

pinkie *or* **pinky** *noun* (*pl.* **pinkies**) the little finger.

pinnacle *noun* **1** a slender spire. **2** a rocky peak. **3** a high point of achievement.

pinpoint *verb trans.* (**pinpointed, pinpointing**) to place, define, or identify precisely.

pinprick *noun* **1** a tiny hole made by or as if by a pin. **2** a slight irritation or annoyance.

pins and needles a prickling sensation in a limb, etc., felt as the flow of blood returns to it after being temporarily obstructed.

pinstripe *noun* a narrow stripe in cloth.

pint (pīnt) *noun* a unit of liquid measure, $\frac{1}{8}$ of a gallon, or 0.473 liter.

pinto bean a stringbean with mottled seeds.

pint-size *or* **pint-sized** *adj.* small.

pinup *noun* a picture of a glamorous person for pinning to a wall.

pinwheel *noun* **1** a toy windmill on a stick. *Also called* **windmill. 2** a Catherine wheel.

pioneer *noun* **1** an explorer or early settler. **2** an innovator or initiator. —*verb intrans.*, *trans.* (**pioneered, pioneering**) to be a pioneer.

pious *adj.* **1** religiously devout. **2** dutiful. **3** ostentatiously virtuous; sanctimonious. ▸ **piously** *adv.* ▸ **piousness** *noun*

pip¹ *noun* the seed of an apple, orange, etc.

pip² *noun* (*usu.* **pips**) a short high-pitched signal sound on a radio, telephone, etc.

pip³ *noun* one of the spots on playing cards, dice, or dominoes.

pipe *noun* **1** a tube for conveying water, gas, oil, etc. **2** a little bowl with a hollow stem for smoking tobacco, etc. **3** *Mus.* **a** a wind instrument consisting of a simple wooden or metal tube. **b** any of the vertical metal tubes through which sound is produced on an organ. —*verb trans.*, *intrans.* (**piped, piping**) **1** to convey (gas, water, oil, etc.) through pipes. **2** *Mus.* to play on a pipe or the pipes. ▸ **piper** *noun*

pipe dream a delightful fantasy or unrealistic hope.

pipeline *noun* pipes laid, usu. underground, to carry oil, natural gas, water, etc., across large distances.

pipette (pī-pĕt′) *noun* a narrow glass tube into which liquid can be sucked for transferring or measuring.

pippin *noun* an eating apple with a green or rosy skin.

piquant (pē′kənt, -känt,) *adj.* **1** having a pleasantly spicy taste or tang. **2** amusing, provocative, or stimulating. ▸ **piquancy** *noun*

pique (pēk) *noun* hurt pride; resentment. —*verb trans.* (**piqued, piquing**) **1** to offend. **2** to arouse (curiosity or interest).

piracy *see* **pirate.**

piranha (pə-rän′ə, -yə) *noun* an extremely aggressive, carnivorous, freshwater fish of S America.

pirate *noun* **1** someone who attacks and robs ships at sea. **2** someone who publishes material without permission, or uses someone else's work illegally. —*verb trans.* (**pirated, pirating**) to publish, reproduce, or use (someone else's literary or artistic work, or ideas) without permission. ▸ **piracy** *noun*

pirouette (pĭr,ə-wĕt′) *noun* a spin executed on the points of the feet in dancing, esp. in ballet.

Pisces (pī′sēz) *noun* **1** the Fishes, the name of a constellation and the 12th sign of the zodiac. **2** a person born between Feb. 20 and Mar. 20, under this sign.

pissed *adj. coarse slang* **1** angry; irritated. **2** drunk.

pistachio *noun* (*pl.* **pistachios**) **1** a small tree whose reddish-brown nutlike fruit contains an edible greenish seed. **2** the seed of this tree. *Also called* **pistachio nut.**

piste (pēst) *noun* a ski slope or track of smooth compacted snow.

pistil *noun* the female reproductive structure in a flowering plant.

pistol *noun* a gun that can be held in one hand when fired.

piston *noun* a device that moves up and down in the cylinder of an engine, driven by the pressure of hot gases or steam.

pit¹ *noun* **1** a big deep hole in the ground. **2** a coal mine. **3** an enclosure in which fighting animals or birds are put. **4** a sunken area in front of a stage, for an orchestra. *Also called* **orchestra pit. 5** a scar left by chickenpox or acne. **6** (**the pits**) *slang* an awful or intolerable situation. —*verb trans.* (**pitted, pitting**) **1** to set or match in competition or opposition. **2** to mark with scars and holes. **3** to put into, or bury in, a pit.

pit² *noun* the stone in a peach, plum, etc. —*verb trans.* (**pitted, pitting**) to remove the stone or stones from (e.g., a fruit).

pita *noun* a flat, rounded bread of Middle Eastern origin that can be opened and filled.

pit bull *or* **pit bull terrier** American Staffordshire terrier.

pitch¹ *verb* (**pitched, pitching**) **1** to set up (a tent or camp). **2** to throw or fling: *pitch a ball.* **3** to fall or cause to fall heavily forward. **4** *of a ship* to plunge and lift alternately at bow and stern. **5** *Mus.* to give a particular pitch to (a note) in singing or playing. **6** to choose a level of difficulty, etc., at which to present (a talk, etc.). **7** *Baseball* to throw to the batter. —*noun* **1** *Sport* a the field or area of play. **b** an act or style of pitching or throwing. **2** a level of intensity: *a high pitch of excitement*. **3** the steepness of a slope. **4** *Mus.* the highness or lowness of a note. **5** the plunging and rising motion of a ship.

pitch² *noun* **1** a thick, black, sticky substance obtained from tar. **2** any of various bituminous or resinous substances. —*verb trans.* (**pitched, pitching**) to coat or treat with pitch.

pitch-black *adj.* intensely black or dark.

pitchblende *noun* a mineral that is the main ore of uranium and radium.

pitcher¹ *noun* a large jug with one or two handles and a lip.

pitcher² *noun Baseball* the player who throws the ball to the batter.

pitchfork *noun* a long-handled fork with two or three sharp prongs, for tossing hay.

piteous *adj.* moving, heart-rending, or pathetic. ▸ **piteously** *adv.*

pitfall *noun* a hidden danger, unsuspected hazard, or unforeseen difficulty.

pith *noun* **1** the soft white tissue beneath the rind of many citrus fruits. **2** the innermost, central, essential, or unchanging part.

pithy *adj.* (**pithier, pithiest**) *of a saying, etc.* brief, forceful, and to the point.

pitiable *adj.* **1** arousing pity. **2** inadequate.

pitiful *adj.* **1** arousing pity. **2** sadly inadequate or ineffective. ▸ **pitifully** *adv.*

pittance (pĭt'ns) *noun* a meager allowance or wage.

pitter-patter *noun* the sound of light footsteps.

pituitary (pĭ-tōō'ə-tĕr,ē, -tyōō'-) *noun* (*pl.* **pituitaries**) a gland at the base of the brain that has a central role in the control of growth, sexual development, etc. —*adj.* relating to this gland.

pit viper a venomous snake, e.g., a rattlesnake, that has two heat-sensitive pits on its head.

pity *noun* **1** a feeling of sorrow for the troubles and sufferings of others. **2** a cause of sorrow or regret. —*verb trans.* (**pitied, pitying, pities**) to feel or show pity for. ▸ **pitiless** *adj.* ▸ **pitying** *adj.* ▸ **pityingly** *adv.*

pivot *noun* a central pin, spindle, or shaft, around which something turns or swivels. —*verb intrans.* (**pivoted, pivoting**) **1** to turn or swivel. ▸ **pivotal** *adj.*

pixel *noun* a dot forming the smallest element of the image on a computer or television screen.

pixie *or* **pixy** *noun* (*pl.* **pixies**) a traditionally mischievous fairy-like being.

pizza *noun* a disk of dough covered with cheese, tomatoes, etc., and baked, made orig. in Italy.

pizzazz *or* **pizzaz** *noun colloq.* boldness, vigor, dash, and flamboyance.

pizzeria *noun* a restaurant that makes and sells pizzas.

pizzicato (pĭt,sĭ-kät'ō) *adj. adv., of music for stringed instruments* played using the fingers to pluck the strings.

pkwy *or* **pky** *abbrev.* parkway.

pl. *abbrev.* **1** (Pl.) *used in street names* Place. **2** *Gram.* plural.

placard (plăk'ərd, -ärd,) *noun* a board or stiff card bearing a notice, advertisement, slogan, message of protest, etc., carried or displayed in public.

placate (plā'kāt,, plăk'āt,) *verb trans.* (**placated, placating**) to pacify or appease (an angry person, etc.). ▸ **placation** *noun* ▸ **placatory** *adj.*

place *noun* **1** a country, region, locality, town, village, etc. **2** *colloq.* one's home or lodging. **3** a seat or space, e.g., at a table. **4** customary position: *put it back in its place.* **5** a position within an order, e.g., of competitors in a contest, etc.: *finished in third place.* **6** one's role, function, duty, etc.: *It is not my place to tell her.* **7** an open square or row of houses. —*verb trans.* (**placed, placing**) **1** to put. **2** to submit: *place an order.* **3** to assign final positions to (contestants, etc.): *was placed fourth.*

placebo (plə-sē'bō) *noun* (*pl.* **placebos**) a substance administered as a drug, having no medicinal content but having a reassuring and therefore beneficial effect.

place kick *Football* a kick executed for, e.g., a field goal, with the ball being propped held on the ground in a fixed position.

placement *noun* **1** the act or process of placing or positioning. **2** the finding of a job or home for someone.

placenta (plə-sĕnt'ə) *noun* (*pl.* **placentas, placentae**) an organ that develops in the womb in pregnancy, linked to the fetus by the umbilical cord, through which it provides nutrients and oxygen, etc.

placid *adj.* calm; tranquil. ▸ **placidity** *noun* ▸ **placidly** *adv.*

plagia.ism *noun* the using of someone else's ideas or words as though they were one's own. ▸ **plagiarist** *noun* ▸ **plagiarize** *verb*

plague (plāg) *noun* **1** an epidemic disease with a high mortality rate. **2** an overwhelming intrusion by something unwelcome: *a plague of tourists.* —*verb trans.* (**plagued, plaguing**) **1** to afflict: *plagued by headaches.* **2** to pester.

plaice *noun* (*pl.* **plaice, plaices**) a flatfish that is an important food fish.

plain adj. 1 all of one color; unpatterned or undecorated. 2 simple. 3 obvious; clear. 4 straightforward; direct: plain dealing. 5 of a person lacking beauty; homely. —noun a large area of relatively flat land. —adv. utterly; quite: plain stupid. ▸ **plainly** adj. ▸ **plainness** noun

plainspoken adj. frank to the point of bluntness.

plaintiff noun the party that brings a charge against another party in a court of law.

plaintive adj. mournful, sad or wistful. ▸ **plaintively** adv. ▸ **plaintiveness** noun

plait (plăt, plāt) verb trans. (**plaited, plaiting**) to arrange (esp. hair) by interweaving three or more lengths. —noun a length of hair or other material so interwoven.

plan noun 1 a thought-out arrangement or method for doing something. 2 (usu. **plans**) intentions. 3 an outline diagram of a floor of a building, the streets of a town, etc., as seen from above. —verb trans., intrans. (**planned, planning**) 1 to devise a scheme for. 2 to make plans, preparations, or arrangements for (something). 3 (**plan (something)** or **plan on (something)**) to intend doing (it). 4 to draw up plans for; to design. ▸ **planner** noun ▸ **planning** noun

plane¹ noun an airplane.

plane² noun 1 Math. a flat surface, real or imaginary. 2 a level surface. 3 a level or standard: on a higher intellectual plane. —adj. 1 flat; level. 2 Math. lying in or concerned with one plane: a plane figure.

plane³ noun a carpenter's tool for shaving away unevennesses in wood. —verb trans. (**planed, planing**) 1 to smooth (a surface, esp. of wood) with this tool. 2 (**plane (something) off** or **away**) to remove (it) with this tool.

plane⁴ noun a large tree with thin bark that is shed in large flakes. Also called **plane tree**.

planet noun a celestial body in orbit around the Sun or another star.

planetarium noun (pl. **planetariums, planetaria**) 1 a projector by means of which the positions and movements of stars and planets can be projected onto a domed ceiling. 2 the building with such a projector.

planetary adj. 1 relating to planets. 2 involving or affecting the entire world.

plangent adj. of a sound deep, ringing, and mournful. ▸ **plangency** noun

plank noun 1 a long flat piece of timber. 2 any of the policies forming the platform of a political party. —verb trans. (**planked, planking**) 1 to equip or cover with planks. 2 colloq. to put (something) down roughly or noisily. 3 to broil or bake and then serve (esp. fish) on a plank.

plankton pl. noun microscopic animals and

plants that float in seas and lakes.

plant noun 1 a a living organism characterized by the ability to manufacture carbohydrates by photosynthesis. b a relatively small organism of this type, e.g., as opposed to a tree. 2 the buildings, equipment, and machinery used in a manufacturing or production industry. —verb trans. (**planted, planting**) 1 a to put (seeds or plants) into the ground to grow. b to put plants or seeds into (ground, a garden, bed, etc.). 2 to introduce (an idea, doubt, etc.) into someone's mind. 3 to place firmly: planted my feet on the deck. 4 to post (someone) as a spy or informant.

plantain¹ (plăn'tn) noun 1 a plant belonging to the banana family. 2 the green-skinned bananalike edible fruit of this plant.

plantain² noun a plant with erect spikes of small tightly clustered flowers.

plantation noun 1 a large estate where crops such as cotton and rice are grown. 2 an area of land planted with a certain kind of tree for commercial purposes.

planter noun 1 the owner or manager of a plantation. 2 a container for houseplants.

plaque (plăk) noun 1 a commemorative inscribed tablet fixed to or set into a wall. 2 a wall ornament made of pottery, etc. 3 a buildup of food debris, bacteria, etc. on the surface of teeth.

plasma noun the colorless liquid component of blood or lymph.

plaster noun 1 a pastelike mixture that is applied to walls and hardens to form a smooth surface. 2 plaster of Paris. 3 a pastelike mixture placed on the body for therapeutic purposes. Also called **sticking plaster**. —verb trans. (**plastered, plastering**) 1 to apply plaster to (walls). 2 colloq. to coat or spread thickly: plaster one's hair with gel. 3 to fix with some wet or sticky substance: hair plastered to his skull. ▸ **plasterer** noun

plasterboard noun board consisting of a layer of plaster between two layers of fiberboard, used for making partitions, ceilings, etc.

plaster of Paris powdered gypsum, mixed with water to make a material that dries hard, used for sculpting and for making casts for broken limbs.

plastic noun 1 any of a large number of synthetic materials that can be molded by heat and/or pressure. 2 colloq. a credit card: paid for the furniture with plastic. —adj. 1 made of plastic. 2 easily molded or shaped. 3 of money in the form of, or funded by, a credit card. ▸ **plasticity** noun

plastic surgery surgery concerned with repairing, restoring, or reconstructing deformed or damaged tissue or body parts.

plate 505 **pleasant**

plate *noun* **1 a** a flat or shallow dish on which to serve food. **b** a plateful. **2** a sheet of metal, glass, or other rigid material. **3** an inscribed flat piece of metal, plastic, etc. **4** a thin coating of gold, silver, or tin applied to a metal. *Also called* **plating. 5** a full-page illustration in a book. **6** *Photog.* a sheet of glass prepared with a light-sensitive coating for receiving an image. **7 a** a sheet of metal with an image engraved on it, or a print taken from it. **b** any of various surfaces set up with type ready for printing. **8** *Dentistry* a denture. —*verb trans.* (**plated, plating**) **1** to coat with a thin layer of metal. **2** to cover with metal plates.

plateau (plă-tō′) *noun* (*pl.* **plateaus, plateaux**) **1** an area of relatively high, flat land. **2** a stable, unvarying condition of prices, etc. after a movement.

plateful *noun* (*pl.* **platefuls**) the amount a plate will hold.

plate glass glass made in tough sheets for store windows, mirrors, etc.

platelet (plāt′lət) *noun* a small disk-shaped cell fragment in blood, responsible for blood clotting.

platform *noun* **1** the raised walkway alongside the track at a railroad or subway station, giving passengers access to trains. **2** the publicly declared principles and intentions of a political party.

plating *noun* plate (sense 6).

platinum *noun Chem.* (SYMBOL **Pt**) a silvery-white precious metal, used to make jewelry, surgical instruments, etc., and as a catalyst.

platitude *noun* an empty or unoriginal comment. ▸ **platitudinous** *adj.*

Platonic (plə-tän′ĭk, plā-) *adj.* **1** relating to the Greek philosopher Plato. **2** (*usu.* **platonic**) of human *love* not involving sexual relations. ▸ **platonically** *adv.*

platoon *noun* a subdivision of a company of soldiers, usu. commanded by a lieutenant.

platter *noun* a large flat dish.

platypus *noun* (*pl.* **platypuses**) an egg-laying amphibious mammal with a long flattened toothless snout, webbed feet, and a broad flat tail, found in Australia. *Also called* **duck-billed platypus.**

plaudit *noun* (*usu.* **plaudits**) an often loud expression of approval.

plausible *adj.* credible, reasonable, or likely. ▸ **plausibility** *noun* ▸ **plausibly** *adv.*

play *verb intrans., trans.* (**played, playing**) **1** *esp. of children* to spend time in recreation. **2** to fiddle or meddle with (something). **3** to take part in (a recreational pursuit, sport, match, etc.). **4** to compete against in a game or sport. **5** (**play** (**something**) **on** (**someone**)) to perpetrate (a trick, practical joke, etc.) on (someone). **6** to act or behave in a

certain way: *play it cool.* **7** to act out (a role) in a play, etc. **8** to perform (music) on an instrument; to perform on (an instrument). —*noun* **1** the condition of engaging in recreation or of participating in games: *children at play.* **2** the playing of a game, performance in a sport, etc. **3** behavior; conduct: *fair play.* **4** a dramatic piece for the stage, or a performance of it. **5** fun; jest: *said those things only in play.* **6** freedom of movement; looseness: *too much play in the brake.* **7** use: *brought all her cunning into play.* —**play on** (**something**) **1** to exploit (someone's fears, feelings, sympathies, etc.), for (one's) own benefit. **2** to make a pun on (it): *played on the two meanings of batter.* ▸ **playable** *adj.*

play-act *verb intrans.* (**play-acted, play-acting**) to behave in an insincere way.

playback *noun* the playing back of a sound recording or film, or an instance of it.

playbill *noun* a poster advertising a play or show.

playboy *noun* a man of wealth, leisure, and frivolous lifestyle.

player *noun* **1** a participant in a game or sport. **2** a performer on a musical instrument. **3** an actor or an actress. **4** a device for playing something.

playful *adj.* **1** given to lively playfulness. **2** humorous. ▸ **playfully** *adv.* ▸ **playfulness** *noun*

playgirl *noun* a woman of wealth, leisure, and frivolous lifestyle.

playground *noun* an area for children's recreation, esp. as part of a school's grounds.

playgroup *noun* a number of children belonging to a supervised group for regular play together.

playing card each of a pack of usu. 52 cards used in card games.

play-off *noun* a match or game played to resolve a draw or other undecided contest.

playwright *noun* an author of plays.

plea *noun* **1** an earnest appeal. **2** *Law* a statement made in a court of law by or on behalf of the defendant. **3** an excuse.

plea-bargain *verb intrans.* (**plea-bargained, plea-bargaining**) *Law* to make a bargain whereby a defendant pleads guilty to a lesser charge if the prosecuting attorney agrees to drop a more serious charge.

plead *verb trans., intrans.* (**pleaded** *or* **pled, pleading**) **1** to appeal earnestly. ▤ EN-TREAT, IMPLORE, PRAY, SUPPLICATE. **2** *Law, of an accused person* to state in a court of law that one is guilty or not guilty. **3** to argue in defense of (it). **4** to give as an excuse: *plead ignorance.* ▸ **pleadingly** *adv.*

pleasant (plĕz′ənt) *adj.* **1** giving pleasure; enjoyable; agreeable. **2** *of a person* friendly. ▸ **pleasantly** *adv.* ▸ **pleasantness** *noun*

pleasantry *noun* (*pl.* **pleasantries**) (*usu.* **pleasantries**) a remark or remarks made for the sake of politeness or friendliness.

please *verb trans., intrans.* (**pleased, pleasing**) **1** to give satisfaction, pleasure, or enjoyment to. **2** to choose; to like: *Do what you please.* —*adv.* used politely to accompany a request, order, acceptance of an offer, etc. ▸ **pleasing** *adj.*

pleasurable *adj.* enjoyable; pleasant.

pleasure (plĕzh'ər) *noun* **1** a feeling of enjoyment or satisfaction. **2** a source of such a feeling. **3** one's will, desire, preference, or inclination. —*adj.* used for or done for pleasure: *a pleasure boat.*

pleat (plēt) *noun* a fold that is sewn or pressed into cloth, etc.

plebeian (plĭ-bē'ən) *noun* a person lacking refinement or culture. —*adj.* coarse; vulgar; unrefined.

plebiscite (plĕb'ə-sīt,) *noun* a vote of all the electors, taken to decide a matter of public importance.

plebs *noun* (*pl.* **plebes**) the common people.

plectrum *noun* a small flat implement used for plucking the strings of a guitar.

pled *see* **plead**.

pledge *noun* **1** a solemn promise. **2** something left as security with someone to whom one owes money, etc. —*verb trans.* (**pledged, pledging**) **1** to promise (money, loyalty, etc.) to someone. **2** to bind or commit (oneself, etc.). **3** to offer or give as a pledge or guarantee.

plenary *adj.* **1** full; complete: *plenary powers.* **2** *of a meeting* attended by all members.

plenitude *noun* abundance; profusion.

plenteous (plĕnt'ē-əs) *adj.* abundant.

plentiful *adj.* existing in large amounts.

plenty *pron.* **1** enough or more than enough. **2** a lot. —*noun* wealth or sufficiency: *times of plenty.* —*adv. colloq.* fully: *plenty wide.*

plethora (plĕth'ə-rə) *noun* a large or excessive amount.

pliable *adj.* **1** easily bent; flexible. **2** easily persuaded or influenced. ▸ **pliability** *noun*

pliant *adj.* **1** bending easily; flexible, or supple. **2** easily influenced. ▸ **pliancy** *noun*

plied *see* **ply**².

pliers *pl. noun* a hinged tool with jaws for gripping, bending, or cutting wire, etc.

plies *see* **ply**¹, **ply**².

plight *noun* a danger, difficulty, or situation of hardship.

plinth *noun* a base or pedestal for a statue or other sculpture, or a vase.

plod *verb intrans.* (**plodded, plodding**) **1** to walk slowly with a heavy tread. **2** to work slowly, methodically, and thoroughly. ▸ **plodder** *noun*

plop *noun* the sound of a small object dropping into water. —*verb intrans., trans.* (**plopped, plopping**) to fall or drop with a sound resembling that of a small object going into water. —*adv.* with a plop.

plot¹ *noun* **1** a secret plan. ▣ CABAL, COLLUSION, CONSPIRACY. **2** the story of a play, film, novel, etc. —*verb trans., intrans.* (**plotted, plotting**) **1** to plan (something, esp. illegal or evil), usu. with others. **2** *Math.* to mark a series of individual points on a graph, or to draw a curve through them. ▸ **plotter** *noun*

plot² *noun* a piece of ground, usu. marked off or having boundaries.

plough *see* **plow**.

plover (pləv'ər, plō'vər) *noun* (*pl.* **plover, plovers**) a wading bird with a short straight bill.

plow *or* **plough** *noun* **1** a bladed farm implement used to turn over the surface of the soil, forming ridges and furrows. **2** any similar implement, esp. one for shoveling snow off roads. —*verb trans., intrans.* (**plowed** *or* **ploughed, plowing** *or* **ploughing**) **1** (*also* **plow (something) up**) to till or turn over (soil, land, etc.) with a plow. **2** to make a furrow or to turn over the surface of the soil with a plow. **3** (*usu.* **plow into (something)**) *colloq., of a vehicle* to crash into (something) at speed. ▸ **plowman** *noun*

plowshare *noun* a blade of a plow.

ploy *noun* a cunningly devised means to an end.

pluck *verb trans., intrans.* (**plucked, plucking**) **1** to pull the feathers off (a bird) before cooking. **2** to remove (something) by pulling: *plucked out a gray hair.* **3** to sound (the strings of a guitar, etc.) using the fingers or a plectrum. —*noun* **1** courage; guts. **2** a little tug.

plucky *adj.* (**pluckier, pluckiest**) *colloq.* spiritedly courageous. ▸ **pluckiness** *noun*

plug *noun* **1 a** a piece of rubber, plastic, etc., used as a stopper, e.g., in a bath or sink. **b** (*often in compounds*) any similar device or piece of material: *earplugs.* **2 a** a device with metal pins on an electrical apparatus, that is pushed into a socket to connect with the power supply. **b** the socket. **3** *colloq.* favorable publicity given to a product, program, etc, e.g., on television. **4** a lump of tobacco for chewing. —*verb trans., intrans.* (**plugged, plugging**) **1** to stop or block up (a hole, etc.). **2** *colloq.* to give favorable publicity to (a product, program, etc). **3** (**plug away** *or* **along**) *colloq.* to work or progress steadily. —**plug (something) in** to connect to the power supply by means of a plug.

plum *noun* **1** a small tree cultivated for its edible fruit or its flowers and foliage. **2** the smooth-skinned fruit of this tree. **3** (*also attributive*) *colloq.* something esp. valued or sought: *a plum job.*

plumage (ploo'mĭj) *noun* a bird's feathers.

plumb *noun* a lead weight hanging on the end of a line, used for measuring water depth. —*adj., adv.* straight, vertical, or perpendicular. —*adv.* **1** *colloq.* exactly: *plumb in the middle.* **2** *colloq.* utterly: *plumb crazy.* —*verb trans., intrans.* (**plumbed, plumbing**) **1** to measure the depth of (water) using a plumb. **2** to penetrate, probe, or understand (a mystery, etc.). **3** to be a plumber; to fit the plumbing of.

plumbago (pləm,bā'gō) *noun* graphite.

plumber (plŭm'ər) *noun* a person who installs and repairs water pipes, and water-, oil-, or gas-using appliances.

plumbing *noun* **1** the system of water and gas pipes in a building, etc. **2** the work or trade of a plumber.

plume *noun* **1** a large and ornate feather. **2** a curling column, e.g., of smoke. —*verb trans.* (**plumed, pluming**) **1** to decorate with plumes. **2** (**plume** (**oneself**) **on** (something)) to pride or congratulate (oneself).

plummet (plŭm'ĭt) *verb intrans.* (**plummeted, plummeting**) to plunge or hurtle downward.

plump[1] *adj.* rounded, chubby, or not unattractively fat. —*verb trans.* (**plumped, plumping**) to shake (cushions or pillows) to give (them) a full soft bulk. ▸ **plumpness** *noun*

plump[2] *verb trans., intrans.* (**plumped, plumping**) to put down, drop, fall, or sit heavily. —*noun* a sudden heavy fall, or the sound of it. —*adv.* with a plump.

plunder *verb trans., intrans.* (**plundered, plundering**) to steal (valuable goods), or loot (a place), esp. with open force during a war. ▸ **plunderer** *noun*

plunge (plənj') *verb intrans., trans.* (**plunged, plunging**) **1** to dive, throw oneself, fall, or rush headlong. **2** to involve oneself rapidly and enthusiastically. **3** to dip briefly into water or other liquid. **4** to dip steeply. —*noun* **1** an act of plunging. **2** *colloq.* a dip or swim.

plunger *noun* an implement consisting of a rubber cup at the end of a long handle, used with thrusting action to clear blocked toilets and drains.

pluperfect *Gram. adj.* denoting a tense, formed in English by *had* and a past participle, referring to action already accomplished at the time of the past action being related, as in *They had often gone there before, but this time they lost their way.* —*noun* the pluperfect tense, or a word in the pluperfect tense.

plural *noun Gram.* the form of a noun, pro-

noun, adjective, or verb used for two or more people, things, etc. *See also* **singular**. —*adj.* **1** *Gram.* denoting or in the plural. **2** consisting of more than one, or of different kinds.

pluralism *noun* the existence within a society of a variety of ethnic, cultural, and religious groups. ▸ **pluralist** *noun* ▸ **pluralistic** *adj.*

plurality *noun* (*pl.* **pluralities**) **1** the fact of being plural. **2** a large number or variety.

plus *prep.* **1** *Math.* with the addition of. **2** in combination with; with the added factor of: *bad luck, plus his own obstinacy.* —*adj.* **1** *Math.* denoting the symbol +. **2** advantageous; bonus: *a plus factor in the marketability of the car.* —*noun* (*pl.* **pluses**) **1** *Math.* the symbol +, denoting addition or positive value. *Also called* **plus sign**. **2** *colloq.* a bonus, advantage, or extra.

plush *adj. colloq.* luxurious, opulent, stylish, or costly.

plutocracy *noun* (*pl.* **plutocracies**) **1** government or domination by the wealthy. **2** a state governed by the wealthy. ▸ **plutocrat** *noun* ▸ **plutocratic** *adj.*

plutonium (ploo-tō'nē-əm) *noun Chem.* (SYMBOL Pu) a highly poisonous, silvery-gray radioactive metal that is used as an energy source for nuclear weapons and some nuclear reactors.

ply[1] *noun* (*pl.* **plies**) **1** thickness measured by the number of strands or layers that compose it: *three-ply wool.* **2** a strand or layer.

ply[2] *verb trans., intrans.* (**plied, plying, plies**) **1** (**ply** (**someone**) **with** (something)) to keep supplying or importuning (someone): *plied them with drinks.* **2** to go regularly to and fro between destinations: *a freighter that plies between Baltimore and Miami.*

plywood *noun* a material made up of thin layers of wood glued together.

PM *or* **P.M.** *abbrev.* **1** Prime Minister. **2** provost marshal.

p.m. *abbrev. post meridiem* (Latin), after midday.

PMS *abbrev.* premenstrual syndrome.

pneumatic *adj.* **1** relating to air or gases. **2** containing or operated by compressed air. ▸ **pneumatically** *adv.*

pneumonia (noo-mōn'yə) *noun* inflammation of one or more lobes of the lungs, usu. as a result of infection.

PO *or* **P.O.** *abbrev.* petty officer.

Po *symbol Chem.* polonium.

poach[1] *verb trans.* (**poached, poaching**) **1** to cook (an egg without its shell) in or over boiling water. **2** to simmer (fish) in milk or other liquid. ▸ **poacher** *noun*

poach[2] *verb trans., intrans.* (**poached, poaching**) **1** to catch (game or fish) illegally on someone else's property. **2** to intrude on

(another's territory or area of responsibility)
▸ **poacher** noun

pock noun **1** a small inflamed area on the skin, containing pus, esp. one caused by smallpox. **2** a pockmark.

pocket noun **1** an enclosed section in or on a garment in which to carry things. **2** one's financial resources. **3** an isolated patch or area: *pockets of unemployment.* **4** a net or pouch hanging from the side of a billiard table, into which balls are played. —*adj.* small enough to be carried in a pocket: *pocket calculators.* —*verb trans.* (**pocketed, pocketing**) **1** to put into one's pocket. **2** *colloq.* to steal: *pocketed the proceeds and fled.*

pocketbook noun **1** a wallet. **2** a handbag or purse. **3** a notebook.

pocketknife noun a penknife.

pockmark noun a small pit or hollow in the skin left by a pock, esp. in chickenpox or smallpox. ▸ **pockmarked** adj.

pod noun **1** the long, dry fruit produced by, e.g., peas, which splits to release its seeds. **2** in an airplane or space vehicle, a detachable container or housing, e.g., for an engine.

podiatry (pə-dī′ə-trē) noun the diagnosis, treatment, and prevention of foot disorders. *Also called* **chiropody.** ▸ **podiatrist** noun

podium noun (*pl.* **podia, podiums**) **1** a small platform for a public speaker, orchestra conductor, etc. **2** a lectern.

poem noun **1** a composition in verse. **2** an object, scene, or creation of inspiring beauty.

poet (pō′ət, -ĭt) noun a writer of poems.

poetic adj. of, relating to, or suitable for poets or poetry. ▸ **poetically** adv.

poet laureate (*pl.* **poets laureate, poet laureates**) a poet officially appointed to produce poems for state occasions.

poetry noun **1** the art of composing poems. **2** poems collectively.

pogrom (pō′grəm, pə-grăm′) noun an organized massacre, orig. of Jews in 19th c Russia.

poignant (poin′yənt) adj. **1** painful to the feelings: *a poignant reminder.* **2** deeply moving. ▸ **poignancy** noun ▸ **poignantly** adv.

poinsettia (poin-sĕt′ə, -sĕt′ē-ə) noun a shrub that has large vermilion petal-like bracts.

point noun **1** a sharp or tapering end or tip. **2** a dot. **b** the dot inserted before a decimal fraction, as in 2.1 = *two point one.* **3** a punctuation mark, esp. a period or an exclamation point. **4** a position, place, or location. **5** a moment. **6** a stage, e.g., in a process. **7 a** a feature or characteristic. **b** a single, usu. small feature, constituent, or characteristic. ▣ DETAIL, ELEMENT, ITEM, PARTICULAR. **8** aim or intention. **9** use or value: *no point in trying.* **10** *Electr.* a socket or power point. **11** a headland or promontory. —*verb trans.*

intrans. (**pointed, pointing**) **1** to turn (something) in a particular direction. ▣ AIM, DIRECT, LEVEL, TRAIN. **2 a** to extend one's finger or a pointed object toward someone or something, so as to direct attention there. **b** *of a sign, etc.* to indicate a certain direction. **3** to extend or face in a certain direction. **4** to indicate or suggest (someone or something): *It points to only one solution.*

point-blank adj. **1** *of a shot* fired at very close range. **2** *of a question, refusal, etc.* direct. —*adv.* **1** at close range. **2** in a blunt, direct manner.

pointed adj. **1** having or ending in a point. **2** *of a remark, etc.* intended to convey a particular meaning or message, though not directly expressing it. ▸ **pointedly** adv.

pointer noun **1** a rod used by a speaker for indicating positions on a wall map, chart, etc. **2** the indicating needle on a measuring instrument. **3** *colloq.* a suggestion or hint.

pointless adj. lacking purpose or meaning. ▸ **pointlessness** noun

point of order (*pl.* **points of order**) a question raised in an assembly as to whether the business is being done according to the rules.

point of sale (*pl.* **points of sale**) (ABBREV. **POS**) a checkout counter. ▸ **point-of-sale** adj.

point of view (*pl.* **points of view**) one's own opinion or way of seeing things.

poise noun **1** self-confidence, calm, or composure. **2** grace of posture or carriage. **3** a state of equilibrium, balance, or stability e.g., between extremes. —*verb trans., intrans.* (**poised, poising**) **1** to balance or suspend. **2** to be in a state of readiness. ▸ **poised** adj.

poison noun a substance that damages tissues or causes death when absorbed or swallowed. —*verb trans.* (**poisoned, poisoning**) **1** to harm or kill with poison. **2** to put poison into (food, etc.). **3** to contaminate or pollute. ▸ **poisoner** noun ▸ **poisonous** adj.

poison ivy, poison oak *and* **poison sumac** *or* **poison elder** various woody vines and shrubs that produce an itching rash on contact with human skin.

poke¹ verb trans., intrans. (**poked, poking**) **1** to thrust (something pointed). **2** to prod or jab. **3** to make (a hole) by prodding.

poke² noun dialect a paper bag.

poker¹ noun a metal rod for stirring a fire to make it burn better.

poker² noun a card game in which players bet on the hands they hold.

pokey¹ or **poky** noun (*pl.* **pokeys** or **pokies**) slang a jail.

pokey² or **poky** adj. (**pokier, pokiest**) colloq. **1** of, e.g., a person slow and dawdling. **2** of a room, house, etc. small and confined or cramped.

polar *adj.* **1 a** relating to Earth's North or South Pole or the regions around them. **b** extremely cold. **2** relating to or having electric or magnetic poles.

polar bear a large white bear found in the Arctic region.

polarity *noun (pl.* **polarities) 1** the state of having two opposite poles: *magnetic polarity.* **2** the tendency to develop or to be drawn in opposite directions; oppositeness or an opposite.

polarize (pō'lə-rīz,) *verb trans., intrans.* (**polarized, polarizing) 1** to give magnetic or electrical polarity to. **2** *of people or opinions* to split according to opposing views. ▸ **polarization** *noun*

Pole *noun* a native or citizen of Poland.

pole[1] *noun* **1** either the North Pole or South Pole. **2** *Geol.* magnetic pole (sense 2). **3** either of the two terminals of a battery.

pole[2] *noun* a usu. cylindrical rod, e.g., one fixed in the ground as a support.

poleax *noun* a long-handled battleax.

polecat *noun* **1** a mammal resembling a large weasel. *Also called* **fitch. 2** a skunk (sense 1)

polemic (pə-lĕm'ĭk) *noun* a piece of writing or a speech fiercely attacking or defending an idea, opinion, etc.; writing or oratory of this sort. —*adj.* (*also* **polemical**) relating to or involving polemic or polemics. ▸ **polemicist** *noun* ▸ **polemics** *noun*

pole vault an athletic event consisting of a jump over a high horizontal bar with the help of a long flexible pole. *See* **track and field athletics.** ▸ **pole-vaulter** *noun*

police (pə-lēs') *noun (pl.* **police) 1 a** the department empowered by a government to keep order, enforce the law, and prevent and detect crime. **b** a body of people constituting such a department. **c** (*pl.*) members of such a body. **2** *Mil.* the cleaning up of a military area, e.g., a barracks. —*verb trans.* (**policed, policing) 1** to keep law and order in (an area). **2** *Mil.* to clean (an area) on a military installation.

police officer, policeman *or* **policewoman** a member of a police force.

police state a state with a repressive government that uses secret police to eliminate opposition.

policy[1] *noun (pl.* **policies) 1** a plan of action, usu. based on certain principles. **2** a course of conduct: *Your best policy is to keep quiet.*

policy[2] *noun (pl.* **policies)** an insurance agreement, or the document confirming it. ▸ **policyholder** *noun*

poliomyelitis (pŏ,lē-ō,mī,ə-līt'ĭs) *or* **polio** *noun* a viral disease of the brain and spinal cord.

Polish (pō'līsh) *adj.* of or relating to Poland, its people, or their language. —*noun* the language of Poland.

polish (păl'ĭsh) *verb trans., intrans.* (**polished, polishing) 1** to make or become smooth and glossy by rubbing. **2** to improve or perfect. **3** to make cultivated, refined, or elegant. —*noun* **1** a substance used for polishing surfaces. **2** a smooth shiny finish; a gloss. **3** an act of polishing. **4** refinement or elegance.

politburo (păl'ət-byŏŏr,ō, pō'lət-) *noun (pl.* **politburos)** the policymaking committee of a former Communist state.

polite *adj.* **1** well-mannered and courteous. **2** well-bred, cultivated, or refined. ▸ **politely** *adv.* ▸ **politeness** *noun*

politic (păl'ə-tĭk) *adj.* **1** *of a course of action* prudent; wise; shrewd. **2** *of a person* cunning; crafty.

political (pə-lĭt'ĭ-kəl) *adj.* **1** of or relating to government or public affairs. **2** relating to politics. ▸ **politically** *adv.*

political asylum protection given by a country to political refugees from a foreign country.

political correctness (ABBREV. **PC**) the avoidance of expressions or actions that may be understood to exclude or denigrate people on the grounds of race, gender, or sexual orientation. ▸ **politically correct**

politician (păl,ə-tĭsh'ən) *noun* **1** someone engaged in politics, esp. as a member of a legislative body. **2** someone who goes in for power-seeking maneuvers.

politicize *verb intrans., trans.* (**politicized, politicizing)** to give a political nature to. ▸ **politicization** *noun*

politico (pə-lĭt'ĭ-kō) *noun (pl.* **politicos)** a politician.

politics *noun* **1** (*sing.*) the science or business of government. **2** (*sing.*) the study of politics, political institutions, etc. **3** (*pl.*) moves and maneuvers concerned with the acquisition of power or getting one's way, e.g., in business.

polka (pōl'kə) *noun* a lively dance performed usu. with a partner; also, a piece of music for it.

polka dot (pō'kə) any of numerous, regularly spaced dots forming a pattern on fabric, etc.

poll (pōl) *noun* **1** (**polls**) a political election. **2** the voting, or votes cast, at an election: *a heavy poll.* **3** a survey of public opinion carried out by directly questioning a representative sample of the populace. *Also called* **opinion poll.** —*verb trans., intrans.* (**polled, polling) 1** to win (a number of votes) in an election. **2** to register the votes of (a population). **3** to cast (one's vote). **4** to conduct an opinion poll among.

pollen *noun* the fine dustlike powder that is produced by the anthers of flowering plants.

pollinate (păl'ə-nāt,) *verb trans.* (**pollinated, pollinating**) to transfer pollen to the stigma of the same flower or another flower in order to achieve fertilization and subsequent development of seed. ▸ **pollination** *noun*

pollster *noun* a person who organizes opinion polls.

poll tax a fixed tax levied on each member of a population, usu. as a precondition to the right to vote.

pollute (pə-lōōt') *verb trans.* (**polluted, polluting**) to contaminate with harmful substances; to make impure. ▸ **pollutant** *noun* ▸ **pollution** *noun*

polo *noun* a game played on horseback by teams of four using long-handled hammers to propel the ball along the ground.

polonium *noun Chem.* (SYMBOL **Po**) a rare radioactive metal.

polo shirt a pullover sports shirt of cotton knit with a high close-fitting neckband.

poltergeist (pōl'tər-gīst,) *noun* a ghost responsible for otherwise unaccountable noises in a household, allegedly given also to shifting objects about.

poly *noun colloq.* polyester.

poly- *combining form* forming words denoting: **1** many or much. **2** *Chem.* polymerized.

polyanthus *noun* (*pl.* **polyanthuses**) a variety of primrose.

polyester *noun* a synthetic resin used to form artificial fibers that are strong, durable, resistant to creasing, and quick-drying.

polyethylene *noun* a waxy translucent thermoplastic used for making food containers and packaging.

polygamy (pə-lĭg'ə-mē) *noun* the state or practice of having more than one spouse at any one time. *See also* monogamy. ▸ **polygamist** *noun* ▸ **polygamous** *adj.*

polyglot *adj.* speaking, using, or written in many languages. —*noun* a person who speaks many languages.

polygon (păl'ī-gän,) *noun Geom.* a two-dimensional figure with three or more straight sides. ▸ **polygonal** *adj.*

polygyny *noun Sociol.* the state or practice of having more than one wife at any one time. ▸ **polygynous** *adj.*

polyhedron *noun* (*pl.* **polyhedrons, polyhedra**) *Geom.* a three-dimensional figure with four or more faces, all of which are polygons. ▸ **polyhedral** *adj.*

polymer *noun Chem.* a very large molecule consisting of a long chain of much smaller molecules (*monomers*) linked end to end to form a series of repeating units. ▸ **polymeric** *adj.* ▸ **polymerization** *noun* ▸ **polymerize** *verb intrans., trans.*

polyp *noun* **1** a tiny tube-shaped sea creature

with a ring of tentacles around its mouth. **2** a small growth with a stalklike base, projecting from a mucous membrane.

polystyrene *noun* a tough transparent thermoplastic used in packaging, ceiling tiles, etc., and can be expanded to form foam.

polysyllabic *adj.* having three or more syllables.

polytechnic *noun* a school in which courses in a large range of subjects, esp. industrial arts and the applied sciences, are taught. —*adj.* offering or receiving coursework in the industrial arts and applied sciences.

polytheism (păl'ī-thē,ĭz,əm) *noun* belief in or worship of more than one god. ▸ **polytheist** *noun* ▸ **polytheistic** *adj.*

polyunsaturated *adj. Chem.* denoting a compound, esp. a fat or oil, that contains two or more double bonds per molecule.

polyurethane (păl,ī-yŏŏr'ə-thān,) *noun* a resin used in e.g. adhesives, paints, varnishes, and foams.

polyvinyl chloride (ABBREV. **PVC**) a tough thermoplastic used in pipes and other molded products, phonograph records, food packaging, waterproof clothing, and insulation for wires and cables.

pomade (pə-mād', -mäd') *noun* a perfumed ointment for the hair and scalp.

pomegranate (păm'ə-grăn,ət, pəm'grăn,-) *noun* **1** a small tree cultivated for its edible fruit and its attractive white, orange, or red flowers. **2** the fruit of this plant.

pommel (pəm'əl, păm'-) *noun* **1** the raised forepart of a saddle. **2** a rounded knob forming the end of a sword hilt. —*verb* (**pommeled** *or* **pommelled**, **pommeling** *or* **pommelling**) to pummel.

pomp *noun* **1** ceremonial grandeur. **2** vain ostentation.

pompom *or* **pompon** *noun* a ball of cut wool or other yarn, used as a trimming on clothes.

pompous *adj.* **1** solemnly self-important. **2** of *language* inappropriately grand and flowery. ▸ **pomposity** *noun* ▸ **pompously** *adv.*

poncho *noun* (*pl.* **ponchos**) an originally S American outer garment made of or like a blanket with a hole in the middle for one's head to go through.

pond *noun* a small body of water, whether natural or artificial.

ponder *verb trans., intrans.* (**pondered, pondering**) to consider or contemplate (something).

ponderous *adj.* **1** *of speech, humor, etc.* heavy-handed, laborious, excessively solemn, or pompous. **2** heavy or cumbersome; lumbering in movement. **3** weighty; important. ▸ **ponderously** *adv.* ▸ **ponderousness** *noun*

ponies *see* pony.

pontiff *noun RC Church* used as a title for a pope.

pontifical *adj.* pertaining to the pope or a bishop.

pontificate *verb intrans.* (păn-tĭf'ĭ-kāt,) (**pontificated, pontificating**) to pronounce one's opinion pompously and arrogantly. —*noun* (păn-tĭf'ĭ-kət) *RC Church* the office of pope or time of being pope.

pontoon *noun* any of a number of flat-bottomed craft, barges, etc., anchored side by side across a river, to support a temporary bridge.

pony *noun* (*pl.* **ponies**) a small breed of horse.

ponytail *noun* a person's hair drawn back and tied at the back of the head.

poodle *noun* a breed of dog with a long curly coat.

pooh *interj. colloq.* used to express scorn or disgust.

pooh-pooh *verb trans.* (**pooh-poohed, pooh-poohing**) *colloq.* to express scorn for (a suggestion, etc.).

pool¹ *noun* **1** a small area of still water. **2** a patch of spilled liquid. **3** a swimming pool.

pool² *noun* **1** a reserve of money, personnel, etc., used as a communal resource. **2** the combined stakes of a group of bettors, which are later paid to the winner. **3** a group of businesses with an arrangement to maintain high prices, so eliminating competition and preserving profits. **4** a game like billiards played with a white cue ball and usu. 15 numbered colored balls. —*verb trans.* (**pooled, pooling**) to put (money or other resources) into a common supply for general use.

poop¹ *noun* the raised, enclosed area at the stern of an old sailing ship.

poop² *verb trans., intrans. colloq.* (**pooped, pooping**) to become exhausted.

poop³ *noun slang* privileged information.

poor *adj.* **1** having insufficient money or means to live comfortably. **2** (**poor in (something)**) not well supplied with (it). **3** not good; unsatisfactory. **4** used in expressing pity or sympathy: *Poor thing!* ▸ **poorly** *adj.*

poor house an institution maintained at public expense for sheltering the homeless.

pop¹ *noun* a sharp explosive noise. —*verb trans., intrans.* (**popped, popping**) **1** to cause to make or to make a pop. **2** to burst with a pop. **3** (*also* **pop out**) to spring out; to protrude. **4** *colloq.* to go quickly: *pop next door for a cup of sugar.* —*adv.* with a pop.

pop² *noun* modern popular music. —*adj.* **1** performing or featuring pop music. **2** popular: *a pop cultural phenomenon.*

pop³ *noun colloq.* a father.

popcorn *noun* corn grains heated until they burst open and puff up.

pope *noun* the Bishop of Rome, the head of the Roman Catholic Church.

pop fly *Baseball* a high, short fly ball.

popgun *noun* a toy gun that fires a cork or pellet with a pop.

popinjay *noun* a dandy or fop.

poplar *noun* a tall, slender tree.

poplin *noun* a strong cotton cloth with a finely ribbed finish.

poppy *noun* (*pl.* **poppies**) a plant with large brightly colored bowl-shaped flowers, one variety of which is a source of opium.

poppycock *noun colloq.* nonsense.

pop-top *noun* the tab of a can that can be pulled up and off to create an opening.

populace (păp'yə-ləs) *noun* ordinary citizens.

popular *adj.* **1** liked or enjoyed by most people. **2** *of beliefs, etc.* accepted by many people. **3** *of a person* generally liked and admired. **4** involving the will or preferences of the public in general. ▸ **popularity** *noun* ▸ **popularly** *adv.*

popularize *verb trans.* (**popularized, popularizing**) to make popular. ▸ **popularization** *noun*

populate (păp'yə-lāt,) *verb trans.* (**populated, populating**) **1** to inhabit or live in (a certain area). **2** to supply (uninhabited places) with inhabitants.

population *noun* **1** all the people living in a particular country, area, etc. **2** the number of people living in a particular area, etc. **3** the total number of animals or plants of the same species living in a certain area.

populous *adj.* thickly populated.

porcelain (pôr'sə-lən) *noun* **1** a fine white translucent earthenware, orig. made in China. **2** objects made of this material.

porch *noun* **1** a verandah. **2** a structure forming a covered entrance to the doorway of a building.

porcupine (pôr'sĭn,) *noun* a large nocturnal rodent with long, sharp spikes.

pore¹ *noun* a small opening in the surface of e.g., in animal skin or the undersurface of leaves, through which substances can pass.

pore² *verb intrans.* (**pored, poring**) (**pore over (something)**) to look at or examine closely and searchingly.

pork *noun* the flesh of a hog used as food.

porker *noun* a pig reared for fresh meat.

porn *noun colloq.* pornography.

pornography *noun* books, pictures, films, etc., designed to be sexually arousing. ▸ **pornographer** *noun* ▸ **pornographic** *adj.*

porous *adj.* **1** having pores or cavities. **2** of such a texture or consistency as to allow the passage of liquids through. ▸ **porosity** *noun*

porphyry *noun* a rock that contains large crystals surrounded by much smaller crystals. ▸ **porphyritic** *adj.*

porpoise (pôr'pəs) *noun* (*pl.* **porpoise, porpoises**) a small whale with a blunt snout and a triangular dorsal fin.

porridge *noun* a dish of oatmeal boiled in water, or of some other cereal boiled in water or milk.

port[1] *noun* **1 a** a harbor. **b** a town or city with a harbor. **2** *Comput.* a point of connection for attaching a peripheral device.

port[2] *noun* the left side of a ship or aircraft.

port[3] *noun* **1** a porthole. **2** an opening in an armored vehicle or in a fortification through which to look or to fire weapons.

port[4] *noun* a fortified Portuguese wine.

portable *adj.* that can be carried. —*noun* a portable radio, television, typewriter, etc.

portage (pôr'ij, pôr-täzh') *noun* **1** the carrying of ships, equipment, etc., overland from one waterway to another. **2** the route used for this transport. —*verb trans., intrans.* (**portaged, portaging**) to transport or travel by portage.

portal *noun* an entrance, gateway, or doorway.

portcullis *noun* a grating fitted into a town gateway or castle entrance, lowered to bar intruders.

portend *verb trans.* (**portended, portending**) to warn of; to be an omen of.

portent *noun* **1** a prophetic sign or omen. **2** a marvel or prodigy.

portentous *adj.* **1** ominous or fateful. **2** weighty, solemn, or pompous.

porter *noun* a person employed to carry luggage or packages, e.g., at a hotel or a railroad station.

portfolio *noun* (*pl.* **portfolios**) **1** a case for carrying papers, drawings, photographs, etc. **2** the post of a government minister with responsibility for a specific department.

porthole (pôrt'hōl,) *noun* a usu. round opening in a ship's side to admit light and air.

portico *noun* (*pl.* **porticoes, porticos**) *Archit.* a colonnade forming a porch or covered way alongside a building.

portion *noun* **1** a piece or part. **2** a share. **3** one's destiny or fate. —*verb trans.* (**portioned, portioning**) (*also* **portion (something) out**) to distribute (it) portion by portion.

portly *adj.* (**portlier, portliest**) *esp. of a man* somewhat stout.

portrait *noun* **1** a drawing, painting, or photograph of a person, esp. of the face only. **2** a written description, movie depiction, etc., of someone or something. ▸ **portraiture** *noun*

portray *verb trans.* (**portrayed, portraying**) **1** to make a portrait of. **2** to describe or depict. **3** to act the part of (a character) in a play, movie, etc. ▸ **portrayal** *noun*

Portuguese *noun* **1** a native or citizen of Portugal. **2** (**the Portuguese**) the people of Portugal. **3** the language of Portugal. —*adj.* relating to Portugal, its inhabitants, or their language.

pose *noun* **1** a position or attitude of the body. **2** insincere behavior intended to make an impression. —*verb intrans., trans.* (**posed, posing**) **1** to take up a position, or position (someone), for a photograph, portrait, etc. **2** to behave in an exaggerated or artificial way. **3** (**pose as** (**someone** *or* **something**)) to pretend to be (someone or something). **4** to cause (a problem, etc.) or present (a threat, etc.).

poser *noun* **1** a poseur. **2** *colloq.* a difficult problem; a puzzle.

poseur (pō-zər') *noun* a person who behaves affectedly or insincerely.

posh *adj.* high-quality, expensive, or stylish.

posit *verb trans.* (**posited, positing**) to lay down, or assume, as a basis for discussion.

position *noun* **1** where something or someone is located or can be found. **2** the right or proper place. **3** a way of sitting, standing, lying, facing, being held or placed, etc.: *an upright position.* **4** an opinion or viewpoint. **5** a job or post: *a senior position at the bank.* **6** importance or status in society. —*verb trans.* (**positioned, positioning**) to put in position; to place.

positive *adj.* **1** sure; certain; convinced. **2** allowing no doubt: *positive proof.* **3** expressing agreement or approval: *a positive response.* **4** optimistic. **5** forceful or determined. **6** *Math.* denoting a number or quantity greater than zero. **7** *Phys., Electr.* having a deficiency of electrons, and so being able to attract them; denoting one of two terminals having the higher electrical potential. **8** *Photog.* having light and shade, or colors, as in the actual image, not reversed, etc. —*noun* **1** *Photog.* a print in which light, shade, and color correspond to those of the actual image. **2** a positive thing, esp. a positive quantity or a positive electrical terminal. ▸ **positively** *noun* ▸ **positiveness** *noun*

posse (päs'ē) *noun* **1** a troop of men at the service of a local sheriff, to aid him or her in law enforcement. **2** a search party.

possess *verb trans.* (**possessed, possessing**) **1** to own. **2** to have as a feature or quality. **3** *of, e.g., an emotion* to take hold of (someone). ▸ **possessor** *noun*

possessed *adj.* controlled or driven by demons, etc.

possession *noun* **1 a** legal claim, right, title, or holding. **b** occupancy of property: *took possession of the new house.* **c** something owned. **d** (**possessions**) one's property or belongings. **2** the crime of possessing something illegally. **3** *Sport* control of a ball, e.g., in football by one or other team in a game.

possessive *adj.* **1** relating to possession. **2** unwilling to share or to allow others the use of things that one owns. **3** inclined to dominate and allow no independence to, e.g., one's child, etc.: *a possessive spouse.* **4** *Gram.* denoting the form of a noun, pronoun, or adjective that shows possession, e.g., *Jack's, its, her.* —*noun Gram.* **1** the possessive form of a word. **2** a word in this form. ▸ **possessively** *adv.*

possibility *noun* (*pl.* **possibilities**) **1** something that is possible. **2** the state of being possible. **3** (**possibilities**) promise or potential.

possible *adj.* **1** able to be done. **2** that may happen. **3** imaginable; conceivable: *a possible explanation.* —*noun* a potentially selectable person or thing. ▸ **possibly** *adv.*

possum *noun dialect* an opossum.

post¹ *noun* a shaft or rod fixed upright in the ground, as a support, marker, etc. —*verb trans.* (**posted, posting**) **1** to put up (a notice, etc.) for public viewing. **2** to announce the name of (someone) among others in a published list.

post² *noun* **1** a job. **2** a position to which one is assigned for military duty. **3** a settlement or establishment. —*verb trans.* (**posted, posting**) to station (someone) somewhere on duty; to transfer (personnel) to a new location.

post³ *noun* **1 a** a mail delivery. **b** letters and parcels delivered by this system; mail. **2** *Brit.* **a** the official system for the delivery of mail. —*verb trans.* (**posted, posting**) **1 a** to put (mail) into a mailbox. **b** to send by post. **2** *Commerce* to enter (an item) in a ledger.

post- *combining form* forming words denoting after: *postwar.*

postage (pōˈstĭj) *noun* the charge for sending a letter, etc., through the mail.

postal *adj.* of or relating to the post office or delivery of mail.

post card a card for writing messages on, often with a picture on one side.

postcode *noun* the UK equivalent of a ZIP Code.

postdate *verb trans.* (**postdated, postdating**) **1** to put a future date on (e.g., a check). **2** to occur at a later date than.

poster *noun* **1** a large notice or advertisement for public display. **2** a large printed picture.

poster color *same as* **poster paint**.

posterior *noun* one's buttocks. —*adj.* placed behind or after.

posterity *noun* **1** future generations. **2** one's descendants.

poster paint *or* **poster color** a water-based paint in a bright opaque color.

Post Exchange *trademark* used for a store on a military installation where members of the armed forces and their dependents can buy merchandise.

postgraduate *noun* a person studying for an advanced degree or qualification after obtaining a lower degree. —*adj.* relating to such a person or degree.

posthaste *adv.* with all speed.

posthumous (päsˈchə-məs) *adj.* **1** published after the death of the author, composer, etc. **2** awarded or coming after death: *posthumous acclaim.* ▸ **posthumously** *adv.*

postman *or* **postwoman** *noun* a person whose job is to deliver mail.

postmark *noun* a mark stamped on mail by the post office, canceling the stamp and showing the date, time, and place of mailing.

postmaster *noun* a man or woman in charge of a local post office.

postmaster general (*pl.* **postmasters general**) the executive who is in charge of a country's postal services.

post meridiem (ABBREV. **p.m.**) after noon.

postmistress *noun* a woman in charge of a local post office.

postmortem **1** an autopsy. **2** an after-the-event discussion.

postnatal *adj.* relating to the period immediately after birth.

post office the government department, or a local or regional office, in charge of postal services.

postoperative *adj.* relating to the period immediately following a surgical operation.

postpaid *adj.* with postage prepaid.

postpone *verb trans.* (**postponed, postponing**) to defer or put off till later. ▸ **postponement** *noun*

postscript *noun* (ABBREV. **P.S., PS**) a message added to a letter as an afterthought, after one's signature.

postulant (päsˈchə-lənt) *noun* a candidate for holy orders or for admission to a religious community. ▸ **postulancy** *noun*

postulate (päsˈchə-lāt,) *verb trans.* (**postulated, postulating**) to assume or suggest as the basis for discussion. ▸ **postulation** *noun*

posture (päsˈchər) *noun* **1** the way one holds one's body in standing, sitting, or walking. **2** a particular position or attitude of the body. **3** an attitude adopted toward a particular issue, etc. —*verb intrans.* (**postured, posturing**) to pose, strike attitudes, etc., so as to draw attention to oneself. ▸ **postural** *adj.* ▸ **posturer** *noun*

posy *noun* (*pl.* **posies**) a small bunch of flowers, or a small flower.

pot¹ *noun* **1** any of various usu. deep, round domestic containers used as cooking or serving utensils or for storage. **2** *Games* the pool of accumulated bets in any gambling game. **3** *Billiards* a shot that pockets a ball. —*verb trans.* (**potted, potting**) **1** to plant in a plant pot. **2** to preserve (food) in a pot. **3** *Billiards* to shoot (a ball) into a pocket. —**go to pot** *colloq.* to degenerate badly.

pot² *noun colloq.* marijuana (sense 1).

potable (pōt'ə-bəl) *adj.* fit for drinking.

potash *noun* **1** any of various compounds of potassium, esp. the fertilizer potassium carbonate. **2** potassium hydroxide.

potassium *noun* (SYMBOL K) a soft silvery-white metal that reacts violently with water.

potassium hydroxide a highly corrosive white crystalline solid that dissolves in water to form a strong alkaline solution. *Also called* **potash**.

potassium nitrate a highly explosive white crystalline solid that is used in the manufacture of fireworks, matches, gun-powder, fertilizers, and as a food preservative. *Also called* **niter, saltpeter**.

potato *noun* (*pl.* **potatoes**) **1** a plant that produces edible tubers. **2** the tuber of this plant, that can be cooked and eaten as a vegetable.

potato chip a deep-fat fried, thin slice of potato, dried, and then salted.

potbelly *noun* (*pl.* **potbellies**) *colloq.* a fat stomach. ▶ **potbellied** *adj.*

potboiler *noun* an inferior work of literature produced by a writer capable of better work, simply to make money and stay in the public view.

potent *adj.* **1** strong; effective; powerful. **2** *of a drug or poison* powerful and swift in effect. **3** *of a male* capable of sexual intercourse. ▶ **potency** *noun*

potential *adj.* possible or likely, though not tested or actual. —*noun* **1** the capabilities, powers, or resources that a person or thing has, though not yet developed. **2** *Phys.* the energy required to move a unit of mass, electric charge, etc., from an infinite distance to the point in a gravitational or electric field where it is to be measured. ▶ **potentially** *adv.*

pothole *noun* **1** a hole worn in a road surface. **2** a vertical cave system or deep hole eroded in limestone.

potion *noun* a draft of medicine, poison, or elixir.

potluck *noun* **1** whatever is available. **2** a meal at which the guests eat dishes brought by everyone.

potpourri (pō,pə-rē') *noun* **1** a fragrant mixture of dried flowers, leaves, etc., placed in containers and used to scent rooms, closets, or drawers. **2** a medley or mixture.

potshot *noun* **1 a** an easy shot made at close

range. **b** a shot made without taking careful aim. **2** irresponsible criticism or an instance of it.

potter *noun* a person who makes pottery.

pottery *noun* **1** vessels or other objects of baked clay. **2** the art of making such objects. **3** a factory where such objects are produced commercially.

pouch *noun* **1** *old use* a purse or small bag. **2** in marsupials such as the kangaroo, a pocket of skin on the belly, in which the young are carried till weaned.

poultice (pōl'tĭs) *noun* a hot, semiliquid mixture spread on a bandage and applied to the skin to reduce inflammation.

poultry *noun* **1** domesticated birds, e.g., chickens, ducks, geese, and turkeys. **2** the meat of such birds.

pounce *verb trans., intrans.* (**pounced, pouncing**) **1** to leap on a victim or prey. **2** to seize on; to grab eagerly. —*noun* an act of pouncing.

pound¹ *noun* **1** (ABBREV. **lb.**) a measure of weight equal to 16 ounces (453.592 grams) avoirdupois, or in terms of apothecary weight, 12 ounces (373.242 grams) troy. **2 a** (fl) the principal currency unit of the United Kingdom, divided into 100 pence. *Also called* **pound sterling**. **b** the English name for the principal currency unit in several other countries, e.g., Malta, and Egypt.

pound² *noun* an enclosure for stray animals.

pound³ *verb trans., intrans.* (**pounded, pounding**) **1** to beat or bang (something) vigorously: *pounded at the door*. **2** to walk or run with heavy thudding steps. **3** to crush or grind to a powder.

poundage (pown'dĭj) *noun* a fee or commission charged per pound in weight or money.

pour *verb trans., intrans.* (**poured, pouring**) **1** to flow or cause to flow in a downward stream. **2** *of a jug, etc.* to discharge (liquid) in a certain way: *doesn't pour very well.* **3** to rain heavily. ▣ LASH. **4** (**pour in** *or* **out**) to flow or issue plentifully. ▶ **pourer** *noun*

pout *verb intrans., trans.* (**pouted, pouting**) **1** to push the lower lip or both lips forward as an indication of sulkiness. **2** *of the lips* to stick out in this way. —*noun* an act of pouting or a pouting expression. ▶ **poutingly** *adv.* ▶ **pouty** *adj.*

poverty *noun* the condition of being poor.

poverty-stricken *adj.* suffering from poverty.

POW *abbrev.* prisoner of war.

powder *noun* **1** a substance in the form of fine dustlike particles. **2** a dustlike cosmetic patted onto the skin. **3** gunpowder. **4** a medicine in the form of fine particles. —*verb trans.* (**powdered, powdering**) **1** to apply powder to; to sprinkle or cover with powder. **2** to reduce to a powder by crushing. ▸ **powdery** *adj.*

powder room a bathroom for women.

power *noun* **1** control and influence exercised over others. **2** the capacity or ability to exert effort. ◼ FORCE, MIGHT, STRENGTH ◼ WEAKNESS. **3** the ability, skill, opportunity, or authority to do something. **4** a right, privilege, or responsibility. **5** political control: *assumed power.* **6** a state that has an influential role in international affairs: *a major world power.* **7** any form of energy, esp. when used as the driving force for a machine, etc.: *nuclear power.* **8** *Math.* exponent (sense 1). **9** *Phys.* the rate of doing work or converting energy from one form into another. —*verb trans.* (**powered, powering**) to supply with power. ▸ **powerful** *adj.* ▸ **powerfully** *adv.* ▸ **powerless** *adj.*

powerboat *noun* a motorboat.

powerhouse *noun* **1** a power station. **2** *colloq.* a forceful or vigorous person.

power of attorney (*pl.* **powers of attorney**) *Law* the right to act for another in legal and business matters.

power plant 1 a power station. **2** the engine and parts making up the unit that supplies the propelling power in a vehicle.

power station a building where electricity is generated on a large scale from another form of energy, e.g., coal, nuclear fuel, moving water. *Also called* **powerhouse, power plant.**

powwow *noun* **1** *colloq.* a meeting for discussion. **2** *Hist.* a meeting or a ritual held by Native Americans.

pox *noun* an infectious viral disease that causes a skin rash of pimples.

pp *abbrev. Mus.* pianissimo.

pp. *abbrev.* pages.

p.p. *per procurationem* (Latin), by the agency of.

P.P.S. *abbrev. post postscriptum* (Latin), after the postscript, i.e., an additional postscript.

PR *abbrev.* public relations.

Pr *symbol Chem.* praseodymium.

practicable *adj.* capable of being done, used, or successfully carried out. ▸ **practicability** *noun* ▸ **practicably** *adv.*

practical *adj.* **1** concerned with action, achieving a purpose, or getting a result, in contrast to mere theory. **2** effective in actual use: *a practical knowledge of German.* **3** designed for efficiency rather than decoration. **4** of, e.g., *clothes* designed for tough or everyday use. **5** *of a person* a sensible and efficient in deciding and acting. **b** good at doing manual jobs. ▸ **practicality** *noun*

practical joke a trick played on someone.

practically (prăk′tĭ-klē) *adv.* **1** almost. **2** in a practical manner.

practical nurse a licensed practical nurse.

practice *noun* **1** the process of carrying something out: *put ideas into practice.* **2** a habit, activity, procedure, or custom. **3** repeated exercise to improve one's technique in an art, sport, etc. **4** a physician's or attorney's business. —*verb trans., intrans.* (**practiced, practicing**) **1** to do exercises repeatedly in (an art, sport, etc.) so as to improve one's performance. **2** to make a habit of. **3** to go in for as a custom. **4** to work at or follow (a profession, esp. medicine or law).

practitioner *noun* someone practicing an art or profession, esp. medicine.

pragmatic *adj.* concerned with what is practicable, expedient, and convenient, rather than with theories and ideals.

pragmatism *noun* a practical, matter-of-fact approach to dealing with problems, etc. ▸ **pragmatist** *noun*

prairie *noun* a treeless, grass-covered plain.

prairie dog a small ground squirrel that has a barking alarm call.

praise *verb trans.* (**praised, praising**) **1** to express admiration or approval of. **2** to worship or glorify (God) with hymns, thanksgiving, etc. —*noun* **1** an often loud expression of approval. ◼ ACCLAIM, ACCLAMATION, APPLAUSE, LAUDATION, PLAUDIT ◼ CRITICISM, DISAPPROVAL. **2** worship of God.

praiseworthy *adj.* deserving praise; commendable.

praline (prä′lĕn,, prô′-) *noun* a candy consisting of nuts in caramelized sugar.

pram *noun Brit.* a baby carriage.

prance *verb intrans.* (**pranced, prancing**) **1** *esp. of a horse* to walk with lively, springing steps. **2** to frisk or skip about. **3** to walk about in a swaggering way. ◼ FLOUNCE, SASHAY, STRUT.

prank *noun* a practical joke. ▸ **prankster** *noun*

praseodymium (prā,zē-ō-dĭm′ē-əm) *noun Chem.* (SYMBOL **Pr**) a soft silvery metallic element that is used in the alloy misch metal.

prate *verb intrans., trans.* (**prated, prating**) to talk or utter foolishly.

prattle *verb intrans., trans.* (**prattled, prattling**) to chatter foolishly; to babble. —*noun* childish or foolish chatter. ▸ **prattler** *noun*

prawn *noun* a small edible shrimplike crustacean.

pray *verb intrans., trans.* (**prayed, praying**) **1** to address one's god with a prayer. **2** to beg for earnestly. **3** to hope desperately.

prayer (prăr, prĕr) *noun* **1** an address to one's god, making a request or giving thanks. **2** the activity of praying. **3** an earnest hope, desire, or entreaty. **4** (**prayers**) a service of worship in which prayers are said.

pre- *prefix* forming words denoting before: **1** in time: *prewar*. **2** in position: *premolar*. **3** in importance: *preeminent*.

preach *verb intrans., trans.* (**preached, preaching**) **1** to deliver (a sermon) as part of a religious service. **2** to give (someone) advice in a tedious, obtrusive manner. **3** to advise; to advocate. ▸ **preacher** *noun*

preamble (prē'ăm,bəl) *noun* an introduction or preface, e.g., to a speech or document.

prearrange *verb trans.* (**prearranged, prearranging**) to arrange in advance.

precarious (prǐ-kăr'ē-əs) *adj.* **1** unsafe; insecure; dangerous. **2** uncertain; chancy: *a precarious diplomatic situation.* ▸ **precariously** *adv.* ▸ **precariousness** *noun*

precaution *noun* a measure taken to ensure a satisfactory outcome, or to avoid a risk or danger. ▸ **precautionary** *adj.*

precede *verb trans., intrans.* (**preceded, preceding**) **1** to go or be before, in time, order, position, rank, or importance. **2** to preface or introduce.

precedence (prĕs'əd-ns) *noun* **1** priority. **2** the fact of preceding, or right to precede others, in order, rank, importance, etc.

precedent *noun* a previous incident, legal case, etc., that is parallel to one under consideration; the measures taken or judgment given in that case, serving as a basis for a decision in the present one.

precept *noun* a guiding rule or principle, esp. of a moral kind.

precinct *noun* **1** (*also* **precincts**) the enclosed grounds of a large building, etc. **2** (*also* **precincts**) the neighborhood or environs of a place. **3 a** any of the districts into which a city is divided for administrative or police purposes. **b** a police station located in and having law-enforcement jurisdiction over such a district.

preciosity *noun* affectedness or exaggerated refinement in speech or manner.

precious (prĕsh'əs) *adj.* **1** valuable. **2** dear; treasured. **3** affected or overly refined. ▸ **preciousness** *noun*

precipice (prĕs'ə-pĭs) *noun* a sheer cliff.

precipitate *verb trans.* (prǐ-sĭp'ə-tāt,) (**precipitated, precipitating**) **1** to cause, or hasten the advent of. **2** to throw or plunge. **3** *Chem.* to form or to cause to form a suspension of small solid particles in a solution. **4** to fall as, e.g., rain. —*adj.* (prǐ-sĭp'ət-ət) of actions or decisions sudden and quick. —(prǐ-sĭp'ət-ət, -ə-tāt,) *noun Chem.* a suspension of small solid particles that are formed in a solution. ▸ **precipitately** *adv.*

Usage See note at *precipitous*.

precipitation *noun* **1** rash haste. **2** rain, snow, sleet, etc. **3** the act of precipitating or process of being precipitated. **4** *Chem.* the formation of a precipitate.

precipitous *adj.* inclined to such a sharp degree as to be almost perpendicular.

> *Usage* Since the use of *precipitous* to mean *precipitate* (i.e., hasty; ill-considered) is considered an error by many people, many careful writers draw a distinction between the two words.

précis (prā-sē') *noun* (*pl.* **précis**) a summary of a piece of writing.

precise *adj.* **1** particular; very: *at this precise moment.* ⊟ EXACT, VERY ⊠ IMPRECISE, NONSPECIFIC. **2** clear; detailed. **3** accurate. ▸ **precisely** *adv.* ▸ **preciseness** *noun*

precision *noun* accuracy.

preclude *verb trans.* (**precluded, precluding**) **1** to rule out, eliminate, or make impossible. **2** to prevent (someone's) involvement in (something). ▸ **preclusion** *noun*

precocious *adj.* of, e.g., a child unusually advanced in mental development, speech, behavior, etc. ▸ **precociously** *adv.* ▸ **precocity** *noun*

preconceive *verb trans.* (**preconceived, preconceiving**) to form (an idea) of something before having direct experience of it. ▸ **preconception** *noun*

precondition *noun* a condition to be satisfied in advance.

precursor *noun* **1** something that is a sign of an approaching event. **2** a chemical compound from which another compound is directly produced.

predate *verb trans.* (**predated, predating**) **1** to write a bygone date on (a document, etc.). **2** to occur at an earlier date than.

predator (prĕd'ət-ər) *noun* an animal that obtains food by catching and eating other animals.

predatory *adj.* **1** of an animal killing and feeding on others. **2** of people exploiting the weakness or good will of others for personal gain.

predecessor (prĕd'ə-sĕs,ər) *noun* **1** the person who preceded one in one's own job or position. **2** the previous version, model, etc., of a particular thing or product.

predestine *verb trans.* (**predestined, predestining**) **1** to destine; to fix by fate.

predetermine *verb trans.* (**predetermined, predetermining**) **1** to decide, settle, or fix in advance. **2** to influence, shape, or cause to tend a certain way.

predicament *noun* a difficulty that one finds oneself in.

predicate *noun* (prĕd'ĭ-kət) *Gram.* the word or words in a sentence that make a statement about the subject. ▸ **predication** *noun*

predicative *adj.* 1 *Gram.*, of an adjective forming part of or only found in a predicate, as *asleep* in *They were asleep*. *See also* **attributive.** 2 relating to predicates. ▸ **predicatively** *adv.*

predict *verb trans.* (**predicted, predicting**) to prophesy, foretell, forecast, or foresee. ▸ **predictability** *noun* ▸ **predictable** *adj.* ▸ **predictably** *adv.* ▸ **prediction** *noun*

predilection (prĕd,l-ĕk'shən) *noun* a special liking or preference.

predispose *verb trans.* (**predisposed, predisposing**) 1 to incline (someone) to react in a particular way. 2 to make susceptible to (esp. illness). ▸ **predisposition** *noun*

predominate (prĭ-dăm'ə-nāt,) *verb intrans. trans.* (**predominated, predominating**) 1 to be more numerous than others. 2 to be more noticeable or prominent than others. 3 to prevail over. ▸ **predominant** *adj.* ▸ **predominantly** *adv.*

preeminent (prē-ĕm'ə-nənt) *adj.* excelling all others; outstanding. ▸ **preeminence** *noun* ▸ **preeminently** *adv.*

preempt (prē-ĕmpt') *verb trans.* (**preempted, preempting**) 1 to forestall and so make pointless (an action planned by someone else). 2 to obtain in advance for oneself. ▸ **preemption** *noun* ▸ **preemptive** *adj.*

preen *verb trans., intrans.* (**preened, preening**) 1 of a bird to clean and smooth (its feathers) with its beak. 2 to groom (oneself), esp. in a vain manner. 3 to pride or congratulate (oneself) on account of (something).

prefab *noun* a prefabricated building, esp. a house.

prefabricate (prē-făb'rĭ-kāt,) *verb trans.* (**prefabricated, prefabricating**) to manufacture standard sections of (a building) for later quick assembly. ▸ **prefabrication** *noun*

preface (prĕf'əs) *noun* an explanatory statement at the beginning of a book. —*verb trans.* (**prefaced, prefacing**) to provide (a book, etc.) with a preface.

prefatory *adj.* 1 relating to or being a preface. 2 introductory: *prefatory remarks.*

prefect (prē'fĕkt,) *noun* a senior pupil with minor disciplinary powers in a school.

prefer (prĭ-fər') *verb trans.* (**preferred, preferring**) 1 (**prefer** (one thing) **to** (another)) to like (it) better: *prefer tea to coffee.* 2 *Law* to submit (a charge, accusation, etc.) to a court of law for consideration.

preferable (prĕf'ə-rə-bəl) *adj.* more desirable, suitable, or advisable. ▸ **preferably** *adv.*

preference (prĕf'rəns, -ərns) *noun* 1 the preferring of one thing, etc., over another. 2 one's choice of or liking for someone or something particular. 3 favorable consideration: *give preference to experienced applicants.*

preferential (prĕf,ə-rĕn'chəl) *adj.* bestowing special favors or advantages.

preferment *noun* promotion to a more responsible position.

prefigure *verb trans.* (**prefigured, prefiguring**) to be an advance sign of something that is to come. ▸ **prefiguration** *noun*

prefix *noun* 1 *Gram.* an element such as *un-, re-, non-,* and *de-* added to the beginning of a word to create a new word. 2 a title such as *Mr., Dr.,* and *Ms.,* used before a person's name. —*verb trans.* (**prefixed, prefixing**) 1 to add as an introduction. 2 to attach as a prefix to a word. 3 to add a prefix to.

pregnant *adj.* 1 carrying an unborn child or young in the womb. 2 of a remark, pause, etc. loaded with a significance very obvious to those present. ▸ **pregnancy** *noun*

prehensile (prē-hĕn'səl, -sĭl,) *adj.* adapted for grasping: *a prehensile tail.*

prehistory *noun* the period before historical records. ▸ **prehistoric** *adj.* ▸ **prehistorically** *adv.*

prejudge *verb trans.* (**prejudged, prejudging**) 1 to form an opinion on (an issue, etc.) before having all the relevant facts. 2 to condemn (someone) unheard. ▸ **prejudgment** *noun*

prejudice (prĕj'ə-dĭs) *noun* 1 a biased opinion, based on insufficient knowledge. 2 unthinking hostility, e.g., toward a particular racial or religious group. —*verb trans.* (**prejudiced, prejudicing**) 1 to cause (someone) to feel prejudice. 2 to harm or endanger. ▸ **prejudicial** *adj.*

prelate (prĕl'ət) *noun* a bishop, an abbot, or another high-ranking ecclesiastic. ▸ **prelacy** *noun*

preliminary *adj.* introductory or preparatory. —*noun* (*pl.* **preliminaries**) (*usu.* **preliminaries**) something done or said by way of introduction or preparation.

prelude *noun* 1 *Mus.* an introductory passage or first movement, e.g., of a fugue or suite. 2 a short musical piece, a poetic composition, etc. 3 an event that precedes and prepares the ground for one of greater significance.

premature *adj.* 1 *Med.*, of, e.g., a human infant born before the expected or normal time. 2 of a decision, etc. hasty. ▸ **prematurely** *adv.*

premeditate *verb trans.* (**premeditated, premeditating**) to plan deliberately; to think out beforehand. ▸ **premeditation** *noun*

premenstrual *adj.* relating to the time just before a menstrual period.

premier *adj.* first in rank; most important; leading. —*noun* a prime minister. ▸ **premiership** *noun*

premiere *noun* the first public performance of a play or showing of a film. —*verb trans*

(premiered, premiering) to present a premiere of.

premise (prěm'ĭs) noun **1** something assumed to be true as a basis for stating something further; in logic, either of the propositions introducing a syllogism. **2 (premises)** a building and its grounds.

premium noun **1** an amount usu. paid annually on an insurance agreement. **2** an extra sum added to wages or to interest.

premolar noun Dentistry any of the four teeth between the canines and first molars.

premonition noun a feeling that something is about to happen before it actually does.

prenatal adj. belonging to the period before childbirth.

preoccupied adj. **(preoccupied by** or **with (something)) 1** lost in thought. **2** having one's attention completely taken up. **3** already occupied: a preoccupied hotel suite.

preoccupy verb trans. **(preoccupied, preoccupying, preoccupies)** to occupy the attention of wholly; to obsess.

preordain verb trans. **(preordained, preordaining)** to decree or determine in advance.

prep colloq. adj. preparatory —noun preparations.

prep. abbrev. Gram. preposition.

preparation noun **1** the process of preparing or state of being prepared. **2** (usu. **preparations)** something done by way of preparing or getting ready.

preparatory adj. preparing for something; introductory.

preparatory school a private secondary school, preparing pupils for college.

prepare verb trans., intrans. **(prepared, preparing) 1** to make or get ready. **2** to make (a meal).

preponderance noun **1** the circumstance of being more numerous. **2** a superior number; a majority. ▸ **preponderant** adj.

preposition noun (ABBREV. **prep.**) Gram. a word such as to, from, into, or against, that deals with the position, movement, relationship, etc., of things or people. ▸ **prepositional** adj.

prepossess verb trans. **(prepossessed, prepossessing) 1** to charm. **2** to win over; to incline or bias.

preposterous adj. laughably senseless. ▸ **preposterously** adv.

prep school a preparatory school.

prepuce noun Anat. the foreskin.

prerecord verb trans. **(prerecorded, prerecording)** to record (a program for radio or television) in advance of its scheduled broadcasting time.

prerequisite noun a preliminary requirement that must be satisfied.

prerogative noun an exclusive right or

privilege arising from one's rank or position.

Pres. abbrev. President.

presage (prěs'ĭj, prĭ-sāj') verb trans. **(presaged, presaging)** to be a warning sign of something to come. —noun a portent, warning, or omen.

presbyter noun **1** in various churches, a member of the clergy. **2** in presbyterian churches, an elder.

presbyterian (prěz'bə-tĭr'ē-ən) adj. **1** denoting church administration by elders. **2 (Presbyterian)** designating a church governed by elders. —noun **(Presbyterian)** a member of a Presbyterian church.

presbytery noun (pl. **presbyteries) 1** an area of local administration of a Presbyterian church. **2** a body of elders, esp. one sitting as a local church court. **3** the eastern section of a church building, beyond the choir. **4** RC Church the residence of a priest.

preschool adj. denoting or relating to children before they are old enough to attend school.

prescient adj. having or showing a knowledge or understanding of what the future will bring. ▸ **prescience** noun

prescribe verb trans. **(prescribed, prescribing) 1** to give an order for (a medicine) as a remedy, esp. by completing a prescription for it. **2** to recommend or set officially (e.g., a text for academic study).

prescription noun **1 a** a set of orders from, e.g., a physician for preparing and taking a medicine, etc. **b** the medicine, etc., so prescribed by a physician. **2** the act of prescribing.

prescriptive adj. **1** laying down rules. **2** of a right, etc. established by custom.

presence noun **1** the state or circumstance of being present. **2** one's attendance, e.g., at an event. **3** someone's company or nearness: in my presence. **4** one's physical bearing, esp. if commanding or authoritative.

present¹ (prěz'ənt) adj. **1** being at the place or occasion in question. **2** existing, detectable, or able to be found. **3** Gram., of the tense of a verb denoting action now, or action that is continuing or habitual. —noun **1** the present time. **2** Gram. the present tense, or a verb in it.

present² (prĭ-zěnt') verb trans., intrans. **(presented, presenting) 1** to give (something) to (someone), esp. formally or ceremonially: presented them with medals. **2** to make (someone) known to (someone): Let me present you to my friends. **3** to offer for consideration: presented several proposals. **4** to set out: She presents her work neatly.

present³ (prěz'ənt) noun a gift.

presentable adj. **1** fit to be seen, appear in company, etc. **2** passable; satisfactory.

presentation (prĕˌzĕnˌtāˈshən, prĕzˌən-) noun 1 the act of presenting. 2 the manner in which something is presented, laid out, explained, or advertised.

presentiment noun a feeling that something, esp. something bad, is about to happen, just before it does.

presently adv. 1 soon; shortly. 2 at the present time; now.

> *Usage* The second meaning of *presently* is objected to by many critics; a safer and more precise choice of wording might be *currently*.

preserve verb trans. (**preserved, preserving**) 1 to save from loss, damage, decay, or deterioration. 2 to treat (food) so that it will last, e.g., by freezing, pickling, etc. 3 to keep safe from danger or death. —noun 1 an area of land or water where animals and plants are protected: *a game preserve.* 2 a jam, pickle, or other form of food in which fruit or vegetables are preserved by cooking in sugar, storing in salt or vinegar, etc. ▶ **preservation** noun ▶ **preservative** noun, adj.

preside verb intrans. (**presided, presiding**) 1 (**preside at** or **over** (**something**)) to take the lead or be in charge at an event or a meeting, etc. 2 to be a dominating presence in.

president (prĕzˈəd-ənt) noun 1 a (often **President**) the elected head of state in a republic. b (**President**) the elected head of state and chief political executive of the USA. 2 the chief officeholder in a club or society. 3 the head of a business organization or corporation. ▶ **presidency** noun ▶ **presidential** adj.

Presidents' Day the third Monday in February, a legal holiday in the USA commemorating the birthdays of George Washington and Abraham Lincoln.

presidium (prĭ-sĭdˈē-əm) noun (pl. **presidia, presidiums**) a standing executive committee in a Communist or former Communist state.

press¹ verb trans., intrans. (**pressed, pressing, presses**) 1 a to push steadily, esp. with the finger. b to act upon by steady thrusting force. ◪ JAM, MASH, PUSH, SQUASH. c to squeeze (e.g., someone's hand) affectionately. 2 to iron (clothes, etc.). 3 a to demand firmly; to ask again and again. ◪ INSIST, PRESSURE, PROD, URGE. b to urge acceptance, discussion, or recognition of: *pressed her claim.* 4 Law to bring (charges) officially against a party. —noun 1 an act of pressing. 2 an apparatus for pressing, flattening, etc. 3 a printing press. 4 a (**the press**) newspapers or journalists in general. b newspaper publicity or reviews received by a show, book, etc.

press² verb trans. (**pressed, pressing, presses**) 1 to force (men) into the army or navy. 2 to put to esp. emergency use.

press agent (ABBREV. P.A., PA) a person who arranges newspaper, radio, and television publicity for an author, performer, or celebrity.

press conference an interview granted to reporters by a politician or another person in the news. *Also called* **news conference.**

press release an official statement given to the press by an organization, etc.

pressure noun 1 the force exerted on a surface divided by the area of the surface to which it is applied. 2 the act of pressing or process of being pressed. 3 force or coercion; forceful persuasion. 4 the need to perform a great deal at speed: *work under pressure.* 5 tension or stress. —verb trans. (**pressured, pressuring**) to repeatedly demand firmly.

pressurize verb trans. (**pressurized, pressurizing**) 1 to adjust the pressure within (an enclosed compartment such as an aircraft cabin) to maintain nearly normal atmospheric pressure. 2 to put pressure on; to force or coerce.

prestidigitator noun someone expert at sleight of hand; a conjurer.

prestige (prĕs-tēzhˈ, -tējˈ) noun 1 elevated professional or social position. 2 fame, distinction, or reputation because of success or rank. ▶ **prestigious** adj.

presto Mus. adj., adv. very fast. —noun (pl. **prestos**) a passage to be played very fast.

presume verb trans., intrans. (**presumed, presuming**) 1 to suppose (something to be the case) though one has no proof. 2 to be so bold as (to do something) without the proper right or knowledge: *wouldn't presume to advise the experts.* ▶ **presumable** ▶ **presumably** adv.

presumption noun 1 the act of presuming. 2 something presumed. 3 grounds or justification for presuming something. ▶ **presumptive** adj.

presumptuous adj. insolent or arrogant. ▶ **presumptuously** adv. ▶ **presumptuousness** noun

presuppose verb trans. (**presupposed, presupposing**) 1 to take for granted; to assume as true. 2 to require as a necessary condition. ▶ **presupposition** noun

pretend (prĭ-tĕndˈ) verb trans., intrans. (**pretended, pretending**) 1 to act as if, or to give the impression that, something is the case when it is not. 2 to imply or claim falsely. 3 to claim to feel; to profess falsely: *pretend friendship toward someone.* —adj. colloq. fake. ▶ **pretender** noun

pretense noun 1 the act of pretending. 2 make-believe. 3 insincere behavior intended

to make an impression. ■ ACT, DISSEM-
BLANCE, MASQUERADE, POSE, SHAM,
SHOW, SIMULATION. **4** a claim, esp. an
unjustified one: *made on pretense to expert
knowledge.* **5** show, affectation, or ostentation; pretentiousness. **6** (*usu.* **pretenses**)
a misleading declaration of intention. **7** show
or semblance.

pretension *noun* **1** foolish vanity, self-
importance, or affectation; pretentiousness.
2 a claim or aspiration.

pretentious *adj.* **1** pompous, self-important,
or foolishly grandiose. **2** showy; ostentatious. ▸ **pretentiously** *adv.* ▸ **pretentiousness** *noun*

preternatural *adj.* **1** departing from the norm.
2 supernatural. ▸ **preternaturally** *adv.*

pretext *noun* a false reason given for doing
something, to disguise the real one.

prettify *verb trans.* (**prettified, prettifying,
prettifies**) to make prettier. ▸ **prettification**
noun

pretty *adj.* (**prettier, prettiest**) **1** facially
attractive. **2** charming to look at. **3** *of music,
sound, etc.* delicately melodious. **4** neat,
elegant, or skillful: *a pretty solution.* —*adv.*
fairly; satisfactorily; rather; decidedly.
▸ **prettily** *adv.* ▸ **prettiness** *noun*

prevail *verb intrans.* (**prevailed, prevailing**)
1 (**prevail over** *or* **against** (someone *or*
something)) to be victorious. **2** to be
common, usual, or generally accepted. **3** to
be predominant. **4** (**prevail on** *or* **upon**
(someone)) to persuade (someone).

prevalent (prĕv'ə-lənt) *adj.* common; widespread. ▸ **prevalence** *noun*

prevaricate (prĭ-vār'ĭ-kāt,) *verb intrans.* (**pre-
varicated, prevaricating**) to avoid stating
the truth or coming directly to the point.
▸ **prevarication** *noun* ▸ **prevaricator** *noun*

prevent *verb trans.* (**prevented, preventing**) to stop (someone from doing something, or something from happening). ▸ **pre-
ventable** *or* **preventible** *adj.* ▸ **prevention**
noun

preventive *or* **preventative** *adj.* tending or
intended to prevent something, e.g., illness.
—*noun* **1** a drug intended to prevent illness.
2 a precautionary measure.

preview *noun* an advance showing of a film,
play, exhibition, etc., before presentation to
the general public. —*verb trans.* (**pre-
viewed, previewing**) to show or view in
advance to a select audience.

previous *adj.* **1** earlier. **2** former. **3** prior: *a
previous engagement.* ▸ **previously** *adv.*

prey (prā) *noun* **1** a creature that a predatory
animal hunts and kills as food. **2** a victim or
victims: *easy prey for muggers.* —*verb
intrans.* (**preyed, preying, preys**) **1** *of an
animal* to attack (it) as prey. **2** a to. bully,

exploit, or terrorize (someone) as a victim. **b**
to afflict (someone).

price *noun* **1** the amount, usu. in money, for
which a thing is sold or offered. **2** that which
one must give up or suffer in gaining
something else. **3** the sum by which one
may be bribed. —*verb trans.* (**priced,
pricing**) **1** to set a price for, or mark a price
on. **2** to find out the price of.

priceless *adj.* too valuable to have a price.

pricey *or* **pricy** *adj.* (**pricier, priciest**) *colloq.*
expensive.

prick *verb trans., intrans.* (**pricked, pricking**)
1 a to pierce slightly with a fine point. **b** to
make (a hole) by this means. **c** to hurt by this
means. **2** to smart or cause to smart. **3** to
mark out (a pattern) in punctured holes.
—*noun* **1** an act of pricking or a feeling of
being pricked; the resultant pain. **2** a
puncture made by pricking.

prickle *noun* **1** a sharp point or thornlike
growth on a plant or animal. **2** a pricking
sensation: *a prickle of fear.* —*verb intrans.,
trans.* (**prickled, prickling**) to cause, affect
with, or be affected by, a pricking sensation.

prickly *adj.* (**pricklier, prickliest**) **1** having
prickles. **2** causing prickling. **3** *colloq., of a
person* irritable; hypersensitive. ▸ **prickli-
ness** *noun*

prickly pear 1 a low-growing cactus with a
prickly, pear-shaped fruit. **2** the fruit of this
plant, edible in some species.

pride *noun* **1** a a feeling of pleasure and
satisfaction at one's own or another's
accomplishments, possessions, etc. **b**
something that inspires this feeling: *That
car's my pride and joy.* **2** personal dignity;
self-respect. **3** too good an opinion of
oneself. **4** a group of lions. —*verb trans.*
(**prided, priding**) (**pride** (oneself) **on**
(something)) to congratulate (oneself) or
be proud on account of (it)

pried, pries *see* pry[1], pry[2].

priest *noun* **1** in some Christian churches, an
ordained minister. **2** in non-Christian
religions, an official who performs sacrifices
and other religious rites. ▸ **priesthood** *noun*
▸ **priestly** *adj.*

priestess *noun* in non-Christian religions, a
female official who performs sacrifices and
other religious rites.

prig *noun* a self-righteously moralistic person.
▸ **priggish** *adj.* ▸ **priggishly** *adv.* ▸ **prig-
gishness** *noun*

prim *adj.* **1** stiffly formal, overly modest, or too
proper. **2** prudishly disapproving. ▸ **primly**
adv. ▸ **primness** *noun*

primacy *noun* (*pl.* **primacies**) **1** the condition
of being first in rank, importance, or order. **2**
the rank, office, or area of jurisdiction of a
primate of a church.

prima donna (prē,mə-dän'ə) **1** a leading female opera singer. **2** someone difficult to please, esp. if given to melodramatic tantrums when displeased.

prima facie (prī,mə-fā'shə, -shē) *adv.* at first sight; on the evidence available. —*adj.* based on first impressions.

primal *adj.* **1** relating to the beginnings of life; original. **2** basic; fundamental.

primarily *adv.* **1** chiefly; mainly. **2** in the first place; initially.

primary *adj.* **1** first or most important; principal. **2** earliest in order or development. **3** basic; fundamental. **4** firsthand; direct. —*noun* (*pl.* **primaries**) **1** something first in order, importance, etc. **2** a preliminary election at the state or local level in which voters choose candidates for political office. Also called **primary election**.

primary color any of the three pigment colors—red, yellow, and blue—which can be combined in various proportions to give all the other colors of the spectrum.

primary election a primary (sense 2).

primary school a school that encompasses the first three or four elementary grades and sometimes kindergarten.

primate (prī'māt,) *noun* **1** an archbishop. **2** *Zool.* an animal belonging to the order that includes human beings, apes, and monkeys.

prime *adj.* **1** chief; fundamental. **2** excellent: *in prime condition.* —*noun* the best, most productive, or most active stage in the life of a person or thing: *in the prime of life.* —*verb trans.* (**primed, priming**) **1** to prepare (something) in some way. **2** to ready (a gun or explosive device) for firing or detonating. **3** to supply (someone) with the necessary facts in advance.

prime meridian the 0° line of longitude, passing through Greenwich, England.

prime minister (ABBREV. **PM, P.M.**) the chief minister of a government.

prime number a whole number that can only be divided by itself and 1, e.g., 3, 5, 7, 11.

primer¹ (prĭm'ər) *noun* a first or introductory book of instruction.

primer² (prī'mər) *noun* **1** a substance for sealing wood before painting. **2** an igniting or detonating device for firing the main charge in a gun or mine.

primeval (prī-mē'vəl) *adj.* belonging to Earth's beginnings.

primitive *adj.* **1** belonging to earliest times, or the earliest stages of development: *primitive tools.* **2** simple, rough, crude, or rudimentary. ▸ **primitively** *adv.*

primordial *adj.* existing from the beginning, esp. of the world; formed earliest: *primordial matter.* ▸ **primordially** *adv.*

primp *verb trans., intrans.* (**primped, primping**) to groom; to preen (oneself).

primrose *noun* a small plant with crinkled leaves and long-stalked, pale yellow or sometimes pink flowers.

prince *noun* **1** the son of a sovereign. **2** a nonreigning male member of a royal or imperial family. **3** a leading or dominant figure in a field, e.g., a wealthy manufacturer. ▸ **princely** *adj.*

princess *noun* **1** a daughter of a sovereign. **2** a nonreigning female member of a royal or imperial family. **3** a noblewoman in certain countries.

principal *adj.* first in rank or importance, chief; main. —*noun* **1** the head of an educational institution. **2** a leading actor, singer, or dancer in a theatrical production. **3** *Law* **a** the person on behalf of whom an agent acts. **b** a person ultimately responsible for fulfilling an obligation. ▸ **principally** *adv.*

principality *noun* (*pl.* **principalities**) a territory ruled by a prince, or one from which he derives his title.

principle *noun* **1** a general truth or assumption from which to argue. **2** (*usu.* **principles**) a basic set of rules, parts, or levels. **3** a scientific law, e.g. as explaining a natural phenomenon. **4** a general rule of morality that guides one's conduct.

principled *adj.* having or proceeding from high moral principles.

print *verb trans., intrans.* (**printed, printing**) **1** to reproduce (text or pictures) on paper with ink. **2** to publish (a book, article, etc.). **3** to write in separate, as opposed to joined-up, letters. **4** to make (a photograph) from a negative. —*noun* **1** a mark produced by or as if by pressure. **2** a fingerprint. **3** lettering with each letter written separately. **4** mechanically printed text. **5** a printed publication. **6** a design printed from an engraved wood block or metal plate. **7** a photograph made from a negative. **8** a fabric with a printed or stamped design. —**print (something) out** to produce a printed version of (something, e.g., computer data).

printer *noun* **1** a person or business engaged in printing books, newspapers, etc. **2** a machine that prints, e.g., photographs. **3** *Comput.* an output device that produces printed copies of text or graphics.

printing *noun* **1** the art or business of producing books, etc., in print. **2** the run of books, etc., printed all at one time. **3** handwriting in which the letters are separately written.

printout *noun Comput.* output in printed form.

prior¹ (prī'ər) *adj.* **1** of an engagement already arranged for the time in question. **2** preceding, e.g., in urgency or importance: *a prior claim.*

prior² *noun* **1** the head of a community of monks and friars. **2** the deputy of the abbot of an abbey.

prioress *noun* **1** the head of a community of nuns. **2** the deputy of the abbess of an abbey.

prioritize (prī-ôr'ə-tīz,, -är'-) *verb trans.* (**prioritized, prioritizing**) to schedule (something) for immediate, or earliest, attention.

> *Usage*Though widely used, *prioritize* is regarded by many critics as a prime instance of business and governmental jargon.

priority *noun* (*pl.* **priorities**) **1** the right to or go first; precedence or preference. **2** something that must be attended to before anything else. **3** the fact or condition of being earlier than others.

priory (prī'ə-rē) *noun* (*pl.* **priories**) a religious house under the supervision of a prior or prioress.

prise *verb same as* **prize²**.

prism *noun* **1** *Geom.* a solid figure in which the two ends are matching parallel polygons (e.g., triangles, squares) and all other surfaces are rectangles or parallelograms. **2** *Optics* a transparent block, usu. of glass and with triangular ends and rectangular sides, that separates a beam of white light into the colors of the visible spectrum. ▸ **prismatic** *adj.*

prison *noun* a secure place of confinement for prisoners in custody. ▣ JAIL, PEN, PENITENTIARY.

prisoner *noun* a person who is under arrest or confined in prison.

prisoner of war (*pl.* **prisoners of war**) (ABBREV. **POW**) someone, specifically a member of the armed forces, who is taken prisoner during a war.

prissy *adj.* (**prissier, prissiest**) insipidly prim and prudish.

pristine (prĭs-tēn') *adj.* **1** unchanged or unspoiled; original. **2** fresh, clean, unused, or untouched: *pristine linens.*

privacy *noun* **1** freedom from intrusion by the public. **2** seclusion.

private (prī'vət) *adj.* **1** not open to or available for the use of the general public. **2** holding no public office: *private individuals.* **3** kept secret. **4** relating to one's personal, as distinct from one's professional, life. **5** *of thoughts or opinions* personal and usu. kept to oneself. **6** *of a place* secluded: *a private garden.* —*noun* (ABBREV. **PVT, Pvt.**) *Mil.* a soldier or Marine of a rank below that of a noncommissioned officer. ▸ **privately** *adv.*

private enterprise the management and financing of industry, etc., by private individuals or companies, not a state.

privateer (prī,və-tīr') *noun Hist.* **1** a privately

owned ship ordered to seize and plunder an enemy's ships in wartime. **2** the commander or crew of such a ship.

privation *noun* the condition of not having or being deprived of life's comforts or necessities, or of something particular.

privatize *verb trans.* (**privatized, privatizing**) to free (a state-owned business) from state ownership into private ownership. ▸ **privatization** *noun. See also* **nationalize.**

privet (prĭv'ət) *noun* a shrub with dark green or yellow leaves and strongly scented creamy-white flowers, that is often used as hedges.

privilege (prĭv'lĭj, -ə-lĭj) *noun* rights, advantages and power enjoyed by people of wealth and high social class. ▸ **privileged** *adj.*

privy (prĭv'ē) *adj.* **1** (**privy to** (**something**)) allowed to share in (secret discussions, etc.), or be in the know about (secret plans, happenings, etc.). **2** secret; hidden; concealed. —*noun* (*pl.* **privies**) a bathroom or an outhouse.

prize¹ *noun* **1** something won, e.g., in a competition or lottery. **2** a reward given in recognition of excellence. **3** something striven for or worth striving for. —*verb trans.* (**prized, prizing**) to value highly.

prize² *or* **prise** *verb trans.* (**prized** *or* **prised, prizing** *or* **prising**) to lever (something) open, off, out, etc.

PRO *or* **P.R.O.** *abbrev.* public relations officer.

pro¹ *adv.* in agreement or favor. —*prep.* in agreement with or in favor of. —*noun* (*pl.* **pros**) a reason, argument, or choice in favor: *pros and cons.*

pro² *noun* (*pl.* **pros**) *colloq.* **1** a professional. **2** an expert.

pro- *prefix* forming words denoting: **1** in favor of; admiring or supporting: *pro-French.* **2** serving in place of: *pronoun.*

probable *adj.* **1** likely to happen. **2** likely to be the case. **3** *of an explanation, etc.* likely to be correct. ▸ **probability** *noun*

probably *adv.* almost certainly.

probate (prō'bāt,) *noun Law* the process of establishing that a will is valid. ▸ **probate** *verb*

probation *noun* **1** the system whereby offenders are allowed limited freedom under supervision on condition of good behavior. **2** in certain types of employment, a period during which a new employee is observed on the job. ▸ **probationary** *adj.* ▸ **probationer** *noun*

probe *noun* **1** a long, slender, usu. metal instrument used by physicians to examine wounds, inspect body cavities, etc. **2** an investigation. **3** an act of probing; a poke or prod. —*verb trans., intrans.* (**probed, probing**) (**probe** *or* **probe into** (**some-**

thing)) **1** to investigate (it) closely. **2** to examine (it) with a probe. **3** to poke or prod (it).

probity *noun* integrity; honesty.

problem *noun* **1** a situation or matter that is difficult to understand or deal with. **2** a person or thing that is difficult to deal with. **3** a puzzle or mathematical question set for solving.

problematic *or* **problematical** *adj.* **1** causing problems. **2** uncertain.

proboscis (prǝ-bǎs'ĭs, -kĭs) *noun* (**proboscises, proboscides**) **1** a flexible, elongated nose or snout, e.g., the trunk of an elephant. **2** the elongated mouth part of certain insects.

procedure (prǝ-sē'jǝr) *noun* **1** the method and order followed in doing something. **2** an established routine for conducting business at a meeting or in a law case. **3** a course of action; a step or measure taken. ▸ **procedural** *adj.* ▸ **procedurally** *adv.*

proceed (prǝ-sēd', prō-) *verb intrans.* (**proceeded, proceeding**) **1** to make one's way. **2** to go on with (something); to continue after stopping. **3** to set about a task, etc.: *instructions on how to proceed.* **4** to begin.

proceeding *noun* **1** a piece of behavior; an action. **2** (**proceedings**) a published record of the business done or papers read at a meeting of a society, etc. **3** (**proceedings**) *Law* legal action.

proceeds (prō'sēdz,) *pl. noun* money made, e.g., from selling.

process (prǎs'ĕs,, prō'sĕs,) *noun* **1** a series of operations performed on something during manufacture, etc. **2** a series of stages passed through, resulting in development or transformation. **3** an operation or procedure: *a slow process.* —*verb trans.* (**processed, processing**) **1** to put through the required process: *process a film.* **2** to analyze (data) by computer.

procession *noun* a file of people or vehicles proceeding ceremonially in orderly formation.

processor *noun* **1** a machine or person that processes something. **2** *Comput.* a central processing unit.

proclaim (prǝ-klām', prō-) *verb trans.* (**proclaimed, proclaiming**) to announce publicly. ▸ **proclamation** *noun*

proclivity *noun* (*pl.* **proclivities**) a tendency or liking.

procrastinate (prō-krǎs'tǝ-nāt,) *verb intrans.* (**procrastinated, procrastinating**) to keep putting off doing something that should be done right away. ▸ **procrastination** *noun* ▸ **procrastinator** *noun*

procreate (prō,krē-āt') *verb trans., intrans.* (**procreated, procreating**) to produce

(offspring); to reproduce. ▸ **procreation** *noun*

proctor *noun* a person who monitors undergraduates as they take examinations.

procurator (prǎk'yǝ-rāt,ǝr) *noun* **1** an agent with power of attorney to manage someone else's affairs. **2**. in the Roman empire, a financial agent or administrator in a province.

procure (prǝ-kyōōr', prō-) *verb trans., intrans.* (**procured, procuring**) **1** to manage to obtain or bring about. **2** to provide (prostitutes) for clients. ▸ **procurement** *noun* ▸ **procurer** *noun*

prod *verb trans.* (**prodded, prodding**) **1** to knock (something) slightly. **2** to prompt or spur into action. —*noun* **1** a poke, jab, or nudge. **2** a reminder, often persistent. **3** a pointed instrument; a goad: *a cattle prod.*

prodigal (prǎd'ĭ-gǝl) *adj.* **1** heedlessly extravagant or wasteful. **2** lavish; generous. —*noun* a squanderer, wastrel, or spendthrift. ▸ **prodigality** *noun* ▸ **prodigally** *adv.*

prodigious (prǝ-dĭj'ǝs) *adj.* **1** extraordinary or marvelous. **2** of exceedingly or excessively large size. ▸ **prodigiously** *adv.*

prodigy *noun* (*pl.* **prodigies**) **1** an extraordinary phenomenon; a wonder. **2** a person, esp. a child or youth, of extraordinary brilliance or talent.

produce *verb trans., intrans.* (prǝ-dōōs') (**produced, producing**) **1** to bring out or present to view. **2** to bear (children, leaves, etc.). **3** to yield (crops, etc.). **4** to make or manufacture (e.g., goods). **5** to direct (a play), arrange (a radio or television program) for presentation, or finance and schedule the making of (a movie). —*noun* (prǎd'ōōs,, prōd'-) foodstuffs derived from crops or livestock, e.g., fruit, vegetables, eggs, and dairy products. ▸ **producer** *noun*

product *noun* **1** something produced; e.g., through manufacture or agriculture. **2** a result. **3** *Math.* the value obtained by multiplying two or more numbers.

production *noun* **1** the act of producing; the process of producing or being produced: *this car goes into production next year.* **2** a quantity produced or rate of producing it. **3** a particular presentation of, e.g., a play, opera, or ballet.

productive *adj.* **1** yielding a lot; fertile; fruitful. **2** useful; profitable. ▸ **productively** *adv.*

productivity *noun* rate and efficiency of work, e.g., in industrial production.

proem (prō'ĕm,, -ǝm) *noun* an introduction, prelude, or preface.

prof *noun colloq.* a professor.

profane (prǝ-fān', prō-) *adj.* **1** showing disrespect for sacred things; irreverent. **2** not sacred or spiritual; temporal or worldly. —*verb trans.* (**profaned, profaning**) **1** to treat (something sacred) irreverently. **2** to violate or defile (something that should be respected). ▸ **profanely** adv.

profanity (prə-fĕn'ət-ē) noun (pl. **profanities**) **1** lack of respect for sacred things. **2** blasphemous language; a blasphemy, swearword, oath, etc.

profess (prə-fĕs', prō-) verb trans. (**professed, professing**) **1** to make an open declaration of (beliefs, etc.). **2** to declare one's adherence to. **3** to claim or pretend: professed ignorance.

profession noun **1** an occupation, esp. one that requires specialist academic and practical training; e.g., medicine or law. **2** the body of people engaged in a particular one of these occupations. **3** an act of professing; a declaration.

professional adj. **1** earning one's living in the performance, practice, or teaching of something that is a pastime for others. **2** belonging to or relating to a trained field of occupation. —noun someone who is skilled in a particular field: media professionals. ▸ **professionalism** noun ▸ **professionally** adj.

professor noun a university or college teacher ranking above associate professor. ▸ **professorship** noun

proffer (prăf'ər) verb trans. (**proffered, proffering**) to offer.

proficient adj. fully trained and competent; expert. ▸ **proficiency** noun ▸ **proficiently** adv.

profile noun **1** a side view, esp. of a face or a head. **2** a brief outline, sketch, assessment, or analysis. —verb trans. (**profiled, profiling**) to produce a brief assessment of (a subject).

profit 1 noun money gained from selling something for more than one paid for it. **2** an excess of income over expenses. **3** advantage or benefit. —verb intrans. (**profited, profiting**) (**profit from** or **by** (**something**)) to benefit from (it).

profitable adj. **1** of a business, etc. making a profit. **2** useful; fruitful. ▸ **profitability** noun ▸ **profitably** adv.

profiteer (prăf,ə-tîr') noun a person who takes advantage of a shortage to make exorbitant profits.. —verb intrans. (**profiteered, profiteering**) to make excessive profits in such a way.

profligate (prăf'lĭ-gət, -găt,) adj. **1** immoral and irresponsible. **2** scandalously extravagant. —noun a person who is extravagant, irresponsible, or dissolute. ▸ **profligacy** noun ▸ **profligately** adv.

pro forma (prō-fôr'mə) done merely as a formality: a pro forma protest of innocence.

profound adj. **1** radical, extensive, and far-reaching. **2** of a feeling deeply felt or rooted: profound grief. **3** of comments, etc. showing understanding or penetration. ▸ **profoundly** adv.

profundity noun (pl. **profundities**) **1** the condition of being profound. **2** depth.

profuse (prə-fyōōs', prō-) adj. **1** offering or providing something in large quantities. **2** copious: profuse apologies. ▸ **profusely** adv.

profusion noun **1** the condition of being profuse. **2** extravagance.

progenitor noun **1** an ancestor, forebear, or forefather. **2** the begetter or originator of a movement, etc.

progeny (prăj'ə-nē) noun (pl. **progeny, progenies**) an offspring or a descendant.

prognosis noun (pl. **prognoses**) **1** an informed forecast of developments in any situation. **2** a physician's prediction on the course of a patient's illness and his or her chances of recovery.

program noun **1 a** the schedule of proceedings for, and list of participants in, a theater performance, entertainment, ceremony, etc. **b** a leaflet or booklet describing these. **2** an agenda, plan, or schedule. **3** a series of planned projects to be undertaken. **4** a scheduled radio or television presentation. **5** (usu. **program**) a set of coded instructions to a computer for the performance of a series of operations. —verb trans. (**programmed, programming**) **1** to include in a program; to schedule. **2** to draw up a program for. **3** Comput. to set (a computer) by program to perform a set of operations. **4** to set so as to operate at the required time: heating programmed to come on at 7:00 p.m. ▸ **programmable** adj.

progress noun (prăg'rəs, -rĕs,) **1** movement while traveling in any direction. **2** the course taken in any direction, degree, or manner. **3** forward movement, esp. toward a goal: the progress made by research. ▣ ADVANCEMENT, HEADWAY, MARCH ▣ RETREAT, RETROGRESSION. —verb intrans. (prə-grĕs') (**progressed, progressing**) **1** to move forward or onward; to proceed toward a goal. **2** to advance or develop. **3** to improve.

progression noun **1** the process of moving forward or advancing in stages. **2** Math. a sequence of numbers, each of which bears a specific relationship to the preceding number.

progressive adj. **1** advanced in outlook; using or favoring new methods. **2** advancing continuously or by stages. **3** of a disease continuously increasing in severity or complication. **4** Gram., of tense formed with the verb be and the present participle, and usu. representing continuing action or a continuing state, as in I am waiting. —noun

1 a person with progressive ideas. **2** *Gram.* a verb in a progressive form. ▸ **progressively** *adv.*

prohibit (prə-hĭb′ĭt, prō-) *verb trans.* (**prohibited, prohibiting**) **1** to debar from doing. ▣ DISALLOW, FORBID, OUTLAW, STOP ▣ ALLOW, PERMIT. **2** to prevent or hinder ▸ **prohibition** *noun* ▸ **prohibitory** *adj.*

prohibitive *adj.* **1** prohibiting. **2** tending to prevent or discourage. **3** *of prices, etc.* unaffordably high.

project *noun* (prăj′ĭkt, -ĕkt,) **1** a plan, scheme, or proposal. **2** a research or study assignment. —*verb intrans., trans.* (prə-jĕkt′) (**projected, projecting**) **1** to jut out; to protrude. **2** to throw forward; to propel. **3** to throw (a shadow or image) onto a surface. **4** to propose or plan. **5** to forecast from present trends and other data. **6** to ascribe (feelings of one's own) to other people. **7** to cause (one's voice) to be heard clearly at some distance. ▸ **projection** *noun*

projectile (prə-jĕk′təl, -tīl,) *noun* an object that is propelled or thrown with force, esp. a missile such as a bullet or rocket.

projector *noun* an instrument that projects an enlarged version of an illuminated image on to a screen. ▸ **projectionist** *noun*

prolapse *noun Med.* the slipping out of place or falling down of a body part, esp. the slipping of the uterus into the vagina.

proletariat (prō,lə-tĕr′ē-ət) *noun* the working class, esp. unskilled laborers and industrial workers. ▸ **proletarian** *noun, adj.*

proliferate (prə-lĭf′ə-rāt,) *verb intrans., trans.* (**proliferated, proliferating**) **1** *of a plant or animal species* to reproduce rapidly. **2** to increase in numbers or amount. ▸ **proliferation** *noun*

prolific *adj.* **1** abundant in growth; producing plentiful fruit or offspring. **2** *of a writer, artist, etc.* constantly productive of new work. ▸ **prolifically** *adv.*

prologue *or* **prolog** *noun* **1 a** a speech addressed to the audience at the beginning of a play. **b** the actor delivering such a speech. **2** a preface to a literary work. **3** an event serving as an introduction or prelude.

prolong *verb trans.* (**prolonged, prolonging**) to make longer; to extend or protract. ▸ **prolongation** *noun*

prom *noun* a formal dance for high-school juniors and/or seniors, usu. given near the end of the school year.

promenade (prăm,ə-nād′, -näd′) *noun* **1** a broad paved walk, esp. along a shore. **2** a stately stroll. —*verb intrans., trans.* (**promenaded, promenading**) **1** to stroll in a stately fashion. **2** to walk (the streets, etc.).

prominent *adj.* **1** jutting out; projecting; protruding; bulging: *prominent eyes.* **2**

noticeable; conspicuous. **3** leading; notable: *took a prominent role.* ▸ **prominence** *noun* ▸ **prominently** *adv.*

promiscuous *adj.* **1** indulging in casual or indiscriminate sex. **2** haphazardly mixed. ▸ **promiscuity** *noun* ▸ **promiscuously** *adv.*

promise *verb trans.* (**promised, promising**) **1** to give an undertaking (to do or not do something). **2** to undertake to give (some one something). **3** to show signs of bringing (something): *clouds that promise rain.* —*noun* **1** an undertaking to give, do, or not do, something. **2** a sign. **3** signs of future excellence. ▸ **promising** *adj.* ▸ **promisingly** *adv.*

promissory (prăm′ə-sôr,ē) *adj.* expressing or containing a promise.

promissory note a signed promise to pay a stated sum of money.

promontory (prăm′ən-tôr,ē) *noun* (*pl.* **promontories**) a usu. hilly part of a coastline that projects into the sea.

promote *verb trans.* (**promoted, promoting**) **1** to raise in rank or grade. ▣ ELEVATE, JUMP, UP, UPGRADE ▣ BUST, DEGRADE, DEMOTE, DOWNGRADE, REDUCE. **2** to contribute to; to increase. **3** to work for the cause of: *promote peace.* **4** to try to boost the sales of (a product) by advertising. **5** to be the organizer or financial backer of (an undertaking). ▸ **promoter** *noun* ▸ **promotion** *noun* ▸ **promotional** *adj.*

prompt *adj.* **1 a** occurring at the arranged time. **b** quick; immediate. **2** instantly willing; unhesitating: *prompt with offers of help.* —*adv.* on time; punctually. —*noun* **1** something serving as a reminder. **2** words supplied by a prompter to an actor. **3** a prompter. —*verb trans., intrans.* (**prompted, prompting**) **1** to cause, lead, or remind (someone) to do something. **2** to produce or elicit (a reaction or response): *What prompted that remark?* **3** to help (an actor) to remember his or her next words by supplying the first few. ▸ **prompter** *noun* ▸ **promptly** *adv.* ▸ **promptness** *noun*

promulgate (prăm′əl-gāt,) *verb trans.* (**promulgated, promulgating**) **1** to make (a decree, etc.) effective by means of an official public announcement. **2** to publicize or promote (an idea, etc.) widely. ▸ **promulgation** *noun* ▸ **promulgator** *noun*

pron. *abbrev. Gram.* pronoun.

prone *adj.* **1** lying flat, esp. face downward. **2** (**prone to (something)**) predisposed to (it), or liable to suffer from (it). **3** inclined or liable to do something. ▸ **proneness** *noun*

prong *noun* a point or spike, esp. one of those making up the head of a fork.

pronoun *noun Gram.* a word such as *she, him, they,* and *it* used in place of, and to refer to, a

noun or noun phrase. ▸ **pronominal** *adj.*
▸ **pronominally** *adv.* .

pronounce *verb trans.* .(**pronounced, pronouncing**) **1** to say or utter (words, sounds,
letters, etc.); to say or sound correctly. **2** to
declare officially, formally, or authoritatively:
pronounced her innocent. **3** to pass or
deliver (judgment). ▸ **pronounceable** *adj.*

pronounced *adj.* noticeable; distinct: *a pronounced limp.*

pronouncement *noun* **1** a formal announcement. **2** a declaration of opinion; a verdict.

pronto *adv. colloq.* immediately.

pronunciation *noun* the act of, or a manner
of, or the usual way of, pronouncing words,
sounds, letters, etc.

proof *noun* **1** evidence, esp. conclusive
evidence, that something is true or a fact. **2**
Law the accumulated evidence on which a
verdict is based. **3** a test, trial, or demonstration: *as a proof of her love.* **4** *Printing* a
trial copy of a sheet of printed text for
examination or correction. —*adj.* able or
designed to withstand, deter, or be free
from: *windproof.* —*verb trans.* (**proofed,
proofing**) **1** to take a proof of (printed
material). **2** to proofread.

proofread *verb trans., intrans.* (**proofread,
proofreading**) to read and mark for correction the proofs of (a text, etc.). ▸ **proof-
reader** *noun*

prop¹ *noun* **1** a rigid support. **2** a person or
thing that one depends on for help or emotional support. —*verb trans.* (**propped,
propping**) (*also* **prop (something) up**) to
support or hold (it) upright with or as if with
a prop.

prop² *noun colloq.* **1** a propeller. **2** *Theat.* an
object used on stage.

propaganda *noun* **1** the organized circulation
by a political group, etc., of information, misinformation, rumor, or opinion, presented so
as to influence public feeling. **2** the material
circulated in this way. ▸ **propagandist** *noun* .

propagate (prăp′ə-gāt,) *verb intrans., trans.*
(**propagated, propagating**) **1** *Bot.* **a** of a
plant to multiply. **b** to grow (new plants) by
natural means or artificially. **2** to spread or
popularize (ideas, etc.). ▸ **propagation**
noun ▸ **propagator** *noun*

propane *noun* a colorless, odorless, flammable gas obtained from petroleum, used as
a fuel and as a solvent and refrigerant.

propel (prə-pĕl′) *verb trans.* (**propelled,
propelling**) **1** to drive or push forward. **2** to
steer or send in a certain direction.

propellant *or* **propellent** *noun* the fuel and
oxidizer that are burned in a rocket in order
to provide thrust.

propeller *noun* a device consisting of a shaft
with radiating blades that rotate to propel an

aircraft or a ship or boat.

propene *noun Chem.* propylene.

propensity *noun* (*pl.* **propensities**) a
tendency or inclination.

proper *adj.* **1** real; genuine. **2** right; correct. **3**
appropriate: *at the proper time.* **4** own
particular; correct: *in its proper place.* **5**
(*used after a noun*) strictly so called; itself:
the city proper. **6** worthy of being called
such; utter: *felt like a proper fool.*
▸ **properly** *adv.*

proper fraction *Math.* a fraction in which the
numerator has a value lower than that of the
denominator. *See also* **improper fraction.**

proper noun *or* **proper name** *Gram.* the
name of a particular person, place, or thing,
typically capitalized. *See also* **common
noun.**

propertied *adj.* owning property, esp. land.

property *noun* (*pl.* **properties**) **1** something
one owns. **2** one's possessions collectively. **3**
the concept of ownership. **4** a quality or
attribute: *the properties of hydrogen.*

prophecy (prăf′ə-sē) *noun* (*pl.* **prophecies**) **1**
the interpretation of divine will or the
foretelling of the future. **2** a prophetic
utterance; a prediction.

prophesy (prăf′ə-sī,) *verb trans., intrans.*
(**prophesied, prophesying, prophesies**)
to foretell (future happenings); to predict.

prophet *noun* **1** a person inspired to express
divine will or reveal the future. **2** (**Prophet**)
Bible any of the writers of prophecy in the
Old Testament, or the books attributed to
them. **3** someone claiming to be able to tell
what will happen in the future.

prophetess *noun* a female prophet.

prophetic *adj.* **1** foretelling the future. **2** of or
relating to prophets or prophecy. ▸ **prophet-
ically** *adv.*

prophylactic *adj.* guarding against or
preventing disease or other mishap. —*noun*
1 a prophylactic drug or device, e.g., a condom. **2** any precautionary measure.

prophylaxis *noun* (*pl.* **prophylaxes**) precautionary measures.

propinquity (prō-pĭng′kwət-ē) *noun* nearness in place or time.

propitiate (prō-pĭsh′ē-āt,) *verb trans.* (**propi-
tiated, propitiating**) to appease or placate.
▸ **propitiation** *noun* ▸ **propitiator** *noun*
▸ **propitiatory** *adj.*

propitious *adj.* favorable; auspicious; advantageous. ▸ **propitiously** *adv.*

proponent *noun* a supporter or advocate.

proportion *noun* **1** a part of a total. **2** the size
of one element or group in relation to the
whole or total. **3** the size of one group or
component in relation to another: *was
mixed in a proportion of two parts to one.* **4**
the correct balance between parts or

elements. **5** (**proportions**) size; dimensions: *a task of huge proportions.* **6** *Math.* correspondence between the ratios of two pairs of quantities, as expressed in *2 is to 8 as 3 is to 12.* —*verb trans.* (**proportioned, proportioning**) to adjust the proportions or to balance the parts of.

proportional *adj.* (often **proportional to** (**something**)) **1** corresponding or matching in size, rate, etc. **2** in correct proportion; proportionate. ► **proportionally** *adv.*

proportionate (prə-pôr'shə-nət) *adj.* (**proportionate to** (**something**)) being in correct proportion. ► **proportionately** *adv.*

propose *verb trans., intrans.* (**proposed, proposing**) **1** to offer (a plan, etc.) for consideration; to suggest. **2** to suggest or nominate (someone for a position, task, etc.). **3** to be the proposer of (the motion in a debate). **4** to intend. **5** (**propose to** (**someone**)) to make (someone) an offer of marriage. ► **proposal** *noun* ► **proposer** *noun*

proposition *noun* **1** a proposal or suggestion. **2** something to be dealt with or undertaken: *an awkward proposition.* **3** *colloq.* an invitation to engage in a sexual act. —*verb trans.* (**propositioned, propositioning**) *colloq.* to propose that (someone) take part in a sex act.

propound *verb trans.* (**propounded, propounding**) to put forward (an idea, theory, etc.) for consideration or discussion.

proprietary (prə-prī'ə-těr,ē) *adj.* **1** *of, e.g., rights* belonging to an owner or proprietor. **2** *of medicines, etc.* marketed under a trade name. **3** privately owned and managed.

proprietor (prə-prī'ət-ər) *noun* **1** an owner, esp. of a store, hotel, business, etc. **2** the rightful owner of a trade name. ► **proprietorship** *noun*

propriety *noun* (*pl.* **proprieties**) **1** socially acceptable behavior; modesty or decorum. **2** moral acceptability; rightness. **3** (**proprieties**) the details of correct behavior; accepted standards of conduct: *observe the proprieties.*

propulsion *noun* the process of driving or of being driven forward; a force that propels.

propylene (prō'pə-lēn,) *noun* a flammable gas that is derived from petroleum and is used in organic synthesis. *Also called* **propene.**

pro rata (prō-rāt'ə, -rät'ə) in proportion; in accordance with a certain rate.

prorogue (prō-rōg') *verb trans., intrans.* (**prorogued, proroguing**) to discontinue the meetings of (a legislative body) for a time, without dissolving (it). ► **prorogation** *noun*

prosaic (prō-zā'ĭk) *adj.* **1** unpoetic; unimaginative. **2** dull, ordinary, and uninteresting. ► **prosaically** *adv.*

proscribe *verb trans.* (**proscribed, proscribing**) **1** to prohibit or condemn (something, e.g., a practice). **2** to outlaw or exile (someone). ► **proscription** *noun* ► **proscriptive** *adj.*

prose *noun* ordinary written or spoken language as distinct from verse or poetry.

prosecute (präs'ə-kyōōt,) *verb trans., intrans.* (**prosecuted, prosecuting**) **1** to bring a criminal action against (someone). **2** to carry on or out: *prosecuting her inquiries.* ► **prosecution** *noun*

prosecutor *or* **prosecuting attorney** (AB-BREV. **P.A., PA**) *noun* an attorney who brings or conducts a criminal action against a specified party.

proselyte (präs'ə-līt,) *noun* a convert, esp. to a doctrine or religion.

prosody (präs'əd-ē) *noun* the study of verse composition, esp. poetic meter. ► **prosodic** *adj.* ► **prosodist** *noun*

prospect *noun* **1** a visualization of something due or likely to happen. **2** an outlook for the future. **3** (**prospects**) opportunities for advancement: *a job with prospects.* **4** a broad physical view. —*verb intrans.* (**prospected, prospecting**) (**prospect for**) **1** to search for (gold, etc.). **2** to hunt for or look out for (e.g., a job). ► **prospector** *noun*

prospective *adj.* likely or expected; future: *prospective buyers.*

prospectus *noun* (**prospectuses**) a document giving information about a project or venture.

prosper *verb intrans.* (**prospered, prospering**) to do well, esp. financially; to thrive or flourish.

prosperous *adj.* wealthy and successful. ► **prosperity** *noun* ► **prosperously** *adv.*

prostate (präs'tāt,) *noun* a muscular gland around the base of the bladder in men, controlled by sex hormones, which produces a fluid that activates sperm during ejaculation. *Also called* **prostate gland**.

prosthesis *noun* (*pl.* **prostheses**) an artificial substitute for a part of the body that is missing. ► **prosthetic** *adj.*

prostitute *noun* a person who accepts money in return for sex acts. —*verb trans.* (**prostituted, prostituting**) to offer (oneself or someone else) as a prostitute. ► **prostitution** *noun*

prostrate (präs'trāt,) *adj.* **1** lying face downward in an attitude of abject submission, humility, or adoration. **2** lying flat. **3** exhausted by illness, grief, etc. —*verb trans.* (**prostrated, prostrating**) **1** to throw (oneself) face down in submission or adoration. **2** to exhaust physically or emotionally. ► **prostration** *noun*

prot- *combining form same as* **proto-**.

protactinium *noun* (SYMBOL **Pa**) a radio-active metallic element.

protagonist *noun* **1** the main character in a play or story. **2** the person, or any of the people, at the center of a story or event. **3** *colloq.* a leader or champion of a movement, cause, etc.

> *Usage* Sense 3 of *protagonist*, a leader or champion, is often considered a mistake by linguistic conservatives. Careful speakers and writers can use *advocate* or *proponent* instead to avoid criticism.

protean (prōt'ē-ən) *adj.* **1** readily able to change shape or appearance; variable; changeable. **2** versatile; diverse.

protect *verb trans.* (**protected, protecting**) **1** to shield from danger. **2** to cover against loss, etc., by insurance.

protection *noun* **1** the act of protecting or the condition of being protected. **2** something that protects. **3** insurance coverage.

protective *adj.* **1** giving or designed to give protection. **2** inclined or tending to protect. ▸ **protectively** *adv.* ▸ **protectiveness** *noun*

protector *noun* **1** a person or thing that protects. **2** a patron or benefactor. **3** a person ruling a country during the childhood of the sovereign, or in the absence of a sovereign.

protectorate *noun* **1** the office or the period of rule of a protector. **2 a** a protectorship of a weak or backward country assumed by a more powerful one. **b** the status of a territory that is so protected without actual annexation.

protégé (prōt'ə-zhā,) or **protege** *noun* a person under the guidance, protection, and patronage of a more important or wiser person.

pro tempore (prō-tĕm'pə-rē) or *colloq.* **pro tem** serving, continuing, or lasting for only a limited period of time.

protest *verb intrans., trans.* (prə-tĕst', prō'tĕst,) (**protested, protesting**) **1** to engage in opposition by arguing against something. **2** to challenge or object to (e.g., a decision or measure). —*noun* (prō'tĕst,) **1** a declaration of disapproval or dissent; an objection. **2** an organized public demonstration of disapproval. ▸ **protester** *noun*

Protestant (prät'ə-stənt) *noun* a member of any of the Christian churches which in the 16th c separated from the Roman Catholic Church; a member of any body descended from these. —*adj.* relating or belonging to Protestants. ▸ **Protestantism** *noun*

protestation *noun* **1** a protest or objection. **2** a solemn declaration or avowal.

proto- or **prot-** *combining form* forming words denoting first; earliest: *prototype*.

protocol *noun* **1** correct formal or diplomatic etiquette or procedure. **2** a first draft of a diplomatic document, e.g., setting out the terms of a treaty. **3** a plan of a scientific experiment or medical procedure: *a treatment protocol*.

proton *noun* any of the positively charged subatomic particles that are found inside the nucleus at the center of an atom. *See also* **electron, neutron**.

protoplasm *noun* the translucent, colorless, semiliquid substance of which living cells are chiefly composed.

prototype *noun* an original model from which later forms are copied, developed, or derived.

protozoan *noun* a single-celled organism, e.g., amoeba, paramecium, many of which are parasitic and some the cause of diseases. *Also called* **protozoon**.—*adj.* relating to protozoans.

protract (prō-trăkt') *verb trans.* (**protracted, protracting**) to cause to last a long time; to prolong.

protractor *noun Geom.* an instrument, usu. a transparent plastic semicircle marked in degrees, for drawing and measuring angles.

protrude *verb intrans., trans.* (**protruded, protruding**) **1** to stick out; to project. **2** to push out or forward. ▸ **protrusion** *noun*

protuberance *noun* a bulging out; a swelling. ▸ **protuberant** *adj.*

proud *adj.* **1** (*often* **proud of (someone** *or* **something)**) feeling pride at (one's own or another's accomplishments, one's possessions, etc.). **2** being a cause or occasion for pride: *a proud day*. **3** arrogant; conceited. **4** concerned about one's dignity and self-respect. **5** honored; delighted. ▸ **proudly** *adv.*

prove *verb trans., intrans.* (*pa p* **proved** *or* **proven;** *pr t* **proving;** *pa t* **proved**) **1** to show to be true, correct, or a fact. **2** to show to be. **3** to turn out to be: *Her advice proved sound.* **4** to show (oneself) to be: *He has proved himself reliable.* ▸ **provable** *adj.*

provenance *noun* the place of origin or the source of, e.g., a work of art.

Provençal (prō-vän-säl') *adj.* of or relating to Provence in the S of France, its inhabitants, or their language. —*noun* **1** a language spoken in Provence, related to French. **2** a native of Provence.

provender (präv'ən-dər) *noun* **1** dry food for livestock, e.g., hay. **2** food.

proverb (präv'ərb,) *noun* a well-known saying that gives advice or expresses a supposed truth. ▸ **proverbial** *adj.* ▸ **proverbially** *adv.*

provide *verb trans., intrans.* (**provided, providing**) **1** to supply. **2** (**provide for** *or* **against (something)**) to be prepared for an emergency, etc. **3** (**provide for (some-**

one)) to support or keep a dependant. ▸ **provider** *noun*

provided (that) *conj.* on the condition or understanding that.

providence *noun* **1** a mysterious power or force believed to operate to keep one from harm, etc.; the benevolent foresight of God. **2 (Providence)** God or Nature regarded as an all-seeing protector of the world. **3** the quality of being provident.

provident *adj.* careful and thrifty in planning ahead. ▸ **providently** *adv.*

providential *adj.* being such because of providence; fortunate; lucky; opportune. ▸ **providentially** *adv.*

province *noun* **1** an administrative division of a country. **2** one's allotted range of duties, or one's field of knowledge or experience. **3 (the provinces)** the parts of a country away from the capital, regarded as culturally unsophisticated.

provincial *adj.* **1** of, belonging to, or relating to a province. **2** relating to or typical of the parts of a country away from the capital. **3** unsophisticated or narrow in outlook. ▸ **provincialism** *noun* ▸ **provincially** *adv.*

provision *noun* **1** the act of providing. **2** something provided or made available. **3** measures taken in advance; preparations. **4 (provisions)** food and other necessaries. —*verb trans.* **(provisioned, provisioning)** to supply with food.

provisional *adj.* serving, continuing, or lasting for only a limited period of time. ▸ **provisionally** *adv.*

proviso (prə-vī'zō) *noun* (*pl.* **provisos**) *Law* a clause stating a condition. ▸ **provisory** *adj.*

provocateur (prō-väk,ə-tər') *noun* an agent provocateur.

provocation *noun* **1** the act of provoking or state of being provoked. **2** a cause of anger, irritation, or indignation.

provocative *adj.* **1** tending or intended to cause anger. **2** sexually arousing or stimulating, esp. by design. ▸ **provocatively** *adv.*

provoke *verb trans.* **(provoked, provoking) 1** to annoy or infuriate, esp. deliberately. **2** to incite: *provoke a riot.* **3** to rouse (someone's anger, etc.). ▸ **provoking** *adj.*

provost marshal (ABBREV. **PM, P.M.**) an officer in charge of military police.

prow *noun* the projecting front part of a ship.

prowess *noun* **1** skill; ability; expertise. **2** valor.

prowl *verb intrans.* **(prowled, prowling) 1** to go about stealthily, e.g., in search of prey. **2** to pace restlessly. —*noun* an act of prowling. ▸ **prowler** *noun*

proximate (präk'sĭ-mat) *adj.* immediately before or after in time, place, or order of occurrence; nearest.

proximity *noun* closeness in space or time.

proxy *noun* (*pl.* **proxies**) **.1 a** a person authorized to act or vote on another's behalf. **b** the agency of such a person. **2** the authority to act or vote for someone else, or a document granting this authority.

prude *noun* a person who is, or affects to be, shocked by improper behavior, mention of sexual matters, etc. ▸ **prudish** *adj.*

prudent (prōōd'nt) *adj.* **1** wise or careful in conduct. **2** shrewd or thrifty in planning ahead. ▸ **prudence** *noun* ▸ **prudential** *adj.* ▸ **prudently** *adv.*

prune¹ *verb trans.* **(pruned, pruning) 1** to cut unwanted growth off (a plant). **2** to decrease (something) in length or scope. —*noun* an act of pruning.

prune² *noun* a dried plum.

prurient *adj.* excessively interested in sexual matters. ▸ **prurience** *noun* ▸ **pruriently** *adv.*

pruritus *noun Med.* severe itching.

Prussian *adj.* relating to Prussia, a former kingdom in northern Germany and Poland. —*noun* a native or inhabitant of Prussia.

pry¹ *verb intrans.* **(pried, prying, pries) 1** to investigate matters that do not concern one. **2** to peer or peep inquisitively.

pry² *verb trans.* **(pried, prying, pries)** to raise or open with a lever.

P.S. *abbrev.* (*also* **PS**) postscript.

psalm (säm, sälm) *noun* a sacred song, esp. one from the Book of Psalms in the Old Testament. ▸ **psalmist** *noun*

psalter (sôl'tər) *noun* **1 (Psalter)** the Book of Psalms. **2** a book containing the Biblical psalms.

PSAT *abbrev.* Preliminary Scholastic Aptitude Test.

pseudo- *or* **pseud-** *combining form* forming words denoting false.

pseudonym (sōōd'ə-nĭm,) *noun* a false name used by an author. ▸ **pseudonymous** *adj.*

psoriasis (sə-rī'ə-sĭs) *noun* a skin disease characterized by red patches covered with white scales.

PST *or* **P.S.T.** *abbrev.* Pacific Standard Time.

psych *verb trans.* **(psyched, psyching)** *colloq.* to undermine the confidence of an opponent, etc.

psych- *combining form same as* **psycho-**.

psyche *noun* one's mind, esp. with regard to the deep feelings and attitudes that account for one's opinions and behavior.

psychedelic *adj.* denoting a state of mind with heightened or altered perceptions and increased mental powers.

psychiatry (sə-kī'ə-trē) *noun* the branch of medicine that is concerned with the study, diagnosis, treatment, and prevention of mental and emotional disorders. ▸ **psychiatric** adj. ▸ **psychiatrist** noun

psychic (sī′kĭk) adj. **1** relating to mental processes or experiences that are not scientifically explainable, e.g., telepathy. **2** of a person sensitive to influences producing scientifically unexplainable experiences.

psycho colloq. noun (pl. **psychos**) a psychopath. —adj. psychopathic.

psycho- or **psych-** combining form forming words denoting the mind and its workings: psychology.

psychoanalysis noun a theory and method of treatment for mental disorders, pioneered by Sigmund Freud, which emphasizes the effects of unconscious motivation and conflict on a person's behavior. ▸ **psychoanalyst** noun ▸ **psychoanalytic** or **psychoanalytical** adj. ▸ **psychoanalyze** verb

psychological warfare propaganda and other methods used in wartime to influence enemy opinion and sap enemy morale.

psychology (sī-kăl′ə-jē) noun **1** the scientific study of the mind and behavior of humans and animals. **2** the ability to understand how people's minds work. ▸ **psychological** adj. ▸ **psychologically** adv. ▸ **psychologist** noun

psychopath (sī′kə-păth,) noun a person with a personality disorder who displays little or no remorse for antisocial acts. ▸ **psychopathic** adj. ▸ **psychopathically** adv. ▸ **psychopathy** noun

psychopathology noun Med. **1** the scientific study of mental disorders, as opposed to the treatment of such disorders. **2** the symptoms of a mental disorder.

psychosis noun (pl. **psychoses**) any of various severe mental disorders in which there is a loss of contact with reality, in the form of delusions or hallucinations. ▸ **psychotic** adj., noun ▸ **psychotically** adv.

psychosomatic adj. Med., of physical symptoms strongly associated with or caused by psychological factors, esp. stress. ▸ **psychosomatically** adv.

psychotherapy noun the treatment of mental disorders and emotional and behavioral problems by psychological means, rather than by drugs or surgery. ▸ **psychotherapist** noun

PT abbrev. physical training.

P.T.[1] or **PT** abbrev. Pacific Time.

P.T.[2] abbrev. physical therapy.

Pt symbol Chem. platinum.

Pt. abbrev. Port.

pt. abbrev. **1** part. **2** pint. **3** point.

pterodactyl (tĕr,ə-dăk′təl) noun an extinct flying reptile with leathery wings.

p.t.o. or **P.T.O.** abbrev. please turn over.

ptomaine (tō′mān,) noun an organic compound containing nitrogen produced during the bacterial decomposition of dead animal and plant matter.

PTV abbrev. Public Television.

Pu symbol Chem. plutonium.

pub noun a place where alcoholic drinks may be bought for consumption on the premises.

puberty (pyōō′bərt-ē) noun **1** the onset of sexual maturity. **2** the period in life when this begins.

pubescence noun **1** the onset of puberty. **2** a soft downy covering on plants. ▸ **pubescent** adj.

pubic adj. relating to the pubis.

pubis noun (pl. **pubes**) one of the two bones forming the lower front part of each side of the pelvis.

public adj. **1** of or concerning the people of a country or community: public opinion. **2** a relating to the organization and administration of a community: a public prosecutor. **b** relating to the community. **c** provided for the use of the community. **d** provided by the state or federal government for those in need: public assistance. **3** well known through exposure in the media. **4** made, done, held, etc., openly, for all to see, hear or participate in: a public announcement. **5** known to all: public knowledge. **6** watched or attended by an audience, spectators, etc.: her last public appearance. —noun (sing., pl.) **1** the people or community. **2** an author's, performer's, etc., audience or group of devotees.

public-address system (ABBREV. **PA**) a system of microphones, amplifiers, and loudspeakers, by means of which public announcements, etc., can be communicated over a large area. Also called **PA system**.

publican noun Bible a tax collector.

publication noun **1** the act of publishing a printed work; the process of publishing or of being published. **2** a book, magazine, newspaper, or other printed and published work.

public company a company whose stock shares are available for purchase by the public.

public defender Law a usu. court-appointed attorney who represents clients unable to afford or find paid defense attorneys.

publicist (pŭb′lə-sĭst) noun a person who engages in publicizing; a press agent.

publicity (pə-blĭs′ət-ē) noun **1 a** advertising or other activity designed to attract public interest in something. **b** public interest so attracted. **2** the condition of being the object of public attention.

publicize verb trans. (**publicized, publicizing**) **1** to make generally or widely known. **2** to advertise.

public relations (ABBREV. **PR**) **1** (sing., pl.) the relationship of an organization, etc., with the public. **2** (*sing.*, *pl.*) the degree of success so achieved.

public school 1 a school funded by local and/or state government for the free education of students. **2** *Brit.* a secondary school run independently of the state, financed by endowments and by pupils' fees.

public-spirited *adj.* acting from or showing concern for the general good of all.

publish *verb trans.*, *intrans.* (**published**, **publishing**) **1** to prepare, produce, market, and distribute (printed material, etc.) for sale to the public. **2** *of an author* to have (one's work) published. **3** to publish the work of (an author).

publisher *noun* **1** a person or company engaged in the business of publishing books, newspapers, music, software, etc. **2** a newspaper proprietor. ▸ **publishing** *noun*

puce (pyoōs) *noun* a color anywhere in the range between deep purplish pink and purplish brown.

puck *noun* a thick disk of hard rubber used in ice hockey in place of a ball.

pucker *verb trans.*, *intrans.* (**puckered**, **puckering**) to gather into creases, folds or wrinkles; to wrinkle. —*noun* a wrinkle, fold, or crease.

puckish *adj.* mischievous; playful.

pudding *noun* **1** a sweet or savory food usu. made with flour and eggs and cooked by steaming, boiling, or baking. **2 a** *Brit.* any sweet food served as dessert. **b** the dessert course.

puddle *noun* a small pool, esp. of rainwater, e.g., on the road.

pudenda *pl. noun* the external sexual organs, esp. of a woman.

pudgy *adj.* (**pudgier**, **pudgiest**) *adj.* plump or chubby.

pueblo *noun* (*pl.* **pueblos**) a town or settlement with buildings made of stone or adobe.

puerile (pyoōr'əl, -īl,) *adj.* childish; silly. ▸ **puerility** *noun*

puerperal (pyoō-ər'pə-rəl) *adj.* connected with childbirth.

puff *noun* **1** a small rush, gust, or blast of air, wind, etc.; also, the sound made by it. **2** a small cloud of smoke, dust, or steam. **3** an act of inhaling and exhaling smoke from a pipe or cigarette. **4** a light pastry. **5** a powder puff. —*verb trans.*, *intrans.* (**puffed**, **puffing**) **1** to blow or breathe in small blasts. **2** *of smoke, steam, etc.* to emerge in small gusts or blasts. **3** to inhale and exhale smoke from, or draw at, (a cigarette, etc.). **4** to pant, or go along panting. **5** (*also* **puff out** *or* **up**) to swell or cause to swell.

puff adder 1 a large viper. **2** the hognose snake.

puffer fish a tropical fish that in response to attacks by predators is able to inflate its spine-covered body to become almost spherical. *Also called* **blowfish**, **swellfish**.

puffin *noun* a short, stout, black and white seabird, with a large triangular bill with red, yellow, and blue stripes.

puff pastry light flaky pastry made with a high proportion of fat.

puffy *adj.* (**puffier**, **puffiest**) swollen as a result of injury or ill health. ▸ **puffiness** *noun*

pug *noun* a small breed of dog having a compact body, a short coat, a flattened face with a short wrinkled snout, and a short curled tail carried over its back.

pugilism (pyoō'jə-lĭz,əm) *noun* the sport of boxing or prizefighting. ▸ **pugilist** *noun*

pugnacious *adj.* given to fighting; quarrelsome, belligerent, or combative. ▸ **pugnaciously** *adv.* ▸ **pugnacity** *noun*

puke *slang verb trans.*, *intrans.* (**puked**, **puking**) to vomit. —*noun* vomit.

pukka *adj. colloq.* **1** superior; high-quality. **2** upper-class; well-bred. **3** genuine.

pull *verb trans.*, *intrans.* (**pulled**, **pulling**) **1** to drag or tug, often with great effort. ⊟ HAUL, LUG, TOW, TUG ⊠ PUSH, SHOVE. **2** to remove or extract a cork, weeds, etc., with a tugging action. **3** to operate (a trigger, lever, or switch) with a tugging action. **4** to tear or take apart with a tugging action. **5** to row (a boat). **6** *of a driver or vehicle* to steer or move in a particular direction: *pulled into the parking lot.* **7** to attract (a crowd, votes, etc.). **8** to strain (a muscle or tendon). —*noun* **1** an act of pulling. **2** attraction; attracting force: *magnetic pull.* **3** useful influence: *has some pull with the department.* **4** a tab, etc., for pulling. **5** a stroke made with an oar. —**pull (something) off** *colloq.* to arrange or accomplish (it) successfully. **pull through** *or* **pull (someone) through** to recover or help (someone) to recover from, e.g., an illness or personal tragedy. **pull up** *of a driver or vehicle* to stop. **pull (someone) up** to reprimand (someone).

pullet *noun* a young female hen in its first laying year.

pulley *noun* (*pl.* **pulleys**) a device for lifting and lowering weights, consisting of a wheel with a grooved rim over which a rope or belt runs.

pullout *noun* a withdrawal from combat, etc.

pullover *noun* a sweater.

pulmonary *adj.* **1** of, relating to, or affecting the lungs. **2** having the function of a lung.

pulp *noun* **1** the flesh of a fruit or vegetable. **2** a soft wet mass of mashed material: *wood pulp.* **3** *Dentistry* the soft inner tissue of a tooth. **4** worthless literature, magazines, etc., printed on poor paper. —*verb trans.*, *intrans.* (**pulped**, **pulping**) to reduce, or be reduced, to a pulp. ▸ **pulpy** *adj.*

pulpit *noun* a small enclosed platform in a church, from which the preacher delivers sermons.

pulsar (pəl'sär,) *noun* a source of electromagnetic radiation in space emitted in brief regular pulses.

pulsate (pəl'sāt,) *verb intrans.* (**pulsated**, **pulsating**) 1 to contract and expand rhythmically. 2 *Phys.* to vary in force or intensity in a regularly recurring pattern. ▸ **pulsation** *noun*

pulse[1] *noun* 1 the rhythmic beat corresponding to the contractions of the heart as it pumps blood around the body. 2 the rate of this beat. 3 a regular throbbing beat in music. 4 *Phys.* a signal, e.g., of light or electric current, of very short duration. —*verb intrans.* (**pulsed**, **pulsing**) to vibrate with a strong, regular rhythm.

pulse[2] the dried seed of a plant of the pea family, used as food, e.g., the pea, lentil.

pulverize *verb trans.*, *intrans.* (**pulverized**, **pulverizing**) 1 a to break into pieces. b to crush or crumble. 2 to defeat utterly; to annihilate. ▸ **pulverization** *noun*

puma (pyōō'mə, pōō'-) *noun* a mountain lion

pumice (pəm'ĭs) *noun* (*in full* **pumice stone**) a very light, porous, white or gray form of solidified lava.

pummel *verb* (**pummeled** *or* **pummelled**, **pummeling** *or* **pummelling**) to beat repeatedly with the fists.

pump[1] *noun* a device for forcing or driving liquids or gases into or out of something. —*verb trans.*, *intrans.* (**pumped**, **pumping**) 1 to raise, force, or drive (liquids or gases) out of or into something with a pump. 2 (*also* **pump** (**something**) **up**) to inflate (a tire, etc.) with a pump. 3 to force in large gushes or flowing amounts: *pumping waste into trenches*. 4 to try to extract information from (someone) by persistent questioning.

pump[2] *noun* a plain, low-cut shoe for women.

pumpernickel *noun* a dark, heavy, coarse rye bread.

pumpkin *noun* 1 a trailing or climbing plant that produces large round orange fruits at ground level. 2 the edible fruit of this plant, which contains pulpy flesh and many seeds, enclosed by a hard leathery orange rind.

pun *noun* a joke consisting of a play on words, esp. one where an association is created between words of similar sound but different meaning, e.g., *Mouse Tales* (= tails).

punch[1] *verb trans.*, *intrans.* (**punched**, **punching**) to hit with one's fist. —*noun* a blow with the fist.

punch[2] *noun* 1 a tool for cutting holes or notch-es, or stamping designs, in leather, paper, metal, etc. 2 a tool for driving nail heads well down into a surface. —*verb trans.*, *intrans.* (**punched**, **punching**) to pierce, notch, or stamp with a punch: *punched our tickets*.

punch[3] *noun* a drink made from fruit juices, alcohol, water, and spice.

punch line the words that conclude a funny story and contain its point.

punchy *adj.* (**punchier**, **punchiest**) *of speech or writing* vigorous and effective.

punctilio *noun* (*pl.* **punctilios**) 1 strictness in observing the finer details of etiquette, ceremony, or correct formal behavior. 2 a fine social detail. ▸ **punctilious** *adj.* ▸ **punctiliously** *adv.*

punctual (pəngk'chə-wəl) *adj.* 1 occurring at the arranged time. ▣ PROMPT, TIMELY ▣ LATE, TARDY, UNPUNCTUAL. 2 making a habit of arriving on time. ▸ **punctuality** *noun*

punctuate (pəngk'chə-wāt,) *verb trans.*, *intrans.* (**punctuated**, **punctuating**) 1 to put punctuation marks into (a piece of writing). 2 to interrupt repeatedly. 3 to give emphasis to.

punctuation *noun* 1 a system of marks used in a text to clarify its meaning for the reader, e.g., commas, colons, and semicolons. 2 the use of such marks.

puncture *noun* a small hole pierced in something with a sharp point. —*verb trans.*, *intrans.* (**punctured**, **puncturing**) to pierce a hole in, or to be pierced.

pundit *noun* an authority or supposed authority on a particular subject, esp. one regularly consulted.

pungent (pən'jənt) *adj.* 1 of a taste or smell sharp and strong. 2 of remarks, wit, etc. cleverly caustic or biting. ▸ **pungency** *noun* ▸ **pungently** *adv.*

punish *verb trans.* (**punished**, **punishing**) 1 to cause (an offender) to suffer for an offense. 2 to impose a penalty for (an offense). 3 *colloq.* to treat roughly. ▸ **punishable** *adj.* ▸ **punishment** *noun*

punitive *adj.* relating to, inflicting, or intended to inflict punishment: *punitive measures*. ▸ **punitively** *adv.*

Punjabi *or* **Panjabi** *noun* a language spoken in the state of Punjab, India, and in Pakistan. —*adj.* relating to or in Punjab.

punk *noun* 1 an antiestablishment movement manifesting itself in aggressive music and bizarreness of dress and hairstyle. 2 a follower of punk styles or punk rock. 3 punk rock. 4 *slang* a worthless or stupid person, often a member of a violent youth gang. —*adj.* 1 relating to or characteristic of punk as a movement. **2** *slang* worthless; inferior: *a punk car.*

punk rock loud, aggressive rock music with violent and often crude lyrics.

punster *noun* a person who makes puns.

punt[1] *noun* a long flat-bottomed open boat with square ends, propelled by a pole pushed against the bed of the river, etc. —*verb intrans., trans.* (**punted, punting**) to propel (a punt, etc.) with a pole.

punt[2] *noun Football* a kick executed with the toe of the boot to a ball as it is dropped directly from the hands and before it hits the ground. —*verb trans., intrans.* (**punted, punting**) to kick in this way.

puny *adj.* (**punier, puniest**) small, weak, or undersized.

pup *noun* **1** a young dog. **2** the young of other animals, e.g., the seal.

pupa *noun* (*pl.* **pupae, pupas**) in the life cycle of insects such as butterflies and moths, the inactive stage during which a larva is transformed into a mature adult. ▸ **pupal** *adj.*

pupil[1] *noun* a schoolchild or student.

pupil[2] *noun* the circular opening in the center of the iris in the eye, through which light passes to the retina.

puppet *noun* **1** a doll that can be made to move in a lifelike way. **2** a person who is being controlled or manipulated by someone else.

puppeteer *noun* a person skilled in manipulating puppets and giving puppet shows. ▸ **puppetry** *noun*

puppy *noun* (*pl.* **puppies**) a young dog.

purblind *adj.* **1** nearly blind; dim-sighted. **2** obtuse; dull-witted.

purchase *verb trans.* (**purchased, purchasing**) to buy. —*noun* **1** the act of buying. **2** something bought. **3** a sure grasp or foothold. **4** *Mech.* the advantage given by a device such as a pulley or lever. ▸ **purchaser** *noun*

purdah (pərd'ə) *noun* the seclusion or veiling of women from public view in some Muslim and Hindu societies.

pure *adj.* **1** consisting of itself only: *pure alcohol.* ▤ NEAT, STRAIGHT, UNADULTERATED, UNDILUTED, UNMIXED ▤ ADULTERATED, DILUTED, IMPURE, MIXED. **2** containing no contaminants and no pollutants. **3** totally virtuous and clean. **4** utter: *pure coincidence.* **5** of unmixed blood or descent. ▸ **purely** *adv.* ▸ **pureness** *noun* ▸ **purity** *noun*

purebred *adj.* denoting an animal or plant that is the offspring of parents of the same breed or variety.

purée (pyŏŏ-rā') *noun* a quantity of fruit or vegetables reduced to a pulp by liquidizing or rubbing through a sieve. —*verb trans.*

(**puréed, puréeing, purées**) to reduce to a purée.

purgative *noun* a medicine that causes the bowels to empty. —*adj., of a medicine, etc.* having the effect of emptying the bowels.

purgatory *noun* **1** (**Purgatory**) *RC Church* a place or state into which the soul passes after death to be cleansed of pardonable sins before going to heaven. **2** a state of discomfort or suffering.

purge *verb trans., intrans.* (**purged, purging**) **1** to rid (e.g., the soul or body) of unwholesome thoughts or substances; to get rid of (impure elements) from (something). **2** to take or give a purgative to empty (the bowels), or the bowels of (a person). —*noun* **1** an act of, or the process of, purging. **2 a** the process of purging the bowels. **b** a medicine to empty the bowels.

purify *verb trans.* (**purified, purifying, purifies**) to make pure. ▸ **purifier** *noun*

Purim (pŏŏr'ĭm) *noun* the Jewish Festival of Lots held about Mar. 1, commemorating the deliverance of the Jews from the plot of Haman to have them massacred, as related in the Book of Esther.

purism *noun* insistence on purity, esp. in language. ▸ **purist** *noun*

puritan *noun* **1** (**Puritan**) *Hist.* a supporter of the 16th-c to 17th-c Protestant movement in England and America that sought to rid church worship of ritual. **2** a person who disapproves generally of luxuries and amusements. ▸ **puritanism** *noun* ▸ **puritanical** *adj.*

purl[1] *noun Knitting* a basic stitch made with the wool passed behind the needle. —*verb trans.* (**purled, purling**) to knit in purl.

purl[2] *verb intrans.* (**purled, purling**) **1** to flow with a murmuring sound. **2** to eddy or swirl.

purlieus (pər'lŏŏ,) *pl. noun* the surroundings or immediate neighborhood of a place.

purloin (pər-loin') *verb trans.* (**purloined, purloining**) to steal, filch, or pilfer.

purple *noun* **1** a color that is a mixture of blue and red. **2** crimson cloth, or a robe made from it worn as a symbol of authority. —*adj.* **1** of either of these colors. **2** *of writing* elaborate: *purple prose.*

purport *noun* (pər'pôrt,) meaning, significance, point, or gist. —*verb intrans.* (pər-pôrt') (**purported, purporting**) to present itself so as to seem or claim: *a work purporting to have been written by Charles I.*

purpose *noun* **1** one's object or aim. **2** the function for which something is intended. **3** determination; resolve: *a woman of purpose.* —*verb trans.* (**purposed, purposing**) to intend (to do something). —**on purpose** with intent; deliberately. ▸ **pur-**

poseful *adj.* ▸ **purposefully** *adv.* ▸ **purposeless** *adj.*

purposely *adv.* on purpose; intentionally.

> **Usage** The adverbs *purposefully* and *purposely* are often confused.

purr *verb intrans., trans.* (**purred, purring**) *of* a cat to make a soft, low, vibrating sound. —*noun* a soft, low, vibrating sound.

purse *noun* **1** a small container for keeping one's money in. **2** a woman's handbag. — *verb trans.* (**pursed, pursing**) to draw (the lips) together in disapproval or deep thought.

purser *noun* a crew member aboard a ship or commercial aircraft who is responsible for keeping account of monetary matters.

pursuance (par-sōō'əns) *noun* the process of pursuing: *in pursuance of his duties.*

pursuant *adj.* (*often* **pursuant to**) conformable to; proceeding from.

pursue *verb trans., intrans.* (**pursued, pursuing**) **1** to chase. **2** to proceed along (a course or route). **3** to put one's efforts into achieving (a goal or aim). ▸ **pursuer** *noun*

pursuit *noun* **1** the act of pursuing: *followed in hot pursuit.* **2** an occupation or hobby.

purulence (pyōōr'yə-ləns) *noun* **1** the condition of being full of or discharging pus. **2** pus. ▸ **purulent** *adj.*

purvey (pər-vā') *verb trans., intrans.* (**purveyed, purveying, purveys**) to supply (goods, merchandise, or provisions). ▸ **purveyance** *noun* ▸ **purveyor** *noun*

purview *noun* **1** scope of responsibility or concern, e.g., of a court of law. **2** the extent of one's knowledge.

pus *noun* the thick, yellowish liquid that forms in abscesses or infected wounds.

push *verb trans., intrans.* (**pushed, pushing**) **1** to act upon by steady thrusting force. **2** to touch or hold and move forward in front of one. **3** to force one's way. **4** (**push (someone) into (something)**) to coax, urge, persuade, or goad (someone) to do (something). **5** to pressure (oneself or another) into working harder, achieving more, etc. **6** to promote products or urge acceptance of ideas. **7** *colloq.* to sell drugs illegally. —*noun* **1** an act of pushing. **2** a burst of effort toward achieving something. **3** determination, aggression, or drive. ▸ **pusher** *noun*

push button a button pressed to operate a machine, etc. ▸ **push-button** *or* **pushbutton** *adj.*

pushover *noun colloq.* **1** someone who is easily defeated or outwitted. **2** a task easily accomplished.

pushup *noun* an exercise performed face down, raising and lowering the body with the arms while keeping the trunk and legs rigid.

pushy *adj.* (**pushier, pushiest**) *colloq.* aggressively self-assertive or ambitious.

pusillanimous (pyōō,sə-lăn'ə-məs) *adj.* timid, cowardly, weak-spirited, or faint-hearted. ▸ **pusillanimity** *noun*

puss[1] *noun colloq.* a cat.

puss[2] *noun slang* the face.

pussy *noun* (*pl.* **pussies**) *colloq.* a cat.

pussyfoot *verb intrans.* (**pussyfooted, pussyfooting, pussyfoots**) **1** to avoid taking a stand or answering (a question) by speaking evasively. **2** to pad about stealthily. ▸ **pussyfooter** *noun*

pussy willow a small N American tree that has silky gray catkins.

pustule (pəs'chōōl,) *noun* a small inflammation on the skin, containing pus. ▸ **pustular** *adj.*

put *verb trans., intrans.* (**put, putting**) **1** to place in or convey to a specified position or situation. **2** to equip something with (something): *put a new lock on a door.* **3** to cause to be. **4** to apply. **5** to set or impose: *put an end to free lunches.* **6** to lay (blame, reliance, emphasis, etc.) on something or someone: *put the onus on us.* **7** to invest or pour (energy, money, or other resources) into something. **8** to submit (questions, ideas, etc.) to someone. **9** to express: *a disaster, to put it mildly.* **10** to write: *don't know what to put in this box.* **11** *Athletics* to throw (the shot). —**put (someone) down** to humiliate, criticize, sneer at, or snub (someone). **put (something) down 1** to put (it) on a surface after holding (it), etc. **2** to crush a revolt, etc. **3** to kill (an animal) painlessly. **put (someone) off 1** to cancel or postpone an engagement with (someone). **2** to cause (someone) to lose enthusiasm or to feel disgust for (something): *Her accident put me off climbing.* **put (someone) out 1** to inconvenience (someone). **2** to offend or annoy (someone). **put (something) out** to extinguish (a light or fire).

putative (pyōō'tət-ĭv) *adj.* generally supposed; assumed.

putdown *or* **put-down** *noun colloq.* a snub or humiliation.

put-on *adj., of an accent, manner, etc.* assumed; pretended. —*noun colloq.* a trick or deception.

putrefy (pyōō'trə-fī,) *verb intrans.* (**putrefied, putrefying, putrefies**) to go bad, rot, or decay, esp. with a foul smell. ▸ **putrefaction** *noun*

putrescent *adj.* decaying; rotting. ▸ **putrescence** *noun*

putrid *adj.* **1** decayed; rotten. **2** stinking; foul; disgusting. **3** *colloq.* repellent; worthless.

putt (pət') *Golf verb trans., intrans.* (**putted, putting**) to send (a ball) gently forward along the ground toward a hole. —*noun* a stroke used in propelling a golf ball gently toward a hole. ▸ **putting** noun

putter noun **1** a golf club used for putting. **2** a person who putts.

putty noun (pl. **putties**) a paste of ground chalk and linseed oil, used for fixing glass in window frames, filling holes in wood, etc.

puzzle verb trans., intrans. (**puzzled, puzzling**) **1** to perplex, mystify, bewilder, or baffle. **2** (**puzzle over (something)**) to brood, ponder, wonder, or worry about (it). **3** (usu. **puzzle (something) out**) to solve (it) after prolonged thought. —noun **1** a baffling problem. **2** a game or toy in the form of something for solving. ▸ **puzzlement** noun ▸ **puzzling** adj.

PVC abbrev. polyvinyl chloride.

PVT or **Pvt.** abbrev. Mil. private.

pygmy or **pigmy** noun (pl. **pygmies**) **1** (**Pygmy**) a member of one of the unusually short peoples of equatorial Africa.. **2** an undersized person; a dwarf. —adj. of a small size: pygmy fig trees.

pyjamas pl. noun Brit. pajamas.

pylon noun **1** a tall steel structure for supporting electric power cables. **2** a post or tower to guide a pilot at an airfield.

pyramid noun **1** a huge ancient Egyptian royal tomb built on a square base with four sloping triangular sides meeting in a point. **2** Geom. a similarly-shaped solid with a square or triangular base. **3** any structure, pile, etc., of similar shape. ▸ **pyramidal** adj.

pyre noun a pile of wood on which a corpse is ceremonially cremated.

pyro- combining form forming words denoting fire: pyromania / pyrotechnics.

pyromania noun an obsessive urge to set fires. ▸ **pyromaniac** noun

pyrotechnics noun **1** (sing.) the art or craft of making fireworks. **2** (pl.) a fireworks display. **3** (pl.) a display of fiery brilliance, e.g., in speech or music.

Pyrrhic victory (pĭr'ĭk) a victory won at so great a cost that it hardly can be regarded as a victory at all.

> After the costly defeat of the Romans by *Pyrrhus*, king of Epirus, in 280 BC

Pythagorean theorem (pǝ-thăg,ǝ-rē'ǝn) Math. a theorem stating that, in a right triangle, the square of the length of the hypotenuse is equal to the sum of the squares of the other two sides.

python noun a nonvenomous snake that kills its prey by coiling its body around it and squeezing until the prey suffocates.

pyx (pĭks) noun Christianity a container in which the consecrated Communion bread is kept.

Qq

Q¹ or **q** noun (pl. **Qs, Q's, q's**) the 17th letter of the English alphabet.

Q² abbrev. Chess queen.

q. abbrev. **1** quart. **2** quarter. **3** quarterly. **4** (also Q) question.

q and a or **Q A** abbrev. question and answer.

qb abbrev. Football quarterback.

Q.E.D. abbrev. quod erat demonstrandum (Latin), which was what had to be proved.

qi or **chi** (chē) noun Chinese Med. an individual person's life force, the free flow of which within the body is believed to ensure physical and spiritual health.

QM abbrev. quartermaster.

qr. abbrev. **1** quarter. **2** quarterly.

qt or **qt.** abbrev. quart.

Q-Tip trademark used to denote a cotton-tipped swab.

qty. abbrev. quantity.

quack¹ noun the characteristic cry of a duck. —verb intrans. (**quacked, quacking**) **1** of a duck to make a characteristic raucous cry. **2** to talk in a loud, silly voice.

quack² noun **1** a medically unqualified person who claims a physician's education, knowledge, skill, and licensure. **2** colloq. a charlatan. ▸ **quackery** noun

quad¹ (kwäd) noun colloq. a quadruplet.

quad² noun colloq. a quadrangle.

quad³ colloq. adj. quadraphonic. —noun quadraphonics.

quadr- or **quadri-** combining form forming words denoting four: quadrangle.

quadrangle noun **1** Geom. a square, rectangle, or other four-sided two-dimensional figure. **2** an open rectangular court within the buildings of a college, school, etc.

quadrant noun **1** Geom. a quarter of the circumference of a circle. **2** Geom. a quarter of a circle, i.e., an area bounded by two radii meeting at right angles. **3** Geom. a quarter of a sphere. **4** Naut., Astron. an instrument incorporating a graduated 90° arc, used for measuring altitude, e.g., of the stars.

quadraphonic *adj.*, *of sound reproduction* using four loudspeakers fed by four separate channels. ▸ **quadraphonics** *noun*

quadratic *Math.* involving the square, but no higher power, of an unknown quantity or variable.

quadrennial *adj.* **1** lasting four years. **2** occurring every four years. ▸ **quadrennially** *adv.*

quadri- *combining form same as* **quadr-**.

quadrilateral *noun Geom.* a four-sided two-dimensional figure. —*adj.* four-sided.

quadrille *noun* a square dance for four couples, in five or six movements; music for it.

quadriplegia *noun* paralysis affecting the arms and legs. ▸ **quadriplegic** *noun, adj.*

quadruped (kwäd′drə-pĕd,) *noun* a four-footed animal, esp. a mammal.

quadruple (kwä-drōō′pəl, -drəp′əl) *verb trans.*, *intrans.* (**quadrupled, quadrupling**) to multiply by four or to increase fourfold. —*adj.* **1** four times as many or much. **2** composed of four parts. **3** *Mus.*, *of time* having four beats to the bar. —*noun* a quadruple number or amount. ▸ **quadruply** *adv.*

quadruplet *noun* each of four children or animals born at one birth.

quadruplicate *verb trans.* (kwä-drōō′plĭ-kāt,) (**quadruplicated, quadruplicating**) to make quadruple or fourfold. —*adj.* (kwä-drōō-′plĭ-kət, -kāt,) copied four times; fourfold.

quaff *verb trans.*, *intrans.* (**quaffed, quaffing**) *literary* to drink eagerly or deeply.

quagmire *noun* an area of soft marshy ground; a swamp.

quahog (kŏ′hôg,, kwô′-, -häg,) *noun* an edible clam of the N American Atlantic coast.

quail[1] *noun* (*pl.* **quail, quails**) a small bird of the partridge family.

quail[2] *verb intrans.* (**quailed, quailing**) to lose courage or feel fear; to flinch.

quaint *adj.* charmingly or pleasingly odd or old-fashioned.

quake[1] *verb intrans.* (**quaked, quaking**) **1** to undergo heavy vibration or jolting particularly as the result of a physical shock. **2** to tremble with fear. —*noun* a shudder or tremor.

quake[2] *noun* a series of shock waves that pass through Earth, often causing the ground to shake.

Quaker (kwā′kər) *noun* a member of a Christian movement, the Society of Friends.

> Originally a nickname given to the group because their founder, George Fox, told to *quake* at the word of God

quaking aspen *see* **aspen**.

qualification *noun* **1** an official record that one has completed a course of training, has

performed satisfactorily in an examination, etc. **2** a skill or ability that fits one for a job, etc. **3** the act, process, or fact of qualifying. **4** an addition to a statement, etc., that restricts it; a condition, limitation, or modification.

qualify *verb intrans.*, *trans.* (**qualified, qualifying, qualifies**) **1** to complete a course of training, pass an examination, etc., that gives one professional status. **2** to make suitable for a task, job, etc.: *is hardly qualified to judge us.* **3** (**qualify for (something)**) to fulfill requirements that give one a right to (an award, privilege, etc.). **4** to be seen as having the right characteristics to be: *What qualifies as news these days?* **5** to add something to (a statement, etc.) that restricts or limits it. **6** to modify, tone down, or restrict. **7** *Gram., of an adjective* to define or describe (a noun). ▸ **qualifier** *noun*

qualitative *adj.* relating to, investigating, or affecting the quality of something.

quality *noun* (*pl.* **qualities**) **1** standard of goodness. **2** high standard; excellence. **3** (*attributive*) of a high quality or standard: *quality newspapers.* **4** a distinguishing element. **5** high social status: *people of quality.*

qualm (kwäm, kwälm) *noun* **1** a sudden feeling of nervousness or apprehension. **2** a scruple, misgiving, or pang of conscience. **3** a feeling of faintness or nausea.

quandary (kwän′drē) *noun* (*pl.* **quandaries**) a situation in which one is at a loss what to do; a dilemma or predicament.

quango *noun* (*pl.* **quangos**) a government-funded body responsible for some area of public concern.

quantify *verb trans.* (**quantified, quantifying, quantifies**) to find out the quantity of; to express as a quantity.

quantitative *adj.* **1** relating to quantity. **2** estimated or measurable in terms of quantity.

quantity *noun* (*pl.* **quantities**) (ABBREV. **qty.**) **1** the property things have that makes them measurable or countable; the size or amount. **2** a specified amount: *a tiny quantity.* **3** *Math.* a value that may be expressed as a number, or the symbol or figure representing it.

quantum *noun* (*pl.* **quanta**) **1** an amount or quantity; something measurable or countable. **2** *Phys.* a tiny indivisible unit of any form of physical energy.

quantum leap *or* **quantum jump** a sudden transition; a spectacular advance.

quantum theory *Phys.* the theory that energy exists in indivisible units or quanta.

quarantine (kwôr′ən-tēn,, kwär′-) *noun* the isolation of people or animals to prevent the spread of an infectious disease that they could be developing; the duration of such isolation. —*verb trans.* (**quarantined, quarantining**) to impose such isolation on; to put into quarantine.

quark *noun Phys.* the name given to a hypothetical particle believed to be the basic component of baryons and mesons.

quarrel (kwôr'əl, kwär'-) *noun* **1** an angry disagreement or argument. **2** a cause of such disagreement; a complaint: **3** a break in a friendship; a breach or rupture. —*verb intrans.* (**quarrel** *or* **quarrelled, quarreling** *or* **quarrelling**) **1** to argue or dispute angrily. **2** to disagree and remain on bad terms. **3** to find fault: *I can't quarrel with her reasoning.*

quarrelsome *adj.* inclined to quarrel or dispute.

quarry¹ *noun* (*pl.* **quarries**) an open excavation for extracting stone or slate for building. —*verb trans.* (**quarried, quarrying, quarries**) **1** to extract (stone, etc.) from a quarry. **2** to excavate a quarry in (land).

quarry² *noun* (*pl.* **quarries**) **1** a hunted animal or bird; prey. **2** someone or something that is the object of pursuit.

quart (kwôrt) *noun* (ABBREV. **q., qt, qt.**) **1 a** a unit of liquid measure in the US Customary system equivalent to $\frac{1}{4}$ gal. or 32 oz. (0.946 liter). **b** a unit of dry measure in the US Customary system equivalent to $\frac{1}{8}$ peck or 2 pts. (1.01 liter). **2** a container that will hold such a measure of liquid or dry material.

quarter *noun* (ABBREV. **q. qr.**) **1** one of four equal parts into which an object or quantity may be divided; the fraction one divided by four. **2** any of the three-month divisions of the year, esp. beginning or ending on a quarter day. **3** a unit of weight equal to 25 lbs. or one forth of a hundredweight. **4** *colloq.* one quarter of a pound, or 4 oz. **5** a US coin valued at 25 cents; 25 cents. **6** a period of 15 minutes; a point of time 15 minutes after , or before any hour. **7** (**Quarter**) a district of a city, etc. **8** (*often* **quarters**) a section of the public; certain people or a certain person. **9** (**quarters**) lodgings or accommodations. **10** mercy shown to someone in one's power, e.g., a defeated enemy: *victors who gave no quarter.* **11** any limb of a four-limbed animal. —*verb trans.* (**quartered, quartering**) **1** to divide into quarters. **2** to accommodate or billet in lodgings. **3** *Hist.* to divide (the body of a hanged traitor, etc.) into four parts. —*adj.* being one of four equal parts: *a quarter hour.*

quarterback *noun* (ABBREV. **qb**) *Football* the player in the backfield who calls the signals for his team's offensive play.

quarterdeck *noun* the stern part of a ship's upper deck.

quarterfinal *noun* (*also* **quarter finals**) the round of a competition involving four participants or teams, preceding the semifinal. ▸ **quarterfinalist** *noun*

quarter horse a strong saddle horse of a breed that was developed in the western USA.

quarterly (ABBREV. **q., qr.**) *adj.* done, occurring, or published once every quarter of a year. —*adv.* once every quarter. —*noun* (*pl.* **quarterlies**) a quarterly publication or college examination.

quartermaster *noun* (ABBREV. **QM**) **1** a commissioned officer in the US Army responsible for the troops' accommodation, food, and clothing. **2** *Naut.* a petty officer in the US Navy responsible for navigation.

quarter note *Mus.* a note with one-fourth the time value of a whole note. *Also called* **crotchet.**

quartet *or* **quartette** (kwôr-tĕt') *noun* **1** *Mus.* **a** an ensemble of four singers or instrumental players. **b** a piece for four such performers to play. **2** a group or set of four.

quarto *noun* (*pl.* **quartos**) *Printing* a size of paper produced by folding a sheet into four leaves or eight pages.

quartz *noun Geol.* one of the commonest minerals, consisting of pure silica.

quartzite *noun Geol.* any of various pale or white metamorphic rocks, composed largely or entirely of quartz.

quash *verb trans.* (**quashed, quashing, quashes**) **1** *Law* **a** to reject or set aside (a verdict, etc.) as invalid, particularly by judicial action. **b** to annul (a law, etc.), particularly by judicial action. **2** to subdue, crush, or suppress (a rebellion, a rumor, etc.).

quasi- *prefix* forming words denoting to some extent; virtually: *a quasiofficial role.*

quatrain *noun Poetry* a verse or poem of four lines.

quatrefoil (kăt'ər-foil,, kă'trə-) *noun* **1** a flower with four petals. **2** a leaf composed of four lobes or leaflets.

quaver *verb intrans., trans.* (**quavered, quavering**) **1** *of someone's voice* to be unsteady; to shake or tremble. **2** to say or sing in a trembling voice. —*noun* **1** *Brit. Mus.* an eighth note. **2** a tremble in the voice. ▸ **quavery** *adj.*

quay (kē, kā) *noun* a wharf for the loading and unloading of ships.

queasy *adj.* (**queasier, queasiest**) **1** feeling slightly sick. **2** *of the stomach or digestion* easily upset. **3** *of the conscience* readily made uneasy. ▸ **queasily** *adv.* ▸ **queasiness** *noun*

Québecois (kā,bĕ,kwä') *adj.* of or pertaining to Quebec, Canada, and esp. its French culture and French-speaking citizenry.

—*noun* an inhabitant or native of Quebec, particularly a French-speaking one.

Quechua (kĕch′wǝ) *noun* a S American language of the Andean-Equatorial group. —*adj.* relating to, spoken, or written in Quechua.

queen *noun* 1 a female, often hereditary, ruler of a nation. 2 the wife of a king. 3 a a leading or dominant female figure in a field. b a place or thing considered supreme in some way. 4 a large female ant, bee, or wasp that lays eggs. 5 *Cards* a face card bearing the image of a queen. 6 *Chess* the most powerful piece. —*verb trans., intrans.* (**queened, queening**) *Chess* 1 to make (a pawn) into a queen. 2 *of a pawn* to be converted into a queen. ▸ **queenly** *adj.* ▸ **queenliness** *noun*

Queen's English standard written or spoken English, generally regarded as the most correct or acceptable form.

queer *adj.* (**queerer, queerest**) 1 odd, strange, or unusual. 2 *colloq.* a slightly crazy. b slightly bizarre, e.g., in behavior. 3 faint or ill: *feeling queer.* 4 *offensive slang, of a man* gay or homosexual. ▸ **queerly** *adv.* ▸ **queerness** *noun*

quell *verb trans.* (**quelled, quelling**) 1 to crush or subdue (riots, disturbances, opposition, etc.). 2 to suppress or overcome (unwanted feelings, etc.).

quench *verb trans.* (**quenched, quenching**) 1 to get rid of (one's thirst) by drinking. 2 to extinguish (a fire). 3 to damp or crush (ardor, enthusiasm, desire, etc.). 4 to cool (a metal) rapidly by plunging (it) into a liquid.

querulous *adj.* 1 inclined to complain. 2 *of a voice, tone, etc.* complaining, grumbling, or whining.

query (kwĭr′ē, kwĕr′ē) *noun* (*pl.* **queries**) 1 a question, esp. one that raises a doubt. 2 a request for information; an inquiry. 3 a notation calling something into question, esp. a question mark. —*verb trans.* (**queried, querying, queried**) 1 to raise a doubt about: *query a bill.* 2 to ask.

quest *noun* 1 a search or hunt. 2 the object of one's search; one's goal. —*verb intrans.* (**quested, questing**) (*often* **quest about for** (**something**)) to search about; to roam around in search of something.

question *noun* (ABBREV. **q., Q**) 1 an utterance that requests information or another answer. 2 a doubt or query. 3 an uncertainty. 4 a problem or difficulty: *the Balkans question.* 5 a problem set for discussion or solution in an examination paper, etc. 6 an investigation or search for information. 7 a matter or issue. 8 an issue on which something is dependent: *a question of time rather than money.* —*verb trans.* (**questioned, questioning**) 1 to ask (someone) questions; to interrogate. 2 to raise doubts about; to query. —**no**

question of no possibility or intention of. **out of the question** impossible and so not worth considering. ▸ **questioner** *noun*

questionable *adj.* 1 a of dubious value or benefit. b suspicious; dubious; suspect: *questionable motives.* 2 not likely to happen. ▣ DOUBTFUL, IMPROBABLE, UNLIKELY ▣ LIKELY, PROBABLE, UNQUESTIONABLE.

question mark 1 the punctuation mark (?) placed after a question. 2 a situation, issue, or set of circumstances regarded as unsettled or in doubt.

questionnaire *noun* a set of questions for distribution to a number of people, as a means of collecting information, surveying opinions, etc.

quetzal (kĕt-säl′) *noun* (*pl.* **quetzals, quetzales**) a bird, native to Central America with brilliant green and crimson plumage.

queue (kyōō) *noun* 1 a line or file of people or vehicles waiting for something. 2 *Comput.* a list of items, e.g., programs or data, held in a system in the order in which they are to be processed. 3 a long braid of hair; a pigtail. —*verb intrans.* (**queued, queuing**) 1 (*also* **queue up**) to form a line or wait in a line. 2 *Comput.* to line up tasks for a computer to process.

quibble *verb intrans.* (**quibbled, quibbling**) 1 to evade the truth by making much over trivial distinctions. 2 to make petty objections and criticisms. —*noun* a trifling objection or petty distinction.

quiche (kēsh) *noun* a tart with a savory filling usu. made with eggs.

quick *adj.* 1 taking little time; speedy. 2 lasting briefly. 3 causing or involving no delay; immediate. 4 intelligent; alert; sharp. 5 *of the temper* easily roused. 6 nimble, deft, or brisk. 7 apt or ready: *quick to take the initiative.* —*adv.* in a fast way; rapidly. —*noun* 1 an area of sensitive flesh, esp. at the base of the fingernail or toenail. 2 (**the quick**) those who are alive: *the quick and the dead.* ▸ **quickly** *adv.* ▸ **quickness** *noun*

quicken *verb intrans., trans.* (**quickened, quickening**) 1 to make or become quicker. 2 to stimulate or stir (someone's interest, imagination, etc.).

quickie *noun colloq.* something quickly dealt with or done.

quicklime *noun* calcium oxide.

quicksand *noun* loose, wet sand that sucks in people or heavy objects standing or placed on it.

quicksilver *noun old use* mercury.

quickstep *noun* a ballroom dance with fast steps; a piece of music for this.

quid¹ *noun Brit.* (*pl.* **quid**) *slang* a pound (sterling).

quid² *noun* a bit of tobacco for chewing.

quiddity *noun* **1** the essence. **2** a trifling detail or point; a quibble.

quid pro quo (*pl.* **quid pro quos**) something given or taken in recompense or retaliation for something else.

quiescent (kwī-ĕs′ənt) *adj.* **1** quiet; silent. **2** in an inactive state, esp. one unlikely to last. ▣ ABEYANT, DORMANT, LATENT ▣ ACTIVE, LIVE, PATENT. ▸ **quiescence** *noun* ▸ **quiescently** *adv.*

quiet *adj.* **1** making little or no noise; soft. **2** lacking noise. **3** saying nothing; silent. **4** *of a person* reserved; unassertive. **5** *of business or trade* not flourishing; poor. **6** secret; private: *had a quiet word with her.* —*noun* absence of or freedom from noise, commotion, etc.; calm, tranquility, or repose. —*verb trans., intrans.* (**quieted, quieting**) to make or become quiet or calm. ▸ **quietly** *adv.* ▸ **quietness** *noun*

quieten *verb trans., intrans.* (**quietened, quietening**) **1** to make or become quiet. **2** to calm (doubts, fears, etc.).

quietude *noun* quietness; tranquility.

quietus (kwī-ĕt′əs) *noun* **1** that which serves to eliminate, repress, or curb. **2** death. **3** release or discharge from debts or duties.

quill *noun* **1** a large stiff feather from a bird's wing or tail; the hollow base part of it. **2** a pen made from a bird's feather. **3** one of the long spines on a porcupine.

quilt *noun* a bedcover containing padding or a filling of feathers, etc., kept in place by intersecting seams. —*verb trans., intrans.* (**quilted, quilting**) to sew (material, garments, etc.) in two layers with a filling, esp. with decorative seaming. ▸ **quilted** *adj.*

quince *noun* the round or pear-shaped fruit of an Asian tree, used to make jellies, preserves, etc.

quinine (kwī′nīn₁) *noun Med.* a bitter-tasting drug, obtained from cinchona bark, that was formerly widely used to treat malaria.

quinquennial *adj.* **1** lasting five years. **2** occurring every five years. ▸ **quinquennially** *adv.*

quinsy *noun* inflammation of the throat with an abscess on the tonsils.

quintal *noun* **1** a metric unit of weight equal to 100 kg. **2** formerly in the British Imperial System, a hundredweight, 112 lbs.

quintessential *adj.* central, essential, or most typical. ▸ **quintessence** *noun* ▸ **quintessentially** *adv.*

quintet *or* **quintette** (kwĭn-tĕt′) *noun* **1** *Mus.* **a** an ensemble of five singers or instrumental players. **b** a piece for five such performers. **2** any group or set of five: *a quintet of kittens.*

quintuple (kwĭn-təp′əl, -tōō′pəl) *verb trans., intrans.* (**quintupling, quintupling**) to multiply by five or to increase fivefold. —*adj.* **1** five times as many or much. **2** composed of five parts. —*noun* a quintuple number or amount.

quintuplet *noun* one of five children born to a mother at one birth.

quip *noun* a witty remark. —*verb intrans., trans.* (**quipped, quipping**) **1** to make quips or a quip. **2** to say in jest.

quire *noun* a paper measure, 25 (formerly 24) sheets.

quirk *noun* **1** an odd habit, mannerism, or aspect of personality. **2** an odd twist in affairs or turn of events; a strange coincidence: *quirks of fate.* ▸ **quirky** *adj.*

quisling *noun* a traitor or collaborator.

After Vidkun *Quisling*, head of the Norwegian fascist party during the German occupation

quit *verb trans., intrans.* (*pa t* and *pa p* **quit** or **quitted**; *pr p* **quitting**) **1** to leave (a place, etc.). **2** to leave, give up, or resign (a job). **3** to bring (activity) to cessation or suspension or to undergo this. ▸ **quitter** *noun*

quitclaim *Law noun* transfer of a deed, title, claim, or right to another party. —*verb trans.* (**quitclaimed, quitclaiming**) to give up and renounce all claim to (e.g., a right).

quite *adv.* **1** to a total degree or extent; completely; entirely: *quite unintelligible.* **2** to a high degree. **3** to some or a limited degree; rather; fairly: *The meal was quite good.* **4** *used in reply* I agree, see your point, etc.

quits *adj. colloq.* even with one another because of repayment made. —**call it quits** to agree to stop a quarrel or dispute, acknowledging that the outcome is even.

quittance (kwĭt′ns) *noun* a person's release from debt or other obligation, or a document acknowledging this.

quiver[1] *verb intrans.* (**quivered, quivering**) to shake or tremble slightly; to shiver. —*noun* a tremble or shiver.

quiver[2] *noun* a long narrow case in which to carry arrows.

quixotic (kwĭk-sät′ĭk) *adj.* **1** absurdly generous or chivalrous. **2** unrealistically romantic or idealistic.

After Don *Quixote*, the knight in Cervantes's 16th-century Spanish romance

quiz *noun* (*pl.* **quizzes**) **1** an entertainment, e.g., on radio or television, in which the knowledge of a panel of contestants is tested; a quiz show. **2** a series of questions as a test of general or specialized knowledge. **3** an interrogation. —*verb trans.* (**quizzed, quizzing**) to question; to interrogate.

quizzical *adj., of a look, expression, etc.* mocking; questioning; amused. ▸ **quizzically** *adv.*

quoin *noun* **1** the angle of a building. **2** a cornerstone.

quoit (koit, kwoit) *noun dialect* **1** (**quoits**) a game in which metal, rubber, or rope rings are thrown at pegs, with the aim of encircling them. **2** a ring of metal, rubber, or rope used in this game.

quondam (kwăn′dăm,) *adj.* having been such previously: *our quondam President.*

quorum *noun* (*pl.* **quorums**) the minimum number of members who must be present at a meeting for its business to be valid.

> From Latin phrase *quorum vos .. esse volumus* 'of whom we wish that you be (one, two, etc.)', used in legal commissions

quota *noun* **1** a total number or quantity that is permitted or required. **2** someone's allocated share; e.g., of work.

quotable *adj.* worth quoting.

quotation *noun* **1** the act of quoting. **2** something quoted. **3** an estimated price for a job submitted by a contractor to a client.

quotation mark each of a pair of punctuation marks (" " or ' ') used to show the beginning and end of a quotation, or on either side of a word or phrase on which attention is to be focused.

quote *verb trans., intrans.* (**quoted, quoting**) **1** to repeat the exact words of. **2** to refer to (a law, etc.) as authority or support. **3** *of a contractor* to submit (a price) for a particular job. —*noun* **1** a quotation. **2** a price quoted. **3** (**quotes**) quotation marks. —*interj. colloq.* used in speech to indicate that one is quoting: *her quote reluctance unquote.*

quotidian (kwō-tĭd′ē-ən) *adj.* everyday; commonplace.

quotient (kwō-shənt) *noun Math.* the number of times one number is contained in another, found by dividing the latter by the former.

Qur'an *noun same as* **Koran.**

q.v. *abbrev. quod vide* (Latin), which see, see this word (used to refer a reader from a word used in a dictionary or encyclopedia text, etc., to the entry dealing with it).

QWERTY (kwərt′ē) *noun* the standard arrangement of keys on a typewriter or keyboard designed for English-language users, with the letters *q w e r t y* at the top left of the letters section of the keyboard.

Rr

R¹ *or* **r** *noun* (*pl.* **Rs, R's, r's**) the 18th letter of the English alphabet.

R² *abbrev.* denoting a movie rating that permits admission only to people of a certain age, typically 17, unless they are accompanied by a parent or a guardian.

R³ *abbrev.* **1** (*also* **r**) registered trademark. **2** River. **3** (*also* **r**) roentgen. **4** *Chess* rook².

r *abbrev.* **1** radius. **2** *Printing* recto. **3** (*also* **R**) *Electr.* resistance (sense 4). **4** right.

R.A. *abbrev.* **1** (*also* **RA**) rear admiral. **2** Regular Army.

Ra *symbol Chem.* radium.

rabbi (răb′ī,) *noun* **1** a Jewish religious leader. **2** a Jewish scholar or teacher of the law.

rabbit *noun* a small, long-eared, burrowing animal with a fluffy white tail.

rabbit warren 1 a system of burrows in which wild rabbits live. **2** *colloq.* a structure, e.g., a house, with many narrow corridors and a confusing layout of small rooms.

rabble *noun* **1** a noisy disorderly crowd. **2** (**the rabble**) the lowest class of people.

rabble-rouser *noun* a person who makes speeches, esp. ones meant to arouse feelings of anger and violence in those listening.

rabid *adj.* **1** *of dogs, etc.* affected with rabies. **2** fanatical; unreasoning. ▸ **rabidity** *noun* ▸ **rabidly** *adv.* ▸ **rabidness** *noun*

rabies *noun* a disease of the central nervous system, transmitted by the bite of an infected animal, which can affect all warm-blooded animals, causing madness and usu. death.

raccoon *or* **racoon** *noun* (*pl.* **raccoons, racoon**) a small, furry, N American animal, with a black striped tail and face.

race¹ *noun* **1** a contest of speed between runners, horses, cars, etc. **2** (**races**) a series of such contests over a fixed course, esp. for horses or dogs. **3** a contest or rivalry, esp. to be the first to do or get something. **4** a strong or rapid current of water in a sea or river. —*verb intrans., trans.* (**raced, racing**) **1** to move with speed, often heedlessly. **2** to take part in a race. **3** to have a race with (someone). **4** to enter (a horse, car, etc.) in a race. **5** (**race around**) to run or move quickly and energetically, often in a disorganized state. **6** to move or cause to move more quickly than usual. **7** to own racehorses, or watch horse-racing as a hobby. ▸ **racer** *noun* ▸ **racing** *noun*

race² noun 1 a major division of humankind having a particular set of physical characteristics, such as size, hair type, or skin color. 2 a tribe, nation, or other group of people thought of as distinct from others. 3 human beings as a group: *the human race.* 4 a group of animals or plants within a species, which have characteristics which make them distinct from other members of that species.

racecourse noun a course or track used for racing horses, cars, bicycles, runners, etc. Also called **racetrack**.

racehorse noun a horse bred and used for racing.

raceme (rā'sĕm,) noun Bot. a flower head consisting of individual flowers attached to a long stem e.g., the bluebell.

racetrack noun a racecourse.

racial adj. 1 relating to a particular race. 2 based on race. ▸ **racially** adv.

racism noun 1 the belief that a particular race is inherently superior to others. 2 abusive, oppressive behavior, discrimination, and prejudice caused by such a belief. ▸ **racist** noun, adj.

rack¹ noun 1 a framework with rails, shelves, hooks, etc., for holding or storing things. 2 a bar with teeth which connects with, and moves, a cogwheel or pinion. 3 Hist. an instrument for torturing people by stretching their bodies. 4 slang a bed or a bunk. —verb trans. (**racked, racking**) 1 to cause pain or suffering to: *was racked with guilt.* 2 Hist. to torture on a rack. —**rack** (**one's**) **brain** to think as hard as (one) can. **rack up** colloq. to accumulate, e.g., points in a game or match.

rack² noun a joint of meat, esp. of lamb, including the neck and front ribs.

rack³ noun same as **wrack**.

racket¹ or **racquet** noun a wooden or metal oval frame with a network of strings stretched across it, used for playing tennis, badminton, squash, etc. See also **bat¹** (sense 1).

racket² noun 1 a loud, confused noise or disturbance; a din. 2 a fraudulent or illegal means of making money.

racketeer noun a person who makes money in an illegal way. —verb intrans. (**racketeered, racketeering**) to make money as a racketeer or to engage in the activities of a racketeer. ▸ **racketeering** noun

raconteur (răk,än,tər') noun a person who tells anecdotes in an amusing or entertaining way.

racoon noun same as **raccoon**.

racquet noun same as **racket¹**.

racquetball noun Sport a ballgame for two or four players, played using rackets with short handles and a hollow rubber ball on a four-walled handball court.

racy adj. (**racier, raciest**) 1 lively or spirited. 2 slightly indecent; risqué. ▸ **racily** adv. ▸ **raciness** noun

rad¹ adj. slang 1 dangerously showy; radical: *the rad moves of a snowboarder.* 2 great, marvelous, or wonderful.

rad² abbrev. Math. radian.

radar (rā'där,) noun 1 Radio a system for detecting the direction, speed, and distance of distant objects by transmitting radio waves and detecting the signals reflected back from the surface of those objects. 2 the equipment for sending out and receiving such radio waves.

radial adj. 1 of lines spreading out from the center of a circle, like rays. 2 of or relating to rays, a radius, or radii. 3 along or in the direction of a radius or radii. ▸ **radially** adv.

radian noun Math. (ABBREV. **rad**) the angle, approximately 57°, formed at the centre of a circle by two radii which are as long as the arc they cut on the circle's circumference.

radiant adj. 1 emitting rays of light or heat. 2 glowing or shining. 3 beaming with great joy, love, hope, or health. 4 transmitted by or as if by radiation. ▸ **radiance** noun ▸ **radiantly** adv.

radiate verb trans., intrans. (rād'ē-āt,) (**radiated, radiating**) 1 to send out rays of (light, heat, electromagnetic radiation, etc.). 2 of light, heat, radiation, etc. to be emitted in rays. 3 to show a lot of (happiness, good health, etc.) clearly: *radiate cheerfulness.* 4 to spread or cause to spread out from a central point as radii. —adj. (rād'ē-ət) having rays, radii, or a radial structure.

radiation noun 1 the sending out of energy in the form of electromagnetic waves or particles, such as x-rays. 2 the energy sent out in this way. 3 the act of radiating.

radiator noun 1 an apparatus for heating, consisting of a series of pipes through which hot water (or steam) is circulated. 2 an apparatus for heating in which wires are made hot by electricity. 3 an apparatus for cooling an engine, consisting of a series of tubes through which water passes, and a fan.

radical adj. 1 concerning or relating to the basic nature of something; fundamental. 2 a far-reaching; thoroughgoing: *radical changes.* b slang dangerously flashy. c slang great, marvelous, or wonderful. 3 in favor of or tending to produce extreme political and social reforms. 4 of a political group or party in favor of extreme reforms. —noun 1 a person who is a member of a radical political group, or who holds radical political views. 2 Chem. a group of atoms which behaves like a single atom. ▸ **radically** adv. ▸ **radicalness** noun

radicalism *noun* the beliefs and opinions of political radicals.

radii *see* radius.

radio *noun* (*pl.* **radios**) 1 the sending and receiving of messages, etc. without connecting wires, using electromagnetic waves. 2 a wireless device that receives, and may also transmit, information in this manner. 3 a message or broadcast that is transmitted in this manner. —*adj.* 1 of or for transmitting or transmitted by radio. 2 controlled by radio. —*verb trans., intrans.* (**radioed, radioing, radios**) 1 to send (a message) to (someone) by radio. 2 to broadcast or communicate by radio.

radio- *combining form* forming words denoting: 1 radio or broadcasting: *radio-telephones.* 2 radioactivity: *radioactive.* 3 rays or radiation: *radiology.*

radioactivity *noun* 1 the spontaneous disintegration of the atomic nuclei of some elements, e.g. uranium, resulting in the giving off of radiation. 2 the subatomic particles or radiation emitted during this process. ▸ **radioactive** *adj.*

radiocarbon *noun* a radioactive isotope of carbon, esp. carbon-14.

radio frequency a frequency of electromagnetic waves used for radio and television broadcasting.

radiogram *noun* 1 a radiograph. 2 *Brit. old use* an apparatus consisting of a radio and a record player.

radiograph *noun* a photograph taken using a form of radiation other than light, such as x-rays or gamma rays, esp. of the inside of the body. *Also called* **radiogram.** ▸ **radiographer** *noun* ▸ **radiography** *noun*

radioisotope *noun Phys.* a naturally occurring or synthetic radioactive isotope of a chemical element.

radiology *noun* the branch of medicine that is concerned with the use of radiation (e.g., x-rays) and radioactive isotopes to diagnose and treat diseases. ▸ **radiological** *adj.* ▸ **radiologist** *noun*

radiophonic *adj.* relating to sound produced electronically.

radiotelephone *noun* a telephone that works by radio waves, used esp. in vehicles.

radio telescope a large, usu. dish-shaped antenna, used to study distant stars, galaxies, etc., by detecting the radio waves they emit.

radiotherapy *noun* treatment of disease, esp. cancer, by x-rays and other forms of radiation.

radio wave *Phys.* an electromagnetic wave that has a low frequency and a long wavelength, widely used for communication.

radish *noun* a plant of the mustard family, with pungent-tasting, red-skinned white roots,

which are eaten raw as a salad vegetable.

radium *noun Chem.* (**SYMBOL Ra**) a silvery-white, radioactive metal obtained from uranium ores, esp. pitchblende.

radius *noun* (*pl.* **radii, radiuses**) 1 a straight line running from the center of a circle to a point on its circumference. 2 the length of such a line. 3 a usu. specified distance from a central point, thought of as limiting an area: *within a four mile radius.* 4 *Anat.* the shorter of the two bones in the human forearm.

radon *noun Chem.* (**SYMBOL Rn**) a colorless, highly toxic radioactive gas formed by the decay of radium.

raffia *noun* ribbonlike fiber obtained from the leaves of certain palm trees, used for weaving mats, baskets, etc.

raffish *adj.* slightly shady or disreputable; rakish. ▸ **raffishly** *adv.* ▸ **raffishness** *noun*

raffle *noun* a lottery, often to raise money for charity, in which certain numbered tickets win prizes. —*verb trans.* (**raffled, raffling**) (*also* **raffle off**) to offer as a prize in a raffle.

raft¹ *noun* 1 a flat structure of plastic, rubber, logs, timber, etc., fastened together so as to float on water, used for recreation, sport, transport, or as a platform. 2 a flat, floating mass, e.g., of ice or vegetation. —*verb trans., intrans.* (**rafted, rafting**) 1 to transport by raft. 2 to travel by raft. 3 *Sport* to engage in the water sport of riding a raft down a river, esp. a fast river.

raft² *noun slang* a huge collection, number, or quantity: *asked a whole raft of questions.*

rafter *noun* any of several sloping beams supporting a roof.

rag¹ *noun* 1 a scrap of cloth, esp. a piece that has been worn, or torn off old clothes. 2 (*usu.* **rags**) clothing, or a piece of it, esp. when old and tattered. 3 *colloq.* a newspaper, esp. one regarded as inferior.

rag² *verb trans., intrans.* (**ragged, ragging**) 1 *slang* to tease or to taunt (another). 2 *slang* to scold.

rag³ *noun* a piece of ragtime music.

ragamuffin *noun* a ragged, disreputable child.

rage *noun* 1 violent anger, or a fit of it. 2 violent, stormy action, e.g., of the wind, sea, or a battle. 3 an intense desire or passion for something. 4 a widespread, usu. temporary fashion or craze. —*verb intrans.* (**raged, raging**) 1 to be violently angry. 2 to speak wildly with anger or passion; to rave. 3 *of the wind, sea, a battle, etc* to be stormy. —**all the rage** *colloq.* very much in fashion.

ragged *adj.* 1 *of clothes* old, worn, and tattered. 2 dressed in old, worn, tattered clothing. 3 having a rough and irregular edge; jagged. 4 untidy; straggly. ▸ **raggedly** *adv.* ▸ **raggedness** *noun*

raglan *adj.* **1** *of a sleeve* attached to a garment by two seams running diagonally from the neck to the armpit. **2** *of a garment* having such sleeves.

> Named after Lord *Raglan*, British commander in the Crimean war

ragout (răg-o͞o′) *noun* a highly seasoned stew of meat and vegetables.

ragtime *noun* jazz piano music with a highly syncopated rhythm.

ragweed *noun* a weed with small greenish flower heads that produce such an abundance of pollen that the plant is regarded as a prime cause of hay fever.

ragwort *noun* a common plant with yellow flowers with ragged petals.

raid *noun* **1** a sudden unexpected attack by armed people, troops, etc. **2** a sudden unexpected visit by the police searching for suspected criminals or illicit goods. —*verb trans., intrans.* (**raided, raiding**) **1** to make a raid on. **2** to go on a raid. ▸ **raider** *noun*

rail¹ *noun* **1** a usu. horizontal bar supported by vertical posts, forming a fence or barrier. **2** a horizontal bar on which to hang things. **3** (*often* **the rails** *or* **rails**) either of a pair of lengths of steel forming a track for the wheels of a train. **4** a railroad or a railroad system. —*verb trans.* (**railed, railing**) (**rail (something) off**) to enclose (a space) within a rail or rails.

rail² *verb intrans.* (**railed, railing**) (**rail at** *or* **against (something** *or* **someone)**) to complain or criticize abusively or bitterly.

rail³ *noun* any of various species of small wading birds, usu. living near water, with a short neck and wings, and long legs.

railcar *noun* a railroad car.

railing *noun* **1** (*usu.* **railings**) a fence or barrier. **2** fence-building material.

raillery *noun* good-humored teasing, or an instance of it.

railroad *noun* **1** a track or set of tracks formed by two parallel steel rails fixed to sleepers, for trains to run on. **2** a system of such tracks, plus all the trains, buildings, and people required for it to function. **3** a company responsible for operating such a system. **4** a similar set of tracks for a different type of vehicle: *funicular railroad. Also called* **railway**. —*verb trans.* (**railroaded, railroading**) *colloq.* (**railroad (someone) into (something)** *or* **into doing (something)**) to rush (someone) unfairly into doing (something).

railroad car a passenger car, freight car, or flatcar on a railroad or on a train. *Also called* **railcar**.

railway *noun* a railroad.

raiment *noun* articles of dress for covering the body.

rain *noun* **1** a form of precipitation consisting of water droplets that fall from the clouds. **2** (*also* **rains**) the season of heavy rainfall in tropical countries. **3** a heavy fall, e.g., of complaints or questions. —*verb intrans., trans.* (**rained, raining**) **1** *of precipitation* to fall as water droplets. **2** to fall or cause to fall like droplets of water: *bullets raining down on them.* —**rain out** *of a sports event* to end early or to be canceled altogether because of rain. **right as rain** *colloq.* perfectly all right or in order. ▸ **rainy** *adj.*

rainbow *noun* **1** an arch of all the colors of the spectrum that can be seen in the sky when falling raindrops reflect and refract sunlight. **2** a collection or array of bright colors. **3** a diverse group.

rain check **1** a ticket stub that entitles its holder to admission to, e.g., a rescheduled sports event that has been canceled because of rain. **2** *colloq.* a promise made that an unaccepted invitation or offer will indeed be accepted at some future time.

raincoat *noun* a light waterproof coat worn to keep out the rain.

rainfall *noun* **1** the amount of rain, hail, and snow that falls in a certain place over a certain period. **2** a shower of rain.

rain forest a dense tropical forest, generally dominated by tall broad-leaved evergreen trees.

raise *verb trans.* (**raised, raising**) **1** to move or lift to a high position or level. **2** to put in an upright or standing position. **3** to build. **4** to increase the value, amount, or strength of: *raise prices / raise one's voice.* **5** to put forward for consideration or discussion. **6** to collect, levy, or gather together: *raise revenues via bond issues.* **7** to stir up or incite: *raise a protest.* **8** to bring into being; to provoke. **9** to promote to a higher rank. **10** to awaken or arouse from sleep or death. **11** to grow (vegetables, a crop, etc.). **12** to bring up or rear. **13** to bring to an end or remove: *raise the siege.* **14** to cause (bread or dough) to rise with yeast. **15** *Cards* to bet more than (another player). —*noun* **1** the act of raising or lifting. **2** *colloq.* an increase in salary.

raisin *noun* a dried sweet grape.

raison d'être (rā‚zŌN‚dĕtr′) (*pl.* **raisons d'être**) a purpose or reason that justifies a thing's or person's existence.

Raj (räj) *noun Hist.* the British rule in India (1858–1947).

rajah *or* **raja** *noun Hist.* an Indian prince or king.

rake¹ *noun* **1** a long-handled tool with a comblike part at one end, used for smoothing or breaking up soil, gathering leaves together, etc. **2** a tool with a similar shape or use, e.g., a croupier's tool for gathering money together. —*verb trans.*, *intrans.* (**raked, raking**) **1** to collect, gather, or remove with or as if with a rake. **2** (**rake (something) over**) to make (it) smooth with a rake. **3** to work with a rake. **4** to search (something) carefully. —**rake (something) in** *colloq.* to earn or acquire (it) in large amounts. **rake (something) up** *colloq.* **1** to revive or uncover (something forgotten or lost). **2** to find (it), esp. with difficulty: *raked up enough cash for a holiday.*

rake² *noun* a fashionable man who lives a dissolute, immoral life.

rake³ *verb trans., intrans.* (**raked, raking**) to set or be set at a sloping angle.

rake-off *noun colloq.* a share of the profits, esp. when dishonest or illegal.

rakish *adj.* **1** having a smart, sleek appearance. **2** confident, adventurous, and jaunty in appearance, attitude, or demeanor. ▸ **rakishly** *adv.* ▸ **rakishness** *noun*

rally *verb trans., intrans.* (**rallied, rallying, rallies**) **1** to come or bring together again after being dispersed. **2** to come or bring together for a common cause or action. **3** to revive (one's spirits, strength, abilities, etc.) by making an effort. —*noun* (*pl.* **rallies**) **1** a reassembling of forces to make a new effort. **2** a mass meeting of people with a common cause or interest. **3** *Tennis* a usu. long series of strokes between players before one of them finally wins the point. **4** *Motor Racing* a competition to test skill in driving, usu. held on public roads. —**rally round** *or* **around** to come together to support or help (someone or something): *rallied round to help.*

RAM (răm) *abbrev.* **1** *Comput.* random-access memory. **2** Royal Academy of Music.

ram *noun* **1** an uncastrated male sheep or goat. **2** a battering ram. **3** a pointed device on a warship's prow, for making holes in enemy ships. —*verb trans., intrans.* (**rammed, ramming**) **1** to force down or into position by pushing hard. **2** to strike or crash against violently: *rammed the car into a wall.*

Ramadan (răm'ə-dän,) *noun* **1** the ninth month of the Muslim year, during which Muslims fast between sunrise and sunset. **2** the fast itself.

ramble *verb intrans.* (**rambled, rambling**) **1** to go for a long walk or walks, esp. in the countryside, for pleasure. **2** (*also* **ramble on**) to speak or write in an aimless or confused way. **3** to grow or extend in a straggling, trailing way. —*noun* a walk, esp. in the countryside, for pleasure. ▸ **rambler** *noun.*

rambling *noun* walking for pleasure, usu. in the countryside. —*adj.* **1** that rambles; wandering, straggling. **2** *of speech* disconnected. ▸ **ramblingly** *adv.*

rambunctious *adj.* unruly; boisterous; dis-

orderly. ▸ **rambunctiously** *adv.* ▸ **rambunctiousness** *noun*

ramekin (răm'kĭn, -ə-kĭn) *noun* **1** a small baking dish for a single serving of food served in a ramekin.

ramify *verb intrans., trans.* (**ramified, ramifying, ramifies**) **1** to have a set of consequences, esp. serious or complicated ones. **2** to separate or cause to separate into branches or sections. ▸ **ramification** *noun*

ramp *noun* a sloping surface between two different levels, esp. one that can be used instead of steps.

rampage (răm'pāj,) *verb intrans.* (**rampaged, rampaging**) to rush about angrily, violently, wildly, or excitedly. —**on the rampage** rampaging, often destructively.

rampant *adj.* uncontrolled; unrestrained. ▸ **rampantly** *adv.*

rampart *noun* a broad mound or wall for defense, usu. with a wall or parapet on top.

ramrod *noun* **1** a rod for ramming charge down into, or for cleaning, the barrel of a gun. **2** a person who is strict, stern, and inflexible, both physically and morally.

ramshackle *adj., esp. of buildings* badly made and likely to fall down; rickety.

ran *see* **run**.

ranch *noun* **1** an extensive grassland farm where cattle, horses, or sheep are raised. **2** a ranch house. —*verb intrans.* (**ranched, ranching**) to raise large numbers of sheep, cattle, or horses on a ranch. ▸ **rancher** *noun*

ranch house 1 the dwelling on a ranch lived in by the owner of the property. **2** a one-story, rectangular dwelling with a low-pitched roof.

rancid (răn'sĭd) *adj., of butter, oil, etc.* tasting or smelling sour. ▸ **rancidity** *noun* ▸ **rancidly** *adv.* ▸ **rancidness** *noun*

rancor *noun* the quality or condition of feeling bitter. ▸ **rancorous** *adj.* ▸ **rancorously** *adv.*

rand *noun* (*pl.* **rand, rands**) the standard monetary unit used in South Africa and some neighboring countries.

r&b *or* **R&B** *abbrev.* rhythm and blues.

R & D *abbrev.* research and development.

random *adj.* governed not by plan but by chance. —**at random** without any particular plan, system or purpose. ▸ **randomly** *adv.* ▸ **randomness** *noun*

random-access memory (ABBREV. **RAM**) *Comput.* a temporary memory available to the user that allows programs to be loaded and run, and data to be changed.

randy *adj.* (**randier, randiest**) *colloq.* **1** sexually excited; lusty. **2** ignoring sexual restraint. ▸ **randily** *adv.* ▸ **randiness** *noun*

ranee *noun Hist. same as* **rani**.

rang *see* **ring²**

range *noun* **1 a** an area between limits within which things may move, function, etc.; the limits forming this area. **b** the extent of one's knowledge. ▣ KEN, PURVIEW, REACH. **2 a** number of items, products, etc., forming a distinct series. **3** *Mus.* the distance between the lowest and highest notes which may be produced by an instrument or a singing voice. **4** the distance between a weapon and its target. **5** an area where target practice may take place. **6** a group of mountains forming a distinct series or row. **7** a large area of open land for grazing livestock. **8** the region over which a plant or animal is distributed. **9** an enclosed kitchen fireplace fitted with a large stove with one or more ovens and a flat top surface for heating pans. —*verb trans.* (**ranged, ranging**) **1** to put into a row or rows. **2** to put (someone, oneself, etc.) into a specified category or group. **3** to vary or change between specified limits. **4** (**range over** *or* **through** (**something**)) to roam freely in (it). **5** to stretch or extend in a specified direction or over a specified area: *fires ranging over the prairie.*

ranger *noun* **1** a member of a group of armed men who patrol and police a region. **2** (**Ranger**) a soldier who has been specially trained for raiding and combat; a commando. **3** a warden hired to protect, e.g., a national forest.

rangy (rān′jē) *adj.* (**rangier, rangiest**) having long thin limbs and a slender body.

rani (rän′ē) *or* **ranee** *noun Hist.* the wife or widow of a rajah.

rank¹ *noun* **1** a line or row of people or things. **2** a line of soldiers standing side by side. **3** a position of seniority within, e.g., the armed forces. **4** a distinct class or group, e.g., according to ability. **5** elevated professional or social position. **6** (**the ranks**) ordinary soldiers as opposed to officers. —*verb trans., intrans.* (**ranked, ranking**) **1** to arrange (people or things) in a row or line. **2** to give or have a particular grade, position, or status in relation to others. **3** to have a higher position, status, etc., than (someone else); to outrank (someone else).

rank² *adj.* (**ranker, rankest**) **1** coarsely overgrown and untidy. **2** offensively strong in smell or taste. **3** bold, open, and shocking: *rank disobedience.* **4** complete. ▸ **rankly** *adv.* ▸ **rankness** *noun*

rankle *verb intrans.* (**rankled, rankling**) to continue to cause feelings of annoyance or bitterness: *His curt refusal still rankles.*

ransack *verb trans.* (**ransacked, ransacking**) **1** to search thoroughly and often roughly. **2** to rob or plunder.

ransom *noun* **1** money paid in return for the release of a kidnapped person. **2** the releasing of a kidnapped person in return for this money. —*verb trans.* (**ransomed, ransoming**) **1** to pay a ransom for (someone's) release. **2** to demand a ransom before releasing (someone). ▸ **ransomer** *noun*

rant *verb intrans., trans.* (**ranted, ranting**) **1** to talk in a loud, angry way. **2** to declaim in a loud, pompous, self-important way. —*noun* loud, pompous, empty speech. ▸ **ranter** *noun*

rap¹ *noun* **1** a quick sharp tap or blow, or the sound made by this. **2** *slang* blame or punishment: *he took the rap.* **3 a** a fast rhythmic monologue recited over a musical backing with a pronounced beat. **b** a style of rock music based on rhythmic monologues. *Also called* **rap music.** —*verb trans., intrans.* (**rapped, rapping**) **1** to strike sharply. **2** to make a sharp tapping sound. **3** (*usu.* **rap** (**something**) **out**) to utter (e.g., a command) sharply and quickly. **4** to criticize sharply. **5** to communicate (a message) by raps or knocks. **6** *slang* to talk or have a discussion. **7** to perform a fast rhythmic monologue to music with a pronounced beat. ▸ **rapper** *noun*

rap² *noun* the least bit: *not care a rap.*

rapacious *adj.* **1** greedy and grasping, esp. for money. **2** living by catching prey. ▸ **rapaciously** *adv.* ▸ **rapaciousness** *noun*

rape¹ *noun* **1** the crime of forcing another person to engage in sexual intercourse, against that person's will. **2** violation, despoiling, or abuse. —*verb trans.* (**raped, raping**) to commit rape on. ▸ **rapist** *noun*

rape² *noun* oilseed rape.

rapid *adj.* moving, acting, or happening quickly; fast. —*noun* (**rapids**) a part of a river where the water flows quickly, usu. over dangerous, sharply descending rocks. ▸ **rapidity** *noun* ▸ **rapidly** *adv.* ▸ **rapidness** *noun*

rapid eye movement (ABBREV. **REM**) *Physiol.* a stage of relatively shallow sleep during which the eyes move rapidly from side to side, generally while dreaming.

rapine (răp′ĭn, -ĭn,) *noun* plundering; robbery.

rapport (ra-pôr′) *noun* a feeling of sympathy and understanding; a close emotional bond.

rapprochement (răp,rōsh,män′) *noun* the establishment or renewal of a close, friendly relationship, esp. between states.

rapscallion *noun* a rascal or scamp.

rapt *adj.* **1** enraptured; enchanted. **2** completely absorbed.

raptor *noun* a bird of prey. ▸ **raptorial** *adj.*

rapture *noun* **1** a feeling of immense joy. **2** (**raptures**) great enthusiasm for or pleasure in something. ▸ **rapturous** *adj.*

rare¹ *adj.* **1** done, found, or occurring very seldom. **2** *of the atmosphere at high altitudes* thin; rarefied. **3** unusually good; excellent: *rare abilities.* ▸ **rarity** *noun*

rare² *adj.*, *of meat* cooked on the outside but still raw on the inside.

rarefied *adj.* **1** select; exclusive. **2** esoteric; mysterious; spiritual.

rarefy (răr′ə-fī,, rĕr′-) *verb trans., intrans.* (**rarefied, rarefying, rarefies**) **1** to make or become less dense or solid. **2** to refine or purify.

rarely *adv.* **1** not often. **2** extremely well.

raring *adj.* keen and enthusiastic: *raring to go.*

rascal *noun* **1** a dishonest person; a rogue. **2** a mischievous child.

rase *verb same as* **raze**.

rash¹ *adj.* acting, or done, with little caution or thought; hasty: *rash promises.* ▸ **rashly** *adv.* ▸ **rashness** *noun*

rash² *noun* **1** a temporary outbreak of red spots or patches on the skin, often accompanied by itching. **2** a large number of instances of a thing happening at the same time: *a rash of burglaries.*

rasher *noun* a thin slice of bacon or ham.

rasp *noun* **1** a coarse, rough file. **2** a harsh, rough, grating sound. —*verb trans., intrans.* (**rasped, rasped**) **1** to scrape roughly, esp. with a rasp. **2** to grate on or irritate (e.g., someone's nerves). **3** to speak or utter in a harsh, grating voice. ▸ **rasper** *noun*

raspberry (răz′bĕr,ē) *noun* (*pl.* **raspberries**) **1** a deciduous shrub with upright thorny canes, cultivated for its edible fruit. **2** the edible fruit of this plant. **3** *slang* a coarse sound made by sticking the tongue out and blowing through the lips, usu. to express disapproval.

raspy *adj.* (**raspier, raspiest**) rough.

Rastafarian (răs,tə-fär′ē-ən) *noun* a follower of an orig. West Indian sect, which reveres Haile Selassie, the former Emperor of Ethiopia, as God. —*adj.* relating to or characteristic of Rastafarians.

rat *noun* **1** any of various small rodents, similar to mice, usu. blackish-brown in color with a long scaly tail. **2** *colloq.* a person who is disloyal toward his or her friends, party, etc. —*verb intrans.* (**ratted, ratting**) **1** to hunt rats. **2** (**rat on** (**someone**)) *colloq.* to betray or desert (someone). —**smell a rat** *colloq.* to sense that something is not as it should be.

ratatouille (ră,tă,tōō′ē) *noun* a stew made with tomatoes, peppers, eggplant, zucchini, onions, and garlic.

ratchet *noun* **1** a bar that fits into the notches of a toothed wheel so as to cause the wheel to turn in one direction only. **2** a wheel with a toothed rim. *Also called* **ratchet wheel**. **3** the mechanism including the bar and toothed wheel together.

rate¹ *noun* **1** the amount of something considered in relation to, or measured according to, another amount: *a high yearly suicide rate.* **2** a price or charge, often measured per unit. **3** a price or charge fixed according to a standard scale: *the current exchange rate.* **4** class or rank. **5** speed of movement or change. —*verb trans., intrans.* (**rated, rating**) **1** to give a value to: *rates him number two in the world.* **2** to be worthy of (something). **3** to be placed in a certain class or rank. —**at any rate** in any case; anyway. **at this** *or* **that rate** if this, or that, is or continues to be the case.

rate² *verb trans.* (**rated, rating**) to scold severely.

rate of exchange exchange rate.

rather *adv.* **1** more readily; from preference. **2** more truly or properly: *my mother, or rather my stepmother.* **3** to a certain extent; somewhat. **4** on the contrary. —*interj.* yes indeed; very much.

ratify *verb trans.* (**ratified, ratifying, ratifies**) to give formal consent to (e.g., a treaty, agreement, etc.), esp. by signature. ▸ **ratification** *noun*

rating *noun* **1** a classification according to order, rank, or value. **2** an estimated value of a person's position, esp. as regards credit. **3** (*often* **the ratings**) the proportion of viewers or listeners forming the estimated audience of a television or radio program, used as a measure of that program's popularity.

ratio *noun* (*pl.* **ratios**) **1** the number or degree of one class of things in relation to another, or between one thing and another, expressed as a proportion. **2** *Math.* the number of times one quantity can be divided by another.

ration (răsh′ən, rā′shən) *noun* **1** a fixed allowance of food, clothing, gasoline, etc., during a time of shortage. **2** (**rations**) one's daily allowance of food, esp. in the army. —*verb trans.* (**rationed, rationing**) **1** (**ration** (**something**) **out**) to distribute or share out (something), esp. when in short supply, usu. in fixed amounts. **2** to restrict the supply of provisions to (someone).

rational *adj.* **1** of or based on reason or logic. **2** able to think, form opinions, make judgments, etc. **3** sensible; reasonable. **4** sane. ▸ **rationally** *adv.*

rationale (răsh,ə-năl′) *noun* the underlying principles or reasons on which a decision, belief, action, etc., is based.

rationalism *noun* the theory that an individual's actions and beliefs should be based on reason rather than on intuition or the teachings of others. ▸ **rationalist** *noun* ▸ **rationalistic** *adj.*

rationality *noun* **1** the condition of being rational. **2** the possession or due exercise of reason. **3** the condition of being reasonable.

rationalize *verb trans., intrans.* (**rationalized, rationalizing**) **1 a** to attribute (one's behavior or attitude) to sensible, well-thought-out reasons or motives, esp. after the event. **b** to explain one's behavior, etc., in this way. **2** to make logical or rational. ▸ **rationalization** *noun*

rational number *Math.* a number that can be expressed in the form of a fraction, e.g., $\frac{a}{b}$, where *a* and *b* are whole numbers, and *b* is not zero, e.g., $\frac{4}{5}$.

ratpack *noun slang* a clique, the members of which share common interests.

rat race *colloq.* the fierce competition for success, wealth, etc., in business, society, etc.

rattan *noun* **1** a climbing palm with very long, thin, tough stems. *Also called* **rattan palm. 2** the stripped stem of this plant, widely used to make walking sticks, baskets and other wickerworks. *Also called* **rattan cane.**

rattle *verb intrans., trans.* (**rattled, rattling**) **1** to make a series of short, sharp, hard sounds in quick succession. **2** to cause (e.g., crockery) to make such a noise. **3** to move along rapidly, often with a rattling noise. **4** (*usu.* **rattle on**) to chatter thoughtlessly or idly. **5** (**rattle** (**something**) **off** *or* **rattle through** (**something**)) to say or recite (it) rapidly and unthinkingly. **6** *colloq.* to make anxious or nervous; to upset. —*noun* **1** a series of short sharp sounds made in quick succession. **2** a baby's toy that rattles when it is shaken. **3** the loose horny structures at the end of a rattlesnake's tail. ▸ **rattly** *adj.*

rattler *noun colloq.* a rattlesnake.

rattlesnake *noun* a poisonous American snake that vibrates a series of dry horny structures at the end of its tail, producing a loud rattling sound.

rattletrap *noun colloq.* a broken-down, rickety old vehicle, esp. a car.

ratty *adj.* (**rattier, rattiest**) **1** of or like a rat. **2** in disrepair; shabby: *a ratty old cloak.*

raucous (rô'kəs) *adj.* hoarse; harsh. ▸ **raucously** *adv.* ▸ **raucousness** *noun*

raunchy *adj.* (**raunchier, raunchiest**) *slang* **1** coarsely or openly sexual. **2** full of grime and dirt; unclean. ▸ **raunchily** *adv.*

ravage (răv'ĭj) *verb trans., intrans.* (**ravaged, ravaging**) to cause extensive damage to a place; to destroy. —*noun* (*usu.* **ravages**) damage or destruction: *the ravages of time.*

rave *verb intrans., trans.* (**raved, raving**) **1 a** to talk wildly as if mad or delirious. **b** to say in a wild manner: *raved her displeasure at him.* **2** (**rave about** *or* **over** (**something**)) to talk enthusiastically or passionately about (it). —*noun* **1** extravagant praise. **2** an all-night dance party. —*adj. colloq.* extremely enthusiastic: *rave reviews.*

ravel (răv'əl) *verb trans., intrans.* (**raveled** *or* **ravelled, raveling** *or* **ravelling**) **1** to tangle, or to become tangled up. **2** to untangle, unravel, or untwist (something). **3** to fray:

This fabric ravels easily. —*noun* **1** a tangle or knot. **2** a complication. **3** a loose or broken thread.

raven *noun* a large bird belonging to the crow family, with lustrous blue-black plumage and a hoarse croaking cry. —*adj.* glossy blue-black in color.

ravenous (răv'ə-nəs) *adj.* **1** extremely hungry or greedy. **2** *of hunger, a desire, etc.* intensely strong. **3** living on prey; predatory. ▸ **ravenously** *adv.* ▸ **ravenousness** *noun*

ravine (rə-vēn') *noun* a deep, narrow, steep-sided gorge.

raving *adj., adv.* **1** frenzied; delirious. **2** *colloq.* great; extreme: *a raving beauty.* —*noun* (*usu.* **ravings**) wild, frenzied, or delirious talk.

ravioli *noun* (*pl.* **ravioli, raviolis**) **1** a small, square pasta case with a savory filling of meat, cheese, etc. **2** a dish made with these.

ravish *verb trans.* (**ravished, ravishing**) **1** to cause to be overcome with joy, delight, etc.; to enrapture. **2** *old use* to rape.

ravishing *adj.* having an appearance or qualities that delight the senses. ▸ **ravishingly** *adv.*

raw *adj.* **1** not cooked. **2 a** not processed, purified, or refined. **b** lacking refined manners and sensitivity. **3** *of statistics, data, etc.* having undergone no analysis. **4** *of a person* young and callow. **5** *of a wound, etc.* having a sore, inflamed surface. **6** *of weather* cold and damp. —*noun* a sore, inflamed, or sensitive place. —**in the raw 1** in a natural or crude state. **2** naked. ▸ **rawness** *noun*

rawboned *adj.* lean and gaunt.

raw deal *colloq.* harsh, unfair treatment.

rawhide *noun* **1** untanned leather. **2** a whip made from untanned leather.

raw material any material usu. in its natural state, from which something is made or developed.

ray[1] *noun* **1** a narrow beam of light or radioactive particles. **2** any of a set of lines fanning out from a central point. **3** a small amount of or the beginnings of, esp. hope or understanding.

ray[2] *noun* any of numerous fish with a broad, flattened body, eyes on the top of its head, and a long narrow tail.

rayon *noun* a strong, durable, artificial fiber made from cellulose.

raze *or* **rase** *verb trans.* (**razed** *or* **rased, razing** *or* **rasing**) to destroy or demolish (buildings, a town, etc.) completely.

razor *noun* a sharp-edged instrument used for shaving.

razorbill *noun* a seabird with a sharp-edged bill.

razor edge 1 a very fine, sharp edge. **2** a critical, delicately balanced situation.

razzle-dazzle *noun slang* flashy, dazzling excitement or showiness.

razzmatazz *noun* **1** razzle-dazzle. **2** humbug; double talk.

Rb *symbol Chem.* rubidium.

RBI or rbi *abbrev. Baseball* run(s) batted in.

RC *abbrev.* **1** Red Cross. **2** Roman Catholic.

Rd. *abbrev.* Road.

RDA *abbrev.* recommended daily allowance.

Re² *symbol Chem.* rhenium.

re¹ (rā) *noun* the second note in the solfeggio scale.

re² (rā, rē) *prep.* with regard to; concerning.

re- *prefix* forming words denoting a repetition or reversal of the action of the root word: *reread / rewrite.*

reach *verb trans., intrans.* (**reached, reaching**) **1** to arrive at; to get as far as. **2 a** to be able to touch or get hold of. **b** to bring to fruition (a goal, ambition, etc.), esp. through hard work. **3** to project or extend to a point. **4** to stretch out one's arm to try to touch or get hold of something. **5** *colloq.* to hand or pass: *Reach me the salt, please.* **6** to make contact or communicate with, esp. by telephone. —*noun* **1** the distance one can stretch one's arm, hand, etc.: *within reach.* **2** a distance that can be traveled easily. **3** an act of reaching out. **4** a range of influence or power. **b** the extent of one's knowledge. **5** (*usu.* **reaches**) a section within clear limits, e.g., part of a river or canal between two bends or locks. **6** (*usu.* **reaches**) level or rank: *the upper reaches of government.* ▸ **reachable** *adj.*

react (rē-ākt′) *verb intrans., trans.* (**reacted, reacting**) **1** (**react to** (**something** or **someone**)) to respond in a certain way to (something said or done). **2** (**react against** (**something**)) to respond to (it) in a way that shows dislike or disapproval. **3** to undergo or cause to undergo a chemical reaction.

reactance *noun Electr.* in an electric circuit carrying alternating current, the property of an inductor or capacitor that causes it to oppose the flow of current.

reaction *noun* **1** a reacting or response to something. **2** opposition to change, esp. political change, and a desire to return to a former system. **3** a complete change of opinions, feelings, etc., to the opposite of what they were. **4** a bodily response (e.g., to a drug). **5** *Chem.* the process whereby one or more substances react to form one or more different substances. **6** *Phys.* a nuclear reaction.

reactionary *adj.*, of a person or policies opposed to change or progress and in favor of a return to a former system. —*noun* (*pl.* **reactionaries**) a reactionary person.

reactive *adj.* showing a reaction; liable to react; sensitive to stimuli.

reactor *noun* a nuclear reactor.

read *verb trans., intrans.* (**read, reading**) **1** to look at and understand (printed or written words). **2** to speak (words that are printed or written). **3** to learn or gain knowledge of by reading. **4** to pass one's leisure time reading (books). **5** to interpret or understand the meaning of: *read a map.* **6** to interpret or understand (signs, marks, etc.) without using one's eyes: *read Braille.* **7** to know (a language) well enough to be able to understand something written in it. **8** to have a certain wording: *The letter reads as follows.* **9** to think that (a statement, etc.) has a particular meaning: *I read it as a criticism.* **10** of writing to be, or not be, coherent, fluent, and logical: *an essay that reads well.* **11** of a dial, instrument, etc. to show a particular measurement. **12** to indicate that (a word, phrase, etc.) ought to be replaced by another: *For feed read deed.* **13** to put into a specified condition by reading. **14** to study (a subject) at a university. **15** to hear and understand, esp. when using a two-way radio. **16** (**read** (**something**) **in** or **out**) *Comput.* to transfer data from a disk or other storage device into the main memory of a computer. —*noun* **1** a period or act of reading. **2** *slang* a book, etc., thought of as being interesting or not so: *a good read.* —**read between the lines** to understand a meaning that is implied but not stated. **well** or **widely read** educated, esp. in literature, through reading. ▸ **readable** *adj.* ▸ **readability** *noun* ▸ **readableness** *noun* ▸ **reader** *noun*

readership *noun* the total number of people who read a newspaper, the novels of a particular author, etc.

readily (rĕd′l-ē) *adv.* **1** promptly; willingly. **2** quickly. ▸ **readiness** *noun*

reading *noun* **1** the action of a person who reads. **2** the ability to read: *his reading is poor.* **3** books, material, etc., for reading. **4** an event at which a play, poetry, etc., is read to an audience. **5** the actual word or words that can be read in a text, esp. where more than one version is possible. **6** information, figures, etc., shown by an instrument or meter. **7** an understanding or interpretation. —*adj.* of, for, or fond of reading.

read-only memory *Comput.* (**ABBREV. ROM**) a memory that holds data permanently and allows it to be read and used but not changed.

readout *noun Comput.* data that has been copied from the main memory of a computer into an external storage device, e.g. a disk or tape, or a display device.

ready (rĕd′ē) *adj.* (**readier, readiest**) **1** prepared and available for action or use. **2** willing: *always ready to help.* **3** prompt;

quick: *too ready to find fault.* **4** likely or about to do. —*verb trans.* (**readied, ready-ing, readies**) to make ready.

ready-made *adj.* of *clothes* made to a standard size, not made-to-measure.

ready money *colloq.* money available for immediate use.

ready-to-wear *adj.* (ABBREV. **RTW**) of *clothes* sold finished and in standard sizes.

reagent (rē-ā'jənt) *noun Chem.* a substance which behaves in a characteristic way in chemical reactions, used to detect the presence of other substances.

real *adj.* **1** actually existing; not imaginary. **2** not imitation; genuine. **3** agreeing with or corresponding to fact. **4** great, important, or serious: *a real problem.* —*adv.* really; very. —**for real** *slang* in reality; seriously.

real estate property in the form of houses or land. *Also called* **realty.**

realism *noun* **1** an acceptance of things or a willingness to deal with things as they really are. **2** (**Realism**) the deliberate presentation in art and literature of subject matter as it really is. **3** *Philos.* the theory that physical objects exist even when they are not perceived by the mind. *See also* **idealism** (sense 3). ▶ **realist** *noun*

realistic *adj.* **1** representing things as they really are; lifelike. **2** relating to realism or realists. ▶ **realistically** *adv.*

reality *noun* (*pl.* **realities**) **1** the state or fact of being real. **2** the real nature of something; the truth. **3** that which is real and not imaginary.

realize *verb trans., intrans.* (**realized, realizing**) **1** to begin to know or understand. **2** to make real; to make come true. **3** to cause to seem real; to act out: *realize story on film.* ▶ **realizable** *adj.* ▶ **realization** *noun*

really *adv.* **1** in fact; actually. **2** very; genuinely: *a really lovely day.* —*interj.* used to express surprise, doubt, or mild protest.

realm (rĕlm) *noun* **1** a kingdom. **2** a field of interest, study, or activity.

real number *Math.* any rational or irrational number.

realpolitik (rä-äl'pō,lĭ'tēk,) *noun* politics based on the practical needs of life rather than on moral or ethical ideas.

real time *Comput.* **1** the actual time during which a process involving a computer occurs. **2** the time from which data are input into a computer to the time at which a solution or result is generated. ▶ **real-time** *adj.*

Realtor (rē'əl-tər) *trademark* used to denote a real estate agent who is a member of the National Association of Realtors.

realty *noun* **1** real estate. **2** a real-estate agency.

ream *noun* **1** a number of sheets of paper

equivalent to 20 quires, formerly 480, now usu. 500 or 516. **2** (**reams**) *colloq.* a large amount, esp. of paper or writing.

reap *verb trans., intrans.* (**reaped, reaping**) **1** to cut or gather (grain, etc.). **2** to clear (a field) by cutting a crop. **3** to receive as a consequence of one's actions.

reaper *noun* a person or machine that reaps. —**the grim reaper** *or* **the reaper** the specter of death; death itself.

reapply *verb trans., intrans.* (**reapplied, reapplying, reapplies**) to apply again or afresh.

rear[1] *noun* **1** the back part; the area at the back. **2** that part of an army that is farthest away from the enemy. **3** the buttocks. —*adj.* situated at the back: *a rear window.*

rear[2] *verb trans., intrans.* (**reared, rearing**) **1** to feed, care for, and educate. **2** to breed (animals), or grow (crops). **3** (*also* **rear up**) *esp. of a horse* to rise on the hind legs.

rear admiral (ABBREV. **RADM, R.Adm., R.A., RA**) an officer in the US Navy or Coast Guard ranking above commodore and below vice admiral.

rearguard *noun* a group of soldiers who protect the rear of an army, esp. in retreats.

rearmost (rîr'mōst,) *adj.* last of all.

rearward *adj.* at or to the rear. —*adv.* (*also* **rearwards**) toward the rear.

reason *noun* **1** a justification or motive for an action, belief, etc. **2** an underlying explanation or cause. **3 a** the part of the mind that uses both memory and intelligence in order to think, work out solutions to problems, and assimilate concepts. ▣ INTELLECT, UNDER-STANDING. **b** the power of the mind to perform these operations. **4** sanity. —*verb intrans., trans.* (**reasoned, reasoning**) **1** to use one's mind and reason to form opinions and judgments, reach conclusions, etc. **2** (**reason with** (**someone**)) to try to persuade (someone) by means of argument. **3** (**reason** (**someone**) **into** *or* **out of** (**something**)) to persuade or influence (someone) with argument. **4** (*also* **reason** (**something**) **out**) to think (it) or set (it) out logically. —**by reason of** (**something specified**) because of; as a consequence of (that which is specified). **within reason** within the bounds of what is sensible or possible.

reasonable *adj.* **1** showing reason or good judgment; sensible. **2** willing to listen to reason or argument. **3** in accordance with reason; not extreme or excessive; fair. **4** not costly. **5** satisfactory or equal to what one might expect. ▶ **reasonableness** *noun* ▶ **reasonably** *adv.*

reasoning *noun* **1** the forming of judgments or opinions using reason or careful argument. **2** the opinions or judgments so formed.

reassure *verb trans.* (**reassured, reassuring**) to relieve (someone) of anxiety and so give confidence to. ▸ **reassurance** *noun* ▸ **reassuring** *adj.*

rebate *noun* 1 a return of part of a sum of money paid. 2 a discount.

rebel (rĕb'əl) *noun* 1 a person who opposes or fights against people in authority or oppressive conditions. 2 a person who does not accept the rules of normal behavior, dress, etc. —*adj.* engaged in rebelling or in rebellion. (rĭ-bĕl') —*verb intrans.* (**rebelled, rebelling**) 1 to resist authority or oppressive conditions openly and with force. 2 to reject the accepted rules of behavior, dress, etc. 3 to feel aversion or dislike.

rebellion *noun* an act of rebelling; a revolt.

rebellious *adj.* 1 unwilling to comply with order or to exhibit respect for those in authority. ◨ INSUBORDINATE, MUTINOUS ◪ OBEDIENT, SUBORDINATE. 2 opposed to and fighting against the government of a country. ◨ INSURGENT, INSURRECTIONARY, REVOLTING, SEDITIOUS ◪ LOYAL. ▸ **rebelliously** *adv.* ▸ **rebelliousness** *noun*

rebirth *noun* a revival, renaissance, or renewal, often a spiritual one.

reboot *Comput. verb trans., intrans.* (**rebooted, rebooting**) to restart (a computer), either by switching off at the power source or pressing a reset button, etc.

reborn *adj.* born again, esp. in the sense of having received new spiritual life.

rebound (rē'bownd, rĭ-bownd') *verb intrans.* (**rebounded, rebounding**) 1 a to bounce or spring back or off, as a basketball does. b *Basketball* to regain possession of the ball as it bounces off the backboard or the basket rim after an unsuccessful shot has been made. 2 (**rebound on** *or* **upon** (**someone**)) *of an action* to have a bad effect on the person performing the action. —*noun* 1 an instance of rebounding; a recoil. 2 *Basketball* the act of getting possession of a rebounding ball. —**on the rebound** while still recovering from an emotional shock, esp. the ending of a love affair or attachment.

rebuff (rĭ-bəf') *noun* an unkind or unfriendly refusal to help someone or a rejection of help, advice, etc., from someone. —*verb trans.* (**rebuffed, rebuffing**) to reject or refuse (an offer of or plea for help, a request, etc.) unkindly.

rebuild *verb* (**rebuilt, rebuilding**) to build again or anew.

rebuke (rĭ-byōōk') *verb trans.* (**rebuked, rebuking**) to speak severely to (someone) because he or she has done wrong. —*noun* the act of speaking severely to someone, or being spoken severely to.

rebus (rē'bəs) *noun* (*pl.* **rebuses**) a puzzle in which pictures and symbols are used to represent words and parts of words to form a message or phrase.

rebut *verb trans.* (**rebutted, rebutting**) 1 to disprove (a charge or claim) esp. by offering opposing evidence. 2 to force to turn back; to repel. ▸ **rebuttal** *noun*

recalcitrant *adj.* not willing to accept authority or discipline; stubbornly defiant. ▸ **recalcitrance** *noun*

recall *verb trans.* (rĭ-kôl') (**recalled, recalling**) 1 to order to return. 2 to remember. 3 to cancel or revoke: *recall a license.* 4 to request return of (a product) to its manufacturer, usu. to make needed repairs or other adjustments. —*noun* (rĭ-kôl', rē'kôl,) 1 an act of recalling. 2 the ability to remember accurately and in detail: *total recall.* 3 a request by a manufacturer that a certain product be returned.

recant *verb intrans., trans.* (**recanted, recanting**) 1 to reject one's (usu. religious or political) beliefs, esp. publicly. 2 to withdraw (a statement). ▸ **recantation** *noun*

recap *colloq. verb trans., intrans.* (**recapped, recapping**) to recapitulate. —*noun* a recapitulation.

recapitulate (rē,kə-pĭch'ə-lāt,) *verb trans., intrans.* (**recapitulated, recapitulating**) to go over the chief points of (an argument, statement, etc.) again. ▸ **recapitulation** *noun*

recapture *verb trans.* (**recaptured, recapturing**) 1 to capture again. 2 to convey, produce, or experience (images or feelings from the past). —*noun* the act of recapturing or an instance of being recaptured.

recede *verb intrans.* (**receded, receding**) 1 to go or move back or backward. 2 to become more distant. 3 to grow less. 4 to bend or slope backward. ▸ **receding** *adj.*

receipt (rĭ-sēt') *noun* 1 a written note saying that money or goods have been received. 2 the act of receiving or being received. 3 (*usu.* **receipts**) money received during a given period of time, esp. by a store, theater, or other business.

receive *verb trans., intrans.* (**received, receiving**) 1 to get, be given, or accept. 2 to experience or suffer. 3 to give attention to or consider. 4 to react in a specified way in response to: *received the news well.* 5 to be awarded (an honor). 6 to welcome or greet (guests), esp. formally. 7 to change (radio or television signals) into sounds or pictures.

receiver *noun* 1 a person or thing that receives. 2 *Law* a person who is appointed by a court to take control of the business of a bankrupt party. **3** the part of a telephone that is held to the ear.

receivership *noun* **1** the status of a party or a business that is under the control of an official receiver. **2** the office of receiver.

recent *adj.* happening, done, having appeared, etc., not long ago. ▸ **recently** *adv.*

receptacle *noun* a container.

reception *noun* **1** the act of receiving or being received. **2** a response, or reaction, whether welcome or unwelcome. **3** a formal party or social gathering to welcome guests, esp. after a wedding. **4** the quality of radio or television signals received. **5** an office or desk where visitors or clients are welcomed on arrival, e.g., in a hotel.

receptionist *noun* a person employed in a hotel, business, physician's office, etc., to deal with visitors and guests, take and make telephone calls, etc.

receptive *adj.* able, willing, and quick to understand and accept new ideas. ▸ **receptively** *adv.* ▸ **receptiveness** *noun*

receptor *noun* Biol. **1** an element of the nervous system adapted for reception of stimuli, e.g., a sense organ or sensory nerve ending. **2** a site in or on a cell to which a drug or hormone can become attached, stimulating a reaction inside the cell.

recess (rē'sĕs, rĭ-sĕs') *noun* **1** an open space or alcove set in a wall. **2** (*often* **recesses**) a hidden, inner, or secret place. **3** a temporary break from work, esp. of a court of law. **4** a short break between school classes. —*verb trans.* (**recessed, recessing**) **1** to put into a recess. **2** to make a recess in. **3** to take a break or adjourn.

recession *noun* **1** a temporary decline in economic activity, trade, and prosperity. **2** the act of receding or state of being set back.

recessional *noun* a hymn sung during the departure of the clergy and choir after a service.

recessive *adj.* **1** tending to recede. **2** Genetics of a gene which carries a characteristic which will only be manifest if not overridden by another gene.

recheck *verb trans., intrans.* (**rechecked, rechecking**) to check again. —*noun* a second or further check.

recidivism *noun* the habit of relapsing into crime. ▸ **recidivist** *noun*

recipe (rĕs'ə-pē) *noun* **1** a list of ingredients for and set of instructions on how to prepare and cook a particular kind of meal, cake, etc. **2** (**a recipe for** (**something**)) a way of achieving (something): *a recipe for success.*

recipient *noun* a person or thing that receives.

reciprocal *adj.* **1** given to and received from in return; mutual. **2** Gram., of a pronoun ex-

pressing a relationship between two specified nouns, or expressing mutual action, e.g., *one another* in *John and Mary love one another.* —*noun* Math. the value obtained when 1 is divided by the number concerned, e.g., the reciprocal of 4 is $\frac{1}{4}$. ▸ **reciprocally** *adv.*

reciprocate (rĭ-sĭp'rə-kāt,) *verb trans., intrans.* (**reciprocated, reciprocating**) **1** to return (affection, love, etc.). **2** (**reciprocate with** (**something**)) to give (it) in return. ▸ **reciprocation** *noun*

reciprocity (rĕs,ə-prăs'ət-ē) *noun* **1** reciprocal action. **2** a mutual exchange of privileges or advantages between countries, trade organizations, businesses, etc.

recital *noun* **1** a public performance of music, songs, or dancing, usu. by one person or a small number of people. **2** an oral or written account of an event or series of events. **3** an act of reciting. ▸ **recitalist** *noun*

recitation *noun* Mus. **1** something that is recited from memory. **2** an act of reciting.

recitative (rĕs,ə-ə-tēv') *noun* **1** a style of singing akin to speech, used for narrative sequences in opera or oratorio. **2** a passage sung in this way.

recite *verb trans., intrans.* (**recited, reciting**) **1** to repeat aloud from memory. **2** to make a detailed statement about or list.

reckless *adj.* acting or done without any thought of the consequences; very careless. ▸ **recklessly** *adv.* ▸ **recklessness** *noun*

reckon *verb trans., intrans.* (**reckoned, reckoning**) **1** to work out, find out, or estimate, esp. by mathematical means. **2** to think of as part of or belonging to: *I reckon him among my friends.* **3** to consider or think of in a specified way. **4** *colloq.* to think or suppose. **5** (**reckon on** (**someone** *or* **something**)) to rely on or expect (the one or ones specified): *We reckoned on their support.* **6** to calculate something. —**reckon with** *or* **without** (**something**) to expect, or not expect, trouble or difficulties. (**someone** *or* **something**) **to be reckoned with** (a person or thing) that is not to be ignored.

reckoning *noun* **1** calculation; counting. **2** a settling of accounts, debts, grievances, etc. —**day of reckoning** a time when one has to account for one's actions; a time of judgment.

reclaim *verb trans.* (**reclaimed, reclaiming**) **1** to seek to regain possession of; to claim back. **2** to make (waste land) fit for use, esp. by draining. **3** to recover useful materials from industrial or domestic waste. **4** to reform (someone). ▸ **reclaimable** *adj.* ▸ **reclamation** *noun*

recline *verb intrans., trans.* (**reclined, reclining**) **1** to lean or lie on one's back or side. **2**

to lean or lay (e.g., one's head) in a resting position.

recliner *noun* a comfortable chair with a back that can slope at different angles, and a footrest.

recluse (rĕk'lōōs,, -lōōz,) *noun* a person who lives alone and in seclusion; a hermit.

recognition *noun* the act or state of recognizing or an instance of being recognized.

recognizance *noun* Law a legally binding promise made to a magistrate, judge, or court to do or not do something specified.

recognize *verb trans.* (**recognized, recognizing**) 1 to identify (a person or thing known or experienced before). 2 to admit or be aware of: *recognize one's mistakes.* 3 to show approval of and gratitude for. 4 to accept as valid. ▸ **recognizable** *adj.* ▸ **recognizably** *adv.*

recoil *verb intrans.* (rĭ-koil') (**recoiled, recoiling**) 1 (**recoil at** *or* **from (something)**) to move or jump back or away from (it) quickly or suddenly, usu. in horror or fear. 2 to spring back or rebound. 3 *of a gun* to spring powerfully backward under the force of being fired. —*noun* (rē'koil,, rĭ-koil') the act of recoiling, esp. the backward movement of a gun when fired.

recollect *verb trans.* (**recollected, recollecting**) to remember. ▸ **recollection** *noun*

recommend *verb trans.* (**recommended, recommending**) 1 to advise. 2 to suggest as being suitable to be accepted, chosen, etc.; to commend. ▸ **recommendable** *adj.* ▸ **recommendation** *noun*

recompense (rĕk'əm-pĕns,) *verb trans.* (**recompensed, recompensing**) to pay or give (someone) compensation for injury or hardship suffered or reward for services, etc. —*noun* money, etc., given in compensation.

reconcile *verb trans., intrans.* (**reconciled, reconciling**) 1 a (**reconcile (one person) with (another)**) to put (them) on friendly terms again, esp. after a quarrel. b *of two or more people* to be on friendly terms again. 2 (**reconcile (one thing) with (another)**) to bring (two or more different aims, points of view, etc.), into agreement; to harmonize (them). 3 (**be reconciled to** *or* **reconcile (oneself) to (something)**) to agree to accept an unwelcome fact or situation patiently. ▸ **reconciliation** *noun* ▸ **reconciliatory** *adj.*

recondite (rĕk'ən-dīt,) *adj.* 1 *of a subject or knowledge* little known. 2 dealing with profound, abstruse, or obscure knowledge.

recondition *verb trans.* (**reconditioned, reconditioning**) to repair or restore to original or good working condition.

reconnaissance (rĭ-kän'ə-səns) *noun* 1 a

survey of land, enemy troops, etc., to obtain information about the enemy. 2 a preliminary survey.

reconnoiter *verb trans., intrans.* (**reconnoitered, reconnoitering**) to make a reconnaissance of (land, enemy troops, etc.).

reconsider *verb trans., intrans.* (**reconsidered, reconsidering**) to consider (something) again and possibly change one's opinion or decision. ▸ **reconsideration** *noun*

reconstitute *verb trans.* (**reconstituted, reconstituting**) 1 to put or change back to the original form, e.g., by adding water. 2 to form or make up in a different way. ▸ **reconstitution** *noun*

reconstruct *verb trans.* (**reconstructed, reconstructing**) 1 to create a description or idea (of e.g., a crime) from the evidence available. 2 to rebuild. ▸ **reconstruction** *noun*

record *noun* (pronounced with stress on *rec-*) 1 a formal written report or statement of facts, events, or information. 2 (*often* **records**) information, facts, etc., collected over a usu. long period of time. 3 the state or fact of being recorded. 4 a thin plastic disk used as a recording medium for reproducing music or other sound. 5 *Sport* a performance that is officially recorded as the best of a particular kind or in a particular class. 6 a description of the history and achievements of a person, institution, etc. 7 a list of the crimes of which a person has been convicted. 8 *Comput.* in database systems, a subdivision of a file, consisting of a collection of fields, each of which contains a particular item of information. —*verb trans., intrans.* (pronounced with stress on *-cord*) (**recorded, recording**) 1 to set down in writing or another permanent form, esp. for use in the future. 2 to register (sound, music, speech, etc.) on a record or tape so that it can be listened to in the future. 3 *of a dial, instrument, etc.* to show or register (a particular figure, etc.). —**off the record** *of information, statements, etc.* not intended to be repeated or made public. **on record** as a matter of official or public knowledge.

recorder *noun* 1 something that records, e.g. a tape recorder. 2 *Mus.* a wooden or plastic wind instrument with a tapering mouthpiece and holes that are covered by the player's fingers.

recording *noun* 1 the process of registering sounds or images on a record, tape, etc. 2 sound or images that have been recorded.

recount (rĭ-kownt') *verb trans.* (**recounted, recounting**) to tell (a story, etc.) in detail.

re-count *verb trans.* (rē-kownt') (**re-counted, re-counting**) to count again. —*noun* (rē'-

kownt) the process of re-counting, esp. of votes in a close or disputed election.

recoup (rĭ-kōōp') *verb trans., intrans.* (**recouped, recouping**) **1** to recover or get back (something lost, e.g., money). **2** to compensate (e.g., for something lost).

recourse *noun* **1** a source of help or protection. **2** the right to demand payment.

recover *verb trans., intrans.* (**recovered, recovering**) **1** to get or find again. **2** to regain one's good health, spirits, or composure. **3** to regain a former, usu. better, status or condition. **4** to regain control of (one's emotions, actions, etc.). **5** *Law* to gain (compensation or damages) by legal action. **6** to get money to make up for (expenses, loss, etc.). **7** to obtain (a valuable or usable substance) from a waste product or byproduct. ▸ **recoverable** *adj.* ▸ **recovery** *noun*

recreant (rĕk'rē-ənt) *noun* a cowardly or disloyal person. —*adj.* cowardly or disloyal.

re-create (rē,krē-āt') *verb trans.* (**re-created, re-creating**) to create again; to reproduce.

recreation (rĕk,rē-ā'shən) *noun* a pleasant, enjoyable, often refreshing, activity done in one's spare time. ▸ **recreational** *adj.*

recrimination *noun* an accusation made by an accused person against his or her accuser; counptercharge. ▸ **recriminatory** *adj.*

recrudesce *verb intrans.* (**recrudesced, recrudescing**) *esp. of a disease* to become active again, esp. after a dormant period. ▸ **recrudescence** *noun* ▸ **recrudescent** *adj.*

recruit (rĭ-krōōt') *noun* **1** a newly enlisted member of an army, air force, navy, etc. **2** a new member of a society, group, etc. —*verb trans., intrans.* (**recruited, recruiting**) to enlist (people) as recruits. ▸ **recruitment** *noun*

rectal *adj.* of or relating to the rectum.

rectangle *noun Geom.* a four-sided figure with opposite sides that are equal and four right angles. ▸ **rectangular** *adj.*

rectify *verb trans.* (**rectified, rectifying, rectifies**) to put right or correct (a mistake, etc.). ▸ **rectifiable** *adj.* ▸ **rectification** *noun*

rectilinear *adj.* **1** in or forming a straight line. **2** bounded by straight lines.

rectitude *noun* correctness of behavior or judgment; moral integrity; honesty.

recto *noun* (*pl.* **rectos**) (ABBREV. **r**) *Printing* the right-hand page of an open book. *See also* **verso**.

rector *noun* **1** a cleric who is in charge of a parish. **2** *RC Church* a priest in charge of a congregation or a religious house. **3** the headmaster of some schools, colleges, and universities. ▸ **rectorial** *adj.*

rectory *noun* (*pl.* **rectories**) the residence of a rector.

rectum *noun* (*pl.* **rectums, recta**) the lower part of the alimentary canal, ending at the anus.

recumbent *adj.* lying down; reclining.

recuperable *adj.* recoverable.

recuperate (rĭ-kōō'pə-rāt,) *verb intrans., trans.* (**recuperated, recuperating**) **1** to recover, esp. from illness. **2** to recover (something lost, one's health, etc.). ▸ **recuperation** *noun* ▸ **recuperative** *adj.*

recur *verb intrans.* (**recurred, recurring**) **1** to happen again or at intervals. **2** *of a thought, etc.* to come back into one's mind. ▸ **recurrence** *noun* ▸ **recurrent** *adj.* ▸ **recurrently** *adv.*

recycle *verb trans., intrans.* (**recycled, recycling**) to pass through a series of changes so as to return to a former state, esp. to process waste material so that it can be used again. ▸ **recyclable** *adj.*, *noun* ▸ **recycling** *noun*

red *adj.* (**redder, reddest**) **1** of the color of blood. **2** *of hair or fur* of a color that varies between a golden brown and a deep reddish-brown. **3** *of the eyes* bloodshot or with red rims. **4** having a flushed face, esp. from shame or anger. **5** *of wine* made with black grapes whose skins color the wine. **6** *colloq.* communist. —*noun* **1** the color of blood, or a similar shade. **2** something of this color. **3** the traffic light or a sign indicating that traffic should stop. **4** the debit side of an account. **5** *colloq.* (*often* **Red**) a communist or socialist. —**in the red** showing a financial deficit; in debt. ▸ **redness** *noun*

red blood cell *Med.* a red disk-shaped blood cell in mammals, which carries oxygen to the tissues. *Also called* **erythrocyte, red corpuscle.**

red-blooded *adj.* active; virile.

redbreast *noun* a robin.

redcoat *noun Hist.* a British soldier, esp. one fighting in the American Revolution.

red corpuscle *Med.* a red blood cell.

redden *verb trans., intrans.* (**reddened, reddening**) **1** to make or become red or redder. **2** to blush.

reddish *adj.* somewhat red.

redeem *verb trans.* (**redeemed, redeeming**) **1** to buy back. **2** to recover (e.g., something pawned or mortgaged) by payment or service. **3** to fulfill (a promise). **4** to set (a person) free or save (a person's life) by paying a ransom. **5** to free (someone or oneself) from blame or debt. **6** *of Christ* to free (humanity) from sin by his death on the cross. **7** to make up for (something bad or wrong). **8** to exchange (tokens, vouchers, etc.) for goods. **9** to exchange (bonds, shares, etc.) for cash. ▸ **redeemable** *adj.* ▸ **redeemer** *noun* ▸ **redeeming** *adj.*

redemption *noun* **1** the act of redeeming or state of being redeemed. **2** that which redeems. ▸ **redemptive** *adj.*

redeye *noun slang* a late-night commercial airline flight. ▸ **redeye** *adj.*

red giant *Astron.* a cool, red star that has a large diameter relative to the sun.

red-handed *adj.* in the act of committing a crime: *caught red-handed.*

redhead *noun* a person with red hair.

red herring a subject, idea, clue, etc., introduced to divert attention from the real issue or to mislead someone.

red-hot *adj.* **1** *of metal, etc.* heated until it glows red. **2** feeling or showing passionate or intense emotion or excitement. **3** *of news, information, etc.* completely new and up to date.

redial *verb trans., intrans.* (**redialed** or **redialled, redialing** or **redialling**) to dial (a telephone number) again.

red-letter day a day that will always be remembered because something particularly pleasant or important happened on it.

red light 1 a red warning light, esp. one that warns vehicles to stop. **2** a refusal or rejection.

red-light district *colloq.* a district where prostitutes work.

red-lining *noun* the practice of refusing credit to those living in an area with a bad record of repayment or to those who are regarded as poor credit risks.

redo (rē-dōō′) *verb* (*pa t* **redid;** *pa p* **redone;** *pr p* **redoing;** *3d person sing present* **redoes**) **1** to do again or differently. **2** to redecorate.

redolent *adj.* (**redolent of** or **with (something)**) **1** smelling strongly of (it). **2** suggesting (it) strongly. ▸ **redolence** *noun* ▸ **redolently** *adv.*

redoubt (rĭ-dowt′) *noun* **1** a fortification, esp. a temporary one defending a pass or hilltop. **2** a stronghold.

redoubtable *adj.* **1** causing fear or respect. **2** brave; valiant. ▸ **redoubtably** *adv.*

redound *verb intrans.* (**redounded, redounding**) **1** (**redound to (someone)**) to have a direct, usu. advantageous effect on (the one specified). **2** (**redound on (someone)**) to come back to (the one specified) as a consequence.

red pepper 1 cayenne pepper. **2** the ripe red fruit of the capsicum or sweet pepper plant eaten as a vegetable. *See also* **green pepper.**

redress (rĭ-drĕs′) *verb trans.* (**redressed, redressing**) **1** to set right or compensate for (something wrong). **2** to make even or equal again. —*noun* **1** the act of redressing or of being redressed. **2** money, etc., paid as compensation for loss or wrong done.

redshift *noun Astron.* a shift of lines in the spectrum towards the red end, usu. considered to occur because the source of light is moving away.

red snapper a marine food fish that has a red or reddish body.

red squirrel a N American squirrel that has a tawny or reddish coat.

red tape unnecessary rules and regulations that result in delay.

reduce (rĭ-dōōs′, -dyōōs′) *verb trans., intrans.* (**reduced, reducing**) **1 a** to decrease (something) in length or scope. **b** to become decreased, e.g., in quantity or size. **2** to change into a usu. worse or undesirable state or form: *reduced her to tears.* **3** to downscale in rank or grade. **4** to bring into a state of obedience; to subdue. **5** to make poorer or weaker than was previously the case. **6** to lower the price of. **7** to lose weight by dieting. **8** to convert (a substance) into a simpler form. **9** to simplify by considering only the essential elements. **10** to thicken (a sauce) by boiling off excess liquid. **11** *Chem.* to cause (a substance) to undergo a chemical reaction whereby it gains hydrogen or loses oxygen. **12** *Math.* to convert (a fraction) to a form with numerator and denominator as low in value as possible, e.g., $\frac{3}{8}$ to $\frac{1}{3}$. ▸ **reducer** *noun* ▸ **reducibility** *noun* ▸ **reducible** *adj.* ▸ **reduction** *noun*

redundancy *noun* (*pl.* **redundancies**) **1** being redundant, or an instance of it. **2** in electronic equipment, the duplication of parts or other elements as a fail-safe feature.

redundant *adj.* **1** not needed; superfluous. **2** *of a word or phrase* expressing an idea that is already conveyed by another word or phrase. **3** of or constructed in such a way as to involve electronic redundancy.

reduplicate (rĭ-dōō′plĭ-kāt,, -dyōō′-) *verb trans., intrans.* (**reduplicated, reduplicating**) **1** to repeat, copy, or double. **2** *Linguistics* to repeat (a word or syllable), often with a minor change, to form a new word, as in *riff-raff.* ▸ **reduplication** *noun*

redwood *noun* **1** an extremely large Californian conifer. **2** the soft, reddish-brown wood of this tree.

reed *noun* **1** *Bot.* a tall, stiff grass growing on wet or marshy ground or in shallow water. **2 a** *Mus.* a thin piece of cane or metal in certain musical instruments that vibrates and makes a sound when air passes over it. **b** a wind instrument or organ pipe with reeds.

reedy *adj.* (**reedier, reediest**) **1** full of reeds. **2** having a tone like a reed instrument, esp. in being thin and piping. **3** thin and weak. ▸ **reedily** *adv.* ▸ **reediness** *noun*

reef[1] *noun* **1** in shallow coastal waters, a mass of rock that either projects above the surface at low tide, or is permanently covered by a shallow layer of water. 2 a coral reef.

reef² *Naut. noun* a part of a sail that may be folded in in rough weather or let out in calm weather, so as to alter the area exposed to the wind. —*verb trans.* (**reefed, reefing**) to reduce the area of (a sail) exposed to the wind.

reefer *noun slang* a cigarette containing marijuana.

reek *noun* a strong, highly unpleasant smell. —*verb intrans.* (**reeked, reeking**) 1 to give off a strong, usu. unpleasant smell. 2 (**reek of (something)**) to suggest or hint at (something unpleasant).

reel *noun* 1 a round, wheel-shaped or cylindrical object on which thread, film, fishing lines, etc., can be wound. 2 the quantity of film, thread, etc., wound on one of these. 3 a device for winding and unwinding a fishing line. 4 a lively Scottish, Irish, or American country dance, or the music for it. —*verb trans., intrans.* (**reeled, reeling**) 1 to wind on a reel. 2 (*usu.* **reel (something) in** *or* **up**) to pull (it) in or up using a reel. 3 to stagger or sway; to move unsteadily. 4 to whirl or appear to move. 5 (*also* **reel back**) to be shaken physically or mentally: *reel back in horror.* 6 to dance a reel. —**reel (something) off** to say, repeat, or write (it) rapidly.

re-entry *or* **reentry** *noun* (*pl.* **re-entries**) *Astron.* the return of a spacecraft to Earth's atmosphere.

refectory *noun* (*pl.* **refectories**) a dining hall in a monastery or college.

refer *verb intrans., trans.* (**referred, referring**) 1 (*usu.* **refer to (something** *or* **someone**)) a to talk or write about (the one specified); to mention (that one). b to relate, concern, or apply to (the one specified): *Does this refer to me?* c to look for information in a specified place. 2 to direct (a person, etc.) to an authority for discussion, information, a decision, treatment, etc. 3 to explain (something) as being caused by. 4 to consider as belonging to a specified place, time, or category. ▸ **referable** *adj.*

referee (rĕf,ə-rē′) *noun* 1 an umpire or judge, e.g., of a game or in a dispute. 2 *Law* a person who is appointed by a court of law to determine a case or to investigate a case and then report on it. —*verb trans., intrans.* (**refereed, refereeing**) to judge or determine (something) or to serve in the capacity of a referee.

reference *noun* 1 (*usu.* **reference to (something)**) a mention of (it); an allusion to (it). 2 a a direction in a book to another passage or book where information can be found. b a book or passage referred to. c the act of referring to a book or passage for information. 3 a a written report on a person's character, talents, and abilities, esp. of his or her aptitude for a particular job or position. b a person referred to for such a report. 4 the provision of facts and information. 5 a relation, correspondence, or connection. 6 a standard for measuring or judging. ▸ **referential** *adj.*

referendum *noun* (*pl.* **referendums, referenda**) the act or principle of giving the people of a country the chance to state their opinion on a matter by voting for or against it.

referral *noun* the act of referring someone to an expert.

refill *noun* (rē′fĭl,) a new filling for something that becomes empty through use, or a container for it. —*verb trans.* (rē-fĭl′) (**refilled, refilling**) to fill again. ▸ **refillable** *adj.*

refine *verb trans., intrans.* (**refined, refining**) 1 to make pure by removing dirt, waste substances, etc. 2 to make or become more elegant, polished, or subtle.

refined *adj.* 1 very polite; well-mannered; elegant. 2 having had all the waste substances, etc., removed. 3 improved; polished.

refinement *noun* 1 the act or process of refining. 2 good manners or good taste; polite speech; elegance. 3 an improvement or perfection. 4 a subtle distinction.

refinery (rĭ-fīn′rē, -fī′nə-rē) *noun* (*pl.* **refineries**) a factory or facility where raw materials such as sugar and oil are refined.

refit *verb trans., intrans.* (**re-fitted, refitting**) 1 to repair or fit new parts to (esp. a ship). 2 *of a ship* to be repaired or have new parts fitted.

reflate *verb trans.* (**reflated, reflating**) to increase economic activity. ▸ **reflation** *noun*

reflect (rĭ-flĕkt′) *verb trans., intrans.* (rē-flĭt′) (**reflected, reflecting**) 1 *of a surface* to send back (light, heat, sound, etc.). 2 *of a mirror, etc.* to give an image of. 3 *of a sound, image, etc.* to be thrown or bounced back. 4 to have as a cause or be a consequence of: *Price increases reflect greater demand.* 5 to show or give an idea of: *a poem that reflects the writer's mood.* 6 (**reflect on** *or* **upon (something)**) to consider it carefully. 7 (**reflect on** *or* **upon (someone)**) *of an action, etc.* to bring praise, or blame, to (the one or ones specified). ▸ **reflection** *noun* ▸ **reflective** *adj.* ▸ **reflectively** *adv.*

reflector *noun* a polished surface that reflects light, heat, etc., esp. on the back of a motor vehicle or a bicycle that glows when light shines on it.

reflex (rē′flĕks,) *noun* 1 an immediate automatic response provoked by a given stimulus of which one is not conscious. 2 the

.ability to respond rapidly to a stimulus. **3** reflected light, sound, heat, etc., or a reflected image. —*adj.* **1** occurring as an automatic response without being thought about. **2** bent or turned backward. **3** directed back on the source; reflected. **4** *of a thought* introspective.

reflexive (rĭ-flĕk'sĭv) *adj.* **1** *Gram.* **a** *of a pronoun* showing that the object of a verb is the same as the subject, e.g., in *he cut himself*, *himself* is a reflexive pronoun. **b** *of a verb* used with a reflexive pronoun as object. **2** automatic. ► **reflexively** *adv.*

reflexology *noun* therapy for health problems and illnesses in which the soles of the feet are massaged, based on the belief that different parts of the soles relate to different parts of the body. ► **reflexologist** *noun*

reforest *verb trans.* (**reforested, reforesting**) *Bot.* to replant trees in a cleared area of land that was formerly forested. ► **reforestation** *noun*

reform (rĭ-fôrm') *verb trans., intrans.* (**reformed, reforming**) **1** to improve or remove faults from (a person, behavior, etc.). **2** to give up bad habits, improve one's behavior, etc. **3** to stop or abolish (misconduct, an abuse, etc.). —*noun* **1** a correction or improvement, esp. in a social or political system. **2** improvement in one's behavior or morals. ► **reformable** *adj.* ► **reformative** *adj.* ► **reformer** *noun*

reformation *noun* **1** the act or process of reforming or being reformed; improvement. **2** (**Reformation**) the 16th-c religious movement which began by trying to reform the Roman Catholic Church and which led to the establishment of the Protestant churches in Europe.

reformatory *noun* (*pl.* **reformatories**) a school for reforming the behavior of young offenders. *Also called* **reform school**.

refraction *noun* *Phys.* a change in the direction of a ray of light, sound, etc when it passes from one medium to another in which its speed is different. ► **refract** *verb trans.* ► **refractive** *adj.*

refractory (rĭ-frăk'tə-rē) *adj.* **1** refusing to change or compromise. **2** *of a material* having a high melting point. —*noun* (*pl.* **refractories**) *Chem.* a refractory material. ► **refractoriness** *noun*

refrain[1] *verb intrans.* (**refrained, refraining**) (**refrain from (something)**) to keep oneself from (acting in a certain way); to avoid (it).

refrain[2] (rĭ-frān') *noun* a phrase or group of lines repeated at the end of each stanza or verse in a poem or song.

refresh *verb trans., intrans.* (**refreshed, refreshing**) **1 a** *of food, rest, etc.* to give renewed strength, energy, and enthusiasm

to. **b** to be the source of renewed strength or energy. **c** to revive (someone, oneself, etc.) with food, rest, etc. **2** to provide a new supply of; to replenish. **3** to make cool. **4** to make (one's memory) clearer and stronger by reading or listening to the source of information again. ► **refresher** *noun* ► **refreshing** *adj.*

refreshment *noun* **1** the act of refreshing or state of being refreshed. **2** something that refreshes. **3** (**refreshments**) food and drink.

refrigerant (rĭ-frĭj'ə-rənt) *noun* a liquid used in the cooling mechanism of a refrigerator. —*adj.* serving to cool.

refrigerate (rĭ-frĭj'ə-rāt,) *verb trans.* (**refrigerated, refrigerating**) to make or keep (food) cold or frozen to prevent it from spoiling. ► **refrigeration** *noun*

refrigerator *noun* an insulated cabinet-shaped device which keeps food cold, thereby slowing down its rate of decay.

refuel *verb trans., intrans.* (**refueled** or **refuelled, refueling** or **refuelling**) **1** to supply (an aircraft, ship, etc.) with more fuel. **2** *of an aircraft, etc.* to take on more fuel.

refuge (rĕf'yōōj, -yōōzh,) *noun* **1** shelter or protection from danger or trouble. **2** a place, person, or thing offering such shelter.

refugee (rĕf,yə-jē') *noun* a person who seeks refuge, esp. from religious or political persecution, in another country.

refulgent *adj.* shining brightly; radiant; beaming. ► **refulgence** *noun*

refund *verb trans.* (rĭ-fənd', rē'fənd,) (**refunded, refunding**) to pay (money, etc.) back to (someone). —*noun* (rē'fənd) **1** the paying back of money, etc. **2** the money, etc., paid back. ► **refundable** *adj.*

refurbish *verb trans.* (**refurbished, refurbishing**) to renovate and redecorate. ► **refurbishment** *noun*

refuse[1] (rĭ-fyōōz') *verb trans., intrans.* (**refused, refusing**) **1** to declare oneself unwilling to do what one has been asked or told to do, etc.; to say no. **2** to decline to accept (something). **3** to refuse to allow (access, etc.) or give (permission). **4** to show or express unwillingness. ► **refusal** *noun*

refuse[2] (rĕf'yōōs,, -yōōz,) *noun* any material thrown away; waste; garbage.

refute (rĭ-fyōōt') *verb trans.* (**refuted, refuting**) **1** to prove that (a person, statement, theory, etc.) is wrong. **2** to deny. ► **refutable** *adj.* ► **refutation** *noun*

regain *verb trans.* (**regained, regaining**) **1** to get back again or recover. **2** to get back to (a place).

regal (rē'gəl) *adj.* of, like, or suitable for a king or queen: *a regal pose.* ► **regally** *adv.*

regale (rĭ-gāl') *verb trans.* (**regaled, regaling**) **1** (**regale (someone) with (some-**

thing)) to amuse (someone) with (stories or other entertainment). **2** to entertain (someone) lavishly.

regalia (rĭ-gāl′yə) *pl. noun* **1** objects, such as a crown and scepter, that are a sign of royalty, used at coronations, etc. **2** the ornaments, ceremonial robes, etc., worn as a sign of a person's importance or authority.

regard *verb trans.* (**regarded, regarding**) **1** to consider (someone or something) in a specified way: *regard him as a friend.* **2** to pay attention to; to take notice of. **3** to look at attentively or steadily. **4** to have a connection with or relate to. —*noun* **1** thorough, serious attentiveness. **2** consideration; sympathy. **3** respect and affection. **4** a gaze or look. **5** (**regards**) good wishes; greetings. ▸ **regardful** *adj.*

regarding *prep.* about; concerning.

regardless *adv.* not thinking or caring about costs, dangers, etc.; in spite of everything. —*adj.* (**regardless of (something)**) taking no notice of (it). ▸ **regardlessly** *adv.*

regatta (rĭ-gät′ə -gät′ə) *noun* a meeting for yacht or boat races.

> From the name of a gondola race held on the Grand Canal in Venice

regency *noun* (*pl.* **regencies**) **1** the position of a regent. **2** government or the period of government by a regent.

regenerate *verb trans., intrans.* (rē-jĕn′ə-rāt′) (**regenerated, regenerating**) **1** to make or become morally or spiritually improved. **2** to develop or give new life or energy; to be brought back or bring back to life or original strength again. —*adj.* (rē-jĕn′ə-rət) having been regenerated, esp. in having improved morally, spiritually, or physically. ▸ **regeneration** *noun* ▸ **regenerative** *adj.* ▸ **regenerator** *noun*

regent *noun* a person who governs a country during a monarch's absence, childhood, or illness. —*adj.* acting as regent; ruling.

reggae (rĕg′ā) *noun* popular West Indian music with a strong syncopated beat.

regicide (rĕj′ĭ-sīd′) *noun* **1** the killing of a king. **2** a person who kills a king.

regime *or* **régime** (rā-zhēm′, rĭ-) *noun* **1** a system of government or a particular government. **2** a regimen.

regimen (rĕj′ə-mən) *noun* a course of treatment, esp. of diet and exercise, which is necessary for one's good health.

regiment *noun* (rĕj′ə-mənt) **1** a unit in the US Army or the US Marines consisting of at least two battalions. **2** a large number. —*verb trans.* (rĕj′ə-mĕnt′) (**regimented, regimenting**) **1** to organize or control strictly, usu. too strictly. **2** to form into a regiment or regiments. ▸ **regimental** *adj.* ▸ **regimen-**

tation *noun* ▸ **regimented** *adj.*

region *noun* **1** an area of the world or a country with particular geographical, social, etc., characteristics. **2** an area of the body around or near a specific part, organ, etc.

regional *adj.* **1** of or relating to a region. **2** *of pain* affecting a particular area of the body. ▸ **regionally** *adv.*

register *noun* **1** a written list or record of names, events, etc., or a book containing one. **2** a machine or other device that records and lists information, esp. a cash register. **3** *Mus.* the range of tones produced by a human singing voice or an instrument. **4** *Linguistics* a style of speech or language suitable for and used in a particular situation. —*verb trans., intrans.* (**registered, registering**) **1** to enter (an event, a name, etc.) in an official register. **2** to enter one's name and address in a hotel register on arrival. **3** (**register for (something)**) to enroll formally for (it). **4** to insure (a letter or parcel) against its possible loss in the mail. **5** *of a device* to record and usu. show (speed, information, etc.) automatically. **6** *of a person's face, etc.* to show (a particular feeling). **7** to make an impression on (someone), e.g., being understood, remembered, etc.

registered nurse (ABBREV. **RN**, **R.N.**) a graduate nurse who has passed state licensing boards and who is legally and technically qualified to practice nursing.

registrar *noun* **1** a person who keeps an official register, esp. of births, deaths, and marriages. **2** a senior administrator in a university responsible for student records.

registration *noun* **1** the act or an instance of registering. **2** something registered.

registry *noun* (*pl.* **registries**) **1** an office or place where registers are kept. **2** registration.

regress *verb intrans.* (rĭ-grĕs′) (**regressed, regressing**) to return to a former less perfect, less advanced, etc., state or condition. —*noun* (rĕ′grĕs′) a return to a former less perfect, less advanced, etc., state or condition. ▸ **regressive** *adj.* ▸ **regressively** *adv.*

regression *noun* **1** the act of regressing. **2** *Psychol.* a return to an earlier level of functioning, e.g., to infantile behavior by an adult.

regret (rĭ-grĕt′) *verb trans.* (**regretted, regretting**) to feel sorry, distressed, disappointed, etc., about. —*noun* **1 a** a feeling of sorrow, distress, or disappointment. **b** an expression of sorrow for a mistake or an offense. **2** (**regrets**) a polite expression of disappointment, used esp. when declining an invitation. ▸ **regretful** *adj.* ▸ **regretfully** *adv.* ▸ **regrettable** *adj.* ▸ **regrettably** *adv.*

regroup (rē-grōōp′) *verb intrans., trans.* (**regrouped, regrouping**) **1** to form into a new or different group. **2** to collect one's thoughts and reorganize one's schedule.

regt. *abbrev.* regiment.

regular *adj.* **1** usual; normal; customary. **2** arranged, occurring, acting, etc., in a fixed pattern of predictable or equal intervals of space or time: *at regular intervals.* **3** agreeing with a rule, custom, or normal practice, etc., and accepted as correct. **4** symmetrical or even; having all the faces, sides, or angles, etc., the same. **5** *colloq.* complete; absolute. **6** *Gram.,* of a noun, verb, etc. following one of the usual patterns of formation. **7** *of troops, an army, etc.* of or forming a permanent professional body. **8** *colloq.* behaving in an acceptable, likable way: *He's just a regular guy.* —*noun* **1** a soldier in a professional regular army. **2** *colloq.* a frequent customer. ▸ **regularity** *noun* ▸ **regularly** *adv.*

regularize *verb trans.* (**regularized, regularizing**) to make regular. ▸ **regularization** *noun*

regulate (rĕg′yə-lāt,) *verb trans.* (**regulated, regulating**) **1** to control or adjust something as required. **2** to control or direct (a person, thing, etc.) according to rules. ▸ **regulator** *noun* ▸ **regulatory** *adj.*

regulation *noun* **1** a rule or instruction. **2** the act of regulating or the state of being regulated.

regurgitate (rĭ-gər′jə-tāt,) *verb trans., intrans.* (**regurgitated, regurgitating**) **1** to bring back (food) into the mouth after it has been swallowed. **2** to repeat exactly (something already said). ▸ **regurgitation** *noun*

rehab (rē′hăb,) *colloq. verb trans.* (**rehabbed, rehabbing, rehabs**) to rehabilitate. —*noun* a rehabilitation.

rehabilitate (rē,ə-bĭl′ə-tāt,, rē,hə-) *verb trans.* (**rehabilitated, rehabilitating**) **1** to help (someone) readapt to normal life, esp. by providing vocational training or therapy. **2** to restore to a former state or rank, or to restore former rights or privileges. ▸ **rehabilitation** *noun*

rehash *colloq. verb trans.* (pronounced with stress on the last syllable) (**rehashed, rehashing, rehashes**) to reuse or rework (subject matter that has been used before). —*noun* (pronounced with stress on the first syllable) a reusing or reworking.

rehearsal *noun* **1** the act of rehearsing. **2** a performance of a play, etc., for practice.

rehearse (rĭ-hərs′) *verb trans., intrans.* (**rehearsed, rehearsing**) **1** to practice (a play, piece of music, etc.) before performing (it) in front of an audience. **2** to train (a person) for performing in front of an audience. **3** to repeat or say over again.

reign (rān) *noun* **1** the time during which a

monarch rules. **2** the time during which something rules or is in control: *a reign of terror.* —*verb intrans.* (**reigned, reigning**) **1** to be a monarch. **2** to be present, exist, or dominate.

reigning *adj., of a winner, champion, etc.* holding the title of champion, etc.

reimburse (rē,ĭm-bərs′) *verb trans.* (**reimbursed, reimbursing**) to pay (a person) money to cover (expenses, losses, etc.). ▸ **reimbursement** *noun*

rein *noun* **1** (*usu.* **reins**) each of two straps attached to a bridle for guiding a horse. **2** a means of control or government. —*verb trans.* (**reined, reining**) (*usu.* **rein (someone** *or* **something) in**) to stop or restrain with or as if with reins. —**give a free rein (to)** to permit freedom of action.

reincarnation *noun* **1** in some beliefs, the rebirth of the soul in another body after death. **2** a person after death born into another body. **3** an idea or a principle presented in a different form. ▸ **reincarnate** *verb trans., intrans*

reindeer *noun* (*pl.* **reindeer, reindeers**) a large deer with antlers found in northern Europe, Asia, and America.

reinforce (rē,ĭn-fōrs′) *verb trans.* (**reinforced, reinforcing**) **1 a** to give additional support to. **b** to cause to be generally strong or stronger. **2** to make (an army, force, etc.) stronger by providing more soldiers and weapons, etc. ▸ **reinforcement** *noun*

reinforced concrete *Engineering* concrete in which steel bars, wires, or mesh have been embedded in order to increase its strength.

reinstate *verb trans.* (**reinstated, reinstating**) to restore to a former, more power-ful, position, status, or rank. ▸ **reinstatement** *noun*

reiterate (rē-ĭt′ə-rāt,) *verb trans.* (**reiterated, reiterating**) to repeat, esp. several times. ▸ **reiteration** *noun*

reject (rĭ-jĕkt′) *verb trans.* (**rejected, rejecting**) **1** to refuse to accept, agree to, admit, believe, etc. **2** to throw away or discard. **3** *of the body* to fail to accept (new tissue or an organ from another body). (rē′jĕkt,) —*noun* a person or thing rejected. ▸ **rejection** *noun*

rejoice *verb intrans., trans.* (**rejoiced, rejoicing**) **1** to feel or show great happiness. **2** to give joy to; to make glad. ▸ **rejoice** *noun*

rejoin[1] (rĭ-join′) *verb trans., intrans.* (**rejoined, rejoining**) to say in reply, esp. abruptly or wittily.

rejoin[2] (rē-join′) *verb intrans., trans.* (**rejoined, rejoining**) to join again.

rejoinder *noun* an answer or remark, often one made abruptly or wittily in reply.

rejuvenate (rĭ-jōō'və-nāt,) *verb trans.* (**rejuvenated, rejuvenating**) to make (a person) feel, look, etc., young again. ▸ **rejuvenation** *noun*

relapse *verb intrans.* (rĭ-lăps') (**relapsed, relapsing**) to return to a former bad or undesirable state or condition, such as ill health or bad habits. —*noun* (rĭ-lăps', rē'lăps,) the act or process of relapsing.

relate *verb trans.* (**related, relating**) 1 to tell or narrate (a story). 2 (**relate (one thing) to** *or* **with (another)**) to show or form a connection or relationship between (facts, events, etc.). 3 (**relate to** *or* **with (something)**) to have or form a connection or relationship: *Crime relates to poverty.* 4 (**relate to (something)**) to be concerned with. 5 (**relate to (someone)**) *colloq.* to get on well with (another).

related *adj.* 1 belonging to the same family. 2 connected: *this and related issues.*

relation *noun* 1 a connection or relationship between one person or thing and another. 2 a person who belongs to the same family as another person through birth or marriage; a relative. 3 reference; respect: *in relation to.* 4 a telling or narrating. 5 (**relations**) a social, political, or personal contact between people, countries, etc. b sexual intercourse.

relationship *noun* 1 the state of being related. 2 the friendship, contact, communications, etc., which exist between people, countries, etc. 3 an emotional or sexual affair.

relative (rĕl'ət-ĭv) *noun* a person who is related to someone else by birth or marriage. —*adj.* 1 compared with something else; comparative: *the relative speeds of a car and train.* 2 existing only in relation to something else. 3 (**relative to (something)**) in proportion to (it). 4 relevant. 5 *Gram.* a of a pronoun referring to something real or implied which has already been stated and attaching a subordinate clause to it, as *who* in *the children who are leaving.* b of a clause attached to a preceding word, phrase, etc., by a relative word such as *which* and *who.* ▸ **relatively** *adv.*

relativism *noun* a philosophical position that maintains that there are truths and values, but denies that they are absolute. ▸ **relativist** *noun*

relativity *noun* 1 the condition of being relative to and therefore affected by something else. 2 *Phys.* two theories of motion developed by Albert Einstein, which recognize the dependence of space, time, and other physical measurements on the position and motion of the observer who is making the measurements. *Also called* **general** *or* **special theory of relativity.**

relax *verb trans., intrans.* (**relaxed, relaxing**) 1 to make or become less tense, nervous, or worried. 2 to give or take rest completely from work or effort. 3 to make or become less strict or severe. 4 to lessen the force, strength, or intensity of: *relax one's vigilance.* 5 to become weak or loose. ▸ **relaxation** *noun* ▸ **relaxed** *adj.* ▸ **relaxing** *adj.*

relaxant *noun Med.* a drug that can make a person feel less tense.

relay *noun* (pronounced with stress on the first syllable) 1 a set of people, supply of materials, etc., that replace others doing or being used for some task, etc. 2 *Sport* a relay race. 3 *Electr.* an electrical switching device that, in response to a change in an electric circuit, opens or closes one or more contacts in the same or another circuit. —*verb trans.* (pronounced with stress on either the last or the first syllable) (**relayed, relaying**) 1 to receive and pass on (news, a message, a television program, etc.). 2 to rebroadcast (a program received from another station or source).

relay race *Sport* a race between teams of runners, swimmers, etc., in which each member of the team covers part of the total distance.

release *verb trans.* (**released, releasing**) 1 to free (a prisoner, etc.) from captivity. 2 to relieve (someone) suffering from something unpleasant, a duty, burden, etc. 3 to loosen (one's grip) and stop holding. 4 to make (news, information, etc.) publicly known. 5 to offer (a film, record, book, etc.) for sale, performance, etc. 6 to move (a catch, brake, etc.) so that it no longer prevents something from moving, operating, etc. 7 to give off or emit (heat, gas, etc.). —*noun* 1 the act of releasing or the state of being released. 2 the act of making available for sale, performance, publication, etc. 3 something made available for sale, performance, etc., esp. a new record or film. 4 an item of news made public, or a document containing this. 5 an order or document allowing a prisoner, etc., to be released. 6 a handle or catch that holds and releases part of a mechanism.

relegate (rĕl'ə-gāt,) *verb trans.* (**relegated, relegating**) 1 to move (someone) down to a lower grade, position, status, division, etc. 2 to refer (a decision, etc.) to (someone or something) for action to be taken. ▸ **relegation** *noun*

relent (rĭ-lĕnt') *verb intrans.* (**relented, relenting**) 1 to become less severe or less unkind. 2 to give way and agree to something one initially would not accept.

relentless *adj.* 1 having or displaying no pity; harsh. 2 never stopping. ▸ **relentlessly** *adv.* ▸ **relentlessness** *noun*

relevant adj. having a bearing on the matter in hand. ▸ **relevance** or **relevancy** noun

reliable adj. able to be trusted or relied on. ▸ **reliability** noun ▸ **reliably** adv.

reliant adj. relying on or having confidence in; trusting. ▸ **reliance** noun

relic noun 1 (often **relics**) a part or fragment of an object left after the rest has decayed. 2 an object valued as being a memorial or souvenir of the past. 3 something left from a past time, esp. a custom, belief, or practice. 4 a part of the body of a saint or martyr or a fragment of an object connected with him or her, preserved as holy. 5 (**relics**) the remains of a dead person; a corpse.

relief noun 1 the lessening or removal of pain, worry, oppression, or distress. 2 a the calmness, relaxation, happiness, etc., which follows the lessening or removal of pain, worry, etc. b that which lessens pain, worry, boredom, or monotony. 3 help given to people in need; welfare. 4 a person who takes over a job or task from another person, usu. after a given period of time. 5 a method of sculpture in which figures project from a flat surface. 6 a clear, sharp outline caused by contrast. 7 the variations in height above sea level of an area of land.

relief map a map that shows the variations in the height of the land, either by shading, or by being a three-dimensional model.

relieve verb trans. (**relieved, relieving**) 1 to lessen or stop (a person's pain, worry, boredom, etc.). 2 (**relieve (someone) of (something)**) a to take a physical or mental burden from (someone). b to take or steal (it) from (someone). 3 to give help or assistance to (someone in need). 4 to make less monotonous or tedious, esp. by providing a contrast. 5 to free or dismiss, e.g., from a duty or restriction. 6 to take over a job or task from (someone).

religion noun 1 a belief in or the worship of a god or gods. 2 a particular system of belief or worship, such as Christianity or Judaism. 3 that to which one is totally devoted and which rules one's life: Skiing is his religion.

religious adj. 1 of or relating to religion. 2 following the rules or forms of worship of a particular religion very closely; pious; devout. 3 taking great care to do something properly; conscientious. 4 of or relating to the monastic way of life. —noun (pl. **religious**) a person bound by monastic vows, e.g., a monk. ▸ **religiously** adv.

relinquish verb trans. (**relinquished, relinquishing**) 1 to give up or abandon. 2 to release one's hold of. 3 to renounce possession or control of (a claim, right, etc.). ▸ **relinquishment** noun

reliquary (rĕl′ə-kwĕr˒ē) noun (pl. **reliquar-** ies) a container for holy relics.

relish verb trans. (**relished, relishing**) 1 to enjoy greatly or with discrimination. 2 to look forward to with great pleasure. —noun 1 pleasure; enjoyment. 2 a spicy appetizing flavor, or a sauce or pickle that adds this to food. 3 zest, charm, liveliness, or gusto.

relive (rē-lĭv′) verb trans. (**relived, reliving**) to experience again, esp. in the imagination.

relocate (rē-lō′kāt,) verb trans., intrans. (**re-located, relocating**) to move (a business, one's home, etc.) from one place, town, etc., to another. ▸ **relocation** noun

reluctant adj. not wanting; unwilling. ▸ **reluctance** noun ▸ **reluctantly** adv.

rely verb intrans. (**relied, relying, relies**) (**rely on (someone or something)**) 1 to depend on or need (someone or something). 2 to trust (someone) to do (something).

REM abbrev. Physiol. rapid eye movement.

remain verb intrans. (**remained, remaining**) 1 to be left when something else, another part, etc., has been lost, taken away, used up, etc. 2 to stay in the same place. 3 to be still (the same); to continue to be. 4 to still need (to be done, shown, dealt with, etc.): That remains to be decided.

remainder noun 1 the number or part that is left after the rest has been taken away. 2 Math. a the amount left over when one number cannot be divided exactly by another number. b the amount left when one number is subtracted from another. 3 a copy of a book that is sold at a reduced price when demand for that book has come to an end. —verb trans. (**remaindered, remaindering**) to sell (a book) as a remainder.

remains pl. noun 1 what is left after part has been taken away, eaten, destroyed, etc. 2 a corpse.

remake verb trans. (**rē-māk′**) (pa t and pa p **remade**; pr p **remaking**) to make again, esp. in a new way. —noun (rē′māk,) something made again, esp. a new version of a movie.

remand (rĭ-mănd′) Law verb trans. (**re-manded, remanding**) 1 to send (a person accused of a crime) back into custody. 2 to return (a case) from a higher to a lower court. —noun an act of remanding.

remark verb trans., intrans. 1 to make a comment. 2 (**remark on (something)**) to notice and comment on (it). —noun a comment; an observation.

remarkable adj. worth mentioning; unusual; extraordinary. ▸ **remarkably** adv.

remedial (rə-mēd′e-əl) adj. serving as a remedy; able to or intended to correct or put right. ▸ **remedially** adv.

remedy noun (pl. **remedies**) 1 a drug or treatment that controls or cures a disease. 2 that which solves a problem or gets rid of an undesirable factor or thing. —verb trans. (**remedied, remedying, remedies**) to put right or correct; to be a remedy for.

remember verb trans., intrans. (**remembered, remembering**) 1 to bring to mind (something or someone) that has been previously forgotten. 2 to keep (a fact, idea, etc.) in one's mind. 3 to pass (a person's) good wishes and greetings to: Remember me to your parents. 4 to commemorate.

remembrance noun 1 the act of remembering or of being remembered. 2 something that reminds a person of something or someone else; a souvenir. 3 a memory or recollection.

remind verb trans. (**reminded, reminding**) (**remind (someone) of (something)**) 1 to cause (someone) to remember (it). 2 to make (someone) think about (someone or something else), esp. because of a similarity. ▸ **reminder** noun

reminisce (rĕm,ə-nĭs′) verb intrans. (**reminisced, reminiscing**) to think, talk, or write about things remembered from the past.

reminiscent adj. 1 (**reminiscent of (something or someone)**) similar, so as to remind one of (something or someone else): a painting reminiscent of Turner. 2 of a person thinking often about the past. ▸ **reminiscence** noun

remiss adj. failing to pay attention; careless; negligent. ▸ **remissly** adv. ▸ **remissness** noun

remission noun 1 a lessening in force or effect, esp. in the symptoms of a disease. 2 forgiveness from sin; pardon. 3 an act of remitting.

remit verb trans., intrans. (rĭ-mĭt′) (**remitted, remitting**) 1 to cancel or refrain from demanding (a debt, punishment, etc). 2 to make or become loose, slack, or relaxed. 3 to send (money) in payment. 4 to refer (a matter for decision, etc.) to another authority. 5 to become less severe for a period of time. 6 to send or put back into a previous state. 7 to forgive. —noun (rĭ-mĭt′, rē′mĭt,) 1 an act of remitting. 2 a matter that is remitted for more consideration.

remittance noun 1 the sending of money in payment. 2 the money so sent.

remittent adj. of a disease becoming less severe at times.

remix (rē-mĭks′) verb trans. (**remixed, remixing**) to mix again in a different way, esp. to mix (a record) again, changing the balance of the different parts, etc. —noun (pronounced with stress on the first syllable) a remixed recording.

remnant noun 1 a small piece or amount of something larger, or a small number of a large quantity of things left unsold. 2 a surviving trace or vestige.

remonstrance noun 1 the act of remonstrating. 2 a strong, usu. formal, protest.

remonstrate (rĭ-män′strāt,) verb trans., intrans. (**remonstrated, remonstrating**) 1 (**remonstrate with (someone)**) to protest to (someone), or to task (someone) to task. 2 to engage in opposition by arguing against something. ▸ **remonstration** noun

remorse noun a deep feeling of guilt and regret for something wrong or bad that one has done. ▸ **remorseful** adj. ▸ **remorsefully** adv.

remorseless adj. without pity; cruel. ▸ **remorselessly** adv.

remote adj. 1 far away or distant in time or place. 2 out of the way. 3 operated or controlled from a distance. 4 distantly related. 5 very small or slight: a remote chance. 6 of a person's manner not friendly or interested; aloof. ▸ **remoteness** noun

remote control Electron. 1 the control of machinery or electrical devices from a distance, by means of radio electrical signals. 2 a device used to operate a television set from a distance.

remotely adv. in a remote way or degree: The two issues are not remotely the same.

remove verb trans. (**removed, removing**) 1 to move (a person, thing, etc.) to a different place. 2 to take off (a piece of clothing). 3 to get rid of. 4 to dismiss (from a job, position, etc.). 5 to move to a new house. —noun 1 a removal. 2 the degree of difference separating two things. ▸ **removable** adj. ▸ **removal** noun ▸ **remover** noun

removed adj. 1 separated or distant. 2 of cousins separated by a usu. specified number of generations.

remunerate (rĭ-myōō′nə-rāt,) verb trans. (**remunerated, remunerating**) 1 to pay for services done. 2 to recompense. ▸ **remuneration** noun ▸ **remunerative** adj.

renaissance noun any rebirth or revival.

renal (rēn′l) adj. of, relating to, or in the area of the kidneys.

renascence (rə-näs′əns, -nā′səns) noun a new birth or a rebirth, esp. a cultural rebirth or revival. ▸ **renascent** adj.

rend verb trans., intrans. (pa t and pa p **rent** or **rended**; pr p **rending**) 1 to tear, esp. using force or violence. 2 to become torn, esp. violently.

render verb trans. (**rendered, rendering**) 1 to cause to become: a signature that rendered the contract valid. 2 to give or provide (help, a service, etc.). 3 to pay (money) or perform (a duty), esp. in return for something. 4 (also **render (something) up**) to give up, release, or yield. 5 to express (something) in another language, with the same meaning. **6** to portray or reproduce, esp. in painting or music. **7** to present or submit for payment, approval, consideration, etc.: *rendered her travel expenses.* **8** to melt down (fat).

rendezvous (rän'dĭ-vōō,) *noun* **1** an appointment to meet, or the meeting itself, at a specified time and place. **2** the place where such a meeting is to be; a place where people meet. —*verb intrans.* (**rendezvous, rendezvoused**) to meet at an appointed place.

rendition *noun* **1** a performance or interpretation (of a piece of music or a dramatic role, etc.). **2** an act of translating.

renegade *noun* a person who deserts the religious, political, etc., group to which he or she belongs in order to join a rival or enemy group.

renege (rĭ-nĭg', -nĕg') *verb intrans., trans.* (**reneged, reneging**) **1** (**renege on** (**something**)) to go back on a promise, agreement, one's word, etc. **2** to renounce (a promise, etc.) or desert (a person, faith, etc.). **3** *Cards* to not follow suit when required to. ▸ **reneger** *noun*

renew *verb trans., intrans.* (**renewed, renewing**) **1** to make fresh or like new again; to restore. **2** to begin or begin to do again; to repeat. **3** to begin (an activity) again after a break. **4 a** to make (a license, lease, loan, etc.) valid for a further period of time. **b** to extend (the loan of a library book or a tape). **5** to replenish or replace. ▸ **renewable** *adj.* ▸ **renewal** *noun* ▸ **renewer** *noun*

rennet *noun* a substance obtained from the stomachs of calves and used for curdling milk when making cheese.

renounce *verb trans., intrans.* (**renounced, renouncing**) **1** to give up (a claim, title, right, etc.), esp. formally and publicly. **2** to refuse to recognize or associate with. **3** to give up (a bad habit). **4** *Cards* to fail to follow suit. ▸ **renouncement** *noun*

renovate (rĕn'ə-vāt,) *verb trans.* (**renovated, renovating**) to restore (esp. a building) to a former and better condition. ▸ **renovation** *noun* ▸ **renovator** *noun*

renown *noun* the condition of being widely known. ▸ **renowned** *adj.*

rent¹ *noun* money paid to the owner of property by a tenant in return for the use or occupation of that property. —*verb trans., intrans.* (**rented, renting**) **1** to pay rent for (a building, etc.). **2** (**rent** (**something**) or **rent** (**something**) **out**) to allow the use of (one's property) in return for payment of rent. **3** to be hired out for rent.

rent² *noun* an opening or split made by tearing, often violently. —*verb see* **rend.**

rental *noun* **1** money paid as rent. **2** the act of renting.

renunciation *noun* **1** the act of renouncing. **2** a formal declaration of renouncing.

reorder *verb trans.* (**reordered, reordering**) **1** to order again. **2** to place or arrange in a different order.

Rep. *abbrev.* representative (sense 1b).

rep¹ *noun colloq.* a representative.

rep² *noun colloq.* a repertory theater or company.

rep³ *noun colloq.* one's reputation.

repaid *see* **repay.**

repair¹ *verb trans.* (**repaired, repairing**) **1** to restore (something damaged or broken) to good, working condition. **2** to put right, heal, or make up for (something wrong that has been done). —*noun* **1** the act of repairing. **2** a condition or state: *in good repair.* **3** a part or place that has been mended or repaired. ▸ **repairable** *adj.*

repair² *verb intrans.* (**repaired, repairing**) (**repair to** (**a place**)) to go (there); to take oneself off to (it).

reparable (rĕp'ə-rə-bəl) *adj.* able to be put right.

reparation *noun* **1** the act of making up for (something wrong that has been done). **2** money paid or something done for this purpose. **3** (*usu.* **reparations**) compensation paid after a war by a defeated nation for the damage caused.

repartee (rĕp,ər-tē') *noun* **1** the practice or skill of making spontaneous witty replies. **2** conversation having many such replies.

repast *noun* a sumptuous formal meal.

repatriate (rē-pā'trē-āt,) *verb trans.* (**repatriated, repatriating**) to send (someone) back to the country of (that person's) origin. ▸ **repatriation** *noun*

repay *verb trans.* (*pa t and pa p* **repaid**; *pr p* **repaying**) **1** to pay back (money). **2** to do or give something to (someone) in return for (something done or given to oneself). ▸ **repayable** *adj.* ▸ **repayment** *noun*

repeal *verb trans.* (**repealed, repealing**) to make (a law, etc.) no longer valid. —*noun* the act of repealing (a law, etc.). ▸ **repealable** *adj.*

repeat *verb trans., intrans.* (rĭ-pēt') (**repeated, repeating**) **1** to say, do, etc., again. **2** to tell (something one has heard) to someone else, esp. when one ought not to. **3** to say (something) from memory. **4** to occur again; to recur. —*noun* (rĭ-pēt', rē'pēt,) **1** an act of repeating. **2** something repeated, esp. a television program that has been broadcast before. **3** *Mus.* a passage to be repeated, or a sign marking this. —*adj.* (pronounced with stress on the last syllable) repeated: *a repeat showing.* ▸ **repeatable** *adj.*

repeated *adj.* 1 done again. 2 having been reiterated. ▸ **repeatedly** *adv.*

repel *verb trans., intrans.* (**repelled, repelling**) 1 to force or drive back or away. 2 to cause a feeling of disgust or loathing. 3 to fail to mix with, absorb, or be attracted by (something else). 4 to reject.

repellent *noun* something that repels (e.g., insects). —*adj.* repelling, esp. causing a feeling of disgust or loathing: *a repellant odor.* ▸ **repellently** *adv.*

repent *verb trans., intrans.* (**repented, repenting**) 1 to feel sorrow or regret for (something one has done); to wish some action, etc., undone. 2 to be sorry for all the bad things one has done and decide to live a better life.

repentance *noun* 1 the act of repenting. 2 the state of being penitent. ▸ **repentant** *adj.*

repercussion *noun* 1 (*often* **repercussions**) a usu. bad unforeseen or indirect result or consequence of an action or event. 2 an echo or reverberation. ▸ **repercussive** *adj.*

repertoire (rĕp′ə-twär,, -or-) *noun* 1 the list of songs, plays, operas, etc., that a performer, singer, group of actors, etc., is able or ready to perform. 2 a range or stock of skills, techniques, talents, etc., that someone or something has.

repertory *noun* (*pl.* **repertories**) 1 a repertoire (sense 1). 2 a group of actors who perform a series of plays from their repertoire in the course of a season at one theater. 3 a a theater where a repertory company performs its plays. *Also called* **repertory theater.** b repertory theaters in general.

repetition *noun* 1 the act of repeating or the condition of being repeated. 2 a thing repeated.

repetitious *adj.* having too much repetition. ▸ **repetitiously** *adv.* ▸ **repetitiousness** *noun*

repetitive (rĭ-pĕt′ət-ĭv) *adj.* marked by repetition. ▸ **repetitively** *adv.* ▸ **repetitiveness** *noun*

repine *verb intrans.* (**repined, repining**) to fret or feel discontented.

replace *verb trans.* (**replaced, replacing**) 1 to put (something) back into a previous or proper position. 2 to take the place of or substitute for. ▸ **replaceable** *adj.* ▸ **replacement** *noun*

replay *noun* (rē′plā,) 1 the playing of a tape or recording again. 2 the playing of a tennis match, etc., again. —*verb* (rē-plā′) (**replayed, replaying**) to play (a tape, recording, tennis match, etc.) again.

replenish *verb trans.* (**replenished, replenishing**) to fill up again or stock, esp. with a supply of something which has been used up. ▸ **replenishment** *noun*

replete *adj.* 1 (**replete with (something)**) completely or well supplied with (it). 2 *formal* having eaten enough or more than enough. ▸ **repletion** *noun*

replica *noun* 1 an exact copy, esp. of a work of art. 2 a facsimile; a copy.

replicate (rĕp′lĭ-kāt,) *verb trans., intrans.* (**replicated, replicating**) 1 to make a replica of. 2 to repeat (an experiment).

reply *verb intrans., trans.* (**replied, replying, replies**) 1 to respond in words, writing, or action. 2 to say or do (something) in response. —*noun* (*pl.* **replies**) something said, written, or done in answer or response.

report *noun* 1 a detailed statement or account, esp. after investigation. 2 a detailed, and usu. formal, account of the discussions and decisions of a committee, inquiry, or other group of people. 3 general talk; rumor. 4 character or reputation. 5 a loud explosive noise. —*verb trans., intrans.* (**reported, reporting**) 1 to bring back as an answer, news, or account. 2 to give a formal or official account or description of. 3 a to make a complaint about (someone), esp. to a person in authority. b to make (something) known to a person in authority. 4 (**report for (something)** or **to (someone)**) to present oneself at an appointed place or time, for a particular purpose. 5 (**report to (someone)**) to be responsible to (someone), under (that person's) authority. 6 to account for oneself in a particular way: *report sick.* 7 to act as a news reporter.

report card a written statement of a pupil's schoolwork and social behavior at school.

reportedly *adv.* according to report.

reporter *noun* 1 a person who writes articles and reports for a newspaper, or for broadcast on television or radio. 2 *Law* a court reporter.

repose¹ *noun* a state of rest, calm, or peacefulness. —*verb intrans., trans.* (**reposed, reposing**) 1 to lie resting. 2 to lay (oneself, one's head, etc.) to rest.

repose² *verb trans., intrans.* (**reposed, reposing**) to place (confidence, etc.) in a person or thing: *reposed her trust in him.*

repository *noun* (*pl.* **repositories**) 1 a place or container in which things may be stored, esp. a museum or warehouse. 2 a person or thing thought of as a store of information, knowledge, etc. 3 a trusted person to whom one can confide secrets.

repossess *verb trans.* (**repossessed, repossessing**) *of a creditor* to regain possession of (property or goods), esp. because the debtor has defaulted on payment. ▸ **repossession** *noun*

reprehend *verb trans.* (**reprehended, reprehending**) to find fault with; to blame or reprove.

reprehensible *adj.* deserving blame or criticism. ▸ **reprehensibly** *adv.*

represent *verb trans.* (**represented, representing**) **1** to serve as a symbol or sign for; to stand for or correspond to: *A thesis represents years of hard work.* **2** to speak or act on behalf of. **3** to be a good example of; to typify. **4** to present an image of or portray, esp. through painting or sculpture. **5** to bring clearly to mind: *a film representing all the horrors of war.* **6** to describe in a specified way; to attribute a specified character or quality to. **7** to show, state, or explain.

representation *noun* **1** the act of representing or the state of being represented. **2** a person or thing that represents someone or something else. **3** (*often* **representations**) a strong statement made to present facts, opinions, complaints, or demands. ▸ **representational** *adj.*

representative *adj.* **1** representing or depicting. **2** being a good example; typical. **3** acting as a deputy for someone else. **4** of *government* carried on by elected people. —*noun* **1 a** a person who represents someone or something else, esp. a person who represents, or sells the goods of, a business or company. **b** (ABBREV. **Rep.**) a member of the US House of Representatives or of a state legislature's lower house. **2** a typical example. ▸ **representatively** *adv.* ▸ **representativeness** *noun*

repress *verb trans.* (**repressed, repressing**) **1** to keep (an impulse, etc.) under control. **2** to put down, esp. using force: *repress an insurrection.* **3** to exclude (an unpleasant thought) from one's conscious mind. ▸ **repression** *noun* ▸ **repressive** *adj.* ▸ **repressively** *adv.* ▸ **repressiveness** *noun* ▸ **repressor** *noun*

reprieve *verb trans.* (**reprieved, reprieving**) **1** to delay or cancel the punishment of (a prisoner condemned to death). **2** to give temporary relief from trouble, difficulty, pain, etc. —*noun* **1** the act of delaying or canceling a death sentence. **2** temporary relief, e.g., from trouble, difficulty, or pain.

reprimand *verb trans.* (**reprimanded, reprimanding**) to criticize or rebuke severely, esp. formally. —*noun* severe, usu. formal, criticism or rebuking.

reprint *noun* (pronounced with stress on the first syllable) **1** a copy of a book or an article made by reprinting the original without any changes. **2** an occasion of reprinting. **3** the number of copies of a book or an article so printed. —*verb trans., intrans.* (pronounced with stress on the last syllable) (**reprinted, reprinting**) **1** to print more copies of · (a book). **2** *of a book* to have more copies printed.

reprisal *noun* **1** the act of taking revenge or

retaliating. **2** the usu. forcible taking of foreign land in retaliation for injuries inflicted.

reprise (rĭ-prēz′) *Mus. noun* a repeated passage or theme. —*verb trans.* (**reprised, reprising**) to repeat (an earlier passage or theme) in music.

reproach *verb trans.* (**reproached, reproaching**) to express disapproval of or disappointment with (a person) for a wrongdoing. —*noun* **1** an act of reproaching. **2** (*often* **reproaches**) an expression of disappointment. **3** a cause of disgrace or shame. ▸ **reproachful** *adj.* ▸ **reproachfully** *adv.*

reprobate (rĕp′rə-bāt,) *noun* a person of no moral and ethical principles. —*adj.* unprincipled and immoral.

reproduce *verb trans., intrans.* (**reproduced, reproducing**) **1** to make or produce a copy or imitation of; to duplicate. **2** to make or produce again or anew. **3** to turn out in a specified manner when copied. **4** to produce (new individuals) either sexually or asexually. ▸ **reproducible** *adj.* ▸ **reproduction** *noun* ▸ **reproductive** *adj.* ▸ **reproductively** *adv.*

reproof (rĭ-prōōf′) *noun* blame or criticism; a rebuke.

reprove *verb trans.* (**reproved, reproving**) to blame or condemn (someone) for a fault or some wrong done.

reproving *adj.* disapproving; condemnatory. ▸ **reprovingly** *adv.*

reptile (rĕp′tĭl,) *noun* **1** *Zool.* any of the group of cold-blooded vertebrates which have a body covered with scales or bony plates, e.g. snakes, lizards, and crocodiles. **2** a mean, despicable person. ▸ **reptilian** *adj.*

republic *noun* **1** a form of government in which there is no monarch, and in which supreme power is held by the people or their elected representatives. **2** a country, state, or unit within a state having a similar form of government.

republican *adj.* **1** of or resembling a republic. **2** in favor of or supporting a republican system of government: **3** (**Republican**) of, relating to, or belonging to the Republican Party in the USA. —*noun* **1** a person who favors a republican system of government. **2** (**Republican**) a member or supporter of the Republican Party in the USA. *See also* **democrat** (sense 2). ▸ **republicanism** *noun*

repudiate (rĭ-pyōōd′ē-āt,) *verb trans.* (**repudiated, repudiating**) **1** to deny or reject. **2** to refuse to recognize or have anything to do with; to disown. **3** to refuse to acknowledge or pay (a debt, obligation, etc.). ▸ **repudiation** *noun*

repugnant *adj.* (**repugnant to (someone)**) causing (someone) a feeling of disgust or loathing. ▸ **repugnance** *noun* ▸ **repugnantly** *adv.*

repulse verb trans. (**repulsed, repulsing**) **1** to drive or force back (an enemy). **2** to reject (a person's offer of help, kindness, etc.) with coldness and discourtesy. **3** to cause a feeling of disgust, horror, or loathing in. —noun **1** an act of repulsing or state of being repulsed. **2** a cold, discourteous rejection.

repulsion noun **1** a feeling of disgust, horror, or loathing. **2** a forcing back or being forced back. **3** Phys. a force that tends to push two objects apart, such as that between like electric charges or like magnetic poles.

repulsive adj. causing a feeling of disgust, horror, or loathing. ▸ **repulsively** adv. ▸ **repulsiveness** noun

reputable (rĕp'yət-ə-bəl) adj. well thought of; respected; respectable. ▸ **reputably** adv.

reputation noun **1** a generally held opinion about a person with regard to his or her abilities, moral character, etc. **2** a high opinion generally held about a person or thing; a good name.

repute (rĭ-pyo͞ot') verb trans. (**reputed, reputing**) (**be reputed**) to be generally considered. —noun the condition of being widely known. ▸ **reputed** adj. ▸ **reputedly** adv.

request noun **1** the act of asking for something. **2** something asked for. **3** the state of being asked for or sought after: be in request. —verb trans. (**requested, requesting**) to ask (someone) for (something). —**upon** or **on request** if or when requested.

requiem (rĕk'wē-əm) noun **1** (also **Requiem**) RC Church a mass for the souls of the dead. **2** a piece of music written to accompany a mass for the souls of the dead.

require verb trans. (**required, requiring**) **1** to wish to have; to need. **2** to have as a necessary or essential condition for success, fulfillment, etc. **3** to demand or exact by authority. ▸ **requirement** noun

requisite (rĕk'wə-zĭt) adj. required; necessary; indispensable. —noun a necessity.

requisition noun **1** a usu. written, formal, and authoritative request for supplies or the use of something, esp. by an armed force. **2** the act of formally demanding, requesting, or taking something. —verb trans. (**requisitioned, requisitioning**) to order, take, or demand (supplies, etc.) by official requisition.

requite verb trans. (**requited, requiting**) formal **1** to make a suitable return to or repay (a person) for some act. **2** (**requite** (**one thing**) **for** or **with** (**another**)) to repay (e.g., good with good or evil with evil). ▸ **requital** noun

reran see **rerun**.

reroute verb trans. (**rerouted, rerouting**) to direct (e.g., traffic) along an alternate route.

rerun verb trans. (rē-rən') (pa t **reran**; pa p **rerun**; pr p **rerunning**) **1** to run (a race) again. **2** to broadcast (a series of television or radio programs) again. —noun (rē'rən,) **1** a race that is run again. **2** a series of television or radio programs that are broadcast again.

rescind (rĭ-sĭnd') verb trans. (**rescinded, rescinding**) to annul, or revoke (an order, law, custom, etc.). ▸ **rescindment** noun

rescue verb trans. (**rescued, rescuing**) to free (a person or thing) from danger, evil, trouble, captivity, etc. —noun the act of rescuing or the fact of being rescued. ▸ **rescuer** noun

research (rĭ-sərch', rē'sərch,) noun a detailed, careful investigation into an area of study. —verb trans., intrans. (**researched, researching**) **1** to study (something) using detailed, careful techniques. **2** to carry out research. ▸ **researcher** noun

resemblance (rĭ-zĕm'bləns) noun a likeness: a striking resemblance.

resemble (rĭ-zĕm'bəl) verb trans. (**resembled, resembling**) to be or look like or similar to.

resent verb trans. (**resented, resenting**) to feel anger, bitterness, or ill will toward.

resentful adj. full of or caused by resentment. ▸ **resentfully** adv. ▸ **resentfulness** noun

resentment noun the quality or condition of feeling bitter. ▣ ACRIMONY, BITTERNESS, GALL, RANCOR, RESENTFULNESS.

reservation noun **1** the act of reserving for future use. **2** something (e.g., a hotel room) that has been reserved. **3** (usu. **reservations**) a doubt or objection that prevents one from being able to accept or approve something wholeheartedly. **4** a limiting condition or proviso. **5** an area of land set aside for a particular purpose, esp. in the USA and Canada, for the original inhabitants.

reserve verb trans. (**reserved, reserving**) **1** to obtain or order in advance: reserve a hotel room. **2** to keep back or set aside for the use of a particular person or for a particular purpose. **3** to delay or postpone (a decision, a right, etc.): reserve judgment. —noun **1** something kept back or set aside for later use. **2** the state or condition of being reserved, or an act of reserving. **3** an area of land set aside for a particular purpose, esp. for the protection of animals. **4** shy, cool, cautious, and distant in manner. **5** (also **reserves**) that part of a nation's armed forces that is not part of the regular services, but that can be called up when needed.

reserved adj. **1** having been booked in advance. **2** shy, cool, cautious, and distant.

reservist noun a member of a nation's reserve armed forces.

reservoir (rĕz'əv-wär', -ə-vôr,) *noun* **1** a place, usu. human-made, where water is collected and stored for use by the community. **2** a part of a machine, etc., where liquid is stored. **3** a large store or supply, e.g., of oil or gas underground.

reshuffle *verb trans.* (**reshuffled, reshuffling**) **1** *Cards* to shuffle (cards) again or differently. **2** to reorganize or redistribute (e.g., government posts). —*noun* an act of reshuffling; the result of it.

reside (rĭ-zīd') *verb intrans.* (**resided, residing**) **1** to live or have one's home (in). **2** (**reside in** (someone *or* something)) *of power, authority, a quality, etc.* to be present in or attributable to (the one specified).

residence (rĕz'əd-əns) *noun* **1** a house or dwelling, esp. a large, impressive, and imposing one. **2** the act of living in a place. **3** the period of time one lives in a place.

residency *noun* (*pl.* **residencies**) **1** a residence, often an official dwelling, e.g., of a state governor. **2** a period of advanced, specialized medical training in hospitals for physicians.

resident *noun* **1** a person who lives in a place. **2** a physician undergoing advanced or specialized training in a hospital. —*adj.* **1** living or dwelling in. **2** living or required to live in the place where one works'.

residential *adj.* **1** containing houses rather than factories and businesses. **2** used as a residence. **3** relating to or connected with residence or residences.

residual (rĭ-zĭj'ə-wəl) *adj.* left over; remaining. —*noun* something that remains or is left over.

residue (rĕz'ə-dōō, -dyōō,) *noun* that which remains or is left over when a part has been taken away.

resign (rĭ-zīn') *verb intrans., trans.* (**resigned, resigning**) **1** to give up one's employment or official position. **2** to give up or relinquish (a right, claim, etc.). **3** (**resign** (oneself) **to** (something)) to come to accept (something, esp. something unwelcome) with patience.

resignation (rĕz,ĭg-nā'shən) *noun* **1** an act of resigning. **2** a formal letter or notice of one's intention to resign. **3** the state or quality of having or showing patient, calm acceptance.

resigned *adj.* having or showing patient, calm acceptance of something thought of as inevitable or difficult. ▸ **resignedly** *adv.*

resilient *adj.* **1** *of a person* able to deal readily with or recover quickly from differing circumstances, unexpected difficulties; etc. **2** *of an object* quickly returning to its original shape after being bent, twisted, etc. ▸ **resilience** *or* **resiliency** *noun*

resin (rĕz'ĭn) *noun Chem.* a sticky solid or semi-solid substance produced naturally by certain trees, esp. conifers, or synthetically, and used for making plastics, paints, varnishes, etc. ▸ **resinous** *adj.*

resist *verb trans., intrans.* (**resisted, resisting**) **1** to fight against (someone or something); to refuse to give in or comply. **2** to remain undamaged by or withstand. ▸ **resistible** *adj.*

resistance *noun* **1** the act or an instance of resisting. **2** a measure of the extent to which a living organism can limit the effects of an infection. **3** (ABBREV. **r, R**) *Electr.* a measure of the extent to which a material or an electrical device opposes the flow of an electric current through it. ▸ **resistant** *adj.*

resistor *noun Electr.* a device that introduces a known value of resistance into a circuit, etc.

resolute (rĕz'ə-lōōt,) *adj.* having a fixed purpose or belief, and determined and firm in pursuing it; unwavering. ▸ **resolutely** *adv.* ▸ **resoluteness** *noun*

resolution *noun* **1** the act of making a firm decision. **2** a firm decision. **3** *Law* a decision by a court of law. **4** a formal expression of opinion or will, etc., by a group of people, e.g., at a public meeting. **5** determination or resoluteness. **6** the act of solving or finding the answer to (a problem, question, etc.) **7** the ability of a television screen, photographic film, etc., to reproduce an image in very fine detail.

resolve · *verb trans., intrans.* (**resolved, resolving**) **1** to make a firm decision about (something): *resolved to leave early.* **2** to pass (a resolution), esp. formally by vote. **3** to find an answer to (a problem, question, etc.). **4** to take away or bring an end to (a doubt, fear, etc.). **5** to break up or cause to break up into separate or constituent parts. **6** *of a television screen, photographic film, etc.* to produce an image of in fine detail. —*noun* **1** determination or firm intention. **2** a firm decision; a resolution.

resolved *adj.* having or displaying an unwavering manner.

resonance *noun* **1** the quality or state of being resonant. **2** *Phys.* a phenomenon that occurs when an object or system is made to vibrate at its natural frequency.

resonant *adj.* **1** *of sounds* continuing to sound; echoing or resounding. **2** producing echoing sounds. **3** full of or made stronger by a ringing quality. ▸ **resonantly** *adv.*

resonate *verb intrans., trans.* (**resonated, resonating**) to resound or cause to resound or echo.

resort *verb intrans.* (**resorted, resorting**) (**resort to** (something)) **1** to turn to (it) as a means of solving a problem, etc.; to have recourse to. **2** to go to a place, esp. frequently. —*noun* **1** a place visited by many people, esp. one providing accommodation and recreation for tourists and vacationers. **2** someone or something looked to for help.

resound *verb intrans., trans.* (**resounded, resounding**) **1** *of sounds* to ring or echo. **2** (**resound with** *or* **to** (**something**)) to be filled with echoing or ringing sounds. **3** to be widely known: *Her fame resounds throughout the country.* **4** *of a place* to cause (a sound) to echo or ring. **5** to repeat or spread (the praises of a person or thing).

resounding *adj.* **1** echoing and ringing; reverberating. **2** thorough, clear, and decisive. ▸ **resoundingly** *adv.*

resource *noun* **1** a person or thing that gives help, support, etc., when needed. **2** a means of solving difficulties, problems, etc. **3** skill at finding ways of solving difficulties, problems, etc. **4** a supply of energy, natural materials, or minerals, that may or may not be renewable. **5** (*usu.* **resources**) a means of support, e.g., money and property.

resourceful *adj.* good at finding ways of solving difficulties, problems, etc. ▸ **resourcefully** *adv.* ▸ **resourcefulness** *noun*

respect *noun* **1** good opinion; admiration. **2** the state of being admired or well thought of. **3** (**respect for** (**something** *or* **someone**)) consideration of or attention to (something or someone). **4** (**respects**) a greeting or expression of admiration, esteem, and honor. **5** a particular detail, feature, or characteristic. **6** reference or connection: *In what respect are they different?* —*verb trans.* (**respected, respecting**) **1** to hold (someone or something) in high regard; to have a high opinion of. **2** to show consideration, attention, or thoughtfulness to. ▸ **respectful** *adj.* ▸ **respectfully** *adv.* ▸ **respectfulness** *noun*

respectable *adj.* **1** deserving respect. **2** having a good reputation or character, esp. as regards morals. **3** *of behavior* correct; acceptable. **4** presentable; decent. **5** fairly or relatively good or large. ▸ **respectability** *noun* ▸ **respectably** *adv.*

respecting *prep.* about; concerning.

respective *adj.* belonging to or relating to each person or thing mentioned; particular; separate: *our respective homes.*

respectively *adv.* referring to each person or thing separately and in turn.

respiration *noun* **1** the act of breathing. **2** *Physiol.* the process by which people, animals, living cells, etc. take in oxygen and release carbon dioxide. ▸ **respiratory** *adj.*

respirator *noun* **1** a mask worn over the mouth and nose to prevent poisonous gas, dust, etc., being breathed in. **2** apparatus used to help very ill people breathe when they are unable to do so naturally.

respire *verb intrans., trans.* (**respired, respiring**) **1** to breathe. **2** to release energy as a result of the breakdown of organic compounds such as fats or carbohydrates.

respite (rĕs′pĭt) *noun* **1** a period of rest or relief from or a temporary stopping of something unpleasant, difficult, etc.; a pause. **2** a temporary delay; a reprieve. —*verb trans.* (**respited, respiting**) **1** to grant a respite to. **2** to delay; to postpone.

resplendent *adj.* brilliant or splendid in appearance. ▸ **resplendence** *noun* ▸ **resplendently** *adv.*

respond *verb intrans., trans.* (**responded, responding**) **1** to answer or reply; to say in reply. **2** to act or behave in reply or response. **3** to react favorably or well.

respondent *noun* **1** a person who answers or makes replies. **2** *Law* a defendant, esp. in a divorce suit. —*adj.* making a reply or response; answering.

response *noun* **1** an act of responding, replying, or reacting. **2** a reply or answer. **3** a reaction.

responsibility *noun* (*pl.* **responsibilities**) **1** something or someone for which one is responsible. **2** the state of being responsible or having important duties for which one is responsible.

responsible *adj.* **1** (**responsible for** (**someone** *or* **something**)) having charge or control over (the one or ones specified) and being accountable for (that one or those ones). **2** (**responsible to** (**someone**)) having to account for one's actions to (the one specified). **3** *of a job, position, etc.* having many important duties, esp. the making of important decisions. **4** (**responsible for** (**something**)) being the cause of (it). **5** *of a person* **a** able to be trusted. **b** able to answer for one's own conduct. ▸ **responsibly** *adv.*

responsive *adj.* **1** *of a person* quick to react or respond. **2** reacting well or favorably: *a disease responsive to drugs.* **3** made as or forming a response. ▸ **responsively** *adv.* ▸ **responsiveness** *noun*

rest[1] *noun* **1** a period of relaxation or freedom from work, activity, worry, etc. **2** sleep; repose. **3** calm; tranquility. **4** a state of not moving or working. **5** death thought of as repose: *laid the deceased to rest.* **6** (*often in compounds*) something that holds (something else): *a headrest.* **7** a pause, e.g., in reading, speaking. **8** *Mus.* an interval of silence in a piece of music, or a mark showing this. —*verb trans., intrans.*

(**rested, resting**) **1** to stop or cause to stop working or moving. **2** to relax, esp. by sleeping. **3** to set, place, or lie on or against something for support. **4** to be calm and free from worry. **5** to give or have as a basis or support: *rested her arm on the chair.* **6** to depend or cause to depend or be based on or in. **7** *of the eyes* to remain or cause them to remain looking in a certain direction. **8** *Law* to conclude the calling of witnesses and presentation or arguments in a case at trial: *Your Honor, the defense rests.*

rest² noun (the rest) 1 that which is left when part of something is taken away, finished, etc.; the remainder. **2** the others. —*verb intrans.* (**rested, resting**) to continue to be: *Rest assured we will never give up.*

restaurant (rěs'tə-rŏnt, -ränt,) *noun* a place at which meals may be bought and eaten.

restaurateur (rěs,tə-rə-tər') or **restauranteur** *noun* the owner or manager of a restaurant.

restful *adj.* **1** bringing rest or causing a person to feel calm, peaceful, and rested. **2** relaxed; at rest. ► **restfully** *adv.* ► **restfulness** *noun*

restitution *noun* **1** the act of giving back to the rightful owner something lost or stolen. **2** the paying of compensation for loss or injury.

restive *adj.* **1** unwilling to accept control or authority. **2** restless; nervous. ► **restively** *adv.* ► **restiveness** *noun*

restless *adj.* **1** constantly moving or fidgeting; unable to stay still or quiet. **2** giving no rest. **3** worried, nervous, and uneasy. ► **restlessly** *adv.* ► **restlessness** *noun*

restoration *noun* **1** the act or process of restoring. **2** something restored or given back.

restorative *adj.* tending or helping to restore or improve health, strength, or spirits. —*noun* a food or medicine that serves to restore or improve, e.g., health or strength.

restore *verb trans.* (**restored, restoring**) **1** to return (a building, painting, etc.) to a former condition by repairing or cleaning it. **2** to bring back, or bring back to a normal or proper state. **3** to return (something) lost or stolen to the rightful owner. ► **restorable** *adj.* ► **restorer** *noun*

restrain *verb trans.* (**restrained, restraining**) **1** to prevent (someone, oneself, etc.) from doing something. **2** to keep (one's temper, ambition, etc.) under control. **3** to take away (a person's) freedom.

restrained *adj.* **1** controlling or able to control one's emotions. **2** showing restraint; indulging in no excess.

restraint *noun* **1 a** the act of restraining or state of being restrained. **b** (**restraints**) handcuffs, shackles, etc., used to control a prisoner. **2** a limit or restriction. **3** the ability to remain calm and reasonable. **4** the practice or state of choosing not to do something, e.g., to take no alcohol.

restrict *verb trans.* (**restricted, restricting**) **1** to keep (someone or something) within certain limits. **2** to limit or regulate the use of, esp. to withhold from general use. ► **restriction** *noun*

restricted *adj.* **1** limited in space; narrow; confined. **2** not for general use, circulation, etc.: *a set of restricted radio channels.*

restrictive *adj.* restricting or intended to restrict. ► **restrictively** *adv.*

restroom *noun* a public lavatory.

result *noun* **1** an outcome or consequence. **2** (*often* **results**) an outcome or consequence, positive or favorable: *wanted results, not promises.* **3** a number or quantity obtained by calculation, etc. **4** (**results**) a list of final scores (in a series of sports matches, etc.). —*verb intrans.* (**resulted, resulting**) **1** (**result from (something)**) to be a consequence or outcome of (some action, event, etc.). **2** (**result in (something)**) to end in a specified way.

resultant *adj.* resulting. —*noun Math., Phys.* a single force that is the equivalent of two or more forces acting on an object.

resume (rǐ-zōōm') *verb trans., intrans.* (**resumed, resuming**) **1** to return to or begin again after an interruption. **2** to take back or go to (a former position, etc.): *resume one's seat.* ► **resumption** *noun*

résumé or **resume** (rězʹə-mā,) *noun* **1** a summary. **2** a curriculum vitae.

resurgent *adj.* capable of rising again; that rises again. ► **resurgence** *noun*

resurrect *verb trans.* (**resurrected, resurrecting**) **1** to bring back to life from the dead. **2** to bring back into general use, view, activity, etc.

resurrection *noun* **1** the act of resurrecting or of bringing back into use. **2** the act of coming back to life after death. **3** (**Resurrection**) *Christianity* **a** Christ's coming back to life three days after death on the cross. **b** the coming back to life of all the dead on the Day of Judgment.

resuscitate (rǐ-sǎsʹə-tāt,) *verb trans., intrans.* (**resuscitated, resuscitating**) to bring or come back to consciousness; to revive. ► **resuscitation** *noun*

retail (rēʹtāl,) *noun* the sale of merchandise either individually or in small quantities to customers who will not resell them. —*adj.* relating to or concerned with such sale of goods. —*adv.* by retail; at a retail price: *costs $45 retail.* —*verb trans., intrans.* (**retailed, retailing**) **1 a** to sell (merchandise) to customers. **b** *of merchandise* to be sold in this way. ▸ **retailer** *noun*

retain (rĭ-tān′) *verb trans.* (**retained, retaining**) **1 a** to have in one's possession under one's control. **b** to continue to have, contain, hold, use, etc. **2** to be able to remember. **3** to hold back or keep in place. **4** to secure the services of (a person, esp. an attorney) by paying a preliminary fee.

retainer *noun* **1** a fee paid to secure a person's professional services, esp. those of an attorney. **2** a domestic servant who has been with a family for a long time. **3** *Dentistry* an appliance used to hold the teeth in place after a course of orthodontic treatment has been completed.

retake *verb trans.* (rē-tāk′) (*pa t* **retook**; *pa p* **retaken**; *pr p* **retaking**) **1** to capture again. **2** to take (e.g., an examination) again. **3** to photograph (e.g., a scene in a film) again. —*noun* (rē′tāk,) a second taking.

retaliate (rĭ-tăl′ē-āt,) *verb intrans.* (**retaliated, retaliating**) to repay an injury, wrong, etc., in kind; to get revenge. ▸ **retaliation** *noun* ▸ **retaliatory** *adj.*

retard (rĭ-tärd′) *verb trans.* (**retarded, retarding**) **1** to make slow or delay. **2** to keep back the progress, development, etc.

retardant *adj.* making something slower or delayed.

retardation *noun* the act of retarding or the condition of being retarded.

retarded *adj.* not having made the expected physical or esp. mental development.

retch *verb intrans.* (**retched, retching**) to strain to vomit or almost vomit, but not actually do so. —*noun* an act of retching.

retention *noun* **1** the act of retaining or the state of being retained. **2** the ability to remember experiences and things learned. **3** the failure to get rid of fluid from the body.

retentive *adj.* able to retain or keep, esp. fluid, memories, or information. ▸ **retentively** *adv.* ▸ **retentiveness** *noun*

rethink *verb trans.* (pronounced with stress on the last syllable) (*pa t and pa p* **rethought**; *pr p* **rethinking**) to think about or consider (a plan, etc.) again, usu. with a view to changing one's mind. —*noun* (pronounced with stress on the first syllable) an act of rethinking.

reticent *adj.* not saying very much; not willing to communicate; not communicating everything that one knows. ▸ **reticence** *noun*

retina (rĕt′n-ə) *noun* (*pl.* **retinas, retinae**) *Anat.* the light-sensitive lining at the back of the eye which receives the image from the lens. ▸ **retinal** *adj.*

retinue (rĕt′n-ōō,, -yōō,) *noun* the servants, officials, aides, etc., who travel with and attend to an important person.

retire *verb trans., intrans.* (**retired, retiring**) **1** to stop or cause to stop working permanently, usu. on reaching an age at which a pension can be received. **2** to go away to rest, esp. to go to bed: *retired at eleven.* **3** to go away from or to; to leave: *retire to the drawing room.* **4** to withdraw or cause to withdraw from a sports contest, esp. because of injury. **5** *of a military force, etc.* to move or be moved back away from a dangerous position. ▸ **retirement** *noun*

retired *adj.* **1** having permanently stopped working because of age. **2** secluded and withdrawn.

retiree (rĭ-tī,rē′) *noun* one who is retired from active employment.

retiring *adj.* shy and reserved; disliking public notice. ▸ **retiringly** *adv.*

retook *see* **retake**.

retort (rĭ-tôrt′) *verb intrans., trans.* (**retorted, retorting**) **1** to make a quick and clever or angry reply. **2** to turn (an argument, criticism, blame, etc.) back on the person who first used that argument, criticism, blame, etc. **3** to heat and purify (metal). —*noun* **1** a quick and clever or angry reply. **2** an argument, criticism, blame, etc., that is turned back upon the originator. **3** a glass vessel with a long neck which curves downward, used in distilling.

retouch *verb trans.* (**retouched, retouching**) to improve or repair (a photograph, negative, painting, etc.) by adding extra touches.

retrace *verb trans.* (**retraced, retracing**) **1** to go back over (one's route, path, etc.). **2** to go over (recent events, etc.) again in one's memory. **3** to trace back: *retrace one's roots.*

retract *verb trans., intrans.* (**retracted, retracting**) **1** to withdraw (a statement, claim, etc.) as wrong, offensive, or unjustified. **2** to refuse to acknowledge (a promise, agreement, etc., that one has made). **3** to draw in or back or be drawn in or back. ▸ **retractable** *adj.* ▸ **retraction** *noun*

retractile (rĭ-trăk′təl, -tīl,) *adj. technical, e.g., of a cat's claws* able to be drawn up, in, or back.

retrain *verb trans., intrans.* (**retrained, retraining**) **1** to teach (someone) new skills, e.g., those necessary to qualify them for other employment. **2** to learn new skills.

retreat (rĭ-trēt′) *verb intrans., trans.* (**retreated, retreating**) **1** *of a military force* to move back or away from or to be caused to move back or away from a position or battle. **2** to slope backward; to recede. —*noun* **1 a** the act of retreating, esp. from battle, a military position, danger, etc. **b** a signal to retreat. **2** a place of privacy, safety, and seclusion. **3** a period of retirement from the world, esp. for prayer, meditation, and study.

retrench verb trans., intrans. (**retrenched, retrenching**) to reduce or cut down (e.g., expenses); to economize. ▸ **retrenchment** noun

retrial (rē-trī′əl, rē′trī,əl) noun Law a second trial in a court of law.

retribution (rĕ,trī-byoo′shən) noun deserved punishment, esp. for sin or wrongdoing. ▸ **retributive** adj.

retrieve verb trans., intrans. (**retrieved, retrieving**) 1 to get or bring back again; to recover. 2 to rescue or save: retrieve a situation. 3 Comput. to recover (information) from storage in memory. 4 of a dog to search for and bring back (a ball, stick, etc.). ▸ **retrievable** adj. ▸ **retrieval** noun

retriever noun a breed of dog with a short coat, trained to retrieve game.

retro- prefix forming words meaning: 1 back or backward in time or space. 2 behind.

retroactive adj. applying to or affecting things from a date in the past. ▸ **retroactively** adv. ▸ **retroactivity** noun

retrofit (rĕ,trō-fĭt′, rĕ′trō-fĭt,) verb trans., intrans. (**retrofitted, retrofitting**) 1 to equip (e.g., an aircraft or a car) with devices unavailable at the time of original manufacturing. 2 to substitute modernized or totally new parts in an older system to update it. —noun the act or an instance of retrofitting, or a device, system, or machine so reequipped. —adj. of, relating to, or constituting a retrofit.

retrograde adj. 1 being, tending toward or causing a worse; less advanced or less desirable state. 2 moving or bending backward. —verb intrans. (**retrograded, retrograding**) 1 to move backward. 2 to deteriorate or decline.

retrogress verb intrans. (**retrogressed, retrogressing**) to go back to an earlier, worse, or less advanced condition or state; to deteriorate. ▸ **retrogression** noun ▸ **retrogressive** adj.

retrorocket (rĕ′trō-räk,ət) noun a small rocket motor that is fired in the opposite direction to that in which a spacecraft, artificial satellite, etc., is moving, in order to slow it down.

retrospect (rĕ′trə-spĕkt,) noun (usu. **in retrospect**) a looking back on or a view of what has happened in the past: In retrospect I might have done otherwise. ▸ **retrospect** noun ▸ **retrospective** adj. ▸ **retrospectively** adv.

retrovirus noun any of a group of viruses with genetic material consisting of RNA rather than DNA, including many cancer-causing viruses, as well as the HIV virus.

retry verb trans. (**retried, retrying, retries**) 1 Law to submit to a second trial in a court of law. 2 to make a further attempt.

return verb intrans., trans. (**returned, returning**) 1 to come or go back again to a former place, state, or owner. 2 to send, put back, etc., into a former position. 3 to come back to, in thought or speech. 4 to repay with something of the same value: return a compliment. 5 to answer or reply. 6 Law to report or state officially or formally: return a verdict. 7 to earn or produce (profit, interest, etc.). 8 a Tennis, Badminton to hit (a ball, etc.) served by one's opponent. b Football to run with (the ball). —noun 1 an act of coming back from a place, state, etc. 2 an act of conveying something, esp. to a former place, state, ownership, etc. 3 profit from work, a business, or investment. 4 a statement of a party's income and allowances, used for calculating the tax that must be paid. 5 (usu. **returns**) a statement of the votes polled in an election. 6 an answer or reply. 7 Tennis, Badminton a a ball, etc., hit back after one's opponent's service. b Football the act or an instance of running the ball back: a 45-yd. return after kickoff. —adj. forming, causing, or relating to a return. —**in return** in exchange; in reply; as compensation. ▸ **returnable** adj.

reunion noun 1 a meeting of people (e.g., friends) who have not met for some time. 2 the act of reuniting or state of being reunited.

reunite (rē,yŏŏ-nīt′) verb trans., intrans. (**reunited, reuniting**) to bring or come together after being separated.

Rev. abbrev. Reverend.

rev colloq. noun a revolution in an internal combustion engine. —verb trans., intrans. (**revved, revving**) colloq. (also **rev up**) 1 to increase the speed of (a car engine, etc.). 2 of an engine or vehicle to run faster. 3 (usu. **rev up**) to increase in, e.g., productivity or liveliness.

revamp verb trans. (**revamped, revamping**) to revise, renovate, or patch up, usu. with the aim of improving.

reveal (rĭ-vēl′), verb trans. (**revealed, revealing**) 1 to make known (a secret, etc.). ▣ DISCLOSE, DIVULGE, LEAK ▣ CONCEAL, COVER (UP), HIDE. 2 to allow to be seen; to show: a dress that reveals too much. 3 of a deity to make known through divine inspiration or supernatural means.

revealing adj. 1 that reveals. 2 indicative; significant: made some revealing remarks.

reveille (rĕv′ə-lē) noun a bugle or drum call at daybreak to waken soldiers, etc.

revel verb intrans. (**reveled** or **revelled, reveling** or **revelling**) 1 (**revel in something**) to take great delight in (it). 2 to enjoy oneself in a noisy, lively way. —noun (usu. **revels**) noisy, lively enjoyment, or festivities. ▸ **reveller** or **reveler** noun ▸ **revelry** noun

revelation (rĕv͵ə-lā'shən) *noun* **1** the act of revealing secrets, information, etc. **2** that which is made known or seen. **3** something revealed to humankind by God. ▸ **revelatory** *adj.*

revenge *noun* **1 a** a malicious injury, harm, or wrong perpetrated in return for injury, harm, or wrong received. **b** something done as a means of returning injury, harm, etc., for injury, harm, etc., received. **2** the desire to do such malicious injury, harm, etc. —*verb trans.* (**revenged, revenging**) **1** to do injury, harm, etc., in return for (injury, harm, etc., received). **2** to take revenge on someone on behalf of (oneself or someone else). ▸ **revengeful** *adj.* ▸ **revengefully** *adv.* ▸ **revengefulness** *noun*

revenue *noun* **1** money from any source (e.g., property, shares), esp. the money raised by a government. **2** a government department responsible for collecting public funds.

reverberate (rĭ-vər'bə-rāt͵) *verb intrans., trans.* (**reverberated, reverberating**) **1** of a sound, light, heat, etc. to be echoed, repeated, or reflected again and again. **2** to echo, repeat, or reflect (a sound, light, etc.) again and again. **3** of a story, scandal, etc. to be repeated continually. ▸ **reverberation** *noun*

revere *verb trans.* (**revered, revering**) to feel or show great affection and respect for.

reverence (rĕv'rəns) *noun* great respect, esp. that shown to sacred or holy things.

reverend *adj.* **1** worthy of being revered or respected. **2** (**Reverend**) (ABBREV. **Rev.**) used before proper names as a title for members of the clergy. —*noun colloq.* a member of the clergy.

reverent *adj.* showing or feeling great respect. ▸ **reverently** *adv.*

reverential *adj.* showing great respect or reverence. ▸ **reverentially** *adv.*

reverie *noun* **1** a state of pleasantly dreamy, absent-minded thought. **2** a daydream or absent-minded idea or thought.

reversal *noun* **1** the act of reversing or state of being reversed. **2** a change in fortune, esp. for the worse.

reverse (rĭ-vərs') *verb trans., intrans.* (**reversed, reversing**) **1** to move or cause to move in an opposite or backwards direction. **2** to put into an opposite or contrary position, state, order, etc. **3** to change (a policy, decision, etc.) to the exact opposite or contrary. **4** *Law* to set aside or invalidate (the decision or judgment of a lower court). —*noun* **1** the opposite. **2** an act of changing to an opposite or contrary position, direction, state, etc., or of being changed in this way. **3** the back or rear side, esp. of a book. **4** the side of a coin with the secondary design on it. *See also* **obverse**

(sense 1). **5** a mechanism that makes a machine move in a backward direction. —*adj.* opposite, contrary, or turned around in order, position, or direction.

reversible *adj.* **1** able to be reversed. **2** of clothes able to be worn with either side out.

revert *verb intrans., trans.* (**reverted, reverting**) **1** to return to a topic in thought or conversation. **2** to return to a former, usu. worse, state or practice. **3** *Biol.* to return to an earlier, ancestral, usu. simpler type. **4** *Law, esp. of property* to return to an original owner or his or her heirs after belonging temporarily to someone else. **5** to turn (something) back. ▸ **reversion** *noun*

review *noun* **1** an act of examining, reviewing, or revising, or the state of being examined, reviewed, or revised. **2** a general survey. **3** a survey of the past and past events: *the annual review of the year.* **4** a critical report on a book, play, film, etc. **5** a magazine or newspaper, or a section of one, that contains mainly reviews of books, etc., and other feature articles. **6** a second or additional study or consideration of facts, events, etc. **7** a formal or official inspection of troops, ships, etc. **8** *Law* a reexamination of a case, typically by a higher court of law. —*verb trans., intrans.* (**reviewed, reviewing**) **1** to examine or go over, esp. critically or formally. **2** to look back on and examine (events in the past). **3** to inspect (troops, ships, etc.), esp. formally or officially. **4** to write a critical report on (a book, play, film, etc.). **5** to write reviews. **6** *Law* to reexamine (a case). ▸ **reviewer** *noun*

revile *verb trans., intrans.* (**reviled, reviling**) **1** to abuse or criticize (someone or something) bitterly or scornfully. **2** to speak scornfully or to use abusive language. ▸ **revilement** *noun* ▸ **reviler** *noun*

revise (rĭ-vīz') *verb trans.* (**revised, revising**) **1** to examine again in order to identify and correct faults, or otherwise improve. **2** to correct faults in, make improvements in, and update (a previously printed book), usu. to prepare a new edition. **3** to change or amend (an opinion, etc.). ▸ **reviser** *noun* ▸ **revision** *noun*

revisionism *noun* a policy of revising a doctrine. ▸ **revisionist** *noun*

revitalize *verb trans.* (**revitalized, revitalizing**) to give new life and energy to.

revival *noun* **1** the act of reviving or state of being revived. **2** a renewed interest, esp. in old customs and fashions. **3** a new production or performance, e.g., of an old play. **4 a** a period of renewed religious faith and spirituality. **b** a prayer meeting, evangelistic in nature, held to encourage renewed faith. ▸ **revivalism** *noun* ▸ **revivalist** *noun*

revive verb trans., intrans. (**revived, reviving**) 1 to bring or come back to consciousness, strength, health, vitality, etc. 2 to bring or come back to use, to an active state, to notice, etc.: revive an old play.

revivify verb trans. (**revivified, revivifying, revivifies**) to put new life into. ▸ **revivification** noun

revocable (rĕv'ə-kə-bəl) adj. capable of being revoked or recalled: a revocable permit.

revoke verb trans., intrans. (**revoked, revoking**) to cancel or make (a will, agreement, etc.) no longer valid. ▸ **revocation** noun

revolt verb intrans., trans. (**revolted, revolting**) 1 to rebel against a government, authority, etc. 2 to feel or cause to feel disgust, loathing, or revulsion: That film revolts me. —noun an act of rebelling; a rebellion against authority.

revolting adj. 1 opposed to and fighting against the government of a country. 2 causing a feeling of disgust, loathing, etc.; nauseating. ▸ **revoltingly** adv.

revolution noun 1 the usu. violent overthrow of a government or political system by the governed. 2 a complete, drastic, and usu. far-reaching change in ideas, ways of doing things, etc. 3 a a complete circle or turn around an axis. b an act of turning or moving around an axis.

revolutionary adj. 1 of or resembling a revolution. 2 in favor of and supporting revolution. 3 completely new or different; involving radical change. —noun (pl. **revolutionaries**) a person who takes part in or is in favor of revolution.

revolutionize verb trans. (**revolutionize, revolutionizing**) to cause great, radical, or fundamental changes in.

revolve verb intrans., trans. (**revolved, revolving**) 1 to move or turn, or to cause to move or turn in a circle around a central point; to rotate. 2 (**revolve around** or **about** (**something**)) to have (it) as a center, focus, or main point. 3 to occur in cycles or regularly. ▸ **revolvable** adj.

revolver noun a pistol with a revolving cylinder that holds several bullets, and that can be fired several times without reloading.

revue (rĭ-vyōō') noun an amusing and varied show, with songs, sketches, etc., that are often satirical.

revulsion noun 1 a feeling of complete disgust, distaste, or repugnance. 2 a sudden, often violent change of feeling, esp. from love to hate.

reward noun 1 something given or received in return for work done, a service rendered, good behavior, etc. 2 something given or received in return for good or evil. 3 a sum of money offered usu. for finding or helping to find a criminal, lost property, etc. —verb trans. (**rewarded, rewarding**) to give a reward to (someone) for work done, good behavior, etc.

rewarding adj. giving personal pleasure or satisfaction: a rewarding profession.

rewind verb trans. (**rewound, rewinding**) to wind (tape, film, etc.) back to the beginning.

reword verb trans. (**reworded, rewording**) to express in different words.

rewrite verb trans. (pronounced with stress on the last syllable) (pa t **rewrote**; pa p **rewritten**; pr p **rewriting**) 1 to write again or anew. 2 Comput. to store or copy (data) in the same location from which it was read. —noun (pronounced with stress on the first syllable) the process or result of rewriting.

RF abbrev. Baseball right field; right fielder.

RFD abbrev. rural free delivery.

Rh symbol 1 rhesus. 2 Chem. rhodium.

Rhaetian (rē'shən) noun used as a generic name for the various Romance dialects spoken in Switzerland and N Italy. —adj. relating to these Romance-language dialects.

rhapsody noun (pl. **rhapsodies**) 1 a feeling of joy. ≡ ECSTASY, HEAVEN, PARADISE, RAPTURE ⊠ DEPRESSION, FUNK, MOURNING. 2 an enthusiastic, highly emotional speech or piece of writing. 3 Mus. an emotional piece usu. written to suggest an improvisation. ▸ **rhapsodic** or **rhapsodical** adj. ▸ **rhapsodize** verb

rhenium (rē'nē-əm) noun Chem. (SYMBOL **Re**) a rare silvery-white metallic element used in certain alloys, e.g. those that act as superconductors or that are resistant to high temperatures.

rheostat (rē'ə-stăt,) noun a device which varies the flow of electric current through a circuit.

rhesus (rē'səs) noun a small monkey native to N India. Also called **rhesus monkey.**

rhetoric noun 1 the art of speaking and writing well, elegantly, and effectively, esp. when used to persuade others. 2 language that is full of unnecessarily long or formal words and phrases, and that is also often insincere or meaningless. ▸ **rhetorical** adj.

rhetorical question a question asked to produce an effect and not because the speaker really wants an answer.

rheumatic noun 1 a person affected with rheumatism. 2 (**rheumatics**) colloq. rheumatism, or pain caused by it. —adj. relating to or caused by rheumatism.

rheumatic fever Med. a disease which causes fever, painful swelling of the joints, and possible damage to the heart, found esp. in children.

rheumatism noun a disease marked by painful swelling of the joints and that causes stiffness and pain when moving them.

rheumatoid *adj.* of or like rheumatism or rheumatoid arthritis.

rheumatoid arthritis *Med.* a form of arthritis, particularly common in women, that causes painful swelling and stiffness of the joints.

rhinestone *noun* an imitation diamond usu. made from glass or plastic.

rhino *noun (pl.* **rhinos**) a rhinoceros.

rhinoceros (rī-nǎs'ə-rəs) *noun (pl.* **rhinoceros, rhinoceroses**) a large African herbivorous mammal, with either one or two horns on its snout.

rhizome *noun Bot.* a thick, horizontal underground stem that produces roots and leafy shoots. *Also called* **rootstock.**

rhodium *noun Chem.* (SYMBOL **Rh**) a silvery-white metallic element that is used to make temperature-resistant platinum alloys.

rhododendron *noun* a flowering shrub with thick evergreen leaves and large, showy, colorful flowers.

rhomboid *noun* a four-sided shape with opposite sides and angles equal, two angles being greater and two smaller than a right angle, and two sides being longer than the other two. ► **rhomboidal** *adj.*

rhombus *noun (pl.* **rhombuses, rhombi**) a four-sided shape with all four sides equal, two opposite angles being greater than a right angle and two smaller.

rhubarb *noun* **1** a plant with reddish, sour-tasting stalks which can be cooked, sweetened, and eaten. **2** *colloq.* an argument or a fight.

rhyme *noun* **1** a pattern of words that have the same final sounds at the ends of lines in a poem. **2** the use of such patterns in poetry, etc. **3** a word that has the same sound as another. **4** a short poem, verse, or jingle written in rhyme. —*verb intrans., trans.* (**rhymed, rhyming**) **1** *of words* to have the same final sounds and so form rhymes. **2** to use (a word) as a rhyme for another. **3** to write using rhymes. **4** to put (a story, etc.) into rhyme.

rhythm *noun* **1** a regular repeated pattern, movement, beat, or sequence of events. **2** *Mus.* **a** the regular arrangement of stress, notes of different lengths, and pauses in a piece of music. **b** a particular pattern of stress, notes, etc., in music: *a tango rhythm.* **3** a regular arrangement of sounds and stressed and unstressed syllables in poetry or other writing, suggesting movement; meter. **4** an ability to sing, speak, move, etc., rhythmically. ► **rhythmic** or **rhythmical** *adj.* ► **rhythmically** *adv.*

rhythm and blues (ABBREV. **r&b, R&B**) a style of music that combines certain features of the blues with lively rhythms.

RI *abbrev.* Rhode Island.

rib¹ *noun* **1** any one of the slightly flexible bones that curve around and forward from the spine, forming the chest wall. **2** a cut of meat including one or more ribs. **3** a rod-like bar that supports and strengthens a layer of fabric, membrane, etc., e.g., in an umbrella or insect's wing. **4** a raised ridge in knitted or woven material. **5** one of the pieces of wood that curve around and upward from a ship's keel to form the framework of the hull. —*verb trans., intrans.* (**ribbed, ribbing**) **1** to provide or enclose with ribs. **2** to knit ribs in by alternating plain and purl stitches. ► **ribbed** *adj.* ► **ribbing** *noun*

rib² *verb trans.* (**ribbed, ribbing**) *colloq.* to tease.

ribald (rĭb'əld) *adj., of language, a speaker, humor, etc.* humorous in a vulgar, and often disrespectful, way. ► **ribaldry** *noun*

riband (rĭb'ənd) *noun* a ribbon, esp. one awarded as a prize.

ribbon *noun* **1** a long narrow strip of usu. colored material used for decorating clothes, tying hair and gift packages, etc. **2** a ribbonlike strip. **3** a small piece of colored cloth worn to show membership of a team, or as a sign of having won an award. **4** a narrow strip of inked cloth used to produce print in a typewriter. **5** (**ribbons**) strips or tatters of torn material.

rib cage the chest wall formed by the ribs.

riboflavin (rī,bə-flā'vĭn) *noun Biochem.* a yellow-colored vitamin of the B complex found in green vegetables, milk, egg yolk, and liver. *Also called* **vitamin B².**

ribonucleic acid *Biochem.* RNA.

rice *noun* **1** a grass which grows in wet, marshy ground in warm climates. **2** the edible seeds of this plant.

rich *adj.* **1** having a great deal of money, and material possessions. ▣ AFFLUENT, MONEYED, WEALTHY ▣ IMPOVERISHED, POOR. **2** costly and elaborate: *rich clothes.* **3** high in value or quality: *a rich harvest.* **4 a** (**rich in (something**) having (something) in great quantity or amount. **b** existing in large amounts. **5** *of soil, a region, etc.* productive; fertile. **6** *of colors* vivid and deep. **7** *of a drink, esp. alcoholic* with a full, mellow, well-matured flavor. **8** *of food* heavily seasoned, or containing much fat, oil, or dried fruit. **9** *of an odor* pungent and spicy. **10** *of a voice* full, mellow, and deep. **11** *of a remark or suggestion* unacceptable; outrageous; ridiculous: *That's a bit rich!* ► **richly** *adv.* ► **richness** *noun*

rick *noun* a stack or heap, esp. of hay or corn.

rickets *noun (sing., pl.) Med.* a disease of children caused by a lack of vitamin D, causing the bones to become soft and bend.

rickety *adj.* (**ricketier, ricketiest**) **1** *Med.* affected by or having rickets. **2** unsteady and likely to collapse: *a rickety old deck.*

rickshaw or **ricksha** *noun* a small, two-wheeled, hooded carriage drawn either by a person on foot, or attached to a bicycle or motorcycle.

ricochet (rĭk′ə-shā,) *noun* the action, esp. of a bullet or other missile, of hitting a surface and then rebounding. —*verb intrans.* (**ricocheted** or **ricochetted, ricocheting** or **ricochetting**) *of a missile, e.g., a bullet* to hit a surface and rebound.

ricotta (rĭ-kät′ə) *noun* a soft Italian cheese similar to cottage cheese.

rid *verb trans.* (*pa t* and *pa p* **rid** or **ridded**; *pr p* **ridding**) to free or clear (someone or something) of something undesirable or unwanted.

ridden *see* **ride.**

riddle[1] *noun* a large coarse sieve used e.g., for sifting gravel or grain. —*verb trans.* (**riddled, riddling**) **1** to pass (gravel, grain, etc.) through a riddle. **2** to fill with holes, esp. with gunshot: *a wall riddled with bullet holes.* **3** to spread through; to fill.

riddle[2] *noun* **1** a short, usu. humorous puzzle, that describes something in a mysterious or misleading way, and that has to be solved. **2** a person, thing, or fact that is puzzling .or difficult to understand. —*verb intrans., trans.* (**riddled, riddling**) **1** to speak in riddles. **2** to solve (a riddle).

ride *verb trans., intrans.* (*pa t* **rode**; *pa p* **ridden**; *pr p* **riding**) **1** to sit on and control (a bicycle, horse, etc.). **2** to travel or be carried in a car, train, etc., or on a bicycle, horse, etc. **3** to travel on (a vehicle). **4** to go out on horseback, esp. regularly. **5** to ride a horse in (a race). **6** to move or float on: *a ship riding the waves.* **7** to travel over or across by car, horse, etc. **8** to remain undisturbed or unchanged: *let matters ride.* **9** (**ride on** (**something**)) to depend on (it). —*noun* **1** a journey on horseback or by vehicle. **2** a lift in a motor vehicle. **3** the type of movement felt in a vehicle: *a smooth ride.* **4** a path, esp. one through a woods, for horseback riding. **5** a fairground entertainment, such as a rollercoaster. —**ride** (**something**) **out** to survive or get through (it) safely.

rider *noun* **1** a person who rides. **2** an addition to what has already been said or written, esp. an extra clause added to a document; an amendment, e.g., to a piece of legislation.

ridge *noun* **1** a strip of ground raised on either side of a plowed furrow. **2** a long, narrow, raised area on an otherwise flat surface. **3** the top edge where two upward sloping surfaces meet, e.g., on a roof. **4** *Meteorol.* a long, narrow area of high atmospheric pressure. —*verb trans., intrans.* (**ridged, ridging**) to form or make into ridges.

ridgepole *noun* **1** the beam along the ridge of a roof to which the upper ends of the rafters are attached. **2** the horizontal pole at the top of a tent.

ridicule *noun* language, laughter, behavior, etc., that makes someone or something appear foolish or humiliated; derision; mockery: *held them up to public ridicule.* —*verb trans.* (**ridiculed, ridiculing**) to laugh at, make fun of, or mock.

ridiculous *adj.* laughably senseless. ▣ ABSURD, FOOLISH, IDIOTIC, LUDICROUS, PREPOSTEROUS, RISIBLE, SILLY ▣ SERIOUS. ▶ **ridiculously** *adv.* ▶ **ridiculousness** *noun*

rife *adj.* **1** usu. *of something unfavorable* very common; extensive. **2** (**rife with** (**something**)) having a large amount or number of (something bad or undesirable).

riff *noun Jazz* a short passage of music played repeatedly.

riffle *verb trans., intrans.* (**riffled, riffling**) (**riffle through** (**something**)) to flick or leaf through (the pages of a book, a pile of papers, etc.) rapidly, esp. in a casual search.

riffraff *noun* people regarded as worthless, disreputable, or undesirable.

rifle[1] *noun* a large gun fired from the shoulder, with a long barrel with a spiral groove on the inside that gives the gun greater accuracy. —*verb trans.* (**rifled, rifling**) to cut spiral grooves in (a gun or its barrel).

rifle[2] *verb trans., intrans.* (**rifled, rifling**) **1** to search through (a house, safe, etc.) in order to steal something. **2** to steal (something).

rift *noun* **1** a split or crack, esp. one in the ground. **2** a breaking of friendly relations between previously friendly people. —*verb trans.* (**rifted, rifting**) to tear apart or split.

rig *verb trans.* (**rigged, rigging**) **1** to fit (a ship) with ropes, sails, and rigging. **2** to control or manipulate for dishonest purposes or personal gain: *rig an election.* —*noun* **1** the arrangement of sails, ropes, and masts on a ship. **2** an oil rig. **3** gear or equipment, esp. that used for a specific task. **4** clothing or a uniform worn for a particular occasion or task.

rigamarole *noun* same as **rigmarole.**

rigging *noun* **1** the system of ropes, wires, etc., that support and control a ship's masts and sails. **2** the ropes and wires, etc., that support the structure of an airship or the wings of a biplane.

right *adj.* **1** relating to the side of a person or thing that is toward the east when that person or thing is facing north: **2** on or close to a spectator's right side: *stage right.* **3**

containing or having no mistakes. **4** morally or legally correct or good. **5** suitable; appropriate. **6** in a correct, proper, satisfactory, or healthy condition. **7** of or on the side of fabric, a garment, etc., that is intended to be seen. **8** *Math.* with an axis perpendicular to the base: *a right angle.* **9** relating to the political right. **10** socially acceptable: *knows all the right people.* —*adv.* **1** exactly or precisely. **2** without delay; immediately: *I'll be right over.* **3** all the way; completely. **4** straight; directly: *right to the top.* **5** on or toward the right side. **6** correctly; properly; satisfactorily. —*noun* **1** (*often* **rights**) a power, privilege, etc., that a person may claim legally or morally. **2** (*often* **rights**) a just or legal claim: *mineral rights.* **3** that which is correct, good, or just. **4** fairness, truth, and justice. **5** the right side, part, direction, etc. **6** the members of any political party holding the most conservative views. **7** (**the Right**) people, political parties, etc., in favor of conservative positions and actions. **8** (**rights**) the legal permission to print, publish, film, etc., a book. —*verb trans., intrans.* (**righted, righting**) **1** to put or come back to the correct, esp. upright, position. **2** to avenge or compensate for (something wrong done). **3** to put in order; to correct. —*interj.* used to express agreement, assent, or readiness. —**by rights** rightfully.

right angle an angle of 90°, formed by two lines that are perpendicular to each other. ▸ **right-angled** *adj.*

righteous (rī'chəs) *adj.* **1** free from sin or guilt. **2** of an action morally good; just. ▸ **righteously** *adv.* ▸ **righteousness** *noun*

right field (ABBREV. **RF**) *Baseball* the third of the outfield to the right, facing home plate. ▸ **right-fielder**

rightful *adj.* **1** having a legally just claim. **2** of property, a privilege, etc. held by just right. **3** fair; just; equitable. ▸ **rightfully** *adv.* ▸ **rightfulness** *noun*

right-hand *adj.* **1** on or toward the right. **2** done with the right hand.

right-handed *adj.* **1** having the right hand stronger and more dexterous than the left. **2** for use by right-handed people, or the right hand. **3** of a screw needing to be turned clockwise to be screwed in. ▸ **right-handedly** *adv.* ▸ **right-handedness** *noun*

right-hander *noun* a right-handed person.

rightism *noun* the principles and policies of the political right. ▸ **rightist** *adj., noun*

rightly *adv.* **1** in a correct way; correctly; in a just and fair manner. **2** with good reason; justifiably.

right of way (*pl.* **rights of way**) **1** a the right of the public to use a path that crosses private

property. **b** a path used by this right. **2** the right of one vehicle to proceed before other vehicles coming from different directions at junctions, traffic circles, etc.

right wing 1 the members of a political party who hold the most conservative opinions. **2** *Sport* **a** the right side of a team in a field game. **b** a player playing on this side. ▸ **right-wing** *adj.* ▸ **right-winger** *noun*

rigid *adj.* **1** completely stiff and inflexible. **2** not able to be moved. **3** of a person strictly and inflexibly adhering to one's ideas, opinions and rules. **4** of rules, etc. strictly maintained; not relaxed. ▸ **rigidity** *noun* ▸ **rigidly** *adv.* ▸ **rigidness** *noun*

rigmarole *or* **rigamarole** *noun* **1** an unnecessarily long, complicated series of instructions or procedures. **2** a long, rambling or confused statement or speech.

> Originally *ragman roll*, a Scots term for a long list or catalogue

rigor (rǐg'ər) *noun* **1** stiffness or hardness. **2** severity or strictness, e.g., of temper, behavior, or judgment. **3** strict enforcement of the law or of rules. **4** (*usu.* **rigors**) a harsh or severe condition, esp. of weather or climate. **5** austerity. ▸ **rigorous** *adj.* ▸ **rigorously** *adv.*

rigor mortis (môrt'ĭs) the stiffening of a corpse after death.

rile *verb trans.* (**riled, riling**) to anger or annoy.

rill *noun* a small stream or brook.

rim *noun* **1** a raised, often curved edge or border. **2** the outer circular edge of a wheel to which a tire is mounted. —*verb trans.* (**rimmed, rimming**) to form or provide an edge or rim to. ▸ **rimless** *adj.*

rime *noun* thick white frost. —*verb trans.* (**rimed, riming**) to cover with rime. ▸ **rimy** *adj.*

rind (rīnd) *noun* the thick, hard, outer layer or covering, e.g., on the peel of fruit. —*verb trans.* (**rinded, rinding**) to strip bark from.

ring[1] *noun* **1** a small circle of gold, silver, or other metal or material, worn on a finger. **2** a circle of metal, wood, plastic, etc., for holding, keeping in place, connecting, hanging, etc. **3** an object, mark, or figure that is circular in shape. **4** a circular course. **5** a group of people or things arranged in a circle. **6** an enclosed, usu. circular area for competitions or exhibitions, esp. at a circus. **7** *Sport* **a** a square area marked off by ropes on a platform, where boxers or wrestlers fight. **b** (**the ring**) boxing as a profession. **8** a group of people who act together to control, e.g., drug market, betting, etc. **9** a circular electric element or gas burner on top of a stove. —*verb trans.* (**ringed, ringing**) **1** to make, form, draw, etc., a ring around. **2** to put a ring on the leg of (a bird) as a means of identifying it. **3** to fit a ring in the nose of (a bull) to make it easy to lead.

ring² verb trans., intrans. (pa t **rang**; pa p **rung**; pr p **ringing**) **1** to cause to make, or to make a sound, esp. a ringing, bell-like sound. **2** (**ring (someone) up**) to call (someone) by telephone. **3** (**ring for (someone)**) to ring a bell as a summons to (someone): rang for the maid. **4** of a place or building to be filled with sound. **5** to sound repeatedly; to resound: Criticisms rang in our ears. **6** of the ears to be filled with a buzzing, humming, or ringing sensation or sound. **7** of words, etc. to give a stated impression: His promises rang false. —noun **1** the act or sound of ringing. **2** a the act of ringing a bell. **b** the clear, resonant sound of a bell, or a similarly resonant sound. **3** a telephone call. **4** a suggestion or impression of a particular feeling or quality. —**ring a bell** colloq. to elicit a memory.

ringer noun **1** a person or thing that rings. **2** colloq. a dead ringer. **3** a contestant entered into a race or competition under a false name or other false pretenses. **4** an impostor or fake.

ringleader noun the leader of a group of people who are doing something unlawful or are making trouble.

ringlet noun a long spiral curl of hair.

ringmaster noun a person in charge of performances in a circus ring.

rings see **gymnastics**.

ringside noun **1** the seating area immediately by a boxing, circus, etc., ring. **2** a place that gives a good clear view.

ringworm noun Med. a highly contagious fungal infection in which inflamed and itchy red circular patches form on the skin.

rink noun **1** an area of ice prepared for skating, curling, or ice hockey, or a building containing it. **2** an area of smooth floor for roller skating, or a building containing it.

rinse verb trans. (**rinsed, rinsing**) **1** to wash (soap, detergent, etc.) out of (clothes, hair, dishes, etc.) with clean water. **2** to remove traces of dirt by washing lightly in clean water, usu. without soap. —noun **1** an act of rinsing. **2** liquid used for rinsing. **3** a solution used in hairdressing to give temporary color to the hair. ▸ **rinser** noun

riot noun **1** Law a noisy public disturbance or disorder by a usu. large group of people. **2** uncontrolled, wild revelry and feasting. **3** a striking display (esp. of color). **4** a hilarious person or thing. —verb intrans. (**rioted, rioting**) to take part in a riot. ▸ **rioter** noun

riotous adj. **1** participating in, likely to start, or resembling, a riot. **2** very active, noisy, cheerful, and wild. **3** filled with wild revelry, parties, etc.. riotous living. ▸ **riotously** adv.

▸ **riotousness** noun

R.I.P. abbrev. requiescat in pace (Latin), may he or she rest in peace.

rip verb trans., intrans. (**ripped, ripping**) **1** to tear or come apart violently or roughly. **2** (**rip (something) off** or **out**) to remove (it) quickly and violently. **3** colloq. to rush along or move quickly without restraint. **4** to saw (wood or timber) along the grain. —noun **1** a violent or rough tear or split. **2** an act of ripping. —**rip (someone) off** colloq. **1** to cheat (another) or to steal from (another). **2** to overcharge (another). ▸ **ripper** noun

ripcord noun a cord that releases a parachute from its pack when pulled.

ripe adj. **1** of fruit, etc. fully matured and ready to be picked and eaten. **2** of cheese having been allowed to age in order to develop its full flavor. **3** mature; fully developed. **4** (**ripe for (something)**) a suitable or appropriate to (it). **b** eager or ready for (it). ▸ **ripen** verb ▸ **ripeness** noun

rip-off noun colloq. **1** an act or instance of stealing from, cheating, or defrauding. **2** an item that is outrageously overpriced.

riposte (ri-pōst′) noun **1** a quick, sharp reply; a retort. **2** a fencer's quick return thrust. —verb intrans. (**riposted, riposting**) to answer with a riposte.

ripple noun **1** a slight wave or series of slight waves on the surface of water. **2** a sound that rises and falls quickly and gently like that of rippling water, esp. of laughter or applause. **3** a wavy appearance, e.g., of material. —verb intrans., trans. (**rippled, rippling**) **1** to form or cause to form or flow with ripples or a rippling motion. **2** to make a rippling sound. ▸ **ripply** adj.

rip-roaring adj. wild, noisy, and exciting.

ripsaw noun a saw for cutting along the grain of timber.

rise verb intrans. (pa t **rose**; pa p **risen**; pr p **rising**) **1** to get or stand up, esp. from a sitting, kneeling, or lying position. **2** to get up from bed, esp. after a night's sleep. **3** to move upward; to ascend. **4** to increase in size, amount, volume, strength, degree, intensity, etc. **5** of the Sun, Moon, etc. to appear above the horizon. **6** to stretch or slope upward: ground that rises gently. **7** (**rise up** or **rise against (someone or something)**) to rebel against (the one specified). **8** to move from a lower position, rank, level, etc., to a higher one. **9** to begin or originate: a river that rises in the mountains. **10** (**rise to (something)**) to respond to (something) (e.g., provocation or criticism). —noun **1** an act of rising. **2** an increase in size, amount, volume, strength, status, rank, etc. **3** a piece of rising ground; a slope or hill. **4** a beginning or origin.

riser noun 1 a person who gets out of bed. 2 any of the vertical parts between the horizontal steps of a set of stairs.

risible (rĭz'ə-bəl) adj. 1 laughably senseless. 2 causing laughter. 3 inclined to laughter. ► **risibility** noun

risk noun 1 a the chance or possibility of suffering loss, injury, damage, or failure. b a situation or state in which one is exposed to harm, injury, or loss. 2 a person likely to cause or to sustain loss, injury, or damage. —verb trans. (**risked, risking**) 1 to expose to danger or risk. 2 to take the chance of (risk, danger, etc., occurring): didn't want to risk being late. ► **riskily** adv. ► **riskiness** noun ► **risky** adj.

risqué (rĭs-kā') adj., of a story, joke, etc. bordering on the rude or indecent.

rite noun 1 a religious ceremony or observance. 2 the required words or actions for a religious ceremony.

ritual (rĭch'ə-wəl) noun 1 a the set order or words used in a religious ceremony. b a body of such rituals, esp. of a particular church. c the use of rituals in a religious ceremony. 2 an often repeated series of actions or sets of procedure. —adj. relating to or resembling rites or ritual. ► **ritualism** noun ► **ritualist** noun ► **ritualistic** adj. ► **ritualistically** adv. ► **ritually** adv.

ritzy adj. (**ritzier, ritziest**) colloq. highly elegant, often ostentatiously so.

rival noun 1 a person or group of people competing with another for the same goal or in the same field. 2 a person or thing that equals another in quality, ability, etc. —adj. being a rival. —verb trans. (**rivaled or rivalled, rivaling or rivalling**) 1 to try to gain the same goal as (someone); to be in competition with. 2 to try to equal or to better than. 3 to be able to be compared with as being equal or nearly so. ► **rivalry** noun

riven adj. having been violently torn or split apart.

river noun Geol. a natural flow of water, larger than a stream.

riverboat noun a boat that can be used on rivers.

rivet noun a metal pin or bolt for fastening plates of metal together, with a headless end that can be beaten to form a second head to hold the bolt securely in place. —verb trans. (**riveted, riveting**) 1 to fasten two or more pieces of metal with a metal pin or bolt. 2 to flatten or beat down (the head of a nail, etc.). 3 to fix securely. 4 to attract and hold firmly; to engross (e.g., a person's attention). ► **riveter** noun

riveting adj. fully occupying the mind.

rivulet noun a small stream or river, or something resembling one.

rm. abbrev. room.

RN abbrev. 1 (also **R.N.**) registered nurse. 2 Royal Navy.

Rn symbol Chem. radon.

RNA noun Biochem. ribonucleic acid, an acid found in all living cells that is involved in the development of proteins, and that also holds genetic information. See also **nucleic acid**.

roach[1] noun a silvery freshwater fish of the carp family.

roach[2] noun 1 colloq. a cockroach. 2 slang the butt of a marijuana cigarette.

road noun 1 an open, usu. specially surfaced or paved way, for people, vehicles, or animals to travel on from one place to another. 2 a route or way: the road to ruin.

roadbed noun 1 the foundation of a railroad track. 2 the material laid down to form a road, and that forms a foundation for the road surface.

roadblock noun 1 a barrier put across a road (e.g., by the police) to stop and check vehicles and drivers. 2 an obstacle to progress.

roadhog slang an aggressive and selfish motorist.

roadhouse noun a bar, restaurant, or inn on the side of a road.

roadrunner noun a crested, fast-running N American bird that has a long tail and streaked, brownish feathers.

roadside noun a strip of ground or land beside or along a road.

roadster noun 1 an open sports car for two people. 2 a horse for riding on roads.

road test a test of the operating capability of, e.g., a motor vehicle or a motorist seeking a driver's license. ► **road-test** verb

roadway noun the part of a road or street used by cars.

roadwork noun 1 the building or repairing of a road. 2 fitness training in the form of long runs on roads.

roam verb intrans., trans. (**roamed, roaming**) to ramble or wander about; to wander over or about (a place). —noun the act of roaming; a ramble. ► **roamer** noun

roan adj., usu. of horses or cattle having a reddish-brown or bay coat thickly flecked with gray or white hairs. —noun an animal, esp. a horse, with a coat of this type.

roar verb intrans., trans. (**roared, roaring**) 1 to sound or say loudly and harshly. 2 to emit a loud, growling cry: The lion roared. 3 to laugh loudly and deeply. 4 to make a deep, loud, reverberating sound, as of cannons. 5 to say (something) with a deep, loud cry, esp. as in anger. —noun 1 a loud, deep, prolonged cry, as of lions, a cheering crowd, a person in pain or anger, etc. 2 a loud, deep, prolonged sound, as of cannons.

roaring adj. **1** uttering or emitting roars. **2** thriving, lively, and successful: a roaring business.

roast verb trans., intrans. (**roasted, roasting**) **1** to cook (meat or other food) by exposure to dry heat, esp. in an oven. **2** to dry and make brown (coffee beans, nuts, etc.) by exposure to dry heat. **3** of meat, coffee beans, nuts, etc. to be cooked or dried and made brown by being exposed to dry heat. **4** colloq. to make or become extremely or excessively hot. **5** colloq. to criticize severely. —noun **1** a piece of meat that has been roasted or is suitable for roasting. **2** a party in the open air at which food is roasted and eaten. —adj. roasted: roast beef. ▸ **roaster** noun

roasting colloq. adj. very hot. —noun a dose of severe criticism.

rob verb trans., intrans. (**robbed, robbing**) **1** to steal something from (a person or place), esp. by force or threats. **2** to deprive (someone) of something expected as a right or due. ▸ **robbery** noun

robe noun **1** (often **robes**) a long, loose, flowing garment, esp. one worn for special ceremonies by judges, academics, etc. **2** a dressing gown or bathrobe. —verb trans., intrans. (**robed, robing**) to clothe (oneself or someone else) in robes or a robe.

robin noun **1** a N American thrush with a brick-red breast, larger than the European robin. **2** a small brown European thrush with an orange-red breast. Also called **redbreast**.

robot noun **1** esp. in science fiction, etc., a machine that looks and functions like a human. **2** a machine that can be programmed to perform specific tasks. **3** a person who works efficiently and mechanically, but who lacks human warmth.

robotics noun (sing.) the branch of engineering concerned with the design, construction, operation, and use of industrial robots.

robust adj. **1** strong and healthy; having a strong constitution. **2** strongly built or constructed. **3** of exercise, etc. requiring strength and energy. **4** rough, earthy, and slightly rude. **5** of wine with a full, rich quality. ▸ **robustly** adv. ▸ **robustness** noun

rock¹ noun **1** Geol. **a** a loose or consolidated mass of one or more minerals that forms part of Earth's crust. **b** a large natural mass of this material forming, e.g., a reef. **c** a large stone or boulder; also a stone or a pebble. **2** someone or something that provides a firm foundation or support and can be depended upon. **3** a hard candy usu. in the form of long, cylindrical sticks. **4** slang a precious stone, esp. a diamond. —**on the rocks** colloq. **1** of a marriage broken down; failed. **2** of an alcoholic drink served over ice cubes.

rock² verb trans., intrans. (**rocked, rocking**) **1** to sway or cause to sway gently backward and forward or from side to side: rock a baby to sleep. **2** to undergo heavy vibration or jolting particularly as the result of a physical shock. **3** to disturb, upset, or shock. **4** to dance to or play rock music. —noun **1** a rocking movement. **2** a popular music with a very strong beat, usu. played on electronic instruments and derived from rock 'n' roll. Also called **rock music**. **b** rock 'n' roll. —adj. relating to rock music.

rock-and-roll noun, verb same as **rock 'n' roll**.

rock bottom the lowest possible level. ▸ **rock-bottom** adj.

rocker noun **1** one of usu. two curved supports on which a chair, cradle, etc., rocks. **2** something that rocks on such supports, esp. a rocking chair. **3** a person or thing that rocks. —**off one's rocker** colloq. crazy; mad.

rockery noun (pl. **rockeries**) a rock garden.

rocket noun **1** a cylinder containing flammable material, which when ignited is projected through the air. **2** a projectile or vehicle, esp. a space vehicle, that obtains its thrust from a backward jet of hot gases produced by the burning of a mixture of fuel and oxygen. **3** any one of various plants of the mustard family. —verb intrans., trans. (**rocketed, rocketing**) **1** to move (esp. upward) extremely quickly, as if with the speed of a rocket. **2** to attack with rockets.

rock garden a garden containing plants and rocks arranged in a decorative scheme. Also called **rockery**.

rocking chair a chair that rocks backward and forward on two curved supports.

rocking horse a toy horse mounted on two curved supports on which a child can sit and rock backward and forward.

rock 'n' roll or **rock-and-roll** noun popular music with a lively jive beat and simple melodies. —verb intrans. (**rocked 'n' rolled** or **rocked-and-rolled, rocking 'n' rolling** or **rocking-and-rolling**) **1** to play or dance to this music. **2** slang to get moving, usu. to start driving away from a place.

rock salt common salt occurring as a mass of solid mineral.

rocky¹ adj. (**rockier, rockiest**) **1** full of rocks; made of or resembling rock. **2** full of problems and obstacles. ▸ **rockiness** noun

rocky² adj. (**rockier, rockiest**) shaky; unsteady. ▸ **rockily** adv.

rococo noun an ornamental style, characteristic of the 18th-c Rococo. —adj. florid and elaborate: a rococo speech.

rod noun **1** a long slender stick or bar of wood, metal, etc. **2** a stick or bundle of twigs used for beating as a punishment. **3** a stick, wand, or scepter carried as a symbol of office or authority. **4** a fishing pole. **5** *Anat.* a rod-shaped light-sensitive receptor in the retina of the eye. **6** *slang* a pistol.

rode *see* ride.

rodent *noun* any of the group of relatively small mammals with strong incisors for gnawing, including mice, rats, squirrels, and beavers.

rodeo *noun* (*pl.* **rodeos**) a show or contest of cowboy skills, including riding, lassoing, etc.

roe¹ *noun* **1** the mass of eggs in the body cavity of a female fish. **2** the sperm of a male fish.

roe² *noun* a small deer found in Europe and Asia.

roentgen *or* **röntgen** (rĕnt′gən, rənt′-) (ABBREV. R, r) *noun* a unit for measuring a dose of x-rays.

roger *interj. in radio communications and signaling* used to indicate that a message has been received and understood.

rogue (rōg) *noun* **1** a dishonest person. **2** a person, esp. a child, who is playfully mischievous. —*adj.* of, relating to, resembling, or behaving like a rogue. ▸ **roguery** *noun* ▸ **roguish** *adj.* ▸ **roguishly** *adv.* ▸ **roguishness** *noun*

role *or* **rôle** *noun* **1** an actor's part in a play, movie, etc. **2** a part played in life, business, etc.; a person's function.

role model a person whose life and behavior is taken as an example to follow by someone else.

roll *noun* **1** something flat (e.g., paper, fabric) that is rolled up to form a cylinder or tube. **2 a** a small soft piece of bread for one person. **b** a folded piece of pastry or cake with a specified filling: *a sausage roll.* **3** a rolled mass: *rolls of fat.* **4** an official list of names, e.g., of school pupils. **5** an act of rolling. **6** a swaying or rolling movement. **7** a long, low, prolonged sound. **8** a series of quick beats on a drum. **9** a roller or cylinder used to press, shape, or apply something. —*verb trans., intrans.* (**rolled, rolling**) **1** to cause to move, or to move, by turning over and over as if on an axis, often in a specified direction. **2** to cause to move, or to move on wheels, rollers, etc., or in a vehicle with wheels. **3** (*also* **roll over**) *of a person or animal, etc.,* lying down to turn with a rolling movement to face in another direction. **4** to move or cause to move or flow gently and steadily. **5** e.g., *of a ship* to sway or rock gently from side to side. **6** to walk with a swaying movement. **7** to begin to operate or work, or to cause this: *the cameras rolled.* **8** to move or cause (one's eyes) to move in a circle, esp. in disbelief, despair, or amazement. **9** to form or cause to form a tube or cylinder by winding or being wound around and around. **10** (*also* **roll up** *or* **roll (something) up**) to

wrap (it) or to be wrapped by rolling. **11** (*also* **roll out** *or* **roll (something) out**) to spread (it) out or make (it) flat or flatter, esp. by pressing and smoothing with something heavy. **12** to make a series of long low rumbling sounds. **13** to pronounce (esp. an r sound) with a trill. —**on a roll** *colloq.* experiencing sustained, increasing success.

rollback *noun* a reduction, e.g., in prices, or a retreat, e.g., from a position.

roll call the calling out of names from a list, e.g., at a meeting, to check who is present.

roller *noun* **1** any of a number of cylindrical objects or machines used for flattening, crushing, spreading, printing, applying paint, etc. **2** a rod for rolling cloth, etc., around. **3** a small cylinder on which hair is rolled for curling. **4** a long, heavy ocean wave.

Rollerblades (rō′lər-blādz,) *trademark* used to denote a set of in-line skates.

roller coaster 1 a raised railroad with sharp curves and steep inclines, ridden on for pleasure and excitement. **2** *colloq.* a situation likened to a ride on a roller coaster: *an emotional roller coaster.*

roller skate a series of wheels attached to a framework which can be fitted over one's shoe, or a shoe with wheels attached to the sole. ▸ **roller-skate** *verb* ▸ **roller skater**

rollicking *adj.* boisterous, noisy, and carefree.

rolling pin a wooden, plastic, pottery, etc., cylinder for flattening out dough.

roly-poly *adj.* round and pudgy.

ROM *abbrev. Comput.* read-only memory.

romaine (rō-mān′) *noun same as* cos.

Roman (rō′mən) *adj.* **1** of or related to modern or ancient Rome and the Roman Empire, its history, culture, or inhabitants. **2** of or pertaining to the Roman Catholic Church. **3** (**roman**) *of printing type* set in ordinary upright letters as opposed to italics. —*noun* **1** an inhabitant of modern or ancient Rome. **2** a Roman Catholic. **3** (**roman**) *of printing type* roman letters or typeface.

Roman Catholic *adj.* of or relating to the Christian church that recognizes the pope as its head. —*noun* a member of this church.

romance *noun* **1** a love affair. **2** sentimentalized or idealized love. **3** an atmosphere, the feelings, or behavior associated with romantic love. **4 a** a sentimental account, esp. in writing or on film, of a love affair. **b** such writing, films, etc., as a group or genre. **5** a fictitious story that deals with imaginary, adventurous, and mysterious events, places, etc. **6** a medieval verse narrative dealing with chivalry, highly idealized love, and fantastic adventures. **7** (**Romance**) the group of languages, including French, Spanish, and Italian, that have developed from Latin. —*adj.*

(**Romance**) of or relating to the languages that have developed from Latin. —*verb trans.*, *intrans.* (**romanced,** romancing) 1 to try to win the love of. 2 to talk or write extravagantly, romantically, or fantastically.

Romanesque (rō,mə-nĕsk') *noun* the style of architecture found in W and S Europe from the 9th c to the 12th c. —*adj.* in or relating to this style of architecture.

Romanian *or* **Rumanian** *noun* 1 a native or citizen of Romania. 2 the official language of Romania. —*adj.* of Romania, its people, or their language.

Roman numeral any one of the figures used to represent numbers in the system developed by the ancient Romans, e.g., I (= 1), V (= 5), etc. *See also* **Arabic numeral.**

omantic *adj.* 1 characterized by or inclined toward sentimental and idealized love. 2 dealing with or suggesting adventure, mystery, and sentimentalized love. 3 highly impractical or imaginative, and often also foolish. 4 (*often* **Romantic**) *of literature, art, music, etc.* relating to or in the style of romanticism. —*noun* 1 a romantic person. 2 a person who writes, paints, etc., in the style of Romanticism. ▸ **romantically** *adv.*

Romanticism (rō-mănt'ə-sĭz,əm) *noun* a late 18th-c and early 19th-c movement in art, literature, and music, characterized by an emphasis on feelings and emotions, often using imagery taken from nature, and creating forms that are relatively free from rules and set orders. ▸ **Romanticist** *noun*

romanticize *verb trans., intrans.* (**romanticized, romanticizing**) 1 to make seem romantic. 2 to describe or think of in a romantic, idealized, unrealistic, and sometimes misleading way. 3 to hold romantic ideas or act in a romantic way.

Romany (răm'ə-nē, rō'mə-) *noun* (*pl.* **Romanies**) 1 a Gypsy. 2 the Indic language spoken by Gypsies. —*adj.* of the Gypsies, their language, and culture.

Romeo (rō'mē-ō,) *noun* (*pl.* **Romeos**) an ardent young male lover.

romp *verb intrans.* (**romped, romping**) 1 to play in a lively, boisterous way. 2 to succeed in a race, competition, task, etc., quickly and easily. —*noun* 1 an act of romping; boisterous play. 2 a swift pace. 3 a young person who romps.

rompers *pl. noun* a suit for a baby, with short-legged pants and either a short-sleeved top or a bib top.

rondo *noun* (*pl.* **rondos**) a piece of music with a recurring principal theme.

röntgen *noun same as* **roentgen.**

rood (rōōd) *noun* 1 a cross or crucifix. 2 *literary* the cross on which Christ was crucified.

roof (rōōf, rŏŏf) *noun* (*pl.* **roofs**) 1 the top, usu. rigid, covering of a building or vehicle. 2 the top inner surface of the mouth. 3 a dwelling or home. 4 a high, or the highest, level: *the roof of the world.* —*verb trans., intrans.* (**roofed, roofing**) 1 to cover with a roof. 2 to serve as a roof or shelter for. 3 to make a living putting roofs onto structures or repairing them. ▸ **roofer** *noun*

roofing *noun* materials for building a roof.

rook[1] (rŏŏk) *noun* a large, crow-like bird which nests in colonies in the tops of trees, found in Europe and Asia. —*verb* (**rooked, rooking**) *colloq.* to cheat or defraud, esp. at cards.

rook[2] *noun* (ABBREV. R) *Chess* castle (sense 2).

rookery *noun* (*pl.* **rookeries**) 1 a colony of rooks. 2 a colony, e.g., of penguins or seals.

rookie *noun colloq.* a new or raw recruit.

room *noun* 1 a part of a building that is separated from the rest of the building by having a ceiling, floor, and walls. 2 a space or area that is occupied by or is available to someone or something. 3 all of the people present in a room. 4 opportunity, scope, or possibility: *room for improvement.* 5 (**rooms**) rented lodgings. —*verb intrans.* (**roomed, rooming**) to lodge in or share a room. ▸ **roomful** *noun* ▸ **roominess** *noun* ▸ **roomy** *adj.*

roommate *noun* a person who shares a room with another person.

roost *noun* 1 a branch, perch, etc., on which birds rest at night. 2 a group of birds resting together on the same branch or perch. —*verb intrans.* (**roosted, roosting**) to settle on a roost, esp. for sleep.

rooster *noun* an adult male chicken.

root[1] *noun* 1 *Bot.* the usu. underground part of a plant that secures it in the ground and which absorbs water and nourishment from the soil. 2 the part by which something is attached to or embedded in something larger. 3 *Anat.* the embedded part of a tooth, hair, nail, or similar structure. 4 a basic cause, source, or origin. 5 (**roots**) one's ancestry or family origins. 6 (**roots**) one's feeling of belonging to a community or in a place. 7 *Linguistics* the basic element in a word that remains after all the affixes have been removed, and that may form the basis of a number of related words. *See also* **stem[1]** (sense 4). 8 *Math.* a factor of a quantity that when multiplied by itself a specified number of times produces that quantity again, e.g., 2 is the square root of 4 and the cube root of 8. —*verb trans.* (**rooted, rooting**) 1 to grow roots; to become firmly established. 2 (*also* **root (something) up**) to dig (it) up by the roots. 3 to fix with or as if with roots. 4 to provide with roots. ▸ **rootless** *adj.* ▸ **rootlessness** *noun*

root² *verb intrans.* **(rooted, rooting) 1** *esp. of pigs* to dig up the ground with the snout in search of food. **2** (*usu.* **root around** or **about**) to poke about in looking for something; to rummage. **3** (*usu.* **root (something) out**) to find or extract (it) by rummaging, etc.

root³ *verb intrans.* **(rooted, rooting)** (**root for (that which is specified)**) *colloq.* to support (e.g., a team) with loud cheering and encouragement.

root beer a carbonated soft drink made from the roots of certain plants and flavored with herbs.

root canal *Dentistry* **1** the channel in the root of a tooth that is filled with pulp. **2** a dental procedure in which diseased pulp is removed and the cavity filled with inert material.

rooted *adj.* fixed by or as if by roots; firmly established.

rootstock *noun Bot.* a rhizome.

rope *noun* **1** strong thick cord made by twisting fibers together; also, a length of this cord. **2** a number of objects, esp. pearls or onions, strung together. **3** a hangman's noose. **4** a long, thin, sticky strand. —*verb trans.* **(roped, roping) 1** to tie, fasten, or bind with a rope. **2** (**rope (something) off**) to enclose, separate, or divide (it) with a rope. **3** (*also* **rope up** or **rope (someone) up**) to attach (climbers), or to be attached to a rope for safety. **4** to catch with a rope; to lasso. —**at the end of (one's) rope** *colloq.* at the very limit of (one's) endurance or patience. **know the ropes** to have a thorough knowledge and experience of what needs to be done. **on the ropes** *slang* in a hopeless position; on the verge of total defeat or collapse. ▸ **ropy** or **ropey** *adj.*

Roquefort (rōk′fərt) *trademark* used for a strong, soft, blue-veined cheese made from ewes' milk.

rorqual (rôr′kwəl) any of various baleen whales having a furrowed throat, allowing it to expand when feeding.

Rorschach test (rôr′shäk,) *Psychol.* a test designed to show intelligence, type of personality, mental state, etc., in which the subject is asked to describe the pictures formed by a number of inkblots. *Also called* **inkblot test**.

rosary *noun* (*pl.* **rosaries**) *RC Church* **1** a string of beads used to count prayers as they are recited, used in devotions to the Virgin Mary. **2** a series of prayers with a set form and order counted on a string of beads.

rose¹ *noun* **1 a** any of a family of shrubs with prickly stems and often sweet-smelling flowers. **b** the ornamental flower produced by this plant. **2** a darkish pink color. **3** (**roses**) a light pink, glowing complexion:

put the roses back in one's cheeks. **4** a nozzle with holes, usu. attached to the end of a hose, shower, etc., to make the water come out in a spray. —*adj.* of or resembling roses or a rose, esp. in color or scent.

rose² *see* **rise**.

rosé (rō-zā′). *noun* a light pink wine made by removing the skins of red grapes after fermentation has begun.

roseate (rō′zē-ət, -āt,) *adj.* **1** resembling a rose, esp. in color. **2** unrealistically hopeful or cheerful.

rose-colored *adj.* pink. —**through rose-colored glasses** with an unrealistically hopeful or cheerful view of circumstances.

rose hip the red berrylike fruit of a rose.

rosemary *noun* an evergreen aromatic shrub with stiff needlelike leaves used in cookery and perfumery.

rosette (rō-zĕt′) *noun* **1** a badge or decoration made in colored ribbon to resemble the shape and form of a rose, often awarded as a prize or worn as a sign of affiliation. **2** *Bot.* a circular cluster of leaves arising from a central point.

rosewood *noun* a valuable dark red wood used in making high quality furniture.

Rosh Hashanah (rôsh,häsh,ə-nä′, rôsh,ə-shän′ə) the Jewish festival of the New Year, which falls in September or October.

rosin (räz′ən) *noun* a resin produced by distilling turpentine prepared from dead pine wood, rubbed on the bows of stringed musical instruments, and on the tips of toe shoes to prevent the dancers from slipping. —*verb trans.* **(rosined, rosining)** to rub with rosin.

roster *noun* a list of people showing the order in which they are to do various duties, go on leave, etc. —*verb trans.* **(rostered, rostering)** to put (a name) on a roster.

rostrum *noun* (*pl.* **rostrums, rostra**) **1** a platform on which a public speaker stands. **2** a raised platform. **3** *Zool.* the beak of a bird, or a similar structure in other animals.

rosy *adj.* (**rosier, rosiest**) **1** rose-colored; pink. **2** hopeful; optimistic; cheerful. ▸ **rosily** *adv.* ▸ **rosiness** *noun*

rot *verb trans., intrans.* **(rotted, rotting) 1** to decay or to cause decay. **2** to become corrupt. **3** to become physically weak. —*noun* **1** something that has rotted or decomposed. **2** *colloq.* nonsense; rubbish.

rotary (rōt′ə-rē) *adj.* turning on an axis like a wheel. —*noun* (*pl.* **rotaries**) **1** a traffic circle. **2** any device that rotates about an axis.

rotate (rō′tāt,) *verb trans., intrans.* **(rotated, rotating) 1** to turn or cause to turn on an axis like a wheel. **2** to arrange in an ordered sequence. **3** to take turns according to an ordered sequence.

rotation *noun* **1** an act of rotating or state of being rotated. **2** *Med.* a set period in a sequence during which, e.g., an intern or a medical student, serves on a particular medical or other service: *a pediatric rotation.* **3** one complete turn around an axis. **4** a regular, recurring sequence.

rote *noun* the mechanical use of the memory without necessarily understanding what is memorized.

rotisserie (rō-tǐs′ə-rē) *noun* a cooking apparatus with a spit on which meat, poultry, etc., may be cooked by direct heat.

rotor *noun* **1** a rotating machine part, esp. in an internal combustion engine. **2** a system of blades projecting from a cylinder that rotate at high speed to lift and propel a helicopter.

rototiller *noun* a cultivator driven by a gasoline engine. ▸ **rototill** *verb*

rotten *adj.* **1** having spoiled, decayed, rotted, or fallen to pieces. **2** morally corrupt. **3** *colloq.* miserably unwell: *feeling rotten.* **4** *colloq.* unsatisfactory. **5** *colloq.* unpleasant; disagreeable. ▸ **rottenness** *noun*

rottweiler (rät′wī,lər, rôt′vī,-) *noun* a large breed of dog having a heavy muscular body, and a short black and tan coat.

rotund *adj.* **1** round. **2** plump. **3** impressive or grandiloquent. ▸ **rotundity** *noun*

rotunda *noun* a round, usu. domed, building or hall. ▸ **rotundly** *adv.* ▸ **rotundness** *noun*

rouble *noun* same as **ruble.**

roué (rōō-ā′) *noun* old use a disreputable man.

rouge (rōōzh) *noun* a pink or red powder or cream used to color the cheeks. —*verb intrans., trans.* (**rouged, rouging**) to use rouge, or to apply rouge to (the cheeks).

rough *adj.* **1** *of a surface* not smooth, even, or regular. **2** *of ground* covered with stones, tall grass, bushes and/or scrub. **3** covered with shaggy or coarse hair. **4** harsh or grating. **5** *of a person's character, behavior, etc.* noisy, coarse, or violent. **6** stormy. **7** requiring hard work or considerable physical effort, or involving great difficulty, tension, etc. **8** (**rough on (the one or ones specified)**) unpleasant and hard to bear: *a decision that is rough on everyone.* **9** approximate. **10** not polished or refined: *a rough draft.* **11** *colloq.* slightly unwell and tired, esp. because of heavy drinking or lack of sleep. —*noun* **1** (*often* **the rough**) rough ground, esp. the uncut grass in the side of a golf fairway. **2** an unpleasant or disagreeable side: *take the rough with the smooth.* **3** a crude state. **4** a crude preliminary sketch. **5** a thug or hooligan; a rowdy fellow. —**rough it** *colloq.* to live primitively, without the usual comforts of life. ▸ **roughly** *adv.* ▸ **roughness** *noun*

roughage (rəf′ĭj) *noun* dietary fiber.

roughen *verb trans., intrans.* (**roughened, roughening**) to make or become rough.

rough-hew *verb trans.* (*pa t* **rough-hewed;** *pa p* **rough-hewed** *or* **rough-hewn;** *pr p* **rough-hewing**) to shape crudely and without refining. ▸ **rough-hewn** *adj.*

roughhouse *colloq. noun* a disturbance or brawl. —*verb intrans.* (**roughhoused, roughhousing**) to engage in rowdy or brawling behavior.

roughneck *noun* **1** a worker on an oil rig. **2** a rough and rowdy person.

roughshod *adj., of a horse* having horseshoes with projecting nails which prevent the horse from slipping in wet weather. —**ride roughshod over** to treat (someone) arrogantly and without regard for his or her feelings.

roulette (rōō-lĕt′) *noun* a gambling game in which a ball is dropped into a spinning wheel divided up into compartments with the players betting on which compartment the ball will come to rest in.

round *adj.* **1** shaped like, or similar to, a circle or a ball. **2** not angular; curved and plump. **3** moving in or forming a circle. **4** *of numbers* complete and exact: *a round dozen.* **5** *of a number* without a fraction. **6** *of a number* approximate, without taking minor amounts into account. **7** *of a sum of money* considerable; substantial. —*adv.* **1** in a circular direction or with a circular or revolving movement; around. **2** on all sides so as to surround: *gather round.* **3** in rotation, so as to return to the starting point. **4** to a particular place, esp. a person's home: *come round for supper.* —*prep.* **1** around. **2** throughout: *a tree that stays green round the year.* —*noun* **1** something circular and often flat. **2**. a complete revolution around a circuit or path. **3** the playing of all 18 holes on a golf course in a single session. **4** one of a recurring series of events, actions, etc.: *a round of talks.* **5** a series of regular activities or duties. **6** a regular route followed, esp. for the delivery of something. **7** a stage in a competition. **8** a single period of play, competition, etc., in a group of several, e.g., in boxing. **9** a burst of, e.g., applause or cheering. **10** a single bullet or charge of ammunition. **11** a set of drinks bought at the same time for all the members of a group. **12** *Mus.* an unaccompanied song in which different people all sing the same part continuously but start, and therefore end, at different times. —*verb trans., intrans.* (**rounded, rounding**) **1** to make or become round. **2** to go around. —**in the round 1** with all details shown or considered. **2** *of a theater, chapel, etc.* with the audience or congregation seated on at least three, and often four, sides of the stage or altar. **round (something) off 1** to make corners, angles, etc., smooth. **2** to complete (something) successfully and pleasantly. **round (someone** *or* **something) up** to collect (people or things such as livestock or facts) together. ▸ **roundness** *noun*

roundabout *adj.* deviating from the straight or direct in expression or behavior.

rounded *adj.* curved.

roundhouse *noun* a circular building in which railroad locomotives may be turned around or otherwise switched.

roundly *adv.* plainly and often rudely; bluntly; thoroughly.

round robin a tournament in which each competitor plays each of the others in turn.

roundtable *noun* **1** a meeting or conference at which the participants meet on equal terms. **2 (Round Table)** the table at which King Arthur and his knights sat; round in shape so that no individual knight should have precedence.

roundtrip *noun* a trip to a place and back again, usu. over the same route.

roundup *noun* **1** the herding together of livestock, esp. cattle. **2** a gathering up of people, e.g., by the police. **3** a summary.

roundworm *noun* *Zool.* a nematode.

rouse (rowz) *verb trans., intrans.* (**roused, rousing**) **1** to arouse (someone or oneself) or become aroused from sleep, listlessness, or lethargy. **2** to excite or provoke, or to be excited or provoked.

rousing *adj.* stirring; exciting

roustabout *noun* an unskilled laborer, e.g., on an oil rig or a farm.

rout¹ (rowt) *verb trans.* (**routed, routing**) to defeat completely and cause to flee in confusion. —*noun* **1** a complete, overwhelming defeat. **2** a confused, disorderly retreat. **3** a disorderly, noisy group of people.

rout² *verb trans., intrans.* (**routed, routing**) **1** to dig up, esp. with the snout. **2 (rout (someone) out** *or* **up)** to find or fetch (someone) by searching.

route (rōōt, rowt) *noun* **1** the way traveled on a regular journey. **2 a** a particular group of roads followed to get to a place. **b** a highway or other road. —*verb trans.* (**routed, routing**) to arrange a route for; to send by a selected route.

routine (rōō-tēn′) *noun* **1** a regular or fixed way of doing things. **2** a set series of movements in a dance, performance, etc. **3** *Comput.* a part of a program that performs a specific function. —*adj.* **1** never or rarely changing; regular. **2** done merely as a duty or as per the usual or expected, without genuine care or feeling. ▸ **routinely** *adv.*

rove *verb trans., intrans.* (**roved, roving**) **1** to wander or roam over aimlessly. **2** to keep looking in different directions.

row¹ (rō) *noun* **1** a number of people or things, such as theater seats, numbers, vegetables, etc., arranged in a line. **2** a street with a line of houses on one or both sides.

row² (rō) *verb trans., intrans.* (**rowed, rowing**) **1** to move (a boat) through the water using oars. **2** to carry (people, goods, etc.) in a rowboat. **3 a** to race in rowboats for sport. **b** to compete in (a race) in a rowboat. —*noun* **1** the act of rowing a boat. **2** a trip in a rowboat. ▸ **rower** *noun* ▸ **rowing** *noun*

row³ (row) *noun* **1** a noisy quarrel. **2** a loud, unpleasant noise or disturbance. **3** a severe reprimand. —*verb intrans.* (**rowed, rowing**) to quarrel noisily.

rowan (rō′ən) *noun* mountain ash.

rowboat *noun* a small boat that is propelled usu. by no more than two oars.

rowdy *adj.* (**rowdier, rowdiest**) noisy, rough, and disorderly. —*noun colloq.* a noisy, rough, disorderly person. ▸ **rowdily** *adv.* ▸ **rowdiness** *noun* ▸ **rowdyism** *noun*

rowel (row′əl) *noun* a small spiked wheel on a spur.

royal *adj.* **1** of or suitable for a monarch. **2** belonging to a monarch. **3** regal; magnificent. —*noun colloq.* a member of a monarch's family. ▸ **royally** *adv.*

royal blue a rich, bright, deep-colored blue.

royalist *noun* a supporter of the monarchy. —*adj.* relating to royalists.

royalty *noun* (*pl.* **royalties**) **1** the character, state, office, or power of a monarch. **2** members of a monarch's family, either individually or collectively. **3** a percentage of the profits from each copy of a book, piece of music, invention, etc., sold, performed or used, that is paid to the author, composer, inventor, etc.

rpm *or* **r.p.m.** *abbrev.* revolutions per minute.

RR *abbrev.* **1** railroad. **2** (*also* **R.R.**) Right Reverend. **3** rural route.

R.S.V.P., RSVP *or* **r.s.v.p.** *abbrev. répondez s il vous plaît* (French), please reply.

Ru *symbol Chem.* ruthenium.

rub *verb intrans., trans.* (**rubbed, rubbing**) **1** to move one's hand, an object, etc., back and forward over the surface of (something) with pressure and friction. **2** to move (one's hand, an object, etc.) back and forth over a surface with pressure and friction. **3 (rub against** *or* **on (something))** to move back and forth over (a surface) with pressure and friction. **4 (rub (something) in** *or* **on)** to apply (ointment, lotion, polish, etc.). **5** to clean, polish, dry, or smooth. **6 (rub** *or* **rub (something) away, off, out,** *etc.*) to remove or be removed by pressure and friction. **7** to make (something) sore by pressure and friction. **8** to fray by pressure and friction. —*noun* **1** an act of rubbing. **2**

an obstacle or difficulty. —**rub (something)
down** 1 to rub (one's body, a horse, etc.);
briskly from head to foot, e.g., to dry (it). 2
to prepare (a surface) to receive new paint
or varnish by rubbing the old paint or varnish
off. **rub off on (someone)** to have an effect
on or be passed to (someone else) by close
association. **rub (something) out** to
remove (it) by rubbing.

rubber¹ noun 1 a strong elastic substance
obtained from the latex of various trees or
produced synthetically. 2 a condom. 3 (usu.
rubbers) waterproof rubber or plastic
overshoes; galoshes. 4 something that rubs,
e.g., a device or a machine part. —adj.
of or producing rubber. ▸ **rubbery** adj.

rubber² noun Cards a match, esp. in bridge,
consisting of either three or five games.

rubber band a thin loop of rubber for holding
items together. Also called **elastic band**.

rubberize verb trans. (**rubberized,
rubberizing**) to coat or impregnate (a
substance, esp. a textile) with rubber.

rubberneck slang noun a person, e.g., a
motorist, who stares or gapes, e.g., at a
highway accident. —verb intrans. (**rubber-
necked, rubbernecking**) to stare or gape,
e.g., at an accident scene.

rubber stamp an instrument made of rubber
with figures, letters, names, etc., on it, used
to stamp a name, date, etc.

rubber-stamp verb trans. (**rubber-stamped,
rubber-stamping**) to give automatic or
routine approval of or authorization for.

rubbing noun an impression or copy made by
placing paper over a raised surface and
rubbing the paper with crayon, wax, etc.

rubbish noun 1 garbage. 2 worthless or
useless material or objects. 3 nonsense.
▸ **rubbishy** adj.

rubble noun 1 broken stones, bricks, plaster,
etc., from ruined or demolished buildings. 2
small, rough stones used in building, esp. as
a filling between walls.

rubdown noun an act of rubbing down, esp.
to clean or prepare a surface or to massage
the body.

rubella (roo-bĕl'ə) noun Med. a highly
contagious viral disease characterized by a
reddish-pink rash, and that can cause fetal
abnormalities if contracted in the early
stages of pregnancy. Also called **German
measles**.

rubicund (roo'bĭ-kənd,) adj., esp. of the face
or complexion red or rosy; ruddy.

rubidium noun Chem. (SYMBOL Rb) a silvery-
white, highly reactive metallic element used
in photoelectric cells.

ruble or **rouble** (roo'bəl) noun the standard
unit of currency in the countries of the
former USSR, equal to 100 kopecks.

rubric, noun 1 a heading in a book or
manuscript, esp. one written or underlined
in red. 2 an authoritative rule, esp. one for
the conduct of divine service added in red to
the liturgy.

> From a Latin word for red ink, originally an
> entry in a Biblical text written in red ink

ruby noun (pl. **rubies**) 1 Geol. a deep red
corundum prized as a gemstone. 2 the rich,
deep red color characteristic of this stone.
—adj. of this color.

rucksack noun a bag carried on the back by
means of straps over the shoulders.

ruckus noun colloq. a commotion; a disturbance.

rudder noun 1 a flat piece of metal, wood, etc.,
fixed vertically to a ship's stern for steering. 2
a movable aerofoil attached to the fin of an
aircraft that helps control its movement
along a horizontal plane.

ruddy adj. (**ruddier, ruddiest**) 1 of the face,
complexion, etc. having a healthy, glowing,
rosy, or pink color. 2 red; reddish.

rude adj. 1 lacking or showing a lack of social
manners. ◩ DISCOURTEOUS, ILLMANNERED,
IMPOLITE, INCIVIL, MANNERLESS, UN-
CIVIL, UNCOURTEOUS, UNCOUTH, UN-
MANNERED, UNMANNERLY ◩ COURTEOUS,
MANNERLY, POLITE, WELL-MANNERED. 2
roughly made; lacking refinement or polish.
3 ignorant, uneducated, or primitive. 4
sudden and unpleasant: a rude awakening.
▸ **rudely** adv. ▸ **rudeness** noun

rudiment noun 1 (usu. **rudiments**) a basic set
of rules, parts, or levels. 2 (usu. **rudiments**)
that which is in an early and incomplete stage
of development. ▸ **rudimentary** adj.

rue¹ verb trans. (**rued, ruing**) to wish that (something) had not happened; to regret. ▸ **rueful**
adj. ▸ **ruefully** adv. ▸ **ruefulness** noun

rue² noun an aromatic evergreen shrub having
bluish-green leaves, and is cultivated as a
culinary and medicinal herb.

ruff noun 1 a circular pleated or frilled linen collar
worn around the neck in the late 16th c and
early 17th c. 2 a fringe or frill of feathers or
hair growing on a bird's or other animal's neck.

ruffian noun a violent, brutal, lawless person.
▸ **ruffianly** adj.

ruffle verb trans., intrans. (**ruffled, ruffling**)
1 to make wrinkled or uneven; to spoil the
smoothness of. 2 to make or become
irritated, annoyed, or discomposed. 3 of a
bird to erect (its feathers), usu. in anger or
display. 4 to gather lace, linen, etc., into a
ruff or ruffle. —noun 1 a frill of lace, linen,
etc., worn either around one's neck or
wrists. 2 disturbance of the evenness and
smoothness of a surface or of the peace, a
person's temper, etc. 3 the feathers around
a bird's neck.

rufous (roo′fəs) *adj.*, *esp. of a bird or other animal* reddish or brownish-red in color.

rug *noun* a thick heavy mat or carpet for covering a floor.

Rugby (rəg′bē) *noun* a form of football played with an oval ball that players may pick up and run with and may pass from hand to hand.

Named after *Rugby* School in Warwickshire, where the game was supposedly invented

rugged (rəg′ĭd) *adj.* **1** of hills, ground, etc. having a rough, uneven surface; steep and rocky. **2** *of the face* having features that are strongly marked, irregular and furrowed, and that suggest physical strength. **3** *esp. of a person's character* stern, austere, and unbending. **4** involving physical hardships. ▸ **ruggedly** *adv.* ▸ **ruggedness** *noun*

ruin (roo′ən) *noun* **1** a broken, destroyed, decayed, or collapsed state. **2 a** something that has been broken, destroyed, or that has been caused to decay or collapse. **b** (**ruins**) a building that has collapsed, that has been destroyed, or that is in a state of great disrepair. **3** a complete loss of wealth, social position, power, etc. **4** one that has lost all wealth, social position, or power. **5** a cause of a complete loss of wealth, social position, or power. —*verb* (**ruined, ruining**) **1** to knock down, break into pieces, or bring to ruin. **2** to spoil: *ruined the evening by fighting.* ▸ **ruination** *noun* ▸ **ruinous** *adj.*

rule *noun* **1** a principle, regulation, order, or direction that controls action, function, form, use, etc. **2** government or control, or the period during which government or control is exercised. **3** a general principle, standard, guideline, or custom. **4** a saying that articulates a general truth. **5** a strip of wood, metal, or plastic with a straight edge marked off in units, used for measuring. —*verb trans., intrans.* (**ruled, ruling**) **1** to exercise authority (over); to govern. **2** to keep control of; to restrain. **3** to make an authoritative, usu. official or judicial decision. **4** to be common or prevalent: *Anarchy ruled after the war.* **5** to draw (a straight line). **6** to draw a straight line or a series of parallel lines on (e.g., paper). —**rule (something) out 1** to leave (it) out or not consider (it). **2** to make (it) no longer possible; to preclude (it).

rule of thumb (*pl.* **rules of thumb**) a method of doing something, based on experience rather than theory or careful calculation.

ruler *noun* **1** a person, e.g., a monarch, who rules or governs. **2** a strip of wood, metal, or plastic, with straight edges marked off in units (usu. inches or centimeters), and used for drawing straight lines and measuring.

ruling *noun* an official or authoritative decision, esp. a judicial decision on an issue. —*adj.* **1** governing; controlling. **2** most important or strongest; predominant.

rum *noun* a spirit distilled from fermented molasses or sugar cane.

Rumanian *noun*, *adj. same as* **Romanian.**

rumba *noun* **1** an orig. Cuban dance with pronounced hip movements. **2** music for this dance, with a stressed second beat.

rumble *verb intrans., trans.* (**rumbled, rumbling**) **1** to make a deep, low, grumbling sound. **2** to move making a rumbling noise: *traffic rumbling past.* **3** to say or utter with a rumbling voice or sound. **4** *slang* to participate in an urban street-gang fight. —*noun* **1** a deep, low, grumbling sound. **2** *slang* a street fight, esp. one between urban gangs:

rumen *noun* (*pl.* **rumina, rumens**) *Zool.* the first chamber of the complex stomach of a ruminant animal, such as a cow or sheep.

ruminant *noun* a herbivorous mammal that chews the cud and has a complex stomach with four chambers, e.g., a cow, a sheep, or a goat. —*adj.* **1** of or belonging to this group of mammals. **2** meditating or contemplating.

ruminate (roo′mə-nāt,) *verb intrans.* (**ruminated, ruminating**) **1** *of a ruminant* to chew the cud. **2** to think deeply. ▸ **rumination** *noun* ▸ **ruminative** *adj.*

rummage (rəm′ĭj) *verb intrans., trans.* (**rummaged, rummaging**) **1** to search for something by turning things out or over untidily. **2** to search thoroughly or turn things over untidily in. —*noun* **1** a thorough search. **2** things found by rummaging.

rummage sale a sale of secondhand goods.

rummy *noun Cards* a game in which each player tries to collect sets or sequences of three or more cards.

rumor *noun* **1** an item of news or information that is passed from person to person and that may or may not be true. **2** general talk or gossip; hearsay. —*verb trans.* (**rumored, rumoring**) (*usu.* **be rumored**) to report or spread by rumor.

rump *noun* **1** the rear part of an animal's body. **2** a cut of beef from the rump. *Also called* **rump steak.** **3** a person's buttocks. **4** a small or inferior remnant.

rumple *verb trans., intrans.* (**rumpled, rumpling**) to make or become untidy, creased, or wrinkled. —*noun* a wrinkle or crease.

rumpus *noun* a noisy disturbance, brawl, or uproar.

run *verb intrans., trans.* (*pa t* **ran;** *pa p* **run;** *pr p* **running**) **1** to move on foot in such a way that both or all feet are off the ground together for an instant during each step. **2** to cover or perform by or as if by running: *run a mile.* **3** to move quickly and easily on or as if on wheels. **4** to flee. **5** to move or cause to move in a specified way or direction or with a specified result: *ran the car up the ramp.* **6** of water, etc. to flow. **7** to cause or allow (liquid) to flow. **8** *of a tap, container, etc.* to give out or cause it to give out liquid. **9** to fill (a bath) with water: *ran a hot bath.* **10** to come into a specified condition by or as if by flowing or running: *ran short of time.* **11** to be full of or flow with. **12** to operate or work: *run a machine.* **13** to organize or manage. **14** (**run over, around, up,** *etc.*) to make a brief or casual visit: *ran around the corner to the drugstore.* **15** to travel or cause to travel on a regular route. **16** to continue or cause to continue or extend in a specified direction, for a specified time or distance, or over a specified range: *a play that ran for 10 years.* **17** to continue to have legal force. **18** to drive (someone) in a vehicle, usu. to a specified place. **19** (**run** or **run** (**something**) **over, along, through,** *etc.*) to move or cause (it) to move or pass quickly, lightly, or freely: *She ran her eyes over the report.* **20** to race or finish a race in a specified position: *ran second in the Boston Marathon.* **21** to stand for election. **22** to enter (a contestant) in a race or as a candidate for office. **23** to spread, dissolve, or circulate quickly: *The color in the shirt has run.* **24** to be worded. **25** to be affected by or subjected to; or likely to be affected by: *run a high temperature.* **26** to develop relatively quickly in a specified direction; to tend (toward): *run to fat.* **27** to have as or to be an inherent or recurring part of: *Blue eyes run in the family.* **28** to own, drive, and maintain (a car or other motor vehicle). **29** to publish: *ran the story in the magazine.* **30** (*usu.* **run up**) to accumulate or allow to accumulate: *run up debts.* **31** of stitches to become undone or (of a garment, e.g., hosiery) to have stitches come undone. —*noun* **1** an act of running. **2** the distance covered or the time taken up by an act of running. **3** a rapid running movement. **4** a trip in a vehicle, esp. one taken for pleasure. **5** a continuous, unbroken period or series: *a run of bad luck.* **6** freedom to move about or come and go as one pleases. **7** a high or urgent demand, e.g., for a currency, money, a product, etc.: *a run on the banks.* **8** a route regularly traveled. **9** a row of unraveled stitches, esp. in hosiery. **10** the average type or class: *the usual run of new students.* **11** (**the runs**) *colloq.* diarrhea. **12** a number produced in a single period of production: *a press run of 200,000 units.* **13** *Cards* three or more cards for a series or sequence. **14** an inclined course, esp. one covered with snow used for skiing. **15** a *Baseball* a point scored made by a

batter successfully completing the circuit of four bases. **b** *Football* a player's attempt to carry and advance the ball through the opposing team. **16** (*often in compounds*) an enclosure or pen for domestic fowl or other animals: *a chicken run.* —**on the run** fleeing, esp. from the police. **run along** *colloq.* (*usu.* used as an exclamation) to go away. **run down** of a clock, battery, etc. to cease to work because of a gradual loss of power. **run** (**someone**) **down** of a vehicle or its operator to knock (someone) to the ground. **run** (**someone** or **something**) **down 1** to speak badly of (the one or ones specified), usu. without good reason. **2** to chase or search for (the one or ones specified) until found or captured. **run out of** (**something**) to use up a supply of (it). **run over 1** to go beyond a limit; to overflow. **2** to make a quick brief visit: *I'll run over in 15 minutes.* **run** (**someone**) **over** of a vehicle or driver to knock (someone) down and injure or kill (that one).

runabout *noun* a small car, boat, or aircraft.

runaway *noun* a person or animal that has run away. —*adj.* **1** that is running away or out of control: *a runaway bulldozer.* **2** easily and convincingly won: *a runaway victory.*

rundown *adj.* **1** tired or exhausted; in weakened health. **2** *of a building* shabby; dilapidated. —*noun* **1** a gradual reduction in numbers, size, etc. **2** a brief statement of the main points or items; a summary.

rune *noun* **1** any of the letters of an early alphabet used by the ancient Germanic peoples. **2** a mystical symbol or inscription.

rung¹ *noun* **1** a step on a ladder. **2** a crosspiece on a chair.

rung² *see* **ring²**.

run-in *noun colloq.* a quarrel or an argument.

runnel (rən′l) *noun* a small stream.

runner *noun* **1** one that runs. **2** a *Baseball* one who runs the bases. **b** *Football* a ball carrier. **3** a messenger. **4** a groove or strip along which a drawer, sliding door, etc., slides. **5** either of the strips of metal or wood running the length of a sled, on which it moves. **6** a blade on an ice skate. **7** *Bot.* in certain plants, a long stem that grows horizontally along the surface of the ground. *Also called* **stolon.** **8** a long narrow strip of cloth or carpet used to decorate or cover a table, dresser, floor, etc. **9** a smuggler.

runner-up *noun* (*pl.* **runners-up**) a competitor who finishes in second place.

running *noun* **1** the act of moving quickly. **2** the act of managing, organizing, or operating. **3** *Sport* the sport of someone who runs; the exercise engaged in by someone who runs. —*adj.* **1** of or intended for running. **2** done or performed while running, working, etc.: *running repairs.* **3** continuous: *a running argument.* **4** consecutive: *two days running.* **5** flowing.

running board a footboard along the side of a vehicle.

runny *adj.* (**runnier, runniest**) **1** tending to run or flow with liquid. **2** liquid; watery.

runoff *noun* **1** rainwater that moves over the ground and flows into surface streams and rivers when the ground is saturated with water. **2** an extra race, contest, election, etc., between two people, candidates, or teams that have tied, to decide the winner.

run-of-the-mill *adj.* not special; ordinary.

runt *noun* **1** the smallest animal in a litter. **2** *offensive* an undersized and weak person.

run-through *noun* a practice, rehearsal, or summary.

run-up *noun* an approach or period of preparation, e.g., for an event.

runway *noun* a wide, hard surface from which aircraft take off and on which they land.

rupee (rōō-pē′) *noun* the standard unit of currency in India, Pakistan, Bhutan, Nepal, Sri Lanka, Mauritius, and the Seychelles.

rupture *noun* **1** the act of breaking or bursting, or the state of being broken or burst. **2** a breach of harmony or friendly relations. **3** a hernia. —*verb intrans., trans.* (**ruptured, rupturing**) **1** to become or cause to become disunited. **2** to break, tear, or burst. **3** to cause (someone or oneself) to suffer or to be affected by a hernia.

rural *adj.* of or relating to the countryside.

rural free delivery (ABBREV. **RFD, R.F.D.**) free mail delivery to rural areas.

ruse (rōōz) *noun* a cunningly devised means to an end.

rush¹ *verb trans., intrans.* (**rushed, rushing**) **1 a** to move with speed, impetuously and often heedlessly. ▣ BOLT, CHARGE, CHASE, DASH, FLY, RACE, SHOOT, TEAR ▣ AMBLE, POKE, CRAWL. **b** to cause to hurry: *They rushed me through dinner.* **2** to perform or deal with too quickly or hurriedly. **3** to attack suddenly. **4** (**rush** (**something**) or **rush at** (**something**)) to approach (it) or carry (it) out hastily and impetuously. **5** to force (someone) to act more quickly than he or she wants to. —*noun* **1** a sudden quick movement, esp. forward. **2** a sudden general movement, usu. toward a single goal: *a gold rush.* **3** haste; hurry. **4** a period of great activity: *the pre-Christmas rush.* **5** a sudden demand for something. **6** *slang* a feeling of euphoria after taking a drug. —*adj.* done or needing to be done quickly.

rush² *noun Bot.* a tall grass-like marsh plant.

rusk *noun* a slice of bread that has been rebaked, or a hard dry biscuit resembling this, given as a food to babies.

russet *noun* **1** a reddish-brown color. **2** a variety of apple with a reddish-brown skin. —*adj.* reddish-brown in color.

Russian *noun* **1** a native or citizen of Russia. **2** the Slavic language spoken in Russia and the official language of the former USSR. —*adj.* of Russia, its people, or their language.

rust *noun* **1 a** a reddish-brown coating that forms on the surface of iron or steel that has been exposed to air and moisture. **b** a similar coating that forms on other metals. **2** the color of rust, usu. a reddish-brown. **3** *Bot.* (a fungus causing) a plant disease in which leaves take on a rusty appearance. —*verb trans., intrans.* (**rusted, rusting**) **1** to become or cause to become coated with rust. **2** to become weaker and inefficient, usu. through lack of use. ▸ **rusty** *adj.* ▸ **rustiness** *noun*

rustic *adj.* **1** of or living in the country. **2** having the characteristics of country life or country people, esp. in being simple, unsophisticated, and uncouth. **3** made of rough, untrimmed branches: *rustic furniture.* —*noun* a person from or living in the country. ▸ **rustically** *adv.* ▸ **rusticity** *noun*

rusticate (rəs′tĭ-kāt,) *verb trans., intrans.* (**rusticated, rusticating**) to live, go to live, or send to live in the country.

rustle (rəs′əl) *verb trans., intrans.* (**rustled, rustling**) **1** to make or cause to make a soft whispering sound, as of dry leaves. **2** to move with such a sound. **3** to steal (cattle or horses). —*noun* a quick succession of soft, dry, crisp, whisperlike sounds. —**rustle** (**something**) **up** to arrange, gather together, or prepare quickly. ▸ **rustler** *noun*

rustproof *adj.* that will not rust or will prevent rust from forming.

rut¹ *noun* **1** in many male mammals, a period of sexual excitement that occurs one or more times a year. **2** the time of year when this period of sexual excitement occurs. —*verb intrans.* (**rutted, rutting**) of *male animals* to be in a period of sexual excitement.

rut² *noun* **1** a deep track or furrow in soft ground made by wheels. **2** an established, usu. boring, routine.

rutabaga (rōōt′ə-bā͵gə, rōōt′-) *noun* swede.

ruthenium *noun Chem.* (SYMBOL **Ru**) a silvery-white brittle metallic element that occurs in small amounts in some platinum ores.

ruthless *adj.* having or showing no pity or compassion. ▸ **ruthlessly** *adv.* ▸ **ruthlessness** *noun*

Rx *noun* **1** a medical prescription. **2** any remedy.

rye *noun* **1** a grass-like cereal that produces a grain used for making bread and whiskey, and as food for animals. **2** whiskey distilled from fermented rye.

Ss

S¹ *or* **s** *noun* (*pl.* **Ss, S's, s's**) **1** the 19th letter of the English alphabet. **2** something S-shaped.

S² *abbrev.* **1** saint (sense 1). **2** south. **3** Society.

S³ *symbol Chem.* sulfur.

S. *abbrev.* **1** (*also* **s.**) school¹. **2** sea. **3** (*usu.* **s.**) *Gram.* singular. **4** *of clothing sizes* small.

s *abbrev.* second².

's¹ *suffix* used to form: **1** possessives: *John's*. **2** the plural of numbers and symbols: *3's*.

's² *contr.* **1** is: *He's not here.* **2** has: *She's taken it.* **3** does: *What's he think it is?* **4** us: *Let's go.*

-s¹ *or* **-es** *suffix* forming the plural of nouns: *dogs / churches.*

-s² *or* **-es** *suffix* forming the third person singular present tense of verbs: *walks / misses.*

-s³ *suffix* forming certain adverbs: *works days.*

SA *abbrev.* **1** South Africa. **2** South America.

Sabbath (săb'əth) *noun* (*usu.* **the Sabbath**) a day of the week set aside for religious worship and rest, Saturday among Jews and Sunday among most Christians.

sabbatical *adj.* of or being a period of leave given esp. to teachers in higher education, esp. for study. —*noun* sabbatical leave.

saber *noun* **1** a curved, single-edged cavalry sword. **2** a lightweight fencing sword with a tapering blade.

sable *noun* **1** a small flesh-eating mammal related to the marten. **2** the thick, soft, glossy, dark fur of this animal. — *adj.* **1** *poetic* dark. **2** *Heraldry* black.

sabotage (săb'ə-täzh,) *noun* **1** deliberate damage or destruction, esp. carried out for military or political reasons. **2** action designed to disrupt a plan or scheme. —*verb trans.* (**sabotaged, sabotaging**) to destroy, damage, or disrupt deliberately. ▸ **saboteur** (săb,ə-tər') *noun*

> Originally meaning the destruction of machinery by factory workers, from French *sabot* 'clog'.

SAC *abbrev.* Strategic Air Command.

sac *noun* a baglike part in a plant or animal.

saccharin (săk'ə-rĭn) *noun* a sweet white crystalline substance with no calorie content, used as an artificial sweetener.

saccharine (săk'ə-rĭn, -rēn,, -rīn,) *adj.* overly-sentimental or overly-sweet.

sacerdotal *adj.* of or relating to priests.

sachet (săsh-ā') *noun* **1** a small sealed packet containing a liquid or powder. **2** a small bag containing a scented substance, used to perfume wardrobes, drawers, etc.

sack¹ *noun* **1 a** a large bag, esp. of paper, coarse cloth, or plastic. **b** the amount a sack will hold. **2** *colloq.* (**the sack**) dismissal from employment. **3** (**the sack**) *slang* bed. —*verb trans.* (**sacked, sacking**) **1** *colloq.* to dismiss from employment. **2** to put into sacks.

sack² *verb trans.* (**sacked, sacking**) to plunder and destroy (a town). —*noun* the act of sacking a town.

sackcloth *noun* **1** sacking. **2** a garment made from this fabric, formerly worn in mourning or as a self-punishment for sin.

sacking *noun* **1** coarse cloth used to make sacks. **2** *colloq.* dismissal from employment.

sacra *see* sacrum.

sacrament *noun Christianity* **1** any of various symbolic ceremonies, e.g., marriage or baptism. **2** (**Sacrament**) the service of the Eucharist; the consecrated bread and wine consumed. ▸ **sacramental** *adj.*

sacred *adj.* **1** devoted to a deity and therefore regarded with deep respect. **2** connected with religion or worship: *sacred music.* **3 a** traditional and greatly respected. **b** *of rules, etc.* not to be challenged or broken under any circumstances. **4** dedicated or appropriate to a saint, deity, etc.

sacred cow a thing, esp. a custom or institution, regarded as above criticism.

sacrifice (săk'rĭ-fīs,) *noun* **1** the slaughter of a person or animal as an offering to God or a god; the person or animal slaughtered. **2** any offering made to a deity. **3** a thing of value given up for the sake of another thing or person. —*verb trans.* (**sacrificed, sacrificing**) **1** to offer as a sacrifice. **2** to give up. ▸ **sacrificial** *adj.*

sacrilege *noun* willful damage to or disrespect for something holy or greatly respected by others. ▸ **sacrilegious** *adj.*

sacristan *noun* **1** a person responsible for the safety of the contents of a church. **2** a sexton.

sacristy *noun* (*pl.* **sacristies**) a room in a church for sacred utensils and garments.

sacrosanct *adj.* supremely holy or sacred; not to be violated. ▸ **sacrosanctity** *noun*

sacrum (sā'krəm) *noun* (*pl.* **sacra**) a large triangular bone in the lower back.

sad *adj.* (**sadder, saddest**) **1** feeling unhappy. **2** causing unhappiness. **3** expressing or suggesting unhappiness. **4** very bad: *a sad state.* ▸ **sadly** *adv.* ▸ **sadness** *noun*

sadden *verb trans., intrans.* (**saddened, saddening**) to make or become sad.

saddle *noun* **1** a horseback rider's leather seat. **2** a fixed seat on a bicycle or motorcycle. **3** a cut of meat consisting of the two loins with a section of the backbone. —*verb trans.* (**saddled, saddling**) **1** to put a saddle on (a horse). **2** to burden (someone) with a problem, duty, etc.

saddlery *noun* (*pl.* **saddleries**) **1** the occupation of a saddler. **2** a saddler's shop or stock. **3** a saddle room in a stable, etc.

sadism (sād′ĭz-əm, săd′-) *noun* **1** the practice of gaining sexual pleasure from inflicting pain on others. **2** the inflicting of suffering on others for one's own satisfaction. ▸ **sadist** *noun* ▸ **sadistic** *adj.*

sado-masochism (sād,ō-măs′ə-kĭz,əm) *noun* the practice of deriving sexual pleasure from inflicting pain on oneself and others. ▸ **sado-masochist** *noun* ▸ **sado-masochistic** *adj.*

SAE *or* **sae** *abbrev. Brit.* stamped addressed envelope.

safari *noun* an expedition or tour to hunt or observe wild animals, esp. in Africa.

safari park a large enclosed area in which wild animals roam freely and can be observed by the public from vehicles driven through.

safe *adj.* **1** free from danger. **2** unharmed. **3** giving protection from harm; secure: *a safe place.* **4** involving no risk of loss; assured: *a safe bet.* —*noun* a sturdy metal cabinet for valuables. ▸ **safely** *adv.*

safe-conduct *noun* a document giving official permission to pass or travel without arrest or interference, esp. in wartime.

safecracker *noun* a person who illegally breaks open safes.

safeguard *noun* a device or an arrangement giving protection against danger or harm. —*verb trans.* (**safeguarded, safeguarding**) to ensure the safety of.

safekeeping *noun* care and protection, e.g., for valuables.

safety *noun* (*pl.* **safeties**) **1** the quality or condition of being safe. **2** *Football* two points gained for the defensive team when an offensive player downs the football behind the offensive team's goal line.

safety belt any strap for securing a person and preventing accidents, esp. a seat belt.

safety curtain a fireproof curtain above a theater stage, lowered to control the spread of fire.

safety-deposit box *or* **safe-deposit box** a strongbox in a bank into which valuables can be safely locked. *Also called* **lockbox.**

safety match a match that ignites only when struck on a specially prepared surface.

safety net 1 a large net positioned to catch a trapeze artist, etc., accidentally loss or failing. **2** a measure protecting against loss or failure.

safety pin a U-shaped pin with an attached guard fitting over the point.

safety valve a device in a boiler, etc. that opens when pressure exceeds a certain level.

safflower *noun* a plant with large orange-yellow flowers that yield a dye and seeds that yield an oil used in cooking.

saffron (săf′rən, -răn,) *noun* **1** a species of crocus. **2** the orange powder obtained from the dried stigmas of this plant, used as a food flavoring and as a yellow dye.

sag *verb intrans.* (**sagged, sagging**) **1** to sink or bend, esp. in the middle, under or as if under weight. **2** to hang loosely or bulge through lack of firmness. ▸ **saggy** *adj.*

saga (säg′ə) *noun* **1** a medieval Scandinavian tale of legendary heroes and events. **2** a long, detailed artistic work. **3** *colloq.* a long series of events.

sagacious (sə-gā′shəs) *adj. formal* wise. ▸ **sagacity** *noun*

sage[1] *noun* a man of great wisdom. —*adj.* wise; prudent. ▸ **sagely** *adv.*

sage[2] *noun* **1** a shrub with aromatic gray-green leaves. **2** the leaves of this plant, used in cooking as a seasoning.

sagebrush *noun* a white-flowered aromatic shrub growing in clumps in US deserts.

Sagittarius (săj,ə-tăr′ē-əs, -tĕr′-) *noun* **1** the Archer, the name of a constellation and the ninth sign of the zodiac. **2** a person born between Nov. 22 and Dec. 20, under this sign.

sago *noun* a starchy grain or powder obtained from certain tropical palms.

sahib (sä′hĭb,, -hĕb,) *noun* in India, a term equivalent to Mr. or Sir.

said (sĕd) *verb see* **say.** —*adj. formal* previously mentioned or named: *The said party has denied the accusation.*

sail *noun* **1** a sheet of canvas spread to catch the wind as a means of propelling a ship. **2** a trip in a boat or ship with or without sails. —*verb trans., intrans.* (**sailed, sailing**) **1** to travel by boat or ship: *sail the Pacific.* **2** to control (a boat or ship). **3** to depart by boat or ship: *We sail at 1400 hrs.* **4** (*usu.* **sail along** *or* **past**) to move smoothly and swiftly.

sailboard *noun* a flat hull like a surfboard with a sail attached. ▸ **sailboarding** *noun*

sailcloth *noun* **1** strong cloth, e.g., canvas, used to make sails. **2** heavy cotton cloth.

sailor *noun* any member of a ship's crew, esp. one who is not an officer.

saint *noun* **1** (ABBREV. **S.,** **St.**) a person whose profound holiness is formally recognized after death by a Christian church. **2** *colloq.* a very good and kind person. ▸ **sainthood** *noun* ▸ **saintliness** *noun* ▸ **saintly** *adj.*

Saint Bernard (bər-närd′) a very large dog with a thick brown and white coat.

sake[1] *noun* benefit; behalf; account: *for my sake.* —**for God's** or **heaven's,** *etc.,* sake used to express exasperation, or to beg, e.g., for forgiveness. **for the sake of** for the purpose of; in order to.

sake[2] *or* **saki** (säk′ē) *noun* a Japanese alcoholic drink made from rice.

salaam (sə-läm′) *noun* **1** used as a greeting in Eastern countries, esp. by Muslims. **2** a low bow, a Muslim greeting or show of respect.

salacious *adj.* **1** seeking to arouse sexual desire, esp. obscenely. **2** a ignoring sexual restraint. **b** preoccupied with sex.

salad *noun* a cold dish of raw vegetables or of fruit, usu. served with a dressing.

salamander *noun* a small lizardlike amphibious creature of central and S Europe.

salami *noun* (*pl.* **salamis**) a highly seasoned sausage, usu. served sliced.

salary *noun* (*pl.* **salaries**) a fixed regular payment for esp. nonmanual work, usu. paid monthly or twice a month. ▶ **salaried** *adj.*

> Based on Latin *salarium*, ration money given to Roman legionaries for buying salt

sale *noun* **1** the act or practice of selling. **2** an item sold. **3** (*usu.* **sales**) the value of the items sold. **4** a period during which goods are offered at reduced prices. **5** an event at which goods can be bought. **6** (**sales**) the operations associated with or the staff responsible for selling. —*adj.* **1** intended for selling: *sale goods.* **2** being reduced in cost to the consumer or being such as to reflect this: *sale prices.* ▶ **salable** *or* **saleable** *adj.*

salesclerk *noun* a person who is hired to sell merchandise in a store.

salesman *noun* a man who sells products or merchandise to customers, esp. on commission. ▶ **salesmanship** *noun*

sales tax a tax on retail merchandise.

saleswoman *noun* a woman who sells products or merchandise, esp. on commission.

salient *adj.* **1** striking; outstanding: *the salient points.* **2** *Archit.* jutting out or up.

saline (sā′lēn, -līn,) *adj.* containing sodium chloride; salty. —*noun* a solution of common salt in water. ▶ **salinity** *noun*

saliva (sə-lī′və) *noun* the watery liquid produced by the salivary glands in the mouth to aid digestion. ▶ **salivary** *adj.*

salivate (säl′ə-vāt,) *verb intrans.* (**salivated, salivating**) **1** to have esp. excessive amounts of saliva in the mouth, as at the sight of food. **2** to drool. ▶ **salivation** *noun*

sallow *adj.,* of a person's complexion yellowish-brown, often through poor health. —*verb trans., intrans.* (**sallowed, sallowing**) to make or become sallow.

sally *noun* (*pl.* **sallies**) **1** a sudden attack by troops rushing forward. **2** an excursion. —*verb intrans.* (**sallied, sallying, sallies**) **1** to carry out a sally. **2** (*also* **sally forth**) to rush out or surge forward; to set off.

salmon (säm′ən) *noun* (*pl.* **salmon, salmons**) **1 a** a large silvery marine fish that lays its eggs in fresh water. **b** the edible orange-pink flesh of this fish, highly prized as a food. **2** an orange-pink color. *Also called* **salmon pink.**

salmonella (säl,mə-nĕl′ə) *noun* (*pl.* **salmonellae, salmonellas, salmonella**) **1** (**Salmonella**) any of various types of rod-shaped bacteria that contaminate food. **2** food poisoning caused by such bacteria.

salmon pink salmon (sense 2).

salon (sə-län′) *noun* **1** an establishment where clients go for beauty treatments, esp. a hairdressing salon. **2** a drawing room, esp. in a large continental house. **3** a gathering of arts celebrities in a fashionable household.

saloon *noun* **1** a tavern or a bar. **2** a large public room, e.g., for functions or some other purpose. **3** a large public room on a ship.

salsa (sôl′sə) *noun* **1** a rhythmic dance music of S American origin, mixing jazz with rock. **b** a dance performed to such music. **2** a spicy sauce of Mexican origin, made with tomatoes, onions, and chilies.

salsify *noun* (*pl.* **salsifies**) a purple-flowered Mediterranean plant with a long cylindrical edible root, which is eaten as a vegetable.

salt *noun* **1** sodium chloride, a white crystalline substance used to season and preserve food. **2** a chemical compound in which one or more hydrogen atoms have been replaced by a metal atom or atoms. **3** (**salts**) a substance resembling salt in appearance or taste, esp. a medicine. **4** an experienced sailor. —*verb trans.* (**salted, salting**) **1** to season or preserve (food) with salt. **2** to cover (an icy road) with salt to melt the ice. —*adj.* **1** preserved with salt: *salt pork.* **2** containing salt. **3** tasting of salt. —**rub salt in (someone's) wounds** to add to (someone's) discomfort. **salt (something) away** to store (it) up for future use; to hoard (it). **worth one's salt** worthy of respect. ▶ **salty** *adj.*

saltcellar *noun* a container holding salt for use at the table.

salt marsh marsh (sense 2).

saltpeter *noun Chem.* potassium nitrate.

saltshaker *noun* a container with a perforated top, used for dispensing salt.

saltwater *adj.* pertaining to, consisting of, or living in water that contains salt.

salubrious *adj.* **1** *formal* health-giving: *a salubrious climate.* **2** respectable; pleasant: *not a very salubrious neighborhood.*

salutary *adj.* **1** beneficial, or intended to be so: *a salutary warning.* **2** healthy; wholesome.

salutation *noun* **1 a** an act, gesture, or phrase of greeting. **b** (**salutations**) greetings. **2** an expression used to begin a letter.

salute *verb trans.*, *intrans.* (**saluted**, **saluting**) **1** *Mil.* to pay formal respect to (someone) with a set gesture, esp. with the right arm or a weapon. **2** to pay tribute to: *We salute your bravery.* **3** to greet with a show of friendship or respect. —*noun* **1** *Mil.* a set gesture of respect. **2** a greeting.

salvage (săl'vĭj) *verb trans.* (**salvaged**, **salvaging**) **1** to rescue (e.g., property or a vessel) from potential damage or loss. **2** to recover (a sunken ship). **3** to manage to retain (e.g., one's pride) in adverse circumstances. —*noun* **1** the act of salvaging property, a vessel, etc. **2** property salvaged. **3** payment made as a reward for saving a ship from destruction or loss.

salvation *noun* **1** the act of saving a person or thing from harm. **2** a person or thing that saves another from harm. **3** *Relig.* liberation from the influence of sin, or from its consequences for the human soul.

salve (săv) *noun* **1** ointment to heal or soothe. **2** something that comforts or consoles. —*verb trans.* (**salved**, **salving**) to ease or comfort.

salver *noun* a small ornamented tray, usu. of silver, used in serving drinks.

salvo *noun* (*pl.* **salvos**, **salvoes**) **1** a burst of gunfire from several guns firing at the same time. **2** a sudden round of applause. **3** a ferocious outburst of criticism or insults.

SAM *abbrev.* surface-to-air missile.

Samaritan (sə-măr'ə-t-n) *noun* **1** (*also* **good Samaritan**) a kind or helpful person. **2** *Hist.* an inhabitant of ancient Samaria. —*adj.* relating to Samaria or the Samaritans.

samarium *noun* *Chem.* (SYMBOL **Sm**) a soft silvery metallic element.

samba *noun* **1** a lively Brazilian dance, or a short-stepping ballroom dance developed from it. **2** a piece of music for these.

same *adj.* **1** exactly alike or very similar. **2** being one single one instead of another or others. ◪ IDENTICAL, SELFSAME ◪ DIFFERENT. **3** unchanged or unchanging. —*pron.* (**the same**) the same person or thing, or the one previously mentioned. —*adv.* (**the same**) similarly; likewise: *I feel the same.* ▸ **sameness** *noun*

samovar (săm'ə-vär,) *noun* a Russian urn for boiling water for tea.

Samoyed (sə-moi'əd) *noun* a sturdy dog with a thick white coat and an upward curling tail.

sampan *noun* a small flat-bottomed Asian boat typically propelled by two oars.

sample *noun* a unit or part taken, displayed, or considered as representative of others or of a whole. —*verb trans.* (**sampled**, **sampling**) **1** to take or try as a sample. **2** to get

experience of: *sampled life abroad.*

samurai (săm'ə-rī,) *noun* (*pl.* **samurai**, **samurais**) **1** a member of an aristocratic class of Japanese warriors between the 11th c and 19th c. **2** a two-handed sword with a curved blade. *Also called* **samurai sword**.

sanatorium *or* **sanitarium** *noun* (*pl.* **sanatoriums**, **sanatoria**) **1** a hospital for the chronically ill, or for convalescent patients. **2** a resort for convalescents.

sancta *see* **sanctum**.

sanctify *verb trans.* (**sanctified**, **sanctifying**, **sanctifies**) **1** to make sacred. **2** to free from sin. **3** to declare legitimate or binding in the eyes of the Church: *sanctify a marriage.* ▸ **sanctification** *noun*

sanctimonious *adj.* displaying exaggerated holiness or virtuousness, esp. hypocritically. ▸ **sanctimoniously** *adv.* ▸ **sanctimoniousness** *noun*

sanction *noun* **1** official permission or authority. **2** an economic or military measure taken by one nation to persuade another to adopt a particular policy. **3** a means of encouraging adherence to a social custom, e.g., a penalty or reward. **4** a penalty attached to an offense. —*verb trans.* (**sanctioned**, **sanctioning**) **1** to authorize or confirm formally. **2** to allow or agree to. **3** to encourage. **4** to inflict a penalty on.

sanctity *noun* **1** the quality or condition of being holy or sacred. **2** the quality of deserving to be respected, and not violated: *the sanctity of the home.*

sanctuary *noun* (*pl.* **sanctuaries**) **1** a holy or sacred place. **2** the most sacred area within such a place, e.g., around an altar. **3** a place, historically a church, giving immunity from arrest or other interference. **4** freedom from disturbance: *the sanctuary of the garden.* **5** a nature reserve in which the animals or plants are protected by law.

sanctum *noun* (*pl.* **sanctums**, **sancta**) **1** a sacred place. **2** a place providing total privacy.

sand *noun* **1** small particles consisting of rock and other minerals forming seashores and deserts. **2** (**sands**) an area covered with this substance. —*verb trans.* (**sanded**, **sanding**) to smooth or polish with sandpaper or a sander. ▸ **sandy** *adj.*

sandal *noun* a light shoe with little or no upper and straps attached for holding it on the foot.

sandalwood *noun* **1** an evergreen tree that is grown for its fragrant timber. **2** the hard, pale, fragrant timber obtained from this tree, which also yields an aromatic oil used in perfumes and soap.

sandbag *noun* a sand-filled sack used to form a barrier against gunfire or flood, or as ballast. —*verb trans.* (**sandbagged**, **sandbagging**) **1** to barricade or weigh down with sandbags. **2** *slang* to coerce.

sandbar *noun* a bar of sand in a river, lake, or sea, formed by currents.

sandblast *noun* a jet of sand forced from a tube by air or steam pressure. —*verb trans.* (**sandblasted, sandblasting**) to clean (e.g., stonework) with a blast of sand.

sandbox *noun* a shallow box filled with sand for children to play in.

sandcastle *noun* a pile of sand molded for fun into a castle shape.

sander *noun* a power-driven abrasive tool for sanding wood, etc.

S & L *abbrev.* savings and loan (association).

sandlot *noun* a vacant lot that is often used by youngsters for games.

sandman *noun* a man in folklore who sprinkles sand on children's eyes to make them sleepy.

sandpaper *noun* paper with a coating orig. of sand, now usu. of crushed glass, for smoothing and polishing wood. —*verb trans.* (**sandpapered, sandpapering**) to smooth or polish with sandpaper.

sandpiper *noun* any of various small wading birds with a high-pitched piping call.

sandstone *noun* a soft rock formed from compressed sand.

sandstorm *noun* a strong wind sweeping along clouds of sand.

sandwich *noun* two or more slices of bread or a roll with a filling of cheese, meat, etc. —*verb trans.* (**sandwiched, sandwiching**) to place between two other things.

> After the 18th-century Earl of *Sandwich*, said to have invented it to allow him to gamble without interruption for meals

sane *adj.* **1** sound of mind. **2** sensible. ▸ **sanely** *adv.* ▸ **saneness** *noun*

sang *see* **sing.**

sangfroid (săn-frwä′) *noun* cool-headedness; calmness; composure.

sangria (săng-grē′ə) *noun* a Spanish drink of red wine, fruit juice, and sugar.

sanguinary *adj.* **1** involving much bloodshed; bloody. **2** bloodthirsty.

sanguine *adj.* **1** cheerful and full of hope. **2** *of a complexion* ruddy.

sanitarium *noun same as* **sanatorium.**

sanitary *adj.* **1** promoting good health and the prevention of disease; hygienic. **2** relating to health, esp. waste disposal.

sanitary napkin an absorbent pad worn to catch menstrual fluids.

sanitation *noun* **1** standards of public hygiene. **2** measures taken to preserve public health, esp. waste disposal.

sanitize *verb trans.* (**sanitized, sanitizing**) **1** to make hygienic. **2** to make less controversial by removing potentially offensive elements.

sanity *noun* **1** soundness of mind; the condition of being sane. **2** good sense.

sank *see* **sink.**

Sanskrit (săn′skrĭt) *noun* a language of ancient India, the religious language of Hinduism since ancient times. —*adj.* relating to or expressed in this language.

Santa Claus (săn′tə-klôz,) a jolly old man dressed in red who, in folklore, brings children presents on Christmas Eve or St. Nicholas' Day.

sap *noun* **1** *Bot.* a liquid containing sugars and other nutrients that circulates within plants. **2** vitality. **3** *slang* a weak or easily fooled person. —*verb trans.* (**sapped, sapping**) **1** to drain sap from. **2** to weaken or exhaust.

sapling *noun* a young tree.

sapper *noun* a military engineer, esp. one who lays, detects, disarms, and removes mines.

sapphire *noun* **1** a blue variety of corundum, highly prized as a gemstone. **2** the deep blue color of this stone. —*adj.* of the deep blue color of this stone.

sappy *adj.* (**sappier, sappiest**) **1** *of plants* full of sap. **2** full of energy. **3** *colloq.* foolishly sad or sentimental. **4** *slang* idiotic; foolish.

sapsucker *noun* any of several small N American woodpeckers that drink sap.

sarcasm *noun* **1** an expression of scorn or contempt. **2** the use of such expressions. ▸ **sarcastic** *adj.* ▸ **sarcastically** *adv.*

sarcoma *noun* (*pl.* **sarcomas, sarcomata**) a malignant tumor in connective tissue.

sarcophagus *noun* (*pl.* **sarcophagi, sarcophaguses**) a stone coffin or tomb, esp. one decorated with carvings.

sardine *noun* a young herring or related fish.

Sardinian *noun* **1** a native or citizen of Sardinia. **2** a Romance language spoken in Sardinia. —*adj.* of Sardinia, its people, or their language.

sardonic *adj.* mocking or scornful.

sargasso *noun* (*pl.* **sargassos**) gulfweed.

sari *noun* (*pl.* **saris**) a traditional garment of Hindu women, consisting of a single long piece of fabric wound around the body and draped over one shoulder.

sarong *noun* a Malaysian garment worn by both sexes, a single piece of fabric wrapped around the body from the waist or chest down.

sarsaparilla (săs,pə-rĭl′ə) *noun* **1** a tropical American climbing plant. **2** the root of this plant, dried and used in medicines. **3** a nonalcoholic drink flavored with the root.

sartorial *adj.* relating to tailoring, or to clothes.

SASE *abbrev.* self-addressed stamped envelope.

sash[1] *noun* a broad band of cloth worn around the waist or over one shoulder.

sash[2] *noun* either of two glazed frames forming a sash window.

sashay *verb intrans.* (**sashayed, sashaying, sashays**) *colloq.* to swagger about.

sash window a window consisting of two sashes, one or either of which can slide vertically past the other.

sass *colloq. noun* impertinent speech. —*verb trans.* (**sassed, sassing, sasses**) to speak to or answer impertinently. ▸ **sassy** *adj.*

sassafras *noun* **1** a N American tree of the laurel family. **2** the aromatic dried bark of this tree, which yields a pungent oil used as a food flavoring.

sat *see* **sit**.

Sat. *abbrev.* Saturday.

Satan (sāt'n) *noun* the Devil. ▸ **satanic** *adj.*

Satanism *noun* worship of Satan. ▸ **Satanist** *noun*

satchel *noun* a small briefcaselike bag, e.g., for schoolbooks.

sate *verb trans.* (**sated, sating**) to satisfy (a desire or appetite) to the full or to excess.

satellite *noun* **1** a celestial body that orbits a larger celestial body. **2** a device, esp. a spacecraft, that is launched by a rocket into space and placed in orbit above a planet. **3** a nation or state dependent on a larger neighboring nation-state.

satellite dish a dish antenna.

satiable *adj.* capable of being satisfied.

satiate (sā'shē-āt,) *verb trans.* (**satiated, satiating**) to satisfy fully or to excess. ▸ **satiation** *noun* ▸ **satiety** *noun*

satin *noun* silk or rayon closely woven to produce a shiny finish. ▸ **satiny** *adj.*

satinwood *noun* **1** a shiny light-colored hardwood. **2** the tree that produces it.

satire *noun* **1** a variety of humor aiming at mockery or ridicule, often using sarcasm and irony. **2** any work using this kind of humor. ▸ **satirical** *adj.* ▸ **satirist** *noun* ▸ **satirize** *verb trans.*

satisfaction *noun* **1** the act of satisfying, or the state or feeling of being satisfied. **2** compensation for mistreatment.

satisfactory *adj.* **1** giving satisfaction: *a satisfactory meal.* **2** good enough, but usu. only just. ▸ **satisfactorily** *adv.*

satisfy *verb trans., intrans.* (**satisfied, satisfying, satisfies**) **1** to fulfill the needs, desires, or expectations of; to fulfill (e.g., a desire). **2** to meet the requirements of; to meet (a requirement). **3** to remove the doubts of; to convince. **4** to remove all desire for others; to please: *a taste that satisfies.* **5** to give compensation to.

satrap (sā'trăp,, să'-) *noun* a subordinate ruler.

satsuma *noun* a thin-skinned seedless type of mandarin orange.

saturate (săch'ə-rāt,) *verb trans.* (**saturated, saturating**) **1** to make soaking wet. **2** to fill or cover with a large amount. **3** to add a solid, liquid, or gas to (a solution) until no more of that substance can be dissolved at a given

temperature. ▸ **saturation** *noun*

Saturday (săt'ərd-ē, -ā,) *noun* (ABBREV. **Sat.**) the seventh day of the week.

saturnine *adj. literary* **1** grim-faced; unsmiling. **2** melancholy in character.

satyr *noun* **1** a mythological woodland god, part man, part goat, noted for lechery. **2** a lustful man. ▸ **satyric** *adj.*

sauce *noun* **1** a seasoned liquid in which food is cooked or served or with which food is flavored after serving. **2** added interest or excitement.

sauceboat *noun* a long shallow jug for sauce.

saucepan *noun* a deep cooking pot with a long handle and usu. a lid.

saucer *noun* a small, shallow, round dish for placing under a tea or coffee cup.

saucy *adj.* (**saucier, sauciest**) *colloq.* **1** impertinent or cheeky; attractively bold or forward. **2** *of clothes* pert. ▸ **saucily** *adv.*

sauerkraut *noun* pickled shredded cabbage.

sauna *noun* **1** a steam bath, the steam created by pouring water on hot coals. **2** a building or room equipped for such a bath.

saunter *verb intrans.* (**sauntered, sauntering**) to walk at a leisurely pace, often aimlessly; to stroll. —*noun* **1** a lazy walking pace. **2** a leisurely walk.

sausage *noun* a mass of minced, seasoned meat enclosed in a thin tube-shaped casing.

sauté (sô-tā') *verb trans.* (**sautéed, sautéeing, sautés**) to fry gently for a short time. —*adj.* fried gently and briefly.

savage (săv'īj) *adj.* **1** untamed; uncivilized. **2** ferocious. **3** cruel; barbaric. **4** uncultivated; rugged: *savage terrain.* —*noun* **1** *old use, now offensive* a member of a primitive people. **2** an uncultured, brutish, or cruel person. —*verb trans.* (**savaged, savaging**) to attack with ferocity. ▸ **savagely** *adv.* ▸ **savageness** *noun* ▸ **savagery** *noun*

savanna *or* **savannah** *noun* flat grassland found in the subtropics or the tropics.

savant (sə-vänt') *noun* a male learned person.

savante (sə-vänt') *noun* a female learned person.

save *verb trans., intrans.* (**saved, saving**) **1** to rescue from danger, harm, loss, or failure. **2** (*also* **save (something) up**) to set (it) aside for future use. **3** (*also* **save up**) to set money aside for future use. **4** to use economically so as to avoid waste. **5** to cause or allow to escape potential unpleasantness or inconvenience: *That'll save you the trouble.* **6** *Sport* to prevent (a ball or shot) from reaching the goal; to prevent (a goal) from being scored. **7** *Relig.* to free from the influence or consequences of sin. **8** *Comput.* to transfer (e.g., the contents of a file) from the main memory onto disk or tape for storage. —*noun* an act of saving a ball or shot, or preventing a goal. —*prep.* (*also* **save for**) except. —*conj.* (**save that**) were it not that.

saving *noun* **1** a thing saved, esp. an economy made. **2** (**savings**) money saved up. —*prep. formal* except; save.

savings account a bank account that draws interest.

savings and loan association (ABBREV. **S & L**) a financial institution that invests money mainly in home-mortgage loans.

savings bank a bank that invests depositors' savings and pays interest on them.

savings bond a registered and nontransferable US government bond.

savior *noun* **1** a person who saves someone or something from danger or destruction. **2** a person who frees others from sin or evil. **3** (**the Savior**) *Christianity* Christ.

savoir faire (săv,wär,fãr', -fĕr') **1** expertise. **2** skill, judgment, and tact.

savor *verb trans.* (**savored, savoring**) **1** to taste or smell with relish. **2** to take pleasure in. **3** to flavor or season (food). —*noun* **1** taste or smell of something. **2** a faint but unmistakable quality. **3** a hint or trace.

savory[1] *adj.* **1** having a salty or sharp taste or smell; not sweet. **2** pleasant, esp. morally pleasing or acceptable: *a savory character.* **3** having a very pleasing taste. —*noun* (*pl.* **savories**) a savory food, esp. served as an hors d'oeuvre. ▸ **savoriness** *noun*

savory[2] *noun* (*pl.* **savories**) an aromatic plant of the mint family, whose leaves are widely used as a flavoring in cooking.

savvy *slang verb trans., intrans.* (**savvied, savvying, savvies**) to know or understand. —*noun* **1** common sense; shrewdness. **2** know-how.

saw[1] *see* **see**[1].

saw[2] *noun* a tool with a toothed metal blade for cutting. —*verb trans., intrans.* (*pa t* **sawed**; *pa p* **sawed** *or* **sawn**; *pr p* **sawing**) to cut with or as if with a saw.

sawdust *noun* dust in the form of tiny fragments of wood, made by sawing.

sawed-off shotgun a shotgun with the end of the barrel cut off, making it easier to carry concealed.

sawfish *noun* (*pl.* **sawfish, sawfishes**) a large ray that has a long snout edged with toothlike spikes.

sawhorse *noun* a legged frame that is used to support material being sawed.

sawmill *noun* a factory in which timber is cut into boards, etc.

sawn *see* **saw**[2].

sawyer *noun* a person who saws timber.

sax *noun colloq.* a saxophone.

saxifrage (săk'sĭ-frĭj, -frãj,) *noun* any of a family of rock plants with tufted or mossy leaves and small white, yellow, or red flowers.

Saxon (săk'sən) *noun* a member of a Germanic people that conquered much of England in the 5th and 6th centuries. —*adj.* relating to the Saxons.

saxophone *noun* a wind instrument with a long metal body, finger keys along its length, and an upturned bell. ▸ **saxophonist** *noun*

say *verb* (*pa t and pa p* **said**; *pr p* **saying**) **1** to utter or pronounce. **2** to express in words. **3** to state as an opinion. **4** to suppose: *Say he doesn't come; what then?* **5** to recite or repeat: *say a prayer.* **6** to judge or decide: *difficult to say which is best.* **7** (**say for** *or* **against (something)**) to argue in favor of or against (it). **8** to communicate: *What is the poem trying to say?* **9** to indicate: *The clock says 10 o'clock.* **10** to report or claim: *The hostage is said to be still alive.* **11** to make a statement (about something); to tell: *I'd rather not say.* —*noun* **1** a chance to express an opinion: *You've had your say.* **2** the power to influence a decision: *You have no say in this matter.* —*interj.* used to express surprise, protest, or sudden joy, or to get someone else's attention. —**it goes without saying** it is obvious.

saying *noun* a proverb or maxim.

say-so *noun* **1** the right to make a final decision. **2** an unsupported claim or assertion.

Sb *symbol Chem.* antimony.

SBN *abbrev.* Standard Book Number

S.C. *abbrev. Law* Supreme Court.

Sc *symbol Chem.* scandium.

scab *noun* **1** a crust of dried blood formed over a healing wound. **2** *slang* a worker who defies a union's instruction to strike, or a person hired to replace a striking employee. —*verb intrans.* (**scabbed, scabbing**) **1** (*also* **scab over**) to become covered by a scab. **2** *slang* to work as a scab.

scabbard *noun* a sheath for a sword or dagger.

scabby *adj.* (**scabbier, scabbiest**) **1** covered with scabs. **2** *colloq.* worthless.

scabies *noun Med.* a contagious skin disease that causes severe itching of the skin.

scabrous *adj.* **1** *of skin, etc.* rough and flaky or scaly. **2** *bawdy*; smutty; scandalous.

scad *noun slang* a very large indefinite number: *has scads of hats.*

scaffold *noun* **1** a framework of metal poles and planks used as a temporary platform from which building repair or construction is carried out. **2** a makeshift platform from which a person is executed, esp. by hanging.

scaffolding *noun* **1** a building scaffold or arrangement of scaffolds. **2** materials used for building scaffolds.

scalar (skā'lər, -lãr,) *Math. adj.* denoting a quantity that has magnitude but no direction. —*noun* a scalar quantity. *See also* **vector** (sense 1).

scalawag or **scallywag** *noun colloq.* a rascal.

scald *verb trans.* (**scalded, scalding**) **1** to injure with intensely hot liquid or steam. **2** to treat with hot water so as to sterilize. **3** to heat to just short of boiling point. —*noun* an injury caused by being burned by intensely hot liquid or steam.

scale¹ *noun* **1 a** a series of markings or divisions at regular, known intervals for use in measuring; a system of such markings or divisions. **b** a measuring instrument with such markings. **2** the relationship between actual size and size as represented on a model or drawing. **3** *Mus.* a complete sequence of notes in music. **4** a graded system, e.g., of employees' salaries. **5** extent or level relative to others: *on a grand scale.* —*verb trans.* (**scaled, scaling**) **1** to climb. **2** to change the size of (something) while keeping to the same proportions.

scale² *noun* **1** any of the small thin plates that cover the skin of fish and reptiles. **2** a flaky piece, esp. of skin. **3** tartar on the teeth. **4** a crusty white deposit formed when hard water is heated, e.g., in kettles. —*verb trans., intrans.* (**scaled, scaling**) **1** to remove the scales from (e.g., a fish), or scale from (e.g., a kettle). **2** to remove in thin layers. **3** to come off in thin layers or flakes. ▸ **scaly** *adj.*

scale³ *noun* **1** (**scales**) an instrument for weighing. **2** either of the pans of a balance.

scalene *adj. Math.*, of a triangle having each side a different length.

scallion *noun* an onion having a small bulb and long edible leaves.

scallop, escallop or **scollop** *noun* **1** an edible marine mollusk that has a pair of hinged, fan-shaped, ribbed shells. **2** a shell from this marine mollusk. **3** any of a series of curves that together form a wavy edge, e.g., on fabric. —*verb trans.* (**scalloped, scalloping**) to shape (an edge) in scallops.

scallywag *noun* same as **scalawag.**

scalp *noun* the part of the head usu. covered by hair; the skin covering this part. —*verb trans.* (**scalped, scalping**) **1** to remove the scalp of. **2** *colloq.* to buy up (e.g., theater or concert tickets) for resale at inflated prices.

scalpel *noun* a small surgical knife.

scam *slang noun* a swindle. —*verb trans.* (**scammed, scamming**) to swindle.

scamp *noun* a mischievous child.

scamper *verb intrans.* (**scampered, scampering**) to run quickly taking short steps. —*noun* **1** an act of scampering. **2** a scampering movement or pace.

scampi *noun* **1** (*pl.*) large shrimp. **2** a dish of large shrimp.

scan *verb trans., intrans.* (**scanned, scanning**) **1** to read through or examine carefully. **2** to look over quickly. **3** *Med.* to examine (the body, esp. an internal part of it) by means of e.g. ultrasound. **4** to search (an area) by means of radar or by sweeping a beam of light over it. **5** *Comput.* to examine (data) on a disk. **6 a** to examine the rhythm of (a piece of poetry). **b** of *verse* to conform to a pattern of rhythm. —*noun* **1** the act or an instance of scanning. **2** *Med.* an image obtained by examining the body, esp. an internal part of it, using, e.g., ultrasound. ▸ **scanner** *noun*

scandal *noun* **1** widespread public outrage and loss of reputation; an event or fact causing it. **2** any extremely objectionable fact or situation. **3** malicious gossip.

scandalize *verb trans.* (**scandalized, scandalizing**) to shock or outrage.

scandalmonger *noun* a person who spreads malicious gossip.

scandalous *adj.* **1** disgraceful; outrageous. **2** defamatory. ▸ **scandalously** *adv.*

Scandinavian *noun* **1** a native or citizen of Scandinavia. **2** a group of Germanic languages spoken in Scandinavia. —*adj.* of Scandinavia, its people, or their languages.

scandium *noun Chem.* (**SYMBOL Sc**) a soft, silvery-white metal found in various minerals.

scansion *noun* **1** the act or practice of scanning poetry. **2** a poem's pattern of rhythm.

scant *adj.* **1** in short supply. **2** meager.

scanty *adj.* (**scantier, scantiest**) small in size or amount; barely enough: *scanty clothing.* ▸ **scantily** *adv.* ▸ **scantiness** *noun*

scapegoat *noun* a person made to take the blame for the mistakes of others.

> Literally 'escape goat', after an ancient Jewish ritual of transferring the people's sins to a goat which was afterward let free in the wilderness

scapula (skăp'yə-lə) *noun* (*pl.* **scapulas, scapulae**) *Anat.* the shoulder blade.

scar *noun* **1** a mark left on the skin after a wound has healed. **2** a permanent damaging emotional effect. —*verb trans., intrans.* (**scarred, scarring**) to mark or become marked with scars or a scar.

scarab *noun* **1** a dung beetle regarded as sacred by the ancient Egyptians. **2** an image or carving of this sacred beetle, or a gemstone carved in its shape.

scarce *adj.* **1** rarely found. **2** in short supply. —*adv.* scarcely: *could scarce believe that outlandish tale.* —**make** (**oneself**) **scarce** *colloq.* to leave quickly. ▸ **scarcity** *noun*

scarcely *adv.* **1** only just. **2** hardly ever. **3** not really; not at all: *scarcely a reason to leave.*

Usage The adverb *scarcely* is regarded as a negative, and so if used with another negative (*couldn't scarcely* see through the fog), it is considered incorrect. Say instead: *could scarcely* see through the fog.

scare *verb trans., intrans.* (**scared, scaring**) to make or become afraid. —*noun* **1** a fright. **2** a sudden, widespread, often unwarranted feeling of alarm: *a bomb scare*.

scarecrow *noun* **1** a rough model of a human figure set up in a field, etc., to scare birds from crops. **2** *colloq.* a raggedly dressed person.

scaremonger *noun* a person who causes alarm by spreading rumors of esp. imminent disaster. ▸ **scaremongering** *noun*

scarf¹ *noun* (*pl.* **scarfs, scarves**) a strip or square of fabric worn around the neck, shoulders, or head for warmth or decoration.

scarf² *noun* a glued or bolted joint made between two ends, cut so as to overlap and produce a continuous flush surface. —*verb trans.* (**scarfed, scarfing, scarfs**) to join in this way.

scarify *verb* (**scarified, scarifying, scarifies**) **1** to make scratches or shallow cuts on the surface of. **2** to hurt with severe criticism. ▸ **scarification** *noun*

scarlatina (skär′lə-tē′nə) *noun Med.* scarlet fever.

scarlet *noun* a bright red color. —*adj.* of a bright red color.

scarlet fever an infectious disease causing fever, inflammation of the nose, throat, and mouth, and a rash on the body. *Also called* **scarlatina**.

scarp *noun* an escarpment.

scarves *see* **scarf¹**.

scary *adj.* (**scarier, scariest**) *colloq.* causing fear. ▸ **scarily** *adv.* ▸ **scariness** *noun*

scat¹ *verb intrans.* (**scatted, scatting**) *colloq.* to go away; to run off; to leave at once.

scat² *noun* jazz singing consisting of improvised sounds, not words. —*verb intrans.* (**scatted, scatting**) to sing thus.

scathing (skā′thĭng) *adj.* scornfully critical. ▸ **scathingly** *adv.*

scatology *noun* **1** preoccupation with the obscene, esp. with excrement and related bodily functions. **2** obscene language or literature. **3** *Med.* the study of excrement for the purpose of diagnosis. ▸ **scatological** *adj.*

scatter *verb trans., intrans.* (**scattered, scattering**) **1** to lay or throw haphazardly. **2** to depart or send off in different directions. —*noun* **1** an act of scattering. **2** a quantity of things scattered.

scatterbrain *noun colloq.* a person incapable of organized thought or attention. ▸ **scatterbrained** *adj.*

scattering *noun* **1** dispersion. **2** something scattered. **3** a small number.

scavenge (skăv′ənj) *verb intrans., trans.* (**scavenged, scavenging**) **1** to search among trash and garbage for usable things. **2** *of an animal* to feed on refuse or decaying flesh. ▸ **scavenger** *noun*

Sc.D. *abbrev. Scientiae Doctor* (Latin), Doctor of Science.

scenario *noun* (*pl.* **scenarios**) **1** a rough written outline of a dramatic work, e.g., a film; a synopsis. **2** a hypothetical situation.

scene *noun* **1** the setting in which a real or imaginary event takes place. **2** a unit of action in a play or film. *See also* **act** (sense 5). **3** any of the pieces making up a stage or film set, or the set as a whole. **4** a landscape, situation, etc., as seen by a viewer. **5** an embarrassing display of emotion in public: *Don't make a scene.* **6** *slang* a state of affairs with regard to a particular activity: *the current music scene.* **7** *colloq.* a liked or preferred area of interest or activity: *This is not my scene.*

scenery *noun* (*pl.* **sceneries**) **1** landscape, esp. when attractively rural. **2** the items making up a stage or film set.

scenic *adj.* of, being, or including attractive natural landscapes: *the scenic route.*

scent *noun* **1 a** the distinctive smell of a person, animal, or plant. **b** a trail of this left behind: *dogs on the scent.* **2 a** a sweet odor. **b** perfume. **3** a series of clues or findings on a trail leading to a discovery: *police on the scent of an elusive terrorist.* —*verb trans.* (**scented, scenting**) **1** to discover by the sense of smell; to smell. **2** to be aware of by instinct or intuition; to sense.

scepter *noun* a ceremonial rod carried by a monarch as a symbol of sovereignty.

sceptic *noun same as* **skeptic**.

sch. *abbrev.* school¹.

schedule *noun* **1** a list of activities or events planned to take place at specific times. **2** the state of happening on time according to plan: *behind schedule.* **3** a list or inventory: *a schedule of price changes.* **4** a timetable. —*verb trans.* (**scheduled, scheduling**) **1** to plan (something) to happen at a specific time. **2** to put on a schedule.

schema *noun* (*pl.* **schemata, schemas**) **1** a diagram or plan. **2** an outline or synopsis.

schematic *adj.* **1** following a particular plan or arrangement. **2** in the form of a diagram.

scheme *noun* **1** a plan of action. **2** a careful arrangement of different parts: *a color scheme.* **3** a secret plan to cause harm or damage. **4** a diagram or table. —*verb intrans.* (**schemed, scheming**) to plan secretly, usu. maliciously. ▸ **schemer** *noun*

scherzo noun (pl. **scherzos, scherzi**) Mus. a lively piece, esp. a vigorous or lighthearted movement in a symphony or sonata.

schilling noun the standard unit of currency in Austria.

schism (sĭz'əm, skĭz'-) noun a breakaway group. ▸ **schismatic** adj.

schist (shĭst) noun any metamorphic rock that can be split into roughly parallel layers.

schizo (skĭt'sō) colloq. noun (pl. **schizos**) a schizophrenic. —adj. schizophrenic.

schizoid adj. showing some of the qualities of schizophrenia. —noun a schizoid person.

schizophrenia (skĭt,sə-frē'nē-ə) noun a severe disorder of the mind characterized by feelings of extreme insecurity, a withdrawal into one's own mind, and an inability to distinguish between reality and fantasy. ▸ **schizophrenic** noun, adj.

schlemiel (shlə-mēl') noun slang a bungling dolt.

schlep or **schlepp** (shlĕp) slang verb trans., intrans. (**schlepped, schlepping, schleps** or **schlepps**) **1** to carry, pull, or drag with difficulty. **2** to move slowly and with difficulty. —noun **1** a journey or procedure requiring great effort or involving great difficulty. **2** a clumsy or incompetent person.

schlock noun slang inferior quality; shoddy production.

schmaltz noun colloq. excessive, foolish sentimentality or sadness, e.g., in music or art. ▸ **schmaltzy** adj.

schmo noun (pl. **schmoes, schmos**) slang a stupid, obnoxious person.

schmuck or **shmuck** noun slang a clumsy, stupid, despicable person.

schnapps noun a strong dry alcoholic spirit.

schnauzer noun a dog with a thick wiry coat, marked eyebrows, mustache, and beard.

scholar noun **1** a learned person, esp. an academic. **2** a person who studies; a pupil or student. **3** a person receiving a scholarship. ▸ **scholarly** adj.

scholarship noun **1** a sum of money awarded for the purposes of further study, usu. to an outstanding student. **2** the achievements or methods of a scholar.

scholastic adj. of or relating to learning.

school[1] noun **1** a place where a general education is received esp. as a child or teenager. **2** a place offering instruction in a particular subject: art school. **3** the students and teachers that occupy any such place. **4** the period of the day or year during which such a place is open: stay behind after school. —verb trans. (**schooled, schooling**) **1** to cause (a person) to acquire skill or knowledge (in a subject or activity). **2** to educate in a school. **3** to discipline.

school[2] noun a group of fish, whales, or other marine animals swimming together. Also called **shoal**.

school board a board with members appointed or elected that oversees a local public school system. Also called **board of education.**

schoolchild noun a child who attends a school.

schooling noun education or instruction.

schoolmarm noun a female teacher, esp. one regarded as having old-fashioned manners or attitudes. ▸ **schoolmarmish** adj.

schoolmaster noun a male schoolteacher or head of a school.

schoolmistress noun a female schoolteacher or head of a school.

schoolteacher noun a person who teaches in a school.

schooner noun **1** a fast sailing ship with two or more masts. **2** a large beer glass.

schtick noun slang **1** a theatrical act. **2** a gimmick.

sciatic (sī-ăt'ĭk) adj. **1** relating to the hip or the region around the hip. **2** affected by sciatica.

sciatica noun intense intermittent pain in the lower back, buttocks, and backs of the thighs caused by pressure on the sciatic nerve that runs from the pelvis to the thigh.

science noun **1 a** the systematic observation and investigation of and experimentation with natural phenomena in order to learn about them and formulate laws. **b** the body of knowledge obtained in this way, or any subdivison of it, e.g., chemistry. **2** any knowledge obtained using, or arranged according to, formal principles: the science of foreign relations. **3** acquired skill or technique, as opposed to natural ability. ▸ **scientific** adj. ▸ **scientifically** adv. ▸ **scientist** noun

science fiction (ABBREV. **sf, SF**) fiction presenting a view of life in the future, esp. incorporating space travel.

sci-fi noun colloq. science fiction.

scimitar (sĭm'ət-ər) noun a sword with a curved blade broadening toward the tip.

scintilla noun a hint or trace; an iota.

scintillate (sĭnt'l-āt,) verb intrans. (**scintillated, scintillating**) **1** to sparkle or send out sparks. **2** to capture attention with one's vitality or wit. ▸ **scintillation** noun

scion noun **1** Bot. a piece of plant tissue, usu. a shoot, that is inserted into a cut in the outer stem of another plant when making a graft. **2** a descendant or offspring.

scissors noun (sing., pl.) a one-handed cutting tool with two blades joined in the middle so as to pivot with cutting edges coming together.

sclera noun Anat. the fibrous outer layer of the eyeball.

sclerosis (sklə-rō′sĭs) *noun* (*pl.* **scleroses**) abnormal hardening or thickening of body tissue, organs, or blood vessels, or a disease characterized by this. ▶ **sclerotic** *adj.*

scoff *verb intrans.* (**scoffed, scoffing**) (*often* **scoff at (someone** *or* **something**)) to express scorn or contempt; to jeer. —*noun* an expression of scorn; a jeer.

scold *verb trans.* (**scolded, scolding**) to reprimand angrily. —*noun* a nagging or quarrelsome person. ▶ **scolding** *noun*

scollop *noun, verb* same as **scallop**.

sconce *noun* a candlestick with a handle, or one fixed by a bracket to a wall.

scone *noun* a small, round, flattish, plain cake.

scoop *verb trans.* (**scooped, scooping**) 1 (*also* **scoop (something) up**) to lift or dig (it) with a sweeping circular movement. 2 (*also* **scoop (something) out**) to empty or hollow (it) with such movements. 3 to publish or broadcast a story before (rival newspapers or broadcasters). —*noun* 1 a spoonlike implement for handling or serving food. 2 a shovel-like part of a mechanical digger. 3 a scooping movement. 4 a quantity scooped. 5 a news story printed or aired by one newspaper or broadcast outlet in advance of all others.

scoot *verb intrans.* (**scooted, scooting**) *colloq.* to go quickly.

scooter *noun* 1 a child's toy vehicle consisting of a board on a two-wheeled frame with tall handlebars, propelled by pushing against the ground with one foot while standing on the board with the other. 2 a small-engined motorcycle with a protective front shield curving back at the bottom to form a supporting board for the feet. *Also called* **motor scooter**.

scope *noun* 1 the size and extent e.g., of a subject or topic. 2 the range of topics dealt with. 3 the limits within which there is the freedom or opportunity to act. 4 range of understanding: *details beyond his scope*.

-scope *combining form* forming words denoting an instrument for viewing, examining, or detecting: *telescope*.

scorbutic *adj. Med.* relating to scurvy.

scorch *verb trans., intrans.* (**scorched, scorching, scorches**) to burn or be burned slightly on the surface. —*noun* 1 a scorched area. 2 a mark made by burning slightly on the surface.

scorcher *noun colloq.* an extremely hot day.

score *verb trans., intrans.* (**scored, scoring**) 1 *Sport* **a** to achieve (a point, etc.) in games. **b** to keep a record of points gained during (a game). 2 to make cuts or scratches in the surface of; to mark (e.g., a line) by a shallow cut. 3 (*also* **score (something) out**) to cancel (it) with a line drawn through (it). 4 *Mus.* **a** to break down (music) into parts for individual instruments or voices. **b** to adapt (music) for instruments or voices other than those orig. intended. 5 to achieve a rating; to be judged or regarded. —*noun* 1 *Sport* **a** a number of points, etc., scored. **b** an act of scoring a point, etc. 2 a scratch or shallow cut, esp. made as a mark. 3 a set of 20: *three score.* 4 (**scores**) very many; lots. 5 *Mus.* a written copy of music scored. 6 (**the score**) a reason; grounds: *was accepted on the score of suitability.* 7 a grievance or grudge: *a score to settle.* ▶ **scorer** *noun*

scorn *noun* mocking contempt. —*verb trans.* (**scorned, scorning**) 1 to treat with scorn. 2 to reject with scorn.

scornful *adj.* contemptuous. ▶ **scornfully** *adv.* ▶ **scornfulness** *noun*

Scorpio (skôr′pē-ō͵) *noun* 1 the Scorpion, the name of a constellation and the eighth sign of the zodiac. 2 (*pl.* **Scorpios**) a person born between Oct. 23 and Nov. 21 under this sign.

scorpion *noun* an animal with a long, thin, segmented body and an upward-curling tail with a poisonous sting.

Scot *noun* a native of Scotland.

Scotch *adj.,* of things, esp. products, not usu. of people Scottish. —*noun* Scotch whisky.

scotch *verb trans.* (**scotched, scotching**) to ruin or hinder (e.g., plans).

Scotch whisky whisky distilled in Scotland from barley or other grain. *Also called* **Scotch**.

scot-free *adj.* unpunished or unharmed.

Scots *adj., esp. of law and language* Scottish. —*noun* any of the dialects related to English used in esp. Lowland Scotland.

Scotsman *noun* a male native of Scotland.

Scotswoman *noun* a female native of Scotland.

Scottish *adj.* of Scotland or its people.

scoundrel *noun* a person without principles or morals; a rogue or villain.

scour¹ *verb trans.* (**scoured, scouring**) 1 to clean by rubbing hard. 2 to flush clean with a jet or current of water. —*noun* an act of scouring.

scour² *verb trans.* (**scoured, scouring**) to make an exhaustive search of (e.g., an area).

scourge (skərj′) *noun* 1 a cause of great suffering to many people. 2 a whip used for punishing. —*verb trans.* (**scourged, scourging**) 1 to afflict. 2 to whip.

scout *noun* 1 *Mil.* a person or a group sent out to observe the enemy and bring back information. 2 a talent scout. 3 a Boy or Girl Scout. —*verb intrans.* (**scouted, scouting**) 1 to act as a scout. 2 (*often* **scout around**) *colloq.* to make a search.

scowl *verb intrans.* (**scowled, scowling**) 1 to wrinkle one's forehead in disapproval, worry, etc. 2 to look disapprovingly, angrily, or threateningly. —*noun* a scowling expression.

scrabble *verb intrans.* (**scrabbled, scrabbling**) to scratch, grope, or struggle frantically. —*noun* an act of scrabbling.

scrag *noun* the thin part of a neck of mutton or veal, providing meat of poor quality.

scraggy *adj.* (**scraggier, scraggiest**) scrawny. ▸ **scragginess** *noun*

scram *verb intrans.* (**scrammed, scramming**) *colloq., often as a command* to go away.

scramble *verb trans., intrans.* (**scrambled, scrambling**) 1 to crawl or climb using hands and feet, esp. frantically. 2 to struggle violently against others: *starving people scrambling to grab food.* 3 to cook (eggs) whisked with milk. 4 to throw together haphazardly; to jumble. 5 to transmit (a message) in a distorted form via an electronic scrambler. —*noun* 1 an act of scrambling. 2 a violent struggle to beat others in getting something. 3 a walk or half-climb over rough ground.

scrambler *noun* a device that modifies signals transmitted by radio or telephone so that they can only be made intelligible by means of a special decoding device.

scrap¹ *noun* 1 a small piece; a fragment. 2 the smallest piece or amount: *not a scrap of advice.* 3 waste material, esp. waste metal for recycling or reuse. 4 (**scraps**) leftover pieces of food. —*verb trans.* (**scrapped, scrapping**) to discard as useless, or to abandon as unworkable: *scrap a plan.*

scrap² *colloq. noun* a fight or quarrel. —*verb intrans.* (**scrapped, scrapping**) to fight or quarrel.

scrapbook *noun* a book with blank pages on which newspaper clippings, etc., can be mounted.

scrape *verb trans., intrans.* (**scraped, scraping**) 1 to push or drag (something, esp. a sharp object) along (a hard or rough surface). 2 to move along a surface with a grazing action. 3 a (*also* **scrape** (**something**) **off**) to remove (it) from a surface with such an action. b to damage by such contact: *scraped his elbow.* 4 to make savings through hardship: *scrimp and scrape.* —*noun* 1 an instance or the act of dragging or grazing. 2 a part damaged or cleaned by scraping. 3 *colloq.* a difficult or embarrassing situation; a predicament. 4 *colloq.* a fight or quarrel. ▸ **scraper** *noun*

scrappy *adj.* (**scrappier, scrappiest**) ready for a fight; quarrelsome.

scratch *verb trans., intrans.* (**scratched, scratching**) 1 a to rub or drag (a sharp or pointed object) across (a surface), causing damage or making marks. b to make (e.g., a mark) by such action. 2 to rub (the skin) lightly with the fingernails, e.g., to relieve itching. 3 (*usu.* **scratch** (**something**) **out** *or*

off) to cross (it) out or cancel (it). —*noun* 1 a mark made by scratching. 2 an act of scratching. 3 a superficial wound or minor injury. —*adj.* hastily put together; improvised: *a scratch meal.* —**from scratch** from the beginning. **up to scratch** *colloq.* meeting the required or expected standard. ▸ **scratchily** *adv.* ▸ **scratchy** *adj.*

scrawl *verb trans., intrans.* (**scrawled, scrawling**) to write or draw untidily or hurriedly. —*noun* untidy or illegible handwriting. ▸ **scrawly** *adj.*

scrawny *adj.* (**scrawnier, scrawniest**) very thin and bony. ▸ **scrawniness** *noun*

scream *verb trans., intrans.* (**screamed, screaming**) 1 to utter or cry out in a loud, high-pitched voice, e.g., in fear, pain, or anger. 2 to laugh uproariously. —*noun* 1 a loud piercing cry or other sound. 2 *colloq.* an amusing person or thing.

screech *noun* a harsh, shrill cry, voice, or other noise. —*verb intrans., trans.* (**screeched, screeching**) 1 to utter a screech or as a screech. 2 to make a screech: *brakes that screeched loudly.* ▸ **screechy** *adj.*

screech owl any of various small owls, native to N America, having gray or reddish-brown plumage and a long quavery cry.

screen *noun* 1 a movable set of hinged panels, used, e.g., as a partition or as a decorative object. 2 a single panel used for protection against strong heat or light. 3 the part of a television set on which the images are formed. 4 a white surface onto which movies or slides are projected. 5 *Comput.* the image or the data displayed at any one time on a video terminal or monitor. —*verb trans.* (**screened, screening**) 1 (*usu.* **screen** (**something**) **off**) to separate or partition (it) with a screen. 2 to show at the movies or on television. 3 to subject to an examination, e.g., to test (someone) for reliability.

screenplay *noun* the text of a movie, made up of dialogue, stage directions, etc.

screen test a filmed audition to test an actor's suitability for a movie role.

screenwriter *noun* a writer of screenplays for movies, television, etc. ▸ **screenwriting** *noun*

screw *noun* 1 a nail-shaped fastener with a spiral shaft and a slot in its head. 2 *Naut.* a propeller on a boat or ship. 3 *slang* a prison guard. —*verb trans., intrans.* (**screwed, screwing**) 1 to twist (a screw) into place. 2 to push or pull with a twisting action.

screwball *noun* 1 *slang* a crazy person; an eccentric. 2 *Baseball* a ball that, when pitched to the batter, curves in the direction opposite to that of a curve ball.

screwdriver *noun* a hand tool for twisting a screw into position.

screwy *adj.* (**screwier, screwiest**) *colloq.* crazy; eccentric.

scribble *verb trans., intrans.* (**scribbled, scribbling**) **1** to write quickly or messily. **2** to draw meaningless lines or shapes absentmindedly. —*noun* **1** messy or illegible handwriting. **2** meaningless written lines or shapes. ▸ **scribbler** *noun* ▸ **scribbly** *adj.*

scribe *noun* a person employed to make handwritten copies of documents.

scrimmage (skrĭm'ĭj) *noun* **1** *Football* the contest, involving body contact, between the opposing offensive and defensive teams from the moment the ball is snapped until it is declared by an official to be dead. **2** *Sport* an informal practice session. —*verb intrans.* (**scrimmaged, scrimmaging**) *Sport* to take part in a scrimmage.

scrimp *verb intrans.* (**scrimped, scrimping**) to live economically; to be frugal or sparing.

script *noun* **1** the printed text or the spoken dialogue of a play, movie, or broadcast. **2** a system of characters used for writing; an alphabet: *Chinese script.* **3** handwriting. —*verb trans.* (**scripted, scripting**) to write the script of (a play, movie, or broadcast).

scripture *noun* **1** the sacred writings of a religion. **2** (**Scripture**) the Christian Bible. ▸ **scriptural** *adj.*

scriptwriter *noun* a person who writes scripts for movies or television.

scroll *noun* **1** a roll of parchment or paper written on, now only a ceremonial format. **2** a decorative spiral shape, e.g., in stonework or handwriting. —*verb trans., intrans.* (**scrolled, scrolling**) *Comput.* (*often* **scroll up** *or* **down**) to move (the displayed text on a screen) up or down to bring into view data that cannot be seen all at the same time.

Scrooge *noun* a miser.

scrotum *noun* (*pl.* **scrota, scrotums**) the bag of skin enclosing the testicles in mammals.

scrounge *verb trans., intrans.* (**scrounged, scrounging**) *slang* **1** to get (something) by asking or begging. **2** to get by foraging or salvage. ▸ **scrounger** *noun*

scrub[1] *verb trans., intrans.* (**scrubbed, scrubbing**) **1** to rub hard, esp. with a brush, to remove dirt. **2** to clean by hard rubbing. **3** *colloq.* to cancel or abandon (e.g., plans). —*noun* an act of scrubbing. ▸ **scrubber** *noun*

scrub[2] *noun* **1** an area of land with a poor soil or low rainfall, covered mainly with stunted trees and evergreen shrubs. **2** an undersized domestic animal. **3** *Sport* one who is not a first-string or varsity player. ▸ **scrubby** *adj.*

scruff[1] *noun* the back of the neck; the nape.

scruff[2] *noun colloq.* a scruffy person.

scruffy *adj.* (**scruffier, scruffiest**) shabbily dressed. ▸ **scruffily** *adv.* ▸ **scruffiness** *noun*

scrumptious *adj. colloq.* **1** having a very pleasing taste. **2** delightful.

scrunch *verb trans., intrans.* (**scrunched, scrunching**) **1** to crunch or crumple. **2** to make a crunching sound. —*noun* an act or the sound of scrunching.

scruple (skroo'pəl) *noun* (*usu.* **scruples**) a sense of moral responsibility that makes one reluctant or unwilling to commit a wrong. —*verb intrans.* (**scrupled, scrupling**) to be hesitant or unwilling because of scruples.

scrupulous *adj.* **1** taking care to do nothing morally wrong. **2** giving or showing care and attention to detail. ▸ **scrupulously** *adv.*

scrutinize *verb trans.* (**scrutinized, scrutinizing**) to examine closely and searchingly. ▣ INSPECT, PORE (OVER), STUDY.

scrutiny (skroot'n-ē) *noun* (*pl.* **scrutinies**) **1** a close, thorough examination or inspection. **2** a penetrating or critical look.

scuba (skoo'bə) *noun* a portable breathing device for underwater divers, consisting of one or two cylinders of compressed air connected to a mouthpiece by a tube.

scud *verb intrans.* (**scudded, scudding**) *esp. of clouds* to move quickly.

scuff *verb trans., intrans.* (**scuffed, scuffing**) **1** to graze or scrape, or become grazed or scraped, through wear. **2** to drag (the feet) when walking. —*noun* an area worn away by scuffing.

scuffle *noun* a confused fight or struggle. —*verb intrans.* (**scuffled, scuffling**) to take part in a scuffle.

scull *noun* **1 a** either of a pair of short light oars used by a lone rower. **b** a racing boat propelled by a solitary rower using a pair of such oars. **2** a large single oar at the stern, moved from side to side to propel a boat. —*verb trans.* (**sculled, sculling**) to propel with a scull or sculls. ▸ **sculler** *noun*

scullery *noun* (*pl.* **sculleries**) a room, attached to the kitchen in a large house, where basic kitchen work is done.

sculpt *verb trans., intrans.* (**sculpted, sculpting**) **1** to carve or model (clay, etc.). **2** to create (a solid model), e.g., in clay, etc. **3** to create a solid model of (someone or something), e.g., in clay. ▸ **sculptor** *noun*

sculpture *noun* **1** the art of carving or modeling with clay, wood, stone, plaster, etc. **2** a work or works of art produced in this way. —*verb trans., intrans.* (**sculptured, sculpturing**) to sculpt.

scum *noun* **1** dirt or waste matter floating on the surface of a liquid. **2** *slang* **a** a contemptible person. **b** contemptible people.

scupper *noun* a hole or pipe in a ship's side through which water is drained off the deck.

scurf *noun* dandruff. ► **scurfy** *adj.*

scurrilous *adj.* insulting, abusive, and unjustly damaging to the reputation: *scurrilous charges.* ► **scurrility** *noun*

scurry *verb intrans.* (**scurried, scurrying. scurries**) (**scurry along, away,** *etc.*) to move hurriedly, esp. with short quick steps. —*noun* (*pl.* **scurries**) an act or the sound of scurrying.

scurvy *noun Med.* a disease caused by a lack of vitamin C, marked by swolle.., bleeding gums, and bleeding under the skin. —*adj.* (**scurvier, scurviest**) old vile; contemptible.

scuttle[1] *noun* a container for a small amount of coal, usu. kept near a fireplace.

scuttle[2] *verb intrans.* (**scuttled, scuttling**) to move quickly with short steps; to scurry. —*noun* a scuttling pace or movement.

scuttle[3] *verb* **1** *Naut.* to deliberately sink (a ship) by making holes in it. **2** to ruin (e.g., plans).

scythe (sīth) *noun* a tool with a handle and a long curved blade, used for cutting tall crops or grass by hand. —*verb trans.* (**scythed, scything**) to cut with a scythe.

SE *abbrev.* southeast; southeastern.

Se *symbol Chem.* selenium.

sea *noun* **1 a** the continuous expanse of salt water that covers most of the Earth's surface. **b** any geographical division of this, usu. smaller than an ocean, e.g., the Mediterranean Sea. **c** an area of this with reference to its calmness or turbulence: *choppy seas.* **2** a vast expanse or crowd: *a sea of protesters.* —**at sea 1** in a ship on the sea. **2** confused and disorganized.

sea anemone a sea creature with a round body and petal-like tentacles.

seabed *noun* the bottom or floor of the sea.

seaboard *noun* a coast.

sea change a complete change.

sea dog an old or experienced sailor.

seafarer (sē'fär.ər) *noun* a person who travels by sea; a sailor. ► **seafaring** *adj.*

seafood *noun* shellfish and other edible marine fish.

seagoing *adj.* designed for sea travel.

seagull *noun* any gull of coastal waters.

sea horse a small fish with a horselike head.

seal[1] *noun* **1** a device, e.g., a strip of plastic or metal, serving to keep something closed. **2** a piece of rubber or other material serving to keep a joint airtight or watertight. **3 a** a piece of wax or other material attached to a document and stamped with an official mark to show authenticity. **b** such a mark: *a royal seal.* **c** an engraved metal stamp or ring for making such a mark. —*verb trans.* (**sealed, sealing**) **1** (*also* **seal (something) up**) to make (it) securely closed, airtight, or watertight with a seal. **2** to fix a seal to, or to stamp with a seal. **3** to decide or settle: *seal someone's fate.* —**seal (something) off** to isolate (an area), preventing entry by unauthorized persons.

seal[2] *noun* a streamlined fish-eating marine mammal with webbed flippers. —*verb intrans.* (**sealed, sealing**) to hunt seals.

sealant *noun* a material used for sealing, esp. to protect against weathering or wear.

sea legs ability to resist seasickness and walk steadily on the deck of a rolling ship.

sea level the mean level of the surface of the sea between high and low tides.

sea lion a large seal, found in the Pacific, with small ears, long whiskers, paddlelike forelimbs, and large hind flippers.

seam *noun* **1** a join between edges, esp. one sewn or welded. **2** a layer of coal or ore in the ground. **3** a wrinkle or scar. —*verb trans.* (**seamed, seaming**) **1** to join edge to edge. **2** to scar or wrinkle. ► **seamless** *adj.*

seaman *noun* **1** a sailor; a mariner. **2** (ABBREV. **SMN**) a rank in the US Navy or Coast Guard below petty officer; one having this rank.

seamanship *noun* sailing skills.

seamstress *noun* a woman who sews, esp. professionally.

seamy *adj.* (**seamier, seamiest**) sordid; disreputable. ► **seaminess** *noun*

séance *or* **seance** (sā'äns,, sā-äns') *noun* a meeting at which a person attempts to get in touch with the spirits of dead people in behalf of other people present.

seaplane *noun* an airplane designed to take off from and land on water.

seaport *noun* a coastal town or city with port facilities for seagoing vessels.

sear *verb trans.* (**seared, searing**) **1** to scorch. **2** to wither.

search *verb trans., intrans.* (**searched, searching**) **1** to carry out a thorough exploration to try to find something. **2** to check the clothing or body of (a person) for concealed objects. **3** to examine closely: *search one's conscience.* —*noun* an act of searching.

searchlight *noun* a pivoting exterior light with a powerful beam, used to monitor an area in darkness.

search party a group of people taking part in an organized search for a missing person.

search warrant *Law* a document, issued by a judge, giving a police officer the legal right to search premises.

seascape *noun* a picture of a scene at sea.

seashell *noun* the empty shell of an oyster, mussel, or other mollusk.

seashore *noun* the land immediately adjacent to the sea. *Also called* **seaside.**

seasick *adj.* suffering from nausea brought on by the motion of a ship. ► **seasickness** *noun*

seaside *noun* a seashore.

season *noun* **1** any of the four periods (spring, summer, fall, and winter), into which the year is divided. **2** a period of the year during which some activity is carried out: *the holiday season.* **3** a period having particular characteristics: *our busy season.* —*verb trans.* (**seasoned, seasoning**) **1** to flavor (food) by adding salt, pepper, or other herbs and spices. **2** to prepare (e.g., timber) for use. **3** to make mature: *travelers seasoned by experience.* **4** to tone down or temper: *Season your criticism with objectivity.* **5** to add interest or liveliness to: *seasoned the plot with romance.*

seasonable *adj.* **1** *of weather* appropriate to the season. **2** coming at the right time.

seasonal *adj.* available, happening, or taking place only at certain times of the year.

seasoning *noun* a substance used to season food.

season ticket a ticket giving the right to a specified or unlimited number of visits or journeys during a fixed period.

seat *noun* **1 a** a thing designed for sitting on. **b** the part of such an item on which one sits. **2** a place for sitting, e.g., in a movie theater or concert hall. **3** the human buttocks. **4** the part of a garment covering the buttocks. **5** the base of an object, or any part on which it rests or fits. **6** a position in a legislative body or in local government; a position on a committee or other administrative body. **7** an established center: *seats of learning.* **8** a large country house. **9** a center of authority or jurisdiction: *a town that is the county seat.* —*verb trans.* (**seated, seating**) **1** to assign a seat to, e.g., at a dinner table. **2** to provide seats for: *The car seats six.* **3** to place in a situation or location. **4** to fit firmly and accurately.

seat belt a strap passed across the body and then buckled, to secure a passenger in a seat of a motor vehicle.

seating *noun* the number or arrangement of seats, e.g., in a dining room.

sea urchin a sea creature with a small rounded body protected by a hard spiky shell.

seaward *adj.* facing or moving toward the sea. —*adv.* (*also* **seawards**) toward the sea.

seaweed *noun* **1** *Bot.* any of a number of large marine algae. **2** such plants collectively.

seaworthy *adj.* fit for a voyage at sea. ▶ **seaworthiness** *noun*

Sec. *abbrev.* Secretary.

sec¹ *noun colloq.* a second in time: *Wait a sec.*

sec² *adj.* of wine dry.

sec³ *abbrev.* **1** secant. **2** second² (sense 1).

sec. *abbrev.* second¹.

secant (sē′kənt, -kănt,) *noun* (ABBREV. **sec**) *Math.* **1** a straight line that cuts a curve in

two or more places. **2** for a given angle in a right-angled triangle, the ratio of the length of the hypotenuse to the length of the side adjacent to the angle.

secede (sĭ-sēd′) *verb intrans.* (**seceded, seceding**) to withdraw formally, e.g., from a political or religious body or alliance. ▶ **secession** *noun.*

seclude *verb trans.* (**secluded, secluding**) **1** to keep away from others; to isolate. **2** to keep out of view. ▶ **seclusion** *noun*

second¹ *adj.* (ABBREV. **sec.**) **1** next after the first in order of sequence or importance. **2** alternate: *every second week.* **3** subordinate; inferior: *second to none.* —*noun* **1** a person or thing next in sequence after the first. **2** the second gear in an engine. **3** (**seconds**) flawed merchandise sold at reduced prices. **4** (**seconds**) *colloq.* **a** a second helping of food. **b** the second course of a meal. —*verb trans.* (**seconded, seconding**) **1** to declare formal support for (a proposal, or the person making it). **2** to give support or encouragement of any kind to. —*adv.* in second place: *came second in the race.* ▶ **seconder** *noun*

second² *noun* **1** (ABBREV. **sec, s**) a unit of time, equal to $\frac{1}{60}$ of a minute. **2** (ABBREV. **s**) *Math.* a unit of angular measurement equal to $\frac{1}{360}$ of a degree or $\frac{1}{60}$ of a minute. **3** a moment.

secondary *adj.* **1** of lesser importance. **2** developed from something earlier or original: *a secondary infection.*

second base *Baseball* the second of the three bases, exclusive of home plate. ▶ **second baseman**

second best the next after the best. ▶ **second-best** *adj.*

second class 1 the second highest grade, e.g., of traveling accommodations; the class or category below the first in quality or value. **2** a category of US and Canadian mail consisting of periodicals and newspapers. ▶ **second-class** *adj., adv.*

second cousin a cousin who is a child of one's parent's first cousin.

second-degree *adj.* **1** *Med.* denoting the second most severe type of burn. **2** *of a crime, esp. murder* perpetrated by intent but without malice aforethought, deliberation, or premeditation.

second fiddle *colloq.* a secondary role, or one taking this role.

second-generation *adj.* denoting the stage in technological development marked by use of solid-state circuitry.

secondhand *adj.* **1** previously owned or used by someone else. **2** not coming from the original source, but via an intermediary: *secondhand information.* —*adv.* **1** in a secondhand state. **2** not directly, but from someone else.

secondly adv. in the second place; as a second consideration.

second nature a habit so firmly fixed as to seem an innate part of a person's nature.

second sight the supposed power to see into the future or to see things happening elsewhere.

second thought 1 (second thoughts) doubts. 2 the process of reconsidering and reaching a different decision: *On second thought, I don't think I'll go after all.*

second wind 1 the recovery of normal breathing after exertion. 2 a burst of renewed energy or enthusiasm.

secrecy noun the state or fact of being secret.

secret adj. 1 hidden from or undisclosed to others, or to all but a few. 2 of, relating to, or being those whose activities are unknown to or unobserved by others: *a secret army.* 3 tending to conceal things from others; secretive. —noun 1 a piece of information not revealed or not to be revealed to others. 2 an unknown or un-revealed method of achievement: *the secret of eternal youth.* 3 a fact or purpose that remains unexplained; a mystery. ▸ **secretly** adv.

secretariat noun 1 the administrative department of a large organization, esp. a legislative body. 2 the staff or premises of such an administrative department.

secretary noun (pl. **secretaries**) 1 a person employed to perform administrative or clerical tasks. 2 the member of a club or society responsible for its correspondence and business records. 3 a senior civil servant assisting a government minister or ambassador. 4 a writing desk with a small bookcase on top. ▸ **secretarial** adj.

secretary-general noun (pl. **secretaries-general**) the principal administrative official in a large, esp. political, organization.

secret ballot a kind of voting procedure in which each voter's choices are kept confidential but the overall result is published.

secrete[1] (sĭ-krēt') verb trans. (**secreted, secreting**) of a gland or similar organ to form and release (a substance) for use in the body, or as an excretion. ▸ **secretion** noun ▸ **secretory** adj.

secrete[2] (sĭ-krēt', sē'krət) verb trans. (**secreted, secreting**) to hide away.

secretive adj. inclined not to reveal things to others. ▸ **secretiveness** noun

secret service a government department responsible for the gathering of intelligence about real and potential enemies, and matters of national security.

sect noun a religious or other group whose views and practices differ from those of an established body or from those of a body from which it has separated.

sectarian (sĕk-târ'ē-ən) adj. 1 of, relating to, or belonging to a sect. 2 having, showing, or caused by hostility toward those outside one's own group or belonging to a particular group: *sectarian violence.* —noun a member of a sect. ▸ **sectarianism** noun

section noun 1 any of the parts into which a thing is or can be divided, or from which it is constructed. 2 the surface formed when a plane cuts through a solid geometric figure. —verb trans. (**sectioned, sectioning**) 1 to separate (something) into parts: *sectioned the melon.* 2 Med. to cut or divide (tissue).

sectional adj. 1 made in sections. 2 relating or restricted to a particular group or area.

sector noun 1 a part of an area divided up for military purposes. 2 a separate part into which any sphere of activity, e.g., a nation's economy, can be divided: *the private sector.* 3 a portion of a circle formed by two radii and the part of the circumference lying between them.

secular adj. 1 not religious or ecclesiastical; civil or lay. 2 relating to this world; not heavenly or spiritual. 3 of members of the clergy not bound by vows to a particular religious order. ▸ **secularism** noun

secure (sĭ-kyōōr') adj. 1 free from or providing freedom from danger. 2 free from trouble or worry. 3 firmly fixed or attached. 4 unlikely to be lost or taken away; assured: *a secure job.* —verb trans. (**secured, securing**) 1 to fasten or attach firmly. 2 to get, or to get possession of. 3 to make free from danger or risk. 4 to guarantee. ▸ **securely** adv.

security noun (pl. **securities**) 1 the state of being secure. 2 freedom from the possibility of future financial difficulty. 3 protection from physical harm. 4 something given as a guarantee, e.g., of repayment of a loan. 5 (usu. **securities**) a certificate stating ownership of stocks or shares; the monetary value represented by such certificates.

sedan (sĭ-dăn') noun 1 a closed, two- or four-door automobile having front and back seats. 2 Hist. a large enclosed chair that can be lifted and carried on horizontal poles. Also called **sedan chair.**

sedate[1] (sĭ-dāt') adj. 1 calm and dignified. 2 slow and unexciting. ▸ **sedately** adv.

sedate[2] verb trans. (**sedated, sedating**) to make calm by means of a sedative. ▸ **sedation** noun

sedative (sĕd'ət-ĭv) noun Med. an agent, esp. a drug, that has a calming effect. —adj. of a drug, etc. having a calming effect.

sedentary (sĕd'n-tĕr'ē) adj. 1 of work involving much sitting. 2 of a person spending much time sitting; taking little exercise.

sedge noun any of various grasslike plants of marshy areas.

sediment *noun* **1** insoluble solid particles that have settled at the bottom of a liquid in which they were previously suspended. **2** solid material deposited by the action of gravity, wind, water, or ice and formed into rock.

sedimentary (sĕd,ə-mĕnt'ə-rē) *adj.* **1** relating to or of the nature of sediment. **2** denoting a rock that has formed as a result of the compaction of layers of sediment. *See also* **igneous, metamorphic.**

sedition *noun* speech, writing, or action encouraging public disorder, esp. rebellion against a government. ► **seditious** *adj.*

seduce (sĭ-dōōs', -dyōōs') *verb trans.* **(seduced, seducing) 1** to entice into having sexual relations. **2** to tempt, esp. into wrongdoing. ► **seduction** *noun* ► **seductive** *adj.*

sedulous (sĕj'ə-ləs) *adj. formal* **1** steadily hardworking and conscientious; diligent. **2** painstakingly carried out.

see¹ *verb trans., intrans.* (*pa t* **saw**; *pa p* **seen**; *pr p* **seeing**) **1** to perceive with the eyes. ▣ DESCRY, DETECT, DISCERN, DISTINGUISH, ESPY, MARK, NOTICE, OBSERVE, PERCEIVE, SIGHT, SPY. **2** to have the power of vision. **3** to watch: *see a play.* **4** to understand: *I see what you mean.* **5** to be aware of or know, esp. by looking: *I see from your letter that you're married.* **6** to find out: *wait and see.* **7** to meet up with: *haven't seen her in ages.* **8** to spend time with, esp. romantically: *is seeing a married woman.* **9** to speak to or consult: *I'd like to see the manager.* **10** to receive as a visitor: *The manager refused to see me.* **11** to make sure of something: *See that you lock the door.* **12** (**see to (something)**) to attend to (it). **13** to imagine, esp. to regard as likely: *I just can't see him agreeing.* **14** to consider: *I see her more as a writer than a politician.* **15** (**see (something) in (someone)**) to find an attractive feature in (someone). **16** to be witness to a sight or event: *I don't want to see her hurt.* **17** to escort: *I'll see you home.* **18** to refer to for information: *See page 5.* **—see through (someone)** to discern and understand (someone's hidden motives). **see through (something) 1** to discern (what is implied by an idea or scheme, etc.). **2** to recognize an essential truth underlying (a lie, trick, etc.).

see² *noun* **1** the post of bishop. **2** the area under the authority of a bishop or an archbishop.

seed *noun* (*pl.* **seeds, seed**) **1** *Bot.* the part of the fruit of a plant from which a new plant grows. **2** the origin or beginning. **3** *literary* offspring; descendants. **—verb** *intrans., trans.* (**seeded, seeding**) **1** *of a plant* to produce seeds. **2** to plant (seeds). **3** to remove seeds from (e.g., a fruit). **—go to seed 1** *of a plant* to stop flowering prior to the development of seed. **2** *colloq.* to allow oneself to become unkempt or unhealthy through lack of care. ► **seedless** *adj.*

seedling *noun* a young plant grown from seed.

seedy *adj.* (**seedier, seediest**) **1** *of a fruit, etc.* full of seeds. **2** *of a plant* at the stage of producing seeds. **3** *colloq.* mildly ill. **4** *colloq.* run down; dirty or disreputable.

seeing *noun* the power of vision; the ability to see. **—conj.** (also **seeing that**) given (that); since: *Seeing (that) you are opposed to the plan, I will not pursue it.*

seek *verb trans., intrans.* (**sought, seeking**) **1** to look for. **2** to try to get or achieve: *seek a job.* **3** to try or endeavor: *seeking to please.* **4** to ask for. ► **seeker** *noun*

seem *verb intrans.* (**seemed, seeming**) **1** to appear to the eye. **2** to be apparent; to appear to the mind. **3** to think or believe oneself: *I seem to recognize you.*

seeming *adj.* apparent: *seeming guilt.* ► **seemingly** *adv.*

seemly *adj.* (**seemlier, seemliest**) fitting; suitable: *seemly behavior.*

seen *see* **see¹.**

seep *verb intrans.* (**seeped, seeping**) to escape slowly, through or as if through a narrow opening. ► **seepage** *noun*

seer *noun* **1** a clairvoyant. **2** a prophet.

seersucker *noun* lightweight cotton or linen cloth with a crinkly appearance.

seesaw *noun* **1** a plaything consisting of a plank balanced in the middle, allowing people seated on its ends to propel each other up and down by pushing off the ground with the feet. **2** an alternate up-and-down or back-and-forth movement. **—verb** *intrans.* (**seesawed, seesawing**) to move alternately up and down or back and forth.

seethe (sēth) *verb intrans.* (**seethed, seething**) **1** *of a liquid* to churn and foam because or as if because of boiling. **2** to be extremely agitated.

segment *noun* (sĕg'mənt) **1** a part, section, or portion. **2** a part of a circle or sphere separated off by an intersecting line or plane. **—verb** *trans., intrans.* (sĕg-mĕnt') (**segmented, segmenting**) to divide or be divided into segments. ► **segmentation** *noun*

segregate (sĕg'rə-gāt') *verb trans.* (**segregated, segregating**) to separate (groups or a group) from others or from each other. ► **segregation** *noun* ► **segregationist** *noun*

segue (sā'gwā, sĕg'wā) *verb intrans.* (**segued, seguing**) **1** *Mus.* to make a direct transition from one theme or section to another one. **2** to move directly and smoothly from, e.g., one theme to another.

seismic (sīz'mĭk) *adj.* **1** of or relating to earthquakes. **2** of gigantic proportions: *a seismic change in mood.*

seismograph *noun* an instrument that measures and records the force of earthquakes. ▸ **seismography** *noun*

seismology *noun* the scientific study of earthquakes. ▸ **seismological** *adj.* ▸ **seismologist** *noun*

seize (sēz) *verb trans.* (**seized, seizing**) **1** to take or grab suddenly. **2** to affect suddenly and deeply; to overcome: *They were seized with panic.* **3** to take by force; to capture. **4** to take legal possession of: *seized a contraband shipment.*

seizure *noun* **1** an act or an instance of seizing. **2** a sudden attack of an illness, esp. one producing spasms or loss of movement.

seldom *adv.* hardly ever; rarely.

select *verb trans.* (**selected, selecting**) to choose from among several. —*adj.* **1** picked out in preference to others: *a select group.* **2** to which entrance or membership is restricted; exclusive: *a select country club.* ▸ **selectness** *noun* ▸ **selector** *noun*

selection *noun* **1 a** the act or process of choosing or of being chosen. **b** the right, power, or opportunity to choose. **c** a thing or set of things chosen. **d** a range from which to choose. **2** the process by which certain plants and animals survive while others do not.

selective *adj.* **1** exercising the right to reject some in favor of others. **2** able or tending to select; discriminating. **3** involving only certain people or things. ▸ **selectivity** *noun*

selenium *noun Chem.* (SYMBOL **Se**) a non-metallic, light-sensitive element, used, e.g., in solar batteries.

self *noun* (*pl.* **selves**) **1** personality, or a particular aspect of it. **2** a person as a whole, a combination of characteristics of appearance and behavior: *his usual happy self.* **3** personal interest or advantage. —*pron. colloq.* myself, yourself, himself, or herself.

self- *combining form* forming words denoting: **1** by or for oneself: *self-inflicted.* **2** acting automatically: *self-closing.*

self-absorbed *adj.* involved excessively with oneself or one's own affairs.

self-addressed *adj.* having been addressed by the sender for return to him- or herself.

self-appointed *adj.* acting on one's own authority, without being asked by others.

self-assertive *adj.* always ready to make others aware of one's presence or opinions. ▸ **self-assertion** *noun*

self-assured *adj.* self-confident. ▸ **self-assurance** *noun*

self-centered *adj.* interested only in oneself and in one's own affairs.

self-confidence *noun* **1** total absence of shyness. **2** belief in one's own abilities, etc. ▸ **self-confident** *adj.*

self-conscious *adj.* ill at ease in company as a result of feeling oneself to be observed by others. ▸ **self-consciousness** *noun*

self-contained *adj.* **1** of accommodation of which no part is shared with others. **2** content to be on one's own. **3** complete.

self-control *noun* **1** the practice or state of choosing not to take or do something. **2** the ability to keep one's emotions and impulses in check. ▸ **self-controlled** *adj.*

self-defense *noun* **1** the act or techniques of defending oneself from physical attack. **2** the act of defending one's own rights.

self-denial *noun* the practice or state of not allowing oneself something.

self-destruct *verb intrans.* (**self-destructed, self-destructing**) to destroy itself or oneself. ▸ **self-destruction** *noun*

self-determination *noun* **1** freedom to make one's own decisions without outside interference. **2** a nation's freedom to govern itself, without outside control.

self-discipline *noun* personal control of one's own conduct.

self-effacing *adj.* tending to avoid making others aware of one's achievements, esp. because of shyness or modesty. ▸ **self-effacement** *noun*

self-employed *adj.* working in one's own behalf and under one's own control.

self-esteem *noun* one's opinion, esp. a good opinion, of oneself; self-respect.

self-evident *adj.* clear enough to need no explanation or proof.

self-explanatory *adj.* needing no further explanation; easily understood.

self-expression *noun* the expression of one's personal views, e.g., through, art, or music.

self-fulfilling *adj., of a forecast, etc.* which, simply by being made, has the effect of bringing about the results it predicts.

self-government *noun* the fact or condition of governing itself. ▸ **self-governing** *adj.*

self-image *noun* the conception held by a person about himself or herself.

self-important *adj.* having an exaggerated sense of one's own importance; arrogant and pompous. ▸ **self-importance** *noun*

self-imposed *adj.* forced upon oneself by oneself, not imposed by others.

self-incrimination *noun* incrimination of oneself, esp. in a court of law, by way of one's own testimony.

self-indulgent *adj.* giving in or tending to give in to one's own wishes or whims. ▸ **self-indulgence** *noun*

self-inflicted *adj.* inflicted by oneself or oneself.

self-interest *noun* one's own personal welfare or advantage. ▸ **self-interested** *adj.*

selfish *adj.* tending to be concerned only with personal welfare. ▸ **selfishly** *adv.* ▸ **selfishness** *noun*

selfless *adj.* tending to consider the welfare of others before one's own. ▸ **selflessly** *adv.* ▸ **selflessness** *noun*

self-made *adj.* having achieved wealth or success through one's own efforts.

self-opinionated *adj.* tending to insist that one's own opinions, forcefully stated, are superior to all others.

self-pity *noun* excessive grumbling or moaning about one's own misfortunes.

self-possessed *adj.* calm and controlled, esp. in an emergency. ▸ **self-possession** *noun*

self-preservation *noun* the protection of one's own life or feelings.

self-promotion *noun* publicity about and advertising of oneself by oneself.

self-reliant *adj.* needing and seeking no help from others. ▸ **self-reliance** *noun*

self-respect *noun* respect for oneself and concern for one's dignity and reputation. ▸ **self-respecting** *adj.*

self-restraint *noun* the act of controlling or the capacity to control one's own feelings.

self-righteous *adj.* having too high an opinion of one's own goodness, and intolerant of other people's faults. ▸ **self-righteousness** *noun*

self-rising *adj.*, *of flour* containing an ingredient to make dough or pastry rise.

self-sacrifice *noun* the sacrifice of one's own wishes or interests for the sake of other people's. ▸ **self-sacrificing** *adj.*

selfsame *adj.* being one single one instead of another or others.

self-satisfied *adj.* feeling or showing typically smug satisfaction with oneself or one's accomplishments. ▸ **self-satisfaction** *noun*

self-seeking *adj.* preoccupied with one's own interests and the opportunities for personal advantage. ▸ **self-seeker** *noun*

self-service *noun* a system whereby customers serve themselves. —*adj.* operating such a system.

self-serving *adj.* seeking to benefit oneself, often to the disadvantage of others.

self-starter *noun* *colloq.* a person who requires little supervision in a job, being able to motivate himself or herself.

self-styled *adj.* called or considered so only by oneself: *a self-styled liberal.*

self-sufficient *adj.* able to provide oneself or itself with everything needed to live on or survive. ▸ **self-sufficiency** *noun*

self-willed *adj.* refusing to compromise.

sell *verb trans.*, *intrans.* (pa t and pa p **sold**; pr p **selling**) **1** to give (something) to another

party in exchange for money. **2** to have available for buying: *This store sells VCRs.* **3** (**sell at** *or* **for** (**something**)) to be available for buying at a specified price: *Refrigerators sell for $400 and up.* **4** to be bought by customers; to be in demand: *ice cream sells well in summer.* **5** to cause to be bought; to promote the sale of: *The author's name sells the book.* **6** to persuade (someone) to acquire or agree to something. —**sell out of** (**something**) to sell one's entire stock of (it). **sell out to** (**someone**) to betray one's principles or associates to (another party). **sell** (**someone** *or* **something**) **short** *colloq.* to understate the good qualities of (someone or something). ▸ **seller** *noun*

sell-by date a date on a manufacturer's or distributor's label indicating when a product, esp. food, is considered no longer fit or safe to be sold.

sellout *noun* **1** an event for which all the tickets have been sold. **2** *colloq.* a person who has betrayed his or her principles or the group previously supported.

seltzer *or* **seltzer water** *noun* soda water.

selvage *or* **selvedge** (sĕl′vĭj) *noun* an edge of a length of fabric woven so as to prevent fraying.

selves *see* self.

semantic *adj.* of or relating to meaning. ▸ **semantically** *adv.*

semantics *noun* (*sing.*, *pl.*) the branch of linguistics that deals with meaning.

semaphore *noun* a system of signaling in which flags, lights, or simply the arms are held in positions that represent individual letters and numbers.

semblance *noun* **1** appearance, esp. superficial or deceptive. **2** a hint or trace.

semen (sē′mən) *noun* a thick whitish liquid containing sperm, ejaculated by the penis.

semester *noun* an academic term lasting half an academic year.

semi (sĕm′ē, -ī,) *noun* (*pl.* **semis**) *colloq.* **1** a semitrailer. **2** a semifinal.

semi- *prefix* forming words denoting: **1** half: *semicircular.* **2** partly: *semiconscious.* **3** occurring twice in the stated period: *semiannual.*

Usage See note at *bi-*.

---

semiannual *adj.* happening or published twice a year.

semicircle *noun* **1** one half of a circle. **2** an arrangement in the form of a half a circle. ▸ **semicircular** *adj.*

semicolon *noun* a punctuation mark (;) indicating a pause or division stronger than that marked by a comma and weaker than that marked by a period.

semiconductor *noun Electron.* a substance, such as silicon, that conducts electricity only when heated.

semidetached *adj., of a house* forming part of the same building with another house on one side. —*noun Brit.* a semidetached house.

semifinal *noun* in sports competitions, either of two matches, the winners of which play each other in the final. ▸ **semifinalist** *noun*

seminal *adj.* 1 highly original and at the root of a trend or movement: *seminal writings.* 2 of or relating to seed, semen, or reproduction in general. ▸ **seminally** *adv.*

seminar *noun* 1 a small class for the discussion of a particular topic between students and a professor. 2 a meeting set up for the purpose of discussion.

seminary *noun (pl.* **seminaries**) a college for the training of members of the clergy.

semiotics (sē,mē-ăt′ĭks, sĕm,ē-) *noun (sing.)* the study of human communication, esp. the relationship between words and the objects or concepts to which they refer.

semiprecious *adj., of a gem* considered less valuable than a precious stone.

semiprivate · *adj., e.g., of a hospital room* shared with another or others.

semiprofessional *adj. Sport* 1 engaging only part-time in a sport for which one is paid. 2 *of a sport* engaged in by part-time, paid players. —*noun* 1 *Sport* a semiprofessional player. 2 a person whose job has some but not all professional characteristics.

semiskilled *adj.* having or requiring a degree of training less advanced than that needed for specialized work.

Semitic (sə-mĭt′ĭk) *noun* a group of languages that includes Hebrew, Arabic, and Aramaic. —*adj.* 1 relating to or speaking any such language. 2 relating to the Jews; Jewish.

semitone *noun Mus* half a tone in the scale.

semitrailer *noun* a truck trailer having several sets of wheels only at the rear, the forward section being supported by the truck tractor.

semivowel *noun Linguistics* 1 a speech sound having the qualities of both a vowel and a consonant, such as the sounds represented by the letters *y* and *w.* 2 a letter representing such a sound.

semolina *noun* hard particles of wheat not ground into flour during milling.

senate (sĕn′ət) *noun (often* **Senate**) 1 a law-making body, esp. the upper house of the US Congress. 2 the chief legislative and administrative body in ancient Rome. 3 a governing council in some universities.

senator *noun (often* **Senator**) a member of a senate. ▸ **senatorial** *adj.*

send *verb trans.* (pa t *and* pa p **sent**; pr p **sending**) 1 to cause or order to go or be conveyed or transmitted. 2 to force or propel: *sent me flying.* 3 to cause to become or pass into a specified state: *sent us into fits of laughter.* 4 to bring about, esp. by divine providence. ▸ **sender** *noun*

sendoff *noun* a display of good wishes from an assembled crowd to a departing person or group, e.g., at an airport or a port.

senescent *adj.* growing old; aging.

senile (sē′nĭl,) *adj.* 1 displaying the impairments of mind or body brought on by advanced age. 2 of or caused by advanced age. ▸ **senility** *noun*

senile dementia the progressive mental deterioration brought on by old age. *See also* **dementia**

senior *adj.* 1 (*often* **senior to** (**someone**)) a older than. b higher in rank or authority than. 2 of, relating to, or being a high-school, college, or university student in the last year of study. 3 older than a person of the same name, esp. distinguishing parent from child. 4 of, relating to, or being a senior citizen. —*noun* 1 a person who is older or of a higher rank than another. 2 a student in the final year of study. 3 a senior citizen.

senior citizen a person at or above the age of retirement.

seniority *noun* 1 the state of being senior. 2 a privileged position earned through long service in a profession or with a company.

sensation *noun* 1 awareness of an external or internal stimulus as a result of its perception by sensory receptors or sense organs of the nervous system. 2 a physical feeling: *a burning sensation.* 3 a general feeling. 4 a sudden widespread feeling of excitement or shock; also, the cause of it.

sensational *adj.* 1 causing or intended to cause widespread excitement, intense interest, or shock. 2 outstanding of its kind or class. 3 of or pertaining to the senses. ▸ **sensationally** *adv.*

sensationalism *noun* the practice of deliberately setting out to cause widespread excitement, intense interest, or shock. ▸ **sensationalist** *adj., noun*

sense *noun* 1 any of the faculties of sight, hearing, smell, taste, and touch, used to perceive the physical world or the condition of the body. 2 an awareness of or an ability to make judgments regarding a specified thing: *has a good sense of direction.* 3 (*often* **senses**) soundness of mind: *lost his senses.* 4 practical worth; wisdom: *There's no sense in doing it now.* 5 overall meaning. 6 specific meaning. —*verb trans.* (**sensed**, **sensing**) 1 to detect (a stimulus) by means of any of the five main senses. 2 to be aware of (something) by means other than the five main senses: *I sensed that something was wrong.* 3 to realize or comprehend: *sensed the difference.*

senseless *adj.* **1** unconscious. **2** foolish. ▸ **senselessly** *adv.* ▸ **senselessness** *noun*

sensibility *noun* (*pl.* **sensibilities**) **1** the ability to feel or have sensations. **2** the capacity to be affected emotionally; sensitivity: *sensibility to their grief.* **3** (**sensibilities**) feelings, esp. when easily offended or hurt.

sensible *adj.* **1** having or showing reasonableness or good judgment; wise. **2** perceptible by the senses. **3** able to feel; sensitive: *sensible to pain.* ▸ **sensibly** *adv.*

sensitive *adj.* **1** responding readily, strongly, or painfully: *sensitive to our feelings.* **2** able to feel or respond. **3** easily upset or offended. **4** about which there is much strong feeling or difference of opinion: *sensitive issues.* **5** of *scientific instruments* reacting to or recording very small changes. ▸ **sensitively** *adv.* ▸ **sensitivity** *noun*

sensitize *verb trans.* (**sensitized, sensitizing**) to make sensitive.

sensor *noun Electr.* a device that detects a physical quantity, e.g., light, either recording it or being activated by it to operate a switch.

sensory *adj.* of or pertaining to the senses.

sensual (sĕn'sha-wal) *adj.* **1** of the senses and the body. **2** suggesting, enjoying, or providing physical, esp. sexual, pleasure. **3** pursuing physical pleasures, esp. those derived from sex or food and drink. ▸ **sensuality** *noun*

> *Usage* This word is often confused with *sensuous*.

sensuous *adj.* **1** appealing to or designed to stimulate the senses esthetically. **2** pleasing to the senses. *See note at* **sensual**. ▸ **sensuously** *adv.* ▸ **sensuousness** *noun*

sent *see* **send**.

sentence (sĕn'ns) *noun* **1** a sequence of words forming a meaningful and complete grammatical structure. **2** *Law* a punishment determined by a court or judge. —*verb trans.* (**sentenced, sentencing**) *Law* **1** to announce the punishment to be given to (someone), esp. in a court of law. **2** to condemn to punishment.

sententious (sĕn-tĕn'chəs) *adj.* **1** tending to lecture others on morals. **2** full of, or fond of using, sayings or proverbs. ▸ **sententiousness** *noun*

sentient *adj.* capable of sensation; able to feel. ▸ **sentience** *noun*

sentiment *noun* **1** an emotion, esp. when expressed. **2** emotion, esp. when considered excessive, self-indulgent, or insincere. **3** that which is accepted by a person as true, not always proved. **4** (*sometimes* **sentiments**) opinion, esp. public opinion.

sentimental *adj.* **1 a** easily feeling and expressing tender emotions, esp. love, friendship, and pity. **b** provoking or designed to provoke such emotions, esp. in large measure and without subtlety. **2** closely associated with or moved to tears by fond memories of the past. ▸ **sentimentality** *noun* ▸ **sentimentalize** *verb trans.* ▸ **sentimentally** *adv.*

sentinel (sĕnt'n-əl) *noun* a sentry.

sentry *noun* (*pl.* **sentries**) a guard who controls entry or egress.

sepal *noun Bot.* a leaflike part protecting an unopened flower bud, lying beneath the petals of the unopened flower.

separable *adj.* able to be separated. ▸ **separability** *noun*

separate *verb trans., intrans.* (sĕp'ə-rāt,) (**separated, separating**) **1** to set, take, keep, or force apart (from others or each other). **2** to move apart; to cease to be or live together. **3** to become or cause to become disunited: *powerful political issues that can separate a nation.* ▣ DIVIDE, PART, RUPTURE, SPLIT, SUNDER ▣ COMBINE, FUSE, JOIN, LINK, UNIFY, UNITE. —*adj.* (sĕp'ə-rət) **1** unrelated: *a separate issue.* **2** physically unattached; isolated. —*noun* (sĕp'ə-rət) (*usu.* **separates**) a piece of clothing intended for wear with a variety of others, not part of a suit. ▸, **separately** *adv.* ▸ **separateness** *noun* ▸ **separator** *noun*

separation *noun* **1** the act or process of separating or the state of being separated. **2** a place or line where there is a division. **3** a gap or interval that separates. **4** *Law* an arrangement by which spouses live apart while remaining married.

separatist (sĕp'rət-ĭst) *noun* a person who encourages, or takes action to achieve independence from a country or an established institution. ▸ **separatism** *noun*

sepia (sē'pē-ə) *noun* **1** a yellowish-brown tint used in photography. **2** a dark reddish-brown color. **3** a pigment of this color, obtained from a fluid secreted by the cuttlefish.

sepsis *noun* (*pl.* **sepses**) *Med.* poisoning caused by the spread of harmful bacteria from a point of infection.

September (sĕp-tĕm'bər) *noun* (ABBREV. **Sept., Sept**) the ninth month of the year, following August.

septennial *adj.* **1** occurring once every seven years. **2** lasting seven years.

septet *noun* **1** *Mus.* **a** a group of seven musicians. **b** a piece for seven performers. **2** any group or set of seven.

septic *adj. of a wound* contaminated with harmful bacteria.

septicemia (sĕp͵tə-sē′mē-ə) *noun* blood poisoning.

septic tank an underground tank in which household sewage is broken down by the action of bacteria.

septuagenarian *adj.* aged between 70 and 79. —*noun* a person between the ages of 70 and 79.

septum *noun (pl.* **septa)** *Anat.* any partition between cavities, e.g., nostrils, or areas of soft tissue.

septuplet (sĕp-təp′lət) *noun* any of seven children born at the same time to the same mother.

sepulcher (sĕp′əl-kər) *noun* a grave or burial vault. ▸ **sepulchral** *adj.*

sequel (sē′kwəl) *noun* a book, movie, or play that continues an earlier story.

sequence *noun* **1** a series of things following each other in a particular order; the order followed. **2** *Math.* a set of values in which each is a fixed amount greater or smaller than its predecessor. ▸ **sequential** *adj.*

sequester *verb trans.* **(sequestered, sequestering) 1** to set apart or isolate. **2** to seclude. **3** *Law* **a** to isolate (a jury) during a trial so as to avoid influence or bias. **b** to take temporary possession of (the property of a party) as security against claims.

sequin *noun* a tiny round shiny disk of foil or plastic, sewn on a garment for decoration.

sequoia *noun* the redwood.

sera *see* **serum.**

Serbo-Croatian (sər͵bō-krō-ā′shən) *noun* a Slavonic language spoken in Serbia, Croatia, etc., the main language of the former Yugoslavia.

serenade *Mus. noun* a song or tune traditionally performed at night under a woman's window by her suitor. —*verb trans.* **(serenaded, serenading)** to entertain (a person) with a serenade.

serendipity *noun* the state of frequently making lucky finds. ▸ **serendipitous** *adj.*

serene *adj.* **1** relaxed and in control. **2** showing no indications of turbulence. ▸ **serenely** *adv.* ▸ **serenity** *noun*

serge (sərj′) *noun* a hard-wearing twilled fabric, esp. of wool.

sergeant (sär′jənt) *noun* (ABBREV. **Sgt.) 1** a noncommissioned officer in the US Army, Air Force, or Marines. **2** a police officer ranking below a captain, lieutenant, or inspector.

sergeant major *(pl.* **sergeants major, sergeant majors)** (ABBREV. **Sgt. Maj., SM)** a noncommissioned officer who is the chief administrative assistant of a headquarters in the US Army, Air Force, or Marines.

serial *noun* **1** a story published or broadcast in regular installments. **2** a periodical. —*adj.* **1** appearing in installments. **2** forming a series

or a part of a series. ▸ **serialization** *noun* ▸ **serialize** *verb trans.*

series *noun (pl.* **series) 1** a number of similar, related, or identical things arranged or produced one after the other. **2** a television or radio program in which the same characters appear or a similar subject is addressed, in regularly broadcast shows.

serious *adj.* **1** not lighthearted or flippant; solemn. **2** dealing with important issues: *a serious newspaper.* **b** of such a nature as to appeal to or be understood by sophisticates. **3** severe: *a serious accident.* **4** important; significant; large: *serious differences of opinion.* **5** not joking; earnest; sincere. ▸ **seriously** *adv.* ▸ **seriousness** *noun*

sermon *noun* **1** a public speech about morals, religious duties, or an aspect of religious doctrine, esp. as part of a church service. **2** a lengthy moral or advisory speech. ▸ **sermonize** *verb*

serology (sə-räl′ə-jē) *noun Biol.* the study of blood serum and its constituents.

serotonin (sĕr͵ə-tō′nĭn) *noun Physiol.* a hormone found chiefly in the brain, blood platelets, and intestinal tissues.

serous *adj.* **1** of or relating to serum. **2** resembling serum; watery.

serpent *noun* a snake.

serpentine (sər′pən-tēn͵, -tīn͵) *adj.* **1** snakelike. **2** full of twists and bends.

serration *noun* **1** a saw-edged condition. **2** a sawlike tooth. ▸ **serrated** *adj.*

serried *adj.* closely packed together.

serum (sĭr′əm) *noun (pl.* **serums, sera)** the straw-colored fluid component of blood.

servant *noun* a person employed by another to do household work, etc.

serve *verb trans., intrans.* **(served, serving) 1** to work for the benefit of: *served the community well.* **2** to carry out duties as a member of a body: *serve on a committee.* **3** to be in the armed forces. **4** to give assistance to (customers). **5** to respond to the needs or demands of (someone): *shoes that have served me well.* **6** to bring, distribute, or present (food or drink) to (someone). **7** to provide specified facilities to (someone): *a subway serving the entire city.* **8** to fulfill a need: *There's no chair, but this box will serve.* **9** to put (a ball or shuttlecock) into play in racket sports. **10** *Law* to deliver or present (a legal document). —*noun* an act of serving in a racket game. ▸ **server** *noun*

service *noun* **1** work performed for or in behalf of others; use or usefulness: *did me a great service.* **2** employment or engagement as a member of an organization working to serve or benefit others; such an organization. **3** assistance given to customers. **4** a facility provided: *a bus service.* **5** an occasion of worship or other religious ceremony, the words, etc., used on such an occasion: *the marriage service.* **6** a complete set of dishes. **7** a periodic check of the workings of a vehicle or other machine. **8** *Sport* an act of putting a ball or shuttlecock into play in racket sports; the game in which it is a particular player's turn to do so; the stroke used. **9** (*often* **services**) any of the armed forces. —*verb trans.* (**serviced, servicing**) to subject to a periodic (esp. mechanical) check. ▸ **serviceability** *noun* ▸ **serviceable** *adj.*

serviceman *noun* a male member of any of the armed forces.

service mark (ABBREV. **SM**) *Commerce* a mark used to identify commercial services.

serviceperson *noun* ·**1** a serviceman or servicewoman. **2** a person who maintains equipment.

service station a gasoline station providing additional facilities, e.g., repairs.

servicewoman *noun* a female member of any of the armed forces.

servile (sər'vĭl,) *adj.* **1** slavishly respectful, obedient, or attentive. **2** of, relating to, or suitable for slaves. ▸ **servility** *noun*

serving *noun* a portion of food served at one time; a helping.

servitude *noun* slavery.

servo *noun* (*pl.* **servos**) a device able to perform very powerful mechanical tasks with a relatively small amount of energy. *Also called* **servomechanism.**

sesame (sĕs'ə-mē) *noun* a plant from Southeast Asia with edible seeds.

sessile *adj.* **1** attached directly to the plant, rather than by a stalk. **2** attached directly to the body. **3** *of an animal* immobile.

session *noun* **1 a** a meeting of a court, council, congress, legislature, or parliament. **b** a period during which such meetings are regularly held. **2** a period of time spent engaged in a particular activity. **3** an academic term or year.

sestet *noun* **1** the last six lines of a sonnet. **2** a group of six people or things; a sextet.

set¹ *verb trans., intrans.* (pa t and pa p **set**; pr p **setting**) **1** to put into a certain position or condition: *set free.* **2** to make or become solid, rigid, firm, or motionless. **3** to fix, establish, or settle: *set a date.* **4** to put into a state of readiness: *set the table.* **5** to adjust (an instrument) to the correct reading: *set a clock.* **6** to adjust (a device) so that its controls are activated at a fixed time. **7** to assign as an exercise or duty: *set a test.* **8** to present or fix as a lead to be followed: *set an example.* **9 a** to place on or against a background, or in surroundings: *diamonds that were set in a gold bracelet.* **b** to decorate: *a bracelet set with diamonds.* **10**

to treat (hair) so as to stay firm in the required style. **11** *of the Sun or Moon* to disappear below the horizon. —*noun* **1** form; shape: *the set of his jaw.* **2** posture or bearing. **3** the area within which filmed action takes place; the scenery and props used to create a particular location in filming. **4** the process of setting hair; a hairstyle produced by setting: *a shampoo and set.* —*adj.* **1** allowing no alterations or variations; fixed: *a set menu.* **2** having or displaying an unwavering manner: *a set expression.* ▣ DETERMINED, RESOLUTE, RESOLVED ▣ FALTERING, IRRESOLUTE, VACILLATING, WAVERING. **3** predetermined or conventional: *set phrases.* **4** ready; prepared. **5** about to receive or experience; due: *set for a pay rise.* **6** (**set on (something)**) determined to do (it). **7** assigned; prescribed: *set texts for study.* —**set about (something)** to start or begin (it). **set off** *or* **set out** to begin a journey.

set² *noun* **1** a group of related or similar things regarded as a complete unit. **2** *Math.* a group of related elements: *the set of even numbers.* **3** a complete collection of pieces needed for a particular activity: *a chess set.* **4** *Sport* one of the major divisions of a match, e.g., in tennis, subdivided into games. **5** an instrument for receiving television or radio broadcasts. **6** the songs or tunes performed at a concert.

set³ *or* **sett** *noun* a badger's burrow.

setback *noun* **1** a check or reversal to progress. **2** a disappointment or misfortune.

set piece a carefully prepared performance or sequence of movements.

set square a triangular, usu. plastic, plate used as an aid to drawing lines and angles.

sett *noun same as* **set³**.

settee (sĕ-tē') *noun* a sofa.

setter *noun* a long-haired sporting dog, orig. trained to stand rigidly to indicate the direction of hunted game.

setting *noun* **1** a position at which the controls of an instrument are set. **2 a** a situation or background within or against which action takes place. **b** the scenery and props used in filming a scene. **3** a place setting at a table. **4** a mounting for a jewel.

settle *verb trans., intrans.* (**settled, settling**) **1** to make or become firmly, comfortably, or satisfactorily positioned or established. **2** (**settle (something)** *or* **settle on (something)**) to come to an agreement about (it). **3** to come lightly to rest: *The feather settled on the ground.* **4** (*also* **settle down** *or* **settle (someone) down**) to make or become calm, stable, or disciplined after a period of noisy excitement or upheaval. **5** to establish a permanent home or colony (in). **6** (*also* **settle up**) to pay off or clear (a debt). **7** to sink to the bottom of (something); to sink lower. **8** to transfer ownership of legally: *She settled the estate on her daughter.* —**settle for (something)** to accept (it) as a compromise or in place of something more suitable. ▸ **settler** *noun*

settlement *noun* **1** the act of settling. **2** a community or colony of recently settled people. **3** an agreement, esp. one ending a legal dispute. **4** a settlement house.

settlement house a center that provides certain social services, esp. in a city.

set-to *noun* (*pl.* **set-tos**) a fight or argument.

setup *noun* **1** *colloq.* an arrangement or a set of arrangements. **2** *slang* a trick to get a person unjustly blamed or accused. **3** (*often* **setups**) *colloq.* the utensils needed in mixing alcoholic drinks.

seven *noun* **1** the number or figure 7. **2** the age of 7. **3** any person or thing denoted by the number 7. **4** 7 o'clock. **5** a set of 7 people or things. **6** a score of 7 points. —*adj.* **1** 7 in number. **2** aged 7.

seventeen *noun* **1** the number or figure 17. **2** the age of 17. **3** any person or thing denoted by the number 17. **4** a set of 17 people or things. **5** a score of 17 points. —*adj.* **1** 17 in number. **2** aged 17.

seventeenth *noun, adj.* **1** the one numbered 17 in a series. **2** one of 17 equal parts.

seventh *noun, adj.* **1** the one numbered 7 in a series. **2** one of 7 equal parts.

seventh heaven a state of intense happiness.

seventies *pl. noun* **1** the period of time between one's 70th and 80th birthdays. **2** the range of temperatures between 70 and 80 degrees. **3** the period of time between the 70th and 80th years of a century.

seventieth *noun, adj.* **1** the one numbered 70 in a series. **2** one of 70 equal parts.

seventy *noun* (*pl.* **seventies**) **1** the number or figure 70. **2** the age of 70. **3** a set of 70 people or things. **4** a score of 70 points. —*adj.* **1** 70 in number. **2** aged 70.

sever *verb trans.* (**severed, severing**) **1** to cut off physically. **2** to break off or end. ▸ **severance** *noun*

several *adj.* **1** more than a few, but not a great number. **2** different and distinct; respective: *went their several ways.* —*pron.* quite a few people or things. ▸ **severally** *adv.*

severe *adj.* (**severer, severest**) **1** extreme and difficult to endure. **2** very strict. **3** suggesting seriousness and formality; austere. **4** very important in terms of the consequences. **5** rigorous; demanding. ▸ **severely** *adv.* ▸ **severity** *noun*

sew (sō) *verb trans., intrans.* (*pa t* **sewed**; *pa p* **sewn** *or* **sewed**; *pr p* **sewing**) **1** to stitch, attach, or repair with thread, by hand with a needle or by machine. **2** to make (garments) by stitching pieces of fabric together. ▸ **sewer** *noun*

sewage (sōō-ĭj) *noun* waste matter carried away in drains. *Also called* **sewerage**.

sewer (sōō'ər) *noun* a large underground pipe or channel for carrying away sewage from drains and water from road surfaces.

sewerage (sōō'ə-rĭj, sōōr'ĭj) *noun* **1** a network of sewers. **2** drainage of sewage and surface water using sewers. **3** sewage.

sewing *noun* **1** the act of sewing. **2** something that is being sewn. —*verb see* **sew**.

sex *noun* **1 a** either of the two classes, male and female, into which animals and plants or certain parts of plants are divided according to their role in reproduction. **b** membership of one of these classes, or the attributes that determine this. **2** sexual intercourse, often including other lovemaking activities. —*adj.* **1** of or relating to sexual matters in general: *sex education*. **2** of or based on one's sex: *sex discrimination*. —*verb trans.* (**sexed, sexing, sexes**) to identify the sex of (an animal).

sexagenarian *adj.* aged between 60 and 69. —*noun* a person between the ages of 60 and 69.

sex chromosome a chromosome that carries the genes determining the sex of an organism.

sexism *noun* contempt shown for or unfair treatment of a particular sex, based on prejudice or stereotype. ▸ **sexist** *noun, adj.*

sexless *adj.* **1** neither male nor female. **2** having no desire to engage in sexual activity. **3** sexually unattractive.

sextant (sĕk'stənt) *noun* an instrument like a small telescope mounted on a graded metal arc, used in navigation and surveying for measuring distance by means of angles.

sextet (sĕk-stĕt') *noun* **1** *Mus.* **a** a group of six musicians. **b** a piece for six performers. **2** any group or set of six.

sexton *noun* a person who looks after church property. *Also called* **sacristan**.

sextuple (sĕk-stōō'pəl, -stəp'əl) *adj.* being six times as much or as many. —*verb trans., intrans.* (**sextupled, sextupling**) to multiply or increase by six.

sextuplet *noun* any of six children born at the same time to the same mother.

sexual *adj.* **1** concerned with or suggestive of sex or lovemaking. **2** relating to reproduction involving the fusion of two gametes to form a zygote. **3** of, relating to, or according to membership of the male or female sex.

sexual intercourse **1** human coitus. **2** human sexual union involving genital contact without penetration by the penis.

sexuality noun sexual state, · condition, character, or potency.

sexually transmitted disease (ABBREV. **STD**) any one of various diseases transmitted by sexual intercourse or other physical intimacy.

sexy adj. (**sexier**, **sexiest**) colloq. 1 sexually attractive; arousing sexual desire. 2 currently popular or interesting: sexy new products. ▸ **sexily** adv. ▸ **sexiness** noun

sf or **SF** abbrev. science fiction.

sg abbrev. specific gravity.

Sgt. abbrev. sergeant.

Sgt. Maj. abbrev. sergeant major.

sh interj. used to ask someone to be quiet.

shabby adj. (**shabbier**, **shabbiest**) 1 esp. of clothes or furnishings old and worn; dingy. 2 of a person wearing such clothes. 3 nasty; mean: shabby conduct. ▸ **shabbily** adv. ▸ **shabbiness** noun

shack noun a roughly built cabin; a hut.

shackle noun 1 either of a pair of metal bands, joined by a chain, locked around a prisoner's wrists or ankles to limit movement. 2 something that restricts freedom. —verb trans. (**shackled**, **shackling**) to restrain with, or as if with, shackles.

shad noun (pl. **shad**, **shads**) an edible herring-like fish.

shade noun 1 a the blocking or partial blocking of sunlight, or the dimness caused by it. b an area from which sunlight has been wholly or partially blocked. c such an area represented in a drawing or painting. 2 a supernatural being or form. 3 a device used as a shield from direct light; a lampshade. 4 a color, esp. one similar to but slightly different from a principal color. 5 a small amount: a shade of irony in the passage. —verb trans., intrans. (**shaded**, **shading**) 1 to block or partially block sunlight from. 2 to draw or paint so as to give the impression of shade: shaded the background of the portrait. 3 (often **shade away** or **off**) to change gradually or unnoticeably.

shading noun the representation of areas of shade, e.g., by close parallel lines in a drawing.

shadow noun 1 a dark shape on a surface, produced when an object stands between the surface and a source of light. 2 an area darkened by the blocking out of light. 3 a hint or trace: the shadow of a smile. 4 a sense of gloom or foreboding. 5 a greatly weakened or reduced version: a shadow of her former self. 6 a constant companion. 7 a person following another closely and secretively. —verb trans., intrans. (**shadowed**, **shadowing**) 1 to follow (someone) closely and secretively. 2 to put into darkness by blocking out light. 3 to become clouded or darkened as if by shadows. —adj. having no official status but having

influence nonetheless: a shadow government. ▸ **shadowy** adj.

shadowbox verb intrans. (**shadowboxed**, **shadowboxing**) to box against an imaginary opponent as training. ▸ **shadow-boxing** noun

shady adj. (**shadier**, **shadiest**) 1 sheltered or giving shelter from sunlight. 2 colloq. probably dishonest or illegal: a shady deal.

shaft noun 1 the long straight handle of a tool or weapon. 2 a long straight part, e.g., a revolving rod that transmits motion in vehicle engines. 3 a vertical passageway, esp. one through which an elevator moves. 4 a thing moving or aimed with the directness or violent force of an arrow or missile: a shaft of light.

shag noun 1 a ragged mass of hair. 2 a long coarse pile or nap on fabric. ▸ **shaggy** adj.

shake verb intrans., trans. (pa t **shook**; pa p **shaken**; pr p **shaking**) 1 to undergo heavy vibration or jolting particularly as the result of a physical shock. ▣ JAR, JOLT, QUAKE, ROCK, TREMBLE, TREMOR, VIBRATE. 2 to cause to move in a jerking, rapid manner: shook the latch on the gate. ▣ JIGGLE, JOGGLE. 3 (also **shake** (**something**) **up**) to mix (it) by moving (it) with quick, often violent to-and-fro or up-and-down movements. 4 to wave violently and threateningly: shook her fist. 5 to tremble, totter, or shiver: shook all over in terror. 6 to cause intense shock or agitation within: revelations that shook the nation. 7 (also **shake** (**someone**) **up**) to disturb or upset (someone) greatly. 8 to cause to waver; to weaken: Nothing shook the President's iron resolve. 9 to shake hands. —noun 1 an act or the action of shaking. 2 colloq. a very short while; a moment. 3 (**the shakes**) colloq. a fit of uncontrollable trembling. 4 a milk shake. —**shake a leg** colloq. to hurry up or get moving. **shake** (**something or someone**) **off** 1 to get rid of (the one or ones specified); to free oneself from (them). 2 to escape from (something specified): couldn't shake off my worries about the firm.

shakedown noun slang 1 an act of extortion. 2 slang a complete and careful search.

shaker noun a container from which something, e.g., salt, is dispensed by shaking, or in which something, e.g., a cocktail, is mixed by shaking.

shakeup noun colloq. a fundamental change or reorganization.

shaky adj. (**shakier**, **shakiest**) 1 trembling, as with weakness or illness. 2 not solid, sound, or secure: a shaky political stance.

shale noun a fine-grained rock formed by the compression of clay, silt, or sand.

shall *verb, aux. (pa t* **should**) expressing: **1** the future tense of other verbs, when the subject is *I* or *we*. **2** determination, intention, certainty, and obligation, when the subject is *you, he, she, it*, or *they*: *You shall have what you want.* **3** a question implying future action, often with the sense of an offer or suggestion, esp. when the subject is *I* or *we*: *Shall I give you a hand?* **4** something inevitable: *We shall overcome. See also* **will**[1].

shallot (shə-lät') *noun* a type of small onion.

shallow *adj.* **1** having little depth. **2** not profound or sincere; superficial. —*noun* (*often* **shallows**) a shallow place or part, esp. in water.

shalom (shä-lōm') *noun, interj.* used as a Jewish greeting or farewell.

sham *adj.* false; pretended; insincere: *a sham doctor.* —*verb trans., intrans.* (**shammed, shamming**) to pretend or fake. —*noun* **1 a** something that is not genuine. **b** insincere behavior intended to make an impression. **2** a person who shams; an impostor.

shaman (shä'mən, shā-) *noun* (*pl.* **shamans**) a priest who uses magic, esp. his ability to make his spirit leave his body, to cure illness, commune with gods and spirits, etc. ► **shamanism** *noun* ► **shamanistic** *adj.*

shamble *verb intrans.* (**shambled, shambling**) to walk with slow, awkward, tottering steps. —*noun* a walk or pace characterized by a shambling gait.

shambles *noun* (*sing.*) *colloq.* a confused mess; a state of total disorder.

shame *noun* **1** an embarrassing or degrading sense of guilt, foolishness, or failure as a result of one's own actions or those of another person associated with one. **2** loss of respect or favor, or the cause of it: *resigned the presidency in shame.* ▣ DISGRACE, DISHONOR, DISREPUTE, IGNOMINY, OBLOQUY, OPPROBRIUM ▣ ESTEEM, HONOR, REPUTE, RESPECT. **3** a regrettable or disappointing event or situation. —*verb trans.* (**shamed, shaming**) **1** to cause to feel shame. **2** (**shame** (**someone**) **into** (**something**)) to provoke (someone) into taking action by inspiring feelings of shame. **3** to bring disgrace on. ► **shameful** *adj.* ► **shamefully** *adv.*

shamefaced *adj.* showing shame or embarrassment. ► **shamefacedly** *adv.*

shameless *adj.* **1** showing no shame; incapable of feeling shame. **2** done entirely without shame; blatant. ► **shamelessly** *adv.*

shammy *noun* (*pl.* **shammies**) *same as* **chamois** (sense 2).

shampoo *noun* (*pl.* **shampoos**) **1** a soapy liquid for washing the hair and scalp. **2** a similar liquid for cleaning carpets or upholstery. **3** a treatment with either liquid.

—*verb trans.* (**shampooed, shampooing, shampoos**) to wash or clean with shampoo.

shamrock *noun* a plant with leaves divided into three rounded leaflets, e.g. clover, and used as the national emblem of Ireland.

shandy *noun* (*pl.* **shandies**) a mixture of beer and lemonade.

shanghai *verb* (**shanghaied, shanghaiing, shanghais**) **1** to kidnap and send to sea as a sailor. **2** to trick into an unpleasant situation.

Shangri-la (shăng,rə-lä') *noun* an imaginary earthly paradise.

shank *noun* **1** the lower leg of an animal, esp. a horse, between the knee and the foot. **2** a cut of meat esp. from the upper leg of an animal. **3** a shaft or other long straight part.

shan't *contr.* shall not.

shantey *or* **shanty** *noun same as* **chantey.**

shanty *noun* (*pl.* **shanties**) a hut; a shack.

shape *noun* **1** an outline or form. **2** a person's body or figure. **3** form, person, etc.: *an assistant in the shape of my brother.* **4** a desired form or esp. physical condition: *keep in shape.* **5** condition generally: *in good shape.* **6** an unidentifiable figure: *shapes lurking in the dark.* **7** a mold or pattern. **8** a figure, esp. a geometric one. —*verb trans.* (**shaped, shaping**) **1** to give a particular form to; to fashion. **2** to influence to an important extent: *shaped history.* —**shape up** *colloq.* **1** to appear to be developing in a particular way. **2** to progress or develop well. **take shape** **1** to take on a definite form. **2** to become recognizable as the desired result of plans or theories.

shapeless *adj.* **1** having no regular, describable shape. **2** unattractively shaped. ► **shapelessness** *noun*

shapely *adj.* well proportioned; attractively shaped. ► **shapeliness** *noun*

shard *or* **sherd** *noun* a hard fragment: *shards of glass.*

share[1] *noun* **1** a portion given to or contributed by each of several people or groups. **2 a** a claim to a business and its profits or to a part of these. ▣ INTEREST, STAKE. **b** any one of the units into which the capital stock of a company is divided: *bought 100 shares in the new company.* —*verb trans., intrans.* (**shared, sharing**) **1** (**share** (**something**) *or* **share in** (**something**)) to have joint possession or use of (it), or joint responsibility for (it), with another or others. **2** (*also* **share** (**something**) **out**) to divide (it) into portions, distributed to each of several people or groups.

share[2] *noun* a plowshare.

sharecropper *noun* a farmer who pays a share of the crop the farm produces as rent.

shareholder *noun* a person who owns shares in a company.

shark noun **1** a large, usu. fierce, flesh-eating fish. **2** colloq. a ruthless or dishonest person.

sharkskin noun **1** leather made from a shark's skin. **2** smooth rayon fabric with a dull sheen.

sharp adj. **1** having a thin edge that can cut or a point that can pierce. **2** having a bitter, pungent taste. **3** severely felt: a sharp pain. **4** sudden and acute: a sharp bend. **5 a** quick at learning and understanding. **b** astute but unprincipled or unethical to some degree. **6** abrupt or harsh in speech. **7** easily perceived; clear-cut: in sharp contrast. **8** sarcastic: a sharp retort. **9** colloq. stylish: a sharp dresser. **10** Mus. higher in pitch by a semitone: C sharp. **11** Mus. out of tune by being slightly too high in pitch. —noun **1** Mus. a sharp note; a sign (#) indicating it. **2** colloq. **a** a practiced cheat. **b** an expert. —adv. **1** on the dot; punctually: at 12 o'clock sharp. **2** suddenly: pulled up sharp. **3** Mus. untunefully high. ▸ **sharpener** noun ▸ **sharply** adv. ▸ **sharpness** noun

sharpshooter noun a good marksman.

shatter verb trans., intrans. (**shattered, shattering**) **1** to break into pieces. **2** to destroy completely, or cause to break down: shattered all our hopes. **3** to upset greatly.

shave verb trans., intrans. (pa t **shaved**; pa p **shaved** or **shaven**; pr p **shaving**) **1 a** to cut off (hair) from (the face or other part of the body) with a razor or shaver. **b** to remove a growth of beard in this way. **2** to remove thin slivers from the surface of (esp. wood) with a bladed tool. **3** to graze the surface of or narrowly miss in passing. —noun **1** an act or the process of shaving a growth of beard. **2** a narrow miss or escape: a close shave.

shaver noun **1** an electric device for shaving hair. **2** colloq. a young boy.

shaving noun **1** the removal of hair with a razor. **2** a thin sliver, esp. of wood, taken off with a sharp tool.

shawl noun a large single piece of fabric used as a loose covering for the head or shoulders.

she pron. **1** the female person or animal already referred to. **2** a thing thought of as female, e.g., a ship or a nation, named before or understood from the context. —noun a female person or animal: Is the kitten a she?

s/he pron. (used in gender-neutral contexts) he or she.

sheaf noun (pl. **sheaves**) a bundle, esp. of reaped grain stalks, tied together. —verb trans. (**sheafed, sheafing, sheafs**) to tie up in a bundle.

shear verb trans., intrans. (pa t **sheared**; pa p **sheared** or **shorn**; pr p **shearing**) **1** to clip or cut off with a large pair of clippers. **2** to cut the fleece off (a sheep). **3** (usu. be **shorn of** (**something**)) to be stripped or deprived of (it). —noun (**shears**) (pl.) a two-bladed cutting tool resembling a large pair of scissors. ▸ **shearer** noun

sheath (shēth) noun (pl. **sheaths**) **1** a covering for the blade of a sword or knife. **2** a long, close-fitting covering. **3** a condom. **4** a straight, tight-fitting dress.

sheathe (shēth) verb trans. (**sheathed, sheathing**) to put into, or to protect or cover with, a sheath.

sheaves see sheaf.

shebang (shə-bǎng') noun slang affair; matter: the whole shebang.

shed[1] noun a wooden or metal outbuilding, for working in or for storage or shelter.

shed[2] verb trans. (pa t and pa p **shed**; pr p **shedding**) **1** to release or cause to flow: shed tears. **2** to cast off or get rid of: shed a skin. **3** to cast: shed light on.

she'd contr. **1** she had. **2** she would.

sheen noun glossy shine; luster.

sheep noun (pl. **sheep**) **1** a wild or domesticated herbivorous mammal, kept as a farm animal for its meat, milk, and wool. **2** a meek person who follows unquestioningly.

sheepdog noun a dog used to guard sheep from wild animals or to assist in herding.

sheepish adj. embarrassed because of having done something wrong or foolish. ▸ **sheepishly** adv. ▸ **sheepishness** noun

sheepskin noun **1** a sheep's skin with the wool left on it, or a rug or piece of clothing made from it. **2** colloq. a diploma.

sheer[1] adj. **1** nothing but; absolute: sheer madness. **2** of a cliff, etc. almost perpendicular. **3** so fine as to be almost transparent.

sheer[2] verb intrans. (**sheered, sheering**) to change course suddenly; to swerve.

sheet[1] noun **1** a large broad piece of fabric, esp. for covering the mattress of a bed. **2** any large broad piece or expanse. **3** a piece (of paper).

sheet[2] noun Naut. a controlling rope attached to the lower corner of a sail.

sheet metal metal rolled to a thickness between that of foil and plate.

sheet music music printed on sheets of paper.

sheik or **sheikh** (shēk, shāk) noun **1** the head of an Arab tribe, village, or family. **2** a Muslim leader. ▸ **sheikdom** noun

shelf noun (pl. **shelves**) **1** a usu. narrow horizontal board for laying things on, fixed to a wall or as part of a cupboard, etc. **2** a sandbank or rocky ledge.

shelf life the length of time that a stored product remains usable.

shell noun **1** Bot. the hard protective layer that surrounds the seed, nut, or fruit of some plants. **2** Zool. **a** the tough protective structure that covers the body of certain animals, e.g., mollusks. **b** the protective outer covering of an egg. **3 a** a hard outer case. **b** a thin pastry. **4** a round of ammunition for a large-bore gun. **5** an empty framework or outer case, the early stage of construction or the remains of something, e.g., a building. **6** *Comput.* a program that acts as a user-friendly interface between an operating system and the user. —*verb trans.* (**shelled, shelling**) **1** to remove the shell or shells from. **2** to bombard with, e.g., mortar shells. —**shell out** *colloq.* to pay out.

she'll *contr.* **1** she will. **2** she shall.

shellfish *noun* (*pl.* **shellfish, shellfishes**) a sea creature with a hard outer shell.

shell shock a nervous breakdown caused by prolonged exposure to combat conditions. ▸ **shell-shocked** *adj.*

shelter *noun* **1 a** protection against weather or danger. **b** a place or structure giving such protection. **2** temporary housing for the homeless. —*verb trans., intrans.* (**sheltered, sheltering**) **1** to protect from danger or the effects of weather. **2** to take cover.

shelve *verb trans., intrans.* (**shelved, shelving**) **1** to store on a shelf. **2** to equip with shelves. **3** to postpone the use or implementation of: *shelved the plan.*

shelves *see* **shelf**.

shelving *noun* **1** material for use as shelves. **2** shelves collectively.

shenanigan *noun colloq.* **1** (**shenanigans**) **a** boisterous misbehavior. **b** foolish behavior. **2** a cunningly devised means to an end.

shepherd (shĕp′ərd) *noun* a person who looks after sheep. —*verb trans.* (**shepherded, shepherding**) to guide or herd (a group or crowd).

sherbet *or* **sherbert** *noun* a frozen dessert made of fruit juice, water, sugar, milk, egg whites, and gelatin.

sherd *noun* same as **shard**.

sheriff *noun* the chief police officer in a US county.

sherry *noun* (*pl.* **sherries**) a fortified wine.

she's *contr.* **1** she is. **2** she has.

shiatsu (shē-ät′sōō) *noun Med.* a massage technique that uses the application of pressure to parts of the body. *Also called* **acupressure**.

shibboleth *noun* a custom word, phrase, or pronunciation that characterizes members of a particular group.

> Originally a word giving membership to a group, after a Biblical story in which its correct pronunciation was used as a password

shield *noun* **1** a piece of armor carried to block an attack with a weapon. **2** a representation of this piece of armor. **3** a medal or trophy shaped like this. **4** a protective plate or

screen. —*verb trans.* (**shielded, shielding**) to protect from danger or harm.

shift *verb trans., intrans.* (**shifted, shifting**) **1** to change the position or direction of; to change position or direction. **2** to transfer, switch, or redirect: *shifted the blame to someone else.* **3** to change (gears) in a motor vehicle or on a bicycle. **4** to remove or dislodge. —*noun* **1** a change, or a change of position. **2 a** one of a set of consecutive periods into which a 24-hour working day is divided. **b** the group of workers on duty during any one of these periods. **3** a loose-fitting beltless dress.

shiftless *adj.* **1** having no motivation or initiative. **2** inefficient.

shifty *adj.* (**shiftier, shiftiest**) *of a person or behavior* sly, untrustworthy, or dishonest.

Shiite (shē′īt,) *noun* an adherent of Shia, one branch of Islam. —*adj.* of or relating to Shia.

shilling *noun* in the UK before decimal currency, a monetary unit and coin worth one twentieth of £1, or 12 old pence.

shilly-shally *verb intrans.* (**shilly-shallied, shilly-shallying, shilly-shallies**) to be slow to make up one's mind; to be indecisive.

shimmer *verb intrans.* (**shimmered, shimmering**) to shine quiveringly with reflected light. —*noun* a quivering gleam of reflected light. ▸ **shimmery** *adj.*

shimmy *noun* abnormal vibration, as of a machine. —*verb intrans.* (**shimmied, shimmying, shimmies**) to vibrate in an abnormal way.

shin *noun* **1** the bony front part of the leg below the knee. **2** the lower part of a leg of beef. —*verb trans., intrans.* (**shinned, shinning**) (*usu.* **shin up**) to climb by gripping with the hands and legs.

shinbone *noun* tibia.

shindig *noun colloq.* a lively party.

shine *verb intrans., trans.* (pa t and pa p **shone** *or* **shined**; pr p **shining**) **1** to give out or reflect light. **2** to direct the light from (a source) onto: *shone the flashlight in my face.* **3** to make bright and gleaming by polishing. **4** to be outstandingly impressive: *She shines at math.* —*noun* **1** a shining quality; brightness; luster. **2** sunny weather: *rain or shine.* —**take a shine to (someone)** *colloq.* to like (someone) on first acquaintance.

shingle[1] *noun* a mass of small rounded pebbles that have been worn smooth by the action of water.

shingle[2] *noun* a thin rectangular piece of roofing material. —*verb trans.* (**shingled, shingling**) to roof with shingles.

shingles *noun* (*sing., pl.*) an infectious disease of the nerve cells, producing a rash of painful blisters esp. round the waist.

Shinto (shĭn'tō) *noun* the principal religion of Japan. ▶ **Shintoism** *noun* ▶ **Shintoist** *noun, adj.*

shiny *adj.* (**shinier, shiniest**) reflecting light; polished to brightness.

ship *noun* **1** a large vessel intended for sea travel. **2** *colloq.* a spaceship or airship. —*verb trans.; intrans.* (**shipped, shipping**) **1** to send or transport by ship, or any other means. **2** (**ship (someone) off**) *colloq.* to send (someone) away: *shipped the children off to boarding school.* ▶ **shipper** *noun*

-ship *suffix* forming words denoting: **1** rank, position, or status: *lordship.* **2** a period of office or rule: *during his chairmanship.* **3** a state or condition: *friendship.* **4** a type of skill: *craftsmanship.* **5** a group of individuals: *membership.*

shipmate *noun* a fellow sailor.

shipment *noun* **1** a cargo or consignment. **2** the act or practice of shipping cargo.

shipping *noun* **1** ships as traffic. **2** the commercial transporting of freight, esp. by ship.

shipshape *adj.* in good order; neat and tidy.

shipwreck *noun* **1** the accidental sinking or destruction of a ship. **2** the remains of a sunken or destroyed ship. —*verb trans., intrans.* (**shipwrecked, shipwrecking**) to cause to be, or to be, the victim of accidental sinking or destruction.

shipyard *noun* a place where ships are built and repaired. *Also called* **dockyard.**

shire *noun Brit.* a county.

shirk *verb trans., intrans.* (**shirked, shirking**) to avoid doing (work) or carrying out (a duty). ▶ **shirker** *noun*

shirt *noun* a piece of clothing for the upper body, usu. with a collar and buttons down the front. —**keep (one's) shirt on** *colloq.* to control (one's) temper.

shirtwaist *noun* a woman's bodice or blouse that looks like a shirt.

shish kebab a dish of small pieces of seasoned meat often with sliced vegetables, roasted on small skewers.

shit *obscene noun* **1** feces. **2** the act of defecating. **3** rubbish; nonsense. —*verb intrans.* (*pa t* and *pa p* **shit** or **shat**; *pr p* **shitting**) to defecate. —*interj.* used to express anger or great disappointment.

shiver[1] *verb intrans.* (**shivered, shivering**) to quiver or tremble, e.g., with fear or cold. —*noun* an act of shivering; a shivering movement or sensation. ▶ **shivery** *adj.*

shiver[2] *noun* a small fragment; a splinter. —*verb trans., intrans.* (**shivered, shivering**) to shatter.

shmuck *noun* same as **schmuck.**

shoal[1] *noun* **1** school[2]. **2** a huge crowd; a multitude. —*verb intrans.* (**shoal-ed, shoaling**) to gather or move in a shoal.

shoal[2] *noun* **1** an area of shallow water where sediment has accumulated. **2** such an accumulation of sediment.

shock[1] *noun* **1** a strong emotional disturbance, esp. a feeling of extreme surprise, outrage, or disgust; also, a cause of it. **2** a convulsion caused by the passage of an electric current through the body. **3** a heavy jarring blow or impact. —*verb trans.* (**shocked, shocking**) to cause to feel extreme surprise, outrage, or disgust.

shock[2] *noun* **1** a bushy mass of hair. **2** a number of sheaves of corn propped up against each other to dry.

shock absorber a device that absorbs impact, esp. fitted in motor vehicles to damp the vibrations caused by the wheels passing over bumps in the road.

shocking *adj.* **1** flagrantly wicked or horrible. **2** *colloq.* very bad.

shock wave *Phys.* an intense sound wave, caused by a violent explosion or the movement of an object at a speed greater than that of sound.

shod, shodden *see* **shoe.**

shoddy *adj.* (**shoddier, shoddiest**) **1** poor in quality. **2** of the nature of a cheap imitation. ▶ **shoddily** *adv.* ▶ **shoddiness** *noun*

shoe *noun* **1** a shaped outer covering for the foot, esp. made of leather or other stiff material. **2** something like this footwear in shape or function. **3** a horseshoe. —*verb trans.* (*pa t* **shod**; *pa p* **shod** or **shodden**; *pr p* **shoeing**) to fit (usu. a horse) with shoes.

shoehorn *noun* a curved, shaped piece of metal, plastic, or orig. horn, used for gently levering a foot into a shoe.

shoelace *noun* a string or cord for fastening a shoe. *Also called* **shoestring.**

shoestring *noun* a shoelace. —**on a shoestring** *colloq.* with or using a very small amount of money.

shoetree *noun* a support put inside a shoe to preserve its shape when it is not being worn.

shone *see* **shine.**

shoo *interj.* used to chase away a person or animal. —*verb trans.* (**shooed, shooing**) (**shoo (someone or something) away** or **off**) to chase (someone or something) away by or as if by shouting Shoo!

shook *see* **shake.**

shoot *verb trans., intrans.* (*pa t* and *pa p* **shot**; *pr p* **shooting**) **1** to fire (a gun or other weapon, or bullets, arrows or other missiles). **2** to hit, wound, or kill with a weapon or missile. **3** to direct forcefully and rapidly: *shot questions at them.* **4** to move with speed. **5** *Sport* to strike or throw (a ball, etc.) at a designated goal. **6** to film or take photographs (of). **7** a *colloq.* to pass quickly through: *shoot the rapids.* **b** *slang* to use up or waste: *shot his paycheck on gambling.* 2 Billiards to play a game of (e.g., pool). —*noun* 1 an act of shooting. 2 *Bot.* a new or young plant growth. 3 an outing to hunt animals with firearms; an area of land within which animals are hunted in this way. 4 a session of picture-taking. —**shoot up** 1 to grow or increase very quickly. 2 *slang* to inject heroin, etc. ▸ **shooting** *noun*

shooting star a meteor.

shootout *noun* a gun battle.

shop *noun* 1 a place where goods or services are bought and sold. 2 a place in which esp. manual labor of a particular kind is carried out: *a machine shop.* —*verb intrans.* (**shopped, shopping**) to visit shops in order to buy goods. —**talk shop** *colloq.* to talk about one's work. ▸ **shopper** *noun* ▸ **shopping** *noun*

shop floor 1 the part of a factory where the manual work is carried out. 2 the workers in a factory, as opposed to management.

shopkeeper *noun* a person who owns and manages a shop.

shoplift *verb trans., intrans.* (**shoplifted, shoplifting**) to steal (goods) from shops. ▸ **shoplifter** *noun* ▸ **shoplifting** *noun*

shopping center an area containing a large number of shops of different kinds.

shop steward a worker elected by others to be an official labor union representative in negotiations with the management.

shoptalk *noun* conversations about one's work.

shopworn *adj.* slightly dirty or spoiled from being used as a display in a shop.

shore¹ *noun* 1 land bordering on the sea or any area of water. 2 (**shores**) lands; countries.

shore² *noun* a prop. —*verb trans.* (**shored, shoring**) (*usu.* **shore (something) up**) 1 to support (it) with props. 2 to give support to (it); to sustain or strengthen (it).

shoreline *noun* the line formed where land meets water.

shorn see **shear.**

short *adj.* 1 of little physical length; not long. 2 of little height. 3 brief; concise: *a short speech.* 4 of a temper easily lost. 5 rudely or angrily abrupt; curt. 6 (**short on** or **of** (**something**)) lacking (it); not having enough of (it); deficient: *ran short of money.* 7 of the memory tending not to retain things for long. 8 of pastry crisp and crumbling easily. —*adv.* 1 abruptly: *stopped short.* 2 (**short of**) without going as far as; except: *tried everything short of threats.* —*noun* 1 a short subject. 2 *Electr.* a short circuit. —*verb trans., intrans.* (**shorted, shorting**) *Electr.* to short-circuit. ▸ **shortness** *noun*

shortage (shôrt′lj) *noun* a lack or deficiency.

shortbread *noun* a rich sweet crumbly cookie made with flour, butter, and sugar.

shortcake *noun* a dessert consisting of a cake used as a base, and then topped with fruit.

shortchange *verb trans.* (**shortchanged, shortchanging**) 1 to give (a customer) less than the correct amount of change. 2 *colloq.* to treat unfairly or dishonestly.

short circuit *Electr.* a connection across a circuit with a very low resistance, usu. caused accidentally. ▸ **short-circuit** *verb trans., intrans.*

shortcoming *noun* a slight personal weakness or eccentricity.

shortcut *noun* 1 a quicker route between two places. 2 a method that saves time or effort.

shorten *verb trans., intrans.* (**shortened, shortening**) 1 to decrease (something) in length or scope. 2 to become so reduced.

shortening *noun* butter, lard, or other fat used for making light, flaky pastry.

shortfall *noun* 1 a failure to reach a desired or expected level. 2 the amount or margin by which something is deficient.

shorthand *noun* any of various systems of strokes and dots representing speech sounds and groups of sounds, used as a fast way of recording speech in writing.

shorthanded *adj.* understaffed.

shortie *noun colloq. same as* **shorty**.

shortlist *noun* the best candidates from the total number submitted or nominated, from which the successful candidate will be chosen. —*verb trans.* (**shortlisted, shortlisting**) to place on such a list.

short-lived (shôrt-līvd′, -līvd′) *adj.* lasting only for a short time.

shortly *adv.* 1 soon. 2 in an abrupt manner.

shorts *pl. noun* pants extending from the waist to between the upper thigh and the knee.

short shrift discourteously brief or disdainful consideration.

shortsighted *adj.* 1 affected by myopia. 2 lacking foresight. ▸ **shortsightedness** *noun*

shortstop *noun Baseball* the infield position between second and third base, or the player assigned this position.

short story a work of prose narrative shorter than a novel. *Also called* **story**.

short-tempered *adj.* easily angered.

short-term *adj.* 1 concerned only with the near future. 2 lasting only a short time.

short ton a ton (sense 1).

short wave (ABBREV. **sw**) a radio wave with a wavelength of between 10 and 100 m.

shorty or **shortie** *noun* (*pl.* **shorties**) *colloq.* a shorter-than-average person or thing.

shot¹ *noun* 1 a an act of firing a gun; the sound of a gun being fired. b small metal pellets fired in clusters from a shotgun. c a person considered in terms of ability to shoot: *a* *good shot.* **2** *Sport* **a** an act of shooting or playing a stroke. **b** a heavy metal ball thrown in the shot put. **3 a** a photograph. **b** a single piece of filmed action recorded without a break by one camera. **4** *colloq.* **a** an attempt. **b** a turn or go: *It's my shot now.* **5** *colloq.* an injection of medicine. **6** *colloq.* a drink of alcohol.

shot² *see* **shoot.**

shotgun *noun* a gun with a long, wide, smooth barrel for firing clusters of pellets.

shot put an athletics event in which a heavy metal ball is thrown from the shoulder as far as possible. ▸ **shot-putter** *noun*

should *verb, aux.* expressing: **1** obligation, duty, or recommendation. **2** likelihood or probability: *He should have left by now.* **3** condition: *if I should die.* **4** statements following expressions of feeling or mood: *It seems odd that we should both be here.* **5** (with *first person pronouns*) doubt or polite indirectness: *I should think I'll get the job.* See also **shall.**

shoulder *noun* **1 a** the part of the human body between the neck and upper arm. **b** any object or part resembling a human shoulder. **c** the part of a garment covering this area of the human body. **2** the part of an animal's or bird's body where the foreleg or wing joins the trunk. —*verb trans.* (**shouldered, shouldering**) **1** to bear (e.g., a responsibility). **2** to carry on one's shoulders. **3** to thrust with the shoulder.

shoulder blade the broad flat triangular bone behind either shoulder. *Also called* **scapula.**

shouldn't *contr.* should not.

shout *noun* a loud cry or call. —*verb trans., intrans.* (**shouted, shouting**) (*also* **shout out**) to utter with a loud cry or call; to utter such a cry or call.

shove (shuv') *verb trans., intrans.* (**shoved, shoving**) **1** to push or thrust with force. **2** to place or put, esp. roughly: *shove it in the bag.* —*noun* a forceful push. —**shove off** *colloq.* to go away.

shovel (shuv'əl) *noun* **1** a tool with a deep-sided spadelike blade and a handle, used for lifting and carrying loose material. **2** a machine or device with a scooping action. —*verb trans.* (**shoveled** *or* **shovelled, shoveling** *or* **shovelling**) **1** to lift or carry with or as if with a shovel. **2** to take rapidly, and in huge quantities.

show *verb trans., intrans.* (*pa t* **showed;** *pa p* **shown** *or* **showed;** *pr p* **showing**) **1** to make or become visible or noticeable. **2** to present or give to be viewed. **3** to display or exhibit. **4** to prove, indicate, or reveal. **5** to teach by demonstrating. **6** to lead, guide, or escort: *He will show you to your room.* **7** to give: *Show them some respect.* **8** to demonstrate or give evidence of. —*noun* **1** an entertainment or spectacle. **2** an exhibition. **3 a** insincere behavior intended to make an impression. **b** outward appearance: *all done for show.* —**show off 1** to put on view in such a way as to garner special attention. **2** to behave ostentatiously.

showboat *noun* a floating steamboat theater.

show business the entertainment industry.

showcase *noun* **1** a glass case for displaying objects, e.g., in a museum or shop. **2** a setting in which a person or thing is displayed to good advantage.

showdown *noun colloq.* a contest, such as a fight, to settle a long-term dispute.

shower (show'ər) *noun* **1** a sudden, brief fall of rain, snow, or hail. **2 a** a device producing a stream of water for bathing under, usu. while standing. **b** a room or cubicle fitted with such a device or devices. **c** an act of bathing under such a device. **3** a sudden, esp. heavy, burst or fall: *a shower of abuse.* —*verb trans., intrans.* (**showered, showering**) **1** to cover, bestow, fall, or come abundantly. **2** to bathe under a shower. **3** to rain in showers. ▸ **showery** *adj.*

showing *noun* **1** an act of exhibiting or displaying. **2** a screening of a movie. **3** a performance.

show jumping a competitive sport in which riders on horseback take turns in jumping a variety of obstacles.

showman *noun* **1** a person who owns or manages a circus, a stall at a fairground, or other entertainment. **2** a person skilled in displaying things, esp. personal abilities, so as to attract maximum attention. ▸ **showmanship** *noun*

shown *see* **show.**

showoff *noun colloq.* a person who shows off to attract attention.

showpiece *noun* an excellent example to be copied or admired.

showplace *noun* a noteworthy or esp. beautiful building, etc.

showroom *noun* a room where examples of goods for sale are displayed.

showstopper *noun slang* a performance or performer evoking such a positive reaction from the audience that the show has to be stopped or temporarily interrupted.

showy *adj.* (**showier, showiest**) **1** attractively and impressively bright. **2** ostentatious; gaudy. ▸ **showiness** *noun*

shrank *see* **shrink.**

shrapnel *noun* **1** flying fragments of the casing of any exploding shell. **2** an explosive shell, filled with pellets or metal fragments, detonated in the air.

After Henry *Shrapnel*, 18th-century British general who invented the shell

shred *noun* 1 a thin strip cut or ripped off. 2 the smallest piece or amount: *not a shred of evidence.* —*verb trans.* (pa t and pa p **shredded** or **shred**; pr p **shredding**) to reduce to, or as if to, shreds by, or as if by, cutting or ripping. ► **shredder** *noun*

shrew *noun* 1 a nocturnal mouselike mammal with a long pointed snout. 2 a quarrelsome, scolding woman. ► **shrewish** *adj.*

shrewd *adj.* having or showing good judgment gained from practical experience. ► **shrewdly** *adv.* ► **shrewdness** *noun*

shriek *verb trans., intrans.* (**shrieked, shrieking**) to cry out with a piercing scream. —*noun* a piercing scream.

shrike *noun* a hook-billed songbird that feeds on insects or small birds and animals.

shrill *adj.* high-pitched and piercing. —*verb trans., intrans.* (**shrilled, shrilling**) to utter (something) in such a voice, or to make a high-pitched, piercing sound. ► **shrillness** *noun* ► **shrilly** *adv.*

shrimp *noun* (*pl.* **shrimp, shrimps**) 1 a small edible long-tailed shellfish, smaller than a prawn. 2 *colloq.* a person of very small stature or regarded as being unimportant. —*verb intrans.* (**shrimped, shrimping**) to fish for shrimp. ► **shrimper** *noun*

shrine *noun* 1 a sacred place of worship. 2 the tomb of a saint or other holy person, or a monument erected near it. 3 a place or thing greatly respected because of its associations.

shrink *verb trans., intrans.* (pa t **shrank** or **shrunk**; pa p **shrunk** or **shrunken**; pr p **shrinking**) 1 to make or become smaller. 2 (**shrink from** (**something**)) to move away from (it) in horror or disgust. 3 (**shrink from** (**something**)) to be reluctant to do (it). —*noun slang* a psychiatrist. ► **shrinkage** *noun*

shrivel *verb trans., intrans.* (**shriveled** or **shrivelled, shriveling** or **shrivelling**) (*also* **shrivel up**) to make or become shrunken and wrinkled, esp. through drying out.

shroud *noun* 1 a cloth in which a corpse is wrapped. 2 something that obscures, masks, or hides: *shrouds of fog.* —*verb trans.* (**shrouded, shrouding**) 1 to wrap in a shroud. 2 to obscure, mask, or hide.

shrub *noun* a woody plant, without a main trunk, that branches into several main stems at or just below ground level. ► **shrubbery** *noun* ► **shrubby** *adj.*

shrug *verb trans., intrans.* (**shrugged, shrugging**) to raise (the shoulders) briefly as an indication of doubt or indifference. —*noun* an act of shrugging. —**shrug** (**something**) **off** to dismiss (esp. criticism) lightly.

shrunk, shrunken *see* **shrink**.

shuck *noun* 1 a husk or pod. 2 a clam or an oyster shell. —*verb trans.* (**shucked, shucking**) to remove the husks, pods, or shells of.

shucks *interj. colloq.* used to express mild surprise, disappointment, or frustration.

shudder *verb intrans.* (**shuddered, shuddering**) to tremble, esp. with fear or disgust. —*noun* 1 a trembling movement or feeling derived esp. from fear. 2 a heavy vibration or shaking.

shuffle *verb trans., intrans.* (**shuffled, shuffling**) 1 to move (one's feet) with short quick sliding movements; to walk in this way. 2 to rearrange or mix up roughly or carelessly. 3 *Cards* to jumble up (playing cards) into a random order. —*noun* 1 an act or sound of shuffling. 2 a short quick sliding of the feet.

shun *verb trans.* (**shunned, shunning**) to avoid or keep away from.

shunt *verb trans.* (**shunted, shunting**) 1 to move (a train or railroad car) from one track to another. 2 to change the place or places of. 3 to transfer (e.g., a task) on to someone else. —*noun* 1 the act of shunting or the condition of being shunted. 2 a conductor diverting part of an electric current.

shush *interj.* used to ask someone to be quiet. —*verb trans.* (**shushed, shushing, shushes**) to command to be quiet by or as if by saying Shush!

shut *verb trans., intrans.* (**shut, shutting**) 1 to place or move so as to close an opening: *shut the door.* 2 to close or cause to close over, denying open access to the contents. 3 to not allow access to; to close: *They shut the shop at 5:00 p.m.* —*adj.* not open; closed. —**shut** (**someone**) **out** 1 to prevent (the one specified) from coming into a room, building, etc. 2 *Sport* to prevent (an opposing team) from scoring any points at all in a game. **shut** (**someone**) **up** 1 *colloq.* to make (someone) stop speaking. 2 to confine (someone).

shutdown *noun* a temporary closing, e.g., of a power plant, a factory, or a business.

shuteye (shŭt'ī,) *noun slang* sleep.

shut-in *noun* a patient who is confined indoors as a result of illness or disability.

shutout *noun* 1 *Sport* a game in which one team is prevented from scoring any points whatsoever. 2 a lockout.

shutter *noun* 1 a movable exterior cover for a window, esp. either of a pair of hinged wooden panels. 2 a device in a camera that opens and closes at a variable speed, exposing the film to light.

shuttle *noun* 1 in weaving, the device carrying the horizontal thread backward and forward. 2 the device carrying the lower thread through the loop formed by the upper in a sewing machine. **3** an aircraft, a train, or a bus running a frequent service between two places, usu. at a relatively short distance from one. another. —*verb trans., intrans.* (**shuttled, shuttling**) to move or cause to move or travel back and forth.

shuttlecock *noun Badminton* the cone of feathers or plastic with a rounded cork fixed on its narrow end, hit back and forth across the net.

shy¹ *adj.* (**shier** or **shyer, shiest** or **shyest**) **1** embarrassed or unnerved by the company or attention of others. **2** easily scared; timid. **3** (**shy of (something)**) wary or distrustful of (it). **4** *colloq.* short in payment by a specified amount: *$50 shy.* —*verb intrans.* (**shied, shying, shies**) **1** to jump suddenly aside or back, startled. **2** (*usu.* **shy away**) to move away from, showing reluctance: *shied away from arguing with them.* ▸ **shyly** *adv.* ▸ **shyness** *noun*

shy² *verb trans.* (**shied, shying, shies**) to throw. —*noun* (*pl.* **shies**) a throw.

shyster *noun slang* an unscrupulous or disreputable attorney.

SI *abbrev. Système International (d'Unités)* (French), International System (of Units).

Si *symbol Chem.* silicon.

Siamese (sī,ə-mēz', -mēs') *adj.* Siam (now Thailand) in Southeast Asia, its people, or their language. —*noun* **1** (*pl.* **Siamese**) a native, or citizen of Siam (now Thailand). **2** the language of Siam (now Thailand). **3** (*pl.* **Siamese**) a Siamese cat.

Siamese cat a smooth-haired domestic cat having a fawn-colored coat with darker patches, blue eyes, and a small head.

Siamese twins twins born with a piece of flesh or an organ joining one to the other.

sibling *noun* a brother or sister.

sic¹ *adv.* an indication that a word or phrase in a quotation that appears to be a mistake is in fact quoted accurately.

sic² *verb trans.* (**sicced, siccing**) to incite (esp. a dog) to attack.

sick *adj.* **1** feeling the desire to vomit; vomiting. **2** in poor health. ▣ ILL, UNHEALTHY, UNWELL ▣ FIT, HEALTHY, WELL. **3** relating to ill health: *sick pay.* **4** extremely annoyed; disgusted. **5** mentally deranged. **6** (**sick of (someone** or **something)**) thoroughly weary or fed up with (the one or ones specified). **7** of *humor* exploiting subjects like death· and disease in a disgusting way. ▸ **sickness** *noun*

sickbay *noun* a room where ill or injured people are treated, e.g., aboard a warship.

sicken *verb trans., intrans.* (**sickened, sickening**) **1** to cause to feel like vomiting, or to feel ill. **2** to annoy greatly; to disgust. ▸ **sickening** *adj.* ▸ **sickeningly** *adv.*

sickle *noun* a tool with a short handle and a curved blade for cutting grain crops.

sickly *adj.* (**sicklier, sickliest**) **1** susceptible to illness. **2** of or suggesting illness. **3** inducing the desire to vomit: *a sickly smell.* **4** looking unhealthy: *a sickly plant.* —*adv.* to an extent that suggests illness: *sickly pale.*

side *noun* **1** any of the usu. flat or flattish surfaces that form an outer extent; any of these surfaces other than the top ·and bottom, or other than the front, back, top, and bottom. **2** an edge or border, or the area adjoining it. **3** either of the parts or areas produced when a whole is divided up the middle: *the right side ·of my body.* **4** either of the broad surfaces of a flat or flattish object. **5** any of the lines forming a geometric figure. **6** any of the groups or teams, or opposing positions, in a conflict or competition. **7** an aspect: *saw a different side of him.* **8** the slope of a hill. **9** a part of an area of land; a district. **10** a father's or mother's family or ancestors: *ôn ·her mother's side.* —*adj.* **1** located at the side: *the side entrance.* **2** subsidiary or subordinate: *a side road.* —*verb intrans.* (**sided, siding**) (**side with (someone)**) to adopt (someone's) position or point of view. —**on the side** as a secondary source of income. **side by side 1** close together. **2** with sides touching. **take sides** to support one particular side in an argument.

sideboard *noun* a large piece of furniture consisting of shelves or cabinets mounted above drawers or cupboards.

sideburn *noun* (*usu.* **sideburns**) the short hair growing down in front of a man's ears.

sidecar *noun* a small carriage for passengers, attached to the side of a motorcycle.

side dish a small serving of food accompanying a meal or a main course.

side effect an additional, unexpected, often undesirable effect, esp. of a drug.

sidekick *noun colloq.* a close friend, partner, or deputy.

sidelight *noun* an example or instance of extra information arising out of or accompanying a main topic, issue, or theme.

sideline *noun* **1 a** a line marking either side boundary of an athletic field or other playing area. **b** (**sidelines**) the areas just outside these boundaries; the area to which nonparticipants in any activity are confined. **2** a business, etc., carried on in addition to one's regular work. —*verb trans.* (**sidelined, sidelining**) to relegate to the sidelines.

sidelong *adj., adv.* from or to one side; not direct or directly: *a sidelong glance.*

sidereal (sī-dîr'ē-əl) *adj.* of, relating to, or determined by the stars: *a sidereal year.*

sidesaddle *noun* a horse's saddle enabling a woman in a skirt to sit with both legs on the same side. —*adv.* sitting in this way.

sideshow *noun* an amusement stall at a fair, beside a circus, etc.

sidespin *noun* a rotary movement that causes a ball to take a horizontal spin. *See also* **backspin.**

sidesplitting *adj.* provoking uproarious laughter.

sidestep *verb trans.* (**sidestepped, sidestepping**) 1 to avoid by stepping aside. 2 to avoid taking a stand or answering (a question) by speaking evasively. —*noun* a step taken to one side.

sidestroke *noun* a swimming stroke performed on the side, using a scissors kick and thrusting the arms forward and downward in an alternating pattern.

sideswipe *noun* a blow coming from the side.

sidetrack *verb trans.* (**sidetracked, sidetracking**) to divert the attention of (someone) away from the matter in hand.

sidewalk *noun* the paved walkway running parallel to a street.

sideways *adv., adj.* 1 from, to, or toward one side. 2 with one side foremost.

sidewinder *noun* a rattlesnake that moves with a characteristic winding motion.

siding *noun* 1 a short dead-end railroad line onto which rail cars, etc., can be moved temporarily off a main line. 2 material, e.g., plastic or metal board-shaped pieces, used for surfacing the walls of buildings.

sidle (sīd'l) *verb intrans.* (**sidled, sidling**) to go or move slowly and cautiously.

SIDS (sĭdz) *abbrev.* sudden infant death syndrome.

siege (sēj, sĕzh) *noun* 1 an attempt to capture a military objective, e.g., a city or a fort, by surrounding it with troops and forcing surrender. 2 a similar police operation.

sierra (sē-ĕr'ə) *noun* a mountain range, esp. when jagged.

siesta (sē-ĕs'tə) *noun* a sleep or rest after a midday meal, esp. in hot countries.

sieve (sĭv) *noun* a utensil with a meshed or perforated bottom, used to separate solids from liquids or large particles from smaller ones. —*verb trans.* (**sieved, sieving**) to strain or separate with a sieve.

sift *verb trans.* (**sifted, sifting**) 1 to pass through a sieve in order to separate out lumps or larger particles. 2 to separate by or as if by passing through a sieve. 3 to examine closely and discriminatingly.

sigh *verb intrans., trans.* (**sighed, sighing**) to release a long deep breath, esp. indicating sadness, longing, or relief. —*noun* an act or the sound of sighing.

sight *noun* 1 the power of seeing; vision. 2 a thing seen. 3 one's field of vision, or the opportunity to see things that this provides: *within sight.* 4 (*usu.* **sights**) a place, building, etc., that is particularly interesting to see. 5 a device on a firearm through or along which one looks to take aim. —*verb trans.* (**sighted, sighting**) 1 to apprehend (an image) by using the faculty of vision. 2 a to adjust the sight of (a firearm). b to aim (a firearm) using the sight. ▸ **sighted** *adj.* ▸ **sightless** *adj.*

sight-read *verb trans., intrans.* (**sight-read, sight-reading**) to play or sing from music not previously seen.

sightseeing *noun* visiting places of interest. ▸ **sightsee** *verb intrans.* ▸ **sightseer** *noun*

sign *noun* 1 a printed mark with a meaning; symbol. 2 an indication: *signs of improvement.* 3 a board or panel displaying information for public view. 4 a signal. 5 a sign of the zodiac. —*verb trans., intrans.* (**signed, signing**) 1 to write a signature on. 2 to write (one's name) as a signature. 3 to employ or become employed with the signing of a contract. 4 to give a signal or indication. 5 to communicate using sign language. —**sign off** to bring a broadcast to an end. **sign up** to register (oneself), e.g., as an employee, as a member of the armed forces, or as a volunteer or participant.

signal *noun* 1 a message in the form of a gesture, light, sound, etc., conveying information or indicating the time for action. 2 (*often* **signals**) apparatus used to send such a message. 3 an event that marks the moment for action to be taken. 4 a set of transmitted electrical impulses received as a sound or image, e.g., in television, or the message conveyed by them. —*verb trans.* (**signaled** *or* **signalled, signaling** *or* **signalling**) 1 to transmit (a message) using signals. 2 to indicate. —*adj.* notable: *a signal triumph.* ▸ **signally** *adv.*

signalize *verb trans.* (**signalized, signalizing**) to make notable; distinguish.

signatory *noun* (*pl.* **signatories**) a party, e.g., a person, an organization, or a nation, to a contract, treaty, or other legal document. —*adj.* being a party, e.g., to a contract.

signature (sĭg'nə-chər) *noun* 1 one's name written by oneself as a mark of authorization, etc. 2 *Mus.* an indication of key or time at the beginning of a line.

signet *noun* a small seal used for stamping documents, etc.

significance *noun* 1 meaning. 2 importance.

significant *adj.* 1 having great significance, value, influence, or effect. ▣ CON-SEQUENTIAL, IMPORTANT, MEANINGFUL, MOMENTOUS, SUBSTANTIAL, WEIGHTY ▣

INCONSEQUENTIAL, MINOR, TRIVIAL, UNIM-PORTANT. **2** having some meaning. ▸ **significantly** *adv.*

signify *verb trans., intrans.* (**signified, signifying, signifies**) **1** to be a sign of; to suggest or mean. **2** to be a symbol of; to denote. **3** to be important or significant.

sign language a form of communication using gestures to represent words and ideas.

signpost *noun* **1** a post carrying a sign giving information to motorists or pedestrians. **2** an indicator.

Sikh (sēk) *noun* a follower of a religion founded by Nanak in 16th-century India, worshipping one God. —*adj.* relating to the Sikhs or their beliefs or customs.

silage (sī′lij) *noun* animal fodder made by compressing forage crops, such as grass, and then fermenting them in an airtight silo.

silence *noun* **1** absence of sound, or a period marked by it. **2** failure or unwillingness to disclose information or give away secrets. —*verb trans.* (**silenced, silencing**) to cause to stop speaking giving away information.

silencer *noun* a device attached to a gun barrel to muffle noise upon firing.

silent *adj.* **1** lacking noise. **2** not mentioning or divulging something; not speaking at all. **3** unspoken but expressed: *silent joy.* **4** not pronounced: *the silent p in pneumonia.* —*noun* a silent movie. ▸ **silently** *adv.*

silhouette (sĭl,ə-wĕt′) *noun* **1** a dark shape seen against a light background. **2** an outline drawing of a person, esp. in profile, usu. filled in with black. —*verb trans.* (**silhouetted, silhouetting**) to represent or cause to appear as a silhouette.

> After the 18th-century French finance minister, Etienne de Silhouette, possibly because of his notorious stinginess

silica *noun Geol.* a hard white or colorless glassy solid.

silicate (sĭl′ĭ-kət, -kāt,) *noun Chem.* any of a group of chemical compounds containing silicon, oxygen, and one or more metals.

silicon (SYMBOL **Si**) a nonmetallic element found, e.g., as silica in sand and quartz.

silicone *noun Chem.* a synthetic polymer consisting of chains of alternating silicon and oxygen atoms, with various organic groups linked to the silicon atoms.

silicosis *noun* a lung disease caused by prolonged inhalation of dust containing silica.

silk *noun* **1** a fine soft fiber produced by the silkworm. **2** thread or fabric made from such fibers. ▸ **silken** *adj.* ▸ **silky** *adj.*

silk-screening *noun* a printing technique in which ink is forced through a fine silk or nylon mesh, with areas to be left blank blocked chemically.

silkworm *noun* the caterpillar of the silk moth, domesticated to provide silk on a commercial basis.

sill *noun* the bottom part of a framework around an opening such as a window or door.

sillabub *noun same as* **syllabub**.

silly *adj.* (**sillier, silliest**) **1** laughably senseless. **2** in a dazed state; only partly conscious. ▸ **silliness** *noun*

silo *noun* (pl. **silos**) **1** an airtight tower or a pit for storing silage. **2** a underground chamber housing a guided missile.

silt *noun* fine sand and mud deposited by flowing water. —*verb trans., intrans.* (**silted, silting**) (*often* **silt up**) to cause to become, or to become, blocked by silt.

silvan *adj. same as* **sylvan**.

silver *noun* **1** (SYMBOL **Ag**) *Chem.* a soft, white, lustrous precious metal. **2** coins made of this metal. **3** articles made of or coated with this metal, esp. cutlery and other tableware. **4** a silver medal, e.g., in a sports competition. —*adj.* **1** of a whitish-gray color. **2** denoting a 25th wedding or other anniversary. —*verb trans.* (**silvered, silvering**) **1** to apply a thin coating of silver to. **2** to give a whitish metallic sheen to. ▸ **silvery** *adj.*

silverfish *noun* (pl. **silverfish, silverfishes**) a small wingless silver-colored insect.

silver medal a medal of silver awarded for second place, esp. in sports competitions.

silver-plated *adj.* plated with silver.

silver screen (**the silver screen**) *colloq.* the movie industry or movies in general.

silversmith *noun* a person who makes or repairs articles made of silver.

simian *noun* a monkey or an ape. —*adj.* relating to or resembling monkeys or apes.

similar *adj.* having the same or almost the same characteristics. ▸ **similarity** *noun* ▸ **similarly** *adv.*

simile (sĭm′ə-lē) *noun* a figure of speech in which a thing is described by being likened to something, usu. using *as* or *like*.

similitude *noun formal* similarity.

simmer *verb trans., intrans.* (**simmered, simmering**) **1** to cause to cook, or to cook, gently at just below boiling point. **2** to be near an outburst of emotion, typically anger. —*noun* a simmering state. —**simmer down** to calm down after a commotion, esp. an angry outburst.

simper *verb intrans., trans.* (**simpered, simpering**) **1** to smile in a foolishly weak or deceitful manner. **2** to express in this way. —*noun* a smile indicative of weak silliness or of deceitfulness.

simple *adj.* (**simpler, simplest**) **1** not difficult; easy. **2** not complex; straightforward. **3** not elaborate; basic. **4** down-to-earth; unpretentious. **5** lacking intelligence; gullible.

6 not adulterated; plain: *the simple facts.* **7** *of a sentence* having only one clause. *See also* **compound¹, complex.**

simple interest interest paid only on the principal, not on any accrued interest. *See also* **compound interest.**

simple-minded *adj.* **1** lacking intelligence; foolish. **2** overly simple; unsophisticated. ▸ **simple-mindedness** *noun*

simpleton *noun* a foolish or unintelligent person.

simplicity *noun* a simple state or quality.

simplify *verb trans.* (**simplified, simplifying, simplifies**) to make (something complex or difficult) less complicated or easier to understand. ▸ **simplification** *noun*

simplistic *adj.* unrealistically straightforward or uncomplicated. ▸ **simplistically** *adv.*

simply *adv.* **1** in a straightforward, uncomplicated way. **2** just: *That is simply not true.* **3** absolutely. **4** merely.

simulate (sĭm′yə-lāt,) *verb trans.* (**simulated, simulating**) **1** to produce a convincing recreation of (a real-life event or set of conditions). **2** to pretend to have, do, or feel. ▸ **simulation** *noun*

simulator *noun* a device that simulates required conditions, e.g., for training purposes: *a flight simulator.*

simultaneous *adj.* happening at exactly the same time. ▸ **simultaneously** *adv.*

sin¹ *noun* **1 a** an act that breaks a moral, esp. a religious, law or teaching. **b** the condition of offending a deity by committing a moral offense. **2** an act that offends common standards of morality or decency. **3** a great shame. —*verb intrans.* (**sinned, sinning**) to commit a sin. ▸ **sinful** *adj.*

sin² *abbrev. Math.* sine.

since *conj.* **1** during or throughout the period between now and some earlier stated time. **2** as; because. —*prep.* during or throughout the period between now and some earlier stated time. —*adv.* **1** from that time onward. **2** ago: *five years since.*

sincere *adj.* not pretended or affected; genuine. ▸ **sincerely** *adv.* ▸ **sincerity** *noun*

sine *noun* (ABBREV. **sin**) in trigonometry, in a right-angled triangle, the length of the side opposite an angle divided by the length of the the longest side.

sinecure (sĭn′ə-kyŏŏr′, sī′nə-) *noun* a paid job involving little or no work.

> Literally 'without cure', originally a paid church position which carried no responsibility for curing souls.

sine die (sĭ,nĭ-dī′e, sĭn,ā-dē′ā) with no future time fixed; indefinitely.

sine qua non (sĭn,ə-kwä-nän′, -nōn′) an essential condition or requirement.

sinew (sĭn′yōō) *noun* **1** a tendon. **2** (**sinews**) physical strength; muscle. ▸ **sinewy** *adj.*

sing *verb trans., intrans.* (*pa t* **sang**; *pa p* **sung**; *pr p* **singing**) **1** to speak (words) in a musical, rhythmic fashion, esp. to the accompaniment of music. **2** to cause to pass into a particular state with such sound: *sang the baby to sleep.* **3** to make a musical sound: *a kettle singing on the stove.* **4** *slang* to inform on (someone) or to confess a crime. ▸ **singer** *noun* ▸ **singing** *noun*

sing. *abbrev.* singular.

singe (sĭnj) *verb trans., intrans.* (**singed, singeing**) to burn lightly on the surface; to scorch or become scorched. —*noun* a light surface burn.

single *adj.* **1** of which there is only one; solitary. **2** unmarried, esp. never having been married. **3** for use by one person only: *a single room.* **4** (*used for emphasis*) even one: *not a single person.* —*noun* **1** a single room. **2** a record with only one track on each side. **3** an unmarried person. —*verb trans.* (**singled, singling**) (**single** (someone *or* something) **out**) to pick (the one or ones specified) from among others.

single-breasted *adj., of a coat or jacket* having only one row of buttons and a slight overlap at the front.

single file a line of people one behind the other. *Also called* **Indian file.**

single-handed *adj., adv.* without help from others. ▸ **single-handedly** *adv.*

single-minded *adj.* determinedly pursuing a single aim or object. ▸ **single-mindedly** *adv.* ▸ **single-mindedness** *noun*

singles *pl. noun* **1** a sports match with one player on each side. **2** unmarried people.

singly (sĭng′glē) *adv.* one at a time.

singsong *noun* an informal bout of singing for pleasure. —*adj., of a speaking voice, etc.* having a fluctuating rhythm.

singular *noun Gram.* the form of a noun, pronoun, adjective, or verb used for one person, thing, etc. —*adj.* **1** *Gram.* denoting or in the singular. **2** consisting of one, or of one kind. *See also* **plural.** **3** single, unique. **4** extraordinary; exceptional. **5** strange; odd. ▸ **singularity** *noun* ▸ **singularly** *adv.*

Sinhalese (sĭnh,ə-lēz′) *noun* **1** (*pl.* **Sinhalese**) a native or citizen of Sri Lanka. **2** the official language of Sri Lanka, derived from Sanskrit. —*adj.* of Sri Lanka, its people, or their language.

sinister *adj.* strongly suggesting evil or harm. ▣ BALEFUL, MALIGN.

sink *verb trans., intrans.* (*pa t* **sank** *or* **sunk**; *pa p* **sunk**; *pr p* **sinking**) **1 a** to go under water. ▣ FOUNDER, SUBMERGE, SUBMERSE ▣ FLOAT. **b** to cause to go under and remain under water. **2** to collapse downwardly or inwardly; to fall because of a collapsing base or foundation. **3** to produce the sensation of a downward collapse within the body: *My heart sank at the news.* **4** to embed: *sank the pole into the ground.* **5** to pass steadily and often dangerously into a worse state than what was once the case. **6** (*also* **sink in**) to penetrate or to be absorb-ed. **7** to invest (money) heavily. **8** *colloq.* to ruin the plans of; to ruin (plans): *We are sunk.* **9** *Sport, Games* to send (a ball) into a pocket, hole, or basket. —*noun* a wall-mounted basin with built-in water supply and drainage.

sinker *noun* a weight used to make something, e.g., a fishing line, sink.

sinner *noun* a person who sins or has sinned.

Sino- *combining form* forming words denoting Chinese: *Sino-Soviet.*

sinuous *adj.* **1** having many curves or bends. **2** having a twisting and turning motion.

sinus *noun Anat.* a cavity or depression filled with air, esp. in the bones of the face.

sinusitis *noun* inflammation of the lining of the sinuses.

sip *verb trans., intrans.* (**sipped, sipping**) to drink in very small mouthfuls. —*noun* **1** an act of sipping. **2** an amount sipped.

siphon *or* **syphon** (sī'fən) *noun* an inverted U-tube that can be used to transfer liquid from one container at a higher level into another at a lower level. —*verb trans.* (**siphoned, siphoning**) (*usu.* **siphon (something) off**) **1** to transfer liquid from one container to another using such a device. **2** to take something slowly, continuously, and surreptitiously from a store or fund.

Sir *noun* **1** used as part of the salutation in a formal letter: *Dear Sir or Madam.* **2** (**sir**) used as a polite form of address to a man: *May I help you, sir?*

sire *noun old use* a term of respect used in addressing a king. —*verb trans.* (**sired, siring**) of an animal to father (young).

siren *noun* **1** a device that emits a loud wailing noise, usu. as a warning signal. **2** an irresistible, sexy, often dangerous woman.

sirloin *noun* a fine cut of beef from the upper side of the part of the back in front of the rump.

sis *noun colloq.* sister.

sisal (sī'səl, -zəl) *noun* a strong fiber from the leaves of the agave plant used to make rope.

sissy *noun* (*pl.* **sissies**) a weak, cowardly person.

sister *noun* **1** a woman or girl with the same parents as another person or persons. **2** a woman belonging to the same group, society, church, etc. as another or others. **3** a woman who is a member of a religious group, esp. a nun. —*adj.* of the same origin or design: *a sister ship.* ► **sisterhood** *noun* ► **sisterly** *adj.*

sister-in-law *noun* (*pl.* **sisters-in-law**) **1** the sister of one's husband or wife. **2** the wife of one's brother. **3** the wife of the brother of one's own husband or wife.

sit *verb intrans., trans.* (pa t and pa p **sat**; pr p **sitting**) **1** to rest the body on the buttocks or hindquarters. **2** of a bird to perch or lie. **3** of an object to lie, rest, or hang. **4** to lie unused: *tools sitting in the shed.* **5** to hold a meeting or other session: *Court sits tomorrow.* **6** to be a member, taking regular part in meetings: *sit on a committee.* **7** to take (an examination). **8** to conduct to a seat; to assign a seat to. **9** to be or exist in a specified comparison or relation: *His smoking sits awkwardly with his being a doctor.* **10** to serve as an artist's or photographer's model. —**sit back 1** to sit comfortably, esp. with the back rested. **2** to observe, taking no action, esp. when action is needed. **sit tight 1** to maintain one's position determinedly. **2** to wait patiently. **sit up 1** to bring oneself from a slouching or lying position into an upright sitting position. **2** to take notice suddenly or show a sudden interest. ► **sitter** *noun*

sitar (sī-tär') *noun* a guitarlike instrument of Indian origin, with a long neck, rounded body and two sets of strings.

sitcom *noun* a situation comedy.

sit-down *noun colloq.* a short rest in a seated position. —*adj.* **1** of a meal for which the diners are seated. **2** of a strike in which the workers occupy the workplace until an agreement is reached.

site *noun* **1** the place at which something is situated. **2** an area set aside for a specific activity: *camping site.*

sit-in *noun* an occupation of a building, etc., as a protest.

sitting *noun* **1** a period of continuous action: *wrote it at one sitting.* **2** a turn to eat for any of two or more groups too numerous to eat at the same time in the same place. **3** a period of posing for an artist or a photographer. **4** a session or meeting of an official body. —*adj.* occupying an official position.

sitting room a living room.

situate (sĭch'ə-wāt,) *verb trans.* (**situated, situating**) to put into a certain position or set of circumstances.

situation *noun* **1** a set of circumstances; a state of affairs. **2** a position or location.

situation comedy a television or radio comedy series where the same characters are featured in more or less fixed surroundings.

sit-up *noun* a physical exercise in which, from a lying position, the head and upper body are raised up and over the thighs, often with the hands behind the head.

six *noun* **1** the number or figure 6. **2** the age of 6. **3** any person or thing denoted by the number 6. **4** 6 o'clock. **5** a set of 6 people or things. **6** a score of 6 points. —*adj.* **1** 6 in number. **2** aged 6.

sixteen *noun* **1** the number or figure 16. **2** the age of 16. **3** any person or thing denoted by the number 16. **4** a set of 16 people or things. **5** a score of 16 points. —*adj.* **1** 16 in number. **2** aged 16.

sixteenth *noun, adj.* **1** the one numbered 16 in a series. **2** one of 16 equal parts.

sixth *noun, adj.* **1** the one numbered 6 in a series. **2** one of six equal parts.

sixties *pl. noun* **1** the period of time between one's 60th and 70th birthdays. **2** the range of temperatures between 60 and 70 degrees. **3** the period of time between the 60th and 70th years of a century.

sixtieth *noun, adj.* **1** the one numbered 60 in a series. **2** one of 60 equal parts.

sixty *noun* (*pl.* **sixties**) **1** the number or figure 60. **2** the age of 60. **3** a set of 60 people or things. **4** a score of 60 points. —*adj.* **1** 60 in number. **2** aged 60.

sizable *or* **sizeable** *adj.* fairly large.

size *noun* **1** length, breadth, height, or volume, or a combination of any or all of these. **2** any of a range of graded measure-ments, e.g., of garments. —*verb trans.* (**sized, sizing**) **1** to measure in order to determine size. **2** to sort or arrange according to size. **3** (**size** (**something** *or* **someone**) **up**) to judge the nature, quality, or worth of (someone or something).

sizzle *verb intrans.* (**sizzled, sizzling**) **1** to make a hissing sound when or as if frying in hot fat. **2** *colloq.* to be in a state of intense emotion, esp. anger. —*noun* a hissing sound similar to the sound made by hot grease in a frying pan.

skate[1] *noun* a boot with a steel blade or a set of small wheels fitted to the sole for gliding smoothly over surfaces. —*verb intrans., trans.* (**skated, skating**) to move around on skates. ▸ **skater** *noun* ▸ **skating** *noun*

skate[2] *noun* a large flat edible fish of the ray family.

skateboard *noun* a narrow board mounted on sets of small wheels, for riding on in a standing position. —*verb intrans.* (**skateboarded, skateboarding**) to ride a skateboard. ▸ **skateboarder** *noun*

skedaddle *verb intrans.* (**skedaddled, skedaddling**) *colloq.* to run away quickly.

skeet *noun* trapshooting in which clay pigeons are propelled into the air to be shot.

skein (skān) *noun* a loose coil of wool or thread.

skeleton *noun* **1** the framework of bones that supports and often protects the body of an animal. **2** an initial basic structure or idea upon or around which something else is built. **3** *colloq.* an unhealthily thin person. ▸ **skeletal** *adj.*

skeleton key a key filed in such a way that it can open many different locks.

skeptic *or* **sceptic** *noun* **1** a person who believes that nothing can be known with absolute certainty. **2** a person who questions widely accepted, esp. religious, beliefs. ▸ **skeptical** *or* **sceptical** *adj.* ▸ **skepticism** *or* **scepticism** *noun*

sketch *noun* **1** a rough drawing quickly done. **2** a rough plan or outline. **3** any of several short pieces of comedy presented as a program. —*verb trans., intrans.* (**sketched, sketching**) **1** to do a rough drawing or drawings (of). **2** to give a rough outline of.

sketchy *adj.* (**sketchier, sketchiest**) lacking detail. ▸ **sketchily** *adv.* ▸ **sketchiness** *noun*

skew *adj.* slanted; oblique; askew. —*verb trans., intrans.* (**skewed, skewing**) **1** to slant or cause to slant. **2** to distort.

skewer *noun* a long metal pin pushed through chunks of meat, etc., which are to be roasted. —*verb trans.* (**skewered, skewering**) to fasten or pierce with or as if with a skewer.

ski *noun* (*pl.* **skis**) a long narrow strip of plastic, metal, and formerly wood, upturned at the front, for gliding over snow. —*verb intrans., trans.* (**skied, skiing, skis**) to move on skis, esp. as a sport or leisure activity, either on downhill runs or cross-country. ▸ **skier** *noun* ▸ **skiing** *noun*

skid *verb intrans.* (**skidded, skidding**) **1** *of a wheel, etc.* to slide along without revolving. **2** *of a vehicle* to slide at an angle, esp. out of control. —*noun* an instance of skidding.

skid row the poorest part of a town.

skilful *adj. same as* **skillful**.

ski lift a device for transporting skiers to the top of a slope so that they can ski down.

skill *noun* **1** the quality or degree of being expert; dexterity. **2** a talent or accomplishment.

skilled *adj.* **1** possessing skill; trained, experienced. **2** requiring or showing skill.

skillet *noun* a frying pan.

skillful *or* **skilful** *adj.* having or showing skill. ▸ **skillfully** *adv.*

skim *verb trans., intrans.* (**skimmed, skimming**) **1** to remove (floating matter) from the surface of (a liquid). **2** to brush or cause to brush against or glide lightly over (a surface). **3** (**skim through** (**something**)) to read (it) superficially and quickly.

skim milk milk from which the cream has been removed.

skimp *verb intrans.* (**skimped, skimping**) (**skimp on** (**something**)) to spend, use, or give too little or only just enough of (it).

skimpy *adj.* (**skimpier, skimpiest**) **1** barely enough; inadequate. **2** *of clothes* leaving

much of the body uncovered. ▸ **skimpily**
adv. ▸ **skimpiness** *noun*

skin *noun* **1** the tough flexible covering of the human or animal body. **2** the outer covering of certain fruits and vegetables. **3** complexion: *oily skin.* **4** an animal hide, with or without fur or hair attached. —*verb trans.* (**skinned, skinning**) **1** to strip the skin from. **2** to injure by scraping the skin from. **3** *slang* to cheat or swindle. —**by the skin of (one's) teeth** very narrowly; only just. **get under (some-one's) skin** *colloq.* **1** to annoy and upset (one) greatly. **2** to become a consuming passion.

skin-deep *adj.* superficial.

skin diving underwater swimming with no wet suit and only simple breathing and other equipment. ▸ **skin diver**

skinflint *noun colloq.* a very ungenerous person.

skinny *adj.* (**skinnier, skinniest**) very thin.

skinny-dip *verb intrans.* (**skinny-dipped, skinny-dipping**) *colloq.* to go swimming naked. ▸ **skinny-dipper** *noun*

skintight *adj.*, of *clothing* very tight-fitting.

skip *verb intrans., trans.* (**skipped, skipping**) **1** to go along with light springing steps on alternate feet. **2** to make jumps over a rope, as a game. **3** to omit, leave out, or pass over. **4** *colloq.* not to attend (e.g., a class). —*noun* a skipping movement.

skipper *noun* the captain of a ship, aircraft, or team. —*verb trans.* (**skippered, skippering**) to act as skipper of.

skirmish *noun* **1** a brief battle during a war. **2** a minor fight or dispute. —*verb intrans.* (**skirmished, skirmishing**) to engage in a skirmish.

skirt *noun* **1 a** a woman's garment that hangs from the waist. **b** the part of a woman's dress from the waist down. **2** any part or attachment resembling a skirt, e.g., the flap around the base of a hovercraft. —*verb trans.* (**skirted, skirting**) **1** to border. **2** to pass along or around the edge of. **3** to avoid confronting (e.g., a problem).

skit *noun* a short satirical piece of drama.

skittish *adj.* **1** easily frightened. **2** frequently changing mood. **3** lively and playful.

skulduggery *noun same as* **skullduggery**.

skulk *verb intrans.* (**skulked, skulking**) **1** to hide, or to lurk about. **2** to evade work.

skull *noun* in vertebrates, the hard cartilaginous or bony framework of the head.

skullcap *noun* a small brimless cap fitting closely on the head.

skullduggery *or* **skulduggery** *noun* unscrupulous or dishonest behavior; trickery.

skunk *noun* **1** an animal with a black and white coat, which defends itself by squirting out a foul-smelling liquid. *Also called* **polecat**. **2** a despised person.

sky *noun* (*pl.* **skies**) **1** the apparent dome of space in which the Sun, Moon, and stars can be seen; the heavens. **2** the appearance of this area as a reflection of weather: *dismal skies.* —*verb trans.* (**skied, skying, skies**) to hit (a ball) high into the air.

skydiving *noun* free-falling from an aircraft, often involving performing maneuvers in midair, with a long delay before the parachute is opened. ▸ **skydiver** *noun*

sky-high *adj., adv.* very high: *sky-high prices.*

skyjack *verb trans.* (**skyjacked, skyjacking**) *slang* to hijack (an aircraft).

skylark *noun* a small lark known for its loud song, given in flight. —*verb intrans.* (**skylarked, skylarking**) to lark about.

skylight *noun* a window in a roof or ceiling.

skyline *noun* the outline of buildings, hills, and trees seen against the sky.

skyscraper *noun* an extremely tall building.

skyward *adj.* toward or at the sky. —*adv.* (*also* **skywards**) toward the sky.

slab *noun* a thick, flat, rectangular piece, slice, or other object. —*verb trans.* (**slabbed, slabbing**) to make into or shape into slabs.

slack *adj.* **1** not pulled or stretched tight; loose. **2** giving or showing no care or attention. **3** not busy: *Business is slack.* —*noun* **1** a loosely hanging part. **2** a period of little trade or other activity. —*verb intrans., trans.* (**slacked, slacking**) (*often* **slack off**) **1** to become slower; to slow one's working pace, e.g., through fatigue or laziness. **2** to make or become looser. **3** to become less busy.

slacken *verb trans., intrans.* (**slackened, slackening**) **1** to make or become slack. **2** to make or become less vigorous, rigorous, severe, or intense.

slacker *noun* a person who does not work hard enough; a shirker.

slacks *pl. noun* loose casual trousers.

slag *noun* waste material formed on the surface of molten metal ore.

slain *see* **slay**.

slake *verb trans.* (**slaked, slaking**) **1** to satisfy or quench (thirst, desire, or anger). **2** to cause (lime) to crumble by adding water.

slalom (slāl'əm) *noun* a race, on skis or in vehicles, in and out of obstacles on a winding course.

slam[1] *verb trans., intrans.* (**slammed, slamming**) **1** to shut loudly and with violence. **2** (*usu.* **slam against, into**, *etc.*) *colloq.* to make or cause to make loud heavy contact. —*noun* the act of slamming.

slam[2] *noun Cards* the winning of all tricks, or all but one.

slam-dunk *Basketball noun* a dunk shot. —*verb intrans.; trans.* (**slam-dunked, slam-dunking**) to make a forceful dunk shot; to dunk (the ball) with great force.

slammer noun (**the slammer**) slang prison.

slander noun an untrue and malicious statement about a person, or the act of uttering one. —verb trans. (**slandered, slandering**) to spread a slander about (someone). ▸ **slanderous** adj.

slang noun language used mostly in casual contexts and situations. ▸ **slangy** adj.

slant verb intrans., trans. (**slanted, slanting**) 1 to be at an angle; to slope. 2 to present (information, etc.) in a biased way, or for a particular audience or readership. —noun 1 a sloping position, surface, or line. 2 a bias.

slap noun 1 a blow with the palm of the hand or something else flat. 2 the sound made by such a blow. —verb trans. (**slapped, slapping**) 1 to strike with the open hand or something flat. 2 to bring or send with a slapping sound: slapped the newspaper down on the table. 3 colloq. to apply thickly and carelessly. —a **slap in the face** colloq. an insult or rebuff. **a slap on the wrist** colloq. a mild reprimand.

slapdash adj. careless and hurried.

slaphappy adj. colloq. cheerfully carefree.

slapstick noun comedy in which the humor is derived from boisterous antics of all kinds.

slash verb trans., intrans. (**slashed, slashing**) 1 to make sweeping cuts or cutting strokes. 2 colloq. to reduce suddenly and drastically: slashed defense spending. —noun 1 a long, esp. deep, cut. 2 a sweeping, cutting stroke. 3 Printing a virgule.

slat noun a thin strip, esp. of wood or metal.

slate noun 1 a shiny, dark gray, metamorphic rock that is easily split into thin flat layers. 2 a roofing tile made of this material. 3 formerly a piece of this material on which to write, esp. in school. 4 a dull gray color. —of a dull gray color. —verb trans. (**slated, slating**) 1 to cover (a roof) with slates. 2 to assign, designate, or schedule (someone): She is slated to take over as manager.

slattern noun a woman of dirty or untidy appearance. ▸ **slatternly** adj.

slaughter (slôt′ər) noun 1 cruel and violent murder. 2 the large-scale indiscriminate killing of people or animals. 3 the killing of animals for food. —verb trans. (**slaughtered, slaughtering**) 1 to subject to slaughter. 2 colloq. to defeat resoundingly.

slaughterhouse noun a place where animals are killed to be sold for food; an abattoir.

Slav (släv) noun a member of any of various central and E European peoples speaking Slavonic languages. ▸ **Slavic** adj.

slave noun 1 a person owned by and acting as servant to another, with no personal freedom. 2 a person who works extremely hard for another; a drudge. 3 (**a slave to** (**something**)) a person whose life is dominated by (some activity or thing): a slave to her work. —verb intrans. (**slaved, slaving**) to work hard and ceaselessly. ▸ **slavery** noun

slaver[1] (slā′vər) noun Hist. 1 a person engaging in the buying and selling of slaves. 2 a ship for transporting slaves.

slaver[2] (slă′vər) noun spittle running from the mouth. —verb intrans. (**slavered, slavering**) 1 to let spittle run from the mouth; to dribble. 2 colloq. to talk nonsense.

slavish (slā′vĭsh) adj. 1 rigid in following rules or instructions. 2 very closely copied or imitated. 3 of or resembling a slave. ▸ **slavishly** adv. ▸ **slavishness** noun

Slavonic (slə-văn′ĭk) noun a group of Central and Eastern European languages that includes Russian, Polish, Czech, Slovak, Serbo-Croat, and Slovenian. —adj. of or relating to these languages, the peoples speaking them, or their cultures.

slaw noun coleslaw.

slay verb (pa t slew; pa p slain; pr p slaying) to kill (someone) violently. ▸ **slayer** noun

sleaze noun a disreputable quality, condition, or characteristic.

sleazy adj. (**sleazier, sleaziest**) colloq. cheaply suggestive of sex or crime; disreputable. ▸ **sleaziness** noun

sled noun a vehicle equipped with runners, used to transport people or goods over snow. —verb intrans. (**sledded, sledding**) to ride in or on a sled.

sledge noun a sled. —verb intrans. (**sledged, sledging**) to sled.

sledgehammer noun a large, heavy hammer swung with both arms.

sleek adj. 1 of hair, fur, etc. smooth, soft, and glossy. 2 having a well-fed, prosperous appearance. —verb trans. (**sleeked, sleeking**) to smooth (esp. hair).

sleep noun 1 rest in a state of near unconsciousness. 2 a period of such rest. —verb intrans., trans. (**slept, sleeping**) 1 to rest in a state of sleep. 2 to be motionless, inactive, or dormant. —**sleep on** (**something**) to delay making a decision about (it) until the following morning. **sleep with** (**someone**) to have sexual relations with (someone).

sleeper noun 1 a person who sleeps, esp. in a specified way: a light sleeper. 2 a railroad car providing sleeping accommodation for passengers; a train with such cars. 3 colloq. a record, movie, book, etc., that suddenly becomes popular after initial uninterest.

sleeping bag a large quilted sack in which to sleep, e.g., when camping.

sleeping pill a pill that contains a sedative.

sleeping sickness 1 a disease causing violent fever and extreme drowsiness in both humans and animals in tropical Africa, transmitted by the tsetse fly.

sleepless *adj.* **1** during which one is or was unable to sleep. **2** unable to sleep.

sleepwalking *noun* a condition where a person walks around while asleep. *Also called* **somnambulism.** ▸ **sleepwalk** *verb intrans.* ▸ **sleepwalker** *noun*

sleepy *adj.* **(sleepier, sleepiest) 1** feeling the desire to sleep; drowsy. **2** suggesting sleep or drowsiness: *sleepy music.* **3** characterized by quietness and a lack of activity; *a sleepy village.* ▸ **sleepily** *adv.* ▸ **sleepiness** *noun*

sleepyhead *noun colloq.* **1** a person who often feels sleepy, or who needs a lot of sleep. **2** a person who tends to daydream a lot.

sleet *noun* rain mixed with snow or hail. —*verb intrans.* **(sleeted, sleeting)** to rain with snow or hail. ▸ **sleety** *adj.*

sleeve *noun* **1** the part of a garment that covers the arm. **2** a tubelike cover. **3** the cardboard or paper envelope in which a record is stored. —**up one's sleeve** held secretly in reserve for possible later use. ▸ **sleeveless** *adj.*

sleigh (slā) *noun* a large horse-drawn sled. —*verb intrans.* **(sleighed, sleighing)** to travel by sleigh.

sleight (slīt) *noun* a cunningly devised means to an end.

sleight of hand (*pl.* **sleights of hand**) skill in moving the hands quickly and deceptively, e.g., in performing magic tricks.

slender *adj.* **1** attractively slim. **2** narrow; slight. **3** meager.

slept *see* **sleep.**

sleuth (slooth) *noun* a detective, often a private one. —*verb intrans.* **(sleuthed, sleuthing)** to work as a detective.

slew¹ *see* **slay.**

slew² *or* **slue** *verb intrans., trans.* **(slewed, slewing)** to twist or cause to twist or swing around, esp. suddenly and uncontrollably. —*noun* an act or instance of slewing.

slew³ *noun* a great number of things or items.

slice *noun* **1** a thin broad piece or a wedge, cut off. **2** *colloq.* a share or portion; *a slice of the business.* **3** *Sport* a stroke causing a ball to spin sideways and curve away in a particular direction; the spin so imparted. —*verb trans., intrans.* **(sliced, slicing) 1** to cut up into slices. **2** (*also* **slice (something) off**) to cut (it) off as, or as if in, a slice. **3** *Sport* to strike (a ball) with a slice.

slick *adj.* **1** dishonestly or slyly clever. **2** impressively and only superficially smart or efficient. **3** smooth and glossy; sleek. —*verb trans.* **(slicked, slicking)** to smooth (esp. hair). —*noun* a wide layer of spilled oil, etc. floating on the surface of water.

slicker *noun* **1** a sophisticated, stylish, urbane person. **2** a raincoat or a waterproof poncho or jacket.

slide *verb trans., intrans.* (*pa t and pa p* **slid**; *pr p* **sliding) 1** to cause to move or to move or run smoothly along a surface. **2** to move or place softly and unobtrusively. **3** to lose one's footing; to slip. **4** to pass gradually, esp. through neglect or laziness. —*noun* **1** an act or an instance of sliding. **2** a part that glides smoothly, e.g., the moving part of a trombone. **3** an apparatus for children to play on, usu. with a ladder to climb up and a narrow sloping part to slide down. **4** a small glass plate on which specimens are placed to be viewed through a microscope. **5** a small transparent photograph viewed through a projector.

slide rule *noun* a hand-held mechanical device used to perform numeric calculations.

sliding scale a scale, e.g., of fees charged, that varies according to changes in conditions.

slier, sliest *see* **sly.**

slight *adj.* **1** small in extent, significance, or seriousness. **2** slender. **3** lacking solidity; flimsy. —*verb trans.* **(slighted, slighting)** to insult by ignoring or dismissing abruptly; to snub. ▸ **slightly** *adv.*

slim *adj.* **(slimmer, slimmest) 1** attractively thin; slender. **2** of little thickness or width. **3** slight. —*verb intrans.* **(slimmed, slimming)** to make oneself slim. ▸ **slimmer** *noun*

slime *noun* **1** a thin, unpleasantly slippery or gluey mudlike substance. **2** a mucuslike substance secreted, e.g., by snails.

slimy *adj.* **(slimier, slimiest) 1** like, covered with, or consisting of slime. **2** *colloq.* exaggeratedly and unpleasantly obedient or attentive. **3** vile; disgusting. ▸ **slimily** *adv.* ▸ **sliminess** *noun*

sling *noun* **1** a cloth hoop fastened around the neck, supporting an injured arm. **2** a primitive weapon for launching stones, consisting of a strap or pouch in which the stone is placed and swung around fast. **3** a strap or loop for hoisting, lowering, or carrying a weight. —*verb trans.* **(slung, slinging) 1** *colloq.* to throw, esp. with force. **2** to hang loosely. **3** to launch from a sling.

slingshot *noun* a Y-shaped stick fitted with a rubber band, used for shooting stones, etc. *Also called* **catapult.**

slink *verb intrans.* (*pa t and pa p* **slunk** *or* **slinked**; *pr p* **slinking)** to go or move sneakingly or ashamedly.

slinky *adj.* **(slinkier, slinkiest) 1** *colloq.*, *of clothing* attractively close-fitting. **2** slender. ▸ **slinkily** *adv.* ▸ **slinkiness** *noun*

slip¹ *verb intrans., trans.* **(slipped, slipping) 1** to lose one's footing and slide accidentally. **2** to slide, move, or drop accidentally. **3** to place smoothly, quietly, or secretively. **4** (**slip in, out,** *etc.*) to move quietly and unnoticed. **5** to move or cause to move smoothly with a sliding motion. **6** to pull free from smoothly and swiftly. **7** (*also* **slip up**) to make a slight mistake. **8** *colloq.* to give or pass secretly. —*noun* **1** an instance of losing one's footing and sliding accidentally. **2** a minor, inadvertent mistake. **3** a woman's loose undergarment worn under a dress or skirt. **4** a covering for a pillow. —**give someone the slip** *colloq.* to escape from someone adroitly. **let (something) slip 1** to reveal (it) in speech accidentally. **2** to fail to take advantage of (e.g., an opportunity).

slip *noun* **1 a** a small strip or piece of paper. **b** a small preprinted form. **2** a part of a plant that is cut off for the purpose of grafting. **3** an exceptionally slender person: *a slip of a girl.*

slipcover *noun* a fitted fabric cover for sofas, chairs, etc.

slipknot *noun* a knot undone by simply pulling one end of the line, cord, rope, or string.

slipped disk a painful dislocation of the layer of cartilage between any of the vertebrae.

slipper *noun* a soft loose laceless indoor shoe.

slippery *adj.* **1** so smooth as to cause slipping. **2** difficult to catch or keep hold of. **3** unpredictable or untrustworthy. ▸ **slipperiness** *noun*

slipshod *adj.* giving or showing no care or attention to detail.

slip-up *noun colloq.* a minor mistake.

slit *noun* a long, narrow cut or opening. —*verb trans.* (**slitted, slitting**) **1** to cut a slit in. **2** to cut into strips.

slither *verb intrans.* (**slithered, slithering**) **1** to slide or slip unsteadily while walking, e.g., on ice. **2** to move in a sliding way. —*noun* a slithering movement. ▸ **slithery** *adj.*

sliver *noun* a long, thin piece cut or broken off. —*verb intrans.* (**slivered, slivering**) to become broken or cut into slivers.

slob *noun colloq.* a lazy, untidy, or coarse person. ▸ **slobbish** *adj.* ▸ **slobby** *adj.*

slobber *verb intrans.* (**slobbered, slobbering**) **1** to let saliva dribble from the mouth. **2** (**slobber over (something)**) *colloq.* to express extreme or excessive enthusiasm or admiration for (it). —*noun* saliva dribbled from the mouth.

sloe *noun* the blackthorn fruit or bush.

slog *colloq. verb intrans., trans.* (**slogged, slogging**) **1** to work or toil long and hard. **2** to walk in a slow heavy manner. —*noun* **1** extremely tiring work. **2** a slow heavy walk.

slogan *noun* an advertising or identifying phrase of an organization, product, etc.

sloop *noun* a single-masted sailing boat with fore-and-aft sails.

slop *verb intrans., trans.* (**slopped, slopping**) (*often* **slop around** *or* **about**) **1** to splash or cause to splash or spill violently. **2** *colloq.* to move or behave in an untidy or slovenly way.

—*noun* **1** spilled liquid. **2** (**slops**) unappetizing watery food. **3** (**slops**) waste food. **4** (**slops**) liquid food fed to animals.

slope *noun* **1** an upward or downward slant. **2** a slanting surface; an incline. —*verb intrans.* (**sloped, sloping**) **1** to rise or fall at an angle. **2** to be slanted or inclined.

sloppy *adj.* (**sloppier, sloppiest**) **1** wet or muddy. **2** foolishly sad or sentimental. **3** giving or showing no care or attention to detail. ▸ **sloppily** *adv.* ▸ **sloppiness** *noun*

slosh *verb trans., intrans.* (**sloshed, sloshing**) (*often* **slosh around** *or* **about**) to cause to splash, or to splash or spill noisily. —*noun* the sound of splashing or spilling.

slot *noun* **1** a small, narrow, rectangular opening into which something is fitted or inserted. **2** a time, place, or position within a schedule. —*verb trans.* (**slotted, slotting**) **1** (*also* **slot (something) in**) to fit or insert (it), or place (it) into a slot. **2** to make a slot in.

sloth (slōth, slôth) *noun* **1** a long-haired slow-moving mammal of S America. **2** laziness. ▸ **slothful** *adj.*

slot machine a coin-operated vending, gambling, or video-game machine.

slouch *verb intrans.* (**slouched, slouching**) to sit, stand, or walk in a tired or lazy drooping posture. —*noun* such a posture.

slough[1] (slŏu, slow) *noun* **1** a mud-filled hollow. **2** an area of boggy land; a mire. **3** a state of deep and gloomy emotion.

slough[2] (slǎf) *noun* a part of an animal cast off or molted, esp. a snake's skin. —*verb trans.* (**sloughed, sloughing**) to shed (e.g., a skin).

sloven (slǎv'ən) *noun* a dirty, untidy, careless person. ▸ **slovenliness** *noun* ▸ **slovenly** *adj., adv.*

slow *adj.* **1** not moving fast. **2** taking a long time, or longer than usual or expected. **3** *of a watch* or *clock* showing a time earlier than the correct time. **4** not quickly or easily learning, understanding, or appreciating. **5** progressing at a boringly gentle pace: *a slow novel.* **6** *of business* or *trading* slack. —*adv.* in a slow way: *a clock that runs slow.* —*verb trans., intrans.* (**slowed, slowing**) (*also* **slow down** *or* **up**) to reduce or cause to reduce speed, pace, or rate of progress. ▸ **slowly** *adv.* ▸ **slowness** *noun*

slow motion a speed in film or television that is much slower than real-life movement. ▸ **slow-motion** *adj.*

slowpoke *noun colloq.* a person who moves or acts slowly.

slowworm *noun* a small legless lizard with a snakelike body. *Also called* **blindworm**.

sludge *noun* **1** soft slimy mud. **2** muddy sediment. **3** slush (sense 1). ▸ **sludgy** *adj.*

slue *noun same as* **slew**[2].

slug¹ *noun* a land mollusc similar to a snail, but having no shell.

slug² *noun colloq.* 1 a bullet. 2 a gulped mouthful of liquid, esp. alcohol.

slug³ *colloq. noun* a heavy blow, e.g., with a baseball bat or a fist. —*verb trans.* (**slugged, slugging**) to strike with a heavy blow.

sluggard (slʌg'ərd) *noun old use* a lazy, inactive person.

sluggish *adj.* 1 lacking in energy or vitality. 2 less lively, active, or responsive than usual.

sluice *noun* 1 a **a** channel or drain for water. **b** a valve or sliding gate for controlling the flow in such a channel. *Also called* **sluice gate.** 2 a trough for washing gold or other minerals out of sand, etc. 3 an act of washing down or rinsing. —*verb trans.* (**sluiced, sluicing**) 1 to drain by a sluice. 2 to wash or rinse by throwing water on.

slum *noun* 1 a heavily populated, squalid urban area. 2 a rundown, dirty, usu. overcrowded house. —*verb intrans.* (**slummed, slumming**) to visit slums, esp. out of curiosity. —**slum it** to put up with worse conditions, etc. than one is accustomed to. ‣ **slummy** *adj.*

slumber *noun* sleep. —*verb intrans.* (**slumbered, slumbering**) to sleep. ‣ **slumberous** *adj.*

slump *verb intrans.* (**slumped, slumping**) 1 to drop or sink suddenly and heavily, e.g., with fatigue. 2 *of business or trade* to decline suddenly and sharply. —*noun* a serious decline, e.g., in a nation's economy.

slung *see* **sling**.

slunk *see* **slink**.

slur *verb trans., intrans.* (**slurred, slurring**) 1 to pronounce (words) unclearly. 2 to speak or write about very disparagingly. 3 *Mus.* to sing or play without pauses. —*noun* 1 a disparaging remark. 2 a slurred word or slurring way of speaking. 3 *Mus.* a flowing style of singing or playing.

slurp *verb trans., intrans.* (**slurped, slurping**) to eat or drink noisily with a sucking action. —*noun* a slurping sound.

slush *noun* 1 half-melted snow. 2 a watery half-liquid substance. 3 sickly sentimentality. ‣ **slushy** *adj.*

slush fund a fund of money used for dishonest purposes, esp. by a political party.

slut *noun derog.* 1 a woman who regularly engages in casual sex. 2 a prostitute. 3 an untidy or dirty woman. ‣ **sluttish** *adj.*

sly *adj.* (**slier** *or* **slyer, sliest** *or* **slyest**) 1 cunning. 2 secretively deceitful or dishonest. 3 playfully mischievous. —**on the sly** *colloq.* secretly or furtively. ‣ **slyly** *adv.* ‣ **slyness** *noun*

Sm *symbol Chem.* samarium.

smack¹ *verb trans., intrans.* (**smacked, smacking**) 1 to slap, esp. with the hand. 2 *colloq.* to hit loudly and heavily. 3 to part (the lips) loudly, with relish or in pleasant anticipation. —*noun* 1 an act or the sound of smacking. 2 a loud enthusiastic kiss. —*adv. colloq.* directly; precisely: *drove smack into the tree.*

smack² *verb intrans.* (**smacked, smacking**) (**smack of (something)**) 1 to have the flavor of (it). 2 to have a suggestion or trace of (it). —*noun* 1 distinctive flavor; taste. 2 a hint or trace. 3 *colloq.* heroin.

smack³ *noun* a small single-masted fishing boat.

smacker *noun* 1 *colloq.* a loud enthusiastic kiss. 2 *slang* a US dollar.

small *adj.* 1 little in size or quantity. 2 little in extent, importance, or worth. 3 humble: *small beginnings.* 4 young: *a small child.* 5 humiliated: *made me feel small.* —*noun* a narrow part: *the small of the back.* —*adv.* on a small scale. ‣ **smallness** *noun*

small arms hand-held firearms.

small beer something unimportant.

small calorie a calorie.

small change 1 coins of little value. 2 *slang* something of little or no worth or import.

small fry *colloq.* 1 a person or thing, or people or things, of little importance or influence. 2 young children.

small-minded *adj.* narrow-minded; petty.

smallpox *noun* a highly contagious disease, characterized by fever and a severe rash.

small print fine print.

small talk polite conversation about trivial matters.

smalltime *adj. colloq.* operating on a small scale: *a smalltime criminal.*

smarm *colloq. verb intrans.* (**smarmed, smarming**) to be exaggeratedly and insincerely flattering or respectful. —*noun* exaggerated or insincere flattery. ‣ **smarmily** *adv.* ‣ **smarminess** *noun* ‣ **smarmy** *adj.*

smart *adj.* 1 appealingly elegant or fashionable. 2 good or quick at learning and understanding. 3 expensive and sophisticated: *a smart hotel.* 4 brisk: *walked at a smart pace.* 5 *of a machine, computer, weapon, etc.* intelligent (sense 2): *a smart bomb.* —*verb intrans.* (**smarted, smarting**) 1 to feel or be the cause of a sharp stinging pain. 2 to feel or be the cause of acute irritation or distress. 3 to suffer harsh consequences or punishment. ‣ **smartly** *adv.* ‣ **smartness** *noun*

smart aleck *colloq.* a person who thinks himself or herself cleverer than others; a know-it-all. ‣ **smart-alecky** *adj.*

smarten *verb trans., intrans.* (**smartened, smartening**) (*also* **smarten up**) to make or become smarter; to brighten up.

smash *verb trans., intrans.* (**smashed, smashing**) **1** to destroy or be destroyed by being broken violently into pieces. **2** to strike with violence. **3** to hit (a ball) with a smash. —*noun* **1** an act or the sound of smashing. **2** a powerful overhead stroke in racket sports. **3** *colloq.* a smash hit. —*adv.* with a smashing sound.

smash hit *colloq.* an overwhelming success, esp. a song, film, or play.

smashing *adj. colloq.* excellent; splendid.

smashup *noun colloq.* a violent traffic accident.

smattering *noun* a small amount.

smear *verb trans., intrans.* (**smeared, smearing**) **1** to spread (something sticky or oily) thickly over (a surface). **2** to make or become blurred; to smudge. **3** to say or write damaging things about (someone). —*noun* **1** a greasy mark or patch. **2** damaging criticism; a slur. **3** an amount of a substance placed on a slide for examination under a microscope.

smell *noun* **1** the sense by which one becomes aware of the odor of things. **2** the quality perceived by this sense; odor or scent. **3** an unpleasant odor. **4** an act or instance of smelling something. —*verb trans., intrans.* (*pa t and pa p* **smelled** *or* **smelt;** *pr p* **smelling**) **1** to be aware of or take in the odor of. **2** (**smell of (something)**) **a** to give off an odor of (it). **b** to show signs or traces of (it): *smelling of corruption.* **3** to give off an unpleasant odor. **4** to be aware of by intuition. ▸ **smelliness** *noun* ▸ **smelly** *adj.*

smelling salts (*pl., sing.*) crystals of ammonium carbonate, the odor of which stimulates consciousness after fainting.

smelt[1] *verb trans.* (**smelted, smelting**) to melt (ore) in order to separate the metal it contains. ▸ **smelter** *noun*

smelt[2] *see* **smell**.

smelt[3] *noun* (*pl.* **smelts, smelt**) an edible fish of the salmon family.

smidgen, smidgeon *or* **smidgin** *noun colloq.* a very small amount.

smile *verb intrans., trans.* (**smiled, smiling**) **1** to turn up the corners of the mouth as an expression of pleasure, favor, amusement, etc. **2** (**smile at (someone** *or* **something)**) to react to (another) with such an expression. **3** to show with such an expression: *He smiled his agreement.* —*noun* an act or manner of smiling.

smirch *verb trans.* (**smirched, smirching**) **1** to make dirty; to stain. **2** to damage or sully (a reputation, etc.). —*noun* **1** a stain. **2** a smear on a reputation.

smirk *verb intrans.* (**smirked, smirking**) to smile in a self-satisfied manner. —*noun* a self-satisfied smile.

smite *verb* (*pa t* **smote;** *pa p* **smitten** *or* **smote;** *pr p* **smiting**) **1** to strike or beat with a heavy blow or blows. **2** to afflict.

smith *noun,* (used typically in combination with other words) **1** a person who makes articles in a particular metal: *a silversmith.* **2** a blacksmith. **3** a person who makes skillful use of something: *a wordsmith.*

smithereens (smĭth,ə-rēnz′) *pl. noun colloq.* tiny fragments: *smashed to smithereens.*

smithy (smĭth′ē, smĭth′ē) *noun* (*pl.* **smithies**) a blacksmith's workshop.

smock *noun* a loose shirtlike garment worn over other clothes for protection. —*verb trans.* to apply smocking to.

smocking *noun* decorative stitching used on gathered or tucked material.

smog (smăg, smôg) *noun* fog mixed with smoke and fumes. ▸ **smoggy** *adj.*

smoke *noun* **1** a visible cloud given off by a burning substance. **2** visible fumes or vapors. **3** *colloq.* the act of or time spent smoking tobacco. **4** *colloq.* a cigarette or cigar. —*verb intrans., trans.* (**smoked, smoking**) **1** to give off smoke or visible fumes or vapors. **2** to inhale and then exhale the smoke from burning tobacco or other substances. **3** to preserve or flavor food by exposing it to smoke. —**smoke (someone** *or* **something) out 1** to drive (an animal, etc.) into the open using smoke. **2** to uncover by persistent searching or investigation. ▸ **smokeless** *adj.* ▸ **smoker** *noun* ▸ **smokiness** *noun* ▸ **smoky** *adj.*

smoke screen *or* **smokescreen 1** a cloud of smoke used to conceal, e.g., troops. **2** something said or done to hide or deceive.

smokestack *noun* **1** a tall industrial chimney. **2** a funnel on a ship or steam-powered train.

smolder *verb intrans.* (**smoldered, smoldering**) **1** to burn slowly or without flame. **2** to linger on in a suppressed state.

smooch *colloq. verb intrans.* (**smooched, smooching**) to kiss. —*noun* a kiss.

smooth (smoŏth) *adj.* **1** having an even, regular surface; not rough, coarse, or bumpy. **2** having few or no lumps; of even texture. **3** free from problems or difficulties: *a smooth process.* **4** characterized by steady movement. **5** very elegant or charming, esp. insincerely so. —*verb trans.* (**smoothed, smoothing**) **1** (*also* **smooth (something) down** *or* **out**) to make (it) smooth. **2** (*usu.* **smooth (something) over**) to cause (a difficulty, etc.) to seem less serious or important. **3** to make easier: *smooth the way to promotion.* ▸ **smoothly** *adv.* ▸ **smoothness** *noun*

smorgasbord *noun* an assortment of hot and cold savory dishes served as a buffet.

smote *see* **smite**.

smother *verb trans., intrans.* (**smothered, smothering**) **1** to kill with or die from lack of air; to suffocate. **2** to extinguish (a fire) by cutting off the air supply. **3** to cover with a thick layer. **4** to suppress (e.g., laughter).

smudge *noun* **1** a mark or blot spread by rubbing. **2** a faint or blurred shape. —*verb trans., intrans.* (**smudged, smudging**) **1** to make a smudge on or of. **2** to become a smudge or to become blotted or blurred. ► **smudgy** *adj.*

smug *adj.* (**smugger, smuggest**) arrogantly pleased with oneself; self-satisfied. ► **smugly** *adv.* ► **smugness** *noun*

smuggle *verb trans.* (**smuggled, smuggling**) **1** to take (goods) into or out of a country secretly and illegally. **2** to bring or take secretly, usu. breaking a rule or restriction. ► **smuggler** *noun*

smut *noun* **1** a soot. **b** a speck of dirt or soot. **2** obscene language, pictures, or images. —*verb trans.* (**smutted, smutting**) to dirty or affect with smut. ► **smuttiness** *noun* ► **smutty** *adj.*

Sn *symbol Chem.* tin (sense 1).

snack *noun* a light meal quickly taken, or a bite to eat between meals. —*verb* (**snacked, snacking**) to take a light meal or a bite to eat between meals.

snaffle *noun* a simple bit for a horse.

snafu (snăf-ōō′) *noun colloq.* a confused, chaotic, messy situation.

snag *noun* **1** a problem or drawback. **2 a** a sharp or jagged edge on which clothes, etc., could get caught. **b** a hole or tear in clothes, etc., caused by such catching. **3** a part of a tree submerged in water, hazardous to navigation. —*verb trans.* (**snagged, snagging**) to catch or tear on or as if on a snag.

snail *noun* a small soft-bodied legless creature, with a spiral shell.

snake *noun* **1** a legless crawling reptile with a long narrow body, often having a poisonous bite. **2** any long, flexible, or winding thing or shape. **3** a treacherous person. —*verb intrans.* (**snaked, snaking**) to move windingly or follow a winding course. ► **snakily** *adv.* ► **snaky** *adj.*

snap *verb trans., intrans.* (**snapped, snapping**) **1** to break suddenly and cleanly. **2** to move quickly and forcefully with a sharp sound: *The lid snapped shut.* **3** (**snap at** (**something**)) to make a biting or grasping movement towards (it). **4** to speak abruptly with anger or impatience. **5** *colloq.* to take a photograph of, esp. with simple equipment. **6** *colloq.* to lose one's senses or self-control suddenly. —*noun* **1** the act or sound of snapping. **2** a snapshot. **3** a catch or other fastening that closes with a snapping sound. **4** a crisp cookie. **5** a sudden brief period of cold weather. **6** *Football* the act of quickly passing the ball by the center to a back, an act that starts the play. —*adj.* made without due consideration: *a snap decision.*

snapdragon *noun* a plant having brightly colored two-lipped flowers.

snapper *noun* a deep-bodied edible fish.

snappy *adj.* (**snappier, snappiest**) **1** irritable. **2** smart and fashionable: *a snappy dresser.* **3** lively. **4** fast; quickly. ► **snappily** *adv.* ► **snappiness** *noun*

snapshot *noun* a photograph, esp. taken with simple equipment. *Also called* **snap.**

snare *noun* **1** an animal trap, esp. one with a string or wire noose to catch the animal's foot. **2** something that traps or entangles. —*verb trans.* (**snared, snaring**) to trap or entangle in, or as if in, a snare.

snarl¹ *verb intrans.* (**snarled, snarling**) **1** *of an animal* to growl angrily, showing the teeth. **2** to speak or say aggressively, in anger, or irritation. —*noun* **1** an act of snarling. **2** a snarling sound or facial expression.

snarl² *noun* **1** a knotted or tangled mass. **2** a confused or congested situation or state. —*verb trans., intrans.* (**snarled, snarling**) (*also* **snarl up**) to make or become knotted, tangled, or confused.

snatch *verb trans., intrans.* (**snatched, snatching**) **1** to seize or grab suddenly. **2** to make a sudden grabbing movement. **3** to pull suddenly and forcefully. —*noun* **1** an act or instance of snatching. **2** a fragment overheard or remembered. **3** a brief period.

snazzy *adj.* (**snazzier, snazziest**) *colloq.* fashionably smart or elegant. ► **snazzily** *adv.*

sneak *verb intrans., trans.* (**sneaked, sneaking**) **1** to move or go quietly, avoiding notice. **2** to bring or take secretly: *sneak a look at the letter.* —*noun colloq.* an untrustworthy person. ► **sneakily** *adv.* ► **sneakiness** *noun* ► **sneaky** *adj.*

> *Usage* Although the variant past tense and past participle *snuck* is common at all levels, the preferred form remains *sneaked.*

sneakers *pl. noun* rubber-soled sports or casual shoes. *Also called* **tennis shoes.**

sneer *verb intrans., trans.* (**sneered, sneering**) **1** to show scorn or contempt. **2** to say scornfully or contemptuously. —*noun* an expression of scorn or contempt.

sneeze *verb intrans.* (**sneezed, sneezing**) to blow air out through the nose suddenly, violently, and involuntarily, esp. because of irritation in the nostrils. —*rioun* an act or the sound of sneezing.

snicker *verb intrans.* (**snickered, snickering**) to laugh quietly, esp. in a snide or mocking way. —*noun* a quiet, yet snide or mocking, laugh.

snide *adj.* expressing criticism or disapproval in an indirect way intended to offend.

sniff *verb intrans., trans.* (**sniffed, sniffing**) 1 to draw in air through the nose in short sharp bursts. 2 to smell by inhaling air through the nose in short bursts. —*noun* an act or the sound of sniffing. —**sniff (someone or something) out** to discover or detect (the one or ones specified) by or as if by using the sense of smell.

sniffle *verb intrans.* (**sniffled, sniffling**) to sniff repeatedly, e.g., because of having a cold. —*noun* 1 an act or the sound of sniffling. 2 (**the sniffles**) *colloq.* a slight cold.

sniffy *adj.* (**sniffier, sniffiest**) *colloq.* 1 contemptuous or disdainful. 2 sniffing repeatedly, esp. because of having a cold. ▸ **sniffily** *adv.*

snifter *noun* a pear-shaped goblet for brandy.

snigger *verb intrans.* (**sniggered, sniggering**) to snicker. —*noun* a snicker.

snip *verb trans.* (**snipped, snipping**) to cut, esp. with a quick action with scissors. —*noun* 1 an act of snipping. 2 a small piece snipped off. 3 a small cut or notch.

snipe *noun* (*pl.* **snipe, snipes**) 1 a wading bird with a long, straight bill. 2 a quick verbal attack or criticism. —*verb intrans.* (**sniped, sniping**) (**snipe at (someone)**) 1 to shoot at (someone) from a hidden position. 2 a to criticize (someone) bad-temperedly. b to engage in bad-tempered criticism. ▸ **sniper** *noun*

snippet *noun* a scrap.

snitch *slang noun* 1 a thief. 2 an informer, esp. a police informer. —*verb intrans., trans.* (**snitched, snitching**) 1 to betray others; to inform. 2 to steal; to pilfer. ▸ **snitcher** *noun*

snivel *verb intrans.* (**sniveled** or **snivelled**, **sniveling** or **snivelling**) 1 to whine or complain tearfully. 2 to have a runny nose. —*noun* the act or an instance of sniveling.

snob *noun* a person who places too high a value on social status. ▸ **snobbery** *noun* ▸ **snobbishly** *adv.* ▸ **snobbishness** *noun* ▸ **snobby** *adj.*

> Originally a slang term for 'shoemaker' which changed its meaning to someone of low social class, and later to an ostentatious vulgarian

snooker *noun* pocket billiards in which 15 red balls and 6 balls of other hues are used. *See also* **billiards, pool¹** (sense 5). —*verb trans.* (**snookered, snookering**) 1 in snooker, to force (an opponent) to attempt to hit an obstructed target ball. 2 *slang* to defeat or thwart (oneself or another).

snoop *verb intrans.* (**snooped, snooping**) to go about inquisitively; to pry. —*noun* 1 an act of snooping. 2 a person who snoops. ▸ **snooper** *noun*

snooty *adj.* (**snootier, snootiest**) *colloq.* haughty; snobbish. ▸ **snootily** *adv.* ▸ **snootiness** *noun*

snooze *verb intrans.* (**snoozed, snoozing**) to sleep lightly; to doze. —*noun* a period of light sleep, esp. when brief; a nap.

snore *verb intrans.* (**snored, snoring**) to breathe heavily and with a snorting sound while sleeping. —*noun* an act or the sound of heavy breathing during sleep.

snorkel *noun* 1 a rigid tube through which air can be drawn into the mouth while one is swimming just below the surface. 2 a set of tubes on a submarine extended above the surface of the sea to take in air and release exhaust gases. —*verb intrans.* (**snorkeled, snorkeling**) to swim with a snorkel.

snort *verb intrans., trans.* (**snorted, snorting**) 1 to force air violently and noisily out through the nostrils; to make a similar noise while taking air in. 2 to express contempt or anger with a snort. —*noun* an act or the sound of snorting.

snot *noun slang* 1 mucus from or in the nose. 2 a contemptible person. ▸ **snottily** *adv.* ▸ **snottiness** *noun* ▸ **snotty** *adj.*

snout *noun* 1 the nose and mouthparts of certain animals. 2 *colloq.* the human nose.

snow *noun* 1 frozen water vapor that falls to the ground in soft white flakes. 2 a fall of this. 3 *slang* cocaine or heroin. —*verb intrans.* (**snowed, snowing**) to fall from the sky as frozen precipitation. ▸ **snowy** *adj.*

snowball *noun* a small mass of snow pressed hard together and used as a missile. —*verb trans., intrans.* (**snowballed, snowballing**) 1 to throw snowballs (at). 2 to develop or increase uncontrollably.

snowboard *noun* a board resembling a wheel-less skateboard, used to descend snow-covered slopes. —*verb intrans.* (**snowboarded, snowboarding**) to move down a slope on a snowboard.

snowbound *adj.* shut in by snow.

snowcap *noun* a cap of snow, as on the polar regions or a mountain. ▸ **snowcapped** *adj.*

snowdrift *noun* a bank of snow blown together by the wind.

snowdrop *noun* an early spring plant with drooping white bell-shaped flowers.

snowfall *noun* 1 a fall of snow. 2 an amount of fallen snow.

snowflake *noun* a single, small, feathery clump of crystals of frozen water vapor.

snow goose a white Arctic American goose with black-tipped wings.

snow leopard a large wild cat with fur patterned with black markings. *Also called* **ounce**.

snowman *noun* a human figure made of packed snow.

snowmobile *noun* a motorized vehicle on skis or tracks for traveling on snow. ▸ **snowmobile** *verb intrans.*

snow pea a variety of pea with a thick, soft pod. *Also called* **sugar pea.**

snowplow *noun* **1** a big shovel-like blade for clearing snow off roads or tracks. **2** a vehicle or train fitted with this big blade.

snowshoe *noun* a racketlike framework strapped to the foot for walking over deep snow.

snow tire a tire with studs or deep treads for traveling on snow-covered roads.

snub *verb trans.* (**snubbed, snubbing**) to insult by openly ignoring, rejecting, or otherwise showing contempt. —*noun* an act of snubbing. —*adj.*, of a nose short and flat.

snuff¹ *noun* powdered tobacco for inhaling through the nose. —*verb intrans.* (**snuffed, snuffing**) to take snuff.

snuff² *verb trans.* (**snuffed, snuffing**) **1** (*also* **snuff (something) out**) to extinguish (e.g., a fire, candle, etc.). **2** to snip off the burned part of the wick of (a candle or lamp). —*noun* the burned part of the wick of a lamp or candle.

snuffle *verb intrans., trans.* (**snuffled, snuffling**) **1** to breathe, esp. to breathe in, through a partially blocked nose. **2** to snivel. —*noun* **1** the sound of breathing through a partially blocked nose. **2** (**the snuffles**) *colloq.* a slight cold.

snug *adj.* (**snugger, snuggest**) **1** enjoying or providing warmth, comfort, and shelter; cozy. **2** comfortably close-fitting: *a snug jacket.* ▸ **snugly** *adv.*

snuggle *verb intrans.* (**snuggled, snuggling**) (*usu.* **snuggle down** *or* **in**) to settle oneself into a position of warmth and comfort.

so¹ *adv.* **1** to such an extent. **2** to this, that, or the same extent; as: *This one is not so nice.* **3** extremely: *She is so talented!* **4** in that state or condition: *promised to be faithful, and has remained so.* **5** also; likewise: *So are you.* **6** used to avoid repeating a previous statement: *Because I say so.* —*conj.* **1** therefore; thereafter: *He insulted me, so I objected strongly.* **2** (*also* **so that**) in order that. —*adj.* the case; true: *You think I'm crazy, but it's just not so.* —*interj.* used to express discovery: *So, that's what you've been doing!* —**so as to** in order to; in such a way as to. **so much for** nothing has come of (something); that has disposed of or ruined (something).

so² *noun* same as **sol.**

soak *verb trans., intrans.* (**soaked, soaking**) **1** to stand or leave to stand in a liquid for some time. **2** to make thoroughly wet; to drench. **3** (*also* **soak in** *or* **through**) to penetrate or pass: **4** (*also* **soak (something) up**) to absorb (it). —*noun* an act of soaking. **2** *colloq.* a person who habitually drinks a lot of alcohol.

so-and-so *noun colloq.* **1** a person whose name one does not know or cannot remember. **2** used in place of a vulgar word: *You crafty little so-and-so!*

soap *noun* **1** a mixture of oils or fats, in the form of a liquid, powder, or solid block, used with water to remove dirt. **2** such a substance in the form of a solid block, liquid, or powder. **3** *colloq.* a soap opera. —*verb trans.* (**soaped, soaping**) to apply soap to. ▸ **soapy** *adj.*

soapbox *noun* an improvised platform for public speechmaking.

soap opera a radio or television series dealing with the daily life and troubles of a regular group of characters. *Also called* **soap.**

soapstone *noun* a soft variety of talc, widely used for ornamental carvings.

soapsuds *pl. noun* suds in soapy water.

soar *verb intrans.* (**soared, soaring**) **1** to fly high into the air. **2** to glide through the air at a high altitude. **3** to rise sharply to a great height or level: *temperatures soaring.*

sob *verb intrans., trans.* (**sobbed, sobbing**) to cry uncontrollably with intermittent gulps for breath. —*noun* a gulp for breath between bouts of crying.

sober *adj.* **1** not drunk at all. **2 a** serious or solemn. **b** very important in terms of the consequences. **3** suggesting sedateness or seriousness: *sober clothes.* **4** plain; unembellished: *the sober truth.* —*verb intrans., trans.* (**sobered, sobering**) **1** to become or make someone quieter, less excited, etc. **2** (**sober (someone) up**) to become or make (someone) free from the effects of alcohol.

sobriety (sə-brī′ət-ē) *noun* **1** the condition or quality of being sober. **2** the practice or state of choosing not to take or do something, e.g., alcohol.

sobriquet *or* **soubriquet** (sō′brĭ-kĕt′) *noun* a nickname.

> From a French phrase meaning literally an affectionate chuck under the chin

Soc. *abbrev.* **1** Socialist. **2** Society.

so-called *adj.* called such, but in truth not.

> *Usage* Avoid putting quotations around descriptions following the term so-called: *a so-called statesman* is correct, not *a so-called 'statesman'.*

soccer *noun* a game for two teams of 11 players each, in which the object is to kick or head the ball into the opponent's net.

sociable *adj.* **1** liking the company of others. **2** characterized by friendliness: *a sociable meeting.* ▸ **sociability** *noun* ▸ **sociableness** *noun* ▸ **sociably** *adv.*

social adj. 1 of or for people or society as a whole. 2 relating to the organization and behavior of people in societies or communities: social studies. 3 a tending or needing to live with others. b liking the company of others. 4 promoting friendly gatherings of people: a social club. —noun a social gathering, esp. one organized by a club or other group. ▸ **socially** adv.

socialism noun an economic theory or system where land, industries, transport systems, etc. are owned and run by the state, not private individuals. ▸ **socialist** noun, adj.

socialite noun a person who mixes with people of high social status.

socialize verb intrans., trans. (socialized, socializing) 1 to meet with people on an informal, friendly basis. 2 to circulate among guests at a party. ▸ **socialization** noun

social science the study of the organization and behavior of people in societies and communities. ▸ **social scientist**

social security a system by which payments are made by government to individuals after retirement, in old age, or during periods of unemployment.

social services services provided by the government for the welfare of disadvantaged citizens.

social studies (sing. pl.) a school course including geography, history, government, and sociology.

social work work in any of the services provided by government for the care of its disadvantaged citizens. ▸ **social worker**

society noun (pl. societies) 1 humankind as a whole, or a part of it, such as one nation, considered as a single community. 2 a division of humankind with common characteristics, e.g., of nationality, race, or religion. 3 an organized group or association. 4 rich, fashionable people. 5 company.

Society of Friends the Quakers.

socio- combining form forming words denoting social, of society, or sociology: socioeconomic.

sociology noun the scientific study of the nature, structure, and workings of human society. ▸ **sociological** adj. ▸ **sociologist** noun

sociopath noun a person with a personality disorder, symptoms of which include aggressive antisocial behaviors. ▸ **sociopathic** adj.

sock[1] noun a fabric covering for the foot and ankle, sometimes reaching to the knee.

sock[2] slang verb trans. (socked, socking) to hit with a powerful blow. —noun a powerful blow.

socket noun a specially-shaped hole or set of holes into which something is fitted.

Socratic (sə-krăt'ĭk) adj. relating to the Greek philosopher Socrates, his philosophy, or method of teaching.

sod noun a piece of turf.

soda noun 1 any of various compounds of sodium in everyday use, e.g., sodium bicarbonate. 2 soda water. 3 a soft drink.

soda fountain a counter in a store from which soft drinks, ice cream, and snacks are served.

soda water water made effervescent by the addition of carbon dioxide, widely used as a mixer with alcoholic spirits. Also called **carbonated water, club soda, seltzer, seltzer water.**

sodden adj. 1 thoroughly soaked. 2 made lifeless or sluggish, esp. through excessive consumption of alcohol.

sodium noun (SYMBOL Na) a soft silvery-white metal that occurs mainly as sodium chloride.

sodium bicarbonate baking soda.

sodium chloride Chem. a white crystalline salt, used for, e.g., seasoning and preserving food. Also called **common salt, salt, table salt.**

sodium hydroxide a white crystalline solid, that dissolves in water to form a strongly alkaline solution. Also called **caustic soda, soda.**

sodium nitrate a toxic colorless crystalline solid, used as a food preservative, esp. for cured meats.

sodomy noun 1 a form of intercourse in which the penis is inserted into the anus of a man or woman. 2 copulation between a man or woman and an animal.

sofa noun an upholstered seat with a back and arms, for two or more people.

soft adj. 1 easily yielding or changing shape when pressed; pliable. 2 e.g., of fabric having a smooth surface producing little or no friction. 3 quiet: a soft voice. 4 of little brightness: soft colors. 5 kind or sympathetic. 6 not able to endure rough treatment or hardship. 7 lacking strength of character; easily influenced. 8 mentally weak. 9 weakly sentimental. 10 tender; loving: soft words. 11 colloq. requiring little effort; easy: a soft job. 12 of a drug not severely addictive. 13 having moderate policies or views. —adv. in a soft manner: speaks soft.

softball noun a game similar to baseball, played with a larger, softer ball.

soft drink a nonalcoholic drink.

soften verb trans., intrans. (softened, softening) to make or become soft or softer. —**soften (someone or something) up** to prepare (the one specified) for something unwanted or unwelcome.

softhearted adj. kindhearted and generous.

softie *noun colloq. same as* **softy**.

soft palate the back part of the palate.

soft pedal a pedal on a piano pressed to give a softer tone.

soft sell the use of gentle persuasion as a selling technique.

soft-soap *verb trans.* (**soft-soaped, soft-soaping**) *colloq.* to speak flatteringly to, esp. in order to persuade or deceive.

soft-spoken *adj.* having a soft voice, and usu. a mild manner.

soft spot a fondness.

soft touch *slang* a person easily taken advantage of, esp. financially.

software *noun Comput.* programs, magnetic disks, tapes, etc., as opposed to the computers themselves. *See also* **hardware** (sense 2).

soft water water containing very low levels of calcium and magnesium salts.

softy *or* **softie** *noun* (*pl.* **softies**) *colloq.* **1** a person not able to endure rough treatment or hardship. **2** a weakly sentimental person.

soggy *adj.* (**soggier, soggiest**) **1** thoroughly wet; saturated. **2** *of ground* waterlogged; boggy. ▸ **soggily** *adv.* ▸ **sogginess** *noun*

soh *noun same as* **sol**.

soil¹ *noun* **1** the mixture of fragmented rock and plant and animal debris that lies on the surface of the Earth. **2** country; land.

soil² *verb trans.* (**soiled, soiling**) **1** to make dirty; to stain. **2** to bring discredit on; to sully. —*noun* **1** a stain. **2** dirt. **3** dung.

soiree *or* **soirée** (swä-rā′) *noun* **1** a formal evening party. **2** an evening of entertainment.

sojourn (sō′jəm,, sō-jəm′) *noun* a short stay. —*verb intrans.* (**sojourned, sojourning**) to stay for a short while.

sol, so *or* **soh** *noun* the fifth note of the scale in the solfeggio system of music notation.

solace (säl′əs) *noun* comfort in times of disappointment or sorrow, or a source of this. —*verb trans.* (**solaced, solacing**) **1** to provide with comfort in times of disappointment or sorrow. **2** to bring relief from.

solar (sō′lər) *adj.* of or relating to the Sun. **2** of, by, or using energy from the Sun's rays.

solar battery a battery consisting of a number of solar cells.

solar cell an electric cell that converts solar energy into electricity. *Also called* **photovoltaic cell**.

solar energy energy that is radiated from the Sun, mainly in the form of heat and light.

solarium *noun* (*pl.* **solaria, solariums**) a room constructed chiefly of glass.

solar plexus an area in the abdomen with a concentration of radiating nerves.

solar system the system of the planets, asteroids, and comets, which orbit the Sun.

sold *see* **sell**.

solder (säd′ər) *noun* an alloy with a low melting point applied when molten to join two pieces of metal. —*verb trans.* (**soldered, soldering**) to join (two pieces of metal) by applying a layer of solder between them.

soldier (sōl′jər) *noun* **1** a member of a fighting force, esp. a national army. **2** a member of an army below officer rank. —*verb intrans.* (**soldiered, soldiering**) to serve as a soldier. ▸ **soldierly** *adj.*

sole¹ *noun* **1** the underside of the foot. **2** the underside of a shoe, boot, etc. —*verb trans.* (**soled, soling**) to fit (a shoe or boot) with a sole.

sole² *noun* (*pl.* **sole, soles**) a small edible flat-bodied fish found in warm shallow waters.

sole³ *adj.* **1** only. **2** exclusive. ▸ **solely** *adv.*

solecism (säl′ə-sĭz,əm, sō′lə-) *noun* **1** a mistake in the use of language. **2** an instance of bad or incorrect behavior.

solemn (säl′əm) *adj.* **1** done, made, etc., in earnest. **2** of a very serious and formal nature. **3** glum or somber in appearance, attitude, etc. ▸ **solemnity** *noun* ▸ **solemnly** *adv.*

solemnize (säl′əm-nīz,) *verb trans.* (**solemnized, solemnizing**) **1** to perform (esp. a marriage) with a formal or religious ceremony. **2** to make solemn. ▸ **solemnization** *noun*

solenoid (sō′lə-noid,, säl′ə-) *noun* a cylindrical coil of wire that produces a magnetic field when an electric current is passed through it.

solfeggio (sōl-fĕ′jē-o) *noun* a system of musical notation in which the notes of a scale are represented by syllables, esp. by *do, re, me, fa, soh, la, ti.*

solicit *verb trans., intrans.* (**solicited, soliciting**) **1** to ask for. **2** to require or call for. ▸ **solicitation** *noun*

solicitor *noun* **1** in some US states, a chief law officer. **2** *Brit.* a lawyer who is not a member of the bar.

solicitor general·(*pl.* **solicitors general**) **1** a chief law officer in a US state that has no attorney general. **2** *Brit.* a high ranking law officer.

solicitous *adj.* **1** (**solicitous about** *or* **for** (**someone** *or* **something**)) anxious or concerned about (the one specified). **2** (**solicitous to do something**) willing or eager to do it. ▸ **solicitously** *adv.*

solicitude *noun* **1** anxiety or uneasiness of mind. **2** the state of being solicitous.

solid *adj.* **1** in a form other than a liquid or a gas, and resisting changes in shape. **2** of the same nature or material throughout. **3** a firmly constructed or attached; not easily breaking or loosening. **b** resistant to scratching or indentation. **4** difficult to undermine or destroy; sound: *solid support for the plan.* **5** not hollow. **6** without breaks; continuous: *four solid hours.* **7** competent in degree of quality: *a solid piece of research.* —*noun* **1** a substance that is neither liquid nor gas. **2** *Geom.* a three-dimensional figure. ▸ **solidity** *noun* ▸ **solidly** *adv.*

solidarity *noun* mutual support and unity of interests and actions.

solidify (sə-lĭd′ə-fī,) *verb trans., intrans.* (**solidified, solidifying, solidifies**) to make or become solid. ▸ **solidification** *noun*

soliloquy (sə-lĭl′ə-kwē) *noun* (*pl.* **soliloquies**) a speech in a play, etc., in which a character reveals thoughts or intentions to the audience by talking aloud. ▸ **soliloquize** *verb intrans.*

solitaire (sǎl′ə-tǎr,, -tĕr,) *noun* **1** a puzzle or card game for one player. **2** a single gem in a setting on its own.

solitary *adj.* **1** single; lone. **2** preferring to be alone. **3** remote; secluded. ▸ **solitariness** *noun*

solitude *noun* the state of being alone or secluded.

solo *noun* (*pl.* **solos**) a piece of music or a passage within it for a single voice or instrument, with or without accompaniment. —*adj.* performed alone. —*adv.* alone: *fly solo.* ▸ **soloist** *noun*

solstice *noun* either of the times when the Sun is farthest from the equator.

soluble *adj.* **1** capable of being dissolved in a liquid. **2** capable of being solved or resolved. ▸ **solubility** *noun*

solute (sǎl′yoot,) *noun Chem.* a substance that is dissolved in a solvent.

solution *noun* **1** the process of finding an answer to a problem or puzzle, or the result of this. **2** *Chem.* a liquid which has a solid or gas dissolved in it. **3** the act of dissolving or the state of being dissolved: *in solution.* **4** *Math.* the value that one or more of the variables must have for an equation to be valid.

solve *verb trans.* (**solved, solving**) to discover the answer to (a puzzle) or a way out of (a problem). ▸ **solvable** *adj.*

solvent *adj.* without debts. —*noun* a liquid in which a solid or gas is or may be dissolved. ▸ **solvency** *noun*

somatic *adj.* of or pertaining to the body, as opposed to the mind.

somber *adj.* **1** sad and serious; grave. **2** dark and gloomy. ▸ **somberly** *adv.* ▸ **somberness** *noun*

sombrero *noun* (*pl.* **sombreros**) a man's straw or felt hat with a very wide brim.

some *adj.* **1** denoting an unknown or unspecified amount or number of. **2** of

unknown or unspecified nature or identity. *some problem with the engine.* **3** quite a bit of: *for some time.* **4** at least a little: *tried to feel some excitement.* **5** *colloq.* an excellent or impressive example of: *That was some shot!* —*pron.* **1** certain unspecified things or people. **2** an unspecified amount or number. —*adv.* **1** to an unspecified extent. **2** approximately: *some 20 feet deep.*

-some *suffix* forming words denoting: **1** causing or producing: *troublesome.* **2** inviting: *cuddlesome.* **3** tending to: *quarrelsome.* **4** a group of the specified number of people or things: *a foursome.*

somebody *pron.* **1** an unknown or unspecified person; someone. **2** a person of importance.

someday *adv.* at an unknown or unspecified time in the future.

somehow *adv.* **1** in a way not yet known. **2** for a reason not easy to explain.

someone *pron.* somebody.

someplace *adv.* somewhere.

somersault *noun* a leap or roll in which the whole body turns a complete circle forward or backward. —*verb intrans.* (**somersaulted, somersaulting**) to perform such a leap or roll.

something *pron.* **1** a thing not known or not stated. **2** an amount or number not known or not stated: *40 something.* **3** a person or thing of importance. **4** a certain truth or value: *There is something in what you say.* **5** *colloq.* an impressive person or thing: *She really thinks she's something.* —*adv.* to some degree; rather. —**something else** *colloq.* one that is really remarkable.

sometime *adj.* having been at a past time; former. —*adv.* at an unknown or unspecified time in the future or the past.

sometimes *adv.* now and then; on occasion.

someway *adv.* somehow (sense 1).

somewhat *adv.* a little; rather.

somewhere *adv.* in or to some place or degree, or at some point, not known or not specified. —*noun* an unspecified or unknown site, location, or place.

somnambulism *noun* sleepwalking. ▸ **somnambulist** *noun*

somnolent (sǎm′nə-lənt) *adj.* **1** sleepy or drowsy. **2** causing sleepiness or drowsiness. ▸ **somnolence** *noun*

son *noun* **1** a male child considered in relation to his parents. **2** a man closely associated with, involved with, or influenced by, a person, thing, or place: *a faithful son of the Church.*

sonar *noun* a system for determining the location of underwater objects by transmitting ultrasound signals and measuring the time taken for their echoes to return after they strike an obstacle.

sonata *noun* a piece of classical music, in three or more movements, for a solo instrument.

song *noun* **1** a set of words to be sung, usu. with accompanying music. **2** the musical call of certain birds. **3** singing: *poetry and song*.

songbird *noun* any of various kinds of bird with a musical call.

songster *noun* a talented, esp. male, singer.

songstress *noun* a talented female singer.

sonic *adj.* **1** relating to or using sound or sound waves. **2** traveling at approximately the speed of sound.

sonic boom a loud boom heard when an aircraft passes through the sound barrier.

son-in-law *noun* (*pl.* **sons-in-law**) the husband of one's daughter.

sonnet *noun* a poem with 14 lines.

sonorous *adj.* **1** sounding impressively loud, deep, clear, etc.: *a sonorous bell / a sonorous voice*. **2** *of language* impressively eloquent. ▶ **sonority** *noun* ▶ **sonorousness** *noun*

soon *adv.* **1** in a short time from now or from a stated time. **2** with little delay; quickly. **3** willingly. —**sooner or later** eventually.

soot *noun* a black powdery substance produced when coal or wood is burned. ▶ **sooty** *adj.*

soothe (sooth) *verb trans.* (**soothed, soothing**) **1** to bring relief from (a pain, etc.). **2** to comfort or calm (someone). ▶ **soothing** *adj.*

soothsay *verb intrans.* (**soothsaid, soothsaying**) to foretell or divine. ▶ **soothsayer** *noun*

sop *noun* **1** (*often* **sops**) a piece of food, esp. bread, dipped in a liquid, e.g., soup. **2** something given or done as a bribe or in order to pacify. —*verb trans.* (**sopped, sopping**) (*usu.* **sop (something) up**) to mop or soak (it) up.

sophism (sǎf'ĭz,əm) *noun* a convincing and elaborate but false argument or explanation, esp. one intended to deceive. ▶ **sophist** *noun* ▶ **sophistry** *noun*

sophisticate *verb trans.* (sə-fĭs'tĭ-kāt,) (**sophisticated, sophisticating**) to make sophisticated. —*noun* (sə-fĭs'tĭ-kət, -kāt,) a sophisticated person. ▶ **sophistication** *noun*

sophisticated *adj.* **1** having a broad knowledge and experience of the world, esp. of artistic and intellectual things; appealing to or frequented by sophisticated people. **2** complex and subtle: *sophisticated arguments*.

sophomore (sǎf'môr,) *noun* a second-year student at a school or university.

soporific *adj.* **1** causing sleep. **2** extremely slow and boring: *a soporific speech*. —*noun* a sleep-inducing drug.

soppy *adj.* (**soppier, soppiest**) foolishly sad or sentimental. ▶ **soppily** *adv.* ▶ **soppiness** *noun*

soprano *noun* (*pl.* **sopranos**) **1** a singing voice of the highest pitch for a woman or a boy; also, a person having this voice. **2** a musical part for a person with such a voice.

sorbet (sôr'bət) *noun* a frozen dessert made of fruit juice. *Also called* **water ice**.

sorbitol *noun* a white crystalline carbohydrate used as a sweetener or sugar substitute.

sorcery *noun* magic using the power of supernatural forces. ▶ **sorcerer** *noun* ▶ **sorceress** *noun*

sordid *adj.* **1** repulsively filthy; squalid. **2** morally revolting.

sore *adj.* **1** painful or tender. **2** *colloq.* angry or resentful. —*noun* a diseased spot or area, esp. an ulcer or boil. ▶ **sorely** *adv.*

sorghum *noun* a tropical grass whose grain is used as a cereal and to make molasses.

sorority *noun* (*pl.* **sororities**) a social society for female students. *See also* **fraternity**.

sorrel[1] *noun* a sour-tasting herb, used medicinally and in salads. *Also called* **dock**.

sorrel[2] *adj.* of a reddish-brown or light chestnut color. —*noun* a horse of this color.

sorrow *noun* deep sadness or grief, or a cause of this. —*verb intrans.* (**sorrowed, sorrowing**) to have or express feelings of deep sadness or grief. ▶ **sorrowful** *adj.* ▶ **sorrowfully** *adv.* ▶ **sorrowfulness** *noun*

sorry *adj.* (**sorrier, sorriest**) **1** feeling regret or shame about something one has done, is responsible for, etc. **2** (**sorry for (someone)**) feeling pity or sympathy toward (someone). **3** pitifully bad: *a sorry state*. **4** extremely poor: *a sorry excuse*. —*interj.* **1** used as an apology. **2** used in asking for something just said to be repeated.

sort *noun* **1** a kind, type, or class. **2** *colloq.* a person: *not a bad sort*. —*verb trans.* (**sorted, sorting**) **1** to arrange into different groups according to type or kind. **2** *colloq.* to put right. —**out of sorts** *colloq.* **1** slightly unwell. **2** peevish; bad-tempered. **sort (something) out 1** to separate (it) out from a mixed collection into a group or groups according to kind. **2** to put (it) into order; to arrange (it) methodically. **3** to resolve the difficulties relating to (it).

sortie (sôrt'ē, sôr-tē') *noun* **1** a sudden attack by besieged troops. **2** an operational flight by a single military aircraft. —*verb intrans.* (**sortied, sortieing**) to make a sortie.

SOS *noun* **1** *old use* a ship's or aircraft's call for help, consisting of these letters repeated in Morse code. **2** *colloq.* any call for help.

so-so *adj., adv. colloq.* neither very good nor very bad; passable.

sot *noun* a person who is continually intoxicated. ► **sottish** *adj.*

soubriquet *noun* same as **sobriquet**.

soufflé (sōō-flā′) *noun* a light sweet or savory baked dish, made of whipped egg whites with other ingredients mixed in.

sough (sow, sǝf) *noun* a sighing sound made by the wind blowing through trees. —*verb intrans.* (**soughed, soughing**) to make a sighing sound.

sought see **seek**.

sought-after *adj.* in demand; desired.

soul *noun* 1 the nonphysical part of a person, with personality, emotions, and intellect, widely believed to survive in some form after the death of the body. 2 emotional sensitivity. 3 essential nature. 4 (**the soul of**) a perfect example of: *She is the soul of discretion.* 5 *colloq.* a person: *a kind soul.* 6 soul music. —*adj.* relating to African-American culture: *soul food.* ► **soulless** *adj.*

soul-destroying *adj.* 1 extremely dull, boring, or repetitive. 2 extremely difficult to tolerate or accept emotionally.

soulful *adj.* having or expressing deep feelings, esp. of sadness. ► **soulfully** *adv.*

sound[1] *noun* 1 disturbances in the air caused by vibrations, which are able to be heard. 2 the noise heard as a result of such periodic vibrations. 3 audible quality. 4 the mental impression created by something heard: *I don't like the sound of that.* 5 aural material, e.g., spoken commentary and music, accompanying a film or broadcast. 6 *colloq.* volume or volume control, esp. on a television set. —*verb trans., intrans.* (**sounded, sounding**) 1 to cause to produce, or to produce, a sound or sounds. 2 to create an impression: *That sounds like fun.* 3 to announce or signal with a sound: *sounded the alarm.* 4 *Med.* to examine by tapping or listening. See also **sound**[3] *verb* (sense 2).

sound[2] *adj.* 1 having, showing, or enjoying good health. 2 sensible; well-founded; reliable: *sound advice.* 3 acceptable or approved of. 4 *esp. of punishment, etc.* severe, hard, thorough: *a sound telling-off.* 5 *of sleep* deep and undisturbed. —*adv.* deeply: *sound asleep.* ► **soundly** *adv.*

sound[3] *verb trans.* (**sounded, sounding**) 1 to measure the depth of (esp. the sea). 2 *Med.* to examine (a hollow organ, etc.) with a probe. See also **sound**[1] *verb* (sense 4). —*noun Med.* a probe for examining hollow organs. —**sound (someone) out** to try to discover (someone else's) opinions or intentions.

sound[4] *noun* a narrow passage of water connecting two seas or separating an island and the mainland.

sound barrier the resistance an aircraft meets when it reaches speeds close to the speed of sound.

soundboard *noun* 1 *Mus.* a sounding board (sense 2). 2 *Comput.* a printed circuit board added to a computer to provide or enhance sound effects.

sound-box *noun* the hollow body of a violin, guitar, etc.

sound effects artificially produced sounds matching actions in film, broadcasting, or theater.

sounding board 1 a board over a stage or pulpit directing the speaker's voice toward the audience. 2 *Mus.* a thin board that forms the upper part of the resonating chamber in, e.g., a piano or violin. Also called **soundboard**. 3 a means of testing the acceptability or popularity of ideas or opinions.

soundtrack *noun* 1 a band of magnetic tape along the edge of a cinematographic film, on which the sound is recorded. 2 a recording of the music from a film or broadcast.

sound wall a barrier erected along a freeway, etc. to muffle the noise of traffic. Also called **sound barrier**.

soup *noun* a liquid food made by stewing meat, vegetables, or grains. —**in the soup** *slang* in trouble or difficulty. ► **soupy** *adj.*

soupçon (sōōp-sôn′) *noun* a hint or dash.

soup kitchen a place at which volunteer workers supply free food to needy people.

sour *adj.* 1 having an acid taste or smell. 2 rancid or stale. 3 sullen; miserable. 4 bad, unsuccessful, or inharmonious: *The marriage turned sour.* —*verb intrans., trans.* (**soured, souring**) to make or become sour. ► **sourly** *adv.*

source *noun* 1 the place, thing, person, or circumstance from which something begins or develops. 2 the point at which a river or stream begins. 3 a person, or a book or other document, providing information or evidence: *unnamed sources.*

sour cream cream deliberately made sour by the action of bacteria, for use in cooking.

sourdough (sowr′dō,) *noun* sour, fermented dough that is used in making bread and rolls.

sourpuss *noun colloq.* a sullen person.

souse (sows) *verb trans.* (**soused, sousing**) 1 to plunge into a liquid. 2 to drench. 3 to steep or cook in vinegar or white wine. 4 to pickle. —*noun* 1 an act of sousing. 2 the liquid in which food is soused. 3 a pickled food; pickle. 4 *slang* a drunk.

south (ABBREV. **S**) *noun* (also **the south** or **the South**) the direction to one's right when one faces the rising Sun. —*adj.* 1 in the south; on the side that is on or nearest the south. 2 coming from the direction of the south. —*adv.* toward the south.

southeast (ABBREV. **SE**) *noun* the direction midway between south and east. —*adj.* **1** in the southeast. **2** from the direction of the southeast.

southeaster (sow-thē′stər, sow-ē′-) *noun* a wind blowing from the southeast. ▸ **southeasterly** *adj., adv.*

southeastern *adj.* (ABBREV. **SE**) to the southeast.

southerly (sŭth′ər-lē) *adj.* **1** of a wind, etc. coming from the south. **2** looking, lying, etc., toward the south. —*adv.* to or toward the south. —*noun* (*pl.* **southerlies**) a southerly wind.

southern (sŭth′ərn) *adj.* (ABBREV. **S**) **1** of or in the south. **2** facing or directed toward the south.

southerner or **Southerner** (sŭth′ə-nər) *noun* a person who lives in or comes from the south, esp. the southern part of the USA.

southern lights aurora australis.

southpaw *colloq. noun* a left-handed person, esp. a boxer or baseball pitcher. —*adj.* left-handed.

South Pole 1 the southernmost point of the Earth's axis of rotation, lying in central Antarctica. **2** (**south pole**) the south-seeking pole on a magnet.

southward *adv., adj.* toward the south. ▸ **southwardly** *adv., adj.* ▸ **southwards** *adv.*

southwest (ABBREV. **SW**) *noun* the direction midway between south and west. —*adj.* **1** in the southwest. **2** from the direction of the southwest.

southwester (sowth-wĕs′tər, sow-) *noun* a wind blowing from the southwest. ▸ **southwesterly** *adj., adv.*

southwestern *adj.* (ABBREV. **SW**) to the southwest.

souvenir *noun* a thing bought, kept, or given as a reminder of a place, person, or occasion.

sou'wester (sow-wĕs′tər) *noun* a sailor's waterproof hat with a large flaplike brim at the back.

sovereign (sǎv′rən) —*noun* **1** a supreme ruler or head, esp. a monarch. **2** *Brit.* a former British gold coin worth £1. —*adj.* **1** having supreme power or authority. **2** politically independent. **3** unrivaled; utmost. ▸ **sovereignty** *noun*

soviet (sō′vē-ět,, -ət) *noun* **1** any of the councils that made up the local and national governments in the former Soviet Union. **2** (**Soviet**) a native or inhabitant of the former Soviet Union. —*adj.* (**Soviet**) of the former Soviet Union.

sow¹ (sō) *verb trans.* (*pa t* **sowed**; *pa p* **sown** or **sowed**; *pr p* **sowing**) **1** to plant (seed); to plant (land) with (crops of a particular kind). **2** to introduce or arouse.

sow² (sow) *noun* an adult female hog.

soybean *noun* **1** an Asian bean grown for its edible seeds. **2** the edible seed of this plant, rich in protein and oil.

soy sauce a salty brown sauce made from soybeans.

spa *noun* **1 a** a mineral water spring. **b** a town where such a spring is or was once located. **2** a fashionable resort. **3** a health club.

space *noun* **1 a** the three-dimensional medium in which all matter exists. **b** a portion of this medium; room: *enough space for a pool*. **2** an interval of distance; a gap. **3** an empty place: *a space at our table*. **4** a period of time: *within the space of 10 minutes*. **5** the region of the universe that lies beyond the Earth's atmosphere. *Also called* **outer space**. —*verb trans.* (**spaced**, **spacing**) (*usu.* **space out**) to arrange (things) with intervals, or greater intervals, of distance or time between each.

spacecraft *noun* (*pl.* **spacecraft**) a vehicle for travel in space or for orbiting the Earth.

spaced-out *adj. slang* euphoric or dis-orientated, esp. from the effect of drugs.

space shuttle a reusable, crewed US launch vehicle, used to put a payload into space.

space station a large orbiting spacecraft designed to support crews of astronauts over periods of weeks or months.

space suit a suit designed esp. for use in space travel.

space-time continuum physical reality regarded as having four dimensions: length, breadth, height, and time.

space walk an astronaut's excursion outside a spacecraft while in space.

spacious *adj.* having ample room or space; extending over a large area. ▸ **spaciousness** *noun*

spade¹ *noun* a long-handled digging tool, pushed into the ground with the foot.

spade² *noun Cards* **1** a playing card with a black leaf-shaped emblem on it. **2** (**spades**) a suit of cards with such symbols on them.

spadework *noun* boring, preparatory work.

spadix *noun* (*pl.* **spadices**) *Bot.* a fleshy spike of flowers.

spaghetti (spə-gĕt′ē) *noun* pasta in the form of long, thin, stringlike strands.

span *noun* **1** the length between the supports of a bridge or arch. **2** a measure of length equal to the distance between the extended tips of thumb and little finger. **3** (*often in compounds*) length from end to end in distance or time: *wingspan*. —*verb trans.* (**spanned**, **spanning**) to extend across or over.

spangle *noun* a small piece of glittering material. —*verb trans., intrans.* (**spangled**, **spangling**) **1** to decorate (e.g., clothing) with spangles. **2** to glitter.

Spaniard (spăn'yərd) *noun* a native or citizen of Spain.

spaniel *noun* any of various breeds of dogs having a silky coat and long, drooping ears.

Spanish (spăn'ĭsh) *noun* **1 (the Spanish)** a native or citizen of Spain. **2** the official language of Spain. —*adj.* of Spain, its people, or their language.

Spanish-American *noun* **1** a US resident or citizen of Hispanic origin. **2** a person born or living in Spanish America. —*adj.* of Spanish America, its people, or Hispanic US residents or citizens.

Spanish moss a plant that has dense, gray, threadlike stems falling in matted clusters from the trees and shrubs on which it lives.

spank *verb trans.* (**spanked, spanking**) to smack on the buttocks, usu. as a punishment. —*noun* a smack on the buttocks.

spanking *noun* a series of spanks, esp. as a punishment. —*adv. colloq.* absolutely; strikingly: *spanking new.* —*adj. colloq.* **1** brisk. **2** impressively fine; striking.

spar[1] *noun* a strong thick pole, esp. a mast or beam on a ship.

spar[2] *verb intrans.* (**sparred, sparring**) (*often* **spar with (someone)**) **1** to engage in boxing practice with a partner; to box against an imaginary opponent for practice. **2** to engage in lively, lighthearted argument.

spare *adj.* **1** held in reserve as a replacement. **2** available for use; unoccupied: *a spare seat.* **3** lean; thin. **4** frugal; scanty. —*verb trans.* (**spared, sparing**) **1** to afford to give or give away. **2** to refrain from harming, punishing, killing, or destroying: *spare their feelings.* **3** to avoid causing or bringing on: *spare you the trouble.* **4** to avoid incurring: *no expense spared.* —*noun* a duplicate kept in reserve for use as a replacement.

spare ribs pork ribs with only a small amount of meat on them.

spare tire 1 an extra tire carried in a motor vehicle to replace a punctured one. **2** *colloq.* a band of fat just above a person's waist.

sparing *adj.* economical or frugal. ▸ **sparingly** *adv.*

spark *noun* **1** a tiny red-hot glowing particle thrown off by burning material, or by the friction between two hard surfaces. **2** an electric charge flashing across a gap between two conductors. **3** a trace, hint, or glimmer. **4** a lively, witty, or intelligent person: *a bright spark.* —*verb intrans.* (**sparked, sparking**) to throw off sparks.

sparkle *verb intrans.* (**sparkled, sparkling**) **1** to give off sparks. **2** to shine with tiny points of bright light. **3** of wine, etc. to effervesce. **4** to be impressively lively or witty. —*noun* **1** an act of sparkling; sparkling appearance. **2** liveliness; vivacity; wit.

sparkler *noun* **1** a hand-held firework that gives off sparks. **2** *colloq.* a diamond or other impressive jewel.

sparkplug *noun* in a gasoline engine, a device that ignites the explosive mixture of fuel and air in the cylinder.

sparrow *noun* any of various common small gray or brown birds.

sparse *adj.* thinly scattered or dotted about; scanty. ▸ **sparsely** *adv.* ▸ **sparseness** *noun*

spartan *adj.* **1** e.g., of living conditions harshly basic; austere; frugal. **2** militaristic. —*noun* a spartan person.

spasm *noun* **1** a sudden uncontrollable jerk caused by a contraction of the muscles. **2** a short period of activity; a spell. **3** a sudden burst of emotion: *a spasm of anger.* ▸ **spasmodic** *adj.* ▸ **spasmodically** *adv.*

spastic *noun* a person suffering from repeated muscular spasms. —*adj.* affected by such a condition.

spat[1] *see* **spit**[1].

spat[2] *colloq. noun* a trivial or petty fight or quarrel. —*verb intrans.* (**spatted, spatting**) to engage in a spat.

spat[3] *noun* either of a pair of cloth coverings fitting around the ankles and over the tops of the shoes.

spate *noun* a sudden rush or increased quantity; a burst: *a spate of complaints.*

spathe (spāth) *noun Bot.* a large petal-like bract surrounding some flower heads.

spatial *adj.* of or relating to space.

spatter *verb trans., intrans.* (**spattered, spattering**) to splash in scattered drops or patches. —*noun* **1** a quantity spattered. **2** the act of spattering.

spatula (spăch'ə-lə) *noun* a mixing or spreading tool with a broad, blunt blade.

spawn *noun* the eggs of frogs, fish, and mollusks, laid in water in a soft transparent jellylike mass. —*verb intrans., trans.* (**spawned, spawning**) **1** of frogs, fish, etc. to lay eggs. **2** to give rise to; to lead to.

spay *verb trans.* (**spayed, spaying**) to remove the ovaries from (a female animal).

SPCA *abbrev.* Society for the Prevention of Cruelty to Animals.

SPCC *abbrev.* Society of the Prevention of Cruelty to Children.

speak *verb trans., intrans.* (*pa t* **spoke**; *pa p* **spoken**; *pr p* **speaking**) **1** to utter words; to talk. **2** (*also* **speak to** *or* **with (someone)**) to talk to (someone), or to (each other). **3** to make a speech: *spoke at the convention.* **4** to communicate or to be able to communicate in (a particular language): *speaks German fluently.* **5** (**speak of (something)**) to refer to (it). —**speak out 1** to speak openly; to state one's views forcefully. **2** to speak more loudly. **speak up** to speak more loudly.

speakeasy noun (pl. **speakeasies**) slang a place selling alcohol illicitly during Prohibition.

speaker noun 1 a person who speaks, esp. one making a formal speech. 2 a loudspeaker. 3 (also **Speaker**) the person presiding over a legislative body.

spear noun 1 a weapon consisting of a long pole with a sharp point. 2 a spiky plant shoot. —verb trans. (**speared, spearing**) to pierce with or as if with a spear.

spearfish noun a marlin.

spearhead noun the leading part of an attacking force. —verb trans. (**spear-headed, spearheading**) to lead (a movement, campaign, or attack).

spearmint noun a common variety of mint plant.

special adj. 1 distinct from, esp. better than, others of the same kind. 2 designed for a particular purpose. 3 not ordinary or common: special circumstances. 4 particular; great: made a special effort. —noun a special thing or person, e.g., an extra edition of a newspaper or a train running a particular service.

special effects sound or visual effects that are added to a movie, e.g., for excitement.

Special Forces a division of the US Army made up of troops trained esp. in methods of guerrilla warfare.

specialist noun someone who specializes, esp. a physician in a specific branch of medicine or surgery.

speciality noun (pl. **specialities**) a distinctive feature.

specialize verb intrans., trans. (**specialized, specializing**) 1 (often **specialize in** (something)) to devote all one's efforts to, or reserve one's best efforts for (one particular activity, field of study, etc.). 2 to adapt for a specific purpose. ▸ **specialization** noun

specialty noun (pl. **specialties**) 1 a special skill, pursuit, or occupation. 2 a branch of medicine or surgery in which a physician has had special training. 3 a distinctive item or product: Seafood is this restaurant's specialty.

specie noun money in coin form.

species (spē'sēz, -shēz) noun (pl. **species**) 1 a group of closely related organisms able to breed together. 2 a kind or type.

specific adj. 1 of a particular nature; precisely identified. 2 precise in meaning. —noun (usu. **the specifics**) a specific detail, e.g., of a plan or scheme. ▸ **specifically** adv.

specification noun 1 (often **specifications**) a detailed description of a thing built or constructed. 2 the nature and quality of the parts that a thing is made up of: a car with a hi-tech specification. 3 the act of specifying.

specify verb trans. (**specified, specifying, specifies**) 1 to refer to or identify precisely. 2 to state as a condition or requirement.

specimen noun 1 a sample or example, esp. an object studied or put into a collection. 2 a body sample on which medical tests are carried out.

specious (spē'shəs) adj. seeming to be good, sound, or just, but really false or flawed: specious arguments. ▸ **speciousness** noun

speck noun a small spot, stain, or particle.

speckle noun a little spot, esp. one of several on a different-colored background. —verb trans. (**speckled, speckling**) to mark with speckles.

spectacle noun 1 a thing seen, esp. one that is impressive, wonderful, or ridiculous. 2 a public display or exhibition. 3 (**spectacles**) a pair of eyeglasses.

spectacular adj. 1 impressively striking to see or watch. 2 remarkable. —noun a spectacular show or display. ▸ **spectacularly** adv.

spectator noun a person who watches an event or incident. ▸ **spectate** verb intrans.

specter noun 1 a supernatural being or form. 2 a haunting fear. ▸ **spectral** adj.

spectroscope noun an instrument used to produce, observe, and analyze a spectrum for a particular chemical compound.

spectrum noun (pl. **spectra, spectrums**) 1 Phys. the band of colors produced when white light is split into its constituent wavelengths by passing it through a prism. Also called **visible spectrum**. 2 a full range.

speculate (spĕk'yə-lāt,) verb intrans. (**speculated, speculating**) 1 (often **speculate on** or **about** (something)) to consider the circumstances or possibilities regarding (it), usu. without any factual basis or a definite conclusion. 2 to engage in risky financial transactions, usu. in the hope of making a quick profit. ▸ **speculation** noun ▸ **speculative** adj. ▸ **speculator** noun

sped see **speed**.

speech noun 1 the ability to speak. 2 a way of speaking. 3 spoken language. 4 a talk addressed to other people.

speechless adj. temporarily unable to speak, because of, e.g., surprise, shock, or emotion. ▸ **speechlessly** adv. ▸ **speechlessness** noun

speed noun 1 rate of movement or action. 2 rapidity; quickness. 3 a gear setting on a vehicle: five-speed gearbox. 4 slang amphetamine. —verb intrans. (pa t and pa p **sped** or **speeded**; pr p **speeding**) 1 to move quickly. 2 to drive at a speed higher than the legal limit. ▸ **speedily** adv. ▸ **speediness** noun ▸ **speedy** adj.

speedboat noun a motorboat capable of high speeds.

speed limit the maximum legal speed on a given stretch of road.

speedometer (spĭ-dăm'ət-ər) *noun* an instrument that indicates the speed at which a motor vehicle is traveling.

speedway *noun* a track used for auto or motorcycle races.

speleology (spē,lē-äl'ə-jē) *noun* **1** the scientific study of caves. **2** cave-exploring.

spell[1] *verb trans., intrans.* (pa t and pa p **spelled** or **spelt**; pr p **spelling**) **1** to write or name the letters making up (a word or words) in their correct order. **2** to form (a word) when written in sequence: *B, A, D spells bad.* **3** to indicate clearly. ▸ **speller** *noun*

spell[2] *noun* **1** a set of words that, esp. when spoken, are believed to have magical power. **2** the influence of such power. **3** a strong attracting influence; a fascination.

spell[3] *noun* a period, e.g., of illness, work, or weather, of a particular kind.

spellbound *adj.* completely charmed, as if held by magical power; enthralled; fascinated. ▸ **spellbinding** *adj.*

spelt see **spell**[1].

spelunking (spĭ-lŭng'kĭng) *noun* the activity of exploring caves. ▸ **spelunker** *noun*

spend *verb trans., intrans.* (**spent, spending**) **1** to use up or pay out (money). **2** to use or devote (e.g., time or energy). **3** to use up completely; to exhaust.

spendthrift *noun* a person who spends money carelessly and freely.

spent *verb* see **spend.** —*adj.* used up.

sperm *noun* **1** in animals, any of the millions of fertilizing cells contained in semen. **2** semen.

spermaceti (spər,mə-sĕt'ē, -sĕt'ē) *noun* (pl. **spermacetis**) a white, translucent, waxy solid from the head of the sperm whale.

spermatozoon (spər-măt,ə-zō'än,, -ən) *noun* (pl. **spermatozoa**) a mature sperm cell.

spermicide *noun* a substance that kills sperm, used as contraception.

sperm whale the largest of the toothed whales, with an enormous head and a square snout.

SPF *abbrev.* sun protection factor.

sphagnum *noun* a moss that grows in peat bogs.

sphere (sfĭr) *noun* **1** *Math.* a round solid figure on which all surface points are an equal distance from the center; a globe or ball. **2** a field of activity. **3** range or extent: *sphere of influence.* **4** a class or group within society. ▸ **spherical** *adj.* ▸ **spherically** *adv.*

spheroid *noun Math.* a solid figure that is obtained by rotating an ellipse about either of its axes.

sphincter *noun* a ring of muscle that expands and contracts to open and close the entrance to a cavity in the body.

spice *noun* **1 a** any of numerous strong-smelling vegetable substances, e.g., pepper, ginger, and nutmeg, used to flavor food. **b** such substances collectively. **2** something that adds interest or enjoyment: *Variety is the spice of life.* —*verb trans.* (**spiced, spicing**) **1** to flavor with spice. **2** (also **spice (something) up**) to add interest or enjoyment to (it). ▸ **spicy** *adj.*

spick and span neat, clean, and tidy.

spider *noun* an eight-legged creature, some of which spin silky webs. ▸ **spidery** *adj.*

spider monkey an American tree-dwelling monkey with long thin limbs and a long tail.

spiel (shpēl) *noun colloq.* **1** a long rambling story, esp. given as an excuse. **2** plausible talk, esp. a sales pitch.

spiffy *adj.* (**spiffier, spiffiest**) *colloq.* stylish.

spigot *noun* a water faucet.

spike[1] *noun* **1** a thin sharp point. **2** a large metal nail. **3** a pointed piece of metal, e.g., on railings. **4** (**spikes**) running shoes or golf shoes with spikes on the soles. —*verb trans., intrans.* (**spiked, spiking**) **1** to strike, pierce, or impale with a pointed object. **2** *colloq.* to lace (a drink) with alcohol or a drug. ▸ **spikily** *adv.* ▸ **spikiness** *noun* ▸ **spiky** *adj.*

spike[2] *noun* a long thin flower head with small stalkless flowers along its length.

spikenard (spīk'närd,) *noun* an aromatic Indian plant with purple flowers, or an oil or ointment prepared from it.

spill[1] *verb trans., intrans.* (pa t and pa p **spilled** or **spilt**; pr p **spilling**) **1** to run or cause to run or flow out from a container, esp. accidentally. **2** to come or go in large crowds, esp. quickly. **3** to shed (blood). **4** *colloq.* to throw from a vehicle or saddle. —*noun* **1** an act of spilling. **2** *colloq.* a fall, esp. from a vehicle or horse. ▸ **spillage** *noun*

spill[2] *noun* a thin strip of wood or twisted paper for lighting a fire, candle, etc.

spillway *noun* a channel through which an excess of water, e.g., in a dam, can flow.

spilt see **spill**[1].

spin *verb trans., intrans.* (**spun, spinning**) **1** to rotate or cause to rotate repeatedly, esp. quickly. **2** to draw out and twist (fibers, etc.) into thread. **3** to construct from thread. **4** to throw or strike (a ball) so that it rotates while moving forward, causing deviation through the air or on impact. **5** to have a revolving sensation that disorientates. —*noun* **1** an act of spinning or a spinning motion. **2** rotation in a ball thrown or struck. **3** a nose-first spiral descent in an aircraft, esp. uncontrolled. **4** *colloq.* a short trip in a vehicle, for pleasure.

spinach *noun* a plant of the beet family, grown for its dark green, crinkly, or flat leaves which can be cooked and eaten as a vegetable.

spinal *adj.* of or relating to the spine.

spinal column spine (sense 1).

spinal cord a cordlike mass of nerve tissue running along the spine and connecting the brain to nerves in all other parts of the body.

spindle *noun* **1** a rod with a notched or tapered end, for twisting the thread in spinning. **2** a pin or axis on which something else turns.

spindly *adj.* (**spindlier, spindliest**) long, thin, and frail.

spindrift *noun* spray blown from the crests of waves.

spine *noun* **1** the flexible bony column of the back, consisting of a row of vertebrae connected by cartilage disks. *Also called* **spinal column**. **2** the narrow middle section of a book's cover. **3** *colloq.* strength of character; courage. ▶ **spiny** *adj.*

spineless *adj.* **1** invertebrate. **2** *colloq.* lacking courage or strength of character. ▶ **spinelessness** *noun*

spinet (spĭn′ət) *noun* a small upright piano.

spinnaker (spĭn′ə-kər) *noun* a large triangular sail at the front of a yacht.

spinner *noun* **1** an angler's lure shaped so as to spin in the water when the line is pulled. **2** a person who spins, e.g., improbable stories.

spinneret (spĭn′ə-rĕt′) *noun* a small organ in spiders and some insects from which silk is produced.

spinning wheel a device for spinning thread, consisting of a spindle driven by a hand- or foot-operated wheel.

spinoff *or* **spin-off** *noun* **1** a side effect or byproduct. **2** a thing developed from an earlier product or idea.

spinster *noun* a woman who has never been married. ▶ **spinsterhood** *noun*

spiral (spī′rəl) *noun* **1** the pattern made by a line winding outward from a central point in near-circles of ever increasing size. **2** the pattern made by a line winding downward from a point in near-circles of the same or ever increasing size, as if around a cylinder or cone. **3** a curve or course following such a pattern. **4** a gradual, continuous rise or fall, e.g., of prices. —*adj.* of the shape or nature of a spiral. —*verb intrans.* (**spiraled** *or* **spiralled, spiraling** *or* **spiralling**) to follow a spiral course or pattern. ▶ **spirally** *adv.*

spire *noun* a tall thin structure tapering upward to a point, esp. a church tower.

spirit *noun* **1** the force within a person that is or provides the will to live. **2** this force as an independent part of a person, widely believed to survive the body after death. **3** a supernatural being or form. **4** one's thoughts, concerns, etc., as opposed to one's actual presence: *there in spirit, if not in person.* **5** (*usu.* **spirits**) emotional state; mood: *in*

high spirits. **6** overall atmosphere or feeling: *entered into the spirit of the party.* **7** courage, liveliness, or vivacity. **8** the underlying essential meaning or intention as distinct from literal interpretation. **9** a distilled alcoholic liquid for drinking, e.g. gin. —*verb trans.* (**spirited, spiriting**) (*usu.* **spirit away** *or* **off**) to carry or convey (someone or something) mysteriously or magically.

spirited *adj.* **1** full of courage or liveliness. **2** (*in compounds*) showing a particular kind of spirit, mood, or attitude: *high-spirited.*

spiritual (spĭr′ĭ-chə-wəl) *adj.* **1** of or relating to the spirit or soul, rather than to the body or to physical things. **2** religious: *spiritual leaders.* —*noun* a religious song of southern African-Americans. ▶ **spirituality** *noun* ▶ **spiritually** *adv.*

spiritualism *noun* belief in or the practice of communication with the dead people through a medium. ▶ **spiritualist** *noun*

spirituous *adj.* containing alcohol.

spit[1] *verb intrans., trans.* (pa t and pa p **spat** *or* **spit**; pr p **spitting**) **1** to expel saliva from the mouth. **2** (*also* **spit out**) to force (e.g., food) out of the mouth. **3** to emit in a short explosive burst. **4** to speak or utter with hate or violence. —*noun* saliva expelled from the mouth.

spit[2] *noun* **1** a long thin metal rod on which meat is skewered and held over a fire for roasting. **2** a long narrow strip of land jutting out into the sea.

spite *noun* **1** wishing that distress, injury, or pain will befall another. **2** malicious action or behavior. —*verb trans.* (**spited, spiting**) to annoy or offend intentionally. —**in spite of** regardless of or in opposition to (someone or something). ▶ **spiteful** *adj.* ▶ **spitefully** *adv.* ▶ **spitefulness** *noun*

spittle *noun* saliva.

spittoon *noun* a container in which to spit.

splash *verb trans., intrans.* (**splashed, splashing**) **1** to cause large drops of (a liquid) to be thrown about. **2** of such a substance to fly around or land in large drops. **3** to make wet or dirty with such drops. —*noun* **1** a sound of splashing. **2** an amount splashed. **3** a stain made by splashing. **4** an irregular spot or patch.

splashdown *noun* a landing at sea of a space capsule and its parts.

splat *noun* the sound made by a soft, wet object striking a surface. —*adv.* with this sound: *fell splat on the floor.*

splatter *verb trans., intrans.* (**splattered, splattering**) to splash with or in small scattered drops. —*noun* a splashing sound, esp. when repeated or continuous.

splay *verb trans.* (**splayed, splaying, splays**) to spread (e.g., the fingers).

spleen noun **1** an abdominal organ that purifies the blood. **2** bad temper. ▸ **splenic** or **splenetic** adj.

splendid adj. **1** impressively grand or sumptuous. **2** excellent. ▸ **splendidly** adv. ▸ **splendor** noun

splendiferous (splĕn-dĭf'ə-rəs) adj. colloq. splendid.

splice verb trans. (**spliced, splicing**) **1** to join (two pieces of rope) by weaving strands together. **2** to join (two pieces of film, magnetic tape, etc.) end to end. —noun a join made like this.

splint noun a piece of wood strapped to a broken body part to hold it in position while the bone heals.

splinter noun a small, thin, sharp piece of broken wood, glass, etc. —verb trans., intrans. (**splintered, splintering**) to break into pieces.

split verb trans., intrans. (**split, splitting**) **1** to break or cause to break apart or into pieces, esp. lengthwise. **2** to become or cause to become disunited. **3** (also **split up**) to break or cause (people) to break away from each other through disagreement. **4** slang to go away or leave. —noun **1** a lengthwise break or crack. **2** a separation or division through disagreement.

split-level adj. consisting of more than one level: a split-level brick house.

split pea a dried pea split in half, used in soups and stews.

split second a fraction of a second. ▸ **split-second** adj.

splitting adj., of a headache intense; severe.

splurge noun a spending spree; extravagance. —verb trans., intrans. (**splurged, splurging**) to spend extravagantly.

splutter verb intrans., trans. (**spluttered, spluttering**) **1** to make spitting sounds and throw out drops of liquid, sparks, etc. **2** to speak or say haltingly or incoherently. —noun an act or noise of spluttering.

spoil verb (pa t and pa p **spoiled** or **spoilt**; pr p **spoiling**) **1** to impair, ruin, or make useless or valueless. **2** to make selfish and unable to accept hardship or disappointment by excessive indulgence: spoiled their child. **3** of food to become unfit to eat. —noun (**spoils**) **1** possessions taken by force; plunder. **2** benefits or rewards.

spoilsport noun colloq. a person who spoils, or refuses to join into, the fun of others.

spoilt see spoil.

spoke[1] see speak.

spoke[2] noun any of the radiating rods or bars attaching the rim of a wheel to its center.

spoken verb see speak. —adj. **1** uttered or expressed in speech. **2** (in compounds) speaking in a particular way: soft-spoken.

spokesperson, spokesman, or **spokeswoman** noun a person appointed to speak on behalf of others or of a government, business, etc.

spoliation noun an act or instance of robbing or plundering.

sponge (spənj') noun **1 a** a primitive sea creature with a soft porous skeleton. **b** the soft porous skeleton of this animal. **c** a piece of this material, or a similar synthetic material, used for absorbing moisture and cleansing surfaces. **2** an act of cleaning with a sponge. **3** a sponge cake or pudding. **4** a person who depends upon others for financial and other assistance. Also called **sponger**. —verb trans., intrans. (**sponged, sponging**) **1** to wash or clean with a sponge and water. **2** (**sponge off (someone)**) to live by taking advantage of (others' generosity). ▸ **spongy** adj.

sponge cake a very light cake.

sponsor noun **1** a person or organization that finances an event or broadcast in return for advertising. **2** a person who promises a sum of money to a participant in a forthcoming event. **3** a godparent. —verb trans. (**sponsored, sponsoring**) to act as a sponsor for. ▸ **sponsorship** noun

spontaneous (spän-tā'nē-əs) adj. **1** activated or acting without any prior thought or deliberation. ▣ IMPULSIVE, INSTINCTIVE, INVOLUNTARY ▣ DELIBERATE, PLANNED, PREMEDITATED. **2** occurring naturally or by itself; not caused or influenced from outside. **3** of a manner or style not affected or studied; natural. ▸ **spontaneity** noun

spontaneous combustion the catching fire of a substance as a result of heat generated within it, not applied from outside.

spoof colloq. noun **1** a satirical imitation. **2** a lighthearted hoax. —verb trans. (**spoofed, spoofing**) to subject to a spoof.

spook colloq. noun a supernatural being or form. —verb trans. (**spooked, spooking**) to frighten or startle. ▸ **spooky** adj.

spool noun a small cylinder on which thread, photographic film, tape, etc. is wound.

spoon noun **1** a utensil with a handle and a round or oval shallow bowl-like part, for eating, serving, or stirring food. **2** the amount a spoon will hold. —verb trans., intrans. (**spooned, spooning**) to lift (food) with a spoon. ▸ **spoonful** noun

spoonbill noun a large wading bird.

spoonerism noun a slip in speech where the first sounds of a pair of words are reversed, as in shoving leopard for loving shepherd.

spoon-feed verb trans. **1** to feed (e.g., a baby) with a spoon. **2** to supply (someone) with everything needed or required, making any personal effort unnecessary.

spoor *noun* the track or scent left by an animal.

sporadic *adj.* occurring from time to time, at irregular intervals. ▸ **sporadically** *adv.*

spore *noun* a reproductive structure from which a new organism develops without the need for fusion with another cell.

sport *noun* **1** an activity or competition designed to test physical skills. **b** (*also* **sports**) such activities collectively. **2** good-humored fun: *did it in sport.* **3** *colloq.* a person who cheerfully accepts defeat, inconvenience, or being the butt of jokes: *a good sport.* —*verb trans.* (**sported, sporting**) to wear or display, esp. proudly. ▸ **sporty** *adj.*

sporting *adj.* **1** of or relating to sports. **2** having or displaying fairness or generosity of character. ▸ **sportingly** *adv.*

sportive *adj.* marked by or given to lively playfulness.

sportscast *noun* a broadcast of a sports event or of sporting news. ▸ **sportscaster** *noun*

sportsman *noun* **1** a man who takes part in sports or a sport. **2** a person who plays fair and accepts defeat cheerfully. ▸ **sportsman-like** *adj.* ▸ **sportsmanship** *noun*

sportswoman *noun* **1** a woman who takes part in sports or a sport. **2** a woman who plays fair and accepts defeat cheerfully.

spot *noun* **1** a small mark or stain. **2** a drop of liquid. **3** a small amount, esp. of liquid. **4** an eruption on the skin; a pimple. **5** a place: *a quiet spot.* —*verb trans., intrans.* (**spotted, spotting**) **1** to mark or dirty with spots. **2** to catch sight of. —**on the spot 1** immediately and often without warning: *was fined on the spot.* **2** in an awkward situation, esp. one requiring immediate action or response. ▸ **spottiness** *noun* ▸ **spotty** *adj.*

spot check an inspection made at random and without warning.

spotless *adj.* absolutely clean; unblemished. ▸ **spotlessly** *adv.* ▸ **spotlessness** *noun*

spotlight *noun* **1** a concentrated circle of light on a small area, esp. of a theater stage; also, a lamp casting this light. **2** (**the spotlight**) the attention or gaze of others; public scrutiny. —*verb trans.* (*pa t and pa p* **spotlighted** or **spotlit**; *pr p* **spotlighting**) **1** to illuminate with a spotlight. **2** to direct attention to; to highlight.

spotter *noun* a person who spots, e.g., military targets from an aircraft.

spouse (spows) *noun* a husband or wife.

spout *noun* **1** a projecting tube or lip through which liquid flows or is poured. **2** a jet or stream of liquid. —*verb intrans., trans.* (**spouted, spouting**) **1** to flow or cause to flow out in a jet or stream. **2** to speak or say, esp. at length and boringly.

sprain *verb trans.* (**sprained, spraining**) to injure (a ligament) by sudden overstretching or tearing. —*noun* such an injury.

sprang *see* **spring.**

sprat *noun* a small edible fish of the herring family.

sprawl *verb intrans.* (**sprawled, sprawling**) **1** to sit, lie, or fall lazily with the arms and legs spread out wide. **2** to spread or extend in an irregular, messy way. —*noun* **1** a sprawling position. **2** haphazard urban expansion.

spray[1] *noun* **1** a fine mist of small flying drops of liquid. **2** a device for dispensing a liquid as a mist; an atomizer or aerosol. —*verb trans.* (**sprayed, spraying**) **1** to apply or dispense (a liquid) in a fine mist of droplets. **2** to apply a spray to. **3** to subject to a heavy stream: *sprayed the car with bullets.*

spray[2] *noun* a small branch of a tree or plant with leaves and flowers attached, used for decoration.

spread[2] *verb trans., intrans.* (*pa t and pa p* **spread**; *pr p* **spreading**) **1** to apply or to be capable of being applied in a smooth coating over a surface. **2** (*also* **spread (something) out**) to extend or cause (it) to extend or scatter, often more widely or more thinly. **3** (*also* **spread (something) out**) to open (it) out or unfold (it). **4** to transmit or be transmitted or distributed: *spread rumors.* —*noun* **1** the act or extent of spreading. **2** a food in paste form, e.g., for spreading on bread. **3** a pair of facing pages in a newspaper or magazine. **4** *colloq.* a lavish meal.

spread-eagled *adj.* with arms and legs stretched wide.

spreadsheet *noun* a computer program that enables numerical data to be entered and displayed in a table of rows and columns.

spree *noun* a period of extravagance or excess, esp. in spending money or drinking alcohol.

sprier, spriest *see* **spry.**

sprig *noun* a small shoot or twig.

sprightly *adj.* lively and quickly moving; brisk. ▸ **sprightliness** *noun*

spring *verb intrans., trans.* (*pa t* **sprang** or **sprung**; *pa p* **sprung**; *pr p* **springing**) **1** to leap with a sudden quick launching action. **2** to move suddenly and swiftly by elastic force. **3** (*also* **spring up**) to appear or come into being suddenly. **4** to develop or originate. **5** (**spring something on** (**someone**)) to present or reveal it suddenly and un-expectedly. —*noun* **1** a metal coil that can be stretched or compressed, and returns to its original shape when released. **2** a place from which water emerges from underground. **3** (*also* **Spring**) the season between winter and summer. **5** the ability of a material to return rapidly to its original shape after a distorting force has been removed. ▶ **springy** adj. ▶ **springiness** noun

springboard noun **1** a board that springs up after being jumped on, used by divers and gymnasts as a launching device. **2** something that serves to get things moving.

spring-cleaning noun a thorough cleaning of a house, traditionally carried out in spring. ▶ **spring-clean** verb trans., intrans.

spring tide a tidal pattern that occurs twice a month, when the difference in level between high and low tides is greatest.

springtime noun the season of spring.

sprinkle verb trans. (**sprinkled, sprinkling**) **1** to scatter in tiny drops or particles. **2** to arrange or distribute in a thin scattering. ▶ **sprinkler** noun ▶ **sprinkling** noun.

sprint noun **1** a race at high speed over a short distance. **2** a burst of speed, e.g., at the end of a long race. —verb trans., intrans. (**sprinted, sprinting**) to run at full speed. ▶ **sprinter** noun

sprite noun Folklore an elf or imp.

spritzer noun white wine and soda water.

sprocket noun **1** any of a set of teeth on the rim of a driving wheel, e.g., fitting into the links of a chain or the holes on a strip of film. **2** a wheel with a set of such teeth.

sprout verb trans., intrans. (**sprouted, sprouting**) **1** to develop (a new growth, e.g., of leaves or hair). **2** (also **sprout up**) to grow or develop; to spring up. —noun **1** a shoot or bud. **2** a Brussels sprout.

spruce[1] noun a coniferous evergreen tree.

spruce[2] adj. neat and smart, esp. in appearance and dress.

sprung see spring.

spry adj. (**sprier** or **spryer, spriest** or **spryest**) **1** lively; active. **2** light on one's feet; nimble. ▶ **spryly** adv. ▶ **spryness** noun

spud noun colloq. a potato.

spume (spyo͞om) noun foam or froth. —verb intrans. (**spumed, spuming**) to make spume. ▶ **spumy** adj.

spun see spin.

spunk noun colloq. courage. ▶ **spunky** adj.

spur noun **1** a device with a spiky metal wheel, fitted to the heel of a riding boot, dug into a horse's side to make it go faster. **2** something that encourages greater effort or progress. **3** a spiked part, e.g., on a rooster's leg. **4** a ridge of high land that projects into a valley. —verb trans. (**spurred, spurring**) (usu. **spur** (someone) **on**) to urge (someone) on.

spurge noun a plant producing a bitter, often poisonous, milky juice.

spurious adj. **1** false. **2** based on false or mistaken reasoning. ▶ **spuriously** adv.

spurn verb trans. (**spurned, spurning**) to reject (e.g., a person's love) scornfully.

spurt verb intrans., trans. (**spurted, spurting**) to flow out or cause to flow out in a sudden sharp jet. —noun **1** a jet of liquid suddenly flowing out. **2** a short spell of intensified activity or increased speed.

sputter verb intrans., trans. (**sputtered, sputtering**) **1** to spit out food particles noisily. **2** to spit out (words or expressions) rapidly. **3** to make a popping sound. —noun an act or sound of sputtering.

sputum (spyo͞ot'əm) noun (pl. **sputa**) saliva mixed with mucus that is coughed up from the bronchial passages. Also called **phlegm**.

spy noun (pl. **spies**) **1** a person employed to secretly gather information. **2** a person observing others in secret. —verb (**spied, spying, spies**) **1** (also **spy on**) to act as a spy. **2** to see or spot: spied land.

spyglass noun a small telescope.

spyhole noun a peephole.

sq. abbrev. square.

squab noun a young unfledged bird.

squabble verb intrans. (**squabbled, squabbling**) to quarrel noisily, esp. about something trivial. —noun a noisy, esp. petty quarrel.

squad noun **1** a group of soldiers or police officers. **2** a group of people working together. **3** the players on a sports team.

squad car a police car; a cruiser.

squadron noun **1** the basic aviation unit of the US Air Force, Navy, Marine Corps, and Army. **2** an organization made up of two or more divisions of ships, or two or more Navy divisions or flights of aircraft.

squalid adj. **1** disgustingly filthy and neglected. **2** morally repulsive; sordid. ▶ **squalor** noun

squall (skwôl) noun **1** Meteorol. a storm with sudden, short-lived, violent gusts of wind. **2** a loud cry; a yell. —verb trans., intrans. (**squalled, squalling**) **1** to yell. **2** of a wind to blow in a squall. ▶ **squally** adj.

squamous (skwā'məs) adj. **1** covered with scales; scaly. **2** looking like a scale in flatness.

squander verb trans. (**squandered, squandering**) to use up (money, resources, etc.) wastefully.

square noun **1 a** Geom. a two-dimensional figure with four sides of equal length and four right angles. **b** something shaped like this figure. **2** an open space in a city or town, usu. roughly square-shaped. **3** an L-shaped or T-shaped instrument with which angles can be measured or straight lines drawn. **4** Math. the figure produced when a number is multiplied by itself. **5** colloq. a person with traditional or old-fashioned values or tastes. —adj. **1** shaped in such a way as to have four sides of equal length and four right angles. **2** measured in length and breadth; of an area equal to a square whose sides are the stated length: *One room is 30 feet square.* **3** measuring almost the same in breadth as in length or height: *a man with a square build.* **4** fair; honest: *a square deal.* **5** (**all square**) with each side owing nothing; equal. **6** *colloq.* having traditional or old-fashioned values or tastes. —*verb trans.* (**squared, squaring**) **1** to make square in shape, esp. to make right-angled. **2** to multiply (a number) by itself. **3** (*also* **square up** *or* **square** (**something**) **up**) to pay off or settle a debt. **4** to make the scores (in a match) level. **5** (**square something with someone**) to get someone's approval or permission for it. **6** (**square with** (**something**)) to agree or correspond with (it). —*adv.* **1** in a solid, direct, manner: *hit me square on the jaw.* **2** in a fair, honest manner. ▸ **squarely** *adv.*

square bracket either of a pair of printed brackets [].

square dance a folk dance performed by couples in a square formation.

square meal a good, nourishing meal.

square root *Math.* a number that when multiplied by itself gives a particular number.

squash¹ *verb trans., intrans.* (**squashed, squashing**) **1 a** to act upon by steady thrusting force. **b** to crush or flatten by pressing or squeezing. **2** to force one's body into a confined space. —*noun* **1** a crushed or crowded state. **2** a racket game for two players in a walled indoor court. ▸ **squashy** *adj.*

squash² *noun* (*pl.* **squash**) a marrowlike vegetable of the cucumber family.

squat *verb intrans.* (**squatted, squatting**) **1** to take up, or be sitting in, a low position with the knees fully bent and the weight on the soles of the feet. **2** to occupy an empty building without legal right. —*noun* **1** a squatting position. **2** an empty building unlawfully occupied. —*adj.* short, broad, and sometimes portly. ▸ **squatter** *noun*

squaw *noun offensive* a Native American woman or wife.

squawk *noun* **1** a high-pitched croaking cry, like that of a parrot. **2** a loud protest or complaint. —*verb intrans.* (**squawked, squawking**) **1** to make a high-pitched croaking cry. **2** to complain loudly. ▸ **squawker** *noun* ▸ **squawky** *adj.*

squeak *noun* **1** a short high-pitched cry or sound. **2** (*also* **close squeak**) a narrow escape; a victory or success achieved by the slimmest of margins. —*verb trans., intrans.* (**squeaked, squeaking**) to utter a squeak or to say (something) with a squeak. ▸ **squeakiness** *noun* ▸ **squeaky** *adj.*

squeal *noun* a long high-pitched cry or yelp. —*verb trans., intrans.* (**squealed, squeal-**

ing) **1** to utter a squeal or with a squeal. **2** *colloq.* to inform or tell tales. **3** to complain or protest loudly. ▸ **squealer** *noun*

squeamish *adj.* **1** slightly nauseous. **2** easily made nauseous.

squeegee *noun* a device with a rubber blade for scraping water off a surface.

squeeze *verb trans., intrans.* (**squeezed, squeezing**) **1** to grasp or embrace tightly. **2** to press forcefully, esp. from at least two sides. **3** to press or crush so as to extract (e.g., juice); to extract (e.g., juice) by pressing or crushing. **4** to force one's body into or through a confined space. —*noun* **1** an act of squeezing. **2** a crowded or crushed state. **3** an amount of fruit juice, etc., obtained by squeezing. ▸ **squeezer** *noun*

squelch *noun* a loud gurgling or sucking sound made by contact with a thick sticky substance, e.g., wet mud. —*verb intrans., trans.* (**squelched, squelching**) **1** to make a loud gurgling or sucking sound. **2** to silence (another person or a topic of conversation), usu. by a forceful comment.

squib *noun* **1** a small jumping firework. **2** a satirical criticism or attack; a lampoon.

squid *noun* (*pl.* **squid, squids**) a marine mollusk with a long rounded body and ten trailing tentacles surrounding the mouth.

squiggle *noun* a wavy scribbled line. ▸ **squiggle** *verb trans., intrans.* ▸ **squiggly** *adv.*

squint *noun* **1** *Med.* the condition of having one or both eyes set slightly off-center. **2** *colloq.* a quick look; a peep. —*verb intrans.* (**squinted, squinting**) **1** to be affected by a squint. **2** to look with eyes half-closed; to peer.

squirm *verb intrans.* (**squirmed, squirming**) **1** to wriggle. **2** to feel or show embarrassment, shame, or nervousness. —*noun* a squirming movement.

squirrel (skwər'əl) *noun* **1** a tree-dwelling rodent, with gray or reddish-brown fur and a large bushy tail. **2** an animal of the squirrel family, e.g., a chipmunk or woodchuck.

squirt *verb trans., intrans.* (**squirted, squirting**) to shoot out or cause (a liquid) to shoot out in a narrow jet. —*noun* **1** an act of squirting or an amount of liquid squirted. **2** *colloq.* a small or insignificant person.

squish *noun* a gentle splashing or squelching sound. —*verb trans.* (**squished, squishing**) to make, or move with, this sound.

Sr *symbol Chem.* strontium.

Sr. *abbrev.* **1** (*used after a name*) Senior. **2** (*used before the name of a nun*) Sister.

SSA *abbrev.* Social Security Administration.

SSI *abbrev.* Supplemental Security Income.

St. *abbrev.* **1** saint (sense 1). **2** Street.

st. abbrev. stone (the unit of weight).

stab verb trans., intrans. (**stabbed, stabbing**) **1** to wound or pierce with a pointed instrument or weapon. **2** (**stab at (something)**) to make a quick thrusting movement toward (it) with a sharp object. **3** to produce a sharp piercing sensation. —noun **1** an act of stabbing. **2** a stabbing sensation. **3** colloq. a try.

stabilize verb trans., intrans. (**stabilized, stabilizing**) to make or become stable or more stable. ▸ **stabilization** noun ▸ **stabilizer** noun

stable[1] adj. **1** firmly balanced or fixed. **2** unlikely to be abolished or overthrown. **3** regular or constant: The patient's condition is stable. ▸ **stability** noun

stable[2] noun **1** a building in which horses are kept. **2** a place where horses are bred and trained.

staccato (stə-kät'ō) adj., adv. **1** Mus. with notes played as a series of short, abrupt, audibly separate units. **2** with, or consisting of, a series of short distinct sounds.

stack noun **1** a large, neat pile of hay or straw. **2** any large, neat pile. **3** (usu. **a stack of** or **stacks of something**) colloq. a large amount. **4** a smokestack. —verb trans. (**stacked, stacking**) **1** to arrange in stacks or a stack. **2** to prearrange (playing cards) in a pack so as to allow cheating.

stadium noun (pl. **stadiums, stadia**) a large sports arena.

staff noun **1** (pl. **staffs**) the employees working in an establishment or organization. **2** (pl. **staffs**) the employees working for or assisting a manager. **3** (pl. **staffs** or **staves**) a stick or rod carried in the hand. **4** (pl. **staffs** or **staves**) Mus. a set of lines and spaces on which music is written. —verb trans. (**staffed, staffing**) to provide (an establishment) with staff.

stag noun an adult male deer. —adj. of or for men only; male.

stage noun **1** a platform on which a performance takes place. **2** (**the stage**) the theater as a profession or art form. **3** any of several distinct and successive periods. **4** a part of a journey or route. **5** a stagecoach. —verb trans. (**staged, staging**) **1** to present as a performance; to present a performance of (a play). **2** to prearrange to happen in a particular way. **3** to organize or hold as an event.

stagecoach noun a large horse-drawn coach formerly carrying passengers and mail on regular fixed routes.

stagger verb intrans., trans. (**staggered, staggering**) **1** to walk or move unsteadily. **2** to cause extreme shock or surprise to. **3** to arrange to take place or begin at different times. —noun an act of staggering.

staging noun **1** a temporary platform. **2** the act or process of putting on a play or other spectacle.

stagnant adj. **1** of water not flowing. **2** of water dirty and foul-smelling because of not flowing. **3** not moving or developing: a stagnant economy.

stagnate (stăg'nāt,) verb intrans. (**stagnated, stagnating**) to be or become stagnant. ▸ **stagnation** noun

stagy adj. (**stagier, stagiest**) artificial or affected; theatrical. ▸ **staginess** noun

staid adj. serious or sober in character or manner, esp. to the point of being dull.

stain verb trans., intrans. (**stained, staining**) **1** to make or become marked or discolored, often permanently. **2** to change the color of (e.g., wood) by applying a liquid chemical. —noun **1** a mark or discoloration. **2** a liquid chemical applied (e.g., to wood) to bring about a change of color. **3** a cause of shame or dishonor: a stain on his reputation.

stained glass decorative colored glass used esp. in church windows.

stainless steel an alloy of chromium and steel which is highly resistant to corrosion.

stair noun **1** any of a set of indoor steps connecting the floors of a building. **2** (also **stairs**) a set of these indoor steps.

staircase noun a set of stairs, often including the stairwell. Also called **stairway**.

stairwell noun the vertical shaft containing a staircase. Also called **well**.

stake[1] noun **1** a stick or post, usu. with one end pointed, knocked into the ground as a support. **2** (**the stake**) Hist. a post to which a person was tied to be burned alive as a punishment; the punishment itself. —verb trans. (**staked, staking**) to support or fasten to the ground with a stake. —**stake a claim** to assert or establish a right or ownership.

stake[2] noun **1** a sum of money risked in betting. **2** (**stakes**) a prize, esp. in horseracing. **3** a claim to a business and its profits or to a part of these. —verb trans. (**staked, staking**) **1** to risk as a bet. **2** to give, esp. financial, support to. —**at stake 1** to be won or lost. **2** at risk; in danger.

stakeout noun colloq. a period of undercover surveillance.

stalactite noun an iciclelike mass of limestone attached to the roof of a cave, etc.

stalagmite noun a spiky mass of limestone sticking up from the floor of a cave, etc.

stale adj. **1** of food not fresh; dry and unpalatable. **2** of air musty. **3** lacking freshness and originality, usu. through overuse. **4** out of condition due to overtraining or overstudy. ▸ **staleness** noun

stalemate (stāl'māt,) *noun* a position, in any contest or dispute, from which no progress can be made nor winner emerge; a deadlock.

Stalinism *noun Hist.* the repressive form of rule in the former Soviet Union from 1929–53. ▸ **Stalinist** *noun, adj.*

stalk[1] (stôk) *noun* **1** the main stem of a plant, or the stem that attaches a leaf, flower, or fruit to the plant. **2** a slender connecting part.

stalk[2] *verb trans.* (**stalked, stalking**) **1 a** to hunt stealthily. **b** to follow (another person) persistently and stealthily with the intent to harass, frighten, or injure. **2** to walk or stride stiffly or proudly. ▸ **stalker** *noun*

stall[1] *verb trans., intrans.* (**stalled, stalling**) to delay. —*noun* an act of stalling.

stall[2] *noun* **1** a compartment for a single animal, e.g., in a stable. **2** a platform or stand on which goods or services for sale are displayed or advertised. **3** a church seat with arms. —*verb trans., intrans.* (**stalled, stalling**) *of a motor vehicle or its engine* to cut out or cause it to cut out unintentionally.

stallion *noun* an uncastrated adult male horse.

stalwart (stôl'wərt) *adj.* **1** strong and sturdy. **2** unwavering in commitment and support; reliable. —*noun* a stalwart supporter.

stamen *noun* (*pl.* **stamens, stamina**) *Bot.* the male reproductive structure in a flower.

stamina *noun* the ability or energy to withstand prolonged physical or mental exertion.

stammer *noun* the inability to utter certain speech sounds at the beginning of words, resulting in a repetition of the sound; the resulting repetition. —*verb trans., intrans.* (**stammered, stammering**) to speak or say with a stammer.

stamp *verb trans., intrans.* (**stamped, stamping**) **1** to bring (the foot) down with force. **2** to walk with a heavy tread. **3** to imprint or impress (a mark or design); to imprint or impress (something) with a mark or design. **4** to fix or mark deeply. **5** to prove to be; to characterize. **6** to paste or put a postage or other stamp on. —*noun* **1** a small piece of gummed paper bearing an official mark and indicating that a fee or tax has been paid. **2 a** an instrument for stamping a mark or design; the mark or design stamped. **b** a mark produced by or as if by pressure. ▣ IMPRESSION, IMPRINT. **3** an act of stamping the foot.

stampede (stăm-pēd') *noun* **1** a sudden wild rush of animals, esp. when alarmed. **2** an excited or hysterical rush by a crowd of people. —*verb intrans.* (**stampeded, stampeding**) to rush in a herd or crowd.

stance *noun* **1** position or manner of standing. **2** point of view.

stanch *or* **staunch** (stônch, stänch) *verb trans.* (**stanched, stanching**) to stop the flow of (esp. blood from a wound).

stanchion (stăn'chən) *noun* an upright beam or pole serving as a support.

stand *verb intrans., trans.* (**stood, standing**) **1** (*also* **stand up**) to be in or to move into an upright position supported by the legs or a base. **2** to place or situate or to be placed or situated. **3** to be a particular height: *The tower stands 300 feet tall.* **4** to tolerate or put up with. **5** to be in a particular state or condition: *I stand corrected.* **6** to be in a position (to do something): *We stand to make a lot of money.* **7** to continue to apply or be valid: *The decision stands.* **8** (**stand for** (something)) of a symbol or device to represent or signify (it). **9** to withstand or survive: *stood the test of time.* —*noun* **1** a base on which something is supported. **2** a stall displaying or advertising goods or services for sale. **3** (*often* **stands**) a structure with sitting or standing accommodation for spectators. **4** a rack or other device on which coats, hats, umbrellas, etc., may be hung. **5** an attitude or course of action resolutely adopted: *a stand for peace.* —**stand out** to be noticeable or prominent. **stand up 1** to assume a standing position. **2** to prove to be valid on examination: *an argument that will not stand up.* **stand up for** (someone *or* something) to be outspoken in one's support for or defense of (the one or ones specified). **stand up to** (someone *or* something) to face or resist (e.g., an opponent); to withstand (e.g., hard wear or criticism).

standard *noun* **1** an established or accepted model; a thing with which others are compared so as to be measured or judged. **2** a level of excellence, value, or quality. **3** (*often* **standards**) a principle of behavior or morality adhered to. **4** a flag or other emblem, esp. one carried on a pole. —*adj.* **1** of the normal or accepted kind, without variations or additions. **2** typical; average; unexceptional.

standard-bearer *noun* **1** a person carrying a flag. **2** the leader of a movement or cause.

standardize *verb trans.* (**standardized, standardizing**) to make (all examples) uniform in kind, size, shape, etc.

standby *noun* **1** a state of readiness to act, e.g., in an emergency. **2** a person or thing in this role. —*adj. of air travel* with any spare seats allocated to waiting passengers after the reserved seats have been taken. —*adv.* on a standby basis.

standee (stăn-dē') *noun* a person using standing room, e.g., in a theater.

stand-in noun a substitute, e.g., for a lead performer.

standing noun **1 a** position, status, or reputation. **b** elevated professional or social position. **2** duration: of long standing. —adj. **1** done, taken, etc., in or from a standing position: a standing ovation. **2** regularly used: a standing joke.

standoff noun a draw in, e.g., a contest or a battle.

standoffish adj. unfriendly; aloof. ▸ **standoffishly** adv. ▸ **standoffishness** noun

standpipe noun a vertical water pipe, esp. one providing an emergency supply.

standpoint noun a point of view.

standstill noun a complete stop.

stank see **stink**.

stanza noun Poetry a verse.

stapes (stā'pēz) noun (pl. **stapes**) a small stirrup-shaped bone in the middle ear.

staple¹ noun **1** a U-shaped wire fastener for paper. **2** a U-shaped metal nail. —verb trans. (**stapled, stapling**) to fasten or attach with a staple or staples. ▸ **stapler** noun

staple² adj. **1** principal; main: staple foods. **2** of principal importance as a traded article. —noun a staple product or ingredient.

star noun **1 a** a celestial body consisting of a sphere of gaseous material. **b** any celestial body visible at night. **c** a figure with five or more radiating points, often used as a symbol of rank or excellence. **2 a** a celebrity, esp. from the entertainment world. **b** a principal performer. —verb trans., intrans. (**starred, starring**) **1** to feature or appear as a principal performer. **2** to decorate with stars. ▸ **starry** adj.

starboard (stär'bərd) noun the right side of a ship or aircraft, when facing forward. —adj., adv. of, on, or toward the right side.

starch noun **1** a carbohydrate that occurs in all green plants. **2** a preparation of this substance used to stiffen cloth and to make paper. **3** stiffness of manner; excessive formality. —verb trans. (**starched, starching**) to stiffen with starch. ▸ **starchily** adv. ▸ **starchiness** noun ▸ **starchy** adj.

stardom noun the state of being a celebrity.

stare verb intrans., trans. (**stared, staring**) to look or to look at with a fixed gaze. —noun **1** an act of staring. **2** a fixed gaze.

starfish noun (pl. **starfish, starfishes**) a marine animal with usu. five radiating arms.

stargazer noun colloq. **1** facetious an astronomer or astrologer. **2** a daydreamer.

stark adj. **1** severely bare, harsh, or simple. **2** plain; unembellished: the stark truth. **3** utter; downright.. —adv. to a complete degree; utterly.

starlet noun a young actress, esp. in the movies, regarded as a future star.

starlight noun light from the stars.

starling noun a small common songbird with dark glossy speckled feathers and a short tail.

starlit adj. illuminated by the stars.

starry-eyed adj. **1** overly idealistic or optimistic. **2** radiantly happy or affectionate.

Stars and Stripes (sing., pl.) (**the Stars and Stripes**) the US national flag.

star-studded adj. colloq., featuring many well-known performers.

start verb trans., intrans. **1** to bring or come into being; to begin. **2** (also **start (something) up**) to set or be set in motion, or to put or be put into a working state. **3** (also **start off** or **out**) to be at first. **4** (also **start (something) up**) to establish (it) or set (it) up. **5** (also **start (something) off**) to initiate (it) or get (it) going; to cause or set off. **6** to flinch or shrink back suddenly and sharply, e.g., in surprise. —noun **1** the first or early part. **2** a beginning, origin, or cause. **3** the time or place at which something starts. **4** a sudden flinching or shrinking back. ▸ **starter** noun

startle verb trans. (**startled, startling**) **1** to give a sudden fright to. **2** to surprise.

starve verb trans., intrans. (**starved, starving**) **1** to suffer or cause to suffer extreme ill-health or death, through lack of food. **2** colloq. to be very hungry. **3** (**starve (something or someone) of (something)**) to cause (the one specified) to suffer a severe lack of (something): starved the project of funds. ▸ **starvation** noun

stash slang verb trans. (**stashed, stashing**) to put into a hiding place. —noun a hidden supply or store, or its hiding place.

state noun **1** the condition, e.g., of health, appearance, or emotions, in which a person or thing exists. **2** a territory governed by a single political body; a nation. **3** any of a number of locally governed areas making up a nation or federation under the ultimate control of a central government. **4** (often **State** or **the State**) the political entity of a nation, including the government, the civil service, etc. **5** colloq. an emotionally agitated condition. —adj. **1** relating to, controlled by, or financed by a state: state matters. **2** ceremonial: a state visit by a monarch. —verb trans. (**stated, stating**) to express clearly; to affirm or assert: state an opinion. ▸ **statehood** noun

statecraft noun the governing of a nation.

stateless adj. having no nationality or citizenship. ▸ **statelessness** noun

stately adj. (**statelier, stateliest**) noble, dignified, and impressive in appearance or manner. ▸ **stateliness** noun

statement noun **1** the act of stating. **2** a thing stated, esp. a formal written or spoken declaration. **3** a record sent by a bank to an account holder detailing the holder's transactions within a particular period.

state-of-the-art adj. most modern and best.

stateroom noun a private cabin on a ship.

stateside colloq. adj. of or in the USA. —adv. to or toward the USA.

statesman noun an experienced, distinguished male politician. ▸ **statesmanlike** adj.

statesmanship noun the skill of a statesman or stateswoman.

stateswoman noun an experienced, distinguished, female politician.

static adj. **1** not moving; stationary. **2** not portable; fixed. **3** tending not to move around or change. **4** relating to statics. —noun **1** an accumulation of electric charges that remain at rest instead of moving to form a flow of current. *Also called* **static electricity**. **2** a sharp crackling or hissing sound that interferes with radio and television signals. **3** slang argumentation; criticism.

station noun **1** a stopping point for passenger trains or buses. **2** a local headquarters, e.g., of a police force. **3** a radio or television channel or network affiliate, or the buildings from which broadcasts are transmitted. **4** a position within a class structure: of high social station. **5** a post or place of duty, esp. military or police duty. —verb trans. (**stationed, stationing**) to appoint to a post or place of duty.

stationary (stā'shə-nĕr,ē) adj. **1** not moving; still. **2** not changing.

stationer noun a person or store that sells stationery.

stationery noun paper, envelopes, pens, and other writing materials.

station wagon a car with an extended body, a tailgate, and often a baggage deck.

statistics (stə-tĭs'tĭks) noun **1** (sing.) Math. the branch of mathematics concerned with the collation, classification, and interpretation of numerical data. **2** (**statistic**) an item of numerical information. ▸ **statistical** adj. ▸ **statistically** adv. ▸ **statistician** noun

statue (stăch'ōō) noun a sculpted, molded, or cast figure, esp. of a person or animal.

statuesque (stăch,ə-wĕsk') adj. tall and well-proportioned; dignified and imposing.

statuette (stăch,ə-wĕt') noun a small statue.

stature (stăch'ər) noun **1 a** height of body. **b** the distance from the bottom to the top. **2** elevated professional or social position.

status (stăt'əs, stāt'-) noun **1** a rank or position in relation to others, within society, an organization, etc. **b** elevated professional or social position. **2** legal state, e.g., with regard to adulthood, marriage, or citizenship. **3** importance.

status quo (stăt,ə-skwō', stāt,-) (usu. **the status quo**) the situation at a given moment.

statute (stăch'ōōt,) noun **1** a law. **2** a permanent rule drawn up for an organization.

statutory adj. **1** required or prescribed by law or a rule. **2** usual or regular, as if prescribed by law. ▸ **statutorily** adv.

staunch¹ (stônch, stănch) adj. loyal; trusty; steadfast.

staunch² verb same as **stanch**.

stave noun **1** any of the vertical wooden strips joined to form a barrel or tub. **2** a wooden bar, rod, or shaft, e.g., a rung on a ladder. **3** a verse of a poem or song. —verb trans. (pa t and pa p **staved** or **stove**; pr p **staving**) **1** to smash or crush out of shape. **2** (often **stave (something) in**) to smash a hole in (it). —**stave off** (past tense and past participle **staved**) to preclude by acting in advance.

staves see **staff, stave**.

stay¹ verb intrans., trans. (**stayed, staying, stays**) **1** to remain in the same place or condition. **2** to reside temporarily, e.g., as a guest. **3** to remain or linger in order to share or join in something: stay to dinner. **4** Law to suspend or postpone. —noun **1** a period of temporary residence. **2** Law a postponement of a punishment.

stay² noun **1** a prop or support. **2** any of a number of strips of bone or metal sewn into a corset to stiffen it. **3** (**stays**) a corset.

STD abbrev. sexually transmitted disease.

stead (stĕd) noun **1** the place usu. held or occupied by another. **2** purpose; advantage.

steadfast adj. determinedly unwavering. ▸ **steadfastly** adv. ▸ **steadfastness** noun

steady adj. (**steadier, steadiest**) **1** firmly fixed or balanced. **2** regular; constant; unvarying: steady rain. **3** not easily disrupted or undermined; stable. **4** having a serious or sober character. —verb trans., intrans. (**steadied, steadying, steadies**) to make or become steady or steadier. —adv. in a steady manner. ▸ **steadily** adv. ▸ **steadiness** noun

steak (stāk) noun **1** fine quality beef, or a thick slice of it. **2** beef for stewing or braising in chunks. **3** a thick slice of any meat: salmon steaks.

steal verb trans., intrans. (pa t **stole**; pa p **stolen**; pr p **stealing**) **1** to take away (something) without permission or legal right, esp. secretly. **2** to obtain by cleverness or trickery: steal a kiss. **3** to go stealthily. **4** Baseball to reach a base safely while a pitched ball is in the air. —noun colloq. **1** a thing easily obtained; a bargain. **2** an act of stealing.

stealth (stĕlth) noun **1** softness and quietness of movement, avoiding notice. **2** secretive or deceit-ful behavior. ▸ **stealthily** adv. ▸ **stealthiness** noun ▸ **stealthy** adj.

steam *noun* **1** the gaseous state of water. **2** *colloq.* power, energy, or speed: *run out of steam.* —*verb intrans., trans.* (**steamed, steaming**) **1** to give off steam. **2** to cook or otherwise treat by exposure to steam. **3** to move under the power of steam. —**let off steam** to release anger or energy, built up inside. ▸ **steamy** *adj.*

steamer *noun* **1** a ship with steam-powered engines. **2** a two-tier cooking pot.

steamroller *noun* a large, heavy vehicle for flattening road surfaces, etc. —*verb trans.* (**steamrollered, steamrollering**) *colloq.* **1** to crush (opposition, etc.). **2** to flatten (a road surface, etc.) using a steamroller.

steed *noun literary* a horse.

steel *noun* **1** an iron alloy containing carbon and, in some cases, additional elements. **2** a rough-surfaced rod made of this alloy, on which knives are sharpened by hand. **3** hardness or strength, esp. of character. —*verb trans.* (**steeled, steeling**) (*usu.* **steel oneself**) to harden oneself or prepare oneself emotionally, esp. for something unpleasant. ▸ **steely** *adj.*

steel wool a woolly steel mass for scouring and polishing.

steelworks *noun* (*sing.*) a factory where steel is manufactured.

steep¹ *adj.* **1** almost perpendicular: *steep cliffs.* ▣ ABRUPT, HIGH, PRECIPITOUS, SHEER. **2** of great monetary price. ▸ **steepen** *verb trans., intrans.* ▸ **steeply** *adv.* ▸ **steepness** *noun*

steep² *verb trans., intrans.* (**steeped, steeping**) to soak thoroughly in liquid. —**be steeped in something** to be closely familiar with a subject, etc.

steeple *noun* **1** a tower forming part of a church or temple, esp. one with a spire. **2** the spire itself.

steeplechase *noun* **1** a horserace with hurdles. **2** an athletics event with hurdles and a water jump. —*verb intrans.* (**steeplechased, steeplechasing**) to take part in a steeplechase. ▸ **steeplechaser** *noun*

steeplejack *noun* a person who repairs and/or cleans steeples and tall chimneys.

steer¹ *verb trans., intrans.* (**steered, steering**) **1** to guide or control the direction of (a vehicle or vessel). **2** to guide the course or movements of, e.g., with tuition, persuasion, or force. **3** to follow (a particular course).

steer² *noun* a young bull or male ox, esp. one castrated and raised for beef.

steerage (stîr'ij) *noun* **1** the cheapest accommodation on board a passenger ship. **2** the act or practice of steering.

steering wheel a wheel turned by hand to control the wheels of a vehicle.

stein *noun* a large metal or earthenware beer mug, often with a hinged lid.

stellar *adj.* relating to or like the stars or a star.

stem¹ *noun* **1** the central part of a plant, growing upward from the root, or the part by which a leaf, flower, or fruit is attached to a branch. **2** the long thin supporting part of a wine glass. **3** any long slender part. —*verb intrans.* (**stemmed, stemming**) (**stem from (something or someone)**) to originate with or derive from (the one or ones specified).

stem² *verb* (**stemmed, stemming**) to stop (a flow).

stench *noun* a strong, unpleasant smell.

stencil *noun* **1** a plate with parts cut out to form lettering or a design that is copied onto a surface by laying the plate on the surface and inking or painting over the cut-out parts. **2** the lettering or design produced in this way. —*verb trans.* (**stenciled or stencilled, stenciling or stencilling**) to print or produce by means of a stencil.

stenography *noun* the skill or practice of writing in shorthand. ▸ **stenographer** *noun* ▸ **stenographic** *adj.*

stentorian (stĕn-tôr'ē-ən) or **stentorious** *adj.* powerfully loud.

> Named after *Stentor*, a loud-voiced Greek herald in the *Iliad*

step *noun* **1 a** a single complete action of lifting, then placing down the foot in walking or running. **b** the distance covered in the course of such an action. **c** the sound of a foot being laid on the ground in walking. **2** a movement of the foot, usu. one of a pattern of movements in dancing. **3** (*often* **steps**) a single, often outdoor, stair or any stairlike support. **4** a single action or measure taken towards an end or goal. **5** a degree or stage in a scale or series. —*verb intrans.* (**stepped, stepping**) **1** to move by taking a step or steps. **2** (*usu.* **step on (something)**) to lay one's foot on (it). —**in step 1** walking or marching in unison. **2** in harmony or unison. **out of step** not walking, marching, or being in unison. **step (something) up** to increase the rate, intensity, etc., of (it): *step up the pressure.* **watch one's step 1** to walk with careful steps, avoiding danger. **2** to proceed with caution.

step- *combining form* forming words denoting a relationship through a second or later marriage or partnership: *stepbrother / stepmother.*

step-by-step *adj.* developing or happening slowly, by degrees.

stepchild *noun* a stepson or stepdaughter.

stepdaughter *noun* the daughter of a spouse by a previous marriage.

stepfather *noun* the second or later husband of one's mother.

stepladder *noun* a ladder with flat steps, made freestanding by means of a supporting frame attached by a hinge at the top.

stepmother *noun* the second or later wife of one's father.

stepparent *noun* a stepfather or stepmother.

steppe *noun* an extensive dry, grassy, usu. treeless plain, esp. that in SE Europe and Asia.

steppingstone *noun* 1 a large raised stone in a stream, etc., used for crossing. 2 a means of gradual progress.

-ster *suffix* forming words denoting a person with regard to a characteristic, an activity, membership in a group, etc.: *youngster / trickster.*

stereo *noun* 1 stereophonic reproduction of sound. 2 (*pl.* **stereos**) a hi-fi system giving a stereophonic reproduction of sound. —*adj.* stereophonic.

stereo- *combining form* forming words denoting solid or three-dimensional.

stereophonic *adj. Electron.* relating to reproduced sound by means of two or more independent sound channels to emulate that of a live performance. ▸ **stereophonically** *adv.*

stereoscopic *adj. of certain cameras or microscopes* producing an apparently three-dimensional image by presenting a slightly different view of the same object to each eye. ▸ **stereoscopically** *adv.*

stereotype *noun* 1 an overgeneralized idea, impression, or point of view allowing for no individuality or variation. 2 a person or thing regarded as conforming to such an idea, etc. —*verb trans.* (**stereotyped**, **stereotyping**) to think of or characterize in an over-generalized way. ▸ **stereotypical** *adj.*

> Originally a printing term for a fixed block of type

sterile (stĕr'əl) *adj.* 1 biologically incapable of producing offspring, fruit, or seeds. 2 made free of germs. 3 producing no results; having no new ideas. ▸ **sterility** *noun* ▸ **sterilize** *verb trans.* ▸ **sterilization** *noun*

sterling *noun* British money. —*adj.* 1 of or relating to British money. 2 good quality; worthy; reliable: *of sterling character.* 3 *of silver* of at least 92.5% purity.

> So called after the image of a small star that was impressed on medieval silver pennies

stern¹ *adj.* 1 extremely strict; authoritarian. 2 harsh, severe, or rigorous. 3 unpleasantly serious or unfriendly in appearance or nature. ▸ **sternly** *adv.* ▸ **sternness** *noun*

stern² *noun* the rear of a ship or boat.

sternum *noun* (*pl.* **sternums, sterna**) the broad vertical bone in the center of the chest. *Also called* **breastbone**. ▸ **sternal** *adj.*

steroid (stĕr'oid,, stĭr'-) *noun* 1 a fat-soluble organic compound, widely distributed in living organisms. 2 a drug containing such a compound.

stethoscope *noun* an instrument for listening to sounds made inside the body.

stew *verb trans., intrans.* (**stewed, stewing**) 1 to cook (esp. meat) by long simmering. 2 *colloq.* to be in a state of worry or agitation. —*noun* 1 a dish of food, esp. meat, cooked by stewing. 2 *colloq.* a state of worry or agitation.

steward *noun* 1 an attendant on a passenger ship or aircraft. 2 a person overseeing catering, etc. in a hotel or club. 3 a person employed to manage another's property and affairs. —*verb trans.* (**stewarded**, **stewarding**) to serve as a steward of.

stewardess *noun old use* a female flight attendant.

stick¹ *noun* 1 a thin branch or twig. 2 a long thin piece of wood shaped for a particular purpose. 3 a long thin piece, e.g., of celery. 4 (**the sticks**) *colloq.* a rural area considered remote or unsophisticated.

stick² *verb trans., intrans.* (pa t and pa p **stuck**; pr p **sticking**) 1 to push or thrust (esp. something long and thin or pointed). 2 to fasten by piercing with a pin or other sharp object. 3 to fix, or to be or stay fixed, with an adhesive. 4 to remain persistently: *stuck in my mind.* 5 to make or be made to move; to jam or lock. 6 to confine. 7 (**stick to**) a to remain faithful to (something undertaken, e.g., a promise). b to not stray from (something, e.g., a matter under discussion). 8 *colloq.* to place or put. —**stick around** *slang* to hang around; to remain or linger. **stick out** 1 to project or protrude. 2 to be obvious or noticeable; to stand out. **stick up** *colloq.* 1 to project upward; to stand up. 2 *slang* to rob (someone or something).

sticker *noun* an adhesive label, esp. one displaying a message or advertisement.

sticking plaster plaster (sense 3).

stickler *noun* a person who fastidiously insists on something: *a stickler for accuracy.*

stickup *noun slang* an armed robbery.

sticky *adj.* (**stickier, stickiest**) 1 able or likely to stick to other surfaces. 2 *of the weather* warm and humid. 3 *colloq., of a situation, etc.* difficult; awkward; unpleasant. ▸ **stickiness** *noun*

stiff *adj.* 1 not easily bent or folded; rigid. 2 *of limbs, joints, etc.* lacking suppleness. 3 *of a punishment, etc.* harsh; severe. 4 *of a task, etc.* difficult; arduous. 5 *of a wind* blowing strongly. **6** *of a manner* not natural and relaxed; excessively formal. **7** thick in consistency; viscous. **8** *of an alcoholic drink* strong or powerful. —*adv. colloq.* to an extreme degree: *bored me stiff.* —*noun slang* a corpse. —*verb trans.* (**stiffed, stiffing**) *slang* to cheat (another). ▸ **stiffen** *verb trans., intrans.* ▸ **stiffly** *adv.* ▸ **stiffness** *noun*

stiff-necked *adj.* arrogantly obstinate.

stifle (stī'fəl) *verb intrans., trans.* (**stifled, stifling**) **1** to experience difficulty in breathing, esp. because of heat and lack of air. **2** to kill by stopping the breathing; to smother. **3** to suppress (a feeling or action).

stigma *noun* (*pl.* **stigmas, stigmata**) **1** shame or social disgrace. **2** a blemish or scar on the skin. **3** *Bot.* in a flower, the sticky surface at the tip of the style that receives pollen. **4** (**stigmata**) *Christianity* marks resembling the wounds of Christ's crucifixion.

stigmatize *verb trans.* (**stigmatized, stigmatizing**) to describe or regard as shameful. ▸ **stigmatization** *noun*

stile *noun* a step or set of steps built into a fence or wall.

stiletto (stə-lĕt'ō) *noun* (*pl.* **stilettos**) **1 a** a high thin heel on a woman's shoe. **b** a shoe with such a heel. **2** a dagger with a narrow tapering blade.

still¹ *adj.* **1** motionless; inactive. **2 a** lacking noise. **b** calm; tranquil. —*adv.* **1** up to the present time, or the time in question; yet. **2** even then; nevertheless. **3** quietly and without movement: *sit still.* **4** (*with comparatives*) to a greater degree; even: *older still.* —*verb trans., intrans.* (**stilled, stilling**) **1** to make or become still. **2** to calm, appease, or put an end to. —*noun* **1** tranquility; stillness. **2** a photograph, esp. a scene from a movie, used for publicity purposes. ▸ **stillness** *noun*

still² *noun* an apparatus in which alcoholic spirits are distilled.

stillborn *adj.* dead at birth.

still life (*pl.* **still lifes**) a painting, drawing, or photograph of an object or objects.

stilt *noun* **1** either of a pair of long poles with supports for the feet part way up, on which a person can walk around supported high above the ground. **2** any of a set of props on which a building, jetty, etc., is supported above ground or water level.

stilted *adj., of language* sounding unnatural, esp. overly formal.

stimulant *noun* a drug, etc. that produces an increase in the activity of a particular body system or function.

stimulate (stĭm'yə-lāt,) *verb trans.* (**stimulated, stimulating**) **1** to cause physical activity, or increased activity, in (e.g., an

organ of the body). **2** to excite or arouse the senses of; to animate or invigorate. ▸ **stimulation** *noun*

stimulus *noun* (*pl.* **stimuli**) **1** a change in some aspect of the external or internal environment of an organism that causes a response in the nervous system. **2** an incentive or something that rouses activity.

sting *noun* **1** in certain animals and plants, a defensive puncturing organ that can pierce skin and inject poison. **2** the injection of poison from an animal or plant. **3** a painful wound resulting from the sting of an animal or plant. **4** a sharp tingling pain. —*verb trans., intrans.* (*pa t* and *pa p* **stung**; *pr p* **stinging**) **1** to pierce, poison, or wound with a sting. **2** to produce a sharp tingling pain.

stingray (stĭng'rā,) *noun* a ray with a long, barbed, whiplike tail.

stingy (stĭn'jē) *adj.* (**stingier, stingiest**) ungenerous; mean; miserly. ▸ **stingily** *adv.* ▸ **stinginess** *noun*

stink *noun* **1** a strong, very unpleasant odor. **2** *colloq.* an angry or outraged reaction; a fuss. —*verb intrans., trans.* (*pa t* **stank** or **stunk**; *pa p* **stunk**; *pr p* **stinking**) **1** to give off a foul odor. **2** *colloq.* to be contemptibly bad or unpleasant: *That job stank.* ▸ **stinker** *noun* ▸ **stinky** *adj.*

stint *verb trans., intrans.* (**stinted, stinting**) to limit or restrict, typically in a mean or grudging manner. —*noun* an allotted amount of work.

stipend (stī'pənd) *noun* a salary or allowance. ▸ **stipendiary** (stī-pĕn'dē-ĕr,ē) *adj., noun*

stipple *verb trans.* (**stippled, stippling**) to paint or draw in dots or dabs. —*noun* a pattern so produced.

stipulate (stĭp'yə-lāt,) *verb trans.* (**stipulated, stipulating**) to state as a necessary condition. ▸ **stipulation** *noun*

stir¹ *verb trans., intrans.* (**stirred, stirring**) **1** to mix or agitate (a liquid or semiliquid substance) by repeated circular strokes with a spoon or other utensil. **2** to arouse the emotions of; to move. **3** to make a slight or single movement. **4** to get up after sleeping; to become active after resting. —*noun* **1** an act of stirring. **2** an excited reaction; a commotion: *cause a stir.*

stir² *noun slang* a prison.

stir-crazy *noun slang* emotionally disturbed as a result of being confined, esp. in a prison.

stir-fry *verb trans.* (**stir-fried, stir-frying**) to cook lightly by brisk frying on a high heat with little oil. —*noun* a dish of food so cooked.

stirring *adj.* arousing strong emotions.

stirrup *noun* **1** either of a pair of metal footrests for a horse rider. **2** a strap or loop supporting or passing under a foot:

stitch noun **1 a** a single interlinking loop of thread or yarn in sewing or knitting. **b** a complete movement of the needle or needles creating such a loop. **c** any of various ways in which such loops are interlinked. **2** a sharp pain in the side resulting from physical exertion. —verb trans. (**stitched, stitching, stitches**) (also **stitch (something) up**) to join, close, or decorate (it) with stitches. —**in stitches** colloq. helpless with laughter.

stock noun **1** the total amount of merchandise stored in a place of business, a warehouse, etc. **2** a supply held in reserve. **3** equipment or raw material in use. **4** liquid in which meat or vegetables have been cooked, used as a base for a soup, sauce, etc. **5** the shaped wooden or plastic part of a rifle or similar gun. **6** farm animals; livestock. **7 a** the money raised by a company through the selling of shares. **b** the total shares issued by a company or held by an individual shareholder. **c** a group of shares bought or sold as a unit. **8** ancestry; descent. **9** (**stocks**) Hist. a wooden device into which an offender was fastened to be displayed for public ridicule, held by the head and wrists, or wrists and ankles. **10** reputation; standing. —adj. **1** of a standard type, size, etc., constantly in demand and always kept in stock. **2** of an expression much used, esp. so overused as to be meaningless. —verb trans. (**stocked, stocking**) **1** to keep a stock of (merchandise) for sale. **2** to provide with a supply.

stockade (stäk-ād′) noun a defensive fence or enclosure made from tall heavy posts. —verb trans. (**stockaded, stockading**) to protect or defend with a stockade.

stockbroker noun a person paid to buy and sell stocks and shares for customers.

stock car a car of a standard make that is modified for racing.

stock exchange a market for trading stocks and shares by professional dealers on behalf of customers; also, a building housing this market. Also called **stock market**.

stocking noun either of a pair of close-fitting coverings for women's legs, made of a fine fabric such as nylon.

stockpile noun an accumulated reserve; a supply. —verb trans. (**stockpiled, stockpiling**) to accumulate a usu. large supply, held in reserve for future use.

stockroom noun a storeroom.

stock-still adj., adv. motionless.

stocky adj. (**stockier, stockiest**) of a person or animal broad and strong-looking, esp. when not tall. ▸ **stockily** adv. ▸ **stockiness** noun

stockyard noun a large enclosure in which cattle, etc. are kept temporarily.

stodgy adj. (**stodgier, stodgiest**) **1** boringly conventional or serious. **2** pompous; stuffy. **3** so heavy and starchy as to be indigestible. ▸ **stodgily** adv. ▸ **stodginess** noun

stoic (stō′ĭk) noun a person who seems to be or is indifferent to pain and suffering. —adj. (also **stoical**) **1** accepting suffering or misfortune uncomplainingly. **2** indifferent to both pain and pleasure. ▸ **stoically** adv. ▸ **stoicism** noun

stoke verb trans., intrans. (**stoked, stoking**) **1** to put coal or other fuel into (e.g., a furnace). **2** to arouse or intensify (e.g., passion or enthusiasm). ▸ **stoker** noun

stole[1] see **steal**.

stole[2] noun a woman's scarflike garment, often of fur, worn around the shoulders.

stolen see **steal**.

stolid adj. showing little or no interest or emotion; impassive. ▸ **stolidity** noun ▸ **stolidly** adv. ▸ **stolidness** noun

stomach (stəm′ĭk) noun **1** the large saclike organ into which food passes after it has been swallowed. **2** the area around the abdomen; the belly. —verb trans. (**stomached, stomaching**) colloq. to bear or put up with.

stomachache noun a pain in the abdominal area.

stomp verb intrans. (**stomped, stomping**) to stamp or tread heavily. —noun a lively jazz dance with stamping movements.

stone noun **1** the hard solid material of which rocks are made. **2** a small fragment of rock. **3** a gemstone. **4** the hard seed of any of several fruits. **5** a hard, often painful mass formed within the gall bladder, etc. **6** Brit. (pl. **stone**) a UK measure of weight equal to 14 lbs. (6.35 kg). —verb trans. (**stoned, stoning**) **1** to pelt with stones. **2** to remove the stone from (fruit).

Stone Age noun the earliest period in human history, during which primitive tools and weapons were made of stone.

stoned adj. slang under the influence of drugs or alcohol.

stonewall (stōn′wôl′) verb intrans. (**stonewalled, stonewalling**) **1** to hold up progress intentionally, e.g., by obstructing discussion. **2** to refuse to cooperate or answer questions, e.g., in an official hearing. ▸ **stonewaller** noun

stoneware noun hard, coarse pottery.

stony adj. (**stonier, stoniest**) **1** covered with stones. **2** having a unfriendly or unfeeling appearance or quality. ▸ **stonily** adv.

stood see **stand**.

stooge noun **1** a performer who provides a comedian with opportunities for making jokes, often also the butt of the jokes. **2** an assistant, esp. one exploited.

stool *noun* **1** a seat without a back. **2** a footstool. **3** (*usu.* **stools**) feces or excrement.

stool pigeon *noun* **1** a police informer. **2** a duck hunter's decoy, orig. a pigeon.

stoop¹ *verb intrans.* (**stooped, stooping**) **1** to bend the upper body forward and down. **2** to walk with head and shoulders bent forward. **3** (**stoop to (something**)) to lower oneself to do (it); to condescend to do (it). —*noun* a stooped posture.

stoop² *noun* an open porch; a verandah.

stoop³ *noun* same as **stoup**.

stop *verb trans., intrans.* (**stopped, stopping**) **1** to bring (activity) to cessation or suspension or to undergo this. ⊟ CEASE, DESIST, DISCONTINUE, HALT, QUIT ⊟ BEGIN, START. **2 a** to prevent from doing. **b** to prevent. **3** to withhold or keep back: *stopped all funding*. **4** (*also* **stop (something) up**) to block, plug, or close (it). —*noun* **1** an act of stopping. **2** a place stopped at, e.g., on a bus route. **3** the state of being stopped; a standstill. **4** a device that prevents further movement. **5** *Mus.* a set of organ pipes of uniform tone; a keyboard knob that brings them all into use at once.

stopcock *noun* a valve controlling the flow of liquid in a pipe.

stopgap *noun* a temporary substitute.

stoplight *noun* a red traffic signal indicating that vehicles must stop.

stopover *noun* a brief or temporary stop during a longer journey.

stoppage (stăp′ĭj) *noun* **1** an act of stopping or the state of having been stopped. **2** a stopping of work, as in a strike.

stopper *noun* a cork, plug, or bung.

stopwatch *noun* a watch for accurate recording of elapsed time, e.g., in races, etc.

storage (stôr′ĭj) *noun* **1** the act of storing or the state of being stored. **2** space used for storing things.

store *noun* **1** a commercial establishment where merchandise is sold to the public; a shop. **2** (*also* **stores**) a supply kept in reserve. **3** (*also* **stores**) a place where stocks or supplies are kept. **4** *Comput.* a memory. —*verb trans.* (**stored, storing**) **1** to put aside for future use. **2** (*also* **store (something) up**) to build up a reserve supply of (it). **3** to put something into a warehouse for temporary safekeeping. **4** *Comput.* to put into memory.

storefront *noun* the front wall and windows of a store, facing a street.

storehouse *noun* a place where things are stored.

stork *noun* a large wading bird with long legs.

storm *noun* **1** an outbreak of violent weather, with severe winds and heavy falls of rain often with thunder and lightning. **2** a violent reaction, outburst, or show of feeling: *a storm of disapproval.* **3** a furious burst, e.g., of gunfire or applause. —*verb intrans., trans.* (**stormed, storming**) **1** to go or come loudly and angrily. **2** to say or shout angrily. **3** to make a sudden violent attack on. ▸ **stormy** *adj.*

story¹ *noun* (*pl.* **stories**) **1** a written or spoken description of an event or a series of events, real or imaginary. **2** a short story. **3** the plot of a novel, play, or film. **4** a news article.

story² *noun* (*pl.* **stories**) **1** a level, floor, or other tier of a building. **2** the rooms on such a level of a structure.

stoup *or* **stoop** *noun* a basin for holy water.

stout *adj.* **1** rather fat. **2** designed for hard outdoor wear: *stout boots.* **3** courageous; steadfastly reliable. —*noun* dark malty beer. ▸ **stoutly** *adv.* ▸ **stoutness** *noun*

stouthearted *adj.* steadfastly reliable; courageous. ▸ **stoutheartedly** *adv.* ▸ **stoutheartedness** *noun*

stove¹ *noun* a device fueled by electricity, gas, etc., on and in which to cook food.

stove² *see* **stave**.

stow *verb trans., intrans.* (**stowed, stowing**) (*often* **stow away**) **1** to pack or store, esp. out of sight. **2** to hide on a ship, aircraft etc., in the hope of traveling free.

stowaway *noun* a person who stows away on a ship, etc. —*adj.* **1** traveling as a stowaway. **2** able to be carried or stored easily.

straddle *verb trans.* (**straddled, straddling**) **1** to stand or sit with one leg or part on either side of. **2** *colloq.* to adopt a neutral or noncommittal attitude toward.

straggle *verb intrans.* (**straggled, straggling**) **1** to grow or spread untidily. **2** to lag behind or stray from a main group or course. ▸ **straggler** *noun* ▸ **straggly** *adj.*

straight *adj.* **1** not curved, bent, curly, or wavy. **2** lacking deviations or detours; direct. **3** not sloping, leaning, or twisted; level. **4** frank; open; direct. **5** respectable; honest. **6** in good order; neat; tidy. **7** in a row; successive. **8** consisting of itself only. **9** not comic; serious. **10** *colloq.* conventional in tastes and opinions. **11** *slang* heterosexual. —*adv.* **1** in or into a straight line, position, or posture. **2** following an undeviating course; directly: *went straight home.* **3** honestly; frankly: *talk straight.* **4** without a pause: *slept 10 hours straight.* —*noun* **1** a straight line or part, e.g., of a racetrack. **2** *slang* a heterosexual person. **3** *Cards* a running sequence of five cards, irrespective of suit.

straightaway *noun* a straight stretch, esp. of a road or racecourse. —*adv.* immediately.

straighten *verb trans., intrans.* **(straightened, straightening)** (*often* **straighten out** *or* **up**) **1** to make or become straight. **2** to resolve, disentangle, or put into order.

straightforward *adj.* **1** devoid of difficulties or complications; simple. **2** expressing one's views freely, forthrightly, and sincerely.

straight man a comedian's stooge.

strain¹ *verb trans., intrans.* **(strained, straining) 1** to injure or weaken through overexertion. **2** to make violent efforts. **3** to make extreme use of or demands on. **4 a** to pass through or pour into a sieve or colander. **b** (**strain off**) to remove (something) by the use of a sieve or colander. **5** to stretch or draw tight. —*noun* **1** an injury caused by overexertion, esp. a wrenching of the muscles. **2** an extreme or excessive effort made by, or demand made on, the mind or the body. **3** the fatigue resulting from such an effort. **4** an absence of friendliness and openness; tension.

strain² *noun* **1** a breed of animals or plants. **2** a group of bacteria or viruses of the same species that possess a distinguishing characteristic. **3** an element of a person's character, esp. when inherited.

strainer *noun* a sieve or colander.

strait *noun* **1** (*often* **straits**) a narrow strip of water that links two larger areas of ocean or sea. **2** (**straits**) difficulty; hardship.

straiten *verb trans.* to confine or restrict. —**in straitened circumstances** having very little money or assets.

straitjacket *noun* **1** a jacket with long sleeves crossed at the chest and tied behind, used to restrain the arms of a violent person. **2** a thing that prevents freedom of development or expression.

straitlaced *adj.* strictly correct in moral behavior and attitudes; prudish.

strand¹ *verb trans.* **(stranded, stranding) 1** to run (a ship) aground. **2** to leave in a helpless position, e.g., without transport. —*noun* a shore or beach.

strand² *noun* **1** a single thread, fiber, length of hair, etc. **2** a single element or component part.

strange (strānj) *adj.* **1** not known or experienced before; unfamiliar. **2** not usual, ordinary, or predictable; odd. —*adv.* in a strange manner: *acting strange.* ▸ **strangely** *adv.* ▸ **strangeness** *noun*

stranger *noun* **1** a person whom one does not know. **2** a person from a different place, hometown, family, etc. **3** (**a stranger to**) a person unfamiliar with or inexperienced in (something).

strangle *verb trans.* **(strangled, strangling) 1** to kill or attempt to kill by squeezing the throat with the hands, a cord, etc. **2** to hold back or suppress (e.g., a scream or laughter). ▸ **strangler** *noun*

strangulate (străng'gyə-lāt,) *verb trans.* **(strangulated, strangulating) 1** *Med.* to squeeze so as to stop the flow of blood or air. **2** to strangle. ▸ **strangulation** *noun*

strap *noun* **1** a narrow strip of leather or fabric by which a thing is hung, carried, or fastened. **2** either of a pair of strips of fabric by which a garment hangs from the shoulders. —*verb trans.* **(strapped, strapping)** (**strap in** *or* **up**) to fasten or bind (someone or something) with a strap or straps.

strapping *adj.* tall, strong, and robust.

strata *see* **stratum**.

stratagem *noun* a cunningly devised means to an end.

strategic (strə-tē'jĭk) *adj.* **1** relating to strategy or a strategy. **2** *of weapons* designed for a direct long-range attack on an enemy's homeland, rather than for close-range battlefield use. ▸ **strategically** *adv.*

strategize *verb trans., intrans.* **(strategized, strategizing)** to work out a strategy or strategies.

strategy *noun* (*pl.* **strategies**) **1** the process of or the skill in planning and conducting a military campaign. **2** a long-term plan for future success or development. ▸ **strategist** *noun*

strati *see* **stratus**.

stratify *verb trans.* **(stratified, stratifying, stratifies) 1** *Geol.* to deposit (rock) in layers or strata. **2** to classify or arrange into different grades, levels, or social classes. ▸ **stratification** *noun*

stratosphere (străt'ə-sfīr,) *noun* the layer of the Earth's atmosphere that extends from about 7.5 mi. (12 km) to about 31 mi. (50 km) above its surface, and contains the ozone layer. ▸ **stratospheric** *adj.*

stratum (străt'əm, străt'-) *noun* (*pl.* **strata, stratums**) **1** a layer of sedimentary rock. **2** a level, grade, or social class.

stratus *noun* (*pl.* **strati**) a wide horizontal sheet of low gray layered cloud.

straw *noun* **1** the dried, cut stems and leaves of cereal crops that remain after removal of the grains by threshing. **2** a single stalk. **3** a thin hollow tube for sucking up a drink. **4** a pale yellow color.

strawberry *noun* (*pl.* **strawberries**) **1 a** a trailing plant cultivated for its edible fruit. **b** the juicy red fruit. **2** *slang* a hickey.

straw poll an unofficial vote, esp. taken on the spot, to get some idea of general opinion. *Also called* **straw vote**.

stray *verb intrans.* **(strayed, straying) 1** to wander away from the right path or place, usu. unintentionally. **2** to move away unintentionally from the main or current topic in thought, speech, or writing. **3** to depart from an accepted or required pattern of moral behavior. —*noun* a lost or homeless pet or child. —*adj.* random; casual.

streak *noun* **1** a long irregular stripe or band. **2** a flash of lightning. **3** an element or characteristic: *a cowardly streak.* **4** a short period; a spell: *a lucky streak.* —*verb trans., intrans.* (**streaked, streaking**) **1** to mark with a streak or streaks. **2** to move at great speed; to dash. ▸ **streaky** *adj.*

stream *noun* **1** a very narrow river. **2** a constant flow of liquid. **3** a continuously moving line or mass, e.g., of vehicles. —*verb intrans.* (**streamed, streaming**) **1** to flow or move continuously and in large quantities or numbers. **2** to float or trail in the wind.

streamer *noun* **1** a long paper ribbon used to decorate a room. **2** a roll of colored paper that uncoils when thrown. **3** a long thin flag.

streamline *verb trans.* (**streamlined, streamlining**) **1** to design (e.g., a motor vehicle) in such a way as to minimize resistance to air or fluid flow. **2** to make efficient. ▸ **streamlined** *adj.*

street *noun* **1** a paved public road in a town or city. **2** the road and the buildings together. **3** the people in the buildings or on the pavements.

streetcar *noun* a public conveyance operated on rails that are laid in public streets.

streetwalker *noun* colloq. a prostitute.

streetwise *adj.* colloq. experienced in and able to survive the ruthlessness of urban life.

strength *noun* **1 a** the quality or degree of being physically or mentally strong. **b** the capacity or ability to exert effort. **2** the ability to withstand pressure or force. **3** degree or intensity, e.g., of emotion. **4** potency, e.g., of an alcoholic drink. **5** a highly valued quality or asset.

strengthen *verb trans., intrans.* (**strengthened, strengthening**) to cause to be generally strong or stronger.

strenuous *adj.* requiring or performed with great effort or energy. ▸ **strenuosity** *noun* ▸ **strenuously** *adv.* ▸ **strenuousness** *noun*

streptococcus *noun* (pl. **streptococci**) a bacterium which can cause serious conditions such as pneumonia.

streptomycin (strĕp,tə-mī'sĭn) *noun* an antibiotic used to treat bacterial infections.

stress *noun* **1** physical or mental overexertion. **2** *Phys.* the force exerted on a body that tends to cause that body to deform. **3** a physical and/or emotional reaction that has a harmful effect on the health and functioning of the body. **4** importance, emphasis, or weight laid on or attached to something. **5** emphasis on a particular syllable or word. —*verb trans.* (**stressed,** **stressing**) **1** to put emphasis on. ◨ EMPHASIZE, UNDERLINE, UNDERSCORE ◪ DEEMPHASIZE, DOWNPLAY. **2** to pronounce with emphasis. **3** to subject to mental or physical stress. ▸ **stressful** *adj.* ▸ **stressfully** *adv.* ▸ **stressfulness** *noun*

stretch *verb trans., intrans.* (**stretched, stretching**) **1** to make or become longer or wider by pulling or drawing out. **2** to extend in space or time. **3** (*also* **stretch out**) to straighten and extend (the body or part of the body), e.g., when waking or reaching. **4** to make or become tight or taut. **5** (*also* **stretch out**) to lay (something) out at full length. **6** to be extendable without breaking. **7** to last or cause to last longer through economical use. **8** (*also* **stretch out**) to prolong (something). **9** to make extreme demands on or severely test (e.g., physical abilities). —*noun* **1** an act of stretching, esp. a part of the body. **2** a period of time; a spell. **3** an expanse, e.g., of land. **4** capacity to extend or expand. **5** a straight part on a racetrack or course. **6** *slang* a term of imprisonment. ▸ **stretchiness** *noun* ▸ **stretchy** *adj.*

stretcher *noun* a length of canvas or other sheeting with poles attached, for carrying a sick or wounded patient.

strew *verb trans.* (*pa t* **strewed**; *pa p* **strewn** or **strewed**; *pr p* **strewing**) **1** to scatter untidily. **2** to cover with an untidy scattering.

stria (strī'ə) *noun* (pl. **striae**) any of a series of parallel grooves in rock, or furrows or streaks of color in plants and animals. ▸ **striated** *adj.* ▸ **striation** *noun*

stricken *adj.* deeply affected, esp. by grief or disease. —*verb see* **strike**.

strict *adj.* **1** demanding obedience or close observance of rules; severe. **2** *of instructions, etc.* that must be obeyed to the letter. **3** observing rules or practices very closely. **4** exact; precise: *the strict sense of the word.* ▸ **strictly** *adv.* ▸ **strictness** *noun*

stricture *noun* **1** a severe criticism. **2** *Med.* an abnormal narrowing of a passage.

stride *noun* **1 a** a single long step in walking. **b** the length of such a step. **c** a way of walking in long steps. **2** (*usu.* **strides**) a measure of progress or development. —*verb intrans.* (*pa t* **strode**; *pa p* **stridden**; *pr p* **striding**) **1** to walk with long steps. **2** to take a long step.

strident (strī'dnt) *adj.* **1** *of a sound* loud and harsh. **2** forcefully assertive; compelling. ▸ **stridency** *noun* ▸ **stridently** *adv.*

strife *noun* **1** bitter conflict or fighting. **2** *colloq.* trouble of any sort; hassle.

strike *verb trans., intrans.* (*pa t* **struck**; *pa p* **struck** or **stricken**; *pr p* **striking**) **1** to hit. **2** to make a particular impression on (someone). **3** to come into the mind of; to occur to. **4** to cause (a match) to ignite through friction. **5** *of a clock* to indicate the hours, half hours, and quarter hours with chimes. **6** to happen suddenly: *Disaster struck.* **7** to make a sudden attack. **8** to afflict suddenly; to cause to become through affliction: *struck dumb.* **9** to arrive at or settle (e.g., a bargain or a balance). **10** to find a source of (e.g., oil). **11** (**strike on**) to come upon or arrive at (something, esp. an idea) by chance. **12** to stop working as part of a protest against an employer. —*noun* **1** an act of hitting or dealing a blow. **2 a** a usu. collective on-going refusal to work, as a protest against an employer. **b** a prolonged refusal to engage in a regular or expected activity, e.g., eating, as a protest. **3** a military attack, esp. by air. **4** a discovery of a mineral source, e.g., gold. **5** *Bowling* the knocking down of all pins with a single ball. **6** *Baseball* a ball swung at but missed by the batter. —**strike out 1** to aim blows wildly. **2** *Baseball* **a** *of a batter* to be dismissed by means of three strikes. **b** *of a pitcher* to pitch three strikes to (the one at bat), putting (that player) out. **strike up 1** *of a band, etc.* to begin to play. **2** to start (something, esp. a conversation or friendship). ▸ **striker** *noun*

strikebreaker *noun* a person who continues to work while others strike, or who is brought in to do the job of a striking worker.

striking *adj.* impressive or arresting.

string *noun* **1** thin cord, or a piece of it. **2** any of a set of pieces of stretched wire, catgut, etc. vibrated to produce sound in various musical instruments. **3** (**strings**) the orchestral instruments in which sound is produced in this way, usu. the violins, violas, cellos, and double basses collectively; also the players of these instruments. **4** a set of things, e.g., pearls, threaded together. **5** a series or succession. **6** (**strings**) undesirable conditions or limitations. —*verb trans.* (**strung, stringing**) **1** to equip or provide with a string or strings. **2** to tie with string. **3** to thread (e.g., beads) on a string. **4** (*also* **string out**) to extend in or as if a string. ▸ **stringiness** *noun* ▸ **stringy** *adj.*

stringbean *noun* **1 a** a plant that is cultivated for its slender, green, edible pods. **b** the pod of this plant. **2** *colloq.* a tall thin person or animal.

stringent *adj.* **1** *of rules, terms, etc.* strictly enforced; severe; rigorous. **2** marked by a lack of money: *stringent circumstances.* ▸ **stringency** *noun* ▸ **stringently** *adv.*

stringer *noun* **1** a horizontal beam in a framework. **2** a journalist employed part-time to cover a particular beat or area.

strip *noun* **1** a long narrow piece. **2** a comic strip. **3** an airfield. **4** a striptease performance. —*verb trans., intrans.* (**stripped, stripping**) **1** (*also* **strip off**) to remove (something) by peeling or pulling off; to remove the surface or contents of (something) in this way. **2** (**strip of**) to dispossess (someone) of (something, e.g., property). **3** to remove the clothes of. **4 a** to take one's clothes off. **b** to perform a striptease. **5** (*also* **strip down**) to take (something) completely to pieces. ▸ **stripper** *noun*

stripe *noun* **1** a band of color. **2** a chevron or colored band on a uniform, indicating rank. —*verb trans.* (**striped, striping**) to mark with stripes. ▸ **stripy** *adj.*

stripling *noun* a youth.

strip mining a mining technique where the ore, etc. is exposed through removal of the overlying material.

strip search a thorough search of the body of a person who has been made to take off his or her clothes. ▸ **strip-search** *verb trans.*

striptease *noun* an entertainment in which a person undresses to music in a slow and sexually suggestive way.

strive *verb intrans.* (*pa t* **strove**; *pa p* **striven**; *pr p* **striving**) **1** to try extremely hard; to struggle. **2** to contend; to be in conflict.

strobe lighting equipment for producing a powerful, rapidly flashing light which creates an effect of jerky movement. *Also called* **strobe.**

strode *see* **stride.**

stroke *noun* **1 a** an act of striking; the way a thing is struck, esp. the technique used in striking a ball in sports. **b** a single complete movement in a repeated series, as in swimming or rowing. **c** a specified style of swimming. **2** a single movement with a pen, brush, etc., or the line or daub produced. **3** the total linear distance travelled by a piston in the cylinder of an engine. **4** the striking of a clock, or its sound. **5** a gentle caress or other touching movement. **6** a sudden interruption in the supply of blood to the brain. —*verb trans.* (**stroked, stroking**) **1** to caress in kindness or affection, often repeatedly. **2** to strike (a ball) smoothly.

stroll *verb intrans.* (**strolled, strolling**) to walk in a slow leisurely way. —*noun* a leisurely walk.

stroller *noun* **1** a person who strolls. **2** a wheeled vehicle for a baby or toddler.

strong *adj.* **1** exerting or capable of great force or power. **2** able to withstand rough treatment; robust. **3** *of views, etc.* firmly held or boldly expressed. **4** *of taste, light, etc.* sharply felt or experienced; intense; powerful. **5** *of coffee, alcoholic drinks, etc.*

concentrated. **6** *of an argument* having much force; convincing. **7** *of language* bold or straightforward; rude, offensive, or vulgar. **8** *of a syllable* stressed. ▸ **strongly** *adv*.

strong-arm *colloq. adj.* aggressively forceful.

strongbox *noun* a sturdy lockable box for storing money or valuables; a safe.

stronghold *noun* **1** a fortified place of defense, e.g., a castle. **2** a place from which strong support (e.g., for a political party) emanates.

strongman *noun* **1** a leader of a country with dictatorial power. **2** someone who performs great feats of strength.

strong point a feature or attribute in which a person excels: *Accuracy is his strong point*.

strontium *noun* (SYMBOL **Sr**) a soft, silvery-white, highly reactive metallic element.

strop *noun* a strip of coarse leather, etc. on which razors are sharpened. —*verb trans.* (**stropped, stropping**) to sharpen (a razor) on a strop.

strove *see* **strive**.

struck *see* **strike**.

structure *noun* **1** the way in which the parts of a thing are arranged or organized. **2** a thing built or constructed from smaller parts. —*verb trans.* (**structured, structuring**) to put into an organized form or arrangement. ▸ **structural** *adj*. ▸ **structurally** *adv*.

strudel (strōōd'l) *noun* a baked roll of thin pastry with a filling of fruit, esp. apple.

struggle *verb intrans.* (**struggled, struggling**) **1** to move the body around violently in an attempt to get free. **2** to strive vigorously or make a strenuous effort under difficult conditions. **3** to make one's way with great difficulty. **4** to fight or contend. —*noun* **1** an act of struggling. **2** a fight or contest.

strum *Mus. verb trans., intrans.* (**strummed, strumming**) to play (a stringed instrument, or a tune on it) with sweeps of the fingers or thumb rather than with precise plucking. —*noun* an act of strumming.

strumpet *noun old use* a prostitute, or a woman who engages in casual sex.

strung *see* **string**.

strut¹ *verb intrans.* (**strutted, strutting**) to parade about in a swaggering way. —*noun* a strutting way of walking.

strut² *noun* a bar or rod used to support weight or take pressure; a prop.

strychnine (strĭk'nĭn, -nēn,) *noun* a deadly poison obtained from a tropical Indian tree.

stub *noun* **1** a short piece, e.g., of a cigarette or a pencil, left after the rest has been used up. **2** the part of a check or a ticket kept by the issuer or the recipient as a record of transaction. —*verb trans.* (**stubbed, stubbing**) **1** to accidentally bump the end of (one's toe) against a hard surface. **2** (*also*

stub out) to extinguish (a cigarette, etc.) by pressing the end against a surface.

stubble *noun* **1** the mass of short stalks left in the ground after a crop has been harvested. **2** a short early growth of beard. ▸ **stubbly** *adj*.

stubborn *adj.* **1** refusing to change or compromise. **2** determined; unyielding. **3** difficult to treat, remove, or deal with. ▸ **stubbornly** *adv*. ▸ **stubborness** *noun*

stubby *adj.* (**stubbier, stubbiest**) short and broad or thick-set. ▸ **stubbiness** *noun*

stucco *noun* (*pl.* **stuccoes, stuccos**) plaster or cement used for coating walls, or molding decorative shapes. —*verb trans.* (**stuccoed, stuccoing, stuccoes** *or* **stuccos**) to coat with or mold out of stucco.

stuck *see* **stick²**.

stuck-up *adj. colloq.* snobbish; conceited.

stud¹ *noun* **1** a rivetlike decorative metal knob. **2** any of several projections on the sole of a boot, giving added grip. **3** a fastener, e.g., on a collar or a shirt front. —*verb trans.* (**studded, studding**) **1** to fasten or decorate with studs or a stud. **2** to cover with a dense scattering.

stud² *noun* **1** a male animal, esp. a horse, kept for breeding. **2** *slang* a man who has or claims great sexual energy and prowess.

student *noun* **1** a person following a formal course of study in an educational institution. **2** a person with an informed interest (in a subject): *a student of archaeology*.

studied *adj., of an attitude, expression, etc.* carefully practiced and adopted or produced for effect; affected: *a studied smile*.

studio *noun* (*pl.* **studios**) **1** the workroom of an artist or a photographer. **2 a** a room in which musical recordings, movies, or television or radio programs are made. **b** (**studios**) the premises of a company making any of these.

studio apartment a small apartment with one main room serving as a living, eating, sleeping, and often cooking area.

studious *adj.* **1** having and exhibiting a serious, hard-working approach to study. **2** painstaking or painstakingly carried out. ▸ **studiously** *adv*. ▸ **studiousness** *noun*

study *verb trans., intrans.* (**studied, studying, studies**) **1** to devote oneself to the gaining of knowledge of (a subject); to take an educational course in (a subject). **2 a** to look at or examine closely and searchingly. **b** to think about carefully. —*noun* (*pl.* **studies**) **1** the act or process of studying. **2** (**studies**) work done in the process of acquiring knowledge. **3** a careful, detailed examination or consideration. **4** a private room where quiet work or study is done.

stuff *noun* **1** any material or substance. **2** luggage or equipment; belongings. **3** cloth.

—*verb trans.* (**stuffed, stuffing**) **1** to fill (e.g., a chicken or pepper) with a seasoned mixture of other foods. **2** to fill to capacity or over. **3** to cram or thrust into (something). **4** to feed (oneself) gluttonously.

stuffing *noun* **1** padding used to stuff toys, cushions, etc. **2** a seasoned mixture of foods for stuffing another item of food.

stuffy *adj.* (**stuffier, stuffiest**) **1** poorly ventilated. **2** *colloq.* pompous. **3** *colloq.* boringly conventional or unadventurous. ▸ **stuffily** *adv.* ▸ **stuffiness** *noun*

stultify *verb trans.* (**stultified, stultifying, stultifies**) **1** to dull the mind of, e.g., with tedious tasks. **2** to make (e.g., efforts) appear useless or foolish.

stumble *verb intrans.* (**stumbled, stumbling**) **1** to lose one's balance and pitch forward. **2** to walk unsteadily. **3** to speak with frequent hesitations and mistakes. —*noun* **1** the act or an instance of stumbling. **2** a foolish mistake.

stumbling block an obstacle or source of difficulty.

stump *noun* **1** the part of a felled or fallen tree left in the ground. **2** a short part, e.g., of a limb, left after the larger part has been removed. **3** (**the stump**) a place where campaign speeches are made during an election year. —*verb trans., intrans.* (**stumped, stumping**) **1** to baffle or perplex. **2** to walk stiffly and unsteadily. **3** to travel about giving campaign speeches: *stumping the country.* ▸ **stumpiness** *noun* ▸ **stumpy** *adj.*

stun *verb trans.* (**stunned, stunning**) **1** to make unconscious, e.g., by a blow to the head. **2** to make unable to speak or think clearly, e.g., through shock. **3** *colloq.* to impress greatly; to astound.

stung see **sting**.

stunk see **stink**.

stunner *noun colloq.* a person or thing of overwhelming beauty or attractiveness.

stunning *adj. colloq.* **1** outstandingly beautiful. **2** extremely impressive. ▸ **stunningly** *adv.*

stunt[1] *verb trans.* (**stunted, stunting**) to prevent (growth or development) to the full, or prevent the full growth or development of.

stunt[2] *noun* **1** a daring act or spectacular event intended to show off talent or attract publicity. **2** a dangerous or acrobatic feat performed as part of the action of a movie or television program.

stupefy *verb trans.* (**stupefied, stupefying, stupefies**) **1** to make senseless, e.g., with drugs or alcohol. **2** to amaze or astound. ▸ **stupefaction** *noun*

stupendous *adj.* **1** being so unusual or extreme as to astound. **2** *colloq.* astoundingly huge or excellent. ▸ **stupendously** *adv.*

stupid *adj.* **1** having or showing a lack of common sense or a slowness to understand. **2** *colloq.* trivial; unimportant: *stupid little arguments.* ▸ **stupidity** *noun* ▸ **stupidly** *adv.*

stupor *noun* a state of near-unconsciousness.

sturdy *adj.* (**sturdier, sturdiest**) **1** *of limbs, etc.* thick and strong-looking; robust. **2** healthy; vigorous; hardy. ▸ **sturdily** *adv.* ▸ **sturdiness** *noun*

sturgeon *noun* a large long-snouted fish, the source of caviar.

stutter *noun* a stammer. —*verb trans., intrans.* (**stuttered, stuttering**) to speak or say with a stutter.

sty[1] *noun* (*pl.* **sties**) a pen for hogs.

sty[2] or **stye** *noun* (*pl.* **sties** or **styes**) a swelling or inflammation on the eyelid.

style *noun* **1** a manner or way of doing something. **2** a distinctive manner that characterizes a particular author, painter, etc. **3** kind; type. **4** a striking quality, often elegance. **5** the state of being fashionable: *gone out of style.* **6** a pointed tool used for engraving. **7** *Bot.* the often elongated part of the carpel or a flower that connects the stigma to the ovary. —*verb trans.* (**styled, styling**) **1** to design, shape, or groom in a particular way. **2** to name or designate: *styled herself an expert.* ▸ **stylistic** *adj.* ▸ **stylistically** *adv.*

styli see **stylus**.

stylish *adj.* appealingly elegant or fashionable. ▸ **stylishly** *adv.*

stylist *noun* **1** a trained hairdresser. **2** a writer, artist, etc. who pays a great attention to style.

stylize *verb trans.* (**stylized, stylizing**) to give a distinctive or elaborate style to, esp. creating an impression of unnaturalness.

stylus *noun* (*pl.* **styluses, styli**) **1** the needlelike part of the arm of a record player. **2** the cutting tool used to produce the grooves in a record.

stymie or **stymy** *verb trans.* (**stymied, stymieing** or **stymying, stymies**) to prevent, thwart, or frustrate.

> Originally a golfing term for an opponent's ball in the way of your own

styptic *noun* a substance that stops or prevents bleeding by causing the blood vessels to contract. —*adj.* astringent.

suave (swäv) *adj.* charming, esp. insincerely so. ▸ **suavely** *adv.* ▸ **suavity** *noun*

sub *colloq. noun* **1** a submarine. **2** a substitute player. —*verb intrans., trans.* (**subbed, subbing**) to act as a substitute.

sub- *prefix* forming words denoting: **1** under or below: *submarine*. **2** lower in rank or importance; secondary: *subcontractor*. **3** less than; imperfectly: *subhuman*. **4** a part or division of: *subcommittee*.

subaqua (sŭb-ǎk′wə) *adj.* of, for, or for use in underwater activities.

subatomic *adj.* **1** smaller than an atom. **2** existing or occurring within an atom.

subcompact *noun* a car smaller than a compact.

subconscious *noun* the part of the mind that contains memories, associations, and feelings that can be brought back to conscious awareness. —*adj.* denoting mental processes of which a person is not consciously aware. ▸ **subconsciously** *adv.*

subcontinent *noun* a large part of a continent that is distinctive in some way.

subcontract *noun* a secondary contract, by which the hired person or company hires another to carry out the work. —*verb trans.* (**subcontracted, subcontracting**) to employ (a worker), or pass on (work), under a subcontract. ▸ **subcontractor** *noun*

subculture *noun* the customs, tastes, and activities of a particular group within society.

subcutaneous (sŭb,kyōō-tā′nē-əs) *adj. Med.* under the skin.

subdirectory *noun Comput.* a directory of files contained within another directory.

subdivide *verb trans.* (**subdivided, subdividing**) to divide (a part) into even smaller parts. ▸ **subdivision** *noun*

subdue *verb trans.* (**subdued, subduing**) **1** to overpower and bring under control. **2** to suppress or conquer (feelings or an enemy).

subdued *adj.* **1** of lighting, etc. toned down; soft. **2** of a person uncharacteristically quiet or in low spirits.

subject *noun* (sŭb′jĭkt, -jĕkt) **1 a** a matter or topic under discussion or consideration. **b** the principal idea or focus of attention in a composition or piece of discourse. **2** an area of learning that forms a course of study. **3** a person or thing represented by an artist or writer. **4** a person on whom an experiment or operation is performed. **5** a person under the rule of a monarch or government. **6** *Gram.* a word or phrase referring to the person or thing that performs the action of an active verb or receives the action of a passive verb. *See also* **object¹** (sense 4). —*adj.* (sŭb′jĭkt, -jĕkt) (*often* **subject to**) **1** showing a tendency; prone. **2** exposed; open: *subject to criticism*. **3** governed; dependent: *Our plans are subject to change*. —*verb trans.* (səb-jĕkt′, sŭb′jĕkt,) (**subjected, subjecting**) **1** to cause (someone) to undergo or experience. **2** to make (a person or country) subordinate to or under the control of another. ▸ **subjection** *noun*

subjective *adj.* **1** *Philos.* based on personal thoughts and feelings; not impartial or objective. *See also* **objective** (sense 2a). **2** *Gram.* indicating or referring to the subject of a verb; nominative. ▸ **subjectively** *adv.*

subjugate (sŭb′jə-gāt,) *verb trans.* (**subjugated, subjugating**) to bring under one's control; to make obedient or submissive. ▸ **subjugation** *noun*

subjunctive *Gram. noun* **1** a set of verb forms, or mood, used to express condition, wish, or uncertainty, e.g., *If I were you and I suggest he leave now.* **2** a verb form of this kind. —*adj.* in or of the subjunctive.

sublet (sŭb-lĕt′) *verb trans.* (**sublet, subletting**) to rent out to another person (property, etc. one is renting from someone else).

sublimation *noun* **1** *Chem.* the conversion of a solid directly into a gas or vapor; the reverse process, in which the vapor condenses to form a solid. **2** *Psychol.* the channeling of an undesirable impulse toward the attainment of a more morally or socially acceptable goal. ▸ **sublimate** *verb trans., intrans.*

sublime (sə-blīm′) *adj.* **1** of the highest or noblest nature. **2** overwhelmingly great; supreme. —*verb trans., intrans.* (**sublimed, subliming**) *Chem.* to sublimate. ▸ **sublimely** *adv.* ▸ **sublimity** *noun*

subliminal (sə-blĭm′ən-l) *adj.* existing or occurring below the threshold of ordinary awareness. ▸ **subliminally** *adv.*

submachine gun a lightweight portable machine gun fired from the shoulder or hip.

submarine (sŭb′mə-rēn,, sŭb,mə-rēn′) *noun* a vessel, esp. military, able to travel beneath the surface of the sea. *Also called* **sub**. —*adj.* under the surface of the sea:

submarine sandwich a very large sandwich.

submerge *verb trans., intrans.* (**submerged, submerging**) **1 a** to plunge under the surface of water or other liquid. **b** to go under water. **2** to overwhelm or inundate, e.g., with work.

submerse *verb trans., intrans.* (**submersed, submersing**) **1** to cause to go beneath the surface of a liquid. **2** to go under water. ▸ **submersion** *noun*

submersible *adj., of a vessel* able to operate under water. —*noun* a submersible vessel.

submissive *adj.* willing or tending to submit; meek; obedient. ▸ **submissively** *adv.* ▸ **submissiveness** *noun*

submit *verb intrans., trans.* (**submitted, submitting**) **1** (*also* **submit to**) to give in, esp. to the wishes or control of (another person); to stop resisting. **2** to offer (oneself) as a subject of testing, experimentation, or treatment. **3** to offer or present (e.g., a proposal) for formal consideration. **4** to hand over or deliver. ▸ **submission** *noun*

subnormal *adj.* less than normal, esp. with regard to intelligence.

subordinate *adj.* (sə-bôrd'n-ət) (*often* **subordinate to**) lower in rank or importance (than someone or something). —*noun* a subordinate person or thing. —*verb trans.* (sə-bôrd'n-āt,) (**subordinated, subordinating**) to regard, make, or treat someone or something as subordinate. ▸ **subordination** *noun*

suborn (sə-bôrn') *verb trans.* (**suborned, suborning**) to persuade (someone) to commit a crime or other wrong.

subplot *noun* a subsidiary plot coinciding with the main action in a movie, play, or story.

subpoena (sə-pē'nə) *noun* a written order legally obliging a person to appear in a court of law at a specified time; a summons. —*verb trans.* (**subpoenaed, subpoenaing**) to serve with a subpoena.

subroutine (sŭb'rōō,tēn,) *noun Comput.* a self-contained part of a program that performs a specific task.

subscribe *verb trans., intrans.* (**subscribed, subscribing**) **1** to contribute or undertake to contribute (a sum of money), esp. on a regular basis. **2** (*usu.* **subscribe to**) to undertake to receive (regular issues of a magazine, etc.), in return for payment. **3** (**subscribe to**) to agree with or believe in (a theory, idea, etc.). **4** to write one's name at the bottom of (a document, picture, etc.). ▸ **subscriber** *noun*

subscript (sŭb'skrĭpt,) *Printing adj.,* of a character set below the level of the line, as 2 in H_2O. —*noun* a subscript character.

subscription *noun* **1** a payment made in subscribing. **2** an advance order of a periodical for a set period of time. **3** the act of subscribing; that which is subscribed.

subsequent *adj., adv.* (*also* **subsequent to**) happening after or following (something). ▸ **subsequently** *adv.*

subservient *adj.* **1** ready or eager to submit to the wishes of others, often excessively so. **2** subordinate. ▸ **subservience** *noun*

subset *noun Math.* a set that forms part of a larger set.

subside (səb-sīd') *verb intrans.* (**subsided, subsiding**) **1** of *land, buildings, etc.* to sink to a lower level. **2** of *noise, feelings, etc.* to become less loud or intense. ▸ **subsidence** *noun*

subsidiary (səb-sĭd'ē-ĕr,ē) *adj.* **1** of secondary importance; subordinate. **2** serving as an addition or supplement; auxiliary. —*noun* (*pl.* **subsidiaries**) **1** a subsidiary person or

thing. **2** a company controlled by another, usu. larger, company or other organization.

subsidy *noun* (*pl.* **subsidies**) **1** a sum of money given to another party in order to assist with costs of operation or to keep the prices of something at reasonable levels. **2** financial aid of this kind. ▸ **subsidize** *verb trans.*

subsist *verb intrans.* (**subsisted, subsisting**) **1** (**subsist on**) to live or manage to stay alive by means of (something). **2** (**subsist in**) to be based on or consist of (something).

subsistence *noun* **1** a means of existence; livelihood. **2** (*attributive*) of *wages, etc.* just enough to provide basic necessities.

subsoil *noun* the layer of soil that lies beneath the topsoil.

subsonic *adj.* relating to, being, or traveling at speeds below the speed of sound.

substance *noun* **1** the matter or material that a thing is made of. **2** a particular kind of matter. **3** the essence or basic meaning of something. **4** solid quality or worth. **5** foundation; truth. **6** wealth and influence: *a woman of substance.*

substandard *adj.* below an expected level of quality.

substantial *adj.* **1** having great significance, value, influence, or effect. **2** of real worth. **3** of *food* nourishing. **4** solidly built. **5** relating to actual matter or to actuality. **6** wealthy and influential. ▸ **substantially** *adv.*

substantiate (səb-stăn'chē-āt,) *verb trans.* (**substantiated, substantiating**) to prove or support; to confirm the truth or validity of. ▸ **substantiation** *noun*

substantive (səb'stən-tĭv,) *adj.* **1** of significant importance or value. **2** relating to the essential nature of something. —*noun Gram.* a noun. ▸ **substantively** *adv.*

substitute *noun* a person or thing that takes the place of or is used instead of another. —*verb trans.* (**substituted, substituting**) to use or bring into use as a substitute. —*adj.* acting as a substitute. ▸ **substitution** *noun*

substratum (səb-străt,əm, -străt,-) *noun* (*pl.* **substrata, substratums**) **1** an underlying layer. **2** a foundation or foundation material.

subsume *verb trans.* (**subsumed, subsuming**) to take into or to regard as part of a larger more general group or category.

subtend *verb trans.* (**subtended, subtending**) of *a line or a side of a geometric figure* to be opposite to (an arc or an angle).

subterfuge (sŭb'tər-fyōoj,) *noun* a trick or deception that evades, conceals, or obscures; also, trickery in general.

subterranean (səb,tə-rā'nē-ən) *adj.* existing or operating underground or in secret.

subtext *noun* an unstated message conveyed in a play, movie, book, or picture.

subtitle *noun* **1** (*usu.* **subtitles**) a printed translation of the dialogue of a foreign movie, appearing bit by bit at the bottom of the screen. **2** a second title, usu. expanding on or explaining the main title, e.g., of a book.

subtle *adj.* **1** not straightforwardly or obviously stated or displayed. **2** *of distinctions, etc.* difficult to appreciate or perceive. **3** *of flavors, etc.* extremely faint or delicate. **4** carefully or craftily discreet or indirect. ▸ **subtlety** *noun* ▸ **subtly** *adv.*

subtract *verb trans.* (**subtracted, subtracting**) to take (one number or quantity) from another. ▸ **subtraction** *noun*

suburb *noun* (*often* **suburbs**) a district, esp. residential, on the edge of a town or city. ▸ **suburban** *adj.*

suburbia *noun* suburbs and their inhabitants and way of life regarded collectively.

subvention *noun* a grant or subsidy.

subversive *adj.* likely or tending to subvert or undermine government or authority. —*noun* a subversive person.

subvert (səb-vərt′) *verb trans.* (**subverted, subverting**) **1** to undermine or overthrow (a government or other legally established body). **2** to corrupt (a person); to undermine (a principle, etc.). ▸ **subversion** *noun*

subway *noun* an underground passenger railroad transport system, most often in a large city.

succeed (sək-sēd′) *verb intrans., trans.* (**succeeded, succeeding**) **1** to achieve an aim or purpose. **2** to develop or turn out as planned. **3** to come next after; to follow.

success *noun* **1 a** the quality of succeeding or the state of having succeeded; a favorable development or outcome. **b** a thing that turns out as planned, or that is judged favorably by others. **2 a** attainment of fame, power, or wealth. **b** a person who has attained any such quality. ▸ **successful** *adj.* ▸ **successfully** *adv.*

succession *noun* **1** a series of people or things coming one after the other. **2** the right or order by which one person or thing succeeds another.

successive *adj.* immediately following another or each other. ▸ **successively** *adv.*

successor *noun* a person who follows another, esp. who takes over a job or position.

succinct (sək-sĭngkt′, sə-) *adj.* concise. ▸ **succinctly** *adv.* ▸ **succinctness** *noun*

succor (sək′ər) *noun* help or relief in time of distress or need. —*verb trans.* (**succored, succoring**) to give succor to.

Succoth *noun* same as **Sukkoth**.

succubus *noun* (*pl.* **succubuses, succubi**) an evil female spirit believed by some to have sexual intercourse with sleeping men. *See also* **incubus**.

succulent *noun* a plant that has fleshy stems and leaves adapted for storing water. —*adj.* **1** relating to such plants. **2** *of food* tender and juicy. ▸ **succulence** *noun*

succumb (sə-kəm′) *verb intrans.* (**succumbed, succumbing**) **1** (*often* **succumb to**) to give in (to pressure, temptation, or desire, etc.). **2** to stop living; to cease to be alive.

such *adj.* **1** of that kind, or the same or a similar kind. **2** so great: *I'm such a fool.* —*adv.* very; extremely: *such a lovely present.* —*pron.* a person or thing or people or things like that or those just mentioned: *suitcases, garment bags, and such.* —**such as** for example.

suchlike *adj.* of the same kind. —*pron.* people or things of the same kind: *spoons, ladles, and suchlike.*

suck *verb trans., intrans.* (**sucked, sucking**) **1** (*also* **suck in** *or* **up**) to draw (liquid) into the mouth. **2** to draw liquid from (e.g., a juicy fruit) with the mouth. **3** (*also* **suck in** *or* **up**) to draw (something) in by suction. **4** to draw milk from (a breast or udder) with the mouth. **5** *slang* to be disgusting or very inferior. —*noun* an act or bout of sucking.

sucker *noun* **1** *colloq.* **a** a person easily deceived or taken advantage of. **b** a person who is vulnerable in some way: *a sucker for lending money.* **2 a** an organ in certain animals that is adapted to cling to surfaces by suction, in order to assist in feeding, locomotion, etc. **b** a similar artificial device designed to cling to a surface by creating a vacuum. **3** *Bot.* a shoot arising from an underground stem or root that emerges to form a new plant.

suckle *verb trans., intrans.* (**suckled, suckling**) **1** to feed (offspring) with milk from the breast, teat, or udder. **2** to suck milk from (a breast, teat, or udder).

suckling *noun* a young animal still suckling.

sucrose (sōō′krōs,) *noun Chem.* a sugar extracted from sugar cane and sugar beets for use as a sweetener.

suction *noun* **1** the act or power of sucking. **2** a drawing or adhering force created by a difference or reduction in air pressure.

sudden *adj.* **1** occurring suddenly and quickly. **2** unpredicted or unforeseen. ▸ **suddenly** *adv.* ▸ **suddenness** *noun*

sudden infant death syndrome (ABBREV. SIDS) *Med.* the sudden death of an apparently healthy baby for which no adequate cause can be found. *Also called* **crib death**.

suds *pl. noun* a mass of soapy bubbles.

sue *verb trans., intrans.* (**sued, suing**) to institute legal proceedings against (another).

suede (swād) *noun* soft leather given a velvetlike finish.

suet (sōō′ĕt) *noun* hard fat from around the kidneys of sheep or cattle.

suffer *verb trans., intrans.* (**suffered, suffering**) 1 to undergo, or endure (physical or mental pain or other unpleasantness). 2 (**suffer from**) to be affected by (an illness, etc.). 3 to deteriorate as a result of something. 4 to tolerate: *does not suffer fools gladly.* ▸ **sufferer** *noun* ▸ **suffering** *noun*

sufferance (sŭf′rəns) endurance, misery, or permission: *behavior beyond sufferance.*

suffice (sə-fīs′) *verb intrans., trans.* (**sufficed, sufficing**) 1 to be enough or to be good enough for a particular purpose. 2 to satisfy.

sufficient *adj.* enough; adequate. ▸ **sufficiency** *noun* ▸ **sufficiently** *adv.*

suffix *Gram. noun* an element added to the end of a word to mark a grammatical inflection or create a new word. —*verb trans.* (**suffixed, suffixing**) 1 to attach as a suffix to a word. 2 to add a suffix to.

suffocate (sŭf′ə-kāt,) *verb trans., intrans.* (**suffocated, suffocating**) 1 to kill with or die from lack of air. 2 to experience difficulty in breathing because of heat and lack of air; to stifle. 3 to subject to an oppressive amount of something. ▸ **suffocation** *noun*

suffrage (sŭf′rĭj) *noun* the right to vote in political elections.

suffragette (sŭf,rə-jĕt′) *noun* a woman who campaigned for women's suffrage.

suffuse (sə-fyōōz′) *verb trans.* (**suffused, suffusing**) to cover or spread throughout: *suffused in sunlight.* ▸ **suffusion** *noun*

sugar *noun* 1 a white crystalline water-soluble, sweet-tasting carbohydrate. 2 sucrose. —*verb trans.* (**sugared, sugaring**) 1 to sweeten with sugar. 2 to sprinkle or coat with sugar.

sugar beet *or* **sugarbeet** a variety of beet widely cultivated for its large white conical root which yields sugar.

sugar cane *or* **sugarcane** *noun* a tall tropical grass with thick woody stems from which sugar is obtained.

sugarcoat *verb trans.* (**sugarcoated, sugarcoating**) 1 to coat the surface of (e.g., a cookie) with sugar. 2 to make (something unpleasant) more palatable.

sugar daddy *colloq.* an elderly man with a young girlfriend on whom he lavishes money and gifts.

sugar maple a species of N American maple from whose sap sugar is obtained.

sugar pea *see* **snow pea.**

sugary *adj.* 1 resembling sugar in taste or appearance. 2 containing much or too much sugar. 3 *colloq.* exaggeratedly or insincerely pleasant or affectionate; cloying. ▸ **sugariness** *noun*

suggest (səg-jĕst′) *verb trans.* (**suggested, suggesting**) 1 to put forward as a possibility or recommendation. 2 to make one think of; to create an impression of. 3 to cause one to think or conclude.

suggestible *adj.* easily influenced by suggestions made by others.

suggestion *noun* 1 an act of suggesting. 2 a thing suggested; a proposal or recommendation. 3 a hint or trace.

suggestive *adj.* 1 a (**suggestive of**) causing one to think of (something); creating an impression of (something). b conveying a hint. 2 provoking thoughts or feelings of a sexual nature. ▸ **suggestively** *adv.*

suicide (sōō′ĭ-sīd,) *noun* 1 an act or instance of killing oneself deliberately. 2 a person who deliberately kills himself or herself. 3 the bringing about of one's own downfall, often unintentionally. ▸ **suicidal** *adj.*

suit *noun* 1 a set of clothes, usu. a coat with pants or a skirt, made from the same material and designed to be worn together. 2 an outfit worn on specific occasions or for a specific activity. 3 any of the four groups into which a pack of playing cards is divided. 4 *Law* a lawsuit. —*verb trans., intrans.* (**suited, suiting**) 1 to be acceptable to or what is required by. 2 to be appropriate to, in harmony with, or attractive to.

suitable *adj.* appropriate or agreeable. ▸ **suitability** *noun* ▸ **suitably** *adv.*

suitcase *noun* a portable traveling case for clothes, with flat sides and a handle.

suite (swēt) *noun* 1 a set of rooms forming a self-contained unit within a larger building. 2 a matching set of furniture, bathroom fittings, etc. 3 *Mus.* a set of instrumental movements in related keys.

suitor *noun* 1 *old use* a man courting a woman for love or marriage. 2 *Law* a person who sues; a plaintiff.

Sukkoth *or* **Succoth** (sŏŏk′əs, -ōt) *noun* a Jewish harvest festival.

sulfate (sŭl′fāt,) *noun* a salt of sulfuric acid.

sulfide *noun* a compound containing sulfur and another element.

sulfur *or* **sulphur** *noun* (SYMBOL S) a yellow, solid, nonmetallic element. *Also formerly called* **brimstone.** ▸ **sulfuric** *adj.* ▸ **sulfurous** *adj.*

sulk *verb intrans.* (**sulked, sulking**) to be silent or unsociable out of petty resentment or bad temper. —*noun* (*also* **the sulks**) a bout of sulking.

sulky[1] *adj.* (**sulkier, sulkiest**) inclined to sulk; sulking. ▸ **sulkily** *adv.* ▸ **sulkiness** *noun*

sulky[2] *noun* (*pl.* **sulkies**) a two-wheeled horse-drawn vehicle used in trotting races.

sullen *adj.* **1** silently and stubbornly angry or unsociable. **2** *of skies, etc.* dismal. ▸ **sullenly** *adv.* ▸ **sullenness** *noun*

sully *verb trans.* (**sullied, sullying, sullies**) **1** to affect with something discreditable. **2** to make dirty.

sulphur *noun Chem. same as* **sulfur**.

sultan (sʌlt'n) *noun* the ruler of any of various Muslim countries, esp. a former ruler of the Ottoman empire.

sultana (sʌl-tän'ə, -tǎn'ə) *noun* **1** the wife, mother, sister, or daughter of a sultan. **2** a pale seedless raisin.

sultry *adj.* (**sultrier, sultriest**) **1** *of the weather* hot and humid; close. **2** *of a person* having an appearance or manner suggestive of sexual passion; sensual. ▸ **sultrily** *adv.* ▸ **sultriness** *noun*

sum *noun* **1** the amount produced when numbers or quantities are added together. **2** an arithmetical calculation, esp. of a basic kind. **3** an amount of money. —*verb trans.* (**summed, summing**) (*usu.* **sum up**) **1** to summarize. **2** to express or embody the complete character or nature of. **3** to make a quick assessment of.

summa cum laude used on a diploma, etc. to indicate the recipient has attained the highest possible pass.

summary *noun* (*pl.* **summaries**) a short account outlining the main points. —*adj.* done quickly and without attention to details or formalities. ▸ **summarily** *adv.* ▸ **summarize** *verb trans.*

summation *noun* **1** the process of finding a sum; addition. **2** a final summary.

summer *noun* **1** (*also* **Summer**) the warmest season of the year, between spring and autumn. **2** a time of greatest energy, happiness, etc. —*adj.* of, occurring in, or for use in the summer. ▸ **summery** *adj.*

summerhouse *noun* a small building or shelter designed to provide shade in a park or garden.

summertime *noun* the season of summer.

summit *noun* **1** the highest point of a mountain or hill. **2** the highest attainable level of achievement or development, e.g., in a career. **3** a conference between heads of government or other senior officials.

summon *verb trans.* (**summoned, summoning**) **1** *Law* to order (a person) to come or appear, e.g., in a court of law. **2** to order or call upon (someone) to do something. **3** (**summon up**) to gather or muster (e.g., one's strength or energy).

summons *noun* (*pl.* **summonses**) **1** *Law* a written order legally obliging a person to attend a court of law at a specified time. **2** any authoritative order to come or do something. —*verb trans.* (**summonsed, summonsing**) to serve with a summons.

sumo (soo'mo) *noun* Japanese wrestling.

sump *noun* **1** a small oil reservoir in a vehicle engine. **2** a pit into which liquid drains or is poured.

sumptuous (sʌm'chə-wəs) *adj.* superbly rich and luxurious.

sun *noun* **1** (*usu.* **the Sun**) the central object of the solar system, around which the planets revolve. **2** the heat and light of this star. **3** any star with a system of planets revolving around it. —*verb trans.* (**sunned, sunning**) to expose (oneself) to the sun's rays.

sunbathe *verb intrans.* (**sunbathed, sunbathing**) to expose one's body to the sun, in order to get a suntan.

sunbeam *noun* a ray of light from the Sun.

sun block a preparation that prevents sunburn by filtering out the ultraviolet rays of the Sun.

sunburn *noun* soreness and reddening of the skin caused by overexposure to the Sun's ultraviolet rays.

sundae (sʌn'dē) *noun* a portion of ice cream topped with fruit, nuts, syrup, etc.

Sunday (sʌn'dē, -dā) *noun* (ABBREV. **Sun.**) the first day of the week.

sunder *verb intrans., trans.* (**sundered, sundering**) to become or cause to become disunited.

sundial (sʌn'dīl,) *noun* an instrument that uses sunlight to tell the time, by the position of the shadow that a vertical arm casts on a horizontal plate.

sundown *noun* sunset.

sundry *adj.* various; assorted; miscellaneous. —*noun* (*in pl.* **sundries**) various small unspecified items; oddments.

sunfish *noun* a large ocean fish having a compressed, almost circular body.

sunflower *noun* a tall plant that produces large yellow flowerheads on tall stems, and is widely cultivated for its edible seeds.

sung *see* **sing**.

sunglasses *pl. noun* glasses with tinted lenses, worn to protect the eyes from sunlight.

sunk *verb see* **sink**.

sunken *adj.* **1** situated or fitted at a lower level than the surrounding area: *a sunken garden*. **2** *of the cheeks, etc.* hollow through ill health.

sun lamp a lamp emitting light similar in nature to sunlight, used therapeutically and for artificially tanning the skin.

sunlight *noun* light from the Sun.

sunlit *adj.* lit by the Sun.

Sunnite (sŏŏn'ĭt) *noun* a follower of Sunni, one of the two main branches of the Islamic religion. —*adj.* relating to Sunni.

sunny *adj.* (**sunnier, sunniest**) **1** filled with sunshine or sunlight. **2** cheerful.

sunrise *noun* the Sun's appearance above the horizon in the morning. *Also called* **sunup**.

sunroof *noun* a panel that can be opened in a car roof.

sunscreen *noun* a skin preparation that protects against the Sun's ultraviolet rays.

sunset *noun* the Sun's disappearance below the horizon in the evening. *Also called* **sundown**.

sunshade *noun* an umbrella, awning, or billed cap for protecting one from the sun.

sunshine *noun* **1** fair weather, with the Sun shining brightly. **2** the light or heat of the Sun.

sunspot *noun Astron.* a relatively dark cooler patch on the Sun's surface.

sunstroke *noun* heatstroke.

suntan *noun* browning of the skin through exposure to the sun or a sun lamp.

sunup *noun* sunrise.

sup *verb trans., intrans.* (**supped, supping**) to drink or eat in small mouthfuls. —*noun* a small mouthful; a sip.

super *adj. colloq.* extremely good; excellent. —*interj.* used to express extremely positive feelings, views, or reactions. —*noun colloq.* a superintendent.

super- *combining form* forming words denoting: **1** great or extreme in size or degree: *supertanker*. **2** above or beyond: *supernatural*. **3** outstanding: *superhero*.

superannuated (sŏŏ,pər-ăn'yə-wāt,ĭd) *adj.* **1** made to retire and given a pension; pensioned off. **2** old and no longer fit for use.

superb *adj.* **1** *colloq.* outstandingly excellent. **2** magnificent; majestic. ▸ **superbly** *adv.*

supercharger *noun* a device for increasing the air taken into the cylinder of an internal combustion engine, for greater power output. ▸ **supercharge** *verb trans.*

supercilious *adj.* **1** self-important. **2** arrogantly proud. ▸ **superciliously** *adv.* ▸ **superciliousness** *noun*

superconductivity *noun Phys.* complete loss of electrical resistance at temperatures close to absolute zero. ▸ **superconductor** *noun*

superego (sŏŏ,pə-rē'gō) *noun Psychol.* the part of the mind that is concerned with moral conscience or judgment. *See also* **ego** (sense 3), **id**.

supererogation *noun* an act or instance of doing more than is required.

superficial *adj.* **1** of, on, or near the surface. **2** not thorough or in-depth; cursory. **3** only apparent; not real or genuine. **4** lacking the capacity for sincere emotion or serious thought; shallow. ▸ **superficiality** *noun*

▸ **superficially** *adv.*

superfluous (sə-pər'flə-wəs) *adj.* more than is needed or wanted; surplus.

superhighway *noun* **1** a high-speed, multilane highway. **2** a computer network for global communications.

superhuman (sŏŏ,pər-hyŏŏ'mən, -yŏŏ'-) *adj.* beyond ordinary human ability or knowledge.

superimpose *verb trans.* (**superimposed, superimposing**) to lay or set (one thing) on top of another. ▸ **superimposition** *noun*

superintend *verb trans.* (**superintended, superintending**) to supervise. ▸ **superintendence** *noun* ▸ **superintendent** *noun*

superior *adj.* (*often* **superior to**) **1** higher in rank or position than another or others. **2** better in a particular way than another or others. **3** of high quality. **4** arrogant; self-important. —*noun* **1** a person of higher rank or position than others. **2** the head of a community of nuns or friars. ▸ **superiority** *noun*

superlative (sə-pər'lət-ĭv) *adj.* **1** superior to all others; supreme. **2** *Gram.*, of adjectives and adverbs in the form denoting the greatest degree of the quality in question, using either the suffix *-est* or the word *most*. —*noun Gram.* the superlative form, or an adjective or adverb in this form.

superman *noun* a man with extraordinary strength or ability.

supermarket *noun* a large self-service retail store selling food and other goods.

supernatural *adj.* of, relating to, or being phenomena that cannot be explained by the laws of nature or physics. —*noun* (**the supernatural**) supernatural phenomena.

supernova *noun* (*pl.* **supernovae, supernovas**) a star that suddenly becomes millions of times brighter as a result of a catastrophic explosion.

supernumerary *adj.* additional to the normal or required number; extra. —*noun* (*pl.* **supernumeraries**) **1** a supernumerary person or thing. **2** an actor without a speaking part.

superpower (sŏŏ'pər-pow,ər) *noun* a nation with outstanding political, economic, or military influence.

superscript (sŏŏ'pər-skrĭpt,) *Printing adj.*, of a character set above the level of the line, as 2 in 10^2. —*noun* a superscript character.

supersede (sŏŏ,pər-sēd') *verb trans.* (**superseded, superseding**) **1** to take the place of (often something outdated or no longer valid). **2** to set aside in favor of another.

supersonic *adj.* **1** faster than the speed of sound. **2** *of aircraft* capable of exceeding the speed of sound. ▸ **supersonically** *adv.*

superstar *noun* a widely known person.

superstition *noun* **1** belief in an influence that certain, esp. commonplace, objects, actions, or occurrences have on events, people's lives, etc. **2** a particular opinion or practice based on such belief. **3** widely held but unfounded belief. ▶ **superstitious** *adj.*

superstore *noun* a huge retail store, typically part of a chain, that sells a highly diversified product line in great quantity.

superstructure *noun* a part built above another, esp. a main part.

supertanker *noun* a very large ship designed to transport oil, etc. in large quantities.

supervene (sōō͞,pər-vēn′) *verb intrans.* (**supervened, supervening**) to occur as an esp. unexpected interruption to a process. ▶ **supervention** *noun*

supervise (sōō͞′pər-vīz,) *verb trans.* (**supervised, supervising**) to be in overall charge of; to oversee. ▶ **supervision** *noun* ▶ **supervisor** *noun* ▶ **supervisory** *adj.*

supine (sōō-pīn′) *adj.* **1** lying on one's back. **2** passive or lazy.

supper *noun* a light evening meal.

supplant (sə-plănt′) *verb trans.* (**supplanted, supplanting**) to take the place of, often by force or unfair means.

supple *adj.* exhibiting ease and freedom in body movements. ▶ **supplely** *or* **supply** *adv.* ▶ **suppleness** *noun*

supplement (sŭp′lə-mənt) *noun* a thing added to make something else complete or to make up a deficiency. —*verb trans.* (**supplemented, supplementing**) to add to or to make up a lack of. ▶ **supplementary** *adj.* ▶ **supplementation** *noun*

supplicate (sŭp′lĭ-kāt,) *verb trans., intrans.* (**supplicated, supplicating**) to beg for earnestly. ▶ **supplicant** *noun, adj.* ▶ **supplicate** *noun*

supply *verb trans.* (**supplied, supplying, supplies**) **1** to provide or furnish (someone) (with something). **2** to satisfy (e.g., a need); to make up (a deficiency). —*noun* (*pl.* **supplies**) **1** an act of supplying. **2** an amount supplied. **3** an amount that can be drawn from and used. **4** (**supplies**) necessary food or equipment gathered or taken on a journey, etc. **5** *Econ.* the total amount of a commodity being produced for sale. ▶ **supplier** *noun*

support *verb trans.* (**supported, supporting**) **1** to keep upright or in place; to keep from falling. **2** to bear the weight of. **3** to give active approval and encouragement to. **4** to provide with the means necessary for living or existing. **5** to reinforce the disputed accuracy or validity of (e.g., a claim). —*noun* **1** an act of supporting or the state of being supported. **2** a person, group, or thing that supports. ▶ **supporter** *noun* ▶ **supportive** *adj.*

suppose *verb trans.* (**supposed, supposing**) **1** to consider likely or probable; to regard as certain or probable. **2** to treat (a possibility) as a fact for the purposes of forming an argument or plan.

supposed (sə-pōzd′, -pō′zĭd) *adj.* generally believed to be so or such, but considered doubtful by the speaker. ▶ **supposedly** *adv.*

supposing *conj.* assuming that.

supposition *noun* **1** the act of supposing. **2** something supposed; a mere possibility or assumption, not a fact. ▶ **suppositional** *adj.*

suppository (sə-păz′ə-tôr,ē) *noun* (*pl.* **suppositories**) *Med.* a medicine that can be inserted into the rectum or vagina.

suppress *verb trans.* (**suppressed, suppressing**) **1** to hold in or restrain (feelings, etc.). **2** to put a stop to or crush (e.g., a rebellion). **3** to prevent from broadcasting or circulating; to prevent from being broadcast, circulated, or otherwise made known. ▶ **suppression** *noun* ▶ **suppressor** *noun*

suppurate (sŭp′yə-rāt,) *verb intrans.* (**suppurated, suppurating**) to gather and release pus. ▶ **suppuration** *noun*

supremacy (sōō-prĕm′ə-sē) *noun* **1** supreme power or authority. **2** the state of being supreme. ▶ **supremacist** *noun.*

supreme *adj.* **1** of the highest rank, power, or importance. **2** most excellent; best. **3** greatest in degree. ▶ **supremely** *adv.*

Supreme Court 1 the highest US federal court that has jurisdiction over all other US courts of law. **2** (**supreme court**) the highest court of law in most US states.

sur- *prefix* forming words denoting over, above, beyond.

surcharge (sər′chärj,) *noun* **1** an extra charge. **2** an amount over a permitted load; an overload. —*verb trans.* (**surcharged, surcharging**) **1** to impose a surcharge on. **2** to overload.

sure (shōōr) *adj.* (**surer, surest**) **1** confident beyond doubt in one's belief or knowledge; convinced. **2** guaranteed or certain, e.g., (to happen). **3** (**sure of**) unquestionably destined for or assured of (something). **4** undoubtedly true or accurate: *a sure thing.* **5** reliably stable or secure. —*adv. colloq.* of course; certainly. —**for sure** definitely; undoubtedly. **make sure** to take the necessary action to remove all doubt or risk. ▶ **sureness** *noun*

sure-fire *adj. colloq.* sure to succeed; infallible.

sure-footed *or* **surefooted** *adj.* **1** not stumbling or likely to stumble. **2** not making or not likely to make mistakes.

surely *adv.* **1** without doubt; certainly. **2** *used in questions and exclamations* it must be that; it is hoped or expected that: *Surely you are not leaving already!*

surety (shŏŏr'ət-ē) *noun* (*pl.* **sureties**) **1** security against loss or damage, or a guarantee that a promise will be fulfilled. **2** a thing given as security. **3** a person who agrees to become legally responsible for another person's behavior.

surf *noun* the foam produced by breaking waves. —*verb intrans., trans.* (**surfed, surfing**) **1** *Sport* to ride along the waves on a surfboard. **2** *slang* to explore (e.g., various television programs or various sites on a computer network). ▸ **surfer** *noun*

surface *noun* **1** the upper or outer side of something. **2** the upper level of a body or container of liquid. **3** external appearance, rather than underlying reality. —*verb trans., intrans.* (**surfaced, surfacing**) **1** to form the surface of. **2** to rise to the surface of a liquid. **3** to become apparent; to come to light.

surfboard *noun Sport* a long, narrow fiberglass board that a surfer lies or stands on.

surfeit (sər'fĭt) *noun* **1** an excess. **2** the stuffed or sickened feeling resulting from any excess, esp. overeating or overdrinking. —*verb trans., intrans.* (**surfeited, surfeiting**) to feed or indulge until stuffed or disgusted.

surfing *noun* **1** the sport of riding a surfboard. **2** *slang* sampling or exploration of television programs and channels, or of computer networks.

surge *noun* **1** a sudden powerful mass movement, esp. forward. **2** a sudden sharp increase. **3** a violent rush of emotion. —*verb intrans.* (**surged, surging**) to well up, move, increase, or swell suddenly and with force.

surgeon *noun* a specialist in surgery.

surgery (sər'jə-rē) *noun* (*pl.* **surgeries**) **1 a** the treatment of disease or injury by cutting into the patient's body to operate directly on or to remove the affected part. **b** the skill, craft, or profession of a surgeon. **2** an operating room or laboratory used by a surgeon. ▸ **surgical** *adj.* ▸ **surgically** *adv.*

surly *adj.* (**surlier, surliest**) abrupt and impolite. ▸ **surliness** *noun*

surmise (sər-mīz') *verb trans.* (**surmised, surmising**) to conclude from information available; to infer. —*noun* a conjecture drawn from information available.

surmount *verb trans.* (**surmounted, surmounting**) **1** to overcome (problems, obstacles, etc.). **2** to be set on top of; to crown. ▸ **surmountable** *adj.*

surname (sər'nām,) *noun* a name that is shared by members of a family to identify them. *Also called* **last name.**

surpass *verb trans.* (**surpassed, surpassing**) **1** to go or be beyond in degree or extent; to exceed. **2** to be better than.

surplice (sər'plĭs) *noun* a loose white linen garment worn over ecclesiastical robes.

surplus (sər'pləs,) *noun* an amount exceeding the amount required or used. —*adj.* left over after needs have been met; extra.

surprise (sər-prīz, sə-) *noun* **1** an act of catching someone unawares; the state of being caught unawares. **2** something that catches someone unawares. —*verb trans.* (**surprised, surprising**) **1** to impress greatly with something unusual or unexpected. ▣ AMAZE, ASTONISH, ASTOUND. **2** to come upon unexpectedly or catch unawares. **3** to capture or attack with a sudden unexpected maneuver. ▸ **surprising** *adj.* ▸ **surprisingly** *adv.*

surrealism (sə-rē'ə-lĭz,əm) *noun* a movement in modern art and literature that heightens and distorts perception and registration of reality. ▸ **surreal** *adj.* ▸ **surrealist** *noun, adj.* ▸ **surrealistic** *adj.*

surrender *verb intrans., trans.* (**surrendered, surrendering**) **1** to admit defeat by giving oneself up to an enemy; to yield. **2** (**surrender to**) to allow oneself to be influenced or overcome by (a desire or emotion). **3** to give or hand over, voluntarily or under duress. —*noun* the act of surrendering.

surreptitious (sər,əp-tĭsh'əs) *adj.* done secretly or sneakily. ▸ **surreptitiously** *adv.* ▸ **surreptitiousness** *noun*

surrogate (sər'ə-gət, -gāt,) *adj.* standing in for another. —*noun* a surrogate person or thing. ▸ **surrogacy** *noun*

surround *verb trans.* (**surrounded, surrounding**) **1** to extend all around; to encircle. **2** to make up the particular context or environment of. —*noun* a border or edge, or an ornamental structure fitted around it.

surroundings *pl. noun* the places and things around one; environment.

surtax *noun* an additional tax, esp. on incomes above a certain level.

surveillance *noun* the act of keeping a close watch over a person, e.g., a suspected criminal.

survey *verb trans.* (sər-vā') (**surveyed, surveying, surveys**) **1** to look at or examine at length or in detail in order to get a general view. **2** to examine (a building) in order to assess its condition or value. **3** to measure land heights and distances in (an area) for the purposes of drawing a detailed map. —*noun* (sər'vā,) (*pl.* **surveys**) **1** a detailed investigation, e.g., to find out public opinion or customer preference. **2** an inspection of a building to assess condition or value. **3** collecting of land measurements for mapmaking purposes. ▸ **surveyor** *noun*

survive *verb trans., intrans.* (**survived, surviving**) 1 to remain alive or relatively unharmed in spite of (a dangerous experience). 2 to live on after the death of: *survived her husband by 10 years.* 3 to remain alive or in existence. ▶ **survival** *noun* ▶ **survivalist** *noun* ▶ **survivor** *noun*

susceptible *adj.* 1 (**susceptible to**) prone to (something, e.g., a disease). 2 (**susceptible to**) capable of being influenced by (something, e.g., persuasion). 3 (**susceptible of**) open to or admitting of (something): *susceptible of several interpretations.* ▶ **susceptibility** *noun*

sushi *noun* a Japanese dish of small cakes of cold rice topped with raw fish or vegetables.

suspect *verb trans.* (sə-spĕkt′) (**suspected, suspecting**) 1 to consider likely. 2 to think (a person) possibly guilty of a crime or other wrongdoing. 3 to doubt the truth or genuineness of. —*noun* (sŭs′pĕkt,) a person suspected of committing a crime or other wrongdoing. —*adj.* (sə-spĕkt′, sŭs′pĕkt,) thought to be possibly false or untrue.

suspend *verb trans.* (**suspended, suspending**) 1 to hang or hang up. 2 to bring a halt to, esp. temporarily. 3 to delay or postpone. 4 to remove from a job, etc., temporarily, as punishment or during an investigation of possible misconduct.

suspender *noun* 1 (**suspenders**) elastic straps for holding up men's trousers. *Also called* **braces.** 2 a garter.

suspense *noun* a state of nervous or excited uncertainty. ▶ **suspenseful** *adj.*

suspension *noun* 1 the act of suspending or the state of being suspended. 2 a system of springs and shock absorbers that absorb vibrations in a motor vehicle.

suspension bridge a bridge in which the road or rail surface hangs on vertical cables that are attached to thicker cables stretched between towers.

suspicion *noun* 1 an act of suspecting; a belief or opinion based on intuition or slender evidence. 2 a slight quantity; a trace.

suspicious *adj.* 1 (*often* **suspicious of** or **about**) suspecting or tending to suspect (guilt, other wrongdoing, or danger). 2 arousing suspicion; dubious. ▶ **suspiciously** *adv.*

sustain (sə-stān′) *verb trans.* (**sustained, sustaining**) 1 to maintain the energy, or spirits of; to keep going. 2 to suffer or undergo (e.g., an injury). 3 *Law* to judge (esp. an attorney's objection to an opposing attorney's question or comment in court) to be valid. 4 to bear the weight of. 5 to keep in existence, esp. over a long period.

sustenance *noun* that which keeps up energy or spirits, esp. food and drink.

suture (soo′chər) *noun* 1 the thread used in sewing up wounds. 2 a stitch or seam made with such thread. —*verb trans.* (**sutured, suturing**) to sew up (a wound).

suzerain (soo′zə-rən, -răn,) *noun* 1 a nation or state that has control over another. 2 a feudal lord.

svelte *adj.* of attractively slim build.

SW *abbrev.* southwest; southwestern.

sw *abbrev.* short wave.

swab *noun* 1 a piece of cotton or gauze used to clean wounds, apply antiseptics, etc. 2 a mop used for cleaning floors, ships' decks, etc. 3 *slang* a sailor. —*verb trans.* (**swabbed, swabbing**) to clean with or as if with a swab.

swaddle *verb trans.* (**swaddled, swaddling**) 1 to bandage. 2 *old use* to wrap (a baby) in strips of cloth.

swag *noun slang* stolen goods.

swagger *verb intrans.* (**swaggered, swaggering**) to walk with an air of self-importance, to behave arrogantly. —*noun* a swaggering way of walking or behaving.

swallow[1] *verb trans., intrans.* (**swallowed, swallowing**) 1 to allow (e.g. food) to pass down the throat to the stomach. 2 to move the muscles of the throat as if performing such an action; to gulp. 3 (*also* **swallow up**) to engulf or absorb (something). 4 *colloq.* to believe unquestioningly. —*noun* 1 an act of swallowing. 2 an amount swallowed at one time.

swallow[2] *noun* a small bird having narrow, pointed wings and a deeply forked tail.

swam *verb see* **swim.**

swami (swäm′ē) *noun* a Hindu religious teacher.

swamp *noun* an area of permanently waterlogged ground that has a dense covering of vegetation, esp. trees and shrubs. —*verb trans.* (**swamped, swamping**) 1 to overwhelm or inundate. 2 to cause (a boat) to fill with water. 3 to flood. ▶ **swampy** *adj.*

swan (swän) *noun* a large, graceful aquatic bird with a long slender neck.

swank *colloq. verb intrans.* (**swanked, swanking**) to boast or show off. —*noun* 1 an act of boasting. 2 elegance. —*adj.* appealingly elegant or fashionable. ▶ **swanky** *adj.*

swap (swäp) *or* **swop** *verb trans., intrans.* (**swapped, swapping**) to exchange (one thing) for (another); to engage in such exchange. —*noun* 1 an exchange. 2 a thing exchanged or offered in exchange.

swarm *noun* 1 a large group of insects or other small creatures on the move, esp. bees. 2 a crowd of people on the move. —*verb intrans.* (**swarmed, swarming**) 1 to gather, move, or go in a swarm. 2 to be crowded or overrun with people or things.

swarthy *adj.* **(swarthier, swarthiest)** of dark complexion. ▸ **swarthiness** *noun*

swashbuckler *noun* an adventurer, armed with a sword, who leads a flamboyant life. ▸ **swashbuckling** *adj.*

swastika *noun* a plain cross with the ends bent at right angles, the adopted badge of the Nazi party.

wat *verb trans.* **(swatted, swatting)** to crush (e.g., a fly) with a slapping blow. —*noun* a slapping blow.

swatch *noun* a sample, e.g., of fabric.

swath *or* **swathe** (swăth, swôth) *noun* **1** a strip of grass or corn, etc., cut by a scythe or mower; also, the width of this. **2** a broad strip, esp. of land.

swathe *verb trans.* **(swathed, swathing)** to wrap or bind in fabric, e.g., clothes or bandages. —*noun* a wrapping, esp. of cloth.

sway *verb trans., intrans.* **(swayed, swaying) 1** to swing or cause to swing from side to side, esp. slowly and smoothly. **2** to waver between two opinions or decisions. **3** to persuade to take a particular view or decision. —*noun* **1** a motion from side to side. **2** control or influence.

swear (swěr) *verb intrans., trans.* (*pa t* **swore**; *pa p* **sworn**; *pr p* **swearing) 1** to use indecent or blasphemous language. **2** to promise or assert solemnly or earnestly, by or as if by taking an oath. **3 (swear to)** to solemnly state (something) to be unquestionably true. **4 (swear to)** to bind (someone) to (e.g., a solemn promise): *swore him to secrecy.* —**swear in** to introduce (someone) formally into a post, or onto a witness stand, by requesting an oath be taken. **swear off** *colloq.* to promise to renounce or give (something) up.

sweat (swět) *noun* **1** the moisture that the body gives off through the skin's pores. **2** the state, or an instance, of giving off such moisture. **3** *colloq.* an activity that causes the body to give off such moisture. —*verb intrans., trans.* (*pa t and pa p* **sweated** *or* **sweat**; *pr p* **sweating) 1** to give off sweat. **2** to release a moisture. **3** *colloq.* to be nervous, anxious or afraid. —**sweat it out** *colloq.* to endure a difficult or unpleasant situation to the end. ▸ **sweaty** *adj.*

sweater *noun* a knitted, crocheted, or woven jacket or pullover.

sweatpants *pl. noun* loose style pants.

sweatshirt *noun* a loose, usu. long-sleeved cotton pullover with a fleecy lining.

sweatshop *noun* a workshop or factory in which employees work long hours for poor pay and in poor conditions.

sweatsuit *noun* a loose-fitting suit of a sweatshirt and sweatpants. *Also called* **sweats.**

Swede (swēd) *noun* a native or citizen of Sweden.

swede *noun* a large turnip with yellow flesh. *Also called* **rutabaga.**

Swedish (swēd'ĭsh) *noun* the official language of Sweden. —*adj.* of Sweden, its people, or their language.

sweep *verb trans., intrans.* (*pa t and pa p* **swept**; *pr p* **sweeping) 1** (*also* **sweep up** *or* **sweep (something) up)** to clean (a room, a floor, etc.), or remove (dirt, dust, etc.,), with a brush or broom. **2** to take, carry, or push suddenly and with force. **3** to force or inspire into taking an unwanted or unintended direction or course of action. **4** to lift, gather, or clear with a forceful scooping or brushing movement. **5** to move, pass, or spread smoothly, swiftly, or uncontrollably. **6** to walk impressively or arrogantly. **7** to pass quickly over, making light contact. **8** to extend curvingly and impressively into the distance. **9** *of emotions, etc.* to affect suddenly and overpoweringly. **10** to cast or direct (e.g., one's gaze) with a scanning movement. —*noun* **1** an act of sweeping. **2** a sweeping movement. **3** a sweeping line, e.g., of a road or landscape. **4 (sweeps)** (*sing., pl.*) *colloq.* sweepstakes. **5** *colloq.* a chimney sweep. ▸ **sweeper** *noun*

sweeping *adj.* **1** *of a search, change, etc.* wide-ranging and thorough. **2** *of a statement* too generalized; indiscriminate. **3** *of a victory, etc.* impressive; decisive. —*noun* (*usu.* **sweepings**) a thing or a collection of things swept up. ▸ **sweepingly** *adv.*

sweepstakes *noun* (*sing., pl.*) **1** a system of gambling in which the prize money is the sum of the stakes of all those betting. **2** a horserace in which the winning owner receives sums of money put up by all the other owners.

sweet *adj.* **1** tasting like sugar. **2** pleasing to any of the senses, esp. smell and hearing. **3** likable; charming. —*noun* **1 (sweets)** foods rich in sugar, e.g., candies and pastries. **2** a person one loves or is fond of. ▸ **sweetly** *adv.* ▸ **sweetness** *noun*

sweetbread *noun* the pancreas of a young animal, esp. a calf or a lamb, used as food.

sweetbrier *noun* a fragrant species of wild rose. *Also called* **eglantine.**

sweet cicely (sĭs'ə-lē) myrrh (sense 2).

sweet corn a variety of corn, eaten young while still sweet.

sweeten *verb trans.* **(sweetened, sweetening) 1** to make (food) sweet or sweeter. **2** (*also* **sweeten up**) *colloq.* to make (someone) more agreeable or amenable, e.g., by flattery. ▸ **sweetener** *noun*

sweetheart *noun* **1** used as a term of endearment. **2** a lover. **3** a loved one.

sweetmeat *noun* any small candy or piece of fruit that has been candied.

sweet pea a climbing plant with delicate fragrant brightly-colored flowers.

sweet pepper 1 a fruit consisting of a hollow pod, usu. red, green, or yellow in color. *Also called* **bell pepper**. **2** the plant which produces such fruit.

sweet potato 1 a trailing or climbing plant with large purple funnel-shaped flowers. **2** the edible root of this plant. *Also called* **yam**.

sweet-talk *verb trans.* (**sweet-talked, sweet-talking**) *colloq.* to persuade with flattery. ▸ **sweet talk**

sweet tooth a fondness for sweet foods. ▸ **sweet-toothed** *adj.*

sweet william a plant having dense compact heads of dark red or pink flowers.

swell *verb intrans., trans.* (*pa t* **swelled**; *pa p* **swelled** *or* **swollen**; *pr p* **swelling**) **1** to become or make (something) bigger or fatter. **2** to increase or cause to increase in number, size, or intensity. **3** to become visibly filled with emotion, esp. pride. —*noun* **1** an increase in number, size, or intensity. **2** a heaving of the sea without waves. **3** *colloq.* a person who dresses smartly and fashionably. —*adj. colloq.* excellent.

swelling *noun* an area on the body swollen through injury or infection.

swelter *verb intrans.* (**sweltered, sweltering**) to sweat heavily or feel oppressively hot. —*noun* a sweltering feeling or state.

swept *see* **sweep**.

swerve *verb intrans., trans.* (**swerved, swerving**) **1** to turn or move aside suddenly and sharply, e.g., to avoid a collision. **2** to deviate from a course of action. —*noun* an act of swerving; a swerving movement.

swift *adj.* **1** able to move fast; fast moving. **2** done, given, etc., quickly or promptly. —*noun* a small fast-flying bird with a forked tail. ▸ **swiftly** *adv.* ▸ **swiftness** *noun*

swig *colloq. verb trans., intrans.* (**swigged, swigging**) to drink in gulps, esp. from a bottle. —*noun* a large draft or gulp.

swill *verb trans.* (**swilled, swilling**) **1** to rinse by splashing water round or over. **2** *colloq.* to drink (esp. alcohol) greedily. —*noun* **1** any mushy mixture of scraps fed to hogs. **2** disgusting food or drink. **3** *colloq.* a gulp of alcohol.

swim *verb intrans., trans.* (*pa t* **swam**; *pa p* **swum**; *pr p* **swimming**) **1 a** to go through water by moving the arms and legs, or the tail and fins. **b** to cover (a distance) or cross (a stretch of water) in this way. **2** to feel dizzy: *makes my head swim*. —*noun* **1** a

spell of swimming. **2** the general flow of events. —**in the swim** *colloq.* up to date with and often involved in what is going on around one. ▸ **swimmer** *noun*

swimmingly *adj. colloq.* smoothly and successfully.

swimming pool an artificial pool in which to swim.

swimsuit *noun* a garment worn for swimming. *Also called* **bathing suit**.

swindle *verb trans.* (**swindled, swindling**) to cheat or trick; to obtain by cheating or trickery. —*noun* **1** an act of swindling. **2** something that is not what it is presented as being. ▸ **swindler** *noun*

swine *noun* (*pl.* **swine**) **1** a hog. **2** a despicable person.

swing *verb trans., intrans.* (*pa t and pa p* **swung**; *pr p* **swinging**) **1** to open, close, or move to and fro in a curving motion, pivoting from a fixed point. **2** to move or cause to move or turn with a sweeping or swaying movement or movements. **3** to undergo a sudden sharp change or changes, e.g., of mood. **4** *colloq.* to achieve the successful outcome of; to arrange or fix. **5** *colloq.* to determine or settle the outcome of. **6** *colloq., of a social function* to be lively and exciting. **7** *colloq.* to be promiscuous. **8** *slang* to be hanged by the neck until dead. —*noun* **1** an act, manner, or spell of swinging. **2** a swinging movement. **3** a swinging seat suspended from a frame or branch. **4** a sudden sharp change, e.g., in mood. **5** a swinging stroke with a golf club, cricket bat, etc. **6** usual routine or pace.

swinger *noun colloq.* **1** a person who has a very active social life, esp. with much dancing and drinking. **2** a promiscuous person.

swipe *verb trans.* (**swiped, swiping**) **1** to hit with a heavy sweeping blow. **2** (**swipe at**) to try to hit (someone or something). **3** *colloq.* to steal. —*noun* a heavy sweeping blow.

swirl *verb trans., intrans.* (**swirled, swirling**) to flow or cause to flow or move with a whirling or circling motion. —*noun* a whirling, circling motion.

swish *verb trans., intrans.* (**swished, swishing**) to move or cause to move with a brushing or rustling sound. —*noun* a brushing or rustling sound or movement. —*adj. colloq.* smart and stylish.

Swiss (swĭs) *noun* (*pl.* **Swiss**) **1** a native or citizen of Switzerland. **2** either of the dialects of German and French spoken in Switzerland. —*adj.* of Switzerland, its people, or their dialects.

switch *noun* **1** a manually operated or automatic device that is used to open or close an electric circuit. **2** an exchange; a change. **3** a long flexible twig or cane. **4** a set of railroad tracks in two sections and accompanying mechanical equipment, used to transfer engines and/or cars from one track to another. —*verb trans., intrans.* **(switched, switching) 1 (switch on** or **off)** to turn (an appliance, etc.) on or off by means of a switch. **2** to exchange (one thing or person for another), esp. quickly and without notice. **3** to transfer or change over (e.g., to a different system).

switchblade *noun* a knife whose blade is concealed in its handle and springs out at the touch of a button.

switchboard *noun* **1** a board on which incoming telephone calls are connected electronically or manually. **2** a board from which various pieces of electrical equipment are controlled.

switch hitter *Baseball* a hitter who can bat right- or left-handedly.

swivel (swĭv'əl) *noun* a joint between two parts enabling one part to turn or pivot independently of the other. —*verb trans., intrans.* **(swiveled** or **swivelled, swiveling** or **swivelling)** to turn or pivot on a swivel, or as if on a swivel.

swizzle stick a thin stick used to stir cocktails.

swollen *see* **swell**.

swoon *verb intrans.* **(swooned, swooning) 1** to faint. **2 (swoon over)** to go into raptures or fits of adoration over (someone or something). —*noun* an act of swooning.

swoop *verb intrans.* **(swooped, swooping) 1** to fly down with a fast sweeping movement. **2** to make a sudden forceful attack. —*noun* a swooping movement.

swop *verb, noun same as* **swap**.

sword (sôrd) *noun* **1** a weapon like a large knife. **2 (the sword)** violence or destruction, esp. in war.

swordfish *noun* (*pl.* **swordfish, swordfishes**) a large marine fish with a very long and pointed upper jaw.

swordplay *noun* the activity or art of fencing.

swordsman *noun* a man skilled in fighting with a sword. ▸ **swordsmanship** *noun*

swore *see* **swear**.

sworn *verb see* **swear**. —*adj.* bound or confirmed by or as if by having taken an oath: *sworn enemies.*

swum *see* **swim**.

swung *see* **swing**.

sybarite (sĭb'ə-rīt,) *noun* a person devoted to a life of luxury and pleasure. ▸ **sybaritic** *adj.*

After the ancient Greek city of *Sybaris* in Italy, noted for its luxury

sycamore (sĭk'ə-môr,) *noun* **1** an American plane tree. **2** a maple tree of Europe and Asia. **3** the wood of these trees.

sycophant (sĭk'ə-fənt, -fănt,) *noun* a person who flatters in a servile way. ▸ **sycophancy** *noun* ▸ **sycophantic** *adj.*

syllable (sĭl'ə-bəl) *noun* **1** each of the distinct parts into which a spoken word can be divided, e.g. the word *tiger* has two syllables. **2** the slightest sound: *hardly uttered a syllable.* ▸ **syllabic** *adj.*

syllabub or **sillabub** *noun* a frothy dessert made by whipping a sweetened mixture of cream or milk and wine.

syllabus *noun* (*pl.* **syllabuses, syllabi**) a series of topics prescribed for a course of study; also, a booklet or sheet listing these.

syllogism *noun* an argument in which a conclusion is drawn from two independent statements using logic. ▸ **syllogistic** *adj.*

sylph *noun* **1** *Folklore* a spirit of the air. **2** a slender, graceful woman or girl.

sylvan or **silvan** *adj.* of or relating to woods or woodlands; wooded.

symbiosis *noun* (*pl.* **symbioses**) a close association between two organisms of different species, usu. to the benefit of both. ▸ **symbiotic** *adj.*

symbol *noun* **1** a thing that represents or stands for another, usu. something concrete or material representing an idea or emotion. **2** a letter or sign used to represent a quantity, idea, object, operation, etc. ▸ **symbolic** *adj.* ▸ **symbolically** *adv.* ▸ **symbolize** *verb trans.*

Symbolism *noun* **1 (symbolism)** the use of symbols, esp. to express ideas or emotions in literature, movies, etc. **2** a 19th-c movement in art and literature making extensive use of symbols. ▸ **Symbolist** *noun*

symmetry (sĭm'ə-trē) *noun* (*pl.* **symmetries**) **1** exact similarity between two parts or halves, as if one were a mirror image of the other. **2** the arrangement of parts in pleasing proportion to each other; also, the esthetic satisfaction derived from this arrangement. ▸ **symmetrical** *adj.*

sympathetic *adj.* **1** (*also* **sympathetic to**) feeling or expressing sympathy for (someone or something). **2** amiable, esp. because of being kindhearted. **3** acting or done out of sympathy. **4** in keeping with one's mood or feelings; agreeable. ▸ **sympathetically** *adv.*

sympathize *verb intrans.* **(sympathized, sympathizing) (sympathize with)** to feel or express sympathy for (someone). ▸ **sympathizer** *noun*

sympathy *noun* (*pl.* **sympathies**) **1** a genuine understanding of the sadness or suffering of others, often shown in expressions of sorrow or pity. **2** (*often* **sympathy for** or **with**) loyal or approving support for or agreement with (someone). **3** affection between people resulting from their understanding of each other's personalities.

symphonic *adj. Mus.* suitable for performance by a symphony orchestra.

symphony (sĭm′fə-nē) *noun* (*pl.* **symphonies**) **1** a long musical work in several movements, played by a full orchestra. **2** a pleasing combination of parts, e.g., shapes or colors.

symphony orchestra a large orchestra playing large-scale orchestral music.

symposium *noun* (*pl.* **symposia, symposiums**) **1** a conference held to discuss a particular, esp. academic, subject. **2** a collection of essays by different writers on a single topic.

symptom *noun* **1** *Med.* an indication of the presence of a disease or disorder, esp. something not outwardly visible. **2** an indication of the existence of a usu. unwelcome state or condition. ▸ **symptomatic** *adj.*

synagogue (sĭn′ə-gŏg,) *noun* **1** a Jewish place of worship and religious instruction. **2** a Jewish religious assembly or congregation.

synapse (sĭn′ăps,, sĭ-năps′) *noun* in the nervous system, a region where one nerve cell, or neuron communicates with the next.

sync (sĭngk) *or* **synch** *colloq. noun* synchronization. —*verb trans.* (**synced** *or* **synched, syncing** *or* **synching**) to synchronize.

synchronize *verb trans., intrans.* (**synchronized, synchronizing**) to happen or cause to happen, move, or operate in exact time with (something else or each other). ▸ **synchronization** *noun*

synchronous *adj.* in time with something; synchronized.

syncopate (sĭng′kə-pāt,) *verb trans.* (**syncopated, syncopating**) to alter (musical rhythm) by putting the stress on beats not usu. stressed. ▸ **syncopation** *noun*

syndicate *noun* (sĭn′dĭ-kət) **1** an association of people or groups working together on a single project. **2** a group of business organizations jointly managing or financing a single venture. **3** an association of journalists selling material to a variety of newspapers. —*verb trans.* (sĭn′dĭ-kāt,) (**syndicated, syndicating**) **1** to form into a syndicate. **2** to organize or sell by means of a syndicate. ▸ **syndication** *noun*

syndrome *noun* a complex of symptoms that represent a specific physical or mental illness.

synergy (sĭn′ər-jē) *noun* *Biol.* the phenomenon in which the combined action of two or more compounds is greater than the sum of the individual effects of each.

synod *noun* a local or national council of members of the clergy; also, a meeting of this council.

synonym *noun* a word with the same meaning as another word. ▸ **synonymous** *adj.*

synopsis *noun* (*pl.* **synopses**) *noun* a brief outline or summary, e.g., of the plot of a book. ▸ **synoptic** *adj.*

syntax *noun* the positioning of words in a sentence and their relationship to each other; also, the grammatical rules governing this positioning. ▸ **syntactical** *adj.*

synthesis *noun* (*pl.* **syntheses**) **1 a** the process of putting together separate parts to form a complex whole. **b** the result of such a process. **2** *Chem.* the formation of a complex chemical compound from simpler compounds or elements, esp. via a series of chemical reactions.

synthesize *verb trans.* (**synthesized, synthesizing**) **1** to combine (simple parts) to form (a complex whole). **2** to create by chemical synthesis.

synthesizer *noun* an electronic musical instrument for generating and modifying sounds.

synthetic *adj.* **1** not natural; humanmade. **2** not sincere; sham. ▸ **synthetically** *adv.*

syphilis (sĭf′ə-lĭs) *noun* a sexually transmitted disease. ▸ **syphilitic** *adj.*

syphon *noun, verb* same as **siphon**.

syringe (sə-rĭnj′) *noun* a medical instrument used for injecting or drawing off liquid, consisting of a hollow cylinder with a plunger inside and a thin hollow needle attached. —*verb trans.* (**syringed, syringing**) to inject or draw off using a syringe.

syrup (sĭr′əp, sər′-) *noun* a sweet sticky solution of sugar in water, either obtained from various plants, e.g., sugar cane, maple, or manufactured commercially. ▸ **syrupy** *adj.*

system *noun* **1** a set of interrelated parts forming a complex whole: *a transport system.* **2** an arrangement of mechanical, electrical, or electronic parts functioning as a unit. **3** a way of working; a method. **4** efficiency of organization. **5** one's mind or body regarded as a set of interconnected parts: *got the germs out of my. system.* ▸ **systematic** *adj.* ▸ **systematically** *adv.*

systematize *verb trans.* (**systematized, systematizing**) to organize or arrange in a methodical way. ▸ **systematization** *noun*

systemic *adj.* relating to or affecting the whole body or the whole plant. ▸ **systemically** *adv.*

systems analysis the detailed analysis of all phases of activity of a commercial, industrial, or scientific organization, usu. with a computer, in order to plan more efficient methods and better use of resources. ▸ **systems analyst**

systole (sĭs′tə-lē) *noun* *Physiol.* contraction of the heart muscle, during which blood is pumped into the arteries. *See also* **diastole**. ▸ **systolic** *adj.*

Tt

T¹ *or* **t** *noun* (*pl.* **Ts, T's, t's**) the 20th letter of the English alphabet. —**to a T** perfectly well; exactly: *This apartment suits us to a T.*

T² *symbol Chem.* tritium.

t. *abbrev.* ton (sense 1).

TA *abbrev.* teaching assistant.

Ta *symbol Chem.* tantalum.

tab¹ *noun* **1** a small flap, strip of material, etc., attached to an article, e.g., for identification. **2** a small strip of material attached to a garment for hanging it up. **3** *colloq.* a bill, e.g., in a restaurant. —*verb trans.* (**tabbed, tabbing**) to fix a tab to. —**keep tabs on** (**someone** *or* **something**) *colloq.* to keep a close watch or check on (the one specified). **pick up the tab** to pay a bill in a bar or restaurant.

tab² *noun* a key on a word processor or typewriter that sets margins and columns to arrange information in a table. *Also called* **tabulator.**

Tabasco (tə-băs′kō) *trademark* used for a hot sauce made from a pungent type of red pepper.

tabbouleh (tə-bōō′lə, -lē) *noun* a Mediterranean salad made with cracked wheat, tomatoes, cucumbers, and garlic.

tabby *noun* (*pl.* **tabbies**) **1 a** a gray or brown cat with darker stripes. **b** a female domestic cat. **2** a silk with irregular, wavy, shiny markings. —*adj.* having darker stripes or wavy markings.

tabernacle *noun* **1** (*also* **Tabernacle**) *RC Church* a receptacle in which the consecrated bread and wine are kept. **2** a place of worship.

tabla *noun* a pair of small drums played with the hands in Indian music.

tablature *noun* an old system of musical notation indicating the keys, frets, etc., to be used rather than the pitch to be sounded.

table *noun* **1** a piece of furniture consisting of a flat horizontal surface supported by legs. **2** the people sitting at a table. **3** the food served in a particular house: *She keeps a good table.* **4** a group of words, figures, etc., arranged systematically in columns and rows. ▣ **CHART, TABULATION. 5** a multiplication table. **6** a flat level surface. **7** a slab of stone or wood inscribed with laws. —*verb trans.* (**tabled, tabling**) **1** to postpone discussion of (e.g., a bill) indefinitely. **2** to make or enter into a table; to tabulate. —**turn the tables on** (**someone**) to reverse a situation, so that (the one specified) is at a disadvantage.

tableau *noun* (*pl.* **tableaux, tableaus**) **1** a picture of a group or scene. **2** a group of people on stage forming a silent motionless scene from history, etc. *Also called* **tableau vivant.**

tablecloth *noun* an often decorative cloth for covering a table.

table d'hôte (täb,əl-dōt′) (*pl.* **tables d'hôte**) a meal with a set number of choices offered for a fixed price.

table-hop *verb intrans.* (**table-hopped, table-hopping**) *colloq.* to go from one table to another, e.g., in a restaurant, visiting briefly with the people sitting there.

tableland *noun* a broad high plain or a plateau.

tablespoon *noun* (ABBREV. **tbsp.**) a spoon that is larger than a dessert spoon, used for serving food. ▸ **tablespoonful** *noun*

tablet *noun* **1** a small, solid, measured amount of a medicine; a pill. **2** a solid flat piece of, e.g., soap. **3** a slab of stone or wood on which inscriptions may be carved. **4** a pad of paper on which to write.

table tennis a game based on tennis that is played indoors on a table with small bats and a light hollow ball.

tabloid *noun* a newspaper with a relatively small format, esp. one written in a sensational and informal style. *See also* **broadsheet** (sense 2).

taboo *noun* something that is forbidden for religious reasons or by social custom. —*adj.* forbidden or prohibited.

tabor (tā′bər) *noun* a small, single-headed drum played with one hand.

tabular *adj.* in the form of or according to a table.

tabulate (tăb′yə-lāt,) *verb trans.* (**tabulated, tabulating**) to arrange (information) in tabular form. ▸ **tabulation** *noun*

tabulator *noun* tab².

tachometer (tăk-ăm′ət-ər) *noun* a device that measures the rotations per minute of a rotating shaft.

tachycardia (tăk,ĭ-kärd′ē-ə) *noun* the abnormally rapid beating of the heart.

tacit (tăs′ĭt) *adj.* conveyed indirectly, without words or direct references. ▣ IMPLICIT,

IMPLIED, INFERRED, UNDERSTOOD, UNSPOKEN ⊟ SPOKEN, STATED. ▸ **tacitly** *adv.* ▸ **tacitness** *noun*

taciturn *adj.* markedly restrained in speaking. ⊟ CLOSE-LIPPED, CLOSEMOUTHED, TIGHT-LIPPED, TIGHT-MOUTHED, UN-COMMUNICATIVE ⊟ GARRULOUS, LO-QUACIOUS, TALKATIVE. ▸ **taciturnity** *noun*

tack *noun* 1 a short nail with a sharp point and a broad head. 2 a long, loose, temporary stitch. 3 a the direction of a sailing ship that is sailing into the wind at an angle. b a sailing ship's zigzag course. 4 a direction, course of action, or policy. —*verb trans., intrans.* (**tacked, tacking**) 1 (*also* **tack** (**something) down**) to fasten (it) with tacks. 2 to sew with long, loose, temporary stitches. 3 (*also* **tack** (**something) on**) to attach or add (it) as a supplement. 4 a to sail into the wind at an angle. b to change the tack of (a ship) to the opposite one. 5 to change one's direction, course of action, or policy abruptly.

tackle *noun* 1 a an act of trying to get the ball away from a player or of attempting to stop a player on an opposing team, e.g., in football. b either one of the two linesmen on a football team. 2 the equipment needed for a particular sport or occupation. 3 a system of ropes and pulleys for lifting heavy objects. —*verb trans., intrans.* (**tackled, tackling**) 1 to grasp or seize and struggle with. 2 to try to deal with or solve (a problem). 3 to try to get the ball from (a player on the opposing team).

tacky[1] *adj.* (**tackier, tackiest**) slightly sticky.

tacky[2] *adj.* (**tackier, tackiest**) *colloq.* shabby; vulgar. ▸ **tackiness** *noun*

taco *noun* (*pl.* **tacos**) a thin flat corn tortilla, fried and filled with meat, etc.

tact *noun* the use of skill and judgment in finding the best or most considerate way of dealing with others so as to avoid offense. ⊟ DIPLOMACY, SAVOIR FAIRE, TACTFULNESS ⊟ TACTLESSNESS. ▸ **tactful** *adj.* ▸ **tactfully** *adv.* ▸ **tactfulness** *noun* ▸ **tactless** *adj.* ▸ **tactlessly** *adv.* ▸ **tactlessness** *noun*

tactic *noun* a tactical maneuver.

tactical *adj.* 1 relating to or forming tactics. 2 of a bomb, missile, etc. used to support other military operations. ▸ **tactically** *adv.*

tactics *noun* 1 (*sing.*) the military science of employing and maneuvering troops to win or gain an advantage over an enemy. 2 (*pl.*) the plans, procedure, etc., followed, to gain an end. ▸ **tactician** *noun*

tactile (tăk′təl, -tīl,) *adj.* 1 of or having a sense of touch. 2 perceptible to the sense of touch.

tadpole *noun* the larval stage of many frogs and toads.

tae kwon do (tī′kwän′dō′) a Korean martial art.

taffeta *noun* a stiff, shiny cloth woven from silk or rayon.

taffy *noun* (*pl.* **taffies**) a chewy sweet candy that is made with molasses boiled until extremely thick.

tag[1] *noun* 1 a piece of material, paper, etc., that carries information about the object to which it is attached. 2 a metal or plastic point on the end of a shoelace or cord. 3 a piece of loose-hanging cloth. 4 the final speech in a play, or refrain in a song, added to make the moral clear. *Also called* **tag line**. —*verb trans.* (**tagged, tagging**) 1 to put a tag on. 2 (**tag along, on**, *etc.*) to follow or accompany.

tag[2] *noun* a children's game in which one child chases the others and tries to catch them.

tagliatelle (tăl,yä–těl′ə) *noun* pasta made in the form of long narrow ribbons.

tag line *or* **tagline** 1 a tag[1] (sense 4). 2 a slogan associated with a product or service.

tag sale a collection of personal items sold used.

tahini (tə–hē′nĕ) *noun* a thick paste made from ground sesame seeds.

tai chi (tī′jĕ′) *or* **tai chi chuan** a Chinese system of exercise involving extremely slow and controlled movements.

taiga (tī′gə) *noun* the large area of predominantly coniferous forest located S of the Arctic and sub-Arctic tundra regions.

tail *noun* 1 the part of an animal's body that projects from the rear end of the back. 2 something having a form, function, or position similar to that of an animal's tail. 3 a lower, last, or rear part. 4 (**tails**) the reverse side of a coin. —*verb trans.* (**tailed, tailing**) (**tail** (**someone**) *or* **tail after** (**someone**)) to follow (another) closely. —**tail away** *or* **off** to become gradually smaller or weaker than before. **the tail wagging the dog** *colloq.* a situation in which a small factor controls an entire policy, project, or attempt. **turn tail** to turn around and run away. **with** (**one's**) **tail between** (**one's**) **legs** *colloq.* completely defeated or humiliated. ▸ **tailless** *adj.*

tailback *noun Football* the offensive back who lines up farthest from the line of scrimmage.

tailboard *noun* a tailgate.

tailcoat *noun* a man's formal black jacket, with a long, divided, tapering tail slit to the waist.

tail end the very end or last part.

tailgate *noun* the rear door on a motor vehicle that is opened and then closed during and after loading and unloading. *Also called* **tailboard**.

taillights *pl. noun* the usu. red lights on the rear end of a car, etc.

tailor *noun* a person who makes suits, jackets,

etc., to measure, esp. for men. —*verb trans.*, *intrans.* (**tailored, tailoring**) **1** to make and style (garments) so that they fit well. **2** to make suitable for particular or special circumstances. ▸ **tailored** *adj.*

tailor-made *adj.* **1** made by a tailor to fit a particular person well. **2** well suited or adapted for a particular purpose.

tailspin *noun* an aircraft's spiral dive with the nose facing down.

tail wind a wind blowing in the same direction as that in which a ship, aircraft, etc., is traveling.

taint *verb trans.* (**tainted, tainting**) **1** to affect by pollution, putrefaction, or contamination. **2** to contaminate morally or ethically. **3** to affect with something discreditable. ▣ BESMIRCH, CLOUD, SULLY, TARNISH ▣ CLEAR. —*noun* **1** a spot, mark, or trace of decay, contamination, etc. **2** a corrupt or decayed condition. ▸ **tainted** *adj.*

take *verb trans., intrans.* (pa t **took**, pa p **taken**, pr p **taking**) **1** (*often* take something down, off, out, *etc.*) to reach out for and grasp, pull, etc., (something chosen or known); to grasp, enter, etc., for use. **2** to carry, conduct, or lead to another place. **3** to do or perform. **4** to get, receive, or buy. **5** to agree to have or accept. **6** to accept as true or valid. **7** to adopt or commit (oneself) to. **8** to endure or put up with. **9** to need or require. **10** to use as a means of transport. **11** to make (a written note of (something)). **12** to make (a photographic record); to make a photographic record of (someone or something). **13** to study or teach. **14** to remove, use, or borrow without permission. **15** to proceed to occupy. **16** to come or derive from. **17** to have room or strength to support. **18** to consider as an example. **19** to consider or think of in a particular way; to consider mistakenly (someone) to be (someone *or* something). **20** to capture or win. **21** (**be taken with** (**someone** *or* **something**)) to be charmed and delighted by (the one specified). **22** to eat or drink. **23** to conduct or lead. **24** to be in charge or control of. **25** to react to or receive in a specified way. **26** to feel: *takes pride in her work.* **27** (*also* take (something) away *or* off) to subtract (it). **28** to go down or into: *took the first road on the left.* **29** to deal with or consider. **30** to have or produce the expected or desired effect. **31** to measure: *take someone's temperature.* **32** (**be taken sick** *or* **ill**) to become suddenly ill. —*noun* **1 a** a scene filmed or piece of music recorded during an uninterrupted period of filming or recording. **b** one's understanding, e.g., of a matter: *What's your take on this latest turn of* events? **2** the amount of money taken in a business, etc., over a particular period of time. —**take after** (**someone**) to be like (a parent or other relation) in appearance or character. **take** (**someone**) **apart** to criticize or defeat (someone) severely. **take** (**something**) **apart** to separate (it) into pieces or components. **take** (**someone**) **back 1** to make (someone) remember the past. **2** to receive back (a former partner, etc.), after an estrangement. **take** (**something**) **back 1** to withdraw or retract (a statement or promise). **2** to regain possession of (something). **3** to return (something) to an original or former position. **4** to return (something bought from a shop) for an exchange or refund. **take a degree** to study for and obtain a university or college degree. **take** (**something**) **down 1** to make a written record of (it). **2** to demolish or dismantle (it). **3** to lower (it). **take for granted 1** to treat (someone) casually and with no appreciation. **2** to accept (something) as true or valid without question. **take** (**someone**) **in 1** to give (someone) accommodations or shelter. **2** to deceive (someone). **take** (**something**) **in 1** to include (it). **2** to understand and remember (it). **3** to make (a piece of clothing) smaller. **4** to include a visit to (it). **take it 1** to be able to bear suffering, trouble, difficulty, etc. **2** to assume. **take it from me** you can believe me. **take it or leave it** *colloq.* to accept (something that is at issue) or forget it. **take it out of** (**someone**) *colloq.* to exhaust (someone's) strength or energy. **take it out on** (**someone**) *colloq.* to vent one's anger or frustration on (an innocent person). **take it upon** (**oneself**) to take responsibility. **take off 1** *of an aircraft* to leave the ground. **2** to depart or set out. **3** *colloq.* to become popular and successful. **take** (**something**) **off 1** to remove (something, esp. clothing). **2** to spend (a period of time) away from work on vacation, etc. **take** (**someone**) **on 1** to give (someone) employment. **2** to challenge or compete with (someone). **take** (**something**) **on 1** to agree to do (it). **2** to acquire (a new meaning, quality, etc.). **3** *of an aircraft, ship, etc.* to admit new fuel, cargo, etc., on board. **take** (**someone**) **out 1** to go out with (someone) or escort (that person) in public. **2** *slang* to kill or destroy (someone). **take** (**something**) **out 1** to remove or extract (it). **2** to obtain on application: *take out insurance.* **take over** *or* **take** (**something**) **over** to assume control or ownership of (it). **take to** (**someone** *or* **something**) **1** to develop a liking for (the one specified). **2** to begin to do (something) regularly. **take (something) up 1** to use or occupy (space or time). **2** to become interested in (it) and begin to do (it). **3** to resume (a story, account, etc.) after a pause. **4** to accept (an offer). **take (someone) up on (something) 1** to accept (someone's) (offer, proposal, etc.). **2** to discuss (a point or issue) first raised by (someone). **take up with (someone)** to become friendly with (someone); to begin to associate with (someone).

take-home pay the salary that one actually receives after taxes, etc., have been deducted.

taken *see* take.

takeoff *noun* **1** an instance of an aircraft leaving the ground. **2** an act of imitating or mimicking.

takeout *noun* a cooked dish prepared and bought in a restaurant but taken away and eaten elsewhere.

takeover *noun* the act of taking control of something, esp. a company.

taker *noun* a person who accepts something, esp. a bet.

taking *adj.* attractive; charming. —*noun* **(takings)** the amount of money taken in a shop, etc.

talc (tălk) *noun* **1** a soft mineral form of magnesium silicate. *Also called* **talcum. 2** talcum powder.

talcum powder a fine, often perfumed, powder made from purified talc, used on the body.

tale *noun* **1** a story or narrative. **2** a false or malicious story; a lie. —**tell tales** to disclose secret or private information, esp. about another person's wrongdoing.

talebearer *noun* a person who repeats malicious or false gossip.

talent *noun* **1** a special skill or ability, esp. for art, music, etc. **2** a person with such skill or ability. **3** a measure of weight and unit of currency used, e.g., by the ancient Greeks and Romans. ▸ **talented** *adj.*

talent scout a person whose job it is to discover and recruit talented people, esp. in sports and entertainment.

tali *see* talus.

talisman *noun* (*pl.* **talismans**) a small object that is supposed to have magic powers to protect its owner from evil or work magic; a charm. ▸ **talismanic** *adj.*

talk *verb intrans., trans.* (**talked, talking**) **1** (*often* **talk to** *or* **with** (someone)) to express one's ideas, feelings, and thoughts by means of spoken words. **2** to discuss: *Let's talk business.* **3** to use or be able to use speech. **4** to express in speech: *talk nonsense.* **5** to gossip. **6** to give away secret information. **7** to use (a language) or speak in (it). **8** to get (oneself) into a certain state by

talking: *talked themselves hoarse.* **9** (**talk (someone) into** *or* **out of (something)**) to persuade (someone) by talking to do or not to do (something). **10** to have influence: *Money talks.* **11** to give a talk or lecture. —*noun* **1** a conversation or discussion. **2** (*often* **talks**) a formal discussion or series of negotiations. **3** an informal lecture. **4** gossip or rumor, or the subject of it. **5** impractical discussion or boasting: *His ideas are just talk.* **6** a particular way of speaking or communicating: *baby talk.* —**now you're talking** *colloq.* now you are saying something welcome or of significance. **talk (someone) around** to bring (someone) to one's own way of thinking by talking persuasively. **talk back** to answer rudely or boldly. **talk down to (someone)** to talk condescendingly to (someone). **talk (someone) down** to help (a pilot of an aircraft) to land by sending instructions over the radio. **talk (something) out** to resolve (a problem or difference of opinion) by discussion. **talk (something) over** to discuss (it) thoroughly. **talk (something or someone) up** to speak highly of (someone or something). ▸ **talker** *noun*

talkative *adj.* talking a lot.

talkie *noun old use, colloq.* a movie film with sound.

talking head *slang* a person who is interviewed or provides other commentary on television.

talking point a subject for discussion.

talking-to *noun* (*pl.* **talking-tos**) *colloq.* a scolding.

talk show a television or radio program during which well-known people are interviewed and viewers or listeners may call in with comments or questions.

tall *adj.* **1 a** of above average height. **b** of rather great vertical, upward length or extension. ▣ HIGH ▣ LOW, SHORT. **2** having a stated height: *six feet tall.* **3** difficult to believe: *a tall story.*

tallness *noun* the fact or condition of being tall. ▣ HEIGHT, LOFTINESS, STATURE ▣ LOWNESS, SHORTNESS.

tallow *noun* hard fat from sheep and cattle, used to make candles and soap.

tally *noun* (*pl.* **tallies**) **1** an account or reckoning, e.g., of debts or the score in a game. **2** an identifying mark or label. —*verb intrans., trans.* (**tallied, tallying, tallies**) **1** to agree, correspond, or match. **2** to record or mark (a number, score, etc.).

tally-ho *interj.* used to urge the hounds on at a hunt when a fox has been sighted.

Talmud (tăl′mŏŏd,) *noun* the body of Jewish civil and canon law.

talon *noun* a hooked claw, esp. of a bird of prey.

talus (tā'ləs) *noun* (*pl.* **tali**) the ankle bone.

tamari *noun* a concentrated sauce made of soybeans and salt, used esp. in Japanese cooking.

tamarind *noun* **1** a tropical tree with reddish-yellow flowers, whose fruit is a brown pod. **2** the pod of this tree, containing seeds surrounded by a juicy acidic brown pulp.

tambourine *noun* a small round drum usu. with skin stretched tight on one side only, and small disks of metal set into the rim that jingle when the drum is struck with the hand.

tame *adj.* **1** *of animals* used to living or working with people. **2** docile, meek, and submissive. **3** dull and unexciting. —*verb trans.* (**tamed, taming**) **1** to make (an animal) used to living or working with people. **2** to make meek and humble; to subdue. ▸ **tamable** *adj.* ▸ **tamely** *adv.* ▸ **tameness** *noun* ▸ **tamer** *noun*

tam-o'-shanter *noun* a Scottish flat round cloth or woolen cap.

tamp *verb trans.* (**tamped, tamping**) to drive or force down by repeated blows.

tamper *verb intrans.* (**tampered, tampering**) **1** to interfere or meddle, esp. in a harmful way. **2** to attempt to corrupt or influence, esp. by bribery.

tamperproof *adj.* of packaging designed in such a way that it is difficult or impossible to tamper with.

tampon *noun* a plug of cottonwool or other soft absorbent material inserted into a cavity or wound to absorb blood and other secretions, esp. one for use in the vagina during menstruation.

tan *noun* **1** the brown color of the skin after exposure to the Sun's ultraviolet rays. **2** a tawny brown color. —*adj.* tawny brown in color. —*verb trans., intrans.* (**tanned, tanning**) **1** to make or become brown in the Sun. **2** to convert (hide) into leather by soaking (it) in a solution containing tannin, etc. **3** *colloq.* to beat. ▸ **tanned** *adj.*

tandem *noun* a bicycle for two people, with two seats placed one behind the other. —*adv.* one behind the other: *ride tandem.* —**in tandem** together or in partnership.

tandoori *adj.* cooked in a clay oven.

tang *noun* **1** a strong or sharp taste, flavor, or smell. **2** the pointed end of a knife, sword, etc. ▸ **tangy** *adj.*

tangent *noun* **1** a straight line that touches a curve at one point, and has the same gradient as the curve at the point of contact. **2** a function of an angle in a right-angled triangle, defined as the length of the side opposite the angle divided by the length of the side adjacent to it. —*adj.* being or forming a tangent. —**at a tangent** in a completely different direction or course.

tangential *adj.* **1** of or along a tangent. **2** incidental; peripheral.

tangerine (tăn'jə-rēn') *noun* **1** an edible fruit, smaller than an orange, with sweet flesh surrounded by a loose bright orange rind. **2** the reddish-orange color of a tangerine. —*adj.* of the reddish-orange color of a tangerine.

> Originally meaning 'from Tangiers', from where the fruit was exported in the 19th century

tangible *adj.* **1** able to be felt by touch. **2** relating to actual matter or to actuality. ▸ **tangibility** *noun* ▸ **tangibly** *adv.*

tangle *noun* **1** an untidy or knotted state. **2** a confused or complicated state. —*verb trans., intrans.* (**tangled, tangling**) **1** of hair, fibers, etc. to become or make (them) untidy, knotted, and confused. **2** (**tangle with (someone)**) *colloq.* to become involved with (someone), esp. in conflict or an argument. **3** *colloq.* to trap or hamper the movement of. ▸ **tangled** *adj.*

tango *noun* (*pl.* **tangos**) a dance of Argentinian origin with dramatic stylized body positions and long pauses, or a piece of music for it. —*verb intrans.* (**tangoed, tangoing, tangoes**) to perform this dance.

tank *noun* **1** a large container for storing liquids or gas. **2** a heavy, steel-covered, armored vehicle moving on tracks. —*verb trans., intrans.* (**tanked, tanking**) (often **tank up**) **1** to fill the tank of (a vehicle) with fuel. **2** (often **tank up** or **get tanked up**) *slang* to drink or cause to drink heavily and become very drunk.

tankard *noun* a large drinking mug, used esp. for drinking beer.

tanker *noun* **1** a ship or large truck that transports liquid in bulk. **2** an aircraft that transports fuel.

tank top a sleeveless shirt with wide shoulder straps.

tanner *noun* a person who tans leather. ▸ **tannery** *noun*

tannin *noun* a substance obtained from certain tree barks, etc., used in tanning leather, etc. *Also called* **tannic acid.**

tansy *noun* (*pl.* **tansies**) a plant with tubular yellow flowers.

tantalize *verb trans.* (**tantalized, tantalizing**) to tease (someone) by keeping something wanted just out of reach. ▸ **tantalizing** *adj.* ▸ **tantalizingly** *adv.*

tantalum *noun* *Chem.* (SYMBOL **Ta**) a hard bluish-gray metal that is resistant to corrosion and has a high melting point.

tantamount *adj.* (**tantamount to (something)**) having the same effect or result as (something); equivalent to (it).

tantrum *noun* a fit of childish or petulant bad temper.

Taoism (dow'ĭz,əm) *noun* **1** a Chinese philosophical system advocating a life of simplicity and noninterference with the natural course of events. **2** a religion supposedly based on this system of philosophy. ▸ **Taoist** *noun, adj.*

tap¹ *noun* **1** a quick or light touch or blow, or the sound made by one. **2 a** tap dancing. **b** a piece of metal attached to the sole of a shoe for tap dancing. —*verb trans.* (**tapped, tapping**) **1** to strike or knock lightly. **2** (*also* **tap** (**something**) **out**) to produce (it) by tapping. **3** (**tap at** *or* **on** (**something**)) to strike (it) with a light but audible blow.

tap² *noun* **1** a device consisting of a valve, with a handle for opening and shutting it, attached to a pipe for controlling the flow of liquid or gas. **2** a peg or stopper, esp. in a barrel. **3 a** a receiver for listening to and recording private conversations, attached secretly to a telephone line. **b** an act of attaching such a receiver to a telephone line. **4** a screw for cutting an internal thread. —*verb trans.* (**tapped, tapping**) **1** to get sap from (a tree) by cutting into it. **2** to attach a receiver secretly to (a telephone line) so as to be able to hear private conversations. **3** to start using (a source, supply, etc.). —**on tap 1** stored in casks from which it is served. **2** ready and available for immediate use.

tap dance a dance performed wearing shoes with metal on the soles so that the steps can be heard clearly. ▸ **tap-dance** *verb intrans.* ▸ **tap dancer** ▸ **tap dancing**

tape *noun* **1** a narrow strip of woven cloth used for tying, fastening, etc. **2** a magnetic tape. **b** a tape recording or a videotape. **3** adhesive tape. —*verb trans., intrans.* (**taped, taping**) **1** to fasten, tie, or seal with tape. **2** to record (sounds or images) on magnetic tape.

tape deck a tape recorder and player.

tape measure a length of tape, marked with inches, feet, and yards or centimeters and meters, for measuring.

taper *noun* **1 a** a long thin candle. **b** a long waxed wick for lighting candles or fires. **2** a gradual lessening of width toward one end. —*verb trans., intrans.* (**tapered, tapering**) (*also* **taper off**) **1** to make or become gradually narrower toward one end. **2** to make or become gradually less.

tape recorder a machine that is used to record sound or video signals on magnetic tape, and play them back. ▸ **tape-record** *verb trans.* ▸ **tape recording**

tapestry (tăp'ə-strē) *noun* (*pl.* **tapestries**) a thick woven textile with an ornamental design.

tapeworm *noun* a flatworm that lives as a parasite in the intestines of humans and other vertebrates.

tapioca *noun* hard white grains of starch from the cassava plant, often made into a pudding.

tapir *noun* a mammal, related to the horse and rhinoceros, and similar in size to a donkey.

tappet *noun* a lever or projection that transmits motion from one part of a machine to another.

taproom *noun* a bar serving alcoholic drinks.

taproot *noun* a main root of a plant.

taps *noun* (*sing., pl.*) a bugle call for lights out, also used at military funerals.

tar¹ *noun* a dark, sticky, pungent liquid obtained by distillation of coal or wood, or by petroleum refining. —*verb trans.* (**tarred, tarring**) to cover with or as if with tar. —**tarred with the same brush** having the same faults.

tar² *noun old colloq. use* a sailor.

taramasalata (tăr,ə-mäs,ə-lät'ə) *noun* a creamy pink pâté made from the smoked roe of fish.

tarantella (tăr,ən-tĕl'ə) *noun* a lively country dance from S Italy, or a piece of music for it.

tarantula (tə-răn'chə-lə) *noun* **1** a big European wolf spider. **2** any of a family of large tropical spiders with a fist-sized body and long hairy legs.

tardy *adj.* (**tardier, tardiest**) **1** slow to move, progress, or grow. **2** late. ▸ **tardiness** *noun*

tare¹ *noun* **1** the weight of the wrapping paper or container in which goods are packed. **2** the weight of a vehicle without its fuel, cargo, or passengers.

tare² *noun* **1** any of various plants belonging to the vetch family. **2** (*usu.* **tares**) a weed that grows in cornfields.

target *noun* **1** an object aimed at during shooting practice or competitions, esp. a flat round board marked with concentric circles. **2** an object or area fired or aimed at. **3** a person or thing that is the focus of ridicule or criticism. **4** a result aimed at; a goal. —*verb trans.* (**targeted, targeting**) **1** to direct or aim at (something). **2** to make (a person or thing) the object of an attack.

tariff *noun* **1** the tax or duty to be paid on a particular class of goods imported or exported. **2** a list of such taxes and duties.

tarmac *noun* a surface covered with tarmacadam, esp. an airport runway.

tarmacadam *noun* a mixture of small stones bound together with tar, used to make road or airport runway surfaces.

tarn *noun* a small, often circular, mountain lake.

tarnish *verb trans., intrans.* (**tarnished, tarnishing**) **1** to make (metal) dull and discolored. **2** *of metal* to become dull and discolored. **3** to affect with something discreditable. —*noun* **1** a loss of shine or luster. **2** a discolored or dull film on the surface of metal. ▸ **tarnishable** *adj.*

taro *noun* a plant cultivated in the Pacific islands for its edible rootstock.

tarot (tăr′ō) *noun* **1** a pack of playing cards used for playing several different games or in fortune telling. **2** any of the 22 trump cards in this pack, decorated with allegorical pictures.

tarpaulin *noun* heavy canvas that has been made waterproof; also, a sheet of it.

tarragon *noun* a plant whose leaves are used to season foods.

tarry¹ *verb intrans.* (pronounced like *airy*) (**tarried, tarrying, tarries**) **1** to linger in a place. **2** to be late in coming, doing something, etc.

tarry² *adj.* (pronounced like *tar*) (**tarrier, tarriest**) like tar or covered with tar.

tarsus *noun* the bones forming the upper part of the foot and ankle. ▸ **tarsal** *adj.*

tart¹ *adj.* **1** sharp or sour in taste. **2** brief and sarcastic; cutting. ▸ **tartly** *adv.* ▸ **tartness** *noun*

tart² *noun* **1** a pastry case with a sweet filling such as fruit or jam. **2** *derog. slang* a female prostitute or a promiscuous woman.

tartan *noun* **1** a distinctive checked pattern that can be produced with checks of different widths and different colors. **2** a woolen cloth woven with such a design.

Tartar (tär′ər) *noun* **1** (*also* **Tatar**) a member of a people related to the Turks living esp. in Soviet central Asia. **2** (*also* **Tatar**) the language of this people. **3** (**tartar**) a violent or fierce person. —*adj.* of the Tartars or their language.

tartar *noun* a hard deposit that forms on the teeth.

tartar sauce mayonnaise flavored with chopped pickles, capers, etc., often served as a dressing for fish.

tarty *adj.* (**tartier, tartiest**) *derog. slang,* of a woman blatantly sexual or promiscuous.

task *noun* a piece of work to be done; a chore. —*verb trans.* (**tasked, tasking**) to assign (a piece of work) to. —**take** (**someone**) **to task** to scold or criticize (them).

task force 1 a temporary grouping of different units, e.g., land, sea, and air forces, to undertake a specific mission. **2** a similar grouping of individuals for a specific purpose.

taskmaster *noun* a man who sets and supervises the work of others, esp. strictly or severely.

taskmistress *noun* a woman who sets and supervises the work of others, esp. strictly or severely.

Tasmanian devil a carnivorous burrowing marsupial, found only in remote parts of Tasmania.

tassel *noun* a decoration (e.g., on a cushion or lampshade) consisting of a hanging bunch of threads tied firmly at one end. —*verb trans., intrans.* (**tasseled** *or* **tasselled, tasseling** *or* **tasselling**) to adorn with tassels.

taste *verb trans., intrans.* (**tasted, tasting**) **1** to perceive the flavor of (food, drink, etc.) by means of the sensation produced on the surface of the tongue. **2** to try or test a food or drink by eating or drinking a small amount of it. **3** to be aware of or recognize the flavor of. **4** (**taste of** (**something**)) to have a flavor of (it). **5** to experience. —*noun* **1** the particular sensation produced when food, drink, etc., is placed on the tongue. **2** the quality or flavor of a food, drink, etc., that is perceived by this sense. **3** an act of tasting or a small quantity of food or drink tasted. **4** a first, usu. brief, experience of something. **5** a liking or preference. **6** the ability to judge and appreciate what is suitable as well as being fine, elegant, or beautiful. —**to taste** as needed or desired to give a pleasing flavor: *add water to taste.*

taste bud any one of the cells on the surface of the tongue that are sensitive to flavor.

tasteful *adj.* showing good judgment or taste. ▸ **tastefully** *adv.*

tasteless *adj.* **1** lacking flavor. **2** showing a lack of good taste or judgment.

taster *noun* a person whose job it is to taste and judge the quality of food or drink.

tasting *noun* a social event at which wine or another food or drink is sampled.

tasty *adj.* (**tastier, tastiest**) having a very pleasing taste.

tat *verb trans., intrans.* (**tatted, tatting**) to make (lace for trimming) by hand with a small shuttle.

Tatar (tät′ər) *noun same as* **Tartar** (senses 1, 2).

tatter *noun* (usu. **tatters**) a torn ragged shred of cloth. —**in tatters 1** in a torn and ragged condition. **2** of an argument, etc. completely destroyed.

tattered *adj.* ragged or torn.

tatting *noun* delicate knotted lace trimming.

tattle *noun* idle chatter or gossip. —*verb intrans., trans.* (**tattled, tattling**) **1** to chat or gossip idly. **2** to give away (secrets) by chatting idly or gossiping. ▸ **tattler** *noun*

tattoo¹ (tă-tōō′) *verb trans.* (**tattooed, tattooing, tattoos**) to mark (designs) on (a person) by pricking the skin and putting in indelible dyes. —*noun* (pl. **tattoos**) a design tattooed on the skin. ▸ **tattooer** *noun* ▸ **tattooist** *noun*

tattoo² *noun* (pl. **tattoos**) **1** a signal by drum or bugle calling soldiers to quarters. **2** a rhythmic beating, tapping, or drumming.

From a Dutch term meaning to shut off beer taps at closing time, later applied to a military drumbeat at the end of the day

tatty adj. (**tattier, tattiest**) colloq. shabby and untidy.

taught see **teach**.

taunt verb trans. (**taunted, taunting**) to tease or jeer at in a cruel and hurtful way. —noun a cruel, unpleasant, hurtful or provoking remark.

Originally a phrase taunt for taunt, based on the French tant pour tant meaning 'tit for tat'

taupe (tōp) noun a brownish-gray color. —adj. of a brownish-gray color.

Taurus (tôr′əs) noun 1 the Bull, the name of a constellation and the second sign of the zodiac. 2 a person born between Apr. 21 and May 20, under this sign.

taut adj. 1 pulled or stretched tight. 2 showing nervous strain or anxiety. 3 of a ship in good condition. ▸ **tauten** verb trans., intrans.

tautology noun (pl. **tautologies**) the use of words that repeat the meaning found in other words already used. ▸ **tautological** adj.

tavern noun an inn or public house.

tawdry adj. (**tawdrier, tawdriest**) cheap and showy and of poor quality. ▸ **tawdriness** noun

From St Audrey's lace, once used to make cheap lace neckties

tawny noun a yellowish-brown color. —adj. (**tawnier, tawniest**) of a yellowish-brown color.

tax noun 1 a contribution toward a country's expenses raised by the government from people's salaries, property, etc. 2 a strain, burden, or heavy demand. —verb trans. (**taxed, taxing**) 1 to impose a tax on (a person, goods, etc.). 2 to make a heavy demand on. 3 (**tax someone with something**)) to accuse (someone) of (it). ▸ **taxable** adj.

taxation noun the act or system of imposing taxes.

tax-deductible adj., of expenses, etc. eligible for deduction from taxable income.

tax evasion the intentional avoiding of paying taxes, typically by misstating taxable income.

tax-free adj., adv. requiring or subject to the payment of no tax.

tax haven a country or state with a low rate of taxation compared with one's own.

taxi noun (pl. **taxis**) a car that may be hired together with its driver to carry passengers on usu. short journeys. Also called **taxicab**. —verb intrans. (**taxied, taxiing** or **taxying,**

taxies) 1 of an aircraft to move along the ground slowly before or after takeoff or landing. 2 to travel in a taxi.

taxicab noun a taxi.

taxidermy noun the art of preparing, stuffing, and mounting animal skins. ▸ **taxidermist** noun

taximeter (tăk′sē-mēt,ər) noun a meter fitted to a taxi that monitors the distance traveled and displays the fare due.

taxing adj. requiring a lot of mental or physical effort; demanding.

taxonomy noun the theory and techniques of describing, naming, and classifying living and extinct organisms. ▸ **taxonomic** adj. ▸ **taxonomist** noun

taxpayer noun a person who pays or is liable for tax or taxes.

TB abbrev. tuberculosis.

Tb symbol Chem. terbium.

TBA abbrev. to be announced.

T-bone noun a thick steak from the small end of the loin, containing a T-shaped bone.

tbsp. abbrev. tablespoon.

Tc symbol Chem. technetium.

T cell a lymphocyte involved in cellular immunity.

TD abbrev. touchdown (sense 2).

Te symbol Chem. tellurium.

tea noun 1 a a small evergreen tree or shrub, cultivated in China, India, etc., for its leaves. b the dried leaves of this plant prepared for sale. c a drink prepared by infusing the dried leaves of this plant with boiling water. d a similar drink made from the leaves or flowers of other plants: peppermint tea. 2 a light afternoon meal at which tea, sandwiches, and cakes are served.

tea bag a small bag of thin paper containing tea, infused in boiling water in a pot or cup.

teach verb (pa t and pa p **taught**; pr p **teaching**) 1 to cause (a person) to acquire skill or knowledge in (a subject or activity). ▣ INSTRUCT, SCHOOL, TRAIN, TUTOR ▣ LEARN. 2 to give lessons in (a subject). 3 to cause to learn or understand, esp. by example, experience, or punishment.

teacher noun a person who teaches, esp. professionally in a school.

teach-in noun a series of informal lectures, demonstrations, and discussions on a controversial topic, usu. held on a school campus.

teaching noun 1 the work or profession of a teacher. 2 something that is taught, esp. guidance or doctrine.

teaching hospital a large hospital where medical students are taught.

tea cosy a cover to keep a teapot warm.

teacup noun a medium-sized cup used esp. for drinking tea.

teak *noun* **1** a large evergreen tree, native to S India and Southeast Asia. **2** the heavy yellowish wood of this tree, which is hard and durable.

teal *noun* (*pl.* **teal, teals**) a small duck, native to Europe, Asia, and N America.

tealeaf *noun* (*pl.* **tealeaves**) one of the leaves remaining in the pot or cup after the tea made from them has been drunk.

team *noun* **1** a group of people forming one side in a game. **2** a group of people working together. **3** two or more animals working together, esp. in harness together. —*verb intrans., trans.* (**teamed, teaming**) **1** (*often* **team up with** (*someone*)) to form a team for a common action. **2** to harness (horses, oxen, etc.) together.

team spirit the willingness to work together as part of a team.

teamster *noun* **1** a driver of a team of animals. **2** a truck driver.

teamwork *noun* cooperation between those who are working together on a task.

teapot *noun* a pot with a spout and handle used for making and pouring tea.

tear¹ (tïr) *noun* **1** a drop of clear saline liquid that overflows from the eye in response to irritation or as a result of emotion, esp. sorrow. **2** a tear-shaped drop or blob. —**in tears** engaging in crying; weeping.

tear² (tĕr) *verb trans., intrans.* (*pa t* **tore**; *pa p* **torn**; *pr p* **tearing**) **1** to pull or rip apart by force. **2** (**tear at** (**something**)) to pull (it) violently or with tearing movements. **3** to make (a hole, etc.) by or as if by tearing or ripping. **4** to come apart; to be pulled or ripped apart. **5** (*also* **tear** (**someone**) **away**) to remove or take (someone) by force; to force or persuade (someone) to leave. **6** to move with speed and often heedlessly. —*noun* **1** a rip or a hole caused by tearing. **2** generalized damage: *wear and tear.* —**be torn** to be unable to decide between two or more options. **tear** (**someone**) **apart** to cause (someone) severe suffering or distress. **tear** (**something**) **down** to pull (it) down or demolish (it) using force. **tear into** (**someone**) to attack (someone) physically or verbally. **tear off** *colloq.* to move off at great speed. **tear** (**something**) **up 1** to tear (it) into pieces, esp. to destroy (it). **2** to remove from a fixed position by violence or force.

teardrop *noun* a single tear.

tearful *adj.* **1** inclined to cry or weep. **2** with much crying or weeping. ▸ **tearfully** *adv.* ▸ **tearfulness** *noun*

tear gas a gas that causes stinging, blinding tears, and temporary loss of sight, used e.g., to control riots.

tearjerker *noun colloq.* a sentimental movie, book, etc.

tearoom *noun* a restaurant where tea, coffee, cakes, etc., are served.

tea rose a rose with pink or yellow flowers, said to have a fragrance resembling that of tea.

tease *verb trans., intrans.* (**teased, teasing**) **1** to annoy or irritate deliberately or unkindly. **2** to make fun of playfully or annoyingly. **3** to arouse (someone) sexually without satisfying that desire. **4** to comb wool, hair, etc., to remove tangles and open out the fibers. —*noun* a person or thing that teases. —**tease** (**something**) **out** to clarify (an obscure point) by discussion, etc. ▸ **teasing** *adj.* ▸ **teasingly** *adv.*

teasel *noun* a plant with prickly bracts.

teaser *noun* **1** a puzzle or a tricky problem. **2** a person who enjoys teasing others.

teaspoon *noun* (ABBREV. **tsp.**) a small spoon for use with a teacup.

teat *noun* the nipple of an udder.

technetium (tĕk-nē′shē-əm) *noun Chem.* (SYMBOL **Tc**) a metallic radioactive element that is produced artificially.

technical *adj.* **1** having knowledge of, specializing in, or relating to a practical skill or applied science. **2** relating to a particular subject or requiring knowledge of a particular subject to be understood. **3** according to a strict interpretation of the law or rules. **4** of or showing a quality of technique. ▸ **technically** *adv.*

technicality *noun* (*pl.* **technicalities**) **1** a technical detail or term. **2** a trivial or petty detail caused by a strict interpretation of the law or rules. **3** the state of being technical.

technical knockout (ABBREV. **TKO**) a decision by a referee that a boxer has been defeated even though not having been knocked out.

technician *noun* **1** a person specialized or skilled in a practical art or science. **2** a person employed to do practical work in a laboratory.

Technicolor (tĕk′nĭ-kəl,ər) *trademark* used for a process of producing color motion pictures.

technique *noun* **1** a skill, esp. gained through practice. **2** a practical method or skill. **3** a way of achieving one's purpose skillfully; a knack.

techno *noun* a style of pop music that makes uses of electronic effects.

technobabble *noun colloq.* language that overuses technical jargon.

technocracy *noun* (*pl.* **technocracies**) the government of a country or management of an industry by technical experts. ▸ **technocrat** *noun* ▸ **technocratic** *adj.*

technology *noun* (*pl.* **technologies**) **1** the practical use of scientific knowledge in industry and everyday life. **2** practical sciences as a group. ‣ **technological** adj. ‣ **technologist** noun

tectonics noun (sing.) **1** the study of structures that form Earth's crust and the forces that change it. See also **plate tectonics**. **2** the art or science of building and construction.

teddy noun (pl. **teddies**) **1** a child's stuffed toy bear. Also called **teddy bear 2** a woman's one-piece undergarment consisting of a chemise and panties.

tedious adj. tiresomely long-winded or dull. ‣ **tediously** adv. ‣ **tediousness** noun

tedium noun tediousness; boredom.

tee¹ noun the letter T. See also **T¹**.

tee² noun Golf **1** a small peg with a concave top used to support a ball when the first shot is taken at the beginning of a hole. **2** the small area of level ground where the first shot is taken at the beginning of a hole. —**tee off** Golf to play one's first ball at the beginning of a golf hole. **tee (someone) off** slang to make (someone) angry. **tee up** Golf to place a golf ball on a tee ready for a stroke.

teem verb intrans. (**teemed, teeming**) (**teem with people** or **things**) to be full of (them) or abound in (them).

teen noun **1** (**teens**) the years of a person's life between the ages of 13 and 19. **2** colloq. a teenager.

teenage (tē'nāj,) adj. **1** (also **teenaged**) in one's teens. **2** suitable for people in their teens. ‣ **teenager** noun

teeny adj. (**teenier, teeniest**) colloq. tiny.

teenybopper noun colloq. a young teenager, usu. a girl, who enthusiastically follows the latest trends.

teepee noun same as **tepee**.

tee shirt same as **T-shirt**.

teeter verb intrans. (**teetered, teetering**) **1** to stand or move unsteadily; to wobble. **2** to hesitate or waver.

teeth see **tooth**.

teethe (tēth) verb intrans. (**teethed, teething**) of a baby to cut milk teeth. ‣ **teething** noun

teething ring a small hard ring for a baby to chew on while teething.

teetotal adj. never taking alcoholic drink. ‣ **teetotaler** or **teetotaller** noun

Teflon (tĕf'län,) trademark used to denote a polymer widely used to coat the insides of cooking pans to give them a nonstick surface.

tel. abbrev. telephone.

tele- combining form forming words denoting **1** at, over, or to a distance: telegram. **2** television: telecast. **3** telephone: telemarketing.

telecast verb (pa t and pa p **telecast** or **telecasted**; pr p **telecasting**) to broadcast by television. —noun a television broadcast.

telecommunication or **telecommunications** noun a process or group of processes that allow the transmission of information over long distances by means of electrical or electronic signals, e.g., telephone and radio.

teleconferencing noun the facility for conducting conferences between people in two or more remote locations via video, audio, and/or computer links.

telegenic adj. having physical attributes that project well to a television viewing audience.

telegram noun a message sent by telegraph.

telegraph noun a system of or an instrument for sending messages by way of electrical impulses along a wire. —verb trans., intrans. (**telegraphed, telegraphing**) **1** to send (a message) to (someone) by telegraph. **2** to give a warning of (something that is to happen) without being aware of doing so. ‣ **telegrapher** noun

telegraphy (tə-lĕg'rə-fē) noun the science or practice of sending messages by telegraph.

telekinesis (tĕl,ə-kə-nē'sĭs) noun the moving of objects at a distance without using physical force, e.g., by willpower. ‣ **telekinetic** adj.

telemark noun a downhill ski turn executed on cross-country skis.

telemarketing noun a marketing system that uses the telephone to recruit customers and generate product sales.

telemeter (tĕl'ə-mēt,ər) noun an instrument that is used to take measurements and send the readings obtained, usu. by means of electrical or radio signals, to a location remote from the site of measurement. ‣ **telemetric** adj. ‣ **telemetry** (tə-lĕm'ə-trē) noun

teleology noun the doctrine that the universe, all phenomena, and natural processes are directed toward a goal. ‣ **teleological** adj.

telepathy (tə-lĕp'ə-thē) noun the alleged communication of thoughts directly from one person's mind to another's without using any of the five known senses. ‣ **telepathic** adj. ‣ **telepathically** adv.

telephone noun (ABBREV. **tel.**) **1** an instrument for transmitting human speech in the form of electrical signals or radio waves, enabling people to communicate with each other over a distance. —verb trans., intrans. (**telephoned, telephoning**) **1** to seek or establish contact and speak to (someone) by telephone. **2** to make a telephone call. ‣ **telephonic** adj. ‣ **telephony** (tə-lĕf'ə-nē) noun

telephone book a telephone directory.

telephone booth a small compartment or cubicle containing a telephone for public use.

telephone directory a book listing the names, addresses, and telephone numbers of telephone subscribers in a particular area. *Also called* **telephone book**.

telephotography *noun* the photographing of distant objects with lenses that produce large images. ▸ **telephoto** *adj.* ▸ **telephotographic** *adj.*

telephoto lens a camera lens that produces large images of distant or small objects.

teleprinter *noun* an apparatus with a keyboard that types messages as they are received by telegraph and transmits them as they are typed.

TelePrompTer (těl'ə-prămp'tər) *trademark* used to denote a device placed next to a television or film camera, which displays a script to the speaker.

telescope *noun* an optical instrument containing a powerful magnifying lens or mirror that makes distant objects appear larger. —*verb intrans., trans.* (**telescoped, telescoping**) **1** to collapse part within part like a folding telescope. **2** to crush or compress, or become crushed or compressed, under impact.

telescopic *adj.* **1** of or resembling a telescope. **2** able to be seen only through a telescope. **3** able to discern and magnify distant objects. **4** made in sections that slide into each other. ▸ **telescopically** *adv.*

telethon *noun* a usu. day-long television program broadcast to raise money for a specific charity.

Teletype (těl'ə-tīp,) *trademark* used to denote a type of teleprinter.

televangelist *noun* an evangelical preacher who conducts religious service regularly on television.

televise *verb trans.* (**televised, televising**) to broadcast by television.

television *noun* **1 a** an electronic system that is used to convert moving images and sound into electrical signals, which are then transmitted by radio waves or by cable to a distant receiver that converts the signals back to images and sound. **b** a device with a picture tube and loudspeakers that is used to receive picture and sound signals transmitted in this way. **2** television broadcasting in general.

telex *noun* **1** an international telecommunications network that uses teleprinters and radio and satellite links to enable subscribers to send and receive messages to each other. **2** a teleprinter used in such a network. **3** a message received or sent by such a network. —*verb trans.* (**telexed, telexing**) to send (a message) to (someone) via such a network.

tell *verb trans., intrans.* (**told, telling**) **1** to inform or give information to (someone) in speech or writing. **2** (**tell of** (**something**) *or* **tell** (**someone**) **of** (**something**)) to relate or give an account of (something). **3** to command or instruct. **4** to express in words: *tell lies.* **5** to discover or distinguish: *You can tell it by its smell.* **6** (**tell on** (**someone**)) **a** to give away secrets about (the once specified). **b** to have a noticeable effect on (the one specified). —**all told** with all taken into account; in all. **tell apart** to distinguish between (people or things). **tell** (**someone**) **off** to scold or reprimand (someone).

teller *noun* a bank employee who receives money from and pays it out to members of the public.

telling *adj.* having a marked effect.

telling-off *noun* a scolding.

telltale *noun* **1** a person who spreads gossip and rumors, esp. about another person's misdeeds. **2** a device for recording or monitoring a process, machine, etc. —*adj.* revealing or indicating something secret or hidden.

tellurian (tə-lŏŏr'ē-ən) *adj.* of or living on Earth. —*noun* an inhabitant of Earth.

tellurium *noun Chem.* (SYMBOL **Te**) a brittle silvery-white metalloid element.

temblor (těm'blər) *noun* a series of shock waves that pass through Earth, and may cause the ground to shake.

temerity (tə-měr'ət-ē) *noun* rashness or boldness.

temp *noun colloq.* a person employed on a temporary basis.

temper *noun* **1** a state of the mind in which one emotion predominates. **2** a state of calm; composure: *lose one's temper.* **3** a state of uncontrolled anger: *in a temper.* **4** a tendency to have fits of uncontrolled anger: *a hot temper.* **5** the degree of hardness and toughness of metal or glass. —*verb trans.* (**tempered, tempering**) **1** to make less severe: *Temper firmness with understanding.* **2** to heat (a metal or glass) to a certain temperature and then allow (it) to cool slowly, in order to toughen (it). **3** to tune (a keyboard instrument) so that the pitch is correct.

tempera *noun* an emulsion, esp. one made with egg yolks and water, into which powdered pigments are mixed to produce paint.

temperament *noun* **1** a person's natural character or disposition. **2** an excitable or emotional personality. **3** adjustment made to an instrument's keyboard to obtain the correct pitch.

temperamental *adj.* **1** given to extreme changes of mood. **2** *of a machine, etc.* not working reliably or consistently. **3** of or caused by temperament. ► **temperamentally** adv.

temperance noun **1** moderation and self-restraint, esp. in controlling one's appetite or desires. **2** the practice of choosing not to take alcohol.

temperate (tĕm′pə-rət) adj. **1** self-restrained, esp. in appetite or consumption of alcoholic drink. **2** not excessive; moderate. **3** having temperatures that are mild, and neither tropical nor polar. ► **temperately** adv. ► **temperateness** noun. See also **intemperate**.

temperate zones those parts of Earth having moderate temperatures, lying between the tropics and the polar circles.

temperature noun **1** the degree of hotness or coldness, as measured by a thermometer. **2** a body temperature above normal, regarded as an indicator of ill health.

tempest noun **1** a violent storm with very strong winds. **2** a violent uproar.

tempestuous adj. **1** very stormy. **2** violently emotional; passionate. ► **tempestuousness** noun

tempi see **tempo**.

template or **templet** (tĕm′plət) noun **1** a piece of metal, plastic, or wood cut in a particular shape and used as a pattern when cutting out material, drawing, etc. **2** an established pattern or design to be followed: *the template for a new foreign policy.*

temple¹ noun **1** a building in which people worship, esp. in ancient and non-Christian religions. **2** a building in which meetings of a fraternal, often secret, order are held.

temple² noun either of the flat parts of the head at the side of the forehead.

templet noun same as **template**.

tempo noun (pl. **tempos, tempi**) **1** (pl. **tempi**) the speed at which a piece of music should be or is played. **2** rate or speed.

temporal¹ (tĕm′pə-rəl) adj. of or close to the temples on either side of the head.

temporal² adj. **1** of or relating to time. **2** of worldly or secular life as opposed to religious or spiritual life. ► **temporally** adv.

temporary adj. continuing or lasting for only a limited period of time. ⊟ **ACTING, INTERIM, PRO TEM, PRO TEMPORE, PROVISIONAL** ⊟ **PERMANENT.** ► **temporarily** adv.

temporize verb intrans. (**temporized, temporizing**) **1** to avoid making a decision or committing oneself to a course of action, in order to gain time. **2** to adapt oneself to what the occasion requires.

tempt verb trans. (**tempted, tempting**) **1** to seek to attract and persuade (someone) to do something, esp. something wrong or foolish. **2** to attract or allure. **3** to risk provoking, esp. by doing something fool-

hardy. ► **temptation** noun ► **tempter** noun ► **tempting** adj. ► **temptingly** adv.

temptress noun a very alluring, exciting woman.

tempura (tĕm-pŏŏr′ə, tĕm′pə-rə) noun a Japanese dish of seafood or vegetables deep-fried in batter.

Ten. abbrev. Tennessee.

ten noun **1** the number or figure 10. **2** the age of 10. **3** any person or thing denoted by the number 10. **4** 10 o'clock. **5** a set of 10 people or things. **6** a score of 10 points. —adj. **1** 10 in number. **2** aged 10.

tenable adj. able to be believed, upheld, or maintained. ► **tenability** noun

tenacious adj. **1** holding or sticking firmly. **2** determined; persistent. **3** retaining information extremely well; retentive. ► **tenaciously** adv. ► **tenacity** (tə-năs′ət-ē) noun

tenant noun a person who pays rent to another for the use of property or land. —verb trans. (**tenanted, tenanting**) to occupy as a tenant. ► **tenancy** noun

tenantry noun all of the tenants of an estate or a landlord.

tend¹ verb trans. (**tended, tending**) **1** to take care of; to wait on. **2** (**tend to (something)**) to attend to (it).

tend² verb intrans. (**tended, tending**) **1** (**tend to** or **toward (something)**) to be likely or inclined to (it). **2** to move or slope in a specified direction.

tendency noun (pl. **tendencies**) **1** an inclination to act or think in a particular way. **2** a general course, trend, or drift. **3** a bias.

tendentious (tĕn-dĕn′chəs) adj. having a particular bias, tendency, or underlying purpose. ► **tendentiousness** noun

tender¹ adj. **1** soft and delicate. **2** of meat easily chewed or cut. **3** easily damaged or grieved; sensitive. **4** easily hurt when touched, esp. because of having been hurt before. **5** loving and gentle. **6** easily moved to love, pity, etc. **7** youthful and vulnerable. **8** requiring gentle or careful handling. ► **tenderly** adv. ► **tenderness** noun

tender² verb trans., intrans. (**tendered, tendering**) **1** to offer or present (an apology, resignation, etc.). **2** (**tender for (something)**) to make a formal offer to do (work) for a stated amount of money. —noun a formal offer to do work for a stated amount of money. —**put (something) out to tender** to invite tenders for (a job).

tender³ noun **1** (often in compounds) a person who looks after something or someone. **2** a vessel that carries stores to and from a larger vessel. **3** a railroad car attached to a steam locomotive to carry fuel and water.

tenderfoot *noun* (*pl.* **tenderfoots, tenderfeet**) an inexperienced newcomer or beginner.

tenderhearted *adj.* kind and sympathetic. ▸ **tenderheartedness** *noun*

tenderize *verb trans.* (**tenderized, tenderizing**) to make (meat) tender by pounding it.

tenderloin *noun* a cut from the tenderest part of the loin of pork, beef, etc.

tendinitis *or* **tendonitis** *noun* inflammation of a tendon.

tendon *noun* a cord of strong, fibrous tissue.

tendril *noun* a threadlike extension of a stem or leaf.

tenement *noun* a large building divided into several self-contained apartments, typically of low rent and often in poor structural condition.

tenet *noun* a belief, opinion, or doctrine.

ten-gallon hat a cowboy hat.

tennis *noun* a game for two players or two pairs of players, in which players use rackets to hit a light ball across a net on a rectangular court. *Also called* **lawn tennis**.

tenon *noun* a projection at the end of a piece of wood, etc., formed to fit into a mortise in another piece. —*verb trans.* (**tenoned, tenoning**) 1 to fix with a tenon. 2 to cut a tenon in.

tenor *noun* 1 a singing voice of the highest normal range for an adult man; also, a singer having this voice. 2 the general course or meaning of something written or spoken.

tenpin bowling a form of bowling in which 10 pins are set up at the end of an alley and a ball is rolled at them with the aim of knocking as many down as possible. *Also called* **tenpins**. *See* **bowling** (sense 1).

tense¹ *noun* a verb form that shows the time of its action.

tense² *adj.* 1 feeling anxiety and nervous tension. ▤ EDGY, JITTERY, UNEASY, UPTIGHT ▨ LOOSE, RELAXED. 2 tightly stretched; taut. —*verb trans., intrans.* (**tensed, tensing**) to make or become tense. ▸ **tensely** *adv.* ▸ **tenseness** *noun*

tensile (těn′səl) *adj.* 1 capable of being stretched. 2 relating to stretching or tension.

tension *noun* 1 an act of stretching, the state of being stretched. 2 mental or emotional strain or anxiety. 3 strained relations between people, etc. 4 a force that causes a body to be stretched or elongated. 5 electromotive force.

tent *noun* a shelter of canvas or plastic supported by poles or a frame and fastened to the ground by ropes and pegs. —*verb intrans.* (**tented, tenting**) to camp in a tent.

tentacle *noun* 1 a long, thin, flexible appendage growing on the head or near the mouth of many invertebrate animals (e.g., the octopus). 2 in certain plants, a sticky hair on a leaf that serves to trap insects.

tentative *adj.* 1 not having been made final or completed. 2 uncertain; hesitant. ▸ **tentatively** *adv.* ▸ **tentativeness** *noun*

tenterhook *noun* a sharp hooked nail used for fastening cloth to a drying frame. —**on tenterhooks** in a state of impatient suspense or anxiety.

tenth *noun, adj.* 1 the one numbered 10 in a series. 2 one of ten equal parts.

tenuous *adj.* 1 with little strength or substance; slight. 2 thin; slim. ▸ **tenuously** *adv.* ▸ **tenuousness** *noun*

tenure (těn′yər) *noun* 1 the holding of an office, position, or property. 2 the length of time that an office, position, or property is held. 3 the holding of a position, esp. a college or university teaching job, permanently. ▸ **tenured** *adj.*

tepee *or* **teepee** (tē′pē) *noun* a Native American tent.

tepid *adj.* 1 slightly warm; lukewarm. 2 exhibiting no enthusiasm. ▸ **tepidity** *noun* ▸ **tepidly** *adv.*

tequila (tə-kē′lə) *noun* a Mexican spirit used as the basis for many alcoholic drinks.

ter- *prefix* forming words denoting three, threefold, thrice: *tercentenary*.

terabyte *noun Comput.* a unit of storage capacity equal to 2^{40} or 1,099,511,627,776 bytes.

terbium *noun Chem.* (SYMBOL **Tb**) a silvery metal used in semiconductors and phosphors.

tercentenary *noun* (*pl.* **tercentenaries**) a 300th anniversary. —*adj.* of three hundred years.

tergiversate (tər-jĭv′ər-sāt,) *verb intrans.* (**tergiversated, tergiversating**) to change sides. ▸ **tergiversation** *noun*

term *noun* 1 a word or expression, esp. one used with a precise meaning in a specialized field. 2 (**terms**) a particular way of speaking. 3 a limited or clearly defined period of time. 4 the end of a particular time, esp. the end of pregnancy. 5 (**terms**) a relationship between people or countries: *are on good terms with their cousins.* 6 (**terms**) the rules or conditions of an agreement. 7 (**terms**) fixed charges for work. 8 one of the divisions into which the academic and school year is divided. 9 a quantity that is joined to another by either addition or subtraction. —*verb trans.* (**termed, terming**) to name or call. —**come to terms with** (**someone** *or* **something**) to find a way of living with or tolerating someone or some personal trouble or difficulty. **in terms of** in relation to.

termagant *noun* a scolding, overbearing woman.

terminable *adj.* able to be brought to an end.

terminal *adj.* **1 a** causing death; fatal. **b** having an illness that will cause death. **2** *colloq.* extreme; acute. **3** forming or occurring at an end, boundary, or terminus. —*noun* **1** an arrival and departure building at an airport. **2** a large station at the end of a railroad line or for buses. **3** a point in an electrical device by which it may be connected to another device. **4** a device consisting usu. of a keyboard and visual display unit, which allows a user to communicate with and use a distant computer. ▶ **terminally** *adv.*

terminate (tər′mə-nāt,) *verb trans., intrans.* (**terminated, terminating**) **1** to bring or come to an end. **2** to end or conclude. **3** to end (a pregnancy) artificially before its term. **4** to form a boundary or limit to. **5** to go no further; to stop. ▶ **termination** *noun*

termini *see* **terminus**.

terminology *noun* (*pl.* **terminologies**) the words and phrases used in a particular subject or field.

terminus *noun* (*pl.* **terminuses, termini**) **1** the end of a railroad line or bus route, usu. with a station. **2** an extreme or final point.

termite *noun* an insect, found mainly in the tropics, which causes damage to trees, structural timber of buildings, etc. *Also called* **white ant**.

tern *noun* a sea bird that has gray and white plumage with a black cap, narrow wings, and a long, forked tail.

ternary (tər′nə-rē) *adj.* **1** having three parts. **2** using three as a base.

terpsichorean (tərp,sĭk-ə-rē′ən) *adj.* of or relating to dancing.

terrace (tĕr′əs) *noun* **1** each one of a series of raised level banks of soil, like large steps on the side of a hill, used for cultivation. **2** a row of identical and connected houses, usu. one overlooking a slope, or the street onto which they face. **3** a raised, level, paved area by the side of a house used, e.g., for lawn furniture. —*verb trans.* (**terraced, terracing**) to form into terraces or a terrace.

terra cotta 1 an unglazed brownish-orange earthenware used for pottery, statuettes, etc. **2** the brownish-orange color of this earthenware. ▶ **terra-cotta** *adj.*

terra firma dry land; solid ground.

terrain *noun* a stretch of land, esp. with regard to its physical features.

terrapin *noun* an edible turtle.

terrarium *noun* (*pl.* **terrariums, terraria**) **1** an enclosed area in which small land animals are kept. **2** a large globe-shaped sealed glass jar in which plants are grown.

terrestrial *adj.* **1** relating to dry land or to Earth. **2** denoting animals or plants that are found on dry land. **3** worldly; mundane. **4** *of broadcast signals* sent by a land transmitter, not by satellite.

terrible *adj.* **1** *colloq.* very bad: *a terrible singer.* **2** *colloq.* very great; extreme. **3** extremely and disturbingly frightening.

terribly *adv.* **1** in a terrible way. **2** very.

terrier *noun* a small dog orig. bred to hunt animals in burrows.

terrific *adj.* **1** outstanding of its kind or class. **2** very great or powerful. **3** very frightening; terrifying. ▶ **terrifically** *adv.*

terrify *verb trans.* (**terrified, terrifying, terrifies**) to make very frightened. ▶ **terrified** *adj.* ▶ **terrifying** *adj.*

territorial *adj.* **1** of or relating to a territory. **2** *of birds and other animals* likely to establish its own territory and defend it from others.

territorial waters the sea surrounding a nation-state, considered to belong to that state.

territory *noun* (*pl.* **territories**) **1** a stretch of land; a region. **2 a** the land under the control of a ruler, government, or state. **b** (**Territory**) a US political subdivision that is not a state. **3** an area of knowledge, interest, or activity. **4** an area that a bird or other animal treats as its own and defends against others.

terror *noun* **1** very great fear or dread. **2** something or someone that causes such fear. **3** *colloq.* a troublesome or mischievous child.

terrorism *noun* the systematic, organized, and unlawful use of violence and intimidation to force a government to accept certain demands, perpetrated for political or ideological reasons. ▶ **terrorist** *noun, adj.*

terrorize *verb trans.* (**terrorized, terrorizing**) **1** to frighten greatly. **2** to control (someone) by threatening violence.

terror-stricken *adj.* feeling great fear.

terry *noun* (*pl.* **terries**) an absorbent fabric with uncut loops, used esp. for towels.

terse *adj.* **1** brief and concise. **2** abrupt and rude. ▶ **tersely** *adv.* ▶ **terseness** *noun*

tertiary (tər′shē-ĕr,ē) *adj.* third in order, importance, etc.

tesla *noun* a unit of magnetic flux density.

tessera *noun* (*pl.* **tesserae**) a square piece of stone, glass, etc., used in mosaics.

test *noun* **1 a** a critical examination or trial of qualities, abilities, etc. **b** something used as the basis of such an examination or trial, e.g., a set of questions. **2** something that is used to distinguish, detect, or identify a substance. —*verb trans., intrans.* (**tested, testing**) **1** to examine (someone or something, abilities, qualities, etc), esp. by trial. **2** to examine (a substance) to discover whether another substance is present or not. **3** to achieve a stated result in a test: *Three patients tested positive for the virus.* ▸ **tester** *noun*

testament *noun* **1 a** a written statement of what one wants to be done with one's property after death. **b** a will. **2** proof, evidence, or tribute. **3** a covenant between God and humans. **4 (Testament)** either of the two main divisions of the Bible, the *Old Testament* and the *New Testament.* ▸ **testamentary** (tĕs,tə-mĕnt'ə-rē) *adj.*

testate (tĕs'tāt,, -tət) *adj.* having made and left a valid will.

testator *noun* a man who leaves a will at death.

testatrix *noun* a woman who leaves a will at death.

test case *Law* a case whose outcome will serve as a precedent for all similar cases.

test drive a trial drive of a car by a prospective owner. ▸ **test-drive** *verb*

testes *see* **testis**.

testicle *noun* a testis. ▸ **testicular** (tĕs-tĭk'yə-lər) *adj.*

testify *verb intrans., trans.* **(testified, testifying, testifies) 1** to give evidence in a court of law. **2 (testify to (something))** to serve as evidence or proof of (it). **3** to make a solemn declaration (e.g., of one's faith).

testimonial *noun* **1** a letter or certificate giving details of one's character and qualifications. **2** a gift presented as a sign of respect or as a tribute to someone's personal qualities or services.

testimony *noun* (*pl.* **testimonies**) **1** a statement made under oath, esp. in a court of law. **2** evidence: *Her new invention is a testimony to her intelligence.* **3** a declaration of truth or fact.

testis *noun* (*pl.* **testes**) in male animals, either of the two reproductive glands that produce sperm. *Also called* **testicle**.

testosterone (tĕs-täs'tə-rōn,) *noun* the main male sex hormone, a steroid that is secreted primarily by the testes.

test pilot a pilot who tests new aircraft by flying them.

test tube a thin glass tube closed at one end, used in chemical tests or experiments.

test-tube baby a baby born as a result of fertilization under laboratory conditions of one of the mother's ova by male sperm, followed by implantation of the fertilized ovum in the mother's womb.

testy *adj.* **(testier, testiest)** irritable; bad-tempered. ▸ **testily** *adv.* ▸ **testiness** *noun*

tetanus (tĕt'nəs, -n-əs) *noun* an infectious, potentially fatal disease whose main symptoms are fever and painful muscle spasms that result in rigidity of the mouth and facial muscles. *Also called* **lockjaw**.

tetchy *adj.* **(tetchier, tetchiest)** irritable; peevish. ▸ **tetchily** *adv.* ▸ **tetchiness** *noun*

tête-à-tête (tāt'ə-tāt,) *noun* (*pl.* **tête-à-têtes**) a private conversation between two people. —*adj.* in private.

tether *noun* a rope or chain for tying an animal to a post. —*verb trans.* **(tethered, tethering)** to restrain with a tether. —**at the end of (one's) tether** having reached the limit of (one's) patience, resources, etc.

tetra- *combining form* forming words denoting four: *tetracycline.*

Tetragrammaton (tĕ,trə-grăm'ə-tän,) *noun* the Hebrew name of God written using four letters, either *YHWH* (Yahweh) or *JHVH* (Jehovah).

Teuton (tōōt'n, tyōōt'n) *noun* **1** a speaker of a Germanic language. **2** a member of an ancient Germanic tribe from N Europe. ▸ **Teutonic** (tōō-tän'ĭk, tyōō-) *adj.*

Tex-Mex (tĕks,mĕks') *adj.*, *of food, music, etc.* typically Mexican but with elements taken from US culture.

text *noun* **1** the main body of printed words in a book as opposed to the illustrations, etc. **2** the actual words of an author as opposed to commentary on them. **3** a short passage from the Bible taken as the starting point for a sermon, etc. **4** a book, play, etc., forming part of a course of study. **5** the words written or displayed on a visual display unit.

textbook *noun* a book containing the standard principles and information of a subject being studied.

textile (tĕk'stīl,, -stəl) *noun* a cloth or fabric made by weaving or knitting. —*adj.* of, relating to such cloth.

textual *adj.* relating to, found in, or based on a text. ▸ **textually** *adv.*

texture *noun* **1** the way the surface of a material or substance feels when touched. **2** the structure of a substance as formed by the size and arrangement of the smaller particles that form it. **3** the structure of a piece of music, writing, etc., as formed by the individual parts which form it. ▸ **textural** *adj.* ▸ **textured** *adj.*

Th *symbol Chem.* thorium.

Th. *abbrev.* Thursday.

-th[1] *or* **-eth** *suffix* forming ordinal numbers and fractions from cardinal numbers: *fourth / one-fiftieth.*

-th[2] *suffix* forming nouns denoting an action or process, or a state or condition: *death / filth / width.*

Thai (tī) *noun* the official language of Thailand. —*adj.* of Thailand, its people, or their language.

thalidomide (thə-lĭd'ə-mīd,) *noun* a drug formerly used as a sedative but withdrawn because it was found to cause malformation of a fetus if taken by the mother in early pregnancy.

thallium *noun Chem.* (SYMBOL Tl) a soft bluish-white metal that is used in electronic equipment, etc.

than *conj.* **1** used to introduce the second part of a comparison: *She is older than he is.* **2** used to introduce the less desirable option in a statement of alternatives: *I would rather go swimming than play tennis.* **3** other than: *She was left with no alternative than to resign.* —*prep.* in comparison with: *He married someone older than him.*

thanatology *noun* the study of death, its causes, and related phenomena.

thank *verb trans.* (**thanked, thanking**) **1** to express gratitude to. **2** to hold responsible for: *You have only yourself to thank for your failure.* —*noun* (**thanks**) being grateful or the expression of it. ⊟ APPRECIATION, GRATEFULNESS, GRATITUDE. —**no thanks to** in spite of (the one specified). **thank God** *or* **goodness** *or* **heavens** used to express relief. **thanks to** as a result of; because of. **thank you** used to express polite acknowledgment of, e.g., a gift or offer. ▸ **thankful** *adj.* ▸ **thankfully** *adv.* ▸ **thankfulness** *noun* ▸ **thankless** *adj.* ▸ **thanklessly** *adv.* ▸ **thanklessness** *noun*

thanksgiving *noun* **1** a formal act of giving thanks, esp. to God. **2** (**Thanksgiving** *or* **Thanksgiving Day**) a public holiday for giving thanks nationally, occurring on the fourth Thursday in November in the USA.

that *adj.* (*pl.* **those**) **1** indicating the thing, person, or idea already mentioned, specified, or understood. **2** indicating someone or something that is further away or is in contrast: *not this book, but that one.* —*pron.* (*pl.* **those**) **1** the person, thing, or idea just mentioned, already spoken of, or understood. **2** a relatively distant or more distant person, thing, or idea. —*rel. pron.* used instead of *which, who,* or *whom,* to introduce a relative clause. —*conj.* used to introduce a noun clause, or a clause showing reason, purpose, etc.: *He spoke so quickly that no one could understand.* —*adv.* **1** to the degree or extent shown or understood: *won't reach that far.* **2** *colloq., dialect* to such a degree that; so: *I can't believe they're that unsociable!* —**all that** *colloq.* **1** very: *not all that good.* **2** sexually attractive; irresistible: *He thinks he's all that.* **that's that** that is the end of the matter.

thatch *noun* **1** a roof covering of straw, reeds, etc. **2** thick hair on the head. —*verb trans., intrans.* (**thatched, thatching**) to cover (a roof or building) with thatch. ▸ **thatcher** *noun*

thaw *verb intrans., trans.* (**thawed, thawing**) **1** of snow or ice to melt or cause (it) to melt. **2** (*also* **thaw out** *or* **thaw (something) out**) of anything frozen to become or cause (it) to become unfrozen. **3** to become warm enough to begin to melt snow and ice. **4** (*also* **thaw out** *or* **thaw (something) out**) to become or make more friendly or relaxed. —*noun* an act or process of thawing.

the *definite article* **1** used to refer to a particular person or thing already mentioned, implied, or known. **2** used to refer to a unique person or thing: *the Pope.* **3** used before a singular noun to refer to all the members of that group or class: *a history of the novel.* **4** used before an adjective or noun describing an identified person: *William the Conqueror.* **5** used after a preposition to refer to a unit of quantity, time, etc.: *paid by the hour.* —*adv.* **1** used before comparative adjectives or adverbs to indicate (by) so much or (by) how much: *the sooner the better.* **2** used before superlative adjectives and adverbs to indicate an amount beyond all others: *We like this book the best.*

theater *or* **theatre** *noun* **1** a building designed for the performance of plays, operas, etc. **2** a large room with seats rising in tiers, e.g., for lectures. **3** (*also* **the theater**) the writing and production of plays in general. **4** a scene of action or place where events take place. **5** (**the theater**) the profession of actors and theater companies. **6** a building in which movies are shown commercially.

theatrical *adj.* **1** of or pertaining to theaters or to acting. **2** of behavior, a gesture, etc. artificial and exaggerated. —*noun* (**theatricals**) **1** dramatic performances. **2** histrionics: *Spare us the theatricals and get the job done.* ▸ **theatricality** *noun* ▸ **theatrically** *adv.*

thee *pron. old use, dialect* the objective form of *thou.*

theft *noun* an act of stealing; the crime of stealing.

their *adj.* **1** of or belonging to them. **2** his or her: *Have all the kids got their books with them?*

theirs *pron.* a person or thing that belongs to them. —**of theirs** belonging to them.

theism (thē'ĭz,əm) *noun* the belief in the existence of God or a god. See also **deism**. ▸ **theist** *noun* ▸ **theistic** *adj.*

them *pron.* **1** see **they**. **2** people or things already mentioned or spoken about, or understood or implied.

theme *noun* **1** the subject of a discussion or speech. **2** a short melody that forms the basis of a piece of music and that is developed and repeated with variations. **3** a brief essay.

theme park a large amusement park in which all the rides and attractions are based on a particular theme.

theme song a melody or song associated with and usu. played at the beginning and end of a film, television, or radio program.

themselves *pron.* **1** the reflexive form of *they* and *them*. **2** used for emphasis: *They themselves did it.* **3** their normal selves: *They aren't feeling themselves this morning.* **4** without help; alone.

then *adv.* **1** at that time. **2** soon or immediately after that. **3** in that case; that being so. —*noun* that time: *until then.* —*adj.* being at that time: *the then President of the United States.* —**then and there** at that very time and on that very spot.

thence *adv. formal* **1** from that place or time. **2** therefore.

thenceforth *or* **thenceforward** *adv. formal* from that time or place forward.

theo- *combining form* forming words denoting of God or a god.

theocracy (thē-äk′rə-sē) *noun* (*pl.* **theocracies**) government by priests representing a deity. ▸ **theocratic** *adj.*

theology *noun* (*pl.* **theologies**) **1** the study of God, religion and religious belief. **2** a particular system of religion. ▸ **theologian** *noun* ▸ **theological** *adj.*

theorem (thĭr′əm) *noun* a scientific or mathematical statement that makes certain assumptions in order to explain observed phenomena, and that has been proved to be correct.

theoretical *adj.* **1** concerned with or based on theory rather than on practical knowledge or experience. **2** existing only in theory; hypothetical. ▸ **theoretically** *adv.*

theory (thĭr′ē) *noun* (*pl.* **theories**) **1** a series of ideas and general principles that seek to explain an aspect of the world. **2** an idea or explanation that has not yet been proved. **3** the general, usu. abstract, principles or ideas of a subject. **4** ideal, hypothetical, or abstract reasoning: *a good idea in theory but not in practice.* ▸ **theoretician** *noun* ▸ **theorist** *noun* ▸ **theorize** *verb intrans.*

theosophy (thē-äs′ə-fē) *noun* (*pl.* **theosophies**) a religious philosophy based on the belief that a knowledge of God can be achieved through intuition, mysticism, etc. ▸ **theosophical** *adj.* ▸ **theosophist** *noun*

therapeutic *adj.* **1** of or concerning the curing of disease. **2** bringing a feeling of general well-being. ▸ **therapeutically** *adv.*

therapeutics *noun* (*sing.*) the branch of medicine that is concerned with the cure of diseases.

therapy *noun* (*pl.* **therapies**) the treatment of diseases and disorders by means other than surgery or drugs. ▸ **therapist** *noun*

there *adv.* **1** at, in, or to a place. **2** at that point in speech, a piece of writing, etc. **3** in that respect. **4** used to begin a sentence when the subject of the verb follows the verb instead of coming before it: *There are a lot of mistakes.* —*noun* that place or point: *Let's go on from there.* —*interj.* used to express sympathy, satisfaction, etc., or to comfort. —**then and there** at that very time and on that very spot. **there you are 1** *said when giving something to someone* this is what you want. **2** expressing satisfaction or triumph.

> *Usage* The use of *there* after *that* for emphasis is highly stigmatized and considered an illiteracy.
> The adverbial use of *there* to begin a sentence when the subject of the verb follows the verb is often problematic. Some people erroneously construe *there* as a singular noun; and therefore follow it by a singular verb even when the true subject of the verb is plural, as in the grammatically incorrect sentence *There is too many mistakes.* Note that the verb should in such cases always agree in number with the noun or phrase that follows it, as in the grammatically correct form *There are too many mistakes.*

thereabouts *or* **thereabout** *adv.* near that place, number, or time.

thereafter *adv. formal* from that time on.

thereby *adv.* **1** by that means. **2** in consequence.

therefore *adv.* for that reason; as a consequence.

therein *adv.* in that or it.

thereof *adv.* of or from that or it.

thereon *adv.* on or onto that or it.

thereto *adv.* to that or it; in addition.

thereunder *adv.* under that or it.

thereupon *adv.* immediately after that.

thermal *adj.* **1** of or caused by heat. **2** *of clothing* designed to prevent the loss of heat from the body. —*noun* a rising current of warm air. ▸ **thermally** *adv.*

thermistor (thər′mĭsˌtər) *noun* a device in which the electrical resistance decreases rapidly as its temperature rises.

thermo- *combining form* forming words denoting heat: *thermocouple.*

thermocouple *noun* a device for measuring temperature.

thermodynamics *noun (sing.)* the branch of physics concerned with the study of the relationship between heat and other forms of energy. ▶ **thermodynamic** *adj.* ▶ **thermodynamically** *adv.*

thermometer (thər-măm′ət-ər, thə-) *noun* an instrument for measuring temperature.

thermonuclear *adj.* **1** using or showing nuclear reactions that can be produced only at extremely high temperatures. **2** relating to thermonuclear weapons.

thermonuclear bomb an atomic weapon based on fusion, not fission. *See also* **hydrogen bomb.**

thermoplastic *noun* a polymer that can be repeatedly softened and hardened, without any appreciable change in its properties, by heating and cooling it. —*adj.* denoting such a material.

Thermos (thər′məs) *trademark* used to denote a vacuum flask.

thermosetting *adj., of plastics* becoming permanently hard after a single melting and molding.

thermosphere *noun* the layer of Earth's atmosphere situated above the mesosphere, and in which the temperature rises steadily with increasing height.

thermostat *noun* a device that is used to maintain the temperature of a system at a constant preset level.

thesaurus *noun (pl.* **thesauri, thesauruses)** a book that lists words and their synonyms.

these *see* **this.**

thesis *noun (pl.* **theses) 1** a long written essay or report, esp. one presented for an advanced university degree. **2** a proposition to be supported or upheld in argument. **3** an unproved statement put forward for argument or discussion.

Thespian (thĕs′pē-ən) *adj.* of or relating to drama and the theater. —*noun* an actor or actress.

> Named after *Thespis,* founder of ancient Greek tragedy

they *pron.* **1** the people, animals, or things already spoken about or being indicated. **2** people in general. **3** *colloq.* he or she: *Anyone can help if they want.*

> *Usage* The colloquial usage of *anyone/they* as delineated in sense 3 is entirely acceptable in informal settings, especially in conversation. It is objected to by many in formal speech and writing.

they'd *contr.* **1** they had. **2** they would.

they'll *contr.* **1** they will. **2** they shall.

they're *contr.* they are.

they've *contr.* they have.

thiamine (thī′ə-mĭn, -mēn,) *noun* a member of the vitamin B complex that is found in yeast, beans, and green vegetables. *Also called* **vitamin B1.**

thick *adj.* **1** having a relatively large distance between opposite sides. **2** having a specified distance between opposite sides: *one inch thick.* **3** *of liquids* containing a lot of solid matter; viscous. **4** having many single units placed very close together; dense. **5 (thick with (something))** covered with or full of (it). **6** *of an accent* marked; pronounced. **7** *colloq.* stupid; dull. **8** *colloq.* **(thick with (someone))** very friendly or intimate. **9** *colloq.* excessive: *Now that's a bit thick, don't you think?* —*noun* **(the thick) 1** the busiest or most intense part: *in the thick of the fighting.* **2** the thickest part. —**as thick as thieves** *colloq.* very friendly. **through thick and thin** whatever happens: *I'll stick by you through thick and thin.* ▶ **thickly** *adv.* ▶ **thickness** *noun*

thicken *verb trans., intrans.* **(thickened, thickening) 1** to make or become thick. **2** to become more complicated: *The plot thickens.*

thicket *noun* a dense mass of bushes and trees.

thickset *adj.* **1** heavily built; having a thick, short body. **2** *of shrubs* growing or planted close together.

thick-skinned *adj.* not easily hurt by criticism or insults.

thief *noun (pl.* **thieves)** a person who steals.

thieve *verb intrans.* **(thieved, thieving)** to steal. ▶ **thieving** *noun, adj.*

thievish *adj.* given to stealing.

thigh *noun* the fleshy part of the leg between the knee and hip.

thighbone *see* **femur.**

thimble *noun* a small metal or plastic cap worn on the finger to push a needle when sewing.

thin *adj.* **(thinner, thinnest) 1** having a relatively short distance between opposite sides. **2** narrow or fine. **3** not fat; lean. **4** *of liquids* containing very little solid matter. **5** set far apart; not dense or crowded. **6** lacking in body; weak. **7** not convincing or believable. —*verb trans., intrans.* **(thinned, thinning)** *(usu.* **thin (something) out** or **thin out)** to make or become thin or thinner. ▶ **thinly** *adv.* ▶ **thinness** *noun*

thin air nowhere: *disappeared into thin air.*

thine (thīn) *old use, dialect pron.* something that belongs to you. —*adj.* (used before a vowel instead of *thy*) of or belonging to you.

thing *noun* **1** something that is inanimate, yet has demonstrable physical bulk and existence. ▤ ARTICLE, ITEM, OBJECT. **2** a fact, quality, idea, etc., that can be thought about or referred to. **3** an event, affair, or circumstance. **4** *colloq.* a person or animal: *Poor thing!* **5** a persistent or dominating idea: *has a thing about neatness.* **6** (**things**) personal belongings, esp. clothes. —**do (one's) own thing** *colloq.* to do what (one) likes doing best. **make a thing of (something)** to make a fuss about (it) or exaggerate (its) importance. **one of those things** something that must be accepted or cannot be avoided.

thingamajig *or* **thingamabob** *noun colloq.* something whose name is unknown, forgotten, or deliberately not used.

think *verb intrans.*, *trans.* (**thought**, **thinking**) (*often* **think (something)** *or* **think about** *or* **of (something)**) **1 a** to have or form (ideas) in the mind. **b** to have as a thought in one's mind. **2** to consider, judge, or believe. **3** to intend or plan; to form an idea of. **4** to imagine, expect, or suspect. **5** (**think of (someone** *or* **something)**) to keep (someone) in one's mind; to consider (that person). **6** (**think of (something)** *or* **to do (something)**) to remember (it). **7** (**think of (something)**) to form or have an idea about (it). —*noun colloq.* an act of thinking. —**think better of (something** *or* **someone)** **1** to change one's mind about (the one specified), upon further thought. **2** to think that someone would not be so bad as to do something wrong. **think (something) out 1** to consider or plan (it) carefully. **2** to solve (a problem) by thinking about all the aspects of (it). **think (something) over** to consider all the advantages and disadvantages of (an action, decision, etc.). **think (something) through** to think carefully about all the possible consequences of (a plan, idea, etc.). **think twice about (something)** to hesitate before doing (something); to decide in the end not to do (it). **think (something) up** to invent or devise (it).

thinker *noun* a person who thinks, esp. deeply and constructively.

thinking *noun* **1** the act of using one's mind to produce thoughts. **2** opinion or judgment. —*adj.* using the mind intelligently and constructively.

think tank *colloq.* a group of experts who study a subject or problem in great depth.

thinner *noun* a liquid such as turpentine that is added to paint or varnish to dilute it.

thin-skinned *adj.* easily hurt or upset; sensitive.

thio- *combining form* forming words denoting the presence of sulfur in a compound.

third *adj.* **1** denoting the one numbered 3 in a series. **2** one of three equal parts. **3** being the forward gear that is one faster than second in a gearbox. —*noun* **1** the one numbered 3 in a series. **2** one of three equal parts. **3** (*also* **third gear**) the gear that is one faster than second in a gearbox.

third base *Baseball* **1** the third of the three bases, exclusive of home plate. **2** the position guarded by the third baseman, the infielder at third base.

third class 1 the lowest grade, e.g., of traveling accommodations. **2** the category of mail including all printed matter.

third-class *adj.* of the third class. —*adv.* by third-class mail or transport.

third degree prolonged, intensive interrogation, usu. involving intimidation.

third-degree *adj.* denoting the most serious of the three degrees of burning, with damage to the lower layers of skin tissue.

thirdly *adv.* in the third place; as the third reason, etc.

third party a person who is indirectly involved in a legal action, etc., between two principals.

third person *see* **person** (sense 3).

third-rate *adj.* of very bad or inferior quality.

Third World (*also* **the Third World**) the developing countries in Africa, Asia, and Latin America.

thirst *noun* **1** the need to drink. **2** a strong desire or longing. —*verb intrans.* (**thirsted**, **thirsting**) **1** to have a great desire for something. **2** *old use* to be thirsty.

thirsty *adj.* (**thirstier, thirstiest**) **1** needing to drink. **2** eager or longing. ▸ **thirstily** *adv.*

thirteen *noun* **1** the number or figure 13. **2** the age of 13. **3** any person or thing denoted by the number 13. **4** a set of 13 people or things. **5** a score of 13 points. —*adj.* **1** 13 in number. **2** aged 13.

thirteenth *noun, adj.* **1** the one numbered 13 in a series. **2** one of thirteen equal parts.

thirtieth *noun, adj.* **1** the one numbered 30 in a series. **2** one of thirty equal parts.

thirty *noun* (*pl.* **thirties**) **1** the number or figure 30. **2** the age of 30. **3** any person or thing denoted by the number 30. **4** a set of 30 people or things. **5** a score of 30 points. —*adj.* **1** 30 in number. **2** aged 30.

this *pron.* (*pl.* **these**) **1** a person, animal, thing, or idea already mentioned or otherwise understood from the context. **2** a person, animal, thing, or idea which is nearby, esp. that is closer to the speaker than something else. —*adj.* **1** being the person, animal, thing, or idea which is nearby, esp. closer than something else. **2** being the person, animal, thing, or idea just mentioned or otherwise understood. **3** *colloq.* (used instead of *a* or *the* for emphasis) being a person, animal, thing, or idea not yet mentioned. —*adv.* to a usu. extreme degree or extent: *I didn't think it would be this easy.* —**this and that** *colloq.* various minor unspecified actions, objects, etc.

thistle *noun* a plant with deeply indented leaves with prickly margins, and purplish or yellow flowers.

thistledown *noun* the fluffy hairs attached to thistle seeds.

thither *adv.* to or toward that place.

tho' *conj., adv. colloq.* though.

thole *noun* a pin in the side of a boat to keep an oar in place. *Also called* **thole pin**. *See also* **oarlock**.

Thompson submachine gun a submachine gun of .45 caliber. *Also called* **Tommy gun**.

thong *noun* a narrow strip of leather.

thoracotomy *noun* (*pl.* **thoracotomies**) an incision made surgically into the chest wall.

thorax *noun* (*pl.* **thoraxes**, **thoraces**) the part of the body between the head and abdomen. ▸ **thoracic** *adj.*

thorium *noun Chem.* (*SYMBOL* **Th**) a silvery-gray radioactive metal.

thorn *noun* 1 a hard, sharp point sticking out from the stem of certain plants. 2 a shrub bearing thorns, esp. a hawthorn. 3 a constant irritation or annoyance.

thorny *adj.* (**thornier**, **thorniest**) 1 covered with thorns. 2 full of controversial issues. ▣ NETTLESOME, PRICKLY, SPINY.

thorough *adj.* 1 extremely careful and attending to every detail. 2 carried out with great care and great attention to detail. 3 complete; absolute. ▸ **thoroughly** *adv.* ▸ **thoroughness** *noun*

thoroughbred *noun* an animal, esp. a horse, bred from the best specimens. —*adj. of an animal, esp. a horse* bred from the best specimens; purebred.

thoroughfare *noun* a public road or street.

thoroughgoing *adj.* utter; out-and-out.

those *see* **that**.

thou¹ *pron. old use, dialect* you (singular).

thou² *noun* (*pl.* **thou**, **thous**) *colloq.* a thousand, usu. dollars.

though *conj.* 1 despite the fact that. 2 even if. 3 and yet; but. —*adv.* however. —**as though** as if.

thought *noun* 1 an idea, concept, or opinion. 2 an act of thinking. 3 serious, careful consideration. 4 the faculty or power of reasoning. —*verb see* **think**.

thoughtful *adj.* 1 a exhibiting deep thought. ▣ REFLECTIVE, RUMINATIVE ▣ THOUGHTLESS, UNTHINKING. b thinking deeply. 2 showing careful or serious thought: *a thoughtful reply.* 3 thinking of other people; considerate. ▸ **thoughtfully** *adv.* ▸ **thoughtfulness** *noun*

thoughtless *adj.* 1 not thinking about other people; inconsiderate. 2 showing a lack of careful or serious thought. ▸ **thoughtlessly** *adv.* ▸ **thoughtlessness** *noun*

thousand *noun* 1 the number or figure 1,000. 2 a set of 1,000 people or things. 3 a score of 1,000 points. 4 (*usu.* **thousands**) *colloq.* a large unspecified number or amount. —*adj.* 1,000 in number.

thousandth *noun, adj.* 1 the one numbered 1,000 in a series. 2 one of 1,000 equal parts.

thrall *noun* 1 a person who is in the power of another person or thing; a slave. 2 the state of being in the power of another person or thing; slavery. *Also called* **thralldom**.

thrash *verb trans., intrans.* (**thrashed**, **thrashing**) 1 to beat soundly. 2 to defeat thoroughly. 3 (*usu.* **thrash about**, **around**, *etc.*) to move around violently. 4 to thresh (corn, *etc.*). —**thrash (something) out** to discuss a (problem, *etc.*), thoroughly to try to solve (it). ▸ **thrashing** *noun*

thread *noun* 1 a very thin strand of silk, cotton, *etc.*, esp. when several such strands are twisted together for sewing. 2 any very thin strand of fiber. 3 something like a thread in length and narrowness. 4 the projecting spiral ridge around a screw, bolt, or in a nut. 5 a continuous connecting theme in a story, argument, *etc.* 6 (**threads**) *slang* clothing. —*verb trans., intrans.* (**threaded**, **threading**) 1 to pass a thread through (the eye of a needle). 2 to pass (tape, film, *etc.*) into or through something to put it into its correct position. 3 to string (beads) on a thread or a length of string. 4 to make (one's way) carefully through, e.g., narrow streets. 5 to streak (hair, the sky, *etc.*) with narrow patches of a different color. —**hang by a thread** to be in a very precarious or dangerous state.

threadbare *adj.* 1 worn thin; shabby. 2 wearing such clothes. 3 commonly used and meaningless; hackneyed; feeble.

threat *noun* 1 a warning that one is going to hurt someone. 2 a sign that something unpleasant is about to happen.

threaten *verb trans., intrans.* (**threatened**, **threatening**) 1 to make or be a threat to. 2 to give warning that (something unpleasant is about to happen). 3 *of something unpleasant* to seem likely to happen. ▸ **threatening** *adj.* ▸ **threateningly** *adv.*

three *noun* 1 the number or figure 3. 2 the age of 3. 3 any person or thing denoted by the number 3. 4 3 o'clock. 5 a set of 3 people or things. 6 a score of 3 points. —*adj.* 1 3 in number. 2 aged 3.

three-D or **3-D** *adj.* of, relating to, or being a cinematic medium or production in three dimensions.

three-dimensional *adj.* 1 having or appearing to have three dimensions, i.e., height, width, and depth. 2 *of fictional characters* developed or described in detail and therefore lifelike.

three-legged race a race run between pairs of runners who have their adjacent legs tied together.

three-quarter *adj.* being three-quarters of the full amount or length.

three Rs reading, writing, and arithmetic.

threesome *noun* a group of three.

threnody (thrĕn'əd-ē) *noun* (*pl.* **threnodies**) a song or ode of lamentation.

thresh *verb trans., intrans.* (**threshed, threshing**) to separate the grain or seeds from the stalks of (cereal plants) by beating.

threshold *noun* 1 a piece of wood or stone forming the bottom of a doorway. 2 a doorway. 3 a starting point: *on the threshold of a new career.* 4 the minimum intensity of a stimulus, e.g., pain, that is required to produce a response.

threw *see* **throw**.

thrice *adv.* three times.

thrift *noun* 1 careful management of resources, esp. money. 2 a savings and loan association or savings bank. ▸ **thrifty** *adj.*

thrift shop a store selling preowned items of merchandise.

thrill *verb trans., intrans.* (**thrilled, thrilling**) 1 to cause to feel, or to feel, a sudden strong sensation of excitement or pleasure. ◙ ELECTRIFY. 2 to vibrate or quiver. —*noun* 1 a sudden tingling feeling of excitement or pleasure. 2 something that causes such a feeling. 3 a shivering or trembling feeling caused esp. by fear or distress. ▸ **thrilling** *adj.* ▸ **thrillingly** *adv.*

thriller *noun* an exciting novel, play, or film.

thrive *verb intrans.* (*pa t* **thrived** *or* **throve**; *pa p* **thrived** *or* **thriven**; *pr p* **thriving**) 1 to grow strong and healthy. 2 to prosper or be successful.

throat *noun* 1 the passage that leads from the mouth to the stomach. 2 the front part of the neck. 3 a narrow passageway or opening. —**ram (something) down (someone's) throat** *colloq.* to force (someone) to consider or accept (something undesirable). **stick in (one's) throat** to be impossible to accept.

throaty *adj.* (**throatier, throatiest**) deep and hoarse. *a throaty whisper.* ▸ **throatiness** *noun*

throb *verb intrans.* (**throbbed, throbbing**) 1 to beat, esp. with unusual force. 2 to vibrate with a strong, regular rhythm. ◙ BEAT, PULSATE, PULSE. —*noun* a regular beat; a pulse.

throe *noun* (*usu.* **throes**) a violent pang or spasm. —**in the throes of (something)** in a difficult or painful struggle with (it).

thrombi *see* **thrombus**.

thrombosis *noun* (*pl.* **thromboses**) the formation of a blood clot in a blood vessel.

thrombus *noun* (*pl.* **thrombi**) a blood clot in a blood vessel.

throne *noun* 1 the ceremonial chair of a sovereign or bishop. 2 the office or power of a sovereign.

throng *noun* a crowd; a multitude. —*verb trans., intrans.* (**thronged, thronging**) 1 to crowd or fill. 2 to come together in great numbers.

throttle *noun* a valve that regulates the amount of fuel supplied to an engine. —*verb trans.* (**throttled, throttling**) 1 to injure or kill by choking or strangling. 2 to prevent from being said, expressed, etc.. 3 to control the flow of (fuel) to an engine using a valve. —**throttle back** to reduce the speed of (an engine) by closing the throttle to reduce the amount of fuel supplied to (it).

through *prep.* 1 going from one side or end of to the other. 2 everywhere within: *searched through the house.* 3 from the beginning to the end of. 4 up to and including: *Tuesday through Thursday.* 5 because of: *lost his job through stupidity.* —*adv.* 1 from one side or end to the other. 2 from the beginning to the end: *read the magazine through.* 3 into a position of having completed, esp. successfully. 4 to the core; completely: *soaked through.* 5 in or into communication by telephone: *put the caller through.* —*adj.* going all the way to one's destination without requiring a change of train, etc. —**be through** to have no further prospects or intentions. **be through with (someone)** to have no more to do with (the one specified). **be through with (something)** to have finished or completed (it). **through and through** to a total extent or degree; completely.

throughout *prep.* 1 in all parts of. 2 during the whole of. —*adv.* 1 in every part; everywhere. 2 during the whole time.

throughput *noun* the amount of material put through a process, esp. a computer.

throve *see* **thrive**.

throw *verb trans., intrans.* (*pa t* **threw**; *pa p* **thrown**; *pr p* **throwing**) 1 to propel through the air with force, esp. with a rapid forward movement of the hand and arm. 2 to move into a specified position, esp. suddenly or violently. 3 to put into a specified condition, esp. suddenly. 4 to direct or cast: *throw a glance at someone.* 5 *colloq.* to puzzle or confuse. 6 *of a horse* to make (its rider) fall off. 7 to move (a switch or lever) so as to operate a mechanism. 8 to make (pottery) on a potter's wheel. 9 *colloq.* to lose (a contest) deliberately, esp. in return for a bribe. 10 a to roll (dice) on to a flat surface. b to obtain (a specified number) by throwing dice. **11** to have: *throw a tantrum.* **12** *colloq.* to give (a party). **13** to deliver (a punch). **14** to cause (one's voice) to appear to come from elsewhere. —*noun* **1** an act of throwing. **2** the distance something is thrown. —**throw (something) away 1** to discard (it) or get rid of (it). **2** to fail to take advantage of (it); to waste. **throw (someone) back on (something)** to force (someone) to rely on (it). **throw (something) in 1** to include (it) as part of a bargain at no extra cost. **2** to contribute (a remark) to a discussion, esp. casually. **throw in the towel** *colloq.* to give up or abandon a struggle. **throw (something) off 1** to get rid of (it). **2** to remove (clothing) hurriedly. **throw (something) on** to put on (clothing) hurriedly. **throw (someone) out** to expel (someone). **throw (something) out** to get rid of (it) or reject (it). **throw together** *of circumstances, etc.* to bring (people) into contact by chance. **throw (something) together** to construct (it) hurriedly. **throw up** *colloq.* to vomit. **throw (something) up** to build (it) hurriedly. **throw up (one's) hands** to give up in utter frustration, despair, or horror.

throwaway *adj.* **1** meant to be thrown away after use. **2** said casually.

throwback *noun* reversion to earlier characteristics, or an instance of it.

thrown *see* **throw**.

thru *prep., adv., adj. slang* through.

thrum *verb trans., intrans.* (**thrummed, thrumming**) **1** to strum idly (on a stringed instrument). **2** to drum or tap with the fingers. **3** to hum monotonously.

thrush[1] *noun* a songbird with dull brown upper plumage and a spotted or colored breast.

thrush[2] *noun* **1** a fungal infection, esp. of children, that causes white blisters in the mouth. **2** a similar infection in the vagina.

thrust *verb trans., intrans.* (*pa t and pa p* **thrust**; *pr p* **thrusting**) **1** to push suddenly and violently. **2** (**thrust (something) on** *or* **upon (someone)**) to force (someone) to accept (it); to impose (it) on (someone). **3** (**thrust through (something)**) to pierce or stab (it). **4** (**thrust at (something)**) to make a lunge at (it). **5** (**thrust into** *or* **through**) to force one's way. —*noun* **1** a sudden or violent movement forward; a push or lunge. **2** the force produced by a jet or rocket engine that propels an aircraft or a rocket forward. **3** an attack or lunge with a pointed weapon. **4** the main theme, message or gist, e.g., of an argument. **5** determination; drive.

thruway *noun* a high-speed, multilane road.

thud *noun* a dull sound like that of something heavy falling to the ground. —*verb intrans.*

(**thudded, thudding**) to move or fall with a thud.

thug *noun* a violent or brutal man; a hoodlum. ▸ **thuggish** *adj.*

thuggery *noun* violent, criminal behavior.

thulium *noun Chem.* (**SYMBOL Tm**) a soft silvery-white metal, used as a source of x-rays and gamma rays.

thumb *noun* the two-boned digit on the inner side of the hand. —*verb trans., intrans.* (**thumbed, thumbing**) **1** (**thumb through (something)**) to turn over the pages of (a book, magazine, etc.), to glance at its contents. **2** to ask for or obtain (a lift) in a motor vehicle by signaling to passing drivers with the thumb. —**all thumbs** awkward and clumsy. **thumbs down** a sign indicating failure, rejection, or disapproval. **thumbs up** a sign indicating success, best wishes for success, satisfaction, or approval. **under (someone's) thumb** completely controlled by (someone).

thumb index a series of notches, each with a letter on them, cut into the outer edges of pages of a book for quick reference.

thumbnail *noun* the nail on a thumb. —*adj.* brief and concise.

thumbscrew *noun* an instrument of torture that crushes the thumbs.

thumbtack *noun* a tack with a short shaft and a broad, flat head.

thump *noun* a heavy blow, or the dull sound of such a blow. —*verb trans., intrans.* (**thumped, thumping**) **1** to beat or strike with dull, heavy blows. **2** to throb or beat violently.

thunder *noun* **1** a deep rumbling sound caused by the sudden heating and expansion of gases in the atmosphere by lightning. **2** a loud deep rumbling noise. —*verb intrans., trans.* (**thundered, thundering**) **1** *of thunder* to sound or rumble. **2** to make a noise like thunder while moving. **3** to say or utter in a very loud voice. ▸ **thunderous** *adj.* ▸ **thundery** *adj.*

thunderbolt *noun* **1** a flash of lightning immediately followed by thunder. **2** a sudden and unexpected event.

thunderclap *noun* a crash of thunder.

thundercloud *noun* a large cloud charged with electricity that produces thunder and lightning.

thunderstorm *noun* a storm with thunder and lightning and usu. heavy rain.

thunderstruck *adj.* overcome by surprise; astonished.

Thur. *abbrev.* Thursday.

thurible *noun* a censer.

Thurs. *abbrev.* Thursday.

Thursday (thərz'dē, -dā) *noun* (**ABBREV. Th., Thur., Thurs.**) the fifth day of the week.

thus *adv.* **1** in this manner. **2** to this degree, amount, or distance. **3** therefore; accordingly.

thwack *noun* a blow with something flat, or the noise made by it. —*verb trans.* (**thwacked, thwacking**) to strike (something) with such a noise.

thwart *verb trans.* (**thwarted, thwarting**) to prevent or hinder (a person, plans, etc.). —*noun* a seat for a rower lying across a boat.

thy *adj.* *old use, dialect* of or belonging to you.

thyme (tīm) *noun* a plant of the mint family, cultivated as a culinary herb for its aromatic leaves, which are used as a seasoning.

thymus *noun* (*pl.* **thymuses**) a gland near the base of the neck which produces white blood cells for the immune system. *Also called* **thymus gland**.

thyroid *noun* a gland situated in the neck, which controls growth, development, and metabolic rate. *Also called* **thyroid gland**.

> Based on a Greek word meaning 'doorshaped', because of the shape of the cartilage in the front of the throat.

thyself *pron.* *old use* **1** the reflexive form of *thou* and *thee*. **2** used for emphasis.

Ti *symbol Chem.* titanium.

ti *noun* the seventh note of the scale in the solfeggio system of music notation.

tiara (tē-är′ə, -är′ə) *noun* **1** a women's jeweled ornament for the head. **2** the three-tiered crown worn by the Pope.

Tibetan *noun* **1** a native or citizen of Tibet (or Xizang). **2** the main language of Tibet. —*adj.* of Tibet, its people, or their language.

tibia *noun* (*pl.* **tibiae, tibias**) the inner of the two bones between the knee and ankle. *Also called* **shinbone**.

tic *noun* an habitual twitch of a muscle, esp. of the face.

tick¹ *noun* **1** a usu. soft regular clicking sound, such as that made by a clock. **2** a small mark. —*verb intrans., trans.* (**ticked, ticking**) **1** of a clock to make a sharp, light, clicking sound. **2** (*usu.* **tick away**) of time to pass steadily. **3** to mark (e.g., items listed on a piece of paper) with ticks or a tick. —**tick** (**someone**) **off** *colloq.* to make (someone) angry or annoyed.

tick² *noun* a blood-sucking parasite, closely related to but larger than a mite.

tick³ *noun* **1** the strong cover of a mattress, pillow, or bolster. **2** the strong, usu. striped, cotton fabric from which such covers are made. *Also called* **ticking**.

ticker *noun* **1** that which ticks, e.g., a watch. **2** *colloq.* the heart.

ticker tape *formerly* continuous paper tape with messages, printed by a telegraph instrument.

ticket *noun* **1** a printed piece of paper or card that shows that the holder has paid a fare (e.g., for travel on a bus or train) or for admission (e.g., to a theater or stadium). **2** an official notice issued to someone who has committed a motor vehicle offense. **3** a tag or label. **4 a** a list of candidates running for election in a particular political party. **b** the principles of a particular political party. **5** *slang* a license or permit. **6** *colloq.* exactly what is required: *just the ticket.* —*verb trans.* (**ticketed, ticketing**) to give or attach a ticket to.

ticking *noun* tick³ (sense 2).

tickle *verb trans., intrans.* (**tickled, tickling**) **1** to touch (a person or part of the body) lightly so as to provoke a tingling prickling sensation or laughter. **2** to feel a tingling prickling sensation. **3** *colloq.* to amuse or entertain. —*noun* **1** an act of tickling. **2** a tingling sensation. —**tickled pink** *or* **to death** *colloq.* very pleased or amused.

ticklish *adj.* **1** sensitive to tickling. **2** difficult to manage or deal with. ▸ **ticklishness** *noun*

tidal *adj.* relating to or affected by tides.

tidal wave 1 a tsunami. **2** an unusually large ocean wave. **3** an overwhelming manifestation: *a tidal wave of public criticism.*

tidbit *or* **titbit** *noun* a choice morsel.

tiddlywinks *noun* (*sing.*) a game in which players try to flick small plastic disks into a cup using a larger disk.

tide *noun* **1 a** the twice daily rise and fall of the water level in the oceans and seas. **b** the level of the water, esp. the sea, as affected by this: *high tide.* **2** a sudden or marked trend: *the tide of public opinion.* —*verb intrans., trans.* (**tided, tiding**) **1** to drift with or be carried on the tide. **2** (**tide** (**someone**) **over**) to help (someone) deal with a difficult situation, etc., for a time.

tidewater *noun* water that is affected by the movements of the tides.

tidings *pl. noun* news.

tidy *adj.* (**tidier, tidiest**) **1** neat. **2** methodical. **3** *colloq.* large; considerable: *a tidy sum.* —*verb trans.* (**tidied, tidying, tidies**) (*also* **tidy** (**something**) **away** *or* **up**) to make (it) neat; to put (things) away or arrange (them) neatly. ▸ **tidily** *adv.* ▸ **tidiness** *noun*

tie *verb trans., intrans.* (**tied, tying**) **1 a** to fasten with a string, ribbon, etc. **b** to make (string, ribbon, etc.) into a bow or knot. **c** to be fastened with a string, ribbon, etc. **2** to have the same score or final position as another competitor or entrant (in a game, contest, etc.). **3** to restrict the way (someone) leads his or her life. —*noun* **1** a narrow strip of material worn, esp. by men, around the neck under a shirt collar. **2** a strip of ribbon, rope, etc., for binding and fastening. **3** something that restricts one's freedom. **4** a link or bond: *ties of friendship*. **5** a match, competition, etc., in which the result is an equal score for both sides; also, the score or result achieved. —**tie in with (something)** to be in or be brought into connection; to correspond or be made to correspond. **tie one on** *slang* to have a bout of heavy drinking and get very drunk. **tie (someone) up 1** to bind (someone) securely. **2** to keep (someone) busy. **tie (something) up 1** to attach and fasten (it) securely with string. **2** to block or restrict (progress, movement, or operation). **tie up with (something)** to be in or be brought into connection; to correspond or be made to correspond.

tieback *noun* one of a pair of curtains designed to be tied back against the vertical parts·of the window frame; also, a decorative loop of fabric used to part and drape curtains in this way.

tiebreaker *noun* an extra game or question that decides which of the competitors is to win a match or contest which has ended in a tie.

tie-dyeing *noun* a technique of dyeing fabrics to produce patterns, in which parts of the fabric are tied tightly to stop them absorbing the dye. ▸ **tie-dyed** *adj.*

tie-in *noun* **1** a connection or link. **2** something presented at the same time as something else, esp. a book published to coincide with a movie or television program.

tier (tîr) *noun* any of a series of levels placed one above the other.

tie-up *noun* a temporary delay.

tiff *noun* a petty quarrel. —*verb intrans.* **(tiffed, tiffing)** to squabble.

tiger *noun* **1** the largest member of the cat family, having a tan coat with black stripes and white underparts. **2** a fierce, passionate, or cruel man. ▸ **tigerish** *adj.*

tiger-eye or **tiger's-eye** *noun* a yellow-brown gemstone, consisting of veined quartz.

tiger lily a tall lily having orange petals spotted with black.

tiger's-eye *noun* same as **tiger-eye**.

tight *adj.* **1** fitting very or too closely. **2** stretched so as not to be loose; taut. **3** fixed or held firmly in place. **4** difficult or posing problems: *in a tight spot*. **5** of a contest or match closely or evenly fought. **6** of a schedule, etc. not allowing much time. **7** *colloq.* miserly; mean. **8** *colloq.* drunk. **9** of money in short supply. —*adv.* in a tight manner. ▸ **tighten** *verb* ▸ **tightly** *adv.* ▸ **tightness** *noun*

tight end *Football* an offensive end whose position is close to a tackle.

tightfisted *adj.* mean and ungenerous with money.

tight-lipped *adj.* markedly restrained in speaking.

tightrope *noun* a tightly-stretched rope or wire on which acrobats balance.

tights *pl. noun* a close-fitting garment that covers the feet, legs, and body to the waist, worn by women, dancers, etc.

tightwad *noun slang* a miserly person.

tigress *noun* **1** a female tiger. **2** a fierce, passionate, or cruel woman.

tilde (tĭl′də) *noun* a mark ˜ placed over an *n* in Spanish to show that it is pronounced *ny*.

tile *noun* **1** a flat, thin slab of fired clay, or a similar one of cork or linoleum, used to cover roofs, floors, etc. **2** a tube-shaped piece of clay used for building drains. —*verb trans.* **(tiled, tiling)** to cover with tiles.

tiling *noun* **1** tiles as a group. **2** a tiled area.

till¹ *prep.* up to the time of. —*conj.* up to the time when.

till² *noun* a container or drawer in which money received from customers is put.

till³ *verb trans.* **(tilled, tilling)** to cultivate (land) for the growing of crops.

tillage (tĭl′ĭj) *noun* **1** the cultivating of land for crops. **2** land that has been tilled.

tiller¹ *noun* the lever used to turn the rudder of a boat.

tiller² *noun* a person who·tills land for the cultivation of crops.

tilt *verb trans., intrans.* **(tilted, tilting) 1** to slope or cause to slope. **2** (**tilt at (someone or something)**) to charge at or attack (the one specified). **3 a** to fight on horseback with lances. **b** to point (a lance) or attack with (a lance) as if in a joust. —*noun* **1** a sloping position or angle. **2** a joust. **3** a thrust with a lance during a joust. —**at full tilt** at full speed or with full force.

tilth *noun* the physical condition of the soil surface after cultivation.

timber *noun* **1 a** wood, esp. prepared for building or carpentry. **b** forest or woodland. **2** a wooden beam in the framework of a ship or house. —*verb trans.* **(timbered, timbering)** to provide timber or beams for.

timbered *adj.* built completely or partly of wood.

timberline *noun* the level of high ground above which trees do not grow. *Also called* **tree line.**

timbre (tăm′bər) *noun* the distinctive quality of the tone produced by a musical instrument or voice.

timbrel *noun* a small tambourine.

time *noun* **1** the continuous passing and succession of, e.g., minutes, days, or years. **2** a particular point in time expressed in hours and minutes, or days, months and years. **3** system for reckoning or expressing the·time of day or night: *Pacific Standard*

Time. **4** (*also* **times**) a point or period marked by an event or a particular characteristic. **5** the period required for or spent doing a particular activity. **6** an unspecified interval or period: *stayed there for a time.* **7** one of a number or series of occasions or repeated actions. **8** (**times**) expressing multiplication: *Three times two is six.* **9** a period or occasion characterized by a quality or experience: *had a good time.* **10** *colloq.* a prison sentence: *did time in the federal prison system.* **11** an apprenticeship. **12** the point at which something ends, e.g., a section of a game. **13** the moment at which childbirth or death is expected. **14** a rate of pay for work: *double time.* —*adj.* **1** that can be set to function at a particular moment: *a time switch.* **2** of or pertaining to purchases made on an installment basis. —*verb trans.,* *intrans.* (**timed, timing**) **1** to measure the time taken by (an event, journey, etc.). **2** to arrange, set, or choose the time for. **3** to keep or beat, or cause to keep or beat, time (with). —**ahead of time** earlier than expected. **all in good time** in due course; soon enough. **all the time** on an unceasing level or on a continual basis. **at times** sometimes; occasionally. **behind the times** out-of-date; old-fashioned. **for the time being** for the moment; meanwhile. **from time to time** sometimes; occasionally. **have no time for (someone or something)** to have no interest in or patience with (the one specified); to despise (them). **have the time of (one's) life** to enjoy (oneself) very much. **in good time** early. **in no time** very quickly. **in one's (own) time 1** in (one's) spare time when not at work. **2** at the speed (one) prefers. **in time** early enough. **in time with (someone or something)** at the same speed or rhythm as (the one specified). **make good time** to travel more quickly than one had expected. **no time at all** *colloq.* a very short time. **on time** at the right time; not late. **pass the time of day** to have a brief, casual conversation. **take (one's) time** to work as slowly as one wishes; not to hurry. **take time out from (something)** to take a break from an activity. **time and time again** again and again; repeatedly.

time and motion study a study of the way work is done in a company, with a view to increasing efficiency.

time bomb a bomb that has been set to explode at a particular time.

time capsule a box containing objects chosen as typical of the current age, buried for discovery in the future.

time card a card filled out or stamped by a time clock, indicating a worker's starting and quitting times.

time clock an apparatus with a clock that stamps on time cards the times of starting and quitting of workers.

time-consuming *adj.* taking an inordinately long period of time.

time exposure a photograph taken by exposing the film to the light for a few seconds.

time frame the period during which an event occurs.

time-honored *adj.* respected and upheld because of being a custom or tradition.

timekeeper *noun* a person who records the time, e.g., that is worked by employees or taken by a competitor in a game.

timekeeping *noun* beating, marking, or observing time.

time lag the interval between connected events or phenomena.

timeless *adj.* **1** not belonging to or typical of any particular time. **2** unaffected by time; ageless. ▸ **timelessly** *adv.* ▸ **timelessness** *noun*

time limit a fixed length of time during which something must be done.

timely *adj.* occurring at a suitable moment. ▸ **timeliness** *noun*

time-out *noun* a brief pause or period of rest, e.g., in a game.

timepiece *noun* an instrument for keeping time.

timer *noun* **1** a device like a clock that turns an appliance on or off at preset times. **2** a person or an instrument that records the time taken by someone or something

time-share *noun* **1** time-sharing (sense 1). **2** a vacation property held by time-sharing.

time-sharing *noun* **1** a plan by which a person buys the right to use a vacation home for the same specified period every year for an agreed-upon number of years. *Also called* **time-share. 2** a system that allows many users with individual terminals to use a single computer at the same time.

time signature *Mus.* a sign at the beginning of a piece to show the rhythm it is to be played in, or in the middle of a piece where the rhythm changes.

timetable *noun* a list of the departure and arrival times of trains, buses, etc.

time warp a hypothetical distortion in the time continuum.

timeworn *adj.* worn through long use.

time zone any one of the 24 sections into which the world is divided longitudinally, all places within a given zone generally being at the same standard time.

timid *adj.* easily frightened or alarmed; shy. ▸ **timidity** *noun* ▸ **timidly** *adv.*

timing *noun* the regulating and coordinating of actions and events to achieve the best possible effect.

timorous *adj.* very timid; frightened. ▸ **timorousness** *noun*

timothy *noun* (*pl.* **timothies**) a perennial grass widely used for fodder and pasture.

timpani *or* **tympani** *pl. noun* a set of two or three kettledrums. ▸ **timpanist** *noun*

tin *noun. Chem.* (SYMBOL **Sn**) a soft silvery-white metallic element, used as a thin protective coating for steel, e.g., in cans. —*adj.* made of this metal. —*verb trans.* (**tinned, tinning**) to coat with tin.

tin can a sheet-metal container coated with tin, used in food packaging and storage.

tincture *noun* **1** a slight trace of color; a tinge. **2** a solution of a drug in alcohol for medicinal use. —*verb trans.* (**tinctured, tincturing**) to give a trace of a color, flavor, etc., to.

tinder *noun* dry material that is easily set on fire.

tinder box a volatile, potentially dangerous situation.

tine *noun* a slender prong or tooth, e.g., of a fork or an antler.

tinfoil *noun* tin or other metal in the form of very thin sheets, used for wrapping food.

ting *noun* a high, metallic, tinkling sound.

tinge (tǐnj) *noun* **1** a trace of color. **2** a trace or hint of (e.g., a quality or feeling). —*verb trans.* (**tinged, tingeing** *or* **tinging, tinges**) **1** to give a slight color to. **2** to give a trace or hint of a feeling, quality, etc., to.

tingle *verb trans., intrans.* (**tingled, tingling**) to feel or cause to feel a prickling or slightly stinging sensation. —*noun* a prickling or slightly stinging sensation. ▸ **tingly** *adj.*

tinhorn *noun* a petty dictator.

tinker *noun* **1** a traveling mender of household utensils. **2** a person who likes to repair all manner of devices. —*verb intrans.* (**tinkered, tinkering**) **1** (*often* **tinker around**) to meddle or fiddle with machinery, etc., esp. in an unskilled manner. **2** to work as a tinker.

tinkle *verb intrans.* (**tinkled, tinkling**) to make a sound of or like the ringing of small bells. —*noun* a ringing or jingling sound.

tinny *adj.* (**tinnier, tinniest**) **1** of or resembling tin. **2** not solid or durable; flimsy. **3** *of sound* thin and high-pitched ▸ **tinniness** *noun*

tinsel *noun* **1** a long strip of glittering colored metal threads used as a decoration at Christmas. **2** something cheap and showy.

tint *noun* **1** a variety of a color, esp. one made softer by adding white. **2** a pale or faint color used as a background for printing. **3** a hair dye. —*verb trans.* (**tinted, tinting**) to color slightly.

tintinnabulation *noun* a ringing of bells.

tiny *adj.* (**tinier, tiniest**) very small.

tip¹ *noun* **1** a small pointed end. **2** a small piece forming an end or point. —*verb trans.* (**tipped, tipping**) to put or form a tip on. —**on the tip of** (**one's**) **tongue** about to be or almost said, but not able to be because not quite remembered.

tip² *verb trans., intrans.* (**tipped, tipping**) **1** (*also* **tip up** *or* **tip** (**something**) **up**) to lean or cause to lean. **2** (*also* **tip** (**something**) **out**) to remove or empty (something) from its container by upsetting the container. **3** (*often* **tip over**) to knock or fall over.

tip³ *noun* **1** a gift of money given to a waiter, taxi driver, etc., in return for service done well. **2** a piece of useful information; a helpful hint. —*verb trans.* (**tipped, tipping**) to give a tip to. —**tip** (**someone**) **off** to give (someone) a piece of useful or secret information.

tip⁴ *noun* a light blow or tap. —*verb trans.* (**tipped, tipping**) **1** to hit or strike lightly. **2** *Baseball* to hit a glancing blow to (a pitched ball).

tip-off¹ *noun* a piece of useful or secret information.

tip-off² *noun Basketball* the action of beginning the play at the start of a period with a jump ball.

tippet *noun* a shoulder cape.

tipple *colloq. verb trans., intrans.* (**tippled, tippling**) to drink alcohol regularly. —*noun* a person's favorite alcoholic drink. ▸ **tippler** *noun*

tipstaff *noun* (*pl.* **tipstaves, tipstaffs**) a sheriff's officer.

tipster *noun* a person who gives tips, esp. as to which horses to bet on.

tipsy *adj.* (**tipsier, tipsiest**) *colloq.* slightly drunk. ▸ **tipsiness** *noun*

tiptoe *verb intrans.* (**tiptoed, tiptoeing, tiptoes**) to walk quietly or stealthily on the tips of the toes. —*noun* the tips of the toes. —**on tiptoe** on the tips of the toes.

tiptop *adj. colloq.* excellent; first-class.

tirade *noun* a long angry speech or denunciation.

tire¹ *verb trans., intrans.* (**tired, tiring**) **1** to make or become physically or mentally weary. **2** (**tire of** (**something**)) to lose patience with (it); to become bored with (it). ▸ **tiring** *adj.*

tire² *noun* a thick rubber, air-filled or hollow ring placed over a wheel.

tired *adj.* **1** wearied; exhausted. **2** (**tired of** (**something** *or* **someone**)) no longer interested in (the one specified); bored with (the one specified). ▸ **tiredness** *noun*

tireless *adj.* never becoming weary or exhausted. ▸ **tirelessly** *adv.*

tiresome *adj.* troublesome and irritating; tedious.

'tis *contr.* it is.

tissue *noun* **1** a group of cells with a similar structure and particular function in an animal or a plant. **2 a** thin soft disposable paper or a piece of it for use as a handkerchief. **b** toilet paper. **3** fine thin· soft paper, used for protecting fragile objects. *Also called* **tissue paper. 4** an interwoven mass or collection: *a tissue of lies.*

tissue paper tissue (sense 3).

tit¹ *noun* a small songbird that feeds on insects, seeds, and berries. *Also called* **titmouse.**

tit² *noun* **1** *coarse slang* a woman's breast. **2** *slang* a teat.

Titan *or* **titan** *noun* a person of great importance or influence. ► **titanic** *adj.*

titanium *noun Chem.* (**SYMBOL Ti**) a silvery-white metallic element that is used to make strong, light alloys.

titbit *noun* same as **tidbit.**

tithe (tīth) *noun* **1** (*often* **tithes**) *Hist.* a tenth part of a person's annual income, paid as a tax to support the church or clergy in a parish. **2** a tenth part. —*verb trans., intrans.* (**tithed, tithing**) **1** to demand a tithe from. **2** to pay a tithe. ► **tithable** *adj.*

Titian *noun* a bright reddish-gold color. —*adj.* of a bright reddish-gold color.

titillate (tĭt'l-āt,) *verb trans.* (**titillated, titillating**) to excite gently, esp. in a sexual way. ► **titillation** *noun*

titivate (tĭt'ə-vāt,) *verb trans., intrans.* (**titivated, titivating**) *colloq.* to smarten up or put the finishing touches (to). ► **titivation** *noun*

title *noun* **1** the distinguishing name of a book, piece of music, etc. **2** an often descriptive heading, e.g., of a chapter in a book. **3** a word of address used before a · person's name to show rank, ·occupation, or attainment. **4** (*often* **titles**) written material on film giving credits, dialogue, etc. **5** a right to the possession or ownership of property. **6** *Sport* a championship. **7** a book or other publication. —*verb trans.* (**titled, titling**) to give a title to.

titled *adj.* having a title, esp. one that shows noble rank.

title page the page at the beginning of a book that gives the title, author, etc.

title role the role of the character in a play or film from which that play or film takes its name.

titmouse *noun* (*pl.* **titmice**) tit.

titter *colloq. verb intrans.* (**tittered, tittering**) to giggle or snigger. —*noun* a giggle or snigger.

tittle *noun* **1** a small written or printed sign or mark. **2** a very small particle.

tittle-tattle *noun* idle or petty gossip. —*verb intrans.* (**tittle-tattled, tittle-tattling**) to gossip idly.

titular (tĭch'ə-lər) *adj.* **1** in name only. **2** being or having a title.

tizzy *noun* (*pl.* **tizzies**) *slang* a nervous, confused state.

TKO *abbrev.* technical knockout.

Tl *symbol Chem.* thallium.

TLC *abbrev.* tender loving care.

TM *abbrev.* trademark.

T.M. *abbrev.* transcendental meditation.

Tm *symbol Chem.* thulium.

TNT *abbrev.* trinitrotoluene.

to *prep.* **1** toward; in the direction of. **2** used to express a resulting condition, aim, or purpose. **3** as far as; until. **4** used to introduce the indirect object of a verb. **5** used to express addition. **6** used to express attachment, connection, or possession. **7** before the hour of: *ten minutes to three.* **8** used to express comparison or proportion: *win by two goals to one.* **9** used before an infinitive. —*adv.* **1** into a nearly closed position: *pulled the window to.* **2** back into consciousness: *He came to a few minutes later.* —**to and fro** backward and forward.

toing and froing movement backward and forward in an agitated way.

toad *noun* a tailless amphibian with a short squat head and body and dry skin.

toadstool *noun* a fungus with an umbrella-shaped cap supported by a stem. *See also* **mushroom.**

toady *noun* (*pl.* **toadies**) a person who flatters someone else and does everything he or she wants; a sycophant. —*verb trans., intrans.* (**toadied, toadying, toadies**) (**toady to (someone)**) to flatter (someone) and behave obsequiously toward (that person).

toast *verb trans., intrans.* (**toasted, toasting**) **1 a** to make (esp. bread) brown by exposing it to direct heat. **b** to become brown in this way. **2** to make or become warm by being exposed to heat. **3** to drink ceremonially to the health or success of. —*noun* **1** bread that has been browned by being exposed to direct heat. **2 a** an act of drinking to a person's health or success. **b** the wish conveyed when drinking to someone's health, etc.· **3** a very admired person or thing: *the toast of the town.*

toaster *noun* an electric machine for toasting bread.

toastmaster *noun* a man who announces the toasts to be drunk at a formal dinner.

toastmistress *noun* a woman who announces the toasts to be drunk at a formal dinner.

tobacco *noun* (*pl.* **tobaccos, tobaccoes**) **1** a plant whose large leaves contain nicotine. **2**

the dried leaves of this plant, used to make cigarettes, cigars, etc.

tobacconist *noun* a person or shop that sells tobacco, cigarettes, etc.

-to-be *combining form* forming words denoting of the future, soon to become: *mother-to-be.*

toboggan *noun* a long, runnerless sled, used for riding over snow and ice. —*verb intrans.* (**tobogganed, tobogganing**) to ride on a toboggan.

toccata (tə-kät'ə) *noun* a piece of music for a keyboard instrument intended to show off the performer's skill.

tocsin *noun* an alarm bell or warning signal.

today *noun* **1** this day. **2** the present time. —*adv.* **1** on or during this day. **2** at the present time; nowadays.

toddle *verb intrans.* (**toddled, toddling**) to walk with unsteady steps. —*noun* a toddling walk.

toddler *noun* a very young child who is just beginning to walk.

toddy *noun* (*pl.* **toddies**) a drink made of alcohol, sugar, hot water, etc.

to-do *noun* (*pl.* **to-dos**) *colloq.* a fuss or commotion.

toe *noun* **1** any of the five digits at the end of each foot. **2** the front part of a shoe, sock, etc., covering the toes. **3** the lower, often projecting end of e.g., a tool or an area of land. —*verb trans.* (**toed, toeing**) **1** to kick, strike, or touch with the toes. **2** to provide (e.g., a sock or shoe) with a toe. —**on (one's) toes** alert and ready for action. **toe the line** *colloq.* to act according to the rules. **tread on (someone's) toes** to offend or upset (the person specified).

toecap *noun* a piece of metal or leather covering the toe of a boot or shoe.

toehold *noun* **1** a place to anchor one's toes, e.g., when climbing. **2** a small initial or beginning position.

toenail *noun* a nail covering a toe.

toffee *noun* a sticky candy made from boiling sugar and butter.

tofu *noun* a curd made from soybeans.

tog *verb trans., intrans.* (**togged, togging**) to clothe or dress.

toga *noun* a loose outer garment worn by a citizen of ancient Rome.

together *adv.* **1** with someone or something else. **2** at the same time. **3** so as to be in contact, joined, or united. **4** by action with one or more other people. **5** in or into one place. **6** in a continuous manner; continuously. **7** *colloq.* into a proper order or state of being organized: *got things together.* —*adj. colloq.* well organized; competent. —**together with** in addition to.

togetherness *noun* a feeling of closeness, mutual sympathy and understanding.

toggle *noun* **1** a fastening, e.g., for garments, consisting of a small bar that will pass one way only through a loop of material. **2** a pin, bar, or crosspiece placed through a link in a chain, loop in a rope, etc., to prevent the chain, rope, etc., from slipping. **3** *Comput.* a keyboard command that turns a particular feature alternately on or off. —*verb trans., intrans.* (**toggled, toggling**) **1** to provide or fasten with toggles or a toggle. **2** *Comput.* **a** (**toggle (something) on** *or* **off**) to turn (a particular feature) alternately on and off using the same keyboard command. **b** to move between different features, files, etc., using a keyboard command.

toggle switch 1 an electrical switch consisting of a projecting spring-loaded lever. **2** a key on a computer keyboard that operates in a similar manner, and is used to turn a particular feature on or off.

togs *pl. noun* articles of dress.

toil¹ *verb intrans.* (**toiled, toiling**) **1** to work long and hard. **2** to make progress or move forward with great difficulty or effort. —*noun* long, hard work.

toil² *noun* (*usu.* **toils**) a trap or snare.

toilet *noun* **1 a** a bowl-like receptacle for the body's waste matter, with a water supply for washing this into a drain. **b** a room containing such a receptacle; a bathroom. *Also called* **lavatory. 2** the act of washing, dressing, and arranging one's hair. *Also called* **toilette.**

toilet paper thin absorbent paper used for cleaning the body after urination and defecation.

toiletry *noun* (*pl.* **toiletries**) an article or cosmetic used when washing and making up.

toilette (twä-lĕt') *noun* toilet (sense 2).

toilet water a light perfume.

Tokay (tō-kā', -kī') *noun* a sweet, heavy, aromatic wine.

token *noun* **1** a mark, sign, or distinctive feature. **2** something that serves as a reminder; a keepsake. **3** a small coinlike piece of metal or plastic used instead of money. —*adj.* done as a token and therefore of no real value. —**by the same token** for the same reason.

tokenism *noun* the practice of doing very little of something in pretense that one is committed to it.

told *see* **tell.**

tolerable *adj.* **1** able to be borne or endured. **2** good enough, but usu. only just. ▸ **tolerably** *adv.*

tolerance *noun* **1** the ability to be fair toward and accepting of other people's beliefs or opinions: **2** the ability to endure pain or hardship. **3** the ability of a person to adapt to the effects of a drug.

tolerant *adj.* **1** tolerating the beliefs and opinions of others. **2** capable of enduring unfavorable conditions. **3** able to take drugs without showing serious side effects. ▸ **tolerantly** *adv.*

tolerate (tăl′ə-rāt,) *verb trans.* (**tolerated, tolerating**) **1** to endure (pain or hardship). **2** to be able to resist the effects of (a drug). **3** to treat fairly and accept (a person with different beliefs or opinions). **4** to allow to be done or exist. ▸ **toleration** *noun*

toll¹ (tōl) *verb trans., intrans.* (**tolled, tolling**) **1** to ring (a bell) with slow, measured strokes. **2** *of a bell* to announce or signal by ringing with slow measured strokes: —*noun* the act or sound of tolling.

toll² *noun* **1** a fee or tax paid, e.g., for the use of some bridges, highways, etc. **2** the cost in terms of injury or lost lives caused by a natural disaster, an accident, etc.

tollgate *noun* a barrier across a road or bridge that is not lifted until motorists have paid tolls.

tollhouse cookie a cookie that is made with chocolate chips.

toluene (tăl′yo-wēn,) *noun* a toxic organic compound derived from benzene and used as an industrial solvent, etc.

tom *noun* a male of various animals, esp. a male cat.

tomahawk *noun* a small ax formerly used as a weapon by Native Americans.

tomato *noun* (*pl.* **tomatoes**) **1** a plant whose fruit is a bright red, orange, or yellow edible berry. **2** the large round or egg-shaped fruit of this plant, eaten raw or cooked.

tomb *noun* **1** a chamber or vault for a corpse, often serving as a monument. **2** a hole cut in the ground for a corpse. **3** (**the tomb**) *poetic* death.

tomboy *noun* a girl who likes rough and adventurous games.

tombstone *noun* an ornamental stone placed over a grave, on which the deceased person's name, etc., is engraved.

tomcat *noun* a male cat.

Tom Collins (tăm-kăl′ənz) a cocktail made of gin, carbonated water, sugar, and lime or lemon juice.

Tom, Dick, and Harry anybody at all.

tome *noun* a large, heavy book.

tomfoolery *noun* (*pl.* **tomfooleries**) stupid or foolish behavior.

Tommy gun a Thompson submachine gun.

tommyrot *noun colloq.* absolute nonsense.

tomorrow *noun* **1** the day after today. **2** the future. —*adv.* **1** on the day after today. **2** in the future.

tomtit *noun* a small songbird.

tom-tom *noun* a small-headed drum beaten with the hands.

-tomy *combining form* (*pl.* **-tomies**) forming words denoting removal by surgery: *episiotomy.*

ton *noun* **1** (ABBREV. **t.**) a unit of weight equal to 2,000 lb. (about 907.2 kg). *Also called* **short ton. 2** a unit of weight equal to 2,240 lb. (about 1,016.05 kg). *Also called* **long ton. 3** a unit of weight equal to about 2,204.6 lb. (1,000 kg). *Also called* **metric ton, tonne. 4** a unit used to measure the amount of water a ship displaces, equal to 2,240 lb. or 35 cu. ft. of seawater. **5** (*usu.* **tons**) *colloq.* a lot.

tonal *adj.* of or relating to tone or tonality.

tonality *noun* (*pl.* **tonalities**) **1** the organization of all the notes and chords of a musical piece. **2** the color scheme used in a painting.

tone *noun* **1 a** a musical sound with reference to its quality and pitch. **b** a sound having a definite pitch. **2** a quality or character of the voice expressing a particular mood, etc. **3** the general character or style of spoken or written expression. **4** high quality, style, or character. **5** the quality, tint, or shade of a color. **6** firmness of the body or muscle. —*verb intrans., trans.* (**toned, toning**) **1** (**tone in**) to fit in well; to harmonize. **2** to give tone (to). —**tone down** or **tone (something) down** to become or make (it) softer or less harsh in tone, color, force, etc. **tone up** or **tone (something) up** to become or make (it) stronger, healthier, etc.

tone-deaf *adj.* unable to distinguish accurately between notes of different pitch.

toneless *adj.* without variation in sound, expression, etc. ▸ **tonelessly** *adv.*

tone pad an electronic device similar to a remote control for a television, etc., that allows data to be input into a central computer from a distance.

tone poem a piece of music based on a story or literary or descriptive theme.

tong *noun* a Chinese secret society.

tongs *noun* (*sing., pl.*) a utensil consisting of two arms joined by a hinge or pivot, for lifting objects.

tongue (təng′) *noun* **1** the fleshy muscular organ attached to the floor of the mouth, bearing groups of taste buds on its upper surface. **2** the tongue of some animals, used as food. **3 a** a particular language. **b** a particular manner of speaking: *a sharp tongue.* **4** a narrow strip of land that reaches out into water. **5** the clapper in a bell. **6** a flap in the opening of a shoe or boot. —*verb trans., intrans.* (**tongued, tonguing**) to produce (notes) by tonguing. —**hold (one's) tongue** to say nothing. **tongue in cheek** with humorous intention.

tongue-lashing *noun* a severe scolding.

tongue-tie *noun* a speech impediment caused by an abnormally small fold of skin under the tongue.

tongue-tied *adj.* 1 speechless, esp. because of shyness or embarrassment. 2 affected by tongue-tie.

tongue twister a phrase or sentence that is difficult to say quickly.

tonguing *noun* a way of playing a wind instrument that allows individual notes to be articulated separately by the tongue opening and blocking the passage of air.

tonic *noun* 1 a medicine that increases strength and energy. 2 something that is refreshing or invigorating. 3 a tonic water. b *dialect* a soft drink. 4 the first note of a musical scale, the note on which a key is based. —*adj.* 1 increasing strength and energy. 2 serving to invigorate. 3 *Mus.* of or being the tonic. 4 producing muscular tension.

tonic water a carbonated drink flavored with quinine.

tonight *noun* the night of this present day. —*adv.* on or during the night of the present day.

tonnage (tɒn'ij) *noun* 1 the space available in a ship for carrying cargo, measured in tons. 2 the total carrying capacity of a country's merchant shipping, measured in tons.

tonne (tɒn') *noun* a ton (sense 3).

tonsil *noun* either of two lumps of tissue at the back of the mouth.

tonsillectomy *noun* (*pl.* **tonsillectomies**) a surgical operation to remove the tonsils.

tonsillitis *noun* inflammation of the tonsils.

tonsorial *adj.* relating to barbers or hairdressing.

tonsure (tăn'shər) *noun* 1 a shaved patch on the crown of a monk's or priest's head. 2 the act of shaving the crown of a monk's or priest's head.

too *adv.* 1 to a greater extent or more than is desirable or suitable. 2 in addition; also. 3 what is more; indeed.

took *see* **take**.

tool *noun* 1 an implement, esp. one used for cutting, digging, etc. 2 a thing used in a particular trade or profession. 3 a person who is used or manipulated by another. —*verb trans., intrans.* (**tooled, tooling**) to work or engrave (e.g., stone or leather) with tools.

toolbox *noun* a box for carrying and storing tools.

toolkit *noun* a set of tools, esp. those required for a particular purpose.

toot *noun* a quick, sharp blast of a horn, etc. —*verb trans., intrans.* (**tooted, tooting**) to sound or cause (a horn, etc.) to sound with a quick, sharp blast.

tooth *noun* (*pl.* **teeth**) 1 any of the hard structures embedded in the upper and lower jaw bones that are used for biting and chewing food. 2 one of many equally spaced projections around the edge of a gear wheel. 3 something like a tooth in shape or function, such as one of a series of points on a comb. 4 an appetite or liking: *a sweet tooth.* 5 (**teeth**) enough power or force to be effective. —**in the teeth of (something)** in the very midst of (it). **long in the tooth** *colloq.* old. **set (one's) teeth on edge** to irritate severely. ▸ **toothy** *adj.*

toothache *noun* an ache or pain in a tooth, usu. as a result of tooth decay.

toothbrush *noun* a brush for cleaning the teeth.

toothless *adj.* 1 having no teeth. 2 powerless or ineffective.

toothpaste *noun* a paste used to clean the teeth.

toothpick *noun* a small sharp piece of wood, plastic, etc., for picking food from between the teeth.

toothpowder *noun* a powder used to clean the teeth.

toothsome *adj.* 1 having a very pleasing taste. 2 extremely attractive.

tootle *verb intrans.* (**tootled, tootling**) to toot gently or continuously. —*noun* a tootling sound.

tootsie *noun* (*pl.* **tootsies**) *slang* 1 a foot. 2 a toe.

top¹ *noun* 1 the highest part, point, or level. 2 the highest or most important rank or position. 3 the upper edge or surface. 4 a lid or piece for covering the top of something. 5 a garment for covering the upper half of esp. a woman's body. 6 the highest or loudest degree or pitch: *yelled at the top of his voice.* 7 *Baseball* the first half of any of the innings. —*adj.* at or being the highest or most important. —*verb trans.* (**topped, topping**) 1 to cover or form the top of. 2 to rise above or be better than. 3 to reach the top of. 4 *Golf* to hit the upper half of (the ball). —**from top to toe** from head to foot; completely. **off the top of (one's) head** *slang* with no thought whatsoever. **on top of (something)** 1 in control of (it). 2 in addition to (it). **on top of the world** in the very best of spirits. **top (something) off** to put a finishing or decorative touch to (it).

top² *noun* a toy that spins on a pointed base.

topaz *noun* an aluminum silicate mineral, the pale yellow variety being highly prized as a semiprecious gemstone.

topcoat *noun* a light overcoat.

top-drawer *adj.* of the highest level, of high society.

tope verb intrans. (**toped, toping**) to drink alcohol to excess. ▸ **toper** noun

topflight adj. of the highest quality.

topgallant (tə-găl'ənt, tăp-) noun the mast or sail above the topmast and topsail.

top hat a man's tall, cylindrical hat, often made of silk, worn as part of formal dress.

top-heavy adj. **1** having the upper part large in comparison with the lower. **2** having too many senior staff members in proportion to junior staff members.

topiary noun the art of cutting bushes and hedges into ornamental shapes.

topic noun the principal idea in a composition or piece of discourse.

topical adj. **1** relating to matters of interest at the present time. **2** relating to a particular place; local. **3** of a topic. ▸ **topicality** noun

topknot noun a crest or tuft of hair on the top of a head.

topless adj. **1** of a woman with the breasts exposed. **2** of a place where women go topless.

topmast noun the second mast, usu. directly above the lower mast.

topmost adj. being the highest.

topnotch adj. colloq. of the very best quality.

topography noun (pl. **topographies**) **1** the natural and human-made features on the surface of land, such as rivers, mountains, etc. **2** the mapping or describing of the surface of any object or body. ▸ **topographical** adj.

topper noun slang a top hat.

topping noun something that forms a covering or garnish for food.

topple verb trans., intrans. (**toppled, toppling**) **1** (also **topple over**) to fall or to cause to fall because of being top-heavy. **2** to overthrow or to be overthrown.

topsail (tăp'səl, -sāl,) noun a square sail set across the topmast.

top-secret adj. very secret, esp. officially so categorized, because disclosure of information so classified constitutes a grave threat to national security.

topside noun the surface of the hull of a ship above the waterline.

topsoil noun the uppermost layer of soil, rich in organic matter.

topspin noun a spin given to a ball by hitting it sharply on the upper half with a forward and upward stroke to make it travel higher, farther and more quickly. See also **backspin, sidespin.**

topsy-turvy adj., adv. **1** upside down. **2** in confusion. ▸ **topsy-turviness** noun

Torah (tôr'ə) noun Judaism **1** the whole body of religious law and scholarship. **2** a parchment scroll including the first five books of the Hebrew Scripture. **3** the first five books of the Hebrew Scripture.

torch noun **1** a piece of burning wood, etc., used to give light. **2** a source of heat, light, enlightenment, etc. —**carry a torch for (someone)** to feel (esp. unrequited) love for (someone).

torchlight noun the light of torches or a torch.

tore see **tear²**.

toreador (tôr'ē-ə-dôr,) noun a bullfighter; a matador.

torment noun (tôr'mĕnt,) **1** very great pain, suffering, or anxiety. **2** something that causes great pain, suffering, or anxiety. —verb trans. (tôr-mĕnt', tôr'mĕnt,) (**tormented, tormenting**) **1** to cause great pain, suffering, or anxiety to. **2** to irritate (e.g., a person or an animal). ▸ **tormentor** noun

torn see **tear²**.

tornado noun (pl. **tornadoes, tornados**) a violently destructive storm consisting of a funnel-shaped rotating column of air.

torpedo noun (pl. **torpedoes**) **1** a self-propelled underwater missile that explodes upon impact. **2** a small container holding an explosive charge, used as, e.g., a firework **3** slang a hired assassin. —verb trans. (**torpedoed, torpedoing, torpedoes**) to attack with torpedoes.

torpid adj. **1** lacking in energy. **2** of a hibernating animal dormant. ▸ **torpidity** noun

torpor noun **1** drowsiness, sluggishness, or apathy. **2** a numb state.

torque noun a measure of the tendency of a force to cause an object to rotate about an axis.

torrent noun **1** a great rushing stream or downpour of, e.g., water. **2** a strong flow, e.g., of questions. ▸ **torrential** adj.

torrid adj. **1** of the weather so hot and dry as to scorch the land. **2** intensely emotional; passionate.

torsion noun the act or process of twisting something by applying force to one end while the other is held firm or twisted in the opposite direction. ▸ **torsional** adj.

torso noun (pl. **torsos**) the main part of the human body, without the limbs and head.

tort noun any wrongful act, injury, or damage for which a civil action for damages or compensation may be brought.

torte noun a very rich cake with many thin, iced layers.

tortellini (tôrt,l-ē'nē) noun ring-shaped pasta stuffed, e.g., with cheese or meat.

tortilla (tôr-tē'ə) noun a thin round Mexican corn cake.

tortoise (tôrt'əs) noun a slow-moving toothless reptile with a shell into which the head, short scaly legs, and tail can be withdrawn for safety.

tortoiseshell *noun* **1** the brown and yellow mottled shell of a sea turtle, used in making combs, jewelry, etc.; also, a synthetic product that resembles the shell of a sea turtle. **2** a domestic cat with a mottled orange and brown coat. —*adj.* made of or mottled like tortoiseshell.

tortuous *adj.* **1** full of twists and turns. **2** not straightforward, esp. in being devious or involved. ▸ **tortuousness** *noun*

torture *noun* **1** the infliction of severe pain or mental suffering, esp. as a punishment or as a means of persuading someone to give information. **2** great suffering, or a cause of this. —*verb trans.* (**tortured, torturing**) **1** to subject to torture. **2** to cause to experience great suffering. ▸ **torturous** *adj.* ▸ **torturously** *adv.*

Tory (tôr'ē) *noun* (*pl.* **Tories**) **1** a member or supporter of the British Conservative Party. **2** *Hist.* a supporter of the British Crown during the American Revolution. *Also called* **loyalist.** —*adj.* **1** relating to or supporting the Tories. **2** Conservative. ▸ **Toryism** *noun*

> Originally one of a group of Irish Catholics thrown off their land who waged guerrilla war on British settlers, later applied to any royalist supporter

toss *verb trans., intrans.* (**tossed, tossing**) **1** to throw up into the air. **2** (*usu.* **toss** (**something**) **away, aside, out,** *etc.*) to throw (it) away or discard (it) casually or carelessly. **3** (*also* **toss about, around,** *etc.*) to move restlessly or from side to side repeatedly. **4** (*also* **toss about** *or* **toss** (**something**) **about**) to be thrown or throw (it) from side to side repeatedly and violently. **5** to jerk (the head), esp. as a sign of anger. **6 a** to throw (a spinning coin) into the air and guess which side will land facing up, as a way of settling an issue. **b** to settle an issue with (someone) by tossing a coin: *I'll toss you for the last piece of cake.* **7** to coat (food, esp. salad) by gently mixing it in a dressing. —*noun* **1** an act or an instance of tossing. **2** the tossing of a coin to settle an issue.

tossup *noun* **1** *colloq.* an even chance. **2** an act of tossing a coin.

tot¹ *noun* **1** a small child. **2** a small amount of alcoholic spirits.

tot² *verb trans.* (**totted, totting**) (*also* **tot** (**something**) **up**) to add (it) together.

total *adj.* **1 a** whole; complete. **b** devoid of any qualification. **2** using all possible resources or means. —*noun* the whole or complete amount, e.g., of various things added together. —*verb trans., intrans.* (**totaled** *or* **totalled, totaling** *or* **totalling**) **1** to amount to a specified sum. **2** (*also* **total** (**something**) **up**) to add (it) up to produce a

total. **3** *slang* to destroy (esp. a motor vehicle) completely. ▸ **totality** *noun* ▸ **totally** *adv.*

totalitarian *adj.* of or relating to a system of government by a single party that allows no opposition. —*noun* a ruler with complete and unrestricted power. ▸ **totalitarianism** *noun*

tote *verb trans.* (**toted, toting**) *colloq.* to carry (something).

tote bag a shopping bag.

totem (tōt'əm) *noun* **1 a** a natural object, esp. an animal, used as the badge or sign of a tribe or an individual person among Native Americans. **b** an image or representation of this. **2** an emblem or a symbol that is highly respected. ▸ **totemism** *noun*

totem pole a large wooden pole on which totems are carved and painted.

totter *verb intrans.* (**tottered, tottering**) **1** to move unsteadily. **2** to sway or tremble as if about to fall. **3** *of a system of government, etc.* to be on the verge of collapse. —*noun* an unsteady movement.

toucan *noun* a large bird native to tropical forests, with brightly colored plumage and an enormous colorful bill.

touch *verb trans., intrans.* (**touched, touching**) **1** to bring something (e.g., one's hand) into contact with (something else). **2** to come into contact with (something else). **3** to feel, push, or strike something lightly, esp. with the hand or foot. **4** to be in contact with something else without overlapping. **5** to make (someone) feel pity, sympathy, etc. **6** to have an effect on. **7** to be of concern to. **8** to have dealings with: *I wouldn't touch a job like that.* **9** to use, esp. to eat or drink: *I never touch chocolate.* **10** to be as good as: *No one can touch her at chess.* **11** to mark slightly or delicately. **12** (**touch on** *or* **upon** (**something**)) to speak of or discuss (it) briefly. **13** (**touch** (**someone**) **for** (**something**) *or* **touch** (**someone**) **up for** (**something**)) *slang* to ask for and receive (money) as a loan or gift from (the person specified). —*noun* **1** an act of touching or the sensation of being touched. **2** the sense by which the existence, nature, and quality of objects can be perceived through physical contact with the hands, etc. **3** the particular texture and qualities of an object as perceived through contact with the hands, etc. **4** a small amount or quantity. **5** a slight attack (e.g., of an illness). **6** a detail that adds to or complements the general pleasing effect or appearance: *The artist put the finishing touches to the portrait.* **7** a distinctive or characteristic style. **8** the ability to respond or behave with sensitivity:

The veterinarian has a wonderful touch with animals. **9** contact; communication: *out of touch with recent developments.* **10 (a touch)** *colloq.* a bit; rather. **11** *slang* **a** an act of asking for and receiving money from someone as a gift or loan. **b** a person who can be persuaded to give or lend money: *a soft touch.* —**touch and go** of a very uncertain outcome. **touch base** *or* **bases (with)** *slang* to get in touch (with). **touch down** of an aircraft or spacecraft to land. **touch (something) off** to cause (it) to begin.

touchback *noun Football* a situation in which a defensive team recovers the ball and downs it behind its own goal line.

touchdown *noun* **1** the point of contact of an aircraft with the ground upon landing. **2 (ABBREV. TD)** *Football* the act of carrying, receiving, or getting possession of the ball across the opposing team's goal line in order to score six points.

touché (too-shā') *interj.* **1** used to acknowledge a hit in fencing. **2** used to acknowledge a point scored in an argument.

touched *adj.* **1** feeling pity, sympathy, etc. **2** *colloq.* slightly crazy.

touch football football that is played by people without protective gear, involving touching rather than tackling.

touching *adj.* causing one to feel pity or sympathy. ► **touchingly** *adv.*

touch screen a visual display unit screen that doubles as an input device, and is operated by being touched.

touchstone *noun* a test or standard of judging quality.

touchtone *noun* a telephone operated by push buttons.

touch-type *verb intrans.* (**touch-typed, touch-typing**) to type without looking at the keyboard.

touchy *adj.* (**touchier, touchiest**) *colloq.* **1** easily annoyed or offended. **2** needing to be handled with care and tact. ► **touchiness** *noun*

tough *adj.* **1** not easily cut, broken, torn, or worn out. **2** of food difficult to chew. **3** of people and animals strong and fit. **4** difficult to deal with; testing. **5** severe and determined; resolute. **6** rough and violent. **7** *colloq.* unlucky; unpleasant: *tough luck.* —*noun* a rough, violent person. —**tough it out** *slang* to endure or persevere regardless of difficulties. ► **toughly** *adv.* ► **toughness** *noun*

toughen *verb intrans., trans.* (**toughened, toughening**) (*also* **toughen up** *or* **toughen (someone) up**) to become or to make tough.

toupee (too-pā') *noun* a hairpiece.

tour *noun* **1** an extended journey around a place, stopping at various places along the route. **2** an official period of duty or military service, esp. abroad. —*verb trans., intrans.* (**toured, touring**) to make a tour of (a place).

tour de force (*pl.* **tours de force**) an extremely skillful piece of work.

Tourette's syndrome (too-ĕts') a severe neurological disorder whose symptoms are severe multiple nervous tics and involuntary obscene speech.

tourism *noun* **1** the practice of traveling to and visiting places for pleasure. **2** the industry providing services for tourists.

tourist *noun* a person who travels for pleasure. —*adj.* of or suitable for tourists.

touristy *adj. derog.* designed for or full of tourists.

tourmaline (toor'mə-lĭn, -lēn,) *noun* a mineral used as a semiprecious gemstone.

tournament *noun* a competition between many players for a championship.

tourniquet (toor'nĭ-kət) *noun* a bandage for tying very tightly around an arm or a leg to stop the flow of blood through an artery.

tousle (tow'zəl, -səl) *verb trans.* (**tousled, tousling**) to make (esp. hair) untidy.

tout *verb intrans., trans.* (**touted, touting**) **1** to try persistently to persuade people to buy something, give support, etc. **2** to advertise or praise strongly or aggressively. —*noun* **1** a person who spies on racehorses in training and passes information about their condition, etc., to people wishing to bet on them. **2** a person who touts for trade, esp. persistently or aggressively.

tow¹ (tō) *verb trans.* **1** to drag with great effort. **2** to pull (e.g., a trailer) by rope or cable behind the vehicle one is driving. —*noun* an act of towing. —**in tow 1** (*also* **on** *or* **under tow**) of a vehicle being towed. **2** of a person following or accompanying as a companion.

tow² *noun* fibers of flax or hemp prepared for spinning into rope.

toward *or* **towards** *prep.* **1** in the direction of. **2** in relation or regard to. **3** as a contribution to. **4** just before; near.

Usage Though *toward* and *towards* are equally acceptable in US English with no differences in their meanings, *toward* is more common in US usage, while *towards* is more common in British English.

---

towel *noun* a piece of absorbent cloth or paper for drying oneself, washed dishes, etc. —*verb trans.* (**toweled** *or* **towelled, toweling** *or* **towelling**) to rub or dry with a towel.

towelling *noun* absorbent cotton cloth for making towels.

tower *noun* **1** a tall, narrow structure forming part of a larger, lower building such as a church, or standing alone, built for defense, etc. **2** a multistory building. —*verb intrans.* (**towered, towering**) **1** (*often* **tower above** (**something** *or* **someone**)) to rise high above (the one specified). **2** to appear in an enlarged or threatening form. ▣ LOOM, REAR. —**a tower of strength** a great help or support. **tower over** (**someone**) to be considerably taller than or superior to (the one specified). ▸ **towering** *adj.*

towheaded *adj.* having very fair or tousled hair.

town *noun* **1** an incorporated area with defined boundaries, smaller than a city. **2** a central shopping or business district. —**go out on the town** *colloq.* to enjoy the entertainments offered by a town, esp. its bars and restaurants. **go to town** *colloq.* to do something very thoroughly or with great enthusiasm.

town crier a person whose job it was to make public announcements on the streets of a town.

town hall the building where the official business of a town is conducted.

townhouse *noun* **1** a house connected in a row to another house and sharing a common wall. **2** a person's house in town as opposed to his or her house in the country.

town meeting 1 a legislative assembly made up of the citizens of a town. **2** a televised appearance of a political candidate at which the studio audience asks questions.

township *noun* **1** a subdivision of a county with some degree of local government. **2** *South Afr. Hist.* an urban area inhabited by nonwhites.

towpath *noun* a path beside a canal or river formerly used by horses towing barges.

toxemia *noun* blood poisoning caused by the presence of a bacterial toxin in the bloodstream. ▸ **toxemic** *adj.*

toxic *adj.* **1** poisonous. **2** caused by a poison or toxin. ▸ **toxicity** *noun*

toxicology *noun* the scientific study of poisons. ▸ **toxicologist** *noun*

toxic shock syndrome a potentially fatal condition in women, caused by blood poisoning which is itself caused by a toxin developing in a high-absorbency tampon.

toxin *noun* poison produced naturally by animals, bacteria, etc., esp. in a body.

toy *noun* **1** an object made for a child to play with. **2** anything, esp. a gadget, thought of as being for amusement rather than practical use. **3** something very small, esp. a dwarf breed of dog. —*adj.* **1** made to be played with, esp. in imitation of something real. **2** being a dwarf breed. —*verb intrans.*

(**toyed, toying**) **1** to amuse oneself amorously with (someone). **2** to play with (something) without much interest: *toy with one's food.*

trace¹ *noun* **1** a sign that a person, an animal, or a thing has been in that place. **2 a** a track or footprint. **b** the act or an instance of tracking, esp. one who has disappeared: *put a trace on the delinquent client.* **3** a very small amount that can just be detected. **4** a tracing. **5** a line marked by the moving pen of a recording instrument —*verb trans.* (**traced, tracing**) **1** to track and discover by following clues, a trail, etc. **2** to follow step by step. **3** to make a copy of (a drawing, etc.) by covering it with a sheet of semitransparent paper and drawing over the visible lines. **4** to outline or sketch (a plan, etc.). **5** (*also* **trace back** *or* **trace** (**something**) **back**) to date or be dated back to a specified time. ▸ **tracer** *noun*

trace² *noun* either of two ropes, chains, or straps attached to an animal's collar, etc., for pulling a cart, etc.

tracer bullet a bullet which glows brightly as it travels through the air, indicating the path of the bullet.

tracery *noun* (*pl.* **traceries**) **1** ornamental open stonework used to form a decorative pattern, esp. in a window. **2** a finely patterned decoration or design.

trachea (trā'kē-ə) *noun* (*pl.* **tracheae**) the passage that carries air into and out of the lungs from the larynx. *Also called* **windpipe**.

tracheotomy *noun* (*pl.* **tracheotomies**) a surgical operation in which an incision is made through the front of the neck into the trachea. *Also called* **tracheostomy**.

tracing *noun* a copy of a drawing made on semitransparent paper.

tracing paper thin, semitransparent paper used for tracing drawings.

track *noun* **1 a** a mark or trail left by the passing of a person, animal, or thing, esp. a footprint. **b** a rough path, esp. one beaten by feet. **2** a specially prepared course, esp. for racing. **3** a railroad line, i.e., the parallel rails, the space in between, and the ties and bed below. **4** one of several items, e.g., a song, recorded on a disk or tape. **5** *Comput.* an area that is created on the surface of a magnetic disk during the process of formatting, and within which data can be stored. **6** the line or course of travel or movement. **7** the line or course of thought, etc. **8** the continuous band of metal plates used instead of wheels on many vehicles, e.g., tanks, designed to travel over rough surfaces. —*verb trans., intrans.* (**tracked, tracking**) **1** to follow the marks, footprints, etc., left by (a person or an animal). **2** to follow and plot the course of (a spacecraft, satellite, etc.) by radar. **3** to move a television or film camera in toward or away from the object being filmed. **—in (one's) tracks** exactly where (one) is standing: *a sight that stopped me right in my tracks*. **keep** *or* **lose track of (something)** to keep or fail to keep oneself informed about (its) progress. **make tracks** *colloq.* to set out; to leave. **on the track of (someone** *or* **something)** pursuing or looking for (someone or something). **track (someone** *or* **something) down** to search for and find (someone or something) after a thorough search.

track and field (athletics) athletic events that take place on a running track and the playing field next to it, involving the sports of foot racing, jumping, hurdling, vaulting, and weight throwing. ▶ **track-and-field** *adj.*

trackball *noun* a ball mounted in a small box linked to a computer terminal, rotated with the palm to move a cursor on a screen.

track event a contest involving running, as distinct from a field event. *See also* **field event.**

track light a light that is mounted on, and that can move along, an electrified track.

track record a record of past performance.

track shoe a shoe with a spiked sole worn by a runner.

tracksuit *noun* a warm suit worn by athletes, etc., when exercising.

tract *noun* **1** an area of land. **2** a system in the body with a particular function: *the digestive tract.* **3** a short essay.

tractable *adj.* easily controlled; docile. ▶ **tractability** *noun*

traction *noun* **1** the act of pulling, the state of being pulled, or the force used in pulling. **2** a steady pulling on a muscle or limb using a series of pulleys and weights, to correct a condition or problem. **3** the grip of a wheel, tire, etc., on the surface on which it moves. ▶ **tractive** *adj.*

tractor *noun* **1** a slow-moving motor vehicle with two large rear wheels for pulling farm machinery, etc. **2** the toothed mechanism by which continuous-form paper is advanced through a computer printer.

trade *noun* **1** the buying and selling of goods or services. **2** business and commerce; also, the people involved in it. **3** a personal occupation or job, esp. one requiring skill; a craft. **4** the companies engaged in a particular business or occupation: *the building trade.* **5** customers: *the breakfast trade.* **—verb** *intrans., trans.* (**traded, trading**) **1** (**trade in (something)**) to buy and sell (a particular type of merchandise). **2** to engage in trade (with a person or country). **3** to exchange (one commodity) for another. **—trade**

(something) in to give (it) as part payment for something else. **trade (something) off** to give (it) in exchange for something else. **trade on (something)** to take unfair advantage of (a factor, esp. a person's generosity). ▶ **trader** *noun*

trade-in *noun* a commodity that is traded in exchange for another, esp. a used vehicle.

trademark *noun* (ABBREV. **TM**) **1** a name, word, or symbol officially used to represent a company or individual and shown on all of the merchandise made or sold by that company or individual. **2** a distinguishing characteristic.

trade name a name that· is used by a manufacturer to identify a commercial product. *Also called* **brand name, proprietary name.**

tradeoff *noun* an exchange.

tradesman *noun* a man engaged in trade, esp. a shopkeeper.

tradespeople *pl. noun* people engaged in retail trade.

tradeswoman *noun* a woman engaged in trade, esp. a shopkeeper.

trade union an organization of workers formed to protect their interests. ▶ **trade unionism** ▶ **trade unionist**

trade wind a wind that blows continually toward the Equator and is deflected westward by the eastward rotation of Earth.

trading post a store in a sparsely populated region.

tradition *noun* **1** the handing down of doctrines, beliefs, customs, etc., from generation to generation. **2** a· doctrine, belief, custom, etc., that is passed on. ▶ **traditional** *adj.* ▶ **traditionally** *adv.* ▶ **traditionalism** *noun* ▶ **traditionalist** *noun, adj.*

traduce (trə-dōōs', -dyōōs') *verb trans.* (**traduced, traducing**) to say or write unpleasant things about.

traffic *noun* **1** the vehicles, ships, etc., moving along a route. **2** the movement of vehicles along a route. **3** illegal or dishonest trade. **4** trade; commerce. **5** the transporting of goods. **6** dealings or communication between groups or individuals. **—verb** *trans., intrans.* (**trafficked, trafficking**) **1** (**traffic in (something)**) to deal or trade in (it), esp. illegally. **2** to deal in (a particular type of goods). ▶ **trafficker** *noun*

traffic circle a circular junction that permits the passage of motor vehicles entering from and exiting it to many streets. *Also called* **rotary.**

traffic light a stoplight.

tragedian (trə-jēd'ē-ən) *noun* an·actor who specializes in tragic roles.

tragedienne (trə-jĕd,ē-ĕn′) *noun* an actress who specializes in tragic roles.

tragedy (trăj′əd-ē) *noun* (*pl.* **tragedies**) **1** a serious drama, film, etc., in which the main characters are eventually destroyed through a combination of events, circumstances and personality problems. **2** such plays as a genre. **3** a sad play, film, etc. **4** a disaster. **5** a sad event.

tragic *adj.* **1** sad; intensely distressing. **2** relating to or in the style of tragedy. ▸ **tragically** *adv.*

tragicomedy *noun* (*pl.* **tragicomedies**) a play or an event that includes a mixture of tragedy and comedy. ▸ **tragicomic** *adj.*

trail *verb trans., intrans.* (**trailed, trailing**) **1** to drag or be dragged loosely along the ground. **2** (*usu.* **trail along, behind,** *etc.*) to walk or move along slowly and wearily. **3** to lag behind (a competitor) in a race or contest, often by a stated number of points. **4** to follow the track or footsteps of. —*noun* **1** a track, series of marks, footprints, etc., left by a passing person, animal, or thing. **2** a rough path through a wild area. —**trail off** *or* **away** *of a sound* to become fainter.

trail bike a motorcycle designed for off-road riding.

trailblazer *noun* a person who blazes a trail; a pioneer (*see* **blaze²**). ▸ **trailblazing** *noun, adj.*

trailer *noun* **1** a usu. two-wheeled cart for towing behind a car, e.g., for transporting small boats. **2** a large van, furnished, and pulled by a car, used when parked as a dwelling. **3** brief extracts from a movie, prepared as an advertisement for it.

train *noun* **1** a string of railroad cars with a locomotive. **2** a back part of a long dress that trails behind the wearer. **3** the attendants following or accompanying an important person. **4** a connected series of events, actions, or thoughts. **5** a number of things in a string or connected line. —*verb trans., intrans.* (**trained, training**) **1 a** to cause (a person) to acquire skill or knowledge in (a subject or activity). **b** to prepare (an animal) for (something) through instruction, practice, or exercises. **2** to be taught, or prepare oneself to be taught, through instruction, practice, or exercises. **3** to make (a plant, etc.) grow in a particular direction. ▸ **trainee** *noun* ▸ **trainer** *noun*

training *noun* **1** the process of learning a particular skill and practicing it until the required standard has been reached. **2** the state of being physically fit.

traipse *verb intrans.* (**traipsed, traipsing**) to walk along or about.

trait *noun* a distinguishing element, esp. of a person's character. ◼ ATTRIBUTE, CHARACTERISTIC, FEATURE, QUALITY.

traitor *noun* a person who betrays his or her country to an enemy. ▸ **traitorous** *adj.*

trajectory *noun* (*pl.* **trajectories**) the curved path followed by a projectile.

tram *noun* a truck or wagon running on rails in a mine.

trammel *noun* (*usu.* **trammels**) something that hinders or prevents free action or movement. —*verb trans.* (**trammeled** *or* **trammelled, trammeling** *or* **trammelling**) **1** to catch or entangle. **2** to hinder or prevent the free movement of.

tramp *verb intrans., trans.* (**tramped, tramping**) **1** to walk with firm, heavy footsteps. **2** to make a journey on foot, esp. heavily or wearily. **3** to walk heavily and wearily on or through: *tramp the streets.* —*noun* **1** a person who travels from place to place on foot and who lives by begging. **2** a long, often tiring walk. **3** the sound of heavy, rhythmic footsteps. **4** a tramp steamer. **5** *slang* a promiscuous or immoral woman.

trample *verb trans., intrans.* (**trampled, trampling**) **1** (**trample (something)** *or* **on (something)**) to tread on (it) heavily. **2** to press or be pressed down by treading or being stepped upon. **3** to treat (someone) dismissively or with contempt: *trampled all over them.*

trampoline (trăm,pə-lēn′) *noun* a piece of tough canvas attached to a framework by cords or rope and stretched tight, on which gymnasts, children, etc., may jump. —*verb intrans.* (**trampolined, trampolining**) to jump on a trampoline.

tramp steamer a cargo ship with no fixed or regular route.

tramway *noun* a system of cable cars.

trance *noun* **1** a sleeplike or half-conscious state. **2** a dazed or absorbed state.

tranquil *adj.* quiet; peaceful; undisturbed. ▸ **tranquility** *noun*

tranquilize *verb trans., intrans.* (**tranquilized, tranquilizing**) to make or become calm or less tense, esp. through drugs.

tranquilizer *noun* a drug that acts on the central nervous system and has a calming and relaxing effect.

trans. *abbrev.* translated.

trans- *prefix* forming words denoting **1** on the other side of; across; beyond: *transatlantic.* **2** through: *transdermal.* **3** into another state or place: *transform.*

transact *verb trans.* (**transacted, transacting**) to conduct or carry out (business). ▸ **transaction** *noun*

transatlantic *adj.* **1** crossing the Atlantic. **2** situated on the other side of the Atlantic.

transceiver *noun* a piece of radio equipment that receives and transmits signals.

transcend *verb* (**transcended**, **transcending**) **1** to be beyond the limits of. **2** to be better or greater than; to surpass. ▸ **transcendence** *noun* ▸ **transcendent** *adj.*

transcendental *adj.* going beyond usual human knowledge or experience.

transcendentalism *noun* a philosophical system concerned with what is constant, innate and a priori, independent of and a necessary prerequisite to experience.

transcendental meditation (ABBREV. T.M.) a system of meditation for relieving anxiety, achieving physical and mental relaxation through the usu. silent repetition of a mantra.

transcontinental *adj.* crossing a continent.

transcribe *verb trans.* (**transcribed**, **transcribing**) **1** to write out (a text) in full, e.g., from notes. **2** to copy (a text) from one place to another. **3** to write out (a spoken text). **4** to arrange (a piece) for an instrument or voice that it was not orig. composed for. **5** to record any form of information on a suitable storage medium. **6** to transfer (data) from one storage device to another.

transcript *noun* a written copy.

transcription *noun* **1** the act of transcribing. **2** something transcribed; a transcript.

transducer *noun* a device that converts energy from one form to another.

transept *noun* the part of a cross-shaped church that is at right angles to the nave.

transfer *verb trans., intrans.* (**transferred**, **transferring**) **1** to move from one place, person, or group to another. **2** to change from one vehicle or passenger system to another. **3** to give the right to or ownership of (property) to someone. **4** to move (a design) from one surface to another. —*noun* **1** an act of transferring. **2** a design or picture that can be transferred from one surface to another. **3** a ticket allowing a passenger to continue a journey on another route. ▸ **transferable** *adj.* ▸ **transference** *noun*

transfiguration *noun* **1** a change in appearance, esp. to something more beautiful or glorious. **2** (**Transfiguration**) the radiant change in Christ's appearance, as described in Matthew 17:1–2.

transfigure *verb trans.* (**transfigured**, **transfiguring**) to change the appearance of, esp. so as to make more beautiful or glorious than before.

transfix *verb trans.* (**transfixed**, **transfixing**) **1** to cause (someone) to be unable to move through surprise, fear, etc. **2** to pierce through. ▸ **transfixion** *noun*

transform *verb trans.* (**transformed**, **transforming**) to change the appearance, nature, or function of. ▸ **transformation** *noun*

transformer *noun* an electromagnetic device used to transfer electrical energy from one alternating current circuit to another.

transfuse *verb trans.* (**transfused**, **transfusing**) **1** to transfer (blood or plasma from one person) into the blood vessels of another. **2** to cause to diffuse through. **3** to cause (fluid) to pass from one vessel to another.

transfusion *noun* **1** the introduction of whole blood directly into a person's bloodstream by allowing it to drip through a needle inserted in a vein. **2** the introduction of a component of whole blood or saline solution into a person's bloodstream in a similar manner.

transgress *verb intrans., trans.* (**transgressed**, **transgressing**) **1** to break or violate (divine law, a rule, etc.). **2** to overstep (a limit or boundary). ▸ **transgression** *noun* ▸ **transgressor** *noun*

transient (trăn'shənt, -zhənt) *adj.* lasting, staying, or visiting for a short time only; passing quickly. —*noun* a temporary resident or worker. ▸ **transience** *noun*

transistor *noun* **1** a semiconductor device with three electrodes, used as a switch or to amplify electric current in electronic circuits. **2** a transistor radio using transistors.

transit *noun* **1** the carrying or movement of goods or passengers from place to place. **2** the transport of passengers or goods on public routes, or the system offering such transport. —**in transit** in the process of being taken from or traveling from one place to another.

transit camp a camp for the temporary accommodation of refugees, etc., on the way to their permanent destination.

transition *noun* a change or passage from one place, state, etc., to another. ▸ **transitional** *adj.*

transitive *adj.* of a verb having a direct object.

transit lounge an airport lounge for passengers waiting for a connecting flight.

transitory *adj.* lasting only for a short time.

translate (trăns'lāt, trănz'-) *verb trans., intrans.* (**translated**, **translating**) **1 a** to express (something) in another language. ◨ INTERPRET, PUT, RENDER. **b** to render material from one language into another as a profession. **c** of a written text, etc. to be able to be expressed in another language. **2** to put or express (an idea, etc.) in plainer or simpler terms. **3** to change or be changed into. ▸ **translation** *noun* ▸ **translator** *noun*

transliterate (trăns-lĭt'ə-rāt, trănz,-) *verb trans.* (**transliterated**, **transliterating**) to write (a word, text, etc.) in the letters of another alphabet. ► **transliteration** noun

translucent (trăns-lōō'sənt, trănz,-) adj. **1** admitting light with a small degree of diffusion or distortion; semitransparent. **2** admitting light with little or no diffusion or distortion, thereby making viewed objects entirely visible. ► **translucence** noun ► **translucently** adv.

transmigrate (trăns-mī'grāt,, trănz,-) verb intrans. (**transmigrated, transmigrating**) of a soul in some beliefs to pass into another body at death. ► **transmigration** noun

transmissible adj. capable of being transmitted.

transmission noun **1** an act of transmitting. **2** something transmitted, esp. a radio or television broadcast. **3** the system of parts in a motor vehicle that transfers power from the engine to the wheels.

transmit verb trans., intrans. (**transmitted, transmitting**) **1** to pass or hand on (esp. a message or infection). **2** to send out (signals) by radio waves. **3** to broadcast (a radio or television program). **4** to allow the passage of (e.g., light or sound).

transmitter noun **1** the equipment that converts electrical signals into modulated radio waves for broadcasting. **2** the part of a telephone mouthpiece that converts sound waves into electrical signals.

transmogrify verb trans. (**transmogrified, transmogrifying, transmogrifies**) to transform, often in a surprising or bizarre way. ► **transmogrification** noun

transmute verb trans. (**transmuted, transmuting**) to change the form, substance, or nature of. ► **transmutation** noun

transom noun **1** a horizontal bar of wood or stone placed across the top of a door separating it from a window. **2** a lintel. **3** a small window over the lintel of a door or larger window. Also called **transom window**. **4** a crossbeam in the stern of a boat.

transparency noun (pl. **transparencies**) **1** the state of being transparent. **2** a small photograph on rigid plastic, mounted in a frame and viewed by being placed in a projector.

transparent adj. **1** admitting light with little or no diffusion or distortion, thereby making viewed objects entirely visible. ▤ CLEAR, PELLUCID, TRANSLUCENT ▤ CLOUDY, OPAQUE. **2** easily understood or recognized; obvious: transparent dishonesty. ► **transparently** adv.

transpire verb intrans., trans. (**transpired, transpiring**) **1** to become known. **2** colloq. to happen. **3** of a plant to lose water vapor to the atmosphere by evaporation. **4** to give off in the form of vapor. ► **transpiration** noun

> **Usage** Transpire meaning to happen has long been a usage open to severe criticism, deemed by many as pretentious and etymologically incorrect.

transplant verb trans. (**transplanted, transplanting**) **1** to transfer (an organ, skin, etc.) from one person or part of the body to another. **2** to move (esp. a growing plant) from one place to another. —noun **1** an operation in which an organ, tissue, etc., is transferred from one person to another. **2** something that has been transferred, esp. an organ, skin, or plant. ► **transplantation** noun

transport verb trans. (**transported, transporting**) **1** to carry (goods, passengers, etc.) from one place to another. **2** to send to a penal colony. **3** (usu. be **transported**) to be affected with strong feelings. —noun **1** the transporting of people, goods, etc., from place to place; also, a business for this. **2** a means of being transported from place to place. **3** (often **transports**) strong emotion, esp. of pleasure or delight; ecstasy. ► **transportable** adj. ► **transporter** noun

transportation noun **1** the act of transporting. **2** a means of being transported.

transpose verb trans. (**transposed, transposing**) **1** to cause (two or more things) to change places. **2** to change the position of (a thing) in a sequence or series. **3** to perform or rewrite (music) in a different key. ► **transposable** adj. ► **transposition** noun

transputer (trăns-pyōōt'ər, trănz-) noun a computer chip capable of all the functions of a microprocessor and able to process in parallel.

transsexual noun **1** a person belonging anatomically to one sex who adopts the physical characteristics or social behavior of the opposite sex. **2** a person who has had medical or surgical treatment to alter the external sexual features to resemble those of the opposite sex.

transship verb trans., intrans. (**transshipped, transshipping**) to transfer from one ship or form of transport to another. ► **transshipment** noun

transubstantiate (trăn,səb-stăn'chē-āt,) verb trans. (**transubstantiated, transubstantiating**) to change into another substance.

transubstantiation noun the doctrine that the bread and wine become the actual body and blood of Christ when consecrated during the Eucharist.

transverse *adj.* lying, built, etc., crosswise or at right angles. ▸ **transversely** *adv.*

transvestite *noun* a person, esp. a man, who derives sexual pleasure from wearing the clothes of the opposite sex. ▸ **transvestism** *noun*

trap *noun* **1** a device or hole, usu. with bait attached, for catching animals. **2** a plan or trick for surprising a person into speech or action. **3** a trap door. **4** a bend in a pipe, esp. a drain that fills with liquid to stop foul gases passing up the pipe. **5** a light, two-wheeled carriage. **6** a device for throwing a clay pigeon into the air. **7** (**traps**) drums or other percussion instruments. *See also* **traps**. —*verb trans., intrans.* (**trapped**, **trapping**) **1** to catch (an animal) in a trap. **2** to catch (a person) unawares, esp. with a trick.

trap door a small door or opening in a floor or ceiling.

trapeze *noun* a swinglike apparatus on which gymnasts or acrobats perform tricks.

trapezium *noun* (*pl.* **trapeziums**, **trapezia**) a quadrilateral with no sides parallel.

trapezoid *noun* a quadrilateral with one pair of opposite sides parallel.

trapper *noun* a person who traps animals and sells their fur.

trappings *pl. noun* clothes or ornaments suitable for a particular occasion, ceremony, etc.

traps *pl. noun* personal belongings.

trapshooting *noun* the sport of firing shotguns and rifles at clay pigeons released into the air by spring traps.

trash *noun* **1** material to be thrown away, or that has been thrown away. **2** nonsense. **3** worthless people. ▸ **trashy** *adj.*

trash can a receptacle for household trash.

trattoria (trät,ə-rē'ə) *noun* (*pl.* **trattorias**, **trattorie**) an informal Italian restaurant.

trauma (trow'mə, trô'-) *noun* (*pl.* **traumas**, **traumata**) **1** a physical injury. **2** a state of shock caused by a physical wound or injury. **3** an emotional shock that may have long-term effects. ▸ **traumatic** *adj.* ▸ **traumatically** *adv.* ▸ **traumatize** *verb trans.*

travail (trə-vāl', trăv'āl,) *noun* extremely hard work or labor. —*verb intrans.* to work hard or with pain, esp. in childbirth.

travel *verb intrans., trans.* (**traveled** *or* **travelled**, **traveling** *or* **travelling**) **1** to go from place to place; to journey. **2** to journey through or over (a region, etc.). **3** to be capable of withstanding a long journey: *Her children don't travel well.* **4** of machinery: to move along a fixed course. **5** *colloq.* to move quickly. **6** *Basketball* to run or walk while holding the ball. —*noun* **1** an act of traveling. **2** (*often* **travels**) the process of traveling from one place to another. ▸ **traveler** *or* **traveller** *noun*

travel agency an office dealing in airline, bus, ship, and train tickets, hotel accommodations, etc., for journeys and vacations. ▸ **travel agent**

-traveled *combining form* forming words denoting: **1** having traveled (esp. abroad) a lot. **2** traveled along; frequented: *a well-traveled road.*

traveler's check a check, redeemable internationally, purchased, e.g., from a bank, and valid only when the purchaser countersigns it.

travelogue *noun* a film, etc., about travel, esp. about an individual's trip to a particular place.

traverse *verb trans., intrans.* (trə-vərs') (**traversed**, **traversing**) **1** to go across or through. **2** to move (esp. the barrel of a large gun) to one side while keeping it horizontal. **3** to oppose or thwart. —*noun* (trăv'ərs) **1** an act of traversing. **2** something that lies across. —*adj.* (pronounced with stress on either the first or the second syllable) being or lying across; oblique.

travesty *noun* (*pl.* **travesties**) a contemptibly mocking distortion of something worthy. ▣ CARICATURE, MOCKERY, PARODY. —*verb trans.* (**travestied**, **travestying**, **travesties**) to make a travesty of.

trawl *noun* a large bag-shaped net with a wide mouth, used to catch fish at sea. —*verb trans., intrans.* (**trawled**, **trawling**) **1** to search (the sea, etc.) for (fish) with a trawl. **2** to search through (a large number of things, people, etc.) thoroughly before finding the one required.

trawler *noun* a fishing boat used in trawling.

tray *noun* **1** a flat piece of wood, metal, plastic, etc., usu. with a low edge, for carrying dishes, crockery, etc. **2** a very shallow, lidless box forming a drawer in, e.g., a wardrobe or trunk, or used for displaying articles in a cabinet.

treacherous (trĕch'ə-rəs) *adj.* **1** not able to be trusted. **2** having hidden hazards and dangers. ▸ **treacherousness** *noun*

treachery *noun* (*pl.* **treacheries**) the betrayal of someone or that person's trust; disloyalty, also, an act of betrayal.

tread *verb intrans., trans.* (*pa t* **trod**; *pa p* **trodden** *or* **trod**; *pr p* **treading**) **1** (**tread on** (**something**)) to put a foot or feet on (it); to walk or step on (it). **2** to step or walk on. **3** to crush or press, e.g., into the ground, with a foot or feet; to trample. **4** to wear or form (a path, etc.) by walking. **5** (**tread on** (**someone**)) to suppress (another); to treat (another) cruelly. —*noun* **1** a manner or sound of walking. **2** an act of treading. **3** a mark made by treading; a footprint. **4** the grooved, patterned surface of a tire that grips the road. **5** the part of a wheel that touches a rail. **6** the part of the sole of a shoe that touches the ground. —**tread water 1** to keep oneself afloat and upright in water by making a treading movement with the legs. **2** *colloq.* to progress little.

treadle *noun* a pedal for one or both feet that drives a machine, e.g., a sewing machine.

treadmill *noun* **1** an apparatus for producing motion, consisting of a large wheel turned by people or animals treading on steps inside or around it. **2** a monotonous, dreary routine. **3** an exercise machine consisting of a continuous moving belt whose speed can be regulated to make the user walk, jog, or run.

treason *noun* **1** disloyalty to or betrayal of one's country. **2** a betrayal of trust or an act of disloyalty. ▶ **treasonable** *adj.*

treasure (trězh′ər) *noun* **1** wealth and riches, esp. in the form of gold, silver, jewels, etc., that have been accumulated over a period of time. **2** anything of great value. —*verb trans.* (**treasured**, **treasuring**) to value greatly.

treasurer *noun* **1** the person in a club, etc., who is in charge of the money and accounts. **2** the chief financial officer of a corporation or government.

treasure-trove *noun* **1** treasure or money that is found hidden in the earth and whose owner is unknown. **2** a valuable discovery.

treasury *noun* (*pl.* **treasuries**) **1** a place where treasure is stored. **2** (**Treasury**) the government department in charge of a country's finances. **3** the income or funds of a state, government, etc.

treat *verb trans., intrans.* (**treated**, **treating**) **1** to deal with or behave toward (a person or thing). **2** to care for or deal with (a person, illness, etc.) medically. **3** to put through a process or apply something to. **4** (**treat (someone) to (something)**) to provide (someone) with (food, drink, etc.) at one's own expense. **5** (**treat of (something)**) to deal with or discuss (a subject), esp. in writing. —*noun* **1** an outing, a meal, etc., given as a gift by one person to another. **2** a source of pleasure or enjoyment.

treatise (trēt′ĭs) *noun* a formal piece of writing that deals with a subject in depth.

treatment *noun* **1** the medical or surgical care given to a patient. **2** an act or the manner of dealing with someone or something. —**the full treatment** *colloq.* the appropriate treatment, esp. when lavish or generous.

treaty *noun* (*pl.* **treaties**) a formal agreement between states or governments; also, the document on which such an agreement is set down.

treble *noun* **1** something that is three times as much or as many as something else. **2** a person, esp. a boy, having a soprano singing voice; a part written for this voice. **3** a high-pitched voice or sound. —*adj.* **1** three times as much or as many. **2** for, being, or having a treble voice. —*verb trans., intrans.* (**trebled**, **trebling**) to make or become three times as much.

tree *noun* **1** a tall, woody, perennial plant that typically has one main stem or trunk. **2** something like a tree, esp. in having branches leading from a main trunk. **3** (*also in compounds*) a wooden frame or support for holding things: *a shoe tree.* —*verb trans.* (**treed**, **treeing**) to drive up a tree. ▶ **treeless** *adj.*

tree line a timberline.

treetop *noun* the top of a tree.

trefoil (trē′foil,, trĕf′oil,) *noun* **1** a leaf that is divided into three sections. **2** a carved ornament or decoration with three lobes or sections.

trek *verb intrans.* (**trekked**, **trekking**) **1** to make a journey, often a long, arduous one. **2** *South Afr.* to make a journey by ox wagon. —*noun* **1** the process of traveling from one place to another or an instance of it. **2** *South Afr.* a journey by ox wagon.

trellis *noun* a frame or network of narrow wooden strips used to support climbing plants. —*verb trans.* (**trellised**, **trellising**) to provide or support with a trellis.

tremble *verb intrans.* (**trembled**, **trembling**) **1** to undergo heavy vibration or jolting particularly as the result of a physical shock. **2** to feel fear or anxiety. —*noun* a trembling movement; a shudder.

tremendous *adj.* **1** of exceedingly large size. **2** *colloq.* remarkable; marvelous. ▶ **tremendously** *adv.*

tremolo *noun* (*pl.* **tremolos**) *Mus.* a trembling effect produced by rapidly repeating a note or notes.

tremor *noun* **1** a shaking or quivering. **2** a series of shock waves that pass through Earth, and may cause the ground to shake. **3** a thrill.

tremulous *adj.* **1** trembling, esp. with fear, nervousness, or excitement. **2** *of a line drawn, etc.* written by a shaky hesitant hand and so weak and wavering. ▶ **tremulously** *adv.* ▶ **tremulousness** *noun*

trench *noun* **1** a long narrow ditch dug in the ground, esp. one used to protect soldiers from enemy gunfire. **2** a long narrow depression in Earth's surface, produced by erosion or by movements of Earth's crust. —*verb trans., intrans.* (**trenched**, **trenching**) **1** to dig a trench (in). **2** to provide (a place) with a trench as fortification.

trenchant *adj.* **1** clear, crisp, and keen. **2** forthright; vigorous. ▶ **trenchancy** *noun* ▶ **trenchantly** *adv.*

trench coat a waterproof coat with a belt and epaulettes.

trencher *noun Hist.* a wooden plate for serving food.

trencherman *noun* a person who eats well or heartily.

trend *noun* **1** a general direction or tendency. **2** the current general movement in fashion or taste.

trendsetter *noun* a person who sets a fashion.

trendy *adj. colloq.* (**trendier, trendiest**) following the latest fashions. —*noun* (*pl.* **trendies**) a trendy person.

trepan (trĭ-păn') *noun old use* a trephine.

trephine (trĕ'fĭn,) *noun* a surgical instrument used for removing circular sections of bone during surgery. ▸ **trephine** *verb trans.*

trepidation *noun* fear or nervousness.

trespass *verb intrans.* (**trespassed, trespassing**) (*often* **trespass on** *or* **upon** (**something**)) **1** to enter (someone else's property) without the right or permission to do so. **2** to intrude into a person's time, privacy, rights, etc. **3** to sin. —*noun* **1** the act of entering someone else's property without the right or permission to do so. **2** an intrusion into someone's time, privacy, etc. **3** a sin. **4** *Law* a lawsuit brought for trespassing.

trespasser *noun* **1** a person who trespasses. **2** a sinner.

tress *noun* **1** a long lock or plait of hair. **2** (**tresses**) a woman's or girl's long hair.

trestle *noun* **1** a support, e.g., for a table, consisting of a horizontal beam resting at each end on a pair of legs sloping outward. **2** a bridge, typically for railroad tracks, constructed of vertical, slanted supports and horizontal crosspieces.

trestle table a table consisting of a board or boards supported by trestles.

trews *pl. noun* trousers, esp. of tartan cloth.

tri- *combining form* forming words denoting three, three times, threefold: *triathlon.*

triad *noun* **1** a group of three people or things. **2** *Mus.* a chord consisting of three notes, usually a base note and those notes a third and a fifth above it. **3** any of several Chinese secret societies, esp. one involved in organized crime or drug trafficking. **4** in Welsh literature, a group of three sayings, stories, etc., about related subjects.

triadic *adj.* relating to or consisting of triads.

trial *noun* **1** a legal process by which evidence and applicable law are examined by a court of law in order to determine the issue of specified claims and/or charges. **2** an act of trying or testing; a test. **3** trouble, worry, or vexation, or a cause of it: *Her son is a great trial to her.* **4** *Sport* a preliminary test of a player's or athlete's skill and fitness, esp. before choosing the players or athletes to include in a team. **5** a test of a vehicle's performance held esp. over rough ground or a demanding course. **6** a competition, usu. over rough ground, to test skills in handling high-performance cars or motorcycles. **7** competition testing the skills of animals: *sheepdog trials.* **8** an attempt. —**on trial 1** *Law* being the subject of a legal court action. **2** undergoing tests or examination before being permanently accepted or approved.

trial and error the trying of various methods, alternatives, etc., until the correct or suitable one is found.

trial run a test of, e.g., a vehicle, a piece of machinery, or the strategy of a project, to assess effectiveness.

triangle *noun* **1** *Geom.* a two-dimensional figure with three sides and three angles, whose sum is always 180°; a three-sided polygon. **2** something with a shape similar to this geometric figure. **3** *Mus.* a percussion instrument consisting of a metal bar shaped into a triangle with one corner left open, struck with a small hammer. **4** a sexual relationship or love affair involving three people.

triangular *adj.* **1** in the shape of a triangle. **2** involving three people or parties. ▸ **triangularly** *adv.*

triangularity *noun* a triangular form.

triangulate (trĭ-ăng'gyə-lāt,) *verb trans.* (**triangulated, triangulating**) to survey (an area) by dividing it up into a series of triangles. ▸ **triangulation** *noun*

triathlon *noun* an athletic contest consisting of swimming, running, and cycling. ▸ **triathlete** (trĭ-ăth'lēt,) *noun*

tribalism *noun* **1** the system of tribes as a way of organizing society. **2** the feeling of belonging to a tribe.

tribe *noun* **1** a group of families, clans, or communities that are linked by social, economic, and political ties. **2** a group of people with a common interest, profession, etc. ▸ **tribal** *adj.*

tribesman *noun* a man who belongs to a tribe.

tribeswoman *noun* a woman who belongs to a tribe.

tribulation *noun* great sorrow or trouble, or a cause of it.

tribunal *noun* a court of justice.

tribune[1] *noun* a champion or defender of the rights of the common people.

tribune[2] *noun* a dais or stand.

tributary *noun* (*pl.* **tributaries**) **1** a stream or river flowing into a larger river or lake. **2** a person paying tribute to another. —*adj. of a stream or river* flowing into a larger river or lake.

tribute *noun* **1** something given or said as an expression of praise, thanks, or admiration. **2** a sign of something valuable, worthy of praise, etc.: *Her success was a tribute to all her hard work.*

trice *noun* —**in a trice** in a very short time.

triceps *noun* (*pl.* **tricepses, triceps**) the large muscle at the back of the arm that straightens the elbow.

trichinosis (trĭk,ə-nō'sĭs) *noun Med.* a disorder caused by infestation with a parasitic worm, usu. as a result of eating raw or partially cooked pork containing the worm's larvae.

trichloroethanol *see* **chloral hydrate**.

trick *noun* **1** a cunningly devised means to an end. **2** a deceptive appearance, esp. one caused by the light. **3** a mischievous act; a prank. **4** a clever act or feat that astonishes or amuses. **5** a habit or mannerism: *He has a trick of scratching his nose when he's angry.* **6** a special technique: *a trick of the trade.* **7** *Cards* the cards played in one round of a game and that are won by one of the players. **8** *slang* a prostitute's client. —*adj.* intended to deceive or give a certain illusion: *trick photography.* —*verb trans.* (**tricked, tricking**) **1** to cheat, deceive, or defraud. **2** (**trick** (**someone**) **into** *or* **out of** (**something**)) to make (someone) do as one wants by cheating or deception. —**do the trick** *colloq.* to do or be what is necessary to achieve something. **trick or treat** a children's practice of dressing up on Halloween to call at people's houses for small gifts, threatening to play a trick if they are not given one. **up to** (**one's**) **old tricks** *colloq.* behaving in (one's) usual deceitful way.

trickery *noun* (*pl.* **trickeries**) an act or the practice of deceiving.

trickle *verb trans., intrans.* (**trickled, trickling**) **1** to flow or cause to flow in a thin, slow stream or drops. **2** to move or go slowly and gradually. —*noun* a thin slow stream, flow, or movement.

trickster *noun* a person who plays tricks.

tricky *adj.* (**trickier, trickiest**) **1** difficult to handle; needing skill and care. **2** inclined to trickery; sly. **3** clever at tricks; resourceful. ▸ **trickily** *adv.* ▸ **trickiness** *noun*

tricolor *noun* a three-colored flag.

tricot (trē′kō) *noun* a hand-knitted woolen fabric.

tricycle *noun* a vehicle with three wheels, driven by pedals.

trident (trĭd′nt) *noun* a spear with three prongs, esp. as carried by a sea god or a Roman gladiator.

tried *adj.* **1** tested and proved to be good or efficient. **2** having had one's patience put to strain: *sorely tried by the difficulties of farm life.* —**tried and true** proved through testing to be worthy.

triennial *adj.* **1** happening once every three years. **2** lasting three years. ▸ **triennially** *adv.*

trier *noun* a person who tries hard.

trifle *noun* **1** something that is of very little value. **2** a very small amount. **3** a dessert made typically of sponge cake soaked in sherry and spread with jam or jelly and fruit and topped with custard and whipped cream. —*verb intrans., trans.* (**trifled, trifling**) **1** (**trifle with** (**someone** *or* **something**)) to treat a (person or a person's feelings) frivolously and insensitively. **2** to act, behave, or talk idly. **3** (**trifle** (**something**) **away**) to spend or pass (time) idly; to waste (an opportunity, etc.).

trifling *adj.* **1** unimportant; trivial. **2** frivolously idle: *that student's trifling ways.*

trig¹ *noun Math. colloq.* trigonometry.

trig² *adj.* neat and fashionable in appearance; also, being in good condition.

trigger *noun* **1** a small lever that releases a catch or spring to set a mechanism going, especially one that is squeezed to fire a gun. **2** that which starts a series of actions or reactions. —*verb trans.* (**triggered, triggering**) (*also* **trigger** (**something**) **off**) to start a series of actions, reactions, or events.

triggerfish *noun* (*pl.* **triggerfish, triggerfishes**) a brightly colored fish marked by an erectile spine on its anterior dorsal fin that moves into and stays in a vertical position when the fish is threatened.

trigger-happy *adj. slang* likely to shoot or react violently without thinking or with very little provocation: *trigger-happy rookies.*

trigonometry *noun Math.* the branch of mathematics that is concerned with the relationships between the sides and angles of triangles. ▸ **trigonometric** *adj.*

trike *noun colloq.* a tricycle.

trilateral *adj.* having or pertaining to three sides, parties, or nations. ▸ **trilaterally** *adv.*

trilateralism *noun* the political-economic policy of supporting friendly relations among three nations.

trilby *noun* (*pl.* **trilbies**) a soft felt hat with an indented crown and narrow brim.

So called because a hat of this shape was worn by an actress in the original stage version of George du Maurier's novel, *Trilby* (1894)

trilingual *adj.* **1** able to speak three languages fluently, as or in the manner of a native speaker. **2** written or spoken in three languages. ▸ **trilingually** *adv.*

trill *noun* **1** *Mus.* a sound produced by playing or singing a note and a note higher than it repeatedly and in rapid succession. **2** a shrill warbling sound made by a songbird. **3** a consonant sound, esp. an *r* sound, produced by rapidly vibrating the tongue. —*verb trans., intrans.* (**trilled, trilling**) to play, sing, or pronounce (something) with a trill.

trillion *noun* **1** a million millions (10^{12}). **2** *Brit. old use* a million million millions (10^{18}). **3** (*also* **trillions**) *colloq.* an enormous number or amount: *a trillion problems / has trillions of shoes in her closet.* ▶ **trillionth** *noun, adj.*

trillium *noun* a plant that has a single cluster of three leaves and three-petaled flowers, typically pink or white. *Also called* **wake-robin.**

trilobite (trīˈlə-bīt,) *noun* **1** *Zool.* an extinct marine arthropod having a flat oval body divided lengthwise into three lobes. **2** the fossilized remains of this marine arthropod.

trilogy *noun* (*pl.* **trilogies**) a group of three plays, novels, poems, operas, etc., that are related, often by theme.

trim *verb trans., intrans.* (**trimmed, trimming**) **1** to make neat and tidy, esp. by clipping. **2** (*also* **trim (something) away** *or* **off**) to remove (it) by or as if by cutting: *trim hundreds of pounds off the cost.* **3** to make less by, or as if by, cutting: *trim costs.* **4** to decorate with ribbons, lace, ornaments, etc. **5** to adjust the balance of (a ship, submarine, or aircraft) by moving its cargo, ballast, etc. **6** *Naut.* to arrange (a ship's sails) to suit the weather conditions. **7** to hold a neutral or middle course between two opposing individuals or groups. **8** to adjust one's behavior to suit current trends and opinions, esp. for self-advancement. —*noun* **1** a haircut that neatens but does not change a person's hairstyle. **2** proper order or condition: *in good trim.* **3** material, ornaments, etc., used as decorations. **4** the decorative additions to a car, including the upholstery, internal and external color scheme, and chrome and leather accessories. **5** *Naut.* **a** the set or balance of a ship on the water. **b** *of a ship* the state of being ready, esp. with the sails in proper order, for sailing. **6** the inclination of an aircraft in flight, especially with reference to the horizon. **7** parts removed by trimming. —*adj.* (**trimmer, trimmest**) **1** in good order; neat and tidy. **2** clean-cut; slim. ▶ **trimly** *adv.* ▶ **trimness** *noun*

trimaran *noun* *Naut.* a boat with three hulls placed side by side.

trimester *noun* a period of three months.

trimmer *noun* **1** a person or thing that trims. **2** a person who adjusts his or her behavior to suit current trends and opinions, esp. for self-advancement. **3** a short horizontal beam on a floor into which the ends of joists are fitted.

trimming *noun* **1** ribbon, lace, or other decorations added to, e.g., clothing. **2** (**trimmings**) the traditional or usual sauce, garnish, accompanying vegetables, etc., served with a particular dish: *Thanksgiving turkey and all the trimmings.* **3** (**trimmings**) parts cut or trimmed off.

trimsize *noun* *Printing* the size of a book in terms of the length and width of its jacket.

Trinitarian (trĭn,ə-târˈē-ən) *noun* a person who believes in the doctrine of the Trinity. —*adj.* relating to or believing in the doctrine of the Trinity. *See also* **Unitarian.**

Trinitarianism *noun* the beliefs of the Trinitarians.

trinitrotoluene (trī,nī,trō-tălˈyə-wēn,) *noun* (ABBREV. TNT) *Chem.* a yellow, highly explosive, crystalline solid that is used as an explosive, and in certain photographic chemicals and dyes.

trinity *noun* (*pl.* **trinities**) **1** the state of being or a group of three. **2** (**Trinity**) in Christian theology, the unity of three persons, the Father, Son, and Holy Spirit, in a single Godhead.

trinket *noun* a cheap ornament or piece of jewelry.

trio *noun* (*pl.* **trios**) **1** a group of three. **2** a group of three instruments, players, or singers.

trip *verb trans., intrans.* (**tripped, tripping**) **1** (*also* **trip over** *or* **up**) to cause to stumble, or to stumble. **2** (*also* **trip up**) to make or cause to make a mistake. **3** (*usu.* **trip along**) to walk or dance with short light steps. **4** to move or flow smoothly and easily: *words tripping off the tongue.* **5** *slang* to experience the hallucinatory effects of a drug, esp. LSD. **6** to activate or cause (a device or mechanism) to be activated. —*noun* **1** the process of traveling from one place to another or an instance of it. ⊟ JOURNEY, PEREGRINATION, TRAVEL(S), TREK. **2** a stumble. **3** a short light step or skip. **4** a striking part or catch that activates a mechanism. **5** an error or blunder. **6** *slang* a hallucinatory experience caused by taking a drug, esp. LSD. **7** *slang* an intensely emotional experience. ▶ **tripper** *noun*

tripartite *adj.* involving or concerning three groups, people, etc.

tripe *noun* **1** parts of the stomach of a cow or sheep, eaten as food. **2** *colloq.* nonsense; rubbish.

triple *adj.* **1** three times as great, as much, or as many. **2** made up of three parts or things. —*verb trans., intrans.* (**tripled, tripling**) to make or become three times as great, much, or many. —*noun* three times the usual amount.

triple jump an athletic event in which competitors try to cover the greatest distance with a type of jump consisting of a hop, skip, and a jump.

triplet *noun* 1 one of three children born to the same mother at the same time. 2 a group or set of three.

triplicate *adj.* (trĭp'lĭ-kət) 1 being one of three identical copies. 2 having been tripled. —*noun* any one of three identical copies. —*verb trans.* (trĭp'lĭ-kāt,) (**triplicated, triplicating**) to make three copies of. ▸ **triplication** *noun*

tripod *noun* a stand with three legs for supporting a camera, a small telescope. etc.

triptych (trĭp'tĭk) *noun* a picture or carving on three panels that are joined together by hinges. *See also* **diptych.**

tripwire *noun* a hidden wire that sets off a mechanism, such as an alarm or a bomb, when someone trips over it.

trireme (trī'rēm,) *noun* an ancient Greek or Roman warship with three banks of rowers on each side.

trisect *verb trans.* (**trisected, trisecting**) to divide into three parts. ▸ **trisection** *noun*

trite *adj., of a remark or phrase* lacking freshness and originality, through overuse. ▸ **triteness** *noun*

tritium (trĭt'ē-əm, trĭsh'-) *noun Chem.* (SYMBOL ^{3}H or T) a radioactive isotope of hydrogen.

triumph *noun* 1 mastery achieved over an opponent. ▣ VICTORY, WIN ▣ DEFEAT. 2 the great joy felt upon winning a great victory. —*verb intrans.* (**triumphed, triumphing**) to win a great victory, or to be highly successful. ▸ **triumphal** *adj.*

triumphant *adj.* 1 having won a great victory. 2 feeling or showing great joy over or celebrating a victory. ▸ **triumphantly** *adv.*

triumvir (trī-ŭm'vər) *noun* (*pl.* **triumvirs, triumviri**) any one of a group of three people sharing office or supreme power.

triumvirate (trī-ŭm'və-rət) *noun* a group of three people sharing office or supreme power.

trivet *noun* 1 a low stand for a hot dish, teapot, etc. 2 a three-legged stand or bracket.

trivia *noun* (*sing., pl.*) unimportant matters or details.

trivial *adj.* of very little importance. ▸ **triviality** *noun* ▸ **trivialize** *verb trans.* ▸ **trivially** *adv.*

trochee (trō'kē) *noun Prosody* a foot consisting of one long syllable followed by one short one.

trod *see* **tread.**

trodden *see* **tread.**

troglodyte *noun* 1 a cave dweller. 2 a reclusive person.

troika *noun* 1 a Russian vehicle drawn by three horses. 2 a team of three horses. 3 a group of three people.

Trojan horse 1 *Comput.* a disruptive part of a program that lies dormant until activated by certain circumstances, causing damage to data. 2 a subversive group that is planted within enemy ranks, to be activated at a prearranged time.

troll[1] (trōl) *noun* an imaginary, ugly, evil-tempered, humanlike creature.

troll[2] *verb trans., intrans.* (**trolled, trolling**) to fish by trailing bait on a line through water. —*noun* the bait used in trolling, or a line holding it.

trolley *noun* (*pl.* **trolleys, trollies**) 1 a streetcar. 2 a small wagon or truck running on rails, e.g., in a mine.

trolley bus a bus that receives power from overhead electric wires.

trollop *noun* a promiscuous or disreputable woman.

trombone *noun* a brass wind instrument on which the pitch of notes is altered by sliding a tube in and out. ▸ **trombonist** *noun*

trompe l'oeil (trônp-lœ'ĭ') (*pl.* **trompe l'oeils**) a painting or decoration that gives a convincing illusion of reality.

troop *noun* 1 (*usu.* **troops**) armed forces; soldiers. 2 a division of a cavalry or armored squadron. 3 a group or collection of people. —*verb intrans.* (**trooped, trooping**) (**troop along, off,** etc.) to move as a group.

trooper *noun* 1 a private soldier, esp. one in a cavalry or armored unit. 2 an officer in a state police force.

troopship *noun* a ship for transporting soldiers.

trope *noun* a word or expression used figuratively.

trophy *noun* (*pl.* **trophies**) 1 a cup, medal, etc., awarded as a prize in a contest. 2 something kept in memory of a victory or success, e.g., in hunting.

tropic *noun* 1 either of two imaginary circles running around Earth at 23° 27′ north (the Tropic of Cancer) or 23° 27′ south (the Tropic of Capricorn) of the Equator. 2 (**tropics**) the part of Earth lying between these two circles.

tropical *adj.* 1 relating to the tropics. 2 very hot; passionate.

tropism (trō'pĭz,əm) *noun* the growth movement of a plant in response to an external stimulus such as gravity or light.

troposphere *noun* the lowest layer of Earth's atmosphere, extending from Earth's surface to a height of about 5 mi. (8 km) over the Poles, and about 11 mi. (17 km) over the Equator.

trot *verb intrans., trans.* (**trotted, trotting**) **1** to move at a fairly fast pace. **2** to cause (a horse) to move in this way. —*noun* the pace at which a horse, etc., moves when trotting. —**trot (something) out** *colloq.* **1** to produce (a story, an excuse, etc.) habitually and unthinkingly. **2** to produce (an item) for proud display.

troth (trãth, trŏth, trôth) *noun* faith or fidelity. —**plight (one's) troth** to promise to be faithful in marriage.

trotter *noun* a horse trained to trot in harness.

troubadour *noun* a lyric poet in S France and N Italy in the 11th c to 13th c who wrote about a highly idealized form of love.

trouble *noun* **1** distress, worry, or concern, or a cause of it. **2** bother or effort, or a cause of it. **3** a problem or difficulty. **4** (*often* **troubles**) public disturbances and unrest. —*verb trans., intrans.* (**troubled, troubling**) **1** to feel or cause to feel distress, worry, concern, etc. **2** to cause physical distress or discomfort to. **3** *used in polite requests* to put to inconvenience. **4** to make any effort. —**in trouble** in difficulties, esp. because of doing something wrong.

troubled *adj.* agitated; disturbed.

troublemaker *noun* a person who continually causes trouble, problems, etc., to others.

troubleshooter *noun* a person who is employed to find and solve problems. ▸ **troubleshooting** *noun*

troublesome *adj.* causing worry or difficulty.

trouble spot a site or source of problems or a difficulty.

troublous *adj. old use, literary* full of troubles; disturbed.

trough *noun* **1** a long, narrow, open container used for feeding livestock. **2** a channel, drain, or gutter. **3** a long, narrow hollow between two ocean waves. **4** a long narrow area of low atmospheric pressure. **5** a low point.

trounce *verb trans.* (**trounced, trouncing**) to beat or defeat completely. ▸ **trouncing** *noun*

troupe (trōōp) *noun* a group or company of performers. ▸ **trouper** *noun*

trousers *pl. noun* an outer garment reaching from the waist and covering each leg separately down to the ankle.

trousseau (trōō-sō′) *noun* (*pl.* **trousseaux**, **trousseaus**) a bride's set of new clothes and linen.

trout *noun* (*pl.* **trout, trouts**) a usu. freshwater fish of the salmon family.

trove *noun* a treasure-trove (sense 1).

trowel *noun* a small hand-held tool with a blade, used for applying and spreading plaster, digging in gardens, etc.

troy *noun* a system of weights used for precious metals and gemstones. *Also called* **troy weight**.

truant *noun* a pupil who stays away from school without permission. —**play truant** to stay away from school without permission. ▸ **truancy** *noun*

truce *noun* **1** an agreement to stop fighting, usu. temporarily. **2** a temporary break in hostilities, feuding, etc.

truck¹ *noun* **1** a heavy motor vehicle for transporting goods. **2** a frame with four or more wheels supporting a railroad car. **3** any wheeled vehicle or cart for moving heavy items. —*verb trans., intrans.* (**trucked, trucking**) **1** to transport by truck. **2** to work as a truck driver. ▸ **trucking** *noun*

truck² *noun* **1** exchange of goods; commercial dealings. **2** *colloq.* small goods or wares. **3** farmer's produce, such as vegetables and fruit, for market. —*verb trans., intrans.* (**trucked, trucking**) to give (goods) in exchange; to barter. —**have no truck with (someone** *or* **something)** to have no part in or dealings with (the one specified).

trucker *noun* a person who drives a truck.

truck farm a farm where vegetables, etc., are raised for market.

truckle *noun* a trundle bed. —*verb intrans.* (**truckled, truckling**) to submit passively or weakly.

truckle bed a trundle bed.

truculent *adj.* aggressively defiant or quarrelsome. ▸ **truculence** *noun*

trudge *verb intrans.* (**trudged, trudging**) (*usu.* **trudge along, over,** *etc.*) to walk with slow and weary steps. —*noun* a long, tiring walk.

true *adj.* (**truer, truest**) **1** agreeing with or corresponding to fact. **2** properly so called; genuine. **3** accurate or exact. **4** faithful; loyal. **5** conforming to a standard, pattern, or expectation: *true to form.* **6** of a *compass bearing* measured according to Earth's axis and not magnetic north. —*adv.* in a truthful manner; truthfully. —*verb trans.* (**trued, truing** *or* **trueing**) to bring or restore (e.g., machinery) into an accurate or required position. —**come true** *of a dream, etc.* to happen in reality. ▸ **trueness** *noun* ▸ **truly** *adv.*

true bill a bill of indictment that has been endorsed by a grand jury.

true-blue *adj.* extremely loyal.

truffle *noun* a dark round fungus that grows underground and is considered a delicacy.

truism *noun* a saying that articulates a general truth.

trump *noun* **1 a** (**trumps**) the suit of cards that has been declared to have a higher value than any other suit. **b** a card of this suit, which has a higher value than a card of the other suits. *Also called* **trump card**. **2** *colloq.* a secret advantage. *Also called* **trump card**. **3**

colloq. a helpful or fine person. —*verb trans.,* *intrans.* (**trumped, trumping**) **1** to defeat (an ordinary card or a trick with no trumps) by playing a trump. **2** to win a surprising victory or advantage over (a person, plan, etc.). —**trump (something) up** to invent or make up (false evidence, accusations, etc.).

trump card 1 *Cards.* trump (sense 1b). **2** *colloq.* trump (sense 2).

trumped-up *adj.* invented or made up; false.

trumpery *noun* (*pl.* **trumperies**) showy but worthless articles. —*adj.* showy but worthless.

trumpet *noun* **1** a brass instrument with a powerful, high, clear tone. **2** something like this instrument in shape or sound. **3** the loud cry of an elephant. —*verb intrans., trans.* (**trumpeted, trumpeting**) **1** *of an elephant* to make a loud cry. **2** to blow a trumpet. **3** to make known or proclaim loudly. ▸ **trumpeter** *noun*

truncate (trəng'kāt,, trən'-) *verb trans.* (**truncated, truncating**) to cut; to shorten. ▸ **truncation** *noun*

truncheon *noun* **1** a short, thick, heavy stick carried by police officers. **2** a staff of office.

trundle *verb trans., intrans.* (**trundled, trundling**) (*often* **trundle along, through,** *etc.*) to move or roll heavily and clumsily.

trundle bed a low bed that can be wheeled under a larger bed for storage. *Also called* **truckle, truckle bed**.

trunk *noun* **1** the main stem of a tree. **2** a person's or animal's body without the head and limbs. **3** a main part. **4** a large box or chest for transporting clothes. **5** the storage compartment in an automobile. **6** the long, muscular nose of an elephant. **7** (**trunks**) men's close-fitting shorts worn esp. for swimming.

trunk line 1 a main telephone line between large towns or cities. **2** a main railroad line.

truss *noun* **1** a framework, e.g., of beams supporting a bridge, etc. **2** a bundle of hay or straw. —*verb trans.* (**trussed, trussing**) (*often* **truss (something** *or* **someone) up**) to tie up or bind (someone or something) tightly.

trust *noun* **1** belief or confidence in or reliance on the truth, goodness, etc. of someone or something. **2** charge or care: *The child was placed in my trust.* **3** the state of being responsible for the conscientious performance of a task. **4** an arrangement by which money or property is managed by one person for the benefit of someone else. **b** an amount of money or property managed by one person for the benefit of another. **5** a group of business firms working together to control the market in a particular commodity. —*verb trans., intrans.* (**trusted, trusting**) **1**

(**trust (someone)** *or* **trust in (someone)**) to have faith in (the one specified); to rely on (that one). **2** to allow (someone) to use or do something in the belief that the person will behave responsibly. **3** (**trust (something** *or* **someone) to (someone)**) to give (someone or something) into the care of (the one specified). **4** to be confident. **5** to give credit to. —**take (something) on trust** to accept or believe (it) without verification.

trustee (trəs,tē') *noun* a person or a bank that manages money or property for someone else. ▸ **trusteeship** *noun*

trustful *adj.* inclined to put trust in others.

trust fund money or property held in trust, e.g., until the owner comes of age.

trusting *adj.* trustful.

trustworthy *adj.* able to be trusted. ▸ **trustworthiness** *noun*

trusty *adj.* (**trustier, trustiest**) able to be trusted. —*noun* (*pl.* **trusties**) a convict given special privileges for good behavior. ▸ **trustiness** *noun*

truth *noun* **1** the state of being true. **2** something that is true. —**to tell the truth** *or* **truth to tell** really; actually.

truthful *adj.* **1** *of a person* telling the truth. **2** true; realistic. ▸ **truthfully** *adv.*

try *verb intrans., trans.* (**tried, trying, tries**) **1** to attempt or make an effort (at); to seek to achieve. **2** (*also* **try (something) out**) to test (it) in order to assess (its) usefulness, value, or quality. **3 a** to judge or conduct the trial of (a party) in a court of law. **b** to examine all the evidence in (a case) in a court of law. **4** to exert strain or stress on. —*noun* (*pl.* **tries**) an attempt or effort. —**try (one's) hand at (something)** to see if (one) can do (it). **try (something) on** to put on (clothes, etc.) to check the fit and appearance. **try (something) out** to test (it).

trying *adj.* causing strain or anxiety.

tryout *noun colloq.* a test or trial.

tryst *noun* **1** an arrangement to meet a lover. **2** the meeting itself.

tsar *or* **tzar** (tsär, sär, zär) *noun* **1** a male sovereign who ruled Russia until 1917. **2** a leading figure in a field. *Also called* **czar**.

tsetse (tsĕt'sĕ, tsĕt'-) *noun* a small blood-sucking fly native to Africa that transmits several serious diseases. *Also called* **tsetse fly**.

T-shirt *or* **tee shirt** *noun* a light casual shirt, often made of stretchy material, with no collar and usu. short sleeves.

tsp. *abbrev.* teaspoon.

T-square *noun* a T-shaped ruler for drawing right angles.

TSR *abbrev. Comput.* terminate-and-stay-resident.

TSS *abbrev.* toxic shock syndrome.

tsunami (tsŏ̄-näm'ē) *noun* (*pl.* **tsunamis**) a fast-moving, highly destructive wave, associated with movement of Earth's surface under the sea. *Also called* **tidal wave.**

Tu, *abbrev.* Tuesday.

tub *noun* 1 a large, low, round container, usu. for holding water. 2 a small, round container for holding cottage cheese, etc. 3 a bath. 4 *colloq.* a slow, clumsy boat.

tuba *noun* an instrument made from brass tubing curved elliptically, with a wide upturned bell.

tubby *adj.* (**tubbier, tubbiest**) *colloq.* plump; pudgy. ▸ **tubbiness** *noun*

tube *noun* 1 a long hollow cylinder used for conveying liquids or as a container. 2 a similar long hollow structure in an animal or plant body. 3 a cylindrical container made from soft metal or plastic, used for holding paste which is gotten out by squeezing. 4 a cathode ray tube. 5 *slang* a television set. —**go down the tubes** *slang* to fail dismally; to be ruined.

tuber *noun* in certain plants, a swollen underground root or stem. ▸ **tuberous** *adj.*

tubercle *noun* a small round swelling or lump, e.g., on a bone.

tuberculin *noun* a preparation used to test for and treat tuberculosis.

tuberculosis *noun* (ABBREV. **TB**) an infectious disease of humans and animals, caused by a bacterium. ▸ **tubercular** *or* **tuberculous** *adj.*

tubing *noun* a length of tube or system of tubes, or material for it.

tubular *adj.* 1 made or consisting of tubes. 2 shaped like a tube.

tuck *verb trans.* (**tucked, tucking**) 1 (**tuck (something) in, up,** *etc.*) to push or fold the outer edges of (something) together or into a specified position, esp. to make (it) secure or neat. 2 (**tuck (someone) in**) to fold the edges of the bedclothes tightly around (someone). 3 to put in a confined or hidden place. 4 to make tucks in (a piece of clothing, etc.). —*noun* a flat fold sewn in a piece of material.

tucker *noun* a piece of material, etc., drawn over the bodice of a low-cut dress.

Tudor (tŏ̄d'ər) *adj.* relating to the royal family that ruled England from 1485 to 1603 or this period in English history.

Tues. *or* **Tue.** *abbrev.* Tuesday.

Tuesday (tŏ̄z'dē, tyŏ̄z'-, -dā) *noun* (ABBREV. **Tu., Tue., Tues.**) the third day of the week.

tuft *noun* a small bunch of grass, hair, feathers, etc., attached or growing together at the base. ▸ **tufted** *adj.*

tug *verb trans., intrans.* (**tugged, tugging**) 1 to drag with great effort. 2 to tow (a ship) with a tugboat. —*noun* 1 a strong sharp pull. 2 a hard struggle. 3 a tugboat.

tugboat *noun* a small boat used to tow larger vessels.

tug of war (*pl.* **tugs of war**) a contest in which two teams pull at opposite ends of a rope, trying to pull their opponents over a center line.

tuition *noun* 1 teaching or instruction. 2 the fee paid for instruction.

tulip *noun* a spring-blooming cup-shaped flower in a variety of bright colors.

> Based on a Persian word for 'turban', because of the similarity in shape

tulle (tŏ̄l) *noun* a thin netted cloth made of silk or rayon.

tumble *verb trans., intrans.* (**tumbled, tumbling**) 1 (*usu.* **tumble down, over,** *etc.*) to fall or cause to fall headlong. 2 to fall suddenly, esp. in value or amount. 3 (**tumble about, around,** *etc.*) to roll over and over or toss around helplessly. 4 to perform as an acrobat, esp. turning somersaults. 5 (**tumble to (something)**) *colloq.* to become aware of (it) suddenly. 6 to dry (wet clothes or washing) in an electric dryer. —*noun* 1 an act of tumbling. 2 a fall. 3 a somersault. 4 a confused state.

tumbledown *adj., of a building* falling to pieces; ramshackle.

tumbler *noun* 1 a large drinking glass. 2 an acrobat, esp. one who performs somersaults. 3 the part of a lock that holds the bolt in place. 4 the revolving drum of an electric or gas clothes dryer.

tumbleweed *noun* a bushy plant whose branching parts break off from the main stem at the end of the growing season and are then blown and rolled considerable distances by the wind.

tumbrel *or* **tumbril** *noun* a two-wheeled cart that tips over backward to empty its load.

tumescent (tŏ̄-mĕs'ənt, tyŏ̄-) *adj.* swollen or becoming swollen. ▸ **tumescence** *noun*

tumid *adj.* 1 swollen or enlarged. 2 bombastic; inflated. ▸ **tumidity** *noun*

tummy *noun* (*pl.* **tummies**) *colloq.* the stomach or abdomen.

tumor *noun* an abnormal growth of tissue that develops within or on the surface of normal body tissue.

tumult *noun* 1 a confused noise of many sounds. 2 a violent or angry commotion or disturbance. 3 the state of feeling confused and usu. violent emotions. ▸ **tumultuous** *adj.*

tun *noun* a large cask.

tuna *noun* (*pl.* **tuna, tunas**) a large marine fish found in warm seas, used as food.

tundra *noun* the relatively flat, treeless zone with permanently frozen subsoil, found in Arctic regions.

tune *noun* **1 a** a pleasing succession of musical notes; a melody. **b** the correct or a standard pitch. **2** harmony; agreement. —*verb trans., intrans.* (**tuned, tuning**) **1** (*also* **tune up**) to adjust (musical instruments) to the correct or a standard pitch. **2** (*also* **tune in**) to adjust (a radio receiver) to pick up signals from a required frequency or station, or for a particular program. **3** to adjust (an engine, a machine, etc.) so that it runs properly and efficiently. —**call the tune** *colloq.* to be in charge. **change (one's) tune** to change (one's) attitude, opinions, etc. **in tune 1** having or producing the correct or a required musical pitch. **2** having the same pitch as other instruments or voices. **out of tune** not in tune. **to the tune of (a specified monetary amount)** *colloq.* amounting to the sum or total of (something specified).

tuneful *adj.* having a pleasant tune; melodious.

tuneless *adj.* without a pleasant tune; not melodious.

tuner *noun* **1** a person whose profession is tuning instruments, esp. pianos. **2 a** a knob, dial, etc., that is used to adjust a radio to different wavelengths corresponding to different stations. **b** a radio that is part of a stereo sound system.

tungsten *noun Chem.* (SYMBOL **W**) a very hard silvery-white metallic element. *Also called* **wolfram**.

tunic *noun* **1** a loose, sleeveless garment reaching to the hips or knees. **2** a close-fitting usu. belted jacket with a high collar, worn as part of a soldier's or police officer's uniform.

tuning fork a two-pronged metal instrument that, when struck and made to vibrate, produces a single note virtually free of overtones, to which voices and instruments can adjust their pitch.

tunnel *noun* **1** an underground passage for pedestrians, vehicles, etc. **2** an underground passage dug by an animal such as a mole. —*verb intrans., trans.* (**tunneled** *or* **tunnelled, tunneling** *or* **tunnelling**) **1** (**tunnel through, under,** *etc.*) to make a tunnel through, under, etc. **2** to pass through or as if through a tunnel. —**(the) light at the end of the tunnel** *slang* the end of a long, arduous period of, e.g., labor.

tunnel vision a medical condition in which one is unable to see objects other than those straight ahead.

tunny *noun* (*pl.* **tunny, tunnies**) a tuna.

tupelo (tōō′rpə-lō̱, tyōō′-) *noun* (*pl.* **tupelos**) a tree that has light, soft wood.

turban *noun* **1** a man's headdress consisting of a long cloth sash wound around the head, worn by Muslims and Sikhs. **2** a woman's hat similar to this.

turbid *adj.* **1** of liquid, etc. not clear; cloudy. **2** confused; disordered. ▸ **turbidity** *noun*

turbine *noun* a balanced wheel that converts the kinetic energy of a moving fluid that passes over the blades into the mechanical energy of rotation.

turbo- *combining form* forming words denoting having or driven by a turbine: *turbocharger.*

turbocharger *noun* a supercharger operated by the exhaust gases of an engine, thereby boosting its power.

turbofan *noun* a jet engine driven by a gas turbine in which part of the power developed is used to drive a fan that blows air out of the exhaust and so increases thrust.

turbojet *noun* a jet engine consisting of a compressor and a turbine in which the gas energy produced is directed through a nozzle to produce thrust.

turboprop *noun* a jet engine in which the turbine drives a propeller.

turbot *noun* (*pl.* **turbot, turbots**) a flatfish highly prized as a food fish.

turbulence *noun* **1** a disturbed, wild, or unruly state. **2** the irregular movement of the atmosphere, causing gusts of wind. ▸ **turbulent** *adj.*

tureen (tə-rēn′) *noun* a large deep dish with a cover from which soup is served.

turf *noun* (*pl.* **turfs**) **1 a** the surface of the soil consisting of grass and matted roots. **b** a piece cut from this surface. **2** a slab of peat, burned for fuel. **3** (**the turf**) horseracing, the racetrack. **4** *slang* area of operation or influence; territory. —*verb trans.* (**turfed, turfing**) to cover with turf.

turgid (tər′jĭd) *adj.* **1** inflated; swollen. **2** sounding important but meaning very little; pompous.

Turk (tərk′) *noun* a native or citizen of Turkey.

turkey *noun* (*pl.* **turkeys**) **1 a** a large game bird, now domesticated, with brownish plumage. **b** the flesh of a turkey used as food, eaten particularly at Christmas and at Thanksgiving. **2** *slang* a stupid or inept person. **3** *slang* a play, movie, etc., that is a complete failure.

Turkish (tər′kĭsh) *noun* the official language of Turkey. —*adj.* of Turkey, its people, or their language.

Turkish bath a bath in which the bather first sweats in a hot room filled with steam, is then washed and massaged, and finally takes a cold shower.

Turkish delight a jellylike candy usu. flavored with rose water and dusted with icing sugar.

turmeric (tɜr'mə-rĭk, tōō'-) *noun* **1** a plant of India and the East Indies, which is cultivated for its aromatic rhizomes. **2** the dried, powdered rhizome of this plant, used as a spice and as a yellow dye.

turmoil *noun* wild confusion, agitation, or disorder.

turn *verb trans., intrans.* (**turned, turning**) **1** to move around in a circle or with a circular movement. **2** to change or cause to change position so that a different side comes to the top or front. **3** to change direction or take a new direction. **4** to direct or point to or be directed or pointed. **5** to go around: *turned the corner.* **6** to become or cause to become, or to change to (something specified). **7** to change or cause to change color. **8** *of milk* to make or become sour. **9** to make into a circular or rounded shape on a lathe or potter's wheel. **10** to perform with a rotating movement: *turn somersaults.* **11** to move or swing around a point or pivots. **12** to pass the age or time of. **13** (**turn to** (**someone** *or* **something**)) to appeal to or have recourse to (someone or something) for help or support. **14** (**turn to** (**something**)) to come to consider or pay attention to (it). **15** (*also* **turn** (**something**) **out**) to tip (it) out. **16** *of the stomach* to feel or cause it to feel nausea or queasiness. **17** *of the head* to become, or to cause it to become giddy. **18** (**turn against** (**someone**) *or* **turn** (**one person**) **against** (**another**)) to become, or to make (the one specified) hostile or unfriendly: —*noun* **1** an act of turning; a complete or partial rotation. **2** a change of direction, course, or position. **3** a point or place where a change of direction occurs. **4** a change in condition, course, etc.: *took a turn for the worse.* **5** an opportunity or duty that comes to each of several people in succession. **6** an act of a stated kind, usu. good or malicious. **7** *colloq.* a sudden feeling of illness, faintness, etc.: *The grisly scene gave me quite a turn.* **8** a short act or performance, e.g., in a variety theater; also, a performer. —**at every turn** at every stage; continually. **by turns** one after another in order. **in turn** one after another in order. **take turns** *or* **take it in turn** *of two or more people* to share a task by acting or working one after the other. **turn around** to turn to face in the opposite direction. **turn** (**something**) **around 1** to receive and deal with (a matter) in the appropriate manner. **2** to cause (an undesirable situation) to reverse itself. **turn** (**someone**) **away** to send (someone) away or reject (that person). **turn back** *or* **turn** (**someone**) **back** to return or cause (someone) to return in the opposite direction. **turn** (**something**)

down to reduce a level of (light, noise, etc.) by turning a control. **turn** (**someone** *or* **something**) **down** to reject (someone or something). **turn in 1** to bend inward. **2** *colloq.* to go to bed. **turn** (**someone** *or* **something**) **in** to hand (someone or something) over to someone in authority. **turn** (**something**) **in** to give or register (a good performance, score, etc.). **turn off** to leave a straight course or a main road. **turn** (**someone**) **off** *slang* to cause (someone) to feel dislike or disgust, or to lose sexual interest. **turn** (**something**) **off** to cause (water, electricity, etc., or a machine) to stop flowing or operating by turning a knob or pushing a button or switch. **turn** (**someone**) **on** *slang* **1** to cause (someone) to feel excitement, pleasure, or esp. sexual interest. **2** to cause (someone) to feel a heightened sense of awareness, esp. with hallucinogenic drugs. **turn** (**something**) **on** to cause (electricity, etc., or a machine) to become operational by turning a knob. **turn on** (**someone**) to attack (another) physically or verbally. **turn on** (**something**) to depend on (it). **turn out 1** to happen or prove to be. **2** to leave home for a public meeting or event. **turn** (**someone**) **out 1** to send (someone) away; to make (that person) leave. **2** to dress or groom (the person specified). **turn** (**something**) **out 1** to put (a light, etc.) out or off by turning a knob. **2** to produce (something). **turn over** to roll over when in a lying position. **turn** (**someone** *or* **something**) **over** to surrender (that person or thing) to an authority. **turn** (**something**) **over 1** to turn (it) so that the hidden or reverse side becomes visible or faces upward. **2** to consider (it) carefully. **turn up 1** to arrive. **2** to be found. **turn** (**something**) **up 1** to increase (the intensity or strength of sound, light, etc., produced by a machine) by turning a knob. **2** to discover (facts, evidence, etc.).

turnabout *noun* **1** an act of turning to face the opposite way. **2** a complete reversal of direction or opinion.

turncoat *noun* a person who turns against or leaves his or her party, principles, etc., and joins the opposing side.

turner *noun* a person who works with a lathe.

turning *noun* **1 a** a place where one road branches off from another. **b** a turnoff (sense 1). **2** the art of using a lathe to form curves in wood, metal, etc.

turning point a time or place at which a turn or significant change is made.

turnip *noun* **1** a plant with edible bright green leaves and an edible root. **2** the roundish root of this plant, which has white or yellowish flesh.

turnkey *noun* (*pl.* **turnkeys**) a jailer. —*adj.* ready for immediate operation or use.

turnoff *noun* 1 a road that branches off from a main road. *Also called* **turning.** 2 *slang* a person or thing that causes dislike or disgust.

turn-on *noun slang* a person or thing that causes excitement, esp. sexual excitement.

turnout *noun* 1 the number of people attending a meeting, event, etc. 2 an outfit or set of clothes.

turnover *noun* 1 **a** the total value of sales in a business during a certain time. **b** the rate at which stock is sold and replenished. **c** the rate at which employees pass through a business. 2 a small pastry with a fruit or jam filling.

turnpike *noun* a toll road.

turnstile *noun* a revolving gate with metal arms that allows only one person to pass through at a time.

turntable *noun* 1 the revolving platform on which a record turns on a record player. 2 a revolving platform for turning railroad engines.

turpentine *noun* 1 a thick oily resin obtained from certain trees, e.g., pines. 2 a clear oil distilled from this resin, used in solvents and paint thinners. *Also called* **oil of turpentine.**

turpitude *noun* depravity; vileness.

turquoise (tərʹkwoiz,) *noun* 1 a hard opaque mineral, light blue or green in color, which is a valuable gemstone. 2 the color of turquoise. —*adj.* of the color of turquoise.

> Literally 'Turkish stone', because first found in Turkestan

turret *noun* 1 a small tower on a castle or other building. 2 a small towerlike structure on warships, etc., on which guns are mounted. 3 that part of a lathe holding the cutting tool.

turtle *noun* a reptile with a short broad body protected by a bony shell into which the head and limbs can be drawn for protection. —**turn turtle** to turn upside down; to capsize.

turtledove *noun* a small slender pigeon known for its soft murmuring calls.

turtleneck *noun* a high, round, close-fitting neck on a garment.

tush (tŏŏsh) *noun slang* the human buttocks.

tusk *noun* one of a pair of long, curved, pointed teeth that project from the mouth of certain animals, including the elephant.

tusker *noun* an elephant, etc., with well-developed tusks.

tussle *noun* a vigorous, sharp struggle or fight. —*verb intrans.* (**tussled, tussling**) to struggle or fight vigorously.

tussock *noun* a clump of grass.

tut *interj.* used to express mild disapproval or rebuke.

tutelage (tŏŏtʹl-ĭj) *noun* 1 the state of being a guardian. 2 tuition or instruction. ▸ **tutelary** *adj.*

tutor *noun* a private teacher. —*verb trans., intrans.* (**tutored, tutoring**) to cause (a person) to acquire skill or knowledge in (a subject).

tutorial *noun* 1 a lesson given by a tutor to an individual student. 2 *Comput.* an instructional program in the use of a system or of software. —*adj.* of or pertaining to a tutor.

tutti-frutti *noun* ice cream flavored with mixed, candied fruits.

tutu *noun* a female ballet dancer's very short, stiff skirt.

tux *noun colloq.* a tuxedo.

tuxedo *noun* (*pl.* **tuxedos**) 1 a dinner jacket. 2 an evening suit for a man that includes such a jacket, and also a bowtie, a cummerbund, and pants.

TV *abbrev.* television.

TVA *abbrev.* Tennessee Valley Authority.

TV dinner a frozen, heat-and-serve meal.

TVP *abbrev.* textured vegetable protein.

twaddle *noun colloq.* senseless or silly writing or talk. —*verb intrans.* (**twaddled, twaddling**) to speak or write nonsense.

twain *noun* two.

twang *noun* 1 a sharp sound like that produced by plucking a tightly-stretched string. 2 a nasal tone of voice. —*verb trans., intrans.* (**twanged, twanging**) to make or cause to make a twang.

tweak *verb trans.* (**tweaked, tweaking**) to pull or twist with a sudden jerk. —*noun* a sudden sharp pull or twist.

tweed *noun* 1 a thick, rough, woolen cloth. 2 (**tweeds**) clothes made of this material. ▸ **tweedy** *adj.*

tweet *noun* a melodious chirping sound. —*verb intrans.* (**tweeted, tweeting**) to chirp melodiously.

tweeter *noun* a loudspeaker used to reproduce high-frequency sounds. *See also* **woofer.**

tweezers *pl. noun* a small pair of pincers for pulling out individual hairs, etc.

twelfth *noun, adj.* 1 the one numbered 12 in a series. 2 one of twelve equal parts.

Twelfth Night the evening before the 12th day after Christmas.

twelve *noun* 1 the number or figure 12. 2 the age of 12. 3 any person or thing denoted by the number 12. 4 12 o'clock. 5 a set of 12 people or things. 6 a score of 12 points. —*adj.* 1 12 in number. 2 aged 12.

twentieth *noun, adj.* 1 the one numbered 20 in a series. 2 one of twenty equal parts.

twenty *noun* (*pl.* **twenties**) **1** the number or figure 20. **2** the age of 20. **3** any person or thing denoted by the number 20. **4** a set of 20 people or things. **5** a score of 20 points. —*adj.* **1** 20 in number. **2** aged 20.

twenty-one *noun* blackjack (sense 1).

twerp *noun colloq.* a meddling, insignificant upstart.

twice *adv.* **1** two times. **2** double in amount.

twiddle *verb trans., intrans.* (**twiddled, twiddling**) **1** to twist (something) around and around. **2** (**twiddle with (something)**) to play with (it) idly. —**twiddle (one's) thumbs** to have nothing to do.

twig *noun* a small shoot of a tree, bush, etc.

twilight *noun* **1 a** the faint light in the sky when the Sun is just below the horizon, esp. immediately after sunset. **b** the time of day when this occurs. **2** a period of decline in strength or importance, esp. after a period of vigorous activity.

twilight zone an indefinite or intermediate state or position.

twill *noun* a strong woven cloth worked to give an appearance of parallel diagonal lines.

twin *noun* **1** either of two children born of the same mother at the same time. **2** either of two people or things that are very like. —*adj.* **1** being one of a pair born of the same mother at the same time. **2** being one of very similar parts.

twin bed a single bed, one of a matching pair.

twine *noun* **1** strong string or cord. **2** a coil or twist. —*verb trans., intrans.* (**twined, twining**) **1** to twist together; to interweave. **2** to twist or coil.

twinge (twĭnj) *noun* **1** a sudden, sharp pain. **2** a sudden, sharp pang of emotional pain or bad conscience.

twinight *adj. Baseball* of, pertaining to, or being a double-header with the first of the two games starting in late afternoon.

twinkle *verb intrans.* (**twinkled, twinkling**) **1** to shine with a bright, flickering light. **2** *of the eyes* to shine or sparkle with amusement or mischief. —*noun* **1** a gleam or sparkle in the eyes. **2** a flicker or glimmer of light.

twinkling *noun* **1** an instant. **2** scintillation of the stars.

twirl *verb trans., intrans.* (**twirled, twirling**) to turn or spin around. —*noun* **1** an act of twirling. **2** a curly mark.

twist *verb trans., intrans.* (**twisted, twisting**) **1** to wind or turn around, esp. by moving along a single part, or different parts in opposite directions. **2** to follow a winding course. **3** to wind around or together. **4** to wrench out of the correct shape or position with a sharp turning movement. **5** to distort the form, nature, or meaning of. **6** to dance the twist. —*noun* **1** an act of twisting. **2** something formed by twisting. **3** a turn or coil; a bend. **4** a sharp turning movement that pulls something out of shape; a wrench. **5** an unexpected event, development, or change. **6** a distortion of form, nature, or meaning. **7** a twisted roll of tobacco. **8** a curl of citrus peel used to flavor a drink. **9** (*usu.* **the twist**) a dance, popular in the 1960s, involving twisting movements of the legs and hips. —**twist (someone's) arm** *colloq.* to apply pressure to (someone) to make (that person) do something that one wants.

twisted *adj. colloq.* mentally sick or perverted.

twister *noun colloq.* a tornado.

twisty *adj.* (**twistier, twistiest**) full of twists or turns.

twit *verb trans.* (**twitted, twitting**) to tease or criticize, usu. pleasantly or affectionately.

twitch *verb intrans., trans.* (**twitched, twitching**) **1** to move jerkily. **2** (**twitch (something**) *or* **twitch at (something**)) to pull it sharply or jerkily. —*noun* **1** a sudden sharp pull or jerking movement. **2** a sudden spasm of a muscle, esp. one caused by nervousness.

twitchy *adj.* (**twitchier, twitchiest**) *colloq.* **1** jerking spasmodically. **2** nervous.

twitter *noun* a light chirping sound made esp. by small birds. —*verb intrans., trans.* (**twittered, twittering**) **1** *of a bird* to make a light, chirping sound. **2** to say with a chirping sound.

two *noun* **1** the number or figure 2; any symbol for this number. **2** the age of 2. **3** any person or thing denoted by the number 2. **4** 2 o'clock. **5** a set of 2 people or things. **6** a playing card with 2 spots. *See also* **deuce**[1] (sense 2). **7** a score of 2 points. —*adj.* **1** 2 in number. **2** aged 2. —**put two and two together** to come to a conclusion from the available evidence.

two-bit *adj. slang* cheap; petty.

two-by-four *noun* a length of planking that is 2 in. (5 cm) thick and 4 in. (10 cm) wide.

two-edged *adj.* having sharp, double edges.

two-faced *adj.* hypocritical; insincere.

twofer (tōō′fər) *noun slang* a coupon with which the holder can get two items for the price of one.

two-fisted *adj. slang* vigorous and enthusiastic.

two-handed *adj.* needing two hands.

two-piece *adj., of a suit* having two parts. —*noun* a suit made of two parts.

twosome *noun* a pair of people; a couple.

two-step *noun* a ballroom dance in duple time.

two-time *verb trans.* (**two-timed, two-timing**) *slang* to deceive or be unfaithful to (a husband, wife, or lover).

two-way *adj.* **1** able to move or allowing movement in two opposite directions. **2** *of a radio, telephone, etc.* able to send and receive messages. **3** *of communication between two people* in which both participate equally and responsibility and gains are shared.

tycoon (tī-kōōn′) *noun* a leading or dominant figure in a field, e.g., a wealthy manufacturer.

Based on a Japanese title for a warlord

tying *see* **tie**.

tympana *see* **tympanum**.

tympani *pl. noun same as* **timpani**.

tympanum (tǐm′pə-nəm) *noun* (*pl.* **tympana**, **tympanums**) **1** the eardrum. **2** a drum or drumhead. ▶ **tympanic** *adj.*

type *noun* **1** a class or group of people, animals, or things that share similar characteristics. **2** a person, esp. of a specified kind. **3** a person, animal, or thing that is a characteristic example of its group or class. **4** *Printing* **a** a small metal block with a raised letter or character on one surface, used for printing. **b** a set of such blocks. **c** printed letters, characters, or words. —*verb trans., intrans.* (**typed**, **typing**) **1** to write (words, text, etc.) using a word processor or typewriter. **2** to be a characteristic example of. **3** to decide the type of (e.g., a blood sample); to classify.

type A *or* **Type A** pertaining to a behavior pattern marked by tension, aggression, and impatience.

type B *or* **Type B** pertaining to a behavior pattern marked by a relaxed demeanor, patience, and friendliness.

typecast *verb trans.* (*pa t and pa p* **typecast**; *pr p* **typecasting**) to cast (an actor or actress) regularly in the same kind of part.

typeface *noun Printing* a set of letters, characters, etc., of a particular design or style.

typescript *noun* a keyboarded or typewritten manuscript or copy.

typesetter *noun* a person, firm, or machine that sets type ready for printing. ▶ **typeset** *verb trans.* ▶ **typesetting** *noun*

typewriter *noun* a machine with a keyboard for writing in characters resembling print. ▶ **typewrite** *verb* ▶ **typewriting** *noun*

typhoid fever (tī′foid,) a serious infection of the digestive system caused by a bacterium and characterized by fever and abdominal pain.

typhoon (tī-fōōn′) *noun* a tropical storm, characterized by revolving winds.

typhus *noun* an infectious disease transmitted to humans by lice, etc. whose main symptoms are fever, severe headache, and a red skin rash.

typical *adj.* (*often* **typical of** (**someone** *or* **something**)) **1** being a characteristic or representative example. **2** showing the usual, expected, undesirable characteristics of behavior, etc. ▶ **typically** *adv.*

typify *verb trans.* (**typified**, **typifying**, **typifies**) **1** to be a characteristic example of. **2** to represent by a type or symbol.

typing *noun* typewriting.

typist *noun* a person who types, esp. as an occupation.

typo *noun* (*pl.* **typos**) *colloq.* an error made in the typesetting of a text.

typography *noun* **1** the art or occupation of composing type and arranging texts for printing. **2** the style of printed matter. ▶ **typographer** *noun* ▶ **typographical** *adj.*

tyrannical *adj.* of or resembling a tyrant; oppressive; despotic.

tyrannize *verb trans., intrans.* (**tyrannized**, **tyrannizing**) to rule or treat (a person or people) in a cruel and oppressive way.

tyrannosaur *noun* an extremely large flesh-eating dinosaur.

tyranny *noun* (*pl.* **tyrannies**) **1** cruel, unjust, and oppressive use of power. **2** absolute, cruel, and oppressive government by a single leader or by a group of people.

tyrant *noun* **1** a ruler with complete and unrestricted power. ▤ DESPOT, DICTATOR, OPPRESSOR, SUPREMO, TOTALITARIAN. **2** a person who uses authority or power cruelly and unjustly.

tyro *noun* (*pl.* **tyros**) a beginner or novice.

tzar (tsär, sär, zär) *noun see* **tsar**.

tzatziki (tsät-sē′kē) *noun* a Greek dip made of yogurt and finely chopped cucumber, flavored with mint and garlic.

Uu

U¹ or **u** noun (pl. **Us, U's, u's**) the 21st letter of the English alphabet.

U² symbol Chem. uranium.

U³ or **U.** abbrev. university.

ubiquitous adj. found or seeming to be found everywhere. ▸ **ubiquity** noun

U-boat noun a German submarine, esp. of World Wars I and II.

udder noun a hanging baglike mammary gland of cows, sheep, goats, etc.

UFO noun (pl. **UFOs, UFO's**) colloq. an unidentified flying object esp. one presumed to be from another planet or outer space.

ugly adj. (**uglier, ugliest**) 1 unpleasant in appearance. 2 morally repulsive or offensive. 3 threatening or involving danger or violence. ▸ **ugliness** noun

uhf or **UHF** abbrev. ultrahigh frequency.

UK or **U. K.** abbrev. United Kingdom.

ukase (yōō-kās', -kāz') noun an edict.

Ukrainian noun 1 a native or citizen of Ukraine. 2 the Slavonic language of Ukraine. —adj. of Ukraine, or its people, or their language.

ukulele (yōō,kǝ-lā'lē) noun a small guitar, usu. with four strings.

ulcer noun 1 an open, often infected, sore. 2 a continuing source of harm or evil. ▸ **ulcerous** adj.

ulcerate (ǝl'sǝ-rāt,) verb trans., intrans. (**ulcerated, ulcerating**) to form an ulcer.

ulna noun (pl. **ulnas, ulnae**) the inner and longer of the two forearm bones. ▸ **ulnar** adj.

ulster noun a man's overcoat.

ult. abbrev. ultimate; ultimately.

ulterior adj. of motives, etc. other than what is apparent or admitted.

ultimate (ǝl'tǝ-mǝt) adj. 1 last or final. 2 greatest or most important. 3 fundamental; basic. 4 colloq. most advanced; best. ▸ **ultimately** adv.

ultimatum (ǝl,tǝ-māt'ǝm) noun (pl. **ultimatums, ultimata**) a final statement or condition, often issued as a warning.

ultra- combining form forming words denoting: 1 beyond in place, range, or limit: ultraviolet. 2 over or overly: ultra-strict.

ultrahigh frequency (ABBREV. **uhf, UHF**) a radio frequency between 300 and 3,000 MHz.

ultramarine noun a deep blue color.

ultrasonic adj. relating to or producing ultrasound. ▸ **ultrasonically** adv.

ultrasound noun sound with wave frequencies above the upper limit of normal human hearing.

ultraviolet (ABBREV. **UV, U.V.**) adj. denoting electromagnetic radiation with wavelengths in the region between violet light and x-rays.

ululate (ǝl'yǝ-lāt,) verb intrans. (**ululated, ululating**) to wail, or lament loudly. ▸ **ululation** noun

umbel noun an umbrella-shaped flower head.

umber noun 1 a dark yellowish-brown mineral used as a pigment. 2 a dark yellowish-brown color.

umbilical cord a tubelike organ attaching a fetus to the placenta for nourishment.

umbra noun (pl. **umbras, umbrae**) 1 the darkest part of a shadow, at the center. 2 a shadow, esp. that cast by the Moon onto Earth during an eclipse of the Sun.

umbrage (ǝm'brij) noun offense or resentment: took umbrage at his remarks.

umbrella noun 1 a canopy device giving shelter against rain, etc. 2 an organization, etc. providing protection or overall cover for a number of others.

> Literally 'little shadow' and originally used to refer to a sunshade

umlaut (ōōm'lowt,) noun in Germanic languages, a change in the pronunciation of a vowel, or {¨} above a vowel to indicate this.

umpire noun a person supervising play in various sports, enforcing the rules and deciding disputes. —verb trans., intrans. (**umpired, umpiring**) to act as umpire in a game or match.

umpteen adj. colloq. very many; innumerable. ▸ **umpteenth** adj.

> Originally umpty, a signaller's slang term for a dash in Morse code

UN abbrev. United Nations.

un- prefix forming words denoting the opposite or reversal of the root word: unplug.

unable adj. not having sufficient strength, skill, or authority to do something.

unabridged adj. involving no condensation or shortening: an unabridged text.

unaccountable adj. 1 impossible to explain. 2 not answerable or accountable.

unaccustomed adj. 1 (**unaccustomed to**) not used or accustomed to (something). 2

not usual or customary: *unaccustomed luxury.*

unadulterated *adj.* consisting of itself only.

unadvised *adj.* 1 not advised; without advice. 2 unwise. ▶ **unadvisedly** *adv.*

unaffected *adj.* 1 sincere or genuine; not pretentious. 2 not affected.

unalloyed *adj.*, pure; sheer.

unanimous (yŏŏ-năn′ə-məs) *adj.* 1 all in complete agreement. 2 *of an opinion, decision, etc.* with no one disagreeing. ▶ **unanimity** *noun*

unarmed *adj.* without weapons.

unassuming *adj.* modest or unpretentious.

unattached *adj.* 1 not in a steady romantic or sexual relationship. 2 not attached, associated, or connected.

unawares *adv.* by surprise; unexpectedly.

unbalanced *adj.* 1 not in a state of physical balance. 2 lacking mental balance. 3 lacking impartiality; biased.

unbeknown (ən,bĭ-nōn′) *or* **unbeknownst** *adv.* (**unbeknown to**) *colloq.* without (someone's) knowledge.

unbelief *noun* lack of, esp. religious belief. ▶ **unbeliever** *noun*

unbend *verb intrans., trans.* 1 to become less formal in manner or behavior. 2 to straighten.

unbending *adj.* strict or severe; inflexible.

unborn *adj.* not yet born.

unbosom *verb trans.* (**unbosomed, unbosoming**) (*often* **unbosom oneself**) to speak openly about feelings, etc.

unbounded *adj.* limitless; infinite.

unbowed *adj.* 1 not bowed. 2 not conquered.

unbridled *adj.* freely felt or expressed.

unburden *verb trans.* to remove a load or burden from.

uncalled-for *adj.*, *of a remark, etc.* not warranted or deserved.

uncanny *adj.* 1 strangely disturbing or frightening. 2 beyond ordinary human ability.

uncertain *adj.* 1 not sure, certain, or confident. 2 not definitely known or decided. 3 not to be depended upon. 4 likely to change. ▶ **uncertainty** *noun*

uncharted *adj.* of *territory, etc.* never having been explored fully or mapped in detail.

uncle *noun* the brother of one's father or mother, or the husband of one's aunt.

Uncle Sam the embodiment of the USA, or its government or people.

uncommon *adj.* 1 rare or unusual. 2 remarkably great; extreme. ▶ **uncommonly** *adv.*

unconcerned *adj.* 1 indifferent. 2 not anxious.

unconditional *adj.* straightforward, with no conditions imposed; absolute. ▶ **unconditionally** *adv.*

unconscionable *adj.* 1 without conscience. 2 outrageous; unreasonable; excessive.

unconscious *adj.* 1 lacking the ability to respond to external stimuli, esp. because of injury or illness. 2 done without thinking. 3 relating to mental activity that is below the conscious level. —*noun* the part of the mind controlling mental activity that is below the conscious level. ▶ **unconsciousness** *noun*

uncouth *adj.* lacking social manners.

uncover *verb trans., intrans.* 1 to remove the cover from. 2 to reveal or discover. 3 to take off one's hat as a mark of respect.

unction *noun* 1 *Christianity* **a** the act of ceremonially anointing a person with oil. **b** the oil so used. 2 ointment of any kind.

unctuous (əngk′chə-wəs, əngksh′wəs) *adj.* 1 insincerely and excessively charming. 2 oily.

uncut *adj.* 1 not cut. 2 *of a book, movie, etc.* with no parts cut out.

under *prep.* 1 below or beneath. 2 at the foot of. 3 less than; short of. 4 lower in rank than. 5 during the administration or reign of. 6 subjected to or receiving: *under consideration.* 7 in the category or classification of. 8 according to: *under the terms of the agreement.* 9 in view of: *under the circumstances.* —*adv.* 1 in or to a lower place, position, or rank. 2 into a state of unconsciousness. —*adj.* 1 lower. 2 subordinate.

under- *combining form* forming words denoting: 1 beneath or below: *underfoot.* 2 insufficient or insufficiently: *underpay.* 3 lower in rank or importance: *undersecretary.*

underachieve *verb intrans.* to be less successful than expected, esp. academically. ▶ **underachiever** *noun*

underage (ən,də-rāj′) *or* **underaged** *adj.* not legally old enough: *an underaged driver.*

underarm *adj., adv.* of a way of bowling, pitching, etc. with the arm kept below the level of the shoulder. —*noun* the armpit.

Some words with **un-** prefix.

unalike *adj.*	**unbelievable** *adj.*	**unclasp**
unappetizing *adj.*	**unbiased** *or* **unbiassed** *adj.*	**unclean** *adj.*
unapproachable *adj.*	**unbidden** *adj., adv.*	**unclear** *adj.*
unassailable *adj.*	**unceremonious** *adj.*	**unclothe** *verb trans.*
unattended *adj.*	**unchain** *verb trans.*	**uncomfortable** *adj.*
unavailing *adj.*	**unchristian** *adj.*	**uncommitted** *adj.*
unbearable *adj.*	**uncircumcised** *adj.*	**uncommunicative** *adj.*
unbecoming *adj.*	**uncivil** *adj.*	**uncompromising** *adj.*

underbelly *noun* **1** the part of an animal's belly facing the ground. **2** a vulnerable part.

undercarriage *noun* **1** the landing gear of an aircraft. **2** the chassis of a road vehicle.

undercharge *verb trans.* to charge (a person) too little money.

underclassman *noun* a freshman or sophomore in a high school or college.

underclothes *pl. noun* underwear.

undercoat *noun* a preparatory or protective layer, e.g. of paint, rustproofing, etc. —*verb trans.* (**undercoated**, **undercoating**) to apply an undercoat to.

undercover *adj.* working or carried out in secret.

undercurrent *noun* **1** an unseen current of water. **2** an underlying trend or opinion.

undercut *verb trans.* **1 a** to offer goods or services at a lower price than (a competitor). **b** to diminish or undermine (the effectiveness or authority of another). **2** to cut the underside of. **3** *Sport* to apply backspin to (a ball).

underdeveloped *adj.* **1** having a relatively low level of productivity and economic growth. **2** unusually immature.

underdog *noun* **1** a less highly regarded competitor, etc. **2** a person dominated by another.

underdone *adj.* not cooked enough.

underestimate *verb trans.* (ən,dər-ĕs′tə-māt,) to make too low an estimate, e.g., in value, capacity, etc. —*noun* (ən,dər-ĕs′tə-mət,) too low an estimate.

underexpose *verb trans.* to expose (photographic film) to insufficient light.

underfoot *adj., adv.* under, or as if under, the feet of a walking or running person.

undergarment *noun* an item of underwear.

undergo *verb trans.* to endure, experience, or be subjected to.

undergraduate (ən,dər-grăj′ə-wət) *noun* a person studying for a first degree at a college or university.

underground *noun* **1** a clandestine political, artistic, etc. group. **2** *Brit.* a subway. —*adj.* **1** existing or operating below the surface of the ground. **2** of or belonging to a political or artistic underground. —*adv.* **1** to a position below ground level. **2** into hiding.

undergrowth *noun* a thick growth of shrubs and bushes among trees.

underhand *adj.* **1** secretively deceitful or dishonest. **2** *Sport* underarm. —*adv.* underarm: *pitched the ball underhand.*

underlie *verb trans.* **1** to lie underneath. **2** to be the hidden cause or meaning of.

underline *verb trans.* **1** to draw a line under (e.g., a word or piece of text). **2** to put emphasis on.

underling *noun* a subordinate.

undermine *verb trans.* to wear away, weaken or destroy, esp. gradually and imperceptibly.

underneath *prep., adv.* beneath or below. —*noun* a lower part or surface.

underpants *pl. noun* undershorts.

underpass *noun* a passage, road, etc. going below a road, railroad, etc.

underpin *verb trans.* **1** to support structurally from beneath. **2** to give support to.

underplay *verb trans.* to understate or reduce the emphasis on.

underrate *verb trans.* to underestimate the value, abilities, etc. of.

underscore *verb trans.* to underline (sense 1 and 2).

undersecretary *noun* a subordinate to a cabinet secretary.

undersell *verb trans.* to sell (goods or services) at a lower price than (a competitor).

undershirt *noun* an undergarment covering the chest.

undershoot *verb trans.* **1** of an aircraft to land short of (a runway). **2** to fall short of.

undershorts *pl. noun* briefs worn by men and boys.

underside *noun* the downward-facing side or surface.

undersigned *noun.* the person or people who signed below.

undersized *adj.* of less than the usual size.

underskirt *noun* a garment worn under a dress or skirt.

understand *verb trans., intrans.* **1** to grasp the meaning, etc. (of). **2** to know, believe, or infer, from information received. **3** to have a sympathetic awareness of the character or nature of. **4** to grasp what is said. ▸ **understandable** *adj.*

understanding *noun* **1** the act of understanding or the ability to understand. **2** a perception or interpretation of information

---

Some words with **un-** prefix.

unconditional *adj.*	**undiluted** *adj.*	**unelected** *adj.*
unconstitutional *adj.*	**undistinctive** *or*	**unemotional** *adj.*
uncork *verb trans.*	**undistinguished** *adj.*	**unemployable** *adj.*
uncouple *verb trans.*	**undocumented** *adj.*	**unequal** *adj.*
uncourteous *adj.*	**uneaten** *adj.*	**unequaled** *adj.*
uncrowned *adj.*	**uneconomic** *adj.*	**uneven** *adj.*
undecided *adj.*	**uneconomical** *adj.*	**uneventful** *adj.*
undeniable *adj.*	**uneducated** *adj.*	**unexampled** *adj.*

received. **3** an informal agreement. **4** a condition agreed upon. —*adj.* sympathetic.

understate *verb trans.* to describe as being less in extent or intensity. ▸ **understatement** *noun*

understood *adj.* conveyed or realized indirectly, without words or direct references.

understudy *verb trans., intrans.* to study (a role), or study the role of (an actor), so as to be able to take over if the need arises. —*noun* (*pl.* **understudies**) a person who understudies.

undertake *verb trans.* **1** to accept (a duty, responsibility, or task). **2** to promise or agree.

undertaker *noun* a person whose job is preparing corpses for burial or cremation, organizing funerals, etc. *Also called* **funeral director, mortician.**

undertaking *noun* **1** a duty, responsibility, or task undertaken. **2** a promise or guarantee. **3** the work of an undertaker.

undertone *noun* **1** a quiet tone of voice. **2** an underlying quality, emotion, or atmosphere. **3** a subdued sound or shade of a color.

undervalue *verb trans.* to place too low a value on.

underwear *noun* clothes worn next to the skin. *Also called* **underclothes.**

underworld *noun* **1** the world of vice and crime. **2** *Mythol.* a world beneath the earth's surface, the home of the souls of the dead.

underwrite *verb trans.* **1** to agree to finance (a commercial venture), and accept the loss in the event of failure. **2** to agree to buy, or find a buyer for, leftover shares from (a sale of shares to the public). **3** to issue an insurance policy, accepting the risk involved. ▸ **underwriter** *noun*

undesirable *adj.* unpleasant or objectionable. —*noun* a person or thing considered undesirable.

undid *verb see* **undo.**

undies (ŭn′dēz) *pl. noun colloq.* items of, esp. women's, underwear.

undo *verb trans., intrans.* (pa t **undid**; pa p **undone**; pr p **undoing**; 3d person sing. pr **undoes**) **1** to open, unfasten, or untie. **2** to cancel or reverse the effect or result of. **3** to bring about the downfall of.

undoing *noun* downfall or ruin, or the cause of it. —*verb see* **undo.**

undone *adj.* **1** unfinished. **2** unfastened. **3** ruined: *I am undone!* —*verb see* **undo.**

undress *verb trans., intrans.* to take the clothes off. —*noun* nakedness or near nakedness.

undue (ŭn,dōō′, -dyōō′) *adj.* inappropriately or unjustifiably great.

undulate (ən′jə-lāt,) *verb intrans.* (**undulated, undulating**) **1** to move in or or as if in waves. **2** to be wavy.

unduly *adv.* to an excessive degree.

undying *adj.* everlasting; eternal.

unearned *adj.* **1** gained through investments, interest on savings, etc. **2** not deserved.

unearth *verb trans.* (**unearthed, unearthing**) **1** to dig up out of the ground. **2** to discover by searching.

unearthly *adj.* **1** weird; ghostly. **2** not of this Earth; heavenly or hellish.

uneasy *adj.* **1** feeling or exhibiting anxiety. **2** unstable. **3** causing anxiety; unsettling. ▸ **uneasily** *adv.* ▸ **uneasiness** *noun*

unemployed *adj.* **1** not having a job. **2** not in use; idle. ▸ **unemployment** *noun*

unequivocal *adj.* clearly stated or expressed; unambiguous. ▸ **unequivocally** *adv.*

unerring *adj.* consistently true or accurate; never making an error or missing the mark.

unfailing *adj.* never weakening or failing; always constant. ▸ **unfailingly** *adv.*

unfeeling *adj.* unsympathetic; hard-hearted.

unfit *adj.* **1** not meeting required standards; not good enough. **2** not fit, esp. physically.

unfledged *adj.* **1** of a bird not yet having adult flight feathers. **2** young and inexperienced.

unfold *verb trans., intrans.* **1** to open or spread out. **2** to develop or to be revealed gradually: *as the plot unfolds.*

unfortunate (ən,fôr′chə-nət) *adj.* having, resulting from, or constituting bad luck; regrettable. —*noun* an unfortunate person. ▸ **unfortunately** *adv.*

unfounded *adj.* not based on fact.

unfrequented (ən,frē-kwĕnt′ĭd, -frē′kwənt-) *adj.* rarely passed through or traveled.

unfurl *verb trans., intrans.* to open out from a rolled-up or tied-up state.

ungainly *adj.* (**ungainlier, ungainliest**) awkward and ungraceful in movement. ▸ **ungainliness** *noun*

Some words with **un-** prefix.

unexceptionable *adj.*	**unfathomable** *adj.*	**unflinching** *adj.*
unexceptional *adj.*	**unfavorable** *adj.*	**unfocused** or
unexpected *adj.*	**unfeigned** *adj.*	**unfocussed** *adj.*
unfair *adj.*	**unfettered** *adj.*	**unforgiving** *adj.*
unfaithful *adj.*	**unfinished** *adj.*	**unfunded** *adj.*
unfamiliar *adj.*	**unflagging** *adj.*	**unfunny** *adj.*
unfashionable *adj.*	**unflappable** *adj.*	**ungovernable** *adj.*
unfasten *verb trans.*	**unflattering** *adj.*	**ungrateful** *adj.*

ungodly adj. 1 wicked or sinful. 2 colloq. outrageous. ▸ **ungodliness** noun

unguent (ong'gwənt) noun an ointment.

ungulate (ong'gyə-lət, -lāt,) adj. hoofed. —noun a hoofed mammal.

unhand verb trans. old use, literary to let go of.

unhappy adj. 1 sad. 2 bringing misfortune. ▸ **unhappily** adv. ▸ **unhappiness** noun

unhealthy adj. 1 in poor health. 2 damaging to health. ▸ **unhealthily** adj. ▸ **unhealthiness** noun

unheard-of adj. unprecedented; unknown.

unhinge (ən,hĭnj') verb trans. (**unhinged, unhinging**) to cause (a person, or a person's mind) to become unbalanced. ▸ **unhinged** adj.

unholy adj. 1 wicked; sinful; irreligious. 2 colloq. outrageous.

unhorse verb trans. (**unhorsed, unhorsing**) 1 to throw or force (a rider) off a horse. 2 to overthrow (e.g., a leader or dictator).

uni- combining form forming words denoting one, a single: unidirectional.

unicameral (yōō,nĭ-kăm'ə-rəl) adj. having only one lawmaking.

UNICEF (yōō'nĭ-sĕf,) abbrev. United Nations Children's Emergency Fund.

unicellular adj. consisting of a single cell.

unicorn noun a mythical horse with a long horn on its forehead.

unicycle noun an acrobat's one-wheeled cycle.

unidentified flying object a UFO.

uniform noun a distinctive set of clothing worn by members of a particular organization or profession. —adj. not changing or varying in form or nature. ▸ **uniformity** noun ▸ **uniformly** adv.

unify verb trans., intrans. (**unified, unifying, unifies**) to bring together to form a single unit. ▸ **unification** noun

unilateral (yōōn,ĭ-lăt'ə-rəl) adj. affecting, involving, or done by only one person or group. ▸ **unilaterally** adv.

uninterested adj. indifferent.

> *Usage* See note at *disinterested*.

union noun 1 the act of uniting or the state of being united. 2 an association of people or groups united in a common, esp. political, purpose. 3 a trade union. 4 agreement or harmony. 5 marriage; wedlock.

unionism noun 1 the principle or policy of combining. 2 the principles and practices of trade unions.

unionist or **Unionist** noun 1 a person supporting or believing in trade unions. 2 a person in favor of political union.

unionize verb trans., intrans. (**unionized, unionizing**) to organize (a work force) into a trade union; to become so organized. ▸ **unionization** noun

Union Jack the national flag of the UK.

union shop a factory, etc., in which only union members are employed. Also called **closed shop**. See also **open shop**.

unique (yōō-nēk') adj. being the only one of its kind; having no equal. ▸ **uniquely** adv. ▸ **uniqueness** noun

> *Usage* The adjective *unique* is considered an absolute; that is to say, it is regarded by most specialists and critics as admitting no comparison (most unique) and no qualification adverbially (more unique than; very or quite unique). Expressions such as nearly unique or almost unique, are, however, acceptable in that they do not involve comparison.

unisex (yōō'nĭ-sĕks,) adj. suited to, for use by, or wearable by both men and women.

unison noun 1 Mus. a sameness of pitch in voices or instruments. b the state of singing or playing all in the same pitch. 2 the state of acting all in the same way at the same time. 3 complete agreement.

unit noun 1 a single item, etc. regarded as the smallest subdivision of a whole. 2 a set of things or people that function together. 3 a standard measure of a physical quantity.

Unitarian (yōō,nə-tăr'ē-ən) noun a member of a Christian group rejecting the Trinity, but holding a broad spectrum of beliefs, and, in the USA, part of the Unitarian Universalist Association. —adj. relating to this religious group or belief. See also **Trinitarian**. ▸ **Unitarianism** noun

unitary adj. 1 of or relating to units or a unit. 2 characterized by unity or uniformity.

Some words with **un-** prefix.

unguarded adj.	**uninspiring** adj.	**unmanageable**
unheard adj.	**uninstructed** adj.	**unmannerly** or
unhesitating adj.	**unkind** adj.	**unmannered** adj.
unhopeful adj.	**unladen** adj.	**unmarried** adj.
unidentified adj.	**unlined** adj.	**unmask** verb trans.
unimpeachable adj.	**unlit** adj.	**unmerciful** adj.
unincisive adj.	**unload** verb trans., intrans.	**unmistakable** adj.
uninspired adj.	**unlock** verb trans., intrans	**unmitigated** adj.

unite (yŏŏ-nīt') *verb trans., intrans.* (**united, uniting**) 1 to make or become a single unit or whole. 2 to bring or come together in a common purpose or belief. 3 to have (e.g., features or characteristics) in combination. ▸ **united** *adj.*

unity *noun* (*pl.* **unities**) 1 the state of being a single unified whole. 2 a single unified whole. 3 agreement or harmony between different members or elements.

univalent (yŏŏ,nī-vā'lənt) *adj. Chem.* monovalent. ▸ **univalence** *noun*

universal *adj.* 1 of or pertaining to the Universe. 2 of, relating to, or affecting the whole world or all people. 3 of, relating to, or affecting all the people or things in a particular group. 4 *colloq.* widespread; general. ▸ **universality** *noun* ▸ **universally** *adv.*

Universal Product Code (ABBREV. **UPC**) a bar code.

universe *noun* 1 (**Universe**) the cosmos, i.e., the whole of space and other matter contained within it. 2 all people.

university *noun* (*pl.* **universities**) an institution of higher learning with the authority to award bachelor's, master's, and doctoral degrees.

unkempt (ən-kĕmpt') *adj.* 1 of hair not combed. 2 messy: *an unkempt yard.*

unknown *adj.* 1 not known; unfamiliar. 2 not at all famous.

unlawful *adj.* against the law. ▣ ILLEGAL, ILLEGITIMATE, ILLICIT, LAWLESS, WRONGFUL ▣ LAWFUL, LEGAL, LEGITIMATE, LICIT, RIGHTFUL. ▸ **unlawfully** *adv.* ▸ **unlawfulness** *noun*

unleaded (ən,lĕd-ĭd) *adj., of gasoline* not containing lead additives.

unlearn *verb trans.* to try actively to forget.

unlearned *adj.* (ən,lər'nĭd) uneducated.

unleash *verb trans.* 1 to release (e.g.; a dog) from a leash. 2 to release or give free expression to (e.g., anger).

unless (ən-lĕs) *conj.* if not; except if.

unlettered *adj.* uneducated; illiterate.

unlike *prep.* 1 different from. 2 not typical or characteristic of. —*adj.* disparate,. e.g., in kind, sort, or character.

unlikely *adj.* 1 probably untrue. 2 not likely to happen. 3 not obviously suitable; improbable. ▸ **unlikelihood** *noun*

unlimited *adj.* not limited or restricted.

unloosen *or* **unloose** *verb trans.* 1 to make less tight. 2 to set free.

unlucky *adj.* 1 bringing, resulting from, or constituting bad luck. 2 having or tending to have bad luck.

unmake *verb trans.* to cancel or destroy.

unmentionable *adj.* not fit to be mentioned or talked about, esp. because considered indecent.

unnerve *verb trans.* (**unnerved, unnerving**) 1 to weaken the courage or confidence of. 2 to cause to feel ill at ease.

unnoticeable *adj.* not easily noticed.

unnumbered *adj.* 1 not having been given a number. 2 too numerous to be counted.

unofficial *adj.* neither official nor acting in an official capacity. ▸ **unofficially** *adv.*

unpack *verb trans.* (**unpacked, unpacking**) 1 to take out of a packed state. 2 to empty (e.g., a suitcase) of packed contents.

unparalleled *adj.* so remarkable as to have no equal or parallel.

unperson (ən'pər'sən) *noun* a nonperson.

unpick *verb trans.* to undo (stitches); to take (a sewn or knitted article) to pieces by undoing the stitching.

unpleasant *adj.* not pleasant; disagreeable.

unpleasantness *noun* 1 the quality of being unpleasant. 2 an unpleasant incident, esp. a disagreement involving open hostility.

unplug *verb trans.* 1 to disconnect (an electrical appliance). 2 to remove a plug or blockage from.

unpopular *adj.* generally disliked. ▸ **unpopularity** *noun*

unpracticed *adj.* 1 having had little or no practice or experience. 2 not or not yet put into practice.

unpretentious *adj.* modest and without affectation.

unprintable *adj.* not fit to be printed.

unqualified *adj.* 1 not having any formal qualifications for a particular job, etc. **b** not competent. 2 complete: *an unqualified success.*

unquote *interj.* used in speech to indicate the end of a quotation.

Some words with **un-** prefix.

unmixed *adj.*	**unprecedented** *adj.*	**unready** *adj.*
unmoved *adj.*	**unpredictable** *adj.*	**unrealistic** *adj.*
unnamed *adj.*	**unprofessional** *adj.*	**unreality** *noun*
unnatural *adj.*	**unprofitable** *adj.*	**unreasonable** *adj.*
unobtrusive *adj.*	**unquestionable** *adj.*	**unremarkable** *adj.*
unoccupied *adj.*	**unquestioning** *adj.*	**unrequited** *adj*
unopposed *adj.,* àdv.	**unquiet** *adj.*	**unreserved** *adj.*
unpalatable *adj.*	**unreadable** *adj.*	**unreservedly** *adv.*

unravel verb trans., intrans. **1** to take or come out of a knitted or woven state back into a strand or strands. **2** to make or become clear after being confusing or obscure.

unreachable adj. inaccessible.

unread (ən,rĕd′) adj. **1** of a book, etc. not read. **2** of a person having read few books.

unreal adj. **1** existing only in the mind or imagination. **2** colloq. exceptionally strange, ridiculous, or excellent.

unrelenting adj. **1** refusing to change one's viewpoint or chosen course of action. **2** never stopping; constant; relentless.

unremitting adj. unrelenting (sense 3).

unrest noun anxiety; unease.

unruly adj. (**unrulier, unruliest**) noisily disobedient or disorderly, esp. habitually. ▸ **unruliness** noun

unsaturated adj. Chem. **1** of an organic chemical compound containing at least one double or triple bond between its carbon atoms: unsaturated fats. **2** of a solution not containing the maximum amount of a solute that could be dissolved in it.

unsavory adj. unpleasant or distasteful.

unscathed (ən,skāthd′) adj. not harmed or injured.

unscramble verb trans. **1** to interpret (a coded or scrambled message). **2** to put in order.

unscrupulous adj. without scruples or moral principles. ▸ **unscrupulously** adv.

unseasoned adj. young and callow.

unselfish adj. having or showing concern for others.

unsettle verb trans. to cause to become ill at ease.

unsettled adj. **1** lacking stability; changing or likely to change. **2** not relaxed or at ease. **3** of a debt unpaid.

unsightly adj. (**unsightlier, unsightliest**) not pleasant to look at.

unsolicited adj. not wanted, needed, or asked for: unsolicited advice.

unsound adj. **1** not reliable. **2** not firm or solid.

unspeakable adj. **1** not able to be expressed in words. **2** too bad, wicked, or obscene to be spoken about.

unsteady adj. **1** tending to move; wobbly. **2** tending to change or fluctuate.

unstop verb trans. **1** to free from being blocked or stopped. **2** to draw out the stopper from.

unstoppable adj. colloq. hard to stop.

unstrung adj. **1** with strings removed. **2** unnerved; upset.

unstudied adj. natural and spontaneous.

unsung adj. not praised or recognized.

unsure adj. uncertain; doubtful.

untaught adj. **1** lacking education or knowledge. **2** not acquired by teaching.

unthinkable adj. inconceivable.

unthinking adj. **1** inconsiderate. **2** careless.

untie (ən,tī′) verb trans. **1** to undo from a tied state. **2** to remove the constraints on.

until prep. **1** up to the time of. **2** up to the time of reaching (a place): slept on the train until Paris. **3** (with a negative) before: not until Wednesday. —conj. **1** up to the time that. **2** (with a negative) before: You'll not do that until I say so.

untimely adj. **1** happening before the proper or expected time. **2** coming at an inappropriate or inconvenient time.

unto prep. to; till.

untold adj. **1** not told. **2** too many to be counted: untold numbers.

untouchable adj. **1** not to be touched or handled. **2** discouraging physical contact. —noun a member of the lowest Indian caste, whose touch was formerly regarded as a contamination.

untoward adj. **1** inconvenient; unfortunate. **2** adverse; unfavorable.

untruth noun **1** the fact of being untrue. **2** a lie.

untutored adj. lacking education or knowledge.

unused (ən,yōōzd′) adj. **1** never used. **2** (**unused to**) not accustomed to (something).

unusual adj. not usual; uncommon; rare. ▸ **unusually** adv.

unvarnished adj., not exaggerated or embellished: the unvarnished truth.

unwell adj. in poor health.

unwieldy adj. (**unwieldier, unwieldiest**) large and awkward to carry or manage.

unwind verb trans., intrans. **1** to take or come out of a coiled or wound position. **2** colloq. to relax.

unwitting adj. **1** not realizing or being aware. **2** done without being realized or intended. ▸ **unwittingly** adv.

Some words with **un-** prefix.

unrighteous adj.	**unscrew** verb trans.	**unskilled** adj.
unrivaled or **unrivalled** adj.	**unseasonable** adj.	**unsociable** or **unsocial** adj.
unroll verb trans., intrans.	**unseat** verb trans.	**unsophisticated** adj.
unruffled adj.	**unseemly** adj.	**unsparing** adj.
unsafe adj.	**unseen** adj.	**unspent** adj.
unsaid adj.	**unshackle** verb trans.	**unspoken** adj.
unschooled adj.	**unshakable** adj.	**unsportsmanlike** adj.
unscientific adj.	**unsigned** adj.	**unstable** adj.

unwonted (ən,wônt'ĭd, -wŏnt'-) *adj.* not usual or habitual.

unwritten *adj.* **1** not recorded in writing or print. **2** *of a rule or law* not formally enforceable, but traditionally accepted and followed.

unzip *verb trans.* to unfasten or open by undoing a zipper.

up *prep.* at or to a higher position on or a position further along: *climbed up the stairs.* —*adv.* **1** at or to a higher position or level: *lift it up.* **2** at or to a place higher up, or a more northerly place: *went up to Montreal.* **3** in or to a more erect position: *stood up.* **4** fully or completely: *use up / eat up.* **5** to a particular or necessary point or degree: *saved up for it.* **6** out of bed: *got up.* **7** close to: *walked up to us.* —*adj.* **1 a** moving or directed to a higher position: *the up escalator.* **b** higher than before: *My grades in math are up.* **2** out of bed: *He's not up yet.* **3** having an advantage; ahead: *$5 up after the first bet.* **4** appearing in court: *up for first-degree murder.* **5** *of the sun* above the horizon. **6 a** *colloq.* going on; happening: *What's up?* **b** amiss; wrong: *is something up?* **7** done; over; finished: *His time is up.* —*verb trans., intrans.* (**upped, upping**) **1** to raise or increase: *has upped the prices.* **2** *colloq.* to proceed boldly or unexpectedly to do (something): *He upped and left.* —*noun* an upward trend.

up-and-coming *adj.* beginning to become successful or well known.

upbeat *adj. colloq.* cheerful; optimistic. —*noun Mus.* the unstressed beat at which a conductor raises the baton.

upbraid *verb trans.* to scold or reproach.

upbringing *noun* the general rearing, instruction, and education of a child.

UPC *abbrev.* Universal Product Code.

up-country *adj., adv.* inland. —*noun* the inland regions of a country.

update *verb trans.* (əp,dāt') to make or bring up to date. —*noun* (əp'dāt) the act or an instance of updating.

up-end *verb trans., intrans.* **1** to turn or to be turned upside down. **2** to put into disarray.

up-front *or* **upfront** *adj. colloq.* **1** candid; open. **2** *of money* paid in advance.

upgrade *verb trans., intrans.* **1** to move up in rank or grade. **2** to improve the quality of. **3** to exchange (something) for a newer, better, version.

upheaval (əp,hē'vəl) *noun* a change or disturbance that greatly disrupts.

uphill *adj.* **1** sloping upward. **2** *of a task, etc.* requiring great effort. —*adv.* up a slope.

uphold *verb trans.* **1** to support (an action), defend (a right), or maintain (the law). **2** to declare or confirm (e.g., a court judgment) as correct or just.

upholstery (ə-pōl'strē) *noun* the springs, stuffing, and covers of a chair or sofa, or the work that goes into fitting furniture with these. ▸ **upholster** *verb* ▸ **upholsterer** *noun*

upkeep *noun* the task of keeping something in good order or condition, or the cost of doing so.

upland (əp'lənd, -lănd,) *noun* (*often* **uplands**) a high or hilly region.

uplift *verb trans.* (əp-lĭft') **1** to fill with an invigorating happiness or optimism. **2** to lift up; to collect. —*noun* (əp'lĭft,) an uplifting influence or effect.

upload *verb intrans., trans. Comput.* to transmit (data or a program) from one computer to a larger system.

upmarket *adj.* high in price, quality, or prestige.

upmost *adj., adv.* uppermost.

upon *prep.* on or onto.

upper *adj.* **1** situated above. **2** high or higher in rank or status. —*noun* **1** the part of a shoe above the sole. **2** *slang* a drug that induces euphoria.

uppercase *or* **upper-case** *adj. Printing* consisting of capital letters as opposed to small letters.

upper class the highest social class; the aristocracy. ▸ **upper-class** *adj.*

upperclassman *noun* a high-school or college junior or senior.

upper crust *colloq.* the upper class.

upper hand (**the upper hand**) a position of advantage or dominance.

upper house the senior, usu. smaller part of a bicameral legislature, such as the US Senate.

uppermost *adj., adv.* at, in, or into the highest or most prominent position.

uppity *adj. colloq.* arrogant or snobbish to the point of being presumptuous.

upright *adj.* **1** standing straight up; vertical. **2** having integrity or moral correctness. —*adv.* into an upright position. —*noun* **1** a vertical post or pole. **2** an upright piano.

Some words with un- prefix.

unsuccessful *adj.*	**untidy** *adj.*	**unwarranted** *adj.*
unsuitable *adj.*	**untrue** *adj.*	**unwed** *adj.*
untangle *verb trans.*	**unutterable** *adj.*	**unwilling** *adj.*
untenable *adj.*	**unveil** *verb trans., intrans.*	**unwise** *adj.*
unthrone *verb trans.*	**unvoiced** *adj.*	**unyielding** *adj.*

upright piano a piano with strings arranged vertically in a case above the keyboard.

uprising *noun* a rebellion or revolt.

uproar *noun* **1** a confused noise of many sounds. **2** an outbreak of angry protest and argumentation.

uproarious *adj.* **1** *of laughter* loud and unrestrained. **2** provoking such laughter. ▸ **uproariously** *adv.*

uproot *verb trans.* **1** to pull (a plant) out of the ground completely, with the roots attached. **2** to move away from or cause (someone) to move away from home.

upscale *adj.* of or designed to appeal to high-income purchasers.

upset *verb* (əp-sĕt′) **1** to excite and trouble (a person). ▣ AGITATE, BOTHER, DISCOMPOSE, DISQUIET, DISTURB, PERTURB ▣ CALM, PACIFY, PLACATE, TRANQUILIZE. **2** to ruin or spoil (e.g., plans). **3** to knock over. —*noun* (əp′sĕt,) **1** a disturbance, e.g., of plans or digestion. **2** an unexpected result or outcome. *adj.* (əp-sĕt′) **1** emotionally distressed. **2** *of a stomach* causing nausea, vomiting, etc. ▸ **upsetting** *adj.*

upshot *noun* the final outcome or ultimate effect.

upside *noun* **1** the upper part or side. **2** *colloq.* a positive or favorable aspect.

upside down *adv.* **1** with the top part at the bottom. **2** in or into complete confusion or disorder. —*adj.* (*also* **upside-down**) upturned or inverted.

upstage *adj., adv.* at or toward the back of a theater stage. —*verb trans.* **1** to force (another actor) to turn away from the audience when speaking. **2** to divert attention onto oneself.

upstairs *adj., adv.* **1** on or to an upper floor. **2** *colloq.* in or to a senior or more senior position. —*noun* (*sing.*) an upper floor.

upstanding *adj.* **1** honest; respectable; trustworthy. **2** in an erect posture.

upstart *noun* an arrogant or presumptuous person.

upstate *adj., adv.* to, in, or from the northern part of a state: *upstate New York.*

upstream *adv.* toward the source of a river or stream; against the current.

upsurge *noun* a sudden sharp rise or increase.

uptake *noun* **quick** *or* **slow on the uptake** *colloq.* quick *or* slow to understand or realize.

uptight *adj. colloq.* **1** anxious; tense. **2** angry; irritated. **3** straitlaced.

up-to-date *or* **up to date** *adj.* knowing or reflecting the latest trends.

uptown *adj., adv.* in or toward the upper part of the city, or away from the city center. —*noun* the upper part of a city, or the part that is away from its center.

upturn *noun* an increase in esp. economic activity; an upward trend. —*verb trans., intrans.* to turn over, up, or upside down.

upward *or* **upwards** *adv.* **1** to or toward a higher position or level. **2** to a more senior position or an earlier period. —*adj.* leading or moving up.

upwind *adv.* against the direction of the wind; into the wind. —*adj.* going against or exposed to the wind.

uranium *noun Chem.* (SYMBOL **U**) a dense, silvery-white, radioactive metallic element.

urban *adj.* of, relating to, or situated in a city or town; not rural.

urbane (ər,bān′) *adj.* having refined manners; courteous. ▸ **urbanely** *adv.*

urbanize *verb trans.* (**urbanized, urbanizing**) to make (a district) less rural and more townlike. ▸ **urbanization** *noun*

urchin *noun* **1** a mischievous child. **2** a dirty, raggedly dressed child. **3** a sea urchin.

> Originally meaning 'hedgehog', the prickly sense of which survives in sea urchin

Urdu (ŏŏr′dŏŏ, ər′-) *noun* the official literary language of Pakistan, related to Hindi but with many words from Arabic and Persian. —*adj.* in or relating to Urdu.

urea (yŏŏ-rē′ə) *noun* a compound formed during amino acid breakdown in the liver of mammals, and excreted in the urine.

ureter (yŏŏr′ət-ər) *noun* either of the two tubes through which urine is carried from the kidneys to the bladder.

urethra (yŏŏbē′thrə) *noun* (*pl.* **urethras, urethrae**) the tube through which urine passes from the bladder out of the body.

urge *verb trans.* (**urged, urging**) **1** to demand firmly; to ask for again and again. **2** to beg or entreat. **3** to advise or recommend earnestly. **4** (*also* **urge on**) to encourage. —*noun* a strong impulse, desire, or motivation.

urgent *adj.* **1** requiring immediate action. ▣ IMPERATIVE, IMPORTUNATE, INSISTENT, INSTANT, PRESSING. **2** *of a request, etc.* forcefully and earnestly made. ▸ **urgency** *noun* ▸ **urgently** *adv.*

urinal *noun* a receptacle designed for men to urinate into, or a room containing one or more of these.

urinate (yŏŏr′ə-nāt,) *verb intrans.* (**urinated, urinating**) to discharge urine.

urine *noun* a liquid, consisting mainly of water containing urea and other waste products, that is produced by the kidney and passed out of the body via the urethra.

URL *abbrev. Comput.* Uniform Resource Locator, a set of characters set off by a colon, two back-slashes, and dots, that forms the address of a user or a document on the World Wide Web.

urn noun 1 a vase with a rounded body, a small narrow neck, and a usu. square base. 2 a receptacle used to contain a dead person's ashes. 3 a container for warming or making large quantities of tea or coffee.

urology noun Med. the diagnosis and treatment of diseases and disorders of the male and female urinary tracts and the male genital tract. ▸ **urologist** noun

ursine (ər'sīn,) adj. of or relating to bears.

US abbrev. 1 Uncle Sam. 2 United States.

us pron. 1 the object form of we. 2 all or any people; one. 3 colloq. used as a predicate nominative: It's us at the front door; open up!

Usage See note at we.

USA abbrev. United States of America.

usable or **useable** adj. capable of being used.

USAF or **U.S.A.F.** abbrev. United States Air Force.

usage (yōo'sĭj) noun 1 the act, way, or manner of using; also, the amount used. 2 custom or practice. 3 the way language is used in practice.

use verb trans. (yōoz) (**used, using**) 1 to put to a particular purpose. 2 to consume. 3 to treat (a person) as a means to benefit oneself. —verb aux. (yōos, yōost) was or were formerly: They used to be friends. —noun (yōos) 1 the act of using. 2 the state of being used or of being able to be used: not in use. 3 a practical purpose to which a thing can be put. 4 the quality of serving a practical purpose: Is this any use? 5 the ability or power to use (e.g., a limb). ▸ **user** noun

useable adj. same as **usable**.

used (yōozd) adj. not new; secondhand.

useful (yōos'fəl) adj. designed for efficiency rather than decorativeness. ▸ **usefulness** noun

useless adj. 1 serving no practical purpose. 2 colloq. not at all proficient at (something).

user-friendly adj. designed to be easy or pleasant to use, or easy to follow or understand.

usher noun 1 a person who shows people to their seats, e.g., in a theater or church. 2 an official who guards a door and maintains order, e.g., in a legislature: 3 an official who escorts people to their seats on ceremonial occasions. —verb trans., intrans. (**ushered, ushering**) 1 to conduct or escort (someone) into or out of a building, room, etc. 2 (**usher in**) to be a portent of; to herald.

USMC or **U.S.M.C.** abbrev. United States Marine Corps.

USN or **U.S.N.** abbrev. United States Navy.

USS or **U.S.S.** abbrev. 1 United States Senate. 2 United States Ship.

USSR or **U.S.S.R.** abbrev. Union of Soviet Socialist Republics.

usual adj. done, happening, etc., most often; customary. —**as usual** as regularly happens. ▸ **usually** adv.

usurp (yōo-sərp', -zərp') verb trans. (**usurped, usurping**) to take (e.g., power) or assume (e.g., authority) by force, without right, or unjustly. ▸ **usurper** noun

usury (yōo'zhə-rē) noun (pl. **usuries**) 1 the practice of lending money at an unfairly or illegally high rate of interest. 2 an unfairly or illegally high rate of interest. ▸ **usurious** adj.

utensil noun an implement or container.

uteri pl. noun see **uterus**.

uterus noun (pl. **uteri, uteruses**) the hollow muscular organ of female mammals, where an embryo or fetus develops and is nourished until birth. Also called **womb**. ▸ **uterine** adj.

utile (yōot'l, yōo'tīl,) adj. designed for efficiency rather than decorativeness.

utilitarian adj. 1 intended to be useful rather than beautiful. 2 caring, often too much, about usefulness and not enough about beauty. 3 of or relating to utilitarianism. —noun a supporter of utilitarianism.

utility (yōo-tĭl'ət-ē) noun (pl. **utilities**) 1 the quality or condition of being useful or of use. 2 a useful thing. 3 a public utility.

utilize (yōot'l-īz,) verb trans. (**utilized, utilizing**) to make practical use of; to use. ▸ **utilization** noun

utmost adj. 1 being the greatest possible. 2 farthest; outermost. —noun the greatest possible degree or extent.

utopia noun an imaginary place or situation of ideal perfection.

Literally 'no place', coined by Thomas More for his fictional book Utopia (1516)

utopian adj. unrealistically ideal. ▸ **utopianism** noun

utter[1] verb trans., intrans. (**uttered, uttering**) to say or give out as a sound. ▸ **utterance** noun

utter[2] adj. complete; total. ⊟ ABSOLUTE, DOWNRIGHT, OUT-AND-OUT, OUTRIGHT, POSITIVE, TOTAL, UNMITIGATED, UNQUALIFIED. ▸ **utterly** adv.

uttermost adj. utmost.

U-turn noun a maneuver in which a vehicle is turned to face the other way in a single continuous movement.

UV or **U.V.** abbrev. ultraviolet.

uvula (yōo'vyə-lə) noun the fleshy part of the soft palate that hangs over the back of the tongue at the entrance to the throat.

uxorious (ək,sôr'ē-əs) adj. greatly or submissively fond of one's wife.

Vv

V¹ or **v** *noun* (*pl.* **Vs, V's, v's**) the 22d letter of the English alphabet.

V² *symbol* volt.

V³ *symbol* **1** *Chem.* vanadium. **2** the Roman numeral for 5.

v. or **v** *abbrev.* **1** *Gram.* verb. **2** *Law* versus. **3** (v) *Printing* verso. **4** very. **5** *vide* (Latin), see; refer to.

vacancy *noun* (*pl.* **vacancies**) **1** the state of being vacant. **2** an unoccupied job or position. **3** an unoccupied room in a hotel or motel.

vacant *adj.* **1** empty or unoccupied. **2** having, showing, or suggesting an absence of thought or concentration. ▸ **vacantly** *adv.*

vacate (vă'kāt,, vā-kāt') *verb trans., intrans.* (**vacated, vacating**) **1** to leave or cease to occupy (a house or an official position). **2** *Law* to annul or make void.

vacation *noun* a time devoted to rest and recreation from employment. —*verb intrans.* (**vacationed, vacationing**) to take a holiday.

vaccinate (văk'sə-nāt,) *verb trans.* (**vaccinated, vaccinating**) to innoculate. ▸ **vaccination** *noun*

vaccine (văk-sēn') *noun* a preparation containing, e.g., dead or weakened bacteria or viruses, that gives immunity to disease.

vacillate (văs'ə-lāt,) *verb intrans.* (**vacillated, vacillating**) to change opinions or decisions frequently. ▸ **vacillation** *noun*

vacuous *adj.* **1** unintelligent; stupid; inane. **2** *of a look or expression* conveying no feeling or meaning; blank. **3** empty. ▸ **vacuously** *adv.*

vacuum *noun* (*pl.* **vacuums, vacua**) **1 a** a space from which all matter has been removed. **b** a space from which all or almost all air or other gas has been removed. **2** a state or feeling of emptiness. —*verb trans., intrans.* (**vacuumed, vacuuming**) *colloq.* to clean with a vacuum cleaner.

vacuum cleaner an electrically powered cleaning device that lifts dust and dirt by suction.

vacuum flask a container for preserving the temperature of liquids, esp. drinks.

vacuum-packed *adj.* sealed in a container from which the air has been removed.

vademecum (vād,ē-mā'kəm, vād,ē-mē'kəm) a handbook of practical information that can be carried for frequent reference.

vagabond *noun* a person who lives an unsettled wandering life.

vagary *noun* (*pl.* **vagaries**) an unpredictable, erratic act or turn of events.

vagina *noun* the muscular canal in female mammals that leads from the womb to the exterior sex organs. ▸ **vaginal** *adj.*

vagrant (vā'grənt) *noun* a person who has no permanent home or place of work. —*adj.* **1** wandering or roving around. **2** uncertain; unsettled. ▸ **vagrancy** *noun*

vague *adj.* **1 a** obscured or made unclear by, or as if by, a mist. **b** imprecise. **2** thinking or expressing without clarity or precision. ▸ **vaguely** *adv.* ▸ **vagueness** *noun*

vain *adj.* **1** having too much pride in one's appearance, achievements, or possessions. **2** having no useful effect or result. —**in vain** without success; fruitlessly. ▸ **vainly** *adj.*

vainglory *noun* **1** extreme boastfulness. **2** too good an opinion of oneself. ▸ **vainglorious** *adj.*

vale *noun* a valley.

valediction (văl,ə-dĭk'shən) *noun* a farewell, or a speech given in farewell. ▸ **valedictory** *adj.*

valence or **valency** *noun Chem.* a number that denotes the combining power of an atom of a particular element

valentine *noun* **1** a card or other message given, on St. Valentine's Day (Feb. 14). **2** the person it is given to.

valet (vă-lā', văl'ā,) *noun* a man's personal servant. —*verb intrans.* (**valeted, valeting**) to work as a valet.

valetudinarian *formal adj.* **1** relating to or affected with a long-term or chronic illness. **2** anxious about one's health. —*noun* **1** a person who is chronically ill. **2** a hypochondriac.

valiant *adj.* brave. ▸ **valiantly** *adv.*

valid *adj.* **1** based on truth or sound reasoning. **2** legally acceptable for use. ▸ **validity** *noun*

validate (văl'ə-dāt,) *verb trans.* (**validated, validating**) to make valid; to confirm the validity of. ▸ **validation** *noun*

valise (və-lēs') *noun* a small overnight case or other such piece of hand luggage.

Valium (văl'ē-əm) *trademark* used to denote diazepam.

valley *noun* (*pl.* **valleys**) **1** a long flat area of land flanked on both sides by hills or mountains. **2** a trough or hollow between ridges.

valor *noun* courage, esp. in battle.

valuable *adj.* of considerable value or usefulness. —*noun* (*usu.* **valuables**) personal possessions of high value.

value *noun* **1** worth in money terms. **2** usefulness or desirability, or the degree of usefulness or desirability. **3** the quality of being a fair exchange: *value for money*. **4** (**values**) moral principles or standards. **5** *Math.* a quantity represented by a symbol or set of symbols. **6** *Mus.* the duration of a note or rest. —*verb trans.* (**valued, valuing**) **1** to consider to be of a certain value, esp. a high value. **2** to assess the value of.

value-added tax (ABBREV. **VAT, V.A.T.**) a tax added onto the price of a product or material at each stage of the manufacturing or distributing process.

valve *noun* **1** a device that regulates the flow of a liquid or gas through a pipe by opening or closing an aperture, or that allows flow in one direction only. **2** in, e.g., the heart and veins, a flap of tissue that allows blood, etc. to flow in one direction only. **3** a finger-operated device controlling the flow of air through some brass instruments. **4** either half of the hinged shell of a bivalve mollusk.

vamoose *verb intrans.* (**vamoosed, vamoosing**) *slang* to depart hurriedly.

vamp[1] *colloq. noun* a woman who flaunts her sexual charm, esp. in order to exploit men. —*verb trans., intrans.* (**vamped, vamping**) to behave like a vamp.

vamp[2] *verb trans.* (**vamped, vamping**) **1** (**vamp up**) to refurbish or modernize (something). **2** *Mus.* to improvise (a simple accompaniment).

vampire *noun* **1** a dead person who supposedly rises from the grave at night to suck the blood of the living. **2** a person who ruthlessly exploits others.

vampire bat a small blood-feeding bat.

van[1] *noun* **1** an enclosed motor vehicle. **2** a commercial road vehicle with storage space in the rear, lighter than a truck.

van[2] *noun* a vanguard.

vanadium (və-nād´ē-əm) *noun Chem.* (SYMBOL **V**) a soft silvery-gray metallic element, used to strengthen steel.

vandal (văn´dəl) *noun* someone who willfully, maliciously, and illegally defaces or destroys the property of another. ▸ **vandalism** *noun* ▸ **vandalize** *verb trans.*

vane *noun* **1** a weathervane. **2** the blade of a windmill, propeller, or revolving fan.

vanguard *noun* **1** *Mil.* the part of a force that advances first. **2** a leading position.

vanilla *noun* a plant of the orchid family or its aromatic, podlike fruit as a food flavoring. —*adj.* flavored with vanilla.

vanish *verb intrans.* (**vanished, vanishing**) **1** to go out of sight or view. ▣ DEMATERIALIZE, DISAPPEAR, EVANESCE, EVAPORATE ▣ APPEAR, MATERIALIZE. **2** to cease to exist.

vanity *noun* (*pl.* **vanities**) **1** too good an opinion of oneself. **2** futility or worthlessness. **3 a** a vanity bag. **b** a dressing table.

vanity bag a woman's small case for cosmetics and makeup. *Also called* **vanity case.**

vanquish *verb trans.* (**vanquished, vanquishing**) to defeat or overcome.

vantage *noun* an advantage, esp. in tennis.

vantage point a position affording a clear overall view or prospect.

vapid *adj.* **1** dull; uninteresting. **2** having little taste, color, or smell. ▸ **vapidity** *noun*

vapor *noun* a gas that can be condensed to a liquid by pressure alone, without being cooled.

vaporize *verb trans., intrans.* (**vaporized, vaporizing**) to convert into vapor. ▸ **vaporization** *noun*

variable *adj.* **1 a** varying. **b** changeable, esp. in one's loyalties. **2** able to be varied or altered. —*noun* **1** a thing that can vary unpredictably in nature or degree. **2** a factor that may change or that may be changed. **3** *Math.* a symbol, usu. a letter, for which one or more values may be substituted. ▸ **variability** *noun*

variance *noun* the state of being different or inconsistent. —**at variance** in disagreement or conflict.

variant *noun* **1** a form of a thing that varies from another form of it. **2** an example that differs from a standard. —*adj.* different; differing from a standard.

variation *noun* **1** the act or process of varying or changing. **2** a thing that varies from a standard. **3** the extent to which a thing varies from a standard.

varicolored *adj.* having different colors.

varicose vein an abnormally swollen and twisted vein.

varied *adj.* having variety; diverse.

variety *noun* (*pl.* **varieties**) **1** a kind or sort. **2** departure from a fixed pattern or routine. **3** a plant or animal differing from another in certain characteristics, but not enough to be classed as a separate species.

variety store a shop selling miscellaneous, usu. low-priced merchandise.

various *adj.* **1** several different. **2** different; disparate.

varmint *noun colloq.* a troublesome animal or person.

varnish *noun* **1** an oil-based liquid containing resin, painted on a surface such as wood to give a hard, transparent, often glossy finish. **2** liquid providing a similar finish, e.g., on the fingernails. **3** a superficial attractiveness or impressiveness. —*verb trans.* (**varnished, varnishing**) **1** to apply varnish to. **2** to make superficially appealing.

varsity *noun colloq.* (*pl.* **varsities**) the principal team representing a college, university, or high school in a sport.

vary *verb intrans., trans.* (**varied, varying, varies**) **1** to change or be of different kinds, esp. according to different circumstances. **2** to make or become less regular or uniform and more diverse.

vas *noun* (*pl.* **vasa**) *Biol.* a vessel, tube, or duct carrying liquid.

vascular *adj.* relating to the blood vessels of animals or the sap-conducting tissues of plants.

vas deferens (văs'dĕf'ə-rənz) (*pl.* **vasa deferentia**) the duct from each testicle that carries sperm to the penis.

vase *noun* an ornamental glass or pottery container, esp. one for holding cut flowers.

vasectomy *noun* (*pl.* **vasectomies**) a surgical operation involving the tying and cutting of the vas deferens in order to produce sterility.

vasoconstrictor *noun Physiol.* something that stimulates blood vessels to contract.

vasodilator *noun Physiol.* something that stimulates blood vessels to dilate.

vast *adj.* extremely great in size, extent, or amount. ▸ **vastly** *adv.* ▸ **vastness** *noun*

VAT or **V.A.T.** *abbrev.* value-added tax.

vat *noun* a large barrel or tank for storing or holding liquids, esp. alcoholic drinks.

Vatican (văt'ĭ-kən) *noun* (*usu.* **the Vatican**) **1** the palace and official residence of the pope in Rome. **2** the papacy.

vaudeville *noun* variety entertainment.

vault[1] *noun* **1** an arched roof or ceiling, esp. in a church. **2** an underground chamber used for storage or as a burial tomb. **3** a fortified room or large secure boxlike structure for storing valuables, e.g., in a bank.

vault[2] *verb trans., intrans.* (**vaulted, vaulting**) to spring or leap over, esp. assisted by the hands or a pole. —*noun* an act of vaulting.

vaunt *verb trans., intrans.* (**vaunted, vaunting**) to boast or behave boastfully about. —*noun* a boast. ▸ **vauntingly** *adv.*

VC or **V.C.** *abbrev.* **1** vice-chairman, vice-chairperson, or vice-chairwoman. **2** vice chancellor.

VCR *abbrev.* video cassette recorder.

VD *abbrev.* venereal disease.

VDU *abbrev. Comput.* visual display unit.

veal *noun* the flesh of a calf, used as food.

vector *noun* **1** *Math.* a quantity that has both magnitude and direction. See also **scalar**. **2** *Med.* an agent, such as an insect, capable of transferring a disease-causing microorganism from one organism to another.

veer *verb intrans.* (**veered, veering**) to move abruptly in a different direction. —*noun* a change of direction.

vegan (vē'gən) *noun* a person who does not eat meat, dairy products, or any foods containing animal fats or extracts, often also avoiding animal-based substances. —*adj.* of or for vegans. ▸ **veganism** *noun*

vegetable *noun* a plant or any of its parts other than fruits and seeds, that is used for food, e.g., roots, tubers, or leaves. —*adj.* relating to plants.

vegetal *adj.* consisting of or relating to vegetables or to plant life in general.

vegetarian *noun* a person who does not eat meat or fish. —*adj.* of or for vegetarians. ▸ **vegetarianism** *noun*

vegetate (vĕj'ə-tāt,) *verb intrans.* (**vegetated, vegetating**) **1** to live a dull, inactive life. **2** to live or grow as a vegetable.

vegetation *noun* **1** plants considered collectively. **2** the plants of a particular area.

vegetative *adj.* **1** of or pertaining to plants or vegetation. **2** *Biol.* denoting asexual reproduction in plants or animals, as through bulbs, corms, tubers, etc., and also through grafting and cuttings. **3** *Bot.* of or relating to the phase of plant growth, as opposed to reproduction.

vehemence (vē'ə-məns) *noun* strong, forceful feeling. ▸ **vehement** *adj.* ▸ **vehemently** *adv.*

vehicle (vē'ĭ-kəl) *noun* **1** a conveyance for transporting people or things, esp. a self-powered one. **2** a person or thing used as a means of communicating ideas or opinions, etc. ▸ **vehicular** (vē-hĭk'yŏŏ-lər) *adj.*

veil *noun* **1** a fabric covering for a woman's head or face, forming part of traditional dress in some societies. **2** (**the veil**) *literary* the vocation of a nun. —*verb trans.* (**veiled, veiling**) **1** to cover, or cover the face of, with a veil. **2** to conceal or partly conceal; to disguise or obscure.

vein *noun* **1** a blood vessel that carries blood to the heart. **2** a thin deposit of a mineral in a fracture or joint in the surrounding rock. **3** a streak of different color, e.g., in cheese. **4** in a leaf, a thin branching tube containing the vascular tissues. **5** in an insect, any of the tubes of chitin that stiffen and support the membranous structure of the wings. **6** a mood or tone: *a sarcastic vein.* ▸ **veined** *adj.* ▸ **veiny** *adj.*

Velcro (vĕl'krō) *trademark* used to denote a fastening material consisting of two nylon surfaces that bond tightly when pressed together but are easily pulled apart.

veldt or **veld** (vĕlt) *noun* a wide, grassy plane with few or no trees, esp. in S Africa.

vellum *noun* **1** thick, cream-colored writing paper. **2** a fine parchment, orig. made from calfskin.

velocity *noun (pl.* **velocities**) **1** rate of motion in a particular direction. **2** speed.

velour (və-lōŏr') *or* **velours** *noun* a fabric with a velvetlike pile.

velvet *noun* **1** a fabric, usu. nylon or silk, with a very short, soft, closely woven pile on one side. **2** the soft skin that covers the growing antlers of deer. —*adj.* **1** made of velvet. **2** soft or smooth like velvet. ▸ **velvety** *adj.*

velveteen *noun* cotton fabric with a velvetlike pile.

Ven. *abbrev.* Venerable.

venal (vēn'l) *adj.* **1** willing to be persuaded by corrupt means, esp. bribery. **2** *of behavior* dishonest; corrupt. ▸ **venality** *noun*

vend *verb trans.* (**vended, vending**) to sell or offer for sale (esp. small wares), typically via vending machines or as a street vender.

vender *or* **vendor** *noun* a seller of goods, esp. on the street, at a sports competition, etc.

vendetta *noun* a long-standing bitter feud or quarrel esp. between two families.

vending machine a coin-operated machine dispensing small wares such as candy, drinks, and cigarettes.

vendor *noun same as* **vender**.

veneer (və-nīr') *noun* **1** a thin layer of wood, etc. fixed to the surface of an inferior material to give an attractive finish. **2** a false or misleading appearance. —*verb trans.* (**veneered, veneering**) to put a veneer on.

venerable *adj.* **1** deserving to be greatly respected or revered. **2** (**Venerable**) **a** a title given to an archdeacon in the Episcopal or Anglican Church. **b** *RC Church* a title given to a person due to be declared a saint.

venerate (vĕn'ə-rāt,) *verb trans.* (**venerated, venerating**) to regard with deep respect or awe; to revere. ▸ **veneration** *noun*

venereal (və-nīr'ē-əl) *adj.,* old *use of a disease or infection* transmitted by sexual intercourse. **2** such diseases.

venereal disease (ABBREV. VD) old *use* a sexually transmitted disease.

Venetian blind a window blind consisting of horizontal slats strung together.

vengeance *noun* punishment inflicted as a revenge.

vengeful *adj.* **1** eager for revenge. **2** carried out in revenge.

venial (vē'nē-əl) *adj., of a sin or weakness* forgivable; excusable. ▸ **veniality** *noun*

venial sin *RC Church* a minor sin, not involving loss of divine grace. *See also* **mortal sin**.

venison *noun* the flesh of a deer, used as food.

venom *noun* **1** a poisonous liquid that some creatures, including scorpions and certain snakes, inject in a bite or sting. **2** spitefulness, esp. in language or tone of voice. ▸ **venomous** *adj.*

venous (vē'nəs) *adj.* relating to or contained in veins.

vent[1] *noun* a slit in a garment, esp. at the back of a jacket or coat.

vent[2] *noun* an opening allowing air, gas, or liquid into or out of a confined space. —*verb trans., intrans.* (**vented, venting**) **1** to make a vent in. **2** to let in or out through a vent. **3** to release (esp. emotion) freely.

ventilate (vĕnt'l-āt,) *verb trans.* (**ventilated, ventilating**) **1** to allow fresh air to circulate throughout. **2** to cause (blood) to take up oxygen. **3** to supply air to (the lungs). **4** to expose to public examination or discussion. ▸ **ventilation** *noun* ▸ **ventilator** *noun*

ventral *adj.* **1** denoting the lower or front surface of an animal. **2** denoting a structure that is situated on or just beneath such a surface. ▸ **ventrally** *adv.*

ventricle *noun* **1** in mammals, either of the two lower chambers of the heart. **2** in vertebrates, any of several fluid-filled cavities within the brain. ▸ **ventricular** *adj.*

ventriloquism *noun* the art or act of speaking in a way that makes the sound appear to come from elsewhere, esp. a dummy's mouth. ▸ **ventriloquist** *noun* ▸ **ventriloquize** *verb* ▸ **ventriloquy** *noun*

> Literally 'stomach speaking' and originally meaning being possessed by a talking evil spirit

venture *noun* **1** an exercise or operation involving danger or uncertainty. **2** a business project, esp. one involving risk or speculation. **3** an enterprise attempted. —*verb trans., intrans.* (**ventured, venturing**) **1 a** to dare. **b** (**venture out** *or* **forth**) to dare to go out, esp. outdoors. **2** to put forward or present in the face of possible opposition: *ventured a different opinion.* ▸ **venturer** *noun*

venturesome *or* **venturous** *adj.* **1** ready to act boldly and take risks. ▤ ADVENTUROUS. **2** involving danger; risky.

venue (vĕn'yōō) *noun* **1** the chosen location for a sports event or entertainment. **2** the place where a court case is to be tried, or the district from which the jurors are chosen. **3** a meeting place.

Venus's-flytrap *or* **Venus flytrap** *noun* an insect-eating plant.

veracious *adj.* truthful. ▸ **veracity** *noun*

veranda *or* **verandah** *noun* a porch or a balcony extending along or around the outside of, e.g., a home.

verb *noun* *Gram.* a word that denotes an action, experience, occurrence, or state; e.g., *do, feel, happen, remain.*

verbal *adj.* **1** relating to or consisting of words: *verbal abuse.* **2** by means of language, spoken or written. **3** spoken, not written; oral: *verbal communication.* **4** *Gram.* relating to verbs. ▸ **verbally** *adv.*

> *Usage* To avoid possible confusion with the sense by means of language, spoken or written, some writers and speakers use *oral* instead of *verbal* in the sense spoken, not written. *See also* **oral** (sense 1).

verbalize *verb trans., intrans.* (**verbalized, verbalizing**) **1** to express in words. **2** to use too many words.

verbatim (vər-bāt'ĭm) *adj., adv.* using exactly the same words; word-for-word: *quoted the President verbatim.*

verbiage (vər'bē-ĭj) *noun* **1** the use of language that is wordy, needlessly complicated, or meaningless. **2** the language so used.

verbose (vər-bōs') *adj.* using too many words. ▸ **verbosity** *noun*

verdant *adj.* **1** covered with lush green grass or other such vegetation. **2** of a rich green color. **3** naïve or unsophisticated; green. ▸ **verdancy** *noun*

verdict *noun* **1** *Law* a decision arrived at by a jury or, in some cases, a judge in a court of law. **2** a decision, opinion, or judgment.

verdigris (vərd'ə-grēs,) *noun* a bluish-green coating on copper, brass, or bronze surfaces when exposed to air and moisture for long periods.

verge¹ *noun* **1** a limit, boundary, or border. **2** a point or stage immediately beyond or after which something exists or occurs: *on the verge of tears.* —*verb intrans.* (**verged, verging**) **1** to serve as the border or boundary of something. **2** (**verge on**) to be close to being or becoming (something specified).

verge² *verb intrans.* (**verged, verging**) **1** to slope or incline in a specified direction. **2** to move or tend to or toward (something).

verify *verb trans.* (**verified, verifying, verifies**) to check or confirm the truth or accuracy of. ▸ **verification** *adv.*

verily *adv., old* truly; really.

verisimilitude *noun* **1** the quality of appearing to be real or true. **2** a statement or proposition that sounds true but may not be.

veritable *adj.* accurately described as such; proper: *a veritable genius.* ▸ **veritably** *adv.*

verity *noun* (*pl.* **verities**) **1** a true statement, esp. one of fundamental wisdom or importance; a maxim. **2** the quality or condition of being truthful.

vermiform *adj.* worm-shaped.

vermiform appendix the appendix (sense 2).

vermilion *noun* **1** a bright scarlet color. **2** a pigment of this color.

vermin *noun* (*pl.* **vermin**) **1** wild animals that spread disease or generally cause a nuisance, esp. rats. **2** detestable people regarded collectively. ▸ **verminous** *adj.*

vermouth (vər-mōōth') *noun* wine flavored with aromatic herbs, orig. wormwood.

vernacular *noun* **1** the form of a language as commonly spoken, as opposed to the formal or literary language. **2** the language or jargon of a particular group. —*adj.* **1** of or in the vernacular. **2** local; native.

vernal *adj.* relating or appropriate to spring.

vernier (vər'nē-ər) *noun* a small sliding device on some measuring instruments, used to measure fractions of units.

veronica *noun* a plant with clusters of small, usu. blue, flowers.

verruca (və-rōō'kə) *noun* (*pl.* **verrucae**) a wart.

versatile (vĕr'sət-l) *adj.* **1** adapting easily to different tasks. **2** having numerous uses or abilities. ▸ **versatility** *noun*

verse *noun* **1 a** a division of a poem; a stanza. **b** poetry as opposed to prose. **c** a poem. **2** *Mus.* a division of a song.

versed *adj.* skilled in (something).

versify *verb* (**versified, versifying, versifies**) **1** to write poetry. **2** to express as, or to turn into, a poem. ▸ **versification** *noun*

version *noun* any of several types or forms in which a thing exists or is available, e.g. a particular edition or translation of a book, or one person's account of an incident.

verso *noun* (*pl.* **versos**) *Printing* the left-hand page of an open book. *See also* **recto.**

versus *prep.* (ABBREV. **v., vs.**) **1** against. **2** *Law* in a lawsuit against.

vertebra (vərt'ə-brə) *noun* (*pl.* **vertebrae, vertebras**) any of the small bones or cartilaginous segments that form the backbone. ▸ **vertebral** (vərt'ə-brəl, vər-tē'brəl) *adj.*

vertebrate (vərt'ə-brət, -brāt,) *noun* an animal that has a backbone, e.g., a fish, amphibian, reptile, bird, or mammal. —*adj.* relating to an animal that has a backbone.

vertex *noun* (*pl.* **vertexes, vertices**) **1** the highest point; the peak or summit. **2** *Math.* **a** the point opposite the base of a geometric figure, e.g., the pointed tip of a cone. **b** the point where the two sides of an angle meet in a polygon, or where three or more surfaces meet in a polyhedron.

vertical *adj.* **1** perpendicular to the horizon; upright. **2** running from top to bottom, as opposed to running from side to side. **3** of or at a vertex. —*noun* a vertical line or direction. ▸ **vertically** *adv.*

vertigo *noun* a dizziness or giddiness felt when the sense of balance is disturbed.

verve *noun* great liveliness or enthusiasm.

very adv. **1** to a high degree or great extent: *You are very kind.* **2** (used with *own*, *same*, and with superlative adjectives) absolutely; truly: *the very same day.* —adj. **1** absolute: *the very top of the peak.* **2** set apart or distinguished from every other: *this very moment.* **3** mere: *shocked by the very thought.* **4** exactly right or appropriate.

very high frequency (ABBREV. **vhf, VHF**) a band of radio frequencies in the range 30 to 300 MHz.

very low frequency (ABBREV. **vlf, VLF**) a band of radio frequencies in the range 3 to 30 kHz.

vesicle noun **1** Biol. a small sac or cavity, esp. one filled with fluid. **2** Med. a small blister.

vessel noun **1** a container, esp. for liquid. **2** a ship or large boat. **3** a tube or duct carrying, e.g., blood or sap.

vest noun a sleeveless garment with front buttons, worn over a dress shirt or sometimes as part of a three-piece suit. *Also called* **waistcoat**. —verb trans., intrans. (**vested, vesting**) **1** to bestow legally or officially: *by the power vested in me.* **2** to give (someone) an immediate right to current or future enjoyment or possession of, e.g., retirement benefits. **3** to put on ecclesiastical robes.

vestal adj. virginal; chaste. —noun a chaste woman, esp. a nun.

vested interest 1 a strong interest in something, esp. because of potential personal gain. **2** a person or party with such an interest.

vestibule noun an entrance hall.

vestige (věs'tĭj) noun **1** a slight amount. **2** a surviving trace of what has almost disappeared.

vestigial adj. Biol. no longer having any function: *a vestigial wing.*

vestment noun **1** any of various garments worn ceremonially by members of the clergy and church choir. **2** a ceremonial robe.

vestry noun (pl. **vestries**) **1** a room in a church where the vestments are kept, often also used for meetings, etc. **2** a committee of elected laypeople who administer the temporal affairs of a church or parish. ► **vestryman** noun ► **vestrywoman** noun

vet¹ noun a doctor of veterinary medicine.

vet² noun colloq. a veteran of military service, esp. a combat veteran.

vetch noun a trailing or climbing plant of the pea family. *Also called* **tare**.

veteran noun **1** a person with many years of experience in a particular activity. **2** an old and experienced member of the armed forces. **3** an ex-serviceman or -woman, esp. one who has served in combat.

Veterans Day Nov. 11, a public holiday in the USA, in honor of veterans of all wars.

veterinary adj. concerned with diseases of animals. —noun (pl. **veterinaries**) colloq. a doctor of veterinary medicine. *Also called* **veterinarian, veterinary surgeon**.

veto (vēt'ō) noun (pl. **vetoes**) **1** the right to reject formally a proposal or forbid an action; the using of such a right. **2** colloq. a prohibition or a refusal of permission. —verb trans. (**vetoed, vetoing, vetoes**) **1** to reject or forbid formally and authoritatively. **2** colloq. to forbid.

> Latin for 'I forbid', a phrase originally used by people's tribunes in the Roman Senate when objecting to proposals

vex verb trans. (**vexed, vexing, vexes**) **1** to annoy or irritate. **2** to worry. ► **vexation** noun ► **vexatious** adj. ► **vexing** adj.

vhf or **VHF** abbrev. very high frequency.

via (vī'ə, vē'ə) prep. by way of or by means of.

viable (vī'ə-bəl) adj. **1** of a plan, etc. having a chance of success. **2** of a plant, etc. able to exist or grow in particular conditions. **3** of a fetus or baby able to survive independently outside the womb. ► **viability** noun

viaduct noun a bridgelike structure of stone arches supporting a road or railroad across a valley, etc.

vial noun a small medicine bottle.

viands (vī'əndz) pl. noun provisions.

vibes¹ pl. noun slang feelings, sensations, or an atmosphere experienced or communicated.

vibes² pl. noun Mus. a vibraphone.

vibrant adj. **1** extremely lively or exciting. **2** of a color strong and bright. **3** having the quality or action of vibrating. ► **vibrancy** noun ► **vibrantly** adv.

vibraphone noun Mus. an instrument in which horizontal metal bars of different lengths are made to resound electrically when struck with hammers. ► **vibraphonist** noun

vibrate (vī'brāt,) verb trans., intrans. (**vibrated, vibrating**) **1 a** to move back and forth very rapidly. **b** to undergo heavy vibration or jolting particularly as the result of a physical shock. **2.** to ring or resound. **3** to swing back and forth. ► **vibratory** adj.

vibration noun **1 a** a jolting motion, or a series of such motions, back and forth, particularly one caused by a physical impact or shock. **b** a single movement back and forth in vibrating. **2** (**vibrations**) slang vibes.

vibrato (və-brät'ō) noun (pl. **vibratos**) a faint trembling effect in singing or the playing of string and wind instruments.

vicar (vĭk'ər) noun **1** the minister of an Anglican parish, or a cleric in charge of a chapel in the Episcopal Church. **2** RC Church a priest who is a representative for a higher-ranking cleric.

vicarage (vĭk′ə-rĭj) *noun* a vicar's residence, benefice, or duties.

vicarious (vī-kâr′ē-əs) *adj.* **1** experienced not directly but through witnessing the experience of another person. **2** undergone on behalf of someone else. **3** standing in for another.

vice[1] *noun* **1 a** an immoral, evil, or depraved habit or activity, esp. involving prostitution or drugs. **b** such activities collectively. **2** a bad habit; a fault in one's character.

vice[2] (vī′sē) *prep.* **1** in place of. **2** following on from or succeeding.

vice[3] *see* **vise.**

vice- (vīs) *combining form* forming words denoting next in rank to, and acting as deputy for: *vice-chairperson.*

vice admiral *or* **vice-admiral** (ABBREV. **V.Adm., VADM**) a commissioned officer in the US Navy or Coast Guard ranking above rear admiral and below admiral.

vice-president *or* **vice president** *noun* (ABBREV. **VP, V.P.**) **1** a corporate officer ranking below the president. **2** (**Vice President**) the person elected to the political rank immediately below that of the President of the United States, who is also designated to serve as President of the US Senate.

viceroy (vīs′roi,) *noun* a male governor of a province or colony ruling in the name of, and with the authority of, a monarch or national government.

vice versa (vī′sĭ-vər′sə, vīs-vər′sə) with the order or correspondence reversed: *from you to me and vice versa.*

vicinity *noun* (*pl.* **vicinities**) **1** a neighborhood. **2** the immediately surrounding area. **3** nearness.

vicious *adj.* **1** violent or ferocious. **2** spiteful or malicious. **3** extremely severe or harsh. **4** *of reasoning, etc.* incorrect or faulty; unsound. ► **viciously** *adv.* ► **viciousness** *noun*

vicissitude *noun* **1** an unpredictable change of fortune or circumstance. **2** (*often* **vicissitudes**) any one of a series of unexpected, usu. unwelcome, changes in life.

victim *noun* a person or animal subjected to death, suffering, mistreatment, or trickery.

victimize *verb trans.* (**victimized, victimizing**) **1** to single out for hostile or unfair treatment. **2** to cause to be a victim. ► **victimization** *noun*

victor *noun* the winner or winning side in a war or contest.

Victorian *adj.* **1** relating to or characteristic of the British queen Victoria or the period of her reign (1837–1901). **2** *of attitudes or values* strict and conventional. —*noun* a person who lived during this period.

victorious *adj.* **1** winning a war or contest. **2** marking or representing a victory. ► **victoriously** *adv.*

victory *noun* (*pl.* **victories**) **1** mastery achieved over an opponent or enemy. **2** an occurrence of it.

victual (vĭt′l) *noun* **1** food fit to eat. **2** (**victuals**) food; provisions.

vicuña (vī-kōōn′yə) *noun* **1** an Andean animal resembling a llama, but smaller and more slender. **2** a cloth or yarn made from the wool of this animal.

vide (vīd′ē, vē′dā) *verb* (as an instruction in a text) see; refer to.

videlicet (vĭ-dĕl′ə-sĕt,) *adv.* (ABBREV. **viz.** (esp. in writing)) that is; namely.

video *noun* (*pl.* **videos**) **1** the recording, reproducing, or broadcasting of visual images on magnetic tape. **2 a** a videocassette. **b** videocassette recorder. **3** a film or program prerecorded on videocassette: *now available on video.* —*adj.* relating to the process of or the equipment for recording by video. —*verb trans.* (**videoed, videoing, videos**) to make a videocassette recording of.

videocassette *noun* a cassette containing videotape, for use in a videocassette recorder.

videocassette recorder (ABBREV. **VCR**) a machine for recording a television broadcast on magnetic tape, also used to play back prerecorded tapes. *Also called* **video recorder.**

videodisk *or* **videodisc** *noun* a rotating flat circular plate from which prerecorded video programs can be played on a television receiver.

video game an electronically operated game involving the manipulation of images produced by a computer program on a visual display unit.

videophone *noun* a telephone with audio and video transmission capabilities.

video recorder a videocassette recorder.

videotape *noun* magnetic tape on which visual images and sound can be recorded.

vie *verb intrans.* (**vied, vying**) (**vie with**) to compete or struggle with (someone) (for some gain or advantage).

Vietnamese (vē-ĕt,no-mēz′, -mēs′) *noun* **1** (*pl.* **Vietnamese**) a native or citizen of Vietnam. **2** a language spoken in Vietnam, Laos, and Cambodia. —*adj.* relating to Vietnam, its people, or their language.

view *noun* **1** an act or opportunity of seeing without obstruction. **2** something, esp. a landscape, seen from a particular point. **3** range or field of vision. **4** a scene recorded in photograph or picture form. **5** a description, impression, or opinion. **6** a way of considering or understanding something. —*verb trans.*, *intrans.* (**viewed, viewing**) **1** to see or look at. **2** to inspect or examine. **3** to consider or regard. **4** to watch (a program) on television. ▸ **viewer** *noun*

viewfinder *noun* a device on a camera showing the field of vision covered by the lens.

viewpoint *noun* an interpretation of facts received; an opinion or point of view.

vigil *noun* a period of staying awake, usu. to guard or watch over a person or thing.

vigilant *adj.* ready for possible trouble or danger; alert; watchful. ▸ **vigilance** *noun*

vigilante (vĭj′ə-lănt′ē) *noun* a self-appointed enforcer of law and order.

vignette (vĭn-yĕt′) *noun* **1** a decorative design on the title page of a book, traditionally of vine leaves. **2** a photographic portrait with the background deliberately faded. **3** a short literary essay, esp. describing a person's character.

vigor *noun* **1** great strength and energy of body or mind. **2** liveliness or forcefulness of action. ▸ **vigorous** *adj.* ▸ **vigorously** *adv.*

vile *adj.* **1** evil or wicked. **2** physically repulsive; disgusting. **3** extremely bad or unpleasant.

vilify *verb trans.* (**vilified, vilifying, vilifies**) to say insulting or abusive things about. ▸ **vilification** *noun*

villa (vĭl′ə) *noun* **1** a large country house or mansion. **2** a good-sized, esp. detached, suburban house.

village *noun* **1** a small town or the residents of a small town. **2** a residential complex for participants in a major, usu. international, sporting event. ▸ **villager** *noun*

villain (vĭl′ən) *noun* **1** the principal wicked character in a story. **2** a violent, wicked, or unscrupulous person. **3** *colloq.* a criminal. ▸ **villainous** *adj.* ▸ **villainy** *noun*

villein (vĭl′ən, -ān,) *noun Hist.* a feudal peasant worker owing allegiance directly to a lord.

vim *noun* energy; liveliness; vitality.

vinaigrette (vĭn,ə-grĕt′) *noun* a salad dressing of oil, vinegar, and seasonings.

vindicate (vĭn′dĭ-kāt,) *verb trans.* (**vindicated, vindicating**) **1** to prove to be blameless or beyond criticism. **2** to show to have been worthwhile or justified. ▸ **vindication** *noun* ▸ **vindicatory** *adj.*

vindictive *adj.* **1** feeling or showing spite or hatred. **2** seeking revenge. **3** serving as revenge or retribution. ▸ **vindictively** *adv.* ▸ **vindictiveness** *noun*

vine *noun* **1** a climbing plant that produces grapes. **2** any climbing or trailing plant.

vinegar (vĭn′ə-gər) *noun* **1** a sour liquid fermented from cider, wine, etc., and used as a food flavoring and preservative. ▸ **vinegary** *adj.*

vineyard (vĭn′yərd) *noun* a plantation of grape-bearing vines, esp. for making wine.

viniculture *noun* the cultivation of grapes for making wine. *Also called* **viticulture**. ▸ **viniculturist** *noun*

vino (vē′nō) *noun slang* wine.

vintage (vĭnt′ĭj) *noun* **1 a** the grape harvest of a particular year. **b** the wine produced from a year's harvest. **c** the time of year when grapes are harvested. **2** a particular period of time. —*adj.* **1** of wine of good quality and from a specified year. **2** typical or characteristic of someone or something: *The remark was vintage Churchill.*

vintner *noun* a wine merchant.

vinyl (vīn′l) *noun* a tough plastic manufactured in various forms, e.g., paint additives, floor coverings, and carpet fibers.

viol *noun* a Renaissance stringed musical instrument, having a fretted fingerboard and played with a bow.

viola[1] (vē-ō′lə) *noun* a musical instrument, larger than the violin and lower in pitch.

viola[2] (vī-ō′lə, vē-) *noun* a plant, e.g., a violet or pansy.

violate (vī,ə-lāt,) *verb trans.* (**violated, violating**) **1** to disregard or break (a law, an agreement, or an oath). **2** to treat (something sacred or private) with disrespect. **3** to disturb or disrupt (e.g., a person's peace or privacy). **4** to rape or sexually abuse. ▸ **violation** *noun* ▸ **violator** *noun*

violent *adj.* **1** marked by or using extreme physical force. **2** using or involving the use of such force to cause physical harm. **3** impulsively aggressive and unrestrained in nature or behavior. **4** intense; extreme; vehement. ▸ **violence** *noun* ▸ **violently** *adv.*

violet *noun* **1** a low-growing plant with purple, bluish, white, or yellow, flowers, e.g., the pansy. **2** a similar but unrelated plant, e.g., the African violet. **3** a bluish-purple color.

violin (vī,ə-lĭn′) *noun* **1** a stringed musical instrument with a shaped body and a neck, held with one end under the chin and played with a bow. **2** a person playing a violin in an orchestra or group. ▸ **violinist** *noun*

violist (vē-ō′lĭst) *noun* a viola- or viol-player.

violoncello (vī,ə-lən-chĕl′ō) *noun* (*pl.* **violoncellos**) a cello. ▸ **violoncellist** *noun*

VIP *abbrev.* very important person.

viper *noun* **1** a poisonous snake with long tubular fangs. **2** an adder (sense 1). **3** a treacherous or spiteful person.

virago *noun* (*pl.* **viragoes, viragos**) a loudly fierce or overbearing woman.

virgin *noun* **1** a person, esp. a woman, who has never had sexual intercourse. **2** (**the Virgin**) *RC Church* Mary, the mother of Jesus Christ. —*adj.* **1** never having had sexual intercourse. **2** in its original state; never having been used.

▸ **virginal** adj. ▸ **virginity** noun

Virgo (vər′gō) noun **1** the sixth sign of the zodiac. **2** (pl. **Virgos**) a person born between Aug. 23 and Sep. 22, under this sign.

virgule (vər′gyōōl,) noun Printing a diagonal punctuation mark (/). Also called **slash, solidus**.

virile (vĭr′əl, -īl,) adj. **1** of a man having a high level of sexual desire. **2** displaying or requiring qualities regarded as typically masculine, esp. physical strength. **3** of a man able to produce children. ▸ **virility** noun

virology noun the study of viruses and viral diseases. ▸ **virologist** noun

virtual adj. **1** being so in effect or in practice, but not in name: a virtual state of war. **2** nearly so. ▸ **virtually** adv.

virtual reality (ABBREV. **VR**) a computer simulation of an environment that gives the user the impression of actually being there and interacting with it, usu. by means of a special sensory helmet and gloves. See also **cyberspace** (sense 1).

virtue noun **1** a quality regarded as morally good. **2** moral goodness; righteousness. **3** an admirable quality or desirable feature. **4** virginity, esp. in women.

virtuosity noun brilliance of technique.

virtuoso noun (pl. **virtuosos, virtuosi**) **1** a person with remarkable artistic, esp. musical, skill. **2** (attributive) highly skillful; brilliant: a virtuoso performance.

virtuous adj. possessing or showing virtue; morally sound. ▸ **virtuously** adv.

virulent adj. **1 a** of a disease having a rapidly harmful effect. **b** of a disease or the organism causing it extremely infectious. **2** highly poisonous. **3** bitterly hostile; acrimonious. ▸ **virulence** noun

virus noun **1** a noncellular microorganism that infects the cells of animals, plants, and bacteria. **2 a** an organism that causes and transmits an infectious disease. **b** a disease caused by such an organism. **3** something that damages or corrupts. **4** a computer virus. ▸ **viral** adj.

visa (vē′zə, -sə) noun a permit stamped into a passport to allow the holder to enter or leave the country issuing it.

visage (vĭz′ĭj) noun **1** the human face, including the expression on it. **2** the usual appearance of something.

vis-à-vis (vē,zä-vē′) prep. in relation to; with regard to. —adv. face-to-face. —noun (pl. **vis-à-vis**) a counterpart or opposite number.

viscera pl. noun the internal organs of the body, esp. those in the abdominal cavity.

visceral adj. **1** relating to the viscera. **2** relating to the feelings, esp. the basic human instincts as distinct from the intellect.

viscid adj. thick; glutinous; viscous.

viscose noun cellulose in a viscous state, able to be made into thread.

viscosity noun a measure of the resistance of a liquid or gas to flow.

viscount (vī′kownt,) noun a member of the British nobility below an earl and above a baron in rank. ▸ **viscountcy** noun

viscountess noun **1** the wife or widow of a viscount. **2** a woman of the rank of viscount in her own right.

viscous adj. of liquid thick and sticky.

vise or **vice** (vīs) noun a tool with metal jaws for gripping an object being worked on.

visibility noun **1** the state or fact of being visible. **2** the range in which one can see clearly in given conditions of light and weather: visibility down to 50 yds.

visible adj. **1** able to be seen. **2** able to be perceived; apparent. ▸ **visibly** adv.

vision noun **1** the ability to see. **2** an image conjured up vividly in the imagination. **3** the ability to perceive what is likely, and plan wisely for it. **4** an image communicated supernaturally, esp. by God. **5** a person or thing of overwhelming beauty.

visionary adj. **1** showing or marked by great foresight or imagination. **2** possible only in the imagination; impracticable; fanciful. **3** capable of seeing supernatural images. —noun (pl. **visionaries**) a visionary person.

visit verb trans., intrans. (**visited, visiting**) **1** to go or come to see (a person or place) socially or professionally. **2** to go or come to stay (with) temporarily. **3** (**visit (something) on**) to inflict (harm, punishment, etc.) on (someone). —noun **1** an act of visiting; a social or professional call. **2** a temporary stay.

visitant noun **1** a supernatural being or form. **2** a migratory bird. Also called **visitor**.

visitation noun **1** an official visit or inspection. **2** an instance of seeing a supernatural vision.

visiting card a card with one's name on it, left during a formal visit or included in a wedding gift. Also called **calling card**.

visitor noun **1** someone who visits another person or a place. **2** a visitant (sense 2).

visor or **vizor** (vī′zər) noun **1 a** the movable part of a helmet, covering all or part of the face. **b** a projecting part of a hat or cap, that shades the eyes. **2** a translucent device shaped like the peak of a cap, worn to shade the eyes from the sun.

vista noun **1** a view into the distance. **2** a mental vision extending far into the future or past.

visual adj. **1** relating to or received through sight or vision: a visual image. **2** creating vivid mental images. —noun a chart, graph, or picture used, e.g., to illustrate a speech or

other presentation. *Also called* **visual aid.**
▸ **visually** *adv.*

visual display terminal (ABBREV. **VDT**) *or* **visual display unit** (ABBREV. **VDU**) a screen on which computerized data and graphics are displayed.

visualize *verb trans.* (**visualized, visualizing**) to form a clear mental image of. ▸ **visualization** *noun*

vital *adj.* **1** relating to or essential for life: *the vital organs.* **2** determining life or death, or success or failure: *a vital error.* **3** of the greatest importance; essential. **4** full of life; energetic. —*noun* (**vitals**) the vital organs, including the brain, heart, and lungs. ▸ **vitally** *adv.*

vitality *noun* **1** liveliness and energy. **2** the state of being alive; the ability to stay alive.

vitalize *verb trans.* (**vitalized, vitalizing**) to fill with life or energy. ▸ **vitalization** *noun*

vital statistics statistics concerning births, marriages, deaths, etc.

vitamin *noun* any of various compounds that occur in many foods and are also manufactured synthetically, and that are essential for the normal growth and functioning of the body.

vitiate (vĭsh′ē-āt,) *verb trans.* (**vitiated, vitiating**) **1** to impair the quality or effectiveness of (e.g., an argument). **2** to make (e.g., a legal contract) ineffectual or invalid. ▸ **vitiation** *noun*

viticulture *noun* viniculture.

vitreous *adj.* relating to or consisting of glass.

vitrify *verb trans., intrans.* (**vitrified, vitrifying, vitrifies**) to make into or become glass or glass-like, esp. by heating. ▸ **vitrification** *noun* ▸ **vitrified** *adj.*

vitriol *noun* **1** concentrated sulfuric acid. **2** a sulfate of a metal, orig. one of a glassy appearance. **3** extremely bitter or hateful speech or criticism. ▸ **vitriolic** *adj.*

vituperate (vī-tōō′pə-rāt, -tyōō′-) *verb trans., intrans.* (**vituperated, vituperating**) **1** to attack with abusive criticism or disapproval. **2** to use abusive language. ▸ **vituperation** *noun* ▸ **vituperative** *adj.*

viva (vē′və) *interj.* long live (the person or thing that follows), used to express strong support or approval.

vivace (vē-väch′ā) *adj., adv. Mus.* in a lively manner.

vivacious (vī-vā′shəs) *adj.* attractively lively and animated. ▸ **vivaciously** *adv.* ▸ **vivacity** *noun*

viva voce (vī,və-vō′sē) in speech; orally.

vivid *adj.* **1** *of a color* strong and bright. **2** creating or providing a clear and immediate mental picture. **3** full of life; vivacious. ▸ **vividly** *adv.* ▸ **vividness** *noun*

viviparous (vī-vĭp′ə-rəs) *adj.* giving birth to live young, as opposed to laying eggs. *See also* **oviparous** ▸ **viviparity** *noun*

vivisection *noun* the practice of dissecting living animals for experimental purposes. ▸ **vivisect** *verb* ▸ **vivisectionist** *noun*

vixen *noun* **1** a female fox. **2** a fierce or spiteful woman.

viz. *adv.* videlicet.

vizier (və-zîr′) *noun* a high-ranking government official in certain Muslim countries.

vizor *noun* same as **visor.**

vlf *or* **VLF** *abbrev.* very low frequency.

vocabulary *noun* (*pl.* **vocabularies**) **1** the words used in speaking or writing a particular language. **2** the words or range of words known to or used by a particular person or group. **3** a list of words with translations in another language alongside.

vocal *adj.* **1** relating to or produced by the voice. **2** expressing opinions or criticism freely and forcefully. —*noun* (**vocals**) the parts of a musical composition that are sung. ▸ **vocally** *adv.*

vocal cords the two folds of tissue within the larynx that vibrate and produce sound.

vocalist *noun* a singer, esp. one who sings with a band or in a pop group.

vocalize *verb trans., intrans.* (**vocalized, vocalizing**) **1** to utter or produce with the voice. **2** to express in words; to articulate. ▸ **vocalization** *noun*

vocation *noun* **1** a particular occupation or profession, esp. regarded as needing dedication and skill. **2** a feeling of being especially suited for a particular type of work. **3** a divine calling to adopt a religious life or perform good works. ▸ **vocational** *adj.* ▸ **vocationally** *adv.*

vocative *Gram. noun* **1** in some languages, the particular form of a word used when a person or thing is addressed directly. **2** a word in such a form. —*adj.* in the vocative.

vociferate (vō-sĭf′ə-rāt,) *verb trans., intrans.* (**vociferated, vociferating**) **1** to exclaim loudly and forcefully. **2** to shout or cry in a loud voice.

vociferous *adj.* **1** loud and forceful, esp. in expressing opinions. **2** expressed loudly and forcefully. ▸ **vociferously** *adv.* ▸ **vociferousness** *noun*

vodka *noun* a clear alcoholic spirit traditionally made from rye, sometimes from potatoes.

vogue *noun* **1** (*usu.* **the vogue**) the current fashion or trend in any sphere. **2** a period of being fashionable or popular.

voice *noun* **1** the ability to speak; the power of speech: *lost his voice.* **2** a way of speaking or singing peculiar to each individual: *couldn't recognize the voice.* **3** a tone of speech reflecting a particular emotion. **4** the sound of a person speaking. **5** the ability to sing, esp. to sing well: *has a lovely voice*. **6** expression in the form of spoken words. **7** a means or medium of expression or communication: *newspapers as the voice of a nation*. **8** *Gram.* the status or function of a verb in being either active or passive. —*verb trans.* (**voiced, voicing**) **1** to express in speech. **2** *Phonetics* to pronounce (a consonant) with a vibration of the vocal cords.

voice box the larynx.

voiced *adj.* **1** expressed in speech. **2** *Phonetics* pronounced with a vibration of the vocal cords, as is z, but not s.

voiceless *adj. Phonetics* not voiced.

voice-over or **voiceover** *noun* the voice of an unseen narrator in a film or television advertisement or program.

void *adj.* **1** not valid or legally binding: *declared the contract null and void*. **2** empty or unoccupied. **3** (**void of**) free from (something). —*noun* **1** an empty space. **2** a space left blank or unfilled. **3** a feeling of absence or emptiness strongly felt. —*verb trans.* (**voided, voiding**) **1** to make empty or clear. **2** to invalidate or nullify: *void a check*. **3** to empty (the bladder or bowels).

voile (voil) *noun* a very thin, semitransparent fabric.

volatile (văl′ət-l) *adj.* **1** changing quickly from a solid or liquid into a vapor. **2** explosive. **3** a easily becoming angry or violent. **b** of a *situation, etc.* liable to change quickly, esp. verging on violence. ▸ **volatility** *noun*

volcanic *adj.* **1** relating to or produced by volcanoes or a volcano. **2** easily erupting into anger or violence: *a volcanic temper*.

volcano (văl-kā′nō, vôl-) *noun* (*pl.* **volcanoes**) **1** a crack or vent in Earth's crust through which lava, gas, steam, ash, or solid rock may be forced out, often forming a hill or mountain with a central crater. **2** a situation, or a person, likely to erupt into anger or violence.

> Named after *Vulcan*, the Roman god of fire

vole *noun* a small mouse-like rodent.

volition *noun* the act of willing or choosing; the exercising of one's will: *did it of her own volition.* ▸ **volitional** *adj.*

volley *noun* (*pl.* **volleys**) **1** a firing of several guns or other weapons simultaneously. **2** an aggressive outburst, esp. of criticism or insults. **3** *Sport* a striking of the ball before it bounces. —*verb trans.* (**volleyed, volleying, volleys**) **1** to fire (weapons) in a volley. **2** *Sport* to strike (a ball) before it bounces.

volleyball *noun* a game for two teams of six players each, in which a large ball is volleyed back and forth over a high net with the hands.

volt *noun* (SYMBOL **V**) the unit of voltage, potential difference, or electromotive force in the International System. ▸ **voltage** *noun*

voltmeter *noun* an instrument that measures voltage.

voluble *adj.* **1** speaking or spoken insistently, uninterruptedly, or with ease. **2** tending to talk at great length. ▸ **volubility** *noun* ▸ **volubly** *adv.*

volume *noun* **1** the amount of space occupied by an object, gas, or liquid. **2** loudness of sound; the control that adjusts it on a radio, stereo, etc. **3** a book, whether complete in itself or one of several forming a larger work. **4** an amount or quantity, esp. when large: *the volume of traffic*. —**speak volumes** to be very significant.

voluminous *adj.* **1** of *clothing* flowing or billowing out; ample. **2** **a** of a *writer* producing great quantities of writing. **b** of *writing* enough to fill many volumes.

voluntary *adj.* **1** done or acting by free choice, not by compulsion. **2** **a** working with no expectation of being paid or otherwise rewarded. **b** of *work* unpaid. **c** of *an organization* staffed by unpaid workers; supported by donations of money freely given. **3** of a *movement, muscle, or limb* produced or controlled by the will. —*noun* (*pl.* **voluntaries**) a piece of music, usu. for organ, played before, during, or after a church service. ▸ **voluntarily** *adv.*

volunteer *verb trans., intrans.* (**volunteered, volunteering**) **1** to offer help or services freely, without being persuaded or forced: *volunteers at the hospital three days a week*. **2** to go into military service by choice, without being conscripted. **3** to give (information, etc.) unasked. **4** *colloq.* to nominate (someone) to perform a task or give help. —*noun* **1** a person who volunteers. **2** a person carrying out voluntary work. **3** a member of a non-professional army of voluntary soldiers.

voluptuary *noun* (*pl.* **voluptuaries**) a person addicted to luxury and sensual pleasures. —*adj.* promoting or characterized by luxury and sensual pleasures.

voluptuous *adj.* **1** relating to or suggestive of pleasure. **2** of a *woman* curvaceous. ▸ **voluptuously** *adv.* ▸ **voluptuousness** *noun*

volute (və-lōōt′) *noun* **1** a spiral. **2** *Archit.* a scroll carved in stone, esp. at the top of a column. **3** one single twist in a spiral shell.

vomit *verb trans., intrans.* (**vomited, vomiting**) **1** to eject (the contents of the stomach) forcefully through the mouth. **2** to emit or throw out with force or violence. —*noun* the contents of the stomach when forcefully ejected.

voodoo *noun* **1** witchcraft of a type orig. practiced by the black peoples of the West Indies and southern US. **2** the beliefs and practices of the religious cult that developed it, including serpent-worship and human sacrifice. ▸ **voodooism** *noun*

voracious *adj.* **1** eating or craving food in large quantities. **2** extremely eager: *a voracious reader*. ▸ **voraciously** *adv.* ▸ **voracity** *noun*

vortex *noun* (*pl.* **vortexes**, **vortices**) **1** a whirlpool or whirlwind; any whirling mass or motion. **2** a situation or activity into which all surrounding people or things are helplessly and dangerously drawn. ▸ **vortical** *adj.*

votary *noun* (*pl.* **votaries**) **1** a person bound by solemn vows to a religious life. **2** a person dedicated to a particular cause or activity.

vote *noun* **1** a formal indication of choice or opinion, e.g., in an election or debate. **2 a** the right to express a choice or opinion, e.g., in a national election. **b** a choice or opinion so expressed: *a vote in favor of tax reform.* **c** the support so given by a certain sector of the population, or to a particular candidate or group. —*verb intrans., trans.* (**voted, voting**) **1** to cast a vote, for or against. **2** to decide, state, grant, or bring about by casting votes. **3** to declare support for by casting a vote. **4** to declare or pronounce by general consent: *The show was voted a success.* **5** *colloq.* to propose or suggest. ▸ **voter** *noun*

votive *adj. Relig.* done or given in thanks to a deity or to fulfill a vow or promise.

vouch *verb trans., intrans.* (**vouched, vouching**) (**vouch for**) to give a firm assurance or guarantee (e.g. of someone or something's authenticity, reliability, etc.).

voucher *noun* **1** a document serving as proof, e.g., of the purchase or receipt of goods. **2** a ticket exchangeable for goods or services of a specified value.

vouchsafe *verb trans., intrans.* (**vouchsafed, vouchsafing**) to agree or condescend (to do, give, grant, or allow).

voussoir (vōō-swär′) *noun* one of the wedge-shaped stones that forms part of the center line of an arch. *Also called* **arch stone**.

vow *noun* a solemn, binding promise, esp. one made to or in the name of a deity. —*verb trans.* (**vowed, vowing**) to promise or declare solemnly; to swear.

vowel *noun* **1** any speech sound made with an open mouth and no contact between mouth,

lips, teeth, or tongue. **2** a letter, used alone or in combination, representing such a sound, e.g., in English, the letters *a, e, i, o, u* and in some words *y.*

vox populi (väk′päp′yə-lē, -lī,) public opinion; popular belief.

voyage (voi′ĭj) *noun* a long journey to a distant place, esp. by air or sea or in space. —*verb intrans.* (**voyaged, voyaging**) to go on a voyage; to travel. ▸ **voyager** *noun*

voyeur (voi-ər′) *noun* **1** a person who derives sensual gratification from furtively watching naked bodies or the sexual activity of others. **2** a person who observes, esp. with fascination or intrusively, the feelings of others. ▸ **voyeurism** *noun* ▸ **voyeuristic** *adj.* ▸ **voyeuristically** *adv.*

VP *abbrev.* vice-president.

VR *abbrev.* virtual reality.

vs. *abbrev.* versus.

vulcanite *noun* hard, black, vulcanized rubber.

vulcanize *verb trans.* (**vulcanized, vulcanizing**) to treat (rubber) with sulfur and heat in order to harden it and increase its elasticity. ▸ **vulcanization** *noun*

vulgar *adj.* **1** lacking refined manners and sensitivity. **2** relating to the commonly spoken form of a language, as opposed to the formal or literary language. ▸ **vulgarly** *adv.*

vulgarism *noun* **1** a vulgar expression in speech. **2** an example of vulgar behavior.

vulgarity *noun* (*pl.* **vulgarities**) coarseness in speech or behavior, or an instance of it.

vulgarize *verb trans.* (**vulgarized, vulgarizing**) **1** to make vulgar. **2** to make, or spoil by making, common or popular. ▸ **vulgarization** *noun*

vulnerable *adj.* **1** easily hurt or harmed physically or emotionally. **2** easily tempted or persuaded. **3** (**vulnerable to**) unprotected against physical or verbal attack from (someone or something). ▸ **vulnerability** *noun*

vulpine (vəl′pīn,) *adj.* **1** relating to or resembling foxes or a fox. **2** cunning.

vulture *noun* **1** a large, bare-headed bird that feeds on carrion. **2** a person who exploits the downfall or death of another.

vulva *noun* the parts surrounding the opening to the vagina; the female genitals.

vying *verb see* **vie.**

Ww

W¹ *or* **w** *noun* (*pl.* **Ws, W's, w's**) the 23d letter of the English alphabet.

W² *abbrev.* **1** watt. **2** west; western.

W³ *symbol* tungsten.

W⁴ *symbol* weight (sense 2).

w. *abbrev.* weight (sense 1).

wacko *or* **whacko** *noun* (*pl.* **wackos**) *slang* an eccentric or crazy person.

wacky *or* **whacky** *adj.* (**wackier, wackiest**) *slang* eccentric; crazy.

wad *noun* **1** a compressed mass of soft material for packing, padding, stuffing, etc. **2** a thick bundle, esp. of banknotes.

waddle *verb intrans.* (**waddled, waddling**) to walk with a sideways swaying motion.

wade *verb trans., intrans.* (**waded, wading**) **1** to walk through deep water. **2** to cross (a river, etc.) by wading.

wader *noun* **1** a bird, e.g., a heron, stork, etc., found along the shorelines. **2** (**waders**) long waterproof boots.

wadi (wäd'ē) *noun* a rocky river bed in N Africa and Arabia, dry except during the rains.

wafer *noun* **1** a thin, light, finely layered cookie. **2** a thin disk of unleavened bread or rice paper served to communicants at Holy Communion.

waffle¹ *noun* a light-textured cake formed into a gridlike pattern.

waffle² *verb intrans.* (**waffled, waffling**) to talk or write in an evasive, vague way. —*noun* evasive, vague talk or writing.

waffle iron a flat, double-sided, hinged mold for cooking waffles.

waft *verb trans., intrans.* (**wafted, wafting**) to float or drift, or cause to float or drift, gently. —*noun* a breeze or whiff.

wag *verb trans., intrans.* (**wagged, wagging**) to move, or cause to move, to and fro vigorously. —*noun* **1** a wagging movement. **2** a habitual joker; a playful rogue.

wage *verb trans.* (**waged, waging**) to fight or undertake (a war, campaign, etc.) —*noun* **1** a regular payment for work or a specified rate of pay. **2** (**wages**) pay. **3** (*often* **wages**) (*sing., pl.*) reward, recompense, or repayment.

wager *noun* a bet on an outcome or result. —*verb trans., intrans.* (**wagered, wagering**) to stake in a bet; to bet.

waggle *verb intrans., trans.* (**waggled, waggling**) to move, or cause to move, to and fro.

wagon *noun* a four-wheeled vehicle, esp. a horse-drawn one. —**on the wagon** *slang* temporarily abstaining from alcohol. ▸ **wagoner** *noun*

wagon train a group of covered wagons traveling across the prairie.

wagtail *noun* a small bird with a tail that flips up and down.

wahine (wä-hē'nē) *noun* **1** a Polynesian woman or wife. **2** *slang* a female surfer.

wahoo¹ *noun* (*pl.* **wahoos**) a deciduous shrub or small tree.

wahoo² *noun* (*pl.* **wahoo, wahoos**) a tropical marine game and food fish.

waif *noun* **1** an orphaned, abandoned, or homeless child. **2** an unclaimed and apparently ownerless animal or thing.

wail *noun* a long, drawn-out, mournful or complaining cry. —*verb intrans., trans.* (**wailed, wailing**) to make, or utter with, such a cry, or any similar sound.

wainscot (wānz'kət, -kōt,) *noun* wooden paneling or boarding covering the lower part of the walls of a room. ▸ **wainscoting** *or* **wainscotting** *noun*

waist *noun* **1** the part of the human body between the ribs and hips or the part of a garment covering this. **2** any middle, often narrowing, part of something.

wait *verb intrans., trans.* (**waited, waiting**) **1** to delay action, or remain in a certain place. **2** to work as a waiter or waitress (at): *wait tables.* —*noun* a delay, postponement, or time spent waiting: *a long wait in the line.* —**wait on** to tend to (a person or a person's needs) or act as a servant or attendant to (someone).

waiter *noun* a man who serves food in a restaurant, etc.

waitperson *noun* a waitron.

waitress *noun* a woman who serves food in a restaurant, etc.

waitron (wā'trän,) *noun* a waiter or waitress who serves food in a restaurant, etc. *Also called* **waitperson.**

waitstaff *or* **wait staff** *noun* the waiters and waitresses of a restaurant, etc. collectively

waive *verb trans.* (**waived, waiving**) **1** to forego or give up (a claim, right, etc.). **2** to refrain from enforcing (a rule, penalty, etc.).

waiver *noun* the relinquishment of a right, etc., or a written statement confirming such relinquishment.

wake[1] *verb trans., intrans.* (*pa t* **woke** *or* **waked**; *pa p* **waked** *or* **woken**; *pr p* **waking**) (*also* **wake up** *or* **wake (someone) up**) **1** to rouse or be roused from sleep. **2** to stir or be stirred out of a state of, e.g., inactivity or lethargy. —*noun* a watch or vigil kept beside a corpse.

wake[2] *noun* a trail of disturbed water left by a passing ship, etc.

wakeful *adj.* **1** not asleep; unable to sleep. **2** *of a night* sleepless. **3** vigilant; alert; watchful.

waken *verb trans., intrans.* (**wakened, wakening**) to rouse or be roused from sleep, or from inactivity or lethargy.

wake-robin *noun* a trillium.

wake-up call *slang* a reminder of possible danger, the need for vigilance, etc.

Waldorf salad (wôl′dôrf,) a salad of apples, walnuts, celery, and mayonnaise.

wale *noun* **1** a raised mark on the skin. **2** a ridge on cloth, e.g., the rib on corduroy. **3** a plank along the top edge of a ship's side.

walk *verb intrans., trans.* (**walked, walking**) **1** to go about (the streets, etc.) or travel (a specified distance) on foot: *walked to school / walked three miles.* **2** to accompany, etc. (someone who is on foot): *walked her home.* **3** to take (a dog) out for exercise. **4** to live or behave in a specified manner: *walk tall.* **5** *slang* to be acquitted of a crime: *Despite the evidence, the defendant walked.* **6** *Baseball* to go to first base, or allow (a batter) to go to first base, after four balls have been pitched. **7** *Basketball* to move illegally while in possession of the ball; to travel. —*noun* **1** a manner or pace of walking: *She slowed to a walk.* **2** an outing or journey on foot. **3** a distance walked or for walking: *a three-minute walk.* **4** a path, esp. a broad, formal one. **5** a route for walking.

walkabout *noun* a casual stroll through a crowd by a celebrity, e.g., a politician.

walkaway *noun slang* an easily won victory, esp. in sports; also, an easily accomplished task. *Also called* **walkover**.

walkie-talkie *noun colloq.* a portable two-way radio carried by police, etc.

walk-in *adj.* large enough to be entered by a person: *a walk-in closet.* —*noun* a person attending, e.g., a physician, hairdresser, etc., without an appointment.

walking papers *slang* a dismissal or a discharge, esp. from a job and usu. for misconduct.

walking stick 1 a stick used for support or balance in walking. **2** a stick insect.

Walkman (wôk′mən, -măn,) *trademark* used to denote a small, portable audiocassette recorder or radio, or a combination of these, with lightweight headphones.

walk of life (*pl.* **walks of life**) an occupation or profession: *people from all walks of life.*

walk-on *adj.* of a part in a play, etc. minor and usu. not involving speaking or singing, etc.

walkout *noun* a sudden departure, esp. of workers on strike.

walkover *noun colloq.* an easy victory.

walk-through *noun* a perfunctory rehearsal.

walkup *or* **walk-up** *noun* an apartment, office, building, etc. without an elevator.

walkway *noun* a paved path or passage for pedestrians.

wall *noun* **1** a construction serving as an enclosure, barrier, form of protection, etc.. *a garden wall / membranous cell walls.* **2** a side of a building or room. **3** something similar to a wall: *a wall of fire.* —*verb trans.* (**walled, walling**) **1** to surround, enclose, or separate with a wall or a structure similar to a wall. **2** (**wall up**) to block with, seal behind, or imprison within bricks or a structure similar to a wall. —**off** *or* **up the wall** *slang* crazy.

wallaby *noun* (*pl.* **wallabies, wallaby**) a plant-eating marsupial similar to, but smaller than, a kangaroo.

wallet *noun* a flat pocketbook for holding banknotes, etc. *Also called* **billfold**.

walleye *noun* **1** an eye in which the iris has a chalky appearance. **2** (*pl.* **walleye, walleyes**) a N American freshwater fish with large, staring eyes. *Also called* **dory, walleyed pike**. **3** an eye that squints away from the nose, so that an abnormal amount of the white shows. ▸ **walleyed** *adj.*

wallflower *noun* **1** a plant with fragrant red, orange, yellow, or white flowers. **2** *colloq.* a person who spends an evening at a dance or other social occasion without a romantic partner.

Walloon (wă-lōōn′) *noun* **1** a member of the French-speaking population of S Belgium. **2** their language, a dialect of French. —*adj.* relating to, or belonging to, the Walloons, or their language.

wallop *colloq. verb trans.* (**walloped, walloping**) **1** to slap, hit, or beat vigorously. **2** to defeat convincingly. —*noun* a slap or hit.

wallow *verb intrans.* (**wallowed, wallowing**) **1** to lie or roll about in water, mud, etc. **2** to revel or luxuriate in admiration, etc. **3** to indulge excessively in self-pity, etc. —*noun* a session of wallowing or a place where animals wallow.

wallpaper *noun* paper used to decorate the interior walls of houses, etc. —*verb trans.* (**wallpapered, wallpapering**) to cover (walls), or the walls of (a room), with wallpaper.

wall-to-wall *adj.* **1** *of carpeting* covering the entire floor of a room. **2** *slang* ever-present; inescapable: *wall-to-wall noise.*

walnut *noun* **1** a tree with large compound leaves. **2** a nut produced by this tree, having a wrinkled seed in a hard shell. **3** the wood of this tree used in furniture-making, etc.

walrus *noun* (*pl.* **walrus, walruses**) a large marine mammal, related to the seal.

walrus mustache a thick, drooping mustache.

waltz *noun* **1** a ballroom dance. **2** a piece of music for this dance. —*verb intrans.* (**waltzed, waltzing, waltzes**) **1** to dance a waltz. **2** *slang* to go or move with easy confidence: *waltzes into work late every day.*

wampum *noun* **1** small shells used as money by Native Americans. **2** *slang* money.

WAN *abbrev. Comput.* wide area network.

wan *adj.* (**wanner, wannest**) pale and pinched-looking from illness, exhaustion, or grief. ▸ **wanly** *adv.* ▸ **wanness** *noun*

wand *noun* **1** a slender rod used by magicians, fairies, etc. for performing magic. **2** a conductor's baton. **3** a rod carried as a symbol of authority.

wander *verb intrans., trans.* (**wandered, wandering**) **1** to walk or travel about, with no particular destination; to ramble: *wandered the streets / wandered around soaking up the atmosphere.* **2** to stray from the right path, the point of an argument, etc. **3** to fail to or be unable to concentrate; to be affected by delirium. —*noun* a ramble or stroll. ▸ **wanderer** *noun*

wandering Jew a trailing plant with variegated foliage, popular as a houseplant.

wanderlust *noun* an urge to roam; a liking for keeping on the move.

wane *verb intrans.* (**waned, waning**) **1** *of the Moon* to appear to grow narrower as the Sun illuminates less of its surface. **2** to decline, esp. in importance, influence, etc. —*noun* a decline: *a career that was on the wane.*

wangle *colloq verb trans.* (**wangled, wangling**) to contrive or obtain by persuasiveness or subtle manipulation: *wangled an invitation.* —*noun* an act of wangling.

wannabe (wän'ə-bē, wən'-) *noun* someone who aspires to be or do something important: *a Presidential wannabe.*

want *verb trans., intrans.* (**wanted, wanting**) **1** to feel a need or desire for. **2** to need or require. **3** to lack. —*noun* **1** a desire, need, or requirement. **2** an absence, or something that is absent. **3** poverty or destitution: *living in want.*

wanted *adj.* sought by the police on suspicion of having committed a crime, etc.

wanting *adj.* **1** missing; lacking. **2** not having enough of (something). **3** not up to standard or requirements.

wanton (wônt'n, wänt'n) *adj.* **1** motivelessly cruel. **2** having no motive or reason. **3** sexually or morally lacking in restraint. —*noun* a wanton person. ▸ **wantonly** *adv.*

wapiti (wäp'ət-ē) *noun* (*pl.* **wapiti, wapitis**) a large N American deer with large, branched antlers. *Also called* **elk.**

war *noun* **1** an openly acknowledged state of armed conflict, esp. between nations. **2** a particular armed struggle. **3** a struggle or campaign: *the war against drug dealing.* **4** fierce rivalry or competition. —*verb intrans.* (**warred, warring**) **1** to fight wars. **2** to conflict or be in conflict.

warble *verb intrans., trans.* (**warbled, warbling**) **1** *of a bird* to sing melodiously. **2** *of a person* to sing or utter in a high, tremulous voice; to trill. —*noun* a song or a trilling noise.

warbler *noun* a small songbird.

war cry **1** a cry used to rally troops, or as a signal for charging. **2** a slogan or watchword.

war dance a dance performed by some peoples going into battle, or after victory.

ward *noun* **1** a hospital room with beds for several patients. **2** a political or administrative division in a town, etc. **3** a person, esp. a minor, under the protection of a guardian or court of law. **4** a projection inside a lock that fits into a notch in its key, ensuring that the lock cannot be turned by the wrong key. **5** *old use* a watch or guard kept over something. —*verb trans.* (**warded, warding**) (*usu.* **ward off** or **against**) to fend off (a blow, illness, etc.).

-ward or **-wards** *combining form* forming words denoting direction: *westward / backward.*

warden *noun* **1** an officer in charge of a prison. **2** a public official responsible for maintaining order, etc.

ward heeler a minor political worker in a designated ward.

wardrobe *noun* **1** a clothes closet. **2** a personal stock of clothes.

wardroom *noun* **1** a dining and recreational area for commissioned officers on board a warship. **2** the commissioned officers aboard a warship, regarded collectively.

-wards *combining form same as* **-ward.**

ware *noun* **1** (**wares**) goods for sale. **2** (*in compounds*) manufactured goods of a specified material or for a specified range of use: *glassware / kitchenware.* **3** (*often in compounds*) a particular type of pottery: *Delftware.* **4** (*often in compounds*) a particular type of computer software: *shareware.*

warehouse *noun* a large building where goods are stored and often packed and dispatched to smaller outlets.

warehouse club a discount club for buying goods.

warfare *noun* **1** the activity of waging war. **2** violent conflict.

warhead *noun* the front part of a missile, rocket, torpedo, etc., where the explosives or chemical or biological agents are housed.

warlike *adj.* **1** aggressive; belligerent. **2** relating to war; military.

warlock *noun* a wizard or sorcerer.

warlord *noun* a military leader with civil power.

warm *adj.* **1** moderately, comfortably, or pleasantly hot. **2** providing and preserving heat: *a warm sweater.* **3** kindhearted and affectionate: *a warm person.* **4** welcoming: *a warm reception.* **5** enthusiastic: *warm support.* **6** suggesting comfort, heat, etc.: *warm colors.* **7** close to guessing correctly or finding something sought: *You're getting warm.* —*verb trans., intrans.* **(warmed, warming) 1** to make or become warm or warmer. **2 (warm to)** to begin to like or feel enthusiasm for (someone or something): *warmed to the idea.* —**warm up 1** to become or make (someone or something) warm or warmer. **2** to become, or make (something) become, livelier. **3** to reach, or bring (an engine, etc.) up to an efficient working temperature. **4** to exercise gently in preparation for a strenuous workout, race, etc. ▸ **warmly** *adv.* ▸ **warmness** *noun*

warm-blooded *adj.* **1** of *animals* able to maintain a fairly constant body temperature no matter what the external temperature might be. **2** passionate, impulsive, or ardent.

warm boot a reboot activated without turning the power supply to a computer off, usu. by a keystroke or a combination of keystrokes.

warm-hearted *adj.* kind and affectionate.

warmonger *noun* a person who tries to incite war, or whips up enthusiasm for it.

warmth *noun* **1** the condition of being warm. **2** affection, kindheartedness, or passion.

warm-up or **warmup** *noun* an act or the process of exercising the body in preparation for an athletic contest, etc.

warn *verb trans.* **(warned, warning) 1** to caution, make aware of, or inform in advance. **2** to advise strongly.

warning *noun* **1** a caution or admonition. **2** something serving as a ominous precursor. —*adj.* intended or serving to warn.

warp *verb intrans., trans.* **(warped, warping)** to become, or cause to become, twisted out of shape, distorted, corrupted, or perverted. —*noun* **1** an unevenness, distortion, or twist, e.g., in wood, a personality, time, etc. **2** a set of threads stretched lengthwise in a loom.

war paint 1 paint put on the face by some peoples when going to war. **2** *slang* cosmetics for the face.

warpath *noun* a march to war, esp. among Native Americans. —**on the warpath 1** setting off to fight. **2** *colloq.* in an angry or fighting mood: *The boss is on the warpath.*

warrant (wôr'ənt, wär'-) *noun* **1** a legal authorization, e.g., to arrest someone, search property, etc. **2** a certificate, etc. that authorizes, guarantees, or confirms. **3** a justification. —*verb trans.* **(warranted, warranting) 1** to justify: *Nothing can warrant that kind of outburst.* **2** to affirm or assert with confidence: *I'll warrant he knows nothing of this.* **3** to guarantee; to confirm as genuine, worthy, etc.

warrant officer (ABBREV. **WO, W.O.**) an Army or Navy officer with a rank between a commissioned and noncommissioned officer.

warranty *noun* (*pl.* **warranties**) an assurance or guarantee.

warren *noun* **1** a number of interconnecting rabbit burrows. **2** a place or building with so many streets, passages, etc. that it is difficult to find one's way.

warrior *noun* a skilled fighter.

warship *noun* a ship equipped with guns, missiles, etc., for deployment in naval battles; a combat ship.

wart *noun* a small skin growth, esp. of the fingers, toes, and face. Also called **verruca.**

wart hog or **warthog** a large wild African pig with curved tusks.

wary *adj.* **(warier, wariest) 1** carefully prudent in the avoidance of risk or danger. **2** distrustful, apprehensive, or suspicious. ▸ **warily** *adv.*

was *see* be.

wash *verb trans., intrans.* **(washed, washing) 1** to clean (oneself, a body part, clothes, etc.), esp. using water and often soap or detergent: *washed and got dressed / washed her hair.* **2** to clean, or be able to be cleaned, in a specified way, etc. **3** to remove, or be removed, through washing: *washed the dirt out / a stain that won't wash off.* **4** to flow against or over a place, land feature, etc.: *Waves washed the shore.* **5** to sweep (something) along: *Flood water washed cars away.* **6** *colloq.* to stand scrutiny or investigation: *That excuse just won't wash.* —*noun* **1** an act or the process of washing or a quantity of clothes, etc., for washing or just washed. **2** the breaking of waves against something; the sound of this. **3** the rough water or disturbed air left by an aircraft or a ship. **4** a lotion or other preparation for cleansing or washing.

washable *adj.* able to be washed without damage.

washbasin *noun* a shallow sink.

washcloth *noun* a facecloth.

washed-out *adj.* **1** *colloq.* pale and tired-looking. **2** faded through washing. **3** expelled or not continuing, esp. due to failure.

washed-up *adj. colloq.* incapable of continuing; no longer functioning or necessary.

washer *noun* **1** a machine for washing, e.g., clothes, dishes. **2** a flat ring of rubber or metal for keeping a joint tight.

washing *noun* clothes to be washed or that have been washed.

washing machine a machine, usu. automatic, for washing clothes.

washing soda sodium carbonate.

washout *noun* **1** *colloq.* a complete failure. **2** an event, esp. a sports event, that has to be stopped or canceled because of rain.

washroom *noun* a usu. public bathroom.

washy *adj.* (**washier, washiest**) *colloq.* **1** *of a drink, etc.* too watery or weak. **2** lacking liveliness or vigor; feeble. **3** *of colors* faded-looking; pallid.

WASP (wǎsp, wôsp) *abbrev.* white Anglo-Saxon Protestant.

wasp *noun* a mainly social insect related to bees and ants.

waspish *adj.* sharp-tongued; caustic.

wassail (wǎs'ol, wǎ-sāl') *noun* **1** a festive bout of drinking. **2** a toast made at such an occasion or a drink used in toasting.

waste *verb trans., intrans.* (**wasted, wasting**) **1** to squander. **2** to fail to use or make the best of · (an opportunity, etc.). **3** (*also* **waste away**) to lose or cause to lose flesh, strength, etc. **4** *old use* to devastate (territory); to lay waste. **5** *slang* to kill: *gangsters who wasted two cops.* —*adj.* **1** rejected as useless or excess to requirements. **2** *of ground* lying unused, uninhabited, or uncultivated. —*noun* **1** an act or instance of wasting. **2** a failure to take advantage of something: *a waste of talent.* **3** material no longer needed or produced as a manufacturing byproduct: *nuclear waste.* **4** garbage; trash. **5** (*often* **wastes**) a tract of uncultivated land, or an expanse of ocean, etc.: *the Arctic wastes.* —**lay waste to** to devastate (an area, etc.). ▸ **wastage** *noun*

wasted *adj.* **1** *slang* under the influence of alcohol, drugs, etc. **2** weak and emaciated.

waste disposal a means of getting rid of waste from domestic, industrial, or agricultural sources, or the process of doing this.

wasteful *adj.* causing waste; extravagant. ▸ **wastefully** *adv.*

wasteland *noun* a desolate, barren region.

wastepaper *noun* paper discarded as trash or intended for recycling.

wastepaper basket a receptacle for discarded paper, etc.

waste pipe a pipe carrying waste material or waste water from a sink, etc.

waste product **1** a useless byproduct of, e.g., a manufacturing process. **2** a substance excreted from the body.

wastrel (wās'trol) *noun* an idle spendthrift.

watch *verb trans., intrans.* (**watched, watching**) **1** to look at or focus attention on (someone or something). **2** to guard, look after, keep track of, or monitor. **3** to take care of or pay proper attention to. —*noun* **1** a small portable instrument for telling the time. **2** an act or the process of watching or guarding. **3** a shift on board a ship when crew members are on duty; those on duty in any shift. **4** a body of sentries on lookout duty; a watchman or body of watchmen. **5** (*often in compounds*) a group of people concerned about a specified issue, or the particular concerns or activities of such a group: ·*neighborhood watch.*

watchdog *noun* **1** a dog kept to guard premises, etc. **2** a person or group of people guarding against unacceptable standards, behavior, etc. —*adj.* denoting a group of people guarding against unacceptable standards, etc.

watchful *adj.* alert, vigilant, and wary.

watchmaker *noun* a person or a firm that makes and repairs watches and clocks.

watchman *noun* a person employed to guard premises at night.

watchnight *noun* New Year's Eve, or a church service lasting through midnight on New Year's Eve.

watchtower *noun* a tower from which a sentry keeps watch.

watchword *noun* **1** a catchphrase or rally call used as inspiration, etc. **2** a password, e.g., to a secure area.

water *noun* **1** a colorless, odorless, tasteless liquid, H_2O. **2** (*also* **waters**) a sea, lake, river, etc. **3** (**waters**) the sea around a country's coasts, considered part of its territory. **4** the level or state of the tide: *at high water.* **5** (**waters**) water at a spa, etc., containing minerals. **6** a body fluid, esp. urine or amniotic fluid. **7** the degree of brilliance and transparency of a diamond. —*verb trans., intrans.* (**watered, watering**) **1** to wet, soak, or sprinkle with water. **2** to irrigate (land). **3** to dilute. **4** to fill with liquid: *my mouth's watering.* **5** to provide (animals) with, or take a supply of, drinking water. **6** to give a wavy appearance to (the surface of) fabric by wetting and pressing. ·

waterbed *noun* a water-filled mattress, or a bed with a water-filled mattress.

waterborne adj. carried by water: water-borne spores.

water buffalo an Asian animal belonging to the cattle family, often domesticated and used for pulling plows, etc. Also called **caraboo.**

water cannon a device that sends out a powerful jet of water, used for dispersing crowds, etc.

water chestnut 1 an aquatic plant or its edible nutlike fruits that are an important food source in many parts of Asia. **2** a tropical aquatic sedge or its edible tubers, used in oriental cookery.

water closet (ABBREV. **W.C.**) a booth or a bathroom with a flush toilet and often a washbasin.

watercolor noun paint thinned with water, or a painting done in such paint.

water cooler a device that cools and dispenses drinking water.

watercourse noun the bed or channel of a stream, river, or canal.

watercress noun an aquatic plant or its pungent-tasting leaves, which are used in salads, soups, etc. See also **nasturtium** (sense 2).

waterfall noun a part of a river, stream, etc. where the water falls more or less vertically.

waterfowl noun an aquatic bird, esp. a duck, goose, or swan, or such birds collectively.

waterfront noun the buildings or part of a town along the edge of a river, lake, etc.

water glass a solution of potassium or sodium silicate in water, used as protective coating.

water hole a pool or spring, esp. in a desert area, where animals can drink. Also called **watering hole.**

water ice a sorbet.

watering can a watering pot.

Watergate noun a scandal, usu. a political one involving deception or misuse of power and a subsequent attempt to cover up events.

watering hole 1 a water hole. **2** slang a club open at night for drinking, dancing, and other entertainment.

watering pot a container with a spout for watering plants.

water lily an aquatic plant with large flat circular leaves and big bowl-shaped flowers that sit on the water's surface.

waterline noun a line, esp. on a boat, showing where the water level comes to.

waterlogged adj. **1** saturated with water. **2** of a vessel filled or saturated with water as to be unmanageable.

Waterloo (wôt̯ər-lōō', wät̯-) noun a final defeat, esp. one from which there can be no recovery: meet his Waterloo.

watermark noun **1** a limit reached by a high or low tide. **2** a distinctive mark on paper, esp. one that indicates the manufacturer.

watermelon noun a plant or its large round edible fruit that has a dark green rind, and juicy red flesh studded with many seeds.

water moccasin a cottonmouth.

water ouzel the dipper (sense 2).

water polo a game for two teams of seven swimmers who try to put the ball in the opposition's goal.

waterproof adj. impenetrable to water.

water rat a small rodent that lives near water.

watershed noun **1** the high land separating two river basins. **2** a crucial point after which events take a different turn.

waterside noun the edge of a river, lake, or sea.

water ski (pl. **water skis**) a ski on which to glide over water, usu. when towed by a motorboat.

water-ski verb intrans. (**water-skied, water-skiing, water-skies**) to travel on water skis. ► **water-skier** noun ► **water-skiing** noun

waterspout noun a tornado that occurs over open water, mainly in the tropics, and consists of a rotating column of water and spray.

water table the level below which porous rocks are saturated with groundwater.

watertight adj. **1** so well sealed as to be impenetrable to water. **2** of an argument, etc. without any apparent flaw or weakness; completely sound.

water tower a tower supporting a water tank, from which water can be distributed at uniform pressure.

waterway noun a channel, e.g., a canal or river, used by ships, etc.

water wheel a wheel that is turned by the force of water on blades or buckets around its rim, used as a source of energy to drive machinery, etc.

water wings an inflatable device that keeps a person, esp. a child learning to swim, buoyant.

waterworks noun **1** (sing., pl.) a place where water is purified and stored for distribution to an area. **2** (pl.) colloq. tears; weeping.

watery adj. **1** of or consisting of water: the watery depths. **2** containing too much water: watery tea. ► **wateriness** noun

watt noun (ABBREV. **W**) a unit of electrical activity or power. ► **wattage** noun

wattle noun **1** interwoven branches, etc. forming a framework. **2** a loose dangling fold of skin, esp. at the throat of certain birds, fish, and lizards. **3** the acacia.

wave verb intrans., trans. (**waved, waving**) **1** to move (a hand, flag, etc.) to and fro; to flutter. **2** to give a signal, esp. by a hand gesture: waved them goodbye. **3** to undulate or curl or cause something to undulate or curl. —noun **1** an undulating or moving ridge, e.g. of hair, sea water, etc. **2** an act of waving, e.g., a hand gesture. **3** a regularly repeated disturbance or displacement in a medium, e.g., water or air, or variation and transfer of energy level: *light waves.* **4** a surge: *a wave of nausea.*

waveband *noun* a range of frequencies in the electromagnetic spectrum occupied by radio or television broadcasting transmission.

wavelength *noun* **1** the distance between two successive peaks or two successive troughs of a radio, light, or electromagnetic wave. **2** the length of radio wave used by a particular broadcasting station. **—on the same wavelength** *slang,* of two or more people speaking or thinking in a way that is mutually compatible.

waver *verb intrans.* (**wavered, wavering**) **1** to falter, lessen, or weaken. **2** to hesitate through indecision.

wavy *adj.* (**wavier, waviest**) of hair, a line, outline, etc. undulating. ▸ **waviness** *noun*

wax¹ *noun* a solid or semisolid organic compound, e.g., paraffin wax, beeswax, or a sticky, yellowish matter that forms in the ears. —*verb trans.* (**waxed, waxing, waxes**) to apply a natural or artificial wax to: *waxed and polished the car.*

wax² *verb intrans.* (**waxed, waxing, waxes**) **1** of the Moon to appear to grow wider as the Sun illuminates more of its surface. **2** to increase in size, strength, power, etc.

wax bean a yellow string bean. *Also called* **butter bean.**

waxen *adj.* made of wax or something similar to wax.

wax paper moisture-proof paper treated with wax, used in food preparation, etc.

waxwing *noun* a songbird with grayish-brown plumage and a black tail.

waxwork *noun* **1** a lifelike model, esp. of a celebrity, made of wax. **2** (**waxworks**) an exhibition of these models.

waxy *adj.* (**waxier, waxiest**) resembling wax in appearance, texture, or feel.

way *noun* **1** a route or course running from one place to another. **2** a route or path ahead; room for passing, moving, or progressing. **3** a journey, distance, or direction. **4** a manner, method, plan, style, approach, etc. **5** a habit, routine, characteristic piece of behavior, etc. **6** a respect, state, or condition. —*adv. colloq.* **1** a long way; far: *way off the mark.* **2** extremely; really: *a way cool movie.* —**give way 1** to collapse, subside, or break down, esp. due to pressure. **2** to yield: *gave way to their demands.* **go out of one's way** to make a special effort.

waybill *noun* a list giving details of goods or passengers being carried.

wayfarer *noun* a traveler, esp. one going on foot.

waylay *verb* (*pa t and pa p* **waylaid**; *pr p* **waylaying**) **1** to lie in wait for and ambush. **2** to wait for and delay with conversation.

way-out *adj. slang* unusual, exotic, or new.

-ways *combining form* forming words denoting direction or manner: *edgeways.*

wayside *noun* the edge of a road, or the area to the side of it. —*adj.* growing, lying, or situated near the edge of a road.

wayward *adj.* undisciplined, headstrong, willful, or rebellious. ▸ **waywardness** *noun*

W.C. *abbrev.* water closet.

we *pron.* used as the subject of a verb: **1** to refer to oneself in company with another or others. **2** to refer to people in general: *the times we live in.* **3** by a royal person, writer, editor, etc. to refer to him- or herself or the authority he or she represents.

> *Usage* When the pronoun referring to oneself in company with another or others is followed by a noun in apposition to it, the correct choice is *we,* not *us: We kids need help,* not *Us kids need help.*

weak *adj.* **1** lacking physical strength; in poor physical health. **2** lacking power. **3** low or dropping in value: *a weak dollar.* **4** too easily influenced by others, or yielding too easily to temptation. **5** lacking full flavor or too dilute: *weak tea.* **6** of an argument, etc. unsound or unconvincing. **7** faint: *a weak signal.* ▸ **weakly** *adv.*

weaken *verb trans., intrans.* (**weakened, weakening**) **1** to make or become weak or weaker. **2** to yield to pressure or persuasion.

weak-kneed *adj.* cowardly; feeble.

weakling *noun* **1** a physically weak person or animal. **2** someone with a specified fault or failing: *a moral weakling.*

weak-minded *adj.* **1** of feeble intelligence. **2** lacking will or determination.

weak moment a lapse of self-discipline.

weakness *noun* **1** the condition of being weak. **2** a fault or failing. **3** a liking: *a weakness for chocolate.*

wealth *noun* **1** riches and property, or the possession of them. **2** abundance of resources. **3** a large quantity or amount. ▸ **wealthy** *adj.*

wean *verb trans., intrans.* (**weaned, weaning**) **1** to introduce (a baby or young mammal) to food other than a mother's milk: *Those kittens are too young to be weaned.* **2** to cause (someone or oneself) to do without something, usu. by gradually withdrawing it: *tried to wean him off drugs.*

weapon *noun* an instrument, e.g., a gun, knife, etc., used for killing, inflicting injury, self-defense, etc. ▸ **weaponry** *noun*

wear verb trans., intrans. (pa t **wore**; pa p **worn**; pr p **wearing**) **1** to be dressed in or to have on one's body: wear a jacket. **2** to adopt (a certain style, haircut, expression, etc.): wears his hair long. **3** to deteriorate or become thin, threadbare, etc., through use: These tires are worn. **4** to make (a hole, bare patch, etc.) in something through heavy use: wore a hole in his sock. **5** to make weary: I'm worn to a frazzle. —noun **1** (often in compounds) clothes suitable for a certain purpose, person, occasion, etc.: skiwear. **2** the amount or type of use something is subjected to: shoes that are meant for heavy wear. **3** deterioration through use: machinery showing signs of wear. —**wear away** to become, or make (something) become, smaller, thinner, etc. **wear off** to become less intense; to disappear gradually. **wear out** to become, or make (something) become, unusable through use. ▸ **wearer** noun

wear and tear damage sustained in the course of continual or normal use.

wearing adj. exhausting: a wearing day in heavy traffic.

wearisome adj. tiring, tedious, or frustrating.

weary (wĭr′ē) adj. (**wearier, weariest**) **1** mentally or physically exhausted. **2** causing mental or physical exhaustion, esp. by being dreary, burdensome, etc.: a weary day at the office. **3** (**weary of**) bored, frustrated, etc. with: I'm weary of the constant interruptions. —verb trans., intrans. (**wearied, wearying**) to make or become weary. ▸ **wearily** adv. ▸ **weariness** noun

weasel noun a small, slender bodied carnivorous mammal.

weather (wĕth′ər) noun the prevailing atmospheric conditions in any area at any time in terms of sunshine, rain, etc. —adj. Naut. on the side exposed to the wind. —verb trans., intrans. (**weathered, weathering**) **1** to expose or be exposed to the effects of wind, sunlight, and precipitation; to alter or be altered in color, texture, shape, etc., through such exposure. **2** to cope with and survive: weathered the crisis well. **3** Naut. to get to the windward side of (a headland, etc.). —**under the weather** colloq. slightly ill.

weatherbeaten adj. **1** of the skin or face tanned or lined by exposure to sunlight and wind. **2** worn or damaged by exposure to the weather.

weatherboard noun clapboard.

weather bound unable to travel or progress because of the weather.

weathercock noun a weathervane in the form of a farmyard cock.

weathering noun physical disintegration and chemical decomposition of rocks, wood, etc. from exposure to wind, rain, etc.

weatherize verb trans. (**weatherized, weatherizing**) to protect (e.g., a house, boat, etc.) against the elements.

weatherproof adj. designed or treated so as to keep out the elements.

weathervane noun a revolving arrow or other device that turns to show the wind direction.

weave verb trans., intrans. (pa t **wove**; pa p **woven**; pr p **weaving**) **1** to make (cloth, a tapestry, etc.) in a loom. **2** to construct (something) by passing flexible strips in and out between fixed canes, etc.: wove a basket. **3** to devise (a story, plot, etc.) or to work (details, etc.) into a story, etc. **4** (pa t and pa p **weaved**) to move to and fro or wind in and out: weaved his way through the crowd. —noun the pattern or compactness of the weaving in a fabric: an open weave. ▸ **weaver** noun

web noun **1** a network of slender threads constructed by a spider to trap insects. **2** an intricate network: a web of lies. **3** a membrane connecting the toes of a swimming bird or animal.

Web noun see **World Wide Web**.

webbed adj. **1** having webs or a web. **2** of fingers or toes partially joined together by a membrane of skin.

webbing noun strong fabric woven into strips for use as belts, straps, etc.

web-footed adj. having webbed feet.

Web page a document on the World Wide Web, usu. having links to other Web pages.

Web site a collection of related Web pages, usu. belonging to the same individual, company, etc. and often prefaced by a home page which allows the user to navigate around the site.

wed verb trans., intrans. (pa t **wedded**; pa p **wed** or **wedded**; pr p **wedding**) **1** to marry. **2** to join in marriage. **3** to unite or combine: wed firmness with compassion.

Wed. abbrev. Wednesday.

wedded adj. **1** (**wedded to**) devoted or committed to (something): wedded to her job. **2** in marriage; married: wedded bliss.

wedding noun **1** a marriage ceremony, often including the associated celebrations. **2** a notable anniversary of a marriage: It's our silver wedding next year.

wedge noun **1** a tapering piece of wood, etc. used to separate, split, etc. things. **2** a wedge-shaped section: a wedge of pizza. **3** a shoe heel in the form of a wedge, tapering toward the sole. **4** Golf a lofting club. **5** see **submarine sandwich**. —verb trans. (**wedged, wedging**) **1** to fix or immobilize in position with, or as if with, a wedge: *wedged the door open.* **2** to thrust or insert: *wedged herself into the corner.* **—drive a wedge between** to cause ill-feeling or division between (e.g., people who were formerly friendly or united).

wedlock *noun* the condition of being married.

Wednesday (wĕnz′dĕ, -dā) *noun* (ABBREV. **Wed.**) the fourth day of the week.

wee *adj.* (**weer, weest**) *Scottish colloq.* **1** small. **2** early: *awake until the wee hours.*

weed *noun* **1** a plant that grows wild and has no specific use or esthetic value. **2** a plant growing where it is not wanted. **3** *colloq.* marijuana. *—verb trans., intrans.* (**weeded, weeding**) **1** to uproot weeds (from a garden, flower bed, lawn, etc.). **2** (*usu.* **weed out**) to identify and eliminate (undesirable, etc. people or things): *weed out the troublemakers.*

weeds *pl. noun* the black mourning clothes worn by a widow.

weedy *adj.* (**weedier, weediest**) **1** overrun with weeds. **2** *of a plant* straggly.

week *noun* **1** a sequence of seven consecutive days, usu. thought of as beginning on Sunday. **2** any period of seven consecutive days. **3** the working days of the week, as distinct from the weekend. **4** the period worked per week: *works a 40-hour week.* *—adv.* by a period of seven days before or after a specified day: *will be here Friday week.*

weekday *noun* any day except Sunday, or except Saturday and Sunday.

weekend *noun* the period from Friday evening through Sunday night.

weekly *adj.* occurring, produced, or issued every week, or once a week. *—adv.* every week; or once a week. *—noun* (*pl.* **weeklies**) a periodical published once a week.

weenie *noun colloq.* a frankfurter.

weeny *adj.* (**weenier, weeniest**) *colloq.* tiny.

weep *verb intrans., trans.* (pa t and pa p **wept**; pr p **weeping**) **1** to shed (tears) as an expression of emotion, esp. grief. **2** to lament or bewail: *We all wept her untimely passing.* **3** *of a wound, etc.* to exude matter; to ooze. *—noun* a bout of weeping.

weeping willow a deciduous tree with long, drooping, branches.

weepy *adj.* (**weepier, weepiest**) **1** shedding tears; tearful. **2** *of a story, etc.* sentimental.

weevil *noun* a type of beetle, some of which are serious pests to crop growers.

weft *noun* the threads that are passed over and under the fixed threads of the warp in a loom. *Also called* **woof.**

weigh (wā) *verb trans., intrans.* (**weighed, weighing**) **1** to measure the weight of. **2** to have a certain weight. **3** (*also* **weigh up**) to consider or assess (facts, possibilities, etc.). **4** to oppress or be a burden. **5** to raise (the

anchor) of a ship before sailing.

weight *noun* **1** (ABBREV. **w., wt.**) the amount that someone or something weighs. **2** *Phys.* (SYMBOL **W**) the gravitational force acting on a body at the surface of the Earth or another planet, star, or moon. **3** a system of units for measuring and expressing weight. **4** something of a standard weight, against which the weight of other things can be measured. **5** a heavy object used to compress, hold down, or counterbalance. **6** a heavy load. **7** *Sport* a heavy object for lifting, throwing, or tossing. **8** a burden. **9** importance, influence, force, etc.: *opinions that carry little weight.* *—verb trans.* (**weighted, weighting**) **1** to add weight to. **2** to burden or oppress. **3** to arrange so as to have an unevenness or bias: *a tax system weighted in favor of the wealthy.* *—pull one's weight* to do one's fair share.

weighted mean mean³ (sense 2b).

weightless *adj.* weighing nothing, esp. in space when not subject to the Earth's gravity. ▸ **weightlessness** *noun*

weightlifting *noun* the sport or exercise of lifting barbells. ▸ **weightlifter** *noun*

weight training muscle-strengthening exercises performed with the aid of weights and pulleys.

weighty *adj.* (**weightier, weightiest**) **1** heavy. **2** having great influence, effect, etc. **3** troublesome or burdensome.

weir (wĭr) *noun* a shallow dam constructed across a river to control its flow.

weird (wĭrd) *adj.* **1** strange, bizarre, or very unusual. **2** spooky or uncanny. ▸ **weirdly** *adv.* ▸ **weirdness** *noun*

weirdo *noun* (*pl.* **weirdos**) *slang* someone who behaves or dresses bizarrely.

welch *verb* same as **welsh.**

welcome *verb trans.* (**welcomed, welcoming**) to receive warmly, gratefully, or with approval: *welcomed her guests / welcomed her help.* *—noun* an act of welcoming. *—adj.* **1** warmly received: *was made welcome.* **2** gladly permitted or encouraged: *You're welcome to borrow it.* **3** much appreciated: *a welcome break from the chores.*

weld *verb trans.* (**welded, welding**) **1** to join (pieces of metal) by heating and melting, or heating and pressure. **2** to unite or blend together. *—noun* a join formed by welding. ▸ **welder** *noun*

welfare *noun* **1** health, comfort, happiness, and general well-being. **2** social work concerned with helping those in need. **3** financial support given to those in need: *a family on welfare.*

welfare state a system in which a government uses tax revenues to look after citizens' welfare, e.g. by the provision of free or subsidized health care, pensions for the elderly, financial support for the sick, etc.

well¹ *adv.* (**better, best**) **1** in a competent, skilled, satisfactory, good, etc. way. **2** thoroughly, properly, carefully, fully, closely, etc. **3** successfully, approvingly, prosperously. **4** by a long way; to some extent. **5** very much: *a project well worth doing.* —*adj.* (**better, best**) having, showing, or enjoying good health. *See syn at* **healthy.** —*interj.* used to express curiosity, surprise, indignation, doubt, etc., or as a means of resuming, continuing, prefacing, etc., esp. in conversation: *Well, after that, I just had to leave.* —**as well 1** in addition. **2** with equally good reason, outcome, etc.: *I might as well give it a try.* **mean well** to have helpful or kindly intentions. **well and truly** thoroughly; completely: *He was well and truly drunk.* **Well done!** used to congratulate someone on an achievement, etc.

well² *noun* **1** a shaft sunk into the ground to obtain a supply of water, oil, gas, etc. **2** a natural spring of water, or a pool fed by it. **3** a source or origin of something. —*verb intrans.* (**welled, welling**) to spring, flow, or flood.

well-appointed *adj., of a house, etc.* well furnished or equipped.

well-balanced *adj.* **1** satisfactorily proportioned. **2** sane, sensible, and stable.

well-being *noun* good health; welfare.

wellborn *adj.* descended from a noble family.

well-bred *adj.* having good manners.

well-disposed *adj.* favorable.

well-done *adj.* cooked thoroughly: *I like my steak well-done.*

well-founded *adj., of suspicions, etc.* based on good grounds; justified.

wellhead *noun* a source.

well-heeled *adj. colloq.* prosperous; wealthy.

well-informed *adj.* **1** having sound, reliable information on a particular matter. **2** full of varied knowledge.

well-intentioned *adj.* having good intentions.

well-known *adj.* familiar or famous.

well-mannered *adj.* polite.

well-meaning *adj.* well-intentioned.

well-meant *adj.* intended well.

wellness *noun* good mental and physical health, the result of a sound diet, good exercise, and regular habits.

> *Usage* The noun *wellness,* often used as an attributive (e.g., in phrases like *wellness programs*), was once objected to as an example of jargon. It has, however, enjoyed such pervasive use in the fields of preventive medicine and sports that it is now considered an unexceptionable item in the lexicon of standard American English.

well-off *adj.* **1** having plenty of money. **2** fortunate: *didn't realize when I was well-off.*

well-nigh *adv.* almost; nearly.

well-oiled *adj.* **1** *colloq.* drunk. **2** smoothly operating from thorough practice: *a well-oiled bureaucracy.*

well-preserved *adj.* **1** in good condition; not decayed. **2** youthful in appearance.

well-read (wĕl‚rĕd′) *adj.* having read many books, etc.; educated.

well-rounded *adj.* complete; fully developed: *a well-rounded education* / *a well-rounded personality.*

wellspring *noun* **1** a spring or fountain. **2** a rich, bountiful, or constant source: *a wellspring of information.*

well-to-do *adj.* financially comfortable; wealthy.

well-turned *adj.* **1** *old use* shapely: *a well-turned ankle.* **2** neatly expressed: *a well-turned phrase.*

well-versed *adj.* thoroughly trained: *She's well-versed in the art of flirting.*

well-wisher *noun* someone who wishes another person well.

well-worn *adj.* **1** showing signs of wear. **2** *of an expression, etc.* too familiar from frequent use; trite.

Welsh (wĕlsh) *noun* **1** the Celtic language of Wales. **2** (**the Welsh**) the people of Wales. —*adj.* of Wales, its people, or the Welsh language. ▸ **Welshman** *noun* ▸ **Welshwoman** *noun*

welsh *or* **welch** *verb intrans.* (**welshed, welshing** *or* **welched, welching**) to fail to pay (a debt) or to fail to fulfill (an obligation, deal, etc.).

Welsh rabbit *or* **Welsh rarebit** a dish of melted cheese served on toast.

welt *noun* **1** a reinforcing band, esp. at the waist of a knitted garment, or around the upper of a shoe. **2** a wale.

welter *noun* a confused mass. —*verb intrans.* (**weltered, weltering**) **1** to lie, roll, or wallow (in something). **2** to be rolled or tossed about.

welterweight *noun* **1** a class for professional boxers weighing between 135 and 147 lbs. (61-66.7 kg), or a similar class but with different weights in amateur boxing and wrestling. **2** a boxer or wrestler of this weight.

wen *noun* a cyst on the skin, usu. of the scalp.

wench *noun old use* **1** a girl or young woman. **2** a prostitute. —*verb intrans.* (**wenched, wenching**) to associate with prostitutes.

wend *verb trans.* (**wended, wending**) to go steadily and purposefully on a route.

went *see* **go¹**.

wept *see* **weep**.

were *see* **be**.

werewolf (wĭr'wŏŏlf., wĕr'-, wər'-) *noun* (*pl.* **werewolves**) a person who allegedly changes into a wolf.

Wesleyan *adj.* relating to John Wesley or to Methodism. —*noun* a Methodist.

west *noun* 1 (ABBREV. **W**) (*also* **the west** *or* **the West**) the direction in which the Sun sets, or any part of the world, a country, town, etc., lying in that direction. 2 (**the West**) the countries of Europe and N America, in contrast to those of Asia. —*adj.* (ABBREV. **W**) 1 in the west; on the side that is on or nearest the west. 2 coming from the direction of the west: *a west wind.* —*adv.* (ABBREV. **W**) toward the west.

westbound *adj.* going or leading toward the west.

westerly *adj.* 1 of a wind, etc. coming from the west. 2 looking, lying, etc., toward the west. —*adv.* to or toward the west. —*noun* (*pl.* **westerlies**) a westerly wind.

western *adj.* (ABBREV. **W**) 1 of or in the west. 2 facing or directed toward the west. —*noun* a movie or story about 19th-c cowboys in the west of the USA.

westerner *or* **Westerner** *noun* a person who lives in or comes from the west, esp. the western part of the USA.

West Indian *noun* a native or citizen of the West Indies. —*adj.* of the West Indies or its people.

wet *adj.* (**wetter, wettest**) 1 covered or soaked in water, rain, or other liquid. 2 of the *weather* rainy. 3 allowing the sale of alcoholic drink. —*noun* 1 moisture. 2 rainy weather; rain. —*verb trans.* (*pa t and pa p* **wet** *or* **wetted**; *pr p* **wetting**) 1 to soak with water or other liquid. 2 to urinate in: *wet the bed.*

wetback *noun* an illegal immigrant worker who has crossed into the USA, esp. from Mexico.

wet blanket a dreary, pessimistic person who dampens the enjoyment of others.

wether (wĕth'ər) *noun* a castrated ram.

wet nurse a woman who breast-feeds another woman's baby.

wet suit a tight-fitting rubber suit permeable by water, but conserving body heat, worn by divers, canoeists, yachtsmen, etc.

whack *verb trans.* (**whacked, whacking**) *colloq.* to hit sharply and resoundingly. —*noun colloq.* 1 a sharp, resounding blow, or the sound of this. 2 an attempt.

whacked *adj. colloq.* (*often* **whacked out**) exhausted, crazy, or drunk.

whacking *adj., adv. colloq.* enormous or enormously.

whacko *noun slang* same as **wacko**.

whacky *adj. slang* same as **wacky**.

whale[1] *noun* a large marine mammal that breathes through a blowhole on the top of its head. —*verb intrans.* (**whaled, whaling**) to hunt whales.

whale[2] *verb trans., intrans.* (**whaled, whaling**) to hit or thrash.

whalebone *noun* a light, flexible, horny substance obtained from the mouths of whales and used in corsets. *Also called* **baleen**.

whale oil oil obtained from whale blubber.

whaler *noun* a person or ship engaged in whaling.

whaling *noun* the activity of hunting and killing whales.

wham *verb trans., intrans.* (**whammed, whamming**) to strike or smash with force. —*noun* a forceful blow or the sound of one.

whammy *noun* (*pl.* **whammies**) *slang* a spell or hex.

wharf *noun* (*pl.* **wharves, wharfs**) a landing stage built along a waterfront for loading and unloading vessels.

wharfage (hwôr'fĭj, wôr'-) *noun* 1 dues paid for the use of a wharf. 2 accommodation for vessels at a wharf.

wharfinger *noun* the owner or supervisor of a wharf.

wharves *see* **wharf**.

what *adj., pron.* 1 used in direct and indirect questions to introduce a request for information or clarification: *What street are we on? / Tell me what you've heard about the matter.* 2 used as an intensifier, esp. in exclamations: *What lies they tell! / What a fool!* 3 the thing or things, etc. that: *What you need is a holiday.* —*adv.* to what extent: *What does that matter?*

whatever *adj., pron.* 1 used as an emphatic form of *what*: *Take whatever you want.* 2 no matter what: *I must finish, whatever happens.* 3 at all: *It has nothing whatever to do with you.* 4 used to express uncertainty: *a didgeridoo, whatever that is.*

whatnot *noun* 1 a stand with shelves for ornaments, etc. 2 *colloq.* other unspecified things: *Bring your reports and whatnot.*

what's-his-name *or* **what's-her-name**, *etc. noun colloq.* a substitute for an unknown or forgotten name.

whatsoever *pron., adj.* of any kind: *offered no encouragement whatsoever.*

wheat *noun* a cereal crop whose grains are ground to make flour. ▸ **wheaten** *adj.*

wheat germ the vitamin-rich embryo of wheat, present in the grain.

wheedle *verb intrans., trans.* (**wheedled, wheedling**) to coax or cajole. ▸ **wheedler** *noun*

wheel *noun* 1 a circular rotating object, e.g., one on which a vehicle moves along the ground, or one used for steering, spinning, etc. **2 (wheels)** *slang* a motor vehicle for personal use: *Do you have wheels tonight?* **3 (wheels)** the workings of an organization, etc.: *The wheels of justice ground slowly.* **4** *Hist.* a circular instrument of torture on which the victim was stretched. **5** a circling or pivoting movement, e.g., of troops. **6** a progression that appears to go around in a circle: *the wheel of fortune.* **7** *slang* an important person: *He's some big wheel in the oil business.* —*verb trans., intrans.* **(wheeled, wheeling) 1** to move or cause to move on wheels: *wheeled up the drive / wheeled the baby round the garden.* **2** to turn or rotate or cause to turn or rotate. —**at or behind the wheel 1** in the driver's seat. **2** in charge. **wheel and deal** *colloq.* to try to succeed by using underhand methods or by having interests in many different ventures, esp. in business. ▸ **wheeler-dealer** *noun*

wheelbarrow *noun* a hand-pushed cart with a wheel in front and two legs at the rear, used for carrying loads, e.g., in the building trade, gardening, etc.

wheelbase *noun* the distance between the front and rear axles of a vehicle.

wheelchair *noun* a chair with wheels that gives mobility to a person whose ability to walk is impaired.

wheelhouse *noun* a shelter on a ship's bridge where the steering gear is housed.

wheelie *noun slang* a trick maneuver where a two-wheeled vehicle is made to travel a short distance on its back wheel only.

wheelwright *noun* a person who makes and repairs wheels.

wheeze *verb intrans.* **(wheezed, wheezing)** to breathe in a labored way, esp. because of a lung disorder. —*noun* **1** a wheezing breath or sound. **2** a joke or prank. ▸ **wheezy** *adj.*

whelk *noun* a large predatory marine mollusk, used as food.

whelp *noun* **1** a young dog or wolf; a puppy. **2** an impudent boy or youth. —*verb intrans.* **(whelped, whelping)** to give birth to puppies or cubs.

when *adv.* at what or which time: *When does the plane arrive? / I cannot remember when I last saw them.* —*conj.* **1** at the time that or during the period that: *It happened when I was abroad.* **2** as soon as: *I'll do it when I've finished this.* **3** at any time that; whenever: *Come when you can.* **4** but just then: *I was about to leave when the telephone rang.* **5** at which time; for at that time: *Call me tomorrow when I'll have more information.* **6** in spite of the fact that; considering that: *Why stand when you can sit?* —*pron.* what or which time: *They stayed talking, until when I can't say.*

whence *adv.* **1** from what place: *She inquired whence they had come.* **2** from what cause or circumstance: *We can't explain whence the mistake arose.* —*conj.* **1** from where: *They returned to the village whence they had come.* **2** from which cause or circumstance: *He has red hair, whence his nickname Red.*

> **Usage** Since the denotation of *from* is included in the definition of *whence*, careful writers and speakers try to avoid the redundancy, e.g., in They returned to the village *from whence* they came, saying simply *whence* they came, archaic Biblical usages notwithstanding.

whenever *conj.* **1** at any or every time that: *He gets furious whenever he fails to get his way.* **2** if ever; no matter when: *I'll be here whenever you need me.* —*adv.* used to indicate an unknown or unspecified time: *at the end of the fourth business quarter, whenever that is.*

where *adv.* **1** in, at, or to which place or direction: *Where is she going? / I don't know where this road takes us.* **2** in what respect: *They showed me where I'd gone wrong.* —*pron.* what place: *Where have you come from?* —*conj., pron.* **1** in, at, or to the, or any, place that; in, at, or to which: *This is the village where I was born.* **2** in any case in which: *We try to keep families together where possible.* **3** the aspect or respect in which: *That's where you are wrong.* **4** and there: *We stopped in Chicago, where we picked up George.*

> **Usage** Use *from* with *where* when *where* refers to a point of origin: *Where* have you come *from?* Avoid the use of *to* prepositionally when *where* refers to a point of destination, except in the colloquial question *Where to?*, usu. asked by, e.g., drivers of their passengers. Thus, it is better to say *Where* is he going?, not *Where* is he going *to?* Avoid the preposition *at* with *where* when *where* refers to the site or location of something specified: *Where* is the bus station? (not *Where* is the bus station *at?*).

whereabouts *noun* (*sing., pl.*) a location: *Her whereabouts is an issue for the police. / His whereabouts are uncertain at this time.*

whereas *conj.* **1** when in fact: *She thought she'd failed, whereas she'd done well.* **2** but; by contrast: *I'm a pessimist, whereas my sister is an optimist.*

whereby *conj.* by means of which: *Triage is a system whereby the most seriously injured patients are treated first.*

wherefore *conj., adv.* for what purpose or reason. —*noun* a reason: *the whys and wherefores of the contract.*

wherein *formal adv.* in what respect: *Wherein have we wronged you?* —*conj.* in which place; also, how: *The villages wherein the peasants live have been bombed. / I will show you wherein you have wronged me.*

whereof *conj.* of which: *Recall the circumstances whereof I told you.*

whereon *adv.* old use on which.

wheresoever *conj. formal* no matter where: *We shall find them, wheresoever they may be.*

whereupon *conj.* at which point: *The lights went out, whereupon a person screamed.*

wherever *conj.* in, at, or to any or every place or situation that: *They were welcomed wherever they went.* —*adv.* 1 no matter where: *I won't lose touch, wherever I go.* 2 used as an emphatic form of where: *Wherever can they be?* 3 used to indicate an unknown place: *the Round House, wherever that is.*

wherewithal *noun* (**the wherewithal**) the means or necessary resources, esp. money. —*pron. old use* with which.

wherry *noun* (*pl.* **wherries**) 1 a long, light rowboat, esp. for transporting passengers. 2 a light barge.

whet *verb trans.* (**whetted, whetting**) 1 to sharpen (a blade) by rubbing it against stone, etc. 2 to intensify (appetite, etc.).

whether *conj.* 1 used to introduce an indirect question or a clause expressing doubt, etc.: *We asked whether it was raining.* 2 used to state certainty where two possibilities apply: *He said he was leaving, whether they offered him a raise or not. / The rules, whether fair or unfair, are not our concern.*

whetstone *noun* a stone for sharpening blades.

whey *noun* the watery content of milk.

which *adj., pron.* 1 used like *what* in seeking to identify or specify a thing or person: *Which twin did you mean?* 2 used to introduce some defining or identifying clauses and to introduce commenting clauses: *The evidence on which it is based is weak. / This house, which lies back from the road, is the one you want. 3 any that: *Tell me which books you'd like to borrow.*

whichever *pron., adj.* 1 the one or ones that; any that: *Take whichever are suitable. / Take whichever coat fits better.* 2 according to which: *at 10:00 or 10:30, whichever is more convenient.* 3 no matter which: *We'll be late, whichever way we go. / I'll be satisfied, whichever you choose.*

whiff *noun* 1 a slight smell. 2 a puff or slight rush: *a whiff of smoke.* 3 a hint: *at the first whiff of scandal.* —*verb trans.; intrans.* to puff.

Whig (hwĭg, wĭg) *noun Hist.* 1 a member of the Whigs, a British political party later known as the Liberal Party. 2 a member of a 19th-c US political party opposing the Democratic Party. *See also* **Tory.**

while *conj.* 1 at the same time as: *She sang while he played the piano.* 2 for as long as; for the whole time that: *guards us while we sleep.* 3 during the time that: *happened while we were abroad.* 4 whereas: *He likes camping, while she prefers sailing.* 5 although: *While I see your point, I still cannot agree.* —*noun* 1 a space or lapse of time: *after a while.* 2 trouble; effort: *Is this worth my while?* —*verb trans.* (**whiled, whiling**) to pass (time) in a leisurely or undemanding way: *whiled away the hours on the beach.*

whim *noun* a sudden, whimsical impulse or change of mind.

whimper *verb intrans., trans.* (**whimpered, whimpering**) 1 to cry feebly or plaintively. 2 to say plaintively. —*noun* a feebly plaintive cry.

whimsical *adj.* 1 delicately fanciful or playful. 2 odd, weird, or fantastic. 3 given to having whims. ▸ **whimsicality** *noun*

whimsy (hwĭm′zē, wĭm′-) *noun* (*pl.* **whimsies**) 1 a quaint, fanciful notion. 2 quaint or bizarre humor.

whine *verb intrans., trans.* (**whined, whining**) 1 to whimper. 2 to cry fretfully. 3 to complain peevishly. 4 to speak in a thin, ingratiating, or servile voice. 5 to say peevishly. —*noun* 1 a. whimper. 2 a continuous high-pitched noise. 3 a thin, ingratiating nasal tone of voice.

whinny *verb intrans.* (**whinnied, whinnying, whinnies**) *of a horse* to neigh softly. —*noun* (*pl.* **whinnies**) a gentle neigh.

whip *noun* 1 a lash with a handle, for driving animals or beating people. 2 a member of a political party in a legislature responsible for other members' discipline, attendance, etc. 3 a dessert of beaten egg whites, cream, and usu. fruit flavoring. 4 a whipping action, motion, or noise. —*verb trans., intrans.* (**whipped, whipping**) 1 to strike or thrash with a whip. 2 to lash with the action, motion, force, etc. of a whip. 3 to take, pull, snatch, move, etc. quickly: *whipped out a revolver / whipped round the corner and was gone.* 4 to rouse into a certain state: *whipped the crowd into a fury.* 5 to beat (egg whites, cream, etc.) until stiff. 6 *colloq.* to outdo, outwit, or defeat. —**whip up** 1 to arouse (support, enthusiasm, or other feelings). 2 to prepare (a meal, etc.) at short notice.

whipcord noun **1** strong, fine, tightly twisted cord. **2** cotton or worsted cloth with a diagonal rib.

whiplash noun **1** the lash of a whip, or the motion it represents. **2** a neck injury caused by the sudden jerking back of the head, esp. as a result of a motor-vehicle collision.

whippersnapper noun colloq. a cheeky young lad.

whippet noun a dog, like a greyhound, but smaller.

whipping boy a scapegoat, esp. someone blamed for the shortcomings of others.

whippoorwill noun a nocturnal US bird noted for its distinctive, repetitive call.

whipsaw noun a crosscut saw with a narrow blade, operated by two people. —verb trans. (pa t **whipsawed**; pa p **whipsawed** or **whipsawn**; pr p **whipsawing**) to attack, jostle, or defeat in two directions at the same time.

whipstock noun the handle of a whip.

whir verb intrans. (**whirred, whirring**) to turn or spin with a humming sound. —noun a humming sound.

whirl verb intrans., trans. (**whirled, whirling**) **1** to spin or revolve, or cause to spin or revolve, rapidly. **2** to reel, esp. from excitement, etc. —noun **1** a circling or spiraling movement or pattern: a whirl of smoke. **2** a round of intense activity: a whirl of parties. **3** a dizzy state.

whirligig (hwər′lĕ-gĭg′, wər′-) noun **1** a spinning toy, esp. a top. **2** a merry-go-round. **3** a dizzying round of activity, progression of events, etc.

whirlpool noun a violent, almost circular eddy of water.

whirlwind noun a violently spiraling column of air. —adj. rapid: a whirlwind romance.

whirlybird noun colloq. a helicopter.

whisk verb trans. (**whisked, whisking**) **1** to beat (egg whites, cream, etc.) until stiff. **2** to sweep, brush, move, or transport rapidly or with short, rapid movements: whisked her into the hospital. —noun **1** a whisking movement or action. **2** a hand-held implement for whisking egg whites, etc.

whisker noun **1** a long coarse hair around the mouth of a cat, mouse, dog, etc. **2** (**whiskers**) a man's beard, esp. the parts growing on the cheeks. **3** the tiniest possible margin: escaped by a whisker.

whiskey or **whisky** noun (pl. **whiskeys** or **whiskies**) an alcoholic spirit distilled from a fermented mash of cereal grains, e.g., barley, wheat, or rye; a drink of this.

Based on Scottish Gaelic uisge beatha, meaning 'water of life'.

whisper verb intrans., trans. (**whispered, whispering**) **1** to speak or say quietly, breathing rather than voicing the words. **2** to speak, say, plot, etc. in secrecy or confidence. **3** to make a soft, rustling sound. —noun **1** a low-toned, quiet, or secretive level of speech. **2** (often **whispers**) a rumor or piece of gossip. **3** a soft, rustling sound.

whist noun a card game, usu. for two pairs of players, in which the object is to try to take the majority of available tricks.

whistle (hwĭs′əl, wĭs′-) noun **1** a sound produced by forcing air through pursed lips or through the teeth, to make a musical noise, attract someone's attention, etc. **2** a similar noise, e.g., made by a bird, a railway locomotive, or kettle. **3** any device for making such a sound, e.g., a small metal device blown by a referee to regulate play on the field, or a simple musical instrument. —verb intrans., trans. (**whistled, whistling**) **1** to produce a whistle or whistle-like noise. **2** to blow a whistle, or play on a whistle. ▸ **whistler** noun

whistleblower, whistle-blower or **whistle blower** noun slang someone, esp. a person inside an organization who exposes illegal or dishonest practices, or someone involved in such things, to the authorities.

whistle-stop adj. of a tour, etc. making a number of brief stops at many different places.

whit noun a little or the least bit.

white adj. **1** of the color of snow, the color that reflects all light. **2** (also **White**) of people belonging to one of the pale-skinned races, esp. one of European origin. **3** abnormally pale, from shock or illness. **4** albino. **5** pale-colored, as distinct from darker types: white wine / white bread. —noun **1** the color of snow: dressed all in white. **2** (often **White**) a white person. **3** (also **egg white**) the clear fluid surrounding the yolk of an egg. **4** the white part of the eyeball, surrounding the iris. **5** Games a white playing-piece in chess or checkers, a white ball in pool, etc. **6** (**whites**) white material, garments, etc., e.g. household linen, white clothes worn in tennis, or as a dress uniform in the US Navy and Coast Guard. ▸ **whiteness** noun

white ant a termite.

whitebread adj. colloq. characterized by or having typically white, middle-class attributes, values, attitudes, etc.

white-collar adj. doing skilled clerical or professional work. See also **blue-collar**.

white elephant a possession that serves no real purpose and is inconvenient or expensive to keep.

white feather a symbol of cowardice.

whitefish *noun* a white-fleshed food fish, e.g., a cod, sole, or haddock.

white flag a signal of surrender, truce, or peace.

white gold an alloy of gold used for jewelry.

white goods large domestic appliances, e.g., washers, driers, dishwashers, and stoves.

Whitehall *noun* a street in London where the Prime Minister and senior government officials have homes with offices nearby, and hence a way of referring to the British government.

white heat an intense heat, or a level of intense excitement, enthusiasm, etc.

white-hot *adj.* intensely hot, exciting, passionate, etc.

White House the residence of the US President, and hence a way of referring to the executive branch of the US government.

white knight a person who rescues a company financially, esp. from a hostile takeover bid.

white-knuckle *adj. slang* causing extreme anxiety, alarm, terror, etc.: *a white-knuckle roller-coaster ride.*

white lead a mixture of lead carbonate and lead hydroxide in the form of a white powder, used as coloring matter.

white lie a lie with no harmful consequences, esp. one told to avoid hurting someone's feelings.

whiten *verb trans., intrans.* (**whitened, whitening**) to make or become white or whiter. ▸ **whitener** *noun*

white noise noise in which there is a large number of frequencies of roughly equal intensity.

white-out *noun* conditions of poor visibility in snowy weather.

white paper a government report.

white sale a sale of household linens.

white slave a girl or woman forced into prostitution.

white sugar refined sugar.

white tie 1 a white bow tie, part of men's formal evening dress. **2** formal evening dress for men.

white wall a motor vehicle tire with a band of white on the part around the hubcap.

whitewash *noun* **1** a mixture of lime and water, for giving a white coating to esp. outside walls. **2** an act or the process of covering up something potentially scandalous or embarrassing, or the result of doing this. **3** *colloq.* a resounding victory over an opponent who fails to score. —*verb trans.* (**whitewashed, whitewashing**) **1** to coat with whitewash. **2** to cover up a potentially embarrassing or scandalous incident, etc. **3** *colloq.* to achieve a resounding victory over an opponent who fails to score.

white whale a small toothed whale. *Also called* **beluga.**

whither *adv.* to which place or wherever.

whiting[1] *noun* an edible marine fish.

whiting[2] *noun* ground white chalk, used in putty, whitewash, and silver cleaners.

whitish *adj.* somewhat or nearly white.

whitlow *noun* an inflammation of the finger or toe, esp. near the nail.

whittle *verb trans., intrans.* (**whittled, whittling**) **1** to cut, carve, or pare (a stick, piece of wood, etc.). **2** (**whittle away**) to consume, eat away at, etc. (something) bit by bit. **3** (**whittle down**) to reduce (something) gradually or persistently.

whiz *or* **whizz** *colloq. verb intrans.* (**whizzed, whizzing, whizzes**) **1** to fly through the air, esp. with a whistling noise. **2** to move fast. —*noun* an expert.

whizz kid *colloq.* someone who achieves success early through ability, inventiveness, dynamism, or ambition.

WHO *abbrev.* World Health Organization.

who (hōō) *pron.* **1** used in direct and indirect questions to introduce a request for formation or clarification as to the identity of a person or people: *Who is at the door?* **2** used like *that* to introduce a subordinate clause: *Anyone who wants this can have it. / Julius Caesar, who was murdered in 44 BC, was a great leader.*

whoa (wō, hwō, hō) *interj.* used as a command to stop, esp. to a horse.

whodunit (hōō-dən'ĭt) *noun slang* a detective novel, play, etc.; a mystery.

whoever (hōō-ĕv'ər) *pron.* **1** used as an emphatic form of *who* or *whom: Whoever is that at the door?* **2** no matter who: *Whoever is appointed faces a huge task.* **3** used to indicate a person whose name is not known: *St. Fiacre, whoever he was.*

whole (hōl) *noun* the complete thing, or something complete in itself. —*adj.* **1** entire or complete: *spent the whole day on it.* **2** unbroken, intact. —*adv. colloq.* completely; altogether: *a whole new approach.* ▸ **wholeness** *noun* ▸ **wholly** *adv.*

wholehearted *adj.* sincere and enthusiastic. ▸ **wholeheartedly** *adv.*

whole hog *slang* the fullest possible extent: *Let's go the whole hog and spend April in Paris.*

whole note a musical note, equal to a semibreve.

wholesale *noun* the sale of goods in large quantities to a retailer. —*adj.* on a huge scale and without discrimination: *wholesale destruction.* —*adv.* of or by a type of selling in quantity to a retailer. *See also* **retail.** ▸ **wholesaler** *noun*

wholesome *adj.* (**wholesomer, wholesomest**) 1 attractively healthy. 2 promoting, or contributing to, the health of the body, mind, or character.

whole-wheat *adj.* containing or made from the whole wheat kernel, including the bran.

whom *pron.* used as the objective of *who: Whom do you want? / To whom are you referring?*

whomever *pron.* used as the object of a verb or preposition to denote any person or people that: *I will write to whomever they appoint.*

whomsoever *pron.* whomever.

whoop (hōōp, whōōp) *noun* 1 a loud cry, e.g., of delight, triumph. 2 a noisy breath typical of whooping cough. —*verb intrans., trans.* (**whooped, whooping**) to utter or say with a whoop. —**whoop it up** *colloq.* to celebrate noisily.

whoopee (wŏŏp′ē, hwŏŏp′ē) *interj. slang* used to express exuberant delight.

whooping cough a highly contagious disease, mainly affecting children, characterized by bouts of violent coughing. *Also called* **pertussis.**

whoops *interj.* used to express surprise or concern, esp. at a mistake.

whop *verb trans.* (**whopped, whopping**) 1 to hit; to beat. 2 to defeat soundly.

whopper *noun slang* 1 something very large: *a whopper of a fish.* 2 a big lie.

whopping *adj., adv. slang* huge; enormous.

whore (hôr) *noun* 1 a prostitute. 2 a woman considered sexually promiscuous. —*verb intrans.* (**whored, whoring**) 1 to make use of prostitutes. 2 to engage in prostitution or promiscuous sex.

whorehouse *noun* a brothel.

whorl (hwôrl, wôrl) *noun* 1 *Bot.* a circular arrangement of several petals, leaves, or other identical structures around the same point on a plant. 2 *Zool.* one of the coils in the spiral shell of a mollusk. 3 a fingerprint in which there is a spiral arrangement of the ridges on the skin.

whose *pron.* used as the possessive of *who: Whose is this jacket? / We do not know whose these are.*

whosoever *pron.* whoever.

why *adv.* for what reason: *Why do you ask?* —*conj.* for or because of which: *There was no reason why I should get involved.* —*interj.* used to express surprise, indignation, etc.: *Why, you little monster!* —*noun* a reason: *the whys and wherefores.*

wick *noun* a string in a candle that burns when lit and draws up the wax into the flame.

wicked *adj.* 1 evil; sinful; immoral. 2 mischievous: *a wicked sense of humor.* 3 very severe: *wicked weather.* 4 *slang* excellent or highly skillful: *went to this new club and it was totally wicked.* ▸ **wickedly** *adv.* ▸ **wickedness** *noun*

wicker *adj.* made of interwoven twigs, canes, rushes, etc. ▸ **wickerwork** *noun*

wicket *noun* 1 *Cricket* three wooden posts topped by two bails and defended by a batsman. 2 a small wire arch in croquet. 3 a small door or gate.

wicketkeeper *noun Cricket* a fielder who stands immediately behind the wicket.

wickiup *noun* a Native American hut.

wide *adj.* 1 large in extent from side to side. 2 measuring a certain amount from side to side. 3 open or apart to the fullest extent. 4 covering a great variety; extensive: *a wide range of stock.* 5 large: *a wide difference.* 6 deviating from the point or off the mark. —*adv.* 1 over an extensive area: *traveling far and wide.* 2 extensively; far apart. 3 off the mark: *shot wide of the target.* ▸ **widely** *adv.*

-wide *combining form* forming words denoting the whole extent of: *nationwide.*

wide-angle lens a camera lens with a viewing angle of over 50°.

wide area network (ABBREV. **WAN**) a network of computers spread over a wide region, linked by means of modems, telephone lines, etc.

widen *verb trans., intrans.* (**widened, widening**) to make or become wide or wider.

wide-open *adj. slang* having no laws or no effective law-enforcement agencies: *a wide-open border town.*

wide-ranging *adj.,* of interests, discussions, etc. covering a large variety of subjects.

widespread *adj.* 1 extending over a wide area. 2 affecting or involving large numbers of people: *widespread agreement.*

widgeon *or* **wigeon** (wĭj′ən) *noun* a freshwater dabbling duck.

widget *noun* a small manufactured item or component; a gadget.

widow *noun* 1 a woman whose husband is dead and who has not remarried. 2 a woman whose husband or partner spends a lot of time following a hobby or interest that does not involve her: *a golf widow.* 3 a last line of a paragraph when it appears in print at the top of a page, or any other undesirably stranded piece of printed text. *See also* **orphan** (sense). —*verb trans.* (**widowed, widowing**) to leave (someone) a widow or widower.

widower *noun* a man whose wife is dead and who has not remarried.

width *noun* 1 extent from side to side. 2 the condition or degree of being wide; wideness. 3 the distance from side to side across a swimming pool.

widthwise *adv., adj.* across the width: *folded widthwise.*

wield *verb trans.* (**wielded, wielding**) **1** to brandish or use (a tool, weapon, etc.). **2** to have or exert (power, authority, etc.).

wife *noun* (*pl.* **wives**) **1** a woman to whom a man is married; a married woman. **2** (*often in compounds*) a woman: *fishwife, housewife.* ▸ **wifely** *adj.*

wig *noun* an artificial covering of hair for the head.

wigeon *noun* same as **widgeon**.

wigger *noun* slang, used disparagingly by Black youths a white teenager who adopts the speech, clothing, mannerisms, music, etc. of Black youth culture, esp. hip-hop.

wiggle *verb intrans., trans.* (**wiggled, wiggling**) to move, esp. jerkily, from side to side or up and down. ▸ **wiggly** *adj.*

wight *noun old use* a person.

wigwam *noun* a Native American tent.

wild *adj.* **1** of animals and plants living or growing in their natural habitat; not domesticated or cultivated. **2** ferocious, fierce, or savage. **3** of land or countryside desolate, rugged, inhospitable, or uninhabitable. **4** unrestrained, uncontrolled, frantic, or distraught. **5** disheveled, disordered, stormy. **6** of a guess, etc. approximate or random. **7** (*usu.* **wild about**) intensely keen on, fond of, or enthusiastic about (someone or something). **8** colloq. furious. **9** slang excellent; terrific. —*noun* **1** (**the wild**) an animal's or plant's natural habitat: *returned the cub to the wild.* **2** (*often* **the wilds**) a lonely, sparsely inhabited region, usu. far away from urban areas: *a cabin in the wilds.* —**run wild 1** of a garden or plants to revert to an overgrown, uncultivated state. **2** of, e.g., children to live a life of freedom, with little discipline or control. ▸ **wildly** *adv.* ▸ **wildness** *noun*

wild boar a boar (sense 1).

wild card 1 Cards a designated card that a holder can assign a chosen value to. **2** slang an unpredictable person or factor. **3** Comput. a symbol, e.g., an asterisk, that can be used to represent any character or set of characters, e.g., during a search.

wildcat *noun* **1** a small or medium-sized nondomestic cat, e.g. an ocelot, or bobcat. **2** a well drilled for oil or natural gas in an area regarded as unproductive. **3** a strike not authorized by a union. —*adj.* **1** of an industrial strike not called or approved by a union. **2** of a business scheme, etc. speculative. **3** of an oil or gas well exploratory; experimental. —*verb trans., intrans.* (**wildcatted, wildcatting**) **1** to prospect for (oil or gas) speculatively. **2** to take part in an unauthorized strike.

wildebeest (wĭl'də-bēst,) *noun* (*pl.* **wildebeest, wildebeests**) the gnu.

wilderness *noun* **1** an uncultivated or uninhabited region. **2** an overgrown tangle of weeds, etc.

wildfire *noun* a fast-spreading, extensive fire that is difficult to control. —**spread like wildfire** of, e.g., disease, rumor, etc. to spread rapidly and extensively.

wildfowl *noun* (*pl.* **wildfowl, wildfowls**) **1** a game bird, esp. a duck or other waterfowl. **2** such birds collectively.

wild-goose chase a search that is bound to be unsuccessful.

wildlife *noun* wild animals, birds, and plants in general.

wild oats indiscretions, high living, or casual sexual relations, or a combination of these, esp. those of a person's youth.

wile *noun* **1** (**wiles**) charming personal ways. **2** a piece of cunning; a ruse, trick, maneuver, or stratagem. —*verb trans., intrans.* (**wiled, wiling**) **1** old use to lure or entice (someone). **2** to pass (time) pleasantly or indolently. See also **wily**.

wilful *adj.* same as **willful**.

will[1] *verb aux.* (*pa t* **would**) **1** used for expressing the future tense, intention, determination, requests, commands, etc.: *I will phone you tomorrow.* **2** used for expressing ability, readiness, inevitability, assumption, or probability: *The table will seat ten people.* / *That will be Ted at the door.* See also **shall**.

will[2] *noun* **1** the power of conscious decision. **2** someone's own preference or determination. **3** desire or determination: *the will to live.* **4** a document detailing the disposal of personal property, etc., after a person's death. —*verb trans.* (**willed, willing**) **1** to compel by, or as if by, exerting one's will: *She willed herself to keep going.* **2** formal to decide. **3** to bequeath in a will: *willed the money to charity.*

willful *or* **wilful** *adj.* **1** deliberate; intentional: *willful destruction.* **2** headstrong, obstinate, or self-willed: *a willful child.* ▸ **willfully** *adv.* ▸ **willfulness** *noun*

willies *pl. noun* (**the willies**) colloq. a feeling of anxiety or unease: *a horror flick that gave me the willies.*

willing *adj.* **1** ready, glad, or not disinclined to do something: *were willing to help.* **2** eager and cooperative: *a willing helper.* **3** voluntary. ▸ **willingly** *adv.* ▸ **willingness** *noun*

will-o'-the-wisp *noun* **1** ignis fatuus. **2** something elusive.

willow *noun* **1** a deciduous tree or shrub with slender flexible branches, or its durable wood. **2** a cricket or baseball bat.

willowy adj. (**willowier, willowiest**) of a person tall, slender, and graceful.

willpower or **will power** noun the determination, persistence, and self-discipline needed to accomplish something.

willy-nilly adv. **1** whether one wishes or not; regardless. **2** haphazardly; randomly.

> From the phrase will I, nill I, meaning 'whether I want or don't want'

wilt verb intrans. (**wilted, wilting**) **1** of a plant to droop or become limp from insufficient water. **2** to droop from fatigue or heat.

wily (wī′lē) adj. (**wilier, wiliest**) cunningly astute. ▸ **wiliness** noun

wimp slang noun a feeble, ineffectual person. —verb intrans. (**wimped, wimping**) (**wimp out**) to back out of doing something through lack of courage. ▸ **wimpish** adj. ▸ **wimpy** adj.

WIMP noun Comput. a user interface consisting of windows, icons, mouse, pull-down menus, allowing the user to click on icons on the screen to operate system commands.

wimple noun a woman's headdress, esp. a nun's.

win verb trans., intrans. (pa t and pa p **won**; pr p **winning**) **1** to be victorious, come first, or beat an opponent, rival, enemy, etc. **2** to compete or fight for and obtain (a victory, prize, etc.). **3** to obtain by struggle, effort, ability, etc. **4** (also **win through** or **out**) to be successful, or succeed in getting, esp. after a struggle. —noun **1** a victory or first place, esp. in a sports match or competition. **2** an amount won, gained, or earned.

wince verb intrans. (**winced, wincing, winces**) to shrink back, start, or grimace, e.g., in pain or anticipation of it. —noun a start or grimace in reaction to pain, etc.

winch noun a machine for hoisting or hauling heavy loads; a windlass. —verb trans. (**winched, winching, winches**) (usu. **winch up** or **in**) to hoist or haul (something) with a winch.

wind[1] (wĭnd) noun **1** the natural movement of air across the Earth's surface. **2** a current of air produced artificially, e.g., by a fan. **3** breath or breath supply: short of wind. **4** scent, e.g., of game, a hunter, etc. **5** flatulence. **6** empty, pompous, or trivial talk. —verb trans. (**winded, winding**) to deprive of breath temporarily: She was winded by her marathon run.

wind[2] (wīnd) verb trans., intrans. (pa t and pa p **wound**; pr p **winding**) **1** to wrap, twist, or coil. **2** to progress on a path with many twists and turns. **3** to tighten the spring of (a clock, watch, or other clockwork device) by turning a knob or key. —**wind up 1** to end up:

wound up in jail. **2** to make (someone) tense, nervous, or excited.

windbag noun slang a person full of pompous, tedious, or trivial talk.

windbreak noun a barrier giving protection from the wind.

windbreaker noun a warm outer jacket.

wind-chill factor a lowering of the air temperature that results from taking the speed and temperature of the wind into account. Also called **chill factor**.

wind cone a windsock.

windfall noun **1** an unexpected financial gain, or other piece of good fortune. **2** a fruit, esp. an apple, blown down from its tree.

wind farm an area with several wind turbines for converting wind energy into electricity.

winding sheet a cloth for wrapping up a corpse; a shroud.

wind instrument a musical instrument, e.g., a clarinet, flute, trumpet, etc., played by blowing air through it.

windjammer noun a large, fast, sailing ship.

windlass (wĭnd′ləs) noun a machine for hauling or hoisting weights.

windmill noun **1** a mechanical device operated by wind-driven revolving sails used esp. for milling flour. **2** a pinwheel (sense 1).

window noun **1** an opening in the wall of a building to let in light and air. **2** any similar opening, e.g. for displaying goods in a shop. **3** a frame, usu. fitted with glass, that goes into such an opening. **4** a space or time for something or into which something can be fitted: a window of opportunity. **5** an enclosed rectangular area on the visual display unit of a computer, which can be used as an independent screen.

window box a box fitted along an exterior window ledge; for growing plants.

window-dressing noun **1** the art of making displays in store windows; a store window display. **2** the art or practice of giving something superficial appeal by skillful presentation; the result of doing this.

window-shop verb intrans. (**window-shopped, window-shopping**) to spend time looking in store windows to see what is on offer, usu. without buying anything.

windpipe noun the trachea.

wind power energy generated from wind, used to drive machinery, generate electricity, etc.

windshield noun the front window of a motor vehicle.

windsock noun a fabric device, e.g., at an airport, that shows the direction and speed of the wind. Also called **wind cone**.

windstorm noun a storm that packs high winds but little or no rain.

windsurfing *noun* the sport of riding the waves on a sailboard. *Also called* **boardsailing, sailboarding, windsailing.**

windswept *adj.* **1** exposed to strong winds. **2** disheveled from or otherwise showing the effects of exposure to wind.

wind-up *noun colloq.* **1** a conclusion. **2** *Baseball* a pitcher's preparatory movements prior to releasing the ball.

windward (wĭn'dwərd) *noun* the side of a boat, etc., facing the wind. —*adj., adv.* toward or on the side facing the wind.

windy *adj.* (**windier, windiest**) **1** exposed to or characterized by strong wind: *a windy day.* **2** using too many words..

wine *noun* **1** an alcoholic drink made from the fermented juice of grapes, or one made from other fruits or plants. **2** the dark red color of red wine. —*adj.* of the dark red color of red wine.

winery *noun* (*pl.* **wineries**) a place where wine is prepared and stored.

wineskin *noun* the skin of a goat or sheep sewn up and used for holding wine.

winetasting *noun* a social gathering at which people sample and compare various wines.

wing *noun* **1** a bird's or bat's forelimb that is adapted for flight. **2** a membranous projection that enables an insect to fly. **3** any similar structure, e.g. on either side of the body of an aircraft, an extension on the fruit of the elm or maple tree. **4** a part of a building projecting from a central or main section. **5** (**wings**) the areas at the sides of a stage. **6** an edge or margin of something, e.g., a soccer pitch, a political party, etc. or other body: *plays on the wing / the conservative wing.* —*verb trans.* (**winged, winging**) **1** to wound, usu. superficially. **2** (**wing one's,** etc. **way**) to travel by flying, or as if by flying, quickly: *a letter is winging its way to you.* **3** *poetic* to fly over, or skim lightly. **4** *colloq.* to improvise; to do or say without preparation or forethought: *forgot my notes, so I just had to wing it.* —**on the wing 1** in flight; flying. **2** while doing something else: *had lunch on the wing.* **under someone's wing** under the protection or guidance of someone.

wing chair an armchair that has a high back with forward-projecting side parts.

wingding *noun colloq.* a wild, lively party.

wingspan *noun* the distance from the tip of one wing to the tip of another, e.g., of an aircraft, bird, etc. *Also called* **wing spread.**

wink *verb intrans., trans.* (**winked, winking**) **1** to shut an eye briefly, usu. as an informal, esp. conspiratorial, signal. **2** (**wink at**) to ignore or pretend not to notice (an offense, improper procedure, etc.). —*noun* an act of winking. *See also* **forty winks.**

winkle *noun* a periwinkle.

winner *noun* a person, animal, vehicle, etc., that wins a competition or contest.

winning *adj.* **1** attractive or charming: *a winning smile.* **2** securing victory: *the winning shot.* —*noun* (**winnings**) money won, esp. in gambling. ▸ **winningly** *adv.*

winnow *verb trans.* (**winnowed, winnowing**) **1** to separate chaff from (grain) by blowing a current of air through it or fanning (it). **2** to weed out; to sift (evidence, etc.).

wino *noun* (*pl.* **winos**) *slang* a person who is habitually drunk, esp. on cheap wine, usu. someone living rough.

winsome *adj.* charming; captivating: *a winsome smile.*

winter *noun* **1** (*also* **Winter**) the coldest season of the year, between autumn and spring. **2** a period of adversity, etc. **3** a person's old age. —*adj.* of or belonging to winter. —*verb intrans.* (**wintered, wintering**) to spend the winter in a specified place, usu. other than one's normal home.

wintergreen *noun* **1** an evergreen plant with oval leaves and drooping bell-shaped flowers. **2** an aromatic oil obtained from the leaves of this plant, used medicinally and as a food flavoring. *Also called* **oil of wintergreen.**

winterize *verb trans.* (**winterized, winterizing**) to prepare (e.g., a residence) or equip (e.g., a motor vehicle) for the cold and precipitation characteristic of winter.

winter sports sports, e.g., skiing, tobogganing, skating, etc., held on snow or ice.

wintertime *noun* the season of winter.

wintry *adj.* (**wintrier, wintriest**) **1** like or characteristic of winter. **2** unfriendly, cold, or hostile. ▸ **wintriness** *noun*

wipe *verb trans.* (**wiped, wiping**) **1** to clean or dry with a cloth, etc. **2** to dry (dishes). **3** to remove dirt, etc. from: *wiped his feet on the doormat.* **4** *Comput.* to erase (data, software, etc.) from a tape or disk. **5** to remove or get rid of: *wiped the incident from his memory.* —**wipe out 1** to remove or get rid of: *wipe out an unpleasant memory.* **2** to destroy, obliterate, or wreck. **3** *colloq.* to kill or murder: *an entire family wiped out in a house fire.* **4** of a skier, surfer, etc. to lose balance and fall over.

wire *noun* **1 a** a narrow, flexible strand of metal. **b** a length of this, usu. wrapped in insulating material, for conveying an electric current. **2** *colloq.* a hidden microphone. **3** a telegram. —*verb trans.* (**wired, wiring**) **1** to send a telegram to; to send (a message, money, etc.) by telegram. **2** (*also* **wire up**) to fit with a wire or wires; to connect (an electrical device, etc.) to a power source. **3** *colloq.* to fit (a room, etc) with surveillance equipment. —**down to the wire** *colloq.* to the finish or the very last minute. **get one's,** etc. **wires crossed** to misunderstand or be confused about something.

wired *adj.* **1** *colloq.* fitted with a hidden microphone or hidden surveillance equipment. **2** *slang* extremely nervous, edgy, etc., esp. from too much caffeine, etc. **3** *slang* extremely drunk or stoned. **4** *colloq.* using computers, esp. connected to the Internet: *a wired business getting customer orders from its Web site.*

wire-haired *adj.*, of a breed of dog having a coarse, usu. wavy coat.

wireless *noun* **1** *Brit. old use* a radio. **2** wireless telegraphy. —*adj.* of or relating to cellular phone technology.

wireless telegraphy the transmission of signals by means of electromagnetic waves.

wiretap *verb trans.* (**wiretapped, wiretapping**) to connect a surreptitious listening device to (a telephone). ▸ **wiretapper** *noun* ▸ **wiretapping** *noun*

wiring *noun* a system of connected wires, e.g., in an electrical appliance, house, etc.

wiry *adj.* (**wirier, wiriest**) **1** of slight build, but strong and agile. **2** resembling wire. **3** of hair coarse and wavy.

wisdom *noun* **1** the ability to make sensible judgments and decisions, esp. on the basis of one's knowledge and experience; prudence and common sense. **2** learning; knowledge. **3** the weight of informed opinion: *current wisdom.*

wisdom tooth any of the third molar teeth.

wise¹ *adj.* **1** having or showing wisdom; sensible. **2** learned. **3** astute; shrewd. **4** (*in compounds*) knowing the ways of: *streetwise.* ▸ **wisely** *adv.*

wise² *noun old use* way: *He is in no wise to blame.*

-wise *combining form* forming words denoting: **1** in a specified direction, manner, etc.: *clockwise.* **2** *colloq.* with respect to: *businesswise.*

> *Usage* Although extremely productive, the use of the second sense of -*wise* is considered inelegant and should be avoided in all but informal contexts.

wiseacre (wīˈzā,kər) *noun slang* someone who assumes an air of superior wisdom.

wisecrack *noun slang* a smart, clever, or knowing remark.

wise guy *slang* **1** someone full of smart comments; a know-it-all. **2** a member of the Mafia.

wise man 1 a man whose wisdom is respected. **2** one of the Magi.

wish *verb trans., intrans.* (**wished; wishing**) **1** to desire or long for: *I wish I had an*

interesting job like yours. **2** to make a specified desire known: *We wished them a good journey.* —*noun* **1** a strong desire or longing for a specified thing; a specified thing that someone desires or longs for. **2** (**wishes**) a means of expressing one's good thoughts for someone: *Best wishes to your parents.* —**make a wish** to think of something strongly desired or longed for in the hope that the context will increase its chances of being fulfilled.

wishbone *noun* **1** a V-shaped bone in the breast of poultry. **2** *Football* a V-shaped offensive formation.

wishful thinking an overly optimistic expectation that something will happen.

wishy-washy *adj.* **1** lacking character. **2** of colors, etc. pale and insipid. **3** watery; weak.

wisp *noun* **1** a thin, fine tuft or shred. **2** something slight or insubstantial. ▸ **wispy** *adj.*

wisteria or **wistaria** (wĭsˈtîr,ē-ə) *noun* a deciduous climbing shrub with clusters of lilac, violet, or white flowers.

wistful *adj.* sadly or vainly yearning, or expressive of this. ▸ **wistfully** *adv.* ▸ **wistfulness** *noun*

wit¹ *noun* **1** a natural ability to be amusing. **2** a person with this ability. **3** (*also* **wits**) intelligence; mental faculties, sharpness, or reasoning: *used her wit to outfox her chess opponent / had her wits about her.*

wit² —**to wit** that is to say; namely (used esp. to introduce conditions in legal documents).

witch *noun* **1** a person, esp. a woman, supposed to have magic powers, esp. evil ones. **2** a frighteningly ugly or wicked-old woman.

witchcraft *noun* magic or sorcery practiced by witches.

witch doctor a member of a society or community who is believed to have magic powers, and who can use them to cure or harm people.

witch elm *same as* **wych elm.**

witchery *noun* **1** the activities of witches. **2** a bewitching or spellbinding influence.

witch hazel a shrub with yellow flowers, or an astringent lotion produced from its bark and used to treat bruises, etc.

witch hunt a political, moral, etc. crusade against a person or group.

with (wĭth, wĭth) *prep.* **1** in the company of; accompanying; carrying; beside: *went with her / plays with electronic games.* **2** by means of; using: *raised it with a crowbar / said it with feeling.* **3** in; by: *plastered with mud / filled with garbage.* **4** having; regarding; because of: *a man with a limp / shaking with fear.* **5** against; despite: *quarreled with her brother / With all his* money he's *still unhappy*. **6** in the same direction as; at the same time as: *drift with the current / Discretion comes with age*. —**with it** *slang, old use* fashionable; trendy.

withal (with-ôl', with-) *adv*. **1** as well; into the bargain. **2** for all that; nevertheless.

withdraw *verb* · *intrans*., *trans*. (pa t **withdrew**; pa p **withdrawn**; pr p **withdrawing**) **1** to move or pull back; to retreat or retire. **2** to take (funds) from, e.g., a bank account, etc. **3** to back out or pull out of (something); to discontinue or cancel. **4** to retract (something said). **5** (**withdraw from**) to stop taking (an addictive drug, etc.). ▶ **withdrawal** *noun*

withdrawn *adj*. unresponsive, shy, or reserved. —*verb see* **withdraw**.

withdrew *see* **withdraw**.

withe (with, with) *noun* a pliable branch or twig, esp. of willow.

wither (with'ər) *verb intrans*., *trans*. (**withered, withering**) to shrivel up or cause to shrivel up, fade, die, disappear, etc.

withering *adj*., *of a glance, remark, etc.* bitterly contemptuous.

withers (with'ərz) *pl. noun* the ridge between the shoulder blades of a horse.

withhold *verb trans*. (pa t and pa p **withheld**; pr p **withholding**) to refuse to give or grant.

within *prep*. **1** enclosed by; inside. **2** not outside the limits of; not beyond. **3** in less than (a certain time or distance, etc). —*adv*. inside.

without *prep*. **1** not having the company of; deprived of; not having, using, etc.: *went home without him / I can't live without her / books without covers*. **2** not giving, showing, encountering, etc.: *complied without a murmur / managed without difficulty*. **3** *old use* outside: *armed knights without the walls*. —*adv*. **1** outside or on the outside; externally. **2** with something lacking: *just had to do without*.

withstand *verb trans*. (**withstood, withstanding**) to resist or brave successfully.

witless *adj*. stupid. ▶ **witlessness** *noun*

witness *noun* **1** someone who sees (something) firsthand. **2** someone who gives evidence in a court of law or who adds his or her signature to a legal or other document, etc. **3** proof or evidence. —*verb trans*., *intrans*. (**witnessed, witnessing, witnesses**) **1** to see firsthand. **2** to sign (e.g., a legal or other document) as genuine. **3** to testify.

witness stand an enclosed area where a witness sits to give evidence in a court of law.

witticism *noun* a witty remark.

wittingly *adv*. knowingly; consciously.

witty *adj*. (**wittier, wittiest**) **1** eliciting or intended to elicit amusement and laughter. **2** able or apt to be clever and amusing. ▶ **wittily** *adv*. ▶ **wittiness** *noun*

wives *see* **wife**.

wizard (wiz'ərd) *noun* **1** a man supposed to have magic powers; a magician or sorcerer. **2** *colloq*. (**wizard at, with**, *or* **in**) a person skilled at something: *a wizard at chess*.

wizened (wiz'ənd) *adj*. shriveled or wrinkled, esp. with age.

woad *noun* a plant of the mustard family or a blue dye obtained from its leaves.

wobble *verb intrans*., *trans*. (**wobbled, wobbling**) **1** to rock or cause to rock, sway, or shake unsteadily. **2** to tremble. —*noun* a wobbling, rocking, or swaying motion. ▶ **wobbly** *adj*.

woe *noun* **1** extreme grief, misery, or sorrow. **2** affliction; calamity.

woebegone (wō'bĭ-gôn,) *adj*. dismally sorrowful.

woeful *adj*. **1** mournful; sorrowful. **2** causing woe. **3** *colloq*. disgraceful; terrible: *a woeful performance*. ▶ **woefully** *adv*.

wok *noun* a deep-sided pan used in oriental cooking.

woke *see* **wake**[1]

woken *see* **wake**[1]

wold *noun* a tract of open, rolling upland, esp. in England.

wolf (woolf) *noun* (*pl*. **wolves**) **1** a wild carnivorous mammal of the dog family. **2** *colloq*. a man with an insatiable appetite for sexual conquests. —*verb trans*., *intrans*. (**wolfed, wolfing, wolfs**) (*usu*. **wolf down**) *colloq*. to eat (something) greedily. —**cry wolf** to give a false alarm.

wolfhound *noun* a large dog formerly used for hunting wolves.

wolfram *noun* tungsten.

wolfsbane *noun* **1** monkshood. **2** a poisonous herb. *See also* **aconite**.

wolverine (wool,və-rēn') *noun* a burrowing carnivorous mammal related to the weasel. *Also called* **glutton**.

wolves *see* **wolf**.

woman *noun* (*pl*. **women**) **1** an adult human female, as opposed to an adult male. **2** women generally. **3** *colloq*. a wife or girlfriend. **4** feminine instincts: *The woman in her longed for a child*. —*adj. old use* female: *a woman doctor*.

Usage The use of *woman* as an adjective before terms denoting professions is now considered condescending, if not offensive.

-woman *combining form* forming words denoting: **1** a woman associated with a specified activity: *policewoman*. **2** a woman who is a native of a specified country or place: *Frenchwoman.*

womanhood *noun* **1** the state of being an adult female. **2** women collectively.

womanish *adj.* **1** associated with women. **2** effeminate.

womanize *verb intrans.* (**womanized, womanizing**) to seek out the company of women, or have casual affairs with women, esp. habitually. ▸ **womanizer** *noun*

womankind *noun* women considered as a group.

womanly *.adj.* (**womanlier, womanliest**) displaying or having qualities considered admirable in a woman; suitable for a woman.

womb (wŏŏm) *noun* the uterus.

wombat (wäm'băt,) *noun* a burrowing Australian marsupial.

women *see* **woman.**

womenfolk *pl. noun* **1** women generally. **2** the female members of a family or society. **3** a man's female relations.

women's movement a movement for the promotion of the rights of women, esp. in education, the workplace, and the home.

won *see* **win.**

wonder *noun* **1** astonishment, amazement, awe, or bafflement. **2** a cause of astonishment, amazement, awe, or bafflement; a marvel. —*verb. trans., intrans.* (**wondered, wondering**) **1** to speculate, have a doubt or doubts, or be curious. **2** (*also* **wonder at**) to feel astonishment, etc. (at something); to marvel. ▸ **wondrous** *adj.* ▸ **wondrously** *adv.*

wonderful *adj.* **1** arousing wonder; extraordinary. **2** outstanding of its kind or class. ▸ **wonderfully** *adv.*

wonderland *noun* a place full of marvelous things.

wonderment *noun* **1** surprise. **2** curiosity: *gazed in wonderment.*

wonk *noun slang* an overly enthusiastic student; a nerd; a grind.

wont (wônt, wŏnt) *adj.* habitually inclined, or accustomed. —*noun* a habit. ▸ **wonted** *adj.*

won ton (wän'tän,) **1** a dumpling filled with minced meat, usu. served in a soup. **2** an oriental dish consisting of a soup with filled dumplings.

woo *verb trans., intrans.* (**wooed, wooing, woos**) to seek the love of (a romantic partner) or seek favor with (voters, etc.). ▸ **wooer** *noun*

wood *noun* **1** hard tissue formed in the trunks and branches of trees and shrubs. **2** this material used for building, making furniture, etc. **3** (*also* **woods**) an area of land dominated by trees.

wood alcohol *Chem.* methanol.

woodbine *noun* **1** a honeysuckle with yellow flowers. **2** a Virginia creeper.

woodchuck *noun* a common burrowing rodent. *Also called* **groundhog.**

woodcock *noun* (*pl.* **woodcock, woodcocks**) a long-billed game bird.

woodcut *noun* a design cut into a wooden block, or a print taken from it.

woodcutter *noun* a person who fells trees and chops wood.

wooded *adj.* covered with trees.

wooden *adj.* **1** made of wood. **2** *of an actor, performance, etc.* stiff, unnatural, and inhibited; lacking expression and liveliness.

wooden-headed *adj.* dull-witted or stubborn.

wooden Indian a wooden figure of a Native American man, formerly used as a business sign to denote a cigar store.

woodland *noun* (*also* **woodlands**) an area of land more sparsely covered with trees than a forest.

woodpecker *noun* a bird that uses its beak to bore into trees in search of insects, and to drill nest holes.

wood pigeon a large pigeon found mainly in wooded areas. *Also called* **ringdove.**

wood pulp crushed wood fibers used in making paper.

woodruff *noun* a white-flowered, sweet-smelling plant.

woodwind *noun* an orchestral instrument, e.g. a flute, oboe, clarinet, or bassoon, or the section of the orchestra composed of these instruments and those who play them.

woodwork *noun* **1** the art of making things out of wood; carpentry. **2** the wooden parts of a structure.

woodworm *noun* a beetle larva that bores into wood.

woody *adj.* (**woodier, woodiest**) **1** wooded. **2** resembling or composed of wood.

woody nightshade a plant with small oval poisonous berries that turn yellow and then red as they ripen.

woof¹ (wŏŏf) *noun* the sound of a dog's bark. —*verb intrans.* (**woofed, woofing, woofs**) to give a bark.

woof² (wŏŏf, wŏŏf) *noun Weaving* the weft.

woofer (wŏŏf'ər) *noun* a large loudspeaker for reproducing low-frequency sounds. *See also* **tweeter.**

wool *noun* **1** the soft wavy hair of sheep, etc. **2** fibers of this spun into yarn for knitting, weaving, etc.

woolen *or* **woollen** *adj.* made of or relating to wool or its production, etc. —*noun* (often **woolens**) a woolen, esp. knitted, garment.

woolgathering *noun* absent-mindedness; daydreaming.

woolly or **wooly** adj. (**woollier, woolliest**) **1** made of, like, or covered with wool or wool-like fibers, etc.; fluffy and soft. **2** vague and muddled: *woolly thinking.* —noun colloq. a woolen, usu. knitted, garment.

woozy adj. (**woozier, wooziest**) colloq. feeling dazed, dizzy, or confused, with senses blurred and hazy. ▸ **woozily** adv.

Worcestershire sauce (wŏŏs′tər-shĭr′, -shər) a strong-tasting, spicy sauce made from a variety of ingredients including vinegar and soy sauce.

word noun **1** the smallest unit of spoken or written language that can be used independently. **2** a brief conversation, statement, message, or other communication: *I'd like a word with you.* **3** a solemn promise: *I give you my word.* **4** an order or command; a signal, password, or watchword: *She expects her word to be obeyed.* **5** (**words**) spoken or written language; a song lyric; actors' lines. **6** (**words**) a quarrel: *had words about it.* **7** (**the Word**) the teachings in the Christian bible. **8** Comput. the largest unit of data that a particular microprocessor can handle in a single operation. —verb trans. (**worded, wording**) to express (something) in words: *worded her refusal tactfully.* ☰ COUCH, FORMULATE, PHRASE. —**word for word** repeated in exactly the same words.

wording noun choice of words.

word processing (ABBREV. **WP**) the production of text using a word processor.

word processor (ABBREV. **WP**) Comput. a program for inputting, processing, storing, and retrieving text.

wordy adj. (**wordier, wordiest**) using too many words. ☰ DIFFUSE, LONG-WINDED, PROLIX, VERBOSE, WINDY ☰ CONCISE, CONDENSED, LACONIC, PITHY, SUC-CINCT, TERSE. ▸ **wordily** adv.

wore see **wear**.

work noun **1** physical or mental effort; labor; toil. **2** employment, esp. regular paid employment. **3** a place of employment: *leaves work at 4:30 pm.* **4** tasks, chores, activities, or the results of mental or physical labor: *work to be done in the garden.* **5** an artistic creation: *the works of Milton.* **6** (in compounds) something made in a specified material, using a specified method, or the production or quality of such things: *needlework.* **7** (**works**) a place where a manufacturing process is carried out: *steel works.* **8** (**works**) colloq. the operating parts of something, e.g., a watch, machine, etc. **9** (**the works**) colloq. everything possible, available, etc.: *a headache, fever, nausea, the works.* —verb intrans., trans. (**worked, working**) **1** to perform mental or physical

work. **2** to be employed. **3** to operate, esp. satisfactorily or in a particular way; to be successful or effective: *Does this radio work?* / *It is worked by electricity.* **4** to shape, fashion, cultivate, knead, sew, etc.: *worked metal* / *worked the soil.* **5** to achieve (miracles, wonders, etc.). **6** colloq. to manipulate (a system, rules, etc.) to one's advantage. **7** to move or shift or cause to move or shift gradually: *worked her way to the front of the line.* —**work out 1** to come to a successful conclusion: *If things work out, we will make millions.* **2** to exercise: *works out at the gym.* **3** to solve or resolve: *worked out where he'd gone wrong.*

workable adj. **1** able to be carried out; feasible or practicable. **2** of a metal, etc. able to be worked; malleable. ▸ **workability** noun

workaday adj. **1** ordinary; commonplace. **2** suitable for a work day; practical.

workaholic noun colloq. a person who works excessively long hours or who is addicted to working.

workbench noun a table for a mechanic, craftsman, etc.

workday noun a working day, or the part of a working day during which work is done.

worker noun **1** a person who works. **2** a person employed in manual work. **3** an employee as opposed to an employer. **4** a sterile male honeybee, ant, etc. whose function is to maintain the colony and forage for food. See also **drone** (sense 2).

worker's compensation payments made by an employer to an employee who is disabled or otherwise injured in a job-related situation, required by US law.

work force or **workforce** the number of workers engaged in a particular industry, factory, etc.; the total number of workers potentially available.

workhouse noun Hist. an institution where the poor were housed and given work to do.

working noun **1** (also **workings**) operation or mode of operation. **2** (**workings**) the steps, usu. noted down, by which the answer to a mathematical problem is reached. **3** (**workings**) excavations at a mine or quarry. —adj. effective or functioning properly.

working class a social class below middle class, comprised of wage-earners, esp. in manual labor.

workman noun a skilled person performing a craft.

workmanlike adj. performed in a competent way; efficient, but not exceptional.

workmanship noun the skill of a craftsman, esp. where evident in the appearance of a finished product.

work of art (pl. **works of art**) a painting, sculpture, etc. of high quality.

workout *noun* a session of physical exercise.

workshop *noun* **1** a room or building where construction, repairs, etc. are carried out. **2** a session where people meet to discuss, learn, practice, etc. a specified topic: *a dance workshop.*

work station a computer terminal and the immediate surrounding area.

world *noun* **1** the Earth. **2** another planet or potentially habitable celestial body. **3** the people inhabiting Earth; humankind; human affairs: *the present state of the world.* **4** (also **World**) a group of countries characterized in a certain way: *the Third World.* **5** (also **World**) the people of a particular period, and their culture: *the Ancient World.* **6** a state of existence; a particular area of activity, etc.: *the world of politics.* **7** *colloq.* a great deal, number, quantity, etc.: *did her a world of good.* —*adj.* relating to, affecting, or important throughout the whole world: *world championships.*

world-beater *noun* someone or something of supreme quality.

world-class *adj.* **1** *colloq., often used facetiously* outstandingly good: *a world-class idiot.* **2** showing or being of the highest standard in the world.

worldly *adj.* (**worldlier, worldliest**) **1** material: *worldly possessions.* **2** sophisticated. ▸ **worldliness** *noun*

worldly-wise *adj.* knowledgeable about life.

world music popular music from non-Western, esp. African, cultures.

worldwide *adj., adv.* extending or known throughout the world.

World Wide Web, World-Wide Web or **Worldwide Web** (ABBREV. **WWW**) *Comput.* the complete set of interlinked hypertext documents, called Web pages, that can be accessed on the Internet. *Also called* **Web.**

worm *noun* **1** a soft-bodied limbless invertebrate. **2** a similar but unrelated animal, e.g., the larva of certain insects. **3** a mean, contemptible, weak, or worthless person. **4** a spiral thread of a screw, etc. **5** (**worms**) a disease characterized by the presence of parasitic worms in the intestines of humans or animals. **6** *Comput.* an unauthorized program designed to sabotage a system, esp. by reproducing itself throughout a computer network. —*verb trans.* (**wormed, worming**) **1** (**worm one's way**) to wriggle or maneuver oneself gradually: *wormed their way to the front.* **2** (**worm one's way into**) to insinuate oneself into (someone's favor, affections, etc.). **3** (also **worm out**) to extract (information, etc.) little by little: *wormed the secret out of*

them. **4** to treat (an animal that has worms), esp. to rid it of the parasitic organisms. ▸ **wormy** *adj.*

WORM *abbr. Comput.* Write Once Read Many.

wormeaten *adj.* **1** of *furniture, etc.* riddled with wormholes. **2** old and worn-out.

worm gear 1 a gear consisting of a shaft with a spiral thread that engages with and drives a toothed wheel. **2** (also **worm wheel**) the toothed wheel driven in this way.

wormhole *noun* a hole left by a burrowing worm, in, e.g., furniture, books, fruit, etc.

wormwood *noun* **1** a bitter-tasting herb used for flavoring absinthe and tonics. **2** old use acute bitterness or chagrin, or a cause of it.

worn *verb* see **wear.** —*adj.* **1** weary. **2** showing signs of deterioration through long use or wear; threadbare.

worried *adj.* anxious, concerned, or fretting; expressing anxiety or concern.

worrier *noun* a person who worries, esp. habitually so.

worrisome *adj. old use* causing worry.

worry *verb intrans., trans.* (**worried, worrying, worries**) **1** to be anxious. **2** to cause anxiety to. **3** to bother or harass. **4** to tear and pull about with the teeth. —*noun* (*pl.* **worries**) anxiety or a cause of anxiety.

worry beads a string of beads for manipulating, used to calm the nerves.

worse *adj., adv. see* **bad, badly, ill.**

worsen *verb intrans., trans.* (**worsened, worsening**) to become or make worse.

worship *verb trans., intrans.* (**worshiped** or **worshipped, worshiping** or **worshipping**) **1** to honor (a god) with praise, prayer, hymns, etc. **2** to love, admire, glorify, or exalt: *worships money.* —*noun* **1** the activity of worshiping or a religious service. **2** (**Worship**) a respectful title or form of address. ▸ **worshipful** *adj.* ▸ **worshiper** or **worshipper** *noun*

worst *adj., adv. see* **bad, badly, ill.** —*verb trans.* (**worsted, worsting**) to get the better of; to defeat.

worsted (wŏŏs'tĭd, wûr'stĭd) *noun* a fine, strong woolen yarn, or a fabric woven from it.

wort (wûrt', wôrt) *noun, combining form* a plant: *liverwort.*

worth *noun* **1** value; importance; usefulness. **2** financial value. —*adj.* **1** having a value of. **2** *colloq.* having money and property to the value of: *She's worth two million.* **3** justifying, deserving, meriting, or warranting.

worthless *adj.* of no value, merit, or importance; useless or undeserving. ▸ **worthlessly** *adv.* ▸ **worthlessness** *noun*

worthwhile *adj.* useful, beneficial, or rewarding.

worthy *adj.* (**worthier, worthiest**) 1 admirable; excellent; deserving: *support worthy causes.* 2 (**worthy of**) deserving (something) or suitable to (someone). —*noun* (*pl.* **worthies**) an esteemed person; a dignitary. ▸ **worthily** *adv.* ▸ **worthiness** *noun*

would *verb aux. see* **will¹**.

would-be *adj.* hoping or aspiring to be: *a would-be actor.*

wound¹ (wownd) *see* **wind²**.

wound² (woōnd) *noun* 1 an external injury on a human, animal, or plant. 2 an incision made by a surgeon. 3 an injury caused to pride, feelings, reputation, etc. —*verb trans.*, *intrans.* (**wounded, wounding**) 1 to inflict a wound (on someone or something). 2 to injure (feelings, etc.).

wove *see* **weave**.

woven *see* **weave**.

wow¹ *colloq. interj.* used as an exclamation of astonishment or admiration. —*noun* a huge success. —*verb trans.* (**wowed, wowing**) to impress greatly.

wow² *noun* a repeated distortion in the reproduction of a transmitted sound.

WP *abbrev.* word processing; word processor.

wrack or **rack** *noun* 1 destruction. 2 a wreck or wreckage. —**wrack and ruin** a state of decay or neglect: *let the old house go to wrack and ruin.*

wraith *noun* an insubstantial supernatural being or form.

wrangle *verb intrans.*, *trans.* (**wrangled, wrangling**) 1 to quarrel or argue noisily or bitterly. 2 to round up (cattle, etc.). —*noun* a bitter dispute. ▸ **wrangler** *noun*

wrap *verb* (**wrapped, wrapping**) 1 to fold or wind around (something). 2 (*also* **wrap up**) to cover or enfold (with or in something). —*noun* 1 a shawl or stole for the shoulders. 2 a protective covering. 3 a point at which the filming of a movie or a movie scene ends, or a completed movie or movie sequence. —**wrap up 1** to dress warmly. 2 to conclude or finish (something). **wrapped up in** engrossed in.

wraparound *adj.* 1 of clothing designed to wrap around the body. 2 of a computer facility having the ability to treat text, etc. as continuous, even if it is evoked at a point other than at the start of a document, etc. 3 of word processing software automatically inputting text in the following line when the end of a line is reached.

wrapper *noun* 1 a covering, e.g., around a packet, candy, etc. 2 housecoat.

wrapping *noun* (*usu.* **wrappings**) any of various covers, wrappers, or packing materials.

wrasse (răs) *noun* a marine fish.

wrath *noun* anger; fury. ▸ **wrathful** *adj.*

wreak *verb trans.* (**wreaked, wreaking**) to inflict (havoc, damage, revenge, etc.).

wreath (rēth) *noun* 1 a ring-shaped garland of flowers and foliage placed on a grave as a tribute, or hung up as a decoration. 2 a victor's crown of esp. laurel leaves.

wreathe (rēth) *verb trans.*, *intrans.* (**wreathed, wreathing**) 1 to coil, twine, or intertwine. 2 to hang or encircle with flowers, etc.

wreck *noun* 1 destruction or ruin, esp. accidental. 2 a crashed aircraft, ruined vehicle, sunken ship, or a person in a physically, mentally, or emotionally unhealthy state. —*verb trans.* (**wrecked, wrecking**) to cause the destruction or ruin of. ▣ DEMOLISH, DESTROY, RUIN, SHATTER, SMASH. ▸ **wreckage** *noun*

wrecker *noun* 1 someone who wrecks. 2 a vehicle that takes away crashed motor vehicles.

wren *noun* a very small songbird with short wings and an erect tail.

wrench *verb trans.* (**wrenched, wrenching**) 1 to pull or tug sharply. 2 to sprain (an ankle, etc.). —*noun* 1 a violent pull or twist. 2 a tool for gripping and turning nuts and bolts. 3 a sprain.

wrest *verb trans.* (**wrested, wresting**) to remove or seize by pulling or wrenching.

wrestle *verb trans.*, *intrans.* (**wrestled, wrestling**) 1 to fight by trying to grip, throw, and pinion one's opponent; to do this as a sport; to force to a position in this way. 2 to struggle intensely. —*noun* 1 a spell of wrestling. 2 a struggle. ▸ **wrestler** *noun* ▸ **wrestling** *noun*

wretch *noun* 1 a miserable, unfortunate, pitiful creature. 2 a shamelessly wicked person.

wretched *adj.* 1 pitiable. 2 miserable; unhappy; distressed; distraught. 3 inferior; poor; lowly. ▸ **wretchedly** *adv.* ▸ **wretchedness** *noun*

wriggle *verb intrans.*, *trans.* (**wriggled, wriggling**) 1 to twist to and fro; to squirm. 2 to get out of or into (something) by insinuation, manipulation, etc.: *wriggled out of doing his chores.* —*noun* a squirming action. ▸ **wriggler** *noun* ▸ **wriggly** *adj.*

wright *noun* (*usu. in compounds*) a maker or repairer: *playwright / shipwright.*

wring *verb trans.* (*pa t and pa p* **wrung**; *pr p* **wringing**) 1 (*often* **wring out**) to twist or squeeze (liquid) from (something). 2 to obtain (information, consent, etc.) by force or coercion. 3 to break (a bird's neck) by twisting. 4 to clasp and twist (one's hands) in distress. 5 to tear at or distress (a heart). —*noun* a twist or squeeze. —**wringing wet** saturated.

wringer noun a hand-turned device or a machine for squeezing out water, e.g., from wet clothes.

wrinkle noun 1 a crease or line in the skin, esp. of the face, appearing with advancing age. 2 a slight crease or ridge in a surface. 3 slang an innovation. —verb intrans., trans. (**wrinkled, wrinkling**) to develop, or cause to develop, wrinkles.

wrinkly adj. having many wrinkles. —noun (pl. **wrinklies**) colloq. an old person.

wrist noun a joint between the hand and the forearm, or the region surrounding this.

wristlet noun a decorative or supporting band for the wrist.

wristwatch noun a watch worn strapped to the wrist.

writ noun a legal document stipulating an order.

write verb trans., intrans. (pa t **wrote**; pa p **written**; pr p **writing**) 1 to form or put (letters, etc.) on paper, etc. by hand, usu. with a pen or pencil. 2 to compose or create (a book, music, etc.); to compose novels, articles, etc. as a living. 3 to compose (a letter, etc.); to say in a letter, etc. 4 Comput. to transfer (data) to a memory or storage device. —**write off** to damage (a vehicle, etc.) beyond repair. 2 to cancel (a debt). 3 to discontinue (a project, etc.). 4 to dismiss (something) as being of no importance.

write-off noun something written off, e.g., a motor vehicle involved in an accident, or a debt that has been canceled.

writer noun 1 a person who writes, esp. as a living; an author. 2 someone who has written a particular thing.

writer's cramp painful numbness of the hand brought on by extensive writing.

write-up noun a written or published account, esp. a review.

writhe (rīth) verb intrans. (**writhed, writhing**) to twist violently to and fro, esp. in pain.

writing noun 1 written or printed words. 2 handwriting.

written see **write**.

wrong adj. 1 not correct. 2 mistaken. 3 not appropriate or suitable. 4 not good; not sensible; unjustifiable. 5 morally bad. 6 defective or faulty. 7 amiss. 8 intended as the inner, unseen, side: iron it on the wrong side. 9 unsuitable or unacceptable: get in with the wrong crowd. —adv. 1 incorrectly. 2 improperly; badly. 3 amiss. —noun 1 whatever is not right or just: know right from wrong. 2 an injury done to someone else: did her wrong. —verb trans. (**wronged, wronging**) 1 to treat unjustly. 2 to judge unfairly. —**go wrong** 1 to fail to go as intended. 2 to make an error. 3 to stray morally. 4 to stop functioning properly. **in the wrong** guilty of an error or injustice. ▸ **wrongly** adv.

wrongdoer noun a person guilty of an illegal or immoral act. ▸ **wrongdoing** noun

wrongful adj. unjust or unlawful. ▸ **wrongfully** adv.

wrongheaded adj. unreasonably stubborn; obstinately refusing to compromise. ▸ **wrongheadedness** noun

wrote see **write**.

wroth (rôth) adj. old use full of wrath; angry.

wrought (rôt) adj. 1 old use made, formed, shaped, or fashioned. 2 decorated or ornamented. 3 of metal beaten into shape, as distinct from being cast.

wrought iron a malleable form of iron with a very low carbon content. ▸ **wrought-iron** adj.

wrought-up adj. overly excited; agitated.

wrung see **wring**.

wry adj. (**wrier** or **wryer, wriest** or **wryest**) 1 ironic: a wry sense of humor. 2 twisted to one side; awry; distorted.

wryneck noun 1 a small woodpecker. 2 a neck condition causing the head to be held in a distorted position; torticollis.

wt. abbrev. weight (sense 1).

wurst (wɜrst', wŏŏrst) noun a large German sausage.

WWW noun World Wide Web.

wych elm or **witch elm** (wĭch) a deciduous tree of the elm family, native to Europe and Asia.

WYSBYGI abbrev. Comput. what you see before you get it.

WYSIWYG (wĭz'ē-wĭg,) abbrev. Comput. what you see is what you get.

Xx

X¹ *or* **x** *noun (pl.* **Xs, X's, x's) 1** the 24th letter of the English alphabet. **2** something in the shape of an X. **3** an unknown or unnamed person. **4** a mark used by someone who is unable to sign his or her name.

X² *abbrev.* a movie classified as suitable for people over the age of 17.

X³ *symbol* **1** *Math.* **(x)** an unknown quantity. **2** the Roman numeral for 10.

XC *or* **X-C** *abbrev. Sport* cross-country.

X-chromosome *noun* a female sex chromosome. *See also* **Y-chromosome.**

Xe *symbol Chem.:* xenon.

xenon (zē'năn¸, zĕn'ăn¸) *noun* (SYMBOL **Xe**) an inert gas, one of the rare or noble gases.

xenophobia (zĕn¸ə-fō'bē-ə, zē¸nə-) *noun* intense fear or dislike of foreigners or strangers. ▶ **xenophobic** *adj.*

Xer (ĕks'ər) *noun* a member of **Generation X.**

xerography (zĭr-ăg'rə-fē) *noun* an electrostatic printing process used to make photocopies of printed documents, etc.

xerophyte *noun* a plant, e.g., a desert cactus, that is adapted to grow under conditions where water is very scarce.

Xerox (zĭr'äks¸) *trademark* denoting a photocopying process or machine using xerography. —*noun* a copy made using xerography. —*verb trans.* **(xerox) (xeroxed, xeroxing, xeroxes)** to copy (a document) using xerography.

XL *abbrev.* extra large.

Xmas (krĭs'məs, ĕk'sməs) *noun colloq.* the period of celebration surrounding Dec. 25.

X-rated *adj.* suitable or meant for adults only, esp. because of a high level of explicit sexual references: *an X-rated magazine.*

x-ray *or* **X-ray** *noun* **1** **(x-rays)** electromagnetic radiations of very short wavelength and high energy able to pass through many substances which light cannot penetrate, used for producing photographic images of the interior of solids, esp. as an aid to diagnosis and in radiotherapy. **2** a photograph taken using x-rays. **3** a medical examination using x-rays. —*verb trans.* **(x-rayed, x-raying)** to take a photograph of, using x-rays.

xylem (zī'ləm) *noun* the plant tissue that transports water and mineral nutrients from the roots to all other parts of the plant.

xylophone *noun* a musical instrument consisting of a series of wooden or metal bars of different lengths, played by striking these with wooden hammers.

Yy

Y¹ or **y** noun (pl. **Ys, Y's, y's**) 1 the 25th letter of the English alphabet. 2 something shaped like the letter Y.

Y² symbol 1 Chem. yttrium. 2 Math. (y) the second of two unknown quantities.

Y³ abbrev. yen.

-y suffix 1 forming diminutives or nouns used as terms of affection: daddy. 2 forming adjectives and nouns denoting having the nature of: foggy.

yacht (yät) noun a boat or small ship, usu. with sails and an engine, for racing or cruising. ▸ **yachting** noun ▸ **yachtsman** noun ▸ **yachtswoman** noun

yack verb, noun same as yak².

yahoo (yā′hōō,) noun a uncivilized and uncultured person.

yak¹ noun (pl. **yaks, yak**) a large shaggy-coated ox native to Tibet.

yak² or **yack** colloq. verb intrans. (**yakked, yakking**) to talk at length, often foolishly or annoyingly. —noun persistent foolish or annoying chatter.

yakitori (yäk,ĭ-tôr′ē) noun a Japanese dish of grilled skewered chicken.

yam noun 1 a climbing plant or its thick starchy edible tuber. 2 a sweet potato (sense 2).

yammer verb intrans., trans. (**yammered, yammering**) 1 to complain, or make (a complaint), in a loud, whining way. 2 to talk loudly and at length. —noun an act or the sound of yammering.

yang noun the positive, masculine force of traditional Chinese philosophy, opposite to and complementing **yin**.

Yank (yăngk) noun colloq. a Yankee.

> Originally a nickname for Dutch settlers in New England in the 18th century, possibly because of the Dutch forename Jan

yank noun a sudden sharp pull. —verb trans., intrans. (**yanked, yanking**) to pull or tug sharply. ▤ JERK, WRENCH.

Yankee (yăng′kē) noun 1 a person from the USA. 2 a person from the NE states of the USA. 3 a Union soldier or sympathizer during the Civil War.

yap verb intrans. (**yapped, yapping**) 1 of a dog to give a high-pitched bark. 2 colloq. to talk continually in a shrill voice. —noun a short high-pitched bark. ▸ **yappy** adj.

yapok noun a small aquatic opossum of tropical America.

yard¹ noun 1 (ABBREV. **yd.**) a unit of length equal to 3 ft. (0.99144 m). 2 a long beam hung on a mast, from which to hang a sail.

yard² noun 1 (often in compounds) an area of enclosed ground near a building. 2 (often in compounds) an area of enclosed ground used for a special business purpose: a shipyard. 3 an area of garden around a home, usu. grassed.

yardage (yärd′ĭj) noun length as measured in yards.

yardarm noun Naut. either of the tapering end sections of a yard.

yard goods merchandise sold by measures, e.g., fabric, timber, etc.

yardsale noun a sale of used domestic equipment, books, toys, clothes, etc. held on the lawn of a house.

yardstick noun 1 a standard for comparison. 2 a stick exactly one yard long, used for measuring.

yare adj. 1 of a ship or boat easy to sail or manage. 2 agile, fit, or lively.

yarmulka or **yarmulke** (yäm′ə-kə, yär′məl-) noun a skullcap worn by Jewish men and boys.

yarn noun 1 spun thread. 2 a story, often a long, convoluted, or embellished one. —verb intrans. to tell a story, often in turn: sat up drinking and yarning.

yarrow noun a plant with aromatic segmented leaves and a dense, flat-topped cluster of flower heads.

yashmak noun a veil worn in public by Muslim women.

yaw verb intrans. (**yawed, yawing**) of a ship, aircraft, etc. to deviate from, or fail to keep to, its direct or planned course. —noun an act of yawing.

yawl noun a small fishing boat or sail boat, esp. one with two masts.

yawn verb intrans. (**yawned, yawning**) 1 to open the mouth wide and take a deep involuntary breath when tired or bored. 2 of a hole, gap, etc. to be or become wide open. —noun 1 an act of yawning. 2 colloq. a boring or tiresome event, person, etc.

yaws noun (sing., pl.) an infectious skin disease chiefly of children in tropical countries, causing red swellings.

Yb *symbol Chem.* ytterbium.

Y-chromosome *noun* the male chromosome. *See also* **X-chromosome**.

yd. *abbrev.* yard¹ (sense 1).

ye¹ *pron. old use* you (plural).

ye² (yē, yə, <u>th</u>ə, <u>th</u>ē) *definite article old use* the: *Ye Olde Englishe Tea Shoppe.*

yea (yā) *interj.* yes. —*noun* an affirmative response: *The yeas were greater than the nays.*

yeah *interj. colloq.* yes.

year *noun* **1** the time the Earth, or another planet, takes to go once around the Sun. **2** the period from Jan. 1 to Dec. 31, being 365 days, except in a leap year, when it is 366 days. **3** any period of 12 months. **4** a period of less than 12 months during which an activity is carried on: *The academic year runs from September to May.* **5** a period of study comprising an academic year: *in her third year.* **6** (**years**) **a** age. **b** *colloq.* a very long time. **c** a period of time gone by or to come. ▸ **yearly** *adj., adv.*

year book 1 a book of information updated and published every year, esp. one recording the events, etc., of the previous year. **2** an annual (sense 2).

yearling *noun* an animal that is one year old.

yearn (yərn') *verb intrans.* (**yearned, yearning**) to feel a great desire or longing for something: *yearned to go home.* ▸ **yearning** *noun*

yeast *noun* a single-celled fungus; a preparation of many of these used as a fermenting agent in beer, etc., and as a raising agent in bread, etc.

yeasty *adj.* (**yeastier, yeastiest**) **1** tasting of or smelling of yeast. **2** frothy. **3** trivial.

yech *or* **yecch** (yəкн') *interj.* used to express disgust.

yell *noun* a loud shout or cry. —*verb intrans., trans.* (**yelled, yelling**) to shout or cry out.

yellow *adj.* **1** of the color of gold, butter, egg yolk, a lemon, etc. **2** having or displaying a contemptible lack of courage. **3** of a newspaper, journalism, etc. sensational.—*noun* **1** the color of egg yolk, etc. **2** something of the color of egg yolk, etc. —*verb trans., intrans.* (**yellowed, yellowing**) to make or become yellow.

yellow-bellied *adj. slang* yellow (sense 2). ▸ **yellowbelly** *noun*

yellow dog contract *slang* an employment contract, now illegal, where an employee agrees not to join a union.

yellow fever an acute viral disease of tropical America and West Africa.

yellow jacket a small wasp.

yellow pages *or* **Yellow Pages** a telephone directory for businesses, services, etc.

yelp *verb intrans.* (**yelped, yelping**) to give a sharp, sudden cry. —*noun* a yelping cry.

yen¹ *colloq. noun* a desire. —*verb intrans.* (**yenned, yenning**) to feel a longing for.

yen² *noun* (*pl.* **yen**) the standard unit of Japanese currency.

yenta *noun slang* a meddling, gossipy person, usu. a woman.

yeoman (yō'mən) *noun* **1** *Hist.* a farmer who owned and worked his own land. **2** an attendant or servant. **3** a petty officer in the US Navy doing chiefly clerical work.

yep *interj. colloq.* yes.

yes *interj.* used to express agreement or consent. —*noun* (*pl.* **yeses**) an expression of agreement or consent.

yes man someone who always agrees with superiors, employers, etc., esp. to curry favor with them.

yesterday *noun* **1** the day before today. **2** the recent past. —*adv.* **1** on the day before today. **2** in the recent past.

yesteryear *noun literary* **1** the past in general. **2** last year.

yet *adv.* **1** up till now or then; by now or by that time: *He had not yet arrived.* **2** at this time; now: *You can't leave yet.* **3** at some time in the future: *She may yet make a success of it.* **4** even; still: *yet bigger problems.* —*conj.* but; however; nevertheless: *He said he would do it, yet he has neglected to do so.*

yeti (yĕt'ē) *noun* an apelike creature supposed to live in the Himalayas. *Also called* **abominable snowman**.

yew *noun* a coniferous evergreen tree or shrub, or its reddish-brown wood.

YHA *abbrev.* Youth Hostels Association.

Yiddish (yĭd'ĭsh) *noun* a language spoken by many Jews, based on medieval German, with elements from Hebrew and other languages. —*adj.* of the Yiddish language.

yield *verb trans., intrans.* (**yielded, yielding**) **1** to produce (a natural product): *Contented cows yield more milk.* **2** to give or produce: *Shares yield dividends.* **3** to give up or give in; to surrender. **4** to break or give way under force or pressure. —*noun* an amount produced.

yielding *adj.* **1** submissive. **2** flexible. **3** able to or tending to give way.

yin *noun* the negative, feminine force of traditional Chinese philosophy, opposite to and complementing **yang**.

YMCA *abbrev.* Young Men's Christian Association.

YMHA *abbrev.* Young Men's Hebrew Association.

yo *interj. colloq.* used to attract another's attention or as a greeting.

yodel *verb trans., intrans.* (**yodeled** *or* **yodelled, yodeling** *or* **yodelling**) to sing (a melody, etc.), changing frequently from a normal to a falsetto voice and back again.

—*noun* an act or sound of yodeling. ▸ **yodeler** *noun*

yoga *noun* **1** a Hindu philosophy concerned with obtaining spiritual insight and serenity. **2** a system of physical and mental exercises designed to help achieve this.

yogi *noun* a person who practices the yoga philosophy and the physical and mental disciplines associated with it.

yogurt, yoghurt *or* **yoghourt** *noun* a semi-liquid food made from fermented milk, often flavored with fruit.

yoke *noun* **1** a frame joining a pair of oxen, etc. at the neck while they pull a plow, cart, etc. **2** a frame across a person's shoulders for carrying buckets. **3** something oppressive; a great burden: *the yoke of slavery.* **4** the part of a garment that fits over the shoulders and round the neck. —*verb trans.* (**yoked, yoking**) **1** to join (two oxen, etc.) with a frame. **2** to join or unite.

yokel *noun* an unsophisticated, usu. male, person from the country.

yolk *noun* the yellow part of a bird's or reptile's egg.

Yom Kippur (yŏm,kĭ-pŏŏr′, yŏm,-, -kĭp′ər) an annual Jewish high holy day devoted to repentance for past sins and marked by fasting and prayer. *Also called* **Day of Atonement**.

yon *adj. poetic* that or those over there.

yonder *adj., adv.* situated in or at that place over there.

yore *adv.* long ago: *in the days of yore.*

Yorkshire pudding (yôrk′shər) a baked batter pudding, usu. served with roast beef.

you *pron.* **1** used to refer to a person or the people, etc. being addressed, etc. **2** any or every person: *You don't often see that nowadays.*

young *adj.* **1** in the first part of life, growth, development, etc. **2** in the early stages: *The evening is still young.* —*pl. noun* **1** offspring: *Some birds feed their young on insects.* **2** (**the young**) young people in general. ▸ **youngish** *adj.*

young blood young people, esp. when thought of in terms of their fresh ideas, approaches, etc.

youngster *noun* a young person.

Young Turk a young, progressive, often reformist, member of a group, esp. a political party.

your *adj.* belonging to you.

yours *pron.* something belonging to you.

yourself *pron.* (*pl.* **yourselves**) the reflexive or emphatic form of *you.*

youth *noun* **1** the period of time between childhood and adulthood. **2** the qualities associated with this time, esp. vigor, enthusiasm, rashness, etc. **3** a boy or young man. **4** (*pl.*) young people in general. **5** the early stages of something. ▸ **youthful** *adj.* ▸ **youthfulness** *noun*

youth hostel a lodging place providing simple overnight accommodation for traveling young people. ▸ **youth hosteler**

yowl *noun* a long, wailing cry or howl made esp. by a cat. —*verb intrans.* (**yowled, yowling**) to make this noise.

yo-yo *noun* (*pl.* **yo-yos**) a toy consisting of a pair of joined disks with a string that is used to make it repeatedly wind and unwind. —*verb intrans.* (**yo-yoed, yo-yoing, yo-yoes**) to rise and fall or fluctuate repeatedly: *prices yo-yoing in an unstable economy.*

ytterbium *noun* (SYMBOL **Yb**) a soft, silvery, lustrous metallic element.

yttrium *noun* (SYMBOL **Y**) a silvery-gray metallic element.

yuan (yōō-än′) *noun* the standard currency of the People's Republic of China.

yucca *noun* an evergreen plant with a short thick trunk and stiff, sword-shaped leaves.

yuck *interj. slang* used to indicate extreme disgust. ▸ **yucky** *adj.*

Yule (yōōl) *noun* the period of celebration around Dec. 25.

yummy *adj.* (**yummier, yummiest**) *slang* delicious.

yuppie *or* **yuppy** *noun* (*pl.* **yuppies**) *colloq.* an ambitious, young professional person with a well-paid job.

YWCA *abbrev.* Young Women's Christian Association.

YWHA *abbrev.* Young Women's Hebrew Association.

Zz

Z¹ or **z** noun (pl. **Zs, Z's, z's**) **1** the 26th letter of the English alphabet. **2** something shaped like the letter Z.

Z² symbol **1** Electr. impedance (sense 1). **2** Math. (**z**) a third unknown quantity.

zabaglione (zäb,əl-yō'ně) noun a whipped dessert made from custard and wine.

zany adj. (**zanier, zaniest**) amusingly crazy.

> After the name of a clownish character in the Italian commedia dell'arte

zap verb trans., intrans: (**zapped, zapping**) colloq. **1** to hit, destroy, shoot, etc., esp. suddenly. **2** Comput. to delete (data), usu. with no hope of recovery. **3** to change television channels frequently using a remote-control device. **4** to move quickly or suddenly. **5** to cook in a microwave oven. —noun an act or sound or the process of zapping.

zeal noun great, sometimes excessive, enthusiasm. ≣ ARDOR, FERVOR, FIRE, PASSION ≣ APATHY, INDIFFERENCE.

zealot (zĕl'ət) noun a committed or fanatical supporter of something.

zealous adj. greatly enthusiastic; fervent. ► **zealously** adv.

zebra noun a black-and-white striped African mammal of the horse family.

zebu noun a species of Asian and African domestic cattle with a prominent shoulder hump. Also called **Brahman cattle**.

zee noun the letter Z.

Zeitgeist (tsīt'gīst,, zīt'-) noun a German word meaning spirit of the time, used to denote the prevailing tastes and moral, intellectual, etc. climate characterizing a particular age.

Zen noun a form of Buddhism with an emphasis on meditation as a means of attaining enlightenment. Also called **Zen Buddhism**.

zenith noun **1** the point in the sky that is directly above an observer or place. **2** the highest point in something: the zenith of her career.

zephyr noun a light, gentle breeze.

zeppelin noun a large cigar-shaped airship.

zero noun (pl. **zeros, zeroes**) **1** the number or figure 0. **2** the lowest point on a scale, e.g., on a thermometer. See also **absolute zero**. —adj. **1** of no measurable size or importance.

2 slang not any; not did zero work all week. —verb trans. (**zeroed, zeroing, zeroes**) to set to zero on a scale. —**zero in on 1** to aim for or move toward (something). **2** to focus attention on (something).

zero hour the exact time set for something to happen or begin.

zero population growth (ABBREV. **ZPG**) the theory or practice of limiting the number of births in a given population to a level where they equal the number of deaths.

zero-sum game a situation in which one side's or one person's gain has to be matched by another side's or person's loss.

zero tolerance a rigorous clampdown on crime or socially unacceptable behavior, by the strict application of relevant laws.

zest noun **1** keen enjoyment; enthusiasm. **2** something that adds to one's enjoyment. **3** the peel of an orange or lemon, used for flavoring.

zeugma (zōōg'mə) noun a figure of speech where one word, usu. an adjective or verb, is linked to two others, usu. nouns, for rhetorical effect, as in She plays the piano and the field.

ziggurat noun a pyramid-like temple of ancient Mesopotamia.

zigzag noun **1** one of two or more sharp bends, e.g., in a road. **2** a road, path, etc., with a number of such bends. —adj. having sharp bends to right and left. —verb trans., intrans. (**zigzagged, zigzagging**) to move, or cause to move, in a zigzag path or manner.

zilch noun slang nothing.

zillion noun colloq. a very large, unspecified number.

zinc noun (SYMBOL **Zn**) a brittle bluish-white metallic element.

zinc ointment a soothing antiseptic ointment containing zinc oxide.

zinc oxide an oxide of zinc used as an antiseptic.

zine or **'zine** noun slang a magazine, usu. produced by desktop publishing methods and aimed at a special-interest group.

zing noun **1** a short, high-pitched humming sound, esp. as made by a bullet, etc. **2** colloq. vitality. —verb intrans., trans. (**zinged, zinging**) to move very quickly, esp. making a high-pitched hum.

zinger noun colloq. a sharply witty remark.

zinnia *noun* a plant with brightly colored daisy-like flower heads.

Zionism *noun* a movement which worked for the establishment of a national homeland in Palestine for Jews and now supports the state of Israel. ▸ **Zionist** *noun, adj.*

zip *noun* 1 *Brit.* a zipper. 2 a whizzing sound. 3 *colloq.* energy; vitality. 4 *colloq.* absolutely nothing: *got zip for all my efforts.* —*verb trans., intrans.* (**zipped, zipping**) 1 (*also* **zip up**) to fasten, or to be fastened, with a zipper. 2 to make, or move with, a whizzing sound. 3 *colloq.* to move with speed: *zipped down to the store.* 4 *Comput.* to compress (a file).

ZIP code 1 a five- or nine-digit number designating a specific US postal district and allocated in order to speed up mail sorting and delivery. 2 the system of ZIP code numbers.

zip gun *slang* a crudely crafted, homemade handgun.

zipper *noun* a fastening device, e.g., on clothes, in which two rows of metal or nylon teeth are made to fit into each other when a sliding tab is pulled along them.

zippy *adj.* (**zippier, zippiest**) *colloq.* lively; quick.

zircon *noun* a relatively common mineral used as a gemstone.

zirconium *noun* (SYMBOL **Zr**) a silvery-gray metallic element.

zit *noun colloq.* a pimple.

zither *noun* a stringed musical instrument with a flat wooden sound box played with the fingers or a plectrum while resting on a table or on the player's knees.

ziti *noun* tubular pasta of a medium size.

zloty *noun* (*pl.* **zloty, zlotys, zloties**) the standard unit of currency in Poland.

Zn *symbol Chem.* zinc.

zodiac *noun* 1 a band of sky that extends to about 8° either side of the ecliptic and which includes the paths of the main planets, the Sun, and the Moon. 2 *Astrol.* this band, divided into 12 equal parts, each containing one of the zodiacal signs, Aries, Taurus, Gemini, Cancer, Leo, Virgo, Libra, Scorpio, Sagittarius, Capricorn, Aquarius, and Pisces. 3 a chart or diagram, usu. circular, representing this band for either astronomical or astrological purposes. ▸ **zodiacal** *adj.*

zombie *or* **zombi** *noun* 1 a voodoo god in the form of a snake. 2 a corpse supposedly brought back to life again by magic.

> After the name of a voodoo snake god

zone *noun* 1 an area or region of a country, town, etc., esp. one marked out for a special purpose or by a particular feature. 2 any of the five horizontal bands (Frigid, North Temperate, Torrid, South Temperate, and South Frigid) into which Earth's surface is divided by the Arctic Circle, the Tropic of Cancer, the Tropic of Capricorn, and the Antarctic Circle. —*verb trans., intrans.* (**zoned, zoning**) 1 (**zone off**) to divide (something) into zones. 2 to assign to a particular zone. ▸ **zonal** *adj.*

zonked *adj.* 1 *colloq.* exhausted. 2 *slang* under the influence of drugs or alcohol.

zoo *noun* (*pl.* **zoos**) 1 a place where wild animals are kept for the public to see, and for study, breeding, etc. 2 *colloq.* a disorderly place.

zoology (zō-äl′ə-jē) *noun* the branch of science that involves the study of animals. ▸ **zoological** *adj.* ▸ **zoologically** *adv.*

zoom *verb intrans., trans.* (**zoomed, zooming**) 1 to move, or cause to move, very quickly, making a loud, low-pitched, buzzing sound. 2 to move very quickly. —*noun* the act, sound, or result of zooming.

zoom lens a camera lens designed for changing from long shots to close-ups or vice versa with minimal loss of focus.

zoophyte (zō′ə-fīt,) *noun* an animal, such as a sponge or coral, that resembles a plant.

zoot suit a man's suit with tapering trousers, and a long, loose coat with heavily padded shoulders and wide lapels, popular in the 1940s.

zorch *verb trans.* (**zorched, zorching, zorches**) *Comput. slang, said by computer hackers* to attack.

Zoroastrianism *noun* an ancient religion of Persian origin based on the belief in two opposing divinities, one good and the other evil, and the ultimate triumph of the good one. ▸ **Zoroastrian** *noun, adj.*

ZPG *abbrev.* zero population growth.

Zr *symbol Chem.* zirconium.

zucchini *noun* (*pl.* **zucchini, zucchinis**) a variety of summer squash, used as a vegetable.

Zulu (zōō′lōō) *noun* 1 (*pl.* **Zulu, Zulus**) a member of a SE African people. 2 the language of this people. —*adj.* of the Zulus, or their language.

zydeco (zīd′ə-kō,) *noun* a type of popular Cajun blues dance music, featuring guitars, washboards, and accordions.

zygote *noun* a cell formed as a result of the fertilization of an ovum or egg cell by a sperm or pollen grain.

zymotic *adj.* 1 relating to or causing fermentation. 2 relating to, causing, or resembling an infectious disease.

Common Irregular Verbs

infinitive	past tense	past participle
be	was, were	been
bear	bore	borne
beat	beat	beaten
become	became	become
begin	began	begun
bend	bent	bent
bind	bound	bound
bite	bit	bitten
bleed	bled	bled
blow	blew	blown
break	broke	broken
bring	brought	brought
broadcast	broadcast	broadcast
build	built	built
burn	burnt, burned	burnt, burned
burst	burst	burst
buy	bought	bought
catch	caught	caught
choose	chose	chosen
come	came	come
cost	cost	cost
creep	crept	crept
cut	cut	cut
deal	dealt	dealt
dig	dug	dug
do	did	done
draw	drew	drawn
dream	dreamt, dreamed	dreamt, dreamed
drink	drank	drunk
drive	drove	driven
eat	ate	eaten
fall	fell	fallen
feed	fed	fed
feel	felt	felt
fight	fought	fought
find	found	found
fly	flew	flown
forbid	forbade	forbidden
forget	forgot	forgotten
forgive	forgave	forgiven
freeze	froze	frozen
get	got	got
give	gave	given
go	went	gone
grind	ground	ground

infinitive	past tense	past participle
grow	grew	grown
hang	hung	hung
have	had	had
hear	heard	heard
hide	hid	hidden
hit	hit	hit
hold	held	held
hurt	hurt	hurt
keep	kept	kept
kneel	knelt, kneeled	knelt, kneeled
know	knew	known
lay	laid	laid
lead	led	led
lean	leant, leaned	leant, leaned
leap	leapt, leaped	leapt, leaped
learn	learnt, learned	learnt, learned
leave	left	left
lend	lent	lent
let	let	let
lie	lay	lain
light	lit	lit
lose	lost	lost
make	made	made
mean	meant	meant
meet	met	met
mistake	mistook	mistaken
pay	paid	paid
put	put	put
read	read	read
ride	rode	ridden
ring	rang	rung
rise	rose	risen
run	ran	run
saw	sawed	sawn
say	said	said
see	saw	seen
sell	sold	sold
send	sent	sent
set	set	set
sew	sewed	sewn
shake	shook	shaken
shine	shone	shone
shoot	shot	shot
show	showed	shown, showed
shrink	shrank	shrunk
shut	shut	shut
sing	sang	sung
sink	sank	sunk

infinitive	past tense	past participle
sit	sat	sat
sleep	slept	slept
slide	slid	slid
smell	smelt, smelled	smelt, smelled
sow	sowed	sown
speak	spoke	spoken
spell	spelt, spelled	spelt, spelled
spend	spent	spent
spill	spilt, spilled	spilt, spilled
spin	spun	spun
spit	spat	spat
split	split	split
spoil	spoilt, spoiled	spoilt, spoiled
spread	spread	spread
stand	stood	stood
steal	stole	stolen
stick	stuck	stuck
strike	struck	struck
sweep	swept	swept
swell	swelled	swollen, swelled
swim	swam	swum
swing	swung	swung
take	took	taken
teach	taught	taught
tear	tore	torn
tell	told	told
think	thought	thought
throw	threw	thrown
understand	understood	understood
undo	undid	undone
upset	upset	upset
wake	woke	woken
wear	wore	worn
weep	wept	wept
win	won	won
wind	wound	wound
write	wrote	written